Mergent

HANDBOOK OF
COMMON STOCKS

2019-2020 Winter

MERGENT
BUSINESS PRESS
by FTSE Russell

INTRODUCTION

Mergent's Handbook of Common Stocks provides quick and easy access to basic financial and business information on more than 900 stocks that are included in the Russell 1000, S&P 500, S&P 400 and Mergent's Dividend Achievers. The Tab Section provides one-line information on New York Stock Exchange companies.

The price charts, statistics, and analyses are presented in a format that provides the investor with the necessary perspective for acting on investment advice or suggestions. It also affords investors the opportunity to make investment decisions on their own.

Statistics and analyses are revised quarterly. Every effort is made to secure the most current operating results and dividend information available. In the case of year-end results, preliminary results are shown and analyzed as they are received. Full statistical presentations of annual report information are shown in the following edition. The schedule below describes the publication dates and company reporting periods usually covered in each edition.

The Winter Edition (published in January) covers quarterly reports and preliminary annual reports through September 30.

The Spring Edition (published in April) covers quarterly reports and preliminary annual reports through December 31.

The Summer Edition (published in July) covers quarterly reports and preliminary annual reports through March 31.

The Fall Edition (published in October) covers quarterly reports and preliminary annual reports through June 30.

Note: For various reasons, some companies may not report in time to meet our publication deadlines. Company reports received close to press time are shown in the Addenda. The remainder of late reports are published and analyzed in the next edition of the Handbook.

The special section on these opening pages contains a number of features, including a guide on how to use this book, a classification of companies by their major line of business based on their NAIC code, outstanding stock price movements by company, plus long-term charts on popular stock market averages. The Addenda provide the latest developments available just prior to publication but after the company reports have been completed.

TABLE OF CONTENTS

Page

HOW TO USE THIS BOOK

The presentation of historical data and analytical comments provides the answers to four basic questions for each company:

1. What does the company do?
   (See G.)
2. How has it done in the past?
   (See B, J.)
3. How is it doing now?
   (See C, D, H.)
4. How will it fare in the future?
   (See I.)

A. CAPSULE STOCK INFORMATION shows where the stock is traded and its symbol, a recent price and price/earnings ratio, plus the yield afforded by the indicated dividend based on a recent price. The indicated dividend is the current annualized dividend based on the most recent price. Some companies are designated as Dividend Achievers. Dividend Achievers have, by *Mergent's* criteria, increased their cash dividend payments for at least ten consecutive years, adjusting for splits. The number of years of consecutive increases is given for each Dividend Achiever.

B. LONG-TERM PRICE CHART illustrates the pattern of monthly stock price movements, fully adjusted for stock dividends and splits. The chart points out the degree of volatility in the price movement of the company's stock and what its long-term trend has been. It also shows how it has performed long-term relative to an initial investment in the S&P 500 Index equal to the price of the company's stock at the beginning of the period shown in the price chart. It indicates areas of price support and resistance, plus other technical points to be considered by the investor. The bars at the base of the long-term price chart indicate the monthly trading volume. Monthly trading volume offers the individual an opportunity to recognize at what periods stock accumulation occurs and what percent of a company's outstanding shares are traded.

PRICE SCORES – Above each company's price/volume chart are its *Mergent's Price Scores*. These are basic measures of the stock's performance. Each stock is measured against the New York Stock Exchange Composite Index.

A score of 100 indicates that the stock did as well as the New York Stock Exchange Composite Index during the time period. A score of less than 100 means that the stock did not do as well; a score of more than 100 means that the stock outperformed the NYSE Composite Index. All stock prices are adjusted for splits and stock dividends. The time periods measured for each company conclude with the date of the recent price shown in the top line of each company's profile.

The *7 YEAR PRICE SCORE* mirrors the common stock's price growth over the previous seven years. The higher the price score, the better the relative performance. It is based on the ratio of the latest 12-month average price to the current seven-year average. This ratio is then indexed against the same ratio for the market as a whole (the New York Stock Exchange Composite Index), which is taken as 100.

The *12 MONTH PRICE SCORE* is a similar measurement but for a shorter period of time. It is based on the ratio of the latest two-month average price to the current 12-month average. As was done for the Long-Term Price Score, this ratio is also indexed to the same ratio for the market as a whole.

C. INTERIM EARNINGS (Per Share) – Figures are reported after the effect of extraordinary items, discontinued operations and cumulative effects of accounting changes. Each figure is for the quarterly period indicated. These figures are essentially as reported by the company, although all figures are adjusted for all stock dividends and splits.

ILLUSTRATIVE INC.

Exchange	**A**	Symbol	Price	52Wk Range	Yield	P/E	Div Acheiver
NYS		1000	$143.53 (9/30/2019)	159.40-118.95	2.79	18.89	56 Years

*7 Year Price Score 114.57 *NYSE Composite Index=100 *12 Month Price Score 101.11

Interim Earnings (Per Share)

Qtr.	Mar	Jun	Sep	Dec
2014	1.11	3.66	1.34	1.19
2015	1.21	1.30	1.39	1.23
2016	1.29	1.46	1.50	1.45
2017	1.54	1.69	1.85	(0.21)
2018	1.90	1.97	1.90	1.83

Interim Dividends (Per Share) **C**

Amt	Decl	Ex	Rec	Pay
0.78Q	05/04/2018	06/28/2018	06/29/2018	07/11/2018
1.00Q	08/03/2018	09/27/2018	09/28/2018	10/09/2018
1.00Q	11/01/2018	12/28/2018	12/31/2018	01/10/2019
1.00Q	02/15/2019	03/28/2019	03/29/2019	04/10/2019

Indicated Div: $4.00 (Div. Reinv. Plan) **D**

B

TRADING VOLUME (thousand shares)

Valuation Analysis **Institutional Holding** **E** **F**

Forecast EPS	$7.94 (09/30/2019)	No of Institutions	1693
Market Cap	$47.1 Billion	Shares	356,365,632
Book Value	$3.3 Billion	% Held	64.67
Price/Book	14.47		
Price/Sales	3.19		

Business Summary: Industrial Machinery & Equipment (MIC: 7.2.1 SIC: 3569 NAIC: 333999) **G**

IllUSTRATIVE INC. is a global manufacturer of industrial products and equipment. Co.'s segments include: Automotive Original Equipment Manufacturer, which produces components and fasteners for automotive-related applications; Food Equipment, which is engaged in commercial food equipment; Test and Measurement and Electronics, which produces equipment, consumables, and related software for testing and measuring of materials and structures, as well as equipment and consumables used in the production of electronic subassemblies and microelectronics; and Welding, which produces arc welding equipment, consumables and accessories for an array of industrial and commercial applications.

Recent Developments: For the year ended June 30, 2019, net income increased 51.9% to US$2.56 billion from US$1.69 billion in the prior year. Revenues were US$14.77 billion, up 3.2% from US$14.31 billion the year before. Operating income was US$3.58 billion versus US$3.49 billion in the prior year, an increase of 2.8%. Direct operating expenses rose 3.6% to US$8.60 billion from US$8.31 billion in the comparable period the year before. Indirect operating expenses increased 2.3% to US$2.58 billion from US$2.52 billion in the equivalent prior-year period. **H**

Prospects: Our evaluation of Illustrative Inc. as of Jan. 21, 2018 is the result of our systematic analysis on three basic characteristics: earnings strength, relative valuation, and recent stock price movement. The company has managed to produce a neutral trend in earnings per share over the past 5 quarters and while recent estimates for the company have been mixed, I000 has posted better than expected results. Based on operating earnings yield, the company is about fairly valued when compared to all of the companies in our coverage universe. Share price changes over the past year indicates that I000 will perform well over the near term. **I**

Financial Data

(US$ in Thousands)	12/31/2018	12/31/2017	12/31/2016	12/31/2015	12/31/2014	12/31/2013	12/31/2012	12/31/2011
Earnings Per Share	7.60	4.86	5.70	5.13	7.28	3.74	6.06	4.19
Cash Flow Per Share	8.39	6.98	6.47	6.25	4.02	5.67	4.40	3.98
Tang Book Value Per Share	N.M.	N.M.	N.M.	N.M.	0.92	6.55	6.09	5.35
Dividends Per Share	3.560	2.860	2.400	2.070	1.810	1.600	1.480	1.400
Dividend Payout %	46.84	58.85	42.11	40.35	24.86	42.78	24.42	33.41
Income Statement								
Total Revenue	14,768,000	14,314,000	13,599,000	13,405,000	14,484,000	14,135,000	17,924,000	17,786,583
EBITDA	4,077,000	3,947,000	3,516,000	3,372,000	265,135,000	3,099,000	3,485,000	3,334,240
Depn & Amortn	461,000	462,000	470,000	475,000	262,242,000	549,000	611,000	589,669
Income Before Taxes	3,394,000	3,270,000	2,847,000	2,723,000	2,708,000	2,361,000	3,633,000	2,592,714
Income Taxes	831,000	1,583,000	873,000	820,000	809,000	717,000	1,108,000	575,700
Net Income	2,563,000	1,687,000	2,035,000	1,899,000	2,946,000	1,679,000	2,870,000	2,071,384
Average Shares	337,100	346,800	357,100	370,100	404,600	449,300	473,200	494,646
Balance Sheet								
Current Assets	5,778,000	7,278,000	6,123,000	6,720,000	8,076,000	9,816,000	7,960,000	6,849,346
Total Assets	14,870,000	16,780,000	15,201,000	15,729,000	17,678,000	19,966,000	19,309,000	17,983,514
Current Liabilities	3,542,000	3,053,000	2,760,000	2,368,000	3,533,000	6,034,000	2,651,000	2,976,727
Long-Term Obligations	6,029,000	7,478,000	7,177,000	6,896,000	5,981,000	2,793,000	4,589,000	3,488,198
Total Liabilities	11,616,000	12,195,000	10,947,000	10,505,000	10,859,000	10,263,000	8,748,000	7,965,723
Stockholders' Equity	3,254,000	4,585,000	4,254,000	5,224,000	6,819,000	9,703,000	10,561,000	10,017,791
Shares Outstanding	328,100	341,500	346,900	363,710	382,900	430,200	455,100	483,608
Statistical Record								
Return on Assets %	16.20	10.55	13.12	11.37	15.65	8.55	15.35	12.10
Return on Equity %	65.39	38.17	42.82	31.54	35.66	16.57	27.82	21.37
EBITDA Margin %	27.61	27.57	25.85	25.15	1,830.54	21.92	19.44	18.75
Net Margin %	17.36	11.79	14.96	14.17	20.34	11.88	16.01	11.65
Asset Turnover	0.93	0.90	0.88	0.80	0.77	0.72	0.96	1.04
Current Ratio	1.63	2.38	2.22	2.84	2.29	1.63	3.00	2.30
Debt to Equity	1.85	1.63	1.69	1.32	0.88	0.29	0.43	0.35
Price Range	178.88-118.95	169.25-121.61	127.93-81.05	99.81-80.09	97.21-76.78	84.08-59.77	62.95-47.79	59.02-40.15
P/E Ratio	23.54-15.65	34.83-25.02	22.44-14.22	19.46-15.61	13.35-10.55	22.48-15.98	10.39-7.89	14.09-9.58
Average Yield %	2.43	2.00	2.21	2.24	2.10	2.27	2.61	2.74

J

Address: Harlem Avenue, Glenview, IL 60025 **Telephone:** 847-000-0000 **K**	**Web Site:** www.com **Officers:** E. Scott S- Chairman, Chief Executive Officer, Vice-Chairman, President, Chief Operating Officer Chris A. O'- Vice-Chairman, Executive Vice President	**Auditors:** Deloitte & Touche LLP **Investor Contact:** 800-000-0000 **Transfer Agents:** Computershare Trust Company, N.A., Providence, RI

HOW TO USE THIS BOOK

D. INTERIM DIVIDENDS (Per Share) – The cash dividends are the actual dollar amounts declared by the company. No adjustments have been made for stock dividends and splits. **Ex-Dividend Date**: a stockholder must purchase the stock prior to this date in order to be entitled to the dividend. The **Record Date** indicates the date on which the shareholder had to have been a holder of record in order to qualify for the dividend. The **Payable Date** indicates the date the company paid or intends to pay the dividend. The cash amount shown in the first column is followed by a letter (example "Q" for quarterly) to indicate the frequency of the dividend. A notation of "Dividend payment suspended" indicates that dividend payments have been suspended within the most recent ten years.
Indicated Dividend This is the annualized amount (fully adjusted for splits) of the latest regular cash dividend. Companies with Dividend Reinvestment Plans are indicated here.

E. VALUATION ANALYSIS is a tool for evaluating a company's stock. Included are: Forecast Earnings Per Share (EPS), Market Capitalization, Book Value, Price/Book and Price/Sales.

F. INSTITUTIONAL HOLDINGS – indicates the number of investment companies, insurance companies, mutual funds, bank trust and college endowment funds holding the stock and the total number of shares held as last reported.

G. BUSINESS SUMMARY explains what a company does in terms of the products or services it sells, its markets, and the position the company occupies in its industry. For a quick reference, included are the Company's Standard Industrial Classification (SIC), North American Industry Classification (NAIC) and Mergent's Industry Classification (MIC).

H. RECENT DEVELOPMENTS – This section captures what has happened in the most recent quarter for which results are available. It provides recently released sales, earnings and expense figures.

I. PROSPECTS – This section focuses on what is anticipated for the immediate future, as well as the outlook for the next few years, based on analysis by Mergent.

J. FINANCIAL DATA (fully adjusted for stock dividends and splits) is provided for at least the past seven fiscal years preceded by the most recent three-, six- and nine-month results if available.
Fiscal Years are the annual financial reporting periods as determined by each company. Annual prices and dividends are displayed based on the Company's fiscal year.

Per Share Data:
The Earnings Per Share figure is based on a trailing 12-month period. Earnings per share, and all per share figures, are adjusted for subsequent stock dividends and splits.
Cash Flow Per Share represents the annualized cash flow from operating activities (or for quarters, TTM cash flow from operating activities) divided by the average shares outstanding.
Tangible Book Value Per Share is calculated as stockholders equity (the value of common shares, paid-in capital and retained earnings) minus preferred stock and intangibles such as goodwill, patents and excess acquisition costs, divided by shares outstanding. It demonstrates the underlying cash value of each common share if the company were to be liquidated as of that date.

Dividends Per Share is the total of cash payments made per share to shareholders for the trailing 12-month period.

HOW TO USE THIS BOOK

Dividend Payout % is the proportion of earnings available for common stock that is paid to common shareholders in the form of cash dividends. It is significant because it indicates what percentage of earnings is being reinvested in the business for internal growth.

EDITOR'S NOTE: TTM net income is net income for the last 365 days (normally four reported quarters) ended on the quarterly balance sheet date. Where that last 365 days does not exactly equate to the last four reported quarters the net income for any included partial quarter is adjusted on a pro-rata basis.

INCOME STATEMENT, BALANCE SHEET AND STATISTICAL RECORD

Includes pertinent earnings and balance sheet information essential to analyzing a corporation's performance. The comparisons provide the necessary historical perspective to intelligently review the various operating and financial trends. Generic definitions follow.

Income Statement:
Total Revenues consists of all revenues from operations.
EBITDA represents earnings before, interest, taxes, depreciation and amortization, and special items.
Depreciation and Amortization includes all non-cash charges such as depletion and amortization as well as depreciation.
Income Before Taxes is the remaining income *after* deducting all costs, expenses, property charges, interest etc. but *before* deducting income taxes.
Income Taxes includes the amount charged against earnings to provide for current and deferred income taxes.
Net Income consists of all revenues less all expenses (operating and non-operating), and is presented before preference and common dividends.

Average Shares Outstanding is the weighted average number of shares including common equivalent shares outstanding during the year, as reported by the corporation and fully adjusted for all stock dividends and splits. The use of *average shares* minimizes the distortion in *earnings per share* which could result from issuance of a large amount of stock or the company's purchase of a large amount of its own stock during the year.

Balance Sheet:
Current Assets includes the short-term assets expected to be realized or consumed within one year. Normally includes cash and cash equivalents, short term investments, receivables, prepayments and inventories.
Total Assets represents all of the assets of the company, including tangible and intangible, and current and non-current.
Current Liabilities are all of the obligations of the company normally expected to be paid within one year. Includes bank overdrafts, short-term debt, payables and accruals.
Long-Term Obligations are the total long-term debts (due beyond one year) reported by the company, including bonds, capital lease obligations, notes, mortgages, debentures, etc.
Total Liabilities represents all liabilities of the company, whether current or non-current.
Stockholders' Equity is the sum of all capital stock accounts – paid in capital (including additional premium), retained earnings, and all other capital balances.
Shares Outstanding is the number of shares outstanding as of the date of the company's quarterly/annual report, exclusive of treasury stock and adjusted for subsequent stock dividends and splits.

Statistical Record:
Return on Assets % represents the ratio of annualized net income (or for Mos, TTM net income) to average total assets. This ratio

represents how effectively assets are being used to produce a profit.

Return on Equity % is the ratio of annualized net income (or for Mos, TTM net income) to average stockholders' equity, expressed as a percentage. This ratio illustrates how effectively the investment of the stockholders is being utilized to earn a profit.

EBITDA Margin % represents earnings before interest, taxes, depreciation and amortization as a percentage of total revenue.

Net Margin % is net income expressed as a percentage of total revenues.

Asset Turnover is annualized total revenue (or for Mos, TTM total revenue) divided by average total assets. A measure of efficiency for the use of assets.

Current Ratio represents current assets divided by current liabilities. The higher the figure the better the company is able to meet its current liabilities out of its current assets. A key measure of liquidity for industrial companies.

Debt to Equity is the ratio of long-term obligations to stockholders' equity.

Price Ranges are based on each Company's fiscal year. Where actual stock sales did not take place, a range of lowest bid and highest asked prices is shown.

Price/Earnings Ratio is shown as a range. The figures are calculated by dividing the stock's highest price for the year and its lowest price by the year's earnings per share. Growth stocks tend to command higher P/Es than cyclical stocks.

Average Yield % is the ratio of annual dividends to the real average of the prices over the fiscal year.

EDITOR'S NOTE: In order to preserve the historical relationships between prices, earnings and dividends, figures are not restated to reflect subsequent events. Figures are presented in U.S. dollars unless otherwise indicated.

K. ADDITIONAL INFORMATION on each stock includes the officers of the company, investor relations contact, address, telephone number, web site and transfer agents.

OTHER DEFINITIONS

Factors Pertaining Especially to Real Estate Investment Trusts

Property Income is income from property rental and other associated activities.

Non-Property Income includes interest income and other income not from property activities.

Factors Pertaining Especially to Utilities

PPE Turnover represents annualized total revenue (or for Mos, TTM total revenue) divided by average net property, plant and equipment.

Factors Pertaining Especially to Banks

Interest Income is all interest income, including income from loans and leases, securities and deposits.

Interest Expense is all interest expense, including from loans and leases, securities and deposits.

Net Interest Income is interest income less interest expense. This figure is presented before provision for losses.

Provision for Losses represents the amount charged against earnings to increase the provision made for losses on loans and leases.

Non-Interest Income is any income that is not interest-related. Such income could include trading revenue and gains on the sale of assets.

Non-Interest Expense is all expenses that are not interest-related, including employment costs, office costs, marketing costs, etc.

Net Loans & Leases includes all loans and leases net of provisions for losses. May include commercial, agricultural, real estate, consumer and foreign loans.

Total Deposits are all time and demand deposits entrusted to a bank.

Net Interest Margin % is net interest income before provisions expressed as a percentage of total interest income. A key measure of bank profitability.

Efficiency Ratio % is non-interest expense expressed as a percentage of total revenue.

Loans to Deposits are net loans and leases divided by total deposits. A key measure of bank liquidity.

Factors Pertaining Especially to Insurance Companies

Premium Income is the amount of insurance premiums received from policyholders. This is the primary revenue source for insurance companies.

Benefits and Claims represents the payments made to policyholders under the terms of insurance contracts.

Loss Ratio % is benefits and claims expressed as a percentage of premium income. A key ratio of insurance company profitability.

ABBREVIATIONS AND SYMBOLS

A...Annual
ASE..............American Stock Exchange
()...Deficit
(Div. Reinv. Plan)..Dividend Reinvest Plan offered
E...Extra
M..Monthly
N/A..............................Not Applicable
N.M.............................Not Meaningful
NMS................ National Market Systems
NYS...............New York Stock Exchange
Q..Quarterly
S...................................Semi-Annual
Sp...........................Special Dividend
U...........................Frequency Unknown

FORDS TOP 50 COMPANIES BY REVENUES

Company Name	Ticker Symbol	Total Revenue ($000,000)	Net Income ($000,000)	Book Value	Industry
WALMART	WMT	$514,405	$6,670	$25.71	Department Stores
ROYAL DUTCH A	RDSA	$396,556	$23,352	$49.31	Integrated Int'l Oil
BP PLC	BP	$303,282	$9,383	$27.75	Integrated Int'l Oil
EXXON MOBIL	XOM	$290,212	$20,840	$44.88	Integrated Int'l Oil
TOYOTA MOTOR	TM	$272,933	$17,002	$129.60	Auto & Truck Mfg.
APPLE	AAPL	$260,174	$55,256	$22.57	Computers
BERKSHIRE HATHAW	BRKB	$247,837	$4,021	$164.80	Insurance
AMAZON.COM	AMZN	$232,887	$10,073	$119.77	Specialty Retailers
UNITEDHEALTH GRP	UNH	$226,247	$11,986	$60.48	Medical Services
MCKESSON CORP	MCK	$214,319	$34	$42.50	Drugs
DAIMLER AG	DDAIF	$199,915	$12,617	$69.71	Auto & Truck Mfg.
CVS HEALTH	CVS	$194,579	-$594	$48.47	Drug Stores
TOTAL SA	TOT	$184,651	$11,446	$45.03	Integrated Int'l Oil
AMERISOURCEBERGN	ABC	$179,589	$855	$14.48	Drugs
AT&T INC	T	$170,756	$19,370	$25.33	Telecommunications
CHEVRON	CVX	$166,339	$14,824	$82.93	Integrated Int'l Oil
FORD MOTOR	F	$160,338	$3,677	$9.00	Auto & Truck Mfg.
COSTCO WHOLESALE	COST	$152,703	$3,659	$36.36	Department Stores
GENERAL MOTORS	GM	$147,049	$8,014	$32.31	Auto & Truck Mfg.
CARDINAL HEALTH	CAH	$145,534	$1,363	$3.13	Drugs
HONDA MOTOR	HMC	$143,472	$5,511	$43.69	Auto & Truck Mfg.
WALGREENS BOOTS	WBA	$136,866	$3,982	$27.07	Drug Stores
ALPHABET	GOOGL	$136,819	$30,736	$293.77	Computers
J P MORGAN CHASE	JPM	$131,412	$32,474	$76.88	Banks
VERIZON COMMUNIC	VZ	$130,863	$15,528	$14.34	Telecommunications
MICROSOFT	MSFT	$125,843	$39,240	$14.49	Computers
GEN ELECTRIC	GE	$121,615	-$22,354	$3.25	Diversified Mfg.
KROGER	KR	$121,162	$3,110	$11.63	Food Stores
FANNIE MAE	FNMA	$120,101	$15,959	-$117.43	Finance & Leasing
VALERO ENERGY	VLO	$117,033	$3,122	$51.86	Integrated Domestic Oil
PHILLIPS 66	PSX	$114,217	$5,595	$57.35	Integrated Domestic Oil
BANK OF AMERICA	BAC	$110,584	$28,147	$27.50	Banks
HOME DEPOT	HD	$108,203	$11,121	-$0.23	Specialty Retailers
NISSAN MOTOR	NSANY	$104,514	$2,882	$29.25	Auto & Truck Mfg.
BOEING	BA	$101,127	$10,460	-$7.38	Aerospace
WELLS FARGO & CO	WFC	$101,060	$22,393	$40.90	Banks
CITIGROUP	C	$97,120	$18,045	$82.24	Banks
MARATHON PETROL	MPC	$97,102	$2,780	$52.81	Integrated Domestic Oil
PETROBRAS	PBR	$96,164	$7,173	$12.24	Integrated Int'l Oil
SIEMENS AG	SIEGY	$95,223	$5,644	$32.78	Diversified Mfg.
COMCAST	CMCSA	$94,507	$11,731	$17.81	Broadcasting
DEUTSCHE TELEKOM	DTEGY	$94,421	$4,149	$7.38	Telecommunications
ANTHEM	ANTM	$92,105	$3,750	$126.81	Medical Services
DELL TECHNOL	DELL	$90,621	-$2,310	-$1.61	Computers
HSBC HLDGS PLC	HSBC	$88,667	$13,727	$48.50	Banks
HITACHI	HTHIY	$88,079	$3,408	$63.06	Radio/TV & Electronics
DUPONT DE NEMOUR	DD	$85,977	$3,844	$55.63	Chemicals
ENI SPA	E	$85,046	$4,045	$32.40	Integrated Int'l Oil
JOHNSON JOHNSON	JNJ	$81,581	$15,297	$24.30	Medical Supplies & Equip.
EQUINOR ASA	EQNR	$79,593	$7,535	$13.69	Integrated Int'l Oil

SHORT-TERM PRICE SCORES: COMPANY RANKINGS

25 Highest	SHORT TERM PRICE SCORE	LONG TERM PRICE SCORE	52 WEEK HIGH	52 WEEK LOW	RECENT PRICE
Sonic Automotive, Inc.	132.1	88.5	34.44	13.75	31.00
Carvana Co	128.9	. . .	98.44	30.19	92.05
Anixter International Inc	125.8	74.0	92.97	52.84	92.10
Target Corp	125.7	105.0	129.21	65.53	128.21
Tenet Healthcare Corp.	124.8	61.7	38.75	17.14	38.03
Lithia Motors Inc	124.5	108.0	163.68	76.33	147.00
RingCentral Inc	123.6	. . .	176.70	78.42	168.67
Group 1 Automotive, Inc.	123.3	90.8	109.25	52.72	100.00
Murphy USA Inc	122.9	. . .	120.84	73.54	117.00
Universal Health Realty Income Trust	122.6	122.8	121.97	60.24	117.36
Tiffany & Co.	122.3	92.6	133.80	79.59	133.65
Asbury Automotive Group Inc	122.2	109.6	122.67	66.39	111.79
Ubiquiti Inc	121.3	190.7	198.30	95.95	188.98
Arconic Inc	121.1	80.6	31.80	16.86	30.77
Jabil Inc	120.6	106.5	43.43	23.12	41.33
Western Union Co	120.4	92.8	27.87	16.87	26.78
Cable One Inc	119.9	. . .	1,547.51	803.24	1,488.47
Vistra Energy Corp	119.2	154.7	27.37	4.55	22.99
KBR Inc	118.9	93.1	30.67	15.18	30.50
XPO Logistics, Inc.	118.9	110.0	85.67	46.20	79.70
ADT Inc (DE)	118.6	. . .	9.57	4.35	7.93
World Fuel Services Corp.	118.5	73.5	43.99	21.27	43.42
Owens & Minor, Inc.	117.9	16.0	8.22	2.47	5.17
KB HOME	117.7	113.2	36.80	19.10	34.27
Leggett & Platt, Inc.	117.4	83.6	55.18	35.45	50.83
25 Lowest					
Superior Energy Services, Inc.	17.8	10.4	54.80	0.85	5.01
Whiting Petroleum Corp	34.1	13.6	30.35	4.49	7.34
Antero Resources Corp	40.1	. . .	10.94	1.94	2.85
Tupperware Brands Corp	42.3	27.6	38.13	7.36	8.58
Chesapeake Energy Corp.	43.6	15.6	3.44	0.56	0.83
Valaris plc	45.9	9.5	19.12	3.52	6.56
RPC, Inc.	52.4	40.7	12.89	3.45	5.24
PG&E Corp (Holding Co)	53.4	27.2	24.40	3.80	10.87
Range Resources Corp	55.3	14.5	11.87	3.33	4.85
QEP Resources Inc	59.1	27.9	9.00	2.71	4.50
Fluor Corp.	59.7	44.6	41.56	16.10	18.88
EQT Corp	61.3	35.8	21.73	8.44	10.90
GrubHub Inc	61.3	. . .	86.08	33.11	48.64
O-I Glass Inc	63.3	55.8	20.40	8.50	11.93
Wayfair Inc	64.3	. . .	171.57	79.87	90.37
Southwestern Energy Company	64.4	14.5	4.82	1.58	2.42
Cars.com Inc	65.6	. . .	27.37	8.28	12.22
Chemours Co (The)	66.1	. . .	40.58	11.93	18.09
Callon Petroleum Co. (DE)	66.5	55.9	8.58	3.58	4.83
Granite Construction Inc	66.8	73.9	48.43	23.54	27.67
Diamond Offshore Drilling, Inc.	69.0	24.1	12.41	4.99	7.19
Meredith Corp	69.1	79.4	60.44	31.94	32.47
SM Energy Co.	69.3	27.7	21.14	7.20	11.24
Plantronics, Inc.	70.5	65.8	53.26	22.92	27.34
Teradata Corp (DE)	70.5	78.2	49.28	25.23	26.77

Ranking by Total Revenues
Based on most recent fiscal year-end figures.

Rank	Company Name	Revenues ($Mill)	Rank	Company Name	Revenues ($Mill)
1.	Walmart Inc	514,405.0	26.	Dell Technologies Inc	90,621.0
2.	Exxon Mobil Corp	290,212.0	27.	Johnson & Johnson	81,581.0
3.	Berkshire Hathaway Inc	247,837.0	28.	Intl. Bus. Machines Corp	79,591.0
4.	UnitedHealth Group Inc	226,247.0	29.	Target Corp	75,356.0
5.	McKesson Corp	214,319.0	30.	United Parcel Service Inc	71,861.0
6.	CVS Health Corporation	194,579.0	31.	Lowe's Companies Inc	71,309.0
7.	AmerisourceBergen Corp	179,589.1	32.	FedEx Corp	69,693.0
8.	AT&T Inc	170,756.0	33.	Disney (Walt) Co. (The)	69,570.0
9.	Chevron Corporation	166,339.0	34.	MetLife Inc	67,941.0
10.	Ford Motor Co. (DE)	160,338.0	35.	Procter & Gamble Co.	67,684.0
11.	General Motors Co	147,049.0	36.	United Technologies Corp	66,501.0
12.	Cardinal Health, Inc.	145,534.0	37.	Archer Daniels Midland Co	64,341.0
13.	JPMorgan Chase & Co	131,412.0	38.	Prudential Financial Inc	62,992.0
14.	Verizon Communications	130,863.0	39.	Centene Corp	60,116.0
15.	General Electric Co	121,615.0	40.	Sysco Corp	60,113.9
16.	Kroger Co (The)	121,162.0	41.	HP Inc	58,756.0
17.	Valero Energy Corp	117,033.0	42.	Humana Inc.	56,912.0
18.	Phillips 66	114,217.0	43.	Caterpillar Inc.	54,722.0
19.	Bank of America Corp	110,584.0	44.	Energy Transfer LP	54,087.0
20.	Home Depot Inc	108,203.0	45.	Lockheed Martin Corp	53,762.0
21.	Boeing Co. (The)	101,127.0	46.	Pfizer Inc	53,647.0
22.	Wells Fargo & Co (New)	101,060.0	47.	Morgan Stanley	50,193.0
23.	Citigroup Inc	97,120.0	48.	Cigna Corp (New)	48,650.0
24.	Marathon Petroleum Corp	97,102.0	49.	American Intl. Group	47,389.0
25.	Anthem Inc	92,105.0	50.	HCA Healthcare Inc	46,677.0

Ranking by Net Income
Based on most recent fiscal year-end figures.

Rank	Company Name	Net Income ($Mill)	Rank	Company Name	Net Income ($Mill)
1.	JPMorgan Chase & Co	32,474.0	26.	NextEra Energy Inc	6,638.0
2.	Bank of America Corp	28,147.0	27.	Coca-Cola Co (The)	6,434.0
3.	Wells Fargo & Co (New)	22,393.0	28.	ConocoPhillips	6,257.0
4.	Exxon Mobil Corp	20,840.0	29.	Merck & Co Inc	6,220.0
5.	AT&T Inc	19,370.0	30.	Caterpillar Inc.	6,147.0
6.	Citigroup Inc	18,045.0	31.	Capital One Financial Corp	6,015.0
7.	Verizon Communications	15,528.0	32.	Union Pacific Corp	5,966.0
8.	Johnson & Johnson	15,297.0	33.	McDonald's Corp	5,924.3
9.	Chevron Corporation	14,824.0	34.	Mastercard Inc	5,859.0
10.	Visa Inc	12,080.0	35.	AbbVie Inc	5,687.0
11.	UnitedHealth Group Inc	11,986.0	36.	Phillips 66	5,595.0
12.	Pfizer Inc	11,153.0	37.	3M Co	5,349.0
13.	Home Depot Inc	11,121.0	38.	PNC Financial Services Grp	5,301.0
14.	Oracle Corp	11,083.0	39.	United Technologies Corp	5,269.0
15.	Disney (Walt) Co. (The)	11,054.0	40.	MetLife Inc	5,123.0
16.	Boeing Co. (The)	10,460.0	41.	Lockheed Martin Corp	5,046.0
17.	Morgan Stanley	8,748.0	42.	Bristol-Myers Squibb Co.	4,920.0
18.	Intl. Bus. Machines Corp	8,728.0	43.	United Parcel Service Inc	4,791.0
19.	General Motors Co	8,014.0	44.	Accenture plc	4,779.1
20.	Philip Morris International	7,911.0	45.	Medtronic PLC	4,631.0
21.	US Bancorp (DE)	7,096.0	46.	Linde plc	4,381.0
22.	Altria Group Inc	6,963.0	47.	BlackRock Inc	4,305.0
23.	American Express Co.	6,921.0	48.	Bank of New York Mellon	4,266.0
24.	Honeywell International Inc	6,765.0	49.	Enterprise Products Partners	4,172.4
25.	Walmart Inc	6,670.0	50.	Occidental Petroleum Corp	4,131.0

Ranking by Total Assets

Based on most recent fiscal year-end figures.

Rank	Company Name	Assets ($Mill)	Rank	Company Name	Assets ($Mill)
1.	JPMorgan Chase & Co	2,622,532.0	26.	CVS Health Corporation	196,456.0
2.	Bank of America Corp	2,354,507.0	27.	Disney (Walt) Co. (The)	193,984.0
3.	Citigroup Inc	1,917,383.0	28.	American Express Co.	188,602.0
4.	Wells Fargo & Co (New)	1,895,883.0	29.	Ally Financial Inc	178,869.0
5.	Morgan Stanley	853,531.0	30.	Chubb Ltd	167,771.0
6.	Prudential Financial Inc	815,078.0	31.	Citizens Financial Group	160,518.0
7.	Berkshire Hathaway Inc	707,794.0	32.	BlackRock Inc	159,573.0
8.	MetLife Inc	687,538.0	33.	Pfizer Inc	159,422.0
9.	AT&T Inc	531,864.0	34.	Voya Financial Inc	154,682.0
10.	American International Grp	491,984.0	35.	Cigna Corp (New)	153,226.0
11.	US Bancorp (DE)	467,374.0	36.	Johnson & Johnson	152,954.0
12.	PNC Financial Services Grp	382,315.0	37.	UnitedHealth Group Inc	152,221.0
13.	Capital One Financial Corp	372,538.0	38.	Duke Energy Corp	145,392.0
14.	Bank of New York Mellon	362,873.0	39.	AFLAC Inc	140,406.0
15.	Exxon Mobil Corp	346,196.0	40.	KeyCorp	139,613.0
16.	General Electric Co	309,129.0	41.	Ameriprise Financial Inc	137,216.0
17.	Lincoln National Corp.	298,147.0	42.	United Technologies Corp	134,211.0
18.	Schwab (Charles) Corp	296,482.0	43.	Regions Financial Corp	125,688.0
19.	Verizon Communications	264,829.0	44.	Intl. Bus. Machines Corp	123,382.0
20.	Ford Motor Co. (DE)	256,540.0	45.	M & T Bank Corp	120,097.4
21.	Chevron Corporation	253,863.0	46.	Boeing Co. (The)	117,359.0
22.	State Street Corp.	244,626.0	47.	Southern Company (The)	116,914.0
23.	General Motors Co	227,339.0	48.	Procter & Gamble Co.	115,095.0
24.	Truist Financial Corp	225,697.0	49.	Allstate Corp	112,249.0
25.	Walmart Inc	219,295.0	50.	Dell Technologies Inc	111,820.0

Ranking by Market Capitalization

Based on most recent fiscal year-end figures and closing prices at 12/31/2019

Rank	Company Name	Market Cap ($Mill)	Rank	Company Name	Market Cap ($Mill)
1.	JPMorgan Chase & Co	437,226.0	26.	Salesforce.Com Inc	144,261.7
2.	Johnson & Johnson	383,911.2	27.	Accenture plc	138,333.1
3.	Walmart Inc	337,169.9	28.	Philip Morris International	132,389.4
4.	Visa Inc	321,812.0	29.	AbbVie Inc	130,934.8
5.	Bank of America Corp	316,807.7	30.	Thermo Fisher Scientific Inc	130,270.0
6.	Procter & Gamble Company	308,434.7	31.	United Technologies Corp	129,283.2
7.	Mastercard Inc	297,828.4	32.	Honeywell International Inc	126,472.4
8.	Exxon Mobil Corp	295,246.6	33.	Lilly (Eli) & Co	126,190.0
9.	AT&T Inc	285,479.4	34.	NIKE Inc	125,863.0
10.	UnitedHealth Group Inc	278,521.0	35.	Union Pacific Corp	125,504.4
11.	Disney (Walt) Co. (The)	260,680.9	36.	Intl. Bus. Machines Corp	118,710.8
12.	Verizon Communications	253,937.2	37.	NextEra Energy Inc	118,362.0
13.	Berkshire Hathaway Inc	240,346.5	38.	Linde plc	114,364.8
14.	Home Depot Inc	238,215.7	39.	Danaher Corp	110,241.8
15.	Coca-Cola Co (The)	237,146.6	40.	Lockheed Martin Corp	109,833.0
16.	Citigroup Inc	232,128.6	41.	Bristol-Myers Squibb Co.	104,583.8
17.	Merck & Co Inc	231,557.3	42.	American Express Co.	101,866.5
18.	Chevron Corporation	227,869.0	43.	American Tower Corp	101,796.6
19.	Wells Fargo & Co (New)	227,539.5	44.	3M Co	101,450.4
20.	Pfizer Inc	216,826.9	45.	General Electric Co	97,466.4
21.	Boeing Co. (The)	183,334.9	46.	CVS Health Corporation	96,648.6
22.	Oracle Corp	169,941.2	47.	Altria Group Inc	93,238.2
23.	Abbott Laboratories	153,608.1	48.	US Bancorp (DE)	92,602.6
24.	Medtronic PLC	152,065.8	49.	Lowe's Companies Inc	91,793.1
25.	McDonald's Corp	148,818.8	50.	Fidelity NationalInform.Svcs	85,484.8

Ranking by Current Yield
Based on closing prices at 12/31/2019

Rank	Company Name	Yield %	Rank	Company Name	Yield %
1.	NGL Energy Partners LP	13.76	26.	CenturyLink Inc	7.57
2.	DCP Midstream LP	12.74	27.	Apple Hospitality REIT Inc	7.38
3.	New Residential Investment	12.41	28.	Six Flags Entertainment	7.36
4.	Holly Energy Partners LP	12.14	29.	Meredith Corp	7.08
5.	Vector Group Ltd	11.95	30.	Invesco Ltd	6.84
6.	GEO Group Inc (The) (New)	11.56	31.	Signet Jewelers Ltd	6.81
7.	Annaly Capital Management	11.15	32.	Altria Group Inc	6.73
8.	Macerich Co (The)	11.14	33.	L Brands, Inc	6.62
9.	MFA Financial, Inc.	10.46	34.	Magellan Midstream Partner	6.54
10.	Global Partners LP	10.32	35.	Ford Motor Co. (DE)	6.45
11.	CoreCivic Inc	10.13	36.	Williams Cos Inc (The)	6.41
12.	Chimera Investment Corp	9.73	37.	EPR Properties	6.37
13.	Westwood Holdings Group	9.72	38.	Omega Healthcare Investors	6.33
14.	Tanger Factory Outlet Center	9.64	39.	Enterprise Products Partners	6.32
15.	Energy Transfer LP	9.51	40.	Helmerich & Payne, Inc.	6.25
16.	Macquarie Infrastructure	9.34	41.	TC PipeLines, LP	6.15
17.	Colony Capital Inc (New)	9.26	42.	VEREIT Inc	5.95
18.	Targa Resources Corp	8.92	43.	SITE Centers Corp	5.71
19.	Macy's Inc	8.88	44.	N.Y. Community Bancorp	5.66
20.	Taubman Centers Inc	8.68	45.	Simon Property Group, Inc.	5.57
21.	Park Hotels & Resorts Inc	8.50	46.	Chemours Co (The)	5.53
22.	Iron Mountain Inc (New)	7.76	47.	Philip Morris International	5.50
23.	Starwood Property Trust Inc.	7.72	48.	Ventas Inc	5.49
24.	Occidental Petroleum Corp	7.67	49.	The Gap Inc	5.49
25.	Tenneco Inc	7.63	50.	Kimco Realty Corp	5.41

Ranking by Return on Equity
Based on most recent fiscal year-end figures.

Rank	Company Name	Return on Equity %	Rank	Company Name	Return on Equity %
1.	Boeing Co. (The)	3,014.41	26.	Boeing Co. (The)	3,014.41
2.	Moody's Corp.	1,981.24	27.	Moody's Corp.	1,981.24
3.	Lockheed Martin Corp	1,419.41	28.	Lockheed Martin Corp	1,419.41
4.	Kimberly-Clark Corp.	603.85	29.	Kimberly-Clark Corp.	603.85
5.	Wyndham Destinations Inc	442.11	30.	Wyndham Destinations Inc	442.11
6.	MSCI Inc	433.13	31.	MSCI Inc	433.13
7.	NGL Energy Partners LP	309.86	32.	NGL Energy Partners LP	309.86
8.	S&P Global Inc	292.46	33.	S&P Global Inc	292.46
9.	United Parcel Service Inc	238.30	34.	United Parcel Service Inc	238.30
10.	Burlington Stores Inc	203.13	35.	Burlington Stores Inc	203.13
11.	Insperity Inc	188.08	36.	Insperity Inc	188.08
12.	Energizer Holdings Inc	170.62	37.	Ubiquiti Inc	155.51
13.	Clorox Co (The)	127.63	38.	Clorox Co (The)	127.63
14.	Mastercard Inc	107.87	39.	Mastercard Inc	107.87
15.	Chemours Co (The)	106.19	40.	Chemours Co (The)	106.19
16.	Pitney Bowes Inc	104.51	41.	Pitney Bowes Inc	104.51
17.	Hershey Company (The)	101.77	42.	Hershey Company (The)	101.77
18.	LiveRamp Holdings Inc	98.90	43.	LiveRamp Holdings Inc	98.90
19.	Allison Transmission Hldgs	94.81	44.	Allison Transmission Hldgs	94.81
20.	Block (H & R), Inc.	90.35	45.	Block (H & R), Inc.	90.35
21.	Mettler-Toledo International	90.14	46.	Mettler-Toledo International	90.14
22.	BWX Technologies inc	87.11	47.	BWX Technologies inc	87.11
23.	CBS Corp	81.97	48.	Scotts Miracle-Gro Co	85.85
24.	Zoetis Inc	72.21	49.	Zoetis Inc	72.21
25.	Booz Allen Hamilton Hldg	68.05	50.	Fair Isaac Corp	69.42

Ranking by High P/E Ratio

Based on closing prices at 12/31/2019

Rank	Company Name	P/E Ratio	Rank	Company Name	P/E Ratio
1.	Live Nation Entertainment	7,147.00	26.	Becton, Dickinson & Co	89.70
2.	GrubHub Inc	1,621.33	27.	Kosmos Energy Ltd (DE)	89.14
3.	ServiceNow Inc	1,568.44	28.	Eagle Materials Inc	87.39
4.	Terex Corp.	1,489.00	29.	Procter & Gamble Company	86.98
5.	FedEx Corp	387.72	30.	World Wrestling Entertainmt	85.72
6.	Teradata Corp (DE)	223.08	31.	UDR Inc	85.05
7.	JBG SMITH Properties	189.95	32.	Veeva Systems Inc	83.44
8.	Paramount Group Inc	174.00	33.	FedEx Corp	82.24
9.	Salesforce.Com Inc	173.02	34.	Universal Health Realty Inc.	81.59
10.	Healthcare Trust Of America	168.22	35.	MGM Resorts International	81.53
11.	Alexandria Real Estate Eq.	158.41	36.	Tyler Technologies, Inc.	80.52
12.	Healthcare Realty Trust, Inc.	151.68	37.	Crown Castle International	80.35
13.	Switch Inc	148.20	38.	American Campus Commun.	80.13
14.	Under Armour Inc	144.00	39.	Wex Inc	79.87
15.	Invitation Homes Inc	136.23	40.	Camden Property Trust	67.69
16.	Wex Inc	135.14	41.	Campbell Soup Co	67.03
17.	Hudson Pacific Properties	129.83	42.	American Tower Corp	67.01
18.	Penumbra Inc	128.34	43.	DaVita Inc	65.60
19.	IQVIA Holdings Inc	127.69	44.	Edwards Lifesciences Corp	64.30
20.	World Wrestling Entertain.	124.75	45.	Paramount Group Inc	63.57
21.	Digital Realty Trust Inc	119.74	46.	Mid-America Apart Commu	62.81
22.	CoreLogic Inc.	112.08	47.	Welltower Inc	61.25
23.	Lindsay Corp	111.62	48.	Douglas Emmett Inc	61.19
24.	Retail Properties of America	103.08	49.	Elanco Animal Health Inc	60.43
25.	GoDaddy Inc	102.91	50.	Cars.com Inc	59.87

Ranking by Low P/E Ratio

Based on closing prices at 12/31/2019

Rank	Company Name	P/E Ratio	Rank	Company Name	P/E Ratio
1.	Southwestern Energy Co.	1.22	26.	Spirit Airlines Inc	7.97
2.	Chesapeake Energy Corp.	1.69	27.	Taubman Centers Inc	8.01
3.	United States Steel Corp.	3.22	28.	Sally Beauty Holdings Inc	8.08
4.	Murphy Oil Corp	3.30	29.	Delta Air Lines Inc (DE)	8.19
5.	SolarWinds Corp	3.34	30.	The Gap Inc	8.26
6.	LiveRamp Holdings Inc	3.92	31.	Devon Energy Corp.	8.35
7.	Tupperware Brands Corp	4.09	32.	Equity Commonwealth	8.44
8.	Vornado Realty Trust	4.23	33.	Foot Locker, Inc.	8.46
9.	Big Lots, Inc.	4.46	34.	Global Partners LP	8.51
10.	Callon Petroleum Co. (DE)	4.60	35.	Santander Consumer USA	8.59
11.	Macy's Inc	5.47	36.	ConocoPhillips	8.86
12.	SM Energy Co.	5.71	37.	VMware Inc	8.95
13.	CNX Resources Corp	5.75	38.	Whirlpool Corp	9.01
14.	Unum Group	5.90	39.	Comerica, Inc.	9.09
15.	General Motors Co	5.96	40.	Lennar Corp	9.10
16.	Whiting Petroleum Corp	6.17	41.	Capital One Financial Corp	9.12
17.	Synchrony Financial	6.57	42.	Cabot Oil & Gas Corp.	9.21
18.	Delek US Holdings Inc	6.75	43.	HanesBrands Inc	9.28
19.	MetLife Inc	6.82	44.	Evercore Inc	9.30
20.	Spectrum Brands Holdings	6.91	45.	Allison Transmission Hldgs	9.38
21.	NACCO Industries Inc	7.40	46.	Ashland Global Holdings Inc	9.53
22.	Chemours Co (The)	7.51	47.	Discover Financial Services	9.58
23.	OneMain Holdings Inc	7.54	48.	Nucor Corp.	9.60
24.	Ally Financial Inc	7.55	49.	American Eagle Outfitters	9.67
25.	WPX Energy Inc	7.76	50.	Air Lease Corp	9.68

CLASSIFICATION BY INDUSTRY

Company	SIC	Industry	Company	SIC	Industry
OMNICOM	7311	Advertising	DANA INC	3714	Auto Parts
INTERPUBLIC	7311	Advertising	GENUINE PARTS	5013	Auto Parts
BOEING	3721	Aerospace	LEAR	3714	Auto Parts
CURTISS-WRIGHT	3599	Aerospace	BORGWARNER INC	3714	Auto Parts
GEN DYNAMICS	3721	Aerospace	TENNECO	3714	Auto Parts
HEICO	3724	Aerospace	AUTOLIV	3714	Auto Parts
LOCKHEED MARTIN	5088	Aerospace	WABCO HOLDINGS	3711	Auto Parts
RAYTHEON	3812	Aerospace	ALLISON TRANSMIS	3714	Auto Parts
TELEDYNE TECH	3812	Aerospace	APTIV PLC	3714	Auto Parts
NORTHROP GRUMMAN	3721	Aerospace	EATON CORP PLC	3590	Auto Parts
TRANSDIGM GROUP	3728	Aerospace	FLOWERS FOODS	2051	Bakery Products
SPIRIT AEROSYST	3728	Aerospace	ASSOC BANC-CORP	6022	Banks
AIR LEASE	7359	Aerospace	SYNOVUS FINL	6021	Banks
HUNTINGTON INGAL	3721	Aerospace	COMERICA	6021	Banks
DEERE	3523	Agricultural Machinery	U S BANCORP	6022	Banks
LINDSAY	3523	Agricultural Machinery	M + T BANK	6022	Banks
AGCO	3523	Agricultural Machinery	FIRST HORIZN NTL	6021	Banks
DELTA AIR LINES	4512	Airlines	FNB CORP	6035	Banks
SOUTHWEST AIR	4512	Airlines	CULLEN/FROST	6021	Banks
ALASKA AIR GROUP	4512	Airlines	BANK OF HAWAII	6022	Banks
FEDEX CORP	4513	Airlines	BANK OF AMERICA	6021	Banks
UNITED PARCEL SV	4210	Airlines	WELLS FARGO & CO	6021	Banks
SPIRIT AIRLINES	4512	Airlines	KEYCORP	6021	Banks
ARCONIC	3350	Aluminum	BB+T CORP	6021	Banks
ALCOA CORP	3350	Aluminum	STATE STREET	6022	Banks
PVH	2300	Apparel	BANCORPSOUTH BAN	6022	Banks
V F CORP	2300	Apparel	PNC FINANCIAL	6021	Banks
RALPH LAUREN	2329	Apparel	COMM BANK SYSTEM	6712	Banks
CARTERS	2300	Apparel	SUNTRUST BANKS	6021	Banks
UNDER ARMOUR	2300	Apparel	CITIZENS FINL	6022	Banks
HANESBRANDS	5600	Apparel	CITIGROUP	6021	Banks
CAPRI HOLDINGS	3100	Apparel	PROSPERITY BANCS	6022	Banks
FORD MOTOR	3711	Auto & Truck Mfg.	STERLING BCP	6036	Banks
OSHKOSH	3711	Auto & Truck Mfg.	FIRST REPUBLIC	6021	Banks
HARLEY-DAVIDSON	3751	Auto & Truck Mfg.	REGIONS FINL	6021	Banks
NAVISTAR INTL	3711	Auto & Truck Mfg.	BNK OF NY MELLON	6022	Banks
GENERAL MOTORS	3711	Auto & Truck Mfg.	BANKUNITED INC	6035	Banks
			MOLSON COORS	2082	Brewing

CLASSIFICATION BY INDUSTRY

Company	SIC	Industry	Company	SIC	Industry
BOSTON BEER CO	2082	Brewing	CELANESE CORP	2820	Chemicals
TEGNA	4833	Broadcasting	HUNTSMAN CORP	2800	Chemicals
CBS	4841	Broadcasting	CF INDUSTRIES	2879	Chemicals
DISNEY WALT	7812	Broadcasting	UNIVAR SOLUTIONS	5169	Chemicals
ARMSTRONG WORLD	5039	Building Materials	ELEMENT SOLUTION	2890	Chemicals
CRANE	5031	Building Materials	CHEMOURS	2800	Chemicals
MASCO CORP	3432	Building Materials	INGEVITY	2800	Chemicals
OWENS CORNING	3290	Building Materials	ASHLAND GLOBAL	5169	Chemicals
FLOOR & DECOR	5211	Building Materials	VALVOLINE	2990	Chemicals
FORTUNE BR HOME	1520	Building Materials	LINDE PLC	2819	Chemicals
ARCHER-DANIELS	2070	Bulk Food Processing	NACCO INDUST	1221	Coal
INGREDION	2046	Bulk Food Processing	CACI	7373	Computers
BUNGE LTD	2070	Bulk Food Processing	HP INC	3570	Computers
MARTIN MAR MATLS	5032	Cement	IBM	3570	Computers
EAGLE MATERIALS	3241	Cement	NCR CORP	3578	Computers
VULCAN MATERIALS	5032	Cement	LIVERAMP HOLDING	7374	Computers
AIR PRODUCTS	2819	Chemicals	TERADATA	3571	Computers
CABOT CORP	2892	Chemicals	TYLER TECHNOL	7372	Computers
ECOLAB	2842	Chemicals	JUNIPER NETWORKS	3661	Computers
FMC	2879	Chemicals	ALLIANCE DATA	7389	Computers
FULLER H B	2891	Chemicals	SALESFORCE.COM	7372	Computers
INTL FLAV + FRAG	2860	Chemicals	GLOBAL PAYMENTS	7389	Computers
OLIN	2819	Chemicals	VMWARE	7372	Computers
PPG INDUSTRIES	2851	Chemicals	FIDELITY NAT INF	7389	Computers
QUAKER CHEM	2899	Chemicals	SYNNEX	3577	Computers
STEPAN	2819	Chemicals	WEX	7500	Computers
SHERWIN-WILLIAMS	2851	Chemicals	PALO ALTO NETWOR	3577	Computers
RPM INTL	2851	Chemicals	ORACLE CORP	7372	Computers
SENSIENT TECH	2819	Chemicals	EPAM SYSTEMS	7371	Computers
SCOTTS MIRACLE	2873	Chemicals	SERVICENOW	7372	Computers
MINERALS TECH	2819	Chemicals	RINGCENTRAL	7374	Computers
EASTMAN CHEMICAL	2821	Chemicals	VEEVA SYSTEMS	7372	Computers
ALBEMARLE	2819	Chemicals	GENPACT	8742	Computers
GRACE W R	2800	Chemicals	HUBSPOT	7374	Computers
POLYONE CORP	2821	Chemicals	TWITTER	7370	Computers
WESTLAKE CHEMICA	2869	Chemicals	TWILIO	7372	Computers
NEWMARKET CORP	2869	Chemicals	ZENDESK	7372	Computers
MOSAIC	2899	Chemicals	ACCENTURE PLC	7389	Computers
			SQUARE	7372	Computers

CLASSIFICATION BY INDUSTRY

Company	SIC	Industry	Company	SIC	Industry
GUIDEWIRE SOFTWA	7379	Computers	HOWARD HUGHES	6552	Construction & Real Estate
SCIENCE APPLICA	7373	Computers	TRI POINTE GROUP	1531	Construction & Real Estate
GRUBHUB	7372	Computers	FREEPORT-MCMORAN	1021	Copper
ARISTA NETWORKS	5045	Computers	SOUTHERN COPPER	1021	Copper
GODADDY	7373	Computers	AVON PRODUCTS	2844	Cosmetics & Toiletries
HEWLETT PACK ENT	3570	Computers	LAUDER ESTEE	2844	Cosmetics & Toiletries
CONDUENT	7389	Computers	COTY	2844	Cosmetics & Toiletries
CARS.COM	7374	Computers	DEAN FOODS	2024	Dairy Products
SOLARWINDS	7372	Computers	TARGET CORP	5331	Department Stores
XEROX HOLDINGS	3577	Computers	DILLARDS INC	5311	Department Stores
HERSHEY CO	2064	Confectionery	DOLLAR GENERAL	5331	Department Stores
TOOTSIE ROLL	2064	Confectionery	NORDSTROM	5311	Department Stores
CATERPILLAR	3531	Const. & Mat'l Handling	WALMART	5411	Department Stores
TEREX	3537	Const. & Mat'l Handling	BIG LOTS	5331	Department Stores
COLFAX	3563	Const. & Mat'l Handling	MACYS	5311	Department Stores
INGERSOLL-RAND	3560	Const. & Mat'l Handling	KOHLS	5311	Department Stores
MASTEC	1623	Construction & Real Estate	PENNEY J C	5311	Department Stores
JACOBS ENGINEER	1611	Construction & Real Estate	CONSTELLATION BR	2084	Distilling
DYCOM INDUSTRIES	1623	Construction & Real Estate	GEN ELECTRIC	3612	Diversified Mfg.
EMCOR GROUP	1731	Construction & Real Estate	MSA SAFETY	3842	Diversified Mfg.
TOLL BROTHERS	1531	Construction & Real Estate	3M COMPANY	5112	Diversified Mfg.
KB HOME	1531	Construction & Real Estate	PENTAIR PLC	3550	Diversified Mfg.
PULTEGROUP	1531	Construction & Real Estate	UNITED TECH	3724	Diversified Mfg.
GRANITE CONST	1611	Construction & Real Estate	ITT INC	3594	Diversified Mfg.
D R HORTON	1531	Construction & Real Estate	TEXTRON	3721	Diversified Mfg.
NVR INC	1531	Construction & Real Estate	BRADY CORP	2819	Diversified Mfg.
LENNAR	1520	Construction & Real Estate	HONEYWELL INTL	3822	Diversified Mfg.
JONES LANG LASAL	6531	Construction & Real Estate	CARLISLE	3061	Diversified Mfg.
QUANTA SERVICES	1731	Construction & Real Estate	CVS HEALTH	5912	Drug Stores
FLUOR CORP	8700	Construction & Real Estate	RITE AID	5912	Drug Stores
CBRE GROUP	6500	Construction & Real Estate	BRISTOL-MYERS SQ	2834	Drugs
MACQUARIE INFRAS	5172	Construction & Real Estate	LILLY ELI	2834	Drugs
REALOGY	6531	Construction & Real Estate	PFIZER	2834	Drugs
			MERCK	2834	Drugs
			CARDINAL HEALTH	5122	Drugs
			MCKESSON CORP	5122	Drugs
			NU SKIN ENTERPRS	2834	Drugs

CLASSIFICATION BY INDUSTRY

Company	SIC	Industry	Company	SIC	Industry
AMERISOURCEBERGN	5122	Drugs	DUKE ENERGY	4911	Electric Utilities
HERBALIFE NUTRIT	2834	Drugs	AVANGRID	4911	Electric Utilities
PRESTIGE CONSUME	2834	Drugs	VISTRA ENERGY	4911	Electric Utilities
ABBVIE	2834	Drugs	EMERSON ELECTRIC	3823	Electrical Equipment
ZOETIS	2834	Drugs	HUBBELL	3679	Electrical Equipment
ALLERGAN PLC	2834	Drugs	REGAL BELOIT	3568	Electrical Equipment
CATALENT	2834	Drugs	SMITH A O	3621	Electrical Equipment
ELANCO ANIMAL	2834	Drugs	DANAHER	3823	Electrical Equipment
AMER ELEC POWER	4911	Electric Utilities	AMPHENOL	3678	Electrical Equipment
ENTERGY	4911	Electric Utilities	BELDEN	3357	Electrical Equipment
MDU RESOURCES	4932	Electric Utilities	WESCO INTL	5063	Electrical Equipment
EVERSOURCE ENERG	4911	Electric Utilities	ROCKWELL AUTOMAT	3823	Electrical Equipment
NORTHWESTERN	4931	Electric Utilities	AMETEK	3629	Electrical Equipment
SOUTHERN CO	4911	Electric Utilities	ACUITY BRANDS	5160	Electrical Equipment
HAWAIIAN ELEC IN	4911	Electric Utilities	ENERSYS	5063	Electrical Equipment
DOMINION ENERGY	4911	Electric Utilities	FORTIVE	3823	Electrical Equipment
NEXTERA ENERGY	4911	Electric Utilities	ARROW ELECTRONIC	5065	Electronics & Instruments
PINNACLE WEST	4911	Electric Utilities	BADGER METER	3824	Electronics & Instruments
WEC ENERGY GROUP	4931	Electric Utilities	CORNING	3229	Electronics & Instruments
PORTLAND GEN ELE	4911	Electric Utilities	DIEBOLD NIXDORF	3578	Electronics & Instruments
PUB SERV ENTER	4911	Electric Utilities	PERKINELMER	3826	Electronics & Instruments
CMS ENERGY	4931	Electric Utilities	ANIXTER INTL	5063	Electronics & Instruments
EDISON INTL	4911	Electric Utilities	MOTOROLA SOLUTIO	3663	Electronics & Instruments
AES CORP	4991	Electric Utilities	TELEFLEX	3841	Electronics & Instruments
PPL CORP	4911	Electric Utilities	THERMO FISHER SC	3829	Electronics & Instruments
DTE ENERGY	4911	Electric Utilities	VISHAY INTERTECH	3679	Electronics & Instruments
AMEREN	4931	Electric Utilities	L3HARRIS TECHNOL	3571	Electronics & Instruments
PG+E CORP	4931	Electric Utilities	GRAINGER W W	5961	Electronics & Instruments
NRG ENERGY	4911	Electric Utilities	ROPER TECHNOL	3561	Electronics & Instruments
OGE ENERGY	4911	Electric Utilities	JABIL CIRCUIT	3672	Electronics & Instruments
FIRSTENERGY	4911	Electric Utilities	CIENA	7373	Electronics & Instruments
SEMPRA ENERGY	4932	Electric Utilities	WATERS	3826	Electronics & Instruments
CONSOL EDISON	4931	Electric Utilities	METTLER TOLEDO	3826	Electronics & Instruments
IDACORP	4911	Electric Utilities	AGILENT TECH	3826	Electronics & Instruments
PNM RESOURCES	4931	Electric Utilities			
EXELON	4931	Electric Utilities			
NISOURCE	4923	Electric Utilities			
CENTERPOINT	4911	Electric Utilities			
BLACK HILLS	4911	Electric Utilities			

CLASSIFICATION BY INDUSTRY

Company	SIC	Industry	Company	SIC	Industry
DOLBY LABORATORI	3651	Electronics & Instruments	FEDERATED INVEST	6282	Fund Management
TE CONNECTIVITY	5065	Electronics & Instruments	LAZARD	6199	Fund Management
KEYSIGHT TECH	3823	Electronics & Instruments	BLACKROCK	6211	Fund Management
			KKR & CO	6282	Fund Management
ILLINOIS TOOL	3560	Fabricated Metals	COLONY CAPITAL	6500	Fund Management
KENNAMETAL	3541	Fabricated Metals	SNAP-ON INC	3825	Home Appliances
TIMKEN	3562	Fabricated Metals	WHIRLPOOL	3633	Home Appliances
VALMONT INDUST	3444	Fabricated Metals	TORO	3524	Home Appliances
HEXCEL CORP	3496	Fabricated Metals	HNI CORP	2522	Home Furnishings
RELIANCE STEEL	5051	Fabricated Metals	LEGGETT + PLATT	2511	Home Furnishings
AMER EXPRESS	6153	Finance & Leasing	MOHAWK	2273	Home Furnishings
EQUIFAX	7320	Finance & Leasing	TEMPUR SEALY	2510	Home Furnishings
GATX	4700	Finance & Leasing	MGM RESORTS INTL	7011	Hotel & Motel
ALLY FINANCIAL	6172	Finance & Leasing	CHOICE HOTELS	7011	Hotel & Motel
RYDER SYSTEM	7510	Finance & Leasing	LAS VEGAS SANDS	7011	Hotel & Motel
JEFFERIES FINANC	6822	Finance & Leasing	WYNDHAM DESTINAT	7011	Hotel & Motel
FAIR ISAAC	7389	Finance & Leasing	HYATT HOTELS	7011	Hotel & Motel
CAPITAL ONE FINL	6021	Finance & Leasing	MARRIOTT VACAT	7011	Hotel & Motel
UNITED RENTALS	7359	Finance & Leasing	HILTON GRAND VAC	7000	Hotel & Motel
MASTERCARD	7389	Finance & Leasing	WYNDHAM HOTELS	7011	Hotel & Motel
WESTWOOD HLDGS	6199	Finance & Leasing	CUMMINS INC	3519	Industrial Machinery
FLEETCOR TECHNOL	7389	Finance & Leasing	DOVER	3560	Industrial Machinery
EVERCORE	6199	Finance & Leasing	FLOWSERVE	3561	Industrial Machinery
HERC HOLDINGS	7359	Finance & Leasing	GORMAN-RUPP	3561	Industrial Machinery
WESTERN UNION	6099	Finance & Leasing	GRACO	3561	Industrial Machinery
BROADRIDGE FINL	6199	Finance & Leasing	PARKER-HANNIFIN	3492	Industrial Machinery
DISCOVER FINL	2621	Finance & Leasing	TENNANT	3589	Industrial Machinery
VISA	7389	Finance & Leasing	IDEX CORP	3561	Industrial Machinery
TRANSUNION	7320	Finance & Leasing	MSC INDUSTRIAL	5084	Industrial Machinery
SANTANDER CONSUM	6141	Finance & Leasing	BWX TECHNOLOGIES	3510	Industrial Machinery
ONEMAIN HOLDINGS	6141	Finance & Leasing	XYLEM	3561	Industrial Machinery
SYNCHRONY FINL	6199	Finance & Leasing	WELBILT	3556	Industrial Machinery
KROGER	5411	Food Stores	GARDNER DENVER	3560	Industrial Machinery
LOUISIANA-PACIFC	2493	Forest Products	AFLAC	6311	Insurance
FRANKLIN RES	6282	Fund Management	AMER INTL GROUP	6331	Insurance
EATON VANCE	6282	Fund Management	UNUM GROUP	6321	Insurance
AMERIPRISE FINL	6282	Fund Management	BERKLEY W R	6331	Insurance
INVESCO LTD	6282	Fund Management	CNA FINANCIAL	6331	Insurance
AFFILIATED MGRS	6282	Fund Management	CORELOGIC	6035	Insurance

CLASSIFICATION BY INDUSTRY

Company	SIC	Industry	Company	SIC	Industry
LINCOLN NATL	6311	Insurance	MURPHY OIL	2911	Integrated Domestic Oil
LOEWS	6331	Insurance	OCCIDENTAL PET	1311	Integrated Domestic Oil
MARSH MCLENNAN	6411	Insurance	VALERO ENERGY	2911	Integrated Domestic Oil
MERCURY GENERAL	6331	Insurance	ONEOK	4924	Integrated Domestic Oil
OLD REPUBLIC	6351	Insurance	ENGY TRANSFER LP	4922	Integrated Domestic Oil
BROWN + BROWN	6411	Insurance	HOLLY ENERGY LP	4610	Integrated Domestic Oil
PROGRESSIVE	6331	Insurance	DCP MIDSTREAM LP	4922	Integrated Domestic Oil
RLI	6331	Insurance	KINDER MORGAN	4922	Integrated Domestic Oil
TRAVELERS COS	6331	Insurance	MARATHON PETROL	2911	Integrated Domestic Oil
GLOBE LIFE	6311	Insurance	PBF ENERGY	2911	Integrated Domestic Oil
GALLAGHER ART	6411	Insurance	PHILLIPS 66	2911	Integrated Domestic Oil
ALLEGHANY CORP	6361	Insurance	DELEK US HOLDING	2911	Integrated Domestic Oil
WHITE MOUNTAINS	6162	Insurance	CHEVRON	2911	Integrated Int'l Oil
KEMPER	6331	Insurance	MARATHON OIL	2911	Integrated Int'l Oil
HARTFORD FINL	6411	Insurance	CONOCOPHILLIPS	1311	Integrated Int'l Oil
CHUBB LTD	6331	Insurance	STANLEY BLACK&DE	3423	Machine Tools
REINSURANCE GRP	6321	Insurance	KIRBY	4424	Maritime
ALLSTATE	6399	Insurance	HORMEL FOODS	2011	Meat Packing
RENAISSANCERE	6331	Insurance	TYSON FOODS	2015	Meat Packing
HANOVER INSUR	6331	Insurance	CHEMED CORP	8082	Medical Services
AMERICAN EQUITY	6311	Insurance	HUMANA	6324	Medical Services
AMER FINL GROUP	6331	Insurance	TENET HEALTHCARE	8062	Medical Services
EVEREST RE GROUP	6321	Insurance	UNIVERSAL HEALTH	8062	Medical Services
MARKEL	6331	Insurance	UNITEDHEALTH GRP	6324	Medical Services
METLIFE INC	6411	Insurance	ENCOMPASS HEALTH	8093	Medical Services
PROASSURANCE	6331	Insurance	HCA HEALTHCARE	8062	Medical Services
PRUDENTIAL FINL	6311	Insurance	MEDNAX	8069	Medical Services
CNO FINANCIAL	6321	Insurance	LAB CORP OF AMER	8071	Medical Services
ASSURANT	6321	Insurance	DAVITA INC	8092	Medical Services
ASSURED GUARANTY	6351	Insurance	QUEST DIAGNOSTIC	8071	Medical Services
GENWORTH FINL	6311	Insurance	CENTENE CORP	6324	Medical Services
FIDELITY NAT FIN	6361	Insurance	COMM HEALTH SYST	8062	Medical Services
FIRST AMER FINL	6361	Insurance	ANTHEM	6324	Medical Services
PRIMERICA	6311	Insurance	MOLINA HEALTHCAR	6324	Medical Services
VOYA FINANCIAL	6311	Insurance	WELLCARE HEALTH	6324	Medical Services
HESS	2911	Integrated Domestic Oil	BROOKDALE SR LIV	8050	Medical Services
HOLLYFRONTIER	2911	Integrated Domestic Oil			
WILLIAMS COS	4922	Integrated Domestic Oil			

CLASSIFICATION BY INDUSTRY

Company	SIC	Industry	Company	SIC	Industry
GENESIS HEALTH	8051	Medical Services	BRINK'S COMPANY	7382	Misc. & Divers. Services
CIGNA	6321	Medical Services	ROLLINSINC	7342	Misc. & Divers. Services
ABBOTT LABS	2834	Medical Supplies & Equip.	SERVICE CP INTL	7261	Misc. & Divers. Services
BAXTER INTL	3841	Medical Supplies & Equip.	GRAHAM HOLDINGS	8200	Misc. & Divers. Services
BECTONDICKINSON	3841	Medical Supplies & Equip.	ROBERT HALF	7363	Misc. & Divers. Services
BIO-RAD LABS A	3826	Medical Supplies & Equip.	ADTALEM GLOBAL	8221	Misc. & Divers. Services
CANTEL MEDICAL	5047	Medical Supplies & Equip.	GARTNER INC	8741	Misc. & Divers. Services
HIL-ROM HOLDINGS	3845	Medical Supplies & Equip.	SJW GROUP	4941	Misc. & Divers. Services
OWENS + MINOR	5047	Medical Supplies & Equip.	ABM INDUSTRIES	7349	Misc. & Divers. Services
WEST PHARMACEUT	3069	Medical Supplies & Equip.	WORLD FUEL SVCS	5172	Misc. & Divers. Services
JOHNSON JOHNSON	2834	Medical Supplies & Equip.	CLEAN HARBORS	4955	Misc. & Divers. Services
VARIAN MED SYST	3559	Medical Supplies & Equip.	WASTE MANAGEMENT	4953	Misc. & Divers. Services
STRYKER	3841	Medical Supplies & Equip.	AECOM	8711	Misc. & Divers. Services
HAEMONETICS	3841	Medical Supplies & Equip.	MANPOWERGROUP	7363	Misc. & Divers. Services
COOPER COMPANIES	3851	Medical Supplies & Equip.	ASGN INC	7363	Misc. & Divers. Services
BOSTON SCIENTIFC	3841	Medical Supplies & Equip.	INSPERITY	7363	Misc. & Divers. Services
RESMED	3841	Medical Supplies & Equip.	FACTSET RESEARCH	7375	Misc. & Divers. Services
EDWARDS LIFESCIE	8731	Medical Supplies & Equip.	MAXIMUS	8742	Misc. & Divers. Services
CHARLES RVR LABS	2836	Medical Supplies & Equip.	CALIF WATER SVC	4941	Misc. & Divers. Services
ZIMMER BIOMET	3842	Medical Supplies & Equip.	AMER STATES WATR	4941	Misc. & Divers. Services
GLOBUS MED INC	3841	Medical Supplies & Equip.	MOODY'S CORP	7323	Misc. & Divers. Services
PENUMBRA	3841	Medical Supplies & Equip.	REPUBLIC SERVICE	4953	Misc. & Divers. Services
AVANOS MEDICAL	3842	Medical Supplies & Equip.	LEIDOS HOLDINGS	8700	Misc. & Divers. Services
MEDTRONIC PLC	3845	Medical Supplies & Equip.	KBR INC	1600	Misc. & Divers. Services
STERIS PLC	3842	Medical Supplies & Equip.	MSCI	2721	Misc. & Divers. Services
BALL CORP	3411	Metal & Glass Containers	AMER WATER WORKS	4941	Misc. & Divers. Services
OWENS-ILLINOIS	3221	Metal & Glass Containers	HILLENBRAND	5084	Misc. & Divers. Services
APTARGROUP	3089	Metal & Glass Containers	SERVICEMASTER	7342	Misc. & Divers. Services
CROWN HLDGS	3411	Metal & Glass Containers	BRIGHT HORIZONS	8351	Misc. & Divers. Services
BLOCK H + R	7200	Misc. & Divers. Services	BOOZ ALLEN HAMIL	8748	Misc. & Divers. Services
AQUA AMERICA	4941	Misc. & Divers. Services	NIELSEN HLDG PLC	7389	Misc. & Divers. Services

CLASSIFICATION BY INDUSTRY

Company	SIC	Industry	Company	SIC	Industry
ADT	7381	Misc. & Divers. Services	CONCHO RESOURCES	1311	Oil Producers
NEWMONT GOLDCORP	1041	Misc. Metals & Mining	ANTERO RESOURCES	1311	Oil Producers
COMPASS MINERALS	1400	Misc. Metals & Mining	OASIS PETROLEUM	1311	Oil Producers
THOR INDUST	3716	Mobile Homes	KOSMOS ENERGY	1311	Oil Producers
SOUTHWSTRN ENERG	4923	Natural Gas Utilities	WPX ENERGY	1311	Oil Producers
CHESAPEAKE UTIL	4923	Natural Gas Utilities	MATADOR RESOURCE	1311	Oil Producers
EQT	4923	Natural Gas Utilities	LAREDO PETROLEUM	1311	Oil Producers
NATL FUEL GAS	4924	Natural Gas Utilities	PARSLEY ENERGY	1311	Oil Producers
SOUTH JERSEY IND	4924	Natural Gas Utilities	HELMERICH PAYNE	1381	Oil Well Drilling
NEW JERSEY RES	4924	Natural Gas Utilities	VALARIS PLC	1381	Oil Well Drilling
ATMOS ENERGY	4924	Natural Gas Utilities	DIAMND OFFSHR DR	1381	Oil Well Drilling
UGI	4932	Natural Gas Utilities	NABORS INDUST	1381	Oil Well Drilling
TC PIPELINES LP	4922	Natural Gas Utilities	TRANSOCEAN LTD	1381	Oil Well Drilling
SPIRE INC	4924	Natural Gas Utilities	HALLIBURTON	1389	Oil Well Equip. & Services
TARGA RESOURCE	4922	Natural Gas Utilities	OCEANEERING INTL	1389	Oil Well Equip. & Services
ONE GAS	4924	Natural Gas Utilities	RPC INC	5084	Oil Well Equip. & Services
SOUTHWEST GAS HO	4923	Natural Gas Utilities	BUCKEYE PARTNERS	4613	Oil Well Equip. & Services
NWEST NAT HLD	4924	Natural Gas Utilities	SUPERIOR ENERGY	1389	Oil Well Equip. & Services
AVERY DENNISON	2671	Office Equip. & Supplies	NATL OILWELL VAR	3533	Oil Well Equip. & Services
DELUXE CORP	2782	Office Equip. & Supplies	DRIL-QUIP	3533	Oil Well Equip. & Services
PITNEY-BOWES	3579	Office Equip. & Supplies	MAGELLAN M PN LP	4610	Oil Well Equip. & Services
APACHE	1311	Oil Producers	NOW INC	3533	Oil Well Equip. & Services
NOBLE ENERGY	1311	Oil Producers	CAMPBELL SOUP	2032	Packaged Food
RANGE RESOURCES	1311	Oil Producers	CONAGRA BRANDS	2038	Packaged Food
CONTL RESOURCES	1311	Oil Producers	GEN MILLS	2043	Packaged Food
EOG RESOURCES	1311	Oil Producers	KELLOGG	2043	Packaged Food
CABOT OIL + GAS	1311	Oil Producers	MCCORMICK + CO	2099	Packaged Food
SM ENERGY	1311	Oil Producers	SMUCKER J M	2033	Packaged Food
CHESAPEAKE ENRGY	1311	Oil Producers	SPECTRUM BRANDS	3639	Packaged Food
CALLON PETROLEUM	1311	Oil Producers	TREEHOUSE FOODS	2035	Packaged Food
PIONEER NAT RES	1311	Oil Producers	POST HOLDINGS	2043	Packaged Food
ENTERPRISE PROD	1311	Oil Producers	INTL PAPER	2621	Paper
CNX RESOURCES	1311	Oil Producers	DOMTAR CORP	2621	Paper
DEVON ENERGY	1311	Oil Producers	WESTROCK	2653	Paper
QEP RESOURCES	1311	Oil Producers	GREIF INC A	2657	Paper Prod. & Containers
CIMAREX ENERGY	1311	Oil Producers	PACKAGING CORP	2650	Paper Prod. & Containers
WHITING PETROLEU	1311	Oil Producers			

CLASSIFICATION BY INDUSTRY

Company	SIC	Industry	Company	SIC	Industry
SONOCO PRODUCTS	2631	Paper Prod. & Containers	PS BUSINESS PARK	6798	Real Estate Invest. Trusts
SEALED AIR	3081	Paper Prod. & Containers	NATL HEALTH INV	6798	Real Estate Invest. Trusts
BERRY GLOBAL GRP	3089	Paper Prod. & Containers	KIMCO REALTY	6798	Real Estate Invest. Trusts
GRAPHIC PACKAG	2657	Paper Prod. & Containers	OMEGA HEALTHCARE	6798	Real Estate Invest. Trusts
VERITIV	5110	Paper Prod. & Containers	TAUBMAN CENTERS	6798	Real Estate Invest. Trusts
WATSCO	5070	Plumbing, Heating, & AC	SITE CENTERS	6798	Real Estate Invest. Trusts
LENNOX INTL	3585	Plumbing, Heating, & AC	EQUITY LIFESTYLE	6798	Real Estate Invest. Trusts
DONALDSON CO	3564	Pollution Control Equip.	VORNADO REALTY	6798	Real Estate Invest. Trusts
S&P GLOBAL	2731	Publishing	TANGER FACTORY	6798	Real Estate Invest. Trusts
MEREDITH	2721	Publishing	HEALTHCARE RLTY	6798	Real Estate Invest. Trusts
NEW YORK TIMES	2711	Publishing	EQUITY RESIDENTL	6798	Real Estate Invest. Trusts
PLANTRONICS	3651	Radio/TV & Electronics	CAMDEN PROPERTY	6798	Real Estate Invest. Trusts
TRINITY INDUST	3743	Railroad Equipment	MACERICH CO	6798	Real Estate Invest. Trusts
WABTEC	3743	Railroad Equipment	SUN COMMUNITIES	6798	Real Estate Invest. Trusts
KANSAS CITY SO	4011	Railroads	MID-AMER APARTMT	6798	Real Estate Invest. Trusts
UNION PACIFIC	4011	Railroads	AVALONBAY COMM	6798	Real Estate Invest. Trusts
NORFOLK SOUTHERN	4011	Railroads	ESSEX PROPERTY	6798	Real Estate Invest. Trusts
GENESEE + WYOMNG	4011	Railroads	HIGHWOODS PROP	6798	Real Estate Invest. Trusts
FEDERAL RLTY INV	6798	Real Estate Invest. Trusts	LIBERTY PPTY TR	6798	Real Estate Invest. Trusts
RAYONIER	6798	Real Estate Invest. Trusts	FIRST IND RLTY	6798	Real Estate Invest. Trusts
UDR	6798	Real Estate Invest. Trusts	APT INV AND MGMT	6798	Real Estate Invest. Trusts
WEYERHAEUSER	2411	Real Estate Invest. Trusts	GEO GROUP	8744	Real Estate Invest. Trusts
REALTY INCOME	6798	Real Estate Invest. Trusts	MACK-CALI REALTY	6798	Real Estate Invest. Trusts
VENTAS	6798	Real Estate Invest. Trusts	LIFE STORAGE	6798	Real Estate Invest. Trusts
NATL RETAIL PROP	6798	Real Estate Invest. Trusts	IRON MOUNTAIN	6798	Real Estate Invest. Trusts
HCP	6798	Real Estate Invest. Trusts	W P CAREY	6500	Real Estate Invest. Trusts
WELLTOWER	6798	Real Estate Invest. Trusts	KILROY REALTY	6798	Real Estate Invest. Trusts
DUKE REALTY	6798	Real Estate Invest. Trusts	URSTADT BIDDLE	6798	Real Estate Invest. Trusts
BRANDYWINE RLTY	6798	Real Estate Invest. Trusts	ALEXANDRIA RE EQ	6798	Real Estate Invest. Trusts
UNIV HEALTH RLTY	6798	Real Estate Invest. Trusts	BOSTON PROPERTIE	6798	Real Estate Invest. Trusts
EQUITY COMMONWEA	6798	Real Estate Invest. Trusts	S L GREEN	6512	Real Estate Invest. Trusts
WEINGARTEN RLTY	6798	Real Estate Invest. Trusts			
CORP OFFICE PROP	6798	Real Estate Invest. Trusts			

CLASSIFICATION BY INDUSTRY

Company	SIC	Industry	Company	SIC	Industry
PIEDMONT OFFICE	6512	Real Estate Invest. Trusts	OUTFRONT MEDIA	7311	Real Estate Invest. Trusts
ANNALY CAPITAL	6189	Real Estate Invest. Trusts	BRIXMOR PROPERTY	6798	Real Estate Invest. Trusts
EPR PROPERTIES	6798	Real Estate Invest. Trusts	PARAMOUNT GROUP	6798	Real Estate Invest. Trusts
PROLOGIS	6798	Real Estate Invest. Trusts	URBAN EDGE PROP	6500	Real Estate Invest. Trusts
CROWN CASTLE INT	6798	Real Estate Invest. Trusts	PARK HOTELS & RE	7011	Real Estate Invest. Trusts
AMER TOWER REIT	6798	Real Estate Invest. Trusts	INVITATION HOMES	6519	Real Estate Invest. Trusts
MFA FINANCIAL	6798	Real Estate Invest. Trusts	JBG SMITH PROPER	6798	Real Estate Invest. Trusts
SIMON PROPERTY	6798	Real Estate Invest. Trusts	SIX FLAGS ENT	7990	Recreation
HOST HOTELS	7011	Real Estate Invest. Trusts	VAIL RESORTS	7011	Recreation
CORECIVIC	8744	Real Estate Invest. Trusts	CARNIVAL	4489	Recreation
RETAIL PROPERT	6798	Real Estate Invest. Trusts	ROYAL CARIBBEAN	4489	Recreation
COLUMBIA PROPERT	6798	Real Estate Invest. Trusts	WORLD WRESTLING	7900	Recreation
AMER CAMPUS	6798	Real Estate Invest. Trusts	LIVE NATION ENT	7929	Recreation
MEDICAL PROP	6798	Real Estate Invest. Trusts	CINEMARK HLDINGS	7830	Recreation
EXTRA SPACE STOR	6798	Real Estate Invest. Trusts	PLANET FITNESS	7997	Recreation
DIGITAL REALTY	6798	Real Estate Invest. Trusts	BRUNSWICK	3519	Recreation Products
CUBESMART	6798	Real Estate Invest. Trusts	POLARIS	5599	Recreation Products
SPIRIT REALTY	6798	Real Estate Invest. Trusts	MCDONALDS	5812	Restaurants & Fast Food
HEALTHCARE TRUST	6798	Real Estate Invest. Trusts	BRINKER INTL	5812	Restaurants & Fast Food
DOUGLAS EMMETT	6798	Real Estate Invest. Trusts	DARDEN RESTAURNT	5812	Restaurants & Fast Food
CHIMERA INVEST	6798	Real Estate Invest. Trusts	YUM! BRANDS	5812	Restaurants & Fast Food
APPLE HOSPITALIT	6798	Real Estate Invest. Trusts	CHIPOTLE MEX GRL	5810	Restaurants & Fast Food
STARWOOD PROPERT	6798	Real Estate Invest. Trusts	DOMINO'S PIZZA	5140	Restaurants & Fast Food
HUDSON PACIFIC	6531	Real Estate Invest. Trusts	YUM CHINA	5812	Restaurants & Fast Food
CORESITE REALTY	6798	Real Estate Invest. Trusts	WEBSTER FINL CRP	6035	Savings & Loans
VEREIT	6798	Real Estate Invest. Trusts	NEW YORK COMM BC	6036	Savings & Loans
STORE CAPITAL	6798	Real Estate Invest. Trusts	SCHWAB CHARLES	6211	Securities Brokerage
EMPIRE STATE REA	6798	Real Estate Invest. Trusts	LEGG MASON	6211	Securities Brokerage
ALEX & BALDWIN	6798	Real Estate Invest. Trusts	RAYMOND JAMES	6211	Securities Brokerage
NEW RESIDENTIAL	6798	Real Estate Invest. Trusts	MORGAN STANLEY	6211	Securities Brokerage
AMER HOMES 4 REN	6798	Real Estate Invest. Trusts	INTERCONTEXCH	6200	Securities Brokerage
			NIKE B	3021	Shoes
			DECKERS OUTDOOR	3021	Shoes
			SKECHERS USA	5130	Shoes

CLASSIFICATION BY INDUSTRY

Company	SIC	Industry	Company	SIC	Industry
CLOROX	2842	Soap & Household Prod.	GAMESTOP	5734	Specialty Retailers
COLGATE-PALMOLIV	2844	Soap & Household Prod.	SALLY BEAUTY HLD	5990	Specialty Retailers
KIMBERLY-CLARK	2621	Soap & Household Prod.	KAR AUCTION SVCS	5500	Specialty Retailers
PROCTER & GAMBLE	2834	Soap & Household Prod.	MURPHY USA	5500	Specialty Retailers
CHURCH + DWIGHT	2842	Soap & Household Prod.	BURLINGTON STORE	5311	Specialty Retailers
TUPPERWARE BRAND	3089	Soap & Household Prod.	WAYFAIR	5961	Specialty Retailers
EDGEWELL PERSONA	2844	Soap & Household Prod.	CARVANA	5500	Specialty Retailers
ENERGIZER	3690	Soap & Household Prod.	CARPENTER TECH	3312	Steel
COCA-COLA	2086	Soft Drinks	COMMERCIAL METAL	5051	Steel
KEURIG DR PEPPER	2080	Soft Drinks	NUCOR	3312	Steel
GAP	5651	Specialty Retailers	WORTHINGTON IND	3312	Steel
LOWES COMPANIES	5722	Specialty Retailers	AK STEEL	3312	Steel
TIFFANY	5944	Specialty Retailers	ALLEGHENY TECH	3674	Steel
TJX	5651	Specialty Retailers	U S STEEL CORP	3312	Steel
AUTONATION	5511	Specialty Retailers	CENTURYLINK	4813	Telecommunications
HOME DEPOT	5251	Specialty Retailers	SPRINT	4813	Telecommunications
L BRANDS	5621	Specialty Retailers	VERIZON COMMUNIC	4813	Telecommunications
AARONS	7359	Specialty Retailers	AT&T INC	4899	Telecommunications
WILLIAMS-SONOMA	5719	Specialty Retailers	U S CELLULAR	4812	Telecommunications
BEST BUY	5731	Specialty Retailers	TELEPHONE + DATA	4812	Telecommunications
SIGNET JEWELERS	5944	Specialty Retailers	ZAYO GROUP	3669	Telecommunications
FOOT LOCKER	5331	Specialty Retailers	CABLE ONE	4841	Telecommunications
AUTOZONE	5531	Specialty Retailers	COOPER TIRE	3011	Tire & Rubber
AMER EAGLE OUTF	5651	Specialty Retailers	VECTOR GROUP	2111	Tobacco
PENSKE AUTO GRP	5531	Specialty Retailers	UNIVERSAL CORP	5159	Tobacco
LITHIA MOTORS	5511	Specialty Retailers	ALTRIA GROUP	2111	Tobacco
GROUP 1 AUTOMOTI	5511	Specialty Retailers	PHILIP MORRIS	2111	Tobacco
SONIC AUTOMOTIVE	5511	Specialty Retailers	XPO LOGISTICS	4700	Trucking
DICKS SPORTING	5940	Specialty Retailers	SYSCO	5142	Vending & Food Services
ASBURY AUTOMOTIV	5500	Specialty Retailers	ARAMARK	5812	Vending & Food Services
ADV AUTO PARTS	5531	Specialty Retailers	PERFORMANCE FOOD	5141	Vending & Food Services
CARMAX	5731	Specialty Retailers	US FOODS	5140	Vending & Food Services

DOW JONES INDUSTRIAL AVERAGE

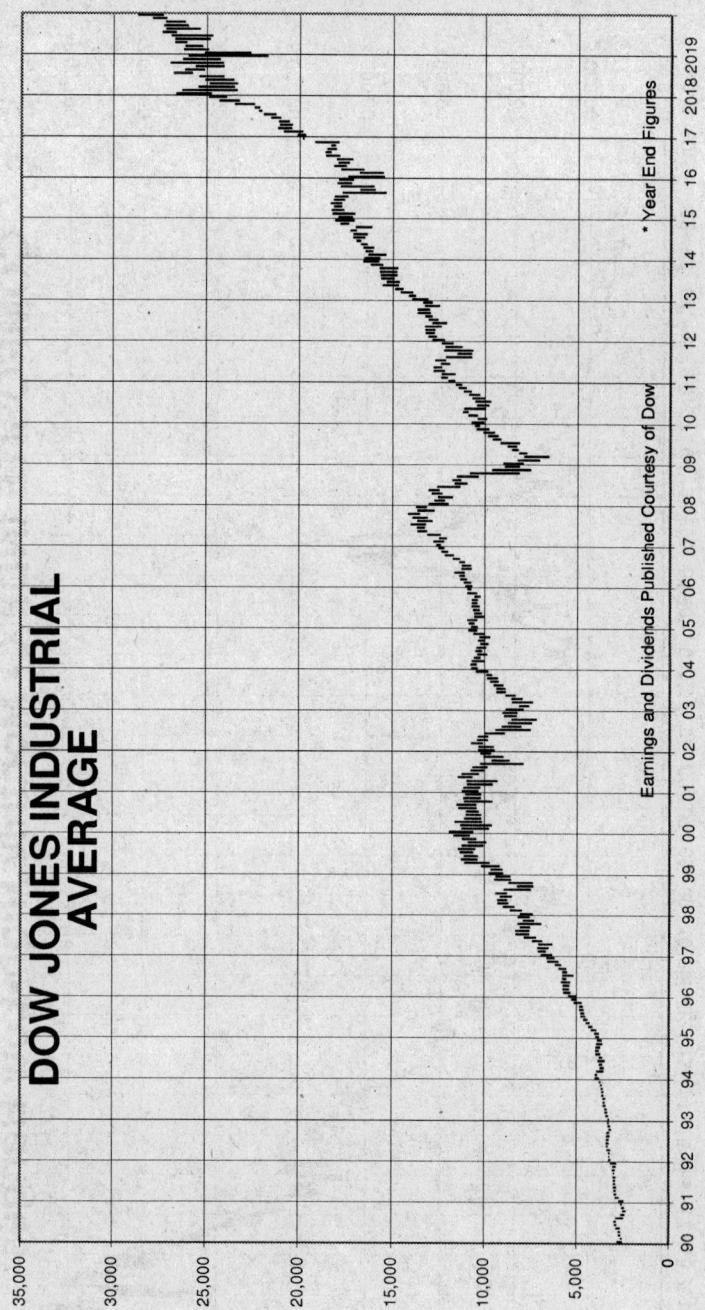

Earnings and Dividends Published Courtesy of Dow   * Year End Figures

27a

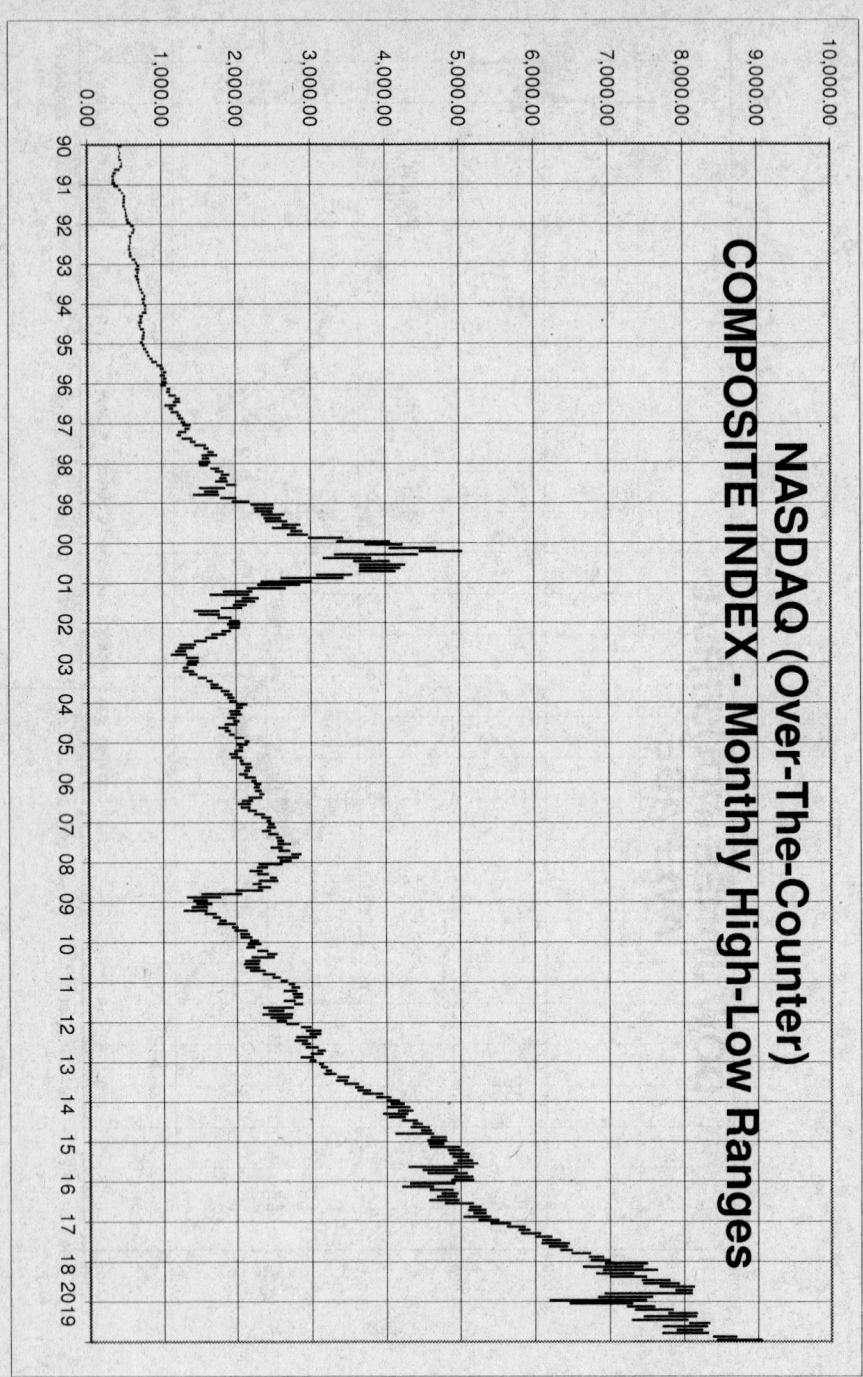

NASDAQ (Over-The-Counter)
COMPOSITE INDEX - Monthly High-Low Ranges

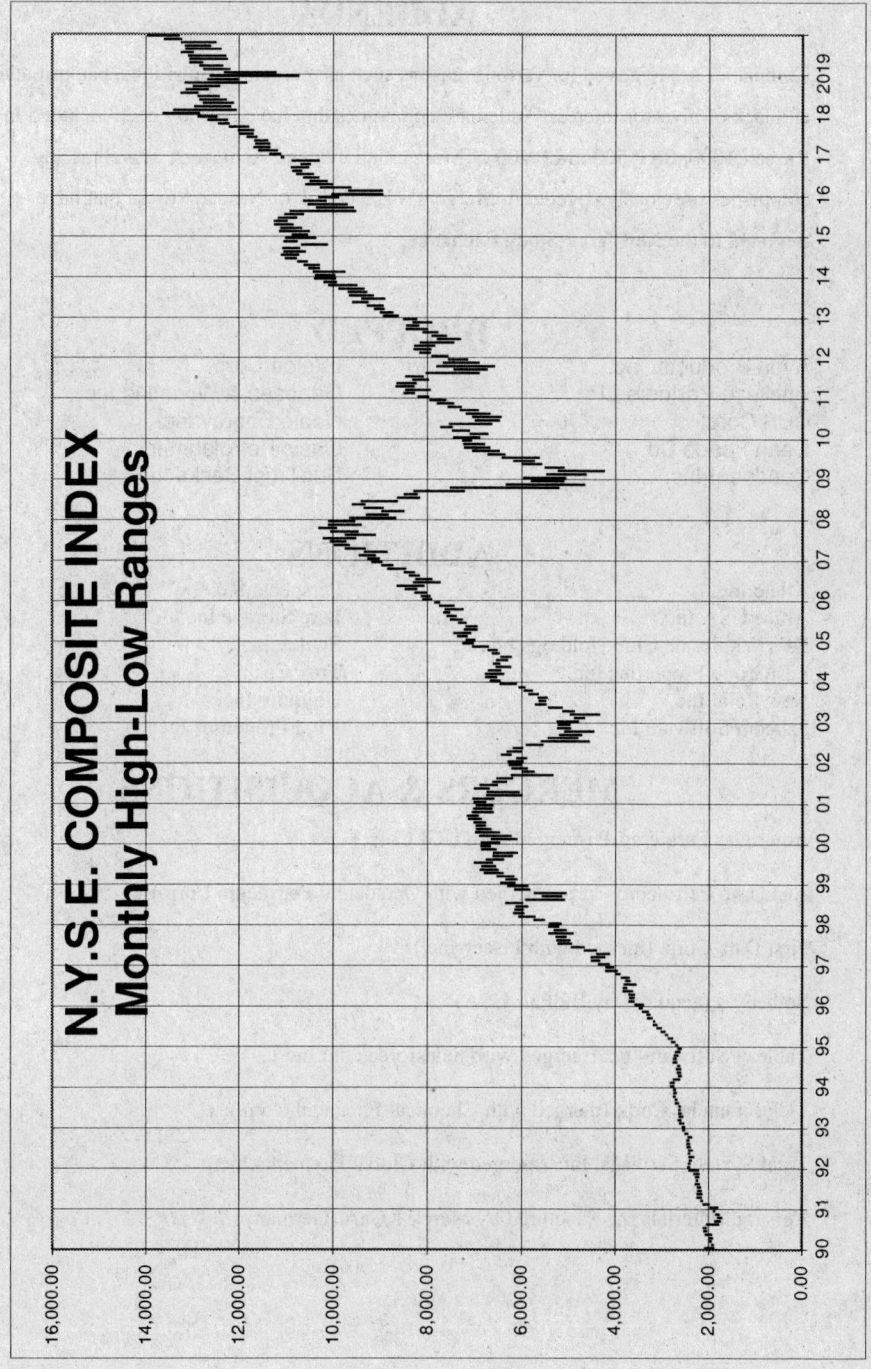

N.Y.S.E. COMPOSITE INDEX
Monthly High-Low Ranges

ADDENDA

Companies are removed for various reasons such as mergers, acquisitions, bankruptcies and lack of investor interest. Added are companies that have recently been included in the Russell 1000, S&P 500, S&P 400 or Mergent's Dividend Achievers, as well as any companies previously covered in Mergent's Handbook of Nasdaq Stocks that have migrated to the New York Stock Exchange.

DROPPED

Avon Products, Inc.
Buckeye Partners LP
CBS Corp
Dean Foods Co
Conduent Inc.

Exelon Corp.
Genesee & Wyoming Inc.
Noble Energy Inc.
Oasis Petroleum Inc.
SunTrust Banks Inc.

ADDITIONS

Allete Inc.
Altice USA Inc.
BJ's Wholesale Club Holdings Inc.
EastGroup Properties Inc.
New Relic Inc.
Paycom Software Inc.

Perspecta Inc.
Pure Storage Inc.
Switch Inc.
Trex Co.
Ubiquity Inc.
VICI Properties Inc.

MERGERS & ACQUISITIONS

AmeriGas Partners LP (merged with UGI Corp.)

Anadarko Petroleum Corp. (merged with Occidental Petroleum Corp.)

First Data Corp. (merged with Fiserv Inc.)

Sotheby's (acquired by BidFair USA)

Tableau Software Inc. (merged with Salesforce.com Inc.)

TCF Financial Corp. (merged with Chemical Financial Corp.)

Total System Services, Inc. (merged with Global Payments Inc.)

Versum Materials Inc. (acquired by Merck KGaA (Germany)

ADDENDA
RECENT DIVIDEND INCREASES

Company	Amount	Frequency	Date	Company	Amount	Frequency	Date
Aaron's Inc	0.04	Q	12/18/2019	Group 1 Automotive, Inc.	0.29	Q	11/29/2019
ADT Inc (DE)	0.70	Q	12/12/2019	Healthcare Trust Of America Inc	0.32	Q	10/2/2019
Agilent Technologies, Inc.	0.18	Q	12/30/2019	Hewlett Packard Enterprise Co	0.12	Q	12/10/2019
Air Lease Corp	0.15	Q	12/19/2019	Hillenbrand Inc	0.21	Q	12/16/2019
Alexandria Real Estate Equities Inc	1.03	Q	12/30/2019	HollyFrontier Corp	0.35	Q	11/26/2019
Ameren Corp	0.50	Q	12/10/2019	Honeywell International Inc	0.90	Q	11/14/2019
American Electric Power Co Inc	0.70	Q	11/7/2019	Horton (DR) Inc	0.18	Q	11/26/2019
American Equity Investment Life Holding	0.30	Q	12/2/2019	Host Hotels & Resorts Inc	0.20	Q	12/30/2019
American Express Co.	0.43	Q	10/3/2019	HP Inc	0.18	Q	12/10/2019
American Financial Group Inc	1.80	Q	11/14/2019	Hubbell Inc.	0.91	Q	11/27/2019
American Tower Corp (New)	1.01	Q	12/26/2019	Huntington Ingalls Industries, Inc.	1.03	Q	11/27/2019
Armstrong World Industries Inc	0.20	Q	11/6/2019	Idacorp Inc	0.67	Q	11/4/2019
Associated Banc-Corp	0.18	Q	11/29/2019	International Paper Co	0.51	Q	11/14/2019
Assurant Inc	0.63	Q	11/22/2019	Iron Mountain Inc (New)	0.62	Q	12/13/2019
Atmos Energy Corp.	0.58	Q	11/22/2019	JPMorgan Chase & Co	0.90	Q	10/3/2019
Bank of Hawaii Corp	0.67	Q	11/27/2019	Kansas City Southern	0.40	Q	12/30/2019
Becton, Dickinson & Co	0.79	Q	12/9/2019	Kemper Corp (DE)	0.28	Q	11/15/2019
Black Hills Corporation	0.54	Q	11/15/2019	Lauder (Estee) Cos., Inc. (The)	0.48	Q	11/27/2019
Booz Allen Hamilton Holding Corp.	0.27	Q	11/13/2019	Lockheed Martin Corp	2.40	Q	11/29/2019
Boston Properties Inc	0.98	Q	12/30/2019	M & T Bank Corp	1.10	Q	11/29/2019
Brady Corp	0.22	Q	10/9/2019	Magellan Midstream Partners LP	1.02	Q	11/6/2019
Brown & Brown Inc	0.09	Q	11/7/2019	Marriott Vacations Worldwide Corp.	0.54	Q	12/20/2019
Brown-Forman Corp	0.17	Q	12/4/2019	Masco Corp.	0.14	Q	10/10/2019
Brunswick Corp.	0.24	Q	11/18/2019	MAXIMUS Inc.	0.28	Q	11/14/2019
Cabot Oil & Gas Corp.	0.10	Q	11/5/2019	McCormick & Co Inc	0.62	Q	12/30/2019
Columbia Property Trust Inc	0.21	Q	12/13/2019	McDonald's Corp	1.25	Q	11/29/2019
ConocoPhillips	0.42	Q	10/16/2019	MDU Resources Group Inc	0.21	Q	12/11/2019
Crown Castle International Corp (New)	1.20	Q	12/12/2019	Merck & Co Inc	0.61	Q	12/13/2019
Delek US Holdings Inc (New)	0.30	Q	11/15/2019	Mercury General Corp.	0.63	Q	12/11/2019
Dolby Laboratories Inc	0.22	Q	11/25/2019	Motorola Solutions Inc	0.64	Q	12/12/2019
Douglas Emmett Inc	0.28	Q	12/30/2019	NIKE Inc	0.25	Q	11/29/2019
DTE Energy Co	1.01	Q	12/13/2019	Northwest Natural Holding Co	0.48	Q	10/30/2019
Duke Realty Corp	0.24	Q	11/13/2019	Nucor Corp.	0.40	Q	12/30/2019
Eastman Chemical Co	0.66	Q	12/13/2019	OGE Energy Corp.	0.39	Q	10/9/2019
Eaton Vance Corp	0.38	Q	10/30/2019	Omega Healthcare Investors, Inc.	0.67	Q	10/30/2019
Ecolab Inc	0.47	Q	12/16/2019	ONEOK Inc	0.92	Q	11/1/2019
Edison International	0.64	Q	12/30/2019	Oshkosh Corp (New)	0.30	Q	11/15/2019
Emerson Electric Co.	0.50	Q	11/14/2019	Park Hotels & Resorts Inc	0.55	Q	12/30/2019
Entergy Corp	0.93	Q	11/6/2019	Penske Automotive Group Inc	0.41	Q	11/7/2019
Enterprise Products Partners L.P.	0.44	Q	10/30/2019	Pinnacle West Capital Corp	0.78	Q	11/1/2019
Equity Commonwealth	3.50	Q	10/4/2019	PolyOne Corp.	0.20	Q	12/12/2019
Everest Re Group Ltd	1.55	Q	12/3/2019	Prosperity Bancshares Inc.	0.46	Q	12/13/2019
Fidelity National Financial Inc	0.33	Q	12/16/2019	PulteGroup Inc	0.12	Q	12/17/2019
FMC Corp.	0.44	Q	12/30/2019	RLI Corp	1.00	Q	11/27/2019
Franklin Resources Inc	0.27	Q	12/30/2019	Rockwell Automation, Inc.	1.02	Q	11/8/2019
Global Partners LP	0.52	Q	11/7/2019	Rollins, Inc.	0.11	Q	11/7/2019
Global Payments Inc	0.20	Q	12/12/2019	RPM International Inc (DE)	0.36	Q	10/11/2019
Gorman-Rupp Company (The)	0.15	Q	11/14/2019	Sensient Technologies Corp.	0.39	Q	11/1/2019

ADDENDA

RECENT DIVIDEND DECREASES

Company	Amount	Frequency	Date
Accenture plc	0.80	Q	10/16/2019
Berkley (WR) Corp	0.11	Q	11/21/2019
Fluor Corp.	0.10	Q	12/3/2019
Hanover Insurance Group Inc	0.65	Q	12/13/2019
Nielsen Holdings PLC	0.06	Q	11/20/2019
OneMain Holdings Inc	0.25	Q	11/25/2019

RECENT AND PENDING NAME CHANGES

OLD NAME	NEW NAME
BB&T	Trust Financial Corp.
HCP Inc.	Healthpeak Properties Inc.
Molson Coors Brewing Co	Molson Coors Beverage Co.
Owens-Illinois, Inc.	O-I Glass Inc.
Newmont Goldcorp Corp	Newmont Corp.

RECENT DIVIDEND STOCK CHANGES

Name	Change	EX	Record	Payable
Equity Lifestyle Properties Inc	100%	10/16/2019	10/1/2019	10/15/2019
Superior Energy Services	1-for 10	12/20/2019	. . . .	. . . .

The 2019 Dividend Achievers

Companies listed below qualified for the 2019-2020 Winter Edition of Mergent's Dividend Achievers
Also shown are total numbers of consecutive years of dividend growth.

Company Name	Years of Growth	Company Name	Years of Growth
3M Co	58	Donaldson Co. Inc.	21
Aaron's, Inc.	13	Dover Corp	61
Abbott Laboratories	43	Duke Energy Corp	12
ABM Industries, Inc.	52	Eaton Vance Corp	35
AFLAC Inc.	34	Ecolab, Inc.	24
Air Products & Chemicals, Inc.	34	Edison International	12
Albemarle Corp.	22	Emerson Electric Co.	60
Altria Group Inc	51	Energy Transfer LP	11
American Equity Investment Life Holding Co	13	Enterprise Products Partners L.P.	18
American Financial Group Inc	11	Equity Lifestyle Properties Inc	12
American States Water Co.	63	Erie Indemnity Co.	21
Ameriprise Financial Inc	11	Essex Property Trust, Inc.	22
AmerisourceBergen Corp.	12	Evercore Inc.	10
Amtrust Financial	10	Eversource Energy	17
Analog Devices, Inc.	13	Exxon Mobil Corp.	34
AptarGroup Inc.	23	FactSet Research Systems Inc.	17
Aqua America Inc	25	Federal Realty Investment Trust (MD)	49
Archer Daniels Midland Co.	42	FedEx Corp	13
Assurant Inc	12	Flowers Foods, Inc.	13
AT&T Inc	32	Franklin Resources, Inc.	27
Atlantic Tele-Network, Inc.	17	Fuller (H.B.) Company	49
Atmos Energy Corp.	29	General Dynamics Corp.	25
Atrion Corp.	13	General Mills, Inc.	13
Automatic Data Processing Inc.	41	Genuine Parts Co.	60
Badger Meter, Inc.	24	Globe Life Inc.	11
Becton, Dickinson and Co.	44	Gorman-Rupp Co. (The)	44
Bemis Co Inc	33	Graco Inc.	17
Berkley (W. R.) Corp.	15	Grainger (W.W.) Inc.	45
Best Buy Inc	13	Hanover Insurance Group Inc	11
Black Hills Corporation	45	Hasbro, Inc.	13
Brady Corp.	32	Helmerich & Payne, Inc.	40
Brown & Brown, Inc.	23	Hillenbrand Inc.	10
Brown-Forman Corp.	32	Holly Energy Partners LP	12
California Water Service Group (DE)	49	Hormel Foods Corp.	50
Cardinal Health, Inc.	20	Illinois Tool Works, Inc.	54
Carlisle Companies Inc.	40	International Business Machines Corp.	21
Caterpillar Inc.	23	International Flavors & Fragrances Inc.	14
CenterPoint Energy, Inc	11	ITT Corporation	14
Chemed Corp	10	Johnson & Johnson	52
Chesapeake Utilities Corp.	13	Kellogg Co	12
Chevron Corporation	29	Kimberly-Clark Corp.	42
Church & Dwight Co., Inc.	20	Kroger Co	10
Clorox Co.	40	L3Harris Tecnologies	17
Coca-Cola Co (The)	54	Leggett & Platt, Inc.	45
Colgate-Palmolive Co.	54	Lindsay Corp	14
Community Bank System, Inc.	25	Lockheed Martin Corp.	14
Compass Minerals International Inc	12	Lowe's Companies Inc	55
Consolidated Edison, Inc.	42	Magellan Midstream Partners LP	15
CSX Corp.	12	McCormick & Co., Inc.	30
Cullen/Frost Bankers, Inc.	23	McDonald's Corp	40
Cummins, Inc.	11	MDU Resources Group Inc.	26
CVS Health Corporation	13	Mercury General Corp.	30
Digital Realty Trust, Inc.	12	Meredith Corp.	23
Dominion Energy	13		

The 2019 Dividend Achievers (continued)

Companies listed below qualified for the 2019-2020 WinterEdition of Mergent's Dividend Achievers
Also shown are total numbers of consecutive years of dividend growth.

Company Name	Years of Growth	Company Name	Years of Growth
MSA Safety Inc	46	South Jersey Industries, Inc.	17
MSC Industrial Direct Co., Inc.	13	Southern Company (The)	15
Nacco Industries	10	Southwest Gas Holdings	10
National Fuel Gas Co. (NJ)	45	Spire Inc.	13
National Health Investors, Inc.	14	Stanley Black & Decker, Inc.	49
National Healthcare Corp.	11	Stepan Co.	49
National Retail Properties Inc	27	Stryker Corp.	24
New Jersey Resources Corp	21	Sunoco Logistics Partners L.P.	14
Newmarket Corp	10	Sysco Corp.	40
NextEra Energy Inc	21	Tanger Factory Outlet Centers, Inc.	23
NIKE, Inc	15	Target Corp	45
Northrop Grumman Corp	13	TC PipeLines, LP	17
Northwest Natural Gas Co.	61	Telephone & Data Systems, Inc.	42
Northwest Natural Holding Co.	62	Tennant Co.	44
Northwestern Corp.	11	Texas Instruments Inc.	13
NU Skin Enterprises, Inc.	15	The Gap, Inc.	12
Nucor Corp.	44	Tiffany & Co.	14
Occidental Petroleum Corp	14	TJX Companies, Inc.	20
OGE Energy	10	Tompkins Financial Corp	20
Old Republic International Corp.	35	Tootsie Roll Industries Inc	53
Omega Healthcare Investors, Inc.	14	Toro Co. (The)	13
Oneok Inc.	14	TransMontaigne Partners L.P.	11
Owens & Minor, Inc.	19	Travelers Companies Inc (The)	11
Polaris Inc.	21	UGI Corp.	29
Portland General Electric	10	Union Pacific	10
PPG Industries, Inc.	45	United Bankshares, Inc.	35
PPL Corp	17	United Technologies Corp.	23
Procter & Gamble Co.	63	Universal Corp.	46
Prosperity Bancshares Inc.	17	Universal Health Realty Income Trust	29
Quaker Chemical Corp	10	Urstadt Biddle Properties Inc	18
Raytheon Co.	12	Vector Group Ltd	18
Realty Income Corp.	22	Verizon Communications Inc	12
Regal Beloit Corp	12	VF Corp.	44
Republic Services, Inc.	13	W.P. Carey Inc	18
RLI Corp.	40	Walgreens Boots Alliance Inc	41
Robert Half International Inc.	12	Walmart Inc.	41
Rollins, Inc.	14	Waste Management, Inc. (DE)	13
Roper Industries, Inc	24	WEC Energy Group Inc	13
RPM International Inc (DE)	43	Welltower Inc	13
Ryder System, Inc.	12	West Pharmaceutical Services, Inc.	24
Sensient Technologies Corp.	11	Westlake Chemical Corp	12
Sherwin-Williams Co.	37	Westwood Holdings Group, Inc.	14
SJW Corp.	49	Wiley (John) & Sons Inc.	23
Smith (A.O.) Corp	24	Williams Sonoma Inc	10
Smucker (J.M.) Co.	19	Yum! Brands, Inc.	12
Sonoco Products Co.	33		

AARON'S INC

Exchange	Symbol	Price	52Wk Range	Yield	P/E	Div Acheiver
NYS	AAN	$57.11 (12/31/2019)	78.14-42.05	0.28	19.63	15 Years

*7 Year Price Score 132.65 *NYSE Composite Index=100 *12 Month Price Score 99.85

Interim Earnings (Per Share)

Qtr.	Mar	Jun	Sep	Dec
2016	0.68	0.53	0.40	0.30
2017	0.74	0.51	0.35	2.46
2018	0.73	0.54	0.62	0.89
2019	0.82	0.62	0.58	...

Interim Dividends (Per Share)

Amt	Decl	Ex	Rec	Pay
0.035Q	02/21/2019	03/18/2019	03/19/2019	04/05/2019
0.035Q	05/08/2019	06/17/2019	06/18/2019	07/08/2019
0.035Q	08/08/2019	09/18/2019	09/19/2019	10/04/2019
0.04Q	11/05/2019	12/18/2019	12/19/2019	01/06/2020

Indicated Div: $0.16

Valuation Analysis

		Institutional Holding	
Forecast EPS	$3.81	No of Institutions	
(01/15/2020)		422	
Market Cap	$3.8 Billion	Shares	
Book Value	$1.9 Billion	83,826,288	
Price/Book	2.05	% Held	
Price/Sales	0.97	N/A	

Business Summary: Retail - Furniture & Home Furnishings (MIC: 2.1.6 SIC: 5712 NAIC: 442110)

Aaron's is a provider of lease-purchase solutions. Co. is engaged in the sales and lease ownership and specialty retailing of furniture, consumer electronics, home appliances and accessories through its Co.-operated and franchised stores in several states and Canada as well as its e-commerce platform, Aarons.com. Co.'s stores carry brands such as Samsung®, Hewlett-Packard®, LG®, Whirlpool®, Simmons®, Philips® and Ashley®. Co.'s operating segments include Progressive Leasing, a virtual lease-to-own company that provides lease-purchase solutions; Aaron's Business, which provides consumer electronics and accessories; and Dent-A-Med, Inc., which provides a variety of revolving credit products.

Recent Developments: For the quarter ended Sep 30 2019, net income decreased 9.0% to US$39.8 million from US$43.7 million in the year-earlier quarter. Revenues were US$963.8 million, up 1.1% from US$953.1 million the year before. Operating income was US$55.5 million versus US$57.3 million in the prior-year quarter, a decrease of 3.1%. Direct operating expenses declined 23.5% to US$30.7 million from US$40.1 million in the comparable period the year before. Indirect operating expenses increased 2.6% to US$877.7 million from US$855.7 million in the equivalent prior-year period.

Prospects: Our evaluation of Aaron's Inc as of October 4th, 2019 is the result of our systematic analysis on three basic characteristics: earnings strength, relative valuation, and recent stock price movement. The company has managed to produce a neutral trend in earnings per share over the past 5 quarters. Additionally, recent analyst estimates for the company have been unchanged while AAN has posted results that exceeded analysts' expectations. Based on operating earnings yield, the company is undervalued when compared to all of the companies we cover. Share price changes over the past year indicates that AAN will perform well over the near term.

Financial Data

(US$ in Thousands)	9 Mos	6 Mos	3 Mos	12/31/2018	12/31/2017	12/31/2016	12/31/2015	12/31/2014
Earnings Per Share	2.91	2.95	2.87	2.78	4.06	1.91	1.86	1.08
Cash Flow Per Share	5.11	4.94	4.82	5.16	2.25	6.42	2.30	(0.68)
Tang Book Value Per Share	13.90	13.42	12.74	11.89	12.42	9.90	7.59	5.45
Dividends Per Share	0.140	0.135	0.130	0.125	0.113	0.102	0.094	0.086
Dividend Payout %	4.81	4.58	4.53	4.50	2.77	5.37	5.05	7.96
Income Statement								
Total Revenue	2,944,052	1,980,244	1,012,103	3,828,923	3,383,708	3,207,716	3,179,756	2,725,239
EBITDA	1,655,521	1,111,026	601,785	329,390	313,080	292,713	286,274	191,698
Depn & Amortn	1,464,887	975,688	526,622	61,200	54,800	53,600	52,000	53,700
Income Before Taxes	178,792	127,127	70,308	252,204	239,577	218,422	213,120	121,704
Income Taxes	40,263	28,399	14,230	55,994	(52,959)	79,139	77,411	43,471
Net Income	138,529	98,728	56,078	196,210	292,536	139,283	135,709	78,233
Average Shares	68,652	68,793	68,773	70,597	72,121	73,013	73,043	72,723
Balance Sheet								
Current Assets	1,597,353	1,548,197	1,581,821	1,635,430	1,626,078	1,630,070	1,617,652	1,409,286
Total Assets	3,219,620	3,180,198	3,237,966	2,826,692	2,692,264	2,615,736	2,658,875	2,456,844
Current Liabilities	630,415	595,884	609,613	373,732	372,870	360,193	374,326	358,690
Long-Term Obligations	347,107	347,767	408,286	424,752	368,798	497,829	610,450	606,082
Total Liabilities	1,351,965	1,330,640	1,424,458	1,065,984	964,260	1,134,138	1,292,257	1,233,323
Stockholders' Equity	1,867,655	1,849,558	1,813,508	1,760,708	1,728,004	1,481,598	1,366,618	1,223,521
Shares Outstanding	67,150	67,547	67,677	67,184	70,019	71,448	72,600	72,488
Statistical Record								
Return on Assets %	6.77	7.04	6.72	7.11	11.02	5.27	5.31	3.65
Return on Equity %	11.03	11.36	11.21	11.25	18.23	9.75	10.48	6.62
EBITDA Margin %	56.23	56.11	59.46	8.60	9.25	9.13	9.00	7.03
Net Margin %	4.71	4.99	5.54	5.12	8.65	4.34	4.27	2.87
Asset Turnover	1.33	1.35	1.30	1.39	1.27	1.21	1.24	1.27
Current Ratio	2.53	2.60	2.59	4.38	4.36	4.53	4.32	3.93
Debt to Equity	0.19	0.19	0.23	0.24	0.21	0.34	0.45	0.50
Price Range	65.47-39.55	61.59-39.55	55.45-39.33	55.45-37.59	47.54-26.92	33.97-20.33	40.46-21.74	35.90-23.27
P/E Ratio	22.50-13.59	20.88-13.41	19.32-13.70	19.95-13.52	11.71-6.63	17.79-10.64	21.75-11.69	33.24-21.55
Average Yield %	0.26	0.27	0.27	0.27	0.31	0.41	0.29	0.30

Address: 400 Galleria Parkway S.E., Suite 300, Atlanta, GA 30339-3182 Telephone: 678-402-3000	Web Site: www.aarons.com Officers: Ray M. Robinson - Chairman John W. Robinson - President, Chief Executive Officer, Executive Vice President	Auditors: Ernst & Young LLP Investor Contact: 678-402-3116 Transfer Agents: Computershare Investor Services, Canton, MA

1

ABBVIE INC

Exchange	Symbol	Price	52Wk Range	Yield	P/E
NYS	ABBV	$88.54 (12/31/2019)	92.19-62.98	5.33	39.00

*7 Year Price Score 95.15 *NYSE Composite Index=100 *12 Month Price Score 105.72

Interim Earnings (Per Share)

Qtr.	Mar	Jun	Sep	Dec
2016	0.83	0.98	0.97	0.85
2017	1.06	1.19	1.01	0.03
2018	1.74	1.26	1.81	(1.13)
2019	1.65	0.49	1.26	...

Interim Dividends (Per Share)

Amt	Decl	Ex	Rec	Pay
1.07Q	02/21/2019	04/12/2019	04/15/2019	05/15/2019
1.07Q	06/20/2019	07/12/2019	07/15/2019	08/15/2019
1.07Q	09/06/2019	10/11/2019	10/15/2019	11/15/2019
1.18Q	11/01/2019	01/14/2020	01/15/2020	02/14/2020

Indicated Div: $4.72 (Div. Reinv. Plan)

Valuation Analysis

Forecast EPS	$8.93 (01/16/2020)
Market Cap	$130.9 Billion
Book Value	N/A
Price/Book	N/A
Price/Sales	3.98

Institutional Holding

No of Institutions	2508
Shares	1,209,694,464
% Held	65.26

Business Summary: Pharmaceuticals (MIC: 4.1.1 SIC: 2834 NAIC: 325412)

AbbVie is a research-based biopharmaceutical company. Co.'s products are focused on treating conditions such as chronic autoimmune diseases in rheumatology, gastroenterology and dermatology; oncology, including blood cancers; virology, including hepatitis C virus and human immunodeficiency virus; neurological disorders, such as Parkinson's disease; metabolic diseases, including thyroid disease and complications associated with cystic fibrosis; pain associated with endometriosis; as well as other serious health conditions. Co. has medicines in clinical development across immunology, oncology and neuroscience, with additional targeted investment in cystic fibrosis and women's health.

Recent Developments: For the quarter ended Sep 30 2019, net income decreased 31.4% to US$1.88 billion from US$2.75 billion in the year-earlier quarter. Revenues were US$8.48 billion, up 3.0% from US$8.24 billion the year before. Operating income was US$2.62 billion versus US$3.16 billion in the prior-year quarter, a decrease of 17.2%. Direct operating expenses rose 4.6% to US$1.92 billion from US$1.84 billion in the comparable period the year before. Indirect operating expenses increased 21.6% to US$3.94 billion from US$3.24 billion in the equivalent prior-year period.

Prospects: Our evaluation of AbbVie Inc. as of October 4th, 2019 is the result of our systematic analysis on three basic characteristics: earnings strength, relative valuation, and recent stock price movement. The company has managed to produce a neutral trend in earnings per share over the past 5 quarters. However, recent analyst estimates for the company have been raised and ABBV has posted results that exceeded analysts' expectations. Based on operating earnings yield, the company is undervalued when compared to all of the companies we cover. Share price changes over the past year indicates that ABBV will perform very poorly over the near term.

Financial Data

(US$ in Thousands)	9 Mos	6 Mos	3 Mos	12/31/2018	12/31/2017	12/31/2016	12/31/2015	12/31/2014
Earnings Per Share	2.27	2.82	3.59	3.66	3.30	3.63	3.13	1.10
Cash Flow Per Share	9.08	9.06	9.32	8.71	6.24	4.33	4.64	2.23
Dividends Per Share	4.170	4.060	3.950	3.590	2.560	2.280	2.020	1.660
Dividend Payout %	183.70	143.97	110.03	98.09	77.58	62.81	64.54	150.91
Income Statement								
Total Revenue	24,562,000	16,083,000	7,828,000	32,753,000	28,216,000	25,638,000	22,859,000	19,960,000
EBITDA	7,914,000	4,990,000	3,372,000	8,106,000	10,232,000	10,038,000	8,167,000	3,546,000
Depn & Amortn	1,508,000	1,005,000	503,000	1,765,000	1,501,000	1,189,000	836,000	786,000
Income Before Taxes	5,352,000	3,351,000	2,544,000	5,197,000	7,727,000	7,884,000	6,645,000	2,369,000
Income Taxes	271,000	154,000	88,000	(490,000)	2,418,000	1,931,000	1,501,000	595,000
Net Income	5,081,000	3,197,000	2,456,000	5,687,000	5,309,000	5,953,000	5,144,000	1,774,000
Average Shares	1,483,000	1,484,000	1,483,000	1,546,000	1,603,000	1,631,000	1,637,000	1,610,000
Balance Sheet								
Current Assets	20,166,000	15,100,000	14,413,000	16,945,000	21,223,000	16,187,000	16,314,000	16,088,000
Total Assets	59,441,000	57,142,000	56,769,000	59,352,000	70,786,000	66,099,000	53,050,000	27,547,000
Current Liabilities	17,493,000	16,941,000	13,904,000	17,239,000	16,641,000	9,781,000	10,894,000	11,400,000
Long-Term Obligations	33,126,000	31,619,000	35,066,000	35,066,000	30,953,000	36,440,000	29,240,000	10,565,000
Total Liabilities	67,667,000	65,708,000	64,595,000	67,798,000	65,689,000	61,463,000	49,105,000	25,805,000
Stockholders' Equity	(8,226,000)	(8,566,000)	(7,826,000)	(8,446,000)	5,097,000	4,636,000	3,945,000	1,742,000
Shares Outstanding	1,478,782	1,478,370	1,578,237	1,478,824	1,592,131	1,592,512	1,609,892	1,591,389
Statistical Record								
Return on Assets %	5.18	6.93	8.50	8.74	7.76	9.97	12.76	6.25
Return on Equity %	...	...	...	...	109.09	138.37	180.90	56.91
EBITDA Margin %	32.22	31.03	43.08	24.75	36.26	39.15	35.73	17.77
Net Margin %	20.69	19.88	31.37	17.36	18.82	23.22	22.50	8.89
Asset Turnover	0.52	0.55	0.52	0.50	0.41	0.43	0.57	0.70
Current Ratio	1.15	0.89	1.04	0.98	1.28	1.65	1.50	1.41
Debt to Equity	...	...	...	...	6.07	7.86	7.41	6.06
Price Range	96.01-62.98	98.84-65.70	106.23-77.14	123.21-77.85	98.21-60.00	67.39-51.18	71.23-48.27	69.71-46.46
P/E Ratio	42.30-27.74	35.05-23.30	29.59-21.49	33.66-21.27	29.76-18.18	18.56-14.10	22.76-15.42	63.37-42.24
Average Yield %	5.27	4.73	4.36	3.68	3.41	3.76	3.25	2.99

Address: 1 North Waukegan Road, North Chicago, IL 60064-6400 **Telephone:** 847-932-7900	**Web Site:** www.abbvie.com **Officers:** Richard A. Gonzalez - Chairman, Chief Executive Officer Laura J. Schumacher - Vice-Chairman, Chief Legal Officer, Corporate Secretary, Executive Vice President, General Counsel	**Auditors:** Ernst & Young LLP **Investor Contact:** 847-932-7900 **Transfer Agents:** Computershare Trust Company, N.A., Canton, MA

ABBOTT LABORATORIES

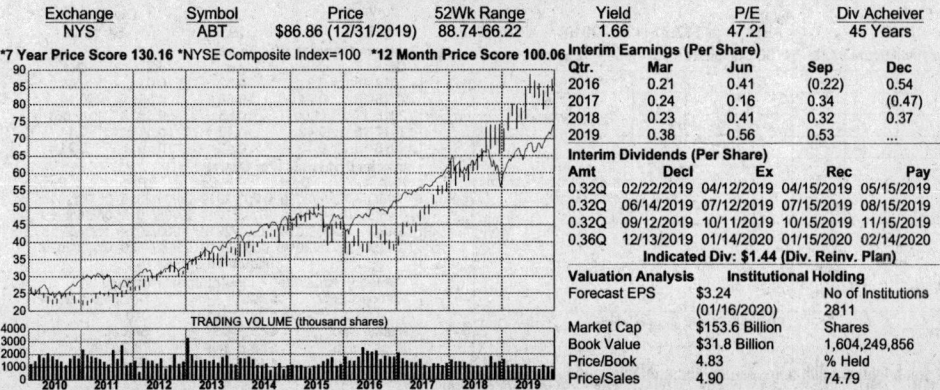

Exchange	Symbol	Price	52Wk Range	Yield	P/E	Div Acheiver
NYS	ABT	$86.86 (12/31/2019)	88.74-66.22	1.66	47.21	45 Years

*7 Year Price Score 130.16 *NYSE Composite Index=100 *12 Month Price Score 100.06

Interim Earnings (Per Share)

Qtr.	Mar	Jun	Sep	Dec
2016	0.21	0.41	(0.22)	0.54
2017	0.24	0.16	0.34	(0.47)
2018	0.23	0.41	0.32	0.37
2019	0.38	0.56	0.53	...

Interim Dividends (Per Share)

Amt	Decl	Ex	Rec	Pay
0.32Q	02/22/2019	04/12/2019	04/15/2019	05/15/2019
0.32Q	06/14/2019	07/12/2019	07/15/2019	08/15/2019
0.32Q	09/12/2019	10/11/2019	10/15/2019	11/15/2019
0.36Q	12/13/2019	01/14/2020	01/15/2020	02/14/2020

Indicated Div: $1.44 (Div. Reinv. Plan)

Valuation Analysis   **Institutional Holding**

Forecast EPS	$3.24	No of Institutions
	(01/16/2020)	2811
Market Cap	$153.6 Billion	Shares
Book Value	$31.8 Billion	1,604,249,856
Price/Book	4.83	% Held
Price/Sales	4.90	74.79

Business Summary: Medical Instruments & Equipment (MIC: 4.3.1 SIC: 2834 NAIC: 325412)

Abbott Laboratories discovers, develops, manufactures and sells of a range of health care products. Co.'s reportable segments are: established pharmaceutical products, which include a range of generic pharmaceuticals; diagnostic products, which include a range of diagnostic systems and tests; nutritional products, which include a range of pediatric and adult nutritional products; and Cardiovascular and neuromodulation products, which include a range of rhythm management, electrophysiology, heart failure, vascular and structural heart devices for the treatment of cardiovascular diseases, as well as neuromodulation devices for the management of chronic pain and movement disorders.

Recent Developments: For the quarter ended Sep 30 2019, income from continuing operations increased 73.9% to US$960.0 million from US$552.0 million in the year-earlier quarter. Net income increased 70.5% to US$960.0 million from US$563.0 million in the year-earlier quarter. Revenues were US$8.08 billion, up 5.5% from US$7.66 billion the year before. Operating income was US$1.20 billion versus US$995.0 million in the prior-year quarter, an increase of 20.4%. Direct operating expenses rose 6.1% to US$3.36 billion from US$3.17 billion in the comparable period the year before. Indirect operating expenses increased 0.7% to US$3.52 billion from US$3.50 billion in the equivalent prior-year period.

Prospects: Our evaluation of Abbott Laboratories as of October 4th, 2019 is the result of our systematic analysis on three basic characteristics: earnings strength, relative valuation, and recent stock price movement. The company has produced a positive trend in earnings per share over the past 5 quarters. However, recent analyst estimates for the company have been unchanged, while ABT has posted results that exceeded analysts' expectations. Based on operating earnings yield, the company is fairly valued when compared to all of the companies we cover. Share price changes over the past year indicates that ABT will perform well over the near term.

Financial Data
(US$ in Thousands)

	9 Mos	6 Mos	3 Mos	12/31/2018	12/31/2017	12/31/2016	12/31/2015	12/31/2014
Earnings Per Share	1.84	1.63	1.48	1.33	0.27	0.94	2.92	1.49
Cash Flow Per Share	3.10	3.23	3.35	3.58	3.20	2.16	1.98	2.42
Tang Book Value Per Share	N.M.	N.M.	N.M.	N.M.	N.M.	5.65	4.08	3.49
Dividends Per Share	1.240	1.200	1.160	1.120	1.060	1.040	0.960	0.880
Dividend Payout %	67.39	73.62	78.38	84.21	392.59	110.64	32.88	59.06
Income Statement								
Total Revenue	23,590,000	15,514,000	7,535,000	30,578,000	27,390,000	20,853,000	20,405,000	20,247,000
EBITDA	5,532,000	3,532,000	1,533,000	6,872,000	6,032,000	3,098,000	4,713,000	4,139,000
Depn & Amortn	2,258,000	1,504,000	753,000	3,278,000	3,021,000	1,353,000	1,472,000	1,548,000
Income Before Taxes	2,837,000	1,734,000	632,000	2,873,000	2,231,000	1,413,000	3,183,000	2,518,000
Income Taxes	199,000	56,000	(40,000)	539,000	1,878,000	350,000	577,000	797,000
Net Income	2,638,000	1,678,000	672,000	2,368,000	477,000	1,400,000	4,423,000	2,284,000
Average Shares	1,784,167	1,781,417	1,776,573	1,770,000	1,749,000	1,483,000	1,506,000	1,527,000
Balance Sheet								
Current Assets	16,119,000	15,195,000	14,409,000	14,632,000	20,147,000	26,776,000	14,155,000	15,261,000
Total Assets	68,539,000	68,427,000	67,610,000	67,173,000	76,250,000	52,666,000	41,247,000	41,275,000
Current Liabilities	10,491,000	9,062,000	9,113,000	9,012,000	8,912,000	6,660,000	9,186,000	10,532,000
Long-Term Obligations	17,639,000	18,982,000	18,845,000	19,359,000	27,210,000	20,681,000	5,871,000	3,408,000
Total Liabilities	36,722,000	36,741,000	36,685,000	36,649,000	45,353,000	32,128,000	20,036,000	19,749,000
Stockholders' Equity	31,817,000	31,686,000	30,925,000	30,524,000	30,897,000	20,538,000	21,211,000	21,526,000
Shares Outstanding	1,768,455	1,767,397	1,764,181	1,755,619	1,743,602	1,472,869	1,472,665	1,508,035
Statistical Record								
Return on Assets %	4.70	4.23	3.79	3.30	0.74	2.97	10.72	5.42
Return on Equity %	10.53	9.30	8.41	7.71	1.85	6.69	20.70	9.78
EBITDA Margin %	23.45	22.77	20.35	22.47	22.02	14.86	23.10	20.44
Net Margin %	11.18	10.82	8.92	7.74	1.74	6.71	21.68	11.28
Asset Turnover	0.45	0.45	0.44	0.43	0.42	0.44	0.49	0.48
Current Ratio	1.54	1.68	1.58	1.62	2.26	4.02	1.54	1.45
Debt to Equity	0.55	0.60	0.61	0.63	0.88	1.01	0.28	0.16
Price Range	88.74-65.56	85.00-60.81	80.06-57.57	74.27-56.27	57.47-39.05	45.29-36.34	51.20-39.06	46.37-35.85
P/E Ratio	48.23-35.63	52.15-37.31	54.09-38.90	55.84-42.31	212.85-144.63	48.18-38.66	17.53-13.38	31.12-24.06
Average Yield %	1.61	1.66	1.71	1.74	2.18	2.57	2.07	2.15

Address: 100 Abbott Park Road, Abbott Park, IL 60064-6400 Telephone: 224-667-6100	Web Site: www.abbott.com Officers: Miles D. White - Executive Chairman, Chairman, Chief Executive Officer Robert B. Ford - President, Chief Executive Officer, Chief Operating Officer, Division Officer	Auditors: Ernst & Young LLP Investor Contact: 847-937-7300 Transfer Agents: Computershare Trust Company, NA, Providence, RI

ABM INDUSTRIES, INC.

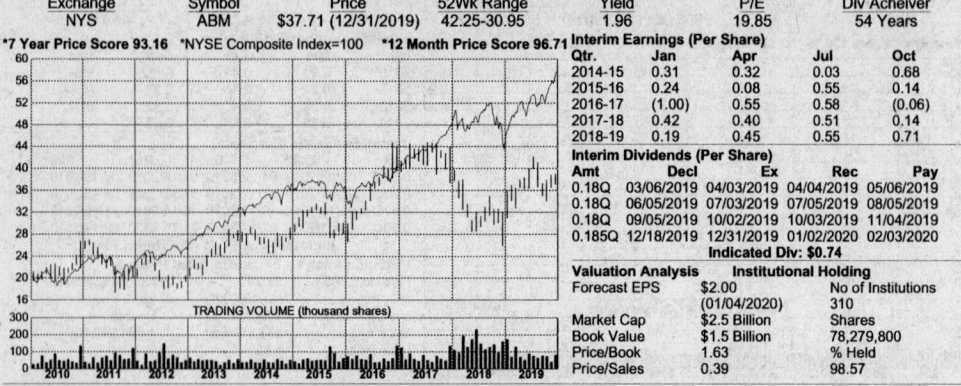

Exchange	Symbol	Price	52Wk Range	Yield	P/E	Div Acheiver
NYS	ABM	$37.71 (12/31/2019)	42.25-30.95	1.96	19.85	54 Years

*7 Year Price Score 93.16 *NYSE Composite Index=100 *12 Month Price Score 96.71

Interim Earnings (Per Share)

Qtr.	Jan	Apr	Jul	Oct
2014-15	0.31	0.32	0.03	0.68
2015-16	0.24	0.08	0.55	0.14
2016-17	(1.00)	0.55	0.58	(0.06)
2017-18	0.42	0.40	0.51	0.14
2018-19	0.19	0.45	0.55	0.71

Interim Dividends (Per Share)

Amt	Decl	Ex	Rec	Pay
0.18Q	03/06/2019	04/03/2019	04/04/2019	05/06/2019
0.18Q	06/05/2019	07/03/2019	07/05/2019	08/05/2019
0.18Q	09/05/2019	10/02/2019	10/03/2019	11/04/2019
0.185Q	12/18/2019	12/31/2019	01/02/2020	02/03/2020

Indicated Div: $0.74

Valuation Analysis

Institutional Holding	
Forecast EPS $2.00 (01/04/2020)	No of Institutions 310
Market Cap $2.5 Billion	Shares
Book Value $1.5 Billion	78,279,800
Price/Book 1.63	% Held
Price/Sales 0.39	98.57

Business Summary: Sanitation Services (MIC: 7.5.3 SIC: 7349 NAIC: 561720)

ABM Industries is a provider of integrated facility solutions. Co.'s segments include: Business and Industry, which encompasses janitorial, facilities engineering, and parking services for commercial real estate properties, sports and entertainment venues, and hospitals and non-acute healthcare facilities; Aviation, which supports airlines and airports with services ranging from parking and janitorial to passenger assistance, catering logistics, air cabin maintenance, and transportation; and Education, which delivers janitorial, custodial, landscaping and grounds, facilities engineering, and parking services for public school districts, private schools, colleges, and universities.

Recent Developments: For the year ended Oct 31 2019, income from continuing operations increased 33.0% to US$127.5 million from US$95.9 million a year earlier. Net income increased 30.3% to US$127.4 million from US$97.8 million in the prior year. Revenues were US$6.50 billion, up 0.9% from US$6.44 billion the year before. Operating income was US$208.3 million versus US$138.6 million in the prior year, an increase of 50.3%. Indirect operating expenses decreased 0.2% to US$6.29 billion from US$6.30 billion in the equivalent prior-year period.

Prospects: Our evaluation of ABM Industries Inc. as of October 4th, 2019 is the result of our systematic analysis on three basic characteristics: earnings strength, relative valuation, and recent stock price movement. The company has managed to produce a neutral trend in earnings per share over the past 5 quarters. However, recent analyst estimates for the company have been reduced while ABM has posted results that exceeded analysts' expectations. Based on operating earnings yield, the company is undervalued when compared to all of the companies we cover. Share price changes over the past year indicates that ABM will perform over the near term.

Financial Data

(US$ in Thousands)	10/31/2019	10/31/2018	10/31/2017	10/31/2016	10/31/2015	10/31/2014	10/31/2013	10/31/2012
Earnings Per Share	1.90	1.47	0.07	1.01	1.33	1.32	1.30	1.14
Cash Flow Per Share	3.94	4.85	0.10	1.48	2.56	2.15	2.47	2.78
Tang Book Value Per Share	N.M.	N.M.	N.M.	N.M.	0.51	N.M.	N.M.	N.M.
Dividends Per Share	0.720	0.700	0.680	0.660	0.640	0.620	0.600	0.580
Dividend Payout %	37.89	47.62	971.43	65.35	48.12	46.97	46.15	50.88
Income Statement								
Total Revenue	6,498,600	6,442,200	5,453,600	5,144,700	4,897,800	5,032,800	4,809,281	4,300,265
EBITDA	315,700	251,100	172,000	112,300	130,600	185,900	179,378	147,117
Depn & Amortn	107,400	112,500	70,100	57,600	57,000	57,300	60,353	50,864
Income Before Taxes	157,200	84,500	82,700	44,300	63,400	117,900	106,133	86,254
Income Taxes	32,700	(8,200)	8,800	(10,400)	18,300	48,800	39,552	29,931
Net Income	127,400	97,800	3,800	57,200	76,300	75,600	72,900	62,582
Average Shares	66,900	66,400	58,300	56,900	57,400	57,100	56,067	54,914
Balance Sheet								
Current Assets	1,275,400	1,171,000	1,235,500	993,700	947,200	927,200	864,632	767,427
Total Assets	3,692,600	3,627,500	3,812,600	2,281,200	2,149,800	2,192,900	2,119,236	1,869,251
Current Liabilities	902,400	792,500	757,800	599,200	568,200	526,400	508,524	473,910
Long-Term Obligations	744,200	902,000	1,161,300	268,300	158,000	319,800	314,870	215,000
Total Liabilities	2,150,600	2,172,900	2,436,900	1,307,200	1,142,300	1,224,100	1,201,729	1,018,853
Stockholders' Equity	1,542,000	1,454,600	1,375,700	974,000	1,007,500	968,800	917,507	850,398
Shares Outstanding	66,571	66,004	65,502	55,599	56,105	55,691	55,477	54,393
Statistical Record								
Return on Assets %	3.48	2.63	0.12	2.57	3.51	3.51	3.66	3.33
Return on Equity %	8.50	6.91	0.32	5.76	7.72	8.02	8.25	7.58
EBITDA Margin %	4.86	3.90	3.15	2.18	2.67	3.69	3.73	3.42
Net Margin %	1.96	1.52	0.07	1.11	1.56	1.50	1.52	1.46
Asset Turnover	1.78	1.73	1.79	2.32	2.26	2.33	2.41	2.29
Current Ratio	1.41	1.48	1.63	1.66	1.67	1.76	1.70	1.62
Debt to Equity	0.48	0.62	0.84	0.28	0.16	0.33	0.34	0.25
Price Range	42.25-25.90	44.01-28.46	44.79-38.22	40.42-26.58	33.80-26.70	29.43-24.57	28.99-18.27	24.50-17.95
P/E Ratio	22.24-13.63	29.94-19.36	639.86-546.00	40.02-26.32	25.41-20.08	22.30-18.61	22.30-14.05	21.49-15.75
Average Yield %	2.00	2.05	1.62	1.97	2.10	2.29	2.59	2.79

Address: One Liberty Plaza, 7th Floor, New York, NY 10006 Telephone: 212-297-0200	Web Site: www.abm.com Officers: Sudhakar Kesavan - Chairman Scott B. Salmirs - President, Chief Executive Officer, Executive Vice President	Auditors: KPMG LLP Investor Contact: 212-297-0200 Transfer Agents: Computershare, Providence, RI

4

ACCENTURE PLC

Exchange	Symbol	Price	52Wk Range	Yield	P/E	Div Acheiver
NYS	ACN	$210.57 (12/31/2019)	212.22-135.79	1.52	28.11	13 Years

*7 Year Price Score 125.12 *NYSE Composite Index=100 *12 Month Price Score 104.35

Interim Earnings (Per Share)

Qtr.	Nov	Feb	May	Aug
2016-17	1.58	1.33	1.05	1.48
2017-18	1.79	1.37	1.60	1.58
2018-19	1.96	1.73	1.93	1.74
2019-20	2.09	...	...	...

Interim Dividends (Per Share)

Amt	Decl	Ex	Rec	Pay
1.46Q	09/27/2018	10/17/2018	10/18/2018	11/15/2018
1.46Q	03/26/2019	04/10/2019	04/11/2019	05/15/2019
0.80Q	09/26/2019	10/16/2019	10/17/2019	11/15/2019
0.80Q	12/19/2019	01/15/2020	01/16/2020	02/14/2020

Indicated Div: $3.20

Valuation Analysis

		Institutional Holding	
Forecast EPS	N/A	No of Institutions	1837
Market Cap	$133.8 Billion	Shares	554,251,648
Book Value	$15.2 Billion	% Held	73.66
Price/Book	8.82		
Price/Sales	3.04		

TRADING VOLUME (thousand shares)

Business Summary: Business Services (MIC: 7.5.2 SIC: 7389 NAIC: 561499)

Accenture is a services company. Co.'s operating groups are: Communications, Media and Technology, which serves communications, media, high tech, software and platform companies; Financial Services, which serves the banking, capital markets and insurance industries; Health and Public Service, which serves healthcare payers and providers, government departments and agencies, public service organizations, educational institutions and non-profit organizations; Products, which serves a set of interconnected consumer-relevant industries such as life sciences; and Resources, which serves the chemicals, energy, forest products, metals and mining, utilities and related industries.

Recent Developments: For the quarter ended Nov 30 2019, net income increased 6.5% to US$1.38 billion from US$1.29 billion in the year-earlier quarter. Revenues were US$11.36 billion, up 7.1% from US$10.61 billion the year before. Operating income was US$1.77 billion versus US$1.63 billion in the prior-year quarter, an increase of 8.5%. Direct operating expenses rose 5.5% to US$7.71 billion from US$7.31 billion in the comparable period the year before. Indirect operating expenses increased 12.7% to US$1.88 billion from US$1.67 billion in the equivalent prior-year period.

Prospects: Our evaluation of Accenture PLC as of October 4th, 2019 is the result of our systematic analysis on three basic characteristics: earnings strength, relative valuation, and recent stock price movement. The company has managed to produce a neutral trend in earnings per share over the past 5 quarters. However, recent analyst estimates for the company have been reduced while ACN has posted results that exceeded analysts' expectations. Based on operating earnings yield, the company is fairly valued when compared to all of the companies we cover. Share price changes over the past year indicates that ACN will perform well over the near term.

Financial Data

(US$ in Thousands)	3 Mos	08/31/2019	08/31/2018	08/31/2017	08/31/2016	08/31/2015	08/31/2014	08/31/2013
Earnings Per Share	7.49	7.36	6.34	5.44	6.45	4.76	4.52	4.93
Cash Flow Per Share	10.05	10.39	9.59	8.02	7.30	6.53	5.50	5.12
Tang Book Value Per Share	13.95	12.89	7.79	6.21	6.14	4.93	5.08	4.71
Dividends Per Share	2.260	2.920	2.660	2.420	2.200	2.040	1.860	1.620
Dividend Payout %	30.17	39.67	41.96	44.49	34.11	42.86	41.15	32.86
Income Statement								
Total Revenue	11,358,958	43,215,013	41,603,428	36,765,478	34,797,661	32,914,424	31,874,678	30,394,285
EBITDA	2,178,160	6,628,048	6,194,766	4,956,454	6,318,398	5,037,040	4,611,862	4,645,433
Depn & Amortn	399,458	440,796	423,471	362,817	729,052	645,923	326,910	324,997
Income Before Taxes	1,800,647	6,251,797	5,808,093	4,616,032	5,603,572	4,410,530	4,297,701	4,339,294
Income Taxes	425,479	1,405,556	1,593,499	981,100	1,253,969	1,136,741	1,121,743	784,775
Net Income	1,356,968	4,779,112	4,059,907	3,445,149	4,111,892	3,053,581	2,941,498	3,281,878
Average Shares	649,389	650,204	655,296	660,463	667,770	678,757	692,389	712,763
Balance Sheet								
Current Assets	15,606,104	15,450,601	13,585,559	12,097,289	11,976,222	11,579,394	11,904,442	11,844,178
Total Assets	33,170,712	29,789,880	24,449,083	22,689,890	20,609,004	18,266,058	17,930,452	16,867,049
Current Liabilities	11,199,408	11,061,896	10,151,751	9,824,279	8,878,924	8,532,199	8,158,079	8,160,990
Long-Term Obligations	15,935	16,247	19,676	22,163	24,457	25,587	26,403	25,600
Total Liabilities	18,003,574	15,380,872	14,084,330	13,740,413	13,053,742	12,132,333	12,198,417	11,906,863
Stockholders' Equity	15,167,138	14,409,008	10,364,753	8,949,477	7,555,262	6,133,725	5,732,035	4,960,186
Shares Outstanding	635,589	636,383	639,689	636,088	642,590	650,036	656,556	666,355
Statistical Record								
Return on Assets %	16.24	17.62	17.23	15.91	21.10	16.87	16.91	19.57
Return on Equity %	34.92	38.58	42.04	41.75	59.91	51.47	55.02	72.08
EBITDA Margin %	19.18	15.34	14.89	13.48	18.16	15.30	14.47	15.28
Net Margin %	11.95	11.06	9.76	9.37	11.82	9.28	9.23	10.80
Asset Turnover	1.47	1.59	1.77	1.70	1.79	1.82	1.83	1.81
Current Ratio	1.39	1.40	1.34	1.23	1.35	1.36	1.46	1.45
Debt to Equity	N.M.	N.M.	N.M.	N.M.	N.M.	N.M.	N.M.	0.01
Price Range	201.25-133.67	198.74-133.67	169.77-129.77	130.76-109.80	119.65-92.29	105.20-75.85	85.40-70.28	83.09-61.06
P/E Ratio	26.87-17.85	27.00-18.16	26.78-20.47	24.04-20.18	18.55-14.31	22.10-15.93	18.89-15.55	16.85-12.39
Average Yield %	1.35	1.71	1.73	2.00	2.03	2.26	2.35	2.22

Address: 1 Grand Canal Square, Grand Canal Harbour, Dublin, 2 Telephone: 164-620-00	Web Site: www.accenture.com Officers: David P. Rowland - Executive Chairman, Senior Vice President, Interim Chief Executive Officer, Chief Financial Officer Julie Spellman Sweet - Chief Executive Officer, Chief Compliance Officer, General Counsel, Secretary, Region Officer	Auditors: KPMG LLP Investor Contact: 353-140-78203 Transfer Agents: Computershare, Canton, MA

ACUITY BRANDS INC (HOLDING COMPANY)

Exchange	Symbol	Price	52Wk Range	Yield	P/E
NYS	AYI	$138.00 (12/31/2019)	146.33-111.45	0.38	17.81

*7 Year Price Score 68.44   *NYSE Composite Index=100   *12 Month Price Score 96.22

TRADING VOLUME (thousand shares)

Interim Earnings (Per Share)

Qtr.	Nov	Feb	May	Aug
2016-17	1.86	1.53	1.90	2.14
2017-18	1.70	2.33	1.80	2.67
2018-19	1.98	1.67	2.22	2.42
2019-20	1.44	...	...	...

Interim Dividends (Per Share)

Amt	Decl	Ex	Rec	Pay
0.13Q	03/29/2019	04/16/2019	04/17/2019	05/01/2019
0.13Q	06/28/2019	07/16/2019	07/17/2019	08/01/2019
0.13Q	09/27/2019	10/17/2019	10/18/2019	11/01/2019
0.13Q	01/08/2020	01/16/2020	01/20/2020	02/03/2020

Indicated Div: $0.52 (Div. Reinv. Plan)

Valuation Analysis / Institutional Holding

Forecast EPS	$9.66	No of Institutions
	(01/17/2020)	593
Market Cap	$5.5 Billion	Shares
Book Value	$2.0 Billion	47,264,568
Price/Book	2.74	% Held
Price/Sales	1.53	90.56

Business Summary: Electrical Equipment (MIC: 7.3.1 SIC: 3648 NAIC: 335129)

Acuity Brands is a provider of lighting and building management solutions and services for commercial, institutional, industrial, infrastructure, and residential applications. Co.'s lighting and building management solutions include devices such as luminaires, lighting controls, controllers for various building systems, power supplies, prismatic skylights, and drivers, as well as integrated systems designed for various indoor and outdoor applications. In addition, Co. provides services across applications that primarily relate to monitoring and controlling lighting and building management systems through network technologies and the commissioning of control systems.

Recent Developments: For the quarter ended Nov 30 2019, net income decreased 28.4% to US$57.0 million from US$79.6 million in the year-earlier quarter. Revenues were US$834.7 million, down 10.5% from US$932.6 million the year before. Operating income was US$83.6 million versus US$116.4 million in the prior-year quarter, a decrease of 28.2%. Direct operating expenses declined 15.3% to US$478.9 million from US$565.1 million in the comparable period the year before. Indirect operating expenses increased 8.4% to US$272.2 million from US$251.1 million in the equivalent prior-year period.

Prospects: Our evaluation of Acuity Brands Inc. as of October 4th, 2019 is the result of our systematic analysis on three basic characteristics: earnings strength, relative valuation, and recent stock price movement. The company has managed to produce a neutral trend in earnings per share over the past 5 quarters. However, recent analyst estimates for the company have been reduced and AYI has posted results that fell short of analysts' expectations. Based on operating earnings yield, the company is undervalued when compared to all of the companies we cover. Share price changes over the past year indicates that AYI will perform well over the near term.

Financial Data
(US$ in Thousands)

	3 Mos	08/31/2019	08/31/2018	08/31/2017	08/31/2016	08/31/2015	08/31/2014	08/31/2013
Earnings Per Share	7.75	8.29	8.52	7.43	6.63	5.09	4.05	2.95
Cash Flow Per Share	12.47	12.46	8.64	7.34	7.93	6.70	5.45	3.14
Tang Book Value Per Share	6.33	12.31	6.19	7.54	7.54	13.16	8.40	4.18
Dividends Per Share	0.520	0.520	0.520	0.520	0.520	0.520	0.520	0.520
Dividend Payout %	6.71	6.27	6.10	7.00	7.84	10.22	12.84	17.63
Income Statement								
Total Revenue	834,700	3,672,700	3,680,100	3,505,100	3,291,300	2,706,700	2,393,500	2,089,100
EBITDA	106,400	515,700	511,200	571,700	517,700	409,500	329,600	253,300
Depn & Amortn	24,200	57,500	51,800	46,600	40,900	34,400	31,800	29,000
Income Before Taxes	73,900	424,900	425,900	492,600	444,600	343,600	265,700	193,100
Income Taxes	16,900	94,500	76,300	170,900	153,800	121,500	89,900	65,700
Net Income	57,000	330,400	349,600	321,700	290,800	222,100	175,800	127,400
Average Shares	39,600	39,800	41,000	43,300	43,800	43,400	43,000	42,500
Balance Sheet								
Current Assets	1,206,400	1,441,800	1,211,100	1,245,600	1,322,900	1,436,500	1,186,700	913,500
Total Assets	3,305,200	3,172,400	2,988,800	2,899,600	2,948,000	2,429,600	2,168,100	1,903,800
Current Liabilities	572,600	596,100	682,700	600,900	672,500	520,900	470,500	386,200
Long-Term Obligations	347,100	347,500	356,400	356,500	355,000	352,400	353,600	353,200
Total Liabilities	1,317,900	1,253,500	1,272,000	1,234,000	1,288,200	1,069,600	1,004,600	910,300
Stockholders' Equity	1,987,300	1,918,900	1,716,800	1,665,600	1,659,800	1,360,000	1,163,500	993,500
Shares Outstanding	39,522	39,452	39,990	41,871	43,736	43,305	42,862	42,486
Statistical Record								
Return on Assets %	9.74	10.73	11.87	11.00	10.79	9.66	8.63	7.00
Return on Equity %	16.47	18.18	20.67	19.35	19.21	17.60	16.30	13.94
EBITDA Margin %	12.75	14.04	13.89	16.31	15.73	15.13	13.77	12.12
Net Margin %	6.83	9.00	9.50	9.18	8.84	8.21	7.34	6.10
Asset Turnover	1.13	1.19	1.25	1.20	1.22	1.18	1.18	1.15
Current Ratio	2.11	2.42	1.77	2.07	1.97	2.76	2.52	2.37
Debt to Equity	0.17	0.18	0.21	0.21	0.21	0.26	0.30	0.36
Price Range	146.33-105.80	165.06-105.80	185.73-110.22	275.12-162.78	279.15-169.87	211.15-117.71	143.65-84.43	88.34-59.86
P/E Ratio	18.88-13.65	19.91-12.76	21.80-12.94	37.03-21.91	42.10-25.62	41.48-23.13	35.47-20.85	29.95-20.29
Average Yield %	0.40	0.40	0.35	0.25	0.23	0.32	0.44	0.72

Address: 1170 Peachtree Street, N.E., Suite 2300, Atlanta, GA 30309-7676
Telephone: 404-853-1400
Fax: 404-853-1300

Web Site: www.acuitybrands.com
Officers: Vernon J. Nagel - Executive Chairman, Chairman, President, Chief Executive Officer Richard K. Reece - President, Executive Vice President, Executive Vice President (frmr), Chief Financial Officer

Auditors: Ernst & Young LLP
Investor Contact: 404-853-1400
Transfer Agents: Computershare Shareowner Services, Pittsburgh, PA

ADT INC (DE)

Exchange	Symbol	Price	52Wk Range	Yield	P/E
NYS	ADT	$7.93 (12/31/2019)	9.57-4.35	1.77	N/A

*7 Year Price Score N/A   ***NYSE Composite Index=100**   ***12 Month Price Score 118.60**

Interim Earnings (Per Share)

Qtr.	Mar	Jun	Sep	Dec
2017	(0.22)	(0.14)	(0.10)	0.99
2018	(0.22)	(0.09)	(0.31)	(0.19)
2019	(0.09)	(0.14)	(0.25)	...

Interim Dividends (Per Share)

Amt	Decl	Ex	Rec	Pay
0.035Q	04/25/2019	06/10/2019	06/11/2019	07/02/2019
0.035Q	08/06/2019	09/10/2019	09/11/2019	10/02/2019
0.70Q	11/12/2019	12/12/2019	12/13/2019	12/23/2019
0.035Q	11/12/2019	12/12/2019	12/13/2019	01/03/2020

Indicated Div: $0.14

Valuation Analysis

		Institutional Holding	
Forecast EPS	$0.99	No of Institutions	
		(01/17/2020)	194
Market Cap	$5.9 Billion	Shares	
Book Value	$3.7 Billion		732,656,896
Price/Book	1.60	% Held	
Price/Sales	1.19		97.44

TRADING VOLUME (thousand shares)

Business Summary: Services (MIC: 6.1.2 SIC: 7382 NAIC: 561621)

ADT is a provider of monitored security and interactive home and business automation solutions in the United States and Canada. Co.'s monitored security and automation offerings involve the installation and monitoring of security and premises automation systems designed to detect intrusion; control access; sense movement, smoke, fire, carbon monoxide, flooding, temperature, and other environmental conditions and hazards; and address personal emergencies. Co.'s products and services include interactive technologies to allow its customers to remotely monitor and manage their residential and commercial environments by adding automation capabilities to its monitored security systems.

Recent Developments: For the quarter ended Sep 30 2019, net loss amounted to US$181.6 million versus a net loss of US$235.5 million in the year-earlier quarter. Revenues were US$1.30 billion, up 13.3% from US$1.15 billion the year before. Operating loss was US$51.2 million versus an income of US$121.8 million in the prior-year quarter. Direct operating expenses rose 35.4% to US$356.6 million from US$263.3 million in the comparable period the year before. Indirect operating expenses increased 30.4% to US$995.2 million from US$763.2 million in the equivalent prior-year period.

Prospects: Our evaluation of ADT Inc. as of October 4th, 2019 is the result of our systematic analysis on three basic characteristics: earnings strength, relative valuation, and recent stock price movement. The company has enjoyed a very positive trend in earnings per share over the past 5 quarters. However, recent analyst estimates for the company have been mixed and ADT has posted results that exceeded analysts' expectations. Based on operating earnings yield, the company is overvalued when compared to all of the companies we cover. Share price changes over the past year indicates that ADT will perform very poorly over the near term.

Financial Data

(US$ in Thousands)	9 Mos	6 Mos	3 Mos	12/31/2018	12/31/2017	12/31/2016	12/31/2015	06/30/2015
Earnings Per Share	(0.67)	(0.73)	(0.68)	(0.81)	0.53	(0.84)	(0.08)	(185,910.00)
Cash Flow Per Share	2.49	2.41	2.37	2.39	2.48	0.96	0.00	696,847.51
Dividends Per Share	0.140	0.140	0.105	0.140	...	...	...	...
Income Statement								
Total Revenue	3,827,374	2,526,804	1,243,060	4,581,673	4,315,502	2,949,766	311,567	237,709
EBITDA	12,282	85,098	63,967	196,586	2,179,491	(254,247)	(36,449)	60,689
Depn & Amortn	(19,962)	(12,712)	(6,107)	166,000	1,868,336	27,000	3,000	49,126
Income Before Taxes	(433,733)	(215,736)	(88,831)	(632,618)	(421,686)	(802,738)	(84,618)	(17,566)
Income Taxes	(81,576)	(45,209)	(22,361)	(23,463)	(764,313)	(266,151)	(30,365)	1,025
Net Income	(352,157)	(170,527)	(66,470)	(609,155)	342,627	(536,587)	(54,253)	(18,591)
Average Shares	739,852	749,575	756,252	747,710	641,074	640,725	640,723	10.00
Balance Sheet								
Current Assets	1,319,167	582,475	606,545	854,017	455,886	388,356	141,693	...
Total Assets	16,947,089	16,977,169	17,033,697	17,208,608	17,014,820	17,176,481	2,319,515	...
Current Liabilities	1,474,017	1,390,978	1,382,169	1,012,490	896,252	852,539	171,959	...
Long-Term Obligations	9,638,118	9,481,059	9,347,601	9,944,112	10,121,126	9,469,682	1,330,145	...
Total Liabilities	13,235,905	13,087,310	12,885,666	12,983,803	13,581,708	13,371,505	1,616,618	...
Stockholders' Equity	3,711,184	3,889,859	4,148,031	4,224,805	3,433,112	3,804,976	702,897	...
Shares Outstanding	750,032	746,360	767,005	766,881	641,118	641,046	640,722	...
Statistical Record								
Return on Assets %	N.M.	N.M.	N.M.	N.M.	2.00	N.M.	...	...
Return on Equity %	N.M.	N.M.	N.M.	N.M.	9.47	N.M.	...	...
EBITDA Margin %	0.32	3.37	5.15	4.29	50.50	N.M.	N.M.	25.53
Net Margin %	N.M.	N.M.	N.M.	N.M.	7.94	N.M.	N.M.	N.M.
Asset Turnover	0.30	0.28	0.27	0.27	0.25	0.30	...	...
Current Ratio	0.89	0.42	0.44	0.84	0.51	0.46	0.82	...
Debt to Equity	2.60	2.44	2.25	2.35	2.95	2.49	1.89	...
Price Range	9.20-4.35	9.48-5.85	9.56-6.01	12.86-6.01	...	...	...	...
Average Yield %	2.09	1.86	1.31	1.59	...	...	...	...

Address: 1501 Yamato Road, Boca Raton, FL 33431 Telephone: 561-322-7235	Web Site: www.adt.com Officers: Marc E. Becker - Chairman James D. DeVries - President, Chief Executive Officer	Auditors: PricewaterhouseCoopers LLP Transfer Agents: American Stock Transfer

ADTALEM GLOBAL EDUCATION INC

Exchange	Symbol	Price	52Wk Range	Yield	P/E
NYS	ATGE	$34.97 (12/31/2019)	51.38-29.70	N/A	17.23

*7 Year Price Score 98.08   *NYSE Composite Index=100   *12 Month Price Score 73.16

Interim Earnings (Per Share)

Qtr.	Sep	Dec	Mar	Jun
2016-17	0.39	0.23	0.62	0.67
2017-18	0.20	(1.33)	0.63	1.00
2018-19	(0.16)	0.29	0.64	0.84
2019-20	0.26	...	...	...

Interim Dividends (Per Share)

Dividend Payment Suspended

Valuation Analysis — **Institutional Holding**

Forecast EPS	$2.47	No of Institutions
	(01/08/2020)	363
Market Cap	$1.9 Billion	Shares
Book Value	$1.3 Billion	68,656,152
Price/Book	1.44	% Held
Price/Sales	1.58	N/A

Business Summary: Educational Services (MIC: 2.2.2 SIC: 8221 NAIC: 611310)

Adtalem Global Education provides educational services. Co.'s institutions and companies provide an array of programs across medical and healthcare, financial services and business and law. Co.'s segments include: Medical and Healthcare, which includes Chamberlain University and Medical and Veterinary Schools that provide educational programs in nursing and health professions, respectively; Financial Services, which includes Becker Professional Education that provides education serving the accounting and finance professions; and Business and Law, which includes Adtalem Education of Brazil institution that focuses in business, engineering, healthcare, law, management, medical and technology.

Recent Developments: For the quarter ended Sep 30 2019, income from continuing operations was US$17.4 million compared with a loss of US$4.9 million in the year-earlier quarter. Net income amounted to US$14.3 million versus a net loss of US$9.6 million in the year-earlier quarter. Revenues were US$254.6 million, up 7.5% from US$236.9 million the year before. Operating income was US$25.7 million versus a loss of US$3.2 million in the prior-year quarter. Direct operating expenses rose 14.8% to US$128.0 million from US$111.5 million in the comparable period the year before. Indirect operating expenses decreased 21.6% to US$100.8 million from US$128.6 million in the equivalent prior-year period.

Prospects: Our evaluation of Adtalem Global Education Inc. as of October 4th, 2019 is the result of our systematic analysis on three basic characteristics: earnings strength, relative valuation, and recent stock price movement. The company has enjoyed a very positive trend in earnings per share over the past 5 quarters. However, recent analyst estimates for the company have been unchanged, while ATGE has posted results that exceeded analysts' expectations. Based on operating earnings yield, the company is undervalued when compared to all of the companies we cover. Share price changes over the past year indicates that ATGE will perform very well over the near term.

Financial Data
(US$ in Thousands)

	3 Mos	06/30/2019	06/30/2018	06/30/2017	06/30/2016	06/30/2015	06/30/2014	06/30/2013
Earnings Per Share	2.03	1.60	0.54	1.91	(0.05)	2.14	2.07	1.65
Cash Flow Per Share	3.14	3.50	3.89	3.59	3.61	3.15	4.14	4.07
Tang Book Value Per Share	6.31	1.79	5.72	6.48	10.41	11.14	11.29	9.63
Dividends Per Share	...	...	...	0.180	0.360	0.360	0.340	0.340
Dividend Payout %	...	...	...	9.42	...	16.82	16.43	20.61
Income Statement								
Total Revenue	254,613	1,239,687	1,231,211	1,809,800	1,843,537	1,909,943	1,923,371	1,964,375
EBITDA	49,887	237,577	260,300	210,801	67,257	241,918	264,007	250,039
Depn & Amortn	24,123	51,741	52,824	72,188	79,400	85,008	82,739	83,111
Income Before Taxes	21,114	170,181	198,683	134,394	(17,298)	153,660	179,367	164,969
Income Taxes	3,706	34,157	84,102	10,420	(14,542)	18,537	27,699	39,227
Net Income	14,361	95,168	33,769	122,283	(3,166)	139,899	134,032	106,786
Average Shares	56,140	59,330	62,280	64,019	64,371	65,277	64,853	64,611
Balance Sheet								
Current Assets	456,113	504,700	688,000	471,207	518,105	601,057	577,091	442,164
Total Assets	2,460,324	2,242,696	2,344,961	2,314,035	2,096,996	2,074,193	1,997,636	1,857,018
Current Liabilities	412,475	311,631	365,781	377,327	361,836	321,909	316,812	316,217
Long-Term Obligations	327,600	398,094	290,073	125,000	...	...	...	...
Total Liabilities	1,133,131	851,166	825,675	644,996	514,909	489,383	464,243	459,862
Stockholders' Equity	1,327,193	1,391,530	1,519,286	1,669,039	1,582,087	1,584,810	1,533,393	1,397,156
Shares Outstanding	54,649	55,303	59,893	62,371	62,549	63,623	63,624	62,946
Statistical Record								
Return on Assets %	4.95	4.15	1.45	5.54	N.M.	6.87	6.95	5.78
Return on Equity %	8.60	6.54	2.12	7.52	N.M.	8.97	9.15	7.76
EBITDA Margin %	19.59	19.16	21.14	11.65	3.65	12.67	13.73	12.73
Net Margin %	5.64	7.68	2.74	6.76	N.M.	7.32	6.97	5.44
Asset Turnover	0.50	0.54	0.53	0.82	0.88	0.94	1.00	1.06
Current Ratio	1.11	1.62	1.88	1.25	1.43	1.87	1.82	1.40
Debt to Equity	0.25	0.29	0.19	0.07	...	...	...	...
Price Range	58.16-38.02	58.16-42.90	49.90-31.35	40.65-17.84	32.02-15.84	49.18-29.98	45.99-28.32	34.03-18.35
P/E Ratio	28.65-18.73	36.35-26.81	92.41-58.06	21.28-9.34	...	22.98-14.01	22.22-13.68	20.62-11.12
Average Yield %	...	...	...	0.60	1.58	0.89	0.93	1.29

Address: 500 West Monroe Street, Chicago, IL 60661	**Web Site:** www.adtalem.com	**Auditors:** PricewaterhouseCoopers LLP
Telephone: 866-374-2678	**Officers:** Lisa W. Wardell - Chairman, President, Chief Executive Officer Michael O. Randolfi - Senior Vice President, Chief Financial Officer	**Investor Contact:** 630-353-3800
		Transfer Agents: Computershare Investor Services, L.L.C.

8

ADVANCE AUTO PARTS INC

Exchange	Symbol	Price	52Wk Range	Yield	P/E
NYS	AAP	$160.16 (12/31/2019)	181.43-134.89	0.15	25.83

*7 Year Price Score 95.75   *NYSE Composite Index=100   *12 Month Price Score 95.12

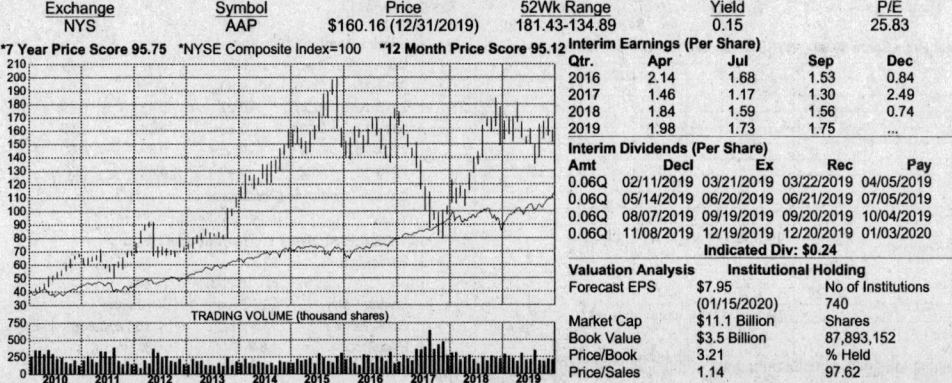

Interim Earnings (Per Share)

Qtr.	Apr	Jul	Sep	Dec
2016	2.14	1.68	1.53	0.84
2017	1.46	1.17	1.30	2.49
2018	1.84	1.59	1.56	0.74
2019	1.98	1.73	1.75	...

Interim Dividends (Per Share)

Amt	Decl	Ex	Rec	Pay
0.06Q	02/11/2019	03/21/2019	03/22/2019	04/05/2019
0.06Q	05/14/2019	06/20/2019	06/21/2019	07/05/2019
0.06Q	08/07/2019	09/19/2019	09/20/2019	10/04/2019
0.06Q	11/08/2019	12/19/2019	12/20/2019	01/03/2020

Indicated Div: $0.24

Valuation Analysis   **Institutional Holding**

Forecast EPS	$7.95	No of Institutions
(01/15/2020)		740
Market Cap	$11.1 Billion	Shares
Book Value	$3.5 Billion	87,893,152
Price/Book	3.21	% Held
Price/Sales	1.14	97.62

Business Summary: Retail - Automotive (MIC: 2.1.4 SIC: 5531 NAIC: 441310)

Advance Auto Parts is an automotive aftermarket parts provider in North America, serving both professional installers and do-it-yourself customers as well as independently owned operators. Co.'s stores and branches provide a selection of brand name, original equipment manufacturer and private label automotive replacement parts, accessories, batteries, and maintenance items for domestic and imported cars, vans, sport utility vehicles and light and heavy duty trucks. Co. operates stores and distribution branches within the U.S., with additional locations in Canada, Puerto Rico and the U.S. Virgin Islands under the trade names Advance Auto Parts, Carquest, Autopart International, and Worldpac.

Recent Developments: For the quarter ended Oct 5 2019, net income increased 6.8% to US$123.7 million from US$115.8 million in the year-earlier quarter. Revenues were US$2.31 billion, up 1.6% from US$2.27 billion the year before. Operating income was US$172.3 million versus US$154.2 million in the prior-year quarter, an increase of 11.7%. Direct operating expenses rose 2.5% to US$1.30 billion from US$1.27 billion in the comparable period the year before. Indirect operating expenses decreased 1.5% to US$839.6 million from US$852.7 million in the equivalent prior-year period.

Prospects: Our evaluation of Advance Auto Parts Inc. as of October 4th, 2019 is the result of our systematic analysis on three basic characteristics: earnings strength, relative valuation, and recent stock price movement. The company has managed to produce a neutral trend in earnings per share over the past 5 quarters. However, recent analyst estimates for the company have been reduced and AAP has posted results that fell short of analysts' expectations. Based on operating earnings yield, the company is fairly valued when compared to all of the companies we cover. Share price changes over the past year indicates that AAP will perform very poorly over the near term.

Financial Data

(US$ in Thousands)	9 Mos	6 Mos	3 Mos	12/29/2018	12/30/2017	12/31/2016	01/02/2016	01/03/2015
Earnings Per Share	6.20	6.01	5.87	5.73	6.42	6.20	6.40	6.71
Cash Flow Per Share	11.91	11.98	12.00	11.03	8.16	6.83	9.45	9.56
Tang Book Value Per Share	28.14	30.21	28.27	27.74	24.66	17.42	10.69	3.55
Dividends Per Share	0.240	0.240	0.240	0.240	0.240	0.240	0.240	0.240
Dividend Payout %	3.87	3.99	4.09	4.19	3.74	3.87	3.75	3.58
Income Statement								
Total Revenue	7,596,389	5,284,283	2,952,036	9,580,554	9,373,784	9,567,679	9,737,018	9,843,861
EBITDA	729,334	503,843	275,587	813,452	785,960	1,014,726	1,042,024	1,089,842
Depn & Amortn	179,565	123,257	69,885	201,600	206,900	215,981	223,728	235,040
Income Before Taxes	517,707	356,967	190,758	555,264	520,259	738,835	752,888	781,394
Income Taxes	126,718	89,647	48,258	131,417	44,754	279,213	279,490	287,569
Net Income	390,989	267,320	142,500	423,847	475,505	459,622	473,398	493,825
Average Shares	70,664	72,008	72,103	73,991	74,110	73,856	73,733	73,414
Balance Sheet								
Current Assets	5,826,648	5,962,471	5,781,838	6,082,454	5,426,892	5,172,764	4,940,746	4,741,040
Total Assets	11,106,802	11,267,946	11,081,511	9,040,648	8,482,301	8,315,033	8,134,565	7,962,358
Current Liabilities	4,463,913	4,372,405	4,298,877	3,885,950	3,480,097	3,676,046	3,797,477	3,743,066
Long-Term Obligations	747,136	746,951	746,767	1,045,720	1,044,327	1,042,949	1,213,161	1,636,311
Total Liabilities	7,651,860	7,596,644	7,534,288	5,489,835	5,067,105	5,398,841	5,673,917	5,959,446
Stockholders' Equity	3,454,942	3,671,302	3,547,223	3,550,813	3,415,196	2,916,192	2,460,648	2,002,912
Shares Outstanding	69,275	71,386	71,737	72,460	73,936	73,749	73,314	73,074
Statistical Record								
Return on Assets %	4.43	4.34	4.36	4.85	5.68	5.60	5.90	7.18
Return on Equity %	12.49	11.91	12.11	12.20	15.06	17.14	21.27	27.61
EBITDA Margin %	9.60	9.53	9.34	8.49	8.38	10.61	10.70	11.07
Net Margin %	5.15	5.06	4.83	4.42	5.07	4.80	4.86	5.02
Asset Turnover	0.97	0.96	0.98	1.10	1.12	1.17	1.21	1.43
Current Ratio	1.31	1.36	1.34	1.57	1.56	1.41	1.30	1.27
Debt to Equity	0.22	0.20	0.21	0.29	0.31	0.36	0.49	0.82
Price Range	184.72-134.89	184.72-139.34	184.72-103.76	184.72-103.76	174.79-79.38	176.78-136.19	200.38-143.00	161.22-110.22
P/E Ratio	29.79-21.76	30.74-23.18	31.47-17.68	32.24-18.11	27.23-12.36	28.51-21.97	31.31-22.34	24.03-16.43
Average Yield %	0.15	0.15	0.15	0.16	0.17	0.20	0.15	0.18

Address: 2635 East Millbrook Road, Raleigh, NC 27604	**Web Site:** www.AdvanceAutoParts.com	**Auditors:** DELOITTE & TOUCHE LLP
Telephone: 540-362-4911	**Officers:** Jeffrey C. Smith - Chairman Thomas R. Greco - President, Chief Executive Officer	**Investor Contact:** 540-561-6444
		Transfer Agents: BNY Mellon Shareowner Services, Pittsburgh, PA

AECOM

Exchange	Symbol	Price	52Wk Range	Yield	P/E
NYS	ACM	$43.13 (12/31/2019)	43.84-26.37	N/A	N/A

*7 Year Price Score 89.00   ***NYSE Composite Index=100**   ***12 Month Price Score 115.19**

Interim Earnings (Per Share)

Qtr.	Dec	Mar	Jun	Sep
2014-15	(0.73)	0.00	(0.11)	0.01
2015-16	(0.13)	0.27	0.43	0.05
2016-17	0.30	0.65	0.64	0.55
2017-18	0.69	(0.75)	0.37	0.52
2018-19	0.32	0.49	0.52	(3.00)

Interim Dividends (Per Share)

No Dividends Paid

Valuation Analysis **Institutional Holding**

Forecast EPS	$3.32	No of Institutions
	(01/16/2020)	442
Market Cap	$6.8 Billion	Shares
Book Value	$3.7 Billion	158,613,888
Price/Book	1.84	% Held
Price/Sales	0.34	87.07

Business Summary: Construction Services (MIC: 7.5.4 SIC: 8711 NAIC: 541330)

AECOM designs, builds, finances and operates infrastructure assets for governments, businesses and organizations. Co. provides: planning, consulting, architectural and engineering design services to commercial and government clients in transportation, facilities, environmental, energy, water and government markets; construction services, including building construction and energy, infrastructure and industrial construction; as well as program and facilities management and maintenance, training, logistics, consulting, technical assistance, and systems integration and information technology services, for agencies of the United States government and for other national governments.

Recent Developments: For the year ended Sep 30 2019, net loss amounted to US$184.0 million versus net income of US$197.1 million in the prior year. Revenues were US$20.17 billion, up 0.1% from US$20.16 billion the year before. Operating income was US$25.1 million versus US$424.9 million in the prior year, a decrease of 94.1%. Direct operating expenses declined 0.7% to US$19.36 billion from US$19.50 billion in the comparable period the year before. Indirect operating expenses increased 249.2% to US$788.4 million from US$225.8 million in the equivalent prior-year period.

Prospects: Our evaluation of AECOM as of October 4th, 2019 is the result of our systematic analysis on three basic characteristics: earnings strength, relative valuation, and recent stock price movement. The company has enjoyed a very positive trend in earnings per share over the past 5 quarters. However, recent analyst estimates for the company have been mixed and ACM has posted results that fell short of analysts' expectations. Based on operating earnings yield, the company is undervalued when compared to all of the companies we cover. Share price changes over the past year indicates that ACM will perform well over the near term.

Financial Data

(US$ in Thousands)	09/30/2019	09/30/2018	09/30/2017	09/30/2016	09/30/2015	09/30/2014	09/30/2013	09/30/2012
Earnings Per Share	(1.66)	0.84	2.13	0.62	(1.04)	2.33	2.35	(0.52)
Cash Flow Per Share	4.95	4.87	4.47	5.25	5.11	3.71	4.06	3.86
Tang Book Value Per Share	N.M.	N.M.	N.M.	N.M.	N.M.	1.64	1.32	2.78
Income Statement								
Total Revenue	20,173,329	20,155,512	18,203,402	17,410,825	17,989,880	8,356,783	8,153,495	8,218,180
EBITDA	125,384	522,370	676,010	451,385	233,182	366,806	426,892	91,029
Depn & Amortn	164,500	158,500	157,100	171,700	191,300	69,100	70,700	77,100
Income Before Taxes	(265,110)	96,351	287,600	21,523	(257,745)	256,864	311,455	(31,167)
Income Taxes	(130)	(19,643)	7,706	(37,917)	(80,237)	82,024	92,578	74,416
Net Income	(261,050)	136,468	339,390	96,109	(154,845)	229,854	239,243	(58,567)
Average Shares	157,044	162,261	159,135	156,073	149,605	98,657	101,942	111,875
Balance Sheet								
Current Assets	7,534,645	7,127,322	6,682,222	6,000,771	6,246,085	3,434,113	3,131,602	3,147,293
Total Assets	14,461,591	14,681,131	14,396,956	13,726,745	14,014,298	6,123,377	5,665,623	5,664,568
Current Liabilities	6,461,754	6,129,677	5,578,379	5,304,756	4,836,052	2,455,769	2,053,549	2,078,402
Long-Term Obligations	3,285,755	3,483,746	3,702,109	3,758,966	4,446,527	939,565	1,089,060	907,141
Total Liabilities	10,771,015	10,588,351	10,400,830	10,359,824	10,606,550	3,936,860	3,644,180	3,495,104
Stockholders' Equity	3,690,576	4,092,780	3,996,126	3,366,921	3,407,748	2,186,517	2,021,443	2,169,464
Shares Outstanding	157,482	156,983	157,529	153,901	151,263	96,715	96,016	107,041
Statistical Record								
Return on Assets %	N.M.	0.94	2.41	0.69	N.M.	3.90	4.22	N.M.
Return on Equity %	N.M.	3.37	9.22	2.83	N.M.	10.92	11.42	N.M.
EBITDA Margin %	0.62	2.59	3.71	2.59	1.30	4.39	5.24	1.11
Net Margin %	N.M.	0.68	1.86	0.55	N.M.	2.75	2.93	N.M.
Asset Turnover	1.38	1.39	1.29	1.25	1.79	1.42	1.44	1.43
Current Ratio	1.17	1.16	1.20	1.13	1.29	1.40	1.52	1.51
Debt to Equity	0.89	0.85	0.93	1.12	1.30	0.43	0.54	0.42
Price Range	38.43-24.92	39.62-32.09	40.13-26.92	36.17-23.15	35.36-24.92	38.13-27.47	35.20-18.87	24.06-14.91
P/E Ratio	...	47.17-38.20	18.84-12.64	58.34-37.34		16.36-11.79	14.98-8.03	...

Address: 1999 Avenue of the Stars, Suite 2600, Los Angeles, CA 90067 Telephone: 213-593-8000	Web Site: www.aecom.com Officers: Michael S. Burke - Chairman, President, Chief Executive Officer Daniel R. Tishman - Vice-Chairman	Auditors: Ernst & Young LLP Investor Contact: 212-973-2982 Transfer Agents: Computershare Investor Services, LLC, Canton, MA

AES CORP.

Exchange	Symbol	Price	52Wk Range	Yield	P/E
NYS	AES	$19.90 (12/31/2019)	20.04-14.17	2.88	26.18

*7 Year Price Score 107.03 *NYSE Composite Index=100 *12 Month Price Score 104.44

Interim Earnings (Per Share)

Qtr.	Mar	Jun	Sep	Dec
2016	0.19	(0.73)	0.26	(1.43)
2017	(0.04)	0.08	0.23	(2.03)
2018	1.03	0.44	0.15	0.19
2019	0.23	0.02	0.32	...

Interim Dividends (Per Share)

Amt	Decl	Ex	Rec	Pay
0.137Q	04/15/2019	04/30/2019	05/01/2019	05/15/2019
0.137Q	07/16/2019	07/31/2019	08/01/2019	08/15/2019
0.137Q	10/16/2019	10/31/2019	11/01/2019	11/15/2019
0.143Q	12/09/2019	01/30/2020	01/31/2020	02/14/2020
		Indicated Div: $0.57		

Valuation Analysis   **Institutional Holding**

Forecast EPS	$1.34	No of Institutions
	(01/17/2020)	848
Market Cap	$13.2 Billion	Shares
Book Value	$4.0 Billion	780,850,880
Price/Book	3.28	% Held
Price/Sales	1.27	93.01

Business Summary: Electric Utilities (MIC: 3.1.1 SIC: 4911 NAIC: 221121)

AES is a holding company. Through its subsidiaries, Co. operates a portfolio of electricity generation and distribution businesses. The first business line is generation, where Co. owns and/or operates power plants to generate and sell power to customers, such as utilities, industrial users, and other intermediaries. The second business line is utilities, where Co. owns and/or operates utilities to generate or purchase, distribute, transmit and sell electricity to end-user customers in the residential, commercial, industrial and governmental sectors within a defined service area. In certain circumstances, Co.'s utilities also generate and sell electricity on the wholesale market.

Recent Developments: For the quarter ended Sep 30 2019, income from continuing operations increased 55.2% to US$298.0 million from US$192.0 million in the year-earlier quarter. Net income increased 56.0% to US$298.0 million from US$191.0 million in the year-earlier quarter. Revenues were US$2.63 billion, down 7.5% from US$2.84 billion the year before. Direct operating expenses declined 11.2% to US$1.92 billion from US$2.17 billion in the comparable period the year before. Indirect operating expenses decreased 4.7% to US$41.0 million from US$43.0 million in the equivalent prior-year period.

Prospects: Our evaluation of AES Corp. as of October 4th, 2019 is the result of our systematic analysis on three basic characteristics: earnings strength, relative valuation, and recent stock price movement. The company has enjoyed a very positive trend in earnings per share over the past 5 quarters. However, recent analyst estimates for the company have been mixed and AES has posted results that fell short of analysts' expectations. Based on operating earnings yield, the company is undervalued when compared to all of the companies we cover. Share price changes over the past year indicates that AES will perform well over the near term.

Financial Data

(US$ in Millions)	9 Mos	6 Mos	3 Mos	12/31/2018	12/31/2017	12/31/2016	12/31/2015	12/31/2014
Earnings Per Share	0.76	0.59	1.01	1.81	(1.76)	(1.71)	0.44	1.06
Cash Flow Per Share	3.65	3.68	3.80	3.54	3.77	4.36	3.11	2.49
Tang Book Value Per Share	3.77	3.89	3.91	3.91	2.84	3.13	3.47	3.71
Dividends Per Share	0.539	0.533	0.526	0.520	0.480	0.440	0.400	0.200
Dividend Payout %	70.99	90.34	52.13	28.73	...	...	90.91	18.87
Income Statement								
Total Revenue	7,758	5,133	2,650	10,736	10,530	13,586	14,963	17,146
EBITDA	2,216	1,361	786	3,724	2,702	2,209	3,138	3,886
Depn & Amortn	774	512	246	960	1,005	1,105	1,104	1,204
Income Before Taxes	896	472	354	2,018	771	137	1,122	1,576
Income Taxes	302	172	115	708	990	(188)	465	419
Net Income	381	171	154	1,203	(1,161)	(1,130)	306	769
Average Shares	667	667	667	665	660	662	689	724
Balance Sheet								
Current Assets	5,470	5,517	5,855	5,015	6,398	6,411	6,866	7,826
Total Assets	33,423	33,238	33,471	32,521	33,112	36,119	36,850	38,966
Current Liabilities	4,991	4,042	4,357	4,399	6,028	5,272	6,950	6,997
Long-Term Obligations	17,879	18,668	18,445	17,636	17,801	19,160	18,278	18,725
Total Liabilities	29,397	29,134	29,347	28,434	29,810	32,543	33,163	34,616
Stockholders' Equity	4,026	4,104	4,124	4,087	3,302	3,576	3,687	4,350
Shares Outstanding	663	663	663	662	660	659	666	703
Statistical Record								
Return on Assets %	1.54	1.22	2.04	3.67	N.M.	N.M.	0.81	1.94
Return on Equity %	12.40	9.67	16.48	32.56	N.M.	N.M.	7.61	17.56
EBITDA Margin %	28.56	26.51	29.66	34.69	25.66	16.26	20.97	22.66
Net Margin %	4.91	3.33	5.81	11.21	N.M.	N.M.	2.05	4.49
Asset Turnover	0.31	0.32	0.32	0.33	0.30	0.37	0.39	0.43
Current Ratio	1.10	1.36	1.34	1.14	1.06	1.22	0.99	1.12
Debt to Equity	4.44	4.55	4.47	4.32	5.39	5.36	4.96	4.30
Price Range	18.41-13.82	18.41-12.63	18.41-11.29	16.01-10.06	11.95-10.23	13.26-8.54	13.94-8.83	15.57-12.79
P/E Ratio	24.22-18.18	31.20-21.41	18.23-11.18	8.85-5.56	...	...	31.68-20.07	14.69-12.07
Average Yield %	3.33	3.43	3.66	4.02	4.28	3.87	3.33	1.40

Address: 4300 Wilson Boulevard, Arlington, VA 22203	Web Site: www.aes.com	Auditors: Ernst & Young LLP
Telephone: 703-522-1315	Officers: John B. Morse - Chairman Andres R. Gluski - President, Chief Executive Officer, Executive Vice President, Chief Operating Officer	Investor Contact: 703-682-6451
Fax: 703-528-4510		Transfer Agents: Computershare Investor Services, Canton, MA

AFFILIATED MANAGERS GROUP INC.

Exchange	Symbol	Price	52Wk Range	Yield	P/E
NYS	AMG	$84.74 (12/31/2019)	115.53-71.80	1.51	N/A

*7 Year Price Score 47.06   ***NYSE Composite Index=100**   ***12 Month Price Score 86.38**

TRADING VOLUME (thousand shares)

Interim Earnings (Per Share)

Qtr.	Mar	Jun	Sep	Dec
2016	1.92	1.97	2.00	2.69
2017	2.13	2.22	2.22	5.46
2018	2.77	2.16	2.34	(2.75)
2019	(3.87)	2.11	1.71	...

Interim Dividends (Per Share)

Amt	Decl	Ex	Rec	Pay
0.32Q	02/04/2019	02/13/2019	02/14/2019	03/01/2019
0.32Q	05/06/2019	05/15/2019	05/16/2019	05/30/2019
0.32Q	07/29/2019	08/07/2019	08/08/2019	08/22/2019
0.32Q	10/28/2019	11/06/2019	11/07/2019	11/21/2019

Indicated Div: $1.28

Valuation Analysis | **Institutional Holding**

Forecast EPS	$14.04	No of Institutions
	(01/16/2020)	627
Market Cap	$5.0 Billion	Shares
Book Value	$3.1 Billion	63,771,472
Price/Book	1.61	% Held
Price/Sales	2.20	87.33

Business Summary: Wealth Management (MIC: 5.5.2 SIC: 6282 NAIC: 523920)

Affiliated Managers Group is a global asset management company with equity investments in boutique investment management firms (Affiliates). Co. provides centralized assistance to its Affiliates in strategic matters, marketing, distribution, product development and operations. Through its Affiliates, Co. provides a range of strategies designed to assist institutional, retail and clients worldwide in attaining their investment objectives. In addition, Co. manages investment strategies that address the needs of institutional clients, including foundations and endowments, defined benefit and defined contribution plans for corporations and municipalities, and multi-employer plans.

Recent Developments: For the quarter ended Sep 30 2019, net income decreased 19.7% to US$162.1 million from US$201.9 million in the year-earlier quarter. Revenues were US$549.0 million, down 8.7% from US$601.3 million the year before. Indirect operating expenses decreased 11.4% to US$373.4 million from US$421.6 million in the equivalent prior-year period.

Prospects: Our evaluation of Affiliated Managers Group Inc. as of October 4th, 2019 is the result of our systematic analysis on three basic characteristics: earnings strength, relative valuation, and recent stock price movement. The company has enjoyed a very positive trend in earnings per share over the past 5 quarters. However, recent analyst estimates for the company have been mixed and AMG has posted results that exceeded analysts' expectations. Based on operating earnings yield, the company is undervalued when compared to all of the companies we cover. Share price changes over the past year indicates that AMG will perform poorly over the near term.

Financial Data

(US$ in Thousands)	9 Mos	6 Mos	3 Mos	12/31/2018	12/31/2017	12/31/2016	12/31/2015	12/31/2014
Earnings Per Share	(2.80)	(2.17)	(2.12)	4.52	12.03	8.57	9.28	8.01
Cash Flow Per Share	17.48	17.11	17.68	21.28	20.90	18.91	22.19	25.31
Dividends Per Share	1.260	1.240	1.220	1.200	0.800	...	...	...
Dividend Payout %	...	...	...	26.55	6.65	...	...	...
Income Statement								
Total Revenue	1,684,000	1,135,100	543,100	2,378,400	2,305,000	2,194,600	2,484,500	2,510,900
EBITDA	661,600	438,700	211,100	931,200	972,400	873,600	992,600	977,600
Depn & Amortn	72,000	50,900	29,600	136,800	106,700	134,500	142,300	139,100
Income Before Taxes	532,200	349,900	163,300	713,800	764,900	645,800	801,700	731,800
Income Taxes	4,400	(26,100)	(61,800)	181,300	58,400	235,600	256,900	227,900
Net Income	(6,800)	(93,100)	(200,800)	243,600	689,500	472,800	516,000	452,100
Average Shares	50,400	51,000	51,900	53,800	58,600	57,000	57,200	58,400
Balance Sheet								
Current Assets	1,123,400	1,132,300	1,084,600	1,286,500	1,116,100	1,084,000	1,304,200	1,316,300
Total Assets	7,679,000	7,727,800	7,677,000	8,219,100	8,702,100	8,749,100	7,784,800	7,698,100
Current Liabilities	648,000	607,100	576,500	746,600	807,200	729,300	729,400	808,300
Long-Term Obligations	1,792,600	1,791,400	1,780,700	1,522,200	1,550,300	1,808,000	1,589,600	1,591,800
Total Liabilities	4,609,000	4,502,500	4,536,600	4,761,700	4,879,900	5,129,500	4,947,700	5,071,100
Stockholders' Equity	3,070,000	3,225,300	3,140,400	3,457,400	3,822,200	3,619,600	2,837,100	2,627,000
Shares Outstanding	58,500	50,700	58,500	58,500	58,500	58,500	55,800	54,600
Statistical Record								
Return on Assets %	N.M.	N.M.	N.M.	2.88	7.90	5.70	6.67	6.45
Return on Equity %	N.M.	N.M.	N.M.	6.69	18.53	14.61	18.89	18.99
EBITDA Margin %	39.29	38.65	38.87	39.15	42.19	39.81	39.95	38.93
Net Margin %	N.M.	N.M.	N.M.	10.24	29.91	21.54	20.77	18.01
Asset Turnover	0.28	0.28	0.28	0.28	0.26	0.26	0.32	0.36
Current Ratio	1.73	1.87	1.88	1.72	1.38	1.49	1.79	1.63
Debt to Equity	0.58	0.56	0.57	0.44	0.41	0.50	0.56	0.61
Price Range	138.00-74.49	160.01-83.82	183.93-90.24	215.76-90.24	206.51-141.34	179.01-117.80	228.02-144.01	216.88-179.30
P/E Ratio	...	...	...	47.73-19.96	17.17-11.75	20.89-13.75	24.57-15.52	27.08-22.38
Average Yield %	1.26	1.07	0.92	0.78	0.46	...	...	...

Address: 777 South Flagler Drive, West Palm Beach, FL 33401 **Telephone:** 800-345-1100	**Web Site:** www.amg.com **Officers:** Sean M. Healey - Executive Chairman, Chairman, Chief Executive Officer Jay C. Horgen - President, Chief Executive Officer, Chief Financial Officer, Treasurer	**Auditors:** PricewaterhouseCoopers LLP **Investor Contact:** 617-747-3300 **Transfer Agents:** American Stock Transfer & Trust Company, New York, NY

AFLAC INC

*7 Year Price Score 114.03 *NYSE Composite Index=100 *12 Month Price Score 98.60

Interim Earnings (Per Share)

Qtr.	Mar	Jun	Sep	Dec
2016	0.87	0.66	0.77	0.92
2017	0.73	0.90	0.90	3.25
2018	0.91	1.07	1.09	0.69
2019	1.23	1.09	1.04	...

Interim Dividends (Per Share)

Amt	Decl	Ex	Rec	Pay
0.27Q	01/31/2019	02/19/2019	02/20/2019	03/01/2019
0.27Q	04/25/2019	05/21/2019	05/22/2019	06/03/2019
0.27Q	07/25/2019	08/20/2019	08/21/2019	09/03/2019
0.27Q	10/24/2019	11/19/2019	11/20/2019	12/02/2019

Indicated Div: $1.08 (Div. Reinv. Plan)

Valuation Analysis | **Institutional Holding**

Forecast EPS	$4.43	No of Institutions
	(01/17/2020)	1501
Market Cap	$38.9 Billion	Shares
Book Value	$29.4 Billion	595,166,080
Price/Book	1.32	% Held
Price/Sales	1.78	59.67

Business Summary: Life & Health (MIC: 5.2.2 SIC: 6321 NAIC: 524113)

Aflac is a holding company. Through its subsidiaries, Co. sells supplemental health and life insurance in the U.S. and Japan. Co.'s insurance business is marketed and administered through its subsidiary, American Family Life Assurance Company of Columbus (Aflac), in the U.S. and through its subsidiary, Aflac Life Insurance Japan Ltd., in Japan. Most of Aflac's policies are individually underwritten and marketed through independent agents. Aflac U.S. markets and administers group products through Co.'s subsidiary, Continental American Insurance Company, branded as Aflac Group Insurance. Co.'s insurance operations in the U.S. and Japan service the two markets for Co.'s insurance business.

Recent Developments: For the quarter ended Sep 30 2019, net income decreased 8.0% to US$777.0 million from US$845.0 million in the year-earlier quarter. Revenues were US$5.54 billion, down 0.7% from US$5.58 billion the year before. Net premiums earned were US$4.74 billion versus US$4.64 billion in the prior-year quarter, an increase of 2.2%. Net investment income rose 7.6% to US$936.0 million from US$870.0 million a year ago.

Prospects: Our evaluation of AFLAC Inc. as of October 4th, 2019 is the result of our systematic analysis on three basic characteristics: earnings strength, relative valuation, and recent stock price movement. The company has produced a positive trend in earnings per share over the past 5 quarters. However, recent analyst estimates for the company have been unchanged, while AFL has posted results that exceeded analysts' expectations. Based on operating earnings yield, the company is undervalued when compared to all of the companies we cover. Share price changes over the past year indicates that AFL will perform well over the near term.

Financial Data (US$ in Thousands)	9 Mos	6 Mos	3 Mos	12/31/2018	12/31/2017	12/31/2016	12/31/2015	12/31/2014
Earnings Per Share	4.05	4.10	4.08	3.77	5.77	3.21	2.92	3.25
Cash Flow Per Share	7.59	7.47	8.41	7.81	7.74	7.26	7.87	7.26
Tang Book Value Per Share	40.04	38.14	34.90	31.06	31.50	25.24	20.86	20.73
Dividends Per Share	1.070	1.060	1.050	1.040	0.870	0.830	0.790	0.750
Dividend Payout %	26.42	25.85	25.74	27.59	15.08	25.86	27.01	23.08
Income Statement								
Premium Income	14,109,000	9,373,000	4,691,000	18,677,000	18,531,000	19,225,000	17,570,000	19,072,000
Total Revenue	16,704,000	11,168,000	5,657,000	21,758,000	21,667,000	22,559,000	20,872,000	22,728,000
Benefits & Claims	8,958,000	5,932,000	2,967,000	12,000,000	12,181,000	12,919,000	11,746,000	12,937,000
Income Before Taxes	3,388,000	2,351,000	1,242,000	3,983,000	4,018,000	4,067,000	3,862,000	4,491,000
Income Taxes	865,000	606,000	314,000	1,063,000	(586,000)	1,408,000	1,329,000	1,540,000
Net Income	2,523,000	1,745,000	928,000	2,920,000	4,604,000	2,659,000	2,533,000	2,951,000
Average Shares	743,842	748,849	755,790	774,650	797,860	827,842	866,344	908,000
Balance Sheet								
Total Assets	154,137,000	151,400,000	145,679,000	140,406,000	137,217,000	129,819,000	118,296,000	119,767,000
Total Liabilities	124,699,000	123,159,000	119,630,000	116,944,000	112,619,000	109,337,000	100,588,000	101,420,000
Stockholders' Equity	29,438,000	28,241,000	26,049,000	23,462,000	24,598,000	20,482,000	17,708,000	18,347,000
Shares Outstanding	735,130	740,465	746,487	755,286	780,910	811,620	848,760	884,890
Statistical Record								
Return on Assets %	2.09	2.12	2.14	2.10	3.45	2.14	2.13	2.45
Return on Equity %	11.57	11.97	12.44	12.15	20.43	13.89	14.05	17.90
Loss Ratio %	63.49	63.29	63.25	64.25	65.73	67.20	66.85	67.83
Net Margin %	15.10	15.63	16.40	13.42	21.25	11.79	12.14	12.98
Price Range	56.89-41.70	55.34-41.70	50.25-41.70	48.04-41.63	44.63-33.57	37.14-27.77	32.99-27.61	33.40-27.90
P/E Ratio	14.05-10.30	13.50-10.17	12.32-10.22	12.74-11.04	7.73-5.82	11.57-8.65	11.30-9.46	10.28-8.58
Average Yield %	2.17	2.23	2.23	2.32	2.23	2.45	2.55	2.44

Address: 1932 Wynnton Road, Columbus, GA 31999 Telephone: 706-323-3431 Fax: 706-596-3488	Web Site: www.aflac.com Officers: Daniel P. Amos - Chairman, President, Chief Executive Officer Frederick John Crawford - President, Chief Operating Officer, Executive Vice President, Chief Financial Officer	Auditors: KPMG LLP Investor Contact: 706-596-3264 Transfer Agents: Aflac Incorporated Shareholder Services, Columbus, GA

AGCO CORP.

Exchange	Symbol	Price	52Wk Range	Yield	P/E
NYS	AGCO	$77.25 (12/31/2019)	80.68-54.35	0.83	19.26

*7 Year Price Score 101.54 *NYSE Composite Index=100 *12 Month Price Score 103.70

Interim Earnings (Per Share)

Qtr.	Mar	Jun	Sep	Dec
2016	0.09	0.61	0.50	0.76
2017	(0.13)	1.14	0.76	0.55
2018	0.30	1.14	0.89	1.25
2019	0.84	1.82	0.10	...

Interim Dividends (Per Share)

Amt	Decl	Ex	Rec	Pay
0.15Q	01/25/2019	02/14/2019	02/15/2019	03/15/2019
0.16Q	04/25/2019	05/14/2019	05/15/2019	06/14/2019
0.16Q	07/12/2019	08/14/2019	08/15/2019	09/16/2019
0.16Q	10/24/2019	11/14/2019	11/15/2019	12/16/2019

Indicated Div: $0.64

Valuation Analysis

Forecast EPS $5.08 (01/14/2020)
Market Cap $5.9 Billion
Book Value $3.0 Billion
Price/Book 1.97
Price/Sales 0.64

Institutional Holding

No of Institutions 584
Shares 80,972,656
% Held 77.84

Business Summary: Industrial Machinery & Equipment (MIC: 7.2.1 SIC: 3523 NAIC: 333111)

AGCO is a manufacturer and distributor of agricultural equipment and related replacement parts. Co. sells a range of agricultural equipment, including tractors, combines, self-propelled sprayers, hay tools, forage equipment, seeding and tillage equipment, implements, and grain storage and protein production systems. Co.'s products are used in the agricultural equipment industry and are marketed under the Challenger®, Fendt®, GSI®, Massey Ferguson® and Valtra® brands. Co. distributes its products through independent dealers and distributors. In addition, Co. provides retail and wholesale financing through its finance joint ventures with Cooperatieve Centrale Raiffeisen-Boerenleenbank B.A.

Recent Developments: For the quarter ended Sep 30 2019, net income decreased 91.1% to US$6.3 million from US$70.7 million in the year-earlier quarter. Revenues were US$2.11 billion, down 4.8% from US$2.21 billion the year before. Operating income was US$105.9 million versus US$111.3 million in the prior-year quarter, a decrease of 4.9%. Direct operating expenses declined 4.7% to US$1.66 billion from US$1.74 billion in the comparable period the year before. Indirect operating expenses decreased 5.0% to US$344.3 million from US$362.4 million in the equivalent prior-year period.

Prospects: Our evaluation of AGCO Corp. as of October 4th, 2019 is the result of our systematic analysis on three basic characteristics: earnings strength, relative valuation, and recent stock price movement. The company has generated a negative trend in earnings per share over the past 5 quarters. However, recent analyst estimates for the company have been unchanged while AGCO has posted results that exceeded analysts' expectations. Based on operating earnings yield, the company is undervalued when compared to all of the companies we cover. Share price changes over the past year indicates that AGCO will perform well over the near term.

Financial Data

(US$ in Thousands)	9 Mos	6 Mos	3 Mos	12/31/2018	12/31/2017	12/31/2016	12/31/2015	12/31/2014
Earnings Per Share	-4.01	4.80	4.12	3.58	2.32	1.96	3.06	4.36
Cash Flow Per Share	6.83	7.67	8.19	7.56	7.27	4.53	6.03	4.69
Tang Book Value Per Share	13.20	13.49	11.92	11.29	10.55	9.97	14.51	19.09
Dividends Per Share	0.620	0.610	0.600	0.600	0.560	0.520	0.480	0.440
Dividend Payout %	15.46	12.71	14.56	16.76	24.14	26.53	15.69	10.09
Income Statement								
Total Revenue	6,527,800	4,418,400	1,995,800	9,352,000	8,306,500	7,410,500	7,467,300	9,723,700
EBITDA	555,700	403,600	146,100	704,000	608,700	531,600	584,900	877,800
Depn & Amortn	204,800	137,800	68,300	289,900	279,800	274,600	260,100	280,400
Income Before Taxes	335,000	256,300	74,300	360,300	283,800	204,900	279,400	539,000
Income Taxes	155,800	72,600	19,400	110,900	133,600	92,200	72,500	187,700
Net Income	213,500	205,900	65,100	285,500	186,400	160,100	266,400	410,400
Average Shares	76,700	77,200	77,500	79,700	80,200	81,700	87,100	94,200
Balance Sheet								
Current Assets	3,956,600	4,161,600	3,961,300	3,537,400	3,627,700	3,165,700	2,898,300	3,527,900
Total Assets	8,079,200	8,415,100	8,204,300	7,626,400	7,971,700	7,168,400	6,501,300	7,395,900
Current Liabilities	3,027,700	3,228,900	3,054,700	2,766,700	2,650,600	2,144,900	2,185,400	2,216,900
Long-Term Obligations	1,269,200	1,308,100	1,404,300	1,275,300	1,618,100	1,610,000	928,800	997,600
Total Liabilities	5,102,600	5,350,400	5,248,600	4,693,500	4,942,100	4,392,300	3,663,000	3,947,400
Stockholders' Equity	2,976,600	3,064,700	2,955,700	2,932,900	3,029,600	2,776,100	2,838,300	3,448,500
Shares Outstanding	75,915	76,313	76,742	76,536	79,553	79,465	83,814	89,146
Statistical Record								
Return on Assets %	3.90	4.57	3.92	3.66	2.46	2.34	3.83	5.18
Return on Equity %	10.61	12.52	10.86	9.58	6.42	5.69	8.47	11.00
EBITDA Margin %	8.51	9.13	7.32	7.53	7.33	7.17	7.83	9.03
Net Margin %	3.27	4.66	3.26	3.05	2.24	2.16	3.57	4.22
Asset Turnover	1.14	1.12	1.12	1.20	1.10	1.08	1.07	1.23
Current Ratio	1.31	1.29	1.30	1.28	1.37	1.48	1.33	1.59
Debt to Equity	0.43	0.43	0.48	0.43	0.53	0.58	0.33	0.29
Price Range	80.21-50.07	77.85-50.07	69.55-50.07	74.11-50.07	75.48-58.03	60.66-44.02	57.87-42.72	59.19-42.08
P/E Ratio	20.00-12.49	16.22-10.43	16.88-12.15	20.70-13.99	32.53-25.01	30.95-22.46	18.91-13.96	13.58-9.65
Average Yield %	0.93	0.96	0.98	0.96	0.84	1.03	0.98	0.87

Address: 4205 River Green Parkway, Duluth, GA 30096
Telephone: 770-813-9200

Web Site: www.agcocorp.com
Officers: Martin H. Richenhagen - Chairman, President, Chief Executive Officer Torsten Dehner - Senior Vice President, Region Officer, Division Officer

Auditors: KPMG LLP
Investor Contact: 770-232-8229
Transfer Agents: Computershare Trust Company, N.A., Canton, MA

AGILENT TECHNOLOGIES, INC.

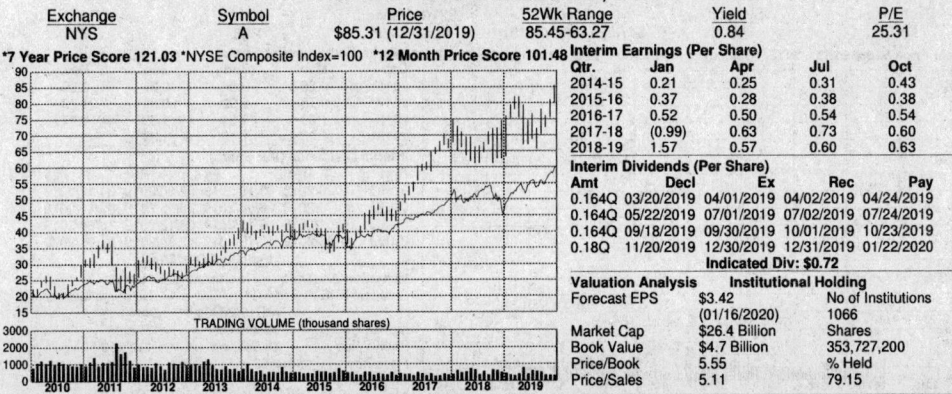

Exchange	Symbol	Price	52Wk Range	Yield	P/E
NYS	A	$85.31 (12/31/2019)	85.45-63.27	0.84	25.31

*7 Year Price Score 121.03 *NYSE Composite Index=100 *12 Month Price Score 101.48

Interim Earnings (Per Share)

Qtr.	Jan	Apr	Jul	Oct
2014-15	0.21	0.25	0.31	0.43
2015-16	0.37	0.28	0.38	0.38
2016-17	0.52	0.50	0.54	0.54
2017-18	(0.99)	0.63	0.73	0.60
2018-19	1.57	0.57	0.60	0.63

Interim Dividends (Per Share)

Amt	Decl	Ex	Rec	Pay
0.164Q	03/20/2019	04/01/2019	04/02/2019	04/24/2019
0.164Q	05/22/2019	07/01/2019	07/02/2019	07/24/2019
0.164Q	09/18/2019	09/30/2019	10/01/2019	10/23/2019
0.18Q	11/20/2019	12/30/2019	12/31/2019	01/22/2020

Indicated Div: $0.72

Valuation Analysis

		Institutional Holding	
Forecast EPS	$3.42	No of Institutions	
	(01/16/2020)	1066	
Market Cap	$26.4 Billion	Shares	
Book Value	$4.7 Billion	353,727,200	
Price/Book	5.55	% Held	
Price/Sales	5.11	79.15	

Business Summary: Medical Instruments & Equipment (MIC: 4.3.1 SIC: 3826 NAIC: 334516)

Agilent Technologies is engaged in life sciences, diagnostics and applied chemical markets. Co.'s segments are: Life Sciences and Applied Markets Business, which provides instruments and software that enable customers to identify, quantify and analyze the physical and biological properties of substances and products; Diagnostics and Genomics Business, which includes the genomics, nucleic acid contract manufacturing and research and development, pathology, companion diagnostics, reagent partnership and biomolecular analysis businesses; and Agilent CrossLab Business, which spans the entire lab with its consumables and services portfolio to improve customer outcomes.

Recent Developments: For the year ended Oct 31 2019, net income increased 238.9% to US$1.07 billion from US$316.0 million in the prior year. Revenues were US$5.16 billion, up 5.1% from US$4.91 billion the year before. Operating income was US$941.0 million versus US$904.0 million in the prior year, an increase of 4.1%. Direct operating expenses rose 5.6% to US$2.36 billion from US$2.23 billion in the comparable period the year before. Indirect operating expenses increased 5.0% to US$1.86 billion from US$1.78 billion in the equivalent prior-year period.

Prospects: Our evaluation of Agilent Technologies Inc. as of October 4th, 2019 is the result of our systematic analysis on three basic characteristics: earnings strength, relative valuation, and recent stock price movement. The company has managed to produce a neutral trend in earnings per share over the past 5 quarters. Additionally, recent analyst estimates for the company have been unchanged while A has posted results that exceeded analysts' expectations. Based on operating earnings yield, the company is fairly valued when compared to all of the companies we cover. Share price changes over the past year indicates that A will perform in line with the market over the near term.

Financial Data

(US$ in Millions)	10/31/2019	10/31/2018	10/31/2017	10/31/2016	10/31/2015	10/31/2014	10/31/2013	10/31/2012
Earnings Per Share	3.37	0.97	2.10	1.40	1.20	1.49	2.10	3.27
Cash Flow Per Share	3.25	3.39	2.76	2.43	1.47	2.14	3.38	3.52
Tang Book Value Per Share	0.16	3.47	5.79	4.07	4.09	5.17	3.98	3.09
Dividends Per Share	0.656	0.596	0.528	0.460	0.400	0.528	0.460	0.300
Dividend Payout %	19.47	61.44	25.14	32.86	33.33	35.44	21.90	9.17
Income Statement								
Total Revenue	5,163	4,914	4,472	4,202	4,038	6,981	6,782	6,858
EBITDA	1,068	1,085	954	700	637	944	1,140	1,306
Depn & Amortn	111	102	94	95	98	194	181	171
Income Before Taxes	919	946	803	544	480	646	859	1,043
Income Taxes	(152)	630	119	82	42	142	135	(110)
Net Income	1,071	316	684	462	401	504	724	1,153
Average Shares	318	325	326	329	335	338	345	353
Balance Sheet								
Current Assets	3,189	3,848	4,169	3,635	3,686	5,500	4,983	4,629
Total Assets	9,452	8,541	8,426	7,802	7,479	10,831	10,686	10,536
Current Liabilities	2,080	1,171	1,263	945	976	1,702	1,602	1,893
Long-Term Obligations	1,791	1,799	1,801	1,912	1,655	2,762	2,699	2,112
Total Liabilities	4,704	3,974	3,595	3,559	3,312	5,533	5,400	5,354
Stockholders' Equity	4,748	4,567	4,831	4,243	4,167	5,298	5,286	5,182
Shares Outstanding	309	317	322	323	331	334	332	346
Statistical Record								
Return on Assets %	11.90	3.72	8.43	6.03	4.38	4.68	6.82	11.74
Return on Equity %	23.00	6.72	15.08	10.96	8.47	9.52	13.83	24.23
EBITDA Margin %	20.69	22.08	21.33	16.66	15.78	13.52	16.81	19.04
Net Margin %	20.74	6.43	15.30	10.99	9.93	7.22	10.68	16.81
Asset Turnover	0.57	0.58	0.55	0.55	0.44	0.65	0.64	0.70
Current Ratio	1.53	3.29	3.30	3.85	3.78	3.23	3.11	2.45
Debt to Equity	0.38	0.39	0.37	0.45	0.40	0.52	0.51	0.41
Price Range	82.00-62.61	74.82-61.13	68.03-43.21	48.44-34.80	43.55-33.37	43.57-35.79	37.89-25.56	32.79-23.55
P/E Ratio	24.33-18.58	77.13-63.02	32.40-20.58	34.60-24.86	36.29-27.81	29.24-24.02	18.04-12.17	10.03-7.20
Average Yield %	0.90	0.89	0.95	1.08	1.01	1.31	1.46	1.46

Address: 5301 Stevens Creek Blvd., Santa Clara, CA 95051	**Web Site:** www.agilent.com	**Auditors:** PricewaterhouseCoopers LLP
Telephone: 800-227-9770	**Officers:** Koh Boon Hwee - Chairman Michael R. (Mike) McMullen - President, Chief Executive Officer, Senior Vice President, Division Officer	**Investor Contact:** 408-345-8948
Fax: 408-345-8474		**Transfer Agents:** ComputerShare Investor Services, Chicago, IL

AIR LEASE CORP

Exchange	Symbol	Price	52Wk Range	Yield	P/E
NYS	AL	$47.52 (12/31/2019)	48.42-29.65	1.26	9.68

*7 Year Price Score 91.71   *NYSE Composite Index=100   *12 Month Price Score 109.57

Interim Earnings (Per Share)

Qtr.	Mar	Jun	Sep	Dec
2016	0.85	0.84	0.86	0.89
2017	0.78	0.92	0.90	4.23
2018	1.00	1.04	1.32	1.24
2019	1.23	1.10	1.34	...

Interim Dividends (Per Share)

Amt	Decl	Ex	Rec	Pay
0.13Q	02/20/2019	03/19/2019	03/20/2019	04/10/2019
0.13Q	05/08/2019	06/04/2019	06/05/2019	07/11/2019
0.13Q	08/07/2019	09/12/2019	09/13/2019	10/04/2019
0.15Q	11/06/2019	12/19/2019	12/20/2019	01/06/2020

Indicated Div: $0.60

Valuation Analysis

Forecast EPS	$5.04
	(01/16/2020)
Market Cap	$5.4 Billion
Book Value	$5.5 Billion
Price/Book	0.98
Price/Sales	2.79

Institutional Holding

No of Institutions	387
Shares	112,959,624
% Held	99.16

Business Summary: Miscellaneous Transportation Services (MIC: 7.4.5 SIC: 7359 NAIC: 532411)

Air Lease is an aircraft leasing company. Co. is mainly engaged in purchasing new commercial jet transport aircraft directly from aircraft manufacturers, such as The Boeing Company and Airbus S.A.S., and leasing those aircraft to airlines. In addition to its leasing activities, Co. sells aircraft from its operating lease portfolio to third parties, including other leasing companies, financial services companies, and airlines. Co. also provides fleet management services to investors and owners of aircraft portfolios. Co. provides aircraft to airline customers in various geographical regions, such as Asia, the Pacific Rim, Latin America, the Middle East, Europe, Africa, and North America.

Recent Developments: For the quarter ended Sep 30 2019, net income increased 6.3% to US$155.8 million from US$146.6 million in the year-earlier quarter. Revenues were US$530.9 million, up 17.8% from US$450.7 million the year before. Indirect operating expenses increased 24.3% to US$337.1 million from US$271.3 million in the equivalent prior-year period.

Prospects: Our evaluation of Air Lease Corp as of October 4th, 2019 is the result of our systematic analysis on three basic characteristics: earnings strength, relative valuation, and recent stock price movement. The company has managed to produce a neutral trend in earnings per share over the past 5 quarters. However, recent analyst estimates for the company have been reduced and AL has posted results that fell short of analysts' expectations. Based on operating earnings yield, the company is undervalued when compared to all of the companies we cover. Share price changes over the past year indicates that AL will perform in line with the market over the near term.

Financial Data

(US$ in Thousands)	9 Mos	6 Mos	3 Mos	12/31/2018	12/31/2017	12/31/2016	12/31/2015	12/31/2014
Earnings Per Share	4.91	4.89	4.83	4.60	6.82	3.44	2.34	2.38
Cash Flow Per Share	12.09	11.87	11.43	11.98	10.27	9.90	8.19	7.53
Tang Book Value Per Share	48.47	47.46	46.56	43.32	39.83	32.89	29.44	27.07
Dividends Per Share	0.520	0.490	0.460	0.430	0.325	0.225	0.170	0.130
Dividend Payout %	10.59	10.02	9.52	9.35	4.77	6.54	7.26	5.46
Income Statement								
Total Revenue	1,468,348	937,446	466,051	1,679,702	1,516,380	1,419,055	1,222,840	1,050,493
EBITDA	1,411,746	902,039	447,895	1,564,855	1,405,253	1,319,121	1,056,857	952,023
Depn & Amortn	565,468	363,263	175,191	581,985	508,352	452,682	397,760	336,657
Income Before Taxes	529,267	335,480	174,944	640,138	609,530	580,238	392,953	394,776
Income Taxes	107,081	69,081	36,850	129,303	(146,622)	205,313	139,562	138,778
Net Income	422,186	266,399	138,094	510,835	756,152	374,925	253,391	255,998
Average Shares	113,263	112,807	112,380	112,363	111,657	110,798	110,628	110,192
Balance Sheet								
Current Assets	336,423	288,102	298,242	2,132,258	1,871,058	1,581,478	1,244,238	1,434,891
Total Assets	21,609,701	20,484,348	19,178,935	18,481,808	15,614,164	13,975,616	12,355,098	10,774,784
Current Liabilities	420,444	453,536	366,826	1,372,710	1,165,322	1,113,110	1,069,313	889,124
Long-Term Obligations	13,751,872	12,859,244	11,869,671	11,538,905	9,698,785	8,713,874	7,712,421	6,714,362
Total Liabilities	16,147,528	15,184,464	14,005,118	13,674,908	11,486,722	10,593,429	9,335,186	8,002,722
Stockholders' Equity	5,462,173	5,299,884	5,173,817	4,806,900	4,127,442	3,382,187	3,019,912	2,772,062
Shares Outstanding	112,701	111,666	111,118	110,949	103,621	102,844	102,582	102,392
Statistical Record								
Return on Assets %	2.86	2.92	3.07	3.00	5.11	2.84	2.19	2.55
Return on Equity %	11.28	11.44	11.45	11.44	20.14	11.68	8.75	9.67
EBITDA Margin %	96.15	96.22	96.10	93.16	92.67	92.96	86.43	90.63
Net Margin %	28.75	28.42	29.63	30.41	49.87	26.42	20.72	24.37
Asset Turnover	0.10	0.10	0.10	0.10	0.10	0.11	0.11	0.10
Current Ratio	0.80	0.64	0.81	1.55	1.61	1.42	1.16	1.61
Debt to Equity	2.52	2.43	2.29	2.40	2.35	2.58	2.55	2.42
Price Range	45.97-28.73	46.96-28.73	46.96-28.73	50.34-28.73	48.31-34.64	37.02-22.73	40.21-29.83	42.44-30.27
P/E Ratio	9.36-5.85	9.60-5.88	9.72-5.95	10.94-6.25	7.08-5.08	10.76-6.61	17.18-12.75	17.83-12.72
Average Yield %	1.35	1.25	1.13	1.00	0.82	0.75	0.48	0.36

Address: 2000 Avenue of the Stars, Suite 1000N, Los Angeles, CA 90067 **Telephone:** 310-553-0555	**Web Site:** www.airleasecorp.com **Officers:** Steven F. Udvar-Házy - Executive Chairman, Chairman, Chief Executive Officer John L. Plueger - President, Chief Executive Officer, Chief Operating Officer	**Auditors:** KPMG LLP **Investor Contact:** 310-553-0555 **Transfer Agents:** American Stock Transfer & Trust Company, LLC, Seattle, WA

AIR PRODUCTS & CHEMICALS INC

Exchange	Symbol	Price	52Wk Range	Yield	P/E	Div Acheiver
NYS	APD	$234.99 (12/31/2019)	241.31-154.62	1.97	29.60	36 Years

*7 Year Price Score 121.09 *NYSE Composite Index=100 *12 Month Price Score 105.02

Interim Earnings (Per Share)

Qtr.	Dec	Mar	Jun	Sep
2014-15	1.50	1.33	1.47	1.58
2015-16	1.67	(2.17)	1.59	1.80
2016-17	1.37	9.70	0.46	2.13
2017-18	0.70	1.89	2.15	2.05
2018-19	1.57	1.90	2.20	2.26

Interim Dividends (Per Share)

Amt	Decl	Ex	Rec	Pay
1.16Q	01/24/2019	03/29/2019	04/01/2019	05/13/2019
1.16Q	05/14/2019	06/28/2019	07/01/2019	08/12/2019
1.16Q	07/18/2019	09/30/2019	10/01/2019	11/11/2019
1.16Q	11/26/2019	12/31/2019	01/02/2020	02/10/2020

Indicated Div: $4.64 (Div. Reinv. Plan)

Valuation Analysis / Institutional Holding

Forecast EPS	$9.45	No of Institutions
	(01/17/2020)	1566
Market Cap	$51.8 Billion	Shares
Book Value	$11.1 Billion	246,845,840
Price/Book	4.69	% Held
Price/Sales	5.81	84.16

Business Summary: Specialty Chemicals (MIC: 8.3.2 SIC: 2813 NAIC: 325120)

Air Products and Chemicals serves customers globally with a portfolio of products, services, and solutions that include atmospheric gases, process and other gases, equipment, and services. Co. is a supplier of hydrogen and is engaged in helium and liquefied natural gas (LNG) process technology and equipment. Co. also develops, engineers, builds, owns and operates industrial gas projects, including gasification projects that convert abundant natural resources into syngas for the production of power, fuels and chemicals. Co. designs and manufactures equipment for air separation, hydrocarbon recovery and purification, LNG, and liquid helium and liquid hydrogen transport and storage.

Recent Developments: For the year ended Sep 30 2019, income from continuing operations increased 21.4% to US$1.81 billion from US$1.49 billion a year earlier. Net income increased 18.0% to US$1.81 billion from US$1.53 billion in the prior year. Revenues were US$8.92 billion, down 0.1% from US$8.93 billion the year before. Operating income was US$2.14 billion versus US$1.97 billion in the prior year, an increase of 9.1%. Direct operating expenses declined 3.5% to US$5.98 billion from US$6.19 billion in the comparable period the year before. Indirect operating expenses increased 3.1% to US$799.0 million from US$775.1 million in the equivalent prior-year period.

Prospects: Our evaluation of Air Products & Chemicals Inc. as of October 4th, 2019 is the result of our systematic analysis on three basic characteristics: earnings strength, relative valuation, and recent stock price movement. The company has enjoyed a very positive trend in earnings per share over the past 5 quarters. However, recent analyst estimates for the company have been unchanged, while APD has posted results that exceeded analysts' expectations. Based on operating earnings yield, the company is fairly valued when compared to all of the companies we cover. Share price changes over the past year indicates that APD will perform very well over the near term.

Financial Data (US$ in Thousands)	09/30/2019	09/30/2018	09/30/2017	09/30/2016	09/30/2015	09/30/2014	09/30/2013	09/30/2012
Earnings Per Share	7.94	6.78	13.65	2.89	5.88	4.61	4.68	5.44
Cash Flow Per Share	13.48	11.65	11.62	12.48	11.34	10.28	7.41	8.33
Tang Book Value Per Share	44.63	43.87	41.20	25.04	26.05	25.82	22.12	19.38
Dividends Per Share	4.580	5.200	3.620	3.390	3.200	3.020	2.770	2.500
Dividend Payout %	57.68	76.70	26.52	117.30	54.42	65.51	59.19	45.96
Income Statement								
Total Revenue	8,918,900	8,930,200	8,187,600	9,524,400	9,894,900	10,439,000	10,180,400	9,611,700
EBITDA	3,260,800	2,911,400	2,298,300	2,985,900	2,560,400	2,233,600	2,182,700	2,094,200
Depn & Amortn	1,049,700	940,700	843,200	893,000	900,400	914,800	864,700	817,200
Income Before Taxes	2,074,100	1,840,200	1,336,000	1,983,600	1,561,100	1,203,100	1,182,600	1,158,700
Income Taxes	480,100	524,300	260,900	586,500	415,900	366,000	307,900	287,300
Net Income	1,760,000	1,497,800	3,000,400	631,100	1,277,900	991,700	994,200	1,167,300
Average Shares	221,600	220,800	218,000	218,300	217,300	215,220	212,300	214,700
Balance Sheet								
Current Assets	4,618,300	5,082,200	5,876,700	4,317,300	2,910,800	3,294,800	3,439,100	3,415,800
Total Assets	18,942,800	19,178,300	18,467,200	18,055,300	17,438,100	17,779,100	17,850,500	16,941,800
Current Liabilities	1,820,900	2,338,300	2,489,000	3,283,300	3,648,100	2,963,000	3,227,600	2,689,900
Long-Term Obligations	3,227,400	2,951,700	6,804,800	9,836,200	7,898,200	9,649,000	10,112,600	9,168,400
Total Liabilities	7,889,200	8,320,800	8,381,000	10,975,700	10,189,100	10,413,300	10,808,000	10,464,600
Stockholders' Equity	11,053,600	10,857,500	10,086,200	7,079,600	7,249,000	7,365,800	7,042,100	6,477,200
Shares Outstanding	220,415	219,515	218,346	217,350	215,359	213,538	211,179	212,475
Statistical Record								
Return on Assets %	9.23	7.96	16.43	3.55	7.26	5.57	5.72	7.45
Return on Equity %	16.06	14.30	34.96	8.78	17.49	13.77	14.71	18.97
EBITDA Margin %	36.56	32.60	28.07	31.35	25.88	21.40	21.44	21.79
Net Margin %	19.73	16.77	36.65	6.63	12.91	9.50	9.77	12.14
Asset Turnover	0.47	0.47	0.45	0.54	0.56	0.59	0.59	0.61
Current Ratio	2.54	2.17	2.36	1.31	0.80	1.11	1.07	1.27
Debt to Equity	0.29	0.27	0.67	1.39	1.09	1.31	1.44	1.42
Price Range	231.81-148.91	174.00-152.20	151.53-132.26	145.52-107.53	146.19-110.04	126.03-94.84	101.71-71.27	85.68-68.29
P/E Ratio	29.20-18.75	25.66-22.45	11.10-9.69	50.35-37.21	24.86-18.71	27.34-20.57	21.73-15.23	15.75-12.55
Average Yield %	2.40	3.20	2.54	2.68	2.43	2.74	3.30	3.20

Address: 7201 Hamilton Boulevard, Allentown, PA 18195-1501	Web Site: www.airproducts.com	Auditors: KPMG LLP
Telephone: 610-481-4911	Officers: Seifollah (Seifi) Ghasemi - Chairman, President, Chief Executive Officer M. Scott Crocco -	Investor Contact: 610-481-7461
Fax: 610-481-5900	Executive Vice President, Chief Financial Officer, Senior Vice President, Vice President, Controller, Principal Accounting Officer	Transfer Agents: Broadridge Corporate Issuer Services, Inc., Brentwood, NY

AK STEEL HOLDING CORP.

Exchange	Symbol	Price	52Wk Range	Yield	P/E
NYS	AKS	$3.29 (12/31/2019)	3.52-1.72	N/A	10.28

*7 Year Price Score 44.45   *NYSE Composite Index=100   *12 Month Price Score 106.69

Interim Earnings (Per Share)

Qtr.	Mar	Jun	Sep	Dec
2016	(0.08)	0.08	0.21	(0.29)
2017	0.19	0.19	(0.02)	(0.35)
2018	0.09	0.18	0.21	0.11
2019	(0.01)	0.21	0.01	...

Interim Dividends (Per Share)

Dividend Payment Suspended

Valuation Analysis / **Institutional Holding**

Forecast EPS	$0.35	No of Institutions
	(01/17/2020)	390
Market Cap	$1.0 Billion	Shares
Book Value	$134.6 Million	238,585,040
Price/Book	7.73	% Held
Price/Sales	0.16	59.64

TRADING VOLUME (thousand shares)

Business Summary: Non-Precious Metals (MIC: 8.2.2 SIC: 3312 NAIC: 331111)

AK Steel Holding is a producer of flat-rolled carbon, stainless and electrical steels products primarily for the automotive, infrastructure and manufacturing, and distributors and converters markets through its wholly-owned subsidiary, AK Steel Corporation. Co.'s other subsidiaries also provide customer solutions with carbon and stainless steel tubing products, solutions, tool design, hot- and cold-stamped steel components and assemblies. Co. sells its carbon steel products mainly to customers in North America, and it sells its electrical and stainless steel products primarily in North America and Europe. Co. also produces metallurgical coal through its AK Coal Resources, Inc. subsidiary.

Recent Developments: For the quarter ended Sep 30 2019, net income decreased 76.6% to US$19.9 million from US$84.9 million in the year-earlier quarter. Revenues were US$1.54 billion, down 11.5% from US$1.74 billion the year before. Operating income was US$51.1 million versus US$114.8 million in the prior-year quarter, a decrease of 55.5%. Direct operating expenses declined 8.1% to US$1.37 billion from US$1.49 billion in the comparable period the year before. Indirect operating expenses decreased 12.0% to US$118.4 million from US$134.6 million in the equivalent prior-year period.

Prospects: Our evaluation of AK Steel Holding Corp. as of October 4th, 2019 is the result of our systematic analysis on three basic characteristics: earnings strength, relative valuation, and recent stock price movement. The company has suffered a very negative trend in earnings per share over the past 5 quarters. However, recent analyst estimates for the company have been mixed and AKS has posted results that exceeded analysts' expectations. Based on operating earnings yield, the company is undervalued when compared to all of the companies we cover. Share price changes over the past year indicates that AKS will perform very poorly over the near term.

Financial Data

(US$ in Thousands)	9 Mos	6 Mos	3 Mos	12/31/2018	12/31/2017	12/31/2016	12/31/2015	12/31/2014
Earnings Per Share	0.32	0.52	0.49	0.59	0.02	(0.03)	(2.86)	(0.65)
Cash Flow Per Share	0.97	0.99	0.92	1.16	0.63	1.32	1.13	(2.18)
Tang Book Value Per Share	0.43	0.43	0.30	N.M.	...	...	...	...
Income Statement								
Total Revenue	4,913,700	3,378,200	1,697,700	6,818,200	6,080,500	5,882,500	6,692,900	6,505,700
EBITDA	395,700	282,900	107,900	609,700	428,900	441,900	6,200	320,200
Depn & Amortn	173,100	117,500	60,500	220,200	226,000	216,600	216,000	201,900
Income Before Taxes	110,600	90,400	9,500	237,900	50,600	61,400	(382,800)	(26,400)
Income Taxes	2,700	2,400	1,400	(6,200)	(17,000)	3,200	63,400	7,700
Net Income	65,100	62,300	(4,500)	186,000	6,200	(7,800)	(509,000)	(96,900)
Average Shares	316,800	316,500	315,600	315,600	319,700	230,000	177,200	148,100
Balance Sheet								
Current Assets	2,066,200	2,160,200	2,229,400	2,201,300	1,833,900	1,823,700	1,806,200	2,025,700
Total Assets	4,604,600	4,687,000	4,770,100	4,515,700	4,296,100	4,036,000	4,084,400	4,858,500
Current Liabilities	1,001,600	1,066,900	1,087,700	1,128,600	1,001,000	865,300	1,042,600	1,125,200
Long-Term Obligations	1,969,700	1,946,200	2,037,700	1,993,700	2,110,100	1,816,600	2,354,100	2,452,500
Total Liabilities	4,470,000	4,551,400	4,676,100	4,415,800	4,512,100	4,308,200	5,062,000	5,351,000
Stockholders' Equity	134,600	135,600	94,000	99,900	(216,000)	(272,200)	(977,600)	(492,500)
Shares Outstanding	316,382	316,342	316,306	315,535	314,884	314,160	177,893	177,215
Statistical Record								
Return on Assets %	2.17	3.57	3.31	4.22	0.15	N.M.	N.M.	N.M.
Return on Equity %	85.11	198.54	408.01	...	...	...	...	...
EBITDA Margin %	8.05	8.37	6.36	8.94	7.05	7.51	0.09	4.92
Net Margin %	1.32	1.84	N.M.	2.73	0.10	N.M.	N.M.	N.M.
Asset Turnover	1.45	1.49	1.49	1.55	1.46	1.44	1.50	1.54
Current Ratio	2.06	2.02	2.05	1.95	1.83	2.11	1.73	1.80
Debt to Equity	14.63	14.35	21.68	19.96	...	...	...	...
Price Range	4.94-1.72	5.36-1.72	5.36-2.16	6.65-2.16	11.11-4.14	10.95-1.83	5.97-2.04	11.19-5.20
P/E Ratio	15.44-5.38	10.31-3.31	10.94-4.41	11.27-3.66	555.50-207.00	...	...	...

Address: 9227 Centre Pointe Drive, West Chester, OH 45069 **Telephone:** 513-425-5000 **Fax:** 513-425-5220	**Web Site:** www.aksteel.com **Officers:** Kirk W. Reich - President, Vice President, Chief Operating Officer, Division Officer Roger K. Newport - Chief Executive Officer, Executive Vice President, Senior Vice President, Vice President, Vice President, Chief Financial Officer	**Auditors:** Ernst & Young LLP **Investor Contact:** 513-425-5270 **Transfer Agents:** Computershare Investor Services, LLC, Canton, MA

ALASKA AIR GROUP, INC.

Exchange	Symbol	Price	52Wk Range	Yield	P/E
NYS	ALK	$67.75 (12/31/2019)	71.91-53.60	2.07	13.77

*7 Year Price Score 84.64   *NYSE Composite Index=100   *12 Month Price Score 103.42

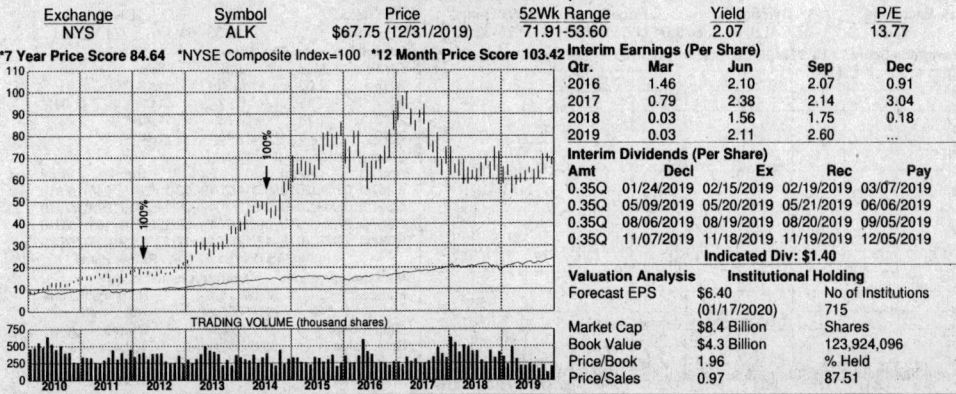

Interim Earnings (Per Share)

Qtr.	Mar	Jun	Sep	Dec
2016	1.46	2.10	2.07	0.91
2017	0.79	2.38	2.14	3.04
2018	0.03	1.56	1.75	0.18
2019	0.03	2.11	2.60	...

Interim Dividends (Per Share)

Amt	Decl	Ex	Rec	Pay
0.35Q	01/24/2019	02/15/2019	02/19/2019	03/07/2019
0.35Q	05/09/2019	05/20/2019	05/21/2019	06/06/2019
0.35Q	08/06/2019	08/19/2019	08/20/2019	09/05/2019
0.35Q	11/07/2019	11/18/2019	11/19/2019	12/05/2019

Indicated Div: $1.40

Valuation Analysis   **Institutional Holding**

Forecast EPS	$6.40 (01/17/2020)	No of Institutions	715
Market Cap	$8.4 Billion	Shares	
Book Value	$4.3 Billion		123,924,096
Price/Book	1.96	% Held	
Price/Sales	0.97		87.51

Business Summary: Airlines/Air Freight (MIC: 7.4.4 SIC: 4512 NAIC: 481111)

Alaska Air Group operates two airlines, Alaska Airlines, Inc. (Alaska) and Horizon Air Industries, Inc. (Horizon). Co.'s operation also includes McGee Air Services, an aviation services provider. Co. operates in three segments: Mainline, which includes scheduled air transportation on Alaska's Boeing or Airbus jet aircraft for passengers and cargo throughout the U.S., and in parts of Canada, Mexico, and Costa Rica; Regional, which includes Horizon's and other third-party carriers' scheduled air transportation for passengers across a shorter distance network within the U.S. under capacity purchase agreements (CPA); and Horizon, which includes the capacity sold to Alaska under CPA.

Recent Developments: For the quarter ended Sep 30 2019, net income increased 48.4% to US$322.0 million from US$217.0 million in the year-earlier quarter. Revenues were US$2.39 billion, up 8.0% from US$2.21 billion the year before. Operating income was US$422.0 million versus US$297.0 million in the prior-year quarter, an increase of 42.1%. Direct operating expenses declined 1.0% to US$988.0 million from US$998.0 million in the comparable period the year before. Indirect operating expenses increased 6.8% to US$979.0 million from US$917.0 million in the equivalent prior-year period.

Prospects: Our evaluation of Alaska Air Group Inc. as of October 4th, 2019 is the result of our systematic analysis on three basic characteristics: earnings strength, relative valuation, and recent stock price movement. The company has enjoyed a very positive trend in earnings per share over the past 5 quarters. However, recent analyst estimates for the company have been mixed and ALK has posted results that exceeded analysts' expectations. Based on operating earnings yield, the company is undervalued when compared to all of the companies we cover. Share price changes over the past year indicates that ALK will perform in line with the market over the near term.

Financial Data

(US$ in Thousands)	9 Mos	6 Mos	3 Mos	12/31/2018	12/31/2017	12/31/2016	12/31/2015	12/31/2014
Earnings Per Share	4.92	4.07	3.52	3.52	8.35	6.54	6.56	4.42
Cash Flow Per Share	12.90	12.17	11.01	9.70	12.90	11.19	12.34	7.60
Tang Book Value Per Share	17.73	15.45	13.57	13.65	13.37	6.92	19.26	16.18
Dividends Per Share	1.370	1.340	1.310	1.280	1.200	1.100	0.800	0.500
Dividend Payout %	27.85	32.92	37.22	36.36	14.37	16.82	12.20	11.31
Income Statement								
Total Revenue	6,553,000	4,164,000	1,876,000	8,264,000	7,933,000	5,931,000	5,598,000	5,368,000
EBITDA	1,108,000	583,000	121,000	1,018,000	1,631,000	1,711,000	1,619,000	1,276,000
Depn & Amortn	317,000	211,000	106,000	398,000	372,000	363,000	320,000	294,000
Income Before Taxes	773,000	357,000	6,000	585,000	1,207,000	1,345,000	1,312,000	975,000
Income Taxes	185,000	91,000	2,000	148,000	173,000	531,000	464,000	370,000
Net Income	588,000	266,000	4,000	437,000	1,034,000	814,000	848,000	605,000
Average Shares	124,067	124,301	123,915	123,975	123,854	124,389	129,372	136,801
Balance Sheet								
Current Assets	2,202,000	2,218,000	2,001,000	1,787,000	2,146,000	2,050,000	1,663,000	1,756,000
Total Assets	12,983,000	12,951,000	12,640,000	10,912,000	10,740,000	9,962,000	6,533,000	6,181,000
Current Liabilities	3,346,000	3,534,000	3,386,000	2,942,000	2,700,000	2,535,000	1,806,000	1,671,000
Long-Term Obligations	1,444,000	1,538,000	1,664,000	1,617,000	2,262,000	2,645,000	571,000	686,000
Total Liabilities	8,731,000	8,978,000	8,894,000	7,161,000	7,019,000	7,031,000	4,122,000	4,054,000
Stockholders' Equity	4,252,000	3,973,000	3,746,000	3,751,000	3,721,000	2,931,000	2,411,000	2,127,000
Shares Outstanding	123,277	123,338	123,504	123,194	123,060	123,328	125,175	131,481
Statistical Record								
Return on Assets %	5.12	4.22	3.72	4.04	9.99	9.84	13.34	10.07
Return on Equity %	15.19	13.38	12.16	11.70	31.09	30.39	37.37	29.11
EBITDA Margin %	16.91	14.00	6.45	12.32	20.56	28.85	28.92	23.77
Net Margin %	8.97	6.39	0.21	5.29	13.03	13.72	15.15	11.27
Asset Turnover	0.72	0.70	0.71	0.76	0.77	0.72	0.88	0.89
Current Ratio	0.66	0.63	0.59	0.61	0.79	0.81	0.92	1.05
Debt to Equity	0.34	0.39	0.44	0.43	0.61	0.90	0.24	0.32
Price Range	74.74-53.60	74.74-53.60	74.74-53.60	75.01-57.58	100.24-61.68	91.56-55.66	86.33-58.77	59.77-36.59
P/E Ratio	15.19-10.89	18.36-13.17	21.23-15.23	21.31-16.36	12.00-7.39	14.00-8.51	13.16-8.96	13.52-8.28
Average Yield %	2.20		2.13	2.08	1.99	1.43	1.53	1.12	1.06

Address: 19300 International Boulevard, Seattle, WA 98188 **Telephone:** 206-392-5040	**Web Site:** www.alaskaair.com **Officers:** Bradley D. Tilden - Chairman, President, Chief Executive Officer Shane R. Tackett - Executive Vice President, Chief Financial Officer	**Auditors:** KPMG LLP **Investor Contact:** 206-392-5260 **Transfer Agents:** Computershare Trust Company N.A., Providence, RI

ALBEMARLE CORP.

Exchange	Symbol	Price	52Wk Range	Yield	P/E	Div Acheiver
NYS	ALB	$73.04 (12/31/2019)	92.28-59.30	2.01	13.53	24 Years

*7 Year Price Score 77.63 *NYSE Composite Index=100 *12 Month Price Score 88.28

Interim Earnings (Per Share)

Qtr.	Mar	Jun	Sep	Dec
2016	2.02	(2.78)	1.13	5.31
2017	0.45	0.92	1.06	(1.94)
2018	1.18	2.73	1.20	1.23
2019	1.26	1.45	1.46	...

Interim Dividends (Per Share)

Amt	Decl	Ex	Rec	Pay
0.367Q	02/26/2019	03/14/2019	03/15/2019	04/01/2019
0.367Q	05/08/2019	06/13/2019	06/14/2019	07/01/2019
0.367Q	07/24/2019	09/12/2019	09/13/2019	10/01/2019
0.367Q	10/29/2019	12/12/2019	12/13/2019	01/02/2020

Indicated Div: $1.47 (Div. Reinv. Plan)

Valuation Analysis — **Institutional Holding**

Forecast EPS	$6.06	No of Institutions
	(01/17/2020)	785
Market Cap	$7.7 Billion	Shares
Book Value	$3.8 Billion	122,479,664
Price/Book	2.02	% Held
Price/Sales	2.20	87.78

Business Summary: Specialty Chemicals (MIC: 8.3.2 SIC: 2819 NAIC: 325998)

Albemarle is a global developer, manufacturer and marketer of chemicals across a range of end markets including energy storage, petroleum refining, consumer electronics, construction, automotive, lubricants, pharmaceuticals, crop protection and custom chemistry services. Co.'s segments include: Lithium, which develops and manufactures a range of basic lithium compounds and lithium specialties and reagents; Bromine Specialties, which includes products used in fire safety solutions and other chemicals applications; and Catalysts, which includes Clean Fuels Technologies, fluidized catalytic cracking catalysts and additives, and performance catalyst solutions.

Recent Developments: For the quarter ended Sep 30 2019, net income increased 19.6% to US$171.6 million from US$143.5 million in the year-earlier quarter. Revenues were US$879.7 million, up 13.1% from US$777.7 million the year before. Operating income was US$186.1 million versus US$163.8 million in the prior-year quarter, an increase of 13.7%. Direct operating expenses rose 14.6% to US$569.9 million from US$497.2 million in the comparable period the year before. Indirect operating expenses increased 5.9% to US$123.7 million from US$116.8 million in the equivalent prior-year period.

Prospects: Our evaluation of Albemarle Corp. as of October 4th, 2019 is the result of our systematic analysis on three basic characteristics: earnings strength, relative valuation, and recent stock price movement. The company has enjoyed a very positive trend in earnings per share over the past 5 quarters. However, recent analyst estimates for the company have been reduced, while ALB has posted results that exceeded analysts' expectations. Based on operating earnings yield, the company is undervalued when compared to all of the companies we cover. Share price changes over the past year indicates that ALB will perform very poorly over the near term.

Financial Data

(US$ in Thousands)	9 Mos	6 Mos	3 Mos	12/31/2018	12/31/2017	12/31/2016	12/31/2015	12/31/2014
Earnings Per Share	5.40	5.14	6.42	6.34	0.49	5.68	3.00	1.69
Cash Flow Per Share	4.86	4.92	4.53	5.04	2.74	6.51	3.24	6.26
Tang Book Value Per Share	18.31	17.56	16.35	15.45	14.86	16.89	N.M.	13.74
Dividends Per Share	1.438	1.405	1.373	1.340	1.280	1.220	1.160	1.100
Dividend Payout %	26.62	27.33	21.38	21.14	261.22	21.48	38.67	65.09
Income Statement								
Total Revenue	2,596,863	1,717,116	832,064	3,374,950	3,071,976	2,677,203	3,651,335	2,445,548
EBITDA	676,666	447,348	215,728	1,017,106	731,648	759,245	671,609	352,437
Depn & Amortn	156,718	102,231	49,283	170,000	169,500	178,800	180,700	97,900
Income Before Taxes	484,653	320,930	153,859	794,701	446,798	515,264	358,187	213,179
Income Taxes	93,266	67,925	37,514	144,826	431,817	96,263	29,122	18,484
Net Income	442,837	287,767	133,569	693,562	54,850	643,675	334,906	133,316
Average Shares	106,299	106,316	106,356	109,458	112,380	113,239	111,556	79,102
Balance Sheet								
Current Assets	1,969,752	2,036,637	1,987,176	1,998,421	2,477,563	3,306,618	1,831,003	3,348,850
Total Assets	8,141,603	8,094,414	7,871,062	7,581,674	7,750,772	8,161,207	9,615,014	5,223,103
Current Liabilities	1,421,243	1,399,981	1,278,191	1,183,173	1,200,925	1,140,103	1,616,685	1,139,886
Long-Term Obligations	1,381,984	1,398,419	1,393,904	1,397,916	1,415,360	2,121,718	3,174,674	2,223,035
Total Liabilities	4,305,044	4,293,613	4,198,788	3,996,353	4,076,223	4,366,145	6,360,622	3,863,638
Stockholders' Equity	3,836,559	3,800,801	3,672,274	3,585,321	3,674,549	3,795,062	3,254,392	1,359,465
Shares Outstanding	106,031	105,971	105,950	105,616	110,546	112,523	112,219	78,030
Statistical Record								
Return on Assets %	7.33	7.00	9.01	9.05	0.69	7.22	4.51	3.03
Return on Equity %	15.54	14.60	18.61	19.11	1.47	18.21	14.52	8.93
EBITDA Margin %	26.06	26.05	25.93	30.14	23.82	28.36	18.39	14.41
Net Margin %	17.05	16.76	16.05	20.55	1.79	24.04	9.17	5.45
Asset Turnover	0.45	0.44	0.44	0.44	0.39	0.30	0.49	0.56
Current Ratio	1.39	1.45	1.55	1.69	2.06	2.90	1.13	2.94
Debt to Equity	0.36	0.37	0.38	0.39	0.39	0.56	0.98	1.64
Price Range	107.99-59.30	107.99-63.30	107.99-72.69	137.45-73.13	144.58-88.05	91.80-47.71	64.38-41.78	72.62-53.16
P/E Ratio	20.00-10.98	21.01-12.32	16.82-11.32	21.68-11.53	295.06-179.69	16.16-8.40	21.46-13.93	42.97-31.46
Average Yield %	1.81	1.62	1.49	1.35	1.11	1.65	2.16	1.71

Address: 4250 Congress Street, Suite 900, Charlotte, NC 28209 **Telephone:** 980-299-5700	**Web Site:** www.albemarle.com **Officers:** Luther C. Kissam - Chairman, President, President (frmr), Chief Executive Officer, Principal Financial Officer, Principal Executive Officer Scott A. Tozier - Executive Vice President, Chief Financial Officer, Senior Vice President, Chief Risk Officer, Principal Accounting Officer, Chief Accounting Officer	**Auditors:** PricewaterhouseCoopers LLP **Investor Contact:** 980-299-5700 **Transfer Agents:** Wells Fargo Bank, N.A. Shareowner Services, St. Paul, MN

ALCOA CORPORATION

Exchange	Symbol	Price	52Wk Range	Yield	P/E
NYS	AA	$21.51 (12/31/2019)	30.98-16.73	N/A	N/A

*7 Year Price Score N/A   *NYSE Composite Index=100   *12 Month Price Score 84.31

Interim Earnings (Per Share)

Qtr.	Mar	Jun	Sep	Dec
2016	(1.15)	(0.29)	(0.04)	(0.76)
2017	1.21	0.40	0.60	(1.05)
2018	0.80	0.39	(0.22)	0.23
2019	(1.07)	(2.17)	(1.19)	...

Interim Dividends (Per Share)

No Dividends Paid

Valuation Analysis   **Institutional Holding**

Forecast EPS	$0.27	No of Institutions
	(01/17/2020)	412
Market Cap	$4.0 Billion	Shares
Book Value	$4.5 Billion	168,856,800
Price/Book	0.88	% Held
Price/Sales	0.35	85.77

Business Summary: Metal Products (MIC: 8.2.3 SIC: 3353 NAIC: 331315)

Alcoa is a vertically integrated aluminum company comprised of bauxite mining, alumina refining, aluminum production (smelting, casting, and rolling), and energy generation. Co. has operating locations (through direct and indirect ownership) in countries around the world, situated primarily in Australia, Brazil, Canada, Europe, and the U.S.

Recent Developments: For the quarter ended Sep 30 2019, net loss amounted to US$147.0 million versus net income of US$195.0 million in the year-earlier quarter. Revenues were US$2.57 billion, down 24.3% from US$3.39 billion the year before. Direct operating expenses declined 14.7% to US$2.12 billion from US$2.49 billion in the comparable period the year before. Indirect operating expenses increased 10.9% to US$499.0 million from US$450.0 million in the equivalent prior-year period.

Prospects: Our evaluation of Alcoa Corporation as of October 4th, 2019 is the result of our systematic analysis on three basic characteristics: earnings strength, relative valuation, and recent stock price movement. The company has suffered a very negative trend in earnings per share over the past 5 quarters. In addition, recent analyst estimates for the company have been reduced while AA has posted results that exceeded analysts' expectations. Based on operating earnings yield, the company is overvalued when compared to all of the companies we cover. Share price changes over the past year indicates that AA will perform very poorly over the near term.

Financial Data
(US$ in Thousands)

	9 Mos	6 Mos	3 Mos	12/31/2018	12/31/2017	12/31/2016	12/31/2015	12/31/2014
Earnings Per Share	(4.20)	(3.23)	(0.67)	1.20	1.16	(2.19)	...	...
Cash Flow Per Share	5.16	5.77	3.03	2.41	6.65	(1.69)	...	...
Tang Book Value Per Share	24.46	26.38	27.80	29.17	24.42	30.91	...	...
Income Statement								
Total Revenue	7,997,000	5,430,000	2,719,000	13,403,000	11,652,000	9,318,000	11,199,000	13,147,000
EBITDA	517,000	348,000	306,000	2,469,000	2,015,000	799,000	713,000	1,200,000
Depn & Amortn	530,000	346,000	172,000	733,000	752,000	718,000	780,000	954,000
Income Before Taxes	(103,000)	(58,000)	104,000	1,614,000	1,159,000	(162,000)	(337,000)	(63,000)
Income Taxes	361,000	266,000	150,000	726,000	600,000	184,000	402,000	284,000
Net Income	(822,000)	(601,000)	(199,000)	227,000	217,000	(400,000)	(863,000)	(256,000)
Average Shares	186,000	186,000	185,000	189,000	187,000	183,000	...	...
Balance Sheet								
Current Assets	3,643,000	3,818,000	4,114,000	4,134,000	4,238,000	3,181,000	2,566,000	2,917,000
Total Assets	14,670,000	15,349,000	15,956,000	15,938,000	17,447,000	16,741,000	16,413,000	18,680,000
Current Liabilities	2,455,000	2,531,000	2,803,000	2,919,000	3,252,000	2,821,000	2,404,000	2,735,000
Long-Term Obligations	1,805,000	1,804,000	1,802,000	1,801,000	1,388,000	1,424,000	207,000	313,000
Total Liabilities	10,131,000	10,454,000	10,799,000	10,549,000	12,924,000	11,087,000	6,971,000	8,081,000
Stockholders' Equity	4,539,000	4,895,000	5,157,000	5,389,000	4,523,000	5,654,000	9,442,000	10,599,000
Shares Outstanding	185,572	185,557	185,534	184,770	185,200	182,930		
Statistical Record								
Return on Assets %	N.M.	N.M.	N.M.	1.36	1.27	N.M.	N.M.	...
Return on Equity %	N.M.	N.M.	N.M.	4.58	4.26	N.M.	N.M.	...
EBITDA Margin %	6.46	6.41	11.25	18.42	17.29	8.57	6.37	9.13
Net Margin %	N.M.	N.M.	N.M.	1.69	1.86	N.M.	N.M.	N.M.
Asset Turnover	0.74	0.76	0.79	0.80	0.68	0.56	0.64	...
Current Ratio	1.48	1.51	1.47	1.42	1.30	1.13	1.07	1.07
Debt to Equity	0.40	0.37	0.35	0.33	0.31	0.25	0.02	0.03
Price Range	43.11-16.73	48.29-21.17	60.23-25.15	60.23-25.15	54.14-28.83	32.05-22.91	...	...
P/E Ratio	...	...	...	50.19-20.96	46.67-24.85		...	...

Address: 201 Isabella Street, Suite 500, Pittsburgh, PA 15212-5858 **Telephone:** 412-315-2900	**Web Site:** www.alcoa.com **Officers:** Michael G. Morris - Chairman, Chairman (frmr) Roy C. Harvey - President, Chief Executive Officer	**Auditors:** PricewaterhouseCoopers LLP **Transfer Agents:** Computershare Trust Company, N.A.

21

ALEXANDER & BALDWIN INC (REIT)

Exchange	Symbol	Price	52Wk Range	Yield	P/E
NYS	ALEX	$20.96 (12/31/2019)	25.44-18.38	3.63	N/A

*7 Year Price Score 55.45   *NYSE Composite Index=100   *12 Month Price Score 89.13

Interim Earnings (Per Share)

Qtr.	Mar	Jun	Sep	Dec
2016	(0.15)	(0.01)	(0.03)	0.01
2017	0.14	0.09	0.13	3.98
2018	0.66	0.03	0.20	(1.91)
2019	0.12	(0.01)	(0.69)	...

Interim Dividends (Per Share)

Amt	Decl	Ex	Rec	Pay
0.145Q	02/26/2019	03/08/2019	03/11/2019	03/26/2019
0.165Q	04/26/2019	05/09/2019	05/10/2019	06/06/2019
0.19Q	08/01/2019	08/09/2019	08/12/2019	09/05/2019
0.19Q	10/24/2019	11/08/2019	11/12/2019	12/05/2019

Indicated Div: $0.76

Valuation Analysis

		Institutional Holding	
Forecast EPS	$-0.48	No of Institutions	
	(01/14/2020)	N/A	
Market Cap	$1.5 Billion	Shares	
Book Value	$1.1 Billion	N/A	
Price/Book	1.35	% Held	
Price/Sales	2.42	N/A	

Business Summary: REITs (MIC: 5.3.1 SIC: 6798 NAIC: 525930)

Alexander & Baldwin is a real estate company. Co. operates in three segments: Commercial Real Estate, which owns, operates and manages retail, industrial and office properties in Hawaii and on the Mainland, and leases urban land in Hawaii to third-party lessees; Land Operations, which engages in planning, zoning, financing, constructing, purchasing, managing, selling, and investing in real property, renewable energy and diversified agribusiness activities; and Materials and Construction, which includes asphalt paving as prime contractor and subcontractor, imports and sells liquid asphalt, and manufactures and sells precast concrete products.

Recent Developments: For the quarter ended Sep 30 2019, loss from continuing operations was US$50.8 million compared with income of US$15.8 million in the year-earlier quarter. Net loss amounted to US$50.9 million versus net income of US$15.6 million in the year-earlier quarter. Revenues were US$89.1 million, down 25.4% from US$119.4 million the year before. Revenues from property income fell 14.5% to US$51.2 million from US$59.9 million in the corresponding quarter a year earlier.

Prospects: Our evaluation of Alexander & Baldwin Inc. (REIT) as of October 4th, 2019 is the result of our systematic analysis on three basic characteristics: earnings strength, relative valuation, and recent stock price movement. The company has generated a negative trend in earnings per share over the past 5 quarters. However, recent analyst estimates for the company have been unchanged while ALEX has posted results that fell short of analysts' expectations. Based on operating earnings yield, the company is overvalued when compared to all of the companies we cover. Share price changes over the past year indicates that ALEX will perform in line with the market over the near term.

Financial Data
(US$ in Thousands)

	9 Mos	6 Mos	3 Mos	12/31/2018	12/31/2017	12/31/2016	12/31/2015	12/31/2014
Earnings Per Share	(2.49)	(1.60)	(1.56)	(1.02)	4.34	(0.18)	0.54	1.25
Cash Flow Per Share	5.20	5.04	4.52	4.39	(0.03)	2.26	2.63	0.80
Tang Book Value Per Share	15.34	15.54	15.73	14.96	10.25	21.71	22.06	21.26
Dividends Per Share	0.500	0.310	0.145	11.650	15.920	0.250	...	...
Dividend Payout %	...	...	...	...	366.82		...	...
Income Statement								
Total Revenue	327,600	238,500	129,400	644,400	425,500	387,500	570,500	560,000
EBITDA	15,500	45,500	26,800	12,100	56,400	165,200	117,000	106,700
Depn & Amortn	36,600	23,400	10,900	32,500	32,300	106,100	43,800	55,000
Income Before Taxes	(43,700)	7,100	8,400	(52,900)	600	35,300	47,600	28,800
Income Taxes	(1,100)	(1,100)	(1,100)	16,300	(218,200)	2,600	16,500	(1,400)
Net Income	(41,600)	8,200	9,000	(72,000)	228,300	(10,200)	29,600	61,400
Average Shares	72,300	72,200	72,500	70,600	53,000	49,400	49,300	49,300
Balance Sheet								
Current Assets	169,200	164,700	201,300	180,700	274,800	138,300	152,500	175,900
Total Assets	2,121,700	2,184,500	2,249,600	2,225,200	2,231,200	2,156,300	2,243,500	2,329,900
Current Liabilities	222,500	182,400	214,500	129,400	926,800	165,100	184,700	183,000
Long-Term Obligations	732,400	727,700	775,000	739,100	585,200	472,700	497,800	631,500
Total Liabilities	996,900	996,600	1,049,500	1,014,700	1,576,800	936,200	1,008,300	1,126,000
Stockholders' Equity	1,124,800	1,187,900	1,200,100	1,210,500	654,400	1,220,100	1,235,200	1,203,900
Shares Outstanding	72,300	72,241	72,135	72,000	49,300	49,000	48,900	48,800
Statistical Record								
Return on Assets %	N.M.	N.M.	N.M.	N.M.	10.41	N.M.	1.29	2.66
Return on Equity %	N.M.	N.M.	N.M.	N.M.	24.36	N.M.	2.43	5.18
EBITDA Margin %	4.73	19.08	20.71	1.88	13.25	42.63	20.51	19.05
Net Margin %	N.M.	3.44	6.96	N.M.	53.65	N.M.	5.19	10.96
Asset Turnover	0.29	0.30	0.29	0.29	0.19	0.18	0.25	0.24
Current Ratio	0.76	0.90	0.94	1.40	0.30	0.84	0.83	0.96
Debt to Equity	0.65	0.61	0.65	0.61	0.89	0.39	0.40	0.52
Price Range	25.44-17.78	25.44-17.78	25.44-17.78	29.15-17.78	46.87-27.62	46.09-29.30	43.52-33.34	44.56-34.74
P/E Ratio	...	...	...	...	10.80-6.36	...	80.59-61.74	35.65-27.79
Average Yield %	2.22	1.37	0.65	51.20	37.60	0.66	...	...

Address: 822 Bishop Street, Honolulu, HI 96813	**Web Site:** www.alexanderbaldwin.com	**Auditors:** Deloitte & Touche LLP
Telephone: 808-525-6611	**Officers:** Stanley M. Kuriyama - Chairman, President, Chief Executive Officer Christopher J. Benjamin - President, Chief Executive Officer, Chief Operating Officer	**Transfer Agents:** Computershare Shareowner Services LLC

ALEXANDRIA REAL ESTATE EQUITIES INC

Exchange	Symbol	Price	52Wk Range	Yield	P/E
NYS	ARE	$161.58 (12/31/2019)	162.52-111.37	2.55	158.41

*7 Year Price Score 115.83 *NYSE Composite Index=100 *12 Month Price Score 103.38

Interim Earnings (Per Share)

Qtr.	Mar	Jun	Sep	Dec
2016	(0.05)	(1.72)	0.07	(0.30)
2017	0.29	0.35	0.55	0.38
2018	1.32	0.51	1.99	(0.33)
2019	1.11	0.68	(0.44)	...

Interim Dividends (Per Share)

Amt	Decl	Ex	Rec	Pay
0.97Q	03/04/2019	03/28/2019	03/29/2019	04/15/2019
1.00Q	06/03/2019	06/27/2019	06/28/2019	07/15/2019
1.00Q	09/04/2019	09/27/2019	09/30/2019	10/15/2019
1.03Q	12/05/2019	12/30/2019	12/31/2019	01/15/2020

Indicated Div: $4.12

Valuation Analysis

Forecast EPS	$2.06
	(01/16/2020)
Market Cap	$18.6 Billion
Book Value	$7.8 Billion
Price/Book	2.39
Price/Sales	12.71

Institutional Holding

No of Institutions	632
Shares	135,193,824
% Held	98.72

Business Summary: REITs (MIC: 5.3.1 SIC: 6798 NAIC: 525930)

Alexandria Real Estate Equities is an urban office real estate investment trust. Co. is engaged in the business of providing space for lease to the life science and technology industries. Co.'s properties are similar in that they provide space for lease to the life science and technology industries, consist of improvements that are generic and reusable for the life science and technology industries, are primarily located in AAA urban innovation cluster locations, and have similar economic characteristics. Co. operates in locations, including Greater Boston, San Francisco, New York City, San Diego, Seattle, Maryland, and Research Triangle Park.

Recent Developments: For the quarter ended Sep 30 2019, net loss amounted to US$36.0 million versus net income of US$219.4 million in the year-earlier quarter. Revenues were US$390.5 million, up 14.2% from US$341.8 million the year before. Revenues from property income rose 14.6% to US$385.8 million from US$336.5 million in the corresponding quarter a year earlier.

Prospects: Our evaluation of Alexandria Real Estate Equities Inc. as of October 4th, 2019 is the result of our systematic analysis on three basic characteristics: earnings strength, relative valuation, and recent stock price movement. The company has produced a positive trend in earnings per share over the past 5 quarters. However, recent analyst estimates for the company have been mixed and ARE has posted results that fell short of analysts' expectations. Based on operating earnings yield, the company is overvalued when compared to all of the companies we cover. Share price changes over the past year indicates that ARE will perform well over the near term.

Financial Data

(US$ in Thousands)	9 Mos	6 Mos	3 Mos	12/31/2018	12/31/2017	12/31/2016	12/31/2015	12/31/2014
Earnings Per Share	1.02	3.45	3.28	3.52	1.58	(1.99)	1.63	1.01
Cash Flow Per Share	5.90	5.57	5.21	5.54	4.92	5.14	4.79	4.70
Tang Book Value Per Share	67.15	67.61	67.54	65.56	58.88	53.37	49.73	48.43
Dividends Per Share	3.940	3.870	3.800	3.730	3.450	3.230	3.050	2.880
Dividend Payout %	386.27	112.17	115.85	105.97	218.35	...	187.12	285.15
Income Statement								
Total Revenue	1,123,182	732,698	358,842	1,327,459	1,128,097	921,706	843,474	726,877
EBITDA	251,855	186,340	85,500	979,895	713,677	376,287	516,121	410,164
Depn & Amortn	(16,982)	(12,172)	(5,716)	463,588	406,365	319,039	265,802	232,277
Income Before Taxes	140,655	116,533	52,116	358,812	178,667	(49,705)	144,506	98,588
Net Income	160,724	207,926	129,159	379,312	169,093	(65,901)	144,217	101,574
Average Shares	112,120	111,501	111,054	103,321	92,063	76,103	71,528	71,169
Balance Sheet								
Current Assets	463,638	247,453	325,450	281,928	287,448	151,110	164,455	123,443
Total Assets	17,058,154	16,039,470	15,480,206	14,464,956	12,103,953	10,354,888	8,911,120	8,136,036
Current Liabilities	1,356,851	1,271,796	1,281,789	1,091,987	855,977	808,585	651,361	547,899
Long-Term Obligations	6,737,683	6,356,205	5,843,503	5,478,255	4,764,807	4,164,025	3,965,795	3,678,579
Total Liabilities	9,267,922	8,410,450	7,913,629	7,122,991	6,154,287	5,459,092	4,936,033	4,307,597
Stockholders' Equity	7,790,232	7,629,020	7,566,577	7,341,965	5,949,666	4,895,796	3,975,087	3,828,439
Shares Outstanding	115,150	111,985	111,180	111,011	99,783	87,665	72,548	71,463
Statistical Record								
Return on Assets %	0.87	2.68	2.63	2.86	1.51	N.M.	1.69	1.30
Return on Equity %	1.86	5.63	5.42	5.71	3.12	N.M.	3.70	2.62
EBITDA Margin %	22.42	25.43	23.83	73.82	63.26	40.83	61.19	56.43
Net Margin %	14.31	28.38	35.99	28.57	14.99	N.M.	17.10	13.97
Asset Turnover	0.09	0.10	0.10	0.10	0.10	0.10	0.10	0.09
Current Ratio	0.34	0.19	0.25	0.26	0.34	0.19	0.25	0.23
Debt to Equity	0.86	0.83	0.77	0.75	0.80	0.85	1.00	0.96
Price Range	155.23-110.28	152.76-110.28	143.83-110.28	129.93-110.28	134.03-108.18	114.52-71.65	102.42-83.40	90.19-63.62
P/E Ratio	152.19-108.12	44.28-31.97	43.85-33.62	36.91-31.33	84.83-68.47	...	62.83-51.17	89.30-62.99
Average Yield %	2.89	2.95	3.01	3.00	2.90	3.28	3.30	3.75

Address: 26 North Euclid Avenue, Pasadena, CA 91101
Telephone: 626-578-0777

Web Site: www.are.com
Officers: Joel S. Marcus - Executive Chairman, Chairman, President, Chief Executive Officer Stephen A. Richardson - Co-Chief Executive Officer, Chief Operating Officer, Region Officer

Auditors: Ernst & Young LLP
Investor Contact: 626-396-4828
Transfer Agents: American Stock Transfer & Trust Company, LLC, Brooklyn, NY

ALLEGHANY CORP.

Exchange	Symbol	Price	52Wk Range	Yield	P/E
NYS	Y	$799.57 (12/31/2019)	802.01-605.83	1.25	78.31

*7 Year Price Score 109.04 *NYSE Composite Index=100 *12 Month Price Score 105.52

Interim Earnings (Per Share)

Qtr.	Mar	Jun	Sep	Dec
2016	9.96	4.99	10.09	4.51
2017	9.67	6.60	(20.90)	9.95
2018	11.04	19.44	19.07	(46.91)
2019	30.39	20.46	6.27	...

Interim Dividends (Per Share)

Amt	Decl	Ex	Rec	Pay
10.00U	02/21/2018	03/02/2018	03/05/2018	03/15/2018

Indicated Div: $10.00

Valuation Analysis

Forecast EPS	$37.95
	(01/16/2020)
Market Cap	$11.5 Billion
Book Value	$8.8 Billion
Price/Book	1.30
Price/Sales	1.45

Institutional Holding

No of Institutions	509
Shares	15,263,254
% Held	75.84

Business Summary: General Insurance (MIC: 5.2.1 SIC: 6331 NAIC: 524126)

Alleghany is an insurance holding company. Co. classifies its businesses into three reportable segments: reinsurance segment, which consists of property and casualty reinsurance operations conducted by its Transatlantic Holdings, Inc.'s reinsurance operating subsidiaries; insurance segment, which consists of property and casualty insurance operations conducted in the U.S. by Alleghany Insurance Holdings LLC through RSUI Group, Inc.; and Alleghany Capital segment, which owns and manages a portfolio of middle market businesses primarily through Co.'s wholly-owned subsidiary, Alleghany Capital Corporation and its subsidiaries.

Recent Developments: For the quarter ended Sep 30 2019, net income decreased 65.0% to US$101.3 million from US$289.5 million in the year-earlier quarter. Revenues were US$2.16 billion, down 0.8% from US$2.18 billion the year before. Net premiums earned were US$1.39 billion versus US$1.23 billion in the prior-year quarter, an increase of 13.4%. Net investment income rose 16.1% to US$147.8 million from US$127.3 million a year ago.

Prospects: Our evaluation of Alleghany Corp. as of October 4th, 2019 is the result of our systematic analysis on three basic characteristics: earnings strength, relative valuation, and recent stock price movement. The company has enjoyed a very positive trend in earnings per share over the past 5 quarters. However, recent analyst estimates for the company have been unchanged, while Y has posted results that exceeded analysts' expectations. Based on operating earnings yield, the company is fairly valued when compared to all of the companies we cover. Share price changes over the past year indicates that Y will perform in line with the market over the near term.

Financial Data
(US$ in Thousands)

	9 Mos	6 Mos	3 Mos	12/31/2018	12/31/2017	12/31/2016	12/31/2015	12/31/2014
Earnings Per Share	10.21	23.01	21.99	2.62	5.85	29.59	35.13	41.40
Cash Flow Per Share	35.15	29.56	23.56	26.72	28.92	51.23	20.54	22.72
Tang Book Value Per Share	538.40	527.82	500.50	458.58	501.62	472.17	463.26	450.23
Dividends Per Share	...	...	...	10.000	...	...	...	...
Dividend Payout %				381.68				
Income Statement								
Premium Income	4,043,298	2,653,317	1,297,309	4,976,190	4,954,990	4,975,777	4,230,286	4,410,647
Total Revenue	6,739,886	4,579,929	2,321,256	6,887,160	6,424,655	6,131,019	4,999,478	5,231,809
Benefits & Claims	2,497,037	1,589,301	792,498	3,520,431	3,620,197	2,917,166	2,339,790	2,494,565
Income Before Taxes	1,061,905	932,603	556,414	39,592	36,690	647,805	757,368	931,909
Income Taxes	207,878	179,868	108,512	(15,062)	(63,802)	187,141	195,173	251,777
Net Income	826,118	735,686	440,227	39,539	90,133	456,921	560,315	679,239
Average Shares	14,422	14,439	14,485	15,062	15,410	15,442	15,879	16,405
Balance Sheet								
Total Assets	26,490,831	26,356,378	25,793,057	25,344,896	25,384,317	23,756,591	22,846,333	23,489,436
Total Liabilities	17,662,173	17,670,464	17,556,570	17,652,186	16,870,254	15,816,646	15,291,626	16,016,008
Stockholders' Equity	8,828,658	8,685,914	8,236,487	7,692,710	8,514,063	7,939,945	7,554,707	7,473,428
Shares Outstanding	14,405	14,430	14,447	14,576	15,390	15,410	15,544	16,054
Statistical Record								
Return on Assets %	0.44	1.20	1.21	0.16	0.37	1.96	2.42	2.90
Return on Equity %	1.31	3.61	3.71	0.49	1.10	5.88	7.46	9.44
Loss Ratio %	61.76	59.90	61.09	70.75	73.06	58.63	55.31	56.56
Net Margin %	12.26	16.06	18.97	0.57	1.40	7.45	−11.21	12.98
Price Range	797.91-580.75	693.19-575.06	656.06-564.59	656.06-562.45	656.22-523.19	616.13-450.94	515.25-440.61	482.00-363.60
P/E Ratio	78.15-56.88	30.13-24.99	29.83-25.67	250.40-214.68	112.17-89.43	20.82-15.24	14.67-12.54	11.64-8.78
Average Yield %	...	...	...	1.65	...	...	...	...

Address: 1411 Broadway, 34th Floor, New York, NY 10018 **Telephone:** 212-752-1356	**Web Site:** www.alleghany.com **Officers:** Jefferson W. Kirby - Chairman Weston M. Hicks - President, Chief Executive Officer	**Auditors:** Ernst & Young LLP **Transfer Agents:** Computershare Trust Company, N.A., Providence, RI

ALLEGHENY TECHNOLOGIES, INC

Exchange	Symbol	Price	52Wk Range	Yield	P/E
NYS	ATI	$20.66 (12/31/2019)	29.26-17.25	N/A	11.87

*7 Year Price Score 76.52 *NYSE Composite Index=100 *12 Month Price Score 91.24

TRADING VOLUME (thousand shares)

Interim Earnings (Per Share)

Qtr.	Mar	Jun	Sep	Dec
2016	(0.94)	(0.18)	(4.95)	0.10
2017	0.16	0.09	(1.12)	0.04
2018	0.42	0.52	0.37	0.30
2019	0.12	0.54	0.78	...

Interim Dividends (Per Share)

Dividend Payment Suspended

Valuation Analysis		Institutional Holding	
Forecast EPS	$1.17	No of Institutions	
	(01/17/2020)	488	
Market Cap	$2.6 Billion	Shares	
Book Value	$2.2 Billion	168,900,256	
Price/Book	1.20	% Held	
Price/Sales	0.63	96.02	

Business Summary: Non-Precious Metals (MIC: 8.2.2 SIC: 3317 NAIC: 331210)

Allegheny Technologies manufactures specialty materials and components, ranging from alloy development to finished components, as well as producing powders for use in jet engine forgings and 3D-printed aerospace products. Co.'s segments are: High Performance Materials & Components, which produces a range of materials and components, including advanced metallic powder alloys, made from titanium and titanium-based alloys, nickel-based alloys and superalloys; and Flat Rolled Products, which nickel-based alloys, specialty alloys, titanium and titanium-based alloys, and stainless steel in a variety of product forms including plate, sheet, engineered strip, and Precision Rolled Strip® products.

Recent Developments: For the quarter ended Sep 30 2019, net income increased 107.4% to US$115.3 million from US$55.6 million in the year-earlier quarter. Revenues were US$1.02 billion, unchanged from the year before. Operating income was US$94.5 million versus US$94.9 million in the prior-year quarter, a decrease of 0.4%. Direct operating expenses declined 0.1% to US$859.0 million from US$859.8 million in the comparable period the year before. Indirect operating expenses decreased 0.5% to US$65.2 million from US$65.5 million in the equivalent prior-year period.

Prospects: Our evaluation of Allegheny Technologies Inc. as of October 4th, 2019 is the result of our systematic analysis on three basic characteristics: earnings strength, relative valuation, and recent stock price movement. The company has generated a negative trend in earnings per share over the past 5 quarters. However, recent analyst estimates for the company have been mixed and ATI has posted results that exceeded analysts' expectations. Based on operating earnings yield, the company is undervalued when compared to all of the companies we cover. Share price changes over the past year indicates that ATI will perform poorly over the near term.

Financial Data

(US$ in Thousands)	9 Mos	6 Mos	3 Mos	12/31/2018	12/31/2017	12/31/2016	12/31/2015	12/31/2014
Earnings Per Share	1.74	1.33	1.31	1.61	(0.83)	(5.97)	(3.53)	(0.03)
Cash Flow Per Share	2.11	2.01	2.47	3.14	0.20	(0.41)	1.22	0.52
Tang Book Value Per Share	13.04	11.91	11.09	10.75	9.60	6.55	13.11	16.72
Dividends Per Share	...	...	...	...	...	0.240	0.620	0.720
Income Statement								
Total Revenue	3,103,900	2,085,200	1,004,800	4,046,600	3,525,100	3,134,600	3,719,600	4,223,400
EBITDA	409,900	229,700	80,600	505,100	182,500	(439,700)	(177,900)	286,800
Depn & Amortn	114,600	77,600	38,700	156,400	135,200	170,300	189,900	176,600
Income Before Taxes	220,400	101,400	17,100	247,700	(86,500)	(734,000)	(478,000)	1,500
Income Taxes	10,300	6,600	800	11,000	(6,800)	(106,600)	(112,100)	(8,700)
Net Income	201,100	90,100	15,000	222,400	(91,900)	(640,900)	(377,900)	(2,600)
Average Shares	146,700	146,400	126,100	145,900	110,100	107,300	107,300	107,100
Balance Sheet								
Current Assets	2,422,400	2,261,400	2,177,900	2,246,700	1,915,700	1,766,500	1,867,600	2,482,100
Total Assets	5,628,900	5,549,300	5,491,000	5,501,800	5,185,400	5,170,000	5,751,700	6,582,600
Current Liabilities	763,300	759,200	760,000	836,900	712,600	708,700	686,500	959,900
Long-Term Obligations	1,541,700	1,537,100	1,536,200	1,535,500	1,530,600	1,771,900	1,491,800	1,509,100
Total Liabilities	3,460,900	3,522,900	3,556,800	3,616,100	3,446,000	3,814,800	3,668,900	3,984,200
Stockholders' Equity	2,168,000	2,026,400	1,934,200	1,885,700	1,739,400	1,355,200	2,082,800	2,598,400
Shares Outstanding	126,085	126,079	126,034	125,684	125,857	108,925	109,174	108,710
Statistical Record								
Return on Assets %	4.40	3.32	3.31	4.16	N.M.	N.M.	N.M.	N.M.
Return on Equity %	11.68	9.20	9.49	12.27	N.M.	N.M.	N.M.	N.M.
EBITDA Margin %	13.21	11.02	8.02	12.48	5.18	N.M.	N.M.	6.79
Net Margin %	6.48	4.32	1.49	5.50	N.M.	N.M.	N.M.	N.M.
Asset Turnover	0.75	0.76	0.75	0.76	0.68	0.57	0.60	0.63
Current Ratio	3.17	2.98	2.87	2.68	2.69	2.49	2.72	2.59
Debt to Equity	0.71	0.76	0.79	0.81	0.88	1.31	0.72	0.58
Price Range	29.47-17.25	29.75-21.21	29.75-21.21	29.77-21.21	25.84-14.89	18.94-7.62	37.45-10.46	46.23-29.86
P/E Ratio	16.94-9.91	22.37-15.95	22.71-16.19	18.49-13.17	...	...	...	...
Average Yield %	...	...	...	...	...	1.61	2.52	1.92

Address: 1000 Six PPG Place, Pittsburgh, PA 15222-5479 Telephone: 412-394-2800	Web Site: www.atimetals.com Officers: Richard (Rich) J. Harshman - Executive Chairman, Chairman, President, Chief Executive Officer Diane C. Creel - Chairman	Auditors: Ernst & Young LLP Investor Contact: 412-394-3004 Transfer Agents: Computershare

ALLERGAN PLC

Exchange	Symbol	Price	52Wk Range	Yield	P/E
NYS	AGN	$191.17 (12/31/2019)	191.58-115.73	1.55	N/A

*7 Year Price Score 63.45   ***NYSE Composite Index=100**   ***12 Month Price Score 111.53**

Interim Earnings (Per Share)

Qtr.	Mar	Jun	Sep	Dec
2016	0.47	(1.44)	38.58	0.74
2017	(7.86)	(2.37)	(12.07)	9.09
2018	(0.99)	(1.39)	(0.11)	(12.76)
2019	(7.25)	(5.37)	(2.40)	...

Interim Dividends (Per Share)

Amt	Decl	Ex	Rec	Pay
0.74Q	01/25/2019	02/14/2019	02/15/2019	03/15/2019
0.74Q	05/02/2019	05/13/2019	05/14/2019	06/14/2019
0.74Q	07/19/2019	08/12/2019	08/13/2019	09/13/2019
0.74Q	10/23/2019	11/12/2019	11/13/2019	12/13/2019

Indicated Div: $2.96

Valuation Analysis   **Institutional Holding**

Forecast EPS	N/A	No of Institutions
		1233
Market Cap	$62.7 Billion	Shares
Book Value	$58.5 Billion	307,291,232
Price/Book	1.07	% Held
Price/Sales	3.97	81.13

Business Summary: Pharmaceuticals (MIC: 4.1.1 SIC: 2834 NAIC: 325412)

Allergan is a pharmaceutical company focused on developing, manufacturing and commercializing pharmaceutical, device, biologic, surgical and regenerative medicine products for patients around the world. Co. operates and manages its business in three operating segments: U.S. Specialized Therapeutics, which provides eye care, neurosciences and urology therapeutic products; U.S. General Medicine, which focuses on newly developed pharmaceutical products; and International, which provides an array of aesthetics products outside of the U.S. Co.'s portfolio of products include Alloderm® for skin graft and Alphagan®/Combigan® as selective alpha2 agonist.

Recent Developments: For the quarter ended Sep 30 2019, net loss amounted to US$785.6 million versus a net loss of US$36.3 million in the year-earlier quarter. Revenues were US$4.05 billion, up 3.6% from US$3.91 billion the year before. Operating loss was US$596.6 million versus an income of US$257.5 million in the prior-year quarter. Direct operating expenses rose 7.1% to US$639.0 million from US$596.8 million in the comparable period the year before. Indirect operating expenses increased 31.1% to US$4.01 billion from US$3.06 billion in the equivalent prior-year period.

Prospects: Our evaluation of Allergan PLC as of October 4th, 2019 is the result of our systematic analysis on three basic characteristics: earnings strength, relative valuation, and recent stock price movement. The company has produced a positive trend in earnings per share over the past 5 quarters. However, recent analyst estimates for the company have been mixed and AGN has posted results that exceeded analysts' expectations. Based on operating earnings yield, the company is undervalued when compared to all of the companies we cover. Share price changes over the past year indicates that AGN will perform poorly over the near term.

Financial Data

(US$ in Thousands)	9 Mos	6 Mos	3 Mos	12/31/2018	12/31/2017	12/31/2016	12/31/2015	12/31/2014
Earnings Per Share	(27.78)	(25.49)	(21.51)	(15.26)	(13.19)	38.18	10.01	(7.42)
Cash Flow Per Share	21.55	17.04	16.31	16.74	17.60	3.69	12.32	10.21
Dividends Per Share	2.940	2.920	2.900	2.880	2.800	...	...	...
Income Statement								
Total Revenue	11,737,900	7,687,200	3,597,100	15,787,400	15,940,700	14,570,600	15,071,000	13,062,300
EBITDA	345,900	(656,300)	(843,900)	(5,794,600)	(9,187,000)	(1,452,600)	(3,119,700)	(1,078,300)
Depn & Amortn	4,503,000	2,906,700	1,451,500	196,300	171,500	153,700	128,600	230,900
Income Before Taxes	(4,696,700)	(3,929,200)	(2,475,900)	(6,856,900)	(10,386,400)	(2,832,000)	(4,430,200)	(1,712,100)
Income Taxes	251,100	233,000	(68,600)	(1,770,700)	(6,670,400)	(1,897,000)	(1,561,900)	(81,900)
Net Income	(4,953,800)	(4,167,000)	(2,408,000)	(5,096,400)	(4,125,500)	14,973,400	3,915,200	(1,630,500)
Average Shares	328,000	327,800	332,000	337,000	333,800	384,900	367,800	219,700
Balance Sheet								
Current Assets	9,593,600	8,572,800	6,289,300	6,475,400	11,376,700	17,857,900	8,615,400	6,881,700
Total Assets	94,408,900	95,480,700	98,036,300	101,787,600	118,341,900	128,986,300	135,840,700	52,529,100
Current Liabilities	9,638,700	8,303,700	8,849,200	5,727,900	9,848,100	7,874,700	8,328,300	5,018,600
Long-Term Obligations	18,786,000	19,609,300	19,554,100	22,929,400	25,843,500	29,970,800	40,293,400	14,846,300
Total Liabilities	35,933,700	35,806,000	36,494,300	36,673,500	44,520,800	52,793,600	59,249,300	24,198,000
Stockholders' Equity	58,475,200	59,674,700	61,542,000	65,114,100	73,821,100	76,192,700	76,591,400	28,331,100
Shares Outstanding	328,100	327,900	327,800	332,600	330,200	334,900	394,500	247,600
Statistical Record								
Return on Assets %	N.M.	N.M.	N.M.	N.M.	N.M.	11.28	4.16	N.M.
Return on Equity %	N.M.	N.M.	N.M.	N.M.	N.M.	19.55	7.46	N.M.
EBITDA Margin %	2.95	N.M.	N.M.	N.M.	N.M.	N.M.	N.M.	N.M.
Net Margin %	N.M.	N.M.	N.M.	N.M.	N.M.	102.76	25.98	N.M.
Asset Turnover	0.16	0.15	0.15	0.14	0.13	0.11	0.16	0.35
Current Ratio	1.00	1.03	0.71	1.13	1.16	2.27	1.03	1.37
Debt to Equity	0.32	0.33	0.32	0.32	0.35	0.39	0.53	0.52
Price Range	193.46-115.73	193.46-115.73	193.46-129.82	193.46-129.82	256.15-163.58	312.50-188.47	339.50-252.10	270.61-167.93
P/E Ratio	...	...	...	...	...	8.18-4.94	33.92-25.18	...
Average Yield %	1.93	1.85	1.77	1.70	1.27	...	...	...

Address: Clonshaugh Business and Technology Park, Dublin, 07054 **Telephone:** 862-261-7000	**Web Site:** www.allergan.com **Officers:** Brenton L. Saunders - Chairman, President, Chief Executive Officer Maria Teresa Hilado - Executive Vice President, Chief Financial Officer, Chief Financial Officer	**Auditors:** PricewaterhouseCoopers LLP **Investor Contact:** 862-261-7488 **Transfer Agents:** American Stock Transfer and Trust Company, New York, NY

ALLETE INC

Exchange	Symbol	Price	52Wk Range	Yield	P/E
NYS	ALE	$81.17 (12/31/2019)	88.17-73.16	2.90	21.25

*7 Year Price Score 108.80 *NYSE Composite Index=100   *12 Month Price Score 93.66

Interim Earnings (Per Share)

Qtr.	Mar	Jun	Sep	Dec
2016	0.93	0.50	0.81	0.89
2017	0.97	0.72	0.88	0.81
2018	0.99	0.61	0.59	1.19
2019	1.37	0.66	0.60	...

Interim Dividends (Per Share)

Amt	Decl	Ex	Rec	Pay
0.588Q	02/01/2019	02/14/2019	02/15/2019	03/01/2019
0.588Q	04/24/2019	05/14/2019	05/15/2019	06/01/2019
0.588Q	07/25/2019	08/14/2019	08/15/2019	09/01/2019
0.588Q	10/24/2019	11/14/2019	11/15/2019	12/01/2019

Indicated Div: $2.35

Valuation Analysis

		Institutional Holding	
Forecast EPS	$3.55	No of Institutions	430
(01/15/2020)		Shares	
Market Cap	$4.2 Billion		52,100,120
Book Value	$2.2 Billion	% Held	
Price/Book	1.90	N/A	
Price/Sales	3.03		

Business Summary: Electric Utilities (MIC: 3.1.1 SIC: 4931 NAIC: 221122)

Allete is an energy company. Co.'s segments are: Regulated Operations, which include its regulated utilities, Minnesota Power, and Superior Water, Light and Power Company, and its investment in American Transmission Company LLC; ALLETE Clean Energy, Inc., which focuses on developing, acquiring, and operating renewable energy projects; and U.S. Water Services Holding Company, which provides integrated water management for industry by combining chemical, equipment, engineering and service. Co.'s Corporate and Other is comprised of BNI Energy, Inc., Co.'s coal mining operations in North Dakota, and Co.'s investment in Nobles 2, ALLETE Properties, LLC, Co.'s Florida real estate investment.

Recent Developments: For the quarter ended Sep 30 2019, net income increased 1.6% to US$31.2 million from US$30.7 million in the year-earlier quarter. Revenues were US$288.3 million, down 17.2% from US$348.0 million the year before. Operating income was US$37.0 million versus US$43.3 million in the prior-year quarter, a decrease of 14.5%. Direct operating expenses declined 21.2% to US$189.3 million from US$240.1 million in the comparable period the year before. Indirect operating expenses decreased 4.0% to US$62.0 million from US$64.6 million in the equivalent prior-year period.

Prospects: Our evaluation of Allete Inc. as of October 4th, 2019 is the result of our systematic analysis on three basic characteristics: earnings strength, relative valuation, and recent stock price movement. The company has generated a negative trend in earnings per share over the past 5 quarters. In addition, recent analyst estimates for the company have been reduced and ALE has posted results that fell short of analysts' expectations. Based on operating earnings yield, the company is fairly valued when compared to all of the companies we cover. Share price changes over the past year indicates that ALE will perform well over the near term.

Financial Data

(US$ in Thousands)	9 Mos	6 Mos	3 Mos	12/31/2018	12/31/2017	12/31/2016	12/31/2015	12/31/2014
Earnings Per Share	3.82	3.81	3.76	3.38	3.38	3.14	2.92	2.90
Cash Flow Per Share	6.02	6.47	7.58	8.44	7.93	6.72	7.04	6.29
Tang Book Value Per Share	42.68	42.79	42.57	37.52	36.04	33.89	32.71	35.04
Dividends Per Share	2.322	2.295	2.268	2.240	2.140	2.080	2.020	1.960
Dividend Payout %	60.80	60.24	60.31	66.27	63.31	66.24	69.18	67.59
Income Statement								
Total Revenue	935,900	647,600	357,200	1,498,600	1,419,300	1,339,700	1,486,400	1,136,800
EBITDA	316,700	223,400	134,000	409,100	404,100	418,000	378,000	325,300
Depn & Amortn	151,500	98,200	49,700	200,100	171,900	190,600	165,900	135,700
Income Before Taxes	116,300	92,400	67,800	141,100	164,400	157,100	150,500	142,600
Income Taxes	(4,300)	(1,900)	2,900	(15,500)	14,700	19,800	25,300	36,700
Net Income	135,900	104,700	70,500	174,100	172,200	155,300	141,100	124,800
Average Shares	51,800	51,700	51,700	51,500	51,000	49,500	48,400	43,100
Balance Sheet								
Current Assets	296,100	397,300	556,400	334,300	367,500	294,500	371,000	418,800
Total Assets	5,275,800	5,176,500	5,218,800	5,165,000	5,080,000	4,906,400	4,907,100	4,360,800
Current Liabilities	483,300	296,600	322,400	405,100	351,200	399,500	275,400	416,000
Long-Term Obligations	1,404,900	1,505,900	1,525,000	1,428,500	1,439,200	1,370,400	1,568,700	1,272,800
Total Liabilities	3,068,000	2,971,500	3,020,100	3,009,200	3,011,800	3,013,400	3,086,900	2,751,400
Stockholders' Equity	2,207,800	2,205,000	2,198,700	2,155,800	2,068,200	1,893,000	1,820,200	1,609,400
Shares Outstanding	51,700	51,500	51,624	51,509	51,117	49,560	49,075	45,929
Statistical Record								
Return on Assets %	3.77	3.82	3.76	3.40	3.45	3.16	3.04	3.18
Return on Equity %	9.11	9.11	9.01	8.24	8.69	8.34	8.23	8.45
EBITDA Margin %	33.84	34.50	37.51	27.30	28.47	31.20	25.43	28.62
Net Margin %	14.52	16.17	19.74	11.62	12.13	11.59	9.49	10.98
Asset Turnover	0.27	0.28	0.29	0.29	0.28	0.27	0.32	0.29
Current Ratio	0.61	1.34	1.73	0.83	1.05	0.74	1.35	1.01
Debt to Equity	0.64	0.68	0.69	0.66	0.70	0.72	0.86	0.79
Price Range	88.17-73.16	85.80-73.16	83.83-70.90	82.32-67.19	80.50-62.18	66.23-48.77	59.19-45.66	57.95-44.39
P/E Ratio	23.08-19.15	22.52-19.20	22.30-18.86	24.36-19.88	23.82-18.40	21.09-15.53	20.27-15.64	19.98-15.31
Average Yield %	2.86	2.91	2.95	2.99	2.96	3.56	3.96	3.93

Address: 30 West Superior Street, Duluth, MN 55802-2093 **Telephone:** 218-279-5000	**Web Site:** www.allete.com **Officers:** Alan R. Hodnik - Chairman, President, Chief Executive Officer Bethany M. Owen - President, Senior Vice President, Chief Legal Officer, Chief Administrative Officer	**Auditors:** PricewaterhouseCoopers LLP **Investor Contact:** 218-723-3953 **Transfer Agents:** Wells Fargo Bank, N.A., South St. Paul, MN

ALLIANCE DATA SYSTEMS CORP.

Exchange	Symbol	Price	52Wk Range	Yield	P/E
NYS	ADS	$112.20 (12/31/2019)	181.51-100.00	2.25	13.12

*7 Year Price Score 52.64   ***NYSE Composite Index=100**   ***12 Month Price Score 70.75**

Interim Earnings (Per Share)

Qtr.	Mar	Jun	Sep	Dec
2016	2.35	1.24	3.55	0.22
2017	2.58	2.47	4.20	4.87
2018	2.95	3.93	5.39	5.24
2019	2.80	2.64	(2.13)	...

Interim Dividends (Per Share)

Amt	Decl	Ex	Rec	Pay
0.63Q	02/07/2019	02/20/2019	02/21/2019	03/19/2019
0.63Q	04/25/2019	05/13/2019	05/14/2019	06/18/2019
0.63Q	07/18/2019	09/03/2019	09/04/2019	09/26/2019
0.63Q	10/24/2019	11/13/2019	11/14/2019	12/17/2019

Indicated Div: $2.52

Valuation Analysis / Institutional Holding

Forecast EPS	$16.86	No of Institutions	
	(01/17/2020)	739	
Market Cap	$5.2 Billion	Shares	
Book Value	$1.5 Billion		56,623,088
Price/Book	3.46	% Held	
Price/Sales	0.84		74.78

Business Summary: Business Services (MIC: 7.5.2 SIC: 7389 NAIC: 561499)

Alliance Data Systems is a provider of data-driven marketing and loyalty solutions. Co. provides a portfolio of outsourced marketing solutions, including customer loyalty programs, database marketing services, end-to-end marketing services, analytics and creative services, direct marketing services and private label and co-brand retail credit card programs. Co. focuses on facilitating and managing interactions between its clients and their customers through all consumer marketing channels, including in-store, online, email, social media, mobile, direct mail and telephone. Co.'s products and services are reported under three segments: LoyaltyOne®, Epsilon and Card Services.

Recent Developments: For the quarter ended Sep 30 2019, income from continuing operations decreased 57.9% to US$121.6 million from US$288.7 million in the year-earlier quarter. Net loss amounted to US$107.6 million versus net income of US$296.5 million in the year-earlier quarter. Revenues were US$1.44 billion, up 1.0% from US$1.42 billion the year before. Operating income was US$304.2 million versus US$479.8 million in the prior-year quarter, a decrease of 36.6%. Direct operating expenses rose 5.1% to US$687.5 million from US$654.0 million in the comparable period the year before. Indirect operating expenses increased 54.1% to US$445.9 million from US$289.3 million in the equivalent prior-year period.

Prospects: Our evaluation of Alliance Data Systems Corp. as of October 4th, 2019 is the result of our systematic analysis on three basic characteristics: earnings strength, relative valuation, and recent stock price movement. The company has managed to produce a neutral trend in earnings per share over the past 5 quarters. However, recent analyst estimates for the company have been reduced and ADS has posted results that fell short of analysts' expectations. Based on operating earnings yield, the company is undervalued when compared to all of the companies we cover. Share price changes over the past year indicates that ADS will perform poorly over the near term.

Financial Data

(US$ in Thousands)	9 Mos	6 Mos	3 Mos	12/31/2018	12/31/2017	12/31/2016	12/31/2015	12/31/2014
Earnings Per Share	8.55	16.07	17.36	17.49	14.10	7.34	8.85	7.87
Cash Flow Per Share	46.31	49.18	51.24	50.18	46.85	35.54	27.57	23.84
Tang Book Value Per Share	8.36	24.28	21.03	N.M.	N.M.	N.M.	N.M.	N.M.
Dividends Per Share	2.460	2.400	2.340	2.280	2.080	0.520	...	...
Dividend Payout %	28.77	14.93	13.48	13.04	14.75	7.08	...	...
Income Statement								
Total Revenue	4,120,300	2,682,700	1,334,200	7,791,200	7,719,400	7,138,100	6,439,746	5,302,940
EBITDA	1,031,000	716,300	367,900	2,283,700	2,061,200	1,708,200	1,698,049	1,368,994
Depn & Amortn	32,600	22,100	11,000	389,400	415,700	442,700	436,189	270,527
Income Before Taxes	571,000	406,800	207,400	1,223,700	1,081,100	837,000	931,676	837,941
Income Taxes	128,800	86,100	33,100	260,600	292,400	319,400	326,248	321,801
Net Income	180,500	288,100	149,100	963,100	788,700	515,800	596,541	506,293
Average Shares	50,400	52,600	53,200	55,100	55,900	58,900	62,301	62,445
Balance Sheet								
Current Assets	24,783,600	28,273,900	27,035,900	24,711,700	24,705,600	19,589,300	16,250,417	13,814,776
Total Assets	27,157,800	30,739,700	29,433,100	30,387,700	30,684,800	25,514,100	22,421,830	20,263,977
Current Liabilities	11,812,100	10,606,700	10,596,700	11,484,000	10,146,700	9,229,500	6,405,559	6,305,483
Long-Term Obligations	2,693,600	5,515,100	5,720,000	10,527,500	13,415,700	10,103,300	10,136,018	8,134,248
Total Liabilities	25,660,900	28,348,000	27,193,600	28,055,600	28,829,500	23,855,900	20,411,800	17,867,597
Stockholders' Equity	1,496,900	2,391,700	2,239,500	2,332,100	1,855,300	1,658,200	2,010,030	2,396,380
Shares Outstanding	46,100	50,900	52,300	53,400	55,400	57,400	60,877	63,812
Statistical Record								
Return on Assets %	1.64	2.91	3.22	3.15	2.81	2.15	2.80	3.02
Return on Equity %	24.57	38.55	44.72	46.00	44.90	28.05	27.08	31.14
EBITDA Margin %	25.02	26.70	27.57	29.31	26.70	23.93	26.37	25.82
Net Margin %	4.38	10.74	11.18	12.36	10.22	7.23	9.26	9.55
Asset Turnover	0.22	0.22	0.25	0.26	0.27	0.30	0.30	0.32
Current Ratio	2.10	2.67	2.55	2.15	2.43	2.12	2.54	2.19
Debt to Equity	1.80	2.31	2.55	4.51	7.23	6.09	5.04	3.39
Price Range	237.84-122.05	248.69-134.42	248.69-144.46	276.37-144.46	264.57-210.43	276.57-177.12	309.91-247.05	294.27-233.67
P/E Ratio	27.82-14.27	15.48-8.36	14.33-8.32	15.80-8.26	18.76-14.92	37.68-24.13	35.02-27.92	37.39-29.69
Average Yield %	1.49	1.27	1.14	1.02	0.88	0.24	...	...

Address: 3075 Loyalty Circle,	Web Site: www.alliancedata.com	Auditors: DELOITTE & TOUCHE LLP
Columbus, OH 43219	Officers: Robert A. Minicucci - Chairman Charles L.	Investor Contact: 212-850-5721
Telephone: 614-729-4000	Horn - Vice-Chairman, Acting Chief Executive	Transfer Agents: ComputerShare
	Officer, Executive Vice President, Chief Financial	Investor Services, Providence, RI
	Officer	

ALLISON TRANSMISSION HOLDINGS INC

Exchange	Symbol	Price	52Wk Range	Yield	P/E
NYS	ALSN	$48.32 (12/31/2019)	51.69-41.39	1.24	9.38

*7 Year Price Score 111.24 *NYSE Composite Index=100   *12 Month Price Score 97.09

Interim Earnings (Per Share)

Qtr.	Mar	Jun	Sep	Dec
2016	0.28	0.36	0.27	0.36
2017	0.52	0.63	0.75	1.46
2018	1.08	1.29	1.27	1.14
2019	1.32	1.46	1.23	...

Interim Dividends (Per Share)

Amt	Decl	Ex	Rec	Pay
0.15Q	02/21/2019	03/01/2019	03/04/2019	03/15/2019
0.15Q	05/09/2019	05/17/2019	05/20/2019	05/31/2019
0.15Q	08/12/2019	08/22/2019	08/23/2019	08/30/2019
0.15Q	11/04/2019	11/14/2019	11/15/2019	11/27/2019

Indicated Div: $0.60

Valuation Analysis / **Institutional Holding**

Forecast EPS	$4.75	No of Institutions
	(01/16/2020)	470
Market Cap	$5.8 Billion	Shares
Book Value	$743.0 Million	208,569,232
Price/Book	7.77	% Held
Price/Sales	2.12	61.83

Business Summary: Auto Parts (MIC: 1.8.2 SIC: 3714 NAIC: 336350)

Allison Transmission Holdings is a holding company. Through its subsidiaries, Co. manufactures fully-automatic transmissions for medium- and heavy-duty commercial vehicles and medium- and heavy-tactical U.S. defense vehicles. Co.'s transmissions are in used various applications, including on-highway trucks (distribution, refuse, construction, fire and emergency), buses (mainly school, transit and electric hybrid-transit), motorhomes, off-highway vehicles and equipment (mainly energy, mining and construction) and defense vehicles (wheeled and tracked). Co. also sells replacement parts, support equipment and other products to service the installed base of vehicles utilizing its transmissions.

Recent Developments: For the quarter ended Sep 30 2019, net income decreased 10.8% to US$149.0 million from US$167.0 million in the year-earlier quarter. Revenues were US$669.0 million, down 3.3% from US$692.0 million the year before. Operating income was US$224.0 million versus US$246.0 million in the prior-year quarter, a decrease of 8.9%. Direct operating expenses declined 0.9% to US$321.0 million from US$324.0 million in the comparable period the year before. Indirect operating expenses increased 1.6% to US$124.0 million from US$122.0 million in the equivalent prior-year period.

Prospects: Our evaluation of Allison Transmission Holding as of October 4th, 2019 is the result of our systematic analysis on three basic characteristics: earnings strength, relative valuation, and recent stock price movement. The company has generated a negative trend in earnings per share over the past 5 quarters. However, recent analyst estimates for the company have been unchanged while ALSN has posted results that exceeded analysts' expectations. Based on operating earnings yield, the company is undervalued when compared to all of the companies we cover. Share price changes over the past year indicates that ALSN will perform in line with the market over the near term.

Financial Data
(US$ in Thousands)

	9 Mos	6 Mos	3 Mos	12/31/2018	12/31/2017	12/31/2016	12/31/2015	12/31/2014
Earnings Per Share	5.15	5.19	5.02	4.78	3.36	1.27	1.03	1.25
Cash Flow Per Share	7.31	7.35	6.97	6.29	4.42	3.51	3.30	3.10
Dividends Per Share	0.600	0.600	0.600	0.600	0.600	0.600	0.600	0.510
Dividend Payout %	11.65	11.56	11.95	12.55	17.86	47.24	58.25	40.80
Income Statement								
Total Revenue	2,081,000	1,412,000	675,000	2,713,000	2,262,000	1,840,200	1,985,800	2,127,400
EBITDA	861,000	591,000	288,000	1,090,000	800,000	618,100	588,700	699,100
Depn & Amortn	126,000	82,000	41,000	164,000	170,000	175,900	185,400	192,600
Income Before Taxes	634,000	440,000	211,000	805,000	527,000	341,300	288,800	368,100
Income Taxes	137,000	92,000	44,000	166,000	23,000	126,400	106,500	139,500
Net Income	497,000	348,000	167,000	639,000	504,000	214,900	182,300	228,600
Average Shares	121,000	124,000	127,000	134,000	150,000	168,800	177,200	182,300
Balance Sheet								
Current Assets	748,000	705,000	881,000	725,000	632,000	547,600	616,800	758,000
Total Assets	4,471,000	4,355,000	4,392,000	4,237,000	4,205,000	4,218,600	4,408,400	4,804,200
Current Liabilities	477,000	468,000	465,000	426,000	417,000	342,200	304,600	345,900
Long-Term Obligations	2,513,000	2,514,000	2,514,000	2,523,000	2,534,000	2,146,800	2,352,700	2,502,600
Total Liabilities	3,728,000	3,687,000	3,646,000	3,578,000	3,516,000	3,138,300	3,219,800	3,406,400
Stockholders' Equity	743,000	668,000	746,000	659,000	689,000	1,080,300	1,188,600	1,397,800
Shares Outstanding	119,528	120,503	125,255	126,251	139,990	163,795	171,157	179,488
Statistical Record								
Return on Assets %	14.71	15.53	15.14	15.14	11.97	4.97	3.96	4.75
Return on Equity %	90.26	104.25	90.22	94.81	56.97	18.89	14.10	16.12
EBITDA Margin %	41.37	41.86	42.67	40.18	35.37	33.59	29.65	32.86
Net Margin %	23.88	24.65	24.74	23.55	22.28	11.68	9.18	10.75
Asset Turnover	0.62	0.65	0.63	0.64	0.54	0.43	0.43	0.44
Current Ratio	1.57	1.51	1.89	1.70	1.52	1.60	2.02	2.19
Debt to Equity	3.38	3.76	3.37	3.83	3.68	1.99	1.98	1.79
Price Range	53.37-40.83	53.44-39.86	53.44-38.05	53.44-37.45	44.08-32.81	35.02-21.58	33.90-24.64	34.38-26.46
P/E Ratio	10.36-7.93	10.30-7.68	10.65-7.58	11.18-7.83	13.12-9.76	27.57-16.99	32.91-23.92	27.50-21.17
Average Yield %	1.30	1.29	1.32	1.36	1.60	2.15	2.24	1.68

Address: One Allison Way,	Web Site: www.allisontransmission.com	Auditors: PricewaterhouseCoopers LLP
Indianapolis, IN 46222	Officers: Lawrence E. (Larry) Dewey - Chairman,	Investor Contact: 317-242-5000
Telephone: 317-242-5000	President, Chief Executive Officer David S. Graziosi -	Transfer Agents: American Stock
	President, Chief Executive Officer, Executive Vice	Transfer & Trust Company, LLC,
	President, Chief Financial Officer, Assistant Secretary	Brooklyn, NY

ALLSTATE CORP

Exchange	Symbol	Price	52Wk Range	Yield	P/E
NYS	ALL	$112.45 (12/31/2019)	112.62-80.30	1.78	14.04

*7 Year Price Score 110.49 *NYSE Composite Index=100 *12 Month Price Score 103.80

Interim Earnings (Per Share)

Qtr.	Mar	Jun	Sep	Dec
2016	0.57	0.64	1.31	2.16
2017	1.79	1.49	1.74	3.34
2018	2.63	1.80	2.37	(0.84)
2019	3.74	2.44	2.67	...

Interim Dividends (Per Share)

Amt	Decl	Ex	Rec	Pay
0.50Q	02/08/2019	02/27/2019	02/28/2019	04/01/2019
0.50Q	05/21/2019	05/30/2019	05/31/2019	07/01/2019
0.50Q	07/17/2019	08/29/2019	08/30/2019	10/01/2019
0.50Q	11/15/2019	11/27/2019	11/29/2019	01/02/2020

Indicated Div: $2.00 (Div. Reinv. Plan)

Valuation Analysis / **Institutional Holding**

Forecast EPS	$10.55	No of Institutions
	(01/17/2020)	1492
Market Cap	$36.5 Billion	Shares
Book Value	$26.1 Billion	355,062,496
Price/Book	1.40	% Held
Price/Sales	0.86	69.23

Business Summary: General Insurance (MIC: 5.2.1 SIC: 6331 NAIC: 524126)

Allstate is a holding company. Through its subsidiaries, Co. is engaged in the property and casualty insurance business in the U.S. and Canada. Co.'s segments include: Allstate Protection, which provides private passenger auto, homeowners, other personal lines and commercial insurance; Service Businesses, which includes SquareTrade that provides consumer protection plans and related technical support; Allstate Life, which provides interest-sensitive and variable life insurance products, as well as distributes non-proprietary retirement products; and Allstate Benefits, which provides voluntary benefits products, including life, accident, critical illness, and other health insurance products.

Recent Developments: For the quarter ended Sep 30 2019, net income decreased 4.9% to US$931.0 million from US$979.0 million in the year-earlier quarter. Revenues were US$11.07 billion, up 5.8% from US$10.47 billion the year before. Net premiums earned were US$9.72 billion versus US$9.21 billion in the prior-year quarter, an increase of 5.6%. Net investment income rose 4.3% to US$880.0 million from US$844.0 million a year ago.

Prospects: Our evaluation of Allstate Corp. as of October 4th, 2019 is the result of our systematic analysis on three basic characteristics: earnings strength, relative valuation, and recent stock price movement. The company has enjoyed a very positive trend in earnings per share over the past 5 quarters. However, recent analyst estimates for the company have been mixed and ALL has posted results that exceeded analysts' expectations. Based on operating earnings yield, the company is undervalued when compared to all of the companies we cover. Share price changes over the past year indicates that ALL will perform in line with the market over the near term.

Financial Data
(US$ in Millions)

	9 Mos	6 Mos	3 Mos	12/31/2018	12/31/2017	12/31/2016	12/31/2015	12/31/2014
Earnings Per Share	8.01	7.71	7.07	5.96	8.36	4.67	5.05	6.27
Cash Flow Per Share	16.03	15.50	15.82	14.88	11.92	10.68	9.02	7.50
Tang Book Value Per Share	63.21	66.66	56.88	50.76	52.46	48.11	44.78	46.27
Dividends Per Share	1.960	1.920	1.880	1.840	1.480	1.320	1.200	1.120
Dividend Payout %	24.47	24.90	26.59	30.87	17.70	28.27	23.76	17.86
Income Statement								
Premium Income	28,756	19,037	9,430	36,513	34,678	33,582	32,467	31,086
Total Revenue	33,203	22,134	10,990	39,815	38,524	36,534	35,653	35,239
Benefits & Claims	1,521	1,008	497	24,812	23,852	24,078	22,837	21,193
Income Before Taxes	3,858	2,698	1,620	2,744	3,991	2,754	3,282	4,236
Income Taxes	784	555	328	492	802	877	1,111	1,386
Net Income	3,074	2,143	1,292	2,252	3,189	1,877	2,171	2,850
Average Shares	333	336	337	353	367	377	406	438
Balance Sheet								
Total Assets	121,073	118,374	115,834	112,249	112,422	108,610	104,656	108,533
Total Liabilities	94,933	93,898	92,416	90,937	89,871	88,037	84,631	86,229
Stockholders' Equity	26,140	24,476	23,418	21,312	22,551	20,573	20,025	22,304
Shares Outstanding	325	300	333	332	355	366	381	418
Statistical Record								
Return on Assets %	2.38	2.37	2.24	2.00	2.89	1.76	2.04	2.46
Return on Equity %	11.27	11.53	11.00	10.27	14.79	9.22	10.26	13.02
Loss Ratio %	5.29	5.29	5.27	67.95	68.78	71.70	70.34	68.18
Net Margin %	9.26	9.68	11.76	5.66	8.28	5.14	6.09	8.09
Price Range	108.68-77.27	103.55-77.27	102.03-77.27	104.43-77.27	104.91-73.09	74.58-57.70	72.58-56.99	71.00-49.55
P/E Ratio	13.57-9.65	13.43-10.02	14.43-10.93	17.52-12.96	12.55-8.74	15.97-12.36	14.37-11.29	11.32-7.90
Average Yield %	2.05	2.04	2.02	1.94	1.68	1.96	1.82	1.89

Address: 2775 Sanders Road, Northbrook, IL 60062
Telephone: 847-402-5000

Web Site: www.allstate.com
Officers: Thomas J. Wilson - Chairman, President, Chief Executive Officer Don Civgin - Vice-Chairman, Senior Vice President, Chief Financial Officer

Auditors: Deloitte & Touche LLP
Investor Contact: 800-416-8803
Transfer Agents: Wells Fargo Bank, N.A. Shareowner Services, St. Paul, MN

ALLY FINANCIAL INC

Exchange	Symbol	Price	52Wk Range	Yield	P/E
NYS	ALLY	$30.56 (12/31/2019)	35.05-22.66	2.49	7.55

*7 Year Price Score N/A   *NYSE Composite Index=100   *12 Month Price Score 99.61

Interim Earnings (Per Share)

Qtr.	Mar	Jun	Sep	Dec
2016	0.49	0.71	0.43	0.52
2017	0.46	0.55	0.63	0.41
2018	0.57	0.81	0.88	0.70
2019	0.92	1.46	0.97	...

Interim Dividends (Per Share)

Amt	Decl	Ex	Rec	Pay
0.17Q	04/15/2019	04/30/2019	05/01/2019	05/15/2019
0.17Q	07/16/2019	07/31/2019	08/01/2019	08/15/2019
0.17Q	10/08/2019	10/31/2019	11/01/2019	11/15/2019
0.19Q	01/14/2020	01/30/2020	01/31/2020	02/14/2020

Indicated Div: $0.76

Valuation Analysis

		Institutional Holding	
Forecast EPS	$3.70	No of Institutions	602
	(01/17/2020)	Shares	
Market Cap	$11.7 Billion		402,176,832
Book Value	$14.5 Billion	% Held	
Price/Book	0.81	N/A	
Price/Sales	1.03		

Business Summary: Credit & Lending (MIC: 5.4.1 SIC: 6141 NAIC: 522291)

Ally Financial is a digital-financial services and financial holding company. Through its subsidiaries, Co. provides a range of financial services and insurance products to automotive dealerships and consumers. Co.'s online bank provides mortgage-lending services and a variety of deposit and other banking products, including savings, money-market and checking accounts, certificates of deposit, and individual retirement accounts. Co. also supports the Ally CashBack Credit Card. Additionally, Co. provides securities-brokerage and investment-advisory services through Ally Invest. Co.'s corporate-finance business provides capital for equity sponsors and middle-market companies.

Recent Developments: For the quarter ended Sep 30 2019, income from continuing operations increased 1.9% to US$381.0 million from US$374.0 million in the year-earlier quarter. Net income increased 1.9% to US$381.0 million from US$374.0 million in the year-earlier quarter. Net interest income increased 5.0% to US$1.42 billion from US$1.35 billion in the year-earlier quarter. Provision for loan losses was US$263.0 million versus US$233.0 million in the prior-year quarter, an increase of 12.9%. Non-interest income rose 3.8% to US$413.0 million from US$398.0 million, while non-interest expense advanced 1.7% to US$1.07 billion.

Prospects: Our evaluation of Ally Financial Inc as of October 4th, 2019 is the result of our systematic analysis on three basic characteristics: earnings strength, relative valuation, and recent stock price movement. The company has managed to produce a neutral trend in earnings per share over the past 5 quarters. However, recent analyst estimates for the company have been raised and ALLY has posted results that exceeded analysts' expectations. Based on operating earnings yield, the company is undervalued when compared to all of the companies we cover. Share price changes over the past year indicates that ALLY will perform well over the near term.

Financial Data
(US$ in Millions)

	9 Mos	6 Mos	3 Mos	12/31/2018	12/31/2017	12/31/2016	12/31/2015	12/31/2014
Earnings Per Share	4.05	3.96	3.31	2.95	2.04	2.15	(2.66)	1.83
Cash Flow Per Share	10.09	10.01	10.23	9.76	8.99	9.47	10.55	7.07
Tang Book Value Per Share	37.05	35.84	33.67	32.18	30.33	28.00	26.44	29.46
Dividends Per Share	0.660	0.640	0.600	0.560	0.400	0.160	...	...
Dividend Payout %	16.30	16.16	18.13	18.98	19.61	7.44	...	...
Income Statement								
Total Revenue	8,689	5,785	2,899	10,466	9,866	9,835	9,539	9,667
Income Before Taxes	1,480	980	486	1,622	1,507	1,581	1,393	1,246
Income Taxes	140	21	111	359	581	470	496	321
Net Income	1,337	956	374	1,263	929	1,067	1,289	1,150
Average Shares	392	399	405	427	455	482	482	481
Balance Sheet								
Total Assets	181,485	180,448	180,117	178,869	167,148	163,728	158,581	151,828
Total Liabilities	167,035	166,132	166,418	165,601	153,654	150,411	145,142	136,429
Stockholders' Equity	14,450	14,316	13,699	13,268	13,494	13,317	13,439	15,399
Shares Outstanding	383	392	399	404	437	467	481	480
Statistical Record								
Return on Assets %	0.92	0.92	0.79	0.73	0.56	0.66	0.83	0.76
Return on Equity %	11.82	11.80	10.36	9.44	6.93	7.95	8.94	7.77
Net Margin %	15.39	16.53	12.90	12.07	9.42	10.85	13.51	11.90
Asset Turnover	0.06	0.06	0.06	0.06	0.06	0.06	0.06	0.06
Price Range	35.05-20.74	30.99-20.74	28.13-20.74	30.83-20.74	29.41-18.22	20.40-14.90	23.88-18.33	27.90-20.12
P/E Ratio	8.65-5.12	7.83-5.24	8.50-6.27	10.45-7.03	14.42-8.93	9.49-6.93	...	15.25-10.99
Average Yield %	2.33	2.38	2.29	2.08	1.78	0.88	...	...

Address: Ally Detroit Center, 500 Woodward Avenue, Floor 10, Detroit, MI 48226
Telephone: 866-710-4623

Web Site: www.ally.com
Officers: Franklin (Fritz) W. Hobbs - Chairman Jeffrey J. Brown - Chief Executive Officer, Senior Executive Vice President, Division Officer

Auditors: DELOITTE & TOUCHE LLP
Investor Contact: 866-710-4623
Transfer Agents: Computershare Limited

ALTICE USA INC

Exchange	Symbol	Price	52Wk Range	Yield	P/E
NYS	ATUS	$27.34 (12/31/2019)	31.61-16.52	N/A	54.68

*7 Year Price Score N/A   *NYSE Composite Index=100   *12 Month Price Score 104.25

Interim Earnings (Per Share)

Qtr.	Mar	Jun	Sep	Dec
2017	(0.12)	(0.72)	(0.25)	3.26
2018	(0.17)	(0.13)	0.04	0.29
2019	(0.04)	0.13	0.12	...

Interim Dividends (Per Share)

Amt	Decl	Ex	Rec	Pay
2.035U	05/14/2018	06/07/2018	05/22/2018	06/06/2018

Valuation Analysis   **Institutional Holding**

Forecast EPS	$0.40	No of Institutions	
	(01/17/2020)	370	
Market Cap	$17.4 Billion	Shares	
Book Value	$2.3 Billion	360,954,880	
Price/Book	7.58	% Held	
Price/Sales	1.79	48.56	

Business Summary: Radio & Television (MIC: 2.3.1 SIC: 4841 NAIC: 515210)

Altice USA is a holding company. Through its subsidiaries, Co. is a broadband communications and video services provider and markets its services under Optimum and Suddenlink brands. Co. delivers broadband, pay television, telephony services, proprietary content and advertising services to customers in and around the New York metropolitan area and in the south-central U.S., with the majority of its customers located in Texas, West Virginia, Louisiana, Arkansas, North Carolina, Oklahoma, Arizona, California, Missouri and Ohio. Co. also provides fiber connectivity, bandwidth and managed services to enterprise customers through its Lightpath business and advertising time to advertisers.

Recent Developments: For the quarter ended Sep 30 2019, net income increased 129.4% to US$77.4 million from US$33.7 million in the year-earlier quarter. Revenues were US$2.44 billion, up 0.9% from US$2.42 billion the year before. Operating income was US$471.5 million versus US$505.6 million in the prior-year quarter, a decrease of 6.7%. Direct operating expenses rose 3.8% to US$820.9 million from US$790.5 million in the comparable period the year before. Indirect operating expenses increased 2.2% to US$1.15 billion from US$1.12 billion in the equivalent prior-year period.

Prospects: Our evaluation of Altice USA Inc as of October 4th, 2019 is the result of our systematic analysis on three basic characteristics: earnings strength, relative valuation, and recent stock price movement. The company has generated a negative trend in earnings per share over the past 5 quarters. However, recent analyst estimates for the company have been unchanged and ATUS has posted results in line with analysts' expectations. Based on operating earnings yield, the company is overvalued when compared to all of the companies we cover. Share price changes over the past year indicates that ATUS will perform over the near term.

Financial Data

(US$ in Thousands)	9 Mos	6 Mos	3 Mos	12/31/2018	12/31/2017	12/31/2016
Earnings Per Share	0.50	0.42	0.16	0.03	2.18	(8,320.00)
Cash Flow Per Share	4.00	3.95	3.71	3.44	2.88	11,844.55
Dividends Per Share	...	...	2.035	2.035	1.290	...
Dividend Payout %	...	...	1,271.88	6,783.33	59.17	...
Income Statement						
Total Revenue	7,286,310	4,847,648	2,396,567	9,566,608	9,326,570	6,017,212
EBITDA	1,431,804	900,739	364,746	3,035,490	1,858,530	1,398,481
Depn & Amortn	82,398	53,876	26,066	1,508,125	1,588,668	1,046,896
Income Before Taxes	195,053	79,786	(47,784)	(18,061)	(1,331,349)	(1,091,145)
Income Taxes	56,445	18,574	(22,586)	(38,655)	(2,852,967)	(259,666)
Net Income	138,607	61,368	(24,999)	18,833	1,520,031	(832,030)
Average Shares	646,006	668,648	695,528	730,088	696,055	100
Balance Sheet						
Current Assets	817,779	742,919	711,042	903,254	853,560	1,704,919
Total Assets	33,773,508	33,779,651	33,559,373	33,613,808	34,775,225	36,474,249
Current Liabilities	1,879,347	2,518,940	1,801,820	2,021,191	2,492,983	3,704,933
Long-Term Obligations	23,895,580	22,980,286	23,137,835	22,653,975	21,347,954	22,428,098
Total Liabilities	31,475,226	31,079,095	30,366,064	29,812,860	29,049,634	34,376,547
Stockholders' Equity	2,298,282	2,700,556	3,193,309	3,800,948	5,725,591	2,097,702
Shares Outstanding	636,827	655,226	679,784	709,040	737,068	100
Statistical Record						
Return on Assets %	1.04	0.91	0.36	0.06	4.27	...
Return on Equity %	11.45	9.12	2.78	0.40	38.86	...
EBITDA Margin %	19.65	18.58	15.22	31.73	19.93	23.24
Net Margin %	1.90	1.27	N.M.	0.20	16.30	N.M.
Asset Turnover	0.29	0.29	0.28	0.28	0.26	...
Current Ratio	0.44	0.29	0.39	0.45	0.34	0.46
Debt to Equity	10.40	8.51	7.25	5.96	3.73	10.69
Price Range	29.89-14.61	25.03-14.61	22.24-14.61	23.27-14.61	34.30-17.85	...
P/E Ratio	59.78-29.22	59.60-34.79	139.00-91.31	775.67-487.00	15.73-8.19	...
Average Yield %	...	...	11.01	10.98	4.83	...

Address: 1 Court Square West, Long Island City, NY 11101 **Telephone:** 516-803-2300	**Web Site:** www.alticeusa.com **Officers:** Patrick Drahi - Chairman Dexter Goei - Chairman, Chief Executive Officer, Holding/Parent Company Officer	**Auditors:** KPMG LLP **Transfer Agents:** American Stock Transfer & Trust Company, LLC

ALTRIA GROUP INC

Exchange	Symbol	Price	52Wk Range	Yield	P/E	Div Acheiver
NYS	MO	$49.91 (12/31/2019)	57.73-40.12	6.73	53.10	53 Years

*7 Year Price Score 75.49   *NYSE Composite Index=100   *12 Month Price Score 94.91

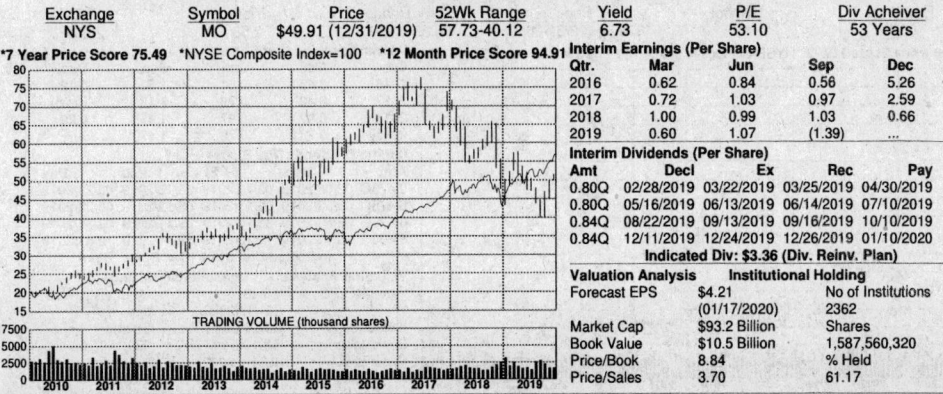

Interim Earnings (Per Share)

Qtr.	Mar	Jun	Sep	Dec
2016	0.62	0.84	0.56	5.26
2017	0.72	1.03	0.97	2.59
2018	1.00	0.99	1.03	0.66
2019	0.60	1.07	(1.39)	...

Interim Dividends (Per Share)

Amt	Decl	Ex	Rec	Pay
0.80Q	02/28/2019	03/22/2019	03/25/2019	04/30/2019
0.80Q	05/16/2019	06/13/2019	06/14/2019	07/10/2019
0.84Q	08/22/2019	09/13/2019	09/16/2019	10/10/2019
0.84Q	12/11/2019	12/24/2019	12/26/2019	01/10/2020

Indicated Div: $3.36 (Div. Reinv. Plan)

Valuation Analysis

		Institutional Holding	
Forecast EPS	$4.21 (01/17/2020)	No of Institutions	2362
Market Cap	$93.2 Billion	Shares	1,587,560,320
Book Value	$10.5 Billion	% Held	61.17
Price/Book	8.84		
Price/Sales	3.70		

Business Summary: Tobacco Products (MIC: 1.3.1 SIC: 2111 NAIC: 312221)

Altria Group is a holding company. Co.'s subsidiaries include: Philip Morris USA Inc., which is engaged in the manufacture and sale of cigarettes; John Middleton Co., which is engaged in the manufacture and sale of machine-made cigars and pipe tobacco; Sherman Group Holdings, LLC and its subsidiaries, which are engaged in the manufacture and sale of cigarettes and the sale of cigars; and UST LLC, which through its subsidiaries, including U.S. Smokeless Tobacco Company LLC and Ste. Michelle Wine Estates Ltd., is engaged in the manufacture and sale of smokeless tobacco products and wine. The products of Co.'s tobacco subsidiaries include smokeable tobacco products and machine-made cigars.

Recent Developments: For the quarter ended Sep 30 2019, net loss amounted to US$2.60 billion versus net income of US$1.94 billion in the year-earlier quarter. Revenues were US$6.86 billion, up 0.3% from US$6.84 billion the year before. Operating income was US$2.94 billion versus US$2.56 billion in the prior-year quarter, an increase of 15.1%. Direct operating expenses declined 6.2% to US$3.36 billion from US$3.58 billion in the comparable period the year before. Indirect operating expenses decreased 20.8% to US$553.0 million from US$698.0 million in the equivalent prior-year period.

Prospects: Our evaluation of Altria Group Inc. as of October 4th, 2019 is the result of our systematic analysis on three basic characteristics: earnings strength, relative valuation, and recent stock price movement. The company has produced a positive trend in earnings per share over the past 5 quarters. However, recent analyst estimates for the company have been mixed and MO has posted results that fell short of analysts' expectations. Based on operating earnings yield, the company is undervalued when compared to all of the companies we cover. Share price changes over the past year indicates that MO will perform in line with the market over the near term.

Financial Data

(US$ in Thousands)	9 Mos	6 Mos	3 Mos	12/31/2018	12/31/2017	12/31/2016	12/31/2015	12/31/2014
Earnings Per Share	0.94	3.36	3.28	3.68	5.31	7.28	2.67	2.56
Cash Flow Per Share	3.80	3.71	4.20	4.45	2.56	1.94	2.96	2.36
Dividends Per Share	3.240	3.200	3.100	3.000	2.540	2.350	2.170	2.000
Dividend Payout %	344.68	95.24	94.51	81.52	47.83	32.28	81.27	78.13
Income Statement								
Total Revenue	19,103,000	12,247,000	5,628,000	25,364,000	25,576,000	25,744,000	25,434,000	24,522,000
EBITDA	2,275,000	4,386,000	1,867,000	9,305,000	10,189,000	21,987,000	8,342,000	7,764,000
Depn & Amortn	163,000	106,000	53,000	189,000	188,000	183,000	204,000	188,000
Income Before Taxes	1,123,000	3,584,000	1,430,000	8,451,000	9,296,000	21,057,000	7,321,000	6,768,000
Income Taxes	1,473,000	999,000	395,000	2,374,000	(399,000)	7,608,000	2,835,000	2,704,000
Net Income	516,000	3,116,000	1,120,000	6,963,000	10,222,000	14,239,000	5,241,000	5,070,000
Average Shares	1,868,000	1,870,000	1,874,000	1,888,000	1,921,000	1,952,000	1,961,000	1,978,000
Balance Sheet								
Current Assets	4,291,000	4,483,000	6,262,000	4,299,000	4,344,000	7,260,000	6,086,000	6,878,000
Total Assets	52,913,000	57,501,000	59,233,000	55,638,000	43,202,000	45,932,000	32,535,000	34,475,000
Current Liabilities	7,662,000	7,952,000	10,119,000	21,193,000	6,792,000	7,375,000	7,078,000	7,673,000
Long-Term Obligations	26,903,000	27,096,000	27,024,000	11,898,000	13,030,000	13,881,000	12,915,000	13,693,000
Total Liabilities	42,368,000	43,037,000	45,154,000	40,851,000	27,825,000	33,162,000	29,655,000	31,461,000
Stockholders' Equity	10,545,000	14,464,000	14,079,000	14,787,000	15,377,000	12,770,000	2,880,000	3,014,000
Shares Outstanding	1,868,125	1,868,089	1,871,754	1,874,057	1,901,259	1,943,272	1,960,059	1,971,474
Statistical Record								
Return on Assets %	3.65	12.53	12.00	14.09	22.94	36.19	15.64	14.62
Return on Equity %	13.56	41.70	42.00	46.17	72.63	181.47	177.84	142.16
EBITDA Margin %	11.91	35.81	33.17	36.69	39.84	85.41	32.80	31.66
Net Margin %	2.70	25.44	19.90	27.45	39.97	55.31	20.61	20.68
Asset Turnover	0.52	0.50	0.48	0.51	0.57	0.65	0.76	0.71
Current Ratio	0.56	0.56	0.62	0.20	0.64	0.98	0.86	0.90
Debt to Equity	2.55	1.87	1.92	0.80	0.85	1.09	4.48	4.54
Price Range	65.87-40.12	65.87-43.33	65.87-43.33	71.56-47.56	77.71-61.22	69.87-57.20	61.53-47.54	51.27-34.00
P/E Ratio	70.07-42.68	19.60-12.90	20.08-13.21	19.45-12.92	14.63-11.53	9.60-7.86	23.04-17.81	20.03-13.28
Average Yield %	6.25	5.79	5.48	4.98	3.64	3.68	4.03	4.75

Address: 6601 West Broad Street, Richmond, VA 23230	Web Site: www.altria.com	Auditors: PricewaterhouseCoopers LLP
Telephone: 804-274-2200	Officers: Howard A. Willard - Chairman, Chief Executive Officer, Executive Vice President, Chief Operating Officer, Chief Financial Officer William F. Gifford - Vice-Chairman, Executive Vice President, Chief Financial Officer	Investor Contact: 804-484-8222 Transfer Agents: Computershare Trust Company, N.A., Providence, RI

AMEREN CORP

Exchange	Symbol	Price	52Wk Range	Yield	P/E
NYS	AEE	$76.80 (12/31/2019)	80.38-63.53	2.58	23.63

*7 Year Price Score 119.72 *NYSE Composite Index=100 *12 Month Price Score 96.30

Interim Earnings (Per Share)

Qtr.	Mar	Jun	Sep	Dec
2016	0.43	0.61	1.52	0.12
2017	0.42	0.79	1.18	(0.25)
2018	0.62	0.97	1.45	0.28
2019	0.78	0.72	1.47	...

Interim Dividends (Per Share)

Amt	Decl	Ex	Rec	Pay
0.475Q	02/08/2019	03/12/2019	03/13/2019	03/29/2019
0.475Q	05/03/2019	06/11/2019	06/12/2019	06/28/2019
0.475Q	08/09/2019	09/10/2019	09/11/2019	09/30/2019
0.495Q	10/11/2019	12/10/2019	12/11/2019	12/31/2019

Indicated Div: $1.98 (Div. Reinv. Plan)

Valuation Analysis

		Institutional Holding	
Forecast EPS	$3.28	No of Institutions	
	(01/17/2020)	844	
Market Cap	$18.9 Billion	Shares	
Book Value	$8.1 Billion	229,159,792	
Price/Book	2.34	% Held	
Price/Sales	3.14	76.38	

Business Summary: Electric Utilities (MIC: 3.1.1 SIC: 4931 NAIC: 221111)

Ameren is a public utility holding company. Through its subsidiary, Union Electric Company, Co. operates a rate-regulated electric generation, transmission, and distribution business and a rate-regulated natural gas distribution business in Missouri. Through its subsidiary, Ameren Illinois Company, Co. operates rate-regulated electric transmission, electric distribution, and natural gas distribution businesses in Illinois. Through its Ameren Transmission Company of Illinois subsidiary, Co. operates a Federal Energy Regulatory Commission rate-regulated electric transmission business. Co. also has other subsidiaries that conduct other activities, such as providing shared services.

Recent Developments: For the quarter ended Sep 30 2019, net income increased 1.9% to US$366.0 million from US$359.0 million in the year-earlier quarter. Revenues were US$1.66 billion, down 3.8% from US$1.72 billion the year before. Operating income was US$520.0 million versus US$533.0 million in the prior-year quarter, a decrease of 2.4%. Direct operating expenses declined 6.2% to US$891.0 million from US$950.0 million in the comparable period the year before. Indirect operating expenses increased 2.9% to US$248.0 million from US$241.0 million in the equivalent prior-year period.

Prospects: Our evaluation of Ameren Corp. as of October 4th, 2019 is the result of our systematic analysis on three basic characteristics: earnings strength, relative valuation, and recent stock price movement. The company has generated a negative trend in earnings per share over the past 5 quarters. However, recent analyst estimates for the company have been mixed and AEE has posted results that fell short of analysts' expectations. Based on operating earnings yield, the company is fairly valued when compared to all of the companies we cover. Share price changes over the past year indicates that AEE will perform well over the near term.

Financial Data

(US$ in Thousands)	9 Mos	6 Mos	3 Mos	12/31/2018	12/31/2017	12/31/2016	12/31/2015	12/31/2014
Earnings Per Share	3.25	3.23	3.48	3.32	2.14	2.68	2.59	2.40
Cash Flow Per Share	8.75	9.08	9.39	8.90	8.67	8.73	8.31	6.39
Tang Book Value Per Share	31.10	30.02	29.70	29.53	27.92	27.58	26.94	25.98
Dividends Per Share	1.900	1.883	1.865	1.847	1.778	1.715	1.655	1.610
Dividend Payout %	58.46	58.28	53.59	55.65	83.06	63.99	63.90	67.08
Income Statement								
Total Revenue	4,594,000	2,935,000	1,556,000	6,291,000	6,177,000	6,076,000	6,098,000	6,053,000
EBITDA	1,232,000	658,000	337,000	2,479,000	2,436,000	2,328,000	2,158,000	2,087,000
Depn & Amortn	70,000	42,000	28,000	1,053,000	974,000	945,000	896,000	813,000
Income Before Taxes	897,000	439,000	220,000	1,058,000	1,105,000	1,041,000	948,000	970,000
Income Taxes	158,000	66,000	27,000	237,000	576,000	382,000	363,000	377,000
Net Income	734,000	370,000	191,000	815,000	523,000	653,000	630,000	586,000
Average Shares	247,500	247,200	246,400	245,800	244,200	243,400	243,600	244,400
Balance Sheet								
Current Assets	1,495,000	1,514,000	1,422,000	1,533,000	1,612,000	1,593,000	1,917,000	2,046,000
Total Assets	28,546,000	28,103,000	27,509,000	27,215,000	25,945,000	24,699,000	23,640,000	22,676,000
Current Liabilities	2,285,000	2,752,000	2,392,000	2,687,000	2,940,000	2,674,000	2,093,000	2,249,000
Long-Term Obligations	8,651,000	8,222,000	8,221,000	7,859,000	7,094,000	6,595,000	6,880,000	6,120,000
Total Liabilities	20,484,000	20,312,000	19,804,000	19,584,000	18,761,000	17,596,000	16,694,000	15,963,000
Stockholders' Equity	8,062,000	7,791,000	7,705,000	7,631,000	7,184,000	7,103,000	6,946,000	6,713,000
Shares Outstanding	246,000	245,800	245,600	244,500	242,600	242,600	242,600	242,600
Statistical Record								
Return on Assets %	2.89	2.90	3.19	3.07	2.07	2.69	2.72	2.68
Return on Equity %	10.20	10.48	11.45	11.00	7.32	9.27	9.22	8.84
EBITDA Margin %	26.82	22.42	21.66	39.41	39.44	38.31	35.39	34.48
Net Margin %	15.98	12.61	12.28	12.96	8.47	10.75	10.33	9.68
Asset Turnover	0.22	0.22	0.23	0.24	0.24	0.25	0.26	0.28
Current Ratio	0.65	0.55	0.59	0.57	0.55	0.60	0.92	0.91
Debt to Equity	1.07	1.06	1.07	1.03	0.99	0.93	0.99	0.91
Price Range	80.38-63.24	77.45-59.97	74.75-55.33	70.71-52.59	64.54-51.69	53.77-42.13	46.54-37.51	47.92-35.40
P/E Ratio	24.73-19.46	23.98-18.57	21.48-15.90	21.30-15.84	30.16-24.15	20.06-15.72	17.97-14.48	19.97-14.75
Average Yield %	2.65	2.76	2.91	3.05	3.11	3.50	3.96	4.02

| Address: 1901 Chouteau Avenue, St. Louis, MO 63103 | Web Site: www.ameren.com | Auditors: PricewaterhouseCoopers LLP |
| Telephone: 314-621-3222 | Officers: Warner L. Baxter - Chairman, President, Chief Executive Officer Michael L. Moehn - Executive Vice President, Chief Financial Officer | Transfer Agents: Ameren Services Company, St. Louis, MO |

AMERICAN CAMPUS COMMUNITIES INC

Exchange	Symbol	Price	52Wk Range	Yield	P/E
NYS	ACC	$47.03 (12/31/2019)	50.73-40.19	4.00	61.88

*7 Year Price Score 90.54   *NYSE Composite Index=100   *12 Month Price Score 96.07

Interim Earnings (Per Share)

Qtr.	Mar	Jun	Sep	Dec
2016	0.36	0.14	0.07	0.19
2017	0.25	(0.02)	(0.01)	0.29
2018	0.18	0.33	(0.02)	0.34
2019	0.21	0.07	0.14	...

Interim Dividends (Per Share)

Amt	Decl	Ex	Rec	Pay
0.46Q	01/22/2019	01/31/2019	02/01/2019	02/15/2019
0.47Q	05/01/2019	05/10/2019	05/13/2019	05/24/2019
0.47Q	07/31/2019	08/09/2019	08/12/2019	08/23/2019
0.47Q	10/30/2019	11/07/2019	11/11/2019	11/22/2019

Indicated Div: $1.88

Valuation Analysis   **Institutional Holding**

Forecast EPS	$0.60	No of Institutions
	(01/17/2020)	497
Market Cap	$6.5 Billion	Shares
Book Value	$3.3 Billion	161,617,616
Price/Book	1.94	% Held
Price/Sales	6.92	84.80

Business Summary: REITs (MIC: 5.3.1 SIC: 6798 NAIC: 525930)

American Campus Communities is a real estate investment trust. Through American Campus Communities Operating Partnership, L.P., Co. is an owners, managers and developers of student housing properties. Co. has four reportable segments: Owned Properties, which includes off-campus properties that are located in close proximity to the school campus; On-Campus Participating Properties, which includes on-campus properties that are operated under long-term ground/facility leases; Development Services, which consists of development and construction management services; and Property Management Services, which includes third-party management contracts in which Co. is responsible for operations.

Recent Developments: For the quarter ended Sep 30 2019, net income amounted to US$19.3 million versus a net loss of US$2.7 million in the year-earlier quarter. Revenues were US$227.7 million, up 6.7% from US$213.5 million the year before. Revenues from property income rose 3.9% to US$218.0 million from US$209.8 million in the corresponding quarter a year earlier.

Prospects: Our evaluation of American Campus Communities Inc. as of October 4th, 2019 is the result of our systematic analysis on three basic characteristics: earnings strength, relative valuation, and recent stock price movement. The company has managed to produce a neutral trend in earnings per share over the past 5 quarters: Additionally, recent analyst estimates for the company have been unchanged while ACC has posted results that fell short of analysts' expectations. Based on operating earnings yield, the company is overvalued when compared to all of the companies we cover. Share price changes over the past year indicates that ACC will perform well over the near term.

Financial Data
(US$ in Thousands)

	9 Mos	6 Mos	3 Mos	12/31/2018	12/31/2017	12/31/2016	12/31/2015	12/31/2014
Earnings Per Share	0.76	0.60	0.86	0.84	0.50	0.75	1.02	0.58
Cash Flow Per Share	2.79	2.59	2.55	2.75	2.37	2.38	2.33	2.47
Tang Book Value Per Share	24.25	24.64	25.07	25.42	25.56	26.05	24.66	24.35
Dividends Per Share	1.860	1.850	1.840	1.820	1.740	1.660	1.580	1.500
Dividend Payout %	244.74	308.33	213.95	216.67	348.00	221.33	154.90	258.62
Income Statement								
Total Revenue	687,207	459,502	242,131	880,810	796,447	786,361	753,381	733,915
EBITDA	146,129	97,161	59,082	218,947	141,787	175,879	206,371	151,286
Depn & Amortn	990	321	83	3,000	4,500	900	3,700	2,400
Income Before Taxes	61,897	42,256	31,732	121,553	71,110	101,773	119,303	62,692
Income Taxes	983	678	364	2,429	989	1,150	1,242	1,308
Net Income	60,249	40,026	29,640	117,095	69,038	99,061	115,991	62,839
Average Shares	138,375	138,243	138,152	137,722	136,002	130,018	114,032	105,711
Balance Sheet								
Current Assets	113,147	98,172	93,911	115,082	73,942	55,385	68,809	67,144
Total Assets	7,668,982	7,382,897	7,325,448	7,038,846	6,897,370	5,865,913	6,025,947	5,834,748
Current Liabilities	86,295	67,079	58,439	88,767	53,741	76,614	71,988	70,629
Long-Term Obligations	3,363,469	3,241,362	3,109,423	3,027,599	3,024,519	2,125,297	2,967,980	2,972,719
Total Liabilities	4,338,907	4,002,898	3,886,524	3,557,795	3,412,385	2,420,928	3,255,751	3,225,194
Stockholders' Equity	3,330,075	3,379,999	3,438,924	3,481,051	3,484,985	3,444,985	2,770,196	2,609,554
Shares Outstanding	137,326	137,200	137,188	136,967	136,362	132,225	112,350	107,175
Statistical Record								
Return on Assets %	1.46	1.19	1.69	1.68	1.08	1.66	1.96	1.10
Return on Equity %	3.16	2.44	3.50	3.36	1.99	3.18	4.31	2.40
EBITDA Margin %	21.26	21.14	24.40	24.86	17.80	22.37	27.39	20.61
Net Margin %	8.77	8.71	12.24	13.29	8.67	12.60	15.40	8.56
Asset Turnover	0.13	0.13	0.13	0.13	0.12	0.13	0.13	0.13
Current Ratio	1.31	1.46	1.61	1.30	1.38	0.72	0.96	0.95
Debt to Equity	1.01	0.96	0.90	0.87	0.87	0.62	1.07	1.14
Price Range	49.11-39.13	48.42-39.13	48.12-36.85	43.83-34.80	51.43-40.23	54.55-39.33	44.84-32.26	41.88-32.21
P/E Ratio	64.62-51.49	80.70-65.22	55.95-42.85	52.18-41.43	102.86-80.46	72.73-52.44	43.96-31.63	72.21-55.53
Average Yield %	4.12	4.22	4.38	4.52	3.73	3.50	3.98	3.95

Address: 12700 Hill Country Blvd., Suite T-200, Austin, TX 78738 **Telephone:** 512-732-1000	**Web Site:** www.americancampus.com **Officers:** Edward Lowenthal - Chairman James C. Hopke - President, Executive Vice President, Executive Vice President, Executive Vice President (frmr), Chief Operating Officer	**Auditors:** Ernst & Young LLP **Investor Contact:** 512-732-1041 **Transfer Agents:** Wells Fargo Bank N.A., Mendota Heights, MN

AMERICAN EAGLE OUTFITTERS, INC.

Exchange	Symbol	Price	52Wk Range	Yield	P/E
NYS	AEO	$14.70 (12/31/2019)	24.12-14.13	3.74	9.67

*7 Year Price Score 89.91 ***NYSE Composite Index=100** ***12 Month Price Score 78.66**

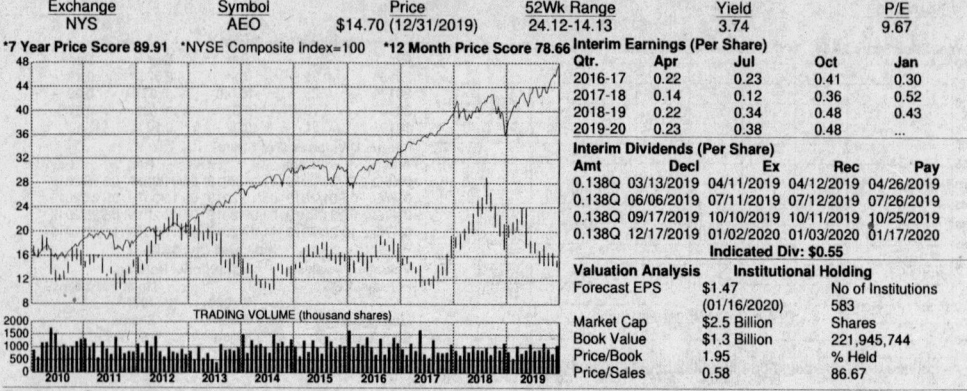

Interim Earnings (Per Share)

Qtr.	Apr	Jul	Oct	Jan
2016-17	0.22	0.23	0.41	0.30
2017-18	0.14	0.12	0.36	0.52
2018-19	0.22	0.34	0.48	0.43
2019-20	0.23	0.38	0.48	...

Interim Dividends (Per Share)

Amt	Decl	Ex	Rec	Pay
0.138Q	03/13/2019	04/11/2019	04/12/2019	04/26/2019
0.138Q	06/06/2019	07/11/2019	07/12/2019	07/26/2019
0.138Q	09/17/2019	10/10/2019	10/11/2019	10/25/2019
0.138Q	12/17/2019	01/02/2020	01/03/2020	01/17/2020

Indicated Div: $0.55

Valuation Analysis **Institutional Holding**

Forecast EPS	$1.47	No of Institutions
	(01/16/2020)	583
Market Cap	$2.5 Billion	Shares
Book Value	$1.3 Billion	221,945,744
Price/Book	1.95	% Held
Price/Sales	0.58	86.67

Business Summary: Retail - Apparel and Accessories (MIC: 2.1.5 SIC: 5651 NAIC: 448140)

American Eagle Outfitters is a multi-brand retailer. Co. operates retail stores and online at www.ae.com and www.aerie.com. Co. provides a range of apparel and accessories for men and women under the American Eagle Outfitters brand, and intimates, apparel and personal care products for women under the Aerie brand. Co. operates stores in the U.S., Canada, Mexico, Hong Kong, and China. Co. also has license agreements with third-parties to operate American Eagle Outfitters and Aerie stores throughout Asia, Europe, India, Latin America and the Middle East. Co. also operates two other brands, Tailgate, a vintage, sports-inspired apparel brand, and Todd Snyder New York, a menswear brand.

Recent Developments: For the quarter ended Nov 2 2019, net income decreased 5.5% to US$80.8 million from US$85.5 million in the year-earlier quarter. Revenues were US$1.07 billion, up 6.2% from US$1.00 billion the year before. Operating income was US$103.1 million versus US$108.6 million in the prior-year quarter, a decrease of 5.1%. Direct operating expenses rose 9.1% to US$659.4 million from US$604.2 million in the comparable period the year before. Indirect operating expenses increased 4.5% to US$304.0 million from US$290.9 million in the equivalent prior-year period.

Prospects: Our evaluation of American Eagle Outfitters Inc. as of October 4th, 2019 is the result of our systematic analysis on three basic characteristics: earnings strength, relative valuation, and recent stock price movement. The company has enjoyed a very positive trend in earnings per share over the past 5 quarters. However, recent analyst estimates for the company have been mixed and AEO has posted results that exceeded analysts' expectations. Based on operating earnings yield, the company is undervalued when compared to all of the companies we cover. Share price changes over the past year indicates that AEO will perform poorly over the near term.

Financial Data (US$ in Thousands)	9 Mos	6 Mos	3 Mos	02/02/2019	02/03/2018	01/28/2017	01/30/2016	01/31/2015
Earnings Per Share	1.52	1.52	1.48	1.47	1.13	1.16	1.11	0.42
Cash Flow Per Share	2.33	2.47	2.53	2.59	2.20	2.02	1.76	1.75
Tang Book Value Per Share	7.22	6.94	6.89	7.13	6.68	6.27	5.45	5.55
Dividends Per Share	0.550	0.550	0.550	0.550	0.500	0.500	0.500	0.500
Dividend Payout %	36.18	36.18	37.16	37.41	44.25	43.10	45.05	119.05
Income Statement								
Total Revenue	2,993,581	1,927,169	886,290	4,035,720	3,795,549	3,609,865	3,521,848	3,282,867
EBITDA	379,974	228,727	97,378	509,365	446,142	487,906	462,487	292,031
Depn & Amortn	136,355	90,787	45,350	164,265	158,969	152,644	140,616	132,529
Income Before Taxes	243,619	137,940	52,028	345,100	287,173	335,262	321,871	159,502
Income Taxes	57,125	32,206	11,276	83,198	83,010	122,813	108,580	70,715
Net Income	186,494	105,734	40,752	261,902	204,163	212,449	218,138	80,322
Average Shares	168,693	171,781	174,073	178,035	180,156	183,835	196,237	195,135
Balance Sheet								
Current Assets	1,078,574	1,020,073	950,603	1,046,253	968,530	901,229	723,375	890,513
Total Assets	3,452,252	3,359,159	3,255,353	1,903,378	1,816,313	1,782,660	1,612,246	1,696,908
Current Liabilities	810,152	763,646	649,797	542,645	485,221	493,783	463,682	459,093
Total Liabilities	2,191,867	2,130,582	2,013,602	615,823	569,522	578,091	560,870	557,162
Stockholders' Equity	1,260,385	1,228,577	1,241,751	1,287,555	1,246,791	1,204,569	1,051,376	1,139,746
Shares Outstanding	166,974	168,962	171,870	172,436	177,316	181,886	180,135	194,516
Statistical Record								
Return on Assets %	9.67	10.26	10.54	14.12	11.25	12.55	13.22	4.75
Return on Equity %	20.55	21.48	21.45	20.72	16.52	18.89	19.97	6.99
EBITDA Margin %	12.69	11.87	10.99	12.62	11.75	13.52	13.13	8.90
Net Margin %	6.23	5.49	4.60	6.49	5.38	5.89	6.19	2.45
Asset Turnover	1.56	1.60	1.64	2.18	2.09	2.13	2.13	1.94
Current Ratio	1.33	1.34	1.46	1.93	2.00	1.83	1.56	1.94
Price Range	24.12-14.38	28.99-16.30	28.99-17.12	28.99-17.10	19.37-10.62	19.37-13.12	18.35-13.24	14.85-10.28
P/E Ratio	15.87-9.46	19.07-10.72	19.59-11.57	19.72-11.63	17.14-9.40	16.70-11.31	16.53-11.93	35.36-24.48
Average Yield %	2.91	2.61	2.46	2.50	3.58	3.05	3.08	3.93

Address: 77 Hot Metal Street, Pittsburgh, PA 15203-2329 **Telephone:** 412-432-3300	**Web Site:** www.ae.com **Officers:** Jay L. Schottenstein - Executive Chairman, Chief Executive Officer, Chairman, Interim Chief Executive Officer Michael R. Rempell - Executive Vice President, Chief Operating Officer	**Auditors:** Ernst & Young LLP **Investor Contact:** 412-432-3300 **Transfer Agents:** Computershare Trust Company, N.A., Providence, RI

AMERICAN ELECTRIC POWER CO INC

Exchange	Symbol	Price	52Wk Range	Yield	P/E
NYS	AEP	$94.51 (12/31/2019)	95.72-72.77	2.96	21.93

*7 Year Price Score 112.73 *NYSE Composite Index=100 *12 Month Price Score 99.40

Interim Earnings (Per Share)

Qtr.	Mar	Jun	Sep	Dec
2016	1.02	1.02	(1.56)	0.76
2017	1.20	0.76	1.10	0.81
2018	0.92	1.07	1.17	0.74
2019	1.16	0.93	1.48	...

Interim Dividends (Per Share)

Amt	Decl	Ex	Rec	Pay
0.67Q	01/22/2019	02/07/2019	02/08/2019	03/08/2019
0.67Q	04/23/2019	05/09/2019	05/10/2019	06/10/2019
0.67Q	07/23/2019	08/08/2019	08/09/2019	09/10/2019
0.70Q	10/22/2019	11/07/2019	11/08/2019	12/10/2019

Indicated Div: $2.80 (Div. Reinv. Plan)

Valuation Analysis

		Institutional Holding	
Forecast EPS	$4.20 (01/17/2020)	No of Institutions	1534
Market Cap	$46.7 Billion	Shares	
Book Value	$19.8 Billion		446,234,592
Price/Book	2.36	% Held	
Price/Sales	2.96		74.11

Business Summary: Electric Utilities (MIC: 3.1.1 SIC: 4911 NAIC: 221122)

American Electric Power Company is a public utility holding company. The public utility subsidiaries of Co. provide electric service, consisting of generation, transmission and distribution, on an integrated basis to their retail customers. The service areas of Co.'s public utility subsidiaries cover portions of the states of Arkansas, Indiana, Kentucky, Louisiana, Michigan, Ohio, Oklahoma, Tennessee, Texas, Virginia and West Virginia. Transmission networks are interconnected with distribution facilities in the territories served.

Recent Developments: For the quarter ended Sep 30 2019, net income increased 26.6% to US$733.9 million from US$579.7 million in the year-earlier quarter. Revenues were US$4.32 billion, down 0.4% from US$4.33 billion the year before. Operating income was US$958.2 million versus US$668.6 million in the prior-year quarter, an increase of 43.3%. Direct operating expenses declined 13.6% to US$2.39 billion from US$2.77 billion in the comparable period the year before. Indirect operating expenses increased 7.7% to US$965.7 million from US$896.8 million in the equivalent prior-year period.

Prospects: Our evaluation of American Electric Power Company Inc. as of October 4th, 2019 is the result of our systematic analysis on three basic characteristics: earnings strength, relative valuation, and recent stock price movement. The company has managed to produce a neutral trend in earnings per share over the past 5 quarters. In addition, recent analyst estimates for the company have been mixed and AEP has posted results that exceeded analysts' expectations. Based on operating earnings yield, the company is fairly valued when compared to all of the companies we cover. Share price changes over the past year indicates that AEP will perform over the near term.

Financial Data
(US$ in Thousands)

	9 Mos	6 Mos	3 Mos	12/31/2018	12/31/2017	12/31/2016	12/31/2015	12/31/2014
Earnings Per Share	4.31	4.00	4.14	3.90	3.88	1.24	4.17	3.34
Cash Flow Per Share	9.40	10.16	10.60	10.60	8.68	9.18	9.68	9.44
Tang Book Value Per Share	39.95	39.02	38.89	38.55	37.09	35.27	36.33	34.18
Dividends Per Share	2.680	2.630	2.580	2.530	2.390	2.270	2.150	2.030
Dividend Payout %	62.18	65.75	62.32	64.87	61.60	183.06	51.56	60.78
Income Statement								
Total Revenue	11,945,400	7,630,400	4,056,800	16,195,700	15,424,900	16,380,100	16,453,200	17,020,000
EBITDA	2,599,900	1,540,000	881,000	5,358,300	5,837,500	3,443,700	5,651,500	5,448,000
Depn & Amortn	71,600	46,100	25,100	2,400,400	2,126,300	2,090,900	2,154,700	2,073,000
Income Before Taxes	1,746,700	987,400	600,100	1,973,500	2,816,200	475,600	2,622,900	2,490,000
Income Taxes	30,700	(9,900)	44,500	115,300	969,700	(73,700)	919,600	942,000
Net Income	1,767,600	1,034,100	572,800	1,923,800	1,912,600	610,900	2,047,100	1,634,000
Average Shares	495,461	495,382	494,484	493,758	492,611	491,662	490,574	488,899
Balance Sheet								
Current Assets	4,166,400	4,061,300	3,914,800	4,113,900	4,253,100	6,033,900	4,072,400	4,478,000
Total Assets	73,900,700	72,550,000	70,722,000	68,802,800	64,729,100	63,467,700	61,683,100	59,633,000
Current Liabilities	8,611,200	8,357,100	7,990,600	8,648,800	8,271,300	9,498,000	7,108,500	7,967,000
Long-Term Obligations	24,553,500	24,174,400	22,898,200	21,648,200	19,419,600	17,378,400	17,740,900	16,181,000
Total Liabilities	54,113,700	53,232,200	51,479,500	49,735,000	46,430,200	46,070,700	43,791,400	42,813,000
Stockholders' Equity	19,787,000	19,317,800	19,242,500	19,067,800	18,298,900	17,397,000	17,891,700	16,820,000
Shares Outstanding	493,936	493,757	493,427	493,245	492,005	491,711	491,052	489,402
Statistical Record								
Return on Assets %	3.01	2.83	3.00	2.88	2.98	0.97	3.37	2.82
Return on Equity %	10.97	10.38	10.82	10.30	10.72	3.45	11.79	9.93
EBITDA Margin %	21.76	20.18	21.72	33.08	37.84	21.02	34.35	32.01
Net Margin %	14.80	13.55	14.12	11.88	12.40	3.73	12.44	9.60
Asset Turnover	0.22	0.23	0.24	0.24	0.24	0.26	0.27	0.29
Current Ratio	0.48	0.49	0.49	0.48	0.51	0.64	0.57	0.56
Debt to Equity	1.24	1.25	1.19	1.14	1.06	1.00	0.99	0.96
Price Range	94.59-70.22	91.55-68.87	85.98-62.93	80.36-62.93	77.63-62.12	71.27-57.64	64.57-52.54	62.91-46.08
P/E Ratio	21.95-16.29	22.89-17.22	20.77-15.20	20.61-16.14	20.01-16.01	57.48-46.48	15.48-12.60	18.84-13.80
Average Yield %	3.23	3.37	3.52	3.60	3.41	3.54	3.79	3.84

Address: 1 Riverside Plaza, Columbus, OH 43215-2373 **Telephone:** 614-716-1000 **Fax:** 614-223-1823	**Web Site:** www.aep.com **Officers:** Nicholas K. Akins - Chairman, President, Chief Executive Officer David M. Feinberg - Executive Vice President, Senior Vice President, Secretary, General Counsel	**Auditors:** PricewaterhouseCoopers LLP **Investor Contact:** 614-716-2819 **Transfer Agents:** Computershare Trust Company, N.A., Providence, RI

AMERICAN EQUITY INVESTMENT LIFE HOLDING CO

Exchange	Symbol	Price	52Wk Range	Yield	P/E	Div Acheiver
NYS	AEL	$29.93 (12/31/2019)	32.89-20.70	1.00	34.40	15 Years

*7 Year Price Score 91.79   ***NYSE Composite Index=100**   ***12 Month Price Score 98.89**

Interim Earnings (Per Share)

Qtr.	Mar	Jun	Sep	Dec
2016	(0.55)	0.18	(0.09)	1.42
2017	0.60	0.30	0.63	0.40
2018	1.55	1.03	1.85	0.59
2019	(0.33)	0.20	0.41	...

Interim Dividends (Per Share)

Amt	Decl	Ex	Rec	Pay
0.24A	11/17/2016	12/01/2016	12/05/2016	12/20/2016
0.26A	11/16/2017	11/28/2017	11/29/2017	12/12/2017
0.28A	11/15/2018	11/27/2018	11/28/2018	12/12/2018
0.30A	11/22/2019	12/03/2019	12/03/2019	12/12/2019

Indicated Div: $0.30

Valuation Analysis / Institutional Holding

Forecast EPS	$5.64	No of Institutions
	(01/17/2020)	377
Market Cap	$2.7 Billion	Shares
Book Value	$4.1 Billion	104,418,664
Price/Book	0.66	% Held
Price/Sales	1.43	93.47

Business Summary: Life & Health (MIC: 5.2.2 SIC: 6311 NAIC: 524113)

American Equity Investment Life Holding is a holding company. Co. is engaged in the development and sale of fixed index and fixed rate annuity products. Through its wholly-owned life insurance subsidiaries, American Equity Investment Life Insurance Company, American Equity Investment Life Insurance Company of New York and Eagle Life Insurance Company, Co. issues fixed index annuity products, which allows policyholders to earn index credits based on the performance of a particular index without the risk of loss of their principal; and fixed rate deferred annuity products, which includes annual reset and multi-year rate guaranteed products.

Recent Developments: For the quarter ended Sep 30 2019, net income decreased 77.9% to US$37.4 million from US$169.3 million in the year-earlier quarter. Revenues were US$643.4 million, down 46.1% from US$1,19 billion the year before. Net premiums earned were US$68.8 million versus US$65.6 million in the prior-year quarter, an increase of 4.9%. Net investment income rose 7.5% to US$590.4 million from US$549.4 million a year ago.

Prospects: Our evaluation of American Equity Investment Life Holding Co as of October 4th, 2019 is the result of our systematic analysis on three basic characteristics: earnings strength, relative valuation, and recent stock price movement. The company has suffered a very negative trend in earnings per share over the past 5 quarters. However, recent analyst estimates for the company have been mixed and AEL has posted results that exceeded analysts' expectations. Based on operating earnings yield, the company is undervalued when compared to all of the companies we cover. Share price changes over the past year indicates that AEL will perform very poorly over the near term.

Financial Data
(US$ in Thousands)

	9 Mos	6 Mos	3 Mos	12/31/2018	12/31/2017	12/31/2016	12/31/2015	12/31/2014
Earnings Per Share	0.87	2.31	3.14	5.01	1.93	0.97	2.72	1.58
Cash Flow Per Share	19.13	22.59	17.59	0.48	21.60	16.63	6.40	9.51
Tang Book Value Per Share	45.35	38.46	32.38	26.55	31.91	26.04	23.90	28.13
Dividends Per Share	0.280	0.280	0.280	0.280	0.260	0.240	0.220	0.200
Dividend Payout %	32.18	12.12	8.92	5.59	13.47	24.74	8.09	12.66
Income Statement								
Total Revenue	2,350,510	1,707,114	1,000,720	1,547,098	3,891,652	2,220,282	1,518,937	2,168,973
Income Before Taxes	34,738	(16,267)	(39,463)	565,742	316,271	130,247	337,314	196,064
Income Taxes	8,798	(4,847)	(9,453)	107,726	141,626	47,004	117,484	70,041
Net Income	25,940	(11,420)	(30,010)	458,016	174,645	83,243	219,830	126,023
Average Shares	91,710	91,785	91,743	91,422	90,311	85,605	80,961	79,893
Balance Sheet								
Total Assets	68,329,993	66,371,304	64,482,164	61,625,564	62,030,736	56,053,472	49,041,163	43,989,734
Total Liabilities	64,203,277	62,873,829	61,542,627	59,226,463	59,180,579	53,761,877	47,096,628	41,849,858
Stockholders' Equity	4,126,716	3,497,475	2,939,537	2,399,101	2,850,157	2,291,595	1,944,535	2,139,876
Shares Outstanding	91,006	90,936	90,784	90,369	89,331	88,001	81,354	76,062
Statistical Record								
Return on Assets %	0.12	0.33	0.46	0.74	0.30	0.16	0.47	0.30
Return on Equity %	2.41	7.15	10.46	17.45	6.79	3.92	10.76	7.15
Net Margin %	1.10	N.M.	N.M.	29.60	4.49	3.75	14.47	5.81
Asset Turnover	0.03	0.04	0.04	0.03	0.07	0.04	0.03	0.05
Price Range	36.13-20.70	37.57-25.73	37.57-25.73	37.57-25.73	32.22-22.34	24.03-12.81	29.67-22.76	29.46-20.43
P/E Ratio	41.53-23.79	16.26-11.14	11.96-8.19	7.50-5.14	16.69-11.58	24.77-13.21	10.91-8.37	18.65-12.93
Average Yield %	0.97	0.88	0.86	0.84	0.97	1.41	0.83	0.83

Address: 6000 Westown Parkway, West Des Moines, IA 50266 **Telephone:** 515-221-0002	**Web Site:** www.american-equity.com **Officers:** Anant Bhalla - President, Chief Executive Officer Ronald James Grensteiner - Executive Vice President	**Auditors:** KPMG LLP **Investor Contact:** 515-221-0002 **Transfer Agents:** Computershare Trust Company, N.A., Providence, RI

AMERICAN EXPRESS CO.

Exchange	Symbol	Price	52Wk Range	Yield	P/E
NYS	AXP	$124.49 (12/31/2019)	128.57-93.43	1.38	15.05

*7 Year Price Score 110.57 *NYSE Composite Index=100   *12 Month Price Score 98.55

Interim Earnings (Per Share)

Qtr.	Mar	Jun	Sep	Dec
2016	1.45	2.10	1.20	0.89
2017	1.34	1.47	1.50	(1.33)
2018	1.86	1.84	1.88	2.32
2019	1.80	2.07	2.08	...

Interim Dividends (Per Share)

Amt	Decl	Ex	Rec	Pay
0.39Q	03/11/2019	04/04/2019	04/05/2019	05/10/2019
0.39Q	05/08/2019	07/03/2019	07/05/2019	08/09/2019
0.43Q	09/23/2019	10/03/2019	10/04/2019	11/08/2019
0.43Q	12/12/2019	01/02/2020	01/03/2020	02/10/2020

Indicated Div: $1.72

Valuation Analysis | **Institutional Holding**

Forecast EPS	$8.18 (01/17/2020)	No of Institutions 2284
Market Cap	$102.2 Billion	Shares
Book Value	$23.0 Billion	869,752,448
Price/Book	4.44	% Held
Price/Sales	2.21	78.71

Business Summary: Credit & Lending (MIC: 5.4.1 SIC: 6153 NAIC: 522210)

American Express is a payments company. Co.'s principal products and services are charge and credit card products and travel-related services provided to consumers and businesses. Co.'s range of products and services includes: charge card, credit card and other payment and financing products; merchant acquisition and processing, servicing and settlement, and point-of-sale marketing and information products and services for merchants; network services; other fee services, including fraud prevention services and the design and operation of customer loyalty programs; expense management products and services; and travel-related services.

Recent Developments: For the quarter ended Sep 30 2019, net income increased 6.1% to US$1.76 billion from US$1.65 billion in the year-earlier quarter. Net interest income increased 12.3% to US$2.20 billion from US$1.96 billion in the year-earlier quarter. Provision for loan losses was US$879.0 million versus US$817.0 million in the prior-year quarter, an increase of 7.6%. Non-interest income rose 7.4% to US$8.79 billion from US$8.18 billion, while non-interest expense advanced 8.8% to US$7.84 billion.

Prospects: Our evaluation of American Express Co. as of October 4th, 2019 is the result of our systematic analysis on three basic characteristics: earnings strength, relative valuation, and recent stock price movement. The company has produced a positive trend in earnings per share over the past 5 quarters. However, recent analyst estimates for the company have been mixed and AXP has posted results that exceeded analysts' expectations. Based on operating earnings yield, the company is undervalued when compared to all of the companies we cover. Share price changes over the past year indicates that AXP will perform well over the near term.

Financial Data
(US$ in Thousands)

	9 Mos	6 Mos	3 Mos	12/31/2018	12/31/2017	12/31/2016	12/31/2015	12/31/2014
Earnings Per Share	8.27	8.07	7.84	7.91	2.97	5.65	5.05	5.56
Cash Flow Per Share	11.13	18.36	18.33	10.43	15.33	8.79	10.98	10.52
Tang Book Value Per Share	28.05	27.75	26.54	22.36	16.67	18.48	17.68	16.42
Dividends Per Share	1.560	1.520	1.480	1.440	1.310	1.190	1.100	0.980
Dividend Payout %	18.86	18.84	18.88	18.20	44.11	21.06	21.78	17.63
Income Statement								
Total Revenue	34,854,000	22,988,000	11,259,000	43,281,000	35,583,000	33,823,000	34,441,000	35,999,000
Income Before Taxes	6,443,000	4,177,000	1,958,000	8,122,000	7,414,000	8,096,000	7,938,000	8,991,000
Income Taxes	1,377,000	866,000	408,000	1,201,000	4,678,000	2,688,000	2,775,000	3,106,000
Net Income	5,066,000	3,311,000	1,550,000	6,921,000	2,736,000	5,408,000	5,163,000	5,885,000
Average Shares	827,000	836,000	843,000	859,000	886,000	935,000	1,003,000	1,051,000
Balance Sheet								
Total Assets	194,184,000	197,603,000	197,193,000	188,602,000	181,159,000	158,893,000	161,184,000	159,103,000
Total Liabilities	171,159,000	174,511,000	174,975,000	166,312,000	162,932,000	138,392,000	140,511,000	138,430,000
Stockholders' Equity	23,025,000	23,092,000	22,218,000	22,290,000	18,227,000	20,501,000	20,673,000	20,673,000
Shares Outstanding	821,000	832,000	837,000	847,000	859,000	904,000	969,000	1,023,000
Statistical Record								
Return on Assets %	3.69	3.65	3.63	3.74	1.61	3.37	3.22	3.77
Return on Equity %	31.81	31.72	32.69	34.16	14.13	26.20	24.97	29.30
Net Margin %	14.53	14.40	13.77	15.99	7.69	15.99	14.99	16.35
Asset Turnover	0.24	0.24	0.23	0.23	0.21	0.21	0.22	0.23
Price Range	128.57-89.50	124.92-89.50	113.55-89.50	112.89-88.34	99.70-75.32	75.32-51.11	93.04-67.87	95.84-80.24
P/E Ratio	15.55-10.82	15.48-11.09	14.48-11.42	14.27-11.17	33.57-25.36	13.33-9.05	18.42-13.44	17.24-14.43
Average Yield %	1.39	1.41	1.44	1.43	1.55	1.86	1.41	1.09

Address: 200 Vesey Street, New York, NY 10285 **Telephone:** 212-640-2000 **Fax:** 212-640-0404	**Web Site:** www.americanexpress.com **Officers:** Stephen J. Squeri - Chairman, Chief Executive Officer, Vice-Chairman, Division Officer Jeffrey C. Campbell - Executive Vice President, Chief Financial Officer	**Auditors:** PricewaterhouseCoopers LLP **Transfer Agents:** Computershare Shareowner Services LLC, Canton, MA

AMERICAN FINANCIAL GROUP INC

Exchange	Symbol	Price	52Wk Range	Yield	P/E	Div Acheiver
NYS	AFG	$109.65 (12/31/2019)	111.58-89.10	1.64	15.15	13 Years

*7 Year Price Score 105.39 *NYSE Composite Index=100 *12 Month Price Score 101.17

Interim Earnings (Per Share)

Qtr.	Mar	Jun	Sep	Dec
2016	1.14	0.62	1.23	4.35
2017	1.72	1.61	0.13	1.84
2018	1.60	2.31	2.26	(0.32)
2019	3.63	2.31	1.62	...

Interim Dividends (Per Share)

Amt	Decl	Ex	Rec	Pay
0.40Q	07/01/2019	07/12/2019	07/15/2019	07/25/2019
0.45Q	10/01/2019	10/11/2019	10/15/2019	10/25/2019
1.80Sp	11/04/2019	11/14/2019	11/15/2019	11/25/2019
0.45Q	01/02/2020	01/14/2020	01/15/2020	01/27/2020

Indicated Div: $1.80 (Div. Reinv. Plan)

Valuation Analysis — **Institutional Holding**

Forecast EPS	$8.60	No of Institutions
	(01/17/2020)	555
Market Cap	$9.9 Billion	Shares
Book Value	$6.3 Billion	76,767,736
Price/Book	1.56	% Held
Price/Sales	1.27	65.26

Business Summary: General Insurance (MIC: 5.2.1 SIC: 6331 NAIC: 524126)

American Financial Group is a holding company. Through its subsidiary, Great American Insurance Group, Co. is engaged primarily in property and casualty insurance, focusing on commercial products for businesses, and in the sale of traditional fixed, fixed-indexed and variable-indexed annuities in the retail, financial institutions, registered investment advisor and education markets. Co.'s property and casualty insurance segments consist of property and transportation, specialty casualty, and specialty financial. Co.'s annuity segment sells fixed, fixed-indexed and variable-indexed annuities in the retail, financial institutions, broker-dealer and registered investment advisor markets.

Recent Developments: For the quarter ended Sep 30 2019, net income decreased 29.6% to US$143.0 million from US$203.0 million in the year-earlier quarter. Revenues were US$2.12 billion, up 5.7% from US$2.01 billion the year before. Net premiums earned were US$1.45 billion versus US$1.33 billion in the prior-year quarter, an increase of 8.6%.

Prospects: Our evaluation of American Financial Group Inc. as of October 4th, 2019 is the result of our systematic analysis on three basic characteristics: earnings strength, relative valuation, and recent stock price movement. The company has enjoyed a very positive trend in earnings per share over the past 5 quarters. In addition, recent analyst estimates for the company have been raised, and AFG has posted results that exceeded analysts' expectations. Based on operating earnings yield, the company is undervalued when compared to all of the companies we cover. Share price changes over the past year indicates that AFG will perform in line with the market over the near term.

Financial Data
(US$ in Thousands)

	9 Mos	6 Mos	3 Mos	12/31/2018	12/31/2017	12/31/2016	12/31/2015	12/31/2014
Earnings Per Share	7.24	7.88	7.88	5.85	5.28	7.33	3.94	4.97
Cash Flow Per Share	27.74	23.82	24.00	23.40	20.55	13.20	15.49	13.73
Tang Book Value Per Share	67.84	65.43	60.89	53.34	58.12	54.27	50.22	53.34
Dividends Per Share	4.600	4.550	4.500	4.450	4.787	2.152	2.030	1.910
Dividend Payout %	63.54	57.74	57.11	76.07	90.67	29.37	51.52	38.43
Income Statement								
Premium Income	3,832,000	2,384,000	1,179,000	4,889,000	4,601,000	4,352,000	4,328,000	3,986,000
Total Revenue	6,107,000	3,984,000	2,024,000	7,150,000	6,865,000	6,498,000	6,145,000	5,713,000
Benefits & Claims	3,285,000	2,082,000	1,012,000	4,041,000	3,873,000	3,595,000	3,558,000	3,306,000
Income Before Taxes	849,000	672,000	413,000	639,000	724,000	787,000	565,000	626,000
Income Taxes	171,000	137,000	87,000	122,000	247,000	119,000	195,000	220,000
Net Income	686,000	539,000	329,000	530,000	475,000	649,000	352,000	452,000
Average Shares	91,100	91,000	90,700	90,600	89,800	88,500	89,400	91,000
Balance Sheet								
Total Assets	69,067,000	67,697,000	66,132,000	63,456,000	60,658,000	55,072,000	49,859,000	47,535,000
Total Liabilities	62,746,000	61,607,000	60,467,000	58,486,000	55,328,000	50,156,000	45,267,000	42,656,000
Stockholders' Equity	6,321,000	6,090,000	5,665,000	4,970,000	5,330,000	4,916,000	4,592,000	4,879,000
Shares Outstanding	90,127	89,917	89,637	89,291	88,275	86,924	87,474	87,708
Statistical Record								
Return on Assets %	0.99	1.10	1.13	0.85	0.82	1.23	0.72	1.01
Return on Equity %	11.44	12.78	13.16	10.29	9.27	13.61	7.43	9.54
Loss Ratio %	85.73	87.33	85.84	82.65	84.18	82.61	82.21	82.94
Net Margin %	11.23	13.53	16.25	7.41	6.92	9.99	5.73	7.91
Price Range	112.06-85.28	114.34-85.28	114.76-85.28	120.49-85.28	109.06-85.86	88.12-65.14	75.17-58.04	62.36-52.93
P/E Ratio	15.48-11.78	14.51-10.82	14.56-10.82	20.60-14.58	20.66-16.26	12.02-8.89	19.08-14.73	12.55-10.65
Average Yield %	4.60	4.46	4.30	4.10	4.83	2.93	3.03	3.28

Address: 301 East Fourth Street, Cincinnati, OH 45202 **Telephone:** 513-579-2121	**Web Site:** www.afginc.com **Officers:** Carl H. Lindner - Co-President, Co-Chief Executive Officer S. Craig Lindner - Co-President, Co-Chief Executive Officer	**Auditors:** Ernst & Young LLP **Investor Contact:** 513-579-6739 **Transfer Agents:** American Stock Transfer & Trust Company, New York, NY

AMERICAN HOMES 4 RENT

Exchange	Symbol	Price	52Wk Range	Yield	P/E
NYS	AMH	$26.21 (12/31/2019)	27.06-19.47	0.76	97.07

*7 Year Price Score N/A   *NYSE Composite Index=100   *12 Month Price Score 101.96

Interim Earnings (Per Share)

Qtr.	Mar	Jun	Sep	Dec
2016	(0.02)	(0.04)	(0.09)	0.01
2017	(0.01)	0.00	0.01	(0.08)
2018	0.02	(0.05)	0.05	0.06
2019	0.05	0.08	0.08	...

Interim Dividends (Per Share)

Amt	Decl	Ex	Rec	Pay
0.05Q	02/21/2019	03/14/2019	03/15/2019	04/01/2019
0.05Q	05/09/2019	06/13/2019	06/14/2019	07/01/2019
0.05Q	08/02/2019	09/12/2019	09/13/2019	09/30/2019
0.05Q	11/07/2019	12/31/2019	01/02/2020	01/07/2020

Indicated Div: $0.20

Valuation Analysis   **Institutional Holding**

Forecast EPS	$0.27 (01/16/2020)	No of Institutions	N/A
Market Cap	$7.9 Billion	Shares	
Book Value	$5.3 Billion	N/A	
Price/Book	1.48	% Held	N/A
Price/Sales	6.98		

Business Summary: REITs (MIC: 5.3.1 SIC: 6798 NAIC: 525930)

American Homes 4 Rent is a real estate investment trust focused on acquiring, renovating, leasing and operating single-family homes as rental properties. American Homes 4 Rent, L.P. and its consolidated subsidiaries is the entity through which Co. conducts substantially all of its business and owns, directly or through subsidiaries, substantially all of its assets. Co.'s portfolio of single-family properties is internally managed through its proprietary property management platform.

Recent Developments: For the quarter ended Sep 30 2019, net income increased 36.7% to US$41.4 million from US$30.3 million in the year-earlier quarter. Revenues were US$298.3 million, up 6.5% from US$280.1 million the year before. Revenues from property income rose 5.3% to US$293.1 million from US$278.2 million in the corresponding quarter a year earlier.

Prospects: Our evaluation of American Homes 4 Rent as of October 4th, 2019 is the result of our systematic analysis on three basic characteristics: earnings strength, relative valuation, and recent stock price movement. The company has generated a negative trend in earnings per share over the past 5 quarters. However, recent analyst estimates for the company have been unchanged while AMH has posted results that exceeded analysts' expectations. Based on operating earnings yield, the company is overvalued when compared to all of the companies we cover. Share price changes over the past year indicates that AMH will perform well over the near term.

Financial Data
(US$ in Thousands)

	9 Mos	6 Mos	3 Mos	12/31/2018	12/31/2017	12/31/2016	12/31/2015	12/31/2014
Earnings Per Share	0.27	0.24	0.11	0.08	(0.08)	(0.14)	(0.40)	(0.34)
Cash Flow Per Share	1.51	1.50	1.50	1.40	1.46	1.19	0.96	0.82
Tang Book Value Per Share	17.34	17.31	17.33	17.30	17.54	16.73	15.10	15.74
Dividends Per Share	0.200	0.200	0.200	0.200	0.200	0.200	0.200	0.200
Dividend Payout %	74.07	83.33	181.82	250.00	...	...	...	...
Income Statement								
Total Revenue	859,368	561,064	279,204	1,072,855	960,399	878,889	630,576	398,874
EBITDA	450,035	296,993	66,816	536,038	470,859	401,447	265,196	152,305
Depn & Amortn	239,288	159,112	1,810	300,700	281,747	260,154	223,731	165,516
Income Before Taxes	114,796	73,395	33,091	112,438	76,492	10,446	(47,948)	(33,092)
Net Income	103,667	66,365	30,065	108,273	80,999	6,695	(62,301)	(48,057)
Average Shares	301,032	299,991	297,444	294,268	264,254	234,010	210,600	196,348
Balance Sheet								
Current Assets	334,312	316,898	345,560	175,214	182,823	250,241	168,968	185,985
Total Assets	9,140,121	9,142,623	9,191,038	9,001,481	8,608,768	8,107,210	6,807,786	6,227,351
Current Liabilities	295,817	306,043	271,741	573,428	595,080	568,751	291,591	486,723
Long-Term Obligations	2,837,115	2,841,057	2,943,925	2,454,311	2,137,864	2,600,839	2,580,962	1,571,034
Total Liabilities	3,814,842	3,830,159	3,931,168	3,749,516	3,459,139	3,914,274	3,548,441	2,777,250
Stockholders' Equity	5,325,279	5,312,464	5,259,870	5,251,965	5,149,629	4,192,936	3,259,345	3,450,101
Shares Outstanding	300,711	300,462	297,227	296,649	286,749	243,375	207,870	211,473
Statistical Record								
Return on Assets %	1.49	1.39	1.30	1.23	0.97	0.09	N.M.	N.M.
Return on Equity %	2.55	2.39	2.27	2.08	1.73	0.18	N.M.	N.M.
EBITDA Margin %	52.37	52.93	23.93	49.96	49.03	45.68	42.06	38.18
Net Margin %	12.06	11.83	10.77	10.09	8.43	0.76	N.M.	N.M.
Asset Turnover	0.12	0.12	0.12	0.12	0.11	0.12	0.10	0.08
Current Ratio	1.13	1.04	1.27	0.31	0.31	0.44	0.58	0.38
Debt to Equity	0.53	0.53	0.56	0.47	0.42	0.62	0.79	0.46
Price Range	25.89-19.08	25.37-19.08	23.24-19.08	23.24-18.73	23.77-20.34	22.84-13.21	17.48-15.30	18.51-15.87
P/E Ratio	95.89-70.67	105.71-79.50	211.27-173.45	290.50-234.13	...	...	...	...
Average Yield %	0.87	0.90	0.94	0.96	0.90	1.07	1.21	1.16

Address: 30601 Agoura Road, Suite 200, Agoura Hills, CA 91301 **Telephone:** 805-413-5300	**Web Site:** www.americanhomes4rent.com **Officers:** Tamara Hughes Gustavson - Chairman David P. Singelyn - Chief Executive Officer, Interim Chief Financial Officer	**Auditors:** Ernst & Young LLP **Transfer Agents:** American Stock Transfer & Trust Company, LLC

AMERICAN INTERNATIONAL GROUP INC

Exchange	Symbol	Price	52Wk Range	Yield	P/E
NYS	AIG	$51.33 (12/31/2019)	57.89-38.75	N/A	25.29

*7 Year Price Score 76.38 ***NYSE Composite Index=100** ***12 Month Price Score 99.71**

Interim Earnings (Per Share)

Qtr.	Mar	Jun	Sep	Dec
2016	(0.16)	1.68	0.42	(2.70)
2017	1.18	1.19	(1.91)	(7.14)
2018	1.01	1.02	(1.41)	(0.68)
2019	0.75	1.24	0.72	...

Interim Dividends (Per Share)

Amt	Decl	Ex	Rec	Pay
0.32Q	02/13/2019	03/14/2019	03/15/2019	03/29/2019
0.32Q	05/06/2019	06/13/2019	06/14/2019	06/28/2019
0.32Q	08/07/2019	09/16/2019	09/17/2019	09/30/2019
0.32Q	11/01/2019	12/11/2019	12/12/2019	12/26/2019

Indicated Div: $1.28

Valuation Analysis / **Institutional Holding**

Forecast EPS	$4.56	No of Institutions	
	(01/18/2020)	1365	
Market Cap	$44.7 Billion	Shares	
Book Value	$65.6 Billion	1,031,888,000	
Price/Book	0.68	% Held	
Price/Sales	0.88	N/A	

Business Summary: General Insurance (MIC: 5.2.1 SIC: 6331 NAIC: 524126)

American International Group is a holding company. Through its subsidiaries, Co. provides property casualty insurance, life insurance, retirement products, and other financial services. Co.'s business operations include: General Insurance, which provides insurance products and services for commercial and personal insurance customers; Life and Retirement, which brings together a portfolio of life insurance, retirement and institutional products provided through a multichannel distribution network; and Other Operations, which include Blackboard U.S. Holdings, Inc., a subsidiary focused on delivering commercial insurance solutions using digital technology, data analytics and automation.

Recent Developments: For the quarter ended Sep 30 2019, income from continuing operations was US$973.0 million compared with a loss of US$1.22 billion in the year-earlier quarter. Net income amounted to US$973.0 million versus a net loss of US$1.26 billion in the year-earlier quarter. Revenues were US$12.91 billion, up 12.4% from US$11.49 billion the year before. Net premiums earned were US$7.62 billion versus US$7.67 billion in the prior-year quarter, a decrease of 0.7%. Net investment income fell 1.0% to US$2.91 billion from US$2.94 billion a year ago.

Prospects: Our evaluation of American International Group Inc. as of October 4th, 2019 is the result of our systematic analysis on three basic characteristics: earnings strength, relative valuation, and recent stock price movement. The company has enjoyed a very positive trend in earnings per share over the past 5 quarters. However, recent analyst estimates for the company have been mixed and AIG has posted results that exceeded analysts' expectations. Based on operating earnings yield, the company is undervalued when compared to all of the companies we cover. Share price changes over the past year indicates that AIG will perform in line with the market over the near term.

Financial Data
(US$ in Thousands)

	9 Mos	6 Mos	3 Mos	12/31/2018	12/31/2017	12/31/2016	12/31/2015	12/31/2014
Earnings Per Share	2.03	(0.10)	(0.32)	(0.01)	(6.54)	(0.78)	1.65	5.20
Cash Flow Per Share	(0.79)	(0.99)	0.03	0.07	(9.23)	2.18	2.21	3.51
Tang Book Value Per Share	74.85	73.63	69.33	65.04	72.49	76.66	75.10	77.69
Dividends Per Share	1.280	1.280	1.280	1.280	1.280	1.280	0.810	0.500
Dividend Payout %	63.05	...	...	...	...	...	49.09	9.62
Income Statement								
Premium Income	23,117,000	15,500,000	8,070,000	30,614,000	31,374,000	34,393,000	36,655,000	37,254,000
Total Revenue	37,931,000	25,017,000	12,456,000	47,389,000	49,520,000	52,367,000	58,327,000	64,406,000
Benefits & Claims	19,373,000	12,481,000	6,679,000	27,412,000	29,972,000	32,437,000	31,345,000	28,281,000
Income Before Taxes	4,251,000	2,991,000	1,154,000	257,000	1,466,000	(74,000)	3,281,000	10,501,000
Income Taxes	950,000	663,000	217,000	154,000	7,526,000	185,000	1,059,000	2,927,000
Net Income	2,419,000	1,763,000	654,000	(6,000)	(6,084,000)	(849,000)	2,196,000	7,529,000
Average Shares	895,814	888,325	877,512	910,141	930,561	1,091,085	1,334,464	1,447,553
Balance Sheet								
Total Assets	525,122,000	522,269,000	512,922,000	491,984,000	498,301,000	498,264,000	496,943,000	515,581,000
Total Liabilities	459,519,000	457,730,000	452,135,000	435,623,000	433,130,000	421,964,000	407,285,000	408,683,000
Stockholders' Equity	65,603,000	64,539,000	60,787,000	56,361,000	65,171,000	76,300,000	89,658,000	106,898,000
Shares Outstanding	869,949	869,901	869,736	866,609	899,044	995,335	1,193,916	1,375,926
Statistical Record								
Return on Assets %	0.35	N.M.	N.M.	N.M.	N.M.	N.M.	0.43	1.42
Return on Equity %	2.89	N.M.	N.M.	N.M.	N.M.	N.M.	2.23	7.26
Loss Ratio %	83.80	80.52	82.76	89.54	95.53	94.31	85.51	75.91
Net Margin %	6.38	7.05	5.25	(0.01)	(12.29)	(1.62)	3.76	11.69
Price Range	57.89-36.59	55.56-36.59	56.31-36.59	64.80-36.59	67.20-58.11	66.70-48.79	64.54-48.87	56.51-46.88
P/E Ratio	28.52-18.02	...	...	...	...	...	39.12-29.62	10.87-9.02
Average Yield %	2.67	2.69	2.63	2.43	2.05	2.23	1.38	0.95

Address: 175 Water Street, New York, NY 10038 **Telephone:** 212-770-7000	**Web Site:** www.aig.com **Officers:** Douglas M. Steenland - Chairman Brian Duperreault - President, Chief Executive Officer	**Auditors:** PricewaterhouseCoopers LLP **Transfer Agents:** Wells Fargo Bank, N.A. Shareowner Services, St. Paul, MN

AMERICAN STATES WATER CO

*7 Year Price Score 139.06 *NYSE Composite Index=100 *12 Month Price Score 105.77

Interim Earnings (Per Share)

Qtr.	Mar	Jun	Sep	Dec
2016	0.28	0.45	0.59	0.30
2017	0.34	0.62	0.57	0.35
2018	0.29	0.44	0.62	0.37
2019	0.35	0.72	0.76	...

Interim Dividends (Per Share)

Amt	Decl	Ex	Rec	Pay
0.275Q	01/29/2019	02/14/2019	02/15/2019	03/01/2019
0.275Q	05/01/2019	05/15/2019	05/16/2019	06/03/2019
0.305Q	07/30/2019	08/14/2019	08/15/2019	09/03/2019
0.305Q	10/29/2019	11/14/2019	11/15/2019	12/02/2019

Indicated Div: $1.22 (Div. Reinv. Plan)

Valuation Analysis	Institutional Holding
Forecast EPS $2.04	No of Institutions
(01/16/2020)	418
Market Cap $3.2 Billion	Shares
Book Value $595.9 Million	33,920,532
Price/Book 5.36	% Held
Price/Sales 6.76	73.46

Business Summary: Water Utilities (MIC: 3.2.1 SIC: 4941 NAIC: 221310)

American States Water is a holding company. Co. is the parent company of Golden State Water Company (GSWC) and American States Utility Services, Inc. (ASUS). Co. has three segments: water, electric and contracted services. Within the segments, Co. has two principal business units: water and electric service utility operations conducted through GSWC, and contracted services conducted through ASUS and its subsidiaries. GSWC is engaged in the purchase, production, distribution and sale of water as well as distributes electricity in California. ASUS, through its subsidiaries has contracted with the U.S. government to provides water and/or wastewater services at various military installations.

Recent Developments: For the quarter ended Sep 30 2019, net income increased 22.0% to US$28.0 million from US$23.0 million in the year-earlier quarter. Revenues were US$134.5 million, up 8.3% from US$124.2 million the year before. Operating income was US$42.7 million versus US$34.0 million in the prior-year quarter, an increase of 25.8%. Direct operating expenses rose 6.4% to US$62.3 million from US$58.5 million in the comparable period the year before. Indirect operating expenses decreased 6.8% to US$29.5 million from US$31.7 million in the equivalent prior-year period.

Prospects: Our evaluation of American States Water Co. as of October 4th, 2019 is the result of our systematic analysis on three basic characteristics: earnings strength, relative valuation, and recent stock price movement. The company has produced a positive trend in earnings per share over the past 5 quarters. However, recent analyst estimates for the company have been mixed and AWR has posted results that exceeded analysts' expectations. Based on operating earnings yield, the company is overvalued when compared to all of the companies we cover. Share price changes over the past year indicates that AWR will perform over the near term.

Financial Data

(US$ in Thousands)	9 Mos	6 Mos	3 Mos	12/31/2018	12/31/2017	12/31/2016	12/31/2015	12/31/2014
Earnings Per Share	2.20	2.06	1.78	1.72	1.88	1.62	1.60	1.57
Cash Flow Per Share	3.06	3.16	3.55	3.72	3.95	2.65	2.54	4.22
Tang Book Value Per Share	16.15	15.68	15.23	15.16	14.42	13.49	12.73	13.21
Dividends Per Share	1.130	1.100	1.080	1.060	0.994	0.914	0.874	0.831
Dividend Payout %	51.36	53.40	60.67	61.63	52.87	56.42	54.63	52.93
Income Statement								
Total Revenue	360,876	226,380	101,733	436,816	440,603	436,087	458,641	465,791
EBITDA	131,149	79,198	32,427	142,406	168,406	154,822	161,519	161,547
Depn & Amortn	26,727	17,640	10,890	40,663	39,273	39,109	42,674	41,751
Income Before Taxes	88,188	50,777	16,162	81,888	108,341	94,478	98,215	99,106
Income Taxes	20,546	11,141	3,310	18,017	38,974	34,735	37,731	38,048
Net Income	67,642	39,636	12,852	63,871	69,367	59,743	60,484	61,058
Average Shares	36,996	36,963	36,951	36,936	36,844	36,750	37,614	38,880
Balance Sheet								
Current Assets	132,469	122,025	116,776	131,468	155,463	166,875	132,697	209,451
Total Assets	1,604,381	1,567,283	1,526,097	1,501,433	1,416,734	1,470,493	1,348,600	1,378,298
Current Liabilities	119,847	106,346	107,630	146,585	156,662	177,944	123,507	99,290
Long-Term Obligations	281,001	281,014	281,070	380,158	324,941	325,252	325,541	325,798
Total Liabilities	1,008,434	988,496	964,597	943,210	886,789	976,196	882,655	871,497
Stockholders' Equity	595,947	578,787	561,500	558,223	529,945	494,297	465,945	506,801
Shares Outstanding	36,839	36,831	36,795	36,757	36,680	36,571	36,501	38,286
Statistical Record								
Return on Assets %	5.31	5.08	4.47	4.38	4.81	4.23	4.44	4.54
Return on Equity %	14.16	13.66	12.07	11.74	13.55	12.41	12.44	12.22
EBITDA Margin %	36.34	34.98	31.87	32.60	38.22	35.50	35.22	34.68
Net Margin %	18.74	17.51	12.63	14.62	15.74	13.70	13.19	13.11
Asset Turnover	0.31	0.31	0.30	0.30	0.31	0.31	0.34	0.35
Current Ratio	1.11	1.15	1.08	0.90	0.99	0.94	1.07	2.11
Debt to Equity	0.47	0.49	0.50	0.68	0.61	0.66	0.70	0.64
Price Range	94.18-58.90	75.38-58.12	72.08-51.51	69.19-50.34	57.91-41.22	47.18-37.62	43.57-36.00	38.71-27.15
P/E Ratio	42.81-26.77	36.59-28.21	40.49-28.94	40.23-29.27	30.80-21.93	29.12-23.22	27.23-22.50	24.66-17.29
Average Yield %	1.56	1.66	1.74	1.81	2.05	2.21	2.21	2.64

AMERICAN TOWER CORP

Exchange	Symbol	Price	52Wk Range	Yield	P/E
NYS	AMT	$229.82 (12/31/2019)	241.07-156.74	1.76	64.02

*7 Year Price Score 138.44 ***NYSE Composite Index=100** ***12 Month Price Score 100.47**

Interim Earnings (Per Share)

Qtr.	Mar	Jun	Sep	Dec
2016	0.58	0.37	0.55	0.47
2017	0.67	0.80	0.69	0.51
2018	0.63	0.69	0.83	0.62
2019	0.89	0.96	1.12	...

Interim Dividends (Per Share)

Amt	Decl	Ex	Rec	Pay
0.90Q	03/07/2019	04/10/2019	04/11/2019	04/26/2019
0.92Q	05/22/2019	06/18/2019	06/19/2019	07/12/2019
0.95Q	09/16/2019	09/26/2019	09/27/2019	10/17/2019
1.01Q	12/12/2019	12/26/2019	12/27/2019	01/14/2020

Indicated Div: $4.04

Valuation Analysis — **Institutional Holding**

Forecast EPS	$4.00	No of Institutions
(01/17/2020)		1720
Market Cap	$101.8 Billion	Shares
Book Value	$5.2 Billion	503,010,752
Price/Book	19.42	% Held
Price/Sales	13.07	N/A

Business Summary: REITs (MIC: 5.3.1 SIC: 6798 NAIC: 525930)

American Tower is a holding company. Through its subsidiaries, Co. is a real estate investment trusts and an independent owner, operator and developer of multitenant communications real estate. Co.'s primary business is the leasing of space on communications sites to wireless service providers, radio and television broadcast companies, wireless data providers, government agencies and municipalities and tenants in a number of other industries. Co. also provides tower-related services, including site acquisition, zoning and permitting and structural analysis, which primarily support its site leasing business, including the addition of new tenants and equipment on its sites.

Recent Developments: For the quarter ended Sep 30 2019, net income increased 33.9% to US$505.3 million from US$377.3 million in the year-earlier quarter. Revenues were US$1.95 billion, up 9.4% from US$1.79 billion the year before.

Prospects: Our evaluation of Americann Tower REIT, Inc. as of October 4th, 2019 is the result of our systematic analysis on three basic characteristics: earnings strength, relative valuation, and recent stock price movement. The company has enjoyed a very positive trend in earnings per share over the past 5 quarters. However, recent analyst estimates for the company have been mixed and AMT has posted results that exceeded analysts' expectations. Based on operating earnings yield, the company is overvalued when compared to all of the companies we cover. Share price changes over the past year indicates that AMT will perform very well over the near term.

Financial Data

(US$ in Thousands)	9 Mos	6 Mos	3 Mos	12/31/2018	12/31/2017	12/31/2016	12/31/2015	12/31/2014
Earnings Per Share	3.59	3.30	3.03	2.77	2.67	1.98	1.41	2.00
Cash Flow Per Share	9.08	8.68	8.48	8.53	6.83	6.34	5.21	5.39
Dividends Per Share	3.610	3.450	3.150	3.150	2.620	2.170	1.810	1.400
Dividend Payout %	100.56	104.55	103.96	113.72	98.13	109.60	128.37	70.00
Income Statement								
Total Revenue	5,656,600	3,703,000	1,813,400	7,440,100	6,663,900	5,785,668	4,771,516	4,100,048
EBITDA	3,142,100	2,045,000	1,013,000	2,808,600	2,795,000	2,565,307	2,059,623	1,973,189
Depn & Amortn	1,117,600	751,600	376,300	883,100	835,500	758,900	661,400	551,800
Income Before Taxes	1,447,500	905,500	441,600	1,154,600	1,256,100	1,125,860	829,962	865,704
Income Taxes	100,300	63,600	34,000	(110,100)	30,700	155,501	157,955	62,505
Net Income	1,325,100	826,500	397,400	1,236,400	1,238,900	956,425	685,074	824,910
Average Shares	445,829	445,337	444,621	442,960	431,688	429,283	423,015	400,086
Balance Sheet								
Current Assets	2,362,000	2,232,400	2,062,300	2,385,100	2,038,100	1,689,870	996,468	947,968
Total Assets	39,307,200	39,072,700	38,926,800	33,010,400	33,214,300	30,879,150	26,904,272	21,331,545
Current Liabilities	4,787,400	4,821,600	4,411,900	4,689,900	2,512,100	1,631,269	1,200,029	1,929,692
Long-Term Obligations	19,040,000	18,615,900	19,107,100	18,405,100	19,430,300	18,294,659	17,068,807	13,711,084
Total Liabilities	34,066,800	33,595,200	33,579,800	27,674,300	26,972,800	24,115,255	20,252,593	17,377,985
Stockholders' Equity	5,240,400	5,477,500	5,347,000	5,336,100	6,241,500	6,763,895	6,651,679	3,953,560
Shares Outstanding	442,835	442,386	441,968	441,060	428,820	427,102	423,885	396,698
Statistical Record								
Return on Assets %	4.43	4.07	3.68	3.73	3.87	3.30	2.84	3.97
Return on Equity %	30.27	26.68	23.09	21.36	19.05	14.22	12.92	22.03
EBITDA Margin %	55.55	55.23	55.86	37.75	41.94	44.34	43.16	48.13
Net Margin %	23.43	22.32	21.91	16.62	18.59	16.53	14.36	20.12
Asset Turnover	0.22	0.21	0.20	0.22	0.21	0.20	0.20	0.20
Current Ratio	0.49	0.46	0.47	0.51	0.81	1.04	0.83	0.49
Debt to Equity	3.63	3.40	3.57	3.45	3.11	2.70	2.57	3.47
Price Range	241.07-140.68	217.52-140.38	197.06-135.10	167.63-133.00	152.72-103.01	117.84-83.66	104.06-87.01	105.01-78.83
P/E Ratio	67.15-39.19	65.92-42.54	65.04-44.59	60.52-48.01	57.20-38.58	59.52-42.25	73.80-61.71	52.51-39.41
Average Yield %	1.92	2.03	2.04	2.16	2.01	2.05	1.89	1.55

Address: 116 Huntington Avenue, Boston, MA 02116 **Telephone:** 617-375-7500	**Web Site:** www.americantower.com **Officers:** James D. (Jim) Taiclet - Chairman, President, Chief Executive Officer, Chief Operating Officer Thomas (Tom) A. Bartlett - Executive Vice President, Chief Financial Officer, Treasurer	**Auditors:** DELOITTE & TOUCHE LLP **Investor Contact:** 617-375-7500 **Transfer Agents:** Computershare

AMERICAN WATER WORKS CO, INC.

Exchange	Symbol	Price	52Wk Range	Yield	P/E
NYS	AWK	$122.85 (12/31/2019)	129.50-88.77	1.63	35.00

*7 Year Price Score 131.39 *NYSE Composite Index=100 *12 Month Price Score 100.80

TRADING VOLUME (thousand shares)

Interim Earnings (Per Share)

Qtr.	Mar	Jun	Sep	Dec
2016	0.46	0.77	0.83	0.57
2017	0.52	0.73	1.13	(0.01)
2018	0.59	0.91	1.04	0.62
2019	0.62	0.94	1.33	...

Interim Dividends (Per Share)

Amt	Decl	Ex	Rec	Pay
0.50Q	04/17/2019	05/10/2019	05/13/2019	06/04/2019
0.50Q	07/26/2019	08/08/2019	08/09/2019	09/04/2019
0.50Q	10/29/2019	11/08/2019	11/12/2019	12/04/2019
0.50Q	12/06/2019	02/06/2020	02/07/2020	03/04/2020

Indicated Div: $2.00

Valuation Analysis | **Institutional Holding**

Forecast EPS	$3.61	No of Institutions
(01/17/2020)		1056
Market Cap	$22.2 Billion	Shares
Book Value	$6.2 Billion	194,241,440
Price/Book	3.59	% Held
Price/Sales	6.24	85.22

Business Summary: Water Utilities (MIC: 3.2.1 SIC: 4941 NAIC: 221310)

American Water Works is a holding company. Through its subsidiaries, Co. is a water and wastewater utility company. Co.'s Regulated Businesses provide water and wastewater services to residential, commercial, industrial, public authority, fire service and sale for resale customers. Co.'s Market-Based Businesses segments include Homeowner Services Group, which provides warranty protection programs to residential and commercial customers; Military Services Group, which provides water and wastewater services on military installations; and its Keystone Clearwater Solutions, LLC subsidiary, which provides water transfer services for shale natural gas exploration and production companies.

Recent Developments: For the quarter ended Sep 30 2019, net income increased 29.7% to US$240.0 million from US$185.0 million in the year-earlier quarter. Revenues were US$1.01 billion, up 3.8% from US$976.0 million the year before. Operating income was US$406.0 million versus US$335.0 million in the prior-year quarter, an increase of 21.2%. Direct operating expenses rose 1.3% to US$395.0 million from US$390.0 million in the comparable period the year before. Indirect operating expenses decreased 15.5% to US$212.0 million from US$251.0 million in the equivalent prior-year period.

Prospects: Our evaluation of American Water Works Co. Inc. as of October 4th, 2019 is the result of our systematic analysis on three basic characteristics: earnings strength, relative valuation, and recent stock price movement. The company has enjoyed a very positive trend in earnings per share over the past 5 quarters. However, recent analyst estimates for the company have been mixed and AWK has posted results that exceeded analysts' expectations. Based on operating earnings yield, the company is fairly valued when compared to all of the companies we cover. Share price changes over the past year indicates that AWK will perform very well over the near term.

Financial Data

(US$ in Thousands)	9 Mos	6 Mos	3 Mos	12/31/2018	12/31/2017	12/31/2016	12/31/2015	12/31/2014
Earnings Per Share	3.51	3.22	3.19	3.15	2.38	2.62	2.64	2.35
Cash Flow Per Share	7.40	7.41	7.38	7.70	8.14	7.15	6.59	6.13
Tang Book Value Per Share	25.11	24.21	23.69	23.27	22.45	21.75	21.02	20.66
Dividends Per Share	1.910	1.865	1.820	1.780	1.620	1.465	1.330	1.210
Dividend Payout %	54.42	57.92	57.05	56.51	68.07	55.92	50.38	51.49
Income Statement								
Total Revenue	2,708,000	1,695,000	813,000	3,440,000	3,357,000	3,302,000	3,159,000	3,011,328
EBITDA	1,574,000	937,000	424,000	1,634,000	1,714,000	1,530,000	1,495,000	1,349,306
Depn & Amortn	593,000	371,000	179,000	497,000	460,000	435,000	405,000	356,952
Income Before Taxes	697,000	379,000	152,000	787,000	912,000	770,000	782,000	709,814
Income Taxes	174,000	96,000	39,000	222,000	486,000	302,000	306,000	279,973
Net Income	523,000	283,000	113,000	567,000	426,000	468,000	476,000	423,108
Average Shares	181,000	181,000	181,000	180,000	179,000	179,000	180,000	179,806
Balance Sheet								
Current Assets	799,000	741,000	691,000	781,000	720,000	784,000	657,000	661,369
Total Assets	22,238,000	21,854,000	21,464,000	21,223,000	19,482,000	18,482,000	17,241,000	16,130,956
Current Liabilities	1,488,000	1,317,000	2,156,000	2,094,000	2,325,000	2,392,000	1,533,000	1,240,998
Long-Term Obligations	8,640,000	8,642,000	7,562,000	7,569,000	6,490,000	5,749,000	5,862,000	5,432,744
Total Liabilities	16,048,000	15,827,000	15,532,000	15,532,000	15,359,000	14,097,000	13,264,000	11,215,365
Stockholders' Equity	6,190,000	6,027,000	5,932,000	5,864,000	5,385,000	5,218,000	5,049,000	4,915,591
Shares Outstanding	180,769	180,651	180,513	180,684	178,444	178,096	178,282	179,462
Statistical Record								
Return on Assets %	2.95	2.75	2.79	2.79	2.24	2.61	2.85	2.71
Return on Equity %	10.54	9.90	10.09	10.08	8.04	9.09	9.55	8.78
EBITDA Margin %	58.12	55.28	52.15	47.50	51.06	46.34	47.33	44.81
Net Margin %	19.31	16.70	13.90	16.48	12.69	14.17	15.07	14.05
Asset Turnover	0.17	0.17	0.17	0.17	0.18	0.18	0.19	0.19
Current Ratio	0.54	0.56	0.32	0.37	0.31	0.33	0.43	0.53
Debt to Equity	1.40	1.43	1.27	1.29	1.21	1.10	1.16	1.11
Price Range	129.50-86.31	118.40-85.28	107.20-78.35	97.80-76.06	92.25-70.57	84.76-59.44	60.61-48.63	55.86-41.16
P/E Ratio	36.89-24.59	36.77-26.48	33.61-24.56	31.05-24.15	38.76-29.65	32.35-22.69	22.96-18.42	23.77-17.51
Average Yield %	1.82	1.92	2.02	2.07	2.01	2.02	2.45	2.53

Address: 1 Water Street, Camden, NJ 08102-1658 **Telephone:** 856-955-4001	**Web Site:** www.amwater.com **Officers:** Karl F. Kurz - Chairman Susan N. Story - President, Chief Executive Officer, Senior Vice President, Chief Financial Officer	**Auditors:** PricewaterhouseCoopers LLP **Investor Contact:** 856-566-4005 **Transfer Agents:** American Stock Transfer & Trust Company, Brooklyn, NY

AMERIPRISE FINANCIAL INC

Exchange	Symbol	Price	52Wk Range	Yield	P/E	Div Acheiver
NYS	AMP	$166.58 (12/31/2019)	168.43-104.37	2.33	11.75	13 Years

*7 Year Price Score 96.47   *NYSE Composite Index=100   *12 Month Price Score 108.60

Interim Earnings (Per Share)

Qtr.	Mar	Jun	Sep	Dec
2016	2.09	1.97	1.30	2.44
2017	2.52	2.50	3.24	1.20
2018	3.91	3.10	3.43	3.75
2019	2.82	3.57	4.04	...

Interim Dividends (Per Share)

Amt	Decl	Ex	Rec	Pay
0.90Q	01/30/2019	02/14/2019	02/15/2019	02/28/2019
0.97Q	04/24/2019	05/03/2019	05/06/2019	05/17/2019
0.97Q	07/24/2019	08/02/2019	08/05/2019	08/16/2019
0.97Q	10/23/2019	11/01/2019	11/04/2019	11/15/2019

Indicated Div: $3.88 (Div. Reinv. Plan)

Valuation Analysis		Institutional Holding	
Forecast EPS	$16.16	No of Institutions	
	(01/17/2020)	1150	
Market Cap	$21.2 Billion	Shares	
Book Value	$6.0 Billion	150,766,288	
Price/Book	3.54	% Held	
Price/Sales	1.65	71.78	

Business Summary: Wealth Management (MIC: 5.5.2 SIC: 6282 NAIC: 523930)

Ameriprise Financial is a holding company. Through its subsidiaries, Co. provides a range of products and services to individual and institutional clients. Co. has the following segments: Advice and Wealth Management, which provides financial planning and advice, as well as brokerage services, primarily to retail clients through its financial advisors; Asset Management, which provides investment management and advice and investment products to clients through its subsidiaries; Annuities, which provides RiverSource variable and fixed annuity products to individual clients; and Protection, which provides a variety of products including life, disability income and property casualty insurance.

Recent Developments: For the quarter ended Sep 30 2019, net income increased 8.0% to US$543.0 million from US$503.0 million in the year-earlier quarter. Revenues were US$3.32 billion, up 0.8% from US$3.29 billion the year before. Direct operating expenses declined 2.6% to US$1.80 billion from US$1.85 billion in the comparable period the year before. Indirect operating expenses increased 2.3% to US$872.0 million from US$852.0 million in the equivalent prior-year period.

Prospects: Our evaluation of Ameriprise Financial Inc. as of October 4th, 2019 is the result of our systematic analysis on three basic characteristics: earnings strength, relative valuation, and recent stock price movement. The company has produced a positive trend in earnings per share over the past 5 quarters. However, recent analyst estimates for the company have been reduced, while AMP has posted results that exceeded analysts' expectations. Based on operating earnings yield, the company is undervalued when compared to all of the companies we cover. Share price changes over the past year indicates that AMP will perform poorly over the near term.

Financial Data

(US$ in Millions)	9 Mos	6 Mos	3 Mos	12/31/2018	12/31/2017	12/31/2016	12/31/2015	12/31/2014
Earnings Per Share	14.18	13.57	13.10	14.20	9.44	7.81	8.48	8.30
Cash Flow Per Share	30.61	23.42	21.45	17.84	11.04	11.82	14.16	12.52
Tang Book Value Per Share	47.07	45.93	43.54	40.99	40.90	40.66	42.20	44.37
Dividends Per Share	3.740	3.670	3.600	3.530	3.240	2.920	2.590	2.260
Dividend Payout %	26.38	27.04	27.48	24.86	34.32	37.39	30.54	27.23
Income Statement								
Total Revenue	9,680	6,363	3,118	12,835	12,027	11,696	12,170	12,268
EBITDA	1,994	1,260	569	2,875	2,562	1,982	2,679	3,019
Depn & Amortn	132	91	46	146	141	149	150	144
Income Before Taxes	1,698	1,057	470	2,484	2,214	1,592	2,142	2,547
Income Taxes	268	170	75	386	734	278	455	545
Net Income	1,430	887	395	2,098	1,480	1,314	1,562	1,619
Average Shares	134	138	140	147	156	168	184	195
Balance Sheet								
Current Assets	5,392	4,361	3,347	9,282	8,405	7,796	8,133	8,055
Total Assets	149,513	148,678	144,403	137,216	147,470	139,821	145,342	148,810
Current Liabilities	15,420	15,160	13,317	13,608	12,463	11,963	10,440	9,387
Long-Term Obligations	4,771	4,811	5,125	4,610	5,099	5,236	10,246	9,929
Total Liabilities	143,516	142,648	138,560	131,628	141,472	133,529	138,125	140,686
Stockholders' Equity	5,997	6,030	5,843	5,588	5,998	6,292	7,217	8,124
Shares Outstanding	127	131	134	136	146	154	171	183
Statistical Record								
Return on Assets %	1.34	1.32	1.31	1.47	1.03	0.92	1.06	1.10
Return on Equity %	33.90	33.08	32.51	36.22	24.08	19.40	20.36	19.85
EBITDA Margin %	20.60	19.80	18.25	22.40	21.30	16.95	22.01	24.61
Net Margin %	14.77	13.94	12.67	16.35	12.31	11.23	12.83	13.20
Asset Turnover	0.09	0.09	0.09	0.09	0.08	0.08	0.08	0.08
Current Ratio	0.35	0.29	0.25	0.68	0.67	0.65	0.78	0.86
Debt to Equity	0.80	0.80	0.88	0.82	0.85	0.83	1.42	1.22
Price Range	153.53-97.58	153.53-97.58	151.97-97.58	182.04-97.58	171.70-111.55	118.90-76.27	137.81-103.08	136.76-101.47
P/E Ratio	10.83-6.88	11.31-7.19	11.60-7.45	12.82-6.87	18.19-11.82	15.22-9.77	16.25-12.16	16.48-12.23
Average Yield %	2.80	2.73	2.69	2.46	2.35	3.00	2.12	1.92

Address: 1099 Ameriprise Financial Center, Minneapolis, MN 55474 Telephone: 612-671-3131	Web Site: www.ameriprise.com Officers: James M. Cracchiolo - Chairman, Chief Executive Officer Walter Stanley Berman - Executive Vice President, Chief Financial Officer	Auditors: PricewaterhouseCoopers LLP Investor Contact: 612-671-2080 Transfer Agents: Computershare Trust Company, N.A, Providence, RI

46

AMERISOURCEBERGEN CORP.

Exchange	Symbol	Price	52Wk Range	Yield	P/E	Div Acheiver
NYS	ABC	$85.02 (12/31/2019)	91.70-71.06	1.88	21.04	14 Years

*7 Year Price Score 83.07   *NYSE Composite Index=100   *12 Month Price Score 98.70

Interim Earnings (Per Share)

Qtr.	Dec	Mar	Jun	Sep
2014-15	(0.91)	(2.33)	0.89	1.65
2015-16	1.46	2.68	1.56	0.63
2016-17	1.11	1.86	0.23	(1.56)
2017-18	3.90	1.29	1.25	1.09
2018-19	1.84	0.13	1.43	0.62

Interim Dividends (Per Share)

Amt	Decl	Ex	Rec	Pay
0.40Q	02/05/2019	02/15/2019	02/19/2019	03/04/2019
0.40Q	05/08/2019	05/17/2019	05/20/2019	06/03/2019
0.40Q	08/08/2019	08/16/2019	08/19/2019	09/03/2019
0.40Q	11/07/2019	11/15/2019	11/18/2019	12/02/2019

Indicated Div: $1.60

Valuation Analysis

		Institutional Holding	
Forecast EPS	$7.54	No of Institutions	
	(01/17/2020)	1071	
Market Cap	$17.6 Billion	Shares	
Book Value	$2.9 Billion	191,320,576	
Price/Book	6.11	% Held	
Price/Sales	0.10	63.01	

Business Summary: Pharmaceuticals (MIC: 4.1.1 SIC: 5122 NAIC: 424210)

AmerisourceBergen is a pharmaceutical sourcing and distribution services company. Co.'s Pharmaceutical Distribution Services reportable segment provides pharmaceutical distribution and additional services to physicians who focus on a variety of disease states, especially oncology, and to other healthcare providers, including hospitals and dialysis clinics. Additionally, this segment provides data analytics, outcomes research, and additional services for biotechnology and pharmaceutical manufacturers. This segment also provides pharmacy management, staffing and additional consulting services, and supply management software to a variety of retail and institutional healthcare providers.

Recent Developments: For the year ended Sep 30 2019, net income decreased 47.1% to US$854.1 million from US$1.62 billion in the prior year. Revenues were US$179.59 billion, up 6.9% from US$167.94 billion the year before. Direct operating expenses rose 6.8% to US$174.45 billion from US$163.33 billion in the comparable period the year before. Indirect operating expenses increased 25.4% to US$4.03 billion from US$3.21 billion in the equivalent prior-year period.

Prospects: Our evaluation of AmerisourceBergen Corp. as of October 4th, 2019 is the result of our systematic analysis on three basic characteristics: earnings strength, relative valuation, and recent stock price movement. The company has produced a positive trend in earnings per share over the past 5 quarters. However, recent analyst estimates for the company have been unchanged, while ABC has posted results that exceeded analysts' expectations. Based on operating earnings yield, the company is undervalued when compared to all of the companies we cover. Share price changes over the past year indicates that ABC will perform well over the near term.

Financial Data

(US$ in Thousands)	09/30/2019	09/30/2018	09/30/2017	09/30/2016	09/30/2015	09/30/2014	09/30/2013	09/30/2012
Earnings Per Share	4.04	7.53	1.64	6.32	(0.62)	1.17	1.84	2.80
Cash Flow Per Share	11.15	6.48	6.89	14.94	18.00	6.44	3.41	5.15
Dividends Per Share	1.600	1.520	1.460	1.360	1.160	0.940	0.840	0.520
Dividend Payout %	39.60	20.19	89.02	21.52	...	80.34	45.65	18.57
Income Statement								
Total Revenue	179,589,121	167,939,635	153,143,826	146,849,686	135,961,803	119,569,127	87,959,167	79,489,596
EBITDA	1,445,977	1,712,933	1,325,492	1,763,360	561,085	912,379	1,037,045	1,377,084
Depn & Amortn	321,102	318,483	262,420	232,538	187,935	162,089	138,690	118,529
Income Before Taxes	967,106	1,219,751	917,887	1,390,910	274,149	673,428	824,458	1,163,131
Income Taxes	112,971	(438,469)	553,403	(37,019)	409,036	389,398	331,023	454,945
Net Income	855,365	1,658,405	364,484	1,427,929	(134,887)	276,484	433,707	718,986
Average Shares	211,840	220,336	221,602	225,959	217,786	235,405	235,345	256,903
Balance Sheet								
Current Assets	28,132,054	25,894,372	24,303,299	22,851,847	20,334,488	16,800,205	14,393,651	10,987,151
Total Assets	39,171,980	37,669,838	35,316,470	33,656,200	27,736,157	21,532,183	18,918,638	15,444,126
Current Liabilities	29,581,294	27,869,687	26,818,165	25,281,308	22,700,765	17,250,160	14,870,635	11,214,482
Long-Term Obligations	4,354,398	4,510,828	3,781,960	3,870,244	3,493,048	1,995,623	1,396,606	1,446,770
Total Liabilities	36,293,063	34,737,014	33,252,009	31,526,796	27,102,637	19,575,284	16,598,893	12,987,414
Stockholders' Equity	2,878,917	2,932,824	2,064,461	2,129,404	633,520	1,956,899	2,319,745	2,456,712
Shares Outstanding	206,760	213,217	217,993	220,050	206,891	221,908	229,994	235,394
Statistical Record								
Return on Assets %	2.23	4.54	1.06	4.64	N.M.	1.37	2.52	4.71
Return on Equity %	29.44	66.37	17.38	103.08	N.M.	12.93	18.16	26.94
EBITDA Margin %	0.81	1.02	0.87	1.20	0.41	0.76	1.18	1.73
Net Margin %	0.48	0.99	0.24	0.97	N.M.	0.23	0.49	0.90
Asset Turnover	4.67	4.60	4.44	4.77	5.52	5.91	5.12	5.21
Current Ratio	0.95	0.93	0.91	0.90	0.90	0.97	0.97	0.98
Debt to Equity	1.51	1.54	1.83	1.82	5.51	1.02	0.60	0.59
Price Range	93.76-70.76	105.48-73.23	96.38-69.03	105.02-73.66	115.48-75.02	78.33-61.10	62.23-38.99	42.08-35.57
P/E Ratio	23.21-17.51	14.01-9.73	58.77-42.09	16.62-11.66	...	66.95-52.22	33.82-21.19	15.03-12.70
Average Yield %	1.93	1.72	1.72	1.54	1.15	1.34	1.67	1.37

Address: 1300 Morris Drive, Chesterbrook, PA 19087-5594	**Web Site:** www.amerisourcebergen.com	**Auditors:** Ernst & Young LLP
Telephone: 610-727-7000	**Officers:** Steven H. Collis - Chairman, President, Chief Executive Officer John G. Chou - Executive Vice President, Chief Legal Officer, Chief Business Officer, Senior Vice President, General Counsel, Secretary	**Investor Contact:** 610-727-3693
Fax: 610-647-0141		**Transfer Agents:** Computershare, Louisville, KY

AMETEK INC

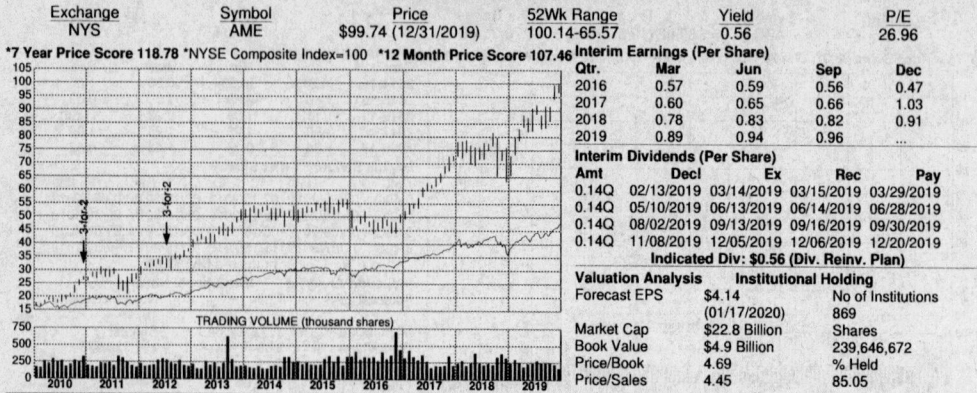

Exchange	Symbol	Price	52Wk Range	Yield	P/E
NYS	AME	$99.74 (12/31/2019)	100.14-65.57	0.56	26.96

*7 Year Price Score 118.78 ***NYSE Composite Index=100** ***12 Month Price Score 107.46**

Interim Earnings (Per Share)

Qtr.	Mar	Jun	Sep	Dec
2016	0.57	0.59	0.56	0.47
2017	0.60	0.65	0.66	1.03
2018	0.78	0.83	0.82	0.91
2019	0.89	0.94	0.96	...

Interim Dividends (Per Share)

Amt	Decl	Ex	Rec	Pay
0.14Q	02/13/2019	03/14/2019	03/15/2019	03/29/2019
0.14Q	05/10/2019	06/13/2019	06/14/2019	06/28/2019
0.14Q	08/02/2019	09/13/2019	09/16/2019	09/30/2019
0.14Q	11/08/2019	12/05/2019	12/06/2019	12/20/2019

Indicated Div: $0.56 (Div. Reinv. Plan)

Valuation Analysis

		Institutional Holding	
Forecast EPS	$4.14	No of Institutions	869
	(01/17/2020)		
Market Cap	$22.8 Billion	Shares	239,646,672
Book Value	$4.9 Billion		
Price/Book	4.69	% Held	85.05
Price/Sales	4.45		

Business Summary: Electrical Equipment (MIC: 7.3.1 SIC: 3629 NAIC: 335999)

AMETEK is a global manufacturer of electronic instruments and electromechanical devices with operations in North America, Europe, Asia and South America. Co.'s products are marketed and sold through Electronic Instruments (EIG) and Electromechanical (EMG) operating groups. EIG is engaged in the design and manufacture of process control instruments for the oil and gas, petrochemical, pharmaceutical, semiconductor, automation, and food and beverage industries. EMG is a supplier of automation solutions, thermal management systems, specialty metals and electrical interconnects. Products supplied include its motion control products as well as its electrical connectors and electronics packaging.

Recent Developments: For the quarter ended Sep 30 2019, net income increased 15.4% to US$220.7 million from US$191.2 million in the year-earlier quarter. Revenues were US$1.28 billion, up 7.0% from US$1.19 billion the year before. Operating income was US$301.1 million versus US$265.3 million in the prior-year quarter, an increase of 13.5%. Direct operating expenses rose 5.1% to US$823.3 million from US$783.0 million in the comparable period the year before. Indirect operating expenses increased 5.3% to US$152.3 million from US$144.7 million in the equivalent prior-year period.

Prospects: Our evaluation of Ametek Inc. as of October 4th, 2019 is the result of our systematic analysis on three basic characteristics: earnings strength, relative valuation, and recent stock price movement. The company has enjoyed a very positive trend in earnings per share over the past 5 quarters. However, recent analyst estimates for the company have been mixed and AME has posted results that exceeded analysts' expectations. Based on operating earnings yield, the company is fairly valued when compared to all of the companies we cover. Share price changes over the past year indicates that AME will perform in line with the market over the near term.

Financial Data

(US$ in Thousands)	9 Mos	6 Mos	3 Mos	12/31/2018	12/31/2017	12/31/2016	12/31/2015	12/31/2014
Earnings Per Share	3.70	3.56	3.45	3.34	2.94	2.19	2.45	2.37
Cash Flow Per Share	4.69	4.34	4.16	4.01	3.62	3.25	2.80	2.96
Dividends Per Share	0.560	0.560	0.560	0.560	0.360	0.360	0.360	0.330
Dividend Payout %	15.14	15.73	16.23	16.77	12.24	16.44	14.69	13.92
Income Statement								
Total Revenue	3,853,736	2,577,103	1,287,691	4,845,872	4,300,170	3,840,087	3,974,295	4,021,964
EBITDA	1,037,139	686,338	337,091	1,155,325	1,077,985	967,123	966,882	948,484
Depn & Amortn	169,935	114,673	57,500	85,400	183,227	179,716	68,707	63,724
Income Before Taxes	801,768	527,537	256,938	987,745	796,729	693,103	806,380	804,832
Income Taxes	161,248	107,766	52,670	209,812	115,259	-180,945	215,521	220,372
Net Income	640,520	419,771	204,268	777,933	681,470	512,158	590,859	584,460
Average Shares	229,560	229,328	228,686	232,712	231,845	233,730	241,586	247,102
Balance Sheet								
Current Assets	2,272,184	2,127,153	1,924,644	1,836,144	1,934,655	1,928,190	1,619,613	1,578,604
Total Assets	9,219,709	9,069,602	8,891,483	8,662,288	7,796,064	7,100,674	6,664,530	6,420,963
Current Liabilities	1,110,519	978,558	1,007,228	1,258,704	1,138,663	924,441	1,025,172	936,144
Long-Term Obligations	2,229,252	2,368,690	2,368,197	2,273,837	1,866,166	2,062,644	1,556,045	1,427,825
Total Liabilities	4,353,744	4,402,821	4,434,862	4,420,366	3,768,431	3,844,161	3,409,904	3,181,402
Stockholders' Equity	4,865,965	4,666,781	4,456,621	4,241,922	4,027,633	3,256,513	3,254,626	3,239,561
Shares Outstanding	228,592	228,345	227,840	227,110	231,193	229,378	235,515	241,335
Statistical Record								
Return on Assets %	9.83	9.55	9.45	9.45	9.15	7.42	9.03	9.50
Return on Equity %	18.17	18.27	18.49	18.81	18.71	15.69	18.20	18.33
EBITDA Margin %	26.91	26.63	26.18	23.84	25.07	25.18	24.33	23.58
Net Margin %	16.62	16.29	15.86	16.05	15.85	13.34	14.87	14.53
Asset Turnover	0.59	0.59	0.59	0.59	0.58	0.56	0.61	0.65
Current Ratio	2.05	2.17	1.91	1.46	1.70	2.09	1.58	1.69
Debt to Equity	0.46	0.51	0.53	0.54	0.46	0.63	0.48	0.44
Price Range	92.11-63.35	90.84-63.35	82.97-63.35	81.53-63.35	72.87-49.18	53.59-43.88	57.50-47.90	54.20-46.12
P/E Ratio	24.89-17.12	25.52-17.79	24.05-18.36	24.41-18.97	24.79-16.73	24.47-20.04	23.47-19.55	22.87-19.46
Average Yield %	0.70	0.72	0.75	0.75	0.59	0.75	0.67	0.64

Address: 1100 Cassatt Road, Berwyn, PA 19312-1177 **Telephone:** 610-647-2121 **Fax:** 610-647-0211	**Web Site:** www.ametek.com **Officers:** David A. Zapico - Chairman, Chief Executive Officer, Executive Vice President, Chief Operating Officer, Division Officer William J. Burke - Executive Vice President, Chief Financial Officer, Senior Vice President, Comptroller, Treasurer	**Auditors:** Ernst & Young LLP **Transfer Agents:** American Stock Transfer & Trust Co., New York, NY

AMPHENOL CORP.

Exchange	Symbol	Price	52Wk Range	Yield	P/E
NYS	APH	$108.23 (12/31/2019)	108.28-75.07	0.92	28.41

*7 Year Price Score 118.36 *NYSE Composite Index=100 *12 Month Price Score 103.93

Interim Earnings (Per Share)

Qtr.	Mar	Jun	Sep	Dec
2016	0.50	0.65	0.71	0.75
2017	0.71	0.80	0.88	(0.33)
2018	0.84	0.91	1.01	1.09
2019	0.87	0.93	0.92	...

Interim Dividends (Per Share)

Amt	Decl	Ex	Rec	Pay
0.23Q	01/30/2019	03/18/2019	03/19/2019	04/10/2019
0.23Q	05/02/2019	06/18/2019	06/19/2019	07/11/2019
0.25Q	07/23/2019	09/16/2019	09/17/2019	10/09/2019
0.25Q	10/30/2019	12/16/2019	12/17/2019	01/08/2020

Indicated Div: $1.00

Valuation Analysis

		Institutional Holding	
Forecast EPS	$3.66	No of Institutions	982
	(01/15/2020)		
Market Cap	$32.0 Billion	Shares	
Book Value	$4.2 Billion	338,969,984	
Price/Book	7.71	% Held	
Price/Sales	3.86	91.57	

TRADING VOLUME (thousand shares)

Business Summary: Electrical Equipment (MIC: 7.3.1 SIC: 3678 NAIC: 334417)

Amphenol is a designer, manufacturer and marketer of electrical, electronic and fiber optic connectors, interconnect systems, antennas, sensors and sensor-based products and coaxial and specialty cable. Co.'s segments include: Interconnect Products and Assemblies, which designs, manufactures and markets a range of connector and connector systems, and other products, including antennas and sensors, used in a range of applications in a set of end markets; and Cable Products and Solutions, which designs, manufactures and markets cable, products and components for use primarily in the broadband communications and information technology markets as well as certain applications in other markets.

Recent Developments: For the quarter ended Sep 30 2019, net income decreased 11.7% to US$282.3 million from US$319.6 million in the year-earlier quarter. Revenues were US$2.10 billion, down 1.3% from US$2.13 billion the year before. Operating income was US$413.6 million versus US$444.2 million in the prior-year quarter, a decrease of 6.9%. Direct operating expenses was unchanged at US$1.44 billion versus the comparable period the year before. Indirect operating expenses increased 1.8% to US$248.3 million from US$244.0 million in the equivalent prior-year period.

Prospects: Our evaluation of Amphenol Corp. as of October 4th, 2019 is the result of our systematic analysis on three basic characteristics: earnings strength, relative valuation, and recent stock price movement. The company has managed to produce a neutral trend in earnings per share over the past 5 quarters. In addition, recent analyst estimates for the company have been mixed and APH has posted results that fell short of analysts' expectations. Based on operating earnings yield, the company is fairly valued when compared to all of the companies we cover. Share price changes over the past year indicates that APH will perform poorly over the near term.

Financial Data
(US$ in Thousands)

	9 Mos	6 Mos	3 Mos	12/31/2018	12/31/2017	12/31/2016	12/31/2015	12/31/2014
Earnings Per Share	3.81	3.90	3.88	3.85	2.06	2.61	2.41	2.21
Cash Flow Per Share	4.91	4.64	4.45	3.69	3.74	3.49	3.33	2.81
Tang Book Value Per Share	N.M.	N.M.	N.M.	N.M.	N.M.	N.M.	1.77	0.94
Dividends Per Share	0.940	0.920	0.920	0.880	0.700	0.580	0.530	0.450
Dividend Payout %	24.67	23.59	23.71	22.86	33.98	22.22	21.99	20.36
Income Statement								
Total Revenue	6,074,400	3,973,800	1,958,500	8,202,000	7,011,300	6,286,400	5,568,700	5,345,500
EBITDA	1,418,100	942,200	464,800	1,989,800	1,651,300	1,419,200	1,274,300	1,200,800
Depn & Amortn	235,400	163,400	85,600	299,700	226,800	217,000	171,600	168,100
Income Before Taxes	1,093,200	719,100	349,500	1,588,400	1,352,400	1,141,100	1,052,800	972,500
Income Taxes	250,000	158,300	79,600	371,500	691,700	308,500	280,500	257,300
Net Income	836,300	556,000	267,500	1,205,000	650,500	822,900	763,500	709,100
Average Shares	306,200	308,700	308,600	312,600	316,500	315,200	316,500	320,430
Balance Sheet								
Current Assets	4,232,200	4,222,100	4,127,500	4,571,600	4,656,000	3,591,200	3,850,000	3,504,100
Total Assets	10,683,600	10,634,000	10,208,100	10,044,900	10,003,900	8,498,700	7,458,400	7,027,000
Current Liabilities	2,122,600	2,052,900	1,649,200	2,451,300	1,579,400	1,635,200	1,008,400	1,045,600
Long-Term Obligations	3,545,400	3,569,400	3,554,800	2,806,400	3,541,500	2,635,500	2,813,200	2,672,300
Total Liabilities	6,528,300	6,485,700	6,085,000	6,027,900	6,014,100	4,823,800	4,219,900	4,119,600
Stockholders' Equity	4,155,300	4,148,300	4,123,100	4,017,000	3,989,800	3,674,900	3,238,500	2,907,400
Shares Outstanding	296,100	297,200	298,000	298,500	305,700	308,300	308,000	309,884
Statistical Record								
Return on Assets %	11.50	12.02	12.31	12.02	7.03	10.29	10.54	10.75
Return on Equity %	28.77	30.61	30.04	30.10	16.97	23.74	24.85	24.59
EBITDA Margin %	23.35	23.71	23.73	24.26	23.55	22.58	22.88	22.46
Net Margin %	13.77	13.99	13.66	14.69	9.28	13.09	13.71	13.27
Asset Turnover	0.81	0.83	0.85	0.82	0.76	0.79	0.77	0.81
Current Ratio	1.99	2.06	2.50	1.86	2.95	2.20	3.82	3.35
Debt to Equity	0.85	0.86	0.86	0.70	0.89	0.72	0.87	0.92
Price Range	105.38-75.07	105.38-75.07	96.99-75.07	96.99-75.65	91.04-66.60	68.83-45.42	60.20-49.06	55.45-42.34
P/E Ratio	27.66-19.70	27.02-19.25	25.00-19.35	25.19-19.65	44.19-32.33	26.37-17.40	24.98-20.36	25.09-19.16
Average Yield %	1.03	1.01	1.04	0.99	0.91	1.10	0.98	0.93

Address: 358 Hall Avenue, Wallingford, CT 06492	Web Site: www.amphenol.com	Auditors: DELOITTE & TOUCHE LLP
Telephone: 203-265-8900	Officers: Martin H. Loeffler - Chairman, Executive Chairman Richard Adam Norwitt - President, Chief Executive Officer	Transfer Agents: Computershare Trust Company, N.A., Providence, RI
Fax: 203-265-8746		

ANIXTER INTERNATIONAL INC

Exchange	Symbol	Price	52Wk Range	Yield	P/E
NYS	AXE	$92.10 (12/31/2019)	92.97-52.84	N/A	15.48

*7 Year Price Score 74.00 ***NYSE Composite Index=100** ***12 Month Price Score 125.76**

Interim Earnings (Per Share)

Qtr.	Mar	Jun	Sep	Dec
2016	0.68	0.61	1.21	1.09
2017	0.91	1.18	1.11	0.01
2018	0.94	1.02	1.40	1.22
2019	1.14	1.86	1.73	...

Interim Dividends (Per Share)

Dividend Payment Suspended

Valuation Analysis **Institutional Holding**

Forecast EPS	$6.92	No of Institutions
	(01/15/2020)	342
Market Cap	$3.1 Billion	Shares
Book Value	$1.8 Billion	41,388,336
Price/Book	1.80	% Held
Price/Sales	0.36	87.96

Business Summary: Electrical Equipment (MIC: 7.3.1 SIC: 5063 NAIC: 423610)

Anixter International is engaged in the distribution of network and security solutions, electrical and electronic solutions, and utility power solutions through Anixter Inc. and its subsidiaries. The Network and Security Solutions segment supplies products and customized supply chain solutions. The Electrical and Electronic Solutions segment supplies wire and cable, control, lighting and electrical bulk products and customized supply chain solutions. The Utility Power Solutions segment supplies electrical transmission and distribution products, power plant maintenance, repair and operations supplies and smart-grid products, and arranges materials management and procurement outsourcing.

Recent Developments: For the quarter ended Sep 27 2019, net income increased 24.6% to US$59.3 million from US$47.6 million in the year-earlier quarter. Revenues were US$2.22 billion, up 2.0% from US$2.18 billion the year before. Operating income was US$101.8 million versus US$89.5 million in the prior-year quarter, an increase of 13.7%. Direct operating expenses rose 1.2% to US$1.78 billion from US$1.75 billion in the comparable period the year before. Indirect operating expenses increased 3.0% to US$344.6 million from US$334.6 million in the equivalent prior-year period.

Prospects: Our evaluation of Anixter International Inc. as of October 4th, 2019 is the result of our systematic analysis on three basic characteristics: earnings strength, relative valuation, and recent stock price movement. The company has produced a positive trend in earnings per share over the past 5 quarters. However, recent analyst estimates for the company have been mixed and AXE has posted results that exceeded analysts' expectations. Based on operating earnings yield, the company is undervalued when compared to all of the companies we cover. Share price changes over the past year indicates that AXE will perform very poorly over the near term.

Financial Data
(US$ in Thousands)

	9 Mos	6 Mos	3 Mos	12/28/2018	12/29/2017	12/30/2016	01/01/2016	01/02/2015
Earnings Per Share	5.95	5.62	4.78	4.58	3.21	3.59	3.81	5.84
Cash Flow Per Share	7.06	0.15	2.79	4.09	5.49	8.37	2.78	3.17
Tang Book Value Per Share	16.15	14.14	11.75	10.20	8.98	3.36	N.M.	16.62
Income Statement								
Total Revenue	6,593,300	4,371,100	2,108,500	8,400,200	7,927,400	7,622,800	6,190,500	6,445,500
EBITDA	337,100	218,000	94,500	368,500	376,600	341,700	294,300	378,600
Depn & Amortn	55,100	36,600	18,100	69,000	64,300	65,500	47,600	35,700
Income Before Taxes	223,700	141,600	56,000	223,200	237,600	197,500	182,900	294,800
Income Taxes	61,800	39,000	16,900	66,900	128,600	76,400	86,000	100,000
Net Income	161,900	102,600	39,100	156,300	109,000	120,500	127,600	194,800
Average Shares	34,300	34,200	34,200	34,100	34,000	33,600	33,400	33,300
Balance Sheet								
Current Assets	3,139,400	3,199,800	3,158,100	3,172,000	2,833,800	2,688,500	2,727,800	2,589,800
Total Assets	4,868,500	4,910,700	4,869,700	4,653,100	4,252,200	4,093,600	4,142,000	3,586,500
Current Liabilities	1,640,200	1,535,700	1,501,600	1,629,000	1,350,800	1,263,900	1,156,200	1,030,500
Long-Term Obligations	1,083,200	1,303,000	1,368,300	1,251,800	1,247,900	1,378,800	1,642,900	1,207,700
Total Liabilities	3,117,100	3,212,800	3,249,000	3,082,700	2,793,200	2,801,400	2,962,600	2,453,500
Stockholders' Equity	1,751,400	1,697,900	1,620,700	1,570,400	1,459,000	1,292,200	1,179,400	1,133,000
Shares Outstanding	34,194	34,085	34,071	33,862	33,657	33,437	33,278	33,141
Statistical Record								
Return on Assets %	4.29	4.08	3.57	3.52	2.62	2.93	3.31	6.06
Return on Equity %	12.29	11.98	10.49	10.35	7.95	9.78	11.07	18.08
EBITDA Margin %	5.11	4.99	4.48	4.39	4.75	4.48	4.75	5.87
Net Margin %	2.46	2.35	1.85	1.86	1.37	1.58	2.06	3.02
Asset Turnover	1.84	1.84	1.87	1.89	1.90	1.86	1.61	2.00
Current Ratio	1.91	2.08	2.10	1.95	2.10	2.13	2.36	2.51
Debt to Equity	0.62	0.77	0.84	0.80	0.86	1.07	1.39	1.07
Price Range	70.30-50.44	74.70-50.44	79.15-50.44	85.35-50.44	88.00-63.15	83.65-38.29	88.18-56.66	107.51-76.57
P/E Ratio	11.82-8.48	13.29-8.98	16.56-10.55	18.64-11.01	27.41-19.67	23.30-10.67	23.14-14.87	18.41-13.11

Address: 2301 Patriot Blvd., Glenview, IL 60026	**Web Site:** www.anixter.com	**Auditors:** Ernst & Young LLP
Telephone: 224-521-8000	**Officers:** Samuel (Sam) Zell - Chairman William A. (Bill) Galvin - President, Chief Executive Officer, Chief Operating Officer, Division Officer	**Investor Contact:** 224-521-8895
		Transfer Agents: Wells Fargo Shareowner Services, Mendota Heights, MN

ANNALY CAPITAL MANAGEMENT INC

Exchange	Symbol	Price	52Wk Range	Yield	P/E
NYS	NLY	$9.42 (12/31/2019)	10.47-8.19	11.15	N/A

*7 Year Price Score 71.63 *NYSE Composite Index=100 *12 Month Price Score 93.55

Interim Earnings (Per Share)

Qtr.	Mar	Jun	Sep	Dec
2016	(0.96)	(0.32)	0.70	1.89
2017	0.41	(0.01)	0.31	0.65
2018	1.12	0.49	0.29	(1.94)
2019	(0.63)	(1.24)	(0.54)	...

Interim Dividends (Per Share)

Amt	Decl	Ex	Rec	Pay
0.30Q	03/14/2019	03/28/2019	03/29/2019	04/30/2019
0.25Q	06/13/2019	06/27/2019	06/28/2019	07/31/2019
0.25Q	09/09/2019	09/27/2019	09/30/2019	10/31/2019
0.25Q	12/12/2019	12/30/2019	12/31/2019	01/31/2020

Indicated Div: $1.05 (Div. Reinv. Plan)

Valuation Analysis

Forecast EPS	$0.99
	(01/17/2020)
Market Cap	$13.5 Billion
Book Value	$15.2 Billion
Price/Book	0.89
Price/Sales	N/A

Institutional Holding

No of Institutions	947
Shares	968,016,960
% Held	70.61

Business Summary: REITs (MIC: 5.3.1 SIC: 6798 NAIC: 525930)

Annaly Capital Management is a real estate investment trust. Co. is externally managed by Annaly Management Company LLC. Co. is capital manager that invests in and finances residential and commercial assets. Co. owns a portfolio of real estate related investments, including mortgage pass-through certificates, collateralized mortgage obligations, credit risk transfer securities, other securities representing interests in or obligations backed by pools of mortgage loans, residential mortgage loans, and mortgage servicing rights. Co.'s investment groups include: Annaly Agency Group, Annaly Residential Credit Group, Annaly Commercial Real Estate Group, and Annaly Middle Market Lending Group.

Recent Developments: For the quarter ended Sep 30 2019, net loss amounted to US$747.2 million versus net income of US$385.4 million in the year-earlier quarter. Revenues were US$79.0 million, down 92.1% from US$1.01 billion the year before.

Prospects: Our evaluation of Annaly Capital Management Inc. as of October 4th, 2019 is the result of our systematic analysis on three basic characteristics: earnings strength, relative valuation, and recent stock price movement. The company has managed to produce a neutral trend in earnings per share over the past 5 quarters. In addition, recent analyst estimates for the company have been mixed and NLY has posted results that fell short of analysts' expectations. Based on operating earnings yield, the company is undervalued when compared to all of the companies we cover. Share price changes over the past year indicates that NLY will perform poorly over the near term.

Financial Data

(US$ in Thousands)	9 Mos	6 Mos	3 Mos	12/31/2018	12/31/2017	12/31/2016	12/31/2015	12/31/2014
Earnings Per Share	(4.35)	(3.52)	(1.79)	(0.06)	1.37	1.39	0.42	(0.96)
Cash Flow Per Share	(1.92)	(0.93)	0.25	2.17	6.50	7.05	(3.34)	6.47
Tang Book Value Per Share	8.87	8.98	9.25	8.89	10.75	10.41	11.62	13.00
Dividends Per Share	1.100	1.150	1.200	1.200	2.485	3.169	3.169	3.169
Dividend Payout %	...	...	...	...	181.40	227.97	754.46	...
Income Statement								
Interest Income	2,713,083	1,793,784	866,186	3,332,563	2,493,126	2,210,951	2,170,697	2,632,647
Interest Expense	2,164,817	1,397,912	647,695	1,897,860	1,008,354	657,752	471,596	512,659
Net Interest Income	548,266	395,872	218,491	1,434,703	1,484,772	1,553,199	1,699,101	2,119,988
Non-Interest Income	(3,703,057)	(2,862,725)	(981,424)	(1,053,057)	315,350	128,348	(1,035,068)	(2,747,604)
Non-Interest Expense	228,283	162,145	83,737	329,873	224,124	250,356	200,240	209,338
Income Before Taxes	(3,383,074)	(2,628,998)	(846,670)	51,773	1,575,998	1,431,191	463,793	(836,954)
Income Taxes	(10,241)	(3,334)	2,581	(2,375)	6,982	(1,595)	(1,954)	5,325
Net Income	(3,372,539)	(2,625,480)	(849,150)	54,408	1,569,604	1,433,756	466,556	(842,083)
Average Shares	1,453,359	1,456,038	1,398,614	1,209,601	1,066,351	970,102	947,276	947,539
Balance Sheet								
Net Loans & Leases	3,946,614	3,546,468	3,879,324	4,585,975	1,438,322	456,714	278,600	...
Total Assets	128,956,120	131,800,776	119,172,549	105,787,527	101,760,050	87,905,046	75,190,893	88,355,367
Total Liabilities	113,736,824	116,098,095	103,396,332	91,675,415	86,894,577	75,336,866	63,294,919	75,026,876
Stockholders' Equity	15,219,296	15,702,681	15,776,217	14,112,112	14,865,473	12,568,180	11,895,974	13,328,491
Shares Outstanding	1,437,964	1,456,263	1,448,103	1,313,763	1,159,585	1,018,913	935,929	947,643
Statistical Record								
Return on Assets %	N.M.	N.M.	N.M.	0.05	1.66	1.75	0.57	N.M.
Return on Equity %	N.M.	N.M.	N.M.	0.38	11.44	11.69	3.70	N.M.
Net Interest Margin %	16.58	19.12	25.22	43.05	59.55	70.25	78.27	80.53
Efficiency Ratio %	83.75	...	...	14.47	7.98	10.70	17.63	...
Price Range	10.47-8.19	10.72-8.81	10.72-9.71	11.67-9.71	12.66-10.08	11.25-8.69	11.04-9.06	11.92-9.97
P/E Ratio	...	...	...	...	9.24-7.36	8.09-6.25	26.29-21.57	...
Average Yield %	11.37	11.44	11.68	11.56	21.35	30.57	31.33	28.13

Address: 1211 Avenue of the Americas, New York, NY 10036 Telephone: 212-696-0100 Fax: 212-696-9809	Web Site: www.annaly.com Officers: Thomas Hamilton - Chairman Glenn A. Votek - President, Interim Chief Executive Officer, Chief Financial Officer	Auditors: Ernst & Young LLP Transfer Agents: Computershare Shareowner Services LLC, Jersey City, NJ

ANTHEM INC

Exchange	Symbol	Price	52Wk Range	Yield	P/E
NYS	ANTM	$302.03 (12/31/2019)	317.42-234.82	1.06	18.38

*7 Year Price Score 136.43 ***NYSE Composite Index=100** ***12 Month Price Score 98.01**

Interim Earnings (Per Share)

Qtr.	Mar	Jun	Sep	Dec
2016	2.63	2.91	2.30	1.37
2017	3.73	3.16	2.80	4.65
2018	4.99	3.98	3.62	1.61
2019	5.91	4.36	4.55	...

Interim Dividends (Per Share)

Amt	Decl	Ex	Rec	Pay
0.80Q	01/29/2019	03/15/2019	03/18/2019	03/29/2019
0.80Q	04/23/2019	06/07/2019	06/10/2019	06/25/2019
0.80Q	07/23/2019	09/09/2019	09/10/2019	09/25/2019
0.80Q	10/22/2019	12/04/2019	12/05/2019	12/20/2019

Indicated Div: $3.20

Valuation Analysis

Forecast EPS	$19.42
	(01/15/2020)
Market Cap	$76.6 Billion
Book Value	$31.3 Billion
Price/Book	2.45
Price/Sales	0.77

Institutional Holding

No of Institutions	1265
Shares	
258,901,984	
% Held	0.03

Business Summary: Life & Health (MIC: 5.2.2 SIC: 6324 NAIC: 524114)

Anthem is an insurance holding company. Co. provides network-based managed care plans to Large Group, Small Group, Individual, Medicaid and Medicare markets. Co.'s managed care plans include preferred provider organizations, health maintenance organizations, point-of-service plans, indemnity plans and other hybrid plans, and hospital only and limited benefit products. In addition, Co. provides managed care services to self-funded customers, including claims processing. Co. also provides other insurance products and services such as dental, vision, life and disability insurance benefits, as well as services to the federal government in connection with the Federal Employee Program®.

Recent Developments: For the quarter ended Sep 30 2019, net income increased 23.2% to US$1.18 billion from US$960.0 million in the year-earlier quarter. Revenues were US$26.67 billion, up 14.7% from US$23.25 billion the year before. Net premiums earned were US$23.79 billion versus US$21.45 billion in the prior-year quarter, an increase of 10.9%. Net investment income fell 3.2% to US$242.0 million from US$250.0 million a year ago.

Prospects: Our evaluation of Anthem Inc. as of October 4th, 2019 is the result of our systematic analysis on three basic characteristics: earnings strength, relative valuation, and recent stock price movement. The company has managed to produce a neutral trend in earnings per share over the past 5 quarters. In addition, recent analyst estimates for the company have been mixed and ANTM has posted results that exceeded analysts' expectations. Based on operating earnings yield, the company is undervalued when compared to all of the companies we cover. Share price changes over the past year indicates that ANTM will perform well over the near term.

Financial Data

(US$ in Thousands)	9 Mos	6 Mos	3 Mos	12/31/2018	12/31/2017	12/31/2016	12/31/2015	12/31/2014
Earnings Per Share	16.43	15.50	15.12	14.19	14.35	9.21	9.38	8.99
Cash Flow Per Share	20.36	16.12	12.61	14.83	16.00	12.16	15.65	12.21
Tang Book Value Per Share	8.18	5.68	2.23	N.M.	N.M.	N.M.	N.M.	N.M.
Dividends Per Share	3.150	3.100	3.050	3.000	2.700	2.600	2.500	1.750
Dividend Payout %	19.17	20.00	20.17	21.14	18.82	28.23	26.65	19.47
Income Statement								
Total Revenue	76,806,000	50,132,000	24,666,000	92,105,000	90,039,400	84,863,000	79,156,500	73,874,100
Income Before Taxes	4,887,000	3,398,000	1,945,000	5,068,000	3,963,800	4,555,400	4,631,000	4,368,100
Income Taxes	1,014,000	708,000	394,000	1,318,000	121,000	2,085,600	2,071,000	1,808,000
Net Income	3,873,000	2,690,000	1,551,000	3,750,000	3,842,800	2,469,800	2,560,000	2,569,700
Average Shares	260,000	261,000	262,300	264,200	267,800	268,100	272,900	285,900
Balance Sheet								
Total Assets	77,809,000	75,851,000	74,523,000	71,571,000	70,540,000	65,083,100	61,717,800	62,065,000
Total Liabilities	46,477,000	45,058,000	44,525,000	43,030,000	44,037,100	39,982,700	38,673,700	37,813,700
Stockholders' Equity	31,332,000	30,793,000	29,998,000	28,541,000	26,502,900	25,100,400	23,044,100	24,251,300
Shares Outstanding	253,780	255,876	257,354	257,395	256,084	263,747	261,238	268,109
Statistical Record								
Return on Assets %	5.65	5.43	5.40	5.28	5.67	3.88	4.14	4.23
Return on Equity %	14.23	13.69	14.00	13.63	14.89	10.23	10.83	10.49
Net Margin %	5.04	5.37	6.29	4.07	4.27	2.91	3.23	3.48
Price Range	317.42-236.25	317.42-236.25	317.42-220.13	296.25-215.63	234.96-142.79	147.66-117.22	171.04-123.26	129.16-84.25
P/E Ratio	19.32-14.38	20.48-15.24	20.99-14.56	20.88-15.20	16.37-9.95	16.03-12.73	18.23-13.14	14.37-9.37
Average Yield %	1.13	1.13	1.16	1.20	1.45	1.95	1.70	1.62

Address: 220 Virginia Avenue, Indianapolis, IN 46204 **Telephone:** 800-331-1476	**Web Site:** www.antheminc.com **Officers:** Elizabeth E. Tallett - Chairman Gail Koziara Boudreaux - President, Chief Executive Officer	**Auditors:** Ernst & Young LLP **Investor Contact:** 212-476-1473 **Transfer Agents:** EquiServe Trust Company, N.A., Providence, RI

ANTERO RESOURCES CORP

Exchange	Symbol	Price	52Wk Range	Yield	P/E
NYS	AR	$2.85 (12/31/2019)	10.94-1.94	N/A	47.50

*7 Year Price Score N/A   *NYSE Composite Index=100   *12 Month Price Score 40.09

Interim Earnings (Per Share)

Qtr.	Mar	Jun	Sep	Dec
2016	(0.02)	(2.12)	0.77	(1.62)
2017	0.85	(0.02)	(0.43)	1.53
2018	0.05	(0.43)	(0.49)	(0.39)
2019	3.17	0.14	(2.86)	...

Interim Dividends (Per Share)

No Dividends Paid

Valuation Analysis		Institutional Holding	
Forecast EPS	$-0.46	No of Institutions	
	(01/17/2020)	349	
Market Cap	$866.9 Million	Shares	
Book Value	$7.4 Billion	510,626,464	
Price/Book	0.12	% Held	
Price/Sales	0.19	92.21	

Business Summary: Production & Extraction (MIC: 9.1.1 SIC: 1311 NAIC: 211111)

Antero Resources is an oil and natural gas company engaged in the exploration, development and production of natural gas, natural gas liquids (NGLs), and oil properties located in the Appalachian Basin. Co. focuses on unconventional reservoirs, which can be characterized as fractured shale formations. Co.'s drilling operations are focused in the Marcellus Shale and Utica Shale of the Appalachian Basin. Co. operates in the following industry segments: the exploration, development and production of natural gas, NGLs, and oil; gathering and processing; water handling and treatment; and marketing of excess firm transportation capacity. All of Co.'s operations are conducted in the U.S.

Recent Developments: For the quarter ended Sep 30 2019, net loss amounted to US$878.9 million versus a net loss of US$78.0 million in the year-earlier quarter. Revenues were US$1.12 billion, up 3.9% from US$1.08 billion the year before. Operating loss was US$985.9 million versus an income of US$4.8 million in the prior-year quarter. Direct operating expenses rose 42.5% to US$776.9 million from US$545.1 million in the comparable period the year before. Indirect operating expenses increased 152.1% to US$1.33 billion from US$526.7 million in the equivalent prior-year period.

Prospects: Our evaluation of Antero Resources Corp as of October 4th, 2019 is the result of our systematic analysis on three basic characteristics: earnings strength, relative valuation, and recent stock price movement. The company has suffered a very negative trend in earnings per share over the past 5 quarters. However, recent analyst estimates for the company have been mixed and AR has posted results that fell short of analysts' expectations. Based on operating earnings yield, the company is undervalued when compared to all of the companies we cover. Share price changes over the past year indicates that AR will perform well over the near term.

Financial Data
(US$ in Thousands)

	9 Mos	6 Mos	3 Mos	12/31/2018	12/31/2017	12/31/2016	12/31/2015	12/31/2014
Earnings Per Share	0.06	2.43	1.86	(1.26)	1.94	(2.88)	3.43	2.57
Cash Flow Per Share	5.77	6.47	6.74	6.59	6.36	4.20	3.67	3.81
Tang Book Value Per Share	24.48	26.98	26.86	24.84	25.76	19.89	21.42	16.73
Income Statement								
Total Revenue	3,455,952	2,337,071	1,037,407	4,139,626	3,655,574	1,744,525	3,954,858	2,720,632
EBITDA	1,213,280	1,956,728	1,613,512	80,905	748,593	(983,857)	1,797,986	1,758,515
Depn & Amortn	726,827	484,397	241,177	9,000	10,000	8,900	7,700	479,167
Income Before Taxes	312,585	1,346,217	1,300,385	(214,838)	469,892	(1,246,309)	1,555,886	1,119,297
Income Taxes	33,332	305,959	288,710	(128,857)	(295,051)	(496,376)	575,890	445,672
Net Income	142,067	1,020,931	978,763	(397,517)	615,070	(848,816)	941,364	673,587
Average Shares	307,781	309,137	308,788	316,036	316,283	294,945	274,143	262,068
Balance Sheet								
Current Assets	729,500	713,049	544,896	806,613	833,087	402,587	1,248,236	1,252,160
Total Assets	16,120,288	17,330,880	17,288,730	15,519,464	15,261,490	14,255,550	14,155,224	11,573,495
Current Liabilities	1,171,168	1,221,107	1,266,781	853,540	762,096	817,388	707,270	1,155,105
Long-Term Obligations	3,703,828	3,602,379	3,475,950	5,461,688	4,800,090	4,703,973	4,708,513	4,362,550
Total Liabilities	8,673,590	8,991,180	8,995,932	7,853,656	7,112,309	7,992,925	8,220,832	7,189,702
Stockholders' Equity	7,446,698	8,339,700	8,292,798	7,665,808	8,149,181	6,262,625	5,934,392	4,383,793
Shares Outstanding	304,161	309,123	308,741	308,594	316,379	314,877	277,035	262,071
Statistical Record								
Return on Assets %	0.13	4.51	3.46	N.M.	4.17	N.M.	7.32	7.41
Return on Equity %	0.27	9.09	6.88	N.M.	8.54	N.M.	18.25	16.88
EBITDA Margin %	35.11	83.73	155.53	1.95	20.48	N.M.	45.46	64.64
Net Margin %	4.11	43.68	94.35	N.M.	16.83	N.M.	23.80	24.76
Asset Turnover	0.28	0.27	0.25	0.27	0.25	0.12	0.31	0.30
Current Ratio	0.62	0.58	0.43	0.95	1.09	0.49	1.76	1.08
Debt to Equity	0.50	0.43	0.42	0.71	0.59	0.75	0.79	1.00
Price Range	19.48-2.80	22.44-5.37	22.44-7.81	22.44-9.08	26.16-17.65	30.10-19.77	45.65-19.12	67.41-38.60
P/E Ratio	324.67-46.67	9.23-2.21	12.06-4.20	...	13.48-9.10	...	13.31-5.57	26.23-15.02

Address: 1615 Wynkoop Street, Denver, CO 80202 **Telephone:** 303-357-7310	**Web Site:** www.anteroresources.com **Officers:** Paul M. Rady - Chairman, Chief Executive Officer Glen C. Warren - President, Chief Financial Officer, Secretary	**Auditors:** KPMG LLP **Transfer Agents:** American Stock Transfer & Trust Company, LLC

APACHE CORP

Exchange	Symbol	Price	52Wk Range	Yield	P/E
NYS	APA	$25.59 (12/31/2019)	37.09-18.38	3.91	N/A

*7 Year Price Score 40.44   *NYSE Composite Index=100   *12 Month Price Score 78.96

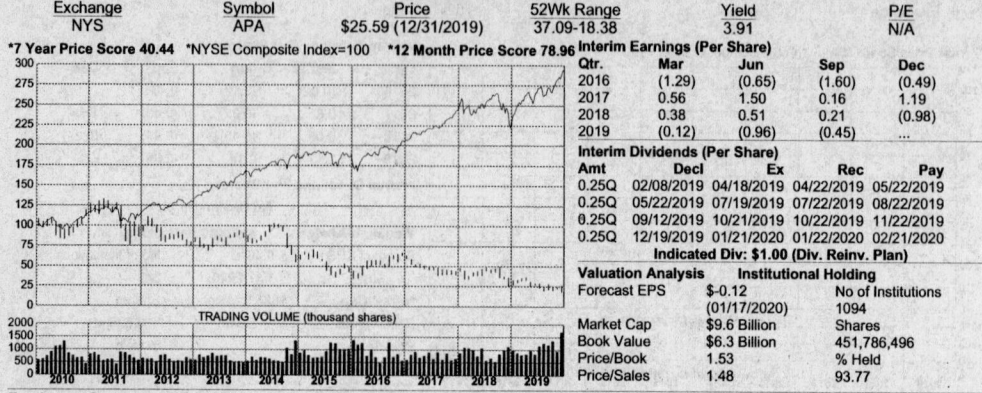

Interim Earnings (Per Share)

Qtr.	Mar	Jun	Sep	Dec
2016	(1.29)	(0.65)	(1.60)	(0.49)
2017	0.56	1.50	0.16	1.19
2018	0.38	0.51	0.21	(0.98)
2019	(0.12)	(0.96)	(0.45)	...

Interim Dividends (Per Share)

Amt	Decl	Ex	Rec	Pay
0.25Q	02/08/2019	04/18/2019	04/22/2019	05/22/2019
0.25Q	05/22/2019	07/19/2019	07/22/2019	08/22/2019
0.25Q	09/12/2019	10/21/2019	10/22/2019	11/22/2019
0.25Q	12/19/2019	01/21/2020	01/22/2020	02/21/2020

Indicated Div: $1.00 (Div. Reinv. Plan)

Valuation Analysis

Institutional Holding	
Forecast EPS	$-0.12
	(01/17/2020)
Market Cap	$9.6 Billion
Book Value	$6.3 Billion
Price/Book	1.53
Price/Sales	1.48

No of Institutions
1094
Shares
451,786,496
% Held
93.77

Business Summary: Production & Extraction (MIC: 9.1.1 SIC: 1311 NAIC: 211111)

Apache is an independent energy company that explores for, develops, and produces natural gas, crude oil, and natural gas liquids. Co. had exploration and production operations in three geographic areas: the U.S., Egypt, and offshore the U.K. in the North Sea. Co. also has exploration interests in Suriname.

Recent Developments: For the quarter ended Sep 30 2019, net loss amounted to US$117.0 million versus net income of US$161.0 million in the year-earlier quarter. Revenues were US$1.48 billion, down 25.5% from US$1.98 billion the year before. Direct operating expenses declined 12.2% to US$416.0 million from US$474.0 million in the comparable period the year before. Indirect operating expenses decreased 5.1% to US$1.05 billion from US$1.10 billion in the equivalent prior-year period.

Prospects: Our evaluation of Apache Corp. as of October 4th, 2019 is the result of our systematic analysis on three basic characteristics: earnings strength, relative valuation, and recent stock price movement. The company has suffered a very negative trend in earnings per share over the past 5 quarters. However, recent analyst estimates for the company have been mixed and APA has posted results that exceeded analysts' expectations. Based on operating earnings yield, the company is overvalued when compared to all of the companies we cover. Share price changes over the past year indicates that APA will perform very poorly over the near term.

Financial Data

(US$ in Thousands)	9 Mos	6 Mos	3 Mos	12/31/2018	12/31/2017	12/31/2016	12/31/2015	12/31/2014
Earnings Per Share	(2.51)	(1.85)	(0.38)	0.11	3.41	(3.71)	(61.20)	(14.06)
Cash Flow Per Share	8.31	9.29	10.00	9.89	6.37	6.39	7.89	22.03
Tang Book Value Per Share	16.76	17.42	18.59	19.03	19.47	16.44	6.79	68.66
Dividends Per Share	1.000	1.000	1.000	1.000	1.000	1.000	1.000	0.950
Dividend Payout %	...	...	...	909.09	29.33	...	...	...
Income Statement								
Total Revenue	4,715,000	3,238,000	1,635,000	7,424,000	6,423,000	5,354,000	6,366,000	13,851,000
EBITDA	2,276,000	1,456,000	908,000	3,747,000	3,594,000	1,352,000	1,406,000	7,382,000
Depn & Amortn	1,959,000	1,248,000	646,000	2,405,000	2,280,000	2,618,000	29,372,000	10,158,000
Income Before Taxes	27,000	13,000	165,000	958,000	918,000	(1,682,000)	(28,226,000)	(2,906,000)
Income Taxes	462,000	331,000	167,000	672,000	(585,000)	(442,000)	(5,469,000)	1,637,000
Net Income	(577,000)	(407,000)	(47,000)	40,000	1,304,000	(1,405,000)	(23,119,000)	(5,403,000)
Average Shares	377,000	377,000	376,000	384,000	383,000	379,000	378,000	384,000
Balance Sheet								
Current Assets	1,971,000	2,791,000	2,504,000	2,687,000	3,725,000	3,241,000	3,752,000	6,415,000
Total Assets	21,405,000	21,806,000	21,751,000	21,582,000	21,922,000	22,519,000	18,842,000	55,952,000
Current Liabilities	1,921,000	2,262,000	2,374,000	2,201,000	2,564,000	1,843,000	1,841,000	3,664,000
Long-Term Obligations	8,393,000	8,157,000	8,094,000	8,054,000	7,934,000	8,544,000	8,777,000	11,245,000
Total Liabilities	15,104,000	15,255,000	14,762,000	14,452,000	14,506,000	16,281,000	16,276,000	30,015,000
Stockholders' Equity	6,301,000	6,551,000	6,989,000	7,130,000	7,416,000	6,238,000	2,566,000	25,937,000
Shares Outstanding	376,022	375,956	375,910	374,696	380,954	379,439	378,034	376,504
Statistical Record								
Return on Assets %	N.M.	N.M.	N.M.	0.18	5.87	N.M.	N.M.	N.M.
Return on Equity %	N.M.	N.M.	N.M.	0.55	19.10	N.M.	N.M.	N.M.
EBITDA Margin %	48.27	44.97	55.54	50.47	55.96	25.25	22.09	53.30
Net Margin %	N.M.	N.M.	N.M.	0.54	20.30	N.M.	N.M.	N.M.
Asset Turnover	0.30	0.32	0.34	0.34	0.29	0.26	0.17	0.24
Current Ratio	1.03	1.23	1.05	1.22	1.45	1.76	2.04	1.75
Debt to Equity	1.33	1.25	1.16	1.13	1.07	1.37	3.42	0.43
Price Range	49.30-19.93	49.30-25.40	49.30-25.40	49.30-25.40	63.78-38.37	67.35-34.38	71.40-36.20	103.48-55.20
P/E Ratio	...	...	...	448.18-230.91	18.70-11.25	...	...	...
Average Yield %	3.22	2.75	2.56	2.44	2.09	1.87	1.84	1.11

Address: One Post Oak Central, 2000 Post Oak Boulevard, Suite 100, Houston, TX 77056-4400 **Telephone:** 713-296-6000	**Web Site:** www.apachecorp.com **Officers:** John J. Christmann - President, Chief Executive Officer, Vice President, Region Officer P. Anthony Lannie - Executive Vice President, General Counsel, Interim Chief Financial Officer	**Auditors:** Ernst & Young LLP **Investor Contact:** 281-302-2286 **Transfer Agents:** Wells Fargo Bank, N.A., South St. Paul, MN

APARTMENT INVESTMENT & MANAGEMENT CO

Exchange	Symbol	Price	52Wk Range	Yield	P/E
NYS	AIV	$51.65 (12/31/2019)	55.23-43.67	N/A	21.98

*7 Year Price Score 102.47 *NYSE Composite Index=100 *12 Month Price Score 98.51

Interim Earnings (Per Share)

Qtr.	Mar	Jun	Sep	Dec
2016	0.15	1.45	0.07	1.06
2017	0.07	0.10	0.11	1.72
2018	0.54	0.02	3.72	0.06
2019	1.88	0.40	0.01	...

Interim Dividends (Per Share)

Amt	Decl	Ex	Rec	Pay
0.38Q	05/02/2018	05/17/2018	05/18/2018	05/31/2018
0.38Q	08/01/2018	08/16/2018	08/17/2018	08/31/2018
0.38Q	10/31/2018	11/15/2018	11/16/2018	11/30/2018
1-for-1.03119	...	02/21/2019	...	...

Valuation Analysis

		Institutional Holding	
Forecast EPS	$2.49	No of Institutions	
	(01/17/2020)	560	
Market Cap	$7.7 Billion	Shares	
Book Value	$1.7 Billion	197,666,160	
Price/Book	4.51	% Held	
Price/Sales	8.39	N/A	

Business Summary: REITs (MIC: 5.3.1 SIC: 6798 NAIC: 525930)

Apartment Investment and Management is a self-administered and self-managed real estate investment trust, focused on the ownership, management, redevelopment and limited development of apartment communities located in the U.S. Co., through its wholly-owned subsidiaries, AIMCO-GP, Inc. and AIMCO-LP Trust, owns a majority of the ownership interests in AIMCO Properties, L.P. (the Aimco Operating Partnership). Co. conducts all of its business and owns all of its assets through the Aimco Operating Partnership. Co.'s Real Estate portfolio includes garden style, apartment communities located in various states and the District of Columbia.

Recent Developments: For the quarter ended Sep 30 2019, net income decreased 99.3% to US$4.0 million from US$603.9 million in the year-earlier quarter. Revenues were US$229.8 million, down 5.2% from US$242.5 million the year before. Revenues from property income fell 100.0% to nil from US$234.0 million in the corresponding quarter a year earlier.

Prospects: Our evaluation of Apartment Investment & Management Co. as of October 4th, 2019 is the result of our systematic analysis on three basic characteristics: earnings strength, relative valuation, and recent stock price movement. The company has produced a positive trend in earnings per share over the past 5 quarters. However, recent analyst estimates for the company have been mixed and AIV has posted results that fell short of analysts' expectations. Based on operating earnings yield, the company is overvalued when compared to all of the companies we cover. Share price changes over the past year indicates that AIV will perform well over the near term.

Financial Data

(US$ in Thousands)	9 Mos	6 Mos	3 Mos	12/31/2018	12/31/2017	12/31/2016	12/31/2015	12/31/2014
Earnings Per Share	2.35	6.06	5.69	4.34	2.02	2.75	1.57	2.12
Cash Flow Per Share	2.51	2.57	2.75	2.62	2.60	2.49	2.39	2.28
Tang Book Value Per Share	11.45	11.85	11.82	10.89	10.09	10.97	9.65	7.34
Dividends Per Share	2.800	2.410	2.020	1.567	1.485	1.361	1.217	1.072
Dividend Payout %	119.05	39.74	35.53	36.10	73.47	49.44	77.63	50.48
Income Statement								
Total Revenue	684,262	454,435	230,235	972,410	1,005,437	995,854	981,310	984,363
EBITDA	760,692	623,093	426,524	1,280,105	573,527	590,993	568,089	547,943
Depn & Amortn	283,027	185,489	93,565	386,809	371,850	338,126	311,487	286,422
Income Before Taxes	363,319	362,445	294,276	703,576	15,394	64,275	63,866	47,428
Income Taxes	(1,942)	1,154	2,981	(13,027)	(32,126)	(25,208)	(27,524)	(20,047)
Net Income	340,571	338,592	274,133	666,227	315,774	430,410	248,710	309,249
Average Shares	148,636	148,599	144,445	151,332	152,053	151,660	150,864	141,585
Balance Sheet								
Current Assets	93,225	65,907	198,389	72,595	142,541	131,150	137,745	120,416
Total Assets	6,539,178	6,240,804	6,283,769	6,190,004	6,079,040	6,232,818	6,144,194	6,097,028
Current Liabilities	...	...	...	...	...	36,677	36,123	41,919
Long-Term Obligations	4,254,710	3,997,447	3,929,023	4,075,665	4,088,911	3,884,632	3,873,160	4,135,139
Total Liabilities	4,833,719	4,477,586	4,400,133	4,490,585	4,415,896	4,438,915	4,521,803	4,869,293
Stockholders' Equity	1,705,459	1,763,218	1,883,636	1,699,419	1,663,144	1,793,903	1,622,391	1,227,735
Shares Outstanding	148,884	148,827	148,758	144,623	152,434	152,143	151,598	141,975
Statistical Record								
Return on Assets %	5.47	14.33	13.66	10.86	5.13	6.94	4.06	5.08
Return on Equity %	18.17	54.23	48.21	39.63	18.27	25.13	17.45	28.18
EBITDA Margin %	111.17	137.11	185.26	131.64	57.04	59.35	57.89	55.66
Net Margin %	49.77	74.51	119.07	68.51	31.41	43.22	25.34	31.42
Asset Turnover	0.14	0.15	0.15	0.16	0.16	0.16	0.16	0.16
Current Ratio	...	...	...	...	...	3.58	3.81	2.87
Debt to Equity	2.49	2.27	2.09	2.40	2.46	2.17	2.39	3.37
Price Range	52.35-43.16	51.69-42.78	51.42-39.87	48.83-39.19	47.98-43.74	49.07-36.56	42.47-35.94	39.52-26.52
P/E Ratio	22.28-18.36	8.53-7.06	9.04-7.01	11.25-9.03	23.75-21.65	17.85-13.29	27.05-22.89	18.64-12.51
Average Yield %	5.71	5.07	4.45	3.60	3.24	3.14	3.07	3.22

Address: 4582 South Ulster Street, Suite 1700, Denver, CO 80237 **Telephone:** 303-757-8101 **Fax:** 303-759-3226	**Web Site:** www.aimco.com **Officers:** Terry Considine - Chairman, Chief Executive Officer Paul L. Beldin - Executive Vice President, Chief Financial Officer, Senior Vice President, Chief Accounting Officer	**Auditors:** Ernst & Young LLP **Investor Contact:** 303-691-4350 **Transfer Agents:** Computershare Trust Company, N.A., Providence, RI

APPLE HOSPITALITY REIT INC

Exchange	Symbol	Price	52Wk Range	Yield	P/E
NYS	APLE	$16.25 (12/31/2019)	16.79-14.20	7.38	20.06

*7 Year Price Score N/A *NYSE Composite Index=100 *12 Month Price Score 95.40

Interim Earnings (Per Share)

Qtr.	Mar	Jun	Sep	Dec
2016	0.20	0.31	0.07	0.19
2017	0.15	0.39	0.28	(0.01)
2018	0.18	0.29	0.27	0.15
2019	0.17	0.28	0.21	...

Interim Dividends (Per Share)

Amt	Decl	Ex	Rec	Pay
0.10M	09/19/2019	10/01/2019	10/02/2019	10/15/2019
0.10M	10/21/2019	11/01/2019	11/04/2019	11/18/2019
0.10M	11/21/2019	12/02/2019	12/03/2019	12/16/2019
0.10M	12/19/2019	01/02/2020	01/03/2020	01/15/2020

Indicated Div: $1.20

Valuation Analysis

		Institutional Holding	
Forecast EPS	$0.79	No of Institutions	
	(01/17/2020)	306	
Market Cap	$3.6 Billion	Shares	
Book Value	$3.3 Billion	157,203,600	
Price/Book	1.09	% Held	
Price/Sales	2.86	60.38	

Business Summary: REITs (MIC: 5.3.1 SIC: 6798 NAIC: 525930)

Apple Hospitality REIT is a real estate investment trust that invests in real estate, primarily in the lodging sector, in the U.S. Co. owns hotels located in urban, suburban and developing markets throughout several states. All of Co.'s hotels operate under Marriott, Hilton or Hyatt brands. The hotels are operated and managed under separate management agreements with hotel management companies, none of which are affiliated with Co.

Recent Developments: For the quarter ended Sep 30 2019, net income decreased 25.6% to US$46.2 million from US$62.1 million in the year-earlier quarter. Revenues were US$331.7 million, down 0.1% from US$332.2 million the year before. Revenues from property income fell 0.2% to US$307.3 million from US$307.8 million in the corresponding quarter a year earlier.

Prospects: Our evaluation of Apple Hospitality REIT Inc as of October 4th, 2019 is the result of our systematic analysis on three basic characteristics: earnings strength, relative valuation, and recent stock price movement. The company has managed to produce a neutral trend in earnings per share over the past 5 quarters. However, recent analyst estimates for the company have been raised and APLE has posted results that fell short of analysts' expectations. Based on operating earnings yield, the company is fairly valued when compared to all of the companies we cover. Share price changes over the past year indicates that APLE will perform in line with the market over the near term.

Financial Data

(US$ in Thousands)	9 Mos	6 Mos	3 Mos	12/31/2018	12/31/2017	12/31/2016	12/31/2015	12/31/2014
Earnings Per Share	0.81	0.87	0.88	0.90	0.82	0.76	0.65	0.04
Cash Flow Per Share	1.78	1.80	1.82	1.76	1.72	1.73	1.56	1.47
Tang Book Value Per Share	14.86	14.97	15.04	15.22	15.53	15.78	15.18	16.13
Dividends Per Share	1.200	1.100	1.200	1.300	1.100	1.200	0.800	...
Dividend Payout %	148.15	126.44	136.36	144.44	134.15	157.89	123.08	...
Income Statement								
Total Revenue	976,626	644,904	303,787	1,270,555	1,238,622	1,041,025	898,314	803,896
EBITDA	337,025	228,013	101,801	441,340	407,181	333,272	278,767	145,437
Depn & Amortn	143,946	96,059	47,950	183,482	176,499	148,163	127,449	113,112
Income Before Taxes	146,969	100,603	38,357	206,673	183,339	145,083	118,186	8,802
Income Taxes	505	362	206	587	847	431	898	1,969
Net Income	146,464	100,241	38,151	206,086	182,492	144,652	117,288	6,833
Average Shares	223,901	223,899	223,932	229,659	223,526	190,856	180,261	171,488
Balance Sheet								
Current Assets	...	...	...	33,632	29,791	29,425	22,651	32,526
Total Assets	4,990,427	4,988,839	5,024,387	4,928,672	4,902,338	4,979,883	3,722,775	3,779,749
Current Liabilities	107,763	88,949	88,926	107,420	109,057	124,856	77,614	55,555
Long-Term Obligations	1,555,728	1,547,822	1,568,434	1,412,242	1,222,196	1,337,963	998,103	709,570
Total Liabilities	1,663,491	1,636,771	1,657,360	1,519,662	1,331,253	1,462,819	1,075,717	765,125
Stockholders' Equity	3,326,936	3,352,068	3,367,027	3,409,010	3,571,085	3,517,064	2,647,058	3,014,624
Shares Outstanding	223,856	223,869	223,868	223,997	229,961	222,938	174,368	186,910
Statistical Record								
Return on Assets %	3.63	3.93	4.04	4.19	3.69	3.32	3.13	0.26
Return on Equity %	5.25	5.69	5.84	5.90	5.15	4.68	4.14	0.32
EBITDA Margin %	34.51	35.36	33.51	34.74	32.87	32.01	31.03	18.09
Net Margin %	15.00	15.54	12.56	16.22	14.73	13.90	13.06	0.85
Asset Turnover	0.26	0.25	0.26	0.26	0.25	0.24	0.24	0.31
Current Ratio	...	...	...	0.31	0.27	0.24	0.29	0.59
Debt to Equity	0.47	0.46	0.47	0.41	0.34	0.38	0.38	0.24
Price Range	17.39-13.85	18.36-13.85	19.21-13.85	20.12-13.85	20.64-17.59	20.59-17.26	20.68-16.38	...
P/E Ratio	21.47-17.10	21.10-15.92	21.83-15.74	22.36-15.39	25.17-21.45	27.09-22.71	31.82-25.20	...
Average Yield %	7.51	6.68	7.06	7.40	5.77	6.32	4.23	...

Address: 814 East Main Street, Richmond, VA 23219 **Telephone:** 804-344-8121	**Web Site:** www.applehospitalityreit.com **Officers:** Glade M. Knight - Executive Chairman, Chief Executive Officer Justin G. Knight - President, Chief Executive Officer	**Auditors:** Ernst & Young LLP

APTARGROUP INC.

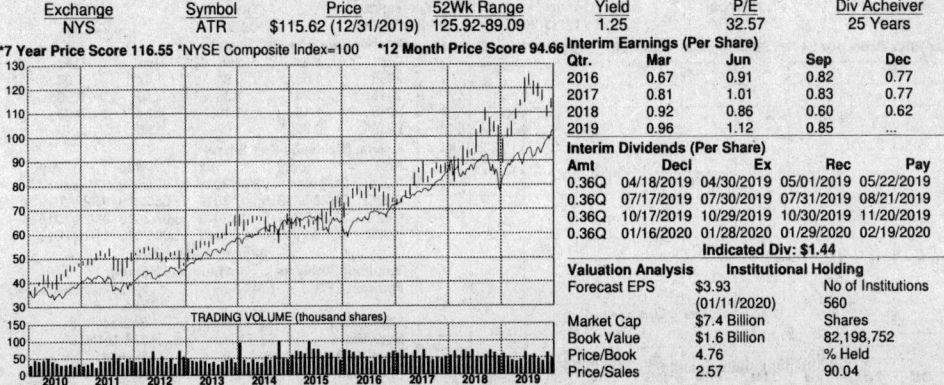

Exchange	Symbol	Price	52Wk Range	Yield	P/E	Div Acheiver
NYS	ATR	$115.62 (12/31/2019)	125.92-89.09	1.25	32.57	25 Years

7 Year Price Score 116.55 *NYSE Composite Index=100* **12 Month Price Score 94.66**

Interim Earnings (Per Share)

Qtr.	Mar	Jun	Sep	Dec
2016	0.67	0.91	0.82	0.77
2017	0.81	1.01	0.83	0.77
2018	0.92	0.86	0.60	0.62
2019	0.96	1.12	0.85	...

Interim Dividends (Per Share)

Amt	Decl	Ex	Rec	Pay
0.36Q	04/18/2019	04/30/2019	05/01/2019	05/22/2019
0.36Q	07/17/2019	07/30/2019	07/31/2019	08/21/2019
0.36Q	10/17/2019	10/29/2019	10/30/2019	11/20/2019
0.36Q	01/16/2020	01/28/2020	01/29/2020	02/19/2020

Indicated Div: $1.44

Valuation Analysis | **Institutional Holding**

Forecast EPS	$3.93 (01/11/2020)	No of Institutions 560
Market Cap	$7.4 Billion	Shares
Book Value	$1.6 Billion	82,198,752
Price/Book	4.76	% Held
Price/Sales	2.57	90.04

Business Summary: Plastics (MIC: 8.4.2 SIC: 3089 NAIC: 326199)

AptarGroup is a supplier of a range of dispensing, sealing and active packaging solutions for the beauty, personal care, home care, prescription drug, consumer health care, injectables, food and beverage markets. Co.'s primary products are dispensing pumps, which dispense a spray or lotion from non-pressurized containers; closures, which are plastic caps that allow a product to be dispensed without removing the cap; aerosol valves, which dispense product from pressurized containers; and elastomeric primary packaging components, which include stoppers for infusion, antibiotic, lyophilization and diagnostic vials, pre-filled syringe components, as well as dropper bulbs and syringe plungers.

Recent Developments: For the quarter ended Sep 30 2019, net income increased 45.5% to US$56.8 million from US$39.0 million in the year-earlier quarter. Revenues were US$701.3 million, up 5.3% from US$665.8 million the year before. Operating income was US$90.2 million versus US$61.1 million in the prior-year quarter, an increase of 47.7%. Direct operating expenses rose 2.0% to US$444.2 million from US$435.4 million in the comparable period the year before. Indirect operating expenses decreased 1.5% to US$166.8 million from US$169.3 million in the equivalent prior-year period.

Prospects: Our evaluation of AptarGroup Inc. as of October 4th, 2019 is the result of our systematic analysis on three basic characteristics: earnings strength, relative valuation, and recent stock price movement. The company has managed to produce a neutral trend in earnings per share over the past 5 quarters. However, recent analyst estimates for the company have been reduced while ATR has posted results that exceeded analysts' expectations. Based on operating earnings yield, the company is fairly valued when compared to all of the companies we cover. Share price changes over the past year indicates that ATR will perform over the near term.

Financial Data (US$ in Thousands)	9 Mos	6 Mos	3 Mos	12/31/2018	12/31/2017	12/31/2016	12/31/2015	12/31/2014
Earnings Per Share	3.55	3.30	3.04	3.00	3.41	3.17	3.09	2.85
Cash Flow Per Share	7.57	5.99	5.40	5.02	5.20	5.20	5.19	4.84
Tang Book Value Per Share	8.95	9.10	8.19	7.24	12.49	10.81	12.89	11.85
Dividends Per Share	1.400	1.380	1.340	1.320	1.280	1.220	1.140	1.090
Dividend Payout %	39.44	41.82	44.08	44.00	37.54	38.49	36.89	38.25
Income Statement								
Total Revenue	2,188,399	1,487,121	744,460	2,764,761	2,469,283	2,330,934	2,317,149	2,597,809
EBITDA	441,925	302,731	145,049	448,111	472,936	458,767	458,955	451,343
Depn & Amortn	144,574	95,356	47,489	156,292	142,755	145,485	134,647	146,893
Income Before Taxes	274,221	192,186	90,094	266,249	295,054	280,688	295,289	288,218
Income Taxes	80,684	55,180	27,000	71,254	74,796	74,893	95,276	94,677
Net Income	193,669	136,919	63,004	194,745	220,030	205,590	199,348	191,658
Average Shares	66,702	66,232	65,349	64,958	64,596	64,849	64,492	67,292
Balance Sheet								
Current Assets	1,324,728	1,418,541	1,329,445	1,330,808	1,670,073	1,270,170	1,294,994	1,213,938
Total Assets	3,465,139	3,588,716	3,415,634	3,377,735	3,137,823	2,606,785	2,438,726	2,437,190
Current Liabilities	648,837	670,934	623,916	689,170	527,748	542,955	411,900	604,738
Long-Term Obligations	1,075,153	1,148,261	1,141,062	1,125,993	1,191,146	772,737	762,524	588,892
Total Liabilities	1,911,483	2,007,610	1,948,238	1,955,179	1,826,085	1,432,835	1,289,315	1,333,783
Stockholders' Equity	1,553,656	1,581,106	1,467,396	1,422,556	1,311,738	1,173,950	1,149,411	1,103,407
Shares Outstanding	63,900	64,000	63,100	62,916	61,860	62,146	62,516	61,931
Statistical Record								
Return on Assets %	6.82	6.36	5.92	5.98	7.66	8.13	8.18	7.77
Return on Equity %	15.91	14.79	13.82	14.24	17.70	17.65	17.70	14.84
EBITDA Margin %	20.19	20.36	19.48	16.21	19.15	19.68	19.81	17.37
Net Margin %	8.85	9.21	8.46	7.04	8.91	8.82	8.60	7.38
Asset Turnover	0.84	0.83	0.84	0.85	0.86	0.92	0.95	1.05
Current Ratio	2.04	2.11	2.13	1.93	3.16	2.34	3.14	2.01
Debt to Equity	0.69	0.73	0.78	0.79	0.91	0.66	0.66	0.53
Price Range	125.92-89.09	124.34-89.09	111.97-87.93	111.97-81.38	90.09-71.64	80.46-66.70	75.72-61.38	68.38-56.18
P/E Ratio	35.47-25.10	37.68-27.00	36.83-28.92	37.32-27.13	26.42-21.01	25.38-21.04	24.50-19.86	23.99-19.71
Average Yield %	1.28	1.32	1.35	1.37	1.55	1.61	1.71	1.69

Address: 265 Exchange Drive, Suite 100, Crystal Lake, IL 60014 **Telephone:** 815-477-0424 **Fax:** 815-477-0481	**Web Site:** www.aptar.com **Officers:** George L. Fotiades - Chairman Heidi Tlili - Division Officer	**Auditors:** PricewaterhouseCoopers LLP **Investor Contact:** 815-477-0424 **Transfer Agents:** Wells Fargo Shareowner Services, South St. Paul, MN

APTIV PLC

Exchange	Symbol	Price	52Wk Range	Yield	P/E
NYS	APTV	$94.97 (12/31/2019)	97.86-60.42	0.93	24.48

*7 Year Price Score 102.34 ***NYSE Composite Index=100** ***12 Month Price Score 107.71**

Interim Earnings (Per Share)

Qtr.	Mar	Jun	Sep	Dec
2016	1.53	0.94	1.07	1.03
2017	1.24	1.38	1.48	0.96
2018	1.15	1.10	0.84	0.93
2019	0.92	1.07	0.96	...

Interim Dividends (Per Share)

Amt	Decl	Ex	Rec	Pay
0.22Q	01/24/2019	02/05/2019	02/06/2019	02/20/2019
0.22Q	04/25/2019	05/07/2019	05/08/2019	05/22/2019
0.22Q	07/25/2019	08/06/2019	08/07/2019	08/21/2019
0.22Q	10/24/2019	11/05/2019	11/06/2019	11/20/2019

Indicated Div: $0.88

Valuation Analysis

		Institutional Holding	
Forecast EPS	N/A	No of Institutions	734
Market Cap	$24.3 Billion	Shares	275,161,856
Book Value	$3.6 Billion	% Held	N/A
Price/Book	6.81		
Price/Sales	1.69		

Business Summary: Auto Parts (MIC: 1.8.2 SIC: 3714 NAIC: 336399)

Aptiv is a technology and mobility company primarily serving the automotive sector. Co. designs and manufactures vehicle components and provide electrical, electronic and active safety technology solutions to the global automotive and commercial vehicle markets, creating the software and hardware foundation for vehicle features and functionality. Co.'s Signal and Power Solutions segment provides design, manufacture and assembly of the vehicle's electrical architecture, including engineered component products. Co.'s Advanced Safety and User Experience segment provides components, systems and advanced software development for passenger safety, security, comfort and vehicle operation.

Recent Developments: For the quarter ended Sep 30 2019, net income increased 9.1% to US$252.0 million from US$231.0 million in the year-earlier quarter. Revenues were US$3.56 billion, up 2.1% from US$3.49 billion the year before. Operating income was US$320.0 million versus US$323.0 million in the prior-year quarter, a decrease of 0.9%. Direct operating expenses rose 1.7% to US$2.88 billion from US$2.83 billion in the comparable period the year before. Indirect operating expenses increased 8.8% to US$357.0 million from US$328.0 million in the equivalent prior-year period.

Prospects: Our evaluation of Aptiv PLC as of October 4th, 2019 is the result of our systematic analysis on three basic characteristics: earnings strength, relative valuation, and recent stock price movement. The company has produced a positive trend in earnings per share over the past 5 quarters. However, recent analyst estimates for the company have been reduced, while APTV has posted results that exceeded analysts' expectations. Based on operating earnings yield, the company is undervalued when compared to all of the companies we cover. Share price changes over the past year indicates that APTV will perform in line with the market over the near term.

Financial Data

(US$ in Millions)	9 Mos	6 Mos	3 Mos	12/31/2018	12/31/2017	12/31/2016	12/31/2015	12/31/2014
Earnings Per Share	3.88	3.76	3.79	4.02	5.06	4.59	5.06	4.48
Cash Flow Per Share	6.56	5.93	6.01	6.16	5.49	7.09	5.97	7.11
Tang Book Value Per Share	1.18	N.M.	N.M.	N.M.	0.51	N.M.	N.M.	3.80
Dividends Per Share	0.880	0.880	0.880	0.880	1.380	1.160	1.000	1.000
Dividend Payout %	22.68	23.40	23.22	21.89	27.27	25.27	19.76	22.32
Income Statement								
Total Revenue	10,761	7,202	3,575	14,435	12,884	16,661	15,165	17,023
EBITDA	1,513	1,010	485	1,976	1,817	2,150	2,077	2,316
Depn & Amortn	543	364	175	522	429	570	447	486
Income Before Taxes	858	573	275	1,334	1,255	1,425	1,508	1,705
Income Taxes	102	64	33	250	223	242	263	282
Net Income	760	514	240	1,067	1,355	1,257	1,450	1,351
Average Shares	256	257	259	265	268	273	286	301
Balance Sheet								
Current Assets	5,385	4,854	4,819	4,777	5,641	5,419	5,121	5,224
Total Assets	12,939	13,108	13,019	12,480	12,169	12,292	11,973	10,746
Current Liabilities	3,875	3,991	4,014	3,694	3,540	4,148	3,927	3,889
Long-Term Obligations	3,939	3,997	3,995	4,038	4,132	3,959	3,956	2,417
Total Liabilities	9,374	9,589	9,601	9,021	8,870	9,891	9,723	8,236
Stockholders' Equity	3,565	3,519	3,418	3,459	3,299	2,401	2,250	2,510
Shares Outstanding	255	256	257	259	265	269	278	291
Statistical Record								
Return on Assets %	7.97	7.73	7.82	8.66	11.08	10.33	12.76	12.40
Return on Equity %	28.08	27.92	29.05	31.58	47.54	53.91	60.92	49.84
EBITDA Margin %	14.06	14.02	13.57	13.69	14.10	12.90	13.70	13.61
Net Margin %	7.06	7.14	6.71	7.39	10.52	7.54	9.56	7.94
Asset Turnover	1.14	1.13	1.12	1.17	1.05	1.37	1.34	1.56
Current Ratio	1.39	1.22	1.20	1.29	1.59	1.31	1.30	1.34
Debt to Equity	1.10	1.14	1.17	1.17	1.25	1.65	1.76	0.96
Price Range	91.15-60.08	98.45-60.08	102.93-60.08	102.93-60.08	88.77-56.57	71.81-47.75	74.68-55.77	62.10-48.83
P/E Ratio	23.49-15.48	26.18-15.98	27.16-15.85	25.60-14.95	17.54-11.18	15.64-10.40	14.76-11.02	13.86-10.90
Average Yield %	1.16	1.11	1.08	1.01	1.87	2.03	1.49	1.77

Address: 5 Hanover Quay, Grand Canal Dock, Dublin, D02 VY79
Telephone: 125-970-13

Web Site: www.delphi.com
Officers: Rajiv L. Gupta - Chairman Kevin P. Clark - President, Chief Executive Officer, Executive Vice President, Senior Vice President, Chief Operating Officer, Chief Financial Officer

Auditors: Ernst & Young LLP
Investor Contact: 248-813-2494
Transfer Agents: Computershare Trust Company, N.A., Providence

AQUA AMERICA INC

Exchange	Symbol	Price	52Wk Range	Yield	P/E	Div Acheiver
NYS	WTR	$46.94 (12/31/2019)	47.08-32.83	2.00	67.06	27 Years

*7 Year Price Score 107.82 *NYSE Composite Index=100 *12 Month Price Score 104.78

Interim Earnings (Per Share)

Qtr.	Mar	Jun	Sep	Dec
2016	0.29	0.33	0.41	0.28
2017	0.28	0.34	0.43	0.30
2018	0.29	0.37	0.44	(0.02)
2019	0.09	0.25	0.38	...

Interim Dividends (Per Share)

Amt	Decl	Ex	Rec	Pay
0.219Q	02/04/2019	02/14/2019	02/15/2019	03/01/2019
0.219Q	05/02/2019	05/16/2019	05/17/2019	06/01/2019
0.234Q	07/25/2019	08/15/2019	08/16/2019	09/01/2019
0.234Q	10/31/2019	11/14/2019	11/15/2019	12/01/2019

Indicated Div: $0.94 (Div. Reinv. Plan)

Valuation Analysis / **Institutional Holding**

Forecast EPS	$1.48	No of Institutions
	(01/16/2020)	760
Market Cap	$10.1 Billion	Shares
Book Value	$3.9 Billion	169,832,896
Price/Book	2.62	% Held
Price/Sales	11.65	80.54

Business Summary: Water Utilities (MIC: 3.2.1 SIC: 4941 NAIC: 221310)

Aqua America is the holding company for regulated utilities providing water or wastewater services in Pennsylvania, Ohio, Texas, Illinois, North Carolina, New Jersey, Indiana, and Virginia. Co.'s operating subsidiary, Aqua Pennsylvania, Inc., provides water or wastewater services and its service territory is located in the suburban areas in counties north and west of the City of Philadelphia as well as in other counties in Pennsylvania. Co.'s other regulated utility subsidiaries provide similar services in other states. In addition, Co.'s market-based activities are conducted through Aqua Infrastructure, LLC and Aqua Resources Inc.

Recent Developments: For the quarter ended Sep 30 2019, net income increased 13.1% to US$88.5 million from US$78.2 million in the year-earlier quarter. Revenues were US$243.6 million, up 7.7% from US$226.1 million the year before. Operating income was US$106.5 million versus US$104.3 million in the prior-year quarter, an increase of 2.1%. Direct operating expenses rose 19.5% to US$82.0 million from US$68.6 million in the comparable period the year before. Indirect operating expenses increased 3.6% to US$55.1 million from US$53.2 million in the equivalent prior-year period.

Prospects: Our evaluation of Aqua America Inc. as of October 4th, 2019 is the result of our systematic analysis on three basic characteristics: earnings strength, relative valuation, and recent stock price movement. The company has managed to produce a neutral trend in earnings per share over the past 5 quarters. In addition, recent analyst estimates for the company have been mixed and WTR has posted results that exceeded analysts' expectations. Based on operating earnings yield, the company is fairly valued when compared to all of the companies we cover. Share price changes over the past year indicates that WTR will perform well over the near term.

Financial Data

(US$ in Thousands)	9 Mos	6 Mos	3 Mos	12/31/2018	12/31/2017	12/31/2016	12/31/2015	12/31/2014
Earnings Per Share	0.70	0.76	0.88	1.08	1.35	1.32	1.14	1.31
Cash Flow Per Share	1.32	1.31	2.02	2.07	2.15	2.23	2.10	2.06
Tang Book Value Per Share	17.65	17.48	10.87	10.99	10.78	10.19	9.58	9.19
Dividends Per Share	0.891	0.876	0.862	0.847	0.792	0.739	0.686	0.634
Dividend Payout %	127.33	115.26	97.92	78.46	58.67	55.95	60.18	48.40
Income Statement								
Total Revenue	663,650	420,024	201,132	838,091	809,525	819,875	814,204	779,903
EBITDA	338,739	189,486	75,135	421,172	480,964	465,765	453,755	442,543
Depn & Amortn	118,113	78,624	39,074	146,032	136,302	130,987	125,290	123,054
Income Before Taxes	146,504	59,703	8,211	176,238	256,321	254,184	251,929	243,092
Income Taxes	(11,894)	(10,341)	(8,170)	(13,669)	16,914	20,978	14,962	25,219
Net Income	160,316	71,827	16,924	191,988	239,738	234,182	201,790	233,239
Average Shares	232,464	219,790	178,552	178,399	178,175	177,846	177,517	177,763
Balance Sheet								
Current Assets	2,178,893	2,117,920	143,775	147,172	131,246	128,650	128,370	152,522
Total Assets	9,340,970	9,180,350	7,080,950	6,964,496	6,332,463	6,158,991	5,741,038	5,406,752
Current Liabilities	352,123	398,949	434,099	398,977	284,488	301,536	193,199	225,335
Long-Term Obligations	2,909,998	2,761,117	2,474,599	2,398,464	2,007,753	1,737,605	1,743,612	1,560,655
Total Liabilities	5,478,408	5,355,576	5,088,365	4,955,132	4,374,842	4,308,923	4,015,108	3,751,409
Stockholders' Equity	3,862,562	3,824,774	1,992,585	2,009,364	1,957,621	1,850,068	1,725,930	1,655,343
Shares Outstanding	215,828	215,775	178,369	178,091	177,713	177,394	176,544	176,753
Statistical Record								
Return on Assets %	1.95	1.86	2.34	2.89	3.84	3.93	3.62	4.46
Return on Equity %	5.30	5.02	7.97	9.68	12.59	13.06	11.94	14.62
EBITDA Margin %	51.04	45.11	37.36	50.25	59.41	56.81	55.73	56.74
Net Margin %	24.16	17.10	8.41	22.91	29.61	28.56	24.78	29.91
Asset Turnover	0.11	0.11	0.13	0.13	0.13	0.14	0.15	0.15
Current Ratio	6.19	5.31	0.33	0.37	0.46	0.43	0.66	0.68
Debt to Equity	0.75	0.72	1.24	1.19	1.03	0.94	1.01	0.94
Price Range	45.24-32.37	41.95-32.37	38.02-32.37	38.65-32.37	39.33-29.54	35.66-28.67	30.51-24.49	28.05-22.59
P/E Ratio	64.63-46.24	55.20-42.59	43.20-36.78	35.79-29.97	29.13-21.88	27.02-21.72	26.76-21.48	21.41-17.24
Average Yield %	2.35	2.40	2.44	2.41	2.37	2.35	2.56	2.55

Address: 762 W. Lancaster Avenue, Bryn Mawr, PA 19010-3489 **Telephone:** 610-527-8000	**Web Site:** www.aquaamerica.com **Officers:** Christopher H. Franklin - Chairman, Chief Executive Officer, President, Executive Vice President, Senior Vice President, Executive Vice President, Region Officer, Senior Vice President, Division Officer, Chief Executive Officer, Division Officer, Region Officer Richard Scott (Rick) Fox - Executive Vice President, Division Officer	**Auditors:** PricewaterhouseCoopers LLP **Investor Contact:** 610-527-8000 **Transfer Agents:** Computershare Trust Company, N.A., Providence, RI

ARAMARK

Exchange	Symbol	Price	52Wk Range	Yield	P/E
NYS	ARMK	$43.40 (12/31/2019)	45.12-28.68	1.01	24.38

*7 Year Price Score N/A *NYSE Composite Index=100 *12 Month Price Score 112.58

Interim Earnings (Per Share)
Qtr.	Dec	Mar	Jun	Sep
2014-15	0.35	0.24	0.14	0.23
2015-16	0.38	0.27	0.18	0.34
2016-17	0.50	0.28	0.26	0.45
2017-18	1.16	0.11	0.29	0.68
2018-19	0.99	0.12	0.33	0.34

Interim Dividends (Per Share)
Amt	Decl	Ex	Rec	Pay
0.11Q	01/30/2019	02/13/2019	02/14/2019	02/28/2019
0.11Q	05/01/2019	05/15/2019	05/16/2019	05/30/2019
0.11Q	07/31/2019	08/14/2019	08/15/2019	08/29/2019
0.11Q	11/19/2019	11/29/2019	12/02/2019	12/09/2019

Indicated Div: $0.44

Valuation Analysis
		Institutional Holding	
Forecast EPS	$2.34	No of Institutions	
(01/17/2020)		439	
Market Cap	$10.8 Billion	Shares	
Book Value	$3.3 Billion	275,089,568	
Price/Book	3.24	% Held	
Price/Sales	0.66	100.79	

Business Summary: Hotels, Restaurants & Travel (MIC: 2.2.1 SIC: 5812 NAIC: 722110)

Aramark is a provider of food, facilities and uniform services. Co. manages its Food and Support Services (FSS) business in segments split between its United States and International operations. Co.'s FSS segments manage a number of interrelated services-including food, hospitality, procurement and facility services-for school districts, colleges and universities, healthcare facilities, businesses, sports, entertainment and recreational venues, conference and convention centers, national and state parks and correctional institutions. Co.'s Uniform and Career Apparel segment provides employee uniform solution, including design, sourcing and manufacturing, delivery, cleaning and maintenance.

Recent Developments: For the year ended Sep 27 2019, net income decreased 21.1% to US$448.5 million from US$568.4 million in the prior year. Revenues were US$16.23 billion, up 2.8% from US$15.79 billion the year before. Operating income was US$891.2 million versus US$818.4 million in the prior year, an increase of 8.9%. Direct operating expenses rose 3.8% to US$14.53 billion from US$14.00 billion in the comparable period the year before. Indirect operating expenses decreased 17.4% to US$803.5 million from US$973.3 million in the equivalent prior-year period.

Prospects: Our evaluation of Aramark as of October 4th, 2019 is the result of our systematic analysis on three basic characteristics: earnings strength, relative valuation, and recent stock price movement. The company has managed to produce a neutral trend in earnings per share over the past 5 quarters. In addition, recent analyst estimates for the company have been mixed and ARMK has posted results that exceeded analysts' expectations. Based on operating earnings yield, the company is fairly valued when compared to all of the companies we cover. Share price changes over the past year indicates that ARMK will perform poorly over the near term.

Financial Data
(US$ in Thousands)	09/27/2019	09/28/2018	09/29/2017	09/30/2016	10/02/2015	10/03/2014	09/27/2013	09/28/2012
Earnings Per Share	1.78	2.24	1.49	1.16	0.96	0.63	0.33	0.49
Cash Flow Per Share	4.00	4.27	4.32	3.34	2.88	1.73	3.46	3.41
Dividends Per Share	0.440	0.420	0.412	0.380	0.345	0.225	...	...
Dividend Payout %	24.72	18.75	27.65	32.76	35.94	35.71		
Income Statement								
Total Revenue	16,227,341	15,789,633	14,604,412	14,415,829	14,329,135	14,832,913	13,945,657	13,505,426
EBITDA	1,301,399	1,085,686	1,038,595	975,609	849,925	799,681	748,924	815,174
Depn & Amortn	421,400	270,000	237,900	234,800	226,600	239,900	239,100	236,600
Income Before Taxes	556,172	471,876	520,642	430,931	341,996	229,677	90,629	124,968
Income Taxes	107,706	(96,564)	146,455	142,699	105,020	80,218	19,233	18,066
Net Income	448,549	567,885	373,923	287,806	235,946	148,956	69,356	103,551
Average Shares	252,010	253,352	251,557	248,763	246,616	237,451	209,370	209,707
Balance Sheet								
Current Assets	2,658,387	2,901,425	2,653,139	2,492,571	2,379,123	2,464,976	2,287,165	2,185,501
Total Assets	13,736,321	13,720,102	11,006,229	10,582,072	10,224,050	10,455,693	10,267,106	10,487,354
Current Liabilities	2,705,298	2,490,159	2,368,095	2,184,745	2,180,988	2,378,873	2,389,253	2,163,674
Long-Term Obligations	6,612,239	7,213,077	5,190,331	5,223,514	5,212,290	5,355,789	5,758,229	5,971,305
Total Liabilities	10,416,274	10,690,544	8,547,168	8,421,066	8,340,691	8,737,657	9,363,399	9,554,337
Stockholders' Equity	3,320,047	3,029,558	2,459,061	2,161,006	1,883,359	1,718,036	903,707	933,017
Shares Outstanding	247,756	246,744	245,593	244,713	239,917	233,910	201,798	202,573
Statistical Record								
Return on Assets %	3.28	4.61	3.47	2.77	2.29	1.41	0.67	...
Return on Equity %	14.17	20.75	16.23	14.27	13.14	11.18	7.57	...
EBITDA Margin %	8.02	6.88	7.11	6.77	5.93	5.39	5.37	6.04
Net Margin %	2.76	3.60	2.56	2.00	1.65	1.00	0.50	0.77
Asset Turnover	1.19	1.28	1.36	1.39	1.39	1.41	1.35	...
Current Ratio	0.98	1.17	1.12	1.14	1.09	1.04	0.96	1.01
Debt to Equity	1.99	2.38	2.11	2.42	2.77	3.12	6.37	6.40
Price Range	43.12-27.50	45.99-36.61	41.48-33.08	38.21-29.57	33.49-25.35	29.89-22.70	...	...
P/E Ratio	24.22-15.45	20.53-16.34	27.84-22.20	32.94-25.49	34.89-26.41	47.44-36.03	...	...
Average Yield %	1.27	1.21	1.10	1.03	1.14	1.12	0.84	...

Address: 2400 Market Street, Philadelphia, PA 19103	**Web Site:** www.aramark.com	**Auditors:** KPMG LLP
Telephone: 215-238-3000	**Officers:** Stephen I. Sadove - Chairman Paul C. Hilal - Vice-Chairman	**Investor Contact:** 215-238-3000
		Transfer Agents: Computershare Trust Company, N.A.

ARCHER DANIELS MIDLAND CO.

Exchange	Symbol	Price	52Wk Range	Yield	P/E	Div Acheiver
NYS	ADM	$46.35 (12/31/2019)	46.35-36.76	3.02	22.07	44 Years

*7 Year Price Score 80.99   ***NYSE Composite Index=100**   ***12 Month Price Score 99.36**

Interim Earnings (Per Share)

Qtr.	Mar	Jun	Sep	Dec
2016	0.39	0.48	0.58	0.72
2017	0.59	0.48	0.34	1.38
2018	0.70	1.00	0.94	0.55
2019	0.41	0.42	0.72	...

Interim Dividends (Per Share)

Amt	Decl	Ex	Rec	Pay
0.35Q	02/05/2019	02/15/2019	02/19/2019	03/12/2019
0.35Q	05/01/2019	05/14/2019	05/15/2019	06/05/2019
0.35Q	08/08/2019	08/21/2019	08/22/2019	09/12/2019
0.35Q	11/07/2019	11/20/2019	11/21/2019	12/12/2019

Indicated Div: $1.40 (Div. Reinv. Plan)

Valuation Analysis		Institutional Holding	
Forecast EPS	$2.53	No of Institutions	
	(01/17/2020)	1193	
Market Cap	$25.8 Billion	Shares	
Book Value	$18.9 Billion	594,984,896	
Price/Book	1.37	% Held	
Price/Sales	0.40	76.60	

Business Summary: Food (MIC: 1.2.1 SIC: 2041 NAIC: 311211)

Archer Daniels Midland is a producer of food and beverage ingredients, and other products made from a variety of agricultural products. Co.'s segments are: Origination, which buys, stores, cleans, and transports agricultural commodities and resells these commodities as food and feed ingredients and as raw materials for the agricultural processing industry; Oilseeds, which is engaged in the origination, merchandising, crushing, and further processing of oilseeds into vegetable oils and protein meals; Carbohydrate Solutions, which is engaged in corn and wheat wet and dry milling and other activities; and Nutrition, which manufactures, sells, and distributes specialty products.

Recent Developments: For the quarter ended Sep 30 2019, net income decreased 23.9% to US$408.0 million from US$536.0 million in the year-earlier quarter. Revenues were US$16.73 billion, up 5.9% from US$15.80 billion the year before. Direct operating expenses rose 6.1% to US$15.65 billion from US$14.74 billion in the comparable period the year before. Indirect operating expenses increased 17.9% to US$631.0 million from US$535.0 million in the equivalent prior-year period.

Prospects: Our evaluation of Archer Daniels Midland Co. as of October 4th, 2019 is the result of our systematic analysis on three basic characteristics: earnings strength, relative valuation, and recent stock price movement. The company has generated a negative trend in earnings per share over the past 5 quarters. However, recent analyst estimates for the company have been unchanged while ADM has posted results that fell short of analysts' expectations. Based on operating earnings yield, the company is undervalued when compared to all of the companies we cover. Share price changes over the past year indicates that ADM will perform poorly over the near term.

Financial Data
(US$ in Thousands)

	9 Mos	6 Mos	3 Mos	12/31/2018	12/31/2017	12/31/2016	12/31/2015	12/31/2014
Earnings Per Share	2.10	2.32	2.90	3.19	2.79	2.16	2.98	3.43
Cash Flow Per Share	(8.44)	(7.64)	(5.74)	(8.48)	3.89	2.50	4.01	7.60
Tang Book Value Per Share	24.19	24.03	23.99	26.73	25.84	23.51	23.88	25.58
Dividends Per Share	1.385	1.370	1.355	1.340	1.280	1.200	1.120	0.960
Dividend Payout %	65.95	59.05	46.72	42.01	45.88	55.56	37.58	27.99
Income Statement								
Total Revenue	48,327,000	31,601,000	15,304,000	64,341,000	60,828,000	62,346,000	67,702,000	81,201,000
EBITDA	1,720,000	1,006,000	511,000	2,556,000	2,179,000	2,518,000	2,930,000	3,853,000
Depn & Amortn	742,000	493,000	245,000	812,000	802,000	787,000	799,000	850,000
Income Before Taxes	813,000	398,000	214,000	1,542,000	1,153,000	1,530,000	1,894,000	2,758,000
Income Taxes	212,000	117,000	81,000	245,000	534,000	7,000	438,000	877,000
Net Income	875,000	468,000	233,000	1,810,000	1,595,000	1,279,000	1,849,000	2,248,000
Average Shares	563,000	566,000	566,000	567,000	572,000	591,000	621,000	656,000
Balance Sheet								
Current Assets	19,178,000	19,548,000	20,262,000	20,588,000	19,925,000	21,045,000	21,829,000	26,028,000
Total Assets	41,804,000	42,616,000	43,151,000	40,833,000	39,963,000	39,769,000	40,157,000	44,027,000
Current Liabilities	12,020,000	12,602,000	13,361,000	11,776,000	12,570,000	13,173,000	13,505,000	15,602,000
Long-Term Obligations	7,631,000	7,701,000	7,675,000	7,698,000	6,623,000	6,504,000	5,779,000	5,558,000
Total Liabilities	22,931,000	23,661,000	24,256,000	21,852,000	21,650,000	22,596,000	22,258,000	24,452,000
Stockholders' Equity	18,873,000	18,955,000	18,895,000	18,981,000	18,313,000	17,173,000	17,899,000	19,575,000
Shares Outstanding	557,000	558,000	560,000	559,000	557,000	573,000	595,000	637,000
Statistical Record								
Return on Assets %	2.92	3.24	3.92	4.48	4.00	3.19	4.39	5.12
Return on Equity %	6.29	7.00	8.77	9.71	8.99	7.27	9.87	11.32
EBITDA Margin %	3.56	3.18	3.34	3.97	3.58	4.04	4.33	4.75
Net Margin %	1.81	1.48	1.52	2.81	2.62	2.05	2.73	2.77
Asset Turnover	1.58	1.56	1.52	1.59	1.53	1.56	1.61	1.85
Current Ratio	1.60	1.55	1.52	1.75	1.59	1.60	1.62	1.67
Debt to Equity	0.40	0.41	0.41	0.41	0.36	0.38	0.32	0.28
Price Range	51.79-36.76	51.79-38.32	51.79-39.62	51.79-39.62	46.97-38.96	47.72-30.51	53.17-34.18	53.71-38.23
P/E Ratio	24.66-17.50	22.32-16.52	17.86-13.66	16.24-12.42	16.84-13.96	22.09-14.12	17.84-11.47	15.66-11.15
Average Yield %	3.25	3.05	2.95	2.93	2.99	2.96	2.44	2.08

Address: 77 West Wacker Drive, Suite 4600, Chicago, IL 60601 **Telephone:** 312-634-8100	**Web Site:** www.adm.com **Officers:** Juan R. Luciano - Chairman, President, Chief Executive Officer, Executive Vice President, Chief Operating Officer Ray G. Young - Executive Vice President, Chief Financial Officer, Senior Vice President	**Auditors:** Ernst & Young LLP **Investor Contact:** 217-424-5656 **Transfer Agents:** Hickory Point Bank & Trust, fsb, Decatur, IL

ARCONIC INC

Exchange	Symbol	Price	52Wk Range	Yield	P/E
NYS	ARNC	$30.77 (12/31/2019)	31.80-16.86	0.26	39.96

*7 Year Price Score 80.63 ***NYSE Composite Index=100** ***12 Month Price Score 121.07**

Interim Earnings (Per Share)

Qtr.	Mar	Jun	Sep	Dec
2016	0.00	0.27	0.33	(2.91)
2017	0.65	0.43	0.22	(1.59)
2018	0.29	0.24	0.32	0.44
2019	0.39	0.24	0.21	...

Interim Dividends (Per Share)

Amt	Decl	Ex	Rec	Pay
0.06Q	01/29/2019	02/07/2019	02/08/2019	02/25/2019
0.02Q	03/11/2019	05/02/2019	05/03/2019	05/25/2019
0.02Q	07/11/2019	08/01/2019	08/02/2019	08/25/2019
0.02Q	09/26/2019	11/07/2019	11/08/2019	11/25/2019

Indicated Div: $0.08

Valuation Analysis   **Institutional Holding**

Forecast EPS	$2.11	No of Institutions
	(01/16/2020)	911
Market Cap	$13.3 Billion	Shares
Book Value	$4.7 Billion	505,287,392
Price/Book	2.84	% Held
Price/Sales	0.93	N/A

Business Summary: Non-Precious Metals (MIC: 8.2.2 SIC: 3334 NAIC: 331312)

Arconic is engaged in lightweight metals engineering and manufacturing. Co.'s segments include: Engineered Products and Solutions, which produces products that are used mainly in the aerospace (commercial and defense), industrial, commercial transportation, and power generation end markets; Global Rolled Products, which produces aluminum sheet and plate for a variety of end markets, and also produces aseptic foil for the packaging end market; and Transportation and Construction Solutions, which produces products that are used in the commercial transportation and nonresidential building and construction end markets, and also produces aluminum products for the industrial products end market.

Recent Developments: For the quarter ended Sep 30 2019, net income decreased 41.0% to US$95.0 million from US$161.0 million in the year-earlier quarter. Revenues were US$3.56 billion, up 1.0% from US$3.52 billion the year before. Operating income was US$326.0 million versus US$345.0 million in the prior-year quarter, a decrease of 5.5%. Direct operating expenses declined 2.8% to US$2.80 billion from US$2.88 billion in the comparable period the year before. Indirect operating expenses increased 45.3% to US$433.0 million from US$298.0 million in the equivalent prior-year period.

Prospects: Our evaluation of Arconic Inc. as of October 4th, 2019 is the result of our systematic analysis on three basic characteristics: earnings strength, relative valuation, and recent stock price movement. The company has enjoyed a very positive trend in earnings per share over the past 5 quarters. However, recent analyst estimates for the company have been mixed and ARNC has posted results that exceeded analysts' expectations. Based on operating earnings yield, the company is undervalued when compared to all of the companies we cover. Share price changes over the past year indicates that ARNC will perform very well over the near term.

Financial Data

(US$ in Thousands)	9 Mos	6 Mos	3 Mos	12/31/2018	12/31/2017	12/31/2016	12/31/2015	12/31/2014
Earnings Per Share	0.77	0.88	1.39	1.30	(0.28)	(2.31)	(0.93)	0.63
Cash Flow Per Share	0.75	0.73	0.84	0.45	1.55	1.98	3.77	4.32
Tang Book Value Per Share	N.M.	N.M.	N.M.	0.20	N.M.	N.M.	12.43	15.45
Dividends Per Share	0.160	0.200	0.240	0.240	0.240	0.090	...	...
Dividend Payout %	20.78	22.73	17.27	18.46	...	...	...	...
Income Statement								
Total Revenue	10,791,000	7,232,000	3,541,000	14,014,000	12,960,000	12,394,000	22,534,000	23,906,000
EBITDA	913,000	492,000	479,000	1,799,000	1,498,000	2,022,000	2,099,000	2,415,000
Depn & Amortn	407,000	276,000	137,000	576,000	551,000	1,132,000	1,280,000	1,372,000
Income Before Taxes	271,000	62,000	257,000	868,000	470,000	407,000	337,000	589,000
Income Taxes	110,000	(4,000)	70,000	226,000	544,000	1,476,000	445,000	320,000
Net Income	161,000	66,000	187,000	642,000	(74,000)	(941,000)	(322,000)	268,000
Average Shares	457,000	445,000	489,000	503,000	451,000	438,000	419,666	393,333
Balance Sheet								
Current Assets	5,908,000	6,018,000	6,053,000	6,581,000	6,378,000	5,892,000	7,953,000	8,269,000
Total Assets	17,484,000	17,913,000	18,361,000	18,693,000	18,718,000	20,038,000	36,528,000	37,399,000
Current Liabilities	4,460,000	3,621,000	3,659,000	3,520,000	2,824,000	2,749,000	5,211,000	5,541,000
Long-Term Obligations	4,905,000	5,901,000	5,899,000	5,896,000	6,806,000	8,044,000	9,044,000	8,769,000
Total Liabilities	12,788,000	13,059,000	13,195,000	13,120,000	13,808,000	14,923,000	24,482,000	25,093,000
Stockholders' Equity	4,696,000	4,854,000	5,166,000	5,573,000	4,910,000	5,115,000	12,046,000	12,306,000
Shares Outstanding	432,941	440,188	448,629	483,270	481,416	438,519	436,720	405,554
Statistical Record								
Return on Assets %	2.12	2.46	3.75	3.43	N.M.	N.M.	N.M.	0.73
Return on Equity %	7.54	8.85	13.15	12.25	N.M.	N.M.	N.M.	2.34
EBITDA Margin %	8.46	6.80	13.53	12.84	11.56	16.31	9.31	10.10
Net Margin %	1.49	0.91	5.28	4.58	N.M.	N.M.	N.M.	1.12
Asset Turnover	0.80	0.79	0.77	0.75	0.67	0.44	0.61	0.65
Current Ratio	1.32	1.66	1.65	1.87	2.26	2.14	1.53	1.49
Debt to Equity	1.04	1.22	1.14	1.06	1.39	1.57	0.75	0.71
Price Range	27.31-16.14	25.82-16.14	23.75-16.14	30.84-16.14	30.55-19.19	25.49-15.19	38.47-17.62	39.66-22.76
P/E Ratio	35.47-20.96	29.34-18.34	17.09-11.61	23.72-12.42	...	...	...	62.95-36.13
Average Yield %	0.74	0.98	1.21	1.11	0.94	0.43	...	...

Address: 201 Isabelle Street, Suite 200, Pittsburgh, PA 15212-5872	Web Site: www.arconic.com	Auditors: PricewaterhouseCoopers LLP
Telephone: 412-553-1940	Officers: John C. Plant - Chairman, Chief Executive Officer Kenneth J. (Ken) Giacobbe - Executive Vice President, Chief Financial Officer, Division Officer	Investor Contact: 212-836-2758 Transfer Agents: Computershares

ARISTA NETWORKS INC

Exchange	Symbol	Price	52Wk Range	Yield	P/E
NYS	ANET	$203.40 (12/31/2019)	328.54-185.30	N/A	21.41

*7 Year Price Score N/A   *NYSE Composite Index=100   *12 Month Price Score 73.93

Interim Earnings (Per Share)

Qtr.	Mar	Jun	Sep	Dec
2016	0.48	0.53	0.69	0.79
2017	1.07	1.30	1.68	1.29
2018	1.79	(2.08)	2.08	2.11
2019	2.47	2.33	2.59	...

Interim Dividends (Per Share)

No Dividends Paid

Valuation Analysis / **Institutional Holding**

Forecast EPS	$9.54	No of Institutions
	(01/17/2020)	666
Market Cap	$15.5 Billion	Shares
Book Value	$2.7 Billion	49,018,444
Price/Book	5.85	% Held
Price/Sales	6.33	62.37

TRADING VOLUME (thousand shares)

Business Summary: Computer Hardware & Equipment (MIC: 6.2.1 SIC: 5045 NAIC: 423430)

Arista Networks is a supplier of cloud networking solutions that use software products to address the needs of internet companies, cloud service providers and data centers and campuses for enterprise support. Co.'s cloud networking solutions consist of its Extensible Operating System, or EOS, a set of network applications and its Ethernet switching and routing platforms. The programmability of EOS has enabled Co. to create a set of software applications that address the requirements of cloud networking, including workflow automation, and has also enabled Co. to integrate with a range of third-party applications for virtualization, management, automation, orchestration and network services.

Recent Developments: For the quarter ended Sep 30 2019, net income increased 24.0% to US$208.9 million from US$168.5 million in the year-earlier quarter. Revenues were US$654.4 million, up 16.2% from US$563.3 million the year before. Operating income was US$228.6 million versus US$180.8 million in the prior-year quarter, an increase of 26.5%. Direct operating expenses rose 17.6% to US$237.1 million from US$201.7 million in the comparable period the year before. Indirect operating expenses increased 4.3% to US$188.7 million from US$180.8 million in the equivalent prior-year period.

Prospects: Our evaluation of Arista Networks Inc as of October 4th, 2019 is the result of our systematic analysis on three basic characteristics: earnings strength, relative valuation, and recent stock price movement. The company has managed to produce a neutral trend in earnings per share over the past 5 quarters. In addition, recent analyst estimates for the company have been mixed and ANET has posted results that exceeded analysts' expectations. Based on operating earnings yield, the company is fairly valued when compared to all of the companies we cover. Share price changes over the past year indicates that ANET will perform in line with the market over the near term.

Financial Data

(US$ in Thousands)	9 Mos	6 Mos	3 Mos	12/31/2018	12/31/2017	12/31/2016	12/31/2015	12/31/2014
Earnings Per Share	9.50	8.99	4.58	4.06	5.35	2.50	1.67	1.29
Cash Flow Per Share	12.19	7.10	6.29	6.73	8.74	1.91	3.04	2.36
Tang Book Value Per Share	33.43	31.61	29.97	26.84	22.55	15.64	11.57	8.48
Income Statement								
Total Revenue	1,858,160	1,203,745	595,424	2,151,369	1,646,186	1,129,167	837,591	584,106
EBITDA	630,615	407,558	196,258	318,202	497,740	264,761	162,561	135,513
Depn & Amortn	(6,032)	5,240	2,631	26,700	20,200	19,400	13,400	10,000
Income Before Taxes	675,098	427,323	205,525	288,801	474,760	242,225	146,009	121,508
Income Taxes	75,923	37,043	5,646	(39,314)	51,559	58,036	24,907	34,658
Net Income	599,175	390,280	201,029	328,115	423,201	184,189	121,102	86,850
Average Shares	80,753	81,335	81,201	80,844	78,977	73,222	71,411	54,590
Balance Sheet								
Current Assets	3,240,420	3,028,518	2,900,974	2,714,802	2,266,429	1,526,126	974,328	679,479
Total Assets	3,619,825	3,441,292	3,332,444	3,081,983	2,460,860	1,729,007	1,159,890	811,023
Current Liabilities	548,189	525,020	543,193	606,504	529,905	459,553	235,011	144,373
Long-Term Obligations	...	...	...	35,431	37,673	39,593	41,210	42,547
Total Liabilities	963,821	915,732	932,077	938,594	798,946	621,187	371,738	255,365
Stockholders' Equity	2,656,004	2,525,560	2,400,367	2,143,389	1,661,914	1,107,820	788,152	555,658
Shares Outstanding	76,368	76,555	76,453	75,668	73,706	70,811	68,132	65,528
Statistical Record								
Return on Assets %	23.98	23.24	13.01	11.84	20.20	12.72	12.29	14.78
Return on Equity %	33.44	34.35	18.12	17.25	30.56	19.38	18.02	27.42
EBITDA Margin %	33.94	33.86	32.96	14.79	30.24	23.45	19.41	23.20
Net Margin %	32.25	32.42	33.76	15.25	25.71	16.31	14.46	14.87
Asset Turnover	0.76	0.75	0.77	0.78	0.79	0.78	0.85	0.99
Current Ratio	5.91	5.77	5.34	4.48	4.28	3.32	4.15	4.71
Debt to Equity	...	...	...	0.02	0.02	0.04	0.05	0.08
Price Range	328.54-188.90	328.54-188.90	315.02-188.90	308.58-188.90	243.55-88.23	98.00-53.00	87.68-56.71	93.31-55.00
P/E Ratio	34.58-19.88	36.55-21.01	68.78-41.24	76.00-46.53	45.52-16.49	39.20-21.20	52.50-33.96	72.33-42.64

Address: 5453 Great America Parkway, Santa Clara, CA 95054 **Telephone:** 408-547-5500	**Web Site:** www.arista.com **Officers:** Andreas Bechtolsheim - Chairman, Chief Development Officer, Interim Chief Financial Officer Jayshree Ullal - President, Chief Executive Officer	**Auditors:** Ernst & Young LLP **Transfer Agents:** Computershare Trust Company, N.A., Canton, MA

ARMSTRONG WORLD INDUSTRIES INC

Exchange	Symbol	Price	52Wk Range	Yield	P/E
NYS	AWI	$93.97 (12/31/2019)	102.48-58.21	0.85	23.20

*7 Year Price Score 134.20 *NYSE Composite Index=100 *12 Month Price Score 102.11

Interim Earnings (Per Share)

Qtr.	Mar	Jun	Sep	Dec
2016	(0.18)	0.30	1.26	0.49
2017	0.56	0.77	0.92	0.62
2018	0.51	0.89	1.46	0.70
2019	0.78	1.09	1.48	...

Interim Dividends (Per Share)

Amt	Decl	Ex	Rec	Pay
0.175Q	02/20/2019	03/04/2019	03/05/2019	03/20/2019
0.175Q	04/24/2019	05/08/2019	05/09/2019	05/23/2019
0.175Q	07/24/2019	08/07/2019	08/08/2019	08/22/2019
0.20Q	10/23/2019	11/06/2019	11/07/2019	11/21/2019

Indicated Div: $0.80

Valuation Analysis / **Institutional Holding**

Forecast EPS	$4.54	No of Institutions
	(01/17/2020)	379
Market Cap	$4.6 Billion	Shares
Book Value	$367.3 Million	60,109,868
Price/Book	12.39	% Held
Price/Sales	4.42	93.51

Business Summary: Construction Materials (MIC: 8.5.1 SIC: 5039 NAIC: 327993)

Armstrong World Industries is a producer of ceiling systems for use primarily in the construction and renovation of commercial and residential buildings. Co. designs, manufactures and sells ceiling systems (primarily mineral fiber, fiberglass wool and metal). Co.'s segments are: Mineral Fiber, which produces suspended mineral fiber and soft fiber ceiling systems for use in commercial and residential settings and includes its joint venture, Worthington Armstrong Venture, that manufactures suspension system (grid) products and ceiling component products; and Architectural Specialties, which produces and sources ceilings and walls for use in commercial settings.

Recent Developments: For the quarter ended Sep 30 2019, income from continuing operations increased 41.3% to US$90.7 million from US$64.2 million in the year-earlier quarter. Net income decreased 3.9% to US$73.2 million from US$76.2 million in the year-earlier quarter. Revenues were US$277.1 million, up 6.4% from US$260.5 million the year before. Operating income was US$113.3 million versus US$81.3 million in the prior-year quarter, an increase of 39.4%. Direct operating expenses rose 1.7% to US$165.4 million from US$162.6 million in the comparable period the year before. Indirect operating income amounted to US$1.6 million compared with an expense of US$16.6 million in the equivalent prior-year period.

Prospects: Our evaluation of Armstrong World Industries Inc. as of October 4th, 2019 is the result of our systematic analysis on three basic characteristics: earnings strength, relative valuation, and recent stock price movement. The company has generated a negative trend in earnings per share over the past 5 quarters. However, recent analyst estimates for the company have been mixed and AWI has posted results that exceeded analysts' expectations. Based on operating earnings yield, the company is fairly valued when compared to all of the companies we cover. Share price changes over the past year indicates that AWI will perform over the near term.

Financial Data

(US$ in Thousands)	9 Mos	6 Mos	3 Mos	12/31/2018	12/31/2017	12/31/2016	12/31/2015	12/31/2014
Earnings Per Share	4.05	4.03	3.83	3.56	2.86	1.87	1.68	1.14
Cash Flow Per Share	3.40	3.29	3.94	3.96	3.20	0.89	3.67	3.80
Tang Book Value Per Share	N.M.	N.M.	N.M.	N.M.	N.M.	N.M.	5.04	2.68
Dividends Per Share	0.700	0.525	0.350	0.175	...	...	...	...
Dividend Payout %	17.28	13.03	9.14	4.92	...	...	...	...
Income Statement								
Total Revenue	791,200	514,100	242,100	975,300	893,600	1,234,500	2,420,000	2,515,300
EBITDA	202,900	146,500	56,400	282,100	277,900	207,600	219,200	293,000
Depn & Amortn	14,700	33,800	15,100	79,400	89,200	89,200	118,300	129,400
Income Before Taxes	156,600	92,800	30,900	167,800	155,100	71,200	57,800	120,100
Income Taxes	48,800	32,800	13,400	53,100	1,500	50,400	71,300	83,200
Net Income	166,800	93,600	39,100	185,900	154,800	104,700	94,200	63,800
Average Shares	49,500	49,800	49,500	52,100	53,900	55,700	55,900	55,400
Balance Sheet								
Current Assets	296,700	695,600	749,000	752,800	648,900	406,200	880,800	811,500
Total Assets	1,509,700	1,890,000	1,942,600	1,873,500	1,873,500	1,758,000	2,691,900	2,606,200
Current Liabilities	142,200	581,500	589,900	549,500	269,900	224,100	436,300	388,100
Long-Term Obligations	650,500	734,600	749,700	764,800	817,700	848,600	950,900	1,003,000
Total Liabilities	1,142,400	1,646,900	1,662,300	1,612,300	1,454,200	1,491,600	1,923,100	1,957,100
Stockholders' Equity	367,300	243,100	280,300	261,200	419,300	266,400	768,800	649,100
Shares Outstanding	48,431	48,661	48,640	48,808	52,772	54,428	55,359	55,126
Statistical Record								
Return on Assets %	11.47	11.00	10.47	9.92	8.53	4.69	3.56	2.31
Return on Equity %	57.69	63.16	57.65	54.64	45.15	20.17	13.29	9.65
EBITDA Margin %	25.64	28.50	23.30	28.92	31.10	16.82	9.06	11.65
Net Margin %	21.08	18.21	16.15	19.06	17.32	8.48	3.89	2.54
Asset Turnover	0.59	0.55	0.53	0.52	0.49	0.55	0.91	0.91
Current Ratio	2.09	1.20	1.27	1.37	2.40	1.81	2.02	2.09
Debt to Equity	1.77	3.02	2.67	2.93	1.95	3.19	1.24	1.55
Price Range	100.12-55.13	98.15-55.13	79.42-54.95	72.20-54.95	60.55-38.80	45.51-31.45	51.99-38.75	53.19-39.27
P/E Ratio	24.72-13.61	24.35-13.68	20.74-14.35	20.28-15.44	21.17-13.57	24.34-16.82	30.95-23.06	46.65-34.44
Average Yield %	0.88	0.72	0.53	0.28	...	...	...	...

Address: 2500 Columbia Avenue, Lancaster, PA 17603	Web Site: www.armstrong.com	Auditors: KPMG LLP
Telephone: 717-397-0611	Officers: David S. Cookson - Senior Vice President Victor (Vic) D. Grizzle - President, Chief Executive Officer, Executive Vice President, Division Officer	Investor Contact: 717-396-6354 Transfer Agents: American Stock Transfer & Trust Company, New York, NY

ARROW ELECTRONICS, INC.

Exchange	Symbol	Price	52Wk Range	Yield	P/E
NYS	ARW	$84.74 (12/31/2019)	86.10-62.66	N/A	N/A

*7 Year Price Score 96.64   *NYSE Composite Index=100   *12 Month Price Score 102.69

Interim Earnings (Per Share)

Qtr.	Mar	Jun	Sep	Dec
2016	1.14	1.45	1.28	1.81
2017	1.26	1.11	1.50	0.61
2018	1.56	1.92	1.99	2.63
2019	1.63	(6.48)	1.10	...

Interim Dividends (Per Share)

No Dividends Paid

Valuation Analysis		Institutional Holding	
Forecast EPS	$7.46	No of Institutions	
	(01/14/2020)	556	
Market Cap	$6.9 Billion	Shares	
Book Value	$4.7 Billion	106,958,512	
Price/Book	1.48	% Held	
Price/Sales	0.23	86.43	

TRADING VOLUME (thousand shares)

Business Summary: Electrical Equipment (MIC: 7.3.1 SIC: 3679 NAIC: 334419)

Arrow Electronics is a provider of products, services, and solutions to industrial and commercial users of electronic components and enterprise computing solutions. Co.'s customer base consists of original equipment manufacturers, value-added resellers, Managed Service Providers, contract manufacturers, and other commercial customers. Co. has two segments: the global components, which markets and distributes electronic components and provides a range of capabilities throughout the life cycle of technology products and services; and the global enterprise computing solutions, which provides computing solutions and services, including data-center, cloud, security, and analytics solutions.

Recent Developments: For the quarter ended Sep 28 2019, net income decreased 47.8% to US$93.0 million from US$178.2 million in the year-earlier quarter. Revenues were US$7.08 billion, down 5.5% from US$7.49 billion the year before. Operating income was US$173.2 million versus US$290.3 million in the prior-year quarter, a decrease of 40.3%. Direct operating expenses declined 4.4% to US$6.28 billion from US$6.57 billion in the comparable period the year before. Indirect operating expenses decreased 1.2% to US$625.6 million from US$633.5 million in the equivalent prior-year period.

Prospects: Our evaluation of Arrow Electronics Inc. as of October 4th, 2019 is the result of our systematic analysis on three basic characteristics: earnings strength, relative valuation, and recent stock price movement. The company has managed to produce a neutral trend in earnings per share over the past 5 quarters. Additionally, recent analyst estimates for the company have been unchanged while ARW has posted results that exceeded analysts' expectations. Based on operating earnings yield, the company is undervalued when compared to all of the companies we cover. Share price changes over the past year indicates that ARW will perform poorly over the near term.

Financial Data

(US$ in Thousands)	9 Mos	6 Mos	3 Mos	12/31/2018	12/31/2017	12/31/2016	12/31/2015	12/31/2014
Earnings Per Share	(1.12)	(0.23)	8.17	8.10	4.48	5.68	5.20	4.98
Cash Flow Per Share	7.57	9.85	0.22	3.12	1.40	3.90	6.92	6.82
Tang Book Value Per Share	29.01	29.00	28.73	27.32	25.03	18.94	15.22	18.24
Income Statement								
Total Revenue	21,578,657	14,500,539	7,155,991	29,676,768	26,812,508	23,825,261	23,282,020	22,768,674
EBITDA	(91,148)	(271,541)	268,859	1,359,098	1,047,395	1,057,559	1,023,575	989,978
Depn & Amortn	34,749	27,629	19,090	232,622	192,721	199,020	203,028	197,978
Income Before Taxes	(279,323)	(402,714)	197,788	911,705	690,864	707,824	685,146	676,015
Income Taxes	30,878	1,538	53,907	187,799	287,126	190,674	191,697	184,943
Net Income	(316,100)	(408,231)	140,735	716,195	401,962	522,750	497,726	498,045
Average Shares	83,397	84,652	86,319	88,444	89,766	92,033	95,686	99,947
Balance Sheet								
Current Assets	11,839,648	12,110,356	12,253,884	13,608,300	12,417,759	10,316,721	9,186,471	9,032,607
Total Assets	15,689,711	16,024,369	16,830,752	17,784,445	16,462,809	14,206,366	13,021,930	12,442,856
Current Liabilities	7,371,641	7,377,961	7,034,125	8,790,428	7,956,569	6,689,222	6,056,152	5,838,021
Long-Term Obligations	2,942,293	3,157,274	3,575,891	3,239,115	2,933,045	2,696,334	2,380,575	2,075,453
Total Liabilities	10,998,892	11,255,644	11,381,749	12,459,455	11,511,270	9,792,928	8,879,487	8,288,886
Stockholders' Equity	4,690,819	4,768,725	5,449,003	5,324,990	4,951,539	4,413,438	4,142,443	4,153,970
Shares Outstanding	81,764	83,141	85,173	85,191	87,691	88,913	90,923	95,895
Statistical Record								
Return on Assets %	N.M.	N.M.	4.36	4.18	2.62	3.83	3.91	4.07
Return on Equity %	N.M.	N.M.	13.61	13.94	8.58	12.19	12.00	11.95
EBITDA Margin %	N.M.	N.M.	3.76	4.58	3.91	4.44	4.40	4.35
Net Margin %	N.M.	N.M.	1.97	2.41	1.50	2.19	2.14	2.19
Asset Turnover	1.81	1.83	1.82	1.73	1.75	1.75	1.83	1.86
Current Ratio	1.61	1.64	1.74	1.55	1.56	1.54	1.52	1.55
Debt to Equity	0.63	0.66	0.66	0.61	0.59	0.61	0.57	0.50
Price Range	86.10-62.66	86.10-62.66	81.99-63.25	86.94-63.25	83.96-69.97	72.44-46.66	64.67-50.79	62.71-46.42
P/E Ratio	...	...	10.04-7.74	10.73-7.81	18.74-15.62	12.75-8.21	12.44-9.77	12.59-9.32

Address: 9201 East Dry Creek Road, Centennial, CO 80112 **Telephone:** 303-824-4000	**Web Site:** www.arrow.com **Officers:** Michael J. Long - Chairman, President, Chief Executive Officer, Chief Operating Officer Christopher D. (Chris) Stansbury - Senior Vice President, Chief Financial Officer, Vice President, Principal Accounting Officer	**Auditors:** Ernst & Young LLP **Investor Contact:** 303-824-4000 **Transfer Agents:** Wells Fargo Shareowner Services, South St. Paul, MN

ASBURY AUTOMOTIVE GROUP INC

Exchange	Symbol	Price	52Wk Range	Yield	P/E
NYS	ABG	$111.79 (12/31/2019)	122.67-66.39	N/A	11.97

*7 Year Price Score 109.58 *NYSE Composite Index=100 *12 Month Price Score 122.19

Interim Earnings (Per Share)

Qtr.	Mar	Jun	Sep	Dec
2016	1.27	1.65	1.47	3.03
2017	1.61	1.52	1.48	2.02
2018	1.93	2.11	2.18	2.06
2019	2.11	2.84	2.33	...

Interim Dividends (Per Share)

No Dividends Paid

Valuation Analysis		Institutional Holding	
Forecast EPS	$9.23	No of Institutions	
	(01/15/2020)	291	
Market Cap	$2.2 Billion	Shares	
Book Value	$600.0 Million	26,356,276	
Price/Book	3.60	% Held	
Price/Sales	0.30	64.84	

Business Summary: Retail - Automotive (MIC: 2.1.4 SIC: 5599 NAIC: 441229)

Asbury Automotive Group is an automotive retailer with store operations conducted by its subsidiaries. Co. owns and operates new vehicle franchises, representing various brands of automobiles. Co.'s stores provide a range of automotive products and services, including new and used vehicles; parts and service, including vehicle repair and maintenance services, replacement parts, and collision repair services; and finance and insurance products, including arranging vehicle financing through third parties and aftermarket products, such as extended service contracts, guaranteed asset protection insurance, prepaid maintenance, and credit life and disability insurance.

Recent Developments: For the quarter ended Sep 30 2019, net income increased 1.6% to US$45.0 million from US$44.3 million in the year-earlier quarter. Revenues were US$1.84 billion, up 4.8% from US$1.76 billion the year before. Operating income was US$82.2 million versus US$80.8 million in the prior-year quarter, an increase of 1.7%. Direct operating expenses rose 4.7% to US$1.55 billion from US$1.48 billion in the comparable period the year before. Indirect operating expenses increased 6.9% to US$210.9 million from US$197.2 million in the equivalent prior-year period.

Prospects: Our evaluation of Asbury Automotive Group Inc. as of October 4th, 2019 is the result of our systematic analysis on three basic characteristics: earnings strength, relative valuation, and recent stock price movement. The company has managed to produce a neutral trend in earnings per share over the past 5 quarters. In addition, recent analyst estimates for the company have been mixed and ABG has posted results that exceeded analysts' expectations. Based on operating earnings yield, the company is undervalued when compared to all of the companies we cover. Share price changes over the past year indicates that ABG will perform over the near term.

Financial Data
(US$ in Thousands)

	9 Mos	6 Mos	3 Mos	12/31/2018	12/31/2017	12/31/2016	12/31/2015	12/31/2014
Earnings Per Share	9.34	9.19	8.46	8.28	6.62	7.40	6.41	3.71
Cash Flow Per Share	13.16	7.41	2.06	0.50	12.80	6.31	5.91	2.82
Tang Book Value Per Share	13.58	14.33	11.62	11.69	8.83	4.85	5.47	10.25
Income Statement								
Total Revenue	5,316,300	3,474,300	1,670,800	6,874,400	6,456,500	6,527,800	6,588,300	5,867,700
EBITDA	275,200	187,200	83,600	344,600	319,800	374,000	366,000	262,700
Depn & Amortn	17,600	11,800	5,800	33,700	32,100	30,700	29,500	26,400
Income Before Taxes	186,700	127,200	53,700	224,800	209,100	267,800	273,400	183,000
Income Taxes	45,900	31,400	12,800	56,800	70,000	100,600	104,000	71,000
Net Income	140,800	95,800	40,900	168,000	139,100	167,200	169,200	111,600
Average Shares	19,300	19,300	19,400	20,300	21,000	22,600	26,400	30,100
Balance Sheet								
Current Assets	1,448,000	1,529,500	1,628,600	1,553,000	1,302,100	1,332,400	1,343,000	1,276,700
Total Assets	2,816,500	2,814,000	2,904,900	2,695,400	2,356,700	2,336,100	2,305,900	2,192,000
Current Liabilities	1,235,100	1,272,600	1,416,800	1,303,300	1,058,200	1,104,900	1,007,800	1,041,100
Long-Term Obligations	867,800	871,200	874,700	866,500	862,600	912,700	940,400	678,700
Total Liabilities	2,216,500	2,257,700	2,400,300	2,222,200	1,962,500	2,056,400	1,991,400	1,747,100
Stockholders' Equity	600,000	556,300	504,600	473,200	394,200	279,700	314,500	444,900
Shares Outstanding	19,304	19,350	19,407	19,345	20,813	21,253	24,810	28,523
Statistical Record								
Return on Assets %	6.80	6.77	6.33	6.65	5.93	7.18	7.52	5.47
Return on Equity %	33.52	35.86	36.34	38.74	41.28	56.12	44.56	23.86
EBITDA Margin %	5.18	5.39	5.00	5.01	4.95	5.73	5.56	4.48
Net Margin %	2.65	2.76	2.45	2.44	2.15	2.56	2.57	1.90
Asset Turnover	2.66	2.63	2.60	2.72	2.75	2.80	2.93	2.88
Current Ratio	1.17	1.20	1.15	1.19	1.21	1.21	1.33	1.23
Debt to Equity	1.45	1.57	1.73	1.83	2.19	3.26	2.99	1.53
Price Range	102.56-59.04	84.34-59.04	77.40-59.04	77.40-59.04	69.45-50.15	67.44-45.07	95.54-66.76	77.56-45.42
P/E Ratio	10.98-6.32	9.18-6.42	9.15-6.98	9.35-7.13	10.49-7.58	9.11-6.09	14.90-10.41	20.91-12.24

Address: 2905 Premiere Parkway N.W., Suite 300, Duluth, GA 30097 **Telephone:** 770-418-8200	**Web Site:** www.asburyauto.com **Officers:** David W. Hult - President, Chief Executive Officer, Executive Vice President, Chief Operating Officer George A. Villasana - Senior Vice President, General Counsel, Secretary, Vice President	**Auditors:** Ernst & Young LLP **Investor Contact:** 770-418-8210 **Transfer Agents:** Computershare Trust Company, N.A.

ASGN INC

Exchange	Symbol	Price	52Wk Range	Yield	P/E
NYS	ASGN	$70.97 (12/31/2019)	71.67-50.73	N/A	20.75

*7 Year Price Score 109.55 ***NYSE Composite Index=100** ***12 Month Price Score 102.72**

Interim Earnings (Per Share)

Qtr.	Mar	Jun	Sep	Dec
2016	0.32	0.48	0.55	0.45
2017	0.42	0.62	0.66	1.27
2018	0.55	0.63	0.93	0.87
2019	0.66	0.81	1.08	...

Interim Dividends (Per Share)

No Dividends Paid

Valuation Analysis — **Institutional Holding**

Forecast EPS	$4.65	No of Institutions	
(01/17/2020)		386	
Market Cap	$3.7 Billion	Shares	
Book Value	$1.3 Billion	59,281,224	
Price/Book	2.81	% Held	
Price/Sales	0.98	N/A	

Business Summary: Business Services (MIC: 7.5.2 SIC: 7363 NAIC: 561320)

ASGN is a provider of information technology and staffing services in the technology, digital, engineering and life sciences fields across commercial and government sectors. Co. provides services through three segments: Apex, which provides technical, scientific, digital and creative services and solutions to clients across the U.S. and Canada; the Oxford segment, which provides technical, digital, engineering and life sciences resources and consulting services in select skill and geographic markets; and the Oxford segment, which provides technical, digital, engineering and life sciences resources and consulting services in select skill and geographic markets.

Recent Developments: For the quarter ended Sep 30 2019, income from continuing operations increased 17.1% to US$57.5 million from US$49.1 million in the year-earlier quarter. Net income increased 16.9% to US$57.4 million from US$49.1 million in the year-earlier quarter. Revenues were US$1.00 billion, up 10.6% from US$906.4 million the year before. Operating income was US$90.9 million versus US$74.2 million in the prior-year quarter, an increase of 22.5%. Direct operating expenses rose 11.8% to US$711.3 million from US$636.3 million in the comparable period the year before. Indirect operating expenses increased 2.3% to US$200.5 million from US$195.9 million in the equivalent prior-year period.

Prospects: Our evaluation of ASGN INC as of October 4th, 2019 is the result of our systematic analysis on three basic characteristics: earnings strength, relative valuation, and recent stock price movement. The company has generated a negative trend in earnings per share over the past 5 quarters. In addition, recent analyst estimates for the company have been reduced and ASGN has posted results that fell short of analysts' expectations. Based on operating earnings yield, the company is undervalued when compared to all of the companies we cover. Share price changes over the past year indicates that ASGN will perform in line with the market over the near term.

Financial Data
(US$ in Thousands)

	9 Mos	6 Mos	3 Mos	12/31/2018	12/31/2017	12/31/2016	12/31/2015	12/31/2014
Earnings Per Share	3.42	3.27	3.09	2.98	2.97	1.81	1.84	1.42
Cash Flow Per Share	5.60	5.62	5.26	5.49	3.74	3.68	2.25	1.80
Income Statement								
Total Revenue	2,898,700	1,896,000	923,700	3,399,781	2,625,924	2,440,413	2,065,008	1,859,922
EBITDA	265,700	162,900	76,500	355,154	283,380	251,954	199,624	183,971
Depn & Amortn	38,800	26,900	13,800	95,006	58,644	62,228	51,267	37,701
Income Before Taxes	185,700	107,500	48,200	204,175	197,093	157,399	121,913	133,540
Income Taxes	50,200	29,500	13,300	46,191	39,219	60,203	50,491	54,527
Net Income	135,400	78,000	34,900	157,706	157,675	97,201	97,650	77,184
Average Shares	53,400	53,400	53,200	53,061	53,205	53,747	53,005	54,294
Balance Sheet								
Current Assets	747,100	697,100	691,400	686,372	499,523	437,524	414,208	385,904
Total Assets	2,831,600	2,799,000	2,814,600	2,687,851	1,810,129	1,752,667	1,767,307	1,274,174
Current Liabilities	353,400	326,500	313,700	308,249	166,717	162,499	160,350	165,566
Long-Term Obligations	985,200	1,026,000	1,107,700	1,100,424	575,213	640,355	755,508	396,875
Total Liabilities	1,500,100	1,515,300	1,587,300	1,505,789	818,738	883,728	982,513	639,766
Stockholders' Equity	1,331,500	1,283,700	1,227,300	1,182,062	991,391	868,939	784,794	634,408
Shares Outstanding	52,700	52,800	52,800	52,511	52,151	52,716	53,024	51,386
Statistical Record								
Return on Assets %	6.60	6.32	7.00	7.01	8.85	5.51	6.42	6.09
Return on Equity %	14.73	14.71	14.49	14.51	16.95	11.72	13.76	12.11
EBITDA Margin %	9.17	8.59	8.28	10.45	10.79	10.32	9.67	9.89
Net Margin %	4.67	4.11	3.78	4.64	6.00	3.98	4.73	4.15
Asset Turnover	1.39	1.36	1.56	1.51	1.47	1.38	1.36	1.47
Current Ratio	2.11	2.14	2.20	2.23	3.00	2.69	2.58	2.33
Debt to Equity	0.74	0.80	0.90	0.93	0.58	0.74	0.96	0.63
Price Range	77.32-50.73	93.69-50.73	93.69-51.74	93.69-51.74	64.74-43.21	45.77-29.68	47.64-31.27	38.92-26.39
P/E Ratio	22.61-14.83	28.65-15.51	30.32-16.74	31.44-17.36	21.80-14.55	25.29-16.40	25.89-16.99	27.41-18.58

Address: 26745 Malibu Hills Road, Calabasas, CA 91301 Telephone: 818-878-7900	Web Site: www.onassignment.com Officers: Jeremy M. Jones - Chairman Theodore S. Hanson - President, Chief Executive Officer, Executive Vice President	Auditors: Deloitte & Touche LLP Investor Contact: 818-878-7900 Transfer Agents: Computershare, Canton, MA

ASHLAND GLOBAL HOLDINGS INC

Exchange	Symbol	Price	52Wk Range	Yield	P/E
NYS	ASH	$76.53 (12/31/2019)	80.53-69.30	1.44	9.53

*7 Year Price Score 104.65 *NYSE Composite Index=100   *12 Month Price Score 92.90

Interim Earnings (Per Share)

Qtr.	Dec	Mar	Jun	Sep
2015-16	1.35	1.38	1.13	(4.33)
2016-17	(0.01)	1.47	(0.54)	(0.92)
2017-18	(0.07)	1.15	0.56	0.15
2018-19	(0.76)	1.19	1.05	6.53

Interim Dividends (Per Share)

Amt	Decl	Ex	Rec	Pay
0.25Q	01/31/2019	02/28/2019	03/01/2019	03/15/2019
0.275Q	05/22/2019	05/31/2019	06/03/2019	06/15/2019
0.275Q	07/17/2019	08/29/2019	08/30/2019	09/15/2019
0.275Q	11/14/2019	11/29/2019	12/02/2019	12/15/2019

Indicated Div: $1.10

Valuation Analysis / **Institutional Holding**

Forecast EPS	$2.90	No of Institutions
	(01/17/2020)	N/A
Market Cap	$4.6 Billion	Shares
Book Value	$3.6 Billion	N/A
Price/Book	1.29	% Held
Price/Sales	1.84	N/A

Business Summary: Specialty Chemicals (MIC: 8.3.2 SIC: 5169 NAIC: 325199)
Ashland Global Holdings is a holding company. Through its subsidiaries, Co. is engaged in providing chemical solutions to customers in a range of consumer and industrial markets. Co.'s reportable segments are: Specialty Ingredients, which is a provider in cellulose ethers, vinyl pyrrolidones and biofunctionals and uses natural, synthetic and semisynthetic polymers derived from cellulose ethers, vinyl pyrrolidones, acrylic polymers, polyester and polyurethane-based adhesives, and plant and seed extract; and Intermediates and Solvents, which is a producer of 1,4 butanediol and related derivatives, including n-methylpyrrolidone.

Recent Developments: For the year ended Sep 30 2019, income from continuing operations increased 26.3% to US$24.0 million from US$19.0 million a year earlier. Net income increased 343.0% to US$505.0 million from US$114.0 million in the prior year. Revenues were US$2.49 billion, down 3.7% from US$2.59 billion the year before. Operating income was US$166.0 million versus US$102.0 million in the prior year, an increase of 62.7%. Direct operating expenses was unchanged at US$1.73 billion versus the comparable period the year before. Indirect operating expenses decreased 21.0% to US$601.0 million from US$761.0 million in the equivalent prior-year period.

Prospects: Our evaluation of Ashland Global Holdings Inc. as of October 4th, 2019 is the result of our systematic analysis on three basic characteristics: earnings strength, relative valuation, and recent stock price movement. The company has produced a positive trend in earnings per share over the past 5 quarters. In addition, recent analyst estimates for the company have been raised, and ASH has posted results that exceeded analysts' expectations. Based on operating earnings yield, the company is fairly valued when compared to all of the companies we cover. Share price changes over the past year indicates that ASH will perform in line with the market over the near term.

Financial Data

(US$ in Millions)	09/30/2019	09/30/2018	09/30/2017	09/30/2016	09/30/2015	09/30/2014
Earnings Per Share	8.03	1.79	0.01	(0.46)	4.48	3.00
Cash Flow Per Share	3.68	5.46	4.11	11.13	1.31	7.53
Tang Book Value Per Share	3.73	N.M.	N.M.	N.M.	N.M.	...
Dividends Per Share	1.050	0.950	1.230	1.560	1.460	1.360
Dividend Payout %	13.08	53.07	12,300.00	...	32.59	45.33
Income Statement						
Total Revenue	2,493	3,743	3,260	4,948	5,387	6,121
EBITDA	381	455	342	552	569	343
Depn & Amortn	203	217	219	260	263	304
Income Before Taxes	66	106	(105)	108	146	(118)
Income Taxes	46	9	7	133	(22)	(188)
Net Income	505	114	1	(29)	309	233
Average Shares	63	64	62	64	69	78
Balance Sheet						
Current Assets	1,433	1,712	1,903	2,866	3,093	3,561
Total Assets	7,251	8,252	8,618	9,697	10,054	10,951
Current Liabilities	757	1,075	968	1,216	1,442	1,687
Long-Term Obligations	1,501	2,275	2,584	3,055	3,348	2,942
Total Liabilities	3,680	4,846	5,212	6,350	7,017	7,368
Stockholders' Equity	3,571	3,406	3,406	3,347	3,037	3,583
Shares Outstanding	60	62	62	62	67	...
Statistical Record						
Return on Assets %	6.51	1.35	0.01	N.M.	2.94	2.02
Return on Equity %	14.48	3.35	0.03	N.M.	9.34	5.73
EBITDA Margin %	15.28	12.16	10.49	11.16	10.56	5.60
Net Margin %	20.26	3.05	0.03	N.M.	5.74	3.81
Asset Turnover	0.32	0.44	0.36	0.50	0.51	0.53
Current Ratio	1.89	1.59	1.97	2.36	2.14	2.11
Debt to Equity	0.42	0.67	0.76	0.91	1.10	0.82
Price Range	84.21-65.28	86.11-65.08	67.45-52.62	60.33-43.67	64.35-47.16	53.51-41.63
P/E Ratio	10.49-8.13	48.11-36.36	N.M.	...	14.36-10.53	17.84-13.88
Average Yield %	1.37	1.27	2.05	2.92	2.53	2.81

Address: 50 E. RiverCenter Boulevard, Covington, KY 41011 **Telephone:** 859-815-3333	**Web Site:** www.ashland.com **Officers:** Guillermo Novo - Chairman, Chief Executive Officer J. Kevin Willis - Senior Vice President, Chief Financial Officer	**Auditors:** Ernst & Young LLP **Transfer Agents:** Wells Fargo Shareowner Services, Mendota Heights, MN

ASSOCIATED BANC-CORP

Exchange	Symbol	Price	52Wk Range	Yield	P/E
NYS	ASB	$22.04 (12/31/2019)	23.67-18.64	3.27	11.08

*7 Year Price Score 85.79   *NYSE Composite Index=100   *12 Month Price Score 96.08

Interim Earnings (Per Share)

Qtr.	Mar	Jun	Sep	Dec
2016	0.27	0.31	0.34	0.34
2017	0.35	0.36	0.41	0.31
2018	0.40	0.50	0.48	0.51
2019	0.50	0.49	0.49	...

Interim Dividends (Per Share)

Amt	Decl	Ex	Rec	Pay
0.17Q	02/05/2019	02/28/2019	03/01/2019	03/15/2019
0.17Q	04/30/2019	05/31/2019	06/03/2019	06/17/2019
0.17Q	07/30/2019	08/30/2019	09/03/2019	09/16/2019
0.18Q	10/29/2019	11/29/2019	12/02/2019	12/16/2019

Indicated Div: $0.72 (Div. Reinv. Plan)

Valuation Analysis / Institutional Holding

Forecast EPS	$1.91	No of Institutions
(01/16/2020)		393
Market Cap	$3.5 Billion	Shares
Book Value	$3.9 Billion	141,362,960
Price/Book	0.90	% Held
Price/Sales	2.22	76.66

Business Summary: Banking (MIC: 5.1.1 SIC: 6022 NAIC: 522110)

Associated Banc is a bank holding company. Through its subsidiaries, Co. provides banking and nonbanking products and services. Co. has three segments: Corporate and Commercial Specialty, which includes lending solutions, deposit and cash management solutions, and financial services; Community, Consumer, and Business, which includes lending solutions, deposit and transactional solutions, investable funds solutions, trust and investment management accounts, insurance and benefits-related products and services, and fiduciary services; and Risk Management and Shared Services, which includes corporate risk management, credit administration, finance, treasury, and operations and technology.

Recent Developments: For the quarter ended Sep 30 2019, net income decreased 3.0% to US$83.3 million from US$85.9 million in the year-earlier quarter. Net interest income decreased 5.9% to US$206.4 million from US$219.4 million in the year-earlier quarter. Provision for loan losses was US$2.0 million versus a credit for loan losses of US$5.0 million in the prior-year quarter. Non-interest income rose 14.2% to US$100.9 million from US$88.3 million, while non-interest expense declined 1.7% to US$200.9 million.

Prospects: Our evaluation of Associated Banc-Corp. as of October 4th, 2019 is the result of our systematic analysis on three basic characteristics: earnings strength, relative valuation, and recent stock price movement. The company has managed to produce a neutral trend in earnings per share over the past 5 quarters. However, recent analyst estimates for the company have been reduced while ASB has posted results that exceeded analysts' expectations. Based on operating earnings yield, the company is undervalued when compared to all of the companies we cover. Share price changes over the past year indicates that ASB will perform poorly over the near term.

Financial Data

(US$ in Thousands)	9 Mos	6 Mos	3 Mos	12/31/2018	12/31/2017	12/31/2016	12/31/2015	12/31/2014
Earnings Per Share	1.99	1.98	1.99	1.89	1.42	1.26	1.19	1.16
Cash Flow Per Share	4.17	2.78	2.68	2.97	3.04	4.22	2.02	1.35
Tang Book Value Per Share	14.62	14.18	13.85	13.45	13.26	12.38	11.70	11.51
Dividends Per Share	0.680	0.660	0.640	0.620	0.500	0.450	0.410	0.370
Dividend Payout %	34.17	33.33	32.16	32.80	35.21	35.71	34.45	31.90
Income Statement								
Interest Income	903,500	612,081	305,948	1,154,137	886,605	791,568	753,662	736,745
Interest Expense	267,969	182,914	90,401	274,557	145,385	84,295	77,384	55,778
Net Interest Income	635,531	429,167	215,547	879,580	741,220	707,273	676,278	680,967
Provision for Losses	16,000	14,000	6,000	...	26,000	70,000	37,500	16,000
Non-Interest Income	287,890	187,040	91,203	355,567	332,680	352,883	328,409	290,319
Non-Interest Expense	590,379	389,450	191,671	821,799	709,133	702,560	697,399	679,241
Income Before Taxes	317,042	212,756	109,078	413,349	338,767	287,596	269,788	276,045
Income Taxes	62,356	41,409	22,392	79,786	109,503	87,322	81,487	85,536
Net Income	254,686	171,347	86,686	333,562	229,264	200,274	188,301	190,509
Average Shares	160,382	163,672	165,433	169,732	153,647	149,961	150,603	158,254
Balance Sheet								
Net Loans & Leases	22,689,537	23,156,611	23,010,137	22,781,670	20,604,655	19,896,865	18,564,994	17,482,479
Total Assets	32,596,460	33,272,628	33,700,866	33,647,859	30,483,594	29,139,315	27,715,021	26,821,774
Total Deposits	24,422,562	25,274,222	25,533,057	24,897,393	22,785,962	21,888,448	21,007,665	18,763,504
Total Liabilities	28,675,605	29,372,835	29,864,996	29,866,971	27,246,151	26,048,003	24,777,775	24,021,523
Stockholders' Equity	3,920,855	3,899,794	3,835,870	3,780,888	3,237,443	3,091,312	2,937,246	2,800,251
Shares Outstanding	159,290	162,661	163,903	164,440	152,843	152,120	151,239	151,541
Statistical Record								
Return on Assets %	1.04	1.03	1.05	1.04	0.77	0.70	0.69	0.75
Return on Equity %	8.91	9.03	9.29	9.51	7.25	6.63	6.56	6.69
Net Interest Margin %	70.81	69.78	70.45	76.21	83.60	89.35	89.73	92.43
Efficiency Ratio %	51.22	49.20	48.26	54.43	58.16	61.39	64.45	66.13
Loans to Deposits	0.93	0.92	0.90	0.92	0.90	0.91	0.88	0.93
Price Range	26.55-18.64	28.35-18.72	28.85-18.72	28.85-18.72	26.50-21.25	25.15-15.48	20.84-16.62	19.36-15.58
P/E Ratio	13.34-9.37	14.32-9.45	14.50-9.41	15.26-9.90	18.66-14.96	19.96-12.29	17.51-13.97	16.69-13.43
Average Yield %	3.13	2.81	2.58	2.42	2.04	2.36	2.16	2.08

Address: 433 Main Street, Green Bay, WI 54301	Web Site: www.associatedbank.com	Auditors: KPMG LLP
	Officers: William R. Hutchinson - Chairman Philip B. Flynn - President, Chief Executive Officer	Investor Contact: 920-491-7059
Telephone: 920-491-7500		Transfer Agents: Wells Fargo Shareowner Services, Saint Paul, MN

ASSURANT INC

Exchange	Symbol	Price	52Wk Range	Yield	P/E
NYS	AIZ	$131.08 (12/31/2019)	133.55-88.66	1.92	32.53

*7 Year Price Score 110.47 *NYSE Composite Index=100 *12 Month Price Score 111.16

Interim Earnings (Per Share)

Qtr.	Mar	Jun	Sep	Dec
2016	3.34	2.70	2.37	0.67
2017	2.53	2.16	(1.05)	5.66
2018	1.96	1.09	0.76	0.26
2019	2.52	2.21	(0.96)	...

Interim Dividends (Per Share)

Amt	Decl	Ex	Rec	Pay
0.60Q	05/08/2019	05/24/2019	05/28/2019	06/18/2019
0.60Q	07/19/2019	08/23/2019	08/26/2019	09/16/2019
0.63Q	11/08/2019	11/22/2019	11/25/2019	12/16/2019
0.63Q	01/14/2020	02/21/2020	02/24/2020	03/16/2020

Indicated Div: $2.52

Valuation Analysis / **Institutional Holding**

Forecast EPS	$8.66	No of Institutions
	(01/17/2020)	611
Market Cap	$8.0 Billion	Shares
Book Value	$5.7 Billion	73,957,232
Price/Book	1.41	% Held
Price/Sales	0.81	90.22

Business Summary: Life & Health (MIC: 5.2.2 SIC: 6321 NAIC: 524114)

Assurant is a holding company. Through its subsidiaries, Co. is a provider of risk management solutions in the housing and lifestyle markets. Co. operates in North America, Latin America, Europe and Asia Pacific through three segments: Global Housing, which consists of lender-placed insurance, multi-family housing and voluntary manufactured housing, homeowners and flood insurance; Global Lifestyle, which consists of connected living, including mobile device protection products and related services, extended service contracts and assistance services, global automotive, and global financial services; and Global Preneed, which provides pre-funded funeral insurance in Canada and the U.S.

Recent Developments: For the quarter ended Sep 30 2019, net loss amounted to US$53.2 million versus net income of US$53.0 million in the year-earlier quarter. Revenues were US$2.50 billion, up 10.1% from US$2.27 billion the year before. Net premiums earned were US$2.02 billion versus US$1.85 billion in the prior-year quarter, an increase of 8.7%. Net investment income rose 11.7% to US$169.5 million from US$151.8 million a year ago.

Prospects: Our evaluation of Assurant Inc. as of October 4th, 2019 is the result of our systematic analysis on three basic characteristics: earnings strength, relative valuation, and recent stock price movement. The company has enjoyed a very positive trend in earnings per share over the past 5 quarters. However, recent analyst estimates for the company have been mixed and AIZ has posted results that exceeded analysts' expectations. Based on operating earnings yield, the company is undervalued when compared to all of the companies we cover. Share price changes over the past year indicates that AIZ will perform in line with the market over the near term.

Financial Data

(US$ in Thousands)	9 Mos	6 Mos	3 Mos	12/31/2018	12/31/2017	12/31/2016	12/31/2015	12/31/2014
Earnings Per Share	4.03	5.75	4.63	3.98	9.39	9.13	2.05	6.44
Cash Flow Per Share	22.17	19.45	15.64	11.09	9.65	2.19	3.73	5.46
Tang Book Value Per Share	8.47	4.42	N.M.	34.97	58.46	54.11	51.83	57.12
Dividends Per Share	2.400	2.360	2.320	2.280	2.150	2.030	1.370	1.060
Dividend Payout %	59.55	41.04	50.11	57.29	22.90	22.23	66.83	16.46
Income Statement								
Total Revenue	7,480,400	4,981,100	2,435,600	8,057,600	6,415,000	7,531,780	10,325,494	10,381,653
Income Before Taxes	375,700	400,300	217,000	333,500	444,500	848,588	201,181	744,137
Income Taxes	117,700	89,100	48,400	80,900	(75,100)	283,238	59,626	273,230
Net Income	255,000	309,800	165,700	251,000	519,600	565,350	141,555	470,907
Average Shares	61,804	65,288	65,777	59,545	55,311	61,934	69,017	73,152
Balance Sheet								
Total Assets	43,751,500	43,139,500	42,237,000	41,089,300	31,843,000	29,709,128	30,043,128	31,562,466
Total Liabilities	38,092,900	37,409,300	36,796,400	35,977,300	27,572,400	25,611,028	25,519,161	26,381,159
Stockholders' Equity	5,658,600	5,730,200	5,440,600	5,112,000	4,270,600	4,098,100	4,523,967	5,181,307
Shares Outstanding	60,758	61,207	61,678	61,908	52,417	55,941	65,850	69,299
Statistical Record								
Return on Assets %	0.65	0.91	0.84	0.69	1.69	1.89	0.46	1.54
Return on Equity %	5.18	7.05	6.29	5.35	12.42	13.08	2.92	9.40
Net Margin %	3.41	6.22	6.80	3.12	8.10	7.51	1.37	4.54
Asset Turnover	0.22	0.22	0.24	0.22	0.21	0.25	0.34	0.34
Price Range	127.50-82.65	110.30-82.65	110.30-82.65	110.30-82.65	106.27-87.74	93.74-66.23	86.81-59.86	69.52-60.81
P/E Ratio	31.64-20.51	19.18-14.37	23.82-17.85	27.71-20.77	11.32-9.34	10.27-7.25	42.35-29.20	10.80-9.44
Average Yield %	2.33	2.36	2.35	2.34	2.18	2.42	1.92	1.60

Address: 28 Liberty Street, 41st Floor, New York, NY 10005 **Telephone:** 212-859-7000	**Web Site:** www.assurant.com **Officers:** Alan B. Colberg - President, Chief Executive Officer, Executive Vice President Keith Meier - Executive Vice President, Division Officer	**Auditors:** PricewaterhouseCoopers LLP **Investor Contact:** 212-859-7197 **Transfer Agents:** Computershare, Providence, RI

ASSURED GUARANTY LTD

Exchange	Symbol	Price	52Wk Range	Yield	P/E
NYS	AGO	$49.02 (12/31/2019)	50.51-37.88	1.47	14.17

*7 Year Price Score 116.57 *NYSE Composite Index=100 *12 Month Price Score 104.72

Interim Earnings (Per Share)

Qtr.	Mar	Jun	Sep	Dec
2016	0.43	1.09	3.60	1.50
2017	2.49	1.24	1.72	0.48
2018	1.68	0.67	1.47	0.85
2019	0.52	1.39	0.70	...

Interim Dividends (Per Share)

Amt	Decl	Ex	Rec	Pay
0.18Q	02/27/2019	03/12/2019	03/13/2019	03/27/2019
0.18Q	05/08/2019	05/21/2019	05/22/2019	06/05/2019
0.18Q	08/07/2019	08/20/2019	08/21/2019	09/04/2019
0.18Q	11/06/2019	11/19/2019	11/20/2019	12/04/2019

Indicated Div: $0.72

Valuation Analysis   **Institutional Holding**

Forecast EPS	N/A	No of Institutions	423
Market Cap	$4.7 Billion	Shares	
Book Value	$6.7 Billion		124,396,384
Price/Book	0.71	% Held	
Price/Sales	5.37		78.04

Business Summary: General Insurance (MIC: 5.2.1 SIC: 6351 NAIC: 524298)

Assured Guaranty is a Bermuda-based holding company that provides, through its operating subsidiaries, credit protection products to the U.S. and international public finance including infrastructure and structured finance markets. Co. markets its financial guaranty insurance directly to issuers and underwriters of public finance and structured finance securities as well as to investors in such obligations. Co. guarantees obligations issued in the U.S. and the U.K, and also guarantees obligations issued in other countries and regions. Co.'s financial guaranty direct and assumed businesses provide credit protection on public finance, infrastructure and structured finance obligations.

Recent Developments: For the quarter ended Sep 30 2019, net income decreased 57.1% to US$69.0 million from US$161.0 million in the year-earlier quarter. Revenues were US$206.0 million, down 25.1% from US$275.0 million the year before. Net premiums earned were US$123.0 million versus US$142.0 million in the prior-year quarter, a decrease of 13.4%. Net investment income fell 11.1% to US$88.0 million from US$99.0 million a year ago.

Prospects: Our evaluation of Assured Guaranty Ltd. as of October 4th, 2019 is the result of our systematic analysis on three basic characteristics: earnings strength, relative valuation, and recent stock price movement. The company has managed to produce a neutral trend in earnings per share over the past 5 quarters. In addition, recent analyst estimates for the company have been mixed and AGO has posted results that exceeded analysts' expectations. Based on operating earnings yield, the company is undervalued when compared to all of the companies we cover. Share price changes over the past year indicates that AGO will perform in line with the market over the near term.

Financial Data
(US$ in Thousands)

	9 Mos	6 Mos	3 Mos	12/31/2018	12/31/2017	12/31/2016	12/31/2015	12/31/2014
Earnings Per Share	3.46	4.23	3.51	4.68	5.96	6.56	7.08	6.26
Cash Flow Per Share	(2.60)	(1.78)	1.00	4.20	3.59	(1.06)	(0.35)	3.34
Tang Book Value Per Share	68.94	67.35	65.21	63.23	58.95	50.82	43.96	36.37
Dividends Per Share	0.700	0.680	0.660	0.640	0.570	0.520	0.480	0.440
Dividend Payout %	20.23	16.08	18.80	13.68	9.56	7.93	6.78	7.03
Income Statement								
Total Revenue	667,000	461,000	195,000	1,002,000	1,739,000	1,677,000	2,207,000	1,994,000
Income Before Taxes	323,000	237,000	56,000	580,000	991,000	1,017,000	1,431,000	1,531,000
Income Taxes	61,000	44,000	4,000	59,000	261,000	136,000	375,000	443,000
Net Income	265,000	196,000	54,000	521,000	730,000	881,000	1,056,000	1,088,000
Average Shares	98,900	101,900	104,000	111,300	122,300	134,100	149,000	173,600
Balance Sheet								
Total Assets	13,367,000	13,581,000	13,551,000	13,603,000	14,433,000	14,151,000	14,544,000	14,925,000
Total Liabilities	6,715,000	6,859,000	6,882,000	7,048,000	7,594,000	7,647,000	8,481,000	9,167,000
Stockholders' Equity	6,652,000	6,722,000	6,669,000	6,555,000	6,839,000	6,504,000	6,063,000	5,758,000
Shares Outstanding	96,495	99,801	102,270	103,672	116,020	127,988	137,928	158,306
Statistical Record								
Return on Assets %	2.60	3.21	2.74	3.72	5.11	6.12	7.17	6.97
Return on Equity %	5.33	6.66	5.62	7.78	10.94	13.98	17.87	20.01
Net Margin %	39.73	42.52	27.69	52.00	41.98	52.53	47.85	54.56
Asset Turnover	0.07	0.07	0.07	0.07	0.12	0.12	0.15	0.13
Price Range	47.70-36.29	47.70-35.84	45.34-34.99	42.72-33.01	45.38-33.65	38.86-22.04	29.52-23.62	26.65-20.73
P/E Ratio	13.79-10.49	11.28-8.48	12.92-9.97	9.13-7.05	7.61-5.65	5.92-3.36	4.17-3.34	4.26-3.31
Average Yield %	1.65	1.64	1.68	1.69	1.44	1.87	1.82	1.84

Address: 30 Woodbourne Avenue, Hamilton, HM 08 **Telephone:** 441-279-5700	**Web Site:** www.assuredguaranty.com **Officers:** Francisco L. Borges - Chairman Dominic J. Frederico - President, Chief Executive Officer	**Auditors:** PricewaterhouseCoopers LLP **Investor Contact:** 441-279-5700 **Transfer Agents:** Mellon Investor Services LLC

AT&T INC

Exchange	Symbol	Price	52Wk Range	Yield	P/E	Div Acheiver
NYS	T	$39.08 (12/31/2019)	39.63-28.54	5.32	17.52	34 Years

*7 Year Price Score 78.38   *NYSE Composite Index=100   *12 Month Price Score 107.38

Interim Earnings (Per Share)

Qtr.	Mar	Jun	Sep	Dec
2016	0.61	0.55	0.54	0.40
2017	0.56	0.63	0.49	3.07
2018	0.75	0.81	0.65	0.66
2019	0.56	0.51	0.50	...

Interim Dividends (Per Share)

Amt	Decl	Ex	Rec	Pay
0.51Q	03/29/2019	04/09/2019	04/10/2019	05/01/2019
0.51Q	06/28/2019	07/09/2019	07/10/2019	08/01/2019
0.51Q	09/26/2019	10/09/2019	10/10/2019	11/01/2019
0.52Q	12/13/2019	01/09/2020	01/10/2020	02/03/2020

Indicated Div: $2.08 (Div. Reinv. Plan)

Valuation Analysis

		Institutional Holding	
Forecast EPS	$3.56	No of Institutions	
	(01/17/2020)	3276	
Market Cap	$285.4 Billion	Shares	
Book Value	$183.0 Billion	4,804,148,736	
Price/Book	1.56	% Held	
Price/Sales	1.57	N/A	

Business Summary: Services (MIC: 6.1.2 SIC: 4899 NAIC: 517110)

AT&T is a holding company. Through its subsidiaries, Co. is a provider of telecommunications, media and technology services globally. Co. has four reportable segments: Communications, which provides wireless and wireline telecom, video and broadband services to consumers located in the U.S. or in U.S. territories and businesses globally; WarnerMedia, which includes media and entertainment businesses that principally develop, produce and distribute feature films, television content, and other content globally; Latin America, which provides entertainment services in Latin America and wireless services in Mexico; and Xandr, which develops digital advertising services.

Recent Developments: For the quarter ended Sep 30 2019, net income decreased 18.0% to US$3.95 billion from US$4.82 billion in the year-earlier quarter. Revenues were US$44.59 billion, down 2.5% from US$45.74 billion the year before. Operating income was US$7.90 billion versus US$7.27 billion in the prior-year quarter, an increase of 8.7%. Direct operating expenses declined 2.7% to US$20.15 billion from US$20.71 billion in the comparable period the year before. Indirect operating expenses decreased 6.9% to US$16.53 billion from US$17.76 billion in the equivalent prior-year period.

Prospects: Our evaluation of AT&T Inc. as of October 4th, 2019 is the result of our systematic analysis on three basic characteristics: earnings strength, relative valuation, and recent stock price movement. The company has managed to produce a neutral trend in earnings per share over the past 5 quarters. Additionally, recent analyst estimates for the company have been unchanged while T has posted results that fell short of analysts' expectations. Based on operating earnings yield, the company is undervalued when compared to all of the companies we cover. Share price changes over the past year indicates that T will perform poorly over the near term.

Financial Data

(US$ in Thousands)	9 Mos	6 Mos	3 Mos	12/31/2018	12/31/2017	12/31/2016	12/31/2015	12/31/2014
Earnings Per Share	2.23	2.38	2.68	2.85	4.76	2.10	2.37	1.19
Cash Flow Per Share	6.66	6.80	6.25	6.43	6.35	6.36	6.38	6.02
Dividends Per Share	2.030	2.020	2.010	2.000	1.960	1.920	1.880	1.840
Dividend Payout %	91.03	84.87	75.00	70.18	41.18	91.43	79.32	154.62
Income Statement								
Total Revenue	134,372,000	89,784,000	44,827,000	170,756,000	160,546,000	163,786,000	146,801,000	132,447,000
EBITDA	28,726,000	19,900,000	10,016,000	52,980,000	41,328,000	45,285,000	44,022,000	31,171,000
Depn & Amortn	7,059,000	5,199,000	2,497,000	20,102,000	19,761,000	20,661,000	19,289,000	17,773,000
Income Before Taxes	15,294,000	10,411,000	5,378,000	24,921,000	15,267,000	19,714,000	20,613,000	9,785,000
Income Taxes	3,059,000	2,122,000	1,023,000	4,920,000	(14,708,000)	6,479,000	7,005,000	3,442,000
Net Income	11,509,000	7,809,000	4,096,000	19,370,000	29,450,000	12,976,000	13,345,000	6,224,000
Average Shares	7,356,001	7,353,001	7,342,001	6,806,001	6,182,999	6,188,999	5,645,999	5,220,999
Balance Sheet								
Current Assets	50,695,000	47,218,000	46,472,000	51,427,000	79,146,000	38,369,000	35,992,000	32,028,000
Total Assets	548,796,000	546,914,000	548,384,000	531,864,000	444,097,000	403,821,000	402,672,000	292,829,000
Current Liabilities	68,126,000	66,376,000	64,652,000	64,420,000	81,389,000	50,576,000	47,816,000	37,282,000
Long-Term Obligations	153,568,000	157,790,000	163,942,000	166,250,000	125,972,000	113,681,000	118,515,000	76,011,000
Total Liabilities	365,747,000	362,657,000	363,272,000	347,775,000	303,236,000	280,686,000	280,001,000	206,459,000
Stockholders' Equity	183,049,000	184,257,000	185,112,000	184,089,000	140,861,000	123,135,000	122,671,000	86,370,000
Shares Outstanding	7,303,375	7,305,030	7,297,226	7,281,629	6,139,424	6,138,993	6,144,939	5,186,912
Statistical Record								
Return on Assets %	3.02	3.21	3.78	3.97	6.95	3.21	3.84	2.18
Return on Equity %	8.92	9.47	11.36	11.92	22.31	10.53	12.77	7.02
EBITDA Margin %	21.38	22.16	22.34	31.03	25.74	27.65	29.99	23.53
Net Margin %	8.57	8.70	9.14	11.34	18.34	7.92	9.09	4.70
Asset Turnover	0.34	0.34	0.36	0.35	0.38	0.41	0.42	0.46
Current Ratio	0.74	0.71	0.72	0.80	0.97	0.76	0.75	0.86
Debt to Equity	0.84	0.86	0.89	0.90	0.89	0.92	0.97	0.88
Price Range	38.74-27.36	34.12-27.36	36.14-27.36	39.16-27.36	43.02-32.86	43.47-33.51	36.18-31.80	36.74-31.86
P/E Ratio	17.37-12.27	14.34-11.50	13.49-10.21	13.74-9.60	9.04-6.90	20.70-15.96	15.27-13.42	30.87-26.77
Average Yield %	6.33	6.44	6.33	6.01	5.08	4.89	5.56	5.32

Address: 208 S. Akard St., Dallas, TX 75202 Telephone: 210-821-4105	Web Site: www.att.com Officers: Randall L. Stephenson - Chairman, President, Chief Executive Officer, Senior Executive Vice President, Chief Financial Officer, Chief Operating Officer John T. Stankey - President, Group President, Chief Operating Officer, Chief Strategy Officer	Auditors: Ernst & Young LLP Investor Contact: 210-351-2058 Transfer Agents: Computershare Trust Company, N.A, Providence, RI

ATMOS ENERGY CORP.

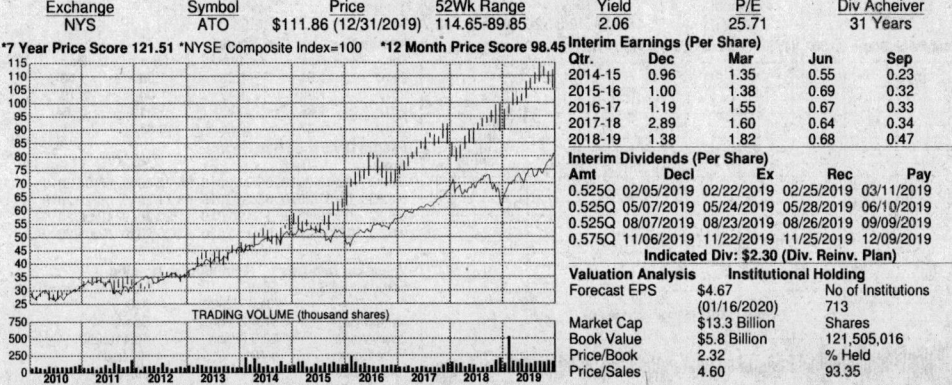

Exchange	Symbol	Price	52Wk Range	Yield	P/E	Div Acheiver
NYS	ATO	$111.86 (12/31/2019)	114.65-89.85	2.06	25.71	31 Years

*7 Year Price Score 121.51 *NYSE Composite Index=100 *12 Month Price Score 98.45

Interim Earnings (Per Share)

Qtr.	Dec	Mar	Jun	Sep
2014-15	0.96	1.35	0.55	0.23
2015-16	1.00	1.38	0.69	0.32
2016-17	1.19	1.55	0.67	0.33
2017-18	2.89	1.60	0.64	0.34
2018-19	1.38	1.82	0.68	0.47

Interim Dividends (Per Share)

Amt	Decl	Ex	Rec	Pay
0.525Q	02/05/2019	02/22/2019	02/25/2019	03/11/2019
0.525Q	05/07/2019	05/24/2019	05/28/2019	06/10/2019
0.525Q	08/07/2019	08/23/2019	08/26/2019	09/09/2019
0.575Q	11/06/2019	11/22/2019	11/25/2019	12/09/2019

Indicated Div: $2.30 (Div. Reinv. Plan)

Valuation Analysis / **Institutional Holding**

Forecast EPS	$4.67	No of Institutions	
	(01/16/2020)	713	
Market Cap	$13.3 Billion	Shares	
Book Value	$5.8 Billion	121,505,016	
Price/Book	2.32	% Held	
Price/Sales	4.60	93.35	

TRADING VOLUME (thousand shares)

Business Summary: Gas Utilities (MIC: 3.3.1 SIC: 4924 NAIC: 221210)

Atmos Energy is engaged in the regulated natural gas distribution and pipeline and storage businesses. Co. delivers natural gas through regulated sales and transportation arrangements to residential, commercial, public-authority and industrial customers. Co.'s segments are: Distribution, which is comprised of its regulated natural gas distribution and related sales operations; and Pipeline and Storage, which consists of the pipeline and storage operations of its Atmos Pipeline-Texas Division (APT) and its natural gas transmission operations in Louisiana. APT has intrastate pipeline operations in Texas with a focus on the natural gas-producing areas of central, northern and eastern Texas.

Recent Developments: For the year ended Sep 30 2019, income from continuing operations decreased 15.2% to US$511.4 million from US$603.1 million a year earlier. Net income decreased 15.2% to US$511.4 million in the prior year. Revenues were US$2.90 billion, down 6.9% from US$3.12 billion the year before. Operating income was US$746.1 million versus US$727.9 million in the prior year, an increase of 2.5%. Direct operating expenses declined 26.5% to US$858.8 million from US$1.17 billion in the comparable period the year before. Indirect operating expenses increased 6.3% to US$1.30 billion from US$1.22 billion in the equivalent prior-year period.

Prospects: Our evaluation of Atmos Energy Corp. as of October 4th, 2019 is the result of our systematic analysis on three basic characteristics: earnings strength, relative valuation, and recent stock price movement. The company has managed to produce a neutral trend in earnings per share over the past 5 quarters. In addition, recent analyst estimates for the company have been mixed and ATO has posted results in line with analysts' expectations. Based on operating earnings yield, the company is fairly valued when compared to all of the companies we cover. Share price changes over the past year indicates that ATO will perform well over the near term.

Financial Data

(US$ in Thousands)	09/30/2019	09/30/2018	09/30/2017	09/30/2016	09/30/2015	09/30/2014	09/30/2013	09/30/2012
Earnings Per Share	4.35	5.43	3.73	3.38	3.09	2.96	2.64	2.37
Cash Flow Per Share	8.27	10.13	8.17	7.66	8.21	7.58	6.77	6.49
Tang Book Value Per Share	42.06	36.30	29.86	26.17	24.16	23.35	20.29	17.93
Dividends Per Share	2.100	1.940	1.800	1.680	1.560	1.480	1.400	1.380
Dividend Payout %	48.28	35.73	48.26	49.70	50.49	50.00	53.03	58.23
Income Statement								
Total Revenue	2,901,848	3,115,546	2,759,735	3,349,949	4,142,136	4,940,916	3,886,257	3,438,483
EBITDA	1,154,382	1,078,873	1,043,909	959,521	903,011	861,070	739,289	678,173
Depn & Amortn	400,920	361,083	319,633	293,096	276,005	254,956	237,607	246,577
Income Before Taxes	650,309	611,144	604,094	550,477	510,765	476,819	373,297	290,422
Income Taxes	138,903	8,080	221,383	200,373	195,690	187,002	142,599	98,226
Net Income	511,406	603,064	396,421	350,104	315,075	289,817	243,194	216,717
Average Shares	117,461	111,012	106,100	103,524	101,892	97,608	91,711	91,172
Balance Sheet								
Current Assets	458,031	478,853	539,646	681,686	630,985	775,840	683,266	827,962
Total Assets	13,367,619	11,874,437	10,749,596	10,010,889	9,092,945	8,594,704	7,940,401	7,495,675
Current Liabilities	1,209,440	1,915,131	1,013,443	1,788,281	1,154,823	910,650	978,486	1,275,954
Long-Term Obligations	3,529,452	2,493,665	3,067,045	2,188,779	2,455,388	2,455,986	2,455,671	1,956,305
Total Liabilities	7,617,396	7,104,486	6,850,930	6,547,830	5,898,148	5,508,472	5,359,992	5,136,432
Stockholders' Equity	5,750,223	4,769,951	3,898,666	3,463,059	3,194,797	3,086,232	2,580,409	2,359,243
Shares Outstanding	119,338	111,273	106,104	103,930	101,478	100,388	90,640	90,239
Statistical Record								
Return on Assets %	4.05	5.33	3.82	3.66	3.56	3.51	3.15	2.92
Return on Equity %	9.72	13.91	10.77	10.49	10.03	10.23	9.85	9.37
EBITDA Margin %	39.78	34.63	37.83	28.64	21.80	17.43	19.02	19.72
Net Margin %	17.62	19.36	14.36	10.45	7.61	5.87	6.26	6.30
Asset Turnover	0.23	0.28	0.27	0.35	0.47	0.60	0.50	0.46
Current Ratio	0.38	0.25	0.53	0.38	0.55	0.85	0.70	0.65
Debt to Equity	0.61	0.52	0.79	0.63	0.77	0.80	0.95	0.83
Price Range	114.65-89.33	94.77-78.03	88.69-68.96	81.32-57.82	58.81-47.35	53.40-41.08	45.19-33.20	36.94-30.60
P/E Ratio	26.36-20.54	17.45-14.37	23.78-18.49	24.06-17.11	19.03-15.32	18.04-13.88	17.12-12.58	15.59-12.91
Average Yield %	2.07	2.23	2.27	2.39	2.89	3.11	3.52	4.11

Address: Three Lincoln Centre, Suite 1800, 5430 LBJ Freeway, Dallas, TX 75240 **Telephone:** 972-934-9227 **Fax:** 972-855-3075	**Web Site:** www.atmosenergy.com **Officers:** Kim R. Cocklin - Executive Chairman, President, Chief Executive Officer John K. Akers - President, Executive Vice President, Senior Vice President, Chief Executive Officer	**Auditors:** Ernst & Young LLP **Investor Contact:** 972-855-3729 **Transfer Agents:** American Stock Transfer & Trust Company, New York, NY

AUTOLIV INC

Exchange	Symbol	Price	52Wk Range	Yield	P/E
NYS	ALV	$84.41 (12/31/2019)	86.79-61.57	2.94	34.31

*7 Year Price Score 80.36 *NYSE Composite Index=100 *12 Month Price Score 103.98

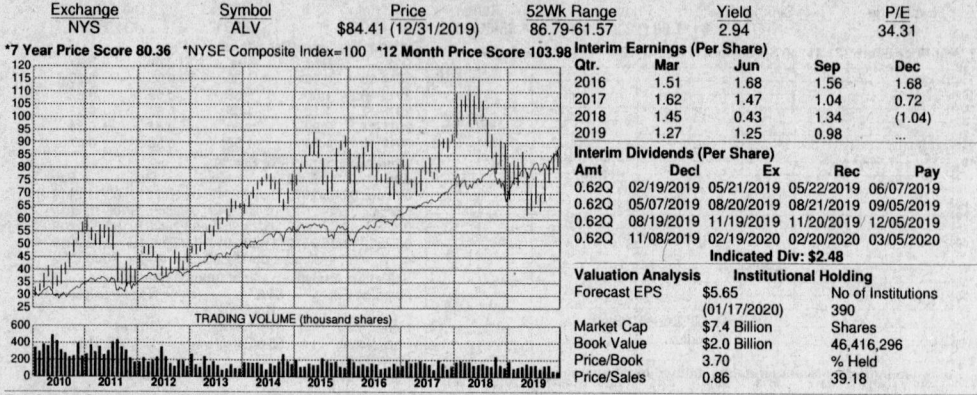

Interim Earnings (Per Share)

Qtr.	Mar	Jun	Sep	Dec
2016	1.51	1.68	1.56	1.68
2017	1.62	1.47	1.04	0.72
2018	1.45	0.43	1.34	(1.04)
2019	1.27	1.25	0.98	...

Interim Dividends (Per Share)

Amt	Decl	Ex	Rec	Pay
0.62Q	02/19/2019	05/21/2019	05/22/2019	06/07/2019
0.62Q	05/07/2019	08/20/2019	08/21/2019	09/05/2019
0.62Q	08/19/2019	11/19/2019	11/20/2019	12/05/2019
0.62Q	11/08/2019	02/19/2020	02/20/2020	03/05/2020

Indicated Div: $2.48

Valuation Analysis

		Institutional Holding	
Forecast EPS	$5.65	No of Institutions	
	(01/17/2020)	390	
Market Cap	$7.4 Billion	Shares	
Book Value	$2.0 Billion	46,416,296	
Price/Book	3.70	% Held	
Price/Sales	0.86	39.18	

Business Summary: Auto Parts (MIC: 1.8.2 SIC: 3714 NAIC: 336399)

Autoliv is a holding company. Through its subsidiaries, Autoliv AB and Autoliv ASP, Inc., Co. develops, manufactures and supplies automotive safety systems to the automotive industry with a range of product offerings, primarily passive safety systems. Passive safety systems are primarily to improve vehicle safety. Passive safety systems include modules and components for frontal-impact airbag protection systems, side-impact airbag protection systems, seatbelts, steering wheels, inflator technologies, battery cable cutters, pedestrian protection systems and child seats. Co.'s business is conducted in the following geographical regions, Europe, the Americas, China, Japan and the Rest of Asia.

Recent Developments: For the quarter ended Sep 30 2019, net income decreased 27.1% to US$86.0 million from US$118.0 million in the year-earlier quarter. Revenues were US$2.03 billion, unchanged from the year before. Operating income was US$153.8 million versus US$192.5 million in the prior-year quarter, a decrease of 20.1%. Direct operating expenses was unchanged at US$1.65 billion versus the comparable period the year before. Indirect operating expenses increased 16.4% to US$225.3 million from US$193.6 million in the equivalent prior-year period.

Prospects: Our evaluation of Autoliv Inc. as of October 4th, 2019 is the result of our systematic analysis on three basic characteristics: earnings strength, relative valuation, and recent stock price movement. The company has produced a positive trend in earnings per share over the past 5 quarters. However, recent analyst estimates for the company have been reduced, and ALV has posted results that fell short of analysts' expectations. Based on operating earnings yield, the company is undervalued when compared to all of the companies we cover. Share price changes over the past year indicates that ALV will perform very poorly over the near term.

Financial Data

(US$ in Thousands)	9 Mos	6 Mos	3 Mos	12/31/2018	12/31/2017	12/31/2016	12/31/2015	12/31/2014
Earnings Per Share	2.46	2.82	2.00	2.18	4.87	6.42	5.17	5.06
Cash Flow Per Share	7.08	7.58	8.36	6.78	10.70	9.82	8.51	7.74
Tang Book Value Per Share	6.64	6.97	6.21	5.29	25.08	18.07	18.86	19.90
Dividends Per Share	2.480	2.480	2.480	2.460	2.380	2.300	2.220	2.120
Dividend Payout %	100.81	87.94	124.00	112.84	48.87	35.83	42.94	41.90
Income Statement								
Total Revenue	6,356,400	4,328,700	2,174,000	8,678,200	10,382,600	10,073,600	9,169,600	9,240,500
EBITDA	495,700	342,400	172,400	1,010,000	1,015,200	1,242,100	1,052,400	1,024,100
Depn & Amortn	8,600	5,700	2,800	342,000	425,900	383,000	319,000	305,400
Income Before Taxes	437,200	303,200	152,600	608,800	535,500	801,200	671,000	660,100
Income Taxes	131,900	83,500	42,100	234,900	203,500	242,200	218,200	198,000
Net Income	611,800	441,000	222,800	190,400	427,100	567,100	456,800	467,800
Average Shares	87,300	87,300	87,400	87,300	87,700	88,400	88,400	92,400
Balance Sheet								
Current Assets	2,908,800	3,052,200	3,111,100	3,285,400	4,204,700	4,140,900	4,038,300	4,136,200
Total Assets	6,589,500	6,785,500	6,772,600	6,721,600	8,549,900	8,234,400	7,525,500	7,442,900
Current Liabilities	2,304,800	2,418,400	2,738,500	2,865,500	2,654,900	2,597,600	2,226,400	2,138,600
Long-Term Obligations	1,815,100	1,850,200	1,598,100	1,609,000	1,321,700	1,323,600	1,499,400	1,521,200
Total Liabilities	4,602,800	4,761,400	4,812,100	4,837,900	4,514,800	4,557,200	4,069,900	4,015,800
Stockholders' Equity	1,986,700	2,024,100	1,960,500	1,883,700	4,035,100	3,677,200	3,455,600	3,427,100
Shares Outstanding	87,200	87,200	87,224	87,144	86,972	88,230	88,107	88,726
Statistical Record								
Return on Assets %	7.80	6.89	3.66	2.49	5.09	7.18	6.10	6.49
Return on Equity %	25.86	23.27	9.29	6.43	11.08	15.86	13.27	12.63
EBITDA Margin %	7.80	7.91	7.93	11.64	9.78	12.33	11.48	11.08
Net Margin %	9.62	10.19	10.25	2.19	4.11	5.63	4.98	5.06
Asset Turnover	1.28	1.26	1.10	1.14	1.24	1.27	1.23	1.28
Current Ratio	1.26	1.26	1.14	1.15	1.58	1.59	1.81	1.93
Debt to Equity	0.91	0.91	0.82	0.85	0.33	0.36	0.43	0.44
Price Range	90.81-61.57	106.88-61.57	115.08-67.97	115.08-69.78	93.37-69.35	90.60-67.92	94.23-69.57	77.82-62.15
P/E Ratio	36.91-25.03	37.90-21.83	57.54-33.98	52.79-32.01	19.17-14.24	14.11-10.58	18.23-13.46	15.38-12.28
Average Yield %	3.28	3.03	2.74	2.55	2.93	2.91	2.69	2.97

Address: Klarabergsviadukten 70, Section B7, Stockholm, SE-111 64
Telephone: 858-720-600

Web Site: www.autoliv.com
Officers: Hasse Johansson - Chairman Svante Mogefors - Executive Vice President

Auditors: Ernst & Young AB
Investor Contact: 248-223-8107
Transfer Agents: Computershare Trust Company, N.A., Providence, RI

AUTONATION, INC.

Exchange	Symbol	Price	52Wk Range	Yield	P/E
NYS	AN	$48.63 (12/31/2019)	52.99-32.87	N/A	11.42

*7 Year Price Score 72.86   *NYSE Composite Index=100   *12 Month Price Score 110.96

Interim Earnings (Per Share)

Qtr.	Mar	Jun	Sep	Dec
2016	0.89	1.08	1.05	1.13
2017	0.97	0.86	1.00	1.61
2018	1.01	1.07	1.23	1.03
2019	1.01	1.12	1.10	...

Interim Dividends (Per Share)

No Dividends Paid

Valuation Analysis   Institutional Holding

Forecast EPS	$4.34	No of Institutions
	(01/17/2020)	437
Market Cap	$4.3 Billion	Shares
Book Value	$3.0 Billion	83,312,880
Price/Book	1.45	% Held
Price/Sales	0.20	62.72

Business Summary: Retail - Automotive (MIC: 2.1.4 SIC: 5511 NAIC: 441110)

AutoNation, through its subsidiaries, is an automotive retailer. Co. provides a range of automotive products and services, including new vehicles, used vehicles, parts and service, which includes automotive repair and maintenance services as well as wholesale parts and collision businesses, and automotive finance and insurance products, which include vehicle service and other protection products, and the arranging of financing for vehicle purchases through third-party finance sources.Co. owns and operates new vehicle franchises from stores located in the U.S., predominantly in main metropolitan markets in the Sunbelt region. Co. has three segments: Domestic, Import, and Premium Luxury.

Recent Developments: For the quarter ended Sep 30 2019, income from continuing operations decreased 11.0% to US$100.0 million from US$112.3 million in the year-earlier quarter. Net income decreased 11.2% to US$99.5 million from US$112.0 million in the year-earlier quarter. Revenues were US$5.46 billion, up 2.1% from US$5.35 billion the year before. Operating income was US$193.5 million versus US$203.6 million in the prior-year quarter, a decrease of 5.0%. Direct operating expenses rose 1.8% to US$4.57 billion from US$4.49 billion in the comparable period the year before. Indirect operating expenses increased 6.5% to US$693.9 million from US$651.7 million in the equivalent prior-year period.

Prospects: Our evaluation of AutoNation Inc. as of October 4th, 2019 is the result of our systematic analysis on three basic characteristics: earnings strength, relative valuation, and recent stock price movement. The company has managed to produce a neutral trend in earnings per share over the past 5 quarters. In addition, recent analyst estimates for the company have been mixed and AN has posted results that exceeded analysts' expectations. Based on operating earnings yield, the company is undervalued when compared to all of the companies we cover. Share price changes over the past year indicates that AN will perform well over the near term.

Financial Data

(US$ in Thousands)	9 Mos	6 Mos	3 Mos	12/31/2018	12/31/2017	12/31/2016	12/31/2015	12/31/2014
Earnings Per Share	4.26	4.39	4.34	4.34	4.43	4.15	3.89	3.52
Cash Flow Per Share	7.13	7.18	6.32	5.62	5.52	4.99	4.50	4.14
Tang Book Value Per Share	10.27	9.01	7.62	6.75	2.92	1.99	4.65	3.55
Income Statement								
Total Revenue	15,786,800	10,325,600	4,981,800	21,412,800	21,534,600	21,609,000	20,862,000	19,108,800
EBITDA	595,900	398,500	194,000	949,700	1,016,900	1,042,000	1,003,900	934,700
Depn & Amortn	3,900	2,600	1,300	171,600	164,200	148,800	132,100	112,600
Income Before Taxes	401,400	264,300	126,100	529,400	636,500	702,300	722,700	682,300
Income Taxes	108,300	71,200	34,000	133,500	201,500	270,600	279,000	262,500
Net Income	292,300	192,800	92,000	396,000	434,600	430,500	442,600	418,700
Average Shares	90,400	90,200	90,700	91,300	98,200	103,800	113,900	118,900
Balance Sheet								
Current Assets	4,398,800	4,663,600	4,831,800	4,884,000	4,797,500	4,714,800	4,711,400	3,999,200
Total Assets	10,451,800	10,699,500	10,914,300	10,665,100	10,271,500	10,060,000	9,558,300	8,399,700
Current Liabilities	5,195,000	5,590,300	5,898,500	5,658,100	5,635,700	5,829,200	5,169,100	3,882,000
Long-Term Obligations	1,575,800	1,576,200	1,575,900	1,926,200	1,959,200	1,611,100	1,753,700	2,103,400
Total Liabilities	7,455,100	7,816,600	8,128,500	7,949,100	7,902,200	7,749,700	7,209,000	6,327,600
Stockholders' Equity	2,996,700	2,882,900	2,785,800	2,716,000	2,369,300	2,310,300	2,349,300	2,072,100
Shares Outstanding	89,212	89,075	89,204	90,022	91,559	100,652	110,804	113,313
Statistical Record								
Return on Assets %	3.74	3.79	3.73	3.78	4.28	4.38	4.93	5.13
Return on Equity %	13.71	14.77	15.00	15.57	18.57	18.43	20.02	20.26
EBITDA Margin %	3.77	3.86	3.89	4.44	4.72	4.82	4.81	4.89
Net Margin %	1.85	1.87	1.85	1.85	2.02	1.99	2.12	2.19
Asset Turnover	2.06	2.01	2.00	2.05	2.12	2.20	2.32	2.34
Current Ratio	0.85	0.83	0.82	0.86	0.85	0.81	0.91	1.03
Debt to Equity	0.53	0.55	0.57	0.71	0.83	0.70	0.75	1.02
Price Range	52.02-32.87	50.48-32.87	51.06-32.87	62.00-33.24	56.25-38.72	59.66-40.26	66.20-56.12	61.23-46.84
P/E Ratio	12.21-7.72	11.50-7.49	11.76-7.57	14.29-7.66	12.70-8.74	14.38-9.70	17.02-14.43	17.39-13.31

Address: 200 SW 1st Avenue, Fort Lauderdale, FL 33301 Telephone: 954-769-6000	Web Site: www.autonation.com Officers: Michael (Mike) J. Jackson - Executive Chairman, Chairman, President (frmr), Chief Executive Officer, President Cheryl S. Miller - President, Executive Vice President, Chief Executive Officer, Chief Financial Officer	Auditors: KPMG LLP Investor Contact: 954-769-7342 Transfer Agents: Computershare Trust Company, N.A.

AUTOZONE, INC.

Exchange	Symbol	Price	52Wk Range	Yield	P/E
NYS	AZO	$1191 (12/31/2019)	1250.00-811.37	N/A	18.53

*7 Year Price Score 126.16 *NYSE Composite Index=100 *12 Month Price Score 106.23

TRADING VOLUME (thousand shares)

Interim Earnings (Per Share)

Qtr.	Nov	Feb	May	Aug
2017-18	10.00	10.38	13.42	15.02
2018-19	13.47	11.49	15.99	22.51
2019-20	14.30	...	...	...

Interim Dividends (Per Share)

No Dividends Paid

Valuation Analysis		Institutional Holding	
Forecast EPS	$65.85	No of Institutions	
	(01/14/2020)	1010	
Market Cap	$28.2 Billion	Shares	
Book Value	N/A		28,270,344
Price/Book	N/A	% Held	
Price/Sales	2.35		81.78

Business Summary: Retail - Automotive (MIC: 2.1.4 SIC: 5531 NAIC: 441310)

AutoZone is a retailer and a distributor of automotive replacement parts and accessories. Co. operates stores in the United States, including Puerto Rico and Saint Thomas, Mexico, and Brazil. Each store carries a product line for cars, sport utility vehicles, vans and light trucks, including new and remanufactured automotive hard parts, maintenance items, accessories and non-automotive products. In addition, Co. has a commercial sales program that provides commercial credit and delivery of parts and other products to local, regional and national repair garages, dealers, service stations and public sector accounts. Co. also sells the ALLDATA brand automotive diagnostic and repair software.

Recent Developments: For the quarter ended Nov 23 2019, net income decreased 0.3% to US$350.3 million from US$351.4 million in the year-earlier quarter. Revenues were US$2.79 billion, up 5.7% from US$2.64 billion the year before. Operating income was US$500.0 million versus US$487.8 million in the prior-year quarter, an increase of 2.5%. Direct operating expenses rose 5.5% to US$1.29 billion from US$1.22 billion in the comparable period the year before. Indirect operating expenses increased 7.7% to US$1.00 billion from US$929.7 million in the equivalent prior-year period.

Prospects: Our evaluation of AutoZone Inc. as of October 4th, 2019 is the result of our systematic analysis on three basic characteristics: earnings strength, relative valuation, and recent stock price movement. The company has managed to produce a neutral trend in earnings per share over the past 5 quarters. In addition, recent analyst estimates for the company have been mixed and AZO has posted results that exceeded analysts' expectations. Based on operating earnings yield, the company is undervalued when compared to all of the companies we cover. Share price changes over the past year indicates that AZO will perform over the near term.

Financial Data

(US$ in Thousands)	3 Mos	08/31/2019	08/25/2018	08/26/2017	08/27/2016	08/29/2015	08/30/2014	08/31/2013
Earnings Per Share	64.29	63.43	48.77	44.07	40.70	36.03	31.57	27.79
Cash Flow Per Share	89.07	83.88	77.35	55.40	52.92	48.46	40.43	38.73
Income Statement								
Total Revenue	2,793,038	11,863,743	11,221,077	10,888,676	10,635,676	10,187,340	9,475,313	9,147,530
EBITDA	502,218	2,594,256	2,164,333	2,411,489	2,365,772	2,229,200	2,088,346	2,008,588
Depn & Amortn	2,195	378,119	353,477	331,420	305,377	276,149	258,123	235,490
Income Before Taxes	456,280	2,031,333	1,636,329	1,925,489	1,912,714	1,802,612	1,662,714	1,587,683
Income Taxes	105,942	414,112	298,793	644,620	671,707	642,371	592,970	571,203
Net Income	350,338	1,617,221	1,337,536	1,280,869	1,241,007	1,160,241	1,069,744	1,016,480
Average Shares	24,493	25,498	27,424	29,065	30,488	32,206	33,882	36,581
Balance Sheet								
Current Assets	5,156,975	5,028,685	4,635,869	4,611,255	4,239,573	3,970,294	3,580,612	3,278,013
Total Assets	12,700,456	9,895,913	9,346,980	9,259,781	8,599,787	8,102,349	7,517,858	6,892,089
Current Liabilities	5,868,236	5,512,141	5,028,681	4,766,301	4,690,320	4,712,873	4,541,094	4,169,150
Long-Term Obligations	5,287,324	5,206,344	5,005,930	5,081,238	4,924,119	4,624,876	4,162,890	4,013,267
Total Liabilities	14,476,546	11,609,764	10,867,335	10,688,158	10,387,325	9,803,739	9,139,715	8,579,408
Stockholders' Equity	(1,776,090)	(1,713,851)	(1,520,355)	(1,428,377)	(1,787,538)	(1,701,390)	(1,621,857)	(1,687,319)
Shares Outstanding	23,655	24,038	25,742	27,833	29,118	30,659	32,304	34,293
Statistical Record								
Return on Assets %	14.54	16.54	14.42	14.38	14.90	14.90	14.89	15.20
EBITDA Margin %	17.98	21.87	19.29	22.15	22.24	21.88	22.04	21.96
Net Margin %	12.54	13.63	11.92	11.76	11.67	11.39	11.29	11.11
Asset Turnover	1.08	1.21	1.21	1.22	1.28	1.31	1.32	1.37
Current Ratio	0.88	0.91	0.92	0.97	0.90	0.84	0.79	0.79
Price Range	1187.65-809.07	1180.00-714.71	796.95-522.38	809.87-493.15	815.98-695.46	750.13-501.78	543.84-411.89	448.58-344.99
P/E Ratio	18.47-12.58	18.60-11.27	16.34-10.71	18.38-11.19	20.05-17.09	20.82-13.93	17.23-13.05	16.14-12.41

Address: 123 South Front Street, Memphis, TN 38103 **Telephone:** 901-495-6500	**Web Site:** www.autozone.com **Officers:** William C. (Bill) Rhodes - Chairman, President, Chief Executive Officer William T. Giles - Executive Vice President, Chief Financial Officer	**Auditors:** Ernst & Young LLP **Investor Contact:** 901-495-6500 **Transfer Agents:** ComputerShare Investor Services, Providence, RI

AVALONBAY COMMUNITIES, INC.

Exchange	Symbol	Price	52Wk Range	Yield	P/E
NYS	AVB	$209.70 (12/31/2019)	222.04-169.20	2.90	29.00

*7 Year Price Score 99.73   *NYSE Composite Index=100   *12 Month Price Score 98.47

Interim Earnings (Per Share)

Qtr.	Mar	Jun	Sep	Dec
2016	1.73	1.44	2.59	1.76
2017	1.72	1.20	1.72	1.72
2018	1.03	1.84	1.39	2.79
2019	1.23	1.21	2.00	...

Interim Dividends (Per Share)

Amt	Decl	Ex	Rec	Pay
1.52Q	02/04/2019	03/28/2019	03/29/2019	04/15/2019
1.52Q	05/16/2019	06/27/2019	06/28/2019	07/15/2019
1.52Q	09/19/2019	09/27/2019	09/30/2019	10/15/2019
1.52Q	11/20/2019	12/30/2019	12/31/2019	01/15/2020

Indicated Div: $6.08 (Div. Reinv. Plan)

Valuation Analysis

		Institutional Holding	
Forecast EPS	$5.63	No of Institutions	
	(01/17/2020)	798	
Market Cap	$29.3 Billion	Shares	
Book Value	$10.8 Billion	163,624,096	
Price/Book	2.71	% Held	
Price/Sales	12.68	93.39	

Business Summary: REITs (MIC: 5.3.1 SIC: 6798 NAIC: 525930)

AvalonBay Communities is a real estate investment trust. Co. develops, redevelops, acquires, owns and operates multifamily communities primarily in New England, the New York/New Jersey metro area, the Mid-Atlantic, the Pacific Northwest, and Northern and Southern California. Co. owns or holds a direct or indirect ownership interest in: operating apartment communities containing apartment homes in various states and the District of Columbia; communities under development; and rights to develop an additional communities.

Recent Developments: For the quarter ended Sep 30 2019, net income increased 45.4% to US$279.7 million from US$192.4 million in the year-earlier quarter. Revenues were US$587.6 million, up 2.0% from US$576.0 million the year before.

Prospects: Our evaluation of AvalonBay Communities Inc. as of October 4th, 2019 is the result of our systematic analysis on three basic characteristics: earnings strength, relative valuation, and recent stock price movement. The company has managed to produce a neutral trend in earnings per share over the past 5 quarters. In addition, recent analyst estimates for the company have been mixed and AVB has posted results that fell short of analysts' expectations. Based on operating earnings yield, the company is overvalued when compared to all of the companies we cover. Share price changes over the past year indicates that AVB will perform well over the near term.

Financial Data
(US$ in Thousands)

	9 Mos	6 Mos	3 Mos	12/31/2018	12/31/2017	12/31/2016	12/31/2015	12/31/2014
Earnings Per Share	7.23	6.62	7.25	7.05	6.35	7.52	5.51	5.21
Cash Flow Per Share	9.58	9.45	9.74	9.44	9.13	8.34	7.91	6.79
Tang Book Value Per Share	76.57	76.10	76.11	76.77	75.22	74.07	71.83	68.51
Dividends Per Share	6.030	5.980	5.930	5.880	5.680	5.400	5.000	4.640
Dividend Payout %	83.40	90.33	81.79	83.40	89.45	71.81	90.74	89.06
Income Statement								
Total Revenue	1,731,060	1,143,446	566,184	2,284,535	2,158,628	2,045,255	1,856,028	1,685,061
EBITDA	1,295,892	780,304	389,146	1,810,915	1,589,868	1,687,995	1,327,114	1,143,050
Depn & Amortn	517,667	342,822	169,764	631,196	584,150	531,434	477,923	442,682
Income Before Taxes	628,830	339,580	171,490	958,745	806,057	969,051	673,576	519,750
Income Taxes	11,178	(6)	12	(160)	141	305	1,861	9,368
Net Income	618,324	338,647	170,366	974,525	876,921	1,034,002	742,038	683,567
Average Shares	139,852	139,618	138,832	138,289	138,066	137,461	134,593	131,237
Balance Sheet								
Current Assets	334,754	330,044	195,207	249,680	234,592	362,048	535,405	634,702
Total Assets	19,060,467	18,932,575	18,639,983	18,380,200	18,414,821	17,867,271	16,931,305	16,176,723
Current Liabilities	439,379	429,300	441,110	309,254	297,683	280,727	264,474	244,027
Long-Term Obligations	7,361,279	7,352,217	7,040,067	7,040,263	7,329,470	7,030,880	6,456,948	6,525,852
Total Liabilities	8,246,042	8,182,575	7,905,984	7,747,594	8,026,775	7,695,855	7,090,779	7,130,318
Stockholders' Equity	10,814,425	10,750,000	10,733,999	10,632,606	10,388,046	10,171,416	9,840,526	9,046,405
Shares Outstanding	139,660	139,656	139,403	138,508	138,094	137,330	137,002	132,050
Statistical Record								
Return on Assets %	5.32	4.88	5.38	5.30	4.83	5.93	4.48	4.34
Return on Equity %	9.47	8.67	9.52	9.27	8.53	10.31	7.86	7.75
EBITDA Margin %	74.86	68.24	68.73	79.27	73.65	82.53	71.50	67.83
Net Margin %	35.72	29.62	30.09	42.66	40.62	50.56	39.98	40.57
Asset Turnover	0.12	0.12	0.12	0.12	0.12	0.12	0.11	0.11
Current Ratio	0.76	0.77	0.44	0.81	0.79	1.29	2.02	2.60
Debt to Equity	0.68	0.68	0.66	0.66	0.71	0.69	0.66	0.72
Price Range	216.16-168.84	210.47-168.84	200.92-157.76	191.67-153.90	199.10-169.61	191.00-159.75	185.54-159.08	169.20-117.53
P/E Ratio	29.90-23.35	31.79-25.50	27.71-21.76	27.19-21.83	31.35-26.71	25.40-21.24	33.67-28.87	32.48-22.56
Average Yield %	3.08	3.18	3.32	3.42	3.07	3.06	2.91	3.26

Address: Ballston Tower, 671 N. Glebe Road, Suite 800, Arlington, VA 22203 **Telephone:** 703-329-6300 **Fax:** 703-329-9130	**Web Site:** www.avalonbay.com **Officers:** Timothy J. Naughton - Chairman, President, Chief Executive Officer William M. McLaughlin - Executive Vice President, Executive Vice President (frmr)	**Auditors:** Ernst & Young LLP **Investor Contact:** 703-317-4681 **Transfer Agents:** Computershare, Pittsburgh, PA

AVANGRID INC

Exchange	Symbol	Price	52Wk Range	Yield	P/E
NYS	AGR	$51.16 (12/31/2019)	52.63-47.76	3.44	26.65

*7 Year Price Score N/A *NYSE Composite Index=100 *12 Month Price Score 93.62

Interim Earnings (Per Share)

Qtr.	Mar	Jun	Sep	Dec
2016	0.69	0.33	0.35	0.68
2017	0.77	0.39	0.32	(0.25)
2018	0.79	0.34	0.40	0.38
2019	0.70	0.36	0.48	...

Interim Dividends (Per Share)

Amt	Decl	Ex	Rec	Pay
0.44Q	02/13/2019	03/07/2019	03/08/2019	04/01/2019
0.44Q	04/11/2019	06/06/2019	06/07/2019	07/01/2019
0.44Q	07/16/2019	09/05/2019	09/06/2019	10/01/2019
0.44Q	12/02/2019	12/11/2019	12/12/2019	01/02/2020

Indicated Div: $1.76

Valuation Analysis

Forecast EPS	$2.23
	(01/17/2020)
Market Cap	$15.8 Billion
Book Value	$15.2 Billion
Price/Book	1.04
Price/Sales	2.47

Institutional Holding

No of Institutions	311
Shares	47,926,096
% Held	14.54

Business Summary: Electric Utilities (MIC: 3.1.1 SIC: 4911 NAIC: 221119)

Avangrid is an energy services holding company engaged in the regulated energy distribution business through its subsidiary, Avangrid Networks, Inc. (Networks), and in the renewable energy generation business through its subsidiary, Avangrid Renewables Holding, Inc. (ARHI). ARHI in turn holds subsidiaries including Avangrid Renewables, LLC (Renewables). Networks owns and operates its regulated utility businesses through its subsidiaries, including electric transmission and distribution and natural gas distribution, transportation and sales. Renewables operates a portfolio of renewable energy generation facilities primarily using onshore wind power and also solar, biomass and thermal power.

Recent Developments: For the quarter ended Sep 30 2019, net income increased 3.7% to US$139.0 million from US$134.0 million in the year-earlier quarter. Revenues were US$1.49 billion, down 3.8% from US$1.55 billion the year before. Operating income was US$239.0 million versus US$253.0 million in the prior-year quarter, a decrease of 5.5%. Direct operating expenses declined 5.3% to US$867.0 million from US$916.0 million in the comparable period the year before. Indirect operating expenses increased 1.1% to US$381.0 million from US$377.0 million in the equivalent prior-year period.

Prospects: Our evaluation of Avangrid Inc as of October 4th, 2019 is the result of our systematic analysis on three basic characteristics: earnings strength, relative valuation, and recent stock price movement. The company has produced a positive trend in earnings per share over the past 5 quarters. However, recent analyst estimates for the company have been reduced, and AGR has posted results that fell short of analysts' expectations. Based on operating earnings yield, the company is fairly valued when compared to all of the companies we cover. Share price changes over the past year indicates that AGR will perform well over the near term.

Financial Data

(US$ in Thousands)	9 Mos	6 Mos	3 Mos	12/31/2018	12/31/2017	12/31/2016	12/31/2015	12/31/2014
Earnings Per Share	1.92	1.84	1.82	1.92	1.23	2.04	1.05	1.70
Cash Flow Per Share	5.55	5.25	4.88	5.79	5.70	5.03	5.35	5.48
Tang Book Value Per Share	37.89	37.83	37.90	37.71	37.61	37.05	36.85	43.25
Dividends Per Share	1.760	1.760	1.752	1.744	1.728	1.728	...	...
Dividend Payout %	91.67	95.65	96.26	90.83	140.49	84.71	...	...
Income Statement								
Total Revenue	4,729,000	3,242,000	1,842,000	6,478,000	5,963,000	6,018,000	4,367,000	4,594,000
EBITDA	839,000	575,000	348,000	1,911,000	1,205,000	2,056,000	1,209,000	1,512,000
Depn & Amortn	51,000	32,000	14,000	840,000	802,000	779,000	641,000	563,000
Income Before Taxes	562,000	389,000	256,000	768,000	123,000	1,009,000	301,000	706,000
Income Taxes	103,000	70,000	41,000	170,000	(259,000)	379,000	34,000	282,000
Net Income	477,000	327,000	217,000	595,000	381,000	630,000	267,000	424,000
Average Shares	309,517	309,512	309,712	309,712	309,661	309,817	254,605	243,000
Balance Sheet								
Current Assets	1,880,000	1,803,000	1,998,000	1,963,000	2,260,000	2,252,000	2,474,000	2,299,000
Total Assets	33,547,000	33,141,000	32,608,000	32,167,000	31,671,000	31,309,000	30,743,000	24,252,000
Current Liabilities	2,848,000	2,812,000	3,153,000	3,004,000	3,114,000	2,712,000	2,035,000	1,773,000
Long-Term Obligations	6,718,000	6,282,000	5,487,000	5,368,000	5,196,000	4,510,000	4,530,000	2,516,000
Total Liabilities	18,397,000	18,006,000	17,450,000	17,063,000	16,594,000	16,200,000	15,690,000	11,812,000
Stockholders' Equity	15,150,000	15,135,000	15,158,000	15,104,000	15,077,000	15,109,000	15,053,000	12,440,000
Shares Outstanding	309,005	309,005	309,005	309,005	309,005	308,993	308,864	243,000
Statistical Record								
Return on Assets %	1.83	1.77	1.77	1.86	1.21	2.03	0.97	1.79
Return on Equity %	3.94	3.77	3.75	3.94	2.52	4.17	1.94	3.47
EBITDA Margin %	17.74	17.74	18.89	29.50	20.21	34.16	27.68	32.91
Net Margin %	10.09	10.09	11.78	9.18	6.39	10.47	6.11	9.23
Asset Turnover	0.20	0.20	0.20	0.20	0.19	0.19	0.16	0.19
Current Ratio	0.66	0.64	0.63	0.65	0.73	0.83	1.22	1.30
Debt to Equity	0.44	0.42	0.36	0.36	0.34	0.30	0.30	0.20
Price Range	53.08-46.16	54.13-46.16	54.26-46.16	54.26-45.83	53.07-37.80	46.49-35.62	38.40-33.26	...
P/E Ratio	27.65-24.04	29.42-25.09	29.81-25.36	28.26-23.87	43.15-30.73	22.79-17.46	36.57-31.68	...
Average Yield %	3.53	3.53	3.49	3.49	3.79	4.26	...	...

Address: 180 Marsh Hill Road, Orange, CT 06477	**Web Site:** www.avangrid.com	**Auditors:** KPMG LLP
Telephone: 207-629-1200	**Officers:** Peter Church - Senior Vice President Ignacio Sanchez Galan - Chairman	**Transfer Agents:** Broadridge Corporate Issuer Solutions, Inc., Philadelphia, PA

AVANOS MEDICAL INC

Exchange	Symbol	Price	52Wk Range	Yield	P/E
NYS	AVNS	$33.70 (12/31/2019)	51.04-31.89	N/A	N/A

*7 Year Price Score N/A   *NYSE Composite Index=100   *12 Month Price Score 84.61

Interim Earnings (Per Share)

Qtr.	Mar	Jun	Sep	Dec
2016	0.30	0.14	0.19	0.22
2017	0.27	0.36	0.35	0.71
2018	0.43	0.73	0.09	(0.05)
2019	(0.43)	(0.17)	(0.24)	...

Interim Dividends (Per Share)

No Dividends Paid

Valuation Analysis   Institutional Holding

Forecast EPS	$1.04	No of Institutions	
	(01/16/2020)	402	
Market Cap	$1.6 Billion	Shares	
Book Value	$1.3 Billion	51,322,964	
Price/Book	1.27	% Held	
Price/Sales	2.37	N/A	

TRADING VOLUME (thousand shares)

Business Summary: Medical Instruments & Equipment (MIC: 4.3.1 SIC: 3842 NAIC: 339113)

Avanos Medical is a medical technology company focused on delivering medical device solutions to healthcare providers and patients in more than 90 countries with manufacturing facilities in the United States, Mexico, France, Germany and Tunisia. Co. provides a portfolio of product offerings focused on respiratory and digestive health, along with surgical and interventional pain management. These products include post-operative pain management solutions, minimally invasive interventional (or chronic) pain therapies, closed airway suction systems and enteral feeding tubes. Products are sold under the ON-Q, COOLIEF, MICROCUFF, MIC-KEY, HOMEPUMP, CORTRAK, GAME READY and other brand names.

Recent Developments: For the quarter ended Sep 30 2019, loss from continuing operations was US$11.5 million compared with income of US$4.2 million in the year-earlier quarter. Net loss amounted to US$11.5 million versus net income of US$4.2 million in the year-earlier quarter. Revenues were US$171.4 million, up 3.8% from US$165.1 million the year before. Operating loss was US$18.1 million versus an income of US$7.0 million in the prior-year quarter. Direct operating expenses rose 26.5% to US$76.4 million from US$60.4 million in the comparable period the year before. Indirect operating expenses increased 15.8% to US$113.1 million from US$97.7 million in the equivalent prior-year period.

Prospects: Our evaluation of Avanos Medical Inc. as of October 4th, 2019 is the result of our systematic analysis on three basic characteristics: earnings strength, relative valuation, and recent stock price movement. The company has generated a negative trend in earnings per share over the past 5 quarters. However, recent analyst estimates for the company have been mixed and AVNS has posted results in line with analysts' expectations. Based on operating earnings yield, the company is fairly valued when compared to all of the companies we cover. Share price changes over the past year indicates that AVNS will perform very poorly over the near term.

Financial Data

(US$ in Thousands)	9 Mos	6 Mos	3 Mos	12/31/2018	12/31/2017	12/31/2016	12/31/2015	12/31/2014
Earnings Per Share	(0.89)	(0.56)	0.34	1.22	1.69	0.85	(9.15)	0.58
Cash Flow Per Share	(1.66)	(2.74)	(4.11)	(3.08)	3.08	4.04	2.09	3.18
Tang Book Value Per Share	5.80	7.05	7.01	7.28	6.43	N.M.	0.59	N.M.
Income Statement								
Total Revenue	507,800	336,400	164,200	652,300	611,600	1,592,300	1,574,400	1,672,100
EBITDA	(41,700)	(27,100)	(21,000)	14,000	(24,100)	130,400	(337,700)	147,300
Depn & Amortn	10,800	7,300	3,600	13,500	19,000	43,000	40,000	53,000
Income Before Taxes	(57,500)	(37,200)	(25,900)	(18,100)	(72,200)	55,300	(410,500)	91,200
Income Taxes	(17,700)	(8,900)	(5,600)	(9,600)	(40,100)	15,500	15,800	64,100
Net Income	(39,800)	(28,300)	(20,300)	57,500	79,300	39,800	(426,300)	27,100
Average Shares	47,700	47,600	47,500	47,200	46,800	47,000	46,600	46,538
Balance Sheet								
Current Assets	546,500	572,500	660,000	713,600	1,160,700	593,500	676,000	684,900
Total Assets	1,807,700	1,783,400	1,834,000	1,833,400	2,195,900	2,071,800	2,000,200	2,527,600
Current Liabilities	218,100	187,000	238,400	264,300	389,800	324,400	315,200	356,000
Long-Term Obligations	247,900	247,800	305,600	247,700	541,100	579,000	578,100	632,300
Total Liabilities	540,800	506,500	553,900	536,200	980,500	969,300	944,900	1,036,400
Stockholders' Equity	1,266,900	1,276,900	1,280,100	1,297,200	1,215,400	1,102,500	1,055,300	1,491,200
Shares Outstanding	47,719	47,653	47,504	47,444	46,920	46,681	46,614	46,535
Statistical Record								
Return on Assets %	N.M.	N.M.	0.84	2.85	3.72	1.95	N.M.	...
Return on Equity %	N.M.	N.M.	1.34	4.58	6.84	3.68	N.M.	...
EBITDA Margin %	N.M.	N.M.	N.M.	2.15	N.M.	8.19	N.M.	8.81
Net Margin %	N.M.	N.M.	N.M.	8.81	12.97	2.50	N.M.	1.62
Asset Turnover	0.37	0.36	0.33	0.32	0.29	0.78	0.70	...
Current Ratio	2.51	3.06	2.77	2.70	2.98	1.83	2.14	1.92
Debt to Equity	0.20	0.19	0.24	0.19	0.45	0.53	0.55	0.42
Price Range	66.67-32.06	72.65-37.68	72.65-39.84	72.65-41.16	48.63-35.52	39.06-23.29	50.41-27.00	45.47-35.82
P/E Ratio	...	...	213.68-117.18	59.55-33.74	28.78-21.02	45.95-27.40	...	78.40-61.76

Address: 5405 Windward Parkway, Suite 100 South, Alpharetta, GA 30004 **Telephone:** 844-428-2667	**Web Site:** www.avanos.com **Officers:** Ronald W. Dollens - Chairman Joseph Fralin Woody - Chief Executive Officer	**Auditors:** DELOITTE & TOUCHE LLP **Transfer Agents:** Computershare

AVERY DENNISON CORP

Exchange	Symbol	Price	52Wk Range	Yield	P/E
NYS	AVY	$130.82 (12/31/2019)	133.89-87.07	1.77	47.06

*7 Year Price Score 123.20 *NYSE Composite Index=100 *12 Month Price Score 109.19

Interim Earnings (Per Share)

Qtr.	Mar	Jun	Sep	Dec
2016	0.98	0.88	0.98	0.69
2017	1.25	1.34	1.20	(0.66)
2018	1.40	1.07	1.69	1.12
2019	(1.74)	1.69	1.71	...

Interim Dividends (Per Share)

Amt	Decl	Ex	Rec	Pay
0.52Q	01/30/2019	03/05/2019	03/06/2019	03/20/2019
0.58Q	04/25/2019	06/04/2019	06/05/2019	06/19/2019
0.58Q	07/24/2019	09/03/2019	09/04/2019	09/18/2019
0.58Q	10/24/2019	12/03/2019	12/04/2019	12/18/2019

Indicated Div: $2.32 (Div. Reinv. Plan)

Valuation Analysis

		Institutional Holding	
Forecast EPS	$6.55	No of Institutions	
	(01/16/2020)	805	
Market Cap	$10.9 Billion	Shares	
Book Value	$1.1 Billion	103,709,192	
Price/Book	10.34	% Held	
Price/Sales	1.55	83.09	

Business Summary: Containers & Packaging (MIC: 8.1.3 SIC: 2671 NAIC: 326112)

Avery Dennison is engaged in the production of pressure-sensitive materials and a variety of tickets, tags, labels and other converted products. Co. sells its pressure-sensitive materials to label printers and converters that convert the materials into labels and other products through embossing, printing, stamping and die-cutting. Co. sells other pressure-sensitive materials in converted form as tapes and reflective sheeting. Co. also manufactures and sells a variety of other converted products and items not involving pressure-sensitive components, such as fasteners, tickets, tags, radio-frequency identification inlays and tags, and imprinting equipment and related solutions.

Recent Developments: For the quarter ended Sep 28 2019, net income decreased 3.3% to US$144.6 million from US$149.5 million in the year-earlier quarter. Revenues were US$1.76 billion, unchanged from the year before. Direct operating expenses declined 0.8% to US$1.29 billion from US$1.30 billion in the comparable period the year before. Indirect operating expenses increased 0.2% to US$291.8 million from US$291.2 million in the equivalent prior-year period.

Prospects: Our evaluation of Avery Dennison Corp. as of October 4th, 2019 is the result of our systematic analysis on three basic characteristics: earnings strength, relative valuation, and recent stock price movement. The company has managed to produce a neutral trend in earnings per share over the past 5 quarters. However, recent analyst estimates for the company have been reduced while AVY has posted results that exceeded analysts' expectations. Based on operating earnings yield, the company is undervalued when compared to all of the companies we cover. Share price changes over the past year indicates that AVY will perform well over the near term.

Financial Data

(US$ in Thousands)	9 Mos	6 Mos	3 Mos	12/29/2018	12/30/2017	12/31/2016	01/02/2016	01/03/2015
Earnings Per Share	2.78	2.76	2.14	5.28	3.13	3.54	2.95	2.60
Cash Flow Per Share	8.78	5.78	5.66	5.26	7.38	6.59	5.22	3.92
Tang Book Value Per Share	0.09	N.M.	N.M.	N.M.	N.M.	0.74	2.60	3.07
Dividends Per Share	2.200	2.140	2.080	2.010	1.760	1.600	1.460	1.340
Dividend Payout %	79.14	77.54	97.20	38.07	56.23	45.20	49.49	51.54
Income Statement								
Total Revenue	5,297,200	3,535,800	1,740,100	7,159,000	6,613,800	6,086,500	5,966,900	6,330,300
EBITDA	275,600	32,700	(220,400)	754,800	779,100	654,500	594,600	563,200
Depn & Amortn	133,400	89,400	44,500	141,500	126,600	117,500	125,200	135,500
Income Before Taxes	84,200	(95,700)	(284,400)	554,800	589,500	477,100	408,900	364,400
Income Taxes	(58,900)	(93,500)	(138,400)	85,400	307,700	156,400	134,500	113,300
Net Income	141,100	(3,500)	(146,900)	467,400	281,800	320,700	274,300	248,900
Average Shares	84,800	85,100	84,300	88,600	90,100	90,700	92,900	95,700
Balance Sheet								
Current Assets	2,333,400	2,377,200	2,323,700	2,298,000	2,237,900	1,904,800	1,775,400	1,921,300
Total Assets	5,338,700	5,389,700	5,353,700	5,177,500	5,136,900	4,396,400	4,133,700	4,360,200
Current Liabilities	2,267,900	2,278,500	2,040,500	1,994,000	1,971,800	2,004,300	1,459,100	1,597,800
Long-Term Obligations	1,483,700	1,503,300	1,759,900	1,771,600	1,316,300	713,400	963,600	945,300
Total Liabilities	4,281,300	4,327,200	4,361,800	4,222,400	4,090,700	3,470,900	3,168,000	3,293,700
Stockholders' Equity	1,057,400	1,062,500	991,900	955,100	1,046,200	925,500	965,700	1,066,500
Shares Outstanding	83,584	84,227	84,399	84,723	88,011	88,308	89,967	90,458
Statistical Record								
Return on Assets %	4.53	4.61	3.67	9.09	5.93	7.54	6.48	5.46
Return on Equity %	22.64	23.33	18.76	46.84	28.66	34.01	27.07	19.14
EBITDA Margin %	5.20	0.92	N.M.	10.54	11.78	10.75	9.96	8.90
Net Margin %	2.66	N.M.	N.M.	6.53	4.26	5.27	4.60	3.93
Asset Turnover	1.34	1.34	1.34	1.39	1.39	1.43	1.41	1.39
Current Ratio	1.03	1.04	1.14	1.15	1.13	0.95	1.22	1.20
Debt to Equity	1.40	1.41	1.77	1.85	1.26	0.77	1.00	0.89
Price Range	120.48-83.79	116.37-83.79	114.68-83.79	122.68-83.79	117.10-70.14	78.84-58.16	66.18-51.07	52.67-41.28
P/E Ratio	43.34-30.14	42.16-30.36	53.59-39.15	23.23-15.87	37.41-22.41	22.27-16.43	22.43-17.31	20.26-15.88
Average Yield %	2.09	2.07	2.07	1.90	1.94	2.22	2.49	2.74

Address: 207 Goode Avenue, Glendale, CA 91203 **Telephone:** 626-304-2000	**Web Site:** www.averydennison.com **Officers:** Mitchell R. Butier - Chairman, President, Chief Executive Officer, Senior Vice President, Chief Financial Officer, Chief Operating Officer Gregory S. Lovins - Senior Vice President, Chief Financial Officer, Vice President, Interim Chief Financial Officer, Treasurer	**Auditors:** PricewaterhouseCoopers LLP **Investor Contact:** 626-304-2000 **Transfer Agents:** Broadridge Corporate Issuer Solutions, Inc., Brentwood, NY

BADGER METER INC

Exchange	Symbol	Price	52Wk Range	Yield	P/E	Div Achiever
NYS	BMI	$64.93 (12/31/2019)	66.08-47.88	1.05	41.09	26 Years

*7 Year Price Score 123.64 *NYSE Composite Index=100 *12 Month Price Score 103.96

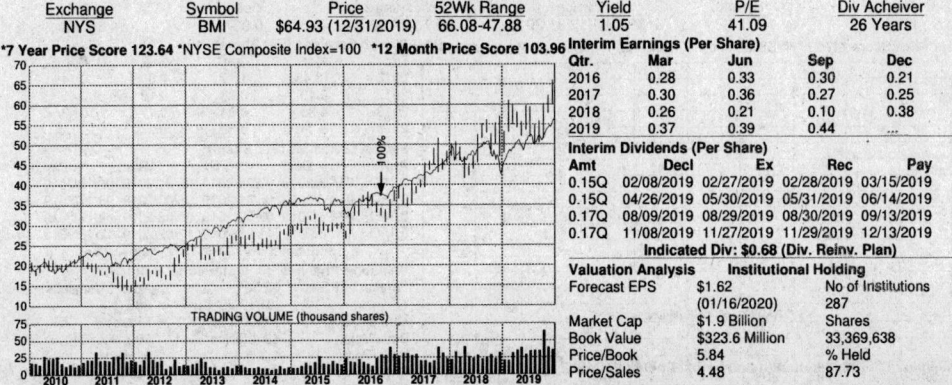

Interim Earnings (Per Share)

Qtr.	Mar	Jun	Sep	Dec
2016	0.28	0.33	0.30	0.21
2017	0.30	0.36	0.27	0.25
2018	0.26	0.21	0.10	0.38
2019	0.37	0.39	0.44	...

Interim Dividends (Per Share)

Amt	Decl	Ex	Rec	Pay
0.15Q	02/08/2019	02/27/2019	02/28/2019	03/15/2019
0.15Q	04/26/2019	05/30/2019	05/31/2019	06/14/2019
0.17Q	08/09/2019	08/29/2019	08/30/2019	09/13/2019
0.17Q	11/08/2019	11/27/2019	11/29/2019	12/13/2019

Indicated Div: $0.68 (Div. Reinv. Plan)

Valuation Analysis

	Institutional Holding
Forecast EPS $1.62 (01/16/2020)	No of Institutions 287
Market Cap $1.9 Billion	Shares
Book Value $323.6 Million	33,369,638
Price/Book 5.84	% Held
Price/Sales 4.48	87.73

Business Summary: Electronic Instruments & Related Products (MIC: 6.2.3 SIC: 3824 NAIC: 334514)

Badger Meter is an innovator, manufacturer and marketer of products incorporating flow measurement, control and communication solutions serving markets worldwide. Co.'s product lines fall into two categories: sales of water meters, radios and related technologies to municipal water utilities (municipal water) and sales of meters, valves and other products for industrial applications in water, wastewater, and other industries (flow instrumentation). Co. provides flow measurement, control and communication portfolios in the market. This portfolio carries brand names including Recordall®, Hedland®, Dynasonics®, Blancett®, and Research Control®.

Recent Developments: For the quarter ended Sep 30 2019, net income increased 346.2% to US$12.7 million from US$2.9 million in the year-earlier quarter. Revenues were US$108.6 million, down 1.8% from US$110.6 million the year before. Operating income was US$16.4 million versus US$15.7 million in the prior-year quarter, an increase of 4.5%. Direct operating expenses rose 0.4% to US$67.0 million from US$66.7 million in the comparable period the year before. Indirect operating expenses decreased 10.6% to US$25.2 million from US$28.2 million in the equivalent prior-year period.

Prospects: Our evaluation of Badger Meter Inc. as of October 4th, 2019 is the result of our systematic analysis on three basic characteristics: earnings strength, relative valuation, and recent stock price movement. The company has generated a negative trend in earnings per share over the past 5 quarters. However, recent analyst estimates for the company have been raised and BMI has posted results that fell short of analysts' expectations. Based on operating earnings yield, the company is fairly valued when compared to all of the companies we cover. Share price changes over the past year indicates that BMI will perform in line with the market over the near term.

Financial Data

(US$ in Thousands)	9 Mos	6 Mos	3 Mos	12/31/2018	12/31/2017	12/31/2016	12/31/2015	12/31/2014
Earnings Per Share	1.58	1.24	1.06	0.95	1.19	1.11	0.90	1.03
Cash Flow Per Share	2.81	2.62	2.46	2.08	1.72	1.94	1.25	1.25
Tang Book Value Per Share	6.95	6.65	6.31	6.07	5.18	5.32	4.37	3.63
Dividends Per Share	0.620	0.600	0.580	0.560	0.490	0.430	0.390	0.370
Dividend Payout %	39.24	48.39	54.72	58.95	41.18	38.74	43.33	35.92
Income Statement								
Total Revenue	317,069	208,423	104,881	433,732	402,440	393,761	377,698	364,768
EBITDA	63,693	41,638	20,522	48,363	67,678	61,480	52,362	54,938
Depn & Amortn	18,011	12,360	6,242	11,354	12,056	10,715	9,993	8,891
Income Before Taxes	45,402	29,064	14,151	35,852	54,833	49,844	41,152	44,912
Income Taxes	10,499	6,882	3,327	8,062	20,262	17,549	15,214	15,234
Net Income	34,903	22,182	10,824	27,790	34,571	32,295	25,938	29,678
Average Shares	29,193	29,211	29,238	29,189	29,111	29,050	28,894	28,756
Balance Sheet								
Current Assets	191,541	175,544	171,223	164,659	158,623	151,012	149,328	141,105
Total Assets	417,490	404,861	403,249	392,691	391,727	349,699	355,480	341,158
Current Liabilities	58,845	54,307	57,924	60,015	93,109	75,838	104,544	107,075
Total Liabilities	93,851	88,409	94,636	89,188	114,275	93,490	123,205	126,827
Stockholders' Equity	323,639	316,452	308,613	303,503	277,452	256,209	232,275	214,331
Shares Outstanding	29,111	29,113	29,114	29,118	29,118	29,118	29,049	28,922
Statistical Record								
Return on Assets %	11.27	9.00	7.78	7.09	9.33	9.13	7.45	9.03
Return on Equity %	14.91	11.99	10.54	9.57	12.96	13.19	11.62	14.45
EBITDA Margin %	20.09	19.98	19.57	11.15	16.82	15.61	13.86	15.06
Net Margin %	11.01	10.64	10.32	6.41	8.59	8.20	6.87	8.14
Asset Turnover	1.03	1.05	1.09	1.11	1.09	1.11	1.08	1.11
Current Ratio	3.26	3.23	2.96	2.74	1.70	1.99	1.43	1.32
Price Range	61.05-46.99	61.05-45.40	61.05-41.50	56.97-41.50	51.60-34.60	38.55-26.61	32.79-27.66	30.02-23.79
P/E Ratio	38.64-29.74	49.23-36.61	57.59-39.15	59.97-43.68	43.36-29.08	34.73-23.97	36.43-30.73	29.15-23.10
Average Yield %	1.15	1.12	1.14	1.14	1.18	1.26	1.30	1.41

Address: 4545 W. Brown Deer Road, Milwaukee, WI 53233 **Telephone:** 414-355-0400	**Web Site:** www.badgermeter.com **Officers:** Kenneth C. (Ken) Bockhorst - Chairman, President, Chief Executive Officer, Senior Vice President, Chief Operating Officer Robert A. Wrocklage - Senior Vice President, Vice President, Chief Financial Officer, Treasurer	**Auditors:** Ernst & Young LLP **Investor Contact:** 414-371-5702 **Transfer Agents:** American Stock Transfer & Trust Company, LLC, New York, NY

BALL CORP

Exchange	Symbol	Price	52Wk Range	Yield	P/E
NYS	BLL	$64.67 (12/31/2019)	80.78-44.26	0.93	39.92

*7 Year Price Score 137.97 ***NYSE Composite Index=100** ***12 Month Price Score 96.51**

Interim Earnings (Per Share)

Qtr.	Mar	Jun	Sep	Dec
2016	(0.45)	1.17	0.00	0.14
2017	0.19	0.28	0.13	0.45
2018	0.35	0.34	0.17	0.43
2019	0.34	0.58	0.27	...

Interim Dividends (Per Share)

Amt	Decl	Ex	Rec	Pay
0.10Q	01/23/2019	02/28/2019	03/01/2019	03/15/2019
0.15Q	04/24/2019	05/31/2019	06/03/2019	06/17/2019
0.15Q	07/24/2019	08/30/2019	09/03/2019	09/17/2019
0.15Q	10/23/2019	11/29/2019	12/02/2019	12/16/2019

Indicated Div: $0.60 (Div. Reinv. Plan)

Valuation Analysis   **Institutional Holding**

Forecast EPS	$2.50	No of Institutions
	(01/17/2020)	882
Market Cap	$21.3 Billion	Shares
Book Value	$3.4 Billion	302,757,504
Price/Book	6.33	% Held
Price/Sales	1.84	76.41

Business Summary: Metal Products (MIC: 8.2.3 SIC: 3411 NAIC: 332431)

Ball is a supplier of metal packaging to the beverage, personal care and household products industries. Co. provides aerospace and other technologies and services. Co.'s main product line is aluminum beverage containers. Co. also produces aerosol containers, extruded aluminum aerosol containers and aluminum slugs. Co.'s segments are: beverage packaging, North and Central America, beverage packaging, South America, and beverage packaging, Europe, all of which are engaged in manufacturing and selling metal beverage containers; and aerospace, which manufactures and sells aerospace and other related products and provides services used in the defense, civil space and commercial space industries.

Recent Developments: For the quarter ended Sep 30 2019, net income increased 55.9% to US$92.0 million from US$59.0 million in the year-earlier quarter. Revenues were US$2.95 billion, unchanged from the year before. Operating income was US$198.0 million versus US$268.0 million in the prior-year quarter, a decrease of 26.1%. Direct operating expenses was unchanged at US$2.36 billion versus the comparable period the year before. Indirect operating expenses increased 24.1% to US$392.0 million from US$316.0 million in the equivalent prior-year period.

Prospects: Our evaluation of Ball Corp. as of October 4th, 2019 is the result of our systematic analysis on three basic characteristics: earnings strength, relative valuation, and recent stock price movement. The company has enjoyed a very positive trend in earnings per share over the past 5 quarters. However, recent analyst estimates for the company have been mixed and BLL has posted results in line with analysts' expectations. Based on operating earnings yield, the company is fairly valued when compared to all of the companies we cover. Share price changes over the past year indicates that BLL will perform very well over the near term.

Financial Data

(US$ in Thousands)	9 Mos	6 Mos	3 Mos	12/31/2018	12/31/2017	12/31/2016	12/31/2015	12/31/2014
Earnings Per Share	1.62	1.52	1.28	1.29	1.05	0.81	1.00	1.65
Cash Flow Per Share	3.61	4.16	4.52	4.54	4.22	0.61	3.67	3.66
Dividends Per Share	0.500	0.450	0.400	0.400	0.365	0.260	0.260	0.260
Dividend Payout %	30.86	29.61	31.25	31.01	34.76	31.90	26.13	15.76
Income Statement								
Total Revenue	8,755,000	5,802,000	2,785,000	11,635,000	10,983,000	9,061,000	7,997,000	8,570,000
EBITDA	1,094,000	782,000	343,000	1,433,000	1,311,000	812,000	852,500	1,078,100
Depn & Amortn	368,000	254,000	122,000	498,000	509,000	349,000	247,300	239,500
Income Before Taxes	485,000	366,000	140,000	633,000	514,000	125,000	345,500	645,600
Income Taxes	73,000	41,000	10,000	185,000	165,000	(126,000)	47,000	149,900
Net Income	406,000	314,000	117,000	454,000	374,000	263,000	280,900	470,000
Average Shares	340,632	341,637	342,676	352,321	356,985	322,884	281,968	284,860
Balance Sheet								
Current Assets	3,829,000	4,533,000	4,399,000	3,940,000	3,758,000	3,653,000	2,184,000	2,313,500
Total Assets	16,237,000	17,109,000	16,923,000	16,554,000	17,169,000	16,173,000	9,777,000	7,571,000
Current Liabilities	3,773,000	4,134,000	4,035,000	4,095,000	4,107,000	2,969,000	2,141,600	2,006,800
Long-Term Obligations	6,623,000	6,916,000	6,719,000	6,510,000	6,518,000	7,310,000	5,054,200	2,993,800
Total Liabilities	12,872,000	13,649,000	13,377,000	13,096,000	13,228,000	12,738,000	8,525,700	6,537,900
Stockholders' Equity	3,365,000	3,460,000	3,546,000	3,458,000	3,941,000	3,435,000	1,251,300	1,033,100
Shares Outstanding	329,196	331,840	334,469	335,258	349,881	349,730	284,578	273,932
Statistical Record								
Return on Assets %	3.41	3.03	2.57	2.69	2.24	2.02	3.24	6.11
Return on Equity %	15.90	14.26	11.77	12.27	10.14	11.19	24.59	42.10
EBITDA Margin %	12.50	13.48	12.32	12.32	11.94	8.96	10.66	12.58
Net Margin %	4.64	5.41	4.20	3.90	3.41	2.90	3.51	5.48
Asset Turnover	0.71	0.67	0.67	0.69	0.66	0.70	0.92	1.11
Current Ratio	1.01	1.10	1.09	0.96	0.92	1.23	1.02	1.15
Debt to Equity	1.97	2.00	1.89	1.88	1.65	2.13	4.04	2.90
Price Range	80.78-42.35	69.99-35.76	58.84-35.25	50.50-35.25	42.93-35.77	41.01-31.95	38.58-30.25	35.08-24.14
P/E Ratio	49.86-26.14	46.05-23.53	45.97-27.54	39.15-27.33	40.89-34.06	50.63-39.44	38.58-30.25	21.26-14.63
Average Yield %	0.84	0.89	0.89	0.90	0.97	0.92	0.71	0.86

Address: 10 Longs Peak Drive, P.O.	Web Site: www.ball.com	Auditors: PricewaterhouseCoopers LLP
Box 5000, Broomfield, CO 80021-2510	Officers: John A. Hayes - Chairman, President, Chief	Investor Contact: 303-460-3537
Telephone: 303-469-3131	Executive Officer Scott C. Morrison - Senior Vice	Transfer Agents: Computershare,
	President, Chief Financial Officer, Treasurer	Providence, RI

BANCORPSOUTH BANK (TUPELO, MS)

Exchange	Symbol	Price	52Wk Range	Yield	P/E
NYS	BXS	$31.41 (12/31/2019)	33.17-26.14	2.36	14.61

*7 Year Price Score 94.08   *NYSE Composite Index=100   *12 Month Price Score 101.03

Interim Earnings (Per Share)

Qtr.	Mar	Jun	Sep	Dec
2016	0.24	0.37	0.40	0.41
2017	0.41	0.41	0.43	0.42
2018	0.54	0.55	0.67	0.47
2019	0.52	0.53	0.63	...

Interim Dividends (Per Share)

Amt	Decl	Ex	Rec	Pay
0.17Q	01/23/2019	03/14/2019	03/15/2019	04/01/2019
0.17Q	04/24/2019	06/13/2019	06/14/2019	07/01/2019
0.185Q	07/24/2019	09/12/2019	09/13/2019	10/01/2019
0.185Q	10/23/2019	12/12/2019	12/13/2019	01/02/2020

Indicated Div: $0.74 (Div. Reinv. Plan)

Valuation Analysis

		Institutional Holding	
Forecast EPS	$2.27	No of Institutions	
	(01/17/2020)	289	
Market Cap	$3.3 Billion	Shares	
Book Value	$2.5 Billion	83,775,760	
Price/Book	1.32	% Held	
Price/Sales	3.24	N/A	

Business Summary: Banking (MIC: 5.1.1 SIC: 6022 NAIC: 522110)

BancorpSouth Bank conducts commercial banking and financial services to individuals and small-to-medium size businesses. Co.'s segments are: Mortgage, which includes the mortgage banking activities of originating mortgage loans, selling mortgage loans in the secondary market and servicing the mortgage loans; Insurance Agencies, which serves as agents in the sale of commercial lines of insurance and lines of property and casualty, life, health and employee benefits products and services; Wealth Management, which includes credit related products; and General Corporate and Other, which includes other activities not allocated to the segments.

Recent Developments: For the quarter ended Sep 30 2019, net income decreased 4.4% to US$63.8 million from US$66.7 million in the year-earlier quarter. Net interest income increased 17.2% to US$166.6 million from US$142.1 million in the year-earlier quarter. Non-interest income rose 5.3% to US$75.4 million from US$71.6 million, while non-interest expense advanced 12.1% to US$159.6 million.

Prospects: Our evaluation of BancorpSouth Bank as of October 4th, 2019 is the result of our systematic analysis on three basic characteristics: earnings strength, relative valuation, and recent stock price movement. The company has managed to produce a neutral trend in earnings per share over the past 5 quarters. In addition, recent analyst estimates for the company have been mixed and BXS has posted results that fell short of analysts' expectations. Based on operating earnings yield, the company is undervalued when compared to all of the companies we cover. Share price changes over the past year indicates that BXS will perform poorly over the near term.

Financial Data

(US$ in Thousands)	9 Mos	6 Mos	3 Mos	12/31/2018	12/31/2017	12/31/2016	12/31/2015	12/31/2014
Earnings Per Share	2.15	2.19	2.21	2.23	1.67	1.41	1.33	1.21
Cash Flow Per Share	1.84	2.17	2.52	2.26	1.98	1.52	1.39	1.48
Tang Book Value Per Share	15.33	15.17	14.92	14.62	15.44	14.95	14.27	13.40
Dividends Per Share	0.700	0.680	0.650	0.620	0.530	0.450	0.350	0.250
Dividend Payout %	32.56	31.05	29.41	27.80	31.74	31.91	26.32	20.66
Income Statement								
Interest Income	571,200	372,196	181,133	653,493	512,991	483,179	464,378	450,257
Interest Expense	92,030	59,625	28,579	78,271	38,955	29,727	28,696	33,595
Net Interest Income	479,170	312,571	152,554	575,222	474,036	453,452	435,682	416,662
Provision for Losses	1,500	1,000	500	4,500	3,000	4,000	(13,000)	...
Non-Interest Income	205,984	130,552	64,220	282,037	268,033	279,030	277,968	269,146
Non-Interest Expense	467,256	307,642	149,968	587,634	507,446	532,038	539,911	518,406
Income Before Taxes	216,398	134,481	66,306	265,125	231,623	196,444	186,739	167,402
Income Taxes	47,986	29,826	14,708	43,808	78,590	63,716	59,248	50,652
Net Income	168,412	104,655	51,598	221,317	153,033	132,728	127,491	116,750
Average Shares	101,493	100,888	99,717	99,135	91,755	94,455	96,124	96,302
Balance Sheet								
Net Loans & Leases	14,233,389	13,718,734	13,092,939	13,132,379	11,074,811	10,855,182	10,404,227	9,711,508
Total Assets	19,850,225	18,936,814	18,314,183	18,001,540	15,298,518	14,724,388	13,798,662	13,326,369
Total Deposits	16,025,756	15,136,648	14,692,609	14,069,966	11,915,596	11,688,141	11,331,161	10,972,339
Total Liabilities	17,360,798	16,609,694	16,087,598	15,795,803	13,585,033	13,000,505	12,143,218	11,720,310
Stockholders' Equity	2,489,427	2,327,120	2,226,585	2,205,737	1,713,485	1,723,883	1,655,444	1,606,059
Shares Outstanding	104,775	100,651	99,066	99,797	90,312	93,696	94,162	96,254
Statistical Record								
Return on Assets %	1.16	1.21	1.24	1.33	1.02	0.93	0.94	0.89
Return on Equity %	9.36	9.93	10.24	11.29	8.90	7.83	7.82	7.49
Net Interest Margin %	83.72	83.75	84.22	88.02	92.41	93.85	93.82	92.54
Efficiency Ratio %	58.16	61.26	61.12	62.81	64.97	69.80	72.73	72.06
Loans to Deposits	0.89	0.91	0.89	0.93	0.93	0.93	0.92	0.89
Price Range	33.17-24.55	35.10-24.55	35.15-24.55	35.20-24.55	34.20-27.55	31.60-18.96	26.93-19.76	25.90-19.62
P/E Ratio	15.43-11.42	16.03-11.21	15.90-11.11	15.78-11.01	20.48-16.50	22.41-13.45	20.25-14.86	21.40-16.21
Average Yield %	2.41	2.23	2.06	1.92	1.73	1.91	1.45	1.09

Address: One Mississippi Plaza, 201 South Spring Street, Tupelo, MS 38804 **Telephone:** 662-680-2000	**Web Site:** www.bancorpsouth.com **Officers:** James D. Rollins - Chairman, Chief Executive Officer Christopher A. Bagley - President, Chief Operating Officer, Interim Chief Financial Officer, Treasurer	**Auditors:** KPMG LLP **Investor Contact:** 662-680-2000 **Transfer Agents:** Computershare, Canton, MA

BANK OF AMERICA CORP

Exchange	Symbol	Price	52Wk Range	Yield	P/E
NYS	BAC	$35.22 (12/31/2019)	35.52-24.56	2.04	13.04

*7 Year Price Score 117.09 *NYSE Composite Index=100 *12 Month Price Score 107.26

Interim Earnings (Per Share)

Qtr.	Mar	Jun	Sep	Dec
2016	0.21	0.36	0.41	0.40
2017	0.41	0.46	0.48	0.21
2018	0.62	0.63	0.66	0.70
2019	0.70	0.74	0.56	...

Interim Dividends (Per Share)

Amt	Decl	Ex	Rec	Pay
0.15Q	01/30/2019	02/28/2019	03/01/2019	03/29/2019
0.15Q	04/24/2019	06/06/2019	06/07/2019	06/28/2019
0.18Q	07/25/2019	09/05/2019	09/06/2019	09/27/2019
0.18Q	10/22/2019	12/05/2019	12/06/2019	12/27/2019

Indicated Div: $0.72 (Div. Reinv. Plan)

Valuation Analysis

		Institutional Holding	
Forecast EPS	$3.05	No of Institutions	
	(01/17/2020)	2979	
Market Cap	$319.8 Billion	Shares	
Book Value	$268.4 Billion	7,646,970,880	
Price/Book	1.19	% Held	
Price/Sales	2.79	59.50	

Business Summary: Banking (MIC: 5.1.1 SIC: 6021 NAIC: 522110)

Bank of America is a bank and a financial holding company. Through its subsidiaries, Co. provides a range of banking, investing, asset management and other financial and risk management products and services. Co.'s segments include: Consumer Banking, which provides credit, banking and investment products and services; Global Wealth and Investment Management, which provides investment management, brokerage, banking and retirement products; Global Banking, which provides lending-related products and services, integrated working capital management and treasury solutions, and underwriting and advisory services; and Global Markets, which provides sales and trading services and research services.

Recent Developments: For the quarter ended Sep 30 2019, net income decreased 19.4% to US$5.78 billion from US$7.17 billion in the year-earlier quarter. Net interest income increased 1.0% to US$12.19 billion from US$12.06 billion in the year-earlier quarter. Provision for loan losses was US$779.0 million versus US$716.0 million in the prior-year quarter, an increase of 8.8%. Non-interest income fell 0.4% to US$10.62 billion from US$10.66 billion, while non-interest expense advanced 16.6% to US$15.17 billion.

Prospects: Our evaluation of Bank of America Corp. as of October 4th, 2019 is the result of our systematic analysis on three basic characteristics: earnings strength, relative valuation, and recent stock price movement. The company has generated a negative trend in earnings per share over the past 5 quarters. In addition, recent analyst estimates for the company have been reduced while BAC has posted results that exceeded analysts' expectations. Based on operating earnings yield, the company is undervalued when compared to all of the companies we cover. Share price changes over the past year indicates that BAC will perform in line with the market over the near term.

Financial Data

(US$ in Millions)	9 Mos	6 Mos	3 Mos	12/31/2018	12/31/2017	12/31/2016	12/31/2015	12/31/2014
Earnings Per Share	2.70	2.80	2.69	2.61	1.56	1.50	1.31	0.36
Cash Flow Per Share	(1.21)	1.48	1.47	3.91	1.02	1.78	2.65	2.54
Tang Book Value Per Share	19.37	19.03	18.37	18.00	16.87	16.61	15.16	13.91
Dividends Per Share	0.630	0.600	0.570	0.540	0.390	0.250	0.200	0.120
Dividend Payout %	23.33	21.43	21.19	20.69	25.00	16.67	15.27	33.33
Income Statement								
Interest Income	54,310	36,394	18,170	66,769	57,579	51,057	49,800	50,886
Interest Expense	17,559	11,830	5,795	19,337	12,912	9,961	10,549	10,934
Net Interest Income	36,751	24,564	12,375	47,432	44,667	41,096	39,251	39,952
Provision for Losses	2,649	1,870	1,013	3,282	3,396	3,597	3,161	2,275
Non-Interest Income	32,144	21,524	10,629	43,815	42,685	42,605	43,256	44,295
Non-Interest Expense	41,661	26,492	13,224	53,381	54,743	54,951	57,192	75,117
Income Before Taxes	24,585	17,726	8,767	34,584	29,213	25,153	22,154	6,855
Income Taxes	4,149	3,067	1,456	6,437	10,981	7,247	6,266	2,022
Net Income	20,436	14,659	7,311	28,147	18,232	17,906	15,888	4,833
Average Shares	9,353	9,559	9,787	10,236	10,779	11,036	11,215	10,584
Balance Sheet								
Net Loans & Leases	973,288	959,689	942,335	947,661	937,786	904,512	898,220	879,808
Total Assets	2,426,330	2,395,892	2,377,164	2,354,507	2,281,234	2,187,702	2,144,316	2,104,534
Total Deposits	1,392,836	1,375,093	1,379,337	1,381,476	1,309,545	1,260,934	1,197,259	1,118,936
Total Liabilities	2,157,943	2,124,484	2,110,154	2,089,182	2,014,088	1,920,862	1,888,111	1,861,063
Stockholders' Equity	268,387	271,408	267,010	265,325	267,146	266,840	256,205	243,471
Shares Outstanding	9,079	9,342	9,568	9,669	10,287	10,052	10,380	10,516
Statistical Record								
Return on Assets %	1.16	1.24	1.21	1.21	0.82	0.82	0.75	0.23
Return on Equity %	10.45	10.87	10.70	10.57	6.83	6.83	6.36	2.03
Net Interest Margin %	68.02	66.88	68.11	71.04	77.58	80.49	78.82	78.51
Efficiency Ratio %	53.16	45.56	45.92	48.27	54.60	58.67	61.46	78.92
Loans to Deposits	0.70	0.70	0.68	0.69	0.72	0.72	0.75	0.79
Price Range	30.89-22.73	31.80-22.73	31.80-22.73	32.84-22.73	29.88-22.05	23.16-11.16	18.45-15.15	18.13-14.51
P/E Ratio	11.44-8.42	11.36-8.12	11.82-8.45	12.58-8.71	19.15-14.13	15.44-7.44	14.08-11.56	50.36-40.31
Average Yield %	2.23	2.09	2.14	1.82	1.58	1.62	1.24	0.73

Address: Bank of America Corporate Center, 100 N. Tryon Street, Charlotte, NC 28255 Telephone: 704-386-5681	Web Site: www.bankofamerica.com Officers: Brian T. Moynihan - Chairman, President, Chief Executive Officer, Division Officer Thong M. Nguyen - Vice-Chairman, Division Officer	Auditors: PricewaterhouseCoopers LLP Investor Contact: 800-521-3984 Transfer Agents: Computershare Trust Company, N.A., Providence, RI

BANK OF HAWAII CORP

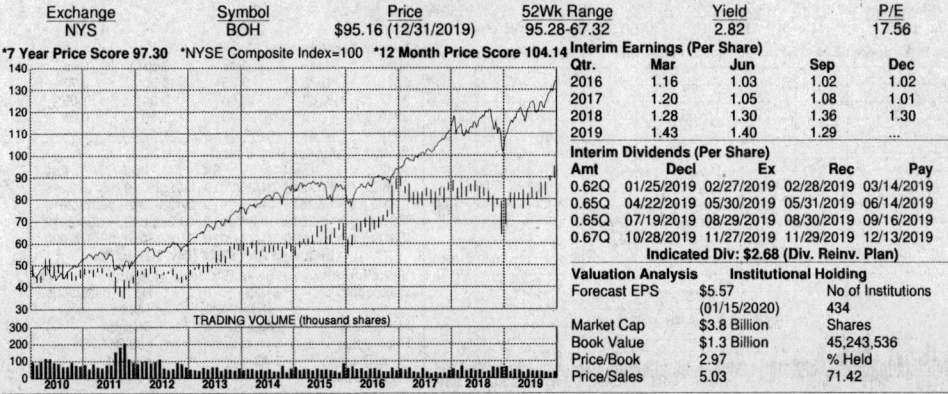

Exchange	Symbol	Price	52Wk Range	Yield	P/E
NYS	BOH	$95.16 (12/31/2019)	95.28-67.32	2.82	17.56

*7 Year Price Score 97.30 *NYSE Composite Index=100 *12 Month Price Score 104.14

Interim Earnings (Per Share)

Qtr.	Mar	Jun	Sep	Dec
2016	1.16	1.03	1.02	1.02
2017	1.20	1.05	1.08	1.01
2018	1.28	1.30	1.36	1.30
2019	1.43	1.40	1.29	...

Interim Dividends (Per Share)

Amt	Decl	Ex	Rec	Pay
0.62Q	01/25/2019	02/27/2019	02/28/2019	03/14/2019
0.65Q	04/22/2019	05/30/2019	05/31/2019	06/14/2019
0.65Q	07/19/2019	08/29/2019	08/30/2019	09/16/2019
0.67Q	10/28/2019	11/27/2019	11/29/2019	12/13/2019

Indicated Div: $2.68 (Div. Reinv. Plan)

Valuation Analysis

		Institutional Holding	
Forecast EPS	$5.57	No of Institutions	
	(01/15/2020)	434	
Market Cap	$3.8 Billion	Shares	
Book Value	$1.3 Billion	45,243,536	
Price/Book	2.97	% Held	
Price/Sales	5.03	71.42	

TRADING VOLUME (thousand shares)

Business Summary: Banking (MIC: 5.1.1 SIC: 6022 NAIC: 522110)

Bank of Hawaii is a bank holding company. Through its subsidiary, Bank of Hawaii, Co. provides financial products and services primarily to customers in Hawaii, Guam, and other Pacific Islands. Co. has four segments: Retail Banking, which provides loan and lease, deposit, and retail insurance products; Commercial Banking, which provides corporate banking, commercial real estate loans, commercial lease financing, auto dealer financing, and deposit products; Investment Services and Private Banking, which includes trust services, investment management, and institutional investment advisory services; and Treasury and Other, which consists of corporate asset and liability management activities.

Recent Developments: For the quarter ended Sep 30 2019, net income decreased 8.6% to US$52.1 million from US$56.9 million in the year-earlier quarter. Net interest income increased 1.5% to US$124.9 million from US$123.0 million in the year-earlier quarter. Provision for loan losses was US$4.3 million versus US$3.8 million in the prior-year quarter, an increase of 11.8%. Non-interest income rose 12.1% to US$46.5 million from US$41.5 million, while non-interest expense advanced 10.8% to US$100.3 million.

Prospects: Our evaluation of Bank of Hawaii Corp. as of October 4th, 2019 is the result of our systematic analysis on three basic characteristics: earnings strength, relative valuation, and recent stock price movement. The company has managed to produce a neutral trend in earnings per share over the past 5 quarters. However, recent analyst estimates for the company have been reduced while BOH has posted results that exceeded analysts' expectations. Based on operating earnings yield, the company is undervalued when compared to all of the companies we cover. Share price changes over the past year indicates that BOH will perform in line with the market over the near term.

Financial Data

(US$ in Thousands)	9 Mos	6 Mos	3 Mos	12/31/2018	12/31/2017	12/31/2016	12/31/2015	12/31/2014
Earnings Per Share	5.42	5.49	5.39	5.23	4.33	4.23	3.70	3.69
Cash Flow Per Share	6.50	7.14	6.35	7.62	4.14	5.30	5.41	4.77
Tang Book Value Per Share	30.61	30.24	29.55	29.21	27.73	25.95	24.53	22.84
Dividends Per Share	2.540	2.490	2.440	2.340	2.040	1.890	1.800	1.800
Dividend Payout %	46.86	45.36	45.27	44.74	47.11	44.68	48.65	48.78
Income Statement								
Interest Income	442,296	294,213	145,642	550,173	503,794	457,900	432,110	417,633
Interest Expense	68,466	45,279	20,805	63,821	46,556	40,321	38,023	37,977
Net Interest Income	373,830	248,934	124,837	486,352	457,238	417,579	394,087	379,656
Provision for Losses	11,250	7,000	3,000	13,425	16,900	4,750	1,000	(4,864)
Non-Interest Income	135,636	89,129	43,679	168,923	185,417	197,343	186,219	180,017
Non-Interest Expense	286,131	185,782	93,057	371,624	357,691	350,578	348,104	326,899
Income Before Taxes	212,085	145,281	72,459	270,226	268,064	259,594	231,202	237,638
Income Taxes	44,315	29,563	13,660	50,624	83,392	78,133	70,498	74,596
Net Income	167,770	115,718	58,799	219,602	184,672	181,461	160,704	163,042
Average Shares	40,450	40,769	41,213	41,999	42,607	42,879	43,454	44,125
Balance Sheet								
Net Loans & Leases	10,809,082	10,674,163	10,460,495	10,353,068	9,708,832	8,908,011	7,780,913	6,794,037
Total Assets	17,672,140	17,688,845	17,446,413	17,143,974	17,089,052	16,492,367	15,455,016	14,787,208
Total Deposits	15,340,752	15,488,821	15,267,310	15,027,242	14,883,968	14,320,240	13,251,103	12,633,089
Total Liabilities	16,380,650	16,402,897	16,176,723	15,875,774	15,857,184	15,330,830	14,338,756	13,732,122
Stockholders' Equity	1,291,490	1,285,948	1,269,690	1,268,200	1,231,868	1,161,537	1,116,260	1,055,086
Shares Outstanding	40,359	40,687	41,078	41,499	42,401	42,635	43,282	43,724
Statistical Record								
Return on Assets %	1.28	1.30	1.30	1.28	1.10	1.13	1.06	1.13
Return on Equity %	17.42	17.88	17.87	17.57	15.43	15.89	14.80	15.78
Net Interest Margin %	84.34	83.53	85.71	88.40	90.76	91.19	91.20	90.91
Efficiency Ratio %	51.57	47.79	49.15	51.68	51.90	53.50	56.30	54.70
Loans to Deposits	0.70	0.69	0.69	0.69	0.65	0.62	0.59	0.54
Price Range	87.55-63.92	86.07-63.92	88.33-63.92	88.62-63.92	90.36-75.00	89.31-55.26	69.22-54.53	61.52-53.53
P/E Ratio	16.15-11.79	15.68-11.64	16.39-11.86	16.94-12.22	20.87-17.32	21.11-13.06	18.71-14.74	16.67-14.51
Average Yield %	3.19	3.13	3.03	2.85	2.47	2.67	2.85	3.12

Address: 130 Merchant Street, Honolulu, HI 96813 **Telephone:** 888-643-3888	**Web Site:** www.boh.com **Officers:** Peter S. Ho - Chairman, President, Chief Executive Officer, Chief Banking Officer Wayne Y. Hamano - Vice-Chairman, Chief Commercial Officer	**Auditors:** Ernst & Young LLP **Investor Contact:** 808-694-8430 **Transfer Agents:** Computershare Investor Services, LLC, Canton, MA

BANK OF NEW YORK MELLON CORP

Exchange	Symbol	Price	52Wk Range	Yield	P/E
NYS	BK	$50.33 (12/31/2019)	53.98-40.95	2.46	13.04

*7 Year Price Score 92.24 *NYSE Composite Index=100 *12 Month Price Score 97.32

Interim Earnings (Per Share)

Qtr.	Mar	Jun	Sep	Dec
2016	0.73	0.75	0.90	0.77
2017	0.83	0.88	0.94	1.08
2018	1.10	1.03	1.06	0.84
2019	0.94	1.01	1.07	...

Interim Dividends (Per Share)

Amt	Decl	Ex	Rec	Pay
0.28Q	04/17/2019	04/26/2019	04/29/2019	05/10/2019
0.31Q	07/17/2019	07/26/2019	07/29/2019	08/09/2019
0.31Q	10/16/2019	10/25/2019	10/28/2019	11/08/2019
0.31Q	01/16/2020	01/24/2020	01/27/2020	02/07/2020

Indicated Div: $1.24 (Div. Reinv. Plan)

Valuation Analysis

		Institutional Holding	
Forecast EPS	$4.23	No of Institutions	
	(01/17/2020)	1464	
Market Cap	$46.4 Billion	Shares	
Book Value	$41.1 Billion	890,267,584	
Price/Book	1.13	% Held	
Price/Sales	2.31	73.74	

Business Summary: Banking (MIC: 5.1.1 SIC: 6022 NAIC: 522110)

Bank of New York Mellon is a bank holding company. Through its subsidiaries, Co. provides a range of financial products and services in domestic and international markets. Co.'s segments include: Investment Services, which provides business services and technology solutions to entities including financial institutions, corporations, foundations and endowments, public funds and government agencies; Investment Management, in which its investment personnel deliver a portfolio of investment services independently, and through its global distribution network, to institutional and retail clients; and Other, which includes corporate treasury activities, derivatives and other trading activity.

Recent Developments: For the quarter ended Sep 30 2019, net income decreased 6.6% to US$1.04 billion from US$1.11 billion in the year-earlier quarter. Net interest income decreased 18.1% to US$730.0 million from US$891.0 million in the year-earlier quarter. Credit for loan losses was US$16.0 million versus US$3.0 million in the prior-year quarter, an increase of 433.3%. Non-interest income fell 1.5% to US$3.13 billion from US$3.18 billion, while non-interest expense declined 5.4% to US$2.59 billion.

Prospects: Our evaluation of Bank of New York Mellon Corp. as of October 4th, 2019 is the result of our systematic analysis on three basic characteristics: earnings strength, relative valuation, and recent stock price movement. The company has managed to produce a neutral trend in earnings per share over the past 5 quarters. In addition, recent analyst estimates for the company have been mixed and BK has posted results that exceeded analysts' expectations. Based on operating earnings yield, the company is undervalued when compared to all of the companies we cover. Share price changes over the past year indicates that BK will perform poorly over the near term.

Financial Data

(US$ in Thousands)	9 Mos	6 Mos	3 Mos	12/31/2018	12/31/2017	12/31/2016	12/31/2015	12/31/2014
Earnings Per Share	3.86	3.85	3.87	4.04	3.72	3.15	2.71	2.15
Cash Flow Per Share	6.16	2.01	6.13	5.98	4.49	5.84	3.74	1.98
Tang Book Value Per Share	16.81	16.74	16.14	15.49	15.03	12.32	11.67	11.22
Dividends Per Share	1.150	1.120	1.080	1.040	0.860	0.720	0.680	1.240
Dividend Payout %	29.79	29.09	27.91	25.74	23.12	22.86	25.09	57.67
Income Statement								
Total Revenue	15,138,000	10,065,000	4,978,000	19,213,000	16,617,000	15,674,000	15,494,000	16,046,000
Income Before Taxes	3,765,000	2,478,000	1,193,000	5,192,000	4,610,000	4,725,000	4,235,000	3,563,000
Income Taxes	747,000	501,000	237,000	938,000	496,000	1,177,000	1,013,000	912,000
Net Income	3,001,000	1,963,000	946,000	4,266,000	4,090,000	3,547,000	3,158,000	2,567,000
Average Shares	935,677	953,928	965,960	1,007,141	1,040,290	1,072,013	1,112,511	1,137,480
Balance Sheet								
Total Assets	373,168,000	381,168,000	346,132,000	362,873,000	371,758,000	333,469,000	393,780,000	385,303,000
Total Liabilities	332,048,000	339,635,000	304,907,000	322,235,000	330,507,000	294,658,000	355,743,000	347,862,000
Stockholders' Equity	41,120,000	41,533,000	41,225,000	40,638,000	41,251,000	38,811,000	38,037,000	37,441,000
Shares Outstanding	922,198	942,662	957,517	960,425	1,013,442	1,047,488	1,085,342	1,118,227
Statistical Record								
Return on Assets %	1.07	1.08	1.12	1.16	1.16	0.97	0.81	0.34
Return on Equity %	9.39	9.53	9.74	10.42	10.22	9.21	8.37	3.42
Net Margin %	19.82	19.50	19.00	22.20	24.61	22.63	20.38	16.00
Asset Turnover	0.06	0.05	0.05	0.05	0.05	0.04	0.04	0.02
Price Range	53.98-40.95	55.64-42.69	57.72-44.49	58.42-44.49	54.97-43.87	49.17-32.74	45.26-35.66	41.53-30.91
P/E Ratio	13.98-10.61	14.45-11.09	14.91-11.50	14.46-11.01	14.78-11.79	15.61-10.39	16.70-13.16	19.32-14.38
Average Yield %	2.40	2.24	2.08	1.96	1.72	1.79	1.65	3.40

Address: 240 Greenwich Street, New York, NY 10286 **Telephone:** 212-495-1784	**Web Site:** www.bnymellon.com **Officers:** Thomas P. (Todd) Gibbons - Vice-Chairman, Interim Chief Executive Officer, Senior Executive Vice President, Chief Financial Officer, Division Officer Bridget E. Engle - Senior Executive Vice President, Chief Information Officer	**Auditors:** KPMG LLP **Investor Contact:** 412-234-4633 **Transfer Agents:** Computershare Shareowner Services LLC, Jersey City, NJ

BANKUNITED INC.

Exchange	Symbol	Price	52Wk Range	Yield	P/E
NYS	BKU	$36.56 (12/31/2019)	37.10-29.94	2.30	13.39

*7 Year Price Score 83.51   *NYSE Composite Index=100   *12 Month Price Score 98.18

Interim Earnings (Per Share)

Qtr.	Mar	Jun	Sep	Dec
2016	0.51	0.52	0.47	0.59
2017	0.57	0.60	0.62	3.79
2018	0.77	0.82	0.90	0.50
2019	0.65	0.81	0.77	...

Interim Dividends (Per Share)

Amt	Decl	Ex	Rec	Pay
0.21Q	03/19/2019	04/11/2019	04/12/2019	04/30/2019
0.21Q	06/26/2019	07/11/2019	07/12/2019	07/31/2019
0.21Q	09/12/2019	10/11/2019	10/15/2019	10/31/2019
0.21Q	12/19/2019	01/13/2020	01/14/2020	01/31/2020

Indicated Div: $0.84

Valuation Analysis / Institutional Holding

Forecast EPS	$2.96	No of Institutions	
	(01/16/2020)	328	
Market Cap	$3.5 Billion	Shares	
Book Value	$2.9 Billion	119,267,848	
Price/Book	1.19	% Held	
Price/Sales	2.27	85.32	

Business Summary: Banking (MIC: 5.1.1 SIC: 6035 NAIC: 522120)

BankUnited is a bank holding company. Through its subsidiary, BankUnited, National Association (the Bank), Co. provides a range of banking and related services to individual and corporate customers. The Bank also provides certain commercial lending and deposit products through national platform. Co.'s lending products include small business loans, commercial real estate loans, equipment loans and leases, term loans, formula-based loans, municipal and non-profit loans and leases, commercial lines of credit, and residential mortgage warehouse lines of credit. Co.'s deposit products include checking accounts, money market deposit accounts, savings accounts and certificates of deposit.

Recent Developments: For the quarter ended Sep 30 2019, net income decreased 21.7% to US$76.2 million from US$97.3 million in the year-earlier quarter. Net interest income decreased 26.3% to US$185.7 million from US$252.0 million in the year-earlier quarter. Provision for loan losses was US$1.8 million versus US$1.2 million in the prior-year quarter, an increase of 53.3%. Non-interest income fell 2.3% to US$37.9 million from US$38.7 million, while non-interest expense declined 29.0% to US$121.3 million.

Prospects: Our evaluation of BankUnited Inc as of October 4th, 2019 is the result of our systematic analysis on three basic characteristics: earnings strength, relative valuation, and recent stock price movement. The company has produced a positive trend in earnings per share over the past 5 quarters. However, recent analyst estimates for the company have been reduced, while BKU has posted results that exceeded analysts' expectations. Based on operating earnings yield, the company is undervalued when compared to all of the companies we cover. Share price changes over the past year indicates that BKU will perform poorly over the near term.

Financial Data

(US$ in Thousands)	9 Mos	6 Mos	3 Mos	12/31/2018	12/31/2017	12/31/2016	12/31/2015	12/31/2014
Earnings Per Share	2.73	2.86	2.87	2.99	5.58	2.09	2.35	1.95
Cash Flow Per Share	8.86	8.64	7.93	7.94	3.02	2.98	2.13	(0.50)
Tang Book Value Per Share	29.78	29.27	28.92	28.71	27.59	22.47	20.90	19.52
Dividends Per Share	0.840	0.840	0.840	0.840	0.840	0.840	0.630	1.050
Dividend Payout %	30.77	29.37	29.27	28.09	15.05	40.19	26.81	53.85
Income Statement								
Total Revenue	1,081,908	720,650	358,084	1,581,166	1,362,365	1,165,634	983,040	867,909
Income Before Taxes	299,468	199,067	90,185	415,650	404,461	335,444	296,893	293,250
Income Taxes	75,826	51,644	24,213	90,784	(209,812)	109,703	45,233	89,035
Net Income	223,642	147,423	65,972	324,866	614,273	225,741	251,660	204,215
Average Shares	94,262	96,622	97,964	104,077	105,857	103,656	102,972	100,595
Balance Sheet								
Total Assets	32,950,535	33,092,265	32,702,976	32,164,326	30,346,986	27,880,151	23,883,467	19,210,529
Total Liabilities	30,041,260	30,224,355	29,779,586	29,240,493	27,320,924	25,461,722	21,639,569	17,157,995
Stockholders' Equity	2,909,275	2,867,910	2,923,390	2,923,833	3,026,062	2,418,429	2,243,898	2,052,534
Shares Outstanding	95,070	95,315	98,404	99,141	106,848	104,166	103,626	101,656
Statistical Record								
Return on Assets %	0.86	0.92	0.97	1.04	2.11	0.87	1.17	1.19
Return on Equity %	9.23	9.96	10.26	10.92	22.56	9.66	11.71	10.26
Net Margin %	20.67	20.46	18.42	20.55	45.09	19.37	25.60	23.53
Asset Turnover	0.05	0.05	0.05	0.05	0.05	0.04	0.05	0.05
Price Range	36.96-28.22	42.67-28.22	44.24-28.22	44.24-28.22	40.90-30.50	38.22-28.13	39.34-26.74	35.38-27.66
P/E Ratio	13.54-10.34	14.92-9.87	15.41-9.83	14.80-9.44	7.33-5.47	18.29-13.46	16,74-11.38	18.14-14.18
Average Yield %	2.50	2.38	2.27	2.17	2.36	2.57	1.82	3.30

Address: 14817 Oak Lane, Miami Lakes, FL 33016 Telephone: 305-569-2000	Web Site: www.bankunited.com Officers: John Adam Kanas - Chairman, President, Chief Executive Officer Rajinder P. Singh - President, Chief Executive Officer, Chief Operating Officer	Auditors: KPMG LLP Investor Contact: 305-569-2000 Transfer Agents: Registrar and Transfer Company

BAXTER INTERNATIONAL INC

Exchange	Symbol	Price	52Wk Range	Yield	P/E
NYS	BAX	$83.62 (12/31/2019)	89.78-64.48	1.05	28.25

*7 Year Price Score 125.59 *NYSE Composite Index=100 *12 Month Price Score 96.97

Interim Earnings (Per Share)

Qtr.	Mar	Jun	Sep	Dec
2016	6.12	2.19	0.24	0.46
2017	0.49	0.48	0.45	(0.13)
2018	0.71	0.63	1.00	0.64
2019	0.66	0.66	...	...

Interim Dividends (Per Share)

Amt	Decl	Ex	Rec	Pay
0.19Q	02/19/2019	02/28/2019	03/01/2019	04/01/2019
0.22Q	05/07/2019	06/06/2019	06/07/2019	07/01/2019
0.22Q	07/16/2019	08/29/2019	08/30/2019	10/01/2019
0.22Q	11/19/2019	12/05/2019	12/06/2019	01/02/2020

Indicated Div: $0.88 (Div. Reinv. Plan)

Valuation Analysis

		Institutional Holding	
Forecast EPS	$3.39	No of Institutions	
	(01/24/2020)	1628	
Market Cap	$42.7 Billion	Shares	
Book Value	$7.8 Billion	573,905,088	
Price/Book	5.46	% Held	
Price/Sales	3.85	77.30	

Business Summary: Medical Instruments & Equipment (MIC: 4.3.1 SIC: 3841 NAIC: 339112)

Baxter International, through its subsidiaries, provides a portfolio of healthcare products, including acute and chronic dialysis therapies; sterile intravenous solutions; infusion systems and devices; parenteral nutrition therapies; inhaled anesthetics; generic injectable pharmaceuticals; and surgical hemostat and sealant products. These products are used by hospitals, kidney dialysis centers, nursing homes, rehabilitation centers, doctors' offices and by patients at home under physician supervision. Co. manages its business based on three geographic segments: Americas (North and South America), Europe, Middle East and Africa and Asia-Pacific.

Recent Developments: For the quarter ended June 30 2019, net income was unchanged at US$343.0 million versus US$343.0 million the year-earlier quarter. Revenues were US$2.84 billion, unchanged from the year before. Operating income was US$355.0 million versus US$384.0 million in the prior-year quarter, a decrease of 7.6%. Direct operating expenses rose 4.9% to US$1.68 billion from US$1.60 billion in the comparable period the year before. Indirect operating expenses decreased 6.0% to US$804.0 million from US$855.0 million in the equivalent prior-year period.

Prospects: Our evaluation of Baxter International Inc. as of October 4th, 2019 is the result of our systematic analysis on three basic characteristics: earnings strength, relative valuation, and recent stock price movement. The company has managed to produce a neutral trend in earnings per share over the past 5 quarters. Additionally, recent analyst estimates for the company have been unchanged while BAX has posted results that exceeded analysts' expectations. Based on operating earnings yield, the company is fairly valued when compared to all of the companies we cover. Share price changes over the past year indicates that BAX will perform well over the near term.

Financial Data

(US$ in Millions)	6 Mos	3 Mos	12/31/2018	12/31/2017	12/31/2016	12/31/2015	12/31/2014	12/31/2013
Earnings Per Share	2.96	2.93	2.97	1.29	9.01	1.76	4.56	3.66
Cash Flow Per Share	3.64	3.50	3.93	3.38	3.02	3.02	5.93	5.89
Tang Book Value Per Share	6.88	6.42	6.70	8.59	8.50	8.78	4.00	3.62
Dividends Per Share	0.790	0.760	0.730	0.610	0.505	1.270	2.050	1.920
Dividend Payout %	26.69	25.94	24.58	47.29	5.60	72.16	44.96	52.46
Income Statement								
Total Revenue	5,472	2,632	11,127	10,561	10,163	9,968	16,671	15,259
EBITDA	1,185	604	2,499	2,033	5,820	1,313	3,589	3,445
Depn & Amortn	393	195	785	761	800	759	1,005	823
Income Before Taxes	754	391	1,669	1,217	4,954	428	2,439	2,494
Income Taxes	64	44	63	493	(12)	35	493	537
Net Income	690	347	1,624	717	4,965	968	2,497	2,012
Average Shares	519	522	546	555	551	549	547	549
Balance Sheet								
Current Assets	7,218	6,087	5,919	7,263	6,574	11,796	10,351	10,004
Total Assets	17,544	16,350	15,641	17,111	15,546	20,975	25,917	25,869
Current Liabilities	2,597	3,327	2,836	2,821	2,744	5,750	6,042	5,906
Long-Term Obligations	5,157	3,451	3,473	3,509	2,779	3,935	7,606	8,126
Total Liabilities	9,732	8,704	7,847	7,987	7,256	12,129	17,797	17,406
Stockholders' Equity	7,812	7,646	7,794	9,124	8,290	8,846	8,120	8,463
Shares Outstanding	510	510	512	541	539	547	542	543
Statistical Record								
Return on Assets %	9.27	9.52	9.92	4.39	27.12	4.13	9.64	8.70
Return on Equity %	18.95	18.90	19.20	8.23	57.79	11.41	30.12	26.13
EBITDA Margin %	21.66	22.95	22.46	19.25	57.27	13.17	21.53	22.58
Net Margin %	12.61	13.18	14.60	6.79	48.85	9.71	14.98	13.19
Asset Turnover	0.65	0.67	0.68	0.65	0.56	0.43	0.64	0.66
Current Ratio	2.78	1.83	2.09	2.57	2.40	2.05	1.71	1.69
Debt to Equity	0.66	0.45	0.45	0.38	0.34	0.44	0.94	0.96
Price Range	82.41-61.45	81.31-61.45	77.80-61.45	66.05-44.44	49.16-34.76	42.13-32.27	41.83-36.12	40.43-34.71
P/E Ratio	27.84-20.76	27.75-20.97	26.20-20.69	51.20-34.45	5.46-3.86	23.94-18.34	9.17-7.92	11.05-9.48
Average Yield %	1.08	1.07	1.04	1.05	1.15	3.39	5.22	5.10

Address: One Baxter Parkway,	Web Site: www.baxter.com	Auditors: PricewaterhouseCoopers LLP
Deerfield, IL 60015	Officers: Jose E. Almeida - Chairman, President,	Transfer Agents: Computershare Trust
Telephone: 224-948-2000	Chief Executive Officer James K. Saccaro - Executive	Company, N.A., Providence, RI
Fax: 847-948-2964	Vice President, Chief Financial Officer	

BECTON, DICKINSON & CO

Exchange	Symbol	Price	52Wk Range	Yield	P/E	Div Acheiver
NYS	BDX	$271.97 (12/31/2019)	273.49-211.20	1.16	69.03	46 Years

*7 Year Price Score 118.57 *NYSE Composite Index=100 *12 Month Price Score 99.03

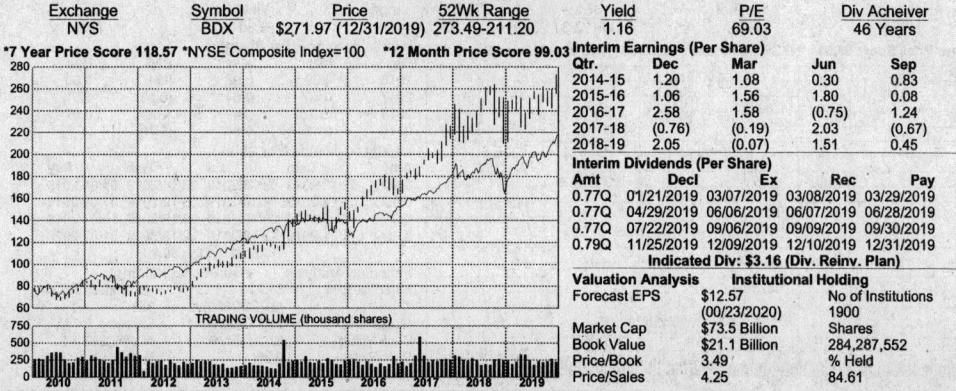

Interim Earnings (Per Share)

Qtr.	Dec	Mar	Jun	Sep
2014-15	1.20	1.08	0.30	0.83
2015-16	1.06	1.56	1.80	0.08
2016-17	2.58	1.58	(0.75)	1.24
2017-18	(0.76)	(0.19)	2.03	(0.67)
2018-19	2.05	(0.07)	1.51	0.45

Interim Dividends (Per Share)

Amt	Decl	Ex	Rec	Pay
0.77Q	01/21/2019	03/07/2019	03/08/2019	03/29/2019
0.77Q	04/29/2019	06/06/2019	06/07/2019	06/28/2019
0.77Q	07/22/2019	09/06/2019	09/09/2019	09/30/2019
0.79Q	11/25/2019	12/09/2019	12/10/2019	12/31/2019

Indicated Div: $3.16 (Div. Reinv. Plan)

Valuation Analysis

		Institutional Holding	
Forecast EPS	$12.57	No of Institutions	
	(00/23/2020)	1900	
Market Cap	$73.5 Billion	Shares	
Book Value	$21.1 Billion	284,287,552	
Price/Book	3.49	% Held	
Price/Sales	4.25	84.61	

Business Summary: Medical Instruments & Equipment (MIC: 4.3.1 SIC: 3841 NAIC: 339112)

Becton, Dickinson and Company is a medical technology company engaged in the development, manufacture and sale of a range of medical supplies, devices, laboratory equipment and diagnostic products. Co.'s segments are: BD Medical, which produces an array of medical technologies and devices that are used to help improve healthcare delivery in a range of settings; BD Life Sciences, which provides products for the safe collection and transport of diagnostics specimens, and instruments and reagent systems to detect a range of infectious diseases, healthcare-associated infections and cancers; and BD Interventional, which provides vascular, urology, oncology and surgical products.

Recent Developments: For the year ended Sep 30 2019, net income increased 296.5% to US$1.23 billion from US$311.0 million in the prior year. Revenues were US$17.29 billion, up 8.2% from US$15.98 billion the year before. Operating income was US$1.76 billion versus US$1.51 billion in the prior year, an increase of 16.6%. Direct operating expenses rose 3.3% to US$9.00 billion from US$8.71 billion the year before. Indirect operating expenses increased 13.3% to US$6.53 billion from US$5.76 billion in the equivalent prior-year period.

Prospects: Our evaluation of Becton, Dickinson and Co. as of October 4th, 2019 is the result of our systematic analysis on three basic characteristics: earnings strength, relative valuation, and recent stock price movement. The company has produced a positive trend in earnings per share over the past 5 quarters. However, recent analyst estimates for the company have been reduced, while BDX has posted results that exceeded analysts' expectations. Based on operating earnings yield, the company is fairly valued when compared to all of the companies we cover. Share price changes over the past year indicates that BDX will perform in line with the market over the near term.

Financial Data

(US$ in Thousands)	09/30/2019	09/30/2018	09/30/2017	09/30/2016	09/30/2015	09/30/2014	09/30/2013	09/30/2012
Earnings Per Share	3.94	0.60	4.60	4.49	3.35	5.99	6.49	5.59
Cash Flow Per Share	12.34	11.09	11.65	12.00	8.54	9.03	8.80	8.22
Tang Book Value Per Share	N.M.	N.M.	N.M.	N.M.	N.M.	14.79	14.07	9.65
Dividends Per Share	3.080	3.000	2.920	2.640	2.400	2.180	1.980	1.800
Dividend Payout %	78.17	500.00	63.48	58.80	71.64	36.39	30.51	32.20
Income Statement								
Total Revenue	17,290,000	15,983,000	12,093,000	12,483,000	10,282,000	8,446,000	8,054,000	7,708,382
EBITDA	4,056,000	3,792,000	2,509,000	2,555,000	1,986,000	2,173,000	1,809,000	2,067,671
Depn & Amortn	2,253,000	1,978,000	1,088,000	1,114,000	891,000	562,000	546,000	510,938
Income Before Taxes	1,176,000	1,173,000	976,000	1,074,000	739,000	1,522,000	1,165,000	1,472,408
Income Taxes	(57,000)	862,000	(124,000)	97,000	44,000	337,000	236,000	362,880
Net Income	1,233,000	311,000	1,100,000	976,000	695,000	1,185,000	1,293,000	1,169,927
Average Shares	274,775	264,621	223,588	217,536	207,509	197,709	199,193	209,181
Balance Sheet								
Current Assets	6,664,000	7,411,000	18,633,000	6,367,000	6,045,000	6,131,000	5,873,000	5,322,071
Total Assets	51,765,000	53,904,000	37,734,000	25,586,000	26,820,000	12,447,000	12,149,000	11,360,909
Current Liabilities	5,655,000	7,216,000	3,342,000	4,400,000	4,386,000	2,235,000	2,130,000	1,978,055
Long-Term Obligations	18,081,000	18,894,000	18,664,000	10,550,000	11,370,000	3,769,000	3,763,000	3,761,112
Total Liabilities	30,684,000	32,909,000	24,783,000	17,953,000	19,656,000	7,396,000	7,106,000	7,225,020
Stockholders' Equity	21,081,000	20,994,000	12,948,000	7,633,000	7,164,000	5,053,000	5,043,000	4,135,889
Shares Outstanding	270,427	268,224	227,942	213,291	210,695	191,892	193,999	196,911
Statistical Record								
Return on Assets %	2.33	0.68	3.47	3.71	3.54	9.64	11.00	10.71
Return on Equity %	5.86	1.83	10.69	13.16	11.38	23.47	28.17	26.03
EBITDA Margin %	23.46	23.73	20.75	20.47	19.32	25.73	22.46	26.82
Net Margin %	7.13	1.95	9.10	7.82	6.76	14.03	16.05	15.18
Asset Turnover	0.33	0.35	0.38	0.48	0.52	0.69	0.69	0.71
Current Ratio	1.18	1.03	5.58	1.45	1.38	2.74	2.76	2.69
Debt to Equity	0.86	0.90	1.44	1.38	1.59	0.75	0.75	0.91
Price Range	264.38-209.85	262.40-193.73	205.63-162.80	181.55-132.19	153.86-113.60	120.33-98.33	104.50-74.63	79.91-70.65
P/E Ratio	67.10-53.26	437.33-322.88	44.70-35.39	40.43-29.44	45.93-33.91	20.09-16.42	16.10-11.50	14.30-12.64
Average Yield %	1.27	1.30	1.59	1.67	1.72	1.93	2.18	2.39

Address: 1 Becton Drive, Franklin Lakes, NJ 07417-1880	Web Site: www.bd.com	Auditors: Ernst & Young LLP
Telephone: 201-847-6800	Officers: Vincent A. Forlenza - Executive Chairman, Chairman, President, Chief Executive Officer, Chief Operating Officer Thomas E. Polen - President, Chief Executive Officer, Executive Vice President, Chief Operating Officer, Division Officer	Investor Contact: 180-028-46845 Transfer Agents: Computershare Trust Company, N.A., Canton, MA

BELDEN INC

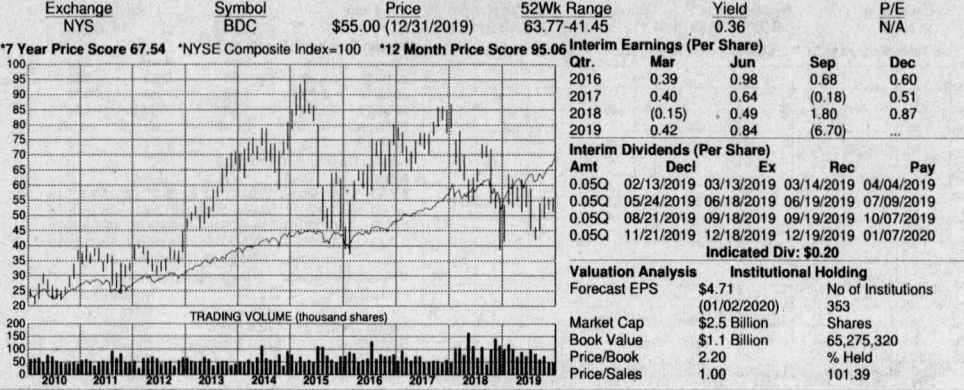

Exchange	Symbol	Price	52Wk Range	Yield	P/E
NYS	BDC	$55.00 (12/31/2019)	63.77-41.45	0.36	N/A

*7 Year Price Score 67.54   *NYSE Composite Index=100   *12 Month Price Score 95.06

Interim Earnings (Per Share)

Qtr.	Mar	Jun	Sep	Dec
2016	0.39	0.98	0.68	0.60
2017	0.40	0.64	(0.18)	0.51
2018	(0.15)	0.49	1.80	0.87
2019	0.42	0.84	(6.70)	...

Interim Dividends (Per Share)

Amt	Decl	Ex	Rec	Pay
0.05Q	02/13/2019	03/13/2019	03/14/2019	04/04/2019
0.05Q	05/24/2019	06/18/2019	06/19/2019	07/09/2019
0.05Q	08/21/2019	09/18/2019	09/19/2019	10/07/2019
0.05Q	11/21/2019	12/18/2019	12/19/2019	01/07/2020

Indicated Div: $0.20

Valuation Analysis

		Institutional Holding	
Forecast EPS	$4.71	No of Institutions	
	(01/02/2020)	353	
Market Cap	$2.5 Billion	Shares	
Book Value	$1.1 Billion	65,275,320	
Price/Book	2.20	% Held	
Price/Sales	1.00	101.39	

Business Summary: Electrical Equipment (MIC: 7.3.1 SIC: 3357 NAIC: 335921)

Belden is a signal transmission solutions company. Co. operates its business under the two segments: Enterprise Solutions (Enterprise) and Industrial Solutions (Industrial). The Enterprise segment provides network infrastructure solutions, as well as cabling and connectivity solutions for broadcast, commercial audio/video, and security applications. The Industrial segment provides networking components and machine connectivity products.

Recent Developments: For the quarter ended Sep 29 2019, net loss amounted to US$297.0 million versus net income of US$85.9 million in the year-earlier quarter. Revenues were US$620.3 million, down 5.4% from US$655.8 million the year before. Operating loss was US$280.5 million versus an income of US$131.3 million in the prior-year quarter. Direct operating expenses declined 2.5% to US$384.9 million from US$394.9 million in the comparable period the year before. Indirect operating expenses increased 298.1% to US$515.9 million from US$129.6 million in the equivalent prior-year period.

Prospects: Our evaluation of Belden Inc. as of October 4th, 2019 is the result of our systematic analysis on three basic characteristics: earnings strength, relative valuation, and recent stock price movement. The company has produced a positive trend in earnings per share over the past 5 quarters. However, recent analyst estimates for the company have been unchanged, while BDC has posted results that exceeded analysts' expectations. Based on operating earnings yield, the company is undervalued when compared to all of the companies we cover. Share price changes over the past year indicates that BDC will perform very poorly over the near term.

Financial Data
(US$ in Thousands)

	9 Mos	6 Mos	3 Mos	12/31/2018	12/31/2017	12/31/2016	12/31/2015	12/31/2014
Earnings Per Share	(4.57)	3.93	3.58	3.08	1.37	2.65	1.54	1.69
Cash Flow Per Share	6.25	8.64	8.30	7.11	6.05	7.46	5.58	4.48
Dividends Per Share	0.200	0.200	0.210	0.210	0.200	0.200	0.200	0.200
Dividend Payout %	...	5.09	5.87	6.82	14.60	7.55	12.99	11.83
Income Statement								
Total Revenue	1,845,023	1,224,705	587,175	2,585,368	2,388,643	2,356,672	2,309,222	2,308,265
EBITDA	(68,254)	177,321	81,033	428,318	331,846	367,096	289,174	261,290
Depn & Amortn	105,152	70,709	36,041	146,429	149,597	145,585	150,391	102,126
Income Before Taxes	(215,967)	78,251	30,799	220,330	99,348	126,461	38,170	77,591
Income Taxes	13,580	10,783	5,621	59,619	6,495	(1,185)	(26,568)	7,114
Net Income	(229,607)	67,402	25,202	160,894	93,210	128,003	66,204	74,449
Average Shares	44,444	39,611	39,660	40,956	42,643	42,557	42,953	43,997
Balance Sheet								
Current Assets	1,122,657	1,116,458	1,129,742	1,258,724	1,372,071	1,478,952	843,164	1,414,150
Total Assets	3,441,995	3,822,980	3,757,958	3,779,321	3,840,613	3,806,803	3,315,841	3,262,827
Current Liabilities	577,488	590,021	572,056	716,922	678,928	570,279	549,263	525,359
Long-Term Obligations	1,403,670	1,457,571	1,519,583	1,463,200	1,560,748	1,620,161	1,750,521	1,765,422
Total Liabilities	2,303,295	2,394,770	2,327,047	2,392,174	2,406,378	2,346,490	2,491,742	2,455,641
Stockholders' Equity	1,138,700	1,428,210	1,430,911	1,387,147	1,434,235	1,460,313	824,099	807,186
Shares Outstanding	45,457	45,452	39,454	39,396	42,019	42,180	41,981	42,464
Statistical Record								
Return on Assets %	N.M.	5.27	4.88	4.22	2.44	3.58	2.01	2.48
Return on Equity %	N.M.	14.16	13.48	11.41	6.44	11.18	8.12	9.06
EBITDA Margin %	N.M.	14.48	13.80	16.57	13.89	15.58	12.52	11.32
Net Margin %	N.M.	5.50	4.29	6.22	3.90	5.43	2.87	3.23
Asset Turnover	0.70	0.68	0.68	0.68	0.62	0.66	0.70	0.77
Current Ratio	1.94	1.89	1.97	1.76	2.02	2.59	1.54	2.69
Debt to Equity	1.23	1.02	1.06	1.05	1.09	1.11	2.12	2.19
Price Range	72.06-38.68	73.64-38.68	73.64-38.68	87.00-38.68	86.29-64.68	80.48-37.15	95.14-45.10	80.96-58.56
P/E Ratio	...	18.74-9.84	20.57-10.80	28.25-12.56	62.99-47.21	30.37-14.02	61.78-29.29	47.91-34.65
Average Yield %	0.37	0.34	0.35	0.32	0.26	0.32	0.28	0.28

Address: 1 North Brentwood Boulevard, 15th Floor, St. Louis, MO 63105 **Telephone:** 314-854-8000 **Fax:** 314-854-8001	**Web Site:** www.belden.com **Officers:** John S. Stroup - Chairman, President, Chief Executive Officer Brian E. Anderson - Senior Vice President, General Counsel, Corporate Secretary	**Auditors:** Ernst & Young LLP **Investor Contact:** 314-854-8054 **Transfer Agents:** American Stock Transfer & Trust Company, Brooklyn, NY

BERKLEY (WR) CORP

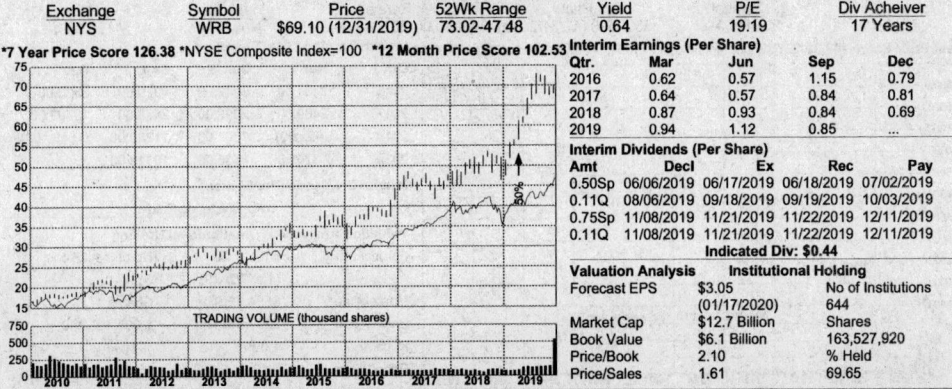

Exchange	Symbol	Price	52Wk Range	Yield	P/E	Div Acheiver
NYS	WRB	$69.10 (12/31/2019)	73.02-47.48	0.64	19.19	17 Years

*7 Year Price Score 126.38 *NYSE Composite Index=100 *12 Month Price Score 102.53

Interim Earnings (Per Share)

Qtr.	Mar	Jun	Sep	Dec
2016	0.62	0.57	1.15	0.79
2017	0.64	0.57	0.84	0.81
2018	0.87	0.93	0.84	0.69
2019	0.94	1.12	0.85	...

Interim Dividends (Per Share)

Amt	Decl	Ex	Rec	Pay
0.50Sp	06/06/2019	06/17/2019	06/18/2019	07/02/2019
0.11Q	08/06/2019	09/18/2019	09/19/2019	10/03/2019
0.75Sp	11/08/2019	11/21/2019	11/22/2019	12/11/2019
0.11Q	11/08/2019	11/21/2019	11/22/2019	12/11/2019

Indicated Div: $0.44

Valuation Analysis

		Institutional Holding	
Forecast EPS	$3.05	No of Institutions	
(01/17/2020)		644	
Market Cap	$12.7 Billion	Shares	
Book Value	$6.1 Billion	163,527,920	
Price/Book	2.10	% Held	
Price/Sales	1.61	69.65	

Business Summary: General Insurance (MIC: 5.2.1 SIC: 6331 NAIC: 524126)

W. R. Berkley is an insurance holding company. Co. operates in two segments of the property casualty insurance business: Insurance, which includes commercial insurance business, including excess and surplus lines, admitted lines and specialty personal lines throughout the U.S., as well as insurance business in the U.K., Continental Europe, South America, Canada, Mexico, Scandinavia, Asia and Australia; and Reinsurance, which provides reinsurance business on a facultative and treaty basis, primarily in the U.S., the U.K., Continental Europe, Australia, the Asia-Pacific region and South Africa.

Recent Developments: For the quarter ended Sep 30 2019, net income increased 0.4% to US$165.2 million from US$164.4 million in the year-earlier quarter. Revenues were US$1.97 billion, up 1.4% from US$1.94 billion the year before. Net premiums earned were US$1.68 billion versus US$1.60 billion in the prior-year quarter, an increase of 4.6%. Net investment income fell 13.1% to US$161.7 million from US$186.1 million a year ago.

Prospects: Our evaluation of Berkley (W. R.) Corp. as of October 4th, 2019 is the result of our systematic analysis on three basic characteristics: earnings strength, relative valuation, and recent stock price movement. The company has generated a negative trend in earnings per share over the past 5 quarters. However, recent analyst estimates for the company have been mixed and WRB has posted results that exceeded analysts' expectations. Based on operating earnings yield, the company is fairly valued when compared to all of the companies we cover. Share price changes over the past year indicates that WRB will perform over the near term.

Financial Data

(US$ in Thousands)	9 Mos	6 Mos	3 Mos	12/31/2018	12/31/2017	12/31/2016	12/31/2015	12/31/2014
Earnings Per Share	3.60	3.59	3.41	3.33	2.84	3.12	2.58	3.24
Cash Flow Per Share	5.62	4.74	3.77	3.26	3.80	4.60	4.74	3.83
Tang Book Value Per Share	32.05	31.69	30.53	28.77	28.71	26.97	24.04	23.35
Dividends Per Share	1.253	1.577	1.400	1.393	1.033	1.007	0.313	0.953
Dividend Payout %	34.78	43.88	41.10	41.80	36.38	32.26	12.14	29.42
Income Statement								
Premium Income	4,916,507	3,239,697	1,592,856	6,371,505	6,311,419	6,293,348	6,040,609	5,744,418
Total Revenue	5,926,122	3,960,406	1,937,022	7,691,651	7,684,764	7,654,184	7,206,457	7,128,928
Benefits & Claims	3,058,950	2,017,479	988,650	3,974,702	4,002,348	3,845,800	3,656,270	3,490,567
Income Before Taxes	706,157	503,175	229,439	812,094	772,770	896,438	732,030	952,196
Income Taxes	141,965	104,134	47,825	163,028	219,433	292,953	227,923	302,593
Net Income	562,638	397,431	180,722	640,749	549,094	601,916	503,694	648,884
Average Shares	193,589	193,059	192,669	192,395	193,526	192,829	195,283	200,478
Balance Sheet								
Total Assets	26,218,511	26,487,903	25,585,260	24,895,977	24,299,917	23,364,844	21,730,967	21,716,691
Total Liabilities	20,162,215	20,511,143	19,825,308	19,458,126	18,888,573	18,317,636	17,130,721	17,126,746
Stockholders' Equity	6,056,296	5,976,760	5,759,952	5,437,851	5,411,344	5,047,208	4,600,246	4,589,945
Shares Outstanding	183,674	183,168	183,024	182,993	182,272	181,790	184,961	190,123
Statistical Record								
Return on Assets %	2.72	2.71	2.61	2.60	2.30	2.66	2.32	3.07
Return on Equity %	12.09	12.13	11.69	11.81	10.50	12.44	10.96	14.54
Loss Ratio %	62.22	62.27	62.07	62.38	63.41	61.11	60.53	60.76
Net Margin %	9.49	10.04	9.33	8.33	7.15	7.86	6.99	9.10
Price Range	73.02-46.37	66.88-46.37	56.48-46.37	53.62-45.17	48.65-41.69	44.50-31.97	38.94-32.27	35.97-25.29
P/E Ratio	20.28-12.88	18.63-12.92	16.56-13.60	16.10-13.57	17.13-14.68	14.26-10.25	15.09-12.51	11.10-7.80
Average Yield %	2.13	2.92	2.74	2.80	2.26	2.66	0.89	3.13

Address: 475 Steamboat Road, Greenwich, CT 06830 **Telephone:** 203-629-3000	**Web Site:** www.wrberkley.com **Officers:** William R. Berkley - Executive Chairman, Chairman, Chief Executive Officer W. Robert Berkley - President, Chief Executive Officer, Chief Operating Officer	**Auditors:** KPMG LLP **Investor Contact:** 203-629-3040 **Transfer Agents:** Wells Fargo Bank, N.A., Mendota Heights, MN

BERKSHIRE HATHAWAY INC

Exchange	Symbol	Price	52Wk Range	Yield	P/E
NYS	BRK A	$339590 (12/31/2019)	340380.00-287000.00	N/A	20.58

*7 Year Price Score 108.31 *NYSE Composite Index=100 *12 Month Price Score 100.29

TRADING VOLUME (thousand shares)

Interim Earnings (Per Share)

Qtr.	Mar	Jun	Sep	Dec
2016	3401.00	3042.00	4379.00	3823.00
2017	2469.00	2592.00	2473.00	19793.00
2018	(692.00)	7301.00	11280.00	(15439.00)
2019	13209.00	8608.00	10119.00	...

Interim Dividends (Per Share)

No Dividends Paid

Valuation Analysis / Institutional Holding

Valuation Analysis		Institutional Holding	
Forecast EPS	$15527.00	No of Institutions	
	(11/17/2019)	3117	
Market Cap	$554.1 Billion	Shares	
Book Value	$397.6 Billion	1,065,403,840	
Price/Book	1.39	% Held	
Price/Sales	2.19	18.55	

Business Summary: General Insurance (MIC: 5.2.1 SIC: 6331 NAIC: 524126)

Berkshire Hathaway is a holding company owning subsidiaries engaged in a number of business activities. Co.'s segments include: Insurance and Reinsurance Businesses, which provide insurance and reinsurance of property and casualty and life, accident and health risks; Railroad Business, which operates railroad systems in North America; Utilities and Energy Businesses, which generate, transmit, store, distribute and supply energy; Manufacturing Businesses, which include industrial products, building products and consumer products; and Service and Retailing Businesses, where service business provides grocery and foodservice distribution, and retailing business includes automotive operations.

Recent Developments: For the quarter ended Sep 30 2019, net income decreased 11.0% to US$16.66 billion from US$18.71 billion in the year-earlier quarter. Revenues were US$64.97 billion, up 2.4% from US$63.45 billion the year before. Net premiums earned were US$15.32 billion versus US$14.33 billion in the prior-year quarter, an increase of 6.9%.

Prospects: Our evaluation of Berkshire Hathaway Inc. as of October 4th, 2019 is the result of our systematic analysis on three basic characteristics: earnings strength, relative valuation, and recent stock price movement. The company has produced a positive trend in earnings per share over the past 5 quarters. However, recent analyst estimates for the company have been mixed and BRK.B has posted results that fell short of analysts' expectations. Based on operating earnings yield, the company is fairly valued when compared to all of the companies we cover. Share price changes over the past year indicates that BRK.B will perform in line with the market over the near term.

Financial Data
(US$ in Thousands)

	9 Mos	6 Mos	3 Mos	12/31/2018	12/31/2017	12/31/2016	12/31/2015	12/31/2014
Earnings Per Share	16,497.00	17,658.00	16,351.00	2,446.00	27,326.00	14,645.00	14,656.00	12,092.00
Cash Flow Per Share	22,936.29	23,285.56	22,820.17	22,752.23	27,833.87	19,738.16	19,164.63	19,477.25
Tang Book Value Per Share	175,025.95	165,382.94	156,772.55	143,930.05	142,578.70	103,406.82	111,777.28	109,230.64
Income Statement								
Premium Income	44,505,000	29,182,000	14,319,000	57,418,000	60,597,000	45,881,000	41,294,000	41,253,000
Total Revenue	189,248,000	124,276,000	60,678,000	247,837,000	242,137,000	223,604,000	210,821,000	194,673,000
Benefits & Claims	34,946,000	22,912,000	11,078,000	45,605,000	54,509,000	36,037,000	31,940,000	31,587,000
Income Before Taxes	64,959,000	45,114,000	27,479,000	6,168,000	20,900,000	32,744,000	34,946,000	28,105,000
Income Taxes	13,333,000	9,501,000	5,915,000	(321,000)	(21,515,000)	9,240,000	10,532,000	7,935,000
Net Income	52,258,000	35,734,000	21,661,000	4,021,000	44,940,000	24,074,000	24,083,000	19,872,000
Average Shares	1,633	1,634	1,639	1,643	1,644	1,643	1,643	1,643
Balance Sheet								
Total Assets	788,482,000	760,108,000	738,724,000	707,794,000	702,095,000	620,854,000	552,257,000	526,186,000
Total Liabilities	390,873,000	377,564,000	369,847,000	359,091,000	353,799,000	337,853,000	296,707,000	286,016,000
Stockholders' Equity	397,609,000	382,544,000	368,877,000	348,703,000	348,296,000	283,001,000	255,550,000	240,170,000
Shares Outstanding	1,631	1,634	1,635	1,640	1,644	1,644	1,643	1,642
Statistical Record								
Return on Assets %	3.52	3.92	3.72	0.57	6.79	4.09	4.47	3.93
Return on Equity %	6.95	7.80	7.49	1.15	14.24	8.92	9.72	8.60
Loss Ratio %	78.52	78.51	77.37	79.43	89.95	78.54	77.35	76.57
Net Margin %	27.61	28.75	35.70	1.62	18.56	10.77	11.42	10.21
Price Range	335630-282640	335630-282000	335630-281600	335630-281600	299360-238100	249711-187000	226680-192200	229300-164075
P/E Ratio	20.34-17.13	19.01-15.97	20.53-17.22	137.22-115.13	10.96-8.71	17.05-12.77	15.47-13.11	18.96-13.57

Address: 3555 Farnam Street, Omaha, NE 68131 **Telephone:** 402-346-1400	**Web Site:** www.berkshirehathaway.com **Officers:** Warren E. Buffett - Chairman, Chief Executive Officer Charles T. Munger - Vice-Chairman	**Auditors:** DELOITTE & TOUCHE LLP **Transfer Agents:** Wells Fargo Bank, N.A., St. Paul, MN

BERRY GLOBAL GROUP INC

Exchange	Symbol	Price	52Wk Range	Yield	P/E
NYS	BERY	$47.49 (12/31/2019)	58.83-37.37	N/A	15.83

*7 Year Price Score 101.63 *NYSE Composite Index=100   *12 Month Price Score 89.99

Interim Earnings (Per Share)

Qtr.	Dec	Mar	Jun	Sep
2014-15	0.11	0.31	(0.11)	0.39
2015-16	0.03	0.47	0.76	0.61
2016-17	0.40	0.54	0.79	0.81
2017-18	1.20	0.66	0.81	1.00
2018-19	0.66	0.55	0.10	1.69

Interim Dividends (Per Share)

No Dividends Paid

Valuation Analysis		Institutional Holding	
Forecast EPS	$4.07	No of Institutions	
	(01/17/2020)	433	
Market Cap	$6.3 Billion	Shares	
Book Value	$1.6 Billion	141,568,384	
Price/Book	3.88	% Held	
Price/Sales	0.71	96.67	

Business Summary: Plastics (MIC: 8.4.2 SIC: 3089 NAIC: 326199)

Berry Global Group is a supplier of a range of non-woven products used within consumer and industrial end markets. Co.'s segments are: Consumer Packaging International, which includes recycling, bottles and canisters, containers, polythene films, and technical components product groups; Consumer Packaging North America, which includes containers and pails, foodservice, and tubes product groups; Engineered Materials, which includes stretch and shrink films, converter films, food and consumer films, retail bags, polyvinyl chloride films, and agriculture films product groups; and Health, and Hygiene and Specialties, which includes health products, hygiene products, and specialties products.

Recent Developments: For the year ended Sep 28 2019, net income decreased 18.5% to US$404.0 million from US$496.0 million in the prior year. Revenues were US$8.88 billion, up 12.8% from US$7.87 billion the year before. Operating income was US$974.0 million versus US$761.0 million in the prior year, an increase of 28.0%. Direct operating expenses rose 12.8% to US$7.26 billion from US$6.44 billion in the comparable period the year before. Indirect operating expenses decreased 3.7% to US$645.0 million from US$670.0 million in the equivalent prior-year period.

Prospects: Our evaluation of Berry Global Group Inc. as of October 4th, 2019 is the result of our systematic analysis on three basic characteristics: earnings strength, relative valuation, and recent stock price movement. The company has generated a negative trend in earnings per share over the past 5 quarters. In addition, recent analyst estimates for the company have been reduced and BERY has posted results that fell short of analysts' expectations. Based on operating earnings yield, the company is undervalued when compared to all of the companies we cover. Share price changes over the past year indicates that BERY will perform well over the near term.

Financial Data
(US$ in Millions)

	09/28/2019	09/29/2018	09/30/2017	10/01/2016	09/26/2015	09/27/2014	09/28/2013	09/29/2012
Earnings Per Share	3.00	3.67	2.56	1.89	0.70	0.51	0.48	0.02
Cash Flow Per Share	9.17	7.66	7.66	6.98	5.36	4.55	4.10	5.76
Income Statement								
Total Revenue	8,878	7,869	7,095	6,489	4,881	4,958	4,647	4,766
EBITDA	1,432	1,274	1,239	1,124	663	646	670	687
Depn & Amortn	613	538	521	525	350	358	341	355
Income Before Taxes	490	477	449	308	122	67	85	4
Income Taxes	86	(19)	109	72	36	4	28	2
Net Income	404	496	340	236	86	62	57	2
Average Shares	134	135	132	125	123	121	119	86
Balance Sheet								
Current Assets	3,757	2,285	2,004	1,792	1,383	1,432	1,337	1,233
Total Assets	16,469	9,131	8,476	7,653	5,028	5,268	5,135	5,106
Current Liabilities	2,039	1,237	1,134	1,031	705	767	684	646
Long-Term Obligations	11,261	5,806	5,608	5,712	3,648	3,860	3,875	4,431
Total Liabilities	14,851	7,700	7,464	7,435	5,096	5,385	5,334	5,561
Stockholders' Equity	1,618	1,431	1,012	218	(68)	(117)	(199)	(455)
Shares Outstanding	132	131	130	122	119	117	115	83
Statistical Record								
Return on Assets %	3.16	5.65	4.23	3.66	1.68	1.20	1.12	0.04
Return on Equity %	26.57	40.72	55.44	309.58	...	...	...	...
EBITDA Margin %	16.13	16.19	17.46	17.32	13.58	13.03	14.42	14.41
Net Margin %	4.55	6.30	4.79	3.64	1.76	1.25	1.23	0.04
Asset Turnover	0.70	0.90	0.88	1.01	0.95	0.96	0.91	0.93
Current Ratio	1.84	1.85	1.77	1.74	1.96	1.87	1.95	1.91
Debt to Equity	6.96	4.06	5.54	26.20	...	...	...	...
Price Range	58.83-38.21	61.03-45.68	58.77-42.81	45.97-28.42	36.80-23.14	26.21-18.12	24.99-13.48	...
P/E Ratio	19.61-12.74	16.63-12.45	22.96-16.72	24.32-15.04	52.57-33.06	51.39-35.53	52.06-28.08	...

Address: 101 Oakley Street, Evansville, IN 47710
Telephone: 812-424-2904

Web Site: www.berryplastics.com
Officers: Thomas E. (Tom) Salmon - Chairman, President, Chief Executive Officer, Chief Operating Officer, Division Officer James M. Till - Executive Vice President, Controller

Auditors: Ernst & Young LLP
Investor Contact: 812-.30-6.2964
Transfer Agents: Computershare Trust Company, N.A.

BEST BUY INC

Exchange	Symbol	Price	52Wk Range	Yield	P/E	Div Acheiver
NYS	BBY	$87.80 (12/31/2019)	88.64-52.50	2.28	15.68	15 Years

*7 Year Price Score 123.47 *NYSE Composite Index=100 *12 Month Price Score 108.94

Interim Earnings (Per Share)

Qtr.	Apr	Jul	Oct	Jan
2016-17	0.70	0.61	0.61	1.89
2017-18	0.60	0.67	0.78	1.21
2018-19	0.72	0.86	0.99	2.63
2019-20	0.98	0.89	1.10	...

Interim Dividends (Per Share)

Amt	Decl	Ex	Rec	Pay
0.50Q	02/27/2019	03/19/2019	03/20/2019	04/10/2019
0.50Q	05/24/2019	06/12/2019	06/13/2019	07/05/2019
0.50Q	08/30/2019	09/18/2019	09/19/2019	10/10/2019
0.50Q	11/27/2019	12/16/2019	12/17/2019	01/07/2020

Indicated Div: $2.00 (Div. Reinv. Plan)

Valuation Analysis — **Institutional Holding**

Forecast EPS	$5.94	No of Institutions
	(01/16/2020)	983
Market Cap	$22.8 Billion	Shares
Book Value	$3.1 Billion	254,854,688
Price/Book	7.30	% Held
Price/Sales	0.53	67.87

Business Summary: Retail - Appliances and Electronics (MIC: 2.1.7 SIC: 5731 NAIC: 443112)

Best Buy provides computing and mobile phones, consumer electronics, appliances, entertainment, services and other products. Co. operates two reportable segments: Domestic, which is comprised of the operations in all states, districts and territories of the U.S. under various brand names including Best Buy, bestbuy.com, Best Buy Direct, Best Buy Express, Best Buy Mobile, Geek Squad, GreatCall, Magnolia and Pacific Kitchen and Home; and International, which is comprised of all operations in Canada and Mexico under the brand names Best Buy, Best Buy Express, Best Buy Mobile, Geek Squad and the domain names bestbuy.ca and bestbuy.com.mx.

Recent Developments: For the quarter ended Nov 2 2019, net income increased 5.8% to US$293.0 million from US$277.0 million in the year-earlier quarter. Revenues were US$9.76 billion, up 1.8% from US$9.59 billion the year before. Operating income was US$395.0 million versus US$322.0 million in the prior-year quarter, an increase of 22.7%. Direct operating expenses rose 1.9% to US$7.40 billion from US$7.27 billion in the comparable period the year before. Indirect operating expenses decreased 1.8% to US$1.97 billion from US$2.00 billion in the equivalent prior-year period.

Prospects: Our evaluation of Best Buy Inc. as of October 4th, 2019 is the result of our systematic analysis on three basic characteristics: earnings strength, relative valuation, and recent stock price movement. The company has managed to produce a neutral trend in earnings per share over the past 5 quarters. In addition, recent analyst estimates for the company have been mixed and BBY has posted results that exceeded analysts' expectations. Based on operating earnings yield, the company is undervalued when compared to all of the companies we cover. Share price changes over the past year indicates that BBY will perform poorly over the near term.

Financial Data

(US$ in Thousands)	9 Mos	6 Mos	3 Mos	02/02/2019	02/03/2018	01/28/2017	01/30/2016	01/31/2015
Earnings Per Share	5.60	5.49	5.46	5.20	3.26	3.81	2.56	3.49
Cash Flow Per Share	8.50	7.21	8.24	8.74	7.01	8.01	3.83	5.55
Tang Book Value Per Share	8.24	21.15	21.70	9.00	11.26	13.77	12.15	12.84
Dividends Per Share	1.950	1.900	1.850	1.800	1.360	1.570	1.430	0.720
Dividend Payout %	34.82	34.61	33.88	34.62	41.72	41.21	55.86	20.63
Income Statement								
Total Revenue	28,442,000	18,678,000	9,142,000	42,879,000	42,151,000	39,403,000	39,528,000	40,339,000
EBITDA	1,683,000	1,072,000	548,000	2,731,000	2,575,000	2,542,000	2,047,000	2,133,000
Depn & Amortn	607,000	401,000	200,000	770,000	683,000	654,000	657,000	656,000
Income Before Taxes	1,026,000	637,000	330,000	1,888,000	1,817,000	1,816,000	1,310,000	1,387,000
Income Taxes	230,000	134,000	65,000	424,000	818,000	609,000	503,000	141,000
Net Income	796,000	503,000	265,000	1,464,000	1,000,000	1,228,000	897,000	1,233,000
Average Shares	265,200	269,400	271,500	281,400	307,100	322,600	350,700	353,600
Balance Sheet								
Current Assets	10,175,000	8,192,000	8,014,000	8,870,000	9,829,000	10,516,000	9,886,000	11,729,000
Total Assets	16,926,000	14,978,000	14,550,000	12,901,000	13,049,000	13,856,000	13,519,000	15,256,000
Current Liabilities	9,726,000	7,576,000	7,171,000	7,513,000	7,817,000	7,122,000	6,925,000	7,777,000
Long-Term Obligations	1,239,000	1,247,000	1,193,000	1,332,000	811,000	1,321,000	1,339,000	1,580,000
Total Liabilities	13,801,000	11,693,000	11,196,000	9,595,000	9,437,000	9,147,000	9,141,000	10,261,000
Stockholders' Equity	3,125,000	6,570,000	6,708,000	3,306,000	3,612,000	4,709,000	4,378,000	4,995,000
Shares Outstanding	260,000	265,000	267,000	265,703	282,988	311,108	323,779	351,468
Statistical Record								
Return on Assets %	9.59	11.23	11.42	11.31	7.31	9.00	6.25	8.45
Return on Equity %	49.89	23.41	22.45	42.44	23.65	27.10	19.19	27.53
EBITDA Margin %	5.92	5.74	5.99	6.37	6.11	6.45	5.18	5.29
Net Margin %	2.80	2.69	2.90	3.41	2.37	3.12	2.27	3.06
Asset Turnover	2.71	3.19	3.22	3.31	3.08	2.89	2.75	2.76
Current Ratio	1.05	1.08	1.12	1.18	1.26	1.48	1.43	1.51
Debt to Equity	0.40	0.19	0.18	0.40	0.22	0.28	0.31	0.32
Price Range	77.86-48.24	82.60-48.24	82.60-48.24	82.60-48.24	78.06-42.14	49.31-26.93	41.77-25.87	39.91-22.78
P/E Ratio	13.90-8.61	15.05-8.79	15.13-8.84	15.88-9.28	23.94-12.93	12.94-7.07	16.32-10.11	11.44-6.53
Average Yield %	2.93	2.77	2.65	2.54	2.42	4.36	4.13	2.35

Address: 7601 Penn Avenue South, Richfield, MN 55423	**Web Site:** www.bestbuy.com	**Auditors:** Deloitte & Touche LLP
Telephone: 612-291-1000	**Officers:** Hubert Joly - Executive Chairman, Chairman, President, Chief Executive Officer Richard M. Schulze - Chairman Emeritus, Chairman	**Investor Contact:** 612-291-1000 **Transfer Agents:** Computershare, Providence, RI

BIG LOTS, INC.

Exchange	Symbol	Price	52Wk Range	Yield	P/E
NYS	BIG	$28.72 (12/31/2019)	39.33-19.16	4.18	4.46

*7 Year Price Score 55.28   *NYSE Composite Index=100   *12 Month Price Score 76.59

Interim Earnings (Per Share)

Qtr.	Apr	Jul	Oct	Jan
2016-17	0.79	0.50	0.03	1.96
2017-18	1.15	0.67	0.10	2.43
2018-19	0.74	0.59	(0.16)	2.64
2019-20	0.39	0.16	3.25	...

Interim Dividends (Per Share)

Amt	Decl	Ex	Rec	Pay
0.30Q	03/06/2019	03/21/2019	03/22/2019	04/05/2019
0.30Q	05/29/2019	06/13/2019	06/14/2019	06/28/2019
0.30Q	08/28/2019	09/12/2019	09/13/2019	09/27/2019
0.30Q	12/04/2019	12/13/2019	12/16/2019	12/30/2019

Indicated Div: $1.20

Valuation Analysis — **Institutional Holding**

Forecast EPS	$3.80	No of Institutions
	(00/22/2020)	428
Market Cap	$1.1 Billion	Shares
Book Value	$762.3 Million	56,100,924
Price/Book	1.47	% Held
Price/Sales	0.21	57.08

Business Summary: Retail - General Merchandise/Department Stores (MIC: 2.1.1 SIC: 5331 NAIC: 452990)

Big Lots is a discount retailer. Co.'s primary merchandising categories include Furniture (upholstery, mattress, and case goods departments), Seasonal (Christmas trim, lawn and garden, and summer departments), Soft Home (fashion bedding, utility bedding, bath, window, decorative textile, home organization, and frames departments), Food (beverage and grocery, candy and snacks departments), Consumables (health, beauty and cosmetics, plastics, paper, chemical, and pet departments), Hard Home (small appliances, table top, food preparation, stationery, greeting cards, and home maintenance departments), and Electronics, Toys, and Accessories (electronics, toys, jewelry, and hosiery departments).

Recent Developments: For the quarter ended Nov 2 2019, net income amounted to US$127.0 million versus a net loss of US$6.6 million in the year-earlier quarter. Revenues were US$1.17 billion, up 1.6% from US$1.15 billion the year before. Operating income was US$170.5 million versus a loss of US$9.6 million in the prior-year quarter. Direct operating expenses rose 2.1% to US$704.6 million from US$690.2 million in the comparable period the year before. Indirect operating expenses decreased 37.5% to US$292.9 million from US$468.7 million in the equivalent prior-year period.

Prospects: Our evaluation of Big Lots Inc. as of October 4th, 2019 is the result of our systematic analysis on three basic characteristics: earnings strength, relative valuation, and recent stock price movement. The company has managed to produce a neutral trend in earnings per share over the past 5 quarters. In addition, recent analyst estimates for the company have been mixed and BIG has posted results that exceeded analysts' expectations. Based on operating earnings yield, the company is undervalued when compared to all of the companies we cover. Share price changes over the past year indicates that BIG will perform poorly over the near term.

Financial Data

(US$ in Thousands)	9 Mos	6 Mos	3 Mos	02/02/2019	02/03/2018	01/28/2017	01/30/2016	01/31/2015
Earnings Per Share	6.44	3.03	3.46	3.83	4.38	3.32	2.80	2.06
Cash Flow Per Share	7.03	7.23	4.87	5.75	5.75	6.90	6.80	5.81
Tang Book Value Per Share	19.53	16.53	16.61	17.31	15.97	14.70	14.67	14.92
Dividends Per Share	1.200	1.200	1.200	1.200	1.000	0.840	0.760	0.510
Dividend Payout %	18.63	39.60	34.68	31.33	22.83	25.30	27.14	24.76
Income Statement								
Total Revenue	3,716,198	2,548,210	1,295,796	5,238,105	5,270,980	5,200,439	5,190,582	5,177,078
EBITDA	478,215	216,115	116,445	342,951	419,165	369,732	353,233	344,188
Depn & Amortn	269,136	177,168	89,890	125,000	117,100	120,400	122,700	119,700
Income Before Taxes	195,422	30,649	22,822	207,613	295,354	244,241	226,850	221,900
Income Taxes	46,722	8,931	7,282	50,719	105,522	91,458	83,842	85,239
Net Income	148,700	21,718	15,540	156,894	189,832	152,828	142,873	114,276
Average Shares	39,094	39,077	40,002	40,962	43,300	45,974	50,964	55,552
Balance Sheet								
Current Assets	1,261,552	1,040,438	1,069,092	1,128,003	1,021,973	994,379	994,432	1,038,429
Total Assets	3,421,746	3,192,295	3,045,645	2,023,347	1,651,726	1,607,707	1,640,370	1,635,891
Current Liabilities	977,244	951,408	855,469	638,560	589,608	678,595	678,448	587,829
Long-Term Obligations	501,115	467,800	470,400	374,100	199,800	106,400	62,300	62,100
Total Liabilities	2,659,422	2,547,752	2,397,314	1,330,306	982,139	957,077	919,900	846,341
Stockholders' Equity	762,324	644,543	648,331	693,041	669,587	650,630	720,470	789,550
Shares Outstanding	39,036	39,001	39,042	40,042	41,925	44,259	49,101	52,912
Statistical Record								
Return on Assets %	9.24	4.91	5.92	8.56	11.46	9.44	8.75	6.79
Return on Equity %	37.89	19.71	21.11	23.09	28.29	22.35	18.98	13.55
EBITDA Margin %	12.87	8.48	8.99	6.55	7.95	7.11	6.81	6.65
Net Margin %	4.00	0.85	1.20	3.00	3.60	2.94	2.75	2.21
Asset Turnover	1.91	2.11	2.21	2.86	3.18	3.21	3.18	3.08
Current Ratio	1.29	1.09	1.25	1.77	1.73	1.47	1.47	1.77
Debt to Equity	0.66	0.73	0.73	0.54	0.30	0.16	0.09	0.08
Price Range	44.90-20.13	50.13-23.70	50.13-26.74	58.75-26.74	64.22-46.45	56.02-36.19	50.96-35.88	50.80-25.71
P/E Ratio	6.97-3.13	16.54-7.82	14.49-7.73	15.34-6.98	14.66-10.61	16.87-10.90	18.20-12.81	24.66-12.48
Average Yield %	3.97	3.43	3.07	2.84	1.94	1.75	1.68	1.22

Address: 4900 E. Dublin-Granville Road, Columbus, OH 43081	**Web Site:** www.biglots.com	**Auditors:** DELOITTE & TOUCHE LLP
Telephone: 614-278-6800	**Officers:** James R. Chambers - Chairman Bruce K. Thorn - President, Chief Executive Officer	**Investor Contact:** 614-278-6622
Fax: 614-278-6666		**Transfer Agents:** Computershare Investor Services, Canton, MA

BIO-RAD LABORATORIES INC

Exchange	Symbol	Price	52Wk Range	Yield	P/E
NYS	BIO	$370.03 (12/31/2019)	374.20-224.30	N/A	29.56

*7 Year Price Score 135.06 *NYSE Composite Index=100 *12 Month Price Score 109.59

Interim Earnings (Per Share)

Qtr.	Mar	Jun	Sep	Dec
2016	0.42	0.61	0.62	(0.70)
2017	0.41	0.17	0.91	2.58
2018	21.77	8.87	8.89	(27.40)
2019	28.74	19.86	(8.68)	...

Interim Dividends (Per Share)

No Dividends Paid

Valuation Analysis		Institutional Holding	
Forecast EPS	$7.20	No of Institutions	
	(01/15/2020)	480	
Market Cap	$11.1 Billion	Shares	
Book Value	$5.1 Billion	23,178,824	
Price/Book	2.16	% Held	
Price/Sales	4.81	64.14	

Business Summary: Biotechnology (MIC: 4.1.2 SIC: 3826 NAIC: 334516)

Bio-Rad Laboratories is a manufacturer and distributor of its own life science research and clinical diagnostics products. Co. has two primary segments: Life Science, which is engaged in the life sciences market and develops, manufactures and markets reagents, apparatus and laboratory instruments; and Clinical Diagnostics, which designs, manufactures, sells and supports test systems, informatics systems, test kits and quality controls that serve clinical laboratories in the diagnostics market. Co. sells its products and services to a client base comprised of scientific research, healthcare, education and government customers.

Recent Developments: For the quarter ended Sep 30 2019, net loss amounted to US$258.8 million versus net income of US$269.3 million in the year-earlier quarter. Revenues were US$560.6 million, up 2.8% from US$545.1 million the year before. Operating income was US$57.5 million versus US$36.3 million in the prior-year quarter, an increase of 58.4%. Direct operating expenses declined 1.9% to US$253.6 million from US$258.4 million in the comparable period the year before. Indirect operating expenses decreased 0.3% to US$249.6 million from US$250.4 million in the equivalent prior-year period.

Prospects: Our evaluation of Bio-Rad Laboratories Inc. as of October 4th, 2019 is the result of our systematic analysis on three basic characteristics: earnings strength, relative valuation, and recent stock price movement. The company has generated a negative trend in earnings per share over the past 5 quarters. However, recent analyst estimates for the company have been mixed and BIO has posted results that exceeded analysts' expectations. Based on operating earnings yield, the company is overvalued when compared to all of the companies we cover. Share price changes over the past year indicates that BIO will perform in line with the market over the near term.

Financial Data

(US$ in Thousands)	9 Mos	6 Mos	3 Mos	12/31/2018	12/31/2017	12/31/2016	12/31/2015	12/31/2014
Earnings Per Share	12.52	30.09	19.10	12.10	4.07	0.95	3.85	3.05
Cash Flow Per Share	13.51	12.26	9.67	9.57	3.50	7.33	6.38	9.46
Tang Book Value Per Share	157.68	171.94	150.70	123.07	75.54	65.86	60.64	49.21
Income Statement								
Total Revenue	1,687,231	1,126,598	553,979	2,289,415	2,160,153	2,068,172	2,019,441	2,175,044
EBITDA	1,582,703	1,905,194	1,123,752	648,121	249,319	191,702	289,239	290,088
Depn & Amortn	31,100	19,800	10,000	138,100	148,700	142,900	131,800	149,900
Income Before Taxes	1,561,651	1,896,867	1,127,266	512,659	97,805	41,560	145,847	131,557
Income Taxes	356,462	432,862	262,071	147,045	(24,444)	13,435	32,754	42,712
Net Income	1,205,189	1,464,005	865,195	365,614	122,249	28,125	113,093	88,845
Average Shares	29,831	30,154	30,104	30,228	30,034	29,646	29,409	29,133
Balance Sheet								
Current Assets	2,047,632	2,087,940	2,031,643	2,023,478	1,976,649	1,844,524	1,777,596	1,716,367
Total Assets	7,177,116	7,646,945	6,862,914	5,611,068	4,273,012	3,850,504	3,711,542	3,341,278
Current Liabilities	434,040	445,977	444,306	450,795	502,696	471,322	441,351	446,761
Long-Term Obligations	437,808	437,680	437,606	438,937	434,581	434,186	435,707	435,710
Total Liabilities	2,045,924	2,160,135	1,999,059	1,590,737	1,342,762	1,263,745	1,221,039	1,156,123
Stockholders' Equity	5,131,192	5,486,810	4,863,855	4,020,331	2,930,250	2,586,759	2,490,503	2,185,155
Shares Outstanding	29,934	29,800	29,820	29,800	29,785	29,576	29,359	29,069
Statistical Record								
Return on Assets %	5.42	12.90	8.78	7.40	3.01	0.74	3.21	2.64
Return on Equity %	7.51	17.87	12.28	10.52	4.43	1.10	4.84	4.06
EBITDA Margin %	93.80	169.11	202.85	28.31	11.54	9.27	14.32	13.34
Net Margin %	71.43	129.95	156.18	15.97	5.66	1.36	5.60	4.08
Asset Turnover	0.33	0.33	0.35	0.46	0.53	0.55	0.57	0.65
Current Ratio	4.72	4.68	4.57	4.49	3.93	3.91	4.03	3.84
Debt to Equity	0.09	0.08	0.09	0.11	0.15	0.17	0.17	0.20
Price Range	345.24-220.10	326.15-220.10	326.15-220.10	326.15-220.10	271.30-182.91	183.46-123.93	151.93-113.77	133.73-106.48
P/E Ratio	27.58-17.58	10.84-7.31	17.08-11.52	26.95-18.19	66.66-44.94	193.12-130.45	39.46-29.55	43.85-34.91

Address: 1000 Alfred Nobel Drive, Hercules, CA 94547 Telephone: 510-724-7000	Web Site: www.bio-rad.com Officers: Norman D. Schwartz - Chairman, President, Chief Executive Officer Michael Crowley - Executive Vice President	Auditors: KPMG LLP Investor Contact: 510-741-6104 Transfer Agents: Computershare, Canton, MA

BJ'S WHOLESALE CLUB HOLDINGS INC

Exchange	Symbol	Price	52Wk Range	Yield	P/E
NYS	BJ	$22.74 (12/31/2019)	28.91-21.13	N/A	14.77

*7 Year Price Score N/A   *NYSE Composite Index=100   *12 Month Price Score 89.54

TRADING VOLUME (thousand shares)

Interim Earnings (Per Share)

Qtr.	Apr	Jul	Oct	Jan
2017-18	(0.67)	0.22	0.25	0.72
2018-19	0.15	(0.05)	0.39	0.50
2019-20	0.25	0.39	0.40	...

Interim Dividends (Per Share)

Dividend Payment Suspended

Valuation Analysis / Institutional Holding

Forecast EPS	$1.46	No of Institutions
	(01/22/2020)	258
Market Cap	$3.1 Billion	Shares
Book Value	N/A	142,347,280
Price/Book	N/A	% Held
Price/Sales	0.24	101.34

Business Summary: Retail - General Merchandise/Department Stores (MIC: 2.1.1 SIC: 5331 NAIC: 452990)

BJ's Wholesale Club holding is a holding company. Through its subsidiary, Co. is a warehouse club operator. Co. delivers value to its members, consistently providing 25% or more savings on a representative basket of manufacturer-branded groceries compared. Co. provides a curated assortment focused on perishable products, continuously refreshed general merchandise, gasoline and other ancillary services to deliver a shopping experience. Co. operates warehouse club in New York, Florida, Massachusetts, New Jersey, Pennsylvania, Connecticut, Virginia, Maryland, North Carolina, New Hampshire, Ohio, Georgia, Delaware, Maine, Rhode Island and South Carolina.

Recent Developments: For the quarter ended Nov 2 2019, income from continuing operations increased 1.2% to US$55.2 million from US$54.6 million in the year-earlier quarter. Net income increased 1.2% to US$55.1 million from US$54.4 million in the year-earlier quarter. Revenues were US$3.23 billion, up 0.2% from US$3.22 billion the year before. Operating income was US$100.9 million versus US$90.3 million in the prior-year quarter, an increase of 11.7%. Direct operating expenses declined 0.7% to US$2.61 billion from US$2.63 billion in the comparable period the year before. Indirect operating expenses increased 3.0% to US$516.7 million from US$501.8 million in the equivalent prior-year period.

Prospects: Our evaluation of BJs Wholesale Club Holdings as of October 4th, 2019 is the result of our systematic analysis on three basic characteristics: earnings strength, relative valuation, and recent stock price movement. The company has generated a negative trend in earnings per share over the past 5 quarters. However, recent analyst estimates for the company have been unchanged while BJ has posted results that exceeded analysts' expectations. Based on operating earnings yield, the company is undervalued when compared to all of the companies we cover. Share price changes over the past year indicates that BJ will perform over the near term.

Financial Data

(US$ in Thousands)	9 Mos	6 Mos	3 Mos	02/02/2019	02/03/2018	01/28/2017	01/30/2016
Earnings Per Share	1.54	1.53	1.09	1.05	0.54	0.48	0.26
Cash Flow Per Share	2.93	3.21	2.97	3.67	2.34	3.38	1.82
Dividends Per Share	...	...	...	...	8.310	...	...
Dividend Payout %	...	...	...	...	1,538.89	...	...
Income Statement							
Total Revenue	9,718,382	6,488,978	3,143,136	13,007,347	12,754,589	12,350,537	12,467,553
EBITDA	274,324	172,069	72,005	472,232	392,796	411,435	381,127
Depn & Amortn	3,969	2,646	1,323	168,779	172,524	195,416	194,331
Income Before Taxes	188,081	114,851	42,893	138,918	23,548	72,668	36,703
Income Taxes	42,507	24,473	6,808	11,826	(28,427)	27,968	12,049
Net Income	145,413	90,321	35,798	127,261	50,301	44,224	24,104
Average Shares	138,191	139,516	140,462	121,134	92,264	90,736	90,241
Balance Sheet							
Current Assets	1,542,408	1,265,264	1,343,224	1,337,206	1,336,604	1,264,395	...
Total Assets	5,478,081	5,152,087	5,226,716	3,239,285	3,273,856	3,232,219	...
Current Liabilities	2,051,807	1,611,065	1,673,912	1,577,688	1,469,587	1,200,341	...
Long-Term Obligations	1,339,700	1,540,602	1,543,537	1,577,745	2,534,368	2,042,159	...
Total Liabilities	5,582,567	5,316,673	5,375,025	3,441,369	4,293,275	3,571,285	...
Stockholders' Equity	(104,486)	(164,586)	(148,309)	(202,084)	(1,019,419)	(339,066)	...
Shares Outstanding	137,217	136,762	139,054	137,317	87,073	87,073	87,073
Statistical Record							
Return on Assets %	4.69	4.99	3.51	3.92	1.52	...	...
EBITDA Margin %	2.82	2.65	2.29	3.63	3.08	3.33	3.06
Net Margin %	1.50	1.39	1.14	0.98	0.39	0.36	0.19
Asset Turnover	2.94	3.14	3.08	4.01	3.86	...	...
Current Ratio	0.75	0.79	0.80	0.85	0.91	1.05	...
Price Range	28.91-19.83	31.45-19.83	31.45-19.83	31.45-19.83	...	...	...
P/E Ratio	18.77-12.88	20.56-12.96	28.85-18.19	29.95-18.89	...	...	...

Address: 25 Research Drive, Westborough, MA 01581 Telephone: 774-512-7400	Web Site: www.bjs.com Officers: Christopher J. Baldwin - Chairman, President, Chief Executive Officer Lee Delaney - President, Executive Vice President, Chief Commercial Officer	Auditors: PricewaterhouseCoopers LLP Transfer Agents: American Stock Transfer & Trust Company, LLC

BLACK HILLS CORPORATION

Exchange	Symbol	Price	52Wk Range	Yield	P/E	Div Acheiver
NYS	BKH	$78.54 (12/31/2019)	81.64-61.27	2.72	21.40	47 Years

*7 Year Price Score 106.48 ***NYSE Composite Index=100** ***12 Month Price Score 97.29**

Interim Earnings (Per Share)

Qtr.	Mar	Jun	Sep	Dec
2016	0.77	0.01	0.26	0.33
2017	1.39	0.40	0.50	0.92
2018	2.46	0.40	0.31	1.51
2019	1.73	0.24	0.19	...

Interim Dividends (Per Share)

Amt	Decl	Ex	Rec	Pay
0.505Q	01/30/2019	02/14/2019	02/15/2019	03/01/2019
0.505Q	04/29/2019	05/16/2019	05/17/2019	06/01/2019
0.505Q	07/31/2019	08/16/2019	08/19/2019	09/01/2019
0.535Q	10/29/2019	11/15/2019	11/18/2019	12/01/2019

Indicated Div: $2.14 (Div. Reinv. Plan)

Valuation Analysis **Institutional Holding**

Forecast EPS	$3.50
(01/17/2020)	
Market Cap	$4.8 Billion
Book Value	$2.3 Billion
Price/Book	2.07
Price/Sales	2.74

No of Institutions	441
Shares	68,732,248
% Held	99.39

Business Summary: Electric Utilities (MIC: 3.1.1 SIC: 4911 NAIC: 221121)

Black Hills is a utility holding company, which operates in four segments: Electric Utilities, which generates, transmits and distributes electricity to customers in South Dakota, Wyoming, Colorado and Montana; Gas Utilities, which serves natural gas utility customers in Arkansas, Colorado, Iowa, Nebraska, Kansas and Wyoming; Power Generation, which produces electric power from its wind, natural gas and coal generating plants and sells the electric capacity and energy primarily to its utilities under long-term contracts; and Mining, which produces coal at its mine near Gillette, WY, and sells the coal primarily under long-term contracts to mine-mouth electric generation facilities.

Recent Developments: For the quarter ended Sep 30 2019, income from continuing operations decreased 29.4% to US$15.4 million from US$21.8 million in the year-earlier quarter. Net income decreased 26.5% to US$15.4 million from US$20.9 million in the year-earlier quarter. Revenues were US$325.5 million, up 1.1% from US$322.0 million the year before. Operating income was US$70.6 million versus US$65.1 million in the prior-year quarter, an increase of 8.4%. Direct operating expenses declined 3.0% to US$190.1 million from US$195.9 million in the comparable period the year before. Indirect operating expenses increased 6.4% to US$64.9 million from US$61.0 million in the equivalent prior-year period.

Prospects: Our evaluation of Black Hills Corp. as of October 4th, 2019 is the result of our systematic analysis on three basic characteristics: earnings strength, relative valuation, and recent stock price movement. The company has generated a negative trend in earnings per share over the past 5 quarters. However, recent analyst estimates for the company have been mixed and BKH has posted results that fell short of analysts' expectations. Based on operating earnings yield, the company is fairly valued when compared to all of the companies we cover. Share price changes over the past year indicates that BKH will perform over the near term.

Financial Data

(US$ in Thousands)	9 Mos	6 Mos	3 Mos	12/31/2018	12/31/2017	12/31/2016	12/31/2015	12/31/2014
Earnings Per Share	3.67	3.79	3.95	4.66	3.21	1.37	(0.71)	2.89
Cash Flow Per Share	8.14	7.74	8.26	8.98	8.05	6.16	9.45	7.29
Tang Book Value Per Share	16.54	16.43	16.00	14.46	7.51	5.75	21.54	22.82
Dividends Per Share	2.020	1.990	1.960	1.930	1.810	1.680	1.620	1.560
Dividend Payout %	55.04	52.51	49.62	41.42	56.39	122.63	...	53.98
Income Statement								
Total Revenue	1,257,246	931,698	597,810	1,754,268	1,680,266	1,572,974	1,304,605	1,393,570
EBITDA	271,323	217,826	161,349	599,411	613,030	419,042	193,413	412,428
Depn & Amortn	6,326	4,219	2,007	204,173	196,507	195,223	161,734	150,210
Income Before Taxes	162,528	144,625	124,625	255,882	281,742	93,106	(49,522)	194,177
Income Taxes	22,078	19,577	17,263	(23,667)	73,367	10,475	(22,160)	65,395
Net Income	130,131	118,391	103,808	258,442	177,034	72,970	(32,111)	128,781
Average Shares	61,104	60,606	60,060	55,486	55,120	53,271	45,288	44,598
Balance Sheet								
Current Assets	377,421	369,673	484,570	503,833	570,782	466,814	822,151	454,036
Total Assets	7,274,950	7,081,453	7,037,572	6,963,327	6,658,902	6,515,444	4,655,501	4,279,806
Current Liabilities	691,124	488,401	591,015	648,230	649,101	527,932	422,029	651,281
Long-Term Obligations	3,049,235	3,049,672	2,950,299	2,950,835	3,109,400	3,211,189	1,866,866	1,267,589
Total Liabilities	4,945,472	4,764,703	4,758,413	4,781,739	4,949,928	4,900,805	3,189,634	2,903,782
Stockholders' Equity	2,329,478	2,316,750	2,279,159	2,181,588	1,708,974	1,614,639	1,465,867	1,376,024
Shares Outstanding	61,454	61,066	60,354	60,004	53,540	53,382	51,192	44,671
Statistical Record								
Return on Assets %	3.11	3.25	3.36	3.79	2.69	1.30	N.M.	3.16
Return on Equity %	10.46	10.73	11.19	13.29	10.65	4.72	N.M.	9.60
EBITDA Margin %	21.58	23.38	26.99	34.17	36.48	26.64	14.83	29.60
Net Margin %	10.35	12.71	17.36	14.73	10.54	4.64	N.M.	9.24
Asset Turnover	0.25	0.26	0.26	0.26	0.26	0.28	0.29	0.34
Current Ratio	0.55	0.76	0.82	0.78	0.88	0.88	1.95	0.70
Debt to Equity	1.31	1.32	1.29	1.35	1.82	1.99	1.27	0.92
Price Range	81.64-57.24	81.64-56.71	74.39-52.69	67.81-50.66	71.88-57.44	64.08-45.57	53.12-37.29	61.39-47.48
P/E Ratio	22.25-15.60	21.54-14.96	18.83-13.34	14.55-10.87	22.39-17.89	46.77-33.26	...	21.24-16.43
Average Yield %	2.84	2.98	3.16	3.31	2.75	2.87	3.54	2.84

Address: 7001 Mount Rushmore Road, Rapid City, SD 57702 **Telephone:** 605-721-1700	**Web Site:** www.blackhillscorp.com **Officers:** David R. Emery - Executive Chairman, Chairman, President, Chief Executive Officer Linden R. Evans - President, Chief Executive Officer, Chief Operating Officer, Division Officer	**Auditors:** DELOITTE & TOUCHE LLP **Investor Contact:** 605-721-1171 **Transfer Agents:** Wells Fargo Shareowner Services, St. Paul, MN

BLACKROCK INC

Exchange	Symbol	Price	52Wk Range	Yield	P/E
NYS	BLK	$502.70 (12/31/2019)	503.24-377.98	2.63	19.39

*7 Year Price Score 97.57 *NYSE Composite Index=100 *12 Month Price Score 103.38

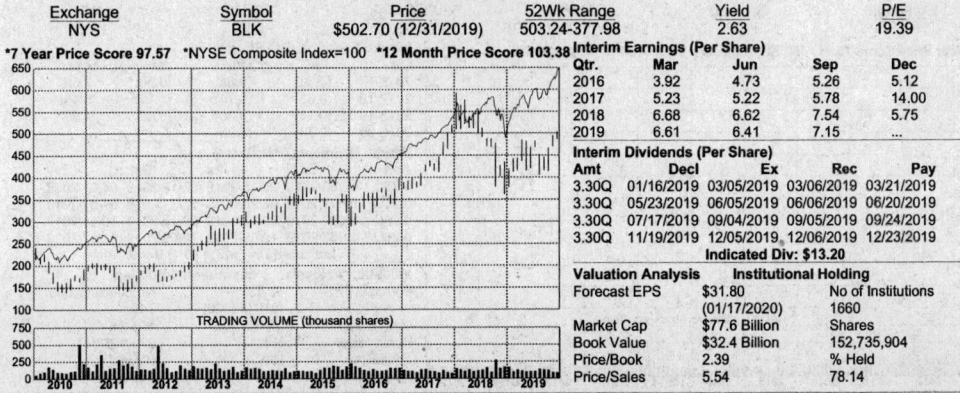

Interim Earnings (Per Share)

Qtr.	Mar	Jun	Sep	Dec
2016	3.92	4.73	5.26	5.12
2017	5.23	5.22	5.78	14.00
2018	6.68	6.62	7.54	5.75
2019	6.61	6.41	7.15	...

Interim Dividends (Per Share)

Amt	Decl	Ex	Rec	Pay
3.30Q	01/16/2019	03/05/2019	03/06/2019	03/21/2019
3.30Q	05/23/2019	06/05/2019	06/06/2019	06/20/2019
3.30Q	07/17/2019	09/04/2019	09/05/2019	09/24/2019
3.30Q	11/19/2019	12/05/2019	12/06/2019	12/23/2019

Indicated Div: $13.20

Valuation Analysis | **Institutional Holding**

Forecast EPS	$31.80 (01/17/2020)	No of Institutions 1660
Market Cap	$77.6 Billion	Shares
Book Value	$32.4 Billion	152,735,904
Price/Book	2.39	% Held
Price/Sales	5.54	78.14

Business Summary: Finance Intermediaries & Services (MIC: 5.5.1 SIC: 6211 NAIC: 523120)

BlackRock is an investment management firm. Co. provides a range of investment and technology services to institutional and retail clients worldwide. Products are provided directly and through intermediaries in a variety of vehicles, including open-end and closed-end mutual funds, iShares® exchange-traded funds, separate accounts, collective investment trusts and other pooled investment vehicles. Co. also provides technology services, including the investment and risk management technology platform, Aladdin®, Aladdin Wealth, Cachematrix and FutureAdvisor, as well as advisory services and solutions to a base of institutional and wealth management clients.

Recent Developments: For the quarter ended Sep 30 2019, net income decreased 7.0% to US$1.12 billion from US$1.20 billion in the year-earlier quarter. Revenues were US$3.69 billion, up 3.2% from US$3.58 billion the year before. Operating income was US$1.50 billion versus US$1.40 billion in the prior-year quarter, an increase of 7.6%. Indirect operating expenses increased 0.5% to US$2.19 billion from US$2.18 billion in the equivalent prior-year period.

Prospects: Our evaluation of BlackRock Inc. as of October 4th, 2019 is the result of our systematic analysis on three basic characteristics: earnings strength, relative valuation, and recent stock price movement. The company has managed to produce a neutral trend in earnings per share over the past 5 quarters. In addition, recent analyst estimates for the company have been mixed and BLK has posted results that fell short of analysts' expectations. Based on operating earnings yield, the company is undervalued when compared to all of the companies we cover. Share price changes over the past year indicates that BLK will perform in line with the market over the near term.

Financial Data
(US$ in Thousands)

	9 Mos	6 Mos	3 Mos	12/31/2018	12/31/2017	12/31/2016	12/31/2015	12/31/2014
Earnings Per Share	25.92	26.31	26.52	26.58	30.23	19.04	19.79	19.25
Cash Flow Per Share	13.85	16.00	18.90	19.18	23.61	13.06	18.05	18.31
Tang Book Value Per Share	N.M.	N.M.	N.M.	6.40	7.60	N.M.	N.M.	N.M.
Dividends Per Share	13.030	12.860	12.440	12.020	10.000	9.160	8.720	7.720
Dividend Payout %	50.27	48.88	46.91	45.22	33.08	48.11	44.06	40.10
Income Statement								
Total Revenue	10,562,000	6,870,000	3,346,000	14,198,000	12,491,000	11,155,000	11,401,000	11,081,000
EBITDA	4,305,000	2,782,000	1,390,000	5,766,000	5,703,000	4,888,000	5,049,000	4,901,000
Depn & Amortn	68,000	40,000	15,000	204,000	221,000	223,000	243,000	274,000
Income Before Taxes	4,153,000	2,693,000	1,358,000	5,378,000	5,277,000	4,460,000	4,602,000	4,395,000
Income Taxes	961,000	620,000	298,000	1,076,000	270,000	1,290,000	1,250,000	1,131,000
Net Income	3,175,000	2,056,000	1,053,000	4,305,000	4,970,000	3,172,000	3,345,000	3,294,000
Average Shares	156,447	156,360	159,348	161,948	164,415	166,579	169,038	171,112
Balance Sheet								
Current Assets	7,502,000	6,783,000	6,662,000	8,959,000	9,593,000	8,441,000	8,320,000	7,843,000
Total Assets	163,872,000	163,347,000	165,008,000	159,573,000	220,217,000	220,177,000	225,261,000	239,808,000
Current Liabilities	2,752,000	2,355,000	1,955,000	3,280,000	3,314,000	2,974,000	3,039,000	2,900,000
Long-Term Obligations	5,932,000	5,964,000	4,966,000	4,979,000	5,014,000	4,915,000	4,930,000	4,938,000
Total Liabilities	131,465,000	131,454,000	133,699,000	127,199,000	188,392,000	191,079,000	196,758,000	212,442,000
Stockholders' Equity	32,407,000	31,893,000	31,309,000	32,374,000	31,825,000	29,098,000	28,503,000	27,366,000
Shares Outstanding	154,349	154,543	154,500	157,553	159,977	161,534	163,461	164,786
Statistical Record								
Return on Assets %	2.42	2.34	2.24	2.27	2.26	1.42	1.44	1.43
Return on Equity %	12.66	13.12	13.49	13.41	16.32	10.98	11.97	12.24
EBITDA Margin %	40.76	40.49	41.54	40.61	45.66	43.82	44.29	44.23
Net Margin %	30.06	29.93	31.47	30.32	39.79	28.44	29.34	29.73
Asset Turnover	0.08	0.08	0.07	0.07	0.06	0.05	0.05	0.05
Current Ratio	2.73	2.88	3.41	2.73	2.89	2.84	2.74	2.70
Debt to Equity	0.18	0.19	0.16	0.15	0.16	0.17	0.17	0.18
Price Range	485.24-361.77	512.49-361.77	551.86-361.77	593.26-361.77	518.86-371.64	398.45-289.72	380.33-293.52	364.40-286.39
P/E Ratio	18.72-13.96	19.48-13.75	20.81-13.64	22.32-13.61	17.16-12.29	20.93-15.22	19.22-14.83	18.93-14.88
Average Yield %	3.02	2.91	2.70	2.44	2.36	2.62	2.51	2.42

Address: 55 East 52nd Street, New York, NY 10055 Telephone: 212-810-5300	Web Site: www.blackrock.com Officers: Laurence D. Fink - Chairman, Chief Executive Officer Robert S. (Rob) Kapito - President	Auditors: Deloitte & Touche LLP Transfer Agents: Computershare, Jersey City, NJ

BLOCK (H & R), INC.

Exchange	Symbol	Price	52Wk Range	Yield	P/E
NYS	HRB	$23.48 (12/31/2019)	29.30-23.02	4.43	12.10

*7 Year Price Score 75.41   *NYSE Composite Index=100   *12 Month Price Score 89.94

Interim Earnings (Per Share)
Qtr.	Jul	Oct	Jan	Apr
2016-17	(0.56)	(0.68)	(0.50)	3.66
2017-18	(0.63)	(0.74)	(1.18)	5.45
2018-19	(0.74)	(0.86)	(0.62)	4.25
2019-20	(0.74)	(0.95)	...	...

Interim Dividends (Per Share)
Amt	Decl	Ex	Rec	Pay
0.25Q	03/06/2019	03/15/2019	03/18/2019	04/01/2019
0.26Q	06/11/2019	06/20/2019	06/21/2019	07/01/2019
0.26Q	08/22/2019	09/12/2019	09/13/2019	10/01/2019
0.26Q	11/07/2019	12/06/2019	12/09/2019	01/02/2020

Indicated Div: $1.04 (Div. Reinv. Plan)

Valuation Analysis
Forecast EPS	$2.43
	(01/10/2020)
Market Cap	$4.6 Billion
Book Value	N/A
Price/Book	N/A
Price/Sales	1.47

Institutional Holding
No of Institutions	740
Shares	274,481,344
% Held	98.03

Business Summary: Miscellaneous Consumer Services (MIC: 2.2.3 SIC: 7291 NAIC: 541213)

H&R Block provides assisted, do-it-yourself, and virtual tax return preparation solutions through various channels (including in-person, online and mobile applications, virtual, and desktop software) and distributes Co.-branded products and services to the general public in the U.S., Canada, Australia, and their respective territories. Co. also provides additional services, such as Refund Transfers, its Peace of Mind® Extended Service Plan (POM), H&R Block Emerald Prepaid Mastercard®, H&R Block Emerald Advance® lines of credit, Tax Identity Shield®, and Refund Advance loans. For its Canadian clients Co. also provides POM, H&R Block Instant Refund™, and H&R Block Pay With Refund® services.

Recent Developments: For the quarter ended Oct 31 2019, loss from continuing operations was US$183.6 million compared with a loss of US$170.9 million in the year-earlier quarter. Net loss amounted to US$188.0 million versus a net loss of US$176.3 million in the year-earlier quarter. Revenues were US$160.8 million, up 8.0% from US$148.9 million the year before. Direct operating expenses rose 1.0% to US$253.2 million from US$250.8 million in the comparable period the year before. Indirect operating expenses increased 32.7% to US$150.3 million from US$113.3 million in the equivalent prior-year period.

Prospects: Our evaluation of Block (H & R) Inc. as of October 4th, 2019 is the result of our systematic analysis on three basic characteristics: earnings strength, relative valuation, and recent stock price movement. The company has generated a negative trend in earnings per share over the past 5 quarters. However, recent analyst estimates for the company have been unchanged while HRB has posted results that exceeded analysts' expectations. Based on operating earnings yield, the company is undervalued when compared to all of the companies we cover. Share price changes over the past year indicates that HRB will perform well over the near term.

Financial Data
(US$ in Thousands)	6 Mos	3 Mos	04/30/2019	04/30/2018	04/30/2017	04/30/2016	04/30/2015	04/30/2014
Earnings Per Share	1.94	2.03	2.04	2.91	1.91	1.49	1.71	1.72
Cash Flow Per Share	2.73	2.47	2.95	4.07	2.58	2.13	2.28	2.96
Tang Book Value Per Share	...	N.M.	N.M.	N.M.	...	N.M.	3.48	2.79
Dividends Per Share	1.020	1.010	1.000	0.960	0.880	0.800	0.800	0.800
Dividend Payout %	52.58	49.75	49.02	32.99	46.07	53.69	46.78	46.51
Income Statement								
Total Revenue	311,163	150,362	3,094,881	3,159,931	3,036,314	3,038,153	3,078,658	3,024,295
EBITDA	(355,032)	(155,464)	709,199	854,643	821,608	730,693	889,351	851,816
Depn & Amortn	81,262	38,605	93,500	103,400	103,200	100,800	101,300	84,700
Income Before Taxes	(468,420)	(207,114)	545,160	668,732	629,287	569,479	742,805	767,116
Income Taxes	(139,142)	(61,390)	99,904	41,823	208,370	185,926	256,061	267,019
Net Income	(338,246)	(150,247)	422,509	613,149	408,945	374,267	473,663	475,157
Average Shares	198,079	202,037	206,724	210,213	214,095	250,818	277,136	276,027
Balance Sheet								
Current Assets	601,412	946,705	1,993,359	1,891,713	1,346,039	1,222,298	2,951,301	3,114,006
Total Assets	2,756,741	3,110,000	3,299,945	3,140,949	2,694,108	2,857,775	4,515,420	4,693,529
Current Liabilities	1,263,957	732,969	923,001	843,651	939,280	1,039,605	1,878,289	2,313,116
Long-Term Obligations	980,299	1,493,289	1,492,629	1,494,609	1,493,017	1,501,925	505,298	505,837
Total Liabilities	2,832,488	2,819,196	2,758,418	2,747,238	2,754,991	2,834,672	2,682,471	3,136,980
Stockholders' Equity	(75,747)	290,804	541,527	393,711	(60,883)	23,103	1,832,949	1,556,549
Shares Outstanding	195,245	200,958	201,959	209,254	207,171	220,517	275,275	274,228
Statistical Record								
Return on Assets %	16.56	14.87	13.12	21.02	14.73	10.12	10.29	10.29
Return on Equity %	...	176.02	90.35	368.45	...	40.22	27.95	33.70
EBITDA Margin %	N.M.	N.M.	22.92	27.05	27.06	24.05	28.89	28.17
Net Margin %	N.M.	N.M.	13.65	19.40	13.47	12.32	15.39	15.71
Asset Turnover	1.25	1.08	0.96	1.08	1.09	0.82	0.67	0.66
Current Ratio	0.48	1.29	2.16	2.24	1.43	1.18	1.57	1.35
Debt to Equity	...	5.14	2.76	3.80	...	65.01	0.28	0.32
Price Range	29.30-23.11	29.30-23.53	29.60-22.50	31.51-23.86	24.79-19.46	37.40-20.24	35.64-27.64	32.19-26.05
P/E Ratio	15.10-11.91	14.43-11.59	14.51-11.03	10.83-8.20	12.98-10.19	25.10-13.58	20.84-16.16	18.72-15.15
Average Yield %	3.93	3.85	3.88	3.54	3.88	2.47	2.48	2.76

Address: One H&R Block Way, Kansas City, MO 64105 **Telephone:** 816-854-3000	**Web Site:** www.hrblock.com **Officers:** Robert A. Gerard - Chairman Jeffrey J. Jones - President, Chief Executive Officer, Chief Executive Officer - Designate	**Auditors:** Deloitte & Touche LLP **Transfer Agents:** Wells Fargo Shareowner Services, St. Paul, MN

BOEING CO. (THE)

Exchange	Symbol	Price	52Wk Range	Yield	P/E
NYS	BA	$325.76 (12/31/2019)	440.62-310.90	2.52	50.19

*7 Year Price Score 147.47 *NYSE Composite Index=100 *12 Month Price Score 90.60

Interim Earnings (Per Share)

Qtr.	Mar	Jun	Sep	Dec
2016	1.83	(0.37)	3.60	2.57
2017	2.34	2.89	3.06	5.16
2018	4.15	3.73	4.07	5.90
2019	3.75	(5.21)	2.05	...

Interim Dividends (Per Share)

Amt	Decl	Ex	Rec	Pay
2.055Q	04/29/2019	05/09/2019	05/10/2019	06/07/2019
2.055Q	06/24/2019	08/08/2019	08/09/2019	09/06/2019
2.055Q	10/21/2019	11/07/2019	11/08/2019	12/06/2019
2.055Q	12/16/2019	02/13/2020	02/14/2020	03/06/2020

Indicated Div: $8.22

Valuation Analysis / Institutional Holding

Valuation Analysis		Institutional Holding	
Forecast EPS	$0.60	No of Institutions	2767
	(01/17/2020)		
Market Cap	$183.3 Billion	Shares	487,000,288
Book Value	N/A	% Held	64.42
Price/Book	N/A		
Price/Sales	2.11		

Business Summary: Aerospace (MIC: 7.1.1 SIC: 3721 NAIC: 336411)

Boeing is an aerospace firm. Co. operates in four reportable segments: Commercial Airplanes, which develops, produces and markets commercial jet aircraft; Defense, Space and Security, which engages in the research, development, production and modification of manned and unmanned military aircraft and weapons systems, surveillance and engagement, strategic defense and intelligence systems, satellite systems and space exploration; Global Services, which provides parts, maintenance, modifications, logistics support, training, data analytics and information-based services; and Boeing Capital, which facilitates, arranges, structures and provides selective financing solutions.

Recent Developments: For the quarter ended Sep 30 2019, net income decreased 50.6% to US$1.17 billion from US$2.36 billion in the year-earlier quarter. Revenues were US$19.98 billion, down 20.5% from US$25.15 billion the year before. Operating income was US$1.26 billion versus US$2.23 billion in the prior-year quarter, a decrease of 43.5%. Direct operating expenses declined 19.5% to US$16.93 billion from US$21.04 billion in the comparable period the year before. Indirect operating expenses decreased 4.7% to US$1.79 billion from US$1.88 billion in the equivalent prior-year period.

Prospects: Our evaluation of Boeing Co. as of October 4th, 2019 is the result of our systematic analysis on three basic characteristics: earnings strength, relative valuation, and recent stock price movement. The company has generated a negative trend in earnings per share over the past 5 quarters. In addition, recent analyst estimates for the company have been reduced while BA has posted results that exceeded analysts' expectations. Based on operating earnings yield, the company is fairly valued when compared to all of the companies we cover. Share price changes over the past year indicates that BA will perform poorly over the near term.

Financial Data

(US$ in Millions)	9 Mos	6 Mos	3 Mos	12/31/2018	12/31/2017	12/31/2016	12/31/2015	12/31/2014
Earnings Per Share	6.49	8.51	17.45	17.85	13.43	7.61	7.44	7.38
Cash Flow Per Share	4.81	17.18	26.40	26.42	22.12	16.48	13.63	12.17
Tang Book Value Per Share	...	...	N.M.	N.M.	N.M.	N.M.	N.M.	0.96
Dividends Per Share	7.875	7.530	7.185	6.840	5.680	4.360	3.640	2.920
Dividend Payout %	121.34	88.48	41.17	38.32	42.29	57.29	48.92	39.57
Income Statement								
Total Revenue	58,648	38,668	22,917	101,127	93,392	94,571	96,114	90,762
EBITDA	2,209	245	2,957	13,524	11,751	6,989	8,513	8,597
Depn & Amortn	1,643	1,067	521	1,556	1,548	1,418	1,357	1,414
Income Before Taxes	86	(1,099)	2,313	11,493	9,843	5,265	6,881	6,850
Income Taxes	(291)	(301)	184	1,144	1,850	673	1,979	1,691
Net Income	374	(793)	2,149	10,460	8,197	4,895	5,176	5,446
Average Shares	569	565	571	585	610	642	695	736
Balance Sheet								
Current Assets	101,656	95,111	89,509	87,830	65,161	62,488	68,234	67,785
Total Assets	132,598	126,261	120,209	117,359	92,333	89,997	94,408	99,198
Current Liabilities	91,846	92,189	83,615	81,590	56,269	50,134	50,412	56,717
Long-Term Obligations	20,298	14,859	11,363	10,657	9,782	9,568	8,730	8,141
Total Liabilities	136,714	131,583	120,084	117,020	91,978	89,180	88,073	90,533
Stockholders' Equity	(4,116)	(5,322)	125	339	355	817	6,335	8,665
Shares Outstanding	562	562	563	567	591	617	666	706
Statistical Record								
Return on Assets %	3.07	4.17	8.67	9.98	8.99	5.29	5.35	5.68
Return on Equity %	...	...	1,504.38	3,014.41	1,398.81	136.51	69.01	46.27
EBITDA Margin %	3.77	0.63	12.90	13.37	12.58	7.39	8.86	9.47
Net Margin %	0.64	N.M.	9.38	10.34	8.78	5.18	5.39	6.00
Asset Turnover	0.70	0.77	0.86	0.96	1.02	1.02	0.99	0.95
Current Ratio	1.11	1.03	1.07	1.08	1.16	1.25	1.35	1.20
Debt to Equity	...	...	90.90	31.44	27.55	11.71	1.38	0.94
Price Range	440.62-294.16	440.62-294.16	440.62-294.16	392.30-294.16	297.90-156.97	157.81-108.44	158.31-125.49	144.37-118.34
P/E Ratio	67.89-45.33	51.78-34.57	25.25-16.86	21.98-16.48	22.18-11.69	20.74-14.25	21.28-16.87	19.56-16.04
Average Yield %	2.17	2.08	2.02	1.98	2.64	3.27	2.54	2.27

Address: 100 North Riverside Plaza, Chicago, IL 60606-1596	Web Site: www.boeing.com	Auditors: DELOITTE & TOUCHE LLP
Telephone: 312-544-2000	Officers: David L. Calhoun - Chairman, President, Chief Executive Officer Gregory D. Smith - Executive Vice President, Executive Vice President (frmr), Vice President, Interim Chief Executive Officer, Chief Financial Officer, Chief Accounting Officer, Corporate Controller	Investor Contact: 312-544-2000 Transfer Agents: Computershare Trust Company, N.A., Providence, RI

BOOZ ALLEN HAMILTON HOLDING CORP.

Exchange	Symbol	Price	52Wk Range	Yield	P/E
NYS	BAH	$71.13 (12/31/2019)	77.10-43.97	1.52	22.30

*7 Year Price Score 152.21 *NYSE Composite Index=100 *12 Month Price Score 106.82

Interim Earnings (Per Share)

Qtr.	Jun	Sep	Dec	Mar
2016-17	0.45	0.41	0.37	0.44
2017-18	0.53	0.47	0.47	0.58
2018-19	0.72	0.64	0.92	0.64
2019-20	0.83	0.80	...	...

Interim Dividends (Per Share)

Amt	Decl	Ex	Rec	Pay
0.23Q	02/01/2019	02/13/2019	02/14/2019	02/28/2019
0.23Q	05/23/2019	06/13/2019	06/14/2019	06/28/2019
0.23Q	07/25/2019	08/13/2019	08/14/2019	08/30/2019
0.27Q	10/30/2019	11/13/2019	11/14/2019	12/02/2019

Indicated Div: $1.08

Valuation Analysis / **Institutional Holding**

Forecast EPS	$3.15	No of Institutions	
(01/16/2020)		539	
Market Cap	$10.0 Billion	Shares	
Book Value	$840.2 Million	239,141,904	
Price/Book	11.88	% Held	
Price/Sales	1.41	87.64	

Business Summary: Business Services (MIC: 7.5.2 SIC: 8742 NAIC: 541611)

Booz Allen Hamilton Holding is a holding company. Co. provides management and technology consulting, analytics, engineering, digital solutions, mission operations, and cyber knowledge to U.S. and international governments, corporations, and non-profit organizations. Co.'s services are: Consulting, which focuses on solving client problems and developing mission-oriented solutions; Analytics, which includes decision analytics, automation, and data science solutions; Digital Solutions, which develops, designs, and implements solutions; Engineering, which delivers engineering services and solutions; and Cyber, which focuses on active prevention, detection, and cost effectiveness.

Recent Developments: For the quarter ended Sep 30 2019, net income increased 23.3% to US$114.3 million from US$92.7 million in the year-earlier quarter. Revenues were US$1.82 billion, up 12.7% from US$1.61 billion the year before. Operating income was US$172.0 million versus US$143.8 million in the prior-year quarter, an increase of 19.7%. Direct operating expenses rose 12.8% to US$1.38 billion from US$1.23 billion in the comparable period the year before. Indirect operating expenses increased 8.4% to US$263.8 million from US$243.3 million in the equivalent prior-year period.

Prospects: Our evaluation of Booz Allen Hamilton Holding as of October 4th, 2019 is the result of our systematic analysis on three basic characteristics: earnings strength, relative valuation, and recent stock price movement. The company has managed to produce a neutral trend in earnings per share over the past 5 quarters. However, recent analyst estimates for the company have been raised and BAH has posted results that exceeded analysts' expectations. Based on operating earnings yield, the company is fairly valued when compared to all of the companies we cover. Share price changes over the past year indicates that BAH will perform over the near term.

Financial Data (US$ in Thousands)	6 Mos	3 Mos	03/31/2019	03/31/2018	03/31/2017	03/31/2016	03/31/2015	03/31/2014
Earnings Per Share	3.19	3.03	2.91	2.05	1.67	1.94	1.52	1.54
Cash Flow Per Share	3.51	4.13	3.52	2.53	2.58	1.70	2.13	2.35
Dividends Per Share	0.880	0.840	0.800	0.700	0.620	0.540	1.460	2.400
Dividend Payout %	27.59	27.72	27.49	34.15	37.13	27.84	96.05	155.84
Income Statement								
Total Revenue	3,644,753	1,825,176	6,704,037	6,171,853	5,804,284	5,405,738	5,274,770	5,478,693
EBITDA	357,516	182,236	652,720	568,373	520,498	500,377	510,450	516,417
Depn & Amortn	2,459	1,219	47,800	48,100	46,300	50,100	52,700	57,600
Income Before Taxes	304,007	155,830	515,403	438,004	411,900	379,462	385,918	380,787
Income Taxes	72,296	38,444	96,874	132,893	159,410	85,368	153,349	148,599
Net Income	231,711	117,386	418,529	305,111	252,490	294,094	232,569	232,188
Average Shares	141,362	141,129	143,156	147,750	150,274	149,719	150,375	148,681
Balance Sheet								
Current Assets	2,163,403	2,116,399	1,699,340	1,488,719	1,294,480	1,189,771	1,163,208	1,255,977
Total Assets	4,568,858	4,513,650	3,831,841	3,603,366	3,373,105	3,010,171	2,877,493	2,940,818
Current Liabilities	1,210,569	1,211,514	1,179,239	1,036,166	1,101,401	939,913	848,994	917,104
Long-Term Obligations	2,044,821	2,063,321	1,701,837	1,755,419	1,470,174	1,484,448	1,569,272	1,585,231
Total Liabilities	3,728,675	3,764,827	3,156,475	3,048,738	2,799,514	2,601,683	2,690,995	2,769,182
Stockholders' Equity	840,183	748,823	675,366	554,628	573,591	408,488	186,498	171,636
Shares Outstanding	140,373	140,218	140,027	143,446	148,887	147,992	149,089	149,295
Statistical Record								
Return on Assets %	10.92	10.60	11.26	8.75	7.91	9.96	7.99	7.59
Return on Equity %	60.99	63.66	68.05	54.09	51.42	98.59	129.88	116.55
EBITDA Margin %	9.81	9.98	9.74	9.21	8.97	9.26	9.68	9.43
Net Margin %	6.36	6.43	6.24	4.94	4.35	5.44	4.41	4.24
Asset Turnover	1.71	1.69	1.80	1.77	1.82	1.83	1.81	1.79
Current Ratio	1.79	1.75	1.44	1.44	1.18	1.27	1.37	1.37
Debt to Equity	2.43	2.76	2.52	3.17	2.56	3.63	8.41	9.24
Price Range	77.10-43.46	66.21-43.46	58.14-37.88	40.02-31.90	38.20-27.24	31.13-24.45	30.46-20.82	22.16-12.90
P/E Ratio	24.17-13.62	21.85-14.34	19.98-13.02	19.52-15.56	22.87-16.31	16.05-12.60	20.04-13.70	14.39-8.38
Average Yield %	1.51	1.59	1.67	1.91	1.93	1.94	5.87	13.04

Address: 8283 Greensboro Drive, McLean, VA 22102 **Telephone:** 703-902-5000	**Web Site:** www.boozallen.com **Officers:** Ralph W. Shrader - Chairman, President, Chief Executive Officer Horacio D. Rozanski - President, Chief Executive Officer, Executive Vice President, Chief Operating Officer	**Auditors:** Ernst & Young LLP **Investor Contact:** 703-377-5332 **Transfer Agents:** Computershare, Jersey City, NJ

BORGWARNER INC

Exchange	Symbol	Price	52Wk Range	Yield	P/E
NYS	BWA	$43.38 (12/31/2019)	46.31-30.88	1.57	11.92

*7 Year Price Score 70.71 *NYSE Composite Index=100 *12 Month Price Score 105.32

Interim Earnings (Per Share)

Qtr.	Mar	Jun	Sep	Dec
2016	0.75	0.76	0.39	(1.35)
2017	0.89	1.01	0.88	(0.69)
2018	1.07	1.30	0.98	1.10
2019	0.77	0.83	0.94	...

Interim Dividends (Per Share)

Amt	Decl	Ex	Rec	Pay
0.17Q	02/14/2019	02/28/2019	03/01/2019	03/15/2019
0.17Q	04/25/2019	05/31/2019	06/03/2019	06/17/2019
0.17Q	07/25/2019	08/30/2019	09/03/2019	09/16/2019
0.17Q	11/14/2019	11/29/2019	12/02/2019	12/16/2019

Indicated Div: $0.68

Valuation Analysis | **Institutional Holding**

Forecast EPS	$3.93 (01/17/2020)	No of Institutions 767
Market Cap	$9.0 Billion	Shares
Book Value	$4.5 Billion	225,267,824
Price/Book	2.01	% Held
Price/Sales	0.88	89.84

Business Summary: Auto Parts (MIC: 1.8.2 SIC: 3714 NAIC: 336350)

BorgWarner is a holding company. Through its subsidiaries, Co. is a global product provider in technology solutions for combustion, hybrid and electric vehicles. Co. manufactures and sells these products worldwide, primarily to original equipment manufacturers of light vehicles (passenger cars, sport-utility vehicles, vans and light trucks). Co.'s segments are: Engine, which provides turbochargers, eBoosters, timing systems, emissions systems, thermal systems, gasoline ignition technology, cabin heaters, battery heaters and battery charging; and Drivetrain, which provides rotating electrical components, power electronics, clutching systems, control modules and all-wheel drive systems.

Recent Developments: For the quarter ended Sep 30 2019, net income decreased 4.1% to US$207.0 million from US$215.9 million in the year-earlier quarter. Revenues were US$2.49 billion, up 0.5% from US$2.48 billion the year before. Operating income was US$276.0 million versus US$278.0 million in the prior-year quarter, a decrease of 0.7%. Direct operating expenses rose 0.3% to US$1.97 billion from US$1.96 billion in the comparable period the year before. Indirect operating expenses increased 4.4% to US$248.0 million from US$237.6 million in the equivalent prior-year period.

Prospects: Our evaluation of Borg Warner Inc. as of October 4th, 2019 is the result of our systematic analysis on three basic characteristics: earnings strength, relative valuation, and recent stock price movement. The company has generated a negative trend in earnings per share over the past 5 quarters. In addition, recent analyst estimates for the company have been reduced and BWA has posted results that fell short of analysts' expectations. Based on operating earnings yield, the company is undervalued when compared to all of the companies we cover. Share price changes over the past year indicates that BWA will perform poorly over the near term.

Financial Data

(US$ in Thousands)	9 Mos	6 Mos	3 Mos	12/31/2018	12/31/2017	12/31/2016	12/31/2015	12/31/2014
Earnings Per Share	3.64	3.68	4.15	4.44	2.08	0.55	2.70	2.86
Cash Flow Per Share	6.79	6.26	5.48	5.41	5.61	4.82	3.87	3.53
Tang Book Value Per Share	10.82	10.30	9.62	9.28	6.37	4.96	5.71	9.98
Dividends Per Share	0.680	0.680	0.680	0.680	0.590	0.530	0.520	0.510
Dividend Payout %	18.68	18.48	16.39	15.32	28.37	96.36	19.26	17.83
Income Statement								
Total Revenue	7,609,000	5,117,000	2,566,000	10,529,600	9,799,300	9,071,000	8,023,200	8,305,100
EBITDA	1,123,000	736,000	371,000	1,630,600	1,484,900	617,300	1,259,900	1,294,100
Depn & Amortn	324,000	214,000	107,000	431,300	407,800	391,400	320,200	330,400
Income Before Taxes	765,000	499,000	253,000	1,147,000	1,012,400	147,600	886,800	932,800
Income Taxes	230,000	164,000	91,000	211,300	580,300	30,300	280,400	292,600
Net Income	526,000	332,000	160,000	930,700	439,900	118,500	609,700	655,800
Average Shares	206,300	206,800	207,100	209,496	211,548	215,328	225,648	228,924
Balance Sheet								
Current Assets	3,987,000	3,849,000	3,719,000	3,804,600	3,543,200	2,911,600	3,135,300	2,970,800
Total Assets	10,199,000	10,231,000	10,104,000	10,095,300	9,787,600	8,834,700	8,841,500	7,228,000
Current Liabilities	2,525,000	2,313,000	2,299,000	2,398,900	2,425,200	2,091,800	2,357,300	2,168,200
Long-Term Obligations	1,656,000	1,929,000	1,923,000	1,940,700	2,103,700	2,043,600	2,124,600	716,300
Total Liabilities	5,742,000	5,837,000	5,830,000	5,869,800	6,070,800	5,616,400	5,287,800	3,611,800
Stockholders' Equity	4,457,000	4,394,000	4,274,000	4,225,500	3,716,800	3,218,300	3,553,700	3,616,200
Shares Outstanding	206,493	206,514	207,266	208,214	210,812	212,262	219,324	226,430
Statistical Record								
Return on Assets %	7.59	7.65	8.60	9.36	4.72	1.34	7.59	9.27
Return on Equity %	17.74	18.33	21.15	23.44	12.69	3.49	17.01	18.28
EBITDA Margin %	14.76	14.38	14.46	15.49	15.15	6.81	15.70	15.58
Net Margin %	6.91	6.49	6.24	8.84	4.49	1.31	7.60	7.90
Asset Turnover	1.02	1.02	1.02	1.06	1.05	1.02	1.00	1.17
Current Ratio	1.58	1.66	1.62	1.59	1.46	1.39	1.33	1.37
Debt to Equity	0.37	0.44	0.45	0.46	0.57	0.63	0.60	0.20
Price Range	44.23-30.88	46.36-33.20	53.91-33.20	57.91-33.20	55.68-37.99	43.23-27.69	63.01-38.89	67.38-50.24
P/E Ratio	12.15-8.48	12.60-9.02	12.99-8.00	13.04-7.48	26.77-18.26	78.60-50.35	23.34-14.40	23.56-17.57
Average Yield %	1.76	1.68	1.58	1.47	1.30	1.53	1.00	0.86

Address: 3850 Hamlin Road, Auburn Hills, MI 48326	Web Site: www.borgwarner.com	Auditors: PricewaterhouseCoopers LLP
Telephone: 248-754-9200	Officers: Frederic B. Lissalde - President, Chief Executive Officer, Executive Vice President, Chief Operating Officer, Vice President Tonit M. Calaway - Executive Vice President, Chief Legal Officer, Secretary, Chief Human Resources Officer	Investor Contact: 248-754-0881 Transfer Agents: BNY Mellon Shareowner Services, Jersey City, NJ

BOSTON BEER CO INC (THE)

Exchange	Symbol	Price	52Wk Range	Yield	P/E
NYS	SAM	$377.85 (12/31/2019)	441.26-233.45	N/A	38.21

*7 Year Price Score 123.66 *NYSE Composite Index=100 *12 Month Price Score 103.93

TRADING VOLUME (thousand shares)

Interim Earnings (Per Share)

Qtr.	Mar	Jun	Sep	Dec
2016	0.53	2.06	2.48	1.74
2017	0.45	2.35	2.78	2.55
2018	0.78	1.98	3.21	1.86
2019	2.02	2.36	3.65	...

Interim Dividends (Per Share)

No Dividends Paid

Valuation Analysis / Institutional Holding

Forecast EPS	$9.62	No of Institutions
	(01/10/2020)	398
Market Cap	$4.5 Billion	Shares
Book Value	$719.0 Million	12,677,785
Price/Book	6.32	% Held
Price/Sales	3.87	75.17

Business Summary: Beverages (MIC: 1.2.2 SIC: 2082 NAIC: 312120)

Boston Beer Company is engaged in the business of selling alcohol beverages throughout the U.S. and in selected international markets. Co.'s brands include Samuel Adams®, Twisted Tea®, Angry Orchard® Hard Cider, and Truly Hard Seltzer, as well as craft beer brands brewed by its subsidiary A&S Brewing Collaborative LLC and its affiliates. Co. produces alcohol beverages including malt beverages, hard cider and hard seltzer at Co.-owned breweries and its cidery and under contract arrangements at other brewery locations. Co. sells its products in the U.S., Canada, Europe, Israel, Australia, New Zealand, the Caribbean, the Pacific Rim, Mexico, and Central and South America.

Recent Developments: For the quarter ended Sep 28 2019, net income increased 17.7% to US$44.7 million from US$38.0 million in the year-earlier quarter. Revenues were US$378.5 million, up 23.3% from US$306.9 million the year before. Operating income was US$59.8 million versus US$46.7 million in the prior-year quarter, an increase of 28.1%. Direct operating expenses rose 27.4% to US$190.6 million from US$149.6 million in the comparable period the year before. Indirect operating expenses increased 15.8% to US$128.0 million from US$110.5 million in the equivalent prior-year period.

Prospects: Our evaluation of Boston Beer Co. Inc. as of October 4th, 2019 is the result of our systematic analysis on three basic characteristics: earnings strength, relative valuation, and recent stock price movement. The company has generated a negative trend in earnings per share over the past 5 quarters. In addition, recent analyst estimates for the company have been reduced while SAM has posted results that exceeded analysts' expectations. Based on operating earnings yield, the company is overvalued when compared to all of the companies we cover. Share price changes over the past year indicates that SAM will perform over the near term.

Financial Data

(US$ in Thousands)	9 Mos	6 Mos	3 Mos	12/29/2018	12/30/2017	12/31/2016	12/26/2015	12/27/2014
Earnings Per Share	9.89	9.45	9.07	7.82	8.09	6.79	7.25	6.69
Cash Flow Per Share	16.51	14.29	16.27	14.10	11.33	12.10	12.89	10.92
Tang Book Value Per Share	41.72	44.85	42.08	39.71	36.13	35.81	35.87	33.09
Income Statement								
Total Revenue	948,524	570,058	251,651	995,649	862,992	906,446	959,934	903,007
EBITDA	168,233	93,409	42,054	166,794	166,793	186,253	198,354	180,373
Depn & Amortn	41,841	26,089	12,863	51,800	51,200	49,300	43,400	34,800
Income Before Taxes	126,864	67,930	29,828	116,286	116,142	137,121	155,010	145,594
Income Taxes	30,585	16,380	6,134	23,623	17,093	49,772	56,596	54,851
Net Income	96,279	51,550	23,694	92,663	99,049	87,349	98,414	90,743
Average Shares	12,150	11,684	11,636	11,734	12,180	12,796	13,520	13,484
Balance Sheet								
Current Assets	209,392	178,756	260,860	231,571	168,348	201,238	223,603	207,462
Total Assets	1,016,176	813,330	704,020	639,851	569,624	623,297	645,400	605,161
Current Liabilities	166,484	188,266	132,002	120,514	101,758	101,519	111,160	110,170
Long-Term Obligations	...	...	...	...	...	411	471	528
Total Liabilities	297,196	290,529	214,202	179,534	146,101	176,715	184,179	169,021
Stockholders' Equity	718,980	522,801	489,818	460,317	423,523	446,582	461,221	436,140
Shares Outstanding	12,034	11,573	11,552	11,498	11,621	12,368	12,756	13,069
Statistical Record								
Return on Assets %	14.40	15.56	16.68	15.36	16.65	13.55	15.78	17.34
Return on Equity %	20.47	23.07	23.10	21.03	22.83	18.93	21.99	24.65
EBITDA Margin %	17.74	16.39	16.71	16.75	19.33	20.55	20.66	19.97
Net Margin %	10.15	9.04	9.42	9.31	11.48	9.64	10.25	10.05
Asset Turnover	1.43	1.54	1.65	1.65	1.45	1.41	1.54	1.73
Current Ratio	1.26	0.95	1.98	1.92	1.65	1.98	2.01	1.88
Price Range	441.26-233.45	377.76-233.45	327.15-187.45	327.15-163.05	194.60-129.90	204.25-146.42	323.99-197.05	297.78-203.81
P/E Ratio	44.62-23.60	39.97-24.70	36.07-20.67	41.84-20.85	24.05-16.06	30.08-21.56	44.69-27.18	44.51-30.46

Address: One Design Center Place, Suite 850, Boston, MA 02210	**Web Site:** www.bostonbeer.com	**Auditors:** Deloitte & Touche LLP
Telephone: 617-368-5000	**Officers:** C. James Koch - Chairman David A. Burwick - President, Chief Executive Officer	**Investor Contact:** 617-368-5060
Fax: 617-368-5500		**Transfer Agents:** Computershare Shareowner Services LLC, Jersey City, NJ

BOSTON PROPERTIES INC

Exchange	Symbol	Price	52Wk Range	Yield	P/E
NYS	BXP	$137.86 (12/31/2019)	139.87-109.15	2.84	41.15

*7 Year Price Score 88.69 *NYSE Composite Index=100 *12 Month Price Score 98.18

Interim Earnings (Per Share)

Qtr.	Mar	Jun	Sep	Dec
2016	1.18	0.63	0.50	0.95
2017	0.63	0.87	0.76	0.67
2018	1.14	0.83	0.77	0.96
2019	0.63	1.06	0.70	...

Interim Dividends (Per Share)

Amt	Decl	Ex	Rec	Pay
0.95Q	03/18/2019	03/28/2019	03/29/2019	04/30/2019
0.95Q	06/10/2019	06/27/2019	06/28/2019	07/31/2019
0.95Q	09/10/2019	09/27/2019	09/30/2019	10/31/2019
0.98Q	12/17/2019	12/30/2019	12/31/2019	01/30/2020

Indicated Div: $3.92

Valuation Analysis

		Institutional Holding	
Forecast EPS	$3.31	No of Institutions	
	(01/17/2020)	761	
Market Cap	$21.3 Billion	Shares	
Book Value	$5.7 Billion	183,266,208	
Price/Book	3.75	% Held	
Price/Sales	7.33	89.75	

Business Summary: REITs (MIC: 5.3.1 SIC: 6798 NAIC: 525930)

Boston Properties is a real estate investment trust, and developer, owner and manager of office properties. Co.'s properties are concentrated in five markets: Boston, Los Angeles, New York, San Francisco and Washington, DC. Co. is a real estate company, with substantial in-house knowledge and resources in acquisitions, development, financing, capital markets, construction management, property management, marketing, leasing, accounting, risk management, tax and legal services. Co. manages Boston Properties Limited Partnership, which is the entity through which Co. conducts substantially all of its business and owns (either directly or through subsidiaries) substantially all of its assets.

Recent Developments: For the quarter ended Sep 30 2019, net income decreased 6.0% to US$141.4 million from US$150.4 million in the year-earlier quarter. Revenues were US$743.6 million, up 8.3% from US$686.3 million the year before. Revenues from property income rose 9.6% to US$717.8 million from US$654.9 million in the corresponding quarter a year earlier.

Prospects: Our evaluation of Boston Properties Inc. as of October 4th, 2019 is the result of our systematic analysis on three basic characteristics: earnings strength, relative valuation, and recent stock price movement. The company has enjoyed a very positive trend in earnings per share over the past 5 quarters. However, recent analyst estimates for the company have been mixed and BXP has posted results that fell short of analysts' expectations. Based on operating earnings yield, the company is fairly valued when compared to all of the companies we cover. Share price changes over the past year indicates that BXP will perform well over the near term.

Financial Data

(US$ in Thousands)	9 Mos	6 Mos	3 Mos	12/31/2018	12/31/2017	12/31/2016	12/31/2015	12/31/2014
Earnings Per Share	3.35	3.42	3.19	3.70	2.93	3.26	3.73	2.83
Cash Flow Per Share	7.76	7.47	7.32	7.45	5.89	6.73	5.21	4.54
Tang Book Value Per Share	35.45	35.69	36.48	36.79	36.38	36.32	35.87	35.90
Dividends Per Share	3.800	3.800	3.650	3.500	3.050	2.700	3.850	7.100
Dividend Payout %	113.43	111.11	114.42	94.59	104.10	82.82	103.22	250.88
Income Statement								
Total Revenue	2,203,061	1,459,508	725,767	2,717,076	2,602,076	2,550,820	2,490,821	2,396,998
EBITDA	725,574	483,654	228,807	1,734,158	1,535,614	1,588,549	1,472,991	1,429,565
Depn & Amortn	1,821	1,213	605	645,649	617,547	694,403	639,542	628,573
Income Before Taxes	428,462	286,443	130,946	710,341	543,586	481,297	401,253	345,249
Net Income	378,075	267,681	100,730	582,847	462,439	512,785	583,106	443,611
Average Shares	154,820	154,874	154,844	154,682	154,390	153,977	153,844	153,308
Balance Sheet								
Current Assets	2,009,797	2,323,536	1,578,416	1,760,184	1,459,130	1,311,774	1,650,256	2,988,994
Total Assets	21,288,575	21,268,275	20,501,604	20,256,477	19,372,233	18,851,643	18,379,456	19,886,767
Current Liabilities	669,867	673,137	583,408	531,026	554,186	672,765	792,415	1,289,267
Long-Term Obligations	12,259,522	12,218,487	11,378,334	11,007,757	10,271,611	9,796,133	9,216,513	10,086,984
Total Liabilities	15,609,540	15,552,422	14,664,986	14,373,306	13,558,276	13,065,348	12,670,021	14,189,469
Stockholders' Equity	5,679,035	5,715,853	5,836,618	5,883,171	5,813,957	5,786,295	5,709,435	5,697,298
Shares Outstanding	154,572	154,563	154,515	154,458	154,325	153,790	153,579	153,113
Statistical Record								
Return on Assets %	2.55	2.62	2.52	2.94	2.42	2.75	3.05	2.22
Return on Equity %	9.16	9.31	8.62	9.97	7.97	8.90	10.22	7.72
EBITDA Margin %	32.93	33.14	31.53	63.82	59.01	62.28	59.14	59.64
Net Margin %	17.16	18.34	13.88	21.45	17.77	20.10	23.41	18.51
Asset Turnover	0.14	0.14	0.14	0.14	0.14	0.14	0.13	0.12
Current Ratio	3.00	3.45	2.71	3.31	2.63	1.95	2.08	2.32
Debt to Equity	2.16	2.14	1.95	1.87	1.77	1.69	1.61	1.77
Price Range	138.77-109.09	138.77-109.09	135.67-109.09	132.48-109.09	139.88-117.70	143.61-108.18	144.74-108.65	136.28-100.37
P/E Ratio	41.42-32.56	40.58-31.90	42.53-34.20	35.81-29.48	47.74-40.17	44.05-33.18	38.80-29.13	48.16-35.47
Average Yield %	2.96	2.97	2.93	2.85	2.41	2.12	2.99	6.00

Address: Prudential Center, 800 Boylston Street, Suite 1900, Boston, MA 02199-8103 **Telephone:** 617-236-3300	**Web Site:** www.bostonproperties.com **Officers:** Mortimer B. Zuckerman - Chairman Emeritus, Chairman, Executive Chairman, Chief Executive Officer Douglas T. Linde - President	**Auditors:** PricewaterhouseCoopers LLP **Investor Contact:** 617-236-3322 **Transfer Agents:** Computershare Trust Company, N.A., Providence, RI

BOSTON SCIENTIFIC CORP.

Exchange	Symbol	Price	52Wk Range	Yield	P/E
NYS	BSX	$45.22 (12/31/2019)	45.37-32.91	N/A	58.73

*7 Year Price Score 145.21 ***NYSE Composite Index=100** ***12 Month Price Score 101.22**

Interim Earnings (Per Share)

Qtr.	Mar	Jun	Sep	Dec
2016	0.15	(0.15)	0.17	0.09
2017	0.21	0.11	0.20	(0.44)
2018	0.21	0.40	0.31	0.27
2019	0.30	0.11	0.09	...

Interim Dividends (Per Share)

No Dividends Paid

Valuation Analysis — **Institutional Holding**

Forecast EPS	$1.57	No of Institutions
	(01/16/2020)	1115
Market Cap	$63.0 Billion	Shares
Book Value	$9.7 Billion	1,515,003,008
Price/Book	6.50	% Held
Price/Sales	6.06	92.43

Business Summary: Medical Instruments & Equipment (MIC: 4.3.1 SIC: 3841 NAIC: 339112)

Boston Scientific is a developer, manufacturer and marketer of medical devices that are used in a range of interventional medical fields. Co.'s businesses include: Endoscopy, which develops and manufactures devices to diagnose and treat gastrointestinal and pulmonary conditions; Urology and Pelvic Health, which develops and manufactures devices to treat various urological and pelvic conditions; Cardiac Rhythm Management, which develops and manufactures implantable devices that monitor the heart and deliver electricity to treat cardiac abnormalities; and Neuromodulation, which develops and manufactures devices to treat various neurological movement disorders and manage chronic pain.

Recent Developments: For the quarter ended Sep 30 2019, net income decreased 70.8% to US$126.0 million from US$432.0 million in the year-earlier quarter. Revenues were US$2.71 billion, up 13.1% from US$2.39 billion the year before. Operating income was US$383.0 million versus US$388.0 million in the prior-year quarter, a decrease of 1.3%. Direct operating expenses rose 15.6% to US$777.0 million from US$672.0 million in the comparable period the year before. Indirect operating expenses increased 16.1% to US$1.55 billion from US$1.33 billion in the equivalent prior-year period.

Prospects: Our evaluation of Boston Scientific Corp. as of October 4th, 2019 is the result of our systematic analysis on three basic characteristics: earnings strength, relative valuation, and recent stock price movement. The company has managed to produce a neutral trend in earnings per share over the past 5 quarters. Additionally, recent analyst estimates for the company have been unchanged while BSX has posted results that exceeded analysts' expectations. Based on operating earnings yield, the company is fairly valued when compared to all of the companies we cover. Share price changes over the past year indicates that BSX will perform well over the near term.

Financial Data

(US$ in Thousands)	9 Mos	6 Mos	3 Mos	12/31/2018	12/31/2017	12/31/2016	12/31/2015	12/31/2014
Earnings Per Share	0.77	0.99	1.28	1.19	0.08	0.25	(0.18)	(0.09)
Cash Flow Per Share	0.83	0.84	0.34	0.22	1.04	0.71	0.45	0.96
Income Statement								
Total Revenue	7,831,000	5,124,000	2,493,000	9,823,000	9,048,000	8,386,000	7,477,000	7,380,000
EBITDA	1,178,000	921,000	628,000	1,956,000	1,436,000	675,000	(97,000)	(11,000)
Depn & Amortn	220,000	142,000	69,000	296,000	279,000	270,000	274,000	287,000
Income Before Taxes	693,000	602,000	457,000	1,422,000	933,000	177,000	(650,000)	(509,000)
Income Taxes	(11,000)	24,000	33,000	(249,000)	828,000	(170,000)	(411,000)	(390,000)
Net Income	704,000	578,000	424,000	1,671,000	104,000	347,000	(239,000)	(119,000)
Average Shares	1,412,200	1,408,600	1,408,400	1,401,400	1,392,700	1,377,200	1,341,200	1,324,300
Balance Sheet								
Current Assets	4,847,000	6,334,000	6,234,000	4,003,000	3,822,000	3,239,000	3,471,000	3,606,000
Total Assets	26,756,000	24,309,000	23,802,000	20,999,000	19,042,000	18,096,000	18,133,000	17,042,000
Current Liabilities	4,254,000	4,850,000	4,479,000	5,260,000	5,654,000	3,587,000	2,430,000	2,846,000
Long-Term Obligations	9,591,000	7,591,000	7,590,000	4,803,000	3,815,000	5,420,000	5,674,000	3,859,000
Total Liabilities	17,058,000	14,884,000	14,570,000	12,273,000	12,029,000	11,363,000	11,813,000	10,585,000
Stockholders' Equity	9,699,000	9,425,000	9,233,000	8,726,000	7,012,000	6,733,000	6,320,000	6,457,000
Shares Outstanding	1,393,776	1,391,532	1,390,583	1,384,581	1,373,496	1,362,104	1,346,647	1,327,451
Statistical Record								
Return on Assets %	4.63	6.36	8.36	8.35	0.56	1.91	N.M.	N.M.
Return on Equity %	12.12	16.26	22.10	21.24	1.51	5.30	N.M.	N.M.
EBITDA Margin %	15.04	17.97	25.19	19.91	15.87	8.05	N.M.	N.M.
Net Margin %	8.99	11.28	17.01	17.01	1.15	4.14	N.M.	N.M.
Asset Turnover	0.44	0.46	0.46	0.49	0.49	0.46	0.43	0.44
Current Ratio	1.14	1.31	1.39	0.76	0.68	0.90	1.43	1.27
Debt to Equity	0.99	0.81	0.82	0.55	0.54	0.80	0.90	0.60
Price Range	43.45-31.73	42.98-31.73	40.75-26.84	39.04-25.20	29.80-21.88	24.48-16.07	18.94-13.22	13.98-11.37
P/E Ratio	56.43-41.21	43.41-32.05	31.84-20.97	32.81-21.18	372.50-273.50	97.92-64.28	...	...

Address: 300 Boston Scientific Way, Marlborough, MA 01752-1234 Telephone: 508-683-4000	Web Site: www.bostonscientific.com Officers: Michael F. Mahoney - Chairman, President, Chief Executive Officer Kevin J. Ballinger - Executive Vice President, Senior Vice President, Division Officer	Auditors: Ernst & Young LLP Investor Contact: 508-650-8023 Transfer Agents: Computershare Shareowner Services, Providence, RI

BRADY CORP

Exchange	Symbol	Price	52Wk Range	Yield	P/E	Div Acheiver
NYS	BRC	$57.26 (12/31/2019)	58.87-43.01	1.52	22.19	34 Years

*7 Year Price Score 120.28 *NYSE Composite Index=100 *12 Month Price Score 107.89

Interim Earnings (Per Share)

Qtr.	Oct	Jan	Apr	Jul
2016-17	0.44	0.49	0.43	0.48
2017-18	0.49	0.08	0.49	0.66
2018-19	0.58	0.55	0.65	0.68
2019-20	0.70	...	...	...

Interim Dividends (Per Share)

Amt	Decl	Ex	Rec	Pay
0.212Q	02/19/2019	04/08/2019	04/09/2019	04/30/2019
0.212Q	05/21/2019	07/09/2019	07/10/2019	07/31/2019
0.218Q	09/05/2019	10/09/2019	10/10/2019	10/31/2019
0.218Q	11/19/2019	01/09/2020	01/10/2020	01/31/2020

Indicated Div: $0.87 (Div. Reinv. Plan)

Valuation Analysis		Institutional Holding	
Forecast EPS	$2.63 (01/16/2020)	No of Institutions	287
Market Cap	$3.1 Billion	Shares	
Book Value	$876.5 Million		53,473,296
Price/Book	3.48	% Held	
Price/Sales	2.64		82.13

Business Summary: Manufacturing (MIC: 6.1.1 SIC: 3999 NAIC: 339950)

Brady is a manufacturer and supplier of identification solutions and workplace safety products that identify and protect premises, products and people. Co. is organized within two segments: Identification Solutions, which includes industrial and healthcare identification products in several categories, including facility identification and protection, product identification, wire identification, people identification, patient identification, and custom wristbands; and Workplace Safety, which includes workplace safety and compliance products in several categories, including safety and compliance signs, tags, and labels, informational signage, asset tracking labels, and first aid products.

Recent Developments: For the quarter ended Oct 31 2019, net income increased 22.4% to US$37.5 million from US$30.6 million in the year-earlier quarter. Revenues were US$286.9 million, down 2.1% from US$293.2 million the year before. Operating income was US$40.9 million versus US$40.6 million in the prior-year quarter, an increase of 0.7%. Direct operating expenses declined 0.8% to US$145.5 million from US$146.7 million in the comparable period the year before. Indirect operating expenses decreased 5.1% to US$100.5 million from US$105.9 million in the equivalent prior-year period.

Prospects: Our evaluation of Brady Corp. as of October 4th, 2019 is the result of our systematic analysis on three basic characteristics: earnings strength, relative valuation, and recent stock price movement. The company has managed to produce a neutral trend in earnings per share over the past 5 quarters. However, recent analyst estimates for the company have been raised and BRC has posted results that exceeded analysts' expectations. Based on operating earnings yield, the company is fairly valued when compared to all of the companies we cover. Share price changes over the past year indicates that BRC will perform poorly over the near term.

Financial Data

(US$ in Thousands)	3 Mos	07/31/2019	07/31/2018	07/31/2017	07/31/2016	07/31/2015	07/31/2014	07/31/2013
Earnings Per Share	2.58	2.46	1.73	1.84	1.58	0.06	(0.89)	(3.02)
Cash Flow Per Share	3.43	3.08	2.77	2.82	2.74	1.82	1.80	2.80
Tang Book Value Per Share	8.07	7.62	5.58	4.08	2.26	1.67	2.48	1.09
Dividends Per Share	0.855	0.850	0.830	0.820	0.810	0.800	0.780	0.760
Dividend Payout %	33.14	34.55	47.98	44.57	51.27	1,333.33	...	...
Income Statement								
Total Revenue	286,947	1,160,645	1,173,851	1,113,316	1,120,625	1,171,731	1,225,034	1,152,109
EBITDA	319,326	185,497	174,192	152,326	140,544	63,506	(12,082)	(33,380)
Depn & Amortn	277,055	18,023	19,009	20,190	23,375	27,355	26,727	48,725
Income Before Taxes	41,570	164,644	152,015	126,632	109,345	24,995	(53,109)	(98,746)
Income Taxes	4,072	33,386	60,955	30,987	29,235	20,093	(4,963)	42,070
Net Income	37,498	131,258	91,060	95,645	80,110	2,987	(45,968)	(154,535)
Average Shares	53,736	53,323	52,524	51,956	50,769	51,383	51,866	51,330
Balance Sheet								
Current Assets	593,908	573,279	471,339	407,814	407,424	408,582	463,842	512,490
Total Assets	1,231,222	1,157,308	1,056,931	1,050,223	1,043,964	1,062,897	1,253,665	1,438,683
Current Liabilities	255,947	241,945	190,927	187,198	166,727	209,247	291,945	323,497
Long-Term Obligations	...	...	52,618	104,536	211,982	200,774	159,296	201,150
Total Liabilities	354,687	306,534	304,819	350,083	440,366	475,209	520,589	607,886
Stockholders' Equity	876,535	850,774	752,112	700,140	603,598	587,688	733,076	830,797
Shares Outstanding	53,303	52,997	51,932	51,353	50,459	51,319	51,322	52,173
Statistical Record								
Return on Assets %	11.99	11.86	8.64	9.13	7.58	0.26	N.M.	N.M.
Return on Equity %	16.75	16.38	12.54	14.67	13.41	0.45	N.M.	N.M.
EBITDA Margin %	111.28	15.98	14.84	13.68	12.54	5.42	N.M.	N.M.
Net Margin %	13.07	11.31	7.76	8.59	7.15	0.25	N.M.	N.M.
Asset Turnover	1.00	1.05	1.11	1.06	1.06	1.01	0.91	0.76
Current Ratio	2.32	2.37	2.47	2.18	2.44	1.95	1.59	1.58
Debt to Equity	...	...	0.07	0.15	0.35	0.34	0.22	0.24
Price Range	58.55-40.06	51.73-36.85	40.65-31.95	39.80-31.86	32.64-19.52	28.91-21.19	35.54-24.26	36.33-26.34
P/E Ratio	22.69-15.53	21.03-14.98	23.50-18.47	21.63-17.32	20.66-12.35	481.83-353.17	...	...
Average Yield %	1.79	1.90	2.21	2.27	3.20	3.12	2.69	2.38

Address: 6555 West Good Hope Road, Milwaukee, WI 53223	**Web Site:** www.bradycorp.com	**Auditors:** DELOITTE & TOUCHE LLP
Telephone: 414-358-6600	**Officers:** Conrad G. Goodkind - Chairman J. Michael Nauman - President, Chief Executive Officer	**Investor Contact:** 414-438-6940 **Transfer Agents:** Wells Fargo Bank Minnesota, N.A., St. Paul, MN

BRANDYWINE REALTY TRUST

Exchange	Symbol	Price	52Wk Range	Yield	P/E
NYS	BDN	$15.75 (12/31/2019)	16.14-12.51	4.83	20.45

*7 Year Price Score 81.84   *NYSE Composite Index=100   *12 Month Price Score 96.25

Interim Earnings (Per Share)

Qtr.	Mar	Jun	Sep	Dec
2016	0.25	(0.02)	0.03	(0.08)
2017	0.11	0.02	0.11	0.41
2018	0.25	0.07	(0.24)	0.68
2019	0.02	0.03	0.04	...

Interim Dividends (Per Share)

Amt	Decl	Ex	Rec	Pay
0.19Q	02/21/2019	04/03/2019	04/04/2019	04/18/2019
0.19Q	05/22/2019	07/03/2019	07/05/2019	07/19/2019
0.19Q	09/10/2019	10/02/2019	10/03/2019	10/17/2019
0.19Q	12/11/2019	01/07/2020	01/08/2020	01/22/2020

Indicated Div: $0.76 (Div. Reinv. Plan)

Valuation Analysis

		Institutional Holding	
Forecast EPS	$0.12 (01/16/2020)	No of Institutions	391
Market Cap	$2.8 Billion	Shares	
Book Value	$1.7 Billion		239,846,896
Price/Book	1.64	% Held	
Price/Sales	4.85		97.58

Business Summary: REITs (MIC: 5.3.1 SIC: 6798 NAIC: 525930)

Brandywine Realty Trust is a self-administered and self-managed real estate investment trust that provides leasing, property management, development, redevelopment, acquisition and other tenant-related services for a portfolio of office, residential, retail and mixed-use properties. Co.'s properties and the properties owned by the Real Estate Ventures are located in or near Philadelphia, PA; Metropolitan Washington, D.C.; Southern New Jersey; Wilmington, DE; and Austin, TX. In addition, Co. conducts its third-party real estate management services business primarily through wholly-owned management company subsidiaries.

Recent Developments: For the quarter ended Sep 30 2019, net income amounted to US$6.8 million versus a net loss of US$43.5 million in the year-earlier quarter. Revenues were US$145.3 million, up 7.7% from US$135.0 million the year before. Revenues from property income rose 7.9% to US$144.2 million from US$133.6 million in the corresponding quarter a year earlier.

Prospects: Our evaluation of Brandywine Realty Trust as of October 4th, 2019 is the result of our systematic analysis on three basic characteristics: earnings strength, relative valuation, and recent stock price movement. The company has generated a negative trend in earnings per share over the past 5 quarters. However, recent analyst estimates for the company have been mixed and BDN has posted results that fell short of analysts' expectations. Based on operating earnings yield, the company is overvalued when compared to all of the companies we cover. Share price changes over the past year indicates that BDN will perform in line with the market over the near term.

Financial Data

(US$ in Thousands)	9 Mos	6 Mos	3 Mos	12/31/2018	12/31/2017	12/31/2016	12/31/2015	12/31/2014
Earnings Per Share	0.77	0.49	0.53	0.76	0.65	0.19	(0.21)	
Cash Flow Per Share	1.29	1.22	1.17	1.27	1.04	0.98	1.10	1.14
Tang Book Value Per Share	9.05	9.13	9.37	9.55	9.90	10.24	10.43	11.39
Dividends Per Share	0.750	0.740	0.730	0.720	0.640	0.620	0.600	0.600
Dividend Payout %	97.40	151.02	137.74	94.74	98.46	326.32	...	
Income Statement								
Total Revenue	433,378	288,047	143,896	544,345	520,493	525,463	602,631	596,982
EBITDA	85,640	58,181	28,436	408,768	397,918	330,475	305,294	344,407
Depn & Amortn	1,462	3,324	2,485	179,831	185,173	191,624	219,936	210,946
Income Before Taxes	22,515	13,730	5,453	152,943	129,537	52,004	(29,929)	6,814
Income Taxes	46	46	29	423	(628)	...	...	
Net Income	17,500	10,728	4,009	136,324	120,850	40,191	(30,401)	6,975
Average Shares	176,750	176,690	176,464	179,641	176,808	176,010	178,162	166,202
Balance Sheet								
Current Assets	212,757	220,174	205,010	204,479	389,877	355,989	218,912	410,310
Total Assets	4,020,432	4,048,474	4,115,929	4,098,521	3,995,448	4,099,213	4,554,511	4,859,173
Current Liabilities	153,549	132,665	146,482	187,621	182,123	165,056	158,518	184,369
Long-Term Obligations	2,078,255	2,096,536	2,094,797	2,028,046	1,930,828	2,013,112	2,384,717	2,451,308
Total Liabilities	2,329,690	2,330,655	2,346,579	2,278,268	2,166,268	2,232,869	2,620,586	2,718,346
Stockholders' Equity	1,690,742	1,717,819	1,769,350	1,820,253	1,829,180	1,866,344	1,933,925	2,140,827
Shares Outstanding	176,194	176,197	176,001	176,873	178,285	175,140	174,688	179,293
Statistical Record								
Return on Assets %	3.50	2.22	2.35	3.37	2.99	0.93	N.M.	0.14
Return on Equity %	8.05	5.02	5.31	7.47	6.54	2.11	N.M.	0.35
EBITDA Margin %	19.76	20.20	19.76	75.09	76.45	62.89	50.66	57.69
Net Margin %	4.04	3.72	2.79	25.04	23.22	7.65	N.M.	1.17
Asset Turnover	0.14	0.14	0.14	0.13	0.13	0.12	0.13	0.12
Current Ratio	1.39	1.66	1.40	1.09	2.14	2.16	1.38	2.23
Debt to Equity	1.23	1.22	1.18	1.11	1.11	1.06	1.23	1.15
Price Range	16.14-12.36	17.12-12.36	17.12-12.36	18.15-12.36	18.58-15.74	16.87-11.29	17.00-11.72	16.29-13.77
P/E Ratio	20.96-16.05	34.94-25.22	32.30-23.32	23.88-16.26	28.58-24.22	88.79-59.42	...	N.M.
Average Yield %	5.08	4.85	4.73	4.55	3.76	4.15	4.23	4.00

Address: 2929 Walnut Street, Suite 1700, Philadelphia, PA 19104 **Telephone:** 610-325-5600	**Web Site:** www.brandywinerealty.com **Officers:** Gerard H. Sweeney - President, Chief Executive Officer Thomas E. Wirth - Executive Vice President, Chief Financial Officer, Principal Accounting Officer	**Auditors:** PricewaterhouseCoopers LLP **Investor Contact:** 610-832-7702 **Transfer Agents:** Computershare, Providence, RI

BRIGHT HORIZONS FAMILY SOLUTIONS, INC

Exchange	Symbol	Price	52Wk Range	Yield	P/E
NYS	BFAM	$150.29 (12/31/2019)	166.75-107.49	N/A	49.93

*7 Year Price Score 154.27 *NYSE Composite Index=100 *12 Month Price Score 100.93

Interim Earnings (Per Share)

Qtr.	Mar	Jun	Sep	Dec
2016	0.40	0.50	0.37	0.28
2017	0.68	0.54	0.51	0.85
2018	0.62	0.68	0.57	0.78
2019	0.71	0.83	0.69	...

Interim Dividends (Per Share)

No Dividends Paid

Valuation Analysis

		Institutional Holding	
Forecast EPS	$3.64	No of Institutions	
	(01/17/2020)	N/A	
Market Cap	$8.7 Billion	Shares	
Book Value	$894.5 Million	N/A	
Price/Book	9.73	% Held	
Price/Sales	4.31	N/A	

Business Summary: Services (MIC: 6.1.2 SIC: 8351 NAIC: 624410)

Bright Horizons Family Solutions is a provider of child care and early education, back-up care and educational advisory services. Co. provides services under contracts with employers, who provide child care, as well as other dependent care solutions and educational advisory services. Co.'s service offerings include full-service center-based child care and early education, back-up care, and educational advisory services. Co. operates child care and early education centers across a range of customer industries with the capacity to serve children and their families in the U.S., as well as in the U.K., the Netherlands, Canada and India.

Recent Developments: For the quarter ended Sep 30 2019, net income increased 22.8% to US$41.3 million from US$33.6 million in the year-earlier quarter. Revenues were US$511.6 million, up 8.5% from US$471.6 million the year before. Operating income was US$62.6 million versus US$55.5 million in the prior-year quarter, an increase of 12.9%. Direct operating expenses rose 7.8% to US$386.4 million from US$358.5 million in the comparable period the year before. Indirect operating expenses increased 8.7% to US$62.6 million from US$57.6 million in the equivalent prior-year period.

Prospects: Our evaluation of Bright Horizons Family Solutions Inc as of October 4th, 2019 is the result of our systematic analysis on three basic characteristics: earnings strength, relative valuation, and recent stock price movement. The company has produced a positive trend in earnings per share over the past 5 quarters. However, recent analyst estimates for the company have been unchanged, while BFAM has posted results that exceeded analysts' expectations. Based on operating earnings yield, the company is overvalued when compared to all of the companies we cover. Share price changes over the past year indicates that BFAM will perform over the near term.

Financial Data
(US$ in Thousands)

	9 Mos	6 Mos	3 Mos	12/31/2018	12/31/2017	12/31/2016	12/31/2015	12/31/2014
Earnings Per Share	3.01	2.89	2.74	2.66	2.59	1.55	1.50	1.07
Cash Flow Per Share	5.65	5.13	5.13	5.10	4.01	3.59	2.80	2.66
Income Statement								
Total Revenue	1,541,402	1,029,818	501,758	1,903,182	1,740,905	1,569,841	1,458,445	1,352,999
EBITDA	225,458	154,202	71,072	340,064	300,200	271,363	260,291	224,319
Depn & Amortn	25,086	16,459	8,162	100,969	94,761	85,242	78,689	77,399
Income Before Taxes	165,746	114,072	50,962	191,587	161,400	143,197	140,156	112,314
Income Taxes	33,123	22,703	8,920	33,606	4,437	48,437	46,229	40,279
Net Income	132,623	91,369	42,042	157,981	156,963	94,760	93,927	72,035
Average Shares	59,132	58,939	58,752	59,000	60,253	60,594	62,360	67,244
Balance Sheet								
Current Assets	228,129	187,140	187,635	193,891	192,461	154,399	152,713	223,158
Total Assets	3,211,226	3,193,479	3,196,536	2,524,306	2,468,644	2,359,017	2,150,541	2,141,076
Current Liabilities	469,991	453,325	514,256	483,785	460,655	387,580	305,343	279,423
Long-Term Obligations	1,030,254	1,032,459	1,034,664	1,036,870	1,046,011	1,054,009	905,661	911,627
Total Liabilities	2,316,731	2,315,117	2,359,524	1,744,829	1,719,584	1,671,150	1,422,933	1,390,117
Stockholders' Equity	894,495	878,362	837,012	779,477	749,060	687,867	727,608	750,959
Shares Outstanding	57,917	57,898	57,773	57,494	58,013	58,910	60,008	61,534
Statistical Record								
Return on Assets %	6.28	6.05	5.70	6.33	6.50	4.19	4.38	3.39
Return on Equity %	21.41	21.09	20.67	20.67	21.85	13.35	12.71	8.78
EBITDA Margin %	14.63	14.97	14.16	17.87	17.24	17.29	17.85	16.58
Net Margin %	8.60	8.87	8.38	8.30	9.02	6.04	6.44	5.32
Asset Turnover	0.71	0.70	0.68	0.76	0.72	0.69	0.68	0.64
Current Ratio	0.49	0.41	0.36	0.40	0.42	0.40	0.50	0.80
Debt to Equity	1.15	1.18	1.24	1.33	1.40	1.53	1.24	1.21
Price Range	166.75-105.39	150.87-103.54	127.11-94.88	123.75-91.78	94.71-68.01	72.30-60.59	68.58-44.22	47.14-35.94
P/E Ratio	55.40-35.01	52.20-35.83	46.39-34.63	46.52-34.50	36.57-26.26	46.65-39.09	45.72-29.48	44.06-33.59

Address: 200 Talcott Avenue, Watertown, MA 02472 **Telephone:** 617-673-8000	**Web Site:** www.brighthorizons.com **Officers:** David H. Lissy - Executive Chairman, Chief Executive Officer Stephen H. Kramer - President, Chief Executive Officer, Chief Development Officer	**Auditors:** DELOITTE & TOUCHE LLP **Transfer Agents:** Wells Fargo Shareowner Services SM, St. Paul, MN

BRINKER INTERNATIONAL, INC.

Exchange	Symbol	Price	52Wk Range	Yield	P/E
NYS	EAT	$42.00 (12/31/2019)	51.04-37.01	3.62	11.23

*7 Year Price Score 76.74 *NYSE Composite Index=100 *12 Month Price Score 99.31

Interim Earnings (Per Share)

Qtr.	Sep	Dec	Mar	Jun
2016-17	0.42	0.69	0.86	1.01
2017-18	0.20	0.54	1.02	0.98
2018-19	0.64	0.83	1.31	1.21
2019-20	0.39	...	...	...

Interim Dividends (Per Share)

Amt	Decl	Ex	Rec	Pay
0.38Q	01/28/2019	03/07/2019	03/08/2019	03/28/2019
0.38Q	04/30/2019	06/06/2019	06/07/2019	06/27/2019
0.38Q	08/12/2019	09/05/2019	09/06/2019	09/26/2019
0.38Q	10/28/2019	12/05/2019	12/06/2019	12/26/2019

Indicated Div: $1.52

Valuation Analysis

		Institutional Holding	
Forecast EPS	$4.27	No of Institutions	467
	(01/17/2020)		
Market Cap	$1.6 Billion	Shares	
Book Value	N/A		62,871,052
Price/Book	N/A	% Held	69.51
Price/Sales	0.48		

Business Summary: Hotels, Restaurants & Travel (MIC: 2.2.1 SIC: 5812 NAIC: 722110)

Brinker International is engaged in owning, developing, operating and franchising the Chili's® Grill & Bar (Chili's) and Maggiano's Little Italy® (Maggiano's) restaurant brands. Chili's operates in the bar and grill category of casual dining. Chili's menu includes burgers, fajitas, baby back ribs and margaritas. Chili's To Go menu is available online, by calling the restaurant, or through its mobile app. Maggiano's is a casual restaurant brand providing Italian-American cuisine. Dishes are served in both a la carte and family style. Co. provides a range of lunch and dinner options, complimented by a wine list and cocktails.

Recent Developments: For the quarter ended Sep 25 2019, net income decreased 43.6% to US$14.9 million from US$26.4 million in the year-earlier quarter. Revenues were US$786.0 million, up 4.3% from US$753.8 million the year before. Operating income was US$31.2 million versus US$46.9 million in the prior-year quarter, a decrease of 33.5%. Direct operating expenses rose 5.0% to US$679.6 million from US$647.2 million in the comparable period the year before. Indirect operating expenses increased 26.0% to US$75.2 million from US$59.7 million in the equivalent prior-year period.

Prospects: Our evaluation of Brinker International Inc. as of October 4th, 2019 is the result of our systematic analysis on three basic characteristics: earnings strength, relative valuation, and recent stock price movement. The company has managed to produce a neutral trend in earnings per share over the past 5 quarters. In addition, recent analyst estimates for the company have been mixed and EAT has posted results that exceeded analysts' expectations. Based on operating earnings yield, the company is undervalued when compared to all of the companies we cover. Share price changes over the past year indicates that EAT will perform poorly over the near term.

Financial Data
(US$ in Thousands)

	3 Mos	06/26/2019	06/27/2018	06/28/2017	06/29/2016	06/24/2015	06/25/2014	06/26/2013
Earnings Per Share	3.74	3.96	2.72	2.94	3.42	3.05	2.26	2.20
Cash Flow Per Share	6.66	5.57	6.24	6.20	6.71	5.86	5.45	4.06
Tang Book Value Per Share	...	...	...	...	...	...	N.M.	0.11
Dividends Per Share	1.520	1.520	1.520	1.360	1.280	1.120	0.960	0.800
Dividend Payout %	40.64	38.38	55.88	46.26	37.43	36.72	42.48	36.36
Income Statement								
Total Revenue	786,000	3,217,900	3,135,417	3,150,837	3,257,489	3,002,278	2,905,452	2,846,098
EBITDA	69,800	234,400	231,140	260,043	475,329	458,525	380,460	390,914
Depn & Amortn	38,100	1,000	1,932	1,988	156,368	145,242	136,081	131,481
Income Before Taxes	16,800	171,800	170,222	208,508	286,387	284,277	216,288	230,315
Income Taxes	1,900	16,900	44,340	57,685	85,642	87,583	62,249	66,956
Net Income	14,900	154,900	125,882	150,823	200,745	196,694	154,039	163,359
Average Shares	38,100	39,100	46,264	51,250	58,684	64,404	68,152	74,158
Balance Sheet								
Current Assets	173,700	177,000	156,284	154,392	176,774	189,717	210,854	198,591
Total Assets	2,491,000	1,258,300	1,347,340	1,413,700	1,472,716	1,435,873	1,490,604	1,452,603
Current Liabilities	516,400	421,600	434,340	446,428	432,443	418,475	466,110	390,211
Long-Term Obligations	1,313,800	1,206,600	1,499,624	1,319,829	1,113,949	970,825	832,302	780,121
Total Liabilities	3,076,100	2,036,500	2,065,649	1,907,381	1,685,815	1,514,333	1,427,510	1,303,246
Stockholders' Equity	(585,100)	(778,200)	(718,309)	(493,681)	(213,099)	(78,460)	63,094	149,357
Shares Outstanding	37,400	37,500	40,797	48,440	55,420	60,585	64,558	67,444
Statistical Record								
Return on Assets %	7.68	11.92	9.14	10.48	13.58	13.48	10.50	11.34
Return on Equity %	...	...	...	...	...	...	145.41	71.34
EBITDA Margin %	8.88	7.28	7.37	8.25	14.59	15.27	13.09	13.74
Net Margin %	1.90	4.81	4.01	4.79	6.16	6.55	5.30	5.74
Asset Turnover	1.74	2.48	2.28	2.19	2.20	2.06	1.98	1.98
Current Ratio	0.34	0.42	0.36	0.35	0.41	0.45	0.45	0.51
Debt to Equity	...	...	...	...	...	...	13.19	5.22
Price Range	53.48-37.01	53.48-37.31	52.12-29.89	55.19-36.93	59.90-43.42	63.12-44.16	55.00-38.19	41.60-28.71
P/E Ratio	14.30-9.90	13.51-9.42	19.16-10.99	18.77-12.56	17.51-12.70	20.70-14.48	24.34-16.90	18.91-13.05
Average Yield %	3.49	3.36	4.08	2.89	2.60	2.04	2.08	2.32

Address: 3000 Olympus Blvd, Dallas, TX 75019	**Web Site:** www.brinker.com	**Auditors:** KPMG LLP
Telephone: 972-980-9917	**Officers:** Joseph M. (Joe) DePinto - Chairman Wyman T. Roberts - President, Chief Executive Officer	**Investor Contact:** 972-980-9917
		Transfer Agents: Computershare, Canton, MA

BRINKS CO (THE)

Exchange	Symbol	Price	52Wk Range	Yield	P/E
NYS	BCO	$90.68 (12/31/2019)	94.30-64.15	0.66	69.22

*7 Year Price Score 138.34 *NYSE Composite Index=100 *12 Month Price Score 105.70

Interim Earnings (Per Share)

Qtr.	Mar	Jun	Sep	Dec
2016	(0.06)	0.01	0.48	0.25
2017	0.67	0.28	0.38	(1.01)
2018	0.43	(2.11)	0.34	0.69
2019	0.27	0.25	0.10	...

Interim Dividends (Per Share)

Amt	Decl	Ex	Rec	Pay
0.15Q	05/01/2019	05/16/2019	05/17/2019	06/03/2019
0.15Q	07/12/2019	07/26/2019	07/29/2019	09/03/2019
0.15Q	10/14/2019	11/07/2019	11/08/2019	12/02/2019
0.15Q	01/16/2020	02/06/2020	02/07/2020	03/02/2020

Indicated Div: $0.60

Valuation Analysis

		Institutional Holding	
Forecast EPS	$3.93	No of Institutions	
	(01/17/2020)	408	
Market Cap	$4.5 Billion	Shares	
Book Value	$169.2 Million	64,855,352	
Price/Book	26.80	% Held	
Price/Sales	1.24	100.90	

Business Summary: Business Services (MIC: 7.5.2 SIC: 4731 NAIC: 488510)

Brink's is engaged in total cash management, route-based logistics and payment solutions including cash-in-transit, automated teller machine (ATM) services, cash management services, including vault outsourcing, money processing, and safe services, and international transportation of valuables. Co.'s service offerings, among others, include: cash-in-transit services, which include the transportation of cash between businesses and financial institutions; ATM services, which provide customers who own and operate ATMs a variety of service options; global services, which provide transportation of commodities; and CompuSafe® service, which provides a closed-loop system.

Recent Developments: For the quarter ended Sep 30 2019, income from continuing operations decreased 62.4% to US$7.1 million from US$18.9 million in the year-earlier quarter. Net income decreased 64.4% to US$6.7 million from US$18.8 million in the year-earlier quarter. Revenues were US$928.4 million, up 8.9% from US$852.4 million the year before. Operating income was US$52.5 million versus US$67.0 million in the prior-year quarter, a decrease of 21.6%. Direct operating expenses rose 9.5% to US$714.4 million from US$652.6 million in the comparable period the year before. Indirect operating expenses increased 21.6% to US$161.5 million from US$132.8 million in the equivalent prior-year period.

Prospects: Our evaluation of Brink's Co as of October 4th, 2019 is the result of our systematic analysis on three basic characteristics: earnings strength, relative valuation, and recent stock price movement. The company has produced a positive trend in earnings per share over the past 5 quarters. However, recent analyst estimates for the company have been unchanged, while BCO has posted results that exceeded analysts' expectations. Based on operating earnings yield, the company is fairly valued when compared to all of the companies we cover. Share price changes over the past year indicates that BCO will perform in line with the market over the near term.

Financial Data
(US$ in Thousands)

	9 Mos	6 Mos	3 Mos	12/31/2018	12/31/2017	12/31/2016	12/31/2015	12/31/2014
Earnings Per Share	1.31	1.55	(0.81)	(0.65)	0.32	0.68	(0.24)	(1.71)
Cash Flow Per Share	7.30	5.56	5.39	7.15	4.97	3.34	4.24	2.88
Tang Book Value Per Share	N.M.	N.M.	N.M.	N.M.	N.M.	2.64	2.13	3.67
Dividends Per Share	0.600	0.600	0.600	0.600	0.550	0.400	0.400	0.400
Dividend Payout %	45.80	38.71	...	...	171.88	58.82	...	...
Income Statement								
Total Revenue	2,747,400	1,819,000	905,000	3,488,900	3,347,000	3,020,600	3,061,400	3,562,300
EBITDA	279,300	190,500	94,700	134,600	239,700	167,500	81,100	(27,400)
Depn & Amortn	139,500	96,600	47,800	34,200	28,900	23,200	24,900	5,500
Income Before Taxes	72,100	50,500	24,000	40,600	181,100	126,500	40,600	(53,300)
Income Taxes	37,100	22,400	9,700	70,000	157,700	78,500	66,500	36,700
Net Income	31,600	26,200	13,700	(33,300)	16,700	34,500	(11,900)	(83,900)
Average Shares	51,100	50,900	50,900	50,900	51,800	50,600	49,300	49,000
Balance Sheet								
Current Assets	1,246,100	1,244,600	1,154,300	1,206,500	1,488,200	843,700	777,700	907,600
Total Assets	3,702,600	3,732,400	3,602,000	3,236,000	3,059,600	1,994,800	1,946,700	2,192,200
Current Liabilities	888,600	888,800	845,400	849,400	834,900	753,300	641,800	728,400
Long-Term Obligations	1,660,800	1,887,600	1,834,100	1,471,600	1,139,600	247,600	358,100	373,300
Total Liabilities	3,533,400	3,538,200	3,436,700	3,082,300	2,742,200	1,657,700	1,628,800	1,758,200
Stockholders' Equity	169,200	194,200	165,300	153,700	317,400	337,100	317,900	434,000
Shares Outstanding	50,000	50,000	49,900	49,700	50,500	50,000	48,900	48,600
Statistical Record								
Return on Assets %	1.93	2.38	N.M.	N.M.	0.66	1.75	N.M.	N.M.
Return on Equity %	33.89	37.63	N.M.	N.M.	5.10	10.51	N.M.	N.M.
EBITDA Margin %	10.17	10.47	10.46	3.86	7.16	5.55	2.65	N.M.
Net Margin %	1.15	1.44	1.51	N.M.	0.50	1.14	N.M.	N.M.
Asset Turnover	1.06	1.08	1.05	1.11	1.32	1.53	1.48	1.52
Current Ratio	1.40	1.40	1.37	1.42	1.78	1.12	1.21	1.25
Debt to Equity	9.82	9.72	11.10	9.57	3.59	0.73	1.13	0.86
Price Range	92.96-59.10	85.56-59.10	84.50-59.10	87.85-59.10	87.00-41.30	45.10-26.04	33.54-22.41	35.57-20.10
P/E Ratio	70.96-45.11	55.20-38.13	...	...	271.88-129.06	66.32-38.29	...	...
Average Yield %	0.79	0.81	0.82	0.81	0.82	1.19	1.39	1.49

Address: 1801 Bayberry Court, Richmond, VA 23226-8100 Telephone: 804-289-9600	Web Site: www.brinks.com Officers: Douglas A. Pertz - President, Chief Executive Officer Ronald J. (Ron) Domanico - Executive Vice President, Chief Financial Officer	Auditors: DELOITTE & TOUCHE LLP Investor Contact: 804-289-9708 Transfer Agents: Computershare, Providence, RI

BRISTOL-MYERS SQUIBB CO.

Exchange	Symbol	Price	52Wk Range	Yield	P/E
NYS	BMY	$64.19 (12/31/2019)	64.19-42.77	2.80	18.61

*7 Year Price Score 74.44   *NYSE Composite Index=100   *12 Month Price Score 111.39

TRADING VOLUME (thousand shares)

Interim Earnings (Per Share)

Qtr.	Mar	Jun	Sep	Dec
2016	0.71	0.70	0.72	0.53
2017	0.94	0.56	0.51	(1.41)
2018	0.91	0.23	1.16	0.71
2019	1.04	0.87	0.83	...

Interim Dividends (Per Share)

Amt	Decl	Ex	Rec	Pay
0.41Q	03/07/2019	04/04/2019	04/05/2019	05/01/2019
0.41Q	06/13/2019	07/03/2019	07/05/2019	08/01/2019
0.41Q	09/11/2019	10/03/2019	10/04/2019	11/01/2019
0.45Q	12/05/2019	01/02/2020	01/03/2020	02/03/2020

Indicated Div: $1.80

Valuation Analysis

		Institutional Holding	
Forecast EPS	$4.35	No of Institutions	
	(01/17/2020)	2583	
Market Cap	$104.6 Billion	Shares	
Book Value	$17.6 Billion	1,638,505,856	
Price/Book	5.93	% Held	
Price/Sales	4.33	82.53	

Business Summary: Pharmaceuticals (MIC: 4.1.1 SIC: 2834 NAIC: 325412)

Bristol-Myers Squibb is engaged in the discovery, development, licensing, manufacturing, marketing, distribution and sale of biopharmaceutical products. Co.'s products are sold worldwide, primarily to wholesalers, retail pharmacies, hospitals, government entities and the medical profession. Co. manufactures products in the U.S., Puerto Rico and in four foreign countries. Co. has products in the following therapeutic classes: oncology; cardiovascular; and immunoscience. Co.'s products include: Opdivo; Eliquis; Orencia; Sprycel; Yervoy; Empliciti; Baraclude; the Reyataz Franchise; the Sustiva Franchise; and the Hepatitis C Franchise.

Recent Developments: For the quarter ended Sep 30 2019, net income decreased 28.6% to US$1.37 billion from US$1.91 billion in the year-earlier quarter. Revenues were US$6.01 billion, up 5.6% from US$5.69 billion the year before. Direct operating expenses rose 9.8% to US$1.81 billion from US$1.65 billion in the comparable period the year before. Indirect operating expenses increased 6.5% to US$2.54 billion from US$2.38 billion in the equivalent prior-year period.

Prospects: Our evaluation of Bristol-Myers Squibb Co. as of October 4th, 2019 is the result of our systematic analysis on three basic characteristics: earnings strength, relative valuation, and recent stock price movement. The company has managed to produce a neutral trend in earnings per share over the past 5 quarters. However, recent analyst estimates for the company have been raised and BMY has posted results that exceeded analysts' expectations. Based on operating earnings yield, the company is undervalued when compared to all of the companies we cover. Share price changes over the past year indicates that BMY will perform very poorly over the near term.

Financial Data

(US$ in Millions)	9 Mos	6 Mos	3 Mos	12/31/2018	12/31/2017	12/31/2016	12/31/2015	12/31/2014
Earnings Per Share	3.45	3.78	3.14	3.01	0.61	2.65	0.93	1.20
Cash Flow Per Share	5.18	4.39	3.77	3.64	3.21	1.70	1.10	1.90
Tang Book Value Per Share	6.22	5.21	4.68	3.94	2.26	4.76	3.57	3.66
Dividends Per Share	1.630	1.620	1.610	1.600	1.560	1.140	1.490	1.450
Dividend Payout %	47.25	42.86	51.27	53.16	255.74	43.02	160.22	120.83
Income Statement								
Total Revenue	18,200	12,193	5,920	22,561	20,776	19,427	16,560	15,879
EBITDA	6,053	3,929	2,048	6,656	6,009	6,530	2,761	3,127
Depn & Amortn	557	252	199	505	682	448	500	543
Income Before Taxes	5,119	3,509	1,804	5,968	5,131	5,915	2,077	2,381
Income Taxes	584	601	264	1,021	4,156	1,408	446	352
Net Income	4,495	3,142	1,710	4,920	1,007	4,457	1,565	2,004
Average Shares	1,634	1,637	1,637	1,637	1,652	1,680	1,679	1,670
Balance Sheet								
Current Assets	40,191	37,716	17,093	17,160	14,854	13,704	10,415	14,608
Total Assets	57,433	55,163	34,834	34,986	33,551	33,707	31,748	33,749
Current Liabilities	10,489	9,711	8,841	10,654	9,563	8,841	8,017	8,461
Long-Term Obligations	24,390	24,433	5,635	5,646	6,975	5,716	6,550	7,242
Total Liabilities	39,785	39,114	19,616	20,955	21,810	17,530	17,482	18,897
Stockholders' Equity	17,648	16,049	15,218	14,031	11,741	16,177	14,266	14,852
Shares Outstanding	1,629	1,635	1,635	1,624	1,625	1,664	1,669	1,661
Statistical Record								
Return on Assets %	12.41	14.13	15.15	14.36	2.99	13.58	4.78	5.54
Return on Equity %	36.15	43.74	36.73	38.18	7.21	29.20	10.75	13.36
EBITDA Margin %	33.26	32.22	34.59	29.50	28.92	33.61	16.67	19.69
Net Margin %	24.70	25.77	28.89	21.81	4.85	22.94	9.45	12.62
Asset Turnover	0.53	0.54	0.69	0.66	0.62	0.59	0.51	0.44
Current Ratio	3.83	3.88	1.93	1.61	1.55	1.55	1.30	1.73
Debt to Equity	1.38	1.52	0.37	0.40	0.59	0.35	0.46	0.49
Price Range	63.23-42.77	63.23-44.62	63.23-45.12	68.98-48.76	65.35-46.82	76.77-49.23	70.71-57.30	61.30-46.59
P/E Ratio	18.33-12.40	16.73-11.80	20.14-14.37	22.92-16.20	107.13-76.75	28.97-18.58	76.03-61.61	51.08-38.83
Average Yield %	3.31	3.09	2.97	2.77	2.71	1.80	2.31	2.78

Address: 430 E. 29th Street, 14th Floor, New York, NY 10016	Web Site: www.bms.com	Auditors: Deloitte & Touche LLP
Telephone: 212-546-4000	Officers: Giovanni Caforio - Chairman, Chief Executive Officer, Executive Vice President, Chief Commercial Officer, Chief Operating Officer, Division Officer Sandra ("Sandy") Leung - Executive Vice President, Senior Vice President, General Counsel, Corporate Secretary	Investor Contact: 609-252-4611
Fax: 212-546-4020		Transfer Agents: EQ Shareowner Services

BRIXMOR PROPERTY GROUP INC

Exchange	Symbol	Price	52Wk Range	Yield	P/E
NYS	BRX	$21.61 (12/31/2019)	22.71-14.17	5.28	22.28

*7 Year Price Score N/A   *NYSE Composite Index=100   *12 Month Price Score 109.42

Interim Earnings (Per Share)

Qtr.	Mar	Jun	Sep	Dec
2016	0.20	0.21	0.19	0.30
2017	0.23	0.25	0.27	0.23
2018	0.20	0.26	0.49	0.26
2019	0.21	0.23	0.27	...

Interim Dividends (Per Share)

Amt	Decl	Ex	Rec	Pay
0.28Q	02/11/2019	04/04/2019	04/05/2019	04/15/2019
0.28Q	04/29/2019	07/03/2019	07/05/2019	07/15/2019
0.28Q	07/29/2019	10/03/2019	10/04/2019	10/15/2019
0.285Q	10/28/2019	01/03/2020	01/06/2020	01/15/2020

Indicated Div: $1.14 (Div. Reinv. Plan)

Valuation Analysis

		Institutional Holding	
Forecast EPS	$0.92	No of Institutions	
	(01/17/2020)	403	
Market Cap	$6.4 Billion	Shares	
Book Value	$2.8 Billion	339,750,528	
Price/Book	2.33	% Held	
Price/Sales	5.49	97.95	

Business Summary: REITs (MIC: 5.3.1 SIC: 6798 NAIC: 525930)

Brixmor Property Group is a holding company and an internally-managed real estate investment trust. Brixmor Operating Partnership LP and subsidiaries (the Operating Partnership) is the entity through which Co. conducts substantially all of its operations and owns substantially all of its assets. Through the Operating Partnership, Co. is engaged in the ownership, management, leasing, acquisition, disposition and redevelopment of retail shopping centers. Co.'s portfolio is comprised of shopping centers.

Recent Developments: For the quarter ended Sep 30 2019, net income decreased 45.1% to US$80.9 million from US$147.3 million in the year-earlier quarter. Revenues were US$293.0 million, down 4.4% from US$306.5 million the year before. Revenues from property income fell 4.4% to US$292.7 million from US$306.2 million in the corresponding quarter a year earlier.

Prospects: Our evaluation of Brixmor Property Group Inc as of October 4th, 2019 is the result of our systematic analysis on three basic characteristics: earnings strength, relative valuation, and recent stock price movement. The company has enjoyed a very positive trend in earnings per share over the past 5 quarters. In addition, recent analyst estimates for the company have been raised, and BRX has posted results that exceeded analysts' expectations. Based on operating earnings yield, the company is fairly valued when compared to all of the companies we cover. Share price changes over the past year indicates that BRX will perform in line with the market over the near term.

Financial Data

(US$ in Thousands)	9 Mos	6 Mos	3 Mos	12/31/2018	12/31/2017	12/31/2016	12/31/2015	12/31/2014
Earnings Per Share	0.97	1.19	1.22	1.21	0.98	0.91	0.65	0.36
Cash Flow Per Share	1.82	1.72	1.72	1.79	1.81	1.88	1.79	1.97
Tang Book Value Per Share	9.26	9.28	9.37	9.50	9.55	9.60	9.59	9.79
Dividends Per Share	1.115	1.110	1.105	1.100	1.040	0.980	0.900	0.727
Dividend Payout %	114.95	93.28	90.57	90.91	106.12	107.69	138.46	201.94
Income Statement								
Total Revenue	875,109	582,144	291,139	1,234,340	1,283,180	1,275,772	1,265,980	1,236,599
EBITDA	361,330	231,053	111,674	589,424	538,293	526,064	482,117	402,055
Depn & Amortn	6,352	4,499	2,255	8,634	16,566	22,270	40,343	29,264
Income Before Taxes	212,714	131,860	62,900	366,284	295,432	277,665	197,077	110,581
Net Income	212,714	131,860	62,900	366,284	300,293	275,628	193,720	89,002
Average Shares	298,879	298,893	299,029	302,339	305,281	305,060	305,017	244,588
Balance Sheet								
Current Assets	254,804	234,939	239,797	427,625	490,396	403,872	400,625	410,941
Total Assets	8,160,161	8,220,523	8,183,930	8,242,421	9,153,926	9,319,685	9,498,007	9,702,402
Current Liabilities	548,288	530,805	518,094	520,459	569,340	553,636	603,439	679,102
Long-Term Obligations	4,852,510	4,925,537	4,873,065	4,885,863	5,676,238	5,838,889	5,974,266	6,042,997
Total Liabilities	5,400,798	5,456,342	5,391,159	5,406,322	6,245,578	6,396,801	6,628,224	6,798,692
Stockholders' Equity	2,759,363	2,764,181	2,792,771	2,836,099	2,908,348	2,922,884	2,869,783	2,903,710
Shares Outstanding	297,846	297,846	297,987	298,488	304,620	304,343	299,138	296,552
Statistical Record								
Return on Assets %	3.49	4.18	4.29	4.21	3.25	2.92	2.02	0.90
Return on Equity %	10.30	12.69	13.02	12.75	10.30	9.49	6.71	3.38
EBITDA Margin %	41.29	39.69	38.36	47.75	41.95	41.23	38.08	32.51
Net Margin %	24.31	22.65	21.60	29.67	23.40	21.60	15.30	7.20
Asset Turnover	0.14	0.14	0.14	0.14	0.14	0.14	0.13	0.12
Current Ratio	0.46	0.44	0.46	0.82	0.86	0.73	0.66	0.61
Debt to Equity	1.76	1.78	1.74	1.72	1.95	2.00	2.08	2.08
Price Range	20.29-14.17	18.59-14.17	18.53-13.98	18.73-13.98	25.29-17.47	28.96-21.10	27.39-22.23	25.24-20.13
P/E Ratio	20.92-14.61	15.62-11.91	15.19-11.46	15.48-11.55	25.81-17.83	31.82-23.19	42.14-34.20	70.11-55.92
Average Yield %	6.41	6.49	6.70	6.78	5.21	3.80	3.62	3.23

Address: 450 Lexington Avenue, New York, NY 10017 Telephone: 212-869-3000	Web Site: www.brixmor.com Officers: John G. Schreiber - Chairman James M. Taylor - President, Chief Executive Officer	Auditors: Deloitte & Touche LLP Investor Contact: 212-869-3000 Transfer Agents: Computershare Trust Company, N.A., Canton, MA

BROADRIDGE FINANCIAL SOLUTIONS INC

Exchange	Symbol	Price	52Wk Range	Yield	P/E	Div Acheiver
NYS	BR	$123.54 (12/31/2019)	134.87-93.65	1.75	31.68	11 Years

*7 Year Price Score 138.53 *NYSE Composite Index=100 *12 Month Price Score 97.84

Interim Earnings (Per Share)

Qtr.	Sep	Dec	Mar	Jun
2016-17	0.28	0.25	0.63	1.55
2017-18	0.42	0.52	0.90	1.72
2018-19	0.64	0.42	1.45	1.55
2019-20	0.48	...	...	...

Interim Dividends (Per Share)

Amt	Decl	Ex	Rec	Pay
0.485Q	02/06/2019	03/14/2019	03/15/2019	04/03/2019
0.485Q	04/30/2019	06/13/2019	06/14/2019	07/03/2019
0.54Q	07/31/2019	09/12/2019	09/13/2019	10/03/2019
0.54Q	11/15/2019	12/12/2019	12/13/2019	01/03/2020

Indicated Div: $2.16

Valuation Analysis / Institutional Holding

Forecast EPS	$5.13	No of Institutions
	(01/15/2020)	957
Market Cap	$14.2 Billion	Shares
Book Value	$1.1 Billion	141,262,640
Price/Book	12.38	% Held
Price/Sales	3.26	84.88

Business Summary: Finance Intermediaries & Services (MIC: 5.5.1 SIC: 7389 NAIC: 561499)

Broadridge Financial Solutions is a holding company. Through its subsidiaries, Co. provides investor communications and technology-driven solutions to financial services clients. Co.'s services include investor communications, securities processing, data and analytics, and customer communications solutions. Co. has two segments: Investor Communication Solutions, which involves the processing and distribution of proxy materials to investors in equity securities and mutual funds, as well as the facilitation of related vote processing; and Global Technology and Operations, which provides securities processing solutions for capital markets, wealth management, and asset management firms.

Recent Developments: For the quarter ended Sep 30 2019, net income decreased 27.1% to US$55.9 million from US$76.7 million in the year-earlier quarter. Revenues were US$948.6 million, down 2.5% from US$972.8 million the year before. Operating income was US$73.1 million versus US$100.1 million in the prior-year quarter, a decrease of 27.0%. Direct operating expenses declined 1.6% to US$727.5 million from US$739.0 million in the comparable period the year before. Indirect operating expenses increased 10.7% to US$148.0 million from US$133.7 million in the equivalent prior-year period.

Prospects: Our evaluation of Broadridge Financial Solutions Inc. as of October 4th, 2019 is the result of our systematic analysis on three basic characteristics: earnings strength, relative valuation, and recent stock price movement. The company has generated a negative trend in earnings per share over the past 5 quarters. However, recent analyst estimates for the company have been mixed and BR has posted results that exceeded analysts' expectations. Based on operating earnings yield, the company is fairly valued when compared to all of the companies we cover. Share price changes over the past year indicates that BR will perform well over the near term.

Financial Data

(US$ in Thousands)	3 Mos	06/30/2019	06/30/2018	06/30/2017	06/30/2016	06/30/2015	06/30/2014	06/30/2013
Earnings Per Share	3.90	4.06	3.56	2.70	2.53	2.32	2.12	1.69
Cash Flow Per Share	5.47	5.32	5.94	4.37	3.69	3.60	3.24	2.22
Dividends Per Share	1.995	1.940	1.460	1.320	1.200	1.080	0.840	0.720
Dividend Payout %	51.15	47.78	41.01	48.89	47.43	46.55	39.62	42.60
Income Statement								
Total Revenue	948,600	4,362,200	4,329,900	4,142,600	2,897,000	2,694,200	2,558,000	2,430,800
EBITDA	127,800	802,300	747,100	662,100	570,300	530,300	475,500	392,400
Depn & Amortn	50,900	153,200	144,800	126,100	70,500	63,300	58,100	57,000
Income Before Taxes	63,800	607,300	563,700	493,300	474,000	444,400	395,500	323,200
Income Taxes	7,900	125,200	133,100	161,400	161,400	151,800	132,500	111,100
Net Income	55,900	482,100	427,900	326,800	307,500	287,100	263,000	212,100
Average Shares	117,100	118,800	120,400	120,800	121,600	124,000	124,100	125,400
Balance Sheet								
Current Assets	1,095,100	1,042,300	991,100	989,600	1,289,100	861,400	880,600	807,000
Total Assets	4,220,100	3,880,700	3,304,700	3,149,800	2,879,800	2,368,100	2,192,100	2,018,200
Current Liabilities	1,040,900	802,600	777,300	744,900	693,000	508,900	484,400	469,500
Long-Term Obligations	1,368,800	1,470,400	1,053,400	1,102,100	897,600	689,400	524,100	524,500
Total Liabilities	3,076,600	2,753,200	2,210,400	2,146,000	1,834,300	1,440,300	1,230,400	1,202,200
Stockholders' Equity	1,143,400	1,127,500	1,094,300	1,003,800	1,045,500	927,800	961,700	816,000
Shares Outstanding	114,600	114,300	116,300	116,500	118,300	118,200	119,500	119,000
Statistical Record								
Return on Assets %	12.14	13.42	13.26	10.84	11.69	12.59	12.49	10.59
Return on Equity %	38.81	43.40	40.79	31.89	31.08	30.39	29.59	25.45
EBITDA Margin %	13.47	18.39	17.25	15.98	19.69	19.68	18.59	16.14
Net Margin %	5.89	11.05	9.88	7.89	10.61	10.66	10.28	8.73
Asset Turnover	1.14	1.21	1.34	1.37	1.10	1.18	1.22	1.21
Current Ratio	1.05	1.30	1.28	1.33	1.86	1.69	1.82	1.72
Debt to Equity	1.20	1.30	0.96	1.10	0.86	0.74	0.54	0.64
Price Range	134.87-91.79	137.72-91.79	119.63-72.28	77.65-60.56	65.36-49.64	55.53-39.11	42.13-26.93	27.97-20.41
P/E Ratio	34.58-23.54	33.92-22.61	33.60-20.30	28.76-22.43	25.83-19.62	23.94-16.86	19.87-12.70	16.55-12.08
Average Yield %	1.74	1.70	1.55	1.93	2.12	2.29	2.36	3.04

Address: 5 Dakota Drive, Lake Success, NY 11042	Web Site: www.broadridge.com	Auditors: Deloitte & Touche LLP
Telephone: 516-472-5400	Officers: Richard J. (Rich) Daly - Executive Chairman, President, Chief Executive Officer Timothy C. (Tim) Gokey - President, Chief Operating Officer, Senior Vice President, Chief Development Officer, Chief Executive Officer	Investor Contact: 516-472-5400 Transfer Agents: Broadridge Corporate Issuer Solutions, Inc.

BROOKDALE SENIOR LIVING INC

Exchange	Symbol	Price	52Wk Range	Yield	P/E
NYS	BKD	$7.27 (12/31/2019)	8.66-6.02	N/A	N/A

*7 Year Price Score 31.04   *NYSE Composite Index=100   *12 Month Price Score 92.85

Interim Earnings (Per Share)

Qtr.	Mar	Jun	Sep	Dec
2016	(0.26)	(0.19)	(0.28)	(1.45)
2017	(0.68)	(0.25)	(2.22)	0.08
2018	(2.45)	(0.88)	(0.20)	0.70
2019	(0.23)	(0.30)	(0.42)	...

Interim Dividends (Per Share)

No Dividends Paid

Valuation Analysis — **Institutional Holding**

Forecast EPS	$-1.18	No of Institutions
	(00/23/2020)	293
Market Cap	$1.4 Billion	Shares
Book Value	$788.4 Million	203,872,176
Price/Book	1.78	% Held
Price/Sales	0.34	90.56

Business Summary: Hospitals & Health Care Facilities (MIC: 4.2.1 SIC: 8052 NAIC: 623311)

Brookdale Senior Living is a holding company. Through its subsidiaries, Co. is an operator of senior living communities. Co.'s Community offerings include: independent living, which is for middle to upper income seniors; assisted living and memory care, which provides housing and assistance to mid-acuity frail and elderly residents; and continuing care retirement, which provides living arrangements and services to accommodate various physical ability and health. Through its Health Care Services segment Co. provides home health, hospice and outpatient therapy services, and education and wellness programs, to residents of its communities and to seniors living outside of its communities.

Recent Developments: For the quarter ended Sep 30 2019, net loss amounted to US$78.5 million versus a net loss of US$37.1 million in the year-earlier quarter. Revenues were US$1.01 billion, down 9.9% from US$1.12 billion the year before. Operating loss was US$20.2 million versus an income of US$3.6 million in the prior-year quarter. Direct operating expenses rose 1.4% to US$615.7 million from US$607.1 million in the comparable period the year before. Indirect operating expenses decreased 18.8% to US$413.5 million from US$509.4 million in the equivalent prior-year period.

Prospects: Our evaluation of Brookdale Senior Living Inc. as of October 4th, 2019 is the result of our systematic analysis on three basic characteristics: earnings strength, relative valuation, and recent stock price movement. The company has produced a positive trend in earnings per share over the past 5 quarters. However, recent analyst estimates for the company have been mixed and BKD has posted results that fell short of analysts' expectations. Based on operating earnings yield, the company is overvalued when compared to all of the companies we cover. Share price changes over the past year indicates that BKD will perform in line with the market over the near term.

Financial Data

(US$ in Thousands)	9 Mos	6 Mos	3 Mos	12/31/2018	12/31/2017	12/31/2016	12/31/2015	12/31/2014
Earnings Per Share	(0.25)	(0.03)	(0.61)	(2.82)	(3.07)	(2.18)	(2.48)	(1.01)
Cash Flow Per Share	0.87	0.88	0.86	1.09	1.97	1.96	1.59	1.64
Tang Book Value Per Share	3.06	3.44	3.69	4.23	5.00	6.79	8.52	10.64
Income Statement								
Total Revenue	3,070,450	2,061,501	1,042,044	4,531,426	4,747,116	4,976,980	4,960,608	3,831,706
EBITDA	287,557	212,992	114,582	145,719	227,637	495,966	558,601	445,043
Depn & Amortn	281,428	188,528	95,702	444,300	479,400	514,200	721,000	529,100
Income Before Taxes	(174,083)	(95,832)	(41,401)	(569,004)	(573,294)	(400,918)	(549,560)	(330,902)
Income Taxes	(488)	1,312	679	(49,456)	(16,515)	5,378	(92,209)	(181,305)
Net Income	(176,523)	(98,065)	(42,595)	(528,258)	(571,419)	(404,397)	(457,477)	(148,990)
Average Shares	185,516	186,140	186,747	187,468	186,155	185,653	184,333	148,185
Balance Sheet								
Current Assets	628,500	655,929	750,624	774,016	901,872	619,504	497,943	614,789
Total Assets	7,374,203	7,459,482	7,630,773	6,467,260	7,675,449	9,217,687	10,048,564	10,521,363
Current Liabilities	1,058,060	969,598	1,101,724	773,331	1,095,776	731,142	840,148	877,762
Long-Term Obligations	5,343,562	5,447,341	5,429,935	4,197,095	4,539,790	5,829,912	6,196,809	5,993,691
Total Liabilities	6,585,837	6,598,758	6,712,675	5,448,357	6,144,721	7,139,705	7,589,676	7,639,639
Stockholders' Equity	788,366	860,724	918,098	1,018,903	1,530,728	2,077,982	2,458,888	2,881,724
Shares Outstanding	193,073	193,110	194,573	192,356	191,275	190,045	188,338	187,037
Statistical Record								
EBITDA Margin %	9.37	10.33	11.00	3.22	4.80	9.97	11.26	11.61
Asset Turnover	0.60	0.60	0.59	0.64	0.56	0.52	0.48	0.50
Current Ratio	0.59	0.68	0.68	1.00	0.82	0.85	0.59	0.70
Debt to Equity	6.78	6.33	5.91	4.12	2.97	2.81	2.52	2.08
Price Range	9.62-6.02	10.05-6.02	10.05-6.33	10.26-6.33	16.27-8.81	19.30-11.27	38.74-17.69	36.86-26.37

Address: 111 Westwood Place, Suite 400, Brentwood, TN 37027 **Telephone:** 615-221-2250	**Web Site:** www.brookdale.com **Officers:** Lucinda M. (Cindy) Baier - President, Chief Executive Officer, Chief Financial Officer T. Andrew (Andy) Smith - President, Chief Executive Officer, Executive Vice President, General Counsel, Secretary	**Auditors:** Ernst & Young LLP **Investor Contact:** 615-564-8104 **Transfer Agents:** American Stock Transfer & Trust Company, New York, NY

BROWN & BROWN INC

Exchange	Symbol	Price	52Wk Range	Yield	P/E	Div Acheiver
NYS	BRO	$39.48 (12/31/2019)	40.25-26.73	0.86	28.20	25 Years

*7 Year Price Score 129.25 *NYSE Composite Index=100 **12 Month Price Score 108.28

Interim Earnings (Per Share)

Qtr.	Mar	Jun	Sep	Dec
2016	0.22	0.23	0.25	0.20
2017	0.25	0.23	0.27	0.66
2018	0.32	0.26	0.38	0.26
2019	0.40	0.33	0.41	....

Interim Dividends (Per Share)

Amt	Decl	Ex	Rec	Pay
0.08Q	01/24/2019	02/05/2019	02/06/2019	02/20/2019
0.08Q	04/22/2019	05/07/2019	05/08/2019	05/17/2019
0.08Q	07/18/2019	08/06/2019	08/07/2019	08/14/2019
0.085Q	10/24/2019	11/07/2019	11/08/2019	11/20/2019

Indicated Div: $0.34

Valuation Analysis

		Institutional Holding	
Forecast EPS	$1.38	No of Institutions	
	(01/16/2020)	509	
Market Cap	$11.2 Billion	Shares	
Book Value	$3.3 Billion	228,470,160	
Price/Book	3.36	% Held	
Price/Sales	4.80	71.47	

Business Summary: Brokers & Intermediaries (MIC: 5.2.3 SIC: 6411 NAIC: 524210)

Brown & Brown is an insurance agency, wholesale brokerage, insurance programs and service organization. Co. markets and sells insurance products and services, primarily in the property, casualty and employee benefits areas. Co.'s segments are Retail, which sells commercial packages, group medical, workers' compensation, property risk and general liability insurance; National Programs, which provides Professional Programs, Personal Lines Programs, Commercial Programs, Public Entity-Related Programs, and National Flood Program; Wholesale Brokerage, which markets and sells excess and surplus commercial insurance products and services; and Services, which provides insurance-related services.

Recent Developments: For the quarter ended Sep 30 2019, net income increased 8.9% to US$115.5 million from US$106.1 million in the year-earlier quarter. Revenues were US$618.7 million, up 16.5% from US$530.9 million the year before.

Prospects: Our evaluation of Brown & Brown Inc. as of October 4th, 2019 is the result of our systematic analysis on three basic characteristics: earnings strength, relative valuation, and recent stock price movement. The company has managed to produce a neutral trend in earnings per share over the past 5 quarters. Additionally, recent analyst estimates for the company have been unchanged while BRO has posted results that exceeded analysts' expectations. Based on operating earnings yield, the company is fairly valued when compared to all of the companies we cover. Share price changes over the past year indicates that BRO will perform well over the near term.

Financial Data

(US$ in Thousands)	9 Mos	6 Mos	3 Mos	12/31/2018	12/31/2017	12/31/2016	12/31/2015	12/31/2014
Earnings Per Share	1.40	1.37	1.30	1.22	1.41	0.91	0.85	0.70
Cash Flow Per Share	2.41	2.19	1.81	2.09	1.62	1.37	1.49	1.37
Dividends Per Share	0.320	0.315	0.310	0.305	0.278	0.251	0.226	0.205
Dividend Payout %	22.86	22.99	23.85	25.00	19.75	27.61	26.62	29.08
Income Statement								
Total Revenue	1,813,182	1,194,499	619,280	2,014,246	1,881,347	1,766,629	1,660,509	1,575,796
EBITDA	569,140	368,368	196,401	525,842	510,738	483,980	462,707	389,052
Depn & Amortn	97,455	64,835	32,683	22,800	22,700	21,000	20,900	20,895
Income Before Taxes	423,880	272,042	148,520	462,462	449,722	423,499	402,559	339,749
Income Taxes	101,885	65,553	34,624	118,207	50,092	166,008	159,241	132,853
Net Income	321,995	206,489	113,896	344,255	399,630	257,491	243,318	206,896
Average Shares	275,075	274,402	275,014	275,521	277,586	275,608	280,224	285,782
Balance Sheet								
Current Assets	2,606,937	2,291,548	1,994,748	2,167,311	2,242,156	1,760,737	1,537,389	1,570,108
Total Assets	7,680,664	7,164,767	6,806,289	6,688,668	5,747,550	5,287,343	5,012,739	4,956,458
Current Liabilities	2,148,924	1,907,110	1,647,073	1,782,986	1,987,474	1,445,157	1,328,547	1,269,153
Long-Term Obligations	1,513,560	1,426,777	1,439,998	1,456,990	856,141	1,018,372	1,079,878	1,152,846
Total Liabilities	4,366,141	3,984,136	3,707,858	3,688,100	3,164,851	2,927,132	2,862,963	2,842,713
Stockholders' Equity	3,314,523	3,180,631	3,098,431	3,000,568	2,582,699	2,360,211	2,149,776	2,113,745
Shares Outstanding	282,498	281,456	282,048	279,583	276,210	280,208	277,970	286,972
Statistical Record								
Return on Assets %	5.87	6.00	5.91	5.54	7.24	4.99	4.88	4.81
Return on Equity %	12.65	12.84	12.52	12.33	16.17	11.39	11.41	10.04
EBITDA Margin %	31.39	30.84	31.71	26.11	27.15	27.40	27.87	24.69
Net Margin %	17.76	17.29	18.39	17.09	21.24	14.58	14.65	13.13
Asset Turnover	0.34	0.35	0.34	0.32	0.34	0.34	0.33	0.37
Current Ratio	1.21	1.20	1.21	1.22	1.13	1.22	1.16	1.24
Debt to Equity	0.46	0.45	0.46	0.49	0.33	0.43	0.50	0.55
Price Range	36.89-26.07	33.50-26.07	31.34-24.84	31.34-24.84	25.97-20.66	22.56-14.44	17.23-15.37	16.63-14.14
P/E Ratio	26.35-18.62	24.45-19.03	24.11-19.11	25.69-20.36	18.41-14.65	24.79-15.86	20.28-18.08	23.76-20.20
Average Yield %	1.03	1.07	1.09	1.10	1.22	1.38	1.39	1.32

Address: 220 South Ridgewood Avenue, Daytona Beach, FL 32114 **Telephone:** 386-252-9601	**Web Site:** www.bbinsurance.com **Officers:** J. Hyatt Brown - Chairman James C. Hays - Vice-Chairman	**Auditors:** DELOITTE & TOUCHE LLP **Investor Contact:** 386-252-9601 **Transfer Agents:** American Stock Transfer & Trust Co., Brooklyn, NY

BROWN-FORMAN CORP

Exchange	Symbol	Price	52Wk Range	Yield	P/E	Div Acheiver
NYS	BF B	$67.60 (12/31/2019)	68.81-45.35	1.03	37.98	34 Years

*7 Year Price Score 111.82 ***NYSE Composite Index=100** ***12 Month Price Score 111.20**

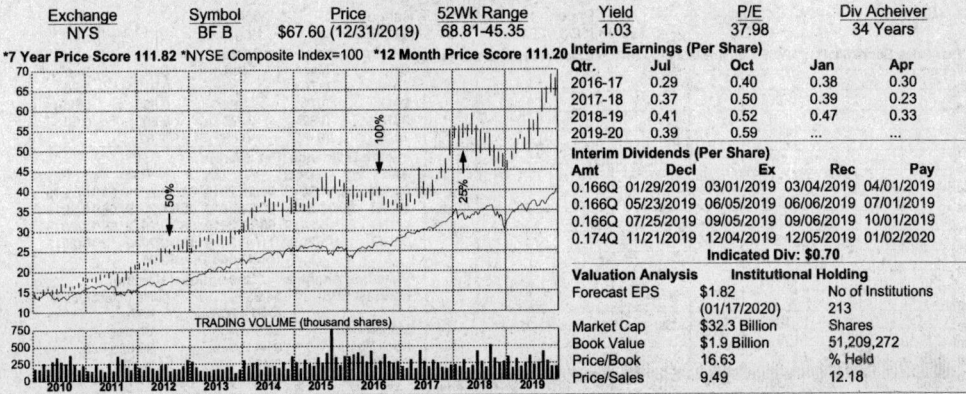

Interim Earnings (Per Share)

Qtr.	Jul	Oct	Jan	Apr
2016-17	0.29	0.40	0.38	0.30
2017-18	0.37	0.50	0.39	0.23
2018-19	0.41	0.52	0.47	0.33
2019-20	0.39	0.59	...	...

Interim Dividends (Per Share)

Amt	Decl	Ex	Rec	Pay
0.166Q	01/29/2019	03/01/2019	03/04/2019	04/01/2019
0.166Q	05/23/2019	06/05/2019	06/06/2019	07/01/2019
0.166Q	07/25/2019	09/05/2019	09/06/2019	10/01/2019
0.174Q	11/21/2019	12/04/2019	12/05/2019	01/02/2020

Indicated Div: $0.70

Valuation Analysis **Institutional Holding**

Forecast EPS	$1.82	No of Institutions
	(01/17/2020)	213
Market Cap	$32.3 Billion	Shares
Book Value	$1.9 Billion	51,209,272
Price/Book	16.63	% Held
Price/Sales	9.49	12.18

Business Summary: Beverages (MIC: 1.2.2 SIC: 2084 NAIC: 312130)

Brown-Forman primarily manufactures, bottles, imports, exports, markets, and sells a variety of alcoholic beverages under various brands. Co. has a portfolio of spirit, ready-to-drink (RTD) cocktail, and wine brands. Co.'s principal brands are: Jack Daniel's Tennessee Whiskey, Jack Daniel's RTDs, Jack Daniel's Tennessee Honey, Gentleman Jack Rare Tennessee Whiskey, Jack Daniel's Tennessee Fire, Jack Daniel's Single Barrel Collection, Jack Daniel's Tennessee Rye, Jack Daniel's Sinatra Select, Jack Daniel's No. 27 Gold Tennessee Whiskey, Jack Daniel's Bottled-in-Bond, Woodford Reserve Kentucky Bourbon, Woodford Reserve Double Oaked, Woodford Reserve Kentucky Rye Whiskey, and Finlandia Vodkas.

Recent Developments: For the quarter ended Oct 31 2019, net income increased 13.3% to US$282.0 million from US$249.0 million in the year-earlier quarter. Revenues were US$989.0 million, up 8.7% from US$910.0 million the year before. Operating income was US$352.0 million versus US$332.0 million in the prior-year quarter, an increase of 6.0%. Direct operating expenses rose 15.6% to US$370.0 million from US$320.0 million in the comparable period the year before. Indirect operating expenses increased 3.5% to US$267.0 million from US$258.0 million in the equivalent prior-year period.

Prospects: Our evaluation of Brown-Forman Corp. as of October 4th, 2019 is the result of our systematic analysis on three basic characteristics: earnings strength, relative valuation, and recent stock price movement. The company has managed to produce a neutral trend in earnings per share over the past 5 quarters. Additionally, recent analyst estimates for the company have been unchanged while BF.B has posted results that exceeded analysts' expectations. Based on operating earnings yield, the company is fairly valued when compared to all of the companies we cover. Share price changes over the past year indicates that BF.B will perform well over the near term.

Financial Data

(US$ in Thousands)	6 Mos	3 Mos	04/30/2019	04/30/2018	04/30/2017	04/30/2016	04/30/2015	04/30/2014
Earnings Per Share	1.78	1.71	1.73	1.48	1.37	2.09	1.28	1.22
Cash Flow Per Share	1.50	1.56	1.65	1.32	1.32	1.03	1.15	1.22
Tang Book Value Per Share	1.10	0.53	0.52	N.M.	N.M.	0.76	1.32	1.38
Dividends Per Share	0.664	0.656	1.648	1.608	1.172	0.524	0.484	0.436
Dividend Payout %	37.30	38.36	95.26	108.65	85.55	25.10	37.69	35.62
Income Statement								
Total Revenue	1,755,000	766,000	3,324,000	3,248,000	2,994,000	3,089,000	3,134,000	2,991,000
EBITDA	634,000	265,000	1,194,000	1,103,000	1,047,000	1,589,000	1,078,000	1,021,000
Depn & Amortn	36,000	18,000	72,000	64,000	58,000	56,000	51,000	50,000
Income Before Taxes	559,000	228,000	1,042,000	977,000	933,000	1,489,000	1,002,000	947,000
Income Taxes	91,000	42,000	207,000	260,000	264,000	422,000	318,000	288,000
Net Income	468,000	186,000	835,000	717,000	669,000	1,067,000	684,000	659,000
Average Shares	480,481	480,088	488,077	484,248	488,076	510,700	532,707	537,705
Balance Sheet								
Current Assets	3,039,000	2,837,000	2,719,000	2,555,000	2,351,000	2,233,000	2,254,000	2,177,000
Total Assets	5,553,000	5,322,000	5,139,000	4,976,000	4,625,000	4,183,000	4,193,000	4,103,000
Current Liabilities	771,000	867,000	703,000	821,000	970,000	791,000	958,000	561,000
Long-Term Obligations	2,288,000	2,267,000	2,290,000	2,341,000	1,689,000	1,230,000	748,000	997,000
Total Liabilities	3,611,000	3,659,000	3,492,000	3,660,000	3,255,000	2,621,000	2,288,000	2,071,000
Stockholders' Equity	1,942,000	1,663,000	1,647,000	1,316,000	1,370,000	1,562,000	1,905,000	2,032,000
Shares Outstanding	477,818	477,539	477,172	481,001	480,107	494,355	521,750	533,637
Statistical Record								
Return on Assets %	15.96	15.87	16.51	14.94	15.19	25.41	16.49	17.05
Return on Equity %	49.67	54.17	56.36	53.39	45.63	61.38	34.75	36.01
EBITDA Margin %	36.13	34.60	35.92	33.96	34.97	51.44	34.40	34.14
Net Margin %	26.67	24.28	25.12	22.08	22.34	34.54	21.83	22.03
Asset Turnover	0.64	0.64	0.66	0.68	0.68	0.74	0.76	0.77
Current Ratio	3.94	3.27	3.87	3.11	2.42	2.82	2.35	3.88
Debt to Equity	1.18	1.36	1.39	1.78	1.23	0.79	0.39	0.49
Price Range	65.52-45.35	57.58-45.35	59.22-45.35	56.52-37.82	40.85-35.17	44.32-36.09	38.82-33.44	36.19-26.60
P/E Ratio	36.81-25.48	33.67-26.52	34.23-26.21	38.19-25.55	29.82-25.67	21.21-17.27	30.33-26.13	29.67-21.80
Average Yield %	1.24	1.29	3.15	3.43	3.08	1.31	1.33	1.45

Address: 850 Dixie Highway, Louisville, KY 40210
Telephone: 502-585-1100
Fax: 502-774-7876

Web Site: www.brown-forman.com
Officers: Geo. Garvin Brown - Chairman, Executive Vice President Lawson E. Whiting - President, Executive Vice President, Senior Vice President, Chief Executive Officer, Chief Operating Officer, Chief Brands Officer, Chief Strategy Officer

Auditors: PricewaterhouseCoopers LLP
Transfer Agents: Computershare, Providence, RI

BRUNSWICK CORP.

Exchange	Symbol	Price	52Wk Range	Yield	P/E
NYS	BC	$59.98 (12/31/2019)	61.57-41.48	1.60	N/A

*7 Year Price Score 84.41 *NYSE Composite Index=100 *12 Month Price Score 110.63

Interim Earnings (Per Share)

Qtr.	Mar	Jun	Sep	Dec
2016	0.70	1.17	0.93	0.20
2017	0.71	1.32	0.88	(1.29)
2018	0.82	0.90	0.80	0.50
2019	(0.42)	0.89	(2.82)	...

Interim Dividends (Per Share)

Amt	Decl	Ex	Rec	Pay
0.21Q	02/14/2019	02/25/2019	02/26/2019	03/15/2019
0.21Q	05/08/2019	05/20/2019	05/21/2019	06/14/2019
0.21Q	07/16/2019	08/19/2019	08/20/2019	09/13/2019
0.24Q	10/15/2019	11/18/2019	11/19/2019	12/13/2019

Indicated Div: $0.96

Valuation Analysis | **Institutional Holding**

Forecast EPS	$4.25	No of Institutions
	(01/17/2020)	492
Market Cap	$4.9 Billion	Shares
Book Value	$1.4 Billion	99,685,728
Price/Book	3.49	% Held
Price/Sales	1.06	91.15

Business Summary: Leisure Equipment (MIC: 1.6.1 SIC: 3511 NAIC: 333611)

Brunswick is a designer, manufacturer, and marketer of recreation products including marine engines, boats, fitness equipment, and active recreation products. Co.'s segments include: Marine Engine, which manufactures and markets a range of outboard, sterndrive, and inboard engine and propulsion systems; Boat, which manufactures and markets fiberglass sport boats, cruisers, pontoon, utility, deck, inflatable, and heavy-gauge aluminum, among others; and Fitness, which designs, manufactures, and distributes a portfolio of cardiovascular fitness equipment (including treadmills, total body cross-trainers, stair climbers, and stationary exercise bicycles) and strength-training equipment.

Recent Developments: For the quarter ended Sep 28 2019, loss from continuing operations was US$232.9 million compared with income of US$75.2 million in the year-earlier quarter. Net loss amounted to US$239.3 million versus net income of US$70.0 million in the year-earlier quarter. Revenues were US$976.6 million, down 6.5% from US$1.04 billion the year before. Operating income was US$119.7 million versus US$98.2 million in the prior-year quarter, an increase of 21.9%. Direct operating expenses declined 8.6% to US$699.7 million from US$765.8 million in the comparable period the year before. Indirect operating expenses decreased 12.7% to US$157.2 million from US$180.1 million in the equivalent prior-year period.

Prospects: Our evaluation of Brunswick Corp. as of October 4th, 2019 is the result of our systematic analysis on three basic characteristics: earnings strength, relative valuation, and recent stock price movement. The company has generated a negative trend in earnings per share over the past 5 quarters. However, recent analyst estimates for the company have been unchanged while BC has posted results that exceeded analysts' expectations. Based on operating earnings yield, the company is undervalued when compared to all of the companies we cover. Share price changes over the past year indicates that BC will perform very poorly over the near term.

Financial Data

(US$ in Thousands)	9 Mos	6 Mos	3 Mos	12/31/2018	12/31/2017	12/31/2016	12/31/2015	12/31/2014
Earnings Per Share	(1.85)	1.77	1.78	3.01	1.62	3.00	2.56	2.58
Cash Flow Per Share	3.76	3.17	3.71	3.85	4.48	4.61	3.48	2.53
Tang Book Value Per Share	5.01	6.15	2.94	1.95	10.43	9.65	10.21	8.94
Dividends Per Share	0.840	0.820	0.800	0.780	0.685	0.615	0.525	0.450
Dividend Payout %	...	46.33	44.94	25.91	42.28	20.50	20.51	17.44
Income Statement								
Total Revenue	3,190,800	2,214,200	1,275,900	5,159,200	4,510,000	4,488,500	4,105,700	3,838,700
EBITDA	202,300	341,500	9,600	507,200	450,800	508,200	423,000	393,000
Depn & Amortn	101,500	66,400	39,800	149,600	89,800	97,100	85,900	78,300
Income Before Taxes	43,800	235,300	(49,600)	314,500	337,200	385,400	311,500	286,100
Income Taxes	93,800	50,500	(11,400)	59,100	156,000	115,300	87,800	93,000
Net Income	(198,100)	41,200	(36,300)	265,300	146,400	276,000	241,400	245,700
Average Shares	85,000	87,300	87,500	88,200	90,100	92,000	94,300	95,100
Balance Sheet								
Current Assets	1,693,600	2,011,400	1,937,800	1,880,200	1,846,700	1,688,500	1,984,900	1,967,800
Total Assets	3,654,400	4,040,800	4,329,800	4,285,700	3,358,200	3,284,700	3,152,500	3,134,400
Current Liabilities	904,000	1,015,700	1,205,700	1,256,500	1,035,100	964,900	908,100	900,100
Long-Term Obligations	1,152,700	1,307,200	1,329,400	1,179,500	431,800	436,500	442,500	450,200
Total Liabilities	2,236,200	2,503,500	2,802,900	2,703,100	1,875,300	1,844,600	1,871,200	1,962,900
Stockholders' Equity	1,418,200	1,537,300	1,526,900	1,582,600	1,482,900	1,440,100	1,281,300	1,171,500
Shares Outstanding	82,406	85,687	87,063	86,757	87,537	89,317	90,813	92,694
Statistical Record								
Return on Assets %	N.M.	4.14	4.04	6.94	4.41	8.55	7.68	8.12
Return on Equity %	N.M.	10.18	10.38	17.31	10.02	20.23	19.68	22.24
EBITDA Margin %	6.34	15.42	0.75	9.83	10.00	11.32	10.30	10.24
Net Margin %	N.M.	1.86	N.M.	5.14	3.25	6.15	5.88	6.40
Asset Turnover	1.19	1.34	1.35	1.35	1.36	1.39	1.31	1.27
Current Ratio	1.87	1.98	1.61	1.50	1.78	1.75	2.19	2.19
Debt to Equity	0.81	0.85	0.87	0.75	0.29	0.30	0.35	0.38
Price Range	67.02-41.48	69.22-41.48	69.22-42.61	69.22-42.61	63.42-48.63	56.03-37.98	56.39-46.50	51.94-38.95
P/E Ratio	...	39.11-23.44	38.89-23.94	23.00-14.16	39.15-30.02	18.68-12.66	22.03-18.16	20.13-15.10
Average Yield %	1.68	1.50	1.37	1.29	1.20	1.31	1.01	1.03

Address: 26125 N. Riverwoods Blvd., Suite 500, Mettawa, IL 60045-3420 Telephone: 847-735-4700	Web Site: www.brunswick.com Officers: Manuel A. (Manny) Fernandez - Chairman William L. Metzger - Senior Vice President, Chief Financial Officer, Vice President, Treasurer	Auditors: DELOITTE & TOUCHE LLP Investor Contact: 847-735-4612 Transfer Agents: ComputerShare Investor Services, Providence, RI

BUNGE LTD.

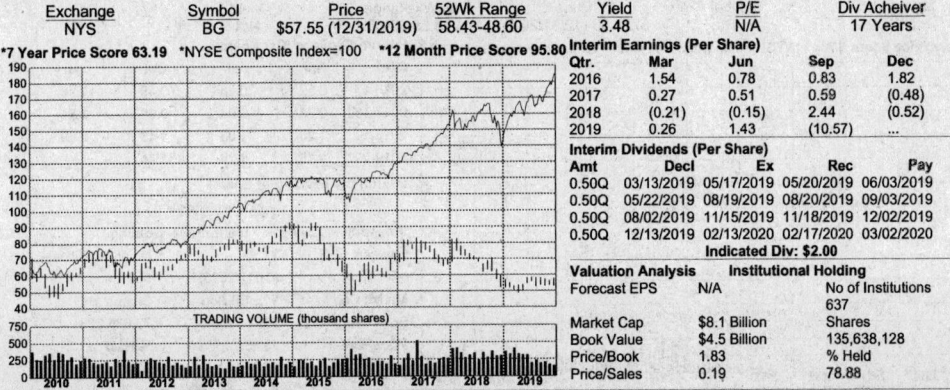

Exchange	Symbol	Price	52Wk Range	Yield	P/E	Div Acheiver
NYS	BG	$57.55 (12/31/2019)	58.43-48.60	3.48	N/A	17 Years

*7 Year Price Score 63.19   *NYSE Composite Index=100   *12 Month Price Score 95.80

Interim Earnings (Per Share)

Qtr.	Mar	Jun	Sep	Dec
2016	1.54	0.78	0.83	1.82
2017	0.27	0.51	0.59	(0.48)
2018	(0.21)	(0.15)	2.44	(0.52)
2019	0.26	1.43	(10.57)	...

Interim Dividends (Per Share)

Amt	Decl	Ex	Rec	Pay
0.50Q	03/13/2019	05/17/2019	05/20/2019	06/03/2019
0.50Q	05/22/2019	08/19/2019	08/20/2019	09/03/2019
0.50Q	08/02/2019	11/15/2019	11/18/2019	12/02/2019
0.50Q	12/13/2019	02/13/2020	02/17/2020	03/02/2020

Indicated Div: $2.00

Valuation Analysis   **Institutional Holding**

Forecast EPS	N/A	No of Institutions: 637
Market Cap	$8.1 Billion	Shares
Book Value	$4.5 Billion	135,638,128
Price/Book	1.83	% Held
Price/Sales	0.19	78.88

Business Summary: Food (MIC: 1.2.1 SIC: 2079 NAIC: 311225)

Bunge is a holding company. Through its subsidiaries, Co. is an agribusiness and food company. Co.'s segments include: Agribusiness, which is principally involved in the purchase, storage, transportation, processing and sale of agricultural commodities and commodity products; Food and Ingredients, which consist of two reportable business segments: edible oil and milling products; Sugar and Bioenergy, which produces and sells sugar and ethanol derived from sugarcane, as well as energy derived from the sugar and ethanol production process; and Fertilizer, which is involved in producing, blending and distributing fertilizer products for the agricultural industry in South America.

Recent Developments: For the quarter ended Sep 30 2019, loss from continuing operations was US$1.48 billion compared with income of US$367.0 million in the year-earlier quarter. Net loss amounted to US$1.48 billion versus net income of US$374.0 million in the year-earlier quarter. Revenues were US$10.32 billion, down 9.5% from US$11.41 billion the year before. Direct operating expenses rose 7.7% to US$11.30 billion from US$10.49 billion in the comparable period the year before. Indirect operating expenses decreased 1.2% to US$329.0 million from US$333.0 million in the equivalent prior-year period.

Prospects: Our evaluation of Bunge Ltd. as of October 4th, 2019 is the result of our systematic analysis on three basic characteristics: earnings strength, relative valuation, and recent stock price movement. The company has suffered a very negative trend in earnings per share over the past 5 quarters. However, recent analyst estimates for the company have been mixed and BG has posted results that exceeded analysts' expectations. Based on operating earnings yield, the company is fairly valued when compared to all of the companies we cover. Share price changes over the past year indicates that BG will perform poorly over the near term.

Financial Data

(US$ in Millions)	9 Mos	6 Mos	3 Mos	12/31/2018	12/31/2017	12/31/2016	12/31/2015	12/31/2014
Earnings Per Share	(9.40)	3.61	2.03	1.64	0.89	5.01	5.07	3.17
Cash Flow Per Share	5.00	7.00	(0.88)	(8.97)	7.17	13.58	4.25	9.57
Tang Book Value Per Share	17.40	33.18	28.49	28.76	39.96	41.18	35.14	49.08
Dividends Per Share	2.000	2.000	2.000	1.960	1.760	1.600	1.440	1.280
Dividend Payout %	...	55.40	98.52	119.51	197.75	31.94	28.40	40.38
Income Statement								
Total Revenue	30,357	20,034	9,938	45,743	45,794	42,679	43,455	57,161
EBITDA	(495)	803	295	1,329	1,035	1,696	1,784	1,570
Depn & Amortn	428	294	139	565	580	-517	518	576
Income Before Taxes	(1,150)	360	88	456	230	996	1,051	734
Income Taxes	70	98	38	179	56	220	296	249
Net Income	(1,229)	259	45	267	160	745	791	515
Average Shares	141	150	141	141	141	148	152	147
Balance Sheet								
Current Assets	10,826	11,107	11,239	11,068	10,403	11,092	10,916	13,081
Total Assets	18,634	20,424	20,535	19,425	18,871	19,188	17,922	21,432
Current Liabilities	7,369	7,457	8,053	7,172	6,215	7,684	7,340	8,704
Long-Term Obligations	4,581	4,039	3,821	4,203	4,160	3,069	2,934	2,855
Total Liabilities	14,174	14,093	14,435	13,252	11,723	12,044	11,481	12,986
Stockholders' Equity	4,460	6,331	6,100	6,173	7,148	7,144	6,441	8,446
Shares Outstanding	141	128	141	141	140	139	142	145
Statistical Record								
Return on Assets %	N.M.	2.63	1.53	1.39	0.84	4.00	4.02	2.14
Return on Equity %	N.M.	8.96	5.06	4.01	2.24	10.94	10.63	5.63
EBITDA Margin %	N.M.	4.01	2.97	2.91	2.26	3.97	4.11	2.75
Net Margin %	N.M.	1.29	0.45	0.58	0.35	1.75	1.82	0.90
Asset Turnover	2.09	2.02	2.07	2.39	2.41	2.29	2.21	2.37
Current Ratio	1.47	1.49	1.40	1.54	1.67	1.44	1.49	1.50
Debt to Equity	1.03	0.64	0.63	0.68	0.58	0.43	0.46	0.34
Price Range	70.77-48.60	70.77-48.60	75.70-50.23	82.55-52.06	83.22-65.15	73.61-47.79	92.85-61.81	92.91-73.51
P/E Ratio	...	19.60-13.46	37.29-24.74	50.34-31.74	93.51-73.20	14.69-9.54	18.31-12.19	29.31-23.19
Average Yield %	...	3.41	3.16	2.85	2.39	2.59	1.79	1.58

Address: 50 Main Street, White Plains, NY 10606 **Telephone:** 914-684-2800	**Web Site:** www.bunge.com **Officers:** Gregory A. Heckman - Chief Executive Officer, Acting Chief Executive Officer Deborah Borg - Executive Vice President, Chief Human Resources Officer, Chief Communications Officer	**Auditors:** Deloitte & Touche LLP **Investor Contact:** 914-684-2800 **Transfer Agents:** Computershare Investor Services LLC

BURLINGTON STORES INC

Exchange	Symbol	Price	52Wk Range	Yield	P/E
NYS	BURL	$228.03 (12/31/2019)	229.58-139.89	N/A	34.87

*7 Year Price Score N/A   *NYSE Composite Index=100   *12 Month Price Score 113.62

Interim Earnings (Per Share)

Qtr.	Apr	Jul	Oct	Jan
2016-17	0.52	0.28	0.45	1.76
2017-18	0.73	0.66	0.65	3.44
2018-19	1.20	1.03	1.12	2.69
2019-20	1.15	1.26	1.44	...

Interim Dividends (Per Share)

No Dividends Paid

Valuation Analysis

		Institutional Holding	
Forecast EPS	$7.33	No of Institutions	
	(01/17/2020)	552	
Market Cap	$15.1 Billion	Shares	
Book Value	$391.6 Million	78,635,328	
Price/Book	38.58	% Held	
Price/Sales	2.13	90.12	

Business Summary: Retail - Apparel and Accessories (MIC: 2.1.5 SIC: 5311 NAIC: 452111)

Burlington Stores is a holding company. Through its indirect subsidiary, Burlington Coat Factory Warehouse Corporation sells merchandise including: women's ready-to-wear apparel, accessories, footwear, menswear, youth apparel, baby, home, coats, beauty, toys and gifts. Co. operates stores under the names Burlington Stores, Cohoes Fashions, Super Baby Depot, MJM Designer Shoes and an online store. Cohoes Fashions provides products similar to those offered by Burlington Stores. MJM Designer Shoes provides moderately priced designer and fashion shoes. The Super Baby Depot stores provides baby clothing, accessories, furniture and other merchandise in the middle to higher price range.

Recent Developments: For the quarter ended Nov 2 2019, net income increased 25.5% to US$96.5 million from US$76.8 million in the year-earlier quarter. Revenues were US$1.78 billion, up 8.6% from US$1.64 billion the year before. Direct operating expenses rose 8.3% to US$1.02 billion from US$944.4 million in the comparable period the year before. Indirect operating expenses increased 5.8% to US$639.2 million from US$604.5 million in the equivalent prior-year period.

Prospects: Our evaluation of Burlington Stores Inc as of October 4th, 2019 is the result of our systematic analysis on three basic characteristics: earnings strength, relative valuation, and recent stock price movement. The company has generated a negative trend in earnings per share over the past 5 quarters. However, recent analyst estimates for the company have been raised and BURL has posted results that exceeded analysts' expectations. Based on operating earnings yield, the company is fairly valued when compared to all of the companies we cover. Share price changes over the past year indicates that BURL will perform well over the near term.

Financial Data

(US$ in Thousands)	9 Mos	6 Mos	3 Mos	02/02/2019	02/03/2018	01/28/2017	01/30/2016	01/31/2015
Earnings Per Share	6.54	6.22	5.99	6.04	5.48	3.01	1.99	0.87
Cash Flow Per Share	11.24	10.66	9.59	9.60	8.75	8.57	4.43	4.09
Tang Book Value Per Share	1.60	0.44	N.M.	N.M.	N.M.	...	...	...
Income Statement								
Total Revenue	5,077,799	3,296,216	1,634,194	6,668,479	6,110,043	5,590,950	5,129,843	4,849,634
EBITDA	348,992	217,124	107,661	758,774	669,257	551,073	448,175	336,981
Depn & Amortn	945	641	330	195,200	181,500	161,700	150,300	148,200
Income Before Taxes	309,093	189,678	93,960	507,584	428,980	333,212	238,876	105,036
Income Taxes	50,302	27,346	16,195	92,839	44,128	117,339	88,394	39,081
Net Income	258,791	162,332	77,765	414,745	384,852	215,873	150,482	65,955
Average Shares	67,159	67,274	67,730	68,679	70,288	71,721	75,443	75,865
Balance Sheet								
Current Assets	1,415,145	1,185,909	1,251,801	1,271,900	1,100,433	928,324	932,982	987,483
Total Assets	5,507,587	5,046,437	5,065,239	3,079,172	2,812,829	2,574,483	2,580,147	2,624,569
Current Liabilities	1,607,646	1,315,768	1,343,890	1,247,742	1,119,631	996,834	886,588	933,117
Long-Term Obligations	982,348	1,079,775	1,133,385	983,643	1,113,808	1,128,843	1,303,497	1,249,276
Total Liabilities	5,115,999	4,731,300	4,786,691	2,756,462	2,726,055	2,624,295	2,679,169	2,690,520
Stockholders' Equity	391,588	315,137	278,548	322,710	86,774	(49,812)	(99,022)	(65,951)
Shares Outstanding	66,249	66,270	66,366	67,145	67,871	70,180	72,071	75,254
Statistical Record								
Return on Assets %	10.17	10.62	10.39	14.12	14.06	8.40	5.80	2.52
Return on Equity %	151.51	180.83	210.31	203.13	2,048.74	...	...	...
EBITDA Margin %	6.87	6.59	6.59	11.38	10.95	9.86	8.74	6.95
Net Margin %	5.10	4.92	4.76	6.22	6.30	3.86	2.93	1.36
Asset Turnover	1.62	1.74	1.72	2.27	2.23	2.18	1.98	1.85
Current Ratio	0.88	0.90	0.93	1.02	0.98	0.93	1.05	1.06
Debt to Equity	2.51	3.43	4.07	3.05	12.84	...	...	...
Price Range	205.56-139.89	182.92-139.89	176.66-135.61	175.64-113.05	127.61-80.27	89.68-49.71	61.02-40.70	51.60-24.26
P/E Ratio	31.43-21.39	29.41-22.49	29.49-22.64	29.08-18.72	23.29-14.65	29.79-16.51	30.66-20.45	59.31-27.89

Address: 2006 Route 130 North, Burlington, NJ 08016 **Telephone:** 609-387-7800	**Web Site:** www.burlingtonstores.com **Officers:** Thomas A. Kingsbury - Executive Chairman, Chairman, President, Chief Executive Officer Jennifer Vecchio - President, Chief Merchandising Officer, Executive Vice President.	**Auditors:** Deloitte & Touche LLP **Transfer Agents:** American Stock Transfer & Trust Company, LLC, Brooklyn, NY

BWX TECHNOLOGIES INC

Exchange	Symbol	Price	52Wk Range	Yield	P/E
		$62.08 (12/31/2019)	63.70-38.10	1.10	29.01

*7 Year Price Score 113.39 *NYSE Composite Index=100 *12 Month Price Score 108.42

Interim Earnings (Per Share)

Qtr.	Mar	Jun	Sep	Dec
2016	0.46	0.55	0.39	0.36
2017	0.55	0.61	0.46	(0.16)
2018	0.66	0.60	0.78	0.23
2019	0.51	0.62	0.78	...

Interim Dividends (Per Share)

Amt	Decl	Ex	Rec	Pay
0.17Q	02/22/2019	03/08/2019	03/11/2019	03/28/2019
0.17Q	05/01/2019	05/16/2019	05/17/2019	06/06/2019
0.17Q	07/30/2019	08/15/2019	08/16/2019	09/06/2019
0.17Q	11/04/2019	11/19/2019	11/20/2019	12/13/2019

Indicated Div: $0.68

Valuation Analysis / **Institutional Holding**

Forecast EPS	$2.55	No of Institutions
	(01/17/2020)	393
Market Cap	$5.9 Billion	Shares
Book Value	$354.5 Million	117,975,912
Price/Book	16.68	% Held
Price/Sales	3.16	N/A

Business Summary: Industrial Machinery & Equipment (MIC: 7.2.1 SIC: 3511 NAIC: 333611)

BWX Technologies is a manufacturer of nuclear components, a developer of nuclear technologies and a service provider. Co. operates three segments: Nuclear Operations Group, which engineers, designs and manufactures precision naval nuclear components, reactors and nuclear fuel for the U.S. Department of Energy/National Nuclear Security Administration's Naval Nuclear Propulsion Program; Nuclear Services Group, which provides services including nuclear materials processing and management and operating services; and Nuclear Power Group, which designs and manufactures commercial nuclear steam generators, heat exchangers, pressure vessels, reactor components and other auxiliary equipment.

Recent Developments: For the quarter ended Sep 30 2019, net income decreased 3.9% to US$75.0 million from US$78.1 million in the year-earlier quarter. Revenues were US$506.0 million, up 18.9% from US$425.5 million the year before. Operating income was US$98.5 million versus US$50.4 million in the prior-year quarter, an increase of 95.4%. Direct operating expenses rose 9.6% to US$357.7 million from US$326.3 million in the comparable period the year before. Indirect operating expenses increased 2.1% to US$49.8 million from US$48.8 million in the equivalent prior-year period.

Prospects: Our evaluation of BWX Technologies Inc. as of October 4th, 2019 is the result of our systematic analysis on three basic characteristics: earnings strength, relative valuation, and recent stock price movement. The company has managed to produce a neutral trend in earnings per share over the past 5 quarters. Additionally, recent analyst estimates for the company have been unchanged while BWXT has posted results that exceeded analysts' expectations. Based on operating earnings yield, the company is fairly valued when compared to all of the companies we cover. Share price changes over the past year indicates that BWXT will perform in line with the market over the near term.

Financial Data

(US$ in Thousands)	9 Mos	6 Mos	3 Mos	12/31/2018	12/31/2017	12/31/2016	12/31/2015	12/31/2014
Earnings Per Share	2.14	2.14	2.12	2.27	1.47	1.76	1.22	0.27
Cash Flow Per Share	2.82	2.09	1.79	1.71	2.24	2.33	3.09	0.69
Tang Book Value Per Share	N.M.	N.M.	N.M.	N.M.	N.M.	N.M.	0.37	4.77
Dividends Per Share	0.670	0.660	0.650	0.640	0.420	0.360	0.320	0.400
Dividend Payout %	31.31	30.84	30.66	28.19	28.57	20.45	26.23	148.15
Income Statement								
Total Revenue	1,393,685	887,685	416,454	1,799,889	1,687,738	1,550,573	1,415,529	2,923,019
EBITDA	285,046	174,593	78,605	323,746	342,942	297,341	242,819	63,161
Depn & Amortn	46,028	30,833	15,122	48,600	47,300	48,400	55,300	92,900
Income Before Taxes	212,699	126,067	55,195	249,802	282,168	241,199	207,669	(36,290)
Income Taxes	52,009	32,501	13,767	52,840	147,415	73,656	80,416	(15,991)
Net Income	182,666	107,856	48,978	226,958	147,844	183,057	131,465	29,388
Average Shares	95,811	95,677	95,821	100,019	100,369	103,840	107,583	108,761
Balance Sheet								
Current Assets	621,450	587,380	577,564	542,448	873,090	693,571	647,294	1,473,802
Total Assets	1,826,420	1,756,480	1,716,786	1,655,096	1,712,339	1,579,815	1,382,139	2,856,936
Current Liabilities	333,740	315,392	325,760	377,348	528,126	439,876	353,780	819,636
Long-Term Obligations	849,589	855,690	856,005	753,617	481,059	497,724	285,000	285,000
Total Liabilities	1,471,944	1,462,350	1,473,937	1,419,434	1,426,945	1,429,797	1,116,423	1,858,232
Stockholders' Equity	354,476	294,130	242,849	235,662	285,394	150,018	265,716	998,704
Shares Outstanding	95,250	95,167	95,135	95,246	99,417	99,290	105,297	106,688
Statistical Record								
Return on Assets %	11.49	11.87	12.87	13.48	8.98	12.33	6.20	1.08
Return on Equity %	54.78	60.88	71.26	87.11	67.91	87.82	20.79	2.72
EBITDA Margin %	20.45	19.67	18.87	17.99	20.32	19.18	17.15	2.16
Net Margin %	13.11	12.15	11.76	12.61	8.76	11.81	9.29	1.01
Asset Turnover	1.05	1.02	1.08	1.07	1.03	1.04	0.67	1.07
Current Ratio	1.86	1.86	1.77	1.44	1.65	1.58	1.83	1.80
Debt to Equity	2.40	2.91	3.52	3.20	1.69	3.32	1.07	0.29
Price Range	63.18-36.76	66.81-36.76	70.94-36.76	70.94-36.76	62.45-39.22	40.52-27.09	32.23-19.33	25.39-19.81
P/E Ratio	29.52-17.18	31.22-17.18	33.46-17.34	31.25-16.19	42.48-26.68	23.02-15.39	26.42-15.84	94.05-73.38
Average Yield %	1.32	1.25	1.14	1.05	0.82	1.02	1.28	1.77

Address: 800 Main Street, 4th Floor, Lynchburg, VA 24504	Web Site:	Auditors: Deloitte & Touche LLP
Telephone: 980-365-4300	Officers: Rex D. Geveden - President, Chief Executive Officer, Chief Operating Officer David S. Black - Senior Vice President, Chief Financial Officer, Vice President, Chief Accounting Officer	Investor Contact: 704-625-4944 Transfer Agents: Computershare Trust Company, N.A., Canton, MA

CABLE ONE INC

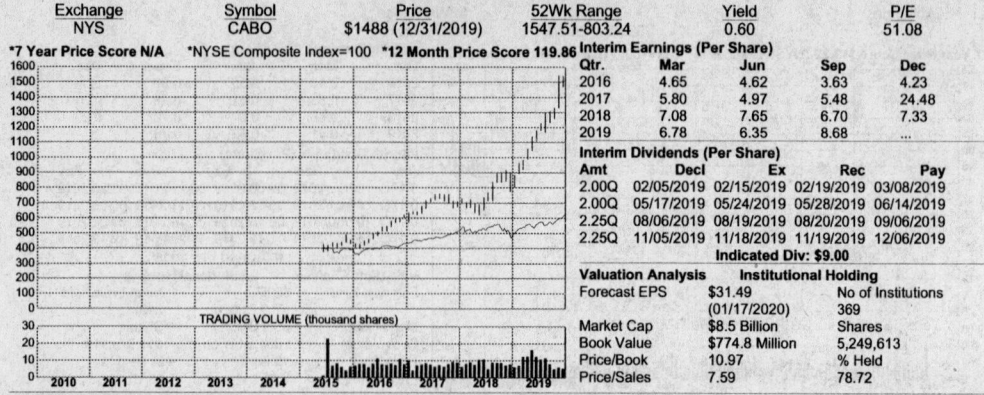

Exchange	Symbol	Price	52Wk Range	Yield	P/E
NYS	CABO	$1488 (12/31/2019)	1547.51-803.24	0.60	51.08

*7 Year Price Score N/A   *NYSE Composite Index=100   *12 Month Price Score 119.86

Interim Earnings (Per Share)

Qtr.	Mar	Jun	Sep	Dec
2016	4.65	4.62	3.63	4.23
2017	5.80	4.97	5.48	24.48
2018	7.08	7.65	6.70	7.33
2019	6.78	6.35	8.68	...

Interim Dividends (Per Share)

Amt	Decl	Ex	Rec	Pay
2.00Q	02/05/2019	02/15/2019	02/19/2019	03/08/2019
2.00Q	05/17/2019	05/24/2019	05/28/2019	06/14/2019
2.25Q	08/06/2019	08/19/2019	08/20/2019	09/06/2019
2.25Q	11/05/2019	11/18/2019	11/19/2019	12/06/2019

Indicated Div: $9.00

Valuation Analysis

		Institutional Holding	
Forecast EPS	$31.49 (01/17/2020)	No of Institutions	369
Market Cap	$8.5 Billion	Shares	5,249,613
Book Value	$774.8 Million	% Held	78.72
Price/Book	10.97		
Price/Sales	7.59		

Business Summary: Business Services (MIC: 7.5.2 SIC: 4841 NAIC: 515210)

Cable One is a provider of data, video and voice services in Western, Midwestern and Southern states. Co. provides these broadband services to residential and business customers in more than 750 communities. The markets Co. serves are primarily non-metropolitan, secondary markets, with majority of its customers located in seven states: Arizona, Idaho, Illinois, Mississippi, Missouri, Oklahoma and Texas. Co.'s product lines include residential data services, residential video services, residential voice services, business services, and advertising.

Recent Developments: For the quarter ended Sep 30 2019, net income increased 30.1% to US$49.8 million from US$38.3 million in the year-earlier quarter. Revenues were US$285.0 million, up 6.2% from US$268.3 million the year before. Operating income was US$80.1 million versus US$63.3 million in the prior-year quarter, an increase of 26.6%. Direct operating expenses rose 3.2% to US$94.9 million from US$92.0 million in the comparable period the year before. Indirect operating expenses decreased 2.7% to US$110.0 million from US$113.0 million in the equivalent prior-year period.

Prospects: Our evaluation of Cable ONE Inc. as of October 4th, 2019 is the result of our systematic analysis on three basic characteristics: earnings strength, relative valuation, and recent stock price movement. The company has generated a negative trend in earnings per share over the past 5 quarters. However, recent analyst estimates for the company have been raised and CABO has posted results that fell short of analysts' expectations. Based on operating earnings yield, the company is overvalued when compared to all of the companies we cover. Share price changes over the past year indicates that CABO will perform over the near term.

Financial Data

(US$ in Thousands)	9 Mos	6 Mos	3 Mos	12/31/2018	12/31/2017	12/31/2016	12/31/2015	12/31/2014
Earnings Per Share	29.14	27.16	28.46	28.77	40.72	17.14	15.19	147,309.00
Cash Flow Per Share	76.61	74.67	73.57	71.74	57.13	43.73	42.10	...
Dividends Per Share	8.250	8.000	7.750	7.500	6.500	6.000	1.500	...
Dividend Payout %	28.31	29.46	27.23	26.07	15.96	35.01	9.87	...
Income Statement								
Total Revenue	849,246	564,255	278,605	1,072,295	960,029	819,625	807,266	814,812
EBITDA	364,123	236,690	120,317	458,399	410,265	335,528	302,110	372,009
Depn & Amortn	148,427	102,709	50,818	186,000	173,600	142,200	140,600	134,000
Income Before Taxes	163,005	97,369	51,403	211,984	189,801	163,107	145,420	238,009
Income Taxes	38,036	22,235	12,664	47,224	(44,227)	64,168	56,387	90,700
Net Income	124,969	75,134	38,739	164,760	234,028	98,939	89,033	147,309
Average Shares	5,741	5,730	5,716	5,725	5,747	5,770	5,860	...
Balance Sheet								
Current Assets	196,118	155,716	242,369	317,863	242,384	185,937	166,353	50,121
Total Assets	2,608,327	2,549,452	2,624,237	2,303,234	2,218,329	1,397,271	1,408,595	1,262,040
Current Liabilities	153,179	143,048	141,204	133,713	170,604	111,143	126,832	95,623
Long-Term Obligations	1,278,110	1,280,637	1,385,475	1,142,056	1,160,682	530,886	545,301	...
Total Liabilities	1,833,568	1,786,544	1,855,202	1,527,876	1,546,913	942,760	973,249	408,752
Stockholders' Equity	774,759	762,908	769,035	775,358	671,416	454,511	435,346	853,288
Shares Outstanding	5,709	5,706	5,699	5,703	5,731	5,708	5,833	...
Statistical Record								
Return on Assets %	6.85	6.51	6.73	7.29	12.95	7.03	...	11.74
Return on Equity %	21.97	21.02	22.17	22.78	41.57	22.18	...	17.45
EBITDA Margin %	42.88	41.95	43.19	42.75	42.73	40.94	37.42	45.66
Net Margin %	14.72	13.32	13.90	15.37	24.38	12.07	11.03	18.08
Asset Turnover	0.46	0.46	0.45	0.47	0.53	0.58	...	0.65
Current Ratio	1.28	1.09	1.72	2.38	1.42	1.67	1.31	0.52
Debt to Equity	1.65	1.68	1.80	1.47	1.73	1.17	1.25	...
Price Range	1308.65-774.10	1182.88-712.91	985.99-619.00	918.65-619.00	762.27-570.00	623.87-396.52	490.48-376.91	...
P/E Ratio	44.91-26.56	43.55-26.25	34.64-21.75	31.93-21.52	18.72-14.00	36.40-23.13	32.29-24.81	...
Average Yield %	0.80	0.87	0.96	0.99	0.94	1.18	0.35	...

Address: 210 E. Earll Drive, Phoenix, AZ 85012 **Telephone:** 602-364-6000	**Web Site:** www.cableone.net **Officers:** Julia M. Laulis - Chairman, President, Chief Executive Officer, Chief Operating Officer Eric Michael Lardy - Senior Vice President	**Auditors:** PricewaterhouseCoopers LLP **Transfer Agents:** Computershare Trust Company, N.A.

CABOT CORP.

Exchange	Symbol	Price	52Wk Range	Yield	P/E
NYS	CBT	$47.52 (12/31/2019)	50.23-37.69	2.95	18.07

*7 Year Price Score 75.75 ***NYSE Composite Index=100** ***12 Month Price Score 100.65**

Interim Earnings (Per Share)

Qtr.	Dec	Mar	Jun	Sep
2014-15	0.69	0.41	(7.04)	0.61
2015-16	(0.11)	0.76	0.88	0.83
2016-17	0.85	1.18	0.71	1.02
2017-18	(1.98)	(2.80)	1.40	1.51
2018-19	1.14	0.39	0.55	0.55

Interim Dividends (Per Share)

Amt	Decl	Ex	Rec	Pay
0.35Q	05/08/2019	05/30/2019	05/31/2019	06/14/2019
0.35Q	07/12/2019	08/29/2019	08/30/2019	09/13/2019
0.35Q	11/08/2019	11/27/2019	11/29/2019	12/13/2019
0.35Q	01/10/2020	02/27/2020	02/28/2020	03/13/2020

Indicated Div: $1.40

Valuation Analysis / Institutional Holding

Forecast EPS	$3.80 (01/17/2020)	No of Institutions 432
Market Cap	$2.7 Billion	Shares 63,251,580
Book Value	$998.0 Million	% Held 78.67
Price/Book	2.72	
Price/Sales	0.81	

Business Summary: Specialty Chemicals (MIC: 8.3.2 SIC: 2895 NAIC: 325182)

Cabot is a specialty chemicals and performance materials company. Co.'s principal products are rubber and specialty grade carbon blacks, specialty compounds, fumed metal oxides, activated carbons, inkjet colorants, and aerogel. Co.'s segments are: Reinforcement Materials, which combines the rubber blacks and elastomer composites product lines; Performance Chemicals, which combines its specialty grades of carbon black, fumed metal oxides and aerogel product lines in its Performance Additives business, and combines its specialty compounds and inkjet product lines in its Formulated Solutions business; and Purification Solutions, which represents Co.'s activated carbon business.

Recent Developments: For the year ended Sep 30 2019, net income amounted to US$186.0 million versus a net loss of US$74.0 million in the prior year. Revenues were US$3.34 billion, up 2.9% from US$3.24 billion the year before. Operating income was US$306.0 million versus US$144.0 million in the prior year, an increase of 112.5%. Direct operating expenses rose 7.4% to US$2.65 billion from US$2.47 billion in the comparable period the year before. Indirect operating expenses decreased 39.6% to US$379.0 million from US$628.0 million in the equivalent prior-year period.

Prospects: Our evaluation of Cabot Corp. as of October 4th, 2019 is the result of our systematic analysis on three basic characteristics: earnings strength, relative valuation, and recent stock price movement. The company has enjoyed a very positive trend in earnings per share over the past 5 quarters. However, recent analyst estimates for the company have been reduced, while CBT has posted results that exceeded analysts' expectations. Based on operating earnings yield, the company is undervalued when compared to all of the companies we cover. Share price changes over the past year indicates that CBT will perform very poorly over the near term.

Financial Data

(US$ in Thousands)	09/30/2019	09/30/2018	09/30/2017	09/30/2016	09/30/2015	09/30/2014	09/30/2013	09/30/2012
Earnings Per Share	2.63	(1.85)	3.80	2.36	(5.27)	3.03	2.36	5.99
Cash Flow Per Share	6.18	4.83	5.46	6.26	7.87	4.89	6.57	6.53
Tang Book Value Per Share	14.23	15.95	19.21	15.79	14.84	16.45	17.77	15.83
Dividends Per Share	1.360	1.290	1.230	1.040	0.880	0.840	0.800	0.760
Dividend Payout %	51.71	...	32.37	44.07	...	27.72	33.90	12.69
Income Statement								
Total Revenue	3,337,000	3,242,000	2,717,000	2,411,000	2,871,000	3,647,000	3,463,000	3,300,000
EBITDA	447,000	303,000	479,000	397,000	(159,000)	544,000	438,000	440,000
Depn & Amortn	142,000	142,000	147,000	154,000	169,000	184,000	176,000	153,000
Income Before Taxes	255,000	117,000	288,000	194,000	(377,000)	308,000	205,000	245,000
Income Taxes	70,000	193,000	29,000	34,000	(45,000)	92,000	58,000	55,000
Net Income	157,000	(113,000)	241,000	149,000	(334,000)	199,000	153,000	388,000
Average Shares	58,800	61,700	62,700	62,900	63,400	65,100	64,500	64,200
Balance Sheet								
Current Assets	1,210,000	1,386,000	1,262,000	1,089,000	1,048,000	1,364,000	1,495,000	1,443,000
Total Assets	3,004,000	3,244,000	3,314,000	3,044,000	3,075,000	4,084,000	4,233,000	4,399,000
Current Liabilities	599,000	952,000	742,000	398,000	441,000	630,000	844,000	919,000
Long-Term Obligations	1,024,000	719,000	661,000	918,000	970,000	1,004,000	1,020,000	1,172,000
Total Liabilities	2,006,000	2,090,000	1,834,000	1,770,000	1,841,000	2,142,000	2,282,000	2,586,000
Stockholders' Equity	998,000	1,154,000	1,480,000	1,274,000	1,234,000	1,942,000	1,951,000	1,813,000
Shares Outstanding	57,080	60,366	61,884	62,210	62,458	64,382	63,970	63,347
Statistical Record								
Return on Assets %	5.03	N.M.	7.58	4.86	N.M.	4.79	3.54	10.26
Return on Equity %	14.59	N.M.	17.50	11.85	N.M.	10.22	8.13	23.45
EBITDA Margin %	13.40	9.35	17.63	16.47	N.M.	14.92	12.65	13.33
Net Margin %	4.70	N.M.	8.87	6.18	N.M.	5.46	4.42	11.76
Asset Turnover	1.07	0.99	0.85	0.79	0.80	0.88	0.80	0.87
Current Ratio	2.02	1.46	1.70	2.74	2.38	2.17	1.77	1.57
Debt to Equity	1.03	0.62	0.45	0.72	0.79	0.52	0.52	0.65
Price Range	64.45-37.69	68.48-53.79	60.90-48.21	53.41-31.56	50.77-30.90	60.30-42.48	43.93-32.41	44.66-23.27
P/E Ratio	24.51-14.33	...	16.03-12.69	22.63-13.37	...	19.90-14.02	18.61-13.73	7.46-3.88
Average Yield %	2.97	2.09	2.27	2.33	2.11	1.58	2.09	2.07

Address: Two Seaport Lane, Suite 1300, Boston, MA 02210 **Telephone:** 617-345-0100	**Web Site:** www.cabotcorp.com **Officers:** Sean D. Keohane - President, Chief Executive Officer, Executive Vice President, Division Officer Karen A. Kalita - Senior Vice President, General Counsel	**Auditors:** DELOITTE & TOUCHE LLP **Investor Contact:** 617-342-6090 **Transfer Agents:** Computershare Trust Company, N.A., Providence, RI

CABOT OIL & GAS CORP.

Exchange	Symbol	Price	52Wk Range	Yield	P/E
NYS	COG	$17.41 (12/31/2019)	27.43-15.71	2.30	9.21

*7 Year Price Score 66.43   *NYSE Composite Index=100   *12 Month Price Score 74.09

Interim Earnings (Per Share)

Qtr.	Mar	Jun	Sep	Dec
2016	(0.12)	(0.14)	(0.02)	(0.64)
2017	0.23	0.05	0.04	(0.09)
2018	0.25	0.09	0.28	0.62
2019	0.62	0.43	0.22	...

Interim Dividends (Per Share)

Amt	Decl	Ex	Rec	Pay
0.09Q	04/25/2019	05/14/2019	05/15/2019	05/29/2019
0.09Q	07/25/2019	08/07/2019	08/08/2019	08/22/2019
0.10Q	10/24/2019	11/05/2019	11/06/2019	11/15/2019
0.10Q	01/03/2020	01/23/2020	01/24/2020	02/07/2020

Indicated Div: $0.40

Valuation Analysis

		Institutional Holding	
Forecast EPS	$1.68 (01/17/2020)	No of Institutions	854
Market Cap	$7.1 Billion	Shares	462,745,568
Book Value	$2.2 Billion	% Held	84.29
Price/Book	3.21		
Price/Sales	3.06		

Business Summary: Production & Extraction (MIC: 9.1.1 SIC: 1311 NAIC: 211111)

Cabot Oil & Gas is an independent oil and gas company engaged in the development, exploitation, exploration and production of oil and gas properties. Co. operates in one segment, natural gas and oil development, exploitation, exploration and production, in the continental U.S. Co.'s operations are primarily concentrated in one unconventional play—the Marcellus Shale in northeast Pennsylvania.

Recent Developments: For the quarter ended Sep 30 2019, net income decreased 26.1% to US$90.4 million from US$122.3 million in the year-earlier quarter. Revenues were US$429.1 million, down 21.3% from US$545.2 million the year before. Operating income was US$129.8 million versus US$176.1 million in the prior-year quarter, a decrease of 26.3%. Direct operating expenses declined 31.3% to US$164.9 million from US$240.0 million in the comparable period the year before. Indirect operating expenses increased 4.1% to US$134.5 million from US$129.2 million in the equivalent prior-year period.

Prospects: Our evaluation of Cabot Oil & Gas Corp. as of October 4th, 2019 is the result of our systematic analysis on three basic characteristics: earnings strength, relative valuation, and recent stock price movement. The company has generated a negative trend in earnings per share over the past 5 quarters. In addition, recent analyst estimates for the company have been reduced while COG has posted results that exceeded analysts' expectations. Based on operating earnings yield, the company is undervalued when compared to all of the companies we cover. Share price changes over the past year indicates that COG will perform poorly over the near term.

Financial Data

(US$ in Thousands)	9 Mos	6 Mos	3 Mos	12/31/2018	12/31/2017	12/31/2016	12/31/2015	12/31/2014
Earnings Per Share	1.89	1.95	1.61	1.24	0.22	(0.91)	(0.28)	0.25
Cash Flow Per Share	3.63	3.48	3.35	2.48	1.94	0.86	1.79	2.97
Tang Book Value Per Share	5.43	5.60	5.48	4.94	5.48	5.52	4.85	5.19
Dividends Per Share	0.320	0.290	0.260	0.250	0.170	0.080	0.080	0.080
Dividend Payout %	16.93	14.87	16.15	20.16	77.27	...	...	32.00
Income Statement								
Total Revenue	1,604,909	1,175,798	641,681	2,188,148	1,764,219	1,155,677	1,357,150	2,173,011
EBITDA	736,330	605,941	353,904	1,192,311	527,772	26,425	529,888	740,620
Depn & Amortn	3,219	2,464	1,089	422,110	573,591	595,211	626,665	637,514
Income Before Taxes	692,809	576,729	340,634	697,000	(127,949)	(657,122)	(193,688)	29,321
Income Taxes	158,679	132,957	77,871	141,094	(328,828)	(242,475)	(73,382)	(72,067)
Net Income	534,130	443,772	262,763	557,043	100,393	(417,124)	(113,891)	104,468
Average Shares	414,462	424,349	425,189	447,568	465,551	456,847	413,696	417,601
Balance Sheet								
Current Assets	421,679	631,330	680,191	544,545	764,957	715,881	144,786	413,447
Total Assets	4,442,665	4,563,729	4,481,547	4,198,829	4,727,344	5,122,569	5,261,899	5,437,716
Current Liabilities	294,785	234,026	240,315	287,264	630,050	257,812	235,552	499,018
Long-Term Obligations	1,132,790	1,219,555	1,219,338	1,226,104	1,217,891	1,520,530	2,005,000	1,752,000
Total Liabilities	2,229,089	2,218,925	2,160,608	2,110,670	2,203,439	2,554,902	3,252,711	3,294,983
Stockholders' Equity	2,213,576	2,344,804	2,320,939	2,088,159	2,523,905	2,567,667	2,009,188	2,142,733
Shares Outstanding	407,924	418,388	423,367	422,684	460,611	465,150	413,875	413,022
Statistical Record								
Return on Assets %	18.77	18.77	15.58	12.48	2.04	N.M.	N.M.	2.01
Return on Equity %	37.57	37.39	29.72	24.16	3.94	N.M.	N.M.	4.81
EBITDA Margin %	45.88	51.53	55.15	54.49	29.92	2.29	39.04	34.08
Net Margin %	33.28	37.74	40.95	25.46	5.69	N.M.	N.M.	4.81
Asset Turnover	0.54	0.54	0.52	0.49	0.36	0.22	0.25	0.42
Current Ratio	1.43	2.70	2.83	1.90	1.21	2.78	0.61	0.83
Debt to Equity	0.51	0.52	0.53	0.59	0.48	0.59	1.00	0.82
Price Range	27.43-16.16	27.43-21.18	26.59-21.18	29.12-21.18	29.44-20.77	26.50-15.48	35.40-15.03	41.61-28.48
P/E Ratio	14.51-8.55	14.07-10.86	16.52-13.16	23.48-17.08	133.82-94.41	...	...	166.44-113.92
Average Yield %	1.37	1.18	1.08	1.04	0.69	0.35	0.30	0.23

Address: Three Memorial City Plaza, 840 Gessner Road, Suite 1400, Houston, TX 77024 **Telephone:** 281-589-4600 **Fax:** 281-589-4653	**Web Site:** www.cabotog.com **Officers:** Dan O. Dinges - Chairman, President, Chief Executive Officer Scott C. Schroeder - Executive Vice President, Chief Financial Officer	**Auditors:** PricewaterhouseCoopers LLP **Investor Contact:** 281-589-4993 **Transfer Agents:** Wells Fargo Bank N.A., Mendota Heights, MN

CACI INTERNATIONAL INC

Exchange	Symbol	Price	52Wk Range	Yield	P/E
NYS	CACI	$249.99 (12/31/2019)	251.63-140.81	N/A	24.95

*7 Year Price Score 143.49 *NYSE Composite Index=100 *12 Month Price Score 110.09

Interim Earnings (Per Share)

Qtr.	Sep	Dec	Mar	Jun
2016-17	1.47	1.69	1.61	1.76
2017-18	1.67	5.66	2.56	2.05
2018-19	3.10	2.71	2.69	1.96
2019-20	2.66	...	...	...

Interim Dividends (Per Share)

No Dividends Paid

Valuation Analysis		Institutional Holding	
Forecast EPS	$12.25	No of Institutions	
	(01/16/2020)	516	
Market Cap	$6.2 Billion	Shares	
Book Value	$2.4 Billion	31,201,264	
Price/Book	2.57	% Held	
Price/Sales	1.20	87.92	

TRADING VOLUME (thousand shares)

Business Summary: IT Services (MIC: 6.3.1 SIC: 7373 NAIC: 541512)

CACI International is a holding company. Through its subsidiaries, Co. is a provider of information solutions and services to the United States government. Co.'s information solutions and services support national security missions and government modernization/transformation for intelligence, defense, and federal civilian customers. Co. provides its services and solutions to its domestic customers in the following market areas, among others: business systems, command and control, communications, cyber security, enterprise information technology (IT), health, and intelligence services. Co.'s international operations provide a mix of IT services and proprietary data and software products.

Recent Developments: For the quarter ended Sep 30 2019, net income decreased 13.8% to US$68.0 million from US$78.8 million in the year-earlier quarter. Revenues were US$1.36 billion, up 16.9% from US$1.17 billion the year before. Operating income was US$100.2 million versus US$99.6 million in the prior-year quarter, an increase of 0.6%. Direct operating expenses rose 12.3% to US$878.9 million from US$782.8 million in the comparable period the year before. Indirect operating expenses increased 35.6% to US$384.4 million from US$283.5 million in the equivalent prior-year period.

Prospects: Our evaluation of Caci International Inc. as of October 4th, 2019 is the result of our systematic analysis on three basic characteristics: earnings strength, relative valuation, and recent stock price movement. The company has managed to produce a neutral trend in earnings per share over the past 5 quarters. However, recent analyst estimates for the company have been raised and CACI has posted results that fell short of analysts' expectations. Based on operating earnings yield, the company is fairly valued when compared to all of the companies we cover. Share price changes over the past year indicates that CACI will perform well over the near term.

Financial Data

(US$ in Thousands)	3 Mos	06/30/2019	06/30/2018	06/30/2017	06/30/2016	06/30/2015	06/30/2014	06/30/2013
Earnings Per Share	10.02	10.46	11.93	6.53	5.76	5.17	5.38	6.35
Cash Flow Per Share	23.11	22.36	13.21	11.53	9.97	9.32	8.48	10.84
Income Statement								
Total Revenue	1,363,392	4,986,341	4,467,860	4,354,617	3,744,053	3,313,452	3,564,562	3,681,990
EBITDA	100,746	414,267	371,400	324,761	288,350	259,081	280,103	291,941
Depn & Amortn	589	36,400	30,700	27,500	23,600	22,700	22,700	21,100
Income Before Taxes	83,346	327,909	298,664	248,619	223,612	201,623	219,245	245,023
Income Taxes	15,369	62,305	(2,507)	84,948	80,813	75,327	83,326	92,347
Net Income	67,977	265,604	301,171	163,671	142,799	126,195	135,316	151,689
Average Shares	25,532	25,395	25,255	25,069	24,802	24,388	25,155	23,885
Balance Sheet								
Current Assets	1,042,268	1,031,520	931,191	879,902	921,838	676,460	735,849	727,975
Total Assets	5,438,184	5,086,843	4,034,206	3,911,082	3,987,341	3,257,116	3,359,138	2,501,265
Current Liabilities	773,624	691,722	538,981	526,744	565,176	399,681	422,587	742,494
Long-Term Obligations	1,551,951	1,618,093	1,015,420	1,177,598	1,402,079	1,029,335	1,238,728	300,790
Total Liabilities	3,013,068	2,715,512	1,927,454	2,117,496	2,380,163	1,776,979	2,002,255	1,296,362
Stockholders' Equity	2,425,116	2,371,331	2,106,752	1,793,586	1,607,178	1,480,137	1,356,883	1,204,903
Shares Outstanding	24,958	24,880	24,704	24,462	24,323	24,184	23,500	23,222
Statistical Record								
Return on Assets %	5.26	5.82	7.58	4.14	3.93	3.81	4.62	6.20
Return on Equity %	11.04	11.86	15.44	9.63	9.23	8.90	10.56	12.82
EBITDA Margin %	7.39	8.31	8.31	7.46	7.70	7.82	7.86	7.93
Net Margin %	4.99	5.33	6.74	3.76	3.81	3.81	3.80	4.12
Asset Turnover	1.07	1.09	1.12	1.10	1.03	1.00	1.22	1.50
Current Ratio	1.35	1.49	1.73	1.67	1.63	1.69	1.74	0.98
Debt to Equity	0.64	0.68	0.48	0.66	0.87	0.70	0.91	0.25
Price Range	233.85-139.42	209.66-139.42	172.75-122.90	133.20-88.63	110.34-73.58	90.76-68.30	80.31-61.30	65.04-48.65
P/E Ratio	23.34-13.91	20.04-13.33	14.48-10.30	20.40-13.57	19.16-12.77	17.56-13.21	14.93-11.39	10.24-7.66

Address: 1100 North Glebe Road, Arlington, VA 22201 Telephone: 703-841-7800 Fax: 703-841-7882	Web Site: www.caci.com Officers: J. Phillip London - Executive Chairman, Chairman John S. Mengucci - President, Chief Executive Officer, Chief Operating Officer	Auditors: Ernst & Young LLP Investor Contact: 703-841-7800 Transfer Agents: American Stock Transfer and Trust Corporation, Brooklyn, NY

CALIFORNIA WATER SERVICE GROUP (DE)

Exchange	Symbol	Price	52Wk Range	Yield	P/E	Div Acheiver
NYS	CWT	$51.56 (12/31/2019)	57.02-44.86	1.53	34.37	51 Years

*7 Year Price Score 131.15 *NYSE Composite Index=100 ***12 Month Price Score 94.74**

Interim Earnings (Per Share)

Qtr.	Mar	Jun	Sep	Dec
2016	(0.02)	0.24	0.48	0.31
2017	0.02	0.39	0.70	0.29
2018	(0.05)	0.27	0.72	0.43
2019	(0.16)	0.35	0.88	...

Interim Dividends (Per Share)

Amt	Decl	Ex	Rec	Pay
0.198Q	01/30/2019	02/08/2019	02/11/2019	02/22/2019
0.198Q	04/24/2019	05/03/2019	05/06/2019	05/17/2019
0.198Q	07/31/2019	08/09/2019	08/12/2019	08/23/2019
0.198Q	10/30/2019	11/07/2019	11/11/2019	11/22/2019

Indicated Div: $0.79 (Div. Reinv. Plan)

Valuation Analysis

		Institutional Holding	
Forecast EPS	$1.40	No of Institutions	
	(01/10/2020)	369	
Market Cap	$2.5 Billion	Shares	
Book Value	$757.8 Million	44,181,924	
Price/Book	3.28	% Held	
Price/Sales	3.49	74.78	

Business Summary: Water Utilities (MIC: 3.2.1 SIC: 4941 NAIC: 221310)

California Water Service Group is a holding company. Through its subsidiaries, Co. is engaged in the production, purchase, storage, treatment, testing, distribution and sale of water for domestic, industrial, public and irrigation uses, and for fire protection. Co. also provides non-regulated water-related services under agreements with municipalities and other private companies. The non-regulated services include full water system operation, billing and meter reading services. Non-regulated operations also include the lease of communication antenna sites, lab services, and promotion of other non-regulated services.

Recent Developments: For the quarter ended Sep 30 2019, net income increased 17.3% to US$42.4 million from US$36.2 million in the year-earlier quarter. Revenues were US$232.5 million, up 5.1% from US$221.3 million the year before. Operating income was US$51.6 million versus US$47.3 million in the prior-year quarter, an increase of 9.0%. Direct operating expenses rose 4.3% to US$112.2 million from US$107.5 million in the comparable period the year before. Indirect operating expenses increased 3.5% to US$68.8 million from US$66.4 million in the equivalent prior-year period.

Prospects: Our evaluation of California Water Service Group as of October 4th, 2019 is the result of our systematic analysis on three basic characteristics: earnings strength, relative valuation, and recent stock price movement. The company has produced a positive trend in earnings per share over the past 5 quarters. However, recent analyst estimates for the company have been unchanged, while CWT has posted results that fell short of analysts' expectations. Based on operating earnings yield, the company is overvalued when compared to all of the companies we cover. Share price changes over the past year indicates that CWT will perform over the near term.

Financial Data

(US$ in Thousands)	9 Mos	6 Mos	3 Mos	12/31/2018	12/31/2017	12/31/2016	12/31/2015	12/31/2014
Earnings Per Share	1.50	1.34	1.26	1.36	1.40	1.01	0.94	1.19
Cash Flow Per Share	3.90	3.59	3.55	3.72	3.08	3.32	3.02	2.68
Tang Book Value Per Share	15.69	14.97	14.78	15.14	14.39	13.69	13.36	13.05
Dividends Per Share	0.780	0.770	0.760	0.750	0.720	0.690	0.670	0.650
Dividend Payout %	52.00	57.46	60.32	55.15	51.43	68.32	71.28	54.62
Income Statement								
Total Revenue	537,679	305,142	126,111	698,196	666,890	609,370	588,368	597,499
EBITDA	164,575	77,928	22,506	208,700	209,481	170,036	160,783	174,346
Depn & Amortn	68,522	45,744	22,893	86,806	79,512	66,074	64,007	64,119
Income Before Taxes	65,304	10,686	(10,631)	84,173	96,109	73,479	69,545	83,465
Income Taxes	13,524	1,330	(2,991)	18,589	28,928	24,804	24,528	26,727
Net Income	51,780	9,356	(7,640)	65,584	67,181	48,675	45,017	56,738
Average Shares	48,141	48,136	48,086	48,060	48,009	47,956	47,880	47,829
Balance Sheet								
Current Assets	212,056	206,030	192,725	188,702	227,873	142,069	127,578	154,124
Total Assets	3,023,254	2,964,595	2,900,662	2,837,704	2,740,375	2,411,745	2,246,095	2,187,351
Current Liabilities	333,944	331,389	384,043	321,166	490,959	250,230	148,455	217,706
Long-Term Obligations	807,478	807,693	710,602	710,027	515,793	531,745	512,287	419,233
Total Liabilities	2,265,459	2,241,431	2,186,533	2,107,547	2,046,913	1,752,274	1,603,940	1,560,725
Stockholders' Equity	757,795	723,164	714,129	730,157	693,462	659,471	642,155	626,626
Shares Outstanding	48,145	48,140	48,134	48,064	48,012	47,964	47,875	47,806
Statistical Record								
Return on Assets %	2.46	2.24	2.15	2.35	2.61	2.08	2.03	2.74
Return on Equity %	9.86	9.15	8.67	9.21	9.93	7.46	7.10	9.26
EBITDA Margin %	30.61	25.54	17.85	29.89	31.41	27.90	27.33	29.18
Net Margin %	9.63	3.07	N.M.	9.39	10.07	7.99	7.65	9.50
Asset Turnover	0.24	0.24	0.25	0.25	0.26	0.26	0.27	0.29
Current Ratio	0.64	0.62	0.50	0.59	0.46	0.57	0.86	0.71
Debt to Equity	1.07	1.12	1.00	0.97	0.74	0.81	0.80	0.67
Price Range	57.02-40.47	54.67-39.90	54.67-35.65	48.77-35.40	45.60-32.50	36.80-22.96	25.96-19.68	26.09-20.44
P/E Ratio	38.01-26.98	40.80-29.78	43.39-28.29	35.86-26.03	32.57-23.21	36.44-22.73	27.62-20.94	21.92-17.18
Average Yield %	1.57	1.66	1.74	1.83	1.90	2.31	2.87	2.78

Address: 1720 North First Street, San Jose, CA 95112	**Web Site:** www.calwatergroup.com	**Auditors:** DELOITTE & TOUCHE LLP
Telephone: 408-367-8200	**Officers:** Peter C. Nelson - Chairman, President, Chief Executive Officer Martin A. Kropelnicki - President, Chief Executive Officer, Vice President, Chief Financial Officer, Chief Operating Officer	**Investor Contact:** 408-367-8200
		Transfer Agents: American Stock Transfer & Trust Company, Brooklyn, NY

CALLON PETROLEUM CO. (DE)

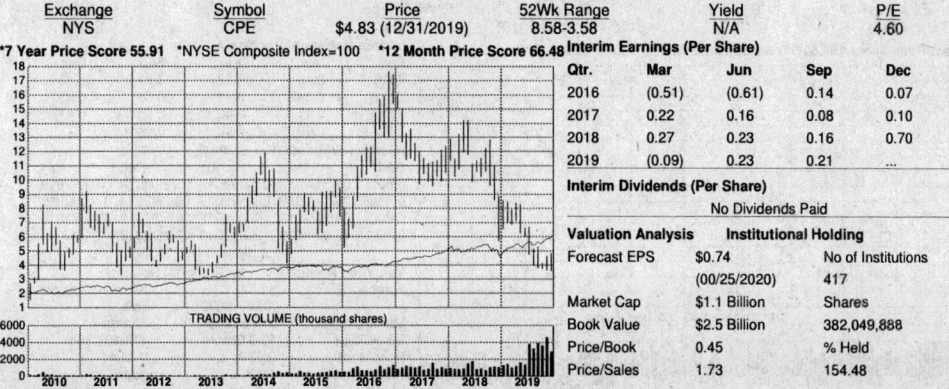

Exchange	Symbol	Price	52Wk Range	Yield	P/E
NYS	CPE	$4.83 (12/31/2019)	8.58-3.58	N/A	4.60

*7 Year Price Score 55.91   *NYSE Composite Index=100   *12 Month Price Score 66.48

Interim Earnings (Per Share)

Qtr.	Mar	Jun	Sep	Dec
2016	(0.51)	(0.61)	0.14	0.07
2017	0.22	0.16	0.08	0.10
2018	0.27	0.23	0.16	0.70
2019	(0.09)	0.23	0.21	...

Interim Dividends (Per Share)

No Dividends Paid

Valuation Analysis / **Institutional Holding**

Forecast EPS	$0.74	No of Institutions	
	(00/25/2020)	417	
Market Cap	$1.1 Billion	Shares	
Book Value	$2.5 Billion	382,049,888	
Price/Book	0.45	% Held	
Price/Sales	1.73	154.48	

TRADING VOLUME (thousand shares)

Business Summary: Production & Extraction (MIC: 9.1.1 SIC: 1311 NAIC: 211111)

Callon Petroleum is an independent oil and natural gas company focused on the acquisition and development of unconventional onshore oil and natural gas reserves in the Permian Basin. The Permian Basin is located in West Texas and southeastern New Mexico and is comprised of three primary sub-basins: the Midland Basin, the Delaware Basin, and the Central Basin Platform.

Recent Developments: For the quarter ended Sep 30 2019, net income increased 47.2% to US$55.8 million from US$37.9 million in the year-earlier quarter. Revenues were US$155.4 million, down 3.6% from US$161.2 million the year before. Operating income was US$52.5 million versus US$72.8 million in the prior-year quarter, a decrease of 27.8%. Direct operating expenses rose 9.5% to US$31.5 million from US$28.8 million in the comparable period the year before. Indirect operating expenses increased 19.6% to US$71.3 million from US$59.6 million in the equivalent prior-year period.

Prospects: Our evaluation of Callon Petroleum Co. as of October 4th, 2019 is the result of our systematic analysis on three basic characteristics: earnings strength, relative valuation, and recent stock price movement. The company has generated a negative trend in earnings per share over the past 5 quarters. In addition, recent analyst estimates for the company have been reduced and CPE has posted results that fell short of analysts' expectations. Based on operating earnings yield, the company is undervalued when compared to all of the companies we cover. Share price changes over the past year indicates that CPE will perform very poorly over the near term.

Financial Data

(US$ in Thousands)	9 Mos	6 Mos	3 Mos	12/31/2018	12/31/2017	12/31/2016	12/31/2015	12/31/2014
Earnings Per Share	1.05	1.00	1.00	1.35	0.56	(0.78)	(3.77)	0.65
Cash Flow Per Share	2.15	2.16	1.98	2.16	1.14	0.94	1.32	2.10
Tang Book Value Per Share	10.81	10.88	10.66	10.74	9.20	8.62	4.53	7.85
Income Statement								
Total Revenue	475,477	320,099	153,047	587,624	366,474	200,851	137,512	151,862
EBITDA	125,351	50,137	(23,216)	312,048	124,756	(79,163)	(179,689)	71,508
Depn & Amortn	2,218	1,479	738	1,078	900	793	865	836
Income Before Taxes	120,915	47,179	(24,692)	308,470	121,697	(91,827)	(201,665)	60,900
Income Taxes	29,444	11,542	(5,149)	8,110	1,273	(14)	38,474	23,134
Net Income	91,471	35,637	(19,543)	300,360	120,424	(91,813)	(240,139)	37,766
Average Shares	228,469	228,411	227,784	217,596	202,102	126,258	65,708	45,961
Balance Sheet								
Current Assets	165,373	138,096	170,998	222,625	144,860	725,126	62,252	60,457
Total Assets	4,016,923	3,915,497	4,108,834	3,979,173	2,693,296	2,267,587	788,594	876,770
Current Liabilities	301,011	291,933	323,937	314,916	205,773	131,550	87,877	98,812
Long-Term Obligations	1,190,654	1,095,260	1,319,867	1,189,473	620,196	390,219	328,565	335,000
Total Liabilities	1,548,271	1,431,625	1,680,389	1,533,965	837,330	534,185	425,836	443,035
Stockholders' Equity	2,468,652	2,483,872	2,428,445	2,445,208	1,855,966	1,733,402	362,758	433,735
Shares Outstanding	228,372	228,263	227,884	227,582	201,836	201,041	80,087	55,225
Statistical Record								
Return on Assets %	6.41	6.19	6.48	9.00	4.85	N.M.	N.M.	5.81
Return on Equity %	10.41	9.71	10.37	13.97	6.71	N.M.	N.M.	10.60
EBITDA Margin %	26.36	15.66	N.M.	53.10	34.04	N.M.	N.M.	47.09
Net Margin %	19.24	11.13	N.M.	51.11	32.86	N.M.	N.M.	24.87
Asset Turnover	0.17	0.17	0.18	0.18	0.15	0.13	0.17	0.23
Current Ratio	0.55	0.47	0.53	0.71	0.70	5.51	0.71	0.61
Debt to Equity	0.48	0.44	0.54	0.49	0.33	0.23	0.91	0.77
Price Range	12.84-3.78	12.84-5.71	14.26-5.71	14.26-5.71	16.07-9.54	17.64-5.23	10.01-4.78	11.94-4.14
P/E Ratio	12.23-3.60	12.84-5.71	14.26-5.71	10.56-4.23	28.70-17.04	...	...	18.37-6.37

Address: One Briarlake Plaza, 2000 W. Sam Houston Parkway S., Suite 2000, Houston, TX 77042 **Telephone:** 281-589-5200	**Web Site:** www.callon.com **Officers:** L. Richard Flury - Chairman Joseph C. Gatto - President, Chief Executive Officer, Chief Financial Officer, Senior Vice President, Treasurer	**Auditors:** Grant Thornton LLP **Investor Contact:** 601-442-1601 **Transfer Agents:** American Stock Transfer & Trust Company, New York, NY

CAMDEN PROPERTY TRUST

Exchange	Symbol	Price	52Wk Range	Yield	P/E
NYS	CPT	$106.10 (12/31/2019)	114.96-84.28	3.02	63.15

*7 Year Price Score 104.60 *NYSE Composite Index=100   *12 Month Price Score 99.73

Interim Earnings (Per Share)

Qtr.	Mar	Jun	Sep	Dec
2016	0.46	4.92	3.21	0.45
2017	0.39	0.43	0.38	0.93
2018	0.41	0.40	0.40	0.41
2019	0.40	0.43	0.44	...

Interim Dividends (Per Share)

Amt	Decl	Ex	Rec	Pay
0.80Q	01/31/2019	03/28/2019	03/29/2019	04/17/2019
0.80Q	06/14/2019	06/27/2019	06/28/2019	07/17/2019
0.80Q	09/16/2019	09/27/2019	09/30/2019	10/17/2019
0.80Q	12/02/2019	12/13/2019	12/16/2019	01/17/2020

Indicated Div: $3.20

Valuation Analysis | **Institutional Holding**

Forecast EPS	$1.64	No of Institutions
	(01/17/2020)	553
Market Cap	$11.3 Billion	Shares
Book Value	$3.6 Billion	112,108,304
Price/Book	3.15	% Held
Price/Sales	11.03	86.93

Business Summary: REITs (MIC: 5.3.1 SIC: 6798 NAIC: 525930)

Camden Property Trust is a real estate investment trust. Co. and all its consolidated subsidiaries are primarily engaged in the ownership, management, development, redevelopment, acquisition, and construction of multifamily apartment communities. Co.'s properties provide residents with a variety of amenities common to multifamily rental properties. Co.'s operating properties are located in the following locations: Phoenix/Scottsdale, AZ; Los Angeles/Orange County, and San Diego/Inland Empire, CA; Denver, CO; Washington DC Metro; Southeast Florida, Orlando, and Tampa/St. Petersburg, FL; Atlanta, GA; Charlotte, and Raleigh, NC; and Austin, Corpus Christi, Dallas/Fort Worth, and Houston, TX.

Recent Developments: For the quarter ended Sep 30 2019, net income increased 12.0% to US$44.8 million from US$40.0 million in the year-earlier quarter. Revenues were US$263.6 million, up 6.7% from US$247.1 million the year before. Revenues from property income rose 7.8% to US$260.7 million from US$241.8 million in the corresponding quarter a year earlier.

Prospects: Our evaluation of Camden Property Trust as of October 4th, 2019 is the result of our systematic analysis on three basic characteristics: earnings strength, relative valuation, and recent stock price movement. The company has enjoyed a very positive trend in earnings per share over the past 5 quarters. However, recent analyst estimates for the company have been mixed and CPT has posted results that fell short of analysts' expectations. Based on operating earnings yield, the company is overvalued when compared to all of the companies we cover. Share price changes over the past year indicates that CPT will perform well over the near term.

Financial Data

(US$ in Thousands)	9 Mos	6 Mos	3 Mos	12/31/2018	12/31/2017	12/31/2016	12/31/2015	12/31/2014
Earnings Per Share	1.68	1.64	1.61	1.63	2.13	9.05	2.76	3.27
Cash Flow Per Share	5.42	4.97	5.26	5.29	4.75	4.93	4.75	4.75
Tang Book Value Per Share	33.67	33.96	34.35	32.12	33.14	30.82	28.87	28.85
Dividends Per Share	3.170	3.140	3.110	3.080	3.000	7.250	2.800	2.640
Dividend Payout %	188.69	191.46	193.17	188.96	140.85	80.11	101.45	80.73
Income Statement								
Total Revenue	785,841	522,250	260,766	957,302	928,691	891,024	900,260	858,589
EBITDA	431,958	283,948	138,423	539,491	545,986	793,167	608,360	628,446
Depn & Amortn	250,734	164,920	80,274	300,946	263,974	250,146	257,082	238,989
Income Before Taxes	122,800	79,838	37,977	154,282	195,262	449,876	253,966	296,194
Income Taxes	709	396	168	1,424	1,224	1,617	1,872	1,903
Net Income	124,609	81,012	38,613	156,128	196,422	819,823	249,315	292,089
Average Shares	99,066	98,997	97,041	95,366	92,515	89,903	89,490	88,468
Balance Sheet								
Current Assets	162,925	154,943	11,747	66,523	401,843	369,854	41,688	185,793
Total Assets	6,648,646	6,621,602	6,285,394	6,219,586	6,173,748	6,028,152	6,037,612	6,056,907
Current Liabilities	326,111	268,663	238,626	276,206	252,639	256,015	242,851	256,767
Long-Term Obligations	2,477,400	2,476,880	2,124,783	2,321,603	2,204,598	2,480,588	2,724,687	2,743,539
Total Liabilities	3,063,768	3,005,979	2,632,566	2,908,163	2,768,385	3,013,279	3,221,055	3,241,305
Stockholders' Equity	3,584,878	3,615,623	3,652,828	3,311,423	3,405,363	3,014,873	2,816,557	2,815,602
Shares Outstanding	106,472	106,466	106,347	103,080	102,769	97,818	97,571	97,604
Statistical Record								
Return on Assets %	2.55	2.49	2.50	2.52	3.22	13.55	4.12	5.00
Return on Equity %	4.73	4.57	4.42	4.65	6.12	28.04	8.85	10.61
EBITDA Margin %	54.97	54.37	53.08	56.36	58.79	89.02	67.58	73.20
Net Margin %	15.86	15.51	14.81	16.31	21.15	92.01	27.69	34.02
Asset Turnover	0.16	0.16	0.16	0.15	0.15	0.15	0.15	0.15
Current Ratio	0.50	0.58	0.05	0.24	1.59	1.44	0.17	0.72
Debt to Equity	0.69	0.69	0.58	0.70	0.65	0.82	0.97	0.97
Price Range	111.78-84.28	107.67-84.28	101.68-82.96	95.52-78.55	95.70-79.06	90.67-70.55	81.28-69.45	77.87-56.88
P/E Ratio	66.54-50.17	65.65-51.39	63.16-51.53	58.60-48.19	44.93-37.12	10.02-7.80	29.45-25.16	23.81-17.39
Average Yield %	3.18	3.28	3.38	3.47	3.44	8.87	3.68	3.77

Address: 11 Greenway Plaza, Suite 2400, Houston, TX 77046	Officers: D. Keith Oden - Executive Vice-Chairman, President Richard J. Campo - Chairman, Chief Executive Officer	Auditors: Deloitte & Touche LLP
Telephone: 713-354-2500		Investor Contact: 713-354-2549
		Transfer Agents: American Stock Transfer and Trust Company, New York, NY

CAMPBELL SOUP CO

Exchange	Symbol	Price	52Wk Range	Yield	P/E
NYS	CPB	$49.42 (12/31/2019)	49.46-32.26	2.83	82.37

*7 Year Price Score 72.16 *NYSE Composite Index=100 *12 Month Price Score 109.76

Interim Earnings (Per Share)

Qtr.	Oct	Jan	Apr	Jul
2016-17	0.94	0.33	0.58	1.04
2017-18	0.91	0.95	(1.31)	0.31
2018-19	0.64	(0.20)	0.28	(0.03)
2019-20	0.55	...	...	...

Interim Dividends (Per Share)

Amt	Decl	Ex	Rec	Pay
0.35Q	03/27/2019	04/10/2019	04/11/2019	04/29/2019
0.35Q	06/26/2019	07/11/2019	07/12/2019	07/29/2019
0.35Q	09/25/2019	10/09/2019	10/10/2019	10/28/2019
0.35Q	11/21/2019	01/07/2020	01/08/2020	01/27/2020

Indicated Div: $1.40 (Div. Reinv. Plan)

Valuation Analysis

Institutional Holding	
Forecast EPS	$2.54	No of Institutions
	(01/17/2020)	870
Market Cap	$16.0 Billion	Shares
Book Value	$1.2 Billion	206,451,408
Price/Book	12.88	% Held
Price/Sales	1.98	47.43

Business Summary: Food (MIC: 1.2.1 SIC: 2032 NAIC: 311422)

Campbell Soup is a manufacturer and marketer of food and beverage products. Co.'s reportable segments are: Meals and Beverages, which includes the retail and foodservice businesses in the United States and Canada, and the meals and shelf-stable beverages business in Latin America; Snacks, which consists of Pepperidge Farm cookies, crackers, fresh bakery and frozen products in United States retail, including Milano cookies and Goldfish crackers, and Snyder's of Hanover pretzels, Lance sandwich crackers, Cape Cod and Kettle Brand potato chips, Late July snacks, Snack Factory Pretzel Crisps, Pop Secret popcorn, Emerald nuts, and other snacking products in the United States and Canada.

Recent Developments: For the quarter ended Oct 27 2019, income from continuing operations decreased 6.1% to US$169.0 million from US$180.0 million in the year-earlier quarter. Net income decreased 14.4% to US$166.0 million from US$194.0 million in the year-earlier quarter. Revenues were US$2.18 billion, down 0.9% from US$2.20 billion the year before. Operating income was US$317.0 million versus US$326.0 million in the prior-year quarter, a decrease of 2.8%. Direct operating expenses declined 2.1% to US$1.45 billion from US$1.48 billion in the comparable period the year before. Indirect operating expenses increased 5.3% to US$421.0 million from US$400.0 million in the equivalent prior-year period.

Prospects: Our evaluation of Campbell Soup Co. as of October 4th, 2019 is the result of our systematic analysis on three basic characteristics: earnings strength, relative valuation, and recent stock price movement. The company has enjoyed a very positive trend in earnings per share over the past 5 quarters. However, recent analyst estimates for the company have been mixed and CPB has posted results that exceeded analysts' expectations. Based on operating earnings yield, the company is fairly valued when compared to all of the companies we cover. Share price changes over the past year indicates that CPB will perform in line with the market over the near term.

Financial Data

(US$ in Thousands)	3 Mos	07/28/2019	07/29/2018	07/30/2017	07/31/2016	08/02/2015	08/03/2014	07/28/2013
Earnings Per Share	0.60	0.70	0.86	2.89	1.81	2.21	2.59	1.44
Cash Flow Per Share	4.48	4.66	4.35	4.24	4.75	3.80	2.82	3.25
Dividends Per Share	1.400	1.400	1.400	1.400	1.248	1.248	1.248	1.160
Dividend Payout %	233.33	200.00	162.79	48.44	68.95	56.47	48.19	80.56
Income Statement								
Total Revenue	2,183,000	8,107,000	8,685,000	7,890,000	7,961,000	8,082,000	8,268,000	8,052,000
EBITDA	328,000	1,368,000	829,000	1,699,000	1,248,000	1,381,000	1,479,000	1,473,000
Depn & Amortn	11,000	389,000	360,000	299,000	288,000	286,000	287,000	393,000
Income Before Taxes	237,000	625,000	272,000	1,293,000	849,000	990,000	1,073,000	955,000
Income Taxes	68,000	151,000	11,000	406,000	286,000	299,000	347,000	275,000
Net Income	166,000	211,000	261,000	887,000	563,000	691,000	818,000	458,000
Average Shares	303,000	302,000	302,000	307,000	311,000	313,000	316,000	317,000
Balance Sheet								
Current Assets	2,053,000	1,967,000	2,296,000	1,900,000	1,908,000	2,092,000	2,100,000	2,221,000
Total Assets	13,110,000	13,148,000	14,529,000	7,726,000	7,837,000	8,089,000	8,113,000	8,323,000
Current Liabilities	3,435,000	3,385,000	3,594,000	2,395,000	2,555,000	2,806,000	2,989,000	3,282,000
Long-Term Obligations	6,706,000	7,103,000	7,998,000	2,499,000	2,314,000	2,552,000	2,244,000	2,544,000
Total Liabilities	11,871,000	12,045,000	13,165,000	6,089,000	6,312,000	6,709,000	6,498,000	7,106,000
Stockholders' Equity	1,239,000	1,103,000	1,364,000	1,637,000	1,525,000	1,380,000	1,615,000	1,217,000
Shares Outstanding	323,000	301,000	301,000	301,000	308,000	310,000	313,000	312,000
Statistical Record								
Return on Assets %	1.32	1.53	2.35	11.43	7.09	8.55	9.79	6.18
Return on Equity %	13.84	17.15	17.44	56.26	38.87	46.27	56.83	43.43
EBITDA Margin %	15.03	16.87	9.55	21.53	15.68	17.09	17.89	18.29
Net Margin %	7.60	2.60	3.01	11.24	7.07	8.55	9.89	5.69
Asset Turnover	0.58	0.59	0.78	1.02	1.00	1.00	0.99	1.09
Current Ratio	0.60	0.58	0.64	0.79	0.75	0.75	0.70	0.68
Debt to Equity	5.41	6.44	5.86	1.53	1.52	1.85	1.39	2.09
Price Range	47.96-32.26	43.08-32.26	54.19-33.19	63.84-50.96	67.55-46.15	49.31-41.60	47.89-38.60	48.14-32.47
P/E Ratio	79.93-53.77	61.54-46.09	63.01-38.59	22.09-17.63	37.32-25.50	22.31-18.82	18.49-14.90	33.43-22.55
Average Yield %	3.53	3.65	3.13	2.44	2.20	2.75	2.87	2.93

Address: 1 Campbell Place, Camden, NJ 08103-1799
Telephone: 856-342-4800
Fax: 856-342-3878

Web Site: www.campbellsoupcompany.com
Officers: Keith R. McLoughlin - Chairman, Interim President, Interim Chief Executive Officer Mark A. Clouse - President, Chief Executive Officer

Auditors: PricewaterhouseCoopers LLP
Investor Contact: 180-084-02865
Transfer Agents: Computershare Trust Company, N.A., Providence, RI

CANTEL MEDICAL CORP

Exchange	Symbol	Price	52Wk Range	Yield	P/E
NYS	CMD	$70.90 (12/31/2019)	92.54-64.30	0.30	70.90

*7 Year Price Score 99.10 ***NYSE Composite Index=100** ***12 Month Price Score 92.29**

Interim Earnings (Per Share)
Qtr.	Oct	Jan	Apr	Jul
2016-17	0.45	0.43	0.42	0.41
2017-18	0.55	0.78	0.45	0.41
2018-19	0.46	0.45	0.20	0.21
2019-20	0.14	...	...	...

Interim Dividends (Per Share)
Amt	Decl	Ex	Rec	Pay
0.085S	06/27/2018	07/16/2018	07/17/2018	07/31/2018
0.10S	12/19/2018	01/16/2019	01/17/2019	01/31/2019
0.10S	06/26/2019	07/16/2019	07/17/2019	07/31/2019
0.105S	12/18/2019	01/16/2020	01/17/2020	01/31/2020

Indicated Div: $0.21

Valuation Analysis
		Institutional Holding	
Forecast EPS	$2.80	No of Institutions	
	(01/14/2020)	350	
Market Cap	$3.0 Billion	Shares	
Book Value	$732.2 Million	47,057,340	
Price/Book	4.12	% Held	
Price/Sales	3.18	94.49	

Business Summary: Medical Instruments & Equipment (MIC: 4.3.1 SIC: 3841 NAIC: 339112)

Cantel Medical is a provider of infection prevention products and services in the healthcare market. Co. has four segments: Medical, which designs, develops, manufactures, sells and installs products and services comprising a circle of infection prevention solutions; Life Sciences, which designs, develops, manufactures, sells, and installs water purification systems; Dental, which designs, manufactures, sells, supplies and distributes infection prevention healthcare products; and Dialysis, which designs, develops, manufactures, sells and services reprocessing systems and sterilants for dialyzers, as well as dialysate concentrates and supplies utilized for renal dialysis

Recent Developments: For the quarter ended Oct 31 2019, net income decreased 70.0% to US$5.8 million from US$19.2 million in the year-earlier quarter. Revenues were US$257.2 million, up 14.0% from US$225.6 million the year before. Operating income was US$14.4 million versus US$27.7 million in the prior-year quarter, a decrease of 47.9%. Direct operating expenses rose 17.5% to US$141.4 million from US$120.3 million in the comparable period the year before. Indirect operating expenses increased 30.8% to US$101.4 million from US$77.6 million in the equivalent prior-year period.

Prospects: Our evaluation of Cantel Medical Corp. as of October 4th, 2019 is the result of our systematic analysis on three basic characteristics: earnings strength, relative valuation, and recent stock price movement. The company has produced a positive trend in earnings per share over the past 5 quarters. In addition, recent analyst estimates for the company have been raised, and CMD has posted results that exceeded analysts' expectations. Based on operating earnings yield, the company is fairly valued when compared to all of the companies we cover. Share price changes over the past year indicates that CMD will perform over the near term.

Financial Data
(US$ in Thousands)	3 Mos	07/31/2019	07/31/2018	07/31/2017	07/31/2016	07/31/2015	07/31/2014	07/31/2013
Earnings Per Share	1.00	1.32	2.18	1.71	1.44	1.15	1.04	0.95
Cash Flow Per Share	1.04	1.61	3.03	2.61	1.94	1.44	1.58	1.28
Tang Book Value Per Share	N.M.	3.40	2.48	2.11	1.49	1.90	1.22	0.82
Dividends Per Share	0.200	0.200	0.170	0.140	0.120	0.100	0.090	0.074
Dividend Payout %	20.00	15.15	7.80	8.19	8.33	8.70	8.65	7.75
Income Statement								
Total Revenue	257,246	918,155	871,922	770,157	664,755	565,004	488,749	425,026
EBITDA	34,285	106,334	140,275	125,581	109,240	89,247	79,173	70,390
Depn & Amortn	19,861	21,510	17,473	15,045	11,989	10,692	8,245	7,202
Income Before Taxes	8,705	75,319	117,513	106,233	93,931	76,191	68,611	60,354
Income Taxes	2,938	20,277	26,472	34,855	33,978	28,238	25,346	21,115
Net Income	5,767	55,042	91,041	71,378	59,953	47,953	43,265	39,239
Average Shares	42,168	41,757	41,635	41,542	41,390	41,202	40,911	40,556
Balance Sheet								
Current Assets	449,732	351,796	338,243	257,371	222,742	188,361	163,909	150,660
Total Assets	1,906,046	1,070,366	963,708	786,373	694,532	584,031	536,145	487,671
Current Liabilities	183,397	151,400	134,783	106,779	96,335	70,624	66,499	59,151
Long-Term Obligations	875,755	220,851	187,302	126,000	116,000	78,500	80,500	85,000
Total Liabilities	1,173,855	408,829	354,841	262,441	240,162	177,398	170,899	166,539
Stockholders' Equity	732,191	661,537	608,867	523,932	454,370	406,633	365,246	321,132
Shares Outstanding	42,576	41,771	41,706	41,728	41,708	41,604	41,442	41,138
Statistical Record								
Return on Assets %	2.88	5.41	10.40	9.64	9.35	8.56	8.45	8.51
Return on Equity %	6.14	8.67	16.07	14.59	13.89	12.43	12.61	13.14
EBITDA Margin %	13.33	11.58	16.09	16.31	16.43	15.80	16.20	16.56
Net Margin %	2.24	5.99	10.44	9.27	9.02	8.49	8.85	9.23
Asset Turnover	0.66	0.90	1.00	1.04	1.04	1.01	0.95	0.92
Current Ratio	2.45	2.32	2.51	2.41	2.31	2.67	2.46	2.55
Debt to Equity	1.20	0.33	0.31	0.24	0.26	0.19	0.22	0.26
Price Range	92.54-64.30	97.71-64.30	129.78-73.30	85.85-68.19	73.88-48.38	55.68-33.53	37.71-25.86	26.86-16.40
P/E Ratio	92.54-64.30	74.02-48.71	59.53-33.62	50.20-39.88	51.31-33.60	48.42-29.16	36.26-24.87	28.27-17.26
Average Yield %	0.26	0.25	0.17	0.18	0.19	0.23	0.27	0.36

Address: 150 Clove Road, Little Falls, NJ 07424	**Web Site:** www.cantelmedical.com	**Auditors:** DELOITTE & TOUCHE LLP
Telephone: 973-890-7220	**Officers:** Charles M. Diker - Chairman George L. Fotiades - Vice-Chairman, President, Chief Executive Officer	**Investor Contact:** 212-554-5466
Fax: 973-890-7270		**Transfer Agents:** American Stock Transfer & Trust Company, New York, NY

CAPITAL ONE FINANCIAL CORP

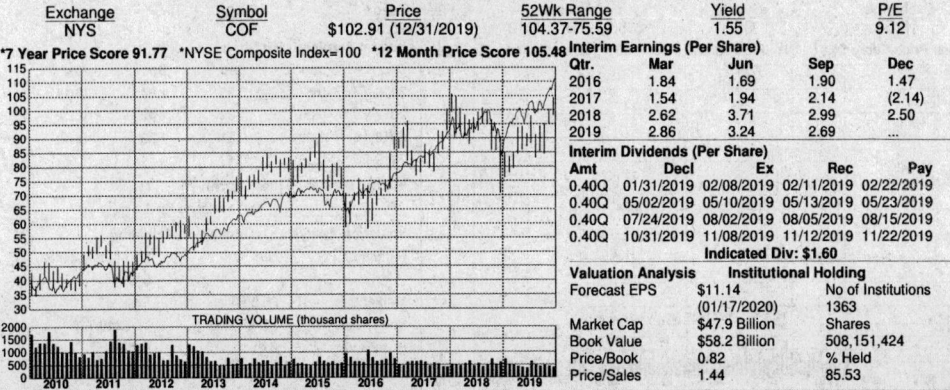

Exchange	Symbol	Price	52Wk Range	Yield	P/E
NYS	COF	$102.91 (12/31/2019)	104.37-75.59	1.55	9.12

*7 Year Price Score 91.77   *NYSE Composite Index=100   *12 Month Price Score 105.48

Interim Earnings (Per Share)

Qtr.	Mar	Jun	Sep	Dec
2016	1.84	1.69	1.90	1.47
2017	1.54	1.94	2.14	(2.14)
2018	2.62	3.71	2.99	2.50
2019	2.86	3.24	2.69	...

Interim Dividends (Per Share)

Amt	Decl	Ex	Rec	Pay
0.40Q	01/31/2019	02/08/2019	02/11/2019	02/22/2019
0.40Q	05/02/2019	05/10/2019	05/13/2019	05/23/2019
0.40Q	07/24/2019	08/02/2019	08/05/2019	08/15/2019
0.40Q	10/31/2019	11/08/2019	11/12/2019	11/22/2019

Indicated Div: $1.60

Valuation Analysis

		Institutional Holding	
Forecast EPS	$11.14	No of Institutions	
	(01/17/2020)	1363	
Market Cap	$47.9 Billion	Shares	
Book Value	$58.2 Billion	508,151,424	
Price/Book	0.82	% Held	
Price/Sales	1.44	85.53	

Business Summary: Banking (MIC: 5.1.1 SIC: 6021 NAIC: 522110)

Capital One Financial is a financial services holding company. Through its subsidiaries, Co. provides an array of financial products and services. Co.'s segments are: Credit Card, which consists of Co.'s domestic consumer and small business card lending, and international card businesses in Canada and the U.K.; Consumer Banking, which consists of Co.'s branch-based deposit gathering and lending activities for consumers and small businesses, national deposit gathering and national auto lending; and Commercial Banking, which consists of Co.'s lending, deposit gathering, capital markets and treasury management services to commercial real estate and commercial and industrial customers.

Recent Developments: For the quarter ended Sep 30 2019, income from continuing operations decreased 11.5% to US$1.33 billion from US$1.50 billion in the year-earlier quarter. Net income decreased 11.3% to US$1.33 billion from US$1.50 billion in the year-earlier quarter. Net interest income decreased 0.8% to US$5.74 billion from US$5.79 billion in the year-earlier quarter. Provision for loan losses was US$1.38 billion versus US$1.27 billion in the prior-year quarter, an increase of 9.1%. Non-interest income rose 3.9% to US$1.22 billion from US$1.18 billion, while non-interest expense advanced 2.6% to US$3.87 billion.

Prospects: Our evaluation of Capital One Financial Corp. as of October 4th, 2019 is the result of our systematic analysis on three basic characteristics: earnings strength, relative valuation, and recent stock price movement. The company has managed to produce a neutral trend in earnings per share over the past 5 quarters. In addition, recent analyst estimates for the company have been mixed and COF has posted results that exceeded analysts' expectations. Based on operating earnings yield, the company is undervalued when compared to all of the companies we cover. Share price changes over the past year indicates that COF will perform in line with the market over the near term.

Financial Data

(US$ in Thousands)	9 Mos	6 Mos	3 Mos	12/31/2018	12/31/2017	12/31/2016	12/31/2015	12/31/2014
Earnings Per Share	11.29	11.59	12.06	11.82	3.49	6.89	7.07	7.59
Cash Flow Per Share	35.06	34.83	34.62	27.04	29.29	23.42	18.69	16.52
Tang Book Value Per Share	93.64	87.64	82.91	79.37	70.43	68.71	62.22	56.15
Dividends Per Share	1.600	1.600	1.600	1.600	1.600	1.600	1.500	1.200
Dividend Payout %	14.17	13.81	13.27	13.54	45.85	23.22	21.22	15.81
Income Statement								
Interest Income	21,243,000	14,168,000	7,092,000	27,176,000	25,222,000	22,891,000	20,459,000	19,397,000
Interest Expense	3,969,000	2,631,000	1,301,000	4,301,000	2,762,000	2,018,000	1,625,000	1,579,000
Net Interest Income	17,274,000	11,537,000	5,791,000	22,875,000	22,460,000	20,873,000	18,834,000	17,818,000
Provision for Losses	4,418,000	3,035,000	1,693,000	5,856,000	7,551,000	6,459,000	4,536,000	3,541,000
Non-Interest Income	3,892,000	2,670,000	1,292,000	5,201,000	4,777,000	4,628,000	4,579,000	4,472,000
Non-Interest Expense	11,322,000	7,450,000	3,671,000	14,902,000	14,194,000	13,558,000	12,996,000	12,180,000
Income Before Taxes	5,426,000	3,722,000	1,719,000	7,318,000	5,492,000	5,484,000	5,881,000	6,569,000
Income Taxes	1,071,000	696,000	309,000	1,293,000	3,375,000	1,714,000	1,869,000	2,146,000
Net Income	4,370,000	3,037,000	1,412,000	6,015,000	1,982,000	3,751,000	4,050,000	4,428,000
Average Shares	471,800	473,000	471,600	483,100	488,600	509,800	548,000	571,900
Balance Sheet								
Net Loans & Leases	243,563,000	239,156,000	233,865,000	239,871,000	247,942,000	240,126,000	225,625,000	204,559,000
Total Assets	378,810,000	373,619,000	373,191,000	372,538,000	365,693,000	357,033,000	334,048,000	308,854,000
Total Deposits	257,148,000	254,535,000	255,107,000	249,764,000	243,702,000	236,768,000	217,721,000	205,548,000
Total Liabilities	320,575,000	317,852,000	319,710,000	320,870,000	316,963,000	309,519,000	286,764,000	263,801,000
Stockholders' Equity	58,235,000	55,767,000	53,481,000	51,668,000	48,730,000	47,514,000	47,284,000	45,053,000
Shares Outstanding	465,720	470,333	469,596	467,717	485,525	480,218	527,259	553,391
Statistical Record								
Return on Assets %	1.52	1.57	1.65	1.63	0.55	1.08	1.26	1.46
Return on Equity %	10.34	10.98	11.84	11.98	4.12	7.89	8.77	10.20
Net Interest Margin %	81.09	81.20	81.66	84.17	89.05	91.18	92.06	91.86
Efficiency Ratio %	46.67	44.70	43.79	46.03	47.31	49.27	51.91	51.03
Loans to Deposits	0.95	0.94	0.92	0.96	1.02	1.01	1.04	1.00
Price Range	98.08-70.78	100.90-70.78	100.90-70.78	105.71-70.78	100.50-76.92	90.62-58.15	91.71-71.55	84.95-68.66
P/E Ratio	8.69-6.27	8.71-6.11	8.37-5.87	8.94-5.99	28.80-22.04	13.15-8.44	12.97-10.12	11.19-9.05
Average Yield %	1.84		1.84	1.69	1.86	2.24	1.88	1.53

Address: 1680 Capital One Drive, McLean, VA 22102 **Telephone:** 703-720-1000	**Web Site:** www.capitalone.com **Officers:** Richard D. Fairbank - Chairman, President, Chief Executive Officer Sheldon F. Hall - Senior Vice President, Chief Risk Officer, Division Officer	**Auditors:** Ernst & Young LLP **Investor Contact:** 703-720-2455 **Transfer Agents:** ComputerShare Investor Services, Providence, RI

CAPRI HOLDINGS LTD

Exchange	Symbol	Price	52Wk Range	Yield	P/E
NYS	CPRI	$38.15 (12/31/2019)	49.83-25.57	N/A	17.18

*7 Year Price Score 54.87 *NYSE Composite Index=100 *12 Month Price Score 91.40

TRADING VOLUME (thousand shares)

Interim Earnings (Per Share)

Qtr.	Jun	Sep	Dec	Mar
2016-17	0.83	0.95	1.64	(0.11)
2017-18	0.80	1.32	1.42	0.29
2018-19	1.22	0.91	1.33	0.12
2019-20	0.30	0.47	...	...

Interim Dividends (Per Share)

No Dividends Paid

Valuation Analysis — **Institutional Holding**

Forecast EPS	N/A	No of Institutions 515
Market Cap	$5.8 Billion	Shares
Book Value	$2.4 Billion	164,248,720
Price/Book	2.41	% Held
Price/Sales	1.04	N/A

Business Summary: Retail - Apparel and Accessories (MIC: 2.1.5 SIC: 3199 NAIC: 316999)

Capri Holdings is a designer, marketer, distributor and retailer of branded women's and men's accessories, apparel and footwear bearing the Versace, Jimmy Choo and Michael Kors tradenames and related trademarks and logos. Co.'s brands cover a range of fashion categories including women's and men's accessories, footwear and ready-to-wear, as well as wearable technology, watches, jewelry, eyewear and a line of fragrance products. Co. sells its Versace, Jimmy Choo and Michael Kors products through retail and wholesale channels of distribution in three principal geographic markets: the Americas (U.S., Canada and Latin America), Europe, Middle East and Africa and Asia.

Recent Developments: For the quarter ended Sep 28 2019, net income decreased 46.7% to US$73.0 million from US$137.0 million in the year-earlier quarter. Revenues were US$1.44 billion, up 15.1% from US$1.25 billion the year before. Operating income was US$75.0 million versus US$190.0 million in the prior-year quarter, a decrease of 60.5%. Direct operating expenses rose 15.9% to US$568.0 million from US$490.0 million in the comparable period the year before. Indirect operating expenses increased 39.4% to US$799.0 million from US$573.0 million in the equivalent prior-year period.

Prospects: Our evaluation of Capri Holdings Ltd. as of October 4th, 2019 is the result of our systematic analysis on three basic characteristics: earnings strength, relative valuation, and recent stock price movement. The company has managed to produce a neutral trend in earnings per share over the past 5 quarters. In addition, recent analyst estimates for the company have been mixed and CPRI has posted results that exceeded analysts' expectations. Based on operating earnings yield, the company is undervalued when compared to all of the companies we cover. Share price changes over the past year indicates that CPRI will perform very poorly over the near term.

Financial Data

(US$ in Thousands)	6 Mos	3 Mos	03/30/2019	03/31/2018	04/01/2017	04/02/2016	03/28/2015	03/29/2014
Earnings Per Share	2.22	2.66	3.58	3.82	3.29	4.44	4.28	3.22
Cash Flow Per Share	4.44	4.27	4.65	7.00	6.21	6.49	4.24	3.13
Tang Book Value Per Share	N.M.	N.M.	N.M.	N.M.	6.77	10.80	10.85	8.54
Income Statement								
Total Revenue	2,788,000	1,346,000	5,238,000	4,718,600	4,493,700	4,712,100	4,371,469	3,310,843
EBITDA	238,000	112,000	847,000	946,400	890,400	1,346,200	1,387,438	1,084,640
Depn & Amortn	102,000	48,000	188,000	182,300	197,700	172,200	131,400	76,600
Income Before Taxes	120,000	51,000	621,000	741,800	688,600	1,172,300	1,255,823	1,007,647
Income Taxes	2,000	6,000	79,000	149,700	137,100	334,600	374,800	346,162
Net Income	118,000	45,000	543,000	591,900	552,500	839,100	881,023	661,485
Average Shares	152,576	152,334	151,614	155,102	168,123	189,054	205,865	205,638
Balance Sheet								
Current Assets	1,895,000	1,710,000	1,729,000	1,262,100	1,164,700	1,669,800	2,017,431	1,777,169
Total Assets	8,393,000	8,308,000	6,650,000	4,059,000	2,409,600	2,566,800	2,691,893	2,216,973
Current Liabilities	1,803,000	1,668,000	1,542,000	960,300	565,800	435,500	330,081	308,370
Long-Term Obligations	1,796,000	1,917,000	1,936,000	674,400	...	2,300	...	...
Total Liabilities	5,988,000	5,987,000	4,221,000	2,041,300	817,000	571,100	450,928	410,842
Stockholders' Equity	2,405,000	2,321,000	2,429,000	2,017,700	1,592,600	1,995,700	2,240,965	1,806,131
Shares Outstanding	151,633	151,565	150,932	149,698	155,833	176,441	199,656	204,261
Statistical Record								
Return on Assets %	5.39	6.55	10.17	18.35	22.27	31.40	35.99	37.83
Return on Equity %	14.70	18.43	24.49	32.88	30.88	38.97	43.66	46.49
EBITDA Margin %	8.54	8.32	16.17	20.06	19.81	28.57	31.74	32.76
Net Margin %	4.23	3.34	10.37	12.54	12.29	17.81	20.15	19.98
Asset Turnover	0.89	0.88	0.98	1.46	1.81	1.76	1.79	1.89
Current Ratio	1.05	1.03	1.12	1.31	2.06	3.83	6.11	5.76
Debt to Equity	0.75	0.83	0.80	0.33	...	N.M.	...	...
Price Range	68.56-25.57	75.41-32.48	75.41-36.03	68.14-33.05	56.35-36.02	66.26-35.57	97.01-64.33	99.84-52.36
P/E Ratio	30.88-11.52	28.35-12.21	21.06-10.06	17.84-8.65	17.13-10.95	14.92-8.01	22.67-15.03	31.01-16.26

Address: 33 Kingsway, London, WC2B 6UF **Telephone:** 207-632-8600	**Web Site:** www.michaelkors.com **Officers:** John D. Idol - Chairman, Chief Executive Officer Michael David Kors - Honorary Chairman, Chief Creative Officer	**Auditors:** Ernst & Young LLP **Investor Contact:** 203-682-8200 **Transfer Agents:** American Stock Transfer & Trust Company, LLC, Brooklyn, NY

CARDINAL HEALTH, INC.

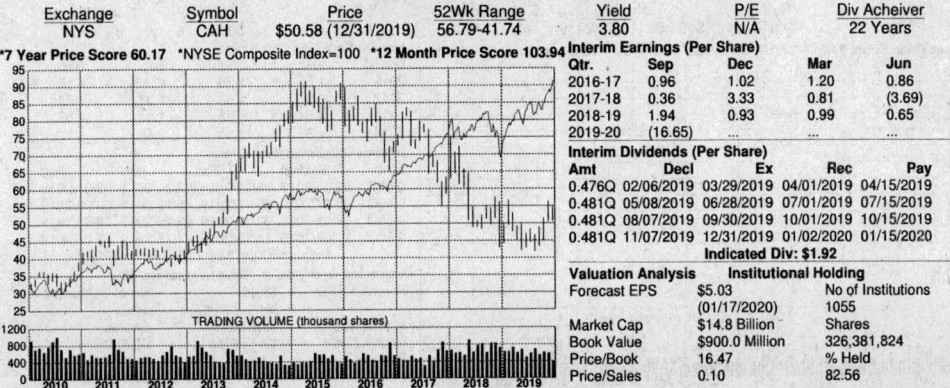

Exchange	Symbol	Price	52Wk Range	Yield	P/E	Div Acheiver
NYS	CAH	$50.58 (12/31/2019)	56.79-41.74	3.80	N/A	22 Years

*7 Year Price Score 60.17 *NYSE Composite Index=100 *12 Month Price Score 103.94

Interim Earnings (Per Share)
Qtr.	Sep	Dec	Mar	Jun
2016-17	0.96	1.02	1.20	0.86
2017-18	0.36	3.33	0.81	(3.69)
2018-19	1.94	0.93	0.99	0.65
2019-20	(16.65)	...	...	...

Interim Dividends (Per Share)
Amt	Decl	Ex	Rec	Pay
0.476Q	02/06/2019	03/29/2019	04/01/2019	04/15/2019
0.481Q	05/08/2019	06/28/2019	07/01/2019	07/15/2019
0.481Q	08/07/2019	09/30/2019	10/01/2019	10/15/2019
0.481Q	11/07/2019	12/31/2019	01/02/2020	01/15/2020

Indicated Div: $1.92

Valuation Analysis / Institutional Holding
Forecast EPS	$5.03	No of Institutions
	(01/17/2020)	1055
Market Cap	$14.8 Billion	Shares
Book Value	$900.0 Million	326,381,824
Price/Book	16.47	% Held
Price/Sales	0.10	82.56

Business Summary: Pharmaceuticals (MIC: 4.1.1 SIC: 5122 NAIC: 424210)

Cardinal Health is a healthcare services and products company providing customized solutions for hospitals, healthcare systems, pharmacies, ambulatory surgery centers, clinical laboratories and physician offices. Co.'s segments include: Pharmaceutical and Medical. Co.'s Pharmaceutical segment distributes branded and generic pharmaceutical, specialty pharmaceutical and over-the-counter healthcare and consumer products in the United States. Co.'s Medical segment manufactures, sources and distributes Cardinal Health branded medical, surgical and laboratory products, which are sold in the United States, Canada, Europe, Asia and other markets.

Recent Developments: For the quarter ended Sep 30 2019, net loss amounted to US$4.92 billion versus net income of US$594.0 million in the year-earlier quarter. Revenues were US$37.34 billion, up 6.0% from US$35.21 billion the year before. Operating loss was US$5.26 billion versus an income of US$816.0 million in the prior-year quarter. Direct operating expenses rose 6.3% to US$35.66 billion from US$33.55 billion in the comparable period the year before. Indirect operating expenses increased 715.9% to US$6.94 billion from US$851.0 million in the equivalent prior-year period.

Prospects: Our evaluation of Cardinal Health Inc. as of October 4th, 2019 is the result of our systematic analysis on three basic characteristics: earnings strength, relative valuation, and recent stock price movement. The company has managed to produce a neutral trend in earnings per share over the past 5 quarters. However, recent analyst estimates for the company have been reduced while CAH has posted results that exceeded analysts' expectations. Based on operating earnings yield, the company is undervalued when compared to all of the companies we cover. Share price changes over the past year indicates that CAH will perform poorly over the near term.

Financial Data
(US$ in Thousands)

	3 Mos	06/30/2019	06/30/2018	06/30/2017	06/30/2016	06/30/2015	06/30/2014	06/30/2013
Earnings Per Share	(14.08)	4.53	0.81	4.03	4.32	3.62	3.38	0.97
Cash Flow Per Share	5.76	9.07	8.84	3.74	9.06	7.65	7.40	5.06
Tang Book Value Per Share	N.M.	N.M.	N.M.	N.M.	N.M.	0.73	1.58	1.18
Dividends Per Share	1.915	1.910	1.863	1.809	1.610	1.415	1.250	1.090
Dividend Payout %	...	42.16	230.06	44.89	37.27	39.07	36.98	112.37
Income Statement								
Total Revenue	37,341,000	145,534,000	136,809,000	129,976,000	121,546,000	102,531,000	91,084,000	101,093,000
EBITDA	(5,044,000)	2,500,000	547,000	2,439,000	2,731,000	2,362,000	2,196,000	1,270,000
Depn & Amortn	234,000	455,000	446,000	314,000	277,000	254,000	265,000	259,000
Income Before Taxes	(5,344,000)	1,751,000	(228,000)	1,924,000	2,276,000	1,967,000	1,798,000	888,000
Income Taxes	(423,000)	386,000	(487,000)	630,000	845,000	755,000	635,000	553,000
Net Income	(4,922,000)	1,363,000	256,000	1,288,000	1,427,000	1,215,000	1,166,000	334,000
Average Shares	296,000	301,000	315,000	320,000	330,000	335,000	345,000	344,000
Balance Sheet								
Current Assets	23,715,000	25,747,000	24,553,000	28,345,000	21,956,000	21,752,000	17,939,000	17,770,000
Total Assets	39,179,000	40,963,000	39,951,000	40,112,000	34,122,000	30,142,000	26,033,000	25,819,000
Current Liabilities	22,549,000	24,109,000	22,893,000	21,221,000	19,701,000	17,243,000	15,115,000	14,590,000
Long-Term Obligations	7,360,000	7,579,000	8,012,000	9,068,000	4,952,000	5,211,000	3,171,000	3,686,000
Total Liabilities	38,279,000	34,635,000	33,892,000	33,304,000	27,568,000	23,886,000	19,632,000	19,844,000
Stockholders' Equity	900,000	6,328,000	6,059,000	6,808,000	6,554,000	6,256,000	6,401,000	5,975,000
Shares Outstanding	293,000	299,000	309,000	316,000	322,000	328,000	337,000	339,000
Statistical Record								
Return on Assets %	N.M.	3.37	0.64	3.47	4.43	4.33	4.50	1.33
Return on Equity %	N.M.	22.01	3.98	19.28	22.22	19.20	18.84	5.47
EBITDA Margin %	N.M.	1.72	0.40	1.88	2.25	2.30	2.41	1.26
Net Margin %	N.M.	0.94	0.19	0.99	1.17	1.19	1.28	0.33
Asset Turnover	3.73	3.60	3.42	3.50	3.77	3.65	3.51	4.04
Current Ratio	1.05	1.07	1.07	1.34	1.11	1.26	1.19	1.22
Debt to Equity	8.18	1.20	1.32	1.33	0.76	0.83	0.50	0.62
Price Range	57.63-41.74	57.63-42.07	78.69-48.83	84.92-65.17	90.85-73.69	91.50-68.56	73.54-47.02	48.76-37.75
P/E Ratio	...	12.72-9.29	97.15-60.28	21.07-16.17	21.03-17.06	25.28-18.94	21.76-13.91	50.27-38.92
Average Yield %	3.95	3.83	2.89	2.35	1.95	1.74	2.01	2.54

Address: 7000 Cardinal Place, Dublin, OH 43017 **Telephone:** 614-757-5000	**Web Site:** www.cardinalhealth.com **Officers:** Gregory B. Kenny - Chairman Michael C. Kaufmann - Chief Executive Officer, Chief Financial Officer, Interim Chief Financial Officer, Division Officer	**Auditors:** Ernst & Young LLP **Investor Contact:** 614-757-7115 **Transfer Agents:** Computershare Trust Company, N.A., Canton, MA

133

CARLISLE COMPANIES INC.

Exchange	Symbol	Price	52Wk Range	Yield	P/E	Div Acheiver
NYS	CSL	$161.84 (12/31/2019)	163.07-99.04	1.24	20.38	34 Years

*7 Year Price Score 113.17 *NYSE Composite Index=100 *12 Month Price Score 110.01

Interim Earnings (Per Share)

Qtr.	Mar	Jun	Sep	Dec
2016	1.05	1.75	(0.15)	1.16
2017	0.94	1.58	1.37	1.82
2018	4.94	1.85	1.64	1.53
2019	1.36	2.65	2.40	...

Interim Dividends (Per Share)

Amt	Decl	Ex	Rec	Pay
0.40Q	02/05/2019	02/19/2019	02/20/2019	03/01/2019
0.40Q	05/07/2019	05/14/2019	05/15/2019	06/03/2019
0.50Q	08/01/2019	08/19/2019	08/20/2019	09/03/2019
0.50Q	11/04/2019	11/15/2019	11/18/2019	12/02/2019

Indicated Div: $2.00 (Div. Reinv. Plan)

Valuation Analysis | **Institutional Holding**

Forecast EPS	$8.04	No of Institutions
	(01/17/2020)	564
Market Cap	$9.1 Billion	Shares
Book Value	$2.7 Billion	60,458,536
Price/Book	3.41	% Held
Price/Sales	1.93	81.64

Business Summary: Rubber Products (MIC: 8.4.1 SIC: 3069 NAIC: 326299)

Carlisle Companies designs, manufactures and markets commercial roofing, energy, agriculture, mining, construction, aerospace and defense electronics, medical technology, transportation, general industrial, protective coatings, wood and auto refinishing. Co.'s segments are: Carlisle Construction Materials, which designs, manufactures and sells thermoplastic polyolefin and ethylene propylene diene monomer rubber; Carlisle Interconnect Technologies, which engineers, manufactures and sells wire, contacts and cable assemblies and satellite communication equipment; and Carlisle Fluid Technologies, which designs, manufactures and sells liquid and powder finishing equipment and system components.

Recent Developments: For the quarter ended Sep 30 2019, income from continuing operations increased 43.8% to US$139.3 million from US$96.9 million in the year-earlier quarter. Net income increased 38.3% to US$137.9 million from US$99.7 million in the year-earlier quarter. Revenues were US$1.28 billion, up 8.4% from US$1.18 billion the year before. Operating income was US$191.0 million versus US$140.0 million in the prior-year quarter, an increase of 36.4%. Direct operating expenses rose 3.8% to US$900.4 million from US$867.1 million in the comparable period the year before. Indirect operating expenses increased 8.5% to US$189.2 million from US$174.3 million in the equivalent prior-year period.

Prospects: Our evaluation of Carlisle Companies Inc. as of October 4th, 2019 is the result of our systematic analysis on three basic characteristics: earnings strength, relative valuation, and recent stock price movement. The company has enjoyed a very positive trend in earnings per share over the past 5 quarters. However, recent analyst estimates for the company have been reduced, while CSL has posted results that exceeded analysts' expectations. Based on operating earnings yield, the company is undervalued when compared to all of the companies we cover. Share price changes over the past year indicates that CSL will perform well over the near term.

Financial Data

(US$ in Thousands)	9 Mos	6 Mos	3 Mos	12/31/2018	12/31/2017	12/31/2016	12/31/2015	12/31/2014
Earnings Per Share	7.94	7.18	6.38	10.02	5.71	3.82	4.82	3.82
Cash Flow Per Share	12.82	9.46	7.23	5.62	7.27	8.25	8.16	4.61
Tang Book Value Per Share	2.03	N.M.	N.M.	3.24	N.M.	7.99	5.08	9.72
Dividends Per Share	1.700	1.600	1.570	1.540	1.440	1.300	1.100	0.940
Dividend Payout %	21.41	22.28	24.61	15.37	25.22	34.03	22.82	24.61
Income Statement								
Total Revenue	3,667,300	2,386,700	1,071,900	4,479,500	4,089,900	3,675,400	3,543,200	3,204,000
EBITDA	666,600	422,900	164,200	585,800	586,600	516,200	575,400	473,000
Depn & Amortn	151,500	100,000	49,100	86,400	84,900	75,100	73,500	64,700
Income Before Taxes	471,700	294,500	101,400	445,900	468,200	410,500	467,900	376,100
Income Taxes	102,000	64,100	24,000	87,300	102,900	159,700	148,300	124,400
Net Income	370,200	232,300	79,400	611,100	365,500	250,100	319,700	251,300
Average Shares	57,335	57,566	57,870	60,786	63,551	64,883	65,804	65,304
Balance Sheet								
Current Assets	2,107,400	1,922,200	1,877,300	2,056,700	1,644,600	1,355,200	1,319,500	1,611,500
Total Assets	5,541,100	5,396,700	5,301,700	5,249,200	5,299,800	3,965,800	3,954,100	3,758,700
Current Liabilities	692,200	649,900	633,200	595,600	658,600	513,500	605,900	392,200
Long-Term Obligations	1,590,200	1,589,400	1,588,500	1,587,800	1,586,200	596,400	598,700	749,800
Total Liabilities	2,860,100	2,813,500	2,777,000	2,651,800	2,771,500	1,498,900	1,606,700	1,553,700
Stockholders' Equity	2,681,000	2,583,200	2,524,700	2,597,400	2,528,300	2,466,900	2,347,400	2,205,000
Shares Outstanding	56,494	56,420	56,802	57,957	61,839	64,257	64,051	64,691
Statistical Record								
Return on Assets %	8.35	7.76	7.05	11.59	7.89	6.30	8.29	6.93
Return on Equity %	17.02	15.99	14.52	23.84	14.63	10.36	14.05	11.99
EBITDA Margin %	18.18	17.72	15.32	13.08	14.34	14.04	16.24	14.76
Net Margin %	10.09	9.73	7.41	13.64	8.94	6.80	9.02	7.84
Asset Turnover	0.86	0.86	0.85	0.85	0.88	0.93	0.92	0.88
Current Ratio	3.04	2.96	2.96	3.45	2.50	2.64	2.18	4.11
Debt to Equity	0.59	0.62	0.63	0.61	0.63	0.24	0.26	0.34
Price Range	149.29-93.18	141.42-93.18	128.82-93.18	128.82-93.18	115.91-92.40	115.96-77.82	104.60-84.11	91.54-71.67
P/E Ratio	18.80-11.74	19.70-12.98	20.19-14.61	12.86-9.30	20.30-16.18	30.36-20.37	21.70-17.45	23.96-18.76
Average Yield %	1.38	1.35	1.41	1.40	1.39	1.29	1.16	1.14

Address: 16430 North Scottsdale Road, Suite 400, Scottsdale, AZ 85254 Telephone: 480-781-5000	Web Site: www.carlisle.com Officers: David A. Roberts - Chairman, President, Chief Executive Officer D. Christian Koch - President, Chief Executive Officer, Chief Operating Officer, Region Officer	Auditors: DELOITTE & TOUCHE LLP Investor Contact: 800-897-9071 Transfer Agents: Computershare Investor Services, LLC, Chicago, IL

CARMAX INC.

Exchange	Symbol	Price	52Wk Range	Yield	P/E
NYS	KMX	$87.67 (12/31/2019)	100.15-58.38	N/A	16.99

*7 Year Price Score 108.16 *NYSE Composite Index=100 *12 Month Price Score 112.69

Interim Earnings (Per Share)

Qtr.	May	Aug	Nov	Feb
2016-17	0.90	0.84	0.72	0.81
2017-18	1.13	0.98	0.81	0.67
2018-19	1.33	1.24	1.09	1.13
2019-20	1.59	1.40	1.04	...

Interim Dividends (Per Share)

No Dividends Paid

Valuation Analysis

		Institutional Holding	
Forecast EPS	$5.15	No of Institutions	
	(01/17/2020)	837	
Market Cap	$14.4 Billion	Shares	
Book Value	$3.7 Billion	215,253,344	
Price/Book	3.88	% Held	
Price/Sales	0.73	74.71	

Business Summary: Retail - Automotive (MIC: 2.1.4 SIC: 5521 NAIC: 441120)

CarMax is a holding company. Through its subsidiaries, Co. is engaged as a retailer of used vehicles. Co. operates in two segments: CarMax Sales Operations, which sells used vehicles, purchases used vehicles from customers and other sources, sells related products and services, and arranges financing options for customers; and CarMax Auto Finance, which consists of finance operation that provides vehicle financing to customer buying retail vehicles from Co. Co.'s products and services include retail merchandising, wholesale auctions, extended protection plans, reconditioning and service, and customer credit.

Recent Developments: For the quarter ended Nov 30 2019, net income decreased 9.0% to US$173.2 million from US$190.3 million in the year-earlier quarter. Revenues were US$4.79 billion, up 11.5% from US$4.30 billion the year before. Direct operating expenses rose 12.1% to US$4.18 billion from US$3.73 billion in the comparable period the year before. Indirect operating expenses increased 20.1% to US$386.1 million from US$321.4 million in the equivalent prior-year period.

Prospects: Our evaluation of Carmax Inc. as of October 4th, 2019 is the result of our systematic analysis on three basic characteristics: earnings strength, relative valuation, and recent stock price movement. The company has managed to produce a neutral trend in earnings per share over the past 5 quarters. However, recent analyst estimates for the company have been raised and KMX has posted results that exceeded analysts' expectations. Based on operating earnings yield, the company is undervalued when compared to all of the companies we cover. Share price changes over the past year indicates that KMX will perform well over the near term.

Financial Data

(US$ in Thousands)	9 Mos	6 Mos	3 Mos	02/28/2019	02/28/2018	02/28/2017	02/29/2016	02/28/2015
Earnings Per Share	5.16	5.21	5.05	4.79	3.60	3.26	3.03	2.73
Cash Flow Per Share	(0.42)	(0.44)	(0.15)	0.93	(0.44)	(2.46)	(0.73)	(4.49)
Tang Book Value Per Share	22.58	21.90	20.88	20.04	18.45	16.66	14.92	15.11
Income Statement								
Total Revenue	15,357,497	10,567,469	5,366,318	18,173,100	17,120,209	15,875,118	15,149,675	14,268,716
EBITDA	759,156	569,029	304,588	1,358,398	1,292,953	1,203,521	1,173,302	1,099,504
Depn & Amortn	158,226	103,468	51,506	169,800	158,600	140,700	127,000	105,700
Income Before Taxes	884,353	656,794	351,257	1,112,806	1,063,608	1,006,405	1,009,944	969,331
Income Taxes	210,854	156,451	84,513	270,393	399,496	379,435	386,516	371,973
Net Income	673,499	500,343	266,744	842,413	664,112	626,970	623,428	597,358
Average Shares	166,534	167,272	167,643	175,884	184,470	192,215	205,540	218,691
Balance Sheet								
Current Assets	3,450,244	3,384,939	3,283,745	3,214,013	3,061,444	2,873,630	2,471,781	2,599,038
Total Assets	20,487,230	20,140,254	19,714,476	18,717,867	17,486,272	16,279,356	14,481,576	13,198,201
Current Liabilities	1,421,041	1,396,704	1,485,402	1,311,509	1,174,058	1,105,787	1,005,193	997,173
Long-Term Obligations	14,604,254	14,384,129	14,027,714	13,806,325	12,752,812	11,826,438	10,342,323	8,818,750
Total Liabilities	16,789,177	16,528,697	16,261,721	15,360,839	14,169,423	13,170,776	11,576,790	10,041,416
Stockholders' Equity	3,698,053	3,611,557	3,452,755	3,357,028	3,316,849	3,108,580	2,904,786	3,156,785
Shares Outstanding	163,795	164,885	165,395	167,478	179,747	186,548	194,712	208,869
Statistical Record								
Return on Assets %	4.45	4.61	4.65	4.65	3.93	4.08	4.49	4.80
Return on Equity %	24.28	24.90	25.47	25.25	20.67	20.85	20.51	18.45
EBITDA Margin %	4.94	5.38	5.68	7.47	7.55	7.58	7.74	7.71
Net Margin %	4.39	4.73	4.97	4.64	3.88	3.95	4.12	4.19
Asset Turnover	1.01	1.00	1.00	1.00	1.01	1.03	1.09	1.15
Current Ratio	2.43	2.42	2.21	2.45	2.61	2.60	2.46	2.61
Debt to Equity	3.95	3.98	4.06	4.11	3.84	3.80	3.56	2.79
Price Range	100.15-56.72	91.34-56.72	80.68-56.72	80.68-56.72	76.81-55.37	68.60-45.70	74.73-42.15	68.30-42.88
P/E Ratio	19.41-10.99	17.53-10.89	15.98-11.23	16.84-11.84	21.34-15.38	21.04-14.02	24.66-13.91	25.02-15.71

Address: 12800 Tuckahoe Creek Parkway, Richmond, VA 23238 Telephone: 804-747-0422	Web Site: www.carmax.com Officers: William D. (Bill) Nash - President, Chief Executive Officer, Executive Vice President, Senior Vice President, Vice President Thomas W. Reedy - Executive Vice President, Executive Vice President (frmr), Senior Vice President, Chief Financial Officer	Auditors: KPMG LLP Investor Contact: 804-935-4591 Transfer Agents: American Stock Transfer & Trust Company, LLC, Brooklyn, NY

CARNIVAL CORP

Exchange	Symbol	Price	52Wk Range	Yield	P/E
NYS	CCL	$50.83 (12/31/2019)	58.85-40.13	3.93	11.47

*7 Year Price Score 82.38   *NYSE Composite Index=100   *12 Month Price Score 87.66

Interim Earnings (Per Share)

Qtr.	Feb	May	Aug	Nov
2015-16	0.18	0.80	1.93	0.84
2016-17	0.48	0.52	1.83	0.75
2017-18	0.54	0.78	2.41	0.72
2018-19	0.48	0.65	2.58	...

Interim Dividends (Per Share)

Amt	Decl	Ex	Rec	Pay
0.50Q	04/17/2019	05/23/2019	05/24/2019	06/14/2019
0.50Q	07/11/2019	08/22/2019	08/23/2019	09/13/2019
0.50Q	10/14/2019	11/21/2019	11/22/2019	12/13/2019
0.50Q	01/15/2020	02/20/2020	02/21/2020	03/13/2020

Indicated Div: $2.00 (Div. Reinv. Plan)

Valuation Analysis   **Institutional Holding**

Forecast EPS	$4.55	No of Institutions
	(01/17/2020)	1167
Market Cap	$34.9 Billion	Shares
Book Value	$25.3 Billion	504,795,456
Price/Book	1.38	% Held
Price/Sales	1.70	56.47

Business Summary: Hotels, Restaurants & Travel (MIC: 2.2.1 SIC: 4489 NAIC: 487210)

Carnival is a leisure travel company. Co. operates in four segments: North America and Australia (NAA), Europe and Asia (EA), Cruise Support, and Tour and Other. Co.'s NAA segment includes Carnival Cruise Line, Princess Cruises, Holland America Line, P&O Cruises (Australia), and Seabourn. Co.'s EA segment includes Costa Cruises, AIDA Cruises, P&O Cruises (the U.K.), and Cunard. Co.'s Cruise Support segment includes its portfolio of port destinations and other services, all of which are operated for the benefit of its cruise brands. Co.'s Tour and Other segment represents the hotels and transportation operations of Holland America Princess Alaska Tours and other operations.

Recent Developments: For the quarter ended Aug 31 2019, net income increased 4.3% to US$1.78 billion from US$1.71 billion in the year-earlier quarter. Revenues were US$6.53 billion, up 11.9% from US$5.84 billion the year before. Operating income was US$1.89 billion versus US$1.79 billion in the prior-year quarter, an increase of 5.4%. Direct operating expenses rose 19.4% to US$3.53 billion from US$2.96 billion in the comparable period the year before. Indirect operating expenses increased 2.5% to US$1.11 billion from US$1.08 billion in the equivalent prior-year period.

Prospects: Our evaluation of Carnival Corp. as of October 4th, 2019 is the result of our systematic analysis on three basic characteristics: earnings strength, relative valuation, and recent stock price movement. The company has managed to produce a neutral trend in earnings per share over the past 5 quarters. However, recent analyst estimates for the company have been reduced while CCL has posted results that exceeded analysts' expectations. Based on operating earnings yield, the company is undervalued when compared to all of the companies we cover. Share price changes over the past year indicates that CCL will perform in line with the market over the near term.

Financial Data (US$ in Thousands)	9 Mos	6 Mos	3 Mos	11/30/2018	11/30/2017	11/30/2016	11/30/2015	11/30/2014
Earnings Per Share	4.43	4.26	4.39	4.44	3.59	3.72	2.26	1.59
Cash Flow Per Share	8.02	8.15	8.08	7.83	7.37	6.87	5.85	4.42
Tang Book Value Per Share	30.92	29.03	29.11	29.23	27.92	25.36	25.29	25.60
Dividends Per Share	2.000	2.000	2.000	1.950	1.600	1.350	1.100	1.000
Dividend Payout %	45.15	46.95	45.56	43.92	44.57	36.29	48.67	62.89
Income Statement								
Total Revenue	16,043,000	9,511,000	4,673,000	18,881,000	17,510,000	16,389,000	15,714,000	15,884,000
EBITDA	4,372,000	1,952,000	901,000	5,404,000	4,701,000	4,783,000	3,634,000	3,160,000
Depn & Amortn	1,607,000	1,059,000	516,000	2,017,000	1,846,000	1,738,000	1,626,000	1,635,000
Income Before Taxes	2,624,000	797,000	338,000	3,207,000	2,666,000	2,828,000	1,799,000	1,245,000
Income Taxes	56,000	10,000	2,000	54,000	60,000	49,000	42,000	9,000
Net Income	2,567,000	787,000	336,000	3,152,000	2,606,000	2,779,000	1,757,000	1,236,000
Average Shares	691,000	693,000	695,000	710,000	725,000	747,000	779,000	778,000
Balance Sheet								
Current Assets	2,712,000	2,835,000	2,101,000	2,225,000	1,596,000	1,689,000	2,451,000	1,503,000
Total Assets	44,001,000	44,512,000	43,930,000	42,401,000	40,778,000	38,936,000	39,237,000	39,532,000
Current Liabilities	8,932,000	10,377,000	9,642,000	9,204,000	8,800,000	7,072,000	6,956,000	6,921,000
Long-Term Obligations	8,893,000	9,080,000	9,134,000	7,897,000	6,993,000	8,357,000	7,413,000	7,363,000
Total Liabilities	18,707,000	20,405,000	19,688,000	17,957,000	16,562,000	16,339,000	15,466,000	15,244,000
Stockholders' Equity	25,295,000	24,108,000	24,241,000	24,443,000	24,216,000	22,597,000	23,771,000	24,288,000
Shares Outstanding	687,000	690,000	691,000	696,000	718,000	726,000	772,000	777,000
Statistical Record								
Return on Assets %	7.14	6.89	7.26	7.58	6.54	7.09	4.46	3.10
Return on Equity %	12.25	12.44	12.74	12.96	11.13	11.95	7.31	5.06
EBITDA Margin %	27.25	20.52	19.28	28.62	26.85	29.18	23.13	19.89
Net Margin %	16.00	8.27	7.19	16.69	14.88	16.96	11.18	7.78
Asset Turnover	0.48	0.46	0.45	0.45	0.44	0.42	0.40	0.40
Current Ratio	0.30	0.27	0.22	0.24	0.18	0.24	0.35	0.22
Debt to Equity	0.35	0.38	0.38	0.32	0.29	0.37	0.31	0.30
Price Range	67.17-43.03	67.17-46.21	67.85-46.21	71.94-54.07	69.48-49.88	55.14-41.92	54.08-42.39	44.16-33.88
P/E Ratio	15.16-9.71	15.77-10.85	15.46-10.53	16.20-12.18	19.35-13.89	14.82-11.27	23.93-18.76	27.77-21.31
Average Yield %	3.70	3.49	3.32	3.08	2.60	2.79	2.29	2.59

Address: 3655 N.W. 87th Avenue, Miami, FL 33178-2428 Telephone: 305-599-2600	Web Site: www.carnivalcorporation.com Officers: Micky Meir Arison - Chairman, Chief Executive Officer, Associate/Affiliate Company Officer Arnold W. Donald - President, Chief Executive Officer, Associate/Affiliate Company Officer	Auditors: PricewaterhouseCoopers LLP Investor Contact: 305-406-5539 Transfer Agents: ComputerShare Investor Services, Providence, RI

CARPENTER TECHNOLOGY CORP.

Exchange	Symbol	Price	52Wk Range	Yield	P/E
NYS	CRS	$49.78 (12/31/2019)	55.88-35.61	1.61	13.71

*7 Year Price Score 85.46 *NYSE Composite Index=100 *12 Month Price Score 102.84

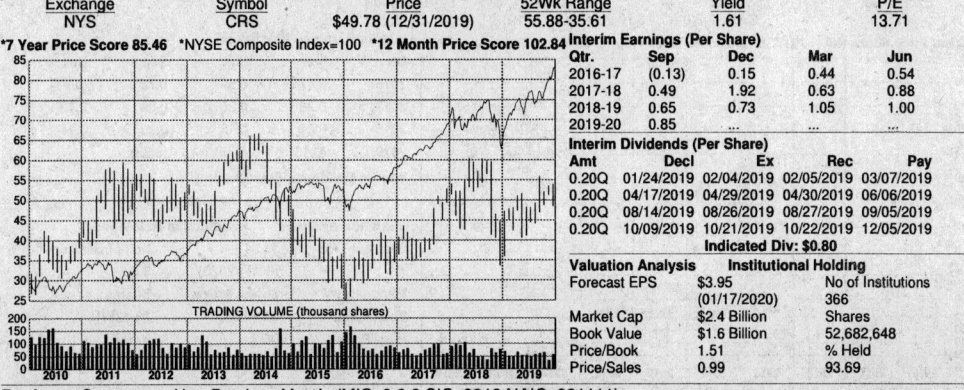

Interim Earnings (Per Share)

Qtr.	Sep	Dec	Mar	Jun
2016-17	(0.13)	0.15	0.44	0.54
2017-18	0.49	1.92	0.63	0.88
2018-19	0.65	0.73	1.05	1.00
2019-20	0.85	...	...	...

Interim Dividends (Per Share)

Amt	Decl	Ex	Rec	Pay
0.20Q	01/24/2019	02/04/2019	02/05/2019	03/07/2019
0.20Q	04/17/2019	04/29/2019	04/30/2019	06/06/2019
0.20Q	08/14/2019	08/26/2019	08/27/2019	09/05/2019
0.20Q	10/09/2019	10/21/2019	10/22/2019	12/05/2019

Indicated Div: $0.80

Valuation Analysis

		Institutional Holding	
Forecast EPS	$3.95	No of Institutions	
	(01/17/2020)	366	
Market Cap	$2.4 Billion	Shares	
Book Value	$1.6 Billion	52,682,648	
Price/Book	1.51	% Held	
Price/Sales	0.99	93.69	

Business Summary: Non-Precious Metals (MIC: 8.2.2 SIC: 3312 NAIC: 331111)

Carpenter Technology is a producer and distributor of alloys, including titanium alloys, powder metals, stainless steels, alloy steels, and tool steels as well as drilling tools. Co.'s alloy-based materials and process solutions are used for applications in the aerospace, defense, transportation, energy, medical, industrial and consumer markets as well as additive manufacturing processes and soft magnetics applications. Co. also produces metal powders and parts. Co. has two business segments: Specialty Alloys Operations, which consists of Co.'s alloy and stainless steel manufacturing operations; and Performance Engineered Products, which consists of Co.'s differentiated operations.

Recent Developments: For the quarter ended Sep 30 2019, net income increased 30.8% to US$41.2 million from US$31.5 million in the year-earlier quarter. Revenues were US$585.4 million, up 2.3% from US$572.4 million the year before. Operating income was US$59.8 million versus US$45.0 million in the prior-year quarter, an increase of 32.9%. Direct operating expenses declined 1.6% to US$472.8 million from US$480.7 million in the comparable period the year before. Indirect operating expenses increased 13.1% to US$52.8 million from US$46.7 million in the equivalent prior-year period.

Prospects: Our evaluation of Carpenter Technology Corp. as of October 4th, 2019 is the result of our systematic analysis on three basic characteristics: earnings strength, relative valuation, and recent stock price movement. The company has generated a negative trend in earnings per share over the past 5 quarters. However, recent analyst estimates for the company have been mixed and CRS has posted results that exceeded analysts' expectations. Based on operating earnings yield, the company is undervalued when compared to all of the companies we cover. Share price changes over the past year indicates that CRS will perform poorly over the near term.

Financial Data

(US$ in Thousands)	3 Mos	06/30/2019	06/30/2018	06/30/2017	06/30/2016	06/30/2015	06/30/2014	06/30/2013
Earnings Per Share	3.63	3.43	3.92	0.99	0.23	1.11	2.47	2.73
Cash Flow Per Share	4.67	4.87	4.43	2.75	5.33	5.37	4.50	4.07
Tang Book Value Per Share	24.89	23.73	24.45	18.61	17.10	19.81	21.94	18.01
Dividends Per Share	0.800	0.800	0.720	0.720	0.720	0.720	0.720	0.720
Dividend Payout %	22.04	23.32	18.37	72.73	313.04	64.86	29.15	26.37
Income Statement								
Total Revenue	585,400	2,380,200	2,157,700	1,797,600	1,813,400	2,226,700	2,173,000	2,271,700
EBITDA	90,100	350,000	292,900	205,500	155,200	223,800	305,900	321,300
Depn & Amortn	30,600	108,100	104,700	105,800	106,500	107,200	93,300	85,100
Income Before Taxes	54,100	216,000	160,200	70,200	20,900	89,000	195,800	215,500
Income Taxes	12,900	49,000	(28,300)	23,200	10,200	30,400	63,600	70,300
Net Income	41,200	167,000	188,500	47,000	11,300	58,700	132,800	146,100
Average Shares	48,300	48,100	47,600	47,100	48,200	52,700	53,600	53,400
Balance Sheet								
Current Assets	1,309,600	1,236,200	1,178,800	1,093,600	1,010,700	1,070,400	1,194,500	1,281,500
Total Assets	3,341,500	3,187,800	3,007,000	2,878,100	2,794,300	2,905,900	3,057,500	2,882,900
Current Liabilities	466,600	416,000	363,300	396,000	298,800	322,100	430,600	421,200
Long-Term Obligations	550,900	550,600	545,700	550,000	611,300	607,100	604,300	604,200
Total Liabilities	1,764,500	1,667,700	1,521,100	1,679,500	1,689,400	1,580,000	1,553,200	1,579,800
Stockholders' Equity	1,577,000	1,520,100	1,485,900	1,198,600	1,104,900	1,325,900	1,504,300	1,303,100
Shares Outstanding	47,719	47,470	47,191	46,753	46,600	50,318	53,137	52,773
Statistical Record								
Return on Assets %	5.57	5.39	6.41	1.66	0.40	1.97	4.47	5.30
Return on Equity %	11.52	11.11	14.04	4.08	0.93	4.15	9.46	12.14
EBITDA Margin %	15.39	14.70	13.57	11.43	8.56	10.05	14.08	14.14
Net Margin %	7.04	7.02	8.74	2.61	0.62	2.64	6.11	6.43
Asset Turnover	0.75	0.77	0.73	0.63	0.63	0.75	0.73	0.82
Current Ratio	2.81	2.97	3.24	2.76	3.38	3.32	2.77	3.04
Debt to Equity	0.35	0.36	0.37	0.46	0.55	0.46	0.40	0.46
Price Range	59.63-33.55	60.26-33.55	60.43-36.96	43.63-31.25	40.56-25.16	64.32-35.69	66.64-45.59	55.70-43.77
P/E Ratio	16.43-9.24	17.57-9.78	15.42-9.43	44.07-31.57	176.35-109.39	57.95-32.15	26.98-18.46	20.40-16.03
Average Yield %	1.73	1.65	1.48	1.91	2.17	1.55	1.21	1.47

Address: 1735 Market Street, 15th Floor, Philadelphia, PA 19103 **Telephone:** 610-208-2000	**Web Site:** www.cartech.com **Officers:** Gregory A. Pratt - Chairman, Interim Executive Chairman, Interim President, Interim Chief Executive Officer Tony R. Thene - President, Chief Executive Officer, Senior Vice President, Chief Financial Officer	**Auditors:** PricewaterhouseCoopers LLP **Investor Contact:** 610-208-3476 **Transfer Agents:** American Stock Transfer & Trust Company

137

CARS.COM INC

Exchange	Symbol	Price	52Wk Range	Yield	P/E
NYS	CARS	$12.22 (12/31/2019)	27.37-8.28	N/A	N/A

*7 Year Price Score N/A   *NYSE Composite Index=100   *12 Month Price Score 65.65

Interim Earnings (Per Share)

Qtr.	Mar	Jun	Sep	Dec
2016	0.47	0.59	0.72	(0.41)
2017	0.38	0.35	0.29	2.12
2018	0.01	0.18	0.23	0.14
2019	(0.13)	(0.09)	(6.38)	...

Interim Dividends (Per Share)

No Dividends Paid

Valuation Analysis — **Institutional Holding**

Valuation Analysis		Institutional Holding	
Forecast EPS	$1.31	No of Institutions	
	(00/24/2020)	304	
Market Cap	$814.8 Million	Shares	
Book Value	$1.1 Billion	73,136,184	
Price/Book	0.71	% Held	
Price/Sales	1.32	107.51	

Business Summary: IT Services (MIC: 6.3.1 SIC: 7374 NAIC: 518210)

Cars.com is engaged in a digital automotive marketplace that connects car shoppers with sellers and original equipment manufacturers (OEMs), providing shoppers with the resources and information to make informed buying decisions. Co.'s portfolio of brands includes Cars.com, Dealer Inspire and DealerRater, in addition to Auto.com, PickupTrucks.com and NewCars.com. Dealer Inspire and DealerRater provide digital solutions for car dealers, including dealer websites, technology and reputation management solutions that improve automotive selling for local dealerships and national OEM brands.

Recent Developments: For the quarter ended Sep 30 2019, net loss amounted to US$426.2 million versus net income of US$15.8 million in the year-earlier quarter. Revenues were US$152.1 million, down 10.2% from US$169.3 million the year before. Operating loss was US$447.7 million versus an income of US$28.3 million in the prior-year quarter. Direct operating expenses rose 5.4% to US$25.1 million from US$23.8 million in the comparable period the year before. Indirect operating expenses increased 390.5% to US$574.7 million from US$117.2 million in the equivalent prior-year period.

Prospects: Our evaluation of Cars.com Inc. as of October 4th, 2019 is the result of our systematic analysis on three basic characteristics: earnings strength, relative valuation, and recent stock price movement. The company has generated a negative trend in earnings per share over the past 5 quarters. In addition, recent analyst estimates for the company have been reduced while CARS has posted results that exceeded analysts' expectations. Based on operating earnings yield, the company is undervalued when compared to all of the companies we cover. Share price changes over the past year indicates that CARS will perform poorly over the near term.

Financial Data

(US$ in Thousands)	9 Mos	6 Mos	3 Mos	12/31/2018	12/31/2017	12/31/2016	12/31/2015	12/31/2014
Earnings Per Share	(6.46)	0.15	0.42	0.55	3.13	1.37	...	...
Cash Flow Per Share	1.84	2.15	2.59	2.33	2.59	2.77	...	...
Income Statement								
Total Revenue	454,495	302,405	154,198	662,127	626,262	633,106	596,510	145,939
EBITDA	(380,401)	42,901	18,201	97,446	145,333	251,787	230,496	34,382
Depn & Amortn	68,835	45,823	22,136	12,800	10,800	74,829	72,658	18,164
Income Before Taxes	(472,225)	(18,199)	(11,501)	56,929	122,162	176,958	157,838	16,218
Income Taxes	(31,011)	(3,142)	(2,470)	18,120	(102,281)	588	...	...
Net Income	(441,214)	(15,057)	(9,031)	38,809	224,443	176,370	157,838	16,218
Average Shares	66,769	66,779	67,584	70,547	71,727	71,598	...	...
Balance Sheet								
Current Assets	129,572	112,844	140,872	153,937	142,639	119,541	98,517	...
Total Assets	2,059,879	2,527,392	2,580,266	2,600,549	2,511,039	2,547,266	2,473,667	...
Current Liabilities	121,805	112,518	119,956	110,710	90,149	71,984	88,370	...
Long-Term Obligations	630,913	644,046	652,178	665,306	557,194	...	...	...
Total Liabilities	918,394	958,244	987,596	973,626	831,911	129,981	169,148	...
Stockholders' Equity	1,141,485	1,569,148	1,592,670	1,626,923	1,679,128	2,417,285	2,304,519	...
Shares Outstanding	66,678	66,672	67,455	68,262	71,627	...	...	...
Statistical Record								
Return on Assets %	N.M.	0.39	1.10	1.52	8.87	7.01	...	...
Return on Equity %	N.M.	0.63	1.76	2.35	10.96	7.45	...	...
EBITDA Margin %	N.M.	14.19	11.80	14.72	23.21	39.77	38.64	23.56
Net Margin %	N.M.	N.M.	N.M.	5.86	35.84	27.86	26.46	11.11
Asset Turnover	0.26	0.25	0.25	0.26	0.25	0.25	...	...
Current Ratio	1.06	1.00	1.17	1.39	1.58	1.66	1.11	...
Debt to Equity	0.55	0.41	0.41	0.41	0.33	...	...	...
Price Range	27.38-8.28	32.47-19.42	32.47-20.14	32.47-20.14	29.98-22.00	...	...	...
P/E Ratio	...	216.47-129.47	77.31-47.95	59.04-36.62	9.58-7.03	...	...	...

Address: 300 S. Riverside Plaza, Suite 1000, Chicago, IL 60606 **Telephone:** 312-601-5000	**Web Site:** www.cars.com **Officers:** Scott E. Forbes - Chairman T. Alex Vetter - President, Chief Executive Officer	**Auditors:** Ernst & Young LLP **Transfer Agents:** Wells Fargo Shareowner Services, Mendota Heights, MN

CARTER'S INC

Exchange	Symbol	Price	52Wk Range	Yield	P/E
NYS	CRI	$109.34 (12/31/2019)	111.14-78.23	1.83	18.66

*7 Year Price Score 87.65   *NYSE Composite Index=100   *12 Month Price Score 104.22

Interim Earnings (Per Share)

Qtr.	Mar	Jun	Sep	Dec
2016	1.04	0.71	1.60	1.74
2017	0.95	0.78	1.71	2.81
2018	0.89	0.79	1.53	2.80
2019	0.75	0.97	1.34	...

Interim Dividends (Per Share)

Amt	Decl	Ex	Rec	Pay
0.50Q	02/14/2019	03/11/2019	03/12/2019	03/22/2019
0.50Q	05/16/2019	05/28/2019	05/29/2019	06/14/2019
0.50Q	08/22/2019	08/30/2019	09/03/2019	09/20/2019
0.50Q	11/21/2019	12/02/2019	12/03/2019	12/13/2019

Indicated Div: $2.00

Valuation Analysis | **Institutional Holding**

Forecast EPS	$6.55	No of Institutions
(01/15/2020)		474
Market Cap	$4.8 Billion	Shares
Book Value	$812.7 Million	63,909,296
Price/Book	5.96	% Held
Price/Sales	1.38	102.90

Business Summary: Apparel, Footwear & Accessories (MIC: 1.4.2 SIC: 5641 NAIC: 448130)

Carter's is a marketer of apparel for babies and young children. Under its Carter's brand, Co. designs, sources, and markets products for sizes newborn to 14. Under its OshKosh B'gosh brand, Co. designs, sources, and markets apparel, mainly on playclothes for children in sizes newborn to 14. Under its Skip Hop brand, Co. designs, sources, and markets products that are sold primarily to families with young children. Co.'s Skip Hop brand focuses on its diaper bags. The Skip Hop brand offering also includes products for playtime, travel, mealtime, kid's bags, bathtime, and homegear. Co.'s reportable segments are U.S. Retail, U.S. Wholesale, and International.

Recent Developments: For the quarter ended Sep 28 2019, net income decreased 16.0% to US$60.3 million from US$71.8 million in the year-earlier quarter. Revenues were US$943.3 million, up 2.1% from US$923.9 million the year before. Operating income was US$83.9 million versus US$103.6 million in the prior-year quarter, a decrease of 19.0%. Direct operating expenses rose 0.9% to US$541.1 million from US$536.5 million in the comparable period the year before. Indirect operating expenses increased 12.1% to US$318.3 million from US$283.9 million in the equivalent prior-year period.

Prospects: Our evaluation of Carter Holdings Inc. as of October 4th, 2019 is the result of our systematic analysis on three basic characteristics: earnings strength, relative valuation, and recent stock price movement. The company has generated a negative trend in earnings per share over the past 5 quarters. However, recent analyst estimates for the company have been mixed and CRI has posted results that exceeded analysts' expectations. Based on operating earnings yield, the company is undervalued when compared to all of the companies we cover. Share price changes over the past year indicates that CRI will perform well over the near term.

Financial Data

(US$ in Thousands)	9 Mos	6 Mos	3 Mos	12/29/2018	12/30/2017	12/31/2016	01/02/2016	01/03/2015
Earnings Per Share	5.86	6.05	5.87	6.00	6.24	5.08	4.50	3.62
Cash Flow Per Share	9.25	8.00	7.30	7.74	6.94	7.42	5.96	5.28
Tang Book Value Per Share	4.69	4.25	4.67	5.09	4.52	6.19	7.52	5.45
Dividends Per Share	1.950	1.900	1.850	1.800	1.480	1.320	0.880	0.760
Dividend Payout %	33.28	31.40	31.52	30.00	23.72	25.98	19.56	20.99
Income Statement								
Total Revenue	2,418,764	1,475,442	741,057	3,462,269	3,400,410	3,199,184	3,013,879	2,893,868
EBITDA	272,710	165,023	77,080	479,634	505,147	495,970	463,136	405,093
Depn & Amortn	71,902	47,602	23,933	89,617	84,416	73,419	68,417	74,937
Income Before Taxes	173,078	99,457	43,746	355,975	391,032	396,070	368,188	302,906
Income Taxes	34,423	21,054	9,280	73,907	88,268	137,964	130,366	108,236
Net Income	138,655	78,403	34,466	282,068	302,764	258,106	237,822	194,670
Average Shares	44,432	45,038	45,371	46,648	48,146	50,375	52,334	53,093
Balance Sheet								
Current Assets	1,223,645	1,041,006	971,027	1,042,958	1,017,669	1,057,086	1,131,465	1,041,458
Total Assets	2,899,580	2,747,160	2,679,944	2,058,858	2,067,999	1,946,597	2,009,113	1,893,096
Current Liabilities	484,168	473,071	361,754	327,421	328,624	277,609	262,718	247,971
Long-Term Obligations	1,461,242	1,293,027	1,317,334	593,264	617,306	580,376	584,431	586,000
Total Liabilities	2,086,846	1,919,263	1,830,540	1,189,425	1,210,906	1,158,473	1,134,062	1,106,412
Stockholders' Equity	812,734	827,897	849,404	869,433	857,093	788,124	875,051	786,684
Shares Outstanding	44,287	44,868	45,379	45,629	47,178	48,948	51,764	52,712
Statistical Record								
Return on Assets %	10.56	11.62	11.77	13.71	15.12	13.09	12.22	10.34
Return on Equity %	33.16	34.27	32.16	32.76	36.91	31.12	28.70	25.75
EBITDA Margin %	11.27	11.18	10.40	13.85	14.86	15.50	15.37	14.00
Net Margin %	5.73	5.31	4.65	8.15	8.90	8.07	7.89	6.73
Asset Turnover	1.38	1.44	1.48	1.68	1.70	1.62	1.55	1.54
Current Ratio	2.53	2.20	2.68	3.19	3.10	3.81	4.31	4.20
Debt to Equity	1.80	1.56	1.55	0.68	0.72	0.74	0.67	0.74
Price Range	108.12-75.76	117.47-75.76	117.47-75.76	122.77-75.76	117.59-78.32	111.47-84.16	108.98-80.98	87.31-64.84
P/E Ratio	18.45-12.93	19.42-12.52	20.01-12.91	20.46-12.63	18.84-12.55	21.94-16.57	24.22-18.00	24.12-17.91
Average Yield %	2.11	1.98	1.88	1.71	1.61	1.36	0.94	1.00

Address: Phipps Tower, 3438 Peachtree Road NE., Suite 1800, Atlanta, GA 30326
Telephone: 678-791-1000

Web Site: www.carters.com
Officers: Michael D. Casey - Chairman, Chief Executive Officer, President Brian J. Lynch - President, Executive Vice President

Auditors: PricewaterhouseCoopers LLP
Investor Contact: 404-745-2889
Transfer Agents: American Stock Transfer & Trust Company, LLC, Brooklyn, NY

CARVANA CO

Exchange	Symbol	Price	52Wk Range	Yield	P/E
NYS	CVNA	$92.05 (12/31/2019)	98.44-30.19	N/A	N/A

*7 Year Price Score N/A ***NYSE Composite Index=100** ***12 Month Price Score 128.93**

Interim Earnings (Per Share)

Qtr.	Mar	Jun	Sep	Dec
2016	(0.19)	(0.13)	(0.16)	(0.68)
2017	(0.44)	(0.28)	(0.29)	(0.45)
2018	(0.53)	(0.41)	(0.50)	(0.81)
2019	(0.69)	(0.58)	(0.78)	...

Interim Dividends (Per Share)

No Dividends Paid

Valuation Analysis | **Institutional Holding**

Forecast EPS	$-2.10	No of Institutions
	(01/17/2020)	264
Market Cap	$13.9 Billion	Shares
Book Value	$105.5 Million	64,898,248
Price/Book	132.19	% Held
Price/Sales	4.08	61.95

Business Summary: Retail - Automotive (MIC: 2.1.4 SIC: 5511 NAIC: 441110)

Carvana is a holding company. Through its subsidiaries, Co. is an e-commerce platform for buying and selling used cars. On Co.'s platform, consumers can research and identify a vehicle using its 360-degree vehicle imaging technology, obtain financing and warranty coverage, purchase the vehicle, and schedule delivery or pick-up, all from their desktop or mobile devices. Co. uses proprietary algorithms to support its nationally pooled inventory of over 14,000 vehicles, inspect and recondition its vehicles and operates its own logistics network to deliver cars directly to customers. Customers in certain markets also have the option to pick up their vehicle at one of Co.'s vending machines.

Recent Developments: For the quarter ended Sep 30 2019, net loss amounted to US$92.2 million versus a net loss of US$64.4 million in the year-earlier quarter. Revenues were US$1.09 billion, up 104.7% from US$534.9 million the year before. Direct operating expenses rose 100.4% to US$957.3 million from US$477.6 million in the comparable period the year before. Indirect operating expenses increased 79.6% to US$208.0 million from US$115.8 million in the equivalent prior-year period.

Prospects: Our evaluation of Carvana Co. as of October 4th, 2019 is the result of our systematic analysis on three basic characteristics: earnings strength, relative valuation, and recent stock price movement. The company has enjoyed a very positive trend in earnings per share over the past 5 quarters. However, recent analyst estimates for the company have been mixed and CVNA has posted results that exceeded analysts' expectations. Based on operating earnings yield, the company is overvalued when compared to all of the companies we cover. Share price changes over the past year indicates that CVNA will perform very well over the near term.

Financial Data
(US$ in Thousands)

	9 Mos	6 Mos	3 Mos	12/31/2018	12/31/2017	12/31/2016	12/31/2015	12/31/2014
Earnings Per Share	(2.86)	(2.58)	(2.41)	(2.24)	(1.31)	(1.10)	(0.42)	(0.17)
Cash Flow Per Share	(11.75)	(11.51)	(12.03)	(13.79)	(13.12)	(2.32)	(0.55)	(0.33)
Tang Book Value Per Share	0.58	0.77	0.25	0.38	0.22	1.23	0.60	...
Income Statement								
Total Revenue	2,836,309	1,741,455	755,234	1,955,467	858,870	365,148	130,392	41,679
EBITDA	(153,077)	(93,420)	(58,369)	(207,227)	(145,057)	(84,825)	(32,568)	(13,430)
Depn & Amortn	29,869	18,272	8,579	22,500	11,600	4,700	2,800	1,700
Income Before Taxes	(238,899)	(146,655)	(82,596)	(254,745)	(164,316)	(93,112)	(36,780)	(15,238)
Net Income	(94,176)	(55,159)	(28,549)	(61,754)	(62,841)	(93,112)	(36,780)	(15,238)
Average Shares	49,787	46,038	41,352	30,043	15,241	103,286	96,582	91,522
Balance Sheet								
Current Assets	1,097,958	957,542	876,786	662,854	489,718	275,241	119,218	...
Total Assets	1,684,321	1,474,404	1,338,401	991,013	641,137	335,833	136,012	...
Current Liabilities	507,453	249,835	630,030	329,511	306,031	196,418	70,808	...
Long-Term Obligations	776,580	743,132	479,039	425,349	48,469	4,404	...	...
Total Liabilities	1,578,789	1,340,656	1,283,628	917,605	515,401	200,822	70,808	...
Stockholders' Equity	105,532	133,748	54,773	73,408	125,736	135,011	65,204	...
Shares Outstanding	151,546	151,113	145,595	145,544	132,760	110,026	108,931	...
Statistical Record								
Asset Turnover	2.36	2.43	2.28	2.40	1.76	1.54	...	...
Current Ratio	2.16	3.83	1.39	2.01	1.60	1.40	1.68	...
Debt to Equity	7.36	5.56	8.75	5.79	0.39	0.03	...	...
Price Range	84.61-29.84	75.23-29.84	70.82-22.38	70.82-17.01	23.39-8.72	...	...	...

Address: 1930 W. Rio Salado Parkway, Tempe, AZ 85281 Telephone: 480-719-8809	Web Site: www.carvana.com Officers: Ernest C. (Ernie) Garcia - Chairman, President, Chief Executive Officer Mark W. Jenkins - Chief Financial Officer	Auditors: Grant Thornton LLP Transfer Agents: American Stock Transfer & Trust Company, LLC, Brookly, NY

CATALENT INC

Exchange	Symbol	Price	52Wk Range	Yield	P/E
NYS	CTLT	$56.30 (12/31/2019)	58.05-29.84	N/A	59.89

*7 Year Price Score N/A   *NYSE Composite Index=100   *12 Month Price Score 105.22

Interim Earnings (Per Share)

Qtr.	Sep	Dec	Mar	Jun
2016-17	0.04	0.14	0.21	0.49
2017-18	0.03	(0.16)	0.14	0.62
2018-19	(0.10)	0.33	0.22	0.44
2019-20	(0.05)	...	...	...

Interim Dividends (Per Share)

No Dividends Paid

Valuation Analysis		Institutional Holding	
Forecast EPS	$1.97	No of Institutions	
	(01/17/2020)	376	
Market Cap	$8.2 Billion	Shares	
Book Value	$1.6 Billion	171,336,448	
Price/Book	4.99	% Held	
Price/Sales	3.13	100.51	

Business Summary: Pharmaceuticals (MIC: 4.1.1 SIC: 2834 NAIC: 325412)

Catalent is a holding company. Through its subsidiaries, Co. is a provider of delivery technologies and development solutions for drugs, biologics and consumer health products. Co. operates in four segments: Softgel Technologies, which provides formulation, development and manufacturing services for soft capsules; Biologics and Specialty Drug Delivery, which provides drug substance development and manufacturing; Oral Drug Delivery, which provides various formulation development and manufacturing technologies; and Clinical Supply Services, which provides manufacturing, packaging, storage, distribution, project management, and inventory management for drugs and biologics in clinical trials.

Recent Developments: For the quarter ended Sep 30 2019, net income amounted to US$100,000 versus a net loss of US$14.4 million in the year-earlier quarter. Revenues were US$664.7 million, up 20.5% from US$551.8 million the year before. Operating income was US$34.4 million versus US$20.4 million in the prior-year quarter, an increase of 68.6%. Direct operating expenses rose 20.8% to US$487.0 million from US$403.3 million in the comparable period the year before. Indirect operating expenses increased 11.9% to US$143.3 million from US$128.1 million in the equivalent prior-year period.

Prospects: Our evaluation of Catalent Inc as of October 4th, 2019 is the result of our systematic analysis on three basic characteristics: earnings strength, relative valuation, and recent stock price movement. The company has generated a negative trend in earnings per share over the past 5 quarters. However, recent analyst estimates for the company have been unchanged while CTLT has posted results that exceeded analysts' expectations. Based on operating earnings yield, the company is fairly valued when compared to all of the companies we cover. Share price changes over the past year indicates that CTLT will perform over the near term.

Financial Data
(US$ in Thousands)

	3 Mos	06/30/2019	06/30/2018	06/30/2017	06/30/2016	06/30/2015	06/30/2014	06/30/2013
Earnings Per Share	0.94	0.90	0.63	0.87	0.89	1.75	0.21	(0.62)
Cash Flow Per Share	1.59	1.72	2.85	2.40	1.24	1.44	2.38	1.84
Income Statement								
Total Revenue	664,700	2,518,000	2,463,400	2,075,400	1,848,100	1,830,800	1,827,700	1,800,300
EBITDA	91,600	411,600	390,900	327,900	327,600	311,800	331,000	331,500
Depn & Amortn	62,100	140,400	127,500	102,200	94,200	94,300	100,500	152,200
Income Before Taxes	(6,800)	160,300	152,000	135,600	144,900	112,500	67,400	(23,900)
Income Taxes	(6,900)	22,900	68,400	25,800	33,700	(97,700)	49,500	24,100
Net Income	100	137,400	83,600	109,800	111,500	212,200	16,200	(46,700)
Average Shares	145,663	145,954	133,201	126,737	125,870	121,348	76,123	74,970
Balance Sheet								
Current Assets	1,266,800	1,395,800	1,240,300	1,059,800	790,200	737,500	687,500	677,900
Total Assets	6,119,500	6,184,000	4,531,100	3,454,300	3,091,100	3,145,400	3,090,200	3,056,800
Current Liabilities	615,800	670,700	576,900	469,000	391,200	399,000	453,000	410,300
Long-Term Obligations	2,858,700	2,882,800	2,649,400	2,055,100	1,832,800	1,864,100	2,685,400	2,656,600
Total Liabilities	4,470,200	3,895,800	3,444,400	2,730,800	2,455,200	2,511,400	3,461,400	3,467,500
Stockholders' Equity	1,649,300	2,288,200	1,086,700	723,500	635,900	634,000	(371,200)	(410,700)
Shares Outstanding	146,235	145,738	133,423	125,049	124,712	124,319	74,821	74,796
Statistical Record								
Return on Assets %	2.86	2.56	2.09	3.36	3.57	6.81	0.53	N.M.
Return on Equity %	9.56	8.14	9.24	16.15	17.51	161.49	...	...
EBITDA Margin %	13.78	16.35	15.87	15.80	17.73	17.03	18.11	18.41
Net Margin %	0.02	5.46	3.39	5.29	6.03	11.59	0.89	N.M.
Asset Turnover	0.50	0.47	0.62	0.63	0.59	0.59	0.59	0.58
Current Ratio	2.06	2.08	2.15	2.26	2.02	1.85	1.52	1.65
Debt to Equity	1.73	1.26	2.44	2.84	2.88	2.94	...	...
Price Range	58.05-29.84	54.21-29.84	47.39-33.75	38.02-21.85	34.21-20.86	31.96-19.85	...	...
P/E Ratio	61.76-31.74	60.23-33.16	75.22-53.57	43.70-25.11	38.44-23.44	18.26-11.34	...	...

Address: 14 Schoolhouse Road,	Web Site: www.catalent.com	Auditors: Ernst & Young LLP
Somerset, NJ 08873	Officers: John R. Chiminski - Chairman, Chief	Transfer Agents: Computershare Trust
Telephone: 732-537-6200	Executive Officer Alessandro Maselli - President,	Company, N.A.
	Chief Operating Officer, Division Officer	

CATERPILLAR INC.

Exchange	Symbol	Price	52Wk Range	Yield	P/E	Div Acheiver
NYS	CAT	$147.68 (12/31/2019)	148.50-113.38	2.79	14.00	25 Years

*7 Year Price Score 104.49 *NYSE Composite Index=100 *12 Month Price Score 102.83

Interim Earnings (Per Share)

Qtr.	Mar	Jun	Sep	Dec
2016	0.46	0.93	0.48	(1.99)
2017	0.32	1.35	1.77	(2.18)
2018	2.74	2.82	2.88	1.81
2019	3.25	2.83	2.66	...

Interim Dividends (Per Share)

Amt	Decl	Ex	Rec	Pay
0.86Q	04/10/2019	04/18/2019	04/22/2019	05/20/2019
1.03Q	05/02/2019	07/19/2019	07/22/2019	08/20/2019
1.03Q	10/09/2019	10/18/2019	10/21/2019	11/20/2019
1.03Q	12/11/2019	01/17/2020	01/21/2020	02/20/2020

Indicated Div: $4.12 (Div. Reinv. Plan)

Valuation Analysis

		Institutional Holding	
Forecast EPS	$10.85	No of Institutions	
	(01/17/2020)	2193	
Market Cap	$81.6 Billion	Shares	
Book Value	$15.0 Billion	472,843,008	
Price/Book	5.46	% Held	
Price/Sales	1.48	60.26	

Business Summary: Construction Services (MIC: 7.5.4 SIC: 3531 NAIC: 333120)

Caterpillar manufactures construction and mining equipment, diesel and natural gas engines, industrial gas turbines and diesel-electric locomotives. Co.'s operating segments include: Construction Industries, which provides machinery for infrastructure, forestry and building construction applications; Resource Industries, which provides machinery for mining, quarry, waste, and material handling applications; Energy and Transportation, which provides reciprocating engines, turbines, diesel-electric locomotives and related parts across various related industries; and Financial Products Segment, which provides financing alternatives to customers and dealers for Co.'s products.

Recent Developments: For the quarter ended Sep 30 2019, net income decreased 13.5% to US$1.49 billion from US$1.73 billion in the year-earlier quarter. Revenues were US$12.76 billion, down 5.6% from US$13.51 billion the year before. Operating income was US$2.02 billion versus US$2.14 billion in the prior-year quarter, a decrease of 5.4%. Direct operating expenses declined 5.0% to US$8.57 billion from US$9.02 billion in the comparable period the year before. Indirect operating expenses decreased 7.8% to US$2.17 billion from US$2.35 billion in the equivalent prior-year period.

Prospects: Our evaluation of Caterpillar Inc. as of October 4th, 2019 is the result of our systematic analysis on three basic characteristics: earnings strength, relative valuation, and recent stock price movement. The company has managed to produce a neutral trend in earnings per share over the past 5 quarters. However, recent analyst estimates for the company have been reduced and CAT has posted results that fell short of analysts' expectations. Based on operating earnings yield, the company is undervalued when compared to all of the companies we cover. Share price changes over the past year indicates that CAT will perform poorly over the near term.

Financial Data

(US$ in Thousands)	9 Mos	6 Mos	3 Mos	12/31/2018	12/31/2017	12/31/2016	12/31/2015	12/31/2014
Earnings Per Share	10.55	10.77	10.76	10.26	1.26	(0.11)	3.50	5.88
Cash Flow Per Share	11.79	12.65	11.78	11.09	9.64	9.57	11.23	13.05
Tang Book Value Per Share	12.99	12.25	13.01	10.29	9.01	8.13	9.23	11.51
Dividends Per Share	3.610	3.440	3.360	3.280	3.100	3.080	2.940	2.600
Dividend Payout %	34.22	31.94	31.23	31.97	246.03	...	84.00	44.22
Income Statement								
Total Revenue	40,656,000	27,898,000	13,466,000	54,722,000	45,462,000	38,537,000	47,011,000	55,184,000
EBITDA	9,104,000	6,318,000	3,198,000	11,383,000	7,814,000	3,947,000	6,654,000	8,986,000
Depn & Amortn	1,933,000	1,288,000	641,000	2,435,000	2,555,000	2,707,000	2,705,000	2,795,000
Income Before Taxes	6,447,000	4,442,000	2,264,000	7,822,000	4,082,000	139,000	2,855,000	5,083,000
Income Taxes	1,470,000	952,000	387,000	1,698,000	3,339,000	192,000	742,000	1,380,000
Net Income	4,995,000	3,501,000	1,881,000	6,147,000	754,000	(67,000)	2,102,000	3,695,000
Average Shares	561,200	573,100	578,800	599,400	599,300	584,300	601,300	628,900
Balance Sheet								
Current Assets	39,160,000	39,789,000	39,126,000	38,603,000	36,244,000	31,967,000	34,418,000	38,867,000
Total Assets	77,993,000	79,187,000	78,726,000	78,509,000	76,962,000	74,704,000	78,497,000	84,681,000
Current Liabilities	27,201,000	27,735,000	27,388,000	28,218,000	26,931,000	26,132,000	26,303,000	27,877,000
Long-Term Obligations	25,588,000	24,764,000	24,240,000	25,000,000	23,847,000	22,818,000	25,247,000	27,784,000
Total Liabilities	63,041,000	64,350,000	63,289,000	64,470,000	63,265,000	61,567,000	63,688,000	67,935,000
Stockholders' Equity	14,952,000	14,837,000	15,437,000	14,039,000	13,697,000	13,137,000	14,809,000	16,746,000
Shares Outstanding	552,658	562,589	571,702	575,542	597,625	586,486	582,321	606,166
Statistical Record								
Return on Assets %	7.74	7.94	8.12	7.91	0.99	N.M.	2.58	4.36
Return on Equity %	39.24	42.24	41.53	44.33	5.62	N.M.	13.32	19.68
EBITDA Margin %	22.39	22.65	23.75	20.80	17.19	10.24	14.15	16.28
Net Margin %	12.29	12.55	13.97	11.23	1.66	N.M.	4.47	6.70
Asset Turnover	0.70	0.70	0.71	0.70	0.60	0.50	0.58	0.65
Current Ratio	1.44	1.43	1.43	1.37	1.35	1.22	1.31	1.39
Debt to Equity	1.71	1.67	1.57	1.78	1.74	1.74	1.70	1.66
Price Range	158.22-112.34	158.22-112.34	158.92-112.34	170.89-112.34	158.42-91.39	97.33-57.91	91.88-63.79	111.40-86.17
P/E Ratio	15.00-10.65	14.69-10.43	14.77-10.44	16.66-10.95	125.73-72.53	...	26.25-18.23	18.95-14.65
Average Yield %	2.77	2.56	2.43	2.27	2.75	3.92	3.73	2.58

Address: 510 Lake Cook Road, Suite 100, Deerfield, IL 60015 **Telephone:** 224-551-4000	**Web Site:** www.caterpillar.com **Officers:** Donald James (Jim) Umpleby - Chairman, Group President, Chief Executive Officer Ramin Younessi - Group President	**Auditors:** PricewaterhouseCoopers LLP **Investor Contact:** 309-675-4549 **Transfer Agents:** ComputerShare, College Station, TX

CBRE GROUP INC

Exchange	Symbol	Price	52Wk Range	Yield	P/E
NYS	CBRE	$61.29 (12/31/2019)	61.29-37.89	N/A	20.16

*7 Year Price Score 117.73 *NYSE Composite Index=100 *12 Month Price Score 105.84

Interim Earnings (Per Share)

Qtr.	Mar	Jun	Sep	Dec
2016	0.24	0.36	0.31	0.78
2017	0.38	0.58	0.58	0.49
2018	0.44	0.67	0.85	1.15
2019	0.48	0.66	0.75	...

Interim Dividends (Per Share)

No Dividends Paid

Valuation Analysis		Institutional Holding	
Forecast EPS	$3.74	No of Institutions	
	(01/15/2020)	860	
Market Cap	$20.6 Billion	Shares	
Book Value	$5.5 Billion	394,533,088	
Price/Book	3.73	% Held	
Price/Sales	0.89	N/A	

Business Summary: Property, Real Estate & Development (MIC: 5.3.2 SIC: 6531 NAIC: 531210)

CBRE Group is a holding company. Through its subsidiaries, Co. is a commercial real estate services and investment firm. Co. provides services to both occupiers of and investors in real estate. For occupiers, Co. provides facilities management, project management, transaction and consulting services, among others. For investors, Co. provides capital markets, property leasing, investment management, property management, valuation and development services, among others. Co. provides commercial real estate services under the CBRE brand name, investment management services under the CBRE Global Investors brand name and development services under the Trammell Crow Company brand name.

Recent Developments: For the quarter ended Sep 30 2019, net income decreased 11.5% to US$258.1 million from US$291.7 million in the year-earlier quarter. Revenues were US$5.93 billion, up 12.6% from US$5.26 billion the year before.

Prospects: Our evaluation of CBRE Group Inc. as of October 4th, 2019 is the result of our systematic analysis on three basic characteristics: earnings strength, relative valuation, and recent stock price movement. The company has managed to produce a neutral trend in earnings per share over the past 5 quarters. In addition, recent analyst estimates for the company have been mixed and CBRE has posted results that exceeded analysts' expectations. Based on operating earnings yield, the company is undervalued when compared to all of the companies we cover. Share price changes over the past year indicates that CBRE will perform over the near term.

Financial Data

(US$ in Thousands)	9 Mos	6 Mos	3 Mos	12/31/2018	12/31/2017	12/31/2016	12/31/2015	12/31/2014
Earnings Per Share	3.04	3.14	3.15	3.10	2.03	1.69	1.63	1.45
Cash Flow Per Share	2.29	2.70	2.91	3.33	2.10	1.34	1.96	2.00
Tang Book Value Per Share	1.66	1.05	0.26	N.M.	N.M.	N.M.	N.M.	N.M.
Income Statement								
Total Revenue	16,774,684	10,849,583	5,135,510	21,340,088	14,209,608	13,071,589	10,855,810	9,049,918
EBITDA	776,785	457,723	167,407	1,345,827	1,246,847	971,375	966,650	904,150
Depn & Amortn	7,196	5,705	4,175	192,800	166,000	151,200	137,200	122,800
Income Before Taxes	701,951	406,226	142,040	1,054,342	953,886	683,375	716,881	675,548
Income Taxes	169,867	106,399	43,878	313,058	466,147	296,662	320,853	263,759
Net Income	644,739	388,140	164,409	1,063,219	691,479	571,973	547,132	484,503
Average Shares	341,100	340,508	340,158	343,122	340,783	338,424	336,414	334,171
Balance Sheet								
Current Assets	7,058,835	6,885,217	6,996,860	6,754,210	5,452,527	5,122,450	5,305,223	3,524,504
Total Assets	15,040,942	14,719,135	14,693,008	13,456,793	11,483,830	10,779,587	11,017,943	7,647,105
Current Liabilities	6,027,970	5,887,449	6,010,082	5,803,380	4,606,645	4,525,429	4,994,157	2,875,634
Long-Term Obligations	1,748,264	1,766,564	1,760,181	1,767,260	1,999,603	2,548,126	2,645,111	1,852,416
Total Liabilities	9,529,113	9,372,498	9,603,629	8,517,996	7,464,400	7,765,100	8,305,291	5,387,275
Stockholders' Equity	5,511,829	5,346,637	5,089,379	4,938,797	4,019,430	3,014,487	2,712,652	2,259,830
Shares Outstanding	335,755	336,329	336,266	336,912	339,459	337,279	334,230	332,991
Statistical Record								
Return on Assets %	7.41	7.87	8.10	8.53	6.21	5.23	5.86	6.62
Return on Equity %	20.31	21.89	22.81	23.74	19.66	19.92	22.01	23.32
EBITDA Margin %	4.63	4.22	3.26	6.31	8.77	7.43	8.90	9.99
Net Margin %	3.84	3.58	3.20	4.98	4.87	4.38	5.04	5.35
Asset Turnover	1.65	1.64	1.64	1.71	1.28	1.20	1.16	1.24
Current Ratio	1.17	1.17	1.16	1.16	1.18	1.13	1.06	1.23
Debt to Equity	0.32	0.33	0.35	0.36	0.50	0.85	0.98	0.82
Price Range	55.73-37.64	52.17-37.64	50.89-37.64	49.98-37.64	44.20-30.04	34.58-23.32	38.92-30.93	35.06-25.47
P/E Ratio	18.33-12.38	16.61-11.99	16.16-11.95	16.12-12.14	21.77-14.80	20.46-13.80	23.88-18.98	24.18-17.57

Address: 400 South Hope Street, 25th Floor, Los Angeles, CA 90071 **Telephone:** 213-613-3333	**Web Site:** www.cbre.com **Officers:** Brandon B. Boze - Chairman Robert E. Sulentic - President, Chief Executive Officer	**Auditors:** KPMG LLP **Investor Contact:** 213-613-3732 **Transfer Agents:** Broadridge Corporate Issuer Solutions, Inc., Edgewood, NY

CELANESE CORP (DE)

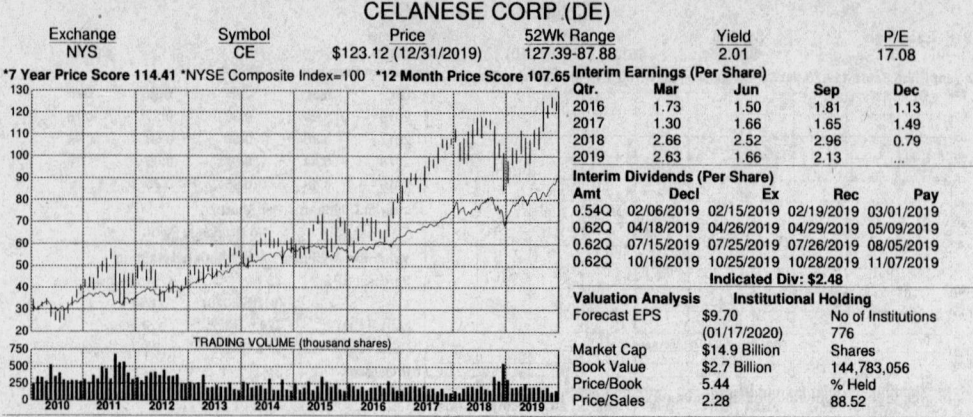

Exchange	Symbol	Price	52Wk Range	Yield	P/E
NYS	CE	$123.12 (12/31/2019)	127.39-87.88	2.01	17.08

*7 Year Price Score 114.41 *NYSE Composite Index=100 *12 Month Price Score 107.65

Interim Earnings (Per Share)

Qtr.	Mar	Jun	Sep	Dec
2016	1.73	1.50	1.81	1.13
2017	1.30	1.66	1.65	1.49
2018	2.66	2.52	2.96	0.79
2019	2.63	1.66	2.13	...

Interim Dividends (Per Share)

Amt	Decl	Ex	Rec	Pay
0.54Q	02/06/2019	02/15/2019	02/19/2019	03/01/2019
0.62Q	04/18/2019	04/26/2019	04/29/2019	05/09/2019
0.62Q	07/15/2019	07/25/2019	07/26/2019	08/05/2019
0.62Q	10/16/2019	10/25/2019	10/28/2019	11/07/2019

Indicated Div: $2.48

Valuation Analysis — **Institutional Holding**

Forecast EPS	$9.70	No of Institutions
	(01/17/2020)	776
Market Cap	$14.9 Billion	Shares
Book Value	$2.7 Billion	144,783,056
Price/Book	5.44	% Held
Price/Sales	2.28	88.52

Business Summary: Specialty Chemicals (MIC: 8.3.2 SIC: 5169 NAIC: 424690)

Celanese is a holding company. Through its subsidiaries, Co. is a technology and specialty materials company. Co. is a producer of engineered polymers and a producer of acetyl products, which are intermediate chemicals. Co.'s segments are: Engineered Materials, which develops, produces and supplies a portfolio of specialty polymers for automotive and medical applications, as well as industrial products and consumer electronics; Acetate Tow, which is a producer and supplier of acetate tow and acetate flake, primarily used in filter products applications; and Acetyl Chain, which includes the chain of intermediate chemistry, emulsion polymers and ethylene vinyl acetate polymers businesses.

Recent Developments: For the quarter ended Sep 30 2019, income from continuing operations decreased 33.8% to US$270.0 million from US$408.0 million in the year-earlier quarter. Net income decreased 34.1% to US$265.0 million from US$402.0 million in the year-earlier quarter. Revenues were US$1.59 billion, down 10.4% from US$1.77 billion the year before. Operating income was US$260.0 million versus US$374.0 million in the prior-year quarter, a decrease of 30.5%. Direct operating expenses declined 6.6% to US$1.17 billion from US$1.26 billion in the comparable period the year before. Indirect operating expenses increased 8.5% to US$154.0 million from US$142.0 million in the equivalent prior-year period.

Prospects: Our evaluation of Celanese Corp. as of October 4th, 2019 is the result of our systematic analysis on three basic characteristics: earnings strength, relative valuation, and recent stock price movement. The company has managed to produce a neutral trend in earnings per share over the past 5 quarters. However, recent analyst estimates for the company have been reduced while CE has posted results that exceeded analysts' expectations. Based on operating earnings yield, the company is undervalued when compared to all of the companies we cover. Share price changes over the past year indicates that CE will perform poorly over the near term.

Financial Data

(US$ in Thousands)	9 Mos	6 Mos	3 Mos	12/31/2018	12/31/2017	12/31/2016	12/31/2015	12/31/2014
Earnings Per Share	7.21	8.04	8.90	8.91	6.09	6.18	2.00	4.00
Cash Flow Per Share	12.15	12.46	13.50	11.60	5.82	6.14	5.71	6.21
Tang Book Value Per Share	11.37	11.75	12.95	12.62	11.66	11.36	10.55	12.67
Dividends Per Share	2.320	2.240	2.160	2.080	1.740	1.380	1.150	0.930
Dividend Payout %	32.18	27.86	24.27	23.34	28.57	22.33	57.50	23.25
Income Statement								
Total Revenue	4,865,000	3,279,000	1,687,000	7,155,000	6,140,000	5,389,000	5,674,000	6,802,000
EBITDA	863,000	570,000	354,000	1,739,000	1,317,000	1,283,000	782,000	1,133,000
Depn & Amortn	18,000	12,000	6,000	343,000	305,000	290,000	357,000	292,000
Income Before Taxes	762,000	501,000	318,000	1,277,000	892,000	875,000	307,000	695,000
Income Taxes	127,000	74,000	46,000	292,000	213,000	122,000	201,000	314,000
Net Income	809,000	546,000	337,000	1,207,000	843,000	900,000	304,000	624,000
Average Shares	123,299	125,847	128,215	135,416	138,317	145,668	152,287	156,166
Balance Sheet								
Current Assets	2,843,000	2,876,000	2,884,000	2,874,000	2,792,000	2,472,000	2,787,000	2,698,000
Total Assets	9,414,000	9,506,000	9,574,000	9,313,000	9,538,000	8,357,000	8,586,000	8,818,000
Current Liabilities	1,533,000	1,408,000	1,822,000	1,779,000	1,559,000	1,077,000	1,550,000	1,338,000
Long-Term Obligations	3,359,000	3,444,000	2,933,000	2,970,000	3,315,000	2,890,000	2,468,000	2,608,000
Total Liabilities	6,667,000	6,642,000	6,527,000	6,329,000	6,651,000	5,769,000	6,208,000	6,000,000
Stockholders' Equity	2,747,000	2,864,000	3,047,000	2,984,000	2,887,000	2,588,000	2,378,000	2,818,000
Shares Outstanding	121,333	123,740	126,612	128,095	135,769	140,660	146,782	152,902
Statistical Record								
Return on Assets %	9.44	10.84	12.20	12.81	9.42	10.59	3.49	7.00
Return on Equity %	28.88	33.50	37.49	41.12	30.79	36.15	11.70	22.62
EBITDA Margin %	17.74	17.38	20.98	24.30	21.45	23.81	13.78	16.66
Net Margin %	16.63	16.65	19.98	16.87	13.73	16.70	5.36	9.17
Asset Turnover	0.68	0.70	0.72	0.76	0.69	0.63	0.65	0.76
Current Ratio	1.85	2.04	1.58	1.62	1.79	2.30	1.80	2.02
Debt to Equity	1.22	1.20	0.96	1.00	1.15	1.12	1.04	0.93
Price Range	125.49-84.41	118.11-84.41	118.11-84.41	118.11-84.41	108.50-79.51	83.30-55.81	73.72-53.41	66.05-48.83
P/E Ratio	17.40-11.71	14.69-10.50	13.27-9.48	13.26-9.47	17.82-13.06	13.48-9.03	36.86-26.70	16.51-12.21
Average Yield %	2.25	2.16	2.05	1.94	1.83	2.03	1.81	1.59

Address: 222 W. Las Colinas Blvd., Suite 900N, Irving, TX 75039-5421 Telephone: 972-443-4000	Web Site: www.celanese.com Officers: Mark C. Rohr - Executive Chairman, Chairman, President, Chief Executive Officer Lori J. Ryerkerk - President, Chief Executive Officer	Auditors: KPMG LLP Investor Contact: 972-443-4965 Transfer Agents: ComputerShare Investor Services, Providence, RI

CENTENE CORP

Exchange	Symbol	Price	52Wk Range	Yield	P/E
NYS	CNC	$62.87 (12/31/2019)	65.89-42.73	N/A	19.46

*7 Year Price Score 124.48 *NYSE Composite Index=100 *12 Month Price Score 101.68

TRADING VOLUME (thousand shares)

Interim Earnings (Per Share)

Qtr.	Mar	Jun	Sep	Dec
2016	(0.07)	0.48	0.41	0.78
2017	0.40	0.73	0.58	0.65
2018	0.95	0.75	0.04	0.57
2019	1.24	1.18	0.23	...

Interim Dividends (Per Share)

No Dividends Paid

Valuation Analysis / Institutional Holding

Valuation Analysis		Institutional Holding	
Forecast EPS	$4.42	No of Institutions	
	(01/15/2020)	975	
Market Cap	$26.4 Billion	Shares	
Book Value	$12.3 Billion	440,802,944	
Price/Book	2.14	% Held	
Price/Sales	0.36	97.85	

Business Summary: Hospitals & Health Care Facilities (MIC: 4.2.1 SIC: 6324 NAIC: 524114)

Centene is an insurance holding company. Through its subsidiaries, Co. is a multi-national healthcare enterprise that provides a portfolio of services to government sponsored and commercial healthcare programs, focusing on under-insured and uninsured individuals. Co. operates in two segments: Managed Care, which provides health plan coverage, including Medicaid, the State Children's Health Insurance Program, Long-Term Services and Supports, Foster Care, Medicare-Medicaid Plans, the Supplemental Security Income Program, and the Health Insurance Marketplace; and Specialty Services, which consists of Co.'s specialty companies providing auxiliary healthcare services and products.

Recent Developments: For the quarter ended Sep 30 2019, net income increased 500.0% to US$96.0 million from US$16.0 million in the year-earlier quarter. Revenues were US$18.98 billion, up 17.3% from US$16.18 billion the year before.

Prospects: Our evaluation of Centene Corp. as of October 4th, 2019 is the result of our systematic analysis on three basic characteristics: earnings strength, relative valuation, and recent stock price movement. The company has managed to produce a neutral trend in earnings per share over the past 5 quarters. In addition, recent analyst estimates for the company have been mixed and CNC has posted results that exceeded analysts' expectations. Based on operating earnings yield, the company is undervalued when compared to all of the companies we cover. Share price changes over the past year indicates that CNC will perform in line with the market over the near term.

Financial Data

(US$ in Thousands)	9 Mos	6 Mos	3 Mos	12/31/2018	12/31/2017	12/31/2016	12/31/2015	12/31/2014
Earnings Per Share	3.23	3.04	2.61	2.26	2.35	1.72	1.44	1.13
Cash Flow Per Share	3.63	5.19	1.70	3.16	4.32	5.78	2.76	5.26
Tang Book Value Per Share	7.99	6.93	5.69	4.03	2.03	N.M.	4.82	3.67
Income Statement								
Total Revenue	55,776,000	36,800,000	18,444,000	60,116,000	48,382,000	40,607,000	22,760,000	16,560,000
EBITDA	2,015,000	1,676,000	849,000	2,159,000	1,706,000	1,622,000	818,000	557,000
Depn & Amortn	194,000	129,000	65,000	448,000	317,000	248,000	78,000	65,000
Income Before Taxes	1,522,000	1,347,000	685,000	1,368,000	1,134,000	1,157,000	697,000	457,000
Income Taxes	415,000	336,000	166,000	474,000	326,000	599,000	339,000	196,000
Net Income	1,112,000	1,017,000	522,000	900,000	828,000	562,000	355,000	271,000
Average Shares	419,956	419,671	419,752	398,506	353,404	327,950	246,132	240,720
Balance Sheet								
Current Assets	13,457,000	13,596,000	13,616,000	11,998,000	8,703,000	8,365,000	3,605,000	3,034,000
Total Assets	34,252,000	34,368,000	33,569,000	30,901,000	21,855,000	20,197,000	7,339,000	5,838,000
Current Liabilities	13,280,000	12,653,000	13,143,000	11,971,000	9,332,000	8,623,000	3,629,000	2,900,000
Long-Term Obligations	6,975,000	7,047,000	6,775,000	6,648,000	4,695,000	4,651,000	1,216,000	888,000
Total Liabilities	21,941,000	22,214,000	22,029,000	19,984,000	15,005,000	14,302,000	5,182,000	4,094,000
Stockholders' Equity	12,311,000	12,154,000	11,540,000	10,917,000	6,850,000	5,895,000	2,157,000	1,744,000
Shares Outstanding	419,667	413,527	413,305	412,478	346,874	343,838	240,685	236,866
Statistical Record								
Return on Assets %	4.14	4.05	3.68	3.41	3.94	4.07	5.39	5.79
Return on Equity %	11.78	11.22	11.36	10.13	12.99	13.92	18.20	18.20
EBITDA Margin %	3.61	4.55	4.60	3.59	3.53	3.99	3.59	3.36
Net Margin %	1.99	2.76	2.83	1.50	1.71	1.38	1.56	1.64
Asset Turnover	2.21	2.20	2.23	2.28	2.30	2.94	3.45	3.54
Current Ratio	1.01	1.07	1.04	1.00	0.93	0.97	0.99	1.05
Debt to Equity	0.57	0.58	0.59	0.61	0.69	0.79	0.56	0.51
Price Range	73.42-43.13	73.44-47.01	73.44-52.12	73.44-49.69	51.51-29.16	37.70-25.34	40.74-25.96	26.79-13.91
P/E Ratio	22.73-13.35	24.16-15.46	28.14-19.97	32.50-21.99	21.92-12.41	21.92-14.73	28.29-18.03	23.71-12.31

Address: 7700 Forsyth Boulevard, St. Louis, MO 63105 **Telephone:** 314-725-4477 **Fax:** 314-725-5180	**Web Site:** www.centene.com **Officers:** Michael F. Neidorff - Chairman, Chairman (frmr), President, President (frmr), Chief Executive Officer, Chief Executive Officer (frmr) Mark J. Brooks - Executive Vice President, Senior Vice President, Chief Information Officer	**Auditors:** KPMG LLP **Transfer Agents:** Broadridge Corporate Issuer Solutions, Inc., Philadelphia, PA

CENTERPOINT ENERGY, INC

Exchange	Symbol	Price	52Wk Range	Yield	P/E	Div Acheiver
NYS	CNP	$27.27 (12/31/2019)	31.40-24.39	4.22	21.64	13 Years

*7 Year Price Score 96.80 *NYSE Composite Index=100 *12 Month Price Score 85.65

Interim Earnings (Per Share)

Qtr.	Mar	Jun	Sep	Dec
2016	0.36	(0.01)	0.41	0.24
2017	0.44	0.31	0.39	2.99
2018	0.38	(0.17)	0.35	0.18
2019	0.28	0.33	0.47	...

Interim Dividends (Per Share)

Amt	Decl	Ex	Rec	Pay
0.287Q	12/12/2018	02/20/2019	02/21/2019	03/14/2019
0.287Q	04/25/2019	05/15/2019	05/16/2019	06/13/2019
0.287Q	07/31/2019	08/14/2019	08/15/2019	09/12/2019
0.287Q	10/17/2019	11/20/2019	11/21/2019	12/12/2019

Indicated Div: $1.15 (Div. Reinv. Plan)

Valuation Analysis

		Institutional Holding	
Forecast EPS	$1.69	No of Institutions	
	(01/16/2020)	883	
Market Cap	$13.7 Billion	Shares	
Book Value	$8.3 Billion	484,209,728	
Price/Book	1.64	% Held	
Price/Sales	1.13	93.25	

Business Summary: Electric Utilities (MIC: 3.1.1 SIC: 4911 NAIC: 221111)

CenterPoint Energy is a holding company. Through its subsidiaries, CenterPoint Energy Houston Electric, LLC (Houston Electric) and CenterPoint Energy Resources Corp. (CERC Corp.), Co. owns and operates electric transmission and distribution and natural gas distribution facilities and supplies natural gas to commercial and industrial customers and electric and natural gas utilities. CenterPoint Energy Services, Inc., a subsidiary of CERC Corp., provides a variety of natural gas management services to gas utilities, large industrial customers, electric generators, smaller commercial and industrial customers, municipalities, educational institutions, government facilities and hospitals.

Recent Developments: For the quarter ended Sep 30 2019, net income increased 70.9% to US$270.0 million from US$158.0 million in the year-earlier quarter. Revenues were US$2.74 billion, up 24.0% from US$2.21 billion the year before. Operating income was US$392.0 million versus US$226.0 million in the prior-year quarter, an increase of 73.5%. Direct operating expenses rose 21.5% to US$1.90 billion from US$1.57 billion in the comparable period the year before. Indirect operating expenses increased 6.4% to US$448.0 million from US$421.0 million in the equivalent prior-year period.

Prospects: Our evaluation of Centerpoint Energy Inc. as of October 4th, 2019 is the result of our systematic analysis on three basic characteristics: earnings strength, relative valuation, and recent stock price movement. The company has enjoyed a very positive trend in earnings per share over the past 5 quarters. However, recent analyst estimates for the company have been mixed and CNP has posted results that exceeded analysts' expectations. Based on operating earnings yield, the company is undervalued when compared to all of the companies we cover. Share price changes over the past year indicates that CNP will perform in line with the market over the near term.

Financial Data

(US$ in Thousands)	9 Mos	6 Mos	3 Mos	12/31/2018	12/31/2017	12/31/2016	12/31/2015	12/31/2014
Earnings Per Share	1.26	1.14	0.64	0.74	4.13	1.00	(1.61)	1.42
Cash Flow Per Share	3.07	3.22	3.83	4.76	3.30	4.46	4.34	3.25
Tang Book Value Per Share	2.13	1.93	1.77	10.88	8.86	6.03	6.10	8.62
Dividends Per Share	1.140	1.130	1.120	1.110	1.070	1.030	0.990	0.950
Dividend Payout %	90.48	99.12	175.00	150.00	25.91	103.00	...	66.90
Income Statement								
Total Revenue	9,071,000	6,329,000	3,531,000	10,589,000	9,614,000	7,528,000	7,386,000	9,226,000
EBITDA	995,000	582,000	278,000	1,870,000	2,224,000	2,033,000	1,930,000	2,061,000
Depn & Amortn	41,000	26,000	16,000	1,243,000	1,036,000	1,126,000	970,000	1,013,000
Income Before Taxes	534,000	279,000	129,000	207,000	798,000	478,000	503,000	577,000
Income Taxes	113,000	51,000	22,000	146,000	(729,000)	254,000	(438,000)	274,000
Net Income	634,000	364,000	169,000	368,000	1,792,000	432,000	(692,000)	611,000
Average Shares	505,080	504,831	503,944	452,465	434,000	431,000	430,000	432,000
Balance Sheet								
Current Assets	3,416,000	3,326,000	3,419,000	7,025,000	3,395,000	2,923,000	2,689,000	3,268,000
Total Assets	34,642,000	34,189,000	33,902,000	27,009,000	22,736,000	21,829,000	21,334,000	23,200,000
Current Liabilities	3,434,000	2,996,000	3,139,000	3,302,000	3,069,000	3,080,000	2,467,000	3,475,000
Long-Term Obligations	14,014,000	14,121,000	13,759,000	8,682,000	8,195,000	7,532,000	7,901,000	8,009,000
Total Liabilities	26,296,000	25,932,000	25,686,000	18,951,000	18,048,000	18,369,000	17,873,000	18,652,000
Stockholders' Equity	8,346,000	8,257,000	8,216,000	8,058,000	4,688,000	3,460,000	3,461,000	4,548,000
Shares Outstanding	502,235	502,214	502,168	501,197	431,044	430,682	430,000	430,000
Statistical Record								
Return on Assets %	2.65	2.28	1.32	1.48	8.04	2.00	N.M.	2.71
Return on Equity %	10.88	9.93	5.69	5.77	43.99	12.45	N.M.	13.77
EBITDA Margin %	10.97	9.20	7.87	17.66	23.13	27.01	26.13	22.34
Net Margin %	6.99	5.75	4.79	3.48	18.64	5.74	N.M.	6.62
Asset Turnover	0.43	0.41	0.39	0.43	0.43	0.35	0.33	0.41
Current Ratio	0.99	1.11	1.09	2.13	1.11	0.95	1.09	0.94
Debt to Equity	1.68	1.71	1.67	1.08	1.75	2.18	2.28	1.76
Price Range	31.40-26.96	31.40-26.92	31.40-24.92	29.34-24.92	30.45-24.59	24.84-16.90	23.63-16.14	25.54-21.54
P/E Ratio	24.92-21.40	27.54-23.61	49.06-38.94	39.65-33.68	7.37-5.95	24.84-16.90	...	17.99-15.17
Average Yield %	3.91	3.90	3.99	4.06	3.80	4.70	5.05	3.95

Address: 1111 Louisiana, Houston, TX 77002	Web Site: www.centerpointenergy.com	Auditors: DELOITTE & TOUCHE LLP
Telephone: 713-207-1111	Officers: Milton Carroll - Executive Chairman, Chairman Scott M. Prochazka - President, Chief Executive Officer, Executive Vice President, Chief Operating Officer	Investor Contact: 713-207-6500 Transfer Agents: CenterPoint Energy Investor Services

CENTURYLINK INC

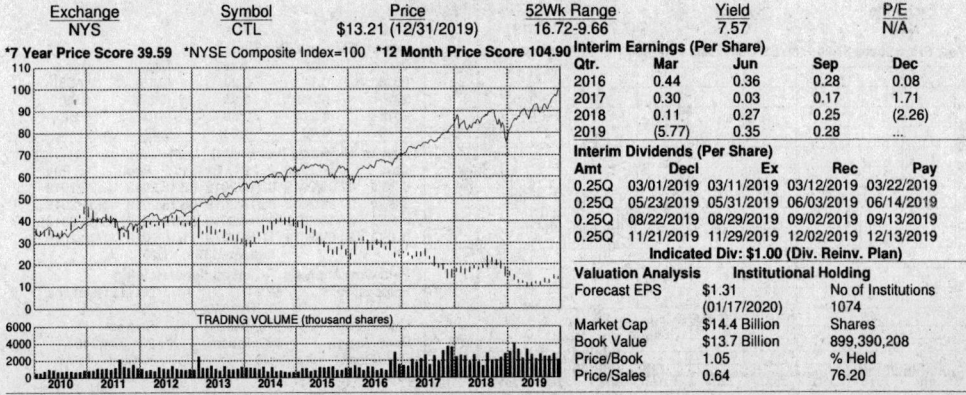

Exchange	Symbol	Price	52Wk Range	Yield	P/E
NYS	CTL	$13.21 (12/31/2019)	16.72-9.66	7.57	N/A

*7 Year Price Score 39.59   *NYSE Composite Index=100   *12 Month Price Score 104.90

Interim Earnings (Per Share)

Qtr.	Mar	Jun	Sep	Dec
2016	0.44	0.36	0.28	0.08
2017	0.30	0.03	0.17	1.71
2018	0.11	0.27	0.25	(2.26)
2019	(5.77)	0.35	0.28	...

Interim Dividends (Per Share)

Amt	Decl	Ex	Rec	Pay
0.25Q	03/01/2019	03/11/2019	03/12/2019	03/22/2019
0.25Q	05/23/2019	05/31/2019	06/03/2019	06/14/2019
0.25Q	08/22/2019	08/29/2019	09/02/2019	09/13/2019
0.25Q	11/21/2019	11/29/2019	12/02/2019	12/13/2019

Indicated Div: $1.00 (Div. Reinv. Plan)

Valuation Analysis / Institutional Holding

Forecast EPS	$1.31	No of Institutions
	(01/17/2020)	1074
Market Cap	$14.4 Billion	Shares
Book Value	$13.7 Billion	899,390,208
Price/Book	1.05	% Held
Price/Sales	0.64	76.20

Business Summary: Services (MIC: 6.1.2 SIC: 4813 NAIC: 517110)

CenturyLink is a holding company. Through its subsidiaries, Co. is a communications company engaged primarily in providing an array of services to its residential and business customers. Co. has following two segments: Business, which provides products and services including IP and data services suite of products, transport and infrastructure, voice services, and IT and managed services to domestic and global enterprises, small and medium businesses, federal, state and local governments and wholesale customers, including other communication providers; and Consumer, which provides broadband, local and long-distance voice, video and other ancillary services to residential customers.

Recent Developments: For the quarter ended Sep 30 2019, net income increased 11.0% to US$302.0 million from US$272.0 million in the year-earlier quarter. Revenues were US$5.61 billion, down 3.6% from US$5.82 billion the year before. Operating income was US$950.0 million versus US$894.0 million in the prior-year quarter, an increase of 6.3%. Direct operating expenses declined 3.1% to US$2.59 billion from US$2.67 billion in the comparable period the year before. Indirect operating expenses decreased 8.3% to US$2.07 billion from US$2.25 billion in the equivalent prior-year period.

Prospects: Our evaluation of CenturyLink, Inc. as of October 4th, 2019 is the result of our systematic analysis on three basic characteristics: earnings strength, relative valuation, and recent stock price movement. The company has generated a negative trend in earnings per share over the past 5 quarters. However, recent analyst estimates for the company have been mixed and CTL has posted results that exceeded analysts' expectations. Based on operating earnings yield, the company is undervalued when compared to all of the companies we cover. Share price changes over the past year indicates that CTL will perform very poorly over the near term.

Financial Data

(US$ in Thousands)	9 Mos	6 Mos	3 Mos	12/31/2018	12/31/2017	12/31/2016	12/31/2015	12/31/2014
Earnings Per Share	(7.40)	(7.43)	(7.51)	(1.63)	2.21	1.16	1.58	1.36
Cash Flow Per Share	6.31	6.22	6.13	6.60	6.18	8.52	9.29	9.13
Dividends Per Share	1.290	1.580	1.870	2.160	2.160	2.160	2.160	2.160
Dividend Payout %	...	...	...	...	97.74	186.21	136.71	158.82
Income Statement								
Total Revenue	16,831,000	11,225,000	5,647,000	23,443,000	17,656,000	17,470,000	17,900,000	18,031,000
EBITDA	41,000	(2,100,000)	(4,316,000)	3,953,000	4,731,000	5,029,000	5,464,000	5,379,000
Depn & Amortn	3,619,000	2,384,000	1,188,000	3,339,000	2,710,000	2,691,000	2,836,000	2,958,000
Income Before Taxes	(5,115,000)	(5,525,000)	(6,027,000)	(1,563,000)	540,000	1,020,000	1,316,000	1,110,000
Income Taxes	377,000	269,000	138,000	170,000	(849,000)	394,000	438,000	338,000
Net Income	(5,492,000)	(5,794,000)	(6,165,000)	(1,733,000)	1,389,000	626,000	878,000	772,000
Average Shares	1,074,790	1,072,813	1,068,878	1,065,866	628,693	540,679	555,093	569,739
Balance Sheet								
Current Assets	4,589,000	3,878,000	3,820,000	3,820,000	4,194,000	5,162,000	2,650,000	3,576,000
Total Assets	64,728,000	64,508,000	64,788,000	70,256,000	75,611,000	47,017,000	47,604,000	50,147,000
Current Liabilities	6,589,000	6,495,000	5,373,000	5,531,000	4,857,000	5,349,000	4,604,000	3,918,000
Long-Term Obligations	33,381,000	33,193,000	34,858,000	35,409,000	37,283,000	18,185,000	18,722,000	20,121,000
Total Liabilities	51,054,000	50,816,000	51,245,000	50,428,000	52,120,000	33,618,000	33,544,000	35,124,000
Stockholders' Equity	13,674,000	13,692,000	13,543,000	19,828,000	23,491,000	13,399,000	14,060,000	15,023,000
Shares Outstanding	1,090,326	1,090,137	1,090,445	1,080,167	1,069,169	546,545	543,800	568,517
Statistical Record								
Return on Assets %	N.M.	N.M.	N.M.	N.M.	2.27	1.32	1.80	1.51
Return on Equity %	N.M.	N.M.	N.M.	N.M.	7.53	4.55	6.04	4.79
EBITDA Margin %	0.24	N.M.	N.M.	16.86	26.80	28.79	30.53	29.83
Net Margin %	N.M.	N.M.	N.M.	N.M.	7.87	3.58	4.91	4.28
Asset Turnover	0.33	0.33	0.33	0.32	0.29	0.37	0.37	0.35
Current Ratio	0.70	0.60	0.71	0.69	0.86	0.97	0.58	0.91
Debt to Equity	2.44	2.42	2.57	1.79	1.59	1.36	1.33	1.34
Price Range	21.99-9.66	23.98-9.66	23.98-11.56	23.98-14.52	27.31-13.62	32.80-22.24	40.52-24.38	41.81-28.09
P/E Ratio	...	...	...	...	12.36-6.16	28.28-19.17	25.65-15.43	30.74-20.65
Average Yield %	9.20	9.69	10.36	11.44	9.88	7.73	6.87	5.92

Address: 100 CenturyLink Drive, Monroe, LA 71203 **Telephone:** 318-388-9000 **Fax:** 318-789-8656	**Web Site:** www.centurylink.com **Officers:** T. Michael Glenn - Chairman Jeffrey K. Storey - President, Chief Executive Officer, Chief Operating Officer	**Auditors:** KPMG LLP **Investor Contact:** 800-833-1188 **Transfer Agents:** Computershare Trust Company, Providence, RI

CF INDUSTRIES HOLDINGS INC

Exchange	Symbol	Price	52Wk Range	Yield	P/E
NYS	CF	$47.74 (12/31/2019)	52.68-39.01	2.51	21.90

*7 Year Price Score 87.94   *NYSE Composite Index=100   *12 Month Price Score 96.78

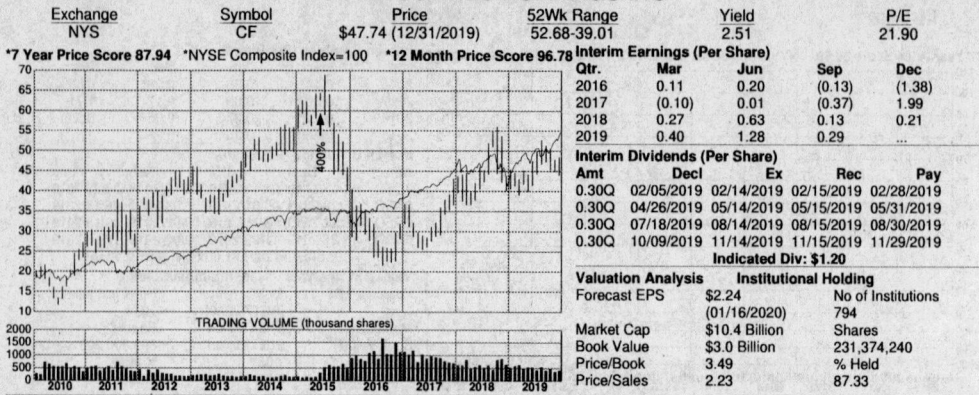

Interim Earnings (Per Share)

Qtr.	Mar	Jun	Sep	Dec
2016	0.11	0.20	(0.13)	(1.38)
2017	(0.10)	0.01	(0.37)	1.99
2018	0.27	0.63	0.13	0.21
2019	0.40	1.28	0.29	...

Interim Dividends (Per Share)

Amt	Decl	Ex	Rec	Pay
0.30Q	02/05/2019	02/14/2019	02/15/2019	02/28/2019
0.30Q	04/26/2019	05/14/2019	05/15/2019	05/31/2019
0.30Q	07/18/2019	08/14/2019	08/15/2019	08/30/2019
0.30Q	10/09/2019	11/14/2019	11/15/2019	11/29/2019

Indicated Div: $1.20

Valuation Analysis

		Institutional Holding	
Forecast EPS	$2.24	No of Institutions	
	(01/16/2020)	794	
Market Cap	$10.4 Billion	Shares	
Book Value	$3.0 Billion	231,374,240	
Price/Book	3.49	% Held	
Price/Sales	2.23	87.33	

Business Summary: Agricultural Chemicals (MIC: 8.3.3 SIC: 2879 NAIC: 325320)

CF Industries Holdings is a global fertilizer and chemical company. Co.'s reportable segments consist of the following segments: ammonia, which produces anhydrous ammonia; granular urea, which produces granular urea that is produced from ammonia and carbon dioxide; urea ammonium nitrate solution (UAN), which produces UAN, a liquid fertilizer product; ammonium nitrate (AN), which produces AN that is used as nitrogen fertilizer and is also used by industrial customers for commercial explosives and blasting systems; and Other, which includes the following products diesel exhaust fluid, urea liquor, nitric acid, as well as compound fertilizer products.

Recent Developments: For the quarter ended Sep 30 2019, net income increased 60.6% to US$114.0 million from US$71.0 million in the year-earlier quarter. Revenues were US$1.04 billion, unchanged from the year before. Operating income was US$188.0 million versus US$136.0 million in the prior-year quarter, an increase of 38.2%. Direct operating expenses declined 6.6% to US$810.0 million from US$867.0 million in the comparable period the year before. Indirect operating expenses increased 8.1% to US$40.0 million from US$37.0 million in the equivalent prior-year period.

Prospects: Our evaluation of CF Industries Holdings Inc. as of October 4th, 2019 is the result of our systematic analysis on three basic characteristics: earnings strength, relative valuation, and recent stock price movement. The company has produced a positive trend in earnings per share over the past 5 quarters. However, recent analyst estimates for the company have been mixed and CF has posted results that exceeded analysts' expectations. Based on operating earnings yield, the company is fairly valued when compared to all of the companies we cover. Share price changes over the past year indicates that CF will perform poorly over the near term.

Financial Data

(US$ in Thousands)	9 Mos	6 Mos	3 Mos	12/31/2018	12/31/2017	12/31/2016	12/31/2015	12/31/2014
Earnings Per Share	2.18	2.02	1.37	1.24	1.53	(1.19)	2.96	5.42
Cash Flow Per Share	6.65	7.20	6.81	6.44	6.99	2.64	5.12	5.50
Tang Book Value Per Share	2.92	3.26	2.69	2.72	5.18	4.30	7.06	8.76
Dividends Per Share	1.200	1.200	1.200	1.200	1.200	1.200	1.200	1.000
Dividend Payout %	55.05	59.41	87.59	96.77	78.43	...	40.54	18.46
Income Statement								
Total Revenue	3,541,000	2,503,000	1,001,000	4,429,000	4,130,000	3,685,000	4,308,300	4,743,200
EBITDA	1,489,000	1,065,000	342,000	1,604,000	271,000	190,000	1,289,600	2,375,400
Depn & Amortn	648,000	430,000	183,000	865,000	102,000	89,000	65,400	53,900
Income Before Taxes	671,000	524,000	103,000	511,000	(134,000)	(94,000)	1,092,600	2,144,200
Income Taxes	113,000	94,000	(8,000)	119,000	(575,000)	(81,000)	395,800	773,000
Net Income	438,000	373,000	90,000	290,000	358,000	(277,000)	699,900	1,390,300
Average Shares	220,700	222,300	224,600	233,800	233,900	233,100	236,100	256,500
Balance Sheet								
Current Assets	1,669,000	1,488,000	1,412,000	1,274,000	1,465,000	2,655,000	1,127,100	2,614,500
Total Assets	12,902,000	12,863,000	12,942,000	12,661,000	13,463,000	15,131,000	12,738,900	11,338,200
Current Liabilities	1,245,000	1,042,000	826,000	705,000	580,000	686,000	1,215,200	979,700
Long-Term Obligations	4,204,000	4,203,000	4,700,000	4,698,000	4,692,000	5,778,000	5,592,700	4,592,500
Total Liabilities	9,922,000	9,797,000	9,987,000	9,703,000	9,884,000	11,783,000	8,703,700	7,128,500
Stockholders' Equity	2,980,000	3,066,000	2,955,000	2,958,000	3,579,000	3,348,000	4,035,200	4,209,700
Shares Outstanding	217,841	218,919	221,524	222,818	233,287	233,114	233,081	241,673
Statistical Record								
Return on Assets %	3.74	3.50	2.40	2.22	2.50	N.M.	5.81	12.63
Return on Equity %	15.18	13.65	9.68	8.87	10.34	N.M.	16.98	29.94
EBITDA Margin %	42.05	42.55	34.17	36.22	6.56	5.16	29.93	50.08
Net Margin %	12.37	14.90	8.99	6.55	8.67	N.M.	16.25	29.31
Asset Turnover	0.36	0.36	0.34	0.34	0.29	0.26	0.36	0.43
Current Ratio	1.34	1.43	1.71	1.81	2.53	3.87	0.93	2.67
Debt to Equity	1.41	1.37	1.59	1.59	1.31	1.73	1.39	1.09
Price Range	56.06-39.01	56.06-39.01	56.06-36.62	56.06-36.49	43.07-25.51	40.81-21.43	68.92-40.07	56.55-44.98
P/E Ratio	25.72-17.89	27.75-19.31	40.92-26.73	45.21-29.43	28.15-16.67	...	23.28-13.54	10.43-8.30
Average Yield %	2.65	2.62	2.69	2.72	3.73	4.22	2.13	1.99

Address: 4 Parkway North, Suite 400, Deerfield, IL 60015	**Web Site:** www.cfindustries.com	**Auditors:** KPMG LLP
Telephone: 847-405-2400	**Officers:** Stephen A. Furbacher - Chairman W. Anthony Will - President, Chief Executive Officer, Senior Vice President, Vice President	**Investor Contact:** 847-405-2550 **Transfer Agents:** Computershare, Providence, RI

CHARLES RIVER LABORATORIES INTERNATIONAL INC.

Exchange	Symbol	Price	52Wk Range	Yield	P/E
NYS	CRL	$152.76 (12/31/2019)	152.76-104.82	N/A	32.64

*7 Year Price Score 129.40 *NYSE Composite Index=100 *12 Month Price Score 100.09

Interim Earnings (Per Share)

Qtr.	Mar	Jun	Sep	Dec
2016	0.78	0.73	0.79	0.93
2017	0.97	1.12	1.08	(0.62)
2018	1.08	1.10	1.22	1.23
2019	1.11	0.88	1.46	...

Interim Dividends (Per Share)

No Dividends Paid

Valuation Analysis		Institutional Holding	
Forecast EPS	$6.55	No of Institutions	
	(01/15/2020)	577	
Market Cap	$7.5 Billion	Shares	
Book Value	$1.5 Billion	63,305,344	
Price/Book	4.87	% Held	
Price/Sales	2.95	97.36	

Business Summary: Biotechnology (MIC: 4.1.2 SIC: 8731 NAIC: 541710)

Charles River Laboratories International is a contract research organization engaged in laboratory animal medicine and science to develop a portfolio of discovery and safety assessment services. Co. has three reportable segments: Research Models and Services, which supplies research models to the drug development industry; Discovery and Safety Assessment, which provides discovery and safety assessment services that include both in vivo and in vitro studies, supporting laboratory services, and non-clinical consulting and program management to support product development; and Manufacturing Support, which includes its microbial solutions, avian vaccine services and biologics testing solutions.

Recent Developments: For the quarter ended Sep 28 2019, income from continuing operations increased 20.8% to US$73.6 million from US$60.9 million in the year-earlier quarter. Net income increased 20.8% to US$73.6 million from US$60.9 million in the year-earlier quarter. Revenues were US$668.0 million, up 14.1% from US$585.3 million the year before. Operating income was US$92.8 million versus US$84.4 million in the prior-year quarter, an increase of 10.0%. Direct operating expenses rose 14.3% to US$421.8 million from US$369.1 million in the comparable period the year before. Indirect operating expenses increased 16.3% to US$153.3 million from US$131.8 million in the equivalent prior-year period.

Prospects: Our evaluation of Charles River Laboratories International Inc. as of October 4th, 2019 is the result of our systematic analysis on three basic characteristics: earnings strength, relative valuation, and recent stock price movement. The company has produced a positive trend in earnings per share over the past 5 quarters. However, recent analyst estimates for the company have been mixed and CRL has posted results that exceeded analysts' expectations. Based on operating earnings yield, the company is fairly valued when compared to all of the companies we cover. Share price changes over the past year indicates that CRL will perform well over the near term.

Financial Data

(US$ in Thousands)	9 Mos	6 Mos	3 Mos	12/29/2018	12/30/2017	12/31/2016	12/26/2015	12/27/2014
Earnings Per Share	4.68	4.44	4.66	4.62	2.54	3.23	3.13	2.66
Cash Flow Per Share	9.02	8.23	8.17	9.23	6.72	6.29	6.22	5.42
Tang Book Value Per Share	N.M.	N.M.	N.M.	N.M.	N.M.	N.M.	0.29	3.64
Income Statement								
Total Revenue	1,930,088	1,262,137	604,569	2,266,096	1,857,601	1,681,432	1,363,302	1,297,662
EBITDA	299,812	197,459	95,509	506,371	457,212	376,015	304,386	284,848
Depn & Amortn	65,611	41,806	19,411	161,730	131,170	126,699	94,929	96,457
Income Before Taxes	198,519	125,284	66,290	281,681	296,955	222,921	195,428	177,595
Income Taxes	24,970	25,287	10,602	54,463	171,369	66,835	43,391	47,671
Net Income	171,671	98,861	55,133	226,373	123,355	154,765	149,313	126,698
Average Shares	49,715	49,662	49,462	49,018	48,564	47,958	47,634	47,558
Balance Sheet								
Current Assets	972,407	1,010,058	866,182	897,836	826,625	656,832	559,234	606,898
Total Assets	4,582,562	4,625,484	3,926,637	3,855,879	2,929,922	2,711,800	2,068,497	1,885,192
Current Liabilities	681,646	635,598	529,759	558,222	463,504	429,593	311,761	296,170
Long-Term Obligations	1,999,461	2,148,699	1,649,887	1,636,598	1,114,105	1,207,696	845,997	745,958
Total Liabilities	3,050,249	3,170,418	2,528,523	2,538,547	1,884,842	1,875,032	1,335,430	1,212,989
Stockholders' Equity	1,532,313	1,455,066	1,398,114	1,317,332	1,045,080	836,768	733,067	672,203
Shares Outstanding	48,837	48,799	48,747	48,209	47,402	47,363	46,698	47,327
Statistical Record								
Return on Assets %	5.52	5.16	6.61	6.69	4.38	6.37	7.57	7.20
Return on Equity %	16.61	16.60	18.04	19.22	13.15	19.40	21.31	19.35
EBITDA Margin %	15.53	15.64	15.80	22.35	24.61	22.36	22.33	21.95
Net Margin %	8.89	7.83	9.12	9.99	6.64	9.20	10.95	9.76
Asset Turnover	0.60	0.58	0.69	0.67	0.66	0.69	0.69	0.74
Current Ratio	1.43	1.59	1.64	1.61	1.78	1.53	1.79	2.05
Debt to Equity	1.30	1.48	1.18	1.24	1.07	1.44	1.15	1.11
Price Range	148.55-104.82	148.55-104.82	146.73-102.37	137.23-98.19	118.09-76.53	88.44-67.10	84.20-61.59	65.59-50.74
P/E Ratio	31.74-22.40	33.46-23.61	31.49-21.97	29.70-21.25	46.49-30.13	27.38-20.77	26.90-19.68	24.66-19.08

Address: 251 Ballardvale Street, Wilmington, MA 01887 Telephone: 781-222-6000	Web Site: www.criver.com Officers: James C. Foster - Chairman, President, President (frmr), Chief Executive Officer David Ross Smith - Corporate Executive Vice President, Chief Financial Officer, Chief Accounting Officer	Auditors: PricewaterhouseCoopers LLP Investor Contact: 781-222-6000 Transfer Agents: ComputerShare Investor Services, Providence, RI

CHEMED CORP

Exchange	Symbol	Price	52Wk Range	Yield	P/E	Div Acheiver
NYS	CHE	$439.26 (12/31/2019)	441.41-265.79	0.29	34.89	10 Years

*7 Year Price Score 162.82 *NYSE Composite Index=100 *12 Month Price Score 109.49

Interim Earnings (Per Share)

Qtr.	Mar	Jun	Sep	Dec
2016	1.45	1.48	1.62	1.94
2017	1.78	(1.35)	2.13	3.26
2018	2.66	3.27	3.06	3.25
2019	2.70	3.08	3.56	...

Interim Dividends (Per Share)

Amt	Decl	Ex	Rec	Pay
0.30Q	02/22/2019	03/01/2019	03/04/2019	03/22/2019
0.30Q	05/20/2019	05/29/2019	05/30/2019	06/19/2019
0.32Q	08/02/2019	08/09/2019	08/12/2019	09/03/2019
0.32Q	11/01/2019	11/07/2019	11/11/2019	12/02/2019

Indicated Div: $1.28

Valuation Analysis / **Institutional Holding**

Forecast EPS	$13.81	No of Institutions	
	(11/12/2019)	536	
Market Cap	$7.0 Billion	Shares	
Book Value	$672.4 Million	20,492,156	
Price/Book	10.41	% Held	
Price/Sales	3.73	89.50	

Business Summary: Diagnostic & Health Related Services (MIC: 4.2.2 SIC: 8082 NAIC: 621610)

Chemed purchases, operates and divests subsidiaries engaged in business activities. Co. conducts its business operations in two segments: the VITAS segment (VITAS) and the Roto-Rooter segment (Roto-Rooter). The VITAS segment provides hospice and palliative care services to its patients through a network of physicians, registered nurses, home health aides, social workers, clergy and volunteers. The Roto-Rooter segment provides plumbing, drain cleaning, water restoration and other related services to residential and commercial customers.

Recent Developments: For the quarter ended Sep 30 2019, net income increased 15.0% to US$58.9 million from US$51.2 million in the year-earlier quarter. Revenues were US$480.6 million, up 8.2% from US$444.2 million the year before. Operating income was US$64.9 million versus US$61.7 million in the prior-year quarter, an increase of 5.2%. Direct operating expenses rose 7.5% to US$328.2 million from US$305.3 million in the comparable period the year before. Indirect operating expenses increased 13.5% to US$87.5 million from US$77.1 million in the equivalent prior-year period.

Prospects: Our evaluation of Chemed Corp. as of October 4th, 2019 is the result of our systematic analysis on three basic characteristics: earnings strength, relative valuation, and recent stock price movement. The company has managed to produce a neutral trend in earnings per share over the past 5 quarters. However, recent analyst estimates for the company have been raised and CHE has posted results that exceeded analysts' expectations. Based on operating earnings yield, the company is fairly valued when compared to all of the companies we cover. Share price changes over the past year indicates that CHE will perform over the near term.

Financial Data

(US$ in Thousands)	9 Mos	6 Mos	3 Mos	12/31/2018	12/31/2017	12/31/2016	12/31/2015	12/31/2014
Earnings Per Share	12.59	12.09	12.28	12.23	5.86	6.48	6.33	5.57
Cash Flow Per Share	18.42	17.27	18.52	17.88	10.12	8.24	10.17	6.42
Tang Book Value Per Share	N.M.	2.55	0.60	0.79	0.54	N.M.	N.M.	N.M.
Dividends Per Share	1.220	1.200	1.180	1.160	1.080	1.000	0.920	0.840
Dividend Payout %	9.69	9.93	9.61	9.48	18.43	15.43	14.53	15.08
Income Statement								
Total Revenue	1,416,231	935,618	462,034	1,782,648	1,666,724	1,576,881	1,543,388	1,456,282
EBITDA	215,002	136,988	61,596	249,319	125,162	184,386	187,390	175,369
Depn & Amortn	29,973	19,750	9,786	5,400	4,400	4,000	3,900	4,400
Income Before Taxes	182,014	115,091	50,787	239,600	116,917	177,054	180,126	162,754
Income Taxes	27,671	19,695	6,120	34,056	18,740	68,311	69,852	63,437
Net Income	154,343	95,396	44,667	205,544	98,177	108,743	110,274	99,317
Average Shares	16,555	16,449	16,525	16,803	16,742	16,789	17,422	17,840
Balance Sheet								
Current Assets	167,795	180,178	159,155	159,840	176,046	169,900	150,808	174,564
Total Assets	1,232,585	1,094,072	1,069,831	975,529	920,026	880,059	852,325	859,932
Current Liabilities	251,501	223,669	217,100	191,670	193,522	171,832	171,336	175,554
Long-Term Obligations	130,000	85,000	100,000	89,200	91,200	100,000	83,750	141,250
Total Liabilities	560,205	475,503	481,821	384,195	379,672	355,960	339,072	408,576
Stockholders' Equity	672,380	618,569	588,010	591,334	540,354	524,099	513,253	451,356
Shares Outstanding	15,929	15,841	15,859	15,873	16,038	16,186	16,797	16,890
Statistical Record								
Return on Assets %	18.87	19.88	20.70	21.69	10.91	12.52	12.88	11.33
Return on Equity %	33.64	34.21	37.48	36.33	18.45	20.91	22.86	22.06
EBITDA Margin %	15.18	14.64	13.33	13.99	7.51	11.69	12.14	12.04
Net Margin %	10.90	10.20	9.67	11.53	5.89	6.90	7.14	6.82
Asset Turnover	1.69	1.82	1.82	1.88	1.85	1.82	1.80	1.66
Current Ratio	0.67	0.81	0.73	0.83	0.91	0.99	0.88	0.99
Debt to Equity	0.19	0.14	0.17	0.15	0.17	0.19	0.16	0.31
Price Range	439.82-265.79	360.84-265.79	333.26-265.79	333.26-246.98	247.53-162.11	161.01-126.08	158.74-101.14	110.83-73.31
P/E Ratio	34.93-21.11	29.85-21.98	27.14-21.64	27.25-20.19	42.24-27.66	24.85-19.46	25.08-15.98	19.90-13.16
Average Yield %	0.36	0.38	0.38	0.39	0.54	0.72	0.70	0.89

Address: 255 E. Fifth Street, Suite 2600, Cincinnati, OH 45202 **Telephone:** 513-762-6690	**Web Site:** **Officers:** George J. Walsh - Chairman Kevin J. McNamara - President, Chief Executive Officer	**Auditors:** PricewaterhouseCoopers LLP **Investor Contact:** 800-224-3633 **Transfer Agents:** Wells Fargo Bank, N.A., Shareowner Services, St. Paul, MN

CHEMOURS CO (THE)

Exchange	Symbol	Price	52Wk Range	Yield	P/E
NYS	CC	$18.09 (12/31/2019)	40.58-11.93	5.53	7.51

*7 Year Price Score N/A   *NYSE Composite Index=100   *12 Month Price Score 66.06

Interim Earnings (Per Share)

Qtr.	Mar	Jun	Sep	Dec
2016	0.28	(0.10)	1.11	(1.26)
2017	0.79	0.84	1.08	1.19
2018	1.58	1.53	1.51	0.83
2019	0.55	0.57	0.46	...

Interim Dividends (Per Share)

Amt	Decl	Ex	Rec	Pay
0.25Q	02/13/2019	02/26/2019	02/27/2019	03/15/2019
0.25Q	04/30/2019	05/15/2019	05/16/2019	06/14/2019
0.25Q	07/31/2019	08/15/2019	08/16/2019	09/16/2019
0.25Q	10/30/2019	11/14/2019	11/15/2019	12/16/2019

Indicated Div: $1.00

Valuation Analysis

		Institutional Holding	
Forecast EPS	$2.38	No of Institutions	598
	(01/16/2020)		
Market Cap	$3.0 Billion	Shares	
Book Value	$837.0 Million		148,552,848
Price/Book	3.53	% Held	
Price/Sales	0.52		67.29

Business Summary: Specialty Chemicals (MIC: 8.3.2 SIC: 2899 NAIC: 325998)

Chemours is a provider of performance chemicals. Co. has three reportable segments: Titanium Technologies, Fluoroproducts and Chemical Solutions. Co.'s Titanium Technologies segment is a producer of titanium dioxide, a white pigment used to deliver whiteness, brightness, opacity and protection in a variety of applications. Co.'s Fluoroproducts segment is a provider of fluoroproducts, including refrigerants and industrial fluoropolymer resins. Co.'s Chemical Solutions segment is a provider of industrial chemicals used in gold production, industrials, and consumer applications. Co.'s key products include refrigerants, sodium cyanide, intermediates, and titanium dioxide pigment.

Recent Developments: For the quarter ended Sep 30 2019, net income decreased 72.4% to US$76.0 million from US$275.0 million in the year-earlier quarter. Revenues were US$1.39 billion, down 14.6% from US$1.63 billion the year before. Direct operating expenses declined 4.8% to US$1.10 billion from US$1.15 billion in the comparable period the year before. Indirect operating expenses decreased 5.6% to US$184.0 million from US$195.0 million in the equivalent prior-year period.

Prospects: Our evaluation of The Chemours Company as of October 4th, 2019 is the result of our systematic analysis on three basic characteristics: earnings strength, relative valuation, and recent stock price movement. The company has generated a negative trend in earnings per share over the past 5 quarters. In addition, recent analyst estimates for the company have been reduced and CC has posted results that fell short of analysts' expectations. Based on operating earnings yield, the company is undervalued when compared to all of the companies we cover. Share price changes over the past year indicates that CC will perform poorly over the near term.

Financial Data

(US$ in Millions)	9 Mos	6 Mos	3 Mos	12/31/2018	12/31/2017	12/31/2016	12/31/2015	12/31/2014
Earnings Per Share	2.41	3.46	4.42	5.45	3.91	0.04	(0.50)	...
Cash Flow Per Share	3.11	3.43	5.36	6.44	3.46	3.26	1.01	...
Tang Book Value Per Share	4.04	3.95	3.82	4.88	3.79	N.M.	N.M.	...
Dividends Per Share	1.000	1.000	0.920	0.840	0.120	0.120	0.580	...
Dividend Payout %	41.49	28.90	20.81	15.41	3.07	300.00	...	...
Income Statement								
Total Revenue	4,173	2,784	1,376	6,638	6,183	5,400	5,717	6,432
EBITDA	694	482	227	1,583	1,363	454	186	784
Depn & Amortn	233	156	77	276	269	281	264	254
Income Before Taxes	305	223	99	1,112	879	(40)	(210)	530
Income Taxes	65	50	13	159	165	(18)	(98)	149
Net Income	265	189	94	995	746	7	(90)	400
Average Shares	165	166	172	182	190	183	180	...
Balance Sheet								
Current Assets	2,827	2,832	2,847	3,293	3,493	2,553	2,301	1,962
Total Assets	7,456	7,433	7,325	7,362	7,293	6,060	6,298	5,978
Current Liabilities	1,643	1,448	1,572	1,709	1,648	1,771	1,466	1,407
Long-Term Obligations	4,007	4,190	3,965	3,959	4,097	3,529	3,915	...
Total Liabilities	6,619	6,610	6,515	6,348	6,433	5,960	6,172	2,309
Stockholders' Equity	837	823	810	1,014	860	100	126	3,669
Shares Outstanding	163	163	164	170	182	182	181	...
Statistical Record								
Return on Assets %	5.45	8.22	10.70	13.58	11.17	0.11	...	6.90
Return on Equity %	41.27	65.91	87.66	106.19	155.42	6.18	...	11.62
EBITDA Margin %	16.63	17.31	16.50	23.85	22.04	8.41	3.25	12.19
Net Margin %	6.35	6.79	6.83	14.99	12.07	0.13	N.M.	6.22
Asset Turnover	0.75	0.80	0.85	0.91	0.93	0.87	...	1.11
Current Ratio	1.72	1.96	1.81	1.93	2.12	1.44	1.57	1.39
Debt to Equity	4.79	5.09	4.90	3.90	4.76	35.29	31.07	...
Price Range	41.64-11.93	47.90-21.09	52.62-25.34	54.49-25.34	57.23-21.22	26.96-3.12	20.85-4.72	...
P/E Ratio	17.28-4.95	13.84-6.10	11.90-5.73	10.00-4.65	14.64-5.43	674.00-78.00	...	...
Average Yield %	3.53	2.83	2.27	1.92	0.28	1.04	6.49	...

Address: 1007 Market Street, Wilmington, DE 19801 **Telephone:** 302-773-1000	**Web Site:** www.chemours.com **Officers:** Richard H. Brown - Chairman Mark P. Vergnano - President, Chief Executive Officer, Holding/Parent Company Officer	**Auditors:** PricewaterhouseCoopers LLP **Transfer Agents:** Computershare Trust Company, N.A.

CHESAPEAKE ENERGY CORP.

Exchange	Symbol	Price	52Wk Range	Yield	P/E
NYS	CHK	$0.83 (12/31/2019)	3.44-0.56	N/A	1.68

*7 Year Price Score 15.60   *NYSE Composite Index=100   *12 Month Price Score 43.64

Interim Earnings (Per Share)

Qtr.	Mar	Jun	Sep	Dec
2016	(1.44)	(2.48)	(1.54)	(0.98)
2017	0.08	0.47	(0.05)	0.34
2018	0.29	(0.04)	0.07	0.53
2019	(0.03)	0.05	(0.06)	...

Interim Dividends (Per Share)

Dividend Payment Suspended

Valuation Analysis

		Institutional Holding	
Forecast EPS	$-0.29	No of Institutions	
	(01/15/2020)	772	
Market Cap	$1.6 Billion	Shares	
Book Value	$4.7 Billion	1,471,592,576	
Price/Book	0.34	% Held	
Price/Sales	0.17	84.06	

Business Summary: Production & Extraction (MIC: 9.1.1 SIC: 1311 NAIC: 211111)

Chesapeake Energy is a holding company. Through its subsidiaries, Co. is an independent exploration and production company engaged in the acquisition, exploration and development of properties to produce oil, natural gas and natural gas liquid from underground reservoirs. Co. owns a portfolio of onshore U.S. liquids and natural gas assets. Co. has positions in the resource plays of the Eagle Ford Shale in South Texas, the stacked pay in the Powder River Basin in Wyoming and the Anadarko Basin in northwestern Oklahoma. Co.'s natural gas resource plays are the Marcellus Shale in the northern Appalachian Basin in Pennsylvania and the Haynesville/Bossier Shales in northwestern Louisiana.

Recent Developments: For the quarter ended Sep 30 2019, net loss amounted to US$61.0 million versus a net loss of US$146.0 million in the year-earlier quarter. Revenues were US$2.09 billion, down 13.9% from US$2.42 billion the year before. Operating income was US$46.0 million versus US$82.0 million in the prior-year quarter, a decrease of 43.9%. Direct operating expenses declined 13.2% to US$460.0 million from US$530.0 million in the comparable period the year before. Indirect operating expenses decreased 12.7% to US$1.58 billion from US$1.81 billion in the equivalent prior-year period.

Prospects: Our evaluation of Chesapeake Energy Corp. as of October 4th, 2019 is the result of our systematic analysis on three basic characteristics: earnings strength, relative valuation, and recent stock price movement. The company has suffered a very negative trend in earnings per share over the past 5 quarters. However, recent analyst estimates for the company have been mixed and CHK has posted results that fell short of analysts' expectations. Based on operating earnings yield, the company is overvalued when compared to all of the companies we cover. Share price changes over the past year indicates that CHK will perform poorly over the near term.

Financial Data

(US$ in Thousands)	9 Mos	6 Mos	3 Mos	12/31/2018	12/31/2017	12/31/2016	12/31/2015	12/31/2014
Earnings Per Share	0.49	0.62	0.53	0.85	0.90	(6.45)	(22.43)	1.87
Cash Flow Per Share	0.93	1.08	1.30	2.20	0.82	(0.27)	1.86	7.03
Tang Book Value Per Share	1.57	1.55	1.49	...	...	...	...	20.87
Dividends Per Share	...	...	...	...	...	...	0.175	0.350
Dividend Payout %	...	...	...	...	...	...	...	18.72
Income Statement								
Total Revenue	6,669,000	4,582,000	2,196,000	10,231,000	9,496,000	7,872,000	12,764,000	20,951,000
EBITDA	1,886,000	1,198,000	345,000	2,499,000	2,376,000	(3,186,000)	(16,552,000)	6,204,000
Depn & Amortn	1,672,000	1,099,000	519,000	1,145,000	995,000	1,107,000	2,229,000	2,915,000
Income Before Taxes	(299,000)	(237,000)	(335,000)	867,000	955,000	(4,589,000)	(19,098,000)	3,200,000
Income Taxes	(315,000)	(314,000)	(314,000)	(10,000)	2,000	(190,000)	(4,463,000)	1,144,000
Net Income	16,000	77,000	(21,000)	873,000	949,000	(4,401,000)	(14,685,000)	1,917,000
Average Shares	1,698,000	1,628,000	1,380,000	909,000	906,000	764,000	662,000	772,000
Balance Sheet								
Current Assets	1,403,000	1,384,000	1,365,000	1,598,000	1,525,000	2,142,000	2,480,000	7,468,000
Total Assets	16,579,000	16,540,000	16,637,000	10,947,000	12,425,000	13,028,000	17,357,000	40,751,000
Current Liabilities	2,348,000	2,220,000	2,930,000	2,828,000	2,356,000	3,648,000	3,685,000	5,863,000
Long-Term Obligations	9,133,000	9,701,000	9,167,000	7,341,000	9,921,000	9,938,000	10,383,000	11,184,000
Total Liabilities	11,883,000	12,349,000	12,540,000	10,603,000	12,921,000	14,488,000	15,219,000	23,848,000
Stockholders' Equity	4,696,000	4,191,000	4,097,000	344,000	(496,000)	(1,460,000)	2,138,000	16,903,000
Shares Outstanding	1,948,527	1,628,878	1,633,624	910,468	906,492	895,058	663,357	663,329
Statistical Record								
Return on Assets %	3.62	4.67	3.89	7.47	7.46	N.M.	N.M.	4.65
Return on Equity %	23.33	34.12	28.84	...	...	N.M.	N.M.	11.65
EBITDA Margin %	28.28	26.15	15.71	24.43	25.02	N.M.	N.M.	29.61
Net Margin %	0.24	1.68	N.M.	8.53	9.99	N.M.	N.M.	9.15
Asset Turnover	0.67	0.70	0.69	0.88	0.75	0.52	0.44	0.51
Current Ratio	0.60	0.62	0.47	0.57	0.65	0.59	0.67	1.27
Debt to Equity	1.94	2.31	2.24	21.34	...	...	4.86	0.66
Price Range	4.87-1.29	5.40-1.73	5.40-1.73	5.40-1.73	7.18-3.51	8.05-1.59	21.26-3.72	29.50-16.71
P/E Ratio	9.94-2.63	8.71-2.79	10.19-3.26	6.35-2.04	7.98-3.90	...	...	15.78-8.94
Average Yield %	...	...	...	...	...	...	1.51	1.42

Address: 6100 North Western Avenue, Oklahoma City, OK 73118 Telephone: 405-848-8000	Web Site: www.chk.com Officers: R. Brad Martin - Chairman Archie W. Dunham - Chairman Emeritus	Auditors: PricewaterhouseCoopers LLC Investor Contact: 405-935-4763 Transfer Agents: Computershare Trust Company, N.A., Canton, MA

CHESAPEAKE UTILITIES CORP.

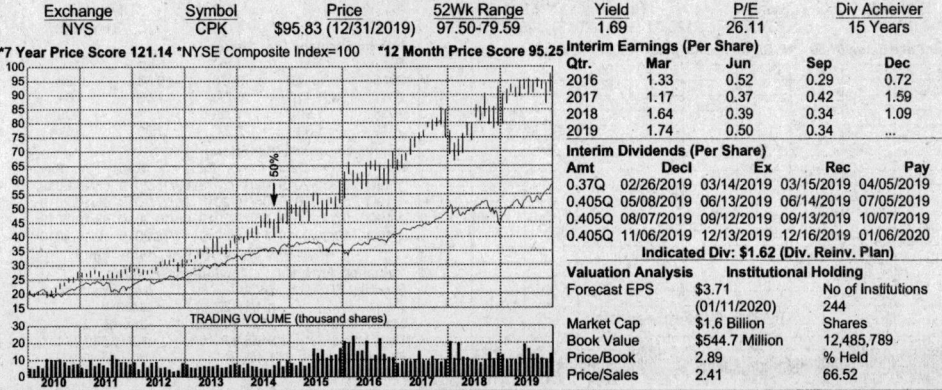

Exchange	Symbol	Price	52Wk Range	Yield	P/E	Div Acheiver
NYS	CPK	$95.83 (12/31/2019)	97.50-79.59	1.69	26.11	15 Years

*7 Year Price Score 121.14 *NYSE Composite Index=100 *12 Month Price Score 95.25

Interim Earnings (Per Share)

Qtr.	Mar	Jun	Sep	Dec
2016	1.33	0.52	0.29	0.72
2017	1.17	0.37	0.42	1.59
2018	1.64	0.39	0.34	1.09
2019	1.74	0.50	0.34	...

Interim Dividends (Per Share)

Amt	Decl	Ex	Rec	Pay
0.37Q	02/26/2019	03/14/2019	03/15/2019	04/05/2019
0.405Q	05/08/2019	06/13/2019	06/14/2019	07/05/2019
0.405Q	08/07/2019	09/12/2019	09/13/2019	10/07/2019
0.405Q	11/06/2019	12/13/2019	12/16/2019	01/06/2020

Indicated Div: $1.62 (Div. Reinv. Plan)

Valuation Analysis / **Institutional Holding**

Forecast EPS	$3.71 (01/11/2020)
No of Institutions	244
Market Cap	$1.6 Billion
Shares	
Book Value	$544.7 Million
	12,485,789
Price/Book	2.89
% Held	
Price/Sales	2.41
	66.52

Business Summary: Gas Utilities (MIC: 3.3.1 SIC: 4923 NAIC: 221210)

Chesapeake Utilities is an energy company engaged in regulated and unregulated energy businesses. Co. operates within two segments: Regulated Energy and Unregulated Energy. Co.'s regulated energy businesses consist of: regulated natural gas distribution operations; regulated natural gas transmission operations; and regulated electric distribution operations. Co.'s unregulated energy segment includes a propane operations; its natural gas marketing operation providing natural gas supply; its unregulated natural gas transmission/supply operation; its Combined Heat and Power Plant that generates electricity and steam; and its subsidiary that provides mobile compressed natural gas utility.

Recent Developments: For the quarter ended Sep 30 2019, income from continuing operations increased 2.5% to US$6.2 million from US$6.1 million in the year-earlier quarter. Net income increased 1.5% to US$5.6 million from US$5.5 million in the year-earlier quarter. Revenues were US$92.6 million, down 0.8% from US$93.4 million the year before. Operating income was US$14.4 million versus US$12.9 million in the prior-year quarter, an increase of 11.5%. Direct operating expenses declined 5.8% to US$61.9 million from US$65.7 million in the comparable period the year before. Indirect operating expenses increased 10.4% to US$16.4 million from US$14.9 million in the equivalent prior-year period.

Prospects: Our evaluation of Chesapeake Utilities Corp. as of October 4th, 2019 is the result of our systematic analysis on three basic characteristics: earnings strength, relative valuation, and recent stock price movement. The company has managed to produce a neutral trend in earnings per share over the past 5 quarters. Additionally, recent analyst estimates for the company have been unchanged while CPK has posted results that fell short of analysts' expectations. Based on operating earnings yield, the company is fairly valued when compared to all of the companies we cover. Share price changes over the past year indicates that CPK will perform well over the near term.

Financial Data

(US$ in Thousands)	9 Mos	6 Mos	3 Mos	12/31/2018	12/31/2017	12/31/2016	12/31/2015	12/31/2014
Earnings Per Share	3.67	3.67	3.56	3.45	3.55	2.86	2.72	2.47
Cash Flow Per Share	7.48	6.89	7.36	8.97	6.74	6.62	6.97	5.45
Tang Book Value Per Share	31.70	31.27	31.22	29.70	28.11	26.32	22.35	20.08
Dividends Per Share	1.550	1.515	1.480	1.435	1.280	1.202	1.133	1.067
Dividend Payout %	42.23	41.28	41.57	41.59	36.06	42.05	41.64	43.18
Income Statement								
Total Revenue	347,630	358,519	227,616	717,489	617,583	498,860	459,244	498,834
EBITDA	82,295	65,390	46,083	102,540	93,200	90,989	85,029	76,096
Depn & Amortn	6,380	4,322	2,135	8,535	8,122	7,334	6,978	6,577
Income Before Taxes	59,332	49,703	38,238	77,574	72,433	73,016	68,045	60,037
Income Taxes	15,355	12,735	9,574	20,994	14,309	28,341	26,905	23,945
Net Income	42,589	36,968	28,664	56,580	58,124	44,675	41,140	36,092
Average Shares	16,453	16,445	16,432	16,419	16,383	15,613	15,143	14,604
Balance Sheet								
Current Assets	114,875	124,242	153,640	191,537	178,587	141,151	112,538	122,373
Total Assets	1,714,240	1,681,042	1,682,797	1,693,671	1,417,434	1,229,219	1,068,586	904,469
Current Liabilities	446,247	512,415	508,569	528,234	413,000	334,051	279,593	194,235
Long-Term Obligations	375,810	275,924	285,998	316,020	197,395	136,954	149,340	158,486
Total Liabilities	1,169,529	1,136,658	1,139,138	1,175,232	931,140	783,133	710,448	604,147
Stockholders' Equity	544,711	544,384	543,659	518,439	486,294	446,086	358,138	300,322
Shares Outstanding	16,403	16,403	16,397	16,378	16,344	16,303	15,270	14,588
Statistical Record								
Return on Assets %	3.75	3.84	3.75	3.64	4.39	3.88	4.17	4.14
Return on Equity %	11.47	11.46	11.13	11.26	12.47	11.08	12.50	12.46
EBITDA Margin %	23.67	18.24	20.25	14.29	15.09	18.24	18.51	15.25
Net Margin %	12.25	10.31	12.59	7.89	9.41	8.96	8.96	7.24
Asset Turnover	0.41	0.45	0.45	0.46	0.47	0.43	0.47	0.57
Current Ratio	0.26	0.24	0.30	0.36	0.43	0.42	0.40	0.63
Debt to Equity	0.69	0.51	0.53	0.61	0.41	0.31	0.42	0.53
Price Range	95.84-78.14	95.49-78.14	93.80-69.40	93.12-66.65	85.55-63.40	70.00-53.54	60.31-45.54	52.60-37.78
P/E Ratio	26.11-21.29	26.02-21.29	26.35-19.49	26.99-19.32	24.10-17.86	24.48-18.72	22.17-16.74	21.30-15.30
Average Yield %	1.73	1.73	1.77	1.81	1.71	1.93	2.21	2.44

Address: 909 Silver Lake Boulevard, Dover, DE 19904
Telephone: 302-734-6799

Web Site: www.chpk.com
Officers: John R. Schimkaitis - Chairman, Vice-Chairman, President, Chief Executive Officer Jeffry M. Householder - President, Chief Executive Officer

Auditors: Baker Tilly Virchow Krause, LLP
Investor Contact: 888-742-5275
Transfer Agents: Computershare Trust Company, N.A., Providence, RI

CHEVRON CORPORATION

Exchange	Symbol	Price	52Wk Range	Yield	P/E	Div Acheiver
NYS	CVX	$120.51 (12/31/2019)	126.68-108.57	3.95	17.29	31 Years

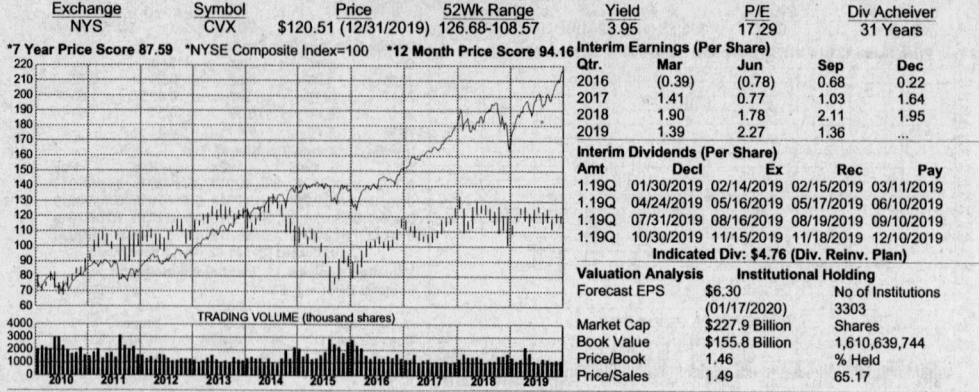

*7 Year Price Score 87.59   *NSYE Composite Index=100   *12 Month Price Score 94.16

Interim Earnings (Per Share)

Qtr.	Mar	Jun	Sep	Dec
2016	(0.39)	(0.78)	0.68	0.22
2017	1.41	0.77	1.03	1.64
2018	1.90	1.78	2.11	1.95
2019	1.39	2.27	1.36	...

Interim Dividends (Per Share)

Amt	Decl	Ex	Rec	Pay
1.19Q	01/30/2019	02/14/2019	02/15/2019	03/11/2019
1.19Q	04/24/2019	05/16/2019	05/17/2019	06/10/2019
1.19Q	07/31/2019	08/16/2019	08/19/2019	09/10/2019
1.19Q	10/30/2019	11/15/2019	11/18/2019	12/10/2019

Indicated Div: $4.76 (Div. Reinv. Plan)

Valuation Analysis   **Institutional Holding**

Forecast EPS	$6.30	No of Institutions
	(01/17/2020)	3303
Market Cap	$227.9 Billion	Shares
Book Value	$155.8 Billion	1,610,639,744
Price/Book	1.46	% Held
Price/Sales	1.49	65.17

Business Summary: Refining & Marketing (MIC: 9.1.2 SIC: 2911 NAIC: 324110)

Chevron is engaged in energy and chemicals operations. Upstream operations consist primarily of, among others, exploring for, developing and producing crude oil and natural gas; processing, liquefaction, transportation and regasification associated with liquefied natural gas transporting, storage and marketing of natural gas; and a gas-to-liquids plant. Downstream operations consist primarily of, among others, refining crude oil into petroleum products; marketing of crude oil and refined products; and manufacturing and marketing of commodity petrochemicals, plastics for industrial uses and fuel and lubricant additives.

Recent Developments: For the quarter ended Sep 30 2019, net income decreased 36.4% to US$2.58 billion from US$4.06 billion in the year-earlier quarter. Revenues were US$36.12 billion, down 17.9% from US$43.99 billion the year before. Direct operating expenses declined 19.4% to US$19.88 billion from US$24.68 billion in the comparable period the year before. Indirect operating expenses decreased 10.5% to US$12.19 billion from US$13.61 billion in the equivalent prior-year period.

Prospects: Our evaluation of Chevron Corporation as of October 4th, 2019 is the result of our systematic analysis on three basic characteristics: earnings strength, relative valuation, and recent stock price movement. The company has generated a negative trend in earnings per share over the past 5 quarters. In addition, recent analyst estimates for the company have been reduced and CVX has posted results that fell short of analysts' expectations. Based on operating earnings yield, the company is undervalued when compared to all of the companies we cover. Share price changes over the past year indicates that CVX will perform well over the near term.

Financial Data

(US$ in Millions)	9 Mos	6 Mos	3 Mos	12/31/2018	12/31/2017	12/31/2016	12/31/2015	12/31/2014
Earnings Per Share	6.97	7.72	7.23	7.74	4.85	(0.27)	2.45	10.14
Cash Flow Per Share	16.38	17.23	16.22	16.14	10.90	6.84	10.42	16.72
Tang Book Value Per Share	80.03	80.01	79.03	78.85	75.39	74.53	78.67	80.03
Dividends Per Share	4.690	4.620	4.550	4.480	4.320	4.290	4.280	4.210
Dividend Payout %	67.29	59.84	62.93	57.88	89.07	...	174.69	41.52
Income Statement								
Total Revenue	110,166	74,050	35,200	166,339	141,722	114,472	138,477	211,970
EBITDA	27,350	18,743	8,276	40,742	28,877	17,498	25,879	47,995
Depn & Amortn	12,789	8,428	4,094	19,419	19,349	19,457	21,037	16,793
Income Before Taxes	13,941	9,892	3,957	20,575	9,221	(2,160)	4,842	31,202
Income Taxes	4,429	2,960	1,315	5,715	(48)	(1,729)	132	11,892
Net Income	9,534	6,954	2,649	14,824	9,195	(497)	4,587	19,241
Average Shares	1,893	1,902	1,900	1,914	1,898	1,873	1,875	1,898
Balance Sheet								
Current Assets	33,988	33,087	33,671	34,021	28,560	29,619	35,347	42,232
Total Assets	256,537	255,878	256,809	253,863	253,806	260,078	266,103	266,026
Current Liabilities	30,233	28,829	29,951	27,171	27,737	31,785	26,464	31,926
Long-Term Obligations	25,056	25,061	26,064	28,733	33,571	35,286	33,664	24,028
Total Liabilities	100,696	99,483	101,764	99,309	105,682	114,522	113,387	110,998
Stockholders' Equity	155,841	156,395	155,045	154,554	148,124	145,556	152,716	155,028
Shares Outstanding	1,890	1,898	1,904	1,902	1,904	1,891	1,882	1,879
Statistical Record								
Return on Assets %	5.17	5.73	5.39	5.84	3.58	N.M.	1.72	7.40
Return on Equity %	8.57	9.55	9.06	9.80	6.26	N.M.	2.98	12.65
EBITDA Margin %	24.83	25.31	23.51	24.49	20.38	15.29	18.69	22.64
Net Margin %	8.65	9.39	7.53	8.91	6.49	N.M.	3.31	9.08
Asset Turnover	0.59	0.62	0.64	0.66	0.55	0.43	0.52	0.82
Current Ratio	1.12	1.15	1.12	1.25	1.03	0.93	1.34	1.32
Debt to Equity	0.16	0.16	0.17	0.19	0.23	0.24	0.22	0.15
Price Range	126.82-100.99	127.83-100.99	130.39-100.99	133.60-100.99	125.98-103.04	118.77-78.98	112.78-70.02	134.85-100.86
P/E Ratio	18.20-14.49	16.56-13.08	18.03-13.97	17.26-13.05	25.98-21.25	...	46.03-28.58	13.30-9.95
Average Yield %	3.94	3.88	3.79	3.73	3.88	4.30	4.44	3.49

Address: 6001 Bollinger Canyon Road, San Ramon, CA 94583-2324 **Telephone:** 925-842-1000 **Fax:** 925-894-6017	**Web Site:** www.chevron.com **Officers:** Michael K. Wirth - Chairman, Vice-Chairman, Chief Executive Officer, Executive Vice President Christine L. Cavallo - Assistant Secretary, Managing Counsel	**Auditors:** PricewaterhouseCoopers LLP **Investor Contact:** 925-842-5690 **Transfer Agents:** Computershare, Providence, RI

CHIMERA INVESTMENT CORP

Exchange	Symbol	Price	52Wk Range	Yield	P/E
NYS	CIM	$20.56 (12/31/2019)	21.37-17.82	9.73	34.85

*7 Year Price Score 95.43 *NYSE Composite Index=100 *12 Month Price Score 100.46

TRADING VOLUME (thousand shares)

Interim Earnings (Per Share)

Qtr.	Mar	Jun	Sep	Dec
2016	0.44	0.39	0.92	1.16
2017	0.84	0.56	0.69	0.52
2018	1.22	0.58	0.79	(0.63)
2019	0.54	0.21	0.47	...

Interim Dividends (Per Share)

Amt	Decl	Ex	Rec	Pay
0.50Q	02/12/2019	03/28/2019	03/29/2019	04/30/2019
0.50Q	04/30/2019	06/27/2019	06/28/2019	07/30/2019
0.50Q	07/30/2019	09/26/2019	09/27/2019	10/31/2019
0.50Q	10/29/2019	12/30/2019	12/31/2019	01/31/2020

Indicated Div: $2.00 (Div. Reinv. Plan)

Valuation Analysis   **Institutional Holding**

Forecast EPS	$2.11	No of Institutions
	(01/17/2020)	420
Market Cap	$3.8 Billion	Shares
Book Value	$4.0 Billion	137,751,536
Price/Book	0.96	% Held
Price/Sales	3.55	N/A

Business Summary: REITs (MIC: 5.3.1 SIC: 6798 NAIC: 525930)

Chimera Investment is a real estate investment trust engaged in investing in mortgage assets. Co.'s investment portfolio includes: Residential Mortgage Loans, which invests in residential mortgage loans through direct and secondary market purchases from banks, non-bank financial institutions, and federally chartered corporations; Residential Mortgage-Backed Securities, which invests in mortgage pass-through certificates issued or guaranteed by the Government National Mortgage Association, Federal National Mortgage Association or Federal Home Loan Mortgage Corporation; Agency mortgage-backed securities; and Other Real-Estate Related Assets.

Recent Developments: For the quarter ended Sep 30 2019, net income decreased 32.4% to US$106.3 million from US$157.3 million in the year-earlier quarter. Revenues were US$325.9 million, down 8.8% from US$357.4 million the year before.

Prospects: Our evaluation of Chimera Investment Corp. as of October 4th, 2019 is the result of our systematic analysis on three basic characteristics: earnings strength, relative valuation, and recent stock price movement. The company has managed to produce a neutral trend in earnings per share over the past 5 quarters. However, recent analyst estimates for the company have been reduced and CIM has posted results that fell short of analysts' expectations. Based on operating earnings yield, the company is undervalued when compared to all of the companies we cover. Share price changes over the past year indicates that CIM will perform in line with the market over the near term.

Financial Data
(US$ in Thousands)

	9 Mos	6 Mos	3 Mos	12/31/2018	12/31/2017	12/31/2016	12/31/2015	12/31/2014
Earnings Per Share	0.59	0.91	1.28	1.96	2.61	2.92	1.25	2.85
Cash Flow Per Share	(1.80)	(0.83)	0.20	1.59	2.60	2.94	1.99	0.89
Tang Book Value Per Share	21.34	21.20	21.12	19.80	19.35	16.64	15.70	17.55
Dividends Per Share	2.000	2.000	2.000	2.000	2.000	2.440	1.440	1.800
Dividend Payout %	338.98	219.78	156.25	102.04	76.63	83.56	115.20	63.16
Income Statement								
Total Revenue	961,658	635,763	350,313	1,198,997	1,168,349	992,902	603,111	768,360
EBITDA	313,929	192,851	118,382	428,713	513,018	557,001	271,308	528,190
Depn & Amortn	30,540	15,789	235	16,985	(11,758)	4,975	20,958	(61,017)
Income Before Taxes	283,389	177,062	118,147	411,728	524,776	552,026	250,350	589,207
Income Taxes	156	155	...	91	108	83	1,000.00	2
Net Income	283,233	176,907	118,147	411,637	524,668	551,943	250,349	589,205
Average Shares	188,440	188,271	188,199	187,748	188,287	188,024	199,650	205,508
Balance Sheet								
Current Assets	286,495	250,486	1,660,074	170,928	164,358	257,411	180,309	235,719
Total Assets	28,632,289	27,637,730	29,337,903	27,708,639	21,222,070	16,684,908	15,344,646	19,155,005
Current Liabilities	16,697,296	15,642,563	17,106,787	15,373,010	7,975,145	6,267,110	8,127,509	10,425,034
Long-Term Obligations	7,939,949	8,026,217	8,277,939	8,615,331	9,594,437	7,275,221	4,249,911	5,095,278
Total Liabilities	24,637,245	23,668,780	25,384,726	24,004,810	17,587,093	13,561,375	12,398,458	15,547,315
Stockholders' Equity	3,995,044	3,968,950	3,953,177	3,703,829	3,634,977	3,123,533	2,946,188	3,607,690
Shares Outstanding	187,158	187,157	187,144	187,052	187,809	187,739	187,711	205,546
Statistical Record								
Return on Assets %	0.67	0.91	1.15	1.68	2.77	3.44	1.45	4.52
Return on Equity %	4.56	6.08	7.63	11.22	15.53	18.14	7.64	16.98
EBITDA Margin %	32.64	30.33	33.79	35.76	43.91	56.10	44.98	68.74
Net Margin %	29.45	27.83	33.73	34.33	44.91	55.59	41.51	76.68
Asset Turnover	0.04	0.04	0.04	0.05	0.06	0.06	0.03	0.06
Current Ratio	0.02	0.02	0.10	0.01	0.02	0.04	0.02	0.02
Debt to Equity	1.99	2.02	2.09	2.33	2.64	2.33	1.44	1.41
Price Range	20.37-17.00	19.39-17.00	19.39-17.00	19.21-16.24	20.83-17.09	17.64-11.39	16.45-12.86	16.95-14.95
P/E Ratio	34.53-28.81	21.31-18.68	15.15-13.28	9.80-8.29	7.98-6.55	6.04-3.90	13.16-10.29	5.95-5.25
Average Yield %	10.63	10.72	10.86	11.04	10.60	16.17	9.79	11.36

Address: 520 Madison Avenue, 32nd Floor, New York, NY 10022	**Web Site:** www.chimerareit.com	**Auditors:** Ernst & Young LLP
Telephone: 212-626-2300	**Officers:** Matthew Lambiase - President, Chief Executive Officer Choudhary Yarlagadda - Chief Operating Officer	**Investor Contact:** 866-315-9930
		Transfer Agents: Computershare Shareowner Services LLC, Jersey City, NJ

CHIPOTLE MEXICAN GRILL INC

Exchange	Symbol	Price	52Wk Range	Yield	P/E
NYS	CMG	$837.11 (12/31/2019)	851.54-431.79	N/A	76.38

*7 Year Price Score 115.32   *NYSE Composite Index=100   *12 Month Price Score 105.53

Interim Earnings (Per Share)

Qtr.	Mar	Jun	Sep	Dec
2016	(0.88)	0.87	0.27	0.54
2017	1.60	2.32	0.69	1.55
2018	2.13	1.68	1.36	1.14
2019	3.13	3.22	3.47	...

Interim Dividends (Per Share)

No Dividends Paid

Valuation Analysis   Institutional Holding

Forecast EPS	$13.88	No of Institutions
	(01/17/2020)	880
Market Cap	$23.3 Billion	Shares
Book Value	$1.6 Billion	31,063,212
Price/Book	14.34	% Held
Price/Sales	4.33	91.64

Business Summary: Hotels, Restaurants & Travel (MIC: 2.2.1 SIC: 5812 NAIC: 722110)

Chipotle Mexican Grill together with its subsidiaries operates Chipotle Mexican Grill restaurants, which feature a relevant menu of burritos, burrito bowls (a burrito without the tortilla), tacos, and salads. Co. operates Chipotle restaurants throughout the U.S., international Chipotle restaurants, and non-Chipotle restaurants. Co. uses various herbs, spices and seasonings to prepare its meats and vegetables. Co. also serves tortilla chips that are seasoned with lime juice and salt, with sides of guacamole, salsas, or queso. In addition to sodas, fruit and tea drinks, and organic milk, most of Co.'s restaurants also provide a selection of beer and margaritas.

Recent Developments: For the quarter ended Sep 30 2019, net income increased 158.0% to US$98.6 million from US$38.2 million in the year-earlier quarter. Revenues were US$1.40 billion, up 14.6% from US$1.23 billion the year before. Operating income was US$115.6 million versus US$58.0 million in the prior-year quarter, an increase of 99.4%. Direct operating expenses rose 11.6% to US$1.11 billion from US$996.3 million in the comparable period the year before. Indirect operating expenses increased 3.2% to US$176.3 million from US$170.8 million in the equivalent prior-year period.

Prospects: Our evaluation of Chipotle Mexican Grill Inc. as of October 4th, 2019 is the result of our systematic analysis on three basic characteristics: earnings strength, relative valuation, and recent stock price movement. The company has enjoyed a very positive trend in earnings per share over the past 5 quarters. In addition, recent analyst estimates for the company have been raised, and CMG has posted results that exceeded analysts' expectations. Based on operating earnings yield, the company is overvalued when compared to all of the companies we cover. Share price changes over the past year indicates that CMG will perform very well over the near term.

Financial Data
(US$ in Thousands)

	9 Mos	6 Mos	3 Mos	12/31/2018	12/31/2017	12/31/2016	12/31/2015	12/31/2014
Earnings Per Share	10.96	8.85	7.31	6.31	6.17	0.77	15.10	14.13
Cash Flow Per Share	23.91	22.61	21.77	22.34	16.39	11.90	21.98	21.98
Tang Book Value Per Share	57.57	54.69	52.73	51.25	47.90	47.91	68.86	64.15
Income Statement								
Total Revenue	4,146,145	2,742,448	1,308,217	4,864,985	4,476,412	3,904,384	4,501,223	4,108,269
EBITDA	463,424	307,619	148,266	470,415	439,091	185,107	900,235	824,777
Depn & Amortn	117,622	77,438	38,105	201,979	163,348	146,368	130,368	110,474
Income Before Taxes	357,289	237,257	113,290	268,436	275,743	38,739	769,867	714,303
Income Taxes	79,547	58,097	25,158	91,883	99,490	15,801	294,265	268,929
Net Income	277,742	179,160	88,132	176,553	176,253	22,938	475,602	445,374
Average Shares	28,388	28,300	28,118	27,962	28,561	29,770	31,494	31,512
Balance Sheet								
Current Assets	954,756	832,402	837,746	814,794	629,535	522,374	814,647	878,479
Total Assets	4,937,937	4,659,307	4,625,482	2,265,518	2,045,692	2,026,103	2,725,066	2,546,285
Current Liabilities	634,019	548,268	581,667	449,990	323,893	281,793	279,942	245,710
Total Liabilities	3,315,490	3,121,258	3,141,683	824,179	681,247	623,610	597,092	533,916
Stockholders' Equity	1,622,447	1,538,049	1,483,799	1,441,339	1,364,445	1,402,493	2,127,974	2,012,369
Shares Outstanding	27,801	27,724	27,722	27,697	28,026	28,814	30,584	31,027
Statistical Record								
Return on Assets %	8.64	7.35	6.11	8.19	8.66	0.96	18.04	19.55
Return on Equity %	20.26	17.02	14.41	12.58	12.74	1.30	22.97	25.09
EBITDA Margin %	11.18	11.22	11.33	9.67	9.81	4.74	20.00	20.08
Net Margin %	6.70	6.53	6.74	3.63	3.94	0.59	10.57	10.84
Asset Turnover	1.50	1.53	1.49	2.26	2.20	1.64	1.71	1.80
Current Ratio	1.51	1.52	1.44	1.81	1.94	1.85	2.91	3.58
Price Range	843.64-385.84	740.59-385.84	710.31-311.16	525.89-251.33	496.14-268.70	533.69-359.92	757.77-479.85	692.69-476.28
P/E Ratio	76.97-35.20	83.68-43.60	97.17-42.57	83.34-39.83	80.41-43.55	693.10-467.43	50.18-31.78	49.02-33.71

Address: 610 Newport Center Drive, Suite 1300, Newport Beach, CA 92660 **Telephone:** 303-595-4000	**Web Site:** www.chipotle.com **Officers:** M. Steven (Steve) Ells - Chairman, Chief Executive Officer, Co-Chief Executive Officer, Executive Chairman Brian R. Niccol - Chief Executive Officer	**Auditors:** Ernst & Young LLP **Investor Contact:** 303-595-4000 **Transfer Agents:** Wells Fargo Shareowner Services, Mendota Heights, MN

CHOICE HOTELS INTERNATIONAL, INC.

Exchange	Symbol	Price	52Wk Range	Yield	P/E
NYS	CHH	$103.43 (12/31/2019)	104.85-70.10	0.87	27.29

*7 Year Price Score 116.90 *NYSE Composite Index=100 *12 Month Price Score 106.71

Interim Earnings (Per Share)

Qtr.	Mar	Jun	Sep	Dec
2016	0.35	0.68	0.84	0.56
2017	0.51	0.79	0.84	(0.12)
2018	0.44	1.40	1.41	0.56
2019	0.54	1.33	1.36	...

Interim Dividends (Per Share)

Amt	Decl	Ex	Rec	Pay
0.215Q	02/25/2019	04/01/2019	04/02/2019	04/17/2019
0.215Q	04/19/2019	07/01/2019	07/02/2019	07/17/2019
0.215Q	09/13/2019	10/01/2019	10/02/2019	10/17/2019
0.225Q	12/13/2019	12/31/2019	01/02/2020	01/16/2020

Indicated Div: $0.90

Valuation Analysis | **Institutional Holding**

Forecast EPS	$4.26	No of Institutions
	(01/16/2020)	309
Market Cap	$5.8 Billion	Shares
Book Value	N/A	38,753,244
Price/Book	N/A	% Held
Price/Sales	5.28	N/A

Business Summary: Hotels, Restaurants & Travel (MIC: 2.2.1 SIC: 7011 NAIC: 721110)

Choice Hotels International is a hotel franchisor. Co. franchises lodging properties under the following proprietary brand names: Comfort Inn®, Comfort Suites®, Quality®, Clarion®, Clarion Pointe™, Sleep Inn®, Econo Lodge®, Rodeway Inn®, MainStay Suites®, Suburban Extended Stay Hotel®, WoodSpring Suites®, Cambria® Hotels, and Ascend Hotel Collection®. Co.'s primary segment is the hotel franchising business. Co.'s domestic franchising operations are conducted through direct franchising relationships while its international franchise operations are conducted through a combination of direct franchising and master franchising relationships.

Recent Developments: For the quarter ended Sep 30 2019, net income decreased 4.7% to US$76.2 million from US$80.0 million in the year-earlier quarter. Revenues were US$310.7 million, up 6.6% from US$291.5 million the year before. Operating income was US$102.4 million versus US$111.2 million in the prior-year quarter, a decrease of 7.9%. Direct operating expenses rose 14.5% to US$158.4 million from US$138.3 million in the comparable period the year before. Indirect operating expenses increased 18.7% to US$49.9 million from US$42.0 million in the equivalent prior-year period.

Prospects: Our evaluation of Choice Hotels International Inc. as of October 4th, 2019 is the result of our systematic analysis on three basic characteristics: earnings strength, relative valuation, and recent stock price movement. The company has managed to produce a neutral trend in earnings per share over the past 5 quarters. However, recent analyst estimates for the company have been raised and CHH has posted results that exceeded analysts' expectations. Based on operating earnings yield, the company is fairly valued when compared to all of the companies we cover. Share price changes over the past year indicates that CHH will perform over the near term.

Financial Data

(US$ in Thousands)	9 Mos	6 Mos	3 Mos	12/31/2018	12/31/2017	12/31/2016	12/31/2015	12/31/2014
Earnings Per Share	3.79	3.84	3.91	3.80	2.02	2.46	2.22	2.10
Cash Flow Per Share	5.18	5.00	4.63	4.33	4.59	2.71	2.81	3.19
Dividends Per Share	0.860	0.645	0.645	0.860	0.860	0.830	0.790	0.750
Dividend Payout %	22.69	16.80	16.50	22.63	42.57	33.74	35.59	35.71
Income Statement								
Total Revenue	846,736	536,004	218,320	1,041,304	1,007,356	924,641	859,878	757,970
EBITDA	285,707	171,362	58,070	322,537	272,862	245,999	230,439	217,241
Depn & Amortn	32,481	20,671	10,822	5,500	5,200	5,600	4,300	3,100
Income Before Taxes	226,108	133,784	38,650	278,581	228,543	199,488	184,886	174,416
Income Taxes	35,848	26,163	6,398	56,903	109,104	60,609	55,956	52,285
Net Income	180,709	104,470	30,081	216,355	114,893	139,371	128,029	123,160
Average Shares	55,626	55,560	55,657	56,601	56,526	56,155	57,273	58,256
Balance Sheet								
Current Assets	260,264	276,864	250,671	243,784	402,933	344,873	310,953	351,414
Total Assets	1,374,262	1,214,277	1,173,816	1,138,370	927,607	852,468	717,010	647,220
Current Liabilities	316,304	321,008	303,871	318,439	294,497	263,668	208,016	200,098
Long-Term Obligations	875,843	784,280	804,730	753,514	725,292	839,409	812,945	782,082
Total Liabilities	1,430,997	1,336,937	1,359,293	1,322,142	1,139,709	1,163,817	1,112,909	1,076,071
Stockholders' Equity	(56,735)	(122,660)	(185,477)	(183,772)	(212,102)	(311,349)	(395,899)	(428,801)
Shares Outstanding	55,715	55,696	55,673	55,679	56,679	56,299	56,336	57,337
Statistical Record								
Return on Assets %	16.74	18.47	19.89	20.94	12.91	17.71	18.77	20.75
EBITDA Margin %	33.74	31.97	26.60	30.97	27.09	26.60	26.80	28.66
Net Margin %	21.34	19.49	13.78	20.78	11.41	15.07	14.89	16.25
Asset Turnover	0.86	0.92	0.94	1.01	1.13	1.18	1.26	1.28
Current Ratio	0.82	0.86	0.82	0.77	1.37	1.31	1.49	1.76
Price Range	94.38-66.86	87.01-66.86	84.30-66.86	84.60-66.86	78.70-53.50	56.70-41.85	64.85-46.62	57.34-43.71
P/E Ratio	24.90-17.64	22.66-17.41	21.56-17.10	22.26-17.59	38.96-26.49	23.05-17.01	29.21-21.00	27.30-20.81
Average Yield %	1.06	0.82	0.83	1.09	1.33	1.71	1.43	1.52

Address: 1 Choice Hotels Circle, Suite 400, Rockville, MD 20850 **Telephone:** 301-592-5000	**Web Site:** www.choicehotels.com **Officers:** Stewart Bainum - Chairman Patrick S. Pacious - President, Chief Executive Officer, Executive Vice President, Chief Operating Officer	**Auditors:** Ernst & Young LLP **Investor Contact:** 301-592-5026 **Transfer Agents:** Computershare, Providence, RI

CHUBB LTD

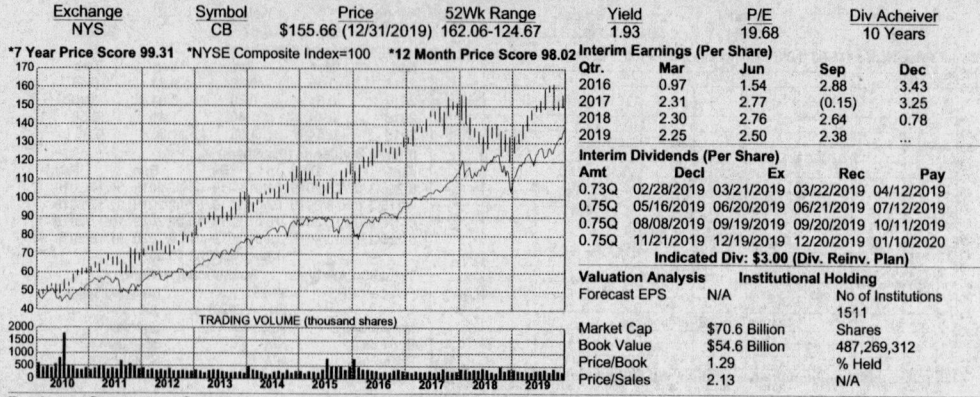

Exchange	Symbol	Price	52Wk Range	Yield	P/E	Div Acheiver
NYS	CB	$155.66 (12/31/2019)	162.06-124.67	1.93	19.68	10 Years

*7 Year Price Score 99.31 *NYSE Composite Index=100 *12 Month Price Score 98.02

Interim Earnings (Per Share)

Qtr.	Mar	Jun	Sep	Dec
2016	0.97	1.54	2.88	3.43
2017	2.31	2.77	(0.15)	3.25
2018	2.30	2.76	2.64	0.78
2019	2.25	2.50	2.38	...

Interim Dividends (Per Share)

Amt	Decl	Ex	Rec	Pay
0.73Q	02/28/2019	03/21/2019	03/22/2019	04/12/2019
0.75Q	05/16/2019	06/20/2019	06/21/2019	07/12/2019
0.75Q	08/08/2019	09/19/2019	09/20/2019	10/11/2019
0.75Q	11/21/2019	12/19/2019	12/20/2019	01/10/2020

Indicated Div: $3.00 (Div. Reinv. Plan)

Valuation Analysis

		Institutional Holding	
Forecast EPS	N/A	No of Institutions	1511
Market Cap	$70.6 Billion	Shares	487,269,312
Book Value	$54.6 Billion	% Held	
Price/Book	1.29	N/A	
Price/Sales	2.13		

Business Summary: General Insurance (MIC: 5.2.1 SIC: 6331 NAIC: 524130)

Chubb, through its subsidiaries, is an insurance and reinsurance organization. Co. provides commercial and personal property and casualty insurance, personal accident and supplemental health insurance, reinsurance, and life insurance. Co. provides commercial insurance products and service offerings such as risk management programs, loss control, and engineering and claims management, as well as insurance products ranging from Directors & Officers and professional liability to various specialty-casualty and umbrella and excess casualty lines. Co. also provides personal lines insurance coverage including homeowners, automobile, valuables, umbrella liability, and recreational marine products.

Recent Developments: For the quarter ended Sep 30 2019, net income decreased 11.4% to US$1.09 billion from US$1.23 billion in the year-earlier quarter. Revenues were US$9.05 billion, up 3.4% from US$8.75 billion the year before. Net premiums earned were US$8.33 billion versus US$7.91 billion in the prior-year quarter, an increase of 5.3%. Net investment income rose 6.1% to US$873.0 million from US$823.0 million a year ago.

Prospects: Our evaluation of Chubb Ltd. as of October 4th, 2019 is the result of our systematic analysis on three basic characteristics: earnings strength, relative valuation, and recent stock price movement. The company has produced a positive trend in earnings per share over the past 5 quarters. However, recent analyst estimates for the company have been unchanged, while CB has posted results that exceeded analysts' expectations. Based on operating earnings yield, the company is undervalued when compared to all of the companies we cover. Share price changes over the past year indicates that CB will perform well over the near term.

Financial Data

(US$ in Thousands)	9 Mos	6 Mos	3 Mos	12/31/2018	12/31/2017	12/31/2016	12/31/2015	12/31/2014
Earnings Per Share	7.91	8.17	8.43	8.49	8.19	8.87	8.62	8.42
Cash Flow Per Share	14.28	13.10	13.62	11.82	9.64	11.41	11.87	13.40
Tang Book Value Per Share	73.19	70.68	67.52	62.93	62.78	56.18	72.26	72.61
Dividends Per Share	2.960	2.940	2.920	2.900	2.820	2.740	2.660	2.700
Dividend Payout %	37.42	35.99	34.64	34.16	34.43	34.89	30.86	32.07
Income Statement								
Premium Income	23,355,000	15,028,000	7,137,000	30,064,000	29,034,000	28,749,000	17,213,000	17,426,000
Total Revenue	25,448,000	16,403,000	7,876,000	32,717,000	32,243,000	31,469,000	18,987,000	19,171,000
Benefits & Claims	14,380,000	9,170,000	4,294,000	18,657,000	19,130,000	16,640,000	10,027,000	10,166,000
Income Before Taxes	3,907,000	2,314,000	1,206,000	4,143,000	3,304,000	4,686,000	3,183,000	3,256,000
Income Taxes	626,000	396,000	188,000	695,000	(139,000)	815,000	462,000	634,000
Net Income	3,281,000	2,190,000	1,040,000	3,962,000	3,861,000	4,135,000	2,834,000	2,853,000
Average Shares	458,150	460,169	461,536	466,802	471,196	465,949	328,835	338,986
Balance Sheet								
Total Assets	175,148,000	174,516,000	171,347,000	167,771,000	167,022,000	159,786,000	102,366,000	98,248,000
Total Liabilities	120,576,000	120,714,000	118,992,000	117,459,000	115,850,000	111,511,000	73,231,000	68,661,000
Stockholders' Equity	54,572,000	53,802,000	52,355,000	50,312,000	51,172,000	48,275,000	29,135,000	29,587,000
Shares Outstanding	453,533	456,077	458,179	459,203	463,833	465,968	324,563	328,659
Statistical Record								
Return on Assets %	2.12	2.21	2.31	2.37	2.36	3.15	2.83	2.96
Return on Equity %	6.89	7.21	7.56	7.81	7.76	10.65	9.65	9.77
Loss Ratio %	61.57	61.02	60.17	62.06	65.89	57.88	58.25	58.34
Net Margin %	12.89	13.35	13.20	12.11	11.97	13.14	14.93	14.88
Price Range	161.44-120.19	150.94-120.19	140.12-120.19	156.15-120.19	155.19-128.48	133.32-108.00	119.47-99.72	117.58-92.19
P/E Ratio	20.41-15.19	18.47-14.71	16.62-14.26	18.39-14.16	18.95-15.69	15.03-12.18	13.86-11.57	13.96-10.95
Average Yield %	2.10	2.17	2.24	2.14	1.98	2.27	2.43	2.60

Address: Baerengasse 32, Zurich, CH-8001 Telephone: 434-567-600	Web Site: www.acegroup.com Officers: John W. Keogh - Executive Vice Chairman, Chief Operating Officer, Vice-Chairman Evan G. Greenberg - Chairman, President, Chief Executive Officer, Vice-Chairman, Chief Operating Officer	Auditors: PricewaterhouseCoopers LLP Investor Contact: +12-128-274445

CHURCH & DWIGHT CO INC

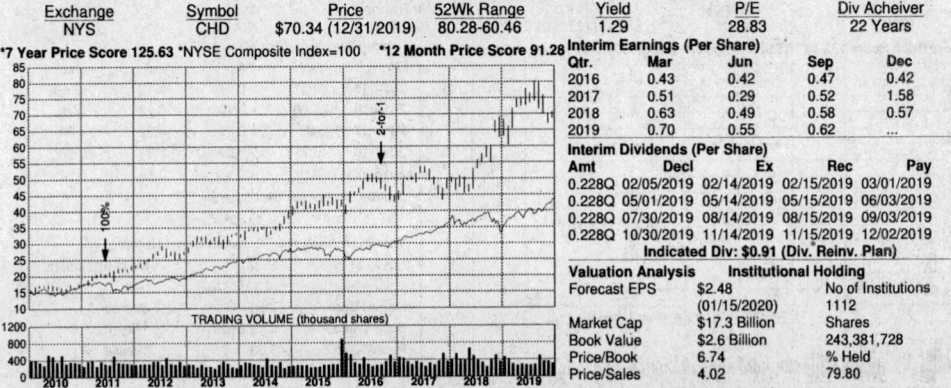

Exchange	Symbol	Price	52Wk Range	Yield	P/E	Div Acheiver
NYS	CHD	$70.34 (12/31/2019)	80.28-60.46	1.29	28.83	22 Years

*7 Year Price Score 125.63 ***NYSE Composite Index=100** ***12 Month Price Score 91.28**

Interim Earnings (Per Share)

Qtr.	Mar	Jun	Sep	Dec
2016	0.43	0.42	0.47	0.42
2017	0.51	0.29	0.52	1.58
2018	0.63	0.49	0.58	0.57
2019	0.70	0.55	0.62	...

Interim Dividends (Per Share)

Amt	Decl	Ex	Rec	Pay
0.228Q	02/05/2019	02/14/2019	02/15/2019	03/01/2019
0.228Q	05/01/2019	05/14/2019	05/15/2019	06/03/2019
0.228Q	07/30/2019	08/14/2019	08/15/2019	09/03/2019
0.228Q	10/30/2019	11/14/2019	11/15/2019	12/02/2019

Indicated Div: $0.91 (Div. Reinv. Plan)

Valuation Analysis / **Institutional Holding**

Forecast EPS	$2.48	No of Institutions	
(01/15/2020)		1112	
Market Cap	$17.3 Billion	Shares	
Book Value	$2.6 Billion	243,381,728	
Price/Book	6.74	% Held	
Price/Sales	4.02	79.80	

Business Summary: Household & Personal Products (MIC: 1.7.1 SIC: 2841 NAIC: 325611)

Church & Dwight develops, manufactures and markets a range of consumer household and personal care products and specialty products focused on animal productivity, chemicals and cleaners. Co. provides ARM & HAMMER baking soda, cat litter, laundry detergent, carpet deodorizer and other baking soda based products; TROJAN condoms, lubricants and vibrators; OXICLEAN stain removers, cleaning solutions, laundry detergents and bleach alternatives; SPINBRUSH battery-operated toothbrushes; FIRST RESPONSE home pregnancy and ovulation test kits; NAIR depilatories; ORAJEL oral analgesic; and L'IL CRITTERS and VITAFUSION gummy dietary supplements for children and adults, respectively.

Recent Developments: For the quarter ended Sep 30 2019, net income increased 7.5% to US$157.3 million from US$146.3 million in the year-earlier quarter. Revenues were US$1.09 billion, up 5.0% from US$1.04 billion the year before. Operating income was US$216.8 million versus US$204.2 million in the prior-year quarter, an increase of 6.2%. Direct operating expenses rose 0.7% to US$581.7 million from US$577.5 million in the comparable period the year before. Indirect operating expenses increased 13.7% to US$290.9 million from US$255.9 million in the equivalent prior-year period.

Prospects: Our evaluation of Church & Dwight Co. Inc. as of October 4th, 2019 is the result of our systematic analysis on three basic characteristics: earnings strength, relative valuation, and recent stock price movement. The company has managed to produce a neutral trend in earnings per share over the past 5 quarters. Additionally, recent analyst estimates for the company have been unchanged while CHD has posted results that exceeded analysts' expectations. Based on operating earnings yield, the company is fairly valued when compared to all of the companies we cover. Share price changes over the past year indicates that CHD will perform over the near term.

Financial Data

(US$ in Thousands)	9 Mos	6 Mos	3 Mos	12/31/2018	12/31/2017	12/31/2016	12/31/2015	12/31/2014
Earnings Per Share	2.44	2.40	2.34	2.27	2.90	1.75	1.53	1.50
Cash Flow Per Share	3.29	3.21	3.03	3.11	2.72	2.54	2.31	2.00
Dividends Per Share	0.900	0.890	0.880	0.870	0.760	0.710	0.670	0.620
Dividend Payout %	36.89	37.08	37.61	38.33	26.21	40.57	43.65	41.20
Income Statement								
Total Revenue	3,213,500	2,124,100	1,044,700	4,145,900	3,776,200	3,493,100	3,394,800	3,297,600
EBITDA	776,000	511,600	279,800	854,100	795,400	784,100	730,000	697,800
Depn & Amortn	129,900	82,900	38,600	64,400	60,900	59,700	58,300	57,100
Income Before Taxes	590,500	392,000	223,400	710,300	681,900	696,700	641,200	613,300
Income Taxes	124,500	81,200	49,400	150,900	(50,700)	246,900	225,000	211,000
Net Income	471,500	314,200	175,700	568,600	743,400	459,000	410,400	413,900
Average Shares	252,900	252,700	251,900	250,700	256,100	262,100	267,200	275,000
Balance Sheet								
Current Assets	908,800	925,900	913,700	1,078,200	1,000,200	756,800	906,000	1,032,500
Total Assets	6,610,100	6,662,600	5,960,600	6,069,200	6,014,800	4,354,100	4,256,900	4,381,300
Current Liabilities	1,142,100	1,184,700	1,133,300	1,326,300	935,000	1,001,900	872,700	905,300
Long-Term Obligations	1,809,600	1,809,600	1,509,400	1,508,800	2,103,400	693,400	692,800	698,600
Total Liabilities	4,050,800	4,057,800	3,461,300	3,615,400	3,796,800	2,376,200	2,233,700	2,279,400
Stockholders' Equity	2,559,300	2,604,800	2,499,300	2,453,800	2,218,000	1,977,900	2,023,200	2,101,900
Shares Outstanding	245,296	246,960	246,066	246,885	247,629	253,962	259,908	266,703
Statistical Record								
Return on Assets %	9.77	9.61	9.85	9.41	14.34	10.63	9.50	9.58
Return on Equity %	25.01	25.00	25.27	24.34	35.43	22.88	19.90	18.81
EBITDA Margin %	24.15	24.09	26.78	20.60	21.06	22.45	21.50	21.16
Net Margin %	14.67	14.79	16.82	13.71	19.69	13.14	12.09	12.55
Asset Turnover	0.68	0.67	0.70	0.69	0.73	0.81	0.79	0.76
Current Ratio	0.80	0.78	0.81	0.81	1.07	0.76	1.04	1.14
Debt to Equity	0.71	0.69	0.60	0.61	0.95	0.35	0.34	0.33
Price Range	80.28-54.87	77.98-52.94	71.95-45.41	69.18-45.41	53.80-43.32	51.67-39.12	45.28-38.78	40.27-31.03
P/E Ratio	32.90-22.49	32.49-22.06	30.75-19.41	30.48-20.00	18.55-14.94	29.53-22.35	29.60-25.35	26.84-20.69
Average Yield %	1.29	1.37	1.51	1.60	1.55	1.52	1.58	1.79

Address: 500 Charles Ewing Boulevard, Ewing, NJ 08628 **Telephone:** 609-806-1200 **Fax:** 609-497-7269	**Web Site:** www.churchdwight.com **Officers:** James R. Craigie - Chairman, Chief Executive Officer Matthew Thomas Farrell - President, Chief Executive Officer, Executive Vice President, Chief Financial Officer, Chief Operating Officer	**Auditors:** DELOITTE & TOUCHE LLP **Investor Contact:** 609-497-7111 **Transfer Agents:** Computershare Inc., Canton, MA

CIENA CORP

Exchange	Symbol	Price	52Wk Range	Yield	P/E
NYS	CIEN	$42.69 (12/31/2019)	45.95-32.87	N/A	26.52

*7 Year Price Score 132.14 *NYSE Composite Index=100 *12 Month Price Score 91.43

Interim Earnings (Per Share)

Qtr.	Jan	Apr	Jul	Oct
2014-15	(0.17)	0.17	0.19	(0.12)
2015-16	(0.08)	0.10	0.23	0.25
2016-17	0.03	0.25	0.39	6.84
2017-18	(3.29)	0.09	0.34	0.35
2018-19	0.21	0.33	0.55	0.51

Interim Dividends (Per Share)
No Dividends Paid

Valuation Analysis

		Institutional Holding	
Forecast EPS	$2.60	No of Institutions	
	(01/15/2020)	640	
Market Cap	$6.6 Billion	Shares	
Book Value	$2.2 Billion	174,870,016	
Price/Book	3.03	% Held	
Price/Sales	1.85	N/A	

Business Summary: IT Services (MIC: 6.3.1 SIC: 7373 NAIC: 541512)

Ciena is a networking systems, services and software company, providing solutions that enable a range of network operators to deploy and manage networks that deliver services to businesses and consumers. Co. provides hardware, software and services that support the transport, switching, aggregation, service delivery and management of video, data and voice traffic on communications networks. Co.'s solutions are used by communications service providers, cable and multiservice operators, Web-scale providers, submarine network operators, governments, enterprises, research and education institutions and other network operators.

Recent Developments: For the year ended Oct 31 2019, net income amounted to US$253.4 million versus a net loss of US$344.7 million in the prior year. Revenues were US$3.57 billion, up 15.4% from US$3.09 billion the year before. Operating income was US$346.8 million versus US$229.9 million in the prior year, an increase of 50.8%. Direct operating expenses rose 14.1% to US$2.03 billion from US$1.78 billion in the comparable period the year before. Indirect operating expenses increased 10.2% to US$1.20 billion from US$1.08 billion in the equivalent prior-year period.

Prospects: Our evaluation of CIENA Corp. as of October 4th, 2019 is the result of our systematic analysis on three basic characteristics: earnings strength, relative valuation, and recent stock price movement. The company has managed to produce a neutral trend in earnings per share over the past 5 quarters. However, recent analyst estimates for the company have been raised and CIEN has posted results that exceeded analysts' expectations. Based on operating earnings yield, the company is fairly valued when compared to all of the companies we cover. Share price changes over the past year indicates that CIEN will perform over the near term.

Financial Data

(US$ in Thousands)	10/31/2019	10/31/2018	10/31/2017	10/31/2016	10/31/2015	10/31/2014	10/31/2013	10/31/2012
Earnings Per Share	1.61	(2.49)	7.53	0.51	0.10	(0.38)	(0.83)	(1.45)
Cash Flow Per Share	2.65	1.59	1.65	2.09	2.21	0.85	0.44	1.08
Tang Book Value Per Share	11.41	9.61	12.36	2.52	1.19	...	...	...
Income Statement								
Total Revenue	3,572,131	3,094,286	2,801,687	2,600,573	2,445,669	2,288,289	2,082,546	1,833,923
EBITDA	450,905	304,522	322,061	269,682	202,050	125,295	89,203	45,951
Depn & Amortn	113,936	101,106	112,913	130,998	125,966	103,751	119,608	125,797
Income Before Taxes	313,190	148,781	156,126	86,718	23,764	(26,673)	(80,191)	(134,699)
Income Taxes	59,756	493,471	(1,105,827)	14,134	12,097	13,964	5,240	9,322
Net Income	253,434	(344,690)	1,261,953	72,584	11,667	(40,637)	(85,431)	(144,021)
Average Shares	157,612	143,738	169,919	150,704	120,101	105,783	102,350	99,341
Balance Sheet								
Current Assets	2,381,802	2,142,602	2,006,311	2,013,192	1,864,210	1,693,190	1,395,802	1,415,690
Total Assets	3,893,346	3,756,523	3,951,711	2,882,442	2,695,051	2,072,632	1,802,770	1,881,143
Current Liabilities	845,940	963,003	1,037,743	891,862	667,034	781,136	615,055	684,970
Long-Term Obligations	745,690	754,695	657,095	1,050,289	1,285,433	1,279,380	1,212,019	1,225,806
Total Liabilities	1,720,585	1,827,189	1,815,369	2,116,101	2,074,175	2,142,247	1,885,447	1,970,115
Stockholders' Equity	2,172,761	1,929,334	2,136,342	766,341	620,876	(69,615)	(82,677)	(88,972)
Shares Outstanding	154,403	154,318	143,043	139,767	135,612	106,979	103,705	100,601
Statistical Record								
Return on Assets %	6.63	N.M.	36.93	2.60	0.49	N.M.	N.M.	N.M.
Return on Equity %	12.36	N.M.	86.95	10.44	4.23	...	...	...
EBITDA Margin %	12.62	9.84	11.50	10.37	8.26	5.48	4.28	2.51
Net Margin %	7.09	N.M.	45.04	2.79	0.48	N.M.	N.M.	N.M.
Asset Turnover	0.93	0.80	0.82	0.93	1.03	1.18	1.13	0.95
Current Ratio	2.82	2.22	1.93	2.26	2.79	2.17	2.27	2.07
Debt to Equity	0.34	0.39	0.31	1.37	2.07	...	...	...
Price Range	45.95-30.64	32.07-19.57	27.50-19.21	25.30-15.73	26.03-14.81	26.20-14.16	27.67-12.42	17.98-10.38
P/E Ratio	28.54-19.03	...	3.65-2.55	49.61-30.84	260.30-148.10	...	...	...

Address: 7035 Ridge Road, Hanover, MD 21076 **Telephone:** 410-694-5700 **Fax:** 410-694-5750	**Web Site:** www.ciena.com **Officers:** Patrick H. Nettles - Executive Chairman Gary B. Smith - President, Chief Executive Officer	**Auditors:** PricewaterhouseCoopers LLP **Transfer Agents:** Computershare Trust Company, N.A., Providence, RI

CIGNA CORP

Exchange	Symbol	Price	52Wk Range	Yield	P/E
NYS	CI	$204.49 (12/31/2019)	206.47-145.49	0.02	18.21

*7 Year Price Score 102.79 *NYSE Composite Index=100 *12 Month Price Score 107.78

TRADING VOLUME (thousand shares)

Interim Earnings (Per Share)

Qtr.	Mar	Jun	Sep	Dec
2016	2.00	1.97	1.76	1.47
2017	2.30	3.15	2.21	1.10
2018	3.72	3.29	3.14	0.40
2019	3.56	3.70	3.57	...

Interim Dividends (Per Share)

Amt	Decl	Ex	Rec	Pay
0.04A	02/27/2019	03/08/2019	03/11/2019	04/10/2019

Indicated Div: $0.04 (Div. Reinv. Plan)

Valuation Analysis

Forecast EPS	$16.94
	(01/17/2020)
Market Cap	$76.4 Billion
Book Value	$44.7 Billion
Price/Book	1.71
Price/Sales	0.59

Institutional Holding

No of Institutions	N/A
Shares	N/A
% Held	N/A

Business Summary: Diagnostic & Health Related Services (MIC: 4.2.2 SIC: 6324 NAIC: 524114)

Cigna is a global health service organization. Co.'s segments are: Integrated Medical, which includes its employer-sponsored medical coverage and Medicare offerings for seniors and individual insurance offerings to non-seniors both on and off the public health insurance exchanges; Health Services, which consists of the pharmacy benefit management business and its home delivery operations; International Markets, which provides a range of medical and supplemental health, life, and accident benefits to individuals and employers; and Group Disability and Other, which includes its commercial long- and short-term disability products, and its term life and universal life group insurance products.

Recent Developments: For the quarter ended Sep 30 2019, net income increased 74.9% to US$1.35 billion from US$774.0 million in the year-earlier quarter. Revenues were US$38.56 billion, up 236.5% from US$11.46 billion the year before. Net premiums earned were US$9.94 billion versus US$8.99 billion in the prior-year quarter, an increase of 10.5%. Net investment income fell 1.7% to US$349.0 million from US$355.0 million a year ago.

Prospects: Our evaluation of Cigna Corp. as of October 4th, 2019 is the result of our systematic analysis on three basic characteristics: earnings strength, relative valuation, and recent stock price movement. The company has produced a positive trend in earnings per share over the past 5 quarters. In addition, recent analyst estimates for the company have been raised, and CI has posted results that exceeded analysts' expectations. Based on operating earnings yield, the company is undervalued when compared to all of the companies we cover. Share price changes over the past year indicates that CI will perform poorly over the near term.

Financial Data

(US$ in Millions)	9 Mos	6 Mos	3 Mos	12/31/2018	12/31/2017	12/31/2016	12/31/2015	12/31/2014
Earnings Per Share	11.23	10.80	10.39	10.54	8.77	7.19	8.04	7.83
Cash Flow Per Share	18.19	13.18	13.01	15.28	16.29	15.72	10.61	7.56
Tang Book Value Per Share	N.M.	N.M.	N.M.	N.M.	31.03	30.14	23.45	18.46
Dividends Per Share	0.040	0.040	0.040	0.040	0.040	0.040	0.040	0.040
Dividend Payout %	0.36	0.37	0.38	0.38	0.46	0.56	0.50	0.51
Income Statement								
Premium Income	29,709	19,774	9,971	36,113	32,307	30,626	29,642	27,214
Total Revenue	115,321	76,765	37,946	48,650	41,616	39,668	37,876	34,914
Benefits & Claims	22,930	15,196	7,620	...	25,406	24,486	23,290	21,334
Income Before Taxes	5,309	3,546	1,788	3,581	3,606	2,979	3,327	3,304
Income Taxes	1,173	764	416	935	1,374	1,136	1,250	1,210
Net Income	4,127	2,776	1,368	2,637	2,237	1,867	2,094	2,102
Average Shares	378	380	384	250	255	259	260	268
Balance Sheet								
Total Assets	154,847	154,401	154,348	153,226	61,753	59,360	57,088	55,896
Total Liabilities	110,151	110,586	111,940	112,198	48,018	45,637	45,053	45,122
Stockholders' Equity	44,696	43,815	42,408	41,028	13,735	13,723	12,035	10,774
Shares Outstanding	373	377	379	380	243	256	256	259
Statistical Record								
Return on Assets %	3.59	3.39	2.84	2.45	3.69	3.20	3.71	3.81
Return on Equity %	14.18	12.61	10.92	9.63	16.29	14.46	18.36	19.70
Loss Ratio %	77.18	76.85	76.42	...	78.64	79.95	78.57	78.39
Net Margin %	3.58	3.62	3.61	5.42	5.38	4.71	5.53	6.02
Price Range	224.84-145.49	224.84-145.49	224.84-159.69	226.22-164.00	211.73-135.72	146.55-116.03	169.77-101.06	105.20-75.64
P/E Ratio	20.02-12.96	20.82-13.47	21.64-15.37	21.46-15.56	24.14-15.48	20.38-16.14	21.12-12.57	13.44-9.66
Average Yield %	0.02	0.02	0.02	0.02	0.02	0.03	0.03	0.04

Address: 900 Cottage Grove Road, Bloomfield, CT 06002 **Telephone:** 860-226-6000 **Fax:** 860-226-6741	**Web Site:** www.cigna.com **Officers:** Isaiah Harris - Chairman David M. Cordani - President, Chief Executive Officer	**Auditors:** PricewaterhouseCoopers LLP **Investor Contact:** 215-761-1414 **Transfer Agents:** Computershare Shareowner Services, Providence, RI

CIMAREX ENERGY CO

Exchange	Symbol	Price	52Wk Range	Yield	P/E
NYS	XEC	$52.49 (12/31/2019)	76.42-37.63	1.52	10.41

*7 Year Price Score 47.78 *NYSE Composite Index=100 *12 Month Price Score 78.44

Interim Earnings (Per Share)

Qtr.	Mar	Jun	Sep	Dec
2016	(2.00)	(2.91)	(0.14)	0.42
2017	1.38	1.02	0.96	1.83
2018	1.96	1.48	1.56	3.32
2019	0.26	1.07	0.39	...

Interim Dividends (Per Share)

Amt	Decl	Ex	Rec	Pay
0.20Q	02/20/2019	05/14/2019	05/15/2019	05/31/2019
0.20Q	05/09/2019	08/14/2019	08/15/2019	08/30/2019
0.20Q	08/29/2019	11/14/2019	11/15/2019	11/29/2019
0.20Q	12/06/2019	02/13/2020	02/14/2020	02/28/2020

Indicated Div: $0.80

Valuation Analysis

		Institutional Holding	
Forecast EPS	$4.09	No of Institutions	
	(01/17/2020)	685	
Market Cap	$5.3 Billion	Shares	
Book Value	$4.0 Billion	123,444,248	
Price/Book	1.35	% Held	
Price/Sales	2.29	97.75	

Business Summary: Production & Extraction (MIC: 9.1.1 SIC: 1311 NAIC: 211111)

Cimarex Energy is an independent oil and gas exploration and production company. Co.'s operations are mainly located in Oklahoma, Texas, and New Mexico. Co.'s operations are focused in two main areas: the Permian Basin and the Mid-Continent. Co.'s Permian Basin region encompasses west Texas and southeast New Mexico. Co.'s Mid-Continent region consists of Oklahoma and the Texas Panhandle.

Recent Developments: For the quarter ended Sep 30 2019, net income decreased 72.7% to US$40.5 million from US$148.4 million in the year-earlier quarter. Revenues were US$582.3 million, down 1.6% from US$591.5 million the year before. Operating income was US$63.8 million versus US$196.7 million in the prior-year quarter, a decrease of 67.6%. Direct operating expenses rose 13.4% to US$154.9 million from US$136.6 million in the comparable period the year before. Indirect operating expenses increased 40.8% to US$363.6 million from US$258.2 million in the equivalent prior-year period.

Prospects: Our evaluation of Cimarex Energy Co as of October 4th, 2019 is the result of our systematic analysis on three basic characteristics: earnings strength, relative valuation, and recent stock price movement. The company has generated a negative trend in earnings per share over the past 5 quarters. In addition, recent analyst estimates for the company have been reduced and XEC has posted results that fell short of analysts' expectations. Based on operating earnings yield, the company is undervalued when compared to all of the companies we cover. Share price changes over the past year indicates that XEC will perform very poorly over the near term.

Financial Data

(US$ in Thousands)	9 Mos	6 Mos	3 Mos	12/31/2018	12/31/2017	12/31/2016	12/31/2015	12/31/2014
Earnings Per Share	5.04	6.21	6.62	8.32	5.19	(4.62)	(25.92)	5.78
Cash Flow Per Share	13.81	15.16	14.78	16.54	11.73	6.40	7.44	18.90
Tang Book Value Per Share	31.62	31.69	30.72	28.30	20.41	18.29	22.96	44.30
Dividends Per Share	0.760	0.720	0.680	0.580	0.320	0.400	0.640	0.620
Dividend Payout %	15.08	11.59	10.27	6.97	6.17	...	...	10.73
Income Statement								
Total Revenue	1,705,725	1,123,420	576,957	2,339,017	1,918,249	1,257,345	1,452,619	2,424,176
EBITDA	263,489	198,778	46,771	1,660,349	1,179,900	(130,304)	(2,948,304)	1,648,862
Depn & Amortn	2,285	1,502	719	590,473	446,031	465,936	778,923	806,021
Income Before Taxes	233,350	177,744	34,389	1,022,507	681,996	(658,264)	(3,782,384)	805,901
Income Taxes	57,198	42,119	8,073	230,656	187,667	(227,215)	(1,373,436)	298,697
Net Income	176,152	135,625	26,316	791,851	494,329	(431,049)	(2,408,948)	507,204
Average Shares	99,735	99,665	95,932	93,820	93,509	93,379	92,992	85,810
Balance Sheet								
Current Assets	556,579	520,056	596,208	1,424,139	935,635	969,304	1,077,930	931,804
Total Assets	7,619,205	7,595,934	7,557,192	6,062,084	5,042,639	4,681,693	5,243,286	8,725,293
Current Liabilities	796,699	814,667	909,914	708,707	679,574	522,352	410,067	776,327
Long-Term Obligations	1,984,734	1,984,230	2,170,083	1,488,554	1,486,920	1,487,939	1,485,620	1,500,000
Total Liabilities	3,648,027	3,652,421	3,714,210	2,732,298	2,474,361	2,321,629	2,445,608	4,224,661
Stockholders' Equity	3,971,178	3,943,513	3,842,982	3,329,786	2,568,278	2,360,064	2,797,678	4,500,632
Shares Outstanding	101,820	101,473	101,407	95,755	95,437	95,123	94,820	87,592
Statistical Record								
Return on Assets %	7.33	9.14	9.86	14.26	10.17	N.M.	N.M.	6.35
Return on Equity %	14.07	17.57	19.16	26.85	20.06	N.M.	N.M.	11.90
EBITDA Margin %	15.45	17.69	8.11	70.98	61.51	N.M.	N.M.	68.02
Net Margin %	10.33	12.07	4.56	33.85	25.77	N.M.	N.M.	20.92
Asset Turnover	0.35	0.36	0.37	0.42	0.39	0.25	0.21	0.30
Current Ratio	0.70	0.64	0.66	2.01	1.38	1.86	2.63	1.20
Debt to Equity	0.50	0.50	0.56	0.45	0.58	0.63	0.53	0.33
Price Range	100.44-37.63	102.10-54.37	102.39-57.32	128.66-57.32	142.47-91.33	143.25-75.60	129.44-85.27	148.77-92.73
P/E Ratio	19.93-7.47	16.44-8.76	15.47-8.66	15.46-6.89	27.45-17.60	...	...	25.74-16.04
Average Yield %	1.15	0.93	0.80	0.62	0.28	0.35	0.58	0.51

Address: 1700 Lincoln Street, Suite 3700, Denver, CO 80203 **Telephone:** 303-295-3995	**Web Site:** www.cimarex.com **Officers:** Thomas E. Jorden - Chairman, President, Executive Vice President, Chief Executive Officer, Principal Executive Officer Krista L. Johnson - Division Officer	**Auditors:** KPMG LLP **Investor Contact:** 303-295-3995 **Transfer Agents:** Continental Stock Transfer & Trust Company, New York, NY

CINEMARK HOLDINGS INC

Exchange	Symbol	Price	52Wk Range	Yield	P/E
NYS	CNK	$33.85 (12/31/2019)	42.39-33.05	4.02	21.42

*7 Year Price Score 87.27   *NYSE Composite Index=100   *12 Month Price Score 86.57

Interim Earnings (Per Share)

Qtr.	Mar	Jun	Sep	Dec
2016	0.50	0.46	0.56	0.66
2017	0.68	0.44	0.33	0.81
2018	0.53	0.70	0.43	0.17
2019	0.28	0.86	0.27	...

Interim Dividends (Per Share)

Amt	Decl	Ex	Rec	Pay
0.34Q	02/22/2019	03/07/2019	03/08/2019	03/22/2019
0.34Q	05/23/2019	06/07/2019	06/10/2019	06/24/2019
0.34Q	08/15/2019	09/03/2019	09/04/2019	09/18/2019
0.34Q	11/21/2019	12/03/2019	12/04/2019	12/18/2019

Indicated Div: $1.36

Valuation Analysis / **Institutional Holding**

Forecast EPS	$1.98	No of Institutions
	(01/17/2020)	488
Market Cap	$4.0 Billion	Shares
Book Value	$1.5 Billion	144,383,136
Price/Book	2.67	% Held
Price/Sales	1.20	102.69

Business Summary: Entertainment (MIC: 2.3.2 SIC: 7832 NAIC: 512131)

Cinemark Holdings is a holding company. Through its subsidiaries, Co. is engaged in the motion picture exhibition industry, with theatres in the U.S., Brazil, Argentina, Chile, Colombia, Peru, Ecuador, Honduras, El Salvador, Nicaragua, Costa Rica, Panama, Guatemala, Bolivia, Curacao and Paraguay. Co. provides a variety of content at its theatres. Co. monitors upcoming films and other content and works with film distributors to license the content. Co. plays films from various genres, such as animated films, family films, dramas, comedies, horror and action films. Co. provides content in both 2-D and 3-D formats in its theatres, and in various locations, Co. provides its large format, XD.

Recent Developments: For the quarter ended Sep 30 2019, net income decreased 36.9% to US$32.0 million from US$50.6 million in the year-earlier quarter. Revenues were US$821.8 million, up 9.0% from US$754.2 million the year before. Operating income was US$58.5 million versus US$82.7 million in the prior-year quarter, a decrease of 29.3%. Direct operating expenses rose 11.6% to US$430.4 million from US$385.7 million in the comparable period the year before. Indirect operating expenses increased 16.5% to US$332.9 million from US$285.8 million in the equivalent prior-year period.

Prospects: Our evaluation of Cinemark Holdings Inc. as of October 4th, 2019 is the result of our systematic analysis on three basic characteristics: earnings strength, relative valuation, and recent stock price movement. The company has enjoyed a very positive trend in earnings per share over the past 5 quarters. However, recent analyst estimates for the company have been reduced, while CNK has posted results that exceeded analysts' expectations. Based on operating earnings yield, the company is undervalued when compared to all of the companies we cover. Share price changes over the past year indicates that CNK will perform in line with the market over the near term.

Financial Data

(US$ in Thousands)	9 Mos	6 Mos	3 Mos	12/31/2018	12/31/2017	12/31/2016	12/31/2015	12/31/2014
Earnings Per Share	1.58	1.74	1.58	1.83	2.26	2.19	1.87	1.66
Cash Flow Per Share	5.19	4.99	4.97	4.80	4.57	3.90	3.96	3.97
Dividends Per Share	1.340	1.320	1.300	1.280	1.160	1.080	1.000	1.000
Dividend Payout %	84.81	75.86	82.28	69.95	51.33	49.32	53.48	60.24
Income Statement								
Total Revenue	2,494,296	1,672,479	714,723	3,221,735	2,991,547	2,918,765	2,852,609	2,626,990
EBITDA	464,909	343,405	123,707	648,422	644,154	637,692	610,472	548,557
Depn & Amortn	188,575	123,670	61,769	257,826	235,093	207,091	186,898	173,138
Income Before Taxes	197,179	166,310	34,706	271,492	309,392	328,684	319,541	267,320
Income Taxes	64,152	50,099	11,917	95,429	79,358	103,819	128,939	96,064
Net Income	165,052	133,699	32,728	213,827	264,180	255,091	216,869	192,610
Average Shares	116,600	116,548	116,418	116,342	116,059	115,783	115,399	114,966
Balance Sheet								
Current Assets	594,768	662,551	544,506	559,030	657,570	676,317	715,151	741,010
Total Assets	5,751,603	5,902,248	5,790,748	4,481,838	4,470,893	4,306,633	4,126,497	4,151,980
Current Liabilities	639,779	700,195	656,978	474,689	468,913	443,225	439,793	414,407
Long-Term Obligations	1,898,044	1,902,311	1,906,516	2,005,094	2,031,532	2,016,722	1,981,882	2,016,552
Total Liabilities	4,267,900	4,386,969	4,338,806	3,038,100	3,077,098	3,044,815	3,026,789	3,039,180
Stockholders' Equity	1,483,703	1,515,279	1,451,942	1,443,738	1,393,795	1,261,818	1,099,708	1,112,800
Shares Outstanding	117,150	117,151	117,107	116,830	116,475	116,210	115,924	115,700
Statistical Record								
Return on Assets %	3.64	3.93	3.62	4.78	6.02	6.03	5.24	4.64
Return on Equity %	12.55	13.71	12.67	15.07	19.90	21.54	19.60	17.46
EBITDA Margin %	18.64	20.53	17.31	20.13	21.53	21.85	21.40	20.88
Net Margin %	6.62	7.99	4.58	6.64	8.83	8.74	7.60	7.33
Asset Turnover	0.65	0.62	0.62	0.72	0.68	0.69	0.69	0.63
Current Ratio	0.93	0.95	0.83	1.18	1.40	1.53	1.63	1.79
Debt to Equity	1.28	1.26	1.31	1.39	1.46	1.60	1.80	1.81
Price Range	42.41-35.23	42.41-34.41	42.41-33.75	43.31-33.73	44.58-32.29	42.23-27.15	45.52-31.56	36.37-27.73
P/E Ratio	26.84-22.30	24.37-19.78	26.84-21.36	23.67-18.43	19.73-14.29	19.28-12.40	24.34-16.88	21.91-16.70
Average Yield %	3.43	3.42	3.41	3.38	2.99	2.99	2.62	3.07

Address: 3900 Dallas Parkway, Suite 500, Plano, TX 75093	Web Site: www.cinemark.com	Auditors: Deloitte & Touche LLP
Telephone: 972-665-1000	Officers: Lee Roy Mitchell - Chairman Mark Zoradi - Chief Executive Officer	Investor Contact: 972-665-1500
		Transfer Agents: Wells Fargo Shareholder Services

CITIGROUP INC

Exchange	Symbol	Price	52Wk Range	Yield	P/E
NYS	C	$79.89 (12/31/2019)	79.89-52.06	N/A	10.61

*7 Year Price Score 97.53   *NYSE Composite Index=100   *12 Month Price Score 106.20

Interim Earnings (Per Share)

Qtr.	Mar	Jun	Sep	Dec
2016	1.10	1.24	1.24	1.14
2017	1.35	1.28	1.42	(7.03)
2018	1.68	1.63	1.73	1.64
2019	1.87	1.95	2.07	...

Interim Dividends (Per Share)

Amt	Decl	Ex	Rec	Pay
0.45Q	04/17/2019	05/03/2019	05/06/2019	05/24/2019
0.51Q	07/17/2019	08/02/2019	08/02/2019	08/23/2019
0.51Q	10/22/2019	11/01/2019	11/04/2019	11/22/2019
0.51Q	01/15/2020	01/31/2020	02/03/2020	02/28/2020

Indicated Div: $2.04

Valuation Analysis

Forecast EPS	$8.58
	(01/17/2020)
Market Cap	$174.4 Billion
Book Value	$196.4 Billion
Price/Book	0.89
Price/Sales	1.70

Institutional Holding

No of Institutions	2426
Shares	2,410,993,408
% Held	N/A

TRADING VOLUME (thousand shares)

Business Summary: Banking (MIC: 5.1.1 SIC: 6021 NAIC: 522110)

Citigroup is a financial services holding company whose businesses provide consumers, corporations, governments and institutions with a range of financial products and services, including consumer banking and credit, corporate and investment banking, securities brokerage, trade and securities services and wealth management. Co. operates via two primary business segments: Global Consumer Banking, which provides banking services to retail customers through retail banking, including commercial banking, and Citi-branded cards and Citi retail services; and Institutional Clients Group, which includes banking and markets and securities services.

Recent Developments: For the quarter ended Sep 30 2019, income from continuing operations increased 6.7% to US$4.94 billion from US$4.63 billion in the year-earlier quarter. Net income increased 6.6% to US$4.93 billion from US$4.63 billion in the year-earlier quarter. Net interest income decreased 1.4% to US$11.64 billion from US$11.80 billion in the year-earlier quarter. Provision for loan losses was US$2.07 billion versus US$1.95 billion in the prior-year quarter, an increase of 6.3%. Non-interest income rose 5.3% to US$6.93 billion from US$6.59 billion, while non-interest expense advanced 1.4% to US$10.48 billion.

Prospects: Our evaluation of Citigroup Inc. as of October 4th, 2019 is the result of our systematic analysis on three basic characteristics: earnings strength, relative valuation, and recent stock price movement. The company has managed to produce a neutral trend in earnings per share over the past 5 quarters. However, recent analyst estimates for the company have been reduced while C has posted results that exceeded analysts' expectations. Based on operating earnings yield, the company is undervalued when compared to all of the companies we cover. Share price changes over the past year indicates that C will perform poorly over the near term.

Financial Data

(US$ in Thousands)	9 Mos	6 Mos	3 Mos	12/31/2018	12/31/2017	12/31/2016	12/31/2015	12/31/2014
Earnings Per Share	7.53	7.19	6.87	6.68	(2.98)	4.72	5.40	2.20
Cash Flow Per Share	(12.82)	(3.99)	(3.26)	14.82	(3.18)	18.62	13.23	14.99
Tang Book Value Per Share	68.81	67.41	65.32	63.54	59.96	64.03	60.03	56.24
Dividends Per Share	1.860	1.800	1.670	1.540	0.960	0.420	0.160	0.040
Dividend Payout %	24.70	25.03	24.31	23.05	...	8.90	2.96	1.82
Income Statement								
Interest Income	57,965,000	38,788,000	19,076,000	70,828,000	61,204,000	57,615,000	58,551,000	61,683,000
Interest Expense	22,615,000	15,079,000	7,317,000	24,266,000	16,517,000	12,511,000	11,921,000	13,690,000
Net Interest Income	35,350,000	23,709,000	11,759,000	46,562,000	44,687,000	45,104,000	46,630,000	47,993,000
Provision for Losses	6,113,000	4,042,000	1,968,000	7,354,000	7,503,000	6,749,000	7,108,000	6,828,000
Non-Interest Income	20,558,000	13,625,000	6,817,000	26,292,000	26,762,000	24,771,000	29,724,000	28,889,000
Non-Interest Expense	31,596,000	21,115,000	10,596,000	42,055,000	41,185,000	41,649,000	44,420,000	55,690,000
Income Before Taxes	18,199,000	12,177,000	6,012,000	23,445,000	22,761,000	21,477,000	24,826,000	14,364,000
Income Taxes	3,727,000	2,648,000	1,275,000	5,357,000	29,388,000	6,444,000	7,440,000	6,864,000
Net Income	14,422,000	9,509,000	4,710,000	18,045,000	(6,798,000)	14,912,000	17,242,000	7,313,000
Average Shares	2,237,100	2,289,000	2,342,400	2,494,800	2,698,500	2,888,300	3,007,700	3,037,000
Balance Sheet								
Net Loans & Leases	679,213,000	676,204,000	670,017,000	671,881,000	654,679,000	612,309,000	604,991,000	628,641,000
Total Assets	2,014,802,000	1,988,226,000	1,958,413,000	1,917,383,000	1,842,465,000	1,792,077,000	1,731,210,000	1,842,530,000
Total Deposits	1,087,769,000	1,045,467,000	1,030,355,000	1,013,170,000	959,822,000	929,406,000	907,887,000	899,332,000
Total Liabilities	1,818,429,000	1,790,867,000	1,762,161,000	1,721,163,000	1,641,725,000	1,566,957,000	1,509,353,000	1,631,996,000
Stockholders' Equity	196,373,000	197,359,000	196,252,000	196,220,000	200,740,000	225,120,000	221,857,000	210,534,000
Shares Outstanding	2,183,194	2,259,057	2,312,468	2,368,468	2,569,909	2,772,392	2,953,279	3,023,918
Statistical Record								
Return on Assets %	0.95	0.95	0.93	0.96	N.M.	0.84	0.96	0.39
Return on Equity %	9.53	9.28	9.11	9.09	N.M.	6.65	7.98	3.53
Net Interest Margin %	60.70	60.62	61.64	65.74	73.01	78.29	79.64	77.81
Efficiency Ratio %	40.14	39.66	40.92	43.30	46.82	50.55	50.32	61.49
Loans to Deposits	0.62	0.65	0.65	0.66	0.68	0.66	0.67	0.70
Price Range	73.01-49.26	74.79-49.26	74.79-49.26	80.08-49.26	77.10-55.68	61.09-34.98	60.34-46.95	56.37-45.68
P/E Ratio	9.70-6.54	10.40-6.85	10.89-7.17	11.99-7.37	...	12.94-7.41	11.17-8.69	25.62-20.76
Average Yield %	2.86	2.74	2.22	2.22	1.46	0.91	0.30	0.08

Address: 388 Greenwich Street, New York, NY 10013 **Telephone:** 212-559-1000	**Web Site:** www.citigroup.com **Officers:** John Cunningham Dugan - Chairman Michael S. Helfer - Vice-Chairman, General Counsel, Corporate Secretary	**Auditors:** KPMG LLP **Investor Contact:** 212-559-2718 **Transfer Agents:** Computershare Trust Company, N.A., Providence, RI	

CITIZENS FINANCIAL GROUP INC

	Exchange	Symbol	Price	52Wk Range	Yield	P/E
	NYS	CFG	$40.61 (12/31/2019)	40.75-29.73	3.84	10.72

*7 Year Price Score N/A *NYSE Composite Index=100 *12 Month Price Score 102.94

Interim Earnings (Per Share)

Qtr.	Mar	Jun	Sep	Dec
2016	0.41	0.46	0.56	0.55
2017	0.61	0.63	0.68	1.33
2018	0.78	0.88	0.91	0.95
2019	0.92	0.95	0.97	...

Interim Dividends (Per Share)

Amt	Decl	Ex	Rec	Pay
0.32Q	04/17/2019	04/30/2019	05/01/2019	05/15/2019
0.36Q	07/19/2019	07/30/2019	07/31/2019	08/14/2019
0.36Q	10/18/2019	10/29/2019	10/30/2019	11/13/2019
0.39Q	01/15/2020	01/28/2020	01/29/2020	02/12/2020

Indicated Div: $1.56

Valuation Analysis / Institutional Holding

Forecast EPS	$3.79	No of Institutions
	(01/17/2020)	807
Market Cap	$18.0 Billion	Shares
Book Value	$21.9 Billion	495,904,896
Price/Book	0.83	% Held
Price/Sales	2.24	83.32

Business Summary: Banking (MIC: 5.1.1 SIC: 6022 NAIC: 522110)

Citizens Financial Group is a bank holding company. Co.'s principal business activity is banking, conducted through its subsidiaries Citizens Bank, National Association and Citizens Bank of Pennsylvania. Co.'s operating segments are: Consumer Banking and Commercial Banking. In Consumer Banking, Co. provides mobile and online banking, a 24/7 customer contact center and automated teller machines. Consumer Banking products and services include banking, lending, savings, and wealth management. In Commercial Banking, Co. provides corporate, institutional and not-for-profit clients a range of wholesale banking products and services including lending and deposits, and capital markets.

Recent Developments: For the quarter ended Sep 30 2019, net income increased 1.4% to US$449.0 million from US$443.0 million in the year-earlier quarter. Net interest income was unchanged at US$1.15 billion versus the year-earlier quarter. Provision for loan losses was US$101.0 million versus US$78.0 million in the prior-year quarter, an increase of 29.5%. Non-interest income rose 18.5% to US$493.0 million from US$416.0 million, while non-interest expense advanced 6.9% to US$973.0 million.

Prospects: Our evaluation of Citizens Financial Group Inc as of October 4th, 2019 is the result of our systematic analysis on three basic characteristics: earnings strength, relative valuation, and recent stock price movement. The company has managed to produce a neutral trend in earnings per share over the past 5 quarters. However, recent analyst estimates for the company have been reduced while CFG has posted results that exceeded analysts' expectations. Based on operating earnings yield, the company is undervalued when compared to all of the companies we cover. Share price changes over the past year indicates that CFG will perform in line with the market over the near term.

Financial Data

(US$ in Thousands)	9 Mos	6 Mos	3 Mos	12/31/2018	12/31/2017	12/31/2016	12/31/2015	12/31/2014
Earnings Per Share	3.79	3.73	3.66	3.52	3.25	1.97	1.55	1.55
Cash Flow Per Share	3.43	2.03	3.33	3.69	3.75	2.85	2.29	2.50
Tang Book Value Per Share	30.80	30.23	28.97	28.01	26.76	24.66	23.73	22.70
Dividends Per Share	1.270	1.180	1.080	0.980	0.640	0.460	0.400	0.100
Dividend Payout %	33.51	31.64	29.51	27.84	19.69	23.35	25.81	6.45
Income Statement								
Interest Income	4,688,000	3,150,000	1,570,000	5,758,000	4,920,000	4,266,000	3,854,000	3,664,000
Interest Expense	1,217,000	824,000	410,000	1,226,000	747,000	508,000	452,000	363,000
Net Interest Income	3,471,000	2,326,000	1,160,000	4,532,000	4,173,000	3,758,000	3,402,000	3,301,000
Provision for Losses	283,000	182,000	85,000	326,000	321,000	369,000	302,000	319,000
Non-Interest Income	1,383,000	890,000	428,000	1,596,000	1,534,000	1,497,000	1,422,000	1,678,000
Non-Interest Expense	2,861,000	1,888,000	937,000	3,619,000	3,474,000	3,352,000	3,259,000	3,392,000
Income Before Taxes	1,710,000	1,146,000	566,000	2,183,000	1,912,000	1,534,000	1,263,000	1,268,000
Income Taxes	369,000	254,000	127,000	462,000	260,000	489,000	423,000	403,000
Net Income	1,341,000	892,000	439,000	1,721,000	1,652,000	1,045,000	840,000	865,000
Average Shares	447,134	459,304	462,520	480,430	503,685	523,930	538,220	557,724
Balance Sheet								
Net Loans & Leases	118,632,000	117,816,000	117,622,000	116,738,000	110,099,000	107,058,000	98,191,000	92,496,000
Total Assets	164,362,000	162,749,000	161,342,000	160,518,000	152,336,000	149,520,000	138,208,000	132,857,000
Total Deposits	124,714,000	124,004,000	123,916,000	119,575,000	115,089,000	109,804,000	102,539,000	95,707,000
Total Liabilities	142,511,000	140,732,000	139,811,000	139,701,000	132,066,000	129,773,000	118,562,000	113,589,000
Stockholders' Equity	21,851,000	22,017,000	21,531,000	20,817,000	20,270,000	19,747,000	19,646,000	19,268,000
Shares Outstanding	443,913	457,903	461,116	466,007	490,812	511,954	527,774	545,884
Statistical Record								
Return on Assets %	1.12	1.13	1.13	1.10	1.09	0.72	0.62	0.68
Return on Equity %	8.57	8.47	8.52	8.38	8.26	5.29	4.32	4.50
Net Interest Margin %	74.45	73.80	73.89	78.71	84.82	88.09	88.27	90.09
Efficiency Ratio %	47.91	46.57	46.90	49.21	53.83	58.16	61.77	63.50
Loans to Deposits	0.95	0.95	0.95	0.98	0.96	0.97	0.96	0.97
Price Range	39.23-27.94	41.50-27.94	43.24-27.94	47.87-27.94	42.63-32.08	36.46-18.14	28.32-22.63	25.51-21.80
P/E Ratio	10.35-7.37	11.13-7.49	11.81-7.63	13.60-7.94	13.12-9.87	18.51-9.21	18.27-14.60	16.46-14.06
Average Yield %	3.64	3.26	2.84	2.42	1.75	1.90	1.57	0.42

Address: One Citizens Plaza, Providence, RI 02903 **Telephone:** 401-456-7000 **Fax:** 401-455-5927	**Web Site:** www.citizensbank.com **Officers:** Bruce Van Saun - Chairman, Chief Executive Officer John F. Woods - Vice-Chairman, Executive Vice President, Chief Financial Officer	**Auditors:** DELOITTE & TOUCHE LLP **Transfer Agents:** Common Stock is Computershare Trust Company, N.A.

CLEAN HARBORS INC

Exchange	Symbol	Price	52Wk Range	Yield	P/E
NYS	CLH	$85.75 (12/31/2019)	86.86-49.35	N/A	53.26

*7 Year Price Score 105.65 *NYSE Composite Index=100 *12 Month Price Score 110.34

Interim Earnings (Per Share)

Qtr.	Mar	Jun	Sep	Dec
2016	(0.36)	0.07	(0.18)	(0.22)
2017	(0.37)	0.45	0.21	1.47
2018	(0.22)	0.54	0.55	0.29
2019	0.02	0.65	0.65	...

Interim Dividends (Per Share)

No Dividends Paid

Valuation Analysis | **Institutional Holding**

Forecast EPS	$1.93	No of Institutions
	(01/07/2020)	414
Market Cap	$4.8 Billion	Shares
Book Value	$1.2 Billion	65,682,028
Price/Book	3.87	% Held
Price/Sales	1.41	88.58

Business Summary: Sanitation Services (MIC: 7.5.3 SIC: 4953 NAIC: 562112)

Clean Harbors is a provider of environmental, energy and industrial services throughout North America. Co. collects, transports, treats and disposes of hazardous and non-hazardous waste, including resource recovery, physical treatment, fuel blending, incineration, landfill disposal, wastewater treatment, lab chemical disposal, explosives management and CleanPack® services. Co.'s Safety-Kleen business provides an array of environmental services and complementary products to a range of customers including automobile repair shops, car and truck dealers, metal fabricators, machine manufacturers, fleet maintenance shops and other automotive, industrial and retail customers.

Recent Developments: For the quarter ended Sep 30 2019, net income increased 17.0% to US$36.4 million from US$31.1 million in the year-earlier quarter. Revenues were US$891.7 million, up 5.8% from US$843.2 million the year before. Operating income was US$80.4 million versus US$65.7 million in the prior-year quarter, an increase of 22.2%. Direct operating expenses rose 5.5% to US$612.8 million from US$580.7 million in the comparable period the year before. Indirect operating expenses increased 0.9% to US$198.5 million from US$196.8 million in the equivalent prior-year period.

Prospects: Our evaluation of Clean Harbors Inc. as of October 4th, 2019 is the result of our systematic analysis on three basic characteristics: earnings strength, relative valuation, and recent stock price movement. The company has generated a negative trend in earnings per share over the past 5 quarters. However, recent analyst estimates for the company have been mixed and CLH has posted results that exceeded analysts' expectations. Based on operating earnings yield, the company is overvalued when compared to all of the companies we cover. Share price changes over the past year indicates that CLH will perform in line with the market over the near term.

Financial Data

(US$ in Thousands)	9 Mos	6 Mos	3 Mos	12/31/2018	12/31/2017	12/31/2016	12/31/2015	12/31/2014
Earnings Per Share	1.61	1.51	1.40	1.16	1.76	(0.69)	0.76	(0.47)
Cash Flow Per Share	7.35	6.84	6.29	6.65	5.01	4.50	6.80	4.93
Tang Book Value Per Share	5.11	4.49	3.85	3.83	4.26	2.10	2.37	4.76
Income Statement								
Total Revenue	2,541,185	1,649,517	780,839	3,300,303	2,944,978	2,755,226	3,275,137	3,401,636
EBITDA	372,630	232,601	93,617	439,876	395,897	339,241	420,199	355,590
Depn & Amortn	199,608	133,400	66,900	264,300	251,400	247,000	234,000	239,400
Income Before Taxes	113,341	59,222	6,953	94,482	58,689	8,716	109,646	38,522
Income Taxes	39,752	22,002	5,977	28,846	(42,050)	48,589	65,544	66,850
Net Income	73,589	37,220	976	65,636	100,739	(39,873)	44,102	(28,328)
Average Shares	56,165	56,066	56,082	56,340	57,200	57,532	58,434	60,311
Balance Sheet								
Current Assets	1,300,584	1,213,186	1,148,122	1,202,158	1,154,056	1,092,871	921,196	1,126,433
Total Assets	4,021,862	3,955,321	3,882,054	3,738,321	3,706,570	3,681,920	3,431,428	3,704,278
Current Liabilities	680,042	633,690	597,510	602,278	503,817	504,668	517,120	572,471
Long-Term Obligations	1,555,257	1,562,989	1,564,005	1,565,021	1,625,537	1,633,272	1,382,543	1,395,000
Total Liabilities	2,786,067	2,745,854	2,710,089	2,568,565	2,518,368	2,597,679	2,335,146	2,441,407
Stockholders' Equity	1,235,795	1,209,467	1,171,965	1,169,756	1,188,202	1,084,241	1,096,282	1,262,871
Shares Outstanding	55,807	55,859	55,827	55,847	56,501	57,297	57,593	58,903
Statistical Record								
Return on Assets %	2.31	2.21	2.09	1.76	2.73	N.M.	1.24	N.M.
Return on Equity %	7.40	7.15	6.84	5.57	8.87	N.M.	3.74	N.M.
EBITDA Margin %	14.66	14.10	11.99	13.33	13.44	12.31	12.83	10.45
Net Margin %	2.90	2.26	0.12	1.99	3.42	N.M.	1.35	N.M.
Asset Turnover	0.87	0.87	0.88	0.89	0.80	0.77	0.92	0.89
Current Ratio	1.91	1.91	1.92	2.00	2.29	2.17	1.78	1.97
Debt to Equity	1.26	1.29	1.33	1.34	1.37	1.51	1.26	1.10
Price Range	78.07-46.83	76.00-46.83	72.04-45.45	72.03-45.45	61.33-49.98	57.78-39.35	58.87-40.22	64.51-44.98
P/E Ratio	48.49-29.09	50.33-31.01	51.46-32.46	62.09-39.18	34.85-28.40	...	77.46-52.92	...

Address: 42 Longwater Drive, Norwell, MA 02061-9149
Telephone: 781-792-5000

Web Site: www.cleanharbors.com
Officers: Alan S. McKim - Chairman, President, Chief Executive Officer Michael Louis Battles - Executive Vice President, Chief Financial Officer, Chief Accounting Officer, Corporate Controller, Senior Vice President

Auditors: DELOITTE & TOUCHE LLP
Investor Contact: 617-542-5300
Transfer Agents: American Stock Transfer & Trust Company, New York, NY

CLOROX CO (THE)

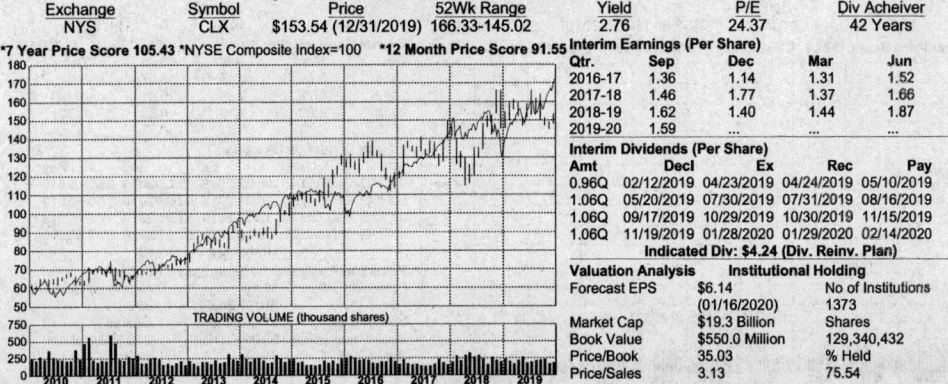

Exchange	Symbol	Price	52Wk Range	Yield	P/E	Div Acheiver
NYS	CLX	$153.54 (12/31/2019)	166.33-145.02	2.76	24.37	42 Years

*7 Year Price Score 105.43 *NYSE Composite Index=100 *12 Month Price Score 91.55

Interim Earnings (Per Share)

Qtr.	Sep	Dec	Mar	Jun
2016-17	1.36	1.14	1.31	1.52
2017-18	1.46	1.77	1.37	1.66
2018-19	1.62	1.40	1.44	1.87
2019-20	1.59	...	...	...

Interim Dividends (Per Share)

Amt	Decl	Ex	Rec	Pay
0.96Q	02/12/2019	04/23/2019	04/24/2019	05/10/2019
1.06Q	05/20/2019	07/30/2019	07/31/2019	08/16/2019
1.06Q	09/17/2019	10/29/2019	10/30/2019	11/15/2019
1.06Q	11/19/2019	01/28/2020	01/29/2020	02/14/2020

Indicated Div: $4.24 (Div. Reinv. Plan)

Valuation Analysis

		Institutional Holding	
Forecast EPS	$6.14	No of Institutions	
	(01/16/2020)	1373	
Market Cap	$19.3 Billion	Shares	
Book Value	$550.0 Million	129,340,432	
Price/Book	35.03	% Held	
Price/Sales	3.13	75.54	

Business Summary: Household & Personal Products (MIC: 1.7.1 SIC: 2842 NAIC: 325612)

Clorox is a manufacturer and marketer of consumer products. Co. sells its products through mass retailers, grocery outlets, warehouse clubs, dollar stores, home hardware centers, drug, pet and military stores, third-party and owned e-commerce channels, and distributors. Co. has four reportable segments: Cleaning, which consists of laundry, home care and other products; Household, which consists of charcoal, bags, wraps and containers, cat litter, and digestive health products; Lifestyle, which consists of food products, water-filtration systems and filters, natural personal care products, and dietary supplements; and International, which consists of products sold outside the United States.

Recent Developments: For the quarter ended Sep 30 2019, net income decreased 3.3% to US$203.0 million from US$210.0 million in the year-earlier quarter. Revenues were US$1.51 billion, down 3.6% from US$1.56 billion the year before. Direct operating expenses declined 4.7% to US$843.0 million from US$885.0 million in the comparable period the year before. Indirect operating expenses decreased 1.2% to US$405.0 million from US$410.0 million in the equivalent prior-year period.

Prospects: Our evaluation of Clorox Co. as of October 4th, 2019 is the result of our systematic analysis on three basic characteristics: earnings strength, relative valuation, and recent stock price movement. The company has managed to produce a neutral trend in earnings per share over the past 5 quarters. However, recent analyst estimates for the company have been reduced while CLX has posted results that exceeded analysts' expectations. Based on operating earnings yield, the company is fairly valued when compared to all of the companies we cover. Share price changes over the past year indicates that CLX will perform over the near term.

Financial Data
(US$ in Thousands)

	3 Mos	06/30/2019	06/30/2018	06/30/2017	06/30/2016	06/30/2015	06/30/2014	06/30/2013
Earnings Per Share	6.30	6.32	6.26	5.33	4.92	4.37	4.23	4.30
Cash Flow Per Share	7.98	7.77	7.53	6.73	5.99	6.71	5.92	5.91
Dividends Per Share	3.940	3.840	3.480	3.200	3.080	2.960	2.840	2.560
Dividend Payout %	62.54	60.76	55.59	60.04	62.60	67.73	67.14	59.53
Income Statement								
Total Revenue	1,506,000	6,214,000	6,124,000	5,973,000	5,761,000	5,655,000	5,591,000	5,623,000
EBITDA	327,000	1,285,000	1,288,000	1,261,000	1,216,000	1,154,000	1,116,000	1,124,000
Depn & Amortn	44,000	182,000	167,000	163,000	165,000	165,000	169,000	171,000
Income Before Taxes	258,000	1,009,000	1,042,000	1,014,000	968,000	893,000	847,000	834,000
Income Taxes	55,000	204,000	231,000	330,000	335,000	315,000	299,000	279,000
Net Income	203,000	820,000	823,000	701,000	648,000	580,000	558,000	572,000
Average Shares	127,465	129,792	131,581	131,566	131,717	132,776	131,742	132,969
Balance Sheet								
Current Assets	1,266,000	1,305,000	1,311,000	1,514,000	1,485,000	1,429,000	1,395,000	1,420,000
Total Assets	5,397,000	5,116,000	5,060,000	4,573,000	4,518,000	4,164,000	4,258,000	4,311,000
Current Liabilities	1,458,000	1,440,000	1,200,000	1,809,000	1,558,000	1,405,000	1,638,000	1,134,000
Long-Term Obligations	2,287,000	2,287,000	2,284,000	1,391,000	1,797,000	1,796,000	1,595,000	2,170,000
Total Liabilities	4,847,000	4,557,000	4,334,000	4,031,000	4,221,000	4,046,000	4,104,000	4,165,000
Stockholders' Equity	550,000	559,000	726,000	542,000	297,000	118,000	154,000	146,000
Shares Outstanding	125,495	125,686	127,982	129,014	129,355	128,614	128,796	130,366
Statistical Record								
Return on Assets %	15.55	16.12	17.09	15.42	14.89	13.77	13.02	13.20
Return on Equity %	132.52	127.63	129.81	167.10	311.44	426.47	372.00	10,400.00
EBITDA Margin %	21.71	20.68	21.03	21.11	21.11	20.41	19.96	19.99
Net Margin %	13.48	13.20	13.44	11.74	11.25	10.26	9.98	10.17
Asset Turnover	1.18	1.22	1.27	1.31	1.32	1.34	1.30	1.30
Current Ratio	0.87	0.91	1.09	0.84	0.95	1.02	0.85	1.25
Debt to Equity	4.16	4.09	3.15	2.57	6.05	15.22	10.36	14.86
Price Range	166.36-142.18	166.36-129.53	149.69-114.80	141.15-112.25	138.39-104.02	111.93-86.39	95.83-81.49	89.53-70.10
P/E Ratio	26.41-22.57	26.32-20.50	23.91-18.34	26.48-21.06	28.13-21.14	25.61-19.77	22.65-19.26	20.82-16.30
Average Yield %	2.53	2.54	2.64	2.49	2.50	2.91	3.23	3.27

Address: 1221 Broadway, Oakland, CA 94612-1888 **Telephone:** 510-271-7000	**Web Site:** www.thecloroxcompany.com **Officers:** Benno O. Dorer - Chairman, Chief Executive Officer, Executive Vice President, Senior Vice President, Division Officer Jon M. Balousek - Executive Vice President, Senior Vice President, Division Officer	**Auditors:** Ernst & Young LLP **Transfer Agents:** Computershare, Providence, RI

CMS ENERGY CORP

Exchange	Symbol	Price	52Wk Range	Yield	P/E	Div Acheiver
NYS	CMS	$62.84 (12/31/2019)	65.04-48.31	2.59	28.69	11 Years

*7 Year Price Score 117.64   *NYSE Composite Index=100   *12 Month Price Score 100.65

Interim Earnings (Per Share)

Qtr.	Mar	Jun	Sep	Dec
2016	0.59	0.45	0.67	0.28
2017	0.71	0.33	0.61	(0.01)
2018	0.86	0.49	0.59	0.38
2019	0.75	0.33	0.73	...

Interim Dividends (Per Share)

Amt	Decl	Ex	Rec	Pay
0.383Q	04/18/2019	05/02/2019	05/03/2019	05/31/2019
0.383Q	07/18/2019	08/01/2019	08/02/2019	08/30/2019
0.383Q	10/17/2019	10/31/2019	11/01/2019	11/27/2019
0.407Q	01/16/2020	02/06/2020	02/07/2020	02/28/2020

Indicated Div: $1.63

Valuation Analysis

		Institutional Holding	
Forecast EPS	$2.49	No of Institutions	
	(01/17/2020)	822	
Market Cap	$17.8 Billion	Shares	
Book Value	$5.0 Billion	333,578,016	
Price/Book	3.60	% Held	
Price/Sales	2.59	93.05	

Business Summary: Electric Utilities (MIC: 3.1.1 SIC: 4931 NAIC: 221119)

CMS Energy is a holding company. Co. has several subsidiaries, including Consumers Energy Company (Consumers), an electric and gas utility, and CMS Enterprises Company (CMS Enterprises), primarily a domestic independent power producer and marketer. Consumers serves individuals and businesses operating in the alternative energy, automotive, chemical, food, and metal products industries, as well as a diversified group of other industries. CMS Enterprises, through its subsidiaries and equity investments, is engaged in domestic independent power production, including the development and operation of renewable generation, and the marketing of independent power production.

Recent Developments: For the quarter ended Sep 30 2019, net income increased 22.5% to US$207.0 million from US$169.0 million in the year-earlier quarter. Revenues were US$1.55 billion, down 3.3% from US$1.60 billion the year before. Operating income was US$351.0 million versus US$294.0 million in the prior-year quarter, an increase of 19.4%. Direct operating expenses declined 11.8% to US$910.0 million from US$1.03 billion in the comparable period the year before. Indirect operating expenses increased 4.4% to US$285.0 million from US$273.0 million in the equivalent prior-year period.

Prospects: Our evaluation of CMS Energy Corp. as of October 4th, 2019 is the result of our systematic analysis on three basic characteristics: earnings strength, relative valuation, and recent stock price movement. The company has enjoyed a very positive trend in earnings per share over the past 5 quarters. However, recent analyst estimates for the company have been mixed and CMS has posted results that fell short of analysts' expectations. Based on operating earnings yield, the company is fairly valued when compared to all of the companies we cover. Share price changes over the past year indicates that CMS will perform well over the near term.

Financial Data

(US$ in Millions)	9 Mos	6 Mos	3 Mos	12/31/2018	12/31/2017	12/31/2016	12/31/2015	12/31/2014
Earnings Per Share	2.19	2.05	2.21	2.32	1.64	1.98	1.89	1.74
Cash Flow Per Share	5.42	5.20	5.70	6.03	6.09	5.85	5.95	5.35
Tang Book Value Per Share	17.47	17.09	17.12	16.78	15.77	15.23	14.21	13.34
Dividends Per Share	1.505	1.480	1.455	1.430	1.330	1.240	1.160	1.080
Dividend Payout %	68.72	72.20	65.84	61.64	81.10	62.63	61.38	62.07
Income Statement								
Total Revenue	5,050	3,504	2,059	6,873	6,583	6,399	6,456	7,179
EBITDA	1,730	1,139	681	1,990	2,178	2,053	1,916	1,801
Depn & Amortn	729	514	298	778	881	811	750	685
Income Before Taxes	618	374	262	765	871	813	782	714
Income Taxes	110	68	48	115	424	273	271	250
Net Income	513	306	213	657	460	551	523	477
Average Shares	284	284	283	282	280	278	276	274
Balance Sheet								
Current Assets	2,305	2,254	2,376	2,468	2,475	2,280	2,320	2,597
Total Assets	26,009	25,292	24,793	24,529	23,050	21,622	20,340	19,185
Current Liabilities	2,165	2,386	2,106	2,624	2,784	2,655	2,302	2,014
Long-Term Obligations	12,121	11,322	11,196	10,684	9,214	8,750	8,559	8,139
Total Liabilities	21,052	20,441	19,935	19,774	18,609	17,369	16,402	15,515
Stockholders' Equity	4,957	4,851	4,858	4,755	4,441	4,253	3,938	3,670
Shares Outstanding	283	283	283	283	281	279	277	275
Statistical Record								
Return on Assets %	2.49	2.40	2.64	2.76	2.06	2.62	2.65	2.61
Return on Equity %	12.80	12.24	13.31	14.29	10.58	13.42	13.75	13.39
EBITDA Margin %	34.26	32.51	33.07	28.95	33.09	32.08	29.68	25.09
Net Margin %	10.16	8.73	10.34	9.56	6.99	8.61	8.10	6.64
Asset Turnover	0.28	0.29	0.29	0.29	0.29	0.30	0.33	0.39
Current Ratio	1.06	0.94	1.13	0.94	0.89	0.86	1.01	1.29
Debt to Equity	2.45	2.33	2.30	2.25	2.07	2.06	2.17	2.22
Price Range	65.04-48.14	59.15-46.78	56.23-42.63	53.48-41.77	50.55-41.51	46.17-35.61	38.20-31.39	36.42-26.12
P/E Ratio	29.70-21.98	28.85-22.82	25.44-19.29	23.05-18.00	30.82-25.31	23.32-17.98	20.21-16.61	20.93-15.01
Average Yield %	2.73	2.85	2.95	3.04	2.87	2.99	3.35	3.60

Address: One Energy Plaza, Jackson, MI 49201 **Telephone:** 517-788-0550	**Web Site:** www.cmsenergy.com **Officers:** John G. Russell - Chairman, President, Chief Executive Officer Patricia K. Poppe - President, Chief Executive Officer, Division Officer, Principal Executive Officer	**Auditors:** PricewaterhouseCoopers LLP **Investor Contact:** 517-788-1868 **Transfer Agents:** Investor Services Department, Jackson, MI

CNA FINANCIAL CORP

Exchange	Symbol	Price	52Wk Range	Yield	P/E
NYS	CNA	$44.81 (12/31/2019)	49.89-42.35	3.12	19.07

*7 Year Price Score 91.60 *NYSE Composite Index=100 *12 Month Price Score 91.86

Interim Earnings (Per Share)

Qtr.	Mar	Jun	Sep	Dec
2016	0.25	0.77	1.26	0.89
2017	0.96	1.00	0.53	0.82
2018	1.07	0.99	1.23	(0.31)
2019	1.25	1.02	0.39	...

Interim Dividends (Per Share)

Amt	Decl	Ex	Rec	Pay
0.35Q	02/11/2019	02/22/2019	02/25/2019	03/14/2019
0.35Q	04/29/2019	05/10/2019	05/13/2019	05/30/2019
0.35Q	08/02/2019	08/16/2019	08/19/2019	09/05/2019
0.35Q	10/25/2019	11/07/2019	11/11/2019	12/02/2019

Indicated Div: $1.40

Valuation Analysis / Institutional Holding

Forecast EPS	$3.55	No of Institutions
	(01/16/2020)	298
Market Cap	$12.2 Billion	Shares
Book Value	$12.1 Billion	275,198,080
Price/Book	1.00	% Held
Price/Sales	1.17	99.21

Business Summary: General Insurance (MIC: 5.2.1 SIC: 6331 NAIC: 524126)

CNA Financial is an insurance holding company. Co.'s insurance products primarily include commercial property and casualty coverages, including surety. Co.'s services include warranty, risk management information services and claims administration. Co.'s products and services are primarily marketed through independent agents, brokers and managing general underwriters to a variety of customers. Co.'s commercial property and casualty insurance operations are reported in three business segments: Specialty, Commercial and International. Co.'s operations outside of Property & Casualty Operations are reported in two business segments: Life & Group and Corporate & Other.

Recent Developments: For the quarter ended Sep 30 2019, net income decreased 68.2% to US$107.0 million from US$336.0 million in the year-earlier quarter. Revenues were US$2.69 billion, up 2.4% from US$2.62 billion the year before. Net premiums earned were US$1.89 billion versus US$1.85 billion in the prior-year quarter, an increase of 2.0%. Net investment income was unchanged at US$487.0 million versus a year ago.

Prospects: Our evaluation of CNA Financial Corp. as of October 4th, 2019 is the result of our systematic analysis on three basic characteristics: earnings strength, relative valuation, and recent stock price movement. The company has produced a positive trend in earnings per share over the past 5 quarters. However, recent analyst estimates for the company have been mixed and CNA has posted results that exceeded analysts' expectations. Based on operating earnings yield, the company is undervalued when compared to all of the companies we cover. Share price changes over the past year indicates that CNA will perform well over the near term.

Financial Data

(US$ in Thousands)	9 Mos	6 Mos	3 Mos	12/31/2018	12/31/2017	12/31/2016	12/31/2015	12/31/2014
Earnings Per Share	2.35	3.19	3.16	2.98	3.30	3.17	1.77	2.55
Cash Flow Per Share	4.93	5.11	4.77	4.52	4.63	5.22	5.13	5.34
Tang Book Value Per Share	44.12	43.99	41.65	40.78	44.60	43.71	42.94	46.83
Dividends Per Share	3.400	3.400	3.350	3.300	3.100	3.000	3.000	2.000
Dividend Payout %	144.68	106.58	106.01	110.74	93.94	94.64	169.49	78.43
Income Statement								
Premium Income	5,517,000	3,627,000	1,803,000	7,312,000	6,988,000	6,924,000	6,921,000	7,212,000
Total Revenue	7,990,000	5,305,000	2,695,000	10,134,000	9,542,000	9,366,000	9,101,000	9,692,000
Benefits & Claims	...	...	...	5,572,000	5,310,000	5,283,000	5,384,000	5,591,000
Income Before Taxes	888,000	761,000	419,000	964,000	1,310,000	1,137,000	549,000	1,207,000
Income Taxes	161,000	141,000	77,000	151,000	411,000	278,000	70,000	319,000
Net Income	727,000	620,000	342,000	813,000	899,000	859,000	479,000	691,000
Average Shares	272,600	272,400	272,600	272,500	272,100	271,100	270,700	270,600
Balance Sheet								
Total Assets	60,450,000	59,963,000	58,477,000	57,152,000	56,567,000	55,233,000	55,047,000	55,566,000
Total Liabilities	48,327,000	47,876,000	47,022,000	45,935,000	44,323,000	43,264,000	43,291,000	42,772,000
Stockholders' Equity	12,123,000	12,087,000	11,455,000	11,217,000	12,244,000	11,969,000	11,756,000	12,794,000
Shares Outstanding	271,478	271,456	271,527	271,456	271,205	270,495	270,274	269,980
Statistical Record								
Return on Assets %	1.09	1.48	1.49	1.43	1.61	1.55	0.87	1.23
Return on Equity %	5.44	7.42	7.55	6.93	7.43	7.22	3.90	5.43
Loss Ratio %	...	...	...	76.20	75.99	76.30	77.79	77.52
Net Margin %	9.10	11.69	12.69	8.02	9.42	9.17	5.26	7.13
Price Range	49.89-42.04	48.61-42.04	50.47-42.04	55.08-42.04	54.98-40.21	42.07-28.21	43.40-34.24	43.08-36.29
P/E Ratio	21.23-17.89	15.24-13.18	15.97-13.30	18.48-14.11	16.66-12.18	13.27-8.90	24.52-19.34	16.89-14.23
Average Yield %	7.44	7.51	7.29	6.88	6.49	8.96	7.82	5.01

Address: 151 N. Franklin, Chicago, IL 60606	**Web Site:** www.cna.com	**Auditors:** DELOITTE & TOUCHE LLP
Telephone: 312-822-5000	**Officers:** Dino E. Robusto - Chairman, Chief Executive Officer James Michael Anderson - Chief	**Investor Contact:** 312-822-4278
Fax: 312-822-6419	Financial Officer, Executive Vice President, Senior Vice President, Head	**Transfer Agents:** Wells Fargo Bank, N.A., St. Paul, MN

CNO FINANCIAL GROUP INC

Exchange	Symbol	Price	52Wk Range	Yield	P/E
NYS	CNO	$18.13 (12/31/2019)	19.18-14.09	2.43	18.13

*7 Year Price Score 76.28   *NYSE Composite Index=100   *12 Month Price Score 101.58

Interim Earnings (Per Share)

Qtr.	Mar	Jun	Sep	Dec
2016	0.25	0.34	0.11	1.32
2017	0.36	0.48	0.59	(0.41)
2018	0.50	0.61	(3.22)	0.17
2019	0.32	0.24	0.27	...

Interim Dividends (Per Share)

Amt	Decl	Ex	Rec	Pay
0.10Q	02/20/2019	03/08/2019	03/11/2019	03/25/2019
0.11Q	05/10/2019	06/07/2019	06/10/2019	06/24/2019
0.11Q	08/07/2019	09/09/2019	09/10/2019	09/24/2019
0.11Q	11/14/2019	12/09/2019	12/10/2019	12/24/2019

Indicated Div: $0.44

Valuation Analysis

		Institutional Holding	
Forecast EPS	$1.81	No of Institutions	371
	(01/17/2020)	Shares	
Market Cap	$2.8 Billion	212,425,168	
Book Value	$4.6 Billion	% Held	N/A
Price/Book	0.61		
Price/Sales	0.74		

Business Summary: Life & Health (MIC: 5.2.2 SIC: 6321 NAIC: 524114)

CNO Financial Group is a holding company for a group of insurance companies that develop, market and administer health insurance, annuity, individual life insurance and other insurance products. Co. focuses on serving middle-income pre-retiree and retired Americans. Co.'s segments are: Bankers Life, which markets and distributes Medicare supplement insurance, interest-sensitive life insurance, life insurance, fixed annuities and long-term care insurance products; Washington National, which underwrites and markets supplemental health (including accident insurance products) and life insurance; and Colonial Penn, which markets mainly graded benefit and simplified issue life insurance.

Recent Developments: For the quarter ended Sep 30 2019, net income amounted to US$42.0 million versus a net loss of US$529.8 million in the year-earlier quarter. Revenues were US$944.0 million, down 36.3% from US$1.48 billion the year before. Net premiums earned were US$620.0 million versus US$656.9 million in the prior-year quarter, a decrease of 5.6%.

Prospects: Our evaluation of CNO Financial Group Inc. as of October 4th, 2019 is the result of our systematic analysis on three basic characteristics: earnings strength, relative valuation, and recent stock price movement. The company has produced a positive trend in earnings per share over the past 5 quarters. However, recent analyst estimates for the company have been unchanged, and CNO has posted results in line with analysts' expectations. Based on operating earnings yield, the company is undervalued when compared to all of the companies we cover. Share price changes over the past year indicates that CNO will perform poorly over the near term.

Financial Data

(US$ in Thousands)	9 Mos	6 Mos	3 Mos	12/31/2018	12/31/2017	12/31/2016	12/31/2015	12/31/2014
Earnings Per Share	1.00	(2.49)	(2.12)	(1.90)	1.02	2.01	1.39	0.24
Cash Flow Per Share	4.63	2.47	2.41	1.92	3.61	4.29	3.85	0.57
Tang Book Value Per Share	29.92	27.12	23.99	20.78	29.05	25.82	22.49	23.06
Dividends Per Share	0.420	0.410	0.400	0.390	0.350	0.310	0.270	0.240
Dividend Payout %	42.00	...	...	...	34.31	15.42	19.42	100.00
Income Statement								
Premium Income	1,857,600	1,237,600	619,300	2,593,100	2,647,300	2,601,100	2,556,000	2,629,700
Total Revenue	2,946,800	2,002,800	1,023,000	4,313,500	4,297,200	3,985,100	3,811,900	4,144,700
Benefits & Claims	1,816,700	1,233,900	623,500	2,278,600	2,602,700	2,390,500	2,308,300	2,586,200
Income Before Taxes	166,800	113,300	65,600	(264,800)	480,500	353,200	367,700	175,100
Income Taxes	35,400	23,900	13,800	50,200	304,900	(5,000)	97,000	123,700
Net Income	131,400	89,400	51,800	(315,000)	175,600	358,200	270,700	51,400
Average Shares	155,260	159,735	162,189	165,457	172,144	178,323	195,166	217,655
Balance Sheet								
Total Assets	33,279,800	32,716,000	32,314,400	31,439,800	33,110,300	31,975,200	31,125,100	31,184,200
Total Liabilities	28,726,500	28,463,800	28,476,500	28,068,900	28,262,800	27,488,300	26,986,600	26,496,000
Stockholders' Equity	4,553,300	4,252,200	3,837,900	3,370,900	4,847,500	4,486,900	4,138,500	4,688,200
Shares Outstanding	152,183	156,768	159,955	162,201	166,857	173,753	184,028	203,324
Statistical Record								
Return on Assets %	0.49	N.M.	N.M.	N.M.	0.54	1.13	0.87	0.16
Return on Equity %	3.91	N.M.	N.M.	N.M.	3.76	8.28	6.13	1.07
Loss Ratio %	97.80	99.70	100.68	87.87	98.32	91.90	90.31	98.35
Net Margin %	4.46	4.46	5.06	(7.30)	4.09	8.99	7.10	1.24
Price Range	21.65-13.83	22.26-13.83	22.73-13.83	26.38-13.83	25.50-18.73	20.39-15.00	20.77-14.99	19.15-15.57
P/E Ratio	21.65-13.83	...	...	...	25.00-18.36	10.14-7.46	14.94-10.78	79.79-64.88
Average Yield %	2.49	2.25	2.08	1.87	1.60	1.78	1.49	1.38

Address: 11825 N. Pennsylvania Street, Carmel, IN 46032 **Telephone:** 317-817-6100	**Web Site:** www.cnoinc.com **Officers:** Gary C. Bhojwani - President, Chief Executive Officer Bruce K. Baude - Executive Vice President, Chief Operating Officer, Chief Technology Officer	**Auditors:** PricewaterhouseCoopers LLP **Investor Contact:** 317-817-2893 **Transfer Agents:** American Stock Transfer & Trust Company, Brooklyn, NY

CNX RESOURCES CORP

Exchange	Symbol	Price	52Wk Range	Yield	P/E
NYS	CNX	$8.85 (12/31/2019)	13.53-6.19	N/A	5.75

*7 Year Price Score 39.76   ***NYSE Composite Index=100**   ***12 Month Price Score 85.12**

TRADING VOLUME (thousand shares)

Interim Earnings (Per Share)

Qtr.	Mar	Jun	Sep	Dec
2016	(0.43)	(2.05)	0.11	(1.34)
2017	(0.17)	0.73	(0.11)	1.20
2018	2.35	0.19	0.59	0.53
2019	(0.44)	0.84	0.61	...

Interim Dividends (Per Share)

Dividend Payment Suspended

Valuation Analysis

		Institutional Holding	
Forecast EPS	$0.66	No of Institutions	
	(01/15/2020)	443	
Market Cap	$1.7 Billion	Shares	
Book Value	$4.4 Billion	229,152,720	
Price/Book	0.37	% Held	
Price/Sales	0.89	N/A	

Business Summary: Production & Extraction (MIC: 9.1.1 SIC: 1311 NAIC: 211111)

CNX Resources is an oil and natural gas company. Co. is focused on the exploration, development, production, gathering, processing and acquisition of natural gas properties in the Appalachian Basin. Co.'s operations are centered on unconventional shale formations, primarily the Marcellus Shale and Utica Shale. Co. operates, develops and explores for natural gas in Appalachia (Pennsylvania, West Virginia, Ohio, and Virginia).

Recent Developments: For the quarter ended Sep 30 2019, net income decreased 1.9% to US$144.0 million from US$146.8 million in the year-earlier quarter. Revenues were US$530.0 million, up 33.5% from US$397.1 million the year before. Direct operating expenses rose 24.2% to US$128.0 million from US$103.1 million in the comparable period the year before. Indirect operating expenses decreased 1.2% to US$170.6 million from US$172.7 million in the equivalent prior-year period.

Prospects: Our evaluation of CNX Resources Corp. as of October 4th, 2019 is the result of our systematic analysis on three basic characteristics: earnings strength, relative valuation, and recent stock price movement. The company has suffered a very negative trend in earnings per share over the past 5 quarters. In addition, recent analyst estimates for the company have been reduced while CNX has posted results that exceeded analysts' expectations. Based on operating earnings yield, the company is undervalued when compared to all of the companies we cover. Share price changes over the past year indicates that CNX will perform poorly over the near term.

Financial Data

(US$ in Thousands)	9 Mos	6 Mos	3 Mos	12/31/2018	12/31/2017	12/31/2016	12/31/2015	12/31/2014
Earnings Per Share	1.54	1.52	0.87	3.71	1.65	(3.70)	(1.64)	0.70
Cash Flow Per Share	5.66	5.20	4.74	4.17	2.83	2.04	2.21	4.07
Tang Book Value Per Share	18.97	18.28	16.92	17.27	17.43	16.55	20.53	23.14
Dividends Per Share	...	...	...	...	...	0.010	0.145	0.250
Dividend Payout %	...	...	...	...	...	...	...	35.71
Income Statement								
Total Revenue	1,413,460	883,463	278,431	1,730,434	1,455,131	2,026,375	3,114,401	3,726,804
EBITDA	470,522	237,606	(38,732)	1,122,723	692,060	264,024	349,970	977,879
Depn & Amortn	6,057	4,408	1,707	501,784	412,036	598,503	649,601	571,191
Income Before Taxes	350,137	157,275	(76,210)	475,005	118,581	(525,955)	(498,900)	183,124
Income Taxes	78,133	29,231	(11,559)	215,557	(176,458)	10,010	(134,425)	14,347
Net Income	190,679	75,140	(87,337)	796,533	380,747	(848,102)	(374,885)	163,090
Average Shares	188,430	192,780	197,475	214,628	230,951	229,387	229,186	231,580
Balance Sheet								
Current Assets	345,726	460,094	364,966	501,686	852,504	626,139	804,763	1,166,350
Total Assets	9,286,258	9,146,697	8,777,361	8,592,170	6,931,913	9,183,981	10,929,902	11,759,530
Current Liabilities	621,624	623,245	588,495	522,975	441,679	940,014	1,680,937	1,147,961
Long-Term Obligations	2,649,634	2,628,944	2,442,764	2,391,504	2,207,373	2,762,069	2,748,205	3,275,878
Total Liabilities	4,851,279	4,821,041	4,561,848	4,262,212	3,032,014	5,385,586	6,227,875	6,430,072
Stockholders' Equity	4,434,979	4,325,656	4,215,513	4,329,958	3,899,899	3,798,395	4,702,027	5,329,458
Shares Outstanding	186,586	187,559	196,052	198,663	223,743	229,443	229,054	230,265
Statistical Record								
Return on Assets %	3.34	3.48	2.15	10.26	4.73	N.M.	N.M.	1.41
Return on Equity %	6.69	7.00	4.24	19.36	9.89	N.M.	N.M.	3.16
EBITDA Margin %	33.29	26.89	N.M.	64.88	47.56	13.03	11.24	26.24
Net Margin %	13.49	8.51	N.M.	46.03	26.17	N.M.	N.M.	4.38
Asset Turnover	0.21	0.20	0.18	0.22	0.18	0.20	0.27	0.32
Current Ratio	0.56	0.74	0.62	0.96	1.93	0.67	0.48	1.02
Debt to Equity	0.60	0.61	0.58	0.55	0.57	0.73	0.58	0.61
Price Range	15.85-6.19	17.98-6.83	17.98-9.78	17.98-10.92	16.30-11.35	18.39-4.16	28.64-5.42	39.58-26.80
P/E Ratio	10.29-4.02	11.83-4.49	20.67-11.24	4.85-2.94	9.88-6.88	...	...	56.54-38.28
Average Yield %	...	...	...	...	...	0.08	0.85	0.75

Address: CNX Center, 1000 CONSOL Energy Drive, Suite 400, Canonsburg, PA 15317-6506 **Telephone:** 724-485-4000	**Web Site:** www.cnx.com **Officers:** William N. Thorndike - Chairman Nicholas J. DeIuliis - President, Chief Executive Officer, Executive Vice President, Chief Operating Officer	**Auditors:** Ernst & Young LLP **Investor Contact:** 724-485-3157 **Transfer Agents:** ComputerShare, College Station, TX

COCA-COLA CO (THE)

Exchange	Symbol	Price	52Wk Range	Yield	P/E	Div Acheiver
NYS	KO	$55.35 (12/31/2019)	55.77-44.69	2.89	30.58	56 Years

*7 Year Price Score 96.02 *NYSE Composite Index=100 *12 Month Price Score 99.91

Interim Earnings (Per Share)

Qtr.	Mar	Jun	Sep	Dec
2016	0.34	0.79	0.24	0.12
2017	0.27	0.32	0.33	(0.63)
2018	0.32	0.54	0.44	0.21
2019	0.39	0.61	0.60	...

Interim Dividends (Per Share)

Amt	Decl	Ex	Rec	Pay
0.40Q	02/21/2019	03/14/2019	03/15/2019	04/01/2019
0.40Q	04/25/2019	06/13/2019	06/14/2019	07/01/2019
0.40Q	07/18/2019	09/13/2019	09/16/2019	10/01/2019
0.40Q	10/17/2019	11/29/2019	12/02/2019	12/16/2019

Indicated Div: $1.60 (Div. Reinv. Plan)

Valuation Analysis

		Institutional Holding	
Forecast EPS	$2.10	No of Institutions	
	(01/17/2020)	2945	
Market Cap	$237.1 Billion	Shares	
Book Value	$18.7 Billion	3,444,001,536	
Price/Book	12.67	% Held	
Price/Sales	6.86	67.90	

Business Summary: Beverages (MIC: 1.2.2 SIC: 2086 NAIC: 312111)

Coca-Cola is a nonalcoholic beverage company. Co. owns or licenses and markets nonalcoholic beverage brands, which Co. groups into the following category clusters: sparkling soft drinks; water, enhanced water and sports drinks; juice, dairy and plant-based beverages; tea and coffee; and energy drinks. Co.'s nonalcoholic sparkling soft drink brands include Coca-Cola, Diet Coke, Fanta and Sprite. Co. markets, manufactures and sells beverage concentrates and syrups, including fountain syrups; and finished sparkling soft drinks and other nonalcoholic beverages. Co.'s operating segments are Europe, Middle East and Africa; Latin America; North America; Asia Pacific; and Bottling Investments.

Recent Developments: For the quarter ended Sep 27 2019, net income increased 42.4% to US$2.59 billion from US$1.82 billion in the year-earlier quarter. Revenues were US$9.51 billion, up 8.3% from US$8.78 billion the year before. Operating income was US$2.50 billion versus US$2.61 billion in the prior-year quarter, a decrease of 4.4%. Direct operating expenses rose 12.6% to US$3.77 billion from US$3.35 billion in the comparable period the year before. Indirect operating expenses increased 15.1% to US$3.24 billion from US$2.82 billion in the equivalent prior-year period.

Prospects: Our evaluation of Coca-Cola Co as of October 4th, 2019 is the result of our systematic analysis on three basic characteristics: earnings strength, relative valuation, and recent stock price movement. The company has managed to produce a neutral trend in earnings per share over the past 5 quarters. Additionally, recent analyst estimates for the company have been unchanged while KO has posted results that exceeded analysts' expectations. Based on operating earnings yield, the company is fairly valued when compared to all of the companies we cover. Share price changes over the past year indicates that KO will perform well over the near term.

Financial Data

(US$ in Thousands)	9 Mos	6 Mos	3 Mos	12/31/2018	12/31/2017	12/31/2016	12/31/2015	12/31/2014
Earnings Per Share	1.81	1.65	1.58	1.50	0.29	1.49	1.67	1.60
Cash Flow Per Share	2.25	2.16	1.73	1.72	1.64	2.03	2.42	2.42
Tang Book Value Per Share	N.M.	N.M.	N.M.	N.M.	0.10	0.45	0.33	0.90
Dividends Per Share	1.590	1.580	1.570	1.560	1.480	1.400	1.320	1.220
Dividend Payout %	87.85	95.76	99.37	104.00	510.34	93.96	79.04	76.25
Income Statement								
Total Revenue	28,198,000	18,691,000	8,020,000	31,856,000	35,410,000	41,863,000	44,294,000	45,998,000
EBITDA	8,806,000	5,620,000	2,377,000	8,596,000	7,021,000	8,989,000	11,112,000	10,181,000
Depn & Amortn	965,000	602,000	275,000	1,017,000	1,186,000	1,597,000	1,753,000	1,736,000
Income Before Taxes	7,558,000	4,812,000	1,999,000	7,342,000	5,671,000	7,301,000	9,116,000	8,556,000
Income Taxes	1,446,000	943,000	486,000	1,623,000	5,560,000	1,586,000	2,239,000	2,201,000
Net Income	6,878,000	4,285,000	1,678,000	6,434,000	1,248,000	6,527,000	7,351,000	7,098,000
Average Shares	4,320,999	4,304,999	4,305,999	4,298,999	4,323,999	4,366,999	4,404,999	4,449,999
Balance Sheet								
Current Assets	23,117,000	24,360,000	28,540,000	30,634,000	36,545,000	34,010,000	33,395,000	32,986,000
Total Assets	87,433,000	89,996,000	88,347,000	83,216,000	87,896,000	87,270,000	90,093,000	92,023,000
Current Liabilities	25,100,000	29,382,000	27,943,000	29,223,000	27,194,000	26,532,000	26,930,000	32,374,000
Long-Term Obligations	31,012,000	29,296,000	29,400,000	25,364,000	31,182,000	29,684,000	28,407,000	19,063,000
Total Liabilities	68,720,000	71,815,000	70,612,000	66,235,000	70,824,000	64,208,000	64,539,000	61,703,000
Stockholders' Equity	18,713,000	18,181,000	17,735,000	16,981,000	17,072,000	23,062,000	25,554,000	30,320,000
Shares Outstanding	4,284,000	4,275,000	4,268,000	4,268,000	4,259,000	4,288,000	4,323,999	4,365,999
Statistical Record								
Return on Assets %	8.89	7.83	7.43	7.52	1.42	7.34	8.07	7.80
Return on Equity %	41.91	38.54	36.12	37.79	6.22	26.78	26.31	22.36
EBITDA Margin %	31.23	30.07	29.64	26.98	19.83	21.47	25.09	22.13
Net Margin %	24.39	22.93	20.92	20.20	3.52	15.59	16.60	15.43
Asset Turnover	0.40	0.37	0.36	0.37	0.40	0.47	0.49	0.51
Current Ratio	0.92	0.83	1.02	1.05	1.34	1.28	1.24	1.02
Debt to Equity	1.66	1.61	1.66	1.49	1.83	1.29	1.11	0.63
Price Range	55.77-44.64	51.92-43.47	50.51-41.55	50.51-41.55	47.43-40.44	46.89-40.17	43.84-37.99	44.83-37.10
P/E Ratio	30.81-24.66	31.47-26.35	31.97-26.30	33.67-27.70	163.55-139.45	31.47-26.96	26.25-22.75	28.02-23.19
Average Yield %	3.23	3.34	3.42	3.44	3.34	3.22	3.20	2.99

Address: One Coca-Cola Plaza, Atlanta, GA 30313	**Web Site:** www.coca-colacompany.com	**Auditors:** Ernst & Young LLP
Telephone: 404-676-2121	**Officers:** James Quincey - Chairman, President, Chief Executive Officer, Chief Operating Officer, Region Officer Brian John Smith - President, Chief Operating Officer, Region Officer	**Investor Contact:** 404-676-7563
Fax: 404-676-6792		**Transfer Agents:** Computershare Trust Company, N.A., Providence, RI

COLGATE-PALMOLIVE CO.

Exchange	Symbol	Price	52Wk Range	Yield	P/E	Div Acheiver
NYS	CL	$68.84 (12/31/2019)	75.57-58.97	2.50	25.50	56 Years

*7 Year Price Score 84.89 *NYSE Composite Index=100 *12 Month Price Score 92.25

Interim Earnings (Per Share)

Qtr.	Mar	Jun	Sep	Dec
2016	0.59	0.67	0.78	0.68
2017	0.64	0.59	0.68	0.37
2018	0.72	0.73	0.60	0.70
2019	0.65	0.67	...	

Interim Dividends (Per Share)

Amt	Decl	Ex	Rec	Pay
0.43Q	03/14/2019	04/17/2019	04/19/2019	05/15/2019
0.43Q	06/20/2019	07/17/2019	07/18/2019	08/15/2019
0.43Q	09/11/2019	10/22/2019	10/23/2019	11/15/2019
0.43Q	01/09/2020	01/22/2020	01/23/2020	02/14/2020

Indicated Div: $1.72 (Div. Reinv. Plan)

Valuation Analysis

		Institutional Holding	
Forecast EPS	$2.83	No of Institutions	
	(01/17/2020)	2094	
Market Cap	$59.0 Billion	Shares	
Book Value	N/A	796,185,024	
Price/Book	N/A	% Held	
Price/Sales	3.81	74.81	

Business Summary: Household & Personal Products (MIC: 1.7.1 SIC: 2844 NAIC: 325620)

Colgate-Palmolive manufactures and markets a variety of products in the U.S. and around the world. Co. has two product segments: Oral, Personal and Home Care; and Pet Nutrition. Oral, Personal and Home Care products include toothpaste, toothbrushes and mouthwash, bar and liquid hand soaps, shower gels, shampoos, conditioners, deodorants and antiperspirants, skin care products, dishwashing detergents, fabric conditioners, household cleaners, and other similar items. Pet Nutrition products include specialty pet nutrition products manufactured and marketed by Hill's Pet Nutrition.

Recent Developments: For the quarter ended Sep 30 2019, net income increased 11.6% to US$627.0 million from US$562.0 million in the year-earlier quarter. Revenues were US$3.93 billion, up 2.2% from US$3.85 billion the year before. Operating income was US$856.0 million versus US$874.0 million in the prior-year quarter, a decrease of 2.1%. Direct operating expenses rose 2.3% to US$1.61 billion from US$1.58 billion in the comparable period the year before. Indirect operating expenses increased 4.7% to US$1.46 billion from US$1.40 billion in the equivalent prior-year period.

Prospects: Our evaluation of Colgate-Palmolive Co. as of October 4th, 2019 is the result of our systematic analysis on three basic characteristics: earnings strength, relative valuation, and recent stock price movement. The company has managed to produce a neutral trend in earnings per share over the past 5 quarters. Additionally, recent analyst estimates for the company have been unchanged while CL has posted results that fell short of analysts' expectations. Based on operating earnings yield, the company is fairly valued when compared to all of the companies we cover. Share price changes over the past year indicates that CL will perform well over the near term.

Financial Data

(US$ in Thousands)	9 Mos	6 Mos	3 Mos	12/31/2018	12/31/2017	12/31/2016	12/31/2015	12/31/2014
Earnings Per Share	2.70	2.63	2.68	2.75	2.28	2.72	1.52	2.36
Cash Flow Per Share	3.52	3.50	3.53	3.51	3.46	3.51	3.27	3.60
Dividends Per Share	1.700	1.690	1.680	1.660	1.590	1.550	1.500	1.420
Dividend Payout %	62.96	64.26	62.69	60.36	69.74	56.99	98.68	60.17
Income Statement								
Total Revenue	11,678,000	7,750,000	3,884,000	15,544,000	15,454,000	15,195,000	16,034,000	17,277,000
EBITDA	2,930,000	1,971,000	982,000	3,656,000	3,613,000	3,860,000	2,814,000	3,582,000
Depn & Amortn	386,000	256,000	128,000	59,000	35,000	33,000	33,000	32,000
Income Before Taxes	2,431,000	1,637,000	814,000	3,454,000	3,476,000	3,728,000	2,755,000	3,526,000
Income Taxes	586,000	419,000	214,000	906,000	1,313,000	1,152,000	1,215,000	1,194,000
Net Income	1,724,000	1,146,000	560,000	2,400,000	2,024,000	2,441,000	1,384,000	2,180,000
Average Shares	861,200	861,900	863,200	873,000	887,800	898,400	909,700	924,300
Balance Sheet								
Current Assets	4,349,000	4,255,000	4,133,000	3,793,000	4,639,000	4,338,000	4,384,000	4,863,000
Total Assets	15,026,000	13,151,000	12,883,000	12,161,000	12,676,000	12,123,000	11,958,000	13,459,000
Current Liabilities	4,231,000	3,782,000	3,865,000	3,341,000	3,408,000	3,305,000	3,534,000	3,946,000
Long-Term Obligations	7,646,000	6,640,000	6,655,000	6,354,000	6,566,000	6,520,000	6,269,000	5,644,000
Total Liabilities	15,350,000	13,498,000	13,435,000	12,263,000	12,736,000	12,366,000	12,257,000	12,314,000
Stockholders' Equity	(324,000)	(347,000)	(552,000)	(102,000)	(60,000)	(243,000)	(299,000)	1,145,000
Shares Outstanding	857,044	858,006	858,514	862,912	874,701	883,108	892,738	906,712
Statistical Record								
Return on Assets %	16.89	17.63	17.87	19.33	16.32	20.22	10.89	15.95
Return on Equity %	...	...	...	...	...	...	327.19	126.38
EBITDA Margin %	25.09	25.43	25.28	23.52	23.38	25.40	17.55	20.73
Net Margin %	14.76	14.79	14.42	15.44	13.10	16.06	8.63	12.62
Asset Turnover	1.12	1.19	1.19	1.25	1.25	1.26	1.26	1.26
Current Ratio	1.03	1.13	1.07	1.14	1.36	1.31	1.24	1.23
Debt to Equity	...	...	...	...	...	...	...	4.93
Price Range	75.57-57.88	73.99-57.88	72.44-57.88	77.50-57.88	77.23-64.53	75.27-62.45	71.46-60.37	71.00-60.17
P/E Ratio	27.99-21.44	28.13-22.01	27.03-21.60	28.18-21.05	33.87-28.30	27.67-22.96	47.01-39.72	30.08-25.50
Average Yield %	2.51	2.55	2.59	2.49	2.20	2.21	2.23	2.15

Address: 300 Park Avenue, New York, NY 10022	**Web Site:** www.colgatepalmolive.com	**Auditors:** PricewaterhouseCoopers LLP
Telephone: 212-310-2000	**Officers:** Ian M. Cook - Chairman, Executive Chairman, President, Chief Executive Officer Noel R.	**Investor Contact:** 212-310-2575
Fax: 212-310-3284	Wallace - President, Chief Executive Officer, Chief Operating Officer, Division Officer, Region Officer	**Transfer Agents:** Computershare, Providence, RI

COLFAX CORP

Exchange	Symbol	Price	52Wk Range	Yield	P/E
NYS	CFX	$36.38 (12/31/2019)	36.46-20.19	N/A	N/A

*7 Year Price Score 57.84 *NYSE Composite Index=100 *12 Month Price Score 114.88

Interim Earnings (Per Share)

Qtr.	Mar	Jun	Sep	Dec
2016	0.18	0.32	0.23	0.31
2017	0.31	0.43	0.37	0.11
2018	0.20	0.31	0.26	0.39
2019	(0.39)	(3.45)	0.08	...

Interim Dividends (Per Share)

No Dividends Paid

Valuation Analysis

		Institutional Holding	
Forecast EPS	$1.98	No of Institutions	
	(01/17/2020)	324	
Market Cap	$4.3 Billion	Shares	
Book Value	$3.0 Billion	123,328,976	
Price/Book	1.44	% Held	
Price/Sales	1.14	94.33	

Business Summary: Industrial Machinery & Equipment (MIC: 7.2.1 SIC: 3563 NAIC: 333912)

Colfax is a technology company that provides air and gas handling and fabrication technology products and services to customers under the Howden and ESAB brands. Co. has two segments: Air and Gas Handling, which designs, manufactures, installs and maintains air and gas handling products for use in a range of markets, including power generation, oil, gas and petrochemical, mining, wastewater, and general industrial and other; and Fabrication Technology, which formulates, develops, manufactures and supplies consumable products and equipment for use in the cutting, joining and automated welding of steels, aluminum and other metals and metal alloys.

Recent Developments: For the quarter ended Sep 27 2019, income from continuing operations decreased 77.4% to US$3.8 million from US$16.7 million in the year-earlier quarter. Net income decreased 63.7% to US$12.8 million from US$35.2 million in the year-earlier quarter. Revenues were US$846.5 million, up 61.5% from US$524.0 million the year before. Operating income was US$67.9 million versus US$35.1 million in the prior-year quarter, an increase of 93.6%. Direct operating expenses rose 35.6% to US$478.4 million from US$352.7 million in the comparable period the year before. Indirect operating expenses increased 120.4% to US$300.3 million from US$136.2 million in the equivalent prior-year period.

Prospects: Our evaluation of Colfax Corp. as of October 4th, 2019 is the result of our systematic analysis on three basic characteristics: earnings strength, relative valuation, and recent stock price movement. The company has generated a negative trend in earnings per share over the past 5 quarters. In addition, recent analyst estimates for the company have been reduced while CFX has posted results that exceeded analysts' expectations. Based on operating earnings yield, the company is undervalued when compared to all of the companies we cover. Share price changes over the past year indicates that CFX will perform very poorly over the near term.

Financial Data

(US$ in Thousands)	9 Mos	6 Mos	3 Mos	12/31/2018	12/31/2017	12/31/2016	12/31/2015	12/31/2014
Earnings Per Share	(3.37)	(3.19)	0.57	1.16	1.22	1.04	1.34	3.02
Cash Flow Per Share	1.41	1.49	1.17	1.88	1.78	2.00	2.45	3.18
Income Statement								
Total Revenue	2,439,085	1,592,566	1,007,668	3,666,812	3,300,184	3,647,047	3,967,053	4,624,476
EBITDA	268,689	164,336	25,818	280,654	81,451	317,215	375,345	504,053
Depn & Amortn	190,577	120,469	44,832	53,800	52,300	79,200	90,700	94,500
Income Before Taxes	(8,708)	(11,125)	(48,135)	182,802	(11,986)	207,999	236,902	358,248
Income Taxes	6,840	8,193	(3,578)	(21)	42,554	62,808	49,724	(62,025)
Net Income	(510,783)	(521,257)	(52,023)	140,196	151,090	128,111	167,739	392,098
Average Shares	137,050	136,945	133,713	120,795	123,229	123,198	124,869	122,666
Balance Sheet								
Current Assets	3,499,132	3,636,593	2,408,657	1,958,441	2,069,832	1,785,597	1,759,765	2,099,463
Total Assets	9,591,272	9,899,253	10,502,407	6,603,872	6,709,697	6,385,459	6,732,919	7,245,098
Current Liabilities	1,505,677	1,598,555	1,571,628	1,199,345	1,097,380	1,106,674	1,116,344	1,285,535
Long-Term Obligations	4,002,365	4,078,232	4,037,146	1,192,408	1,055,305	1,286,738	1,411,755	1,529,389
Total Liabilities	6,609,264	6,804,455	6,924,907	3,334,112	3,209,282	3,488,588	3,662,944	4,098,272
Stockholders' Equity	2,982,008	3,094,798	3,577,500	3,269,760	3,500,415	2,896,871	3,069,975	3,146,826
Shares Outstanding	117,756	117,667	117,558	117,275	123,245	122,780	123,486	123,730
Statistical Record								
Return on Assets %	N.M.	N.M.	0.73	2.11	2.31	1.95	2.40	5.67
Return on Equity %	N.M.	N.M.	1.77	4.14	4.72	4.28	5.40	13.85
EBITDA Margin %	11.02	10.32	2.56	7.65	2.47	8.70	9.46	10.90
Net Margin %	N.M.	N.M.	N.M.	3.82	4.58	3.51	4.23	8.48
Asset Turnover	0.47	0.46	0.44	0.55	0.50	0.55	0.57	0.67
Current Ratio	2.32	2.27	1.53	1.63	1.89	1.61	1.58	1.63
Debt to Equity	1.34	1.32	1.13	0.36	0.30	0.44	0.46	0.49
Price Range	36.52-19.20	36.52-19.20	36.52-19.20	41.76-19.20	43.16-34.88	39.75-19.29	53.47-22.00	74.92-47.20
P/E Ratio	...	64.07-33.68	36.52-19.20	36.00-16.55	35.38-28.59	38.22-18.55	39.90-16.42	24.81-15.63

Address: 420 National Business Parkway, 5th Floor, Annapolis Junction, MD 20701 **Telephone:** 301-323-9000	**Web Site:** www.colfaxcorp.com **Officers:** Mitchell P. Rales - Chairman Matthew L. Trerotola - President, Chief Executive Officer	**Auditors:** Ernst & Young LLP **Investor Contact:** 301-323-9090 **Transfer Agents:** Registrar and Transfer Company, Cranford, NJ

COLONY CAPITAL INC

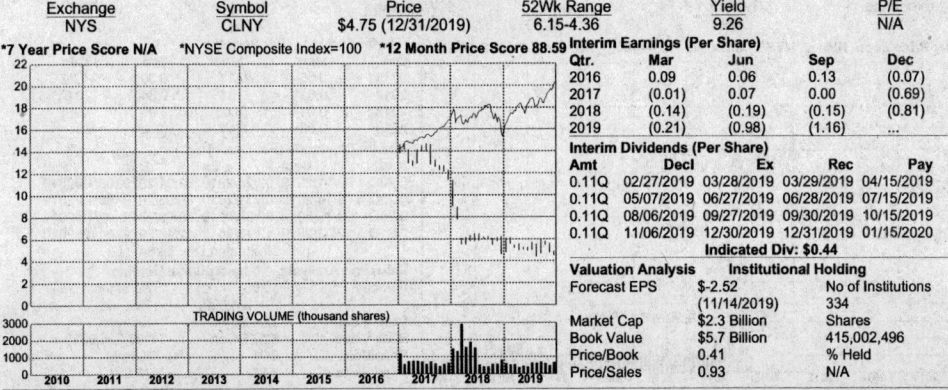

Exchange	Symbol	Price	52Wk Range	Yield	P/E
NYS	CLNY	$4.75 (12/31/2019)	6.15-4.36	9.26	N/A

*7 Year Price Score N/A   *NYSE Composite Index=100   *12 Month Price Score 88.59

Interim Earnings (Per Share)

Qtr.	Mar	Jun	Sep	Dec
2016	0.09	0.06	0.13	(0.07)
2017	(0.01)	0.07	0.00	(0.69)
2018	(0.14)	(0.19)	(0.15)	(0.81)
2019	(0.21)	(0.98)	(1.16)	...

Interim Dividends (Per Share)

Amt	Decl	Ex	Rec	Pay
0.11Q	02/27/2019	03/28/2019	03/29/2019	04/15/2019
0.11Q	05/07/2019	06/27/2019	06/28/2019	07/15/2019
0.11Q	08/06/2019	09/27/2019	09/30/2019	10/15/2019
0.11Q	11/06/2019	12/30/2019	12/31/2019	01/15/2020

Indicated Div: $0.44

Valuation Analysis

		Institutional Holding	
Forecast EPS	$-2.52	No of Institutions	
	(11/14/2019)	334	
Market Cap	$2.3 Billion	Shares	
Book Value	$5.7 Billion	415,002,496	
Price/Book	0.41	% Held	
Price/Sales	0.93	N/A	

Business Summary: REITs (MIC: 5.3.1 SIC: 6531 NAIC: 531390)

Colony Capital is a holding company. Through its subsidiaries, Co. is an investment management firm focused on real estate. Co.'s segments are: Healthcare, which includes senior housing, skilled nursing facilities, medical office buildings and hospitals; industrial, which invests in light industrial assets; hospitality, which includes extended stay hotels and select service hotels; CLNC, which represents its investment in Colony Credit Real Estate, Inc.; other equity and debt, which includes its real estate and real estate-related debt and equity investments; and investment management, which raises, invests and manages funds on behalf of a set of institutional and individual investors.

Recent Developments: For the quarter ended Sep 30 2019, loss from continuing operations was US$626.2 million compared with a loss of US$28.7 million in the year-earlier quarter. Net loss amounted to US$565.8 million versus a net loss of US$17.4 million in the year-earlier quarter. Revenues were US$652.5 million, up 9.0% from US$598.7 million the year before. Revenues from property income fell 6.6% to US$462.2 million from US$494.9 million in the corresponding quarter a year earlier.

Prospects: Our evaluation of Colony Capital Inc. as of October 4th, 2019 is the result of our systematic analysis on three basic characteristics: earnings strength, relative valuation, and recent stock price movement. The company has suffered a very negative trend in earnings per share over the past 5 quarters. However, recent analyst estimates for the company have been mixed and CLNY has posted results that fell short of analysts' expectations. Based on operating earnings yield, the company is overvalued when compared to all of the companies we cover. Share price changes over the past year indicates that CLNY will perform very poorly over the near term.

Financial Data

(US$ in Thousands)	9 Mos	6 Mos	3 Mos	12/31/2018	12/31/2017	12/31/2016	12/31/2015	12/31/2014
Earnings Per Share	(3.16)	(2.15)	(1.36)	(1.28)	(0.64)	0.21	0.60	0.10
Cash Flow Per Share	0.73	0.91	0.99	1.02	1.03	0.92	0.84	0.25
Tang Book Value Per Share	5.91	7.05	8.09	8.40	9.69	N.M.	0.92	1.03
Dividends Per Share	0.440	0.440	0.440	0.440	2.213	0.400	0.400	0.100
Dividend Payout %	...	...	...	...	...	190.48	66.67	100.00
Income Statement								
Total Revenue	1,773,993	1,121,498	632,903	2,665,276	2,796,734	398,542	435,821	259,142
EBITDA	(467,373)	16,323	93,791	501,737	851,555	164,833	201,022	22,661
Depn & Amortn	513,468	334,637	161,322	471,460	453,300	75,121	59,253	900
Income Before Taxes	(980,841)	(318,314)	(67,531)	(565,414)	(176,567)	63,798	140,991	21,761
Income Taxes	13,751	3,783	1,111	(59,781)	(98,399)	11,022	21,869	1,622
Net Income	(1,044,544)	(516,728)	(74,976)	(519,607)	(197,891)	42,281	119,794	19,100
Average Shares	479,776	479,228	478,874	496,993	532,600	185,111	193,119	194,408
Balance Sheet								
Current Assets	892,473	888,367	876,486	855,661	1,422,426	241,011	220,077	198,950
Total Assets	22,123,994	22,658,538	23,221,033	22,215,249	24,785,650	850,627	374,821	266,987
Current Liabilities	751,171	693,521	775,103	300,018	470,095	91,165	197,148	65,239
Long-Term Obligations	8,666,108	8,739,667	10,712,788	10,039,957	10,827,810	468,425	...	...
Total Liabilities	16,460,263	16,296,820	16,352,328	15,209,197	16,377,725	666,515	199,756	65,239
Stockholders' Equity	5,663,731	6,361,718	6,868,705	7,006,052	8,407,925	184,112	175,065	201,748
Shares Outstanding	487,752	487,747	485,509	484,081	543,335	193,639	189,898	196,686
Statistical Record								
Return on Assets %	N.M.	N.M.	N.M.	N.M.	N.M.	6.88	37.33	12.79
Return on Equity %	N.M.	N.M.	N.M.	N.M.	N.M.	23.48	63.58	16.60
EBITDA Margin %	N.M.	1.46	14.82	18.82	30.45	41.36	46.12	8.74
Net Margin %	N.M.	N.M.	N.M.	N.M.	N.M.	10.61	27.49	7.37
Asset Turnover	0.11	0.11	0.11	0.11	0.22	0.65	1.36	1.74
Current Ratio	1.19	1.28	1.13	2.85	3.03	2.64	1.12	3.05
Debt to Equity	1.53	1.37	1.56	1.43	1.29	2.54	...	...
Price Range	6.24-4.36	6.50-4.60	6.50-4.60	11.37-4.60	14.70-11.41	...	...	...
Average Yield %	8.13	7.78	7.52	6.79	16.60	...	...	...

Address: 515 South Flower Street, 44th Floor, Los Angeles, CA 90071 **Telephone:** 310-282-8820	**Web Site:** www.clns.com **Officers:** Thomas J. Barrack - Executive Chairman, Chief Executive Officer Darren J. Tangen - President	**Auditors:** Ernst & Young LLP **Transfer Agents:** American Stock Transfer & Trust Company, LLC, Brookly, NY

COLUMBIA PROPERTY TRUST INC

Exchange	Symbol	Price	52Wk Range	Yield	P/E
NYS	CXP	$20.91 (12/31/2019)	23.09-18.73	4.02	67.45

*7 Year Price Score N/A   *NYSE Composite Index=100   *12 Month Price Score 91.24

Interim Earnings (Per Share)

Qtr.	Mar	Jun	Sep	Dec
2016	0.05	0.11	0.30	0.22
2017	0.61	0.01	0.84	(0.01)
2018	0.01	(0.03)	0.05	0.04
2019	0.03	0.41	(0.17)	...

Interim Dividends (Per Share)

Amt	Decl	Ex	Rec	Pay
0.20Q	02/11/2019	02/28/2019	03/01/2019	03/15/2019
0.20Q	05/14/2019	05/31/2019	06/03/2019	06/18/2019
0.20Q	08/13/2019	08/30/2019	09/03/2019	09/18/2019
0.21Q	12/03/2019	12/13/2019	12/16/2019	01/07/2020

Indicated Div: $0.84

Valuation Analysis   **Institutional Holding**

Forecast EPS	$0.08	No of Institutions
	(01/16/2020)	289
Market Cap	$2.4 Billion	Shares
Book Value	$2.7 Billion	107,395,032
Price/Book	0.91	% Held
Price/Sales	8.27	76.59

Business Summary: REITs (MIC: 5.3.1 SIC: 6798 NAIC: 525930)

Columbia Property Trust is a real estate investment trust that owns and operates commercial real estate properties. Co. conducts its business primarily through Columbia Property Trust Operating Partnership, L.P., which acquires, redevelops, owns, leases, and operates real properties directly, through wholly owned subsidiaries, or through unconsolidated joint ventures. Co. typically acquires, develops, or redevelops office properties. These properties are located primarily in New York, San Francisco, Washington, D.C., and Atlanta.

Recent Developments: For the quarter ended Sep 30 2019, net loss amounted to US$20.3 million versus net income of US$6.4 million in the year-earlier quarter. Revenues were US$71.9 million, down 1.9% from US$73.3 million the year before.

Prospects: Our evaluation of Columbia Property Trust Inc as of October 4th, 2019 is the result of our systematic analysis on three basic characteristics: earnings strength, relative valuation, and recent stock price movement. The company has managed to produce a neutral trend in earnings per share over the past 5 quarters. However, recent analyst estimates for the company have been raised and CXP has posted results that exceeded analysts' expectations. Based on operating earnings yield, the company is overvalued when compared to all of the companies we cover. Share price changes over the past year indicates that CXP will perform well over the near term.

Financial Data

(US$ in Thousands)	9 Mos	6 Mos	3 Mos	12/31/2018	12/31/2017	12/31/2016	12/31/2015	12/31/2014
Earnings Per Share	0.31	0.53	0.09	0.08	1.45	0.68	0.36	0.74
Cash Flow Per Share	1.21	1.22	1.01	0.83	0.51	1.56	1.79	1.90
Tang Book Value Per Share	22.87	23.21	22.99	23.20	20.78	20.04	20.40	21.03
Dividends Per Share	0.800	0.800	0.800	0.800	0.800	1.200	1.200	1.200
Dividend Payout %	258.06	150.94	888.89	1,000.00	55.17	176.47	333.33	162.16
Income Statement								
Total Revenue	220,112	148,163	75,433	297,943	289,000	473,543	566,065	540,797
EBITDA	94,267	80,418	40,598	132,925	129,040	188,826	231,811	206,241
Depn & Amortn	78,204	52,054	26,755	81,795	80,394	108,543	131,490	117,766
Income Before Taxes	(17,217)	5,373	1,749	1,525	(2,341)	19,962	22,279	20,039
Income Taxes	18	16	7	37	(213)	445	378	662
Net Income	30,974	51,260	3,513	9,491	176,041	84,281	44,619	92,635
Average Shares	116,821	116,823	116,880	118,311	121,159	123,228	124,847	124,918
Balance Sheet								
Current Assets	149,959	14,885	22,311	107,535	103,930	288,059	153,377	273,224
Total Assets	3,925,801	4,044,795	4,223,729	4,173,993	4,511,539	4,299,793	4,678,118	4,738,878
Current Liabilities	53,281	43,403	37,962	72,457	148,963	167,755	136,113	106,276
Long-Term Obligations	1,145,225	1,224,223	1,409,930	1,323,846	1,784,941	1,534,438	1,845,830	1,800,066
Total Liabilities	1,228,267	1,302,064	1,504,865	1,432,977	1,979,603	1,797,025	2,063,924	2,005,400
Stockholders' Equity	2,697,534	2,742,731	2,718,864	2,741,016	2,531,936	2,502,768	2,614,194	2,733,478
Shares Outstanding	116,908	116,908	116,879	116,698	119,789	122,184	124,363	124,973
Statistical Record								
Return on Assets %	0.88	1.51	0.26	0.22	4.00	1.87	0.95	1.99
Return on Equity %	1.31	2.26	0.41	0.36	6.99	3.29	1.67	3.36
EBITDA Margin %	42.83	54.28	53.82	44.61	44.65	39.88	40.95	38.14
Net Margin %	14.07	34.60	4.66	3.19	60.91	17.80	7.88	17.13
Asset Turnover	0.07	0.07	0.07	0.07	0.07	0.11	0.12	0.12
Current Ratio	2.81	0.34	0.59	1.48	0.70	1.72	1.13	2.57
Debt to Equity	0.42	0.45	0.52	0.48	0.70	0.61	0.71	0.66
Price Range	23.53-18.13	24.23-18.13	24.23-18.13	24.23-18.13	23.43-20.62	24.63-19.81	27.67-21.16	29.13-23.12
P/E Ratio	75.90-58.48	45.72-34.21	269.22-201.44	302.88-226.63	16.16-14.22	36.22-29.13	76.86-58.78	39.36-31.24
Average Yield %	3.70	3.62	3.64	3.65	3.63	5.46	4.81	4.67

Address: 315 Park Avenue South, New York, NY 10010 **Telephone:** 212-687-0800	**Web Site:** www.columbiapropertytrust.com **Officers:** John L. Dixon - Chairman E. Nelson Mills - President, Chief Executive Officer	**Auditors:** DELOITTE & TOUCHE LLP **Transfer Agents:** DST Systems Inc

COMERICA, INC.

Exchange	Symbol	Price	52Wk Range	Yield	P/E
NYS	CMA	$71.75 (12/31/2019)	88.31-58.80	3.74	9.09

*7 Year Price Score 100.35 *NYSE Composite Index=100 ***12 Month Price Score 92.26**

Interim Earnings (Per Share)

Qtr.	Mar	Jun	Sep	Dec
2016	0.34	0.58	0.84	0.92
2017	1.11	1.13	1.26	0.64
2018	1.59	1.87	1.86	1.88
2019	2.11	1.94	1.96	...

Interim Dividends (Per Share)

Amt	Decl	Ex	Rec	Pay
0.67Q	01/22/2019	03/14/2019	03/15/2019	04/01/2019
0.67Q	04/23/2019	06/13/2019	06/14/2019	07/01/2019
0.67Q	07/23/2019	09/12/2019	09/13/2019	10/01/2019
0.67Q	11/05/2019	12/12/2019	12/13/2019	01/01/2020

Indicated Div: $2.68 (Div. Reinv. Plan)

Valuation Analysis   Institutional Holding

Forecast EPS	$7.75	No of Institutions
	(01/16/2020)	831
Market Cap	$10.3 Billion	Shares
Book Value	$7.2 Billion	157,967,632
Price/Book	1.44	% Held
Price/Sales	2.69	68.21

Business Summary: Banking (MIC: 5.1.1 SIC: 6021 NAIC: 522110)

Comerica is a financial holding company, engaged in lending to and accepting deposits from businesses and individuals. Co.'s segments are: Business Bank, which provides commercial loans and lines of credit, deposits, cash management, capital market products, international trade finance, letters of credit, foreign exchange management services and loan syndication services; Retail Bank, which provides consumer lending, consumer deposit gathering and mortgage loan origination; and Wealth Management, which provides products and services consisting of fiduciary services, private banking, retirement services, investment management and advisory services, investment banking and brokerage services.

Recent Developments: For the quarter ended Sep 30 2019, net income decreased 8.2% to US$292.0 million from US$318.0 million in the year-earlier quarter. Net interest income decreased 2.2% to US$586.0 million from US$599.0 million in the year-earlier quarter. Non-interest income rose 9.4% to US$256.0 million from US$234.0 million, while non-interest expense declined 3.8% to US$435.0 million.

Prospects: Our evaluation of Comerica Inc. as of October 4th, 2019 is the result of our systematic analysis on three basic characteristics: earnings strength, relative valuation, and recent stock price movement. The company has generated a negative trend in earnings per share over the past 5 quarters. In addition, recent analyst estimates for the company have been reduced and CMA has posted results that fell short of analysts' expectations. Based on operating earnings yield, the company is undervalued when compared to all of the companies we cover. Share price changes over the past year indicates that CMA will perform very poorly over the near term.

Financial Data

(US$ in Thousands)	9 Mos	6 Mos	3 Mos	12/31/2018	12/31/2017	12/31/2016	12/31/2015	12/31/2014
Earnings Per Share	7.89	7.79	7.72	7.20	4.14	2.68	2.84	3.16
Cash Flow Per Share	10.33	9.39	8.22	9.62	6.34	2.86	4.90	3.57
Tang Book Value Per Share	49.95	48.89	47.67	46.89	46.07	44.47	43.03	41.35
Dividends Per Share	2.610	2.540	2.210	1.840	1.090	0.890	0.830	0.790
Dividend Payout %	33.08	32.61	28.63	25.56	26.33	33.21	29.23	25.00
Income Statement								
Interest Income	2,148,000	1,437,000	710,000	2,619,000	2,182,000	1,909,000	1,784,000	1,750,000
Interest Expense	353,000	228,000	104,000	267,000	121,000	112,000	95,000	95,000
Net Interest Income	1,795,000	1,209,000	606,000	2,352,000	2,061,000	1,797,000	1,689,000	1,655,000
Provision for Losses	66,000	31,000	(13,000)	(1,000)	74,000	248,000	147,000	27,000
Non-Interest Income	744,000	488,000	238,000	976,000	1,107,000	1,051,000	1,050,000	868,000
Non-Interest Expense	1,292,000	857,000	433,000	1,794,000	1,860,000	1,930,000	1,842,000	1,658,000
Income Before Taxes	1,181,000	809,000	424,000	1,535,000	1,234,000	670,000	750,000	870,000
Income Taxes	252,000	172,000	85,000	300,000	491,000	193,000	229,000	277,000
Net Income	929,000	637,000	339,000	1,235,000	743,000	477,000	521,000	593,000
Average Shares	148,000	153,000	160,000	171,000	178,000	177,000	181,000	185,000
Balance Sheet								
Net Loans & Leases	50,839,000	51,144,000	49,655,000	49,492,000	48,461,000	48,358,000	48,450,000	47,999,000
Total Assets	72,848,000	72,537,000	70,690,000	70,818,000	71,567,000	72,978,000	71,877,000	69,190,000
Total Deposits	56,809,000	55,537,000	54,091,000	55,561,000	57,903,000	58,985,000	59,853,000	57,486,000
Total Liabilities	65,648,000	65,214,000	63,281,000	63,311,000	63,604,000	65,182,000	64,317,000	61,788,000
Stockholders' Equity	7,200,000	7,323,000	7,409,000	7,507,000	7,963,000	7,796,000	7,560,000	7,402,000
Shares Outstanding	144,136	149,797	155,417	160,083	172,858	175,313	175,707	179,018
Statistical Record								
Return on Assets %	1.72	1.75	1.81	1.73	1.03	0.66	0.74	0.88
Return on Equity %	16.54	16.43	16.78	15.97	9.43	6.20	6.96	8.15
Net Interest Margin %	82.42	82.94	85.35	89.81	94.45	94.13	94.67	94.57
Efficiency Ratio %	44.98	43.40	45.68	49.90	56.55	65.20	65.00	63.33
Loans to Deposits	0.89	0.92	0.92	0.89	0.84	0.82	0.81	0.83
Price Range	92.72-58.80	99.43-64.45	100.31-64.45	102.21-64.45	87.74-64.46	70.03-31.02	52.65-40.41	52.37-43.06
P/E Ratio	11.75-7.45	12.76-8.27	12.99-8.35	14.20-8.95	21.19-15.57	26.13-11.57	18.54-14.23	16.57-13.63
Average Yield %	3.48	3.08	2.52	2.01	1.49	1.95	1.82	1.63

Address: Comerica Bank Tower, 1717 Main Street, MC 6404, Dallas, TX 75201	**Web Site:** www.comerica.com	**Auditors:** Ernst & Young LLP
	Officers: Curtis C. Farmer - Chairman, Vice-Chairman, President, Executive Vice President, Chief Executive Officer John D. Buchanan - Executive Vice President, Chief Legal Officer, Corporate Secretary	**Investor Contact:** 214-462-6831
Telephone: 214-462-6831		**Transfer Agents:** Wells Fargo Shareowner Services, St. Paul, MN

COMMERCIAL METALS CO.

Exchange	Symbol	Price	52Wk Range	Yield	P/E
NYS	CMC	$22.27 (12/31/2019)	22.60-13.35	2.16	10.12

*7 Year Price Score 81.15 *NYSE Composite Index=100 *12 Month Price Score 114.92

Interim Earnings (Per Share)

Qtr.	Nov	Feb	May	Aug
2016-17	0.05	0.26	0.34	(0.26)
2017-18	0.31	0.09	0.34	0.43
2018-19	0.17	0.12	0.66	0.72
2019-20	0.70	...	...	...

Interim Dividends (Per Share)

Amt	Decl	Ex	Rec	Pay
0.12Q	03/20/2019	04/04/2019	04/05/2019	04/18/2019
0.12Q	06/19/2019	07/03/2019	07/05/2019	07/18/2019
0.12Q	10/22/2019	11/05/2019	11/06/2019	11/20/2019
0.12Q	01/02/2020	01/14/2020	01/15/2020	01/30/2020

Indicated Div: $0.48

Valuation Analysis / **Institutional Holding**

Forecast EPS	$2.49	No of Institutions
	(01/17/2020)	400
Market Cap	$2.6 Billion	Shares
Book Value	$1.7 Billion	134,506,848
Price/Book	1.55	% Held
Price/Sales	0.45	91.89

Business Summary: Non-Precious Metals (MIC: 8.2.2 SIC: 3312 NAIC: 331111)

Commercial Metals, together with its subsidiaries, manufactures, recycles and markets steel and metal products, related materials and services. Co. has four reportable segments: Americas Recycling, which processes scrap metals for use as a raw material by Co. and other manufacturers of new metal products; Americas Mills, which operates electric arc furnace (EAF) mini mills, EAF micro mills, rerolling mill, scrap metal shredders, and scrap metal processing facilities; Americas Fabrication, which includes warehouses that sell or rent products for the installation of concrete; and International Mill, which consists of an EAF mini mill, recycling and fabrication operations located in Poland.

Recent Developments: For the quarter ended Nov 30 2019, income from continuing operations increased 326.1% to US$82.8 million from US$19.4 million in the year-earlier quarter. Net income increased 322.2% to US$83.3 million from US$19.7 million in the year-earlier quarter. Revenues were US$1.38 billion, up 8.4% from US$1.28 billion the year before. Direct operating expenses rose 2.5% to US$1.15 billion from US$1.12 billion in the comparable period the year before. Indirect operating expenses decreased 4.3% to US$128.1 million from US$133.9 million in the equivalent prior-year period.

Prospects: Our evaluation of Commercial Metals Co. as of October 4th, 2019 is the result of our systematic analysis on three basic characteristics: earnings strength, relative valuation, and recent stock price movement. The company has enjoyed a very positive trend in earnings per share over the past 5 quarters. However, recent analyst estimates for the company have been mixed and CMC has posted results that exceeded analysts' expectations. Based on operating earnings yield, the company is undervalued when compared to all of the companies we cover. Share price changes over the past year indicates that CMC will perform very poorly over the near term.

Financial Data

(US$ in Thousands)	3 Mos	08/31/2019	08/31/2018	08/31/2017	08/31/2016	08/31/2015	08/31/2014	08/31/2013
Earnings Per Share	2.20	1.66	1.17	0.39	0.47	1.20	0.97	0.66
Cash Flow Per Share	4.57	0.31	1.36	1.51	5.08	2.69	1.17	1.27
Tang Book Value Per Share	13.80	13.23	12.21	11.54	11.35	10.83	10.81	10.26
Dividends Per Share	0.480	0.480	0.480	0.480	0.480	0.480	0.480	0.480
Dividend Payout %	21.82	28.92	41.03	123.08	102.13	40.00	49.48	72.73
Income Statement								
Total Revenue	1,384,708	5,829,002	4,643,723	4,569,675	4,610,526	5,988,605	7,039,959	6,889,575
EBITDA	118,334	423,720	338,000	202,465	266,764	447,470	350,959	326,622
Depn & Amortn	(8,331)	83,887	131,659	113,414	119,343	125,182	128,407	124,078
Income Before Taxes	110,087	268,460	165,384	45,004	85,190	244,528	144,811	132,936
Income Taxes	27,332	69,681	30,147	12,454	12,647	83,206	42,724	57,979
Net Income	83,348	198,093	138,506	46,332	54,762	141,634	115,551	77,315
Average Shares	119,773	119,124	118,145	117,364	116,623	117,949	118,607	117,552
Balance Sheet								
Current Assets	2,014,583	2,080,005	2,077,205	1,713,900	2,048,125	2,307,101	2,553,791	2,366,195
Total Assets	3,808,351	3,758,771	3,328,304	2,975,131	3,130,869	3,372,302	3,688,520	3,494,801
Current Liabilities	601,964	694,590	541,943	608,438	821,118	617,348	891,153	781,109
Long-Term Obligations	1,179,443	1,227,214	1,138,619	805,580	757,948	1,277,882	1,281,042	1,278,814
Total Liabilities	2,106,850	2,134,910	1,834,907	1,574,374	1,763,597	2,053,101	2,340,040	2,224,802
Stockholders' Equity	1,701,501	1,623,861	1,493,397	1,400,757	1,367,272	1,319,201	1,348,480	1,269,999
Shares Outstanding	118,649	117,924	117,015	115,793	114,635	115,635	117,829	117,010
Statistical Record								
Return on Assets %	6.96	5.59	4.39	1.52	1.68	4.01	3.22	2.23
Return on Equity %	16.41	12.71	9.57	3.35	4.07	10.62	8.83	6.14
EBITDA Margin %	8.55	7.27	7.28	4.43	5.79	7.47	4.99	4.74
Net Margin %	6.02	3.40	2.98	1.01	1.19	2.37	1.64	1.12
Asset Turnover	1.58	1.64	1.47	1.50	1.41	1.70	1.96	1.99
Current Ratio	3.35	2.99	3.83	2.82	2.49	3.74	2.87	3.03
Debt to Equity	0.69	0.76	0.76	0.58	0.55	0.97	0.95	1.01
Price Range	21.76-13.35	21.60-13.35	26.13-17.57	24.34-14.77	18.30-12.91	18.54-12.99	20.58-14.91	17.41-12.74
P/E Ratio	9.89-6.07	13.01-8.04	22.33-15.02	62.41-37.87	38.94-27.47	15.45-10.83	21.22-15.37	26.38-19.30
Average Yield %	2.80	2.75	2.20	2.51	3.07	3.02	2.61	3.21

Address: 6565 North MacArthur Blvd.,	Web Site: www.cmc.com	Auditors: DELOITTE & TOUCHE LLP
Irving, TX 75039	Officers: Barbara R. Smith - Chairman, President,	Investor Contact: 214-689-4300
Telephone: 214-689-4300	Chief Executive Officer, Chief Operating Officer,	Transfer Agents: StockTrans®, a
Fax: 214-689-5886	Chief Financial Officer, Senior Vice President Tracy	Broadridge Company
	L. Porter - Executive Vice President, Senior Vice	
	President, Chief Operating Officer, Division Officer	

COMMUNITY BANK SYSTEM INC

Exchange	Symbol	Price	52Wk Range	Yield	P/E	Div Acheiver
NYS	CBU	$70.94 (12/31/2019)	71.07-56.94	2.31	22.24	27 Years

*7 Year Price Score 112.71 *NYSE Composite Index=100 *12 Month Price Score 101.11

Interim Earnings (Per Share)

Qtr.	Mar	Jun	Sep	Dec
2016	0.55	0.58	0.61	0.58
2017	0.57	0.35	0.68	1.43
2018	0.78	0.86	0.83	0.78
2019	0.80	0.86	0.75	...

Interim Dividends (Per Share)

Amt	Decl	Ex	Rec	Pay
0.38Q	02/21/2019	03/14/2019	03/15/2019	04/10/2019
0.38Q	05/16/2019	06/13/2019	06/14/2019	07/10/2019
0.41Q	08/21/2019	09/13/2019	09/16/2019	10/10/2019
0.41Q	11/20/2019	12/12/2019	12/13/2019	01/10/2020

Indicated Div: $1.64 (Div. Reinv. Plan)

Valuation Analysis

Institutional Holding	
Forecast EPS $3.28 (01/14/2020)	No of Institutions 289
Market Cap $3.7 Billion	Shares
Book Value $1.8 Billion	45,723,404
Price/Book 1.99	% Held
Price/Sales 6.05	72.54

Business Summary: Banking (MIC: 5.1.1 SIC: 6021 NAIC: 522110)

Community Bank System is a financial holding company which wholly-owns two subsidiaries: Community Bank, N.A. (the Bank), and Benefit Plans Administrative Services, Inc. Co. also sponsors two unconsolidated subsidiary business trusts formed for the purpose of issuing mandatorily-redeemable preferred securities which are considered Tier I capital under regulatory capital adequacy guidelines. The Bank's operates as a financial services enterprise providing a range of banking and other financial services to retail, commercial, and municipal customers.

Recent Developments: For the quarter ended Sep 30 2019, net income decreased 9.0% to US$39.2 million from US$43.1 million in the year-earlier quarter. Net interest income increased 5.9% to US$91.3 million from US$86.2 million in the year-earlier quarter. Provision for loan losses was US$1.8 million versus US$2.2 million in the prior-year quarter, a decrease of 20.9%. Non-interest income rose 2.3% to US$57.1 million from US$55.8 million, while non-interest expense advanced 13.7% to US$96.9 million.

Prospects: Our evaluation of Community Bank System Inc. as of October 4th, 2019 is the result of our systematic analysis on three basic characteristics: earnings strength, relative valuation, and recent stock price movement. The company has managed to produce a neutral trend in earnings per share over the past 5 quarters. In addition, recent analyst estimates for the company have been mixed and CBU has posted results that exceeded analysts' expectations. Based on operating earnings yield, the company is undervalued when compared to all of the companies we cover. Share price changes over the past year indicates that CBU will perform in line with the market over the near term.

Financial Data

(US$ in Thousands)	9 Mos	6 Mos	3 Mos	12/31/2018	12/31/2017	12/31/2016	12/31/2015	12/31/2014
Earnings Per Share	3.19	3.27	3.27	3.24	3.03	2.32	2.19	2.22
Cash Flow Per Share	3.55	3.87	3.79	4.33	3.88	2.97	2.84	3.04
Tang Book Value Per Share	19.35	19.57	18.51	17.68	15.98	16.14	15.00	14.75
Dividends Per Share	1.550	1.520	1.480	1.440	1.320	1.260	1.220	1.160
Dividend Payout %	48.59	46.48	45.26	44.44	43.56	54.31	55.71	52.25
Income Statement								
Interest Income	285,680	187,033	92,681	362,733	329,455	285,187	259,622	256,220
Interest Expense	19,245	11,874	5,822	17,678	13,780	11,291	11,202	11,792
Net Interest Income	266,435	175,159	86,859	345,055	315,675	273,896	248,420	244,428
Provision for Losses	5,573	3,822	2,422	10,837	10,984	8,076	6,447	7,178
Non-Interest Income	173,496	116,402	55,696	224,059	202,423	155,625	123,299	119,020
Non-Interest Expense	276,757	179,828	88,652	345,289	347,149	266,848	233,055	226,580
Income Before Taxes	157,601	107,911	51,481	212,988	159,965	154,597	132,217	129,690
Income Taxes	31,422	20,950	9,535	44,347	9,248	50,785	40,987	38,337
Net Income	126,179	86,961	41,946	168,641	150,717	103,812	91,230	91,353
Average Shares	52,246	52,188	52,061	51,748	49,470	44,485	41,401	41,029
Balance Sheet								
Net Loans & Leases	6,803,768	6,234,760	6,217,191	6,231,920	6,209,635	4,903,745	4,756,906	4,191,907
Total Assets	11,597,297	10,745,388	10,916,467	10,607,295	10,746,198	8,666,437	8,552,669	7,489,440
Total Deposits	9,168,285	8,488,205	8,619,662	8,322,371	8,444,420	7,075,954	6,873,474	5,935,264
Total Liabilities	9,756,876	8,935,878	9,159,339	8,893,512	9,110,883	7,468,337	7,412,022	6,501,536
Stockholders' Equity	1,840,421	1,809,510	1,757,128	1,713,783	1,635,315	1,198,100	1,140,647	987,904
Shares Outstanding	51,660	51,570	51,471	51,257	50,696	44,437	43,774	40,747
Statistical Record								
Return on Assets %	1.50	1.60	1.56	1.58	1.55	1.20	1.14	1.25
Return on Equity %	9.52	9.86	10.06	10.07	10.64	8.85	8.57	9.80
Net Interest Margin %	92.53	93.59	93.72	95.13	95.82	96.04	95.69	95.40
Efficiency Ratio %	62.24	58.80	59.75	58.84	65.27	60.54	60.86	60.38
Loans to Deposits	0.74	0.73	0.72	0.75	0.74	0.69	0.69	0.71
Price Range	67.47-54.72	67.47-54.72	66.52-52.61	66.52-51.22	62.32-49.11	62.24-34.47	43.13-33.60	39.91-32.84
P/E Ratio	21.15-17.15	20.63-16.73	20.34-16.09	20.53-15.81	20.57-16.21	26.83-14.86	19.69-15.34	17.98-14.79
Average Yield %	2.49	2.43	2.43	2.43	2.38	2.87	3.27	3.18

Address: 5790 Widewaters Parkway, DeWitt, NY 13214-1883 Telephone: 315-445-2282	Web Site: www.communitybankna.com Officers: Sally A. Steele - Chairman Mark E. Tryniski - President, Chief Executive Officer	Auditors: PricewaterhouseCoopers LLP Investor Contact: 315-445-3121 Transfer Agents: American Stock Transfer & Trust Company LLC, Brooklyn, NY

COMMUNITY HEALTH SYSTEMS, INC.

Exchange	Symbol	Price	52Wk Range	Yield	P/E
NYS	CYH	$2.90 (12/31/2019)	5.13-1.81	N/A	N/A

*7 Year Price Score 13.84 *NYSE Composite Index=100 *12 Month Price Score 90.69

Interim Earnings (Per Share)

Qtr.	Mar	Jun	Sep	Dec
2016	0.10	(12.91)	(0.71)	(1.99)
2017	(1.79)	(1.22)	(0.98)	(18.01)
2018	(0.22)	(0.97)	(2.88)	(2.91)
2019	(1.04)	(1.47)	(0.15)	...

Interim Dividends (Per Share)

Dividend Payment Suspended

Valuation Analysis — **Institutional Holding**

Forecast EPS	$-1.78	No of Institutions
	(01/16/2020)	341
Market Cap	$341.8 Million	Shares
Book Value	N/A	142,316,928
Price/Book	N/A	% Held
Price/Sales	0.03	82.86

Business Summary: Hospitals & Health Care Facilities (MIC: 4.2.1 SIC: 8062 NAIC: 622110)

Community Health Systems is a holding company. Through its subsidiaries, Co. operates general acute care hospitals and outpatient facilities. Co. provides healthcare services through the hospitals that it owns and operates and affiliated businesses in non-urban and selected urban markets. Services provided through Co.'s hospitals and affiliated businesses include general acute care, emergency room, general and specialty surgery, critical care, internal medicine, obstetrics, diagnostic, psychiatric and rehabilitation services. Co. also provides additional outpatient services at urgent care centers, occupational medicine clinics, imaging centers, cancer centers and ambulatory surgery centers.

Recent Developments: For the quarter ended Sep 30 2019, net income amounted to US$2.0 million versus a net loss of US$308.0 million in the year-earlier quarter. Revenues were US$3.25 billion, down 5.9% from US$3.45 billion the year before. Operating income was US$184.0 million versus US$74.0 million in the prior-year quarter, an increase of 148.6%. Indirect operating expenses decreased 9.3% to US$3.06 billion from US$3.38 billion in the equivalent prior-year period.

Prospects: Our evaluation of Community Health Systems Inc. as of October 4th, 2019 is the result of our systematic analysis on three basic characteristics: earnings strength, relative valuation, and recent stock price movement. The company has produced a positive trend in earnings per share over the past 5 quarters. However, recent analyst estimates for the company have been mixed and CYH has posted results that exceeded analysts' expectations. Based on operating earnings yield, the company is overvalued when compared to all of the companies we cover. Share price changes over the past year indicates that CYH will perform very poorly over the near term.

Financial Data

(US$ in Thousands)	9 Mos	6 Mos	3 Mos	12/31/2018	12/31/2017	12/31/2016	12/31/2015	12/31/2014
Earnings Per Share	(5.57)	(8.30)	(7.80)	(6.99)	(22.00)	(15.54)	1.37	0.82
Cash Flow Per Share	0.22	3.91	2.66	2.43	6.92	10.24	8.05	14.47
Income Statement								
Total Revenue	9,925,000	6,679,000	3,376,000	14,155,000	15,353,000	18,438,000	19,437,000	18,639,000
EBITDA	911,000	575,000	311,000	939,000	(1,057,000)	304,000	2,495,000	1,341,000
Depn & Amortn	456,000	305,000	153,000	700,000	861,000	1,100,000	1,174,000	75,000
Income Before Taxes	(327,000)	(252,000)	(99,000)	(737,000)	(2,849,000)	(1,758,000)	348,000	294,000
Income Taxes	(71,000)	3,000	7,000	(11,000)	(449,000)	(104,000)	116,000	82,000
Net Income	(302,000)	(285,000)	(118,000)	(788,000)	(2,459,000)	(1,721,000)	158,000	92,000
Average Shares	113,891	113,862	113,257	112,728	111,769	110,730	115,272	112,549
Balance Sheet								
Current Assets	3,382,000	3,484,000	3,595,000	3,549,000	4,068,000	4,666,000	5,166,000	5,566,000
Total Assets	15,895,000	16,132,000	16,309,000	15,859,000	17,450,000	21,944,000	26,861,000	27,421,000
Current Liabilities	2,355,000	2,503,000	2,508,000	2,392,000	2,356,000	2,887,000	3,072,000	3,589,000
Long-Term Obligations	13,286,000	13,393,000	13,385,000	13,392,000	13,880,000	14,789,000	16,822,000	16,681,000
Total Liabilities	17,743,000	17,965,000	17,972,000	17,394,000	18,217,000	20,329,000	22,842,000	23,418,000
Stockholders' Equity	(1,848,000)	(1,833,000)	(1,663,000)	(1,535,000)	(767,000)	1,615,000	4,019,000	4,003,000
Shares Outstanding	117,858	118,051	118,073	116,248	114,651	113,876	112,757	116,725
Statistical Record								
Return on Assets %	N.M.	N.M.	N.M.	N.M.	N.M.	N.M.	0.58	0.41
Return on Equity %	...	...	...	...	N.M.	N.M.	3.94	2.60
EBITDA Margin %	9.18	8.61	9.21	6.63	N.M.	1.65	12.84	7.19
Net Margin %	N.M.	N.M.	N.M.	N.M.	N.M.	N.M.	0.81	0.49
Asset Turnover	0.83	0.83	0.82	0.85	0.78	0.75	0.72	0.84
Current Ratio	1.44	1.39	1.43	1.48	1.73	1.62	1.68	1.55
Debt to Equity	...	...	...	...	...	9.16	4.19	4.17
Price Range	5.13-1.81	5.13-2.50	5.13-2.62	6.18-2.62	10.32-3.99	21.84-4.66	52.71-20.73	47.29-28.99
P/E Ratio	...	...	...	...	...	...	38.48-15.13	57.67-35.35

Address: 4000 Meridian Boulevard, Franklin, TN 37067	Web Site: www.chs.net	Auditors: Deloitte & Touche LLP
Telephone: 615-465-7000	Officers: Wayne T. Smith - Chairman, President, Chief Executive Officer, Principal Executive Officer	Investor Contact: 615-465-7000
	Tim L. Hingtgen - President, Chief Operating Officer, Executive Vice President	Transfer Agents: Registrar and Transfer Company, Cranford, NJ

COMPASS MINERALS INTERNATIONAL INC

Exchange	Symbol	Price	52Wk Range	Yield	P/E	Div Acheiver
NYS	CMP	$60.96 (12/31/2019)	61.00-39.75	4.72	36.29	14 Years

*7 Year Price Score 61.14   ***NYSE Composite Index=100**   ***12 Month Price Score 100.16**

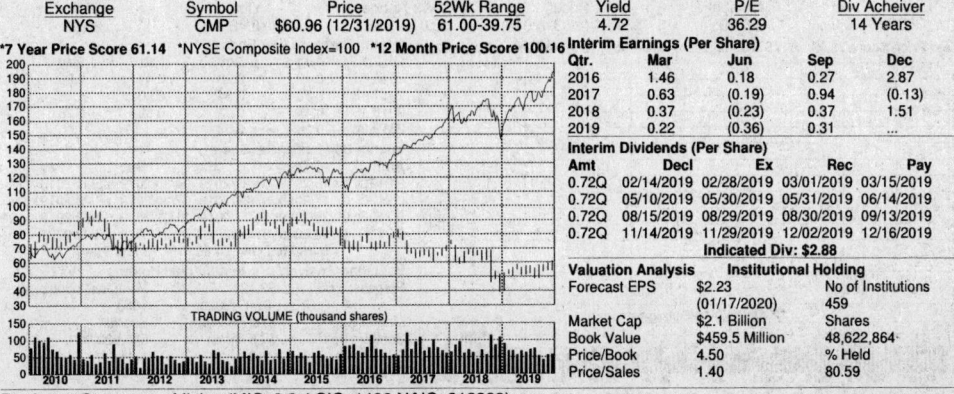

Interim Earnings (Per Share)

Qtr.	Mar	Jun	Sep	Dec
2016	1.46	0.18	0.27	2.87
2017	0.63	(0.19)	0.94	(0.13)
2018	0.37	(0.23)	0.37	1.51
2019	0.22	(0.36)	0.31	...

Interim Dividends (Per Share)

Amt	Decl	Ex	Rec	Pay
0.72Q	02/14/2019	02/28/2019	03/01/2019	03/15/2019
0.72Q	05/10/2019	05/30/2019	05/31/2019	06/14/2019
0.72Q	08/15/2019	08/29/2019	08/30/2019	09/13/2019
0.72Q	11/14/2019	11/29/2019	12/02/2019	12/16/2019

Indicated Div: $2.88

Valuation Analysis

		Institutional Holding	
Forecast EPS	$2.23	No of Institutions	459
	(01/17/2020)		
Market Cap	$2.1 Billion	Shares	
Book Value	$459.5 Million		48,622,864
Price/Book	4.50	% Held	
Price/Sales	1.40		80.59

Business Summary: Mining (MIC: 8.2.4 SIC: 1499 NAIC: 212399)

Compass Minerals International is a holding company. Through its wholly owned subsidiaries, Co. is a provider of minerals, including salt, specialty plant nutrition products, and specialty chemicals. Co. has three reportable segments: Salt, which produces, markets and sells salt and magnesium chloride and sodium chloride; Plant Nutrition North America, which includes sales of sulfate of potash specialty fertilizer and specialty plant nutrients; and Plant Nutrition South America, which manufactures, distributes and markets an array of specialty plant nutrients and supplements developed and formulated from primary and secondary nutrients, specialty plant nutrients and biostimulants.

Recent Developments: For the quarter ended Sep 30 2019, net income decreased 17.2% to US$10.6 million from US$12.8 million in the year-earlier quarter. Revenues were US$341.3 million, up 5.8% from US$322.5 million the year before. Operating income was US$30.1 million versus US$32.6 million in the prior-year quarter, a decrease of 7.7%. Direct operating expenses rose 5.5% to US$264.9 million from US$251.1 million in the comparable period the year before. Indirect operating expenses increased 19.3% to US$46.3 million from US$38.8 million in the equivalent prior-year period.

Prospects: Our evaluation of Compass Minerals International Inc. as of October 4th, 2019 is the result of our systematic analysis on three basic characteristics: earnings strength, relative valuation, and recent stock price movement. The company has enjoyed a very positive trend in earnings per share over the past 5 quarters. However, recent analyst estimates for the company have been mixed and CMP has posted results that fell short of analysts' expectations. Based on operating earnings yield, the company is fairly valued when compared to all of the companies we cover. Share price changes over the past year indicates that CMP will perform very poorly over the near term.

Financial Data

(US$ in Thousands)	9 Mos	6 Mos	3 Mos	12/31/2018	12/31/2017	12/31/2016	12/31/2015	12/31/2014
Earnings Per Share	1.68	1.74	1.87	2.02	1.25	4.79	4.69	6.44
Cash Flow Per Share	3.44	3.31	4.17	5.63	4.34	4.94	4.09	7.24
Tang Book Value Per Share	0.68	1.63	2.21	2.17	4.32	4.36	14.73	14.25
Dividends Per Share	2.880	2.880	2.880	2.880	2.880	2.780	2.640	2.400
Dividend Payout %	171.43	165.52	154.01	142.57	230.40	58.04	56.29	37.27
Income Statement								
Total Revenue	990,200	648,900	403,700	1,493,600	1,364,400	1,138,000	1,098,700	1,282,500
EBITDA	64,100	30,700	29,500	278,200	279,200	325,100	315,500	391,100
Depn & Amortn	2,100	1,400	700	139,100	124,400	92,300	79,500	79,200
Income Before Taxes	11,300	(3,700)	12,600	76,600	101,900	198,700	214,500	291,800
Income Taxes	5,300	500	4,900	8,800	60,000	34,600	55,300	73,900
Net Income	6,400	(4,200)	7,600	68,800	42,700	162,700	159,200	217,900
Average Shares	33,884	33,883	33,874	33,848	33,820	33,780	33,692	33,581
Balance Sheet								
Current Assets	695,400	625,200	619,200	721,200	737,500	715,000	512,300	702,700
Total Assets	2,329,800	2,320,900	2,308,600	2,367,900	2,571,000	2,466,500	1,628,900	1,637,200
Current Liabilities	277,900	276,400	286,000	283,300	268,000	372,000	170,800	237,700
Long-Term Obligations	1,358,200	1,275,900	1,225,600	1,321,200	1,330,400	1,194,800	722,100	622,500
Total Liabilities	1,870,300	1,798,000	1,769,800	1,827,700	1,876,400	1,749,400	989,200	983,600
Stockholders' Equity	459,500	522,900	538,800	540,200	694,600	717,100	639,700	653,600
Shares Outstanding	33,884	33,882	33,873	33,853	33,827	33,789	33,701	33,609
Statistical Record								
Return on Assets %	2.45	2.59	2.70	2.79	1.70	7.92	9.75	14.33
Return on Equity %	11.59	11.10	10.56	11.14	6.05	23.92	24.62	36.08
EBITDA Margin %	6.47	4.73	7.31	18.63	20.46	28.57	28.72	30.50
Net Margin %	0.65	N.M.	1.88	4.61	3.13	14.30	14.49	16.99
Asset Turnover	0.63	0.63	0.62	0.60	0.54	0.55	0.67	0.84
Current Ratio	2.50	2.26	2.17	2.55	2.75	1.92	3.00	2.96
Debt to Equity	2.96	2.44	2.27	2.45	1.92	1.67	1.13	0.95
Price Range	69.03-39.00	69.90-39.00	69.90-39.00	75.65-39.00	83.60-60.10	81.85-66.62	95.60-72.12	97.20-77.09
P/E Ratio	41.09-23.21	40.17-22.41	37.38-20.86	37.45-19.31	66.88-48.08	17.09-13.91	20.38-15.38	15.09-11.97
Average Yield %	5.43	5.15	4.89	4.58	4.16	3.76	3.08	2.76

Address: 9900 West 109th Street, Suite 100, Overland Park, KS 66210 **Telephone:** 913-344-9200	**Web Site:** www.compassminerals.com **Officers:** Kevin S. Crutchfield - President, Chief Executive Officer James D. Standen - Interim Chief Financial Officer, Chief Financial Officer, Principal Financial Officer, Principal Accounting Officer, Treasurer, Vice President	**Auditors:** Ernst & Young LLP **Investor Contact:** 913-344-9200 **Transfer Agents:** Computershare Trust Company, N.A., Providence, RI

CONAGRA BRANDS INC

Exchange	Symbol	Price	52Wk Range	Yield	P/E
NYS	CAG	$34.24 (12/31/2019)	35.07-20.85	2.48	20.88

*7 Year Price Score 73.09 ***NYSE Composite Index=100** ***12 Month Price Score 103.44**

TRADING VOLUME (thousand shares)

Interim Earnings (Per Share)

Qtr.	Aug	Nov	Feb	May
2016-17	0.42	0.28	0.41	0.35
2017-18	0.36	0.54	0.90	0.18
2018-19	0.45	0.31	0.50	0.25
2019-20	0.36	0.53	...	...

Interim Dividends (Per Share)

Amt	Decl	Ex	Rec	Pay
0.212Q	04/15/2019	04/29/2019	04/30/2019	05/31/2019
0.212Q	07/17/2019	07/29/2019	07/30/2019	08/29/2019
0.212Q	09/20/2019	10/31/2019	11/01/2019	12/03/2019
0.212Q	12/10/2019	01/30/2020	01/31/2020	03/03/2020

Indicated Div: $0.85 (Div. Reinv. Plan)

Valuation Analysis

		Institutional Holding	
Forecast EPS	$2.12	No of Institutions	
	(01/17/2020)	1053	
Market Cap	$16.7 Billion	Shares	
Book Value	$7.6 Billion	540,950,208	
Price/Book	2.19	% Held	
Price/Sales	1.58	87.71	

Business Summary: Food (MIC: 1.2.1 SIC: 2038 NAIC: 311412)

Conagra Brands is a packaged goods food company. Co.'s segments are: Grocery and Snacks, which includes branded, shelf stable food products sold in various retail channels; Refrigerated and Frozen, which includes branded, temperature controlled food products sold in various retail channels; International, which includes branded food products sold in retail and foodservice channels outside of the U.S.; Foodservice, which includes customized food products for sale to restaurants and other foodservice establishments; Pinnacle Foods, which includes and private-label food products; and Commercial Foods, which included commercially branded and private label food and ingredients, among others.

Recent Developments: For the quarter ended Nov 24 2019, income from continuing operations increased 94.7% to US$261.5 million from US$134.3 million in the year-earlier quarter. Net income increased 97.5% to US$261.5 million from US$132.4 million in the year-earlier quarter. Revenues were US$2.82 billion, up 18.3% from US$2.38 billion the year before. Direct operating expenses rose 18.5% to US$2.02 billion from US$1.71 billion in the comparable period the year before. Indirect operating expenses decreased 24.9% to US$358.5 million from US$477.6 million in the equivalent prior-year period.

Prospects: Our evaluation of Conagra Brands Inc. as of October 4th, 2019 is the result of our systematic analysis on three basic characteristics: earnings strength, relative valuation, and recent stock price movement. The company has produced a positive trend in earnings per share over the past 5 quarters. However, recent analyst estimates for the company have been mixed and CAG has posted results that exceeded analysts' expectations. Based on operating earnings yield, the company is undervalued when compared to all of the companies we cover. Share price changes over the past year indicates that CAG will perform poorly over the near term.

Financial Data

(US$ in Thousands)	6 Mos	3 Mos	05/26/2019	05/27/2018	05/28/2017	05/29/2016	05/31/2015	05/25/2014
Earnings Per Share	1.64	1.42	1.52	1.98	1.46	(1.56)	(0.60)	0.70
Cash Flow Per Share	2.65	2.54	2.54	2.37	2.73	2.79	3.42	3.69
Dividends Per Share	0.850	0.850	0.850	0.850	0.900	1.000	1.000	1.000
Dividend Payout %	51.83	59.86	55.92	42.93	61.64	...	...	142.86
Income Statement								
Total Revenue	5,211,500	2,390,700	9,538,400	7,938,300	7,826,900	11,642,900	15,832,400	17,702,600
EBITDA	906,000	369,900	1,263,800	1,068,400	958,600	4,551,400	(55,100)	1,066,800
Depn & Amortn	193,400	96,700	49,100	34,900	33,600	3,670,000	108,500	111,400
Income Before Taxes	468,500	150,500	823,300	874,800	729,500	583,600	(495,500)	576,400
Income Taxes	72,600	(11,500)	218,800	174,600	254,700	225,400	234,000	298,200
Net Income	434,300	173,800	678,300	808,400	639,300	(677,000)	(252,600)	303,100
Average Shares	488,300	487,900	445,600	407,400	436,000	438,500	426,100	427,500
Balance Sheet								
Current Assets	3,029,600	2,728,000	2,733,800	1,938,900	2,013,200	3,576,700	3,667,700	4,230,800
Total Assets	22,492,600	22,354,500	22,213,800	10,389,500	10,096,300	13,390,600	17,542,200	19,366,400
Current Liabilities	3,425,800	2,449,900	2,142,600	2,336,200	1,720,500	2,532,400	3,310,200	2,642,400
Long-Term Obligations	9,295,900	10,323,400	10,655,700	3,231,500	2,769,200	4,917,800	6,888,900	8,767,600
Total Liabilities	14,880,500	14,914,400	14,829,200	6,713,300	6,105,500	9,677,000	13,016,200	14,107,900
Stockholders' Equity	7,612,100	7,440,100	7,384,600	3,676,200	3,990,800	3,713,600	4,526,000	5,258,500
Shares Outstanding	486,813	486,654	486,085	390,828	416,519	438,064	428,204	421,915
Statistical Record								
Return on Assets %	3.53	4.10	4.17	7.91	5.46	N.M.	N.M.	1.53
Return on Equity %	10.82	12.06	12.30	21.15	16.64	N.M.	N.M.	5.78
EBITDA Margin %	17.38	15.47	13.25	13.46	12.25	39.09	N.M.	6.03
Net Margin %	8.33	7.27	7.11	10.18	8.17	N.M.	N.M.	1.71
Asset Turnover	0.46	0.61	0.59	0.78	0.67	0.75	0.84	0.89
Current Ratio	0.88	1.11	1.28	0.83	1.17	1.41	1.11	1.60
Debt to Equity	1.22	1.39	1.44	0.88	0.69	1.32	1.52	1.67
Price Range	32.60-20.85	38.25-20.85	38.94-20.85	39.95-32.43	41.50-33.23	36.13-29.12	30.27-22.36	28.97-21.99
P/E Ratio	19.88-12.71	26.94-14.68	25.62-13.72	20.18-16.38	28.42-22.76	...	...	41.39-31.42
Average Yield %	3.12	2.93	2.73	2.36	2.38	3.04	3.74	3.96

Address: 222 West Merchandise Mart Plaza, Suite 1300, Chicago, IL 60654
Telephone: 312-549-5000

Web Site: www.conagrabrands.com
Officers: Richard H. Lenny - Chairman Sean M. Connolly - President, Chief Executive Officer

Auditors: KPMG LLP
Investor Contact: 402-240-4154
Transfer Agents: Wells Fargo Shareowner Services, St. Paul, MN

CUBESMART

Exchange	Symbol	Price	52Wk Range	Yield	P/E
NYS	CUBE	$31.48 (12/31/2019)	36.31-28.07	4.19	34.22

*7 Year Price Score 105.81 *NYSE Composite Index=100 *12 Month Price Score 90.17

Interim Earnings (Per Share)

Qtr.	Mar	Jun	Sep	Dec
2016	0.08	0.11	0.13	0.13
2017	0.14	0.18	0.21	0.22
2018	0.19	0.21	0.23	0.25
2019	0.19	0.26	0.22	...

Interim Dividends (Per Share)

Amt	Decl	Ex	Rec	Pay
0.32Q	02/19/2019	03/29/2019	04/01/2019	04/15/2019
0.32Q	05/14/2019	06/28/2019	07/01/2019	07/15/2019
0.32Q	07/23/2019	09/30/2019	10/01/2019	10/15/2019
0.33Q	12/12/2019	12/31/2019	01/02/2020	01/15/2020

Indicated Div: $1.32

Valuation Analysis / **Institutional Holding**

Forecast EPS	$0.86	No of Institutions
(01/17/2020)		410
Market Cap	$6.1 Billion	Shares
Book Value	$1.8 Billion	252,632,048
Price/Book	3.36	% Held
Price/Sales	9.64	N/A

Business Summary: REITs (MIC: 5.3.1 SIC: 6798 NAIC: 525930)

CubeSmart is a self-administered and self-managed real estate company focused primarily on the ownership, operation, management, acquisition, and development of self-storage properties in the U.S. Co.'s self-storage facilities provide storage space for its residential and commercial customers. Co.'s customers rent storage cubes for their use on a month-to-month basis. Additionally, some of Co.'s stores provide outside storage areas for vehicles and boats. Co.'s stores are designed to accommodate both residential and commercial customers, with features such as aisles and load-bearing capabilities for truck access.

Recent Developments: For the quarter ended Sep 30 2019, net income decreased 1.6% to US$42.6 million from US$43.3 million in the year-earlier quarter. Revenues were US$166.5 million, up 8.6% from US$153.4 million the year before.

Prospects: Our evaluation of CubeSmart as of October 4th, 2019 is the result of our systematic analysis on three basic characteristics: earnings strength, relative valuation, and recent stock price movement. The company has managed to produce a neutral trend in earnings per share over the past 5 quarters. Additionally, recent analyst estimates for the company have been unchanged while CUBE has posted results that exceeded analysts' expectations. Based on operating earnings yield, the company is fairly valued when compared to all of the companies we cover. Share price changes over the past year indicates that CUBE will perform over the near term.

Financial Data

(US$ in Thousands)	9 Mos	6 Mos	3 Mos	12/31/2018	12/31/2017	12/31/2016	12/31/2015	12/31/2014
Earnings Per Share	0.92	0.93	0.88	0.88	0.74	0.45	0.42	0.14
Cash Flow Per Share	1.71	1.72	1.68	1.65	1.63	1.47	1.28	1.11
Tang Book Value Per Share	9.37	9.26	9.02	9.09	8.93	9.15	9.33	8.69
Dividends Per Share	1.280	1.260	1.240	1.220	1.110	0.900	0.690	0.550
Dividend Payout %	139.13	135.48	140.91	138.64	150.00	200.00	164.29	392.86
Income Statement								
Total Revenue	478,409	311,862	152,845	597,944	558,943	510,039	444,521	376,963
EBITDA	297,827	192,422	92,732	376,461	344,906	308,456	279,340	210,616
Depn & Amortn	124,566	80,500	39,066	145,663	148,319	164,442	154,113	129,003
Income Before Taxes	117,321	74,876	35,525	166,353	136,997	91,038	79,167	32,621
Net Income	127,072	84,918	35,498	163,889	134,288	87,905	77,712	26,379
Average Shares	193,817	190,543	187,984	185,495	181,448	179,533	170,191	150,863
Balance Sheet								
Current Assets	15,251	15,383	6,541	38,268	37,594	20,843	96,458	14,413
Total Assets	3,950,330	3,947,469	3,814,189	3,752,972	3,545,336	3,475,028	3,114,834	2,786,339
Current Liabilities	213,647	227,034	229,618	211,015	199,127	143,415	124,122	97,736
Long-Term Obligations	1,824,273	1,852,834	1,792,112	1,747,094	1,634,990	1,595,743	1,262,212	1,173,851
Total Liabilities	2,136,688	2,173,580	2,116,820	2,043,294	1,916,202	1,819,646	1,471,507	1,338,313
Stockholders' Equity	1,813,642	1,773,889	1,697,369	1,709,678	1,629,134	1,655,382	1,643,327	1,448,026
Shares Outstanding	193,554	191,626	188,137	187,145	182,215	180,083	174,667	163,956
Statistical Record								
Return on Assets %	4.62	4.67	4.47	4.49	3.83	2.66	2.63	1.03
Return on Equity %	9.99	10.17	9.97	9.82	8.18	5.32	5.03	2.08
EBITDA Margin %	62.25	61.70	60.67	62.96	61.71	60.48	62.84	55.87
Net Margin %	26.56	27.23	23.22	27.41	24.03	17.23	17.48	7.00
Asset Turnover	0.17	0.16	0.16	0.16	0.16	0.15	0.15	0.15
Current Ratio	0.07	0.07	0.03	0.18	0.19	0.15	0.78	0.15
Debt to Equity	1.01	1.04	1.06	1.02	1.00	0.96	0.77	0.81
Price Range	36.31-27.29	34.49-27.29	32.97-27.29	32.97-25.34	29.65-22.94	33.30-23.88	31.42-22.07	22.92-15.63
P/E Ratio	39.47-29.66	37.09-29.34	37.47-31.01	37.47-28.80	40.07-31.00	74.00-53.07	74.81-52.55	163.71-111.64
Average Yield %	4.01	4.09	4.12	4.16	4.26	3.10	2.71	2.96

Address: 5 Old Lancaster Road, Malvern, PA 19355 **Telephone:** 610-535-5000	**Web Site:** www.cubesmart.com **Officers:** Christopher P. Marr - President, Chief Executive Officer, Chief Operating Officer, Chief Investment Officer, Treasurer Timothy M. Martin - Chief Financial Officer, Treasurer, Senior Vice President, Chief Accounting Officer	**Auditors:** KPMG LLP **Investor Contact:** 610-293-5700 **Transfer Agents:** American Stock Transfer & Trust Co., LLC, Brooklyn, NY

CONCHO RESOURCES INC

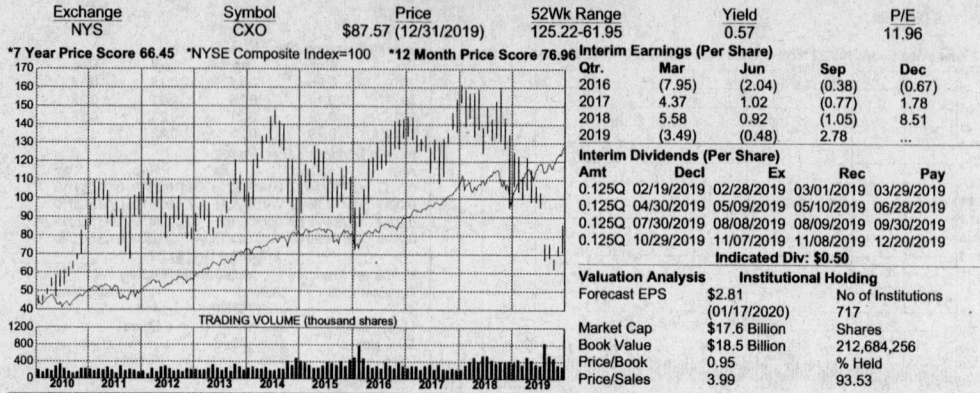

Exchange	Symbol	Price	52Wk Range	Yield	P/E
NYS	CXO	$87.57 (12/31/2019)	125.22-61.95	0.57	11.96

*7 Year Price Score 66.45   *NYSE Composite Index=100   *12 Month Price Score 76.96

Interim Earnings (Per Share)

Qtr.	Mar	Jun	Sep	Dec
2016	(7.95)	(2.04)	(0.38)	(0.67)
2017	4.37	1.02	(0.77)	1.78
2018	5.58	0.92	(1.05)	8.51
2019	(3.49)	(0.48)	2.78	...

Interim Dividends (Per Share)

Amt	Decl	Ex	Rec	Pay
0.125Q	02/19/2019	02/28/2019	03/01/2019	03/29/2019
0.125Q	04/30/2019	05/09/2019	05/10/2019	06/28/2019
0.125Q	07/30/2019	08/08/2019	08/09/2019	09/30/2019
0.125Q	10/29/2019	11/07/2019	11/08/2019	12/20/2019

Indicated Div: $0.50

Valuation Analysis

		Institutional Holding	
Forecast EPS	$2.81	No of Institutions	
	(01/17/2020)	717	
Market Cap	$17.6 Billion	Shares	
Book Value	$18.5 Billion	212,684,256	
Price/Book	0.95	% Held	
Price/Sales	3.99	93.53	

Business Summary: Production & Extraction (MIC: 9.1.1 SIC: 1311 NAIC: 211111)

Concho Resources is an independent oil and natural gas company engaged in the acquisition, development, exploration and production of oil and natural gas properties. Co.'s operations are primarily focused in the Permian Basin of Southeast New Mexico and West Texas. Co. is actively developing its resource base utilizing development projects, which include long-lateral wells and multi-well pad locations, throughout its operating areas. Co.'s operating areas include: the Midland Basin and the Delaware Basin, which includes its assets in the Northern Delaware Basin, Southern Delaware Basin and New Mexico Shelf.

Recent Developments: For the quarter ended Sep 30 2019, net income amounted to US$558.0 million versus a net loss of US$199.0 million in the year-earlier quarter. Revenues were US$1.12 billion, down 6.5% from US$1.19 billion the year before. Operating income was US$822.0 million versus a loss of US$225.0 million in the prior-year quarter. Direct operating expenses rose 12.2% to US$275.0 million from US$245.0 million in the comparable period the year before. Indirect operating expenses decreased 98.5% to US$18.0 million from US$1.17 billion in the equivalent prior-year period.

Prospects: Our evaluation of Concho Resources Inc. as of October 4th, 2019 is the result of our systematic analysis on three basic characteristics: earnings strength, relative valuation, and recent stock price movement. The company has generated a negative trend in earnings per share over the past 5 quarters. In addition, recent analyst estimates for the company have been reduced and CXO has posted results that fell short of analysts' expectations. Based on operating earnings yield, the company is fairly valued when compared to all of the companies we cover. Share price changes over the past year indicates that CXO will perform well over the near term.

Financial Data

(US$ in Thousands)	9 Mos	6 Mos	3 Mos	12/31/2018	12/31/2017	12/31/2016	12/31/2015	12/31/2014
Earnings Per Share	7.32	3.49	4.89	13.25	6.41	(10.85)	0.54	4.88
Cash Flow Per Share	13.86	14.41	13.52	14.97	11.51	10.25	7.48	15.38
Tang Book Value Per Share	81.34	78.36	78.82	82.52	59.77	52.02	53.56	46.49
Dividends Per Share	0.375	0.250	0.125	...	...	...	...	...
Dividend Payout %	5.12	7.16	2.56	...	...	...	...	...
Income Statement								
Total Revenue	3,346,000	2,231,000	1,104,000	4,151,000	2,586,000	1,634,988	1,803,573	2,660,147
EBITDA	1,316,000	1,000	(377,000)	3,060,000	1,048,000	(2,114,418)	330,955	2,052,361
Depn & Amortn	1,434,000	945,000	465,000	22,000	21,000	20,600	18,300	979,740
Income Before Taxes	(259,000)	(1,039,000)	(889,000)	2,889,000	881,000	(2,338,536)	97,271	855,960
Income Taxes	(25,000)	(247,000)	(194,000)	603,000	(75,000)	(876,090)	31,371	317,785
Net Income	(234,000)	(792,000)	(695,000)	2,286,000	956,000	(1,462,446)	65,900	538,175
Average Shares	199,454	199,185	199,148	171,249	147,956	134,755	120,373	109,132
Balance Sheet								
Current Assets	2,017,000	860,000	1,027,000	1,409,000	592,000	546,494	1,314,550	1,188,396
Total Assets	26,132,000	25,478,000	26,168,000	26,294,000	13,732,000	12,119,326	12,641,876	11,799,963
Current Liabilities	1,340,000	1,403,000	1,660,000	1,356,000	1,165,000	753,186	596,420	1,427,193
Long-Term Obligations	4,349,000	4,350,000	4,567,000	4,194,000	2,691,000	2,740,580	3,332,188	3,517,320
Total Liabilities	7,621,000	7,519,000	8,109,000	7,526,000	4,817,000	4,496,633	5,699,325	6,519,175
Stockholders' Equity	18,511,000	17,959,000	18,059,000	18,768,000	8,915,000	7,622,693	6,942,551	5,280,788
Shares Outstanding	201,044	200,598	200,599	200,257	148,726	146,058	129,137	113,004
Statistical Record								
Return on Assets %	4.98	2.59	3.73	11.42	7.40	N.M.	0.54	5.03
Return on Equity %	7.16	3.75	5.44	16.52	11.56	N.M.	1.08	11.91
EBITDA Margin %	39.33	0.04	N.M.	73.72	40.53	N.M.	18.35	77.15
Net Margin %	N.M.	N.M.	N.M.	55.07	36.97	N.M.	3.65	20.23
Asset Turnover	0.17	0.22	0.21	0.21	0.20	0.13	0.15	0.25
Current Ratio	1.51	0.61	0.62	1.04	0.51	0.73	2.20	0.83
Debt to Equity	0.23	0.24	0.25	0.22	0.30	0.36	0.48	0.67
Price Range	159.96-66.64	159.96-94.90	159.96-94.90	161.66-94.90	153.92-108.05	143.25-72.52	128.31-86.67	148.00-83.01
P/E Ratio	21.85-9.10	45.83-27.19	32.71-19.41	12.20-7.16	24.01-16.86	...	237.61-160.50	30.33-17.01
Average Yield %	0.35	0.20	0.09	...	...	...	...	...

Address: One Concho Center, 600 West Illinois Avenue, Midland, TX 79701 **Telephone:** 432-683-7443 **Fax:** 432-683-7441	**Web Site:** www.concho.com **Officers:** Timothy A. (Tim) Leach - Chairman, President, Chief Executive Officer Jack F. Harper - President, Chief Financial Officer, Executive Vice President, Treasurer, Senior Vice President, Chief of Staff	**Auditors:** Grant Thornton LLP **Investor Contact:** 432-685-2533 **Transfer Agents:** American Stock Transfer & Trust Company, New York, NY

CONOCOPHILLIPS

Exchange	Symbol	Price	52Wk Range	Yield	P/E
NYS	COP	$65.03 (12/31/2019)	70.65-50.42	2.58	8.86

*7 Year Price Score 85.61 *NYSE Composite Index=100 *12 Month Price Score 93.24

Interim Earnings (Per Share)

Qtr.	Mar	Jun	Sep	Dec
2016	(1.18)	(0.86)	(0.84)	(0.03)
2017	0.47	(2.78)	0.34	1.28
2018	0.75	1.39	1.59	1.60
2019	1.60	1.40	2.74	...

Interim Dividends (Per Share)

Amt	Decl	Ex	Rec	Pay
0.305Q	01/30/2019	02/08/2019	02/11/2019	03/01/2019
0.305Q	05/01/2019	05/10/2019	05/13/2019	06/03/2019
0.305Q	07/11/2019	07/19/2019	07/22/2019	09/03/2019
0.42Q	10/07/2019	10/16/2019	10/17/2019	12/02/2019

Indicated Div: $1.68 (Div. Reinv. Plan)

Valuation Analysis | **Institutional Holding**

Forecast EPS	$3.63	No of Institutions
	(01/17/2020)	2352
Market Cap	$71.4 Billion	Shares
Book Value	$35.1 Billion	1,038,974,848
Price/Book	2.03	% Held
Price/Sales	1.83	65.88

Business Summary: Production & Extraction (MIC: 9.1.1 SIC: 1311 NAIC: 211111)

ConocoPhillips is an exploration and production company engaged in exploring for, produceing, transporting and marketing crude oil, bitumen, natural gas, liquefied natural gas and natural gas liquids. Co.'s segments include: Alaska, which operates in Alaska; Lower 48, which operates in the U.S. and the Gulf of Mexico; Canada, which operates in northeastern Alberta and western Canada; Europe and North Africa, which consists of operations and exploration activities in Norway, the U.K. and Libya; Asia Pacific and Middle East, which has activities in China, Indonesia, Malaysia, Australia, Qatar, Timor-Leste and Brunei; and Other International, which has activities in Colombia and Chile.

Recent Developments: For the quarter ended Sep 30 2019, net income increased 64.0% to US$3.07 billion from US$1.87 billion in the year-earlier quarter. Revenues were US$10.09 billion, down 0.7% from US$10.17 billion the year before. Direct operating expenses declined 17.5% to US$4.04 billion from US$4.90 billion in the comparable period the year before. Indirect operating expenses increased 8.3% to US$2.56 billion from US$2.36 billion in the equivalent prior-year period.

Prospects: Our evaluation of ConocoPhillips as of October 4th, 2019 is the result of our systematic analysis on three basic characteristics: earnings strength, relative valuation, and recent stock price movement. The company has generated a negative trend in earnings per share over the past 5 quarters. In addition, recent analyst estimates for the company have been reduced and COP has posted results that fell short of analysts' expectations. Based on operating earnings yield, the company is undervalued when compared to all of the companies we cover. Share price changes over the past year indicates that COP will perform poorly over the near term.

Financial Data

(US$ in Thousands)	9 Mos	6 Mos	3 Mos	12/31/2018	12/31/2017	12/31/2016	12/31/2015	12/31/2014
Earnings Per Share	7.34	6.19	6.18	5.32	(0.70)	(2.91)	(3.58)	5.51
Cash Flow Per Share	10.74	11.53	11.79	11.09	5.80	3.53	6.10	13.53
Tang Book Value Per Share	32.03	29.70	29.07	28.06	26.00	28.27	32.17	42.16
Dividends Per Share	1.220	1.200	1.180	1.160	1.060	1.000	2.940	2.840
Dividend Payout %	16.62	19.39	19.09	21.80	...	...	...	51.54
Income Statement								
Total Revenue	28,530,000	18,437,000	10,057,000	38,727,000	32,584,000	24,360,000	30,935,000	55,517,000
EBITDA	13,422,000	8,179,000	4,466,000	16,664,000	5,328,000	4,777,000	2,794,000	18,367,000
Depn & Amortn	4,602,000	3,036,000	1,546,000	5,956,000	6,845,000	9,062,000	9,113,000	8,329,000
Income Before Taxes	8,238,000	4,745,000	2,687,000	9,973,000	(2,615,000)	(5,530,000)	(7,239,000)	9,390,000
Income Taxes	1,724,000	1,302,000	841,000	3,668,000	(1,822,000)	(1,971,000)	(2,868,000)	3,583,000
Net Income	6,469,000	3,413,000	1,833,000	6,257,000	(855,000)	(3,615,000)	(4,428,000)	6,869,000
Average Shares	1,113,250	1,131,242	1,146,515	1,175,538	1,221,038	1,245,440	1,241,919	1,245,863
Balance Sheet								
Current Assets	15,217,000	15,800,000	13,683,000	13,274,000	16,512,000	8,609,000	8,789,000	15,068,000
Total Assets	70,340,000	71,261,000	71,498,000	69,980,000	73,362,000	89,772,000	97,484,000	116,539,000
Current Liabilities	5,942,000	8,996,000	7,370,000	7,395,000	9,397,000	6,909,000	9,256,000	11,537,000
Long-Term Obligations	14,799,000	14,809,000	14,832,000	14,856,000	17,128,000	26,186,000	23,453,000	22,383,000
Total Liabilities	35,194,000	38,285,000	38,639,000	38,041,000	42,755,000	54,798,000	57,722,000	64,628,000
Stockholders' Equity	35,146,000	32,976,000	32,859,000	31,939,000	30,607,000	34,974,000	39,762,000	51,911,000
Shares Outstanding	1,097,268	1,110,141	1,130,175	1,138,349	1,177,107	1,237,269	1,235,995	1,231,352
Statistical Record								
Return on Assets %	11.83	10.19	10.13	8.73	N.M.	N.M.	N.M.	5.86
Return on Equity %	24.85	22.31	22.72	20.01	N.M.	N.M.	N.M.	13.21
EBITDA Margin %	47.05	44.36	44.41	43.03	16.35	19.61	9.03	33.08
Net Margin %	22.67	18.51	18.23	16.16	N.M.	N.M.	N.M.	12.37
Asset Turnover	0.55	0.56	0.56	0.54	0.40	0.26	0.29	0.47
Current Ratio	2.56	1.76	1.86	1.79	1.76	1.25	0.95	1.31
Debt to Equity	0.42	0.45	0.45	0.47	0.56	0.75	0.59	0.43
Price Range	79.89-50.42	79.89-57.01	79.89-57.01	79.89-52.00	56.23-42.50	52.64-31.88	69.88-42.19	86.76-61.69
P/E Ratio	10.88-6.87	12.91-9.21	12.93-9.22	15.02-9.78	...	...	...	15.75-11.20
Average Yield %	1.92	1.78	1.72	1.76	2.22	2.35	5.05	3.83

Address: 925 N. Eldridge Parkway, Houston, TX 77079	**Web Site:** www.conocophillips.com	**Auditors:** Ernst & Young LLP
Telephone: 281-293-1000	**Officers:** Ryan M. Lance - Chairman, Chief Executive Officer, Division Officer Kelly B. Rose - Senior Vice President, General Counsel, Corporate Secretary	**Investor Contact:** 212-207-1996
		Transfer Agents: Computershare, Canton, MA

CONSOLIDATED EDISON INC

Exchange	Symbol	Price	52Wk Range	Yield	P/E	Div Acheiver
NYS	ED	$90.47 (12/31/2019)	94.65-74.45	3.38	21.34	44 Years

*7 Year Price Score 99.99   *NYSE Composite Index=100   *12 Month Price Score 96.93

Interim Earnings (Per Share)

Qtr.	Mar	Jun	Sep	Dec
2016	1.05	0.77	1.62	0.66
2017	1.27	0.57	1.48	1.63
2018	1.37	0.60	1.39	1.05
2019	1.31	0.46	1.42	...

Interim Dividends (Per Share)

Amt	Decl	Ex	Rec	Pay
0.74Q	04/18/2019	05/14/2019	05/15/2019	06/17/2019
0.74Q	07/18/2019	08/13/2019	08/14/2019	09/16/2019
0.74Q	10/17/2019	11/12/2019	11/13/2019	12/16/2019
0.765Q	01/16/2020	02/18/2020	02/19/2020	03/16/2020

Indicated Div: $3.06 (Div. Reinv. Plan)

Valuation Analysis / Institutional Holding

Forecast EPS	$4.30	No of Institutions
	(01/17/2020)	1318
Market Cap	$30.0 Billion	Shares
Book Value	$18.0 Billion	243,771,936
Price/Book	1.67	% Held
Price/Sales	2.39	64.20

Business Summary: Electric Utilities (MIC: 3.1.1 SIC: 4931 NAIC: 221121)

Consolidated Edison is a holding company. Through its subsidiaries, Co. is engaged in provision of energy services. Co.'s subsidiaries: Consolidated Edison Company of New York, Inc.'s principal business operations are its regulated electric, gas and steam delivery businesses; Orange & Rockland Utilities, Inc.'s principal business operations are its regulated electric and gas delivery businesses; Con Edison Clean Energy Businesses, Inc. develops, owns and operates renewable and energy infrastructure projects and provides energy-related products and services to wholesale and retail customers; and Con Edison Transmission, Inc. is engaged in electric and gas transmission projects.

Recent Developments: For the quarter ended Sep 30 2019, net income increased 15.6% to US$503.0 million from US$435.0 million in the year-earlier quarter. Revenues were US$3.37 billion, up 1.1% from US$3.33 billion the year before. Operating income was US$867.0 million versus US$826.0 million in the prior-year quarter, an increase of 5.0%. Direct operating expenses declined 5.6% to US$1.46 billion from US$1.55 billion in the comparable period the year before. Indirect operating expenses increased 8.6% to US$1.04 billion from US$957.0 million in the equivalent prior-year period.

Prospects: Our evaluation of Consolidated Edison Inc. as of October 4th, 2019 is the result of our systematic analysis on three basic characteristics: earnings strength, relative valuation, and recent stock price movement. The company has produced a positive trend in earnings per share over the past 5 quarters. However, recent analyst estimates for the company have been mixed and ED has posted results that fell short of analysts' expectations. Based on operating earnings yield, the company is fairly valued when compared to all of the companies we cover. Share price changes over the past year indicates that ED will perform well over the near term.

Financial Data

(US$ in Thousands)	9 Mos	6 Mos	3 Mos	12/31/2018	12/31/2017	12/31/2016	12/31/2015	12/31/2014
Earnings Per Share	4.24	4.21	4.35	4.42	4.94	4.12	4.05	3.71
Cash Flow Per Share	9.20	9.73	9.35	8.65	10.96	11.48	11.18	9.67
Tang Book Value Per Share	47.99	47.18	46.79	45.58	47.93	45.07	43.08	41.46
Dividends Per Share	2.935	2.910	2.885	2.860	2.760	2.680	2.600	2.520
Dividend Payout %	69.22	69.12	66.32	64.71	55.87	65.05	64.20	67.92
Income Statement								
Total Revenue	9,623,000	6,258,000	3,514,000	12,337,000	12,033,000	12,075,000	12,554,000	12,919,000
EBITDA	2,054,000	1,202,000	771,000	3,923,000	3,943,000	3,645,000	3,529,000	3,424,000
Depn & Amortn	(88,000)	(59,000)	(29,000)	1,321,000	1,217,000	1,006,000	1,078,000	1,173,000
Income Before Taxes	1,370,000	751,000	553,000	1,783,000	1,997,000	1,943,000	1,798,000	1,660,000
Income Taxes	243,000	127,000	108,000	401,000	472,000	698,000	605,000	568,000
Net Income	1,048,000	576,000	424,000	1,382,000	1,525,000	1,245,000	1,193,000	1,092,000
Average Shares	333,200	329,200	323,400	312,900	308,800	301,900	294,400	294,000
Balance Sheet								
Current Assets	3,581,000	3,707,000	3,781,000	3,864,000	3,537,000	3,406,000	3,836,000	3,854,000
Total Assets	55,940,000	55,602,000	55,066,000	53,920,000	48,111,000	48,255,000	45,642,000	44,308,000
Current Liabilities	6,219,000	5,969,000	6,348,000	6,207,000	4,902,000	3,843,000	4,720,000	3,781,000
Long-Term Obligations	18,356,000	18,317,000	17,758,000	17,495,000	14,731,000	14,735,000	12,006,000	11,631,000
Total Liabilities	37,981,000	37,893,000	37,697,000	37,194,000	32,693,000	33,957,000	32,590,000	31,732,000
Stockholders' Equity	17,959,000	17,709,000	17,369,000	16,726,000	15,418,000	14,298,000	13,052,000	12,576,000
Shares Outstanding	332,000	332,000	327,000	321,000	310,000	305,000	293,000	292,876
Statistical Record								
Return on Assets %	2.62	2.56	2.65	2.71	3.17	2.64	2.65	2.57
Return on Equity %	8.15	8.05	8.35	8.60	10.26	9.08	9.31	8.80
EBITDA Margin %	21.34	19.21	21.94	31.80	32.77	30.19	28.11	26.50
Net Margin %	10.89	9.20	12.07	11.20	12.67	10.31	9.50	8.45
Asset Turnover	0.24	0.24	0.24	0.24	0.25	0.26	0.28	0.30
Current Ratio	0.58	0.62	0.60	0.62	0.72	0.89	0.81	1.02
Debt to Equity	1.02	1.03	1.02	1.05	0.96	1.03	0.92	0.92
Price Range	94.65-74.45	89.65-74.41	85.68-71.39	83.93-71.39	89.66-72.64	81.67-64.27	71.40-57.21	68.50-52.46
P/E Ratio	22.32-17.56	21.29-17.67	19.70-16.41	18.99-16.15	18.15-14.70	19.82-15.60	17.63-14.13	18.46-14.14
Average Yield %	3.52	3.60	3.68	3.68	3.40	3.62	4.11	4.39

Address: 4 Irving Place, New York, NY 10003	Web Site: www.conedison.com	Auditors: PricewaterhouseCoopers LLP
Telephone: 212-460-4600	Officers: John McAvoy - Chairman, President, Chief Executive Officer Robert N. Hoglund - Senior Vice President, Chief Financial Officer	Investor Contact: 212-460-6611 Transfer Agents: Computershare, Pittsburgh, PA

CONSTELLATION BRANDS INC

Exchange	Symbol	Price	52Wk Range	Yield	P/E
NYS	STZ	$189.75 (12/31/2019)	212.54-150.94	1.58	45.83

*7 Year Price Score 107.70 *NYSE Composite Index=100   *12 Month Price Score 93.14

Interim Earnings (Per Share)

Qtr.	May	Aug	Nov	Feb
2016-17	1.55	1.75	1.98	2.25
2017-18	2.00	2.48	2.44	4.62
2018-19	3.77	5.87	1.56	6.36
2019-20	(1.30)	(2.77)	1.85	...

Interim Dividends (Per Share)

Amt	Decl	Ex	Rec	Pay
0.75Q	04/03/2019	05/09/2019	05/10/2019	05/24/2019
0.75Q	06/27/2019	08/12/2019	08/13/2019	08/27/2019
0.75Q	10/02/2019	11/07/2019	11/08/2019	11/22/2019
0.75Q	01/07/2020	02/10/2020	02/11/2020	02/25/2020

Indicated Div: $3.00

Valuation Analysis

		Institutional Holding	
Forecast EPS	$8.71	No of Institutions	1376
	(01/17/2020)		
Market Cap	$36.2 Billion	Shares	
Book Value	$11.7 Billion		181,309,824
Price/Book	3.09	% Held	
Price/Sales	4.40		70.82

Business Summary: Beverages (MIC: 1.2.2 SIC: 2084 NAIC: 312130)

Constellation Brands is an international beverage alcohol company. Co. is a producer and marketer of beer, wine and spirits with operations in the U.S., Mexico, New Zealand, Italy and Canada. Co. has two segments: Beer, in which Co. is engaged in the U.S. beer market that includes the imported, craft, domestic super premium, and alternative beverage alcohol categories and it has the right to import, market and sell these Mexican beer brands in the U.S.; and Wine and Spirits, in which its wine portfolio is supported by grapes purchased from independent growers, primarily in the U.S., New Zealand and Chile, and vineyard holdings in the U.S., New Zealand and Italy.

Recent Developments: For the quarter ended Nov 30 2019, net income increased 17.4% to US$366.5 million from US$312.1 million in the year-earlier quarter. Revenues were US$2.00 billion, up 1.4% from US$1.97 billion the year before. Operating income was US$267.2 million versus US$556.5 million in the prior-year quarter, a decrease of 52.0%. Direct operating expenses rose 0.9% to US$1.01 billion from US$1.00 billion in the comparable period the year before. Indirect operating expenses increased 74.2% to US$720.3 million from US$413.5 million in the equivalent prior-year period.

Prospects: Our evaluation of Constellation Brands Inc. as of October 4th, 2019 is the result of our systematic analysis on three basic characteristics: earnings strength, relative valuation, and recent stock price movement. The company has managed to produce a neutral trend in earnings per share over the past 5 quarters. In addition, recent analyst estimates for the company have been mixed and STZ has posted results that exceeded analysts' expectations. Based on operating earnings yield, the company is fairly valued when compared to all of the companies we cover. Share price changes over the past year indicates that STZ will perform well over the near term.

Financial Data

(US$ in Thousands)	9 Mos	6 Mos	3 Mos	02/28/2019	02/28/2018	02/28/2017	02/29/2016	02/28/2015
Earnings Per Share	4.14	3.85	12.49	17.57	11.55	7.52	5.18	4.17
Cash Flow Per Share	12.25	12.14	12.20	11.79	9.92	8.51	7.17	5.61
Tang Book Value Per Share	6.37	4.69	8.20	6.61	N.M.	N.M.	N.M.	N.M.
Dividends Per Share	2.990	2.980	2.970	2.960	2.080	1.600	1.240	...
Dividend Payout %	72.22	77.40	23.78	16.85	18.01	21.28	23.94	...
Income Statement								
Total Revenue	6,440,600	4,441,200	2,097,200	8,116,000	7,585,000	7,331,500	6,548,400	6,028,000
EBITDA	1,884,200	1,532,500	709,300	2,857,600	2,574,000	2,693,300	1,985,000	1,697,800
Depn & Amortn	277,200	192,700	86,600	447,100	386,500	293,900	221,000	202,000
Income Before Taxes	1,277,700	1,113,600	508,100	2,043,400	1,855,500	2,066,100	1,450,100	1,158,100
Income Taxes	(1,046,500)	(387,600)	(185,400)	685,900	11,900	554,200	440,600	343,400
Net Income	(410,200)	(770,600)	(245,400)	3,435,900	2,318,900	1,535,100	1,054,900	839,300
Average Shares	194,856	168,310	168,118	195,532	200,745	204,099	203,821	201,224
Balance Sheet								
Current Assets	3,469,900	3,537,500	3,580,900	3,684,000	3,474,000	3,230,000	2,977,600	2,910,800
Total Assets	27,093,700	27,555,100	28,951,100	29,231,500	20,538,700	18,602,400	16,965,000	15,144,500
Current Liabilities	2,460,200	2,195,900	2,939,300	3,163,800	1,944,700	2,697,600	2,272,300	1,130,700
Long-Term Obligations	11,339,700	12,159,800	11,745,800	11,759,800	9,417,600	7,720,700	6,816,200	7,137,500
Total Liabilities	15,384,300	16,177,600	16,776,500	16,680,500	12,492,600	11,711,200	10,405,400	9,373,800
Stockholders' Equity	11,709,400	11,377,500	12,174,600	12,551,000	8,046,100	6,891,200	6,559,600	5,770,700
Shares Outstanding	190,818	190,591	191,571	191,278	191,306	194,598	199,458	194,541
Statistical Record								
Return on Assets %	3.02	2.99	9.40	13.81	11.85	8.63	6.55	5.70
Return on Equity %	7.22	6.82	21.53	33.36	31.05	22.83	17.06	15.61
EBITDA Margin %	29.26	34.51	33.82	35.21	33.94	36.74	30.31	28.17
Net Margin %	N.M.	N.M.	N.M.	42.33	30.57	20.94	16.11	13.92
Asset Turnover	0.30	0.32	0.31	0.33	0.39	0.41	0.41	0.41
Current Ratio	1.41	1.61	1.22	1.16	1.79	1.20	1.31	2.57
Debt to Equity	0.97	1.07	0.96	0.94	1.17	1.12	1.04	1.24
Price Range	212.54-150.94	228.67-150.94	233.02-150.94	234.22-150.94	228.57-155.79	171.24-138.71	154.36-110.91	115.78-77.97
P/E Ratio	51.34-36.46	59.39-39.21	18.66-12.08	13.33-8.59	19.79-13.49	22.77-18.45	29.80-21.41	27.76-18.70
Average Yield %	1.59	1.56	1.50	1.43	1.06	1.01	0.97	...

Address: 207 High Point Drive, Building 100, Victor, NY 14564 **Telephone:** 585-678-7100	**Web Site:** www.cbrands.com **Officers:** Robert Sands - Executive Chairman, President, Chief Executive Officer Richard Sands - Executive Chairman, Executive Vice-Chairman	**Auditors:** KPMG LLP **Investor Contact:** 188-892-22150 **Transfer Agents:** Computershare Shareowner Services, College Station, TX

CONTINENTAL RESOURCES INC.

Exchange	Symbol	Price	52Wk Range	Yield	P/E
NYS	CLR	$34.30 (12/31/2019)	51.82-27.30	N/A	16.41

*7 Year Price Score 67.50   *NYSE Composite Index=100   *12 Month Price Score 79.75

Interim Earnings (Per Share)

Qtr.	Mar	Jun	Sep	Dec
2016	(0.54)	(0.32)	(0.30)	0.07
2017	0.00	(0.17)	0.03	2.25
2018	0.63	0.65	0.84	0.53
2019	0.50	0.63	0.43	...

Interim Dividends (Per Share)

No Dividends Paid

Valuation Analysis		Institutional Holding	
Forecast EPS	$2.20	No of Institutions	
	(01/17/2020)	562	
Market Cap	$12.8 Billion	Shares	
Book Value	$6.6 Billion	84,672,072	
Price/Book	1.95	% Held	
Price/Sales	2.78	18.97	

Business Summary: Production & Extraction (MIC: 9.1.1 SIC: 1311 NAIC: 211111)

Continental Resources is an independent crude oil and natural gas company engaged in the exploration, development, and production of crude oil and natural gas mainly in the North, South and East regions of the U.S. The North region consists of properties north of Kansas and west of the Mississippi River and includes North Dakota Bakken, Montana Bakken, and the Red River units. The South region includes all properties south of Nebraska and west of the Mississippi River including various plays in the South Central Oklahoma Oil Province and Sooner Trend Anadarko Canadian Kingfisher areas of Oklahoma. The East region is comprised of undeveloped leasehold acreage east of the Mississippi River.

Recent Developments: For the quarter ended Sep 30 2019, net income decreased 49.9% to US$157.4 million from US$314.2 million in the year-earlier quarter. Revenues were US$1.10 billion, down 13.9% from US$1.28 billion the year before. Operating income was US$278.7 million versus US$491.3 million in the prior-year quarter, a decrease of 43.3%. Direct operating expenses rose 7.3% to US$271.2 million from US$252.8 million in the comparable period the year before. Indirect operating expenses increased 3.0% to US$554.2 million from US$538.1 million in the equivalent prior-year period.

Prospects: Our evaluation of Continental Resources Inc. as of October 4th, 2019 is the result of our systematic analysis on three basic characteristics: earnings strength, relative valuation, and recent stock price movement. The company has generated a negative trend in earnings per share over the past 5 quarters. In addition, recent analyst estimates for the company have been reduced and CLR has posted results that fell short of analysts' expectations. Based on operating earnings yield, the company is undervalued when compared to all of the companies we cover. Share price changes over the past year indicates that CLR will perform poorly over the near term.

Financial Data (US$ in Thousands)	9 Mos	6 Mos	3 Mos	12/31/2018	12/31/2017	12/31/2016	12/31/2015	12/31/2014
Earnings Per Share	2.09	2.50	2.52	2.64	2.11	(1.08)	(0.96)	2.64
Cash Flow Per Share	8.84	8.91	8.83	9.29	5.60	3.03	5.03	9.10
Tang Book Value Per Share	17.63	17.29	16.78	16.34	13.68	11.49	12.52	13.35
Income Statement								
Total Revenue	3,436,814	2,332,617	1,124,234	4,709,586	3,120,828	1,980,273	2,680,167	4,801,618
EBITDA	2,428,005	1,670,073	802,881	3,448,952	2,121,400	1,397,675	1,524,448	3,214,277
Depn & Amortn	1,465,856	983,183	496,561	1,859,118	1,670,838	1,709,567	1,746,454	1,368,311
Income Before Taxes	757,751	550,582	238,483	1,296,802	156,067	(632,454)	(535,085)	1,562,038
Income Taxes	177,386	127,639	51,990	307,102	(633,380)	(232,775)	(181,417)	584,697
Net Income	581,695	423,533	186,976	988,317	789,447	(399,679)	(353,668)	977,341
Average Shares	370,676	374,009	374,474	374,838	373,768	370,380	369,540	370,758
Balance Sheet								
Current Assets	1,225,684	1,413,675	1,484,062	1,412,361	1,251,725	913,233	822,339	1,389,601
Total Assets	15,771,355	15,829,422	15,633,923	15,297,947	14,199,651	13,811,776	14,919,808	15,145,070
Current Liabilities	1,371,769	1,368,346	1,445,451	1,387,509	1,330,242	932,393	923,028	1,952,013
Long-Term Obligations	5,568,413	5,767,316	5,766,647	5,765,989	6,351,405	6,577,697	7,115,644	5,995,837
Total Liabilities	9,219,370	9,345,919	9,310,213	9,152,814	9,068,448	9,509,780	10,250,908	10,177,226
Stockholders' Equity	6,551,985	6,483,503	6,323,710	6,145,133	5,131,203	4,301,996	4,668,900	4,967,844
Shares Outstanding	371,730	374,943	376,768	376,021	375,219	374,492	372,959	372,005
Statistical Record								
Return on Assets %	5.07	6.12	6.28	6.70	5.64	N.M.	N.M.	7.22
Return on Equity %	12.50	15.49	16.14	17.53	16.74	N.M.	N.M.	21.91
EBITDA Margin %	70.65	71.60	71.42	73.23	67.98	70.58	56.88	66.94
Net Margin %	16.93	18.16	16.63	20.99	25.30	N.M.	N.M.	20.35
Asset Turnover	0.30	0.31	0.31	0.32	0.22	0.14	0.18	0.35
Current Ratio	0.89	1.03	1.03	1.02	0.94	0.98	0.89	0.71
Debt to Equity	0.85	0.89	0.91	0.94	1.24	1.53	1.52	1.21
Price Range	71.79-28.08	71.79-35.00	71.79-36.20	71.79-36.20	53.41-30.03	58.01-16.04	52.63-20.00	80.64-30.95
P/E Ratio	34.35-13.44	28.72-14.00	28.49-14.37	27.19-13.71	25.31-14.23	...	...	30.55-11.72

Address: 20 N. Broadway, Oklahoma City, OK 73102 Telephone: 405-234-9000	Web Site: www.clr.com Officers: Harold G. Hamm - Executive Chairman, Chairman, Chief Executive Officer Jeffrey B. Hume - Vice-Chairman, President, Chief Operating Officer	Auditors: Grant Thornton LLP Investor Contact: 405-234-9127 Transfer Agents: American Stock Transfer & Trust Company, New York

COOPER COMPANIES, INC. (THE)

Exchange	Symbol	Price	52Wk Range	Yield	P/E
NYS	COO	$321.29 (12/31/2019)	341.49-246.18	0.02	34.44

*7 Year Price Score 127.75 *NYSE Composite Index=100 *12 Month Price Score 97.05

Interim Earnings (Per Share)

Qtr.	Jan	Apr	Jul	Oct
2014-15	1.25	1.23	0.91	0.75
2015-16	1.05	1.52	1.79	1.23
2016-17	1.53	2.12	2.09	1.78
2017-18	(2.50)	1.23	2.03	2.02
2018-19	2.07	2.45	2.40	2.42

Interim Dividends (Per Share)

Amt	Decl	Ex	Rec	Pay
0.03S	07/12/2018	07/20/2018	07/23/2018	08/07/2018
0.03S	01/07/2019	01/18/2019	01/22/2019	02/08/2019
0.03S	07/10/2019	07/22/2019	07/23/2019	08/07/2019
0.03S	01/07/2020	01/22/2020	01/23/2020	02/10/2020

Indicated Div: $0.06

Valuation Analysis / Institutional Holding

Valuation Analysis		Institutional Holding	
Forecast EPS	$12.83 (01/17/2020)	No of Institutions	746
Market Cap	$15.8 Billion	Shares	
Book Value	$3.6 Billion		61,878,800
Price/Book	4.35	% Held	95.80
Price/Sales	5.95		

Business Summary: Medical Instruments & Equipment (MIC: 4.3.1 SIC: 3851 NAIC: 339115)

Cooper Companies is a global medical device company. Co. operates through CooperVision and CooperSurgical business units. CooperVision is a manufacturer providing products for contact lens wearers. CooperVision designs its products for astigmatism, presbyopia, myopia, ocular dryness and eye fatigues with a collection of spherical, toric and multifocal contact lenses. CooperVision is engaged in myopia management and specialty eye care markets with products, such as orthokeratology and scleral lenses. CooperSurgical focuses on improving the health of women, babies and families through a portfolio of products and services including medical devices, fertility, diagnostics and contraception.

Recent Developments: For the year ended Oct 31 2019, net income increased 233.6% to US$466.7 million from US$139.9 million in the prior year. Revenues were US$2.65 billion, up 4.8% from US$2.53 billion the year before. Operating income was US$546.7 million versus US$403.1 million in the prior year, an increase of 35.6%. Direct operating expenses declined 0.4% to US$896.6 million from US$900.5 million in the comparable period the year before. Indirect operating expenses decreased 1.6% to US$1.21 billion from US$1.23 billion in the equivalent prior-year period.

Prospects: Our evaluation of Cooper Companies Inc. as of October 4th, 2019 is the result of our systematic analysis on three basic characteristics: earnings strength, relative valuation, and recent stock price movement. The company has managed to produce a neutral trend in earnings per share over the past 5 quarters. Additionally, recent analyst estimates for the company have been unchanged while COO has posted results that exceeded analysts' expectations. Based on operating earnings yield, the company is fairly valued when compared to all of the companies we cover. Share price changes over the past year indicates that COO will perform over the near term.

Financial Data
(US$ in Thousands)

	10/31/2019	10/31/2018	10/31/2017	10/31/2016	10/31/2015	10/31/2014	10/31/2013	10/31/2012
Earnings Per Share	9.33	2.81	7.52	5.59	4.14	5.51	5.96	5.05
Cash Flow Per Share	14.44	13.62	12.14	10.47	8.07	9.46	8.56	6.56
Tang Book Value Per Share	N.M.	N.M.	6.48	1.93	1.23	N.M.	17.05	12.55
Dividends Per Share	0.060	0.060	0.060	0.060	0.060	0.060	0.060	0.060
Dividend Payout %	0.64	2.14	0.80	1.07	1.45	1.09	1.01	1.19
Income Statement								
Total Revenue	2,653,400	2,532,800	2,139,000	1,966,814	1,797,060	1,717,776	1,587,725	1,445,136
EBITDA	691,200	561,300	495,800	382,613	380,147	442,700	446,788	398,437
Depn & Amortn	145,800	146,700	68,400	60,790	146,559	138,201	125,349	111,214
Income Before Taxes	477,400	331,900	394,000	295,633	215,485	296,534	312,271	275,452
Income Taxes	10,700	192,000	21,100	20,699	10,341	24,705	15,365	26,808
Net Income	466,700	139,900	372,900	273,917	203,523	269,856	296,151	248,339
Average Shares	50,000	49,700	49,600	49,026	49,179	48,960	49,685	49,152
Balance Sheet								
Current Assets	1,163,400	1,090,900	953,200	934,458	841,818	791,617	747,241	657,860
Total Assets	6,274,500	6,112,800	4,858,700	4,475,918	4,460,610	4,458,340	3,137,261	2,941,384
Current Liabilities	1,110,600	536,500	396,100	536,455	569,172	442,182	321,253	262,552
Long-Term Obligations	1,262,600	1,985,700	1,149,300	1,107,448	1,105,764	1,280,833	301,670	348,422
Total Liabilities	2,646,100	2,805,200	1,683,000	1,776,051	1,793,101	1,888,462	732,726	748,633
Stockholders' Equity	3,628,400	3,307,600	3,175,700	2,699,867	2,667,509	2,569,878	2,404,535	2,192,751
Shares Outstanding	49,100	49,200	48,800	48,785	48,268	48,143	47,995	48,440
Statistical Record								
Return on Assets %	7.54	2.55	7.99	6.11	4.56	7.11	9.74	8.90
Return on Equity %	13.46	4.32	12.69	10.18	7.77	10.85	12.88	11.99
EBITDA Margin %	26.05	22.16	23.18	19.45	21.15	25.77	28.14	27.57
Net Margin %	17.59	5.52	17.43	13.93	11.33	15.71	18.65	17.18
Asset Turnover	0.43	0.46	0.46	0.44	0.40	0.45	0.52	0.52
Current Ratio	1.05	2.03	2.41	1.74	1.48	1.79	2.33	2.51
Debt to Equity	0.35	0.60	0.36	0.41	0.41	0.50	0.13	0.16
Price Range	341.49-232.70	279.25-217.88	254.90-159.50	189.90-121.01	189.09-137.62	164.29-117.30	134.97-89.40	100.67-56.64
P/E Ratio	36.60-24.94	99.37-77.54	33.90-21.21	33.97-21.65	45.67-33.24	29.82-21.29	22.65-15.00	19.93-11.22
Average Yield %	0.02	0.02	0.03	0.04	0.04	0.04	0.05	0.08

Address: 6140 Stoneridge Mall Road, Suite 590, Pleasanton, CA 94588
Telephone: 925-460-3600
Fax: 925-460-3648

Web Site: www.coopercos.com
Officers: Albert G. (Al) White - President, Chief Executive Officer, Chief Financial Officer, Executive Vice President, Chief Strategy Officer, Vice President, Treasurer Holly R. Sheffield - Executive Vice President, Chief Strategy Officer

Auditors: KPMG LLP
Investor Contact: 925-460-3663
Transfer Agents: American Stock Tranfer & Trust Company, Brooklyn, NY

COOPER TIRE & RUBBER CO.

Exchange	Symbol	Price	52Wk Range	Yield	P/E
NYS	CTB	$28.75 (12/31/2019)	35.20-22.69	1.46	32.30

*7 Year Price Score 75.07 *NYSE Composite Index=100 *12 Month Price Score 92.67

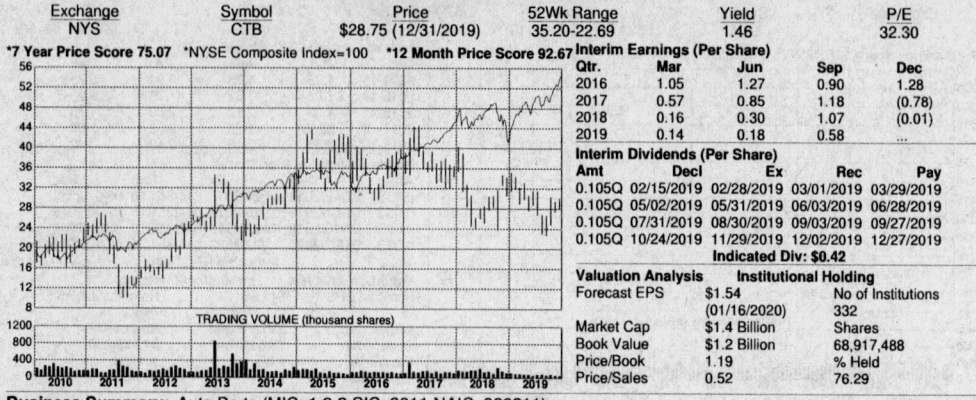

Interim Earnings (Per Share)

Qtr.	Mar	Jun	Sep	Dec
2016	1.05	1.27	0.90	1.28
2017	0.57	0.85	1.18	(0.78)
2018	0.16	0.30	1.07	(0.01)
2019	0.14	0.18	0.58	...

Interim Dividends (Per Share)

Amt	Decl	Ex	Rec	Pay
0.105Q	02/15/2019	02/28/2019	03/01/2019	03/29/2019
0.105Q	05/02/2019	05/31/2019	06/03/2019	06/28/2019
0.105Q	07/31/2019	08/30/2019	09/03/2019	09/27/2019
0.105Q	10/24/2019	11/29/2019	12/02/2019	12/27/2019

Indicated Div: $0.42

Valuation Analysis

		Institutional Holding	
Forecast EPS	$1.54	No of Institutions	
	(01/16/2020)	332	
Market Cap	$1.4 Billion	Shares	
Book Value	$1.2 Billion	68,917,488	
Price/Book	1.19	% Held	
Price/Sales	0.52	76.29	

Business Summary: Auto Parts (MIC: 1.8.2 SIC: 3011 NAIC: 326211)

Cooper Tire & Rubber is a manufacturer and marketer of replacement tires. In its Americas Tire Operations segment, Co. manufactures and markets passenger car and light truck tires, mainly for sale in the U.S. replacement market, and also supplies passenger car tires to the North American, Mexican, Central American and South American markets. In its International Tire Operations segment, Co.'s U.K. entity manufactures and markets passenger car, light truck, motorcycle and racing tires and tire retread material for domestic and global markets, and its Serbian entity manufactures passenger car and light truck tires mainly for the European markets and for export to the North American segment.

Recent Developments: For the quarter ended Sep 30 2019, net income decreased 47.7% to US$29.0 million from US$55.4 million in the year-earlier quarter. Revenues were US$704.1 million, down 4.5% from US$737.7 million the year before. Operating income was US$52.8 million versus US$81.2 million in the prior-year quarter, a decrease of 35.0%. Direct operating expenses declined 1.3% to US$589.8 million from US$597.7 million in the comparable period the year before. Indirect operating expenses increased 4.9% to US$61.6 million from US$58.7 million in the equivalent prior-year period.

Prospects: Our evaluation of Cooper Tire & Rubber Co. as of Jan. 21, 2018 is the result of our systematic analysis on three basic characteristics: earnings strength, relative valuation, and recent stock price movement. The company has managed to produce a neutral trend in earnings per share over the past 5 quarters and while recent estimates for the company have been mixed, CTB has posted better than expected results. Based on operating earnings yield, the company is undervalued when compared to all of the companies in our coverage universe. Share price changes over the past year indicates that CTB will perform very poorly over the near term.

Financial Data

(US$ in Thousands)	9 Mos	6 Mos	3 Mos	12/31/2018	12/31/2017	12/31/2016	12/31/2015	12/31/2014
Earnings Per Share	0.89	1.38	1.50	1.51	1.81	4.51	3.69	3.42
Cash Flow Per Share	4.11	4.66	4.69	5.05	3.39	5.67	5.27	5.20
Tang Book Value Per Share	21.46	21.08	20.94	20.63	18.44	16.65	14.81	11.82
Dividends Per Share	0.420	0.420	0.420	0.420	0.420	0.420	0.420	0.420
Dividend Payout %	47.19	30.43	28.00	27.81	23.20	9.31	11.38	12.28
Income Statement								
Total Revenue	2,002,428	1,298,293	619,163	2,808,062	2,854,656	2,924,869	2,972,901	3,424,809
EBITDA	109,381	57,608	27,580	319,846	450,843	562,634	523,215	550,230
Depn & Amortn	27,314	18,240	9,131	183,823	182,232	173,315	167,578	175,073
Income Before Taxes	65,355	28,624	13,515	114,058	243,925	367,093	334,028	348,519
Income Taxes	19,908	12,186	6,337	33,495	147,180	115,799	118,224	111,697
Net Income	45,146	15,801	6,979	76,586	95,400	248,381	212,766	213,578
Average Shares	50,358	50,362	50,378	50,597	52,673	55,090	57,623	62,401
Balance Sheet								
Current Assets	1,378,874	1,371,103	1,384,223	1,456,732	1,388,317	1,420,518	1,334,630	1,427,552
Total Assets	2,696,616	2,704,073	2,677,168	2,634,205	2,607,735	2,619,395	2,436,176	2,489,931
Current Liabilities	764,851	751,087	715,850	760,344	505,353	500,814	433,003	511,365
Long-Term Obligations	120,657	120,624	121,305	121,284	295,987	297,094	296,412	298,931
Total Liabilities	1,487,506	1,511,724	1,490,528	1,462,162	1,480,639	1,543,381	1,456,928	1,646,139
Stockholders' Equity	1,209,110	1,192,349	1,186,640	1,172,043	1,127,096	1,076,014	979,248	843,792
Shares Outstanding	50,183	50,169	50,150	50,073	50,941	52,999	55,832	58,151
Statistical Record								
Return on Assets %	1.68	2.59	2.81	2.92	3.65	9.80	8.64	8.17
Return on Equity %	3.76	5.98	6.47	6.66	8.66	24.10	23.34	23.28
EBITDA Margin %	5.46	4.44	4.45	11.39	15.79	19.24	17.60	16.07
Net Margin %	2.25	1.22	1.13	2.73	3.34	8.49	7.16	6.24
Asset Turnover	1.04	1.05	1.06	1.07	1.09	1.15	1.21	1.31
Current Ratio	1.80	1.83	1.93	1.92	2.75	2.84	3.08	2.79
Debt to Equity	0.10	0.10	0.10	0.10	0.26	0.28	0.30	0.35
Price Range	35.20-22.69	35.20-23.68	35.20-23.68	40.35-23.68	44.45-32.00	40.30-29.53	43.69-31.46	34.98-22.27
P/E Ratio	39.55-25.49	25.51-17.16	23.47-15.79	26.72-15.68	24.56-17.68	8.94-6.55	11.84-8.53	10.23-6.51
Average Yield %	1.41	1.38	1.43	1.39	1.13	1.19	1.10	1.49

Address: 701 Lima Avenue, Findlay, OH 45840
Telephone: 419-423-1321
Fax: 419-424-4305

Web Site: www.coopertire.com
Officers: Bradley E. Hughes - President, Chief Executive Officer, Senior Vice President, Vice President, Chief Operating Officer, Chief Financial Officer, Treasurer Christopher J. Eperjesy - Senior Vice President, Chief Financial Officer

Auditors: Ernst & Young LLP
Investor Contact: 419-424-4165
Transfer Agents: Computershare Inc., Canton, MA

CORECIVIC INC

Exchange	Symbol	Price	52Wk Range	Yield	P/E
NYS	CXW	$17.38 (12/31/2019)	24.07-14.86	10.13	11.00

*7 Year Price Score 54.29 *NYSE Composite Index=100 *12 Month Price Score 80.74

Interim Earnings (Per Share)

Qtr.	Mar	Jun	Sep	Dec
2016	0.39	0.49	0.47	0.52
2017	0.42	0.38	0.35	0.35
2018	0.32	0.33	0.34	0.35
2019	0.41	0.41	0.41	...

Interim Dividends (Per Share)

Amt	Decl	Ex	Rec	Pay
0.44Q	02/21/2019	03/29/2019	04/01/2019	04/15/2019
0.44Q	05/16/2019	06/28/2019	07/01/2019	07/16/2019
0.44Q	08/15/2019	09/30/2019	10/01/2019	10/15/2019
0.44Q	12/12/2019	01/03/2020	01/06/2020	01/15/2020

Indicated Div: $1.76

Valuation Analysis

		Institutional Holding	
Forecast EPS	$1.56	No of Institutions	419
	(11/21/2019)		
Market Cap	$2.1 Billion	Shares	
Book Value	$1.4 Billion	132,023,224	
Price/Book	1.50	% Held	
Price/Sales	1.05	N/A	

Business Summary: REITs (MIC: 5.3.1 SIC: 6798 NAIC: 525930)

CoreCivic is a real estate investment trust. Co. is the owner of partnership correctional, detention, and residential reentry facilities and prison operators in the U.S. Through three segments, CoreCivic Safety, CoreCivic Community, and CoreCivic Properties, Co. provides a range of solutions to government partners that serve the public good through corrections and detention management, a network of residential reentry centers to help address America's recidivism crisis, and government real estate solutions. In addition to providing fundamental residential services, Co.'s correctional, detention, and residential reentry facilities provide a variety of rehabilitation and educational programs.

Recent Developments: For the quarter ended Sep 30 2019, net income increased 19.5% to US$49.0 million from US$41.0 million in the year-earlier quarter. Revenues were US$508.5 million, up 9.9% from US$462.7 million the year before.

Prospects: Our evaluation of CoreCivic Inc. as of October 4th, 2019 is the result of our systematic analysis on three basic characteristics: earnings strength, relative valuation, and recent stock price movement. The company has enjoyed a very positive trend in earnings per share over the past 5 quarters. However, recent analyst estimates for the company have been mixed and CXW has posted results that fell short of analysts' expectations. Based on operating earnings yield, the company is undervalued when compared to all of the companies we cover. Share price changes over the past year indicates that CXW will perform well over the near term.

Financial Data (US$ in Thousands)	9 Mos	6 Mos	3 Mos	12/31/2018	12/31/2017	12/31/2016	12/31/2015	12/31/2014
Earnings Per Share	1.58	1.51	1.43	1.34	1.50	1.87	1.88	1.66
Cash Flow Per Share	2.87	2.57	2.46	2.72	2.89	3.19	3.42	3.65
Tang Book Value Per Share	11.21	11.20	11.21	10.73	11.57	11.74	11.82	12.34
Dividends Per Share	1.750	1.740	1.730	1.720	1.680	2.040	2.160	2.040
Dividend Payout %	110.76	115.23	120.98	128.36	112.00	109.09	114.89	122.89
Income Statement								
Total Revenue	1,482,880	974,358	484,064	1,835,766	1,765,498	1,849,785	1,793,087	1,646,867
EBITDA	218,493	146,184	74,117	400,313	406,186	461,727	431,311	355,500
Depn & Amortn	2,566	1,712	857	152,000	145,700	165,800	151,400	114,000
Income Before Taxes	152,854	102,374	51,824	167,560	191,951	228,172	230,215	201,965
Income Taxes	5,942	4,456	2,484	8,353	13,911	8,253	8,361	6,943
Net Income	146,912	97,918	49,340	159,207	178,040	219,919	221,854	195,022
Average Shares	119,189	119,262	118,918	118,716	118,465	117,791	117,785	117,312
Balance Sheet								
Current Assets	380,645	392,109	355,331	373,525	327,490	298,824	342,058	365,985
Total Assets	3,748,845	3,738,891	3,670,380	3,655,660	3,272,398	3,271,604	3,356,018	3,127,191
Current Liabilities	714,802	671,601	346,065	366,396	290,838	272,193	324,595	318,988
Long-Term Obligations	1,521,785	1,569,118	1,828,114	1,806,372	1,452,717	1,435,169	1,447,077	1,200,000
Total Liabilities	2,365,644	2,356,300	2,287,966	2,240,601	1,820,790	1,812,641	1,893,270	1,645,691
Stockholders' Equity	1,383,201	1,382,591	1,382,414	1,415,059	1,451,608	1,458,963	1,462,748	1,481,500
Shares Outstanding	119,096	119,096	119,068	118,674	118,204	117,554	117,232	116,764
Statistical Record								
Return on Assets %	5.13	5.12	4.92	4.60	5.44	6.62	6.84	6.36
Return on Equity %	13.41	12.82	12.13	11.11	12.23	15.01	15.07	13.07
EBITDA Margin %	14.73	15.00	15.31	21.81	23.01	24.96	24.05	21.59
Net Margin %	9.91	10.05	10.19	8.67	10.08	11.89	12.37	11.84
Asset Turnover	0.54	0.55	0.54	0.53	0.54	0.56	0.55	0.54
Current Ratio	0.53	0.58	1.03	1.02	1.13	1.10	1.05	1.15
Debt to Equity	1.10	1.13	1.32	1.28	1.00	0.98	0.99	0.81
Price Range	24.20-15.80	25.96-17.38	25.96-17.38	25.96-17.64	35.03-21.77	35.02-13.18	42.10-24.62	38.33-31.13
P/E Ratio	15.32-10.00	17.19-11.51	18.15-12.15	19.37-13.16	23.35-14.51	18.73-7.05	22.39-13.10	23.09-18.75
Average Yield %	8.67	7.89	7.88	7.67	5.98	7.77	6.40	6.00

Address: 5501 Virginia Way, Brentwood, TN 37027 **Telephone:** 615-263-3000	**Web Site:** www.cca.com **Officers:** Mark A. Emkes - Chairman Damon T. Hininger - President, Chief Executive Officer	**Auditors:** Ernst & Young LLP **Investor Contact:** 615-263-3005 **Transfer Agents:** American Stock Transfer and Trust Company LLC, New York, NY

CORELOGIC INC.

Exchange	Symbol	Price	52Wk Range	Yield	P/E
NYS	CLGX	$43.71 (12/31/2019)	48.93-32.80	N/A	112.08

*7 Year Price Score 90.65   *NYSE Composite Index=100   *12 Month Price Score 94.35

Interim Earnings (Per Share)

Qtr.	Mar	Jun	Sep	Dec
2016	0.31	0.45	0.39	0.04
2017	0.18	0.48	0.36	0.76
2018	0.34	0.71	0.27	0.15
2019	0.02	(0.07)	0.29	...

Interim Dividends (Per Share)

No Dividends Paid

Valuation Analysis		Institutional Holding	
Forecast EPS	$2.73	No of Institutions	
	(01/17/2020)	354	
Market Cap	$3.5 Billion	Shares	
Book Value	$932.9 Million	86,563,000	
Price/Book	3.73	% Held	
Price/Sales	2.00	N/A	

Business Summary: IT Services (MIC: 6.3.1 SIC: 7374 NAIC: 519190)

CoreLogic is a property information, analytics and data-enabled software platforms and services provider. Co. provides its clients a database covering real property and mortgage information, judgments and liens, eviction information, non-prime lending records, credit information, and tax information, among other data types. Co.'s segments are: Property Intelligence and Risk Management Solutions, which delivers housing market and property-level insights, predictive analytics and risk management solutions; and Underwriting and Workflow Solutions, which provides mortgage origination and monitoring solutions, including underwriting-related solutions and data-enabled valuations and appraisals.

Recent Developments: For the quarter ended Sep 30 2019, income from continuing operations increased 79.9% to US$40.5 million from US$22.5 million in the year-earlier quarter. Net income increased 3.3% to US$23.2 million from US$22.5 million in the year-earlier quarter. Revenues were US$459.0 million, up 1.6% from US$451.8 million the year before. Operating income was US$73.7 million versus US$59.8 million in the prior-year quarter, an increase of 23.3%. Direct operating expenses declined 1.0% to US$228.2 million from US$230.4 million in the comparable period the year before. Indirect operating expenses decreased 2.8% to US$157.1 million from US$161.6 million in the equivalent prior-year period.

Prospects: Our evaluation of CoreLogic Inc. as of October 4th, 2019 is the result of our systematic analysis on three basic characteristics: earnings strength, relative valuation, and recent stock price movement. The company has produced a positive trend in earnings per share over the past 5 quarters. However, recent analyst estimates for the company have been mixed and CLGX has posted results that exceeded analysts' expectations. Based on operating earnings yield, the company is fairly valued when compared to all of the companies we cover. Share price changes over the past year indicates that CLGX will perform in line with the market over the near term.

Financial Data
(US$ in Thousands)

	9 Mos	6 Mos	3 Mos	12/31/2018	12/31/2017	12/31/2016	12/31/2015	12/31/2014
Earnings Per Share	0.39	0.37	1.15	1.48	1.78	1.19	1.41	0.79
Cash Flow Per Share	4.39	4.07	3.98	4.39	4.59	4.71	3.69	3.54
Income Statement								
Total Revenue	1,336,203	877,246	417,708	1,788,378	1,851,117	1,952,557	1,528,110	1,405,040
EBITDA	177,685	76,656	50,676	332,023	314,616	303,957	308,216	241,940
Depn & Amortn	83,511	56,406	28,738	91,400	83,900	82,200	73,700	68,300
Income Before Taxes	36,765	(17,656)	3,213	166,649	168,892	163,974	173,226	106,658
Income Taxes	508	(13,973)	1,058	45,691	18,172	54,524	57,394	29,770
Net Income	19,298	(3,885)	1,687	121,864	152,162	106,550	127,844	73,200
Average Shares	80,914	80,473	81,277	82,275	85,234	89,122	90,564	92,429
Balance Sheet								
Current Assets	424,260	420,132	396,339	403,520	430,268	391,887	542,266	500,625
Total Assets	4,138,455	4,150,512	4,213,996	4,168,990	4,077,413	3,907,534	3,701,050	3,516,362
Current Liabilities	660,243	647,357	614,402	587,092	613,366	668,421	614,476	550,590
Long-Term Obligations	1,636,272	1,667,021	1,709,501	1,752,241	1,683,524	1,496,889	1,315,511	1,319,211
Total Liabilities	3,205,594	3,197,020	3,214,725	3,168,492	3,069,537	2,904,550	2,651,560	2,502,195
Stockholders' Equity	932,861	953,492	999,271	1,000,498	1,007,876	1,002,984	1,049,490	1,014,167
Shares Outstanding	79,519	80,133	80,633	80,092	80,885	84,368	88,228	89,343
Statistical Record								
Return on Assets %	0.77	0.75	2.30	2.96	3.81	2.79	3.54	2.25
Return on Equity %	3.25	3.15	9.49	12.14	15.13	10.35	12.39	7.11
EBITDA Margin %	13.30	8.74	12.13	18.57	17.00	15.57	20.17	17.22
Net Margin %	1.44	N.M.	0.40	6.81	8.22	5.46	8.37	5.21
Asset Turnover	0.42	0.42	0.43	0.43	0.46	0.51	0.42	0.43
Current Ratio	0.64	0.65	0.65	0.69	0.70	0.59	0.88	0.91
Debt to Equity	1.75	1.75	1.71	1.75	1.67	1.49	1.25	1.30
Price Range	48.93-32.09	54.90-32.09	55.48-32.09	55.48-32.09	49.10-35.01	42.56-32.19	42.18-30.75	35.86-26.00
P/E Ratio	125.46-82.28	148.38-86.73	48.24-27.90	37.49-21.68	27.58-19.67	35.76-27.05	29.91-21.81	45.39-32.91

Address: 40 Pacifica, Irvine, CA 92618
Telephone: 949-214-1000

Web Site: www.corelogic.com
Officers: Paul F. Folino - Chairman Frank D. Martell - President, Chief Executive Officer, Chief Financial Officer, Chief Operating Officer

Auditors: PricewaterhouseCoopers LLP
Investor Contact: 703-610-5410
Transfer Agents: Wells Fargo Shareowner Services, South Saint Paul, MN

CORESITE REALTY CORP

Exchange	Symbol	Price	52Wk Range	Yield	P/E
NYS	COR	$112.12 (12/31/2019)	122.38-84.51	4.35	53.90

*7 Year Price Score 125.91   *NYSE Composite Index=100   *12 Month Price Score 97.55

Interim Earnings (Per Share)

Qtr.	Mar	Jun	Sep	Dec
2016	0.37	0.37	0.36	0.44
2017	0.48	0.46	0.46	0.44
2018	0.59	0.57	0.52	0.54
2019	0.54	0.53	0.47	...

Interim Dividends (Per Share)

Amt	Decl	Ex	Rec	Pay
1.10Q	03/07/2019	03/28/2019	03/29/2019	04/15/2019
1.22Q	05/16/2019	06/27/2019	06/28/2019	07/15/2019
1.22Q	09/04/2019	09/27/2019	09/30/2019	10/15/2019
1.22Q	12/11/2019	12/30/2019	12/31/2019	01/15/2020

Indicated Div: $4.88

Valuation Analysis

		Institutional Holding	
Forecast EPS	$2.05	No of Institutions	430
	(01/17/2020)		
Market Cap	$4.2 Billion	Shares	
Book Value	$180.2 Million		42,338,888
Price/Book	23.45	% Held	
Price/Sales	7.47		95.96

Business Summary: REITs (MIC: 5.3.1 SIC: 6798 NAIC: 525930)

CoreSite Realty is a real estate investment trust. Through its controlling interest in CoreSite, L.P., Co. is engaged in the business of ownership, acquisition, construction and operation of data centers in the U.S., including San Francisco Bay area, Los Angeles, the Northern Virginia area (including Washington D.C.), the New York area, Boston, Chicago, Denver and Miami. Co.'s data centers are buildings that house networking, storage and communications technology infrastructure, including servers, storage devices, switches, routers and fiber optic transmission equipment. These buildings are designed to provide the power, cooling and network connectivity necessary to operate this equipment.

Recent Developments: For the quarter ended Sep 30 2019, net income decreased 9.5% to US$22.6 million from US$25.0 million in the year-earlier quarter. Revenues were US$144.9 million, up 4.1% from US$139.2 million the year before. Revenues from property income rose 7.8% to US$19.1 million from US$17.7 million in the corresponding quarter a year earlier.

Prospects: Our evaluation of CoreSite Realty Corp. as of October 4th, 2019 is the result of our systematic analysis on three basic characteristics: earnings strength, relative valuation, and recent stock price movement. The company has managed to produce a neutral trend in earnings per share over the past 5 quarters. In addition, recent analyst estimates for the company have been mixed and COR has posted results that fell short of analysts' expectations. Based on operating earnings yield, the company is overvalued when compared to all of the companies we cover. Share price changes over the past year indicates that COR will perform well over the near term.

Financial Data

(US$ in Thousands)	9 Mos	6 Mos	3 Mos	12/31/2018	12/31/2017	12/31/2016	12/31/2015	12/31/2014
Earnings Per Share	2.08	2.13	2.17	2.22	1.84	1.54	1.03	0.66
Cash Flow Per Share	6.98	6.85	7.05	7.40	6.20	5.27	5.65	4.70
Tang Book Value Per Share	3.59	4.16	4.74	5.31	6.84	7.95	8.33	7.32
Dividends Per Share	4.640	4.450	4.260	4.140	3.580	2.390	1.790	1.470
Dividend Payout %	223.08	208.92	196.31	186.49	194.57	155.19	173.79	222.73
Income Statement								
Total Revenue	426,692	281,801	138,895	544,392	481,821	400,352	333,292	272,420
EBITDA	207,381	137,784	68,158	264,599	232,314	183,276	63,600	44,839
Depn & Amortn	102,249	66,295	32,725	122,320	107,502	88,659	(520)	(556)
Income Before Taxes	74,337	51,680	25,935	106,753	100,665	82,040	57,022	40,090
Income Taxes	45	32	30	(10)	174	119	163	38
Net Income	56,646	39,196	19,661	77,922	74,855	58,709	34,706	22,765
Average Shares	37,132	36,618	36,547	35,137	34,058	32,732	25,706	21,740
Balance Sheet								
Current Assets	31,033	32,594	28,442	21,063	34,122	29,554	19,089	20,952
Total Assets	2,046,742	2,001,444	1,932,862	1,853,667	1,532,659	1,451,303	1,162,543	1,075,425
Current Liabilities	194,522	183,583	171,304	144,994	136,074	122,062	111,821	73,803
Long-Term Obligations	1,572,266	1,505,007	1,409,828	1,333,522	939,570	690,450	391,007	318,500
Total Liabilities	1,866,546	1,801,696	1,711,157	1,611,112	1,251,639	1,015,577	746,426	752,838
Stockholders' Equity	180,196	199,748	221,705	242,555	281,020	435,726	416,117	322,587
Shares Outstanding	37,688	36,890	36,901	36,708	34,240	33,896	30,650	21,757
Statistical Record								
Return on Assets %	3.95	4.11	4.33	4.60	5.02	4.48	3.10	2.18
Return on Equity %	34.36	33.79	31.38	29.77	20.89	13.75	9.40	6.95
EBITDA Margin %	48.60	48.89	49.07	48.60	48.22	45.78	19.08	16.46
Net Margin %	13.28	13.91	14.16	14.31	15.54	14.66	10.41	8.36
Asset Turnover	0.29	0.30	0.31	0.32	0.32	0.31	0.30	0.26
Current Ratio	0.16	0.18	0.17	0.15	0.25	0.24	0.17	0.28
Debt to Equity	8.73	7.53	6.36	5.50	3.34	1.58	0.94	0.99
Price Range	121.89-82.91	119.68-82.91	117.12-82.91	117.12-82.91	119.54-80.61	91.49-55.30	60.10-39.05	39.56-29.90
P/E Ratio	58.60-39.86	56.19-38.92	53.97-38.21	52.76-37.35	64.97-43.81	59.41-35.91	58.35-37.91	59.94-45.30
Average Yield %	4.37	4.20	4.10	3.95	3.48	3.24	3.59	4.39

Address: 1001 17th Street, Suite 500, Denver, CO 80202 **Telephone:** 866-777-2673	**Web Site:** www.coresite.com **Officers:** Robert G. Stuckey - Chairman Paul E. Szurek - President, Chief Executive Officer	**Auditors:** KPMG LLP

CORNING INC

Exchange	Symbol	Price	52Wk Range	Yield	P/E
NYS	GLW	$29.11 (12/31/2019)	35.08-27.07	2.75	21.89

*7 Year Price Score 106.74 *NYSE Composite Index=100 *12 Month Price Score 88.79

Interim Earnings (Per Share)

Qtr.	Mar	Jun	Sep	Dec
2016	(0.36)	1.87	0.26	1.42
2017	0.07	0.42	0.39	(1.55)
2018	(0.72)	0.78	0.67	0.31
2019	0.55	0.09	0.38	...

Interim Dividends (Per Share)

Amt	Decl	Ex	Rec	Pay
0.20Q	02/06/2019	02/27/2019	02/28/2019	03/29/2019
0.20Q	05/02/2019	05/30/2019	05/31/2019	06/28/2019
0.20Q	07/17/2019	08/29/2019	08/30/2019	09/30/2019
0.20Q	10/02/2019	11/14/2019	11/15/2019	12/13/2019

Indicated Div: $0.80

Valuation Analysis / **Institutional Holding**

Forecast EPS	$1.74	No of Institutions
	(01/16/2020)	1566
Market Cap	$22.4 Billion	Shares
Book Value	$13.0 Billion	803,944,064
Price/Book	1.72	% Held
Price/Sales	1.91	65.03

Business Summary: Electrical Equipment (MIC: 7.3.1 SIC: 3211 NAIC: 327211)

Corning is a provider of glass. Co.'s segments are: Display Technologies, which manufactures glass substrates for displays, including organic light-emitting diode and liquid crystal displays that are used in televisions, notebook computers and flat panel desktop monitors; Optical Communications, which consists of carrier network and enterprise network; Specialty Materials, which manufactures products that provide material formulations for glass, glass ceramics and fluoride crystals; Environmental Technologies, which manufactures ceramic substrates and filter products for emissions control in mobile applications; and Life Sciences, which provides consumables, general labware and equipment.

Recent Developments: For the quarter ended Sep 30 2019, net income decreased 46.1% to US$337.0 million from US$625.0 million in the year-earlier quarter. Revenues were US$2.93 billion, down 2.5% from US$3.01 billion the year before. Operating income was US$365.0 million versus US$522.0 million in the prior-year quarter, a decrease of 30.1%. Direct operating expenses rose 7.9% to US$1.92 billion from US$1.78 billion in the comparable period the year before. Indirect operating expenses decreased 8.2% to US$652.0 million from US$710.0 million in the equivalent prior-year period.

Prospects: Our evaluation of Corning Inc. as of October 4th, 2019 is the result of our systematic analysis on three basic characteristics: earnings strength, relative valuation, and recent stock price movement. The company has managed to produce a neutral trend in earnings per share over the past 5 quarters. However, recent analyst estimates for the company have been reduced while GLW has posted results that exceeded analysts' expectations. Based on operating earnings yield, the company is undervalued when compared to all of the companies we cover. Share price changes over the past year indicates that GLW will perform in line with the market over the near term.

Financial Data

(US$ in Thousands)	9 Mos	6 Mos	3 Mos	12/31/2018	12/31/2017	12/31/2016	12/31/2015	12/31/2014
Earnings Per Share	1.33	1.62	2.31	1.13	(0.66)	3.23	1.00	1.73
Cash Flow Per Share	...	2.57	2.83	3.58	2.24	2.46	2.30	3.61
Tang Book Value Per Share	9.90	10.20	10.37	10.49	12.63	14.28	12.75	13.84
Dividends Per Share	0.780	0.760	0.740	0.720	0.620	0.540	0.480	0.400
Dividend Payout %	58.65	46.91	32.03	63.72	...	16.72	48.00	23.12
Income Statement								
Total Revenue	8,686,000	5,752,000	2,812,000	11,290,000	10,116,000	9,390,000	9,111,000	9,715,000
EBITDA	1,348,000	1,542,000	930,000	2,559,000	2,564,000	4,730,000	2,490,000	4,599,000
Depn & Amortn	85,000	715,000	335,000	1,293,000	1,158,000	1,195,000	1,184,000	1,200,000
Income Before Taxes	1,118,000	733,000	550,000	1,113,000	1,296,000	3,408,000	1,187,000	3,302,000
Income Taxes	271,000	200,000	76,000	437,000	2,154,000	(3,000)	147,000	1,096,000
Net Income	928,000	591,000	499,000	1,066,000	(497,000)	3,695,000	1,339,000	2,472,000
Average Shares	897,000	789,000	908,000	941,000	1,021,000	1,144,000	1,343,000	1,427,000
Balance Sheet								
Current Assets	6,156,000	6,311,000	6,349,000	7,034,000	8,827,000	9,048,000	8,269,000	10,238,000
Total Assets	27,329,000	27,575,000	27,321,000	27,505,000	27,494,000	27,899,000	28,547,000	30,063,000
Current Liabilities	3,600,000	3,416,000	3,059,000	3,311,000	3,209,000	2,751,000	2,814,000	2,324,000
Long-Term Obligations	6,225,000	6,080,000	6,018,000	5,994,000	4,749,000	3,646,000	3,910,000	3,227,000
Total Liabilities	14,295,000	14,150,000	13,714,000	13,713,000	11,796,000	10,006,000	9,759,000	8,484,000
Stockholders' Equity	13,034,000	13,425,000	13,607,000	13,792,000	15,698,000	17,893,000	18,788,000	21,579,000
Shares Outstanding	768,000	779,000	782,000	788,000	858,000	926,000	1,130,000	1,274,000
Statistical Record								
Return on Assets %	4.54	5.61	7.95	3.88	N.M.	13.06	4.57	8.45
Return on Equity %	9.06	11.05	15.37	7.23	N.M.	20.09	6.63	11.57
EBITDA Margin %	15.52	26.81	33.07	22.67	25.35	50.37	27.33	47.34
Net Margin %	10.68	10.27	17.75	9.44	N.M.	39.35	14.70	25.45
Asset Turnover	0.44	0.44	0.43	0.41	0.37	0.33	0.31	0.33
Current Ratio	1.71	1.85	2.08	2.12	2.75	3.29	2.94	4.41
Debt to Equity	0.48	0.45	0.44	0.43	0.30	0.20	0.21	0.15
Price Range	35.74-27.07	36.13-27.35	36.13-26.35	36.13-26.35	32.64-24.19	24.94-16.69	25.00-15.97	23.32-17.05
P/E Ratio	26.87-20.35	22.30-16.88	15.64-11.41	31.97-23.32	...	7.72-5.17	25.00-15.97	13.48-9.86
Average Yield %	2.46	2.35	2.37	2.35	2.13	2.55	2.36	1.97

Address: One Riverfront Plaza, Corning, NY 14831 **Telephone:** 607-974-9000	**Web Site:** www.corning.com **Officers:** Wendell P. Weeks - Chairman, President, Chief Executive Officer Lawrence D. McRae - Vice-Chairman, Corporate Development Officer, Executive Vice President, Senior Vice President	**Auditors:** PricewaterhouseCoopers LLP **Investor Contact:** 888-267-6464 **Transfer Agents:** ComputerShare Investor Services, Chicago, IL

CORPORATE OFFICE PROPERTIES TRUST

Exchange	Symbol	Price	52Wk Range	Yield	P/E
NYS	OFC	$29.38 (12/31/2019)	30.13-21.03	3.74	19.85

*7 Year Price Score 82.88   ***NYSE Composite Index=100**   ***12 Month Price Score 99.49**

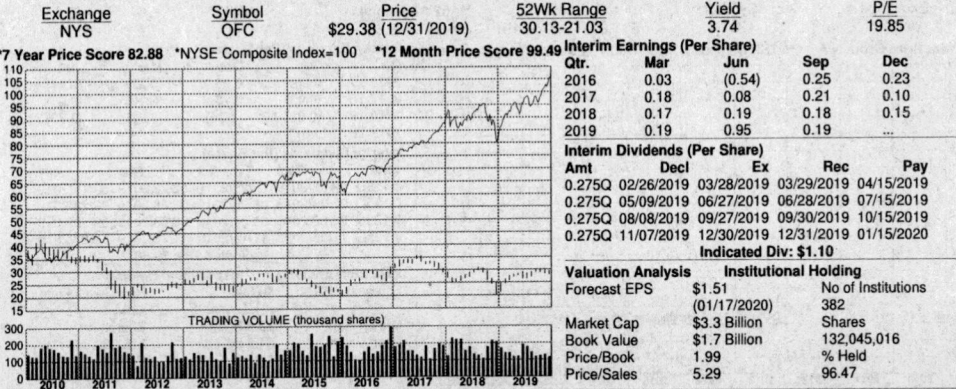

Interim Earnings (Per Share)

Qtr.	Mar	Jun	Sep	Dec
2016	0.03	(0.54)	0.25	0.23
2017	0.18	0.08	0.21	0.10
2018	0.17	0.19	0.18	0.15
2019	0.19	0.95	0.19	...

Interim Dividends (Per Share)

Amt	Decl	Ex	Rec	Pay
0.275Q	02/26/2019	03/28/2019	03/29/2019	04/15/2019
0.275Q	05/09/2019	06/27/2019	06/28/2019	07/15/2019
0.275Q	08/08/2019	09/30/2019	09/30/2019	10/15/2019
0.275Q	11/07/2019	12/30/2019	12/31/2019	01/15/2020

Indicated Div: $1.10

Valuation Analysis

		Institutional Holding	
Forecast EPS	$1.51	No of Institutions	382
	(01/17/2020)		
Market Cap	$3.3 Billion	Shares	132,045,016
Book Value	$1.7 Billion	% Held	96.47
Price/Book	1.99		
Price/Sales	5.29		

Business Summary: REITs (MIC: 5.3.1 SIC: 6798 NAIC: 525930)

Corporate Office Properties Trust is a real estate investment trust. Through Corporate Office Properties, L.P. and subsidiaries, Co. is engaged in owning, managing, leasing, developing and acquiring office and data center properties. The majority of Co.'s portfolio is in locations that support the U.S. Government and its contractors, most of whom are engaged in national security, defense and information technology (IT) related activities servicing priority missions (Defense/IT Locations). Co. also owns a portfolio of office properties located in select urban/urban-like submarkets in the Greater Washington, DC/Baltimore region.

Recent Developments: For the quarter ended Sep 30 2019, net income increased 14.4% to US$23.2 million from US$20.3 million in the year-earlier quarter. Revenues were US$159.4 million, up 16.0% from US$137.4 million the year before. Revenues from property income rose 1.4% to US$129.5 million from US$127.7 million in the corresponding quarter a year earlier.

Prospects: Our evaluation of Corporate Office Properties Trust as of October 4th, 2019 is the result of our systematic analysis on three basic characteristics: earnings strength, relative valuation, and recent stock price movement. The company has enjoyed a very positive trend in earnings per share over the past 5 quarters. However, recent analyst estimates for the company have been mixed and OFC has posted results that exceeded analysts' expectations. Based on operating earnings yield, the company is overvalued when compared to all of the companies we cover. Share price changes over the past year indicates that OFC will perform in line with the market over the near term.

Financial Data

(US$ in Thousands)	9 Mos	6 Mos	3 Mos	12/31/2018	12/31/2017	12/31/2016	12/31/2015	12/31/2014
Earnings Per Share	1.48	1.47	0.71	0.69	0.57	(0.03)	1.74	0.25
Cash Flow Per Share	1.93	1.90	1.90	1.74	2.33	2.45	2.17	2.20
Tang Book Value Per Share	14.37	14.55	13.96	13.99	13.10	12.92	13.19	12.96
Dividends Per Share	1.100	1.100	1.100	1.100	1.100	1.100	1.100	1.100
Dividend Payout %	74.32	74.83	154.93	159.42	192.98	...	63.22	440.00
Income Statement								
Total Revenue	483,441	324,010	148,940	578,112	612,820	574,328	625,466	586,473
EBITDA	310,507	236,430	74,636	283,726	269,552	184,019	345,394	258,146
Depn & Amortn	108,402	72,328	36,127	137,116	134,228	132,719	140,025	136,086
Income Before Taxes	153,807	131,088	22,121	75,583	64,659	(26,419)	120,812	34,590
Income Taxes	(113)	18	194	(363)	1,098	244	199	310
Net Income	148,907	127,650	20,859	74,703	70,091	11,439	178,300	40,255
Average Shares	111,943	113,105	110,218	104,125	99,155	94,502	97,667	88,263
Balance Sheet								
Current Assets	158,514	164,774	43,790	37,532	56,133	262,844	100,454	48,703
Total Assets	3,855,369	3,803,469	3,775,859	3,656,005	3,578,484	3,780,885	3,909,312	3,670,257
Current Liabilities	200,562	211,019	169,057	153,790	162,706	169,815	159,081	183,908
Long-Term Obligations	1,862,301	1,784,362	1,876,149	1,824,569	1,844,186	1,904,001	2,077,752	1,920,057
Total Liabilities	2,198,980	2,131,189	2,165,484	2,070,594	2,192,447	2,257,826	2,364,787	2,218,834
Stockholders' Equity	1,656,389	1,672,280	1,610,375	1,585,411	1,386,037	1,523,059	1,544,525	1,451,423
Shares Outstanding	112,059	111,949	111,939	110,241	101,292	98,498	94,531	93,255
Statistical Record								
Return on Assets %	4.49	4.47	2.13	2.07	1.90	0.30	4.70	1.10
Return on Equity %	10.44	10.65	5.18	5.03	4.82	0.74	11.90	2.80
EBITDA Margin %	64.23	72.97	50.11	49.08	43.99	32.04	55.22	44.02
Net Margin %	30.80	39.40	14.00	12.92	11.44	1.99	28.51	6.86
Asset Turnover	0.17	0.16	0.16	0.16	0.17	0.15	0.17	0.16
Current Ratio	0.79	0.78	0.26	0.24	0.34	1.55	0.63	0.26
Debt to Equity	1.12	1.07	1.17	1.15	1.33	1.25	1.35	1.32
Price Range	30.11-20.34	30.94-20.34	30.94-20.34	30.94-20.34	35.79-29.01	31.34-20.04	30.75-20.34	29.29-23.69
P/E Ratio	20.34-13.74	21.05-13.84	43.58-28.65	44.84-29.48	62.79-50.89	...	17.67-11.69	117.16-94.76
Average Yield %	4.11	4.05	4.05	4.07	4.03	3.35	4.10	4.36	4.06

Address: 6711 Columbia Gateway Drive, Suite 300, Columbia, MD 21046	Web Site: www.copt.com	Auditors: ProcewaterhouseCoopers LLP
Telephone: 443-285-5400	Officers: Thomas F. Brady - Chairman Stephen E. Budorick - President, Chief Executive Officer, Executive Vice President, Chief Operating Officer	Investor Contact: 443-285-5400
Fax: 443-285-7650		Transfer Agents: Wells Fargo Shareowner Services, St. Paul, MN

COTY, INC.

Exchange	Symbol	Price	52Wk Range	Yield	P/E
NYS	COTY	$11.25 (12/31/2019)	13.73-6.56	4.44	N/A

*7 Year Price Score N/A   *NYSE Composite Index=100   *12 Month Price Score 103.44

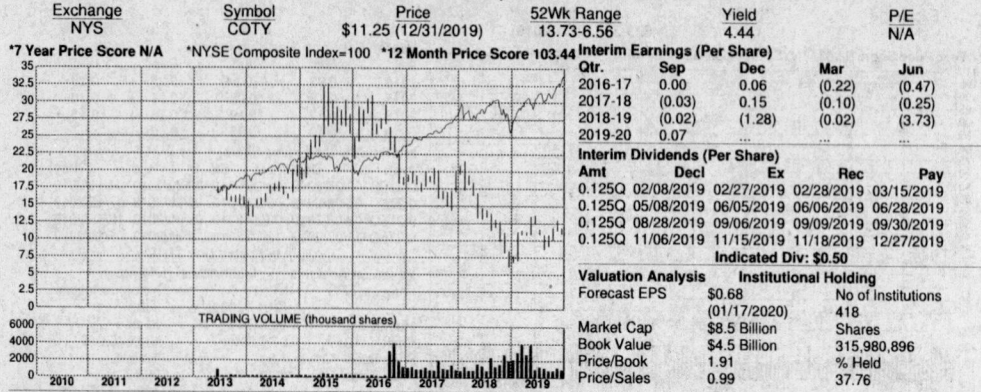

Interim Earnings (Per Share)

Qtr.	Sep	Dec	Mar	Jun
2016-17	0.00	0.06	(0.22)	(0.47)
2017-18	(0.03)	0.15	(0.10)	(0.25)
2018-19	(0.02)	(1.28)	(0.02)	(3.73)
2019-20	0.07	...	...	...

Interim Dividends (Per Share)

Amt	Decl	Ex	Rec	Pay
0.125Q	02/08/2019	02/27/2019	02/28/2019	03/15/2019
0.125Q	05/08/2019	06/05/2019	06/06/2019	06/28/2019
0.125Q	08/28/2019	09/06/2019	09/09/2019	09/30/2019
0.125Q	11/06/2019	11/15/2019	11/18/2019	12/27/2019

Indicated Div: $0.50

Valuation Analysis

Forecast EPS	$0.68
	(01/17/2020)
Market Cap	$8.5 Billion
Book Value	$4.5 Billion
Price/Book	1.91
Price/Sales	0.99

Institutional Holding

No of Institutions	418
Shares	315,980,896
% Held	37.76

Business Summary: Miscellaneous Consumer Goods (MIC: 1.6.3 SIC: 7231 NAIC: 812112)

Coty and its subsidiaries are a beauty company. Co. manufactures, markets, sells and distributes beauty products, including fragrances, color cosmetics, hair care products and skin and body related products. Co. is organized into three divisions, which is also its operating and reportable segments: Consumer Beauty, Luxury and Professional Beauty. Consumer Beauty is primarily focused on color cosmetics, retail hair coloring and styling products, body care and mass fragrances. Luxury is primarily focused on fragrances, skincare and cosmetics. Professional Beauty is primarily focused on hair and nail care products for salon personnel.

Recent Developments: For the quarter ended Sep 30 2019, net income amounted to US$56.3 million versus a net loss of US$10.1 million in the year-earlier quarter. Revenues were US$1.94 billion, down 4.4% from US$2.03 billion the year before. Operating income was US$126.0 million versus a loss of US$20.7 million in the prior-year quarter. Direct operating expenses declined 8.7% to US$738.4 million from US$809.1 million in the comparable period the year before. Indirect operating expenses decreased 13.2% to US$1.08 billion from US$1.24 billion in the equivalent prior-year period.

Prospects: Our evaluation of Coty, Inc. as of October 4th, 2019 is the result of our systematic analysis on three basic characteristics: earnings strength, relative valuation, and recent stock price movement. The company has generated a negative trend in earnings per share over the past 5 quarters. However, recent analyst estimates for the company have been unchanged and COTY has posted results in line with analysts' expectations. Based on operating earnings yield, the company is undervalued when compared to all of the companies we cover. Share price changes over the past year indicates that COTY will perform poorly over the near term.

Financial Data

(US$ in Thousands)	3 Mos	06/30/2019	06/30/2018	06/30/2017	06/30/2016	06/30/2015	06/30/2014	06/30/2013
Earnings Per Share	(4.96)	(5.04)	(0.23)	(0.66)	0.44	0.64	(0.26)	0.42
Cash Flow Per Share	1.01	0.85	0.55	1.18	1.45	1.49	1.41	1.22
Dividends Per Share	0.500	0.500	0.500	0.650	0.250	0.200	0.200	0.150
Dividend Payout %	...	...	...	...	56.82	31.25	...	35.71
Income Statement								
Total Revenue	1,942,800	8,648,500	9,398,000	7,650,300	4,349,100	4,395,200	4,551,600	4,649,100
EBITDA	325,300	(3,119,900)	496,700	(159,400)	373,100	462,500	189,400	564,600
Depn & Amortn	205,300	382,500	384,200	280,000	152,400	156,200	165,000	169,400
Income Before Taxes	46,400	(3,778,100)	(152,500)	(658,000)	138,800	233,300	(44,100)	318,700
Income Taxes	(9,900)	(8,500)	(24,700)	(259,500)	(40,400)	(26,100)	20,100	116,800
Net Income	52,300	(3,784,200)	(168,800)	(422,200)	156,900	232,500	(97,400)	168,000
Average Shares	758,900	751,200	749,700	642,800	354,200	362,900	381,700	396,400
Balance Sheet								
Current Assets	3,132,700	3,272,700	3,651,000	3,581,500	1,938,400	1,856,400	2,784,800	2,416,900
Total Assets	17,283,500	17,665,400	22,630,200	22,548,200	7,100,200	6,018,900	6,592,500	6,470,000
Current Liabilities	3,237,400	3,477,100	4,044,000	3,803,600	1,855,200	1,526,200	1,597,300	1,463,200
Long-Term Obligations	7,453,500	7,469,900	7,305,400	6,928,300	4,001,000	2,605,900	3,260,100	2,590,100
Total Liabilities	12,828,500	13,078,500	13,780,500	13,233,500	6,740,000	5,049,100	5,748,700	4,976,000
Stockholders' Equity	4,455,000	4,586,900	8,849,700	9,314,700	360,200	969,800	843,800	1,494,000
Shares Outstanding	757,000	754,200	750,700	747,900	337,100	360,800	353,900	383,800
Statistical Record								
Return on Assets %	N.M.	N.M.	N.M.	N.M.	2.39	3.69	N.M.	2.66
Return on Equity %	N.M.	N.M.	N.M.	N.M.	23.53	25.64	N.M.	13.31
EBITDA Margin %	16.74	N.M.	5.29	N.M.	8.58	10.52	4.16	12.14
Net Margin %	2.69	N.M.	N.M.	N.M.	3.61	5.29	N.M.	3.61
Asset Turnover	0.43	0.43	0.42	0.52	0.66	0.70	0.70	0.73
Current Ratio	0.97	0.94	0.90	0.94	1.04	1.22	1.74	1.65
Debt to Equity	1.67	1.63	0.83	0.74	11.11	2.69	3.86	1.73
Price Range	13.73-6.11	14.44-6.11	21.53-13.11	29.75-17.05	32.68-21.79	32.45-15.94	17.85-13.25	17.52-16.61
P/E Ratio	...	...	...	...	74.27-49.52	50.70-24.91	...	41.71-39.55
Average Yield %	4.83	4.55	2.85	3.07	0.91	0.96	1.26	0.88

Address: 350 Fifth Avenue, New York, NY 10118	**Web Site:** www.coty.com	**Auditors:** DELOITTE & TOUCHE LLP
Telephone: 212-389-7300	**Officers:** Peter Harf - Chairman, Chairman (frmr), Chief Executive Officer Pierre Laubies - Chief Executive Officer	**Investor Contact:** 212-389-7300

CRANE CO.

Exchange	Symbol	Price	52Wk Range	Yield	P/E
NYS	CR	$86.38 (12/31/2019)	88.91-69.66	1.81	15.68

*7 Year Price Score 96.21   *NYSE Composite Index=100   *12 Month Price Score 95.43

Interim Earnings (Per Share)

Qtr.	Mar	Jun	Sep	Dec
2016	0.93	1.15	1.07	(1.09)
2017	1.05	1.14	1.13	(0.48)
2018	1.13	1.32	1.59	1.46
2019	1.36	1.50	1.19	...

Interim Dividends (Per Share)

Amt	Decl	Ex	Rec	Pay
0.39Q	01/28/2019	02/27/2019	02/28/2019	03/11/2019
0.39Q	04/29/2019	05/30/2019	05/31/2019	06/10/2019
0.39Q	07/22/2019	08/29/2019	08/30/2019	09/09/2019
0.39Q	10/28/2019	11/27/2019	11/29/2019	12/09/2019

Indicated Div: $1.56

Valuation Analysis / Institutional Holding

Forecast EPS	$6.01	No of Institutions
(01/16/2020)		493
Market Cap	$5.2 Billion	Shares
Book Value	$1.7 Billion	52,747,616
Price/Book	3.05	% Held
Price/Sales	1.58	69.07

Business Summary: Industrial Machinery & Equipment (MIC: 7.2.1 SIC: 3499 NAIC: 332999)

Crane is a manufacturer of engineered industrial products. Co.'s segments are: Fluid Handling, which is a provider of engineered fluid handling equipment; Payment and Merchandising Technologies, which provides payment acceptance products, designs and manufactures vending equipment and related solutions, and supplies banknotes and banknote security features; Aerospace and Electronics, which supplies components and systems for the commercial aerospace and military aerospace and defense markets; and Engineered Materials, which manufactures fiberglass-reinforced plastic panels and coils, primarily for use in the manufacturing of recreational vehicles, truck bodies, truck trailers.

Recent Developments: For the quarter ended Sep 30 2019, net income decreased 25.2% to US$72.6 million from US$97.1 million in the year-earlier quarter. Revenues were US$772.3 million, down 9.8% from US$855.8 million the year before. Operating income was US$109.3 million versus US$123.9 million in the prior-year quarter, a decrease of 11.8%. Direct operating expenses declined 9.3% to US$494.4 million from US$544.8 million in the comparable period the year before. Indirect operating expenses decreased 9.9% to US$168.6 million from US$187.1 million in the equivalent prior-year period.

Prospects: Our evaluation of Crane Co. as of October 4th, 2019 is the result of our systematic analysis on three basic characteristics: earnings strength, relative valuation, and recent stock price movement. The company has managed to produce a neutral trend in earnings per share over the past 5 quarters. However, recent analyst estimates for the company have been reduced while CR has posted results that exceeded analysts' expectations. Based on operating earnings yield, the company is undervalued when compared to all of the companies we cover. Share price changes over the past year indicates that CR will perform poorly over the near term.

Financial Data
(US$ in Thousands)

	9 Mos	6 Mos	3 Mos	12/31/2018	12/31/2017	12/31/2016	12/31/2015	12/31/2014
Earnings Per Share	5.51	5.91	5.73	5.50	2.84	2.07	3.89	3.23
Cash Flow Per Share	6.04	5.59	4.00	6.94	5.35	5.42	3.95	4.50
Dividends Per Share	1.520	1.480	1.440	1.400	1.320	1.320	1.320	1.260
Dividend Payout %	27.59	25.04	25.13	25.45	46.48	63.77	33.93	39.01
Income Statement								
Total Revenue	2,445,600	1,673,300	831,700	3,345,500	2,786,000	2,748,000	2,740,500	2,924,997
EBITDA	433,900	301,200	143,400	532,700	442,100	238,900	411,300	360,365
Depn & Amortn	84,200	56,300	27,700	72,700	41,000	40,200	39,100	41,700
Income Before Taxes	316,600	222,900	104,400	411,400	367,500	164,100	336,500	281,156
Income Taxes	70,500	49,400	21,900	75,900	195,000	40,300	106,500	87,587
Net Income	245,900	173,400	82,400	335,600	171,800	122,800	228,900	192,672
Average Shares	60,800	60,800	60,700	61,000	60,400	59,300	58,800	59,603
Balance Sheet								
Current Assets	1,456,900	1,379,900	1,371,300	1,362,900	1,518,500	1,315,700	1,203,500	1,195,184
Total Assets	4,158,500	4,141,800	4,142,300	4,042,700	3,593,500	3,428,000	3,341,600	3,450,785
Current Liabilities	649,000	634,600	703,700	740,200	837,500	520,800	572,800	640,025
Long-Term Obligations	934,900	940,300	940,200	942,300	494,100	745,300	749,300	749,213
Total Liabilities	2,461,000	2,469,800	2,551,700	2,518,500	2,248,300	2,294,200	2,202,200	2,391,033
Stockholders' Equity	1,697,500	1,672,000	1,590,600	1,524,200	1,345,200	1,133,800	1,139,400	1,059,752
Shares Outstanding	59,978	59,948	59,888	59,508	59,411	58,964	58,109	58,121
Statistical Record								
Return on Assets %	8.10	8.70	8.09	8.79	4.89	3.62	6.74	5.50
Return on Equity %	20.78	23.08	23.01	23.39	13.86	10.77	20.82	17.02
EBITDA Margin %	17.74	18.00	17.24	15.92	15.87	8.69	15.01	12.32
Net Margin %	10.05	10.36	9.91	10.03	6.17	4.47	8.35	6.59
Asset Turnover	0.79	0.82	0.78	0.88	0.79	0.81	0.81	0.83
Current Ratio	2.24	2.17	1.95	1.84	1.81	2.53	2.10	1.87
Debt to Equity	0.55	0.56	0.59	0.62	0.37	0.66	0.66	0.71
Price Range	99.68-67.48	99.68-67.48	99.68-67.48	99.94-67.48	90.46-71.55	77.36-43.14	69.78-45.27	76.33-53.63
P/E Ratio	18.09-12.25	16.87-11.42	17.40-11.78	18.17-12.27	31.85-25.19	37.37-20.84	17.94-11.64	23.63-16.60
Average Yield %	1.84	1.74	1.68	1.58	1.69	2.32	2.33	1.87

Address: 100 First Stamford Place, Stamford, CT 06902
Telephone: 203-363-7300

Web Site:
Officers: R. S. Evans - Chairman Max H. Mitchell - President, Chief Executive Officer, Executive Vice President, Chief Operating Officer

Auditors: DELOITTE & TOUCHE LLP
Investor Contact: 203-363-7352
Transfer Agents: First Chicago Trust Company of New York, Jersey City, NJ

CROWN CASTLE INTERNATIONAL CORP

Exchange	Symbol	Price	52Wk Range	Yield	P/E
NYS	CCI	$142.15 (12/31/2019)	149.07-105.67	3.38	71.79

*7 Year Price Score 114.00 *NYSE Composite Index=100 *12 Month Price Score 98.19

Interim Earnings (Per Share)

Qtr.	Mar	Jun	Sep	Dec
2016	0.11	0.22	0.26	0.36
2017	0.33	0.31	0.21	0.17
2018	0.21	0.36	0.33	0.44
2019	0.44	0.52	0.58	...

Interim Dividends (Per Share)

Amt	Decl	Ex	Rec	Pay
1.125Q	02/21/2019	03/14/2019	03/15/2019	03/29/2019
1.125Q	05/16/2019	06/13/2019	06/14/2019	06/28/2019
1.125Q	08/08/2019	09/12/2019	09/13/2019	09/30/2019
1.20Q	10/16/2019	12/12/2019	12/13/2019	12/31/2019

Indicated Div: $4.80

Valuation Analysis

Forecast EPS	$2.01
	(01/17/2020)
Market Cap	$59.1 Billion
Book Value	$11.3 Billion
Price/Book	5.22
Price/Sales	10.13

Institutional Holding

No of Institutions	1265
Shares	449,103,424
% Held	N/A

Business Summary: REITs (MIC: 5.3.1 SIC: 6798 NAIC: 525930)

Crown Castle International is a holding company. Through its subsidiaries, Co. owns, operates and leases shared communications infrastructure that is geographically dispersed throughout the U.S., including towers and other structures, such as rooftops (collectively, towers), and fiber primarily supporting small cell networks (small cells) and fiber solutions. Co.'s towers, fiber and small cells assets are collectively referred to herein as communications infrastructure. Co.'s core business is providing access, including space or capacity, to its shared communications infrastructure via long-term contracts in various forms, including lease, license, sublease and service agreements.

Recent Developments: For the quarter ended Sep 30 2019, net income increased 65.9% to US$272.0 million from US$164.0 million in the year-earlier quarter. Revenues were US$1.51 billion, up 10.1% from US$1.38 billion the year before. Revenues from property income rose 6.4% to US$1.26 billion from US$1.18 billion in the corresponding quarter a year earlier.

Prospects: Our evaluation of Crown Castle International Corp. as of October 4th, 2019 is the result of our systematic analysis on three basic characteristics: earnings strength, relative valuation, and recent stock price movement. The company has managed to produce a neutral trend in earnings per share over the past 5 quarters. However, recent analyst estimates for the company have been raised and CCI has posted results that exceeded analysts' expectations. Based on operating earnings yield, the company is overvalued when compared to all of the companies we cover. Share price changes over the past year indicates that CCI will perform over the near term.

Financial Data

(US$ in Thousands)	9 Mos	6 Mos	3 Mos	12/31/2018	12/31/2017	12/31/2016	12/31/2015	12/31/2014
Earnings Per Share	1.98	1.73	1.57	1.34	1.01	0.95	4.42	1.04
Cash Flow Per Share	6.29	6.29	6.17	6.06	5.35	5.22	5.39	5.01
Dividends Per Share	4.500	4.425	4.350	4.275	3.900	3.605	3.345	0.820
Dividend Payout %	227.27	255.78	277.07	319.03	386.14	379.47	75.68	78.85
Income Statement								
Total Revenue	4,418,000	2,904,000	1,426,000	5,423,000	4,355,605	3,921,225	3,663,851	3,689,884
EBITDA	1,250,000	801,000	383,000	2,427,000	1,957,414	1,720,790	1,773,951	1,718,209
Depn & Amortn	1,000	1,000	1,000	1,100,000	914,900	832,700	774,900	757,400
Income Before Taxes	744,000	466,000	216,000	690,000	470,593	373,854	473,829	388,134
Income Taxes	15,000	10,000	6,000	19,000	26,043	16,881	(51,457)	(10,640)
Net Income	729,000	456,000	210,000	671,000	444,550	356,973	1,520,992	390,513
Average Shares	418,000	418,000	417,000	415,000	383,221	340,879	334,062	333,265
Balance Sheet								
Current Assets	1,253,000	1,294,000	1,193,000	1,229,000	1,133,780	1,324,761	981,245	931,502
Total Assets	38,344,000	38,147,000	37,778,000	32,785,000	32,229,570	22,675,092	22,036,245	21,143,276
Current Liabilities	1,734,000	1,698,000	1,565,000	1,417,000	1,292,082	961,355	855,369	898,935
Long-Term Obligations	17,750,000	17,471,000	17,120,000	16,575,000	16,044,369	12,069,393	12,143,019	11,807,526
Total Liabilities	27,019,000	26,624,000	26,032,000	20,751,000	19,890,488	15,117,977	14,947,024	14,427,051
Stockholders' Equity	11,325,000	11,523,000	11,746,000	12,034,000	12,339,082	7,557,115	7,089,221	6,716,225
Shares Outstanding	416,000	416,000	416,000	415,000	406,280	360,536	333,771	333,856
Statistical Record								
Return on Assets %	2.65	2.36	2.19	2.06	1.62	1.59	7.04	1.87
Return on Equity %	7.97	6.92	6.24	5.51	4.47	4.86	22.03	5.72
EBITDA Margin %	28.29	27.58	26.86	44.75	44.94	43.88	48.42	46.57
Net Margin %	16.50	15.70	14.73	12.37	10.21	9.10	41.51	10.58
Asset Turnover	0.16	0.16	0.16	0.17	0.16	0.17	0.17	0.18
Current Ratio	0.72	0.76	0.76	0.87	0.88	1.38	1.15	1.04
Debt to Equity	1.57	1.52	1.46	1.38	1.30	1.60	1.71	1.76
Price Range	149.07-103.54	136.92-103.54	128.00-100.82	117.47-100.82	114.03-84.36	102.56-78.22	88.71-76.58	84.75-68.96
P/E Ratio	75.29-52.29	79.14-59.85	81.53-64.22	87.66-75.24	112.90-83.52	107.96-82.34	20.07-17.33	81.49-66.31
Average Yield %	3.64	3.79	3.94	3.94	3.92	4.01	4.04	1.07

Address: 1220 Augusta Drive, Suite 600, Houston, TX 77057-2261	**Web Site:** www.crowncastle.com	**Auditors:** PricewaterhouseCoopers LLP
Telephone: 713-570-3000	**Officers:** J. Landis Martin - Chairman Jay A. Brown - President, Chief Executive Officer, Chief Financial Officer, Senior Vice President, Treasurer	**Investor Contact:** 713-570-3050
		Transfer Agents: Mellon Investor Services LLC, Jersey City, NJ

CROWN HOLDINGS INC

Exchange	Symbol	Price	52Wk Range	Yield	P/E
NYS	CCK	$72.54 (12/31/2019)	76.62-41.23	N/A	20.43

*7 Year Price Score 98.94 *NYSE Composite Index=100 *12 Month Price Score 114.05

Interim Earnings (Per Share)

Qtr.	Mar	Jun	Sep	Dec
2016	0.57	1.21	1.31	0.47
2017	0.77	0.94	1.32	(0.64)
2018	0.67	0.99	1.23	0.40
2019	0.77	1.02	1.36	...

Interim Dividends (Per Share)

No Dividends Paid

Valuation Analysis   Institutional Holding

Forecast EPS	$5.03	No of Institutions
(01/17/2020)		614
Market Cap	$9.8 Billion	Shares
Book Value	$1.6 Billion	172,963,680
Price/Book	6.07	% Held
Price/Sales	0.85	93.41

Business Summary: Metal Products (MIC: 8.2.3 SIC: 3411 NAIC: 332431)

Crown Holdings is engaged in the design, manufacture and sale of packaging products for consumer goods and industrial products. Co.'s packaging for consumer goods include steel and aluminum cans for food, beverage, household and other consumer products, glass bottles for beverage products, metal vacuum closures and steel crowns. Co.'s packaging for industrial products includes steel and plastic strap consumables and equipment, paper-based protective packaging, and plastic film consumables and equipment. Co.'s products include the SuperEnd® and 360 End™ beverage can ends, its Easylift™ aperture steel food can ends, and PeelSeam™ and PeelFit™ aluminum foil laminated ends.

Recent Developments: For the quarter ended Sep 30 2019, net income increased 5.7% to US$204.0 million from US$193.0 million in the year-earlier quarter. Revenues were US$3.08 billion, down 2.8% from US$3.17 billion the year before. Operating income was US$352.0 million versus US$365.0 million in the prior-year quarter, a decrease of 3.6%. Direct operating expenses declined 3.0% to US$2.58 billion from US$2.66 billion in the comparable period the year before. Indirect operating expenses increased 2.6% to US$156.0 million from US$152.0 million in the equivalent prior-year period.

Prospects: Our evaluation of Crown Holdings Inc. as of October 4th, 2019 is the result of our systematic analysis on three basic characteristics: earnings strength, relative valuation, and recent stock price movement. The company has managed to produce a neutral trend in earnings per share over the past 5 quarters. In addition, recent analyst estimates for the company have been mixed and CCK has posted results that fell short of analysts' expectations. Based on operating earnings yield, the company is undervalued when compared to all of the companies we cover. Share price changes over the past year indicates that CCK will perform over the near term.

Financial Data
(US$ in Thousands)

	9 Mos	6 Mos	3 Mos	12/31/2018	12/31/2017	12/31/2016	12/31/2015	12/31/2014
Earnings Per Share	3.55	3.42	3.39	3.28	2.38	3.56	2.82	2.79
Cash Flow Per Share	7.50	6.24	4.90	4.27	5.62	6.70	6.93	6.65
Income Statement								
Total Revenue	8,874,000	5,790,000	2,755,000	11,151,000	8,698,000	8,284,000	8,762,000	9,097,000
EBITDA	1,339,000	871,000	395,000	1,528,000	1,313,000	1,247,000	1,135,000	952,000
Depn & Amortn	366,000	245,000	122,000	425,000	247,000	247,000	237,000	190,000
Income Before Taxes	695,000	438,000	178,000	740,000	829,000	769,000	639,000	516,000
Income Taxes	190,000	136,000	48,000	216,000	401,000	186,000	178,000	41,000
Net Income	423,000	240,000	103,000	439,000	323,000	496,000	393,000	387,000
Average Shares	135,000	134,800	134,400	133,880	135,610	139,310	139,140	138,500
Balance Sheet								
Current Assets	4,082,000	4,214,000	4,024,000	4,079,000	3,074,000	2,841,000	3,049,000	3,624,000
Total Assets	15,337,000	15,565,000	15,357,000	15,262,000	10,663,000	9,599,000	10,020,000	9,708,000
Current Liabilities	3,632,000	3,608,000	3,342,000	3,913,000	3,250,000	2,896,000	2,908,000	2,926,000
Long-Term Obligations	8,042,000	8,549,000	8,814,000	8,517,000	5,217,000	4,717,000	5,255,000	5,007,000
Total Liabilities	13,718,000	14,271,000	14,223,000	14,325,000	10,062,000	9,233,000	9,876,000	9,589,000
Stockholders' Equity	1,619,000	1,294,000	1,134,000	937,000	601,000	366,000	144,000	119,000
Shares Outstanding	135,527	135,527	135,338	135,173	134,275	139,840	139,441	139,000
Statistical Record								
Return on Assets %	3.10	2.96	3.18	3.39	3.19	5.04	3.98	4.36
Return on Equity %	37.19	43.98	47.60	57.09	66.80	193.98	298.86	629.27
EBITDA Margin %	15.09	15.04	14.34	13.70	15.10	15.05	12.95	10.46
Net Margin %	4.77	4.15	3.74	3.94	3.71	5.99	4.49	4.25
Asset Turnover	0.76	0.76	0.82	0.86	0.86	0.84	0.89	1.03
Current Ratio	1.12	1.17	1.20	1.04	0.95	0.98	1.05	1.24
Debt to Equity	4.97	6.61	7.77	9.09	8.68	12.89	36.49	42.08
Price Range	68.58-39.63	61.20-39.63	55.91-39.63	59.26-39.63	61.17-52.48	57.09-44.21	56.63-44.31	52.31-40.12
P/E Ratio	19.32-11.16	17.89-11.59	16.49-11.69	18.07-12.08	25.70-22.05	16.04-12.42	20.08-15.71	18.75-14.38

Address: 770 Township Line Road, Yardley, PA 19067	**Web Site:** www.crowncork.com	**Auditors:** PricewaterhouseCoopers LLP
Telephone: 215-698-5100	**Officers:** John W. Conway - Chairman, President, Chief Executive Officer, Chief Operating Officer	**Investor Contact:** 215-698-5341
	Timothy J. Donahue - President, Chief Executive Officer, Executive Vice President, Chief Financial Officer, Chief Operating Officer	**Transfer Agents:** Wells Fargo Shareowner Services, St. Paul, MN

CULLEN/FROST BANKERS, INC.

Exchange	Symbol	Price	52Wk Range	Yield	P/E	Div Acheiver
NYS	CFR	$97.78 (12/31/2019)	105.70-80.32	2.90	13.85	25 Years

*7 Year Price Score 95.34   *NYSE Composite Index=100   *12 Month Price Score 94.94

Interim Earnings (Per Share)

Qtr.	Mar	Jun	Sep	Dec
2016	1.07	1.11	1.24	1.28
2017	1.28	1.29	1.41	1.53
2018	1.61	1.68	1.78	1.82
2019	1.79	1.72	1.73	...

Interim Dividends (Per Share)

Amt	Decl	Ex	Rec	Pay
0.67Q	01/31/2019	02/27/2019	02/28/2019	03/15/2019
0.71Q	04/25/2019	05/30/2019	05/31/2019	06/14/2019
0.71Q	07/24/2019	08/29/2019	08/30/2019	09/13/2019
0.71Q	10/31/2019	11/27/2019	11/29/2019	12/13/2019

Indicated Div: $2.84

Valuation Analysis | **Institutional Holding**

Forecast EPS	$6.83	No of Institutions
(01/14/2020)		518
Market Cap	$6.1 Billion	Shares
Book Value	$3.9 Billion	67,230,704
Price/Book	1.58	% Held
Price/Sales	4.10	81.81

Business Summary: Banking (MIC: 5.1.1 SIC: 6021 NAIC: 522110)

Cullen/Frost Bankers is a financial holding company and a bank holding company. Through its subsidiaries, Co. provides a range of products and services throughout various Texas markets. Co. provides commercial and consumer banking services, as well as trust and investment management, insurance, brokerage, mutual funds, leasing, treasury management, capital markets advisory and item processing services. Co. serves a variety of industries including, among others, energy, manufacturing, services, construction, retail, telecommunications, healthcare, military and transportation. Co.'s operations are managed along two reportable operating segments: Banking and Frost Wealth Advisors.

Recent Developments: For the quarter ended Sep 30 2019, net income decreased 5.1% to US$111.8 million from US$117.8 million in the year-earlier quarter. Net interest income increased 4.7% to US$253.0 million from US$241.7 million in the year-earlier quarter. Provision for loan losses was US$8.0 million versus US$2.7 million in the prior-year quarter, an increase of 201.9%. Non-interest income rose 1.8% to US$89.2 million from US$87.7 million, while non-interest expense advanced 7.8% to US$208.9 million.

Prospects: Our evaluation of Cullen/Frost Bankers Inc. as of October 4th, 2019 is the result of our systematic analysis on three basic characteristics: earnings strength, relative valuation, and recent stock price movement. The company has managed to produce a neutral trend in earnings per share over the past 5 quarters. However, recent analyst estimates for the company have been reduced and CFR has posted results in line with analysts' expectations. Based on operating earnings yield, the company is undervalued when compared to all of the companies we cover. Share price changes over the past year indicates that CFR will perform poorly over the near term.

Financial Data
(US$ in Thousands)

	9 Mos	6 Mos	3 Mos	12/31/2018	12/31/2017	12/31/2016	12/31/2015	12/31/2014
Earnings Per Share	7.06	7.11	7.07	6.90	5.51	4.70	4.28	4.29
Cash Flow Per Share	10.99	9.56	7.90	8.83	8.45	7.00	6.27	4.62
Tang Book Value Per Share	49.24	46.92	44.24	40.74	39.28	34.60	33.60	32.32
Dividends Per Share	2.760	2.720	2.680	2.580	2.250	2.150	2.100	2.030
Dividend Payout %	39.09	38.26	37.91	37.39	40.83	45.74	49.07	47.32
Income Statement								
Interest Income	855,731	569,458	281,321	1,051,198	892,947	788,412	749,496	701,471
Interest Expense	102,824	69,558	34,852	93,306	26,525	12,076	12,864	14,537
Net Interest Income	752,907	499,900	246,469	957,892	866,422	776,336	736,632	686,934
Provision for Losses	25,404	17,403	11,003	21,613	35,460	51,673	51,845	16,314
Non-Interest Income	268,647	179,423	96,785	351,286	336,470	349,708	328,730	320,144
Non-Interest Expense	613,873	405,009	201,800	778,884	759,069	732,960	693,718	654,740
Income Before Taxes	382,277	256,911	130,451	508,681	408,363	341,411	319,799	336,024
Income Taxes	42,359	28,829	13,955	53,763	44,214	37,150	40,471	58,047
Net Income	339,918	228,082	116,496	454,918	364,149	304,261	279,328	277,977
Average Shares	63,158	63,554	63,827	64,686	64,662	62,968	63,473	62,973
Balance Sheet								
Net Loans & Leases	14,498,369	14,324,220	14,269,989	13,967,601	12,990,301	11,822,347	11,350,672	10,887,993
Total Assets	33,098,176	31,818,863	31,664,566	32,292,966	31,747,880	30,196,319	28,567,118	28,277,775
Total Deposits	27,083,582	25,985,023	26,294,863	27,149,204	26,872,389	25,811,575	24,343,595	24,135,930
Total Liabilities	29,216,719	28,077,556	28,070,988	28,924,049	28,450,017	27,193,791	25,676,775	25,426,372
Stockholders' Equity	3,881,457	3,741,307	3,593,578	3,368,917	3,297,863	3,002,528	2,890,343	2,851,403
Shares Outstanding	62,536	62,638	63,081	62,985	63,475	63,474	61,982	63,149
Statistical Record								
Return on Assets %	1.43	1.49	1.47	1.42	1.18	1.03	0.98	1.06
Return on Equity %	12.77	13.20	13.60	13.65	11.56	10.30	9.73	10.36
Net Interest Margin %	88.38	87.96	87.61	91.12	97.03	98.47	98.28	97.93
Efficiency Ratio %	55.62	54.81	53.37	55.54	61.74	64.40	64.34	64.09
Loans to Deposits	0.54	0.55	0.54	0.51	0.48	0.46	0.47	0.45
Price Range	107.01-80.32	115.95-82.72	120.77-82.72	120.77-82.72	101.40-81.59	88.77-42.55	80.10-59.40	81.67-68.06
P/E Ratio	15.16-11.38	16.31-11.63	17.08-11.70	17.50-11.99	18.40-14.81	18.89-9.05	18.71-13.88	19.04-15.86
Average Yield %	2.88	2.68	2.55	2.42	2.44	3.27	3.05	2.66

Address: 111 W. Houston Street, San Antonio, TX 78205 Telephone: 210-220-4011 Fax: 210-220-5578	Web Site: www.frostbank.com Officers: Phillip D. (Phil) Green - Chairman, President, Chief Executive Officer, Group Executive Vice President, Chief Financial Officer Paul H. Bracher - President	Auditors: Ernst & Young LLP Investor Contact: 210-220-5632 Transfer Agents: American Stock Transfer & Trust Company, LLC, Brooklyn, NY

CUMMINS, INC.

Exchange	Symbol	Price	52Wk Range	Yield	P/E	Div Acheiver
NYS	CMI	$178.96 (12/31/2019)	186.44-130.74	2.93	11.14	13 Years

*7 Year Price Score 95.64   *NYSE Composite Index=100   *12 Month Price Score 106.09

Interim Earnings (Per Share)

Qtr.	Mar	Jun	Sep	Dec
2016	1.87	2.40	1.72	2.24
2017	2.36	2.53	2.71	(1.63)
2018	1.96	3.32	4.28	3.62
2019	4.20	4.27	3.97	...

Interim Dividends (Per Share)

Amt	Decl	Ex	Rec	Pay
1.14Q	02/12/2019	02/21/2019	02/22/2019	03/07/2019
1.14Q	05/14/2019	05/23/2019	05/24/2019	06/05/2019
1.311Q	07/09/2019	08/20/2019	08/21/2019	09/03/2019
1.311Q	10/07/2019	11/13/2019	11/14/2019	12/02/2019

Indicated Div: $5.24 (Div. Reinv. Plan)

Valuation Analysis   **Institutional Holding**

Forecast EPS	$14.88	No of Institutions
	(01/15/2020)	1494
Market Cap	$27.4 Billion	Shares
Book Value	$7.8 Billion	160,032,352
Price/Book	3.51	% Held
Price/Sales	1.14	76.28

Business Summary: Auto Parts (MIC: 1.8.2 SIC: 3519 NAIC: 333618)

Cummins is a diesel engine manufacturer. Co.'s segments include: Engine, which manufactures and markets a range of diesel and natural gas powered engines; Distribution, which consists of product lines that service and/or distribute the range of Co.'s products and services; Components, which supplies aftertreatment systems, turbochargers, transmissions, filtration products, electronics and fuel systems for commercial diesel and natural gas applications; Power Systems, which includes power generation, industrial, and generator technologies product lines; and Electrified Power, which designs, manufactures, sells and supports electrified power systems ranging from fully electric to hybrid.

Recent Developments: For the quarter ended Sep 29 2019, net income decreased 11.7% to US$616.0 million from US$698.0 million in the year-earlier quarter. Revenues were US$5.77 billion, down 2.9% from US$5.94 billion the year before. Operating income was US$699.0 million versus US$803.0 million in the prior-year quarter, a decrease of 13.0%. Direct operating expenses declined 2.7% to US$4.27 billion from US$4.39 billion in the comparable period the year before. Indirect operating expenses increased 6.3% to US$795.0 million from US$748.0 million in the equivalent prior-year period.

Prospects: Our evaluation of Cummins Inc. as of October 4th, 2019 is the result of our systematic analysis on three basic characteristics: earnings strength, relative valuation, and recent stock price movement. The company has generated a negative trend in earnings per share over the past 5 quarters. However, recent analyst estimates for the company have been mixed and CMI has posted results that fell short of analysts' expectations. Based on operating earnings yield, the company is undervalued when compared to all of the companies we cover. Share price changes over the past year indicates that CMI will perform in line with the market over the near term.

Financial Data

(US$ in Thousands)	9 Mos	6 Mos	3 Mos	12/31/2018	12/31/2017	12/31/2016	12/31/2015	12/31/2014
Earnings Per Share	16.06	16.37	15.42	13.15	5.97	8.23	7.84	9.02
Cash Flow Per Share	21.38	19.85	18.49	14.66	13.67	11.42	11.56	12.41
Tang Book Value Per Share	35.90	39.62	36.83	33.63	31.41	36.05	37.65	38.02
Dividends Per Share	4.731	4.560	4.500	4.440	4.210	4.000	3.510	2.810
Dividend Payout %	29.46	27.86	29.18	33.76	70.52	48.60	44.77	31.15
Income Statement								
Total Revenue	17,993,000	12,225,000	6,004,000	23,771,000	20,428,000	17,509,000	19,110,000	19,221,000
EBITDA	2,535,000	1,763,000	870,000	3,307,000	2,895,000	2,410,000	2,485,000	2,826,000
Depn & Amortn	15,000	10,000	5,000	475,000	467,000	434,000	419,000	351,000
Income Before Taxes	2,471,000	1,716,000	845,000	2,753,000	2,365,000	1,930,000	2,025,000	2,434,000
Income Taxes	501,000	362,000	176,000	566,000	1,371,000	474,000	555,000	698,000
Net Income	1,960,000	1,338,000	663,000	2,141,000	999,000	1,394,000	1,399,000	1,651,000
Average Shares	156,600	158,000	157,700	162,773	167,270	169,336	178,406	183,079
Balance Sheet								
Current Assets	10,228,000	10,450,000	10,091,000	9,818,000	8,928,000	7,707,000	7,947,000	9,055,000
Total Assets	20,346,000	20,254,000	19,846,000	19,062,000	18,075,000	15,011,000	15,134,000	15,776,000
Current Liabilities	6,725,000	6,289,000	6,427,000	6,384,000	5,677,000	4,325,000	3,803,000	4,021,000
Long-Term Obligations	1,619,000	1,624,000	1,605,000	1,597,000	1,588,000	1,568,000	1,576,000	1,589,000
Total Liabilities	12,536,000	11,976,000	12,026,000	11,714,000	10,816,000	8,136,000	7,728,000	8,027,000
Stockholders' Equity	7,810,000	8,278,000	7,820,000	7,348,000	7,259,000	6,875,000	7,406,000	7,749,000
Shares Outstanding	153,200	157,800	157,500	158,000	165,700	168,200	175,200	182,200
Statistical Record								
Return on Assets %	12.91	13.32	12.97	11.53	6.04	9.22	9.05	10.82
Return on Equity %	33.85	33.50	32.59	29.31	14.14	19.47	18.46	21.64
EBITDA Margin %	14.09	14.42	14.49	13.91	14.17	13.76	13.00	14.70
Net Margin %	10.89	10.94	11.04	9.01	4.89	7.96	7.32	8.59
Asset Turnover	1.23	1.24	1.27	1.28	1.23	1.16	1.24	1.26
Current Ratio	1.52	1.66	1.57	1.54	1.57	1.78	2.09	2.25
Debt to Equity	0.21	0.20	0.21	0.22	0.22	0.23	0.21	0.21
Price Range	175.37-125.49	171.60-125.49	170.83-125.49	192.50-125.49	180.35-137.42	146.46-83.52	147.85-85.21	160.55-123.70
P/E Ratio	10.92-7.81	10.48-7.67	11.08-8.14	14.64-9.54	30.21-23.02	17.80-10.15	18.86-10.87	17.80-13.71
Average Yield %	3.08	3.06	3.09	2.95	2.65	3.44	2.80	1.95

Address: 500 Jackson Street, P.O. Box 3005, Columbus, IN 47202-3005
Telephone: 812-377-5000
Fax: 812-377-4937

Web Site: www.cummins.com
Officers: Norman Thomas Linebarger - Chairman, President, Chief Executive Officer, Executive Vice President, Vice President, Chief Financial Officer, Chief Operating Officer, Division Officer Livingston L. Satterthwaite - President, Vice President, Chief Operating Officer, Division Officer

Auditors: PricewaterhouseCoopers LLP
Investor Contact: 812-377-3121
Transfer Agents: Wells Fargo Shareowner Services

CURTISS-WRIGHT CORP.

Exchange	Symbol	Price	52Wk Range	Yield	P/E
NYS	CW	$140.89 (12/31/2019)	143.48-99.45	0.48	20.24

*7 Year Price Score 116.26 *NYSE Composite Index=100 *12 Month Price Score 107.22

Interim Earnings (Per Share)

Qtr.	Mar	Jun	Sep	Dec
2016	0.73	0.88	1.02	1.52
2017	0.73	1.13	1.43	1.51
2018	0.98	1.68	1.68	1.89
2019	1.29	1.86	1.92	...

Interim Dividends (Per Share)

Amt	Decl	Ex	Rec	Pay
0.15Q	02/06/2019	03/27/2019	03/28/2019	04/11/2019
0.17Q	05/15/2019	06/19/2019	06/20/2019	07/05/2019
0.17Q	09/11/2019	10/02/2019	10/03/2019	10/17/2019
0.17Q	11/14/2019	11/27/2019	11/29/2019	12/06/2019

Indicated Div: $0.68

Valuation Analysis

		Institutional Holding	
Forecast EPS	$7.22	No of Institutions	
	(01/17/2020)	442	
Market Cap	$6.0 Billion	Shares	
Book Value	$1.7 Billion	45,668,848	
Price/Book	3.54	% Held	
Price/Sales	2.42	74.38	

Business Summary: Industrial Machinery & Equipment (MIC: 7.2.1 SIC: 3599 NAIC: 333999)

Curtiss-Wright is a manufacturing and service company that designs, manufactures, and overhauls components and provides engineered products and services. Co.'s segments are: Commercial/Industrial, which provides engineered products and services including industrial vehicle products, sensors, valves and surface technology services; Defense, which provides Commercial Off-the-Shelf embedded computing board-level modules, integrated subsystems, instrumentation and control systems, turret aiming and stabilization products, and weapons handling systems; and Power, which provides hardware, pumps, valves, fastening systems, containment doors, airlock hatches, and spent fuel management products.

Recent Developments: For the quarter ended Sep 30 2019, net income increased 10.8% to US$82.5 million from US$74.5 million in the year-earlier quarter. Revenues were US$614.9 million, up 3.3% from US$595.4 million the year before. Operating income was US$105.6 million versus US$97.0 million in the prior-year quarter, an increase of 8.8%. Direct operating expenses rose 4.3% to US$388.8 million from US$372.9 million in the comparable period the year before. Indirect operating expenses decreased 4.0% to US$120.5 million from US$125.5 million in the equivalent prior-year period.

Prospects: Our evaluation of Curtiss-Wright Corp. as of October 4th, 2019 is the result of our systematic analysis on three basic characteristics: earnings strength, relative valuation, and recent stock price movement. The company has managed to produce a neutral trend in earnings per share over the past 5 quarters. Additionally, recent analyst estimates for the company have been unchanged while CW has posted results that exceeded analysts' expectations. Based on operating earnings yield, the company is undervalued when compared to all of the companies we cover. Share price changes over the past year indicates that CW will perform in line with the market over the near term.

Financial Data
(US$ in Thousands)

	9 Mos	6 Mos	3 Mos	12/31/2018	12/31/2017	12/31/2016	12/31/2015	12/31/2014
Earnings Per Share	6.96	6.72	6.54	6.22	4.80	4.15	3.05	2.31
Cash Flow Per Share	9.28	8.18	8.31	7.66	8.80	9.51	3.48	6.91
Tang Book Value Per Share	4.12	2.48	0.69	0.31	2.31	1.55	N.M.	2.73
Dividends Per Share	0.620	0.620	0.600	0.600	0.560	0.520	0.520	0.520
Dividend Payout %	8.91	9.23	9.17	9.65	11.67	12.53	17.05	22.51
Income Statement								
Total Revenue	1,832,190	1,217,310	578,314	2,411,835	2,271,026	2,108,931	2,205,683	2,243,126
EBITDA	378,001	240,679	103,316	449,622	402,690	371,809	375,932	349,338
Depn & Amortn	76,998	51,600	25,793	59,400	61,600	62,600	64,700	66,600
Income Before Taxes	277,820	173,847	70,251	356,239	299,619	267,961	275,194	246,944
Income Taxes	59,645	38,182	14,658	80,490	84,728	78,579	82,946	76,995
Net Income	218,175	135,665	55,593	275,749	214,891	187,329	145,461	113,338
Average Shares	42,995	43,024	43,058	44,316	44,761	45,045	47,616	49,075
Balance Sheet								
Current Assets	1,416,286	1,336,652	1,238,739	1,343,966	1,401,860	1,414,811	1,316,620	1,571,075
Total Assets	3,482,309	3,426,640	3,328,802	3,255,385	3,236,321	3,037,781	3,029,378	3,399,511
Current Liabilities	648,105	637,869	603,268	687,328	590,997	675,262	525,187	571,993
Long-Term Obligations	761,057	761,476	761,894	762,313	813,989	815,630	953,083	953,279
Total Liabilities	1,781,169	1,774,344	1,743,222	1,724,604	1,708,521	1,746,590	1,773,955	1,921,078
Stockholders' Equity	1,701,140	1,652,296	1,585,580	1,530,781	1,527,800	1,291,191	1,255,423	1,478,433
Shares Outstanding	42,689	42,715	42,801	42,772	44,123	44,181	44,621	47,904
Statistical Record								
Return on Assets %	8.91	8.80	8.84	8.50	6.85	6.16	4.53	3.31
Return on Equity %	18.12	18.15	18.18	18.03	15.25	14.67	10.64	7.48
EBITDA Margin %	20.63	19.77	17.87	18.64	17.73	17.63	17.04	15.57
Net Margin %	11.91	11.14	9.61	11.43	9.46	8.88	6.59	5.05
Asset Turnover	0.73	0.74	0.75	0.74	0.72	0.69	0.69	0.65
Current Ratio	2.19	2.10	2.05	1.96	2.37	2.10	2.51	2.75
Debt to Equity	0.45	0.46	0.48	0.50	0.53	0.63	0.76	0.64
Price Range	138.41-97.15	140.25-97.15	142.06-97.15	142.06-97.15	124.20-83.41	107.06-63.70	77.08-61.97	73.16-58.77
P/E Ratio	19.89-13.96	20.87-14.46	21.72-14.85	22.84-15.62	25.88-17.38	25.80-15.35	25.27-20.32	31.67-25.44
Average Yield %	0.53	0.53	0.49	0.48	0.56	0.62	0.75	0.78

Address: 130 Harbour Place Drive, Suite 300, Davidson, NC 28036
Telephone: 704-869-4600

Web Site: www.curtisswright.com
Officers: David C. Adams - Chairman, Chief Executive Officer, President, Vice President, Co-Chief Operating Officer, Chief Operating Officer Thomas P. Quinly - Vice President, Chief Operating Officer

Auditors: Deloitte & Touche LLP
Investor Contact: 973-541-3700
Transfer Agents: Broadridge Corporate Issuer Solutions, Inc., Brentwood, NY

CVS HEALTH CORPORATION

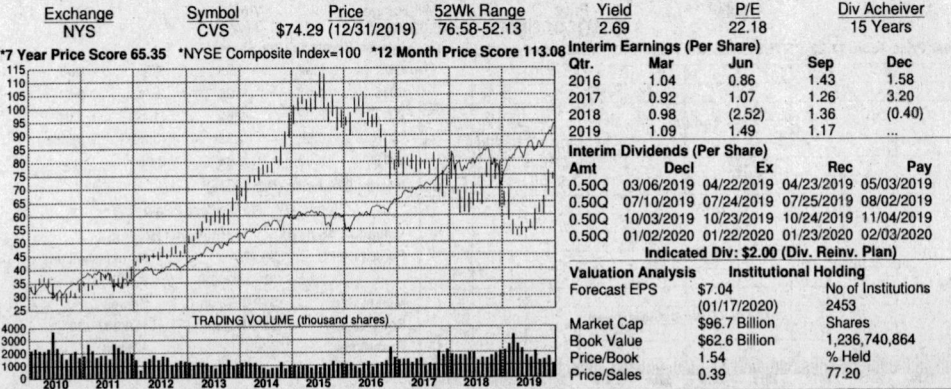

Exchange	Symbol	Price	52Wk Range	Yield	P/E	Div Acheiver
NYS	CVS	$74.29 (12/31/2019)	76.58-52.13	2.69	22.18	15 Years

*7 Year Price Score 65.35   ***NYSE Composite Index=100**   ***12 Month Price Score 113.08**

Interim Earnings (Per Share)

Qtr.	Mar	Jun	Sep	Dec
2016	1.04	0.86	1.43	1.58
2017	0.92	1.07	1.26	3.20
2018	0.98	(2.52)	1.36	(0.40)
2019	1.09	1.49	1.17	...

Interim Dividends (Per Share)

Amt	Decl	Ex	Rec	Pay
0.50Q	03/06/2019	04/22/2019	04/23/2019	05/03/2019
0.50Q	07/10/2019	07/24/2019	07/25/2019	08/02/2019
0.50Q	10/03/2019	10/23/2019	10/24/2019	11/04/2019
0.50Q	01/02/2020	01/22/2020	01/23/2020	02/03/2020

Indicated Div: $2.00 (Div. Reinv. Plan)

Valuation Analysis

Forecast EPS	$7.04
	(01/17/2020)
Market Cap	$96.7 Billion
Book Value	$62.6 Billion
Price/Book	1.54
Price/Sales	0.39

Institutional Holding

No of Institutions	2453
Shares	
	1,236,740,864
% Held	77.20

Business Summary: Diagnostic & Health Related Services (MIC: 4.2.2 SIC: 5912 NAIC: 446110)

CVS Health, together with its subsidiaries, is a health company. Co.'s segments include: Pharmacy Services, which provides a range of pharmacy benefit management solutions, including plan design offerings and administration, and formulary management; Retail/Long-Term Care (LTC), which sells prescription drugs and an assortment of general merchandise, provides health care services through its MinuteClinic® walk-in medical clinics and conducts LTC pharmacy operations; and Health Care Benefits, which provides a range of voluntary and consumer-directed health insurance products and related services, including medical, pharmacy, dental, and Medicare Advantage and Medicare Supplement plans.

Recent Developments: For the quarter ended Sep 30 2019, income from continuing operations increased 10.0% to US$1.53 billion from US$1.39 billion in the year-earlier quarter. Net income increased 10.0% to US$1.53 billion from US$1.39 billion in the year-earlier quarter. Revenues were US$64.81 billion, up 36.5% from US$47.49 billion the year before. Operating income was US$2.93 billion versus US$2.57 billion in the prior-year quarter, an increase of 13.8%. Direct operating expenses rose 2.4% to US$40.44 billion from US$39.50 billion in the comparable period the year before. Indirect operating expenses increased 296.1% to US$21.45 billion from US$5.41 billion in the equivalent prior-year period.

Prospects: Our evaluation of CVS Health Corp. as of October 4th, 2019 is the result of our systematic analysis on three basic characteristics: earnings strength, relative valuation, and recent stock price movement. The company has managed to produce a neutral trend in earnings per share over the past 5 quarters. Additionally, recent analyst estimates for the company have been unchanged while CVS has posted results that exceeded analysts' expectations. Based on operating earnings yield, the company is undervalued when compared to all of the companies we cover. Share price changes over the past year indicates that CVS will perform very poorly over the near term.

Financial Data

(US$ in Thousands)	9 Mos	6 Mos	3 Mos	12/31/2018	12/31/2017	12/31/2016	12/31/2015	12/31/2014
Earnings Per Share	3.35	3.54	(0.47)	(0.57)	6.44	4.90	4.63	3.96
Cash Flow Per Share	9.75	8.35	6.52	8.49	7.85	9.36	7.52	7.01
Tang Book Value Per Share	N.M.	N.M.	N.M.	N.M.	N.M.	N.M.	N.M.	0.04
Dividends Per Share	2.000	2.000	2.000	2.000	2.000	1.700	1.400	1.100
Dividend Payout %	59.70	56.50	...	...	31.06	34.69	30.24	27.78
Income Statement								
Total Revenue	189,887,000	125,077,000	61,646,000	194,579,000	184,765,000	177,526,000	153,290,000	139,367,000
EBITDA	12,239,000	8,267,000	3,832,000	5,725,000	11,009,000	11,395,000	10,954,000	9,678,000
Depn & Amortn	3,275,000	2,183,000	1,111,000	1,700,000	1,700,000	1,700,000	1,500,000	1,400,000
Income Before Taxes	6,663,000	4,530,000	1,939,000	1,406,000	8,268,000	8,637,000	8,616,000	7,678,000
Income Taxes	1,776,000	1,172,000	512,000	2,002,000	1,637,000	3,317,000	3,386,000	3,033,000
Net Income	4,887,000	3,357,000	1,421,000	(594,000)	6,622,000	5,317,000	5,237,000	4,644,000
Average Shares	1,305,000	1,302,000	1,302,000	1,044,000	1,024,000	1,079,000	1,126,000	1,169,000
Balance Sheet								
Current Assets	48,185,000	46,901,000	47,857,000	45,243,000	31,229,000	31,042,000	30,378,000	25,983,000
Total Assets	220,113,000	218,904,000	219,768,000	196,456,000	95,131,000	94,462,000	93,657,000	74,252,000
Current Liabilities	52,544,000	49,376,000	50,631,000	44,009,000	30,648,000	26,250,000	23,169,000	19,027,000
Long-Term Obligations	64,206,000	66,941,000	67,888,000	71,444,000	22,181,000	25,615,000	26,267,000	11,695,000
Total Liabilities	157,499,000	157,622,000	160,082,000	138,231,000	57,440,000	57,632,000	56,461,000	36,294,000
Stockholders' Equity	62,614,000	61,282,000	59,686,000	58,225,000	37,691,000	36,830,000	37,196,000	37,958,000
Shares Outstanding	1,301,000	1,299,000	1,298,000	1,295,000	1,014,000	1,061,000	1,101,000	1,140,000
Statistical Record								
Return on Assets %	2.54	2.46	N.M.	N.M.	6.99	5.64	6.24	6.37
Return on Equity %	9.01	8.93	N.M.	N.M.	17.77	14.33	13.94	12.24
EBITDA Margin %	6.45	6.61	6.22	2.94	5.96	6.42	7.15	6.94
Net Margin %	2.57	2.68	2.31	N.M.	3.58	3.00	3.42	3.33
Asset Turnover	1.39	1.29	1.19	1.33	1.95	1.88	1.83	1.91
Current Ratio	0.92	0.95	0.95	1.03	1.02	1.18	1.31	1.37
Debt to Equity	1.03	1.09	1.14	1.23	0.59	0.70	0.71	0.31
Price Range	80.80-52.13	80.80-52.13	80.80-52.36	83.63-60.60	83.92-66.80	106.10-73.53	113.45-91.56	98.25-65.44
P/E Ratio	24.12-15.56	22.82-14.73	...	...	13.03-10.37	21.65-15.01	24.50-19.78	24.81-16.53
Average Yield %	3.21	3.06	2.92	2.82	2.58	1.83	1.38	1.40

Address: One CVS Drive, Woonsocket, RI 02895	**Web Site:** www.cvshealth.com	**Auditors:** Ernst & Young LLP
Telephone: 401-765-1500	**Officers:** David W. Dorman - Chairman Larry J. Merlo - President, Chief Executive Officer	**Investor Contact:** 800-201-0938
Fax: 401-762-2137		**Transfer Agents:** Computershare, Providence, RI

DAVITA INC

Exchange	Symbol	Price	52Wk Range	Yield	P/E
NYS	DVA	$75.03 (12/31/2019)	75.03-43.42	N/A	28.42

*7 Year Price Score 71.20 *NYSE Composite Index=100 *12 Month Price Score 115.03

Interim Earnings (Per Share)

Qtr.	Mar	Jun	Sep	Dec
2016	0.47	0.26	2.76	0.81
2017	2.29	0.65	(1.14)	1.61
2018	0.98	1.53	(0.82)	(0.85)
2019	0.90	1.64	0.95	...

Interim Dividends (Per Share)

No Dividends Paid

Valuation Analysis		Institutional Holding	
Forecast EPS	$5.27	No of Institutions	
	(01/14/2020)	675	
Market Cap	$10.0 Billion	Shares	
Book Value	$2.3 Billion	150,953,920	
Price/Book	4.33	% Held	
Price/Sales	0.89	64.45	

Business Summary: Diagnostic & Health Related Services (MIC: 4.2.2 SIC: 8092 NAIC: 621492)

DaVita consists of two primary divisions, DaVita Kidney Care (Kidney Care) and DaVita Medical Group (DMG). Kidney Care is comprised of Co.'s U.S. dialysis and related lab services, its ancillary services and strategic initiatives, including its international operations and its corporate administrative support. Co.'s U.S. dialysis and related lab services business is its principal line of business, which is a provider of kidney dialysis services in the U.S. for patients suffering from chronic kidney failure, also known as end stage renal disease. Co.'s DMG division is a patient- and physician-focused integrated healthcare delivery and management company providing outcomes-based medical care.

Recent Developments: For the quarter ended Sep 30 2019, income from continuing operations increased 81.2% to US$208.5 million from US$115.1 million in the year-earlier quarter. Net income amounted to US$201.7 million versus a net loss of US$96.7 million in the year-earlier quarter. Revenues were US$2.90 billion, up 2.0% from US$2.85 billion the year before. Operating income was US$378.3 million versus US$289.0 million in the prior-year quarter, an increase of 30.9%. Direct operating expenses declined 3.5% to US$1.99 billion from US$2.06 billion in the comparable period the year before. Indirect operating expenses increased 8.1% to US$534.6 million from US$494.5 million in the equivalent prior-year period.

Prospects: Our evaluation of Davita Inc. as of October 4th, 2019 is the result of our systematic analysis on three basic characteristics: earnings strength, relative valuation, and recent stock price movement. The company has enjoyed a very positive trend in earnings per share over the past 5 quarters. However, recent analyst estimates for the company have been mixed and DVA has posted results that exceeded analysts' expectations. Based on operating earnings yield, the company is undervalued when compared to all of the companies we cover. Share price changes over the past year indicates that DVA will perform in line with the market over the near term.

Financial Data

(US$ in Thousands)	9 Mos	6 Mos	3 Mos	12/31/2018	12/31/2017	12/31/2016	12/31/2015	12/31/2014
Earnings Per Share	2.64	0.87	0.76	0.92	3.47	4.29	1.25	3.33
Cash Flow Per Share	11.82	9.61	9.32	10.37	10.11	9.71	7.35	6.87
Income Statement								
Total Revenue	8,489,895	5,585,817	2,743,112	11,404,851	10,876,634	14,745,105	13,781,837	12,795,106
EBITDA	1,610,717	1,096,364	493,267	2,115,196	2,383,189	2,435,967	1,588,675	2,125,042
Depn & Amortn	456,685	300,770	148,528	574,799	544,129	545,734	475,484	428,309
Income Before Taxes	802,258	532,409	213,220	1,052,962	1,408,426	1,475,851	704,811	1,286,439
Income Taxes	197,938	132,684	56,746	258,400	323,859	455,813	295,726	446,343
Net Income	566,110	422,840	149,289	159,394	663,618	879,874	269,732	723,114
Average Shares	151,295	166,799	166,780	172,364	191,348	204,924	216,251	216,927
Balance Sheet								
Current Assets	3,998,718	6,390,629	9,225,076	8,424,159	8,744,358	3,980,228	4,503,280	3,876,797
Total Assets	17,451,830	19,930,960	22,605,944	19,110,252	18,948,193	18,741,257	18,514,875	17,942,715
Current Liabilities	2,206,640	5,706,944	8,230,877	4,891,161	3,041,177	2,696,445	2,399,138	2,088,652
Long-Term Obligations	8,014,475	5,377,798	5,787,013	8,172,847	9,158,018	8,947,327	9,001,308	8,383,280
Total Liabilities	15,133,254	15,881,662	18,730,590	15,406,810	14,258,164	14,093,210	13,644,095	12,772,202
Stockholders' Equity	2,318,576	4,049,298	3,875,354	3,703,442	4,690,029	4,648,047	4,870,780	5,170,513
Shares Outstanding	133,888	164,472	166,396	166,387	182,462	194,554	209,754	215,640
Statistical Record								
Return on Assets %	2.26	0.69	0.63	0.84	3.52	4.71	1.48	4.13
Return on Equity %	13.55	3.27	3.07	3.80	14.21	18.44	5.37	15.06
EBITDA Margin %	18.97	19.63	17.98	18.55	21.91	16.52	11.53	16.61
Net Margin %	6.67	7.57	5.44	1.40	6.10	5.97	1.96	5.65
Asset Turnover	0.61	0.57	0.54	0.60	0.58	0.79	0.76	0.73
Current Ratio	1.81	1.12	1.12	1.72	2.88	1.48	1.88	1.86
Debt to Equity	3.46	1.33	1.49	2.21	1.95	1.92	1.85	1.62
Price Range	76.08-43.42	76.08-43.42	76.08-48.73	80.03-48.73	72.36-53.89	78.44-55.16	84.23-67.79	78.07-62.74
P/E Ratio	28.82-16.45	87.45-49.91	100.11-64.12	86.99-52.97	20.85-15.53	18.28-12.86	67.38-54.23	23.44-18.84

Address: 2000 16th Street, Denver, CO 80202	Web Site: www.davita.com	Auditors: KPMG LLP
Telephone: 720-631-2100	Officers: Kent J. Thiry - Executive Chairman, Chairman, Chief Executive Officer, Co-Chairman Javier J. Rodriguez - Chief Executive Officer, Division Officer, President, Senior Vice President	Investor Contact: 310-536-2585 Transfer Agents: Computershare

DANAHER CORP

Exchange	Symbol	Price	52Wk Range	Yield	P/E
NYS	DHR	$153.48 (12/31/2019)	153.48-97.62	0.44	45.41

*7 Year Price Score 135.10 *NYSE Composite Index=100 *12 Month Price Score 102.73

Interim Earnings (Per Share)

Qtr.	Mar	Jun	Sep	Dec
2016	1.09	0.94	0.56	1.06
2017	0.72	0.79	0.81	1.21
2018	0.80	0.95	0.93	1.06
2019	0.46	0.97	0.89	...

Interim Dividends (Per Share)

Amt	Decl	Ex	Rec	Pay
0.17Q	03/08/2019	03/28/2019	03/29/2019	04/26/2019
0.17Q	05/07/2019	06/27/2019	06/28/2019	07/26/2019
0.17Q	09/10/2019	09/26/2019	09/27/2019	10/25/2019
0.17Q	12/10/2019	12/26/2019	12/27/2019	01/31/2020

Indicated Div: $0.68

Valuation Analysis · **Institutional Holding**

Forecast EPS	$4.38	No of Institutions
(01/17/2020)		1932
Market Cap	$110.2 Billion	Shares
Book Value	$32.5 Billion	654,823,872
Price/Book	3.39	% Held
Price/Sales	5.39	80.54

Business Summary: Medical Instruments & Equipment (MIC: 4.3.1 SIC: 3823 NAIC: 334513)

Danaher designs, manufactures and markets medical, industrial and commercial products and services, Co. has four segments: Life Sciences, which provides research tools to study the basic building blocks of life, including genes and proteins; Diagnostics, which provides analytical instruments, reagents, consumables, software and services to hospitals, physicians' offices, and reference laboratories; Dental, which provides products that are used to diagnose, treat and prevent disease and ailments of the teeth, gums and supporting bone; and Environmental and Applied Solutions, which provides products and services that help protect resources and keep global food and water supplies safe.

Recent Developments: For the quarter ended Sep 27 2019, net income increased 1.5% to US$673.9 million from US$663.7 million in the year-earlier quarter. Revenues were US$5.04 billion, up 3.8% from US$4.85 billion the year before. Operating income was US$834.8 million versus US$830.7 million in the prior-year quarter, an increase of 0.5%. Direct operating expenses rose 3.1% to US$2.23 billion from US$2.16 billion in the comparable period the year before. Indirect operating expenses increased 6.1% to US$1.97 billion from US$1.86 billion in the equivalent prior-year period.

Prospects: Our evaluation of Danaher Corp. as of October 4th, 2019 is the result of our systematic analysis on three basic characteristics: earnings strength, relative valuation, and recent stock price movement. The company has managed to produce a neutral trend in earnings per share over the past 5 quarters. In addition, recent analyst estimates for the company have been mixed and DHR has posted results that exceeded analysts' expectations. Based on operating earnings yield, the company is fairly valued when compared to all of the companies we cover. Share price changes over the past year indicates that DHR will perform over the near term.

Financial Data

(US$ in Thousands)	9 Mos	6 Mos	3 Mos	12/31/2018	12/31/2017	12/31/2016	12/31/2015	12/31/2014
Earnings Per Share	3.38	3.42	3.40	3.74	3.53	3.65	4.74	3.63
Cash Flow Per Share	5.67	5.62	5.51	5.74	5.00	5.08	5.45	5.35
Dividends Per Share	0.670	0.660	0.650	0.640	0.560	0.570	0.540	0.400
Dividend Payout %	19.82	19.30	19.12	17.11	15.86	15.62	11.39	11.02
Income Statement								
Total Revenue	15,073,800	10,036,500	4,879,900	19,893,000	18,329,700	16,882,400	20,563,100	19,913,800
EBITDA	3,445,200	2,278,300	1,057,400	4,042,500	3,671,800	3,340,500	4,055,000	4,140,400
Depn & Amortn	986,900	659,200	328,400	601,500	577,800	545,000	573,500	552,600
Income Before Taxes	2,460,100	1,617,100	721,400	3,292,800	2,938,800	2,611,300	3,324,000	3,481,800
Income Taxes	721,100	552,000	387,600	641,900	469,000	457,900	725,300	883,400
Net Income	1,733,100	1,065,100	333,800	2,650,900	2,492,100	2,553,700	3,357,400	2,598,400
Average Shares	729,300	727,900	718,500	710,200	706,100	699,800	708,500	716,100
Balance Sheet								
Current Assets	20,353,700	11,603,700	10,080,400	7,093,800	6,850,000	6,665,100	7,836,700	9,431,300
Total Assets	61,531,100	53,322,000	51,774,400	47,832,500	46,648,600	45,295,300	48,222,200	36,991,700
Current Liabilities	5,934,000	5,008,000	4,632,800	4,841,500	4,792,300	6,874,000	6,170,400	5,396,400
Long-Term Obligations	16,536,200	10,144,400	9,458,200	9,688,500	10,327,400	9,674,200	12,025,200	3,401,500
Total Liabilities	29,028,800	21,120,800	20,217,800	19,618,100	20,290,400	22,292,500	24,531,900	13,613,600
Stockholders' Equity	32,502,300	32,201,200	31,556,600	28,214,400	26,358,200	23,002,800	23,690,300	23,378,100
Shares Outstanding	718,200	717,300	715,800	701,500	696,600	692,200	686,800	704,300
Statistical Record								
Return on Assets %	4.54	4.88	4.89	5.61	5.42	5.45	7.88	7.25
Return on Equity %	8.24	8.33	8.23	9.72	10.10	10.91	14.27	11.36
EBITDA Margin %	22.86	22.70	21.67	20.32	20.03	19.79	19.72	20.79
Net Margin %	11.50	10.61	6.84	13.33	13.60	15.13	16.33	13.05
Asset Turnover	0.37	0.40	0.41	0.42	0.40	0.36	0.48	0.56
Current Ratio	3.43	2.32	2.18	1.47	1.43	0.97	1.27	1.75
Debt to Equity	0.51	0.32	0.30	0.34	0.39	0.42	0.51	0.15
Price Range	146.47-94.85	143.73-94.85	132.29-94.85	109.54-92.16	94.62-78.78	81.84-63.35	73.78-62.06	65.98-54.34
P/E Ratio	43.33-28.06	42.03-27.73	38.91-27.90	29.29-24.64	26.80-22.32	22.42-17.36	15.57-13.09	18.18-14.97
Average Yield %	0.54	0.58	0.62	0.63	0.65	0.76	0.81	0.68

Address: 2200 Pennsylvania Avenue, N.W., Suite 800W, Washington, DC 20037-1701	**Web Site:** www.danaher.com **Officers:** Steven M. Rales - Chairman Thomas Patrick (Tom) Joyce - President, Chief Executive Officer, Executive Vice President	**Auditors:** Ernst & Young LLP **Investor Contact:** 202-828-0850 **Transfer Agents:** Computershare, Providence, RI
Telephone: 202-828-0850		
Fax: 202-828-0860		

DARDEN RESTAURANTS, INC.

Exchange	Symbol	Price	52Wk Range	Yield	P/E
NYS	DRI	$109.01 (12/31/2019)	127.57-98.32	3.23	21.67

*7 Year Price Score 130.40 *NYSE Composite Index=100 *12 Month Price Score 93.31

Interim Earnings (Per Share)

Qtr.	Aug	Nov	Feb	May
2016-17	0.87	0.64	1.32	0.98
2017-18	0.93	0.67	1.73	1.39
2018-19	1.32	0.92	1.79	1.67
2019-20	1.37	0.20	...	...

Interim Dividends (Per Share)

Amt	Decl	Ex	Rec	Pay
0.75Q	03/21/2019	04/09/2019	04/10/2019	05/01/2019
0.88Q	06/19/2019	07/09/2019	07/10/2019	08/01/2019
0.88Q	09/19/2019	10/09/2019	10/10/2019	11/01/2019
0.88Q	12/19/2019	01/09/2020	01/10/2020	02/03/2020

Indicated Div: $3.52 (Div. Reinv. Plan)

Valuation Analysis

		Institutional Holding	
Forecast EPS	$6.40	No of Institutions	
	(01/17/2020)	1041	
Market Cap	$13.2 Billion	Shares	
Book Value	$2.3 Billion	144,153,808	
Price/Book	5.83	% Held	
Price/Sales	1.53	89.33	

TRADING VOLUME (thousand shares)

Business Summary: Hotels, Restaurants & Travel (MIC: 2.2.1 SIC: 5812 NAIC: 722110)

Darden Restaurants is a restaurant company. Co. owns and operates restaurants through subsidiaries in the U.S. and Canada under the Olive Garden®, LongHorn Steakhouse®, Cheddar's Scratch Kitchen®, Yard House®, The Capital Grille®, Seasons 52®, Bahama Breeze®, and Eddie V's Prime Seafood® trademarks. Co. has four reportable segments: Olive Garden; LongHorn Steakhouse; Fine Dining (which includes The Capital Grille and Eddie V's); and Other Business (which includes Cheddar's Scratch Kitchen, Yard House, Seasons 52, Bahama Breeze and results from its franchise operations).

Recent Developments: For the quarter ended Nov 24 2019, income from continuing operations decreased 78.1% to US$25.4 million from US$115.9 million in the year-earlier quarter. Net income decreased 78.6% to US$24.7 million from US$115.6 million in the year-earlier quarter. Revenues were US$2.06 billion, up 4.2% from US$1.97 billion the year before. Operating income was US$160.2 million versus US$148.1 million in the prior-year quarter, an increase of 8.2%. Direct operating expenses rose 4.0% to US$1.65 billion from US$1.59 billion in the comparable period the year before. Indirect operating expenses increased 2.8% to US$245.3 million from US$238.6 million in the equivalent prior-year period.

Prospects: Our evaluation of Darden Restaurants Inc. as of October 4th, 2019 is the result of our systematic analysis on three basic characteristics: earnings strength, relative valuation, and recent stock price movement. The company has managed to produce a neutral trend in earnings per share over the past 5 quarters. In addition, recent analyst estimates for the company have been mixed and DRI has posted results that exceeded analysts' expectations. Based on operating earnings yield, the company is fairly valued when compared to all of the companies we cover. Share price changes over the past year indicates that DRI will perform well over the near term.

Financial Data

(US$ in Thousands)	6 Mos	3 Mos	05/26/2019	05/27/2018	05/28/2017	05/29/2016	05/31/2015	05/25/2014
Earnings Per Share	5.03	5.75	5.69	4.73	3.80	2.90	5.47	2.15
Cash Flow Per Share	10.45	10.70	10.29	8.25	7.41	6.46	6.74	4.25
Tang Book Value Per Share	1.02	1.88	2.10	0.49	N.M.	4.00	7.00	5.37
Dividends Per Share	3.260	3.130	3.000	2.520	2.240	2.100	2.200	2.200
Dividend Payout %	64.81	54.43	52.72	53.28	58.95	72.41	40.22	102.33
Income Statement								
Total Revenue	4,190,300	2,133,900	8,510,400	8,080,100	7,170,200	6,933,500	6,764,000	6,285,600
EBITDA	382,200	287,700	1,169,200	1,081,500	951,400	916,000	695,500	627,100
Depn & Amortn	173,800	86,200	336,700	314,700	273,900	293,800	327,900	318,200
Income Before Taxes	184,200	190,400	782,300	605,700	637,300	449,700	175,300	174,600
Income Taxes	(13,000)	18,600	63,700	1,900	154,800	90,000	(21,100)	(8,600)
Net Income	195,300	170,600	713,400	596,000	479,100	375,000	709,500	286,200
Average Shares	123,700	124,600	125,400	126,000	126,000	129,300	129,700	133,200
Balance Sheet								
Current Assets	535,500	670,300	892,600	553,600	799,800	820,300	1,056,400	1,976,400
Total Assets	9,742,700	9,719,600	5,892,800	5,469,600	5,504,200	4,582,600	5,994,700	7,100,700
Current Liabilities	1,557,500	1,548,600	1,474,100	1,384,500	1,289,200	1,187,100	1,196,700	1,618,500
Long-Term Obligations	928,200	928,000	927,700	926,500	936,600	440,000	1,452,300	2,533,400
Total Liabilities	7,469,000	7,338,200	3,500,200	3,274,800	3,402,500	2,630,600	3,661,200	4,943,800
Stockholders' Equity	2,273,700	2,381,300	2,392,600	2,194,800	2,101,700	1,952,000	2,333,500	2,156,900
Shares Outstanding	121,510	122,601	123,100	123,500	125,400	126,200	126,700	132,300
Statistical Record								
Return on Assets %	8.20	9.43	12.59	10.89	9.53	7.11	10.66	4.09
Return on Equity %	27.71	30.83	31.19	27.82	23.70	17.55	31.09	13.61
EBITDA Margin %	9.12	13.48	13.74	13.38	13.27	13.21	10.28	9.98
Net Margin %	4.66	7.99	8.38	7.38	6.68	5.41	10.49	4.55
Asset Turnover	1.13	1.13	1.50	1.48	1.43	1.31	1.02	0.90
Current Ratio	0.34	0.43	0.61	0.40	0.62	0.69	0.88	1.22
Debt to Equity	0.41	0.39	0.39	0.42	0.45	0.23	0.62	1.17
Price Range	127.57-96.71	126.62-96.71	124.78-87.41	99.31-77.05	88.40-59.68	67.78-53.93	62.44-39.18	48.94-40.99
P/E Ratio	25.36-19.23	22.02-16.82	21.93-15.36	21.00-16.29	23.26-15.71	23.37-18.60	11.41-7.16	22.76-19.07
Average Yield %	2.83	2.75	2.73	2.86	3.15	3.39	4.41	4.89

Address: 1000 Darden Center Drive, Orlando, FL 32837 **Telephone:** 407-245-4000	**Web Site:** www.darden.com **Officers:** Charles M. (Chuck) Sonsteby - Chairman Eugene I. (Gene) Lee - President, President (frmr), Chief Executive Officer, Interim Chief Executive Officer, Division Officer	**Auditors:** KPMG LLP **Investor Contact:** 800-832-7336 **Transfer Agents:** Wells Fargo Shareowner Services, Mendota Heights, MN

DANA INC

Exchange	Symbol	Price	52Wk Range	Yield	P/E
NYS	DAN	$18.20 (12/31/2019)	20.74-11.71	2.20	10.96

*7 Year Price Score 71.51   *NYSE Composite Index=100   *12 Month Price Score 97.78

Interim Earnings (Per Share)
Qtr.	Mar	Jun	Sep	Dec
2016	0.30	0.36	0.39	3.31
2017	0.51	0.47	0.46	(0.74)
2018	0.73	0.85	0.65	0.68
2019	0.68	(0.47)	0.77	...

Interim Dividends (Per Share)
Amt	Decl	Ex	Rec	Pay
0.10Q	02/13/2019	02/28/2019	03/01/2019	03/22/2019
0.10Q	05/01/2019	05/16/2019	05/17/2019	06/07/2019
0.10Q	07/30/2019	08/15/2019	08/16/2019	09/06/2019
0.10Q	10/22/2019	11/07/2019	11/08/2019	11/29/2019

Indicated Div: $0.40

Valuation Analysis
		Institutional Holding	
Forecast EPS	$3.03	No of Institutions	418
	(01/17/2020)		
Market Cap	$2.6 Billion	Shares	
Book Value	$1.8 Billion	171,576,352	
Price/Book	1.46	% Held	
Price/Sales	0.30	N/A	

Business Summary: Auto Parts (MIC: 1.8.2 SIC: 3714 NAIC: 336399)

Dana is a provider of high technology drive and motion products, sealing solutions, thermal-management technologies and fluid-power products. Co.'s segments are: Light Vehicle Driveline Technologies, which include light trucks, sport utility vehicles, crossover utility vehicles, vans, and passenger cars; Commercial Vehicle Driveline Technologies, which include medium/heavy duty trucks, buses, and specialty vehicles; Off-Highway Drive and Motion Technologies, which include construction, earth moving, agricultural, mining, forestry, material handling, and industrial stationary; and Power Technologies, which include medium/heavy vehicle market, and off-highway market.

Recent Developments: For the quarter ended Sep 30 2019, net income increased 16.7% to US$112.0 million from US$96.0 million in the year-earlier quarter. Revenues were US$2.16 billion, up 9.4% from US$1.98 billion the year before. Direct operating expenses rose 11.2% to US$1.88 billion from US$1.69 billion in the comparable period the year before. Indirect operating expenses increased 3.8% to US$135.0 million from US$130.0 million in the equivalent prior-year period.

Prospects: Our evaluation of Dana Inc. as of October 4th, 2019 is the result of our systematic analysis on three basic characteristics: earnings strength, relative valuation, and recent stock price movement. The company has managed to produce a neutral trend in earnings per share over the past 5 quarters. However, recent analyst estimates for the company have been reduced and DAN has posted results that fell short of analysts' expectations. Based on operating earnings yield, the company is undervalued when compared to all of the companies we cover. Share price changes over the past year indicates that DAN will perform poorly over the near term.

Financial Data
(US$ in Thousands)	9 Mos	6 Mos	3 Mos	12/31/2018	12/31/2017	12/31/2016	12/31/2015	12/31/2014
Earnings Per Share	1.66	1.54	2.86	2.91	0.71	4.36	0.99	1.84
Cash Flow Per Share	4.30	3.56	4.03	3.92	3.82	2.62	2.55	3.23
Tang Book Value Per Share	7.15	6.55	5.51	6.34	4.91	6.66	3.64	4.94
Dividends Per Share	0.400	0.400	0.400	0.400	0.240	0.240	0.230	0.200
Dividend Payout %	24.10	25.97	13.99	13.75	33.80	5.50	23.23	10.87
Income Statement								
Total Revenue	6,633,000	4,469,000	2,163,000	8,143,000	7,209,000	5,826,000	6,060,000	6,617,000
EBITDA	434,000	209,000	218,000	849,000	704,000	497,000	566,000	576,000
Depn & Amortn	252,000	164,000	78,000	270,000	233,000	182,000	174,000	213,000
Income Before Taxes	98,000	(11,000)	115,000	494,000	380,000	215,000	292,000	260,000
Income Taxes	(27,000)	(32,000)	20,000	78,000	283,000	(424,000)	82,000	(70,000)
Net Income	141,000	30,000	98,000	427,000	111,000	640,000	159,000	319,000
Average Shares	144,800	144,000	144,800	146,500	146,900	146,800	160,000	173,500
Balance Sheet								
Current Assets	3,273,000	3,370,000	3,443,000	2,907,000	2,882,000	2,284,000	2,474,000	2,954,000
Total Assets	7,231,000	7,346,000	7,284,000	5,918,000	5,644,000	4,860,000	4,326,000	4,930,000
Current Liabilities	1,990,000	2,064,000	2,113,000	1,747,000	1,702,000	1,253,000	1,091,000	1,261,000
Long-Term Obligations	2,482,000	2,560,000	2,572,000	1,755,000	1,759,000	1,595,000	1,553,000	1,613,000
Total Liabilities	5,440,000	5,630,000	5,850,000	4,573,000	4,631,000	3,703,000	3,598,000	3,850,000
Stockholders' Equity	1,791,000	1,716,000	1,434,000	1,345,000	1,013,000	1,157,000	728,000	1,080,000
Shares Outstanding	143,923	143,913	143,901	144,663	144,984	143,938	150,068	166,070
Statistical Record								
Return on Assets %	3.66	3.39	6.30	7.39	2.11	13.90	3.44	6.34
Return on Equity %	15.91	15.73	32.86	36.22	10.23	67.72	17.59	26.71
EBITDA Margin %	6.54	4.68	10.08	10.43	9.77	8.53	9.34	8.70
Net Margin %	2.13	0.67	4.53	5.24	1.54	10.99	2.62	4.82
Asset Turnover	1.31	1.27	1.23	1.41	1.37	1.26	1.31	1.32
Current Ratio	1.64	1.63	1.63	1.66	1.69	1.82	2.27	2.34
Debt to Equity	1.39	1.49	1.79	1.30	1.74	1.38	2.13	1.49
Price Range	20.74-11.71	21.45-12.98	26.73-12.98	34.88-12.98	33.04-17.57	19.74-10.09	23.20-13.11	24.60-17.21
P/E Ratio	12.49-7.05	13.93-8.43	9.35-4.54	11.99-4.46	46.54-24.75	4.53-2.31	23.43-13.24	13.37-9.35
Average Yield %	2.42	2.26	2.08	1.81	1.01	1.74	1.20	0.93

Address: 3939 Technology Drive, Maumee, OH 43537
Telephone: 419-887-3000
Fax: 419-887-5200

Web Site: www.dana.com
Officers: James K. Kamsickas - Chairman, President, Chief Executive Officer Jonathan M. Collins - Executive Vice President, Senior Vice President, Chief Financial Officer

Auditors: PricewaterhouseCoopers LLP
Investor Contact: 800-537-8823
Transfer Agents: Wells Fargo Shareowner Services

DCP MIDSTREAM LP

Exchange	Symbol	Price	52Wk Range	Yield	P/E
NYS	DCP	$24.49 (12/31/2019)	33.99-20.64	12.74	N/A

*7 Year Price Score 61.62   ***NYSE Composite Index=100**   ***12 Month Price Score 76.23**

Interim Earnings (Per Share)

Qtr.	Mar	Jun	Sep	Dec
2016	0.36	0.12	0.78	0.38
2017	0.41	0.33	(0.41)	0.10
2018	0.08	0.07	0.18	0.28
2019	0.14	0.43	(1.59)	...

Interim Dividends (Per Share)

Amt	Decl	Ex	Rec	Pay
0.78Q	01/23/2019	02/01/2019	02/04/2019	02/14/2019
0.78Q	04/23/2019	05/02/2019	05/03/2019	05/15/2019
0.78Q	07/23/2019	08/01/2019	08/02/2019	08/14/2019
0.78Q	10/22/2019	10/31/2019	11/01/2019	11/14/2019

Indicated Div: $3.12

Valuation Analysis   **Institutional Holding**

Forecast EPS	$-0.72	No of Institutions	
	(01/17/2020)	223	
Market Cap	$3.5 Billion	Shares	
Book Value	N/A	94,317,504	
Price/Book	N/A	% Held	
Price/Sales	0.42	53.73	

Business Summary: Equipment & Services (MIC: 9.1.3 SIC: 4922 NAIC: 486210)

DCP Midstream is a limited partnership that owns, operates, acquires and develops a portfolio of midstream energy assets. Co.'s operations are organized into two reportable segments: Logistics and Marketing and Gathering and Processing. Co.'s Logistics and Marketing segment includes transporting, trading, marketing and storing natural gas and natural gas liquids (NGLs), fractionating NGLs and wholesale propane logistics. Co.'s Gathering and Processing segment consists of gathering, compressing, treating, and processing natural gas, producing and fractionating NGLs, and recovering condensate.

Recent Developments: For the quarter ended Sep 30 2019, net loss amounted to US$177.0 million versus net income of US$82.0 million in the year-earlier quarter. Revenues were US$1.70 billion, down 38.4% from US$2.76 billion the year before. Operating loss was US$211.0 million versus an income of US$66.0 million in the prior-year quarter. Direct operating expenses declined 40.7% to US$1.50 billion from US$2.52 billion in the comparable period the year before. Indirect operating expenses increased 144.1% to US$415.0 million from US$170.0 million in the equivalent prior-year period.

Prospects: Our evaluation of DCP Midstream L.P. as of October 4th, 2019 is the result of our systematic analysis on three basic characteristics: earnings strength, relative valuation, and recent stock price movement. The company has enjoyed a very positive trend in earnings per share over the past 5 quarters. However, recent analyst estimates for the company have been mixed and DCP has posted results that exceeded analysts' expectations. Based on operating earnings yield, the company is fairly valued when compared to all of the companies we cover. Share price changes over the past year indicates that DCP will perform very poorly over the near term.

Financial Data

(US$ in Thousands)	9 Mos	6 Mos	3 Mos	12/31/2018	12/31/2017	12/31/2016	12/31/2015	12/31/2014
Earnings Per Share	(0.74)	1.03	0.67	0.61	0.43	1.64	0.91	2.84
Cash Flow Per Share	5.29	6.12	5.98	4.62	6.25	5.00	5.67	4.92
Dividends Per Share	3.120	3.120	3.120	3.120	3.120	3.120	3.120	3.005
Dividend Payout %	...	302.91	465.67	511.48	725.58	190.24	342.86	105.81
Income Statement								
Total Revenue	5,696,000	3,997,000	2,199,000	9,822,000	8,462,000	1,497,000	1,898,000	3,642,000
EBITDA	196,000	309,000	134,000	582,000	589,000	310,000	256,000	555,000
Depn & Amortn	298,000	200,000	101,000	378,000	367,000	112,000	109,000	101,000
Income Before Taxes	(323,000)	(33,000)	(36,000)	(65,000)	(67,000)	104,000	55,000	368,000
Income Taxes	2,000	1,000	1,000	3,000	2,000	...	(5,000)	6,000
Net Income	16,000	194,000	75,000	298,000	229,000	312,000	228,000	423,000
Average Shares	143,300	143,300	143,300	143,300	143,300	114,700	114,600	106,600
Balance Sheet								
Current Assets	1,059,000	823,000	1,082,000	1,271,000	1,322,000	227,000	306,000	590,000
Total Assets	14,034,000	14,033,000	14,187,000	14,266,000	13,878,000	5,161,000	5,477,000	5,739,000
Current Liabilities	1,692,000	1,803,000	2,404,000	1,904,000	1,488,000	734,000	200,000	601,000
Long-Term Obligations	5,165,000	4,750,000	4,236,000	4,782,000	4,707,000	1,750,000	2,424,000	2,061,000
Total Liabilities	7,247,000	6,908,000	7,003,000	6,998,000	6,470,000	2,560,000	2,705,000	2,746,000
Shares Outstanding	143,329	143,317	143,317	143,317	143,309	114,749	114,742	113,949
Statistical Record								
Return on Assets %	0.77	2.63	2.23	2.12	2.41	5.85	4.07	8.24
EBITDA Margin %	3.44	7.73	6.09	5.93	6.96	20.71	13.49	15.24
Net Margin %	0.28	4.85	3.41	3.03	2.71	20.84	12.01	11.61
Asset Turnover	0.58	0.67	0.71	0.70	0.89	0.28	0.34	0.71
Current Ratio	0.63	0.46	0.45	0.67	0.89	0.31	1.53	0.98
Price Range	43.59-23.49	45.57-25.35	45.57-25.35	45.57-25.35	41.57-29.79	39.07-15.60	47.49-20.93	57.56-41.18
P/E Ratio	...	44.24-24.61	68.01-37.84	74.70-41.56	96.67-69.28	23.82-9.51	52.19-23.00	20.27-14.50
Average Yield %	9.88	8.84	8.41	8.09	8.79	10.13	9.48	5.76

Address: 370 17th Street, Suite 2500, Denver, CO 80202 **Telephone:** 303-595-3331	**Web Site:** www.dcpmidstream.com **Officers:** Wouter T. van Kempen - Chairman, Chief Executive Officer Sean P. O'Brien - Group Vice President, Chief Financial Officer	**Auditors:** DELOITTE & TOUCHE LLP **Investor Contact:** 303-633-2913 **Transfer Agents:** American Stock Transfer & Trust Company

DECKERS OUTDOOR CORP.

Exchange NYS	Symbol DECK	Price $168.86 (12/31/2019)	52Wk Range 179.06-113.30	Yield N/A	P/E 17.64

*7 Year Price Score 147.17 *NYSE Composite Index=100 *12 Month Price Score 102.59

TRADING VOLUME (thousand shares)

Interim Earnings (Per Share)

Qtr.	Jun	Sep	Dec	Mar
2016-17	(1.84)	1.21	1.27	(0.48)
2017-18	(1.32)	1.54	2.69	0.67
2018-19	(1.00)	2.48	6.68	0.85
2019-20	(0.67)	2.71	...	...

Interim Dividends (Per Share)

No Dividends Paid

Valuation Analysis / **Institutional Holding**

Forecast EPS	$9.07	No of Institutions
	(01/15/2020)	529
Market Cap	$4.7 Billion	Shares
Book Value	$916.3 Million	35,384,008
Price/Book	5.16	% Held
Price/Sales	2.26	72.23

Business Summary: Apparel, Footwear & Accessories (MIC: 1.4.2 SIC: 3021 NAIC: 316211)

Deckers Outdoor is engaged in designing, marketing and distributing footwear, apparel and accessories. Co. markets its products primarily under five brands. The UGG brand is comprised of a line of footwear, apparel and accessories for women, men and children. The HOKA brand is a line of footwear and apparel. The Teva brand's product line includes sandals, shoes, and boots. Sanuk brand is comprised of casual shoe and sandal categories. Other brands consist of Koolaburra by UGG brand, a casual footwear fashion using sheepskin and other plush materials. Co.'s retail stores are primarily UGG brand concept and UGG brand outlet stores.

Recent Developments: For the quarter ended Sep 30 2019, net income increased 4.6% to US$77.8 million from US$74.4 million in the year-earlier quarter. Revenues were US$542.2 million, up 8.0% from US$501.9 million the year before. Operating income was US$97.1 million versus US$90.4 million in the prior-year quarter, an increase of 7.4%. Direct operating expenses rose 7.7% to US$269.2 million from US$250.0 million in the comparable period the year before. Indirect operating expenses increased 8.9% to US$175.9 million from US$161.5 million in the equivalent prior-year period.

Prospects: Our evaluation of Deckers Outdoor Corp. as of October 4th, 2019 is the result of our systematic analysis on three basic characteristics: earnings strength, relative valuation, and recent stock price movement. The company has generated a negative trend in earnings per share over the past 5 quarters. However, recent analyst estimates for the company have been mixed and DECK has posted results that exceeded analysts' expectations. Based on operating earnings yield, the company is undervalued when compared to all of the companies we cover. Share price changes over the past year indicates that DECK will perform over the near term.

Financial Data

(US$ in Thousands)	6 Mos	3 Mos	03/31/2019	03/31/2018	03/31/2017	03/31/2016	03/31/2015	03/31/2014
Earnings Per Share	9.57	9.34	8.84	3.58	0.18	3.70	4.66	(0.08)
Cash Flow Per Share	10.68	10.48	12.13	10.31	6.21	3.85	4.93	5.61
Tang Book Value Per Share	30.49	32.15	33.62	28.54	27.36	23.63	21.67	19.34
Income Statement								
Total Revenue	819,044	276,839	2,020,437	1,903,339	1,790,147	1,875,197	1,817,057	294,716
EBITDA	85,858	(20,980)	372,794	270,796	52,183	212,303	274,445	10,278
Depn & Amortn	19,966	10,345	45,227	48,572	52,628	50,024	49,293	10,569
Income Before Taxes	67,618	(29,605)	328,934	220,696	(6,986)	156,885	221,139	(742)
Income Taxes	9,159	(10,254)	64,626	106,302	(12,696)	34,620	59,359	1,943
Net Income	58,459	(19,351)	264,308	114,394	5,710	122,265	161,780	(2,685)
Average Shares	28,705	29,089	29,903	31,996	32,355	33,039	34,733	34,621
Balance Sheet								
Current Assets	1,135,031	1,188,493	1,095,405	910,690	820,821	785,765	686,593	623,862
Total Assets	1,691,659	1,751,056	1,427,206	1,264,379	1,191,780	1,278,068	1,169,933	1,064,204
Current Liabilities	465,847	441,745	250,524	189,166	159,051	238,498	167,542	122,215
Long-Term Obligations	30,592	30,747	30,901	31,504	32,082	32,631	33,154	...
Total Liabilities	775,355	755,777	382,076	323,600	237,525	310,597	232,921	175,355
Stockholders' Equity	916,304	995,279	1,045,130	940,779	954,255	967,471	937,012	888,849
Shares Outstanding	27,975	28,965	29,141	30,447	31,987	32,020	33,292	34,624
Statistical Record								
Return on Assets %	17.90	17.55	19.64	9.31	0.46	9.96	14.48	N.M.
Return on Equity %	31.63	29.02	26.62	12.07	0.59	12.80	17.72	N.M.
EBITDA Margin %	10.48	N.M.	18.45	14.23	2.92	11.32	15.10	3.49
Net Margin %	7.14	N.M.	13.08	6.01	0.32	6.52	8.90	N.M.
Asset Turnover	1.34	1.30	1.50	1.55	1.45	1.53	1.63	1.03
Current Ratio	2.44	2.69	4.37	4.81	5.16	3.29	4.10	5.10
Debt to Equity	0.03	0.03	0.03	0.03	0.03	0.03	0.04	...
Price Range	179.06-102.49	176.19-102.49	148.59-86.58	98.29-55.78	68.57-44.99	76.58-42.27	99.38-66.05	88.56-47.35
P/E Ratio	18.71-10.71	18.86-10.97	16.81-9.79	27.46-15.58	380.94-249.94	20.70-11.42	21.33-14.17	...

Address: 250 Coromar Drive, Goleta, CA 93117	Web Site: www.deckers.com	Auditors: KPMG LLP
Telephone: 805-967-7611	Officers: Michael F. Devine - Chairman David Powers - President, Chief Executive Officer, Division Officer	Investor Contact: 203-.68-2.8200 Transfer Agents: Mellon Investor Services LLC, South Hackensack, NJ

DEERE & CO.

Exchange	Symbol	Price	52Wk Range	Yield	P/E
NYS	DE	$173.26 (12/31/2019)	179.80-134.82	1.75	17.07

*7 Year Price Score 119.86 *NYSE Composite Index=100 *12 Month Price Score 100.68

Interim Earnings (Per Share)

Qtr.	Jan	Apr	Jul	Oct
2014-15	1.12	2.03	1.53	1.10
2015-16	0.80	1.56	1.55	0.90
2016-17	0.61	2.49	1.97	1.57
2017-18	(1.66)	3.67	2.78	2.42
2018-19	1.54	3.52	2.81	2.28

Interim Dividends (Per Share)

Amt	Decl	Ex	Rec	Pay
0.76Q	02/27/2019	03/28/2019	03/29/2019	05/01/2019
0.76Q	05/29/2019	06/27/2019	06/28/2019	08/01/2019
0.76Q	08/27/2019	09/27/2019	09/30/2019	11/08/2019
0.76Q	12/04/2019	12/30/2019	12/31/2019	02/10/2020

Indicated Div: $3.04 (Div. Reinv. Plan)

Valuation Analysis

		Institutional Holding	
Forecast EPS	$9.40	No of Institutions	
	(01/17/2020)	1720	
Market Cap	$54.3 Billion	Shares	
Book Value	$11.4 Billion	271,556,480	
Price/Book	4.75	% Held	
Price/Sales	1.38	65.08	

Business Summary: Industrial Machinery & Equipment (MIC: 7.2.1 SIC: 3523 NAIC: 332212)

Deere & Co. operates the following segments: Agriculture and Turf, which manufactures and distributes a line of agriculture and turf equipment and related service parts, including utility tractors, tractor loaders, combines, cotton pickers, cotton strippers, and sugarcane harvesters; Construction and Forestry, which manufactures and distributes a range of machines and service parts used in construction, earthmoving, road building, material handling and timber harvesting, including backhoe loaders and crawler dozers and loaders; and Financial Services, which finances sales and leases by Co.'s dealers of new and used agriculture and turf equipment and construction and forestry equipment.

Recent Developments: For the year ended Nov 3 2019, net income increased 37.4% to US$3.26 billion from US$2.37 billion in the prior year. Revenues were US$39.26 billion, up 5.1% from US$37.36 billion the year before. Direct operating expenses rose 4.8% to US$28.00 billion from US$26.71 billion in the comparable period the year before. Indirect operating expenses increased 6.1% to US$5.70 billion from US$5.37 billion in the equivalent prior-year period.

Prospects: Our evaluation of Deere & Co. as of October 4th, 2019 is the result of our systematic analysis on three basic characteristics: earnings strength, relative valuation, and recent stock price movement. The company has managed to produce a neutral trend in earnings per share over the past 5 quarters. In addition, recent analyst estimates for the company have been mixed and DE has posted results that fell short of analysts' expectations. Based on operating earnings yield, the company is undervalued when compared to all of the companies we cover. Share price changes over the past year indicates that DE will perform poorly over the near term.

Financial Data

(US$ in Thousands)	11/03/2019	10/28/2018	10/29/2017	10/31/2016	10/31/2015	10/31/2014	10/31/2013	10/31/2012
Earnings Per Share	10.15	7.24	6.68	4.81	5.77	8.63	9.09	7.63
Cash Flow Per Share	10.61	5.66	6.92	11.91	11.21	9.71	8.45	2.93
Tang Book Value Per Share	22.72	20.80	25.81	17.79	18.80	23.74	25.00	15.00
Dividends Per Share	3.040	2.580	2.400	2.400	2.400	2.220	1.990	1.790
Dividend Payout %	29.95	35.64	35.93	49.90	41.59	25.72	21.89	23.46
Income Statement								
Total Revenue	39,258,000	37,357,700	29,737,700	26,644,000	28,862,800	36,066,900	37,795,400	36,157,100
EBITDA	6,333,000	6,028,300	4,779,300	3,688,700	4,152,100	6,157,400	6,861,700	6,072,200
Depn & Amortn	779,000	754,000	726,000	701,000	692,000	696,000	637,000	555,000
Income Before Taxes	4,088,000	4,070,700	3,153,800	2,224,000	2,780,100	4,797,400	5,483,400	4,734,400
Income Taxes	852,000	1,726,900	971,100	700,100	840,100	1,626,500	1,945,900	1,659,400
Net Income	3,253,000	2,368,400	2,159,100	1,523,900	1,940,000	3,161,700	3,537,300	3,064,700
Average Shares	320,600	327,300	323,300	316,600	336,000	366,100	389,200	401,500
Balance Sheet								
Current Assets	17,176,000	17,305,000	18,851,400	12,176,600	12,492,000	14,019,600	15,316,900	16,942,400
Total Assets	73,011,000	70,108,000	65,786,300	57,981,400	57,947,600	61,336,400	59,521,300	56,265,800
Current Liabilities	24,903,000	25,259,200	22,692,600	19,236,100	20,408,600	21,232,500	21,979,000	19,092,000
Long-Term Obligations	30,229,000	27,237,000	25,891,000	23,760,000	23,833,000	24,381,000	21,578,000	22,453,000
Total Liabilities	61,598,000	58,820,200	56,229,000	51,461,400	51,204,200	52,273,800	49,255,500	49,423,700
Stockholders' Equity	11,413,000	11,287,800	9,557,300	6,520,000	6,743,400	9,062,600	10,265,800	6,842,100
Shares Outstanding	313,140	318,455	321,841	314,767	316,687	345,504	373,802	387,805
Statistical Record								
Return on Assets %	4.47	3.50	3.51	2.62	3.25	5.23	6.11	5.85
Return on Equity %	28.20	22.79	27.01	22.92	24.55	32.72	41.35	44.81
EBITDA Margin %	16.13	16.14	16.07	13.84	14.39	17.07	18.15	16.79
Net Margin %	8.29	6.34	7.26	5.72	6.72	8.77	9.36	8.48
Asset Turnover	0.54	0.55	0.48	0.46	0.48	0.60	0.65	0.69
Current Ratio	0.69	0.69	0.83	0.63	0.61	0.66	0.70	0.89
Debt to Equity	2.65	2.41	2.71	3.64	3.53	2.69	2.10	3.28
Price Range	176.11-130.56	171.49-131.28	133.25-88.06	88.30-71.78	97.33-72.89	94.53-80.01	95.05-80.90	88.40-70.59
P/E Ratio	17.35-12.86	23.69-18.13	19.95-13.18	18.36-14.92	16.87-12.63	10.95-9.27	10.46-8.90	11.59-9.25
Average Yield %	1.93	1.72	2.10	2.98	2.73	2.54	2.31	2.26

Address: One John Deere Place, Moline, IL 61265	**Web Site:** www.johndeere.com	**Auditors:** DELOITTE & TOUCHE LLP
Telephone: 309-765-8000	**Officers:** Samuel R. Allen - Chairman, President, Chief Executive Officer, Chief Operating Officer,	**Investor Contact:** 309-765-4491
Fax: 309-765-9929	Division Officer Ryan D. Campbell - Senior Vice President, Chief Financial Officer	**Transfer Agents:** ComputerShare, College Station, TX

DELEK US HOLDINGS INC

Exchange	Symbol	Price	52Wk Range	Yield	P/E
NYS	DK	$33.53 (12/31/2019)	43.32-30.17	3.58	6.75

*7 Year Price Score 95.99   *NYSE Composite Index=100   *12 Month Price Score 94.06

TRADING VOLUME (thousand shares)

Interim Earnings (Per Share)

Qtr.	Mar	Jun	Sep	Dec
2016	(0.47)	(0.11)	(2.61)	0.70
2017	0.18	(0.61)	1.29	2.87
2018	(0.43)	0.89	2.03	1.39
2019	1.90	1.00	0.68	...

Interim Dividends (Per Share)

Amt	Decl	Ex	Rec	Pay
0.27Q	02/19/2019	03/04/2019	03/05/2019	03/19/2019
0.28Q	05/06/2019	05/17/2019	05/20/2019	06/03/2019
0.29Q	07/29/2019	08/16/2019	08/19/2019	09/03/2019
0.30Q	11/04/2019	11/15/2019	11/18/2019	12/02/2019

Indicated Div: $1.20

Valuation Analysis

		Institutional Holding	
Forecast EPS	$3.42	No of Institutions	N/A
	(01/17/2020)		
Market Cap	$2.5 Billion	Shares	N/A
Book Value	$1.7 Billion	% Held	N/A
Price/Book	1.47		
Price/Sales	0.25		

Business Summary: Refining & Marketing (MIC: 9.1.2 SIC: 2911 NAIC: 324110)

Delek US Holdings is a holding company. Through its subsidiaries, Co. is engaged in the downstream energy business focused on petroleum refining, the transportation, storage and wholesale distribution of crude oil, intermediate and refined products and convenience store retailing. Co.'s segments are: refining, which produces petroleum-based products used in transportation and industrial markets; logistics, which gathers, transports and stores crude oil and markets, distributes, transports and stores refined products; and retail, which provides gasoline and diesel, food products, tobacco products, non-alcoholic and alcoholic beverages, general merchandise and money orders to the public.

Recent Developments: For the quarter ended Sep 30 2019, income from continuing operations decreased 67.7% to US$60.0 million from US$185.8 million in the year-earlier quarter. Net income decreased 67.8% to US$60.0 million from US$186.3 million in the year-earlier quarter. Revenues were US$2.33 billion, down 15.7% from US$2.77 billion the year before. Operating income was US$87.4 million versus US$255.2 million in the prior-year quarter, a decrease of 65.8%. Direct operating expenses declined 11.2% to US$2.15 billion from US$2.42 billion in the comparable period the year before. Indirect operating expenses increased 5.9% to US$97.3 million from US$91.9 million in the equivalent prior-year period.

Prospects: Our evaluation of Delek US Holdings Inc. as of October 4th, 2019 is the result of our systematic analysis on three basic characteristics: earnings strength, relative valuation, and recent stock price movement. The company has suffered a very negative trend in earnings per share over the past 5 quarters. In addition, recent analyst estimates for the company have been reduced while DK has posted results that exceeded analysts' expectations. Based on operating earnings yield, the company is undervalued when compared to all of the companies we cover. Share price changes over the past year indicates that DK will perform poorly over the near term.

Financial Data

(US$ in Thousands)	9 Mos	6 Mos	3 Mos	12/31/2018	12/31/2017	12/31/2016	12/31/2015	12/31/2014
Earnings Per Share	4.97	6.32	6.21	3.95	4.00	(2.49)	0.32	3.35
Cash Flow Per Share	10.76	12.17	11.37	6.77	4.64	4.32	2.96	5.39
Tang Book Value Per Share	9.98	10.13	10.04	8.59	9.07	15.38	16.92	15.92
Dividends Per Share	1.100	1.060	1.030	0.960	0.300	0.600	0.600	1.000
Dividend Payout %	22.13	16.77	16.59	24.30	7.50	...	187.50	29.85
Income Statement								
Total Revenue	7,014,500	4,680,200	2,199,900	10,233,100	7,267,100	4,197,900	5,762,000	8,324,300
EBITDA	590,100	356,400	270,100	784,900	526,000	(179,800)	215,000	477,600
Depn & Amortn	149,300	3,200	46,300	189,000	149,500	115,100	132,700	110,200
Income Before Taxes	354,400	297,500	197,600	475,800	286,700	(347,800)	25,100	327,600
Income Taxes	83,800	70,400	45,800	101,900	(29,200)	(171,500)	(16,600)	101,600
Net Income	277,900	226,600	149,300	340,100	288,800	(153,700)	19,400	198,600
Average Shares	75,702	77,280	78,446	86,768	72,303	61,921	61,320	59,355
Balance Sheet								
Current Assets	2,864,400	2,787,300	2,760,700	2,420,300	2,611,800	1,402,200	988,800	1,247,400
Total Assets	6,793,300	6,573,200	6,371,800	5,760,600	5,935,200	2,985,100	3,324,900	2,891,400
Current Liabilities	2,226,700	2,058,700	1,860,900	1,663,500	2,671,700	940,500	759,700	857,200
Long-Term Obligations	1,935,400	1,852,300	1,729,100	1,751,300	875,400	748,500	880,500	533,300
Total Liabilities	5,102,200	4,858,700	4,646,300	4,128,000	4,284,600	1,993,200	2,171,600	1,889,700
Stockholders' Equity	1,691,100	1,714,500	1,725,500	1,632,600	1,650,600	991,900	1,153,300	1,001,700
Shares Outstanding	74,287	75,445	76,953	78,000	80,770	61,954	62,137	57,271
Statistical Record								
Return on Assets %	6.08	8.17	8.42	5.82	6.48	N.M.	0.62	6.94
Return on Equity %	23.09	31.50	31.36	20.72	21.86	N.M.	1.80	20.51
EBITDA Margin %	8.41	7.62	12.28	7.67	7.24	N.M.	3.73	5.74
Net Margin %	3.96	4.84	6.79	3.32	3.97	N.M.	0.34	2.39
Asset Turnover	1.52	1.56	1.62	1.75	1.63	1.33	1.85	2.91
Current Ratio	1.29	1.35	1.48	1.45	0.98	1.49	1.30	1.46
Debt to Equity	1.14	1.08	1.00	1.07	0.53	0.75	0.76	0.53
Price Range	43.34-29.54	55.42-29.54	59.81-29.54	59.81-29.54	35.08-20.88	24.89-11.88	40.86-22.45	35.77-25.87
P/E Ratio	8.72-5.94	8.77-4.67	9.63-4.76	15.14-7.48	8.77-5.22	...	127.69-70.16	10.68-7.72
Average Yield %	3.03	2.68	2.41	2.22	1.17	3.67	1.84	3.25

Address: 7102 Commerce Way, Brentwood, TN 37027 Telephone: 615-771-6701	Web Site: www.Delekus.com Officers: Ezra Uzi Yemin - Chairman, President, Chief Executive Officer Avigal Soreq - Executive Vice President, Chief Commercial Officer	Auditors: Ernst & Young LLP Investor Contact: 615-435-1366 Transfer Agents: American Stock Transfer & Trust Company, Brooklyn, NY

DELL TECHNOLOGIES INC

Exchange	Symbol	Price	52Wk Range	Yield	P/E
NYS	DVMT	$51.39 (12/31/2019)	69.80-42.62	N/A	10.89

*7 Year Price Score N/A *NYSE Composite Index=100 *12 Month Price Score 88.94

Interim Earnings (Per Share)

Qtr.	Apr	Jul	Oct	Jan
2016-17	0.14	1.41	(4.51)	(0.53)
2017-18	(2.57)	(1.97)	(2.05)	(0.50)
2018-19	(1.95)	(1.45)	(1.84)	(0.79)
2019-20	0.38	4.47	0.66	...

Interim Dividends (Per Share)

No Dividends Paid

Valuation Analysis   **Institutional Holding**

Forecast EPS	$7.34	No of Institutions
	(01/17/2020)	704
Market Cap	$37.6 Billion	Shares
Book Value	N/A	181,562,544
Price/Book	N/A	% Held
Price/Sales	0.41	N/A

TRADING VOLUME (thousand shares)

Business Summary: Internet & Software (MIC: 6.3.2 SIC: 3571 NAIC: 334111)

Dell Technologies is a holding company. Through its subsidiaries, Co. designs, develops, manufactures, markets, sells, and supports a range of products and services. Co.'s reportable segments are: Infrastructure Solutions Group, which includes servers, networking, and storage, as well as services and third-party software and peripherals; Client Solutions Group, which includes desktops, thin client products, and notebooks, as well as services and third-party software and peripherals; and VMware, which provides compute, cloud management, networking and security, storage and availability, and other end-user computing offerings.

Recent Developments: For the quarter ended Nov 1 2019, net income amounted to US$552.0 million versus a net loss of US$895.0 million in the year-earlier quarter. Revenues were US$22.84 billion, up 1.6% from US$22.48 billion the year before. Operating income was US$836.0 million versus a loss of US$356.0 million in the prior-year quarter. Direct operating expenses declined 5.0% to US$15.72 billion from US$16.54 billion in the comparable period the year before. Indirect operating expenses decreased 0.1% to US$6.29 billion from US$6.30 billion in the equivalent prior-year period.

Prospects: Our evaluation of Dell Technologies Inc. as of October 4th, 2019 is the result of our systematic analysis on three basic characteristics: earnings strength, relative valuation, and recent stock price movement. The company has produced a positive trend in earnings per share over the past 5 quarters. However, recent analyst estimates for the company have been mixed and DELL has posted results that exceeded analysts' expectations. Based on operating earnings yield, the company is undervalued when compared to all of the companies we cover. Share price changes over the past year indicates that DELL will perform in line with the market over the near term.

Financial Data

(US$ in Thousands)	9 Mos	6 Mos	3 Mos	02/01/2019	02/02/2018	02/03/2017	01/29/2016	01/30/2015
Earnings Per Share	4.72	2.22	(3.70)	(6.04)	(7.08)	(4.22)	(2.72)	(3.02)
Cash Flow Per Share	11.24	9.96	9.09	8.98	8.87	3.18	5.35	6.31
Income Statement								
Total Revenue	68,122,000	45,278,000	21,908,000	90,621,000	78,660,000	61,642,000	50,911,000	54,142,000
EBITDA	6,550,000	4,245,000	610,000	5,914,000	1,312,000	(1,656,000)	714,000	885,000
Depn & Amortn	4,608,000	3,114,000	43,000	6,100,000	7,000,000	3,700,000	2,000,000	2,100,000
Income Before Taxes	(95,000)	(254,000)	(143,000)	(2,361,000)	(5,688,000)	(5,356,000)	(1,286,000)	(1,215,000)
Income Taxes	(5,208,000)	(4,815,000)	(472,000)	(180,000)	(1,833,000)	(1,619,000)	(118,000)	(107,000)
Net Income	4,208,000	3,709,000	293,000	(2,310,000)	(3,728,000)	(1,672,000)	(1,104,000)	(1,221,000)
Average Shares	750,000	751,000	751,000	582,000	567,000	470,000	405,000	404,000
Balance Sheet								
Current Assets	34,772,000	35,316,000	33,655,000	36,138,000	38,957,000	30,773,000	23,573,000	...
Total Assets	116,814,000	115,520,000	109,892,000	111,820,000	122,281,000	118,206,000	45,122,000	...
Current Liabilities	49,055,000	47,020,000	43,479,000	44,972,000	45,892,000	38,135,000	25,310,000	...
Long-Term Obligations	44,727,000	45,973,000	48,640,000	49,201,000	43,998,000	43,061,000	10,650,000	...
Total Liabilities	117,684,000	116,945,000	114,582,000	116,389,000	112,571,000	104,732,000	43,550,000	...
Stockholders' Equity	(870,000)	(1,425,000)	(4,690,000)	(4,569,000)	9,710,000	13,474,000	1,572,000	...
Shares Outstanding	731,000	724,000	719,000	719,000	769,000	778,000	405,000	...
Statistical Record								
Return on Assets %	3.28	2.12	N.M.	N.M.	N.M.	N.M.	...	...
Return on Equity %	88.67	55.12	N.M.	N.M.	N.M.	N.M.	...	...
EBITDA Margin %	9.62	9.38	2.78	6.53	1.67	N.M.	1.40	1.63
Net Margin %	6.18	8.19	1.34	N.M.	N.M.	N.M.	N.M.	N.M.
Asset Turnover	0.77	0.77	0.78	0.78	0.66	0.74	...	...
Current Ratio	0.71	0.75	0.77	0.80	0.85	0.81	0.93	...
Debt to Equity	...	...	...	...	4.53	3.20	6.77	...
Price Range	69.80-42.62	69.80-42.62	68.70-42.62	49.65-42.62	...	...	...	...
P/E Ratio	14.79-9.03	31.44-19.20	...	...	...	...	...	...

Address: One Dell Way, Round Rock, TX 78682	**Web Site:** www.delltechnologies.com	**Auditors:** PricewaterhouseCoopers LLP
Telephone: 800-289-3355	**Officers:** Michael S. Dell - Chairman, Chief Executive Officer Marius A. Haas - President, Chief Commercial Officer	**Investor Contact:** 800-289-3355

DELTA AIR LINES INC (DE)

Exchange	Symbol	Price	52Wk Range	Yield	P/E
NYS	DAL	$58.48 (12/31/2019)	63.16-45.61	2.75	8.19

*7 Year Price Score 103.84 *NYSE Composite Index=100 *12 Month Price Score 97.97

Interim Earnings (Per Share)

Qtr.	Mar	Jun	Sep	Dec
2016	1.21	2.03	1.70	0.87
2017	0.82	1.68	1.64	0.82
2018	0.77	1.47	1.91	1.53
2019	1.09	2.21	2.31	...

Interim Dividends (Per Share)

Amt	Decl	Ex	Rec	Pay
0.35Q	02/07/2019	02/28/2019	03/01/2019	03/22/2019
0.35Q	04/18/2019	05/01/2019	05/02/2019	05/23/2019
0.403Q	07/11/2019	07/24/2019	07/25/2019	08/15/2019
0.403Q	10/09/2019	10/23/2019	10/24/2019	11/14/2019

Indicated Div: $1.61

Valuation Analysis

		Institutional Holding	
Forecast EPS	$7.25 (01/17/2020)	No of Institutions	1446
Market Cap	$37.8 Billion	Shares	
Book Value	$15.1 Billion		726,728,832
Price/Book	2.51	% Held	
Price/Sales	0.82		0.02

Business Summary: Airlines/Air Freight (MIC: 7.4.4 SIC: 4512 NAIC: 481111)

Delta Air Lines provides scheduled air transportation for passengers and cargo throughout the U.S. and around the world. Co.'s route network is centered around a system of hub and main markets at airports in Amsterdam, Atlanta, Boston, Detroit, London-Heathrow, Los Angeles, Mexico City, Minneapolis-St. Paul, New York-LaGuardia, New York-JFK, Paris-Charles de Gaulle, Salt Lake City, Sao Paulo, Seattle, Seoul-Incheon and Tokyo-Narita. Each of these operations includes flights that gather and distribute traffic from markets in the geographic region surrounding the hub or main market to domestic and international cities and to other hubs or main markets.

Recent Developments: For the quarter ended Sep 30 2019, net income increased 13.1% to US$1.50 billion from US$1.32 billion in the year-earlier quarter. Revenues were US$12.56 billion, up 5.1% from US$11.95 billion the year before. Operating income was US$2.07 billion versus US$1.65 billion in the prior-year quarter, an increase of 25.9%. Direct operating expenses declined 0.4% to US$5.16 billion from US$5.18 billion in the comparable period the year before. Indirect operating expenses increased 3.9% to US$5.33 billion from US$5.13 billion in the equivalent prior-year period.

Prospects: Our evaluation of Delta Air Lines Inc. as of October 4th, 2019 is the result of our systematic analysis on three basic characteristics: earnings strength, relative valuation, and recent stock price movement. The company has produced a positive trend in earnings per share over the past 5 quarters. However, recent analyst estimates for the company have been reduced, while DAL has posted results that exceeded analysts' expectations. Based on operating earnings yield, the company is undervalued when compared to all of the companies we cover. Share price changes over the past year indicates that DAL will perform over the near term.

Financial Data

(US$ in Thousands)	9 Mos	6 Mos	3 Mos	12/31/2018	12/31/2017	12/31/2016	12/31/2015	12/31/2014
Earnings Per Share	7.14	6.74	6.00	5.67	4.95	5.79	5.63	0.78
Cash Flow Per Share	13.67	12.44	11.46	10.15	7.15	9.57	9.95	5.92
Tang Book Value Per Share	0.72	N.M.	N.M.	N.M.	N.M.	N.M.	N.M.	N.M.
Dividends Per Share	1.452	1.400	1.355	1.310	1.015	0.675	0.450	0.300
Dividend Payout %	20.34	20.77	22.58	23.10	20.51	11.66	7.99	38.46
Income Statement								
Total Revenue	35,568,000	23,008,000	10,472,000	44,438,000	41,244,000	39,639,000	40,704,000	40,362,000
EBITDA	6,988,000	4,339,000	1,644,000	7,762,000	8,297,000	8,924,000	9,438,000	3,422,000
Depn & Amortn	1,960,000	1,328,000	615,000	2,300,000	2,200,000	1,900,000	1,800,000	1,700,000
Income Before Taxes	4,800,000	2,853,000	946,000	5,151,000	5,701,000	6,636,000	7,157,000	1,072,000
Income Taxes	1,131,000	680,000	216,000	1,216,000	2,124,000	2,263,000	2,631,000	413,000
Net Income	3,669,000	2,173,000	730,000	3,935,000	3,577,000	4,373,000	4,526,000	659,000
Average Shares	648,000	652,000	667,000	694,000	723,000	755,000	804,000	845,000
Balance Sheet								
Current Assets	6,944,000	7,134,000	7,196,000	6,340,000	7,844,000	7,451,000	9,056,000	12,465,000
Total Assets	63,219,000	62,518,000	61,841,000	60,266,000	53,292,000	51,261,000	53,134,000	54,121,000
Current Liabilities	20,211,000	21,164,000	21,323,000	18,578,000	18,573,000	15,239,000	17,526,000	16,879,000
Long-Term Obligations	7,923,000	7,710,000	7,710,000	14,054,000	6,592,000	6,201,000	6,766,000	8,561,000
Total Liabilities	48,151,000	48,560,000	48,930,000	46,579,000	39,382,000	38,974,000	42,284,000	45,308,000
Stockholders' Equity	15,068,000	13,958,000	12,911,000	13,687,000	13,910,000	12,287,000	10,850,000	8,813,000
Shares Outstanding	646,742	650,200	654,996	679,944	707,197	730,737	778,783	825,258
Statistical Record								
Return on Assets %	7.98	7.67	7.10	6.93	6.84	8.35	8.44	1.24
Return on Equity %	32.80	33.83	32.34	28.52	27.31	37.70	46.04	6.44
EBITDA Margin %	19.65	18.86	15.70	17.47	20.12	22.51	23.19	8.48
Net Margin %	10.32	9.44	6.97	8.86	8.67	11.03	11.12	1.63
Asset Turnover	0.78	0.77	0.78	0.78	0.79	0.76	0.76	0.76
Current Ratio	0.34	0.34	0.34	0.34	0.42	0.49	0.52	0.74
Debt to Equity	0.53	0.55	0.60	1.03	0.47	0.50	0.62	0.97
Price Range	63.16-45.61	60.71-45.61	60.71-45.61	60.71-47.96	56.43-44.03	51.78-33.36	52.26-40.00	49.23-27.47
P/E Ratio	8.85-6.39	9.01-6.77	10.12-7.60	10.71-8.46	11.40-8.89	8.94-5.76	9.28-7.10	63.12-35.22
Average Yield %	2.65	2.60	2.55	2.40	2.03	1.56	0.98	0.80

Address: Post Office Box 20706, Atlanta, GA 30320-6001
Telephone: 404-715-2600

Web Site: www.delta.com
Officers: Glen W. Hauenstein - President, Executive Vice President, Chief Revenue Officer, Executive Vice President (frmr) Edward H. Bastian - Chief Executive Officer, President, Executive Vice President, Chief Financial Officer, Senior Vice President, Vice President, Controller, Division Officer

Auditors: Ernst & Young LLP
Investor Contact: 404-715-2170
Transfer Agents: Wells Fargo Shareowner Services, St. Paul, MN

DELUXE CORP

Exchange	Symbol	Price	52Wk Range	Yield	P/E
NYS	DLX	$49.92 (12/31/2019)	53.75-36.85	2.40	N/A

*7 Year Price Score 65.39 *NYSE Composite Index=100 *12 Month Price Score 106.04

Interim Earnings (Per Share)

Qtr.	Mar	Jun	Sep	Dec
2016	1.18	1.18	1.19	1.10
2017	1.16	1.22	0.59	1.74
2018	1.31	1.25	(0.67)	1.23
2019	0.93	0.75	(7.49)	...

Interim Dividends (Per Share)

Amt	Decl	Ex	Rec	Pay
0.30Q	01/22/2019	02/15/2019	02/19/2019	03/04/2019
0.30Q	04/30/2019	05/17/2019	05/20/2019	06/03/2019
0.30Q	08/05/2019	08/16/2019	08/19/2019	09/03/2019
0.30Q	10/24/2019	11/15/2019	11/18/2019	12/02/2019

Indicated Div: $1.20

Valuation Analysis

		Institutional Holding	
Forecast EPS	$6.69	No of Institutions	439
	(01/17/2020)	Shares	
Market Cap	$2.1 Billion	Shares	49,426,500
Book Value	$525.5 Million	% Held	79.43
Price/Book	4.00		
Price/Sales	1.04		

Business Summary: Printing (MIC: 7.5.5 SIC: 2761 NAIC: 323116)

Deluxe is engaged in providing payment solutions. Co.'s product and service offerings are comprised of: Marketing solutions and other services, which include digital printing and web-to-print solutions, hosting and domain name services, logo and web design, and search engine marketing and optimization; Checks, in which Co. is a provider of checks; and Forms, accessories and other products, which provides printed forms to small businesses, including deposit tickets, billing forms, work orders, job proposals, purchase orders, invoices and personnel forms, as well as computer forms, envelopes, office supplies, ink stamps and labels.

Recent Developments: For the quarter ended Sep 30 2019, net loss amounted to US$318.5 million versus a net loss of US$31.1 million in the year-earlier quarter. Revenues were US$493.6 million, up 0.1% from US$493.2 million the year before. Operating loss was US$340.7 million versus a loss of US$17.3 million in the prior-year quarter. Direct operating expenses rose 3.1% to US$203.7 million from US$197.6 million in the comparable period the year before. Indirect operating expenses increased 101.6% to US$630.6 million from US$312.8 million in the equivalent prior-year period.

Prospects: Our evaluation of Deluxe Corp. as of October 4th, 2019 is the result of our systematic analysis on three basic characteristics: earnings strength, relative valuation, and recent stock price movement. The company has produced a positive trend in earnings per share over the past 5 quarters. In addition, recent analyst estimates for the company have been raised, and DLX has posted results that exceeded analysts' expectations. Based on operating earnings yield, the company is undervalued when compared to all of the companies we cover. Share price changes over the past year indicates that DLX will perform poorly over the near term.

Financial Data

(US$ in Thousands)	9 Mos	6 Mos	3 Mos	12/31/2018	12/31/2017	12/31/2016	12/31/2015	12/31/2014
Earnings Per Share	(4.58)	2.24	2.74	3.16	4.72	4.65	4.36	3.96
Cash Flow Per Share	7.72	6.85	6.91	7.24	7.03	6.56	6.23	5.63
Dividends Per Share	1.200	1.200	1.200	1.200	1.200	1.200	1.200	1.150
Dividend Payout %	...	53.57	43.80	37.97	25.42	25.81	27.52	29.04
Income Statement								
Total Revenue	1,486,645	993,051	499,065	1,998,025	1,965,556	1,849,062	1,772,817	1,674,082
EBITDA	(105,677)	196,148	107,745	485,371	563,622	531,356	485,646	448,627
Depn & Amortn	113,291	76,617	42,206	245,628	229,436	168,668	137,400	114,917
Income Before Taxes	(246,219)	100,991	56,238	212,631	312,827	340,386	327,947	297,181
Income Taxes	(1,498)	27,219	15,048	63,001	82,672	111,004	109,318	97,387
Net Income	(244,721)	73,772	41,190	149,630	230,155	229,382	218,629	199,794
Average Shares	42,533	43,554	44,065	46,991	48,448	48,975	49,825	50,262
Balance Sheet								
Current Assets	425,716	445,077	431,148	450,046	392,966	398,230	325,988	318,890
Total Assets	1,888,963	2,314,038	2,322,411	2,305,096	2,208,827	2,184,338	1,844,402	1,688,391
Current Liabilities	361,847	349,634	356,449	392,050	425,770	415,684	751,043	467,248
Long-Term Obligations	924,000	951,000	946,000	911,073	665,260	722,806	196,222	393,401
Total Liabilities	1,363,436	1,419,889	1,424,848	1,389,683	1,193,814	1,303,368	1,099,333	1,040,894
Stockholders' Equity	525,527	894,149	897,563	915,413	1,015,013	880,970	745,069	647,497
Shares Outstanding	42,099	49,928	43,638	44,647	47,953	48,546	49,019	49,742
Statistical Record								
Return on Assets %	N.M.	4.33	5.55	6.63	10.48	11.36	12.38	12.27
Return on Equity %	N.M.	10.14	13.08	15.50	24.28	28.14	31.40	33.36
EBITDA Margin %	N.M.	19.75	21.59	24.29	28.67	28.74	27.39	26.80
Net Margin %	N.M.	7.43	8.25	7.49	11.71	12.41	12.33	11.93
Asset Turnover	0.97	0.87	0.87	0.89	0.89	0.92	1.00	1.03
Current Ratio	1.18	1.27	1.21	1.15	0.92	0.96	0.43	0.68
Debt to Equity	1.76	1.06	1.05	1.00	0.66	0.82	0.26	0.61
Price Range	55.43-36.85	66.80-36.85	76.61-36.96	77.69-36.96	76.84-67.03	73.04-51.00	69.57-53.36	63.54-45.52
P/E Ratio	...	29.82-16.45	27.96-13.49	24.59-11.70	16.28-14.20	15.71-10.97	15.96-12.24	16.05-11.49
Average Yield %	2.68	2.46	2.15	1.91	1.69	1.89	1.93	2.08

Address: 3680 Victoria St. N., Shoreview, MN 55126-2966
Telephone: 651-483-7111
Fax: 651-483-7337

Web Site: www.deluxe.com
Officers: Martyn R. Redgrave - Chairman Barry McCarthy - President, Chief Executive Officer

Auditors: PricewaterhouseCoopers LLP
Investor Contact: 651-787-1068
Transfer Agents: Wells Fargo Bank Minnesota, N.A., St. Paul, MN

DEVON ENERGY CORP.

Exchange	Symbol	Price	52Wk Range	Yield	P/E
NYS	DVN	$25.97 (12/31/2019)	35.16-19.80	1.39	8.35

*7 Year Price Score 48.04 ***NYSE Composite Index=100** ***12 Month Price Score 83.25**

TRADING VOLUME (thousand shares)

Interim Earnings (Per Share)

Qtr.	Mar	Jun	Sep	Dec
2016	(6.44)	(3.04)	1.89	0.70
2017	1.07	0.80	0.43	(0.61)
2018	(0.38)	(0.83)	5.14	2.39
2019	(0.74)	1.19	0.27	...

Interim Dividends (Per Share)

Amt	Decl	Ex	Rec	Pay
0.09Q	02/19/2019	06/13/2019	06/14/2019	06/28/2019
0.09Q	06/05/2019	09/12/2019	09/13/2019	09/27/2019
0.09Q	09/11/2019	12/12/2019	12/13/2019	12/27/2019
0.09Q	12/04/2019	03/12/2020	03/13/2020	03/31/2020

Indicated Div: $0.36

Valuation Analysis

		Institutional Holding	
Forecast EPS	$1.41	No of Institutions	
	(01/17/2020)	1139	
Market Cap	$10.0 Billion	Shares	
Book Value	$6.5 Billion	446,301,920	
Price/Book	1.54	% Held	
Price/Sales	1.12	64.18	

Business Summary: Production & Extraction (MIC: 9.1.1 SIC: 1311 NAIC: 211111)

Devon Energy is an independent energy company engaged primarily in the exploration, development and production of oil, natural gas and natural gas liquids. Co.'s operations are concentrated in various North American onshore areas in the U.S. and Canada. Co.'s areas of operation include Barnett Shale, Delaware Basin, Eagle Ford, Heavy Oil, Rockies Oil, and the STACK development, located primarily in Oklahoma's Canadian, Kingfisher and Blaine counties.

Recent Developments: For the quarter ended Sep 30 2019, income from continuing operations decreased 10.9% to US$139.0 million from US$156.0 million in the year-earlier quarter. Net income decreased 95.7% to US$109.0 million from US$2.56 billion in the year-earlier quarter. Revenues were US$1.85 billion, down 14.3% from US$2.16 billion the year before. Direct operating expenses declined 11.8% to US$368.0 million from US$417.0 million in the comparable period the year before. Indirect operating expenses decreased 26.7% to US$1.29 billion from US$1.75 billion in the equivalent prior-year period.

Prospects: Our evaluation of Devon Energy Corp. as of October 4th, 2019 is the result of our systematic analysis on three basic characteristics: earnings strength, relative valuation, and recent stock price movement. The company has suffered a very negative trend in earnings per share over the past 5 quarters. However, recent analyst estimates for the company have been raised and DVN has posted results that exceeded analysts' expectations. Based on operating earnings yield, the company is fairly valued when compared to all of the companies we cover. Share price changes over the past year indicates that DVN will perform poorly over the near term.

Financial Data

(US$ in Thousands)	9 Mos	6 Mos	3 Mos	12/31/2018	12/31/2017	12/31/2016	12/31/2015	12/31/2014
Earnings Per Share	3.11	7.98	5.96	6.10	1.70	(6.52)	(35.55)	3.91
Cash Flow Per Share	7.88	6.61	4.66	4.51	5.59	3.43	13.23	14.77
Tang Book Value Per Share	14.18	14.37	16.01	18.59	13.09	3.75	4.83	37.25
Dividends Per Share	0.340	0.330	0.320	0.300	0.240	0.420	0.960	0.940
Dividend Payout %	10.93	4.14	5.37	4.92	14.12	...	...	24.04
Income Statement								
Total Revenue	4,996,000	3,149,000	1,501,000	10,734,000	13,949,000	12,197,000	13,145,000	19,566,000
EBITDA	1,151,000	555,000	32,000	2,578,000	2,970,000	(987,000)	(17,622,000)	7,904,000
Depn & Amortn	1,176,000	774,000	459,000	1,658,000	2,074,000	1,986,000	3,129,000	3,319,000
Income Before Taxes	(25,000)	(219,000)	(427,000)	920,000	896,000	(3,877,000)	(21,268,000)	4,059,000
Income Taxes	16,000	(39,000)	(110,000)	156,000	(182,000)	(173,000)	(6,065,000)	2,368,000
Net Income	287,000	178,000	(317,000)	3,064,000	898,000	(3,302,000)	(14,454,000)	1,607,000
Average Shares	394,000	411,000	428,000	497,000	523,000	507,000	407,000	407,000
Balance Sheet								
Current Assets	2,846,000	5,167,000	2,703,000	4,437,000	4,791,000	3,772,000	4,026,000	6,498,000
Total Assets	14,394,000	16,649,000	18,077,000	19,566,000	30,241,000	25,913,000	29,532,000	50,637,000
Current Liabilities	1,658,000	3,467,000	1,968,000	2,226,000	3,315,000	2,616,000	3,295,000	5,935,000
Long-Term Obligations	4,539,000	4,557,000	6,084,000	5,785,000	10,291,000	10,154,000	12,137,000	9,830,000
Total Liabilities	7,852,000	9,655,000	10,220,000	10,380,000	20,987,000	19,986,000	22,483,000	29,098,000
Stockholders' Equity	6,542,000	6,994,000	7,857,000	9,186,000	9,254,000	5,927,000	7,049,000	21,539,000
Shares Outstanding	386,700	409,300	415,500	449,000	525,000	523,000	418,000	409,000
Statistical Record								
Return on Assets %	8.31	16.87	12.42	12.30	3.20	N.M.	N.M.	3.44
Return on Equity %	18.60	51.49	35.13	33.23	11.83	N.M.	N.M.	7.65
EBITDA Margin %	23.04	17.62	2.13	24.02	21.29	N.M.	N.M.	40.40
Net Margin %	5.74	5.65	N.M.	28.54	6.44	N.M.	N.M.	8.21
Asset Turnover	0.52	0.42	0.42	0.43	0.50	0.44	0.33	0.42
Current Ratio	1.72	1.49	1.37	1.99	1.45	1.44	1.22	1.09
Debt to Equity	0.69	0.65	0.77	0.63	1.11	1.71	1.72	0.46
Price Range	40.65-20.98	45.61-20.98	45.61-20.98	45.61-20.98	49.01-29.54	48.33-18.65	69.03-28.67	79.50-52.66
P/E Ratio	13.07-6.75	5.72-2.63	7.65-3.52	7.48-3.44	28.83-17.38	...	...	20.33-13.47
Average Yield %	1.20	1.01	0.91	0.81	0.64	1.17	1.81	1.39

Address: 333 West Sheridan Avenue, Oklahoma City, OK 73102-5015 **Telephone:** 405-235-3611	**Web Site:** www.devonenergy.com **Officers:** Duane C. Radtke - Vice-Chairman David A. Hager - President, Chief Executive Officer, Executive Vice President, Chief Operating Officer	**Auditors:** KPMG LLP **Investor Contact:** 405-552-4505 **Transfer Agents:** Computershare Trust Company, N.A., Providence, RI

DIAMOND OFFSHORE DRILLING, INC.

Exchange	Symbol	Price	52Wk Range	Yield	P/E
NYS	DO	$7.19 (12/31/2019)	12.41-4.99	N/A	N/A

*7 Year Price Score 24.11   *NYSE Composite Index=100   *12 Month Price Score 68.97

Interim Earnings (Per Share)

Qtr.	Mar	Jun	Sep	Dec
2016	0.64	(4.30)	0.10	0.84
2017	0.17	0.12	0.08	(0.24)
2018	0.14	(0.50)	(0.37)	(0.57)
2019	(0.53)	(0.83)	(0.69)	...

Interim Dividends (Per Share)

Dividend Payment Suspended

Valuation Analysis		Institutional Holding	
Forecast EPS	$-2.84	No of Institutions	
	(01/17/2020)	413	
Market Cap	$990.0 Million	Shares	
Book Value	$3.3 Billion	170,942,112	
Price/Book	0.30	% Held	
Price/Sales	1.06	109.67	

TRADING VOLUME (thousand shares)

Business Summary: Equipment & Services (MIC: 9.1.3 SIC: 1381 NAIC: 213111)

Diamond Offshore Drilling provides contract drilling services to the energy industry around the globe. Co.'s fleet enables it to provide services in the floater market on a worldwide basis. Co.'s contracts to provide offshore drilling services vary in their terms and provisions. The principal markets for Co.'s offshore contract drilling services are: the Gulf of Mexico, including the U.S., and Mexico; South America, principally offshore Brazil, and Trinidad and Tobago; Australia and Southeast Asia, including Malaysia, Indonesia, Myanmar and Vietnam; Europe, principally offshore the U.K., and Norway; East and West Africa; and the Mediterranean.

Recent Developments: For the quarter ended Sep 30 2019, net loss amounted to US$95.1 million versus a net loss of US$51.1 million in the year-earlier quarter. Revenues were US$254.0 million, down 11.3% from US$286.3 million the year before. Operating loss was US$72.8 million versus a loss of US$23.0 million in the prior-year quarter. Direct operating expenses rose 9.8% to US$213.0 million from US$194.0 million in the comparable period the year before. Indirect operating expenses decreased 1.3% to US$113.9 million from US$115.3 million in the equivalent prior-year period.

Prospects: Our evaluation of Diamond Offshore Drilling Inc. as of Jan. 21, 2018 is the result of our systematic analysis on three basic characteristics: earnings strength, relative valuation, and recent stock price movement. The company has suffered a very negative trend in earnings per share over the past 5 quarters. However, while recent estimates for the company have been lowered by analysts, DO has posted better than expected results. Based on operating earnings yield, the company is about fairly valued when compared to all of the companies in our coverage universe. Share price changes over the past year indicates that DO will perform very poorly over the near term.

Financial Data

(US$ in Thousands)	9 Mos	6 Mos	3 Mos	12/31/2018	12/31/2017	12/31/2016	12/31/2015	12/31/2014
Earnings Per Share	(2.62)	(2.30)	(1.97)	(1.31)	0.13	(2.72)	(2.00)	2.81
Cash Flow Per Share	0.21	0.72	1.10	1.69	3.60	4.70	5.37	7.22
Tang Book Value Per Share	24.00	24.69	25.53	26.08	27.50	27.34	29.99	32.46
Dividends Per Share	...	...	...	...	...	...	0.500	3.500
Dividend Payout %	...	...	...	...	...	...	...	124.56
Income Statement								
Total Revenue	704,268	450,248	233,542	1,083,215	1,485,746	1,600,342	2,419,393	2,814,671
EBITDA	29,020	13,157	37,019	219,927	438,310	2,627	202,426	1,032,926
Depn & Amortn	263,844	175,151	86,898	331,789	348,695	381,760	493,162	456,483
Income Before Taxes	(321,342)	(218,732)	(77,390)	(226,625)	(21,440)	(468,299)	(381,348)	515,191
Income Taxes	(38,898)	(31,416)	(4,062)	(46,353)	(39,786)	(95,796)	(107,063)	128,180
Net Income	(282,444)	(187,316)	(73,328)	(180,272)	18,346	(372,503)	(274,285)	387,011
Average Shares	137,694	137,691	137,522	137,399	137,265	137,168	137,157	137,523
Balance Sheet								
Current Assets	514,422	590,664	732,802	785,938	886,653	505,807	669,595	899,059
Total Assets	5,871,034	5,977,236	6,112,484	6,035,694	6,250,570	6,371,877	7,164,889	8,021,289
Current Liabilities	279,206	269,449	273,257	236,846	223,288	340,499	625,723	856,646
Long-Term Obligations	1,975,275	1,974,816	1,974,365	1,973,922	1,972,225	1,980,884	1,994,773	1,994,526
Total Liabilities	2,565,710	2,578,339	2,600,608	2,451,041	2,476,309	2,621,743	3,052,119	3,569,726
Stockholders' Equity	3,305,324	3,398,897	3,511,876	3,584,653	3,774,261	3,750,134	4,112,770	4,451,563
Shares Outstanding	137,694	137,690	137,580	137,438	137,227	137,169	137,158	137,147
Statistical Record								
Return on Assets %	N.M.	N.M.	N.M.	N.M.	0.29	N.M.	N.M.	4.72
Return on Equity %	N.M.	N.M.	N.M.	N.M.	0.49	N.M.	N.M.	8.52
EBITDA Margin %	4.12	2.92	15.85	20.30	29.50	0.16	8.37	36.70
Net Margin %	N.M.	N.M.	N.M.	N.M.	1.23	N.M.	N.M.	13.75
Asset Turnover	0.16	0.16	0.17	0.18	0.24	0.24	0.32	0.34
Current Ratio	1.84	2.19	2.68	3.32	3.97	1.49	1.07	1.05
Debt to Equity	0.60	0.58	0.56	0.55	0.52	0.53	0.49	0.45
Price Range	20.80-5.36	20.91-7.39	21.22-8.98	21.22-8.98	19.49-10.22	26.11-14.80	37.23-16.81	56.92-29.37
P/E Ratio	...	...	...	...	149.92-78.62	...	...	20.26-10.45
Average Yield %	...	...	...	...	...	...	1.91	7.82

Address: 15415 Katy Freeway, Houston, TX 77094	Web Site: www.diamondoffshore.com	Auditors: DELOITTE & TOUCHE LLP
Telephone: 281-492-5300	Officers: James S. Tisch - Chairman Marc Gerard Rex Edwards - President, Chief Executive Officer	Investor Contact: 281-492-5393
Fax: 281-492-5316		Transfer Agents: Computershare, Providence, R.I.

DICK'S SPORTING GOODS, INC

Exchange	Symbol	Price	52Wk Range	Yield	P/E
NYS	DKS	$49.49 (12/31/2019)	49.49-31.20	2.22	13.79

*7 Year Price Score 70.48   *NYSE Composite Index=100   *12 Month Price Score 112.92

Interim Earnings (Per Share)

Qtr.	Apr	Jul	Oct	Jan
2016-17	0.50	0.82	0.44	0.81
2017-18	0.52	1.03	0.35	1.10
2018-19	0.59	1.20	0.39	1.06
2019-20	0.61	1.26	0.66	...

Interim Dividends (Per Share)

Amt	Decl	Ex	Rec	Pay
0.275Q	02/27/2019	03/14/2019	03/15/2019	03/29/2019
0.275Q	05/24/2019	06/13/2019	06/14/2019	06/28/2019
0.275Q	08/19/2019	09/12/2019	09/13/2019	09/27/2019
0.275Q	11/21/2019	12/12/2019	12/13/2019	12/31/2019

Indicated Div: $1.10

Valuation Analysis

Forecast EPS	$3.60	
	(01/17/2020)	
Market Cap	$4.2 Billion	
Book Value	$1.7 Billion	
Price/Book	2.43	
Price/Sales	0.48	

Institutional Holding

No of Institutions	527
Shares	93,876,344
% Held	85.57

Business Summary: Retail - Specialty (MIC: 2.1.3 SIC: 5941 NAIC: 451110)

Dick's Sporting Goods is an omni-channel sporting goods retailer offering sports equipment, apparel, footwear and accessories. Co. also owns and operates Golf Galaxy, Field & Stream and other specialty concept stores, and Dick's Team Sports HQ, an all-in-one youth sports digital platform offering scheduling, communications and live scorekeeping through its GameChanger mobile apps, free league management services, custom uniforms and fan wear, and access to donations and sponsorships. Co. provides products to its customers through its retail stores and online. Co. is also involved in local communities, sponsoring teams in various sports.

Recent Developments: For the quarter ended Nov 2 2019, net income increased 52.2% to US$57.6 million from US$37.8 million in the year-earlier quarter. Revenues were US$1.96 billion, up 5.6% from US$1.86 billion the year before. Operating income was US$45.6 million versus US$52.9 million in the prior-year quarter, a decrease of 13.7%. Direct operating expenses rose 3.6% to US$1.38 billion from US$1.33 billion in the comparable period the year before. Indirect operating expenses increased 13.7% to US$535.0 million from US$470.7 million in the equivalent prior-year period.

Prospects: Our evaluation of Dick's Sporting Goods Inc. as of October 4th, 2019 is the result of our systematic analysis on three basic characteristics: earnings strength, relative valuation, and recent stock price movement. The company has produced a positive trend in earnings per share over the past 5 quarters. However, recent analyst estimates for the company have been mixed and DKS has posted results that exceeded analysts' expectations. Based on operating earnings yield, the company is undervalued when compared to all of the companies we cover. Share price changes over the past year indicates that DKS will perform poorly over the near term.

Financial Data

(US$ in Thousands)	9 Mos	6 Mos	3 Mos	02/02/2019	02/03/2018	01/28/2017	01/30/2016	01/31/2015
Earnings Per Share	3.59	3.32	3.26	3.24	3.01	2.56	2.83	2.84
Cash Flow Per Share	3.99	4.20	5.49	7.31	6.86	6.85	5.60	5.10
Tang Book Value Per Share	15.95	15.99	15.72	16.23	15.09	13.99	13.24	12.88
Dividends Per Share	1.050	1.000	0.950	0.900	0.680	0.605	0.550	0.500
Dividend Payout %	29.25	30.12	29.14	27.78	22.59	23.63	19.43	17.61
Income Statement								
Total Revenue	6,142,093	4,179,889	1,920,677	8,436,570	8,590,472	7,921,981	7,270,965	6,814,479
EBITDA	521,972	368,107	148,835	671,768	730,684	670,878	715,387	720,829
Depn & Amortn	201,152	128,711	66,024	229,600	221,300	206,600	180,500	161,600
Income Before Taxes	307,911	230,765	79,730	431,920	501,337	458,422	530,875	556,014
Income Taxes	80,268	60,706	22,205	112,056	177,892	171,026	200,484	211,816
Net Income	227,643	170,059	57,525	319,864	323,445	287,396	330,391	344,198
Average Shares	86,601	89,400	94,388	98,781	107,586	112,216	116,794	121,238
Balance Sheet								
Current Assets	2,876,915	2,466,017	2,439,704	2,122,398	2,006,085	1,995,678	1,812,690	1,850,384
Total Assets	7,206,999	6,915,215	6,911,994	4,187,149	4,203,939	4,058,296	3,559,336	3,436,198
Current Liabilities	2,081,645	1,925,391	1,855,388	1,504,639	1,425,014	1,397,415	1,191,675	1,118,833
Long-Term Obligations	719,300	441,500	369,500	54,781	60,084	4,679	5,324	5,913
Total Liabilities	5,498,097	5,150,129	5,085,959	2,282,988	2,262,438	2,128,807	1,770,149	1,603,973
Stockholders' Equity	1,708,902	1,765,086	1,826,035	1,904,161	1,941,501	1,929,489	1,789,187	1,832,225
Shares Outstanding	83,967	86,776	92,025	93,845	103,028	110,330	111,751	118,106
Statistical Record								
Return on Assets %	5.60	5.56	5.65	7.64	7.70	7.57	9.47	10.61
Return on Equity %	18.57	16.80	17.04	16.68	16.44	15.50	18.30	19.59
EBITDA Margin %	8.50	8.81	7.75	7.96	8.51	8.47	9.84	10.58
Net Margin %	3.71	4.07	3.00	3.79	3.77	3.63	4.54	5.05
Asset Turnover	1.46	1.53	1.50	2.02	2.05	2.09	2.08	2.10
Current Ratio	1.38	1.28	1.31	1.41	1.41	1.43	1.52	1.65
Debt to Equity	0.42	0.25	0.20	0.03	0.03	N.M.	N.M.	N.M.
Price Range	41.18-29.77	41.18-29.77	41.18-29.77	39.43-29.77	53.17-24.39	62.25-36.57	58.98-34.24	57.26-41.90
P/E Ratio	11.47-8.29	12.40-8.97	12.63-9.13	12.17-9.19	17.66-8.10	24.32-14.29	20.84-12.10	20.16-14.75
Average Yield %	2.90	2.78	2.67	2.61	1.83	1.20	1.12	1.03

Address: 345 Court Street, Coraopolis, PA 15108 **Telephone:** 724-273-3400	**Web Site:** www.DICKS.com **Officers:** Edward W. Stack - Chairman, Chief Executive Officer William J. Colombo - Vice-Chairman, Chief Marketing Officer	**Auditors:** DELOITTE & TOUCHE LLP **Transfer Agents:** American Stock Transfer & Trust Company, New York, NY

DIEBOLD NIXDORF INC

Exchange	Symbol	Price	52Wk Range	Yield	P/E
NYS	DBD	$10.56 (12/31/2019)	14.22-2.49	N/A	N/A

*7 Year Price Score 31.77 *NYSE Composite Index=100 *12 Month Price Score 85.58

Interim Earnings (Per Share)

Qtr.	Mar	Jun	Sep	Dec
2016	2.56	(0.32)	(1.44)	(1.14)
2017	(0.78)	(0.41)	(0.47)	(1.43)
2018	(0.94)	(1.82)	(2.79)	(1.91)
2019	(1.74)	(0.66)	(0.46)	...

Interim Dividends (Per Share)

Dividend Payment Suspended

Valuation Analysis | **Institutional Holding**

Forecast EPS	$-0.14	No of Institutions	
	(11/19/2019)	355	
Market Cap	$809.2 Million	Shares	
Book Value	N/A		100,172,696
Price/Book	N/A	% Held	
Price/Sales	0.18		92.19

Business Summary: Computer Hardware & Equipment (MIC: 6.2.1 SIC: 3578 NAIC: 423430)

Diebold Nixdorf is engaged in enabling Connected Commerce. Co. automates, digitizes and transforms the way people bank and shop. Co.'s integrated solutions connect digital and physical channels for consumers. Co.'s operating structure is focused on its two customer segments consisting of Banking and Retail. The products for banking customers consist of cash recyclers and dispensers, deposit terminals, teller automation and kiosk technologies, as well as physical security solutions. The retail product portfolio includes modular, integrated and mobile point of sale and self-checkout terminals that meet automation and omnichannel requirements of consumers.

Recent Developments: For the quarter ended Sep 30 2019, net loss amounted to US$34.8 million versus a net loss of US$244.6 million in the year-earlier quarter. Revenues were US$1.08 billion, down 3.6% from US$1.12 billion the year before. Operating income was US$23.2 million versus a loss of US$160.3 million in the prior-year quarter. Direct operating expenses declined 9.3% to US$807.3 million from US$890.1 million in the comparable period the year before. Indirect operating expenses decreased 36.2% to US$248.3 million from US$389.2 million in the equivalent prior-year period.

Prospects: Our evaluation of Diebold Nixdorf Inc. as of Jan. 21, 2018 is the result of our systematic analysis on three basic characteristics: earnings strength, relative valuation, and recent stock price movement. The company has managed to produce a neutral trend in earnings per share over the past 5 quarters. However, while recent estimates for the company have been mixed, DBD has posted better than expected results. Based on operating earnings yield, the company is undervalued when compared to all of the companies in our coverage universe. Share price changes over the past year indicates that DBD will perform poorly over the near term.

Financial Data

(US$ in Thousands)	9 Mos	6 Mos	3 Mos	12/31/2018	12/31/2017	12/31/2016	12/31/2015	12/31/2014
Earnings Per Share	(4.77)	(7.10)	(8.26)	(7.48)	(3.09)	(0.48)	1.12	1.76
Cash Flow Per Share	3.59	1.11	(0.25)	(1.37)	0.49	0.41	0.57	2.90
Tang Book Value Per Share	...	...	...	...	N.M.	N.M.	3.86	5.56
Dividends Per Share	...	...	...	0.100	0.400	0.963	1.150	1.150
Dividend Payout %	...	...	...	...	...	...	102.68	65.34
Income Statement								
Total Revenue	3,257,100	2,178,300	1,028,100	4,578,600	4,609,300	3,316,300	2,419,300	3,051,053
EBITDA	170,400	94,500	35,300	(264,100)	14,200	(75,100)	119,000	250,211
Depn & Amortn	171,300	115,800	58,400	105,300	92,900	61,800	40,700	48,202
Income Before Taxes	(147,200)	(117,000)	(71,100)	(515,600)	(175,700)	(238,300)	45,800	170,589
Income Taxes	74,800	69,600	60,400	37,200	29,800	(67,600)	(13,700)	53,570
Net Income	(218,700)	(183,000)	(132,700)	(568,700)	(233,100)	(33,000)	73,700	114,417
Average Shares	76,800	76,700	76,400	76,000	75,500	69,100	65,600	65,154
Balance Sheet								
Current Assets	1,870,400	1,937,200	2,137,300	2,203,400	2,508,400	2,619,600	1,643,600	1,655,530
Total Assets	3,889,100	4,104,500	4,327,300	4,311,900	5,250,200	5,270,300	2,249,300	2,342,136
Current Liabilities	1,546,100	1,569,100	1,654,500	1,568,400	1,799,400	1,824,500	955,800	1,027,723
Long-Term Obligations	2,100,300	2,174,100	2,301,600	2,190,000	1,787,100	1,691,400	613,100	479,794
Total Liabilities	4,339,000	4,433,300	4,628,700	4,498,300	4,780,200	4,678,900	1,836,900	1,810,532
Stockholders' Equity	(449,900)	(328,800)	(301,400)	(186,400)	470,000	591,400	412,400	531,604
Shares Outstanding	76,626	76,745	76,572	76,174	75,558	75,144	65,001	64,632
Statistical Record								
Return on Assets %	N.M.	N.M.	N.M.	N.M.	N.M.	N.M.	3.21	5.06
Return on Equity %	...	...	N.M.	N.M.	N.M.	N.M.	15.61	20.28
EBITDA Margin %	5.23	4.34	3.43	N.M.	0.31	N.M.	4.92	8.20
Net Margin %	N.M.	N.M.	N.M.	N.M.	N.M.	N.M.	3.05	3.75
Asset Turnover	1.06	1.03	0.96	0.96	0.88	0.88	1.05	1.35
Current Ratio	1.21	1.23	1.29	1.40	1.39	1.44	1.72	1.61
Debt to Equity	...	...	...	...	3.80	2.86	1.49	0.90
Price Range	14.22-2.49	13.30-2.49	16.30-2.49	18.80-2.49	31.60-16.15	30.09-21.20	37.83-29.36	40.61-32.35
P/E Ratio	...	...	...	...	...	...	33.78-26.21	23.07-18.38
Average Yield %	...	...	...	0.98	1.66	3.77	3.40	3.12

Address: 5995 Mayfair Road, P.O. Box 3077, North Canton, OH 44720-8077 **Telephone:** 330-490-4000	**Web Site:** www.diebold.com **Officers:** Gary G. Greenfield - Chairman Gerrard Schmid - President, Chief Executive Officer	**Auditors:** KPMG LLP **Investor Contact:** 330-490-6319 **Transfer Agents:** Wells Fargo Shareowner Services

DIGITAL REALTY TRUST INC

Exchange	Symbol	Price	52Wk Range	Yield	P/E	Div Acheiver
NYS	DLR	$119.74 (12/31/2019)	135.74-101.83	3.61	119.74	14 Years

*7 Year Price Score 110.28 *NYSE Composite Index=100 *12 Month Price Score 94.92

Interim Earnings (Per Share)

Qtr.	Mar	Jun	Sep	Dec
2016	0.27	0.19	1.25	0.48
2017	0.41	0.36	(0.02)	0.26
2018	0.42	0.32	0.33	0.15
2019	0.46	0.15	0.24	...

Interim Dividends (Per Share)

Amt	Decl	Ex	Rec	Pay
1.08Q	02/21/2019	03/14/2019	03/15/2019	03/29/2019
1.08Q	05/13/2019	06/13/2019	06/14/2019	06/28/2019
1.08Q	08/13/2019	09/12/2019	09/13/2019	09/30/2019
1.08Q	11/19/2019	12/12/2019	12/13/2019	01/15/2020

Indicated Div: $4.32

Valuation Analysis

		Institutional Holding	
Forecast EPS	$1.13 (01/17/2020)	No of Institutions	942
Market Cap	$25.0 Billion	Shares	
Book Value	$9.4 Billion		255,983,888
Price/Book	2.65	% Held	
Price/Sales	7.80		102.00

Business Summary: REITs (MIC: 5.3.1 SIC: 6798 NAIC: 525930)

Digital Realty Trust, through its controlling interest in Digital Realty Trust, L.P. and its subsidiaries are a global provider of data center, colocation and interconnection solutions for customers across a variety of industry verticals ranging from cloud and information technology services, social networking and communications to financial services, manufacturing, energy, healthcare, and consumer products. Digital Realty Trust, L.P., is the entity through which Co., conducts its business of owning, acquiring, developing and operating data centers. Co. operates as a real estate investment trust for federal income tax purposes.

Recent Developments: For the quarter ended Sep 30 2019, net income decreased 25.1% to US$67.6 million from US$90.3 million in the year-earlier quarter. Revenues were US$806.5 million, up 4.9% from US$768.9 million the year before. Revenues from property income rose 4.6% to US$802.5 million from US$766.9 million in the corresponding quarter a year earlier.

Prospects: Our evaluation of Digital Realty Trust Inc. as of October 4th, 2019 is the result of our systematic analysis on three basic characteristics: earnings strength, relative valuation, and recent stock price movement. The company has managed to produce a neutral trend in earnings per share over the past 5 quarters. In addition, recent analyst estimates for the company have been mixed and DLR has posted results that fell short of analysts' expectations. Based on operating earnings yield, the company is overvalued when compared to all of the companies we cover. Share price changes over the past year indicates that DLR will perform in line with the market over the near term.

Financial Data

(US$ in Thousands)	9 Mos	6 Mos	3 Mos	12/31/2018	12/31/2017	12/31/2016	12/31/2015	12/31/2014
Earnings Per Share	1.00	1.09	1.26	1.21	0.99	2.20	1.56	0.99
Cash Flow Per Share	7.02	7.39	7.21	6.72	5.88	6.07	5.78	4.92
Tang Book Value Per Share	23.57	24.07	24.83	20.72	28.05	20.94	19.67	20.87
Dividends Per Share	4.250	4.180	4.110	4.040	3.720	3.520	3.400	3.320
Dividend Payout %	425.00	383.49	326.19	333.88	375.76	160.00	217.95	335.35
Income Statement								
Total Revenue	2,421,778	1,615,312	814,515	3,046,478	2,457,928	2,142,213	1,763,336	1,616,438
EBITDA	1,424,097	962,642	526,934	1,885,048	1,373,224	1,387,107	1,074,431	941,142
Depn & Amortn	940,475	638,421	330,780	1,256,780	879,585	720,930	578,064	557,356
Income Before Taxes	266,711	175,042	116,046	310,220	238,652	425,133	292,551	195,364
Income Taxes	13,726	8,900	4,266	2,084	7,901	10,385	6,451	5,238
Net Income	243,477	176,980	116,812	331,246	248,259	426,187	296,689	200,183
Average Shares	209,801	209,435	208,526	206,035	174,895	150,679	138,865	133,637
Balance Sheet								
Current Assets	311,902	354,474	451,888	434,843	289,528	225,974	252,460	188,807
Total Assets	23,172,765	23,430,091	23,342,067	23,766,695	21,404,345	12,192,585	11,451,267	9,526,784
Current Liabilities	938,740	984,812	922,571	1,381,750	1,179,979	969,072	735,268	720,942
Long-Term Obligations	10,924,035	10,842,578	10,279,656	11,101,479	8,648,618	5,838,607	5,934,241	4,673,127
Total Liabilities	13,735,475	13,867,866	13,253,659	13,892,219	11,001,362	7,096,570	6,951,135	5,648,528
Stockholders' Equity	9,437,290	9,562,225	10,088,408	9,874,476	10,402,983	5,096,015	4,500,132	3,878,256
Shares Outstanding	208,583	208,324	208,214	206,425	205,470	159,019	146,384	135,626
Statistical Record								
Return on Assets %	1.32	1.41	1.52	1.47	1.48	3.60	2.83	2.08
Return on Equity %	3.03	3.21	3.36	3.27	3.20	8.86	7.08	5.35
EBITDA Margin %	58.80	59.59	64.69	61.88	55.87	64.75	60.93	58.22
Net Margin %	10.05	10.96	14.34	10.87	10.10	19.89	16.83	12.38
Asset Turnover	0.14	0.14	0.14	0.13	0.15	0.18	0.17	0.17
Current Ratio	0.33	0.36	0.49	0.31	0.25	0.23	0.34	0.26
Debt to Equity	1.16	1.13	1.02	1.12	0.83	1.15	1.32	1.20
Price Range	129.81-101.83	124.88-101.83	124.30-100.99	124.30-97.95	126.04-99.36	112.10-72.50	77.01-61.52	70.27-49.12
P/E Ratio	129.81-101.83	114.57-93.42	98.65-80.15	102.73-80.95	127.31-100.36	50.95-32.95	49.37-39.44	70.98-49.62
Average Yield %	3.67	3.63	3.67	3.66	3.28	3.80	5.01	5.56

Address: Four Embarcadero Center, Suite 3200, San Francisco, CA 94111 **Telephone:** 415-738-6500 **Fax:** 415-738-6501	**Web Site:** www.digitalrealty.com **Officers:** Laurence A. Chapman - Chairman A. William Stein - Chief Executive Officer, Interim Chief Executive Officer, Chief Financial Officer, Chief Investment Officer	**Auditors:** KPMG LLP **Investor Contact:** 415-738-6500 **Transfer Agents:** American Stock Transfer & Trust Company, New York, NY

DILLARD'S INC.

Exchange	Symbol	Price	52Wk Range	Yield	P/E
NYS	DDS	$73.48 (12/31/2019)	81.62-54.95	0.82	15.40

*7 Year Price Score 69.39 *NYSE Composite Index=100 *12 Month Price Score 99.95

Interim Earnings (Per Share)

Qtr.	Apr	Jul	Oct	Jan
2016-17	2.17	0.35	0.67	1.69
2017-18	2.12	(0.58)	0.50	5.37
2018-19	2.89	(0.10)	0.27	3.15
2019-20	2.99	(1.59)	0.22	...

Interim Dividends (Per Share)

Amt	Decl	Ex	Rec	Pay
0.10Q	02/28/2019	03/28/2019	03/29/2019	05/06/2019
0.10Q	05/20/2019	06/27/2019	06/28/2019	08/05/2019
0.15Q	08/22/2019	09/27/2019	09/30/2019	11/04/2019
0.15Q	11/21/2019	12/30/2019	12/31/2019	02/03/2020

Indicated Div: $0.60

Valuation Analysis — **Institutional Holding**

Forecast EPS	$4.05	No of Institutions
	(01/09/2020)	313
Market Cap	$1.8 Billion	Shares
Book Value	$1.6 Billion	32,958,164
Price/Book	1.13	% Held
Price/Sales	0.28	79.04

Business Summary: Retail - General Merchandise/Department Stores (MIC: 2.1.1 SIC: 5311 NAIC: 452111)

Dillard's is a fashion apparel, cosmetics and home furnishing retailer. Co. operates Dillard's stores, including clearance centers, and an Internet store providing a selection of merchandise including fashion apparel for women, men and children, accessories, cosmetics, home furnishings and other consumer goods. Co. also operates a general contracting construction company, a portion of whose business includes constructing and remodeling stores for Co. Most of Co.'s stores are located in suburban shopping malls and open-air centers. Customers may also purchase Co.'s merchandise online at its website, www.dillards.com, which features online gift registries and a variety of other services.

Recent Developments: For the quarter ended Nov 2 2019, net income decreased 26.4% to US$5.5 million from US$7.4 million in the year-earlier quarter. Revenues were US$1.42 billion, down 2.2% from US$1.45 billion the year before. Direct operating expenses declined 2.9% to US$926.8 million from US$954.9 million in the comparable period the year before. Indirect operating expenses decreased 0.3% to US$494.0 million from US$495.3 million in the equivalent prior-year period.

Prospects: Our evaluation of Dillard's Inc. as of October 4th, 2019 is the result of our systematic analysis on three basic characteristics: earnings strength, relative valuation, and recent stock price movement. The company has suffered a very negative trend in earnings per share over the past 5 quarters. In addition, recent analyst estimates for the company have been reduced and DDS has posted results that fell short of analysts' expectations. Based on operating earnings yield, the company is undervalued when compared to all of the companies we cover. Share price changes over the past year indicates that DDS will perform very poorly over the near term.

Financial Data

(US$ in Thousands)	9 Mos	6 Mos	3 Mos	02/02/2019	02/03/2018	01/28/2017	01/30/2016	01/31/2015
Earnings Per Share	4.77	4.82	6.31	6.23	7.51	4.93	6.91	7.79
Cash Flow Per Share	12.87	14.23	13.69	13.48	9.15	15.11	11.57	14.39
Tang Book Value Per Share	65.28	65.88	67.48	63.70	60.77	53.41	49.98	49.02
Dividends Per Share	0.450	0.400	0.400	0.400	0.340	0.280	0.260	0.240
Dividend Payout %	9.43	8.30	6.34	6.42	4.53	5.68	3.76	3.08
Income Statement								
Total Revenue	4,380,439	2,956,780	1,497,935	6,503,349	6,422,676	6,418,009	6,754,545	6,780,129
EBITDA	250,917	179,846	164,542	484,480	507,269	564,734	719,707	823,074
Depn & Amortn	164,373	107,740	52,533	224,000	232,000	244,000	250,000	251,000
Income Before Taxes	51,523	48,621	100,772	207,962	212,689	257,675	408,784	510,768
Income Taxes	8,130	10,690	22,170	37,730	(7,800)	88,500	140,770	179,480
Net Income	43,393	37,931	78,602	170,263	221,324	169,220	269,370	331,853
Average Shares	24,913	25,584	26,315	27,312	29,487	34,308	39,005	42,603
Balance Sheet								
Current Assets	2,179,984	1,867,881	2,094,944	1,770,532	1,729,851	1,837,921	1,668,883	1,888,442
Total Assets	3,800,063	3,512,079	3,778,988	3,431,369	3,673,169	3,888,136	3,865,625	4,170,071
Current Liabilities	1,330,949	1,006,232	1,179,346	933,535	1,039,701	976,517	751,216	885,323
Long-Term Obligations	566,703	566,981	567,229	567,235	568,309	730,094	822,054	820,704
Total Liabilities	2,187,680	1,866,235	2,042,080	1,752,988	1,965,014	2,170,719	2,070,320	2,150,801
Stockholders' Equity	1,612,383	1,645,844	1,736,908	1,678,381	1,708,155	1,717,417	1,795,305	2,019,270
Shares Outstanding	24,700	24,983	25,739	26,348	28,106	32,157	35,920	41,192
Statistical Record								
Return on Assets %	3.30	3.68	4.45	4.81	5.76	4.38	6.72	8.10
Return on Equity %	7.94	7.86	9.85	10.08	12.71	9.66	14.16	16.59
EBITDA Margin %	5.73	6.08	10.98	7.45	7.90	8.80	10.66	12.14
Net Margin %	0.99	1.28	5.25	2.62	3.45	2.64	3.99	4.89
Asset Turnover	1.65	1.82	1.72	1.84	1.67	1.66	1.69	1.65
Current Ratio	1.64	1.86	1.78	1.90	1.66	1.88	2.22	2.13
Debt to Equity	0.35	0.34	0.33	0.34	0.33	0.43	0.46	0.41
Price Range	81.62-54.95	93.05-56.08	97.51-56.08	97.51-56.08	78.87-46.93	87.74-54.65	142.22-61.24	125.81-83.60
P/E Ratio	17.11-11.52	19.30-11.63	15.45-8.89	15.65-9.00	10.50-6.25	17.80-11.09	20.58-8.86	16.15-10.73
Average Yield %	0.68	0.58	0.54	0.53	0.60	0.42	0.26	0.22

Address: 1600 Cantrell Road, Little Rock, AR 72201
Telephone: 501-376-5200

Web Site: www.dillards.com
Officers: William T. Dillard - Chairman, Chief Executive Officer Alex Dillard - President

Auditors: KPMG LLP
Investor Contact: 501-376-5965
Transfer Agents: Registrar and Transfer Company, Cranford, NJ

DISCOVER FINANCIAL SERVICES

Exchange	Symbol	Price	52Wk Range	Yield	P/E
NYS	DFS	$84.82 (12/31/2019)	92.91-58.41	2.07	9.58

*7 Year Price Score 103.02 *NYSE Composite Index=100 *12 Month Price Score 102.34

Interim Earnings (Per Share)

Qtr.	Mar	Jun	Sep	Dec
2016	1.35	1.47	1.56	1.41
2017	1.43	1.40	1.59	1.00
2018	1.82	1.91	2.05	2.02
2019	2.15	2.32	2.36	...

Interim Dividends (Per Share)

Amt	Decl	Ex	Rec	Pay
0.40Q	01/17/2019	02/20/2019	02/21/2019	03/07/2019
0.40Q	04/18/2019	05/23/2019	05/24/2019	06/06/2019
0.44Q	07/18/2019	08/21/2019	08/22/2019	09/05/2019
0.44Q	10/17/2019	11/20/2019	11/21/2019	12/05/2019

Indicated Div: $1.76

Valuation Analysis / **Institutional Holding**

Valuation Analysis		Institutional Holding	
Forecast EPS	$9.08	No of Institutions	1210
	(01/17/2020)		
Market Cap	$26.7 Billion	Shares	
Book Value	$11.7 Billion	356,376,704	
Price/Book	2.28	% Held	
Price/Sales	1.93	72.42	

Business Summary: Credit & Lending (MIC: 5.4.1 SIC: 6141 NAIC: 522210)

Discover Financial Services is a bank holding, as well as a financial holding company. Co. manages its business activities in two segments: Direct Banking, which includes consumer banking and lending products, specifically Discover-branded credit cards issued to individuals on the Discover Network and other consumer banking products and services, including student loans, personal loans, home equity loans, and deposit products; and Payment Services, which includes the PULSE network, Diners Club International and its Network Partners business, which provides payment transaction processing and settlement services on the Discover Network.

Recent Developments: For the quarter ended Sep 30 2019, net income increased 6.9% to US$770.0 million from US$720.0 million in the year-earlier quarter. Net interest income increased 8.1% to US$2.40 billion from US$2.22 billion in the year-earlier quarter. Provision for loan losses was US$799.0 million versus US$742.0 million in the prior-year quarter, an increase of 7.7%. Non-interest income fell 0.6% to US$498.0 million from US$501.0 million, while non-interest expense advanced 9.1% to US$1.11 billion.

Prospects: Our evaluation of Discover Financial Services as of October 4th, 2019 is the result of our systematic analysis on three basic characteristics: earnings strength, relative valuation, and recent stock price movement. The company has managed to produce a neutral trend in earnings per share over the past 5 quarters. In addition, recent analyst estimates for the company have been mixed and DFS has posted results that exceeded analysts' expectations. Based on operating earnings yield, the company is undervalued when compared to all of the companies we cover. Share price changes over the past year indicates that DFS will perform well over the near term.

Financial Data
(US$ in Thousands)

	9 Mos	6 Mos	3 Mos	12/31/2018	12/31/2017	12/31/2016	12/31/2015	12/31/2014
Earnings Per Share	8.85	8.54	8.13	7.79	5.42	5.77	5.13	4.90
Cash Flow Per Share	17.33	19.50	19.17	15.09	13.93	10.90	8.82	8.28
Tang Book Value Per Share	34.10	32.91	31.60	30.63	27.69	26.60	24.41	22.58
Dividends Per Share	1.640	1.600	1.550	1.500	1.300	1.160	1.080	0.920
Dividend Payout %	18.53	18.74	19.07	19.26	23.99	20.10	21.05	18.78
Income Statement								
Total Revenue	10,430,000	6,892,000	3,395,000	12,848,000	11,545,000	10,497,000	10,002,000	9,611,000
Income Before Taxes	2,911,000	1,917,000	930,000	3,597,000	3,537,000	3,656,000	3,612,000	3,694,000
Income Taxes	662,000	438,000	204,000	855,000	1,438,000	1,263,000	1,315,000	1,371,000
Net Income	2,249,000	1,479,000	726,000	2,742,000	2,099,000	2,393,000	2,297,000	2,323,000
Average Shares	317,000	323,000	328,000	345,000	374,000	406,000	437,498	463,412
Balance Sheet								
Total Assets	110,786,000	110,707,000	110,720,000	109,553,000	100,087,000	92,308,000	86,936,000	83,126,000
Total Liabilities	99,069,000	99,214,000	99,461,000	98,423,000	89,195,000	80,985,000	75,661,000	71,992,000
Stockholders' Equity	11,717,000	11,493,000	11,259,000	11,130,000	10,892,000	11,323,000	11,275,000	11,134,000
Shares Outstanding	314,981	319,475	325,385	331,445	357,920	388,766	421,678	449,188
Statistical Record								
Return on Assets %	2.71	2.70	2.63	2.62	2.18	2.66	2.70	2.86
Return on Equity %	25.83	25.79	25.32	24.90	18.90	21.12	20.50	21.17
Net Margin %	21.56	21.46	21.38	21.34	18.18	22.80	22.97	24.17
Asset Turnover	0.13	0.13	0.12	0.12	0.12	0.12	0.12	0.12
Price Range	92.91-55.09	82.27-55.09	79.99-55.09	81.31-55.09	77.50-57.66	73.18-43.25	65.49-50.60	66.38-52.21
P/E Ratio	10.50-6.22	9.63-6.45	9.84-6.78	10.44-7.07	14.30-10.64	12.68-7.50	12.77-9.86	13.55-10.66
Average Yield %	2.20	2.20	2.17	2.04	1.99	2.07	1.89	1.52

Address: 2500 Lake Cook Road, Riverwoods, IL 60015 **Telephone:** 224-405-0900	**Web Site:** www.discover.com **Officers:** Lawrence A. Weinbach - Independent Chairman Roger C. Hochschild - President, Chief Executive Officer, Chief Operating Officer	**Auditors:** Deloitte & Touche LLP **Investor Contact:** 224-405-4555 **Transfer Agents:** Computershare, Jersey City, NJ

DISNEY (WALT) CO. (THE)

Exchange	Symbol	Price	52Wk Range	Yield	P/E
NYS	DIS	$144.63 (12/31/2019)	151.64-106.33	1.22	21.78

*7 Year Price Score 107.98 ***NYSE Composite Index=100** ***12 Month Price Score 104.77**

Interim Earnings (Per Share)

Qtr.	Dec	Mar	Jun	Sep
2014-15	1.27	1.23	1.45	0.95
2015-16	1.73	1.30	1.59	1.10
2016-17	1.55	1.50	1.51	1.14
2017-18	2.91	1.95	1.96	1.52
2018-19	1.86	3.55	0.97	0.45

Interim Dividends (Per Share)

Amt	Decl	Ex	Rec	Pay
0.84S	06/26/2018	07/06/2018	07/09/2018	07/26/2018
0.88S	11/28/2018	12/07/2018	12/10/2018	01/10/2019
0.88S	06/26/2019	07/05/2019	07/08/2019	07/25/2019
0.88S	12/04/2019	12/13/2019	12/16/2019	01/16/2020

Indicated Div: $1.76

Valuation Analysis / Institutional Holding

Forecast EPS	$5.42	No of Institutions
	(01/17/2020)	N/A
Market Cap	$257.9 Billion	Shares
Book Value	$88.9 Billion	N/A
Price/Book	2.90	% Held
Price/Sales	3.71	N/A

TRADING VOLUME (thousand shares)

Business Summary: Entertainment (MIC: 2.3.2 SIC: 4841 NAIC: 515210)

Walt Disney is an entertainment company. Co.'s segments are: Media Networks, which includes domestic cable networks, broadcast television network and domestic television stations, and television production and distribution; Parks, Experiences and Products, which includes theme parks and resorts, and consumer products operations; Studio Entertainment, which includes motion picture production and distribution, music production and distribution, and post-production services; and Direct-to-Consumer and International, which includes international television networks and channels, direct-to-consumer streaming services, and other digital content distribution platforms and services.

Recent Developments: For the year ended Sep 28 2019, income from continuing operations decreased 16.5% to US$10.91 billion from US$13.07 billion a year earlier. Net income decreased 11.3% to US$11.58 billion from US$13.07 billion in the prior year. Revenues were US$69.57 billion, up 17.1% from US$59.43 billion the year before. Direct operating expenses rose 28.4% to US$42.02 billion from US$32.73 billion in the comparable period the year before. Indirect operating expenses increased 41.8% to US$16.88 billion from US$11.90 billion in the equivalent prior-year period.

Prospects: Our evaluation of Disney (Walt) Co. as of October 4th, 2019 is the result of our systematic analysis on three basic characteristics: earnings strength, relative valuation, and recent stock price movement. The company has managed to produce a neutral trend in earnings per share over the past 5 quarters. However, recent analyst estimates for the company have been reduced and DIS has posted results that fell short of analysts' expectations. Based on operating earnings yield, the company is fairly valued when compared to all of the companies we cover. Share price changes over the past year indicates that DIS will perform over the near term.

Financial Data
(US$ in Thousands)

	09/28/2019	09/29/2018	09/30/2017	10/01/2016	10/03/2015	09/27/2014	09/28/2013	09/29/2012
Earnings Per Share	6.64	8.36	5.69	5.73	4.90	4.26	3.38	3.13
Cash Flow Per Share	3.62	9.56	7.89	8.13	6.34	5.64	5.29	4.45
Tang Book Value Per Share	N.M.	7.19	1.91	5.33	5.74	5.65	5.96	5.41
Dividends Per Share	1.760	1.680	1.560	1.420	1.810	0.860	0.750	0.600
Dividend Payout %	26.51	20.10	27.42	24.78	36.94	20.19	22.19	19.17
Income Statement								
Total Revenue	69,570,000	59,434,000	55,137,000	55,632,000	52,465,000	48,813,000	45,041,000	42,278,000
EBITDA	19,185,000	18,416,000	16,635,000	16,729,000	15,525,000	13,657,000	11,140,000	10,989,000
Depn & Amortn	4,160,000	3,011,000	2,782,000	2,527,000	2,354,000	2,288,000	2,192,000	1,987,000
Income Before Taxes	14,047,000	14,831,000	13,468,000	13,942,000	13,054,000	11,392,000	8,713,000	8,633,000
Income Taxes	3,031,000	1,663,000	4,422,000	5,078,000	5,016,000	4,242,000	2,984,000	3,087,000
Net Income	11,054,000	12,598,000	8,980,000	9,391,000	8,382,000	7,501,000	6,136,000	5,682,000
Average Shares	1,666,000	1,507,000	1,578,000	1,639,000	1,709,000	1,759,000	1,813,000	1,818,000
Balance Sheet								
Current Assets	28,124,000	16,825,000	15,889,000	16,966,000	16,758,000	15,176,000	14,109,000	13,709,000
Total Assets	193,984,000	98,598,000	95,789,000	92,033,000	88,182,000	84,186,000	81,241,000	74,898,000
Current Liabilities	31,341,000	17,860,000	19,595,000	16,842,000	16,334,000	13,292,000	11,704,000	12,813,000
Long-Term Obligations	38,129,000	17,084,000	19,119,000	16,483,000	12,773,000	12,676,000	13,050,000	10,981,000
Total Liabilities	105,107,000	49,825,000	54,474,000	48,768,000	43,657,000	39,228,000	35,812,000	35,139,000
Stockholders' Equity	88,877,000	48,773,000	41,315,000	43,265,000	44,525,000	44,958,000	45,429,000	39,759,000
Shares Outstanding	1,783,000	1,488,000	1,517,000	1,597,000	1,661,000	1,707,000	1,800,000	1,780,000
Statistical Record								
Return on Assets %	7.58	13.00	9.59	10.45	9.57	9.09	7.88	7.75
Return on Equity %	16.11	28.05	21.29	21.45	18.43	16.64	14.45	14.77
EBITDA Margin %	27.58	30.99	30.17	30.07	29.59	27.98	24.73	25.99
Net Margin %	15.89	21.20	16.29	16.88	15.98	15.37	13.62	13.44
Asset Turnover	0.48	0.61	0.59	0.62	0.60	0.59	0.58	0.58
Current Ratio	0.90	0.94	0.81	1.01	1.03	1.14	1.21	1.07
Debt to Equity	0.43	0.35	0.46	0.38	0.29	0.28	0.29	0.28
Price Range	146.39-100.35	116.94-96.93	115.84-90.83	120.07-88.85	121.69-81.74	90.94-63.59	67.67-47.06	52.92-29.00
P/E Ratio	22.05-15.11	13.99-11.59	20.36-15.96	20.95-15.51	24.83-16.68	21.35-14.93	20.02-13.92	16.91-9.27
Average Yield %	1.42	1.59	1.49	1.41	1.77	1.09	1.24	1.41

Address: 500 South Buena Vista Street, Burbank, CA 91521 **Telephone:** 818-560-1000	**Web Site:** www.disney.com **Officers:** Robert A. (Bob) Iger - Chairman, President, Chief Executive Officer Alan N. Braverman - Senior Executive Vice President, General Counsel, Secretary	**Auditors:** PricewaterhouseCoopers LLP **Investor Contact:** 818-553-7200 **Transfer Agents:** Broadridge Corporate Issuer Solutions, Brentwood, NY

DOLBY LABORATORIES INC

Exchange	Symbol	Price	52Wk Range	Yield	P/E
NYS	DLB	$68.80 (12/31/2019)	69.91-57.38	1.28	28.20

*7 Year Price Score 108.54 *NYSE Composite Index=100 *12 Month Price Score 99.65

Interim Earnings (Per Share)

Qtr.	Dec	Mar	Jun	Sep
2014-15	0.40	0.56	0.34	0.46
2015-16	0.30	0.66	0.62	0.22
2016-17	0.51	0.49	0.73	0.22
2017-18	(0.80)	0.66	0.78	0.47
2018-19	0.93	0.70	0.38	0.43

Interim Dividends (Per Share)

Amt	Decl	Ex	Rec	Pay
0.19Q	01/29/2019	02/11/2019	02/12/2019	02/21/2019
0.19Q	04/30/2019	05/13/2019	05/14/2019	05/22/2019
0.19Q	07/30/2019	08/09/2019	08/12/2019	08/20/2019
0.22Q	11/12/2019	11/25/2019	11/26/2019	12/04/2019

Indicated Div: $0.88

Valuation Analysis / **Institutional Holding**

Forecast EPS	$3.46 (01/11/2020)	No of Institutions 456
Market Cap	$6.9 Billion	Shares
Book Value	$2.3 Billion	67,880,928
Price/Book	2.99	% Held
Price/Sales	5.55	56.98

Business Summary: Manufacturing (MIC: 6.1.1 SIC: 3651 NAIC: 334310)

Dolby Laboratories designs and manufactures audio and imaging products for the cinema, television, broadcast, and entertainment industries. Co. has various licensing models: a two-tier model, an integrated licensing model, a patent licensing model, and collaboration arrangements. Co.'s products include cinema imaging products, cinema audio products, Dolby Conference Phone, Dolby Voice Room, and other products. Co. provides various services to support theatrical and television production for cinema exhibition, broadcast, and home entertainment, including equipment training and maintenance, mixing room alignment, equalization, as well as audio, color, and light image calibration.

Recent Developments: For the year ended Sep 27 2019, net income increased 504.0% to US$255.5 million from US$42.3 million in the prior year. Revenues were US$1.24 billion, up 17.7% from US$1.05 billion the year before. Operating income was US$257.1 million versus US$183.5 million in the prior year, an increase of 40.1%. Direct operating expenses rose 26.1% to US$160.9 million from US$127.6 million in the comparable period the year before. Indirect operating expenses increased 10.8% to US$823.7 million from US$743.5 million in the equivalent prior-year period.

Prospects: Our evaluation of Dolby Laboratories Inc. as of October 4th, 2019 is the result of our systematic analysis on three basic characteristics: earnings strength, relative valuation, and recent stock price movement. The company has enjoyed a very positive trend in earnings per share over the past 5 quarters. However, recent analyst estimates for the company have been unchanged, while DLB has posted results that fell short of analysts' expectations. Based on operating earnings yield, the company is fairly valued when compared to all of the companies we cover. Share price changes over the past year indicates that DLB will perform poorly over the near term.

Financial Data

(US$ in Thousands)	09/27/2019	09/28/2018	09/29/2017	09/30/2016	09/25/2015	09/26/2014	09/27/2013	09/28/2012
Earnings Per Share	2.44	1.14	1.95	1.81	1.75	1.99	1.84	2.46
Cash Flow Per Share	3.23	3.42	3.66	3.49	3.03	3.55	2.70	3.66
Tang Book Value Per Share	17.89	16.25	16.01	14.25	13.58	13.38	11.40	13.41
Dividends Per Share	0.760	0.640	0.560	0.480	0.400	...	4.000	...
Dividend Payout %	31.15	56.14	28.72	26.52	22.86	...	217.39	...
Income Statement								
Total Revenue	1,241,620	1,171,924	1,081,454	1,025,738	970,638	960,176	909,674	926,264
EBITDA	313,058	348,895	300,594	282,345	289,621	310,672	284,773	393,376
Depn & Amortn	55,500	54,800	53,400	52,000	48,200	38,100	37,400	30,600
Income Before Taxes	282,307	312,867	256,644	235,904	245,782	276,099	250,646	368,991
Income Taxes	26,802	190,062	54,217	49,502	62,542	67,379	60,344	103,857
Net Income	255,151	122,246	201,802	185,860	181,390	206,103	189,271	264,302
Average Shares	104,572	106,978	103,286	102,424	103,862	103,632	102,788	107,541
Balance Sheet								
Current Assets	1,381,540	1,301,954	1,011,434	759,730	918,330	1,005,851	812,722	970,286
Total Assets	2,821,749	2,659,269	2,533,554	2,310,106	2,133,293	1,984,012	1,737,945	1,960,798
Current Liabilities	306,853	272,127	245,773	213,083	209,681	189,370	172,815	156,840
Total Liabilities	514,398	469,718	396,812	339,850	326,225	273,995	256,835	240,529
Stockholders' Equity	2,307,351	2,189,551	2,136,742	1,970,256	1,807,068	1,710,017	1,481,110	1,720,269
Shares Outstanding	100,141	103,239	102,155	101,422	101,034	102,268	101,739	103,095
Statistical Record								
Return on Assets %	9.34	4.72	8.36	8.23	8.84	11.11	10.26	13.78
Return on Equity %	11.38	5.67	9.85	9.68	10.34	12.95	11.86	15.66
EBITDA Margin %	25.21	29.77	27.80	27.53	29.84	32.36	31.30	42.47
Net Margin %	20.55	10.43	18.66	18.12	18.69	21.47	20.81	28.53
Asset Turnover	0.45	0.45	0.45	0.45	0.47	0.52	0.49	0.48
Current Ratio	4.50	4.78	4.12	3.57	4.38	5.31	4.70	6.19
Price Range	71.58-57.38	71.83-57.38	59.07-45.19	54.54-30.50	45.99-30.91	46.93-34.39	35.60-28.98	45.11-26.28
P/E Ratio	29.34-23.52	63.01-50.33	30.29-23.17	30.13-16.85	26.28-17.66	23.58-17.28	19.35-15.75	18.34-10.68
Average Yield %	1.18	1.00	1.11	1.15	1.02	...	12.23	...

Address: 1275 Market Street, San Francisco, CA 94103-1410 Telephone: 415-558-0200	Web Site: www.dolby.com Officers: Peter Gotcher - Chairman Kevin J. Yeaman - President, Chief Executive Officer	Auditors: KPMG LLP Transfer Agents: Computershare Trust Company, N.A., Providence, RI

DOLLAR GENERAL CORP

Exchange	Symbol	Price	52Wk Range	Yield	P/E
NYS	DG	$155.98 (12/31/2019)	165.80-107.71	0.82	24.45

*7 Year Price Score 136.56 ***NYSE Composite Index=100** ***12 Month Price Score 108.66**

Interim Earnings (Per Share)

Qtr.	Apr	Jul	Oct	Jan
2016-17	1.03	1.08	0.84	1.48
2017-18	1.02	1.08	0.93	2.61
2018-19	1.36	1.52	1.26	1.83
2019-20	1.48	1.65	1.42	...

Interim Dividends (Per Share)

Amt	Decl	Ex	Rec	Pay
0.32Q	03/13/2019	04/08/2019	04/09/2019	04/23/2019
0.32Q	05/29/2019	07/08/2019	07/09/2019	07/23/2019
0.32Q	08/28/2019	10/07/2019	10/08/2019	10/22/2019
0.32Q	12/04/2019	01/06/2020	01/07/2020	01/21/2020

Indicated Div: $1.28

Valuation Analysis

		Institutional Holding	
Forecast EPS	$6.65	No of Institutions	
	(01/16/2020)	1147	
Market Cap	$39.7 Billion	Shares	
Book Value	$6.6 Billion	285,655,264	
Price/Book	5.97	% Held	
Price/Sales	1.46	N/A	

Business Summary: Retail - General Merchandise/Department Stores (MIC: 2.1.1 SIC: 5331 NAIC: 452990)

Dollar General is a discount retailer. Co.'s consumables products includes paper and cleaning products, packaged food, perishables, snacks, health and beauty, pet, and tobacco products. Co.'s seasonal products include decorations, toys, batteries, small electronics, greeting cards, stationery, prepaid phones and accessories, gardening supplies, hardware, automotive and home office supplies. Co.'s home products include kitchen supplies, cookware, small appliances, light bulbs, storage containers, frames, candles, craft supplies and kitchen, bed and bath soft goods. Co.'s apparel includes casual everyday apparel, as well as socks, underwear, disposable diapers, shoes and accessories.

Recent Developments: For the quarter ended Nov 1 2019, net income increased 9.4% to US$365.6 million from US$334.1 million in the year-earlier quarter. Revenues were US$6.99 billion, up 8.9% from US$6.42 billion the year before. Operating income was US$491.4 million versus US$442.1 million in the prior-year quarter, an increase of 11.1%. Direct operating expenses rose 8.9% to US$4.93 billion from US$4.52 billion in the comparable period the year before. Indirect operating expenses increased 8.3% to US$1.57 billion from US$1.45 billion in the equivalent prior-year period.

Prospects: Our evaluation of Dollar General Inc. as of October 4th, 2019 is the result of our systematic analysis on three basic characteristics: earnings strength, relative valuation, and recent stock price movement. The company has managed to produce a neutral trend in earnings per share over the past 5 quarters. However, recent analyst estimates for the company have been raised and DG has posted results that exceeded analysts' expectations. Based on operating earnings yield, the company is fairly valued when compared to all of the companies we cover. Share price changes over the past year indicates that DG will perform over the near term.

Financial Data

(US$ in Thousands)	9 Mos	6 Mos	3 Mos	02/01/2019	02/02/2018	02/03/2017	01/29/2016	01/30/2015
Earnings Per Share	6.38	6.22	6.09	5.97	5.63	4.43	3.95	3.49
Cash Flow Per Share	8.95	8.44	8.37	8.11	6.63	5.61	4.69	4.33
Tang Book Value Per Share	4.36	4.71	4.00	3.39	2.18	N.M.	N.M.	0.56
Dividends Per Share	1.250	1.220	1.190	1.160	1.040	1.000	0.880	...
Dividend Payout %	19.59	19.61	19.54	19.43	18.47	22.57	22.28	...
Income Statement								
Total Revenue	20,596,331	13,604,938	6,623,185	25,625,043	23,470,967	21,986,598	20,368,562	18,909,588
EBITDA	1,953,807	1,335,920	634,722	2,569,387	2,407,616	2,441,749	2,290,568	2,104,993
Depn & Amortn	372,378	245,908	122,485	454,100	403,300	378,300	350,600	335,900
Income Before Taxes	1,506,422	1,039,269	486,304	2,015,416	1,907,280	1,965,628	1,853,024	1,680,861
Income Taxes	329,304	227,701	101,291	425,944	368,320	714,495	687,944	615,516
Net Income	1,177,118	811,568	385,013	1,589,472	1,538,960	1,251,133	1,165,080	1,065,345
Average Shares	257,699	259,102	260,265	266,105	273,362	282,261	295,211	305,681
Balance Sheet								
Current Assets	5,068,542	4,919,138	4,583,769	4,663,020	4,247,852	3,677,771	3,432,410	3,532,609
Total Assets	22,412,790	21,917,529	21,304,284	13,204,038	12,516,911	11,672,298	11,257,885	11,224,104
Current Liabilities	4,506,038	4,312,270	3,956,716	3,015,857	2,964,878	2,622,805	1,995,596	1,987,740
Long-Term Obligations	2,762,490	2,573,483	2,732,105	2,862,740	2,604,613	2,710,576	2,969,175	2,639,427
Total Liabilities	15,764,495	15,168,369	14,731,615	6,786,645	6,391,137	6,266,004	5,880,009	5,514,066
Stockholders' Equity	6,648,295	6,749,160	6,572,669	6,417,393	6,125,774	5,406,294	5,377,876	5,710,038
Shares Outstanding	254,600	257,068	258,322	259,511	268,733	275,212	286,694	303,447
Statistical Record								
Return on Assets %	9.35	9.35	9.53	12.39	12.76	10.74	10.39	9.67
Return on Equity %	25.54	24.82	25.13	25.41	26.76	22.83	21.07	19.23
EBITDA Margin %	9.49	9.82	9.58	10.03	10.26	11.11	11.25	11.13
Net Margin %	5.72	5.97	5.81	6.20	6.56	5.69	5.72	5.63
Asset Turnover	1.53	1.53	1.55	2.00	1.95	1.89	1.82	1.72
Current Ratio	1.12	1.14	1.16	1.55	1.43	1.40	1.72	1.78
Debt to Equity	0.42	0.38	0.42	0.45	0.43	0.50	0.55	0.46
Price Range	165.80-98.85	144.97-98.23	126.38-87.48	117.53-86.05	105.34-68.35	96.71-66.97	81.18-60.02	71.29-53.50
P/E Ratio	25.99-15.49	23.31-15.79	20.75-14.36	19.69-14.41	18.71-12.14	21.83-15.12	20.55-15.19	20.43-15.33
Average Yield %	0.97	1.04	1.10	1.13	1.32	1.25	1.21	...

Address: 100 Mission Ridge, Goodlettsville, TN 37072
Telephone: 615-855-4000
Fax: 615-855-5527

Web Site: www.dollargeneral.com
Officers: Michael M. Calbert - Chairman, Chairman (frmr) John W. Garratt - Executive Vice President, Senior Vice President, Chief Financial Officer, Interim Chief Financial Officer

Auditors: Ernst & Young LLP
Investor Contact: 615-855-4000
Transfer Agents: Wells Fargo Bank, N.A., St. Paul, MN

DOMINION ENERGY INC

Exchange	Symbol	Price	52Wk Range	Yield	P/E	Div Acheiver
NYS	D	$82.82 (12/31/2019)	83.46-67.97	4.43	62.27	15 Years

*7 Year Price Score 88.88   ***NYSE Composite Index=100**   ***12 Month Price Score 100.20**

Interim Earnings (Per Share)
Qtr.	Mar	Jun	Sep	Dec
2016	0.88	0.73	1.10	0.73
2017	1.01	0.62	1.03	2.06
2018	0.77	0.69	1.30	0.97
2019	(0.86)	0.05	1.17	...

Interim Dividends (Per Share)
Amt	Decl	Ex	Rec	Pay
0.917Q	01/25/2019	02/28/2019	03/01/2019	03/20/2019
0.917Q	05/07/2019	06/06/2019	06/07/2019	06/20/2019
0.917Q	07/31/2019	09/05/2019	09/06/2019	09/20/2019
0.917Q	10/31/2019	12/05/2019	12/06/2019	12/20/2019

Indicated Div: $3.67 (Div. Reinv. Plan)

Valuation Analysis / Institutional Holding
Forecast EPS	$4.21	No of Institutions
	(01/17/2020)	1820
Market Cap	$68.2 Billion	Shares
Book Value	$29.3 Billion	642,131,136
Price/Book	2.33	% Held
Price/Sales	4.41	82.61

Business Summary: Electric Utilities (MIC: 3.1.1 SIC: 4911 NAIC: 221121)

Dominion Energy is engaged in producing and transporting energy. Co.'s operations are conducted through various subsidiaries, including Virginia Electric and Power Company, which generates, transmits and distributes electricity for sale in Virginia and northeastern North Carolina; and Dominion Energy Gas Holdings, LLC, which conducts business activities through a regulated interstate natural gas transmission pipeline and underground storage system in the Northeast, mid-Atlantic and Midwest states, regulated gas transportation and distribution operations in Ohio, and gas gathering and processing activities primarily in West Virginia, Ohio and Pennsylvania.

Recent Developments: For the quarter ended Sep 30 2019, net income increased 11.6% to US$985.0 million in the year-earlier quarter. Revenues were US$4.27 billion, up 23.7% from US$3.45 billion the year before. Operating income was US$1.31 billion versus US$1.15 billion in the prior-year quarter, an increase of 14.3%. Direct operating expenses rose 22.8% to US$1.95 billion from US$1.59 billion in the comparable period the year before. Indirect operating expenses increased 40.8% to US$1.01 billion from US$715.0 million in the equivalent prior-year period.

Prospects: Our evaluation of Dominion Energy Inc. as of October 4th, 2019 is the result of our systematic analysis on three basic characteristics: earnings strength, relative valuation, and recent stock price movement. The company has managed to produce a neutral trend in earnings per share over the past 5 quarters. In addition, recent analyst estimates for the company have been mixed and D has posted results that exceeded analysts' expectations. Based on operating earnings yield, the company is fairly valued when compared to all of the companies we cover. Share price changes over the past year indicates that D will perform in line with the market over the near term.

Financial Data
(US$ in Thousands)	9 Mos	6 Mos	3 Mos	12/31/2018	12/31/2017	12/31/2016	12/31/2015	12/31/2014
Earnings Per Share	1.33	1.46	2.10	3.74	4.72	3.44	3.20	2.24
Cash Flow Per Share	5.87	5.81	5.94	7.30	7.15	6.68	7.55	5.90
Tang Book Value Per Share	21.79	20.22	21.27	19.13	15.58	12.08	14.77	13.57
Dividends Per Share	3.587	3.505	3.422	3.340	3.035	2.800	2.590	2.400
Dividend Payout %	269.74	240.07	162.98	89.30	64.30	81.40	80.94	107.14
Income Statement								
Total Revenue	12,097,000	7,828,000	3,858,000	13,366,000	12,586,000	11,737,000	11,683,000	12,436,000
EBITDA	4,181,000	1,931,000	640,000	6,902,000	6,497,000	5,726,000	5,401,000	4,531,000
Depn & Amortn	2,235,000	1,472,000	734,000	2,280,000	2,202,000	1,849,000	1,669,000	1,560,000
Income Before Taxes	574,000	(462,000)	(563,000)	3,129,000	3,090,000	2,867,000	2,828,000	1,778,000
Income Taxes	208,000	157,000	114,000	580,000	(30,000)	655,000	905,000	452,000
Net Income	349,000	(626,000)	(680,000)	2,447,000	2,999,000	2,123,000	1,899,000	1,310,000
Average Shares	813,000	802,600	793,100	654,900	636,000	617,100	593,700	584,500
Balance Sheet								
Current Assets	6,269,000	5,727,000	5,975,000	5,161,000	4,334,000	4,248,000	4,191,000	5,615,000
Total Assets	102,359,000	100,822,000	100,054,000	77,914,000	76,585,000	71,610,000	58,797,000	54,327,000
Current Liabilities	12,191,000	9,503,000	9,776,000	7,647,000	9,636,000	8,115,000	8,120,000	7,198,000
Long-Term Obligations	33,635,000	36,648,000	36,861,000	31,144,000	30,948,000	30,231,000	23,616,000	21,805,000
Total Liabilities	73,073,000	73,125,000	73,145,000	57,807,000	59,443,000	57,005,000	46,133,000	42,772,000
Stockholders' Equity	29,286,000	27,697,000	26,909,000	20,107,000	17,142,000	14,605,000	12,664,000	11,555,000
Shares Outstanding	823,000	803,000	802,000	681,000	645,000	628,000	596,000	585,000
Statistical Record								
Return on Assets %	1.09	0.97	1.42	3.17	4.05	3.25	3.36	2.51
Return on Equity %	4.15	3.80	5.67	13.14	18.89	15.53	15.68	11.17
EBITDA Margin %	34.56	24.67	16.59	51.64	51.62	48.79	46.23	36.43
Net Margin %	2.89	N.M.	N.M.	18.31	23.83	18.09	16.25	10.53
Asset Turnover	0.17	0.16	0.16	0.17	0.17	0.18	0.21	0.24
Current Ratio	0.51	0.60	0.61	0.67	0.45	0.52	0.52	0.78
Debt to Equity	1.15	1.32	1.37	1.55	1.81	2.07	1.86	1.89
Price Range	81.04-67.97	79.22-67.97	77.04-61.75	80.28-61.75	84.91-71.68	78.92-67.47	79.27-64.89	80.23-63.51
P/E Ratio	60.93-51.11	54.26-46.55	36.69-29.40	21.47-16.51	17.99-15.19	22.94-19.61	24.77-20.28	35.82-28.35
Average Yield %	4.79	4.78	4.86	4.73	3.88	3.82	3.65	3.43

Address: 120 Tredegar Street, Richmond, VA 23219	**Web Site:** www.dom.com	**Auditors:** DELOITTE & TOUCHE LLP
Telephone: 804-819-2000	**Officers:** Thomas F. Farrell - Chairman, President, Chief Executive Officer Robert M. Blue - Executive	**Investor Contact:** 804-819-2205
Fax: 804-775-5819	Vice President, Co-Chief Operating Officer, Division Officer	**Transfer Agents:** Dominion Resources Services, Inc. Richmond, VA

DOMINOS PIZZA INC.

Exchange	Symbol	Price	52Wk Range	Yield	P/E
NYS	DPZ	$293.78 (12/31/2019)	296.65-222.45	0.89	32.43

*7 Year Price Score 140.38 ***NYSE Composite Index=100** ***12 Month Price Score 102.44**

Interim Earnings (Per Share)

Qtr.	Mar	Jun	Sep	Dec
2017	1.26	1.32	1.18	2.07
2018	2.00	1.78	1.95	2.62
2019	2.20	2.19	2.05	…

Interim Dividends (Per Share)

Amt	Decl	Ex	Rec	Pay
0.65Q	02/20/2019	03/14/2019	03/15/2019	03/29/2019
0.65Q	04/23/2019	06/13/2019	06/14/2019	06/28/2019
0.65Q	07/10/2019	09/12/2019	09/13/2019	09/30/2019
0.65Q	10/04/2019	12/12/2019	12/13/2019	12/27/2019

Indicated Div: $2.60 (Div. Reinv. Plan)

Valuation Analysis | **Institutional Holding**

Forecast EPS	$9.42	No of Institutions
	(01/17/2020)	661
Market Cap	$12.0 Billion	Shares
Book Value	N/A	53,373,592
Price/Book	N/A	% Held
Price/Sales	3.38	96.12

Business Summary: Hotels, Restaurants & Travel (MIC: 2.2.1 SIC: 5812 NAIC: 722211)

Domino's Pizza is involved in the: retail sales of food through Co.-owned Domino's Pizza stores; sales of food, equipment and supplies to Co.-owned and franchised Domino's Pizza stores; and receipt of royalties, advertising contributions and fees from U.S. Domino's Pizza franchisees. Co.'s menu features pizza products with varying sizes and crust types. Co.'s typical store also provides oven-baked sandwiches, pasta, boneless chicken and wings, bread side items, desserts and soft drink products. International markets vary toppings by country and culture, such as squid topping in Japan, and feature regional specialty items, such as a banana and cinnamon dessert pizza in Brazil.

Recent Developments: For the quarter ended Sep 8 2019, net income increased 2.7% to US$86.4 million from US$84.1 million in the year-earlier quarter. Revenues were US$820.8 million, up 4.4% from US$786.0 million the year before. Operating income was US$143.0 million versus US$132.4 million in the prior-year quarter, an increase of 8.0%. Direct operating expenses rose 2.8% to US$504.6 million from US$490.7 million in the comparable period the year before. Indirect operating expenses increased 6.4% to US$173.2 million from US$162.8 million in the equivalent prior-year period.

Prospects: Our evaluation of Dominos Pizza Inc. as of October 4th, 2019 is the result of our systematic analysis on three basic characteristics: earnings strength, relative valuation, and recent stock price movement. The company has managed to produce a neutral trend in earnings per share over the past 5 quarters. However, recent analyst estimates for the company have been reduced while DPZ has posted results that exceeded analysts' expectations. Based on operating earnings yield, the company is fairly valued when compared to all of the companies we cover. Share price changes over the past year indicates that DPZ will perform in line with the market over the near term.

Financial Data
(US$ in Thousands)

	9 Mos	6 Mos	3 Mos	12/30/2018	12/31/2017	01/01/2017	01/03/2016	12/28/2014
Earnings Per Share	9.06	8.96	8.55	8.35	5.83	4.30	3.47	2.86
Cash Flow Per Share	11.14	10.75	9.97	9.44	7.38	5.92	5.33	3.51
Dividends Per Share	2.400	2.400	2.300	2.200	1.840	1.520	1.240	1.000
Dividend Payout %	26.49	26.79	26.90	26.35	31.56	35.35	35.73	34.97
Income Statement								
Total Revenue	2,468,422	1,647,610	835,963	3,432,867	2,787,979	2,472,628	2,216,528	1,993,833
EBITDA	428,744	284,625	144,605	633,387	576,577	498,600	450,266	386,895
Depn & Amortn	3,288	2,198	1,101	61,698	55,345	44,558	44,827	41,534
Income Before Taxes	325,367	215,122	109,143	428,678	400,153	344,658	306,215	258,623
Income Taxes	53,985	30,113	16,493	66,706	122,248	129,980	113,426	96,036
Net Income	271,382	185,009	92,650	361,972	277,905	214,678	192,789	162,587
Average Shares	42,040	42,236	42,202	43,331	47,677	49,923	55,532	56,931
Balance Sheet								
Current Assets	605,339	643,447	590,543	566,951	579,780	495,873	602,637	428,361
Total Assets	1,160,272	1,177,167	1,148,275	907,385	836,753	716,295	799,845	619,280
Current Liabilities	421,245	412,906	412,013	379,743	398,285	403,698	375,983	265,608
Long-Term Obligations	3,407,101	3,414,988	3,447,819	3,495,691	3,121,490	2,148,990	2,181,460	1,523,546
Total Liabilities	4,095,921	4,081,453	4,123,440	3,947,306	3,572,137	2,599,438	2,600,096	1,838,745
Stockholders' Equity	(2,935,649)	(2,904,286)	(2,975,165)	(3,039,921)	(2,735,384)	(1,883,143)	(1,800,251)	(1,219,465)
Shares Outstanding	40,898	41,232	41,083	40,977	42,898	48,100	49,838	55,553
Statistical Record								
Return on Assets %	36.96	35.72	37.58	41.62	35.79	28.40	26.73	28.49
EBITDA Margin %	17.37	17.28	17.30	18.45	20.68	20.16	20.31	19.40
Net Margin %	10.99	11.23	11.08	10.54	9.97	8.68	8.70	8.15
Asset Turnover	3.43	3.30	3.58	3.95	3.59	3.27	3.07	3.49
Current Ratio	1.44	1.56	1.43	1.49	1.46	1.23	1.60	1.61
Price Range	294.86-222.45	300.67-234.35	300.67-230.32	300.67-186.94	218.88-158.36	172.26-104.16	119.43-94.17	95.93-67.17
P/E Ratio	32.55-24.55	33.56-26.16	35.17-26.94	36.01-22.39	37.54-27.16	40.06-24.22	34.42-27.14	33.54-23.49
Average Yield %	0.91	0.89	0.87	0.86	0.97	1.09	1.16	1.29

Address: 30 Frank Lloyd Wright Drive, Ann Arbor, MI 48105
Telephone: 734-930-3030

Web Site: www.dominos.com
Officers: David A. Brandon - Chairman, Chief Executive Officer Richard E. Allison - Chief Executive Officer, Division Officer, Executive Vice President

Auditors: PricewaterhouseCoopers LLP
Investor Contact: 734-930-3008
Transfer Agents: ComputerShare Investor Services, Providence, RI

DOMTAR CORP

Exchange	Symbol	Price	52Wk Range	Yield	P/E
NYS	UFS	$49.61 (12/31/2019)	70.60-42.45	3.67	15.31

*7 Year Price Score 88.79 ***NYSE Composite Index=100** ***12 Month Price Score 86.30**

Interim Earnings (Per Share)

Qtr.	Mar	Jun	Sep	Dec
2016	0.06	0.29	0.94	0.75
2017	0.32	0.61	1.11	(6.15)
2018	0.86	0.68	1.57	1.37
2019	1.27	0.28	0.32	...

Interim Dividends (Per Share)

Amt	Decl	Ex	Rec	Pay
0.435Q	02/20/2019	04/01/2019	04/02/2019	04/15/2019
0.455Q	05/08/2019	07/01/2019	07/02/2019	07/16/2019
0.455Q	08/07/2019	10/01/2019	10/02/2019	10/15/2019
0.455Q	11/06/2019	12/31/2019	01/02/2020	01/15/2020

Indicated Div: $1.82

Valuation Analysis | **Institutional Holding**

Forecast EPS	$3.15 (01/17/2020)	No of Institutions N/A
Market Cap	$2.9 Billion	Shares
Book Value	$2.4 Billion	N/A
Price/Book	1.20	% Held
Price/Sales	0.55	N/A

Business Summary: Paper & Forest Products (MIC: 8.1.2 SIC: 2621 NAIC: 322121)

Domtar is engaged in designing, manufacturing, marketing and distributing a range of fiber-based products such as communication papers, specialty and packaging papers and absorbent hygiene products. Co.'s segments are: Pulp and Paper, which consists of business papers including copy and electronic imaging papers, computer papers, preprinted forms and digital papers, commercial printing and publishing papers including uncoated freesheet papers, specialty and packaging papers, and pulp products such as softwood, fluff and hardwood kraft; and Personal Care, which designs, manufactures, markets and distributes absorbent hygiene products, including adult incontinence and infant diaper products.

Recent Developments: For the quarter ended Sep 30 2019, net income decreased 79.8% to US$20.0 million from US$99.0 million in the year-earlier quarter. Revenues were US$1.28 billion, down 6.1% from US$1.37 billion the year before. Operating income was US$29.0 million versus US$114.0 million in the prior-year quarter, a decrease of 74.6%. Direct operating expenses declined 1.7% to US$1.04 billion from US$1.06 billion in the comparable period the year before. Indirect operating expenses increased 9.8% to US$213.0 million from US$194.0 million in the equivalent prior-year period.

Prospects: Our evaluation of Domtar Corp. as of October 4th, 2019 is the result of our systematic analysis on three basic characteristics: earnings strength, relative valuation, and recent stock price movement. The company has generated a negative trend in earnings per share over the past 5 quarters. In addition, recent analyst estimates for the company have been reduced and UFS has posted results that fell short of analysts' expectations. Based on operating earnings yield, the company is undervalued when compared to all of the companies we cover. Share price changes over the past year indicates that UFS will perform poorly over the near term.

Financial Data

(US$ in Thousands)	9 Mos	6 Mos	3 Mos	12/31/2018	12/31/2017	12/31/2016	12/31/2015	12/31/2014
Earnings Per Share	3.24	4.49	4.89	4.48	(4.11)	2.04	2.24	6.64
Cash Flow Per Share	8.11	7.32	8.24	8.81	7.16	7.41	7.16	9.78
Tang Book Value Per Share	31.70	32.32	32.03	30.85	29.51	24.25	24.06	25.96
Dividends Per Share	1.760	1.740	1.305	1.740	1.660	1.645	1.600	1.400
Dividend Payout %	54.32	38.75	26.69	38.84	...	80.64	71.43	21.08
Income Statement								
Total Revenue	3,976,000	2,693,000	1,376,000	5,455,000	5,157,000	5,098,000	5,264,000	5,563,000
EBITDA	404,000	301,000	191,000	693,000	(15,000)	552,000	628,000	727,000
Depn & Amortn	219,000	147,000	73,000	289,000	302,000	329,000	340,000	363,000
Income Before Taxes	147,000	128,000	105,000	342,000	(383,000)	157,000	156,000	261,000
Income Taxes	28,000	29,000	24,000	57,000	(125,000)	29,000	14,000	(170,000)
Net Income	118,000	98,000	80,000	283,000	(258,000)	128,000	142,000	431,000
Average Shares	61,700	63,300	63,200	63,100	62,700	62,700	63,400	64,900
Balance Sheet								
Current Assets	1,600,000	1,630,000	1,652,000	1,589,000	1,657,000	1,568,000	1,554,000	1,670,000
Total Assets	4,884,000	4,993,000	5,022,000	4,925,000	5,212,000	5,680,000	5,663,000	6,185,000
Current Liabilities	702,000	740,000	753,000	783,000	741,000	753,000	788,000	926,000
Long-Term Obligations	938,000	824,000	853,000	853,000	1,129,000	1,218,000	1,219,000	1,181,000
Total Liabilities	2,445,000	2,374,000	2,414,000	2,387,000	2,729,000	3,004,000	3,011,000	3,295,000
Stockholders' Equity	2,439,000	2,619,000	2,608,000	2,538,000	2,483,000	2,676,000	2,652,000	2,890,000
Shares Outstanding	59,023	62,906	63,100	62,914	62,695	62,588	62,849	64,010
Statistical Record								
Return on Assets %	4.07	5.60	6.07	5.58	N.M.	2.25	2.40	6.92
Return on Equity %	8.21	11.19	12.12	11.27	N.M.	4.79	5.12	15.20
EBITDA Margin %	10.16	11.18	13.88	12.70	N.M.	10.83	11.93	13.07
Net Margin %	2.97	3.64	5.81	5.19	N.M.	2.51	2.70	7.75
Asset Turnover	1.07	1.08	1.08	1.08	0.95	0.90	0.89	0.89
Current Ratio	2.28	2.20	2.19	2.03	2.24	2.08	1.97	1.80
Debt to Equity	0.38	0.31	0.33	0.34	0.45	0.46	0.46	0.41
Price Range	70.60-42.45	70.92-46.95	70.92-46.95	70.92-47.31	63.91-47.33	54.86-42.41	59.49-44.24	63.73-37.66
P/E Ratio	21.79-13.10	15.80-10.46	14.50-9.60	15.83-10.56	...	26.89-20.79	26.56-19.75	9.60-5.67
Average Yield %	3.05	2.81	2.81	2.12	2.87	3.13	3.37	3.04	2.88

Address: 234 Kingsley Park Drive, Fort Mill, SC 29715 Telephone: 803-802-7500	Web Site: www.domtar.com Officers: John D. Williams - President, Chief Executive Officer Daniel Buron - Senior Vice President, Chief Financial Officer	Auditors: PricewaterhouseCoopers LLP Investor Contact: 514-848-5555 Transfer Agents: ComputerShare Investor Services, Providence, RI

DONALDSON CO. INC.

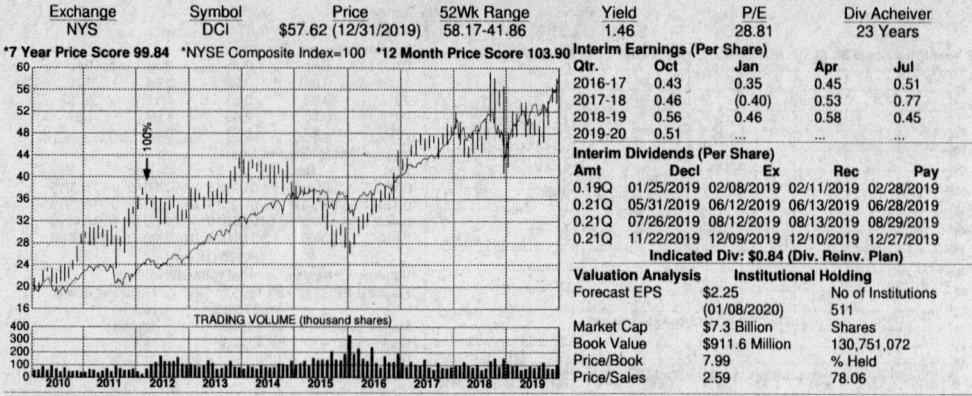

Exchange	Symbol	Price	52Wk Range	Yield	P/E	Div Acheiver
NYS	DCI	$57.62 (12/31/2019)	58.17-41.86	1.46	28.81	23 Years

*7 Year Price Score 99.84 *NYSE Composite Index=100 *12 Month Price Score 103.90

Interim Earnings (Per Share)

Qtr.	Oct	Jan	Apr	Jul
2016-17	0.43	0.35	0.45	0.51
2017-18	0.46	(0.40)	0.53	0.77
2018-19	0.56	0.46	0.58	0.45
2019-20	0.51	...	...	...

Interim Dividends (Per Share)

Amt	Decl	Ex	Rec	Pay
0.19Q	01/25/2019	02/08/2019	02/11/2019	02/28/2019
0.21Q	05/31/2019	06/12/2019	06/13/2019	06/28/2019
0.21Q	07/26/2019	08/12/2019	08/13/2019	08/29/2019
0.21Q	11/22/2019	12/09/2019	12/10/2019	12/27/2019

Indicated Div: $0.84 (Div. Reinv. Plan)

Valuation Analysis

		Institutional Holding	
Forecast EPS	$2.25	No of Institutions	
	(01/08/2020)	511	
Market Cap	$7.3 Billion	Shares	
Book Value	$911.6 Million	130,751,072	
Price/Book	7.99	% Held	
Price/Sales	2.59	78.06	

Business Summary: Industrial Machinery & Equipment (MIC: 7.2.1 SIC: 3564 NAIC: 333411)

Donaldson is a manufacturer of filtration systems and replacement parts. Co. has two operating segments: Engine Products, which consist of replacement filters for both air and liquid filtration applications, air filtration systems, liquid filtration systems for fuel, lube and hydraulic applications, and exhaust and emissions systems and sensors, indicators and monitoring systems; and Industrial Products, which consist of dust, fume and mist collectors, compressed air purification systems, gas and liquid filtration for food, beverage and industrial processes, air filtration systems for gas turbines, polytetrafluoroethylene membrane-based products and air and gas filtration systems.

Recent Developments: For the quarter ended Oct 31 2019, net income decreased 11.9% to US$65.0 million from US$73.8 million in the year-earlier quarter. Revenues were US$672.7 million, down 4.1% from US$701.4 million the year before. Operating income was US$88.7 million versus US$98.7 million in the prior-year quarter, a decrease of 10.1%. Direct operating expenses declined 4.7% to US$441.4 million from US$463.0 million in the comparable period the year before. Indirect operating expenses increased 2.1% to US$142.6 million from US$139.7 million in the equivalent prior-year period.

Prospects: Our evaluation of Donaldson Co. Inc. as of October 4th, 2019 is the result of our systematic analysis on three basic characteristics: earnings strength, relative valuation, and recent stock price movement. The company has generated a negative trend in earnings per share over the past 5 quarters. In addition, recent analyst estimates for the company have been reduced while DCI has posted results that exceeded analysts' expectations. Based on operating earnings yield, the company is fairly valued when compared to all of the companies we cover. Share price changes over the past year indicates that DCI will perform very poorly over the near term.

Financial Data

(US$ in Thousands)	3 Mos	07/31/2019	07/31/2018	07/31/2017	07/31/2016	07/31/2015	07/31/2014	07/31/2013
Earnings Per Share	2.00	2.05	1.36	1.74	1.42	1.49	1.76	1.64
Cash Flow Per Share	2.90	2.70	2.02	2.34	2.13	1.55	2.18	2.13
Tang Book Value Per Share	4.21	4.11	4.50	4.37	3.76	3.81	5.70	6.01
Dividends Per Share	0.800	0.780	0.730	0.700	0.685	0.665	0.575	0.410
Dividend Payout %	40.00	38.05	53.68	40.23	48.24	44.63	32.67	25.00
Income Statement								
Total Revenue	672,700	2,844,900	2,734,200	2,371,900	2,220,300	2,371,213	2,473,466	2,436,948
EBITDA	112,500	468,600	456,000	410,300	346,900	370,660	432,903	417,891
Depn & Amortn	21,200	73,500	71,100	68,800	68,800	66,900	62,000	58,800
Income Before Taxes	86,600	375,200	363,600	322,000	257,400	288,603	360,703	348,181
Income Taxes	21,600	108,000	183,300	89,200	66,600	80,492	100,479	100,804
Net Income	65,000	267,200	180,300	232,800	190,800	208,111	260,224	247,377
Average Shares	128,600	130,300	132,200	134,100	134,800	139,381	147,641	150,455
Balance Sheet								
Current Assets	1,159,100	1,122,600	1,125,700	1,151,000	1,009,700	1,030,716	1,225,277	1,055,662
Total Assets	2,283,300	2,142,600	1,976,600	1,979,700	1,788,600	1,809,534	1,942,411	1,743,556
Current Liabilities	531,100	482,900	469,400	484,100	543,800	560,647	609,580	476,435
Long-Term Obligations	596,800	584,400	499,600	537,300	351,800	389,218	243,726	102,774
Total Liabilities	1,371,700	1,245,300	1,123,600	1,129,600	1,021,200	1,034,765	939,928	658,369
Stockholders' Equity	911,600	897,300	853,000	850,100	767,400	774,769	1,002,483	1,085,187
Shares Outstanding	126,476	127,318	128,772	130,605	132,892	134,598	140,405	146,152
Statistical Record								
Return on Assets %	11.67	12.97	9.11	12.36	10.58	11.09	14.12	14.24
Return on Equity %	29.34	30.53	21.17	28.79	24.68	23.42	24.93	24.80
EBITDA Margin %	16.72	16.47	16.68	17.30	15.62	15.63	17.50	17.15
Net Margin %	9.66	9.39	6.59	9.81	8.59	8.78	10.52	10.15
Asset Turnover	1.27	1.38	1.38	1.26	1.23	1.26	1.34	1.40
Current Ratio	2.18	2.32	2.40	2.38	1.86	1.84	2.01	2.22
Debt to Equity	0.65	0.65	0.59	0.63	0.46	0.50	0.24	0.09
Price Range	56.68-40.71	59.18-40.71	52.18-43.40	47.96-35.64	36.88-26.17	42.91-31.93	43.58-35.15	39.26-32.02
P/E Ratio	28.34-20.36	28.87-19.86	38.37-31.91	27.56-20.48	25.97-18.43	28.80-21.43	24.76-19.97	23.94-19.52
Average Yield %	1.60	1.54	1.56	1.66	2.20	1.75	1.41	1.15

Address: 1400 West 94th Street, Minneapolis, MN 55431
Telephone: 952-887-3131

Web Site: www.donaldson.com
Officers: Tod E. Carpenter - Chairman, President, Chief Executive Officer, Chief Operating Officer, Division Officer Scott J. Robinson - Senior Vice President, Chief Financial Officer, Vice President

Auditors: PricewaterhouseCoopers LLP
Investor Contact: 952-887-3753
Transfer Agents: Wells Fargo Shareowner Services, St. Paul, MN

DOUGLAS EMMETT INC

Exchange	Symbol	Price	52Wk Range	Yield	P/E
NYS	DEI	$43.90 (12/31/2019)	44.80-32.82	2.55	67.54

*7 Year Price Score 101.55 **NYSE Composite Index=100* ***12 Month Price Score 101.03**

Interim Earnings (Per Share)

Qtr.	Mar	Jun	Sep	Dec
2016	0.10	0.12	0.21	0.13
2017	0.12	0.13	0.15	0.17
2018	0.17	0.19	0.18	0.15
2019	0.17	0.20	0.13	...

Interim Dividends (Per Share)

Amt	Decl	Ex	Rec	Pay
0.26Q	03/08/2019	03/28/2019	03/29/2019	04/16/2019
0.26Q	05/30/2019	06/27/2019	06/28/2019	07/12/2019
0.26Q	09/13/2019	09/27/2019	09/30/2019	10/16/2019
0.28Q	12/05/2019	12/30/2019	12/31/2019	01/15/2020

Indicated Div: $1.12

Valuation Analysis / Institutional Holding

Forecast EPS	$0.64	No of Institutions
(01/16/2020)		401
Market Cap	$7.7 Billion	Shares
Book Value	$2.5 Billion	214,753,248
Price/Book	3.14	% Held
Price/Sales	8.38	96.09

Business Summary: REITs (MIC: 5.3.1 SIC: 6798 NAIC: 525930)

Douglas Emmett is a self-administered and self-managed real estate investment trust. Co. owns and operates office and multifamily properties located in premier coastal submarkets in Los Angeles and Honolulu. Co. operates two segments: the acquisition, development, ownership and management of office real estate, and the acquisition, development, ownership and management of multifamily real estate. The services for its office segment include primarily rental of office space and other tenant services, including parking and storage space rental. The services for its multifamily segment include primarily rental of apartments and other tenant services, including parking and storage space rental.

Recent Developments: For the quarter ended Sep 30 2019, net income decreased 33.9% to US$23.4 million from US$35.4 million in the year-earlier quarter. Revenues were US$238.1 million, up 6.6% from US$223.3 million the year before.

Prospects: Our evaluation of Douglas Emmett Inc. as of October 4th, 2019 is the result of our systematic analysis on three basic characteristics: earnings strength, relative valuation, and recent stock price movement. The company has produced a positive trend in earnings per share over the past 5 quarters. However, recent analyst estimates for the company have been mixed and DEI has posted results that exceeded analysts' expectations. Based on operating earnings yield, the company is overvalued when compared to all of the companies we cover. Share price changes over the past year indicates that DEI will perform well over the near term.

Financial Data

(US$ in Thousands)	9 Mos	6 Mos	3 Mos	12/31/2018	12/31/2017	12/31/2016	12/31/2015	12/31/2014
Earnings Per Share	0.65	0.70	0.69	0.68	0.58	0.55	0.39	0.30
Cash Flow Per Share	2.63	2.58	2.63	2.55	2.50	2.27	1.86	1.71
Tang Book Value Per Share	13.95	14.21	13.84	14.08	14.34	12.63	13.07	13.38
Dividends Per Share	1.040	1.030	1.020	1.010	0.940	0.890	0.850	0.810
Dividend Payout %	160.00	147.14	147.83	148.53	162.07	160.65	220.21	270.00
Income Statement								
Total Revenue	692,789	454,720	224,186	881,316	812,052	742,551	635,774	599,539
EBITDA	216,078	145,537	69,026	565,478	520,459	469,013	401,847	380,160
Depn & Amortn	12,256	5,533	2,945	303,464	270,856	241,102	197,639	198,799
Income Before Taxes	96,069	72,648	32,788	128,612	104,427	81,763	68,755	52,854
Net Income	85,155	62,667	28,701	116,086	94,443	85,397	58,384	44,621
Average Shares	175,278	172,498	170,221	169,902	161,230	153,190	150,604	176,221
Balance Sheet								
Current Assets	331,626	443,912	292,710	283,262	294,881	215,036	190,262	102,071
Total Assets	8,520,895	8,677,711	8,215,909	8,261,709	8,292,641	7,613,705	6,066,161	5,954,596
Current Liabilities	232,487	215,378	237,403	277,719	272,395	223,267	157,027	168,196
Long-Term Obligations	4,187,851	4,315,798	4,140,158	4,134,030	4,117,390	4,369,537	3,611,276	3,435,290
Total Liabilities	6,070,025	6,182,559	5,854,211	5,859,377	5,855,117	5,692,562	4,139,950	4,011,138
Stockholders' Equity	2,450,870	2,495,152	2,361,698	2,402,332	2,437,524	1,921,143	1,926,211	1,943,458
Shares Outstanding	175,348	175,222	170,237	170,214	169,564	151,530	146,919	144,869
Statistical Record								
Return on Assets %	1.31	1.40	1.41	1.40	1.19	1.25	0.97	0.76
Return on Equity %	4.51	4.80	4.84	4.80	4.33	4.43	3.02	2.28
EBITDA Margin %	31.19	32.01	30.79	64.16	64.09	63.16	63.21	63.41
Net Margin %	12.29	13.78	12.80	13.17	11.63	11.50	9.18	7.44
Asset Turnover	0.11	0.11	0.11	0.11	0.10	0.11	0.11	0.10
Current Ratio	1.43	2.06	1.23	1.02	1.08	0.96	1.21	0.61
Debt to Equity	1.71	1.73	1.75	1.72	1.69	2.27	1.87	1.77
Price Range	42.86-32.54	42.00-32.54	41.14-32.54	41.08-32.54	41.39-36.46	38.70-24.95	31.79-26.85	29.38-23.29
P/E Ratio	65.94-50.06	60.00-46.49	59.62-47.16	60.41-47.85	71.36-62.86	70.36-45.36	81.51-68.85	97.93-77.63
Average Yield %	2.66	2.68	2.71	2.69	2.42	2.65	2.89	2.96

Address: 1299 Ocean Avenue, Suite 1000, Santa Monica, CA 90401 Telephone: 310-255-7700	Web Site: www.douglasemmett.com Officers: Dan A. Emmett - Chairman Jordan L. Kaplan - President, Chief Executive Officer	Auditors: Ernst & Young LLP Investor Contact: 310-255-7751 Transfer Agents: Computershare Investor Services

DOVER CORP

Exchange	Symbol	Price	52Wk Range	Yield	P/E	Div Acheiver
NYS	DOV	$115.26 (12/31/2019)	115.85-69.79	1.70	26.02	63 Years

*7 Year Price Score 117.13 *NYSE Composite Index=100 *12 Month Price Score 109.13

Interim Earnings (Per Share)

Qtr.	Mar	Jun	Sep	Dec
2016	0.64	0.76	0.83	1.03
2017	1.09	1.04	1.14	1.88
2018	0.84	0.91	1.05	0.96
2019	0.72	1.35	1.40	...

Interim Dividends (Per Share)

Amt	Decl	Ex	Rec	Pay
0.48Q	02/15/2019	02/27/2019	02/28/2019	03/15/2019
0.48Q	05/03/2019	05/30/2019	05/31/2019	06/17/2019
0.49Q	08/01/2019	08/29/2019	08/30/2019	09/16/2019
0.49Q	11/07/2019	11/27/2019	11/29/2019	12/16/2019

Indicated Div: $1.96 (Div. Reinv. Plan)

Valuation Analysis

		Institutional Holding	
Forecast EPS	$5.85	No of Institutions	
	(01/17/2020)	1079	
Market Cap	$16.7 Billion	Shares	
Book Value	$3.0 Billion	165,114,368	
Price/Book	5.55	% Held	
Price/Sales	2.34	80.98	

Business Summary: Industrial Machinery & Equipment (MIC: 7.2.1 SIC: 3559 NAIC: 333319)

Dover is a global manufacturer delivering equipment and components, specialty systems, consumable supplies, software and digital solutions and support services through three operating segments: Engineered Systems, which is focused on the design, manufacture and service of critical equipment and components across its two platforms, the printing and identification and industrials; Fluids, which is focused on the safe handling of critical fluids across the retail fueling, chemical, hygienic, oil and gas and industrial end markets; and Refrigeration and Food Equipment, which is a provider of equipment and systems serving the commercial refrigeration and food equipment end markets.

Recent Developments: For the quarter ended Sep 30 2019, income from continuing operations increased 31.0% to US$206.0 million from US$157.3 million in the year-earlier quarter. Net income increased 31.0% to US$206.0 million from US$157.3 million in the year-earlier quarter. Revenues were US$1.83 billion, up 4.5% from US$1.75 billion the year before. Operating income was US$282.7 million versus US$220.1 million in the prior-year quarter, an increase of 28.5%. Direct operating expenses rose 4.6% to US$1.15 billion from US$1.10 billion in the comparable period the year before. Indirect operating expenses decreased 8.4% to US$390.8 million from US$426.4 million in the equivalent prior-year period.

Prospects: Our evaluation of Dover Corp. as of October 4th, 2019 is the result of our systematic analysis on three basic characteristics: earnings strength, relative valuation, and recent stock price movement. The company has managed to produce a neutral trend in earnings per share over the past 5 quarters. In addition, recent analyst estimates for the company have been mixed and DOV has posted results that exceeded analysts' expectations. Based on operating earnings yield, the company is undervalued when compared to all of the companies we cover. Share price changes over the past year indicates that DOV will perform well over the near term.

Financial Data

(US$ in Thousands)	9 Mos	6 Mos	3 Mos	12/31/2018	12/31/2017	12/31/2016	12/31/2015	12/31/2014
Earnings Per Share	4.43	4.08	3.64	3.75	5.15	3.25	5.46	4.59
Cash Flow Per Share	6.57	5.83	5.37	5.27	5.28	5.54	6.02	5.70
Dividends Per Share	1.930	1.920	1.910	1.900	1.820	1.720	1.640	1.550
Dividend Payout %	43.57	47.06	52.47	50.67	35.34	52.92	30.04	33.77
Income Statement								
Total Revenue	5,360,808	3,535,463	1,724,757	6,992,118	7,830,436	6,794,342	6,956,311	7,752,728
EBITDA	835,225	515,003	201,424	986,181	1,301,834	994,469	1,095,383	1,373,465
Depn & Amortn	97,364	65,219	32,188	138,712	191,285	175,495	167,516	152,079
Income Before Taxes	645,987	388,057	138,318	725,378	973,843	689,332	800,610	1,094,207
Income Taxes	136,191	84,267	32,613	134,233	162,178	180,440	204,729	316,067
Net Income	509,796	303,790	105,705	570,267	811,665	508,892	869,829	775,235
Average Shares	147,051	147,179	146,911	152,133	157,744	156,636	159,172	168,842
Balance Sheet								
Current Assets	2,585,992	2,623,251	2,529,466	2,503,754	3,207,120	2,589,191	2,420,779	2,896,822
Total Assets	8,669,301	8,776,050	8,657,911	8,365,771	10,657,653	10,115,991	8,619,763	9,090,385
Current Liabilities	1,825,302	1,955,115	1,946,922	1,827,421	2,298,193	1,940,318	1,367,182	2,039,354
Long-Term Obligations	2,908,729	2,946,493	2,940,967	2,943,660	2,986,702	3,206,637	2,617,342	2,253,041
Total Liabilities	5,651,659	5,820,779	5,820,458	5,597,105	6,274,473	6,316,245	4,975,188	5,389,660
Stockholders' Equity	3,017,643	2,955,271	2,837,453	2,768,666	4,383,180	3,799,746	3,644,575	3,700,725
Shares Outstanding	145,266	145,437	145,329	144,916	154,823	155,428	155,003	163,011
Statistical Record								
Return on Assets %	7.60	6.99	5.67	6.00	7.81	5.42	9.82	7.78
Return on Equity %	22.59	20.80	14.95	15.95	19.84	13.63	23.68	17.08
EBITDA Margin %	15.58	14.57	11.68	14.10	16.63	14.64	15.75	17.72
Net Margin %	9.51	8.59	6.13	8.16	10.37	7.49	12.50	10.00
Asset Turnover	0.84	0.82	0.74	0.74	0.75	0.72	0.79	0.78
Current Ratio	1.42	1.34	1.30	1.37	1.40	1.33	1.77	1.42
Debt to Equity	0.96	1.00	1.04	1.06	0.68	0.84	0.72	0.61
Price Range	103.39-66.53	100.20-66.53	93.80-66.53	89.36-66.53	81.88-61.62	62.26-42.50	62.77-45.19	73.51-54.69
P/E Ratio	23.34-15.02	24.56-16.31	25.77-18.28	23.83-17.74	15.90-11.97	19.16-13.08	11.50-8.28	16.02-11.92
Average Yield %	2.14	2.22	2.34	2.24	2.36	2.64	3.16	2.35

Address: 3005 Highland Parkway, Downers Grove, IL 60515 **Telephone:** 630-541-1540	**Web Site:** www.dovercorporation.com **Officers:** Michael F. Johnston - Chairman Richard Joseph Tobin - President, Chief Executive Officer	**Auditors:** PricewaterhouseCoopers LLP **Investor Contact:** 212-922-1640 **Transfer Agents:** ComputerShare Investor Services, Providence, RI	

DRIL-QUIP INC

Exchange	Symbol	Price	52Wk Range	Yield	P/E
NYS	DRQ	$46.91 (12/31/2019)	55.63-30.03	N/A	N/A

*7 Year Price Score 55.34 *NYSE Composite Index=100 *12 Month Price Score 95.02

Interim Earnings (Per Share)

Qtr.	Mar	Jun	Sep	Dec
2016	0.97	0.96	0.51	0.03
2017	0.00	0.00	(0.78)	(1.91)
2018	(0.20)	(0.08)	(0.28)	(2.02)
2019	(0.17)	0.05	(0.04)	...

Interim Dividends (Per Share)

No Dividends Paid

Valuation Analysis

Valuation Analysis		Institutional Holding	
Forecast EPS	$0.01	No of Institutions	
	(00/25/2020)	349	
Market Cap	$1.7 Billion	Shares	
Book Value	$1.1 Billion	51,133,400	
Price/Book	1.55	% Held	
Price/Sales	4.20	111.58	

Business Summary: Equipment & Services (MIC: 9.1.3 SIC: 3533 NAIC: 333132)

Dril-Quip designs, manufactures, sells and services drilling and production equipment that is primarily for use in deepwater, harsh environment and severe service applications. Co.'s principal products consist of subsea and surface wellheads, subsea and surface production trees, subsea control systems and manifolds, mudline hanger systems, connectors and associated pipe, drilling and production riser systems, liner hangers, wellhead connectors, diverters and safety valves. Co. also provides technical advisory assistance on an as-requested basis during installation of its products, as well as rework and reconditioning services for customer-owned Co. products.

Recent Developments: For the quarter ended Sep 30 2019, net loss amounted to US$1.3 million versus a net loss of US$10.4 million in the year-earlier quarter. Revenues were US$108.2 million, up 16.1% from US$93.3 million the year before. Operating income was US$222,000 versus a loss of US$14.1 million in the prior-year quarter. Direct operating expenses rose 6.9% to US$76.0 million from US$71.1 million in the comparable period the year before. Indirect operating expenses decreased 11.7% to US$32.0 million from US$36.2 million in the equivalent prior-year period.

Prospects: Our evaluation of Dril-Quip Inc. as of October 4th, 2019 is the result of our systematic analysis on three basic characteristics: earnings strength, relative valuation, and recent stock price movement. The company has enjoyed a very positive trend in earnings per share over the past 5 quarters. However, recent analyst estimates for the company have been mixed and DRQ has posted results in line with analysts' expectations. Based on operating earnings yield, the company is overvalued when compared to all of the companies we cover. Share price changes over the past year indicates that DRQ will perform poorly over the near term.

Financial Data

(US$ in Thousands)	9 Mos	6 Mos	3 Mos	12/31/2018	12/31/2017	12/31/2016	12/31/2015	12/31/2014
Earnings Per Share	(2.18)	(2.42)	(2.55)	(2.58)	(2.69)	2.47	4.98	5.19
Cash Flow Per Share	0.55	0.91	0.98	1.23	2.88	6.55	4.96	3.74
Tang Book Value Per Share	29.08	29.16	29.08	29.05	31.69	34.19	34.90	31.98
Income Statement								
Total Revenue	306,353	198,125	94,317	384,626	455,469	538,731	844,310	930,957
EBITDA	21,896	13,369	2,753	(89,938)	(30,536)	144,459	279,335	309,948
Depn & Amortn	25,155	16,851	8,356	32,800	38,600	31,600	30,500	31,200
Income Before Taxes	3,185	1,083	(3,718)	(114,989)	(65,644)	115,868	249,771	279,380
Income Taxes	8,864	5,452	2,333	(19,294)	34,995	22,647	57,763	70,668
Net Income	(5,679)	(4,369)	(6,051)	(95,695)	(100,639)	93,221	192,008	208,712
Average Shares	35,559	36,210	35,559	37,075	37,457	37,667	38,531	40,190
Balance Sheet								
Current Assets	878,719	868,143	843,340	852,981	1,008,549	1,056,711	1,124,298	1,127,140
Total Assets	1,205,635	1,201,901	1,183,729	1,192,510	1,399,805	1,461,404	1,428,250	1,449,251
Current Liabilities	96,533	87,097	70,729	82,258	99,911	101,480	100,815	198,642
Total Liabilities	112,963	104,773	88,324	96,348	105,344	104,980	103,792	204,059
Stockholders' Equity	1,092,672	1,097,128	1,095,405	1,096,162	1,294,461	1,356,424	1,324,458	1,245,192
Shares Outstanding	36,180	36,207	36,212	36,264	38,132	37,797	37,951	38,932
Statistical Record								
Return on Assets %	N.M.	N.M.	N.M.	N.M.	N.M.	6.43	13.35	14.68
Return on Equity %	N.M.	N.M.	N.M.	N.M.	N.M.	6.94	14.94	16.78
EBITDA Margin %	7.15	6.75	2.92	N.M.	N.M.	26.81	33.08	33.29
Net Margin %	N.M.	N.M.	N.M.	N.M.	N.M.	17.30	22.74	22.42
Asset Turnover	0.32	0.30	0.29	0.30	0.32	0.37	0.59	0.65
Current Ratio	9.10	9.97	11.92	10.37	10.09	10.41	11.15	5.67
Price Range	55.63-26.85	58.25-26.85	58.25-26.85	58.25-26.85	67.10-36.20	65.65-47.50	80.20-55.11	115.81-70.00
P/E Ratio	...	...	...	...	...	26.58-19.23	16.10-11.07	22.31-13.49

Address: 6401 N. Eldridge Parkway, Houston, TX 77041	**Web Site:** www.dril-quip.com	**Auditors:** PricewaterhouseCoopers LLP
Telephone: 713-939-7711	**Officers:** John V. Lovoi - Chairman Blake T. DeBerry - President, Chief Executive Officer, Senior Vice President	**Investor Contact:** 713-939-7711
Fax: 713-939-8063		**Transfer Agents:** Computershare, Jersey City, NJ

DTE ENERGY CO

Exchange	Symbol	Price	52Wk Range	Yield	P/E
NYS	DTE	$129.87 (12/31/2019)	133.80-107.89	3.12	21.83

*7 Year Price Score 110.63 *NYSE Composite Index=100 *12 Month Price Score 94.41

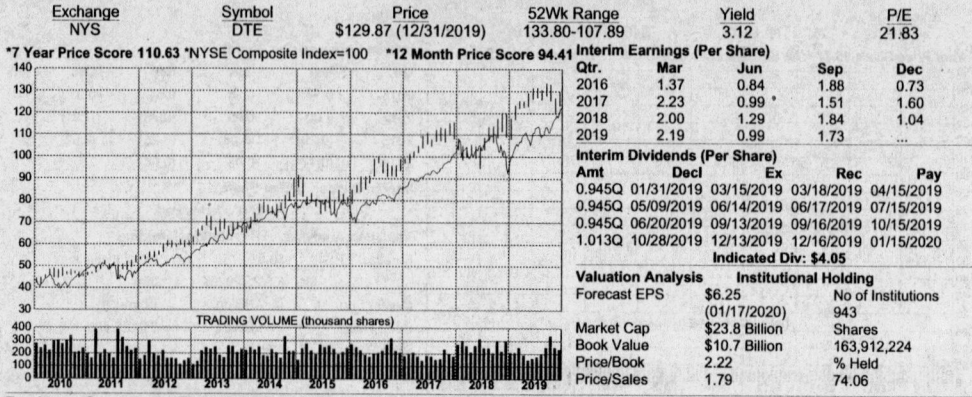

Interim Earnings (Per Share)

Qtr.	Mar	Jun	Sep	Dec
2016	1.37	0.84	1.88	0.73
2017	2.23	0.99	1.51	1.60
2018	2.00	1.29	1.84	1.04
2019	2.19	0.99	1.73	...

Interim Dividends (Per Share)

Amt	Decl	Ex	Rec	Pay
0.945Q	01/31/2019	03/15/2019	03/18/2019	04/15/2019
0.945Q	05/09/2019	06/14/2019	06/17/2019	07/15/2019
0.945Q	06/20/2019	09/13/2019	09/16/2019	10/15/2019
1.013Q	10/28/2019	12/13/2019	12/16/2019	01/15/2020

Indicated Div: $4.05

Valuation Analysis

		Institutional Holding	
Forecast EPS	$6.25	No of Institutions	
	(01/17/2020)	943	
Market Cap	$23.8 Billion	Shares	
Book Value	$10.7 Billion	163,912,224	
Price/Book	2.22	% Held	
Price/Sales	1.79	74.06	

Business Summary: Electric Utilities (MIC: 3.1.1 SIC: 4911 NAIC: 221122)

DTE Energy is a holding company. Co. is engaged in the generation, purchase, distribution and sale of electricity to customers in southeastern Michigan through its DTE Electric Company subsidiary, as well as in the purchase, storage, transportation, distribution and sale of natural gas throughout Michigan and the sale of storage and transportation capacity through its DTE Gas Company subsidiary. Co.'s non-utility operations are: gas storage and pipelines, which consists of natural gas pipeline, gathering, transportation, and storage businesses; power and industrial projects; and energy trading, which consists of energy marketing and trading operations.

Recent Developments: For the quarter ended Sep 30 2019, net income decreased 5.4% to US$317.0 million from US$335.0 million in the year-earlier quarter. Revenues were US$3.12 billion, down 12.1% from US$3.55 billion the year before. Operating income was US$450.0 million versus US$429.0 million in the prior-year quarter, an increase of 4.9%. Direct operating expenses declined 18.0% to US$2.25 billion from US$2.74 billion in the comparable period the year before. Indirect operating expenses increased 11.0% to US$424.0 million from US$382.0 million in the equivalent prior-year period.

Prospects: Our evaluation of DTE Energy Co. as of October 4th, 2019 is the result of our systematic analysis on three basic characteristics: earnings strength, relative valuation, and recent stock price movement. The company has produced a positive trend in earnings per share over the past 5 quarters. However, recent analyst estimates for the company have been mixed and DTE has posted results that fell short of analysts' expectations. Based on operating earnings yield, the company is fairly valued when compared to all of the companies we cover. Share price changes over the past year indicates that DTE will perform well over the near term.

Financial Data

(US$ in Thousands)	9 Mos	6 Mos	3 Mos	12/31/2018	12/31/2017	12/31/2016	12/31/2015	12/31/2014
Earnings Per Share	5.95	6.06	6.36	6.17	6.32	4.83	4.05	5.10
Cash Flow Per Share	13.85	14.28	14.25	14.81	11.83	11.61	10.68	10.39
Tang Book Value Per Share	40.93	39.64	40.42	39.00	35.41	32.79	37.14	35.07
Dividends Per Share	3.780	3.718	3.655	3.600	3.360	3.060	2.840	2.690
Dividend Payout %	63.53	61.34	57.47	58.35	53.16	63.35	70.12	52.75
Income Statement								
Total Revenue	9,521,000	6,402,000	3,514,000	14,212,000	12,607,000	10,630,000	10,337,000	12,301,000
EBITDA	1,528,000	991,000	625,000	1,871,000	1,912,000	1,646,000	1,485,000	1,771,000
Depn & Amortn	45,000	30,000	15,000	108,000	101,000	89,000	98,000	77,000
Income Before Taxes	1,026,000	662,000	462,000	1,216,000	1,287,000	1,105,000	950,000	1,275,000
Income Taxes	122,000	75,000	54,000	98,000	175,000	271,000	230,000	364,000
Net Income	902,000	583,000	401,000	1,120,000	1,134,000	868,000	727,000	905,000
Average Shares	184,000	184,000	183,000	181,000	179,000	179,000	179,000	177,000
Balance Sheet								
Current Assets	2,985,000	2,726,000	2,840,000	3,260,000	3,081,000	2,762,000	2,575,000	3,087,000
Total Assets	38,345,000	36,851,000	36,434,000	36,288,000	33,767,000	32,041,000	28,737,000	27,974,000
Current Liabilities	3,865,000	3,654,000	3,647,000	4,438,000	2,812,000	2,437,000	2,528,000	2,577,000
Long-Term Obligations	13,858,000	13,569,000	12,776,000	12,134,000	12,185,000	11,269,000	8,835,000	8,343,000
Total Liabilities	27,605,000	26,455,000	25,889,000	26,051,000	24,255,000	23,030,000	19,965,000	19,647,000
Stockholders' Equity	10,740,000	10,396,000	10,545,000	10,237,000	9,512,000	9,011,000	8,772,000	8,327,000
Shares Outstanding	183,396	183,301	183,212	181,925	179,386	179,432	179,470	176,991
Statistical Record								
Return on Assets %	2.97	3.11	3.30	3.20	3.45	2.85	2.56	3.36
Return on Equity %	10.44	10.95	11.35	11.34	12.24	9.74	8.50	11.14
EBITDA Margin %	16.05	15.48	17.79	13.16	15.17	15.48	14.37	14.40
Net Margin %	9.47	9.11	11.41	7.88	9.00	8.17	7.03	7.36
Asset Turnover	0.36	0.38	0.40	0.41	0.38	0.35	0.36	0.46
Current Ratio	0.77	0.75	0.78	0.73	1.10	1.13	1.02	1.20
Debt to Equity	1.29	1.31	1.21	1.19	1.28	1.25	1.01	1.00
Price Range	133.80-107.89	131.59-103.15	125.91-94.70	119.95-94.70	115.99-97.10	100.10-78.38	91.54-73.78	90.18-65.10
P/E Ratio	22.49-18.13	21.71-17.02	19.80-14.89	19.44-15.35	18.35-15.36	20.72-16.23	22.60-18.22	17.68-12.76
Average Yield %	3.13	7.21	3.31	3.36	3.15	3.34	3.52	3.55

Address: One Energy Plaza, Detroit, MI 48226-1279
Telephone: 313-235-4000

Web Site: www.dteenergy.com
Officers: Gerard M. Anderson - Executive Chairman, Chairman, President, Chief Executive Officer David E. Meador - Vice-Chairman, Executive Vice President, Chief Financial Officer, Chief Administrative Officer

Auditors: PricewaterhouseCoopers LLP
Investor Contact: 313-235-4000
Transfer Agents: Wells Fargo Bank, N.A.

DUKE ENERGY CORP

Exchange	Symbol	Price	52Wk Range	Yield	P/E	Div Acheiver
NYS	DUK	$91.21 (12/31/2019)	97.17-83.66	4.14	18.88	14 Years

*7 Year Price Score 94.19 *NYSE Composite Index=100 *12 Month Price Score 94.59

Interim Earnings (Per Share)

Qtr.	Mar	Jun	Sep	Dec
2016	1.01	0.74	1.70	(0.33)
2017	1.02	0.98	1.36	1.00
2018	0.88	0.71	1.51	0.65
2019	1.24	1.12	1.82	...

Interim Dividends (Per Share)

Amt	Decl	Ex	Rec	Pay
0.927Q	05/02/2019	05/16/2019	05/17/2019	06/17/2019
0.945Q	07/08/2019	08/15/2019	08/16/2019	09/16/2019
0.945Q	10/25/2019	11/14/2019	11/15/2019	12/16/2019
0.945Q	01/03/2020	02/13/2020	02/14/2020	03/16/2020

Indicated Div: $3.78 (Div. Reinv. Plan)

Valuation Analysis		Institutional Holding	
Forecast EPS	$5.03	No of Institutions	
	(01/17/2020)	2003	
Market Cap	$66.5 Billion	Shares	
Book Value	$46.4 Billion	581,899,840	
Price/Book	1.43	% Held	
Price/Sales	2.65	N/A	

Business Summary: Electric Utilities (MIC: 3.1.1 SIC: 4931 NAIC: 221122)

Duke Energy is a holding company. Through its subsidiaries, Co. operates as an energy company. Co.'s segments include: Electric Utilities and Infrastructure, which provides retail electric service through the generation, transmission, distribution and sale of electricity to customers within the Southeast and Midwest regions of the U.S.; Gas Utilities and Infrastructure, which conducts natural gas operations, as well as owns, operates and has investments in various pipeline transmission and natural gas storage facilities; and Commercial Renewables, which acquires, develops, builds, operates and owns wind and solar renewable generation throughout the continental U.S.

Recent Developments: For the quarter ended Sep 30 2019, income from continuing operations increased 24.6% to US$1.32 billion from US$1.06 billion in the year-earlier quarter. Net income increased 24.1% to US$1.32 billion from US$1.07 billion in the year-earlier quarter. Revenues were US$6.94 billion, up 4.7% from US$6.63 billion the year before. Operating income was US$1.93 billion versus US$1.58 billion in the prior-year quarter, an increase of 22.2%. Direct operating expenses declined 1.8% to US$3.51 billion from US$3.57 billion in the comparable period the year before. Indirect operating expenses increased 1.7% to US$1.50 billion from US$1.48 billion in the equivalent prior-year period.

Prospects: Our evaluation of Duke Energy Corp. Holding Co as of October 4th, 2019 is the result of our systematic analysis on three basic characteristics: earnings strength, relative valuation, and recent stock price movement. The company has enjoyed a very positive trend in earnings per share over the past 5 quarters. However, recent analyst estimates for the company have been mixed and DUK has posted results that exceeded analysts' expectations. Based on operating earnings yield, the company is fairly valued when compared to all of the companies we cover. Share price changes over the past year indicates that DUK will perform well over the near term.

Financial Data

(US$ in Thousands)	9 Mos	6 Mos	3 Mos	12/31/2018	12/31/2017	12/31/2016	12/31/2015	12/31/2014
Earnings Per Share	4.83	4.52	4.11	3.76	4.36	3.11	4.05	2.66
Cash Flow Per Share	9.82	9.53	9.68	10.15	9.48	9.81	9.62	9.32
Tang Book Value Per Share	34.53	34.25	34.00	33.72	31.92	30.87	33.99	34.73
Dividends Per Share	3.728	3.710	3.672	3.635	3.490	3.360	3.240	3.150
Dividend Payout %	77.17	82.08	89.36	96.68	80.05	108.04	80.00	118.42
Income Statement								
Total Revenue	18,976,000	12,036,000	6,163,000	24,521,000	23,565,000	22,743,000	23,459,000	23,925,000
EBITDA	8,739,000	5,358,000	2,726,000	9,760,000	10,166,000	9,524,000	9,256,000	9,076,000
Depn & Amortn	3,831,000	2,483,000	1,238,000	4,696,000	4,046,000	3,880,000	3,613,000	3,507,000
Income Before Taxes	3,251,000	1,790,000	945,000	2,990,000	4,147,000	3,749,000	4,068,000	4,004,000
Income Taxes	424,000	236,000	95,000	448,000	1,196,000	1,156,000	1,326,000	1,669,000
Net Income	3,074,000	1,720,000	900,000	2,666,000	3,059,000	2,152,000	2,816,000	1,883,000
Average Shares	729,000	728,000	727,000	708,000	700,000	691,000	694,000	707,000
Balance Sheet								
Current Assets	9,619,000	9,509,000	9,168,000	9,714,000	8,453,000	8,039,000	8,322,000	11,575,000
Total Assets	155,917,000	153,449,000	151,136,000	145,392,000	137,914,000	132,761,000	121,156,000	120,709,000
Current Liabilities	13,390,000	13,447,000	12,282,000	15,041,000	12,482,000	11,551,000	11,400,000	11,233,000
Long-Term Obligations	56,274,000	55,844,000	55,169,000	51,123,000	49,035,000	45,576,000	37,495,000	37,213,000
Total Liabilities	109,479,000	108,236,000	106,106,000	101,575,000	96,175,000	91,728,000	81,429,000	79,834,000
Stockholders' Equity	46,438,000	45,213,000	45,030,000	43,817,000	41,739,000	41,033,000	39,727,000	40,875,000
Shares Outstanding	729,000	728,000	728,000	727,000	700,000	700,000	688,000	707,000
Statistical Record								
Return on Assets %	2.36	2.22	2.03	1.88	2.26	1.69	2.33	1.60
Return on Equity %	7.89	7.45	6.79	6.23	7.39	5.31	6.99	4.58
EBITDA Margin %	46.05	44.52	44.23	39.80	43.14	41.88	39.46	37.94
Net Margin %	16.20	14.29	14.60	10.87	12.98	9.46	12.00	7.87
Asset Turnover	0.17	0.17	0.17	0.17	0.17	0.18	0.19	0.20
Current Ratio	0.72	0.71	0.75	0.65	0.68	0.70	0.73	1.03
Debt to Equity	1.21	1.24	1.23	1.17	1.17	1.11	0.94	0.91
Price Range	96.28-79.19	91.53-78.09	91.53-72.12	90.90-72.12	91.09-76.50	87.23-71.04	89.36-65.83	86.83-67.13
P/E Ratio	19.93-16.40	20.25-17.28	22.27-17.55	24.18-19.18	20.89-17.55	28.05-22.84	22.06-16.25	32.64-25.24
Average Yield %	4.23	4.33	4.44	4.54	4.15	4.27	4.33	4.27

Address: 550 South Tryon Street, Charlotte, NC 28202-1803	Web Site: www.duke-energy.com	Auditors: Deloitte & Touche LLP
Telephone: 704-382-3853	Officers: Lynn J. Good - Chairman, President, Chief Executive Officer, Vice-Chairman, Group Executive, Chief Financial Officer Steven K. Young - Executive Vice President, Chief Financial Officer, Senior Vice President, Controller, Chief Accounting Officer	Investor Contact: 704-382-4070 Transfer Agents: Duke Energy, Charlotte, NC

DUKE REALTY CORP

Exchange	Symbol	Price	52Wk Range	Yield	P/E
NYS	DRE	$34.67 (12/31/2019)	35.49-25.04	2.71	30.96

*7 Year Price Score 111.61 *NYSE Composite Index=100 *12 Month Price Score 103.17

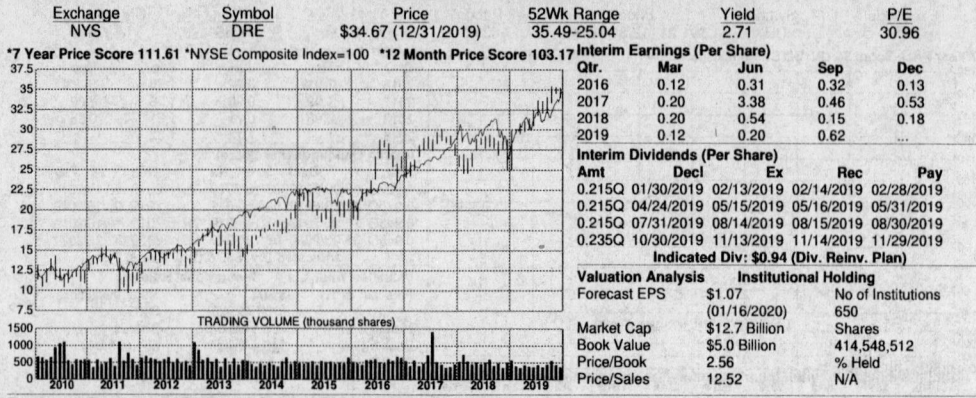

Interim Earnings (Per Share)

Qtr.	Mar	Jun	Sep	Dec
2016	0.12	0.31	0.32	0.13
2017	0.20	3.38	0.46	0.53
2018	0.20	0.54	0.15	0.18
2019	0.12	0.62	...	

Interim Dividends (Per Share)

Amt	Decl	Ex	Rec	Pay
0.215Q	01/30/2019	02/13/2019	02/14/2019	02/28/2019
0.215Q	04/24/2019	05/15/2019	05/16/2019	05/31/2019
0.215Q	07/31/2019	08/14/2019	08/15/2019	08/30/2019
0.235Q	10/30/2019	11/13/2019	11/14/2019	11/29/2019

Indicated Div: $0.94 (Div. Reinv. Plan)

Valuation Analysis		Institutional Holding	
Forecast EPS	$1.07	No of Institutions	
	(01/16/2020)	650	
Market Cap	$12.7 Billion	Shares	
Book Value	$5.0 Billion	414,548,512	
Price/Book	2.56	% Held	
Price/Sales	12.52	N/A	

Business Summary: REITs (MIC: 5.3.1 SIC: 6798 NAIC: 525930)
Duke Realty is a self-administered and self-managed real estate investment trust (REIT) and is the sole general partner of Duke Realty Limited Partnership (Partnership) and its consolidated subsidiaries. Co. and Partnership focuses on the ownership, management and development of bulk distribution (industrial) real estate. Co.'s two reportable operating segments include: the ownership and rental of industrial real estate investments; and the various real estate services such as property management, asset management, maintenance, leasing, development, general contracting and construction management to third-party property owners and joint ventures, as well as Co.'s taxable REIT subsidiary.

Recent Developments: For the quarter ended Sep 30 2019, income from continuing operations increased 328.5% to US$228.4 million from US$53.3 million in the year-earlier quarter. Net income increased 327.0% to US$228.5 million from US$53.5 million in the year-earlier quarter. Revenues were US$241.3 million, up 4.1% from US$231.9 million the year before. Revenues from property income rose 9.4% to US$215.4 million from US$196.9 million in the corresponding quarter a year earlier.

Prospects: Our evaluation of Duke Realty Corp. as of October 4th, 2019 is the result of our systematic analysis on three basic characteristics: earnings strength, relative valuation, and recent stock price movement. The company has managed to produce a neutral trend in earnings per share over the past 5 quarters. In addition, recent analyst estimates for the company have been mixed and DRE has posted results that fell short of analysts' expectations. Based on operating earnings yield, the company is overvalued when compared to all of the companies we cover. Share price changes over the past year indicates that DRE will perform well over the near term.

Financial Data

(US$ in Thousands)	9 Mos	6 Mos	3 Mos	12/31/2018	12/31/2017	12/31/2016	12/31/2015	12/31/2014
Earnings Per Share	1.12	0.65	0.99	1.07	4.56	0.88	1.77	0.60
Cash Flow Per Share	1.43	1.42	1.35	1.35	1.26	1.28	1.10	1.32
Tang Book Value Per Share	13.54	12.87	12.86	12.98	12.72	9.77	9.22	8.31
Dividends Per Share	0.860	0.845	0.830	0.815	1.620	0.730	0.890	0.680
Dividend Payout %	76.79	130.00	83.84	76.17	35.53	82.95	50.28	113.33
Income Statement								
Total Revenue	743,284	501,955	264,929	947,870	780,934	902,244	949,432	1,164,704
EBITDA	647,022	316,947	137,366	694,774	541,813	658,239	611,171	639,454
Depn & Amortn	247,526	162,117	77,554	256,250	242,606	255,419	253,683	290,279
Income Before Taxes	338,627	114,480	40,438	370,752	226,925	265,279	188,581	130,808
Income Taxes	6,465	7,001	385	8,828	(357)	(589)	(3,928)	(844)
Net Income	342,170	115,604	44,551	383,729	1,634,431	312,143	615,310	243,588
Average Shares	367,271	362,926	362,362	363,297	362,011	357,076	352,197	340,446
Balance Sheet								
Current Assets	289,557	172,498	169,096	182,704	193,474	159,375	174,619	211,786
Total Assets	8,262,954	8,014,127	7,962,480	7,804,024	7,388,196	6,772,002	6,917,113	7,754,839
Current Liabilities	231,356	209,192	216,239	226,847	178,939	254,002	263,318	323,687
Long-Term Obligations	2,767,582	2,838,975	2,826,824	2,658,501	2,422,891	2,908,477	3,341,739	4,453,403
Total Liabilities	3,305,021	3,373,530	3,340,870	3,145,823	2,855,352	3,306,184	3,735,181	4,894,514
Stockholders' Equity	4,957,933	4,640,597	4,621,610	4,658,201	4,532,844	3,465,818	3,181,932	2,860,325
Shares Outstanding	366,295	360,625	359,420	358,851	356,361	354,756	345,285	344,112
Statistical Record								
Return on Assets %	5.05	3.00	4.62	5.05	23.08	4.55	8.39	3.14
Return on Equity %	8.43	5.00	7.76	8.35	40.87	9.37	20.37	8.29
EBITDA Margin %	87.05	63.14	51.85	73.30	69.38	72.96	64.37	54.90
Net Margin %	46.03	23.03	16.82	40.48	209.29	34.60	64.81	20.91
Asset Turnover	0.13	0.13	0.13	0.12	0.11	0.13	0.13	0.15
Current Ratio	1.25	0.82	0.78	0.81	1.08	0.63	0.66	0.65
Debt to Equity	0.56	0.61	0.61	0.57	0.53	0.84	1.05	1.56
Price Range	34.10-25.00	32.43-25.00	30.83-25.00	29.39-24.52	30.14-24.04	28.79-18.76	22.58-17.61	20.63-14.53
P/E Ratio	30.45-22.32	49.89-38.46	31.14-25.25	27.47-22.92	6.61-5.27	32.72-21.32	12.76-9.95	34.38-24.22
Average Yield %	2.84	2.34	2.90	2.93	2.97	5.83	3.00	4.40	3.86

Address: 600 East 96th Street, Suite 100, Indianapolis, IN 46240 Telephone: 317-808-6000	Web Site: www.dukerealty.com Officers: James (Jim) B. Connor - Chairman, President, Chief Executive Officer, Senior Executive Vice President, Chief Operating Officer, Region Officer Mark A. Denien - Executive Vice President, Chief Financial Officer, Senior Vice President, Chief Accounting Officer	Auditors: KPMG LLP Investor Contact: 317-808-6060 Transfer Agents: American Stock Transfer & Trust Company, New York, NY

DYCOM INDUSTRIES, INC.

Exchange	Symbol	Price	52Wk Range	Yield	P/E
NYS	DY	$47.15 (12/31/2019)	63.67-40.47	N/A	26.49

*7 Year Price Score 69.46 *NYSE Composite Index=100 *12 Month Price Score 92.15

TRADING VOLUME (thousand shares)

Interim Earnings (Per Share)

Qtr.	Apr	Jul	Oct	Jan
2018-19	0.53	0.94	0.87	(0.37)
2019-20	0.45	0.94	0.76	...

Interim Dividends (Per Share)

No Dividends Paid

Valuation Analysis		Institutional Holding	
Forecast EPS	$2.48	No of Institutions	
	(01/09/2020)	388	
Market Cap	$1.5 Billion	Shares	
Book Value	$880.1 Million	41,175,928	
Price/Book	1.69	% Held	
Price/Sales	0.44	95.97	

Business Summary: Construction Services (MIC: 7.5.4 SIC: 1623 NAIC: 237130)

Dycom Industries is a provider of specialty contracting services. Co. supplies telecommunications providers with a portfolio of specialty services, including program management, engineering, construction, maintenance, installation, and underground facility locating. Co. provides the labor, tools, and equipment necessary to plan, design, engineer, locate, expand, upgrade, install, and maintain the telecommunications infrastructure of its customers. Co. also performs construction and maintenance services for electric and gas utilities and other customers. In addition, Co. provides underground facility locating services for a variety of utility companies, including telecommunication providers.

Recent Developments: For the quarter ended Oct 26 2019, net income decreased 12.9% to US$24.2 million from US$27.8 million in the year-earlier quarter. Revenues were US$884.1 million, up 4.2% from US$848.2 million the year before. Direct operating expenses rose 5.4% to US$724.4 million from US$687.2 million in the comparable period the year before. Indirect operating expenses increased 2.6% to US$117.2 million from US$114.3 million in the equivalent prior-year period.

Prospects: Our evaluation of Dycom Industries Inc. as of October 4th, 2019 is the result of our systematic analysis on three basic characteristics: earnings strength, relative valuation, and recent stock price movement. The company has produced a positive trend in earnings per share over the past 5 quarters. However, recent analyst estimates for the company have been reduced, while DY has posted results that exceeded analysts' expectations. Based on operating earnings yield, the company is fairly valued when compared to all of the companies we cover. Share price changes over the past year indicates that DY will perform poorly over the near term.

Financial Data
(US$ in Thousands)

	9 Mos	6 Mos	3 Mos	01/26/2019	01/27/2018	07/29/2017	07/30/2016	07/25/2015
Earnings Per Share	1.78	1.89	1.89	1.97	2.15	4.92	3.89	2.41
Cash Flow Per Share	0.29	(0.71)	1.39	3.99	10.37	8.20	7.96	4.18
Tang Book Value Per Share	12.98	11.98	10.79	10.10	7.43	5.35	1.57	3.43
Income Statement								
Total Revenue	2,602,079	1,717,964	833,743	3,127,700	1,411,348	3,066,880	2,672,542	2,022,312
EBITDA	275,122	183,028	79,628	289,366	139,071	410,914	346,561	241,940
Depn & Amortn	143,013	94,833	46,917	156,959	72,961	123,125	105,514	79,331
Income Before Taxes	93,870	63,084	20,478	88,038	46,550	250,425	206,327	135,584
Income Taxes	25,466	18,909	6,199	25,131	(22,285)	93,208	77,587	51,260
Net Income	68,404	44,175	14,279	62,907	68,835	157,217	128,740	84,324
Average Shares	31,826	31,820	31,786	31,990	32,054	31,984	33,115	35,026
Balance Sheet								
Current Assets	1,411,930	1,307,847	1,178,515	1,096,440	904,786	938,518	851,234	696,632
Total Assets	2,395,576	2,328,371	2,211,206	2,097,503	1,840,956	1,899,307	1,719,716	1,358,864
Current Liabilities	364,787	356,964	341,655	284,991	259,612	318,538	322,627	226,710
Long-Term Obligations	970,243	932,277	867,376	867,574	733,843	738,265	706,202	521,841
Total Liabilities	1,515,426	1,474,938	1,390,029	1,293,335	1,115,960	1,227,724	1,162,429	851,664
Stockholders' Equity	880,150	853,433	821,177	804,168	724,996	671,583	557,287	507,200
Shares Outstanding	31,520	31,489	31,478	31,430	31,185	31,087	31,420	33,381
Statistical Record								
Return on Assets %	2.49	2.80	2.93	3.20	7.38	8.71	8.23	6.58
Return on Equity %	6.64	7.33	7.65	8.25	19.77	25.66	23.80	17.05
EBITDA Margin %	10.57	10.65	9.55	9.25	9.85	13.40	12.97	11.96
Net Margin %	2.63	2.57	1.71	2.01	4.88	5.13	4.82	4.17
Asset Turnover	1.48	1.55	1.58	1.59	1.51	1.70	1.71	1.58
Current Ratio	3.87	3.66	3.45	3.85	3.49	2.95	2.64	3.07
Debt to Equity	1.10	1.09	1.06	1.08	1.01	1.10	1.27	1.03
Price Range	76.01-40.47	89.93-43.33	116.20-43.33	122.80-49.39	120.60-76.07	108.99-71.34	95.94-48.61	69.62-25.67
P/E Ratio	42.70-22.74	47.58-22.93	61.48-22.93	62.34-25.07	56.09-35.38	22.15-14.50	24.66-12.50	28.89-10.65

Address: 11780 US Highway 1, Suite 600, Palm Beach Gardens, FL 33408	Web Site: www.dycomind.com	Auditors: ProcewaterhouseCoopers LLP
Telephone: 561-627-7171	Officers: Steven E. Nielsen - Chairman, President, Chief Executive Officer Timothy R. Estes - Executive Vice President, Chief Operating Officer	Investor Contact: 561-627-7171
Fax: 561-627-7709		Transfer Agents: American Stock Transfer & Trust Company, New York, NY

EAGLE MATERIALS INC

Exchange	Symbol	Price	52Wk Range	Yield	P/E
NYS	EXP	$90.66 (12/31/2019)	95.44-61.03	0.44	74.31

*7 Year Price Score 82.93 ***NYSE Composite Index=100** ***12 Month Price Score 102.49**

TRADING VOLUME (thousand shares)

Interim Earnings (Per Share)

Qtr.	Jun	Sep	Dec	Mar
2016-17	0.93	1.25	1.17	0.75
2017-18	1.13	1.31	2.08	0.76
2018-19	1.38	1.53	1.24	(2.68)
2019-20	0.94	1.72	...	...

Interim Dividends (Per Share)

Amt	Decl	Ex	Rec	Pay
0.10Q	02/05/2019	04/11/2019	04/12/2019	05/10/2019
0.10Q	05/20/2019	06/20/2019	06/21/2019	07/19/2019
0.10Q	08/08/2019	10/03/2019	10/04/2019	11/08/2019
0.10Q	11/08/2019	12/09/2019	12/10/2019	01/24/2020

Indicated Div: $0.40

Valuation Analysis

		Institutional Holding	
Forecast EPS	$5.40	No of Institutions	
	(01/17/2020)	481	
Market Cap	$3.8 Billion	Shares	
Book Value	$1.0 Billion	51,436,172	
Price/Book	3.73	% Held	
Price/Sales	2.69	83.04	

Business Summary: Construction Materials (MIC: 8.5.1 SIC: 3241 NAIC: 327310)

Eagle Materials, through its subsidiaries, is a supplier of heavy construction materials, light building materials, and materials used for oil and natural gas extraction in the U.S. Co.'s products are commodities that are used in commercial and residential construction; public construction projects; projects to build, expand, and repair roads and highways; and in oil and natural gas extraction. Co.'s business is organized into three sectors: Heavy Materials, which includes the cement and concrete and aggregates segments; Light Materials, which includes the Gypsum wallboard and recycled paperboard segments; and Oil and Gas Proppants, which are used in oil and gas extraction.

Recent Developments: For the quarter ended Sep 30 2019, net income decreased 1.1% to US$71.8 million from US$72.6 million in the year-earlier quarter. Revenues were US$414.5 million, up 8.7% from US$381.5 million the year before. Direct operating expenses rose 9.3% to US$310.0 million from US$283.6 million in the comparable period the year before. Indirect operating expenses amounted to US$159,000 compared with an income of US$679,000 in the equivalent prior-year period.

Prospects: Our evaluation of Eagle Materials Inc. as of October 4th, 2019 is the result of our systematic analysis on three basic characteristics: earnings strength, relative valuation, and recent stock price movement. The company has produced a positive trend in earnings per share over the past 5 quarters. However, recent analyst estimates for the company have been mixed and EXP has posted results that fell short of analysts' expectations. Based on operating earnings yield, the company is undervalued when compared to all of the companies we cover. Share price changes over the past year indicates that EXP will perform in line with the market over the near term.

Financial Data

(US$ in Thousands)	6 Mos	3 Mos	03/31/2019	03/31/2018	03/31/2017	03/31/2016	03/31/2015	03/31/2014
Earnings Per Share	1.22	1.03	1.47	5.28	4.10	3.05	3.71	2.49
Cash Flow Per Share	8.66	7.27	7.51	7.01	6.92	5.36	4.72	3.48
Tang Book Value Per Share	18.74	19.27	21.73	24.41	19.98	18.03	15.91	13.40
Dividends Per Share	0.400	0.400	0.400	0.400	0.400	0.400	0.400	0.400
Dividend Payout %	32.79	38.83	27.21	7.58	9.76	13.11	10.78	16.06
Income Statement								
Total Revenue	785,123	370,597	1,393,241	1,386,520	1,211,220	1,143,492	1,066,368	898,396
EBITDA	202,036	81,944	187,744	365,781	360,764	280,952	289,403	229,575
Depn & Amortn	56,333	27,960	118,200	109,600	86,000	84,200	69,700	67,300
Income Before Taxes	127,282	45,429	41,170	228,543	252,133	180,169	207,960	143,993
Income Taxes	35,974	13,557	10,875	15,330	96,300	66,660	66,074	57,561
Net Income	113,097	41,304	68,860	256,632	198,219	152,592	186,853	124,243
Average Shares	41,833	44,150	46,932	48,645	48,361	50,070	50,372	49,939
Balance Sheet								
Current Assets	487,055	466,517	427,621	458,735	400,624	380,003	366,635	306,960
Total Assets	2,326,211	2,269,078	2,169,163	2,368,003	2,247,124	1,883,635	1,882,591	1,511,529
Current Liabilities	194,775	192,956	179,333	179,329	229,519	120,589	184,576	108,820
Long-Term Obligations	930,426	840,259	655,092	620,922	605,253	499,714	455,714	371,759
Total Liabilities	1,315,456	1,213,812	959,676	950,313	1,043,674	843,104	871,998	680,030
Stockholders' Equity	1,010,755	1,055,266	1,209,487	1,417,690	1,203,450	1,040,531	1,010,593	831,499
Shares Outstanding	41,625	42,924	45,117	48,282	48,453	48,526	50,245	50,053
Statistical Record								
Return on Assets %	1.83	1.87	3.04	11.12	9.60	8.08	11.01	8.32
Return on Equity %	3.52	3.52	5.24	19.58	17.67	14.84	20.29	16.27
EBITDA Margin %	25.73	22.11	13.48	26.38	29.79	24.57	27.14	25.55
Net Margin %	14.41	11.15	4.94	18.51	16.37	13.34	17.52	13.83
Asset Turnover	0.60	0.58	0.61	0.60	0.59	0.61	0.63	0.60
Current Ratio	2.50	2.42	2.38	2.56	1.75	3.15	1.99	2.82
Debt to Equity	0.92	0.80	0.54	0.44	0.50	0.48	0.45	0.45
Price Range	92.70-57.48	109.23-57.48	112.93-57.48	120.30-87.24	108.70-68.78	87.68-46.85	104.73-69.80	90.88-61.72
P/E Ratio	75.98-47.11	106.05-55.81	76.82-39.10	22.78-16.52	26.51-16.78	28.75-15.36	28.23-18.81	36.50-24.79
Average Yield %	0.50	0.49	0.46	0.39	0.46	0.56	0.46	0.54

Address: 5960 Berkshire Lane, Suite 900, Dallas, TX 75225	**Web Site:** www.eaglematerials.com	**Auditors:** Ernst & Young LLP
Telephone: 214-432-2000	**Officers:** Michael R. Nicolais - Chairman, Vice-Chairman Michael Haack - President, Chief Executive Officer, Executive Vice President, Chief Operating Officer	**Investor Contact:** 214-432-2000
Fax: 214-432-2100		**Transfer Agents:** Computershare, Inc., Providence , RI

EASTGROUP PROPERTIES INC

Exchange	Symbol	Price	52Wk Range	Yield	P/E
NYS	EGP	$132.67 (12/31/2019)	137.62-88.69	2.26	53.93

*7 Year Price Score 126.48 *NYSE Composite Index=100 *12 Month Price Score 107.49

Interim Earnings (Per Share)

Qtr.	Mar	Jun	Sep	Dec
2016	0.67	1.35	0.45	0.46
2017	0.38	1.08	0.46	0.51
2018	0.83	0.52	0.64	0.51
2019	0.62	0.73	0.60	...

Interim Dividends (Per Share)

Amt	Decl	Ex	Rec	Pay
0.72Q	03/08/2019	03/28/2019	03/29/2019	04/15/2019
0.72Q	05/23/2019	06/27/2019	06/28/2019	07/15/2019
0.75Q	08/29/2019	09/27/2019	09/30/2019	10/15/2019
0.75Q	12/06/2019	12/27/2019	12/30/2019	01/15/2020

Indicated Div: $3.00

Valuation Analysis

		Institutional Holding	
Forecast EPS	$2.50	No of Institutions	
	(01/17/2020)	414	
Market Cap	$5.1 Billion	Shares	
Book Value	$1.1 Billion		44,662,280
Price/Book	4.61	% Held	
Price/Sales	15.79		95.90

Business Summary: REITs (MIC: 5.3.1 SIC: 6798 NAIC: 525930)

EastGroup Properties is an equity real estate investment trust. Co. is focused on the development, acquisition and operation of industrial properties in key Sunbelt markets throughout the U.S., primarily in the states of Florida, Texas, Arizona, California and North Carolina. Co. has one reportable segment which is industrial properties. These properties are primarily located in key Sunbelt regions of the U.S.

Recent Developments: For the quarter ended Sep 30 2019, net income decreased 2.0% to US$22.6 million from US$23.0 million in the year-earlier quarter. Revenues were US$83.9 million, up 11.4% from US$75.3 million the year before. Revenues from property income rose 11.4% to US$83.9 million from US$75.3 million in the corresponding quarter a year earlier.

Prospects: Our evaluation of EastGroup Properties Inc. as of October 4th, 2019 is the result of our systematic analysis on three basic characteristics: earnings strength, relative valuation, and recent stock price movement. The company has managed to produce a neutral trend in earnings per share over the past 5 quarters. In addition, recent analyst estimates for the company have been mixed and EGP has posted results that fell short of analysts' expectations. Based on operating earnings yield, the company is overvalued when compared to all of the companies we cover. Share price changes over the past year indicates that EGP will perform over the near term.

Financial Data
(US$ in Thousands)

	9 Mos	6 Mos	3 Mos	12/31/2018	12/31/2017	12/31/2016	12/31/2015	12/31/2014
Earnings Per Share	2.46	2.50	2.29	2.49	2.44	2.93	1.49	1.52
Cash Flow Per Share	5.12	5.13	5.06	4.65	4.56	4.25	4.09	3.75
Tang Book Value Per Share	28.36	26.43	24.69	24.37	21.18	18.70	16.73	17.30
Dividends Per Share	2.910	2.880	2.800	2.720	2.520	2.440	2.340	2.220
Dividend Payout %	118.29	115.20	122.27	109.24	103.28	83.28	157.05	146.05
Income Statement								
Total Revenue	244,837	160,899	78,798	300,392	274,150	253,047	235,008	219,829
EBITDA	165,575	111,773	52,118	199,749	187,374	195,100	142,947	141,262
Depn & Amortn	67,303	44,598	20,738	76,007	69,010	63,793	59,882	57,303
Income Before Taxes	72,058	49,483	22,534	88,636	83,589	96,094	48,399	48,473
Net Income	72,053	49,482	22,529	88,506	83,183	95,509	47,866	47,941
Average Shares	37,869	37,019	36,526	35,506	34,047	32,628	32,196	31,452
Balance Sheet								
Current Assets	43,329	42,060	42,515	41,829	37,004	34,830	31,584	29,002
Total Assets	2,400,444	2,295,380	2,171,646	2,131,705	1,953,221	1,825,764	1,666,232	1,575,824
Current Liabilities	122,427	96,381	83,364	86,563	64,967	52,701	44,181	39,439
Long-Term Obligations	1,112,490	1,135,354	1,120,192	1,105,787	1,108,282	1,101,333	1,032,237	933,177
Total Liabilities	1,293,962	1,288,037	1,251,778	1,228,646	1,203,749	1,188,103	1,111,370	1,004,695
Stockholders' Equity	1,106,482	1,007,343	919,868	903,059	749,472	637,661	554,862	571,129
Shares Outstanding	38,409	37,559	36,752	36,501	34,758	33,332	32,421	32,232
Statistical Record								
Return on Assets %	4.04	4.22	3.98	4.33	4.40	5.46	2.95	3.14
Return on Equity %	9.18	9.86	9.73	10.71	11.99	15.97	8.50	8.84
EBITDA Margin %	67.63	69.47	66.14	66.50	68.35	77.10	60.83	64.26
Net Margin %	29.43	30.75	28.59	29.46	30.34	37.74	20.37	21.81
Asset Turnover	0.14	0.15	0.15	0.15	0.15	0.14	0.14	0.14
Current Ratio	0.35	0.44	0.51	0.48	0.57	0.66	0.71	0.74
Debt to Equity	1.01	1.13	1.22	1.22	1.48	1.73	1.86	1.63
Price Range	127.11-88.69	118.19-88.69	112.30-80.99	101.69-78.17	94.97-69.14	75.17-50.11	67.09-52.00	69.50-56.92
P/E Ratio	51.67-36.05	47.28-35.48	49.04-35.37	40.84-31.39	38.92-28.34	25.66-17.10	45.03-34.90	45.72-37.45
Average Yield %	2.67	2.81	2.90	2.97	3.05	3.76	4.01	3.52

Address: 400 W Parkway Place, Suite 100, Ridgeland, MS 39157 **Telephone:** 601-354-3555	**Web Site:** www.eastgroup.net **Officers:** Leland R. Speed - Chairman, Chairman Emeritus David H. Hoster - Chairman, President, Chief Executive Officer	**Auditors:** KPMG LLP **Transfer Agents:** Wells Fargo Shareowner Services, St. Paul, MN

EASTMAN CHEMICAL CO

Exchange	Symbol	Price	52Wk Range	Yield	P/E
NYS	EMN	$79.26 (12/31/2019)	84.60-61.55	3.33	14.28

*7 Year Price Score 78.85   ***NYSE Composite Index=100**   ***12 Month Price Score 98.47**

Interim Earnings (Per Share)

Qtr.	Mar	Jun	Sep	Dec
2016	1.69	1.71	1.56	0.79
2017	1.89	2.00	2.22	3.37
2018	2.00	2.39	2.89	0.28
2019	1.49	1.85	1.93	...

Interim Dividends (Per Share)

Amt	Decl	Ex	Rec	Pay
0.62Q	02/14/2019	03/14/2019	03/15/2019	04/05/2019
0.62Q	05/02/2019	06/14/2019	06/17/2019	07/05/2019
0.62Q	08/01/2019	09/13/2019	09/16/2019	10/04/2019
0.66Q	12/05/2019	12/13/2019	12/16/2019	01/03/2020

Indicated Div: $2.64

Valuation Analysis

	Institutional Holding	
Forecast EPS	$7.00	No of Institutions
	(01/17/2020)	944
Market Cap	$10.8 Billion	Shares
Book Value	$6.0 Billion	133,854,344
Price/Book	1.79	% Held
Price/Sales	1.14	75.48

TRADING VOLUME (thousand shares)

Business Summary: Plastics (MIC: 8.4.2 SIC: 2821 NAIC: 325211)

Eastman Chemical is a global advanced materials and specialty additives company. Co.'s segments include: Additives and Functional Products, which manufactures chemicals for products in the transportation, building and construction, animal nutrition, and other markets; Advanced Materials, which produces and markets polymers, films, and plastics in transportation, consumables, building and construction, durable goods, and health and wellness markets; Chemical Intermediates, which utilizes integration from the cellulose and acetyl, olefins, and alkylamines streams; and Fibers, which manufactures and sells Estron™ acetate tow and Estrobond™ triacetin plasticizers for use in filtration media.

Recent Developments: For the quarter ended Sep 30 2019, net income decreased 35.4% to US$267.0 million from US$413.0 million in the year-earlier quarter. Revenues were US$2.33 billion, down 8.7% from US$2.55 billion the year before. Direct operating expenses declined 3.7% to US$1.75 billion from US$1.82 billion in the comparable period the year before. Indirect operating expenses decreased 0.5% to US$204.0 million from US$205.0 million in the equivalent prior-year period.

Prospects: Our evaluation of Eastman Chemical Co. as of October 4th, 2019 is the result of our systematic analysis on three basic characteristics: earnings strength, relative valuation, and recent stock price movement. The company has generated a negative trend in earnings per share over the past 5 quarters. In addition, recent analyst estimates for the company have been reduced and EMN has posted results that fell short of analysts' expectations. Based on operating earnings yield, the company is undervalued when compared to all of the companies we cover. Share price changes over the past year indicates that EMN will perform very poorly over the near term.

Financial Data

(US$ in Thousands)	9 Mos	6 Mos	3 Mos	12/31/2018	12/31/2017	12/31/2016	12/31/2015	12/31/2014
Earnings Per Share	5.55	6.51	7.05	7.56	9.47	5.75	5.66	4.97
Cash Flow Per Share	11.50	11.26	11.32	10.93	11.44	9.38	10.85	9.42
Dividends Per Share	2.480	2.420	2.360	2.300	2.090	1.890	1.660	1.450
Dividend Payout %	44.68	37.17	33.48	30.42	22.07	32.87	29.33	29.18
Income Statement								
Total Revenue	7,068,000	4,743,000	2,380,000	10,151,000	9,549,000	9,008,000	9,648,000	9,527,000
EBITDA	1,520,000	1,002,000	475,000	1,982,000	1,950,000	1,716,000	1,794,000	1,532,000
Depn & Amortn	462,000	311,000	155,000	437,000	420,000	412,000	402,000	355,000
Income Before Taxes	893,000	580,000	264,000	1,310,000	1,289,000	1,049,000	1,129,000	990,000
Income Taxes	158,000	112,000	55,000	226,000	(99,000)	190,000	275,000	235,000
Net Income	733,000	467,000	209,000	1,080,000	1,384,000	854,000	848,000	751,000
Average Shares	137,800	139,100	140,100	142,900	146,100	148,400	149,800	151,100
Balance Sheet								
Current Assets	3,440,000	3,516,000	3,551,000	3,365,000	3,143,000	2,866,000	2,878,000	3,173,000
Total Assets	16,137,000	16,256,000	16,361,000	15,995,000	15,999,000	15,457,000	15,611,000	16,072,000
Current Liabilities	2,080,000	2,226,000	2,352,000	1,851,000	1,982,000	1,795,000	2,056,000	2,022,000
Long-Term Obligations	5,567,000	5,624,000	5,602,000	5,925,000	6,147,000	6,311,000	6,608,000	7,248,000
Total Liabilities	10,117,000	10,387,000	10,518,000	10,192,000	10,596,000	10,925,000	11,670,000	12,562,000
Stockholders' Equity	6,020,000	5,869,000	5,843,000	5,803,000	5,403,000	4,532,000	3,941,000	3,510,000
Shares Outstanding	135,928	136,943	138,527	139,726	142,915	146,438	147,761	148,596
Statistical Record								
Return on Assets %	4.72	5.62	6.11	6.75	8.80	5.48	5.35	5.38
Return on Equity %	12.85	15.79	17.54	19.28	27.86	20.10	22.76	20.56
EBITDA Margin %	21.51	21.13	19.96	19.53	20.42	19.05	18.59	16.08
Net Margin %	10.37	9.85	8.78	10.64	14.49	9.48	8.79	7.88
Asset Turnover	0.58	0.59	0.61	0.63	0.61	0.58	0.61	0.68
Current Ratio	1.65	1.58	1.51	1.82	1.59	1.60	1.40	1.57
Debt to Equity	0.92	0.96	0.96	1.02	1.14	1.39	1.68	2.06
Price Range	97.36-61.55	103.62-64.92	109.97-67.69	110.84-67.69	93.42-75.92	78.21-58.43	83.75-63.30	90.20-71.49
P/E Ratio	17.54-11.09	15.92-9.97	15.60-9.60	14.66-8.95	9.86-8.02	13.60-10.16	14.80-11.18	18.15-14.38
Average Yield %	3.23	2.89	2.59	2.39	2.49	2.72	2.27	1.75

Address: 200 South Wilcox Drive, Kingsport, TN 37662 Telephone: 423-229-2000	Web Site: www.eastman.com Officers: Mark J. Costa - Chairman, President, Executive Vice President, Chief Executive Officer, Chief Marketing Officer Mark J. Costa - Chairman, President, Executive Vice President, Chief Executive Officer, Chief Marketing Officer	Auditors: PricewaterhouseCoopers LLP Investor Contact: 212-835-1620 Transfer Agents: American Stock Transfer & Trust Company, New York, NY

EATON CORP PLC

Exchange	Symbol	Price	52Wk Range	Yield	P/E
NYS	ETN	$94.72 (12/31/2019)	95.13-66.63	3.00	16.82

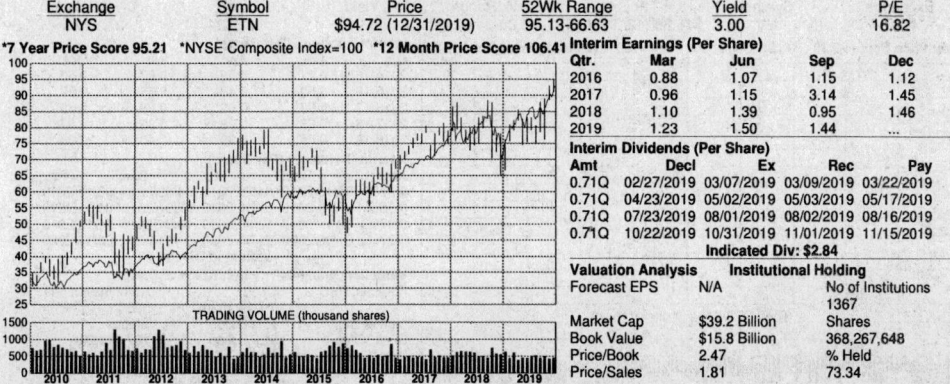

*7 Year Price Score 95.21 *NYSE Composite Index=100 *12 Month Price Score 106.41

Interim Earnings (Per Share)

Qtr.	Mar	Jun	Sep	Dec
2016	0.88	1.07	1.15	1.12
2017	0.96	1.15	3.14	1.45
2018	1.10	1.39	0.95	1.46
2019	1.23	1.50	1.44	...

Interim Dividends (Per Share)

Amt	Decl	Ex	Rec	Pay
0.71Q	02/27/2019	03/07/2019	03/09/2019	03/22/2019
0.71Q	04/23/2019	05/02/2019	05/03/2019	05/17/2019
0.71Q	07/23/2019	08/01/2019	08/02/2019	08/16/2019
0.71Q	10/22/2019	10/31/2019	11/01/2019	11/15/2019

Indicated Div: $2.84

Valuation Analysis

		Institutional Holding	
Forecast EPS	N/A	No of Institutions	1367
Market Cap	$39.2 Billion	Shares	
Book Value	$15.8 Billion		368,267,648
Price/Book	2.47	% Held	
Price/Sales	1.81		73.34

Business Summary: Electrical Equipment (MIC: 7.3.1 SIC: 3599 NAIC: 336399)

Eaton is a power management company providing energy-efficient solutions. Co.'s segments are: Electrical Products and Electrical Systems and Services, which consists of, among others, electrical components, industrial components, residential products, single phase power quality, emergency lighting and fire detection; Hydraulics, which provides hydraulics components, systems and services; Aerospace, which supplies aerospace fuel, hydraulics, and pneumatic systems; Vehicle, which designs, manufactures, markets, and supplies drivetrain, powertrain systems and components; and eMobility, which designs, manufactures, markets, and supplies electrical and electronic components and systems.

Recent Developments: For the quarter ended Sep 30 2019, net income increased 44.7% to US$602.0 million from US$416.0 million in the year-earlier quarter. Revenues were US$5.31 billion, down 1.8% from US$5.41 billion the year before. Direct operating expenses declined 2.4% to US$3.51 billion from US$3.60 billion in the comparable period the year before. Indirect operating expenses were unchanged at US$1.03 billion versus the equivalent prior-year period.

Prospects: Our evaluation of Eaton Corp PLC as of October 4th, 2019 is the result of our systematic analysis on three basic characteristics: earnings strength, relative valuation, and recent stock price movement. The company has managed to produce a neutral trend in earnings per share over the past 5 quarters. However, recent analyst estimates for the company have been reduced while ETN has posted results that exceeded analysts' expectations. Based on operating earnings yield, the company is undervalued when compared to all of the companies we cover. Share price changes over the past year indicates that ETN will perform in line with the market over the near term.

Financial Data
(US$ in Millions)

	9 Mos	6 Mos	3 Mos	12/31/2018	12/31/2017	12/31/2016	12/31/2015	12/31/2014
Earnings Per Share	5.63	5.14	5.03	4.91	6.68	4.21	4.23	3.76
Cash Flow Per Share	8.00	7.71	6.77	6.12	6.00	5.59	5.09	3.96
Dividends Per Share	2.790	2.740	2.690	2.640	2.400	2.280	2.200	1.960
Dividend Payout %	49.56	53.31	53.48	53.77	35.93	54.16	52.01	52.13
Income Statement								
Total Revenue	16,152	10,838	5,305	21,609	20,404	19,747	20,855	22,552
EBITDA	2,910	1,912	890	3,168	4,090	2,846	2,856	2,502
Depn & Amortn	668	442	221	473	476	486	479	514
Income Before Taxes	2,059	1,341	603	2,424	3,368	2,127	2,145	1,761
Income Taxes	299	183	81	278	382	202	164	(42)
Net Income	1,759	1,158	522	2,145	2,985	1,922	1,979	1,793
Average Shares	418	423	425	436	447	456	467	476
Balance Sheet								
Current Assets	8,012	8,126	7,744	7,590	8,337	6,941	6,616	8,100
Total Assets	31,895	32,244	31,649	31,092	32,623	30,419	31,031	33,529
Current Liabilities	4,661	4,450	5,286	5,154	5,075	5,485	4,625	5,355
Long-Term Obligations	8,346	8,390	7,090	6,768	7,167	6,711	7,781	8,024
Total Liabilities	16,047	15,938	15,416	14,985	15,370	15,522	15,845	17,743
Stockholders' Equity	15,848	16,306	16,233	16,107	17,253	14,897	15,186	15,786
Shares Outstanding	413	420	423	423	439	449	458	467
Statistical Record								
Return on Assets %	7.52	6.88	6.78	6.73	9.47	6.24	6.13	5.20
Return on Equity %	14.66	13.37	13.01	12.86	18.57	12.74	12.78	11.01
EBITDA Margin %	18.02	17.64	16.78	14.66	20.05	14.41	13.69	11.09
Net Margin %	10.89	10.68	9.84	9.93	14.63	9.73	9.49	7.95
Asset Turnover	0.68	0.68	0.67	0.68	0.65	0.64	0.65	0.65
Current Ratio	1.72	1.83	1.47	1.47	1.64	1.27	1.43	1.51
Debt to Equity	0.53	0.51	0.44	0.42	0.42	0.45	0.51	0.51
Price Range	88.03-64.86	88.50-64.86	88.50-64.86	88.50-64.86	81.51-66.88	69.86-47.27	73.50-49.74	79.44-58.27
P/E Ratio	15.64-11.52	17.22-12.62	17.59-12.89	18.02-13.21	12.20-10.01	16.59-11.23	17.38-11.76	21.13-15.50
Average Yield %	3.56	3.49	3.47	3.34	3.19	3.69	3.50	2.75

Address: Eaton House, 30 Pembroke Road, Dublin 4, 44114-2584 **Telephone:** 163-729-00	**Web Site:** www.eaton.com **Officers:** Craig Arnold - Chairman, Chief Executive Officer Richard H. Fearon - Vice-Chairman, Chief Financial Officer, Chief Planning Officer	**Auditors:** Ernst & Young LLP **Investor Contact:** 216-523-4205 **Transfer Agents:** Computershare Shareowner Services, Jersey City, NJ

EATON VANCE CORP

Exchange	Symbol	Price	52Wk Range	Yield	P/E	Div Acheiver
NYS	EV	$46.69 (12/31/2019)	48.68-34.05	3.21	13.34	37 Years

*7 Year Price Score 83.36   *NYSE Composite Index=100   *12 Month Price Score 105.50

Interim Earnings (Per Share)

Qtr.	Jan	Apr	Jul	Oct
2014-15	0.21	0.58	0.57	0.53
2015-16	0.50	0.48	0.55	0.57
2016-17	0.53	0.62	0.58	0.69
2017-18	0.63	0.78	0.83	0.87
2018-19	0.75	0.89	0.90	0.96

Interim Dividends (Per Share)

Amt	Decl	Ex	Rec	Pay
0.35Q	04/10/2019	04/29/2019	04/30/2019	05/15/2019
0.35Q	07/10/2019	07/30/2019	07/31/2019	08/15/2019
0.375Q	10/10/2019	10/30/2019	10/31/2019	11/15/2019
0.375Q	01/09/2020	01/30/2020	01/31/2020	02/14/2020

Indicated Div: $1.50

Valuation Analysis		Institutional Holding	
Forecast EPS	$3.50	No of Institutions	
	(01/15/2020)	525	
Market Cap	$5.3 Billion	Shares	
Book Value	$1.2 Billion	107,426,944	
Price/Book	4.48	% Held	
Price/Sales	3.15	65.97	

Business Summary: Wealth Management (MIC: 5.5.2 SIC: 6282 NAIC: 523930)

Eaton Vance is engaged in managing investment funds and providing investment management and advisory services to high-net-worth individuals and institutions. Through its investment affiliates, Co. manages active equity, income, alternative and blended strategies across a range of investment styles and asset classes, including United States, global and international equities, floating-rate bank loans, municipal bonds, global income, high-yield and investment grade bonds, and mortgage-backed securities, as well as a range of systematic investment strategies, including systematic equity, systematic alternatives and managed options strategies.

Recent Developments: For the year ended Oct 31 2019, net income increased 8.8% to US$432.9 million from US$397.9 million in the prior year. Revenues were US$1.68 billion, down 0.5% from US$1.69 billion the year before. Operating income was US$520.9 million versus US$555.2 million in the prior year, a decrease of 6.2%. Direct operating expenses declined 9.0% to US$150.2 million from US$165.0 million in the comparable period the year before. Indirect operating expenses increased 4.1% to US$1.01 billion from US$972.2 million in the equivalent prior-year period.

Prospects: Our evaluation of Eaton Vance Corp. as of October 4th, 2019 is the result of our systematic analysis on three basic characteristics: earnings strength, relative valuation, and recent stock price movement. The company has produced a positive trend in earnings per share over the past 5 quarters. However, recent analyst estimates for the company have been unchanged, while EV has posted results that exceeded analysts' expectations. Based on operating earnings yield, the company is undervalued when compared to all of the companies we cover. Share price changes over the past year indicates that EV will perform poorly over the near term.

Financial Data
(US$ in Thousands)

	10/31/2019	10/31/2018	10/31/2017	10/31/2016	10/31/2015	10/31/2014	10/31/2013	10/31/2012
Earnings Per Share	3.50	3.11	2.42	2.12	1.92	2.44	1.53	1.72
Cash Flow Per Share	4.65	1.16	0.59	3.09	1.94	0.85	1.00	1.59
Tang Book Value Per Share	7.47	6.56	5.58	3.59	2.82	3.05	3.01	3.42
Dividends Per Share	1.425	1.280	1.150	1.075	1.015	0.910	1.820	0.770
Dividend Payout %	40.71	41.16	47.52	50.71	52.86	37.30	118.95	44.77
Income Statement								
Total Revenue	1,683,252	1,702,249	1,529,010	1,342,860	1,403,563	1,450,294	1,357,503	1,209,036
EBITDA	535,269	542,287	483,264	432,158	416,908	546,788	425,313	473,015
Depn & Amortn	17,600	15,000	9,100	10,900	11,400	10,900	13,000	16,900
Income Before Taxes	559,038	543,235	469,169	408,052	369,384	491,149	359,453	403,738
Income Taxes	135,252	156,703	173,666	153,630	143,214	186,710	143,896	142,385
Net Income	400,035	381,938	282,131	241,307	230,299	304,316	193,841	203,465
Average Shares	114,388	122,932	116,418	113,982	118,155	121,595	122,444	115,126
Balance Sheet								
Current Assets	844,236	1,054,030	811,008	610,346	816,015	580,522	668,767	632,423
Total Assets	4,253,629	3,599,328	2,330,901	1,732,576	2,116,471	1,860,086	2,407,249	1,979,491
Current Liabilities	385,883	376,977	320,079	269,937	277,047	275,719	255,222	227,985
Long-Term Obligations	2,237,608	1,492,686	631,441	573,967	970,850	725,637	1,100,415	946,605
Total Liabilities	3,069,510	2,491,897	1,319,505	1,028,787	1,496,240	1,204,910	1,737,465	1,367,419
Stockholders' Equity	1,184,119	1,107,431	1,011,396	703,789	620,231	655,176	669,784	612,072
Shares Outstanding	113,566	116,950	118,520	113,987	115,885	118,261	121,631	116,291
Statistical Record								
Return on Assets %	10.19	12.88	13.89	12.50	11.58	14.26	8.84	10.65
Return on Equity %	34.91	36.05	32.90	36.35	36.11	45.94	30.24	37.84
EBITDA Margin %	31.80	31.86	31.61	32.18	29.70	37.70	31.33	39.12
Net Margin %	23.77	22.44	18.45	17.97	16.41	20.98	14.28	16.83
Asset Turnover	0.43	0.57	0.75	0.70	0.71	0.68	0.62	0.63
Current Ratio	2.19	2.80	2.53	2.26	2.95	2.11	2.62	2.77
Debt to Equity	1.89	1.35	0.62	0.82	1.57	1.11	1.64	1.55
Price Range	46.74-32.65	60.87-42.23	51.90-34.60	40.18-27.18	44.00-33.06	43.63-34.29	44.18-28.14	29.70-21.78
P/E Ratio	13.35-9.33	19.57-13.58	21.45-14.30	18.95-12.82	22.92-17.22	17.88-14.05	28.88-18.39	17.27-12.66
Average Yield %	3.45	2.37	2.54	3.09	2.56	2.38	4.80	2.92

Address: Two International Place,	Web Site: www.eatonvance.com	Auditors: DELOITTE & TOUCHE LLP
Boston, MA 02110	Officers: Thomas E. Faust - Chairman, President,	Investor Contact: 617-482-8260
Telephone: 617-482-8260	Chief Executive Officer Daniel C. Cataldo - Vice	Transfer Agents: ComputerShare
Fax: 617-482-2396	President, Chief Administrative Officer	Investor Services, Providence, RI

ECOLAB INC

Exchange	Symbol	Price	52Wk Range	Yield	P/E	Div Acheiver
NYS	ECL	$192.99 (12/31/2019)	208.57-141.54	0.97	37.04	26 Years

*7 Year Price Score 120.45 *NYSE Composite Index=100 *12 Month Price Score 96.45

Interim Earnings (Per Share)

Qtr.	Mar	Jun	Sep	Dec
2016	0.77	0.87	1.27	1.23
2017	0.86	1.01	1.34	1.93
2018	0.84	1.20	1.48	1.35
2019	1.01	1.26	1.59	...

Interim Dividends (Per Share)

Amt	Decl	Ex	Rec	Pay
0.46Q	02/22/2019	03/18/2019	03/19/2019	04/15/2019
0.46Q	05/02/2019	06/17/2019	06/18/2019	07/15/2019
0.46Q	08/01/2019	09/16/2019	09/17/2019	10/15/2019
0.47Q	12/04/2019	12/16/2019	12/17/2019	01/15/2020

Indicated Div: $1.88 (Div. Reinv. Plan)

Valuation Analysis / Institutional Holding

Valuation Analysis		Institutional Holding	
Forecast EPS	$5.86 (01/15/2020)	No of Institutions	1538
Market Cap	$55.6 Billion	Shares	273,685,248
Book Value	$8.6 Billion	% Held	74.65
Price/Book	6.49		
Price/Sales	3.75		

Business Summary: Specialty Chemicals (MIC: 8.3.2 SIC: 2842 NAIC: 325612)

Ecolab is a provider of water, hygiene and energy technologies and services. Co.'s segments include: Global Industrial, which provides water treatment and process applications, and cleaning and sanitizing solutions in the manufacturing, food and beverage processing, chemical, power generation, pharmaceutical and commercial laundry industries; Global Institutional, which provides cleaning and sanitizing products to the foodservice, hospitality, lodging, healthcare, government, education and retail industries; and Global Energy, which serves the process chemicals and water treatment needs of the global petroleum and petrochemical industries in both upstream and downstream applications.

Recent Developments: For the quarter ended Sep 30 2019, net income increased 7.1% to US$469.3 million from US$438.3 million in the year-earlier quarter. Revenues were US$3.82 billion, up 1.9% from US$3.75 billion the year before. Operating income was US$587.6 million versus US$516.2 million in the prior-year quarter, an increase of 13.8%. Direct operating expenses rose 0.8% to US$2.21 billion from US$2.19 billion in the comparable period the year before. Indirect operating expenses decreased 1.7% to US$1.02 billion from US$1.04 billion in the equivalent prior-year period.

Prospects: Our evaluation of Ecolab Inc. as of October 4th, 2019 is the result of our systematic analysis on three basic characteristics: earnings strength, relative valuation, and recent stock price movement. The company has produced a positive trend in earnings per share over the past 5 quarters. However, recent analyst estimates for the company have been mixed and ECL has posted results that exceeded analysts' expectations. Based on operating earnings yield, the company is fairly valued when compared to all of the companies we cover. Share price changes over the past year indicates that ECL will perform over the near term.

Financial Data

(US$ in Thousands)	9 Mos	6 Mos	3 Mos	12/31/2018	12/31/2017	12/31/2016	12/31/2015	12/31/2014
Earnings Per Share	5.21	5.10	5.04	4.88	5.13	4.14	3.32	3.93
Cash Flow Per Share	8.42	8.38	7.52	7.89	7.22	6.61	6.75	6.05
Dividends Per Share	1.840	1.790	1.740	1.690	1.520	1.420	1.340	1.155
Dividend Payout %	35.32	35.10	34.52	34.63	29.63	34.30	40.36	29.39
Income Statement								
Total Revenue	11,082,700	7,264,800	3,505,400	14,668,200	13,838,300	13,152,800	13,545,100	14,280,500
EBITDA	2,244,800	1,391,700	627,200	2,647,900	2,605,800	2,476,000	2,121,300	2,513,000
Depn & Amortn	728,500	483,800	238,800	621,000	586,000	561,000	560,000	558,000
Income Before Taxes	1,371,300	809,000	339,000	1,804,600	1,764,800	1,650,400	1,317,700	1,698,400
Income Taxes	229,400	136,400	38,600	364,300	242,400	403,300	300,500	476,200
Net Income	1,129,300	665,100	296,500	1,429,100	1,508,400	1,229,600	1,002,100	1,202,800
Average Shares	292,800	292,100	292,300	292,800	294,000	296,700	301,400	305,900
Balance Sheet								
Current Assets	4,870,100	4,853,500	4,751,000	4,677,700	4,596,400	4,279,400	4,447,500	4,871,100
Total Assets	20,835,600	20,827,600	20,927,600	20,074,500	19,962,400	18,330,200	18,641,700	19,466,700
Current Liabilities	3,919,500	4,127,700	4,156,000	3,685,600	3,431,800	3,019,400	4,764,400	4,386,600
Long-Term Obligations	5,966,900	5,987,100	6,008,700	6,301,600	6,758,300	6,145,700	4,260,200	4,864,000
Total Liabilities	12,267,900	12,602,200	12,706,900	12,071,300	12,343,900	11,429,100	11,731,800	12,150,800
Stockholders' Equity	8,567,700	8,225,400	8,220,700	8,003,200	7,618,500	6,901,100	6,909,900	7,315,900
Shares Outstanding	288,200	287,751	288,200	287,714	289,322	291,825	295,967	299,852
Statistical Record								
Return on Assets %	7.47	7.34	7.19	7.14	7.88	6.63	5.26	6.15
Return on Equity %	18.48	18.61	18.69	18.30	20.78	17.76	14.09	16.41
EBITDA Margin %	20.25	19.16	17.89	18.05	18.83	18.82	15.66	17.60
Net Margin %	10.19	9.16	8.46	9.74	10.90	9.35	7.40	8.42
Asset Turnover	0.73	0.72	0.72	0.73	0.72	0.71	0.71	0.73
Current Ratio	1.24	1.18	1.14	1.27	1.34	1.42	0.93	1.11
Debt to Equity	0.70	0.73	0.73	0.79	0.89	0.89	0.62	0.66
Price Range	208.57-137.90	199.69-137.90	176.54-133.97	160.49-127.76	137.42-117.86	124.05-100.14	122.10-98.93	118.07-98.03
P/E Ratio	40.03-26.47	39.15-27.04	35.03-26.58	32.89-26.18	26.79-22.97	29.96-24.19	36.78-29.80	30.04-24.94
Average Yield %	1.05	1.10	1.15	1.17	1.18	1.23	1.18	1.06

Address: 1 Ecolab Place, St. Paul, MN 55102	**Web Site:** www.ecolab.com	**Auditors:** PricewaterhouseCoopers LLP	
Telephone: 800-232-6522	**Officers:** Douglas M. Baker - Chairman, President, Chief Executive Officer, Chief Operating Officer	**Investor Contact:** 651-293-2545	
	Timothy P. Mulhere - Executive Vice President, Region Officer, Executive Vice President (frmr)	**Transfer Agents:** Elavon Financial Services DAC	

EDGEWELL PERSONAL CARE CO

Exchange	Symbol	Price	52Wk Range	Yield	P/E
NYS	EPC	$30.96 (12/31/2019)	46.31-26.61	N/A	N/A

*7 Year Price Score 41.63 *NYSE Composite Index=100 *12 Month Price Score 87.99

Interim Earnings (Per Share)

Qtr.	Dec	Mar	Jun	Sep
2014-15	1.69	(1.41)	(1.17)	(3.54)
2015-16	0.39	1.10	0.61	0.88
2016-17	0.58	1.14	0.95	(2.57)
2017-18	0.12	1.20	0.22	0.36
2018-19	(0.01)	0.89	(8.16)	0.39

Interim Dividends (Per Share)

No Dividends Paid

Valuation Analysis / Institutional Holding

Valuation Analysis		Institutional Holding	
Forecast EPS	$3.13	No of Institutions	
	(01/17/2020)	460	
Market Cap	$1.7 Billion	Shares	
Book Value	$1.3 Billion	70,351,776	
Price/Book	1.29	% Held	
Price/Sales	0.78	N/A	

Business Summary: Household & Personal Products (MIC: 1.7.1 SIC: 2844 NAIC: 325620)

Edgewell Personal Care is a manufacturer and marketer of personal care products. Co.'s segments are: Wet Shave, which manufactures and distributes Schick and Wilkinson Sword razor systems, composed of razor handles and refillable blades, and disposable shave products for men and women; Sun and Skin Care, which markets sun care products under the Banana Boat and Hawaiian Tropic brands; Feminine Care, which provides tampons under the Playtex Gentle Glide® 360°™, Playtex Sport®, Playtex and o.b. brands, and markets pads and liners under the Stayfree and Carefree brands; and All Other, which includes infant care, pet care and miscellaneous other products.

Recent Developments: For the year ended Sep 30 2019, net loss amounted to US$372.2 million versus net income of US$103.3 million in the prior year. Revenues were US$2.14 billion, down 4.2% from US$2.23 billion the year before. Direct operating expenses declined 2.3% to US$1.17 billion from US$1.20 billion in the comparable period the year before. Indirect operating expenses increased 56.1% to US$1.36 billion from US$869.1 million in the equivalent prior-year period.

Prospects: Our evaluation of Edgewell Personal Care Co. as of October 4th, 2019 is the result of our systematic analysis on three basic characteristics: earnings strength, relative valuation, and recent stock price movement. The company has generated a negative trend in earnings per share over the past 5 quarters. However, recent analyst estimates for the company have been unchanged while EPC has posted results that exceeded analysts' expectations. Based on operating earnings yield, the company is undervalued when compared to all of the companies we cover. Share price changes over the past year indicates that EPC will perform very poorly over the near term.

Financial Data

(US$ in Thousands)

	09/30/2019	09/30/2018	09/30/2017	09/30/2016	09/30/2015	09/30/2014	09/30/2013	09/30/2012
Earnings Per Share	(6.88)	1.90	0.10	2.99	(4.44)	5.69	6.47	6.22
Cash Flow Per Share	3.52	4.87	5.17	2.97	2.40	9.23	12.08	9.71
Income Statement								
Total Revenue	2,141,000	2,234,400	2,298,400	2,362,000	2,421,200	4,447,700	4,466,000	4,567,200
EBITDA	(257,800)	306,100	90,400	365,300	(285,200)	716,400	863,100	829,400
Depn & Amortn	69,900	74,300	74,100	73,600	73,700	120,300	164,700	136,700
Income Before Taxes	(390,300)	163,800	(52,900)	219,900	(458,700)	473,500	567,900	565,400
Income Taxes	(18,100)	60,500	(58,600)	41,200	(162,600)	117,400	160,900	156,500
Net Income	(372,200)	103,300	5,700	178,700	(275,300)	356,100	407,000	408,900
Average Shares	54,100	54,500	57,500	59,700	62,000	62,600	62,900	65,700
Balance Sheet								
Current Assets	1,044,400	951,200	1,186,200	1,452,000	1,636,600	2,729,600	2,568,400	2,522,600
Total Assets	3,420,900	3,953,300	4,188,800	4,771,500	4,991,700	6,928,700	6,717,400	6,731,200
Current Liabilities	659,600	717,000	524,400	868,200	666,800	1,573,700	1,153,400	1,307,500
Long-Term Obligations	1,097,800	1,103,800	1,525,400	1,544,200	1,704,000	1,768,900	1,998,800	2,138,600
Total Liabilities	2,117,400	2,208,700	2,447,100	2,942,500	3,127,600	4,406,400	4,263,800	4,661,700
Stockholders' Equity	1,303,500	1,744,600	1,741,700	1,829,000	1,864,100	2,522,300	2,453,600	2,069,500
Shares Outstanding	54,206	54,040	56,017	57,914	60,176	61,824	62,324	61,522
Statistical Record								
Return on Assets %	N.M.	2.54	0.13	3.65	N.M.	5.22	6.05	6.09
Return on Equity %	N.M.	5.93	0.32	9.65	N.M.	14.31	18.00	19.55
EBITDA Margin %	N.M.	13.70	3.93	15.47	N.M.	16.11	19.33	18.16
Net Margin %	N.M.	4.62	0.25	7.57	N.M.	8.01	9.11	8.95
Asset Turnover	0.58	0.55	0.51	0.48	0.41	0.65	0.66	0.68
Current Ratio	1.58	1.33	2.26	1.67	2.45	1.73	2.23	1.93
Debt to Equity	0.84	0.63	0.88	0.84	0.91	0.70	0.81	1.03
Price Range	48.03-26.61	72.56-41.40	81.75-69.72	87.48-69.84	107.28-78.40	92.73-67.59	80.20-52.29	59.13-47.72
P/E Ratio	...	38.19-21.79	817.50-697.20	29.26-23.36	...	16.30-11.88	12.40-8.08	9.51-7.67

Address: 6 Research Drive, Shelton, CT 06484
Telephone: 203-944-5500

Web Site: www.edgewell.com
Officers: Rod R. Little - President, Chief Executive Officer, Chief Financial Officer Daniel J. Sullivan - Chief Financial Officer

Auditors: PricewaterhouseCoopers LLP
Investor Contact: 314-982-2013
Transfer Agents: Continental Stock Transfer & Trust Company, New York, NY

EDISON INTERNATIONAL

Exchange	Symbol	Price	52Wk Range	Yield	P/E	Div Acheiver
NYS	EIX	$75.41 (12/31/2019)	76.36-53.51	3.38	N/A	14 Years

*7 Year Price Score 86.22 *NYSE Composite Index=100 *12 Month Price Score 101.06

Interim Earnings (Per Share)

Qtr.	Mar	Jun	Sep	Dec
2016	0.82	0.84	1.27	1.03
2017	1.10	0.85	1.43	(1.66)
2018	0.67	0.84	1.57	(4.38)
2019	0.85	1.20	1.35	...

Interim Dividends (Per Share)

Amt	Decl	Ex	Rec	Pay
0.613Q	02/28/2019	03/28/2019	03/29/2019	04/30/2019
0.613Q	06/26/2019	07/05/2019	07/08/2019	07/31/2019
0.613Q	08/22/2019	09/27/2019	09/30/2019	10/31/2019
0.637Q	12/12/2019	12/30/2019	12/31/2019	01/31/2020

Indicated Div: $2.55 (Div. Reinv. Plan)

Valuation Analysis | **Institutional Holding**

Forecast EPS	$4.75	No of Institutions
	(01/17/2020)	928
Market Cap	$27.0 Billion	Shares
Book Value	$13.2 Billion	363,578,624
Price/Book	2.05	% Held
Price/Sales	2.18	95.93

Business Summary: Electric Utilities (MIC: 3.1.1 SIC: 4911 NAIC: 221111)

Edison International is a holding company. Through its subsidiary, Southern California Edison Company (SCE), which is an investor-owned public utility, Co. is primarily engaged in the business of supplying and delivering electricity to southern California. Co. is also the parent company of Edison Energy Group, Inc., a holding company for Edison Energy, LLC, which is engaged in the business of providing energy services to commercial and industrial customers. SCE supplies electricity to its customers through transmission and distribution networks. Its transmission facilities include sub-transmission facilities and are located primarily in California but also in Nevada and Arizona.

Recent Developments: For the quarter ended Sep 30 2019, net income decreased 7.7% to US$502.0 million from US$544.0 million in the year-earlier quarter. Revenues were US$3.74 billion, down 12.4% from US$4.27 billion the year before. Operating income was US$636.0 million versus US$739.0 million in the prior-year quarter, a decrease of 13.9%. Direct operating expenses declined 14.5% to US$2.55 billion from US$2.98 billion in the comparable period the year before. Indirect operating expenses increased 1.1% to US$556.0 million from US$550.0 million in the equivalent prior-year period.

Prospects: Our evaluation of Edison International as of October 4th, 2019 is the result of our systematic analysis on three basic characteristics: earnings strength, relative valuation, and recent stock price movement. The company has produced a positive trend in earnings per share over the past 5 quarters. However, recent analyst estimates for the company have been mixed and EIX has posted results that exceeded analysts' expectations. Based on operating earnings yield, the company is undervalued when compared to all of the companies we cover. Share price changes over the past year indicates that EIX will perform in line with the market over the near term.

Financial Data

(US$ in Thousands)	9 Mos	6 Mos	3 Mos	12/31/2018	12/31/2017	12/31/2016	12/31/2015	12/31/2014
Earnings Per Share	(0.98)	(0.76)	(1.12)	(1.30)	1.72	3.97	3.10	4.89
Cash Flow Per Share	0.26	7.85	7.75	9.75	11.00	9.96	13.83	9.96
Tang Book Value Per Share	36.71	32.90	32.31	32.10	35.82	36.82	34.89	33.64
Dividends Per Share	2.450	1.830	2.435	2.428	2.232	1.982	1.732	1.482
Dividend Payout %	...	...	...	...	129.80	49.94	55.89	30.32
Income Statement								
Total Revenue	9,377,000	5,636,000	2,824,000	12,657,000	12,320,000	11,869,000	11,524,000	13,413,000
EBITDA	2,926,000	1,766,000	879,000	1,271,000	3,191,000	3,688,000	3,539,000	4,349,000
Depn & Amortn	1,316,000	837,000	498,000	1,650,000	1,610,000	1,520,000	1,420,000	1,815,000
Income Before Taxes	1,020,000	540,000	196,000	(1,089,000)	949,000	1,590,000	1,568,000	1,979,000
Income Taxes	(212,000)	(190,000)	(112,000)	(739,000)	281,000	177,000	486,000	443,000
Net Income	1,141,000	670,000	278,000	(423,000)	565,000	1,311,000	1,020,000	1,612,000
Average Shares	349,000	327,000	327,000	326,000	328,000	330,000	329,000	329,000
Balance Sheet								
Current Assets	4,662,000	3,936,000	3,999,000	3,359,000	3,729,000	2,123,000	2,654,000	4,019,000
Total Assets	64,212,000	59,521,000	58,793,000	56,715,000	52,580,000	51,319,000	50,310,000	50,186,000
Current Liabilities	6,003,000	5,665,000	5,375,000	5,395,000	7,068,000	5,912,000	4,927,000	5,479,000
Long-Term Obligations	17,066,000	15,883,000	15,683,000	14,632,000	11,642,000	10,175,000	10,964,000	10,234,000
Total Liabilities	51,052,000	48,801,000	48,267,000	46,256,000	40,909,000	39,323,000	38,942,000	39,226,000
Stockholders' Equity	13,160,000	10,720,000	10,526,000	10,459,000	11,671,000	11,996,000	11,368,000	10,960,000
Shares Outstanding	358,522	325,811	325,811	325,811	325,811	325,811	325,811	325,811
Statistical Record								
Return on Assets %	N.M.	N.M.	N.M.	N.M.	1.09	2.57	2.03	3.33
Return on Equity %	N.M.	N.M.	N.M.	N.M.	4.77	11.19	9.14	15.43
EBITDA Margin %	31.20	31.33	31.13	10.04	25.90	31.07	30.71	32.42
Net Margin %	12.17	11.89	9.84	N.M.	4.59	11.05	8.85	12.02
Asset Turnover	0.21	0.23	0.23	0.23	0.24	0.23	0.23	0.28
Current Ratio	0.78	0.69	0.74	0.62	0.53	0.36	0.54	0.73
Debt to Equity	1.30	1.48	1.49	1.40	1.00	0.85	0.96	0.93
Price Range	76.36-47.19	70.54-47.19	70.54-47.19	70.54-47.19	82.64-63.24	78.55-58.28	69.05-55.58	68.27-45.07
P/E Ratio	...	...	...	...	48.05-36.77	19.79-14.68	22.27-17.93	13.96-9.22
Average Yield %	3.83	2.92	3.88	3.84	2.87	2.81	2.82	2.63

Address: 2244 Walnut Grove Avenue,	Web Site: www.edisoninvestor.com	Auditors: PricewaterhouseCoopers LLP
P.O. Box 976, Rosemead, CA 91770	Officers: William P. Sullivan - Chairman Pedro J.	Transfer Agents: Wells Fargo
Telephone: 626-302-2222	Pizarro - President, Chief Executive Officer	Shareowner Services, St. Paul, MN

EDWARDS LIFESCIENCES CORP

Exchange	Symbol	Price	52Wk Range	Yield	P/E
NYS	EW	$233.29 (12/31/2019)	246.26-143.66	N/A	63.74

*7 Year Price Score 164.23 *NYSE Composite Index=100 *12 Month Price Score 113.21

Interim Earnings (Per Share)

Qtr.	Mar	Jun	Sep	Dec
2016	0.66	0.58	0.65	0.72
2017	1.06	0.86	0.79	(0.01)
2018	0.96	1.32	1.06	0.04
2019	1.18	1.14	1.30	...

Interim Dividends (Per Share)

Amt	Decl	Ex	Rec	Pay
100%	11/19/2015	12/14/2015	11/30/2015	12/11/2015

Valuation Analysis | **Institutional Holding**

Forecast EPS	$5.60	No of Institutions
	(01/15/2020)	1281
Market Cap	$48.6 Billion	Shares
Book Value	$3.8 Billion	202,964,544
Price/Book	12.75	% Held
Price/Sales	11.72	N/A

Business Summary: Medical Instruments & Equipment (MIC: 4.3.1 SIC: 3842 NAIC: 339113)

Edwards Lifesciences is engaged in medical treatments for structural heart disease and critical care monitoring. Co. manufactures heart valve systems and repairs products used to replace or repair a patient's diseased or defective heart valve. Co.'s technologies is focused on the less invasive repair or replacement of the mitral and tricuspid valves of the heart. Co. is also engaged in hemodynamic monitoring systems used to measure a patient's cardiovascular function in the hospital setting. Co.'s products and technologies are categorized into four main areas: Transcatheter Aortic Valve Replacement, Surgical Structural Heart, Critical Care, and Transcatheter Mitral and Tricuspid Therapies.

Recent Developments: For the quarter ended Sep 30 2019, net income increased 21.6% to US$274.7 million from US$225.9 million in the year-earlier quarter. Revenues were US$1.09 billion, up 20.7% from US$906.6 million the year before. Operating income was US$294.3 million versus US$248.9 million in the prior-year quarter, an increase of 18.2%. Direct operating expenses rose 30.0% to US$292.4 million from US$224.9 million in the comparable period the year before. Indirect operating expenses increased 17.2% to US$507.3 million from US$432.8 million in the equivalent prior-year period.

Prospects: Our evaluation of Edwards Lifesciences Corp. as of October 4th, 2019 is the result of our systematic analysis on three basic characteristics: earnings strength, relative valuation, and recent stock price movement. The company has produced a positive trend in earnings per share over the past 5 quarters. However, recent analyst estimates for the company have been mixed and EW has posted results that exceeded analysts' expectations. Based on operating earnings yield, the company is overvalued when compared to all of the companies we cover. Share price changes over the past year indicates that EW will perform well over the near term.

Financial Data

(US$ in Thousands)	9 Mos	6 Mos	3 Mos	12/31/2018	12/31/2017	12/31/2016	12/31/2015	12/31/2014
Earnings Per Share	3.66	3.42	3.60	3.38	2.70	2.61	2.25	3.74
Cash Flow Per Share	5.15	4.70	3.74	4.43	4.74	3.30	2.55	4.80
Tang Book Value Per Share	10.92	9.34	9.61	8.11	6.49	8.45	7.75	8.31
Income Statement								
Total Revenue	3,173,900	2,079,900	993,000	3,722,800	3,435,300	2,963,700	2,493,700	2,322,900
EBITDA	909,200	587,200	281,700	834,200	1,111,900	809,900	690,400	1,212,300
Depn & Amortn	65,400	42,300	5,700	74,900	74,100	63,600	58,700	57,500
Income Before Taxes	851,000	549,300	278,000	761,400	1,034,900	737,900	622,400	1,144,000
Income Taxes	84,300	57,300	28,300	39,200	451,300	168,400	127,500	332,900
Net Income	766,700	492,000	249,700	722,200	583,600	569,500	494,900	811,100
Average Shares	212,100	212,100	212,200	213,600	215,900	217,800	220,300	217,000
Balance Sheet								
Current Assets	2,739,700	2,354,700	2,368,800	2,286,900	2,532,100	2,240,000	2,047,900	2,294,600
Total Assets	5,966,300	5,573,500	5,469,300	5,323,700	5,695,800	4,510,000	4,059,300	3,524,300
Current Liabilities	775,800	697,000	646,500	876,600	1,402,900	532,500	476,200	434,400
Long-Term Obligations	594,200	594,100	593,900	593,800	438,400	822,300	599,900	598,100
Total Liabilities	2,151,500	2,073,200	2,021,800	2,183,300	2,739,600	1,891,000	1,556,200	1,332,900
Stockholders' Equity	3,814,800	3,500,300	3,447,500	3,140,400	2,956,200	2,619,000	2,503,100	2,191,400
Shares Outstanding	208,500	207,900	208,400	207,700	209,700	211,600	215,400	215,600
Statistical Record								
Return on Assets %	12.98	12.88	13.55	13.11	11.44	13.26	13.05	25.96
Return on Equity %	21.56	21.75	22.87	23.69	20.94	22.18	21.08	43.25
EBITDA Margin %	28.65	28.23	28.37	22.41	32.37	27.33	27.69	52.19
Net Margin %	24.16	23.65	25.15	19.40	16.99	19.22	19.85	34.92
Asset Turnover	0.70	0.70	0.68	0.68	0.67	0.69	0.66	0.74
Current Ratio	3.53	3.38	3.66	2.61	1.80	4.21	4.30	5.28
Debt to Equity	0.16	0.17	0.17	0.19	0.15	0.31	0.24	0.27
Price Range	226.29-139.22	193.23-137.11	192.15-127.36	174.10-111.58	120.15-89.49	121.36-74.52	82.56-61.93	66.74-32.09
P/E Ratio	61.83-38.04	56.50-40.09	53.38-35.38	51.51-33.01	44.50-33.14	46.50-28.55	36.69-27.52	17.84-8.58

Address: One Edwards Way, Irvine, CA 92614	**Web Site:** www.edwards.com	**Auditors:** PricewaterhouseCoopers LLP
Telephone: 949-250-2500	**Officers:** Michael A. Mussallem - Chairman, Chief Executive Officer Scott B. Ullem - Corporate Vice-President, Chief Financial Officer	**Transfer Agents:** ComputerShare Investor Services, Providence, RI

ELANCO ANIMAL HEALTH INC

Exchange	Symbol	Price	52Wk Range	Yield	P/E
NYS	ELAN	$29.45 (12/31/2019)	34.96-25.29	N/A	95.00

*7 Year Price Score N/A   *NYSE Composite Index=100   *12 Month Price Score 85.83

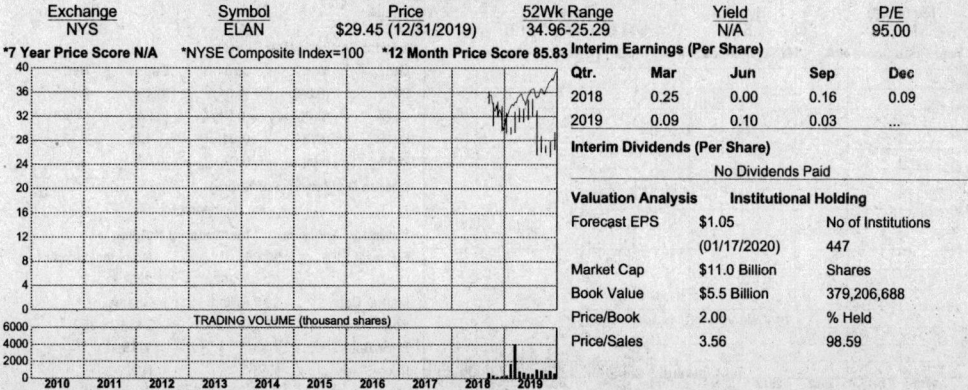

Interim Earnings (Per Share)

Qtr.	Mar	Jun	Sep	Dec
2018	0.25	0.00	0.16	0.09
2019	0.09	0.10	0.03	...

Interim Dividends (Per Share)

No Dividends Paid

Valuation Analysis   **Institutional Holding**

Forecast EPS	$1.05	No of Institutions
	(01/17/2020)	447
Market Cap	$11.0 Billion	Shares
Book Value	$5.5 Billion	379,206,688
Price/Book	2.00	% Held
Price/Sales	3.56	98.59

TRADING VOLUME (thousand shares)

Business Summary: Pharmaceuticals (MIC: 4.1.1 SIC: 2834 NAIC: 325412)

Elanco Animal Health is an animal health company. Co. groups its products into four principal categories: Companion Animal (CA) Disease Prevention, which includes parasiticides and vaccine products for canines and felines; CA Therapeutics, which includes products for the treatment of pain, osteoarthritis, otitis, cardiovascular and dermatology indications in canines and felines; Food Animal (FA) Future Protein and Health, which includes vaccines, antibiotics, parasiticides and other products used in poultry and aquaculture production; and FA Ruminants and Swine, which includes vaccines, antibiotics, implants, parasiticides and other products used in ruminants and swine production.

Recent Developments: For the quarter ended Sep 30 2019, net income decreased 83.4% to US$10.0 million from US$60.2 million in the year-earlier quarter. Revenues were US$771.3 million, up 1.3% from US$761.1 million the year before. Direct operating expenses declined 1.8% to US$411.1 million from US$418.5 million in the comparable period the year before. Indirect operating expenses increased 41.3% to US$372.7 million from US$263.8 million in the equivalent prior-year period.

Prospects: Our evaluation of Elanco Animal Health Incorporated as of October 4th, 2019 is the result of our systematic analysis on three basic characteristics: earnings strength, relative valuation, and recent stock price movement. The company has managed to produce a neutral trend in earnings per share over the past 5 quarters. However, recent analyst estimates for the company have been reduced while ELAN has posted results that exceeded analysts' expectations. Based on operating earnings yield, the company is fairly valued when compared to all of the companies we cover. Share price changes over the past year indicates that ELAN will perform in line with the market over the near term.

Financial Data
(US$ in Thousands)

	9 Mos	6 Mos	3 Mos	12/31/2018	12/31/2017	12/31/2016	12/31/2015
Earnings Per Share	0.31	0.44	0.34	0.28	...	...	...
Cash Flow Per Share	0.64	0.99	1.22	1.55	...	...	...
Tang Book Value Per Share	0.28	N.M.	N.M.	N.M.	...	...	...
Income Statement							
Total Revenue	2,284,000	1,512,700	731,100	3,066,800	2,889,000	2,913,500	2,909,100
EBITDA	291,700	234,800	114,600	422,400	68,400	224,000	(24,900)
Depn & Amortn	149,000	98,300	49,000	278,700	301,000	246,400	234,600
Income Before Taxes	82,500	95,000	44,800	114,100	(232,600)	(22,400)	(259,500)
Income Taxes	5,100	27,600	13,300	27,600	78,100	25,500	(48,700)
Net Income	77,400	67,400	31,500	86,500	(310,700)	(47,900)	(210,800)
Average Shares	373,200	367,000	366,000	313,700		...	...
Balance Sheet							
Current Assets	2,310,400	2,383,500	2,278,300	2,504,900	2,123,700	1,947,400	...
Total Assets	8,823,700	8,856,900	8,747,400	8,956,700	8,940,300	8,099,700	...
Current Liabilities	741,500	777,500	708,200	970,700	632,600	618,900	...
Long-Term Obligations	2,335,600	2,382,000	2,436,600	2,443,300	...	...	...
Total Liabilities	3,336,000	3,591,400	3,551,200	3,759,200	1,149,500	1,071,800	...
Stockholders' Equity	5,487,700	5,265,500	5,196,200	5,197,500	7,790,800	7,027,900	...
Shares Outstanding	372,999	365,707	365,702	365,643	...	...	...
Statistical Record							
Return on Assets %	1.04	1.65	...	0.97	N.M.	...	...
Return on Equity %	1.77	2.24	...	1.33	N.M.	...	...
EBITDA Margin %	12.77	15.52	15.68	13.77	2.37	7.69	N.M.
Net Margin %	3.39	4.46	4.31	2.82	N.M.	N.M.	N.M.
Asset Turnover	0.34	0.35	...	0.34	0.34	...	...
Current Ratio	3.12	3.07	3.22	2.58	3.36	3.15	...
Debt to Equity	0.43	0.45	0.47	0.47	...	...	...
Price Range	34.96-25.62	36.19-29.00	36.19-29.00	36.19-29.63	...	...	...
P/E Ratio	112.77-82.65	82.25-65.91	106.44-85.29	129.25-105.82	...	...	...

Address: 2500 Innovation Way, Greenfield, IN 46140 **Telephone:** 877-352-6261	**Web Site:** www.elanco.com **Officers:** R. David Hoover - Chairman Jeffrey N. Simmons - President, Chief Executive Officer	**Auditors:** Ernst & Young LLP **Transfer Agents:** Computershare Trust Company, N.A.

245

ELEMENT SOLUTIONS INC

Exchange	Symbol	Price	52Wk Range	Yield	P/E
NYS	ESI	$11.68 (12/31/2019)	12.16-8.64	N/A	61.47

*7 Year Price Score N/A   *NYSE Composite Index=100   *12 Month Price Score 102.91

Interim Earnings (Per Share)

Qtr.	Mar	Jun	Sep	Dec
2016	(0.59)	(0.04)	(0.15)	0.06
2017	(0.09)	(0.21)	(0.24)	(0.50)
2018	0.13	0.04	(1.42)	0.12
2019	0.09	0.01	(0.03)	...

Interim Dividends (Per Share)

No Dividends Paid

Valuation Analysis

Forecast EPS	$0.86	No of Institutions
	(01/17/2020)	235
Market Cap	$2.9 Billion	Shares
Book Value	$2.1 Billion	243,928,352
Price/Book	1.38	% Held
Price/Sales	1.58	N/A

Business Summary: Specialty Chemicals (MIC: 8.3.2 SIC: 5169 NAIC: 325998)

Element Solutions is a holding company. Through its subsidiaries, Co. is a specialty chemicals company. Co. manages two segments: Electronics, which develops materials that join electronic circuits, designs and manufactures proprietary liquid chemical processes (bath) to manufacture printed circuit boards, and provides copper interconnects, die attachment, wafer bump processes and photomask technologies; and Industrial and Specialty, which provides specialty chemicals to protect and decorate metal and plastic surfaces, produces and markets photopolymers, and produces, markets and supports water-based hydraulic control fluids for offshore deep-water production and drilling applications.

Recent Developments: For the quarter ended Sep 30 2019, loss from continuing operations was US$6.0 million compared with a loss of US$4.3 million in the year-earlier quarter. Net loss amounted to US$6.9 million versus a net loss of US$405.9 million in the year-earlier quarter. Revenues were US$464.7 million, down 4.9% from US$488.5 million the year before. Operating income was US$66.9 million versus US$59.6 million in the prior-year quarter, an increase of 12.2%. Direct operating expenses declined 7.1% to US$259.0 million from US$278.9 million in the comparable period the year before. Indirect operating expenses decreased 7.5% to US$138.8 million from US$150.0 million in the equivalent prior-year period.

Prospects: Our evaluation of Element Solutions Inc. as of October 4th, 2019 is the result of our systematic analysis on three basic characteristics: earnings strength, relative valuation, and recent stock price movement. The company has enjoyed a very positive trend in earnings per share over the past 5 quarters. However, recent analyst estimates for the company have been unchanged, while ESI has posted results that exceeded analysts' expectations. Based on operating earnings yield, the company is undervalued when compared to all of the companies we cover. Share price changes over the past year indicates that ESI will perform poorly over the near term.

Financial Data

(US$ in Thousands)	9 Mos	6 Mos	3 Mos	12/31/2018	12/31/2017	12/31/2016	12/31/2015	12/31/2014
Earnings Per Share	0.19	(1.20)	(1.17)	(1.13)	(1.04)	(0.65)	(1.52)	(1.94)
Cash Flow Per Share	0.46	0.37	0.48	(0.00)	0.64	0.76	1.58	0.73
Income Statement								
Total Revenue	1,381,200	916,500	459,800	1,961,000	3,775,900	3,585,900	2,542,300	843,200
EBITDA	149,700	71,000	34,500	302,400	130,900	402,600	33,500	26,300
Depn & Amortn	30,800	20,700	10,300	44,600	78,300	75,000	48,900	19,300
Income Before Taxes	45,200	(6,000)	(13,900)	(53,200)	(289,000)	(48,100)	(229,300)	(30,900)
Income Taxes	40,000	(17,200)	(10,400)	23,800	6,600	28,600	75,100	(6,700)
Net Income	17,800	24,700	23,200	(324,400)	(296,200)	(73,700)	(308,600)	(29,900)
Average Shares	254,400	259,600	268,200	288,200	286,100	272,300	203,200	135,300
Balance Sheet								
Current Assets	850,300	926,300	1,001,700	2,482,200	2,340,600	2,071,200	2,270,500	1,578,400
Total Assets	4,273,100	4,440,300	4,572,200	9,401,500	10,252,400	10,054,100	10,190,200	4,557,600
Current Liabilities	289,800	338,000	456,100	1,142,500	1,091,800	1,082,700	1,062,400	242,600
Long-Term Obligations	1,514,200	1,515,300	1,516,500	5,350,700	5,440,600	5,122,900	5,173,600	1,400,800
Total Liabilities	2,151,000	2,207,500	2,315,500	7,292,300	7,509,300	7,318,000	7,440,400	2,098,000
Stockholders' Equity	2,122,100	2,232,800	2,256,700	2,109,200	2,743,100	2,736,100	2,749,800	2,459,600
Shares Outstanding	251,100	258,323	257,442	288,974	287,399	284,221	229,464	182,066
Statistical Record								
Return on Assets %	0.78	N.M.	N.M.	N.M.	N.M.	N.M.	N.M.	N.M.
Return on Equity %	2.54	N.M.	N.M.	N.M.	N.M.	N.M.	N.M.	N.M.
EBITDA Margin %	10.84	7.75	7.50	15.42	3.47	11.23	1.32	3.12
Net Margin %	1.29	2.70	5.05	N.M.	N.M.	N.M.	N.M.	N.M.
Asset Turnover	0.27	0.26	0.32	0.20	0.37	0.35	0.34	0.25
Current Ratio	2.93	2.74	2.20	2.17	2.14	1.91	2.14	6.51
Debt to Equity	0.71	0.68	0.67	2.54	1.98	1.87	1.88	0.57
Price Range	12.67-8.64	13.39-9.31	13.39-9.31	13.39-9.31	14.58-9.45	12.83-5.55	28.35-10.12	28.70-13.83
P/E Ratio	66.68-45.47	...	...	...	...	...	...	...

Address: 500 East Broward Boulevard, Suite 1860, Fort Lauderdale, FL 33394	Web Site: www.platformspecialtyproducts.com	Auditors: PricewaterhouseCoopers LLP
Telephone: 561-207-9600	Officers: Martin E. Franklin - Executive Chairman, Chairman Scot R. Benson - President, Chief Operating Officer, Division Officer	

EMCOR GROUP, INC.

Exchange	Symbol	Price	52Wk Range	Yield	P/E
NYS	EME	$86.30 (12/31/2019)	93.05-58.09	0.37	15.49

*7 Year Price Score 114.34 *NYSE Composite Index=100 ***12 Month Price Score 103.97**

Interim Earnings (Per Share)

Qtr.	Mar	Jun	Sep	Dec
2016	0.56	0.90	0.84	0.67
2017	0.87	0.95	1.09	0.90
2018	0.94	1.21	1.35	1.35
2019	1.28	1.49	1.45	...

Interim Dividends (Per Share)

Amt	Decl	Ex	Rec	Pay
0.08Q	04/03/2019	04/17/2019	04/18/2019	04/30/2019
0.08Q	07/08/2019	07/18/2019	07/19/2019	07/30/2019
0.08Q	10/07/2019	10/17/2019	10/18/2019	10/30/2019
0.08Q	01/06/2020	01/16/2020	01/17/2020	01/31/2020

Indicated Div: $0.32

Valuation Analysis

		Institutional Holding	
Forecast EPS	$5.71	No of Institutions	
	(11/25/2019)	517	
Market Cap	$4.8 Billion	Shares	
Book Value	$2.0 Billion	73,284,144	
Price/Book	2.45	% Held	
Price/Sales	0.54	87.28	

Business Summary: Construction Services (MIC: 7.5.4 SIC: 1731 NAIC: 238210)

EMCOR Group is an electrical and mechanical construction and facilities services firm. In addition, Co. provides a number of building services and industrial services. Co.'s services are provided through its operating subsidiaries and joint venture entities. Co. focuses on providing construction services relating to electrical and mechanical systems all types of facilities and on providing various services relating to the operation, maintenance and management of facilities, including refineries and petrochemical plants. Co. also provides its construction services indirectly by acting as a subcontractor to contractors, systems suppliers, property managers and other subcontractors.

Recent Developments: For the quarter ended Sep 30 2019, income from continuing operations increased 2.4% to US$81.8 million from US$79.9 million in the year-earlier quarter. Net income increased 3.0% to US$81.8 million from US$79.4 million in the year-earlier quarter. Revenues were US$2.29 billion, up 11.8% from US$2.05 billion the year before. Operating income was US$115.7 million versus US$111.8 million in the prior-year quarter, an increase of 3.6%. Direct operating expenses rose 12.3% to US$1.95 billion from US$1.74 billion in the comparable period the year before. Indirect operating expenses increased 11.5% to US$220.2 million from US$197.6 million in the equivalent prior-year period.

Prospects: Our evaluation of EMCOR Group Inc. as of October 4th, 2019 is the result of our systematic analysis on three basic characteristics: earnings strength, relative valuation, and recent stock price movement. The company has managed to produce a neutral trend in earnings per share over the past 5 quarters. However, recent analyst estimates for the company have been raised and EME has posted results that exceeded analysts' expectations. Based on operating earnings yield, the company is undervalued when compared to all of the companies we cover. Share price changes over the past year indicates that EME will perform over the near term.

Financial Data

(US$ in Thousands)	9 Mos	6 Mos	3 Mos	12/31/2018	12/31/2017	12/31/2016	12/31/2015	12/31/2014
Earnings Per Share	5.57	5.47	5.19	4.85	3.82	2.97	2.72	2.52
Cash Flow Per Share	6.80	4.65	4.85	4.66	6.18	4.34	4.25	3.72
Tang Book Value Per Share	8.42	6.99	5.61	4.67	3.63	1.17	2.63	1.27
Dividends Per Share	0.320	0.320	0.320	0.320	0.320	0.320	0.320	0.320
Dividend Payout %	5.75	5.85	6.17	6.60	8.38	10.77	11.76	12.70
Income Statement								
Total Revenue	6,770,671	4,482,930	2,158,728	8,130,631	7,686,999	7,551,524	6,718,726	6,424,965
EBITDA	373,705	246,244	114,326	486,769	419,048	388,266	361,277	364,344
Depn & Amortn	34,500	23,169	11,610	80,943	88,494	79,808	74,195	74,466
Income Before Taxes	330,473	217,021	99,893	395,028	318,749	296,494	278,823	281,645
Income Taxes	92,257	60,639	27,483	109,106	90,699	111,199	106,256	103,528
Net Income	238,216	156,382	72,410	283,531	227,196	181,935	172,286	168,664
Average Shares	56,558	56,499	56,424	58,443	59,618	61,206	63,307	67,062
Balance Sheet								
Current Assets	2,558,113	2,420,635	2,313,861	2,386,207	2,284,509	2,210,847	2,067,419	1,886,603
Total Assets	4,532,721	4,393,578	4,278,324	4,088,807	3,965,904	3,894,170	3,546,470	3,388,967
Current Liabilities	1,793,374	1,704,566	1,673,183	1,734,398	1,650,952	1,511,774	1,413,728	1,283,417
Long-Term Obligations	247,837	276,448	280,438	279,764	294,786	408,296	300,065	316,399
Total Liabilities	2,557,556	2,499,393	2,467,558	2,348,262	2,292,637	2,357,081	2,069,759	1,972,954
Stockholders' Equity	1,975,165	1,894,185	1,810,766	1,740,545	1,673,267	1,537,089	1,476,711	1,416,013
Shares Outstanding	56,147	56,129	56,084	55,983	58,798	59,946	61,067	62,981
Statistical Record								
Return on Assets %	7.41	7.59	7.40	7.04	5.78	4.88	4.97	4.92
Return on Equity %	16.85	17.29	17.17	16.61	14.15	12.04	11.91	11.70
EBITDA Margin %	5.52	5.49	5.30	5.99	5.45	5.14	5.38	5.67
Net Margin %	3.52	3.49	3.35	3.49	2.96	2.41	2.56	2.63
Asset Turnover	2.11	2.12	2.07	2.02	1.96	2.02	1.94	1.87
Current Ratio	1.43	1.42	1.38	1.38	1.38	1.46	1.46	1.47
Debt to Equity	0.13	0.15	0.15	0.16	0.18	0.27	0.20	0.22
Price Range	89.20-57.53	88.10-57.53	81.35-57.53	84.14-57.53	83.64-60.39	73.04-42.47	51.68-39.96	47.79-39.07
P/E Ratio	16.01-10.33	16.11-10.52	15.67-11.08	17.35-11.86	21.90-15.81	24.59-14.30	19.00-14.69	18.96-15.50
Average Yield %	0.42	0.43	0.44	0.42	0.47	0.60	0.69	0.73

Address: 301 Merritt Seven, Norwalk, CT 06851-1092	**Web Site:** www.emcorgroup.com	**Auditors:** Ernst & Young LLP
Telephone: 203-849-7800	**Officers:** Anthony J. Guzzi - Chairman, President, Chief Executive Officer Mark A. Pompa - Executive Vice President, Chief Financial Officer	**Investor Contact:** 203-849-7938
		Transfer Agents: Computershare Shareowner Services, Pittsburgh, PA

EMERSON ELECTRIC CO.

Exchange	Symbol	Price	52Wk Range	Yield	P/E	Div Acheiver
NYS	EMR	$76.26 (12/31/2019)	76.97-56.41	2.62	20.56	62 Years

*7 Year Price Score 89.96   *NYSE Composite Index=100   *12 Month Price Score 104.79

Interim Earnings (Per Share)

Qtr.	Dec	Mar	Jun	Sep
2014-15	0.75	1.42	0.84	0.98
2015-16	0.53	0.57	0.74	0.68
2016-17	0.48	0.45	0.64	0.78
2017-18	0.61	0.76	1.12	0.97
2018-19	0.74	0.84	0.97	1.16

Interim Dividends (Per Share)

Amt	Decl	Ex	Rec	Pay
0.49Q	02/05/2019	02/14/2019	02/15/2019	03/11/2019
0.49Q	05/07/2019	05/16/2019	05/17/2019	06/10/2019
0.49Q	08/06/2019	08/15/2019	08/16/2019	09/10/2019
0.50Q	11/05/2019	11/14/2019	11/15/2019	12/10/2019

Indicated Div: $2.00 (Div. Reinv. Plan)

Valuation Analysis

		Institutional Holding	
Forecast EPS	$3.64	No of Institutions	
	(01/17/2020)	2048	
Market Cap	$46.6 Billion	Shares	
Book Value	$8.2 Billion	569,062,976	
Price/Book	5.66	% Held	
Price/Sales	2.54	67.01	

Business Summary: Electrical Equipment (MIC: 7.3.1 SIC: 3679 NAIC: 334419)

Emerson Electric is a company that brings technology and engineering together to provide solutions for customers in a range of industrial, commercial and consumer markets around the world. Co.'s segments are: Automation Solutions, which provides measurement and analytical instrumentation, valves, actuators and regulators, industrial solutions, and process control systems and solutions; Climate Technologies, which provides products and services for residential heating and cooling, commercial air conditioning, commercial and industrial refrigeration, and cold chain management; and Tools and Home Products, which provides tools for personnel and homeowners and appliance solutions.

Recent Developments: For the year ended Sep 30 2019, income from continuing operations increased 4.7% to US$2.33 billion from US$2.22 billion a year earlier. Net income increased 4.7% to US$2.33 billion from US$2.22 billion in the prior year. Revenues were US$18.37 billion, up 5.5% from US$17.41 billion the year before. Direct operating expenses rose 5.8% to US$10.56 billion from US$9.98 billion in the comparable period the year before. Indirect operating expenses increased 3.8% to US$4.78 billion from US$4.61 billion in the equivalent prior-year period.

Prospects: Our evaluation of Emerson Electric Co. as of October 4th, 2019 is the result of our systematic analysis on three basic characteristics: earnings strength, relative valuation, and recent stock price movement. The company has managed to produce a neutral trend in earnings per share over the past 5 quarters. However, recent analyst estimates for the company have been reduced while EMR has posted results that exceeded analysts' expectations. Based on operating earnings yield, the company is undervalued when compared to all of the companies we cover. Share price changes over the past year indicates that EMR will perform very poorly over the near term.

Financial Data

(US$ in Thousands)	09/30/2019	09/30/2018	09/30/2017	09/30/2016	09/30/2015	09/30/2014	09/30/2013	09/30/2012
Earnings Per Share	3.71	3.46	2.35	2.52	3.99	3.03	2.76	2.67
Cash Flow Per Share	4.88	4.58	2.98	4.46	3.76	5.27	5.08	4.17
Tang Book Value Per Share	N.M.	N.M.	2.36	4.29	N.M.	1.79	1.99	0.60
Dividends Per Share	1.960	1.940	1.920	1.900	1.880	1.720	1.640	1.600
Dividend Payout %	52.83	56.07	81.70	75.40	47.12	56.77	59.42	59.93
Income Statement								
Total Revenue	18,372,000	17,408,000	15,264,000	14,522,000	22,304,000	24,537,000	24,669,000	24,412,000
EBITDA	3,734,000	3,481,000	3,050,000	2,979,000	5,053,000	4,285,000	4,155,000	4,085,000
Depn & Amortn	701,000	655,000	550,000	475,000	721,000	743,000	741,000	746,000
Income Before Taxes	2,859,000	2,667,000	2,335,000	2,316,000	4,161,000	3,348,000	3,196,000	3,115,000
Income Taxes	531,000	443,000	660,000	697,000	1,428,000	1,164,000	1,130,000	1,091,000
Net Income	2,306,000	2,203,000	1,518,000	1,635,000	2,710,000	2,147,000	2,004,000	1,968,000
Average Shares	620,600	635,300	643,400	646,800	676,500	704,100	722,900	734,600
Balance Sheet								
Current Assets	7,139,000	6,619,000	8,252,000	9,960,000	10,049,000	10,867,000	10,999,000	10,126,000
Total Assets	20,497,000	20,390,000	19,589,000	21,743,000	22,088,000	24,177,000	24,711,000	23,818,000
Current Liabilities	5,976,000	6,164,000	5,045,000	8,008,000	7,800,000	8,454,000	7,625,000	7,133,000
Long-Term Obligations	4,277,000	3,137,000	3,794,000	4,062,000	4,289,000	3,559,000	4,055,000	3,787,000
Total Liabilities	12,264,000	11,443,000	10,871,000	14,175,000	14,007,000	14,058,000	14,126,000	13,523,000
Stockholders' Equity	8,233,000	8,947,000	8,718,000	7,568,000	8,081,000	10,119,000	10,585,000	10,295,000
Shares Outstanding	611,000	629,200	641,691	642,796	654,608	696,605	706,660	724,113
Statistical Record								
Return on Assets %	11.28	11.02	7.35	7.44	11.72	8.78	8.26	8.23
Return on Equity %	26.85	24.94	18.64	20.84	29.78	20.74	19.20	18.97
EBITDA Margin %	20.32	20.00	19.98	20.51	22.66	17.46	16.84	16.73
Net Margin %	12.55	12.66	9.94	11.26	12.15	8.75	8.12	8.06
Asset Turnover	0.90	0.87	0.74	0.66	0.96	1.00	1.02	1.02
Current Ratio	1.19	1.07	1.64	1.24	1.29	1.29	1.44	1.42
Debt to Equity	0.52	0.35	0.44	0.54	0.53	0.35	0.38	0.37
Price Range	78.52-55.49	78.41-59.02	64.15-49.41	56.34-42.29	65.77-43.04	70.26-61.79	66.50-47.32	53.37-40.69
P/E Ratio	21.16-14.96	22.66-17.06	27.30-21.03	22.36-16.78	16.48-10.79	23.19-20.39	24.09-17.14	19.99-15.24
Average Yield %	2.98	2.77	3.30	3.75	3.29	2.60	2.93	3.27

Address: 8000 W. Florissant Avenue, P.O. Box 4100, St. Louis, MO 63136 **Telephone:** 314-553-2000	**Web Site:** www.emerson.com **Officers:** David N. Farr - Chairman, President, Chief Executive Officer Michael H. (Mike) Train - President, Division Officer	**Auditors:** KPMG LLP **Investor Contact:** 314-553-2197 **Transfer Agents:** Computershare, Inc., Providence, RI

EMPIRE STATE REALTY TRUST INC

Exchange	Symbol	Price	52Wk Range	Yield	P/E
NYS	ESRT	$13.96 (12/31/2019)	16.14-13.02	3.01	45.03

*7 Year Price Score N/A   *NYSE Composite Index=100   *12 Month Price Score 90.19

TRADING VOLUME (thousand shares)

Interim Earnings (Per Share)

Qtr.	Mar	Jun	Sep	Dec
2016	0.06	0.09	0.12	0.11
2017	0.06	0.10	0.12	0.10
2018	0.06	0.10	0.10	0.13
2019	0.03	0.06	0.09	...

Interim Dividends (Per Share)

Amt	Decl	Ex	Rec	Pay
0.105Q	03/01/2019	03/14/2019	03/15/2019	03/29/2019
0.105Q	05/17/2019	06/13/2019	06/14/2019	06/28/2019
0.105Q	08/09/2019	09/13/2019	09/16/2019	09/30/2019
0.105Q	12/13/2019	12/20/2019	12/23/2019	12/31/2019

Indicated Div: $0.42

Valuation Analysis

	Institutional Holding	
Forecast EPS	$0.18 (01/17/2020)	No of Institutions 243
Market Cap	$2.5 Billion	Shares
Book Value	$1.2 Billion	172,982,576
Price/Book	2.04	% Held
Price/Sales	3.42	89.70

Business Summary: REITs (MIC: 5.3.1 SIC: 6798 NAIC: 525930)

Empire State Realty Trust is a self-administered and self-managed real estate investment trust. Co. owns, manages, operates, acquires and repositions office and retail properties in Manhattan and the greater New York metropolitan area, including the Empire State Building. Co.'s operating partnership, Empire State Realty OP, L.P., conducts substantially all of Co.'s business. Co. has two reportable segments: Real Estate and Observatory. Co.'s real estate segment includes all activities related to the ownership, management, operation, acquisition, repositioning and disposition of its real estate assets. Co.'s observatory segment operates the floor observatories at the Empire State Building.

Recent Developments: For the quarter ended Sep 30 2019, net income decreased 8.4% to US$26.8 million from US$29.2 million in the year-earlier quarter. Revenues were US$192.9 million, up 3.5% from US$186.4 million the year before. Revenues from property income rose 5.6% to US$150.2 million from US$142.2 million in the corresponding quarter a year earlier.

Prospects: Our evaluation of Empire State Realty Trust Inc as of October 4th, 2019 is the result of our systematic analysis on three basic characteristics: earnings strength, relative valuation, and recent stock price movement. The company has managed to produce a neutral trend in earnings per share over the past 5 quarters. Additionally, recent analyst estimates for the company have been unchanged while ESRT has posted results that fell short of analysts' expectations. Based on operating earnings yield, the company is overvalued when compared to all of the companies we cover. Share price changes over the past year indicates that ESRT will perform in line with the market over the near term.

Financial Data

(US$ in Thousands)	9 Mos	6 Mos	3 Mos	12/31/2018	12/31/2017	12/31/2016	12/31/2015	12/31/2014
Earnings Per Share	0.31	0.32	0.36	0.39	0.39	0.38	0.29	0.27
Cash Flow Per Share	1.63	1.46	1.64	1.67	1.21	1.63	1.78	1.41
Tang Book Value Per Share	1.92	1.90	1.96	4.27	4.19	4.25	0.28	N.M.
Dividends Per Share	0.420	0.420	0.420	0.420	0.420	0.400	0.340	0.340
Dividend Payout %	135.48	131.25	116.67	107.69	107.69	105.26	117.24	125.93
Income Statement								
Total Revenue	536,410	343,537	167,293	731,511	712,468	678,000	657,634	635,326
EBITDA	113,087	66,280	27,754	320,926	312,889	290,886	259,688	230,826
Depn & Amortn	5,493	3,965	1,678	130,069	119,490	106,343	108,319	89,505
Income Before Taxes	56,789	28,667	9,126	121,895	124,926	113,396	83,877	74,865
Income Taxes	1,219	(119)	(730)	4,642	6,673	6,146	3,949	4,655
Net Income	33,348	17,232	5,911	66,539	63,583	52,392	34,666	27,143
Average Shares	298,151	298,131	298,049	297,259	298,049	277,568	266,621	254,506
Balance Sheet								
Current Assets	330,319	563,378	654,676	670,813	530,197	615,885	112,565	106,005
Total Assets	3,925,317	4,155,575	4,192,440	4,195,780	3,931,347	3,890,953	3,300,650	3,296,495
Current Liabilities	175,042	164,225	184,545	188,478	157,935	181,247	159,989	137,011
Long-Term Obligations	1,669,177	1,919,405	1,919,172	1,918,933	1,688,721	1,612,331	1,632,416	1,611,652
Total Liabilities	2,695,294	2,931,924	2,959,747	2,949,294	2,755,061	2,728,813	2,767,917	2,819,853
Stockholders' Equity	1,230,023	1,223,651	1,232,693	1,238,482	1,168,282	1,154,136	524,729	468,638
Shares Outstanding	180,149	178,020	176,593	174,910	161,477	155,840	120,023	107,191
Statistical Record								
Return on Assets %	1.39	1.37	1.50	1.64	1.63	1.45	1.05	0.94
Return on Equity %	4.63	4.69	5.17	5.53	5.48	6.22	6.98	6.36
EBITDA Margin %	21.08	19.29	16.59	43.87	43.92	42.90	39.49	36.33
Net Margin %	6.22	5.02	3.53	9.10	8.92	7.73	5.27	4.27
Asset Turnover	0.18	0.18	0.18	0.18	0.18	0.19	0.20	0.22
Current Ratio	1.89	3.43	3.55	3.56	3.36	3.40	0.70	0.77
Debt to Equity	1.36	1.57	1.56	1.55	1.45	1.40	3.11	3.44
Price Range	16.43-13.02	17.74-13.81	17.74-13.81	20.30-13.81	21.92-19.76	22.17-14.67	18.96-15.94	17.88-14.19
P/E Ratio	53.00-42.00	55.44-43.16	49.28-38.36	52.05-35.41	56.21-50.67	58.34-38.61	65.38-54.97	66.22-52.56
Average Yield %	2.77	2.64	2.58	2.48	2.03	2.11	1.91	2.14

Address: 111 West 33rd Street, 12th Floor, New York, NY 10120 **Telephone:** 212-687-8700	**Web Site:** www.empirestaterealtytrust.com **Officers:** Anthony E. Malkin - Chairman, Chief Executive Officer, President John B. Kessler - President, Chief Operating Officer	**Auditors:** Ernst & Young LLP **Transfer Agents:** American Stock Transfer & Trust Company, LLC

ENCOMPASS HEALTH CORP

Exchange	Symbol	Price	52Wk Range	Yield	P/E
NYS	EHC	$69.27 (12/31/2019)	72.09-57.71	1.62	21.58

*7 Year Price Score 115.14 *NYSE Composite Index=100 *12 Month Price Score 104.01

Interim Earnings (Per Share)

Qtr.	Mar	Jun	Sep	Dec
2016	0.61	0.65	0.64	0.69
2017	0.70	0.70	0.67	0.61
2018	0.84	0.92	0.89	0.28
2019	1.03	0.92	0.98	...

Interim Dividends (Per Share)

Amt	Decl	Ex	Rec	Pay
0.27Q	02/21/2019	03/29/2019	04/01/2019	04/15/2019
0.27Q	05/03/2019	06/28/2019	07/01/2019	07/15/2019
0.28Q	07/23/2019	09/30/2019	10/01/2019	10/15/2019
0.28Q	10/25/2019	12/31/2019	01/02/2020	01/15/2020

Indicated Div: $1.12

Valuation Analysis

		Institutional Holding	
Forecast EPS	$3.84	No of Institutions	
	(01/17/2020)	542	
Market Cap	$6.8 Billion	Shares	
Book Value	$1.3 Billion	121,926,840	
Price/Book	5.12	% Held	
Price/Sales	1.51	N/A	

TRADING VOLUME (thousand shares)

Business Summary: Hospitals & Health Care Facilities (MIC: 4.2.1 SIC: 8093 NAIC: 623110)

Encompass Health is a provider of healthcare services, providing both facility-based and home-based patient care through its network of inpatient rehabilitation hospitals, home health agencies, and hospice agencies. Co.'s inpatient rehabilitation hospitals provide specialized rehabilitative care across an array of diagnoses and deliver patient care services. Co.'s home health agencies provide home care services such as skilled nursing, physical, occupational, and speech therapy, medical social work, and home health aide services. Co. also provides hospice services such as pain control and symptom management, and emotional and spiritual support to terminally ill patients and their families.

Recent Developments: For the quarter ended Sep 30 2019, income from continuing operations increased 9.2% to US$119.5 million from US$109.4 million in the year-earlier quarter. Net income increased 9.3% to US$119.5 million from US$109.3 million in the year-earlier quarter. Revenues were US$1.16 billion, up 8.8% from US$1.07 billion the year before. Direct operating expenses rose 9.6% to US$156.6 million from US$142.9 million in the comparable period the year before. Indirect operating expenses increased 10.8% to US$833.1 million from US$751.6 million in the equivalent prior-year period.

Prospects: Our evaluation of Encompass Health Corp. as of October 4th, 2019 is the result of our systematic analysis on three basic characteristics: earnings strength, relative valuation, and recent stock price movement. The company has managed to produce a neutral trend in earnings per share over the past 5 quarters. In addition, recent analyst estimates for the company have been mixed and EHC has posted results that exceeded analysts' expectations. Based on operating earnings yield, the company is undervalued when compared to all of the companies we cover. Share price changes over the past year indicates that EHC will perform poorly over the near term.

Financial Data
(US$ in Thousands)

	9 Mos	6 Mos	3 Mos	12/31/2018	12/31/2017	12/31/2016	12/31/2015	12/31/2014
Earnings Per Share	3.21	3.12	3.12	2.93	2.69	2.59	1.91	2.29
Cash Flow Per Share	6.12	6.96	7.17	7.79	7.01	6.78	5.42	5.13
Dividends Per Share	1.090	1.080	1.060	1.040	0.980	0.940	0.880	0.780
Dividend Payout %	33.96	34.62	33.97	35.49	36.43	36.29	46.07	34.06
Income Statement								
Total Revenue	3,420,600	2,259,000	1,124,000	4,277,300	3,919,000	3,646,000	3,115,700	2,374,300
EBITDA	714,800	466,800	243,700	756,000	754,600	746,600	620,800	565,300
Depn & Amortn	160,300	105,200	52,500	124,200	111,800	102,300	91,000	79,900
Income Before Taxes	439,300	286,700	154,000	484,500	488,400	472,200	386,900	376,200
Income Taxes	88,600	54,300	30,800	118,900	160,600	163,900	141,900	110,700
Net Income	291,100	193,500	102,300	292,300	256,300	247,600	183,100	222,000
Average Shares	99,400	99,300	99,700	99,800	99,300	99,500	101,000	100,700
Balance Sheet								
Current Assets	1,077,400	844,900	682,700	662,100	702,200	654,500	598,700	686,600
Total Assets	6,386,800	5,812,100	5,583,800	5,175,000	4,893,700	4,681,900	4,606,100	3,408,800
Current Liabilities	1,108,600	752,900	768,200	672,500	517,500	475,600	426,400	364,300
Long-Term Obligations	2,961,900	2,719,600	2,521,800	2,478,600	2,545,400	2,979,300	3,134,700	2,110,800
Total Liabilities	5,053,700	4,536,200	4,269,500	3,898,300	3,712,000	3,946,000	3,994,700	2,842,400
Stockholders' Equity	1,333,100	1,275,900	1,314,300	1,276,700	1,181,700	735,900	611,400	566,400
Shares Outstanding	98,600	98,600	99,100	98,926	98,305	88,929	90,130	87,788
Statistical Record								
Return on Assets %	5.54	5.69	5.91	5.81	5.35	5.32	4.57	7.47
Return on Equity %	24.08	24.51	24.75	23.78	26.73	36.65	31.09	44.21
EBITDA Margin %	20.90	20.66	21.68	17.67	19.25	20.48	19.92	23.81
Net Margin %	8.51	8.57	9.10	6.83	6.54	6.79	5.88	9.35
Asset Turnover	0.78	0.81	0.83	0.85	0.82	0.78	0.78	0.80
Current Ratio	0.97	1.12	0.89	0.98	1.36	1.38	1.40	1.88
Debt to Equity	2.22	2.13	1.92	1.94	2.15	4.05	5.13	3.73
Price Range	78.49-57.71	82.35-57.71	82.35-55.68	82.35-49.67	50.10-38.61	43.05-30.91	47.93-33.04	41.74-30.05
P/E Ratio	24.45-17.98	26.39-18.50	26.39-17.85	28.11-16.95	18.62-14.35	16.62-11.93	25.09-17.30	18.23-13.12
Average Yield %	1.68	1.48	1.54	1.57	2.18	2.42	2.21	2.15

Address: 9001 Liberty Parkway, Birmingham, AL 35242
Telephone: 205-967-7116

Web Site: www.encompasshealth.com
Officers: Leo I. Higdon - Chairman Jon F. Hanson - Chairman

Auditors: PricewaterhouseCoopers LLP
Investor Contact: 205-968-6400
Transfer Agents: Computershare Investor Services, Canton, MA

ENERGIZER HOLDINGS INC

Exchange	Symbol	Price	52Wk Range	Yield	P/E
NYS	ENR	$50.22 (12/31/2019)	52.10-33.49	2.39	86.59

*7 Year Price Score N/A   *NYSE Composite Index=100   *12 Month Price Score 104.10

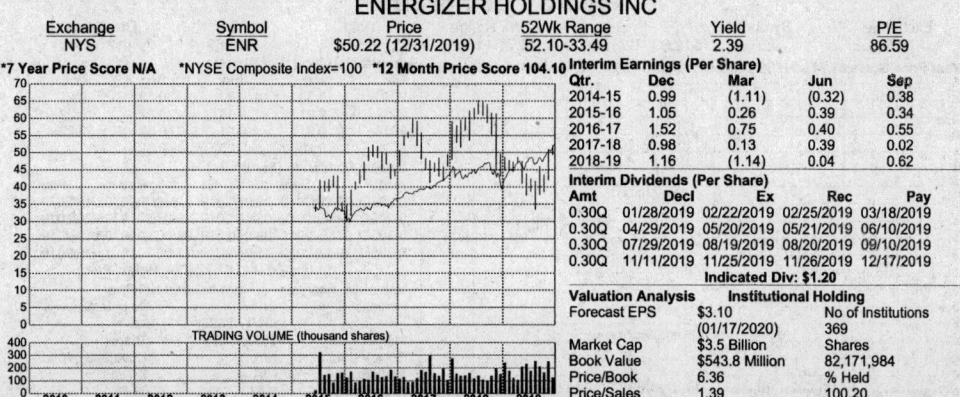

Interim Earnings (Per Share)

Qtr.	Dec	Mar	Jun	Sep
2014-15	0.99	(1.11)	(0.32)	0.38
2015-16	1.05	0.26	0.39	0.34
2016-17	1.52	0.75	0.40	0.55
2017-18	0.98	0.13	0.39	0.02
2018-19	1.16	(1.14)	0.04	0.62

Interim Dividends (Per Share)

Amt	Decl	Ex	Rec	Pay
0.30Q	01/28/2019	02/22/2019	02/25/2019	03/18/2019
0.30Q	04/29/2019	05/20/2019	05/21/2019	06/10/2019
0.30Q	07/29/2019	08/19/2019	08/20/2019	09/10/2019
0.30Q	11/11/2019	11/25/2019	11/26/2019	12/17/2019

Indicated Div: $1.20

Valuation Analysis

	Institutional Holding	
Forecast EPS	$3.10	No of Institutions
	(01/17/2020)	369
Market Cap	$3.5 Billion	Shares
Book Value	$543.8 Million	82,171,984
Price/Book	6.36	% Held
Price/Sales	1.39	100.20

Business Summary: Household & Personal Products (MIC: 1.7.1 SIC: 3692 NAIC: 335912)

Energizer Holdings is a manufacturer, marketer and distributor of household and specialty batteries, portable lights, and automotive appearance, performance, refrigerants and freshener products. Co. provides batteries using various technologies including lithium, alkaline, carbon zinc, nickel metal hydride, zinc air, and silver oxide. Co. manufactures, distributes and markets lighting products including headlights, lanterns, children's lights and area lights. Co. also provides auto care products in the appearance and fragrance categories including protectants, wipes, tire and wheel care products, glass cleaners, leather care products, air fresheners and washes.

Recent Developments: For the year ended Sep 30 2019, income from continuing operations decreased 30.8% to US$64.7 million from US$93.5 million a year earlier. Net income decreased 45.3% to US$51.1 million from US$93.5 million in the prior year. Revenues were US$2.49 billion, up 38.8% from US$1.80 billion the year before. Direct operating expenses rose 54.2% to US$1.49 billion from US$966.8 million in the comparable period the year before. Indirect operating expenses increased 27.5% to US$719.0 million from US$563.9 million in the equivalent prior-year period.

Prospects: Our evaluation of Energizer Holdings Co. as of October 4th, 2019 is the result of our systematic analysis on three basic characteristics: earnings strength, relative valuation, and recent stock price movement. The company has managed to produce a neutral trend in earnings per share over the past 5 quarters. However, recent analyst estimates for the company have been raised and ENR has posted results that fell short of analysts' expectations. Based on operating earnings yield, the company is undervalued when compared to all of the companies we cover. Share price changes over the past year indicates that ENR will perform very poorly over the near term.

Financial Data

(US$ in Thousands)	09/30/2019	09/30/2018	09/30/2017	09/30/2016	09/30/2015	09/30/2014	09/30/2013	09/30/2012
Earnings Per Share	0.58	1.52	3.22	2.04	(0.06)	...	...	...
Cash Flow Per Share	2.25	3.82	3.20	3.12	2.60	...	...	...
Dividends Per Share	1.200	1.160	1.100	1.000	0.250	...	...	...
Dividend Payout %	206.90	76.32	34.16	49.02		...	...	...
Income Statement								
Total Revenue	2,494,500	1,797,700	1,755,700	1,634,200	1,631,600	1,840,400	2,012,200	2,087,700
EBITDA	372,300	311,300	371,300	250,700	114,300	308,200	284,900	381,800
Depn & Amortn	86,700	37,700	44,900	30,700	37,100	40,300	54,800	55,300
Income Before Taxes	73,100	175,200	273,300	165,700	(700)	215,200	162,000	257,600
Income Taxes	8,400	81,700	71,800	38,000	3,300	57,900	47,100	70,600
Net Income	51,100	93,500	201,500	127,700	(4,000)	157,300	114,900	187,000
Average Shares	67,300	61,400	62,600	62,500	62,200	...	...	...
Balance Sheet								
Current Assets	2,036,800	1,171,100	1,020,200	889,500	1,126,500	747,100	753,000	...
Total Assets	5,449,600	3,178,800	1,823,600	1,731,500	1,629,600	1,194,700	1,238,800	...
Current Liabilities	1,069,000	751,200	582,000	533,100	467,800	380,400	395,100	...
Long-Term Obligations	3,461,600	2,206,800	978,500	981,700	995,000			...
Total Liabilities	4,905,800	3,154,300	1,738,500	1,761,500	1,689,700	470,200	501,100	...
Stockholders' Equity	543,800	24,500	85,100	(30,000)	(60,100)	724,500	737,700	...
Shares Outstanding	68,902	59,608	60,708	61,672	62,195	...	...	...
Statistical Record								
Return on Assets %	1.18	3.74	11.34	7.58	N.M.	...	...	...
Return on Equity %	17.98	170.62	731.40	...	N.M.	...	...	...
EBITDA Margin %	14.92	17.32	21.15	15.34	7.01	16.75	14.16	18.29
Net Margin %	2.05	5.20	11.48	7.81	N.M.	8.55	5.71	8.96
Asset Turnover	0.58	0.72	0.99	0.97	1.16	...	...	...
Current Ratio	1.91	1.56	1.75	1.67	2.41	1.96	1.91	...
Debt to Equity	6.37	90.07	11.50	...	...	...	...	...
Price Range	61.57-33.49	65.06-41.83	59.82-41.14	52.35-30.23	42.31-33.00	...	...	...
P/E Ratio	106.16-57.74	42.80-27.52	18.58-12.78	25.66-14.82	...	...	...	...
Average Yield %	2.61	2.09	2.23	2.35	0.64	...	...	...

Address: 533 Maryville University Drive, St. Louis, MO 63141 **Telephone:** 314-985-2000	**Web Site:** www.energizerholdings.com **Officers:** Patrick J. Moore - Chairman, Vice-Chairman Mark S. LaVigne - President, Executive Vice President, Chief Operating Officer	**Auditors:** PricewaterhouseCoopers LLP **Transfer Agents:** Continental Stock Transfer and Trust Company

ENERGY TRANSFER LP

Exchange	Symbol	Price	52Wk Range	Yield	P/E	Div Acheiver
NYS	ET	$12.83 (12/31/2019)	15.74-11.16	9.51	10.69	12 Years

*7 Year Price Score 61.74   ***NYSE Composite Index=100**   ***12 Month Price Score 82.37**

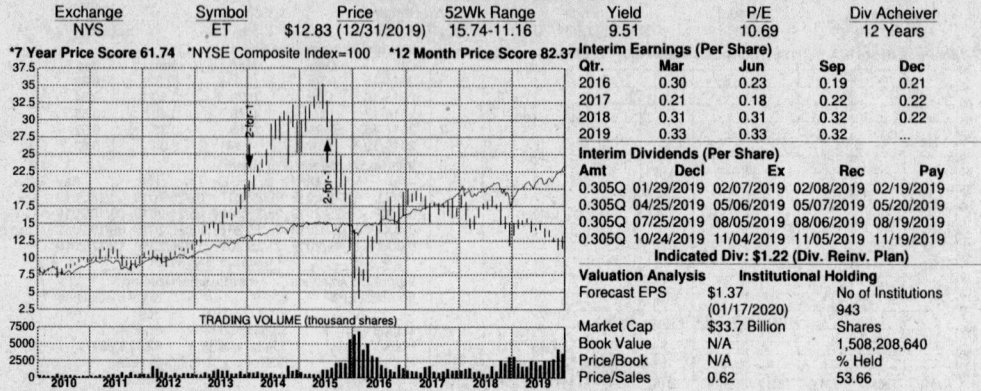

Interim Earnings (Per Share)

Qtr.	Mar	Jun	Sep	Dec
2016	0.30	0.23	0.19	0.21
2017	0.21	0.18	0.22	0.22
2018	0.31	0.31	0.32	0.22
2019	0.33	0.33	0.32	...

Interim Dividends (Per Share)

Amt	Decl	Ex	Rec	Pay
0.305Q	01/29/2019	02/07/2019	02/08/2019	02/19/2019
0.305Q	04/25/2019	05/06/2019	05/07/2019	05/20/2019
0.305Q	07/25/2019	08/05/2019	08/06/2019	08/19/2019
0.305Q	10/24/2019	11/04/2019	11/05/2019	11/19/2019

Indicated Div: $1.22 (Div. Reinv. Plan)

Valuation Analysis   **Institutional Holding**

Forecast EPS	$1.37	No of Institutions
(01/17/2020)		943
Market Cap	$33.7 Billion	Shares
Book Value	N/A	1,508,208,640
Price/Book	N/A	% Held
Price/Sales	0.62	53.66

Business Summary: Equipment & Services (MIC: 9.1.3 SIC: 4922 NAIC: 486210)

Energy Transfer is a holding company. Through its subsidiaries, Co. is engaged in natural gas operations, including natural gas midstream and intrastate transportation and storage and interstate natural gas transportation and storage, and crude oil, natural gas liquid (NGL) and refined products transportation, terminalling services and acquisition and marketing activities. In addition, Co. owns investments in other businesses. Co.'s segments include: intrastate transportation and storage; interstate transportation and storage; midstream; NGL and refined products transportation and services; crude oil transportation and services; investment in Sunoco LP; investment in USAC; and all other.

Recent Developments: For the quarter ended Sep 30 2019, income from continuing operations decreased 16.7% to US$1.16 billion from US$1.39 billion in the year-earlier quarter. Net income decreased 16.5% to US$1.16 billion from US$1.39 billion in the year-earlier quarter. Revenues were US$13.50 billion, down 7.0% from US$14.51 billion the year before. Operating income was US$1.83 billion versus US$1.70 billion in the prior-year quarter, an increase of 7.5%. Direct operating expenses declined 10.8% to US$9.89 billion from US$11.09 billion in the comparable period the year before. Indirect operating expenses increased 3.3% to US$1.78 billion from US$1.72 billion in the equivalent prior-year period.

Prospects: Our evaluation of Energy Transfer L.P. as of October 4th, 2019 is the result of our systematic analysis on three basic characteristics: earnings strength, relative valuation, and recent stock price movement. The company has generated a negative trend in earnings per share over the past 5 quarters. However, recent analyst estimates for the company have been unchanged while ET has posted results that fell short of analysts' expectations. Based on operating earnings yield, the company is undervalued when compared to all of the companies we cover. Share price changes over the past year indicates that ET will perform in line with the market over the near term.

Financial Data
(US$ in Thousands)

	9 Mos	6 Mos	3 Mos	12/31/2018	12/31/2017	12/31/2016	12/31/2015	12/31/2014
Earnings Per Share	1.20	1.20	1.18	1.15	0.83	0.92	1.11	0.57
Cash Flow Per Share	3.12	3.14	2.74	5.27	4.11	3.26	2.89	2.92
Dividends Per Share	1.220	1.220	1.220	1.220	1.150	1.140	1.020	0.750
Dividend Payout %	101.67	101.67	103.39	106.09	138.55	123.91	91.89	130.43
Income Statement								
Total Revenue	40,493,000	26,998,000	13,121,000	54,087,000	40,523,000	37,504,000	42,126,000	55,691,000
EBITDA	7,629,000	5,133,000	2,605,000	7,883,000	4,692,000	3,475,000	4,136,000	3,677,000
Depn & Amortn	2,343,000	1,559,000	774,000	2,538,000	2,204,000	2,089,000	1,776,000	1,223,000
Income Before Taxes	3,539,000	2,406,000	1,241,000	3,290,000	566,000	(446,000)	717,000	1,085,000
Income Taxes	214,000	160,000	126,000	4,000	(1,833,000)	(217,000)	(100,000)	357,000
Net Income	2,580,000	1,748,000	870,000	1,694,000	954,000	995,000	1,189,000	633,000
Average Shares	2,635,500	2,631,000	2,627,900	1,461,400	1,150,800	1,078,600	1,064,400	1,090,800
Balance Sheet								
Current Assets	7,066,000	7,198,000	7,127,000	6,750,000	10,683,000	6,985,000	5,410,000	6,153,000
Total Assets	91,856,000	90,812,000	89,773,000	88,246,000	86,246,000	79,011,000	71,189,000	64,469,000
Current Liabilities	7,037,000	6,429,000	6,695,000	9,310,000	7,897,000	7,277,000	4,910,000	6,782,000
Long-Term Obligations	46,840,000	46,499,000	46,373,000	43,373,000	43,671,000	42,858,000	36,837,000	29,653,000
Total Liabilities	70,938,000	69,978,000	69,119,000	67,687,000	87,442,000	80,705,000	72,121,000	63,805,000
Shares Outstanding	2,627,000	2,623,200	2,619,600	2,619,369	1,079,145	1,046,947	1,046,923	1,080,613
Statistical Record								
Return on Assets %	3.55	3.07	2.56	1.94	1.15	1.32	1.75	1.10
EBITDA Margin %	18.84	19.01	19.85	14.57	11.58	9.27	9.82	6.60
Net Margin %	6.37	6.47	6.63	3.13	2.35	2.65	2.82	1.14
Asset Turnover	0.60	0.62	0.64	0.62	0.49	0.50	0.62	0.97
Current Ratio	1.00	1.12	1.06	0.73	1.35	0.96	1.10	0.91
Price Range	18.09-11.80	18.97-11.80	18.97-11.80	19.18-11.80	19.86-15.15	19.59-4.05	35.24-11.09	32.24-19.62
P/E Ratio	15.08-9.83	15.81-9.83	16.08-10.00	16.68-10.26	23.93-18.25	21.29-4.40	31.75-9.99	56.56-34.43
Average Yield %	8.30	7.79	7.59	7.40	6.47	8.51	3.71	2.85

Address: 8111 Westchester Drive, Suite 600, Dallas, TX 75225
Telephone: 214-981-0700

Web Site: www.energytransfer.com
Officers: Kelcy L. Warren - Chairman John W. McReynolds - President, Chief Financial Officer

Auditors: Grant Thornton LLP
Investor Contact: 214-981-0700
Transfer Agents: American Stock Transfer & Trust, Brooklyn, NY

ENERSYS

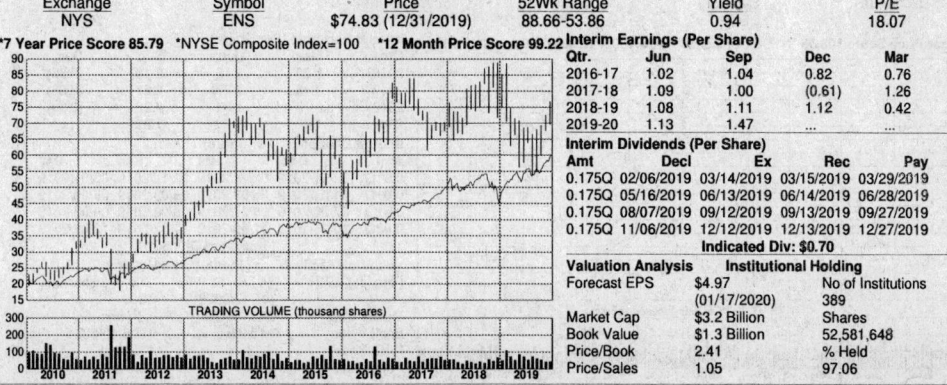

Exchange	Symbol	Price	52Wk Range	Yield	P/E
NYS	ENS	$74.83 (12/31/2019)	88.66-53.86	0.94	18.07

*7 Year Price Score 85.79   *NYSE Composite Index=100   *12 Month Price Score 99.22

Interim Earnings (Per Share)

Qtr.	Jun	Sep	Dec	Mar
2016-17	1.02	1.04	0.82	0.76
2017-18	1.09	1.00	(0.61)	1.26
2018-19	1.08	1.11	1.12	0.42
2019-20	1.13	1.47	...	...

Interim Dividends (Per Share)

Amt	Decl	Ex	Rec	Pay
0.175Q	02/06/2019	03/14/2019	03/15/2019	03/29/2019
0.175Q	05/16/2019	06/13/2019	06/14/2019	06/28/2019
0.175Q	08/07/2019	09/12/2019	09/13/2019	09/27/2019
0.175Q	11/06/2019	12/12/2019	12/13/2019	12/27/2019

Indicated Div: $0.70

Valuation Analysis | **Institutional Holding**

Forecast EPS	$4.97	No of Institutions	
	(01/17/2020)	389	
Market Cap	$3.2 Billion	Shares	
Book Value	$1.3 Billion	52,581,648	
Price/Book	2.41	% Held	
Price/Sales	1.05	97.06	

Business Summary: Electrical Equipment (MIC: 7.3.1 SIC: 5063 NAIC: 423610)

EnerSys is a manufacturer, marketer and distributor of industrial batteries. Co. also manufactures, markets and distributes products such as battery chargers, power equipment, battery accessories, and outdoor cabinet enclosures. Co.'s product lines are: reserve power products, which are used for backup power for the continuous operation of critical applications in telecommunications systems, uninterruptible power systems applications for computer and computer-controlled systems, and other specialty power applications; and motive power products, which are used to provide power for electric industrial forklifts used in manufacturing, warehousing and other material handling applications.

Recent Developments: For the quarter ended Sep 29 2019, net income increased 32.1% to US$62.7 million from US$47.4 million in the year-earlier quarter. Revenues were US$762.1 million, up 15.4% from US$660.5 million the year before. Operating income was US$58.7 million versus US$63.4 million in the prior-year quarter, a decrease of 7.3%. Direct operating expenses rose 13.1% to US$564.8 million from US$499.6 million in the comparable period the year before. Indirect operating expenses increased 42.1% to US$138.6 million from US$97.5 million in the equivalent prior-year period.

Prospects: Our evaluation of Enersys as of October 4th, 2019 is the result of our systematic analysis on three basic characteristics: earnings strength, relative valuation, and recent stock price movement. The company has produced a positive trend in earnings per share over the past 5 quarters. However, recent analyst estimates for the company have been mixed and ENS has posted results that fell short of analysts' expectations. Based on operating earnings yield, the company is undervalued when compared to all of the companies we cover. Share price changes over the past year indicates that ENS will perform very poorly over the near term.

Financial Data

(US$ in Thousands)	6 Mos	3 Mos	03/31/2019	03/31/2018	03/31/2017	03/31/2016	03/31/2015	03/31/2014
Earnings Per Share	4.14	3.78	3.73	2.77	3.64	2.99	3.77	3.02
Cash Flow Per Share	5.16	4.75	4.67	4.95	5.67	6.93	4.26	4.08
Tang Book Value Per Share	5.20	4.28	3.84	16.60	14.29	11.58	11.63	14.01
Dividends Per Share	0.700	0.700	0.700	0.700	0.700	0.700	0.700	0.500
Dividend Payout %	16.91	18.52	18.77	25.27	19.23	23.41	18.57	16.56
Income Statement								
Total Revenue	1,542,367	780,230	2,808,017	2,581,891	2,367,149	2,316,249	2,505,512	2,474,433
EBITDA	169,052	90,213	261,697	309,201	280,280	251,966	318,244	230,545
Depn & Amortn	41,053	20,725	48,618	45,874	45,388	47,686	49,261	49,693
Income Before Taxes	107,004	58,590	182,211	238,326	212,695	181,937	249,339	163,747
Income Taxes	(4,330)	9,954	21,584	118,493	54,472	50,113	67,814	16,980
Net Income	111,334	48,636	160,239	119,594	160,214	136,150	181,188	150,328
Average Shares	42,708	43,118	43,008	43,119	44,012	45,474	48,052	49,788
Balance Sheet								
Current Assets	1,639,810	1,519,869	1,536,648	1,539,587	1,418,915	1,296,239	1,233,418	1,300,700
Total Assets	3,290,813	3,182,418	3,118,193	2,486,925	2,293,029	2,214,488	2,163,047	2,321,858
Current Liabilities	565,639	598,888	612,933	491,530	467,431	451,171	433,371	581,403
Long-Term Obligations	1,117,818	978,632	971,931	579,590	587,705	606,398	495,973	288,132
Total Liabilities	1,975,338	1,889,492	1,835,906	1,291,250	1,189,573	1,201,357	1,122,817	1,065,843
Stockholders' Equity	1,315,475	1,292,926	1,282,287	1,195,675	1,103,456	1,013,131	1,040,230	1,256,015
Shares Outstanding	42,281	42,478	42,620	41,915	43,447	43,189	44,068	46,942
Statistical Record								
Return on Assets %	6.18	5.80	5.72	5.00	7.11	6.20	8.08	6.98
Return on Equity %	14.19	13.23	12.93	10.40	15.14	13.22	15.78	12.40
EBITDA Margin %	10.96	11.56	9.32	11.98	11.84	10.88	12.70	9.32
Net Margin %	7.22	6.23	5.71	4.63	6.77	5.88	7.23	6.08
Asset Turnover	1.05	1.04	1.00	1.08	1.05	1.06	1.12	1.15
Current Ratio	2.90	2.54	2.51	3.13	3.04	2.87	2.85	2.24
Debt to Equity	0.85	0.76	0.76	0.48	0.53	0.60	0.48	0.23
Price Range	88.82-53.86	88.82-56.23	88.82-62.80	83.96-61.45	82.71-52.44	72.75-43.39	71.81-51.83	73.87-42.78
P/E Ratio	21.45-13.01	23.50-14.88	23.81-16.84	30.31-22.18	22.72-14.41	24.33-14.51	19.05-13.75	24.46-14.17
Average Yield %	0.98	0.93	0.90	0.98	1.01	1.17	1.11	0.84

Address: 2366 Bernville Road, Reading, PA 19605
Telephone: 610-208-1991

Web Site: www.enersys.com
Officers: David M. Shaffer - President, Chief Executive Officer Michael J. Schmidtlein - Executive Vice President, Senior Vice President, Chief Financial Officer

Auditors: Ernst & Young LLP
Investor Contact: 610-236-4040
Transfer Agents: Computershare

ENTERGY CORP

Exchange	Symbol	Price	52Wk Range	Yield	P/E
NYS	ETR	$119.80 (12/31/2019)	121.56-84.00	3.11	30.10

*7 Year Price Score 108.86 *NYSE Composite Index=100 *12 Month Price Score 107.00

Interim Earnings (Per Share)

Qtr.	Mar	Jun	Sep	Dec
2016	1.28	3.16	2.16	(9.86)
2017	0.46	2.27	2.21	(2.66)
2018	0.73	1.34	2.92	(0.38)
2019	1.32	1.22	1.82	...

Interim Dividends (Per Share)

Amt	Decl	Ex	Rec	Pay
0.91Q	02/01/2019	02/13/2019	02/14/2019	03/01/2019
0.91Q	04/03/2019	05/08/2019	05/09/2019	06/03/2019
0.91Q	07/26/2019	08/07/2019	08/08/2019	09/03/2019
0.93Q	10/25/2019	11/06/2019	11/07/2019	12/02/2019

Indicated Div: $3.72

Valuation Analysis | **Institutional Holding**

Forecast EPS	$5.35	No of Institutions
	(01/17/2020)	929
Market Cap	$23.9 Billion	Shares
Book Value	$10.3 Billion	206,109,824
Price/Book	2.33	% Held
Price/Sales	2.18	95.40

Business Summary: Electric Utilities (MIC: 3.1.1 SIC: 4911 NAIC: 221122)

Entergy is a holding company. Through its subsidiaries, Co. is an integrated energy company engaged mainly in electric power production and retail distribution operations. Co. owns and operates power plants. Co. operates through two segments: Utility, which generates, transmits, distributes and sells electric power to retail and wholesale customers in Arkansas, Louisiana, Mississippi, and Texas; and Entergy Wholesale Commodities, which includes the ownership, operation, and decommissioning of nuclear power plants, located in the northern U.S., the sale of the electric power produced by its operating plants to wholesale customers, and also provides operations and management services.

Recent Developments: For the quarter ended Sep 30 2019, net income decreased 31.6% to US$369.5 million from US$539.8 million in the year-earlier quarter. Revenues were US$3.14 billion, up 1.2% from US$3.10 billion the year before. Operating income was US$519.9 million versus US$271.0 million in the prior-year quarter, an increase of 91.8%. Direct operating expenses declined 10.3% to US$2.07 billion from US$2.31 billion in the comparable period the year before. Indirect operating expenses increased 5.0% to US$549.7 million from US$523.6 million in the equivalent prior-year period.

Prospects: Our evaluation of Entergy Corp. as of October 4th, 2019 is the result of our systematic analysis on three basic characteristics: earnings strength, relative valuation, and recent stock price movement. The company has suffered a very negative trend in earnings per share over the past 5 quarters. However, recent analyst estimates for the company have been mixed and ETR has posted results that fell short of analysts' expectations. Based on operating earnings yield, the company is fairly valued when compared to all of the companies we cover. Share price changes over the past year indicates that ETR will perform well over the near term.

Financial Data

(US$ in Thousands)	9 Mos	6 Mos	3 Mos	12/31/2018	12/31/2017	12/31/2016	12/31/2015	12/31/2014
Earnings Per Share	3.98	5.08	5.20	4.63	2.28	(3.26)	(0.99)	5.22
Cash Flow Per Share	13.29	12.22	12.29	13.15	14.60	16.72	18.37	21.67
Tang Book Value Per Share	49.61	48.52	46.40	45.95	43.28	44.15	51.56	54.91
Dividends Per Share	3.640	3.620	3.600	3.580	3.500	3.420	3.340	3.320
Dividend Payout %	91.46	71.26	69.23	77.32	153.51	...	...	63.60
Income Statement								
Total Revenue	8,416,367	5,275,792	2,609,584	11,009,452	11,074,481	10,845,645	11,513,251	12,494,921
EBITDA	2,724,566	1,655,694	787,026	2,509,768	3,420,647	1,262,772	1,773,982	4,157,567
Depn & Amortn	1,634,677	1,068,807	530,224	2,040,555	2,078,578	2,123,291	2,117,236	2,127,892
Income Before Taxes	942,069	543,409	301,417	(174,271)	967,923	(1,381,762)	(799,661)	1,549,854
Income Taxes	73,430	44,229	42,771	(1,036,826)	542,570	(817,259)	(642,927)	589,597
Net Income	868,639	499,180	258,646	862,555	425,353	(564,503)	(156,734)	960,257
Average Shares	200,492	194,238	192,234	183,378	180,535	178,885	179,176	180,296
Balance Sheet								
Current Assets	3,661,672	3,283,508	3,407,776	2,958,064	3,285,331	3,684,268	4,067,412	4,389,633
Total Assets	50,506,268	50,565,745	49,605,381	48,275,066	46,707,149	45,904,434	44,647,681	46,527,854
Current Liabilities	5,103,046	4,522,608	4,861,083	5,443,544	5,036,207	3,200,096	3,089,958	3,848,891
Long-Term Obligations	16,938,014	17,204,288	17,167,886	15,538,681	14,337,274	14,492,237	13,138,557	12,529,819
Total Liabilities	40,251,796	40,548,815	40,415,587	39,211,359	38,516,831	37,619,440	35,072,705	36,215,369
Stockholders' Equity	10,254,472	10,016,930	9,189,794	9,063,707	8,190,318	8,284,994	9,574,976	10,312,485
Shares Outstanding	199,087	198,686	189,916	189,056	180,517	179,129	178,389	179,240
Statistical Record								
Return on Assets %	1.63	1.99	2.03	1.82	0.92	N.M.	N.M.	2.14
Return on Equity %	8.55	10.71	11.31	10.00	5.16	N.M.	N.M.	9.48
EBITDA Margin %	32.37	31.38	30.16	22.80	30.89	11.64	15.41	33.27
Net Margin %	10.32	9.46	9.91	7.83	3.84	N.M.	N.M.	7.69
Asset Turnover	0.22	0.22	0.22	0.23	0.24	0.24	0.25	0.28
Current Ratio	0.72	0.73	0.70	0.54	0.65	1.15	1.32	1.14
Debt to Equity	1.65	1.72	1.87	1.71	1.75	1.75	1.37	1.22
Price Range	117.55-80.33	104.26-78.98	96.51-76.05	90.46-72.02	87.42-70.44	82.03-66.56	89.90-61.53	91.16-60.52
P/E Ratio	29.54-20.18	20.52-15.55	18.56-14.62	19.54-15.56	38.34-30.89	...	...	17.46-11.59
Average Yield %	3.80	4.07	4.27	4.42	4.49	4.55	4.58	4.47

Address: 639 Loyola Avenue, New Orleans, LA 70113 **Telephone:** 504-576-4000	**Web Site:** www.entergy.com **Officers:** Leo P. Denault - Chairman, Chief Executive Officer, Executive Vice President, Chief Financial Officer A. Christopher Bakken - Executive Vice President, Chief Nuclear Officer	**Auditors:** Deloitte & Touche LLP **Investor Contact:** 504-576-4879 **Transfer Agents:** Wells Fargo Shareowner Services, St. Paul, MN

ENTERPRISE PRODUCTS PARTNERS L.P.

Exchange	Symbol	Price	52Wk Range	Yield	P/E	Div Acheiver
NYS	EPD	$28.16 (12/31/2019)	30.68-24.59	6.32	12.98	20 Years

*7 Year Price Score 79.31 *NYSE Composite Index=100 *12 Month Price Score 89.33

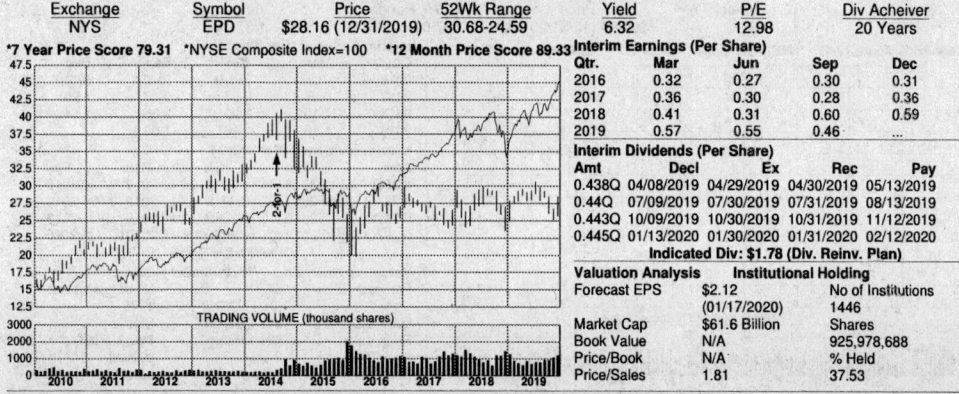

Interim Earnings (Per Share)

Qtr.	Mar	Jun	Sep	Dec
2016	0.32	0.27	0.30	0.31
2017	0.36	0.30	0.28	0.36
2018	0.41	0.31	0.60	0.59
2019	0.57	0.46	...	

Interim Dividends (Per Share)

Amt	Decl	Ex	Rec	Pay
0.438Q	04/08/2019	04/29/2019	04/30/2019	05/13/2019
0.44Q	07/09/2019	07/30/2019	07/31/2019	08/13/2019
0.443Q	10/09/2019	10/30/2019	10/31/2019	11/12/2019
0.445Q	01/13/2020	01/30/2020	01/31/2020	02/12/2020

Indicated Div: $1.78 (Div. Reinv. Plan)

Valuation Analysis / **Institutional Holding**

Valuation Analysis		Institutional Holding	
Forecast EPS	$2.12	No of Institutions	
	(01/17/2020)	1446	
Market Cap	$61.6 Billion	Shares	
Book Value	N/A	925,978,688	
Price/Book	N/A	% Held	
Price/Sales	1.81	37.53	

Business Summary: Equipment & Services (MIC: 9.1.3 SIC: 4922 NAIC: 486210)

Enterprise Products Partners is a provider of midstream energy services to producers and consumers of natural gas, natural gas liquids (NGLs), crude oil, petrochemicals and refined products. Co.'s midstream energy operations include: natural gas gathering, treating, processing, transportation and storage; NGL transportation, fractionation, storage, and export and import terminals; crude oil gathering, transportation, storage, and export and import terminals; petrochemical and refined products transportation, storage, export and import terminals, and related services; and a marine transportation business that operates primarily on the U.S. inland and Intracoastal Waterway systems.

Recent Developments: For the quarter ended Sep 30 2019, net income decreased 21.7% to US$1.04 billion from US$1.33 billion in the year-earlier quarter. Revenues were US$7.96 billion, down 16.9% from US$9.59 billion the year before. Operating income was US$1.47 billion versus US$1.64 billion in the prior-year quarter, a decrease of 10.3%. Direct operating expenses declined 17.8% to US$6.57 billion from US$8.00 billion in the comparable period the year before. Indirect operating income amounted to US$83.8 million compared with an income of US$59.3 million in the equivalent prior-year period.

Prospects: Our evaluation of Enterprise Products Partners L.P. as of October 4th, 2019 is the result of our systematic analysis on three basic characteristics: earnings strength, relative valuation, and recent stock price movement. The company has managed to produce a neutral trend in earnings per share over the past 5 quarters. Additionally, recent analyst estimates for the company have been unchanged while EPD has posted results that exceeded analysts' expectations. Based on operating earnings yield, the company is undervalued when compared to all of the companies we cover. Share price changes over the past year indicates that EPD will perform well over the near term.

Financial Data
(US$ in Thousands)

	9 Mos	6 Mos	3 Mos	12/31/2018	12/31/2017	12/31/2016	12/31/2015	12/31/2014
Earnings Per Share	2.17	2.31	2.07	1.91	1.30	1.20	1.26	1.47
Cash Flow Per Share	3.05	3.02	2.77	2.81	2.18	1.95	2.04	2.25
Dividends Per Share	1.745	1.735	1.725	1.715	1.668	1.590	1.510	1.430
Dividend Payout %	80.41	75.11	83.33	89.79	128.27	132.50	119.84	97.28
Income Statement								
Total Revenue	24,783,900	16,819,800	8,543,500	36,534,200	29,241,500	23,022,300	27,027,900	47,951,200
EBITDA	5,282,600	3,584,100	1,795,900	6,351,700	4,736,000	4,412,700	4,305,700	4,630,900
Depn & Amortn	1,164,600	769,900	380,600	1,436,200	1,296,100	1,215,700	1,161,600	1,114,100
Income Before Taxes	3,167,800	2,246,900	1,138,100	3,818,800	2,455,300	2,214,400	2,182,300	2,597,100
Income Taxes	37,400	22,000	12,300	60,300	25,700	23,400	(2,500)	23,100
Net Income	3,494,400	2,475,200	1,260,500	4,172,400	2,799,300	2,513,100	2,521,200	2,787,400
Average Shares	2,202,300	2,202,600	2,199,500	2,187,000	2,154,300	2,089,100	1,998,600	1,895,200
Balance Sheet								
Current Assets	7,913,800	6,258,900	6,628,600	6,060,700	6,506,400	6,528,200	4,313,000	5,490,700
Total Assets	61,015,300	58,721,800	58,397,500	56,969,800	54,418,100	52,194,000	48,952,000	47,100,700
Current Liabilities	8,669,500	6,264,100	8,592,700	7,167,500	9,295,100	8,250,500	7,166,600	7,873,700
Long-Term Obligations	25,639,200	26,385,000	24,181,600	24,678,100	21,713,700	21,120,900	20,826,700	19,157,400
Total Liabilities	36,519,300	34,282,000	34,339,600	33,116,300	31,870,900	30,147,000	28,656,900	29,037,500
Shares Outstanding	2,189,170	2,189,006	2,188,561	2,184,869	2,161,090	2,117,588	2,012,553	1,937,324
Statistical Record								
Return on Assets %	8.05	8.82	7.96	7.49	5.25	4.96	5.25	6.39
EBITDA Margin %	21.31	21.31	21.02	17.39	16.20	19.17	15.93	9.66
Net Margin %	14.10	14.72	14.75	11.42	9.57	10.92	9.33	5.81
Asset Turnover	0.57	0.62	0.63	0.66	0.55	0.45	0.56	1.10
Current Ratio	0.91	1.00	0.77	0.85	0.70	0.79	0.60	0.70
Price Range	30.68-23.51	29.91-23.51	29.91-23.51	29.91-23.51	29.86-23.89	29.93-19.79	36.83-21.86	41.11-31.84
P/E Ratio	14.14-10.83	12.95-10.18	14.45-11.36	15.66-12.31	22.97-18.38	24.94-16.49	29.23-17.35	27.97-21.66
Average Yield %	6.20	6.17	6.22	6.26	6.25	6.12	5.04	3.91

Address: 1100 Louisiana Street, 10th Floor, Houston, TX 77002
Telephone: 713-381-6500

Web Site: www.enterpriseproducts.com
Officers: Randa Duncan Williams - Chairman Richard H. Bachmann - Vice-Chairman

Auditors: Deloitte & Touche LLP
Investor Contact: 866-230-0745
Transfer Agents: Wells Fargo Shareowner Services, South St. Paul, MN

EOG RESOURCES, INC.

Exchange	Symbol	Price	52Wk Range	Yield	P/E
NYS	EOG	$83.76 (12/31/2019)	107.07-64.44	1.37	16.23

*7 Year Price Score 77.67   *NYSE Composite Index=100   *12 Month Price Score 82.60

Interim Earnings (Per Share)

Qtr.	Mar	Jun	Sep	Dec
2016	(0.86)	(0.53)	(0.35)	(0.24)
2017	0.05	0.04	0.17	4.20
2018	1.10	1.20	2.05	1.54
2019	1.10	1.46	1.06	...

Interim Dividends (Per Share)

Amt	Decl	Ex	Rec	Pay
0.22Q	02/13/2019	04/15/2019	04/16/2019	04/30/2019
0.287Q	05/02/2019	07/16/2019	07/17/2019	07/31/2019
0.287Q	09/12/2019	10/16/2019	10/17/2019	10/31/2019
0.287Q	12/10/2019	01/16/2020	01/17/2020	01/31/2020

Indicated Div: $1.15

Valuation Analysis

		Institutional Holding	
Forecast EPS	$4.81	No of Institutions	
	(01/17/2020)	1475	
Market Cap	$48.7 Billion	Shares	
Book Value	$21.1 Billion	586,817,856	
Price/Book	2.31	% Held	
Price/Sales	2.76	85.99	

Business Summary: Production & Extraction (MIC: 9.1.1 SIC: 1311 NAIC: 211111)

EOG Resources, together with its subsidiaries, explores for, develops, produces and markets crude oil and natural gas primarily in main producing basins in the U.S., The Republic of Trinidad and Tobago, The People's Republic of China, Canada and, from time to time, select other international areas.

Recent Developments: For the quarter ended Sep 30 2019, net income decreased 48.4% to US$615.1 million from US$1.19 billion in the year-earlier quarter. Revenues were US$4.30 billion, down 10.0% from US$4.78 billion the year before. Operating income was US$828.0 million versus US$1.51 billion in the prior-year quarter, a decrease of 45.0%. Direct operating expenses rose 10.7% to US$699.9 million from US$632.0 million in the comparable period the year before. Indirect operating expenses increased 5.0% to US$2.78 billion from US$2.64 billion in the equivalent prior-year period.

Prospects: Our evaluation of EOG Resources Inc. as of October 4th, 2019 is the result of our systematic analysis on three basic characteristics: earnings strength, relative valuation, and recent stock price movement. The company has generated a negative trend in earnings per share over the past 5 quarters. However, recent analyst estimates for the company have been mixed and EOG has posted results that fell short of analysts' expectations. Based on operating earnings yield, the company is undervalued when compared to all of the companies we cover. Share price changes over the past year indicates that EOG will perform in line with the market over the near term.

Financial Data

(US$ in Thousands)	9 Mos	6 Mos	3 Mos	12/31/2018	12/31/2017	12/31/2016	12/31/2015	12/31/2014
Earnings Per Share	5.16	6.15	5.89	5.89	4.46	(1.98)	(8.29)	5.32
Cash Flow Per Share	14.61	14.84	13.56	13.47	7.42	4.25	6.59	15.92
Tang Book Value Per Share	36.31	35.53	34.30	33.39	28.15	24.24	23.54	32.30
Dividends Per Share	0.948	0.845	0.810	0.757	0.670	0.670	0.670	0.511
Dividend Payout %	18.36	13.74	13.75	12.86	15.02	...	...	9.61
Income Statement								
Total Revenue	13,059,727	8,756,272	4,058,642	17,275,399	11,208,320	7,650,632	8,757,428	18,035,340
EBITDA	5,648,989	3,858,315	1,761,737	7,921,458	4,344,941	2,277,593	(3,370,519)	9,193,814
Depn & Amortn	2,790,496	1,836,899	879,595	3,435,408	3,409,387	3,553,417	3,313,644	3,997,041
Income Before Taxes	2,714,059	1,916,602	827,236	4,240,998	661,182	(1,557,505)	(6,921,556)	4,995,315
Income Taxes	615,670	433,335	191,810	821,958	(1,921,397)	(460,819)	(2,397,041)	2,079,828
Net Income	2,098,389	1,483,267	635,426	3,419,040	2,582,579	(1,096,686)	(4,524,515)	2,915,487
Average Shares	581,271	580,247	580,222	580,441	578,693	553,384	545,697	548,539
Balance Sheet								
Current Assets	4,819,731	4,495,521	4,907,885	5,057,390	3,279,108	3,554,603	2,592,244	5,416,021
Total Assets	36,542,269	35,751,501	35,663,535	33,934,474	29,833,078	29,459,433	26,975,244	34,762,687
Current Liabilities	4,473,713	4,414,057	4,301,268	3,728,364	2,725,542	2,027,291	1,819,287	3,384,308
Long-Term Obligations	4,163,115	4,165,284	5,166,050	5,170,169	6,030,836	6,979,779	6,653,685	5,903,354
Total Liabilities	15,417,989	15,121,225	15,759,738	14,570,286	13,549,805	15,477,852	14,032,209	17,050,105
Stockholders' Equity	21,124,280	20,630,276	19,903,797	19,364,188	16,283,273	13,981,581	12,943,035	17,712,582
Shares Outstanding	581,776	580,625	580,314	580,023	578,476	576,700	549,858	548,294
Statistical Record								
Return on Assets %	8.52	10.52	10.29	10.72	8.71	N.M.	N.M.	8.92
Return on Equity %	15.08	18.73	18.59	19.18	17.07	N.M.	N.M.	17.60
EBITDA Margin %	43.26	44.06	43.41	45.85	38.77	29.77	N.M.	50.98
Net Margin %	16.07	16.94	15.66	19.79	23.04	N.M.	N.M.	16.17
Asset Turnover	0.50	0.53	0.53	0.54	0.38	0.27	0.28	0.55
Current Ratio	1.08	1.02	1.14	1.36	1.20	1.75	1.42	1.60
Debt to Equity	0.20	0.20	0.26	0.27	0.37	0.50	0.51	0.33
Price Range	132.35-71.66	132.35-81.88	132.35-82.86	132.35-82.86	109.41-83.15	108.01-60.24	99.74-68.36	117.98-80.87
P/E Ratio	25.65-13.89	21.52-13.31	22.47-14.07	22.47-14.07	24.53-18.64	...	...	22.18-15.20
Average Yield %	1.01	0.81	0.74	0.67	0.70	0.80	0.79	0.52

Address: 1111 Bagby, Sky Lobby 2, Houston, TX 77002 **Telephone:** 713-651-7000	**Web Site:** www.eogresources.com **Officers:** William R. Thomas - Chairman, President, Chief Executive Officer, Senior Executive Vice President Gary L. Thomas - President, Senior Executive Vice President, Chief Operating Officer	**Auditors:** DELOITTE & TOUCHE LLP **Investor Contact:** 713-651-7000 **Transfer Agents:** Computershare Trust Company, N.A., Providence, RI

EPAM SYSTEMS, INC.

Exchange NYS	**Symbol** EPAM	**Price** $212.16 (12/31/2019)	**52Wk Range** 215.86-112.29	**Yield** N/A	**P/E** 49.45

*7 Year Price Score 172.81 *NYSE Composite Index=100 *12 Month Price Score 109.22

TRADING VOLUME (thousand shares)

Interim Earnings (Per Share)

Qtr.	Mar	Jun	Sep	Dec
2016	0.45	0.46	0.49	0.47
2017	0.44	0.68	0.77	(0.58)
2018	1.15	0.89	1.15	1.05
2019	1.06	1.02	1.16	...

Interim Dividends (Per Share)

No Dividends Paid

Valuation Analysis		Institutional Holding	
Forecast EPS	$5.36	No of Institutions	
	(01/17/2020)	474	
Market Cap	$11.7 Billion	Shares	
Book Value	$1.5 Billion		56,973,996
Price/Book	7.81	% Held	
Price/Sales	5.38		93.19

Business Summary: Internet & Software (MIC: 6.3.2 SIC: 7371 NAIC: 541511)

Epam Systems is a provider of software product development and digital platform engineering services to customers located around the world, primarily in North America, Europe, Asia and Australia. Co.'s industry services include financial services, travel and consumer, software and hi-tech, business information and media, life sciences and healthcare, as well as other industries.

Recent Developments: For the quarter ended Sep 30 2019, net income increased 2.1% to US$67.0 million from US$65.6 million in the year-earlier quarter. Revenues were US$588.1 million, up 25.6% from US$468.2 million the year before. Operating income was US$80.6 million versus US$64.6 million in the prior-year quarter, an increase of 24.8%. Direct operating expenses rose 25.4% to US$377.5 million from US$301.1 million in the comparable period the year before. Indirect operating expenses increased 26.8% to US$130.0 million from US$102.5 million in the equivalent prior-year period.

Prospects: Our evaluation of EPAM Systems, Inc. as of October 4th, 2019 is the result of our systematic analysis on three basic characteristics: earnings strength, relative valuation, and recent stock price movement. The company has managed to produce a neutral trend in earnings per share over the past 5 quarters. In addition, recent analyst estimates for the company have been mixed and EPAM has posted results that exceeded analysts' expectations. Based on operating earnings yield, the company is overvalued when compared to all of the companies we cover. Share price changes over the past year indicates that EPAM will perform over the near term.

Financial Data

(US$ in Thousands)	9 Mos	6 Mos	3 Mos	12/31/2018	12/31/2017	12/31/2016	12/31/2015	12/31/2014
Earnings Per Share	4.29	4.28	4.15	4.24	1.32	1.87	1.62	1.40
Cash Flow Per Share	5.21	4.92	5.25	5.45	3.75	3.27	1.57	2.22
Tang Book Value Per Share	22.74	21.71	20.53	19.21	15.30	12.15	8.98	7.43
Income Statement								
Total Revenue	1,661,023	1,072,920	521,333	1,842,912	1,450,448	1,160,132	914,128	730,027
EBITDA	248,157	156,226	73,361	274,790	190,704	136,835	113,318	94,318
Depn & Amortn	40,203	25,732	12,187	28,539	21,000	15,217	11,979	12,134
Income Before Taxes	214,729	134,760	64,250	249,773	174,305	126,466	106,070	86,953
Income Taxes	28,196	15,229	3,496	9,517	101,545	27,200	21,614	17,312
Net Income	186,533	119,531	60,754	240,256	72,760	99,266	84,456	69,641
Average Shares	57,844	57,614	57,236	56,673	54,984	53,215	51,986	49,734
Balance Sheet								
Current Assets	1,364,692	1,285,823	1,244,747	1,199,068	960,033	646,551	528,935	415,087
Total Assets	2,040,163	1,931,451	1,831,435	1,611,802	1,250,256	925,811	778,536	594,026
Current Liabilities	311,470	272,614	282,566	262,829	180,967	116,219	127,911	125,413
Long-Term Obligations	25,000	25,000	25,000	25,031	25,033	25,048	35,000	
Total Liabilities	548,046	509,204	493,210	349,206	275,309	144,399	165,313	129,976
Stockholders' Equity	1,492,117	1,422,247	1,338,225	1,262,596	974,947	781,412	613,223	464,050
Shares Outstanding	54,949	54,779	54,564	54,080	52,983	51,097	50,166	48,303
Statistical Record								
Return on Assets %	13.91	14.75	14.90	16.79	6.69	11.62	12.31	13.56
Return on Equity %	18.34	19.34	19.77	21.47	8.29	14.20	15.68	16.58
EBITDA Margin %	14.94	14.56	14.07	14.91	13.15	11.79	12.40	12.92
Net Margin %	11.23	11.14	11.65	13.04	5.02	8.56	9.24	9.54
Asset Turnover	1.22	1.23	1.22	1.29	1.33	1.36	1.33	1.42
Current Ratio	4.38	4.72	4.41	4.56	5.31	5.56	4.14	3.31
Debt to Equity	0.02	0.02	0.02	0.02	0.03	0.03	0.06	...
Price Range	200.82-106.28	179.36-106.28	173.13-106.28	144.00-104.87	108.93-63.66	78.62-57.00	82.50-45.41	51.95-30.21
P/E Ratio	46.81-24.77	41.91-24.83	41.72-25.61	33.96-24.73	82.52-48.23	42.04-30.48	50.93-28.03	37.11-21.58

Address: 41 University Drive, Suite 202, Newtown, PA 18940 **Telephone:** 267-759-9000	**Web Site:** www.epam.com **Officers:** Arkadiy Dobkin - Chairman, President, Chief Executive Officer Balazs Fejes - Senior Vice President, Chief Technology Officer, Division Officer	**Auditors:** DELOITTE & TOUCHE LLP **Investor Contact:** 267-759-9000Ext.64 **Transfer Agents:** American Stock Transfer & Trust Company, LLC, Brooklyn, NY

EPR PROPERTIES

Exchange	Symbol	Price	52Wk Range	Yield	P/E
NYS	EPR	$70.64 (12/31/2019)	80.28-63.12	6.37	27.27

*7 Year Price Score 97.88 *NYSE Composite Index=100 *12 Month Price Score 90.57

Interim Earnings (Per Share)

Qtr.	Mar	Jun	Sep	Dec
2016	0.77	0.77	0.81	0.82
2017	0.75	1.02	0.77	0.74
2018	0.32	1.15	1.15	0.65
2019	0.79	0.79	0.36	...

Interim Dividends (Per Share)

Amt	Decl	Ex	Rec	Pay
0.375M	09/17/2019	09/27/2019	09/30/2019	10/15/2019
0.375M	10/18/2019	10/30/2019	10/31/2019	11/15/2019
0.375M	11/15/2019	11/27/2019	11/29/2019	12/16/2019
0.375M	12/16/2019	12/30/2019	12/31/2019	01/15/2020

Indicated Div: $4.50 (Div. Reinv. Plan)

Valuation Analysis		Institutional Holding	
Forecast EPS	$2.59	No of Institutions	
	(01/17/2020)	573	
Market Cap	$5.5 Billion	Shares	
Book Value	$3.0 Billion	87,840,144	
Price/Book	1.82	% Held	
Price/Sales	7.99	N/A	

Business Summary: REITs (MIC: 5.3.1 SIC: 6798 NAIC: 525930)

EPR Properties is a real estate investment trust with an investment portfolio that includes entertainment, recreation and education properties. Co.'s segments are: Entertainment, which include investments in megaplex theatres, entertainment retail centers and family entertainment centers; Recreation, which include investments in ski properties, golf entertainment complexes and other recreation facilities; Education, which include investments in public charter schools, early education centers and private schools; and Other, which consist of land under ground lease, property under development and land held for development related to the Resorts World Catskills casino and resort project.

Recent Developments: For the quarter ended Sep 30 2019, net income decreased 63.0% to US$34.0 million from US$91.8 million in the year-earlier quarter. Revenues were US$184.9 million, up 4.8% from US$176.4 million the year before. Revenues from property income rose 14.4% to US$161.3 million from US$140.9 million in the corresponding quarter a year earlier.

Prospects: Our evaluation of EPR Properties as of October 4th, 2019 is the result of our systematic analysis on three basic characteristics: earnings strength, relative valuation, and recent stock price movement. The company has generated a negative trend in earnings per share over the past 5 quarters. However, recent analyst estimates for the company have been mixed and EPR has posted results that fell short of analysts' expectations. Based on operating earnings yield, the company is fairly valued when compared to all of the companies we cover. Share price changes over the past year indicates that EPR will perform well over the near term.

Financial Data

(US$ in Thousands)	9 Mos	6 Mos	3 Mos	12/31/2018	12/31/2017	12/31/2016	12/31/2015	12/31/2014
Earnings Per Share	2.59	3.38	3.74	3.27	3.29	3.17	2.93	2.86
Cash Flow Per Share	5.42	5.83	6.67	6.52	5.49	4.82	4.79	4.61
Tang Book Value Per Share	38.86	39.26	38.59	37.96	39.10	34.11	33.95	33.57
Dividends Per Share	4.455	4.410	4.365	4.320	4.080	3.840	3.630	3.420
Dividend Payout %	172.01	130.47	116.71	132.11	124.01	121.14	123.89	119.58
Income Statement								
Total Revenue	525,102	340,240	164,542	700,731	575,991	493,242	421,017	385,051
EBITDA	397,008	281,285	137,824	553,497	527,519	425,960	359,661	322,977
Depn & Amortn	127,347	82,102	39,743	148,700	129,100	103,900	85,900	63,000
Income Before Taxes	162,917	129,079	64,255	269,290	265,295	224,916	193,846	178,707
Income Taxes	(2,505)	(1,905)	(605)	2,285	2,399	553	482	4,228
Net Income	165,946	131,943	65,349	266,983	262,968	224,982	194,532	179,633
Average Shares	77,664	76,199	74,725	74,337	71,254	63,474	58,328	54,444
Balance Sheet								
Current Assets	220,958	120,370	133,428	116,876	152,679	128,018	73,962	63,690
Total Assets	6,633,290	6,746,655	6,431,231	6,131,390	6,191,493	4,865,022	4,217,270	3,702,048
Current Liabilities	246,522	239,762	237,098	280,313	235,341	193,496	161,482	130,036
Long-Term Obligations	3,101,611	3,216,623	3,045,742	2,986,054	3,028,827	2,485,625	1,981,920	1,645,523
Total Liabilities	3,592,491	3,701,757	3,518,452	3,266,367	3,264,168	2,679,121	2,143,402	1,775,936
Stockholders' Equity	3,040,799	3,044,898	2,912,779	2,865,023	2,927,325	2,185,901	2,073,868	1,926,112
Shares Outstanding	78,239	77,556	75,483	74,347	74,125	63,647	60,823	57,125
Statistical Record								
Return on Assets %	3.45	4.32	4.78	4.33	4.76	4.94	4.91	5.15
Return on Equity %	7.41	9.37	10.46	9.22	10.29	10.53	9.73	9.94
EBITDA Margin %	75.61	82.67	83.76	78.99	91.58	86.36	85.43	83.88
Net Margin %	31.60	38.78	39.72	38.10	45.65	45.61	46.21	46.65
Asset Turnover	0.11	0.11	0.11	0.11	0.10	0.11	0.11	0.11
Current Ratio	0.90	0.50	0.56	0.42	0.65	0.66	0.46	0.49
Debt to Equity	1.02	1.06	1.05	1.04	1.03	1.14	0.96	0.85
Price Range	80.28-63.12	80.28-63.12	77.47-53.04	71.45-53.04	77.56-63.11	84.46-54.09	65.58-49.57	60.80-48.60
P/E Ratio	31.00-24.37	23.75-18.67	20.71-14.18	21.85-16.22	23.57-19.18	26.64-17.06	22.38-16.92	21.26-16.99
Average Yield %	6.03	6.14	6.51	6.80	5.72	5.43	6.33	6.32

Address: 909 Walnut Street, Suite 200, Kansas City, MO 64106 Telephone: 816-472-1700 Fax: 816-472-5794	Web Site: www.eprkc.com Officers: Robert J. Druten - Chairman Gregory K. Silvers - President, Chief Executive Officer, Executive Vice President, Vice President, Chief Operating Officer, Chief Development Officer, Secretary, General Counsel	Auditors: KPMG LLP Transfer Agents: Computershare Trust Company, N. A., Providence, RI

EQT CORP

Exchange	Symbol	Price	52Wk Range	Yield	P/E
NYS	EQT	$10.90 (12/31/2019)	21.73-8.44	1.10	N/A

*7 Year Price Score 35.82   *NYSE Composite Index=100   *12 Month Price Score 61.28

Interim Earnings (Per Share)

Qtr.	Mar	Jun	Sep	Dec
2016	0.04	(1.55)	(0.05)	(1.13)
2017	0.95	0.24	0.13	6.72
2018	(5.99)	0.07	(0.15)	(2.48)
2019	0.75	0.49	(1.41)	...

Interim Dividends (Per Share)

Amt	Decl	Ex	Rec	Pay
0.03Q	01/16/2019	02/14/2019	02/15/2019	03/01/2019
0.03Q	04/17/2019	05/14/2019	05/15/2019	06/01/2019
0.03Q	07/11/2019	08/08/2019	08/09/2019	09/01/2019
0.03Q	10/09/2019	11/07/2019	11/08/2019	12/01/2019

Indicated Div: $0.12

Valuation Analysis | Institutional Holding

Forecast EPS	$0.93	No of Institutions	
	(01/17/2020)	621	
Market Cap	$2.8 Billion	Shares	
Book Value	$10.9 Billion	269,551,776	
Price/Book	0.26	% Held	
Price/Sales	0.64	N/A	

Business Summary: Production & Extraction (MIC: 9.1.1 SIC: 1311 NAIC: 211111)

EQT is a natural gas production company with a focus in the Appalachian Basin and operations throughout Pennsylvania, West Virginia and Ohio.

Recent Developments: For the quarter ended Sep 30 2019, loss from continuing operations was US$361.0 million compared with a loss of US$127.3 million in the year-earlier quarter. Net loss amounted to US$361.0 million versus net income of US$63.4 million in the year-earlier quarter. Revenues were US$951.6 million, down 9.4% from US$1.05 billion the year before. Operating loss was US$161.5 million versus a loss of US$147.5 million in the prior-year quarter. Direct operating expenses rose 2.6% to US$475.8 million from US$463.5 million in the comparable period the year before. Indirect operating expenses decreased 13.2% to US$637.3 million from US$734.0 million in the equivalent prior-year period.

Prospects: Our evaluation of EQT Corp. as of October 4th, 2019 is the result of our systematic analysis on three basic characteristics: earnings strength, relative valuation, and recent stock price movement. The company has generated a negative trend in earnings per share over the past 5 quarters. In addition, recent analyst estimates for the company have been reduced while EQT has posted results that exceeded analysts' expectations. Based on operating earnings yield, the company is undervalued when compared to all of the companies we cover. Share price changes over the past year indicates that EQT will perform in line with the market over the near term.

Financial Data

(US$ in Thousands)	9 Mos	6 Mos	3 Mos	12/31/2018	12/31/2017	12/31/2016	12/31/2015	12/31/2014
Earnings Per Share	(2.65)	(1.39)	(1.81)	(8.60)	8.04	(2.71)	0.56	2.54
Cash Flow Per Share	8.48	10.78	11.54	11.41	8.74	6.36	7.99	9.33
Tang Book Value Per Share	42.58	43.92	43.42	42.76	40.04	33.91	33.29	30.23
Dividends Per Share	0.120	0.120	0.120	0.120	0.120	0.120	0.120	0.120
Dividend Payout %	...	...	...	...	1.49	...	21.43	4.72
Income Statement								
Total Revenue	3,405,001	2,453,425	1,143,173	4,557,868	3,378,015	1,608,348	2,339,762	2,469,710
EBITDA	425,373	533,524	301,140	(2,771,099)	956,235	681,313	1,392,308	1,539,546
Depn & Amortn	47,824	33,092	15,642	77,374	10,940	927,920	819,216	679,298
Income Before Taxes	222,764	393,356	228,925	(3,077,431)	742,523	(394,527)	426,561	723,711
Income Taxes	(9,244)	77,099	38,234	(696,511)	(1,115,619)	(263,464)	104,675	214,092
Net Income	(44,771)	316,257	190,691	(2,244,568)	1,508,529	(452,983)	85,171	386,965
Average Shares	255,235	255,223	255,387	260,932	187,727	166,978	152,939	152,513
Balance Sheet								
Current Assets	1,495,220	1,598,091	1,380,041	1,969,664	1,163,055	1,828,219	2,251,019	1,904,323
Total Assets	20,160,449	20,479,347	20,339,685	20,721,344	29,522,604	15,472,922	13,976,172	12,064,900
Current Liabilities	1,449,710	1,533,288	2,185,490	2,355,001	1,232,237	804,640	795,819	833,479
Long-Term Obligations	5,154,479	4,992,966	4,343,426	4,792,991	7,323,555	3,289,459	2,793,343	2,822,889
Total Liabilities	9,262,824	9,230,872	9,200,097	9,763,115	16,202,986	9,612,641	8,898,381	7,482,085
Stockholders' Equity	10,897,625	11,248,475	11,139,588	10,958,229	13,319,618	5,860,281	5,077,791	4,582,815
Shares Outstanding	255,170	254,796	254,999	254,472	264,320	172,827	152,554	151,596
Statistical Record								
Return on Assets %	N.M.	N.M.	N.M.	N.M.	6.71	N.M.	0.65	3.54
Return on Equity %	N.M.	N.M.	N.M.	N.M.	15.73	N.M.	1.76	8.98
EBITDA Margin %	12.49	21.75	26.34	N.M.	28.31	42.36	59.51	62.34
Net Margin %	N.M.	12.89	16.68	N.M.	44.66	N.M.	3.64	15.67
Asset Turnover	0.18	0.18	0.18	0.18	0.15	0.11	0.18	0.23
Current Ratio	1.03	1.04	0.63	0.84	0.94	2.27	2.83	2.28
Debt to Equity	0.47	0.44	0.39	0.44	0.55	0.56	0.55	0.62
Price Range	25.89-9.82	30.97-14.39	30.97-16.63	32.10-16.63	36.48-27.67	43.18-26.96	50.05-25.99	59.79-41.03
P/E Ratio	...	...	...	...	4.54-3.44	...	89.38-46.41	23.54-16.15
Average Yield %	0.67	0.55	0.50	0.46	0.36	0.33	0.29	0.23

Address: 625 Liberty Avenue, Suite 1700, Pittsburgh, PA 15222 **Telephone:** 412-553-5700	**Web Site:** **Officers:** James E. Rohr - Chairman Toby Z. Rice - President, Chief Executive Officer	**Auditors:** Ernst & Young LLP **Investor Contact:** 412-553-7833 **Transfer Agents:** Computershare, College Station, TX

EQUIFAX INC

Exchange	Symbol	Price	52Wk Range	Yield	P/E
NYS	EFX	$140.12 (12/31/2019)	146.78-91.34	1.11	N/A

*7 Year Price Score 101.63 ***NYSE Composite Index=100** ***12 Month Price Score 102.05**

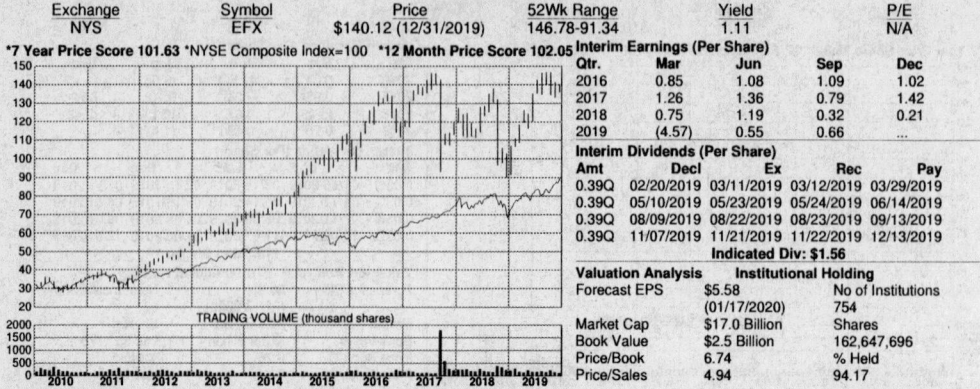

Interim Earnings (Per Share)

Qtr.	Mar	Jun	Sep	Dec
2016	0.85	1.08	1.09	1.02
2017	1.26	1.36	0.79	1.42
2018	0.75	1.19	0.32	0.21
2019	(4.57)	0.55	0.66	...

Interim Dividends (Per Share)

Amt	Decl	Ex	Rec	Pay
0.39Q	02/20/2019	03/11/2019	03/12/2019	03/29/2019
0.39Q	05/10/2019	05/23/2019	05/24/2019	06/14/2019
0.39Q	08/09/2019	08/22/2019	08/23/2019	09/13/2019
0.39Q	11/07/2021	11/21/2019	11/22/2019	12/13/2019

Indicated Div: $1.56

Valuation Analysis

		Institutional Holding	
Forecast EPS	$5.58	No of Institutions	
	(01/17/2020)	754	
Market Cap	$17.0 Billion	Shares	
Book Value	$2.5 Billion	162,647,696	
Price/Book	6.74	% Held	
Price/Sales	4.94	94.17	

Business Summary: Business Services (MIC: 7.5.2 SIC: 7323 NAIC: 561450)

Equifax Inc. is a provider of information solutions and human resources business process outsourcing services for businesses, governments and consumers. Co.'s services are based on databases of consumer and business information. Co. uses statistical techniques, machine learning and proprietary software tools to analyze all available data, creating insights, decision-making solutions and processing services for its clients. Co. also provides information, technology and services to support debt collections and recovery management. Additionally, Co. provides payroll-related and human resource management business process outsourcing services in the U.S.

Recent Developments: For the quarter ended Sep 30 2019, net income increased 108.3% to US$82.5 million from US$39.6 million in the year-earlier quarter. Revenues were US$875.7 million, up 5.0% from US$834.2 million the year before. Operating income was US$121.6 million versus US$64.1 million in the prior-year quarter, an increase of 89.7%. Direct operating expenses declined 0.6% to US$374.5 million from US$376.7 million in the comparable period the year before. Indirect operating expenses decreased 3.5% to US$379.6 million from US$393.4 million in the equivalent prior-year period.

Prospects: Our evaluation of Equifax Inc. as of October 4th, 2019 is the result of our systematic analysis on three basic characteristics: earnings strength, relative valuation, and recent stock price movement. The company has produced a positive trend in earnings per share over the past 5 quarters. However, recent analyst estimates for the company have been mixed and EFX has posted results that exceeded analysts' expectations. Based on operating earnings yield, the company is fairly valued when compared to all of the companies we cover. Share price changes over the past year indicates that EFX will perform well over the near term.

Financial Data

(US$ in Thousands)	9 Mos	6 Mos	3 Mos	12/31/2018	12/31/2017	12/31/2016	12/31/2015	12/31/2014
Earnings Per Share	(3.15)	(3.49)	(2.85)	2.47	4.83	4.04	3.55	2.97
Cash Flow Per Share	2.05	4.68	4.84	5.58	6.79	6.65	6.25	5.08
Dividends Per Share	1.560	1.560	1.560	1.560	1.560	1.320	1.160	1.000
Dividend Payout %	...	...	...	63.16	32.30	32.67	32.68	33.67
Income Statement								
Total Revenue	2,601,800	1,726,100	846,100	3,412,100	3,362,200	3,144,900	2,663,600	2,436,400
EBITDA	(125,800)	(336,000)	(536,600)	775,700	1,130,300	1,089,000	900,400	847,000
Depn & Amortn	248,800	163,100	79,200	315,900	290,900	268,700	200,000	204,200
Income Before Taxes	(456,900)	(553,400)	(642,500)	356,300	746,600	728,200	636,600	574,200
Income Taxes	(53,300)	(67,300)	(88,100)	50,000	148,600	233,100	201,800	200,200
Net Income	(408,000)	(489,100)	(555,900)	299,800	587,300	488,800	429,100	367,400
Average Shares	122,300	122,000	121,600	121,400	121,500	121,100	120,900	123,500
Balance Sheet								
Current Assets	853,000	813,800	864,700	902,300	998,400	672,900	561,600	605,100
Total Assets	7,430,700	7,473,500	7,335,700	7,153,200	7,233,400	6,664,000	4,509,000	4,674,200
Current Liabilities	1,491,800	1,497,900	1,523,000	826,800	1,673,500	1,259,600	603,800	823,100
Long-Term Obligations	2,834,700	2,833,300	2,656,900	2,630,600	1,739,000	2,086,800	1,145,900	1,145,700
Total Liabilities	4,914,900	4,930,100	4,774,000	4,045,400	4,059,000	4,001,300	2,198,100	2,474,100
Stockholders' Equity	2,515,800	2,543,400	2,561,700	3,107,800	3,174,400	2,662,700	2,310,900	2,200,100
Shares Outstanding	121,100	120,900	120,800	120,600	120,100	119,900	118,700	119,400
Statistical Record								
Return on Assets %	N.M.	N.M.	N.M.	4.17	8.45	8.73	9.35	7.97
Return on Equity %	N.M.	N.M.	N.M.	9.54	20.12	19.60	19.02	16.33
EBITDA Margin %	N.M.	N.M.	N.M.	22.73	33.62	34.63	33.80	34.76
Net Margin %	N.M.	N.M.	N.M.	8.79	17.47	15.54	16.11	15.08
Asset Turnover	0.47	0.47	0.47	0.47	0.48	0.56	0.58	0.53
Current Ratio	0.57	0.54	0.57	1.09	0.60	0.53	0.93	0.74
Debt to Equity	1.13	1.11	1.04	0.85	0.55	0.78	0.50	0.52
Price Range	146.78-90.00	138.06-90.00	138.06-90.00	138.06-90.00	146.26-92.98	136.43-93.22	113.61-80.00	82.15-65.04
P/E Ratio	...	...	...	55.89-36.44	30.28-19.25	33.77-23.07	32.00-22.54	27.66-21.90
Average Yield %	1.30	1.33	1.35	1.31	1.23	1.10	1.18	1.36

Address: 1550 Peachtree Street, N.W., Atlanta, GA 30309 **Telephone:** 404-885-8000	**Web Site:** www.equifax.com **Officers:** Bryson R. Koehler - Chief Technology Officer Mark W. Begor - Chief Executive Officer	**Auditors:** Ernst & Young LLP **Investor Contact:** 404-885-8804 **Transfer Agents:** American Stock Transfer & Trust Company, Brookly, NY

EQUITY COMMONWEALTH

Exchange	Symbol	Price	52Wk Range	Yield	P/E
NYS	EQC	$32.83 (12/31/2019)	34.63-29.36	N/A	8.44

*7 Year Price Score 95.09   *NYSE Composite Index=100   *12 Month Price Score 93.58

TRADING VOLUME (thousand shares)

Interim Earnings (Per Share)

Qtr.	Mar	Jun	Sep	Dec
2016	0.31	0.56	0.67	0.08
2017	0.17	(0.06)	0.25	(0.19)
2018	1.48	0.29	0.25	0.11
2019	1.67	1.93	0.18	...

Interim Dividends (Per Share)

Amt	Decl	Ex	Rec	Pay
2.50U	09/26/2018	10/05/2018	10/09/2018	10/23/2018
3.50U	09/24/2019	10/04/2019	10/07/2019	10/23/2019

Valuation Analysis   **Institutional Holding**

Forecast EPS	$3.92	No of Institutions
	(01/15/2020)	403
Market Cap	$4.0 Billion	Shares
Book Value	$3.2 Billion	154,578,304
Price/Book	1.24	% Held
Price/Sales	27.65	N/A

Business Summary: REITs (MIC: 5.3.1 SIC: 6798 NAIC: 525930)

Equity Commonwealth is a real estate investment trust. Co. is engaged in the ownership and operation of office buildings. Co. conducts substantially all of its activities through EQC Operating Trust.

Recent Developments: For the quarter ended Sep 30 2019, net income decreased 27.1% to US$23.9 million from US$32.8 million in the year-earlier quarter. Revenues were US$26.7 million, down 43.0% from US$46.9 million the year before. Revenues from property income fell 45.2% to US$24.0 million from US$43.8 million in the corresponding quarter a year earlier.

Prospects: Our evaluation of Equity Commonwealth as of October 4th, 2019 is the result of our systematic analysis on three basic characteristics: earnings strength, relative valuation, and recent stock price movement. The company has managed to produce a neutral trend in earnings per share over the past 5 quarters. In addition, recent analyst estimates for the company have been mixed and EQC has posted results that fell short of analysts' expectations. Based on operating earnings yield, the company is overvalued when compared to all of the companies we cover. Share price changes over the past year indicates that EQC will perform well over the near term.

Financial Data

(US$ in Thousands)	9 Mos	6 Mos	3 Mos	12/31/2018	12/31/2017	12/31/2016	12/31/2015	12/31/2014
Earnings Per Share	3.89	3.96	2.32	2.15	0.17	1.62	0.56	(0.19)
Cash Flow Per Share	0.93	0.88	0.84	0.73	0.81	1.30	1.41	1.60
Tang Book Value Per Share	25.49	28.83	26.83	25.20	25.60	25.33	23.62	22.64
Dividends Per Share	2.500	2.500	2.500	2.500	...	...	...	0.250
Dividend Payout %	64.27	63.13	107.76	116.28	...	...	...	...
Income Statement								
Total Revenue	101,855	75,120	41,752	197,022	340,571	500,680	714,891	861,857
EBITDA	451,440	441,114	206,983	296,220	129,138	410,332	349,436	119,101
Depn & Amortn	22,725	16,694	8,655	40,386	73,169	102,695	145,888	166,076
Income Before Taxes	477,989	454,614	211,897	276,064	30,166	233,639	102,221	(188,644)
Income Taxes	1,119	1,640	1,300	3,156	500	745	2,364	3,191
Net Income	476,690	452,804	210,518	272,813	29,656	232,894	99,857	24,012
Average Shares	123,564	125,862	125,822	123,385	125,129	126,768	129,437	125,163
Balance Sheet								
Current Assets	3,229,578	3,202,593	3,102,419	2,704,792	2,730,954	2,253,237	2,009,650	644,874
Total Assets	3,731,343	3,702,171	3,713,937	3,530,772	4,236,945	4,526,075	5,244,372	5,761,639
Current Liabilities	477,334	40,457	47,399	62,368	73,955	103,555	133,925	176,248
Long-Term Obligations	25,896	26,091	274,977	274,955	848,578	1,141,667	1,710,324	2,207,665
Total Liabilities	504,518	67,998	323,648	347,971	937,579	1,265,628	1,875,885	2,442,056
Stockholders' Equity	3,226,825	3,634,173	3,390,289	3,182,801	3,299,366	3,260,447	3,368,487	3,319,583
Shares Outstanding	121,924	121,922	121,899	121,572	124,217	123,994	126,349	129,607
Statistical Record								
Return on Assets %	13.04	13.40	7.53	7.02	0.68	4.75	1.81	0.39
Return on Equity %	15.39	14.16	8.71	8.42	0.90	7.01	2.99	0.72
EBITDA Margin %	443.22	587.21	495.74	150.35	37.92	81.95	48.88	13.82
Net Margin %	468.01	602.77	504.21	138.47	8.71	46.52	13.97	2.79
Asset Turnover	0.04	0.04	0.05	0.05	0.08	0.10	0.13	0.14
Current Ratio	6.77	79.16	65.45	43.37	36.93	21.76	15.01	3.66
Debt to Equity	0.01	0.01	0.08	0.09	0.26	0.35	0.51	0.67
Price Range	34.63-28.68	34.01-28.68	33.55-28.68	32.49-28.10	32.51-29.80	31.77-25.41	29.67-25.21	28.06-22.40
P/E Ratio	8.90-7.37	8.59-7.24	14.46-12.36	15.11-13.07	191.24-175.29	19.61-15.69	52.98-45.02	...
Average Yield %	7.77	7.89	7.99	8.13	...	...	...	0.96

Address: Two North Riverside Plaza, Suite 2100, Chicago, IL 60606	**Web Site:** www.eqcre.com	**Auditors:** Ernst & Young LLP
Telephone: 312-646-2800	**Officers:** Samuel (Sam) Zell - Chairman David A. Helfand - President, Chief Executive Officer, Interim Chief Financial Officer	**Investor Contact:** 617-796-8222
Fax: 617-332-2261		**Transfer Agents:** Wells Fargo Bank, National Association, Mendota Heights, MN

EQUITY LIFESTYLE PROPERTIES INC

Exchange	Symbol	Price	52Wk Range	Yield	P/E'	Div Acheiver
NYS	ELS	$70.39 (12/31/2019)	74.08-47.01	1.74	46.62	14 Years

*7 Year Price Score 140.13 *NYSE Composite Index=100 *12 Month Price Score 108.28

Interim Earnings (Per Share)

Qtr.	Mar	Jun	Sep	Dec
2016	0.30	0.21	0.24	0.22
2017	0.33	0.23	0.28	0.26
2018	0.34	0.26	0.32	0.28
2019	0.63	0.26	0.35	...

Interim Dividends (Per Share)

Amt	Decl	Ex	Rec	Pay
0.306Q	04/30/2019	06/27/2019	06/28/2019	07/12/2019
0.306Q	07/30/2019	09/26/2019	09/27/2019	10/11/2019
100%	09/20/2019	10/16/2019	10/01/2019	10/15/2019
0.306Q	10/29/2019	12/26/2019	12/27/2019	01/10/2020

Indicated Div: $1.23

Valuation Analysis / **Institutional Holding**

Forecast EPS	$1.35	No of Institutions
	(01/11/2020)	464
Market Cap	$12.8 Billion	Shares
Book Value	$1.2 Billion	97,680,840
Price/Book	10.27	% Held
Price/Sales	12.54	95.90

Business Summary: REITs (MIC: 5.3.1 SIC: 6798 NAIC: 525930)

Equity Lifestyle Properties is an owner and operator of lifestyle-oriented properties (Properties) consisting primarily of manufactured home and recreational vehicle (RV) communities. Co. has a business model where it owns the land upon which it provides its customers the opportunity to place factory-built homes, cottages, cabins or RVs either on a long-term or short-term basis. Co.'s customers may lease individual developed areas (Sites) or enter right-to-use contracts which provide them access to specific Properties for limited stays. Properties may also have Sites that can accommodate a variety of RVs.

Recent Developments: For the quarter ended Sep 30 2019, net income increased 14.3% to US$68.2 million from US$59.7 million in the year-earlier quarter. Revenues were US$271.2 million, up 5.6% from US$256.7 million the year before. Revenues from property income rose 6.1% to US$248.9 million from US$234.6 million in the corresponding quarter a year earlier.

Prospects: Our evaluation of Equity Lifestyle Properties Inc. as of October 4th, 2019 is the result of our systematic analysis on three basic characteristics: earnings strength, relative valuation, and recent stock price movement. The company has managed to produce a neutral trend in earnings per share over the past 5 quarters. In addition, recent analyst estimates for the company have been mixed and ELS has posted results that fell short of analysts' expectations. Based on operating earnings yield, the company is overvalued when compared to all of the companies we cover. Share price changes over the past year indicates that ELS will perform over the near term.

Financial Data

(US$ in Thousands)	9 Mos	6 Mos	3 Mos	12/31/2018	12/31/2017	12/31/2016	12/31/2015	12/31/2014
Earnings Per Share	1.51	1.48	1.49	1.19	1.09	0.96	0.77	0.70
Cash Flow Per Share	2.42	2.38	2.34	2.31	2.21	2.08	2.10	1.71
Tang Book Value Per Share	6.85	6.79	6.57	6.24	5.82	5.10	4.68	4.62
Dividends Per Share	1.194	1.163	1.131	1.100	0.975	0.850	0.750	0.650
Dividend Payout %	78.80	78.55	76.18	92.44	89.86	88.54	97.40	92.20
Income Statement								
Total Revenue	778,616	507,456	259,090	986,653	925,312	870,435	821,654	776,809
EBITDA	309,747	218,814	146,181	457,941	429,902	405,078	366,852	358,057
Depn & Amortn	2,264	1,536	786	131,501	122,720	118,521	114,698	111,872
Income Before Taxes	229,519	164,861	119,002	221,447	206,612	184,527	146,423	133,890
Net Income	224,179	159,718	113,309	212,612	197,589	173,263	139,371	128,005
Average Shares	192,400	191,860	191,248	190,110	186,850	185,138	183,814	183,022
Balance Sheet								
Current Assets	79,614	126,467	179,033	177,237	112,005	122,235	146,586	139,440
Total Assets	4,137,471	4,014,478	4,008,877	3,925,808	3,610,032	3,478,987	3,420,061	3,446,339
Current Liabilities	556,074	432,528	405,363	384,112	309,973	305,861	281,657	255,066
Long-Term Obligations	2,261,604	2,274,476	2,346,196	2,348,352	2,200,017	2,091,279	2,145,713	2,212,246
Total Liabilities	2,889,712	2,778,405	2,827,051	2,804,256	2,578,078	2,470,444	2,494,993	2,534,346
Stockholders' Equity	1,247,759	1,236,073	1,181,826	1,121,552	1,031,954	1,008,543	925,068	911,993
Shares Outstanding	182,080	182,064	179,992	179,842	177,170	171,058	168,506	167,759
Statistical Record								
Return on Assets %	6.87	6.89	6.90	5.64	5.57	5.01	4.06	3.74
Return on Equity %	23.19	23.43	23.99	19.75	19.37	17.87	15.17	14.18
EBITDA Margin %	39.78	43.12	56.42	46.41	46.46	46.54	44.65	46.09
Net Margin %	28.79	31.47	43.73	21.55	21.35	19.91	16.96	16.48
Asset Turnover	0.26	0.26	0.26	0.26	0.26	0.25	0.24	0.23
Current Ratio	0.14	0.29	0.44	0.46	0.36	0.40	0.52	0.55
Debt to Equity	1.81	1.84	1.99	2.09	2.13	2.07	2.32	2.43
Price Range	68.89-45.80	62.20-44.88	57.57-43.18	51.66-40.77	45.85-35.67	41.58-31.90	33.41-25.77	26.21-18.07
P/E Ratio	45.63-30.33	42.03-30.33	38.64-28.98	43.41-34.26	42.07-32.73	43.31-33.23	43.38-33.47	37.44-25.81
Average Yield %	2.11	2.24	2.34	2.41	2.33	2.33	2.64	2.98

Address: Two North Riverside Plaza, Suite 800, Chicago, IL 60606 **Telephone:** 312-279-1400	**Web Site:** www.equitylifestyleproperties.com **Officers:** Samuel (Sam) Zell - Chairman, Chief Executive Officer, Co-Chairman Marguerite M. Nader - President, Chief Executive Officer, Executive Vice President, Chief Financial Officer	**Auditors:** Ernst & Young LLP **Investor Contact:** 180-024-75279 **Transfer Agents:** American Stock Transfer and Trust Company, LLC, New York, NY

EQUITY RESIDENTIAL

Exchange	Symbol	Price	52Wk Range	Yield	P/E
NYS	EQR	$80.92 (12/31/2019)	88.85-63.76	2.81	37.99

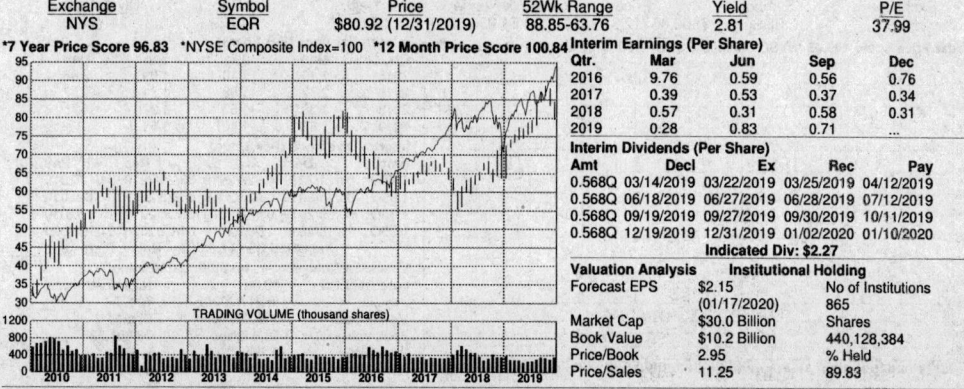

*7 Year Price Score 96.83 *NYSE Composite Index=100 *12 Month Price Score 100.84

Interim Earnings (Per Share)

Qtr.	Mar	Jun	Sep	Dec
2016	9.76	0.59	0.56	0.76
2017	0.39	0.53	0.37	0.34
2018	0.57	0.31	0.58	0.31
2019	0.28	0.83	0.71	...

Interim Dividends (Per Share)

Amt	Decl	Ex	Rec	Pay
0.568Q	03/14/2019	03/22/2019	03/25/2019	04/12/2019
0.568Q	06/18/2019	06/27/2019	06/28/2019	07/12/2019
0.568Q	09/19/2019	09/27/2019	09/30/2019	10/11/2019
0.568Q	12/19/2019	12/31/2019	01/02/2020	01/10/2020

Indicated Div: $2.27

Valuation Analysis | **Institutional Holding**

Forecast EPS	$2.15	No of Institutions	
	(01/17/2020)	865	
Market Cap	$30.0 Billion	Shares	
Book Value	$10.2 Billion	440,128,384	
Price/Book	2.95	% Held	
Price/Sales	11.25	89.83	

Business Summary: REITs (MIC: 5.3.1 SIC: 6798 NAIC: 525930)

Equity Residential is a real estate investment trust focused on the acquisition, development and management of rental apartment properties. Co. is the general partner of, and owns an ownership interest in ERP Operating Limited Partnership (ERPOP). All of Co.'s property ownership, development and related business operations are conducted through ERPOP and those entities/subsidiaries owned or controlled by ERPOP. Co., directly or indirectly through investments in title holding entities, owns all or a portion of properties located in several states and the District of Columbia.

Recent Developments: For the quarter ended Sep 30 2019, net income increased 24.1% to US$277.8 million from US$223.8 million in the year-earlier quarter. Revenues were US$685.1 million, up 4.9% from US$652.9 million the year before.

Prospects: Our evaluation of Equity Residential Properties Trust as of October 4th, 2019 is the result of our systematic analysis on three basic characteristics: earnings strength, relative valuation, and recent stock price movement. The company has produced a positive trend in earnings per share over the past 5 quarters. In addition, recent analyst estimates for the company have been raised, and EQR has posted results that exceeded analysts' expectations. Based on operating earnings yield, the company is overvalued when compared to all of the companies we cover. Share price changes over the past year indicates that EQR will perform well over the near term.

Financial Data

(US$ in Thousands)	9 Mos	6 Mos	3 Mos	12/31/2018	12/31/2017	12/31/2016	12/31/2015	12/31/2014
Earnings Per Share	2.13	2.00	1.48	1.77	1.63	11.68	2.36	1.73
Cash Flow Per Share	3.79	3.68	3.70	3.69	3.45	3.04	3.73	3.67
Tang Book Value Per Share	27.32	27.28	27.02	27.44	27.73	27.86	28.60	28.44
Dividends Per Share	2.243	2.215	2.188	2.160	2.015	13.015	2.210	2.000
Dividend Payout %	105.28	110.75	147.80	122.03	123.62	111.43	93.64	115.61
Income Statement								
Total Revenue	2,017,156	1,332,011	662,494	2,578,434	2,471,406	2,425,800	2,744,965	2,614,748
EBITDA	1,326,552	876,116	422,878	1,631,410	1,586,034	1,551,367	1,771,773	1,671,163
Depn & Amortn	659,565	444,114	216,163	790,117	743,749	705,649	765,895	758,861
Income Before Taxes	370,768	223,969	110,222	431,940	456,005	416,612	558,380	448,485
Income Taxes	749	484	238	878	478	1,613	917	1,394
Net Income	680,613	413,507	104,539	657,535	603,454	4,292,163	870,120	631,308
Average Shares	386,896	386,107	385,184	383,695	382,678	381,992	380,620	377,735
Balance Sheet								
Current Assets	84,596	309,468	93,506	116,313	100,762	219,088	155,115	160,468
Total Assets	21,054,056	20,990,711	20,768,811	20,394,209	20,570,599	20,704,148	23,157,328	22,950,614
Current Liabilities	868,342	460,456	858,509	438,952	430,638	463,348	559,305	507,329
Long-Term Obligations	8,970,867	9,412,041	8,890,063	8,817,939	8,957,291	8,987,258	10,968,498	10,844,861
Total Liabilities	10,871,420	10,837,182	10,721,925	10,221,005	10,328,135	10,475,070	12,686,960	12,582,158
Stockholders' Equity	10,182,636	10,153,529	10,046,886	10,173,204	10,242,464	10,229,078	10,470,368	10,368,456
Shares Outstanding	371,327	370,838	370,462	369,405	368,018	365,870	364,755	362,855
Statistical Record								
Return on Assets %	3.84	3.60	2.67	3.21	2.92	19.52	3.77	2.76
Return on Equity %	7.81	7.32	5.41	6.44	5.90	41.36	8.35	6.05
EBITDA Margin %	65.76	65.77	63.83	63.27	64.18	63.95	64.55	63.91
Net Margin %	33.74	31.04	15.78	25.50	24.42	176.94	31.70	24.14
Asset Turnover	0.13	0.13	0.13	0.13	0.12	0.11	0.12	0.11
Current Ratio	0.10	0.67	0.11	0.26	0.23	0.47	0.28	0.32
Debt to Equity	0.88	0.93	0.88	0.87	0.87	0.88	1.05	1.05
Price Range	86.85-62.67	78.83-62.67	75.63-59.63	72.65-55.26	70.37-59.90	81.59-58.81	81.97-68.95	74.55-51.87
P/E Ratio	40.77-29.42	39.41-31.34	51.10-40.29	41.05-31.22	43.17-36.75	6.99-5.04	34.73-29.22	43.09-29.98
Average Yield %	3.01	3.15	3.27	3.39	3.08	19.16	2.90	3.19

Address: Two North Riverside Plaza, Chicago, IL 60606 **Telephone:** 312-474-1300	**Web Site:** www.equityapartments.com **Officers:** Samuel (Sam) Zell - Chairman Gerald A. Spector - Executive Vice President, Chief Operating Officer, Vice-Chairman	**Auditors:** Ernst & Young LLP **Investor Contact:** 888-879-6356 **Transfer Agents:** Computershare Trust Company, N.A, Providence, RI

ESSEX PROPERTY TRUST INC

Exchange	Symbol	Price	52Wk Range	Yield	P/E	Div Acheiver
NYS	ESS	$300.86 (12/31/2019)	332.54-236.59	2.59	46.29	24 Years

*7 Year Price Score 109.43 *NYSE Composite Index=100 *12 Month Price Score 98.94

Interim Earnings (Per Share)

Qtr.	Mar	Jun	Sep	Dec
2016	1.19	1.10	1.00	2.98
2017	2.72	1.08	1.21	1.57
2018	1.38	1.52	1.22	1.78
2019	1.81	1.40	1.51	...

Interim Dividends (Per Share)

Amt	Decl	Ex	Rec	Pay
1.95Q	02/21/2019	03/28/2019	03/29/2019	04/12/2019
1.95Q	05/15/2019	06/27/2019	06/28/2019	07/12/2019
1.95Q	09/06/2019	09/27/2019	09/30/2019	10/15/2019
1.95Q	12/16/2019	12/31/2019	01/02/2020	01/15/2020

Indicated Div: $7.80 (Div. Reinv. Plan)

Valuation Analysis / **Institutional Holding**

Forecast EPS	$6.09	No of Institutions
	(01/17/2020)	704
Market Cap	$19.9 Billion	Shares
Book Value	$6.2 Billion	78,891,328
Price/Book	3.19	% Held
Price/Sales	13.83	96.61

Business Summary: REITs (MIC: 5.3.1 SIC: 6798 NAIC: 525930)

Essex Property Trust operates as a self-administered and self-managed real estate investment trust. Co. owns all of its interest in its real estate and other investments directly or indirectly through Essex Portfolio, L.P. (the Operating Partnership). Co. is the sole general partner of the Operating Partnership. Co. is engaged primarily in the ownership, operation, management, acquisition, development and redevelopment of primarily apartment communities, located along the West Coast. Co. owns or has an interest in various operating apartment communities, consisting of apartment homes, operating commercial building and active development projects in various stages of development.

Recent Developments: For the quarter ended Sep 30 2019, net income increased 22.7% to US$105.7 million from US$86.1 million in the year-earlier quarter. Revenues were US$366.9 million, up 4.6% from US$350.9 million the year before. Revenues from property income rose 4.6% to US$364.5 million from US$348.6 million in the corresponding quarter a year earlier.

Prospects: Our evaluation of Essex Property Trust Inc. as of October 4th, 2019 is the result of our systematic analysis on three basic characteristics: earnings strength, relative valuation, and recent stock price movement. The company has enjoyed a very positive trend in earnings per share over the past 5 quarters. However, recent analyst estimates for the company have been mixed and ESS has posted results that fell short of analysts' expectations. Based on operating income yield, the company is overvalued when compared to all of the companies we cover. Share price changes over the past year indicates that ESS will perform well over the near term.

Financial Data

(US$ in Thousands)	9 Mos	6 Mos	3 Mos	12/31/2018	12/31/2017	12/31/2016	12/31/2015	12/31/2014
Earnings Per Share	6.50	6.21	6.33	5.90	6.57	6.27	3.49	2.06
Cash Flow Per Share	12.94	12.67	12.39	12.52	11.64	10.85	9.52	8.72
Tang Book Value Per Share	94.20	93.64	94.21	95.11	95.03	94.50	94.28	93.42
Dividends Per Share	7.710	7.620	7.530	7.440	7.000	6.400	5.760	5.110
Dividend Payout %	118.62	122.71	118.96	126.10	106.54	102.07	165.04	248.06
Income Statement								
Total Revenue	1,084,790	717,858	356,223	1,400,053	1,363,899	1,294,001	1,194,407	969,305
EBITDA	389,753	264,315	143,784	981,609	1,017,702	998,708	833,735	583,880
Depn & Amortn	(13,219)	(9,143)	(4,782)	459,660	447,814	412,237	421,673	336,595
Income Before Taxes	275,788	190,331	109,229	324,467	371,598	394,122	226,378	94,545
Income Taxes	1,457	...	...	...	...	4,410	...	...
Net Income	310,468	211,133	118,858	390,153	433,059	414,979	232,120	122,150
Average Shares	65,973	65,821	65,783	66,085	65,898	65,587	65,061	56,696
Balance Sheet								
Current Assets	525,161	344,821	406,310	432,835	352,056	350,461	279,825	237,583
Total Assets	12,997,892	12,671,145	12,578,001	12,383,596	12,495,706	12,217,408	12,005,091	11,562,874
Current Liabilities	382,047	334,348	374,997	314,960	300,691	284,305	272,634	261,248
Long-Term Obligations	6,048,141	5,841,251	5,735,801	5,605,942	5,689,126	5,563,260	5,315,464	5,109,817
Total Liabilities	6,772,792	6,516,238	6,386,744	6,116,523	6,218,300	6,025,230	5,767,358	5,540,202
Stockholders' Equity	6,225,100	6,154,907	6,191,257	6,267,073	6,277,406	6,192,178	6,237,733	6,022,672
Shares Outstanding	66,081	65,726	65,715	65,890	66,054	65,527	65,379	63,682
Statistical Record								
Return on Assets %	3.36	3.25	3.32	3.14	3.50	3.42	1.97	1.46
Return on Equity %	6.83	6.55	...	6.22	6.95	6.66	3.79	3.09
EBITDA Margin %	35.93	36.82	40.36	70.11	74.62	77.18	69.80	60.24
Net Margin %	28.62	29.41	33.37	27.87	31.75	32.07	19.43	12.60
Asset Turnover	0.11	0.11	0.11	0.11	0.11	0.11	0.10	0.12
Current Ratio	1.37	1.03	1.08	1.37	1.17	1.23	1.03	0.91
Debt to Equity	0.97	0.95	0.93	0.89	0.91	0.90	0.85	0.85
Price Range	330.21-236.59	302.91-229.35	292.86-227.40	265.68-217.81	269.39-221.72	240.04-192.26	244.29-206.60	212.86-143.51
P/E Ratio	50.80-36.40	48.78-36.93	46.27-35.92	45.03-36.92	41.00-33.75	38.28-30.66	70.00-59.20	103.33-69.67
Average Yield %	2.74	2.89	3.00	3.09	2.82	2.89	2.57	2.82

Address: 1100 Park Place Suite 200, San Mateo, CA 94403 Telephone: 650-655-7800	Web Site: www.essex.com Officers: George M. Marcus - Chairman Keith R. Guericke - Vice-Chairman, President, Chief Executive Officer	Auditors: KPMG LLP Investor Contact: 650-494-3700 Transfer Agents: Computershare, LLC

EVERCORE INC

Exchange	Symbol	Price	52Wk Range	Yield	P/E	Div Acheiver
NYS	EVR	$74.76 (12/31/2019)	98.02-71.56	3.10	9.30	10 Years

*7 Year Price Score 105.35 *NYSE Composite Index=100 *12 Month Price Score 86.36

Interim Earnings (Per Share)

Qtr.	Mar	Jun	Sep	Dec
2016	0.12	0.55	0.79	0.98
2017	1.76	0.41	1.04	(0.43)
2018	2.10	1.52	1.08	3.63
2019	1.52	1.88	1.01	...

Interim Dividends (Per Share)

Amt	Decl	Ex	Rec	Pay
0.50Q	01/29/2019	02/21/2019	02/22/2019	03/08/2019
0.58Q	04/23/2019	05/30/2019	05/31/2019	06/14/2019
0.58Q	07/23/2019	08/29/2019	08/30/2019	09/13/2019
0.58Q	10/22/2019	11/27/2019	11/29/2019	12/13/2019

Indicated Div: $2.32

Valuation Analysis **Institutional Holding**

Forecast EPS	$7.42	No of Institutions
	(01/16/2020)	460
Market Cap	$2.9 Billion	Shares
Book Value	$764.7 Million	45,594,344
Price/Book	3.86	% Held
Price/Sales	1.39	N/A

Business Summary: Finance Intermediaries & Services (MIC: 5.5.1 SIC: 6211 NAIC: 523110)

Evercore is a holding company. Through its subsidiaries, Co. is an independent investment banking advisory firm. Co. operates through two business segments: Investment Banking, which includes the advisory business which provides advice to clients on mergers, acquisitions, divestitures, shareholder activism and other corporate transactions, and also includes the Evercore ISI business which provides macroeconomic, policy and fundamental equity research and agency-based equity securities trading for institutional investors; and Investment Management, which includes the wealth management business through which Co. provides investment advisory, wealth management and fiduciary services.

Recent Developments: For the quarter ended Sep 30 2019, net income decreased 11.5% to US$52.5 million from US$59.3 million in the year-earlier quarter. Revenues were US$402.2 million, up 5.5% from US$381.3 million the year before. Operating income was US$70.3 million versus US$74.5 million in the prior-year quarter, a decrease of 5.6%. Indirect operating expenses increased 8.2% to US$331.9 million from US$306.7 million in the equivalent prior-year period.

Prospects: Our evaluation of Evercore Inc. as of October 4th, 2019 is the result of our systematic analysis on three basic characteristics: earnings strength, relative valuation, and recent stock price movement. The company has suffered a very negative trend in earnings per share over the past 5 quarters. However, recent analyst estimates for the company have been raised and EVR has posted results that exceeded analysts' expectations. Based on operating earnings yield, the company is undervalued when compared to all of the companies we cover. Share price changes over the past year indicates that EVR will perform well over the near term.

Financial Data
(US$ in Thousands)

	9 Mos	6 Mos	3 Mos	12/31/2018	12/31/2017	12/31/2016	12/31/2015	12/31/2014
Earnings Per Share	8.04	8.11	7.75	8.33	2.80	2.43	0.98	2.08
Cash Flow Per Share	15.86	13.32	11.79	20.93	13.03	10.58	9.60	6.03
Tang Book Value Per Share	16.02	15.07	15.27	15.51	9.98	8.60	7.50	7.27
Dividends Per Share	2.160	2.080	2.000	1.900	1.420	1.270	1.150	1.030
Dividend Payout %	26.87	25.65	25.81	22.81	50.71	52.26	117.35	49.52
Income Statement								
Total Revenue	1,348,571	946,373	415,327	2,064,705	1,704,349	1,440,052	1,223,273	915,858
EBITDA	330,162	238,858	100,424	559,932	443,837	274,334	139,139	179,203
Depn & Amortn	49,174	28,214	16,614	17,855	15,026	13,160	10,469	8,256
Income Before Taxes	280,988	210,644	83,810	542,077	428,811	261,174	128,670	170,947
Income Taxes	60,253	39,851	7,821	108,520	258,442	119,303	77,030	68,756
Net Income	192,252	148,974	67,232	377,240	125,454	107,528	42,863	86,874
Average Shares	42,789	43,376	44,155	45,279	44,826	44,193	43,699	41,843
Balance Sheet								
Current Assets	1,327,398	1,063,564	988,336	1,481,617	1,000,205	925,633	749,464	682,956
Total Assets	2,211,103	1,939,749	1,844,937	2,125,667	1,584,886	1,662,346	1,479,171	1,446,556
Current Liabilities	433,009	411,971	297,592	749,691	464,052	463,421	408,049	385,080
Long-Term Obligations	372,526	168,748	168,679	168,612	175,146	184,647	141,800	127,776
Total Liabilities	1,446,420	1,201,463	1,077,190	1,367,547	1,040,922	1,135,048	974,619	895,275
Stockholders' Equity	764,683	738,286	767,747	758,120	543,964	527,298	504,552	551,281
Shares Outstanding	39,436	39,864	41,068	39,748	39,102	39,190	39,623	36,255
Statistical Record								
Return on Assets %	18.16	20.37	21.39	20.33	7.73	6.83	2.93	6.61
Return on Equity %	49.63	53.12	52.96	57.94	23.42	20.78	8.12	16.49
EBITDA Margin %	24.48	25.24	24.18	27.12	26.04	19.05	11.37	19.57
Net Margin %	14.26	15.74	16.19	18.27	7.36	7.47	3.50	9.49
Asset Turnover	1.08	1.18	1.24	1.11	1.05	0.91	0.84	0.70
Current Ratio	3.07	2.58	3.32	1.98	2.16	2.00	1.84	1.77
Debt to Equity	0.49	0.23	0.22	0.22	0.32	0.35	0.28	0.23
Price Range	98.80-64.90	114.95-64.90	114.95-64.90	114.95-64.90	92.20-67.80	71.55-40.61	59.15-46.88	63.14-45.29
P/E Ratio	12.29-8.07	14.17-8.00	14.83-8.37	13.80-7.79	32.93-24.21	29.44-16.71	60.36-47.84	30.36-21.77
Average Yield %	2.53	2.27	2.21	1.96	1.84	2.43	2.18	1.93

Address: 55 East 52nd Street, New York, NY 10055	Web Site: www.evercore.com	Auditors: Deloitte & Touche LLP
	Officers: John S. Weinberg - Executive Chairman,	Investor Contact: 212-857-3100
Telephone: 212-857-3100	Chairman Roger C. Altman - Senior Chairman,	Transfer Agents: Computershare,
Fax: 212-857-3101	Co-Chairman, Co-Chief Executive Officer	College Station, TX

EVEREST RE GROUP LTD

Exchange	Symbol	Price	52Wk Range	Yield	P/E
NYS	RE	$276.84 (12/31/2019)	279.01-208.80	2.24	27.17

*7 Year Price Score 102.21 *NYSE Composite Index=100 *12 Month Price Score 104.78

Interim Earnings (Per Share)

Qtr.	Mar	Jun	Sep	Dec
2016	4.00	3.67	7.06	8.98
2017	7.07	5.95	(15.73)	13.87
2018	5.11	1.70	5.02	(9.30)
2019	8.54	8.39	2.56	...

Interim Dividends (Per Share)

Amt	Decl	Ex	Rec	Pay
1.40Q	02/20/2019	03/05/2019	03/06/2019	03/20/2019
1.40Q	05/15/2019	05/28/2019	05/29/2019	06/12/2019
1.40Q	08/21/2019	09/03/2019	09/04/2019	09/18/2019
1.55Q	11/20/2019	12/03/2019	12/04/2019	12/24/2019

Indicated Div: $6.20

Valuation Analysis | **Institutional Holding**

Forecast EPS	N/A	No of Institutions
		650
Market Cap	$11.3 Billion	Shares
Book Value	$9.0 Billion	48,380,724
Price/Book	1.26	% Held
Price/Sales	1.44	93.31

Business Summary: General Insurance (MIC: 5.2.1 SIC: 6331 NAIC: 524126)

Everest Re Group is a holding company. Through its subsidiaries, Co. underwrites reinsurance and insurance in the U.S., Bermuda and international markets. Co.'s segments are: U.S. Reinsurance, which writes property and casualty reinsurance and specialty lines of business, including Marine, Aviation, Surety and Accident and Health business; International, which focuses on the international reinsurance markets; Bermuda, which writes property and casualty reinsurance and property and casualty reinsurance; and Insurance, which writes property and casualty insurance, including medical stop loss insurance, directly and through brokers, surplus lines brokers and general agents.

Recent Developments: For the quarter ended Sep 30 2019, net income decreased 47.4% to US$104.4 million from US$198.4 million in the year-earlier quarter. Revenues were US$2.04 billion, up 5.5% from US$1.94 billion the year before. Net premiums earned were US$1.91 billion versus US$1.73 billion in the prior-year quarter, an increase of 10.1%. Net investment income rose 12.2% to US$181.1 million from US$161.4 million a year ago.

Prospects: Our evaluation of Everest Re Group Ltd. as of October 4th, 2019 is the result of our systematic analysis on three basic characteristics: earnings strength, relative valuation, and recent stock price movement. The company has produced a positive trend in earnings per share over the past 5 quarters. However, recent analyst estimates for the company have been reduced, while RE has posted results that exceeded analysts' expectations. Based on operating earnings yield, the company is fairly valued when compared to all of the companies we cover. Share price changes over the past year indicates that RE will perform in line with the market over the near term.

Financial Data
(US$ in Thousands)

	9 Mos	6 Mos	3 Mos	12/31/2018	12/31/2017	12/31/2016	12/31/2015	12/31/2014
Earnings Per Share	10.19	12.65	5.96	2.53	11.36	23.68	22.10	25.91
Cash Flow Per Share	38.56	33.04	21.69	15.11	28.64	33.13	30.14	28.95
Tang Book Value Per Share	220.50	218.06	206.68	194.43	204.95	197.45	178.21	166.75
Dividends Per Share	5.600	5.500	5.400	5.300	5.050	4.700	4.000	3.200
Dividend Payout %	54.96	43.48	90.60	209.49	44.45	19.85	18.10	12.35
Income Statement								
Premium Income	5,455,615	3,549,996	1,732,697	6,931,699	5,937,840	5,320,466	5,481,459	5,169,135
Total Revenue	6,017,083	3,979,058	1,960,083	7,377,206	6,608,071	5,794,346	5,837,889	5,790,589
Benefits & Claims	3,515,104	2,143,180	1,048,550	5,651,403	4,522,581	3,139,629	3,101,915	2,906,534
Income Before Taxes	879,909	791,384	408,791	(226,471)	405,184	1,099,844	1,208,509	1,446,115
Income Taxes	88,092	99,629	59,891	(330,023)	(63,784)	103,500	134,021	187,652
Net Income	791,817	691,755	348,900	103,552	468,968	996,344	977,869	1,199,156
Average Shares	40,746	40,404	40,445	40,586	40,843	41,628	43,877	45,802
Balance Sheet								
Total Assets	27,023,741	26,387,791	25,630,507	24,793,999	23,591,792	21,321,504	21,426,175	20,817,824
Total Liabilities	18,040,483	17,503,631	17,203,878	16,890,195	15,222,560	13,246,108	13,817,590	13,366,704
Stockholders' Equity	8,983,258	8,884,160	8,426,629	7,903,804	8,369,232	8,075,396	7,608,585	7,451,120
Shares Outstanding	40,741	40,741	40,770	40,651	40,835	40,898	42,694	44,685
Statistical Record								
Return on Assets %	1.61	2.05	0.99	0.43	2.09	4.65	4.63	5.90
Return on Equity %	4.78	6.02	2.89	1.27	5.70	12.67	12.99	16.63
Loss Ratio %	64.43	60.37	60.52	81.53	76.17	59.01	56.59	56.23
Net Margin %	13.16	17.38	17.80	1.40	7.10	17.20	16.75	20.71
Price Range	266.76-205.03	253.31-205.03	260.00-205.03	262.67-205.03	271.12-210.36	218.38-169.21	191.54-166.99	176.27-137.48
P/E Ratio	26.18-20.12	20.02-16.21	43.62-34.40	103.82-81.04	23.87-18.52	9.22-7.15	8.67-7.56	6.80-5.31
Average Yield %	2.37	2.35	2.32	2.31	2.12	2.47	2.22	2.01

Address: Seon Place - 4th Floor, 141 Front Street, P.O. Box HM 845, Hamilton, HM 19
Telephone: 441-295-0006
Fax: 441-295-4828

Web Site: www.everestre.com
Officers: Joseph V. Taranto - Chairman, Chief Executive Officer Juan Carlos Andrade Ortiz - President, Chief Executive Officer, Chief Operating Officer

Auditors: PricewaterhouseCoopers LLP
Investor Contact: 908-604-3169
Transfer Agents: Computershare Trust Company, N.A., Providence, RI

EVERSOURCE ENERGY

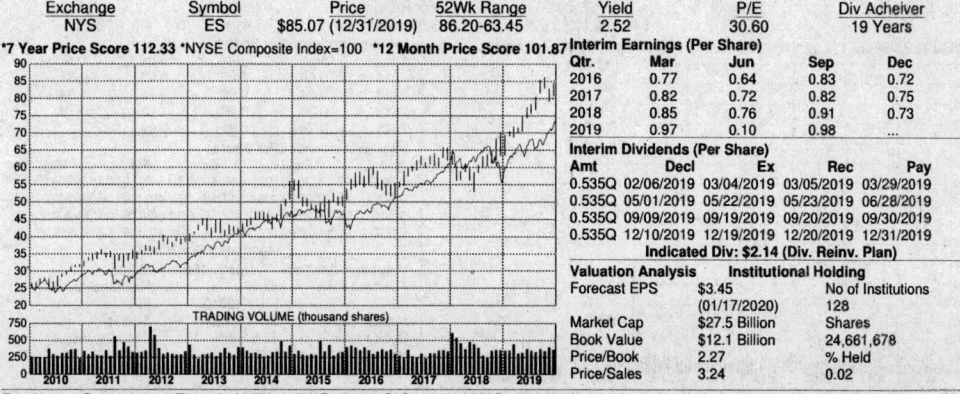

Exchange	Symbol	Price	52Wk Range	Yield	P/E	Div Acheiver
NYS	ES	$85.07 (12/31/2019)	86.20-63.45	2.52	30.60	19 Years

*7 Year Price Score 112.33 *NYSE Composite Index=100 *12 Month Price Score 101.87

Interim Earnings (Per Share)

Qtr.	Mar	Jun	Sep	Dec
2016	0.77	0.64	0.83	0.72
2017	0.82	0.72	0.82	0.75
2018	0.85	0.76	0.91	0.73
2019	0.97	0.10	0.98	...

Interim Dividends (Per Share)

Amt	Decl	Ex	Rec	Pay
0.535Q	02/06/2019	03/04/2019	03/05/2019	03/29/2019
0.535Q	05/01/2019	05/22/2019	05/23/2019	06/28/2019
0.535Q	09/09/2019	09/19/2019	09/20/2019	09/30/2019
0.535Q	12/10/2019	12/19/2019	12/20/2019	12/31/2019

Indicated Div: $2.14 (Div. Reinv. Plan)

Valuation Analysis / **Institutional Holding**

Forecast EPS	$3.45 (01/17/2020)	No of Institutions	128
Market Cap	$27.5 Billion	Shares	24,661,678
Book Value	$12.1 Billion	% Held	0.02
Price/Book	2.27		
Price/Sales	3.24		

Business Summary: Electric Utilities (MIC: 3.1.1 SIC: 4911 NAIC: 221122)

Eversource Energy is a public utility holding company. Through its subsidiaries, Co. has four segments: electric distribution, which are engaged in the distribution of electricity to retail customers in Connecticut, Massachusetts and New Hampshire; electric transmission, which owns and maintains transmission facilities that are part of an interstate power transmission grid over which electricity is transmitted throughout New England; natural gas distribution, which distributes natural gas to communities in Massachusetts and cities and towns in Connecticut; and water distribution, which provides water services in towns and cities in Connecticut, Massachusetts and New Hampshire.

Recent Developments: For the quarter ended Sep 30 2019, net income increased 10.1% to US$320.8 million from US$291.3 million in the year-earlier quarter. Revenues were US$2.18 billion, down 4.2% from US$2.27 billion the year before. Operating income was US$509.2 million versus US$466.0 million in the prior-year quarter, an increase of 9.3%. Direct operating expenses declined 10.6% to US$1.06 billion from US$1.19 billion in the comparable period the year before. Indirect operating expenses decreased 2.2% to US$605.3 million from US$618.6 million in the equivalent prior-year period.

Prospects: Our evaluation of Eversource Energy as of October 4th, 2019 is the result of our systematic analysis on three basic characteristics: earnings strength, relative valuation, and recent stock price movement. The company has managed to produce a neutral trend in earnings per share over the past 5 quarters. Additionally, recent analyst estimates for the company have been unchanged while ES has posted results that fell short of analysts' expectations. Based on operating earnings yield, the company is fairly valued when compared to all of the companies we cover. Share price changes over the past year indicates that ES will perform well over the near term.

Financial Data

(US$ in Thousands)	9 Mos	6 Mos	3 Mos	12/31/2018	12/31/2017	12/31/2016	12/31/2015	12/31/2014
Earnings Per Share	2.78	2.71	3.37	3.25	3.11	2.96	2.76	2.58
Cash Flow Per Share	5.77	6.29	6.40	5.62	6.32	6.83	4.49	5.17
Tang Book Value Per Share	23.77	23.26	22.72	22.28	21.01	22.70	21.54	20.37
Dividends Per Share	2.110	2.080	2.050	2.020	1.900	1.780	1.670	1.570
Dividend Payout %	75.90	76.75	60.83	62.15	61.09	60.14	60.51	60.85
Income Statement								
Total Revenue	6,476,084	4,300,287	2,415,792	8,448,201	7,751,952	7,639,129	7,954,827	7,741,856
EBITDA	2,099,136	1,203,676	789,194	2,648,226	2,769,964	2,621,245	2,464,247	2,272,125
Depn & Amortn	840,392	543,938	285,909	819,930	773,802	715,466	665,856	614,657
Income Before Taxes	859,090	403,100	378,051	1,329,491	1,574,407	1,504,818	1,425,971	1,295,362
Income Taxes	194,435	114,209	83,393	288,972	578,892	554,997	539,967	468,297
Net Income	659,016	340,132	308,678	1,033,000	987,996	942,302	878,485	819,546
Average Shares	326,008	320,388	318,316	317,993	318,031	318,454	318,432	317,417
Balance Sheet								
Current Assets	2,220,905	2,131,697	2,300,864	2,292,224	2,487,099	2,477,672	2,618,786	2,692,465
Total Assets	39,725,394	38,995,906	38,941,007	38,241,256	36,220,386	32,053,173	30,580,309	29,777,975
Current Liabilities	3,748,910	3,512,121	4,559,362	4,112,882	3,589,045	3,638,605	2,989,790	3,134,381
Long-Term Obligations	13,440,165	13,039,180	12,284,330	12,832,031	11,775,889	8,829,354	8,805,574	8,606,017
Total Liabilities	27,603,780	27,041,313	27,303,573	26,754,396	25,134,144	21,341,439	20,228,094	19,801,160
Stockholders' Equity	12,121,614	11,954,593	11,637,434	11,486,817	11,086,242	10,711,734	10,352,215	9,976,815
Shares Outstanding	323,733	323,574	317,347	316,885	316,885	316,885	317,191	316,983
Statistical Record								
Return on Assets %	2.31	2.26	2.82	2.77	2.89	3.00	2.91	2.85
Return on Equity %	7.57	7.41	9.40	9.15	9.07	8.92	8.64	8.37
EBITDA Margin %	32.41	27.99	32.67	31.35	35.73	34.31	30.98	29.35
Net Margin %	10.18	7.91	12.78	12.23	12.75	12.34	11.04	10.59
Asset Turnover	0.22	0.23	0.23	0.23	0.23	0.24	0.26	0.27
Current Ratio	0.59	0.61	0.50	0.56	0.69	0.68	0.88	0.86
Debt to Equity	1.11	1.09	1.06	1.12	1.06	0.82	0.85	0.86
Price Range	85.47-61.09	77.53-58.46	71.95-52.87	70.23-52.87	65.81-54.25	60.25-50.58	56.40-45.41	56.15-41.52
P/E Ratio	30.74-21.97	28.61-21.57	21.35-15.69	21.61-16.27	21.16-17.44	20.35-17.09	20.43-16.45	21.76-16.09
Average Yield %	2.94	3.10	3.25	3.32	3.13	3.22	3.34	3.41

Address: 300 Cadwell Drive, Springfield, MA 01104 **Telephone:** 800-286-5000	**Web Site:** www.eversource.com **Officers:** James J. (Jim) Judge - Chairman, President, Chief Executive Officer, Executive Vice President, Chief Financial Officer Philip J. Lembo - Executive Vice President, Chief Financial Officer, Treasurer, Senior Vice President	**Auditors:** DELOITTE & TOUCHE LLP **Investor Contact:** 860-728-4650 **Transfer Agents:** ComputerShare Investor Services, Providence, RI

EXTRA SPACE STORAGE INC

Exchange	Symbol	Price	52Wk Range	Yield	P/E
NYS	EXR	$105.62 (12/31/2019)	123.52-87.44	3.41	33.32

*7 Year Price Score 117.02 ***NYSE Composite Index=100** ***12 Month Price Score 94.59**

Interim Earnings (Per Share)

Qtr.	Mar	Jun	Sep	Dec
2016	0.66	0.66	0.93	0.67
2017	0.64	0.69	0.74	1.69
2018	0.70	0.75	1.02	0.79
2019	0.74	0.81	0.83	...

Interim Dividends (Per Share)

Amt	Decl	Ex	Rec	Pay
0.86Q	02/14/2019	03/14/2019	03/15/2019	03/29/2019
0.90Q	05/23/2019	06/13/2019	06/14/2019	06/28/2019
0.90Q	08/26/2019	09/13/2019	09/16/2019	09/30/2019
0.90Q	11/11/2019	12/13/2019	12/16/2019	12/31/2019

Indicated Div: $3.60

Valuation Analysis

		Institutional Holding	
Forecast EPS	$3.07	No of Institutions	
	(01/17/2020)	655	
Market Cap	$13.7 Billion	Shares	
Book Value	$2.5 Billion	164,204,016	
Price/Book	5.42	% Held	
Price/Sales	10.68	99.27	

Business Summary: REITs (MIC: 5.3.1 SIC: 6798 NAIC: 525930)

Extra Space Storage is a self-administered and self-managed real estate investment trust that owns, operates, manages, acquires, develops and redevelops self-storage properties. Substantially all of Co.'s business is conducted through Extra Space Storage LP. Co. operates in two segments:self-storage operations, which include rental operations of wholly-owned stores; and tenant reinsurance, which include the reinsurance of risks relating to the loss of goods stored by tenants in Co.'s stores. Co. owns and operates stores in several states, Washington, D.C. and Puerto Rico.

Recent Developments: For the quarter ended Sep 30 2019, net income decreased 17.0% to US$116.0 million from US$139.7 million in the year-earlier quarter. Revenues were US$337.5 million, up 10.0% from US$307.0 million the year before. Revenues from property income rose 9.1% to US$290.9 million from US$266.7 million in the corresponding quarter a year earlier.

Prospects: Our evaluation of Extra Space Storage Inc. as of October 4th, 2019 is the result of our systematic analysis on three basic characteristics: earnings strength, relative valuation, and recent stock price movement. The company has managed to produce a neutral trend in earnings per share over the past 5 quarters. However, recent analyst estimates for the company have been raised and EXR has posted results that exceeded analysts' expectations. Based on operating earnings yield, the company is fairly valued when compared to all of the companies we cover. Share price changes over the past year indicates that EXR will perform over the near term.

Financial Data

(US$ in Thousands)	9 Mos	6 Mos	3 Mos	12/31/2018	12/31/2017	12/31/2016	12/31/2015	12/31/2014
Earnings Per Share	3.17	3.36	3.30	3.27	3.76	2.91	1.56	1.53
Cash Flow Per Share	5.38	5.50	5.32	5.38	4.74	4.30	3.07	2.92
Tang Book Value Per Share	19.49	19.00	18.72	18.99	18.66	17.83	16.81	14.87
Dividends Per Share	3.520	3.480	3.440	3.360	3.120	2.930	2.240	1.810
Dividend Payout %	111.04	103.57	104.24	102.75	82.98	100.69	143.59	118.30
Income Statement								
Total Revenue	972,653	635,148	311,546	1,196,604	1,105,009	991,875	782,270	647,155
EBITDA	647,874	425,093	207,332	822,733	840,297	633,209	419,908	375,990
Depn & Amortn	177,561	117,418	58,855	203,030	185,903	174,906	123,751	109,531
Income Before Taxes	330,969	213,626	101,343	441,872	502,516	330,842	205,476	188,903
Income Taxes	8,580	4,528	1,813	9,244	3,625	15,847	11,148	7,570
Net Income	307,685	199,598	94,770	415,289	479,013	366,127	189,474	178,355
Average Shares	137,318	135,654	134,289	133,159	134,155	125,948	126,918	121,435
Balance Sheet								
Current Assets	66,715	55,644	46,828	72,690	88,891	74,353	244,197	126,293
Total Assets	8,318,430	8,390,719	8,132,514	7,847,978	7,455,137	7,091,446	6,071,407	4,402,107
Current Liabilities	122,658	115,056	99,302	182,461	190,087	468,083	120,916	204,193
Long-Term Obligations	4,812,000	5,038,198	5,001,094	4,730,515	4,460,217	3,941,223	3,499,621	2,232,597
Total Liabilities	5,795,716	5,948,510	5,748,365	5,434,254	5,104,386	4,846,554	3,982,330	2,664,682
Stockholders' Equity	2,522,714	2,442,209	2,384,149	2,413,724	2,350,751	2,244,892	2,089,077	1,737,425
Shares Outstanding	129,410	128,513	127,392	127,103	126,007	125,881	124,119	116,360
Statistical Record								
Return on Assets %	5.08	5.36	5.41	5.43	6.59	5.55	3.62	4.26
Return on Equity %	16.64	18.04	17.84	17.43	20.85	16.85	9.90	10.20
EBITDA Margin %	66.61	66.93	66.55	68.76	76.04	63.84	53.68	58.10
Net Margin %	31.63	31.43	30.42	34.71	43.35	36.91	24.22	27.56
Asset Turnover	0.16	0.16	0.16	0.16	0.15	0.15	0.15	0.15
Current Ratio	0.54	0.48	0.47	0.40	0.47	0.16	2.02	0.62
Debt to Equity	1.91	2.06	2.10	1.96	1.90	1.76	1.68	1.29
Price Range	123.52-84.61	109.73-84.61	102.76-84.61	100.96-77.56	87.86-71.64	94.38-68.78	90.22-58.64	60.12-41.79
P/E Ratio	38.97-26.69	32.66-25.18	31.14-25.64	30.87-23.72	23.37-19.05	32.43-23.64	57.83-37.59	39.29-27.31
Average Yield %	3.45	3.62	3.69	3.72	3.97	3.50	3.10	3.48

Address: 2795 East Cottonwood Parkway, Suite 300, Salt Lake City, UT 84121	Web Site: www.extraspace.com	Auditors: Ernst & Young LLP
	Officers: Kenneth M. Woolley - Chairman, Executive Chairman, Chairman (frmr), Chief Executive Officer Joseph D. (Joe) Margolis - Chief Executive Officer, Chief Investment Officer	Investor Contact: 801-365-4600
Telephone: 801-365-4600		Transfer Agents: American Stock Transfer & Trust Company

EXXON MOBIL CORP

Exchange	Symbol	Price	52Wk Range	Yield	P/E	Div Acheiver
NYS	XOM	$69.78 (12/31/2019)	83.38-66.70	4.99	20.28	36 Years

*7 Year Price Score 71.92   *NYSE Composite Index=100   *12 Month Price Score 89.61

Interim Earnings (Per Share)

Qtr.	Mar	Jun	Sep	Dec
2016	0.43	0.41	0.63	0.41
2017	0.95	0.78	0.93	1.97
2018	1.09	0.92	1.46	1.41
2019	0.55	0.73	...	

Interim Dividends (Per Share)

Amt	Decl	Ex	Rec	Pay
0.82Q	01/30/2019	02/08/2019	02/11/2019	03/11/2019
0.87Q	04/24/2019	05/10/2019	05/13/2019	06/10/2019
0.87Q	07/31/2019	08/12/2019	08/13/2019	09/10/2019
0.87Q	10/30/2019	11/08/2019	11/12/2019	12/10/2019

Indicated Div: $3.48 (Div. Reinv. Plan)

Valuation Analysis

		Institutional Holding	
Forecast EPS	$2.38	No of Institutions	
	(01/17/2020)	3545	
Market Cap	$295.2 Billion	Shares	
Book Value	$189.9 Billion	3,065,313,280	
Price/Book	1.55	% Held	
Price/Sales	1.09	54.49	

Business Summary: Production & Extraction (MIC: 9.1.1 SIC: 1311 NAIC: 211111)

Exxon Mobil operates or markets products in the U.S. and other countries through its divisions and affiliated companies. Co.'s principal business involves exploration for, and production of, crude oil and natural gas and manufacture, trade, transport and sale of crude oil, natural gas, petroleum products, petrochemicals and other products. In the U.S., Co.'s development activities are focused on the onshore U.S., primarily in the Permian Basin of West Texas and New Mexico and the Bakken oil play in North Dakota. Gas development activities are also focused on the Marcellus Shale of Pennsylvania and West Virginia, the Utica Shale of Ohio and the Haynesville Shale of East Texas and Louisiana.

Recent Developments: For the quarter ended Sep 30 2019, net income decreased 49.6% to US$3.25 billion from US$6.45 billion in the year-earlier quarter. Revenues were US$65.05 billion, down 15.1% from US$76.61 billion the year before. Direct operating expenses declined 13.2% to US$44.14 billion from US$50.87 billion in the comparable period the year before. Indirect operating expenses decreased 2.8% to US$16.19 billion from US$16.65 billion in the equivalent prior-year period.

Prospects: Our evaluation of Exxon Mobil Corp. as of October 4th, 2019 is the result of our systematic analysis on three basic characteristics: earnings strength, relative valuation, and recent stock price movement. The company has generated a negative trend in earnings per share over the past 5 quarters. In addition, recent analyst estimates for the company have been reduced while XOM has posted results that exceeded analysts' expectations. Based on operating earnings yield, the company is fairly valued when compared to all of the companies we cover. Share price changes over the past year indicates that XOM will perform in line with the market over the near term.

Financial Data
(US$ in Thousands)

	9 Mos	6 Mos	3 Mos	12/31/2018	12/31/2017	12/31/2016	12/31/2015	12/31/2014
Earnings Per Share	3.44	4.15	4.34	4.88	4.63	1.88	3.85	7.60
Cash Flow Per Share	7.49	7.96	8.39	8.43	7.06	5.27	7.23	10.54
Tang Book Value Per Share	44.89	45.23	45.19	45.27	44.28	40.34	41.10	41.51
Dividends Per Share	3.380	3.330	3.280	3.230	3.060	2.980	2.880	2.700
Dividend Payout %	98.26	80.24	75.58	66.19	66.09	158.51	74.81	35.53
Income Statement								
Total Revenue	197,765,000	132,716,000	63,625,000	290,212,000	244,363,000	226,094,000	268,882,000	411,939,000
EBITDA	28,346,000	18,520,000	9,041,000	50,464,000	39,168,000	30,730,000	40,325,000	69,213,000
Depn & Amortn	14,075,000	9,202,000	4,571,000	18,745,000	19,893,000	22,308,000	18,048,000	17,297,000
Income Before Taxes	13,642,000	8,921,000	4,289,000	30,953,000	18,674,000	7,969,000	21,966,000	51,630,000
Income Taxes	4,598,000	3,124,000	1,883,000	9,532,000	(1,174,000)	(406,000)	5,415,000	18,015,000
Net Income	8,650,000	5,480,000	2,350,000	20,840,000	19,710,000	7,840,000	16,150,000	32,520,000
Average Shares	4,271,000	4,271,000	4,270,000	4,270,000	4,256,000	4,177,000	4,196,000	4,282,000
Balance Sheet								
Current Assets	50,008,000	51,743,000	51,576,000	47,973,000	47,134,000	41,416,000	42,623,000	52,910,000
Total Assets	359,361,000	360,729,000	356,189,000	346,196,000	348,691,000	330,314,000	336,758,000	349,493,000
Current Liabilities	64,195,000	70,287,000	66,632,000	57,138,000	57,771,000	47,638,000	53,976,000	64,633,000
Long-Term Obligations	25,950,000	19,001,000	19,031,000	20,538,000	24,406,000	28,932,000	19,925,000	11,653,000
Total Liabilities	169,446,000	169,352,000	164,967,000	154,402,000	161,003,000	162,989,000	165,947,000	175,094,000
Stockholders' Equity	189,915,000	191,377,000	191,222,000	191,794,000	187,688,000	167,325,000	170,811,000	174,399,000
Shares Outstanding	4,231,000	4,231,000	4,231,094	4,237,000	4,239,000	4,148,000	4,156,000	4,201,000
Statistical Record								
Return on Assets %	4.10	4.99	5.26	6.00	5.81	2.34	4.71	9.34
Return on Equity %	7.70	9.36	9.77	10.98	11.10	4.62	9.36	18.67
EBITDA Margin %	14.33	13.95	14.21	17.39	16.03	13.59	15.00	16.80
Net Margin %	4.37	4.13	3.69	7.18	8.07	3.47	6.01	7.89
Asset Turnover	0.76	0.79	0.81	0.84	0.72	0.68	0.78	1.18
Current Ratio	0.78	0.74	0.77	0.84	0.82	0.87	0.79	0.82
Debt to Equity	0.14	0.10	0.10	0.11	0.13	0.17	0.12	0.07
Price Range	86.51-65.51	86.60-65.51	86.60-65.51	89.07-65.51	90.89-76.10	95.12-73.18	93.37-68.71	104.38-86.41
P/E Ratio	25.15-19.04	20.87-15.79	19.95-15.09	18.25-13.42	19.63-16.44	50.60-38.93	24.25-17.85	13.73-11.37
Average Yield %	4.44	4.24	4.15	4.04	3.74	3.46	3.48	2.78

Address: 5959 Las Colinas Boulevard, Irving, TX 75039-2298	**Web Site:** www.exxonmobil.com	**Auditors:** PricewaterhouseCoopers LLP
Telephone: 972-940-6000	**Officers:** Rex W. Tillerson - Chairman, President, Chief Executive Officer Darren W. Woods - President, Chairman, Senior Vice President, President, Vice President, Chief Executive Officer, Division Officer, Senior Vice President, Vice President, Division Officer	**Investor Contact:** 180-025-21800
Fax: 972-444-1505		**Transfer Agents:** ComputerShare, College Station, TX

FNB CORP

Exchange	Symbol	Price	52Wk Range	Yield	P/E
NYS	FNB	$12.70 (12/31/2019)	12.84-9.84	3.78	10.76

*7 Year Price Score 74.83   *NYSE Composite Index=100   *12 Month Price Score 101.30

Interim Earnings (Per Share)

Qtr.	Mar	Jun	Sep	Dec
2016	0.12	0.19	0.24	0.23
2017	0.09	0.22	0.23	0.06
2018	0.26	0.26	0.30	0.30
2019	0.28	0.29	0.31	...

Interim Dividends (Per Share)

Amt	Decl	Ex	Rec	Pay
0.12Q	02/20/2019	03/04/2019	03/05/2019	03/15/2019
0.12Q	05/15/2019	05/30/2019	05/31/2019	06/15/2019
0.12Q	08/21/2019	09/03/2019	09/04/2019	09/15/2019
0.12Q	10/16/2019	12/02/2019	12/03/2019	12/15/2019

Indicated Div: $0.48

Valuation Analysis / Institutional Holding

Forecast EPS	$1.18	No of Institutions
	(01/16/2020)	455
Market Cap	$4.1 Billion	Shares
Book Value	$4.8 Billion	284,666,336
Price/Book	0.86	% Held
Price/Sales	2.69	74.69

Business Summary: Banking (MIC: 5.1.1 SIC: 6021 NAIC: 522110)

FNB is a financial holding company. Through its subsidiaries, Co. provides a range of financial services, principally to consumers, corporations, governments and small- to medium-sized businesses in its market areas. Commercial banking solutions include corporate banking, small business banking, investment real estate financing, business credit, capital markets and lease financing. Consumer banking products and services include deposit products, mortgage lending, consumer lending and a complete suite of mobile and online banking services. Wealth management services include asset management, private banking and insurance.

Recent Developments: For the quarter ended Sep 30 2019, net income increased 2.0% to US$103.0 million from US$101.0 million in the year-earlier quarter. Net interest income decreased 2.2% to US$229.8 million from US$234.8 million in the year-earlier quarter. Provision for loan losses was US$12.0 million versus US$16.0 million in the prior-year quarter, a decrease of 25.0%. Non-interest income rose 6.7% to US$80.0 million from US$75.0 million, while non-interest expense advanced 4.1% to US$178.0 million.

Prospects: Our evaluation of F.N.B. Corp. as of October 4th, 2019 is the result of our systematic analysis on three basic characteristics: earnings strength, relative valuation, and recent stock price movement. The company has managed to produce a neutral trend in earnings per share over the past 5 quarters. However, recent analyst estimates for the company have been reduced while FNB has posted results that exceeded analysts' expectations. Based on operating earnings yield, the company is undervalued when compared to all of the companies we cover. Share price changes over the past year indicates that FNB will perform very poorly over the near term.

Financial Data

(US$ in Thousands)	9 Mos	6 Mos	3 Mos	12/31/2018	12/31/2017	12/31/2016	12/31/2015	12/31/2014
Earnings Per Share	1.18	1.17	1.14	1.12	0.63	0.78	0.86	0.80
Cash Flow Per Share	0.71	0.54	1.29	1.88	0.92	1.42	1.28	2.67
Tang Book Value Per Share	7.33	7.11	6.91	6.68	6.06	6.47	6.33	5.95
Dividends Per Share	0.480	0.480	0.480	0.480	0.480	0.480	0.480	0.480
Dividend Payout %	40.68	41.03	42.11	42.86	76.19	61.54	55.81	60.00
Income Statement								
Interest Income	941,000	627,000	310,000	1,170,000	980,326	678,963	546,795	508,983
Interest Expense	250,000	166,000	79,000	238,000	133,892	67,451	48,573	42,686
Net Interest Income	691,000	461,000	231,000	932,000	846,434	611,512	498,222	466,297
Provision for Losses	37,000	25,000	14,000	61,000	61,073	55,752	40,441	38,648
Non-Interest Income	220,000	140,000	65,000	276,000	252,449	201,761	162,410	158,274
Non-Interest Expense	519,000	341,000	166,000	695,000	681,541	511,133	390,549	379,253
Income Before Taxes	355,000	235,000	116,000	452,000	356,269	246,388	229,642	206,670
Income Taxes	63,000	46,000	22,000	79,000	157,065	75,497	69,993	62,620
Net Income	292,000	189,000	94,000	373,000	199,204	170,891	159,649	144,050
Average Shares	326,099	325,949	325,828	325,623	303,857	207,768	176,338	169,078
Balance Sheet								
Net Loans & Leases	22,932,000	22,687,000	22,471,000	21,995,000	20,916,277	14,738,884	12,048,428	11,121,112
Total Assets	34,329,000	33,903,000	33,695,000	33,102,000	31,417,635	21,844,817	17,557,662	16,127,090
Total Deposits	24,594,000	23,731,000	23,882,000	23,455,000	22,399,725	16,065,647	12,623,463	11,382,208
Total Liabilities	29,509,000	29,150,000	29,015,000	28,494,000	27,008,441	19,273,200	15,461,480	14,105,634
Stockholders' Equity	4,820,000	4,753,000	4,680,000	4,608,000	4,409,194	2,571,617	2,096,182	2,021,456
Shares Outstanding	324,879	324,807	324,515	324,314	323,465	211,059	175,441	173,992
Statistical Record								
Return on Assets %	1.17	1.18	1.16	1.16	0.75	0.87	0.95	0.97
Return on Equity %	8.40	8.45	8.34	8.27	5.71	7.30	7.75	7.59
Net Interest Margin %	73.25	72.56	74.52	79.66	86.34	90.07	91.12	91.61
Efficiency Ratio %	45.18	44.64	44.27	48.06	55.29	58.04	55.07	56.84
Loans to Deposits	0.93	0.96	0.94	0.94	0.94	0.92	0.95	0.98
Price Range	12.87-9.47	13.81-9.47	14.11-9.47	14.76-9.47	16.30-12.12	16.40-11.18	14.64-11.89	13.65-11.49
P/E Ratio	10.91-8.03	11.80-8.09	12.38-8.31	13.18-8.46	25.87-19.24	21.03-14.33	17.02-13.83	17.06-14.36
Average Yield %	4.18	4.00	3.85	3.66	3.40	3.69	3.60	3.84

Address: One North Shore Center, 12 Federal Street, Pittsburgh, PA 15212
Telephone: 800-555-5455

Web Site: www.fnb-online.com
Officers: Vincent J. Delie - Chairman, President, Chief Executive Officer James L. Dutey - Senior Vice President, Corporate Controller, Principal Accounting Officer

Auditors: Ernst & Young LLP
Investor Contact: 724-983-3429
Transfer Agents: ComputerShare, College Station, TX

FACTSET RESEARCH SYSTEMS INC.

Exchange	Symbol	Price	52Wk Range	Yield	P/E	Div Acheiver
NYS	FDS	$268.30 (12/31/2019)	302.05-194.00	1.07	28.73	19 Years

*7 Year Price Score 126.38 ***NYSE Composite Index=100** ***12 Month Price Score 95.39**

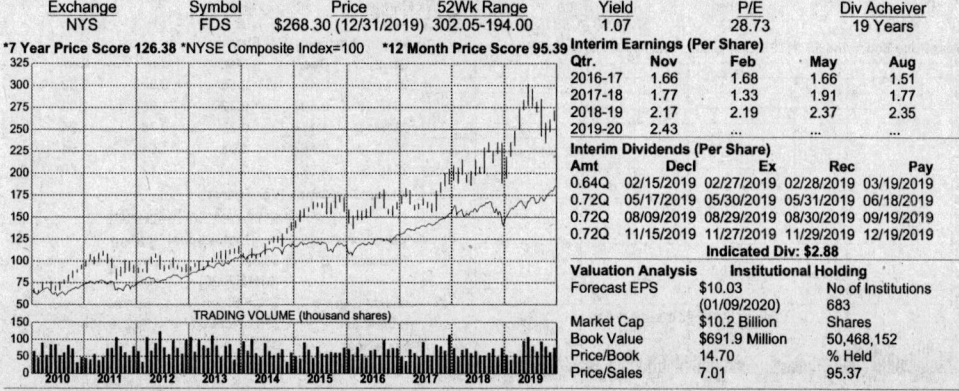

Interim Earnings (Per Share)

Qtr.	Nov	Feb	May	Aug
2016-17	1.66	1.68	1.66	1.51
2017-18	1.77	1.33	1.91	1.77
2018-19	2.17	2.19	2.37	2.35
2019-20	2.43	...	...	...

Interim Dividends (Per Share)

Amt	Decl	Ex	Rec	Pay
0.64Q	02/15/2019	02/27/2019	02/28/2019	03/19/2019
0.72Q	05/17/2019	05/30/2019	05/31/2019	06/18/2019
0.72Q	08/09/2019	08/29/2019	08/30/2019	09/19/2019
0.72Q	11/15/2019	11/27/2019	11/29/2019	12/19/2019

Indicated Div: $2.88

Valuation Analysis   **Institutional Holding**

Forecast EPS	$10.03	No of Institutions	
	(01/09/2020)	683	
Market Cap	$10.2 Billion	Shares	
Book Value	$691.9 Million		50,468,152
Price/Book	14.70	% Held	
Price/Sales	7.01		95.37

Business Summary: IT Services (MIC: 6.3.1 SIC: 7371 NAIC: 541511)

FactSet Research Systems is a provider of integrated financial information, analytical applications and other services for the investment and corporate communities. Co.'s data and technology solutions can be implemented across the investment portfolio lifecycle or as standalone components. Co. is focused on its three segments: United States, Europe, and Asia Pacific. Co. delivers insight and information through the workflow solutions of Research, Analytics and Trading, Content and Technology Solutions, and Wealth. Co. provides insights on global market trends and knowledge on companies and industries, as well as capabilities to monitor portfolio risk and performance and to execute trades.

Recent Developments: For the quarter ended Nov 30 2019, net income increased 11.5% to US$94.0 million from US$84.3 million in the year-earlier quarter. Revenues were US$366.7 million, up 4.3% from US$351.6 million the year before. Operating income was US$113.2 million versus US$100.5 million in the prior-year quarter, an increase of 12.6%. Direct operating expenses declined 1.1% to US$165.0 million from US$166.8 million in the comparable period the year before. Indirect operating expenses increased 5.0% to US$88.5 million from US$84.3 million in the equivalent prior-year period.

Prospects: Our evaluation of FactSet Research Systems Inc. as of October 4th, 2019 is the result of our systematic analysis on three basic characteristics: earnings strength, relative valuation, and recent stock price movement. The company has managed to produce a neutral trend in earnings per share over the past 5 quarters. However, recent analyst estimates for the company have been reduced while FDS has posted results that exceeded analysts' expectations. Based on operating earnings yield, the company is fairly valued when compared to all of the companies we cover. Share price changes over the past year indicates that FDS will perform over the near term.

Financial Data

(US$ in Thousands)	3 Mos	08/31/2019	08/31/2018	08/31/2017	08/31/2016	08/31/2015	08/31/2014	08/31/2013
Earnings Per Share	9.34	9.08	6.78	6.51	8.19	5.71	4.92	4.45
Cash Flow Per Share	12.55	11.20	9.96	8.13	8.08	7.37	6.25	6.15
Tang Book Value Per Share	N.M.	N.M.	N.M.	N.M.	N.M.	4.44	4.39	6.02
Dividends Per Share	2.800	2.720	2.400	2.120	1.880	1.660	1.480	1.320
Dividend Payout %	29.98	29.96	35.40	32.57	22.95	29.07	30.08	29.66
Income Statement								
Total Revenue	366,658	1,435,351	1,350,145	1,221,179	1,127,092	1,006,768	920,335	858,112
EBITDA	126,262	473,435	398,804	378,912	485,429	356,854	329,364	299,310
Depn & Amortn	14,390	35,400	32,600	28,000	23,300	23,100	25,900	28,400
Income Before Taxes	108,741	421,965	351,838	344,312	460,993	333,754	303,464	270,910
Income Taxes	14,784	69,175	84,753	86,053	122,178	92,703	91,921	72,273
Net Income	93,957	352,790	267,085	258,259	338,815	241,051	211,543	198,637
Average Shares	38,587	38,873	39,377	39,642	41,365	42,235	42,970	44,624
Balance Sheet								
Current Assets	546,215	583,812	430,916	409,376	369,276	304,174	249,775	318,034
Total Assets	1,762,232	1,560,130	1,419,447	1,413,315	1,019,161	736,671	663,212	690,197
Current Liabilities	207,650	218,923	221,134	201,139	158,210	139,780	127,291	118,253
Long-Term Obligations	574,219	574,174	574,775	575,000	300,000	35,000	...	...
Total Liabilities	1,070,354	887,874	893,547	853,624	501,780	205,087	152,130	148,418
Stockholders' Equity	691,878	672,256	525,900	559,691	517,381	531,584	511,082	541,779
Shares Outstanding	37,904	38,117	38,192	39,023	40,038	41,316	41,792	43,324
Statistical Record								
Return on Assets %	23.17	23.68	18.86	21.23	38.49	34.44	31.26	28.70
Return on Equity %	58.79	58.89	49.21	47.96	64.42	46.24	40.18	36.31
EBITDA Margin %	34.44	32.98	29.54	31.03	43.07	35.45	35.79	34.88
Net Margin %	25.63	24.58	19.78	21.15	30.06	23.94	22.99	23.15
Asset Turnover	0.93	0.96	0.95	1.00	1.28	1.44	1.36	1.24
Current Ratio	2.63	2.67	1.95	2.04	2.33	2.18	1.96	2.69
Debt to Equity	0.83	0.85	1.09	1.03	0.58	0.07	...	...
Price Range	302.05-188.55	302.05-188.55	229.39-157.03	183.17-151.67	178.81-136.40	173.20-116.34	127.86-101.94	111.60-87.45
P/E Ratio	32.34-20.19	33.27-20.77	33.83-23.16	28.14-23.30	21.83-16.65	30.33-20.37	25.99-20.72	25.08-19.65
Average Yield %	1.10	1.10	1.22	1.28	1.18	1.11	1.37	1.36

Address: 45 Glover Avenue, Norwalk, CT 06850	**Web Site:** www.investor.factset.com	**Auditors:** Ernst & Young LLP
Telephone: 203-810-1000	**Officers:** Philip A. Hadley - Chairman, Chief Executive Officer F. Philip Snow - President, Chief Executive Officer	**Transfer Agents:** Computershare Shareowner Services
Fax: 203-810-1001		

FAIR ISAAC CORP

Exchange	Symbol	Price	52Wk Range	Yield	P/E
NYS	FICO	$374.68 (12/31/2019)	379.35-178.77	N/A	59.10

*7 Year Price Score 184.55 ***NYSE Composite Index=100** ***12 Month Price Score 111.15**

TRADING VOLUME (thousand shares)

Interim Earnings (Per Share)

Qtr.	Dec	Mar	Jun	Sep
2014-15	0.43	0.58	0.62	1.02
2015-16	0.59	0.72	1.08	1.00
2016-17	1.16	0.78	0.78	1.25
2017-18	0.86	1.03	1.04	1.64
2018-19	1.32	1.10	2.12	1.80

Interim Dividends (Per Share)

Dividend Payment Suspended

Valuation Analysis		Institutional Holding	
Forecast EPS	$8.38	No of Institutions	
	(01/15/2020)	550	
Market Cap	$10.8 Billion	Shares	
Book Value	$289.8 Million	36,299,456	
Price/Book	37.43	% Held	
Price/Sales	9.35	79.51	

Business Summary: Business Services (MIC: 7.5.2 SIC: 7389 NAIC: 561499)

Fair Isaac is a provider of analytic, software and data management products and services. Co.'s segments are: Applications, which includes pre-configured decision management applications designed for business problem or process, such as marketing, account origination, customer management, fraud, collections and insurance claims management; Scores, which includes its business-to-business scoring solutions and services, its business-to-consumer scoring solutions and services including myFICO® solutions for consumers, and associated services; and Decision Management Software, which is composed of analytic and decision management software tools and Co.'s FICO® Decision Management Suite.

Recent Developments: For the year ended Sep 30 2019, net income increased 51.9% to US$192.1 million from US$126.5 million in the prior year. Revenues were US$1.16 billion, up 16.0% from US$1.00 billion the year before. Operating income was US$253.5 million versus US$175.4 million in the prior year, an increase of 44.6%. Direct operating expenses rose 7.7% to US$336.8 million from US$312.9 million in the comparable period the year before. Indirect operating expenses increased 11.3% to US$569.7 million from US$511.9 million in the equivalent prior-year period.

Prospects: Our evaluation of Fair, Isaac & Co. Inc. as of October 4th, 2019 is the result of our systematic analysis on three basic characteristics: earnings strength, relative valuation, and recent stock price movement. The company has produced a positive trend in earnings per share over the past 5 quarters. However, recent analyst estimates for the company have been unchanged, while FICO has posted results that exceeded analysts' expectations. Based on operating earnings yield, the company is overvalued when compared to all of the companies we cover. Share price changes over the past year indicates that FICO will perform over the near term.

Financial Data

(US$ in Thousands)	09/30/2019	09/30/2018	09/30/2017	09/30/2016	09/30/2015	09/30/2014	09/30/2013	09/30/2012
Earnings Per Share	6.34	4.57	3.98	3.39	2.65	2.72	2.48	2.64
Cash Flow Per Share	8.98	7.51	7.31	5.93	4.23	5.17	3.85	3.71
Dividends Per Share	...	...	0.040	0.080	0.080	0.080	0.080	0.080
Dividend Payout %	...	...	1.01	2.36	3.02	2.94	3.23	3.03
Income Statement								
Total Revenue	1,160,083	1,032,475	932,169	881,356	838,781	788,985	743,444	676,423
EBITDA	261,950	225,915	189,823	185,184	152,061	173,598	175,746	189,204
Depn & Amortn	6,126	6,594	12,709	13,982	13,673	11,917	13,535	21,544
Income Before Taxes	216,072	188,010	151,324	144,569	109,238	133,131	131,984	136,243
Income Taxes	23,948	45,595	23,068	35,121	22,736	38,252	41,889	44,239
Net Income	192,124	142,415	128,256	109,448	86,502	94,879	90,095	92,004
Average Shares	30,294	31,180	32,245	32,308	32,609	34,864	36,292	36,063
Balance Sheet								
Current Assets	455,706	338,512	310,931	267,638	286,602	288,527	249,188	259,325
Total Assets	1,433,448	1,255,079	1,255,620	1,221,052	1,230,163	1,192,298	1,161,547	1,158,611
Current Liabilities	490,828	422,215	326,655	246,077	243,875	341,404	165,880	209,605
Long-Term Obligations	606,790	528,944	462,801	494,000	516,000	376,000	447,000	455,000
Total Liabilities	1,143,681	991,342	829,083	774,224	793,165	737,684	630,870	684,205
Stockholders' Equity	289,767	263,737	426,537	446,828	436,998	454,614	530,677	474,406
Shares Outstanding	28,944	29,015	30,243	30,935	31,290	32,047	34,786	34,839
Statistical Record								
Return on Assets %	14.29	11.34	10.36	8.91	7.14	8.06	7.77	8.02
Return on Equity %	69.42	41.26	29.37	24.70	19.40	19.26	17.93	19.52
EBITDA Margin %	22.58	21.88	20.36	21.01	18.13	22.00	23.64	27.97
Net Margin %	16.56	13.79	13.76	12.42	10.31	12.03	12.12	13.60
Asset Turnover	0.86	0.82	0.75	0.72	0.69	0.67	0.64	0.59
Current Ratio	0.93	0.80	0.95	1.09	1.18	0.85	1.50	1.24
Debt to Equity	2.09	2.01	1.09	1.11	1.18	0.83	0.84	0.96
Price Range	369.40-171.50	240.03-142.25	145.54-111.42	132.87-81.01	97.25-53.89	64.88-51.00	55.29-40.62	45.95-20.26
P/E Ratio	58.26-27.05	52.52-31.13	36.57-27.99	39.19-23.90	36.70-20.34	23.85-18.75	22.29-16.38	17.41-7.67
Average Yield %	...	...	0.03	0.08	0.10	0.14	0.17	0.20

Address: 181 Metro Drive, Suite 700, San Jose, CA 95110-1346 Telephone: 408-535-1500	Web Site: www.fico.com Officers: Braden R. Kelly - Chairman William J. Lansing - Chief Executive Officer	Auditors: DELOITTE & TOUCHE LLP Investor Contact: 800-213-5542 Transfer Agents: Computershare, College Station, TX

FEDERAL REALTY INVESTMENT TRUST (MD)

Exchange	Symbol	Price	52Wk Range	Yield	P/E	Div Acheiver
NYS	FRT	$128.73 (12/31/2019)	141.16-115.81	3.26	38.09	51 Years

*7 Year Price Score 84.55 *NYSE Composite Index=100 *12 Month Price Score 94.09

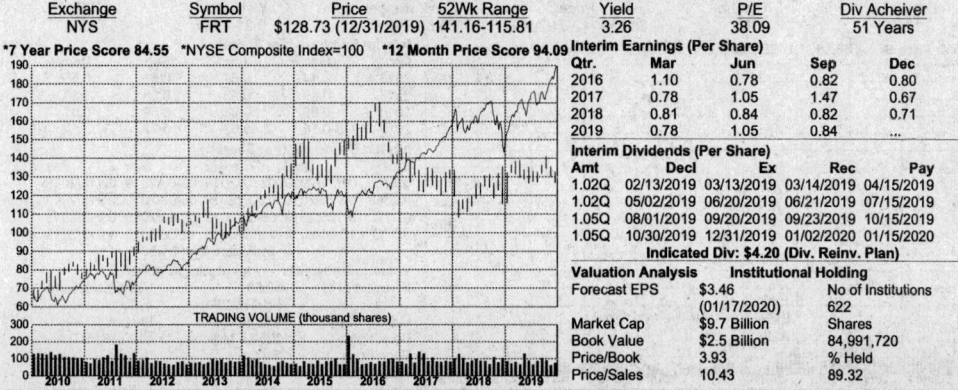

Interim Earnings (Per Share)

Qtr.	Mar	Jun	Sep	Dec
2016	1.10	0.78	0.82	0.80
2017	0.78	1.05	1.47	0.67
2018	0.81	0.84	0.82	0.71
2019	0.78	1.05	0.84	...

Interim Dividends (Per Share)

Amt	Decl	Ex	Rec	Pay
1.02Q	02/13/2019	03/13/2019	03/14/2019	04/15/2019
1.02Q	05/02/2019	06/20/2019	06/21/2019	07/15/2019
1.05Q	08/01/2019	09/23/2019	09/23/2019	10/15/2019
1.05Q	10/30/2019	12/31/2019	01/02/2020	01/15/2020

Indicated Div: $4.20 (Div. Reinv. Plan)

Valuation Analysis / **Institutional Holding**

Forecast EPS	$3.46 (01/17/2020)	No of Institutions 622
Market Cap	$9.7 Billion	Shares
Book Value	$2.5 Billion	84,991,720
Price/Book	3.93	% Held
Price/Sales	10.43	89.32

Business Summary: REITs (MIC: 5.3.1 SIC: 6798 NAIC: 525930)

Federal Realty Investment Trust is an equity real estate investment trust that focuses on the ownership, management, and redevelopment of retail and mixed-use properties located primarily in communities in selected metropolitan markets in the Northeast and Mid-Atlantic regions of the U.S., as well as in California and South Florida. Co. owns or has a majority interest in community and neighborhood shopping centers and mixed-use properties which are operated as primarily retail real estate projects.

Recent Developments: For the quarter ended Sep 30 2019, net income increased 4.6% to US$67.1 million from US$64.2 million in the year-earlier quarter. Revenues were US$233.9 million, up 1.8% from US$229.8 million the year before. Revenues from property income rose 1.9% to US$233.2 million from US$229.0 million in the corresponding quarter a year earlier.

Prospects: Our evaluation of Federal Realty Investment Trust as of October 4th, 2019 is the result of our systematic analysis on three basic characteristics: earnings strength, relative valuation, and recent stock price movement. The company has enjoyed a very positive trend in earnings per share over the past 5 quarters. However, recent analyst estimates for the company have been mixed and FRT has posted results that fell short of analysts' expectations. Based on operating earnings yield, the company is overvalued when compared to all of the companies we cover. Share price changes over the past year indicates that FRT will perform in line with the market over the near term.

Financial Data

(US$ in Thousands)	9 Mos	6 Mos	3 Mos	12/31/2018	12/31/2017	12/31/2016	12/31/2015	12/31/2014
Earnings Per Share	3.38	3.36	3.15	3.18	3.97	3.50	3.03	2.41
Cash Flow Per Share	6.63	6.64	6.70	7.05	6.37	5.90	5.23	5.14
Tang Book Value Per Share	30.60	29.98	29.77	29.44	28.82	27.32	23.80	23.24
Dividends Per Share	4.110	4.080	4.060	4.040	3.960	3.840	3.620	3.300
Dividend Payout %	121.60	121.43	128.89	127.04	99.75	109.71	119.47	136.93
Income Statement								
Total Revenue	696,639	462,692	232,227	915,436	857,348	801,591	744,012	686,090
EBITDA	473,017	319,351	150,715	593,966	536,065	514,580	455,878	431,306
Depn & Amortn	178,327	118,679	59,622	244,245	216,050	193,585	174,796	170,814
Income Before Taxes	212,878	145,523	63,237	240,509	220,365	226,375	188,678	166,645
Net Income	206,511	141,046	60,144	241,907	289,914	249,910	210,219	164,535
Average Shares	74,832	74,713	74,200	73,302	72,233	71,049	68,981	67,492
Balance Sheet								
Current Assets	306,398	244,773	180,782	236,753	255,494	170,021	173,066	192,230
Total Assets	6,607,565	6,383,741	6,351,366	6,289,644	6,275,755	5,423,279	4,911,709	4,546,870
Current Liabilities	323,612	276,474	253,957	274,004	288,930	289,481	228,309	220,420
Long-Term Obligations	3,348,976	3,229,851	3,228,630	3,229,204	3,284,766	2,798,452	2,642,366	2,409,677
Total Liabilities	4,137,637	3,976,575	3,963,208	3,943,753	4,009,049	3,446,546	3,247,960	2,942,469
Stockholders' Equity	2,469,928	2,407,166	2,388,158	2,345,891	2,266,706	1,976,733	1,663,749	1,604,401
Shares Outstanding	75,494	74,950	74,836	74,249	73,090	71,995	69,493	68,605
Statistical Record								
Return on Assets %	4.05	4.07	3.81	3.85	4.96	4.82	4.45	3.75
Return on Equity %	10.92	11.05	10.38	10.49	13.66	13.69	12.86	10.78
EBITDA Margin %	67.90	69.02	64.90	64.88	62.53	64.19	61.27	62.86
Net Margin %	29.64	30.48	25.90	26.43	33.82	31.18	28.25	23.98
Asset Turnover	0.14	0.15	0.15	0.15	0.15	0.15	0.16	0.16
Current Ratio	0.95	0.89	0.71	0.86	0.88	0.59	0.76	0.87
Debt to Equity	1.36	1.34	1.35	1.38	1.45	1.42	1.59	1.50
Price Range	138.92-115.33	138.92-115.33	138.75-111.20	135.55-108.11	145.29-120.52	170.35-136.98	150.27-124.96	137.18-100.90
P/E Ratio	41.10-34.12	41.35-34.32	44.05-35.30	42.63-34.00	36.60-30.36	48.67-39.14	49.59-41.24	56.92-41.87
Average Yield %	3.16	3.16	3.24	3.31	3.02	2.52	2.60	2.75

Address: 1626 East Jefferson Street, Rockville, MD 20852 **Telephone:** 301-998-8100	**Web Site:** www.federalrealty.com **Officers:** Donald C. Wood - President, Chief Executive Officer Daniel Guglielmone - Executive Vice President, Chief Financial Officer, Treasurer	**Auditors:** Grant Thornton LLP **Investor Contact:** 800-658-8980 **Transfer Agents:** American Stock Transfer & Trust Company, New York, NY

FEDERATED INVESTORS INC (PA)

Exchange	Symbol	Price	52Wk Range	Yield	P/E
NYS	FII	$32.59 (12/31/2019)	35.56-25.09	3.31	13.09

*7 Year Price Score 88.50 *NYSE Composite Index=100 *12 Month Price Score 101.04

Interim Earnings (Per Share)

Qtr.	Mar	Jun	Sep	Dec
2016	0.44	0.51	0.54	0.55
2017	0.49	0.53	0.56	1.30
2018	0.60	0.38	0.59	0.61
2019	0.54	0.62	0.72	...

Interim Dividends (Per Share)

Amt	Decl	Ex	Rec	Pay
0.27Q	01/24/2019	02/07/2019	02/08/2019	02/15/2019
0.27Q	04/25/2019	05/07/2019	05/08/2019	05/15/2019
0.27Q	07/25/2019	08/07/2019	08/08/2019	08/15/2019
0.27Q	10/24/2019	11/07/2019	11/08/2019	11/15/2019

Indicated Div: $1.08

Valuation Analysis

		Institutional Holding	
Forecast EPS	$2.58	No of Institutions	
	(01/17/2020)	493	
Market Cap	$3.3 Billion	Shares	
Book Value	$950.5 Million	118,249,096	
Price/Book	3.47	% Held	
Price/Sales	2.58	82.59	

TRADING VOLUME (thousand shares)

Business Summary: Wealth Management (MIC: 5.5.2 SIC: 6282 NAIC: 523930)

Federated Investors is a provider of investment management products and related financial services. Co. sponsors, markets and provides investment-related services to various investment products, including sponsored investment companies and other funds (Federated Funds) and Separate Accounts. Co. markets these funds to banks, broker/dealers and other financial intermediaries who use them to meet the needs of customers and/or clients, including retail investors, corporations and retirement plans. Co. also provides a range of services to support the operation and administration of the Federated Funds. These services include administrative services and shareholder servicing.

Recent Developments: For the quarter ended Sep 30 2019, net income increased 18.7% to US$73.6 million from US$62.0 million in the year-earlier quarter. Revenues were US$340.3 million, up 10.3% from US$308.6 million the year before. Operating income was US$89.3 million versus US$81.9 million in the prior-year quarter, an increase of 9.0%. Indirect operating expenses increased 10.7% to US$251.0 million from US$226.7 million in the equivalent prior-year period.

Prospects: Our evaluation of Federated Investors Inc. as of October 4th, 2019 is the result of our systematic analysis on three basic characteristics: earnings strength, relative valuation, and recent stock price movement. The company has produced a positive trend in earnings per share over the past 5 quarters. However, recent analyst estimates for the company have been mixed and FII has posted results that exceeded analysts' expectations. Based on operating earnings yield, the company is undervalued when compared to all of the companies we cover. Share price changes over the past year indicates that FII will perform over the near term.

Financial Data

(US$ in Thousands)	9 Mos	6 Mos	3 Mos	12/31/2018	12/31/2017	12/31/2016	12/31/2015	12/31/2014
Earnings Per Share	2.49	2.36	2.12	2.18	2.87	2.03	1.62	1.42
Cash Flow Per Share	3.41	1.87	1.80	2.13	2.78	2.54	2.32	1.91
Tang Book Value Per Share	N.M.	N.M.	N.M.	N.M.	0.24	N.M.	N.M.	N.M.
Dividends Per Share	1.080	1.080	1.080	1.060	1.000	2.000	1.000	1.000
Dividend Payout %	43.37	45.76	50.94	48.62	34.84	98.52	61.73	70.42
Income Statement								
Total Revenue	968,869	628,529	307,050	1,135,677	1,102,924	1,143,371	926,609	859,250
EBITDA	259,196	160,686	74,514	314,959	367,874	354,807	288,405	258,963
Depn & Amortn	1,625	1,130	592	12,900	11,100	9,700	9,200	10,000
Income Before Taxes	253,600	156,824	72,522	296,174	352,002	340,934	274,906	239,352
Income Taxes	61,564	38,373	17,911	73,875	57,101	119,420	102,920	89,530
Net Income	190,232	117,270	54,546	220,297	291,341	208,919	169,807	149,236
Average Shares	97,306	97,330	96,995	96,949	97,412	99,117	100,477	100,723
Balance Sheet								
Current Assets	420,872	338,372	278,351	304,101	437,274	359,760	395,828	342,055
Total Assets	1,753,971	1,688,050	1,635,176	1,543,683	1,231,410	1,155,107	1,187,203	1,140,519
Current Liabilities	194,375	151,809	131,692	181,180	128,849	162,538	159,208	149,321
Long-Term Obligations	120,000	125,000	130,000	135,000	170,000	165,750	191,250	216,750
Total Liabilities	803,474	775,522	737,437	686,562	470,195	560,281	539,387	531,025
Stockholders' Equity	950,497	912,528	897,739	857,121	761,215	594,826	647,816	609,494
Shares Outstanding	101,147	101,220	101,249	100,812	101,109	101,998	104,103	104,927
Statistical Record								
Return on Assets %	15.36	16.09	14.95	15.88	24.42	17.79	14.59	13.11
Return on Equity %	28.32	27.86	25.28	27.23	42.97	33.53	27.01	25.39
EBITDA Margin %	26.75	25.57	24.27	27.73	33.35	31.03	31.12	30.14
Net Margin %	19.63	18.66	17.76	19.40	26.42	18.27	18.33	17.37
Asset Turnover	0.78	0.84	0.82	0.82	0.92	0.97	0.80	0.75
Current Ratio	2.17	2.23	2.11	1.68	3.39	2.21	2.49	2.29
Debt to Equity	0.13	0.14	0.14	0.16	0.22	0.28	0.30	0.36
Price Range	35.56-22.17	33.54-22.17	33.33-22.17	36.51-22.17	36.53-25.26	32.93-23.29	35.34-28.29	33.86-25.73
P/E Ratio	14.28-8.90	14.21-9.39	15.72-10.46	16.75-10.17	12.73-8.80	16.22-11.47	21.81-17.46	23.85-18.12
Average Yield %	3.69	4.01	4.20	3.90	3.51	6.89	3.08	3.39

Address: Federated Investors Tower, Pittsburgh, PA 15222-3779 **Telephone:** 412-288-1900	**Web Site:** www.federatedinvestors.com **Officers:** John F. Donahue - Chairman Paul A. Uhlman - Vice President	**Auditors:** Ernst & Young LLP **Transfer Agents:** ComputerShare Investor Services, Providence, RI

FEDEX CORP

Exchange	Symbol	Price	52Wk Range	Yield	P/E	Div Acheiver
NYS	FDX	$151.21 (12/31/2019)	198.15-138.39	1.72	387.72	15 Years

*7 Year Price Score 80.14   *NYSE Composite Index=100   *12 Month Price Score 89.54

Interim Earnings (Per Share)

Qtr.	Aug	Nov	Feb	May
2016-17	2.65	2.59	2.07	3.76
2017-18	2.19	2.84	7.59	4.16
2018-19	3.10	3.51	2.80	(7.38)
2019-20	2.84	2.13	...	...

Interim Dividends (Per Share)

Amt	Decl	Ex	Rec	Pay
0.65Q	02/15/2019	03/08/2019	03/11/2019	04/01/2019
0.65Q	06/10/2019	06/21/2019	06/24/2019	07/08/2019
0.65Q	08/16/2019	09/06/2019	09/09/2019	10/01/2019
0.65Q	11/15/2019	12/06/2019	12/09/2019	01/02/2020

Indicated Div: $2.60 (Div. Reinv. Plan)

Valuation Analysis / **Institutional Holding**

Forecast EPS	$10.80 (01/17/2020)	No of Institutions 1834
Market Cap	$39.5 Billion	Shares
Book Value	$18.7 Billion	225,956,480
Price/Book	2.12	% Held
Price/Sales	0.57	68.63

Business Summary: Airlines/Air Freight (MIC: 7.4.4 SIC: 4513 NAIC: 492110)

FedEx provides transportation, e-commerce and business services through companies under the FedEx brand. These companies are included in the following segments: Federal Express Corporation, including TNT Express B.V., is an express transportation company; FedEx Ground Package System, Inc., which is a provider of small-package ground delivery services; FedEx Freight Corporation, which is a provider of less-than-truckload freight services; and FedEx Corporate Services, Inc., which provides sales, marketing, information technology, communications, customer service, technical support, billing and collections services, and certain back-office functions.

Recent Developments: For the quarter ended Nov 30 2019, net income decreased 40.1% to US$560.0 million from US$935.0 million in the year-earlier quarter. Revenues were US$17.32 billion, down 2.8% from US$17.82 billion the year before. Operating income was US$554.0 million versus US$1.17 billion in the prior-year quarter, a decrease of 52.6%. Direct operating expenses rose 0.1% to US$7.82 billion from US$7.81 billion in the comparable period the year before. Indirect operating expenses increased 1.2% to US$8.95 billion from US$8.84 billion in the equivalent prior-year period.

Prospects: Our evaluation of FedEx Corp. as of October 4th, 2019 is the result of our systematic analysis on three basic characteristics: earnings strength, relative valuation, and recent stock price movement. The company has managed to produce a neutral trend in earnings per share over the past 5 quarters. However, recent analyst estimates for the company have been reduced and FDX has posted results that fell short of analysts' expectations. Based on operating earnings yield, the company is undervalued when compared to all of the companies we cover. Share price changes over the past year indicates that FDX will perform in line with the market over the near term.

Financial Data

(US$ in Thousands)	6 Mos	3 Mos	05/31/2019	05/31/2018	05/31/2017	05/31/2016	05/31/2015	05/31/2014
Earnings Per Share	0.39	1.77	2.03	16.79	11.07	6.51	3.65	6.75
Cash Flow Per Share	21.10	21.07	21.42	17.51	18.53	20.62	18.96	13.89
Tang Book Value Per Share	45.18	43.48	41.69	46.79	33.25	26.50	39.60	39.27
Dividends Per Share	2.600	2.600	2.600	2.000	1.600	1.000	0.800	0.600
Dividend Payout %	666.67	146.89	128.08	11.91	14.45	15.36	21.92	8.89
Income Statement								
Total Revenue	34,372,000	17,048,000	69,693,000	65,450,000	60,319,000	50,365,000	47,453,000	45,567,000
EBITDA	3,636,000	2,012,000	4,584,000	7,963,000	7,958,000	5,655,000	4,448,000	6,031,000
Depn & Amortn	1,780,000	879,000	3,400,000	3,100,000	2,900,000	2,600,000	2,600,000	2,600,000
Income Before Taxes	1,568,000	996,000	655,000	4,353,000	4,579,000	2,740,000	1,627,000	3,289,000
Income Taxes	263,000	251,000	115,000	(219,000)	1,582,000	920,000	577,000	1,192,000
Net Income	1,305,000	745,000	540,000	4,572,000	2,997,000	1,820,000	1,050,000	2,097,000
Average Shares	262,000	262,000	265,000	272,000	270,000	279,000	287,000	310,000
Balance Sheet								
Current Assets	13,198,000	13,017,000	13,086,000	13,341,000	12,628,000	11,989,000	10,941,000	9,683,000
Total Assets	69,954,000	68,452,000	54,403,000	52,330,000	48,552,000	46,064,000	37,069,000	33,070,000
Current Liabilities	10,547,000	9,935,000	9,013,000	9,627,000	7,918,000	8,008,000	5,957,000	5,312,000
Long-Term Obligations	18,691,000	18,726,000	16,617,000	15,243,000	14,909,000	13,838,000	7,249,000	4,736,000
Total Liabilities	51,295,000	50,286,000	36,646,000	32,914,000	32,479,000	32,280,000	22,076,000	17,793,000
Stockholders' Equity	18,659,000	18,166,000	17,757,000	19,416,000	16,073,000	13,784,000	14,993,000	15,277,000
Shares Outstanding	261,119	260,910	260,808	265,924	268,257	265,524	282,430	318,000
Statistical Record								
Return on Assets %	0.12	0.75	1.01	9.06	6.34	4.37	2.99	6.29
Return on Equity %	0.40	2.41	2.91	25.77	20.08	12.61	6.94	12.84
EBITDA Margin %	10.58	11.80	6.58	12.17	13.19	11.23	9.37	13.24
Net Margin %	3.80	4.37	0.77	6.99	4.97	3.61	2.21	4.60
Asset Turnover	1.12	1.16	1.31	1.30	1.28	1.21	1.35	1.37
Current Ratio	1.25	1.31	1.45	1.39	1.59	1.50	1.84	1.82
Debt to Equity	1.00	1.03	0.94	0.79	0.93	1.00	0.48	0.31
Price Range	230.04-138.39	255.73-149.53	265.53-152.70	274.32-193.84	201.02-146.13	184.98-123.18	182.03-139.21	144.53-95.71
P/E Ratio	589.85-354.85	144.48-84.48	130.80-75.22	16.34-11.54	18.16-13.20	28.41-18.92	49.87-38.14	21.41-14.18
Average Yield %	1.54	1.38	1.24	0.86	0.89	0.64	0.49	0.48

Address: 942 South Shady Grove Road, Memphis, TN 38120 Telephone: 901-818-7500	Web Site: www.fedex.com Officers: Frederick W. Smith - Chairman, President, Chief Executive Officer Rajesh Subramaniam - President, Executive Vice President, Chief Operating Officer, Chief Marketing Officer, Chief Communications Officer	Auditors: Ernst & Young LLP Transfer Agents: ComputerShare Investor Services, Providence, RI

FIDELITY NATIONAL FINANCIAL INC

Exchange	Symbol	Price	52Wk Range	Yield	P/E
NYS	FNF	$45.35 (12/31/2019)	48.19-31.37	2.91	16.37

*7 Year Price Score N/A *NYSE Composite Index=100 *12 Month Price Score 107.93

Interim Earnings (Per Share)

Qtr.	Mar	Jun	Sep	Dec
2016	0.26	0.67	0.58	0.83
2017	0.25	0.63	0.62	0.88
2018	0.35	0.90	0.85	0.17
2019	0.74	0.96	0.90	...

Interim Dividends (Per Share)

Amt	Decl	Ex	Rec	Pay
0.31Q	02/13/2019	03/14/2019	03/15/2019	03/29/2019
0.31Q	04/24/2019	06/13/2019	06/14/2019	06/28/2019
0.31Q	07/16/2019	09/13/2019	09/16/2019	09/30/2019
0.33Q	10/29/2019	12/16/2019	12/17/2019	12/31/2019

Indicated Div: $1.32

Valuation Analysis

		Institutional Holding	
Forecast EPS	$3.38	No of Institutions	
	(01/16/2020)	703	
Market Cap	$12.5 Billion	Shares	
Book Value	$5.1 Billion	284,051,744	
Price/Book	2.43	% Held	
Price/Sales	1.60	N/A	

Business Summary: General Insurance (MIC: 5.2.1 SIC: 6361 NAIC: 524127)

Fidelity National Financial is a provider of title insurance, escrow and other title-related services, including trust activities, trustee sales guarantees, recordings and reconveyances and home warranty products and transaction services to the real estate and mortgage industries. Co. has two segments: Title, which consists of the operations of Co.'s title insurance underwriters and related businesses which provides title insurance and escrow and other title-related services including trust activities, trustee sales guarantees, and home warranty products; and Corporate and Other, which consists of the operations of the parent holding company, and Co.'s real estate technology subsidiaries.

Recent Developments: For the quarter ended Sep 30 2019, net income increased 8.0% to US$256.0 million from US$237.0 million in the year-earlier quarter. Revenues were US$2.24 billion, up 7.5% from US$2.09 billion the year before. Net premiums earned were US$1.49 billion versus US$1.30 billion in the prior-year quarter, an increase of 14.7%.

Prospects: Our evaluation of Fidelity National Financial Inc. as of October 4th, 2019 is the result of our systematic analysis on three basic characteristics: earnings strength, relative valuation, and recent stock price movement. The company has enjoyed a very positive trend in earnings per share over the past 5 quarters. In addition, recent analyst estimates for the company have been raised, and FNF has posted results that exceeded analysts' expectations. Based on operating earnings yield, the company is undervalued when compared to all of the companies we cover. Share price changes over the past year indicates that FNF will perform well over the near term.

Financial Data

(US$ in Thousands)	9 Mos	6 Mos	3 Mos	12/31/2018	12/31/2017	12/31/2016	12/31/2015	12/31/2014
Earnings Per Share	2.77	2.72	2.66	2.26	2.38	2.34	1.89	0.75
Cash Flow Per Share	3.56	3.53	3.37	3.45	2.72	4.26	3.31	4.11
Tang Book Value Per Share	7.15	6.43	5.63	5.05	3.95	N.M.	N.M.	N.M.
Dividends Per Share	1.230	1.220	1.210	1.200	1.020	0.880	0.800	0.370
Dividend Payout %	44.40	44.85	45.49	53.10	42.86	37.61	42.33	49.33
Income Statement								
Premium Income	3,858,000	2,371,000	992,000	4,911,000	4,893,000	4,723,000	4,286,000	3,671,000
Total Revenue	6,107,000	3,866,000	1,722,000	7,594,000	7,663,000	9,554,000	9,132,000	8,024,000
Benefits & Claims	174,000	107,000	45,000	221,000	238,000	157,000	246,000	228,000
Income Before Taxes	930,000	617,000	264,000	750,000	864,000	1,072,000	867,000	392,000
Income Taxes	210,000	151,000	65,000	120,000	235,000	372,000	290,000	312,000
Net Income	722,000	472,000	206,000	628,000	771,000	650,000	527,000	583,000
Average Shares	277,000	277,000	277,000	278,000	278,000	280,000	286,000	142,000
Balance Sheet								
Total Assets	10,419,000	10,189,000	9,647,000	9,301,000	9,151,000	14,463,000	13,931,000	13,868,000
Total Liabilities	5,280,000	5,227,000	4,877,000	4,671,000	4,704,000	8,467,000	8,177,000	7,874,000
Stockholders' Equity	5,139,000	4,962,000	4,770,000	4,630,000	4,447,000	5,996,000	5,754,000	5,994,000
Shares Outstanding	275,079	274,416	274,908	275,373	274,431	338,622	347,999	371,777
Statistical Record								
Return on Assets %	7.74	7.74	7.90	6.81	6.53	4.57	3.79	4.78
Return on Equity %	15.59	15.72	15.97	13.84	14.77	11.03	8.97	10.54
Loss Ratio %	4.51	4.51	4.54	4.50	4.86	3.32	5.74	6.21
Net Margin %	11.82	12.21	11.96	8.27	10.06	6.80	5.77	7.27
Price Range	44.96-29.60	41.04-29.60	40.77-29.60	41.85-29.60	40.63-24.17	27.60-21.25	28.73-23.34	25.87-18.83
P/E Ratio	16.23-10.69	15.09-10.88	15.33-11.13	18.52-13.10	17.07-10.16	11.80-9.08	15.20-12.35	34.50-25.10
Average Yield %	3.26	3.31	3.32	3.19	3.19	3.55	3.04	1.76

Address: 601 Riverside Avenue, Jacksonville, FL 32204 Telephone: 904-854-8100	Web Site: www.fnf.com Officers: William P. Foley - Executive Chairman, Chairman Michael J. Nolan - President, Co-Chief Operating Officer, Division Officer	Auditors: Ernst & Young LLP Investor Contact: 904-854-8120 Transfer Agents: Continental Stock Transfer & Trust Company, New York, NY

FIDELITY NATIONAL INFORMATION SERVICES INC

Exchange	Symbol	Price	52Wk Range	Yield	P/E
NYS	FIS	$139.09 (12/31/2019)	139.75-98.31	1.01	65.92

*7 Year Price Score 129.19 *NYSE Composite Index=100 *12 Month Price Score 105.03

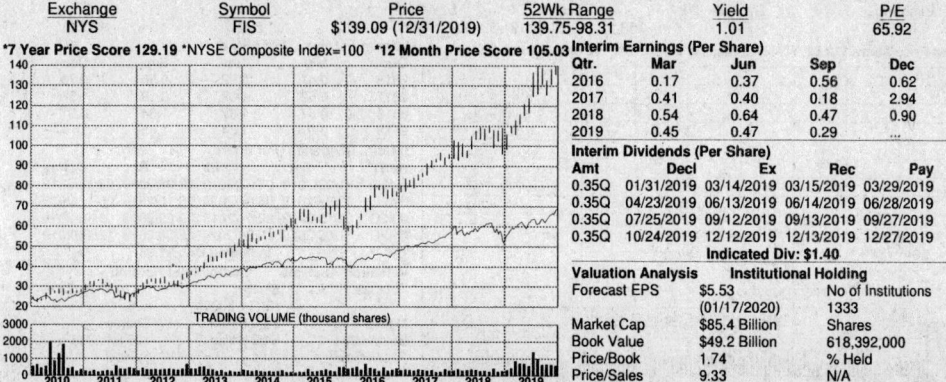

Interim Earnings (Per Share)

Qtr.	Mar	Jun	Sep	Dec
2016	0.17	0.37	0.56	0.62
2017	0.41	0.40	0.18	2.94
2018	0.54	0.64	0.47	0.90
2019	0.45	0.47	0.29	...

Interim Dividends (Per Share)

Amt	Decl	Ex	Rec	Pay
0.35Q	01/31/2019	03/14/2019	03/15/2019	03/29/2019
0.35Q	04/23/2019	06/13/2019	06/14/2019	06/28/2019
0.35Q	07/25/2019	09/12/2019	09/13/2019	09/27/2019
0.35Q	10/24/2019	12/12/2019	12/13/2019	12/27/2019

Indicated Div: $1.40

Valuation Analysis | **Institutional Holding**

Forecast EPS	$5.53	No of Institutions
	(01/17/2020)	1333
Market Cap	$85.4 Billion	Shares
Book Value	$49.2 Billion	618,392,000
Price/Book	1.74	% Held
Price/Sales	9.33	N/A

Business Summary: Business Services (MIC: 7.5.2 SIC: 7389 NAIC: 561499)

Fidelity National Information Services is a provider of financial services technology. Co.'s segments are: Integrated Financial Solutions, which serves the regional and community bank and savings institution for transaction and account processing, payment solutions, channel solutions, digital channels, fraud, risk and compliance solutions, lending and wealth and retirement solutions, and corporate liquidity; Global Financial Solutions, which provides an array of capital markets and asset management and insurance solutions, as well as banking and payments solutions; and Corporate and Other, which includes global commercial services and retail check processing.

Recent Developments: For the quarter ended Sep 30 2019, net income decreased 4.3% to US$156.0 million from US$163.0 million in the year-earlier quarter. Revenues were US$2.82 billion, up 35.4% from US$2.08 billion the year before. Operating income was US$140.0 million versus US$342.0 million in the prior-year quarter, a decrease of 59.1%. Direct operating expenses rose 34.8% to US$1.84 billion from US$1.36 billion in the comparable period the year before. Indirect operating expenses increased 123.3% to US$844.0 million from US$378.0 million in the equivalent prior-year period.

Prospects: Our evaluation of Fidelity National Information Services Inc. as of October 4th, 2019 is the result of our systematic analysis on three basic characteristics: earnings strength, relative valuation, and recent stock price movement. The company has generated a negative trend in earnings per share over the past 5 quarters. However, recent analyst estimates for the company have been mixed and FIS has posted results that fell short of analysts' expectations. Based on operating earnings yield, the company is fairly valued when compared to all of the companies we cover. Share price changes over the past year indicates that FIS will perform over the near term.

Financial Data
(US$ in Thousands)

	9 Mos	6 Mos	3 Mos	12/31/2018	12/31/2017	12/31/2016	12/31/2015	12/31/2014
Earnings Per Share	2.11	2.29	2.46	2.55	3.93	1.72	2.19	2.35
Cash Flow Per Share	4.74	6.14	5.98	6.08	5.28	5.89	3.99	4.09
Dividends Per Share	1.370	1.340	1.310	1.280	1.160	1.040	1.040	0.960
Dividend Payout %	64.93	58.52	53.25	50.20	29.52	60.47	47.49	40.85
Income Statement								
Total Revenue	6,991,000	4,169,000	2,057,000	8,423,000	9,123,000	9,241,000	6,595,200	6,413,800
EBITDA	1,632,000	848,000	419,000	1,585,000	1,553,000	1,474,000	1,359,400	1,341,000
Depn & Amortn	794,000	314,000	156,000	184,000	180,000	185,000	139,100	130,100
Income Before Taxes	596,000	387,000	188,000	1,104,000	1,036,000	906,000	1,036,900	1,053,400
Income Taxes	119,000	72,000	32,000	208,000	(319,000)	317,000	378,800	335,100
Net Income	456,000	302,000	148,000	846,000	1,319,000	568,000	631,500	679,100
Average Shares	524,000	327,000	326,000	332,000	336,000	330,000	288,700	288,700
Balance Sheet								
Current Assets	9,325,000	12,505,000	3,611,000	3,733,000	3,606,000	4,282,000	3,511,400	2,473,100
Total Assets	83,718,000	32,859,000	24,073,000	23,770,000	24,517,000	26,031,000	26,268,800	14,520,500
Current Liabilities	10,901,000	4,170,000	3,521,000	3,125,000	3,923,000	3,151,000	2,363,900	1,598,900
Long-Term Obligations	16,945,000	16,682,000	8,562,000	8,670,000	7,718,000	10,146,000	11,497,800	5,054,600
Total Liabilities	34,523,000	22,874,000	14,177,000	13,555,000	13,682,000	16,290,000	16,947,800	7,963,800
Stockholders' Equity	49,195,000	9,985,000	9,896,000	10,215,000	10,835,000	9,741,000	9,321,000	6,556,700
Shares Outstanding	614,000	324,000	323,000	327,000	333,000	328,000	324,500	284,900
Statistical Record								
Return on Assets %	1.40	2.66	3.35	3.50	5.22	2.17	3.10	4.77
Return on Equity %	2.54	7.38	7.96	8.04	12.82	5.94	7.95	10.34
EBITDA Margin %	23.34	20.34	20.37	18.82	17.02	15.95	20.61	20.91
Net Margin %	6.52	7.24	7.19	10.04	14.46	6.15	9.58	10.59
Asset Turnover	0.17	0.30	0.35	0.35	0.36	0.35	0.32	0.45
Current Ratio	0.86	3.00	1.03	1.19	0.92	1.36	1.49	1.55
Debt to Equity	0.34	1.67	0.87	0.85	0.71	1.04	1.23	0.77
Price Range	139.62-95.83	123.88-95.83	113.10-94.11	110.58-92.74	96.62-76.98	80.84-56.04	73.50-58.52	64.04-48.87
P/E Ratio	66.17-45.42	54.10-41.85	45.98-38.26	43.36-36.37	24.59-19.59	47.00-32.58	33.56-26.72	27.25-20.80
Average Yield %	1.19	1.23	1.25	1.24	1.33	1.46	1.59	1.73

Address: 601 Riverside Avenue, Jacksonville, FL 32204 **Telephone:** 904-438-6000	**Web Site:** www.fisglobal.com **Officers:** Gary A. Norcross - Chairman, President, Corporate Executive Vice President, Chief Operating Officer, Chief Executive Officer Charles D. Drucker - Vice-Chairman	**Auditors:** KPMG LLP **Investor Contact:** 904-438-6000 **Transfer Agents:** Computershare Investor Services, LLC, Chicago, IL

FIRST AMERICAN FINANCIAL CORP

Exchange	Symbol	Price	52Wk Range	Yield	P/E
NYS	FAF	$58.32 (12/31/2019)	64.19-44.12	2.88	11.50

*7 Year Price Score 113.89 *NYSE Composite Index=100 *12 Month Price Score 105.18

Interim Earnings (Per Share)

Qtr.	Mar	Jun	Sep	Dec
2016	0.47	0.92	0.96	0.73
2017	0.52	1.09	0.19	1.96
2018	0.67	1.37	1.34	0.81
2019	0.97	1.64	1.65	...

Interim Dividends (Per Share)

Amt	Decl	Ex	Rec	Pay
0.42Q	01/23/2019	03/07/2019	03/08/2019	03/15/2019
0.42Q	05/07/2019	06/07/2019	06/10/2019	06/17/2019
0.42Q	08/13/2019	09/06/2019	09/09/2019	09/16/2019
0.42Q	11/05/2019	12/06/2019	12/09/2019	12/16/2019

Indicated Div: $1.68

Valuation Analysis | **Institutional Holding**

Forecast EPS	$5.45	No of Institutions
	(01/11/2020)	528
Market Cap	$6.6 Billion	Shares
Book Value	$4.2 Billion	106,861,896
Price/Book	1.54	% Held
Price/Sales	1.11	83.64

Business Summary: General Insurance (MIC: 5.2.1 SIC: 6361 NAIC: 524127)

First American Financial is a holding company. Through its subsidiaries, Co. is engaged in the business of providing financial services through its two segments. The title insurance and services segment provides title insurance, closing and/or escrow services and similar or related services domestically and internationally in connection with residential and commercial real estate transactions. It maintains, manages and provides access to title plant records and images and, in addition, provides banking, trust, document custodial and wealth management services. The specialty insurance segment issues property and casualty insurance policies and sells home warranty products.

Recent Developments: For the quarter ended Sep 30 2019, net income increased 24.2% to US$188.2 million from US$151.5 million in the year-earlier quarter. Revenues were US$1.67 billion, up 8.4% from US$1.54 billion the year before. Net premiums earned were US$1.38 billion versus US$1.26 billion in the prior-year quarter, an increase of 9.5%. Net investment income fell 1.1% to US$78.1 million from US$79.0 million a year ago.

Prospects: Our evaluation of First American Financial Corp. as of October 4th, 2019 is the result of our systematic analysis on three basic characteristics: earnings strength, relative valuation, and recent stock price movement. The company has managed to produce a neutral trend in earnings per share over the past 5 quarters. However, recent analyst estimates for the company have been raised and FAF has posted results that exceeded analysts' expectations. Based on operating earnings yield, the company is undervalued when compared to all of the companies we cover. Share price changes over the past year indicates that FAF will perform well over the near term.

Financial Data
(US$ in Thousands)

	9 Mos	6 Mos	3 Mos	12/31/2018	12/31/2017	12/31/2016	12/31/2015	12/31/2014
Earnings Per Share	5.07	4.76	4.49	4.19	3.76	3.09	2.62	2.15
Cash Flow Per Share	8.13	7.43	6.96	7.04	5.66	4.42	5.08	3.37
Tang Book Value Per Share	26.70	25.29	23.47	22.32	20.44	17.39	16.00	14.48
Dividends Per Share	1.680	1.680	1.640	1.600	1.440	1.200	1.000	0.840
Dividend Payout %	33.14	35.29	36.53	38.19	38.30	38.83	38.17	39.07
Income Statement								
Total Revenue	4,473,397	2,802,201	1,303,581	5,747,844	5,772,363	5,575,846	5,175,456	4,677,949
Income Before Taxes	616,505	371,167	141,670	609,538	445,331	477,581	432,765	350,560
Income Taxes	131,263	74,092	31,866	133,640	23,468	134,105	143,895	116,345
Net Income	483,412	296,230	109,575	474,496	423,049	342,993	288,086	233,534
Average Shares	113,741	113,498	113,224	113,279	112,435	111,156	109,826	108,688
Balance Sheet								
Total Assets	11,804,092	11,443,178	11,160,268	10,630,635	9,573,222	8,831,777	8,254,351	7,666,100
Total Liabilities	7,561,951	7,358,289	7,282,241	6,888,754	6,093,267	5,823,598	5,495,849	5,093,183
Stockholders' Equity	4,242,141	4,084,889	3,878,027	3,741,881	3,479,955	3,008,179	2,758,502	2,572,917
Shares Outstanding	112,336	112,217	112,072	111,496	110,925	109,944	109,098	107,541
Statistical Record								
Return on Assets %	4.96	5.04	4.91	4.70	4.60	4.00	3.62	3.29
Return on Equity %	14.53	14.09	13.82	13.14	13.04	11.86	10.81	9.29
Net Margin %	10.81	10.57	8.41	8.26	7.33	6.15	5.57	4.99
Asset Turnover	0.51	0.54	0.56	0.57	0.63	0.65	0.65	0.66
Price Range	60.33-42.55	57.88-42.55	58.19-42.55	62.09-42.55	57.02-36.83	43.35-32.44	42.36-32.65	34.30-24.92
P/E Ratio	11.90-8.39	12.16-8.94	12.96-9.48	14.82-10.16	15.16-9.80	14.03-10.50	16.17-12.46	15.95-11.59
Average Yield %	3.23	3.28	3.22	3.01	3.16	3.14	2.70	2.99

Address: 1 First American Way, Santa Ana, CA 92707-5913 **Telephone:** 714-250-3000 **Fax:** 714-250-3151	**Web Site:** www.firstam.com **Officers:** Parker S. Kennedy - Executive Chairman, Chairman Dennis J. Gilmore - Chief Executive Officer	**Auditors:** PricewaterhouseCoopers LLP **Investor Contact:** 714-250-5214 **Transfer Agents:** Wells Fargo Shareowner Services

FIRST HORIZON NATIONAL CORP

Exchange	Symbol	Price	52Wk Range	Yield	P/E
NYS	FHN	$16.56 (12/31/2019)	17.28-13.16	3.38	12.64

*7 Year Price Score 84.66   *NYSE Composite Index=100   *12 Month Price Score 101.82

Interim Earnings (Per Share)

Qtr.	Mar	Jun	Sep	Dec
2016	0.20	0.24	0.27	0.23
2017	0.23	0.38	0.28	(0.25)
2018	0.27	0.25	0.83	0.30
2019	0.31	0.35	0.35	...

Interim Dividends (Per Share)

Amt	Decl	Ex	Rec	Pay
0.14Q	01/29/2019	03/14/2019	03/15/2019	04/01/2019
0.14Q	04/23/2019	06/13/2019	06/14/2019	07/01/2019
0.14Q	07/23/2019	09/12/2019	09/13/2019	10/01/2019
0.14Q	10/28/2019	12/12/2019	12/13/2019	01/02/2020

Indicated Div: $0.56

Valuation Analysis

		Institutional Holding	
Forecast EPS	$1.61	No of Institutions	
	(01/16/2020)	547	
Market Cap	$5.2 Billion	Shares	
Book Value	$4.7 Billion	302,266,304	
Price/Book	1.10	% Held	
Price/Sales	2.34	77.90	

Business Summary: Banking (MIC: 5.1.1 SIC: 6021 NAIC: 522110)

First Horizon National is a bank holding company. Through its subsidiary, Co. provides financial services. Co.'s segments are: regional banking, which provides financial products and services, including lending and deposit taking, to consumer and commercial customers; fixed income, which consists of fixed income securities sales, trading, and strategies for institutional clients in the U.S. and abroad, as well as loan sales, portfolio advisory services, and derivative sales; corporate; and nonstrategic, which consists of the run-off consumer lending activities, legacy mortgage banking elements, and the associated ancillary revenues and expenses related to these businesses.

Recent Developments: For the quarter ended Sep 30 2019, net income decreased 58.5% to US$113.9 million from US$274.7 million in the year-earlier quarter. Net interest income decreased 1.6% to US$300.7 million from US$305.7 million in the year-earlier quarter. Provision for loan losses was US$15.0 million versus US$2.0 million in the prior-year quarter, an increase of 650.0%. Non-interest income fell 50.8% to US$171.7 million from US$349.0 million, while non-interest expense advanced 4.6% to US$307.7 million.

Prospects: Our evaluation of First Horizon National Corp. as of October 4th, 2019 is the result of our systematic analysis on three basic characteristics: earnings strength, relative valuation, and recent stock price movement. The company has managed to produce a neutral trend in earnings per share over the past 5 quarters. In addition, recent analyst estimates for the company have been mixed and FHN has posted results that exceeded analysts' expectations. Based on operating earnings yield, the company is undervalued when compared to all of the companies we cover. Share price changes over the past year indicates that FHN will perform poorly over the near term.

Financial Data

(US$ in Thousands)	9 Mos	6 Mos	3 Mos	12/31/2018	12/31/2017	12/31/2016	12/31/2015	12/31/2014
Earnings Per Share	1.31	1.79	1.69	1.65	0.65	0.94	0.34	0.91
Cash Flow Per Share	3.47	1.71	1.77	0.72	(0.07)	0.78	1.57	3.00
Tang Book Value Per Share	9.76	9.47	9.11	8.81	8.01	9.00	8.51	8.63
Dividends Per Share	0.540	0.520	0.500	0.480	0.360	0.280	0.240	0.200
Dividend Payout %	41.22	29.05	29.59	29.09	55.38	29.79	70.59	21.98
Income Statement								
Interest Income	1,220,198	812,704	400,615	1,546,021	989,930	817,909	736,405	709,249
Interest Expense	321,404	214,586	106,107	325,704	147,616	88,825	82,685	81,531
Net Interest Income	898,794	598,118	294,508	1,220,317	842,314	729,084	653,720	627,718
Provision for Losses	37,000	22,000	9,000	7,000	...	11,000	9,000	27,000
Non-Interest Income	470,773	299,038	141,045	722,788	490,219	552,441	517,325	550,044
Non-Interest Expense	904,156	596,484	296,090	1,221,996	1,023,661	925,204	1,053,791	841,211
Income Before Taxes	428,411	278,672	130,463	714,109	308,872	345,321	108,254	309,551
Income Taxes	97,321	61,525	27,058	157,602	131,892	106,810	10,941	78,501
Net Income	322,535	211,475	100,585	545,042	165,515	227,046	85,879	219,523
Average Shares	313,805	315,786	319,581	327,445	244,453	235,292	236,266	236,735
Balance Sheet								
Net Loans & Leases	31,622,527	29,967,167	28,399,799	28,034,257	28,168,751	19,498,700	17,602,602	16,139,003
Total Assets	43,717,684	42,171,770	41,099,003	40,832,258	41,423,388	28,555,231	26,195,136	25,672,887
Total Deposits	31,944,660	32,308,318	32,462,888	32,682,992	30,620,362	22,672,363	19,967,478	18,068,939
Total Liabilities	39,017,072	37,541,120	36,547,913	36,342,309	37,138,331	26,145,578	23,850,981	23,377,350
Stockholders' Equity	4,700,612	4,630,650	4,551,090	4,489,949	4,285,057	2,409,653	2,344,155	2,295,537
Shares Outstanding	311,179	312,478	315,361	318,573	326,736	233,623	238,586	234,219
Statistical Record								
Return on Assets %	1.00	1.40	1.36	1.33	0.47	0.83	0.33	0.89
Return on Equity %	9.19	13.08	12.54	12.42	4.94	9.53	3.70	9.75
Net Interest Margin %	73.79	73.68	73.51	78.93	85.09	89.14	88.77	88.50
Efficiency Ratio %	53.12	52.69	54.66	53.86	69.16	67.52	84.05	66.80
Loans to Deposits	0.99	0.93	0.87	0.86	0.92	0.86	0.88	0.89
Price Range	17.51-12.40	18.85-12.40	19.56-12.40	20.61-12.40	20.76-16.05	20.61-11.62	16.20-12.31	13.91-11.18
P/E Ratio	13.37-9.47	10.53-6.93	11.57-7.34	12.49-7.52	31.94-24.69	21.93-12.36	47.65-36.21	15.29-12.29
Average Yield %	3.56	3.31	2.97	2.66	1.94	1.90	1.65	1.66

Address: 165 Madison Avenue,	Web Site: www.firsthorizon.com	Auditors: KPMG LLP
Memphis, TN 38103	Officers: D. Bryan Jordan - Chairman, President,	Investor Contact: 800-410-4577
Telephone: 901-523-4444	Chief Executive Officer R. Eugene Taylor -	Transfer Agents: Wells Fargo
	Vice-Chairman	

FIRST INDUSTRIAL REALTY TRUST INC

Exchange	Symbol	Price	52Wk Range	Yield	P/E
NYS	FR	$41.51 (12/31/2019)	43.07-28.04	2.22	27.31

*7 Year Price Score 119.83 *NYSE Composite Index=100 *12 Month Price Score 107.13

Interim Earnings (Per Share)

Qtr.	Mar	Jun	Sep	Dec
2016	0.14	0.43	0.27	0.20
2017	0.19	0.32	0.36	0.82
2018	0.30	0.36	0.24	0.40
2019	0.19	0.31	0.62	...

Interim Dividends (Per Share)

Amt	Decl	Ex	Rec	Pay
0.23Q	02/13/2019	03/28/2019	03/29/2019	04/15/2019
0.23Q	05/08/2019	06/27/2019	06/28/2019	07/15/2019
0.23Q	08/06/2019	09/27/2019	09/30/2019	10/21/2019
0.23Q	11/05/2019	12/30/2019	12/31/2019	01/21/2020

Indicated Div: $0.92

Valuation Analysis / **Institutional Holding**

Forecast EPS	$1.31	No of Institutions
	(01/17/2020)	403
Market Cap	$5.3 Billion	Shares
Book Value	$1.7 Billion	164,683,760
Price/Book	3.11	% Held
Price/Sales	12.54	95.13

Business Summary: REITs (MIC: 5.3.1 SIC: 6798 NAIC: 525930)

First Industrial Realty Trust is a self-administered and fully integrated real estate company which owns, manages, acquires, sells, develops and redevelops industrial real estate. Co. is a real estate investment trust. Co.'s in-service portfolio includes all properties that have reached stabilized occupancy, developed and redeveloped properties one year from the date construction is completed and acquired properties that are occupied at acquisition or one year from the acquisition date. Co.'s operations are conducted primarily through First Industrial, L.P., of which Co. is the sole general partner.

Recent Developments: For the quarter ended Sep 30 2019, net income increased 153.7% to US$80.0 million from US$31.5 million in the year-earlier quarter. Revenues were US$106.6 million, up 6.3% from US$100.3 million the year before.

Prospects: Our evaluation of First Industrial Realty Trust Inc. as of October 4th, 2019 is the result of our systematic analysis on three basic characteristics: earnings strength, relative valuation, and recent stock price movement. The company has generated a negative trend in earnings per share over the past 5 quarters. However, recent analyst estimates for the company have been mixed and FR has posted results that fell short of analysts' expectations. Based on operating earnings yield, the company is overvalued when compared to all of the companies we cover. Share price changes over the past year indicates that FR will perform well over the near term.

Financial Data
(US$ in Thousands)

	9 Mos	6 Mos	3 Mos	12/31/2018	12/31/2017	12/31/2016	12/31/2015	12/31/2014
Earnings Per Share	1.52	1.14	1.19	1.31	1.69	1.05	0.67	0.42
Cash Flow Per Share	1.97	1.88	1.71	1.70	1.62	1.50	1.47	1.25
Tang Book Value Per Share	13.11	12.71	12.65	12.79	11.66	10.35	9.37	9.18
Dividends Per Share	0.907	0.895	0.882	0.870	0.840	0.760	0.510	0.410
Dividend Payout %	59.70	78.51	74.16	66.41	49.70	72.38	76.12	97.62
Income Statement								
Total Revenue	315,226	208,636	104,541	403,954	396,402	378,020	365,762	344,599
EBITDA	268,864	142,975	69,537	316,323	363,933	284,936	240,244	186,627
Depn & Amortn	96,710	64,410	32,229	94,626	94,078	95,514	92,955	93,457
Income Before Taxes	132,159	51,841	23,710	167,518	209,494	126,773	76,767	20,004
Income Taxes	3,392	3,148	214	(92)	1,193	1,089	117	238
Net Income	141,914	63,603	23,803	163,239	201,456	121,232	73,802	49,110
Average Shares	126,783	126,489	126,456	124,191	118,787	115,370	110,781	110,325
Balance Sheet								
Current Assets	125,265	115,684	111,323	55,558	51,355	26,218	32,604	18,685
Total Assets	3,376,725	3,254,901	3,178,654	3,142,691	2,941,062	2,793,263	2,718,051	2,581,995
Current Liabilities	209,988	177,338	164,680	155,437	157,833	151,146	148,664	128,596
Long-Term Obligations	1,409,800	1,381,409	1,326,456	1,297,783	1,296,997	1,347,092	1,442,411	1,349,846
Total Liabilities	1,684,178	1,618,357	1,550,335	1,497,177	1,513,262	1,551,822	1,644,951	1,533,045
Stockholders' Equity	1,692,547	1,636,544	1,628,319	1,645,514	1,427,800	1,241,441	1,073,100	1,048,950
Shares Outstanding	126,951	126,487	126,484	126,307	119,883	117,107	111,027	110,600
Statistical Record								
Return on Assets %	5.93	4.57	4.84	5.37	7.03	4.39	2.78	1.90
Return on Equity %	11.61	8.93	9.81	10.62	15.09	10.45	6.96	4.51
EBITDA Margin %	85.29	68.53	66.52	78.31	91.81	75.38	65.68	54.16
Net Margin %	45.02	30.49	22.77	40.41	50.82	32.07	20.18	14.25
Asset Turnover	0.13	0.13	0.13	0.13	0.14	0.14	0.14	0.13
Current Ratio	0.60	0.65	0.68	0.36	0.33	0.17	0.22	0.15
Debt to Equity	0.83	0.84	0.81	0.79	0.91	1.09	1.34	1.29
Price Range	40.07-27.60	37.43-27.60	35.47-27.60	33.87-27.60	32.82-25.35	29.61-19.32	23.08-18.69	21.16-16.42
P/E Ratio	26.36-18.16	32.83-24.21	29.81-23.19	25.85-21.07	19.42-15.00	28.20-18.40	34.45-27.90	50.38-39.10
Average Yield %	2.63	2.72	2.76	2.80	2.87	3.01	2.44	2.21

Address: 1 N. Wacker Drive, Suite 4200, Chicago, IL 60606	Web Site: www.firstindustrial.com	Auditors: PricewaterhouseCoopers LLP
Telephone: 312-344-4300	Officers: Bruce W. Duncan - Chairman, President, Chief Executive Officer Peter E. Baccile - President, Chief Executive Officer	Investor Contact: 312-344-4320
Fax: 312-922-6320		Transfer Agents: Barack Ferrazzano Kirschbaum & Nagelberg LLP

FIRST REPUBLIC BANK (SAN FRANCISCO, CA)

Exchange	Symbol	Price	52Wk Range	Yield	P/E
NYS	FRC	$117.45 (12/31/2019)	117.90-84.34	0.65	23.03

*7 Year Price Score 112.02 *NYSE Composite Index=100 *12 Month Price Score 105.13

Interim Earnings (Per Share)

Qtr.	Mar	Jun	Sep	Dec
2016	0.88	0.97	1.00	1.03
2017	1.01	1.06	1.14	1.10
2018	1.13	1.20	1.19	1.29
2019	1.26	1.24	1.31	...

Interim Dividends (Per Share)

Amt	Decl	Ex	Rec	Pay
0.19Q	04/12/2019	04/24/2019	04/25/2019	05/09/2019
0.19Q	07/16/2019	07/24/2019	07/25/2019	08/08/2019
0.19Q	10/15/2019	10/30/2019	10/31/2019	11/14/2019
0.19Q	01/14/2020	01/29/2020	01/30/2020	02/13/2020

Indicated Div: $0.76

Valuation Analysis / **Institutional Holding**

Forecast EPS	$5.38	No of Institutions	
	(01/17/2020)	689	
Market Cap	$19.8 Billion	Shares	
Book Value	$9.4 Billion	214,376,096	
Price/Book	2.10	% Held	
Price/Sales	4.90	N/A	

Business Summary: Banking (MIC: 5.1.1 SIC: 6029 NAIC: 522110)

First Republic Bank is a commercial bank and trust company. Co. conducts its business through two reportable business segments: Commercial Banking and Wealth Management. The principal business activities of the Commercial Banking segment are accepting funds from the general public, originating loans (primarily real estate secured mortgage loans) and investing in investment securities. Wealth Management segment consists of subsidiary First Republic Investment Management, Inc.; Co.'s money market mutual fund activities through third-party providers and the brokerage activities of First Republic Securities Company, LLC; the Trust Company; and Co.'s foreign exchange activities.

Recent Developments: For the quarter ended Sep 30 2019, net income increased 10.0% to US$234.8 million from US$213.5 million in the year-earlier quarter. Net interest income increased 9.5% to US$695.0 million from US$634.5 million in the year-earlier quarter. Provision for loan losses was US$16.7 million versus US$18.6 million in the prior-year quarter, a decrease of 10.3%. Non-interest income rose 5.8% to US$142.2 million from US$134.4 million, while non-interest expense advanced 10.3% to US$534.0 million.

Prospects: Our evaluation of First Republic Bank as of October 4th, 2019 is the result of our systematic analysis on three basic characteristics: earnings strength, relative valuation, and recent stock price movement. The company has managed to produce a neutral trend in earnings per share over the past 5 quarters. However, recent analyst estimates for the company have been reduced and FRC has posted results that fell short of analysts' expectations. Based on operating earnings yield, the company is undervalued when compared to all of the companies we cover. Share price changes over the past year indicates that FRC will perform poorly over the near term.

Financial Data

(US$ in Thousands)	9 Mos	6 Mos	3 Mos	12/31/2018	12/31/2017	12/31/2016	12/31/2015	12/31/2014
Earnings Per Share	5.10	4.98	4.94	4.81	4.31	3.93	3.18	3.07
Cash Flow Per Share	10.50	8.31	6.48	6.82	6.42	5.72	...	3.64
Tang Book Value Per Share	48.57	47.35	46.49	44.93	40.03	34.94	29.80	26.21
Dividends Per Share	0.740	0.730	0.720	0.710	0.670	0.630	0.590	0.540
Dividend Payout %	14.51	14.66	14.57	14.76	15.55	16.03	18.55	17.59
Income Statement								
Total Revenue	3,062,400	2,010,417	979,335	3,575,051	2,912,079	2,375,685	1,989,145	1,801,364
Income Before Taxes	824,197	537,666	268,344	1,051,742	912,202	827,596	690,668	669,883
Income Taxes	140,198	88,511	41,753	197,914	154,542	154,168	168,523	182,877
Net Income	683,999	449,155	226,591	853,828	757,660	673,428	522,145	487,006
Average Shares	169,346	169,572	169,410	165,612	162,340	154,095	145,510	140,497
Balance Sheet								
Total Assets	111,028,735	105,699,636	101,847,228	99,205,204	87,780,507	73,277,772	58,981,285	48,353,330
Total Liabilities	101,597,529	96,479,993	92,801,244	90,527,427	79,962,206	66,369,120	53,275,602	43,574,863
Stockholders' Equity	9,431,206	9,219,643	9,045,984	8,677,777	7,818,301	6,908,652	5,705,683	4,778,467
Shares Outstanding	168,450	168,176	167,393	164,901	161,695	154,292	146,109	138,268
Statistical Record								
Return on Assets %	0.88	0.90	0.92	0.91	0.94	1.02	0.97	1.08
Return on Equity %	10.12	10.22	10.44	10.35	10.29	10.65	9.96	10.90
Net Margin %	22.34	22.34	23.14	23.88	26.02	28.35	26.25	27.04
Asset Turnover	0.04	0.04	0.04	0.04	0.04	0.04	0.04	0.04
Price Range	106.36-80.23	106.36-80.23	106.20-80.23	106.20-80.23	105.17-86.62	92.14-56.59	69.28-47.62	55.62-45.77
P/E Ratio	20.85-15.73	21.36-16.11	21.50-16.24	22.08-16.68	24.40-20.10	23.45-14.40	21.79-14.97	18.12-14.91
Average Yield %	0.77	0.75	0.74	0.75	0.70	0.87	0.97	1.06

Address: 111 Pine Street, 2nd Floor, San Francisco, CA 94111 **Telephone:** 415-392-1400	**Web Site:** www.firstrepublic.com **Officers:** James H. Herbert - Chairman, Chief Executive Officer Katherine August-deWilde - Vice-Chairman, President, Chief Operating Officer	**Auditors:** KPMG LLP **Investor Contact:** 415-392-1400 **Transfer Agents:** Common and Preferred Stock – Computershare Shareowner Services, LLC

FIRSTENERGY CORP

Exchange	Symbol	Price	52Wk Range	Yield	P/E
NYS	FE	$48.60 (12/31/2019)	48.83-36.71	3.21	22.82

*7 Year Price Score 100.80 *NYSE Composite Index=100 *12 Month Price Score 103.34

Interim Earnings (Per Share)

Qtr.	Mar	Jun	Sep	Dec
2016	0.77	(2.56)	0.89	(13.59)
2017	0.46	0.39	0.89	(5.62)
2018	2.54	0.28	(1.02)	0.24
2019	0.59	0.58	0.72	...

Interim Dividends (Per Share)

Amt	Decl	Ex	Rec	Pay
0.38Q	03/19/2019	05/06/2019	05/07/2019	06/01/2019
0.38Q	07/16/2019	08/06/2019	08/07/2019	09/01/2019
0.38Q	09/17/2019	11/06/2019	11/07/2019	12/01/2019
0.39Q	11/08/2019	02/06/2020	02/07/2020	03/01/2020

Indicated Div: $1.56

Valuation Analysis / Institutional Holding

Valuation Analysis		Institutional Holding	
Forecast EPS	$2.53	No of Institutions	
	(01/17/2020)	936	
Market Cap	$26.3 Billion	Shares	
Book Value	$7.3 Billion	556,963,072	
Price/Book	3.61	% Held	
Price/Sales	2.37	93.78	

Business Summary: Electric Utilities (MIC: 3.1.1 SIC: 4911 NAIC: 221121)

FirstEnergy is a public utility holding company. Co. and its subsidiaries are principally involved in the transmission, distribution and generation of electricity. Co.'s reportable operating segments are comprised of: Regulated Distribution, which distributes electricity through Co.'s utility operating companies and also controls regulated electric generation capacity located primarily in West Virginia, Virginia and New Jersey; and Regulated Transmission, which provides transmission infrastructure owned and operated by the transmission companies and certain of Co.'s utilities to transmit electricity from generation sources to distribution facilities.

Recent Developments: For the quarter ended Sep 30 2019, income from continuing operations decreased 2.5% to US$389.0 million from US$399.0 million in the year-earlier quarter. Net income amounted to US$391.0 million versus a net loss of US$458.0 million in the year-earlier quarter. Revenues were US$2.96 billion, down 3.3% from US$3.06 billion the year before. Operating income was US$681.0 million versus US$710.0 million in the prior-year quarter, a decrease of 4.1%. Direct operating expenses declined 9.2% to US$920.0 million from US$1.01 billion in the comparable period the year before. Indirect operating expenses increased 1.6% to US$1.36 billion from US$1.34 billion in the equivalent prior-year period.

Prospects: Our evaluation of FirstEnergy Corp. as of October 4th, 2019 is the result of our systematic analysis on three basic characteristics: earnings strength, relative valuation, and recent stock price movement. The company has produced a positive trend in earnings per share over the past 5 quarters. However, recent analyst estimates for the company have been unchanged, while FE has posted results that exceeded analysts' expectations. Based on operating earnings yield, the company is undervalued when compared to all of the companies we cover. Share price changes over the past year indicates that FE will perform well over the near term.

Financial Data
(US$ in Thousands)

	9 Mos	6 Mos	3 Mos	12/31/2018	12/31/2017	12/31/2016	12/31/2015	12/31/2014
Earnings Per Share	2.13	0.39	0.09	1.99	(3.88)	(14.49)	1.37	0.71
Cash Flow Per Share	4.81	4.37	3.98	2.87	8.58	7.89	8.17	6.46
Tang Book Value Per Share	3.06	3.06	2.43	2.20	N.M.	1.41	14.17	14.25
Dividends Per Share	1.500	1.480	1.460	1.440	1.440	1.440	1.440	1.440
Dividend Payout %	70.42	379.49	1,622.22	72.36	...	...	105.11	202.82
Income Statement								
Total Revenue	8,362,000	5,399,000	2,883,000	11,261,000	14,017,000	14,562,000	15,026,000	15,049,000
EBITDA	2,996,000	1,954,000	980,000	3,699,000	1,408,000	(6,865,000)	3,190,000	2,346,000
Depn & Amortn	910,000	606,000	297,000	1,136,000	1,138,000	1,313,000	1,282,000	1,220,000
Income Before Taxes	1,366,000	870,000	448,000	1,512,000	(829,000)	(9,232,000)	893,000	171,000
Income Taxes	281,000	174,000	93,000	490,000	895,000	(3,055,000)	315,000	(42,000)
Net Income	1,023,000	632,000	320,000	1,348,000	(1,724,000)	(6,177,000)	578,000	299,000
Average Shares	542,000	533,000	533,000	494,000	444,000	426,000	424,000	421,000
Balance Sheet								
Current Assets	2,616,000	2,386,000	2,314,000	2,392,000	3,108,000	2,950,000	3,040,000	3,876,000
Total Assets	41,506,000	40,884,000	40,490,000	40,063,000	42,257,000	43,148,000	52,187,000	52,166,000
Current Liabilities	4,239,000	3,983,000	4,324,000	4,634,000	4,077,000	7,126,000	5,602,000	5,561,000
Long-Term Obligations	19,422,000	19,053,000	18,814,000	17,751,000	21,115,000	18,192,000	19,192,000	19,176,000
Total Liabilities	34,234,000	33,615,000	33,558,000	33,249,000	38,332,000	36,907,000	39,766,000	39,746,000
Stockholders' Equity	7,272,000	7,269,000	6,932,000	6,814,000	3,925,000	6,241,000	12,421,000	12,420,000
Shares Outstanding	540,311	532,092	531,442	511,915	445,334	442,344	423,560	421,102
Statistical Record								
Return on Assets %	2.87	0.78	0.75	3.28	N.M.	N.M.	1.11	0.58
Return on Equity %	16.42	4.17	4.18	25.10	N.M.	N.M.	4.65	2.38
EBITDA Margin %	35.83	36.19	33.99	32.85	10.04	N.M.	21.23	15.59
Net Margin %	12.23	11.71	11.10	11.97	N.M.	N.M.	3.85	1.99
Asset Turnover	0.27	0.28	0.29	0.27	0.33	0.30	0.29	0.29
Current Ratio	0.62	0.60	0.54	0.52	0.76	0.41	0.54	0.70
Debt to Equity	2.67	2.62	2.71	2.61	5.38	2.91	1.55	1.54
Price Range	48.83-35.84	43.97-34.55	42.00-32.97	39.61-29.40	35.05-28.16	36.60-30.06	41.37-29.12	40.77-30.22
P/E Ratio	22.92-16.83	112.74-88.59	466.67-366.33	19.90-14.77	...	...	30.20-21.26	57.42-42.56
Average Yield %	3.64	3.79	3.94	4.09	4.63	4.32	4.22	4.26

Address: 76 South Main Street, Akron, OH 44308
Telephone: 800-736-3402

Web Site: www.firstenergycorp.com
Officers: Donald T. Misheff - Chairman Charles E. Jones - President, Chief Executive Officer, Division Officer

Auditors: PricewaterhouseCoopers LLP
Investor Contact: 330-384-3859
Transfer Agents: American Stock Transfer & Trust Company, LLC, New York, NY

FLEETCOR TECHNOLOGIES INC

Exchange	Symbol	Price	52Wk Range	Yield	P/E
NYS	FLT	$287.72 (12/31/2019)	308.42-181.60	N/A	27.07

*7 Year Price Score 133.74 ***NYSE Composite Index=100** ***12 Month Price Score 106.12**

Interim Earnings (Per Share)

Qtr.	Mar	Jun	Sep	Dec
2016	1.17	1.21	1.36	1.00
2017	1.31	1.39	2.18	3.04
2018	1.88	1.91	1.71	3.31
2019	1.93	2.90	2.49	...

TRADING VOLUME (thousand shares)

Interim Dividends (Per Share)

No Dividends Paid

Valuation Analysis

Valuation Analysis		Institutional Holding	
Forecast EPS	$11.75	No of Institutions	
	(01/14/2020)	703	
Market Cap	$25.0 Billion	Shares	
Book Value	$3.9 Billion	91,650,064	
Price/Book	6.40	% Held	
Price/Sales	9.63	90.53	

Business Summary: Business Services (MIC: 7.5.2 SIC: 7389 NAIC: 561499)

FleetCor Technologies is provider of commercial payment solutions. Co.'s five primary product lines are Fuel, which provides fuel payment solutions to businesses and government entities who operate vehicle fleets, as well as to main oil companies;Lodging, which provides lodging payment solutions to employees who travel overnight for work purposes; Tolls, which provides an electronic toll and parking payments product; Corporate Payments, which include virtual cards, purchasing cards, travel and entertainment cards; and Gift, which provides gift card product management and processing services. Additionally, Co. provides other payment products including fleet maintenance and employee benefits.

Recent Developments: For the quarter ended Sep 30 2019, net income increased 43.2% to US$225.8 million from US$157.7 million in the year-earlier quarter. Revenues were US$681.0 million, up 9.9% from US$619.6 million the year before. Operating income was US$329.1 million versus US$281.1 million in the prior-year quarter, an increase of 17.1%. Indirect operating expenses increased 4.0% to US$351.9 million from US$338.5 million in the equivalent prior-year period.

Prospects: Our evaluation of FleetCor Technologies Inc. as of October 4th, 2019 is the result of our systematic analysis on three basic characteristics: earnings strength, relative valuation, and recent stock price movement. The company has managed to produce a neutral trend in earnings per share over the past 5 quarters. However, recent analyst estimates for the company have been raised and FLT has posted results that exceeded analysts' expectations. Based on operating earnings yield, the company is fairly valued when compared to all of the companies we cover. Share price changes over the past year indicates that FLT will perform over the near term.

Financial Data

(US$ in Thousands)	9 Mos	6 Mos	3 Mos	12/31/2018	12/31/2017	12/31/2016	12/31/2015	12/31/2014
Earnings Per Share	10.63	9.85	8.86	8.81	7.91	4.75	3.85	4.24
Cash Flow Per Share	13.14	13.64	11.64	10.18	7.42	7.60	8.20	7.21
Income Statement								
Total Revenue	1,949,967	1,268,919	621,825	2,433,492	2,249,538	1,831,546	1,702,865	1,199,390
EBITDA	1,103,787	705,866	336,946	1,509,996	1,312,349	949,306	855,251	657,634
Depn & Amortn	209,441	140,781	68,650	269,230	258,449	198,135	190,240	107,249
Income Before Taxes	779,258	486,501	229,241	1,102,272	946,754	679,275	593,672	521,529
Income Taxes	119,695	52,743	57,134	283,642	153,390	190,534	173,573	144,236
Net Income	659,563	433,758	172,107	811,483	740,200	452,385	362,431	368,707
Average Shares	90,522	90,131	89,244	92,151	93,594	95,213	94,139	86,982
Balance Sheet								
Current Assets	4,440,007	4,386,358	4,172,059	3,875,986	3,549,701	2,527,693	1,945,172	2,137,350
Total Assets	11,914,194	11,975,592	11,514,915	11,202,477	11,318,359	9,626,732	7,891,868	8,674,506
Current Liabilities	3,978,937	4,749,210	4,562,098	4,495,213	4,095,502	3,296,318	2,248,021	2,896,618
Long-Term Obligations	3,307,480	2,676,374	2,708,251	2,748,431	2,902,104	2,521,727	2,061,415	2,168,953
Total Liabilities	8,013,884	8,132,220	7,983,948	7,862,297	7,641,837	6,542,694	5,061,821	5,921,369
Stockholders' Equity	3,900,310	3,843,372	3,530,967	3,340,180	3,676,522	3,084,038	2,830,047	2,753,137
Shares Outstanding	86,770	86,535	86,189	85,845	89,803	91,836	92,376	91,662
Statistical Record								
Return on Assets %	8.23	7.62	6.97	7.21	7.07	5.15	4.38	5.85
Return on Equity %	25.77	24.54	21.80	23.13	21.90	15.26	12.98	18.45
EBITDA Margin %	56.61	55.63	54.19	62.05	58.34	51.83	50.22	54.83
Net Margin %	33.82	34.18	27.68	33.35	32.90	24.70	21.28	30.74
Asset Turnover	0.22	0.22	0.21	0.22	0.21	0.21	0.21	0.19
Current Ratio	1.12	0.92	0.91	0.86	0.87	0.77	0.87	0.74
Debt to Equity	0.85	0.70	0.77	0.82	0.79	0.82	0.73	0.79
Price Range		302.64-175.50	280.85-175.50	246.59-175.50	227.84-175.50	193.38-131.26	175.53-113.39	163.86-137.02	156.05-101.69
P/E Ratio		28.47-16.51	28.51-17.82	27.83-19.81	25.86-19.92	24.45-16.59	36.95-23.87	42.56-35.59	36.80-23.98

Address: 5445 Triangle Parkway, Peachtree Corners, GA 30092 Telephone: 770-449-0479	Web Site: www.fleetcor.com Officers: Ronald F. Clarke - Chairman, Chief Executive Officer Eric R. Dey - Chief Financial Officer	Auditors: Ernst & Young LLP Investor Contact: 770-449-0479 Transfer Agents: American Stock Transfer & Trust Company, LLC, Brooklyn, NY

FLOOR & DECOR HOLDINGS INC

Exchange	Symbol	Price	52Wk Range	Yield	P/E
NYS	FND	$50.81 (12/31/2019)	51.29-25.90	N/A	40.01

*7 Year Price Score N/A   *NYSE Composite Index=100   *12 Month Price Score 105.18

Interim Earnings (Per Share)

Qtr.	Mar	Jun	Sep	Dec
2016	0.08	0.06	0.16	0.19
2017	0.13	0.20	0.22	0.47
2018	0.30	0.38	0.25	0.17
2019	0.29	0.42	0.39	...

Interim Dividends (Per Share)

No Dividends Paid

Valuation Analysis   **Institutional Holding**

Forecast EPS	$1.10	No of Institutions
	(01/15/2020)	260
Market Cap	$5.1 Billion	Shares
Book Value	$723.0 Million	106,761,712
Price/Book	7.10	% Held
Price/Sales	2.63	105.28

Business Summary: Construction Materials (MIC: 8.5.1 SIC: 5211 NAIC: 423310)

Floor & Decor Holdings is a holding company. Through its subsidiaries, Co. is a specialty retailer of hard surface flooring and related accessories. Co.'s customers include installers and commercial businesses, Do It Yourself customers and customers who buy the products for installation. Co.'s primary product categories include Tile, Wood, Laminate/Luxury Vinyl Plank, Natural Stone, Decorative Accessories, and Installation Materials and Tools. In addition to its stores, Co.'s website FloorandDecor.com showcases its products, provides informational training and design ideas and has its products available for sale, which a customer can pick up in store or have delivered.

Recent Developments: For the quarter ended Sep 26 2019, net income increased 54.2% to US$41.0 million from US$26.6 million in the year-earlier quarter. Revenues were US$521.1 million, up 19.5% from US$435.9 million the year before. Operating income was US$31.4 million versus US$34.2 million in the prior-year quarter, a decrease of 8.3%. Direct operating expenses rose 19.3% to US$307.3 million from US$257.7 million in the comparable period the year before. Indirect operating expenses increased 26.7% to US$182.4 million from US$144.0 million in the equivalent prior-year period.

Prospects: Our evaluation of Floor & Decor Holdings Inc. as of October 4th, 2019 is the result of our systematic analysis on three basic characteristics: earnings strength, relative valuation, and recent stock price movement. The company has produced a positive trend in earnings per share over the past 5 quarters. However, recent analyst estimates for the company have been unchanged, while FND has posted results that exceeded analysts' expectations. Based on operating earnings yield, the company is overvalued when compared to all of the companies we cover. Share price changes over the past year indicates that FND will perform over the near term.

Financial Data

(US$ in Thousands)	9 Mos	6 Mos	3 Mos	12/27/2018	12/28/2017	12/29/2016	12/31/2015	12/25/2014
Earnings Per Share	1.27	1.13	1.09	1.11	1.03	0.49	0.31	0.18
Cash Flow Per Share	2.51	2.27	1.76	1.92	1.21	1.08	0.24	0.52
Tang Book Value Per Share	3.82	3.37	2.89	2.54	1.11	N.M.	N.M.	...
Income Statement								
Total Revenue	1,518,454	997,361	477,050	1,709,848	1,384,767	1,050,759	784,012	584,588
EBITDA	170,354	120,567	56,946	181,779	148,584	79,828	70,923	58,440
Depn & Amortn	53,297	34,910	17,184	50,478	36,255	12,512	18,531	24,759
Income Before Taxes	109,935	80,513	36,841	122,384	98,552	54,513	43,006	24,732
Income Taxes	(5,355)	6,197	6,121	6,197	(4,236)	11,474	16,199	9,634
Net Income	115,290	74,316	30,720	116,187	102,788	43,039	26,807	15,098
Average Shares	105,180	104,840	104,321	104,561	99,660	88,430	86,280	85,651
Balance Sheet								
Current Assets	643,709	564,014	527,398	559,458	503,212	336,215	305,190	...
Total Assets	2,156,873	2,011,124	1,873,351	1,234,091	1,067,992	831,166	748,888	...
Current Liabilities	492,432	424,638	398,349	404,285	359,300	243,714	196,574	...
Long-Term Obligations	143,288	140,470	143,252	141,834	185,562	387,243	176,323	...
Total Liabilities	1,433,833	1,340,236	1,253,390	649,782	625,132	696,883	436,523	...
Stockholders' Equity	723,040	670,888	619,961	584,309	442,860	134,283	312,365	...
Shares Outstanding	101,025	99,111	97,997	97,588	95,509	83,518	83,373	83,333
Statistical Record								
Return on Assets %	8.10	7.59	7.80	10.12	10.88	5.46	...	...
Return on Equity %	20.70	19.71	20.77	22.68	35.82	19.32	...	...
EBITDA Margin %	11.22	12.09	11.94	10.63	10.73	7.60	9.05	10.00
Net Margin %	7.59	7.45	6.44	6.80	7.42	4.10	3.42	2.58
Asset Turnover	1.19	1.20	1.21	1.49	1.47	1.33	...	...
Current Ratio	1.31	1.33	1.32	1.38	1.40	1.38	1.55	...
Debt to Equity	0.20	0.21	0.23	0.24	0.42	2.88	0.56	...
Price Range	51.29-24.00	51.79-24.00	57.50-24.00	57.50-24.00	49.59-32.05			
P/E Ratio	40.39-18.90	45.83-21.24	52.75-22.02	51.80-21.62	48.15-31.12			

Address: 2500 Windy Ridge Parkway SE, Atlanta, GA 30339 **Telephone:** 404-471-1634	**Web Site:** www.FloorandDecor.com **Officers:** Norman H. Axelrod - Chairman George Vincent West - Vice-Chairman	**Auditors:** Ernst & Young LLP **Transfer Agents:** American Stock Transfer & Trust Company, LLC

FLOWERS FOODS, INC.

Exchange	Symbol	Price	52Wk Range	Yield	P/E	Div Acheiver
NYS	FLO	$21.74 (12/31/2019)	24.24-18.36	3.50	25.28	15 Years

*7 Year Price Score 88.40   *NYSE Composite Index=100   *12 Month Price Score 93.47

Interim Earnings (Per Share)

Qtr.	Apr	Jul	Sep	Dec
2016	0.28	0.24	0.19	0.06
2017	0.29	0.21	(0.16)	0.37
2018	0.24	0.21	0.19	0.10
2019	0.31	0.25	0.20	...

Interim Dividends (Per Share)

Amt	Decl	Ex	Rec	Pay
0.18Q	02/15/2019	02/28/2019	03/01/2019	03/15/2019
0.19Q	05/23/2019	06/06/2019	06/07/2019	06/21/2019
0.19Q	08/16/2019	08/29/2019	08/30/2019	09/13/2019
0.19Q	11/15/2019	11/27/2019	11/29/2019	12/13/2019

Indicated Div: $0.76 (Div. Reinv. Plan)

Valuation Analysis / Institutional Holding

Forecast EPS	$0.96	No of Institutions
	(01/08/2020)	501
Market Cap	$4.6 Billion	Shares
Book Value	$1.3 Billion	163,538,272
Price/Book	3.56	% Held
Price/Sales	1.13	65.52

Business Summary: Food (MIC: 1.2.1 SIC: 2053 NAIC: 311813)

Flowers Foods is a producers and marketers of bakery products in the U.S. Co. produces a range of breads, buns, rolls, snack cakes, and tortillas. Co. manages its business in two operating segments: direct-store-delivery, which produces fresh breads, buns, rolls, tortillas and snack cakes sold primarily by a network of independent distributors to retail and foodservice customers under the Nature's Own, Dave's Killer Bread, Tastykake, Wonder, and Cobblestone Bread Company brand; and warehouse delivery, which produces fresh snack cakes and frozen breads and rolls and delivers its products fresh or frozen to customers' warehouses nationwide via contract carriers.

Recent Developments: For the quarter ended Oct 5 2019, net income increased 9.4% to US$43.4 million from US$39.6 million in the year-earlier quarter. Revenues were US$966.6 million, up 4.7% from US$923.4 million the year before. Operating income was US$58.7 million versus US$53.5 million in the prior-year quarter, an increase of 9.7%. Direct operating expenses rose 4.8% to US$509.1 million from US$485.7 million in the comparable period the year before. Indirect operating expenses increased 3.8% to US$398.9 million from US$384.3 million in the equivalent prior-year period.

Prospects: Our evaluation of Flowers Foods Inc. as of October 4th, 2019 is the result of our systematic analysis on three basic characteristics: earnings strength, relative valuation, and recent stock price movement. The company has enjoyed a very positive trend in earnings per share over the past 5 quarters. However, recent analyst estimates for the company have been reduced, and FLO has posted results that fell short of analysts' expectations. Based on operating earnings yield, the company is fairly valued when compared to all of the companies we cover. Share price changes over the past year indicates that FLO will perform very well over the near term.

Financial Data

(US$ in Thousands)	9 Mos	6 Mos	3 Mos	12/29/2018	12/30/2017	12/31/2016	01/02/2016	01/03/2015
Earnings Per Share	0.86	0.85	0.81	0.74	0.71	0.78	0.89	0.82
Cash Flow Per Share	1.62	1.68	1.40	1.41	0.71	1.66	1.54	1.47
Tang Book Value Per Share	N.M.	N.M.	N.M.	N.M.	0.21	N.M.	N.M.	0.93
Dividends Per Share	0.740	0.730	0.720	0.710	0.670	0.625	0.568	0.485
Dividend Payout %	86.05	85.88	88.89	95.95	94.37	80.13	63.76	59.15
Income Statement								
Total Revenue	3,206,215	2,239,654	1,263,895	3,951,852	3,920,733	3,926,885	3,778,505	3,748,973
EBITDA	331,182	239,852	134,708	323,324	282,357	380,257	414,679	392,595
Depn & Amortn	111,344	78,148	44,819	118,232	119,445	116,367	116,800	117,200
Income Before Taxes	210,911	155,111	86,065	197,161	149,293	249,537	293,031	268,054
Income Taxes	48,592	36,150	20,199	40,001	(827)	85,761	103,840	92,315
Net Income	162,319	118,961	65,866	157,160	150,120	163,776	189,191	175,739
Average Shares	212,014	211,957	211,884	211,632	210,435	210,354	213,356	213,092
Balance Sheet								
Current Assets	565,827	569,461	577,388	543,724	507,191	476,842	537,515	460,563
Total Assets	3,209,426	3,219,792	3,239,333	2,845,537	2,659,724	2,761,068	2,885,168	2,408,974
Current Liabilities	521,942	494,945	495,145	400,339	393,951	340,624	403,738	315,553
Long-Term Obligations	1,224,262	1,236,544	877,201	990,640	820,141	946,667	933,932	728,940
Total Liabilities	1,916,094	1,925,523	1,971,407	1,587,270	1,409,047	1,550,988	1,642,086	1,285,930
Stockholders' Equity	1,293,332	1,294,269	1,267,926	1,258,267	1,250,677	1,210,080	1,243,082	1,123,044
Shares Outstanding	211,513	211,513	211,460	210,895	210,526	208,422	212,266	209,347
Statistical Record								
Return on Assets %	6.21	6.04	5.81	5.73	2.77	5.82	7.17	7.04
Return on Equity %	14.25	13.84	13.42	12.56	6.10	13.39	16.04	15.72
EBITDA Margin %	10.33	10.71	10.66	8.18	7.20	9.68	10.97	10.47
Net Margin %	5.06	5.31	5.21	3.98	3.83	4.17	5.01	4.69
Asset Turnover	1.38	1.36	1.36	1.44	0.72	1.39	1.43	1.50
Current Ratio	1.08	1.15	1.17	1.36	1.29	1.40	1.33	1.46
Debt to Equity	0.95	0.96	0.69	0.79	0.66	0.78	0.75	0.65
Price Range	24.24-17.96	23.75-17.96	22.71-17.96	22.71-17.96	20.84-17.00	21.85-14.60	27.09-18.85	22.19-17.67
P/E Ratio	28.19-20.88	27.94-21.13	28.04-22.17	30.69-24.27	29.35-23.94	28.01-18.72	30.44-21.18	27.06-21.55
Average Yield %	3.49	3.56	3.57	3.51	3.54	3.54	2.51	2.43

Address: 1919 Flowers Circle, Thomasville, GA 31757
Telephone: 229-226-9110

Web Site: www.flowersfoods.com
Officers: A. Ryals McMullian - President, Chief Executive Officer, Chief Operating Officer, Chief Strategy Officer Karyl H. Lauder - Senior Vice President, Chief Accounting Officer

Auditors: PricewaterhouseCoopers LLP
Investor Contact: 229-227-2348
Transfer Agents: Computershare, Providence, RI

FLOWSERVE CORP

Exchange	Symbol	Price	52Wk Range	Yield	P/E
NYS	FLS	$49.77 (12/31/2019)	53.46-36.43	1.53	26.47

*7 Year Price Score 74.13 *NYSE Composite Index=100 *12 Month Price Score 98.77

Interim Earnings (Per Share)

Qtr.	Mar	Jun	Sep	Dec
2016	0.29	0.48	(0.16)	0.50
2017	0.11	0.32	0.36	(0.81)
2018	0.12	0.10	0.21	0.48
2019	0.44	0.44	0.52	...

Interim Dividends (Per Share)

Amt	Decl	Ex	Rec	Pay
0.19Q	03/07/2019	03/28/2019	03/29/2019	04/12/2019
0.19Q	05/23/2019	06/20/2019	06/21/2019	07/05/2019
0.19Q	08/21/2019	09/19/2019	09/20/2019	10/04/2019
0.19Q	12/13/2019	12/26/2019	12/27/2019	01/10/2020

Indicated Div: $0.76

Valuation Analysis / Institutional Holding

Forecast EPS	$2.18	No of Institutions
	(01/16/2020)	626
Market Cap	$6.5 Billion	Shares
Book Value	$1.7 Billion	150,020,432
Price/Book	3.73	% Held
Price/Sales	1.68	97.15

TRADING VOLUME (thousand shares)

Business Summary: Industrial Machinery & Equipment (MIC: 7.2.1 SIC: 3561 NAIC: 333911)

Flowserve is a manufacturer and aftermarket service provider of flow control systems. Co. develops and manufactures flow control equipment integral to the movement, control and protection of the flow of materials in its customers' processes. Co.'s segments are: Engineered Product Division for long lead time, custom and other engineered pumps and pump systems, mechanical seals, auxiliary systems and replacement parts and related services; Industrial Product Division for engineered and pre-configured industrial pumps and pump systems and related products and services; and Flow Control Division for engineered and industrial valves, control valves, actuators and controls and related services.

Recent Developments: For the quarter ended Sep 30 2019, net income increased 139.7% to US$70.6 million from US$29.4 million in the year-earlier quarter. Revenues were US$996.5 million, up 4.6% from US$952.7 million the year before. Operating income was US$109.6 million versus US$62.2 million in the prior-year quarter, an increase of 76.2%. Direct operating expenses rose 2.9% to US$662.9 million from US$644.2 million in the comparable period the year before. Indirect operating expenses decreased 9.0% to US$224.1 million from US$246.3 million in the equivalent prior-year period.

Prospects: Our evaluation of Flowserve Corp. as of October 4th, 2019 is the result of our systematic analysis on three basic characteristics: earnings strength, relative valuation, and recent stock price movement. The company has generated a negative trend in earnings per share over the past 5 quarters. However, recent analyst estimates for the company have been mixed and FLS has posted results that exceeded analysts' expectations. Based on operating earnings yield, the company is fairly valued when compared to all of the companies we cover. Share price changes over the past year indicates that FLS will perform poorly over the near term.

Financial Data
(US$ in Thousands)

	9 Mos	6 Mos	3 Mos	12/31/2018	12/31/2017	12/31/2016	12/31/2015	12/31/2014
Earnings Per Share	1.88	1.57	1.23	0.91	0.02	1.11	2.00	3.76
Cash Flow Per Share	2.35	2.26	2.67	1.46	2.38	1.74	3.13	4.17
Tang Book Value Per Share	2.94	2.66	2.36	1.95	1.74	1.76	1.66	5.34
Dividends Per Share	0.760	0.760	0.760	0.760	0.570	0.760	0.720	0.640
Dividend Payout %	40.43	48.41	61.79	83.52	2,850.00	68.47	36.00	17.02
Income Statement								
Total Revenue	2,876,679	1,880,135	890,051	3,832,666	3,660,831	3,991,462	4,561,030	4,877,885
EBITDA	361,795	231,472	113,248	312,646	408,154	369,430	575,041	873,024
Depn & Amortn	79,141	54,669	27,466	95,820	101,438	99,897	99,501	93,307
Income Before Taxes	247,123	153,000	73,774	165,131	250,415	212,200	412,335	721,075
Income Taxes	64,646	38,999	16,587	51,224	258,679	75,286	148,922	208,305
Net Income	183,875	115,433	57,261	119,671	2,652	145,060	267,669	518,824
Average Shares	131,846	131,754	131,532	131,271	131,358	130,975	133,811	137,843
Balance Sheet								
Current Assets	2,395,660	2,409,324	2,436,623	2,383,145	2,558,745	2,331,361	2,631,792	2,794,163
Total Assets	4,764,492	4,821,209	4,846,497	4,616,277	4,910,474	4,742,762	5,103,850	4,968,020
Current Liabilities	1,048,196	1,058,871	1,121,431	1,080,975	1,242,908	1,178,141	1,359,962	1,471,875
Long-Term Obligations	1,350,265	1,386,415	1,392,238	1,414,829	1,499,658	1,485,258	1,570,836	1,101,791
Total Liabilities	3,020,157	3,094,898	3,159,698	2,973,962	3,255,887	3,094,528	3,437,373	3,036,458
Stockholders' Equity	1,744,335	1,726,311	1,686,799	1,642,315	1,654,587	1,648,234	1,666,477	1,931,562
Shares Outstanding	130,740	130,850	130,824	130,556	130,322	129,813	129,090	134,349
Statistical Record								
Return on Assets %	5.27	4.37	3.36	2.51	0.05	2.94	5.32	10.37
Return on Equity %	14.71	12.35	9.60	7.26	0.16	8.73	14.88	27.29
EBITDA Margin %	12.58	12.31	12.72	8.16	11.15	9.26	12.61	17.90
Net Margin %	6.39	6.14	6.43	3.12	0.07	3.63	5.87	10.64
Asset Turnover	0.82	0.81	0.79	0.80	0.76	0.81	0.91	0.98
Current Ratio	2.29	2.28	2.17	2.20	2.06	1.98	1.94	1.90
Debt to Equity	0.77	0.80	0.83	0.86	0.91	0.90	0.94	0.57
Price Range	54.88-35.89	56.04-35.89	56.04-35.89	56.04-35.89	51.85-37.58	52.32-35.40	62.86-39.85	81.55-54.80
P/E Ratio	29.19-19.09	35.69-22.86	45.56-29.18	61.58-39.44	N.M.	47.14-31.89	31.43-19.93	21.69-14.57
Average Yield %	1.63	1.62	1.67	1.67	1.26	1.67	1.42	0.88

Address: 5215 N. O'Connor Blvd., Suite 2300, Irving, TX 75039 Telephone: 972-443-6500 Fax: 972-443-6800	Web Site: www.flowserve.com Officers: Roger L. Fix - Chairman Robert Scott Rowe - President, Chief Executive Officer	Auditors: PricewaterhouseCoopers LLP Transfer Agents: Wells Fargo Bank, N.A., Mendota Heights, MN

FLUOR CORP.

Exchange	Symbol	Price	52Wk Range	Yield	P/E
NYS	FLR	$18.88 (12/31/2019)	41.56-16.10	2.12	N/A

*7 Year Price Score 44.62 *NYSE Composite Index=100 *12 Month Price Score 59.67

Interim Earnings (Per Share)
Qtr.	Mar	Jun	Sep	Dec
2016	0.74	0.72	0.03	0.50
2017	0.43	(0.17)	0.67	0.43
2018	(0.13)	0.81	0.55	0.36
2019	(0.42)	(3.96)	(5.29)	...

Interim Dividends (Per Share)
Amt	Decl	Ex	Rec	Pay
0.21Q	02/06/2019	03/01/2019	03/04/2019	04/02/2019
0.21Q	05/02/2019	05/31/2019	06/03/2019	07/02/2019
0.21Q	07/31/2019	09/03/2019	09/03/2019	10/02/2019
0.10Q	10/30/2019	12/03/2019	12/04/2019	01/03/2020

Indicated Div: $0.40

Valuation Analysis
Forecast EPS $-9.35 (01/15/2020)
Market Cap $2.6 Billion
Book Value $1.6 Billion
Price/Book 1.70
Price/Sales 0.16

Institutional Holding
No of Institutions 724
Shares 138,568,352
% Held 81.17

Business Summary: Construction Services (MIC: 7.5.4 SIC: 1629 NAIC: 237990)

Fluor is a holding company. Through its subsidiaries, Co. provides engineering, procurement, construction, fabrication and modularization, operations, maintenance and asset integrity, as well as project management services. Co. serves a set of industries including oil and gas, chemicals and petrochemicals, mining and metals, transportation, power, life sciences and manufacturing. Co. is also a service provider to the U.S. federal government and governments abroad; and it performs operations, maintenance and asset integrity activities for industrial clients. Co. has four segments: Energy & Chemicals; Mining, Industrial, Infrastructure & Power; Diversified Services; and Government.

Recent Developments: For the quarter ended Sep 30 2019, loss from continuing operations was US$771.3 million compared with income of US$82.8 million in the year-earlier quarter. Net loss amounted to US$729.5 million versus net income of US$96.0 million in the year-earlier quarter. Revenues were US$3.94 billion, up 2.5% from US$3.84 billion the year before. Direct operating expenses rose 5.9% to US$3.87 billion from US$3.65 billion in the comparable period the year before. Indirect operating expenses increased 361.0% to US$349.4 million from US$75.8 million in the equivalent prior-year period.

Prospects: Our evaluation of Fluor Corp. as of October 4th, 2019 is the result of our systematic analysis on three basic characteristics: earnings strength, relative valuation, and recent stock price movement. The company has generated a negative trend in earnings per share over the past 5 quarters. In addition, recent analyst estimates for the company have been reduced and FLR has posted results that fell short of analysts' expectations. Based on operating earnings yield, the company is undervalued when compared to all of the companies we cover. Share price changes over the past year indicates that FLR will perform poorly over the near term.

Financial Data
(US$ in Thousands)	9 Mos	6 Mos	3 Mos	12/31/2018	12/31/2017	12/31/2016	12/31/2015	12/31/2014
Earnings Per Share	(9.31)	(3.47)	1.30	1.59	1.36	2.00	2.81	3.20
Cash Flow Per Share	1.71	2.76	2.01	1.15	4.31	5.06	5.86	4.08
Tang Book Value Per Share	7.99	13.13	17.25	17.40	19.85	18.62	20.76	20.17
Dividends Per Share	0.840	0.840	0.840	0.840	0.840	0.840	0.840	0.840
Dividend Payout %	...	...	64.62	52.83	61.76	42.00	29.89	26.25
Income Statement								
Total Revenue	10,622,201	8,287,123	4,192,747	19,166,599	19,520,970	19,036,525	18,114,048	21,531,577
EBITDA	(889,500)	(611,029)	36,341	738,622	651,572	825,156	944,371	1,408,916
Depn & Amortn	169,559	126,717	63,073	216,656	225,269	225,913	189,738	192,594
Income Before Taxes	(1,074,854)	(747,371)	(32,393)	481,752	386,441	546,600	726,552	1,204,909
Income Taxes	368,289	(110,577)	10,915	188,794	121,972	219,151	245,888	352,815
Net Income	(1,355,218)	(613,234)	(58,426)	224,833	191,377	281,401	412,512	510,909
Average Shares	140,163	140,141	139,776	141,272	140,893	140,912	146,722	159,616
Balance Sheet								
Current Assets	5,322,888	5,157,552	5,242,608	5,440,893	5,601,257	5,610,270	5,278,287	5,758,047
Total Assets	7,883,707	8,973,874	9,041,714	8,913,637	9,327,692	9,216,417	7,631,506	8,194,429
Current Liabilities	3,850,371	4,057,696	3,527,893	3,552,513	3,574,170	3,816,029	2,935,352	3,330,853
Long-Term Obligations	1,636,905	1,657,246	1,650,927	1,661,565	1,591,598	1,517,949	992,664	991,685
Total Liabilities	6,324,212	6,599,637	6,089,401	5,950,456	5,985,382	6,091,226	4,634,159	5,083,558
Stockholders' Equity	1,559,495	2,374,237	2,952,313	2,963,181	3,342,310	3,125,191	2,997,347	3,110,871
Shares Outstanding	140,174	140,174	140,108	139,653	139,918	139,258	139,018	148,633
Statistical Record								
Return on Assets %	N.M.	N.M.	1.99	2.47	2.06	3.33	5.21	6.19
Return on Equity %	N.M.	N.M.	6.19	7.13	5.92	9.17	13.51	14.88
EBITDA Margin %	N.M.	N.M.	0.87	3.85	3.34	4.33	5.21	6.54
Net Margin %	N.M.	N.M.	N.M.	1.17	0.98	1.48	2.28	2.37
Asset Turnover	2.00	1.96	2.01	2.10	2.11	2.25	2.29	2.61
Current Ratio	1.38	1.27	1.49	1.53	1.57	1.47	1.80	1.73
Debt to Equity	1.05	0.70	0.56	0.56	0.48	0.49	0.33	0.32
Price Range	60.25-16.35	60.25-27.72	61.48-29.99	61.61-29.99	58.17-37.23	57.14-41.11	61.20-40.94	83.65-56.29
P/E Ratio	...	...	47.29-23.07	38.75-18.86	42.77-27.37	28.57-20.56	21.78-14.57	26.14-17.59
Average Yield %	2.46	2.00	1.80	1.62	1.77	1.66	1.61	1.16

Address: 6700 Las Colinas Boulevard, Irving, TX 75039
Telephone: 469-398-7000

Web Site: www.fluor.com
Officers: Alan L. Boeckmann - Executive Chairman, Chairman Carlos M. Hernandez - Chief Executive Officer, Executive Vice President, Interim Chief Executive Officer, Chief Legal Officer, Corporate Secretary

Auditors: Ernst & Young LLP
Investor Contact: 469-398-7189
Transfer Agents: Computershare, Pittsburgh, PA

FMC CORP.

Exchange	Symbol	Price	52Wk Range	Yield	P/E
NYS	FMC	$99.82 (12/31/2019)	101.49-63.26	1.76	25.79

*7 Year Price Score 113.44 ***NYSE Composite Index=100** ***12 Month Price Score 112.39**

Interim Earnings (Per Share)

Qtr.	Mar	Jun	Sep	Dec
2016	0.36	0.49	0.59	0.12
2017	(0.93)	0.56	0.41	3.95
2018	1.96	0.96	0.54	0.24
2019	1.62	1.32	0.69	...

Interim Dividends (Per Share)

Amt	Decl	Ex	Rec	Pay
0.40Q	02/27/2019	03/28/2019	03/29/2019	04/18/2019
0.40Q	04/30/2019	06/27/2019	06/28/2019	07/18/2019
0.40Q	07/19/2019	09/27/2019	09/30/2019	10/17/2019
0.44Q	12/19/2019	12/30/2019	12/31/2019	01/16/2020

Indicated Div: $1.76

Valuation Analysis

		Institutional Holding	
Forecast EPS	$5.85	No of Institutions	
	(01/17/2020)	758	
Market Cap	$12.9 Billion	Shares	
Book Value	$2.6 Billion	137,465,968	
Price/Book	4.88	% Held	
Price/Sales	2.79	85.64	

Business Summary: Agricultural Chemicals (MIC: 8.3.3 SIC: 2879 NAIC: 325320)

FMC is chemical company serving agricultural, consumer and industrial markets globally. Co.'s segments include: FMC Agricultural Solutions and FMC Lithium. Co.'s FMC Agricultural Solutions segment develops, markets and sells all three primary classes of crop protection chemicals: insecticides, herbicides and fungicides. These products are used in agriculture to improve crop yield and quality by controlling a spectrum of insects, weeds and disease, as well as in non-agricultural markets for pest control. Co.'s FMC Lithium segment manufactures lithium for use in a range of lithium products, which are used primarily in energy storage, specialty polymers and chemical synthesis application.

Recent Developments: For the quarter ended Sep 30 2019, income from continuing operations increased 117.7% to US$110.8 million from US$50.9 million in the year-earlier quarter. Net income increased 19.7% to US$89.5 million from US$74.8 million in the year-earlier quarter. Revenues were US$1.01 billion, up 9.8% from US$923.6 million the year before. Direct operating expenses rose 10.1% to US$581.9 million from US$528.4 million in the comparable period the year before. Indirect operating expenses decreased 6.1% to US$272.5 million from US$290.1 million in the equivalent prior-year period.

Prospects: Our evaluation of FMC Corp. as of October 4th, 2019 is the result of our systematic analysis on three basic characteristics: earnings strength, relative valuation, and recent stock price movement. The company has generated a negative trend in earnings per share over the past 5 quarters. However, recent analyst estimates for the company have been raised and FMC has posted results that exceeded analysts' expectations. Based on operating earnings yield, the company is undervalued when compared to all of the companies we cover. Share price changes over the past year indicates that FMC will perform well over the near term.

Financial Data
(US$ in Thousands)

	9 Mos	6 Mos	3 Mos	12/31/2018	12/31/2017	12/31/2016	12/31/2015	12/31/2014
Earnings Per Share	3.87	3.72	3.36	3.69	3.99	1.56	3.66	2.29
Cash Flow Per Share	(0.12)	(0.39)	1.29	2.74	2.50	3.71	(2.68)	2.80
Tang Book Value Per Share	N.M.	N.M.	N.M.	N.M.	N.M.	2.63	1.62	6.73
Dividends Per Share	1.600	1.365	1.130	0.895	0.660	0.660	0.660	0.600
Dividend Payout %	41.34	36.69	33.63	24.25	16.54	42.31	18.03	26.20
Income Statement								
Total Revenue	3,412,500	2,398,200	1,192,100	4,727,800	2,878,600	3,282,400	3,276,500	4,037,700
EBITDA	815,000	617,400	315,700	965,600	325,500	507,900	23,900	649,300
Depn & Amortn	111,100	74,500	37,300	88,900	65,700	86,400	74,100	103,900
Income Before Taxes	588,400	468,900	243,900	743,600	180,700	338,800	(130,300)	485,900
Income Taxes	75,600	66,900	36,300	88,800	264,100	93,900	47,400	73,500
Net Income	480,600	390,200	215,700	502,100	535,800	209,100	489,000	307,500
Average Shares	131,600	132,269	133,214	135,879	134,255	134,538	133,696	134,282
Balance Sheet								
Current Assets	4,077,600	4,097,000	4,204,100	4,030,200	3,652,700	2,849,200	2,971,900	2,934,400
Total Assets	9,803,800	9,824,500	9,946,000	9,974,300	9,206,300	6,139,300	6,325,900	5,340,500
Current Liabilities	2,521,500	3,230,100	3,337,600	2,993,400	2,209,400	1,438,200	1,453,300	1,910,400
Long-Term Obligations	3,032,400	2,144,300	2,145,000	2,179,000	2,993,000	1,798,800	2,036,300	1,153,400
Total Liabilities	7,154,600	7,060,900	7,185,000	6,853,200	6,524,500	4,181,600	4,460,200	3,810,000
Stockholders' Equity	2,649,200	2,763,600	2,761,000	3,121,100	2,681,800	1,957,700	1,865,700	1,530,500
Shares Outstanding	129,615	130,432	131,657	132,281	134,330	133,690	133,655	133,317
Statistical Record								
Return on Assets %	5.34	5.07	4.48	5.24	6.98	3.35	8.38	5.82
Return on Equity %	18.01	17.20	15.68	17.31	23.10	10.91	28.80	20.16
EBITDA Margin %	23.89	25.74	26.48	20.42	11.31	15.47	0.73	16.08
Net Margin %	14.08	16.27	18.09	10.62	18.61	6.37	14.92	7.62
Asset Turnover	0.48	0.48	0.47	0.49	0.38	0.53	0.56	0.76
Current Ratio	1.62	1.27	1.26	1.35	1.65	1.98	2.04	1.54
Debt to Equity	1.14	0.78	0.78	0.70	1.12	0.92	1.09	0.75
Price Range	91.09-60.74	83.38-60.74	80.07-60.74	85.07-60.74	82.79-49.42	51.13-29.06	55.97-28.54	72.01-44.72
P/E Ratio	23.54-15.69	22.41-16.33	23.83-18.08	23.06-16.46	20.75-12.39	32.77-18.63	15.29-7.80	31.45-19.53
Average Yield %	2.08	1.84	1.54	1.22	0.98	1.67	1.52	1.02

Address: 2929 Walnut Street, Philadelphia, PA 19104	**Web Site:** www.fmc.com	**Auditors:** KPMG LLP
Telephone: 215-299-6000	**Officers:** Pierre R. Brondeau - Executive Chairman, Chairman, President, Chief Executive Officer Mark A. Douglas - President, Chief Executive Officer, Chief Operating Officer, Division Officer	**Investor Contact:** 215-299-6119
Fax: 215-299-5998		**Transfer Agents:** EQ Shareowner Services, Mendota Heights, MN

FOOT LOCKER, INC.

Exchange	Symbol	Price	52Wk Range	Yield	P/E
NYS	FL	$38.99 (12/31/2019)	64.45-34.00	3.90	8.46

*7 Year Price Score 75.53 *NYSE Composite Index=100 *12 Month Price Score 82.10

Interim Earnings (Per Share)

Qtr.	Apr	Jul	Oct	Jan
2016-17	1.39	0.94	1.17	1.41
2017-18	1.36	0.39	0.81	(0.33)
2018-19	1.38	0.75	1.14	1.38
2019-20	1.52	0.55	1.16	...

Interim Dividends (Per Share)

Amt	Decl	Ex	Rec	Pay
0.38Q	02/20/2019	04/17/2019	04/18/2019	05/03/2019
0.38Q	05/21/2019	07/18/2019	07/19/2019	08/02/2019
0.38Q	08/20/2019	10/17/2019	10/18/2019	11/01/2019
0.38Q	11/19/2019	01/16/2020	01/17/2020	01/31/2020

Indicated Div: $1.52

Valuation Analysis   **Institutional Holding**

Forecast EPS	$4.94	No of Institutions	
	(01/11/2020)	747	
Market Cap	$4.1 Billion	Shares	
Book Value	$2.4 Billion	137,509,744	
Price/Book	1.69	% Held	
Price/Sales	0.51	74.95	

Business Summary: Retail - Apparel and Accessories (MIC: 2.1.5 SIC: 5661 NAIC: 448210)

Foot Locker is a retailer of athletically inspired shoes and apparel. Co.'s reportable segments are: North America and International. Co.'s North America operating segment includes the following banners operating in the U.S. and Canada: Foot Locker, Kids Foot Locker, Lady Foot Locker, Champs Sports, Footaction, and SIX:02, including each of their related e-commerce businesses, as well as its Eastbay business that includes internet, catalog, and team sales. Co.'s International operating segment includes the following banners operating in Europe, Asia, Australia, and New Zealand: Foot Locker, Runners Point, Sidestep, and Kids Foot Locker, including each of their related e-commerce businesses.

Recent Developments: For the quarter ended Nov 2 2019, net income decreased 3.8% to US$125.0 million from US$130.0 million in the year-earlier quarter. Revenues were US$1.93 billion, up 3.9% from US$1.86 billion the year before. Operating income was US$164.0 million versus US$144.0 million in the prior-year quarter, an increase of 13.9%. Direct operating expenses rose 3.1% to US$1.31 billion from US$1.27 billion in the comparable period the year before. Indirect operating expenses increased 2.7% to US$456.0 million from US$444.0 million in the equivalent prior-year period.

Prospects: Our evaluation of Foot Locker Inc. as of October 4th, 2019 is the result of our systematic analysis on three basic characteristics: earnings strength, relative valuation, and recent stock price movement. The company has generated a negative trend in earnings per share over the past 5 quarters. However, recent analyst estimates for the company have been mixed and FL has posted results that fell short of analysts' expectations. Based on operating earnings yield, the company is undervalued when compared to all of the companies we cover. Share price changes over the past year indicates that FL will perform very poorly over the near term.

Financial Data

(US$ in Thousands)	9 Mos	6 Mos	3 Mos	02/02/2019	02/03/2018	01/28/2017	01/30/2016	01/31/2015
Earnings Per Share	4.61	4.59	4.79	4.66	2.22	4.91	3.84	3.56
Cash Flow Per Share	7.07	6.16	6.09	6.77	6.29	6.11	5.37	4.96
Tang Book Value Per Share	21.42	20.63	21.57	20.59	19.30	19.11	17.17	16.26
Dividends Per Share	1.485	1.450	1.415	1.380	1.240	1.100	1.000	0.880
Dividend Payout %	32.21	31.59	29.54	29.61	55.86	22.40	26.04	24.72
Income Statement								
Total Revenue	5,784,000	3,852,000	2,078,000	7,939,000	7,782,000	7,766,000	7,412,000	7,151,000
EBITDA	615,000	403,000	274,000	882,000	749,000	1,164,000	989,000	953,000
Depn & Amortn	134,000	90,000	44,000	178,000	173,000	158,000	148,000	139,000
Income Before Taxes	490,000	319,000	234,000	713,000	578,000	1,004,000	837,000	809,000
Income Taxes	133,000	87,000	62,000	172,000	294,000	340,000	296,000	289,000
Net Income	357,000	232,000	172,000	541,000	284,000	664,000	541,000	520,000
Average Shares	107,200	111,100	113,100	116,100	127,900	135,100	140,800	146,000
Balance Sheet								
Current Assets	2,347,000	2,446,000	2,592,000	2,518,000	2,551,000	2,633,000	2,606,000	2,456,000
Total Assets	6,621,000	6,720,000	6,928,000	3,820,000	3,961,000	3,840,000	3,775,000	3,577,000
Current Liabilities	1,237,000	1,229,000	1,290,000	764,000	616,000	612,000	700,000	696,000
Long-Term Obligations	122,000	123,000	123,000	124,000	125,000	127,000	129,000	132,000
Total Liabilities	4,194,000	4,208,000	4,326,000	1,314,000	1,442,000	1,130,000	1,222,000	1,081,000
Stockholders' Equity	2,427,000	2,512,000	2,602,000	2,506,000	2,519,000	2,710,000	2,553,000	2,496,000
Shares Outstanding	105,064	113,199	112,387	112,933	119,829	131,496	136,977	140,864
Statistical Record								
Return on Assets %	10.00	9.86	10.06	13.94	7.16	17.49	14.76	14.76
Return on Equity %	21.12	20.82	21.30	21.59	10.69	25.30	21.49	20.89
EBITDA Margin %	10.63	10.46	13.19	11.11	9.62	14.99	13.34	13.33
Net Margin %	6.17	6.02	8.28	6.81	3.65	8.55	7.30	7.27
Asset Turnover	1.56	1.51	1.47	2.05	1.96	2.05	2.02	2.03
Current Ratio	1.90	1.99	2.01	3.30	4.14	4.30	3.72	3.53
Debt to Equity	0.05	0.05	0.05	0.05	0.05	0.05	0.05	0.05
Price Range	64.45-34.00	64.45-39.34	64.45-40.52	58.92-40.04	77.35-29.24	79.20-51.79	75.76-52.43	57.98-36.73
P/E Ratio	13.98-7.38	14.04-8.57	13.46-8.46	12.64-8.59	34.84-13.17	16.13-10.55	19.73-13.65	16.29-10.32
Average Yield %	2.99	2.81	2.66	2.80	2.37	1.71	1.54	1.74

Address: 330 West 34th Street, New York, NY 10001 **Telephone:** 212-720-3700	**Web Site:** www.footlocker-inc.com **Officers:** Richard A. Johnson - Chairman, President, Chief Executive Officer, Executive Vice President, Chief Operating Officer, Division Officer Stephen D. Jacobs - Executive Vice President, Region Officer	**Auditors:** KPMG LLP **Investor Contact:** 212-720-3700 **Transfer Agents:** Computershare, Providence, R.I.

FORD MOTOR CO. (DE)

Exchange	Symbol	Price	52Wk Range	Yield	P/E
NYS	F	$9.30 (12/31/2019)	10.51-7.65	6.45	22.68

*7 Year Price Score 59.20 *NYSE Composite Index=100 *12 Month Price Score 92.87

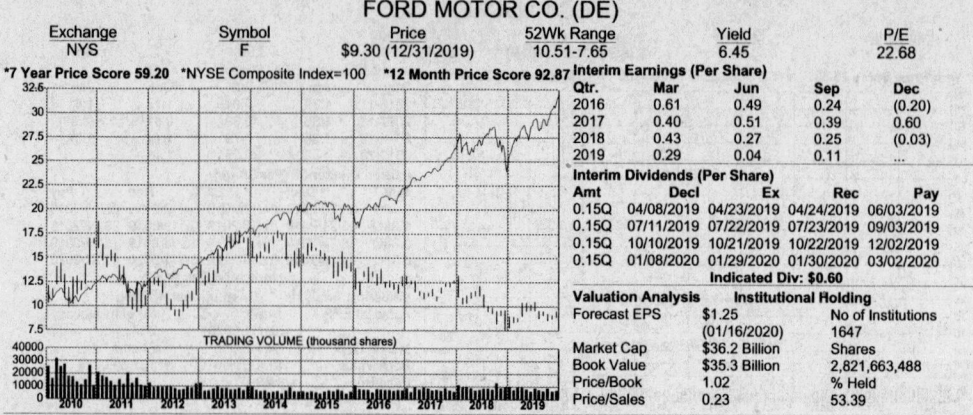

Interim Earnings (Per Share)

Qtr.	Mar	Jun	Sep	Dec
2016	0.61	0.49	0.24	(0.20)
2017	0.40	0.51	0.39	0.60
2018	0.43	0.27	0.25	(0.03)
2019	0.29	0.11	0.04	...

Interim Dividends (Per Share)

Amt	Decl	Ex	Rec	Pay
0.15Q	04/08/2019	04/23/2019	04/24/2019	06/03/2019
0.15Q	07/11/2019	07/22/2019	07/23/2019	09/03/2019
0.15Q	10/10/2019	10/21/2019	10/22/2019	12/02/2019
0.15Q	01/08/2020	01/29/2020	01/30/2020	03/02/2020

Indicated Div: $0.60

Valuation Analysis

		Institutional Holding	
Forecast EPS	$1.25	No of Institutions	
	(01/16/2020)	1647	
Market Cap	$36.2 Billion	Shares	
Book Value	$35.3 Billion	2,821,663,488	
Price/Book	1.02	% Held	
Price/Sales	0.23	53.39	

Business Summary: Autos- Manufacturing (MIC: 1.8.1 SIC: 3711 NAIC: 336111)

Ford Motor designs, manufactures, markets, and services a line of Ford cars, trucks, sport utility vehicles, electrified vehicles, and Lincoln luxury vehicles, provides financial services through its subsidiary, Ford Motor Credit Company LLC (Ford Credit), and is engaged in electrification, autonomous vehicles, and mobility solutions. Co. has three segments: Automotive, which includes the sale of Ford and Lincoln vehicles, service parts, and accessories worldwide; Mobility, which includes its subsidiary, Ford Smart Mobility LLC and its autonomous vehicles business; and Ford Credit, which is comprised of vehicle-related financing and leasing activities.

Recent Developments: For the quarter ended Sep 30 2019, net income decreased 57.4% to US$423.0 million from US$993.0 million in the year-earlier quarter. Revenues were US$36.99 billion, down 1.8% from US$37.67 billion the year before. Operating loss was US$261.0 million versus an income of US$864.0 million in the prior-year quarter. Direct operating expenses rose 2.3% to US$32.28 billion from US$31.57 billion in the comparable period the year before. Indirect operating expenses decreased 5.1% to US$4.97 billion from US$5.23 billion in the equivalent prior-year period.

Prospects: Our evaluation of Ford Motor Co. as of October 4th, 2019 is the result of our systematic analysis on three basic characteristics: earnings strength, relative valuation, and recent stock price movement. The company has enjoyed a very positive trend in earnings per share over the past 5 quarters. However, recent analyst estimates for the company have been reduced, and F has posted results that fell short of analysts' expectations. Based on operating earnings yield, the company is undervalued when compared to all of the companies we cover. Share price changes over the past year indicates that F will perform well over the near term.

Financial Data

(US$ in Millions)	9 Mos	6 Mos	3 Mos	12/31/2018	12/31/2017	12/31/2016	12/31/2015	12/31/2014
Earnings Per Share	0.41	0.55	0.78	0.92	1.90	1.15	1.84	0.80
Cash Flow Per Share	4.05	4.15	3.79	3.78	4.55	4.97	4.07	3.71
Tang Book Value Per Share	9.08	9.05	9.29	9.03	8.78	7.34	7.22	6.27
Dividends Per Share	0.600	0.600	0.600	0.730	0.650	0.850	0.600	0.500
Dividend Payout %	146.34	109.09	76.92	79.35	34.21	73.91	32.61	62.50
Income Statement								
Total Revenue	116,185	79,195	40,342	160,338	156,776	151,800	149,558	144,077
EBITDA	8,046	6,537	3,999	10,163	12,606	10,283	15,681	10,475
Depn & Amortn	(891)	...	...	5,413	4,987	4,667	4,332	4,252
Income Before Taxes	1,654	1,701	1,582	4,222	6,947	5,016	8,434	3,067
Income Taxes	40	482	427	650	520	2,189	2,881	1,156
Net Income	1,719	1,294	1,146	3,677	7,602	4,596	7,373	3,187
Average Shares	4,008	4,014	3,998	3,999	3,999	4,000	4,003	4,046
Balance Sheet								
Current Assets	115,754	118,351	121,195	114,649	115,902	108,461	43,495	39,016
Total Assets	258,157	262,184	263,281	256,540	257,808	237,951	224,925	208,527
Current Liabilities	99,087	98,334	99,237	95,569	94,600	90,281	78,336	73,963
Long-Term Obligations	99,507	103,213	102,612	100,720	102,666	93,301	89,856	79,999
Total Liabilities	222,808	226,087	226,883	220,608	222,918	208,781	196,283	183,722
Stockholders' Equity	35,349	36,097	36,398	35,932	34,890	29,170	28,642	24,805
Shares Outstanding	3,895	3,990	3,919	3,979	3,974	3,975	3,970	3,956
Statistical Record								
Return on Assets %	0.62	0.83	1.16	1.43	3.07	1.98	3.40	1.55
Return on Equity %	4.46	5.98	8.48	10.38	23.73	15.86	27.59	12.45
EBITDA Margin %	6.93	8.25	9.91	6.34	8.04	6.77	10.48	7.27
Net Margin %	1.48	1.63	2.84	2.29	4.85	3.03	4.93	2.21
Asset Turnover	0.61	0.61	0.60	0.62	0.63	0.65	0.69	0.70
Current Ratio	1.17	1.20	1.22	1.20	1.23	1.20	0.56	0.53
Debt to Equity	2.81	2.86	2.82	2.80	2.94	3.20	3.14	3.23
Price Range	10.51-7.63	11.25-7.63	12.11-7.63	13.23-7.63	13.17-10.56	14.09-11.17	16.57-12.90	17.84-13.54
P/E Ratio	25.63-18.61	20.45-13.87	15.53-9.78	14.38-8.29	6.93-5.56	12.25-9.71	9.01-7.01	22.30-16.92
Average Yield %	6.51	6.42	6.15	7.01	5.51	6.73	4.00	3.15

Address: One American Road,	Web Site: www.corporate.ford.com	Auditors: PricewaterhouseCoopers LLP
Dearborn, MI 48126	Officers: William Clay Ford - Executive Chairman,	Investor Contact: 313-845-8540
Telephone: 313-322-3000	Chairman James Patrick (Jim) Hackett - President,	Transfer Agents: Computershare Trust
	Chief Executive Officer	Company, N.A., Providence, RI

FORTIVE CORP

Exchange	Symbol	Price	52Wk Range	Yield	P/E
NYS	FTV	$76.39 (12/31/2019)	89.06-64.24	0.37	10.25

*7 Year Price Score N/A   *NYSE Composite Index=100   *12 Month Price Score 90.99

Interim Earnings (Per Share)

Qtr.	Mar	Jun	Sep	Dec
2016	0.53	0.69	0.65	0.64
2017	0.57	0.68	0.76	0.95
2018	0.74	0.83	0.64	6.00
2019	0.43	0.46	0.56	...

Interim Dividends (Per Share)

Amt	Decl	Ex	Rec	Pay
0.07Q	01/29/2019	02/21/2019	02/22/2019	03/29/2019
0.07Q	04/11/2019	05/30/2019	05/31/2019	06/28/2019
0.07Q	08/15/2019	08/29/2019	08/30/2019	09/27/2019
0.07Q	11/07/2019	11/27/2019	11/29/2019	12/27/2019

Indicated Div: $0.28

Valuation Analysis

		Institutional Holding	
Forecast EPS	$3.44 (01/17/2020)	No of Institutions	929
Market Cap	$25.6 Billion	Shares	
Book Value	$7.2 Billion		301,027,520
Price/Book	3.59	% Held	
Price/Sales	4.05		79.66

Business Summary: Industrial Machinery & Equipment (MIC: 7.2.1 SIC: 3823 NAIC: 334513)

Fortive designs, develops, services, manufactures and markets professional and engineered products, software and services. Co. is comprised of two reportable segments: Professional Instrumentation, which provides products, software and services used to create actionable intelligence by measuring and monitoring a range of physical parameters in industrial applications, including electrical current, radio frequency signals, distance, pressure, temperature, turbidity, radiation, and hazardous gases; and Industrial Technologies, which provides critical technical equipment, components, software and services for manufacturing, repair and transportation markets worldwide.

Recent Developments: For the quarter ended Sep 27 2019, income from continuing operations decreased 3.1% to US$207.3 million from US$214.0 million in the year-earlier quarter. Net income decreased 15.6% to US$207.1 million from US$245.3 million in the year-earlier quarter. Revenues were US$1.86 billion, up 16.2% from US$1.60 billion the year before. Operating income was US$242.1 million versus US$281.6 million in the prior-year quarter, a decrease of 14.0%. Direct operating expenses rose 20.3% to US$932.3 million from US$775.3 million in the comparable period the year before. Indirect operating expenses increased 26.0% to US$685.6 million from US$544.3 million in the equivalent prior-year period.

Prospects: Our evaluation of Fortive Corp. as of October 4th, 2019 is the result of our systematic analysis on three basic characteristics: earnings strength, relative valuation, and recent stock price movement. The company has managed to produce a neutral trend in earnings per share over the past 5 quarters. However, recent analyst estimates for the company have been reduced while FTV has posted results that exceeded analysts' expectations. Based on operating earnings yield, the company is fairly valued when compared to all of the companies we cover. Share price changes over the past year indicates that FTV will perform in line with the market over the near term.

Financial Data

(US$ in Thousands)	9 Mos	6 Mos	3 Mos	12/31/2018	12/31/2017	12/31/2016	12/31/2015	12/31/2014
Earnings Per Share	7.45	7.53	7.90	8.21	2.96	2.51	...	...
Cash Flow Per Share	3.69	3.71	3.97	3.89	3.39	3.28	...	...
Dividends Per Share	0.280	0.280	0.280	0.280	0.280	0.140	...	...
Dividend Payout %	3.76	3.72	3.54	3.41	9.46	5.58	...	...
Income Statement								
Total Revenue	5,317,600	3,457,600	1,592,900	6,452,700	6,656,000	6,224,300	6,178,800	6,337,200
EBITDA	1,057,600	658,700	299,600	1,301,100	1,479,200	1,337,000	1,357,700	1,357,200
Depn & Amortn	309,100	192,300	81,900	125,700	109,000	91,000	88,000	78,000
Income Before Taxes	631,800	396,700	192,400	1,078,400	1,284,200	1,197,000	1,269,700	1,279,200
Income Taxes	85,200	57,400	28,400	160,100	239,700	324,700	405,900	395,800
Net Income	546,100	339,000	164,400	2,913,800	1,044,500	872,300	863,800	883,400
Average Shares	339,900	339,700	339,500	350,700	352,600	347,300		
Balance Sheet								
Current Assets	3,465,900	3,436,300	5,796,300	3,171,200	2,936,800	2,488,700	1,594,100	1,683,400
Total Assets	16,660,400	16,468,100	15,656,200	12,905,600	10,500,600	8,189,800	7,210,600	7,355,600
Current Liabilities	2,916,300	2,791,200	2,639,600	2,192,100	1,602,300	1,466,500	1,323,500	1,285,000
Long-Term Obligations	5,015,600	5,196,500	4,728,300	2,974,700	4,056,200	3,358,000	...	...
Total Liabilities	9,508,700	9,456,500	8,805,500	6,310,100	6,710,300	5,501,900	2,031,100	2,126,300
Stockholders' Equity	7,151,700	7,011,600	6,850,700	6,595,500	3,790,300	2,687,900	5,179,500	5,229,300
Shares Outstanding	335,700	335,400	335,000	334,500	347,800	345,900	...	...
Statistical Record								
Return on Assets %	17.42	18.95	21.41	24.90	11.18	11.30	11.86	...
Return on Equity %	40.96	42.68	51.48	56.11	32.25	22.11	16.60	...
EBITDA Margin %	19.89	19.05	18.81	20.16	22.22	21.48	21.97	21.42
Net Margin %	10.27	9.80	10.32	45.16	15.69	14.01	13.98	13.94
Asset Turnover	0.41	0.44	0.48	0.55	0.71	0.81	0.85	...
Current Ratio	1.19	1.23	2.20	1.45	1.83	1.70	1.20	1.31
Debt to Equity	0.70	0.74	0.69	0.45	1.07	1.25	...	...
Price Range	89.06-63.64	89.06-63.64	87.38-63.64	87.38-63.64	74.65-53.66	55.97-47.49	...	...
P/E Ratio	11.95-8.54	11.83-8.45	11.06-8.06	10.64-7.75	25.22-18.13	22.30-18.92	...	...
Average Yield %	0.36	0.36	0.36	0.36	0.43	0.27	...	...

Address: 6920 Seaway Blvd., Everett, WA 98203 **Telephone:** 425-446-5000	**Web Site:** www.fortive.com **Officers:** Alan G. Spoon - Chairman James A. Lico - President, Chief Executive Officer	**Auditors:** Ernst & Young LLP **Transfer Agents:** Computershare Trust Company, N.A.

291

FORTUNE BRANDS HOME & SECURITY, INC.

Exchange	Symbol	Price	52Wk Range	Yield	P/E
NYS	FBHS	$65.34 (12/31/2019)	65.98-37.66	1.47	22.38

*7 Year Price Score 85.53   *NYSE Composite Index=100   *12 Month Price Score 114.11

TRADING VOLUME (thousand shares)

Interim Earnings (Per Share)

Qtr.	Mar	Jun	Sep	Dec
2016	0.35	0.80	0.78	0.66
2017	0.50	0.88	0.83	0.83
2018	0.49	0.88	0.69	0.60
2019	0.60	0.97	0.75	...

Interim Dividends (Per Share)

Amt	Decl	Ex	Rec	Pay
0.22Q	05/06/2019	05/30/2019	05/31/2019	06/19/2019
0.22Q	07/29/2019	08/29/2019	08/30/2019	09/18/2019
0.22Q	09/23/2019	11/27/2019	11/29/2019	12/18/2019
0.24Q	12/10/2019	02/27/2020	02/28/2020	03/18/2020

Indicated Div: $0.96

Valuation Analysis

		Institutional Holding	
Forecast EPS	$3.58	No of Institutions	
	(01/17/2020)	662	
Market Cap	$9.1 Billion	Shares	
Book Value	$2.3 Billion	150,286,464	
Price/Book	3.89	% Held	
Price/Sales	1.59	79.31	

Business Summary: Household Appliances, Electronics & Goods (MIC: 1.5.1 SIC: 1522 NAIC: 236118)
Fortune Brands Home & Security is a holding company. Through its subsidiaries, Co. provides home and security products. Co.'s segments are: Cabinets, which manufactures cabinetry and vanities, for the kitchen, bath and other parts of the home; Plumbing, which manufactures or assembles and sells faucets, accessories, kitchen sinks and waste disposals; and Doors and Security, which manufactures and sells fiberglass and steel entry door systems, composite decking, railing and fencing, and urethane millwork, as well as manufactures, sources and distributes locks, safety and security devices, and electronic security products and fire resistant safes, security containers and commercial cabinets.

Recent Developments: For the quarter ended Sep 30 2019, income from continuing operations increased 5.8% to US$105.7 million from US$99.9 million in the year-earlier quarter. Net income increased 5.8% to US$105.7 million from US$99.9 million in the year-earlier quarter. Revenues were US$1.46 billion, up 5.7% from US$1.38 billion the year before. Operating income was US$168.0 million versus US$147.1 million in the prior-year quarter, an increase of 14.2%. Direct operating expenses rose 5.4% to US$934.8 million from US$886.9 million in the comparable period the year before. Indirect operating expenses increased 2.7% to US$356.2 million from US$346.8 million in the equivalent prior-year period.

Prospects: Our evaluation of Fortune Brands Home & Security Inc. as of October 4th, 2019 is the result of our systematic analysis on three basic characteristics: earnings strength, relative valuation, and recent stock price movement. The company has managed to produce a neutral trend in earnings per share over the past 5 quarters. In addition, recent analyst estimates for the company have been mixed and FBHS has posted results that fell short of analysts' expectations. Based on operating earnings yield, the company is undervalued when compared to all of the companies we cover. Share price changes over the past year indicates that FBHS will perform poorly over the near term.

Financial Data
(US$ in Thousands)

	9 Mos	6 Mos	3 Mos	12/31/2018	12/31/2017	12/31/2016	12/31/2015	12/31/2014
Earnings Per Share	2.92	2.86	2.77	2.66	3.03	2.62	1.93	0.95
Cash Flow Per Share	4.40	4.14	4.02	4.18	3.92	4.20	2.58	1.57
Tang Book Value Per Share	N.M.	N.M.	N.M.	N.M.	N.M.	N.M.	N.M.	0.85
Dividends Per Share	0.860	0.840	0.820	0.800	0.720	0.640	0.560	0.480
Dividend Payout %	29.45	29.37	29.60	30.08	23.76	24.43	29.02	50.53
Income Statement								
Total Revenue	4,294,100	2,835,100	1,327,900	5,485,100	5,283,300	4,984,900	4,579,400	4,013,600
EBITDA	623,300	417,400	175,400	761,100	814,500	753,900	606,900	498,300
Depn & Amortn	115,100	77,500	38,600	149,600	130,300	122,700	115,100	96,000
Income Before Taxes	436,400	291,700	113,100	537,000	634,800	582,100	459,900	391,900
Income Taxes	109,100	70,100	28,600	147,000	159,500	169,700	153,400	118,300
Net Income	327,800	222,200	84,700	389,600	472,600	413,200	315,000	158,100
Average Shares	140,900	141,300	141,900	146,400	155,800	157,800	163,000	166,300
Balance Sheet								
Current Assets	1,906,700	1,916,900	1,848,000	1,686,100	1,601,700	1,445,200	1,418,700	1,299,100
Total Assets	6,285,600	6,343,400	6,289,200	5,964,600	5,511,400	5,128,500	4,878,600	4,052,900
Current Liabilities	1,376,600	1,695,200	1,238,800	1,492,100	906,800	842,800	757,900	699,600
Long-Term Obligations	1,949,000	1,666,000	2,169,700	1,809,000	1,507,600	1,431,100	1,171,600	643,700
Total Liabilities	3,950,200	3,999,900	4,043,700	3,786,400	2,911,900	2,767,000	2,427,700	1,793,400
Stockholders' Equity	2,335,400	2,343,500	2,245,500	2,178,200	2,599,500	2,361,500	2,450,900	2,259,500
Shares Outstanding	139,151	140,019	139,880	140,498	151,906	153,412	159,906	158,140
Statistical Record								
Return on Assets %	6.63	6.76	6.74	6.79	8.88	8.24	7.05	3.84
Return on Equity %	18.09	18.03	17.35	16.31	19.05	17.13	13.37	6.44
EBITDA Margin %	14.52	14.72	13.21	13.88	15.42	15.12	13.25	12.42
Net Margin %	7.63	7.84	6.38	7.10	8.95	8.29	6.88	3.94
Asset Turnover	0.92	0.94	0.94	0.96	0.99	0.99	1.03	0.98
Current Ratio	1.39	1.13	1.49	1.13	1.77	1.71	1.87	1.86
Debt to Equity	0.83	0.71	0.97	0.83	0.58	0.61	0.48	0.28
Price Range	57.44-35.96	58.00-35.96	59.95-35.96	73.13-35.96	69.32-53.89	64.04-45.27	56.47-43.04	47.83-36.77
P/E Ratio	19.67-12.32	20.28-12.57	21.64-12.98	27.49-13.52	22.88-17.79	24.44-17.28	29.26-22.30	50.35-38.71
Average Yield %	1.77	1.64	1.63	1.45	1.14	1.14	1.16	1.14

Address: 520 Lake Cook Road, Deerfield, IL 60015-5611 **Telephone:** 847-484-4400	**Web Site:** www.fbhs.com **Officers:** Christopher J. Klein - Executive Chairman, President, Chief Executive Officer David M. Thomas - Non-Executive Chairman	**Auditors:** PricewaterhouseCoopers LLP **Transfer Agents:** Wells Fargo Shareowner Services, Mendota Heights, MN

FRANKLIN RESOURCES INC

Exchange	Symbol	Price	52Wk Range	Yield	P/E	Div Acheiver
NYS	BEN	$25.98 (12/31/2019)	35.67-25.80	4.16	11.06	29 Years

*7 Year Price Score 60.05   *NYSE Composite Index=100   *12 Month Price Score 84.05

Interim Earnings (Per Share)

Qtr.	Dec	Mar	Jun	Sep
2014-15	0.91	0.98	0.82	0.59
2015-16	0.74	0.61	0.77	0.82
2016-17	0.77	0.74	0.73	0.76
2017-18	(1.06)	0.78	0.75	0.94
2018-19	0.54	0.72	0.48	0.61

Interim Dividends (Per Share)

Amt	Decl	Ex	Rec	Pay
0.26Q	02/12/2019	03/28/2019	03/29/2019	04/12/2019
0.26Q	06/12/2019	06/27/2019	06/28/2019	07/12/2019
0.26Q	09/05/2019	09/27/2019	09/30/2019	10/11/2019
0.27Q	12/10/2019	12/30/2019	12/31/2019	01/10/2020

Indicated Div: $1.08 (Div. Reinv. Plan)

Valuation Analysis   **Institutional Holding**

Forecast EPS	$2.58	No of Institutions
	(01/15/2020)	885
Market Cap	$13.0 Billion	Shares
Book Value	$9.9 Billion	292,853,408
Price/Book	1.31	% Held
Price/Sales	2.25	43.82

Business Summary: Wealth Management (MIC: 5.5.2 SIC: 6282 NAIC: 523930)

Franklin Resources is a holding company that, together with its subsidiaries, operates as Franklin Templeton®. Co. is an investment management organization that provides investment management and related services to retail, institutional and investors in jurisdictions worldwide through its investment products. Co.'s investment products include its sponsored funds, as well as institutional and separate accounts, and sub-advised products. Co.'s funds include registered and unregistered funds. Co.'s services include fund administration, sales and distribution, and shareholder servicing. Co. also provides sub-advisory services to certain investment products sponsored by other companies.

Recent Developments: For the year ended Sep 30 2019, net income increased 62.3% to US$1.21 billion from US$742.7 million in the prior year. Revenues were US$5.77 billion, down 8.6% from US$6.32 billion the year before. Operating income was US$1.56 billion versus US$2.12 billion in the prior year, a decrease of 26.5%. Direct operating expenses declined 10.8% to US$1.82 billion from US$2.04 billion in the comparable period the year before. Indirect operating expenses increased 11.0% to US$2.40 billion from US$2.16 billion in the equivalent prior-year period.

Prospects: Our evaluation of Franklin Resources Inc. as of October 4th, 2019 is the result of our systematic analysis on three basic characteristics: earnings strength, relative valuation, and recent stock price movement. The company has managed to produce a neutral trend in earnings per share over the past 5 quarters. In addition, recent analyst estimates for the company have been mixed and BEN has posted results that fell short of analysts' expectations. Based on operating earnings yield, the company is undervalued when compared to all of the companies we cover. Share price changes over the past year indicates that BEN will perform in line with the market over the near term.

Financial Data

(US$ in Thousands)	09/30/2019	09/30/2018	09/30/2017	09/30/2016	09/30/2015	09/30/2014	09/30/2013	09/30/2012
Earnings Per Share	2.35	1.39	3.01	2.94	3.29	3.79	3.37	2.98
Cash Flow Per Share	0.40	4.15	2.03	2.95	3.66	3.42	3.22	1.66
Tang Book Value Per Share	13.84	14.57	18.73	17.05	15.88	14.86	12.23	11.09
Dividends Per Share	1.040	3.920	0.800	0.720	1.100	0.480	6.970	1.027
Dividend Payout %	44.26	282.01	26.58	24.49	33.43	12.66	206.82	34.41
Income Statement								
Total Revenue	5,774,500	6,319,100	6,392,200	6,618,000	7,948,700	8,491,400	7,985,000	7,101,000
EBITDA	1,735,100	2,221,900	2,499,300	2,537,500	3,202,000	3,462,400	3,068,900	2,701,700
Depn & Amortn	83,200	78,900	81,500	81,000	81,600	82,600	76,900	67,900
Income Before Taxes	1,658,200	2,170,800	2,441,200	2,443,100	3,091,600	3,341,500	2,952,600	2,609,600
Income Taxes	442,300	1,472,500	759,400	742,100	923,700	997,900	855,900	762,700
Net Income	1,195,700	764,400	1,696,700	1,726,700	2,035,300	2,384,300	2,150,200	1,931,400
Average Shares	504,300	538,000	559,100	583,800	614,900	625,200	634,100	643,200
Balance Sheet								
Current Assets	6,796,600	7,758,500	9,751,600	9,277,600	9,306,800	8,644,100	7,474,400	6,996,500
Total Assets	14,532,200	14,383,500	17,534,000	16,098,800	16,335,700	16,357,100	15,390,300	14,751,500
Current Liabilities	2,022,900	2,092,900	1,114,700	997,300	1,117,800	1,220,200	1,731,800	1,709,100
Long-Term Obligations	747,700	728,500	1,097,600	2,083,400	2,155,300	2,149,000	2,306,000	2,839,100
Total Liabilities	4,625,700	4,484,300	4,914,000	4,163,000	4,494,700	4,773,000	5,317,200	5,550,200
Stockholders' Equity	9,906,500	9,899,200	12,620,000	11,935,800	11,841,000	11,584,100	10,073,100	9,201,300
Shares Outstanding	499,303	519,122	554,865	570,345	603,517	622,893	630,917	636,626
Statistical Record								
Return on Assets %	8.27	4.79	10.09	10.62	12.45	15.02	14.27	13.50
Return on Equity %	12.07	6.79	13.82	14.48	17.38	22.02	22.31	21.73
EBITDA Margin %	30.05	35.16	39.10	38.34	40.28	40.78	38.43	38.05
Net Margin %	20.71	12.10	26.54	26.09	25.61	28.08	26.93	27.20
Asset Turnover	0.40	0.40	0.38	0.41	0.49	0.53	0.53	0.50
Current Ratio	3.36	3.71	8.75	9.30	8.33	7.08	4.32	4.09
Debt to Equity	0.08	0.07	0.09	0.17	0.18	0.19	0.23	0.31
Price Range	35.67-25.93	45.86-30.14	47.28-33.18	41.92-30.67	58.84-36.36	58.51-49.52	56.11-41.55	42.67-30.13
P/E Ratio	15.18-11.03	32.99-21.68	15.71-11.02	14.26-10.43	17.88-11.05	15.44-13.07	16.65-12.33	14.32-10.11
Average Yield %	3.28	10.49	1.93	1.97	2.17	0.88	14.27	2.78

Address: One Franklin Parkway, San Mateo, CA 94403	**Web Site:** www.franklinresources.com	**Auditors:** PricewaterhouseCoopers LLP
Telephone: 650-312-2000	**Officers:** Gregory E. Johnson - Executive Chairman, Chairman, President, Chief Executive Officer Rupert H. Johnson - Vice-Chairman	**Investor Contact:** 650-312-4091
Fax: 650-312-3655		**Transfer Agents:** Computershare, Pittsburgh, PA

FREEPORT-MCMORAN INC

Exchange	Symbol	Price	52Wk Range	Yield	P/E
NYS	FCX	$13.12 (12/31/2019)	14.20-8.51	1.52	87.47

*7 Year Price Score 48.97 *NYSE Composite Index=100 *12 Month Price Score 97.66

Interim Earnings (Per Share)

Qtr.	Mar	Jun	Sep	Dec
2016	(3.35)	(0.38)	0.16	0.29
2017	0.16	0.18	0.19	0.72
2018	0.47	0.59	0.38	0.33
2019	0.02	(0.05)	(0.15)	...

Interim Dividends (Per Share)

Amt	Decl	Ex	Rec	Pay
0.05Q	03/27/2019	04/12/2019	04/15/2019	05/01/2019
0.05Q	06/26/2019	07/12/2019	07/15/2019	08/01/2019
0.05Q	09/25/2019	10/11/2019	10/15/2019	11/01/2019
0.05Q	12/18/2019	01/14/2020	01/15/2020	02/03/2020

Indicated Div: $0.20

Valuation Analysis / **Institutional Holding**

Forecast EPS	$0.01	No of Institutions
	(01/17/2020)	1225
Market Cap	$19.0 Billion	Shares
Book Value	$9.4 Billion	1,238,695,936
Price/Book	2.02	% Held
Price/Sales	1.34	71.26

Business Summary: Mining (MIC: 8.2.4 SIC: 1021 NAIC: 212234)

Freeport-McMoRan is a holding company. Through its subsidiaries, Co. is a mining company. Co. operates assets with proven and probable reserves of copper, gold and molybdenum, and Co. is a publicly traded copper producer. Co.'s portfolio of assets includes the Grasberg minerals district in Indonesia, a copper and gold deposits; and mining operations in the Americas, including the Morenci minerals district in North America and the Cerro Verde operation in South America. Co. has organized its mining operations into four primary divisions: North America copper mines, South America mining, Indonesia mining and Molybdenum mines.

Recent Developments: For the quarter ended Sep 30 2019, loss from continuing operations was US$235.0 million compared with income of US$668.0 million in the year-earlier quarter. Net loss amounted to US$234.0 million versus net income of US$664.0 million in the year-earlier quarter. Revenues were US$3.15 billion, down 35.8% from US$4.91 billion the year before. Operating income of US$38.0 million versus an income of US$1.32 billion in the prior-year quarter. Direct operating expenses declined 14.1% to US$3.03 billion from US$3.53 billion in the comparable period the year before. Indirect operating expenses increased 147.0% to US$163.0 million from US$66.0 million in the equivalent prior-year period.

Prospects: Our evaluation of Freeport-McMoRan Inc. as of October 4th, 2019 is the result of our systematic analysis on three basic characteristics: earnings strength, relative valuation, and recent stock price movement. The company has suffered a very negative trend in earnings per share over the past 5 quarters. In addition, recent analyst estimates for the company have been reduced while FCX has posted results that exceeded analysts' expectations. Based on operating earnings yield, the company is fairly valued when compared to all of the companies we cover. Share price changes over the past year indicates that FCX will perform in line with the market over the near term.

Financial Data

(US$ in Thousands)	9 Mos	6 Mos	3 Mos	12/31/2018	12/31/2017	12/31/2016	12/31/2015	12/31/2014
Earnings Per Share	0.15	0.68	1.32	1.78	1.25	(3.16)	(11.31)	(1.26)
Cash Flow Per Share	0.86	1.57	2.09	2.67	3.24	2.82	2.98	5.42
Tang Book Value Per Share	6.51	6.69	6.74	6.49	5.30	3.98	6.03	17.28
Dividends Per Share	0.200	0.200	0.200	0.150	...	...	0.573	1.250
Dividend Payout %	133.33	29.41	15.15	8.43	...	...	...	...
Income Statement								
Total Revenue	10,491,000	7,338,000	3,792,000	18,628,000	16,403,000	14,830,000	15,877,000	21,438,000
EBITDA	1,362,000	1,066,000	676,000	6,591,000	5,417,000	(107,000)	(9,879,000)	4,069,000
Depn & Amortn	1,021,000	699,000	347,000	1,754,000	1,714,000	2,610,000	3,497,000	3,863,000
Income Before Taxes	(60,000)	89,000	183,000	3,892,000	2,902,000	(3,472,000)	(14,021,000)	(424,000)
Income Taxes	181,000	90,000	105,000	991,000	883,000	371,000	(1,935,000)	324,000
Net Income	(248,000)	(41,000)	31,000	2,602,000	1,817,000	(4,315,000)	(12,195,000)	(1,268,000)
Average Shares	1,452,000	1,451,000	1,457,000	1,458,000	1,454,000	1,318,000	1,082,000	1,039,000
Balance Sheet								
Current Assets	8,347,000	8,730,000	9,045,000	10,720,000	10,779,000	10,435,000	7,462,000	9,045,000
Total Assets	40,943,000	41,086,000	41,059,000	42,216,000	37,302,000	37,317,000	46,577,000	58,795,000
Current Liabilities	3,381,000	3,286,000	3,247,000	3,329,000	5,038,000	4,265,000	4,307,000	5,172,000
Long-Term Obligations	9,915,000	9,912,000	9,902,000	11,124,000	11,703,000	14,795,000	19,779,000	18,492,000
Total Liabilities	31,499,000	31,377,000	31,276,000	32,418,000	29,325,000	31,266,000	38,749,000	40,508,000
Stockholders' Equity	9,444,000	9,709,000	9,783,000	9,798,000	7,977,000	6,051,000	7,828,000	18,287,000
Shares Outstanding	1,451,000	1,451,000	1,451,000	1,449,000	1,448,000	1,445,000	1,246,000	1,039,000
Statistical Record								
Return on Assets %	0.60	2.56	5.00	6.54	4.87	N.M.	N.M.	N.M.
Return on Equity %	2.44	10.43	21.05	29.28	25.91	N.M.	N.M.	N.M.
EBITDA Margin %	12.98	14.53	17.83	35.38	33.02	N.M.	N.M.	18.98
Net Margin %	N.M.	N.M.	0.82	13.97	11.08	N.M.	N.M.	N.M.
Asset Turnover	0.36	0.41	0.45	0.47	0.44	0.35	0.30	0.35
Current Ratio	2.47	2.66	2.79	3.22	2.14	2.45	1.73	1.75
Debt to Equity	1.05	1.02	1.01	1.14	1.47	2.45	2.53	1.01
Price Range	14.20-8.71	18.11-9.71	19.57-9.78	19.99-9.78	19.27-11.21	16.21-3.74	23.66-6.12	39.04-21.03
P/E Ratio	94.67-58.07	26.63-14.28	14.83-7.41	11.23-5.49	15.42-8.97	...	...	...
Average Yield %	1.75	1.58	1.43	0.96	...	...	3.70	3.80

Address: 333 North Central Avenue,	Web Site: www.fcx.com	Auditors: Ernst & Young LLP
Phoenix, AZ 85004-2189	Officers: Richard C. Adkerson - Vice-Chairman,	Investor Contact: 602-366-8400
Telephone: 602-366-8100	President, President (frmr), Chief Executive Officer,	Transfer Agents: Computershare,
	Chief Executive Officer (frmr), Chief Financial Officer	Canton, MA
	Kathleen L. Quirk - Executive Vice President, Chief	
	Financial Officer, Treasurer	

FULLER (HB) COMPANY

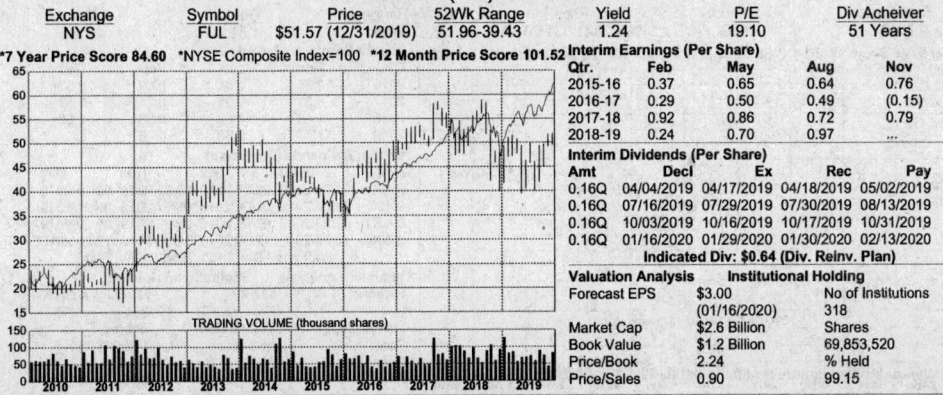

Exchange	Symbol	Price	52Wk Range	Yield	P/E	Div Acheiver
NYS	FUL	$51.57 (12/31/2019)	51.96-39.43	1.24	19.10	51 Years

*7 Year Price Score 84.60 *NYSE Composite Index=100 *12 Month Price Score 101.52

Interim Earnings (Per Share)

Qtr.	Feb	May	Aug	Nov
2015-16	0.37	0.65	0.64	0.76
2016-17	0.29	0.50	0.49	(0.15)
2017-18	0.92	0.86	0.72	0.79
2018-19	0.24	0.70	0.97	...

Interim Dividends (Per Share)

Amt	Decl	Ex	Rec	Pay
0.16Q	04/04/2019	04/17/2019	04/18/2019	05/02/2019
0.16Q	07/16/2019	07/29/2019	07/30/2019	08/13/2019
0.16Q	10/03/2019	10/16/2019	10/17/2019	10/31/2019
0.16Q	01/16/2020	01/29/2020	01/30/2020	02/13/2020

Indicated Div: $0.64 (Div. Reinv. Plan)

Valuation Analysis

		Institutional Holding	
Forecast EPS	$3.00 (01/16/2020)	No of Institutions	318
Market Cap	$2.6 Billion	Shares	
Book Value	$1.2 Billion		69,853,520
Price/Book	2.24	% Held	
Price/Sales	0.90		99.15

Business Summary: Specialty Chemicals (MIC: 8.3.2 SIC: 2891 NAIC: 325520)

H.B. Fuller is a formulator, manufacturer and marketer of adhesives, sealants and other chemical products. Co.'s principal product offering is Industrial adhesives. Co.'s adhesives products are used in manufacturing common consumer and industrial goods, including food and beverage containers, disposable diapers, windows, doors, flooring, roofing, appliances, sportswear, footwear, multi-wall bags, water filtration products, insulation, textiles, automobiles, recreational vehicles, buses, trucks and trailers, marine products, solar energy systems, electronics and products for the aerospace and defense industries. Co. also provides its customers with technical support and solutions.

Recent Developments: For the quarter ended Aug 31 2019, net income increased 31.8% to US$49.7 million from US$37.7 million in the year-earlier quarter. Revenues were US$725.4 million, down 5.8% from US$770.1 million the year before. Direct operating expenses declined 6.7% to US$518.1 million from US$555.1 million in the comparable period the year before. Indirect operating expenses decreased 4.8% to US$140.6 million from US$147.7 million in the equivalent prior-year period.

Prospects: Our evaluation of Fuller (H.B.) Company as of October 4th, 2019 is the result of our systematic analysis on three basic characteristics: earnings strength, relative valuation, and recent stock price movement. The company has managed to produce a neutral trend in earnings per share over the past 5 quarters. However, recent analyst estimates for the company have been reduced and FUL has posted results that fell short of analysts' expectations. Based on operating earnings yield, the company is undervalued when compared to all of the companies we cover. Share price changes over the past year indicates that FUL will perform very poorly over the near term.

Financial Data

(US$ in Thousands)	9 Mos	6 Mos	3 Mos	12/01/2018	12/02/2017	12/03/2016	11/28/2015	11/29/2014
Earnings Per Share	2.70	2.45	2.61	3.29	1.13	2.42	1.69	0.97
Cash Flow Per Share	6.02	...	...	5.02	2.80	3.84	4.20	0.60
Tang Book Value Per Share	N.M.	N.M.	N.M.	N.M.	N.M.	7.30	6.11	8.71
Dividends Per Share	0.630	0.625	0.620	0.615	0.590	0.550	0.510	0.460
Dividend Payout %	23.33	25.51	23.75	18.69	52.21	22.73	30.18	47.42
Income Statement								
Total Revenue	2,157,894	1,432,518	672,935	3,041,002	2,306,043	2,094,605	2,083,660	2,104,454
EBITDA	308,949	184,701	73,631	324,582	149,545	241,928	211,161	145,966
Depn & Amortn	106,538	71,758	36,054	68,636	51,072	49,189	48,305	47,254
Income Before Taxes	132,248	65,272	13,823	156,726	58,699	167,425	138,345	79,312
Income Taxes	38,902	19,581	3,140	(6,356)	9,086	50,436	55,855	34,348
Net Income	98,603	48,885	12,244	171,208	58,242	124,128	86,680	49,773
Average Shares	51,502	52,105	51,901	51,975	51,619	51,270	51,393	51,255
Balance Sheet								
Current Assets	1,080,890	1,108,759	1,092,665	1,087,732	1,144,992	811,253	801,051	765,136
Total Assets	4,032,683	4,149,864	4,166,100	4,175,271	4,360,646	2,058,254	2,042,252	1,869,006
Current Liabilities	457,587	517,576	520,875	546,123	504,913	391,844	349,525	317,199
Long-Term Obligations	2,080,336	2,148,653	2,146,152	2,141,532	2,398,927	588,145	669,606	547,735
Total Liabilities	2,857,084	2,987,282	2,992,407	3,023,504	3,317,019	1,120,378	1,169,332	978,959
Stockholders' Equity	1,175,599	1,162,582	1,173,693	1,151,767	1,043,627	937,876	872,920	890,047
Shares Outstanding	50,953	50,917	50,883	50,732	50,388	50,141	50,074	50,310
Statistical Record								
Return on Assets %	3.36	...	...	4.02	1.81	5.96	4.44	2.67
Return on Equity %	12.15	...	...	15.64	5.88	13.49	9.86	5.48
EBITDA Margin %	14.32	12.89	10.94	10.67	6.48	11.55	10.13	6.94
Net Margin %	4.57	3.41	1.82	5.63	2.53	5.93	4.16	2.37
Asset Turnover	0.70	...	...	0.71	0.72	1.01	1.07	1.13
Current Ratio	2.36	2.14	2.10	1.99	2.27	2.07	2.29	2.41
Debt to Equity	1.77	1.85	1.83	1.86	2.30	0.63	0.77	0.62
Price Range	58.46-39.43	58.97-39.43	58.97-39.83	58.97-42.07	58.64-47.09	48.82-32.71	45.74-32.73	52.74-37.46
P/E Ratio	21.65-14.60	24.07-16.09	22.59-15.26	17.92-12.79	51.89-41.67	20.17-13.52	27.07-19.37	54.37-38.62
Average Yield %	1.34	1.26	1.23	1.18	1.14	1.28	1.25	0.99

Address: 1200 Willow Lake Boulevard, St. Paul, MN 55110-5101	Web Site: www.hbfuller.com	Auditors: KPMG LLP
Telephone: 651-236-5900	Officers: Lee R. Mitau - Chairman R. William Van Sant - Vice-Chairman	Investor Contact: 651-236-5062
Fax: 651-236-5161		Transfer Agents: Wells Fargo Shareholder Services, St. Paul, MN

GALLAGHER (ARTHUR J.) & CO.

Exchange	Symbol	Price	52Wk Range	Yield	P/E
NYS	AJG	$95.23 (12/31/2019)	95.67-70.54	1.81	26.23

*7 Year Price Score 124.53 ***NYSE Composite Index=100** ***12 Month Price Score 102.75**

Interim Earnings (Per Share)

Qtr.	Mar	Jun	Sep	Dec
2016	0.26	0.84	0.69	0.53
2017	0.31	0.95	0.71	0.57
2018	1.48	0.62	0.68	0.62
2019	1.77	0.58	0.66	...

Interim Dividends (Per Share)

Amt	Decl	Ex	Rec	Pay
0.43Q	01/30/2019	02/28/2019	03/01/2019	03/15/2019
0.43Q	04/24/2019	06/06/2019	06/07/2019	06/21/2019
0.43Q	07/24/2019	09/05/2019	09/06/2019	09/20/2019
0.43Q	10/23/2019	12/05/2019	12/06/2019	12/20/2019

Indicated Div: $1.72 (Div. Reinv. Plan)

Valuation Analysis / **Institutional Holding**

Forecast EPS	$3.58	No of Institutions	
	(01/17/2020)	884	
Market Cap	$14.9 Billion	Shares	
Book Value	$4.8 Billion	196,083,360	
Price/Book	3.08	% Held	
Price/Sales	2.09	85.33	

Business Summary: Brokers & Intermediaries (MIC: 5.2.3 SIC: 6411 NAIC: 524210)

Arthur J. Gallagher & Co. is a holding company. Through its subsidiaries, Co. provides insurance brokerage, consulting, and third-party claims settlement and administration services to both domestic and international entities. Co. segments are: brokerage, which provides brokerage and consulting services to companies and entities and, to a lesser extent, individuals, in the areas of insurance placement, risk of loss management, and management of employer sponsored benefit programs; risk management, which provides contract claim settlement, claim administration, loss control services and risk management consulting; and corporate, which is involved in clean energy investments.

Recent Developments: For the quarter ended Sep 30 2019, net income decreased 0.9% to US$137.1 million from US$138.4 million in the year-earlier quarter. Revenues were US$1.83 billion, up 2.6% from US$1.78 billion the year before.

Prospects: Our evaluation of Gallagher (Arthur J.) & Co. as of October 4th, 2019 is the result of our systematic analysis on three basic characteristics: earnings strength, relative valuation, and recent stock price movement. The company has produced a positive trend in earnings per share over the past 5 quarters. However, recent analyst estimates for the company have been reduced, while AJG has posted results that exceeded analysts' expectations. Based on operating earnings yield, the company is fairly valued when compared to all of the companies we cover. Share price changes over the past year indicates that AJG will perform well over the near term.

Financial Data

(US$ in Thousands)	9 Mos	6 Mos	3 Mos	12/31/2018	12/31/2017	12/31/2016	12/31/2015	12/31/2014
Earnings Per Share	3.63	3.65	3.69	3.40	2.54	2.32	2.06	1.97
Cash Flow Per Share	5.53	4.69	4.80	4.19	4.74	3.49	3.79	2.63
Dividends Per Share	1.700	1.680	1.660	1.640	1.560	1.520	1.480	1.440
Dividend Payout %	46.83	46.03	44.99	48.24	61.42	65.52	71.84	73.10
Income Statement								
Total Revenue	5,473,600	3,648,400	1,990,600	6,934,000	6,159,600	5,594,800	5,392,400	4,626,500
EBITDA	681,300	519,300	365,800	607,200	499,200	460,500	387,400	336,800
Depn & Amortn	139,200	92,000	44,000	127,800	121,100	103,600	93,900	69,400
Income Before Taxes	542,100	427,300	321,800	479,400	378,100	356,900	293,500	267,400
Income Taxes	(68,100)	(45,800)	(29,900)	(196,500)	(121,100)	(88,100)	(95,600)	(36,000)
Net Income	570,300	444,200	334,100	633,500	463,100	414,400	356,800	303,400
Average Shares	190,700	189,800	188,400	186,200	182,100	178,400	173,200	154,300
Balance Sheet								
Current Assets	9,328,600	9,547,400	9,669,500	8,118,700	5,170,600	4,416,100	4,335,800	3,811,200
Total Assets	19,173,800	19,200,300	18,631,400	16,334,000	12,897,400	11,489,600	10,913,800	10,010,000
Current Liabilities	8,910,900	8,932,500	8,637,900	7,693,600	4,912,300	4,611,700	4,191,700	3,642,700
Long-Term Obligations	3,815,800	3,815,600	3,690,300	3,091,400	2,691,900	2,144,600	2,075,000	2,125,000
Total Liabilities	14,330,500	14,320,900	13,751,100	11,835,100	8,792,200	7,893,000	7,275,500	6,780,600
Stockholders' Equity	4,843,300	4,879,400	4,880,300	4,498,900	4,105,200	3,596,600	3,638,300	3,229,400
Shares Outstanding	156,500	186,070	185,300	184,000	181,000	178,300	176,900	164,600
Statistical Record								
Return on Assets %	3.90	3.89	3.99	4.33	3.80	3.69	3.41	3.60
Return on Equity %	14.65	14.78	14.77	14.73	12.03	11.42	10.39	11.42
EBITDA Margin %	12.45	14.23	18.38	8.76	8.10	8.23	7.18	7.28
Net Margin %	10.42	12.18	16.78	9.14	7.52	7.41	6.62	6.56
Asset Turnover	0.40	0.40	0.41	0.47	0.51	0.50	0.52	0.55
Current Ratio	1.05	1.07	1.12	1.06	1.05	0.96	1.03	1.05
Debt to Equity	0.79	0.78	0.76	0.69	0.66	0.60	0.57	0.66
Price Range	92.37-68.99	87.82-65.26	80.64-64.77	78.38-62.17	66.96-52.24	52.12-36.24	49.50-40.08	49.39-43.59
P/E Ratio	25.45-19.01	24.06-17.88	21.85-17.55	23.05-18.29	26.36-20.57	22.47-15.62	24.03-19.46	25.07-22.13
Average Yield %	2.09	2.19	2.28	2.33	2.66	3.27	3.23	3.11

Address: 2850 Golf Road, Rolling Meadows, IL 60008 **Telephone:** 630-773-3800	**Web Site:** www.ajg.com **Officers:** J. Patrick (Pat) Gallagher - Chairman, President, Chief Executive Officer Douglas K. (Doug) Howell - Corporate Vice-President, Chief Financial Officer	**Auditors:** Ernst & Young LLP **Investor Contact:** 630-285-3501 **Transfer Agents:** Computershare Investor Services, Canton, MA

GAMESTOP CORP

Exchange	Symbol	Price	52Wk Range	Yield	P/E
NYS	GME	$6.08 (12/31/2019)	15.98-3.21	N/A	N/A

*7 Year Price Score 22.75   *NYSE Composite Index=100   *12 Month Price Score 74.56

Interim Earnings (Per Share)

Qtr.	Apr	Jul	Oct	Jan
2016-17	0.63	0.27	0.49	2.01
2017-18	0.58	0.22	0.59	(1.05)
2018-19	0.28	(0.24)	(4.78)	(1.83)
2019-20	0.07	(4.15)	(1.02)	...

Interim Dividends (Per Share)

Amt	Decl	Ex	Rec	Pay
0.38Q	05/31/2018	06/11/2018	06/12/2018	06/26/2018
0.38Q	09/04/2018	09/17/2018	09/18/2018	10/02/2018
0.38Q	11/27/2018	12/10/2018	12/11/2018	12/21/2018
0.38Q	03/04/2019	03/14/2019	03/15/2019	03/29/2019

Valuation Analysis | **Institutional Holding**

Forecast EPS	$0.00
(01/17/2020)	
Market Cap	$412.8 Million
Book Value	$617.1 Million
Price/Book	0.67
Price/Sales	0.06

No of Institutions	514
Shares	131,653,984
% Held	42.85

TRADING VOLUME (thousand shares)

Business Summary: Retail - Appliances and Electronics (MIC: 2.1.7 SIC: 5734 NAIC: 443120)

GameStop is a multichannel video game and licensed consumer products retailer. Co.'s products and services includes: New Video Game Hardware, which provides video game platforms from manufacturers; New Video Game Software, which provides new video game software for existing and certain prior generation consoles from manufacturers, including Sony, Nintendo and Microsoft; Video Game Accessories, which consist primarily of controllers, gaming headsets, virtual reality products, and memory cards; and Digital, which sells a variety of digital currency and has developed technology to sell downloadable content and full-game downloads in its stores and on its U.S. website.

Recent Developments: For the quarter ended Nov 2 2019, loss from continuing operations was US$83.2 million compared with a loss of US$506.9 million in the year-earlier quarter. Net loss amounted to US$83.4 million versus a net loss of US$488.6 million in the year-earlier quarter. Revenues were US$1.44 billion, down 25.7% from US$1.94 billion the year before. Operating loss was US$45.6 million versus a loss of US$517.9 million in the prior-year quarter. Direct operating expenses declined 27.6% to US$997.4 million from US$1.38 billion in the comparable period the year before. Indirect operating expenses decreased 54.8% to US$486.7 million from US$1.08 billion in the equivalent prior-year period.

Prospects: Our evaluation of GameStop Corp. as of October 4th, 2019 is the result of our systematic analysis on three basic characteristics: earnings strength, relative valuation, and recent stock price movement. The company has enjoyed a very positive trend in earnings per share over the past 5 quarters. However, recent analyst estimates for the company have been reduced, and GME has posted results that fell short of analysts' expectations. Based on operating earnings yield, the company is undervalued when compared to all of the companies we cover. Share price changes over the past year indicates that GME will perform very poorly over the near term.

Financial Data
(US$ in Thousands)

	9 Mos	6 Mos	3 Mos	02/02/2019	02/03/2018	01/28/2017	01/30/2016	01/31/2015
Earnings Per Share	(6.93)	(10.69)	(6.78)	(6.59)	0.34	3.40	3.78	3.47
Cash Flow Per Share	(1.83)	1.08	1.88	3.19	4.22	5.21	6.21	4.29
Tang Book Value Per Share	9.09	8.95	9.07	9.20	3.73	0.21	2.65	4.08
Dividends Per Share	0.760	1.140	1.520	1.520	1.520	1.480	1.440	1.320
Dividend Payout %	...	...	...	...	447.06	43.53	38.10	38.04
Income Statement								
Total Revenue	4,271,900	2,833,400	1,547,700	8,285,300	9,224,600	8,607,900	9,363,800	9,296,000
EBITDA	(404,700)	(383,000)	40,800	(605,300)	274,000	709,400	793,100	762,800
Depn & Amortn	70,100	46,200	23,300	96,700	138,400	151,700	144,900	144,500
Income Before Taxes	(495,500)	(443,900)	9,800	(753,100)	80,300	504,700	625,200	608,300
Income Taxes	(6,200)	(37,800)	2,300	41,700	45,600	151,500	222,400	215,200
Net Income	(491,900)	(408,500)	6,800	(673,000)	34,700	353,200	402,800	393,100
Average Shares	82,100	100,000	102,500	102,100	101,500	103,800	106,700	113,200
Balance Sheet								
Current Assets	1,863,100	1,667,600	1,920,100	3,127,700	2,538,700	2,140,700	1,938,800	2,062,500
Total Assets	3,145,600	2,987,900	3,633,300	4,044,300	5,041,600	4,975,900	4,334,900	4,246,300
Current Liabilities	1,573,500	1,216,800	1,297,300	2,181,100	1,915,600	1,761,500	1,794,400	1,639,700
Long-Term Obligations	419,400	419,100	468,900	471,600	817,900	815,000	350,000	350,600
Total Liabilities	2,528,500	2,178,200	2,341,600	2,708,100	2,827,100	2,721,800	2,253,900	2,178,600
Stockholders' Equity	617,100	809,700	1,291,700	1,336,200	2,214,500	2,254,100	2,081,000	2,067,700
Shares Outstanding	67,900	90,500	102,300	102,000	101,300	101,000	103,300	107,700
Statistical Record								
Return on Assets %	N.M.	N.M.	N.M.	N.M.	0.68	7.61	9.41	9.46
Return on Equity %	N.M.	N.M.	N.M.	N.M.	1.53	16.34	19.47	18.25
EBITDA Margin %	N.M.	N.M.	2.64	N.M.	2.97	8.24	8.47	8.21
Net Margin %	N.M.	N.M.	0.44	N.M.	0.38	4.10	4.30	4.23
Asset Turnover	1.77	2.07	1.99	1.83	1.81	1.85	2.19	2.24
Current Ratio	1.18	1.37	1.48	1.43	1.33	1.22	1.08	1.26
Debt to Equity	0.68	0.52	0.36	0.35	0.37	0.36	0.17	0.17
Price Range	15.98-3.21	17.04-3.78	17.04-8.51	17.04-11.20	26.52-16.00	33.38-20.73	47.44-25.06	46.10-31.92
P/E Ratio	...	...	...	...	78.00-47.06	9.82-6.10	12.55-6.63	13.29-9.20
Average Yield %	8.71	9.98	11.29	10.47	7.22	5.33	3.62	3.36

Address: 625 Westport Parkway, Grapevine, TX 76051
Telephone: 817-424-2000

Web Site: www.gamestop.com
Officers: Daniel A. (Dan) DeMatteo - Executive Chairman, Interim Chief Executive Officer, Interim Chief Executive Officer George E. Sherman - Chief Executive Officer

Auditors: DELOITTE & TOUCHE LLP
Transfer Agents: Computershare, Providence, RI

GARDNER DENVER HOLDINGS INC

Exchange	Symbol	Price	52Wk Range	Yield	P/E
NYS	GDI	$36.68 (12/31/2019)	36.95-20.45	N/A	33.35

*7 Year Price Score N/A   *NYSE Composite Index=100   *12 Month Price Score 106.43

TRADING VOLUME (thousand shares)

Interim Earnings (Per Share)

Qtr.	Mar	Jun	Sep	Dec
2017	(0.05)	(0.83)	0.13	0.81
2018	0.20	0.29	0.35	0.46
2019	0.23	0.21	0.20	...

Interim Dividends (Per Share)

No Dividends Paid

Valuation Analysis		Institutional Holding	
Forecast EPS	$1.57	No of Institutions	
	(01/17/2020)	244	
Market Cap	$7.5 Billion	Shares	
Book Value	$1.8 Billion	211,476,144	
Price/Book	4.19	% Held	
Price/Sales	2.93	102.82	

Business Summary: Industrial Machinery & Equipment (MIC: 7.2.1 SIC: 3569 NAIC: 332710)

Gardner Denver is a holding company. Through its subsidiaries, Co. is a provider of flow control and compression equipment and associated aftermarket parts, consumables and services. Co.'s segments are: Industrials, which designs, manufactures, markets and services air compression, vacuum and blower products; Energy, which designs, manufactures, markets and services positive displacement pumps, liquid ring vacuum pumps, compressors and integrated systems, engineered fluid loading and transfer equipment and associated aftermarket parts, consumables and services; and Medical, which designs, manufactures and market gas, liquid and precision syringe pumps and compressors.

Recent Developments: For the quarter ended Sep 30 2019, net income decreased 42.8% to US$41.3 million from US$72.2 million in the year-earlier quarter. Revenues were US$596.7 million, down 13.4% from US$689.3 million the year before. Operating income was US$72.9 million versus US$117.7 million in the prior-year quarter, a decrease of 38.1%. Direct operating expenses declined 12.1% to US$375.2 million from US$426.9 million in the comparable period the year before. Indirect operating expenses increased 2.7% to US$148.6 million from US$144.7 million in the equivalent prior-year period.

Prospects: Our evaluation of Gardner Denver Holdings Inc. as of October 4th, 2019 is the result of our systematic analysis on three basic characteristics: earnings strength, relative valuation, and recent stock price movement. The company has managed to produce a neutral trend in earnings per share over the past 5 quarters. However, recent analyst estimates for the company have been reduced while GDI has posted results that exceeded analysts' expectations. Based on operating earnings yield, the company is undervalued when compared to all of the companies we cover. Share price changes over the past year indicates that GDI will perform well over the near term.

Financial Data

(US$ in Thousands)	9 Mos	6 Mos	3 Mos	12/31/2018	12/31/2017	12/31/2016	12/31/2015	12/31/2014
Earnings Per Share	1.10	1.25	1.33	1.29	0.10	(0.25)	(2.35)	(0.91)
Cash Flow Per Share	1.91	1.87	2.25	2.20	1.10	1.11	1.15	0.95
Income Statement								
Total Revenue	1,846,100	1,249,400	620,300	2,689,800	2,375,400	1,939,436	2,126,885	2,570,005
EBITDA	363,500	247,100	127,000	629,500	201,800	279,913	(40,807)	211,797
Depn & Amortn	132,900	89,900	45,500	180,400	173,800	172,725	163,024	160,350
Income Before Taxes	162,600	112,400	59,100	349,500	(112,700)	(63,150)	(366,692)	(112,929)
Income Taxes	29,200	20,300	12,000	80,100	(131,200)	(31,860)	(14,704)	22,996
Net Income	133,400	92,100	47,100	269,400	18,400	(36,620)	(351,153)	(135,023)
Average Shares	209,000	208,900	207,700	209,100	188,400	149,184	149,646	148,883
Balance Sheet								
Current Assets	1,494,100	1,463,900	1,398,300	1,331,200	1,463,600	1,188,513	1,157,358	...
Total Assets	4,553,800	4,594,300	4,566,800	4,487,100	4,621,200	4,315,948	4,462,046	...
Current Liabilities	595,800	591,800	616,200	596,400	561,800	497,849	431,279	...
Long-Term Obligations	1,593,800	1,623,500	1,622,300	1,664,200	2,019,300	2,753,794	2,769,459	...
Total Liabilities	2,763,300	2,809,000	2,829,100	2,811,100	3,144,400	4,050,040	4,071,813	...
Stockholders' Equity	1,790,500	1,785,300	1,737,700	1,676,000	1,476,800	265,908	390,233	...
Shares Outstanding	204,543	203,924	200,864	198,169	196,217	148,654	149,669	...
Statistical Record								
Return on Assets %	5.02	5.62	5.87	5.92	0.41	N.M.	...	...
Return on Equity %	13.35	15.42	16.58	17.09	2.11	N.M.	...	...
EBITDA Margin %	19.69	19.78	20.47	23.40	8.50	14.43	N.M.	8.24
Net Margin %	7.23	7.37	7.59	10.02	0.77	N.M.	N.M.	N.M.
Asset Turnover	0.56	0.58	0.58	0.59	0.53	0.44	...	...
Current Ratio	2.51	2.48	2.27	2.23	2.61	2.39	2.68	...
Debt to Equity	0.89	0.91	0.93	0.99	1.37	10.36	7.10	...
Price Range	35.89-18.92	35.89-18.92	34.46-18.92	36.69-18.92	34.43-20.47	...	...	...
P/E Ratio	32.63-17.20	28.71-15.14	25.91-14.23	28.44-14.67	344.30-204.70	...	...	...

Address: 222 East Erie Street, Suite 500, Milwaukee, WI 53202
Telephone: 414-212-4700

Web Site: www.gardnerdenver.com
Officers: Peter M. Stavros – Chairman Vicente Reynal – Chief Executive Officer

Auditors: DELOITTE & TOUCHE LLP
Investor Contact: 414-212-4700
Transfer Agents: American Stock Transfer & Trust Company, LLC

GARTNER INC

Exchange	Symbol	Price	52Wk Range	Yield	P/E
NYS	IT	$154.10 (12/31/2019)	171.04-123.19	N/A	56.45

*7 Year Price Score 120.40 *NYSE Composite Index=100 *12 Month Price Score 100.92

TRADING VOLUME (thousand shares)

Interim Earnings (Per Share)

Qtr.	Mar	Jun	Sep	Dec
2016	0.48	0.57	0.36	0.79
2017	0.43	(1.03)	(0.53)	1.23
2018	(0.22)	0.50	0.13	0.91
2019	0.23	1.13	0.46	...

Interim Dividends (Per Share)

No Dividends Paid

Valuation Analysis

		Institutional Holding	
Forecast EPS	$3.54	No of Institutions	
	(01/08/2020)	629	
Market Cap	$13.8 Billion	Shares	
Book Value	$919.7 Million	152,940,928	
Price/Book	14.99	% Held	
Price/Sales	3.34	94.94	

Business Summary: Business Services (MIC: 7.5.2 SIC: 8741 NAIC: 561110)

Gartner is a research and advisory company. Co.'s principal products and services are delivered through its three business segments: Research, which provides insights and advice across various functional areas of the enterprise through research and other reports, briefings, proprietary tools, access to Co.'s analysts and advisors, peer networking services and membership programs; Conferences, which provides business personnel across the organization the opportunity to learn, share and network; and Consulting, which provides customized solutions to client needs through on-site, day-to-day support, as well as proprietary tools for measuring and improving information technology performance.

Recent Developments: For the quarter ended Sep 30 2019, net income increased 252.1% to US$41.4 million from US$11.8 million in the year-earlier quarter. Revenues were US$1.00 billion, up 8.6% from US$921.7 million the year before. Operating income was US$69.1 million versus US$52.7 million in the prior-year quarter, an increase of 31.1%. Direct operating expenses rose 8.6% to US$365.1 million from US$336.1 million in the comparable period the year before. Indirect operating expenses increased 6.3% to US$566.3 million from US$532.8 million in the equivalent prior-year period.

Prospects: Our evaluation of Gartner Inc. as of October 4th, 2019 is the result of our systematic analysis on three basic characteristics: earnings strength, relative valuation, and recent stock price movement. The company has generated a negative trend in earnings per share over the past 5 quarters. However, recent analyst estimates for the company have been unchanged while IT has posted results that exceeded analysts' expectations. Based on operating earnings yield, the company is overvalued when compared to all of the companies we cover. Share price changes over the past year indicates that IT will perform in line with the market over the near term.

Financial Data

(US$ in Thousands)	9 Mos	6 Mos	3 Mos	12/31/2018	12/31/2017	12/31/2016	12/31/2015	12/31/2014
Earnings Per Share	2.73	2.40	1.77	1.33	0.04	2.31	2.06	2.03
Cash Flow Per Share	5.87	6.19	5.61	5.19	2.88	4.42	4.12	3.88
Income Statement								
Total Revenue	3,041,828	2,041,326	970,444	3,975,454	3,311,494	2,444,540	2,163,056	2,021,441
EBITDA	367,961	247,323	88,230	560,938	237,293	375,544	340,135	324,996
Depn & Amortn	129,135	85,668	42,330	255,609	240,174	61,997	47,142	39,426
Income Before Taxes	165,157	112,059	21,053	181,121	(127,817)	288,431	272,211	274,683
Income Taxes	(432)	(12,142)	258	58,665	(131,096)	94,849	96,576	90,917
Net Income	165,589	124,201	20,795	122,456	3,279	193,582	175,635	183,766
Average Shares	90,887	91,188	91,004	92,122	89,790	83,820	85,056	90,719
Balance Sheet								
Current Assets	1,706,505	1,691,104	1,716,013	1,811,739	2,588,608	1,343,196	1,140,997	1,096,658
Total Assets	6,737,344	6,729,641	6,714,675	6,201,474	7,283,173	2,367,335	2,174,686	1,904,351
Current Liabilities	2,527,263	2,482,151	2,568,918	2,620,935	2,822,585	1,460,249	1,323,492	1,215,218
Long-Term Obligations	2,051,507	2,059,131	2,094,758	2,116,109	2,899,124	664,391	790,000	385,000
Total Liabilities	5,817,687	5,765,839	5,857,778	5,350,717	6,299,708	2,306,457	2,307,086	1,743,180
Stockholders' Equity	919,657	963,802	856,897	850,757	983,465	60,878	(132,400)	161,171
Shares Outstanding	89,477	90,136	90,082	89,702	90,822	82,651	82,338	87,520
Statistical Record								
Return on Assets %	3.94	3.42	2.39	1.82	0.07	8.50	8.61	9.97
Return on Equity %	26.82	23.34	17.66	13.35	0.63	...	1,220.92	70.34
EBITDA Margin %	12.10	12.12	9.09	14.11	7.17	15.36	15.72	16.08
Net Margin %	5.44	6.08	2.14	3.08	0.10	7.92	8.12	9.09
Asset Turnover	0.65	0.63	0.58	0.59	0.69	1.07	1.06	1.10
Current Ratio	0.68	0.68	0.67	0.69	0.92	0.92	0.86	0.90
Debt to Equity	2.23	2.14	2.44	2.49	2.95	10.91	...	2.39
Price Range	171.04-123.06	161.84-123.06	160.00-115.06	160.00-113.41	129.53-90.56	104.93-79.86	93.87-77.92	87.40-62.51
P/E Ratio	62.65-45.08	67.43-51.28	90.40-65.01	120.30-85.27	N.M.	45.42-34.57	45.57-37.83	43.05-30.79

Address: P.O. Box 10212, 56 Top Gallant Road, Stamford, CT 06902-7700 Telephone: 203-316-1111	Web Site: www.gartner.com Officers: James C. Smith - Chairman Eugene A. (Gene) Hall - Chief Executive Officer	Auditors: KPMG LLP Investor Contact: 203-316-6537 Transfer Agents: American Stock Transfer & Trust Company, LLC, New York, NY

GATX CORP

Exchange	Symbol	Price	52Wk Range	Yield	P/E
NYS	GATX	$82.85 (12/31/2019)	85.19-67.99	2.22	14.95

*7 Year Price Score 104.95 *NYSE Composite Index=100 *12 Month Price Score 101.90

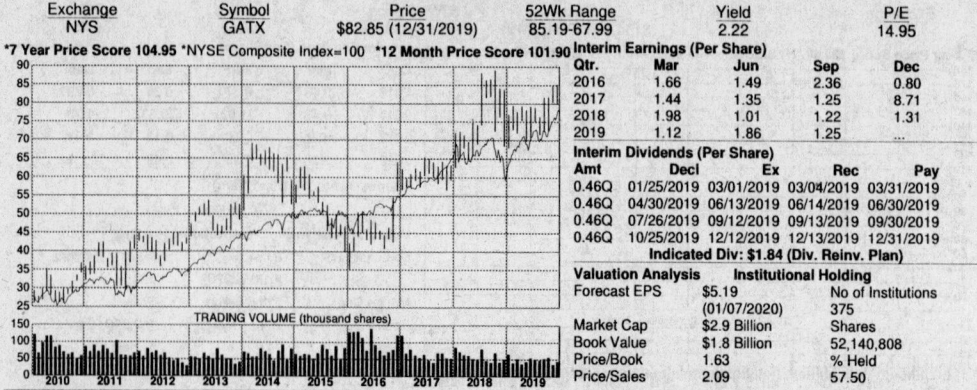

Interim Earnings (Per Share)

Qtr.	Mar	Jun	Sep	Dec
2016	1.66	1.49	2.36	0.80
2017	1.44	1.35	1.25	8.71
2018	1.98	1.01	1.22	1.31
2019	1.12	1.86	1.25	...

Interim Dividends (Per Share)

Amt	Decl	Ex	Rec	Pay
0.46Q	01/25/2019	03/01/2019	03/04/2019	03/31/2019
0.46Q	04/30/2019	06/13/2019	06/14/2019	06/30/2019
0.46Q	07/26/2019	09/12/2019	09/13/2019	09/30/2019
0.46Q	10/25/2019	12/12/2019	12/13/2019	12/31/2019

Indicated Div: $1.84 (Div. Reinv. Plan)

Valuation Analysis / **Institutional Holding**

Forecast EPS	$5.19	No of Institutions
	(01/07/2020)	375
Market Cap	$2.9 Billion	Shares
Book Value	$1.8 Billion	52,140,808
Price/Book	1.63	% Held
Price/Sales	2.09	57.50

Business Summary: Miscellaneous Transportation Services (MIC: 7.4.5 SIC: 4741 NAIC: 488210)

GATX is a railcar lessor, owning fleets in North America, Europe, and Asia. In addition, Co. operates a fleet of U.S.-flagged vessels on the Great Lakes and jointly with Rolls-Royce plc, Co. owns aircraft spare engine lease portfolios. Co. has four business segments: Rail North America, which is composed of Co.'s operations in the U.S., Canada, and Mexico; Rail International, which is composed of Co.'s operations in Europe, India, and Russia; American Steamship Company, which provides waterborne transportation of dry bulk commodities; and Portfolio Management, which is composed primarily of Co.'s ownership in a group of joint ventures with Rolls-Royce plc that lease aircraft spare engines.

Recent Developments: For the quarter ended Sep 30 2019, net income decreased 4.0% to US$45.1 million from US$47.0 million in the year-earlier quarter. Revenues were US$360.7 million, up 3.1% from US$349.7 million the year before. Direct operating expenses rose 5.3% to US$221.4 million from US$210.3 million in the comparable period the year before. Indirect operating expenses decreased 5.3% to US$52.1 million from US$55.0 million in the equivalent prior-year period.

Prospects: Our evaluation of GATX Corp. as of October 4th, 2019 is the result of our systematic analysis on three basic characteristics: earnings strength, relative valuation, and recent stock price movement. The company has managed to produce a neutral trend in earnings per share over the past 5 quarters. Additionally, recent analyst estimates for the company have been unchanged while GATX has posted results that exceeded analysts' expectations. Based on operating earnings yield, the company is undervalued when compared to all of the companies we cover. Share price changes over the past year indicates that GATX will perform poorly over the near term.

Financial Data

(US$ in Thousands)	9 Mos	6 Mos	3 Mos	12/31/2018	12/31/2017	12/31/2016	12/31/2015	12/31/2014
Earnings Per Share	5.54	5.51	4.66	5.52	12.75	6.29	4.69	4.48
Cash Flow Per Share	13.12	13.27	13.58	13.52	12.80	15.42	12.40	9.98
Tang Book Value Per Share	48.64	49.13	47.72	46.57	45.05	32.18	28.60	27.78
Dividends Per Share	1.820	1.800	1.780	1.760	1.680	1.600	1.520	1.320
Dividend Payout %	32.85	32.67	38.20	31.88	13.18	25.44	32.41	29.46
Income Statement								
Total Revenue	1,037,100	676,400	317,000	1,360,900	1,376,900	1,418,300	1,449,900	1,451,000
EBITDA	542,400	365,600	164,400	701,900	697,600	763,700	728,700	676,600
Depn & Amortn	255,600	169,300	82,700	338,200	322,700	310,200	303,300	287,000
Income Before Taxes	146,900	102,700	35,200	195,100	214,400	305,400	270,300	231,200
Income Taxes	35,900	24,000	8,400	34,100	(243,700)	95,700	110,900	75,700
Net Income	154,600	109,500	41,500	211,300	502,000	257,100	205,300	205,000
Average Shares	36,000	36,700	37,100	38,300	39,400	40,900	43,800	45,800
Balance Sheet								
Current Assets	229,000	474,000	447,300	313,700	512,800	538,600	455,200	576,700
Total Assets	8,090,900	8,353,100	8,240,200	7,616,700	7,422,400	7,105,400	6,894,200	6,937,500
Current Liabilities	250,400	178,800	171,700	288,300	158,600	178,600	178,300	238,000
Long-Term Obligations	4,580,200	4,843,100	4,779,100	4,441,000	4,384,200	4,268,100	4,196,800	4,202,100
Total Liabilities	6,304,400	6,518,300	6,431,000	5,828,600	5,629,700	5,758,200	5,614,000	5,623,500
Stockholders' Equity	1,786,500	1,834,800	1,809,200	1,788,100	1,792,700	1,347,200	1,280,200	1,314,000
Shares Outstanding	35,089	35,665	36,203	36,612	37,895	39,442	41,970	44,198
Statistical Record								
Return on Assets %	2.61	2.60	2.25	2.81	6.91	3.66	2.97	3.04
Return on Equity %	11.25	11.26	9.67	11.80	31.98	19.52	15.83	15.12
EBITDA Margin %	52.30	54.05	51.86	51.58	50.66	53.85	50.26	46.63
Net Margin %	14.91	16.19	13.09	15.53	36.46	18.13	14.16	14.13
Asset Turnover	0.18	0.17	0.17	0.18	0.19	0.20	0.21	0.22
Current Ratio	0.91	2.65	2.61	1.09	3.23	3.02	2.55	2.42
Debt to Equity	2.56	2.64	2.64	2.48	2.45	3.17	3.28	3.20
Price Range	89.08-67.99	89.08-67.99	89.08-65.24	89.08-62.71	65.54-56.54	64.17-35.12	62.95-39.87	69.10-51.00
P/E Ratio	16.08-12.27	16.17-12.34	19.12-14.00	16.14-11.36	5.14-4.43	10.20-5.58	13.42-8.50	15.42-11.38
Average Yield %	2.38	2.30	2.32	2.34	2.77	3.47	2.90	2.12

Address: 233 South Wacker Drive, Chicago, IL 60606-7147
Telephone: 312-621-6200

Web Site: www.gatx.com
Officers: Brian A. Kenney - Chairman, President, Chief Executive Officer Robert C. Lyons - Executive Vice President, Senior Vice President, Chief Financial Officer, Division Officer

Auditors: Ernst & Young LLP
Investor Contact: 312-621-6262
Transfer Agents: Computershare, Canton, MA

GENERAL DYNAMICS CORP

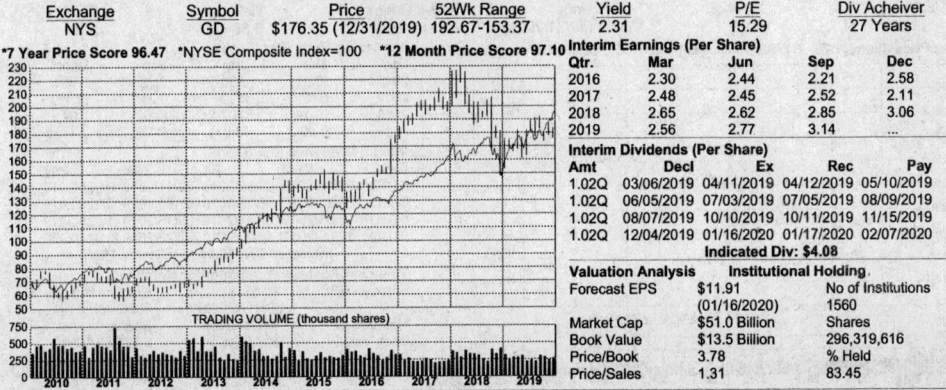

Exchange	Symbol	Price	52Wk Range	Yield	P/E	Div Acheiver
NYS	GD	$176.35 (12/31/2019)	192.67-153.37	2.31	15.29	27 Years

*7 Year Price Score 96.47 *NYSE Composite Index=100 *12 Month Price Score 97.10

Interim Earnings (Per Share)

Qtr.	Mar	Jun	Sep	Dec
2016	2.30	2.44	2.21	2.58
2017	2.48	2.45	2.52	2.11
2018	2.65	2.62	2.85	3.06
2019	2.56	2.77	3.14	...

Interim Dividends (Per Share)

Amt	Decl	Ex	Rec	Pay
1.02Q	03/06/2019	04/11/2019	04/12/2019	05/10/2019
1.02Q	06/05/2019	07/03/2019	07/05/2019	08/09/2019
1.02Q	08/07/2019	10/10/2019	10/11/2019	11/15/2019
1.02Q	12/04/2019	01/16/2020	01/17/2020	02/07/2020

Indicated Div: $4.08

Valuation Analysis | **Institutional Holding**

Forecast EPS	$11.91	No of Institutions
(01/16/2020)		1560
Market Cap	$51.0 Billion	Shares
Book Value	$13.5 Billion	296,319,616
Price/Book	3.78	% Held
Price/Sales	1.31	83.45

Business Summary: Aerospace (MIC: 7.1.1 SIC: 3721 NAIC: 336411)

General Dynamics is an aerospace and defense company. Co. has five operating segments: Aerospace, which provides a family of Gulfstream aircraft and services for business aircraft produced by Gulfstream and other original equipment manufacturers; Combat Systems, which provides combat vehicles, weapons systems and munitions; Information Technology, which provides technology solutions and mission services; Mission Systems, which provides command, control, communications, computers, intelligence, surveillance and reconnaissance products and systems; and Marine Systems, which designs and builds nuclear-powered submarines, surface combatants, and auxiliary and combat-logistics ships.

Recent Developments: For the quarter ended Sep 29 2019, income from continuing operations increased 5.7% to US$913.0 million from US$864.0 million in the year-earlier quarter. Net income increased 7.3% to US$913.0 million from US$851.0 million in the year-earlier quarter. Revenues were US$9.76 billion, up 7.3% from US$9.09 billion the year before. Operating income was US$1.22 billion versus US$1.14 billion in the prior-year quarter, an increase of 7.1%. Direct operating expenses rose 7.6% to US$7.97 billion from US$7.41 billion in the comparable period the year before. Indirect operating expenses increased 3.6% to US$572.0 million from US$552.0 million in the equivalent prior-year period.

Prospects: Our evaluation of General Dynamics Corp. as of October 4th, 2019 is the result of our systematic analysis on three basic characteristics: earnings strength, relative valuation, and recent stock price movement. The company has managed to produce a neutral trend in earnings per share over the past 5 quarters. Additionally, recent analyst estimates for the company have been unchanged while GD has posted results that exceeded analysts' expectations. Based on operating earnings yield, the company is undervalued when compared to all of the companies we cover. Share price changes over the past year indicates that GD will perform well over the near term.

Financial Data

(US$ in Millions)	9 Mos	6 Mos	3 Mos	12/31/2018	12/31/2017	12/31/2016	12/31/2015	12/31/2014
Earnings Per Share	11.53	11.24	11.09	11.18	9.56	9.52	9.08	7.42
Cash Flow Per Share	9.20	8.17	9.90	10.66	12.97	7.19	7.78	11.12
Dividends Per Share	3.900	3.810	3.720	3.630	3.280	2.970	2.690	2.420
Dividend Payout %	33.82	33.90	33.54	32.47	34.31	31.20	29.63	32.61
Income Statement								
Total Revenue	28,577	18,816	9,261	36,193	30,973	31,353	31,469	30,852
EBITDA	3,963	2,549	1,237	5,204	4,621	4,776	4,667	4,384
Depn & Amortn	625	415	205	763	441	454	482	496
Income Before Taxes	2,988	1,898	915	4,085	4,077	4,231	4,102	3,802
Income Taxes	524	347	170	727	1,165	1,169	1,137	1,129
Net Income	2,464	1,551	745	3,345	2,912	2,955	2,965	2,533
Average Shares	290	290	290	299	304	310	326	341
Balance Sheet								
Current Assets	20,151	19,557	18,867	18,189	18,328	15,447	14,571	17,407
Total Assets	48,788	48,074	47,466	45,408	35,046	32,872	31,997	35,355
Current Liabilities	18,227	18,014	15,382	14,739	13,099	12,846	12,445	13,751
Long-Term Obligations	8,989	8,975	11,451	11,444	3,980	2,988	2,898	3,410
Total Liabilities	35,275	35,197	35,232	33,676	23,611	21,896	21,259	23,526
Stockholders' Equity	13,513	12,877	12,234	11,732	11,435	10,976	10,738	11,829
Shares Outstanding	289	288	288	288	296	302	312	332
Statistical Record								
Return on Assets %	7.05	6.95	7.77	8.32	8.58	9.09	8.80	7.16
Return on Equity %	25.68	26.63	27.42	28.88	25.99	27.14	26.28	19.24
EBITDA Margin %	13.87	13.55	13.36	14.38	14.92	15.23	14.83	14.21
Net Margin %	8.62	8.24	8.04	9.24	9.40	9.42	9.42	8.21
Asset Turnover	0.81	0.80	0.90	0.90	0.91	0.96	0.93	0.87
Current Ratio	1.11	1.09	1.23	1.23	1.40	1.20	1.17	1.27
Debt to Equity	0.67	0.70	0.94	0.98	0.35	0.27	0.27	0.29
Price Range	207.16-148.21	207.16-148.21	225.96-148.21	229.95-148.21	213.86-175.32	178.67-124.18	153.28-131.27	145.36-94.46
P/E Ratio	17.97-12.85	18.43-13.19	20.38-13.36	20.57-13.26	22.37-18.34	18.77-13.04	16.88-14.46	19.59-12.73
Average Yield %	2.21	2.13	1.99	1.82	1.67	2.03	1.91	2.04

Address: 11011 Sunset Hills Road, Reston, VA 20190 **Telephone:** 703-876-3000	**Web Site:** www.generaldynamics.com **Officers:** Phebe N. Novakovic - Chairman, President, Chief Executive Officer, Senior Vice President, Chief Operating Officer Jason W. Aiken - Senior Vice President, Vice President, Chief Financial Officer	**Auditors:** KPMG LLP **Investor Contact:** 703-876-3583 **Transfer Agents:** Computershare, Providence, RI

GENERAL ELECTRIC CO

Exchange	Symbol	Price	52Wk Range	Yield	P/E
NYS	GE	$11.16 (12/31/2019)	11.58-7.28	0.36	N/A

*7 Year Price Score 37.79   *NYSE Composite Index=100   *12 Month Price Score 106.48

TRADING VOLUME (thousand shares)

Interim Earnings (Per Share)

Qtr.	Mar	Jun	Sep	Dec
2016	(0.01)	0.30	0.22	0.38
2017	0.07	0.13	0.21	(1.13)
2018	(0.14)	0.07	(2.62)	0.07
2019	0.40	(0.01)	(1.08)	...

Interim Dividends (Per Share)

Amt	Decl	Ex	Rec	Pay
0.01Q	02/15/2019	03/08/2019	03/11/2019	04/25/2019
0.01Q	06/21/2019	06/28/2019	07/01/2019	07/25/2019
0.01Q	09/06/2019	09/13/2019	09/16/2019	10/25/2019
0.01Q	12/06/2019	12/20/2019	12/23/2019	01/27/2020

Indicated Div: $0.04 (Div. Reinv. Plan)

Valuation Analysis   Institutional Holding

Forecast EPS	$0.61	No of Institutions
	(01/17/2020)	2826
Market Cap	$97.5 Billion	Shares
Book Value	$27.9 Billion	6,705,597,952
Price/Book	3.49	% Held
Price/Sales	0.86	60.66

Business Summary: Electrical Equipment (MIC: 7.3.1 SIC: 3699 NAIC: 335999)

General Electric is a technology industrial company. Co.'s segments include: Power, which serves power generation, industrial, government and other customers with products and services related to energy production; Renewable Energy, which makes renewable power sources; Aviation, which designs and produces commercial and military aircraft engines, digital components, electric power and mechanical aircraft systems; Oil and Gas, which provides a mix of oilfield products, services and digital solutions; Healthcare, which provides healthcare technologies; Transportation, which is a supplier to the railroad and marine industries; and Lighting, which focuses on consumer lighting applications.

Recent Developments: For the quarter ended Sep 30 2019, loss from continuing operations was US$1.29 billion compared with a loss of US$23.01 billion in the year-earlier quarter. Net loss amounted to US$9.38 billion versus a net loss of US$22.86 billion in the year-earlier quarter. Revenues were US$23.36 billion, down 0.1% from US$23.39 billion the year before. Direct operating expenses rose 0.3% to US$19.46 billion from US$19.41 billion in the comparable period the year before. Indirect operating expenses decreased 80.5% to US$5.31 billion from US$27.23 billion in the equivalent prior-year period.

Prospects: Our evaluation of General Electric Co as of October 4th, 2019 is the result of our systematic analysis on three basic characteristics: earnings strength, relative valuation, and recent stock price movement. The company has produced a positive trend in earnings per share over the past 5 quarters. However, recent analyst estimates for the company have been mixed and GE has posted results that exceeded analysts' expectations. Based on operating earnings yield, the company is undervalued when compared to all of the companies we cover. Share price changes over the past year indicates that GE will perform in line with the market over the near term.

Financial Data

(US$ in Millions)	9 Mos	6 Mos	3 Mos	12/31/2018	12/31/2017	12/31/2016	12/31/2015	12/31/2014
Earnings Per Share	(0.62)	(2.16)	(2.08)	(2.62)	(0.72)	0.89	(0.61)	1.50
Cash Flow Per Share	0.77	0.27	0.33	0.49	1.20	(0.03)	2.00	2.76
Tang Book Value Per Share	N.M.	N.M.	N.M.	N.M.	N.M.	N.M.	1.71	3.72
Dividends Per Share	0.040	0.150	0.260	0.370	0.840	0.930	0.920	0.890
Dividend Payout %	...	...	...	...	...	104.49	...	59.33
Income Statement								
Total Revenue	68,976	56,117	27,286	121,615	122,092	123,693	117,386	148,589
EBITDA	7,039	6,522	4,120	(4,762)	7,005	20,887	13,302	28,500
Depn & Amortn	4,189	3,398	1,712	10,313	10,927	6,832	1,653	1,789
Income Before Taxes	(422)	1,001	1,275	(20,134)	(8,791)	9,030	8,186	17,229
Income Taxes	1	74	222	583	(3,043)	(464)	6,485	1,772
Net Income	(5,707)	3,716	3,588	(22,355)	(5,786)	8,831	(6,126)	15,233
Average Shares	8,730	8,724	8,726	8,691	8,687	9,130	10,016	10,123
Balance Sheet								
Current Assets	107,256	111,474	112,117	108,000	128,356	138,872	151,993	179,041
Total Assets	263,009	312,109	315,082	309,129	377,945	365,183	492,692	648,349
Current Liabilities	64,255	70,277	71,212	69,211	79,378	81,998	108,197	208,440
Long-Term Obligations	79,369	94,232	95,753	95,234	108,575	105,080	145,301	200,414
Total Liabilities	235,075	276,292	279,505	278,148	313,683	289,356	394,418	520,190
Stockholders' Equity	27,935	35,816	35,577	30,981	64,263	75,828	98,274	128,159
Shares Outstanding	8,733	8,727	8,720	8,702	8,680	8,742	9,379	10,057
Statistical Record								
Return on Assets %	N.M.	N.M.	N.M.	N.M.	N.M.	2.05	N.M.	2.33
Return on Equity %	N.M.	N.M.	N.M.	N.M.	N.M.	10.12	N.M.	11.78
EBITDA Margin %	10.20	11.62	15.10	N.M.	5.74	16.89	11.33	19.18
Net Margin %	N.M.	6.62	13.15	N.M.	N.M.	7.14	N.M.	10.25
Asset Turnover	0.39	0.36	0.36	0.35	0.33	0.29	0.21	0.23
Current Ratio	1.67	1.59	1.57	1.56	1.62	1.69	1.40	0.86
Debt to Equity	2.84	2.63	2.69	3.07	1.69	1.39	1.48	1.56
Price Range	13.08-6.45	13.62-6.45	14.70-6.45	18.28-6.45	30.47-16.69	31.65-26.39	30.07-22.37	26.94-23.02
P/E Ratio	...	...	...	...	...	35.57-29.65	...	17.96-15.35
Average Yield %	0.42	1.47	2.35	2.98	3.36	3.19	3.57	3.56

Address: 41 Farnsworth Street, Boston, MA 02210 Telephone: 617-443-3000	Web Site: www.ge.com Officers: H. Lawrence Culp - Chairman, Chief Executive Officer David Leon Joyce - Vice-Chairman, Division Officer	Auditors: KPMG LLP Investor Contact: 203-373-2460 Transfer Agents: Computershare, Pittsburgh, PA

GENERAL MILLS INC

Exchange	Symbol	Price	52Wk Range	Yield	P/E	Div Acheiver
NYS	GIS	$53.56 (12/31/2019)	55.59-38.43	3.66	15.39	15 Years

*7 Year Price Score 78.53   *NYSE Composite Index=100   *12 Month Price Score 97.88

Interim Earnings (Per Share)

Qtr.	Aug	Nov	Feb	May
2016-17	0.67	0.80	0.61	0.69
2017-18	0.69	0.74	1.62	0.59
2018-19	0.65	0.57	0.74	0.94
2019-20	0.85	0.95	...	...

Interim Dividends (Per Share)

Amt	Decl	Ex	Rec	Pay
0.49Q	02/05/2019	04/09/2019	04/10/2019	05/01/2019
0.49Q	06/25/2019	07/09/2019	07/10/2019	08/01/2019
0.49Q	09/24/2019	10/09/2019	10/10/2019	11/01/2019
0.49Q	11/18/2019	01/09/2020	01/10/2020	02/03/2020

Indicated Div: $1.96 (Div. Reinv. Plan)

Valuation Analysis / Institutional Holding

Valuation Analysis		Institutional Holding	
Forecast EPS	$3.38	No of Institutions	
	(01/15/2020)	1818	
Market Cap	$32.4 Billion	Shares	
Book Value	$7.7 Billion	536,031,808	
Price/Book	4.20	% Held	
Price/Sales	1.93	55.74	

Business Summary: Food (MIC: 1.2.1 SIC: 2043 NAIC: 311230)

General Mills manufactures and markets branded consumer foods. Co.'s segments are: North America Retail, which provides cereals, refrigerated yogurt, soup, meal kits, dessert and baking mixes, frozen pizza and pizza snacks, grain, fruit and savory snacks, and organic products, among others; Convenience Stores and Foodservice, which provides snacks, yogurt, frozen meals and frozen dough products, and baking mixes, among others; Europe and Australia, which includes retail and foodservice businesses in the Europe and Australia region; Asia and Latin America, which consists of retail and foodservice businesses in the Asia and South America regions; and Pets, which includes pet food products.

Recent Developments: For the quarter ended Aug 25 2019, net income increased 33.5% to US$528.5 million from US$395.9 million in the year-earlier quarter. Revenues were US$4.00 billion, down 2.2% from US$4.09 billion the year before. Operating income was US$662.4 million versus US$601.5 million in the prior-year quarter, an increase of 10.1%. Direct operating expenses declined 5.0% to US$2.61 billion from US$2.75 billion in the comparable period the year before. Indirect operating expenses decreased 1.9% to US$727.1 million from US$741.3 million in the equivalent prior-year period.

Prospects: Our evaluation of General Mills Inc. as of October 4th, 2019 is the result of our systematic analysis on three basic characteristics: earnings strength, relative valuation, and recent stock price movement. The company has managed to produce a neutral trend in earnings per share over the past 5 quarters. In addition, recent analyst estimates for the company have been mixed and GIS has posted results that exceeded analysts' expectations. Based on operating earnings yield, the company is undervalued when compared to all of the companies we cover. Share price changes over the past year indicates that GIS will perform well over the near term.

Financial Data
(US$ in Thousands)

	6 Mos	3 Mos	05/26/2019	05/27/2018	05/28/2017	05/29/2016	05/31/2015	05/25/2014
Earnings Per Share	3.48	3.10	2.90	3.64	2.77	2.77	1.97	2.83
Cash Flow Per Share	4.72	4.57	4.69	4.94	3.95	4.40	4.15	4.05
Dividends Per Share	1.960	1.960	1.960	1.960	1.920	1.780	1.670	1.550
Dividend Payout %	56.32	63.23	67.59	53.85	69.31	64.26	84.77	54.77
Income Statement								
Total Revenue	8,423,300	4,002,500	16,865,200	15,740,400	15,619,800	16,563,100	17,630,300	17,909,600
EBITDA	1,841,700	846,700	3,223,900	3,128,100	3,170,000	3,315,500	2,665,600	3,542,800
Depn & Amortn	307,700	154,100	620,100	618,800	603,600	608,100	588,300	585,400
Income Before Taxes	1,295,900	573,900	2,082,000	2,135,600	2,271,300	2,403,600	1,761,900	2,655,000
Income Taxes	222,700	67,200	367,800	57,300	655,200	755,200	586,800	883,300
Net Income	1,101,400	520,600	1,752,700	2,131,000	1,657,500	1,697,400	1,221,300	1,824,400
Average Shares	612,300	611,500	605,400	585,700	598,000	611,900	618,800	645,700
Balance Sheet								
Current Assets	4,478,900	4,261,400	4,186,500	4,123,700	4,061,400	3,937,200	3,785,700	4,393,500
Total Assets	30,452,400	30,313,200	30,111,200	30,624,000	21,812,600	21,712,300	21,964,500	23,145,700
Current Liabilities	7,362,300	6,903,400	7,087,100	7,341,900	5,330,800	5,014,700	4,890,100	5,423,500
Long-Term Obligations	10,953,100	11,619,800	11,624,800	12,668,700	7,642,900	7,057,700	7,607,700	6,423,500
Total Liabilities	22,740,100	22,930,400	23,056,700	24,482,900	17,484,700	16,782,100	16,967,800	16,610,900
Stockholders' Equity	7,712,300	7,382,800	7,054,500	6,141,100	4,327,900	4,930,200	4,996,700	6,534,800
Shares Outstanding	604,600	604,100	601,900	593,100	576,900	596,800	598,700	612,300
Statistical Record								
Return on Assets %	6.96	6.18	5.79	8.15	7.64	7.79	5.33	7.99
Return on Equity %	29.50	27.65	26.64	40.82	35.90	34.29	20.84	27.70
EBITDA Margin %	21.86	21.15	19.12	19.87	20.29	20.02	15.12	19.78
Net Margin %	13.08	13.01	10.39	13.54	10.61	10.25	6.93	10.19
Asset Turnover	0.55	0.55	0.56	0.60	0.72	0.76	0.77	0.78
Current Ratio	0.61	0.62	0.59	0.56	0.76	0.79	0.77	0.81
Debt to Equity	1.42	1.57	1.65	2.06	1.77	1.43	1.52	0.98
Price Range	55.59-36.70	55.20-36.70	53.43-36.70	60.20-41.21	72.64-55.91	65.36-54.12	57.14-48.86	54.40-46.86
P/E Ratio	15.97-10.55	17.81-11.84	18.42-12.66	16.54-11.32	26.22-20.18	23.60-19.54	29.01-24.80	19.22-16.56
Average Yield %	3.95	4.13	4.32	3.71	3.03	3.05	3.14	3.09

Address: Number One General Mills Boulevard, Minneapolis, MN 55426 **Telephone:** 763-764-7600 **Fax:** 763-764-8330	**Web Site:** www.generalmills.com **Officers:** Jeffrey (Jeff) L. Harmening - Chairman, Chief Executive Officer, President, Chief Operating Officer, Executive Vice President, Region Officer Donal L. Mulligan - Executive Vice President, Chief Financial Officer

Auditors: KPMG LLP
Investor Contact: 180-024-55703
Transfer Agents: Wells Fargo Bank, N.A., St. Paul, MN

GENERAL MOTORS CO

Exchange	Symbol	Price	52Wk Range	Yield	P/E
NYS	GM	$36.60 (12/31/2019)	40.88-32.25	4.15	5.96

*7 Year Price Score 87.80   ***NYSE Composite Index=100**   ***12 Month Price Score 92.18**

TRADING VOLUME (thousand shares)

Interim Earnings (Per Share)

Qtr.	Mar	Jun	Sep	Dec
2016	1.24	1.81	1.76	1.19
2017	1.70	1.09	(2.03)	(3.45)
2018	0.72	1.66	1.75	1.40
2019	1.48	1.66	1.60	...

Interim Dividends (Per Share)

Amt	Decl	Ex	Rec	Pay
0.38Q	02/05/2019	03/07/2019	03/08/2019	03/22/2019
0.38Q	04/29/2019	06/06/2019	06/07/2019	06/21/2019
0.38Q	07/31/2019	09/05/2019	09/06/2019	09/20/2019
0.38Q	10/28/2019	12/05/2019	12/06/2019	12/19/2019

Indicated Div: $1.52

Valuation Analysis / Institutional Holding

Forecast EPS	$4.82	No of Institutions
	(01/17/2020)	1383
Market Cap	$51.2 Billion	Shares
Book Value	$44.6 Billion	1,241,011,840
Price/Book	1.15	% Held
Price/Sales	0.35	76.96

Business Summary: Autos- Manufacturing (MIC: 1.8.1 SIC: 3711 NAIC: 336111)

General Motors designs, builds and sells trucks, crossovers, cars and automobile parts worldwide and is investing in and growing a ride-sharing vehicle business. Co. also provides automotive financing services through its subsidiary, General Motors Financial Company, Inc. Co.'s automotive operations serves its customers through its automotive segments: GM North America and GM International. In addition to the vehicles it sells through its dealer network to retail customers, Co. also sells vehicles directly or through its dealer network to fleet customers, including daily rental car companies, commercial fleet customers, leasing companies and governments.

Recent Developments: For the quarter ended Sep 30 2019, income from continuing operations decreased 8.7% to US$2.31 billion from US$2.53 billion in the year-earlier quarter. Net income decreased 8.7% to US$2.31 billion from US$2.53 billion in the year-earlier quarter. Revenues were US$35.47 billion, down 0.9% from US$35.79 billion the year before. Operating income was US$2.30 billion versus US$1.61 billion in the prior-year quarter, an increase of 43.1%. Direct operating expenses declined 1.4% to US$31.16 billion from US$31.60 billion in the comparable period the year before. Indirect operating expenses decreased 22.3% to US$2.01 billion from US$2.58 billion in the equivalent prior-year period.

Prospects: Our evaluation of General Motors Co. as of October 4th, 2019 is the result of our systematic analysis on three basic characteristics: earnings strength, relative valuation, and recent stock price movement. The company has managed to produce a neutral trend in earnings per share over the past 5 quarters. In addition, recent analyst estimates for the company have been mixed and GM has posted results that exceeded analysts' expectations. Based on operating earnings yield, the company is undervalued when compared to all of the companies we cover. Share price changes over the past year indicates that GM will perform over the near term.

Financial Data

(US$ in Millions)

	9 Mos	6 Mos	3 Mos	12/31/2018	12/31/2017	12/31/2016	12/31/2015	12/31/2014
Earnings Per Share	6.14	6.29	6.29	5.53	(2.60)	6.00	5.91	1.65
Cash Flow Per Share	12.31	10.35	10.39	10.81	11.83	10.71	7.55	6.27
Tang Book Value Per Share	27.96	26.17	24.85	23.61	20.78	25.09	21.96	18.04
Dividends Per Share	1,520	1.520	1.520	1.520	1.520	1.520	1.380	1.200
Dividend Payout %	24.76	24.17	24.17	27.49	...	25.33	23.35	72.73
Income Statement								
Total Revenue	106,411	70,938	34,878	147,049	145,588	166,380	152,356	155,929
EBITDA	11,635	7,479	3,141	17,292	21,682	14,312	10,566	7,135
Depn & Amortn	5,600	3,748	1,897	12,847	11,666	4,767	5,220	5,403
Income Before Taxes	6,791	4,524	1,868	6,386	9,731	9,402	5,524	2,152
Income Taxes	932	661	137	474	11,533	2,416	(1,897)	228
Net Income	6,926	4,575	2,157	8,014	(3,864)	9,427	9,687	3,949
Average Shares	1,442	1,438	1,436	1,431	1,492	1,570	1,640	1,687
Balance Sheet								
Current Assets	80,565	81,306	80,090	75,293	68,744	76,203	78,007	83,670
Total Assets	231,529	233,737	233,132	227,339	212,482	221,690	194,520	177,677
Current Liabilities	84,252	84,294	85,303	82,237	76,890	85,181	71,466	65,701
Long-Term Obligations	69,692	73,412	73,812	73,060	67,254	55,600	43,549	31,853
Total Liabilities	186,975	190,921	192,367	188,479	177,481	177,854	154,649	142,220
Stockholders' Equity	44,554	42,816	40,765	38,860	35,001	43,836	39,871	35,457
Shares Outstanding	1,400	1,427	1,418	1,409	1,402	1,497	1,544	1,610
Statistical Record								
Return on Assets %	3.92	4.05	4.04	3.64	N.M.	4.52	5.21	2.30
Return on Equity %	21.72	23.17	24.31	21.70	N.M.	22.46	25.72	10.12
EBITDA Margin %	10.93	10.54	9.01	11.76	14.89	8.60	6.94	4.58
Net Margin %	6.51	6.45	6.18	5.45	N.M.	5.67	6.36	2.53
Asset Turnover	0.63	0.64	0.65	0.67	0.67	0.80	0.82	0.91
Current Ratio	0.96	0.96	0.94	0.92	0.89	0.89	1.09	1.27
Debt to Equity	1.56	1.71	1.81	1.88	1.92	1.27	1.09	0.90
Price Range	40.88-30.56	40.30-30.56	44.85-30.56	44.85-30.56	46.48-32.42	37.66-26.90	38.87-27.28	40.95-29.69
P/E Ratio	6.66-4.98	6.41-4.86	7.13-4.86	8.11-5.53	...	6.28-4.48	6.58-4.62	24.82-17.99
Average Yield %	4.10	4.14	4.09	4.02	4.04	4.85	4.02	3.47

Address: 300 Renaissance Center, Detroit, MI 48265-3000 **Telephone:** 313-667-1500	**Web Site:** www.gm.com **Officers:** Mary T. Barra - Chairman, Chief Executive Officer, Senior Vice President Mark L. Reuss - President, Vice President, Division Officer	**Auditors:** DELOITTE & TOUCHE LLP **Transfer Agents:** Computershare Trust Company, N.A., Providence, RI

GENESIS HEALTHCARE INC

Exchange	Symbol	Price	52Wk Range	Yield	P/E
NYS	GEN	$1.64 (12/31/2019)	1.73-0.98	N/A	N/A

*7 Year Price Score 30.24   *NYSE Composite Index=100   *12 Month Price Score 110.55

Interim Earnings (Per Share)

Qtr.	Mar	Jun	Sep	Dec
2016	(0.48)	(0.26)	(0.23)	0.14
2017	(0.55)	(0.70)	(3.94)	(0.91)
2018	(0.70)	(0.39)	(0.57)	(0.67)
2019	(0.15)	(0.05)	0.40	...

Interim Dividends (Per Share)

No Dividends Paid

Valuation Analysis   **Institutional Holding**

Forecast EPS	$-0.39	No of Institutions
	(01/08/2020)	28
Market Cap	$270.3 Million	Shares
Book Value	N/A	1,463,447
Price/Book	N/A	% Held
Price/Sales	0.06	N/A

Business Summary: Hospitals & Health Care Facilities (MIC: 4.2.1 SIC: 8051 NAIC: 623110)

Genesis Healthcare is a holding company. Co.'s services focus primarily on the medical and physical issues facing elderly patients and are provided by its nursing facilities, assisted/senior living communities, integrated and third-party rehabilitation therapy business, and other ancillary services. Co.'s reportable operating segments comprised of: inpatient services, which includes the operation of skilled nursing facilities and assisted/senior living facilities; rehabilitation therapy services, which includes Co.'s third-party rehabilitation and respiratory therapy services; and other services, which provides a range of other medical services, including physician services.

Recent Developments: For the quarter ended Sep 30 2019, net income amounted to US$58.9 million versus a net loss of US$91.9 million in the year-earlier quarter. Revenues were US$1.12 billion, down 7.7% from US$1.22 billion the year before. Indirect operating expenses decreased 4.9% to US$1.15 billion from US$1.21 billion in the equivalent prior-year period.

Prospects: Our evaluation of Genesis Healthcare Inc. as of October 4th, 2019 is the result of our systematic analysis on three basic characteristics: earnings strength, relative valuation, and recent stock price movement. The company has enjoyed a very positive trend in earnings per share over the past 5 quarters. However, recent analyst estimates for the company have been mixed and GEN has posted results that exceeded analysts' expectations. Based on operating earnings yield, the company is overvalued when compared to all of the companies we cover. Share price changes over the past year indicates that GEN will perform in line with the market over the near term.

Financial Data

(US$ in Thousands)	9 Mos	6 Mos	3 Mos	12/31/2018	12/31/2017	12/31/2016	12/31/2015	12/31/2014
Earnings Per Share	(0.47)	(1.44)	(1.78)	(2.33)	(6.15)	(0.82)	(4.97)	(0.02)
Cash Flow Per Share	0.19	0.40	0.35	0.18	1.28	0.76	0.10	0.69
Tang Book Value Per Share	...	...	...	...	...	...	...	0.20
Income Statement								
Total Revenue	3,430,397	2,306,692	1,161,640	4,976,650	5,373,740	5,732,430	5,619,224	833,256
EBITDA	251,815	129,759	55,998	298,798	(232,260)	624,445	371,445	51,958
Depn & Amortn	86,250	59,529	29,574	210,000	238,200	234,700	218,800	24,300
Income Before Taxes	23,975	(34,261)	(25,092)	(374,940)	(969,842)	(138,799)	(355,164)	(3,582)
Income Taxes	(680)	(111)	51	(2,423)	(10,427)	(17,435)	172,524	(1,248)
Net Income	26,015	(20,082)	(15,263)	(235,231)	(578,982)	(64,013)	(426,195)	(907)
Average Shares	166,002	106,846	103,715	101,007	94,217	152,532	85,755	38,125
Balance Sheet								
Current Assets	784,268	746,628	809,015	875,625	939,907	1,058,987	1,011,493	161,383
Total Assets	4,674,147	4,642,580	4,779,923	4,263,623	4,787,865	5,779,201	6,091,470	650,956
Current Liabilities	1,027,239	964,059	977,194	912,212	899,194	857,560	798,665	115,292
Long-Term Obligations	1,460,628	1,981,275	2,003,476	4,783,814	5,005,175	5,011,424	5,335,573	398,389
Total Liabilities	5,423,209	5,438,584	5,565,420	5,603,143	5,872,092	6,269,524	6,527,777	555,697
Stockholders' Equity	(749,062)	(796,004)	(785,497)	(1,339,520)	(1,084,227)	(490,323)	(436,307)	95,259
Shares Outstanding	164,805	164,778	161,781	161,681	159,406	154,531	153,554	39,994
Statistical Record								
EBITDA Margin %	7.34	5.63	4.82	6.00	N.M.	10.89	6.61	6.24
Net Margin %	0.76	N.M.	N.M.	N.M.	N.M.	N.M.	N.M.	N.M.
Asset Turnover	1.02	1.03	1.01	1.10	1.02	0.96	1.67	1.29
Current Ratio	0.76	0.77	0.83	0.96	1.05	1.23	1.27	1.40
Debt to Equity	...	...	...	...	...	...	...	4.18
Price Range	1.71-0.98	2.38-1.13	2.86-1.16	2.86-0.76	4.69-0.69	4.36-1.38	9.22-3.42	8.91-4.28

Address: 101 East State Street, Kennett Square, PA 19348 **Telephone:** 610-444-6350	**Web Site:** www.genesishcc.com **Officers:** Robert H. Fish - Chief Executive Officer, Chairman George V. Hager - Chief Executive Officer	**Auditors:** KPMG LLP **Transfer Agents:** Wells Fargo Shareowner Services, South St. Paul, MN

GENPACT LTD

Exchange	Symbol	Price	52Wk Range	Yield	P/E
NYS	G	$42.17 (12/31/2019)	42.57-26.43	0.81	27.21

*7 Year Price Score 118.94 *NYSE Composite Index=100 *12 Month Price Score 104.71

Interim Earnings (Per Share)

Qtr.	Mar	Jun	Sep	Dec
2016	0.27	0.31	0.33	0.37
2017	0.26	0.36	0.38	0.35
2018	0.33	0.33	0.38	0.41
2019	0.31	0.38	0.45	...

Interim Dividends (Per Share)

Amt	Decl	Ex	Rec	Pay
0.085Q	02/07/2019	03/07/2019	03/08/2019	03/20/2019
0.085Q	05/09/2019	06/11/2019	06/12/2019	06/21/2019
0.085Q	07/24/2019	09/10/2019	09/11/2019	09/20/2019
0.085Q	10/17/2019	12/06/2019	12/09/2019	12/18/2019

Indicated Div: $0.34

Valuation Analysis / **Institutional Holding**

Forecast EPS	N/A	No of Institutions 420
Market Cap	$8.0 Billion	Shares
Book Value	$1.6 Billion	193,883,568
Price/Book	4.97	% Held
Price/Sales	2.34	92.77

Business Summary: Business Services (MIC: 7.5.2 SIC: 8742 NAIC: 541618)

Genpact is a services firm. Co. provides the following services: finance and accounting services, which include accounts payable and invoice-to-cash; primary industry operations, which help Co.'s clients design, transform and run primary enterprise operations; sourcing, procurement and supply chain services, which provide direct and indirect strategic sourcing and category management; and information technology services, which include end-user computing and infrastructure management. The industries Co. serves include banking and financial services, capital markets, insurance, consumer goods and retail, life sciences and healthcare, infrastructure, manufacturing and services and high tech.

Recent Developments: For the quarter ended Sep 30 2019, net income increased 19.7% to US$88.1 million from US$73.6 million in the year-earlier quarter. Revenues were US$888.8 million, up 18.8% from US$748.0 million the year before. Operating income was US$113.6 million versus US$94.0 million in the prior-year quarter, an increase of 20.8%. Direct operating expenses rose 19.2% to US$573.7 million from US$481.4 million in the comparable period the year before. Indirect operating expenses increased 16.8% to US$201.6 million from US$172.5 million in the equivalent prior-year period.

Prospects: Our evaluation of Genpact Ltd. as of October 4th, 2019 is the result of our systematic analysis on three basic characteristics: earnings strength, relative valuation, and recent stock price movement. The company has produced a positive trend in earnings per share over the past 5 quarters. However, recent analyst estimates for the company have been unchanged, while G has posted results that exceeded analysts' expectations. Based on operating earnings yield, the company is fairly valued when compared to all of the companies we cover. Share price changes over the past year indicates that G will perform over the near term.

Financial Data
(US$ in Thousands)

	9 Mos	6 Mos	3 Mos	12/31/2018	12/31/2017	12/31/2016	12/31/2015	12/31/2014
Earnings Per Share	1.55	1.48	1.43	1.45	1.34	1.28	1.09	0.85
Cash Flow Per Share	2.51	2.16	1.91	1.78	1.85	1.67	1.51	1.23
Tang Book Value Per Share	0.28	0.09	N.M.	N.M.	N.M.	0.73	0.79	0.52
Income Statement								
Total Revenue	2,579,804	1,691,005	809,206	3,000,790	2,736,929	2,570,756	2,461,044	2,279,438
EBITDA	393,223	243,499	112,811	487,520	438,182	426,536	409,892	356,352
Depn & Amortn	74,652	45,943	22,368	88,368	81,321	73,009	76,186	72,572
Income Before Taxes	285,084	174,290	79,320	362,033	325,126	337,343	312,554	254,385
Income Taxes	62,385	39,716	18,483	80,763	59,742	62,098	61,937	57,419
Net Income	222,683	134,563	60,841	282,019	263,111	269,684	239,817	192,002
Average Shares	195,890	194,766	193,394	193,980	197,049	210,126	219,145	225,168
Balance Sheet								
Current Assets	1,556,865	1,459,795	1,394,544	1,355,057	1,433,895	1,227,037	1,195,069	1,188,508
Total Assets	4,097,761	4,012,757	3,904,814	3,529,445	3,449,621	2,885,880	2,793,489	2,742,537
Current Liabilities	1,064,194	1,003,151	1,011,781	976,312	838,784	731,355	594,480	622,114
Long-Term Obligations	950,908	959,151	991,830	977,359	1,009,351	700,652	739,536	651,974
Total Liabilities	2,492,077	2,429,387	2,409,645	2,125,263	2,025,577	1,599,232	1,489,133	1,457,401
Stockholders' Equity	1,605,684	1,583,370	1,495,169	1,404,182	1,424,044	1,286,648	1,304,356	1,285,136
Shares Outstanding	189,346	190,486	189,659	189,346	192,825	198,794	211,472	218,684
Statistical Record								
Return on Assets %	7.99	7.89	7.62	8.08	8.31	9.47	8.66	7.07
Return on Equity %	20.88	19.95	19.44	19.94	19.41	20.76	18.52	14.72
EBITDA Margin %	15.24	14.40	13.94	16.25	16.01	16.59	16.66	15.63
Net Margin %	8.63	7.96	7.52	9.40	9.61	10.49	9.74	8.42
Asset Turnover	0.90	0.90	0.85	0.86	0.86	0.90	0.89	0.84
Current Ratio	1.46	1.46	1.38	1.39	1.71	1.68	2.01	1.91
Debt to Equity	0.59	0.61	0.66	0.70	0.71	0.54	0.57	0.51
Price Range	41.92-25.88	38.15-25.88	35.18-25.88	34.76-25.88	32.66-23.37	28.39-22.70	25.85-18.87	19.30-14.28
P/E Ratio	27.05-16.70	25.78-17.49	24.60-18.10	23.97-17.85	24.37-17.44	22.18-17.73	23.72-17.31	22.71-16.80

Address: Victoria Place, 5th Floor, 31 Victoria Street, Hamilton, HM12 **Telephone:** 441-294-8000	**Web Site:** www.genpact.com **Officers:** Robert G. Scott - Chairman N. V. (Tiger) Tyagarajan - President, Chief Executive Officer	**Auditors:** KPMG **Investor Contact:** 144-129-52244 **Transfer Agents:** Computershare, Providence, RI

GENUINE PARTS CO.

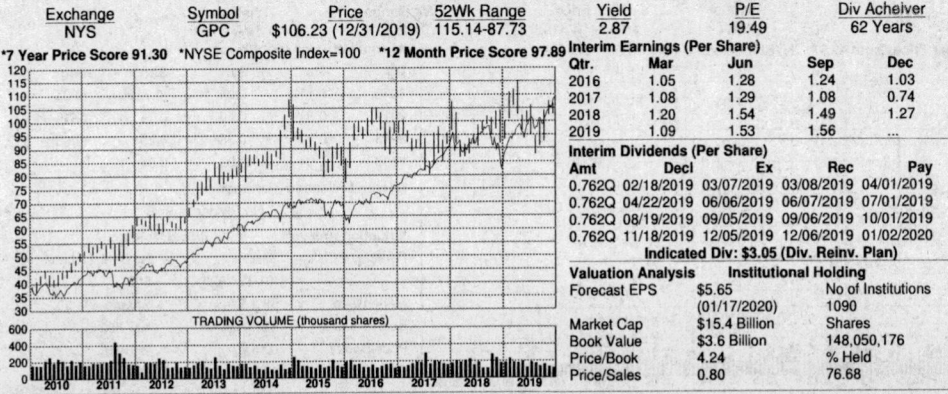

Exchange	Symbol	Price	52Wk Range	Yield	P/E	Div Acheiver
NYS	GPC	$106.23 (12/31/2019)	115.14-87.73	2.87	19.49	62 Years

*7 Year Price Score 91.30 ***NYSE Composite Index=100** ***12 Month Price Score 97.89**

Interim Earnings (Per Share)

Qtr.	Mar	Jun	Sep	Dec
2016	1.05	1.28	1.24	1.03
2017	1.08	1.29	1.08	0.74
2018	1.20	1.54	1.49	1.27
2019	1.09	1.53	1.56	...

Interim Dividends (Per Share)

Amt	Decl	Ex	Rec	Pay
0.762Q	02/18/2019	03/07/2019	03/08/2019	04/01/2019
0.762Q	04/22/2019	06/06/2019	06/07/2019	07/01/2019
0.762Q	08/19/2019	09/05/2019	09/06/2019	10/01/2019
0.762Q	11/18/2019	12/05/2019	12/06/2019	01/02/2020

Indicated Div: $3.05 (Div. Reinv. Plan)

Valuation Analysis **Institutional Holding**

Forecast EPS	$5.65	No of Institutions
(01/17/2020)		1090
Market Cap	$15.4 Billion	Shares
Book Value	$3.6 Billion	148,050,176
Price/Book	4.24	% Held
Price/Sales	0.80	76.68

Business Summary: Auto Parts (MIC: 1.8.2 SIC: 5013 NAIC: 423120)

Genuine Parts is engaged in the distribution of automotive replacement parts, industrial parts and materials, and business products. Co.'s business segments are: Automotive, which distributes automotive parts and accessory items and provides inventory, cataloging, marketing, training and other programs to the automotive aftermarket; Industrial, which distributes industrial replacement parts and related supplies such as bearings, mechanical and electrical power transmission products, industrial automation, and hose, among others; and Business Products, which is engaged in the wholesale distribution of a line of office and other business related products through a customer base of resellers.

Recent Developments: For the quarter ended Sep 30 2019, net income increased 3.3% to US$227.5 million from US$220.2 million in the year-earlier quarter. Revenues were US$5.02 billion, up 6.2% from US$4.72 billion the year before. Direct operating expenses rose 4.7% to US$3.39 billion from US$3.24 billion in the comparable period the year before. Indirect operating expenses increased 13.1% to US$1.34 billion from US$1.19 billion in the equivalent prior-year period.

Prospects: Our evaluation of Genuine Parts Co. as of October 4th, 2019 is the result of our systematic analysis on three basic characteristics: earnings strength, relative valuation, and recent stock price movement. The company has managed to produce a neutral trend in earnings per share over the past 5 quarters. However, recent analyst estimates for the company have been reduced and GPC has posted results that fell short of analysts' expectations. Based on operating earnings yield, the company is undervalued when compared to all of the companies we cover. Share price changes over the past year indicates that GPC will perform in line with the market over the near term.

Financial Data

(US$ in Thousands)	9 Mos	6 Mos	3 Mos	12/31/2018	12/31/2017	12/31/2016	12/31/2015	12/31/2014
Earnings Per Share	5.45	5.38	5.39	5.50	4.18	4.59	4.63	4.61
Cash Flow Per Share	6.63	6.79	7.32	7.81	5.54	6.33	7.64	5.15
Tang Book Value Per Share	N.M.	N.M.	N.M.	N.M.	N.M.	10.91	11.89	12.50
Dividends Per Share	3.007	2.965	2.922	2.880	2.700	2.630	2.460	2.300
Dividend Payout %	55.18	55.11	54.22	52.36	64.59	57.30	53.13	49.89
Income Statement								
Total Revenue	14,686,116	9,671,093	4,736,833	18,735,073	16,308,801	15,339,713	15,280,044	15,341,647
EBITDA	1,088,891	688,951	297,372	1,419,172	1,218,445	1,242,911	1,287,018	1,291,140
Depn & Amortn	197,053	128,131	61,977	241,635	167,691	147,487	141,675	148,313
Income Before Taxes	818,174	513,641	211,512	1,075,612	1,009,268	1,074,340	1,123,681	1,117,739
Income Taxes	206,007	128,961	51,262	265,138	392,511	387,100	418,009	406,453
Net Income	612,167	384,680	160,250	810,474	616,757	687,240	705,672	711,286
Average Shares	146,189	146,736	146,694	147,241	147,701	149,804	152,496	154,375
Balance Sheet								
Current Assets	8,058,671	8,184,670	7,886,391	7,575,690	7,312,893	5,948,431	5,555,316	5,592,525
Total Assets	14,513,190	14,639,472	14,070,530	12,683,040	12,412,381	8,859,400	8,144,771	8,246,238
Current Liabilities	6,372,813	6,498,228	6,545,334	5,900,733	5,474,025	4,244,150	3,940,654	3,584,115
Long-Term Obligations	2,795,878	2,871,106	2,389,244	2,432,133	2,605,713	589,221	287,642	540,040
Total Liabilities	10,870,999	10,974,144	10,519,599	9,232,589	9,000,229	5,665,672	4,998,204	4,944,990
Stockholders' Equity	3,642,191	3,665,328	3,550,931	3,450,451	3,412,152	3,193,728	3,146,567	3,301,248
Shares Outstanding	145,293	146,078	146,063	145,936	146,652	148,410	150,081	153,113
Statistical Record								
Return on Assets %	5.88	5.82	5.92	6.46	5.80	8.06	8.61	8.93
Return on Equity %	22.03	22.06	22.49	23.62	18.67	21.62	21.89	21.39
EBITDA Margin %	7.41	7.12	6.28	7.57	7.47	8.10	8.42	8.42
Net Margin %	4.17	3.98	3.38	4.33	3.78	4.48	4.62	4.64
Asset Turnover	1.42	1.40	1.41	1.49	1.53	1.80	1.86	1.93
Current Ratio	1.26	1.26	1.20	1.28	1.34	1.40	1.41	1.56
Debt to Equity	0.77	0.78	0.67	0.70	0.76	0.18	0.09	0.16
Price Range	115.14-87.73	115.14-90.72	112.03-86.76	107.58-86.52	100.67-80.48	105.24-77.40	106.57-79.53	108.31-77.75
P/E Ratio	21.13-16.10	21.40-16.86	20.78-16.10	19.56-15.73	24.08-19.25	22.93-16.86	23.02-17.18	23.49-16.87
Average Yield %	2.99	2.94	2.99	2.99	2.96	2.75	2.72	2.59

Address: 2999 Wildwood Parkway, Atlanta, GA 30339 **Telephone:** 678-934-5000	**Web Site:** www.genpt.com **Officers:** Paul D. Donahue - Chairman, President, Executive Vice President, Chief Executive Officer, Division Officer Carol B. Yancey - Executive Vice President, Chief Financial Officer, Vice President, Corporate Secretary	**Auditors:** Ernst & Young LLP **Investor Contact:** 770-953-1700 **Transfer Agents:** Computershare, Providence, RI

GENWORTH FINANCIAL, INC. (HOLDING CO)

Exchange	Symbol	Price	52Wk Range	Yield	P/E
NYS	GNW	$4.40 (12/31/2019)	5.01-2.91	N/A	73.33

7 Year Price Score 48.97 *NYSE Composite Index=100* **12 Month Price Score 97.54**

TRADING VOLUME (thousand shares)

Interim Earnings (Per Share)

Qtr.	Mar	Jun	Sep	Dec
2016	0.11	0.34	(0.76)	(0.25)
2017	0.31	0.40	0.21	0.70
2018	0.22	0.38	0.29	(0.65)
2019	0.34	0.33	0.04	...

Interim Dividends (Per Share)

No Dividends Paid

Valuation Analysis

Forecast EPS	$0.83
	(01/17/2020)
Market Cap	$2.2 Billion
Book Value	$14.4 Billion
Price/Book	0.15
Price/Sales	0.26

Institutional Holding

No of Institutions	506
Shares	442,592,576
% Held	69.96

Business Summary: Life & Health (MIC: 5.2.2 SIC: 6311 NAIC: 524113)

Genworth Financial is a holding company. Through its subsidiaries, Co. facilitates homeownership in the U.S. and internationally by providing mortgage insurance products that allow people to purchase homes with low down payments while protecting lenders against the risk of default. Through its homeownership education and assistance programs, Co. also helps people keep their homes when they experience financial difficulties. Co. provides individual and group long-term care insurance products to meet consumer needs for long-term care. Co. has five operating business segments: U.S. Mortgage Insurance, Canada Mortgage Insurance, Australia Mortgage Insurance, U.S. Life Insurance, and Runoff.

Recent Developments: For the quarter ended Sep 30 2019, income from continuing operations increased 31.4% to US$138.0 million from US$105.0 million in the year-earlier quarter. Net income decreased 72.4% to US$58.0 million from US$210.0 million in the year-earlier quarter. Revenues were US$2.02 billion, up 3.5% from US$1.95 billion the year before. Net premiums earned were US$1.02 billion versus US$995.0 million in the prior-year quarter, an increase of 2.0%. Net investment income rose 4.6% to US$816.0 million from US$780.0 million a year ago.

Prospects: Our evaluation of Genworth Financial Inc. as of October 4th, 2019 is the result of our systematic analysis on three basic characteristics: earnings strength, relative valuation, and recent stock price movement. The company has produced a positive trend in earnings per share over the past 5 quarters. However, recent analyst estimates for the company have been mixed and GNW has posted results that exceeded analysts' expectations. Based on operating earnings yield, the company is undervalued when compared to all of the companies we cover. Share price changes over the past year indicates that GNW will perform well over the near term.

Financial Data

(US$ in Millions)	9 Mos	6 Mos	3 Mos	12/31/2018	12/31/2017	12/31/2016	12/31/2015	12/31/2014
Earnings Per Share	0.06	0.31	0.36	0.24	1.63	(0.56)	(1.24)	(2.51)
Cash Flow Per Share	4.50	3.71	3.31	3.26	5.12	3.71	3.20	4.91
Tang Book Value Per Share	28.13	26.81	25.47	24.16	26.29	24.69	25.03	29.45
Income Statement								
Premium Income	3,004	2,240	1,114	4,519	4,004	4,160	4,579	5,431
Total Revenue	6,058	4,360	2,204	8,430	8,295	8,369	8,548	9,565
Income Before Taxes	633	667	342	448	729	320	(15)	(1,276)
Income Taxes	169	219	112	151	(207)	358	(9)	(228)
Net Income	360	342	174	119	817	(277)	(615)	(1,244)
Average Shares	511	508	508	504	501	498	497	496
Balance Sheet								
Total Assets	105,653	104,306	102,188	100,923	105,297	104,658	106,431	111,358
Total Liabilities	91,266	90,549	89,114	88,473	91,879	92,014	93,607	96,435
Stockholders' Equity	14,387	13,757	13,074	12,450	13,418	12,644	12,824	14,923
Shares Outstanding	504	504	503	501	499	498	498	497
Statistical Record								
Return on Assets %	0.03	0.15	0.18	0.12	0.78	N.M.	N.M.	N.M.
Return on Equity %	0.23	1.19	1.39	0.92	6.27	N.M.	N.M.	N.M.
Net Margin %	5.94	7.84	7.89	1.41	9.85	(3.31)	(7.19)	(13.01)
Price Range	5.01-2.91	5.01-2.91	5.01-2.69	4.82-2.69	4.16-3.11	5.22-1.61	9.15-3.47	18.60-7.64
P/E Ratio	83.50-48.50	16.16-9.39	13.92-7.47	20.08-11.21	2.55-1.91	...	...	...

Address: 6620 West Broad Street, Richmond, VA 23230 Telephone: 804-281-6000	Web Site: www.genworth.com Officers: Thomas J. McInerney - President, Chief Executive Officer Kelly L. Groh - Executive Vice President, Chief Financial Officer, Controller	Auditors: KPMG LLP Transfer Agents: Computershare Shareowner Services LLC, College Station, TX

GEO GROUP INC (THE)

Exchange	Symbol	Price	52Wk Range	Yield	P/E
NYS	GEO	$16.61 (12/31/2019)	23.86-13.31	11.56	12.21

*7 Year Price Score 67.72   *NYSE Composite Index=100   *12 Month Price Score 75.33

Interim Earnings (Per Share)

Qtr.	Mar	Jun	Sep	Dec
2016	0.29	0.21	0.39	0.44
2017	0.35	0.25	0.31	0.29
2018	0.29	0.31	0.33	0.28
2019	0.34	0.35	0.39	...

Interim Dividends (Per Share)

Amt	Decl	Ex	Rec	Pay
0.48Q	02/04/2019	02/14/2019	02/15/2019	02/22/2019
0.48Q	04/03/2019	04/12/2019	04/15/2019	04/22/2019
0.48Q	07/09/2019	07/18/2019	07/19/2019	07/26/2019
0.48Q	10/14/2019	10/24/2019	10/25/2019	11/01/2019

Indicated Div: $1.92

Valuation Analysis

		Institutional Holding	
Forecast EPS	$1.50	No of Institutions	379
	(01/03/2020)		
Market Cap	$2.0 Billion	Shares	
Book Value	$1.0 Billion	125,048,232	
Price/Book	2.00	% Held	
Price/Sales	0.82	N/A	

Business Summary: REITs (MIC: 5.3.1 SIC: 6798 NAIC: 525930)

GEO Group is a real estate investment trust. Co. owns, leases and manages correctional, detention and reentry facilities and provides community-based services and youth services in the U.S., Australia, South Africa and the U.K. Co.'s operations include the management and/or ownership of correctional, detention and community-based facilities, and also include the provision of community supervision services for offenders and pretrial defendants, including radio frequency, GPS, and alcohol monitoring devices. Co. also provides transportation services for offender and detainee populations as contracted domestically and in the U.K.

Recent Developments: For the quarter ended Sep 30 2019, net income increased 17.0% to US$45.9 million from US$39.2 million in the year-earlier quarter. Revenues were US$631.6 million, up 8.2% from US$583.5 million the year before.

Prospects: Our evaluation of Geo Group Inc. as of October 4th, 2019 is the result of our systematic analysis on three basic characteristics: earnings strength, relative valuation, and recent stock price movement. The company has enjoyed a very positive trend in earnings per share over the past 5 quarters. However, recent analyst estimates for the company have been mixed and GEO has posted results that fell short of analysts' expectations. Based on operating earnings yield, the company is undervalued when compared to all of the companies we cover. Share price changes over the past year indicates that GEO will perform well over the near term.

Financial Data

(US$ in Thousands)	9 Mos	6 Mos	3 Mos	12/31/2018	12/31/2017	12/31/2016	12/31/2015	12/31/2014
Earnings Per Share	1.36	1.30	1.26	1.20	1.21	1.33	1.25	1.32
Cash Flow Per Share	3.16	2.58	2.57	2.28	3.17	(0.25)	1.29	1.87
Tang Book Value Per Share	0.13	0.20	0.20	0.26	1.33	1.38	1.49	3.56
Dividends Per Share	1.910	1.900	1.890	1.880	1.877	1.733	1.673	0.413
Dividend Payout %	140.44	146.15	150.00	156.67	155.10	130.00	133.51	31.31
Income Statement								
Total Revenue	1,856,212	1,224,633	610,667	2,331,386	2,263,420	2,179,490	1,843,307	1,691,620
EBITDA	235,825	155,234	77,340	368,165	347,185	339,599	323,229	314,531
Depn & Amortn	6,861	5,023	2,563	103,500	98,900	89,900	87,500	79,800
Income Before Taxes	136,234	87,440	42,893	149,317	151,937	149,477	141,171	152,110
Income Taxes	14,509	9,372	4,840	14,117	17,958	7,904	7,389	14,093
Net Income	128,551	82,619	40,705	145,089	146,241	148,715	139,438	143,930
Average Shares	119,282	119,544	119,496	120,747	120,814	111,484	110,992	108,820
Balance Sheet								
Current Assets	517,599	532,884	604,613	591,107	579,709	697,669	438,346	377,406
Total Assets	4,282,879	4,308,138	4,384,066	4,247,463	4,226,908	3,749,409	3,503,342	3,002,208
Current Liabilities	408,605	409,652	708,785	694,583	369,563	504,058	278,624	254,075
Long-Term Obligations	2,666,159	2,678,611	2,452,724	2,416,814	2,552,967	2,181,738	2,118,716	1,604,643
Total Liabilities	3,275,085	3,285,872	3,356,507	3,206,960	3,027,667	2,774,353	2,496,604	1,956,529
Stockholders' Equity	1,007,794	1,022,266	1,027,559	1,040,503	1,199,241	975,056	1,006,738	1,045,679
Shares Outstanding	121,221	121,212	121,186	120,584	124,008	112,547	111,964	111,286
Statistical Record								
Return on Assets %	3.80	3.65	3.52	3.42	3.67	4.09	4.29	4.89
Return on Equity %	15.51	14.68	13.92	12.96	13.45	14.97	13.59	13.91
EBITDA Margin %	12.70	12.68	12.66	15.79	15.34	15.58	17.54	18.59
Net Margin %	6.93	6.75	6.67	6.22	6.46	6.82	7.56	8.51
Asset Turnover	0.58	0.57	0.55	0.55	0.57	0.60	0.57	0.57
Current Ratio	1.27	1.30	0.85	0.85	1.57	1.38	1.57	1.49
Debt to Equity	2.65	2.62	2.39	2.32	2.13	2.24	2.10	1.53
Price Range	24.74-16.42	27.30-18.34	27.54-18.34	27.54-18.94	34.12-23.07	23.95-13.01	30.13-17.67	27.60-20.63
P/E Ratio	18.19-12.07	21.00-14.11	21.86-14.56	22.95-15.78	28.20-19.07	18.01-9.78	24.10-14.14	20.91-15.63
Average Yield %	9.19	8.37	8.08	8.01	6.63	8.67	6.96	1.75

Address: 4955 Technology Way, Boca Raton, FL 33431 **Telephone:** 561-893-0101	**Web Site:** www.geogroup.com **Officers:** George C. Zoley - Chairman, Chief Executive Officer Brian R. Evans - Senior Vice President, Chief Financial Officer	**Auditors:** Grant Thornton LLP **Investor Contact:** 561-893-0101 **Transfer Agents:** Computershare, Providence, RI

GLOBAL PARTNERS LP

Exchange	Symbol	Price	52Wk Range	Yield	P/E
NYS	GLP	$20.16 (12/31/2019)	21.39-16.30	10.32	8.51

*7 Year Price Score 63.37 *NYSE Composite Index=100 *12 Month Price Score 97.37

Interim Earnings (Per Share)

Qtr.	Mar	Jun	Sep	Dec
2016	(0.21)	(0.22)	(3.54)	(1.94)
2017	0.68	0.07	0.44	0.56
2018	1.73	0.19	(0.44)	1.48
2019	0.15	0.38	...	

Interim Dividends (Per Share)

Amt	Decl	Ex	Rec	Pay
0.50Q	01/28/2019	02/07/2019	02/08/2019	02/14/2019
0.51Q	04/29/2019	05/09/2019	05/10/2019	05/15/2019
0.515Q	07/26/2019	08/08/2019	08/09/2019	08/14/2019
0.52Q	10/25/2019	11/07/2019	11/08/2019	11/14/2019

Indicated Div: $2.08

Valuation Analysis

Forecast EPS	$0.72
	(01/15/2020)
Market Cap	$687.4 Million
Book Value	N/A
Price/Book	N/A
Price/Sales	0.05

Institutional Holding

No of Institutions	93
Shares	20,706,158
% Held	37.15

Business Summary: Equipment & Services (MIC: 9.1.3 SIC: 5171 NAIC: 424710)

Global Partners is a master limited partnership that owns, controls or has access to a terminal network of refined petroleum products and renewable fuels. Co.'s segments are: Wholesale, which sells, gathers, blends, stores and transports refined petroleum products, gasoline blendstocks, renewable fuels, crude oil and propane; Gasoline Distribution and Station Operations, which sells branded and unbranded gasoline to gasoline station operators and sub-jobbers; and Commercial, which includes sales and deliveries to end user customers in the public sector and to commercial and industrial end users of unbranded gasoline, home heating oil, diesel, kerosene, residual oil and bunker fuel.

Recent Developments: For the quarter ended Sep 30 2019, net income amounted to US$14.9 million versus a net loss of US$14.5 million in the year-earlier quarter. Revenues were US$3.25 billion, down 6.4% from US$3.47 billion the year before. Operating income was US$50.9 million versus US$8.1 million in the prior-year quarter, an increase of 524.7%. Direct operating expenses declined 8.3% to US$3.06 billion from US$3.33 billion in the comparable period the year before. Indirect operating expenses increased 7.9% to US$136.9 million from US$126.8 million in the equivalent prior-year period.

Prospects: For the Quarter ended Mar. 31, 2017, Co. posted a solid first quarter and continued to position the Partnership for growth. Net income attributable to the Partnership in the first quarter of 2017 was $22.9 million, or $0.68 per diluted limited partner unit, compared with a net loss attributable to the Partnership of $7.0 million, or $0.21 per limited partner unit, in the first quarter of 2016. EBITDA in the first quarter of 2017 was $71.9 million compared with EBITDA of $42.6 million in the comparable period of 2016. Adjusted EBITDA was $60.1 million in the first quarter of 2017 compared with Adjusted EBITDA of $48.7 million in the same period of 2016.

Financial Data

(US$ in Thousands)

	9 Mos	6 Mos	3 Mos	12/31/2018	12/31/2017	12/31/2016	12/31/2015	12/31/2014
Earnings Per Share	2.37	1.55	1.38	2.95	1.74	(5.91)	1.11	3.95
Cash Flow Per Share	9.58	4.49	5.50	5.01	10.37	(3.57)	1.94	12.58
Dividends Per Share	2.000	1.960	1.913	1.875	1.850	1.850	2.735	2.527
Dividend Payout %	84.39	126.45	138.59	63.56	106.32		246.40	63.99
Income Statement								
Total Revenue	9,732,819	6,487,166	2,979,626	12,672,602	8,920,552	8,239,639	10,314,852	17,269,954
EBITDA	110,461	71,312	31,836	293,071	216,184	(49,651)	217,023	233,207
Depn & Amortn	5,015	3,663	2,062	95,900	96,400	102,600	102,300	67,500
Income Before Taxes	37,333	21,627	6,818	108,026	33,554	(238,570)	41,391	117,943
Income Taxes	1,275	462	24	5,623	(23,563)	53	(1,873)	963
Net Income	36,695	21,615	7,126	103,905	58,752	(199,412)	43,563	114,709
Average Shares	34,266	34,286	34,230	33,972	33,634	33,525	32,323	27,502
Balance Sheet								
Current Assets	871,382	931,408	1,009,184	874,908	878,135	1,075,466	867,035	961,223
Total Assets	2,678,245	2,763,915	2,845,990	2,424,291	2,320,169	2,564,020	2,663,675	2,039,977
Current Liabilities	620,568	701,168	780,169	582,752	668,657	799,225	594,734	707,491
Long-Term Obligations	1,186,629	1,177,536	1,181,998	1,034,455	957,774	1,025,850	1,075,564	601,936
Total Liabilities	2,197,724	2,279,321	2,357,999	1,926,960	1,929,216	2,171,365	2,015,886	1,453,035
Shares Outstanding	34,096	33,985	33,753	33,981	33,875	33,773	33,737	30,835
Statistical Record								
Return on Assets %	3.40	2.38	2.00	4.38	2.41	N.M.	1.85	5.13
EBITDA Margin %	1.13	1.10	1.07	2.31	2.42	N.M.	2.10	1.35
Net Margin %	0.38	0.33	0.24	0.82	0.66	N.M.	0.42	0.66
Asset Turnover	4.95	5.25	4.94	5.34	3.65	3.14	4.39	7.73
Current Ratio	1.40	1.33	1.29	1.50	1.31	1.35	1.46	1.36
Price Range	21.39-13.79	21.39-13.79	20.82-13.79	20.82-13.79	21.55-16.05	19.50-12.31	41.82-15.26	45.32-31.68
P/E Ratio	9.03-5.82	13.80-8.90	15.09-9.99	7.06-4.67	12.39-9.22	...	37.68-13.75	11.47-8.02
Average Yield %	10.54	10.47	10.65	10.63	10.09	12.54	8.21	6.37

Address: P.O. Box 9161, 800 South Street, Waltham, MA 02454-9161 **Telephone:** 781-894-8800	**Web Site:** www.globalp.com **Officers:** Richard Slifka - Chairman Eric S. Slifka - President, Chief Executive Officer, Associate/Affiliate Company Officer	**Auditors:** Ernst & Young LLP **Investor Contact:** 781-894-8800 **Transfer Agents:** American Stock Transfer and Trust Company, New Yor, NY

GLOBAL PAYMENTS INC

Exchange	Symbol	Price	52Wk Range	Yield	P/E
NYS	GPN	$182.56 (12/31/2019)	183.49-98.72	0.43	73.02

*7 Year Price Score 161.82 *NYSE Composite Index=100 *12 Month Price Score 110.42

Interim Earnings (Per Share)

Qtr.	Mar	Jun	Sep	Dec
2017	0.32	0.44	0.71	1.54
2018	0.57	0.68	1.11	0.48
2019	0.71	0.77	0.54	...

Interim Dividends (Per Share)

Amt	Decl	Ex	Rec	Pay
0.01Q	02/05/2019	03/14/2019	03/15/2019	03/29/2019
0.01Q	05/02/2019	06/13/2019	06/14/2019	06/28/2019
0.01Q	07/25/2019	09/12/2019	09/13/2019	09/27/2019
0.195Q	10/31/2019	12/12/2019	12/13/2019	12/27/2019

Indicated Div: $0.78

Valuation Analysis / **Institutional Holding**

Forecast EPS	$6.17 (01/17/2020)	No of Institutions	996
Market Cap	$54.9 Billion	Shares	
Book Value	$27.8 Billion		288,788,192
Price/Book	1.98	% Held	
Price/Sales	14.42		87.70

Business Summary: Business Services (MIC: 7.5.2 SIC: 7389 NAIC: 561499)

Global Payments is a provider of payment technology and software solutions. Co.'s payment solutions enables its customers to accept card, electronic, check and digital-based payments. Co.'s offerings include authorization services, settlement and funding services, customer support and help-desk functions, chargeback resolution, terminal rental, sales and deployment, consolidated billing and statements and on-line reporting. Through its wholesale channel, Co. provides payment services to merchants through independent sales organizations. Co.'s credit and debit card transaction processing includes the processing of international card brands, including American Express, JCB, and MasterCard.

Recent Developments: For the quarter ended Sep 30 2019, net income decreased 43.2% to US$105.7 million from US$186.0 million in the year-earlier quarter. Revenues were US$1.11 billion, up 28.9% from US$857.7 million the year before. Operating income was US$174.0 million versus US$223.2 million in the prior-year quarter, a decrease of 22.0%. Direct operating expenses rose 61.4% to US$427.7 million from US$265.0 million in the comparable period the year before. Indirect operating expenses increased 36.5% to US$504.2 million from US$369.5 million in the equivalent prior-year period.

Prospects: Our evaluation of Global Payments Inc. as of October 4th, 2019 is the result of our systematic analysis on three basic characteristics: earnings strength, relative valuation, and recent stock price movement. The company has enjoyed a very positive trend in earnings per share over the past 5 quarters. In addition, recent analyst estimates for the company have been raised, and GPN has posted results that exceeded analysts' expectations. Based on operating earnings yield, the company is fairly valued when compared to all of the companies we cover. Share price changes over the past year indicates that GPN will perform very well over the near term.

Financial Data

(US$ in Thousands)	9 Mos	6 Mos	3 Mos	12/31/2018	12/31/2017	12/31/2016	05/31/2016	05/31/2015
Earnings Per Share	2.50	3.07	2.98	2.84	3.01	0.81	2.04	2.06
Cash Flow Per Share	10.14	5.40	6.67	6.97	3.31	5.59	4.41	3.17
Dividends Per Share	0.040	0.040	0.040	0.040	0.043	0.020	0.040	0.040
Dividend Payout %	1.60	1.30	1.34	1.41	1.44	2.47	1.96	1.94
Income Statement								
Total Revenue	2,924,131	1,818,190	883,039	3,366,366	3,975,163	2,202,896	2,898,150	2,773,718
EBITDA	988,488	664,176	322,814	1,114,740	896,746	432,280	538,633	594,084
Depn & Amortn	393,233	242,958	123,322	377,685	337,878	194,329	113,689	137,487
Income Before Taxes	394,739	305,633	143,345	562,155	392,683	173,344	360,912	417,110
Income Taxes	39,765	56,388	24,140	77,488	(101,387)	35,661	70,695	107,995
Net Income	327,842	232,800	112,341	452,053	468,425	124,931	271,666	278,040
Average Shares	177,543	157,262	158,018	159,271	155,528	154,231	133,167	134,922
Balance Sheet								
Current Assets	4,992,568	4,547,679	4,669,751	3,376,208	4,303,579	3,116,006	2,851,313	3,302,295
Total Assets	45,212,047	14,584,072	14,749,621	13,230,774	12,998,069	10,664,350	10,509,952	5,793,548
Current Liabilities	4,283,152	4,483,582	4,516,222	3,268,620	3,815,590	2,851,956	2,430,707	3,015,904
Long-Term Obligations	8,987,704	5,000,585	5,170,377	5,015,168	4,559,408	4,260,827	4,379,744	1,680,000
Total Liabilities	17,437,413	10,593,468	10,798,808	9,239,367	9,203,542	8,033,559	7,763,476	5,035,572
Stockholders' Equity	27,774,634	3,990,604	3,950,813	3,991,407	3,794,527	2,630,791	2,746,476	757,976
Shares Outstanding	300,544	156,674	157,130	157,961	159,180	152,185	154,421	130,557
Statistical Record								
Return on Assets %	1.37	3.60	3.42	3.45	3.96	2.59	3.32	5.67
Return on Equity %	2.54	12.39	11.97	11.97	11.61	14.58	12.58	15.46	31.68
EBITDA Margin %	33.80	36.53	36.56	33.11	22.56	19.62	18.59	21.42
Net Margin %	11.21	12.80	12.72	13.43	11.78	5.67	9.37	10.02
Asset Turnover	0.13	0.26	0.25	0.26	0.34	0.46	0.35	0.57
Current Ratio	1.17	1.01	1.03	1.03	1.13	1.09	1.17	1.09
Debt to Equity	0.32	1.25	1.31	1.26	1.20	1.62	1.59	2.22
Price Range	174.84-95.37	161.76-95.37	136.52-95.37	128.59-95.37	104.27-70.50	79.23-66.42	77.69-51.09	52.70-33.98
P/E Ratio	69.94-38.15	52.69-31.07	45.81-32.00	45.28-33.58	34.64-23.42	97.81-82.00	38.08-25.04	25.58-16.50
Average Yield %	0.03	0.03	0.03	0.04	0.05	0.03	0.06	0.10

Address: 3550 Lenox Road, Atlanta, GA 30326
Telephone: 770-829-8000

Web Site: www.globalpaymentsinc.com
Officers: M. Troy Woods - Chairman Cameron M. Bready - President, Senior Executive Vice President, Executive Vice President, Chief Financial Officer, Chief Financial Officer (frmr), Chief Operating Officer

Auditors: DELOITTE & TOUCHE LLP
Investor Contact: 770-829-8478
Transfer Agents: Computershare Trust Company, N.A, Canton, MA

GLOBE LIFE INC

Exchange	Symbol	Price	52Wk Range	Yield	P/E	Div Acheiver
NYS	GL PRC	$105.25 (12/31/2019)	106.63-74.53	1.45	15.97	13 Years

*7 Year Price Score 102.66 *NYSE Composite Index=100 *12 Month Price Score 107.74

Interim Earnings (Per Share)

Qtr.	Mar	Jun	Sep	Dec
2016	1.01	1.13	1.25	1.11
2017	1.11	1.18	1.29	8.64
2018	1.49	1.59	1.55	1.45
2019	1.65	1.67	1.82	...

Interim Dividends (Per Share)

Amt	Decl	Ex	Rec	Pay
0.383Q	05/14/2019	08/29/2019	09/01/2019	09/15/2019
0.383Q	05/14/2019	05/30/2019	06/01/2019	06/15/2019
0.383Q	10/28/2019	11/27/2019	12/01/2019	12/15/2019
0.383Q	10/28/2019	02/27/2020	03/01/2020	03/15/2020

Indicated Div: $1.53 (Div. Reinv. Plan)

Valuation Analysis   **Institutional Holding**

Forecast EPS	$6.76	No of Institutions
	(01/17/2020)	756
Market Cap	$11.4 Billion	Shares
Book Value	$7.3 Billion	105,417,096
Price/Book	1.56	% Held
Price/Sales	2.56	N/A

Business Summary: Life & Health (MIC: 5.2.2 SIC: 6311 NAIC: 524113)

Globe Life is an insurance holding company. Through its wholly-owned subsidiaries, Co. provides a variety of life and supplemental health insurance products and annuities to customers. Co.'s segments are: life insurance, which writes a variety of nonparticipating ordinary life insurance products including whole-life insurance, term life insurance, and other life insurance; health insurance, which provides Medicare Supplement and limited-benefit supplemental health insurance products that include primarily critical illness and accident plans; annuity, which includes single-premium and flexible-premium deferred annuities; and investment.

Recent Developments: For the quarter ended Sep 30 2019, income from continuing operations increased 12.9% to US$201.8 million from US$178.7 million in the year-earlier quarter. Net income increased 12.9% to US$201.8 million from US$178.7 million in the year-earlier quarter. Revenues were US$1.14 billion, up 5.3% from US$1.08 billion the year before. Net premiums earned were US$900.0 million versus US$860.8 million in the prior-year quarter, an increase of 4.6%. Net investment income rose 3.3% to US$228.9 million from US$221.6 million a year ago.

Prospects: Our evaluation of Globe Life Inc. as of October 4th, 2019 is the result of our systematic analysis on three basic characteristics: earnings strength, relative valuation, and recent stock price movement. The company has managed to produce a neutral trend in earnings per share over the past 5 quarters. In addition, recent analyst estimates for the company have been mixed and GL has posted results that exceeded analysts' expectations. Based on operating earnings yield, the company is undervalued when compared to all of the companies we cover. Share price changes over the past year indicates that GL will perform poorly over the near term.

Financial Data
(US$ in Thousands)

	9 Mos	6 Mos	3 Mos	12/31/2018	12/31/2017	12/31/2016	12/31/2015	12/31/2014
Earnings Per Share	6.59	6.32	6.24	6.09	12.22	4.49	4.16	4.09
Cash Flow Per Share	12.60	12.29	11.95	11.32	12.28	11.62	8.95	6.61
Tang Book Value Per Share	63.36	57.30	50.96	44.93	50.53	34.95	29.53	33.27
Dividends Per Share	0.665	0.652	0.640	0.630	0.590	0.555	0.405	12.05
Dividend Payout %	10.09	10.32	10.26	10.34	4.83	12.36	9.74	12.39
Income Statement								
Premium Income	2,688,450	1,788,457	890,973	3,421,906	3,282,935	3,137,034	2,998,720	3,209,420
Total Revenue	3,390,956	2,249,677	1,119,216	4,303,751	4,155,573	3,934,629	3,766,065	3,964,296
Benefits & Claims	1,762,811	1,177,119	587,757	2,275,242	2,227,875	2,128,748	2,016,212	2,219,200
Income Before Taxes	704,191	456,861	228,101	863,671	830,648	772,235	766,187	778,468
Income Taxes	130,370	84,858	42,707	162,161	(627,615)	232,645	249,894	235,529
Net Income	573,729	371,911	185,345	701,466	1,454,494	549,779	527,100	542,939
Average Shares	110,913	111,585	112,328	115,248	118,983	122,367	126,757	132,640
Balance Sheet								
Total Assets	25,791,906	24,855,445	24,133,438	23,095,722	23,474,985	21,436,087	19,853,213	20,214,730
Total Liabilities	18,479,375	18,155,047	18,090,012	17,680,545	17,243,564	16,869,226	15,797,661	15,517,264
Stockholders' Equity	7,312,531	6,700,398	6,043,426	5,415,177	6,231,421	4,566,861	4,055,552	4,697,466
Shares Outstanding	108,444	109,222	109,926	110,693	114,593	118,031	122,369	127,930
Statistical Record								
Return on Assets %	3.00	3.00	3.01	3.01	6.48	2.66	2.63	2.83
Return on Equity %	11.49	11.66	12.02	12.05	26.94	12.72	12.04	12.81
Loss Ratio %	65.57	65.82	65.97	66.49	67.86	67.86	67.24	69.15
Net Margin %	16.92	16.53	16.56	16.30	35.00	13.97	14.00	13.70
Price Range	96.20-70.61	89.46-70.61	89.19-70.61	93.32-70.61	91.16-73.00	74.83-48.58	63.12-50.07	82.61-50.32
P/E Ratio	14.60-10.71	14.16-11.17	14.29-11.32	15.32-11.59	7.46-5.97	16.67-10.82	15.17-12.04	20.20-12.30
Average Yield %	0.78	0.77	0.76	0.74	0.75	0.91	0.71	0.95

Address: 3700 South Stonebridge Drive, McKinney, TX 75070 **Telephone:** 972-569-4000	**Web Site:** www.torchmarkcorp.com **Officers:** Gary L. Coleman - Co-Chairman, Co-Chief Executive Officer, Executive Vice President, Chief Financial Officer Larry M. Hutchison - Co-Chairman, Co-Chief Executive Officer, Executive Vice President, General Counsel	**Auditors:** DELOITTE & TOUCHE LLP **Investor Contact:** 972-569-3627 **Transfer Agents:** Wells Fargo Shareowner Services, St. Paul, MN

GLOBUS MEDICAL INC

Exchange	Symbol	Price	52Wk Range	Yield	P/E
NYS	GMED	$58.88 (12/31/2019)	59.50-38.08	N/A	40.61

*7 Year Price Score 126.83 *NYSE Composite Index=100 *12 Month Price Score 111.27

TRADING VOLUME (thousand shares)

Interim Earnings (Per Share)

Qtr.	Mar	Jun	Sep	Dec
2016	0.29	0.27	0.27	0.25
2017	0.30	0.29	0.26	0.25
2018	0.39	0.44	0.35	0.36
2019	0.33	0.38	0.38	...

Interim Dividends (Per Share)

No Dividends Paid

Valuation Analysis

		Institutional Holding	
Forecast EPS	$1.72	No of Institutions	
	(01/14/2020)	N/A	
Market Cap	$5.9 Billion	Shares	
Book Value	$1.3 Billion	N/A	
Price/Book	4.37	% Held	
Price/Sales	7.60	N/A	

Business Summary: Medical Instruments & Equipment (MIC: 4.3.1 SIC: 3841 NAIC: 339112)

Globus Medical is a medical device company that develops and commercializes healthcare solutions for patients with musculoskeletal disorders. Co. is primarily focused on implants for patients with musculoskeletal disorders. Co.'s product categories are: Musculoskeletal Solutions, which consist primarily of implantable devices, biologics, accessories, and surgical instruments used in a range of spinal, orthopedic and neurosurgical procedures; and Enabling Technologies, consisting of computer-assisted intelligent systems designed to improve a surgeon's capabilities and streamline surgical procedures to improve patient care and reduce radiation exposure for all involved.

Recent Developments: For the quarter ended Sep 30 2019, net income increased 8.8% to US$38.3 million from US$35.2 million in the year-earlier quarter. Revenues were US$196.2 million, up 15.9% from US$169.2 million the year before. Operating income was US$42.1 million versus US$38.3 million in the prior-year quarter, an increase of 9.8%. Direct operating expenses rose 19.9% to US$45.4 million from US$37.8 million in the comparable period the year before. Indirect operating expenses increased 16.8% to US$108.8 million from US$93.1 million in the equivalent prior-year period.

Prospects: Our evaluation of Globus Medical Inc as of October 4th, 2019 is the result of our systematic analysis on three basic characteristics: earnings strength, relative valuation, and recent stock price movement. The company has managed to produce a neutral trend in earnings per share over the past 5 quarters. Additionally, recent analyst estimates for the company have been unchanged while GMED has posted results that exceeded analysts' expectations. Based on operating earnings yield, the company is fairly valued when compared to all of the companies we cover. Share price changes over the past year indicates that GMED will perform poorly over the near term.

Financial Data

(US$ in Thousands)	9 Mos	6 Mos	3 Mos	12/31/2018	12/31/2017	12/31/2016	12/31/2015	12/31/2014
Earnings Per Share	1.45	1.42	1.48	1.54	1.10	1.08	1.17	0.97
Cash Flow Per Share	1.63	1.59	1.71	1.86	1.66	1.79	1.28	0.84
Tang Book Value Per Share	11.35	10.82	10.40	9.89	7.92	6.93	6.19	5.26
Income Statement								
Total Revenue	573,701	377,486	182,947	712,969	635,977	563,994	544,753	474,371
EBITDA	121,535	79,432	37,096	230,235	211,995	196,050	195,327	159,686
Depn & Amortn	(1,008)	(736)	(396)	41,630	42,067	38,771	22,522	21,044
Income Before Taxes	135,497	88,744	41,651	188,605	169,928	157,279	172,805	138,642
Income Taxes	25,816	17,370	8,441	32,131	62,580	52,938	60,021	46,157
Net Income	109,681	71,374	33,210	156,474	107,348	104,341	112,784	92,485
Average Shares	102,100	101,582	101,367	101,316	97,887	96,432	96,073	95,457
Balance Sheet								
Current Assets	637,063	583,933	617,568	630,681	620,342	513,766	544,799	470,025
Total Assets	1,452,182	1,390,746	1,335,919	1,300,670	1,078,502	927,637	834,100	703,547
Current Liabilities	94,921	84,184	79,492	96,118	93,073	79,892	82,691	89,412
Total Liabilities	113,387	103,220	98,705	115,154	110,724	95,559	118,776	118,093
Stockholders' Equity	1,338,795	1,287,526	1,237,214	1,185,516	967,778	832,078	715,324	585,454
Shares Outstanding	99,403	99,077	98,982	98,573	96,657	95,929	95,319	94,705
Statistical Record								
Return on Assets %	10.88	11.09	12.19	13.15	10.70	11.81	14.67	14.57
Return on Equity %	11.81	12.02	13.26	14.53	11.93	13.45	17.34	17.49
EBITDA Margin %	21.18	21.04	20.28	32.29	33.33	34.76	35.86	33.66
Net Margin %	19.12	18.91	18.15	21.95	16.88	18.50	20.70	19.50
Asset Turnover	0.57	0.57	0.59	0.60	0.63	0.64	0.71	0.75
Current Ratio	6.71	6.94	7.77	6.56	6.67	6.43	6.59	5.26
Price Range	57.44-38.08	57.44-38.08	57.44-38.08	57.44-41.38	41.64-24.79	27.82-20.65	28.24-20.66	26.95-18.14
P/E Ratio	39.61-26.26	40.45-26.82	38.81-25.73	37.30-26.87	37.85-22.54	25.76-19.12	24.14-17.66	27.78-18.70

Address: 2560 General Armistead Avenue, Audubon, PA 19403 **Telephone:** 610-930-1800 **Fax:** 302-636-5454	**Web Site:** www.globusmedical.com **Officers:** David C. Paul - Chairman, Chief Executive Officer David M. Demski - President, President (frmr), Chief Executive Officer, Chief Operating Officer, Division Officer	**Auditors:** Deloitte & Touche LLP **Investor Contact:** 610-930-1800 **Transfer Agents:** Broadridge Corporate Issuer Solutions, Inc., Philadelphia, PA

GODADDY INC

Exchange	Symbol	Price	52Wk Range	Yield	P/E
NYS	GDDY	$67.92 (12/31/2019)	81.75-60.23	N/A	102.91

*7 Year Price Score N/A   *NYSE Composite Index=100   *12 Month Price Score 90.91

Interim Earnings (Per Share)

Qtr.	Mar	Jun	Sep	Dec
2016	(0.15)	(0.11)	0.05	(0.02)
2017	0.01	0.10	0.17	0.54
2018	0.02	0.11	0.08	0.24
2019	0.07	(0.07)	0.42	...

Interim Dividends (Per Share)

No Dividends Paid

Valuation Analysis

		Institutional Holding	
Forecast EPS	$0.71	No of Institutions	
	(01/17/2020)	458	
Market Cap	$11.7 Billion	Shares	
Book Value	$667.9 Million		175,655,616
Price/Book	17.59	% Held	
Price/Sales	4.05		94.73

TRADING VOLUME (thousand shares)

Business Summary: Internet & Software (MIC: 6.3.2 SIC: 7373 NAIC: 541512)

GoDaddy is a technology provider to small businesses, web design personnel and individuals, delivering cloud-based products and personalized Customer Care. Co. provides hosting, presence and business applications products and services. Co. provides applications and access to relevant third party products helping them connect to their customers, manage and grow their businesses and get found online. Co. has designed and developed a set of cloud-based technology products enabling its customers to establish a digital presence, connect with their customers and manage their ventures.

Recent Developments: For the quarter ended Sep 30 2019, net income increased 444.7% to US$76.8 million from US$14.1 million in the year-earlier quarter. Revenues were US$760.5 million, up 11.9% from US$679.5 million the year before. Operating income was US$91.4 million versus US$37.5 million in the prior-year quarter, an increase of 143.7%. Direct operating expenses rose 16.8% to US$265.0 million from US$226.9 million in the comparable period the year before. Indirect operating expenses decreased 2.6% to US$404.1 million from US$415.1 million in the equivalent prior-year period.

Prospects: Our evaluation of GoDaddy Inc as of October 4th, 2019 is the result of our systematic analysis on three basic characteristics: earnings strength, relative valuation, and recent stock price movement. The company has generated a negative trend in earnings per share over the past 5 quarters. However, recent analyst estimates for the company have been mixed and GDDY has posted results that fell short of analysts' expectations. Based on operating earnings yield, the company is overvalued when compared to all of the companies we cover. Share price changes over the past year indicates that GDDY will perform in line with the market over the near term.

Financial Data

(US$ in Thousands)	9 Mos	6 Mos	3 Mos	12/31/2018	12/31/2017	12/31/2016	12/31/2015	12/31/2014
Earnings Per Share	0.66	0.32	0.50	0.45	0.79	(0.21)	(0.81)	(1.11)
Cash Flow Per Share	3.95	3.66	3.57	3.61	4.37	4.83	4.42	1.40
Income Statement								
Total Revenue	2,207,700	1,447,200	710,000	2,660,100	2,231,900	1,847,900	1,607,300	1,387,262
EBITDA	301,200	154,300	90,900	268,800	278,600	104,700	9,900	(5,558)
Depn & Amortn	160,900	111,000	57,200	97,400	88,800	69,000	61,300	55,574
Income Before Taxes	69,900	(4,200)	9,300	73,000	106,800	(21,500)	(120,600)	(146,129)
Income Taxes	(7,400)	(4,700)	(3,900)	(9,000)	(18,900)	400	(200)	(2,824)
Net Income	76,500	300	12,900	77,100	136,400	(16,500)	(47,400)	(143,305)
Average Shares	181,654	176,007	183,148	181,353	177,054	79,835	58,676	128,567
Balance Sheet								
Current Assets	1,484,600	1,720,400	1,611,800	1,427,300	1,059,500	932,800	693,900	460,882
Total Assets	6,167,600	6,448,900	6,350,600	6,083,400	5,738,300	3,786,900	3,498,800	3,264,805
Current Liabilities	1,969,300	2,020,100	1,970,500	1,886,200	1,810,700	1,262,200	1,113,600	972,749
Long-Term Obligations	2,558,400	2,563,000	2,565,300	2,394,200	2,410,800	1,035,700	1,039,800	1,413,939
Total Liabilities	5,499,700	5,503,800	5,440,200	5,290,700	5,251,800	3,224,400	3,073,000	2,854,414
Stockholders' Equity	667,900	945,100	910,400	792,700	486,500	562,500	425,800	410,391
Shares Outstanding	172,951	178,293	176,768	174,803	167,999	167,112	157,481	129,003
Statistical Record								
Return on Assets %	1.95	0.90	1.41	1.30	2.86	N.M.	N.M.	N.M.
Return on Equity %	17.45	7.10	11.89	12.05	26.01	N.M.	N.M.	N.M.
EBITDA Margin %	13.64	10.66	12.80	10.10	12.48	5.67	0.62	N.M.
Net Margin %	3.47	0.02	1.82	2.90	6.11	N.M.	N.M.	N.M.
Asset Turnover	0.48	0.46	0.45	0.45	0.47	0.51	0.48	0.43
Current Ratio	0.75	0.85	0.82	0.76	0.59	0.74	0.62	0.47
Debt to Equity	3.83	2.71	2.82	3.02	4.96	1.84	2.44	3.45
Price Range	83.07-59.25	84.00-59.25	84.00-59.12	84.00-49.07	51.06-34.41	36.82-24.25	34.24-23.59	...
P/E Ratio	125.86-89.77	262.50-185.16	168.00-118.24	186.67-109.04	64.63-43.56	...	...	...

Address: 14455 N. Hayden Road, Scottsdale, AZ 85260	Web Site: www.godaddy.com	Auditors: Ernst & Young LLP
Telephone: 480-505-8800	Officers: Charles J. (Chuck) Robel - Chairman Aman S. Bhutani - Chief Executive Officer	Transfer Agents: American Stock Transfer & Trust Company, LLC, Brooklyn, NY

GORMAN-RUPP COMPANY (THE)

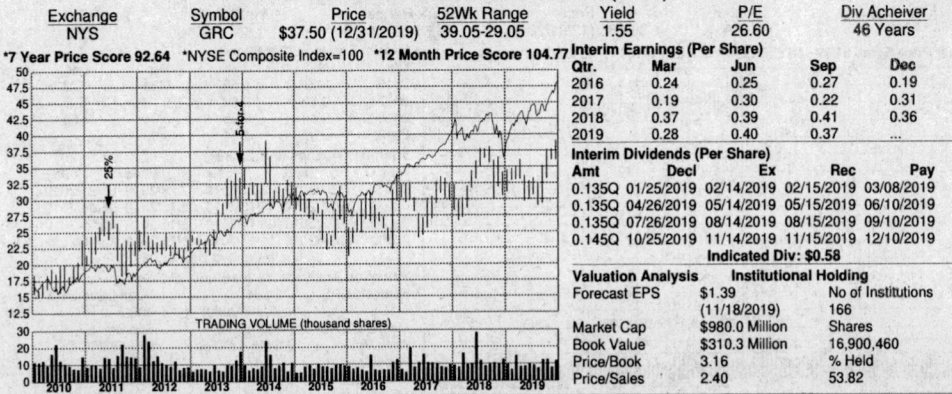

Exchange	Symbol	Price	52Wk Range	Yield	P/E	Div Acheiver
NYS	GRC	$37.50 (12/31/2019)	39.05-29.05	1.55	26.60	46 Years

*7 Year Price Score 92.64   *NYSE Composite Index=100   *12 Month Price Score 104.77

Interim Earnings (Per Share)

Qtr.	Mar	Jun	Sep	Dec
2016	0.24	0.25	0.27	0.19
2017	0.19	0.30	0.22	0.31
2018	0.37	0.39	0.41	0.36
2019	0.28	0.40	0.37	...

Interim Dividends (Per Share)

Amt	Decl	Ex	Rec	Pay
0.135Q	01/25/2019	02/14/2019	02/15/2019	03/08/2019
0.135Q	04/26/2019	05/14/2019	05/15/2019	06/10/2019
0.135Q	07/26/2019	08/14/2019	08/15/2019	09/10/2019
0.145Q	10/25/2019	11/14/2019	11/15/2019	12/10/2019

Indicated Div: $0.58

Valuation Analysis

		Institutional Holding	
Forecast EPS	$1.39	No of Institutions	166
	(11/18/2019)		
Market Cap	$980.0 Million	Shares	
Book Value	$310.3 Million		16,900,460
Price/Book	3.16	% Held	
Price/Sales	2.40		53.82

Business Summary: Industrial Machinery & Equipment (MIC: 7.2.1 SIC: 3561 NAIC: 333911)

Gorman-Rupp designs, manufactures and sells pumps and pump systems for use in water, wastewater, construction, dewatering, industrial, petroleum, original equipment, agriculture, fire protection, heating, ventilating and air conditioning, military and other liquid-handling applications. Co.'s product line consists of pump models ranging in size from 1/4 inches to nearly 15 feet and ranging in several rated capacity. The types of pumps which Co. produces include self-priming centrifugal, standard centrifugal, magnetic drive centrifugal, axial and mixed-flow, vertical turbine line shaft, submersible, high-pressure booster, rotary gear, diaphragm, bellows and oscillating.

Recent Developments: For the quarter ended Sep 30 2019, net income decreased 8.7% to US$9.8 million from US$10.7 million in the year-earlier quarter. Revenues were US$99.3 million, down 3.5% from US$102.9 million the year before. Operating income was US$11.6 million versus US$13.1 million in the prior-year quarter, a decrease of 11.3%. Direct operating expenses declined 2.7% to US$73.5 million from US$75.6 million in the comparable period the year before. Indirect operating expenses were unchanged at US$14.2 million versus the equivalent prior-year period.

Prospects: Our evaluation of Gorman-Rupp Co. as of October 4th, 2019 is the result of our systematic analysis on three basic characteristics: earnings strength, relative valuation, and recent stock price movement. The company has generated a negative trend in earnings per share over the past 5 quarters. However, recent analyst estimates for the company have been unchanged while GRC has posted results that exceeded analysts' expectations. Based on operating earnings yield, the company is fairly valued when compared to all of the companies we cover. Share price changes over the past year indicates that GRC will perform very poorly over the near term.

Financial Data

(US$ in Thousands)	9 Mos	6 Mos	3 Mos	12/31/2018	12/31/2017	12/31/2016	12/31/2015	12/31/2014
Earnings Per Share	1.41	1.45	1.44	1.53	1.02	0.95	0.96	1.38
Cash Flow Per Share	2.41	2.04	1.39	1.58	1.66	2.04	1.55	1.10
Tang Book Value Per Share	10.53	10.32	10.00	9.84	11.02	9.96	9.43	9.22
Dividends Per Share	2.540	2.530	2.520	2.510	0.470	0.430	0.405	0.370
Dividend Payout %	180.14	174.48	175.00	164.05	46.08	45.26	42.19	26.81
Income Statement								
Total Revenue	304,487	205,189	96,859	414,334	379,389	382,071	406,150	434,925
EBITDA	45,147	29,772	12,800	63,616	52,878	52,011	52,548	68,349
Depn & Amortn	10,563	7,095	3,566	13,300	13,500	15,529	15,282	14,615
Income Before Taxes	34,584	22,677	9,242	50,316	39,378	36,482	37,266	53,734
Income Taxes	7,107	4,975	2,020	10,337	12,823	11,599	12,157	17,593
Net Income	27,477	17,702	7,222	39,979	26,555	24,883	25,109	36,141
Average Shares	26,133	26,124	26,118	26,112	26,100	26,087	26,192	26,256
Balance Sheet								
Current Assets	228,246	220,861	207,991	208,686	227,934	203,900	189,391	200,709
Total Assets	387,417	380,596	369,344	368,282	395,015	382,818	364,201	380,904
Current Liabilities	51,202	49,094	45,521	48,465	45,696	49,352	43,460	64,346
Total Liabilities	77,105	75,247	72,397	75,150	69,520	79,930	77,180	98,937
Stockholders' Equity	310,312	305,349	296,947	293,132	325,495	302,888	287,021	281,967
Shares Outstanding	26,133	26,124	26,123	26,117	26,106	26,093	26,083	26,260
Statistical Record								
Return on Assets %	9.11	9.58	9.71	10.48	6.83	6.64	6.74	9.81
Return on Equity %	11.23	11.75	11.94	12.93	8.45	8.41	8.83	13.24
EBITDA Margin %	14.83	14.51	13.22	15.35	13.94	13.61	12.94	15.72
Net Margin %	9.02	8.63	7.46	9.65	7.00	6.51	6.18	8.31
Asset Turnover	1.00	1.04	1.07	1.09	0.98	1.02	1.09	1.18
Current Ratio	4.46	4.50	4.57	4.31	4.99	4.13	4.36	3.12
Price Range	36.53-29.05	38.15-29.67	38.15-28.65	38.15-26.68	33.47-24.07	33.94-21.26	32.12-22.19	39.18-28.87
P/E Ratio	25.91-20.60	26.31-20.46	26.49-19.90	24.93-17.44	32.81-23.60	35.73-22.38	33.46-23.11	28.39-20.92
Average Yield %	7.74	7.42	7.39	7.59	1.59	1.59	1.47	1.16

Address: 600 South Airport Road, Mansfield, OH 44903	Web Site: www.gormanrupp.com	Auditors: Ernst & Young LLP
Telephone: 419-755-1011	Officers: James C. Gorman - Chairman Jeffrey S. Gorman - President, Chief Executive Officer	Investor Contact: 419-755-1397
		Transfer Agents: Broadridge Corporate Issuer Solutions, Inc., Brentwood, NY

GRACE (WR) & CO

Exchange	Symbol	Price	52Wk Range	Yield	P/E
NYS	GRA	$69.85 (12/31/2019)	79.61-63.11	1.55	20.91

*7 Year Price Score 81.69   *NYSE Composite Index=100   *12 Month Price Score 90.39

Interim Earnings (Per Share)

Qtr.	Mar	Jun	Sep	Dec
2016	(0.04)	0.55	0.56	0.22
2017	0.63	0.64	0.70	(1.80)
2018	0.64	0.58	0.24	1.03
2019	0.37	1.14	0.80	...

Interim Dividends (Per Share)

Amt	Decl	Ex	Rec	Pay
0.27Q	02/07/2019	02/27/2019	02/28/2019	03/21/2019
0.27Q	04/25/2019	05/15/2019	05/16/2019	06/06/2019
0.27Q	07/25/2019	08/14/2019	08/15/2019	09/05/2019
0.27Q	10/24/2019	11/13/2019	11/14/2019	12/05/2019

Indicated Div: $1.08

Valuation Analysis / **Institutional Holding**

Forecast EPS	$4.34
	(01/17/2020)
Market Cap	$4.7 Billion
Book Value	$445.4 Million
Price/Book	10.47
Price/Sales	2.36

No of Institutions	409
Shares	67,603,264
% Held	83.97

Business Summary: Specialty Chemicals (MIC: 8.3.2 SIC: 5169 NAIC: 424690)

Grace (W.R.) is engaged in the production and sale of specialty chemicals and specialty materials through two reportable business segments: Grace Catalysts Technologies and Grace Materials Technologies. Grace Catalysts Technologies includes catalysts and related products and technologies used in refining, petrochemical and other chemical manufacturing applications. Grace Materials Technologies includes specialty materials, including silica-based and silica-alumina-based materials, used in consumer/pharma, chemical process, and coatings applications. Co. conducts all of its business through a single wholly owned subsidiary, W. R. Grace & Co.–Conn.

Recent Developments: For the quarter ended Sep 30 2019, net income increased 238.4% to US$53.8 million from US$15.9 million in the year-earlier quarter. Revenues were US$470.5 million, down 4.9% from US$494.9 million the year before. Direct operating expenses declined 4.5% to US$279.5 million from US$292.7 million in the comparable period the year before. Indirect operating expenses decreased 40.8% to US$109.9 million from US$185.6 million in the equivalent prior-year period.

Prospects: Our evaluation of Grace (W.R.) Co. as of October 4th, 2019 is the result of our systematic analysis on three basic characteristics: earnings strength, relative valuation, and recent stock price movement. The company has generated a negative trend in earnings per share over the past 5 quarters. In addition, recent analyst estimates for the company have been reduced while GRA has posted results that exceeded analysts' expectations. Based on operating earnings yield, the company is undervalued when compared to all of the companies we cover. Share price changes over the past year indicates that GRA will perform well over the near term.

Financial Data

(US$ in Thousands)	9 Mos	6 Mos	3 Mos	12/31/2018	12/31/2017	12/31/2016	12/31/2015	12/31/2014
Earnings Per Share	3.34	2.78	2.22	2.49	0.16	1.33	1.99	3.63
Cash Flow Per Share	5.64	5.51	4.85	5.09	4.69	3.81	0.19	(19.55)
Dividends Per Share	1.050	1.020	0.990	0.960	0.840	0.510	...	...
Dividend Payout %	31.44	36.69	44.59	38.55	525.00	38.35	...	...
Income Statement								
Total Revenue	1,453,600	983,100	469,500	1,932,100	1,716,500	1,598,600	3,051,500	3,243,000
EBITDA	331,400	210,000	76,300	374,200	360,600	302,400	499,400	552,900
Depn & Amortn	75,300	49,800	24,900	80,900	96,100	85,700	109,300	112,500
Income Before Taxes	197,900	120,600	31,400	213,100	185,000	136,200	289,200	314,600
Income Taxes	57,000	29,700	10,900	78,100	200,500	59,000	164,700	57,000
Net Income	154,600	100,900	24,700	167,600	11,200	94,100	144,200	276,300
Average Shares	66,800	67,000	66,900	67,300	68,200	70,500	72,600	76,200
Balance Sheet								
Current Assets	1,051,500	1,007,700	980,600	857,300	728,600	654,800	1,184,500	1,690,900
Total Assets	3,779,700	3,726,500	3,646,400	3,565,300	2,907,000	2,911,800	3,676,000	4,095,200
Current Liabilities	704,700	679,500	636,000	514,400	448,200	480,800	707,400	1,182,100
Long-Term Obligations	1,959,300	1,960,400	1,961,600	1,961,000	1,523,800	1,507,600	2,144,300	1,919,000
Total Liabilities	3,334,300	3,345,400	3,298,600	3,234,400	2,650,600	2,543,000	3,468,200	3,729,300
Stockholders' Equity	445,400	381,100	347,800	330,900	256,400	368,800	207,800	365,900
Shares Outstanding	66,735	66,719	66,915	66,792	67,780	68,309	70,533	72,922
Statistical Record								
Return on Assets %	6.13	5.22	4.51	5.18	0.38	2.85	3.71	5.82
Return on Equity %	62.20	55.59	50.66	57.07	3.58	32.55	50.27	59.64
EBITDA Margin %	22.80	21.36	16.25	19.37	21.01	18.92	16.37	17.05
Net Margin %	10.64	10.26	5.26	8.67	0.65	5.89	4.73	8.52
Asset Turnover	0.54	0.56	0.60	0.60	0.59	0.48	0.79	0.68
Current Ratio	1.49	1.48	1.54	1.67	1.63	1.36	1.67	1.43
Debt to Equity	4.40	5.14	5.64	5.93	5.94	4.09	10.32	5.24
Price Range	79.61-59.60	78.60-59.60	78.17-59.60	75.05-59.60	76.60-66.38	79.93-63.12	83.89-68.23	83.47-65.35
P/E Ratio	23.84-17.84	28.27-21.44	35.21-26.85	30.14-23.94	478.75-414.88	60.10-47.46	42.15-34.29	22.99-18.00
Average Yield %	1.48	1.43	1.41	1.39	1.19	0.70	...	...

Address: 7500 Grace Drive, Columbia, MD 21044-4098 **Telephone:** 410-531-4000	**Web Site:** www.grace.com **Officers:** Hudson La Force - President, Senior Vice President, Chief Operating Officer, Chief Financial Officer, Chief Executive Officer Mark A. Shelnitz - Senior Vice President, Vice President, Secretary, General Counsel	**Auditors:** PricewaterhouseCoopers LLP **Investor Contact:** 410-531-4167 **Transfer Agents:** Computershare Shareowner Services LLC, Providence, RI

GRACO INC

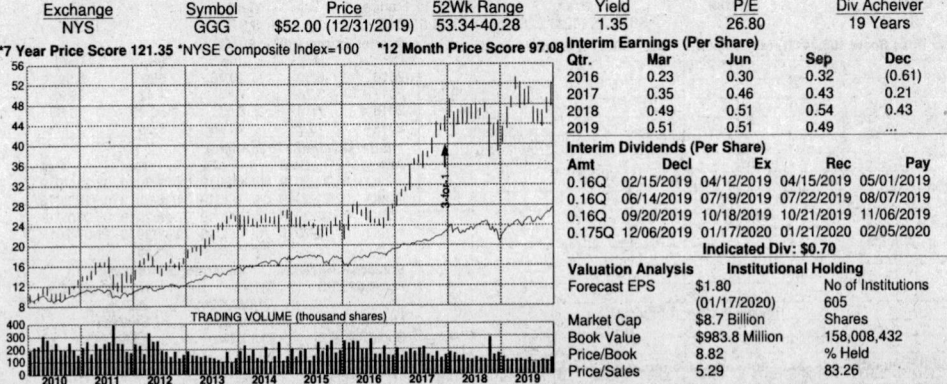

Exchange	Symbol	Price	52Wk Range	Yield	P/E	Div Acheiver
NYS	GGG	$52.00 (12/31/2019)	53.34-40.28	1.35	26.80	19 Years

*7 Year Price Score 121.35 *NYSE Composite Index=100 *12 Month Price Score 97.08

Interim Earnings (Per Share)

Qtr.	Mar	Jun	Sep	Dec
2016	0.23	0.30	0.32	(0.61)
2017	0.35	0.46	0.43	0.21
2018	0.49	0.51	0.54	0.43
2019	0.51	0.51	0.49	...

Interim Dividends (Per Share)

Amt	Decl	Ex	Rec	Pay
0.16Q	02/15/2019	04/12/2019	04/15/2019	05/01/2019
0.16Q	06/14/2019	07/19/2019	07/22/2019	08/07/2019
0.16Q	09/20/2019	10/18/2019	10/21/2019	11/06/2019
0.175Q	12/06/2019	01/17/2020	01/21/2020	02/05/2020

Indicated Div: $0.70

Valuation Analysis / **Institutional Holding**

Forecast EPS	$1.80	No of Institutions
(01/17/2020)		605
Market Cap	$8.7 Billion	Shares
Book Value	$983.8 Million	158,008,432
Price/Book	8.82	% Held
Price/Sales	5.29	83.26

Business Summary: Industrial Machinery & Equipment (MIC: 7.2.1 SIC: 3561 NAIC: 333911)

Graco, together with its subsidiaries, is a manufacturing company. Co. designs, manufactures and markets systems and equipment used to move, measure, control, dispense and spray fluid and powder materials. Co.'s segments are: Industrial, which includes Co.'s Industrial Products and Applied Fluid Technologies divisions and markets equipment and solutions for moving and applying paints, coatings, sealants, adhesives and other fluids; Process, which includes Co.'s Process, Oil and Natural Gas, and Lubrication divisions and markets pumps, valves, meters and accessories; and Contractor, which markets sprayers for architectural coatings for painting, corrosion control, texture and line striping.

Recent Developments:
For the quarter ended Sep 27 2019, net income decreased 9.2% to US$84.1 million from US$92.7 million in the year-earlier quarter. Revenues were US$400.6 million, down 3.7% from US$415.9 million the year before. Operating income was US$103.4 million versus US$114.8 million in the prior-year quarter, a decrease of 9.9%. Direct operating expenses declined 0.7% to US$193.2 million from US$194.5 million in the comparable period the year before. Indirect operating expenses decreased 2.5% to US$104.0 million from US$106.7 million in the equivalent prior-year period.

Prospects:
Our evaluation of Graco Inc. as of October 4th, 2019 is the result of our systematic analysis on three basic characteristics: earnings strength, relative valuation, and recent stock price movement. The company has managed to produce a neutral trend in earnings per share over the past 5 quarters. Additionally, recent analyst estimates for the company have been unchanged while GGG has posted results that fell short of analysts' expectations. Based on operating earnings yield, the company is fairly valued when compared to all of the companies we cover. Share price changes over the past year indicates that GGG will perform well over the near term.

Financial Data

(US$ in Thousands)	9 Mos	6 Mos	3 Mos	12/28/2018	12/29/2017	12/30/2016	12/25/2015	12/26/2014
Earnings Per Share	1.94	1.99	1.99	1.97	1.45	0.24	1.95	1.22
Cash Flow Per Share	2.48	2.17	2.17	2.20	2.02	1.59	1.10	1.34
Tang Book Value Per Share	3.12	2.79	2.30	1.75	1.53	0.80	0.06	0.70
Dividends Per Share	0.613	0.585	0.558	0.530	0.480	0.440	0.400	0.367
Dividend Payout %	31.57	29.40	28.02	26.90	33.10	185.89	20.48	30.14
Income Statement								
Total Revenue	1,233,753	833,198	404,870	1,653,292	1,474,744	1,329,293	1,286,485	1,221,130
EBITDA	352,328	239,587	116,271	456,251	392,796	143,045	518,056	357,906
Depn & Amortn	36,401	24,087	12,013	31,100	29,500	28,800	25,700	24,100
Income Before Taxes	305,343	208,534	100,723	410,766	347,094	96,655	474,713	315,073
Income Taxes	46,325	33,648	13,974	69,712	94,682	55,981	129,000	89,500
Net Income	259,018	174,886	86,749	341,054	252,412	40,674	345,713	225,573
Average Shares	171,777	172,047	170,859	173,213	174,318	170,880	177,021	185,235
Balance Sheet								
Current Assets	772,627	798,893	733,509	723,216	631,926	503,362	509,017	859,507
Total Assets	1,637,424	1,640,547	1,549,047	1,472,741	1,379,205	1,243,109	1,391,352	1,544,778
Current Liabilities	287,527	359,602	354,044	299,803	234,426	177,985	194,616	174,480
Long-Term Obligations	192,101	179,081	173,738	266,391	226,035	305,685	392,695	615,000
Total Liabilities	653,628	714,589	704,609	720,868	656,142	669,289	755,801	948,746
Stockholders' Equity	983,796	925,958	844,438	751,873	723,063	573,820	635,551	596,032
Shares Outstanding	166,780	166,805	166,518	165,170	169,318	167,503	167,297	177,595
Statistical Record								
Return on Assets %	21.31	21.92	22.51	23.98	19.36	3.04	23.61	15.75
Return on Equity %	37.38	41.68	43.56	46.37	39.14	6.62	56.30	36.77
EBITDA Margin %	28.56	28.76	28.72	27.60	26.63	10.76	40.27	29.31
Net Margin %	20.99	20.99	21.43	20.63	17.12	3.06	26.87	18.47
Asset Turnover	1.05	1.06	1.09	1.16	1.13	0.99	0.88	0.85
Current Ratio	2.69	2.22	2.07	2.41	2.70	2.83	2.62	4.93
Debt to Equity	0.20	0.19	0.21	0.35	0.31	0.53	0.62	1.03
Price Range	53.34-37.38	53.34-37.38	49.52-37.38	49.07-37.38	45.63-27.70	28.67-21.19	27.14-21.60	27.14-22.00
P/E Ratio	27.49-19.27	26.80-18.78	24.88-18.78	24.91-18.97	31.47-19.10	119.47-88.28	13.92-11.08	22.25-18.04
Average Yield %	1.33	1.27	1.24	1.18	1.31	1.71	1.66	1.46

Address: 88 - 11th Avenue Northeast, Minneapolis, MN 55413 Telephone: 612-623-6000 Fax: 612-623-6777	Web Site: www.graco.com Officers: Lee R. Mitau - Chairman Patrick J. McHale - President, Chief Executive Officer	Auditors: DELOITTE & TOUCHE LLP Transfer Agents: Wells Fargo Bank, N.A., St. Paul, MN

GRAHAM HOLDINGS CO.

Exchange	Symbol	Price	52Wk Range	Yield	P/E
NYS	GHC	$638.99 (12/31/2019)	744.99-619.77	0.87	14.32

*7 Year Price Score 106.24 *NYSE Composite Index=100 *12 Month Price Score 88.42

Interim Earnings (Per Share)

Qtr.	Mar	Jun	Sep	Dec
2016	6.59	10.76	5.87	6.59
2017	3.75	7.46	4.42	38.25
2018	7.78	8.63	23.28	10.66
2019	15.26	10.65	8.05	...

Interim Dividends (Per Share)

Amt	Decl	Ex	Rec	Pay
1.39Q	01/24/2019	02/06/2019	02/07/2019	02/21/2019
1.39Q	02/21/2019	04/17/2019	04/18/2019	05/16/2019
1.39Q	05/02/2019	07/17/2019	07/18/2019	08/08/2019
1.39Q	09/12/2019	10/16/2019	10/17/2019	11/07/2019

Indicated Div: $5.56

Valuation Analysis

		Institutional Holding	
Forecast EPS	$31.45	No of Institutions	
	(01/08/2020)	397	
Market Cap	$3.4 Billion	Shares	
Book Value	$3.1 Billion	4,804,745	
Price/Book	1.11	% Held	
Price/Sales	1.19	N/A	

Business Summary: Educational Services (MIC: 2.2.2 SIC: 8299 NAIC: 611699)

Graham Holdings is an education and media company, whose operations include educational services; television broadcasting; online, print and local TV news; home health and hospice care; and manufacturing. Co.'s subsidiary, Kaplan, Inc. provides educational services, both domestically and outside the U.S. Co.'s media operations comprise of the ownership and operation of television broadcasting, plus Slate and Foreign Policy magazines; Panoply, a podcast technology and advertising company; and Pinna, an ad-free audio streaming service for children. Co. also owns home health and hospice providers, industrial companies, automotive dealerships and Social Code LLC, a marketing solutions provider.

Recent Developments: For the quarter ended Sep 30 2019, net income decreased 65.6% to US$43.0 million from US$125.1 million in the year-earlier quarter. Revenues were US$738.8 million, up 9.5% from US$674.8 million the year before. Operating income was US$16.3 million versus US$60.7 million in the prior-year quarter, a decrease of 73.2%. Direct operating expenses rose 15.4% to US$517.9 million from US$448.9 million in the comparable period the year before. Indirect operating expenses increased 23.9% to US$204.6 million from US$165.1 million in the equivalent prior-year period.

Prospects: Our evaluation of Graham Holdings Co. as of October 4th, 2019 is the result of our systematic analysis on three basic characteristics: earnings strength, relative valuation, and recent stock price movement. The company has generated a negative trend in earnings per share over the past 5 quarters. However, recent analyst estimates for the company have been unchanged while GHC has posted results that fell short of analysts' expectations. Based on operating earnings yield, the company is undervalued when compared to all of the companies we cover. Share price changes over the past year indicates that GHC will perform over the near term.

Financial Data

(US$ in Thousands)	9 Mos	6 Mos	3 Mos	12/31/2018	12/31/2017	12/31/2016	12/31/2015	12/31/2014
Earnings Per Share	44.62	59.85	57.83	50.20	53.89	29.80	(17.87)	195.03
Cash Flow Per Share	31.68	37.81	43.56	53.82	48.60	46.87	13.06	57.55
Tang Book Value Per Share	247.77	250.67	239.88	237.08	231.68	207.30	231.59	204.94
Dividends Per Share	5.500	5.440	5.380	5.320	5.080	4.840	9.100	10.200
Dividend Payout %	12.33	9.09	9.30	10.60	9.43	16.24	...	5.23
Income Statement								
Total Revenue	2,168,621	1,429,801	692,199	2,695,966	2,591,846	2,481,890	2,586,114	3,535,166
EBITDA	326,928	231,867	118,230	445,698	317,030	382,163	7,530	1,483,888
Depn & Amortn	104,555	68,278	33,876	104,114	103,687	91,271	96,978	222,697
Income Before Taxes	204,539	151,057	78,629	309,035	186,038	258,595	(120,193)	1,226,741
Income Taxes	59,500	44,300	27,600	52,100	(119,700)	81,200	20,500	406,100
Net Income	181,974	138,829	81,748	271,206	302,044	168,590	(100,655)	1,293,843
Average Shares	5,329	5,329	5,326	5,370	5,552	5,589	5,727	6,559
Balance Sheet								
Current Assets	1,534,258	1,485,270	1,477,535	1,532,342	1,735,804	1,871,346	1,860,722	1,690,703
Total Assets	5,487,746	5,212,950	5,197,234	4,764,041	4,937,823	4,432,670	4,352,951	5,752,319
Current Liabilities	988,961	814,564	829,756	812,162	878,612	818,961	725,149	1,050,792
Long-Term Obligations	420,535	497,094	500,238	470,777	486,561	485,719	399,926	399,545
Total Liabilities	2,435,736	2,180,138	2,203,636	1,847,259	2,022,678	1,979,729	1,862,253	2,601,510
Stockholders' Equity	3,052,010	3,032,812	2,993,598	2,916,782	2,915,145	2,452,941	2,490,698	3,150,809
Shares Outstanding	5,314	5,314	5,314	5,300	5,504	5,576	5,803	5,798
Statistical Record								
Return on Assets %	4.61	6.45	6.23	5.59	6.45	3.83	N.M.	22.38
Return on Equity %	7.92	10.85	10.55	9.30	11.25	6.80	N.M.	40.05
EBITDA Margin %	15.08	16.22	17.08	16.53	12.23	15.40	0.29	41.98
Net Margin %	8.39	9.71	11.81	10.06	11.65	6.79	N.M.	36.60
Asset Turnover	0.55	0.56	0.55	0.56	0.55	0.56	0.51	0.61
Current Ratio	1.55	1.82	1.78	1.89	1.98	2.29	2.57	1.61
Debt to Equity	0.14	0.16	0.17	0.16	0.17	0.20	0.16	0.13
Price Range	744.99-553.50	743.43-552.20	687.54-552.20	674.00-552.20	610.10-514.95	541.95-428.09	718.70-471.59	571.19-370.98
P/E Ratio	16.70-12.40	12.42-9.23	11.89-9.55	13.43-11.00	11.32-9.56	18.19-14.37	...	2.93-1.90
Average Yield %	0.82	0.87	0.88	0.90	0.89	0.99	1.50	2.33

Address: 1300 North 17th Street, Arlington, VA 22209	**Web Site:** www.ghco.com	**Auditors:** PricewaterhouseCoopers LLP
Telephone: 703-345-6300	**Officers:** Donald E. Graham - Chairman, Chief Executive Officer Timothy J. O'Shaughnessy - President, Chief Executive Officer	**Investor Contact:** 703-345-6300
		Transfer Agents: ComputerShare Investor Services, Providence, RI

GRAINGER (W.W.) INC.

Exchange	Symbol	Price	52Wk Range	Yield	P/E	Div Acheiver
NYS	GWW	$338.52 (12/31/2019)	338.91-258.54	1.70	19.81	47 Years

*7 Year Price Score 96.92 *NYSE Composite Index=100 *12 Month Price Score 104.39

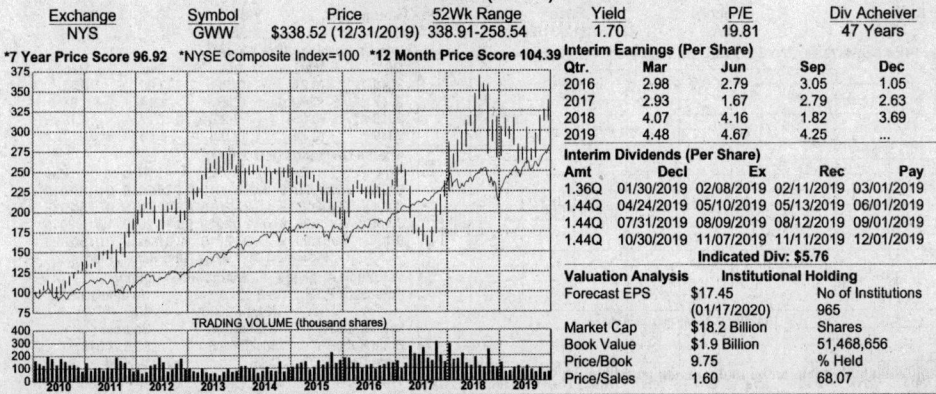

Interim Earnings (Per Share)

Qtr.	Mar	Jun	Sep	Dec
2016	2.98	2.79	3.05	1.05
2017	2.93	1.67	2.79	2.63
2018	4.07	4.16	1.82	3.69
2019	4.48	4.67	4.25	...

Interim Dividends (Per Share)

Amt	Decl	Ex	Rec	Pay
1.36Q	01/30/2019	02/08/2019	02/11/2019	03/01/2019
1.44Q	04/24/2019	05/10/2019	05/13/2019	06/01/2019
1.44Q	07/31/2019	08/09/2019	08/12/2019	09/01/2019
1.44Q	10/30/2019	11/07/2019	11/11/2019	12/01/2019

Indicated Div: $5.76

Valuation Analysis   **Institutional Holding**

Forecast EPS	$17.45	No of Institutions
(01/17/2020)		965
Market Cap	$18.2 Billion	Shares
Book Value	$1.9 Billion	51,468,656
Price/Book	9.75	% Held
Price/Sales	1.60	68.07

Business Summary: Electrical Equipment (MIC: 7.3.1 SIC: 5099 NAIC: 423990)

W.W. Grainger is a distributor of maintenance, repair and operating (MRO) products and services. Co. provides a range of products to its customers including material-handling equipment, safety and security supplies, lighting and electrical products, power and hand tools, pumps and plumbing supplies. Co.'s U.S. segment provides MRO supplies and other related products and services through seCommerce platform, catalogs, branches and sales and service representatives. Co.'s Canadian segment includes Acklands – Grainger Inc. and its subsidiaries. Co.'s Other businesses include Zoro Tools, Inc. in the U.S. and MonotaRO Co., Ltd. in Japan, which operates in Japan and other Asian countries.

Recent Developments: For the quarter ended Sep 30 2019, net income increased 112.2% to US$244.0 million from US$115.0 million in the year-earlier quarter. Revenues were US$2.95 billion, up 4.1% from US$2.83 billion the year before. Operating income was US$338.0 million versus US$189.0 million in the prior-year quarter, an increase of 78.8%. Direct operating expenses rose 5.5% to US$1.85 billion from US$1.75 billion in the comparable period the year before. Indirect operating expenses decreased 14.5% to US$761.0 million from US$890.0 million in the equivalent prior-year period.

Prospects: Our evaluation of Grainger (W.W.) Inc. as of October 4th, 2019 is the result of our systematic analysis on three basic characteristics; earnings strength, relative valuation, and recent stock price movement. The company has managed to produce a neutral trend in earnings per share over the past 5 quarters. However, recent analyst estimates for the company have been reduced and GWW has posted results in line with analysts' expectations. Based on operating earnings yield, the company is undervalued when compared to all of the companies we cover. Share price changes over the past year indicates that GWW will perform very poorly over the near term.

Financial Data

(US$ in Thousands)	9 Mos	6 Mos	3 Mos	12/31/2018	12/31/2017	12/31/2016	12/31/2015	12/31/2014
Earnings Per Share	17.09	14.66	14.15	13.73	10.02	9.87	11.58	11.45
Cash Flow Per Share	20.03	20.17	18.64	18.83	18.32	16.55	15.19	14.05
Tang Book Value Per Share	19.01	19.37	19.84	18.56	10.25	11.64	19.68	40.08
Dividends Per Share	5.600	5.520	5.440	5.360	5.060	4.830	4.590	4.170
Dividend Payout %	32.77	37.65	38.45	39.04	50.50	48.94	39.64	36.42
Income Statement								
Total Revenue	8,639,000	5,692,000	2,799,000	11,221,000	10,424,858	10,137,204	9,973,384	9,964,953
EBITDA	1,270,000	870,000	427,000	1,344,000	1,220,983	1,281,866	1,456,850	1,550,737
Depn & Amortn	171,000	113,000	57,000	162,000	170,000	166,000	162,000	208,326
Income Before Taxes	1,039,000	717,000	351,000	1,100,000	973,095	1,050,251	1,262,445	1,334,386
Income Taxes	261,000	183,000	89,000	258,000	312,881	386,220	465,531	522,090
Net Income	746,000	513,000	253,000	782,000	585,730	605,928	768,996	801,729
Average Shares	54,354	55,378	55,947	56,534	57,983	60,839	65,765	69,205
Balance Sheet								
Current Assets	3,396,000	3,456,000	3,508,000	3,557,000	3,205,989	3,020,229	3,048,642	2,967,549
Total Assets	5,922,000	5,992,000	6,014,000	5,873,000	5,804,254	5,694,307	5,857,755	5,284,252
Current Liabilities	1,572,000	1,452,000	1,462,000	1,501,000	1,506,661	1,628,937	1,788,534	1,261,716
Long-Term Obligations	1,918,000	2,080,000	2,077,000	2,090,000	2,248,036	1,840,946	1,388,414	404,536
Total Liabilities	4,051,000	4,069,000	4,043,000	3,952,000	4,114,122	3,896,372	3,591,121	2,074,380
Stockholders' Equity	1,871,000	1,923,000	1,971,000	1,921,000	1,690,132	1,797,935	2,266,634	3,209,872
Shares Outstanding	53,866	54,571	55,443	55,862	56,328	58,804	62,028	67,432
Statistical Record								
Return on Assets %	16.11	13.89	13.48	13.39	10.19	10.46	13.80	15.20
Return on Equity %	50.15	43.30	42.95	43.31	33.58	29.73	28.08	24.82
EBITDA Margin %	14.70	15.28	15.26	11.98	11.71	12.65	14.61	15.56
Net Margin %	8.64	9.01	9.04	6.97	5.62	5.98	7.71	8.05
Asset Turnover	1.92	1.90	1.89	1.92	1.81	1.75	1.79	1.89
Current Ratio	2.16	2.38	2.40	2.37	2.13	1.85	1.70	2.35
Debt to Equity	1.03	1.08	1.05	1.09	1.33	1.02	0.61	0.13
Price Range	357.96-258.54	369.15-258.56	369.15-266.43	369.15-225.23	258.16-156.25	239.62-182.78	255.22-190.83	269.22-229.29
P/E Ratio	20.95-15.13	25.18-17.64	26.09-18.83	26.89-16.40	25.76-15.59	24.28-18.52	22.04-16.48	23.51-20.03
Average Yield %	1.94	1.81	1.76	1.78	2.50	2.18	2.02	1.67

Address: 100 Grainger Parkway, Lake Forest, IL 60045-5201 **Telephone:** 847-535-1000 **Fax:** 847-535-0878	**Web Site:** www.grainger.com **Officers:** Donald G. Macpherson - Chairman, Chief Executive Officer, Chief Operating Officer Thomas (Tom) B. Okray - Senior Vice President, Chief Financial Officer, Principal Financial Officer	**Auditors:** Ernst & Young LLP **Investor Contact:** 847-535-0409 **Transfer Agents:** Computershare Trust Company, N.A., Providence, RI

GRANITE CONSTRUCTION INC

Exchange	Symbol	Price	52Wk Range	Yield	P/E
NYS	GVA	$27.67 (12/31/2019)	48.43-23.54	1.88	N/A

*7 Year Price Score 73.90 *NYSE Composite Index=100 *12 Month Price Score 66.80

Interim Earnings (Per Share)

Qtr.	Mar	Jun	Sep	Dec
2016	(0.28)	0.35	0.92	0.42
2017	(0.60)	0.35	1.14	0.81
2018	(0.29)	(0.20)	1.17	0.12
2019	(0.74)	(2.09)	0.43	...

Interim Dividends (Per Share)

Amt	Decl	Ex	Rec	Pay
0.13Q	02/06/2019	03/28/2019	03/29/2019	04/15/2019
0.13Q	06/06/2019	06/27/2019	06/28/2019	07/15/2019
0.13Q	09/13/2019	09/27/2019	09/30/2019	10/15/2019
0.13Q	12/04/2019	12/30/2019	12/31/2019	01/15/2020

Indicated Div: $0.52 (Div. Reinv. Plan)

Valuation Analysis — **Institutional Holding**

Forecast EPS	$-2.06	No of Institutions
	(01/14/2020)	357
Market Cap	$1.3 Billion	Shares
Book Value	$1.2 Billion	59,617,316
Price/Book	1.06	% Held
Price/Sales	0.38	101.59

Business Summary: Construction Services (MIC: 7.5.4 SIC: 1629 NAIC: 237990)

Granite Construction is a holding company, which delivers infrastructure solutions for public and private clients. Co.'s segments are: Transportation, which focuses on construction and rehabilitation of roads, pavement preservation, bridges, rail lines, airports and marine ports; Water, which focuses on water-related construction and water management solutions; Specialty, which focuses on construction of various complex projects including infrastructure/site development, mining, public safety, tunnel and power projects; and Materials, which focuses on production of aggregates, asphalt and construction related materials as well as proprietary sanitary and storm water rehabilitation products.

Recent Developments: For the quarter ended Sep 30 2019, net income decreased 62.9% to US$21.9 million from US$59.1 million in the year-earlier quarter. Revenues were US$1.09 billion, up 3.1% from US$1.06 billion the year before. Operating income was US$22.4 million versus US$67.4 million in the prior-year quarter, a decrease of 66.8%. Direct operating expenses rose 9.4% to US$996.7 million from US$911.1 million in the comparable period the year before. Indirect operating expenses decreased 10.4% to US$69.1 million from US$77.1 million in the equivalent prior-year period.

Prospects: Our evaluation of Granite Construction Inc. as of October 4th, 2019 is the result of our systematic analysis on three basic characteristics: earnings strength, relative valuation, and recent stock price movement. The company has suffered a very negative trend in earnings per share over the past 5 quarters. In addition, recent analyst estimates for the company have been reduced and GVA has posted results that fell short of analysts' expectations. Based on operating earnings yield, the company is overvalued when compared to all of the companies we cover. Share price changes over the past year indicates that GVA will perform poorly over the near term.

Financial Data

(US$ in Thousands)	9 Mos	6 Mos	3 Mos	12/31/2018	12/31/2017	12/31/2016	12/31/2015	12/31/2014
Earnings Per Share	(2.28)	(1.54)	0.35	0.96	1.71	1.42	1.52	0.64
Cash Flow Per Share	0.96	1.46	1.88	1.98	3.67	1.84	1.70	1.10
Tang Book Value Per Share	20.47	20.14	22.49	23.40	22.35	21.00	19.93	18.90
Dividends Per Share	0.520	0.520	0.520	0.520	0.520	0.520	0.520	0.520
Dividend Payout %	...	...	148.57	54.17	30.41	36.62	34.21	81.25
Income Statement								
Total Revenue	2,497,451	1,409,341	619,801	3,318,414	2,989,713	2,514,617	2,371,029	2,275,270
EBITDA	(51,285)	(104,476)	(11,492)	162,109	167,214	159,326	173,339	131,883
Depn & Amortn	92,700	61,747	28,846	96,400	63,800	61,000	61,000	64,900
Income Before Taxes	(150,739)	(169,851)	(41,536)	57,220	97,356	89,185	100,217	54,696
Income Taxes	(37,451)	(40,925)	(9,165)	10,414	28,662	30,162	35,179	19,721
Net Income	(111,922)	(132,410)	(34,574)	42,410	.69,098	57,112	60,485	25,346
Average Shares	47,170	46,824	46,699	44,025	40,372	40,225	39,868	39,795
Balance Sheet								
Current Assets	1,504,808	1,402,608	1,316,718	1,415,389	1,232,078	1,088,992	985,222	970,178
Total Assets	2,633,773	2,558,141	2,439,780	2,476,601	1,871,978	1,733,453	1,627,860	1,620,494
Current Liabilities	855,841	809,861	620,101	677,842	655,274	529,934	466,045	462,826
Long-Term Obligations	394,841	366,896	333,290	335,119	178,453	229,498	245,081	275,621
Total Liabilities	1,413,067	1,350,733	1,127,341	1,124,968	926,870	847,465	788,623	826,109
Stockholders' Equity	1,220,706	1,207,408	1,312,439	1,351,633	945,108	885,988	839,237	794,385
Shares Outstanding	46,741	46,838	46,812	46,665	39,871	39,621	39,412	39,186
Statistical Record								
Return on Assets %	N.M.	N.M.	0.92	1.95	3.83	3.39	3.72	1.57
Return on Equity %	N.M.	N.M.	1.73	3.69	7.55	6.60	7.41	3.22
EBITDA Margin %	N.M.	N.M.	N.M.	4.89	5.59	6.34	7.31	5.80
Net Margin %	N.M.	N.M.	N.M.	1.28	2.31	2.27	2.55	1.11
Asset Turnover	1.28	1.31	1.61	1.53	1.66	1.49	1.46	1.41
Current Ratio	1.76	1.73	2.12	2.09	1.88	2.05	2.11	2.10
Debt to Equity	0.32	0.30	0.25	0.25	0.19	0.26	0.29	0.35
Price Range	55.69-26.84	56.77-38.82	59.42-38.82	67.84-38.82	66.66-45.71	61.30-36.25	44.25-29.12	40.29-30.52
P/E Ratio	...	...169.77-110.91	169.77-110.91	70.67-40.44	38.98-26.73	43.17-25.53	29.11-19.16	62.95-47.69
Average Yield %	1.23	1.14	1.06	0.98	0.95	1.11	1.46	1.46

Address: 585 West Beach Street, Watsonville, CA 95076 Telephone: 831-724-1011	Web Site: www.graniteconstruction.com Officers: James H. Roberts - President, Executive Vice President, Chief Executive Officer, Chief Operating Officer (frmr), Interim Chief Operating Officer, Division Officer Kyle T. Larkin - Senior Vice President, California Group Manager	Auditors: PricewaterhouseCoopers LLP Investor Contact: 831-724-1011 Transfer Agents: Computershare, Canton, MA

GRAPHIC PACKAGING HOLDING CO

Exchange	Symbol	Price	52Wk Range	Yield	P/E
NYS	GPK	$16.65 (12/31/2019)	16.86-10.64	1.80	22.50

*7 Year Price Score 91.11 *NYSE Composite Index=100 *12 Month Price Score 111.28

Interim Earnings (Per Share)

Qtr.	Mar	Jun	Sep	Dec
2016	0.18	0.24	0.18	0.11
2017	0.12	0.14	0.15	0.56
2018	0.10	0.16	0.30	0.15
2019	0.19	0.22	0.18	...

Interim Dividends (Per Share)

Amt	Decl	Ex	Rec	Pay
0.075Q	02/21/2019	03/14/2019	03/15/2019	04/05/2019
0.075Q	05/22/2019	06/13/2019	06/15/2019	07/05/2019
0.075Q	07/25/2019	09/12/2019	09/15/2019	10/05/2019
0.075Q	11/14/2019	12/12/2019	12/15/2019	01/05/2020

Indicated Div: $0.30

Valuation Analysis / Institutional Holding

Forecast EPS	$0.87	No of Institutions
(01/17/2020)		389
Market Cap	$4.8 Billion	Shares
Book Value	$1.6 Billion	477,698,976
Price/Book	3.10	% Held
Price/Sales	0.79	95.67

Business Summary: Containers & Packaging (MIC: 8.1.3 SIC: 2657 NAIC: 322212)

Graphic Packaging Holding is a provider of paper-based packaging solutions for a variety of products to food, beverage, and foodservice. Co. operates in three segments: Paperboard Mills, which produces primarily coated unbleached kraft paperboard and coated-recycled paperboard; Americas Paperboard Packaging, which includes paperboard packaging folding cartons sold primarily to Consumer-Packaged Goods (CPG) companies serving the food, beverage, and consumer product markets in the Americas; and Europe Paperboard Packaging, which includes paperboard packaging folding cartons sold primarily to CPG companies serving the food, beverage and consumer product markets in Europe.

Recent Developments: For the quarter ended Sep 30 2019, net income decreased 42.6% to US$70.0 million from US$122.0 million in the year-earlier quarter. Revenues were US$1.58 billion, up 3.3% from US$1.53 billion the year before. Operating income was US$122.7 million versus US$166.4 million in the prior-year quarter, a decrease of 26.3%. Direct operating expenses rose 3.3% to US$1.32 billion from US$1.27 billion in the comparable period the year before. Indirect operating expenses increased 56.4% to US$143.7 million from US$91.9 million in the equivalent prior-year period.

Prospects: Our evaluation of Graphic Packaging Holding Co. as of October 4th, 2019 is the result of our systematic analysis on three basic characteristics: earnings strength, relative valuation, and recent stock price movement. The company has generated a negative trend in earnings per share over the past 5 quarters. However, recent analyst estimates for the company have been mixed and GPK has posted results that exceeded analysts' expectations. Based on operating earnings yield, the company is undervalued when compared to all of the companies we cover. Share price changes over the past year indicates that GPK will perform in line with the market over the near term.

Financial Data

(US$ in Thousands)	9 Mos	6 Mos	3 Mos	12/31/2018	12/31/2017	12/31/2016	12/31/2015	12/31/2014
Earnings Per Share	0.74	0.86	0.80	0.71	0.96	0.71	0.70	0.27
Cash Flow Per Share	0.77	(0.05)	(1.20)	(1.21)	1.66	1.99	1.79	1.60
Dividends Per Share	0.300	0.300	0.300	0.300	0.300	0.225	0.200	...
Dividend Payout %	40.54	34.88	37.50	42.25	31.25	31.69	28.57	...
Income Statement								
Total Revenue	4,640,300	3,058,700	1,505,900	6,023,000	4,403,700	4,298,100	4,160,200	4,240,500
EBITDA	738,800	505,600	251,000	831,800	611,200	636,000	654,700	435,000
Depn & Amortn	337,800	227,300	117,100	360,600	268,500	240,000	227,600	221,600
Income Before Taxes	294,600	207,800	98,900	347,500	253,000	319,400	359,300	132,700
Income Taxes	60,900	44,000	21,000	54,700	(45,500)	93,200	130,400	45,400
Net Income	173,800	121,700	57,900	221,100	300,200	228,000	230,100	89,700
Average Shares	293,700	295,700	298,200	310,100	311,900	321,500	330,700	330,500
Balance Sheet								
Current Assets	1,771,000	1,860,800	1,836,900	1,763,800	1,169,900	1,114,900	1,066,800	1,220,900
Total Assets	7,194,100	7,285,100	7,291,200	7,059,200	4,863,000	4,603,400	4,256,100	4,331,300
Current Liabilities	1,091,800	1,094,000	1,022,200	1,172,300	851,400	779,800	732,200	676,700
Long-Term Obligations	2,935,000	2,997,500	3,129,800	2,905,100	2,213,200	2,088,500	1,838,900	1,942,100
Total Liabilities	5,637,500	5,700,500	5,729,800	5,203,900	3,571,100	3,546,900	3,154,400	3,319,000
Stockholders' Equity	1,556,600	1,584,600	1,561,400	1,855,300	1,291,900	1,056,500	1,101,700	1,012,300
Shares Outstanding	290,244	293,970	295,337	299,891	309,715	313,533	324,688	327,044
Statistical Record								
Return on Assets %	3.05	3.67	3.45	3.71	6.34	5.13	5.36	2.02
Return on Equity %	13.23	15.98	15.24	14.05	25.57	21.07	21.77	8.65
EBITDA Margin %	15.92	16.53	16.67	13.81	13.88	14.80	15.74	10.26
Net Margin %	3.75	3.98	3.84	3.67	6.82	5.30	5.53	2.12
Asset Turnover	0.85	0.85	0.84	1.01	0.93	0.97	0.97	0.95
Current Ratio	1.62	1.70	1.80	1.50	1.37	1.43	1.46	1.80
Debt to Equity	1.89	1.89	2.00	1.57	1.71	1.98	1.67	1.92
Price Range	15.20-10.17	14.96-10.17	16.08-10.17	16.68-10.17	15.83-12.26	14.60-10.74	15.75-12.24	14.05-9.17
P/E Ratio	20.54-13.74	17.40-11.83	20.10-12.71	23.49-14.32	16.49-12.77	20.56-15.13	22.50-17.49	52.04-33.96
Average Yield %	2.34	2.32	2.26	2.12	2.19	1.73	1.41	...

Address: 1500 Riveredge Parkway, Suite 100, Atlanta, GA 30328	Web Site: www.graphicpkg.com	Auditors: PricewaterhouseCoopers LLP
Telephone: 770-240-7200	Officers: Philip R. (Phil) Martens - Chairman Micheal P. Doss - President, Chief Executive Officer, Chief Operating Officer, Executive Vice President, Senior Vice President	Investor Contact: 770-240-7200
		Transfer Agents: Broadridge Corporate Issuer Solutions, Inc., Ardmore, PA

GREIF INC

Exchange	Symbol	Price	52Wk Range	Yield	P/E
NYS	GEF	$44.20 (12/31/2019)	45.27-30.39	3.98	15.29

*7 Year Price Score 68.01   *NYSE Composite Index=100   *12 Month Price Score 106.03

Interim Earnings (Per Share)

Qtr.	Jan	Apr	Jul	Oct
2014-15	0.52	0.35	0.15	0.21
2015-16	(0.19)	0.53	0.78	0.15
2016-17	0.10	0.61	0.74	0.57
2017-18	0.96	0.77	1.15	0.67
2018-19	0.51	0.23	2.65	(1.59)

Interim Dividends (Per Share)

Amt	Decl	Ex	Rec	Pay
0.44Q	02/26/2019	03/15/2019	03/18/2019	04/01/2019
0.44Q	06/04/2019	06/17/2019	06/18/2019	07/01/2019
0.44Q	08/27/2019	09/16/2019	09/17/2019	10/01/2019
0.44Q	12/03/2019	12/17/2019	12/18/2019	01/01/2020

Indicated Div: $1.76

Valuation Analysis

		Institutional Holding	
Forecast EPS	$3.77	No of Institutions	
	(01/15/2020)	314	
Market Cap	$2.1 Billion	Shares	
Book Value	$1.2 Billion	28,527,366	
Price/Book	1.85	% Held	
Price/Sales	0.46	46.45	

Business Summary: Containers & Packaging (MIC: 8.1.3 SIC: 2655 NAIC: 322214)

Greif is a producer of industrial packaging products and services. Co.'s segments are: Rigid Industrial Packaging and Services, which products including steel, fibre and plastic drums, rigid intermediate bulk containers, closure systems for industrial packaging products, and transit protection products; Paper Packaging and Services, which produces and sells containerboard, corrugated sheets, corrugated containers and other corrugated products; Flexible Products and Services, which produces flexible intermediate bulk containers and related services; and Land Management, which is focused on the harvesting and regeneration of Co.'s United States timber properties.

Recent Developments: For the year ended Oct 31 2019, net income decreased 15.4% to US$194.2 million from US$229.5 million in the prior year. Revenues were US$4.60 billion, up 18.6% from US$3.87 billion the year before. Operating income was US$399.1 million versus US$370.5 million in the prior year, an increase of 7.7%. Direct operating expenses rose 17.8% to US$3.64 billion from US$3.08 billion in the comparable period the year before. Indirect operating expenses increased 34.0% to US$560.8 million from US$418.4 million in the equivalent prior-year period.

Prospects: Our evaluation of Greif Bros. Corp. as of October 4th, 2019 is the result of our systematic analysis on three basic characteristics: earnings strength, relative valuation, and recent stock price movement. The company has managed to produce a neutral trend in earnings per share over the past 5 quarters. Additionally, recent analyst estimates for the company have been unchanged while GEF has posted results that exceeded analysts' expectations. Based on operating earnings yield, the company is undervalued when compared to all of the companies we cover. Share price changes over the past year indicates that GEF will perform very poorly over the near term.

Financial Data

(US$ in Thousands)	10/31/2019	10/31/2018	10/31/2017	10/31/2016	10/31/2015	10/31/2014	10/31/2013	10/31/2012
Earnings Per Share	2.89	3.55	2.02	1.28	1.23	1.56	2.52	2.17
Cash Flow Per Share	8.08	5.28	6.38	6.28	4.32	5.49	5.27	9.98
Tang Book Value Per Share	N.M.	5.98	3.32	1.72	1.59	2.00	2.08	0.55
Dividends Per Share	1.760	1.700	1.680	1.680	1.680	1.680	1.680	1.680
Dividend Payout %	60.90	47.89	83.17	131.25	136.59	107.69	66.67	77.42
Income Statement								
Total Revenue	4,595,000	3,873,800	3,638,200	3,323,600	3,616,700	4,239,100	4,353,400	4,269,500
EBITDA	523,500	458,300	367,200	324,000	303,000	369,600	459,400	408,400
Depn & Amortn	149,000	107,500	106,800	107,400	113,400	129,800	131,900	131,400
Income Before Taxes	262,000	299,800	200,300	141,200	114,800	158,000	243,700	187,100
Income Taxes	70,700	73,300	67,200	66,500	48,400	115,000	97,600	56,800
Net Income	171,000	209,400	118,600	74,900	71,900	91,500	147,300	126,100
Average Shares	26,215	25,965	25,822	25,756	25,674	25,552	25,400	25,200
Balance Sheet								
Current Assets	1,249,000	976,700	994,500	920,300	1,008,500	1,154,700	1,094,000	1,064,000
Total Assets	5,426,700	3,194,800	3,232,300	3,153,000	3,315,700	3,667,400	3,882,200	3,856,900
Current Liabilities	825,400	670,200	687,900	659,200	647,000	851,700	801,700	862,000
Long-Term Obligations	2,659,000	884,100	937,800	974,600	1,116,200	1,087,400	1,207,200	1,175,300
Total Liabilities	4,272,300	2,051,500	2,189,900	2,173,800	2,300,100	2,525,300	2,599,000	2,656,100
Stockholders' Equity	1,154,400	1,143,300	1,042,400	979,200	1,015,600	1,142,100	1,283,200	1,200,800
Shares Outstanding	48,265	47,949	47,843	47,791	47,813	47,723	47,576	47,403
Statistical Record								
Return on Assets %	3.97	6.52	3.71	2.31	2.06	2.42	3.81	3.12
Return on Equity %	14.88	19.16	11.73	7.49	6.66	7.55	11.86	10.32
EBITDA Margin %	11.39	11.83	10.09	9.75	8.38	8.72	10.55	9.57
Net Margin %	3.72	5.41	3.26	2.25	1.99	2.16	3.38	2.95
Asset Turnover	1.07	1.21	1.14	1.02	1.04	1.12	1.13	1.06
Current Ratio	1.51	1.46	1.45	1.40	1.56	1.36	1.36	1.23
Debt to Equity	2.30	0.77	0.90	1.00	1.10	0.95	0.94	0.98
Price Range	51.53-30.39	64.87-44.72	61.23-45.59	49.59-24.00	48.17-27.84	55.74-42.68	57.43-40.00	56.50-38.90
P/E Ratio	17.83-10.52	18.27-12.60	30.31-22.57	38.74-18.75	39.16-22.63	35.73-27.36	22.79-15.87	26.04-17.93
Average Yield %	4.54	3.06	3.01	4.66	4.35	3.28	3.36	3.63

Address: 425 Winter Road, Delaware, OH 43015	**Web Site:** www.greif.com	**Auditors:** DELOITTE & TOUCHE LLP
Telephone: 740-549-6000	**Officers:** Michael J. Gasser - Chairman Peter G. Watson - President, Chief Executive Officer, Chief Operating Officer, Division Officer	**Investor Contact:** 740-549-6000
		Transfer Agents: The Bank of NEw York Mellon (Luxembourg) S.A., Luxembourg

GROUP 1 AUTOMOTIVE, INC.

Exchange	Symbol	Price	52Wk Range	Yield	P/E
NYS	GPI	$100.00 (12/31/2019)	109.25-52.72	1.16	11.89

*7 Year Price Score 90.78 *NYSE Composite Index=100 *12 Month Price Score 123.25

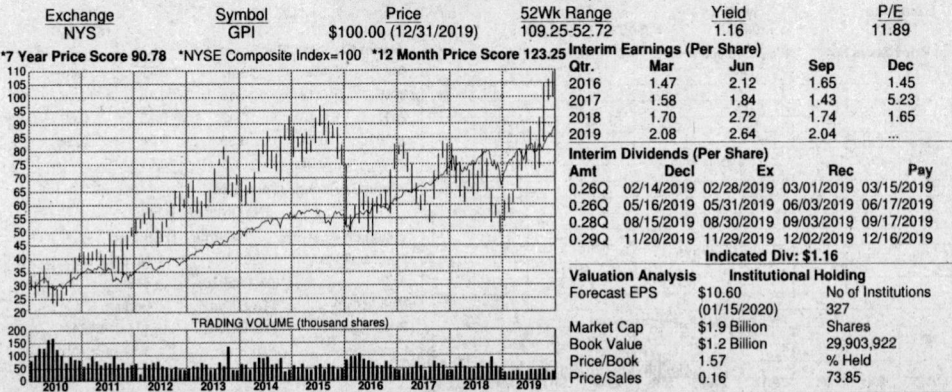

Interim Earnings (Per Share)

Qtr.	Mar	Jun	Sep	Dec
2016	1.47	2.12	1.65	1.45
2017	1.58	1.84	1.43	5.23
2018	1.70	2.72	1.74	1.65
2019	2.08	2.64	2.04	...

Interim Dividends (Per Share)

Amt	Decl	Ex	Rec	Pay
0.26Q	02/14/2019	02/28/2019	03/01/2019	03/15/2019
0.26Q	05/16/2019	05/31/2019	06/03/2019	06/17/2019
0.28Q	08/15/2019	08/30/2019	09/03/2019	09/17/2019
0.29Q	11/20/2019	11/29/2019	12/02/2019	12/16/2019

Indicated Div: $1.16

Valuation Analysis

		Institutional Holding	
Forecast EPS	$10.60	No of Institutions	
	(01/15/2020)	327	
Market Cap	$1.9 Billion	Shares	
Book Value	$1.2 Billion	29,903,922	
Price/Book	1.57	% Held	
Price/Sales	0.16	73.85	

Business Summary: Retail - Automotive (MIC: 2.1.4 SIC: 5511 NAIC: 441110)

Group 1 Automotive is an operator in the automotive retail industry. Through Co.'s dealerships, it sells new and used cars and light trucks; arranges related vehicle financing; sells service and other insurance contracts; provides automotive maintenance and repair services; and sells vehicle parts. Co.'s operations are primarily located in key metropolitan areas in Alabama, California, Florida, Georgia, Kansas, Louisiana, Maryland, Massachusetts, Mississippi, New Hampshire, New Jersey, New Mexico, Oklahoma, South Carolina and Texas in the U.S., in towns of the U.K. and in key metropolitan markets in the states of Sao Paulo, Parana, Mato Grosso do Sul and Santa Catarina in Brazil.

Recent Developments: For the quarter ended Sep 30 2019, net income increased 9.2% to US$38.0 million from US$34.8 million in the year-earlier quarter. Revenues were US$3.12 billion, up 7.9% from US$2.89 billion the year before. Operating income was US$83.3 million versus US$78.2 million in the prior-year quarter, an increase of 6.5%. Direct operating expenses rose 8.1% to US$2.65 billion from US$2.45 billion in the comparable period the year before. Indirect operating expenses increased 7.1% to US$382.3 million from US$356.9 million in the equivalent prior-year period.

Prospects: Our evaluation of Group 1 Automotive Inc. as of October 4th, 2019 is the result of our systematic analysis on three basic characteristics: earnings strength, relative valuation, and recent stock price movement. The company has produced a positive trend in earnings per share over the past 5 quarters. In addition, recent analyst estimates for the company have been raised, and GPI has posted results that exceeded analysts' expectations. Based on operating earnings yield, the company is undervalued when compared to all of the companies we cover. Share price changes over the past year indicates that GPI will perform in line with the market over the near term.

Financial Data

(US$ in Thousands)	9 Mos	6 Mos	3 Mos	12/31/2018	12/31/2017	12/31/2016	12/31/2015	12/31/2014
Earnings Per Share	8.41	8.11	8.19	7.83	10.08	6.67	3.90	3.60
Cash Flow Per Share	12.44	14.51	14.00	13.88	9.74	18.14	6.09	8.48
Dividends Per Share	1.060	1.040	1.040	1.040	0.970	0.910	0.830	0.700
Dividend Payout %	12.60	12.82	12.70	13.28	9.62	13.64	21.28	19.44
Income Statement								
Total Revenue	8,932,400	5,814,065	2,808,376	11,601,358	11,123,721	10,887,612	10,632,505	9,937,889
EBITDA	270,300	185,998	95,368	408,183	399,772	391,434	325,538	298,007
Depn & Amortn	3,100	2,063	8,570	67,100	57,900	51,200	47,200	42,300
Income Before Taxes	164,400	115,409	52,176	205,403	219,003	227,371	182,171	164,400
Income Taxes	38,500	27,536	13,528	47,631	5,561	80,306	88,172	71,396
Net Income	125,900	87,873	38,648	157,772	213,442	147,065	93,999	93,004
Average Shares	17,978	17,930	17,849	19,461	20,425	21,170	23,152	24,885
Balance Sheet								
Current Assets	2,386,500	2,362,134	2,433,071	2,402,366	2,329,186	2,150,587	2,202,955	2,035,219
Total Assets	5,329,000	5,225,761	5,263,491	5,001,075	4,871,065	4,461,903	4,414,929	4,141,492
Current Liabilities	2,397,300	2,335,340	2,436,742	2,386,565	2,198,487	2,053,117	2,039,470	1,922,199
Long-Term Obligations	1,308,000	1,295,720	1,262,582	1,281,489	1,318,184	1,212,809	1,203,436	1,008,837
Total Liabilities	4,142,700	4,061,696	4,135,778	3,905,381	3,746,783	3,531,703	3,496,677	3,163,482
Stockholders' Equity	1,186,300	1,164,065	1,127,713	1,095,694	1,124,282	930,200	918,252	978,010
Shares Outstanding	18,619	18,583	18,521	18,322	20,898	21,405	23,415	24,339
Statistical Record								
Return on Assets %	3.07	3.03	3.11	3.20	4.57	3.30	2.20	2.34
Return on Equity %	13.41	13.13	13.93	14.21	20.78	15.87	9.91	9.11
EBITDA Margin %	3.03	3.20	3.40	3.52	3.59	3.60	3.06	3.00
Net Margin %	1.41	1.51	1.38	1.36	1.92	1.35	0.88	0.94
Asset Turnover	2.32	2.30	2.24	2.35	2.38	2.45	2.49	2.50
Current Ratio	1.00	1.01	1.00	1.01	1.06	1.05	1.08	1.06
Debt to Equity	1.10	1.11	1.12	1.17	1.17	1.30	1.31	1.03
Price Range	92.31-49.33	81.89-49.33	80.24-49.33	82.47-49.33	83.40-53.21	82.35-48.20	96.97-74.61	92.94-60.32
P/E Ratio	10.98-5.87	10.10-6.08	9.80-6.02	10.53-6.30	8.27-5.28	12.35-7.23	24.86-19.13	25.82-16.76
Average Yield %	1.55	1.58	1.62	1.54	1.39	1.49	0.97	0.93

Address: 800 Gessner, Suite 500, Houston, TX 77024 **Telephone:** 713-647-5700 **Fax:** 713-647-5858	**Web Site:** www.group1auto.com **Officers:** Stephen D. Quinn - Chairman Earl J. Hesterberg - President, Chief Executive Officer	**Auditors:** Ernst & Young LLP **Transfer Agents:** American Stock Transfer & Trust Company LLC, Brooklyn, NY

GRUBHUB INC

Exchange	Symbol	Price	52Wk Range	Yield	P/E
NYS	GRUB	$48.64 (12/31/2019)	86.08-33.11	N/A	1621.33

*7 Year Price Score N/A   *NYSE Composite Index=100   *12 Month Price Score 61.31

Interim Earnings (Per Share)

Qtr.	Mar	Jun	Sep	Dec
2016	0.12	0.15	0.15	0.16
2017	0.20	0.17	0.15	0.60
2018	0.34	0.33	0.24	(0.06)
2019	0.07	0.01	0.01	...

Interim Dividends (Per Share)

No Dividends Paid

Valuation Analysis

		Institutional Holding	
Forecast EPS	$0.80	No of Institutions	
	(01/17/2020)	448	
Market Cap	$4.4 Billion	Shares	
Book Value	$1.5 Billion	117,014,464	
Price/Book	2.96	% Held	
Price/Sales	3.53	101.24	

Business Summary: Internet & Software (MIC: 6.3.2 SIC: 7372 NAIC: 511210)

Grubhub and its wholly-owned subsidiaries provide an online and mobile platform for restaurant pick-up and delivery orders. Co. connects diners and restaurants through restaurant technology and platforms. Diners enter their delivery address or use geo-location within the mobile applications and Co. displays the menus and other relevant information for restaurants in its network. Orders may be placed directly online, via mobile applications or over the phone. Co. primarily charges the restaurant a per order commission that is fee based. In several markets, Co. also provides delivery services to restaurants on its platform that do not have their own delivery operations.

Recent Developments: For the quarter ended Sep 30 2019, net income decreased 95.6% to US$1.0 million from US$22.7 million in the year-earlier quarter. Revenues were US$322.1 million, up 30.3% from US$247.2 million the year before. Operating income was US$3.6 million versus US$21.8 million in the prior-year quarter, a decrease of 83.6%. Direct operating expenses rose 43.8% to US$190.9 million from US$132.8 million in the comparable period the year before. Indirect operating expenses increased 37.8% to US$127.6 million from US$92.6 million in the equivalent prior-year period.

Prospects: Our evaluation of GrubHub Inc as of October 4th, 2019 is the result of our systematic analysis on three basic characteristics: earnings strength, relative valuation, and recent stock price movement. The company has produced a positive trend in earnings per share over the past 5 quarters. However, recent analyst estimates for the company have been mixed and GRUB has posted results that fell short of analysts' expectations. Based on operating earnings yield, the company is overvalued when compared to all of the companies we cover. Share price changes over the past year indicates that GRUB will perform poorly over the near term.

Financial Data

(US$ in Thousands)	9 Mos	6 Mos	3 Mos	12/31/2018	12/31/2017	12/31/2016	12/31/2015	12/31/2014
Earnings Per Share	0.03	0.26	0.58	0.85	1.12	0.58	0.44	0.30
Cash Flow Per Share	2.37	1.97	1.85	2.52	1.77	1.15	0.53	0.99
Tang Book Value Per Share	N.M.	N.M.	N.M.	N.M.	0.14	2.59	2.30	1.99
Income Statement								
Total Revenue	970,881	648,828	323,770	1,007,257	683,067	493,331	361,825	253,873
EBITDA	101,541	67,243	33,936	170,856	141,523	119,024	90,578	68,339
Depn & Amortn	82,996	52,286	25,096	85,893	51,773	35,172	28,649	23,355
Income Before Taxes	4,241	6,678	6,028	81,433	89,648	83,852	61,929	44,984
Income Taxes	(4,911)	(1,464)	(862)	2,952	(9,335)	34,295	23,852	20,721
Net Income	9,152	8,142	6,890	78,481	98,983	49,557	38,077	24,263
Average Shares	92,847	92,786	92,918	92,354	88,182	86,135	85,706	81,698
Balance Sheet								
Current Assets	570,382	534,110	376,246	363,775	360,483	396,337	356,274	353,029
Total Assets	2,378,754	2,343,249	2,154,064	2,065,708	1,543,769	1,197,507	1,060,248	979,702
Current Liabilities	244,215	220,656	249,667	223,168	174,548	110,490	89,612	111,005
Long-Term Obligations	492,776	492,723	328,193	335,548	169,645	...	...	...
Total Liabilities	878,043	861,549	692,427	623,369	425,953	225,388	182,652	209,180
Stockholders' Equity	1,500,711	1,481,700	1,461,637	1,442,339	1,117,816	972,119	877,596	770,522
Shares Outstanding	91,412	91,230	91,074	90,756	86,790	85,692	84,979	81,905
Statistical Record								
Return on Assets %	0.18	1.25	2.93	4.35	7.22	4.38	3.73	2.78
Return on Equity %	0.27	1.79	4.17	6.13	9.47	5.34	4.62	3.60
EBITDA Margin %	10.46	10.36	10.48	16.96	20.72	24.13	25.03	26.92
Net Margin %	0.94	1.25	2.13	7.79	14.49	10.05	10.52	9.56
Asset Turnover	0.58	0.57	0.59	0.56	0.50	0.44	0.35	0.29
Current Ratio	2.34	2.42	1.51	1.63	2.07	3.59	3.98	3.18
Debt to Equity	0.33	0.33	0.22	0.23	0.15	...	...	...
Price Range	137.38-55.86	146.73-61.62	146.73-66.15	146.73-66.53	74.09-32.89	43.89-18.34	47.18-22.97	45.21-30.00
P/E Ratio	N.M.	564.35-237.00	252.98-114.05	172.62-78.27	66.15-29.37	75.67-31.62	107.23-52.20	150.70-100.00

Address: 111 W. Washington Street, Suite 2100, Chicago, IL 60602 **Telephone:** 877-585-7878	**Web Site:** www.grubhub.com **Officers:** Brian P. McAndrews - Chairman Adam J. DeWitt - President, Chief Financial Officer, Treasurer	**Auditors:** Crowe LLP **Transfer Agents:** American Stock Transfer & Trust Company, LLC., Brooklyn, NY

GUIDEWIRE SOFTWARE INC

Exchange	Symbol	Price	52Wk Range	Yield	P/E
NYS	GWRE	$109.77 (12/31/2019)	122.51-76.84	N/A	N/A

*7 Year Price Score 128.62 ***NYSE Composite Index=100** ***12 Month Price Score 107.77**

TRADING VOLUME (thousand shares)

Interim Earnings (Per Share)

Qtr.	Oct	Jan	Apr	Jul
2016-17	(0.11)	0.05	(0.02)	0.36
2017-18	(0.12)	(0.59)	(0.62)	1.07
2018-19	0.07	0.01	(0.11)	0.28
2019-20	(0.18)	...	...	...

Interim Dividends (Per Share)

No Dividends Paid

Valuation Analysis		Institutional Holding	
Forecast EPS	$1.17	No of Institutions	
	(01/16/2020)	412	
Market Cap	$9.1 Billion	Shares	
Book Value	$1.6 Billion	99,621,024	
Price/Book	5.72	% Held	
Price/Sales	13.00	110.82	

Business Summary: Internet & Software (MIC: 6.3.2 SIC: 7372 NAIC: 511210)

Guidewire Software provides a technology platform, composed of software, services, and a partner ecosystem, for the property and casualty insurance industry. Guidewire InsurancePlatform™ consists of cloud and on-premise applications to support core operations, data management and analytics, and digital engagement and is connected to various data sources and third party applications. Co.'s operational platforms include: Guidewire InsuranceSuite, which comprises of PolicyCenter, BillingCenter, and ClaimCenter applications; and Guidewire InsuranceNow, which provides policy, billing and claims management functionality to insurers that prefer to subscribe to a cloud-based, all-in-one solution.

Recent Developments: For the quarter ended Oct 31 2019, net loss amounted to US$15.0 million versus net income of US$6.3 million in the year-earlier quarter. Revenues were US$157.0 million, down 12.9% from US$180.3 million the year before. Operating loss was US$24.6 million versus an income of US$2.5 million in the prior-year quarter. Direct operating expenses declined 0.9% to US$80.9 million from US$81.6 million in the comparable period the year before. Indirect operating expenses increased 4.8% to US$100.8 million from US$96.2 million in the equivalent prior-year period.

Prospects: Our evaluation of Guidewire Software Inc as of October 4th, 2019 is the result of our systematic analysis on three basic characteristics: earnings strength, relative valuation, and recent stock price movement. The company has suffered a very negative trend in earnings per share over the past 5 quarters. In addition, recent analyst estimates for the company have been reduced while GWRE has posted results that exceeded analysts' expectations. Based on operating earnings yield, the company is overvalued when compared to all of the companies we cover. Share price changes over the past year indicates that GWRE will perform poorly over the near term.

Financial Data
(US$ in Thousands)

	3 Mos	07/31/2019	07/31/2018	07/31/2017	07/31/2016	07/31/2015	07/31/2014	07/31/2013
Earnings Per Share	...	0.25	(0.25)	0.28	0.20	0.14	0.21	0.25
Cash Flow Per Share	1.52	1.43	1.81	1.85	1.38	0.91	1.15	0.58
Tang Book Value Per Share	14.35	14.20	12.25	9.07	10.13	9.52	9.21	3.67
Income Statement								
Total Revenue	157,010	719,514	661,067	514,284	424,446	380,537	350,246	300,649
EBITDA	(19,552)	9,304	879	34,023	22,432	20,495	23,896	21,214
Depn & Amortn	5,296	9,700	7,700	6,600	6,500	6,000	5,300	4,500
Income Before Taxes	(21,641)	12,452	18	33,277	20,782	16,740	19,946	17,212
Income Taxes	(6,650)	(8,280)	19,683	12,053	5,806	6,855	5,225	1,829
Net Income	(14,991)	20,732	(19,665)	21,224	14,976	9,885	14,721	15,383
Average Shares	82,360	82,681	77,709	75,328	73,765	72,314	69,112	61,943
Balance Sheet								
Current Assets	1,189,725	1,334,974	1,222,507	679,240	707,672	661,644	516,430	210,093
Total Assets	2,199,024	2,166,963	1,978,592	1,078,901	916,178	799,947	757,227	312,270
Current Liabilities	164,686	232,272	225,188	163,616	119,083	104,409	95,386	74,784
Long-Term Obligations	320,477	317,322	305,128	...	...	...	...	...
Total Liabilities	613,499	592,762	554,848	185,620	132,243	110,559	106,541	83,841
Stockholders' Equity	1,585,525	1,574,201	1,423,744	893,281	783,935	689,388	650,686	228,429
Shares Outstanding	82,574	82,140	80,611	75,007	73,039	71,005	69,082	57,909
Statistical Record								
Return on Assets %	0.01	1.00	N.M.	2.13	1.74	1.27	2.75	5.16
Return on Equity %	0.01	1.38	N.M.	2.53	2.03	1.48	3.35	7.46
EBITDA Margin %	N.M.	1.29	0.13	6.62	5.29	5.39	6.82	7.06
Net Margin %	N.M.	2.88	N.M.	4.13	3.53	2.60	4.20	5.12
Asset Turnover	0.33	0.35	0.43	0.52	0.49	0.49	0.65	1.01
Current Ratio	7.22	5.75	5.43	4.15	5.94	6.34	5.41	2.81
Debt to Equity	0.20	0.20	0.21	...	...	...	...	...
Price Range	112.95-74.56	108.38-74.56	95.26-68.36	72.81-49.33	63.79-43.05	60.08-39.76	57.38-34.85	45.47-24.64
P/E Ratio	N.M.	433.52-298.24	...	260.04-176.18	318.95-215.25	429.14-284.00	273.24-165.95	181.88-98.56

Address: 2850 S. Delaware St., Suite 400, San Mateo, CA 94403	Web Site: www.guidewire.com	Auditors: KPMG LLP
Telephone: 650-357-9100	**Officers:** Marcus S. Ryu - Chairman, President, Chief Executive Officer Michael Rosenbaum - Chief Executive Officer	**Investor Contact:** 650-357-5282
Fax: 650-357-9101		**Transfer Agents:** Computershare Shareowner Services LLC, Canton, MA

HAEMONETICS CORP.

Exchange	Symbol	Price	52Wk Range	Yield	P/E
NYS	HAE	$114.90 (12/31/2019)	138.52-81.74	N/A	88.38

*7 Year Price Score 160.64 *NYSE Composite Index=100 *12 Month Price Score 104.89

Interim Earnings (Per Share)

Qtr.	Jun	Sep	Dec	Mar
2016-17	(0.20)	0.38	0.30	(0.99)
2017-18	0.38	0.38	(0.12)	0.22
2018-19	(0.05)	0.35	0.35	0.40
2019-20	(0.17)	0.72	...	...

Interim Dividends (Per Share)

No Dividends Paid

Valuation Analysis — **Institutional Holding**

Forecast EPS	$3.18	No of Institutions
	(01/11/2020)	403
Market Cap	$5.8 Billion	Shares
Book Value	$583.8 Million	64,306,496
Price/Book	9.96	% Held
Price/Sales	5.89	92.95

Business Summary: Medical Instruments & Equipment (MIC: 4.3.1 SIC: 3841 NAIC: 339112)

Haemonetics is a healthcare company. Co. has three product categories: Plasma, which includes plasma collection devices and disposables, plasma donor management software, and anticoagulant and saline sold to plasma customers; Blood Center, which includes blood collection and processing devices and disposables for red cells, platelets and whole blood as well as related donor management software; and Hospital, which is comprised of Hemostasis Management and Cell Processing products, includes devices and methodologies for measuring coagulation characteristics of blood, surgical blood salvage systems, blood cell processing systems, disposables and blood transfusion management software.

Recent Developments: For the quarter ended Sep 28 2019, net income increased 100.2% to US$37.5 million from US$18.7 million in the year-earlier quarter. Revenues were US$252.6 million, up 4.5% from US$241.6 million the year before. Operating income was US$49.7 million versus US$26.1 million in the prior-year quarter, an increase of 90.7%. Direct operating expenses declined 3.2% to US$125.6 million from US$129.7 million in the comparable period the year before. Indirect operating expenses decreased 10.0% to US$77.3 million from US$85.8 million in the equivalent prior-year period.

Prospects: Our evaluation of Haemonetics Corp. as of October 4th, 2019 is the result of our systematic analysis on three basic characteristics: earnings strength, relative valuation, and recent stock price movement. The company has enjoyed a very positive trend in earnings per share over the past 5 quarters. In addition, recent analyst estimates for the company have been raised, and HAE has posted results that exceeded analysts' expectations. Based on operating earnings yield, the company is overvalued when compared to all of the companies we cover. Share price changes over the past year indicates that HAE will perform well over the near term.

Financial Data
(US$ in Thousands)

	6 Mos	3 Mos	03/30/2019	03/31/2018	04/01/2017	04/02/2016	03/28/2015	03/29/2014
Earnings Per Share	1.30	0.93	1.04	0.85	(0.51)	(1.09)	0.32	0.67
Cash Flow Per Share	2.19	2.72	3.10	4.19	3.11	2.36	2.47	2.71
Tang Book Value Per Share	5.12	5.11	6.46	7.34	6.72	4.89	4.78	4.42
Income Statement								
Total Revenue	491,017	238,451	967,579	903,923	886,116	908,832	910,373	938,509
EBITDA	90,906	14,135	160,345	121,857	39,024	3,384	83,765	89,001
Depn & Amortn	54,469	27,437	76,800	57,700	66,500	56,800	52,600	52,600
Income Before Taxes	27,363	(17,725)	73,633	59,632	(27,476)	(53,416)	31,165	36,401
Income Taxes	(1,644)	(9,246)	18,614	14,060	(1,208)	2,163	14,268	1,253
Net Income	29,007	(8,479)	55,019	45,572	(26,268)	(55,579)	16,897	35,148
Average Shares	52,046	51,010	52,942	53,501	51,524	50,910	52,089	52,377
Balance Sheet								
Current Assets	567,789	615,278	576,121	521,177	510,029	488,086	570,277	622,976
Total Assets	1,190,541	1,259,610	1,274,767	1,237,339	1,238,709	1,319,128	1,485,417	1,514,178
Current Liabilities	240,066	293,665	235,759	384,703	211,179	185,551	189,092	216,928
Long-Term Obligations	313,984	318,144	322,454	59,423	253,625	364,529	406,369	392,057
Total Liabilities	606,787	668,644	606,899	484,910	499,099	597,563	659,295	676,290
Stockholders' Equity	583,754	590,966	667,868	752,429	739,610	721,565	826,122	837,888
Shares Outstanding	50,607	50,771	51,019	52,342	52,255	50,932	51,670	52,041
Statistical Record								
Return on Assets %	5.55	3.95	4.39	3.69	N.M.	N.M.	1.13	2.37
Return on Equity %	10.60	7.80	7.77	6.13	N.M.	N.M.	2.04	4.39
EBITDA Margin %	18.51	5.93	16.57	13.48	4.40	0.37	9.20	9.48
Net Margin %	5.91	N.M.	5.69	5.04	N.M.	N.M.	1.86	3.75
Asset Turnover	0.80	0.78	0.77	0.73	0.69	0.64	0.61	0.63
Current Ratio	2.37	2.10	2.44	1.35	2.42	2.63	3.02	2.87
Debt to Equity	0.54	0.54	0.48	0.08	0.34	0.51	0.49	0.47
Price Range	138.52-81.74	120.34-81.74	116.63-71.53	74.41-38.56	41.34-26.13	44.97-29.84	45.38-30.36	45.81-31.84
P/E Ratio	106.55-62.88	129.40-87.89	112.14-68.78	87.54-45.36	...	...	141.81-94.88	68.37-47.52

Address: 400 Wood Road, Braintree, MA 02184-9114 Telephone: 781-848-7100	Web Site: www.haemonetics.com Officers: Richard J. Meelia - Chairman Christopher (Chris) Simon - President, Chief Executive Officer	Auditors: Ernst & Young LLP Investor Contact: 781-356-9402 Transfer Agents: Registrar and Transfer Company, Cranford, NJ

HALLIBURTON COMPANY

Exchange	Symbol	Price	52Wk Range	Yield	P/E
NYS	HAL	$24.47 (12/31/2019)	32.30-17.31	2.94	17.99

*7 Year Price Score 46.72 *NYSE Composite Index=100 *12 Month Price Score 84.45

Interim Earnings (Per Share)

Qtr.	Mar	Jun	Sep	Dec
2016	(2.81)	(3.73)	0.01	(0.16)
2017	(0.04)	0.03	0.42	(0.94)
2018	0.05	0.58	0.50	0.76
2019	0.17	0.09	0.34	...

Interim Dividends (Per Share)

Amt	Decl	Ex	Rec	Pay
0.18Q	02/13/2019	03/05/2019	03/06/2019	03/27/2019
0.18Q	05/15/2019	06/04/2019	06/05/2019	06/26/2019
0.18Q	08/13/2019	09/03/2019	09/04/2019	09/25/2019
0.18Q	11/11/2019	12/04/2019	12/05/2019	12/26/2019

Indicated Div: $0.72

Valuation Analysis / **Institutional Holding**

Forecast EPS	$1.31	No of Institutions	
	(00/25/2020)	1313	
Market Cap	$21.4 Billion	Shares	
Book Value	$9.7 Billion	851,923,200	
Price/Book	2.20	% Held	
Price/Sales	0.93	78.26	

Business Summary: Equipment & Services (MIC: 9.1.3 SIC: 1389 NAIC: 213112)

Halliburton assists its customers throughout the lifecycle of the reservoir, from locating hydrocarbons and managing geological data, to drilling and formation evaluation, well construction and completion, and optimizing production throughout the life of the asset. Co. operates under two segments: Completion and Production, which delivers cementing, stimulation, intervention, pressure control, specialty chemicals, artificial lift and completion products and services; and Drilling and Evaluation, which provides field and reservoir modeling, drilling, evaluation and wellbore placement solutions that enable customers to model, measure, drill and optimize their well construction activities.

Recent Developments: For the quarter ended Sep 30 2019, net income decreased 31.8% to US$296.0 million from US$434.0 million in the year-earlier quarter. Revenues were US$5.55 billion, down 10.1% from US$6.17 billion the year before. Operating income was US$536.0 million versus US$716.0 million in the prior-year quarter, a decrease of 25.1%. Direct operating expenses declined 7.9% to US$4.96 billion from US$5.38 billion in the comparable period the year before. Indirect operating expenses decreased 26.4% to US$53.0 million from US$72.0 million in the equivalent prior-year period.

Prospects: Our evaluation of Halliburton Co. as of October 4th, 2019 is the result of our systematic analysis on three basic characteristics: earnings strength, relative valuation, and recent stock price movement. The company has managed to produce a neutral trend in earnings per share over the past 5 quarters. However, recent analyst estimates for the company have been reduced while HAL has posted results that exceeded analysts' expectations. Based on operating earnings yield, the company is undervalued when compared to all of the companies we cover. Share price changes over the past year indicates that HAL will perform poorly over the near term.

Financial Data

(US$ in Thousands)	9 Mos	6 Mos	3 Mos	12/31/2018	12/31/2017	12/31/2016	12/31/2015	12/31/2014
Earnings Per Share	1.36	1.52	2.01	1.89	(0.53)	(6.69)	(0.79)	4.11
Cash Flow Per Share	2.43	2.33	2.91	3.61	2.84	(1.97)	3.41	4.79
Tang Book Value Per Share	7.89	7.65	7.78	7.69	6.45	8.08	15.60	16.44
Dividends Per Share	0.720	0.720	0.720	0.720	0.720	0.720	0.720	0.630
Dividend Payout %	52.94	47.37	35.82	38.10	...	...	...	15.33
Income Statement								
Total Revenue	17,217,000	11,667,000	5,737,000	23,995,000	20,620,000	15,887,000	23,633,000	32,870,000
EBITDA	2,396,000	1,466,000	751,000	3,974,000	2,831,000	(5,483,000)	1,346,000	7,221,000
Depn & Amortn	1,253,000	836,000	416,000	1,606,000	1,556,000	1,503,000	1,835,000	2,126,000
Income Before Taxes	715,000	343,000	192,000	1,814,000	682,000	(7,625,000)	(936,000)	4,712,000
Income Taxes	190,000	114,000	40,000	157,000	1,131,000	(1,858,000)	(274,000)	1,275,000
Net Income	522,000	227,000	152,000	1,656,000	(463,000)	(5,763,000)	(671,000)	3,500,000
Average Shares	876,000	875,000	873,000	877,000	870,000	861,000	853,000	852,000
Balance Sheet								
Current Assets	11,220,000	11,220,000	11,188,000	11,151,000	10,777,000	11,677,000	21,609,000	15,068,000
Total Assets	26,789,000	26,880,000	26,989,000	25,982,000	25,085,000	27,000,000	36,942,000	32,240,000
Current Liabilities	4,692,000	4,955,000	5,047,000	4,802,000	4,862,000	4,023,000	5,359,000	5,883,000
Long-Term Obligations	11,075,000	11,068,000	11,065,000	10,421,000	10,430,000	12,214,000	14,687,000	7,840,000
Total Liabilities	17,044,000	17,372,000	17,384,000	16,460,000	16,763,000	17,591,000	21,480,000	15,973,000
Stockholders' Equity	9,745,000	9,508,000	9,605,000	9,522,000	8,322,000	9,409,000	15,462,000	16,267,000
Shares Outstanding	876,000	874,000	872,000	871,000	873,000	866,000	856,000	848,000
Statistical Record								
Return on Assets %	4.51	5.04	6.75	6.49	N.M.	N.M.	N.M.	11.39
Return on Equity %	12.66	14.47	19.61	18.56	N.M.	N.M.	N.M.	23.45
EBITDA Margin %	13.92	12.57	13.09	16.56	13.73	N.M.	5.70	21.97
Net Margin %	3.03	1.95	2.65	6.90	N.M.	N.M.	N.M.	10.65
Asset Turnover	0.88	0.90	0.92	0.94	0.79	0.50	0.68	1.07
Current Ratio	2.39	2.26	2.22	2.32	2.22	2.90	4.03	2.56
Debt to Equity	1.14	1.16	1.15	1.09	1.25	1.30	0.95	0.48
Price Range	42.14-17.31	46.26-21.07	54.40-25.14	56.83-25.14	58.21-38.66	55.07-28.48	49.21-33.40	74.02-37.82
P/E Ratio	30.99-12.73	30.43-13.86	27.06-12.51	30.07-13.30	...	...	...	18.01-9.20
Average Yield %	2.61	2.19	1.85	1.65	1.55	1.72	1.75	1.07

Address: 3000 North Sam Houston Parkway East, Houston, TX 77032	Web Site: www.halliburton.com	Auditors: KPMG LLP
Telephone: 281-871-2699	Officers: Jeffrey Allen Miller - Chairman, President, Chief Executive Officer, Executive Vice President, Chief Operating Officer Lance Loeffler - Executive Vice President, Chief Financial Officer	Investor Contact: 888-669-3920 Transfer Agents: Computershare Shareowner Services, Jersey City, NJ

HANESBRANDS INC

Exchange	Symbol	Price	52Wk Range	Yield	P/E
NYS	HBI	$14.85 (12/31/2019)	19.14-12.52	4.04	9.28

*7 Year Price Score 60.95   *NYSE Composite Index=100   *12 Month Price Score 89.88

Interim Earnings (Per Share)

Qtr.	Mar	Jun	Sep	Dec
2016	0.21	0.34	0.45	0.41
2017	0.18	0.47	0.55	(1.03)
2018	0.22	0.39	0.47	0.45
2019	0.22	0.42	0.51	...

Interim Dividends (Per Share)

Amt	Decl	Ex	Rec	Pay
0.15Q	02/07/2019	02/15/2019	02/19/2019	03/12/2019
0.15Q	04/23/2019	05/13/2019	05/14/2019	06/04/2019
0.15Q	07/23/2019	08/12/2019	08/13/2019	09/04/2019
0.15Q	10/22/2019	11/08/2019	11/12/2019	12/03/2019

Indicated Div: $0.60

Valuation Analysis

		Institutional Holding	
Forecast EPS	$1.77	No of Institutions	
	(01/15/2020)	847	
Market Cap	$5.4 Billion	Shares	
Book Value	$1.2 Billion	398,788,704	
Price/Book	4.36	% Held	
Price/Sales	0.77	95.34	

Business Summary: Apparel, Footwear & Accessories (MIC: 1.4.2 SIC: 2389 NAIC: 313312)

Hanesbrands is a marketer of basic innerwear and activewear apparel in the Americas, Europe, Australia and Asia/Pacific under some apparel brands, including Hanes, Champion, Bonds, Maidenform, DIM, Bali, Playtex, Bras N Things, Nur Die/Nur Der, Alternative, L'eggs, JMS/Just My Size, Lovable, Wonderbra, Berlei and Gear for Sports. Co.'s segments are: Innerwear, which includes includes apparel products, such as men's underwear, women's panties, children's underwear, socks and intimate apparel; Activewear, which includes T-shirts, fleece, performance apparel, sport shirts and thermals; and International, which innerwear, activewear, hosiery and home goods products, sold outside of the U.S.

Recent Developments: For the quarter ended Sep 28 2019, net income increased 9.5% to US$187.8 million from US$171.4 million in the year-earlier quarter. Revenues were US$1.87 billion, up 1.0% from US$1.85 billion the year before. Operating income was US$269.8 million versus US$256.9 million in the prior-year quarter, an increase of 5.0%. Direct operating expenses rose 1.6% to US$1.15 billion from US$1.14 billion in the comparable period the year before. Indirect operating expenses decreased 2.9% to US$442.6 million from US$455.8 million in the equivalent prior-year period.

Prospects: Our evaluation of Hanesbrands Inc. as of October 4th, 2019 is the result of our systematic analysis on three basic characteristics: earnings strength, relative valuation, and recent stock price movement. The company has produced a positive trend in earnings per share over the past 5 quarters. However, recent analyst estimates for the company have been mixed and HBI has posted results that exceeded analysts' expectations. Based on operating earnings yield, the company is undervalued when compared to all of the companies we cover. Share price changes over the past year indicates that HBI will perform poorly over the near term.

Financial Data

(US$ in Thousands)	9 Mos	6 Mos	3 Mos	12/29/2018	12/30/2017	12/31/2016	01/02/2016	01/03/2015
Earnings Per Share	1.60	1.56	1.53	1.52	0.17	1.40	1.06	1.32
Cash Flow Per Share	2.05	1.78	1.58	1.77	1.79	1.59	0.57	1.66
Dividends Per Share	0.600	0.600	0.600	0.600	0.600	0.440	0.400	0.300
Dividend Payout %	37.50	38.46	39.22	39.47	352.94	31.43	37.74	22.67
Income Statement								
Total Revenue	5,215,918	3,348,951	1,588,024	6,803,955	6,471,410	6,028,199	5,731,549	5,324,746
EBITDA	725,887	448,444	175,261	973,352	834,192	827,066	695,811	659,557
Depn & Amortn	97,842	82,089	34,674	131,796	122,487	103,175	103,903	98,202
Income Before Taxes	490,373	271,774	92,528	646,881	537,270	571,199	473,873	464,968
Income Taxes	69,143	38,320	13,046	93,797	473,279	34,272	45,018	60,449
Net Income	421,230	233,454	79,482	553,084	61,894	539,382	428,855	404,519
Average Shares	365,597	365,537	365,299	364,505	369,426	384,566	403,659	306,033
Balance Sheet								
Current Assets	3,625,970	3,656,442	3,621,887	3,517,589	3,386,370	3,298,420	2,917,867	2,765,232
Total Assets	7,773,298	7,876,892	7,848,025	7,255,958	6,894,775	6,907,734	5,619,040	5,221,781
Current Liabilities	2,096,904	2,069,817	2,182,435	2,030,242	1,778,745	1,602,922	1,503,909	1,486,602
Long-Term Obligations	3,467,591	3,671,066	3,615,493	3,534,183	3,702,054	3,507,685	2,254,162	1,613,997
Total Liabilities	6,543,056	6,742,042	6,809,987	6,285,675	6,208,573	5,683,820	4,343,149	3,835,009
Stockholders' Equity	1,230,242	1,134,850	1,038,038	970,283	686,202	1,223,914	1,275,891	1,386,772
Shares Outstanding	361,612	361,530	361,471	361,330	360,125	378,687	391,670	300,591
Statistical Record								
Return on Assets %	7.65	7.40	7.29	7.84	0.90	8.64	7.93	8.55
Return on Equity %	55.49	59.57	63.45	66.96	6.50	43.27	32.30	30.41
EBITDA Margin %	13.92	13.39	11.04	14.31	12.89	13.72	12.14	12.39
Net Margin %	8.08	6.97	5.01	8.13	0.96	8.95	7.48	7.60
Asset Turnover	0.92	0.91	0.91	0.96	0.94	0.97	1.06	1.13
Current Ratio	1.73	1.77	1.66	1.73	1.90	2.06	1.94	1.86
Debt to Equity	2.82	3.23	3.48	3.64	5.39	2.87	1.77	1.16
Price Range	19.14-11.62	22.46-11.62	22.46-11.62	23.24-11.62	25.67-18.98	31.18-21.53	34.58-26.54	28.93-16.04
P/E Ratio	11.96-7.26	14.40-7.45	14.68-7.59	15.29-7.64	151.00-111.65	22.27-15.38	32.62-25.03	21.92-12.15
Average Yield %	3.71	3.48	3.41	3.22	2.72	1.66	1.29	1.31

Address: 1000 East Hanes Mill Road,	Web Site: www.Hanes.com	Auditors: PricewaterhouseCoopers LLP
Winston-Salem, NC 27105	Officers: Ronald L. Nelson - Chairman Gerald W.	Investor Contact: 336-519-8080
Telephone: 336-519-8080	Evans - Chief Executive Officer, Chief Operating	Transfer Agents: ComputerShare
	Officer, Co-Chief Operating Officer, Division Officer	Investor Services, Providence, RI

HANOVER INSURANCE GROUP INC

Exchange	Symbol	Price	52Wk Range	Yield	P/E	Div Acheiver
NYS	THG	$136.67 (12/31/2019)	139.27-109.00	1.90	12.89	13 Years

*7 Year Price Score 119.45 *NYSE Composite Index=100 *12 Month Price Score 101.64

Interim Earnings (Per Share)

Qtr.	Mar	Jun	Sep	Dec
2016	1.80	0.05	2.06	(0.30)
2017	1.05	1.83	0.26	1.19
2018	1.57	2.31	2.33	2.88
2019	2.97	1.79	2.96	...

Interim Dividends (Per Share)

Amt	Decl	Ex	Rec	Pay
0.60Q	05/14/2019	06/07/2019	06/10/2019	06/28/2019
0.60Q	09/03/2019	09/12/2019	09/13/2019	09/27/2019
0.65Q	12/05/2019	12/13/2019	12/16/2019	12/27/2019
2.50Sp	12/05/2019	12/13/2019	12/16/2019	12/27/2019

Indicated Div: $2.60

Valuation Analysis   **Institutional Holding**

Forecast EPS	$8.18	No of Institutions
	(01/17/2020)	485
Market Cap	$5.4 Billion	Shares
Book Value	$3.1 Billion	48,684,748
Price/Book	1.75	% Held
Price/Sales	1.14	N/A

Business Summary: General Insurance (MIC: 5.2.1 SIC: 6331 NAIC: 524126)

The Hanover Insurance Group is a holding company. Through its subsidiaries, Co. provides property and casualty insurance products and services. Co. markets its' products and services through independent agents and brokers in the U.S. Co. conducts three operating segments: Commercial Lines, which includes commercial multiple peril, commercial automobile, workers' compensation, and other commercial coverages; Personal Lines, which includes personal automobile, homeowners, and other personal coverages; and Other, which provides investment advisory services to affiliates and also manages assets for unaffiliated institutions such as insurance companies, retirement plans and foundations.

Recent Developments: For the quarter ended Sep 30 2019, income from continuing operations increased 6.9% to US$111.2 million from US$104.0 million in the year-earlier quarter. Net income increased 18.4% to US$118.9 million from US$100.4 million in the year-earlier quarter. Revenues were US$1.21 billion, up 4.1% from US$1.17 billion the year before. Net premiums earned were US$1.12 billion versus US$1.07 billion in the prior-year quarter, an increase of 4.9%. Net investment income rose 3.6% to US$68.8 million from US$66.4 million a year ago.

Prospects: Our evaluation of Hanover Insurance Group Inc. as of October 4th, 2019 is the result of our systematic analysis on three basic characteristics: earnings strength, relative valuation, and recent stock price movement. The company has generated a negative trend in earnings per share over the past 5 quarters. However, recent analyst estimates for the company have been raised and THG has posted results that exceeded analysts' expectations. Based on operating earnings yield, the company is undervalued when compared to all of the companies we cover. Share price changes over the past year indicates that THG will perform well over the near term.

Financial Data (US$ in Thousands)	9 Mos	6 Mos	3 Mos	12/31/2018	12/31/2017	12/31/2016	12/31/2015	12/31/2014
Earnings Per Share	10.60	9.97	10.49	9.09	4.33	3.59	7.40	6.28
Cash Flow Per Share	12.85	12.84	13.72	13.00	16.58	17.19	9.99	12.83
Tang Book Value Per Share	73.43	69.76	67.52	65.62	66.00	63.04	61.82	60.58
Dividends Per Share	7.150	7.090	7.030	2.220	2.040	1.880	1.690	1.520
Dividend Payout %	67.45	71.11	67.02	24.42	47.11	52.37	22.84	24.20
Income Statement								
Premium Income	3,330,200	2,206,100	1,095,100	4,254,400	4,833,400	4,628,100	4,704,800	4,710,300
Total Revenue	3,632,800	2,418,100	1,219,500	4,494,300	5,184,400	4,945,800	5,034,000	5,067,600
Benefits & Claims	2,122,600	1,417,300	699,600	2,724,600	3,128,700	2,964,700	2,884,100	2,927,500
Income Before Taxes	388,700	258,400	148,600	282,500	301,500	192,300	439,400	378,000
Income Taxes	69,900	50,800	26,000	43,500	98,500	36,200	108,600	95,700
Net Income	315,300	196,400	122,400	391,000	186,200	155,100	331,500	282,000
Average Shares	40,200	41,200	41,200	43,000	43,000	43,200	44,800	44,900
Balance Sheet								
Total Assets	12,627,200	12,159,900	11,983,400	12,399,700	15,469,600	14,220,400	13,790,900	13,759,700
Total Liabilities	9,540,400	9,218,800	9,056,400	9,445,000	12,471,900	11,362,900	10,946,500	10,915,700
Stockholders' Equity	3,086,800	2,941,100	2,927,000	2,954,700	2,997,700	2,857,500	2,844,400	2,844,000
Shares Outstanding	39,600	39,600	40,700	42,300	42,500	42,400	43,000	43,900
Statistical Record								
Return on Assets %	3.11	3.05	3.26	2.81	1.25	1.10	2.41	2.08
Return on Equity %	14.46	14.30	15.26	13.14	6.36	5.43	11.66	10.37
Loss Ratio %	63.74	64.24	63.88	64.04	64.73	64.06	61.30	62.15
Net Margin %	8.68	8.12	10.04	8.70	3.59	3.14	6.59	5.56
Price Range	135.71-105.29	130.49-105.29	130.49-105.29	130.49-105.29	108.85-80.59	91.66-74.10	86.58-68.18	73.30-53.14
P/E Ratio	12.80-9.93	13.09-10.56	12.44-10.04	14.36-11.58	25.14-18.61	25.53-20.64	11.70-9.21	11.67-8.46
Average Yield %	5.95	6.00	5.98	1.90	2.19	2.27	2.22	2.44

Address: 440 Lincoln Street, Worcester, MA 01653	Web Site: www.hanover.com	Auditors: PricewaterhouseCoopers LLP
Telephone: 508-855-1000	Officers: John C. Roche - President, Chief Executive Officer, Division Officer Mark Leo Berthiaume - Executive Vice President, Chief Technology Innovation Officer, Chief Administrative Officer	Investor Contact: 508-855-2063
Fax: 508-855-6332		Transfer Agents: ComputerShare Investor Services, Providence, RI

HARLEY-DAVIDSON INC

Exchange	Symbol	Price	52Wk Range	Yield	P/E
NYS	HOG	$37.19 (12/31/2019)	41.04-30.39	4.03	14.30

*7 Year Price Score 57.20 *NYSE Composite Index=100 *12 Month Price Score 98.35

Interim Earnings (Per Share)

Qtr.	Mar	Jun	Sep	Dec
2016	1.36	1.55	0.64	0.28
2017	1.05	1.48	0.40	0.07
2018	1.03	1.45	0.68	0.02
2019	0.80	1.23	0.55	...

Interim Dividends (Per Share)

Amt	Decl	Ex	Rec	Pay
0.375Q	02/27/2019	03/13/2019	03/14/2019	03/29/2019
0.375Q	05/09/2019	05/29/2019	05/30/2019	06/14/2019
0.375Q	09/05/2019	09/16/2019	09/17/2019	09/27/2019
0.375Q	12/03/2019	12/13/2019	12/16/2019	12/27/2019

Indicated Div: $1.50 (Div. Reinv. Plan)

Valuation Analysis **Institutional Holding**

Forecast EPS	$2.67	No of Institutions
	(01/17/2020)	764
Market Cap	$5.7 Billion	Shares
Book Value	$1.8 Billion	183,124,320
Price/Book	3.12	% Held
Price/Sales	1.06	84.89

Business Summary: Autos- Manufacturing (MIC: 1.8.1 SIC: 3751 NAIC: 336991)

Harley-Davidson is the parent company for the groups of companies doing business as Harley-Davidson Motor Company (HDMC) and Harley-Davidson Financial Services (HDFS). Co. has two reportable segments: Motorcycles and Related Products, which consists of HDMC that designs, manufactures and sells at wholesale on-road Harley-Davidson motorcycles as well as motorcycle parts, accessories, general merchandise and related services; and Financial Services, which consists of HDFS that is engaged in the business of financing and servicing wholesale inventory receivables and retail consumer loans, primarily for the purchase of Harley-Davidson motorcycles.

Recent Developments: For the quarter ended Sep 29 2019, net income decreased 24.0% to US$86.6 million from US$113.9 million in the year-earlier quarter. Revenues were US$1.27 billion, down 3.3% from US$1.32 billion the year before. Operating income was US$119.8 million versus US$149.4 million in the prior-year quarter, a decrease of 19.8%. Direct operating expenses declined 1.0% to US$836.0 million from US$844.8 million in the comparable period the year before. Indirect operating expenses decreased 1.5% to US$316.7 million from US$321.5 million in the equivalent prior-year period.

Prospects: Our evaluation of Harley-Davidson Inc. as of October 4th, 2019 is the result of our systematic analysis on three basic characteristics: earnings strength, relative valuation, and recent stock price movement. The company has managed to produce a neutral trend in earnings per share over the past 5 quarters. In addition, recent analyst estimates for the company have been mixed and HOG has posted results that exceeded analysts' expectations. Based on operating earnings yield, the company is undervalued when compared to all of the companies we cover. Share price changes over the past year indicates that HOG will perform very poorly over the near term.

Financial Data

(US$ in Thousands)	9 Mos	6 Mos	3 Mos	12/31/2018	12/31/2017	12/31/2016	12/31/2015	12/31/2014
Earnings Per Share	2.60	2.73	2.95	3.19	3.02	3.83	3.69	3.88
Cash Flow Per Share	5.97	6.08	6.57	7.28	5.84	6.52	5.43	5.30
Tang Book Value Per Share	11.49	11.78	10.90	10.77	10.64	10.61	9.67	13.60
Dividends Per Share	1.495	1.490	1.485	1.480	1.460	1.400	1.240	1.100
Dividend Payout %	57.50	54.58	50.34	46.39	48.34	36.55	33.60	28.35
Income Statement								
Total Revenue	4,289,518	3,016,999	1,384,380	5,716,875	5,647,224	5,996,458	5,995,402	6,228,508
EBITDA	631,375	484,553	199,292	1,072,058	1,207,987	1,359,069	1,463,875	1,466,782
Depn & Amortn	64,335	42,558	21,162	354,545	313,144	305,488	301,595	179,300
Income Before Taxes	543,736	426,480	170,399	686,629	863,839	1,023,911	1,150,163	1,283,320
Income Taxes	133,597	102,904	42,454	155,178	342,080	331,747	397,956	438,709
Net Income	410,139	323,576	127,945	531,451	521,759	692,164	752,207	844,611
Average Shares	156,944	159,425	160,026	166,504	172,932	180,535	203,686	217,706
Balance Sheet								
Current Assets	4,088,997	4,312,161	4,374,081	4,484,442	3,884,742	3,853,852	3,983,154	3,948,095
Total Assets	10,576,230	10,740,316	10,580,613	10,665,664	9,972,672	9,890,240	9,991,167	9,528,097
Current Liabilities	3,698,751	3,742,252	3,590,064	3,597,600	3,158,170	2,862,562	2,752,578	2,389,286
Long-Term Obligations	4,646,449	4,688,541	4,784,210	4,887,667	4,587,258	4,666,975	4,845,388	3,761,528
Total Liabilities	8,740,011	8,829,675	8,783,002	8,891,715	8,128,395	7,970,082	8,151,513	6,618,811
Stockholders' Equity	1,836,219	1,910,641	1,797,611	1,773,949	1,844,277	1,920,158	1,839,654	2,909,286
Shares Outstanding	154,292	156,731	159,072	159,657	168,090	175,947	184,733	211,876
Statistical Record								
Return on Assets %	3.90	4.11	4.65	5.15	5.25	6.94	7.71	8.92
Return on Equity %	20.59	21.51	25.55	29.38	27.72	36.72	31.68	28.54
EBITDA Margin %	14.72	16.06	14.40	18.75	21.39	22.66	24.42	23.55
Net Margin %	9.56	10.73	9.24	9.30	9.24	11.54	12.55	13.56
Asset Turnover	0.52	0.51	0.53	0.55	0.57	0.60	0.61	0.66
Current Ratio	1.11	1.15	1.22	1.25	1.23	1.35	1.45	1.65
Debt to Equity	2.53	2.45	2.66	2.76	2.49	2.43	2.63	1.29
Price Range	45.65-30.39	45.65-31.91	45.94-31.91	55.95-31.91	62.94-44.78	62.07-37.49	66.13-45.12	73.94-55.48
P/E Ratio	17.56-11.69	16.72-11.69	15.57-10.82	17.54-10.00	20.84-14.83	16.21-9.79	17.92-12.23	19.06-14.30
Average Yield %	4.09	3.83	3.68	3.43	2.76	2.82	2.20	1.66

Address: 3700 West Juneau Avenue, Milwaukee, WI 53208 **Telephone:** 414-342-4680	**Web Site:** www.harley-davidson.com **Officers:** Michael J. Cave - Chairman Matthew S. Levatich - President, Chief Executive Officer	**Auditors:** Ernst & Young LLP **Transfer Agents:** Computershare, Inc., Providence, RI

HARTFORD FINANCIAL SERVICES GROUP INC.

Exchange	Symbol	Price	52Wk Range	Yield	P/E
NYS	HIG	$60.77 (12/31/2019)	62.59-42.82	1.97	12.96

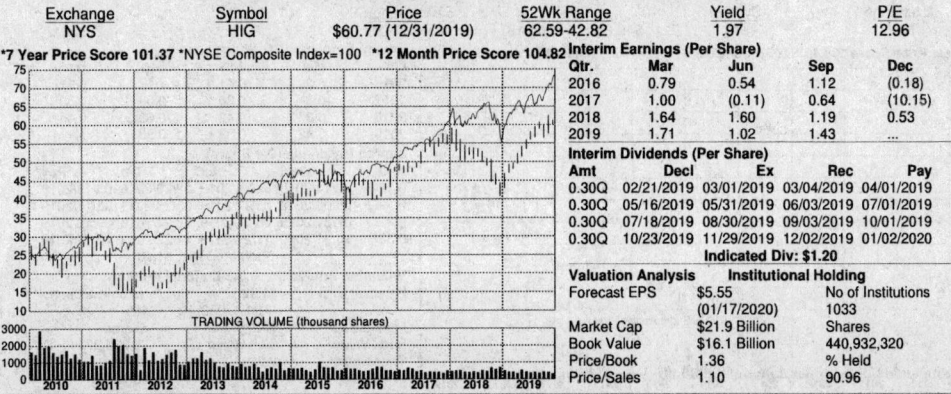

*7 Year Price Score 101.37 *NYSE Composite Index=100 *12 Month Price Score 104.82

Interim Earnings (Per Share)

Qtr.	Mar	Jun	Sep	Dec
2016	0.79	0.54	1.12	(0.18)
2017	1.00	(0.11)	0.64	(10.15)
2018	1.64	1.60	1.19	0.53
2019	1.71	1.02	1.43	...

Interim Dividends (Per Share)

Amt	Decl	Ex	Rec	Pay
0.30Q	02/21/2019	03/01/2019	03/04/2019	04/01/2019
0.30Q	05/16/2019	05/31/2019	06/03/2019	07/01/2019
0.30Q	07/18/2019	08/30/2019	09/03/2019	10/01/2019
0.30Q	10/23/2019	11/29/2019	12/02/2019	01/02/2020

Indicated Div: $1.20

Valuation Analysis		Institutional Holding	
Forecast EPS	$5.55	No of Institutions	
	(01/17/2020)	1033	
Market Cap	$21.9 Billion	Shares	
Book Value	$16.1 Billion	440,932,320	
Price/Book	1.36	% Held	
Price/Sales	1.10	90.96	

Business Summary: General Insurance (MIC: 5.2.1 SIC: 6331 NAIC: 524126)

Hartford Financial Services Group is a holding company. Through its subsidiaries, Co. provides property and casualty insurance, group benefits and mutual funds and exchange-traded products. Co. has five segments: Commercial Lines, which provides workers' compensation, property, automobile, marine, livestock, liability and umbrella coverages; Personal Lines, which provides automobile, homeowners and personal umbrella coverages; Property & Casualty Other Operations, which includes property and casualty operations; Group Benefits, which provides group life, accident and disability coverage; and Hartford Funds, which provides investment products as well as investment management.

Recent Developments: For the quarter ended Sep 30 2019, income from continuing operations increased 25.3% to US$535.0 million from US$427.0 million in the year-earlier quarter. Net income increased 23.8% to US$535.0 million from US$432.0 million in the year-earlier quarter. Revenues were US$5.35 billion, up 10.4% from US$4.84 billion the year before. Net premiums earned were US$4.39 billion versus US$3.99 billion in the prior-year quarter, an increase of 10.2%. Net investment income rose 10.4% to US$490.0 million from US$444.0 million a year ago.

Prospects: Our evaluation of Hartford Financial Services Group Inc. as of October 4th, 2019 is the result of our systematic analysis on three basic characteristics: earnings strength, relative valuation, and recent stock price movement. The company has produced a positive trend in earnings per share over the past 5 quarters. In addition, recent analyst estimates for the company have been raised, and HIG has posted results that exceeded analysts' expectations. Based on operating earnings yield, the company is undervalued when compared to all of the companies we cover. Share price changes over the past year indicates that HIG will perform well over the near term.

Financial Data
(US$ in Thousands)

	9 Mos	6 Mos	3 Mos	12/31/2018	12/31/2017	12/31/2016	12/31/2015	12/31/2014
Earnings Per Share	4.69	4.45	5.03	4.95	(8.61)	2.27	3.96	1.73
Cash Flow Per Share	9.54	7.13	6.69	7.93	6.01	5.31	6.63	4.27
Tang Book Value Per Share	35.20	32.78	33.45	30.13	32.35	43.69	42.67	42.93
Dividends Per Share	1.200	1.200	1.150	1.100	0.940	0.860	0.780	0.660
Dividend Payout %	25.59	26.97	22.86	22.22	...	37.89	19.70	38.15
Income Statement								
Premium Income	12,500,000	8,106,000	3,940,000	15,869,000	14,141,000	13,811,000	13,577,000	13,336,000
Total Revenue	15,379,000	10,032,000	4,940,000	18,955,000	16,974,000	18,300,000	18,377,000	18,614,000
Income Before Taxes	1,884,000	1,231,000	775,000	1,753,000	723,000	804,000	1,978,000	1,699,000
Income Taxes	347,000	229,000	145,000	268,000	985,000	(92,000)	305,000	350,000
Net Income	1,537,000	1,002,000	630,000	1,807,000	(3,131,000)	896,000	1,682,000	798,000
Average Shares	365,400	365,100	364,700	364,100	363,700	394,800	425,200	460,200
Balance Sheet								
Total Assets	70,256,000	69,472,000	63,324,000	62,307,000	225,260,000	223,432,000	228,348,000	245,013,000
Total Liabilities	54,178,000	54,180,000	48,984,000	49,206,000	211,766,000	206,529,000	210,706,000	226,293,000
Stockholders' Equity	16,078,000	15,292,000	14,340,000	13,101,000	13,494,000	16,903,000	17,642,000	18,720,000
Shares Outstanding	360,982	361,605	360,864	359,150	356,835	373,949	401,821	424,415
Statistical Record								
Return on Assets %	2.63	2.50	1.31	1.26	N.M.	0.40	0.71	0.31
Return on Equity %	12.03	11.71	13.39	13.59	N.M.	5.17	9.25	4.24
Net Margin %	9.99	9.99	12.75	9.53	(18.45)	4.90	9.15	4.29
Price Range	60.82-40.76	56.03-40.76	54.58-40.76	59.11-40.76	57.65-47.05	48.58-37.63	49.53-38.90	42.27-32.18
P/E Ratio	12.97-8.69	12.59-9.16	10.85-8.10	11.94-8.23	...	21.40-16.58	12.51-9.82	24.43-18.60
Average Yield %	2.35	2.44	2.34	2.16	1.81	1.97	1.78	1.81

Address: One Hartford Plaza, Hartford, CT 06155 **Telephone:** 860-547-5000	**Web Site:** www.thehartford.com **Officers:** Christopher J. Swift - Chairman, Chief Executive Officer, Executive Vice President, Chief Financial Officer, Principal Accounting Officer Douglas G. (Doug) Elliot - President, Executive Vice President, Division Officer	**Auditors:** DELOITTE & TOUCHE LLP **Investor Contact:** 860-547-8691 **Transfer Agents:** BNY Mellon Shareowner Services, Jersey City, NY

HAWAIIAN ELECTRIC INDUSTRIES INC

Exchange	Symbol	Price	52Wk Range	Yield	P/E
NYS	HE	$46.86 (12/31/2019)	47.42-35.36	2.73	25.47

*7 Year Price Score 108.46 *NYSE Composite Index=100 *12 Month Price Score 100.12

Interim Earnings (Per Share)

Qtr.	Mar	Jun	Sep	Dec
2016	0.30	0.41	1.17	0.41
2017	0.31	0.36	0.55	0.30
2018	0.37	0.42	0.60	0.45
2019	0.42	0.39	0.58	...

Interim Dividends (Per Share)

Amt	Decl	Ex	Rec	Pay
0.32Q	02/14/2019	02/25/2019	02/26/2019	03/13/2019
0.32Q	05/06/2019	05/22/2019	05/23/2019	06/12/2019
0.32Q	07/31/2019	08/21/2019	08/22/2019	09/10/2019
0.32Q	10/31/2019	11/21/2019	11/22/2019	12/10/2019

Indicated Div: $1.28

Valuation Analysis / **Institutional Holding**

Forecast EPS	$1.92	No of Institutions	460
	(01/17/2020)		
Market Cap	$5.1 Billion	Shares	
Book Value	$2.3 Billion		73,235,272
Price/Book	2.24	% Held	55.15
Price/Sales	1.75		

Business Summary: Electric Utilities (MIC: 3.1.1 SIC: 4911 NAIC: 221122)

Hawaiian Electric Industries is a holding company with its subsidiaries principally engaged in electric utility, banking, and renewable/sustainable infrastructure investment businesses operating in the State of Hawaii. Co.'s subsidiary, Hawaiian Electric Company, Inc. and its operating utility subsidiaries are regulated electric public utilities that provide essential electric service to Hawaii's population through the operation of five separate grids that serve communities on the islands of Oahu, Hawaii, and Maui, Lanai and Molokai. Co. also owns ASB Hawaii, Inc. and its subsidiary, American Savings Bank, F.S.B., a financial institution in the State of Hawaii.

Recent Developments: For the quarter ended Sep 30 2019, net income decreased 3.7% to US$63.9 million from US$66.4 million in the year-earlier quarter. Revenues were US$771.5 million, up 0.5% from US$768.0 million the year before. Operating income was US$97.3 million versus US$98.1 million in the prior-year quarter, a decrease of 0.8%. Direct operating expenses rose 0.6% to US$674.2 million from US$670.0 million in the comparable period the year before.

Prospects: Our evaluation of Hawaiian Electric Industries Inc. as of October 4th, 2019 is the result of our systematic analysis on three basic characteristics: earnings strength, relative valuation, and recent stock price movement. The company has managed to produce a neutral trend in earnings per share over the past 5 quarters. In addition, recent analyst estimates for the company have been mixed and HE has posted results that fell short of analysts' expectations. Based on operating earnings yield, the company is fairly valued when compared to all of the companies we cover. Share price changes over the past year indicates that HE will perform well over the near term.

Financial Data

(US$ in Thousands)	9 Mos	6 Mos	3 Mos	12/31/2018	12/31/2017	12/31/2016	12/31/2015	12/31/2014
Earnings Per Share	1.84	1.86	1.89	1.85	1.52	2.29	1.50	1.64
Cash Flow Per Share	5.35	4.81	4.97	4.59	3.87	4.57	3.34	2.96
Tang Book Value Per Share	20.14	19.83	19.60	19.42	18.84	18.59	17.49	17.00
Dividends Per Share	1.270	1.260	1.250	1.240	1.240	1.240	1.240	1.240
Dividend Payout %	69.02	67.74	66.14	67.03	81.58	54.15	82.67	75.61
Income Statement								
Total Revenue	2,148,635	1,377,100	661,615	2,860,849	2,555,625	2,380,654	2,602,982	3,239,542
EBITDA	462,902	292,434	147,311	552,307	551,432	640,773	513,447	508,457
Depn & Amortn	207,860	137,302	67,227	214,036	200,658	194,273	183,966	172,762
Income Before Taxes	189,426	110,733	58,039	254,461	276,580	373,841	254,788	261,922
Income Taxes	36,390	21,587	11,878	50,797	109,393	123,695	93,021	91,712
Net Income	153,036	89,146	46,161	203,664	167,187	250,146	161,767	170,210
Average Shares	109,363	109,255	109,268	109,146	108,933	108,309	106,721	102,937
Balance Sheet								
Current Assets	498,176	516,268	461,281	504,838	534,796	527,620	553,922	558,540
Total Assets	13,517,970	13,537,766	13,360,105	13,104,051	13,099,828	12,425,506	11,790,196	11,184,161
Current Liabilities	6,581,641	6,688,061	6,545,307	6,475,871	6,228,093	5,717,433	5,292,882	4,954,148
Long-Term Obligations	2,014,644	1,995,515	1,970,209	1,989,681	1,874,656	1,811,637	1,915,128	1,797,202
Total Liabilities	11,240,988	11,294,887	11,142,297	10,907,478	10,968,149	10,324,460	9,828,263	9,358,440
Stockholders' Equity	2,276,982	2,242,879	2,217,808	2,196,573	2,131,679	2,101,046	1,961,933	1,825,721
Shares Outstanding	108,972	108,972	108,936	108,879	108,787	108,583	107,460	102,565
Statistical Record								
Return on Assets %	1.54	1.56	1.60	1.55	1.31	2.06	1.41	1.58
Return on Equity %	9.14	9.39	9.63	9.41	7.90	12.28	8.54	9.49
EBITDA Margin %	21.54	21.24	22.27	19.31	21.58	26.92	19.73	15.70
Net Margin %	7.12	6.47	6.98	7.12	6.54	10.51	6.21	5.25
Asset Turnover	0.22	0.22	0.22	0.22	0.20	0.20	0.23	0.30
Current Ratio	0.08	0.08	0.07	0.08	0.09	0.09	0.10	0.11
Debt to Equity	0.88	0.89	0.89	0.91	0.88	0.86	0.98	0.98
Price Range	45.61-35.16	43.93-34.41	41.05-32.69	39.16-31.73	38.35-31.83	34.48-27.74	34.83-27.23	34.62-23.22
P/E Ratio	24.79-19.11	23.62-18.50	21.72-17.30	21.17-17.15	25.23-20.94	15.06-12.11	23.22-18.15	21.11-14.16
Average Yield %	3.14	3.31	3.47	3.54	3.65	4.00	4.05	4.77

Address: 1001 Bishop Street, Suite 2900, Honolulu, HI 96813 **Telephone:** 808-543-5662 **Fax:** 808-543-7966	**Web Site:** www.hei.com **Officers:** Jeffrey N. Watanabe - Chairman Constance H. Lau - President, Chief Executive Officer	**Auditors:** DELOITTE & TOUCHE LLP **Investor Contact:** 808-543-7384 **Transfer Agents:** Continental Stock Transfer & Trust Company, New York, NY

HCA HEALTHCARE INC

Exchange	Symbol	Price	52Wk Range	Yield	P/E
NYS	HCA	$147.81 (12/31/2019)	149.26-112.01	1.08	14.80

*7 Year Price Score 130.52 *NYSE Composite Index=100 *12 Month Price Score 101.47

Interim Earnings (Per Share)

Qtr.	Mar	Jun	Sep	Dec
2016	1.69	1.65	1.59	2.37
2017	1.74	1.75	1.15	1.31
2018	3.18	2.31	2.15	3.01
2019	2.97	2.25	1.76	...

Interim Dividends (Per Share)

Amt	Decl	Ex	Rec	Pay
0.40Q	01/29/2019	02/28/2019	03/01/2019	03/29/2019
0.40Q	04/30/2019	05/31/2019	06/03/2019	06/28/2019
0.40Q	07/29/2019	08/30/2019	09/03/2019	09/30/2019
0.40Q	10/29/2019	11/29/2019	12/02/2019	12/27/2019

Indicated Div: $1.60

Valuation Analysis

		Institutional Holding	
Forecast EPS	$10.50	No of Institutions	939
	(01/15/2020)		
Market Cap	$50.3 Billion	Shares	
Book Value	N/A		280,735,008
Price/Book	N/A	% Held	
Price/Sales	1.00		N/A

Business Summary: Hospitals & Health Care Facilities (MIC: 4.2.1 SIC: 8062 NAIC: 622110)

HCA Healthcare is a holding company. Through its subsidiaries, partnerships and joint ventures (collectively, its affiliates), Co. owns and operates hospitals and related health care entities. These affiliates owned and operated hospitals, freestanding surgery centers and provided outpatient and ancillary services. Co. also operates outpatient health care facilities, which include freestanding ambulatory surgery centers freestanding emergency care facilities, urgent care facilities, walk-in clinics, diagnostic and imaging centers, rehabilitation and physical therapy centers, radiation and oncology therapy centers, physician practices and various other facilities.

Recent Developments: For the quarter ended Sep 30 2019, net income decreased 14.7% to US$764.0 million from US$896.0 million in the year-earlier quarter. Revenues were US$12.69 billion, up 10.9% from US$11.45 billion the year before. Indirect operating expenses increased 12.8% to US$11.72 billion from US$10.38 billion in the equivalent prior-year period.

Prospects: Our evaluation of HCA Healthcare Inc. as of October 4th, 2019 is the result of our systematic analysis on three basic characteristics: earnings strength, relative valuation, and recent stock price movement. The company has managed to produce a neutral trend in earnings per share over the past 5 quarters. In addition, recent analyst estimates for the company have been mixed and HCA has posted results that fell short of analysts' expectations. Based on operating earnings yield, the company is undervalued when compared to all of the companies we cover. Share price changes over the past year indicates that HCA will perform well over the near term.

Financial Data

(US$ in Millions)	9 Mos	6 Mos	3 Mos	12/31/2018	12/31/2017	12/31/2016	12/31/2015	12/31/2014
Earnings Per Share	9.99	10.38	10.44	10.66	5.95	7.30	4.99	4.16
Cash Flow Per Share	21.34	20.07	18.77	19.47	14.98	14.70	11.43	10.21
Dividends Per Share	1.550	1.500	1.450	1.400	...	...	...	...
Dividend Payout %	15.52	14.45	13.89	13.13	...	...	...	...
Income Statement								
Total Revenue	37,813	25,119	12,517	46,677	43,614	41,490	39,678	36,918
EBITDA	5,023	3,593	1,918	9,323	8,137	8,409	7,456	6,979
Depn & Amortn	23	16	8	2,262	2,111	1,946	1,880	1,798
Income Before Taxes	3,614	2,639	1,449	5,306	4,336	4,756	3,911	3,438
Income Taxes	765	550	279	946	1,638	1,378	1,261	1,108
Net Income	2,434	1,822	1,039	3,787	2,216	2,890	2,129	1,875
Average Shares	347	348	350	355	372	395	426	450
Balance Sheet								
Current Assets	10,769	12,869	11,108	10,213	9,977	9,086	9,232	8,930
Total Assets	43,912	45,449	43,379	39,207	36,593	33,758	32,744	31,199
Current Liabilities	7,124	8,961	10,531	7,569	6,158	5,834	5,516	5,480
Long-Term Obligations	34,097	34,120	31,019	32,033	32,858	31,160	30,255	29,307
Total Liabilities	47,477	49,351	47,733	44,157	43,399	41,060	40,343	39,093
Stockholders' Equity	(3,565)	(3,902)	(4,354)	(4,950)	(6,806)	(7,302)	(7,599)	(7,894)
Shares Outstanding	340	341	343	342	350	370	398	420
Statistical Record								
Return on Assets %	8.54	8.76	9.13	9.99	6.30	8.67	6.66	6.25
EBITDA Margin %	13.28	14.30	15.32	19.97	18.66	20.27	18.79	18.90
Net Margin %	6.44	7.25	8.30	8.11	5.08	6.97	5.37	5.08
Asset Turnover	1.22	1.17	1.18	1.23	1.24	1.24	1.24	1.23
Current Ratio	1.51	1.44	1.05	1.35	1.62	1.56	1.67	1.63
Price Range	146.29-112.01	146.29-103.19	146.29-95.32	146.29-84.96	90.49-74.22	82.02-62.83	94.81-64.47	75.00-47.65
P/E Ratio	14.64-11.21	14.09-9.94	14.01-9.13	13.72-7.97	15.21-12.47	11.24-8.61	19.00-12.92	18.03-11.45
Average Yield %	1.18	1.16	1.18	1.22	...	...	...	...

Address: One Park Plaza, Nashville, TN 37203	**Web Site:** www.hcahealthcare.com	**Auditors:** Ernst & Young LLP
Telephone: 615-344-9551	**Officers:** R. Milton Johnson - Chairman, President, Chief Executive Officer, Chief Financial Officer Samuel N. (Sam) Hazen - President, President (frmr), Chief Executive Officer, Chief Operating Officer	**Investor Contact:** 615-344-2688 **Transfer Agents:** Wells Fargo Shareowner Services, St. Paul, MN

HEALTHCARE REALTY TRUST, INC.

Exchange	Symbol	Price	52Wk Range	Yield	P/E
NYS	HR	$33.37 (12/31/2019)	34.77-27.69	3.60	151.68

*7 Year Price Score 92.58 *NSYE Composite Index=100   *12 Month Price Score 97.02

Interim Earnings (Per Share)

Qtr.	Mar	Jun	Sep	Dec
2016	0.09	0.12	0.10	0.47
2017	0.28	0.22	0.02	(0.32)
2018	0.07	0.30	0.05	0.13
2019	0.04	0.03	0.02	...

Interim Dividends (Per Share)

Amt	Decl	Ex	Rec	Pay
0.30Q	02/12/2019	02/21/2019	02/22/2019	03/08/2019
0.30Q	04/30/2019	05/14/2019	05/15/2019	05/30/2019
0.30Q	07/30/2019	08/14/2019	08/15/2019	08/30/2019
0.30Q	10/29/2019	11/13/2019	11/14/2019	11/29/2019

Indicated Div: $1.20 (Div. Reinv. Plan)

Valuation Analysis / Institutional Holding

Forecast EPS	$0.17 (01/17/2020)	No of Institutions	368
Market Cap	$4.4 Billion	Shares	154,091,840
Book Value	$1.8 Billion	% Held	99.58
Price/Book	2.43		
Price/Sales	9.49		

Business Summary: REITs (MIC: 5.3.1 SIC: 6798 NAIC: 525930)

Healthcare Realty Trust is a self-managed and self-administered real estate investment trust that owns, leases, manages, acquires, finances, develops and redevelops real estate properties associated primarily with the delivery of outpatient healthcare services. Co. has gross investments in real estate properties, construction in progress, land held for development and corporate property. Co. provides property management services for healthcare-related properties nationwide.

Recent Developments: For the quarter ended Sep 30 2019, net income decreased 60.3% to US$2.6 million from US$6.5 million in the year-earlier quarter. Revenues were US$119.8 million, up 5.6% from US$113.5 million the year before. Revenues from property income rose 5.6% to US$117.7 million from US$111.5 million in the corresponding quarter a year earlier.

Prospects: Our evaluation of Healthcare Realty Trust Inc. as of October 4th, 2019 is the result of our systematic analysis on three basic characteristics: earnings strength, relative valuation, and recent stock price movement. The company has enjoyed a very positive trend in earnings per share over the past 5 quarters. However, recent analyst estimates for the company have been mixed and HR has posted results that fell short of analysts' expectations. Based on operating earnings yield, the company is overvalued when compared to all of the companies we cover. Share price changes over the past year indicates that HR will perform well over the near term.

Financial Data
(US$ in Thousands)

	9 Mos	6 Mos	3 Mos	12/31/2018	12/31/2017	12/31/2016	12/31/2015	12/31/2014
Earnings Per Share	0.22	0.25	0.52	0.55	0.18	0.78	0.70	0.33
Cash Flow Per Share	1.69	1.58	1.63	1.69	1.52	1.39	1.62	1.32
Tang Book Value Per Share	13.74	13.69	13.98	13.53	14.12	13.99	12.02	12.13
Dividends Per Share	1.200	1.200	1.200	1.200	1.200	1.200	1.200	1.200
Dividend Payout %	545.45	480.00	230.77	218.18	666.67	153.85	171.43	363.64
Income Statement								
Total Revenue	348,774	228,974	112,657	450,389	424,499	411,630	388,471	370,855
EBITDA	55,935	38,808	18,919	287,014	221,274	259,590	230,900	205,776
Depn & Amortn	1,605	1,260	449	164,439	141,776	116,483	106,530	99,384
Income Before Taxes	11,975	9,375	4,891	69,771	23,096	85,756	58,836	33,979
Net Income	11,975	9,375	4,891	69,771	23,092	85,571	69,436	31,887
Average Shares	128,168	127,525	124,231	123,350	118,017	109,387	99,880	96,759
Balance Sheet								
Current Assets	17,098	14,232	21,881	84,281	78,515	127,307	76,302	75,019
Total Assets	3,491,158	3,428,547	3,362,523	3,191,247	3,193,585	3,040,647	2,816,726	2,757,510
Current Liabilities	75,094	60,394	61,519	80,411	70,995	78,880	75,522	70,612
Long-Term Obligations	1,458,224	1,456,974	1,357,404	1,345,984	1,283,880	1,264,370	1,431,494	1,403,692
Total Liabilities	1,685,997	1,659,103	1,556,744	1,474,605	1,403,702	1,387,233	1,573,979	1,536,456
Stockholders' Equity	1,805,161	1,769,444	1,805,779	1,716,642	1,789,883	1,653,414	1,242,747	1,221,054
Shares Outstanding	131,368	129,245	129,214	125,279	125,132	116,417	101,517	98,828
Statistical Record								
Return on Assets %	0.85	0.97	2.00	2.19	0.74	2.91	2.49	1.16
Return on Equity %	1.60	1.82	3.67	3.98	1.34	5.89	5.64	2.59
EBITDA Margin %	16.04	16.95	16.79	63.73	52.13	63.06	59.44	55.49
Net Margin %	3.43	4.09	4.34	15.49	5.44	20.79	17.87	8.60
Asset Turnover	0.14	0.14	0.14	0.14	0.14	0.14	0.14	0.14
Current Ratio	0.23	0.24	0.36	1.05	1.11	1.61	1.01	1.06
Debt to Equity	0.81	0.82	0.75	0.78	0.72	0.76	1.15	1.15
Price Range	33.81-27.10	33.17-27.10	32.80-26.31	32.03-26.31	36.17-29.80	36.50-27.74	30.94-22.11	27.81-21.22
P/E Ratio	153.68-123.18	132.68-108.40	63.08-50.60	58.24-47.84	200.94-165.56	46.79-35.56	44.20-31.59	84.27-64.30
Average Yield %	3.84	3.94	4.08	4.18	3.69	3.80	4.62	4.86

Address: 3310 West End Avenue, Suite 700, Nashville, TN 37203 Telephone: 615-269-8175	Web Site: www.healthcarerealty.com Officers: John Knox Singleton - Chairman Todd J. Meredith - President, Chief Executive Officer, Executive Vice President	Auditors: BDO USA, LLP Transfer Agents: Wells Fargo Shareowner Services, Mendota Heights, MN

HEALTHCARE TRUST OF AMERICA INC

Exchange	Symbol	Price	52Wk Range	Yield	P/E
NYS	HTA	$30.28 (12/31/2019)	31.14-24.73	4.16	168.22

*7 Year Price Score 87.37 ***NYSE Composite Index=100** ***12 Month Price Score 99.53**

Interim Earnings (Per Share)

Qtr.	Mar	Jun	Sep	Dec
2016	0.08	0.09	0.04	0.12
2017	0.09	(0.03)	0.07	0.22
2018	0.05	0.07	0.82	0.08
2019	0.06	0.08	(0.04)	...

Interim Dividends (Per Share)

Amt	Decl	Ex	Rec	Pay
0.31Q	02/14/2019	04/02/2019	04/03/2019	04/10/2019
0.31Q	04/24/2019	07/02/2019	07/03/2019	07/11/2019
0.315Q	07/23/2019	10/02/2019	10/03/2019	10/10/2019
0.315Q	10/28/2019	12/31/2019	01/02/2020	01/09/2020

Indicated Div: $1.26

Valuation Analysis

		Institutional Holding	
Forecast EPS	$0.20	No of Institutions	
	(01/17/2020)	425	
Market Cap	$6.3 Billion	Shares	
Book Value	$3.1 Billion	229,463,168	
Price/Book	2.00	% Held	
Price/Sales	9.12	N/A	

Business Summary: REITs (MIC: 5.3.1 SIC: 6798 NAIC: 525930)

Healthcare Trust of America is a real estate investment trust. Co. focuses on owning and operating medical office buildings that serve healthcare delivery and are located on health system campuses, near university medical centers, or in community core outpatient locations. Co.'s properties include health systems, such as Baylor Scott & White Health, Highmark-Allegheny Health Network, Hospital Corporation of America, Tenet Healthcare System and Community Health Systems.

Recent Developments: For the quarter ended Sep 30 2019, net loss amounted to US$8.6 million versus net income of US$176.3 million in the year-earlier quarter. Revenues were US$175.0 million, down 0.1% from US$175.1 million the year before. Revenues from property income fell 0.1% to US$174.8 million from US$175.0 million in the corresponding quarter a year earlier.

Prospects: Our evaluation of Healthcare Trust Of America as of October 4th, 2019 is the result of our systematic analysis on three basic characteristics: earnings strength, relative valuation, and recent stock price movement. The company has produced a positive trend in earnings per share over the past 5 quarters. However, recent analyst estimates for the company have been unchanged, while HTA has posted results that exceeded analysts' expectations. Based on operating earnings yield, the company is overvalued when compared to all of the companies we cover. Share price changes over the past year indicates that HTA will perform in line with the market over the near term.

Financial Data

(US$ in Thousands)	9 Mos	6 Mos	3 Mos	12/31/2018	12/31/2017	12/31/2016	12/31/2015	12/31/2014
Earnings Per Share	0.18	1.04	1.03	1.02	0.34	0.33	0.26	0.37
Cash Flow Per Share	1.63	1.61	1.59	1.64	1.70	1.49	1.52	1.41
Tang Book Value Per Share	15.10	15.31	15.53	15.38	15.48	11.58	10.53	11.22
Dividends Per Share	1.240	1.235	1.230	1.230	1.210	1.190	1.170	0.290
Dividend Payout %	688.89	118.75	119.42	120.59	355.88	360.61	450.00	78.38
Income Statement								
Total Revenue	515,727	340,723	168,966	696,426	613,990	460,928	403,822	371,505
EBITDA	251,767	181,241	103,713	589,181	390,214	284,776	243,278	243,883
Depn & Amortn	158,900	104,000	66,528	271,441	239,044	175,285	151,614	140,400
Income Before Taxes	20,266	29,265	13,215	215,891	64,795	47,345	33,557	45,994
Net Income	21,236	29,699	13,440	213,463	63,916	45,912	32,931	45,371
Average Shares	205,277	209,005	208,999	210,061	185,278	140,259	128,004	121,168
Balance Sheet								
Current Assets	17,816	29,144	68,475	133,530	118,560	25,045	28,962	31,212
Total Assets	6,322,998	6,240,475	6,242,554	6,188,476	6,449,582	3,747,844	3,172,300	3,041,650
Current Liabilities	157,939	159,853	139,462	185,073	167,852	105,034	94,933	101,042
Long-Term Obligations	2,665,691	2,567,008	2,541,619	2,541,232	2,781,031	1,768,905	1,590,696	1,412,461
Total Liabilities	3,181,312	3,087,533	3,045,060	2,932,452	3,170,800	2,060,570	1,792,876	1,594,511
Stockholders' Equity	3,141,686	3,152,942	3,197,494	3,256,024	3,278,782	1,687,274	1,379,424	1,447,139
Shares Outstanding	207,186	205,117	205,099	205,267	204,892	141,719	127,026	125,087
Statistical Record								
Return on Assets %	0.58	3.48	3.45	3.38	1.25	1.32	1.06	1.57
Return on Equity %	1.13	6.81	6.76	6.53	2.57	2.99	2.33	3.20
EBITDA Margin %	48.82	53.19	61.38	84.60	63.55	61.78	60.24	65.65
Net Margin %	4.12	8.72	7.95	30.65	10.41	9.96	8.15	12.21
Asset Turnover	0.11	0.11	0.11	0.11	0.12	0.13	0.13	0.13
Current Ratio	0.11	0.18	0.49	0.72	0.71	0.24	0.31	0.31
Debt to Equity	0.85	0.81	0.79	0.78	0.85	1.05	1.15	0.98
Price Range	29.57-24.48	29.20-24.48	29.09-24.32	29.83-24.32	32.92-28.69	34.64-26.30	29.94-22.69	27.40-19.66
P/E Ratio	164.28-136.00	28.08-23.54	28.24-23.61	29.25-23.84	96.82-84.38	104.97-79.70	115.15-87.27	74.05-53.14
Average Yield %	4.49	4.49	4.59	4.64	3.95	3.95	4.50	1.22

Address: 16435 N. Scottsdale Road, Suite 320, Scottsdale, AZ 85254 Telephone: 480-998-3478 Fax: 480-991-0755	Web Site: www.htareit.com Officers: Scott D. Peters - Chairman, President, Chief Executive Officer Robert A. Milligan - Executive Vice President, Chief Financial Officer, Secretary, Treasurer	Auditors: Deloitte & Touche LLP Investor Contact: 480-998-3478 Transfer Agents: DST Systems, Inc., Kansas City, MO

HEALTHPEAK PROPERTIES INC

Exchange NYS	Symbol PEAK	Price $34.47 (12/31/2019)	52Wk Range 37.93-26.98	Yield 4.29	P/E 19.59

*7 Year Price Score 75.92   *NYSE Composite Index=100   *12 Month Price Score 99.27

Interim Earnings (Per Share)

Qtr.	Mar	Jun	Sep	Dec
2016	0.25	0.64	0.32	0.12
2017	0.97	0.04	(0.02)	(0.13)
2018	0.08	0.19	0.21	1.75
2019	0.13	(0.03)	(0.09)	...

Interim Dividends (Per Share)

Amt	Decl	Ex	Rec	Pay
0.37Q	01/31/2019	02/15/2019	02/19/2019	02/28/2019
0.37Q	04/25/2019	05/03/2019	05/06/2019	05/21/2019
0.37Q	07/25/2019	08/02/2019	08/05/2019	08/20/2019
0.37Q	10/23/2019	11/01/2019	11/04/2019	11/19/2019

Indicated Div: $1.48 (Div. Reinv. Plan)

Valuation Analysis

		Institutional Holding	
Forecast EPS	$0.09	No of Institutions	
	(01/17/2020)	948	
Market Cap	$17.1 Billion	Shares	
Book Value	$5.9 Billion	579,255,232	
Price/Book	2.87	% Held	
Price/Sales	8.94	N/A	

Business Summary: REITs (MIC: 5.3.1 SIC: 6798 NAIC: 525930)

Healthpeak Properties is a real estate investment trust which invests in real estate serving the healthcare industry. Co. acquires, develops, leases, and manages and disposes of healthcare real estate. Co.'s segments are: senior housing triple-net and senior housing operating portfolio, which include independent living facilities, assisted living facilities, memory care facilities, and continuing care retirement communities; life science, which contains laboratory and office space for biotechnology, medical device and pharmaceutical companies, scientific research institutions, government agencies and other organizations; and medical office.

Recent Developments: For the quarter ended Sep 30 2019, net loss amounted to US$42.3 million versus net income of US$102.9 million in the year-earlier quarter. Revenues were US$538.0 million, up 18.0% from US$456.0 million the year before. Revenues from property income rose 19.1% to US$525.6 million from US$441.2 million in the corresponding quarter a year earlier.

Prospects: Our evaluation of HCP Inc. as of October 4th, 2019 is the result of our systematic analysis on three basic characteristics: earnings strength, relative valuation, and recent stock price movement. The company has generated a negative trend in earnings per share over the past 5 quarters. However, recent analyst estimates for the company have been mixed and HCP has posted results that fell short of analysts' expectations. Based on operating earnings yield, the company is overvalued when compared to all of the companies we cover. Share price changes over the past year indicates that HCP will perform over the near term.

Financial Data

(US$ in Thousands)	9 Mos	6 Mos	3 Mos	12/31/2018	12/31/2017	12/31/2016	12/31/2015	12/31/2014
Earnings Per Share	1.76	2.06	2.28	2.24	0.88	1.34	(1.21)	2.00
Cash Flow Per Share	1.72	1.65	1.70	1.80	1.81	2.59	2.64	2.72
Tang Book Value Per Share	11.38	11.68	11.64	11.81	10.42	10.74	18.65	22.19
Dividends Per Share	1.480	1.480	1.480	1.480	1.480	2.095	2.260	2.180
Dividend Payout %	84.09	71.84	64.91	66.07	168.18	156.34	...	109.00
Income Statement								
Total Revenue	1,465,692	927,721	436,154	1,846,689	1,848,378	2,129,294	2,544,312	2,266,279
EBITDA	201,333	174,124	118,532	1,903,231	1,281,669	830,490	(88,546)	1,332,231
Depn & Amortn	22,703	15,798	6,810	578,674	563,553	(1,197)	(1,295)	(949)
Income Before Taxes	11,131	52,057	62,395	1,058,214	410,400	367,284	(566,847)	893,438
Income Taxes	(11,583)	(5,322)	(3,458)	(17,854)	(1,333)	4,473	(9,011)	250
Net Income	2,010	47,873	61,470	1,061,093	414,169	627,747	(559,235)	922,233
Average Shares	491,203	478,739	479,131	475,387	468,935	467,403	462,795	458,796
Balance Sheet								
Current Assets	212,095	209,892	195,207	188,017	122,936	182,106	456,045	269,125
Total Assets	14,010,210	13,713,093	12,899,501	12,718,553	14,088,461	15,759,265	21,449,849	21,369,940
Current Liabilities	431,493	371,235	352,642	446,246	454,317	475,505	511,512	517,657
Long-Term Obligations	6,600,432	6,290,559	5,763,870	5,567,908	7,880,466	9,189,491	11,069,003	9,759,773
Total Liabilities	8,077,076	7,658,689	7,062,619	6,774,114	8,787,456	10,211,670	12,106,206	10,634,643
Stockholders' Equity	5,933,134	6,054,404	5,836,882	5,944,439	5,301,005	5,547,595	9,343,643	10,735,297
Shares Outstanding	494,848	491,108	477,928	477,496	469,435	468,081	465,488	459,746
Statistical Record								
Return on Assets %	6.15	7.21	8.03	7.92	2.78	3.36	N.M.	4.45
Return on Equity %	15.15	17.48	19.60	18.87	7.64	8.41	N.M.	8.60
EBITDA Margin %	13.74	18.77	27.18	103.06	69.34	39.00	N.M.	58.78
Net Margin %	0.14	5.16	14.09	57.46	22.41	29.48	N.M.	40.69
Asset Turnover	0.14	0.13	0.13	0.14	0.12	0.11	0.12	0.11
Current Ratio	0.49	0.57	0.55	0.42	0.27	0.38	0.89	0.52
Debt to Equity	1.11	1.04	0.99	0.94	1.49	1.66	1.18	0.91
Price Range	35.99-24.71	33.29-24.71	31.85-21.88	30.23-21.64	33.39-25.21	40.33-26.13	48.21-32.75	45.58-36.18
P/E Ratio	20.45-14.04	16.16-12.00	13.97-9.60	13.50-9.66	37.94-28.65	30.10-19.50	...	22.79-18.09
Average Yield %	4.81	5.13	5.49	5.87	4.98	6.11	5.70	5.30

Address: 1920 Main Street, Suite 1200, Irvine, CA 92614 Telephone: 949-407-0700 Fax: 562-733-5200	Web Site: www.hcpi.com Officers: Brian G. Cartwright - Chairman Scott M. Brinker - President, Executive Vice President, Chief Investment Officer	Auditors: Deloitte & Touche LLP Investor Contact: 562-733-5309 Transfer Agents: Wells Fargo Shareowner Services, Saint Paul, MN

HEICO CORP

Exchange	Symbol	Price	52Wk Range	Yield	P/E	Div Acheiver
NYS	HEI	$114.15 (12/31/2019)	145.95-72.97	0.14	47.76	11 Years

*7 Year Price Score 188.04 *NYSE Composite Index=100 *12 Month Price Score 101.96

Interim Earnings (Per Share)

Qtr.	Jan	Apr	Jul	Oct
2014-15	0.21	0.25	0.26	0.29
2015-16	0.24	0.29	0.32	0.33
2016-17	0.30	0.34	0.34	0.39
2017-18	0.48	0.44	0.49	0.50
2018-19	0.58	0.60	0.59	0.63

Interim Dividends (Per Share)

Amt	Decl	Ex	Rec	Pay
25%	06/11/2018	06/28/2018	06/21/2018	06/27/2018
0.07S	12/17/2018	01/02/2019	01/03/2019	01/17/2019
0.07S	06/12/2019	06/28/2019	07/01/2019	07/15/2019
0.08S	12/16/2019	01/08/2020	01/09/2020	01/23/2020

Indicated Div: $0.16

Valuation Analysis   Institutional Holding

Forecast EPS	$2.70	No of Institutions
	(01/11/2020)	537
Market Cap	$15.4 Billion	Shares
Book Value	$1.7 Billion	40,594,192
Price/Book	9.21	% Held
Price/Sales	7.47	33.22

Business Summary: Aerospace (MIC: 7.1.1 SIC: 3724 NAIC: 336412)

HEICO is a holding company. Through its subsidiaries, Co. is engaged as a manufacturer of Federal Aviation Administration-approved jet engine and aircraft component replacement parts. Co. is also a manufacturer of various types of electronic equipment for the aviation, defense, space, medical, telecommunications and electronics industries. Co.'s segments include: Flight Support Group which designs and manufactures jet engine and aircraft component replacement parts for sale; and Electronic Technologies Group, which designs, manufactures and sells various types of electronic, data and microwave, and electro-optical products, including infrared simulation and test equipment.

Recent Developments: For the year ended Oct 31 2019, net income increased 25.9% to US$359.7 million from US$285.7 million in the prior year. Revenues were US$2.06 billion, up 15.6% from US$1.78 billion the year before. Operating income was US$457.1 million versus US$376.2 million in the prior year, an increase of 21.5%. Direct operating expenses rose 14.2% to US$1.24 billion from US$1.09 billion in the comparable period the year before. Indirect operating expenses increased 13.4% to US$356.7 million from US$314.5 million in the equivalent prior-year period.

Prospects: Our evaluation of Heico Corp. as of October 4th, 2019 is the result of our systematic analysis on three basic characteristics: earnings strength, relative valuation, and recent stock price movement. The company has produced a positive trend in earnings per share over the past 5 quarters. In addition, recent analyst estimates for the company have been raised, and HEI has posted results that exceeded analysts' expectations. Based on operating earnings yield, the company is overvalued when compared to all of the companies we cover. Share price changes over the past year indicates that HEI will perform over the near term.

Financial Data

(US$ in Thousands)	10/31/2019	10/31/2018	10/31/2017	10/31/2016	10/31/2015	10/31/2014	10/31/2013	10/31/2012
Earnings Per Share	2.39	1.90	1.37	1.17	1.01	0.92	0.78	0.66
Cash Flow Per Share	3.27	2.48	2.09	1.90	1.33	1.47	1.02	1.07
Dividends Per Share	0.140	0.116	0.097	0.082	0.072	0.241	0.930	0.044
Dividend Payout %	5.86	6.11	7.10	6.99	7.11	26.11	118.69	6.75
Income Statement								
Total Revenue	2,055,647	1,777,721	1,524,813	1,376,258	1,188,648	1,132,311	1,008,757	897,347
EBITDA	485,336	399,387	329,650	285,722	247,390	221,113	197,878	175,207
Depn & Amortn	25,800	23,200	21,900	20,400	17,800	17,100	13,400	11,600
Income Before Taxes	437,841	356,286	297,960	257,050	224,964	198,572	180,761	161,175
Income Taxes	78,100	70,600	90,300	80,900	71,400	59,800	56,200	54,500
Net Income	327,896	259,233	185,985	156,192	133,364	121,293	102,396	85,147
Average Shares	137,350	136,696	135,587	133,144	132,443	131,744	130,824	130,124
Balance Sheet								
Current Assets	813,731	733,808	631,892	584,221	503,612	431,293	441,472	367,911
Total Assets	2,969,211	2,653,396	2,512,431	2,039,475	1,736,387	1,489,214	1,533,015	1,192,846
Current Liabilities	289,138	282,429	249,437	214,421	168,387	152,220	161,286	131,514
Long-Term Obligations	561,049	531,611	673,528	457,814	367,241	328,691	376,818	131,194
Total Liabilities	1,302,669	1,255,145	1,351,351	1,076,096	926,524	789,730	926,669	576,173
Stockholders' Equity	1,666,542	1,398,251	1,161,080	963,379	809,863	699,484	606,346	616,673
Shares Outstanding	134,496	132,931	132,003	131,423	130,611	129,972	129,640	129,060
Statistical Record								
Return on Assets %	11.66	10.04	8.17	8.25	8.27	8.03	7.51	7.96
Return on Equity %	21.40	20.26	17.51	17.57	17.67	18.58	16.74	14.82
EBITDA Margin %	23.61	22.47	21.62	20.76	20.81	19.53	19.62	19.52
Net Margin %	15.95	14.58	12.20	11.35	11.22	10.71	10.15	9.49
Asset Turnover	0.73	0.69	0.67	0.73	0.74	0.75	0.74	0.84
Current Ratio	2.81	2.60	2.53	2.72	2.99	2.83	2.74	2.80
Debt to Equity	0.34	0.38	0.58	0.48	0.45	0.47	0.62	0.21
Price Range	145.95-71.65	93.61-56.79	59.07-34.01	38.01-24.76	32.18-24.32	33.03-23.80	28.39-15.54	19.95-14.01
P/E Ratio	61.07-29.98	49.27-29.89	43.11-24.83	32.49-21.16	31.86-24.08	35.91-25.87	36.40-19.93	30.23-21.23
Average Yield %	0.13	0.16	0.21	0.26	0.25	0.87	4.49	0.26

Address: 3000 Taft Street, Hollywood, FL 33021	**Web Site:** www.heico.com	**Auditors:** DELOITTE & TOUCHE LLP
Telephone: 954-987-4000	**Officers:** Laurans A. Mendelson - Chairman, Chief Executive Officer Eric A. Mendelson - Co-President, Division Officer	**Investor Contact:** 954-987-4000
		Transfer Agents: Computershare Shareowner Services LLC, Providence, RI

HELMERICH & PAYNE, INC.

Exchange	Symbol	Price	52Wk Range	Yield	P/E	Div Acheiver
NYS	HP	$45.43 (12/31/2019)	64.51-36.36	6.25	N/A	42 Years

*7 Year Price Score 60.74   *NYSE Composite Index=100   *12 Month Price Score 79.95

Interim Earnings (Per Share)
Qtr.	Dec	Mar	Jun	Sep
2014-15	1.85	1.37	0.83	(0.19)
2015-16	0.15	0.19	(0.20)	(0.67)
2016-17	(0.33)	(0.45)	(0.21)	(0.21)
2017-18	4.55	(0.12)	(0.08)	0.02
2018-19	0.17	0.55	(1.42)	0.37

Interim Dividends (Per Share)
Amt	Deci	Ex	Rec	Pay
0.71Q	03/06/2019	05/10/2019	05/13/2019	06/03/2019
0.71Q	06/05/2019	08/09/2019	08/12/2019	09/03/2019
0.71Q	09/04/2019	11/07/2019	11/11/2019	12/02/2019
0.71Q	12/13/2019	02/07/2020	02/10/2020	03/02/2020

Indicated Div: $2.84

Valuation Analysis   Institutional Holding
Forecast EPS	$0.38	No of Institutions	
	(01/17/2020)	771	
Market Cap	$4.9 Billion	Shares	
Book Value	$4.0 Billion	133,352,136	
Price/Book	1.23	% Held	
Price/Sales	1.76	90.02	

Business Summary: Equipment & Services (MIC: 9.1.3 SIC: 1381 NAIC: 213111)

Helmerich & Payne provides drilling services and technologies for oil and gas exploration and production companies. Co.'s contract drilling business segments are: United States Land, which operates in Colorado, Louisiana, Ohio, Oklahoma, Montana, New Mexico, North Dakota, Pennsylvania, Texas, Utah, West Virginia and Wyoming; Offshore, which operates in United States federal waters in the Gulf of Mexico; and International Land, which has rigs in Argentina, Bahrain, Colombia and United Arab Emirates. Co.'s drilling technology-based business segment, Helmerich & Payne Technologies, is focused on developing, promoting and commercializing technologies designed to improve the drilling operations.

Recent Developments: For the year ended Sep 30 2019, loss from continuing operations was US$32.5 million compared with income of US$493.0 million a year earlier. Net loss amounted to US$33.7 million versus net income of US$482.7 million in the prior year. Revenues were US$2.80 billion, up 12.5% from US$2.49 billion the year before. Operating income was US$20.6 million versus US$33.0 million in the prior year, a decrease of 37.6%. Direct operating expenses rose 9.4% to US$1.81 billion from US$1.65 billion in the comparable period the year before. Indirect operating expenses increased 20.9% to US$969.3 million from US$801.7 million in the equivalent prior-year period.

Prospects: Our evaluation of Helmerich & Payne Inc. as of October 4th, 2019 is the result of our systematic analysis on three basic characteristics: earnings strength, relative valuation, and recent stock price movement. The company has generated a negative trend in earnings per share over the past 5 quarters. However, recent analyst estimates for the company have been mixed and HP has posted results that exceeded analysts' expectations. Based on operating earnings yield, the company is fairly valued when compared to all of the companies we cover. Share price changes over the past year indicates that HP will perform poorly over the near term.

Financial Data
(US$ in Thousands)	09/30/2019	09/30/2018	09/30/2017	09/30/2016	09/30/2015	09/30/2014	09/30/2013	09/30/2012
Earnings Per Share	(0.34)	4.37	(1.20)	(0.54)	3.87	6.46	6.79	5.34
Cash Flow Per Share	7.84	5.00	3.29	6.96	13.17	10.38	9.38	9.34
Tang Book Value Per Share	35.44	38.94	37.40	42.20	45.44	45.19	41.64	36.28
Dividends Per Share	2.840	2.810	2.800	2.763	2.750	2.438	0.870	0.280
Dividend Payout %	...	64.30	...	...	71.06	37.73	12.81	5.24
Income Statement								
Total Revenue	2,798,490	2,487,268	1,804,741	1,624,232	3,165,441	3,719,707	3,387,614	3,151,802
EBITDA	521,398	615,891	414,777	545,667	1,281,841	1,622,934	1,574,396	1,297,402
Depn & Amortn	556,900	583,802	585,543	598,587	606,992	523,549	455,623	387,549
Income Before Taxes	(51,222)	15,841	(184,598)	(72,667)	665,647	1,096,314	1,114,297	902,580
Income Taxes	(18,712)	(477,169)	(56,735)	(19,677)	243,375	387,548	392,844	328,971
Net Income	(33,656)	482,672	(128,212)	(56,828)	422,225	708,719	736,639	581,045
Average Shares	109,216	109,387	108,500	107,996	108,570	109,141	107,879	108,377
Balance Sheet								
Current Assets	1,115,086	1,115,550	1,235,267	1,572,686	1,439,007	1,277,366	1,258,211	895,228
Total Assets	5,839,515	6,214,867	6,439,988	6,832,019	7,152,012	6,721,861	6,264,827	5,721,085
Current Liabilities	410,238	377,168	344,385	330,120	351,228	507,526	452,273	381,164
Long-Term Obligations	479,356	493,968	492,902	491,847	492,443	40,000	80,000	195,000
Total Liabilities	1,827,292	1,832,132	2,275,397	2,271,094	2,254,560	1,830,884	1,821,100	1,886,087
Stockholders' Equity	4,012,223	4,382,735	4,164,591	4,560,925	4,897,452	4,890,977	4,443,727	3,834,998
Shares Outstanding	108,437	108,993	108,604	108,077	107,767	108,232	106,716	105,697
Statistical Record								
Return on Assets %	N.M.	7.63	N.M.	N.M.	6.09	10.91	12.29	10.81
Return on Equity %	N.M.	11.29	N.M.	N.M.	8.63	15.18	17.80	16.31
EBITDA Margin %	18.63	24.76	22.98	33.60	40.49	43.63	46.48	41.16
Net Margin %	N.M.	19.41	N.M.	N.M.	13.34	19.05	21.75	18.44
Asset Turnover	0.46	0.39	0.27	0.23	0.46	0.57	0.57	0.59
Current Ratio	2.72	2.96	3.59	4.76	4.10	2.52	2.78	2.35
Debt to Equity	0.12	0.11	0.12	0.11	0.10	0.01	0.02	0.05
Price Range	72.94-36.36	74.33-50.02	83.46-42.34	69.77-42.85	97.87-46.50	118.29-68.95	70.82-45.22	65.13-37.39
P/E Ratio	...	17.01-11.45	...	...	25.29-12.02	18.31-10.67	10.43-6.66	12.20-7.00
Average Yield %	5.29	4.40	4.48	4.75	4.01	2.52	1.44	0.54

Address: 1437 South Boulder Avenue, Suite 1400, Tulsa, OK 74119 **Telephone:** 918-742-5531 **Fax:** 918-742-0237	**Web Site:** www.hpinc.com **Officers:** Hans Helmerich - Chairman, President, Chief Executive Officer John W. Lindsay - President, Chief Executive Officer, Executive Vice President, Chief Operating Officer	**Auditors:** Ernst & Young LLP **Investor Contact:** 918-588-5207 **Transfer Agents:** Computershare Investor Services LLC, Providence, RI

HERBALIFE NUTRITION LTD

Exchange	Symbol	Price	52Wk Range	Yield	P/E
NYS	HLF	$47.67 (12/31/2019)	61.47-33.65	N/A	22.49

*7 Year Price Score 113.76 *NYSE Composite Index=100   *12 Month Price Score 91.84

TRADING VOLUME (thousand shares)

Interim Earnings (Per Share)

Qtr.	Mar	Jun	Sep	Dec
2016	0.56	(0.14)	0.51	0.57
2017	0.49	0.81	0.33	(0.34)
2018	0.54	0.62	0.49	0.34
2019	0.66	0.54	0.58	...

Interim Dividends (Per Share)

Dividend Payment Suspended

Valuation Analysis		Institutional Holding	
Forecast EPS	N/A	No of Institutions	
		361	
Market Cap	$6.5 Billion	Shares	
Book Value	N/A	136,599,312	
Price/Book	N/A	% Held	
Price/Sales	1.35	86.21	

Business Summary: Household & Personal Products (MIC: 1.7.1 SIC: 5122 NAIC: 424210)

Herbalife Nutrition is a holding company. Through its subsidiaries, Co. is a nutrition company that sells its products to and through a network of independent members. Co. has four product groups: weight management, which provides meal replacement, protein shakes, drink mixes, weight loss solutions and healthy snacks; targeted nutrition, which provides dietary and nutritional supplements; energy, sports and fitness, which provide products that support a healthy active lifestyle; outer nutrition, which provides facial skin care, body care, and hair care; and literature, promotional and other, which provides start-up kits, sales tools, and educational materials.

Recent Developments: For the quarter ended Sep 30 2019, net income increased 14.5% to US$81.5 million from US$71.2 million in the year-earlier quarter. Revenues were US$1.24 billion, unchanged from the year before. Operating income was US$143.6 million versus US$187.3 million in the prior-year quarter, a decrease of 23.3%. Direct operating expenses rose 11.6% to US$243.4 million from US$218.1 million in the comparable period the year before. Indirect operating expenses increased 2.4% to US$857.5 million from US$837.4 million in the equivalent prior-year period.

Prospects: Our evaluation of Herbalife Nutrition Ltd. as of October 4th, 2019 is the result of our systematic analysis on three basic characteristics: earnings strength, relative valuation, and recent stock price movement. The company has managed to produce a neutral trend in earnings per share over the past 5 quarters. In addition, recent analyst estimates for the company have been mixed and HLF has posted results that fell short of analysts' expectations. Based on operating earnings yield, the company is undervalued when compared to all of the companies we cover. Share price changes over the past year indicates that HLF will perform very poorly over the near term.

Financial Data

(US$ in Thousands)	9 Mos	6 Mos	3 Mos	12/31/2018	12/31/2017	12/31/2016	12/31/2015	12/31/2014
Earnings Per Share	2.12	2.03	2.11	1.98	1.29	1.51	1.99	1.70
Cash Flow Per Share	3.20	3.04	3.87	4.62	3.73	2.21	3.81	2.96
Dividends Per Share	...	...	...	...	...	...	...	0.150
Dividend Payout %	...	...	...	...	...	...	...	8.82
Income Statement								
Total Revenue	3,656,800	2,412,300	1,172,200	4,891,800	4,427,700	4,488,400	4,469,000	4,958,600
EBITDA	548,800	379,500	195,900	706,600	697,600	538,800	663,800	582,000
Depn & Amortn	73,400	49,000	24,400	80,800	80,100	80,700	82,500	81,500
Income Before Taxes	371,400	258,100	135,400	464,200	471,200	364,700	486,400	421,300
Income Taxes	117,100	85,300	39,100	167,600	257,300	104,700	147,300	112,600
Net Income	254,300	172,800	96,300	296,600	213,900	260,000	339,100	308,700
Average Shares	140,000	142,400	145,500	149,500	165,800	172,200	170,600	181,600
Balance Sheet								
Current Assets	1,389,300	1,920,100	1,835,100	1,805,000	1,860,300	1,462,500	1,566,300	1,393,400
Total Assets	2,545,600	3,078,600	2,982,800	2,789,800	2,895,100	2,565,400	2,477,900	2,374,900
Current Liabilities	920,600	1,526,700	1,531,100	1,588,800	906,800	791,500	1,024,400	874,800
Long-Term Obligations	1,779,300	1,776,200	1,775,500	1,774,900	2,165,700	1,438,400	1,392,500	1,711,700
Total Liabilities	3,013,100	3,612,600	3,600,600	3,513,200	3,229,800	2,369,100	2,531,400	2,709,300
Stockholders' Equity	(467,500)	(534,200)	(617,800)	(723,400)	(334,700)	196,300	(53,500)	(334,400)
Shares Outstanding	137,200	141,200	141,100	142,800	164,600	186,200	185,400	184,400
Statistical Record								
Return on Assets %	11.48	10.65	10.44	10.43	7.83	10.28	13.98	12.73
Return on Equity %	...	...	...	...	...	363.15	...	284.46
EBITDA Margin %	15.01	15.73	16.71	14.44	15.76	12.00	14.85	11.74
Net Margin %	6.95	7.16	8.22	6.06	4.83	5.79	7.59	6.23
Asset Turnover	1.83	1.76	1.64	1.72	1.62	1.78	1.84	2.05
Current Ratio	1.51	1.26	1.20	1.14	2.05	1.85	1.53	1.59
Debt to Equity	...	...	...	...	...	7.33	...	...
Price Range	61.47-33.65	61.47-41.25	61.47-48.63	59.40-34.41	39.38-24.59	34.01-21.71	30.39-14.85	40.91-18.58
P/E Ratio	29.00-15.87	30.28-20.32	29.13-23.05	30.00-17.38	30.53-19.07	22.52-14.38	15.27-7.46	24.06-10.93
Average Yield %	...	...	...	...	...	...	...	0.54

Address: P.O. Box 309GT, Ugland House, South Church Street, KY1-1104
Telephone: 213-745-0500

Web Site: www.herbalife.com
Officers: Michael O. Johnson - Chairman, Chief Executive Officer, Executive Chairman, Chief Executive Officer (frmr) John G. DeSimone - Co-President, Chief Strategy Officer, Chief Financial Officer

Auditors: PricewaterhouseCoopers LLP
Transfer Agents: Mellon Investor Services LLC, South Hackensack, NJ

HERC HOLDINGS INC

Exchange	Symbol	Price	52Wk Range	Yield	P/E
NYS	HRI	$48.94 (12/31/2019)	50.39-25.99	N/A	31.17

*7 Year Price Score 63.16 *NYSE Composite Index=100 *12 Month Price Score 106.94

Interim Earnings (Per Share)

Qtr.	Mar	Jun	Sep	Dec
2016	(1.80)	(0.28)	0.11	(0.47)
2017	(1.39)	(0.98)	0.45	7.51
2018	(0.36)	(0.01)	1.60	1.15
2019	(0.23)	0.33	0.32	...

Interim Dividends (Per Share)

No Dividends Paid

Valuation Analysis

		Institutional Holding
Forecast EPS	$2.05	No of Institutions
	(00/24/2020)	342
Market Cap	$1.4 Billion	Shares
Book Value	$593.0 Million	174,220,464
Price/Book	2.38	% Held
Price/Sales	0.70	N/A

Business Summary: Miscellaneous Transportation Services (MIC: 7.4.5 SIC: 7359 NAIC: 532490)

Herc Holdings is an equipment rental supplier. Co. conducts its operations through subsidiaries, including Herc Rentals Inc. Operations are conducted under the Herc Rentals brand in the U.S. and Canada and under the Hertz Equipment Rental brand in other international locations. Co. sells used equipment and contractor supplies such as construction consumables, tools, small equipment and safety supplies; provides repair, maintenance and equipment management services and safety training to certain of its customers; provides equipment re-rental services and provides on-site support to its customers; and provides ancillary services such as equipment transport, cleaning, refueling and labor.

Recent Developments: For the quarter ended Sep 30 2019, net income decreased 79.7% to US$9.4 million from US$46.2 million in the year-earlier quarter. Revenues were US$508.1 million, down 1.6% from US$516.2 million the year before. Direct operating expenses declined 5.7% to US$241.6 million from US$256.1 million in the comparable period the year before. Indirect operating expenses increased 21.6% to US$261.3 million from US$214.9 million in the equivalent prior-year period.

Prospects: Our evaluation of Herc Holdings Inc. as of October 4th, 2019 is the result of our systematic analysis on three basic characteristics: earnings strength, relative valuation, and recent stock price movement. The company has generated a negative trend in earnings per share over the past 5 quarters. However, recent analyst estimates for the company have been mixed and HRI has posted results that fell short of analysts' expectations. Based on operating earnings yield, the company is undervalued when compared to all of the companies we cover. Share price changes over the past year indicates that HRI will perform poorly over the near term.

Financial Data

(US$ in Thousands)	9 Mos	6 Mos	3 Mos	12/31/2018	12/31/2017	12/31/2016	12/31/2015	12/31/2014
Earnings Per Share	1.57	2.85	2.51	2.39	5.60	(0.70)	9.00	(2.70)
Cash Flow Per Share	21.79	20.86	19.62	19.69	12.07	15.27	110.58	114.05
Tang Book Value Per Share	7.29	6.97	6.36	6.60	4.79	N.M.	N.M.	N.M.
Income Statement								
Total Revenue	1,458,900	950,800	475,700	1,976,700	1,754,500	1,554,800	10,535,000	11,046,000
EBITDA	509,200	303,500	139,700	263,100	127,100	124,100	4,005,000	3,945,000
Depn & Amortn	352,400	233,800	116,600	57,300	51,500	44,800	3,042,000	3,320,000
Income Before Taxes	10,400	5,200	(9,800)	68,800	(64,400)	(4,900)	341,000	(23,000)
Income Taxes	(2,000)	2,200	(3,100)	(300)	(224,700)	14,800	68,000	59,000
Net Income	12,400	3,000	(6,700)	69,100	160,300	(19,700)	273,000	(82,000)
Average Shares	29,100	29,100	28,600	28,900	28,600	28,300	30,400	30,266
Balance Sheet								
Current Assets	381,800	367,500	374,400	400,400	474,500	371,700	2,960,000	2,725,000
Total Assets	3,903,100	3,801,500	3,666,400	3,610,200	3,549,700	3,463,300	23,358,000	23,985,000
Current Liabilities	396,200	458,200	335,500	299,200	290,700	242,900	2,153,000	2,290,000
Long-Term Obligations	2,428,800	2,268,100	2,277,300	2,246,200	2,250,000	2,178,600	15,907,000	15,993,000
Total Liabilities	3,310,100	3,217,800	3,100,600	3,037,500	3,039,300	3,145,600	21,339,000	21,521,000
Stockholders' Equity	593,000	583,700	565,800	572,700	510,400	317,700	2,019,000	2,464,000
Shares Outstanding	28,800	28,700	28,600	28,500	28,300	28,300	28,200	30,600
Statistical Record								
Return on Assets %	1.19	2.19	2.00	1.93	4.57	N.M.	1.15	N.M.
Return on Equity %	7.97	15.29	13.60	12.76	38.72	N.M.	12.18	N.M.
EBITDA Margin %	34.90	31.92	29.37	13.31	7.24	7.98	38.02	35.71
Net Margin %	0.85	0.32	N.M.	3.50	9.14	N.M.	2.59	N.M.
Asset Turnover	0.52	0.53	0.56	0.55	0.50	0.12	0.45	0.45
Current Ratio	0.96	0.80	1.12	1.34	1.63	1.53	1.37	1.19
Debt to Equity	4.10	3.89	4.02	3.92	4.41	6.86	7.88	6.49
Price Range	49.45-24.75	60.73-24.75	65.05-24.75	71.47-24.75	65.84-35.01	43.77-21.84	76.96-42.14	97.07-59.61
P/E Ratio	31.50-15.76	21.31-8.68	25.92-9.86	29.90-10.36	11.76-6.25	...	8.55-4.68	...

Address: 27500 Riverview Center Blvd., Bonita Springs, FL 34134 **Telephone:** 239-301-1000	**Web Site:** www.hertz.com **Officers:** Lawrence (Larry) Harris Silber - President, Chief Executive Officer Aaron Birnbaum - Senior Vice President, Chief Operating Officer	**Auditors:** PricewaterhouseCoopers LLP **Investor Contact:** 201-307-2100 **Transfer Agents:** Computershare Trust Company, N.A., Providence, RI

HERSHEY COMPANY (THE)

Exchange	Symbol	Price	52Wk Range	Yield	P/E
NYS	HSY	$146.98 (12/31/2019)	161.40-104.30	2.10	24.42

*7 Year Price Score 107.00 ***NYSE Composite Index=100** ***12 Month Price Score 103.51**

Interim Earnings (Per Share)
Qtr.	Mar	Jun	Sep	Dec
2016	1.06	0.68	1.06	0.54
2017	0.58	0.95	1.28	0.85
2018	1.65	1.11	1.25	1.59
2019	1.45	1.54	1.44	...

Interim Dividends (Per Share)
Amt	Decl	Ex	Rec	Pay
0.722Q	01/29/2019	02/21/2019	02/22/2019	03/15/2019
0.722Q	04/23/2019	05/23/2019	05/24/2019	06/14/2019
0.773Q	07/22/2019	08/22/2019	08/23/2019	09/16/2019
0.773Q	10/22/2019	11/21/2019	11/22/2019	12/16/2019

Indicated Div: $3.09 (Div. Reinv. Plan)

Valuation Analysis
		Institutional Holding	
Forecast EPS	$5.74	No of Institutions	1275
	(01/17/2020)		
Market Cap	$30.8 Billion	Shares	
Book Value	$1.8 Billion	Institutional Holding	142,782,816
Price/Book	17.54	% Held	53.04
Price/Sales	3.89		

Business Summary: Food (MIC: 1.2.1 SIC: 2066 NAIC: 311320)

Hershey is engaged in the production of chocolate and non-chocolate confectionery. Co.'s segments are: North America, which is responsible for Co.'s chocolate and non-chocolate confectionery market position, as well as its grocery and snacks market positions, in the U.S. and Canada; and International and Other, in which Co. has operations and manufactures product in China, Mexico, Brazil, India and Malaysia, and also distributes and sells confectionery products in export markets of Asia, Latin America, Middle East, Europe, Africa and other regions. Co.'s product offerings include chocolate and non-chocolate confectionery products, gum and mint refreshment products, pantry and snack items.

Recent Developments: For the quarter ended Sep 29 2019, net income increased 22.5% to US$325.2 million from US$265.4 million in the year-earlier quarter. Revenues were US$2.13 billion, up 2.6% from US$2.08 billion the year before. Operating income was US$460.8 million versus US$406.3 million in the prior-year quarter, an increase of 13.4%. Direct operating expenses declined 2.1% to US$1.19 billion from US$1.22 billion in the comparable period the year before. Indirect operating expenses increased 5.5% to US$482.5 million from US$457.2 million in the equivalent prior-year period.

Prospects: Our evaluation of Hershey Foods Corp. as of October 4th, 2019 is the result of our systematic analysis on three basic characteristics: earnings strength, relative valuation, and recent stock price movement. The company has managed to produce a neutral trend in earnings per share over the past 5 quarters. In addition, recent analyst estimates for the company have been mixed and HSY has posted results that exceeded analysts' expectations. Based on operating earnings yield, the company is fairly valued when compared to all of the companies we cover. Share price changes over the past year indicates that HSY will perform over the near term.

Financial Data
(US$ in Thousands)	9 Mos	6 Mos	3 Mos	12/31/2018	12/31/2017	12/31/2016	12/31/2015	12/31/2014
Earnings Per Share	6.02	5.83	5.40	5.58	3.66	3.34	2.32	3.77
Cash Flow Per Share	8.10	8.00	10.61	7.62	5.89	4.58	5.54	3.77
Tang Book Value Per Share	N.M.	N.M.	N.M.	N.M.	N.M.	N.M.	N.M.	1.66
Dividends Per Share	2.939	2.888	2.822	2.756	2.548	2.402	2.236	2.040
Dividend Payout %	48.82	49.54	52.26	49.39	69.62	71.92	96.38	54.11
Income Statement								
Total Revenue	5,918,127	3,783,705	2,016,488	7,791,069	7,515,426	7,440,181	7,386,626	7,421,768
EBITDA	1,491,994	974,683	505,721	1,779,910	1,420,542	1,421,359	1,252,548	1,601,107
Depn & Amortn	218,841	144,346	72,329	231,012	211,592	231,735	244,928	211,532
Income Before Taxes	1,166,463	759,103	395,934	1,410,061	1,110,668	1,099,481	901,847	1,306,043
Income Taxes	224,129	141,951	92,053	239,010	354,131	379,437	388,896	459,131
Net Income	942,505	617,198	304,358	1,177,562	782,981	720,044	512,951	846,912
Average Shares	211,312	210,817	210,327	210,989	213,742	215,304	220,651	224,837
Balance Sheet								
Current Assets	2,375,055	2,093,558	2,216,929	2,239,181	2,001,910	1,816,778	1,848,598	2,247,047
Total Assets	8,464,260	7,793,560	7,857,376	7,703,020	5,553,726	5,524,333	5,344,371	5,629,516
Current Liabilities	2,982,374	2,387,427	2,398,185	2,418,566	2,076,543	1,909,443	2,217,912	1,935,647
Long-Term Obligations	2,892,296	2,888,043	3,236,317	3,254,280	2,061,023	2,347,455	1,557,091	1,548,963
Total Liabilities	6,711,098	6,118,440	6,442,639	6,304,299	4,638,388	4,738,477	4,346,374	4,174,454
Stockholders' Equity	1,753,162	1,675,120	1,414,737	1,398,721	915,338	785,856	997,997	1,455,062
Shares Outstanding	209,220	209,659	208,625	209,728	210,860	212,259	216,777	221,044
Statistical Record								
Return on Assets %	15.70	16.02	14.90	17.77	14.14	13.21	9.35	15.42
Return on Equity %	85.63	89.37	94.83	101.77	92.05	80.51	41.82	55.36
EBITDA Margin %	25.21	25.76	25.08	22.85	18.90	19.10	16.96	21.57
Net Margin %	15.93	16.31	15.09	15.11	10.42	9.68	6.94	11.41
Asset Turnover	0.97	1.03	1.03	1.18	1.36	1.37	1.35	1.35
Current Ratio	0.80	0.88	0.92	0.93	0.96	0.95	0.83	1.16
Debt to Equity	1.65	1.72	2.29	2.33	2.25	2.99	1.56	1.06
Price Range	161.40-101.64	138.32-91.04	114.83-89.54	114.06-89.54	115.96-102.87	113.89-83.32	110.78-83.58	108.07-88.15
P/E Ratio	26.81-16.88	23.73-15.62	21.26-16.58	20.44-16.05	31.68-28.11	34.10-24.95	47.75-36.03	28.67-23.38
Average Yield %	2.38	2.62	2.62	2.47	2.75	2.35	2.48	2.09

Address: 19 East Chocolate Avenue, Hershey, PA 17033	Web Site: www.hersheys.com	Auditors: Ernst & Young LLP
Telephone: 717-534-4200	Officers: Charles A. Davis - Chairman Rohit Grover - President	Investor Contact: 800-539-0261
Fax: 717-531-6161		Transfer Agents: Computershare, Providence, RI

HESS CORP

Exchange	Symbol	Price	52Wk Range	Yield	P/E
NYS	HES	$66.81 (12/31/2019)	72.80-40.50	1.50	N/A

*7 Year Price Score 79.70   ***NYSE Composite Index=100**   ***12 Month Price Score 101.96**

Interim Earnings (Per Share)

Qtr.	Mar	Jun	Sep	Dec
2016	(1.72)	(1.29)	(1.12)	(15.81)
2017	(1.07)	(1.46)	(2.02)	(8.57)
2018	(0.38)	(0.48)	(0.18)	(0.06)
2019	0.09	(0.02)	(0.70)	...

Interim Dividends (Per Share)

Amt	Decl	Ex	Rec	Pay
0.25Q	03/06/2019	03/15/2019	03/18/2019	03/29/2019
0.25Q	06/04/2019	06/14/2019	06/17/2019	06/28/2019
0.25Q	09/04/2019	09/13/2019	09/16/2019	09/30/2019
0.25Q	12/04/2019	12/13/2019	12/16/2019	12/31/2019

Indicated Div: $1.00

Valuation Analysis

		Institutional Holding	
Forecast EPS	$-0.67	No of Institutions	
	(01/17/2020)	873	
Market Cap	$20.2 Billion	Shares	
Book Value	$8.9 Billion	325,316,864	
Price/Book	2.27	% Held	
Price/Sales	3.11	N/A	

Business Summary: Production & Extraction (MIC: 9.1.1 SIC: 1311 NAIC: 211111)

Hess is a global exploration and production company engaged in exploration, development, production, transportation, purchase and sale of crude oil, natural gas liquids (NGLs), and natural gas with production operations located primarily in the U.S., Denmark, the Malaysia/Thailand Joint Development Area and Malaysia. Co.'s Midstream operating segment provides fee-based services, including gathering, compressing and processing natural gas and fractionating NGLs; gathering, terminaling, loading and transporting crude oil and NGLs; storing and terminaling propane, and water handling services primarily in the Bakken and Three Forks Shale plays in the Williston Basin area of North Dakota.

Recent Developments: For the quarter ended Sep 30 2019, net loss amounted to US$166.0 million versus net income of US$3.0 million in the year-earlier quarter. Revenues were US$1.52 billion, down 17.1% from US$1.83 billion the year before. Direct operating expenses declined 1.6% to US$791.0 million from US$804.0 million in the comparable period the year before. Indirect operating expenses decreased 14.0% to US$774.0 million from US$900.0 million in the equivalent prior-year period.

Prospects: Our evaluation of Hess Corp. as of October 4th, 2019 is the result of our systematic analysis on three basic characteristics: earnings strength, relative valuation, and recent stock price movement. The company has generated a negative trend in earnings per share over the past 5 quarters. However, recent analyst estimates for the company have been mixed and HES has posted results that exceeded analysts' expectations. Based on operating earnings yield, the company is overvalued when compared to all of the companies we cover. Share price changes over the past year indicates that HES will perform in line with the market over the near term.

Financial Data

(US$ in Thousands)	9 Mos	6 Mos	3 Mos	12/31/2018	12/31/2017	12/31/2016	12/31/2015	12/31/2014
Earnings Per Share	(0.69)	(0.17)	(0.63)	(1.10)	(13.12)	(19.92)	(10.78)	7.53
Cash Flow Per Share	7.40	7.34	6.61	6.50	3.01	2.56	6.99	14.70
Tang Book Value Per Share	28.25	29.34	29.52	31.80	33.93	44.73	66.46	71.18
Dividends Per Share	1.000	1.000	1.000	1.000	1.000	1.000	1.000	1.000
Dividend Payout %	...	...	...	...	...	...	...	13.28
Income Statement								
Total Revenue	4,811,000	3,296,000	1,599,000	6,466,000	5,405,000	4,844,000	6,561,000	11,439,000
EBITDA	2,106,000	1,522,000	765,000	2,502,000	(2,570,000)	(272,000)	38,000	5,983,000
Depn & Amortn	1,536,000	992,000	498,000	1,883,000	2,883,000	3,244,000	3,955,000	3,224,000
Income Before Taxes	285,000	335,000	169,000	220,000	(5,778,000)	(3,854,000)	(4,258,000)	2,436,000
Income Taxes	342,000	226,000	94,000	335,000	(1,837,000)	2,222,000	(1,299,000)	744,000
Net Income	(186,000)	26,000	32,000	(282,000)	(4,074,000)	(6,132,000)	(3,056,000)	2,317,000
Average Shares	302,500	302,200	299,700	298,200	314,100	309,900	283,600	307,700
Balance Sheet								
Current Assets	3,398,000	3,684,000	3,834,000	4,459,000	6,157,000	4,276,000	4,404,000	6,687,000
Total Assets	21,631,000	21,695,000	21,716,000	21,433,000	23,112,000	28,621,000	34,195,000	38,578,000
Current Liabilities	2,344,000	2,332,000	2,271,000	2,203,000	2,435,000	2,251,000	2,628,000	4,851,000
Long-Term Obligations	6,768,000	6,757,000	6,800,000	6,605,000	6,397,000	6,694,000	6,544,000	5,919,000
Total Liabilities	12,723,000	12,401,000	12,374,000	11,804,000	12,061,000	14,087,000	14,809,000	16,373,000
Stockholders' Equity	8,908,000	9,294,000	9,342,000	9,629,000	11,051,000	14,534,000	19,386,000	22,205,000
Shares Outstanding	302,631	304,480	304,280	291,434	315,053	316,523	286,045	285,834
Statistical Record								
Return on Assets %	N.M.	N.M.	N.M.	N.M.	N.M.	N.M.	N.M.	5.70
Return on Equity %	N.M.	N.M.	N.M.	N.M.	N.M.	N.M.	N.M.	9.88
EBITDA Margin %	43.77	46.18	47.84	38.69	N.M.	N.M.	0.58	52.30
Net Margin %	N.M.	0.79	2.00	N.M.	N.M.	N.M.	N.M.	20.26
Asset Turnover	0.30	0.32	0.30	0.29	0.21	0.15	0.18	0.28
Current Ratio	1.45	1.58	1.69	2.02	2.53	1.90	1.68	1.38
Debt to Equity	0.76	0.73	0.73	0.69	0.58	0.46	0.34	0.27
Price Range	74.59-36.43	74.59-36.43	74.59-36.43	74.59-36.43	62.82-38.09	65.14-34.38	78.09-47.44	101.10-65.45
P/E Ratio	...	...	...	...	...	...	...	13.43-8.69
Average Yield %	1.69	1.67	1.68	1.72	2.14	1.90	1.56	1.15

Address: 1185 Avenue of the Americas, New York, NY 10036 Telephone: 212-997-8500	Web Site: www.hess.com Officers: James H. Quigley - Chairman John B. Hess - Chairman, Chief Executive Officer	Auditors: Ernst & Young LLP Investor Contact: 212-536-8940 Transfer Agents: Computershare, Providence, RI

HEWLETT PACKARD ENTERPRISE CO

Exchange	Symbol	Price	52Wk Range	Yield	P/E
NYS	HPE	$15.86 (12/31/2019)	17.46-12.68	3.03	20.60

*7 Year Price Score N/A   *NYSE Composite Index=100   *12 Month Price Score 101.65

Interim Earnings (Per Share)

Qtr.	Jan	Apr	Jul	Oct
2014-15	0.30	0.16	0.13	0.75
2015-16	0.15	0.18	1.32	0.18
2016-17	0.16	(0.37)	0.10	0.32
2017-18	0.89	0.49	0.29	(0.46)
2018-19	0.13	0.30	(0.02)	0.36

Interim Dividends (Per Share)

Amt	Decl	Ex	Rec	Pay
0.113Q	01/31/2019	03/12/2019	03/13/2019	04/03/2019
0.113Q	04/04/2019	06/11/2019	06/12/2019	07/03/2019
0.113Q	06/26/2019	09/10/2019	09/11/2019	10/02/2019
0.12Q	10/23/2019	12/10/2019	12/11/2019	01/02/2020

Indicated Div: $0.48 (Div. Reinv. Plan)

Valuation Analysis / Institutional Holding

Forecast EPS	$1.86	No of Institutions
	(01/16/2020)	912
Market Cap	$20.5 Billion	Shares
Book Value	$17.1 Billion	1,181,490,304
Price/Book	1.20	% Held
Price/Sales	0.70	66.77

Business Summary: IT Services (MIC: 6.3.1 SIC: 7379 NAIC: 541519)

Hewlett Packard Enterprise is a technology company. Co.'s segments are: Hybrid IT, which provides a portfolio of infrastructure and solutions including servers, storage, and HPE Pointnext services; Intelligent Edge, which is comprised of cloud solutions that include wireless local area network, campus and data center switching, software-defined wide-area-networking, security, and associated services to enable secure connectivity; Financial Services, which provides investment solutions for customers that facilitate technology deployment models; and Corporate Investments, which includes Communications and Media Solutions, Hewlett Packard Labs and certain business incubation projects.

Recent Developments: For the year ended Oct 31 2019, income from continuing operations decreased 47.9% to US$1.05 billion from US$2.01 billion a year earlier. Net income decreased 45.0% to US$1.05 billion from US$1.91 billion in the prior year. Revenues were US$29.14 billion, down 5.6% from US$30.85 billion the year before. Operating income was US$1.27 billion versus US$1.74 billion in the prior year, a decrease of 26.7%. Direct operating expenses declined 9.4% to US$19.35 billion from US$21.34 billion in the comparable period the year before. Indirect operating expenses increased 9.6% to US$8.52 billion from US$7.77 billion in the equivalent prior-year period.

Prospects: Our evaluation of Hewlett Packard Enterprise Co. as of October 4th, 2019 is the result of our systematic analysis on three basic characteristics: earnings strength, relative valuation, and recent stock price movement. The company has generated a negative trend in earnings per share over the past 5 quarters. However, recent analyst estimates for the company have been mixed and HPE has posted results that exceeded analysts' expectations. Based on operating earnings yield, the company is undervalued when compared to all of the companies we cover. Share price changes over the past year indicates that HPE will perform poorly over the near term.

Financial Data

(US$ in Millions)	10/31/2019	10/31/2018	10/31/2017	10/31/2016	10/31/2015	10/31/2014	10/31/2013	10/31/2012
Earnings Per Share	0.77	1.23	0.21	1.82	1.34	...	...	...
Cash Flow Per Share	2.95	1.94	0.54	2.88	2.03	...	...	...
Tang Book Value Per Share	N.M.	2.05	3.08	3.71	2.49	...	...	...
Dividends Per Share	0.450	0.375	0.260	0.220	...	...	...	...
Dividend Payout %	58.44	30.49	123.81	12.09	...	...	...	...
Income Statement								
Total Revenue	29,135	30,852	28,871	50,123	52,107	55,123	57,371	61,042
EBITDA	4,574	3,376	3,408	8,471	5,715	6,718	7,692	(8,981)
Depn & Amortn	2,567	2,594	2,521	3,755	3,952	4,106	4,428	4,841
Income Before Taxes	1,533	230	295	4,155	1,470	2,244	2,871	(14,314)
Income Taxes	504	(1,744)	(164)	918	(991)	596	820	447
Net Income	1,049	1,908	344	3,161	2,461	1,648	2,051	(14,761)
Average Shares	1,366	1,553	1,674	1,739	1,834	...	...	...
Balance Sheet								
Current Assets	15,143	17,272	21,444	28,917	31,173	22,031	24,379	...
Total Assets	51,803	55,493	61,406	79,679	81,270	65,071	68,775	...
Current Liabilities	19,159	17,198	18,924	22,531	22,151	19,760	20,912	...
Long-Term Obligations	9,395	10,136	10,182	12,608	15,103	485	617	...
Total Liabilities	34,705	34,254	37,940	48,231	47,735	28,295	30,787	...
Stockholders' Equity	17,098	21,239	23,466	31,448	33,535	36,776	37,988	...
Shares Outstanding	1,294	1,423	1,595	1,666	1,742	...	...	...
Statistical Record								
Return on Assets %	1.96	3.26	0.49	3.92	...	2.46	...	...
Return on Equity %	5.47	8.54	1.25	9.70	...	4.41	...	...
EBITDA Margin %	15.70	10.94	11.80	16.90	10.97	12.19	13.41	N.M.
Net Margin %	3.60	6.18	1.19	6.31	4.72	2.99	3.57	N.M.
Asset Turnover	0.54	0.53	0.41	0.62	...	0.82	...	...
Current Ratio	0.79	1.00	1.13	1.28	1.41	1.11	1.17	...
Debt to Equity	0.55	0.48	0.43	0.40	0.45	0.01	0.02	...
Price Range	16.80-12.27	19.41-13.10	15.14-12.95	13.81-7.17	10.10-8.75	...	...	...
P/E Ratio	21.82-15.94	15.78-10.65	72.10-61.68	7.59-3.94	7.54-6.53	...	...	...
Average Yield %	3.02	2.34	1.86	2.11	...	...	...	...

Address: 6280 America Center Drive, San Jose, CA 95002	**Web Site:** www.hpe.com	**Auditors:** Ernst & Young LLP
Telephone: 650-687-5817	**Officers:** Patricia F. Russo - Chairman Antonio F. Neri - President, Chief Executive Officer, Executive Vice President, Division Officer	**Investor Contact:** 650-687-5817
		Transfer Agents: Wells Fargo Shareowner Services

HEXCEL CORP.

Exchange	Symbol	Price	52Wk Range	Yield	P/E
NYS	HXL	$73.31 (12/31/2019)	85.33-56.18	0.93	21.13

*7 Year Price Score 118.81 *NYSE Composite Index=100 *12 Month Price Score 97.78

Interim Earnings (Per Share)

Qtr.	Mar	Jun	Sep	Dec
2016	0.59	0.70	0.72	0.64
2017	0.70	0.67	0.76	0.96
2018	0.68	0.76	0.91	0.76
2019	0.84	0.94	0.93	...

Interim Dividends (Per Share)

Amt	Decl	Ex	Rec	Pay
0.15Q	01/23/2019	02/04/2019	02/05/2019	02/12/2019
0.15Q	04/23/2019	05/02/2019	05/03/2019	05/10/2019
0.17Q	07/22/2019	08/01/2019	08/02/2019	08/09/2019
0.17Q	10/21/2019	10/31/2019	11/01/2019	11/08/2019

Indicated Div: $0.68

Valuation Analysis

		Institutional Holding	
Forecast EPS	$3.53	No of Institutions	
	(01/17/2020)	613	
Market Cap	$8.0 Billion	Shares	
Book Value	$1.4 Billion	107,684,384	
Price/Book	5.65	% Held	
Price/Sales	3.41	90.07	

Business Summary: Plastics (MIC: 8.4.2 SIC: 2821 NAIC: 325211)

Hexcel is a composites company with two reportable segments. The Composite Materials segment manufactures and markets carbon fibers, fabrics and specialty reinforcements, prepregs and other fiber-reinforced matrix materials, structural adhesives, honeycomb, molding compounds, tooling materials, polyurethane systems and laminates that are incorporated into several applications, including military and commercial aircraft, wind turbine blades, recreational products, transport (cars, boats, trains) and other industrial applications. The Engineered Products segment manufactures and markets composite structures and precision machined honeycomb parts primarily for use in the aerospace industry.

Recent Developments: For the quarter ended Sep 30 2019, net income increased 0.2% to US$80.3 million from US$80.1 million in the year-earlier quarter. Revenues were US$572.5 million, up 5.9% from US$540.5 million the year before. Operating income was US$109.9 million versus US$96.5 million in the prior-year quarter, an increase of 13.9%. Direct operating expenses rose 4.3% to US$414.6 million from US$397.5 million in the comparable period the year before. Indirect operating expenses increased 3.2% to US$48.0 million from US$46.5 million in the equivalent prior-year period.

Prospects: Our evaluation of Hexcel Corp. as of October 4th, 2019 is the result of our systematic analysis on three basic characteristics: earnings strength, relative valuation, and recent stock price movement. The company has managed to produce a neutral trend in earnings per share over the past 5 quarters. Additionally, recent analyst estimates for the company have been unchanged while HXL has posted results that exceeded analysts' expectations. Based on operating earnings yield, the company is fairly valued when compared to all of the companies we cover. Share price changes over the past year indicates that HXL will perform over the near term.

Financial Data

(US$ in Thousands)	9 Mos	6 Mos	3 Mos	12/31/2018	12/31/2017	12/31/2016	12/31/2015	12/31/2014
Earnings Per Share	3.47	3.45	3.27	3.11	3.09	2.65	2.44	2.12
Cash Flow Per Share	4.94	4.95	4.76	4.79	4.73	4.31	3.14	3.29
Tang Book Value Per Share	10.42	13.63	12.81	13.91	15.03	12.83	11.99	11.41
Dividends Per Share	0.620	0.600	0.575	0.550	0.470	0.430	0.400	...
Dividend Payout %	17.87	17.39	17.58	17.68	15.21	16.23	16.39	...
Income Statement								
Total Revenue	1,791,400	1,218,900	609,900	2,189,100	1,973,300	2,004,300	1,861,200	1,855,500
EBITDA	328,900	221,400	104,500	491,300	454,100	453,000	408,800	376,500
Depn & Amortn	1,100	3,500	1,700	120,100	103,500	93,300	76,400	71,200
Income Before Taxes	292,900	194,000	90,800	333,500	323,200	337,600	318,200	297,300
Income Taxes	62,400	44,200	20,600	62,500	42,500	90,300	83,000	89,300
Net Income	233,400	153,100	72,200	276,600	284,000	249,800	237,200	209,400
Average Shares	86,100	86,200	86,000	89,000	91,900	94,200	97,200	98,700
Balance Sheet								
Current Assets	771,600	798,100	782,300	675,800	656,700	607,000	633,800	681,700
Total Assets	3,155,200	3,195,100	3,166,000	2,824,100	2,780,900	2,400,600	2,187,400	2,036,400
Current Liabilities	347,000	359,700	349,900	326,700	262,100	271,900	292,600	310,600
Long-Term Obligations	1,115,200	1,115,800	1,160,000	947,400	805,600	684,400	576,500	415,000
Total Liabilities	1,737,400	1,752,700	1,793,600	1,502,100	1,285,800	1,155,700	1,007,800	886,500
Stockholders' Equity	1,417,800	1,442,400	1,372,400	1,322,000	1,495,100	1,244,900	1,179,600	1,149,900
Shares Outstanding	109,300	85,000	84,800	84,800	89,600	91,400	93,500	95,500
Statistical Record								
Return on Assets %	9.98	9.93	9.49	9.87	10.96	10.86	11.23	10.81
Return on Equity %	21.51	21.06	19.57	19.64	20.73	20.55	20.36	18.13
EBITDA Margin %	18.36	18.16	17.13	22.44	23.01	22.60	21.96	20.29
Net Margin %	13.03	12.56	11.84	12.64	14.39	12.46	12.74	11.29
Asset Turnover	0.78	0.77	0.75	0.78	0.76	0.87	0.88	0.96
Current Ratio	2.22	2.22	2.24	2.07	2.51	2.23	2.17	2.19
Debt to Equity	0.79	0.77	0.85	0.72	0.54	0.55	0.49	0.36
Price Range	85.33-53.76	80.88-53.76	73.26-53.76	73.26-53.76	63.76-49.76	54.97-38.38	54.48-40.38	46.40-36.92
P/E Ratio	24.59-15.49	23.44-15.58	22.40-16.44	23.56-17.29	20.63-16.10	20.74-14.48	22.33-16.55	21.89-17.42
Average Yield %	0.88	0.90	0.87	0.84	0.86	0.97	0.83	...

Address: Two Stamford Plaza, 281 Tresser Boulevard, Stamford, CT 06901-3238 **Telephone:** 203-969-0666	**Web Site:** www.hexcel.com **Officers:** Brett Schneider - Division Officer Nick L. Stanage - Chairman, President, Chief Executive Officer, Chief Operating Officer	**Auditors:** Ernst & Young LLP **Investor Contact:** 203-969-0666 **Transfer Agents:** American Stock Transfer & Trust Company, New York, NY

HIGHWOODS PROPERTIES, INC.

Exchange	Symbol	Price	52Wk Range	Yield	P/E
NYS	HIW	$48.91 (12/31/2019)	48.91-37.96	3.88	39.44

*7 Year Price Score 83.15 *NYSE Composite Index=100 *12 Month Price Score 100.19

Interim Earnings (Per Share)

Qtr.	Mar	Jun	Sep	Dec
2016	4.49	0.32	0.32	0.22
2017	0.31	0.37	0.55	0.55
2018	0.31	0.49	0.32	0.52
2019	0.07	0.38	0.27	...

Interim Dividends (Per Share)

Amt	Decl	Ex	Rec	Pay
0.475Q	02/05/2019	02/15/2019	02/19/2019	03/05/2019
0.475Q	04/18/2019	05/10/2019	05/13/2019	06/04/2019
0.475Q	07/31/2019	08/09/2019	08/12/2019	09/04/2019
0.475Q	10/17/2019	11/07/2019	11/11/2019	12/03/2019

Indicated Div: $1.90

Valuation Analysis

		Institutional Holding	
Forecast EPS	$1.04	No of Institutions	423
	(01/16/2020)		
Market Cap	$5.1 Billion	Shares	
Book Value	$2.2 Billion		120,156,992
Price/Book	2.36	% Held	
Price/Sales	7.00		95.08

TRADING VOLUME (thousand shares)

Business Summary: REITs (MIC: 5.3.1 SIC: 6798 NAIC: 525930)

Highwoods Properties is a real estate investment trust that owns, develops, acquires, leases and manages properties primarily in the business districts of Atlanta, Greensboro, Memphis, Nashville, Orlando, Pittsburgh, Raleigh, Richmond and Tampa. Co.'s primary business is the operation, acquisition and development of office properties. Co. conducts its activities through its subsidiary, Highwoods Realty Limited Partnership. Co. provides a line of real estate services to its customers. Co. provides its customers with services such as build-to-suit construction and space modification, including tenant improvements and expansions.

Recent Developments: For the quarter ended Sep 30 2019, net income decreased 15.6% to US$29.6 million from US$35.0 million in the year-earlier quarter. Revenues were US$187.5 million, up 4.5% from US$179.4 million the year before.

Prospects: Our evaluation of Highwoods Properties Inc. as of October 4th, 2019 is the result of our systematic analysis on three basic characteristics: earnings strength, relative valuation, and recent stock price movement. The company has managed to produce a neutral trend in earnings per share over the past 5 quarters. In addition, recent analyst estimates for the company have been mixed and HIW has posted results that fell short of analysts' expectations. Based on operating earnings yield, the company is fairly valued when compared to all of the companies we cover. Share price changes over the past year indicates that HIW will perform in line with the market over the near term.

Financial Data

(US$ in Thousands)	9 Mos	6 Mos	3 Mos	12/31/2018	12/31/2017	12/31/2016	12/31/2015	12/31/2014
Earnings Per Share	1.24	1.29	1.40	1.64	1.78	5.30	1.00	1.19
Cash Flow Per Share	3.39	3.36	3.31	3.47	3.43	3.10	3.06	2.94
Tang Book Value Per Share	20.45	20.82	20.77	21.42	21.22	20.73	16.36	16.09
Dividends Per Share	1.888	1.875	1.863	1.850	1.760	2.500	1.700	1.700
Dividend Payout %	152.22	145.35	133.04	112.80	98.88	47.17	170.00	142.86
Income Statement								
Total Revenue	543,908	356,433	172,363	720,035	702,737	665,634	604,671	608,468
EBITDA	328,530	218,345	87,056	475,106	482,743	415,770	387,910	397,498
Depn & Amortn	191,940	130,899	60,595	230,232	231,688	224,707	223,384	203,324
Income Before Taxes	76,968	48,351	7,722	175,392	184,259	116,753	80,443	113,761
Net Income	76,444	47,921	7,877	171,835	185,365	524,290	97,078	110,964
Average Shares	106,471	106,445	106,357	106,268	105,594	101,398	97,406	93,800
Balance Sheet								
Current Assets	383,151	279,407	264,606	256,183	312,861	268,832	201,274	214,021
Total Assets	4,890,625	4,742,613	4,726,116	4,675,009	4,623,791	4,561,050	4,493,432	4,004,909
Current Liabilities	272,989	257,338	237,278	218,922	228,215	313,885	248,107	237,633
Long-Term Obligations	2,322,226	2,161,965	2,160,594	2,085,831	2,014,333	1,948,047	2,499,614	2,094,908
Total Liabilities	2,739,963	2,554,482	2,543,432	2,428,289	2,403,973	2,424,695	2,892,125	2,480,698
Stockholders' Equity	2,150,662	2,188,131	2,182,684	2,246,720	2,219,818	2,136,355	1,601,307	1,524,211
Shares Outstanding	103,748	103,704	103,690	103,557	103,266	101,665	96,091	92,907
Statistical Record								
Return on Assets %	2.72	2.88	3.11	3.70	4.04	11.55	2.28	2.84
Return on Equity %	5.95	6.14	6.64	7.69	8.51	27.98	6.21	7.39
EBITDA Margin %	60.40	61.26	50.51	65.98	68.69	62.46	64.15	65.33
Net Margin %	14.05	13.44	4.57	23.86	26.38	78.77	16.05	18.24
Asset Turnover	0.15	0.15	0.15	0.15	0.15	0.15	0.14	0.16
Current Ratio	1.40	1.09	1.12	1.17	1.37	0.86	0.81	0.90
Debt to Equity	1.08	0.99	0.99	0.93	0.91	0.91	1.56	1.37
Price Range	47.19-37.30	51.71-37.30	51.71-37.30	51.71-37.30	53.19-48.87	55.74-39.01	48.14-36.82	45.13-35.82
P/E Ratio	38.06-30.08	40.09-28.91	36.94-26.64	31.53-22.74	29.88-27.46	10.52-7.36	48.14-36.82	37.92-30.10
Average Yield %	4.29	4.13	4.04	4.02	3.44	5.15	3.96	4.21

Address: 3100 Smoketree Court, Suite 600, Raleigh, NC 27604	Web Site: www.highwoods.com	Auditors: DELOITTE & TOUCHE LLP
Telephone: 919-872-4924	Officers: Carlos E. Evans - Chairman Theodore J. Klinck - President, Executive Vice President, Chief Executive Officer, Chief Operating Officer, Chief Investment Officer	Investor Contact: 919-431-1529
Fax: 919-431-1439		Transfer Agents: Wells Fargo Shareholder Services, Mendota Heights, MN

HILL-ROM HOLDINGS, INC.

Exchange	Symbol	Price	52Wk Range	Yield	P/E
NYS	HRC	$113.53 (12/31/2019)	114.01-83.58	0.74	50.46

*7 Year Price Score 132.83 *NYSE Composite Index=100 *12 Month Price Score 98.96

Interim Earnings (Per Share)

Qtr.	Dec	Mar	Jun	Sep
2014-15	0.21	0.45	0.33	(0.17)
2015-16	0.07	0.33	0.68	0.77
2016-17	0.36	0.51	0.09	1.04
2017-18	1.31	0.42	0.67	1.33
2018-19	0.62	0.74	0.48	0.41

Interim Dividends (Per Share)

Amt	Decl	Ex	Rec	Pay
0.21Q	03/06/2019	03/21/2019	03/22/2019	03/29/2019
0.21Q	05/08/2019	06/20/2019	06/21/2019	06/28/2019
0.21Q	07/16/2019	09/19/2019	09/20/2019	09/30/2019
0.21Q	11/05/2019	12/13/2019	12/16/2019	12/31/2019

Indicated Div: $0.84

Valuation Analysis — **Institutional Holding**

Forecast EPS	$5.51	No of Institutions	
	(01/16/2020)	28	
Market Cap	$7.6 Billion	Shares	
Book Value	$1.6 Billion	4,651,597	
Price/Book	4.81	% Held	
Price/Sales	2.60	N/A	

Business Summary: Medical Instruments & Equipment (MIC: 4.3.1 SIC: 3841 NAIC: 339112)

Hill-Rom Holdings is a medical technology company. Co.'s reportable segments are: Patient Support Systems, which include a variety of frames and surfaces (such as medical surgical (med-surg) beds, intensive care unit beds, and bariatric patient beds), patient mobility solutions (such as lifts and other devices used to move patients), non-invasive therapeutic products and surfaces, and its information technologies and software solutions; Front Line Care, which includes its patient monitoring and diagnostics products and its respiratory health products; and Surgical Solutions, which include tables, lights, and pendants utilized within the surgical setting.

Recent Developments: For the year ended Sep 30 2019, net income decreased 39.7% to US$152.2 million from US$252.4 million in the prior year. Revenues were US$2.91 billion, up 2.1% from US$2.85 billion the year before. Operating income was US$316.1 million versus US$289.4 million in the prior year, an increase of 9.2%. Direct operating expenses rose 2.0% to US$1.48 billion from US$1.45 billion in the comparable period the year before. Indirect operating expenses increased 0.4% to US$1.11 billion from US$1.10 billion in the equivalent prior-year period.

Prospects: Our evaluation of Hil-Rom Holdings, Inc. as of October 4th, 2019 is the result of our systematic analysis on three basic characteristics: earnings strength, relative valuation, and recent stock price movement. The company has managed to produce a neutral trend in earnings per share over the past 5 quarters. In addition, recent analyst estimates for the company have been mixed and HRC has posted results that exceeded analysts' expectations. Based on operating earnings yield, the company is fairly valued when compared to all of the companies we cover. Share price changes over the past year indicates that HRC will perform well over the near term.

Financial Data
(US$ in Thousands)

	09/30/2019	09/30/2018	09/30/2017	09/30/2016	09/30/2015	09/30/2014	09/30/2013	09/30/2012
Earnings Per Share	2.25	3.73	1.99	1.86	0.82	1.04	1.74	1.94
Cash Flow Per Share	6.01	5.97	4.74	4.29	3.73	3.65	4.39	4.20
Tang Book Value Per Share	N.M.	N.M.	N.M.	N.M.	N.M.	2.53	4.50	3.07
Dividends Per Share	0.830	0.780	0.710	0.670	0.632	0.595	0.525	0.487
Dividend Payout %	36.89	20.91	35.68	36.02	77.13	57.21	30.17	25.13
Income Statement								
Total Revenue	2,907,300	2,848,000	2,743,700	2,655,200	1,988,200	1,686,100	1,716,200	1,634,800
EBITDA	493,000	488,700	482,700	437,700	201,700	231,400	224,700	243,900
Depn & Amortn	194,800	196,500	210,800	209,000	118,200	106,400	71,200	73,900
Income Before Taxes	208,600	197,200	183,000	138,300	65,100	115,200	144,000	163,500
Income Taxes	56,400	(55,200)	50,700	15,500	18,300	54,600	39,000	42,700
Net Income	152,200	252,400	133,600	124,100	47,700	60,600	105,000	120,800
Average Shares	67,660	67,612	67,225	66,596	58,536	58,523	60,250	62,120
Balance Sheet								
Current Assets	1,663,400	1,155,600	1,166,200	1,082,100	1,141,000	779,300	688,000	681,800
Total Assets	4,919,000	4,360,000	4,528,700	4,262,400	4,457,600	1,752,100	1,586,800	1,627,600
Current Liabilities	1,268,300	662,400	658,700	662,300	578,800	442,300	345,400	378,100
Long-Term Obligations	1,783,100	1,790,400	2,120,400	1,938,400	2,175,200	364,900	225,800	237,500
Total Liabilities	3,345,700	2,743,800	3,170,500	3,035,200	3,310,700	945,600	728,100	815,000
Stockholders' Equity	1,573,300	1,616,200	1,358,200	1,227,200	1,146,900	806,500	858,700	812,600
Shares Outstanding	66,625	67,256	65,813	65,705	65,165	57,439	58,523	60,796
Statistical Record								
Return on Assets %	3.28	5.68	3.04	2.84	1.54	3.63	6.53	8.23
Return on Equity %	9.54	16.97	10.33	10.43	4.88	7.28	12.57	15.50
EBITDA Margin %	16.96	17.16	17.59	16.48	10.14	13.72	13.09	14.92
Net Margin %	5.24	8.86	4.87	4.67	2.40	3.59	6.12	7.39
Asset Turnover	0.63	0.64	0.62	0.61	0.64	1.01	1.07	1.11
Current Ratio	1.31	1.74	1.77	1.63	1.97	1.76	1.99	1.80
Debt to Equity	1.13	1.11	1.56	1.58	1.90	0.45	0.26	0.29
Price Range	107.96-82.86	98.28-75.24	84.17-52.92	61.98-43.29	57.79-40.58	44.39-35.13	37.62-26.40	35.96-25.30
P/E Ratio	47.98-36.83	26.35-20.17	42.30-26.59	33.32-23.27	70.48-49.49	42.68-33.78	21.62-15.17	18.54-13.04
Average Yield %	0.83	0.89	1.04	1.31	1.28	1.49	1.59	1.55

Address: 130 E. Randolph St., Suite 1000, Chicago, IL 60601 Telephone: 312-819-7200 Fax: 812-934-8189	Web Site: www.Hill-Rom.com Officers: William ("Bill") G. Dempsey - Executive Chairman, Chairman John P. Groetelaars - President, Chief Executive Officer	Auditors: PricewaterhouseCoopers LLP Investor Contact: 812-931-2199 Transfer Agents: Computershare Trust Company, N.A., Providence, RI

HILLENBRAND INC

Exchange	Symbol	Price	52Wk Range	Yield	P/E	Div Acheiver
NYS	HI	$33.31 (12/31/2019)	45.78-26.16	2.55	17.35	10 Years

*7 Year Price Score 88.25   *NYSE Composite Index=100   *12 Month Price Score 83.50

Interim Earnings (Per Share)

Qtr.	Dec	Mar	Jun	Sep
2014-15	0.46	0.48	0.50	0.30
2015-16	0.31	0.41	0.48	0.56
2016-17	0.34	0.52	0.52	0.60
2017-18	0.28	(0.34)	0.56	0.70
2018-19	0.45	0.60	0.48	0.40

Interim Dividends (Per Share)

Amt	Decl	Ex	Rec	Pay
0.21Q	02/14/2019	03/14/2019	03/15/2019	03/29/2019
0.21Q	05/08/2019	06/13/2019	06/14/2019	06/28/2019
0.21Q	08/21/2019	09/13/2019	09/16/2019	09/30/2019
0.212Q	12/05/2019	12/16/2019	12/17/2019	12/31/2019

Indicated Div: $0.85

Valuation Analysis / **Institutional Holding**

Forecast EPS	$2.61	No of Institutions
	(00/25/2020)	378
Market Cap	$2.1 Billion	Shares
Book Value	$754.1 Million	67,725,760
Price/Book	2.77	% Held
Price/Sales	1.16	83.22

Business Summary: Industrial Machinery & Equipment (MIC: 7.2.1 SIC: 3999 NAIC: 423830)

Hillenbrand is a global industrial company with several brands that serve a variety of industries. Co.'s segments are: Process Equipment Group, which designs, engineers, manufactures, markets, and services process and material handling equipment and systems for a variety of industries, including plastics, food and pharmaceuticals, chemicals, fertilizers, minerals and mining, energy, wastewater treatment, forest products, and other general industrials; and Batesville®, which is engaged in the death care industry in North America, where it designs, manufactures, distributes, and sells funeral service products and solutions to funeral directors operating funeral homes.

Recent Developments: For the year ended Sep 30 2019, net income increased 55.4% to US$126.2 million from US$81.2 million in the prior year. Revenues were US$1.81 billion, up 2.1% from US$1.77 billion the year before. Direct operating expenses rose 5.0% to US$1.18 billion from US$1.13 billion in the comparable period the year before. Indirect operating expenses decreased 12.8% to US$412.2 million from US$472.5 million in the equivalent prior-year period.

Prospects: Our evaluation of Hillenbrand Inc. as of October 4th, 2019 is the result of our systematic analysis on three basic characteristics: earnings strength, relative valuation, and recent stock price movement. The company has enjoyed a very positive trend in earnings per share over the past 5 quarters. However, recent analyst estimates for the company have been mixed and HI has posted results that fell short of analysts' expectations. Based on operating earnings yield, the company is undervalued when compared to all of the companies we cover. Share price changes over the past year indicates that HI will perform very poorly over the near term.

Financial Data
(US$ in Thousands)

	09/30/2019	09/30/2018	09/30/2017	09/30/2016	09/30/2015	09/30/2014	09/30/2013	09/30/2012
Earnings Per Share	1.92	1.20	1.97	1.77	1.74	1.72	1.01	1.68
Cash Flow Per Share	2.84	3.94	3.87	3.75	1.66	2.84	2.03	2.22
Dividends Per Share	0.840	0.830	0.820	0.810	0.800	0.790	0.780	0.770
Dividend Payout %	43.75	69.17	41.62	45.76	45.98	45.93	77.23	45.83
Income Statement								
Total Revenue	1,807,300	1,770,100	1,590,200	1,538,400	1,596,800	1,667,200	1,553,400	983,200
EBITDA	227,300	193,200	239,300	214,700	214,400	207,200	144,300	164,400
Depn & Amortn	23,200	23,400	25,400	25,600	26,200	26,800	25,300	18,700
Income Before Taxes	176,700	146,500	188,700	163,800	164,400	157,100	95,000	133,300
Income Taxes	50,500	65,300	59,900	47,300	49,100	48,700	28,300	30,100
Net Income	121,400	76,600	126,200	112,800	111,400	109,700	63,400	104,800
Average Shares	63,300	63,800	64,000	63,800	63,900	63,800	63,000	62,400
Balance Sheet								
Current Assets	1,023,200	610,600	593,600	600,300	604,100	637,800	639,400	305,300
Total Assets	2,228,600	1,864,600	1,956,500	1,960,900	1,808,100	1,918,500	2,003,200	1,087,500
Current Liabilities	589,300	531,700	511,700	433,700	404,200	491,100	465,500	151,800
Long-Term Obligations	619,500	344,600	446,900	596,300	518,700	543,500	654,300	271,600
Total Liabilities	1,474,500	1,133,500	1,205,100	1,328,600	1,214,000	1,335,200	1,434,900	581,200
Stockholders' Equity	754,100	731,100	751,400	632,300	594,100	583,300	568,300	506,300
Shares Outstanding	62,700	62,300	63,100	63,000	62,900	62,900	62,900	62,600
Statistical Record								
Return on Assets %	5.93	4.01	6.44	5.97	5.98	5.59	4.10	9.22
Return on Equity %	16.35	10.33	18.24	18.35	18.92	19.05	11.80	22.02
EBITDA Margin %	12.58	10.91	15.05	13.96	13.43	12.43	9.29	16.72
Net Margin %	6.72	4.33	7.94	7.33	6.98	6.58	4.08	10.66
Asset Turnover	0.88	0.93	0.81	0.81	0.86	0.85	1.01	0.86
Current Ratio	1.74	1.15	1.16	1.38	1.49	1.30	1.37	2.01
Debt to Equity	0.82	0.47	0.59	0.94	0.87	0.93	1.15	0.54
Price Range	53.07-26.16	52.70-38.30	39.35-29.10	32.99-24.65	34.71-25.28	33.68-26.13	27.86-18.22	23.90-16.82
P/E Ratio	27.64-13.63	43.92-31.92	19.97-14.77	18.64-13.93	19.95-14.53	19.58-15.19	27.58-18.04	14.23-10.01
Average Yield %	2.11	1.80	2.29	2.72	2.61	2.61	3.30	3.76

Address: One Batesville Boulevard, Batesville, IN 47006 **Telephone:** 812-934-7500	**Web Site:** www.hillenbrand.com **Officers:** F. Joseph Loughrey - Chairman Joe Anthony Raver - President, Chief Executive Officer, Senior Vice President, Division Officer	**Auditors:** Ernst & Young LLP **Investor Contact:** 812-931-6000 **Transfer Agents:** Computershare Trust Company, N. A., Providence, RI

HILTON GRAND VACATIONS INC

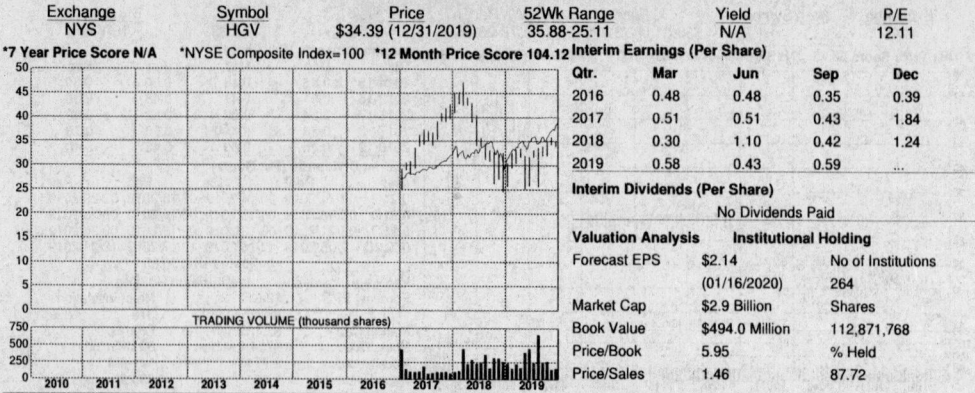

Exchange	Symbol	Price	52Wk Range	Yield	P/E
NYS	HGV	$34.39 (12/31/2019)	35.88-25.11	N/A	12.11

*7 Year Price Score N/A ***NYSE Composite Index=100** ***12 Month Price Score 104.12**

Interim Earnings (Per Share)

Qtr.	Mar	Jun	Sep	Dec
2016	0.48	0.48	0.35	0.39
2017	0.51	0.51	0.43	1.84
2018	0.30	1.10	0.42	1.24
2019	0.58	0.43	0.59	...

Interim Dividends (Per Share)

No Dividends Paid

Valuation Analysis

Forecast EPS	$2.14	No of Institutions
	(01/16/2020)	264
Market Cap	$2.9 Billion	Shares
Book Value	$494.0 Million	112,871,768
Price/Book	5.95	% Held
Price/Sales	1.46	87.72

Institutional Holding

TRADING VOLUME (thousand shares)

Business Summary: Hotels, Restaurants & Travel (MIC: 2.2.1 SIC: 7011 NAIC: 721110)

Hilton Grand Vacations is a timeshare company engaged in developing, marketing, selling and managing timeshare resorts primarily under the Hilton Grand Vacations brand. Co.'s operations primarily consist of: selling vacation ownership intervals (VOIs) for Co. and third parties; operating resorts; financing and servicing loans provided to consumers for their timeshare purchases; and managing Co.'s points-based Hilton Grand Vacations Club exchange program. Co.'s primary products are fee-simple VOIs deeded in perpetuity, developed or acquired by Co. or by third parties. Co. operates its business across two segments: real estate sales and financing, and resort operations and club management.

Recent Developments: For the quarter ended Sep 30 2019, net income increased 22.0% to US$50.0 million from US$41.0 million in the year-earlier quarter. Revenues were US$466.0 million, up 9.1% from US$427.0 million the year before. Direct operating expenses declined 17.2% to US$24.0 million from US$29.0 million in the comparable period the year before. Indirect operating expenses increased 7.5% to US$360.0 million from US$335.0 million in the equivalent prior-year period.

Prospects: Our evaluation of Hilton Grand Vacations Inc. as of October 4th, 2019 is the result of our systematic analysis on three basic characteristics: earnings strength, relative valuation, and recent stock price movement. The company has suffered a very negative trend in earnings per share over the past 5 quarters. However, recent analyst estimates for the company have been mixed and HGV has posted results that fell short of analysts' expectations. Based on operating earnings yield, the company is undervalued when compared to all of the companies we cover. Share price changes over the past year indicates that HGV will perform well over the near term.

Financial Data
(US$ in Millions)

	9 Mos	6 Mos	3 Mos	12/31/2018	12/31/2017	12/31/2016	12/31/2015	12/31/2014
Earnings Per Share	2.84	2.67	3.34	3.05	3.28	1.70	...	...
Cash Flow Per Share	2.26	0.52	(1.81)	(1.64)	3.60	1.59	...	...
Tang Book Value Per Share	4.76	4.26	5.39	5.66	4.50	0.98	...	...
Income Statement								
Total Revenue	1,370	904	450	1,999	1,711	1,583	1,475	1,317
EBITDA	235	152	86	454	354	334	331	324
Depn & Amortn	7	5	2	21	17	12	10	8
Income Before Taxes	195	126	74	403	310	293	292	280
Income Taxes	55	35	20	105	(16)	125	118	113
Net Income	144	94	55	298	327	168	174	167
Average Shares	86	90	95	97	99	99	...	...
Balance Sheet								
Current Assets	2,005	2,004	2,008	1,980	1,989	1,812	1,556	1,445
Total Assets	3,038	2,989	2,961	2,753	2,384	2,180	1,724	1,621
Current Liabilities	455	420	392	425	443	334	304	278
Long-Term Obligations	1,610	1,633	1,520	1,363	1,065	1,184	1,136	1,344
Total Liabilities	2,544	2,539	2,386	2,137	1,866	2,013	1,830	1,994
Stockholders' Equity	494	450	575	616	518	167	(106)	(373)
Shares Outstanding	85	85	91	94	99	98	...	...
Statistical Record								
Return on Assets %	9.02	9.11	12.13	11.60	14.33	8.58	10.40	...
Return on Equity %	50.00	52.74	66.26	52.56	95.47	549.31	...	...
EBITDA Margin %	17.15	16.81	19.11	22.71	20.69	21.10	22.44	24.60
Net Margin %	10.51	10.40	12.22	14.91	19.11	10.61	11.80	12.68
Asset Turnover	0.69	0.71	0.78	0.78	0.75	0.81	0.88	...
Current Ratio	4.41	4.77	5.12	4.66	4.49	5.43	5.12	5.20
Debt to Equity	3.26	3.63	2.64	2.21	2.06	7.09	...	...
Price Range	33.95-24.54	35.65-24.54	44.15-24.54	47.30-24.54	42.71-24.99			
P/E Ratio	11.95-8.64	13.35-9.19	13.22-7.35	15.51-8.05	13.02-7.62	...	...	...

Address: 6355 MetroWest Boulevard, Suite 180, Orlando, FL 32835
Telephone: 407-613-3100

Web Site: www.hiltongrandvacations.com
Officers: Leonard A. Potter - Chairman Mark D. Wang - President, Chief Executive Officer

Auditors: Ernst & Young LLP
Transfer Agents: Wells Fargo Bank

HNI CORP

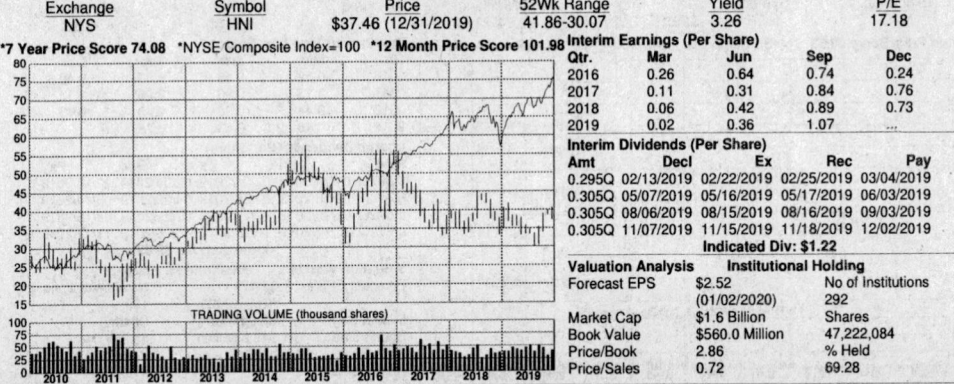

Exchange	Symbol	Price	52Wk Range	Yield	P/E
NYS	HNI	$37.46 (12/31/2019)	41.86-30.07	3.26	17.18

*7 Year Price Score 74.08   *NYSE Composite Index=100   *12 Month Price Score 101.98

Interim Earnings (Per Share)

Qtr.	Mar	Jun	Sep	Dec
2016	0.26	0.64	0.74	0.24
2017	0.11	0.31	0.84	0.76
2018	0.06	0.42	0.89	0.73
2019	0.02	0.36	1.07	...

Interim Dividends (Per Share)

Amt	Decl	Ex	Rec	Pay
0.295Q	02/13/2019	02/22/2019	02/25/2019	03/04/2019
0.305Q	05/07/2019	05/16/2019	05/17/2019	06/03/2019
0.305Q	08/06/2019	08/15/2019	08/16/2019	09/03/2019
0.305Q	11/07/2019	11/15/2019	11/18/2019	12/02/2019

Indicated Div: $1.22

Valuation Analysis

Forecast EPS	$2.52
	(01/02/2020)
Market Cap	$1.6 Billion
Book Value	$560.0 Million
Price/Book	2.86
Price/Sales	0.72

Institutional Holding

No of Institutions	292
Shares	47,222,084
% Held	69.28

Business Summary: Office Equipment & Furniture (MIC: 7.5.1 SIC: 2522 NAIC: 337214)

HNI is a provider of office furniture and hearth products. Co. designs, manufactures and markets a range of office furniture systems and seating across a range of price points. Co.'s office furniture portfolio includes panel-based and freestanding furniture systems and complementary products such as seating, storage, tables and relocatable architectural walls. Co. manufactures and markets prefabricated fireplaces, hearth stoves and related products. Co.'s line of hearth products includes a range of gas, wood and pellet burning fireplaces, inserts, stoves, facings and accessories. Co.'s products are marketed primarily in the U.S. and Canada.

Recent Developments: For the quarter ended Sep 28 2019, net income increased 15.5% to US$46.1 million from US$39.9 million in the year-earlier quarter. Revenues were US$625.4 million, up 2.3% from US$611.1 million the year before. Operating income was US$60.7 million versus US$53.6 million in the prior-year quarter, an increase of 13.1%. Direct operating expenses rose 2.6% to US$387.7 million from US$377.8 million in the comparable period the year before. Indirect operating expenses decreased 1.5% to US$177.0 million from US$179.7 million in the equivalent prior-year period.

Prospects: Our evaluation of HNI Corp. as of October 4th, 2019 is the result of our systematic analysis on three basic characteristics: earnings strength, relative valuation, and recent stock price movement. The company has generated a negative trend in earnings per share over the past 5 quarters. However, recent analyst estimates for the company have been unchanged while HNI has posted results that fell short of analysts' expectations. Based on operating earnings yield, the company is undervalued when compared to all of the companies we cover. Share price changes over the past year indicates that HNI will perform very poorly over the near term.

Financial Data
(US$ in Thousands)

	9 Mos	6 Mos	3 Mos	12/29/2018	12/30/2017	12/31/2016	01/02/2016	01/03/2015
Earnings Per Share	2.18	2.00	2.06	2.11	2.00	1.88	2.32	1.35
Cash Flow Per Share	4.36	3.93	4.34	4.28	3.05	5.04	3.93	3.69
Tang Book Value Per Share	2.59	1.77	1.99	2.29	0.53	4.76	4.51	3.06
Dividends Per Share	1.200	1.190	1.180	1.170	1.130	1.090	1.045	0.990
Dividend Payout %	55.05	59.50	57.28	55.45	56.50	57.98	45.04	73.33
Income Statement								
Total Revenue	1,630,868	1,005,482	479,456	2,257,895	2,175,882	2,203,489	2,304,419	2,222,695
EBITDA	104,833	76,992	9,236	179,236	133,184	190,892	210,176	158,949
Depn & Amortn	17,252	50,067	5,559	51,063	56,494	57,200	46,500	46,100
Income Before Taxes	80,786	22,334	1,566	118,725	70,612	128,911	157,170	104,931
Income Taxes	17,878	5,503	546	25,399	(19,286)	43,273	51,764	43,776
Net Income	62,910	16,832	1,022	93,377	89,795	85,577	105,436	61,471
Average Shares	43,186	43,633	44,088	44,327	44,839	45,502	45,440	45,578
Balance Sheet								
Current Assets	544,567	511,051	484,008	531,883	488,880	433,041	438,370	455,559
Total Assets	1,470,476	1,442,109	1,423,396	1,401,844	1,391,550	1,330,234	1,263,925	1,239,334
Current Liabilities	459,426	423,178	372,860	434,308	489,703	463,473	435,900	457,333
Long-Term Obligations	239,418	285,397	295,876	249,355	240,000	180,000	185,000	197,736
Total Liabilities	910,454	912,925	878,469	838,911	877,482	829,631	786,971	824,747
Stockholders' Equity	560,022	529,184	544,927	562,933	514,068	500,603	476,954	414,587
Shares Outstanding	42,824	42,875	43,339	43,582	43,354	44,078	44,158	44,165
Statistical Record								
Return on Assets %	6.65	6.30	6.64	6.70	6.62	6.62	8.45	5.09
Return on Equity %	17.13	16.91	17.36	17.39	17.75	17.56	23.72	14.21
EBITDA Margin %	6.43	7.66	1.93	7.94	6.12	8.66	9.12	7.15
Net Margin %	3.86	1.67	0.21	4.14	4.13	3.88	4.58	2.77
Asset Turnover	1.56	1.56	1.61	1.62	1.60	1.70	1.85	1.84
Current Ratio	1.19	1.21	1.30	1.22	1.00	0.93	1.01	1.00
Debt to Equity	0.43	0.54	0.54	0.44	0.47	0.36	0.39	0.48
Price Range	44.24-30.07	45.11-33.16	45.11-33.29	45.11-33.29	55.91-32.99	56.26-30.91	57.58-36.06	52.53-31.50
P/E Ratio	20.29-13.79	22.56-16.58	21.90-16.16	21.38-15.78	27.95-16.50	29.93-16.44	24.82-15.54	38.91-23.33
Average Yield %	3.30	3.08	3.04	3.02	2.72	2.47	2.17	2.55

Address: 600 East Second Street, P.O. Box 1109, Muscatine, IA 52761-0071
Telephone: 563-272-7400
Fax: 563-272-7114

Web Site: www.hnicorp.com
Officers: Larry B. Porcellato - Chairman Jeffrey D. Lorenger - President, Executive Vice President, Chief Executive Officer, Division Officer

Auditors: KPMG LLP
Investor Contact: 563-272-7400
Transfer Agents: EQ Shareowner Services, St. Paul, MN

HOLLY ENERGY PARTNERS LP

Exchange	Symbol	Price	52Wk Range	Yield	P/E	Div Acheiver
NYS	HEP	$22.15 (12/31/2019)	30.74-21.26	12.14	10.30	14 Years

*7 Year Price Score 68.53 *NYSE Composite Index=100 *12 Month Price Score 79.82

Interim Earnings (Per Share)

Qtr.	Mar	Jun	Sep	Dec
2016	0.52	0.45	0.33	0.40
2017	0.13	0.36	0.66	1.12
2018	0.44	0.38	0.43	0.45
2019	0.49	0.43	0.78	...

Interim Dividends (Per Share)

Amt	Decl	Ex	Rec	Pay
0.667Q	01/24/2019	02/01/2019	02/04/2019	02/14/2019
0.67Q	04/18/2019	04/26/2019	04/29/2019	05/14/2019
0.672Q	07/18/2019	07/26/2019	07/29/2019	08/13/2019
0.672Q	10/17/2019	10/25/2019	10/28/2019	11/12/2019

Indicated Div: $2.69

Valuation Analysis / Institutional Holding

Forecast EPS	$2.17	No of Institutions
(01/17/2020)		159
Market Cap	$2.3 Billion	Shares
Book Value	$48.6 Million	43,967,048
Price/Book	48.10	% Held
Price/Sales	4.37	51.57

TRADING VOLUME (thousand shares)

Business Summary: Equipment & Services (MIC: 9.1.3 SIC: 4612 NAIC: 486110)

Holly Energy Partners operates a system of petroleum product and crude pipelines, storage tanks, distribution terminals, loading rack facilities and refinery processing units in Texas, New Mexico, Utah, Nevada, Oklahoma, Wyoming, Kansas, Idaho and Washington. Co. has two segments: Pipelines and Terminals, which transports light refined products from HollyFrontier Corporation's (HFC's) Navajo refinery in New Mexico and Delek US Holdings, Inc.'s Big Spring refinery in Texas; and Refinery Processing Unit, which supports HFC's refineries daily operations, which chemically transform crude oil into various petroleum products, including gasoline, diesel, liquefied petroleum gases, asphalt.

Recent Developments: For the quarter ended Sep 30 2019, net income increased 80.9% to US$84.2 million from US$46.5 million in the year-earlier quarter. Revenues were US$135.9 million, up 8.0% from US$125.8 million the year before. Operating income was US$64.1 million versus US$62.9 million in the prior-year quarter, an increase of 1.9%. Direct operating expenses rose 24.8% to US$44.9 million from US$36.0 million in the comparable period the year before. Indirect operating expenses decreased 0.1% to US$26.8 million from US$26.9 million in the equivalent prior-year period.

Prospects: Our evaluation of Holly Energy Partners L.P. as of October 4th, 2019 is the result of our systematic analysis on three basic characteristics: earnings strength, relative valuation, and recent stock price movement. The company has produced a positive trend in earnings per share over the past 5 quarters. However, recent analyst estimates for the company have been unchanged, while HEP has posted results that exceeded analysts' expectations. Based on operating earnings yield, the company is undervalued when compared to all of the companies we cover. Share price changes over the past year indicates that HEP will perform well over the near term.

Financial Data

(US$ in Thousands)	9 Mos	6 Mos	3 Mos	12/31/2018	12/31/2017	12/31/2016	12/31/2015	12/31/2014
Earnings Per Share	2.15	1.80	1.75	1.70	2.28	1.69	1.60	1.20
Cash Flow Per Share	2.90	2.65	2.71	2.81	3.39	4.04	3.97	3.18
Dividends Per Share	2.675	2.663	2.648	2.630	2.505	2.320	2.168	2.045
Dividend Payout %	124.42	147.92	151.29	154.71	109.87	137.28	135.47	170.42
Income Statement								
Total Revenue	401,143	265,248	134,497	506,220	454,362	402,043	358,875	332,545
EBITDA	297,700	177,084	91,690	333,679	318,707	258,674	236,045	201,859
Depn & Amortn	64,007	42,835	21,466	83,300	71,100	62,900	55,400	54,700
Income Before Taxes	179,956	97,076	51,730	180,588	189,650	143,662	143,753	111,061
Income Taxes	36	6	36	26	249	285	228	235
Net Income	179,217	96,872	51,182	178,847	195,040	147,584	137,208	105,525
Average Shares	105,440	105,440	105,440	105,042	70,291	59,872	58,657	58,657
Balance Sheet								
Current Assets	64,200	71,980	66,229	66,474	74,391	56,953	61,142	47,342
Total Assets	2,154,275	2,147,843	2,162,220	2,102,540	2,154,114	1,884,237	1,534,456	1,401,555
Current Liabilities	53,438	53,825	44,388	57,897	55,485	64,735	48,924	44,202
Long-Term Obligations	1,431,869	1,437,710	1,438,054	1,418,900	1,507,308	1,243,912	1,008,752	867,579
Total Liabilities	1,701,134	1,710,099	1,703,162	1,675,105	1,760,155	1,506,003	1,245,784	1,081,193
Stockholders' Equity	48,557	47,722	46,941	...	...	...	...	...
Shares Outstanding	105,440	105,440	105,440	105,440	101,568	62,780	58,657	58,657
Statistical Record								
Return on Assets %	10.64	8.88	8.56	8.40	9.66	8.61	9.35	7.58
Return on Equity %	482.77	410.32	404.93	...	...	...	...	...
EBITDA Margin %	74.21	66.76	68.17	65.92	70.14	64.34	65.77	60.70
Net Margin %	44.68	36.52	38.05	35.33	42.93	36.71	38.23	31.73
Asset Turnover	0.25	0.25	0.24	0.24	0.23	0.23	0.24	0.24
Current Ratio	1.20	1.34	1.49	1.15	1.34	0.88	1.25	1.07
Debt to Equity	29.49	30.13	30.64	...	...	...	...	...
Price Range	32.20-24.95	33.12-26.59	33.12-26.99	33.67-26.50	37.84-30.32	36.83-22.50	36.30-26.62	37.18-28.79
P/E Ratio	14.98-11.60	18.40-14.77	18.93-15.42	19.81-15.59	16.60-13.30	21.79-13.31	22.69-16.64	30.98-23.99
Average Yield %	9.43	9.15	8.96	8.80	7.37	7.21	6.72	6.09

Address: 2828 N. Harwood, Suite 1300, Dallas, TX 75201	Web Site: www.hollyenergy.com	Auditors: Ernst & Young LLP
Telephone: 214-871-3555	Officers: Michael C. Jennings - Chairman, Chief Executive Officer, Chief Executive Officer (frmr), Holding/Parent Company Officer, Associate/Affiliate Company Officer Richard L. Voliva - President, Executive Vice President, Chief Financial Officer, Holding/Parent Company Officer, Associate/Affiliate Company Officer	Investor Contact: 214-954-6511 Transfer Agents: Wells Fargo Shareowner Services, Saint Paul, MN

HOLLYFRONTIER CORP

Exchange	Symbol	Price	52Wk Range	Yield	P/E
NYS	HFC	$50.71 (12/31/2019)	58.25-37.98	2.76	10.10

*7 Year Price Score 92.78   *NYSE Composite Index=100   *12 Month Price Score 99.64

Interim Earnings (Per Share)

Qtr.	Mar	Jun	Sep	Dec
2016	0.12	(2.33)	0.42	0.30
2017	(0.26)	0.33	1.53	2.92
2018	1.50	1.94	1.93	0.82
2019	1.47	1.15	1.58	...

Interim Dividends (Per Share)

Amt	Decl	Ex	Rec	Pay
0.33Q	02/13/2019	02/26/2019	02/27/2019	03/13/2019
0.33Q	05/08/2019	05/17/2019	05/20/2019	06/05/2019
0.33Q	08/01/2019	08/21/2019	08/22/2019	09/04/2019
0.35Q	11/13/2019	11/26/2019	11/27/2019	12/11/2019

Indicated Div: $1.40

Valuation Analysis   **Institutional Holding**

Forecast EPS	$4.94	No of Institutions
	(01/17/2020)	727
Market Cap	$8.2 Billion	Shares
Book Value	$6.0 Billion	178,070,976
Price/Book	1.36	% Held
Price/Sales	0.47	N/A

Business Summary: Refining & Marketing (MIC: 9.1.2 SIC: 2911 NAIC: 324110)

HollyFrontier is a petroleum refiner that produces products such as gasoline, diesel fuel, jet fuel, specialty lubricant products, and specialty and modified asphalt. Co.'s segments are: Refining, which involves the purchase and refining of crude oil and wholesale and branded marketing of refined products; Lubricants and Specialty Products, which includes the production of lubricant products such as base oils, white oils, specialty products and finished lubricants; and Co.'s subsidiary, Holly Energy Partners, L.P., which owns and operates logistics and refinery assets consisting of petroleum product and crude oil pipelines, terminals, tankage, loading rack facilities and processing units.

Recent Developments: For the quarter ended Sep 30 2019, net income decreased 17.7% to US$298.0 million from US$362.1 million in the year-earlier quarter. Revenues were US$4.42 billion, down 7.3% from US$4.77 billion the year before. Operating income was US$426.8 million versus US$503.5 million in the prior-year quarter, a decrease of 15.2%. Direct operating expenses declined 8.8% to US$3.44 billion from US$3.77 billion in the comparable period the year before. Indirect operating expenses increased 12.7% to US$560.2 million from US$497.2 million in the equivalent prior-year period.

Prospects: Our evaluation of HollyFrontier Corp. as of October 4th, 2019 is the result of our systematic analysis on three basic characteristics: earnings strength, relative valuation, and recent stock price movement. The company has generated a negative trend in earnings per share over the past 5 quarters. However, recent analyst estimates for the company have been mixed and HFC has posted results that exceeded analysts' expectations. Based on operating earnings yield, the company is undervalued when compared to all of the companies we cover. Share price changes over the past year indicates that HFC will perform very poorly over the near term.

Financial Data

(US$ in Thousands)	9 Mos	6 Mos	3 Mos	12/31/2018	12/31/2017	12/31/2016	12/31/2015	12/31/2014
Earnings Per Share	5.02	5.37	6.16	6.19	4.52	(1.48)	3.90	1.42
Cash Flow Per Share	11.22	10.60	8.41	8.88	5.40	3.41	5.19	3.85
Tang Book Value Per Share	22.55	21.93	20.71	21.33	17.62	14.99	16.21	16.28
Dividends Per Share	1.320	1.320	1.320	1.320	1.320	1.320	1.310	3.260
Dividend Payout %	26.29	24.58	21.43	21.32	29.20	...	33.59	229.58
Income Statement								
Total Revenue	13,104,690	8,679,862	3,897,247	17,714,666	14,251,299	10,535,700	13,237,920	19,764,327
EBITDA	1,380,601	789,993	281,238	1,942,113	1,256,714	131,854	1,485,685	770,523
Depn & Amortn	224,862	63,784	(110,950)	309,000	286,500	247,900	233,300	261,800
Income Before Taxes	1,065,928	666,261	361,891	1,518,642	856,353	(185,747)	1,212,306	469,507
Income Taxes	279,862	176,841	87,505	347,243	(12,379)	19,414	406,060	141,172
Net Income	711,783	449,970	253,055	1,097,960	805,395	(260,453)	740,101	281,292
Average Shares	165,011	170,547	172,239	176,661	177,196	176,101	188,940	197,428
Balance Sheet								
Current Assets	3,532,766	3,466,397	3,321,338	3,296,379	3,062,828	2,851,009	1,448,065	2,782,998
Total Assets	12,191,328	12,104,491	12,123,430	10,994,601	10,692,154	9,435,661	8,388,299	9,230,640
Current Liabilities	1,705,346	1,664,027	1,669,285	1,168,155	1,422,710	1,083,229	860,615	1,251,403
Long-Term Obligations	2,780,644	2,788,467	2,773,105	2,411,540	2,498,993	2,235,137	1,040,040	1,054,890
Total Liabilities	6,171,120	6,091,344	6,059,390	5,076,030	5,321,325	4,754,267	3,134,884	3,707,056
Stockholders' Equity	6,020,208	6,013,147	6,064,040	5,918,571	5,370,829	4,681,394	5,253,415	5,523,584
Shares Outstanding	161,862	165,898	170,765	172,121	177,407	177,345	180,234	196,086
Statistical Record								
Return on Assets %	7.21	7.99	9.40	10.13	8.00	N.M.	8.40	2.92
Return on Equity %	14.19	15.76	18.60	19.45	16.02	N.M.	13.73	4.88
EBITDA Margin %	10.54	9.10	7.22	10.96	8.82	1.25	11.22	3.90
Net Margin %	5.43	5.18	6.49	6.20	5.65	N.M.	5.59	1.42
Asset Turnover	1.47	1.52	1.52	1.63	1.42	1.18	1.50	2.05
Current Ratio	2.07	2.08	1.99	2.82	2.15	2.63	1.68	2.22
Debt to Equity	0.46	0.46	0.46	0.41	0.47	0.48	0.20	0.19
Price Range	71.35-37.98	76.19-37.98	81.65-46.77	81.65-42.83	51.63-23.90	41.11-22.31	53.80-30.19	52.63-36.11
P/E Ratio	14.21-7.57	14.19-7.07	13.25-7.59	13.19-6.92	11.42-5.29	...	13.79-7.74	37.06-25.43
Average Yield %	2.54	2.30	2.09	2.14	4.12	4.51	3.01	7.06

Address: 2828 N. Harwood, Suite 1300, Dallas, TX 75201
Telephone: 214-871-3555

Web Site: www.hollyfrontier.com
Officers: Franklin Myers - Chairman Michael C. Jennings - Executive Vice Chairman, President, President (frmr), Chief Executive Officer, Chief Executive Officer (frmr), Executive Vice President, Associate/Affiliate Company Officer

Auditors: Ernst & Young LLP
Investor Contact: 214-871-3555
Transfer Agents: Wells Fargo Shareowner Services, Mendota Heights, MN

HOME DEPOT INC

Exchange	Symbol	Price	52Wk Range	Yield	P/E
NYS	HD	$218.38 (12/31/2019)	238.85-168.61	2.49	21.69

*7 Year Price Score 124.82 *NYSE Composite Index=100 *12 Month Price Score 101.81

Interim Earnings (Per Share)

Qtr.	Apr	Jul	Oct	Jan
2016-17	1.44	1.97	1.60	1.45
2017-18	1.67	2.25	1.84	1.53
2018-19	2.08	3.05	2.51	2.10
2019-20	2.27	3.17	2.53	...

Interim Dividends (Per Share)

Amt	Decl	Ex	Rec	Pay
1.36Q	02/25/2019	03/13/2019	03/14/2019	03/28/2019
1.36Q	05/23/2019	06/05/2019	06/06/2019	06/20/2019
1.36Q	08/22/2019	09/04/2019	09/05/2019	09/19/2019
1.36Q	11/21/2019	12/04/2019	12/05/2019	12/19/2019

Indicated Div: $5.44 (Div. Relnv. Plan)

Valuation Analysis / **Institutional Holding**

Forecast EPS	$10.07 (01/16/2020)	No of Institutions 3099
Market Cap	$238.0 Billion	Shares
Book Value	N/A	1,009,791,360
Price/Book	N/A	% Held
Price/Sales	2.15	65.27

Business Summary: Retail - Hardware & Home Improvement (MIC: 2.1.8 SIC: 5251 NAIC: 444130)

The Home Depot is a home improvement retailer. Co. provides its customers an assortment of building materials, home improvement products, lawn and garden products, and decor products and provides a number of services, including home improvement installation services and tool and equipment rental. Co. also maintains a network of distribution and fulfillment centers, as well as a number of e-commerce websites. Co. provides a number of programs for its Professional Customers to meet their particular needs, and for its Do-It-Yourself and Do-It-For-Me customers, Co. provides a number of installation services. Co. also provides tool and equipment rentals for its customers.

Recent Developments: For the quarter ended Nov 3 2019, net income decreased 3.4% to US$2.77 billion from US$2.87 billion in the year-earlier quarter. Revenues were US$27.22 billion, up 3.5% from US$26.30 billion the year before. Operating income was US$3.95 billion versus US$3.87 billion in the prior-year quarter, an increase of 2.0%. Direct operating expenses rose 4.0% to US$17.84 billion from US$17.15 billion in the comparable period the year before. Indirect operating expenses increased 3.0% to US$5.44 billion from US$5.28 billion in the equivalent prior-year period.

Prospects: Our evaluation of Home Depot Inc. as of October 4th, 2019 is the result of our systematic analysis on three basic characteristics: earnings strength, relative valuation, and recent stock price movement. The company has managed to produce a neutral trend in earnings per share over the past 5 quarters. In addition, recent analyst estimates for the company have been mixed and HD has posted results that exceeded analysts' expectations. Based on operating earnings yield, the company is fairly valued when compared to all of the companies we cover. Share price changes over the past year indicates that HD will perform in line with the market over the near term.

Financial Data

(US$ in Thousands)	9 Mos	6 Mos	3 Mos	02/03/2019	01/28/2018	01/29/2017	01/31/2016	02/01/2015
Earnings Per Share	10.07	10.05	9.93	9.73	7.29	6.45	5.46	4.71
Cash Flow Per Share	12.55	12.45	...	11.28	10.24	7.98	7.36	6.18
Tang Book Value Per Share	...	...	...	...	N.M.	1.86	3.37	6.10
Dividends Per Share	5.110	4.780	4.450	4.120	3.560	2.760	2.360	1.880
Dividend Payout %	50.74	47.56	44.81	42.34	48.83	42.79	43.22	39.92
Income Statement								
Total Revenue	84,443,000	57,220,000	26,381,000	108,203,000	100,904,000	94,595,000	88,519,000	83,176,000
EBITDA	14,141,000	9,600,000	4,144,000	17,606,000	16,743,000	15,400,000	13,637,000	12,255,000
Depn & Amortn	1,701,000	1,107,000	547,000	2,076,000	2,062,000	1,973,000	1,863,000	1,786,000
Income Before Taxes	11,604,000	7,937,000	3,324,000	14,556,000	13,698,000	12,491,000	11,021,000	9,976,000
Income Taxes	2,843,000	1,945,000	811,000	3,435,000	5,068,000	4,534,000	4,012,000	3,631,000
Net Income	8,761,000	5,992,000	2,513,000	11,121,000	8,630,000	7,957,000	7,009,000	6,345,000
Average Shares	1,094,000	1,099,000	1,106,000	1,143,000	1,184,000	1,234,000	1,283,000	1,346,000
Balance Sheet								
Current Assets	21,174,000	20,699,000	20,553,000	18,529,000	18,933,000	17,724,000	16,993,000	15,302,000
Total Assets	52,309,000	52,010,000	51,515,000	44,003,000	44,529,000	42,966,000	42,549,000	39,946,000
Current Liabilities	19,565,000	18,798,000	19,673,000	16,716,000	16,194,000	14,133,000	12,526,000	11,269,000
Long-Term Obligations	26,597,000	27,064,000	26,804,000	26,807,000	24,267,000	22,349,000	20,888,000	16,869,000
Total Liabilities	53,391,000	53,170,000	53,658,000	45,881,000	43,075,000	38,633,000	36,233,000	30,624,000
Stockholders' Equity	(1,082,000)	(1,160,000)	(2,143,000)	(1,878,000)	1,454,000	4,333,000	6,316,000	9,322,000
Shares Outstanding	1,090,000	1,096,000	1,101,000	1,105,000	1,158,000	1,203,000	1,252,000	1,307,000
Statistical Record								
Return on Assets %	22.78	22.81	...	24.72	19.78	18.66	17.04	15.81
Return on Equity %	9,331.93	2,639.10	...	...	299.07	149.85	89.89	58.25
EBITDA Margin %	16.75	16.78	15.71	16.27	16.59	16.28	15.41	14.73
Net Margin %	10.38	10.47	9.53	10.28	8.55	8.41	7.92	7.63
Asset Turnover	2.28	2.24	...	2.40	2.31	2.22	2.15	2.07
Current Ratio	1.08	1.10	1.04	1.11	1.17	1.25	1.36	1.36
Debt to Equity	...	...	...	...	16.69	5.16	3.31	1.81
Price Range	237.93-158.14	218.70-158.14	213.85-158.14	213.85-158.14	207.23-136.49	138.77-111.85	134.74-104.43	107.62-74.97
P/E Ratio	23.63-15.70	21.76-15.74	21.54-15.93	21.98-16.25	28.43-18.72	21.51-17.34	24.68-19.13	22.85-15.92
Average Yield %	2.56	2.48	2.34	2.20	2.23	2.11	2.00	2.15

Address: 2455 Paces Ferry Road, Atlanta, GA 30339	Web Site: www.homedepot.com	Auditors: KPMG LLP
Telephone: 770-433-8211	Officers: Craig A. Menear - Chairman, President, Chief Executive Officer, Executive Vice President, Region Officer Carol B. Tome - Executive Vice President, Chief Financial Officer	Investor Contact: 770-384-2871
Fax: 770-431-2707		Transfer Agents: Computershare Trust Company, N.A., Providence, RI

HONEYWELL INTERNATIONAL INC

Exchange	Symbol	Price	52Wk Range	Yield	P/E
NYS	HON	$177.00 (12/31/2019)	182.01-130.07	2.03	20.68

*7 Year Price Score 117.71 *NYSE Composite Index=100 *12 Month Price Score 101.82

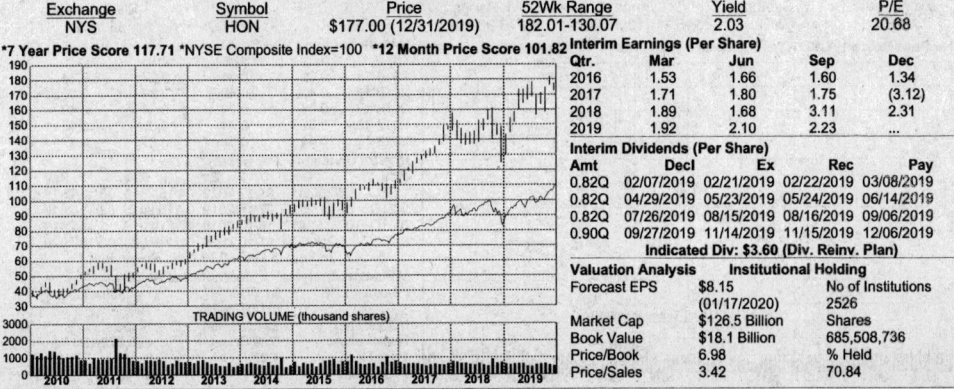

Interim Earnings (Per Share)

Qtr.	Mar	Jun	Sep	Dec
2016	1.53	1.66	1.60	1.34
2017	1.71	1.80	1.75	(3.12)
2018	1.89	1.68	3.11	2.31
2019	1.92	2.10	2.23	...

Interim Dividends (Per Share)

Amt	Decl	Ex	Rec	Pay
0.82Q	02/07/2019	02/21/2019	02/22/2019	03/08/2019
0.82Q	04/29/2019	05/23/2019	05/24/2019	06/14/2019
0.82Q	07/26/2019	08/15/2019	08/16/2019	09/06/2019
0.90Q	09/27/2019	11/14/2019	11/15/2019	12/06/2019

Indicated Div: $3.60 (Div. Reinv. Plan)

Valuation Analysis / Institutional Holding

Valuation Analysis		Institutional Holding	
Forecast EPS	$8.15	No of Institutions	
	(01/17/2020)	2526	
Market Cap	$126.5 Billion	Shares	
Book Value	$18.1 Billion	685,508,736	
Price/Book	6.98	% Held	
Price/Sales	3.42	70.84	

Business Summary: Auto Parts (MIC: 1.8.2 SIC: 3714 NAIC: 336312)

Honeywell International is a technology and manufacturing company. Co.'s segments are: Aerospace, which supplies products, software and services for aircrafts; Honeywell Building Technologies, which provides, among others, products, software, solutions and technologies for building control and optimization, energy management, access control, and video surveillance; Performance Materials and Technologies, which develops and manufactures performance chemicals and materials, process technologies and automation solutions; and Safety and Productivity Solutions, which provides products, software and connected solutions to customers to improve productivity, workplace safety and asset performance.

Recent Developments: For the quarter ended Sep 30 2019, net income decreased 30.1% to US$1.65 billion from US$2.36 billion in the year-earlier quarter. Revenues were US$9.09 billion, down 15.6% from US$10.76 billion the year before. Direct operating expenses declined 20.1% to US$6.04 billion from US$7.56 billion in the comparable period the year before. Indirect operating expenses decreased 15.0% to US$1.30 billion from US$1.52 billion in the equivalent prior-year period.

Prospects: Our evaluation of Honeywell International Inc. as of October 4th, 2019 is the result of our systematic analysis on three basic characteristics: earnings strength, relative valuation, and recent stock price movement. The company has managed to produce a neutral trend in earnings per share over the past 5 quarters. However, recent analyst estimates for the company have been reduced while HON has posted results that exceeded analysts' expectations. Based on operating earnings yield, the company is fairly valued when compared to all of the companies we cover. Share price changes over the past year indicates that HON will perform well over the near term.

Financial Data

(US$ in Thousands)	9 Mos	6 Mos	3 Mos	12/31/2018	12/31/2017	12/31/2016	12/31/2015	12/31/2014
Earnings Per Share	8.56	9.44	9.02	8.98	2.14	6.20	6.04	5.33
Cash Flow Per Share	8.14	8.64	8.81	8.66	7.83	7.17	6.99	6.40
Tang Book Value Per Share	N.M.	N.M.	N.M.	N.M.	N.M.	N.M.	N.M.	3.68
Dividends Per Share	3.280	3.205	3.130	3.055	2.740	2.450	2.148	1.867
Dividend Payout %	38.32	33.95	34.70	34.02	128.04	39.52	35.55	35.04
Income Statement								
Total Revenue	27,213,000	18,127,000	8,884,000	41,802,000	40,534,000	39,302,000	38,581,000	40,306,000
EBITDA	6,876,000	4,400,000	2,112,000	8,308,000	7,745,000	7,374,000	7,434,000	6,665,000
Depn & Amortn	819,000	556,000	261,000	721,000	717,000	726,000	672,000	667,000
Income Before Taxes	5,791,000	3,804,000	1,833,000	7,437,000	6,863,000	6,416,000	6,556,000	5,782,000
Income Taxes	1,151,000	832,000	406,000	659,000	5,204,000	1,601,000	1,739,000	1,489,000
Net Income	4,581,000	2,957,000	1,416,000	6,765,000	1,655,000	4,809,000	4,768,000	4,239,000
Average Shares	726,700	733,000	738,800	753,000	772,100	775,300	789,300	795,200
Balance Sheet								
Current Assets	26,188,000	23,768,000	24,334,000	24,362,000	26,002,000	23,058,000	20,053,000	22,191,000
Total Assets	60,104,000	57,750,000	58,560,000	57,773,000	59,387,000	54,146,000	49,316,000	45,451,000
Current Liabilities	19,915,000	19,894,000	19,593,000	18,924,000	18,861,000	16,331,000	18,371,000	14,773,000
Long-Term Obligations	11,101,000	8,608,000	8,598,000	9,756,000	12,573,000	12,182,000	5,554,000	6,046,000
Total Liabilities	41,988,000	39,873,000	39,786,000	39,586,000	42,106,000	34,774,000	30,743,000	27,575,000
Stockholders' Equity	18,116,000	17,877,000	18,774,000	18,187,000	17,281,000	19,372,000	18,573,000	17,876,000
Shares Outstanding	714,533	719,508	727,742	729,085	750,900	760,800	770,400	782,200
Statistical Record								
Return on Assets %	10.33	11.93	11.28	11.55	2.92	9.27	10.06	9.33
Return on Equity %	34.66	39.55	37.07	38.15	9.03	25.28	26.16	23.87
EBITDA Margin %	25.27	24.27	23.77	19.87	19.11	18.76	19.27	16.54
Net Margin %	16.83	16.31	15.94	16.18	4.08	12.24	12.36	10.52
Asset Turnover	0.61	0.66	0.67	0.71	0.71	0.76	0.81	0.89
Current Ratio	1.31	1.19	1.24	1.29	1.38	1.41	1.09	1.50
Debt to Equity	0.61	0.48	0.46	0.54	0.73	0.63	0.30	0.34
Price Range	178.40-124.83	176.29-124.83	161.15-124.83	161.15-124.83	149.32-111.24	114.13-91.62	102.15-87.19	97.09-81.02
P/E Ratio	20.84-14.58	18.67-13.22	17.87-13.84	17.95-13.90	69.78-51.98	18.41-14.78	16.91-14.44	18.21-15.20
Average Yield %	2.08	2.09	2.14	2.10	2.12	2.30	2.21	2.09

Address: 115 Tabor Road, Morris Plains, NJ 07950 **Telephone:** 973-455-2000 **Fax:** 973-455-4807	**Web Site:** www.honeywell.com **Officers:** Darius Adamczyk - Chairman, President, Chief Executive Officer, Chief Operating Officer, Division Officer Mark R. James - Senior Vice President	**Auditors:** DELOITTE & TOUCHE LLP **Investor Contact:** 973-455-2222 **Transfer Agents:** American Stock Transfer & Trust Company, LLC, Brookly, NY

HORMEL FOODS CORP.

Exchange	Symbol	Price	52Wk Range	Yield	P/E	Div Acheiver
NYS	HRL	$45.11 (12/31/2019)	45.76-38.80	2.06	25.06	52 Years

*7 Year Price Score 107.42 *NYSE Composite Index=100 *12 Month Price Score 98.53

Interim Earnings (Per Share)

Qtr.	Jan	Apr	Jul	Oct
2014-15	0.32	0.34	0.27	0.34
2015-16	0.43	0.40	0.36	0.45
2016-17	0.44	0.39	0.34	0.40
2017-18	0.56	0.44	0.39	0.48
2018-19	0.44	0.52	0.37	0.47

Interim Dividends (Per Share)

Amt	Decl	Ex	Rec	Pay
0.21Q	03/25/2019	04/12/2019	04/15/2019	05/15/2019
0.21Q	05/21/2019	07/12/2019	07/15/2019	08/15/2019
0.21Q	09/23/2019	10/18/2019	10/21/2019	11/15/2019
0.233Q	11/25/2019	01/10/2020	01/13/2020	02/18/2020

Indicated Div: $0.93 (Div. Reinv. Plan)

Valuation Analysis / Institutional Holding

Valuation Analysis		Institutional Holding	
Forecast EPS	$1.77	No. of Institutions	
	(01/07/2020)	799	
Market Cap	$24.1 Billion	Shares	
Book Value	$5.9 Billion	276,072,160	
Price/Book	4.07	% Held	
Price/Sales	2.54	44.18	

Business Summary: Food (MIC: 1.2.1 SIC: 2011 NAIC: 311611)

Hormel Foods is primarily engaged in the production of meat and food products and the marketing of those products throughout the United States and internationally. Co.'s segments are: Grocery Products, which consists of the processing, marketing, and sale of shelf-stable food products; Refrigerated Foods, which consists of the processing, marketing, and sale of branded and unbranded pork, beef, chicken, and turkey products; Jennie-O Turkey Store, which consists of the processing, marketing, and sale of branded and unbranded turkey products; and International and Other, which includes Hormel Foods International Corporation that manufactures, markets, and sells Co.'s products internationally.

Recent Developments: For the year ended Oct 27 2019, net income decreased 3.3% to US$979.1 million from US$1.01 billion in the prior year. Revenues were US$9.50 billion, down 0.5% from US$9.55 billion the year before. Operating income versus US$1.18 billion in the prior year, an increase of 1.4%. Direct operating expenses rose 0.6% from US$7.61 billion from US$7.57 billion in the comparable period the year before. Indirect operating expenses decreased 13.9% to US$688.4 million from US$799.5 million in the equivalent prior-year period.

Prospects: Our evaluation of Hormel Foods Corp. as of October 4th, 2019 is the result of our systematic analysis on three basic characteristics: earnings strength, relative valuation, and recent stock price movement. The company has managed to produce a neutral trend in earnings per share over the past 5 quarters. Additionally, recent analyst estimates for the company have been unchanged while HRL has posted results that exceeded analysts' expectations. Based on operating earnings yield, the company is fairly valued when compared to all of the companies we cover. Share price changes over the past year indicates that HRL will perform in line with the market over the near term.

Financial Data

(US$ in Thousands)	10/27/2019	10/28/2018	10/29/2017	10/30/2016	10/25/2015	10/26/2014	10/27/2013	10/28/2012
Earnings Per Share	1.80	1.86	1.57	1.64	1.27	1.12	0.97	0.93
Cash Flow Per Share	1.73	2.35	1.91	1.85	1.88	1.42	1.21	0.99
Tang Book Value Per Share	4.50	3.14	3.39	3.24	2.78	3.46	3.79	3.93
Dividends Per Share	0.840	0.750	0.680	0.580	0.500	0.400	0.340	0.300
Dividend Payout %	46.67	40.32	43.31	35.37	39.37	35.87	34.87	32.26
Income Statement								
Total Revenue	9,497,317	9,545,700	9,167,519	9,523,224	9,263,863	9,316,256	8,751,654	8,230,670
EBITDA	1,322,274	1,314,460	1,380,239	1,425,565	1,185,009	1,053,431	919,805	854,452
Depn & Amortn	165,210	174,511	139,360	140,355	141,576	139,396	134,329	128,469
Income Before Taxes	1,170,514	1,122,312	1,239,055	1,278,530	1,033,256	904,567	777,994	719,644
Income Taxes	230,567	168,702	431,542	426,698	369,879	316,126	268,431	253,374
Net Income	978,806	1,012,140	846,735	890,052	686,088	602,677	526,211	500,050
Average Shares	545,232	543,869	539,116	542,473	541,002	540,432	540,448	537,782
Balance Sheet								
Current Assets	2,361,413	2,050,100	2,026,523	2,029,912	2,063,032	2,132,771	2,047,413	2,320,684
Total Assets	8,109,004	8,142,292	6,975,908	6,370,067	6,139,831	5,455,619	4,915,880	4,563,966
Current Liabilities	1,105,049	1,138,914	1,058,212	1,053,196	1,214,025	954,692	784,009	786,300
Long-Term Obligations	250,000	624,840	250,000	250,000	250,000	250,000	250,000	250,000
Total Liabilities	2,187,546	2,541,481	2,040,001	1,922,061	2,141,633	1,849,941	1,604,840	1,744,511
Stockholders' Equity	5,921,458	5,600,811	4,935,907	4,448,006	3,998,198	3,605,678	3,311,040	2,819,455
Shares Outstanding	534,488	534,135	528,423	528,483	528,411	527,226	527,316	526,088
Statistical Record								
Return on Assets %	12.08	13.43	12.69	14.00	11.87	11.65	11.13	11.39
Return on Equity %	17.04	19.26	18.05	20.73	18.10	17.47	17.21	18.31
EBITDA Margin %	13.92	13.77	15.06	14.97	12.79	11.31	10.51	10.38
Net Margin %	10.31	10.60	9.24	9.35	7.41	6.47	6.01	6.08
Asset Turnover	1.17	1.27	1.37	1.50	1.60	1.80	1.85	1.87
Current Ratio	2.14	1.80	1.92	1.93	1.70	2.23	2.61	2.95
Debt to Equity	0.04	0.11	0.05	0.06	0.06	0.07	0.08	0.09
Price Range	45.89-38.80	42.44-30.15	38.50-30.27	44.47-33.09	34.24-25.07	26.27-21.11	22.06-14.77	15.34-13.74
P/E Ratio	25.49-21.56	22.82-16.21	24.52-19.28	27.12-20.17	26.96-19.74	23.46-18.85	22.74-15.22	16.49-14.77
Average Yield %	1.99	2.07	1.99	1.52	1.75	1.69	1.77	2.07

Address: 1 Hormel Place, Austin, MN 55912-3680	Web Site: www.hormel.com	Auditors: Ernst & Young LLP
Telephone: 507-437-5611	**Officers:** James P. Snee - Chairman, President, Chief Executive Officer, Chief Operating Officer, Vice President, Group Vice President, Division Officer Glenn R. Leitch - Executive Vice President, Group Vice President, Division Officer	**Investor Contact:** 507-437-5248
Fax: 507-437-5489		**Transfer Agents:** Wells Fargo Shareowner Services, Mendota Heights, MN

HORTON (DR) INC

Exchange	Symbol	Price	52Wk Range	Yield	P/E
NYS	DHI	$52.75 (12/31/2019)	55.91-34.66	1.33	12.30

*7 Year Price Score 116.82 *NYSE Composite Index=100 *12 Month Price Score 109.98

Interim Earnings (Per Share)

Qtr.	Dec	Mar	Jun	Sep
2014-15	0.39	0.40	0.60	0.64
2015-16	0.42	0.52	0.66	0.75
2016-17	0.55	0.60	0.76	0.82
2017-18	0.49	0.91	1.18	1.22
2018-19	0.76	0.93	1.26	1.35

Interim Dividends (Per Share)

Amt	Decl	Ex	Rec	Pay
0.15Q	01/25/2019	02/08/2019	02/11/2019	02/25/2019
0.15Q	04/25/2019	05/10/2019	05/13/2019	05/28/2019
0.15Q	07/30/2019	08/09/2019	08/12/2019	08/26/2019
0.175Q	11/12/2019	11/26/2019	11/27/2019	12/11/2019

Indicated Div: $0.70

Valuation Analysis — Institutional Holding

Forecast EPS	$4.89	No of Institutions	
	(01/14/2020)	962	
Market Cap	$19.4 Billion	Shares	
Book Value	$10.0 Billion	387,006,784	
Price/Book	1.94	% Held	
Price/Sales	1.10	82.69	

Business Summary: Builders (MIC: 2.2.5 SIC: 1531 NAIC: 236117)

D.R. Horton is a homebuilding company. Co.'s business operations consist of homebuilding, a majority-owned residential lot development company, financial services and other activities. Co.'s financial services operations provide mortgage financing and title agency services to homebuyers in its homebuilding markets. Co.'s subsidiary, DHI Mortgage, provides mortgage financing services primarily to its homebuyers and generally sells the mortgages it originates and the related servicing rights to third-party purchasers. Co.'s subsidiary title companies serve as title insurance agents by providing title insurance policies, examination and closing services, primarily to its homebuyers.

Recent Developments: For the year ended Sep 30 2019, net income increased 10.7% to US$1.62 billion from US$1.46 billion in the prior year. Revenues were US$17.59 billion, up 9.5% from US$16.07 billion the year before. Direct operating expenses rose 10.7% to US$13.72 billion from US$12.40 billion in the comparable period the year before. Indirect operating expenses increased 8.5% to US$1.75 billion from US$1.61 billion in the equivalent prior-year period.

Prospects: Our evaluation of Horton (D.R.) Inc. as of October 4th, 2019 is the result of our systematic analysis on three basic characteristics: earnings strength, relative valuation, and recent stock price movement. The company has enjoyed a very positive trend in earnings per share over the past 5 quarters. However, recent analyst estimates for the company have been mixed and DHI has posted results that exceeded analysts' expectations. Based on operating earnings yield, the company is undervalued when compared to all of the companies we cover. Share price changes over the past year indicates that DHI will perform in line with the market over the near term.

Financial Data

(US$ in Thousands)	09/30/2019	09/30/2018	09/30/2017	09/30/2016	09/30/2015	09/30/2014	09/30/2013	09/30/2012
Earnings Per Share	4.29	3.81	2.74	2.36	2.03	1.50	1.33	2.77
Cash Flow Per Share	2.39	1.45	1.16	1.66	1.91	(1.94)	(3.82)	(0.93)
Tang Book Value Per Share	26.76	23.59	20.45	18.00	15.75	13.77	12.45	11.07
Dividends Per Share	0.600	0.500	0.400	0.320	0.250	0.138	0.188	0.150
Dividend Payout %	13.99	13.12	14.60	13.56	12.32	9.17	14.10	5.42
Income Statement								
Total Revenue	17,592,900	16,068,000	14,091,000	12,157,400	10,824,000	8,024,900	6,259,300	4,354,000
EBITDA	2,190,900	2,115,400	1,637,000	1,390,800	1,161,200	840,600	676,700	278,400
Depn & Amortn	66,100	58,200	49,400	50,800	50,300	36,600	22,300	18,800
Income Before Taxes	2,124,800	2,057,200	1,602,100	1,353,500	1,123,400	814,200	657,800	242,900
Income Taxes	506,700	597,700	563,700	467,200	372,700	280,700	195,100	(713,400)
Net Income	1,618,500	1,460,300	1,038,400	886,300	750,700	533,500	462,700	956,300
Average Shares	377,400	383,400	378,900	375,100	369,800	366,600	364,900	359,000
Balance Sheet								
Current Assets	13,024,300	12,074,200	10,366,900	9,778,200	9,376,200	8,549,300	7,397,900	5,821,500
Total Assets	15,606,600	14,114,600	12,184,600	11,558,900	11,151,000	10,222,500	8,856,400	7,248,200
Current Liabilities	1,382,400	1,270,800	911,400	849,200	784,600	747,300	636,400	377,600
Long-Term Obligations	3,399,400	3,203,500	2,871,600	3,271,300	3,811,500	3,682,800	3,509,000	2,493,100
Total Liabilities	5,585,700	5,130,200	4,437,500	4,766,400	5,256,700	5,086,700	4,797,900	3,656,100
Stockholders' Equity	10,020,900	8,984,400	7,747,100	6,792,500	5,894,300	5,115,800	4,058,500	3,592,100
Shares Outstanding	368,431	376,261	374,986	372,923	368,647	364,586	322,943	320,891
Statistical Record								
Return on Assets %	10.89	11.11	8.75	7.78	7.03	5.60	5.75	15.13
Return on Equity %	17.03	17.46	14.28	13.93	13.64	11.63	12.10	30.70
EBITDA Margin %	12.45	13.17	11.62	11.44	10.73	10.47	10.81	6.39
Net Margin %	9.20	9.09	7.37	7.29	6.94	6.65	7.39	21.96
Asset Turnover	1.18	1.22	1.19	1.07	1.01	0.84	0.78	0.69
Current Ratio	9.42	9.50	11.37	11.51	11.95	11.44	11.62	15.42
Debt to Equity	0.34	0.36	0.37	0.48	0.65	0.72	0.86	0.69
Price Range	52.71-32.96	52.87-39.54	39.93-27.28	34.41-23.23	32.21-19.49	25.10-17.69	27.60-17.77	22.37-8.45
P/E Ratio	12.29-7.68	13.88-10.38	14.57-9.96	14.58-9.84	15.87-9.60	16.73-11.79	20.75-13.36	8.08-3.05
Average Yield %	1.43	1.11	1.24	1.05	0.95	0.63	0.86	0.98

Address: 1341 Horton Circle, Arlington, TX 76011 **Telephone:** 817-390-8200	**Web Site:** www.drhorton.com **Officers:** Donald R. Horton - Chairman David V. Auld - President, Chief Executive Officer, Executive Vice President, Chief Operating Officer, Division Officer	**Auditors:** PricewaterhouseCoopers LLP **Investor Contact:** 817-390-8200 **Transfer Agents:** American Stock Transfer & Trust Co., New York, NY

HP INC

Exchange	Symbol	Price	52Wk Range	Yield	P/E
NYS	HPQ	$20.55 (12/31/2019)	23.91-16.03	3.43	9.93

*7 Year Price Score 99.50   *NYSE Composite Index=100   *12 Month Price Score 93.76

Interim Earnings (Per Share)

Qtr.	Jan	Apr	Jul	Oct
2014-15	0.73	0.55	0.47	0.73
2015-16	0.33	0.36	0.45	0.28
2016-17	0.36	0.33	0.41	0.39
2017-18	1.16	0.64	0.54	0.90
2018-19	0.51	0.51	0.78	0.27

Interim Dividends (Per Share)

Amt	Decl	Ex	Rec	Pay
0.16Q	05/15/2019	06/11/2019	06/12/2019	07/03/2019
0.16Q	06/26/2019	09/10/2019	09/11/2019	10/02/2019
0.176Q	11/13/2019	12/10/2019	12/11/2019	01/02/2020
0.176Q	01/16/2020	03/10/2020	03/11/2020	04/01/2020

Indicated Div: $0.70 (Div. Reinv. Plan)

Valuation Analysis

		Institutional Holding	
Forecast EPS	$2.26	No of Institutions	
	(01/17/2020)	1532	
Market Cap	$30.0 Billion	Shares	
Book Value	N/A	1,603,549,952	
Price/Book	N/A	% Held	
Price/Sales	0.51	N/A	

Business Summary: Computer Hardware & Equipment (MIC: 6.2.1 SIC: 3571 NAIC: 334111)

HP is a provider of personal computing and other access devices, imaging and printing products, and related technologies, solutions and services. Co.'s segments are: Personal Systems, which provides commercial and consumer desktop and notebook personal computers, workstations, thin clients, commercial mobility devices, retail point-of-sale systems, displays and other related accessories, software, support and services; Printing, which provides consumer and commercial printer hardware, supplies, solutions and services, as well as scanning devices; and Corporate Investments, which includes HP Labs and certain business incubation and investment projects.

Recent Developments: For the year ended Oct 31 2019, net income decreased 40.8% to US$3.15 billion from US$5.33 billion in the prior year. Revenues were US$58.76 billion, up 0.5% from US$58.47 billion the year before. Operating income was US$3.88 billion versus US$3.83 billion in the prior year, an increase of 1.2%. Direct operating expenses declined 0.5% to US$47.59 billion from US$47.80 billion in the comparable period the year before. Indirect operating expenses increased 6.7% to US$7.29 billion from US$6.84 billion in the equivalent prior-year period.

Prospects: Our evaluation of HP Inc as of October 4th, 2019 is the result of our systematic analysis on three basic characteristics: earnings strength, relative valuation, and recent stock price movement. The company has managed to produce a neutral trend in earnings per share over the past 5 quarters. Additionally, recent analyst estimates for the company have been unchanged while HPQ has posted results that exceeded analysts' expectations. Based on operating earnings yield, the company is undervalued when compared to all of the companies we cover. Share price changes over the past year indicates that HPQ will perform well over the near term.

Financial Data
(US$ in Millions)

	10/31/2019	10/31/2018	10/31/2017	10/31/2016	10/31/2015	10/31/2014	10/31/2013	10/31/2012
Earnings Per Share	2.07	3.26	1.48	1.43	2.48	2.62	2.62	(6.41)
Cash Flow Per Share	3.07	2.80	2.18	1.86	3.58	6.55	6.00	5.34
Dividends Per Share	0.641	0.557	0.531	0.496	0.672	0.610	0.554	0.504
Dividend Payout %	30.96	17.09	35.86	34.69	27.10	23.30	21.16	...
Income Statement								
Total Revenue	58,756	58,472	52,056	48,238	103,355	111,454	112,298	120,357
EBITDA	3,504	3,853	3,939	3,881	9,090	11,485	11,704	(5,973)
Depn & Amortn	739	528	354	332	4,031	4,300	4,573	5,084
Income Before Taxes	2,523	3,013	3,276	3,761	4,732	6,557	6,510	(11,933)
Income Taxes	(629)	(2,314)	750	1,095	178	1,544	1,397	717
Net Income	3,152	5,327	2,526	2,496	4,554	5,013	5,113	(12,650)
Average Shares	1,524	1,634	1,702	1,743	1,836	1,912	1,950	1,974
Balance Sheet								
Current Assets	20,177	21,387	22,318	18,468	51,787	50,145	50,364	50,637
Total Assets	33,467	34,622	32,913	29,010	106,882	103,206	105,676	108,768
Current Liabilities	25,293	25,131	22,412	18,808	42,191	43,735	45,521	46,666
Long-Term Obligations	4,780	4,524	6,747	6,758	21,780	16,039	16,608	21,789
Total Liabilities	34,660	35,261	36,321	32,899	79,114	76,475	78,407	86,332
Stockholders' Equity	(1,193)	(639)	(3,408)	(3,889)	27,768	26,731	27,269	22,436
Shares Outstanding	1,458	1,560	1,650	1,712	1,803	1,839	1,907	1,962
Statistical Record								
Return on Assets %	9.26	15.78	8.16	3.66	4.34	4.80	4.77	N.M.
Return on Equity %	...	...	...	20.85	16.71	18.57	20.57	N.M.
EBITDA Margin %	5.96	6.59	7.57	8.05	8.79	10.30	10.42	N.M.
Net Margin %	5.36	9.11	4.85	5.17	4.41	4.50	4.55	N.M.
Asset Turnover	1.73	1.73	1.68	0.71	0.98	1.07	1.05	1.01
Current Ratio	0.80	0.85	1.00	0.98	1.23	1.15	1.11	1.09
Debt to Equity	...	...	...	...	0.78	0.60	0.61	0.97
Price Range	25.50-16.03	26.42-19.92	22.12-14.35	15.65-9.02	18.49-11.15	17.32-11.06	12.39-5.32	13.57-6.29
P/E Ratio	12.32-7.74	8.10-6.11	14.95-9.70	10.94-6.31	7.45-4.50	6.61-4.22	4.73-2.03	...
Average Yield %	3.15	2.44	2.99	3.90	4.48	4.20	5.93	4.91

Address: 1501 Page Mill Road, Palo Alto, CA 94304 Telephone: 650-857-1501	Web Site: www.hp.com Officers: Charles V. (Chip) Bergh - Chairman Kim M. Rivera - President, Chief Legal Officer, General Counsel, Secretary	Auditors: Ernst & Young LLP Investor Contact: 800-286-5977 Transfer Agents: Wells Fargo Shareowner Services, St. Paul, MN

HOST HOTELS & RESORTS INC

Exchange	Symbol	Price	52Wk Range	Yield	P/E
NYS	HST	$18.55 (12/31/2019)	20.14-15.60	4.31	11.89

*7 Year Price Score 78.88   *NYSE Composite Index=100   *12 Month Price Score 93.59

Interim Earnings (Per Share)

Qtr.	Mar	Jun	Sep	Dec
2016	0.24	0.47	0.14	0.17
2017	0.21	0.28	0.14	0.12
2018	0.34	0.28	0.43	0.41
2019	0.25	0.39	0.51	...

Interim Dividends (Per Share)

Amt	Decl	Ex	Rec	Pay
0.20Q	06/14/2019	06/27/2019	06/28/2019	07/15/2019
0.20Q	09/13/2019	09/27/2019	09/30/2019	10/15/2019
0.05Q	12/13/2019	12/30/2019	12/31/2019	01/15/2020
0.20Q	12/13/2019	12/30/2019	12/31/2019	01/15/2020

Indicated Div: $0.80

Valuation Analysis   **Institutional Holding**

Forecast EPS	$1.25	No of Institutions
	(01/17/2020)	826
Market Cap	$13.3 Billion	Shares
Book Value	$7.5 Billion	938,156,160
Price/Book	1.78	% Held
Price/Sales	2.43	94.29

Business Summary: REITs (MIC: 5.3.1 SIC: 6798 NAIC: 525930)

Host Hotels & Resorts is a real estate investment trust. Co. owns properties and conducts operations through Host Hotels & Resorts, L.P., of which Co. is the sole general partner. Co.'s consolidated lodging portfolio consists of hotels primarily located in the U.S., and with several of the properties located outside of the U.S. in Brazil and Canada. In addition, Co. owns non-controlling interests in domestic and international joint venture and a timeshare venture in Hawaii.

Recent Developments: For the quarter ended Sep 30 2019, net income decreased 1.6% to US$372.0 million from US$378.0 million in the year-earlier quarter. Revenues were US$1.26 billion, down 2.8% from US$1.30 billion the year before.

Prospects: Our evaluation of Host Marriott Corp. as of October 4th, 2019 is the result of our systematic analysis on three basic characteristics: earnings strength, relative valuation, and recent stock price movement. The company has enjoyed a very positive trend in earnings per share over the past 5 quarters. However, recent analyst estimates for the company have been mixed and HST has posted results that exceeded analysts' expectations. Based on operating earnings yield, the company is undervalued when compared to all of the companies we cover. Share price changes over the past year indicates that HST will perform in line with the market over the near term.

Financial Data

(US$ in Millions)	9 Mos	6 Mos	3 Mos	12/31/2018	12/31/2017	12/31/2016	12/31/2015	12/31/2014
Earnings Per Share	1.56	1.48	1.37	1.47	0.76	1.02	0.74	0.96
Cash Flow Per Share	1.75	1.72	1.70	1.76	1.67	1.75	1.56	1.52
Tang Book Value Per Share	10.44	10.23	10.14	10.12	9.43	9.48	9.41	9.71
Dividends Per Share	0.850	0.850	0.850	0.850	0.850	0.850	0.800	0.750
Dividend Payout %	54.49	57.43	62.04	57.82	111.84	83.33	108.11	78.13
Income Statement								
Total Revenue	4,135	2,873	1,390	5,524	5,387	5,430	5,387	5,354
EBITDA	974	562	223	2,383	1,540	1,672	1,477	1,670
Depn & Amortn	5	3	2	951	758	731	737	725
Income Before Taxes	860	488	186	1,271	621	790	510	735
Income Taxes	22	18	2	150	80	40	9	14
Net Income	840	472	186	1,087	564	762	558	732
Average Shares	725	739	740	740	739	743	752	786
Balance Sheet								
Current Assets	2,134	1,270	1,227	1,542	914	374	254	684
Total Assets	13,132	12,525	12,577	12,090	11,693	11,408	11,784	12,207
Current Liabilities	277	248	240	293	283	278	243	298
Long-Term Obligations	4,442	3,864	3,862	3,837	3,954	3,649	4,017	3,992
Total Liabilities	5,633	5,058	5,064	4,596	4,720	4,414	4,720	4,871
Stockholders' Equity	7,499	7,467	7,513	7,494	6,973	6,994	7,064	7,336
Shares Outstanding	718	730	740	740	739	737	750	755
Statistical Record								
Return on Assets %	9.04	8.92	8.28	9.14	4.88	6.55	4.65	5.85
Return on Equity %	15.42	15.02	13.96	15.03	8.08	10.81	7.75	10.05
EBITDA Margin %	23.56	19.56	16.04	43.14	28.59	30.79	27.42	31.19
Net Margin %	20.31	16.43	13.38	19.68	10.47	14.03	10.36	13.67
Asset Turnover	0.43	0.45	0.45	0.46	0.47	0.47	0.45	0.43
Current Ratio	7.70	5.12	5.11	5.26	3.23	1.35	1.05	2.30
Debt to Equity	0.59	0.52	0.51	0.51	0.57	0.52	0.57	0.54
Price Range	20.97-15.60	21.94-15.94	22.25-15.94	22.25-15.94	20.58-17.38	19.18-12.82	24.14-15.20	24.33-18.00
P/E Ratio	13.44-10.00	14.82-10.77	16.24-11.64	15.14-10.84	27.08-22.87	18.80-12.57	32.62-20.54	25.34-18.75
Average Yield %	4.65	4.40	4.31	4.26	4.57	5.24	4.12	3.49

Address: 6903 Rockledge Drive, Suite 1500, Bethesda, MD 20817 **Telephone:** 240-744-1000	**Web Site:** www.hosthotels.com **Officers:** Richard E. Marriott - Chairman James F. Risoleo - President, Chief Executive Officer, Executive Vice President, Chief Investment Officer, Region Officer	**Auditors:** KPMG LLP **Transfer Agents:** Computershare Trust Company, N.A., Providence, RI

HOWARD HUGHES CORP

Exchange	Symbol	Price	52Wk Range	Yield	P/E
NYS	HHC	$126.80 (12/31/2019)	135.00-92.59	N/A	48.77

*7 Year Price Score 79.12 ***NYSE Composite Index=100** ***12 Month Price Score 92.95**

Interim Earnings (Per Share)

Qtr.	Mar	Jun	Sep	Dec
2016	2.69	0.16	0.19	1.01
2017	0.13	0.07	0.24	3.46
2018	0.03	(0.12)	0.54	0.86
2019	0.74	0.31	0.69	...

Interim Dividends (Per Share)

No Dividends Paid

Valuation Analysis / Institutional Holding

Forecast EPS	$1.11	No of Institutions	
	(01/17/2020)	352	
Market Cap	$5.5 Billion	Shares	
Book Value	$3.2 Billion	45,861,240	
Price/Book	1.72	% Held	
Price/Sales	3.70	84.81	

Business Summary: Property, Real Estate & Development (MIC: 5.3.2 SIC: 6552 NAIC: 531312)

Howard Hughes, together with its subsidiaries, operates in three business segments: Operating Assets, Master Planned Communities (MPCs) and Strategic Developments. Co.'s Operating Assets segment includes its investments in joint ventures and other assets, consisting of retail, office, multi-family, hospitality properties and other operating assets and investments. Co.'s MPC segment includes the development and sale of residential and commercial land, primarily in large-scale, long-term projects. Co.'s Strategic Developments segment consists of development or redevelopment projects.

Recent Developments: For the quarter ended Sep 30 2019, net income increased 26.0% to US$30.0 million from US$23.8 million in the year-earlier quarter. Revenues were US$231.2 million, down 10.1% from US$257.2 million the year before.

Prospects: Our evaluation of Howard Hughes Corp as of October 4th, 2019 is the result of our systematic analysis on three basic characteristics: earnings strength, relative valuation, and recent stock price movement. The company has suffered a very negative trend in earnings per share over the past 5 quarters. However, recent analyst estimates for the company have been raised while HHC has posted results in line with analysts' expectations. Based on operating earnings yield, the company is overvalued when compared to all of the companies we cover. Share price changes over the past year indicates that HHC will perform well over the near term.

Financial Data
(US$ in Thousands)

	9 Mos	6 Mos	3 Mos	12/31/2018	12/31/2017	12/31/2016	12/31/2015	12/31/2014
Earnings Per Share	2.60	2.45	2.02	1.32	3.91	4.73	1.60	(0.60)
Cash Flow Per Share	11.30	11.19	5.50	4.89	7.71	1.49	0.61	(1.48)
Tang Book Value Per Share	72.93	72.42	72.33	72.86	73.56	64.53	59.43	56.10
Income Statement								
Total Revenue	1,016,378	785,206	353,890	1,064,537	1,100,120	1,035,005	797,088	634,565
EBITDA	275,043	169,089	93,734	220,324	272,250	410,201	286,603	53,409
Depn & Amortn	127,725	81,947	39,991	113,518	116,401	81,878	82,275	50,683
Income Before Taxes	78,656	44,437	32,990	33,264	95,324	263,958	146,999	16,104
Income Taxes	24,207	15,489	11,016	15,492	(45,801)	118,450	24,001	62,960
Net Income	75,056	45,298	31,821	57,012	168,404	202,303	126,719	(23,531)
Average Shares	43,428	43,271	43,257	43,237	43,089	42,729	42,754	39,464
Balance Sheet								
Current Assets	1,314,115	1,190,227	900,267	963,767	1,064,775	825,933	619,114	721,665
Total Assets	7,947,915	7,709,178	7,416,007	7,355,799	6,729,064	6,367,382	5,721,582	5,119,931
Current Liabilities	890,940	880,819	812,467	936,460	682,568	1,105,125	913,731	898,955
Long-Term Obligations	3,624,684	3,422,490	3,241,985	3,181,213	2,857,945	2,690,747	2,443,962	1,993,470
Total Liabilities	4,756,364	4,545,454	4,255,540	4,223,587	3,546,078	3,799,644	3,361,465	2,896,168
Stockholders' Equity	3,191,551	3,163,724	3,160,467	3,132,212	3,182,986	2,567,738	2,360,117	2,223,763
Shares Outstanding	43,232	43,141	43,139	42,991	43,270	39,790	39,714	39,638
Statistical Record								
Return on Assets %	1.47	1.43	1.23	0.81	2.57	3.34	2.34	N.M.
Return on Equity %	3.57	3.40	2.80	1.81	5.86	8.19	5.53	N.M.
EBITDA Margin %	27.06	21.53	26.49	20.70	24.75	39.63	35.96	8.42
Net Margin %	7.38	5.77	8.99	5.36	15.31	19.55	15.90	N.M.
Asset Turnover	0.19	0.20	0.18	0.15	0.17	0.17	0.15	0.13
Current Ratio	1.47	1.35	1.11	1.03	1.56	0.75	0.68	0.80
Debt to Equity	1.14	1.08	1.03	1.02	0.90	1.05	1.04	0.90
Price Range	135.00-89.85	142.24-89.85	142.24-89.85	142.24-89.85	131.79-105.33	121.71-81.34	159.12-108.49	160.00-118.04
P/E Ratio	51.92-34.56	58.06-36.67	70.42-44.48	107.76-68.07	33.71-26.94	25.73-17.20	99.45-67.81	...

Address: 13355 Noel Road, 22nd Floor, Dallas, TX 75240 Telephone: 214-741-7744 Fax: 214-741-3021	Web Site: www.howardhughes.com Officers: William A. Ackman - Chairman Paul Layne - Chief Executive Officer, Region Officer	Auditors: Ernst & Young LLP Transfer Agents: Computershare, Jersey City, NJ

HUBBELL INC.

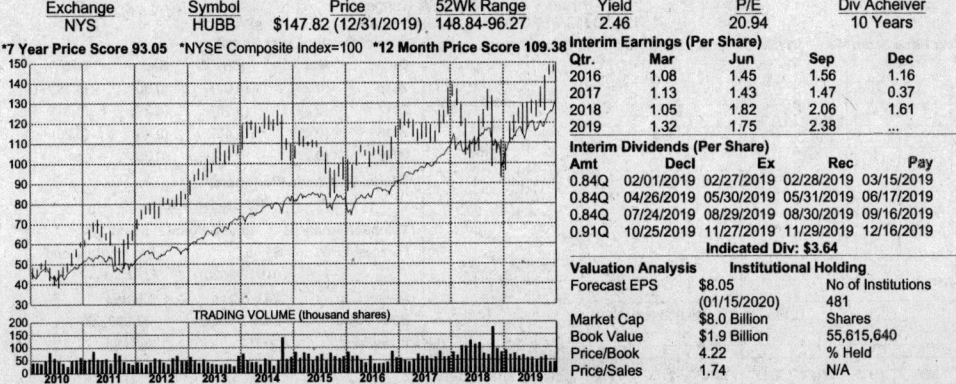

Exchange	Symbol	Price	52Wk Range	Yield	P/E	Div Acheiver
NYS	HUBB	$147.82 (12/31/2019)	148.84-96.27	2.46	20.94	10 Years

*7 Year Price Score 93.05   *NYSE Composite Index=100   *12 Month Price Score 109.38

Interim Earnings (Per Share)

Qtr.	Mar	Jun	Sep	Dec
2016	1.08	1.45	1.56	1.16
2017	1.13	1.43	1.47	0.37
2018	1.05	1.82	2.06	1.61
2019	1.32	1.75	2.38	...

Interim Dividends (Per Share)

Amt	Decl	Ex	Rec	Pay
0.84Q	02/01/2019	02/27/2019	02/28/2019	03/15/2019
0.84Q	04/26/2019	05/30/2019	05/31/2019	06/17/2019
0.84Q	07/24/2019	08/29/2019	08/30/2019	09/16/2019
0.91Q	10/25/2019	11/27/2019	11/29/2019	12/16/2019

Indicated Div: $3.64

Valuation Analysis

		Institutional Holding	
Forecast EPS	$8.05	No of Institutions	
	(01/15/2020)	481	
Market Cap	$8.0 Billion	Shares	
Book Value	$1.9 Billion	55,615,640	
Price/Book	4.22	% Held	
Price/Sales	1.74	N/A	

Business Summary: Electrical Equipment (MIC: 7.3.1 SIC: 3679 NAIC: 334417)

Hubbell is primarily engaged in the design, manufacture and sale of electrical and electronic products for a range of non-residential and residential construction, industrial and utility applications. Co. has two segments: Electrical, which comprised of businesses that sell stock and custom products including application wiring device products, electrical products, connector and grounding products, lighting fixtures and controls, components and assemblies, as well as other electrical equipment; and Power, which consists of operations for the design, manufacture and sale of transmission and distribution components primarily for the electrical utilities industry.

Recent Developments: For the quarter ended Sep 30 2019, net income increased 15.6% to US$132.6 million from US$114.7 million in the year-earlier quarter. Revenues were US$1.20 billion, up 2.1% from US$1.18 billion the year before. Operating income was US$172.9 million versus US$163.8 million in the prior-year quarter, an increase of 5.6%. Direct operating expenses rose 1.4% to US$842.0 million from US$830.7 million in the comparable period the year before. Indirect operating expenses increased 2.1% to US$189.1 million from US$185.2 million in the equivalent prior-year period.

Prospects: Our evaluation of Hubbell Inc. as of October 4th, 2019 is the result of our systematic analysis on three basic characteristics: earnings strength, relative valuation, and recent stock price movement. The company has managed to produce a neutral trend in earnings per share over the past 5 quarters. In addition, recent analyst estimates for the company have been mixed and HUBB has posted results that exceeded analysts' expectations. Based on operating earnings yield, the company is undervalued when compared to all of the companies we cover. Share price changes over the past year indicates that HUBB will perform in line with the market over the near term.

Financial Data

(US$ in Thousands)	9 Mos	6 Mos	3 Mos	12/31/2018	12/31/2017	12/31/2016	12/31/2015	12/31/2014
Earnings Per Share	7.06	6.74	6.81	6.54	4.39	5.24	4.77	5.48
Cash Flow Per Share	10.37	10.58	10.95	9.47	6.92	7.16	5.74	6.66
Tang Book Value Per Share	N.M.	N.M.	N.M.	N.M.	1.55	3.07	7.61	12.47
Dividends Per Share	3.360	3.290	3.220	3.150	2.870	2.590	2.310	2.060
Dividend Payout %	47.59	48.81	47.28	48.17	65.38	49.43	48.43	37.59
Income Statement								
Total Revenue	3,487,700	2,283,700	1,087,300	4,481,700	3,668,800	3,505,200	3,390,400	3,359,400
EBITDA	552,400	330,000	152,100	605,500	545,500	527,200	500,800	566,600
Depn & Amortn	111,100	73,700	36,600	66,100	57,500	53,400	51,200	49,900
Income Before Taxes	389,600	221,600	98,000	467,000	443,100	430,400	418,600	485,500
Income Taxes	85,300	49,900	24,200	100,900	193,200	132,600	136,500	158,300
Net Income	299,000	168,300	72,300	360,200	243,100	293,000	277,300	325,300
Average Shares	54,600	54,600	54,600	54,900	55,100	55,700	58,000	59,200
Balance Sheet								
Current Assets	1,809,900	1,729,000	1,650,600	1,643,700	1,604,100	1,551,300	1,387,800	1,629,400
Total Assets	5,074,300	5,036,000	4,976,100	4,872,100	3,720,600	3,525,000	3,208,700	3,322,800
Current Liabilities	866,200	874,100	847,900	839,300	706,100	589,600	603,100	499,200
Long-Term Obligations	1,714,100	1,722,800	1,731,500	1,737,100	987,100	990,500	595,900	597,600
Total Liabilities	3,171,200	3,200,100	3,168,000	3,091,500	2,086,400	1,932,200	1,468,100	1,395,700
Stockholders' Equity	1,903,100	1,835,900	1,808,100	1,780,600	1,634,200	1,592,800	1,740,600	1,927,100
Shares Outstanding	54,385	54,408	54,508	54,715	54,882	55,532	57,836	58,496
Statistical Record								
Return on Assets %	7.68	7.39	7.52	8.38	6.71	8.68	8.49	9.99
Return on Equity %	21.16	21.01	21.57	21.10	15.07	17.53	15.12	16.97
EBITDA Margin %	15.84	14.45	13.99	13.51	14.87	15.04	14.77	16.87
Net Margin %	8.57	7.37	6.65	8.04	6.63	8.36	8.18	9.68
Asset Turnover	0.92	0.92	0.92	1.04	1.01	1.04	1.04	1.03
Current Ratio	2.09	1.98	1.95	1.96	2.27	2.63	2.30	3.26
Debt to Equity	0.90	0.94	0.96	0.98	0.60	0.62	0.34	0.31
Price Range	137.88-92.76	136.74-92.76	136.74-92.76	139.21-92.76	137.50-109.89	118.54-86.29	116.29-82.96	126.41-101.44
P/E Ratio	19.53-13.14	20.29-13.76	20.08-13.62	21.29-14.18	31.32-25.03	22.62-16.47	24.38-17.39	23.07-18.51
Average Yield %	2.83	2.81	2.82	2.66	2.42	2.48	2.32	1.81

Address: 40 Waterview Drive, Shelton, CT 06484	**Web Site:** www.hubbell.com	**Auditors:** PricewaterhouseCoopers LLP
Telephone: 475-882-4000	**Officers:** David G. Nord - Chairman, President, Chief Executive Officer, Senior Vice President, Chief Financial Officer, Chief Operating Officer Gerben W. Bakker - President, Chief Operating Officer, Division Officer	**Transfer Agents:** Computershare Inc.

HUBSPOT INC

Exchange	Symbol	Price	52Wk Range	Yield	P/E
NYS	HUBS	$158.50 (12/31/2019)	204.88-118.83	N/A	N/A

*7 Year Price Score N/A *NYSE Composite Index=100 *12 Month Price Score 85.64

Interim Earnings (Per Share)

Qtr.	Mar	Jun	Sep	Dec
2016	(0.29)	(0.32)	(0.30)	(0.38)
2017	(0.22)	(0.26)	(0.29)	(0.31)
2018	(0.41)	(0.48)	(0.48)	(0.29)
2019	(0.27)	(0.41)	(0.35)	...

Interim Dividends (Per Share)

No Dividends Paid

Valuation Analysis

		Institutional Holding	
Forecast EPS	$1.45	No of Institutions	
	(01/17/2020)	374	
Market Cap	$6.8 Billion	Shares	
Book Value	$628.4 Million	42,098,556	
Price/Book	10.76	% Held	
Price/Sales	10.98	98.16	

Business Summary: Internet & Software (MIC: 6.3.2 SIC: 7372 NAIC: 511210)

HubSpot provides a cloud-based marketing, sales, and customer service software platform, which it refers to as its Growth Platform. Co.'s Growth Platform features integrated applications that create an adaptable customer experience. These integrated applications include a CRM, search engine optimization, blogging, website content management, messaging, chatbots, social media, marketing automation, email, predictive lead scoring, sales productivity, ticketing and helpdesk tools, customer NPS surveys, analytics, and reporting. Co. also provides other services, which consist of customer on-boarding and training services.

Recent Developments: For the quarter ended Sep 30 2019, net loss amounted to US$15.0 million versus a net loss of US$18.7 million in the year-earlier quarter. Revenues were US$173.6 million, up 31.7% from US$131.8 million the year before. Operating loss was US$14.1 million versus a loss of US$15.1 million in the prior-year quarter. Direct operating expenses rose 29.1% to US$33.3 million from US$25.8 million in the comparable period the year before. Indirect operating expenses increased 27.5% to US$154.4 million from US$121.1 million in the equivalent prior-year period.

Prospects: Our evaluation of HubSpot Inc as of October 4th, 2019 is the result of our systematic analysis on three basic characteristics: earnings strength, relative valuation, and recent stock price movement. The company has generated a negative trend in earnings per share over the past 5 quarters. However, recent analyst estimates for the company have been mixed and HUBS has posted results that exceeded analysts' expectations. Based on operating earnings yield, the company is overvalued when compared to all of the companies we cover. Share price changes over the past year indicates that HUBS will perform over the near term.

Financial Data

(US$ in Thousands)	9 Mos	6 Mos	3 Mos	12/31/2018	12/31/2017	12/31/2016	12/31/2015	12/31/2014
Earnings Per Share	(1.32)	(1.45)	(1.52)	(1.66)	(1.08)	(1.29)	(1.39)	(4.20)
Cash Flow Per Share	2.45	2.28	2.36	2.20	1.35	0.55	(0.01)	(1.08)
Tang Book Value Per Share	13.97	13.87	13.46	5.72	5.04	3.04	3.26	3.22
Income Statement								
Total Revenue	488,674	315,053	151,798	512,980	375,612	270,967	181,943	115,876
EBITDA	(12,222)	(7,370)	(88)	(36,850)	(31,295)	(39,718)	(43,146)	(46,345)
Depn & Amortn	27,384	18,075	8,960	12,900	9,400	5,900	2,700	1,700
Income Before Taxes	(41,769)	(27,033)	(10,387)	(61,960)	(50,039)	(45,029)	(45,641)	(48,321)
Income Taxes	1,675	1,424	713	1,868	(10,325)	533	412	(92)
Net Income	(43,444)	(28,457)	(11,100)	(63,828)	(39,714)	(45,562)	(46,053)	(48,229)
Average Shares	42,531	42,127	40,568	38,529	36,827	35,197	33,222	11,562
Balance Sheet								
Current Assets	1,081,239	1,082,876	1,083,451	712,418	602,501	176,253	145,754	149,509
Total Assets	1,478,881	1,463,492	1,370,125	833,953	712,175	259,755	220,379	174,858
Current Liabilities	280,918	272,913	268,624	237,009	178,296	127,383	91,307	59,428
Long-Term Obligations	334,966	329,457	324,042	318,782	298,447	275	277	78
Total Liabilities	850,529	845,348	771,122	589,312	501,815	141,055	98,671	64,159
Stockholders' Equity	628,352	618,144	599,003	244,641	210,360	118,700	121,708	110,699
Shares Outstanding	42,639	42,276	42,103	39,300	37,503	35,784	34,313	31,430
Statistical Record								
Asset Turnover	0.56	0.53	0.52	0.66	0.77	1.13	0.92	1.03
Current Ratio	3.85	3.97	4.03	3.01	3.38	1.38	1.60	2.52
Debt to Equity	0.53	0.53	0.54	1.30	1.42	N.M.	N.M.	N.M.
Price Range	204.88-114.44	190.57-114.44	176.22-105.30	160.35-89.15	92.95-47.85	59.48-27.52	59.55-32.52	37.00-27.25

Address: 25 First Street, 2nd Floor, Cambridge, MA 02141 **Telephone:** 888-482-7768	**Web Site:** www.hubspot.com **Officers:** Brian Halligan - Chairman, Chief Executive Officer J. Donald Sherman - President, Chief Operating Officer	**Auditors:** PricewaterhouseCoopers LLP **Investor Contact:** 888-482-7768 **Transfer Agents:** Computershare Trust Company, N.A.

HUDSON PACIFIC PROPERTIES INC

Exchange	Symbol	Price	52Wk Range	Yield	P/E
NYS	HPP	$37.65 (12/31/2019)	37.65-27.53	2.66	129.83

*7 Year Price Score 94.80 *NYSE Composite Index=100 *12 Month Price Score 100.11

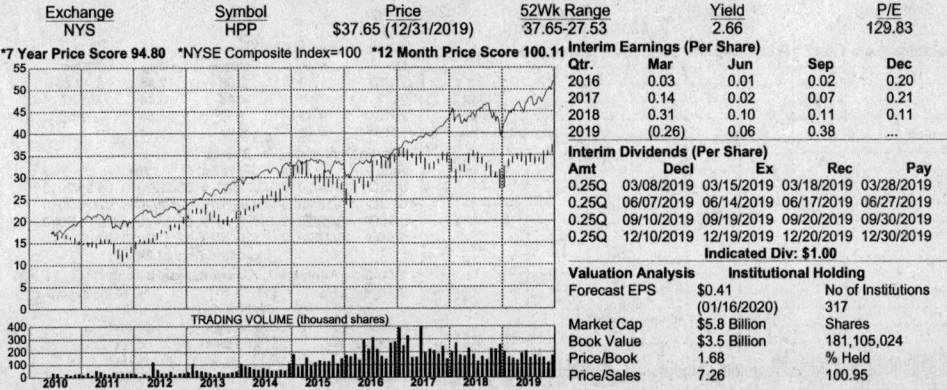

Interim Earnings (Per Share)

Qtr.	Mar	Jun	Sep	Dec
2016	0.03	0.01	0.02	0.20
2017	0.14	0.02	0.07	0.21
2018	0.31	0.10	0.11	0.11
2019	(0.26)	0.06	0.38	...

Interim Dividends (Per Share)

Amt	Decl	Ex	Rec	Pay
0.25Q	03/08/2019	03/15/2019	03/18/2019	03/28/2019
0.25Q	06/07/2019	06/14/2019	06/17/2019	06/27/2019
0.25Q	09/10/2019	09/19/2019	09/20/2019	09/30/2019
0.25Q	12/10/2019	12/19/2019	12/20/2019	12/30/2019

Indicated Div: $1.00

Valuation Analysis **Institutional Holding**

Forecast EPS	$0.41	No of Institutions
	(01/16/2020)	317
Market Cap	$5.8 Billion	Shares
Book Value	$3.5 Billion	181,105,024
Price/Book	1.68	% Held
Price/Sales	7.26	100.95

Business Summary: REITs (MIC: 5.3.1 SIC: 6798 NAIC: 525930)

Hudson Pacific Properties is a holding company. Through its subsidiaries, Co. is a self-administered and self-managed real estate investment trust focused on acquiring, repositioning, developing and operating office and studio properties in submarkets throughout Northern and Southern California and the Pacific Northwest. Co. owns its interests in all of its properties and conducts substantially all of its business through its operating partnership, Hudson Pacific Properties, L.P. Co. has two segments: office properties, which are located in Northern and Southern California and the Pacific Northwest; and studio properties, which are located in Southern California.

Recent Developments: For the quarter ended Sep 30 2019, net income increased 210.6% to US$63.0 million from US$20.3 million in the year-earlier quarter. Revenues were US$208.2 million, up 15.2% from US$180.7 million the year before.

Prospects: Our evaluation of Hudson Pacific Properties Inc as of October 4th, 2019 is the result of our systematic analysis on three basic characteristics: earnings strength, relative valuation, and recent stock price movement. The company has managed to produce a neutral trend in earnings per share over the past 5 quarters. In addition, recent analyst estimates for the company have been mixed and HPP has posted results that fell short of analysts' expectations. Based on operating earnings yield, the company is overvalued when compared to all of the companies we cover. Share price changes over the past year indicates that HPP will perform well over the near term.

Financial Data

(US$ in Thousands)	9 Mos	6 Mos	3 Mos	12/31/2018	12/31/2017	12/31/2016	12/31/2015	12/31/2014
Earnings Per Share	0.29	0.02	0.06	0.63	0.44	0.25	(0.19)	0.15
Cash Flow Per Share	1.62	1.67	1.55	1.38	1.91	2.06	2.03	0.96
Tang Book Value Per Share	22.29	22.17	22.39	23.69	23.39	22.75	18.70	15.50
Dividends Per Share	1.000	1.000	1.000	1.000	1.000	0.800	0.575	0.500
Dividend Payout %	344.83	5,000.00	1,666.67	158.73	227.27	320.00	...	333.33
Income Statement								
Total Revenue	602,263	394,045	197,389	728,418	728,139	639,639	520,850	253,415
EBITDA	121,927	29,905	(11,657)	447,554	469,139	390,843	272,841	125,194
Depn & Amortn	8,586	5,107	1,912	254,324	284,638	271,301	238,380	75,606
Income Before Taxes	38,883	(24,072)	(36,895)	111,781	94,561	43,758	(16,082)	23,686
Net Income	30,590	(29,052)	(39,116)	98,753	68,590	27,984	(16,397)	9,955
Average Shares	156,498	154,687	154,396	155,696	153,882	110,369	85,927	66,509
Balance Sheet								
Current Assets	266,742	246,280	243,044	224,564	215,100	202,325	181,040	109,518
Total Assets	7,428,294	7,486,666	7,373,628	7,070,879	6,622,070	6,678,998	6,254,035	2,340,885
Current Liabilities	261,272	241,990	208,047	289,599	279,549	278,061	254,105	137,634
Long-Term Obligations	2,930,369	3,037,557	2,915,185	2,828,194	2,421,380	2,688,010	2,260,716	918,059
Total Liabilities	3,977,527	4,055,229	3,908,478	3,404,377	2,974,122	3,565,538	4,578,024	1,151,534
Stockholders' Equity	3,450,767	3,431,437	3,465,150	3,666,502	3,647,948	3,113,460	1,676,011	1,189,351
Shares Outstanding	154,414	154,396	154,373	154,371	155,602	136,492	89,153	66,797
Statistical Record								
Return on Assets %	0.65	0.06	0.15	1.44	1.03	0.43	N.M.	0.45
Return on Equity %	1.29	0.11	0.29	2.70	2.03	1.17	N.M.	0.90
EBITDA Margin %	20.24	7.59	N.M.	61.44	64.43	61.10	52.38	49.40
Net Margin %	5.08	N.M.	N.M.	13.56	9.42	4.37	N.M.	3.93
Asset Turnover	0.11	0.11	0.11	0.11	0.11	0.10	0.12	0.11
Current Ratio	1.02	1.02	1.17	0.78	0.77	0.73	0.71	0.80
Debt to Equity	0.85	0.89	0.84	0.77	0.66	0.86	1.35	0.77
Price Range	35.41-27.42	35.68-27.42	36.00-27.42	36.00-27.42	36.65-31.73	35.27-22.97	33.95-27.17	30.34-21.42
P/E Ratio	122.10-94.55	N.M.	600.00-457.00	57.14-43.52	83.30-72.11	141.08-91.88	...	202.27-142.80
Average Yield %	3.04	3.06	3.07	3.08	2.93	2.65	1.90	2.00

Address: 11601 Wilshire Blvd., Ninth Floor, Los Angeles, CA 90025 **Telephone:** 310-445-5700	**Web Site:** **Officers:** Victor J. Coleman - Chairman, President, Chief Executive Officer Mark T. Lammas - Chief Financial Officer, Chief Operating Officer, Treasurer	**Auditors:** Ernst & Young LLP **Investor Contact:** 310-829-5400 **Transfer Agents:** Computershare, Canton, MA

HUMANA INC.

Exchange	Symbol	Price	52Wk Range	Yield	P/E
NYS	HUM	$366.52 (12/31/2019)	371.00-232.89	0.60	19.48

*7 Year Price Score 119.12 *NYSE Composite Index=100 *12 Month Price Score 112.32

Interim Earnings (Per Share)

Qtr.	Mar	Jun	Sep	Dec
2016	1.56	2.06	2.98	(2.66)
2017	7.49	4.46	3.44	1.37
2018	3.53	1.39	4.65	2.58
2019	4.16	6.94	5.14	...

Interim Dividends (Per Share)

Amt	Decl	Ex	Rec	Pay
0.55Q	02/04/2019	03/28/2019	03/29/2019	04/26/2019
0.55Q	04/18/2019	06/27/2019	06/28/2019	07/26/2019
0.55Q	08/22/2019	09/27/2019	09/30/2019	10/25/2019
0.55Q	10/24/2019	12/30/2019	12/31/2019	01/31/2020

Indicated Div: $2.20

Valuation Analysis / **Institutional Holding**

Forecast EPS	$17.78	No of Institutions	
	(01/17/2020)	1085	
Market Cap	$48.5 Billion	Shares	
Book Value	$11.6 Billion	158,812,512	
Price/Book	4.18	% Held	
Price/Sales	0.77	87.67	

Business Summary: Life & Health (MIC: 5.2.2 SIC: 6324 NAIC: 524114)

Humana is a holding company. Through its subsidiaries, Co. is a health and well-being company. Co. manages its business with three segments: Retail, which consists of products sold on a retail basis to individuals including medical and supplemental benefit plans, such as Medicare and state-based Medicaid Contracts; Group and Specialty, which consists of employer group commercial fully-insured medical and specialty health insurance benefits, including dental, vision and life insurance benefits, as well as administrative services only; and Healthcare Services, which includes pharmacy solutions, provider services, clinical care services, clinical programs and predictive modeling, among others.

Recent Developments: For the quarter ended Sep 30 2019, net income increased 7.0% to US$689.0 million from US$644.0 million in the year-earlier quarter. Revenues were US$16.24 billion, up 14.3% from US$14.21 billion the year before. Net premiums earned were US$15.71 billion versus US$13.71 billion in the prior-year quarter, an increase of 14.6%.

Prospects: Our evaluation of Humana Inc. as of October 4th, 2019 is the result of our systematic analysis on three basic characteristics: earnings strength, relative valuation, and recent stock price movement. The company has managed to produce a neutral trend in earnings per share over the past 5 quarters. In addition, recent analyst estimates for the company have been mixed and HUM has posted results that exceeded analysts' expectations. Based on operating earnings yield, the company is undervalued when compared to all of the companies we cover. Share price changes over the past year indicates that HUM will perform in line with the market over the near term.

Financial Data

(US$ in Thousands)	9 Mos	6 Mos	3 Mos	12/31/2018	12/31/2017	12/31/2016	12/31/2015	12/31/2014
Earnings Per Share	18.82	18.33	12.78	12.16	16.81	4.07	8.44	7.36
Cash Flow Per Share	33.30	6.97	(4.56)	15.81	28.04	12.93	5.81	10.49
Tang Book Value Per Share	57.99	58.85	51.42	46.21	47.65	49.65	47.75	39.67
Dividends Per Share	2.150	2.100	2.050	2.000	1.890	0.870	1.150	1.110
Dividend Payout %	11.42	11.46	16.04	16.45	11.24	21.38	13.63	15.08
Income Statement								
Premium Income	47,139,000	31,427,000	15,651,000	54,941,000	52,380,000	53,021,000	52,409,000	45,959,000
Total Revenue	48,593,000	32,352,000	16,107,000	56,912,000	53,767,000	54,379,000	54,289,000	48,500,000
Benefits & Claims	40,168,000	26,811,000	13,493,000	45,882,000	43,496,000	45,007,000	44,269,000	38,166,000
Income Before Taxes	2,863,000	1,975,000	746,000	2,063,000	4,020,000	1,552,000	2,431,000	2,170,000
Income Taxes	684,000	484,000	183,000	391,000	1,572,000	938,000	1,155,000	1,023,000
Net Income	2,195,000	1,506,000	566,000	1,683,000	2,448,000	614,000	1,276,000	1,147,000
Average Shares	134,025	135,579	135,962	138,403	145,585	150,917	151,142	155,874
Balance Sheet								
Total Assets	29,180,000	28,913,000	28,349,000	25,413,000	27,178,000	25,396,000	24,705,000	23,466,000
Total Liabilities	17,579,000	17,041,000	17,508,000	15,252,000	17,336,000	14,711,000	14,359,000	13,820,000
Stockholders' Equity	11,601,000	11,872,000	10,841,000	10,161,000	9,842,000	10,685,000	10,346,000	9,646,000
Shares Outstanding	132,426	135,089	135,035	135,566	137,678	149,305	148,288	149,604
Statistical Record								
Return on Assets %	9.00	7.93	5.69	6.40	9.31	2.44	5.30	5.19
Return on Equity %	22.98	22.69	16.81	16.83	23.85	5.82	12.77	12.10
Loss Ratio %	85.21	85.31	86.21	83.51	83.04	84.89	84.47	83.04
Net Margin %	4.52	4.66	3.51	2.96	4.55	1.13	2.35	2.36
Price Range	353.98-232.89	353.98-232.89	353.98-262.61	353.98-251.28	260.86-195.24	216.76-153.38	214.92-139.09	149.07-95.59
P/E Ratio	18.81-12.37	19.31-12.71	27.70-20.55	29.11-20.66	15.52-11.61	53.26-37.69	25.46-16.48	20.25-12.99
Average Yield %	0.76	0.71	0.67	0.66	0.82	0.49	0.65	0.91

Address: 500 West Main Street, Louisville, KY 40202 **Telephone:** 502-580-1000	**Web Site:** www.humana.com **Officers:** Kurt J. Hilzinger - Chairman Bruce D. Broussard - President, Chief Executive Officer	**Auditors:** PricewaterhouseCoopers LLP **Investor Contact:** 502-580-3644 **Transfer Agents:** American Stock Transfer & Trust Company, LLC, Brooklyn, NY

HUNTINGTON INGALLS INDUSTRIES, INC.

Exchange	Symbol	Price	52Wk Range	Yield	P/E
NYS	HII	$250.88 (12/31/2019)	258.06-188.84	1.64	17.18

*7 Year Price Score 114.83 *NYSE Composite Index=100 *12 Month Price Score 107.12

Interim Earnings (Per Share)

Qtr.	Mar	Jun	Sep	Dec
2016	2.87	2.80	2.27	4.21
2017	2.56	3.21	3.27	1.42
2018	3.48	5.40	5.29	4.94
2019	2.85	3.07	3.74	...

Interim Dividends (Per Share)

Amt	Decl	Ex	Rec	Pay
0.86Q	02/06/2019	02/21/2019	02/22/2019	03/08/2019
0.86Q	04/30/2019	05/23/2019	05/24/2019	06/07/2019
0.86Q	07/30/2019	08/29/2019	08/30/2019	09/13/2019
1.03Q	11/05/2019	11/27/2019	11/29/2019	12/13/2019

Indicated Div: $4.12

Valuation Analysis

		Institutional Holding	
Forecast EPS	$13.82	No of Institutions	
	(01/17/2020)	628	
Market Cap	$10.3 Billion	Shares	
Book Value	$1.7 Billion	43,230,080	
Price/Book	6.03	% Held	
Price/Sales	1.18	78.95	

Business Summary: Defense (MIC: 7.1.2 SIC: 3731 NAIC: 336611)

Huntington Ingalls Industries is a military shipbuilding company and a provider of services to partners in government and industry. Co.'s segments include: Ingalls Shipbuilding, which designs and constructs non-nuclear ships for the U.S. Navy and U.S. Coast Guard, including amphibious assault ships, expeditionary warfare ships, surface combatants, and national security cutters; Newport News Shipbuilding, which is engaged in the designing and constructing nuclear-powered ships, such as aircraft carriers and submarines, and the refueling and overhaul and the inactivation of such ships; and Technical Solutions, which includes businesses that are focused on life-cycle sustainment services.

Recent Developments: For the quarter ended Sep 30 2019, net income decreased 32.8% to US$154.0 million from US$229.0 million in the year-earlier quarter. Revenues were US$2.22 billion, up 6.5% from US$2.08 billion the year before. Operating income was US$214.0 million versus US$290.0 million in the prior-year quarter, a decrease of 26.2%. Direct operating expenses rose 13.1% to US$1.80 billion from US$1.59 billion in the comparable period the year before. Indirect operating expenses increased 1.5% to US$203.0 million from US$200.0 million in the equivalent prior-year period.

Prospects: Our evaluation of Huntington Ingalls Industries Inc. as of October 4th, 2019 is the result of our systematic analysis on three basic characteristics: earnings strength, relative valuation, and recent stock price movement. The company has generated a negative trend in earnings per share over the past 5 quarters. However, recent analyst estimates for the company have been unchanged while HII has posted results that fell short of analysts' expectations. Based on operating earnings yield, the company is undervalued when compared to all of the companies we cover. Share price changes over the past year indicates that HII will perform in line with the market over the near term.

Financial Data

(US$ in Thousands)	9 Mos	6 Mos	3 Mos	12/31/2018	12/31/2017	12/31/2016	12/31/2015	12/31/2014
Earnings Per Share	14.60	16.15	18.48	19.09	10.46	12.14	8.36	6.86
Cash Flow Per Share	23.74	12.52	19.44	20.87	17.81	17.52	17.29	14.67
Tang Book Value Per Share	N.M.	N.M.	N.M.	N.M.	0.73	N.M.	0.83	N.M.
Dividends Per Share	3.440	3.300	3.160	3.020	2.520	2.100	1.700	1.000
Dividend Payout %	23.56	20.43	17.10	15.82	24.09	17.30	20.33	14.58
Income Statement								
Total Revenue	6,487,000	4,268,000	2,080,000	8,176,000	7,441,000	7,068,000	7,020,000	6,957,000
EBITDA	726,000	454,000	218,000	1,232,000	1,071,000	1,044,000	949,000	850,000
Depn & Amortn	163,000	107,000	53,000	203,000	205,000	186,000	180,000	194,000
Income Before Taxes	511,000	313,000	149,000	971,000	772,000	784,000	632,000	507,000
Income Taxes	111,000	67,000	31,000	135,000	293,000	211,000	228,000	169,000
Net Income	400,000	246,000	118,000	836,000	479,000	573,000	404,000	338,000
Average Shares	41,200	41,700	41,400	43,800	45,800	47,200	48,300	49,300
Balance Sheet								
Current Assets	2,025,000	2,123,000	1,922,000	1,745,000	2,195,000	2,142,000	2,284,000	2,546,000
Total Assets	7,184,000	7,230,000	7,000,000	6,383,000	6,374,000	6,352,000	6,024,000	6,269,000
Current Liabilities	1,950,000	1,902,000	1,960,000	1,829,000	1,391,000	1,343,000	1,274,000	1,312,000
Long-Term Obligations	1,721,000	1,877,000	1,680,000	1,283,000	1,279,000	1,278,000	1,273,000	1,592,000
Total Liabilities	5,479,000	5,602,000	5,437,000	4,867,000	4,616,000	4,699,000	4,534,000	4,904,000
Stockholders' Equity	1,705,000	1,628,000	1,563,000	1,516,000	1,758,000	1,653,000	1,490,000	1,365,000
Shares Outstanding	41,000	41,400	41,600	41,900	45,100	46,200	46,900	48,300
Statistical Record								
Return on Assets %	9.15	10.10	11.93	13.11	7.53	9.23	6.57	5.41
Return on Equity %	34.67	41.30	48.64	51.07	28.09	36.36	28.30	23.42
EBITDA Margin %	11.19	10.64	10.48	15.07	14.39	14.77	13.52	12.22
Net Margin %	6.17	5.76	5.67	10.23	6.44	8.11	5.75	4.86
Asset Turnover	1.30	1.26	1.25	1.28	1.17	1.14	1.14	1.11
Current Ratio	1.04	1.12	0.98	0.95	1.58	1.59	1.79	1.94
Debt to Equity	1.01	1.15	1.07	0.85	0.73	0.77	0.85	1.17
Price Range	261.28-177.03	261.28-177.03	265.59-177.03	270.88-177.03	251.96-185.22	187.96-121.41	143.55-103.98	115.48-87.91
P/E Ratio	17.90-12.13	16.18-10.96	14.37-9.58	14.19-9.27	24.09-17.71	15.48-10.00	17.17-12.44	16.83-12.81
Average Yield %	1.61	1.51	1.41	1.29	1.20	1.36	1.22	1.00

Address: 4101 Washington Avenue, Newport News, VA 23607 **Telephone:** 757-380-2000	**Web Site:** www.huntingtoningalls.com **Officers:** Thomas B. Fargo - Chairman C. Michael Petters - President, Chief Executive Officer	**Auditors:** DELOITTE & TOUCHE LLP **Investor Contact:** 757-688-5572 **Transfer Agents:** Computershare Trust Company, N.A., Providence, RI

HUNTSMAN CORP

Exchange	Symbol	Price	52Wk Range	Yield	P/E
NYS	HUN	$24.16 (12/31/2019)	24.94-17.37	2.69	N/A

*7 Year Price Score 81.40   *NYSE Composite Index=100   *12 Month Price Score 101.20

Interim Earnings (Per Share)

Qtr.	Mar	Jun	Sep	Dec
2016	0.24	0.36	0.23	0.53
2017	0.31	0.69	0.60	1.01
2018	1.11	1.71	(0.05)	(1.40)
2019	0.51	0.47	0.13	...

Interim Dividends (Per Share)

Amt	Decl	Ex	Rec	Pay
0.163Q	02/13/2019	03/14/2019	03/15/2019	03/29/2019
0.163Q	05/10/2019	06/13/2019	06/14/2019	06/28/2019
0.163Q	08/08/2019	09/12/2019	09/13/2019	09/30/2019
0.163Q	11/05/2019	12/12/2019	12/13/2019	12/31/2019

Indicated Div: $0.65

Valuation Analysis

		Institutional Holding	
Forecast EPS	$1.81	No of Institutions	
	(01/17/2020)	593	
Market Cap	$5.4 Billion	Shares	
Book Value	$2.5 Billion	213,780,592	
Price/Book	2.19	% Held	
Price/Sales	0.67	70.25	

Business Summary: Specialty Chemicals (MIC: 8.3.2 SIC: 2899 NAIC: 325199)

Huntsman is a manufacturer of differentiated organic chemical products. Co. operates in four segments: Polyurethanes, Performance Products, Advanced Materials and Textile Effects. Co.'s products comprise a range of chemicals and formulations, which Co. markets to a group of consumer and industrial customers. Co.'s products are used in a range of applications, including those in the adhesives, aerospace, automotive, construction products, personal care and hygiene, durable and non-durable consumer products, digital inks, electronics, medical, packaging, coatings and construction, power generation, refining, synthetic fiber, textile chemicals and dyes industries.

Recent Developments: For the quarter ended Sep 30 2019, loss from continuing operations was US$27.0 million compared with income of US$197.0 million in the year-earlier quarter. Net income amounted to US$41.0 million versus a net loss of US$8.0 million in the year-earlier quarter. Revenues were US$1.69 billion, down 14.3% from US$1.97 billion the year before. Operating income was US$152.0 million versus US$223.0 million in the prior-year quarter, a decrease of 31.8%. Direct operating expenses declined 10.3% to US$1.35 billion from US$1.50 billion in the comparable period the year before. Indirect operating expenses decreased 23.0% to US$188.0 million from US$244.0 million in the equivalent prior-year period.

Prospects: Our evaluation of Huntsman Corp. as of October 4th, 2019 is the result of our systematic analysis on three basic characteristics: earnings strength, relative valuation, and recent stock price movement. The company has suffered a very negative trend in earnings per share over the past 5 quarters. In addition, recent analyst estimates for the company have been reduced and HUN has posted results that fell short of analysts' expectations. Based on operating earnings yield, the company is undervalued when compared to all of the companies we cover. Share price changes over the past year indicates that HUN will perform very poorly over the near term.

Financial Data

(US$ in Thousands)	9 Mos	6 Mos	3 Mos	12/31/2018	12/31/2017	12/31/2016	12/31/2015	12/31/2014
Earnings Per Share	(0.29)	(0.47)	0.77	1.39	2.61	1.36	0.38	1.31
Cash Flow Per Share	4.09	3.64	4.35	5.07	5.11	4.59	2.37	3.14
Tang Book Value Per Share	8.93	9.29	9.15	8.70	10.09	4.65	5.23	6.41
Dividends Per Share	0.650	0.650	0.650	0.650	0.500	0.500	0.500	0.500
Dividend Payout %	...	...	84.42	46.76	19.16	36.76	131.58	38.17
Income Statement								
Total Revenue	5,140,000	4,228,000	2,034,000	9,379,000	8,358,000	9,657,000	10,299,000	11,578,000
EBITDA	523,000	571,000	292,000	1,312,000	1,097,000	1,045,000	752,000	1,016,000
Depn & Amortn	201,000	182,000	90,000	310,000	298,000	400,000	377,000	413,000
Income Before Taxes	236,000	330,000	172,000	887,000	634,000	443,000	170,000	398,000
Income Taxes	113,000	102,000	52,000	97,000	64,000	87,000	46,000	51,000
Net Income	259,000	229,000	119,000	337,000	636,000	326,000	93,000	323,000
Average Shares	227,400	232,100	235,100	241,600	243,900	239,600	245,400	246,000
Balance Sheet								
Current Assets	3,729,000	3,013,000	3,136,000	2,958,000	5,979,000	3,555,000	3,834,000	5,039,000
Total Assets	8,115,000	8,500,000	8,640,000	7,953,000	10,244,000	9,189,000	9,820,000	11,002,000
Current Liabilities	1,905,000	1,650,000	1,718,000	1,611,000	3,265,000	1,778,000	1,917,000	2,332,000
Long-Term Obligations	2,204,000	2,277,000	2,323,000	2,224,000	2,258,000	4,136,000	4,626,000	4,939,000
Total Liabilities	5,633,000	5,889,000	6,020,000	5,433,000	7,624,000	7,902,000	8,378,000	9,224,000
Stockholders' Equity	2,482,000	2,611,000	2,620,000	2,520,000	2,620,000	1,287,000	1,442,000	1,778,000
Shares Outstanding	224,690	228,700	232,682	232,994	240,213	236,370	237,080	243,416
Statistical Record								
Return on Assets %	N.M.	N.M.	1.88	3.70	6.55	3.42	0.89	3.20
Return on Equity %	N.M.	N.M.	6.58	13.11	32.56	23.83	5.78	17.19
EBITDA Margin %	10.18	13.51	14.36	13.99	13.13	10.82	7.30	8.78
Net Margin %	5.04	5.42	5.85	3.59	7.61	3.38	0.90	2.79
Asset Turnover	0.86	0.91	0.94	1.03	0.86	1.01	0.99	1.15
Current Ratio	1.96	1.83	1.83	1.84	1.83	2.00	2.00	2.16
Debt to Equity	0.89	0.87	0.89	0.88	0.86	3.21	3.21	2.78
Price Range	27.30-17.37	33.53-17.37	33.53-18.14	35.29-18.14	33.42-19.21	20.33-7.91	24.40-9.33	28.88-21.22
P/E Ratio	...	...	43.55-23.56	25.39-13.05	12.80-7.36	14.95-5.82	64.21-24.55	22.05-16.20
Average Yield %	3.04	2.72	2.46	2.25	1.93	3.38	2.71	1.98

Address: 10003 Woodloch Forest Drive, The Woodlands, TX 77380
Telephone: 281-719-6000

Web Site: www.huntsman.com
Officers: Peter R. Huntsman - Chairman, President, Chief Executive Officer Sean Douglas - Vice President, Treasurer, Executive Vice President, Chief Financial Officer

Auditors: DELOITTE & TOUCHE LLP
Investor Contact: 801-584-5959
Transfer Agents: Computershare, Providence, RI

HYATT HOTELS CORP

Exchange	Symbol	Price	52Wk Range	Yield	P/E
NYS	H	$89.71 (12/31/2019)	90.70-64.57	0.85	19.25

*7 Year Price Score 104.59 *NYSE Composite Index=100 *12 Month Price Score 102.93

Interim Earnings (Per Share)

Qtr.	Mar	Jun	Sep	Dec
2016	0.25	0.49	0.47	0.31
2017	0.54	0.68	0.14	0.61
2018	3.40	0.66	2.09	0.47
2019	0.59	0.80	2.80	...

Interim Dividends (Per Share)

Amt	Decl	Ex	Rec	Pay
0.19Q	02/13/2019	02/26/2019	02/27/2019	03/11/2019
0.19Q	05/17/2019	05/28/2019	05/29/2019	06/10/2019
0.19Q	07/31/2019	08/26/2019	08/27/2019	09/09/2019
0.19Q	10/30/2019	11/25/2019	11/26/2019	12/09/2019

Indicated Div: $0.76

Valuation Analysis / Institutional Holding

Forecast EPS	$1.81	No of Institutions
	(00/22/2020)	300
Market Cap	$9.3 Billion	Shares
Book Value	$3.8 Billion	42,287,784
Price/Book	2.47	% Held
Price/Sales	1.90	31.90

Business Summary: Hotels, Restaurants & Travel (MIC: 2.2.1 SIC: 7011 NAIC: 721110)

Hyatt Hotels is a hospitality company engaged in the development, ownership, operation, management, franchising, licensing or provision of services to a portfolio of properties, consisting of full service hotels, select service hotels, resorts, and other properties, including spas and fitness studios, timeshare, fractional, and other forms of residential and vacation properties. Co. also manages, provides services to, or licenses its trademarks with respect to residential ownership units that are often adjacent to a Hyatt-branded hotel. Additionally, for condominium ownership units, Co. provides services and/or manage the rental programs or homeowner associations associated with such units.

Recent Developments: For the quarter ended Sep 30 2019, net income increased 24.9% to US$296.0 million from US$237.0 million in the year-earlier quarter. Revenues were US$1.22 billion, up 13.1% from US$1.07 billion the year before. Direct operating expenses rose 18.6% to US$1.01 billion from US$849.0 million in the comparable period the year before. Indirect operating expenses increased 3.1% to US$168.0 million from US$163.0 million in the equivalent prior-year period.

Prospects: Our evaluation of Hyatt Hotels Corp. as of October 4th, 2019 is the result of our systematic analysis on three basic characteristics: earnings strength, relative valuation, and recent stock price movement. The company has produced a positive trend in earnings per share over the past 5 quarters. However, recent analyst estimates for the company have been mixed and H has posted results that exceeded analysts' expectations. Based on operating earnings yield, the company is fairly valued when compared to all of the companies we cover. Share price changes over the past year indicates that H will perform well over the near term.

Financial Data

(US$ in Thousands)	9 Mos	6 Mos	3 Mos	12/31/2018	12/31/2017	12/31/2016	12/31/2015	12/31/2014
Earnings Per Share	4.66	3.95	3.81	6.68	1.98	1.52	0.86	2.23
Cash Flow Per Share	4.63	4.65	2.83	3.01	4.97	3.67	3.77	3.09
Tang Book Value Per Share	28.87	27.14	26.74	25.88	22.71	24.30	24.33	26.44
Dividends Per Share	0.720	0.680	0.640	0.600	...	...	...	...
Dividend Payout %	15.45	17.22	16.80	8.98	...	...	...	...
Income Statement								
Total Revenue	3,745,000	2,530,000	1,241,000	4,454,000	4,685,000	4,429,000	4,328,000	4,415,000
EBITDA	623,000	197,000	89,000	1,314,000	620,000	574,000	603,000	869,000
Depn & Amortn	29,000	26,000	20,000	312,000	335,000	315,000	289,000	324,000
Income Before Taxes	595,000	185,000	86,000	943,000	353,000	221,000	258,000	500,000
Income Taxes	148,000	39,000	20,000	182,000	323,000	85,000	70,000	179,000
Net Income	445,000	149,000	63,000	769,000	249,000	204,000	124,000	344,000
Average Shares	105,918	106,953	107,519	115,125	126,346	133,939	143,999	154,350
Balance Sheet								
Current Assets	1,476,000	1,304,000	1,302,000	1,345,000	1,327,000	1,139,000	1,124,000	1,709,000
Total Assets	8,129,000	8,082,000	8,035,000	7,643,000	7,672,000	7,749,000	7,596,000	8,143,000
Current Liabilities	1,044,000	1,114,000	1,105,000	1,061,000	966,000	924,000	1,107,000	730,000
Long-Term Obligations	1,612,000	1,621,000	1,621,000	1,621,000	1,623,000	1,440,000	1,445,000	1,381,000
Total Liabilities	4,373,000	4,440,000	4,413,000	3,973,000	4,137,000	3,846,000	3,605,000	3,516,000
Stockholders' Equity	3,756,000	3,642,000	3,622,000	3,670,000	3,535,000	3,903,000	3,991,000	4,627,000
Shares Outstanding	103,249	104,982	105,517	106,623	118,984	130,815	136,233	149,081
Statistical Record								
Return on Assets %	6.17	5.59	5.26	10.04	3.23	2.65	1.58	4.22
Return on Equity %	12.73	11.72	10.78	21.35	6.70	5.15	2.88	7.32
EBITDA Margin %	16.64	7.79	7.17	29.50	13.23	12.96	13.93	19.68
Net Margin %	11.88	5.89	5.08	17.27	5.31	4.61	2.87	7.79
Asset Turnover	0.62	0.62	0.57	0.58	0.61	0.58	0.55	0.54
Current Ratio	1.41	1.17	1.18	1.27	1.37	1.23	1.02	2.34
Debt to Equity	0.43	0.45	0.45	0.44	0.41	0.37	0.26	0.30
Price Range	80.68-63.49	83.01-63.49	84.24-63.49	84.24-63.49	73.88-50.64	57.69-35.77	61.76-45.86	63.74-45.88
P/E Ratio	17.31-13.62	21.02-16.07	22.11-16.66	12.61-9.50	37.31-25.58	37.95-23.53	71.81-53.33	28.58-20.57
Average Yield %	0.99	0.92	0.86	0.78	...	...	...	...

Address: 150 North Riverside Plaza, 8th Floor, Chicago, IL 60606 **Telephone:** 312-750-1234	**Web Site:** www.hyatt.com **Officers:** Thomas J. Pritzker - Executive Chairman Mark S. Hoplamazian - President, Chief Executive Officer	**Auditors:** DELOITTE & TOUCHE LLP **Investor Contact:** 312-750-1234 **Transfer Agents:** Wells Fargo Shareowner Services, South St. Paul, MN

IDACORP INC

Exchange	Symbol	Price	52Wk Range	Yield	P/E
NYS	IDA	$106.80 (12/31/2019)	113.25-89.94	2.51	25.49

*7 Year Price Score 113.03 *NYSE Composite Index=100   *12 Month Price Score 97.09

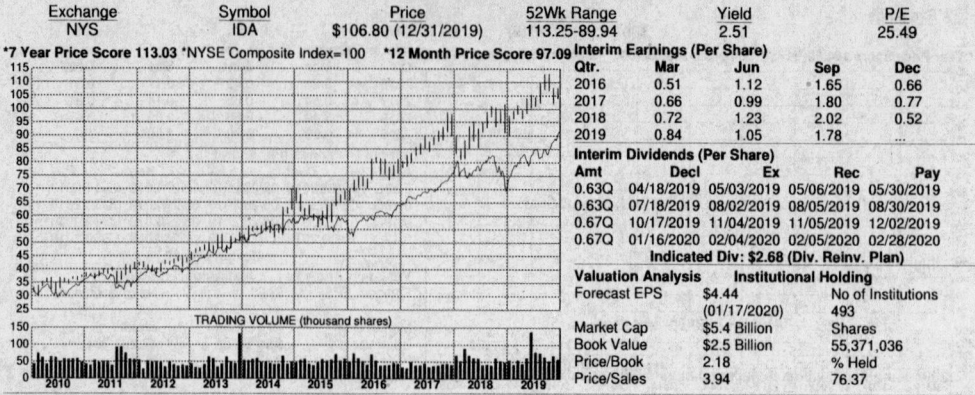

Interim Earnings (Per Share)

Qtr.	Mar	Jun	Sep	Dec
2016	0.51	1.12	1.65	0.66
2017	0.66	0.99	1.80	0.77
2018	0.72	1.23	2.02	0.52
2019	0.84	1.05	1.78	...

Interim Dividends (Per Share)

Amt	Decl	Ex	Rec	Pay
0.63Q	04/18/2019	05/03/2019	05/06/2019	05/30/2019
0.63Q	07/18/2019	08/02/2019	08/05/2019	08/30/2019
0.67Q	10/17/2019	11/04/2019	11/05/2019	12/02/2019
0.67Q	01/16/2020	02/04/2020	02/05/2020	02/28/2020

Indicated Div: $2.68 (Div. Reinv. Plan)

Valuation Analysis   Institutional Holding

Forecast EPS	$4.44	No of Institutions	
	(01/17/2020)	493	
Market Cap	$5.4 Billion	Shares	
Book Value	$2.5 Billion	55,371,036	
Price/Book	2.18	% Held	
Price/Sales	3.94	76.37	

Business Summary: Electric Utilities (MIC: 3.1.1 SIC: 4911 NAIC: 221122)

Idacorp is a holding company. Co.'s principal operating subsidiary, Idaho Power Company (Idaho Power) is an electric utility engaged in the generation, transmission, distribution, sale, and purchase of electric energy and capacity. Idaho Energy Resources Co., a joint venturer in Bridger Coal Company, mines and supplies coal to the Jim Bridger generating plant owned in part by Idaho Power. Co.'s other subsidiaries include: IDACORP Financial Services, Inc., an investor in affordable housing and other real estate investments; and Ida-West Energy Company, an operator of small hydroelectric generation projects.

Recent Developments: For the quarter ended Sep 30 2019, net income decreased 12.1% to US$90.2 million from US$102.6 million in the year-earlier quarter. Revenues were US$386.3 million, down 5.5% from US$408.8 million the year before. Operating income was US$114.2 million versus US$115.2 million in the prior-year quarter, a decrease of 0.9%. Direct operating expenses declined 7.5% to US$262.3 million from US$283.5 million in the comparable period the year before. Indirect operating expenses decreased 2.0% to US$9.9 million from US$10.1 million in the equivalent prior-year period.

Prospects: Our evaluation of Idacorp Inc. as of October 4th, 2019 is the result of our systematic analysis on three basic characteristics: earnings strength, relative valuation, and recent stock price movement. The company has produced a positive trend in earnings per share over the past 5 quarters. However, recent analyst estimates for the company have been unchanged, while IDA has posted results that fell short of analysts' expectations. Based on operating earnings yield, the company is fairly valued when compared to all of the companies we cover. Share price changes over the past year indicates that IDA will perform in line with the market over the near term.

Financial Data

(US$ in Thousands)	9 Mos	6 Mos	3 Mos	12/31/2018	12/31/2017	12/31/2016	12/31/2015	12/31/2014
Earnings Per Share	4.19	4.43	4.61	4.49	4.21	3.94	3.87	3.85
Cash Flow Per Share	8.17	9.13	9.05	9.75	8.70	6.89	7.03	7.27
Tang Book Value Per Share	48.89	47.70	47.24	47.04	44.68	42.55	40.65	38.58
Dividends Per Share	2.520	2.480	2.440	2.400	2.240	2.080	1.920	1.760
Dividend Payout %	60.14	55.98	52.93	53.45	53.21	52.79	49.61	45.71
Income Statement								
Total Revenue	1,053,535	667,214	350,319	1,370,752	1,349,486	1,262,020	1,270,289	1,282,524
EBITDA	394,918	229,532	108,823	477,993	492,439	447,342	449,151	410,942
Depn & Amortn	126,006	83,406	42,234	165,190	162,091	143,661	138,110	132,987
Income Before Taxes	203,216	102,002	44,572	232,460	250,474	221,646	229,107	198,154
Income Taxes	26,506	11,344	4,316	17,386	48,660	36,429	45,760	16,772
Net Income	185,718	95,842	42,686	226,801	212,419	198,288	194,679	193,480
Average Shares	50,558	50,507	50,518	50,510	50,424	50,373	50,292	50,199
Balance Sheet								
Current Assets	604,165	599,453	576,292	597,640	443,601	440,312	462,036	442,101
Total Assets	6,502,319	6,460,853	6,387,815	6,382,754	6,045,405	6,289,897	6,023,314	5,716,853
Current Liabilities	291,082	295,582	273,466	258,592	200,749	249,715	242,306	241,781
Long-Term Obligations	1,836,395	1,835,521	1,835,155	1,834,788	1,746,123	1,744,614	1,725,410	1,614,438
Total Liabilities	4,038,198	4,057,048	4,007,579	4,012,394	3,794,020	4,135,991	3,965,430	3,763,652
Stockholders' Equity	2,464,121	2,403,805	2,380,236	2,370,360	2,251,385	2,153,906	2,057,884	1,953,201
Shares Outstanding	50,397	50,397	50,385	50,393	50,392	50,396	50,340	50,269
Statistical Record								
Return on Assets %	3.31	3.54	3.69	3.65	3.44	3.21	3.32	3.49
Return on Equity %	8.77	9.55	10.06	9.81	9.64	9.39	9.71	10.17
EBITDA Margin %	37.49	34.40	31.06	34.87	36.49	35.45	35.36	32.04
Net Margin %	17.63	14.36	12.18	16.55	15.74	15.71	15.33	15.09
Asset Turnover	0.21	0.22	0.22	0.22	0.22	0.20	0.22	0.23
Current Ratio	2.08	2.03	2.11	2.31	2.21	1.76	1.91	1.83
Debt to Equity	0.75	0.76	0.77	0.77	0.78	0.81	0.84	0.83
Price Range	113.17-89.94	105.62-89.94	101.78-84.98	101.78-81.05	98.81-77.98	81.87-65.73	70.34-55.77	69.99-50.77
P/E Ratio	27.01-21.47	23.84-20.30	22.08-18.43	22.67-18.05	23.47-18.52	20.78-16.68	18.18-14.41	18.18-13.19
Average Yield %	2.51	2.53	2.56	2.61	2.58	2.77	3.05	3.13

Address: 1221 W. Idaho Street, Boise, ID 83702-5627 **Telephone:** 208-388-2200	**Web Site:** www.idacorpinc.com **Officers:** Richard J. Dahl - Chairman Darrel T. Anderson - President, Chief Executive Officer, Executive Vice President, Chief Financial Officer	**Auditors:** Deloitte & Touche LLP **Investor Contact:** 208-388-2664 **Transfer Agents:** Wells Fargo Shareowner Services, Mendota Heights, MN

IDEX CORPORATION

Exchange	Symbol	Price	52Wk Range	Yield	P/E
NYS	IEX	$172.00 (12/31/2019)	173.37-121.42	1.16	30.94

*7 Year Price Score 128.62 *NYSE Composite Index=100 *12 Month Price Score 98.96

Interim Earnings (Per Share)

Qtr.	Mar	Jun	Sep	Dec
2016	0.89	0.99	0.91	0.75
2017	0.99	1.08	1.08	1.21
2018	1.27	1.38	1.37	1.27
2019	1.44	1.48	1.37	...

Interim Dividends (Per Share)

Amt	Decl	Ex	Rec	Pay
0.50Q	05/10/2019	05/16/2019	05/17/2019	05/31/2019
0.50Q	06/18/2019	07/15/2019	07/16/2019	07/31/2019
0.50Q	09/26/2019	10/15/2019	10/16/2019	10/31/2019
0.50Q	11/13/2019	01/14/2020	01/15/2020	01/30/2020

Indicated Div: $2.00 (Div. Reinv. Plan)

Valuation Analysis / **Institutional Holding**

Forecast EPS	$5.82	No of Institutions
	(01/17/2020)	607
Market Cap	$13.1 Billion	Shares
Book Value	$2.2 Billion	89,791,248
Price/Book	6.05	% Held
Price/Sales	5.23	96.61

Business Summary: Industrial Machinery & Equipment (MIC: 7.2.1 SIC: 3561 NAIC: 333911)

IDEX is an applied solutions business. Co. has three reportable business segments: Fluid and Metering Technologies, which designs, produces and distributes positive displacement pumps, flow meters, injectors and other fluid-handling pump modules and systems and provides flow monitoring and other services; Health and Science Technologies, which designs, produces and distributes a range of precision fluidics, rotary lobe pumps, centrifugal and positive displacement pumps, roll compaction and drying systems; and Fire and Safety/Diversified Products, which designs, produces and distributes firefighting pumps, valves, rescue tools, lifting bags and other components and systems.

Recent Developments: For the quarter ended Sep 30 2019, net income decreased 1.1% to US$105.2 million from US$106.4 million in the year-earlier quarter. Revenues were US$624.2 million, up 0.2% from US$622.9 million the year before. Operating income was US$141.8 million versus US$145.1 million in the prior-year quarter, a decrease of 2.3%. Direct operating expenses declined 0.1% to US$342.3 million from US$342.7 million in the comparable period the year before. Indirect operating expenses increased 3.8% to US$140.2 million from US$135.1 million in the equivalent prior-year period.

Prospects: Our evaluation of IDEX Corp. as of October 4th, 2019 is the result of our systematic analysis on three basic characteristics: earnings strength, relative valuation, and recent stock price movement. The company has managed to produce a neutral trend in earnings per share over the past 5 quarters. However, recent analyst estimates for the company have been reduced while IEX has posted results that exceeded analysts' expectations. Based on operating earnings yield, the company is fairly valued when compared to all of the companies we cover. Share price changes over the past year indicates that IEX will perform well over the near term.

Financial Data

(US$ in Thousands)	9 Mos	6 Mos	3 Mos	12/31/2018	12/31/2017	12/31/2016	12/31/2015	12/31/2014
Earnings Per Share	5.56	5.56	5.46	5.29	4.36	3.53	3.62	3.45
Cash Flow Per Share	7.01	6.72	6.58	6.27	5.68	5.26	4.67	4.62
Tang Book Value Per Share	N.M.	0.65	N.M.	N.M.	N.M.	N.M.	N.M.	N.M.
Dividends Per Share	1.860	1.790	1.720	1.660	1.450	1.340	1.240	1.070
Dividend Payout %	33.45	32.19	31.50	31.38	33.26	37.96	34.25	31.01
Income Statement								
Total Revenue	1,888,576	1,264,330	622,231	2,483,666	2,287,312	2,113,043	2,020,668	2,147,767
EBITDA	472,889	322,205	157,256	611,568	546,064	463,166	476,407	477,522
Depn & Amortn	28,760	18,622	9,334	38,495	45,902	49,038	42,426	43,187
Income Before Taxes	410,867	281,651	137,001	528,939	455,273	368,512	392,345	392,440
Income Taxes	82,196	58,174	26,733	118,366	118,016	97,403	109,538	113,054
Net Income	328,671	223,477	110,268	410,573	337,257	271,109	282,807	279,386
Average Shares	76,577	76,387	76,284	77,563	77,333	76,758	77,972	80,728
Balance Sheet								
Current Assets	1,190,624	1,216,882	1,129,228	1,092,532	1,004,043	822,721	862,684	1,075,791
Total Assets	3,713,895	3,640,215	3,551,460	3,473,857	3,399,628	3,154,944	2,805,443	2,908,070
Current Liabilities	370,670	361,791	339,247	364,661	360,975	309,158	309,597	411,968
Long-Term Obligations	848,728	848,555	848,437	848,335	858,788	1,014,235	839,707	765,006
Total Liabilities	1,550,842	1,528,174	1,496,228	1,479,217	1,513,086	1,611,050	1,362,152	1,421,619
Stockholders' Equity	2,163,053	2,112,041	2,055,232	1,994,640	1,886,542	1,543,894	1,443,291	1,486,451
Shares Outstanding	76,036	75,843	75,702	75,952	76,693	76,440	76,534	78,765
Statistical Record								
Return on Assets %	11.74	12.02	11.99	11.95	10.29	9.07	9.90	9.64
Return on Equity %	20.21	20.87	20.72	21.16	19.66	18.10	19.31	18.26
EBITDA Margin %	25.04	25.48	25.27	24.62	23.87	21.92	23.58	22.23
Net Margin %	17.40	17.68	17.72	16.53	14.74	12.83	14.00	13.01
Asset Turnover	0.69	0.70	0.71	0.72	0.70	0.71	0.71	0.74
Current Ratio	3.21	3.36	3.33	3.00	2.78	2.66	2.79	2.61
Debt to Equity	0.39	0.40	0.41	0.43	0.46	0.66	0.58	0.51
Price Range	173.37-118.64	172.14-118.64	156.77-118.64	156.77-118.64	135.57-89.34	95.64-68.33	80.00-68.86	81.58-66.43
P/E Ratio	31.18-21.34	30.96-21.34	28.71-21.73	29.64-22.43	31.09-20.49	27.09-19.36	22.10-19.02	23.65-19.26
Average Yield %	1.24	1.23	1.22	1.18	1.31	1.58	1.64	1.43

Address: 1925 West Field Court, Suite 200, Lake Forest, IL 60045 **Telephone:** 847-498-7070	**Web Site:** www.idexcorp.com **Officers:** Andrew K. Silvernail - Chairman, President, Chief Executive Officer William K. Grogan - Senior Vice President, Chief Financial Officer	**Auditors:** DELOITTE & TOUCHE LLP **Investor Contact:** 847-498-7070 **Transfer Agents:** Computershare, Providence, RI

ILLINOIS TOOL WORKS, INC.

Exchange	Symbol	Price	52Wk Range	Yield	P/E	Div Acheiver
NYS	ITW	$179.63 (12/31/2019)	181.28-123.45	2.38	23.67	56 Years

*7 Year Price Score 110.17 *NYSE Composite Index=100 *12 Month Price Score 109.08

Interim Earnings (Per Share)
Qtr.	Mar	Jun	Sep	Dec
2016	1.29	1.46	1.50	1.45
2017	1.54	1.69	1.85	(0.21)
2018	1.90	1.97	1.90	1.83
2019	1.81	1.91	2.04	...

Interim Dividends (Per Share)
Amt	Decl	Ex	Rec	Pay
1.00Q	02/15/2019	03/28/2019	03/29/2019	04/10/2019
1.00Q	05/03/2019	06/27/2019	06/28/2019	07/10/2019
1.07Q	08/02/2019	09/27/2019	09/30/2019	10/09/2019
1.07Q	10/28/2019	12/30/2019	12/31/2019	01/15/2020

Indicated Div: $4.28 (Div. Reinv. Plan)

Valuation Analysis
		Institutional Holding	
Forecast EPS	$7.61	No of Institutions	
	(01/17/2020)	1700	
Market Cap	$57.7 Billion	Shares	
Book Value	$3.0 Billion	353,604,000	
Price/Book	19.46	% Held	
Price/Sales	4.06	73.03	

Business Summary: Industrial Machinery & Equipment (MIC: 7.2.1 SIC: 3569 NAIC: 333999)

Illinois Tool Works is a global manufacturer of industrial products and equipment. Co.'s segments include: Automotive Original Equipment Manufacturer, which produces components and fasteners for automotive-related applications; Food Equipment, which is engaged in commercial food equipment; Test and Measurement and Electronics, which produces equipment, consumables, and related software for testing and measuring of materials and structures, as well as equipment and consumables used in the production of electronic subassemblies and microelectronics; and Welding, which produces arc welding equipment, consumables and accessories for an array of industrial and commercial applications.

Recent Developments: For the quarter ended Sep 30 2019, net income increased 3.4% to US$660.0 million from US$638.0 million in the year-earlier quarter. Revenues were US$3.48 billion, down 3.7% from US$3.61 billion the year before. Operating income was US$868.0 million versus US$889.0 million in the prior-year quarter, a decrease of 2.4%. Direct operating expenses declined 4.2% to US$2.01 billion from US$2.10 billion in the comparable period the year before. Indirect operating expenses decreased 3.8% to US$604.0 million from US$628.0 million in the equivalent prior-year period.

Prospects: Our evaluation of Illinois Tool Works Inc. as of October 4th, 2019 is the result of our systematic analysis on three basic characteristics: earnings strength, relative valuation, and recent stock price movement. The company has managed to produce a neutral trend in earnings per share over the past 5 quarters. However, recent analyst estimates for the company have been reduced and ITW has posted results that fell short of analysts' expectations. Based on operating earnings yield, the company is fairly valued when compared to all of the companies we cover. Share price changes over the past year indicates that ITW will perform in line with the market over the near term.

Financial Data
(US$ in Thousands)	9 Mos	6 Mos	3 Mos	12/31/2018	12/31/2017	12/31/2016	12/31/2015	12/31/2014
Earnings Per Share	7.59	7.45	7.51	7.60	4.86	5.70	5.13	7.28
Cash Flow Per Share	9.40	9.09	8.83	8.39	6.98	6.47	6.25	4.02
Tang Book Value Per Share	N.M.	N.M.	N.M.	N.M.	N.M.	N.M.	N.M.	0.92
Dividends Per Share	4.070	4.000	3.780	3.560	2.860	2.400	2.070	1.810
Dividend Payout %	53.62	53.69	50.33	46.84	58.85	42.11	40.35	24.86
Income Statement								
Total Revenue	10,640,000	7,161,000	3,552,000	14,768,000	14,314,000	13,599,000	13,405,000	14,484,000
EBITDA	2,948,000	1,950,000	963,000	4,077,000	3,947,000	3,516,000	3,372,000	265,135,000
Depn & Amortn	321,000	217,000	110,000	461,000	462,000	470,000	475,000	262,242,000
Income Before Taxes	2,457,000	1,615,000	790,000	3,394,000	3,270,000	2,847,000	2,723,000	2,708,000
Income Taxes	577,000	395,000	193,000	831,000	1,583,000	873,000	820,000	809,000
Net Income	1,880,000	1,220,000	597,000	2,563,000	1,687,000	2,035,000	1,899,000	2,946,000
Average Shares	324,000	326,600	329,600	337,100	346,800	357,100	370,100	404,600
Balance Sheet								
Current Assets	6,245,000	6,289,000	6,075,000	5,778,000	7,278,000	6,123,000	6,720,000	8,076,000
Total Assets	14,960,000	15,187,000	15,326,000	14,870,000	16,780,000	15,201,000	15,729,000	17,678,000
Current Liabilities	2,223,000	2,188,000	3,961,000	3,542,000	3,053,000	2,760,000	2,368,000	3,533,000
Long-Term Obligations	7,643,000	7,809,000	5,981,000	6,029,000	7,478,000	7,177,000	6,896,000	5,981,000
Total Liabilities	11,994,000	12,096,000	12,130,000	11,616,000	12,195,000	10,947,000	10,505,000	10,859,000
Stockholders' Equity	2,966,000	3,091,000	3,196,000	3,254,000	4,585,000	4,254,000	5,224,000	6,819,000
Shares Outstanding	321,400	323,500	325,800	328,100	341,500	346,900	363,710	382,900
Statistical Record								
Return on Assets %	16.43	16.05	15.93	16.20	10.55	13.12	11.37	15.65
Return on Equity %	76.43	71.70	68.20	65.39	38.17	42.82	31.54	35.66
EBITDA Margin %	27.71	27.23	27.11	27.61	27.57	25.85	25.15	1,830.54
Net Margin %	17.67	17.04	16.81	17.36	11.79	14.96	14.17	20.34
Asset Turnover	0.94	0.93	0.93	0.93	0.90	0.88	0.80	0.77
Current Ratio	2.81	2.87	1.53	1.63	2.38	2.22	2.84	2.29
Debt to Equity	2.58	2.53	1.87	1.85	1.63	1.69	1.32	0.88
Price Range	159.85-118.95	158.33-118.95	159.40-118.95	178.88-118.95	169.25-121.61	127.93-81.05	99.81-80.09	97.21-76.78
P/E Ratio	21.06-15.67	21.25-15.97	21.23-15.84	23.54-15.65	34.83-25.02	22.44-14.22	19.46-15.61	13.35-10.55
Average Yield %	2.84	2.85	2.70	2.43	2.00	2.21	2.24	2.10

Address: 155 Harlem Avenue, Glenview, IL 60025 Telephone: 847-724-7500	Web Site: www.itw.com Officers: E. Scott Santi - Chairman, Chief Executive Officer, Vice-Chairman, President, Chief Operating Officer Christopher A. O'Herlihy - Vice-Chairman, Executive Vice President	Auditors: Deloitte & Touche LLP Investor Contact: 847-657-4104 Transfer Agents: Computershare Trust Company, N.A., Providence, RI

INTERCONTINENTAL EXCHANGE INC

Exchange	Symbol	Price	52Wk Range	Yield	P/E
NYS	ICE	$92.55 (12/31/2019)	94.89-72.15	1.19	25.08

*7 Year Price Score 123.39 *NYSE Composite Index=100 *12 Month Price Score 102.59

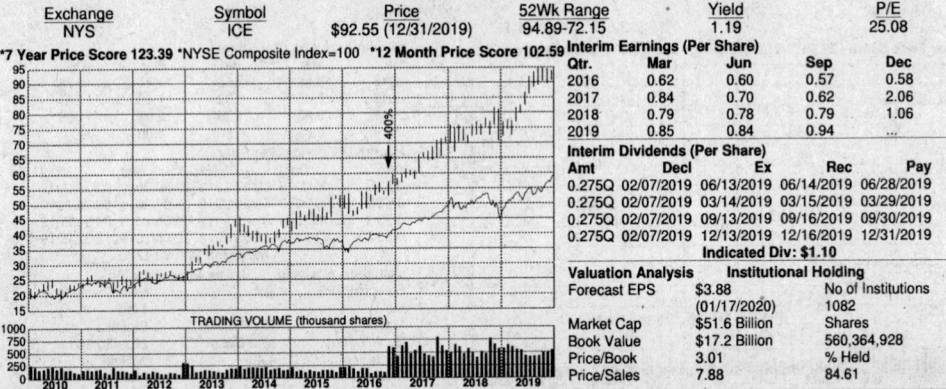

Interim Earnings (Per Share)

Qtr.	Mar	Jun	Sep	Dec
2016	0.62	0.60	0.57	0.58
2017	0.84	0.70	0.62	2.06
2018	0.79	0.78	0.79	1.06
2019	0.85	0.84	0.94	...

Interim Dividends (Per Share)

Amt	Decl	Ex	Rec	Pay
0.275Q	02/07/2019	06/13/2019	06/14/2019	06/28/2019
0.275Q	02/07/2019	03/14/2019	03/15/2019	03/29/2019
0.275Q	02/07/2019	09/13/2019	09/16/2019	09/30/2019
0.275Q	02/07/2019	12/13/2019	12/16/2019	12/31/2019

Indicated Div: $1.10

Valuation Analysis — **Institutional Holding**

Forecast EPS	$3.88	No of Institutions
	(01/17/2020)	1082
Market Cap	$51.6 Billion	Shares
Book Value	$17.2 Billion	560,364,928
Price/Book	3.01	% Held
Price/Sales	7.88	84.61

Business Summary: Finance Intermediaries & Services (MIC: 5.5.1 SIC: 6231 NAIC: 523210)

Intercontinental Exchange is a holding company. Through its subsidiaries, Co. is a global operator of regulated exchanges, clearing houses and listings venues, and a provider of data services for commodity, financial, fixed income and equity markets. Co. operates regulated marketplaces for listing, trading and clearing a range of derivatives contracts and securities across various asset classes, including energy and agricultural commodities, metals, interest rates, equities, exchange traded funds, credit derivatives, bonds and currencies. Co. also provides data services to support the trading, investment, risk management and connectivity needs of customers.

Recent Developments: For the quarter ended Sep 30 2019, net income increased 15.5% to US$537.0 million from US$465.0 million in the year-earlier quarter. Revenues were US$1.66 billion, up 13.7% from US$1.46 billion the year before. Operating income was US$706.0 million versus US$602.0 million in the prior-year quarter, an increase of 17.3%. Direct operating expenses rose 24.3% to US$327.0 million from US$263.0 million in the comparable period the year before. Indirect operating expenses increased 5.4% to US$630.0 million from US$598.0 million in the equivalent prior-year period.

Prospects: Our evaluation of IntercontinentalExchange Inc. as of October 4th, 2019 is the result of our systematic analysis on three basic characteristics: earnings strength, relative valuation, and recent stock price movement. The company has managed to produce a neutral trend in earnings per share over the past 5 quarters. However, recent analyst estimates for the company have been raised and ICE has posted results that exceeded analysts' expectations. Based on operating earnings yield, the company is fairly valued when compared to all of the companies we cover. Share price changes over the past year indicates that ICE will perform well over the near term.

Financial Data

(US$ in Thousands)	9 Mos	6 Mos	3 Mos	12/31/2018	12/31/2017	12/31/2016	12/31/2015	12/31/2014
Earnings Per Share	3.69	3.54	3.48	3.43	4.23	2.37	2.28	1.71
Cash Flow Per Share	4.79	4.76	4.60	4.41	3.54	3.60	2.36	2.57
Dividends Per Share	1.065	1.030	0.995	0.960	0.800	0.680	0.580	0.520
Dividend Payout %	28.86	29.10	28.59	27.99	18.91	28.69	25.46	30.41
Income Statement								
Total Revenue	4,880,000	3,217,000	1,583,000	6,276,000	5,834,000	5,958,000	4,682,000	4,221,000
EBITDA	2,554,000	1,692,000	846,000	3,035,000	2,961,000	2,462,000	1,963,000	1,685,000
Depn & Amortn	473,000	315,000	158,000	293,000	257,000	255,000	213,000	182,000
Income Before Taxes	1,894,000	1,254,000	626,000	2,520,000	2,517,000	2,029,000	1,653,000	1,407,000
Income Taxes	387,000	284,000	134,000	500,000	(25,000)	580,000	358,000	402,000
Net Income	1,485,000	956,000	484,000	1,988,000	2,514,000	1,422,000	1,274,000	981,000
Average Shares	563,000	566,000	570,000	579,000	594,000	599,000	560,000	575,000
Balance Sheet								
Current Assets	68,871,000	64,372,000	67,485,000	66,692,000	53,562,000	57,133,000	53,313,000	50,245,000
Total Assets	95,339,000	90,930,000	93,857,000	92,791,000	78,264,000	82,003,000	77,987,000	68,279,000
Current Liabilities	68,534,000	64,131,000	67,035,000	66,108,000	54,171,000	58,617,000	54,743,000	50,539,000
Long-Term Obligations	6,496,000	6,494,000	6,492,000	6,490,000	4,267,000	3,871,000	4,717,000	2,247,000
Total Liabilities	78,178,000	73,815,000	76,751,000	75,590,000	61,340,000	66,286,000	63,179,000	55,919,000
Stockholders' Equity	17,161,000	17,115,000	17,106,000	17,201,000	16,924,000	15,717,000	14,808,000	12,360,000
Shares Outstanding	558,000	561,000	565,000	569,000	583,000	595,000	595,000	565,000
Statistical Record								
Return on Assets %	2.30	2.33	2.28	2.32	3.14	1.77	1.74	1.47
Return on Equity %	12.33	11.94	11.78	11.65	15.40	9.29	9.38	7.87
EBITDA Margin %	52.34	52.60	53.44	48.36	50.75	41.32	41.93	39.92
Net Margin %	30.43	29.72	30.57	31.68	43.09	23.87	27.21	23.24
Asset Turnover	0.07	0.07	0.07	0.07	0.07	0.07	0.06	0.06
Current Ratio	1.00	1.00	1.01	1.01	0.99	0.97	0.97	0.99
Debt to Equity	0.38	0.38	0.38	0.38	0.25	0.25	0.32	0.18
Price Range	94.89-70.68	86.77-70.68	81.72-69.82	81.72-67.00	72.07-56.22	59.66-45.99	52.83-40.97	45.56-36.69
P/E Ratio	25.72-19.15	24.51-19.97	23.48-20.06	23.83-19.53	17.04-13.29	25.17-19.41	23.17-17.97	26.65-21.46
Average Yield %	1.31	1.33	1.34	1.33	1.29	1.26	1.30	1.23	1.28

Address: 5660 New Northside Drive, Atlanta, GA 30328	Web Site: www.theice.com	Auditors: Ernst & Young LLP
Telephone: 770-857-4700	Officers: Jeffrey C. Sprecher - Chairman, Chief Executive Officer Charles A. Vice - President, Chief Operating Officer, Vice-Chairman	Investor Contact: 770-857-4726
Fax: 770-937-0020		Transfer Agents: Computershare Trust Company, N.A., Providence, RI

INGERSOLL-RAND PLC

Exchange	Symbol	Price	52Wk Range	Yield	P/E
NYS	IR	$132.92 (12/31/2019)	135.01-90.03	1.59	23.78

*7 Year Price Score 125.50 *NYSE Composite Index=100 *12 Month Price Score 104.91

Interim Earnings (Per Share)

Qtr.	Mar	Jun	Sep	Dec
2016	0.58	2.86	1.44	0.76
2017	0.45	1.38	1.43	1.81
2018	0.48	1.79	2.06	1.03
2019	0.82	1.86	1.88	...

Interim Dividends (Per Share)

Amt	Decl	Ex	Rec	Pay
0.53Q	02/06/2019	03/07/2019	03/08/2019	03/29/2019
0.53Q	04/04/2019	06/06/2019	06/07/2019	06/28/2019
0.53Q	06/10/2019	09/05/2019	09/06/2019	09/30/2019
0.53Q	10/03/2019	12/05/2019	12/06/2019	12/31/2019

Indicated Div: $2.12

Valuation Analysis

		Institutional Holding
Forecast EPS	N/A	No of Institutions
		1114
Market Cap	$31.8 Billion	Shares
Book Value	$7.2 Billion	229,480,960
Price/Book	4.40	% Held
Price/Sales	1.95	75.71

Business Summary: Industrial Machinery & Equipment (MIC: 7.2.1 SIC: 3585 NAIC: 333415)

Ingersoll-Rand provides products, services and solutions to enhance energy and air quality in homes and buildings, transport and protect food and perishables. Co.'s Climate segment includes Trane® and American Standard® Heating & Air Conditioning which provide heating, ventilation and air conditioning systems, and commercial and residential building services, parts, support and controls, energy services and building automation and transport temperature control solutions. Co.'s Industrial segment includes compressed air and gas systems and services, power tools, material handling systems, ARO® fluid management equipment, as well as Club Car ® golf, utility and consumer low-speed vehicles.

Recent Developments: For the quarter ended Sep 30 2019, income from continuing operations decreased 17.3% to US$439.0 million from US$531.1 million in the year-earlier quarter. Net income decreased 10.8% to US$463.4 million from US$519.4 million in the year-earlier quarter. Revenues were US$4.34 billion, up 7.8% from US$4.03 billion the year before. Operating income was US$623.2 million versus US$587.0 million in the prior-year quarter, an increase of 6.2%. Direct operating expenses rose 8.0% to US$2.94 billion from US$2.72 billion in the comparable period the year before. Indirect operating expenses increased 8.2% to US$785.3 million from US$725.6 million in the equivalent prior-year period.

Prospects: Our evaluation of Ingersoll-Rand Plc. as of October 4th, 2019 is the result of our systematic analysis on three basic characteristics: earnings strength, relative valuation, and recent stock price movement. The company has produced a positive trend in earnings per share over the past 5 quarters. However, recent analyst estimates for the company have been mixed and IR has posted results that exceeded analysts' expectations. Based on operating earnings yield, the company is fairly valued when compared to all of the companies we cover. Share price changes over the past year indicates that IR will perform well over the near term.

Financial Data

(US$ in Thousands)	9 Mos	6 Mos	3 Mos	12/31/2018	12/31/2017	12/31/2016	12/31/2015	12/31/2014
Earnings Per Share	5.59	5.77	5.70	5.35	5.05	5.65	2.48	3.40
Cash Flow Per Share	6.47	5.88	5.86	5.69	5.98	5.77	3.21	3.60
Dividends Per Share	...	...	...	1.960	1.700	1.360	1.160	1.000
Dividend Payout %	...	...	...	36.64	33.66	24.07	46.77	29.41
Income Statement								
Total Revenue	12,448,000	8,103,700	3,575,900	15,668,200	14,197,600	13,508,900	13,300,700	12,891,400
EBITDA	1,859,200	1,137,900	389,600	2,091,900	1,841,600	1,774,500	1,657,200	1,613,600
Depn & Amortn	291,800	186,900	89,300	217,300	217,300	216,700	209,500	199,900
Income Before Taxes	1,389,900	838,000	248,800	1,660,300	1,417,900	1,344,300	1,235,300	1,201,600
Income Taxes	279,200	166,300	43,000	281,300	80,200	281,500	540,800	293,700
Net Income	1,114,800	656,000	199,900	1,337,600	1,302,600	1,476,200	664,600	931,700
Average Shares	244,600	244,900	245,200	250,100	258,100	261,700	267,800	274,300
Balance Sheet								
Current Assets	6,103,100	6,351,500	7,084,700	5,732,000	6,119,100	5,579,300	4,609,400	5,707,900
Total Assets	20,306,900	20,667,600	19,781,000	17,914,900	18,173,300	17,397,400	16,738,800	17,298,500
Current Liabilities	4,776,100	5,180,200	4,488,500	4,315,700	4,828,000	3,590,300	3,648,400	3,666,100
Long-Term Obligations	4,921,900	4,920,600	5,226,500	3,740,700	2,957,000	3,709,400	3,734,800	3,741,700
Total Liabilities	13,069,300	13,537,100	12,895,200	10,892,200	11,033,000	10,753,600	10,922,100	11,311,100
Stockholders' Equity	7,237,600	7,130,500	6,885,800	7,022,700	7,140,300	6,643,800	5,816,700	5,987,400
Shares Outstanding	239,596	241,576	241,158	241,905	249,479	259,006	261,251	262,899
Statistical Record								
Return on Assets %	7.09	7.30	7.43	7.41	7.32	8.63	3.91	5.33
Return on Equity %	18.82	20.48	20.29	18.89	18.90	23.63	11.26	14.27
EBITDA Margin %	14.94	14.04	10.90	13.35	12.97	13.14	12.46	12.52
Net Margin %	8.96	8.10	5.59	8.54	9.17	10.93	5.00	7.23
Asset Turnover	0.85	0.82	0.83	0.87	0.80	0.79	0.78	0.74
Current Ratio	1.28	1.23	1.58	1.33	1.27	1.55	1.26	1.56
Debt to Equity	0.68	0.69	0.76	0.53	0.41	0.56	0.64	0.62
Price Range	128.13-86.31	126.67-86.31	107.95-80.39	105.63-80.39	95.61-74.90	78.75-48.80	70.91-50.61	64.59-53.57
P/E Ratio	22.92-15.44	21.95-14.96	18.94-14.10	19.74-15.03	18.93-14.83	13.94-8.64	28.59-20.41	19.00-15.76
Average Yield %	...	...	...	2.10	1.98	2.11	1.85	1.66

Address: 170/175 Lakeview Dr., Airside Business Park, Swords
Telephone: 018-707-400

Web Site: www.ingersollrand.com
Officers: Michael W. Lamach - Chairman, Chief Executive Officer, President, Chief Operating Officer David S. Regnery - President, Executive Vice President, Chief Operating Officer

Auditors: PricewaterhouseCoopers LLP
Transfer Agents: The Bank of New York Mellon, New York, NY

INGEVITY CORP

*7 Year Price Score N/A ***NYSE Composite Index=100** ***12 Month Price Score 89.07**

Interim Earnings (Per Share)

Qtr.	Mar	Jun	Sep	Dec
2016	0.19	0.56	(0.17)	0.24
2017	0.45	0.76	0.79	0.97
2018	0.72	1.10	1.16	0.99
2019	0.54	1.34	1.41	...

Interim Dividends (Per Share)

No Dividends Paid

Valuation Analysis | **Institutional Holding**

Forecast EPS	$4.86	No of Institutions
	(01/17/2020)	406
Market Cap	$3.7 Billion	Shares
Book Value	$443.3 Million	46,082,200
Price/Book	8.24	% Held
Price/Sales	2.88	91.56

TRADING VOLUME (thousand shares)

Business Summary: Specialty Chemicals (MIC: 8.3.2 SIC: 5169 NAIC: 424690)

Ingevity is a manufacturer of specialty chemicals and activated carbon materials. Co. reports in two business segments: Performance Materials, which manufactures and sells hardwood-based, chemically activated carbon products, produced through a technical and specialized process primarily for use in gasoline vapor emission control systems in cars, trucks, motorcycles and boats; and Performance Chemicals, which is comprised of four application areas (pavement technologies, oilfield technologies, industrial specialties, and engineered polymers), develops, manufactures, and sells a range of specialty chemicals primarily derived from co-products of the kraft pulping process and caprolactone.

Recent Developments: For the quarter ended Sep 30 2019, net income increased 15.9% to US$59.9 million from US$51.7 million in the year-earlier quarter. Revenues were US$359.9 million, up 15.6% from US$311.2 million the year before. Direct operating expenses rose 14.4% to US$220.4 million from US$192.6 million in the comparable period the year before. Indirect operating expenses increased 21.2% to US$48.6 million from US$40.1 million in the equivalent prior-year period.

Prospects: Our evaluation of Ingevity Corp. as of October 4th, 2019 is the result of our systematic analysis on three basic characteristics: earnings strength, relative valuation, and recent stock price movement. The company has generated a negative trend in earnings per share over the past 5 quarters. However, recent analyst estimates for the company have been mixed and NGVT has posted results that exceeded analysts' expectations. Based on operating earnings yield, the company is undervalued when compared to all of the companies we cover. Share price changes over the past year indicates that NGVT will perform poorly over the near term.

Financial Data

(US$ in Thousands)	9 Mos	6 Mos	3 Mos	12/31/2018	12/31/2017	12/31/2016	12/31/2015	12/31/2014
Earnings Per Share	4.28	4.03	3.79	3.97	2.97	0.83	...	...
Cash Flow Per Share	6.52	6.03	5.62	5.99	4.14	3.04	...	...
Tang Book Value Per Share	N.M.	N.M.	N.M.	1.61	5.42	2.29	...	...
Income Statement								
Total Revenue	989,500	629,600	276,800	1,133,600	972,400	908,300	968,000	1,041,000
EBITDA	270,500	159,500	52,300	293,500	226,100	138,100	187,000	246,000
Depn & Amortn	61,400	39,900	18,500	41,900	35,500	33,200	28,000	27,000
Income Before Taxes	172,800	95,400	22,700	221,800	174,800	87,000	138,000	203,000
Income Taxes	33,400	15,900	...	40,000	29,600	42,600	53,000	70,000
Net Income	139,400	79,500	22,700	169,100	126,500	35,200	80,000	129,000
Average Shares	42,643	42,202	42,237	42,601	42,529	42,271		
Balance Sheet								
Current Assets	499,000	491,600	455,000	422,700	368,700	295,200	299,000	271,000
Total Assets	2,118,800	2,129,500	2,107,200	1,315,200	929,600	832,800	782,000	718,000
Current Liabilities	208,800	216,000	198,300	183,300	153,200	136,900	97,000	139,000
Long-Term Obligations	1,294,400	1,363,300	1,403,200	741,200	444,000	481,300	80,000	86,000
Total Liabilities	1,675,500	1,728,800	1,748,500	976,500	665,700	705,800	265,000	301,000
Stockholders' Equity	443,300	400,700	358,700	338,700	263,900	127,000	517,000	417,000
Shares Outstanding	41,817	41,848	41,823	41,693	42,089	42,115		
Statistical Record								
Return on Assets %	10.64	9.94	9.58	15.07	14.36	...	10.67	...
Return on Equity %	47.39	46.32	48.94	56.12	64.72	...	17.13	...
EBITDA Margin %	27.34	25.33	18.89	25.89	23.25	15.20	19.32	23.63
Net Margin %	14.09	12.63	8.20	14.92	13.01	3.88	8.26	12.39
Asset Turnover	0.74	0.71	0.70	1.01	1.10	...	1.29	...
Current Ratio	2.39	2.28	2.29	2.31	2.41	2.16	3.08	1.95
Debt to Equity	2.92	3.40	3.91	2.19	1.68	3.79	0.15	0.21
Price Range	117.07-73.16	117.07-75.51	117.07-71.50	104.93-69.14	79.59-52.29	54.99-23.50	...	...
P/E Ratio	27.35-17.09	29.05-18.74	30.89-18.87	26.43-17.42	26.80-17.61	66.25-28.31	...	...

Address: 5255 Virginia Avenue, North Charleston, SC 29406	**Web Site:** www.ingevity.com	**Auditors:** PricewaterhouseCoopers LLP
Telephone: 843-740-2300	**Officers:** Richard B. Kelson - Chairman D. Michael Wilson - President, Chief Executive Officer	**Transfer Agents:** Wells Fargo, N.A.

INGREDION INC

Exchange	Symbol	Price	52Wk Range	Yield	P/E
NYS	INGR	$92.95 (12/31/2019)	99.15-73.25	2.71	15.81

*7 Year Price Score 74.17 ***NYSE Composite Index=100** ***12 Month Price Score 94.70**

Interim Earnings (Per Share)

Qtr.	Mar	Jun	Sep	Dec
2016	1.73	1.58	1.93	1.26
2017	1.68	1.78	2.26	1.34
2018	1.90	1.57	1.32	1.37
2019	1.48	1.56	1.47	...

Interim Dividends (Per Share)

Amt	Decl	Ex	Rec	Pay
0.625Q	03/20/2019	03/29/2019	04/01/2019	04/25/2019
0.625Q	05/15/2019	06/28/2019	07/01/2019	07/25/2019
0.63Q	09/18/2019	09/30/2019	10/01/2019	10/25/2019
0.63Q	12/27/2019	12/31/2019	01/02/2020	01/27/2020

Indicated Div: $2.52

Valuation Analysis

	Institutional Holding	
Forecast EPS	$6.52	No of Institutions
	(01/17/2020)	678
Market Cap	$6.2 Billion	Shares
Book Value	$2.6 Billion	82,517,016
Price/Book	2.39	% Held
Price/Sales	1.08	N/A

Business Summary: Food (MIC: 1.2.1 SIC: 2046 NAIC: 311221)

Ingredion provides ingredients solutions. Co. turns corn, tapioca, potatoes, grains, fruits, and vegetables into ingredients and biomaterials for the food, beverage, paper and corrugating, brewing and other industries. Co.'s product lines include starches and sweeteners, animal feed products and edible corn oil. Co.'s starch-based products include both food-grade and industrial starches, and biomaterials. Co.'s sweetener products include glucose syrups, maltose syrups, fructose corn syrup, caramel color, dextrose, polyols, maltodextrins, and glucose and syrup solids. Co.'s products are derived from the processing of corn and other starch-based materials, such as tapioca, potato, and rice.

Recent Developments: For the quarter ended Sep 30 2019, net income increased 4.1% to US$102.0 million from US$98.0 million in the year-earlier quarter. Revenues were US$1.46 billion, up 0.5% from US$1.45 billion the year before. Operating income was US$165.0 million versus US$155.0 million in the prior-year quarter, an increase of 6.5%. Direct operating expenses declined 0.3% to US$1.11 billion from US$1.12 billion in the comparable period the year before. Indirect operating expenses were unchanged at US$179.0 million versus the equivalent prior-year period.

Prospects: Our evaluation of Ingredion Inc as of October 4th, 2019 is the result of our systematic analysis on three basic characteristics: earnings strength, relative valuation, and recent stock price movement. The company has produced a positive trend in earnings per share over the past 5 quarters. However, recent analyst estimates for the company have been reduced, while INGR has posted results that exceeded analysts' expectations. Based on operating earnings yield, the company is undervalued when compared to all of the companies we cover. Share price changes over the past year indicates that INGR will perform poorly over the near term.

Financial Data

(US$ in Thousands)	9 Mos	6 Mos	3 Mos	12/31/2018	12/31/2017	12/31/2016	12/31/2015	12/31/2014
Earnings Per Share	5.88	5.73	5.74	6.17	7.06	6.55	5.51	4.74
Cash Flow Per Share	9.18	9.03	8.55	9.92	10.68	10.63	9.58	9.93
Tang Book Value Per Share	20.31	20.14	18.81	17.09	22.15	17.66	15.82	19.76
Dividends Per Share	2.505	2.500	2.475	2.450	2.200	1.900	1.740	1.680
Dividend Payout %	42.60	43.63	43.12	39.71	31.16	29.01	31.58	35.44
Income Statement								
Total Revenue	4,311,000	2,854,000	1,420,000	5,841,000	5,832,000	5,704,000	5,621,000	5,668,000
EBITDA	589,000	394,000	190,000	940,000	1,046,000	1,001,000	848,000	775,000
Depn & Amortn	158,000	103,000	51,000	247,000	209,000	196,000	194,000	195,000
Income Before Taxes	431,000	291,000	139,000	621,000	769,000	742,000	599,000	520,000
Income Taxes	120,000	82,000	37,000	167,000	237,000	246,000	187,000	157,000
Net Income	304,000	205,000	100,000	443,000	519,000	485,000	402,000	355,000
Average Shares	67,400	67,400	67,400	71,800	73,500	74,100	73,000	74,900
Balance Sheet								
Current Assets	2,342,000	2,215,000	2,170,000	2,138,000	2,415,000	2,252,000	1,950,000	2,144,000
Total Assets	6,095,000	5,998,000	5,932,000	5,728,000	6,080,000	5,782,000	5,074,000	5,091,000
Current Liabilities	957,000	894,000	901,000	946,000	957,000	978,000	742,000	721,000
Long-Term Obligations	2,001,000	1,946,000	1,957,000	1,931,000	1,744,000	1,850,000	1,819,000	1,804,000
Total Liabilities	3,502,000	3,402,000	3,410,000	3,340,000	3,189,000	3,217,000	2,930,000	2,914,000
Stockholders' Equity	2,593,000	2,596,000	2,522,000	2,388,000	2,891,000	2,565,000	2,144,000	2,177,000
Shares Outstanding	66,758	66,720	66,679	66,526	71,994	72,414	71,616	71,322
Statistical Record								
Return on Assets %	6.72	6.71	6.77	7.50	8.75	8.91	7.91	6.79
Return on Equity %	14.66	14.51	14.49	16.78	19.02	20.54	18.61	15.50
EBITDA Margin %	13.66	13.81	13.38	16.09	17.94	17.55	15.09	13.67
Net Margin %	7.05	7.18	7.04	7.58	8.90	8.50	7.15	6.26
Asset Turnover	0.97	0.98	0.97	0.99	0.98	1.05	1.11	1.08
Current Ratio	2.45	2.48	2.41	2.26	2.52	2.30	2.63	2.97
Debt to Equity	0.77	0.75	0.78	0.81	0.60	0.72	0.85	0.83
Price Range	106.19-73.25	113.20-76.16	130.92-88.35	146.04-88.35	141.71-114.09	139.64-86.60	99.34-76.49	86.85-58.88
P/E Ratio	18.06-12.46	19.76-13.29	22.81-15.39	23.67-14.32	20.07-16.16	21.32-13.22	18.03-13.88	18.32-12.42
Average Yield %	2.79	2.61	2.39	2.16	1.78	1.60	2.03	2.27

Address: 5 Westbrook Corporate Center, Westchester, IL 60154	Web Site: www.ingredion.com	Auditors: KPMG LLP
Telephone: 708-551-2600	Officers: Gregory B. Kenny - Chairman James P. (Jim) Zallie - President, Chief Executive Officer, Region Officer, Division Officer	Investor Contact: 708-551-2592
Fax: 708-551-2700		Transfer Agents: Computershare, Providence, RI

INSPERITY INC

Exchange	Symbol	Price	52Wk Range	Yield	P/E
NYS	NSP	$86.04 (12/31/2019)	144.63-68.25	1.39	22.88

*7 Year Price Score 189.19 *NYSE Composite Index=100 *12 Month Price Score 74.73

Interim Earnings (Per Share)

Qtr.	Mar	Jun	Sep	Dec
2016	0.77	0.23	0.33	0.23
2017	0.84	0.33	0.46	0.38
2018	1.18	0.58	0.86	0.59
2019	1.85	0.69	0.63	...

Interim Dividends (Per Share)

Amt	Decl	Ex	Rec	Pay
0.30Q	02/28/2019	03/13/2019	03/14/2019	03/28/2019
0.30Q	05/24/2019	06/07/2019	06/10/2019	06/24/2019
0.30Q	08/23/2019	09/06/2019	09/09/2019	09/23/2019
0.30Q	11/21/2019	12/05/2019	12/06/2019	12/20/2019

Indicated Div: $1.20

Valuation Analysis

		Institutional Holding	
Forecast EPS	$4.14	No of Institutions	465
	(01/07/2020)		
Market Cap	$3.4 Billion	Shares	
Book Value	$41.0 Million		40,308,580
Price/Book	83.96	% Held	
Price/Sales	0.82	N/A	

Business Summary: Business Services (MIC: 7.5.2 SIC: 7363 NAIC: 561330)

Insperity provides an array of human resources (HR) and business solutions. Co.'s HR services offerings are provided through its Workforce Optimization® and Workforce Synchronization™ solutions, which encompass a range of human resources functions, including payroll and employment administration, employee benefits, workers' compensation, government compliance, performance management, and training and development services, along with its cloud-based human capital management platform, its Insperity Premier™ solution. Co. also provides Workforce Acceleration, a human capital management and payroll service solution, as well as a number of other business performance solutions.

Recent Developments: For the quarter ended Sep 30 2019, net income decreased 28.6% to US$25.9 million from US$36.2 million in the year-earlier quarter. Revenues were US$1.04 billion, up 12.8% from US$925.1 million the year before. Operating income was US$34.7 million versus US$48.1 million in the prior-year quarter, a decrease of 27.8%. Direct operating expenses rose 15.0% to US$872.8 million from US$759.1 million in the comparable period the year before. Indirect operating expenses increased 15.2% to US$135.8 million from US$117.9 million in the equivalent prior-year period.

Prospects: Our evaluation of Insperity Inc. as of October 4th, 2019 is the result of our systematic analysis on three basic characteristics: earnings strength, relative valuation, and recent stock price movement. The company has generated a negative trend in earnings per share over the past 5 quarters. However, recent analyst estimates for the company have been unchanged while NSP has posted results that fell short of analysts' expectations. Based on operating earnings yield, the company is fairly valued when compared to all of the companies we cover. Share price changes over the past year indicates that NSP will perform well over the near term.

Financial Data

(US$ in Thousands)	9 Mos	6 Mos	3 Mos	12/31/2018	12/31/2017	12/31/2016	12/31/2015	12/31/2014
Earnings Per Share	3.76	3.99	3.88	3.22	2.01	1.54	0.79	0.53
Cash Flow Per Share	4.01	5.88	6.88	4.48	4.98	3.18	1.34	2.87
Tang Book Value Per Share	0.71	2.97	2.58	1.59	1.29	1.13	3.27	3.74
Dividends Per Share	1.100	1.000	0.900	0.800	1.575	0.485	0.425	1.370
Dividend Payout %	29.26	25.06	23.20	24.84	78.36	31.39	53.80	260.95
Income Statement								
Total Revenue	3,239,714	2,196,326	1,153,010	3,828,549	3,300,223	2,941,347	2,603,614	2,357,788
EBITDA	179,843	137,780	92,152	202,015	148,203	123,040	84,987	70,799
Depn & Amortn	20,929	13,599	6,691	22,979	18,262	16,734	19,401	23,278
Income Before Taxes	162,093	126,908	87,025	182,360	130,141	105,177	65,619	47,627
Income Taxes	31,389	22,063	10,736	46,947	45,739	39,186	26,229	19,623
Net Income	130,704	104,845	76,289	135,413	84,402	65,991	39,390	28,004
Average Shares	40,317	40,916	40,650	41,506	41,271	41,762	48,630	49,424
Balance Sheet								
Current Assets	893,743	919,177	980,081	866,536	778,935	640,322	542,048	569,509
Total Assets	1,292,122	1,316,995	1,350,978	1,191,816	1,063,695	907,174	784,912	796,670
Current Liabilities	761,212	769,848	850,389	772,332	726,481	600,958	487,711	496,451
Long-Term Obligations	239,400	169,400	144,400	144,400	104,400	104,400	...	...
Total Liabilities	1,251,134	1,182,106	1,231,784	1,114,140	997,374	846,649	612,457	592,574
Stockholders' Equity	40,988	134,889	119,194	77,676	66,321	60,525	172,455	204,096
Shares Outstanding	39,997	41,186	41,255	40,934	41,480	42,050	48,530	50,666
Statistical Record								
Return on Assets %	12.79	14.00	13.24	12.01	8.56	7.78	4.98	3.58
Return on Equity %	161.07	131.12	145.67	188.08	133.08	56.49	20.92	12.25
EBITDA Margin %	5.55	6.27	7.99	5.28	4.49	4.18	3.26	3.00
Net Margin %	4.03	4.77	6.62	3.54	2.56	2.24	1.51	1.19
Asset Turnover	3.46	3.45	3.25	3.39	3.35	3.47	3.29	3.02
Current Ratio	1.17	1.19	1.15	1.12	1.07	1.07	1.11	1.15
Debt to Equity	5.84	1.26	1.21	1.86	1.57	1.72	...	...
Price Range	144.63-87.47	131.97-87.47	131.97-67.07	120.80-56.05	59.85-34.73	40.80-21.23	27.46-16.63	18.07-13.51
P/E Ratio	38.47-23.26	33.08-21.92	34.01-17.42	37.52-17.41	29.78-17.28	26.49-13.79	34.76-21.04	34.08-25.48
Average Yield %	0.98	0.89	0.87	0.88	3.65	1.52	1.78	8.78

Address: 19001 Crescent Springs Drive, Kingwood, TX 77339
Telephone: 281-358-8986

Web Site: www.insperity.com
Officers: Paul J. Sarvadi - Chairman, Chief Executive Officer A. Steve Arizpe - President, Executive Vice President, Chief Operating Officer, Chief Operating Officer (frmr)

Auditors: Ernst & Young LLP
Investor Contact: 281-358-8986
Transfer Agents: Computershare, Providence, RI

INTERNATIONAL BUSINESS MACHINES CORP

Exchange	Symbol	Price	52Wk Range	Yield	P/E	Div Acheiver
NYS	IBM	$134.04 (12/31/2019)	151.36-112.91	4.83	15.57	23 Years

*7 Year Price Score 70.56   *NYSE Composite Index=100   *12 Month Price Score 93.31

Interim Earnings (Per Share)

Qtr.	Mar	Jun	Sep	Dec
2016	2.09	2.61	2.98	4.71
2017	1.85	2.48	2.92	(1.10)
2018	1.81	2.61	2.94	2.15
2019	1.78	2.81	1.87	...

Interim Dividends (Per Share)

Amt	Decl	Ex	Rec	Pay
1.57Q	01/29/2019	02/07/2019	02/08/2019	03/09/2019
1.62Q	04/30/2019	05/09/2019	05/10/2019	06/10/2019
1.62Q	07/30/2019	08/08/2019	08/09/2019	09/10/2019
1.62Q	10/29/2019	11/07/2019	11/08/2019	12/10/2019

Indicated Div: $6.48 (Div. Reinv. Plan)

Valuation Analysis

Valuation Analysis		Institutional Holding	
Forecast EPS	$12.80	No of Institutions	
	(01/17/2020)	2880	
Market Cap	$118.7 Billion	Shares	
Book Value	$18.0 Billion	691,830,976	
Price/Book	6.61	% Held	
Price/Sales	1.54	53.48	

Business Summary: IT Services (MIC: 6.3.1 SIC: 7379 NAIC: 541519)

International Business Machines provides integrated solutions and products that utilize data, information technology and business processes. Co.'s business segments, include: Cognitive Solutions, comprises a portfolio that assist clients to identify insights and inform decision-making; Global Business Services, which provides consulting, application management and business process services; Technology Services & Cloud Platforms, which provides infrastructure, technical support and integration software services; Systems, which provides infrastructure platforms to clients; and Global Financing, which encompasses of two primary businesses: financing and remanufacturing and remarketing.

Recent Developments: For the quarter ended Sep 30 2019, income from continuing operations decreased 37.9% to US$1.67 billion from US$2.69 billion in the year-earlier quarter. Net income decreased 37.9% to US$1.67 billion from US$2.69 billion in the year-earlier quarter. Revenues were US$18.03 billion, down 3.9% from US$18.76 billion the year before. Direct operating expenses declined 2.6% to US$9.69 billion from US$9.95 billion in the comparable period the year before. Indirect operating expenses increased 20.1% to US$6.41 billion from US$5.34 billion in the equivalent prior-year period.

Prospects: Our evaluation of International Business Machines Corp. as of October 4th, 2019 is the result of our systematic analysis on three basic characteristics: earnings strength, relative valuation, and recent stock price movement. The company has managed to produce a neutral trend in earnings per share over the past 5 quarters. In addition, recent analyst estimates for the company have been mixed and IBM has posted results that exceeded analysts' expectations. Based on operating earnings yield, the company is undervalued when compared to all of the companies we cover. Share price changes over the past year indicates that IBM will perform poorly over the near term.

Financial Data

(US$ in Thousands)	9 Mos	6 Mos	3 Mos	12/31/2018	12/31/2017	12/31/2016	12/31/2015	12/31/2014
Earnings Per Share	8.61	9.68	9.48	9.52	6.14	12.38	13.42	11.90
Cash Flow Per Share	17.42	18.11	17.32	16.72	17.93	17.70	17.38	16.80
Dividends Per Share	6.380	6.330	6.280	6.210	5.900	5.500	5.000	4.250
Dividend Payout %	74.10	65.39	66.24	65.23	96.09	44.43	37.26	35.71
Income Statement								
Total Revenue	55,370,000	37,342,000	18,182,000	79,591,000	79,139,000	79,919,000	81,741,000	92,793,000
EBITDA	11,271,000	7,711,000	3,469,000	16,281,000	16,412,000	17,233,000	20,196,000	24,872,000
Depn & Amortn	4,409,000	2,740,000	1,446,000	4,480,000	4,541,000	4,381,000	3,855,000	4,492,000
Income Before Taxes	6,173,000	4,651,000	1,883,000	11,342,000	11,400,000	12,330,000	15,945,000	19,986,000
Income Taxes	407,000	558,000	289,000	2,619,000	5,642,000	449,000	2,581,000	4,234,000
Net Income	5,761,000	4,089,000	1,591,000	8,728,000	5,753,000	11,872,000	13,190,000	12,022,000
Average Shares	892,839	890,831	893,910	916,315	937,385	958,714	982,700	1,010,000
Balance Sheet								
Current Assets	38,121,000	77,517,000	52,705,000	49,146,000	49,735,000	43,888,000	42,504,000	49,422,000
Total Assets	149,620,000	154,652,000	130,926,000	123,382,000	125,356,000	117,470,000	110,495,000	117,532,000
Current Liabilities	35,066,000	42,351,000	38,871,000	38,227,000	37,363,000	36,275,000	34,269,000	39,600,000
Long-Term Obligations	57,797,000	58,445,000	39,727,000	35,605,000	39,837,000	34,655,000	33,428,000	35,073,000
Total Liabilities	131,663,000	137,007,000	114,446,000	106,586,000	107,762,000	99,224,000	96,233,000	105,664,000
Stockholders' Equity	17,956,000	17,645,000	16,481,000	16,796,000	17,594,000	18,246,000	14,262,000	11,868,000
Shares Outstanding	885,637	885,875	886,642	892,479	922,179	945,867	965,728	990,523
Statistical Record								
Return on Assets %	5.68	6.32	6.74	7.02	4.74	10.39	11.57	9.86
Return on Equity %	40.87	48.30	49.87	50.76	32.10	72.84	100.96	69.37
EBITDA Margin %	20.36	20.65	19.08	20.46	20.74	21.56	24.71	26.80
Net Margin %	10.40	10.95	8.75	10.97	7.27	14.86	16.14	12.96
Asset Turnover	0.57	0.56	0.61	0.64	0.65	0.70	0.72	0.76
Current Ratio	1.09	1.83	1.36	1.29	1.33	1.21	1.24	1.25
Debt to Equity	3.22	3.31	2.41	2.12	2.26	1.90	2.34	2.96
Price Range	153.75-107.57	153.75-107.57	160.91-107.57	169.12-107.57	181.95-139.70	168.51-117.85	174.40-131.75	197.77-151.41
P/E Ratio	17.86-12.49	15.88-11.11	16.97-11.35	17.76-11.30	29.63-22.75	13.61-9.52	13.00-9.82	16.62-12.72
Average Yield %	4.75	4.67	4.56	4.32	3.74	3.66	3.22	2.33

Address: One New Orchard Road, Armonk, NY 10504 Telephone: 914-499-1900 Fax: 914-765-4190	Web Site: www.ibm.com Officers: Virginia M. (Ginni) Rometty - Chairman, President, Chief Executive Officer, Senior Vice President Michelle H. Browdy - Senior Vice President, Vice President, General Counsel, Secretary, Assistant General Counsel	Auditors: PricewaterhouseCoopers LLP Investor Contact: 914-499-7777 Transfer Agents: Computershare Trust Company, N.A., Providence, RI

INTERNATIONAL FLAVORS & FRAGRANCES INC.

Exchange	Symbol	Price	52Wk Range	Yield	P/E	Div Acheiver
NYS	IFF	$129.02 (12/31/2019)	152.15-106.50	2.33	42.44	16 Years

*7 Year Price Score 93.21   *NYSE Composite Index=100   *12 Month Price Score 94.14

Interim Earnings (Per Share)

Qtr.	Mar	Jun	Sep	Dec
2016	1.47	1.46	1.12	1.00
2017	1.45	1.38	1.39	(0.50)
2018	1.63	1.25	1.17	(0.25)
2019	0.96	1.20	1.13	...

Interim Dividends (Per Share)

Amt	Decl	Ex	Rec	Pay
0.73Q	03/05/2019	03/22/2019	03/25/2019	04/05/2019
0.73Q	04/30/2019	06/21/2019	06/24/2019	07/05/2019
0.75Q	08/05/2019	09/20/2019	09/23/2019	10/04/2019
0.75Q	12/11/2019	12/26/2019	12/27/2019	01/07/2020

Indicated Div: $3.00 (Div. Reinv. Plan)

Valuation Analysis   Institutional Holding

Forecast EPS	$6.17	No of Institutions
	(01/17/2020)	807
Market Cap	$13.8 Billion	Shares
Book Value	$6.1 Billion	126,873,096
Price/Book	2.27	% Held
Price/Sales	2.71	94.17

Business Summary: Specialty Chemicals (MIC: 8.3.2 SIC: 2869 NAIC: 325199)

International Flavors & Fragrances is a creator and manufacturer of tastes and scents (including cosmetic active ingredients). Co.'s products are sold mainly to manufacturers of perfumes and cosmetics, hair and other personal care products, soaps and detergents, cleaning products, dairy, meat and other processed foods, beverages, snacks and savory foods, and sweet and baked goods. Co.'s segments include: Taste, which develops a range of different flavors and taste offerings for its customers; Scent, which has two sources, Fragrance Compounds and Ingredients; and Frutarom, which creates and manufactures a naturals-focused suite of Flavor Compounds and specialty fine ingredients.

Recent Developments: For the quarter ended Sep 30 2019, net income increased 35.6% to US$129.8 million from US$95.7 million in the year-earlier quarter. Revenues were US$1.27 billion, up 39.6% from US$907.5 million the year before. Operating income was US$184.7 million versus US$159.3 million in the prior-year quarter, an increase of 15.9%. Direct operating expenses rose 44.9% to US$734.3 million from US$506.9 million in the comparable period the year before. Indirect operating expenses increased 44.3% to US$348.4 million from US$241.4 million in the equivalent prior-year period.

Prospects: Our evaluation of International Flavors & Fragrances Inc. as of October 4th, 2019 is the result of our systematic analysis on three basic characteristics: earnings strength, relative valuation, and recent stock price movement. The company has enjoyed a very positive trend in earnings per share over the past 5 quarters. However, recent analyst estimates for the company have been reduced, and IFF has posted results that fell short of analysts' expectations. Based on operating earnings yield, the company is fairly valued when compared to all of the companies we cover. Share price changes over the past year indicates that IFF will perform in line with the market over the near term.

Financial Data

(US$ in Thousands)	9 Mos	6 Mos	3 Mos	12/31/2018	12/31/2017	12/31/2016	12/31/2015	12/31/2014
Earnings Per Share	3.04	3.08	3.13	3.79	3.72	5.05	5.16	5.06
Cash Flow Per Share	5.52	5.07	4.44	5.00	4.94	6.70	5.39	6.40
Tang Book Value Per Share	N.M.	N.M.	N.M.	N.M.	1.42	3.29	4.29	9.49
Dividends Per Share	2.940	2.920	2.880	2.840	2.660	2.400	2.060	1.720
Dividend Payout %	96.71	94.81	92.01	74.93	71.51	47.52	39.92	33.99
Income Statement								
Total Revenue	3,856,315	2,588,970	1,297,402	3,977,539	3,398,719	3,116,350	3,023,189	3,088,533
EBITDA	707,549	468,756	218,773	745,294	720,502	679,069	659,963	684,482
Depn & Amortn	143,964	95,534	47,625	164,979	118,094	102,363	74,800	89,354
Income Before Taxes	460,923	304,057	134,576	447,757	537,045	523,717	539,101	549,061
Income Taxes	81,033	53,974	23,362	107,976	241,380	118,686	119,854	134,518
Net Income	372,330	245,206	108,829	337,302	295,665	405,031	419,247	414,543
Average Shares	113,493	112,872	113,389	88,121	79,370	79,981	80,891	81,494
Balance Sheet								
Current Assets	2,898,558	2,990,026	2,925,825	2,941,860	1,896,544	1,609,014	1,455,884	1,710,027
Total Assets	12,984,724	13,348,082	13,211,420	12,889,395	4,598,926	4,016,984	3,721,454	3,494,621
Current Liabilities	1,412,449	1,149,533	1,144,134	1,128,311	768,768	898,297	742,128	518,808
Long-Term Obligations	4,008,134	4,428,675	4,421,430	4,504,417	1,632,186	1,066,855	937,844	934,232
Total Liabilities	6,928,905	7,148,703	7,068,209	6,856,444	2,914,724	2,390,740	2,131,136	1,976,060
Stockholders' Equity	6,055,819	6,199,379	6,143,211	6,032,951	1,684,202	1,626,244	1,590,318	1,518,561
Shares Outstanding	106,775	106,774	106,646	106,619	78,947	79,213	80,022	80,777
Statistical Record								
Return on Assets %	3.43	3.96	3.57	3.86	6.86	10.44	11.62	12.15
Return on Equity %	7.69	8.97	8.06	8.74	17.86	25.12	26.97	27.81
EBITDA Margin %	18.35	18.11	16.86	18.74	21.20	21.79	21.83	22.16
Net Margin %	9.66	9.47	8.39	8.48	8.70	13.00	13.87	13.42
Asset Turnover	0.45	0.52	0.49	0.45	0.79	0.80	0.84	0.90
Current Ratio	2.05	2.60	2.56	2.61	2.47	1.79	1.96	3.30
Debt to Equity	0.66	0.71	0.72	0.75	0.97	0.66	0.59	0.62
Price Range	152.15-106.50	152.15-122.54	148.69-122.13	156.87-122.13	155.44-115.26	142.97-100.49	122.77-98.15	105.43-83.84
P/E Ratio	50.05-35.03	49.40-39.79	47.50-39.02	41.39-32.22	41.78-30.98	28.31-19.90	23.79-19.02	20.84-16.57
Average Yield %	2.19	2.16	2.16	2.08	1.95	1.93	1.81	1.77

Address: 521 West 57th Street, New York, NY 10019-2960 **Telephone:** 212-765-5500	**Web Site:** www.iff.com **Officers:** Andreas Fibig - Chairman, Chief Executive Officer Rustom F. Jilla - Executive Vice President, Chief Financial Officer	**Auditors:** PricewaterhouseCoopers LLP **Investor Contact:** 212-765-5500 **Transfer Agents:** American Stock Transfer & Trust Company, New York, NY

INTERNATIONAL PAPER CO

Exchange	Symbol	Price	52Wk Range	Yield	P/E
NYS	IP	$46.05 (12/31/2019)	47.76-36.74	4.45	13.46

*7 Year Price Score 75.64 *NYSE Composite Index=100 *12 Month Price Score 98.91

Interim Earnings (Per Share)

Qtr.	Mar	Jun	Sep	Dec
2016	0.81	0.10	0.75	0.53
2017	0.50	0.19	0.95	3.49
2018	1.74	0.97	1.37	0.77
2019	1.05	0.73	0.87	...

Interim Dividends (Per Share)

Amt	Decl	Ex	Rec	Pay
0.50Q	05/14/2019	05/24/2019	05/28/2019	06/14/2019
0.50Q	07/09/2019	08/14/2019	08/15/2019	09/16/2019
0.512Q	10/08/2019	11/14/2019	11/15/2019	12/16/2019
0.512Q	01/14/2020	02/20/2020	02/21/2020	03/16/2020

Indicated Div: $2.05 (Div. Reinv. Plan)

Valuation Analysis

		Institutional Holding	
Forecast EPS	$4.38 (01/17/2020)	No of Institutions	1230
Market Cap	$18.1 Billion	Shares	428,494,464
Book Value	$7.4 Billion	% Held	76.97
Price/Book	2.43		
Price/Sales	0.79		

Business Summary: Containers & Packaging (MIC: 8.1.3 SIC: 2621 NAIC: 322121)

International Paper is a producer of renewable fiber-based packaging, pulp and paper products with manufacturing operations in North America, Latin America, Europe, North Africa, India and Russia. Co.'s segments are: Industrial Packaging, which manufactures containerboard, such as linerboard, medium, whitetop, recycled linerboard, recycled medium and saturating kraft; Global Cellulose Fibers, which produces fluff pulp for making absorbent hygiene products like baby diapers, feminine care, adult incontinence and other non-woven products; and Printing Papers, which produces printing and writing papers, such as uncoated papers for use in copiers, desktop and laser printers and digital imaging.

Recent Developments: For the quarter ended Sep 30 2019, income from continuing operations decreased 39.1% to US$342.0 million from US$562.0 million in the year-earlier quarter. Net income decreased 39.1% to US$342.0 million from US$562.0 million in the year-earlier quarter. Revenues were US$5.57 billion, down 5.6% from US$5.90 billion the year before. Direct operating expenses declined 3.0% to US$3.77 billion from US$3.89 billion in the comparable period the year before. Indirect operating expenses decreased 7.0% to US$1.21 billion from US$1.30 billion in the equivalent prior-year period.

Prospects: Our evaluation of International Paper Co. as of October 4th, 2019 is the result of our systematic analysis on three basic characteristics: earnings strength, relative valuation, and recent stock price movement. The company has generated a negative trend in earnings per share over the past 5 quarters. However, recent analyst estimates for the company have been unchanged while IP has posted results that exceeded analysts' expectations. Based on operating earnings yield, the company is undervalued when compared to all of the companies we cover. Share price changes over the past year indicates that IP will perform in line with the market over the near term.

Financial Data

(US$ in Millions)	9 Mos	6 Mos	3 Mos	12/31/2018	12/31/2017	12/31/2016	12/31/2015	12/31/2014
Earnings Per Share	3.42	3.92	4.16	4.85	5.13	2.18	2.23	1.29
Cash Flow Per Share	8.92	8.99	8.23	7.89	4.26	6.01	6.18	7.19
Tang Book Value Per Share	10.28	10.26	10.16	9.95	7.53	2.38	1.33	3.19
Dividends Per Share	2.000	1.975	1.950	1.925	1.863	1.783	1.640	1.450
Dividend Payout %	58.48	50.38	46.88	39.69	36.31	81.77	73.54	112.40
Income Statement								
Total Revenue	16,878	11,310	5,643	23,306	21,743	21,079	22,365	23,617
EBITDA	2,484	1,604	848	3,517	2,620	2,676	3,034	2,787
Depn & Amortn	902	597	297	1,200	1,200	1,200	1,213	1,308
Income Before Taxes	1,204	752	418	1,781	848	956	1,266	872
Income Taxes	371	234	106	445	(1,085)	247	466	123
Net Income	1,060	716	424	2,012	2,144	904	938	555
Average Shares	395	398	403	414	417	415	420	432
Balance Sheet								
Current Assets	7,051	7,388	7,062	6,996	8,277	6,969	6,477	7,959
Total Assets	33,848	34,347	34,178	33,576	33,903	33,345	30,587	28,684
Current Liabilities	4,729	5,049	4,953	4,694	5,102	4,072	3,924	4,909
Long-Term Obligations	10,249	10,331	10,246	10,015	10,846	11,075	8,900	8,631
Total Liabilities	26,407	26,865	26,732	26,214	27,381	29,004	26,703	23,569
Stockholders' Equity	7,441	7,482	7,446	7,362	6,522	4,341	3,884	5,115
Shares Outstanding	392	393	399	400	412	411	412	420
Statistical Record								
Return on Assets %	4.07	4.68	5.01	5.96	6.38	2.82	3.17	1.84
Return on Equity %	19.00	22.25	23.24	28.98	39.47	21.92	20.85	8.40
EBITDA Margin %	14.72	14.18	15.03	15.09	12.05	12.70	13.57	11.80
Net Margin %	6.28	6.33	7.51	8.63	9.86	4.29	4.19	2.35
Asset Turnover	0.67	0.68	0.68	0.69	0.65	0.66	0.75	0.78
Current Ratio	1.49	1.46	1.43	1.49	1.62	1.71	1.65	1.62
Debt to Equity	1.38	1.38	1.38	1.36	1.66	2.55	2.29	1.69
Price Range	50.30-36.74	54.58-37.56	59.01-37.56	65.08-37.56	58.67-49.64	54.28-32.58	57.59-36.80	55.25-44.25
P/E Ratio	14.71-10.74	13.92-9.58	14.19-9.03	13.42-7.74	11.44-9.68	24.90-14.94	25.83-16.50	42.83-34.30
Average Yield %	4.55	4.22	3.97	3.68	3.41	4.09	3.41	3.00

Address: 6400 Poplar Avenue, Memphis, TN 38197
Telephone: 901-419-7000

Web Site: www.internationalpaper.com
Officers: Mark S. Sutton - Chairman, Chief Executive Officer, President, Chief Operating Officer Sharon R. Ryan - Senior Vice President, General Counsel

Auditors: DELOITTE & TOUCHE LLP
Investor Contact: 901-419-1731
Transfer Agents: Computershare Trust Company, N.A., Canton, MA

INTERPUBLIC GROUP OF COMPANIES INC.

Exchange	Symbol	Price	52Wk Range	Yield	P/E
NYS	IPG	$23.10 (12/31/2019)	23.77-19.57	4.07	13.83

*7 Year Price Score 87.81   ***NYSE Composite Index=100**   ***12 Month Price Score 97.12**

Interim Earnings (Per Share)

Qtr.	Mar	Jun	Sep	Dec
2016	0.01	0.38	0.32	0.78
2017	0.05	0.24	0.37	0.80
2018	(0.04)	0.37	0.41	0.84
2019	(0.02)	0.43	0.42	...

Interim Dividends (Per Share)

Amt	Decl	Ex	Rec	Pay
0.235Q	02/13/2019	02/28/2019	03/01/2019	03/15/2019
0.235Q	05/23/2019	05/31/2019	06/03/2019	06/17/2019
0.235Q	08/14/2019	08/30/2019	09/03/2019	09/17/2019
0.235Q	11/19/2019	11/29/2019	12/02/2019	12/16/2019

Indicated Div: $0.94

Valuation Analysis   **Institutional Holding**

Forecast EPS	$1.89 (01/17/2020)	No of Institutions 779
Market Cap	$8.9 Billion	Shares
Book Value	$2.5 Billion	491,202,016
Price/Book	3.62	% Held
Price/Sales	0.88	94.05

Business Summary: Advertising (MIC: 2.3.4 SIC: 7311 NAIC: 541810)

Interpublic Group of Companies is engaged in providing advertising and marketing services. Co. has two reportable segments: Integrated Agency Networks (IAN) and Constituency Management Group (CMG). Within IAN, Co.'s agencies provide a range of communications and marketing services. Co.'s digital agencies provide digital capabilities and serve as main digital partners. In addition, Co.'s domestic integrated agencies provide advertising, marketing communications services and/or marketing services. CMG provides clients with a range of services such as public relations, meeting and event production, sports and entertainment marketing, corporate and brand identity.

Recent Developments: For the quarter ended Sep 30 2019, net income increased 3.0% to US$168.4 million from US$163.5 million in the year-earlier quarter. Revenues were US$2.44 billion, up 6.1% from US$2.30 billion the year before. Operating income was US$280.3 million versus US$261.7 million in the prior-year quarter, an increase of 7.1%. Direct operating expenses rose 5.5% to US$2.08 billion from US$1.97 billion in the comparable period the year before. Indirect operating expenses increased 20.1% to US$78.8 million from US$65.6 million in the equivalent prior-year period.

Prospects: Our evaluation of Interpublic Group of Cos. Inc. as of October 4th, 2019 is the result of our systematic analysis on three basic characteristics: earnings strength, relative valuation, and recent stock price movement. The company has generated a negative trend in earnings per share over the past 5 quarters. However, recent analyst estimates for the company have been unchanged while IPG has posted results that exceeded analysts' expectations. Based on operating earnings yield, the company is undervalued when compared to all of the companies we cover. Share price changes over the past year indicates that IPG will perform in line with the market over the near term.

Financial Data

(US$ in Thousands)	9 Mos	6 Mos	3 Mos	12/31/2018	12/31/2017	12/31/2016	12/31/2015	12/31/2014
Earnings Per Share	1.67	1.66	1.60	1.59	1.46	1.49	1.09	1.12
Cash Flow Per Share	3.40	3.42	3.12	1.47	2.26	1.29	1.65	1.60
Dividends Per Share	0.915	0.890	0.865	0.840	0.720	0.600	0.480	0.380
Dividend Payout %	54.79	53.61	54.06	52.83	49.32	40.27	44.04	33.93
Income Statement								
Total Revenue	7,319,500	4,881,400	2,361,200	9,714,400	7,882,400	7,846,600	7,613,800	7,537,100
EBITDA	641,900	352,400	73,800	1,104,500	1,083,300	1,039,000	956,100	910,500
Depn & Amortn	65,300	48,700	30,500	165,300	135,900	138,300	130,900	132,300
Income Before Taxes	450,500	217,800	1,300	838,000	876,000	830,200	762,200	720,700
Income Taxes	118,700	54,100	10,500	199,200	281,900	198,000	282,800	216,500
Net Income	327,100	161,500	(8,000)	618,900	608,500	579,000	454,600	477,100
Average Shares	391,800	391,200	384,500	389,000	397,300	408,000	415,700	425,400
Balance Sheet								
Current Assets	7,050,000	7,475,400	7,247,000	8,182,900	7,464,100	7,438,000	7,693,100	7,810,200
Total Assets	15,997,600	16,526,900	16,050,000	15,620,300	12,695,200	12,485,200	12,585,100	12,747,200
Current Liabilities	7,398,400	7,731,300	7,531,100	8,123,900	7,678,200	7,706,000	7,584,300	7,463,300
Long-Term Obligations	3,367,100	3,563,800	3,663,700	3,660,200	1,285,600	1,280,700	1,610,300	1,623,500
Total Liabilities	13,528,600	14,103,000	13,734,700	13,227,100	10,494,200	10,468,100	10,619,600	10,630,900
Stockholders' Equity	2,469,000	2,423,900	2,315,300	2,393,200	2,201,000	2,017,100	1,965,500	2,116,300
Shares Outstanding	386,900	386,400	387,039	383,600	383,200	391,600	403,200	413,800
Statistical Record								
Return on Assets %	4.43	4.49	4.42	4.37	4.60	4.84	3.59	3.72
Return on Equity %	28.36	28.92	28.26	26.94	27.45	30.47	22.27	22.03
EBITDA Margin %	8.77	7.22	3.13	11.37	13.74	13.24	12.56	12.08
Net Margin %	4.47	3.31	N.M.	6.37	7.35	7.75	5.97	6.33
Asset Turnover	0.69	0.69	0.70	0.69	0.63	0.62	0.60	0.59
Current Ratio	0.95	0.97	0.96	1.01	0.97	0.97	1.01	1.05
Debt to Equity	1.36	1.47	1.58	1.53	0.58	0.63	0.82	0.77
Price Range	24.65-19.57	24.65-19.75	24.65-19.75	25.33-19.75	25.57-18.45	24.60-20.30	23.65-18.27	20.83-16.05
P/E Ratio	14.76-11.72	14.85-11.90	15.41-12.34	15.93-12.42	17.51-12.64	16.51-13.62	21.70-16.76	18.60-14.33
Average Yield %	4.12	3.96	3.79	3.67	3.20	2.63	2.27	2.06

Address: 909 Third Avenue, New York, NY 10022 **Telephone:** 212-704-1200	**Web Site:** www.interpublic.com **Officers:** Michael I. Roth - Chairman, Chief Executive Officer Ellen Tobi Johnson - Executive Vice President, Senior Vice President, Chief Financial Officer, Treasurer	**Auditors:** PricewaterhouseCoopers LLP **Transfer Agents:** Computershare Shareowner Services LLC, Jersey City, NJ

INVESCO LTD

Exchange	Symbol	Price	52Wk Range	Yield	P/E	Div Acheiver
NYS	IVZ	$17.98 (12/31/2019)	21.97-15.20	6.84	15.37	10 Years

*7 Year Price Score 50.08   ***NYSE Composite Index=100**   ***12 Month Price Score 89.54**

Interim Earnings (Per Share)
Qtr.	Mar	Jun	Sep	Dec
2016	0.38	0.54	0.58	0.55
2017	0.52	0.58	0.65	0.99
2018	0.62	0.59	0.65	0.28
2019	0.44	0.09	0.36	...

Interim Dividends (Per Share)
Amt	Decl	Ex	Rec	Pay
0.30Q	01/29/2019	02/13/2019	02/14/2019	03/01/2019
0.31Q	04/24/2019	05/09/2019	05/10/2019	06/03/2019
0.31Q	07/24/2019	08/14/2019	08/15/2019	09/03/2019
0.31Q	10/23/2019	11/08/2019	11/12/2019	12/02/2019

Indicated Div: $1.23

Valuation Analysis
		Institutional Holding	
Forecast EPS	N/A	No of Institutions	800
Market Cap	$8.2 Billion	Shares	
Book Value	$13.6 Billion		391,475,680
Price/Book	0.60	% Held	
Price/Sales	1.45		N/A

TRADING VOLUME (thousand shares)

Business Summary: Wealth Management (MIC: 5.5.2 SIC: 6282 NAIC: 523930)

Invesco is an independent investment management firm. Co. provides a range of investment capabilities and outcomes, delivered through a set of investment vehicles. Co. has presence in the retail and institutional markets within the investment management industry in North America, EMEA (Europe, Middle East and Africa) and Asia-Pacific. Co.'s asset classes include money market, balanced, equity, fixed income and alternatives. Co.'s distribution channels consist of: Retail, which provides retail products within all of the key asset classes; and Institutional, which provides a suite of domestic and global strategies, including conventional and quantitative equities and financial structures.

Recent Developments: For the quarter ended Sep 30 2019, net income decreased 13.7% to US$242.6 million from US$281.2 million in the year-earlier quarter. Revenues were US$1.72 billion, up 28.2% from US$1.34 billion the year before. Operating income was US$275.1 million versus US$322.1 million in the prior-year quarter, a decrease of 14.6%. Indirect operating expenses increased 41.8% to US$1.45 billion from US$1.02 billion in the equivalent prior-year period.

Prospects: Our evaluation of Invesco Ltd as of October 4th, 2019 is the result of our systematic analysis on three basic characteristics: earnings strength, relative valuation, and recent stock price movement. The company has enjoyed a very positive trend in earnings per share over the past 5 quarters. However, recent analyst estimates for the company have been reduced, while IVZ has posted results that exceeded analysts' expectations. Based on operating earnings yield, the company is undervalued when compared to all of the companies we cover. Share price changes over the past year indicates that IVZ will perform in line with the market over the near term.

Financial Data
(US$ in Thousands)	9 Mos	6 Mos	3 Mos	12/31/2018	12/31/2017	12/31/2016	12/31/2015	12/31/2014
Earnings Per Share	1.17	1.46	1.96	2.14	2.75	2.06	2.26	2.27
Cash Flow Per Share	1.77	1.81	1.96	2.07	3.35	0.31	2.46	2.76
Tang Book Value Per Share	N.M.	N.M.	N.M.	N.M.	1.34	N.M.	0.85	1.16
Dividends Per Share	1.220	1.210	1.200	1.190	1.150	1.110	1.060	0.975
Dividend Payout %	104.27	82.88	61.22	55.61	41.82	53.88	46.90	42.95
Income Statement								
Total Revenue	4,374,600	2,654,000	1,214,600	5,314,100	5,160,300	4,734,400	5,122,900	5,147,100
EBITDA	814,700	440,300	306,500	1,306,900	1,565,300	1,365,800	1,414,600	1,426,500
Depn & Amortn	125,100	76,600	36,300	112,400	99,400	87,300	83,000	76,800
Income Before Taxes	603,000	306,200	241,800	1,104,300	1,384,500	1,197,300	1,327,000	1,362,300
Income Taxes	154,700	80,700	66,200	255,000	268,200	338,300	398,000	390,600
Net Income	449,300	217,800	177,700	882,800	1,127,300	854,200	968,100	988,100
Average Shares	466,900	433,800	388,200	399,900	409,900	415,000	429,300	435,600
Balance Sheet								
Current Assets	21,193,900	21,707,400	22,071,900	20,923,300	22,842,600	17,529,100	16,888,400	12,009,700
Total Assets	37,891,400	38,501,400	32,206,600	30,978,400	31,668,800	25,734,300	25,073,200	20,462,500
Current Liabilities	13,470,000	14,430,700	14,139,500	1,733,700	1,591,800	1,466,700	1,524,400	3,852,600
Long-Term Obligations	7,780,900	7,270,100	7,727,400	7,634,800	6,875,600	6,505,500	7,509,800	6,738,900
Total Liabilities	24,318,200	24,566,700	23,537,300	22,399,600	22,972,700	18,230,500	17,187,900	12,136,500
Stockholders' Equity	13,573,200	13,934,700	8,669,300	8,578,800	8,696,100	7,503,800	7,885,300	8,326,000
Shares Outstanding	453,893	469,793	400,857	397,100	407,100	403,800	417,500	429,900
Statistical Record								
Return on Assets %	1.60	1.70	2.53	2.82	3.93	3.35	4.25	4.97
Return on Equity %	5.00	5.29	9.18	10.22	13.92	11.07	11.94	11.82
EBITDA Margin %	18.62	16.59	25.23	24.59	30.33	28.85	27.61	27.71
Net Margin %	10.27	8.21	14.63	16.61	21.85	18.04	18.90	19.20
Asset Turnover	0.16	0.15	0.16	0.17	0.18	0.19	0.23	0.26
Current Ratio	1.57	1.50	1.56	12.07	14.35	11.95	11.08	3.12
Debt to Equity	0.57	0.52	0.89	0.89	0.79	0.87	0.95	0.81
Price Range	23.24-15.20	27.36-15.71	31.78-15.71	38.40-15.71	37.67-28.92	33.48-23.16	41.85-30.39	41.28-31.77
P/E Ratio	19.86-12.99	18.74-10.76	16.21-8.02	17.94-7.34	13.70-10.52	16.25-11.24	18.52-13.45	18.19-14.00
Average Yield %	6.27	5.61	5.18	4.41	3.43	3.74	2.88	2.61

Address: 1555 Peachtree Street N.E., Suite 1800, Atlanta, GA 30309	Web Site: www.invesco.com	Auditors: PricewaterhouseCoopers LLP
Telephone: 404-892-0896	Officers: Philip A. Taylor - Vice-Chairman, Senior Managing Director, Region Officer Martin L. Flanagan - President, Chief Executive Officer	Investor Contact: 404-439-4605 Transfer Agents: BNY Mellon Shareowner Services, Pittsburg, PA

INVITATION HOMES INC

Exchange	Symbol	Price	52Wk Range	Yield	P/E
NYS	INVH	$29.97 (12/31/2019)	31.09-19.70	1.74	136.23

*7 Year Price Score N/A   ***NYSE Composite Index=100**   ***12 Month Price Score 106.11**

TRADING VOLUME (thousand shares)

Interim Earnings (Per Share)

Qtr.	Mar	Jun	Sep	Dec
2017	(0.08)	0.02	(0.07)	(0.12)
2018	(0.03)	(0.03)	0.00	0.05
2019	0.04	0.07	0.06	...

Interim Dividends (Per Share)

Amt	Deci	Ex	Rec	Pay
0.13Q	02/01/2019	02/12/2019	02/13/2019	02/28/2019
0.13Q	05/03/2019	05/14/2019	05/15/2019	05/31/2019
0.13Q	08/02/2019	08/14/2019	08/15/2019	08/30/2019
0.13Q	11/01/2019	11/12/2019	11/13/2019	11/27/2019

Indicated Div: $0.52

Valuation Analysis   Institutional Holding

Forecast EPS	$0.23	No of Institutions
	(01/14/2020)	396
Market Cap	$16.1 Billion	Shares
Book Value	$8.1 Billion	551,559,040
Price/Book	1.99	% Held
Price/Sales	9.20	100.73

Business Summary: Property, Real Estate & Development (MIC: 5.3.2 SIC: 6519 NAIC: 531190)

Invitation Homes is an owner and operator of single-family homes for lease, providing residents homes in neighborhoods across America. Co. has one reportable segment related to acquiring, renovating, leasing, and operating single-family homes as rental properties, including single-family homes in planned unit developments.

Recent Developments: For the quarter ended Sep 30 2019, net income increased to US$34.0 million from US$1.0 million in the year-earlier quarter. Revenues were US$443.3 million, up 2.1% from US$434.3 million the year before.

Prospects: Our evaluation of Invitation Homes Inc as of October 4th, 2019 is the result of our systematic analysis on three basic characteristics: earnings strength, relative valuation, and recent stock price movement. The company has managed to produce a neutral trend in earnings per share over the past 5 quarters. However, recent analyst estimates for the company have been raised and INVH has posted results that exceeded analysts' expectations. Based on operating earnings yield, the company is overvalued when compared to all of the companies we cover. Share price changes over the past year indicates that INVH will perform well over the near term.

Financial Data

(US$ in Thousands)	9 Mos	6 Mos	3 Mos	12/31/2018	12/31/2017	12/31/2016	12/31/2015	12/31/2014
Earnings Per Share	0.22	0.16	0.09	(0.01)	(0.26)	(0.32)	...	...
Cash Flow Per Share	1.19	1.19	1.20	1.08	0.77	0.48	...	...
Tang Book Value Per Share	14.56	14.66	15.01	15.31	15.80	6.31	...	...
Dividends Per Share	0.500	0.480	0.460	0.440	0.220	...	...	...
Dividend Payout %	227.27	287.50	511.11	...	...	...	...	...
Income Statement								
Total Revenue	1,320,408	877,082	435,500	1,722,962	1,054,456	922,587	836,049	658,722
EBITDA	751,832	503,086	246,282	840,888	414,875	452,312	356,321	173,475
Depn & Amortn	443,075	296,567	148,702	511,988	297,627	263,093	245,065	207,289
Income Before Taxes	30,001	16,830	3,597	(54,695)	(139,722)	(96,829)	(162,480)	(269,626)
Net Income	93,471	59,764	20,822	(4,927)	(105,337)	(78,239)	(160,208)	(269,861)
Average Shares	538,644	525,933	521,817	520,376	339,423	519,372	...	...
Balance Sheet								
Current Assets	326,413	319,455	351,418	359,991	416,562	420,211	493,992	561,715
Total Assets	17,660,018	17,714,153	17,853,619	18,063,428	18,683,638	9,732,351	9,796,978	9,199,653
Current Liabilities	427,295	379,978	344,167	318,598	340,102	174,565	163,986	163,142
Long-Term Obligations	8,655,893	8,964,965	9,080,925	9,249,815	9,651,662	7,570,279	7,725,957	6,564,643
Total Liabilities	9,562,758	9,756,474	9,713,703	9,834,317	10,185,553	7,774,928	7,909,947	6,743,052
Stockholders' Equity	8,097,260	7,957,679	8,139,916	8,229,111	8,498,085	1,957,423	1,887,031	2,456,601
Shares Outstanding	538,356	525,126	524,989	520,647	519,173	310,376	...	...
Statistical Record								
Return on Assets %	0.66	0.47	0.18	N.M.	N.M.	N.M.	N.M.	...
Return on Equity %	1.44	1.05	0.40	N.M.	N.M.	N.M.	N.M.	...
EBITDA Margin %	56.94	57.36	56.55	48.80	39.34	49.03	42.62	26.34
Net Margin %	7.08	6.81	4.78	N.M.	N.M.	N.M.	N.M.	N.M.
Asset Turnover	0.10	0.10	0.09	0.09	0.07	0.09	0.09	...
Current Ratio	0.76	0.84	1.02	1.13	1.22	2.41	3.01	3.44
Debt to Equity	1.07	1.13	1.12	1.12	1.14	3.87	4.09	2.67
Price Range	29.71-19.42	27.75-19.42	24.33-19.42	23.94-19.42	24.10-20.00	...	...	...
P/E Ratio	135.05-88.27	173.44-121.38	270.33-215.78			...	...	...
Average Yield %	2.05	2.07	2.05	1.97	0.99	...	...	...

Address: 1717 Main Street, Suite 2000, Dallas, TX 75201 Telephone: 972-421-3600	Web Site: www.invitationhomes.com Officers: Bryce Blair - Executive Chairman, Chairperson Frederick C. (Fred) Tuomi - President, Chief Executive Officer	Auditors: DELOITTE & TOUCHE LLP Investor Contact: 972-421-3600 Transfer Agents: Computershare Trust Company, N.A.

IQVIA HOLDINGS INC

Exchange	Symbol	Price	52Wk Range	Yield	P/E
NYS	IQV	$154.51 (12/31/2019)	161.46-109.96	N/A	127.69

*7 Year Price Score N/A   *NYSE Composite Index=100   *12 Month Price Score 96.37

TRADING VOLUME (thousand shares)

Interim Earnings (Per Share)

Qtr.	Mar	Jun	Sep	Dec
2016	0.88	0.71	0.82	(1.65)
2017	0.31	0.34	0.38	4.84
2018	0.32	0.29	0.29	0.33
2019	0.29	0.30	0.29	...

Interim Dividends (Per Share)

No Dividends Paid

Valuation Analysis

		Institutional Holding	
Forecast EPS	$6.37	No of Institutions	
	(01/17/2020)	793	
Market Cap	$30.0 Billion	Shares	
Book Value	$6.1 Billion	194,030,528	
Price/Book	4.89	% Held	
Price/Sales	2.75	N/A	

Business Summary: Biotechnology (MIC: 4.1.2 SIC: 8731 NAIC: 541710)

IQVIA Holdings is a provider of analytics, technology solutions and contract research services to the life sciences industry. Co. is managed through three reportable segments: Technology and Analytics Solutions, which provides information, technology solutions and real-world insights and services to life science clients; Research and Development Solutions, which primarily serves biopharmaceutical clients, engaged in research and development and provides clinical research and clinical trial services; and Contract Sales and Medical Solutions, which provides contract sales to both biopharmaceutical clients and the healthcare market.

Recent Developments: For the quarter ended Sep 30 2019, net income increased 3.0% to US$69.0 million from US$67.0 million in the year-earlier quarter. Revenues were US$2.77 billion, up 6.7% from US$2.59 billion the year before. Operating income was US$204.0 million versus US$181.0 million in the prior-year quarter, an increase of 12.7%. Direct operating expenses rose 10.4% to US$1.85 billion from US$1.68 billion in the comparable period the year before. Indirect operating expenses decreased 3.0% to US$713.0 million from US$735.0 million in the equivalent prior-year period.

Prospects: Our evaluation of IQVIA Holdings Inc. as of October 4th, 2019 is the result of our systematic analysis on three basic characteristics: earnings strength, relative valuation, and recent stock price movement. The company has managed to produce a neutral trend in earnings per share over the past 5 quarters. In addition, recent analyst estimates for the company have been mixed and IQV has posted results that exceeded analysts' expectations. Based on operating earnings yield, the company is fairly valued when compared to all of the companies we cover. Share price changes over the past year indicates that IQV will perform over the near term.

Financial Data

(US$ in Thousands)	9 Mos	6 Mos	3 Mos	12/31/2018	12/31/2017	12/31/2016	12/31/2015	12/31/2014
Earnings Per Share	1.21	1.21	1.20	1.24	5.88	0.76	3.08	2.72
Cash Flow Per Share	6.43	6.45	6.02	6.16	4.45	5.75	3.87	3.37
Income Statement								
Total Revenue	8,193,000	5,424,000	2,684,000	10,412,000	9,739,000	6,878,000	5,737,619	5,459,998
EBITDA	597,000	413,000	220,000	859,000	795,000	941,000	781,263	727,069
Depn & Amortn	10,000	6,000	3,000	125,000	125,000	322,000	144,793	127,701
Income Before Taxes	256,000	187,000	109,000	328,000	331,000	479,000	538,995	502,189
Income Taxes	48,000	49,000	41,000	59,000	(987,000)	345,000	158,989	150,056
Net Income	175,000	118,000	58,000	259,000	1,309,000	115,000	387,205	356,383
Average Shares	199,000	200,600	201,700	208,200	222,600	152,000	125,630	131,083
Balance Sheet								
Current Assets	3,995,000	3,978,000	3,999,000	3,874,000	3,450,000	3,337,000	2,411,985	2,146,083
Total Assets	22,892,000	23,068,000	23,109,000	22,549,000	22,742,000	21,208,000	3,926,316	3,305,832
Current Liabilities	3,576,000	3,495,000	3,502,000	3,534,000	2,904,000	2,705,000	1,594,176	1,471,900
Long-Term Obligations	11,444,000	11,299,000	11,187,000	10,907,000	10,122,000	7,108,000	2,419,293	2,292,491
Total Liabilities	16,761,000	16,545,000	16,494,000	15,835,000	14,633,000	12,575,000	4,490,533	4,009,893
Stockholders' Equity	6,131,000	6,523,000	6,615,000	6,714,000	8,109,000	8,633,000	(564,217)	(704,061)
Shares Outstanding	194,000	195,800	197,200	197,500	208,100	235,400	119,377	124,129
Statistical Record								
Return on Assets %	1.08	1.08	1.07	1.14	5.96	0.91	10.71	11.18
Return on Equity %	3.66	3.56	3.35	3.49	15.64	2.84	...	...
EBITDA Margin %	7.29	7.61	8.20	8.25	8.16	13.68	13.62	13.32
Net Margin %	2.14	2.18	2.16	2.49	13.44	1.67	6.75	6.53
Asset Turnover	0.48	0.47	0.45	0.46	0.44	0.55	1.59	1.71
Current Ratio	1.12	1.14	1.14	1.10	1.19	1.23	1.51	1.46
Debt to Equity	1.87	1.73	1.69	1.62	1.25	0.82	...	...
Price Range	161.46-105.70	160.90-99.30	144.45-94.85	130.77-94.85	108.56-75.35	81.06-55.91	79.10-57.07	60.66-45.80
P/E Ratio	133.44-87.36	132.98-82.07	120.38-79.04	105.46-76.49	18.46-12.81	106.66-73.57	25.68-18.53	22.30-16.84

Address: 4820 Emperor Blvd., Durham, NC 27703 **Telephone:** 919-998-2000	**Web Site:** www.quintiles.com **Officers:** Ari Bousbib - Chairman, President, Chief Executive Officer Michael R. McDonnell - Executive Vice President, Chief Financial Officer, Chief Financial Officer	**Auditors:** PricewaterhouseCoopers LLP **Investor Contact:** 919-998-2000 **Transfer Agents:** American Stock Transfer & Trust Company, LLC, Brooklyn, NY

IRON MOUNTAIN INC

Exchange	Symbol	Price	52Wk Range	Yield	P/E
NYS	IRM	$31.87 (12/31/2019)	37.20-29.41	7.76	23.78

*7 Year Price Score 81.22 *NYSE Composite Index=100 *12 Month Price Score 93.67

Interim Earnings (Per Share)

Qtr.	Mar	Jun	Sep	Dec
2016	0.30	(0.06)	0.03	0.19
2017	0.22	0.30	0.09	0.08
2018	0.16	0.33	0.23	0.55
2019	0.10	0.32	0.37	...

Interim Dividends (Per Share)

Amt	Decl	Ex	Rec	Pay
0.611Q	02/07/2019	03/14/2019	03/15/2019	04/02/2019
0.611Q	05/22/2019	06/14/2019	06/17/2019	07/02/2019
0.611Q	07/26/2019	09/13/2019	09/16/2019	10/02/2019
0.619Q	10/31/2019	12/13/2019	12/16/2019	01/02/2020

Indicated Div: $2.47

Valuation Analysis / Institutional Holding

Forecast EPS	$1.02	No of Institutions	734
	(01/17/2020)		
Market Cap	$9.2 Billion	Shares	
Book Value	$1.5 Billion		272,418,272
Price/Book	6.06	% Held	
Price/Sales	2.16		N/A

Business Summary: REITs (MIC: 5.3.1 SIC: 4225 NAIC: 493110)

Iron Mountain is a holding company. Co. operates in six segments: North American Records and Information Management Business, which includes the storage of physical records; North American Data Management Business, which provides storage and rotation of backup computer media; Western European Business, which includes records management, data protection & recovery and information governance and digital solutions; Western European Business, which provides records and information management services; Other International Business, which provides records and information management services throughout the remaining European countries; Global Data Center Business; and Corporate and Other Business.

Recent Developments: For the quarter ended Sep 30 2019, income from continuing operations increased 40.0% to US$108.3 million from US$77.3 million in the year-earlier quarter. Net income increased 64.7% to US$108.3 million from US$65.7 million in the year-earlier quarter. Revenues were US$1.06 billion, unchanged from the year before. Operating income was US$223.5 million versus US$195.6 million in the prior-year quarter, an increase of 14.2%. Direct operating expenses rose 0.7% to US$451.3 million from US$448.0 million in the comparable period the year before. Indirect operating expenses decreased 7.2% to US$387.4 million from US$417.3 million in the equivalent prior-year period.

Prospects: Our evaluation of Iron Mountain Inc. as of October 4th, 2019 is the result of our systematic analysis on three basic characteristics: earnings strength, relative valuation, and recent stock price movement. The company has managed to produce a neutral trend in earnings per share over the past 5 quarters. In addition, recent analyst estimates for the company have been mixed and IRM has posted results in line with analysts' expectations. Based on operating earnings yield, the company is fairly valued when compared to all of the companies we cover. Share price changes over the past year indicates that IRM will perform in line with the market over the near term.

Financial Data

(US$ in Thousands)	9 Mos	6 Mos	3 Mos	12/31/2018	12/31/2017	12/31/2016	12/31/2015	12/31/2014
Earnings Per Share	1.34	1.20	1.21	1.27	0.69	0.42	0.58	1.66
Cash Flow Per Share	3.34	3.39	3.35	3.27	2.71	2.20	2.57	2.42
Dividends Per Share	2.444	2.421	2.397	2.373	2.237	2.005	1.910	5.371
Dividend Payout %	182.39	201.71	198.10	186.89	324.28	477.38	329.31	323.57
Income Statement								
Total Revenue	3,182,994	2,120,770	1,053,863	4,225,761	3,845,578	3,511,453	3,007,976	3,117,693
EBITDA	1,095,739	693,972	313,701	1,219,940	975,963	822,832	727,156	788,647
Depn & Amortn	507,078	342,200	170,236	452,740	406,283	365,526	301,219	304,557
Income Before Taxes	274,234	144,022	41,029	357,911	216,105	146,644	162,066	223,373
Income Taxes	43,127	21,199	10,553	36,263	25,947	44,944	37,713	(97,275)
Net Income	229,677	122,002	29,561	363,351	183,821	104,824	123,241	326,119
Average Shares	287,690	287,481	287,491	286,652	266,845	247,267	212,118	196,749
Balance Sheet								
Current Assets	1,203,893	1,215,103	1,209,850	1,208,114	1,950,315	1,112,107	857,912	917,719
Total Assets	13,577,167	13,720,982	13,689,363	11,852,247	10,972,402	9,486,800	6,350,587	6,570,342
Current Liabilities	1,830,111	1,616,787	1,515,133	1,462,678	1,330,173	1,046,557	841,831	856,736
Long-Term Obligations	8,220,347	8,390,183	8,365,737	8,016,417	6,896,971	6,078,206	4,757,610	4,611,436
Total Liabilities	12,066,337	12,063,161	11,929,962	9,968,067	8,674,964	7,550,253	5,841,746	5,713,987
Stockholders' Equity	1,510,830	1,657,821	1,759,401	1,884,180	2,297,438	1,936,547	508,841	856,355
Shares Outstanding	287,135	287,061	286,829	286,321	283,110	263,682	211,340	209,818
Statistical Record								
Return on Assets %	3.06	2.72	2.71	3.18	1.80	1.32	1.91	4.93
Return on Equity %	22.49	18.70	17.33	17.38	8.68	8.55	18.05	34.26
EBITDA Margin %	34.42	32.72	29.77	28.87	25.38	23.43	24.17	25.30
Net Margin %	7.22	5.75	2.81	8.60	4.78	2.99	4.10	10.46
Asset Turnover	0.33	0.33	0.33	0.37	0.38	0.44	0.47	0.47
Current Ratio	0.66	0.75	0.80	0.83	1.47	1.06	1.02	1.07
Debt to Equity	5.44	5.06	4.75	4.25	3.00	3.14	9.35	5.38
Price Range	37.20-29.41	37.20-30.46	37.20-30.48	37.61-30.48	41.44-33.10	41.25-24.56	41.09-26.13	40.27-25.90
P/E Ratio	27.76-21.95	31.00-25.38	30.74-25.19	29.61-24.00	60.06-47.97	98.21-58.48	70.84-45.05	24.26-15.60
Average Yield %	7.39	7.09	6.97	6.99	6.07	5.85	5.76	6.71

Address: One Federal Street, Boston, MA 02110	**Web Site:** www.ironmountain.com	**Auditors:** DELOITTE & TOUCHE LLP
Telephone: 617-535-4766	**Officers:** Alfred J. Verrecchia - Chairman William L. Meaney - Chief Executive Officer	**Investor Contact:** 617-535-4766
		Transfer Agents: Computershare, Providence, RI

ITT INC

Exchange	Symbol	Price	52Wk Range	Yield	P/E
NYS	ITT	$73.91 (12/31/2019)	74.16-47.07	0.80	21.30

*7 Year Price Score 113.43 *NYSE Composite Index=100 *12 Month Price Score 109.01

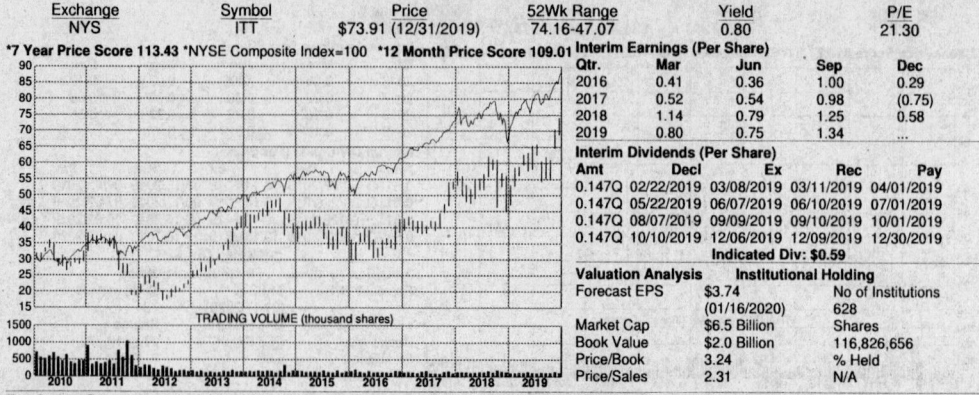

Interim Earnings (Per Share)

Qtr.	Mar	Jun	Sep	Dec
2016	0.41	0.36	1.00	0.29
2017	0.52	0.54	0.98	(0.75)
2018	1.14	0.79	1.25	0.58
2019	0.80	0.75	1.34	...

Interim Dividends (Per Share)

Amt	Decl	Ex	Rec	Pay
0.147Q	02/22/2019	03/08/2019	03/11/2019	04/01/2019
0.147Q	05/22/2019	06/07/2019	06/10/2019	07/01/2019
0.147Q	08/07/2019	09/09/2019	09/10/2019	10/01/2019
0.147Q	10/10/2019	12/06/2019	12/09/2019	12/30/2019

Indicated Div: $0.59

Valuation Analysis / **Institutional Holding**

Forecast EPS	$3.74	No of Institutions	
	(01/16/2020)	628	
Market Cap	$6.5 Billion	Shares	
Book Value	$2.0 Billion	116,826,656	
Price/Book	3.24	% Held	
Price/Sales	2.31	N/A	

Business Summary: Industrial Machinery & Equipment (MIC: 7.2.1 SIC: 3561 NAIC: 333911)

ITT is a manufacturer of engineered components and customized technology solutions for the transportation, industrial, and oil and gas markets. Co. operates through three segments: Motion Technologies, which manufactures brake components and sealing solutions, shock absorbers and damping technologies; Industrial Process, which manufactures engineered fluid process equipment and is a provider of plant optimization and efficiency solutions and aftermarket services and parts; and Connect & Control Technologies, which manufactures harsh-environment connector solutions and critical energy absorption and flow control components.

Recent Developments: For the quarter ended Sep 30 2019, income from continuing operations increased 6.8% to US$118.8 million from US$111.2 million in the year-earlier quarter. Net income increased 6.8% to US$118.7 million from US$111.1 million in the year-earlier quarter. Revenues were US$711.9 million, up 4.6% from US$680.6 million the year before. Operating income was US$152.5 million versus US$137.8 million in the prior-year quarter, an increase of 10.7%. Direct operating expenses rose 5.8% to US$480.6 million from US$454.1 million in the comparable period the year before. Indirect operating expenses decreased 11.2% to US$78.8 million from US$88.7 million in the equivalent prior-year period.

Prospects: Our evaluation of ITT Inc as of October 4th, 2019 is the result of our systematic analysis on three basic characteristics: earnings strength, relative valuation, and recent stock price movement. The company has managed to produce a neutral trend in earnings per share over the past 5 quarters. However, recent analyst estimates for the company have been reduced and ITT has posted results that fell short of analysts' expectations. Based on operating earnings yield, the company is undervalued when compared to all of the companies we cover. Share price changes over the past year indicates that ITT will perform in line with the market over the near term.

Financial Data

(US$ in Thousands)	9 Mos	6 Mos	3 Mos	12/31/2018	12/31/2017	12/31/2016	12/31/2015	12/31/2014
Earnings Per Share	3.47	3.38	3.42	3.76	1.28	2.07	3.88	1.99
Cash Flow Per Share	3.95	4.03	4.24	4.24	2.80	2.69	2.56	2.67
Tang Book Value Per Share	9.36	8.53	8.59	8.85	5.80	5.13	4.12	5.11
Dividends Per Share	0.575	0.562	0.549	0.536	0.512	0.372	0.473	0.440
Dividend Payout %	16.57	16.63	16.05	14.26	40.00	17.97	12.20	22.11
Income Statement								
Total Revenue	2,127,300	1,415,400	695,500	2,745,100	2,585,300	2,405,400	2,485,600	2,654,600
EBITDA	391,800	218,200	111,300	474,200	387,700	331,700	450,500	336,400
Depn & Amortn	61,400	40,700	20,200	82,800	78,300	74,100	70,700	72,900
Income Before Taxes	330,400	177,500	91,100	391,000	309,400	258,400	382,300	262,000
Income Taxes	73,100	39,000	19,700	57,700	194,600	76,000	70,100	71,300
Net Income	256,600	138,100	71,300	333,700	113,500	186,100	351,800	184,500
Average Shares	88,700	88,700	88,600	88,700	89,000	89,900	90,700	92,800
Balance Sheet								
Current Assets	1,706,300	1,702,400	1,678,900	1,645,100	1,478,700	1,401,800	1,497,700	1,636,200
Total Assets	4,064,200	4,041,400	3,937,100	3,846,800	3,700,200	3,601,700	3,723,600	3,631,500
Current Liabilities	888,800	892,400	860,500	872,100	899,400	866,200	953,100	775,400
Long-Term Obligations	74,400	78,500	62,100	...	...	...	...	...
Total Liabilities	2,066,600	2,106,200	2,068,500	2,024,400	2,104,100	2,175,300	2,361,500	2,416,600
Stockholders' Equity	1,997,600	1,935,200	1,868,600	1,822,400	1,596,100	1,426,400	1,362,100	1,214,900
Shares Outstanding	87,600	87,900	87,800	87,600	88,200	88,400	89,500	91,000
Statistical Record								
Return on Assets %	7.80	7.67	7.78	8.84	3.11	5.07	9.57	5.01
Return on Equity %	16.31	16.65	17.23	19.52	7.51	13.31	27.30	15.27
EBITDA Margin %	18.42	15.42	16.00	17.27	15.00	13.79	18.12	12.67
Net Margin %	12.07	9.76	10.25	12.16	4.39	7.74	14.15	6.95
Asset Turnover	0.71	0.71	0.70	0.73	0.71	0.65	0.68	0.72
Current Ratio	1.92	1.91	1.95	1.89	1.64	1.62	1.57	2.11
Debt to Equity	0.04	0.04	0.03	...	...	...	...	...
Price Range	65.86-45.29	65.48-45.29	62.14-45.29	62.14-45.29	54.31-38.01	42.73-29.89	43.40-33.05	49.24-37.55
P/E Ratio	18.98-13.05	19.37-13.40	18.17-13.24	16.53-12.05	42.43-29.70	20.64-14.44	11.19-8.52	24.74-18.87
Average Yield %	1.00	0.99	1.01	0.99	1.19	1.05	1.22	1.00

Address: 1133 Westchester Avenue, White Plains, NY 10604
Telephone: 914-641-2000

Web Site: www.itt.com
Officers: Frank T. MacInnis - Chairman Luca Savi - President, Chief Executive Officer, Executive Vice President, Senior Vice President, Chief Operating Officer, Division Officer

Auditors: Deloitte & Touche LLP
Investor Contact: 914-641-2030
Transfer Agents: Wells Fargo Shareowner Services

JABIL INC

Exchange	Symbol	Price	52Wk Range	Yield	P/E
NYS	JBL	$41.33 (12/31/2019)	43.43-23.12	0.77	31.55

*7 Year Price Score 106.52 *NYSE Composite Index=100 *12 Month Price Score 120.59

Interim Earnings (Per Share)

Qtr.	Nov	Feb	May	Aug
2016-17	0.47	0.11	(0.14)	0.24
2017-18	0.35	0.21	0.25	(0.32)
2018-19	0.76	0.43	0.28	0.34
2019-20	0.26	...	...	...

Interim Dividends (Per Share)

Amt	Decl	Ex	Rec	Pay
0.08Q	01/24/2019	02/14/2019	02/15/2019	03/01/2019
0.08Q	04/18/2019	05/14/2019	05/15/2019	06/03/2019
0.08Q	07/18/2019	08/14/2019	08/15/2019	09/03/2019
0.08Q	10/17/2019	11/14/2019	11/15/2019	12/02/2019

Indicated Div: $0.32

Valuation Analysis — **Institutional Holding**

Forecast EPS	$3.61	No of Institutions	
	(01/17/2020)	584	
Market Cap	$6.3 Billion	Shares	
Book Value	$1.8 Billion	183,121,072	
Price/Book	3.43	% Held	
Price/Sales	0.24	77.25	

Business Summary: Electrical Equipment (MIC: 7.3.1 SIC: 3672 NAIC: 334412)

Jabil is a provider of manufacturing services and solutions. Co. provides electronics design, production and product management services to companies in various industries and end markets. Co.'s manufacturing and supply chain management services and solutions include design, planning, fabrication and assembly, delivery and managing the flow of resources and products. Co.'s segments include: Electronics Manufacturing Services, which utilizes information technology, supply chain design and engineering, technologies centered on primary electronics; and Diversified Manufacturing Services, which provides engineering solutions, with a focus on material sciences, technologies and healthcare.

Recent Developments: For the quarter ended Nov 30 2019, net income decreased 67.2% to US$40.7 million from US$124.1 million in the year-earlier quarter. Revenues were US$7.51 billion, up 15.4% from US$6.51 billion the year before. Operating income was US$152.8 million versus US$216.7 million in the prior-year quarter, a decrease of 29.5%. Direct operating expenses rose 16.1% to US$6.95 billion from US$5.99 billion in the comparable period the year before. Indirect operating expenses increased 32.4% to US$401.1 million from US$302.9 million in the equivalent prior-year period.

Prospects: Our evaluation of Jabil Circuit Inc. as of October 4th, 2019 is the result of our systematic analysis on three basic characteristics: earnings strength, relative valuation, and recent stock price movement. The company has managed to produce a neutral trend in earnings per share over the past 5 quarters. However, recent analyst estimates for the company have been reduced and JBL has posted results that fell short of analysts' expectations. Based on operating earnings yield, the company is undervalued when compared to all of the companies we cover. Share price changes over the past year indicates that JBL will perform very poorly over the near term.

Financial Data

(US$ in Thousands)	3 Mos	08/31/2019	08/31/2018	08/31/2017	08/31/2016	08/31/2015	08/31/2014	08/31/2013
Earnings Per Share	1.31	1.81	0.49	0.69	1.32	1.45	1.19	1.79
Cash Flow Per Share	8.53	7.67	5.42	6.91	4.80	6.40	2.46	5.98
Tang Book Value Per Share	6.02	6.57	6.34	8.22	8.27	8.17	8.32	7.85
Dividends Per Share	0.320	0.320	0.320	0.320	0.320	0.320	0.320	0.320
Dividend Payout %	24.43	17.68	65.31	46.38	24.24	22.07	26.89	17.88
Income Statement								
Total Revenue	7,505,698	25,282,320	22,095,416	19,063,121	18,353,086	17,899,196	15,762,146	18,336,894
EBITDA	157,747	1,389,807	1,278,293	1,142,162	1,211,074	1,069,333	681,594	923,379
Depn & Amortn	16,140	771,833	773,703	760,380	696,621	529,149	485,157	418,154
Income Before Taxes	102,640	450,704	373,401	256,233	387,045	422,046	72,123	386,064
Income Taxes	61,926	161,230	285,860	129,066	132,149	127,861	73,711	15,973
Net Income	40,422	287,111	86,330	129,090	254,095	284,019	241,313	371,482
Average Shares	156,462	158,647	175,044	185,838	192,750	196,005	202,497	207,815
Balance Sheet								
Current Assets	9,252,231	8,345,085	7,549,923	6,626,683	5,848,381	5,866,309	5,359,017	5,820,245
Total Assets	14,444,963	12,970,475	12,045,641	11,095,995	10,322,677	9,603,207	8,479,746	9,153,781
Current Liabilities	9,562,048	8,532,105	7,230,873	6,870,593	5,568,056	5,675,141	4,321,097	4,864,434
Long-Term Obligations	2,115,715	2,121,284	2,493,502	1,632,592	2,074,012	1,346,558	1,669,585	1,690,426
Total Liabilities	12,609,277	11,083,032	10,095,384	8,742,481	7,884,506	7,288,351	6,237,918	6,818,494
Stockholders' Equity	1,835,686	1,887,443	1,950,257	2,353,514	2,438,171	2,314,856	2,241,828	2,335,287
Shares Outstanding	152,300	153,520	164,588	177,727	186,998	192,068	194,113	203,164
Statistical Record								
Return on Assets %	1.50	2.30	0.75	1.21	2.54	3.14	2.74	4.38
Return on Equity %	10.94	14.96	4.01	5.39	10.66	12.47	10.54	16.73
EBITDA Margin %	2.10	5.50	5.79	5.99	6.60	5.97	4.32	5.04
Net Margin %	0.54	1.14	0.39	0.68	1.38	1.59	1.53	2.03
Asset Turnover	1.93	2.02	1.91	1.78	1.84	1.98	1.79	2.16
Current Ratio	0.97	0.98	1.04	0.96	1.05	1.03	1.24	1.20
Debt to Equity	1.15	1.12	1.28	0.69	0.85	0.58	0.74	0.72
Price Range	39.59-21.56	31.95-21.56	31.44-24.38	31.46-20.41	25.93-16.88	24.83-17.66	24.04-15.67	23.90-16.57
P/E Ratio	30.22-16.46	17.65-11.91	64.16-49.76	45.59-29.58	19.64-12.79	17.12-12.18	20.20-13.17	13.35-9.26
Average Yield %	1.08	1.17	1.14	1.21	1.23	1.55	1.49	1.63	1.63

Address: 10560 Dr. Martin Luther King, Jr. Street North, St. Petersburg, FL 33716 Telephone: 727-577-9749	Web Site: www.jabil.com Officers: Timothy L. Main - Chairman, President, Chief Executive Officer Thomas A. Sansone - Vice-Chairman, President	Auditors: Ernst & Young LLP Investor Contact: 727-803-3349 Transfer Agents: Computershare, Providence, RI

JACOBS ENGINEERING GROUP, INC.

Exchange	Symbol	Price	52Wk Range	Yield	P/E
NYS	J	$89.83 (12/31/2019)	97.33-57.30	0.85	14.77

*7 Year Price Score 115.69 *NYSE Composite Index=100 *12 Month Price Score 106.07

Interim Earnings (Per Share)

Qtr.	Dec	Mar	Jun	Sep
2014-15	0.77	0.64	0.73	0.25
2015-16	0.38	0.54	0.57	0.24
2016-17	0.50	0.41	0.74	0.78
2017-18	0.02	0.34	1.05	(0.29)
2018-19	0.86	0.41	3.80	1.06

Interim Dividends (Per Share)

Amt	Decl	Ex	Rec	Pay
0.17Q	05/02/2019	05/16/2019	05/17/2019	06/14/2019
0.17Q	07/11/2019	07/25/2019	07/26/2019	08/23/2019
0.17Q	09/19/2019	10/03/2019	10/04/2019	11/01/2019
0.19Q	01/16/2020	01/30/2020	01/31/2020	02/28/2020

Indicated Div: $0.76

Valuation Analysis / **Institutional Holding**

Forecast EPS	$5.56	No of Institutions
	(01/17/2020)	853
Market Cap	$11.9 Billion	Shares
Book Value	$5.7 Billion	155,036,960
Price/Book	2.09	% Held
Price/Sales	0.94	84.73

Business Summary: Business Services (MIC: 7.5.2 SIC: 8748 NAIC: 541690)

Jacobs Engineering Group provides services including consulting, technical, scientific and project delivery for the government and private sector. Co.'s lines of business are: Critical Mission Solutions, which provides cybersecurity, data analytics, software application development, enterprise and mission information technology, systems integration and other technical consulting solutions to government agencies as well as aerospace, automotive and telecom customers; and People and Places Solutions, which provides end-to-end solutions for its clients' projects, whether connected mobility, water, smart cities, manufacturing or the environment.

Recent Developments: For the year ended Sep 27 2019, income from continuing operations increased to US$314.0 million from US$5.3 million a year earlier. Net income increased 404.3% to US$873.2 million from US$173.1 million in the prior year. Revenues were US$12.74 billion, up 20.4% from US$10.58 billion the year before. Operating income was US$404.9 million versus US$387.4 million in the prior year, an increase of 4.5%. Direct operating expenses rose 21.8% to US$10.26 billion from US$8.42 billion in the comparable period the year before. Indirect operating expenses increased 17.0% to US$2.07 billion from US$1.77 billion in the equivalent prior-year period.

Prospects: Our evaluation of Jacobs Engineering Group Inc. as of October 4th, 2019 is the result of our systematic analysis on three basic characteristics: earnings strength, relative valuation, and recent stock price movement. The company has generated a negative trend in earnings per share over the past 5 quarters. However, recent analyst estimates for the company have been unchanged while JEC has posted results that exceeded analysts' expectations. Based on operating earnings yield, the company is fairly valued when compared to all of the companies we cover. Share price changes over the past year indicates that JEC will perform well over the near term.

Financial Data

(US$ in Thousands)	09/27/2019	09/28/2018	09/29/2017	09/30/2016	10/02/2015	09/26/2014	09/27/2013	09/28/2012
Earnings Per Share	6.08	1.17	2.42	1.73	2.40	2.48	3.23	2.94
Cash Flow Per Share	(2.66)	3.51	4.83	5.68	3.81	5.55	3.48	2.36
Tang Book Value Per Share	N.M.	N.M.	9.02	7.02	7.22	7.61	14.98	11.30
Dividends Per Share	0.510	0.750	0.450	...	...	...	...	...
Dividend Payout %	8.39	64.10	18.60	...	...	...	...	...
Income Statement								
Total Revenue	12,737,868	14,984,646	10,022,788	10,964,157	12,114,832	12,695,157	11,818,376	10,893,778
EBITDA	594,588	821,068	519,017	424,106	591,670	689,322	767,933	699,797
Depn & Amortn	169,269	198,587	122,513	129,971	149,292	145,412	98,874	100,824
Income Before Taxes	350,959	554,705	393,217	286,723	430,137	542,166	661,548	593,336
Income Taxes	36,954	381,563	105,842	72,208	101,255	190,054	221,366	202,382
Net Income	847,979	163,431	293,727	210,463	302,971	328,108	423,093	378,954
Average Shares	139,206	138,712	120,147	121,483	126,110	132,371	130,945	128,692
Balance Sheet								
Current Assets	4,111,768	4,556,584	2,996,180	2,864,470	3,282,976	3,892,071	4,039,558	3,612,077
Total Assets	11,462,711	12,645,795	7,380,859	7,360,022	7,785,926	8,453,659	7,274,144	6,839,433
Current Liabilities	3,073,706	3,145,693	1,926,227	1,782,686	1,981,166	2,349,846	1,887,619	1,747,052
Long-Term Obligations	1,201,245	2,146,877	235,000	385,330	584,434	764,075	415,086	528,260
Total Liabilities	5,748,020	6,791,450	2,952,507	3,094,746	3,494,181	3,984,404	3,061,047	3,116,960
Stockholders' Equity	5,714,691	5,854,345	4,428,352	4,265,276	4,291,745	4,469,255	4,213,097	3,722,473
Shares Outstanding	132,879	142,217	120,385	120,950	123,152	131,752	131,639	129,935
Statistical Record								
Return on Assets %	7.05	1.64	4.00	2.79	3.67	4.18	6.01	5.90
Return on Equity %	14.70	3.19	6.78	4.93	6.80	7.58	10.69	10.80
EBITDA Margin %	4.67	5.48	5.18	3.87	4.88	5.43	6.50	6.42
Net Margin %	6.66	1.09	2.93	1.92	2.50	2.58	3.58	3.48
Asset Turnover	1.06	1.50	1.36	1.45	1.47	1.62	1.68	1.70
Current Ratio	1.34	1.45	1.56	1.61	1.66	1.66	2.14	2.07
Debt to Equity	0.21	0.37	0.05	0.09	0.14	0.17	0.10	0.14
Price Range	93.55-55.24	77.61-55.57	62.17-49.25	55.57-35.06	49.68-36.65	66.81-49.52	62.33-38.43	47.61-31.55
P/E Ratio	15.39-9.09	66.33-47.50	25.69-20.35	32.12-20.27	20.70-15.27	26.94-19.97	19.30-11.90	16.19-10.73
Average Yield %	0.68	1.16	0.82	...	...	...	...	...

Address: 1999 Bryan Street, Suite 1200, Dallas, TX 75201 Telephone: 214-583-8500	Web Site: www.jacobs.com Officers: Steven J. Demetriou - Chairman, President, Chief Executive Officer Kevin C. Berryman - President, Executive Vice President, Chief Financial Officer	Auditors: Ernst & Young LLP Transfer Agents: Wells Fargo Shareowner Services, South St. Paul, MN

JBG SMITH PROPERTIES

Exchange	Symbol	Price	52Wk Range	Yield	P/E
NYS	JBGS	$39.89 (12/31/2019)	43.17-34.39	2.26	189.95

*7 Year Price Score N/A   ***NYSE Composite Index=100**   ***12 Month Price Score 94.46**

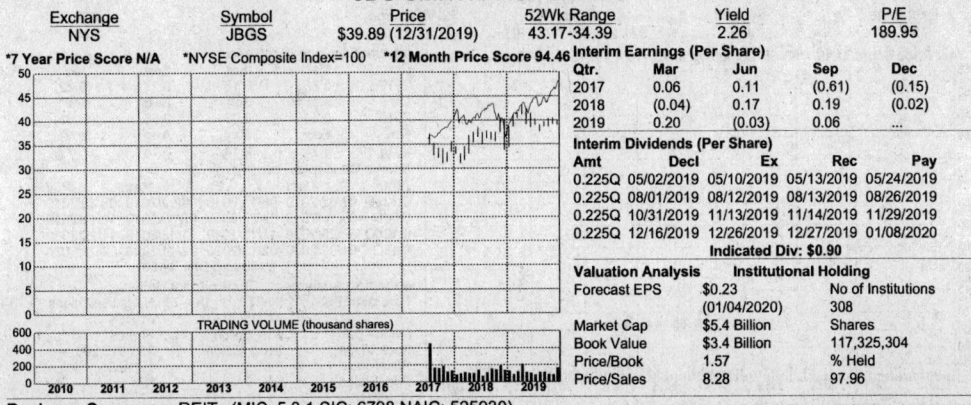

Interim Earnings (Per Share)

Qtr.	Mar	Jun	Sep	Dec
2017	0.06	0.11	(0.61)	(0.15)
2018	(0.04)	0.17	0.19	(0.02)
2019	0.20	(0.03)	0.06	...

Interim Dividends (Per Share)

Amt	Decl	Ex	Rec	Pay
0.225Q	05/02/2019	05/10/2019	05/13/2019	05/24/2019
0.225Q	08/01/2019	08/12/2019	08/13/2019	08/26/2019
0.225Q	10/31/2019	11/13/2019	11/14/2019	11/29/2019
0.225Q	12/16/2019	12/26/2019	12/27/2019	01/08/2020

Indicated Div: $0.90

Valuation Analysis

		Institutional Holding	
Forecast EPS	$0.23	No of Institutions	
	(01/04/2020)	308	
Market Cap	$5.4 Billion	Shares	
Book Value	$3.4 Billion	117,325,304	
Price/Book	1.57	% Held	
Price/Sales	8.28	97.96	

Business Summary: REITs (MIC: 5.3.1 SIC: 6798 NAIC: 525930)

JBG SMITH Properties is a real estate investment trust that owns, operates, invests in and develops real estate assets focusing on urban infill submarkets in and around Washington, DC. Co. owns and operates a portfolio of commercial and multifamily assets. Additionally, Co. has assets under construction comprising commercial assets and multifamily assets, as well as future development assets. In addition, Co.'s third-party asset management and real estate services business provides fee-based real estate services to third parties and the funds. Co. operates in the following business segments: commercial, multifamily and third-party asset management and real estate services.

Recent Developments: For the quarter ended Sep 30 2019, net income decreased 60.1% to US$10.5 million from US$26.4 million in the year-earlier quarter. Revenues were US$167.1 million, up 5.4% from US$158.4 million the year before. Revenues from property income rose 5.4% to US$158.6 million from US$150.4 million in the corresponding quarter a year earlier.

Prospects: Our evaluation of JBG SMITH Properties as of October 4th, 2019 is the result of our systematic analysis on three basic characteristics: earnings strength, relative valuation, and recent stock price movement. The company has managed to produce a neutral trend in earnings per share over the past 5 quarters. In addition, recent analyst estimates for the company have been mixed and JBGS has posted results that fell short of analysts' expectations. Based on operating earnings yield, the company is overvalued when compared to all of the companies we cover. Share price changes over the past year indicates that JBGS will perform well over the near term.

Financial Data

(US$ in Thousands)	9 Mos	6 Mos	3 Mos	12/31/2018	12/31/2017	12/31/2016	12/31/2015	12/31/2014
Earnings Per Share	0.21	0.34	0.54	0.31	(0.70)	0.62	0.49	0.81
Cash Flow Per Share	1.22	1.12	1.40	1.58	0.70	1.34	...	...
Tang Book Value Per Share	23.83	24.00	22.64	24.70	25.18	...	...	...
Dividends Per Share	1.000	1.000	1.000	1.000	0.450	...	...	...
Dividend Payout %	476.19	294.12	185.19	322.58	...	...	...	...
Income Statement								
Total Revenue	482,893	315,816	155,199	644,182	543,013	478,519	470,607	472,923
EBITDA	77,122	54,594	45,224	323,999	135,098	246,512	246,785	250,007
Depn & Amortn	3,858	3,517	1,925	218,845	167,741	133,719	144,188	111,388
Income Before Taxes	34,763	23,799	27,076	45,875	(88,996)	64,299	54,482	82,820
Income Taxes	(689)	(1,121)	(1,172)	(738)	(9,912)	1,083	420	242
Net Income	31,181	21,821	24,861	39,924	(71,753)	61,974	49,628	81,299
Average Shares	134,127	131,754	123,423	119,176	105,359	100,571	100,571	100,571
Balance Sheet								
Current Assets	297,685	348,565	463,440	446,100	385,291	65,643	110,883	...
Total Assets	6,022,264	6,007,275	6,024,694	5,997,285	6,071,807	3,660,640	3,575,878	3,357,744
Current Liabilities	160,031	140,132	134,776	130,960	138,607	324,155	137,004	...
Long-Term Obligations	1,671,296	1,673,057	2,148,790	2,135,510	2,187,980	1,165,014	1,302,956	...
Total Liabilities	2,608,359	2,564,763	3,027,943	3,010,137	3,101,199	1,538,951	1,516,902	...
Stockholders' Equity	3,413,905	3,442,512	2,996,751	2,987,148	2,970,608	2,121,689	2,058,976	1,988,347
Shares Outstanding	134,127	134,127	122,594	120,937	117,955	...	...	...
Statistical Record								
Return on Assets %	0.53	0.76	1.14	0.66	N.M.	1.71	...	...
Return on Equity %	0.98	1.42	2.30	1.34	N.M.	2.96	...	...
EBITDA Margin %	15.97	17.29	29.14	50.30	24.88	51.52	52.44	52.86
Net Margin %	6.46	6.91	16.02	6.20	N.M.	12.95	10.55	17.19
Asset Turnover	0.11	0.11	0.11	0.11	0.11	0.13	...	...
Current Ratio	1.86	2.49	3.44	3.41	2.78	0.20	0.81	...
Debt to Equity	0.49	0.49	0.72	0.71	0.74	0.55	0.63	...
Price Range	43.17-33.75	43.17-33.75	41.59-33.06	40.55-31.04	37.24-31.10	...	...	...
P/E Ratio	205.57-160.71	126.97-99.26	77.02-61.22	130.81-100.13	...	...	...	...
Average Yield %	2.55	2.58	2.67	2.78	1.35	...	...	...

Address: 4445 Willard Avenue, Suite 400, Chevy Chase, MD 20815 **Telephone:** 240-333-3600	**Web Site:** www.jbgsmith.com **Officers:** Steven Roth - Chairman Robert A. Stewart - Executive Vice-Chairman	**Auditors:** DELOITTE & TOUCHE LLP **Investor Contact:** 240-333-3600 **Transfer Agents:** American Stock Transfer & Trust Company, LLC, Brookly, NY

JEFFERIES FINANCIAL GROUP INC

Exchange	Symbol	Price	52Wk Range	Yield	P/E
NYS	JEF	$21.37 (12/31/2019)	21.61-16.25	2.81	N/A

*7 Year Price Score 71.48   *NYSE Composite Index=100   *12 Month Price Score 104.37

Interim Earnings (Per Share)

Qtr.	Mar	Jun	Sep	Dec
2017	0.75	0.16	0.27	(0.72)
Qtr.	Mar	Jun	Sep	Nov
2018	0.34	2.03	0.55	(0.01)
Qtr.	Feb	May	Aug	Nov
2018-19	0.14	2.14	0.15	...

Interim Dividends (Per Share)

Amt	Decl	Ex	Rec	Pay
0.125Q	07/02/2019	08/16/2019	08/19/2019	08/30/2019
0.00Q	09/16/2019	09/27/2019	09/30/2019	10/11/2019
0.125Q	09/26/2019	11/15/2019	11/18/2019	11/29/2019
0.15Q	01/09/2020	02/13/2020	02/14/2020	02/28/2020

Indicated Div: $0.60

Valuation Analysis — **Institutional Holding**

Forecast EPS	$0.97	No of Institutions
(01/15/2020)		671
Market Cap	$6.4 Billion	Shares
Book Value	$10.1 Billion	258,815,200
Price/Book	0.63	% Held
Price/Sales	N/A	N/A

Business Summary: Agricultural Livestock (MIC: 1.1.2 SIC: 5147 NAIC: 311612)

Jefferies Financial Group is a financial holding company. Co.'s Jefferies Group segment operates in two business segments: Capital Markets, which includes investment banking, sales and trading and other related services; and Asset Management, which provides investment management services and overseas and makes capital investments in managed funds and accounts. Co.'s Merchant Banking consists of its various merchant banking businesses and investments, including National Beef Packing Company, Spectrum Brands Holdings, Inc., Linken S.P.A., Vitesse Energy, LLC and JETX Energy LLC, WeWork, HomeFed Corporation, Idaho Timber, FXCM Group, LLC, Foursight Capital and Golden Queen Mining Company.

Recent Developments: For the quarter ended Aug 31 2019, income from continuing operations decreased 72.9% to US$49.4 million from US$182.3 million in the year-earlier quarter. Net income decreased 72.9% to US$49.4 million from US$182.3 million in the year-earlier quarter. Revenues were US$856.8 million, down 25.6% from US$1.15 billion the year before. Direct operating expenses rose 1.1% to US$85.8 million from US$84.9 million in the comparable period the year before. Indirect operating expenses increased 2.2% to US$830.0 million from US$812.1 million in the equivalent prior-year period.

Prospects: Our evaluation of Jefferies Financial Group Inc. as of October 4th, 2019 is the result of our systematic analysis on three basic characteristics: earnings strength, relative valuation, and recent stock price movement. The company has suffered a very negative trend in earnings per share over the past 5 quarters. In addition, recent analyst estimates for the company have been reduced and JEF has posted results that fell short of analysts' expectations. Based on operating earnings yield, the company is overvalued when compared to all of the companies we cover. Share price changes over the past year indicates that JEF will perform poorly over the near term.

Financial Data

(US$ in Thousands)	9 Mos	6 Mos	3 Mos	11/30/2018	12/31/2017	12/31/2016	12/31/2015	12/31/2014
Earnings Per Share	2.42	2.82	2.71	2.90	0.45	0.34	0.74	0.54
Cash Flow Per Share	...	...	...	2.17	2.91	1.64	(2.05)	(2.65)
Tang Book Value Per Share	27.42	27.85	27.38	26.98	21.81	21.53	21.72	20.97
Dividends Per Share	0.625	0.600	0.575	0.450	0.325	0.250	0.250	0.250
Dividend Payout %	25.83	21.28	21.22	15.52	72.22	73.53	33.78	46.30
Income Statement								
Total Revenue	2,786,878	1,930,100	828,443	3,764,034	11,436,393	10,062,617	10,886,458	11,486,485
EBITDA	180,860	215,800	35,797	395,733	1,360,613	437,324	529,740	499,613
Depn & Amortn	(13,252)	(13,669)	(9,225)	67,407	164,039	166,789	172,073	139,744
Income Before Taxes	124,293	183,313	22,004	239,077	1,088,715	161,832	246,255	242,695
Income Taxes	(522,626)	(486,495)	2,302	19,008	760,967	122,109	109,947	165,971
Net Income	767,879	718,127	46,087	1,026,788	171,726	130,001	283,650	208,368
Average Shares	311,897	312,527	318,752	351,275	370,701	371,518	372,431	373,333
Balance Sheet								
Current Assets	33,533,611	33,510,967	34,167,501	15,039,928	14,962,068	12,952,561	12,075,445	15,583,132
Total Assets	49,263,208	48,523,940	48,959,345	47,131,095	47,169,148	45,071,307	46,339,812	52,623,908
Current Liabilities	8,755,895	9,371,892	9,837,767	10,564,832	10,126,211	8,343,947	11,187,884	11,389,283
Long-Term Obligations	10,477,374	9,660,553	9,213,301	7,617,563	7,885,783	7,380,443	7,407,594	8,527,929
Total Liabilities	39,117,766	38,545,069	38,901,393	36,945,229	36,938,151	34,818,207	35,813,601	42,196,750
Stockholders' Equity	10,145,442	9,978,871	10,057,952	10,185,866	10,230,957	10,253,100	10,526,211	10,427,158
Shares Outstanding	299,867	290,686	298,312	307,515	356,227	359,425	362,617	367,498
Statistical Record								
Return on Assets %	...	...	...	2.38	0.37	0.28	0.57	0.41
Return on Equity %	...	...	...	10.99	1.68	1.25	2.71	2.02
EBITDA Margin %	6.49	11.18	4.32	10.51	11.90	4.35	4.87	4.35
Net Margin %	27.55	37.21	5.56	27.28	1.50	1.29	2.61	1.81
Asset Turnover	...	...	...	0.09	0.25	0.22	0.22	0.23
Current Ratio	3.83	3.58	3.47	1.42	1.48	1.55	1.08	1.37
Debt to Equity	1.03	0.97	0.92	0.75	0.77	0.72	0.70	0.82
Price Range	22.18-15.34	23.17-15.34	23.20-15.34	26.22-18.77	25.46-20.84	22.46-13.52	23.59-15.05	26.81-19.69
P/E Ratio	9.17-6.34	8.22-5.44	8.56-5.66	9.04-6.47	56.57-46.32	66.07-39.78	31.87-20.34	49.66-36.47
Average Yield %	3.33	3.05	2.78	2.05	1.37	1.48	1.21	1.05

Address: 520 Madison Avenue, New York, NY 10022	Web Site: www.jefferies.com	Auditors: DELOITTE & TOUCHE LLP
Telephone: 212-460-1900	Officers: Joseph S. Steinberg - Chairman, President	Investor Contact: 212-460-1900
Fax: 212-598-4869	Richard B. Handler - Chief Executive Officer	Transfer Agents: American Stock Transfer & Trust Company, LLC, Brooklyn, NY

JOHNSON & JOHNSON

Exchange	Symbol	Price	52Wk Range	Yield	P/E	Div Acheiver
NYS	JNJ	$145.87 (12/31/2019)	146.44-125.72	2.61	27.78	54 Years

*7 Year Price Score 97.71   ***NYSE Composite Index=100**   ***12 Month Price Score 96.82**

Interim Earnings (Per Share)

Qtr.	Mar	Jun	Sep	Dec
2016	1.54	1.43	1.53	1.38
2017	1.61	1.40	1.37	(3.90)
2018	1.60	1.45	1.44	1.12
2019	1.39	2.08	0.66	...

Interim Dividends (Per Share)

Amt	Decl	Ex	Rec	Pay
0.95Q	04/25/2019	05/24/2019	05/28/2019	06/11/2019
0.95Q	07/15/2019	08/26/2019	08/27/2019	09/10/2019
0.95Q	10/17/2019	11/25/2019	11/26/2019	12/10/2019
0.95Q	01/02/2020	02/24/2020	02/25/2020	03/10/2020

Indicated Div: $3.80 (Div. Reinv. Plan)

Valuation Analysis   **Institutional Holding**

Forecast EPS	$8.65	No of Institutions
	(01/16/2020)	3795
Market Cap	$383.8 Billion	Shares
Book Value	$58.2 Billion	2,329,753,344
Price/Book	6.59	% Held
Price/Sales	4.70	65.96

TRADING VOLUME (thousand shares)

Business Summary: Pharmaceuticals (MIC: 4.1.1 SIC: 2834 NAIC: 325412)

Johnson & Johnson is a holding company engaged in the research and development, manufacture and sale of a range of products in the health care field. Co. has three business segments: Consumer, which includes a range of products used in the baby care, oral care, beauty, over-the-counter pharmaceutical, women's health and wound care markets; Pharmaceutical, which is focused on six therapeutic areas: immunology, infectious diseases and vaccines, neuroscience, oncology, cardiovascular and metabolism and pulmonary hypertension; and Medical Devices, which includes products used in the orthopaedic, surgery, interventional solutions (cardiovascular and neurovascular), and eye health fields.

Recent Developments: For the quarter ended Sep 29 2019, net income decreased 55.4% to US$1.75 billion from US$3.93 billion in the year-earlier quarter. Revenues were US$20.73 billion, up 1.9% from US$20.35 billion the year before. Direct operating expenses rose 4.2% to US$6.87 billion from US$6.59 billion in the comparable period the year before. Indirect operating expenses increased 30.8% to US$12.22 billion from US$9.34 billion in the equivalent prior-year period.

Prospects: Our evaluation of Johnson & Johnson as of October 4th, 2019 is the result of our systematic analysis on three basic characteristics: earnings strength, relative valuation, and recent stock price movement. The company has managed to produce a neutral trend in earnings per share over the past 5 quarters. Additionally, recent analyst estimates for the company have been unchanged while JNJ has posted results that exceeded analysts' expectations. Based on operating earnings yield, the company is undervalued when compared to all of the companies we cover. Share price changes over the past year indicates that JNJ will perform in line with the market over the near term.

Financial Data

(US$ in Millions)	9 Mos	6 Mos	3 Mos	12/30/2018	12/31/2017	01/01/2017	01/03/2016	12/28/2014
Earnings Per Share	5.25	6.03	5.40	5.61	0.47	5.93	5.48	5.70
Cash Flow Per Share	8.83	8.30	8.32	8.30	7.84	6.87	6.84	6.58
Tang Book Value Per Share	N.M.	N.M.	N.M.	N.M.	N.M.	7.66	8.62	7.44
Dividends Per Share	3.700	3.650	3.600	3.540	3.320	3.150	2.950	2.760
Dividend Payout %	70.48	60.53	66.67	63.10	706.38	53.12	53.83	48.42
Income Statement								
Total Revenue	61,312	40,583	20,021	81,581	76,450	71,890	70,074	74,331
EBITDA	18,260	14,927	6,186	25,393	22,022	23,861	23,320	24,927
Depn & Amortn	5,193	3,466	1,761	7,000	3,800	3,700	3,700	3,898
Income Before Taxes	13,110	11,463	4,422	17,999	17,673	19,803	19,196	20,563
Income Taxes	2,001	2,107	673	2,702	16,373	3,263	3,787	4,240
Net Income	11,109	9,356	3,749	15,297	1,300	16,540	15,409	·16,323
Average Shares	2,670	2,692	2,699	2,729	2,746	2,789	2,813	2,864
Balance Sheet								
Current Assets	44,333	41,799	41,987	46,033	43,088	65,032	60,210	59,311
Total Assets	155,521	155,117	150,027	152,954	157,303	141,208	133,411	131,119
Current Liabilities	35,162	31,353	29,111	31,230	30,537	26,287	27,747	25,085
Long-Term Obligations	26,919	27,699	27,660	27,684	30,675	22,442	12,857	15,122
Total Liabilities	97,311	94,332	91,072	93,202	97,143	70,790	62,261	61,367
Stockholders' Equity	58,210	60,785	58,955	59,752	60,160	70,418	71,150	69,752
Shares Outstanding	2,631	2,643	2,656	2,663	2,683	2,707	2,756	2,784
Statistical Record								
Return on Assets %	9.09	10.52	9.57	9.89	0.87	12.08	11.46	12.41
Return on Equity %	23.04	26.41	24.02	25.58	2.00	23.43	21.52	22.76
EBITDA Margin %	29.78	36.78	30.90	31.13	28.81	33.19	33.28	33.54
Net Margin %	18.12	·23.05	18.73	18.75	1.70	23.01	21.99	21.96
Asset Turnover	0.53	0.52	0.53	0.53	0.51	0.53	0.52	0.57
Current Ratio	1.26	1.33	1.44	1.47	1.41	2.47	2.17	2.36
Debt to Equity	0.46	0.46	0.47	0.46	0.51	0.32	0.18	0.22
Price Range	147.84-122.84	147.84-121.58	147.84-119.40	148.14-119.40	143.62-111.76	125.40-95.75	106.39-90.73	109.07-86.62
P/E Ratio	28.16-23.40	24.52-20.16	27.38-22.11	·26.41-21.28	305.57-237.79	21.15-16.15	19.41-16.56	19.14-15.20
Average Yield %	2.72	2.68	2.71	2.66	2.56	2.77	2.96	2.74

Address: One Johnson & Johnson Plaza, New Brunswick, NJ 08933
Telephone: 732-524-0400
Fax: 732-214-0332

Web Site: www.jnj.com
Officers: Alex Gorsky - Chairman, Chief Executive Officer, Division Officer Joaquin Duato - Vice-Chairman, Executive Vice President, Division Officer

Auditors: PricewaterhouseCoopers LLP
Investor Contact: 800-950-5089
Transfer Agents: Computershare Trust Company, N.A., Canton, MA

JONES LANG LASALLE INC

Exchange	Symbol	Price	52Wk Range	Yield	P/E
NYS	JLL	$174.09 (12/31/2019)	174.09-121.89	0.49	17.93

*7 Year Price Score 92.20 ***NYSE Composite Index=100** ***12 Month Price Score 106.55**

Interim Earnings (Per Share)

Qtr.	Mar	Jun	Sep	Dec
2016	0.56	1.73	1.05	3.63
2017	0.24	1.71	1.89	1.71
2018	0.88	2.35	2.93	4.38
2019	0.46	2.40	2.47	...

Interim Dividends (Per Share)

Amt	Decl	Ex	Rec	Pay
0.41S	05/08/2018	05/17/2018	05/18/2018	06/15/2018
0.41S	11/06/2018	11/15/2018	11/16/2018	12/14/2018
0.43S	05/07/2019	05/16/2019	05/17/2019	06/14/2019
0.43S	11/05/2019	11/14/2019	11/15/2019	12/13/2019

Indicated Div: $0.86

Valuation Analysis

Forecast EPS	$13.25
	(01/17/2020)
Market Cap	$9.0 Billion
Book Value	$4.8 Billion
Price/Book	1.88
Price/Sales	0.51

Institutional Holding

No of Institutions	611
Shares	56,728,728
% Held	89.79

Business Summary: Property, Real Estate & Development (MIC: 5.3.2 SIC: 6531 NAIC: 531210)

Jones Lang LaSalle is a professional services firm that engages in real estate and investment management. Co. delivers an array of services across four business segments. Co. manage its Real Estate Services offerings across three geographic business segments: the Americas, Europe, Middle East and Africa (EMEA), and Asia Pacific, and Co. manages its investment management business globally as LaSalle Investment Management. In its Americas, EMEA and Asia Pacific operating segments, Co. provides a range of leasing, capital markets, integrated property and facility management, project management, advisory, consulting, valuations and digital solutions services.

Recent Developments: For the quarter ended Sep 30 2019, net income decreased 5.0% to US$129.3 million from US$136.1 million in the year-earlier quarter. Revenues were US$4.50 billion, up 13.2% from US$3.97 billion the year before.

Prospects: Our evaluation of Jones Lang LaSalle Inc. as of October 4th, 2019 is the result of our systematic analysis on three basic characteristics: earnings strength, relative valuation, and recent stock price movement. The company has generated a negative trend in earnings per share over the past 5 quarters. However, recent analyst estimates for the company have been raised and JLL has posted results that exceeded analysts' expectations. Based on operating earnings yield, the company is undervalued when compared to all of the companies we cover. Share price changes over the past year indicates that JLL will perform in line with the market over the near term.

Financial Data
(US$ in Thousands)

	9 Mos	6 Mos	3 Mos	12/31/2018	12/31/2017	12/31/2016	12/31/2015	12/31/2014
Earnings Per Share	9.71	10.17	10.12	10.54	5.55	6.98	9.65	8.52
Cash Flow Per Share	6.85	8.50	6.81	13.27	17.42	4.74	8.36	11.16
Tang Book Value Per Share	0.49	16.50	14.55	14.40	5.04	N.M.	7.11	9.82
Dividends Per Share	0.840	0.840	0.820	0.820	0.720	0.640	0.560	0.480
Dividend Payout %	8.65	8.26	8.10	7.78	12.97	9.17	5.80	5.63
Income Statement								
Total Revenue	12,582,700	8,087,100	3,820,600	16,318,400	7,932,400	6,803,800	5,965,671	5,429,603
EBITDA	493,900	268,000	71,600	942,100	735,200	633,600	664,756	583,869
Depn & Amortn	145,600	92,000	46,500	217,800	198,300	179,700	134,958	118,205
Income Before Taxes	307,100	152,800	15,500	673,200	480,700	408,600	501,671	437,343
Income Taxes	77,600	35,500	(700)	214,300	267,800	108,000	132,805	97,588
Net Income	260,900	132,000	21,300	484,500	254,200	318,200	438,672	386,063
Average Shares	52,104	46,040	46,019	45,931	45,758	45,528	45,414	45,260
Balance Sheet								
Current Assets	5,590,100	5,030,100	5,027,700	5,206,000	3,354,900	3,299,700	2,650,807	2,118,176
Total Assets	13,077,900	10,580,900	10,552,500	10,025,500	8,014,500	7,629,400	6,205,159	5,075,336
Current Liabilities	4,862,700	4,170,500	4,211,600	4,761,800	3,210,000	2,966,300	2,505,193	2,047,011
Long-Term Obligations	2,371,300	1,708,100	1,709,100	655,600	675,300	1,178,100	529,999	275,000
Total Liabilities	8,293,600	6,758,900	6,810,100	6,334,000	4,771,300	4,839,700	3,516,396	2,688,539
Stockholders' Equity	4,784,300	3,822,000	3,742,400	3,691,500	3,243,200	2,789,700	2,688,763	2,386,797
Shares Outstanding	51,534	45,762	45,739	45,599	45,373	45,213	45,049	44,828
Statistical Record								
Return on Assets %	4.07	4.74	4.71	5.37	3.25	4.59	7.78	7.98
Return on Equity %	11.12	12.92	12.97	13.97	8.43	11.58	17.29	16.91
EBITDA Margin %	3.93	3.31	1.87	5.77	9.27	9.31	11.14	10.75
Net Margin %	2.07	1.63	0.56	2.97	3.20	4.68	7.35	7.11
Asset Turnover	1.54	1.71	1.68	1.81	1.01	0.98	1.06	1.12
Current Ratio	1.15	1.21	1.19	1.09	1.05	1.11	1.06	1.03
Debt to Equity	0.50	0.45	0.46	0.18	0.21	0.42	0.20	0.12
Price Range	167.19-121.89	172.35-121.89	176.43-121.89	177.30-123.19	153.03-99.21	160.19-88.65	179.35-142.69	153.43-101.95
P/E Ratio	17.22-12.55	16.95-11.99	17.43-12.04	16.82-11.69	27.57-17.88	22.95-12.70	18.59-14.79	18.01-11.97
Average Yield %	0.59	0.57	0.54	0.53	0.59	0.57	0.35	0.38

Address: 200 East Randolph Drive, Chicago, IL 60601	**Web Site:** www.jll.com	**Auditors:** KPMG LLP
Telephone: 312-782-5800	**Officers:** Sheila A. Penrose - Chairman Christian Ulbrich - President, Chief Executive Officer, Region Officer	**Investor Contact:** 312-782-5800
Fax: 312-782-4339		**Transfer Agents:** Computershare, Pittsburgh, PA

JPMORGAN CHASE & CO

Exchange	Symbol	Price	52Wk Range	Yield	P/E
NYS	JPM	$139.40 (12/31/2019)	139.40-97.11	2.58	13.73

*7 Year Price Score 118.02 *NYSE Composite Index=100 *12 Month Price Score 110.42

Interim Earnings (Per Share)

Qtr.	Mar	Jun	Sep	Dec
2016	1.35	1.55	1.58	1.71
2017	1.65	1.82	1.76	1.09
2018	2.37	2.29	2.34	2.00
2019	2.65	2.82	2.68	...

Interim Dividends (Per Share)

Amt	Decl	Ex	Rec	Pay
0.80Q	03/19/2019	04/04/2019	04/05/2019	04/30/2019
0.80Q	05/21/2019	07/03/2019	07/05/2019	07/31/2019
0.90Q	09/17/2019	10/03/2019	10/04/2019	10/31/2019
0.90Q	12/10/2019	01/03/2020	01/06/2020	01/31/2020

Indicated Div: $3.60 (Div. Reinv. Plan)

Valuation Analysis / Institutional Holding

Forecast EPS	$10.82 (01/17/2020)	No of Institutions	3599
Market Cap	$437.2 Billion	Shares	2,998,703,872
Book Value	$264.3 Billion	% Held	65.08
Price/Book	1.65		
Price/Sales	3.09		

Business Summary: Banking (MIC: 5.1.1 SIC: 6021 NAIC: 522110)

JPMorgan Chase is a financial holding company. Co.'s activities are organized into four reportable business segments: Consumer and Community Banking, which provides services to consumers and businesses through bank branches, automated teller machines, online, mobile and telephone banking; Corporate and Investment Bank, which consists of Banking and Markets and Investor Services, provides a suite of investment banking, market-making, prime brokerage, and treasury and securities products and services; Commercial Banking, which provides financing to real estate investors and owners; and Asset and Wealth Management, which is engaged in investment and wealth management.

Recent Developments: For the quarter ended Sep 30 2019, net income increased 8.4% to US$9.08 billion from US$8.38 billion in the year-earlier quarter. Net interest income increased 2.3% to US$14.23 billion from US$13.91 billion in the year-earlier quarter. Provision for loan losses was US$1.51 billion versus US$948.0 million in the prior-year quarter, an increase of 59.7%. Non-interest income rose 13.2% to US$15.11 billion from US$13.35 billion, while non-interest expense advanced 5.1% to US$16.42 billion.

Prospects: Our evaluation of J.P. Morgan Chase & Co. as of October 4th, 2019 is the result of our systematic analysis on three basic characteristics: earnings strength, relative valuation, and recent stock price movement. The company has managed to produce a neutral trend in earnings per share over the past 5 quarters. However, recent analyst estimates for the company have been reduced while JPM has posted results that exceeded analysts' expectations. Based on operating earnings yield, the company is undervalued when compared to all of the companies we cover. Share price changes over the past year indicates that JPM will perform poorly over the near term.

Financial Data
(US$ in Millions)

	9 Mos	6 Mos	3 Mos	12/31/2018	12/31/2017	12/31/2016	12/31/2015	12/31/2014
Earnings Per Share	10.15	9.81	9.28	9.00	6.31	6.19	6.00	5.29
Cash Flow Per Share	(23.95)	(24.96)	(9.58)	4.18	(0.70)	5.57	19.85	9.72
Tang Book Value Per Share	58.32	57.21	55.08	53.76	51.16	48.83	45.46	41.92
Dividends Per Share	3.200	2.960	2.720	2.480	2.040	1.840	1.680	1.560
Dividend Payout %	31.53	30.17	29.31	27.56	32.33	29.73	28.00	29.49
Income Statement								
Interest Income	64,113	42,992	21,894	77,442	64,372	55,901	50,973	51,531
Interest Expense	21,034	14,141	7,441	22,383	14,275	9,818	7,463	7,897
Net Interest Income	43,079	28,851	14,453	55,059	50,097	46,083	43,510	43,634
Provision for Losses	4,158	2,644	1,495	4,871	5,290	5,361	3,827	3,139
Non-Interest Income	44,217	29,104	14,670	53,970	49,527	49,585	50,033	50,571
Non-Interest Expense	49,158	32,736	16,395	63,394	58,434	55,771	59,014	61,274
Income Before Taxes	33,980	22,575	11,233	40,764	35,900	34,536	30,702	29,792
Income Taxes	6,069	3,744	2,054	8,290	11,459	9,803	6,260	8,030
Net Income	27,911	18,831	9,179	32,474	24,441	24,733	24,442	21,762
Average Shares	3,208	3,260	3,309	3,415	3,577	3,650	3,733	3,798
Balance Sheet								
Net Loans & Leases	931,983	943,723	942,712	971,109	917,093	880,989	823,744	743,151
Total Assets	2,764,661	2,727,379	2,737,188	2,622,532	2,533,600	2,490,972	2,351,698	2,573,126
Total Deposits	1,525,261	1,524,361	1,493,441	1,470,666	1,443,982	1,375,179	1,279,715	1,363,427
Total Liabilities	2,500,313	2,464,164	2,477,351	2,366,017	2,277,907	2,236,782	2,104,125	2,341,061
Stockholders' Equity	264,348	263,215	259,837	256,515	255,693	254,190	247,573	232,065
Shares Outstanding	3,137	3,198	3,245	3,276	3,426	3,562	3,664	3,715
Statistical Record								
Return on Assets %	1.30	1.29	1.23	1.26	0.97	1.02	0.99	0.87
Return on Equity %	13.37	13.17	12.77	12.68	9.59	9.83	10.19	9.82
Net Interest Margin %	67.36	66.65	66.01	71.10	77.82	82.44	85.36	84.68
Efficiency Ratio %	45.32	45.35	44.84	48.24	51.30	52.87	58.43	60.01
Loans to Deposits	0.61	0.62	0.63	0.66	0.64	0.64	0.64	0.55
Price Range	120.23-92.14	118.63-92.14	118.63-92.14	118.77-92.14	107.83-82.15	87.13-53.07	70.08-54.38	63.15-53.31
P/E Ratio	11.85-9.08	12.09-9.39	12.78-9.93	13.20-10.24	17.09-13.02	14.08-8.57	11.68-9.06	11.94-10.08
Average Yield %	2.95	2.73	2.41	2.24	2.22	2.80	2.63	2.68

Address: 383 Madison Avenue, New York, NY 10179 **Telephone:** 212-270-6000	**Web Site:** www.jpmorganchase.com **Officers:** James (Jamie) Dimon - Chairman, President, Chief Executive Officer Daniel E. Pinto - Co-President, Co-Chief Operating Officer, Division Officer, Region Officer	**Auditors:** PricewaterhouseCoopers LLP **Investor Contact:** 212-270-7325 **Transfer Agents:** Computershare Shareowner Services LLC, Jersey City, NY

JUNIPER NETWORKS INC

Exchange	Symbol	Price	52Wk Range	Yield	P/E
NYS	JNPR	$24.63 (12/31/2019)	28.72-22.64	3.09	23.24

*7 Year Price Score 84.96   *NYSE Composite Index=100   *12 Month Price Score 91.13

Interim Earnings (Per Share)

Qtr.	Mar	Jun	Sep	Dec
2016	0.23	0.36	0.45	0.49
2017	0.28	0.47	0.43	(0.38)
2018	0.10	0.33	0.64	0.55
2019	0.09	0.13	0.29	...

Interim Dividends (Per Share)

Amt	Decl	Ex	Rec	Pay
0.19Q	01/29/2019	02/28/2019	03/01/2019	03/22/2019
0.19Q	04/25/2019	05/31/2019	06/03/2019	06/24/2019
0.19Q	07/25/2019	09/03/2019	09/04/2019	09/25/2019
0.19Q	10/24/2019	11/29/2019	12/02/2019	12/23/2019

Indicated Div: $0.76

Valuation Analysis

		Institutional Holding	
Forecast EPS	$1.71	No of Institutions	
	(01/15/2020)	705	
Market Cap	$8.4 Billion	Shares	
Book Value	$4.6 Billion	378,973,728	
Price/Book	1.81	% Held	
Price/Sales	1.90	80.44	

Business Summary: Peripherals (MIC: 6.2.2 SIC: 3577 NAIC: 334119)

Juniper Networks designs, develops and sells products and services for networks. Co. sells its products in three geographic regions: Americas; Europe, Middle East, and Africa; and Asia Pacific. Co. sells its network products and service offerings across routing, switching, and security technologies. In addition, Co. provides its customers services, including maintenance and support, services, and education and training programs. Co.'s products and services address network requirements for its customers within its vertical: Cloud, Service Provider, and Enterprise. Co.'s portfolio addresses domains in the network: core; edge; access and aggregation; data centers; and campus and branch.

Recent Developments: For the quarter ended Sep 30 2019, net income decreased 55.6% to US$99.3 million from US$223.8 million in the year-earlier quarter. Revenues were US$1.13 billion, down 4.0% from US$1.18 billion the year before. Operating income was US$138.5 million versus US$160.1 million in the prior-year quarter, a decrease of 13.5%. Direct operating expenses declined 3.0% to US$454.7 million from US$468.8 million in the comparable period the year before. Indirect operating expenses decreased 2.0% to US$539.9 million from US$550.9 million in the equivalent prior-year period.

Prospects: Our evaluation of Juniper Networks Inc. as of October 4th, 2019 is the result of our systematic analysis on three basic characteristics: earnings strength, relative valuation, and recent stock price movement. The company has generated a negative trend in earnings per share over the past 5 quarters. However, recent analyst estimates for the company have been mixed and JNPR has posted results that exceeded analysts' expectations. Based on operating earnings yield, the company is undervalued when compared to all of the companies we cover. Share price changes over the past year indicates that JNPR will perform poorly over the near term.

Financial Data

(US$ in Thousands)	9 Mos	6 Mos	3 Mos	12/31/2018	12/31/2017	12/31/2016	12/31/2015	12/31/2014
Earnings Per Share	1.06	1.41	1.61	1.60	0.80	1.53	1.59	(0.73)
Cash Flow Per Share	1.89	1.93	2.15	2.47	3.34	2.89	2.28	1.67
Tang Book Value Per Share	3.25	3.04	4.63	4.61	3.99	4.59	4.04	4.48
Dividends Per Share	0.750	0.740	0.730	0.720	0.400	0.400	0.400	0.200
Dividend Payout %	70.75	52.48	45.34	45.00	50.00	26.14	25.16	...
Income Statement								
Total Revenue	3,237,300	2,104,200	1,001,700	4,647,500	5,027,200	4,990,100	4,857,800	4,627,100
EBITDA	401,200	226,900	93,900	756,400	1,062,800	1,074,200	1,055,200	112,500
Depn & Amortn	155,500	101,700	48,700	193,200	202,800	184,500	141,500	141,900
Income Before Taxes	240,400	122,300	44,500	532,700	811,800	827,400	852,200	(86,300)
Income Taxes	63,800	45,000	13,400	(34,200)	505,600	234,700	218,500	248,000
Net Income	176,600	77,300	31,100	566,900	306,200	592,700	633,700	(334,300)
Average Shares	345,500	349,100	352,700	354,400	384,200	387,800	399,400	457,400
Balance Sheet								
Current Assets	3,187,500	3,758,600	4,309,600	4,581,800	4,184,500	3,971,900	2,912,400	2,971,900
Total Assets	8,753,600	8,903,300	9,137,900	9,363,300	9,833,800	9,656,500	8,619,200	8,403,100
Current Liabilities	1,422,900	1,766,200	1,489,100	1,842,500	1,738,200	1,735,900	1,801,900	1,527,700
Long-Term Obligations	1,687,600	1,490,500	1,789,600	1,789,100	2,136,300	2,133,700	1,648,800	1,349,000
Total Liabilities	4,111,200	4,312,100	4,286,700	4,540,100	5,152,900	4,694,000	4,044,800	3,484,000
Stockholders' Equity	4,642,400	4,591,200	4,851,200	4,823,200	4,680,900	4,962,500	4,574,400	4,919,100
Shares Outstanding	341,000	344,500	352,000	346,400	365,500	381,100	384,000	416,200
Statistical Record								
Return on Assets %	4.13	5.47	6.19	5.91	3.14	6.47	7.45	N.M.
Return on Equity %	7.94	10.95	12.28	11.93	6.35	12.40	13.35	N.M.
EBITDA Margin %	12.39	10.78	9.37	16.28	21.14	21.53	21.72	2.43
Net Margin %	5.46	3.67	3.10	12.20	6.09	11.88	13.05	N.M.
Asset Turnover	0.49	0.50	0.50	0.48	0.52	0.54	0.57	0.49
Current Ratio	2.24	2.13	2.89	2.49	2.41	2.29	1.62	1.95
Debt to Equity	0.36	0.32	0.37	0.37	0.46	0.43	0.36	0.27
Price Range	30.67-22.64	30.67-24.61	30.67-24.07	30.67-24.05	30.89-24.40	28.68-21.24	32.23-21.39	27.95-18.57
P/E Ratio	28.93-21.36	21.75-17.45	19.05-14.95	19.17-15.03	38.61-30.50	18.75-13.88	20.27-13.45	...
Average Yield %	2.80	2.69	2.67	2.65	1.43	1.64	1.52	0.84

Address: 1133 Innovation Way, Sunnyvale, CA 94089 Telephone: 408-745-2000 Fax: 408-745-2100	Web Site: www.juniper.net Officers: Scott G. Kriens - Chairman, Chief Executive Officer Anand Athreya - Executive Vice President, Chief Development Officer	Auditors: Ernst & Young LLP Investor Contact: 408-936-5396 Transfer Agents: Wells Fargo Shareowner Services, Mendota Heights, MN

KANSAS CITY SOUTHERN

Exchange	Symbol	Price	52Wk Range	Yield	P/E
NYS	KSU	$153.16 (12/31/2019)	155.10-92.87	1.04	26.92

*7 Year Price Score 97.56   *NYSE Composite Index=100   *12 Month Price Score 115.35

TRADING VOLUME (thousand shares)

Interim Earnings (Per Share)

Qtr.	Mar	Jun	Sep	Dec
2016	0.99	1.11	1.12	1.20
2017	1.38	1.27	1.23	5.28
2018	1.40	1.45	1.70	1.58
2019	1.02	1.28	1.81	...

Interim Dividends (Per Share)

Amt	Decl	Ex	Rec	Pay
0.36Q	01/31/2019	03/08/2019	03/11/2019	04/03/2019
0.36Q	05/20/2019	06/07/2019	06/10/2019	07/03/2019
0.36Q	08/13/2019	09/06/2019	09/09/2019	10/02/2019
0.40Q	11/12/2019	12/30/2019	12/31/2019	01/22/2020

Indicated Div: $1.60

Valuation Analysis / **Institutional Holding**

Forecast EPS	$6.93	No of Institutions
	(01/17/2020)	872
Market Cap	$15.2 Billion	Shares
Book Value	$4.9 Billion	118,783,600
Price/Book	3.11	% Held
Price/Sales	5.36	84.89

Business Summary: Rail (MIC: 7.4.3 SIC: 4011 NAIC: 482111)

Kansas City Southern is a holding company with domestic and international rail operations in North America. Co. is engaged in the freight rail transportation business operating through a single coordinated rail network under one reportable business segment. Co.'s coordinated rail network comprises approximately 6,700 route miles extending from the midwest and southeast portions of the U.S. south into Mexico and connects with all other Class I railroads, providing shippers with an alternative to other railroad routes and giving direct access to Mexico and the southeast and southwest U.S. through alternate interchange hubs.

Recent Developments: For the quarter ended Sep 30 2019, net income increased 3.8% to US$180.6 million from US$174.0 million in the year-earlier quarter. Revenues were US$747.7 million, up 7.0% from US$699.0 million the year before. Operating income was US$282.0 million versus US$265.4 million in the prior-year quarter, an increase of 6.3%. Direct operating expenses rose 0.2% to US$232.4 million from US$232.0 million in the comparable period the year before. Indirect operating expenses increased 15.7% to US$233.3 million from US$201.6 million in the equivalent prior-year period.

Prospects: Our evaluation of Kansas City Southern Industries Inc. as of October 4th, 2019 is the result of our systematic analysis on three basic characteristics: earnings strength, relative valuation, and recent stock price movement. The company has managed to produce a neutral trend in earnings per share over the past 5 quarters. In addition, recent analyst estimates for the company have been mixed and KSU has posted results that exceeded analysts' expectations. Based on operating earnings yield, the company is fairly valued when compared to all of the companies we cover. Share price changes over the past year indicates that KSU will perform well over the near term.

Financial Data

(US$ in Thousands)	9 Mos	6 Mos	3 Mos	12/31/2018	12/31/2017	12/31/2016	12/31/2015	12/31/2014
Earnings Per Share	5.69	5.58	5.75	6.13	9.16	4.43	4.40	4.55
Cash Flow Per Share	11.06	10.61	10.72	9.29	9.82	8.47	8.29	8.22
Tang Book Value Per Share	49.13	48.30	47.95	47.65	44.09	38.31	36.03	33.96
Dividends Per Share	1.440	1.440	1.440	1.440	1.380	1.320	1.320	1.120
Dividend Payout %	25.31	25.81	25.04	23.49	15.07	29.80	30.00	24.62
Income Statement								
Total Revenue	2,136,500	1,388,800	674,800	2,714,000	2,582,900	2,334,200	2,418,800	2,577,100
EBITDA	924,100	557,000	252,900	1,341,000	1,283,900	1,050,800	1,020,800	1,022,900
Depn & Amortn	262,700	176,200	88,500	346,700	320,900	305,000	284,600	258,100
Income Before Taxes	577,300	324,600	136,200	884,300	862,800	648,100	654,300	692,000
Income Taxes	168,000	93,800	34,700	257,500	(89,600)	182,800	187,300	208,800
Net Income	411,700	231,500	102,800	627,400	962,000	478,100	483,500	502,600
Average Shares	99,699	100,422	100,915	102,270	105,040	107,761	109,915	110,433
Balance Sheet								
Current Assets	613,900	609,700	654,400	635,400	680,100	648,000	537,000	818,300
Total Assets	9,698,400	9,638,100	9,637,700	9,469,800	9,198,700	8,817,500	8,341,000	8,091,000
Current Liabilities	786,200	767,300	480,600	447,000	971,700	744,400	757,600	898,800
Long-Term Obligations	2,394,800	2,401,400	2,677,600	2,679,300	2,235,500	2,271,500	2,045,000	1,841,000
Total Liabilities	4,823,900	4,808,900	4,809,600	4,656,800	4,649,800	4,727,600	4,426,700	4,335,500
Stockholders' Equity	4,874,500	4,829,200	4,828,100	4,813,000	4,548,900	4,089,900	3,914,300	3,755,500
Shares Outstanding	99,111	99,877	100,580	100,896	103,036	106,606	108,461	110,392
Statistical Record								
Return on Assets %	6.00	5.99	6.24	6.72	10.68	5.56	5.88	6.47
Return on Equity %	11.88	11.91	12.41	13.40	22.27	11.91	12.61	14.11
EBITDA Margin %	43.25	40.11	37.48	49.41	49.71	45.02	42.20	39.69
Net Margin %	19.27	16.67	15.23	23.12	37.24	20.48	19.99	19.50
Asset Turnover	0.30	0.29	0.29	0.29	0.29	0.27	0.29	0.33
Current Ratio	0.78	0.79	1.36	1.42	0.70	0.87	0.71	0.91
Debt to Equity	0.49	0.50	0.55	0.56	0.49	0.56	0.52	0.49
Price Range		133.25-90.84	125.25-90.84	119.88-90.84	119.88-90.84	113.44-80.82	99.47-64.35	122.03-70.01	125.88-91.12
P/E Ratio		23.42-15.96	22.45-16.28	20.85-15.80	19.56-14.82	12.38-8.82	22.45-14.53	27.73-15.91	27.67-20.03
Average Yield %	1.27	1.30	1.33	1.33	1.41	1.50	1.35	1.02

Address: 427 West 12th Street, Kansas City, MO 64105	Web Site: www.kcsouthern.com	Auditors: KPMG LLP
Telephone: 816-983-1303	Officers: Robert J. Druten - Chairman Patrick J. Ottensmeyer - President, Chief Executive Officer, Executive Vice President	Investor Contact: 816-983-1551
Fax: 816-556-0297		Transfer Agents: Computershare Trust Company, N.A., Providence, RI

KAR AUCTION SERVICES INC.

Exchange	Symbol	Price	52Wk Range	Yield	P/E
NYS	KAR	$21.79 (12/31/2019)	27.55-17.26	3.49	12.38

*7 Year Price Score 116.99 *NYSE Composite Index=100   *12 Month Price Score 94.40

Interim Earnings (Per Share)

Qtr.	Mar	Jun	Sep	Dec
2016	0.44	0.44	0.39	0.33
2017	0.50	0.41	0.46	1.25
2018	0.66	0.69	0.57	0.50
2019	0.58	0.41	0.27	...

Interim Dividends (Per Share)

Amt	Decl	Ex	Rec	Pay
0.35Q	02/19/2019	03/21/2019	03/22/2019	04/04/2019
0.35Q	05/07/2019	05/31/2019	06/03/2019	06/17/2019
0.19Q	08/06/2019	09/19/2019	09/20/2019	10/03/2019
0.19Q	11/05/2019	12/19/2019	12/20/2019	01/03/2020

Indicated Div: $0.76

Valuation Analysis

		Institutional Holding	
Forecast EPS	$1.15 (01/16/2020)	No of Institutions	507
Market Cap	$2.8 Billion	Shares	
Book Value	$1.6 Billion		169,685,856
Price/Book	1.72	% Held	
Price/Sales	0.83		96.74

Business Summary: Retail - Automotive (MIC: 2.1.4 SIC: 5521 NAIC: 441120)

KAR Auction Services is a holding company. Through its subsidiaries, Co. provides used car auction services and salvage auction services in North America and the U.K. Co.'s segments include: ADESA, Inc. Auctions, which provides whole car auctions and related services to the vehicle remarketing industry in North America through online auctions and auction facilities; Insurance Auto Auctions, Inc., which provides damaged and total loss solutions and salvage vehicle auctions through salvage auction locations throughout North America and Canada; and Automotive Finance Corporation, which provides floorplan financing to independent used vehicle dealers through branches throughout North America.

Recent Developments: For the quarter ended Sep 30 2019, income from continuing operations increased 11.3% to US$34.4 million from US$30.9 million in the year-earlier quarter. Net income decreased 54.5% to US$35.3 million from US$77.5 million in the year-earlier quarter. Revenues were US$701.9 million, up 14.6% from US$612.4 million the year before. Operating income was US$85.7 million versus US$85.6 million in the prior-year quarter, an increase of 0.1%. Direct operating expenses rose 24.3% to US$410.9 million from US$330.7 million in the comparable period the year before. Indirect operating expenses increased 4.7% to US$205.3 million from US$196.1 million in the equivalent prior-year period.

Prospects: Our evaluation of KAR Aucton Services Inc. as of October 4th, 2019 is the result of our systematic analysis on three basic characteristics: earnings strength, relative valuation, and recent stock price movement. The company has generated a negative trend in earnings per share over the past 5 quarters. However, recent analyst estimates for the company have been mixed and KAR has posted results that fell short of analysts' expectations. Based on operating earnings yield, the company is undervalued when compared to all of the companies we cover. Share price changes over the past year indicates that KAR will perform over the near term.

Financial Data

(US$ in Thousands)	9 Mos	6 Mos	3 Mos	12/31/2018	12/31/2017	12/31/2016	12/31/2015	12/31/2014
Earnings Per Share	1.76	2.06	2.34	2.42	2.62	1.60	1.51	·1.19
Cash Flow Per Share	4.66	5.10	5.19	5.58	4.32	2.61	3.39	3.08
Dividends Per Share	1.240	1.400	1.400	1.400	1.310	1.190	1.080	1.020
Dividend Payout %	70.45	67.96	59.83	57.85	50.00	74.38	71.52	85.71
Income Statement								
Total Revenue	2,110,600	1,408,700	1,046,800	3,769,600	3,458,000	3,150,100	2,639,600	2,364,500
EBITDA	265,100	177,100	165,400	783,100	664,000	583,700	506,700	419,000
Depn & Amortn	9,600	7,100	2,600	155,400	102,000	89,600	74,800	67,800
Income Before Taxes	105,500	57,900	105,900	435,700	398,000	355,300	340,500	265,000
Income Taxes	28,400	15,200	28,100	107,700	36,000	132,900	125,900	95,700
Net Income	168,700	133,400	77,800	328,000	362,000	222,400	214,600	169,300
Average Shares	132,400	134,100	133,800	135,700	138,000	139,100	142,300	141,800
Balance Sheet								
Current Assets	3,257,700	3,048,900	3,460,200	3,314,200	3,137,400	2,841,200	2,446,100	2,074,900
Total Assets	6,579,700	6,377,800	8,324,100	7,206,200	6,984,300	6,557,600	5,791,800	5,351,500
Current Liabilities	2,516,200	2,668,400	2,945,600	2,624,800	2,389,200	2,335,000	2,226,100	1,590,600
Long-Term Obligations	1,863,000	1,390,800	2,650,900	2,654,300	2,667,700	2,365,100	1,719,300	1,736,600
Total Liabilities	4,943,900	4,625,200	6,821,600	5,742,000	5,499,400	5,160,300	4,405,700	3,804,400
Stockholders' Equity	1,635,800	1,752,600	1,502,500	1,464,200	1,484,900	1,397,300	1,386,100	1,547,100
Shares Outstanding	128,762	133,445	133,261	132,887	134,315	136,639	137,795	141,316
Statistical Record								
Return on Assets %	3.40	4.10	4.05	4.62	5.35	3.59	3.85	3.23
Return on Equity %	14.76	17.04	20.90	22.24	25.12	15.94	14.63	11.18
EBITDA Margin %	12.56	12.57	15.80	20.77	19.20	18.53	19.20	17.72
Net Margin %	7.99	9.47	7.43	8.70	10.47	7.06	8.13	7.16
Asset Turnover	0.49	0.53	0.50	0.53	0.51	0.51	0.47	0.45
Current Ratio	1.29	1.14	1.17	1.26	1.31	1.22	1.10	1.30
Debt to Equity	1.14	0.79	1.76	1.81	1.80	1.69	1.24	1.12
Price Range	27.55-17.26	25.00-17.26	24.30-17.26	24.30-17.34	19.46-15.25	16.60-12.10	14.95-12.78	13.31-10.00
P/E Ratio	15.65-9.81	12.14-8.38	10.38-7.38	10.04-7.16	7.43-5.82	10.38-7.56	9.90-8.46	11.19-8.41
Average Yield %	5.71	6.65	6.74	6.64	7.67	7.91	7.69	8.81

Address: 11299 N. Illinois Street, Carmel, IN 46032	Web Site: www.karauctionservices.com	Auditors: KPMG LLP
Telephone: 800-923-3725	Officers: James P. Hallett - Chairman, Chief Executive Officer Peter J. Kelly - President, Chief Technology Officer, Division Officer	Investor Contact: 317-249-4390

KB HOME

Exchange	Symbol	Price	52Wk Range	Yield	P/E
NYS	KBH	$34.27 (12/31/2019)	36.80-19.10	1.05	13.65

*7 Year Price Score 113.16 *NYSE Composite Index=100 *12 Month Price Score 117.72

TRADING VOLUME (thousand shares)

Interim Earnings (Per Share)

Qtr.	Feb	May	Aug	Nov
2015-16	0.14	0.17	0.42	0.40
2016-17	0.15	0.33	0.51	0.85
2017-18	(0.82)	0.57	0.87	0.96
2018-19	0.31	0.51	0.73	...

Interim Dividends (Per Share)

Amt	Decl	Ex	Rec	Pay
0.025Q	01/24/2019	02/06/2019	02/07/2019	02/21/2019
0.025Q	04/11/2019	05/01/2019	05/02/2019	05/16/2019
0.09Q	07/15/2019	07/31/2019	08/01/2019	08/15/2019
0.09Q	10/03/2019	11/13/2019	11/14/2019	11/28/2019

Indicated Div: $0.36

Valuation Analysis | Institutional Holding

Forecast EPS	$3.65	No of Institutions
	(01/17/2020)	425
Market Cap	$3.3 Billion	Shares
Book Value	$2.3 Billion	99,424,328
Price/Book	1.46	% Held
Price/Sales	0.76	82.80

Business Summary: Builders (MIC: 2.2.5 SIC: 1531 NAIC: 236117)

KB Home is a homebuilding company. Co. builds a variety of homes designed primarily for first-time and first move-up, as well as second move-up and active adult homebuyers, including attached and detached single-family residential homes, townhomes and condominiums. Co.'s financial services operations provide various insurance products to its homebuyers in the markets where it builds homes and provide title services in certain of those markets. Co.'s financial services operations also provide mortgage banking services, including residential consumer mortgage loan originations, to its homebuyers indirectly through KBHS Home Loans, LLC, a joint venture Co. formed with Stearns Lending, LLC.

Recent Developments: For the quarter ended Aug 31 2019, net income decreased 22.1% to US$68.1 million from US$87.5 million in the year-earlier quarter. Revenues were US$1.16 billion, down 5.3% from US$1.23 billion the year before. Direct operating expenses declined 5.8% to US$944.8 million from US$1.00 billion in the comparable period the year before. Indirect operating expenses increased 11.2% to US$127.6 million from US$114.8 million in the equivalent prior-year period.

Prospects: Our evaluation of KB HOME as of October 4th, 2019 is the result of our systematic analysis on three basic characteristics: earnings strength, relative valuation, and recent stock price movement. The company has produced a positive trend in earnings per share over the past 5 quarters. In addition, recent analyst estimates for the company have been raised, and KBH has posted results that exceeded analysts' expectations. Based on operating earnings yield, the company is undervalued when compared to all of the companies we cover. Share price changes over the past year indicates that KBH will perform poorly over the near term.

Financial Data
(US$ in Thousands)

	9 Mos	6 Mos	3 Mos	11/30/2018	11/30/2017	11/30/2016	11/30/2015	11/30/2014
Earnings Per Share	2.51	2.65	2.71	1.71	1.85	1.12	0.85	9.25
Cash Flow Per Share	1.35	0.69	1.90	2.52	5.98	2.20	1.97	(7.07)
Tang Book Value Per Share	23.50	24.88	22.41	21.95	20.08	18.23	16.51	15.60
Dividends Per Share	0.165	0.100	0.100	0.100	0.100	0.100	0.100	0.100
Dividend Payout %	6.57	3.77	3.69	5.85	5.41	8.93	11.76	1.08
Income Statement								
Total Revenue	2,994,072	1,833,286	811,483	4,547,002	4,368,529	3,594,646	3,032,030	2,400,949
EBITDA	179,104	89,798	34,478	357,584	295,037	163,887	149,353	126,229
Depn & Amortn	3,500	2,597	1,468	2,500	2,800	3,600	3,400	2,400
Income Before Taxes	177,349	88,745	34,115	358,598	287,170	154,916	124,555	93,522
Income Taxes	37,600	13,800	4,500	197,600	109,400	43,700	42,400	(823,400)
Net Income	145,608	77,472	30,011	170,365	180,595	105,615	84,643	918,349
Average Shares	92,842	92,366	96,962	101,059	98,316	96,278	102,857	99,314
Balance Sheet								
Current Assets	4,394,362	4,260,325	4,509,062	4,453,673	4,230,184	4,229,657	4,038,359	3,731,616
Total Assets	5,035,170	4,919,953	5,173,656	5,073,571	5,041,515	5,131,624	5,015,371	4,757,550
Current Liabilities	586,806	530,572	470,799	310,211	296,635	302,920	262,795	238,508
Long-Term Obligations	1,861,918	1,854,556	2,203,589	2,060,263	2,324,845	2,640,149	2,625,536	2,576,525
Total Liabilities	2,772,941	2,724,743	3,045,159	2,986,071	3,115,204	3,408,479	3,324,537	3,161,640
Stockholders' Equity	2,262,229	2,195,210	2,128,497	2,087,500	1,926,311	1,723,145	1,690,834	1,595,910
Shares Outstanding	96,259	88,226	94,994	95,082	95,924	94,504	102,411	102,289
Statistical Record								
Return on Assets %	4.84	5.23	5.36	3.37	3.55	2.08	1.73	23.10
Return on Equity %	11.33	12.74	13.65	8.49	9.90	6.17	5.15	86.15
EBITDA Margin %	5.98	4.90	4.25	7.86	6.75	4.56	4.93	5.26
Net Margin %	4.86	4.23	3.70	3.75	4.13	2.94	2.79	38.25
Asset Turnover	0.87	0.88	0.89	0.90	0.86	0.71	0.62	0.60
Current Ratio	7.49	8.03	9.58	14.36	14.26	13.96	15.37	15.65
Debt to Equity	0.82	0.84	1.04	0.99	1.21	1.53	1.55	1.61
Price Range	28.47-17.61	28.33-17.61	29.93-17.61	38.58-17.61	31.36-15.07	16.62-9.58	17.32-11.87	20.67-13.78
P/E Ratio	11.34-7.02	10.69-6.65	11.04-6.50	22.56-10.30	16.95-8.15	14.84-8.55	20.38-13.96	2.23-1.49
Average Yield %	0.70	0.43	0.41	0.37	0.37	0.47	0.71	0.68	0.58

| Address: 10990 Wilshire Boulevard, Los Angeles, CA 90024 Telephone: 310-231-4000 Fax: 310-231-4222 | Web Site: www.kbhome.com Officers: Jeffrey T. Mezger - Chairman, President, Chief Executive Officer Jeff J. Kaminski - Executive Vice President, Chief Financial Officer | Auditors: Ernst & Young LLP Investor Contact: 310-231-4000 Transfer Agents: ComputerShare Investor Services, Providence, RI |

KBR INC

*7 Year Price Score 93.11 *NYSE Composite Index=100 *12 Month Price Score 118.95

Interim Earnings (Per Share)

Qtr.	Mar	Jun	Sep	Dec
2016	0.30	0.32	(0.44)	(0.61)
2017	0.26	0.54	0.32	1.94
2018	0.97	0.30	0.41	0.31
2019	0.28	0.34	0.39	...

Interim Dividends (Per Share)

Amt	Decl	Ex	Rec	Pay
0.08Q	03/05/2019	03/14/2019	03/15/2019	04/15/2019
0.08Q	05/15/2019	06/14/2019	06/17/2019	07/15/2019
0.08Q	08/21/2019	09/13/2019	09/16/2019	10/15/2019
0.08Q	10/22/2019	12/13/2019	12/16/2019	01/15/2020

Indicated Div: $0.32

Valuation Analysis

		Institutional Holding	
Forecast EPS	$1.69	No of Institutions	
	(01/10/2020)	409	
Market Cap	$4.3 Billion	Shares	
Book Value	$1.8 Billion	185,440,432	
Price/Book	2.41	% Held	
Price/Sales	0.78	98.83	

Business Summary: IT Services (MIC: 6.3.1 SIC: 1629 NAIC: 237990)

KBR is a provider of services and technologies across the asset and program life-cycle within the government services and hydrocarbons industries. Co.'s capabilities include research and development, feasibility and solutions development, technical consulting, systems integration, engineering and design services, process technologies, mission and logistics support solutions, program management, construction services, commissioning and startup services, asset operations and maintenance services. Co.'s business is organized into three core segments, which consist of Government Services, Technology, and Hydrocarbons Services.

Recent Developments: For the quarter ended Sep 30 2019, net income increased 3.6% to US$58.0 million from US$56.0 million in the year-earlier quarter. Revenues were US$1.43 billion, up 11.5% from US$1.28 billion the year before. Operating income was US$104.0 million versus US$99.0 million in the prior-year quarter, an increase of 5.1%. Direct operating expenses rose 11.2% to US$1.26 billion from US$1.13 billion in the comparable period the year before. Indirect operating expenses increased 30.0% to US$65.0 million from US$50.0 million in the equivalent prior-year period.

Prospects: Our evaluation of KBR Inc. as of October 4th, 2019 is the result of our systematic analysis on three basic characteristics: earnings strength, relative valuation, and recent stock price movement. The company has generated a negative trend in earnings per share over the past 5 quarters. However, recent analyst estimates for the company have been unchanged while KBR has posted results that exceeded analysts' expectations. Based on operating earnings yield, the company is undervalued when compared to all of the companies we cover. Share price changes over the past year indicates that KBR will perform over the near term.

Financial Data

(US$ in Thousands)	9 Mos	6 Mos	3 Mos	12/31/2018	12/31/2017	12/31/2016	12/31/2015	12/31/2014
Earnings Per Share	1.32	1.34	1.30	1.99	3.06	(0.43)	1.40	(8.66)
Cash Flow Per Share	2.33	2.00	2.43	1.18	1.37	0.43	0.33	1.16
Tang Book Value Per Share	0.33	0.04	N.M.	N.M.	0.16	N.M.	4.97	3.98
Dividends Per Share	0.320	0.320	0.320	0.320	0.320	0.320	0.320	0.320
Dividend Payout %	24.24	23.88	24.62	16.08	10.46	...	22.86	...
Income Statement								
Total Revenue	4,187,000	2,762,000	1,340,000	4,913,000	4,171,000	4,268,000	5,096,000	6,366,000
EBITDA	336,000	210,000	108,000	414,000	225,000	(27,000)	198,000	(879,000)
Depn & Amortn	76,000	48,000	25,000	31,000	27,000	31,000	35,000	61,000
Income Before Taxes	184,000	111,000	58,000	317,000	177,000	(58,000)	163,000	(940,000)
Income Taxes	58,000	34,000	16,000	88,000	(193,000)	84,000	86,000	421,000
Net Income	144,000	88,000	40,000	281,000	434,000	(61,000)	203,000	(1,262,000)
Average Shares	142,000	141,000	141,000	141,000	141,000	142,000	144,000	146,000
Balance Sheet								
Current Assets	2,107,000	1,980,000	1,971,000	1,959,000	1,425,000	2,047,000	1,844,000	2,544,000
Total Assets	5,402,000	5,318,000	5,317,000	5,072,000	3,674,000	4,144,000	3,412,000	4,199,000
Current Liabilities	1,652,000	1,563,000	1,505,000	1,419,000	1,071,000	1,559,000	1,412,000	2,024,000
Long-Term Obligations	1,196,000	1,199,000	1,240,000	1,243,000	498,000	684,000	51,000	63,000
Total Liabilities	3,605,000	3,544,000	3,544,000	3,354,000	2,445,000	3,387,000	2,347,000	3,257,000
Stockholders' Equity	1,797,000	1,774,000	1,773,000	1,718,000	1,229,000	757,000	1,065,000	942,000
Shares Outstanding	141,706	141,545	141,455	140,900	140,166	142,803	142,058	144,837
Statistical Record								
Return on Assets %	3.64	3.77	3.78	6.43	11.10	N.M.	5.33	N.M.
Return on Equity %	10.87	11.22	11.14	19.07	43.71	N.M.	20.23	N.M.
EBITDA Margin %	8.02	7.60	8.06	8.43	5.39	N.M.	3.89	N.M.
Net Margin %	3.44	3.19	2.99	5.72	10.41	N.M.	3.98	N.M.
Asset Turnover	1.07	1.07	1.08	1.12	1.07	1.13	1.34	1.31
Current Ratio	1.28	1.27	1.31	1.38	1.33	1.31	1.31	1.26
Debt to Equity	0.67	0.68	0.70	0.72	0.41	0.90	0.05	0.07
Price Range	26.79-14.00	24.94-14.00	21.91-14.00	21.91-14.00	21.09-13.63	17.60-11.76	20.60-14.26	33.62-15.23
P/E Ratio	20.30-10.61	18.61-10.45	16.85-10.77	11.01-7.04	6.89-4.45	...	14.71-10.19	...
Average Yield %	1.51	1.62	1.73	1.73	1.94	2.16	1.82	1.35

Address: 601 Jefferson Street, Suite 3400, Houston, TX 77002 **Telephone:** 713-753-2000	**Web Site:** www.kbr.com **Officers:** Lester L. Lyles - Chairman Stuart J.B. Bradie - President, Chief Executive Officer	**Auditors:** KPMG LLP **Investor Contact:** 713-753-5082 **Transfer Agents:** American Stock Transfer & Trust Company, Brooklyn, NY

KELLOGG CO

Exchange	Symbol	Price	52Wk Range	Yield	P/E	Div Acheiver
NYS	K	$69.16 (12/31/2019)	69.16-52.09	3.30	32.32	14 Years

*7 Year Price Score 74.42 *NYSE Composite Index=100 *12 Month Price Score 104.43

Interim Earnings (Per Share)

Qtr.	Mar	Jun	Sep	Dec
2016	0.49	0.79	0.82	(0.15)
2017	0.74	0.80	0.85	1.23
2018	1.27	1.71	1.09	(0.24)
2019	0.82	0.84	0.72	...

Interim Dividends (Per Share)

Amt	Decl	Ex	Rec	Pay
0.56Q	02/22/2019	03/04/2019	03/05/2019	03/15/2019
0.56Q	04/26/2019	05/31/2019	06/03/2019	06/14/2019
0.57Q	07/26/2019	08/30/2019	09/03/2019	09/13/2019
0.57Q	10/18/2019	11/29/2019	12/02/2019	12/16/2019

Indicated Div: $2.28 (Div. Reinv. Plan)

Valuation Analysis | **Institutional Holding**

Forecast EPS	$3.88 (01/15/2020)	No of Institutions 1091
Market Cap	$23.6 Billion	Shares
Book Value	$2.7 Billion	447,803,200
Price/Book	8.65	% Held
Price/Sales	1.73	85.96

Business Summary: Food (MIC: 1.2.1 SIC: 2043 NAIC: 311230)

Kellogg is engaged in the manufacture and marketing of ready-to-eat cereal and convenience foods. Co.'s principal products are snacks, such as crackers, cookies, savory snacks, toaster pastries, cereal bars, granola bars and bites, fruit-flavored snacks; and convenience foods, such as, ready-to-eat cereals, frozen waffles, veggie foods and noodles. Co.'s snacks brands are marketed under brands such as Kellogg's, Keebler, Cheez-It, Pringles, Murray, Austin, Famous Amos, Parati, and RXBAR. Co.'s cereals and cereal bars are generally marketed under the Kellogg's name, with some under the Kashi and Bear Naked brands. Co.'s frozen foods are marketed under the Eggo and Morningstar Farms brands.

Recent Developments: For the quarter ended Sep 28 2019, net income decreased 35.2% to US$248.0 million from US$383.0 million in the year-earlier quarter. Revenues were US$3.37 billion, down 2.8% from US$3.47 billion the year before. Operating income was US$263.0 million versus US$396.0 million in the prior-year quarter, a decrease of 33.6%. Direct operating expenses rose 3.4% to US$2.37 billion from US$2.29 billion in the comparable period the year before. Indirect operating expenses decreased 5.5% to US$737.0 million from US$780.0 million in the equivalent prior-year period.

Prospects: Our evaluation of Kellogg Co as of October 4th, 2019 is the result of our systematic analysis on three basic characteristics: earnings strength, relative valuation, and recent stock price movement. The company has managed to produce a neutral trend in earnings per share over the past 5 quarters. In addition, recent analyst estimates for the company have been mixed and K has posted results that exceeded analysts' expectations. Based on operating earnings yield, the company is undervalued when compared to all of the companies we cover. Share price changes over the past year indicates that K will perform poorly over the near term.

Financial Data

(US$ in Thousands)	9 Mos	6 Mos	3 Mos	12/29/2018	12/30/2017	12/31/2016	01/02/2016	01/03/2015
Earnings Per Share	2.14	2.51	3.38	3.83	3.62	1.96	1.72	1.75
Cash Flow Per Share	4.50	4.73	4.03	4.44	4.74	4.66	4.79	4.93
Dividends Per Share	2.250	2.240	2.220	2.200	2.120	2.040	1.980	1.900
Dividend Payout %	105.14	89.24	65.68	57.44	58.56	104.08	115.12	108.57
Income Statement								
Total Revenue	10,355,000	6,983,000	3,522,000	13,547,000	12,923,000	13,014,000	13,525,000	14,580,000
EBITDA	1,648,000	1,118,000	557,000	2,132,000	2,411,000	1,850,000	1,534,000	1,537,000
Depn & Amortn	360,000	243,000	124,000	516,000	481,000	517,000	534,000	503,000
Income Before Taxes	1,067,000	726,000	359,000	1,329,000	1,674,000	927,000	773,000	825,000
Income Taxes	237,000	146,000	72,000	181,000	412,000	233,000	159,000	186,000
Net Income	815,000	568,000	282,000	1,336,000	1,269,000	694,000	614,000	632,000
Average Shares	342,000	341,000	343,000	348,000	350,000	354,000	356,000	360,000
Balance Sheet								
Current Assets	3,492,000	3,504,000	3,373,000	3,157,000	3,036,000	2,940,000	3,236,000	3,340,000
Total Assets	17,499,000	18,669,000	18,465,000	17,780,000	16,350,000	15,111,000	15,265,000	15,153,000
Current Liabilities	4,389,000	4,989,000	4,978,000	4,529,000	4,479,000	4,474,000	5,739,000	4,364,000
Long-Term Obligations	7,683,000	8,262,000	8,183,000	8,207,000	7,836,000	6,698,000	5,289,000	5,935,000
Total Liabilities	14,772,000	16,019,000	15,932,000	15,179,000	14,138,000	13,201,000	13,137,000	12,364,000
Stockholders' Equity	2,727,000	2,650,000	2,533,000	2,601,000	2,212,000	1,910,000	2,128,000	2,789,000
Shares Outstanding	341,094	341,000	340,000	343,865	345,602	351,069	350,024	356,002
Statistical Record								
Return on Assets %	4.11	4.73	6.68	7.85	8.09	4.58	4.05	4.06
Return on Equity %	25.32	31.49	46.30	55.67	61.74	34.47	25.04	19.63
EBITDA Margin %	15.92	16.01	15.81	15.74	18.66	14.22	11.34	10.54
Net Margin %	7.87	8.13	8.01	9.86	9.82	5.33	4.54	4.33
Asset Turnover	0.77	0.75	0.78	0.80	0.82	0.86	0.89	0.94
Current Ratio	0.80	0.70	0.68	0.70	0.68	0.66	0.56	0.77
Debt to Equity	2.82	3.12	3.23	3.16	3.54	3.51	2.49	2.13
Price Range	71.86-52.09	74.84-52.09	74.84-53.61	74.84-55.82	76.44-58.87	86.98-69.96	73.51-61.31	69.39-56.90
P/E Ratio	33.58-24.34	29.82-20.75	22.14-15.86	19.54-14.57	21.12-16.26	44.38-35.69	42.74-35.65	39.65-32.51
Average Yield %	3.77	3.59	3.46	3.30	3.07	2.67	2.99	2.97

Address: One Kellogg Square, P.O. Box 3599, Battle Creek, MI 49016-3599 **Telephone:** 269-961-2000	**Web Site:** www.kelloggcompany.com **Officers:** Steven A. (Steve) Cahillane - Chairman, Chief Executive Officer, President Gary H. Pilnick - Vice-Chairman, Corporate Development Officer, Chief Legal Officer, Senior Vice President, General Counsel, Secretary	**Auditors:** PricewaterhouseCoopers LLP **Investor Contact:** 269-961-2800 **Transfer Agents:** Wells Fargo Bank, N.A., St. Paul, MN

KEMPER CORP (DE)

Exchange	Symbol	Price	52Wk Range	Yield	P/E
NYS	KMPR	$77.50 (12/31/2019)	90.69-65.03	1.45	12.73

*7 Year Price Score 134.05 *NYSE Composite Index=100 *12 Month Price Score 89.21

Interim Earnings (Per Share)

Qtr.	Mar	Jun	Sep	Dec
2016	(0.04)	0.08	(0.32)	0.60
2017	(0.01)	0.71	0.92	0.71
2018	1.02	0.73	1.40	(0.01)
2019	2.35	1.84	1.91	...

Interim Dividends (Per Share)

Amt	Decl	Ex	Rec	Pay
0.25Q	02/06/2019	02/15/2019	02/19/2019	03/05/2019
0.25Q	05/01/2019	05/10/2019	05/13/2019	05/28/2019
0.25Q	08/07/2019	08/16/2019	08/19/2019	09/03/2019
0.28Q	11/06/2019	11/15/2019	11/18/2019	12/04/2019

Indicated Div: $1.12 (Div. Reinv. Plan)

Valuation Analysis

Forecast EPS	$6.24
	(01/16/2020)
Market Cap	$5.2 Billion
Book Value	$3.9 Billion
Price/Book	1.33
Price/Sales	1.06

Institutional Holding

No of Institutions	383
Shares	52,458,960
% Held	N/A

Business Summary: General Insurance (MIC: 5.2.1 SIC: 6331 NAIC: 524126)

KKemper is an insurance holding company. Through its subsidiaries, Co. provides automobile, homeowners, life, health, and other insurance products to individuals and businesses. Co.'s operating segments are: Preferred Property and Casualty Insurance, which sells preferred automobile insurance, homeowners insurance and other personal insurance; Specialty Property and Casualty Insurance, which provides personal and commercial automobile insurance to consumers who have had difficulty obtaining standard or preferred risk insurance; and Life and Health Insurance, which include individual life, accident, health and property insurance. Co. conducts its operations solely in the U.S.

Recent Developments: For the quarter ended Sep 30 2019, income from continuing operations increased 39.8% to US$129.0 million from US$92.3 million in the year-earlier quarter. Net income increased 39.9% to US$129.0 million from US$92.2 million in the year-earlier quarter. Revenues were US$1.24 billion, up 4.0% from US$1.20 billion the year before. Net premiums earned were US$1.14 billion versus US$1.05 billion in the prior-year quarter, an increase of 7.8%. Net investment income fell 0.3% to US$91.7 million from US$92.0 million a year ago.

Prospects: Our evaluation of Kemper Corp. as of October 4th, 2019 is the result of our systematic analysis on three basic characteristics: earnings strength, relative valuation, and recent stock price movement. The company has generated a negative trend in earnings per share over the past 5 quarters. However, recent analyst estimates for the company have been mixed and KMPR has posted results that exceeded analysts' expectations. Based on operating earnings yield, the company is undervalued when compared to all of the companies we cover. Share price changes over the past year indicates that KMPR will perform in line with the market over the near term.

Financial Data
(US$ in Thousands)

	9 Mos	6 Mos	3 Mos	12/31/2018	12/31/2017	12/31/2016	12/31/2015	12/31/2014
Earnings Per Share	6.09	5.58	4.47	3.22	2.33	0.33	1.65	2.12
Cash Flow Per Share	8.41	8.93	8.55	9.27	4.69	4.69	4.17	2.49
Tang Book Value Per Share	41.72	38.60	34.01	29.92	34.83	32.22	32.52	33.94
Dividends Per Share	0.990	0.980	0.970	0.960	0.960	0.960	0.960	0.960
Dividend Payout %	16.26	17.56	21.70	29.81	41.20	290.91	58.18	45.28
Income Statement								
Premium Income	3,326,600	2,191,400	1,074,800	3,384,400	2,350,000	2,220,000	2,009,600	1,862,200
Total Revenue	3,755,500	2,511,700	1,236,300	3,725,100	2,723,400	2,521,900	2,340,800	2,196,600
Income Before Taxes	504,700	343,200	194,700	199,100	161,100	3,500	100,300	160,200
Income Taxes	98,300	65,800	39,400	10,700	41,200	(9,200)	20,100	47,600
Net Income	406,400	277,400	155,300	190,100	120,900	16,800	85,700	114,500
Average Shares	67,207	66,189	65,606	58,751	51,577	51,214	51,683	53,867
Balance Sheet								
Total Assets	12,819,900	12,616,500	12,182,200	11,544,900	8,376,200	8,210,500	8,036,100	7,833,400
Total Liabilities	8,925,700	8,932,800	8,862,100	8,494,800	6,260,600	6,235,300	6,043,700	5,742,700
Stockholders' Equity	3,894,200	3,683,700	3,320,100	3,050,100	2,115,600	1,975,200	1,992,400	2,090,700
Shares Outstanding	66,641	66,564	64,930	64,756	51,462	51,270	51,326	52,418
Statistical Record								
Return on Assets %	3.36	3.51	2.84	1.91	1.46	0.21	1.08	1.48
Return on Equity %	11.87	13.13	10.83	7.36	5.91	0.84	4.20	5.53
Net Margin %	10.82	-11.04	12.56	5.10	4.44	0.67	3.66	5.21
Price Range	90.69-62.40	90.69-62.40	85.90-55.20	85.90-53.55	70.45-36.70	45.65-23.80	41.44-34.25	40.88-32.97
P/E Ratio	14.89-10.25	16.25-11.18	19.22-12.35	26.68-16.63	30.24-15.75	138.33-72.12	25.12-20.76	19.28-15.55
Average Yield %	1.26	1.25	1.30	1.36	2.00	2.79	2.56	2.62

Address: 200 E. Randolph Street, Suite 3300, Chicago, IL 60601 **Telephone:** 312-661-4600	**Web Site:** www.kemper.com **Officers:** Robert Joseph Joyce - Chairman Joseph P. Lacher - President, Chief Executive Officer	**Auditors:** DELOITTE & TOUCHE LLP **Investor Contact:** 312-661-4930 **Transfer Agents:** Computershare Trust Company, N.A., Providence, RI

KENNAMETAL INC.

Exchange	Symbol	Price	52Wk Range	Yield	P/E
NYS	KMT	$36.89 (12/31/2019)	41.51-27.75	2.17	16.04

*7 Year Price Score 78.00   *NYSE Composite Index=100   *12 Month Price Score 95.97

TRADING VOLUME (thousand shares)

Interim Earnings (Per Share)

Qtr.	Sep	Dec	Mar	Jun
2016-17	(0.27)	0.09	0.48	0.31
2017-18	0.48	0.50	0.61	0.83
2018-19	0.68	0.66	0.82	0.74
2019-20	0.08	...	...	...

Interim Dividends (Per Share)

Amt	Decl	Ex	Rec	Pay
0.20Q	02/04/2019	02/11/2019	02/12/2019	02/26/2019
0.20Q	05/06/2019	05/13/2019	05/14/2019	05/29/2019
0.20Q	08/05/2019	08/12/2019	08/13/2019	08/27/2019
0.20Q	11/04/2019	11/08/2019	11/12/2019	11/26/2019

Indicated Div: $0.80 (Div. Reinv. Plan)

Valuation Analysis

		Institutional Holding	
Forecast EPS	$1.80 (01/15/2020)	No of Institutions	414
Market Cap	$3.1 Billion	Shares	
Book Value	$1.3 Billion		98,291,880
Price/Book	2.35	% Held	
Price/Sales	1.32		97.61

Business Summary: Industrial Machinery & Equipment (MIC: 7.2.1 SIC: 3541 NAIC: 333512)

Kennametal engages in the development and application of tungsten carbides, ceramics, materials and solutions used in metal cutting and extreme wear applications. Co.'s standard and custom product offering spans metalworking and wear applications including turning, milling, hole making, tooling systems and services, as well as other wear components and metallurgical powders. End users of Co.'s metalworking products include manufacturers engaged in a range of industries including: the manufacturers of transportation vehicles and components, machine tools and light and heavy machinery; airframe and aerospace components; and energy-related components for the oil and gas industry.

Recent Developments:
For the quarter ended Sep 30 2019, net income decreased 87.3% to US$7.4 million from US$58.4 million in the year-earlier quarter. Revenues were US$518.1 million, down 11.7% from US$586.7 million the year before. Operating income was US$16.4 million versus US$83.2 million in the prior-year quarter, a decrease of 80.3%. Direct operating expenses rose 0.9% to US$379.1 million from US$375.6 million in the comparable period the year before. Indirect operating expenses decreased 4.2% to US$122.6 million from US$127.9 million in the equivalent prior-year period.

Prospects:
Our evaluation of Kennametal Inc. as of October 4th, 2019 is the result of our systematic analysis on three basic characteristics: earnings strength, relative valuation, and recent stock price movement. The company has generated a negative trend in earnings per share over the past 5 quarters. In addition, recent analyst estimates for the company have been reduced and KMT has posted results that fell short of analysts' expectations. Based on operating earnings yield, the company is undervalued when compared to all of the companies we cover. Share price changes over the past year indicates that KMT will perform poorly over the near term.

Financial Data

(US$ in Thousands)	3 Mos	06/30/2019	06/30/2018	06/30/2017	06/30/2016	06/30/2015	06/30/2014	06/30/2013
Earnings Per Share	2.30	2.90	2.42	0.61	(2.83)	(4.71)	1.99	2.52
Cash Flow Per Share	3.85	3.65	3.40	2.39	2.74	4.43	3.46	3.58
Tang Book Value Per Share	10.23	10.61	8.77	6.51	5.75	8.09	7.76	10.76
Dividends Per Share	0.800	0.800	0.800	0.800	0.800	0.720	0.720	0.640
Dividend Payout %	34.78	27.59	33.06	131.15	...	...	36.18	25.40
Income Statement								
Total Revenue	518,088	2,375,234	2,367,853	2,058,368	2,098,436	2,647,195	2,837,190	2,589,373
EBITDA	50,132	456,281	413,802	218,373	(53,353)	(224,485)	391,482	407,185
Depn & Amortn	31,075	112,052	108,680	107,656	117,466	131,664	130,222	113,104
Income Before Taxes	11,176	311,235	275,041	81,875	(198,571)	(387,615)	228,809	266,609
Income Taxes	3,766	63,359	69,981	29,895	25,313	(16,654)	66,611	59,693
Net Income	6,466	241,925	200,180	49,138	(225,968)	(373,896)	158,366	203,265
Average Shares	83,487	83,291	82,754	81,169	79,835	79,342	79,667	80,612
Balance Sheet								
Current Assets	1,065,389	1,190,827	1,546,166	1,113,901	1,075,341	1,258,546	1,525,196	1,499,473
Total Assets	2,599,405	2,656,269	2,925,737	2,415,496	2,368,793	2,849,529	3,868,086	3,301,039
Current Liabilities	418,719	461,726	886,531	461,478	427,275	482,744	562,756	467,593
Long-Term Obligations	592,858	592,474	591,505	694,991	699,558	735,885	981,666	703,626
Total Liabilities	1,300,839	1,321,097	1,731,412	1,398,202	1,404,470	1,503,722	1,938,830	1,519,213
Stockholders' Equity	1,298,566	1,335,172	1,194,325	1,017,294	964,323	1,345,807	1,929,256	1,781,826
Shares Outstanding	82,833	82,421	81,646	80,665	79,694	79,375	78,672	77,842
Statistical Record								
Return on Assets %	7.50	8.67	7.50	2.05	N.M.	N.M.	4.42	6.42
Return on Equity %	15.18	19.13	18.10	4.96	N.M.	N.M.	8.53	11.87
EBITDA Margin %	9.68	19.21	17.48	10.61	N.M.	N.M.	13.80	15.73
Net Margin %	1.25	10.19	8.45	2.39	N.M.	N.M.	5.58	7.85
Asset Turnover	0.90	0.85	0.89	0.86	0.80	0.79	0.79	0.82
Current Ratio	2.54	2.58	1.74	2.41	2.52	2.61	2.71	3.21
Debt to Equity	0.46	0.44	0.50	0.68	0.73	0.55	0.51	0.39
Price Range	44.34-27.75	44.92-30.75	51.92-33.40	42.40-20.67	34.12-15.91	46.35-30.99	52.07-38.16	43.34-32.19
P/E Ratio	19.28-12.07	15.49-10.60	21.45-13.80	69.51-33.89	...	...	26.17-19.18	17.20-12.77
Average Yield %	2.24	2.13	1.93	2.40	3.23	1.89	1.58	1.65

Address: 600 Grant Street, Suite 5100, Pittsburgh, PA 15219-2706 **Telephone:** 412-248-8000	**Web Site:** www.kennametal.com **Officers:** Lawrence W. Stranghoener - Chairman (frmr), Chairman Christopher (Chris) Rossi - President, Chief Executive Officer	**Auditors:** PricewaterhouseCoopers LLP **Investor Contact:** 724-539-6559 **Transfer Agents:** Computershare, Jersey City, NJ

KEURIG DR PEPPER INC

Exchange	Symbol	Price	52Wk Range	Yield	P/E
NYS	KDP	$28.95 (12/31/2019)	31.21-25.04	N/A	36.19

*7 Year Price Score 34.36 ***NYSE Composite Index=100** ***12 Month Price Score 99.52**

Interim Earnings (Per Share)

Qtr.	Mar	Jun	Sep	Dec
2016	0.96	1.39	1.29	0.90
2017	0.96	1.02	1.11	2.80
2018	0.88	1.30	0.11	0.21
2019	0.16	0.22	0.21	...

Interim Dividends (Per Share)

Amt	Decl	Ex	Rec	Pay
0.15Q	02/14/2019	04/04/2019	04/05/2019	04/19/2019
0.15Q	05/03/2019	07/03/2019	07/05/2019	07/19/2019
0.15Q	09/16/2019	10/03/2019	10/04/2019	10/18/2019
0.15Q	11/14/2019	01/02/2020	01/03/2020	01/17/2020

Valuation Analysis / Institutional Holding

Forecast EPS	$1.22 (01/16/2020)	No of Institutions	577
Market Cap	$40.7 Billion	Shares	332,730,976
Book Value	$22.9 Billion	% Held	N/A
Price/Book	1.78		
Price/Sales	3.70		

TRADING VOLUME (thousand shares)

Business Summary: Beverages (MIC: 1.2.2 SIC: 2086 NAIC: 312111)

Keurig Dr Pepper is a beverage company in North America with a portfolio of flavored (non-cola) carbonated soft drinks (CSDs), non-carbonated beverages (NCBs), including ready-to-drink teas and coffeee, juices, juice drinks, water and mixers, and specialty coffee, and is a producer of single-serve brewing systems. Co. has four segments: Beverage Concentrates, which sells mostly CSDs; Packaged Beverages, which manufactures and sells finished beverages and other products; Latin America Beverages, which manufactures and sells concentrates, syrup and finished beverages; and Coffee Systems, which manufactures and distributes single-serve brewing system, K-Cup pods and other coffee products.

Recent Developments: For the quarter ended Sep 30 2019, net income increased 104.0% to US$304.0 million from US$149.0 million in the year-earlier quarter. Revenues were US$2.87 billion, up 5.1% from US$2.73 billion the year before. Operating income was US$580.0 million versus US$345.0 million in the prior-year quarter, an increase of 68.1%. Direct operating expenses declined 8.9% to US$1.25 billion from US$1.37 billion in the comparable period.the year before. Indirect operating expenses increased 2.5% to US$1.05 billion from US$1.02 billion in the equivalent prior-year period.

Prospects: Our evaluation of Keurig Dr Pepper Inc. as of October 4th, 2019 is the result of our systematic analysis on three basic characteristics: earnings strength, relative valuation, and recent stock price movement. The company has enjoyed a very positive trend in earnings per share over the past 5 quarters. However, recent analyst estimates for the company have been unchanged, while KDP has posted results that exceeded analysts' expectations. Based on operating earnings yield, the company is fairly valued when compared to all of the companies we cover. Share price changes over the past year indicates that KDP will perform well over the near term.

Financial Data
(US$ in Thousands)

	9 Mos	6 Mos	3 Mos	12/31/2018	12/31/2017	12/31/2016	12/31/2015	12/31/2014
Earnings Per Share	0.80	0.70	1.78	0.53	5.89	4.54	3.97	3.56
Cash Flow Per Share	1.67	1.70	1.49	1.48	5.70	5.05	5.19	5.22
Dividends Per Share	0.600	104.200	104.050	104.480	2.320	2.120	1.920	1.640
Dividend Payout %	75.00	14,885.71	5,845.51	19,713.21	39.39	46.70	48.36	46.07
Income Statement								
Total Revenue	8,186,000	5,316,000	2,504,000	7,442,000	6,690,000	6,440,000	6,282,000	6,121,000
EBITDA	2,171,000	1,414,000	647,000	1,476,000	1,532,000	1,618,000	1,491,000	1,379,000
Depn & Amortn	530,000	344,000	163,000	233,000	198,000	191,000	192,000	199,000
Income Before Taxes	1,144,000	731,000	315,000	791,000	1,173,000	1,283,000	1,184,000	1,073,000
Income Taxes	296,000	187,000	85,000	202,000	95,000	434,000	420,000	371,000
Net Income	848,000	544,000	230,000	586,000	1,076,000	847,000	764,000	703,000
Average Shares	1,419,400	1,419,200	1,417,700	1,097,600	182,800	186,600	192,400	197,400
Balance Sheet								
Current Assets	2,269,000	2,221,000	2,162,000	2,159,000	1,117,000	2,736,000	1,817,000	1,211,000
Total Assets	49,400,000	49,547,000	49,291,000	48,918,000	10,022,000	9,791,000	8,869,000	8,273,000
Current Liabilities	6,550,000	6,695,000	6,656,000	5,702,000	1,238,000	1,051,000	1,583,000	1,038,000
Long-Term Obligations	13,147,000	13,164,000	13,246,000	14,506,000	4,400,000	4,468,000	2,875,000	2,588,000
Total Liabilities	26,486,000	26,664,000	26,617,000	26,385,000	7,571,000	7,657,000	6,686,000	5,979,000
Stockholders' Equity	22,914,000	22,883,000	22,674,000	22,533,000	2,451,000	2,134,000	2,183,000	2,294,000
Shares Outstanding	1,406,787	1,406,706	1,406,689	1,405,944	179,743	183,119	187,841	192,957
Statistical Record								
Return on Assets %	2.26	3.20	2.96	1.99	10.86	9.05	8.91	8.53
Return on Equity %	4.93	7.48	6.99	4.69	46.94	39.13	34.13	30.76
EBITDA Margin %	26.52	26.60	25.84	19.83	22.90	25.12	23.73	22.53
Net Margin %	10.36	10.23	9.19	7.87	16.08	13.15	12.16	11.49
Asset Turnover	0.22	0.36	0.33	0.25	0.68	0.69	0.73	0.74
Current Ratio	0.35	0.33	0.32	0.38	0.90	2.60	1.15	1.17
Debt to Equity	0.57	0.58	0.58	0.64	1.80	2.09	1.32	1.13
Price Range	30.91-22.26	123.81-22.19	123.81-22.19	123.81-22.19	98.88-84.47	98.51-82.38	94.99-71.38	74.00-47.22
P/E Ratio	38.64-27.83	176.87-31.70	69.56-12.47	233.60-41.87	16.79-14.34	21.70-18.15	23.93-17.98	20.79-13.26
Average Yield %	2.21	370.40	202.09	145.38	2.53	2.32	2.39	2.77

Address: 53 South Avenue, Burlington, MA 01803 **Telephone:** 802-244-5621	**Web Site:** www.keurig.com **Officers:** Robert ("Bob") James Gamgort - Executive Chairman, President, Chief Executive Officer James L. (Jim) Baldwin - Executive Vice President, Executive Vice President (frmr), Senior Vice President, Chief Legal Officer, General Counsel, Secretary	**Auditors:** DELOITTE & TOUCHE LLP **Investor Contact:** 972-673-7935 **Transfer Agents:** Computershare Investor Services, Canton, MA

KEYCORP

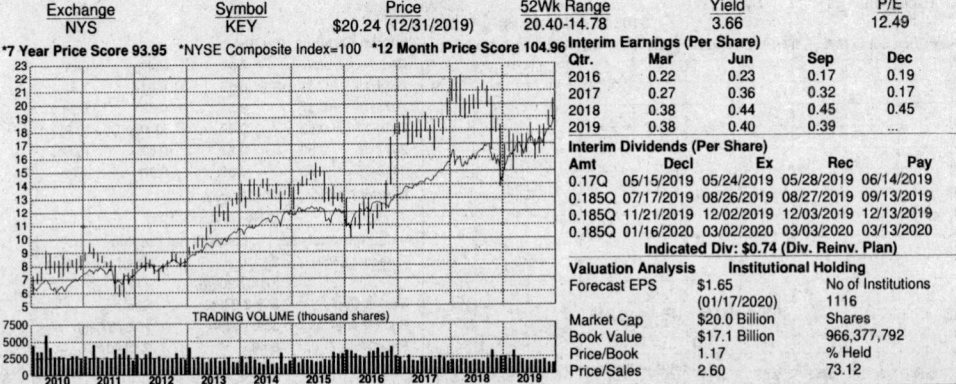

Exchange	Symbol	Price	52Wk Range	Yield	P/E
NYS	KEY	$20.24 (12/31/2019)	20.40-14.78	3.66	12.49

*7 Year Price Score 93.95   *NYSE Composite Index=100   *12 Month Price Score 104.96

Interim Earnings (Per Share)

Qtr.	Mar	Jun	Sep	Dec
2016	0.22	0.23	0.17	0.19
2017	0.27	0.36	0.32	0.17
2018	0.38	0.44	0.45	0.45
2019	0.38	0.40	0.39	...

Interim Dividends (Per Share)

Amt	Decl	Ex	Rec	Pay
0.17Q	05/15/2019	05/24/2019	05/28/2019	06/14/2019
0.185Q	07/17/2019	08/26/2019	08/27/2019	09/13/2019
0.185Q	11/21/2019	12/02/2019	12/03/2019	12/13/2019
0.185Q	01/16/2020	03/02/2020	03/03/2020	03/13/2020

Indicated Div: $0.74 (Div. Reinv. Plan)

Valuation Analysis   Institutional Holding

Forecast EPS	$1.65	No of Institutions
	(01/17/2020)	1116
Market Cap	$20.0 Billion	Shares
Book Value	$17.1 Billion	966,377,792
Price/Book	1.17	% Held
Price/Sales	2.60	73.12

Business Summary: Banking (MIC: 5.1.1 SIC: 6021 NAIC: 522110)

KeyCorp is a holding company. Through its subsidiaries, Co. provides a range of retail and commercial banking, commercial leasing, investment management, consumer finance, commercial mortgage servicing and other servicing, and investment banking products and services to individual, corporate and institutional clients through two main segments: Key Community Bank and Key Corporate Bank. Co.'s bank and trust company subsidiary also provide personal and institutional trust custody services, securities lending, personal financial and planning services, access to mutual funds, treasury services, and international banking services.

Recent Developments: For the quarter ended Sep 30 2019, income from continuing operations decreased 14.3% to US$413.0 million from US$482.0 million in the year-earlier quarter. Net income decreased 13.7% to US$416.0 million from US$482.0 million in the year-earlier quarter. Net interest income decreased 1.4% to US$972.0 million from US$986.0 million in the year-earlier quarter. Provision for loan losses was US$200.0 million versus US$62.0 million in the prior-year quarter, an increase of 222.6%. Non-interest income rose 6.7% to US$650.0 million from US$609.0 million, while non-interest expense declined 2.6% to US$939.0 million.

Prospects: Our evaluation of KeyCorp as of October 4th, 2019 is the result of our systematic analysis on three basic characteristics: earnings strength, relative valuation, and recent stock price movement. The company has generated a negative trend in earnings per share over the past 5 quarters. In addition, recent analyst estimates for the company have been reduced and KEY has posted results that fell short of analysts' expectations. Based on operating earnings yield, the company is undervalued when compared to all of the companies we cover. Share price changes over the past year indicates that KEY will perform poorly over the near term.

Financial Data

(US$ in Thousands)	9 Mos	6 Mos	3 Mos	12/31/2018	12/31/2017	12/31/2016	12/31/2015	12/31/2014
Earnings Per Share	1.62	1.68	1.72	1.71	1.13	0.80	1.05	0.99
Cash Flow Per Share	3.65	2.82	3.25	2.41	1.69	1.82	1.35	1.51
Tang Book Value Per Share	12.42	12.07	11.51	11.10	10.33	9.96	11.16	10.57
Dividends Per Share	0.695	0.680	0.630	0.565	0.380	0.330	0.290	0.250
Dividend Payout %	42.90	40.48	36.63	33.04	33.63	41.25	27.62	25.25
Income Statement								
Interest Income	3,950,000	2,633,000	1,304,000	4,878,000	4,390,000	3,319,000	2,622,000	2,554,000
Interest Expense	1,020,000	675,000	327,000	969,000	613,000	400,000	274,000	261,000
Net Interest Income	2,930,000	1,958,000	977,000	3,909,000	3,777,000	2,919,000	2,348,000	2,293,000
Provision for Losses	336,000	136,000	62,000	246,000	229,000	266,000	166,000	59,000
Non-Interest Income	1,808,000	1,158,000	536,000	2,515,000	2,478,000	2,071,000	1,880,000	1,797,000
Non-Interest Expense	2,921,000	1,982,000	963,000	3,975,000	4,098,000	3,756,000	2,840,000	2,759,000
Income Before Taxes	1,481,000	998,000	488,000	2,203,000	1,928,000	968,000	1,222,000	1,272,000
Income Taxes	239,000	169,000	82,000	344,000	637,000	179,000	303,000	326,000
Net Income	1,248,000	832,000	407,000	1,866,000	1,296,000	791,000	916,000	900,000
Average Shares	998,328	1,007,964	1,016,504	1,054,682	1,088,593	938,536	844,489	878,199
Balance Sheet								
Net Loans & Leases	93,465,000	92,837,000	90,189,000	89,896,000	86,635,000	86,284,000	59,719,000	57,321,000
Total Assets	146,691,000	144,545,000	141,515,000	139,613,000	137,698,000	136,453,000	95,133,000	93,821,000
Total Deposits	111,649,000	109,946,000	108,175,000	107,309,000	105,235,000	104,087,000	71,046,000	71,998,000
Total Liabilities	129,575,000	127,576,000	125,591,000	124,018,000	122,675,000	121,213,000	84,387,000	83,291,000
Stockholders' Equity	17,116,000	16,969,000	15,924,000	15,595,000	15,023,000	15,240,000	10,746,000	10,530,000
Shares Outstanding	988,537	1,003,114	1,013,185	1,019,503	1,069,084	1,079,313	835,751	859,403
Statistical Record								
Return on Assets %	1.21	1.27	1.33	1.35	0.95	0.68	0.97	0.96
Return on Equity %	10.72	11.21	12.02	12.19	8.56	6.07	8.61	8.64
Net Interest Margin %	73.80	73.81	74.92	80.14	86.04	87.95	89.55	89.78
Efficiency Ratio %	47.74	52.23	52.34	53.77	59.67	69.68	63.08	63.41
Loans to Deposits	0.84	0.84	0.83	0.84	0.82	0.83	0.84	0.80
Price Range	20.52-13.82	21.74-13.82	21.74-13.82	22.15-13.82	20.44-16.47	18.54-10.00	15.65-12.16	14.51-12.14
P/E Ratio	12.67-8.53	12.94-8.23	12.64-8.03	12.95-8.08	18.09-14.58	23.17-12.50	14.90-11.58	14.66-12.26
Average Yield %	4.06	3.78	3.36	2.85	2.07	2.60	2.08	1.85

Address: 127 Public Square, Cleveland, OH 44114-1306 Telephone: 216-689-3000	Web Site: www.key.com Officers: Beth E. Mooney - Chairman, Vice-Chairman, President, Chief Executive Officer, Chief Operating Officer Christopher M. Gorman - Chairman, Vice-Chairman, President, Chief Executive Officer, Chief Operating Officer, Division Officer	Auditors: Ernst & Young LLP Investor Contact: 216-689-4221 Transfer Agents: Computershare Investor Services LLC, Providence, RI

KEYSIGHT TECHNOLOGIES INC

Exchange	Symbol	Price	52Wk Range	Yield	P/E
NYS	KEYS	$102.63 (12/31/2019)	109.08-58.32	N/A	31.58

*7 Year Price Score N/A   *NSYE Composite Index=100   *12 Month Price Score 111.15

Interim Earnings (Per Share)

Qtr.	Jan	Apr	Jul	Oct
2014-15	0.41	0.56	0.41	1.62
2015-16	0.37	0.51	0.53	0.54
2016-17	0.63	0.27	(0.10)	(0.22)
2017-18	0.50	0.34	0.63	(0.60)
2018-19	0.60	0.80	0.83	1.02

Interim Dividends (Per Share)

No Dividends Paid

Valuation Analysis		Institutional Holding	
Forecast EPS	$5.13	No of Institutions	
	(01/07/2020)	779	
Market Cap	$19.2 Billion	Shares	
Book Value	$3.0 Billion	182,767,280	
Price/Book	6.40	% Held	
Price/Sales	4.47	89.00	

Business Summary: Industrial Machinery & Equipment (MIC: 7.2.1 SIC: 3823 NAIC: 334513)

Keysight Technologies is a technology company. Co.'s segments are: Communications Solutions Group, which provides electronic design and test software, instruments and systems and related services used in the simulation, design, validation, manufacturing, installation and optimization of electronic equipment; Electronic Industrial Solutions Group, which provides test and measurement solutions and related services across a set of electronic industrial end markets; and Ixia Solutions Group, which helps customers design, validate and support the performance and security of their networks and associated components and applications.

Recent Developments: For the year ended Oct 31 2019, net income increased 276.4% to US$621.0 million from US$165.0 million in the prior year. Revenues were US$4.30 billion, up 11.0% from US$3.88 billion the year before. Operating income was US$711.0 million versus a loss of US$394.0 million in the prior year. Direct operating expenses was unchanged at US$1.77 billion versus the comparable period the year before. Indirect operating expenses decreased 27.2% to US$1.82 billion from US$2.51 billion in the equivalent prior-year period.

Prospects: Our evaluation of Keysight Technologies Inc. as of October 4th, 2019 is the result of our systematic analysis on three basic characteristics: earnings strength, relative valuation, and recent stock price movement. The company has managed to produce a neutral trend in earnings per share over the past 5 quarters. However, recent analyst estimates for the company have been raised and KEYS has posted results that exceeded analysts' expectations. Based on operating earnings yield, the company is fairly valued when compared to all of the companies we cover. Share price changes over the past year indicates that KEYS will perform over the near term.

Financial Data
(US$ in Millions)

	10/31/2019	10/31/2018	10/31/2017	10/31/2016	10/31/2015	10/31/2014	10/31/2013	10/31/2012
Earnings Per Share	3.25	0.86	0.56	1.95	3.00	2.35	...	...
Cash Flow Per Share	5.31	2.97	1.74	2.44	2.22	3.37	...	...
Tang Book Value Per Share	6.97	3.30	N.M.	3.35	2.10	2.14	...	...
Income Statement								
Total Revenue	4,303	3,878	3,189	2,918	2,856	2,933	2,888	3,315
EBITDA	868	(237)	344	495	514	552	566	801
Depn & Amortn	96	103	92	85	81	74	65	55
Income Before Taxes	715	(411)	179	366	388	475	501	746
Income Taxes	94	(576)	77	31	(125)	83	44	(95)
Net Income	621	165	102	335	513	392	457	841
Average Shares	191	191	182	172	171	167	...	...
Balance Sheet								
Current Assets	3,215	2,378	2,177	1,854	1,579	1,850	972	993
Total Assets	6,623	5,824	5,933	3,803	3,508	3,050	2,028	2,133
Current Liabilities	1,003	1,462	819	644	686	769	560	595
Long-Term Obligations	1,788	1,291	2,038	1,100	1,099	1,099	...	...
Total Liabilities	3,619	3,391	3,623	2,290	2,206	2,281	783	828
Stockholders' Equity	3,004	2,433	2,310	1,513	1,302	769	1,245	1,305
Shares Outstanding	187	186	186	169	169	167	...	...
Statistical Record								
Return on Assets %	9.98	2.81	2.10	9.14	15.65	...	21.97	...
Return on Equity %	22.84	6.96	5.34	23.74	49.54	...	35.84	...
EBITDA Margin %	20.17	N.M.	10.79	16.96	18.00	18.82	19.60	24.16
Net Margin %	14.43	4.25	3.20	11.48	17.96	13.37	15.82	25.37
Asset Turnover	0.69	0.66	0.66	0.80	0.87	...	1.39	...
Current Ratio	3.21	1.63	2.66	2.88	2.30	2.41	1.74	1.67
Debt to Equity	0.60	0.53	0.88	0.73	0.84	1.43	...	...
Price Range	104.39-54.35	66.50-41.54	44.67-31.82	33.37-21.18	38.89-29.54	31.50-28.25	...	...
P/E Ratio	32.12-16.72	77.33-48.30	79.77-56.82	17.11-10.86	12.96-9.85	13.40-12.02	...	...

Address: 1400 Fountaingrove Parkway, Santa Rosa, CA 95403 Telephone: 800-829-4444	Web Site: www.keysight.com Officers: Paul N. Clark - Chairman Ronald S. Nersesian - President, Chief Executive Officer	Auditors: PricewaterhouseCoopers LLP Investor Contact: 800-829-4444 Transfer Agents: Computershare Trust Company, N.A.

KILROY REALTY CORP

Exchange	Symbol	Price	52Wk Range	Yield	P/E
NYS	KRC	$83.90 (12/31/2019)	84.50-61.44	2.31	30.40

*7 Year Price Score 94.39 *NYSE Composite Index=100 *12 Month Price Score 102.29

Interim Earnings (Per Share)

Qtr.	Mar	Jun	Sep	Dec
2016	1.84	0.31	0.54	0.28
2017	0.26	0.30	0.67	0.28
2018	0.36	0.27	0.33	1.58
2019	0.36	0.41	0.41	...

Interim Dividends (Per Share)

Amt	Decl	Ex	Rec	Pay
0.455Q	02/12/2019	03/28/2019	03/29/2019	04/17/2019
0.485Q	05/16/2019	06/27/2019	06/28/2019	07/17/2019
0.485Q	09/11/2019	09/27/2019	09/30/2019	10/16/2019
0.485Q	12/10/2019	12/30/2019	12/31/2019	01/15/2020

Indicated Div: $1.94

Valuation Analysis

		Institutional Holding	
Forecast EPS	$1.66	No of Institutions	415
	(01/14/2020)		
Market Cap	$8.9 Billion	Shares	138,194,960
Book Value	$4.3 Billion	% Held	96.66
Price/Book	2.09		
Price/Sales	11.01		

Business Summary: REITs (MIC: 5.3.1 SIC: 6798 NAIC: 525930)

Kilroy Realty is a self-administered real estate investment trust engaged in premier office and mixed-use submarkets along the West Coast. Co. owns, develops, acquires and manages real estate assets, consisting primarily of Class A real estate properties in the coastal regions of Greater Los Angeles, Orange County, San Diego County, the San Francisco Bay Area and Greater Seattle. Co. owns its interests in all of its properties through Kilroy Realty, L.P. (the Operating Partnership) and Kilroy Realty Finance Partnership, L.P. and generally conducts substantially all of its operations through the Operating Partnership.

Recent Developments: For the quarter ended Sep 30 2019, net income increased 26.1% to US$48.3 million from US$38.3 million in the year-earlier quarter. Revenues were US$215.5 million, up 15.5% from US$186.6 million the year before.

Prospects: Our evaluation of Kilroy Realty Corp. as of October 4th, 2019 is the result of our systematic analysis on three basic characteristics: earnings strength, relative valuation, and recent stock price movement. The company has enjoyed a very positive trend in earnings per share over the past 5 quarters. However, recent analyst estimates for the company have been mixed and KRC has posted results that fell short of analysts' expectations. Based on operating earnings yield, the company is overvalued when compared to all of the companies we cover. Share price changes over the past year indicates that KRC will perform well over the near term.

Financial Data

(US$ in Thousands)	9 Mos	6 Mos	3 Mos	12/31/2018	12/31/2017	12/31/2016	12/31/2015	12/31/2014
Earnings Per Share	2.76	2.68	2.54	2.55	1.51	2.97	2.42	1.95
Cash Flow Per Share	3.76	3.83	4.12	4.10	3.54	3.73	3.03	2.95
Tang Book Value Per Share	40.23	38.78	38.77	39.01	37.53	35.94	32.28	28.68
Dividends Per Share	1.880	1.850	1.820	1.790	1.650	3.375	1.400	1.400
Dividend Payout %	68.12	69.03	71.65	70.20	109.27	113.64	57.85	71.79
Income Statement								
Total Revenue	617,219	401,694	201,202	747,298	719,001	642,572	581,275	521,725
EBITDA	172,733	114,434	53,952	526,806	431,652	529,837	455,543	280,123
Depn & Amortn	4,026	4,899	2,743	198,600	190,500	172,000	159,500	153,800
Income Before Taxes	137,307	89,009	41,794	277,926	180,615	303,798	238,604	59,313
Net Income	122,943	79,097	36,903	258,415	164,612	293,788	234,081	180,219
Average Shares	105,359	101,809	101,443	100,482	98,727	93,023	90,395	84,967
Balance Sheet								
Current Assets	679,036	408,839	388,863	479,996	350,789	497,339	270,943	274,582
Total Assets	8,623,815	8,094,721	7,883,987	7,765,707	6,802,838	6,706,633	5,939,469	5,633,736
Current Liabilities	684,542	632,630	615,797	421,974	293,085	424,697	281,315	258,729
Long-Term Obligations	3,394,853	3,275,188	3,085,008	2,932,601	2,347,063	2,320,123	2,238,508	2,469,413
Total Liabilities	4,359,166	4,179,189	3,969,463	3,835,800	3,102,045	3,163,638	2,768,503	2,967,526
Stockholders' Equity	4,264,649	3,915,532	3,914,524	3,929,907	3,700,793	3,542,995	3,170,966	2,666,210
Shares Outstanding	106,011	100,972	100,967	100,746	98,620	93,219	92,258	86,259
Statistical Record								
Return on Assets %	3.50	3.54	3.49	3.55	2.44	4.63	4.05	3.35
Return on Equity %	7.02	7.09	6.82	6.77	4.54	8.73	8.02	7.03
EBITDA Margin %	27.99	28.49	26.81	70.49	60.03	82.46	78.37	53.69
Net Margin %	19.92	19.69	18.34	34.58	22.89	45.72	40.27	34.54
Asset Turnover	0.10	0.10	0.10	0.10	0.11	0.10	0.10	0.10
Current Ratio	0.99	0.65	0.63	1.14	1.20	1.17	0.96	1.06
Debt to Equity	0.80	0.84	0.79	0.75	0.63	0.65	0.71	0.93
Price Range	80.06-59.46	78.36-59.46	77.34-59.46	77.34-59.46	77.91-67.47	76.88-47.38	78.86-62.83	71.10-50.18
P/E Ratio	29.01-21.54	29.24-22.19	30.45-23.41	30.33-23.32	51.60-44.68	25.89-15.95	32.59-25.96	36.46-25.73
Average Yield %	2.56	2.56	2.54	2.52	2.26	5.16	2.00	2.29

Address: 12200 W. Olympic Boulevard, Suite 200, Los Angeles, CA 90064 **Telephone:** 310-481-8400	**Web Site:** www.kilroyrealty.com **Officers:** John B. Kilroy - Chairman, President, Chief Executive Officer Jeffrey C. Hawken - Executive Vice President, Chief Operating Officer	**Auditors:** DELOITTE & TOUCHE LLP **Investor Contact:** 310-481-8400 **Transfer Agents:** Computershare Trust Company, N.A., Canton, MA

KIMBERLY-CLARK CORP.

Exchange	Symbol	Price	52Wk Range	Yield	P/E	Div Acheiver
NYS	KMB	$137.55 (12/31/2019)	142.74-107.87	3.00	23.59	44 Years

*7 Year Price Score 93.10   ***NYSE Composite Index=100**   ***12 Month Price Score 98.56**

Interim Earnings (Per Share)
Qtr.	Mar	Jun	Sep	Dec
2016	1.50	1.56	1.52	1.41
2017	1.57	1.49	1.60	1.74
2018	0.26	1.30	1.29	1.18
2019	1.31	1.40	1.94	...

Interim Dividends (Per Share)
Amt	Decl	Ex	Rec	Pay
1.03Q	01/23/2019	03/07/2019	03/08/2019	04/02/2019
1.03Q	05/02/2019	06/06/2019	06/07/2019	07/02/2019
1.03Q	08/01/2019	09/05/2019	09/06/2019	10/02/2019
1.03Q	11/21/2019	12/05/2019	12/06/2019	01/03/2020

Indicated Div: $4.12 (Div. Reinv. Plan)

Valuation Analysis
Forecast EPS	$6.87 (01/17/2020)
Market Cap	$47.2 Billion
Book Value	N/A
Price/Book	N/A
Price/Sales	2.56

Institutional Holding
No of Institutions	2070
Shares	333,700,576
% Held	69.98

Business Summary: Household & Personal Products (MIC: 1.7.1 SIC: 2679 NAIC: 322299)

Kimberly-Clark is principally engaged in the manufacturing and marketing of a range of products primarily made from natural or synthetic fibers using technologies in fibers, nonwovens and absorbency. Co. is organized into three operating segments: Personal Care, which provides solutions and products such as disposable diapers, training and youth pants, swimpants, baby wipes, feminine and incontinence care products, and other related products; Consumer Tissue, which provides facial and bathroom tissue, paper towels, napkins and related products; and K-C Professional, which provides a range of solutions and supporting products such as wipers, tissue, towels, apparel, soaps and sanitizers.

Recent Developments: For the quarter ended Sep 30 2019, net income increased 47.2% to US$680.0 million from US$462.0 million in the year-earlier quarter. Revenues were US$4.64 billion, up 1.3% from US$4.58 billion the year before. Operating income was US$915.0 million versus US$669.0 million in the prior-year quarter, an increase of 36.8%. Direct operating expenses declined 2.6% to US$3.09 billion from US$3.17 billion in the comparable period the year before. Indirect operating expenses decreased 14.3% to US$640.0 million from US$747.0 million in the equivalent prior-year period.

Prospects: Our evaluation of Kimberly-Clark Corp. as of October 4th, 2019 is the result of our systematic analysis on three basic characteristics: earnings strength, relative valuation, and recent stock price movement. The company has enjoyed a very positive trend in earnings per share over the past 5 quarters. In addition, recent analyst estimates for the company have been raised, and KMB has posted results that exceeded analysts' expectations. Based on operating earnings yield, the company is fairly valued when compared to all of the companies we cover. Share price changes over the past year indicates that KMB will perform well over the near term.

Financial Data
(US$ in Thousands)

	9 Mos	6 Mos	3 Mos	12/31/2018	12/31/2017	12/31/2016	12/31/2015	12/31/2014
Earnings Per Share	5.83	5.18	5.08	4.03	6.40	5.99	2.77	4.04
Cash Flow Per Share	8.03	7.46	7.97	8.53	8.28	8.97	6.34	7.60
Dividends Per Share	4.090	4.060	4.030	4.000	3.880	3.680	3.520	3.360
Dividend Payout %	70.15	78.38	79.33	99.26	60.63	61.44	127.08	83.17
Income Statement								
Total Revenue	13,867,000	9,227,000	4,633,000	18,486,000	18,259,000	18,202,000	18,591,000	19,724,000
EBITDA	2,907,000	1,773,000	878,000	2,948,000	4,023,000	4,022,000	2,359,000	3,383,000
Depn & Amortn	700,000	470,000	234,000	882,000	724,000	705,000	746,000	862,000
Income Before Taxes	2,017,000	1,176,000	582,000	1,813,000	2,991,000	3,009,000	1,335,000	2,255,000
Income Taxes	467,000	275,000	143,000	471,000	776,000	922,000	418,000	856,000
Net Income	1,610,000	939,000	454,000	1,410,000	2,278,000	2,166,000	1,013,000	1,526,000
Average Shares	345,900	346,000	346,000	349,600	355,900	361,700	366,300	377,400
Balance Sheet								
Current Assets	5,064,000	5,321,000	5,255,000	5,041,000	5,211,000	5,115,000	5,426,000	5,559,000
Total Assets	15,033,000	15,347,000	15,204,000	14,518,000	15,151,000	14,602,000	14,842,000	15,526,000
Current Liabilities	6,782,000	6,585,000	7,197,000	6,536,000	5,858,000	5,846,000	6,349,000	6,226,000
Long-Term Obligations	6,198,000	6,701,000	5,990,000	6,247,000	6,472,000	6,439,000	6,106,000	5,630,000
Total Liabilities	15,174,000	15,525,000	15,509,000	14,741,000	14,461,000	14,646,000	14,952,000	14,725,000
Stockholders' Equity	(141,000)	(178,000)	(305,000)	(223,000)	690,000	(44,000)	(110,000)	801,000
Shares Outstanding	343,100	344,216	343,795	344,962	351,106	356,568	360,860	365,336
Statistical Record								
Return on Assets %	13.65	12.04	11.61	9.50	15.31	14.67	6.67	8.86
Return on Equity %	...	...	29,516.67	603.85	705.26	...	293.20	53.27
EBITDA Margin %	20.96	19.22	18.95	15.95	22.03	22.10	12.69	17.15
Net Margin %	11.61	10.18	9.80	7.63	12.48	11.90	5.45	7.74
Asset Turnover	1.25	1.23	1.21	1.25	1.23	1.23	1.22	1.15
Current Ratio	0.75	0.81	0.73	0.77	0.89	0.87	0.85	0.89
Debt to Equity	...	...	...	...	9.38	...	...	7.03
Price Range	142.74-102.30	137.79-102.30	123.90-98.52	123.44-98.52	135.00-109.87	138.13-112.15	129.54-103.35	118.28-98.99
P/E Ratio	24.48-17.55	26.60-19.75	24.39-19.39	30.63-24.45	21.09-17.17	23.06-18.72	46.77-37.31	29.28-24.50
Average Yield %	3.31	3.47	3.64	3.63	3.14	2.91	3.13	3.16

Address: P.O. Box 619100, Dallas, TX 75261-9100
Telephone: 972-281-1200

Web Site: www.kimberly-clark.com
Officers: Michael D. Hsu - Chairman, President, Chief Executive Officer, Chief Operating Officer, Division Officer Maria G. Henry - Senior Vice President, Chief Financial Officer, Principal Accounting Officer

Auditors: DELOITTE & TOUCHE LLP
Investor Contact: 972-281-1440
Transfer Agents: ComputerShare Investor Services, Providence, RI

KIMCO REALTY CORP

Exchange	Symbol	Price	52Wk Range	Yield	P/E
NYS	KIM	$20.71 (12/31/2019)	21.77-14.55	5.41	27.61

*7 Year Price Score 70.93   ***NYSE Composite Index=100**   ***12 Month Price Score 105.85**

TRADING VOLUME (thousand shares)

Interim Earnings (Per Share)

Qtr.	Mar	Jun	Sep	Dec
2016	0.31	0.46	(0.13)	0.16
2017	0.15	0.31	0.24	0.17
2018	0.30	0.36	0.19	0.17
2019	0.24	0.20	0.14	...

Interim Dividends (Per Share)

Amt	Decl	Ex	Rec	Pay
0.28Q	01/31/2019	04/01/2019	04/02/2019	04/15/2019
0.28Q	05/02/2019	07/01/2019	07/02/2019	07/15/2019
0.28Q	07/23/2019	10/01/2019	10/02/2019	10/15/2019
0.28Q	10/24/2019	12/31/2019	01/02/2020	01/15/2020

Indicated Div: $1.12 (Div. Reinv. Plan)

Valuation Analysis   **Institutional Holding**

Forecast EPS	$0.76	No of Institutions
	(01/17/2020)	676
Market Cap	$8.7 Billion	Shares
Book Value	$4.9 Billion	460,634,720
Price/Book	1.78	% Held
Price/Sales	7.62	88.68

Business Summary: REITs (MIC: 5.3.1 SIC: 6798 NAIC: 525930)

Kimco Realty is a self-administered real estate investment trust. Co. and its subsidiaries are engaged principally in the ownership, management, development and operation of open-air shopping centers, which are anchored generally by grocery stores, off-price retailers, discounters or service-oriented tenants. Additionally, Co. provides complementary services on its retail real estate capabilities. Co.'s ownership interests in real estate consist of its consolidated portfolio and portfolios where Co. owns an economic interest, such as properties in Co.'s investment real estate management programs, where Co. partners with institutional investors and also retains management.

Recent Developments: For the quarter ended Sep 30 2019, net income decreased 15.2% to US$85.5 million from US$100.7 million in the year-earlier quarter. Revenues were US$282.9 million, down 0.1% from US$283.1 million the year before. Revenues from property income rose 0.2% to US$279.2 million from US$278.7 million in the corresponding quarter a year earlier.

Prospects: Our evaluation of Kimco Realty Corp. as of October 4th, 2019 is the result of our systematic analysis on three basic characteristics: earnings strength, relative valuation, and recent stock price movement. The company has enjoyed a very positive trend in earnings per share over the past 5 quarters. However, recent analyst estimates for the company have been mixed and KIM has posted results that fell short of analysts' expectations. Based on operating earnings yield, the company is fairly valued when compared to all of the companies we cover. Share price changes over the past year indicates that KIM will perform in line with the market over the near term.

Financial Data

(US$ in Thousands)	9 Mos	6 Mos	3 Mos	12/31/2018	12/31/2017	12/31/2016	12/31/2015	12/31/2014
Earnings Per Share	0.75	0.80	0.96	1.02	0.87	0.79	2.00	0.89
Cash Flow Per Share	1.44	1.43	1.43	1.52	1.45	1.41	1.20	1.54
Tang Book Value Per Share	11.61	12.54	12.61	12.66	12.67	12.37	12.21	11.59
Dividends Per Share	1.120	1.120	1.120	1.120	1.090	1.035	0.975	0.915
Dividend Payout %	149.33	140.00	116.67	109.80	125.29	131.01	48.75	102.81
Income Statement								
Total Revenue	862,754	579,883	295,010	1,164,762	1,200,834	1,170,792	1,166,769	993,897
EBITDA	559,298	386,629	208,286	893,065	696,287	614,416	693,273	577,993
Depn & Amortn	209,440	140,566	71,561	310,380	360,811	355,320	344,527	273,093
Income Before Taxes	218,220	157,571	92,330	399,346	146,329	68,025	168,916	102,107
Income Taxes	(3,580)	286	630	1,600	(880)	72,545	60,230	22,438
Net Income	301,186	217,196	116,169	497,795	426,075	378,850	894,115	424,001
Average Shares	421,002	420,646	420,763	421,379	424,019	419,709	412,851	411,038
Balance Sheet								
Current Assets	332,746	296,360	327,323	338,411	441,535	332,410	372,351	449,943
Total Assets	11,085,131	11,040,903	11,070,200	10,999,100	11,763,726	11,230,600	11,344,171	10,285,728
Current Liabilities	126,203	130,460	130,444	305,165	314,594	270,268	265,241	240,652
Long-Term Obligations	5,312,628	4,905,502	4,868,754	4,873,872	5,478,927	5,066,368	5,376,310	4,620,298
Total Liabilities	6,183,250	5,747,001	5,750,323	5,665,296	6,369,482	5,974,461	6,297,871	5,510,943
Stockholders' Equity	4,901,881	5,293,902	5,319,877	5,333,804	5,394,244	5,256,139	5,046,300	4,774,785
Shares Outstanding	422,230	422,094	422,037	421,388	425,646	425,034	413,430	411,819
Statistical Record								
Return on Assets %	3.51	3.63	4.19	4.37	3.71	3.35	8.27	4.25
Return on Equity %	7.57	7.58	8.75	9.28	8.00	7.33	18.21	9.01
EBITDA Margin %	64.83	66.67	70.60	76.67	57.98	52.48	59.42	58.15
Net Margin %	34.91	37.46	39.38	42.74	35.48	32.36	76.63	42.66
Asset Turnover	0.10	0.10	0.10	0.10	0.10	0.10	0.11	0.10
Current Ratio	2.64	2.27	2.51	1.11	1.40	1.23	1.40	1.87
Debt to Equity	1.08	0.93	0.92	0.91	1.02	0.96	1.07	0.97
Price Range	20.88-14.31	19.13-14.31	18.64-13.24	18.12-13.24	26.07-17.30	28.33-22.26	28.33-22.26	25.91-19.75
P/E Ratio	27.84-19.08	23.91-17.89	19.42-13.79	17.76-12.98	29.97-19.89	40.72-31.28	14.16-11.13	29.11-22.19
Average Yield %	6.40	6.61	6.92	7.11	5.32	3.67	3.85	4.00

Address: 3333 New Hyde Park Road, New Hyde Park, NY 11042 **Telephone:** 516-869-9000	**Web Site:** www.kimcorealty.com **Officers:** Milton Cooper - Executive Chairman Ross Cooper - President, Chief Investment Officer	**Auditors:** PricewaterhouseCoopers LLP **Investor Contact:** 516-869-9000 **Transfer Agents:** Wells Fargo Shareholder Services, St. Paul, MN

KINDER MORGAN INC.

Exchange	Symbol	Price	52Wk Range	Yield	P/E
NYS	KMI	$21.17 (12/31/2019)	21.38-15.38	4.72	23.52

*7 Year Price Score 62.28 *NYSE Composite Index=100 *12 Month Price Score 95.96

Interim Earnings (Per Share)

Qtr.	Mar	Jun	Sep	Dec
2016	0.12	0.15	(0.10)	0.08
2017	0.18	0.15	0.15	(0.47)
2018	0.22	(0.08)	0.31	0.21
2019	0.24	0.23	0.22	...

Interim Dividends (Per Share)

Amt	Decl	Ex	Rec	Pay
0.20Q	01/16/2019	01/30/2019	01/31/2019	02/15/2019
0.25Q	04/17/2019	04/29/2019	04/30/2019	05/15/2019
0.25Q	07/17/2019	07/30/2019	07/31/2019	08/15/2019
0.25Q	10/16/2019	10/30/2019	10/31/2019	11/15/2019

Indicated Div: $1.00 (Div. Reinv. Plan)

Valuation Analysis

		Institutional Holding	
Forecast EPS	$0.96	No of Institutions	
	(01/17/2020)	1437	
Market Cap	$47.9 Billion	Shares	
Book Value	$33.6 Billion	1,716,658,176	
Price/Book	1.43	% Held	
Price/Sales	3.52	63.00	

Business Summary: Equipment & Services (MIC: 9.1.3 SIC: 4923 NAIC: 221210)

Kinder Morgan is an energy infrastructure company. Co.'s segments are: Natural Gas Pipelines, which includes the ownership and operation of, among others, main interstate and intrastate natural gas pipeline and storage systems; Products Pipelines, which includes the ownership and operation of refined petroleum products, NGL and crude oil and condensate pipelines; Terminals, which includes the ownership and/or operation of, among others, liquids and bulk terminal facilities; and carbon dioxide (CO2), which includes the production, transportation and marketing of CO2, the ownership interests in oil fields and gas processing plants in West Texas and crude oil pipeline system in West Texas.

Recent Developments: For the quarter ended Sep 30 2019, net income decreased 48.6% to US$517.0 million from US$1.01 billion in the year-earlier quarter. Revenues were US$3.21 billion, down 8.6% from US$3.52 billion the year before. Operating income was US$951.0 million versus US$1.52 billion in the prior-year quarter, a decrease of 37.2%. Direct operating expenses declined 19.7% to US$1.43 billion from US$1.78 billion in the comparable period the year before. Indirect operating expenses increased 276.9% to US$833.0 million from US$221.0 million in the equivalent prior-year period.

Prospects: Our evaluation of Kinder Morgan, Inc. as of October 4th, 2019 is the result of our systematic analysis on three basic characteristics: earnings strength, relative valuation, and recent stock price movement. The company has enjoyed a very positive trend in earnings per share over the past 5 quarters. However, recent analyst estimates for the company have been mixed and KMI has posted results that fell short of analysts' expectations. Based on operating earnings yield, the company is fairly valued when compared to all of the companies we cover. Share price changes over the past year indicates that KMI will perform well over the near term.

Financial Data

(US$ in Thousands)	9 Mos	6 Mos	3 Mos	12/31/2018	12/31/2017	12/31/2016	12/31/2015	12/31/2014
Earnings Per Share	0.90	0.99	0.68	0.66	0.01	0.25	0.10	0.89
Cash Flow Per Share	2.12	2.07	2.08	2.28	2.06	2.14	2.42	3.93
Tang Book Value Per Share	3.95	3.93	3.90	3.90	3.78	4.02	3.49	3.35
Dividends Per Share	0.900	0.850	0.800	0.725	0.500	0.500	1.930	1.700
Dividend Payout %	100.00	85.86	117.65	109.85	5,000.00	200.00	1,930.00	191.01
Income Statement								
Total Revenue	9,857,000	6,643,000	3,429,000	14,144,000	13,705,000	13,058,000	14,403,000	16,226,000
EBITDA	2,977,000	2,014,000	1,028,000	5,593,000	5,437,000	4,917,000	4,468,000	6,345,000
Depn & Amortn	61,000	40,000	21,000	2,057,000	2,022,000	1,970,000	2,059,000	1,862,000
Income Before Taxes	1,557,000	1,062,000	547,000	1,619,000	1,583,000	1,141,000	358,000	2,685,000
Income Taxes	471,000	320,000	172,000	587,000	1,938,000	917,000	564,000	648,000
Net Income	1,580,000	1,074,000	556,000	1,609,000	183,000	708,000	253,000	1,026,000
Average Shares	2,264,000	2,262,000	2,262,000	2,216,000	2,230,000	2,230,000	2,193,000	1,137,000
Balance Sheet								
Current Assets	2,365,000	2,300,000	2,262,000	5,722,000	2,715,000	3,229,000	2,824,000	3,752,000
Total Assets	76,931,000	76,695,000	76,292,000	78,866,000	79,055,000	80,305,000	84,104,000	83,198,000
Current Liabilities	6,826,000	5,659,000	5,009,000	7,557,000	6,181,000	5,924,000	4,065,000	6,362,000
Long-Term Obligations	32,111,000	33,005,000	33,328,000	33,936,000	35,015,000	37,354,000	42,406,000	40,246,000
Total Liabilities	43,298,000	43,057,000	42,680,000	45,188,000	45,419,000	45,874,000	48,985,000	49,122,000
Stockholders' Equity	33,633,000	33,638,000	33,612,000	33,678,000	33,636,000	34,431,000	35,119,000	34,076,000
Shares Outstanding	2,264,908	2,262,498	2,262,424	2,262,166	2,217,110	2,230,103	2,229,224	2,125,147
Statistical Record								
Return on Assets %	2.66	2.97	2.11	2.04	0.23	0.86	0.30	1.30
Return on Equity %	6.18	6.90	4.88	4.78	0.54	2.03	0.73	4.35
EBITDA Margin %	30.20	30.32	29.98	39.54	39.67	37.66	31.02	39.10
Net Margin %	16.03	16.17	16.21	11.38	1.34	5.42	1.76	6.32
Asset Turnover	0.17	0.18	0.18	0.18	0.17	0.16	0.17	0.20
Current Ratio	0.35	0.41	0.45	0.76	0.44	0.55	0.69	0.59
Debt to Equity	0.95	0.98	0.99	1.01	1.04	1.08	1.21	1.18
Price Range	21.38-14.71	21.38-14.71	20.42-14.71	19.63-14.71	22.94-16.76	23.13-12.01	44.57-14.54	43.01-30.96
P/E Ratio	23.76-16.34	21.60-14.86	30.03-21.63	29.74-22.29	N.M.	92.52-48.04	445.70-145.40	48.33-34.79
Average Yield %	4.72	4.62	4.59	4.24	2.53	2.61	5.52	4.70

Address: 1001 Louisiana Street, Suite 1000, Houston, TX 77002	Web Site: www.kindermorgan.com	Auditors: PricewaterhouseCoopers LLP
Telephone: 713-369-9000	Officers: Richard D. Kinder - Executive Chairman, Chairman, Chief Executive Officer Steven J. Kean - President, Chief Executive Officer, Executive Vice President, Chief Operating Officer	Investor Contact: 713-369-9449
		Transfer Agents: Computershare Investor Services, LLC

KIRBY CORP.

Exchange	Symbol	Price	52Wk Range	Yield	P/E
NYS	KEX	$89.53 (12/31/2019)	89.63-66.60	N/A	46.63

*7 Year Price Score 82.95 *NYSE Composite Index=100 *12 Month Price Score 102.17

TRADING VOLUME (thousand shares)

Interim Earnings (Per Share)

Qtr.	Mar	Jun	Sep	Dec
2016	0.71	0.72	0.59	0.60
2017	0.51	0.48	0.52	4.12
2018	0.54	0.48	0.70	(0.41)
2019	0.74	0.79	0.80	...

Interim Dividends (Per Share)

No Dividends Paid

Valuation Analysis / Institutional Holding

Valuation Analysis		Institutional Holding	
Forecast EPS	$2.90	No of Institutions	
	(01/15/2020)	413	
Market Cap	$5.4 Billion	Shares	
Book Value	$3.4 Billion	76,141,920	
Price/Book	1.59	% Held	95.47
Price/Sales	1.85		

Business Summary: Shipping (MIC: 7.4.2 SIC: 4449 NAIC: 483211)

Kirby is a tank barge operator. Co. has two segments: marine transportation, which provides marine transportation services, operating tank barges and towing vessels transporting bulk liquid products throughout the Mississippi River System, coastwise along all three U.S. coasts, and in Alaska and Hawaii; and Distribution and Services, which sells genuine replacement parts, provides service mechanics to overhaul and repair engines, transmissions, reduction gears and related oilfield services equipment, rebuilds component parts or entire diesel engines, and related equipment used in oilfield services, marine, mining, power generation, on-highway and other industrial applications.

Recent Developments: For the quarter ended Sep 30 2019, net income increased 14.8% to US$48.2 million from US$42.0 million in the year-earlier quarter. Revenues were US$666.8 million, down 5.4% from US$704.8 million the year before. Operating income was US$77.9 million versus US$68.0 million in the prior-year quarter, an increase of 14.6%. Direct operating expenses declined 8.0% to US$458.5 million from US$498.4 million in the comparable period the year before. Indirect operating expenses decreased 5.8% to US$130.4 million from US$138.5 million in the equivalent prior-year period.

Prospects: Our evaluation of Kirby Corp. as of October 4th, 2019 is the result of our systematic analysis on three basic characteristics: earnings strength, relative valuation, and recent stock price movement. The company has managed to produce a neutral trend in earnings per share over the past 5 quarters. However, recent analyst estimates for the company have been reduced while KEX has posted results that exceeded analysts' expectations. Based on operating earnings yield, the company is fairly valued when compared to all of the companies we cover. Share price changes over the past year indicates that KEX will perform very poorly over the near term.

Financial Data

(US$ in Thousands)	9 Mos	6 Mos	3 Mos	12/31/2018	12/31/2017	12/31/2016	12/31/2015	12/31/2014
Earnings Per Share	1.92	1.82	1.51	1.31	5.62	2.62	4.11	4.93
Cash Flow Per Share	7.74	6.39	6.14	5.83	6.39	7.72	9.53	7.74
Tang Book Value Per Share	36.84	35.90	34.89	34.00	32.55	33.63	31.31	29.24
Income Statement								
Total Revenue	2,182,472	1,515,663	744,621	2,970,697	2,214,418	1,770,673	2,147,532	2,566,318
EBITDA	257,703	168,665	82,178	426,714	330,729	478,166	605,469	672,779
Depn & Amortn	29,176	18,903	10,640	266,054	236,534	233,262	225,470	197,312
Income Before Taxes	185,501	121,046	58,337	113,804	72,723	227,214	361,261	454,006
Income Taxes	45,454	29,149	13,880	35,081	(240,889)	84,942	133,742	169,782
Net Income	139,570	91,583	44,296	78,452	313,187	141,406	226,684	282,006
Average Shares	59,906	59,907	59,823	59,689	55,361	53,512	54,826	56,867
Balance Sheet								
Current Assets	958,533	1,054,264	1,118,252	1,096,489	957,082	646,555	640,776	803,154
Total Assets	6,127,885	6,232,890	6,300,692	5,871,594	5,127,427	4,303,499	4,156,266	4,141,909
Current Liabilities	516,991	526,033	582,724	607,782	480,306	358,338	361,917	594,027
Long-Term Obligations	1,434,417	1,594,695	1,667,457	1,410,169	992,403	722,802	778,834	600,000
Total Liabilities	2,756,364	2,913,736	3,038,356	2,658,407	2,016,607	1,894,181	1,887,455	1,887,873
Stockholders' Equity	3,371,521	3,319,154	3,262,336	3,213,187	3,110,820	2,409,318	2,268,811	2,254,036
Shares Outstanding	59,928	59,902	59,873	59,864	59,689	53,855	53,720	56,870
Statistical Record								
Return on Assets %	1.92	1.81	1.50	1.43	6.64	3.33	5.46	7.21
Return on Equity %	3.49	3.35	2.82	2.48	11.35	6.03	10.02	13.23
EBITDA Margin %	11.81	11.13	11.04	14.36	14.94	27.00	28.19	26.22
Net Margin %	6.40	6.04	5.95	2.64	14.14	7.99	10.56	10.99
Asset Turnover	0.48	0.49	0.49	0.54	0.47	0.42	0.52	0.66
Current Ratio	1.85	2.00	1.92	1.80	1.99	1.80	1.77	1.35
Debt to Equity	0.43	0.48	0.51	0.44	0.32	0.30	0.34	0.27
Price Range	86.19-62.29	88.00-62.29	93.30-62.29	93.30-62.29	73.10-60.05	72.71-45.77	83.90-50.86	123.25-80.32
P/E Ratio	44.89-32.44	48.35-34.23	61.79-41.25	71.22-47.55	13.01-10.69	27.75-17.47	20.41-12.37	25.00-16.29

Address: 55 Waugh Drive, Suite 1000, Houston, TX 77007	Web Site: www.kirbycorp.com	Auditors: KPMG LLP
Telephone: 713-435-1000	Officers: David W. Grzebinski - President, Chief Executive Officer, Interim Chief Financial Officer, Chief Operating Officer, Chief Financial Officer, Executive Vice President William G. Harvey - Executive Vice President, Chief Financial Officer	Transfer Agents: Computershare Trust Company, N.A., Providence, RI
Fax: 713-435-1010		

KKR & CO INC

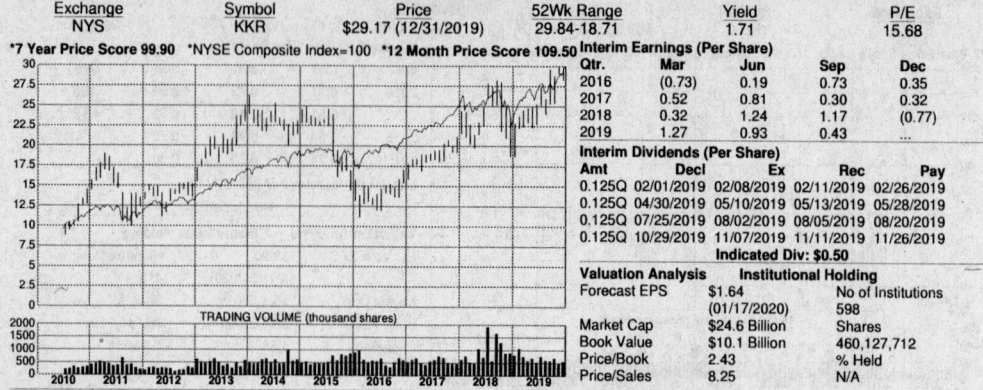

Exchange	Symbol	Price	52Wk Range	Yield	P/E
NYS	KKR	$29.17 (12/31/2019)	29.84-18.71	1.71	15.68

*7 Year Price Score 99.90 *NYSE Composite Index=100 *12 Month Price Score 109.50

Interim Earnings (Per Share)

Qtr.	Mar	Jun	Sep	Dec
2016	(0.73)	0.19	0.73	0.35
2017	0.52	0.81	0.30	0.32
2018	0.32	1.24	1.17	(0.77)
2019	1.27	0.93	0.43	...

Interim Dividends (Per Share)

Amt	Decl	Ex	Rec	Pay
0.125Q	02/01/2019	02/08/2019	02/11/2019	02/26/2019
0.125Q	04/30/2019	05/10/2019	05/13/2019	05/28/2019
0.125Q	07/25/2019	08/02/2019	08/05/2019	08/20/2019
0.125Q	10/29/2019	11/07/2019	11/11/2019	11/26/2019

Indicated Div: $0.50

Valuation Analysis

Forecast EPS	$1.64
	(01/17/2020)
Market Cap	$24.6 Billion
Book Value	$10.1 Billion
Price/Book	2.43
Price/Sales	8.25

Institutional Holding

No of Institutions	598
Shares	460,127,712
% Held	N/A

Business Summary: Finance Intermediaries & Services (MIC: 5.5.1 SIC: 6282 NAIC: 523930)

KKR & Co. is a holding company. Through its subsidiaries, Co. is an investment firm that manages various alternative asset classes including private equity, energy, infrastructure, real estate and credit, with strategic partners that manage hedge funds. Co.'s business lines include: Private Markets, in which Co. manages and sponsors a group of private equity funds that invest capital for long-term appreciation, either through controlling ownership of a company or strategic minority positions; Public Markets, in which Co. operates its combined credit and hedge funds platforms; and Capital Markets, which develops and implements capital solutions for investments or companies seeking financing.

Recent Developments: For the quarter ended Sep 30 2019, net income decreased 75.1% to US$336.6 million from US$1.35 billion in the year-earlier quarter. Revenues were US$790.5 million, down 30.0% from US$1.13 billion the year before. Indirect operating expenses decreased 16.3% to US$619.5 million from US$740.1 million in the equivalent prior-year period.

Prospects: Our evaluation of KKR & Co Inc. as of October 4th, 2019 is the result of our systematic analysis on three basic characteristics: earnings strength, relative valuation, and recent stock price movement. The company has suffered a very negative trend in earnings per share over the past 5 quarters. However, recent analyst estimates for the company have been raised and KKR has posted results that exceeded analysts' expectations. Based on operating earnings yield, the company is undervalued when compared to all of the companies we cover. Share price changes over the past year indicates that KKR will perform in line with the market over the near term.

Financial Data

(US$ in Thousands)	9 Mos	6 Mos	3 Mos	12/31/2018	12/31/2017	12/31/2016	12/31/2015	12/31/2014
Earnings Per Share	1.86	2.60	2.91	2.06	1.95	0.59	1.01	1.16
Cash Flow Per Share	(10.76)	(11.35)	(9.91)	(14.80)	(7.75)	(3.47)	0.86	3.91
Tang Book Value Per Share	11.33	11.04	10.51	9.68	...	...	...	N.M.
Dividends Per Share	0.500	0.545	0.420	0.295	...	...	...	...
Dividend Payout %	26.88	20.96	14.43	14.32	...	...	...	...
Income Statement								
Total Revenue	3,157,829	2,367,344	1,187,480	2,395,836	3,282,265	1,908,093	1,043,768	1,110,008
EBITDA	3,425,735	3,111,384	1,685,216	1,744,045	2,350,847	743,369	4,695,697	4,866,674
Depn & Amortn	...	...	...	7,700	...	...	...	...
Income Before Taxes	3,711,512	3,321,768	1,794,639	2,256,848	2,784,368	975,225	5,341,668	5,458,689
Income Taxes	386,124	332,992	167,593	(194,098)	224,326	24,561	66,636	63,669
Net Income	1,481,607	1,232,053	709,319	1,131,063	1,018,305	309,307	488,482	477,611
Average Shares	559,532	554,643	550,046	533,707	506,288	483,431	482,699	412,049
Balance Sheet								
Current Assets	4,304,914	3,679,552	3,606,936	3,501,334	4,989,487	5,847,564	3,717,047	3,822,265
Total Assets	57,645,049	57,524,065	52,004,019	50,743,375	45,834,719	39,002,897	71,057,759	65,872,745
Current Liabilities	3,440,422	3,178,854	3,047,706	2,600,281	3,810,172	3,221,505	2,676,308	3,174,915
Long-Term Obligations	25,281,202	25,685,785	22,262,369	22,341,192	21,193,859	18,544,075	18,730,017	10,837,784
Total Liabilities	47,527,295	47,648,587	42,681,648	42,093,765	38,648,783	33,063,064	65,510,577	60,473,159
Stockholders' Equity	10,117,754	9,875,478	9,322,371	8,649,610	...	...	...	16,895
Shares Outstanding	842,585	842,585	832,568	833,938	486,174	452,380	457,834	433,330
Statistical Record								
Return on Assets %	2.03	2.82	3.34	2.34	2.40	0.56	0.71	0.81
Return on Equity %	11.47	28.88	33.90	...	...	...	...	...
EBITDA Margin %	108.48	131.43	141.92	72.79	71.62	38.96	449.88	438.44
Net Margin %	46.92	52.04	59.73	47.21	31.02	16.21	46.80	43.03
Asset Turnover	0.06	0.06	0.06	0.05	0.08	0.03	0.02	0.02
Current Ratio	1.25	1.16	1.18	1.35	1.31	1.82	1.39	1.20
Debt to Equity	2.50	2.60	2.39	2.58	...	...	...	641.48
Price Range	29.60-18.68	28.25-18.68	28.25-18.68	28.25-18.68	21.18-15.83	17.13-11.13	24.98-14.45	26.30-19.91
P/E Ratio	15.91-10.04	10.87-7.18	9.71-6.42	13.71-9.07	10.86-8.12	29.03-18.86	24.73-14.31	22.67-17.16
Average Yield %	2.08	2.26	1.78	1.25	...	...	...	...

Address: 9 West 57th Street, Suite 4200, New York, NY 10019
Telephone: 212-750-8300

Web Site: www.kkr.com
Officers: Henry R. Kravis - Co-Chairman, Co-Chief Executive Officer George R. Roberts - Co-Chairman, Co-Chief Executive Officer

Auditors: DELOITTE & TOUCHE LLP
Investor Contact: 877-610-4910
Transfer Agents: American Stock Transfer & Trust Company LLC, Brooklyn, NY

KOHL'S CORP.

Exchange	Symbol	Price	52Wk Range	Yield	P/E
NYS	KSS	$50.95 (12/31/2019)	75.48-44.27	5.26	11.79

*7 Year Price Score 86.79 ***NYSE Composite Index=100** ***12 Month Price Score 84.51**

TRADING VOLUME (thousand shares)

Interim Earnings (Per Share)

Qtr.	Apr	Jul	Oct	Jan
2016-17	0.09	0.77	0.83	1.43
2017-18	0.39	1.24	0.70	2.80
2018-19	0.45	1.76	0.98	1.65
2019-20	0.38	1.51	0.78	...

Interim Dividends (Per Share)

Amt	Decl	Ex	Rec	Pay
0.67Q	02/27/2019	03/19/2019	03/20/2019	04/03/2019
0.67Q	05/15/2019	06/11/2019	06/12/2019	06/26/2019
0.67Q	08/13/2019	09/10/2019	09/11/2019	09/25/2019
0.67Q	11/13/2019	12/10/2019	12/11/2019	12/24/2019
			Indicated Div: $2.68	

Valuation Analysis   **Institutional Holding**

Forecast EPS	$4.76	No of Institutions
	(01/16/2020)	991
Market Cap	$8.0 Billion	Shares
Book Value	$5.4 Billion	200,195,344
Price/Book	1.49	% Held
Price/Sales	0.40	70.22

Business Summary: Retail - General Merchandise/Department Stores (MIC: 2.1.1 SIC: 5311 NAIC: 452111)

Kohl's operates department stores, a website (www.Kohls.com), FILA outlets, and Off-Aisle clearance centers. Co.'s Kohl's stores and website sell proprietary and national brand apparel, footwear, accessories, beauty and home products. Co.'s website includes merchandise that is available in its stores, as well as merchandise that is available only online. Co.'s portfolio includes private brands such as Apt. 9, Croft & Barrow, Jumping Beans, SO and Sonoma Goods for Life and exclusive brands that are developed and marketed through agreements with brands such as Food Network, LC Lauren Conrad, Elle and Simply Vera Vera Wang.

Recent Developments: For the quarter ended Nov 2 2019, net income decreased 23.6% to US$123.0 million from US$161.0 million in the year-earlier quarter. Revenues were US$4.63 billion, unchanged from the year before. Operating income was US$204.0 million versus US$258.0 million in the prior-year quarter, a decrease of 20.9%. Direct operating expenses rose 0.8% to US$2.78 billion from US$2.75 billion in the comparable period the year before. Indirect operating expenses increased 1.7% to US$1.65 billion from US$1.62 billion in the equivalent prior-year period.

Prospects: Our evaluation of Kohl's Corp. as of October 4th, 2019 is the result of our systematic analysis on three basic characteristics: earnings strength, relative valuation, and recent stock price movement. The company has generated a negative trend in earnings per share over the past 5 quarters. In addition, recent analyst estimates for the company have been reduced while KSS has posted results that exceeded analysts' expectations. Based on operating earnings yield, the company is undervalued when compared to all of the companies we cover. Share price changes over the past year indicates that KSS will perform poorly over the near term.

Financial Data
(US$ in Thousands)

	9 Mos	6 Mos	3 Mos	02/02/2019	02/03/2018	01/28/2017	01/30/2016	01/31/2015
Earnings Per Share	4.32	4.52	4.77	4.84	5.12	3.11	3.46	4.24
Cash Flow Per Share	11.08	10.92	11.53	12.88	9.96	12.10	7.66	10.00
Tang Book Value Per Share	34.11	34.28	33.59	33.91	32.30	29.75	29.52	29.81
Dividends Per Share	2.620	2.560	2.500	2.440	2.200	2.000	1.800	1.560
Dividend Payout %	60.65	56.64	52.41	50.41	42.97	64.31	52.02	36.79
Income Statement								
Total Revenue	13,142,000	8,517,000	4,087,000	20,229,000	19,095,000	18,686,000	19,204,000	19,023,000
EBITDA	1,394,000	952,000	348,000	2,262,000	2,407,000	2,121,000	2,318,000	2,575,000
Depn & Amortn	687,000	458,000	230,000	964,000	991,000	938,000	934,000	886,000
Income Before Taxes	550,000	389,000	66,000	1,042,000	1,117,000	875,000	1,057,000	1,349,000
Income Taxes	124,000	86,000	4,000	241,000	258,000	319,000	384,000	482,000
Net Income	426,000	303,000	62,000	801,000	859,000	556,000	673,000	867,000
Average Shares	157,000	159,000	162,000	165,000	168,000	179,000	195,000	204,000
Balance Sheet								
Current Assets	5,781,000	4,678,000	4,635,000	4,835,000	5,331,000	5,247,000	5,076,000	5,698,000
Total Assets	15,739,000	14,542,000	14,466,000	12,469,000	13,340,000	13,574,000	13,606,000	14,431,000
Current Liabilities	4,075,000	2,840,000	2,792,000	2,730,000	2,651,000	2,974,000	2,714,000	2,859,000
Long-Term Obligations	3,188,000	3,125,000	3,080,000	3,384,000	4,388,000	4,480,000	4,581,000	4,651,000
Total Liabilities	10,384,000	9,087,000	9,024,000	6,942,000	7,914,000	8,397,000	8,115,000	8,440,000
Stockholders' Equity	5,355,000	5,455,000	5,442,000	5,527,000	5,426,000	5,177,000	5,491,000	5,991,000
Shares Outstanding	157,000	159,126	162,000	163,000	168,000	174,000	186,000	201,000
Statistical Record								
Return on Assets %	4.68	5.36	5.75	6.22	6.28	4.10	4.81	6.04
Return on Equity %	12.92	13.45	14.58	14.67	15.94	10.45	11.75	14.53
EBITDA Margin %	10.61	11.18	8.51	11.18	12.61	11.35	12.07	13.54
Net Margin %	3.24	3.56	1.52	3.96	4.50	2.98	3.50	4.56
Asset Turnover	1.34	1.45	1.47	1.57	1.40	1.38	1.37	1.32
Current Ratio	1.42	1.65	1.66	1.77	2.01	1.76	1.87	1.99
Debt to Equity	0.60	0.57	0.57	0.61	0.81	0.87	0.83	0.78
Price Range	81.97-44.27	82.05-45.98	82.05-59.40	82.05-58.38	68.83-35.32	59.43-34.49	79.07-42.85	62.50-49.09
P/E Ratio	18.97-10.25	18.15-10.17	17.20-12.45	16.95-12.06	13.44-6.90	19.11-11.09	22.85-12.38	14.74-11.58
Average Yield %	4.40	3.86	3.52	3.51	5.06	4.55	3.05	2.78

Address: N56 W17000 Ridgewood Drive, Menomonee Falls, WI 53051	**Web Site:** www.kohls.com	**Auditors:** Ernst & Young LLP
Telephone: 262-703-7000	**Officers:** Frank V. Sica - Chairman Ratnakar Lavu - Senior Executive Vice President, Chief Technology Officer	**Investor Contact:** 262-703-1440
Fax: 262-703-6373		**Transfer Agents:** Wells Fargo Shareowner Services, St. Paul, MN

KOSMOS ENERGY LTD (DE)

Exchange	Symbol	Price	52Wk Range	Yield	P/E
NYS	KOS	$5.70 (12/31/2019)	7.48-4.07	3.17	13.57

*7 Year Price Score 64.27   *NYSE Composite Index=100   *12 Month Price Score 96.63

Interim Earnings (Per Share)

Qtr.	Mar	Jun	Sep	Dec
2016	(0.15)	(0.28)	(0.15)	(0.15)
2017	(0.07)	(0.02)	(0.16)	(0.31)
2018	(0.13)	(0.26)	(0.31)	0.47
2019	(0.13)	0.04	0.04	...

Interim Dividends (Per Share)

Amt	Decl	Ex	Rec	Pay
0.045Q	02/25/2019	03/06/2019	03/07/2019	03/28/2019
0.045Q	05/06/2019	06/05/2019	06/06/2019	06/27/2019
0.045Q	08/05/2019	09/04/2019	09/05/2019	09/26/2019
0.045Q	11/04/2019	11/29/2019	12/02/2019	12/23/2019

Indicated Div: $0.18

Valuation Analysis / **Institutional Holding**

Forecast EPS	$-0.01	No of Institutions	
	(01/11/2020)	231	
Market Cap	$2.3 Billion	Shares	
Book Value	$891.0 Million	508,904,128	
Price/Book	2.57	% Held	
Price/Sales	1.68	N/A	

Business Summary: Production & Extraction (MIC: 9.1.1 SIC: 1311 NAIC: 211111)

Kosmos Energy is a holding company. Through its subsidiaries, Co. operates as a deepwater independent oil and gas exploration and production company focused along the Atlantic Margins. Co.'s assets include production offshore Ghana, Equatorial Guinea and U.S. Gulf of Mexico, as well as gas development offshore Mauritania and Senegal. Co. also maintains a sustainable exploration program balanced between proven basin infrastructure-led exploration (Equatorial Guinea and U.S. Gulf of Mexico), emerging basins (Mauritania, Senegal and Suriname) and frontier basins (Cote d'Ivoire, Namibia and Sao Tome and Principe).

Recent Developments: For the quarter ended Sep 30 2019, net income amounted to US$16.1 million versus a net loss of US$126.1 million in the year-earlier quarter. Revenues were US$357.0 million, up 42.7% from US$250.2 million the year before. Direct operating expenses rose 73.5% to US$95.5 million from US$55.1 million in the comparable period the year before. Indirect operating expenses decreased 28.4% to US$221.9 million from US$309.8 million in the equivalent prior-year period.

Prospects: Our evaluation of Kosmos Energy Ltd as of October 4th, 2019 is the result of our systematic analysis on three basic characteristics: earnings strength, relative valuation, and recent stock price movement. The company has enjoyed a very positive trend in earnings per share over the past 5 quarters. However, recent analyst estimates for the company have been mixed and KOS has posted results in line with analysts' expectations. Based on operating earnings yield, the company is overvalued when compared to all of the companies we cover. Share price changes over the past year indicates that KOS will perform well over the near term.

Financial Data
(US$ in Thousands)

	9 Mos	6 Mos	3 Mos	12/31/2018	12/31/2017	12/31/2016	12/31/2015	12/31/2014
Earnings Per Share	0.42	0.07	(0.23)	(0.23)	(0.57)	(0.74)	(0.18)	0.72
Cash Flow Per Share	1.42	1.20	0.65	0.64	0.61	0.13	1.15	1.17
Tang Book Value Per Share	2.22	2.20	2.18	2.36	2.30	2.80	3.44	3.46
Dividends Per Share	0.136	0.090	0.045	...	...	...	...	...
Dividend Payout %	32.29	129.14		...	...	...	...	...
Income Statement								
Total Revenue	1,049,694	692,724	296,790	902,369	636,836	385,355	471,556	882,738
EBITDA	522,265	312,909	84,461	293,735	150,892	(118,917)	269,245	812,116
Depn & Amortn	394,100	255,000	111,000	316,300	244,900	131,500	146,600	188,300
Income Before Taxes	27,394	(12,141)	(61,580)	(123,741)	(171,603)	(294,564)	85,436	578,268
Income Taxes	47,398	23,928	(8,674)	43,131	44,937	(10,784)	155,272	298,898
Net Income	(20,004)	(36,069)	(52,906)	(93,991)	(222,792)	(283,780)	(69,836)	279,370
Average Shares	410,992	408,230	401,164	404,585	388,375	385,402	382,610	386,119
Balance Sheet								
Current Assets	550,028	499,714	484,127	509,700	533,602	475,187	734,148	1,010,476
Total Assets	4,468,259	4,465,734	4,501,856	4,088,189	3,192,603	3,341,465	3,203,050	2,972,766
Current Liabilities	472,375	442,649	413,727	384,308	428,730	370,025	456,741	448,771
Long-Term Obligations	2,106,202	2,129,340	2,195,826	2,120,547	1,282,797	1,321,874	860,878	794,269
Total Liabilities	3,577,229	3,581,523	3,625,263	3,146,711	2,295,491	2,260,266	1,877,537	1,633,807
Stockholders' Equity	891,030	884,211	876,593	941,478	897,112	1,081,199	1,325,513	1,338,959
Shares Outstanding	401,494	401,374	401,261	398,651	389,410	386,757	385,090	386,887
Statistical Record								
Return on Assets %	3.76	0.64	N.M.	N.M.	N.M.	N.M.	N.M.	10.51
Return on Equity %	18.13	2.88	N.M.	N.M.	N.M.	N.M.	N.M.	23.97
EBITDA Margin %	49.75	45.17	28.46	32.55	23.69	N.M.	57.10	92.00
Net Margin %	N.M.	N.M.	N.M.	N.M.	N.M.	N.M.	N.M.	31.65
Asset Turnover	0.31	0.34	0.28	0.25	0.19	0.12	0.15	0.33
Current Ratio	1.16	1.13	1.17	1.33	1.24	1.28	1.61	2.25
Debt to Equity	2.36	2.41	2.50	2.25	1.43	1.22	0.65	0.59
Price Range	9.71-3.65	9.71-3.65	9.71-3.65	9.71-3.65	8.53-5.59	7.05-3.50	9.78-4.73	11.23-7.09
P/E Ratio	23.12-8.69	138.71-52.14		...	...	...	...	15.60-9.85
Average Yield %	2.24	1.36	0.66					...

Address: 8176 Park Lane, Dallas, TX 75231	**Web Site:** www.kosmosenergy.com	**Auditors:** Ernst & Young LLP
Telephone: 214-445-9600	**Officers:** Andrew G. Inglis - Chairman, Chief Executive Officer Thomas P. Chambers - Senior Vice President, Chief Financial Officer	**Investor Contact:** 214-445-9669 **Transfer Agents:** Computershare Trust Company, N.A., United States

KROGER CO (THE)

Exchange	Symbol	Price	52Wk Range	Yield	P/E	Div Acheiver
NYS	KR	$28.99 (12/31/2019)	29.80-20.82	2.21	14.72	12 Years

*7 Year Price Score 75.40   *NYSE Composite Index=100   *12 Month Price Score 101.52

TRADING VOLUME (thousand shares)

Interim Earnings (Per Share)

Qtr.	May	Aug	Oct	Jan
2016-17	0.70	0.40	0.41	0.53
2017-18	0.32	0.39	0.44	0.94
2018-19	2.37	0.62	0.39	0.33
2019-20	0.95	0.37	0.32	...

Interim Dividends (Per Share)

Amt	Decl	Ex	Rec	Pay
0.14Q	01/25/2019	02/14/2019	02/15/2019	03/01/2019
0.14Q	03/14/2019	05/14/2019	05/15/2019	06/01/2019
0.16Q	06/27/2019	08/14/2019	08/15/2019	09/01/2019
0.16Q	09/19/2019	11/14/2019	11/15/2019	12/01/2019

Indicated Div: $0.64

Valuation Analysis

		Institutional Holding	
Forecast EPS	$2.19	No of Institutions	1157
	(01/14/2020)		
Market Cap	$23.2 Billion	Shares	845,073,856
Book Value	$8.9 Billion	% Held	71.95
Price/Book	2.61		
Price/Sales	0.19		

Business Summary: Retail - Food & Beverage, Drug & Tobacco (MIC: 2.1.2 SIC: 5411 NAIC: 445110)

Kroger operates as a retailer. Co. also manufacture and process some of the food for sale in its supermarkets. Supermarkets are operated under one of the following formats: combination food and drug stores (combo stores); multi-department stores; marketplace stores; or price impact warehouses. The combo stores provide food and organic sections, pharmacies, general merchandise, pet centers and perishables such as seafood and organic produce. Marketplace provide grocery, pharmacy and health and beauty care departments as well as perishable offering and general merchandise area that includes apparel, home goods and toys.

Recent Developments: For the quarter ended Nov 9 2019, net income decreased 53.6% to US$143.0 million from US$308.0 million in the year-earlier quarter. Revenues were US$27.97 billion, up 0.5% from US$27.83 billion the year before. Operating income was US$254.0 million versus US$647.0 million in the prior-year quarter, a decrease of 60.7%. Direct operating expenses rose 0.2% to US$21.80 billion from US$21.75 billion in the comparable period the year before. Indirect operating expenses increased 9.0% to US$5.92 billion from US$5.43 billion in the equivalent prior-year period.

Prospects: Our evaluation of Kroger Co. as of October 4th, 2019 is the result of our systematic analysis on three basic characteristics: earnings strength, relative valuation, and recent stock price movement. The company has enjoyed a very positive trend in earnings per share over the past 5 quarters. In addition, recent analyst estimates for the company have been raised, and KR has posted results that exceeded analysts' expectations. Based on operating earnings yield, the company is undervalued when compared to all of the companies we cover. Share price changes over the past year indicates that KR will perform poorly over the near term.

Financial Data

(US$ in Thousands)	9 Mos	6 Mos	3 Mos	02/02/2019	02/03/2018	01/28/2017	01/30/2016	01/31/2015
Earnings Per Share	1.97	2.04	2.29	3.76	2.09	2.05	2.06	1.72
Cash Flow Per Share	5.58	5.23	5.09	5.15	3.75	4.55	5.02	4.26
Tang Book Value Per Share	5.93	5.63	5.47	4.44	3.34	2.72	3.15	2.41
Dividends Per Share	0.580	0.580	0.560	0.530	0.490	0.450	0.395	0.340
Dividend Payout %	29.44	28.43	24.45	14.10	23.44	21.95	19.17	19.77
Income Statement								
Total Revenue	93,393,000	65,419,000	37,251,000	121,162,000	122,662,000	115,337,000	109,830,000	108,465,000
EBITDA	4,048,000	3,066,000	1,383,000	7,063,000	4,521,000	5,776,000	5,665,000	5,085,000
Depn & Amortn	1,994,000	1,370,000	197,000	2,465,000	2,436,000	2,340,000	2,089,000	1,948,000
Income Before Taxes	1,591,000	1,369,000	989,000	3,978,000	1,484,000	2,914,000	3,094,000	2,649,000
Income Taxes	398,000	319,000	226,000	900,000	(405,000)	957,000	1,045,000	902,000
Net Income	1,332,000	1,069,000	772,000	3,110,000	1,907,000	1,975,000	2,039,000	1,728,000
Average Shares	807,000	805,000	805,000	818,000	904,000	958,000	980,000	994,000
Balance Sheet								
Current Assets	11,025,000	10,140,000	10,162,000	10,803,000	11,117,000	10,340,000	9,892,000	8,911,000
Total Assets	45,393,000	44,462,000	44,319,000	38,118,000	37,197,000	36,505,000	33,897,000	30,556,000
Current Liabilities	14,118,000	13,350,000	13,575,000	14,274,000	14,197,000	12,860,000	12,971,000	11,403,000
Long-Term Obligations	12,227,000	12,130,000	12,016,000	12,072,000	12,029,000	11,825,000	9,709,000	9,771,000
Total Liabilities	36,478,000	35,751,000	35,738,000	30,232,000	30,266,000	29,807,000	27,077,000	25,144,000
Stockholders' Equity	8,915,000	8,711,000	8,581,000	7,886,000	6,931,000	6,698,000	6,820,000	5,412,000
Shares Outstanding	802,000	802,000	799,000	798,000	870,000	924,000	967,000	974,000
Statistical Record								
Return on Assets %	3.81	4.04	4.59	8.28	5.09	5.63	6.34	5.79
Return on Equity %	19.21	20.45	23.87	42.09	27.53	29.30	33.43	32.10
EBITDA Margin %	4.33	4.69	3.71	5.83	3.69	5.01	5.16	4.69
Net Margin %	1.43	1.63	2.07	2.57	1.55	1.71	1.86	1.59
Asset Turnover	2.91	2.98	2.99	3.23	3.27	3.29	3.42	3.64
Current Ratio	0.78	0.76	0.75	0.76	0.78	0.80	0.76	0.78
Debt to Equity	1.37	1.39	1.40	1.53	1.74	1.77	1.42	1.81
Price Range	31.39-20.82	32.56-20.82	32.56-23.53	32.56-22.98	34.22-19.94	40.65-28.84	42.64-33.66	34.67-17.69
P/E Ratio	15.93-10.57	15.96-10.21	14.22-10.28	8.66-6.11	16.37-9.54	19.83-14.07	20.70-16.34	20.16-10.28
Average Yield %	2.27	2.17	2.01	1.91	1.87	1.30	1.05	1.33

Address: 1014 Vine Street, Cincinnati, OH 45202	**Web Site:** www.thekrogerco.com	**Auditors:** PricewaterhouseCoopers LLP
Telephone: 513-762-4000	**Officers:** W. Rodney McMullen - Chairman, Vice-Chairman, President, Chief Executive Officer, Chief Operating Officer Michael J. Donnelly - Executive Vice President, Executive Vice President (frmr), Senior Vice President, Chief Operating Officer	**Investor Contact:** 513-762-4366
Fax: 513-762-1400		**Transfer Agents:** Wells Fargo Shareowner Services, Saint Paul, MN

LABORATORY CORPORATION OF AMERICA HOLDINGS

Exchange	Symbol	Price	52Wk Range	Yield	P/E
NYS	LH	$169.17 (12/31/2019)	178.10-123.70	N/A	22.23

*7 Year Price Score 100.85 *NYSE Composite Index=100 *12 Month Price Score 99.96

Interim Earnings (Per Share)

Qtr.	Mar	Jun	Sep	Dec
2016	1.55	1.91	1.71	1.77
2017	1.84	1.82	1.74	6.81
2018	1.67	2.27	3.10	1.57
2019	1.86	1.93	2.25	...

Interim Dividends (Per Share)

No Dividends Paid

Valuation Analysis | **Institutional Holding**

Forecast EPS	$11.25	No of Institutions
	(01/16/2020)	1077
Market Cap	$16.5 Billion	Shares
Book Value	$7.2 Billion	118,016,960
Price/Book	2.28	% Held
Price/Sales	1.45	86.06

Business Summary: Diagnostic & Health Related Services (MIC: 4.2.2 SIC: 8071 NAIC: 621511)

Laboratory Corporation of America Holdings is a life sciences company engaged in providing clinical laboratory and end-to-end drug development services. Co. reports its business in two segments: LabCorp Diagnostics, which provides a menu of testing through an integrated network of primary and specialty laboratories across the U.S., supported by an information technology system, logistics, local labs providing testing, and also provides patient access points located throughout the U.S.; and Covance Drug Development, which provides end-to-end drug development, medical device and diagnostic development solutions from early-stage research to clinical development and commercial market access.

Recent Developments: For the quarter ended Sep 30 2019, net income decreased 30.7% to US$221.0 million from US$319.0 million in the year-earlier quarter. Revenues were US$2.93 billion, up 3.4% from US$2.83 billion the year before. Operating income was US$339.9 million versus US$343.4 million in the prior-year quarter, a decrease of 1.0%. Direct operating expenses rose 3.4% to US$2.11 billion from US$2.04 billion in the comparable period the year before. Indirect operating expenses increased 6.9% to US$477.4 million from US$446.5 million in the equivalent prior-year period.

Prospects: Our evaluation of Laboratory Corp. of America Holdings as of October 4th, 2019 is the result of our systematic analysis on three basic characteristics: earnings strength, relative valuation, and recent stock price movement. The company has produced a positive trend in earnings per share over the past 5 quarters. However, recent analyst estimates for the company have been mixed and LH has posted results that exceeded analysts' expectations. Based on operating earnings yield, the company is undervalued when compared to all of the companies we cover. Stock price changes over the past year indicates that LH will perform well over the near term.

Financial Data

(US$ in Thousands)	9 Mos	6 Mos	3 Mos	12/31/2018	12/31/2017	12/31/2016	12/31/2015	12/31/2014
Earnings Per Share	7.61	8.46	8.80	8.61	12.21	7.02	4.34	5.91
Cash Flow Per Share	13.95	12.26	13.35	12.87	14.25	11.44	9.94	8.71
Income Statement								
Total Revenue	8,601,400	5,672,900	2,791,200	11,333,400	10,441,400	9,641,800	8,680,100	6,011,600
EBITDA	1,401,800	912,100	369,600	1,812,400	1,665,500	1,627,800	1,266,900	1,079,500
Depn & Amortn	421,400	277,100	61,200	311,500	306,800	311,100	269,900	157,600
Income Before Taxes	804,100	519,200	251,700	1,256,700	1,123,600	1,097,600	722,100	812,400
Income Taxes	214,400	148,100	68,800	384,400	(139,100)	372,300	294,100	314,100
Net Income	596,700	376,000	185,600	883,700	1,268,200	732,100	436,900	511,200
Average Shares	98,300	98,800	99,500	102,600	103,900	104,300	100,600	86,400
Balance Sheet								
Current Assets	2,987,800	2,848,600	2,885,300	2,835,400	2,682,600	2,478,700	2,663,000	1,692,700
Total Assets	17,847,800	17,744,400	16,970,800	16,185,300	16,568,000	14,247,000	14,221,700	7,301,800
Current Liabilities	2,554,900	2,495,800	2,526,900	1,878,900	2,046,100	1,827,600	1,701,500	976,300
Long-Term Obligations	6,194,100	6,181,200	5,544,300	6,041,900	6,344,600	5,300,000	5,992,100	2,682,700
Total Liabilities	10,616,700	10,600,000	9,859,500	9,213,900	9,738,000	8,741,200	9,277,300	4,481,300
Stockholders' Equity	7,231,100	7,144,400	7,111,300	6,971,400	6,830,000	5,505,800	4,944,400	2,820,500
Shares Outstanding	97,400	97,800	98,700	98,900	101,900	102,700	101,300	84,600
Statistical Record								
Return on Assets %	4.37	4.98	5.30	5.40	8.23	5.13	4.06	7.17
Return on Equity %	10.42	12.03	12.71	12.81	20.56	13.97	11.25	19.25
EBITDA Margin %	16.30	16.08	13.24	15.99	15.95	16.88	14.60	17.96
Net Margin %	6.94	6.63	6.65	7.80	12.15	7.59	5.03	8.50
Asset Turnover	0.66	0.66	0.67	0.69	0.68	0.68	0.81	0.84
Current Ratio	1.17	1.14	1.14	1.51	1.31	1.36	1.57	1.73
Debt to Equity	0.86	0.87	0.78	0.87	0.93	0.96	1.21	0.95
Price Range	178.10-120.82	188.27-120.82	189.41-120.82	189.41-120.82	163.95-129.07	140.98-100.94	128.18-106.86	109.58-87.86
P/E Ratio	23.40-15.88	22.25-14.28	21.52-13.73	22.00-14.03	13.43-10.57	20.08-14.38	29.53-24.62	18.54-14.87

Address: 358 South Main Street, Burlington, NC 27215 **Telephone:** 336-229-1127	**Web Site:** www.labcorp.com **Officers:** David P. King - Executive Chairman, Chairman, President, Chief Executive Officer Adam H. Schechter - President, Chief Executive Officer	**Auditors:** PricewaterhouseCoopers LLP **Investor Contact:** 336-436-5076 **Transfer Agents:** American Stock Transfer & Trust Company, Brooklyn, NY

L BRANDS, INC

Exchange	Symbol	Price	52Wk Range	Yield	P/E
NYS	LB	$18.12 (12/31/2019)	28.87-15.86	6.62	13.83

*7 Year Price Score 33.62   *NYSE Composite Index=100   *12 Month Price Score 73.87

Interim Earnings (Per Share)

Qtr.	Apr	Jul	Oct	Jan
2016-17	0.52	0.87	0.42	2.17
2017-18	0.33	0.48	0.30	2.31
2018-19	0.17	0.36	(0.16)	1.94
2019-20	0.14	0.14	(0.91)	...

Interim Dividends (Per Share)

Amt	Decl	Ex	Rec	Pay
0.30Q	02/07/2019	02/21/2019	02/22/2019	03/08/2019
0.30Q	05/17/2019	05/30/2019	05/31/2019	06/14/2019
0.30Q	08/09/2019	08/22/2019	08/23/2019	09/06/2019
0.30Q	11/08/2019	11/21/2019	11/22/2019	12/06/2019

Indicated Div: $1.20 (Div. Reinv. Plan)

Valuation Analysis

		Institutional Holding	
Forecast EPS	$2.26	No of Institutions	699
	(01/17/2020)		
Market Cap	$5.0 Billion	Shares	
Book Value	N/A		243,835,952
Price/Book	N/A	% Held	
Price/Sales	0.38	N/A	

Business Summary: Retail - Apparel and Accessories (MIC: 2.1.5 SIC: 5621 NAIC: 448120)

L Brands is a holding company. Through its subsidiaries, Co. is a specialty retailer of women's intimate and other apparel, personal care, beauty and home fragrance products. Co. sells its merchandise through company-owned specialty retail stores in the U.S., Canada, the U.K., Ireland and Greater China, and through its websites and other channels. Co.'s other international operations are primarily through franchise, license and wholesale partners. Co. has three reportable segments: Victoria's Secret, Bath & Body Works and Victoria's Secret and Bath & Body Works International. Co. operates the following retail brands: Victoria's Secret, PINK and Bath & Body Works.

Recent Developments: For the quarter ended Nov 2 2019, net loss amounted to US$252.0 million versus a net loss of US$43.0 million in the year-earlier quarter. Revenues were US$2.68 billion, down 3.5% from US$2.78 billion the year before. Operating loss was US$151.0 million versus an income of US$54.0 million in the prior-year quarter. Direct operating expenses rose 4.8% to US$1.94 billion from US$1.85 billion in the comparable period the year before. Indirect operating expenses increased 2.1% to US$892.0 million from US$874.0 million in the equivalent prior-year period.

Prospects: Our evaluation of L Brands, Inc. as of October 4th, 2019 is the result of our systematic analysis on three basic characteristics: earnings strength, relative valuation, and recent stock price movement. The company has managed to produce a neutral trend in earnings per share over the past 5 quarters. However, recent analyst estimates for the company have been reduced while LB has posted results that exceeded analysts' expectations. Based on operating earnings yield, the company is undervalued when compared to all of the companies we cover. Share price changes over the past year indicates that LB will perform very poorly over the near term.

Financial Data

(US$ in Thousands)	9 Mos	6 Mos	3 Mos	02/02/2019	02/03/2018	01/28/2017	01/30/2016	01/31/2015
Earnings Per Share	1.31	2.06	2.28	2.31	3.42	3.98	4.22	3.50
Cash Flow Per Share	4.62	4.81	5.01	5.00	4.87	6.60	6.44	6.13
Dividends Per Share	1.500	1.800	2.100	2.400	2.400	4.400	4.000	2.360
Dividend Payout %	114.50	87.38	92.11	103.90	70.18	110.55	94.79	67.43
Income Statement								
Total Revenue	8,207,000	5,530,000	2,629,000	13,237,000	12,632,000	12,574,000	12,154,000	11,454,000
EBITDA	554,000	592,000	304,000	1,832,000	2,289,000	2,608,000	2,725,000	2,398,000
Depn & Amortn	443,000	295,000	145,000	590,000	571,000	518,000	457,000	438,000
Income Before Taxes	(175,000)	103,000	60,000	857,000	1,312,000	1,696,000	1,934,000	1,636,000
Income Taxes	(1,000)	25,000	20,000	213,000	329,000	538,000	681,000	594,000
Net Income	(174,000)	78,000	40,000	644,000	983,000	1,158,000	1,253,000	1,042,000
Average Shares	276,000	278,000	278,000	279,000	287,000	291,000	297,000	298,000
Balance Sheet								
Current Assets	2,926,000	2,653,000	2,947,000	3,260,000	3,293,000	3,465,000	4,156,000	3,232,000
Total Assets	10,630,000	10,618,000	10,998,000	8,090,000	8,149,000	8,170,000	8,493,000	7,544,000
Current Liabilities	2,543,000	2,216,000	2,197,000	1,986,000	2,031,000	2,014,000	1,875,000	1,679,000
Long-Term Obligations	5,477,000	5,475,000	5,749,000	5,739,000	5,707,000	5,700,000	5,715,000	4,765,000
Total Liabilities	11,872,000	11,551,000	11,900,000	8,959,000	8,902,000	8,899,000	8,752,000	7,526,000
Stockholders' Equity	(1,242,000)	(933,000)	(902,000)	(869,000)	(753,000)	(729,000)	(259,000)	18,000
Shares Outstanding	276,000	276,275	276,000	275,000	280,000	286,000	290,000	292,000
Statistical Record								
Return on Assets %	3.97	6.31	6.79	7.95	11.85	13.94	15.67	14.18
EBITDA Margin %	6.75	10.71	11.56	13.84	18.12	20.74	22.42	20.94
Net Margin %	N.M.	1.41	1.52	4.87	7.78	9.21	10.31	9.10
Asset Turnover	1.42	1.44	1.41	1.63	1.52	1.51	1.52	1.56
Current Ratio	1.15	1.20	1.34	1.64	1.62	1.72	2.22	1.54
Debt to Equity	...	...	...	...	...	...	...	264.72
Price Range	37.02-15.86	37.02-21.50	37.81-24.59	49.87-24.59	62.95-36.06	96.56-59.01	100.22-77.87	87.05-50.87
P/E Ratio	28.26-12.11	17.97-10.44	16.58-10.79	21.59-10.65	18.41-10.54	24.26-14.83	23.75-18.45	24.87-14.53
Average Yield %	6.02	6.48	6.92	7.08	4.92	5.98	4.41	3.63

Address: Three Limited Parkway, Columbus, OH 43230 **Telephone:** 614-415-7000	**Web Site:** www.lb.com **Officers:** Leslie H. Wexner - Chairman, Chief Executive Officer Stuart B. Burgdoerfer - Executive Vice President, Chief Financial Officer	**Auditors:** Ernst & Young LLP **Investor Contact:** 614-415-6400 **Transfer Agents:** American Stock Transfer & Trust Company, Brookly, NY

LAREDO PETROLEUM, INC

Exchange	Symbol	Price	52Wk Range	Yield	P/E
NYS	LPI	$2.87 (12/31/2019)	4.19-2.08	N/A	13.67

*7 Year Price Score 18.42 *NYSE Composite Index=100 *12 Month Price Score 78.90

Interim Earnings (Per Share)

Qtr.	Mar	Jun	Sep	Dec
2016	(0.85)	(0.33)	0.04	(0.07)
2017	0.28	0.25	0.05	1.72
2018	0.36	0.14	0.24	0.64
2019	(0.04)	0.75	(1.14)	...

Interim Dividends (Per Share)

No Dividends Paid

Valuation Analysis

		Institutional Holding	
Forecast EPS	$0.76	No of Institutions	
	(00/25/2020)	252	
Market Cap	$682.1 Million	Shares	
Book Value	$1.1 Billion	331,386,176	
Price/Book	0.63	% Held	
Price/Sales	0.82	98.18	

TRADING VOLUME (thousand shares)

Business Summary: Production & Extraction (MIC: 9.1.1 SIC: 1311 NAIC: 211111)

Laredo Petroleum is an independent energy company focused on the acquisition, exploration and development of oil and natural gas properties, and midstream and marketing services, primarily in the Permian Basin of West Texas. The Permian Basin is comprised of several distinct geological provinces, including the Midland Basin to the east, the Delaware Basin to the west and the Central Platform in the middle. Co.'s primary development and production fairway is located on the east side of the Midland Basin, 35 miles east of Midland, TX. Co.'s acreage is contiguous in the neighboring Texas counties of Howard, Glasscock, Reagan, Sterling and Irion.

Recent Developments: For the quarter ended Sep 30 2019, net loss amounted to US$264.6 million versus net income of US$55.1 million in the year-earlier quarter. Revenues were US$193.6 million, down 30.8% from US$279.7 million the year before. Operating loss was US$350.4 million versus an income of US$104.4 million in the prior-year quarter. Direct operating expenses declined 35.5% to US$61.2 million from US$94.9 million in the comparable period the year before. Indirect operating expenses increased 500.0% to US$482.8 million from US$80.5 million in the equivalent prior-year period.

Prospects: Our evaluation of Laredo Petroleum, Inc. as of October 4th, 2019 is the result of our systematic analysis on three basic characteristics: earnings strength, relative valuation, and recent stock price movement. The company has generated a negative trend in earnings per share over the past 5 quarters. However, recent analyst estimates for the company have been raised and LPI has posted results that exceeded analysts' expectations. Based on operating earnings yield, the company is undervalued when compared to all of the companies we cover. Share price changes over the past year indicates that LPI will perform in line with the market over the near term.

Financial Data
(US$ in Thousands)

	9 Mos	6 Mos	3 Mos	12/31/2018	12/31/2017	12/31/2016	12/31/2015	12/31/2014
Earnings Per Share	0.21	1.59	0.98	1.39	2.29	(1.16)	(11.10)	1.85
Cash Flow Per Share	2.14	2.32	2.03	2.31	1.61	1.58	1.59	3.53
Tang Book Value Per Share	4.54	5.66	4.90	5.02	3.16	0.75	0.61	10.88
Income Statement								
Total Revenue	619,159	425,590	208,947	1,105,775	822,162	597,378	606,640	793,885
EBITDA	(42,925)	204,860	9,862	392,848	636,761	(171,119)	(2,284,387)	556,030
Depn & Amortn	12,122	8,002	3,902	6,100	5,900	5,900	6,500	5,100
Income Before Taxes	(101,550)	165,546	(9,587)	328,844	542,289	(270,142)	(2,393,680)	430,051
Income Taxes	(812)	1,655	(96)	4,249	1,800	...	(176,945)	164,286
Net Income	(100,738)	163,891	(9,491)	324,595	548,974	(260,739)	(2,209,936)	265,573
Average Shares	231,562	231,557	230,476	233,172	240,122	225,512	199,158	143,554
Balance Sheet								
Current Assets	224,732	192,515	172,730	192,752	235,382	154,777	332,232	365,253
Total Assets	2,277,651	2,619,922	2,514,789	2,420,305	2,023,289	1,782,346	1,813,287	3,932,549
Current Liabilities	145,817	170,678	203,622	200,465	277,419	187,945	216,815	425,025
Long-Term Obligations	979,972	1,029,526	1,064,081	983,636	791,855	1,353,909	1,416,226	1,801,295
Total Liabilities	1,198,399	1,275,601	1,343,357	1,246,075	1,257,710	1,601,773	1,681,840	2,369,348
Stockholders' Equity	1,079,252	1,344,321	1,171,432	1,174,230	765,579	180,573	131,447	1,563,201
Shares Outstanding	237,673	237,479	239,191	233,936	242,521	241,929	213,808	143,686
Statistical Record								
Return on Assets %	2.12	15.26	9.93	14.61	28.85	N.M.	N.M.	8.10
Return on Equity %	4.66	32.00	21.63	33.47	116.04	N.M.	N.M.	18.73
EBITDA Margin %	N.M.	48.14	4.72	35.53	77.45	N.M.	N.M.	70.04
Net Margin %	N.M.	38.51	N.M.	29.35	66.77	N.M.	N.M.	33.45
Asset Turnover	0.36	0.38	0.46	0.50	0.43	0.33	0.21	0.24
Current Ratio	1.54	1.13	0.85	0.96	0.85	0.82	1.53	0.86
Debt to Equity	0.91	0.77	0.91	0.84	1.03	7.50	10.77	1.15
Price Range	7.85-2.41	10.15-2.43	11.00-2.83	11.52-3.04	15.21-9.49	15.99-4.10	15.80-7.05	30.98-7.39
P/E Ratio	37.38-11.48	6.38-1.53	11.22-2.89	8.29-2.19	6.64-4.14	...	...	16.75-3.99

Address: 15 W. Sixth Street, Suite 900, Tulsa, OK 74119
Telephone: 918-513-4570

Web Site: www.laredopetro.com
Officers: Randy A. Foutch - Chairman, Chief Executive Officer Mikell Jason Pigott - President, Chief Executive Officer

Auditors: Grant Thornton LLP
Investor Contact: 918-858-5504
Transfer Agents: American Stock Transfer and Trust Company, Brooklyn, NY

LAS VEGAS SANDS CORP

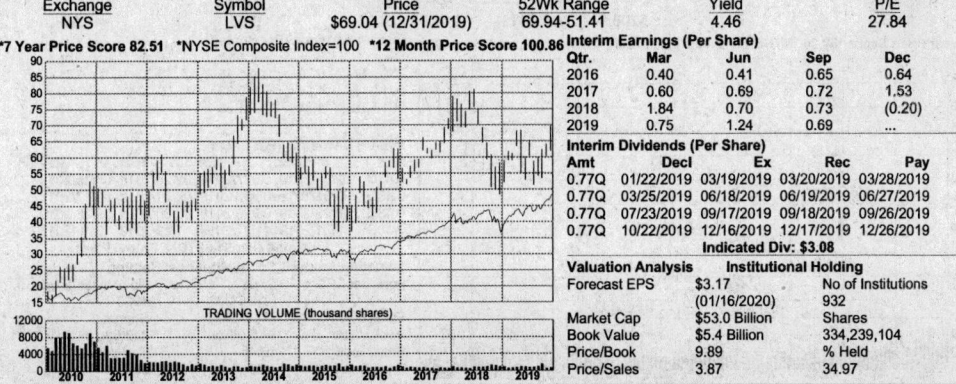

Exchange	Symbol	Price	52Wk Range	Yield	P/E
NYS	LVS	$69.04 (12/31/2019)	69.94-51.41	4.46	27.84

*7 Year Price Score 82.51   ***NYSE Composite Index=100**   ***12 Month Price Score 100.86**

Interim Earnings (Per Share)

Qtr.	Mar	Jun	Sep	Dec
2016	0.40	0.41	0.65	0.64
2017	0.60	0.69	0.72	1.53
2018	1.84	0.70	0.73	(0.20)
2019	0.75	1.24	0.69	...

Interim Dividends (Per Share)

Amt	Decl	Ex	Rec	Pay
0.77Q	01/22/2019	03/19/2019	03/20/2019	03/28/2019
0.77Q	03/25/2019	06/18/2019	06/19/2019	06/27/2019
0.77Q	07/23/2019	09/17/2019	09/18/2019	09/26/2019
0.77Q	10/22/2019	12/16/2019	12/17/2019	12/26/2019

Indicated Div: $3.08

Valuation Analysis / Institutional Holding

Forecast EPS	$3.17	No of Institutions
(01/16/2020)		932
Market Cap	$53.0 Billion	Shares
Book Value	$5.4 Billion	334,239,104
Price/Book	9.89	% Held
Price/Sales	3.87	34.97

Business Summary: Hotels, Restaurants & Travel (MIC: 2.2.1 SIC: 7011 NAIC: 721120)

Las Vegas Sands is a developer of destination properties (integrated resorts) that feature accommodations, gaming, entertainment and retail, convention and exhibition facilities, restaurants and other amenities. Co. owns and operates integrated resorts in Asia and the U.S. Through its ownership of Sands China Ltd., Co. owns and operates properties including The Venetian Macao Resort Hotel, Sands Cotai Central, The Parisian Macao and Four Seasons Hotel Macao, Cotai Strip and the Sands Macao. In Singapore, Co. owns and operates the Marina Bay Sands. Co.'s Las Vegas operating properties is an integrated resort that includes The Venetian Resort Las Vegas and the Sands Expo Center.

Recent Developments: For the quarter ended Sep 30 2019, net income decreased 4.3% to US$669.0 million in US$699.0 million in the year-earlier quarter. Revenues were US$3.25 billion, down 3.6% from US$3.37 billion the year before. Operating income was US$899.0 million versus US$922.0 million in the prior-year quarter, a decrease of 2.5%. Direct operating expenses declined 7.0% to US$1.60 billion from US$1.72 billion in the comparable period the year before. Indirect operating expenses increased 2.9% to US$749.0 million from US$728.0 million in the equivalent prior-year period.

Prospects: Our evaluation of Las Vegas Sands Corp. as of October 4th, 2019 is the result of our systematic analysis on three basic characteristics: earnings strength, relative valuation, and recent stock price movement. The company has enjoyed a very positive trend in earnings per share over the past 5 quarters. However, recent analyst estimates for the company have been mixed and LVS has posted results that fell short of analysts' expectations. Based on operating earnings yield, the company is undervalued when compared to all of the companies we cover. Share price changes over the past year indicates that LVS will perform in line with the market over the near term.

Financial Data

(US$ in Thousands)	9 Mos	6 Mos	3 Mos	12/31/2018	12/31/2017	12/31/2016	12/31/2015	12/31/2014
Earnings Per Share	2.48	2.52	1.98	3.07	3.54	2.10	2.47	3.52
Cash Flow Per Share	4.03	4.01	5.33	5.98	5.74	5.07	4.33	6.00
Tang Book Value Per Share	6.92	7.15	7.06	7.24	8.11	7.64	8.49	8.93
Dividends Per Share	3.060	3.040	3.020	3.000	2.920	2.880	2.600	2.000
Dividend Payout %	123.39	120.63	152.53	97.72	82.49	137.14	105.26	56.82
Income Statement								
Total Revenue	10,230,000	6,980,000	3,646,000	13,729,000	12,882,000	11,410,000	11,688,461	14,583,849
EBITDA	3,345,000	2,456,000	966,000	4,889,000	4,609,000	3,708,000	3,949,486	5,200,486
Depn & Amortn	57,000	36,000	16,000	1,176,000	1,246,000	1,189,000	1,077,469	1,119,237
Income Before Taxes	2,924,000	2,173,000	829,000	3,326,000	3,052,000	2,255,000	2,621,882	3,832,711
Income Taxes	403,000	321,000	85,000	375,000	(209,000)	239,000	236,185	244,640
Net Income	2,069,000	1,536,000	582,000	2,413,000	2,806,000	1,670,000	1,966,236	2,840,629
Average Shares	769,000	772,000	775,000	786,000	792,000	795,000	797,596	808,019
Balance Sheet								
Current Assets	4,808,000	4,957,000	5,055,000	5,566,000	3,207,000	3,098,000	3,609,250	5,190,499
Total Assets	22,427,000	22,594,000	22,313,000	22,547,000	20,687,000	20,469,000	20,987,421	22,361,691
Current Liabilities	3,004,000	3,031,000	2,917,000	3,157,000	2,948,000	2,806,000	2,464,135	2,712,494
Long-Term Obligations	11,877,000	11,909,000	11,888,000	11,874,000	9,344,000	9,428,000	9,372,645	9,892,913
Total Liabilities	17,068,000	17,034,000	16,788,000	16,863,000	14,194,000	14,292,000	14,170,680	15,148,105
Stockholders' Equity	5,359,000	5,560,000	5,525,000	5,684,000	6,493,000	6,177,000	6,816,741	7,213,586
Shares Outstanding	768,000	770,000	773,000	775,463	789,484	794,960	794,645	798,258
Statistical Record								
Return on Assets %	8.30	8.52	7.02	11.16	13.64	8.03	9.07	12.60
Return on Equity %	31.08	30.46	23.88	39.63	44.29	25.63	28.03	38.18
EBITDA Margin %	32.70	35.19	26.49	35.61	35.78	32.50	33.79	35.66
Net Margin %	20.22	22.01	15.96	17.58	21.78	14.64	16.82	19.48
Asset Turnover	0.60	0.61	0.63	0.64	0.63	0.55	0.54	0.65
Current Ratio	1.60	1.64	1.73	1.76	1.09	1.10	1.46	1.91
Debt to Equity	2.22	2.14	2.15	2.09	1.44	1.53	1.37	1.37
Price Range	68.44-48.44	75.12-48.44	81.27-48.44	81.27-48.44	71.97-51.69	62.84-36.97	60.56-36.98	87.81-52.31
P/E Ratio	27.60-19.53	29.81-19.22	41.05-24.46	26.47-15.78	20.33-14.60	29.92-17.60	24.52-14.97	24.95-14.86
Average Yield %	5.25	5.02	4.70	4.43	4.80	5.69	5.08	2.81

Address: 3355 Las Vegas Boulevard South, Las Vegas, NV 89109 Telephone: 702-414-1000	Web Site: www.sands.com Officers: Sheldon G. Adelson - Chairman, Chief Executive Officer, Treasurer Robert G. Goldstein - President, Chief Operating Officer, Executive Vice President	Auditors: DELOITTE & TOUCHE LLP Transfer Agents: American Stock Transfer & Trust Company, New York, NY

LAUDER (ESTEE) COS., INC. (THE)

Exchange	Symbol	Price	52Wk Range	Yield	P/E
NYS	EL	$206.54 (12/31/2019)	207.95-124.91	0.93	40.50

*7 Year Price Score 139.25 ***NYSE Composite Index=100** ***12 Month Price Score 105.14**

Interim Earnings (Per Share)

Qtr.	Sep	Dec	Mar	Jun
2016-17	0.79	1.15	0.80	0.61
2017-18	1.14	0.33	0.99	0.50
2018-19	1.34	1.55	1.51	0.43
2019-20	1.61	...	...	...

Interim Dividends (Per Share)

Amt	Decl	Ex	Rec	Pay
0.43Q	02/04/2019	02/27/2019	02/28/2019	03/15/2019
0.43Q	05/01/2019	05/30/2019	05/31/2019	06/17/2019
0.43Q	08/19/2019	08/29/2019	08/30/2019	09/16/2019
0.48Q	10/31/2019	11/27/2019	11/29/2019	12/16/2019

Indicated Div: $1.92 (Div. Reinv. Plan)

Valuation Analysis / Institutional Holding

Forecast EPS	$5.98 (01/17/2020)	No of Institutions	1263
Market Cap	$74.5 Billion	Shares	247,839,344
Book Value	$4.5 Billion	% Held	53.89
Price/Book	16.45		
Price/Sales	4.89		

Business Summary: Household & Personal Products (MIC: 1.7.1 SIC: 2844 NAIC: 325620)

Estee Lauder Companies is a manufacturer and marketer of skin care, makeup, fragrance and hair care products. Co.'s products are sold under a number of brand names including: Estee Lauder, Clinique, Origins, MzAzC, Bobbi Brown, La Mer, Jo Malone London, Aveda and Too Faced. Co. is also the global licensee for fragrances, cosmetics and/or related products sold under various designer brand names. Co.'s products include skin care, makeup and related items such as compacts, brushes and other makeup tools, fragrance sold in various forms, hair care, and other ancillary products and services.

Recent Developments: For the quarter ended Sep 30 2019, net income increased 19.1% to US$598.0 million from US$502.0 million in the year-earlier quarter. Revenues were US$3.90 billion, up 10.5% from US$3.52 billion the year before. Operating income was US$779.0 million versus US$652.0 million in the prior-year quarter, an increase of 19.5%. Direct operating expenses rose 10.3% to US$908.0 million from US$823.0 million in the comparable period the year before. Indirect operating expenses increased 7.8% to US$2.21 billion from US$2.05 billion in the equivalent prior-year period.

Prospects: Our evaluation of Lauder (Estee) Cos. Inc. as of October 4th, 2019 is the result of our systematic analysis on three basic characteristics: earnings strength, relative valuation, and recent stock price movement. The company has managed to produce a neutral trend in earnings per share over the past 5 quarters. Additionally, recent analyst estimates for the company have been unchanged while EL has posted results that exceeded analysts' expectations. Based on operating earnings yield, the company is fairly valued when compared to all of the companies we cover. Share price changes over the past year indicates that EL will perform over the near term.

Financial Data

(US$ in Thousands)	3 Mos	06/30/2019	06/30/2018	06/30/2017	06/30/2016	06/30/2015	06/30/2014	06/30/2013
Earnings Per Share	5.10	4.82	2.95	3.35	2.96	2.82	3.06	2.58
Cash Flow Per Share	6.82	6.92	6.99	4.90	4.82	5.12	3.98	3.16
Tang Book Value Per Share	4.08	3.64	4.05	3.10	5.44	5.79	7.32	5.76
Dividends Per Share	1.720	1.670	1.480	1.320	1.140	0.920	0.780	1.080
Dividend Payout %	33.73	34.65	50.17	39.40	38.51	32.62	25.49	41.86
Income Statement								
Total Revenue	3,895,000	14,863,000	13,683,000	11,824,000	11,262,300	10,780,400	10,968,800	10,181,700
EBITDA	903,000	2,877,000	2,521,000	2,120,000	2,011,500	2,006,300	2,205,700	1,878,900
Depn & Amortn	125,000	495,000	469,000	428,000	401,200	400,000	378,100	329,800
Income Before Taxes	760,000	2,307,000	1,980,000	1,617,000	1,555,200	1,560,600	1,776,800	1,475,200
Income Taxes	162,000	513,000	863,000	361,000	434,400	467,200	567,700	451,400
Net Income	595,000	1,785,000	1,108,000	1,249,000	1,114,600	1,088,900	1,204,100	1,019,800
Average Shares	368,600	370,400	375,700	373,000	376,600	385,700	393,100	394,900
Balance Sheet								
Current Assets	7,022,000	7,212,000	6,168,000	4,964,000	4,225,100	4,468,500	4,825,200	4,297,200
Total Assets	15,431,000	13,156,000	12,567,000	11,568,000	9,223,300	8,239,200	7,868,800	7,145,200
Current Liabilities	4,590,000	4,605,000	3,310,000	2,823,000	2,680,500	2,135,600	2,056,700	1,934,600
Long-Term Obligations	2,895,000	2,896,000	3,361,000	3,383,000	1,910,000	1,607,500	1,324,700	1,326,000
Total Liabilities	10,901,000	8,770,000	7,879,000	7,184,000	5,651,400	4,596,000	4,013,900	3,858,300
Stockholders' Equity	4,530,000	4,386,000	4,688,000	4,384,000	3,571,900	3,643,200	3,854,900	3,286,900
Shares Outstanding	360,702	361,102	367,145	368,103	367,759	374,882	382,884	387,994
Statistical Record								
Return on Assets %	13.44	13.88	9.18	12.01	12.73	13.52	16.04	14.85
Return on Equity %	42.08	39.34	24.43	31.40	30.81	29.04	33.72	33.88
EBITDA Margin %	23.18	19.36	18.42	17.93	17.86	18.61	20.11	18.45
Net Margin %	15.28	12.01	8.10	10.56	9.90	10.10	10.98	10.02
Asset Turnover	1.09	1.16	1.13	1.14	1.29	1.34	1.46	1.48
Current Ratio	1.53	1.57	1.86	1.76	1.58	2.09	2.35	2.22
Debt to Equity	0.64	0.66	0.72	0.77	0.53	0.44	0.34	0.40
Price Range	207.03-122.46	183.95-122.46	158.03-93.86	98.19-75.84	97.13-75.73	90.22-70.40	76.77-64.71	71.80-50.56
P/E Ratio	40.59-24.01	38.16-25.41	53.57-31.82	29.31-22.64	32.81-25.58	31.99-24.96	25.09-21.15	27.83-19.60
Average Yield %	1.07		1.04	1.52	1.30	1.17	1.10	1.73

Address: 767 Fifth Avenue, New York, NY 10153	**Web Site:** www.elcompanies.com	**Auditors:** KPMG LLP
Telephone: 212-572-4200	**Officers:** William P. Lauder - Executive Chairman Leonard A. Lauder - Chairman Emeritus, Chairman	**Investor Contact:** 800-308-2334 **Transfer Agents:** Computershare, Providence, RI

414

LAZARD LTD

Exchange	Symbol	Price	52Wk Range	Yield	P/E	Div Acheiver
NYS	LAZ	$39.96 (12/31/2019)	41.16-31.16	4.70	15.08	11 Years

7 Year Price Score 70.24 **NYSE Composite Index=100** **12 Month Price Score 98.79**

Interim Earnings (Per Share)

Qtr.	Mar	Jun	Sep	Dec
2016	0.50	0.61	0.85	0.96
2017	0.81	0.91	0.82	(0.64)
2018	1.21	1.13	0.82	0.90
2019	0.80	0.55	0.40	...

Interim Dividends (Per Share)

Amt	Decl	Ex	Rec	Pay
0.44Q	02/04/2019	02/14/2019	02/15/2019	03/01/2019
0.47Q	04/24/2019	05/03/2019	05/06/2019	05/17/2019
0.47Q	07/24/2019	08/02/2019	08/05/2019	08/16/2019
0.47Q	10/30/2019	11/07/2019	11/11/2019	11/22/2019

Indicated Div: $1.88

Valuation Analysis / Institutional Holding

Forecast EPS	N/A	No of Institutions 406
Market Cap	$4.2 Billion	Shares
Book Value	$613.4 Million	100,013,560
Price/Book	6.89	% Held
Price/Sales	1.61	69.30

TRADING VOLUME (thousand shares)

Business Summary: Finance Intermediaries & Services (MIC: 5.5.1 SIC: 6282 NAIC: 523930)

Lazard is a financial advisory and asset management firm. Co. focuses primarily on two business segments: Financial Advisory, which provides a range of financial advisory services regarding mergers and acquisitions and other strategic matters, restructurings, capital structure, capital raising, shareholder advisory and various other financial matters; and Asset Management, which provides a range of global investment solutions and investment management services in equity and fixed income strategies, alternative investments and private equity funds to corporations, public funds, sovereign entities, endowments and foundations, labor funds, financial intermediaries and private clients.

Recent Developments: For the quarter ended Sep 30 2019, net income decreased 55.7% to US$48.2 million from US$108.7 million in the year-earlier quarter. Revenues were US$611.1 million, down 4.6% from US$640.8 million the year before. Operating income was US$52.4 million versus US$138.7 million in the prior-year quarter, a decrease of 62.2%. Direct operating expenses rose 39.7% to US$20.0 million from US$14.3 million in the comparable period the year before. Indirect operating expenses increased 10.4% to US$538.7 million from US$487.8 million in the equivalent prior-year period.

Prospects: Our evaluation of Lazard Ltd. as of October 4th, 2019 is the result of our systematic analysis on three basic characteristics: earnings strength, relative valuation, and recent stock price movement. The company has produced a positive trend in earnings per share over the past 5 quarters. However, recent analyst estimates for the company have been reduced, while LAZ has posted results that exceeded analysts' expectations. Based on operating earnings yield, the company is undervalued when compared to all of the companies we cover. Share price changes over the past year indicates that LAZ will perform poorly over the near term.

Financial Data

(US$ in Thousands)	9 Mos	6 Mos	3 Mos	12/31/2018	12/31/2017	12/31/2016	12/31/2015	12/31/2014
Earnings Per Share	2.65	3.07	3.65	4.06	1.91	2.92	7.40	3.20
Cash Flow Per Share	6.64	6.40	5.15	5.87	8.35	4.81	7.08	6.02
Tang Book Value Per Share	2.31	2.26	2.91	4.83	6.79	6.99	7.86	2.94
Dividends Per Share	2.320	2.730	2.260	3.030	2.810	2.690	2.350	1.200
Dividend Payout %	87.55	88.93	61.92	74.63	147.12	92.12	31.76	37.50
Income Statement								
Total Revenue	1,923,552	1,312,479	661,678	2,884,833	2,697,829	2,383,663	2,404,767	2,363,017
EBITDA	600,366	456,489	228,086	698,972	866,458	585,972	21,986	560,316
Depn & Amortn	326,645	235,141	108,423	18,206	41,012	68,511	38,606	40,851
Income Before Taxes	273,721	221,348	119,663	680,766	825,446	517,461	(16,620)	519,465
Income Taxes	55,536	51,359	23,187	148,317	565,599	123,769	(1,009,552)	85,402
Net Income	209,523	162,819	97,042	527,125	253,583	387,698	986,373	427,277
Average Shares	113,881	116,175	120,820	129,767	132,479	132,633	133,244	133,813
Balance Sheet								
Current Assets	2,956,736	2,965,616	2,884,077	2,977,419	3,026,422	2,245,765	2,054,105	1,875,226
Total Assets	5,551,879	5,507,473	5,499,477	4,997,241	4,928,677	4,556,508	4,486,766	3,332,236
Current Liabilities	1,824,615	1,812,320	1,625,661	1,869,952	1,709,667	1,113,149	1,186,512	942,468
Long-Term Obligations	1,678,921	1,678,131	1,759,297	1,434,260	1,190,383	1,195,805	1,007,378	1,060,365
Total Liabilities	4,938,437	4,888,671	4,798,256	4,080,390	3,728,874	3,320,521	3,173,311	2,625,492
Stockholders' Equity	613,442	618,802	701,221	916,851	1,199,803	1,235,987	1,313,455	706,744
Shares Outstanding	105,815	108,004	111,919	112,191	119,018	122,137	125,512	122,315
Statistical Record								
Return on Assets %	6.15	7.56	9.30	10.62	5.35	8.55	25.23	13.47
Return on Equity %	38.43	45.79	54.72	49.81	20.82	30.33	97.65	67.45
EBITDA Margin %	31.21	34.78	34.47	24.23	32.12	24.58	0.91	23.71
Net Margin %	10.89	12.41	14.67	18.27	9.40	16.26	41.02	18.08
Asset Turnover	0.50	0.52	0.56	0.58	0.57	0.53	0.62	0.75
Current Ratio	1.62	1.64	1.77	1.59	1.77	2.02	1.73	1.99
Debt to Equity	2.74	2.71	2.51	1.56	0.99	0.97	0.77	1.50
Price Range	48.16-31.16	54.30-31.16	56.05-33.98	59.40-33.98	52.50-40.61	45.01-27.00	58.78-41.47	54.96-41.37
P/E Ratio	18.17-11.76	17.69-10.15	15.36-9.31	14.63-8.37	27.49-21.26	15.41-9.25	7.94-5.60	17.18-12.93
Average Yield %	11.70	6.39	5.02	6.12	6.24	7.45	4.65	2.44

Address: Clarendon House, 2 Church Street, Hamilton, HM 11	**Web Site:** www.lazard.com	**Auditors:** DELOITTE & TOUCHE LLP
Telephone: 441-295-1422	**Officers:** Kenneth M. Jacobs - Chairman, Chief Executive Officer Evan L. Russo - Chief Financial Officer, Associate/Affiliate Company Officer	**Investor Contact:** 212-632-6637 **Transfer Agents:** Computershare, Pittsburgh, PA

LEAR CORP.

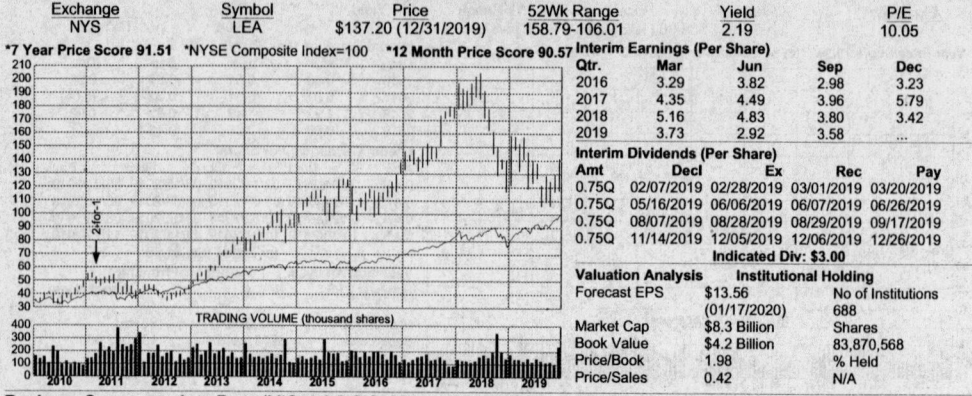

Exchange	Symbol	Price	52Wk Range	Yield	P/E
NYS	LEA	$137.20 (12/31/2019)	158.79-106.01	2.19	10.05

*7 Year Price Score 91.51 ***NYSE Composite Index=100** ***12 Month Price Score 90.57**

Interim Earnings (Per Share)

Qtr.	Mar	Jun	Sep	Dec
2016	3.29	3.82	2.98	3.23
2017	4.35	4.49	3.96	5.79
2018	5.16	4.83	3.80	3.42
2019	3.73	2.92	3.58	...

Interim Dividends (Per Share)

Amt	Decl	Ex	Rec	Pay
0.75Q	02/07/2019	02/28/2019	03/01/2019	03/20/2019
0.75Q	05/16/2019	06/06/2019	06/07/2019	06/26/2019
0.75Q	08/07/2019	08/28/2019	08/29/2019	09/17/2019
0.75Q	11/14/2019	12/05/2019	12/06/2019	12/26/2019

Indicated Div: $3.00

Valuation Analysis

		Institutional Holding	
Forecast EPS	$13.56	No of Institutions	
	(01/17/2020)	688	
Market Cap	$8.3 Billion	Shares	
Book Value	$4.2 Billion	83,870,568	
Price/Book	1.98	% Held	
Price/Sales	0.42	N/A	

Business Summary: Auto Parts (MIC: 1.8.2 SIC: 3714 NAIC: 336360)

Lear is a supplier to the global automotive industry. Co. is engaged in supplying seating, electrical distribution systems and electronic modules, as well as related sub-systems, components and software, to automotive manufacturers. Co.'s business is organized under two reporting segments: Seating, which consists of the design, development, engineering, assembly and delivery of seat systems, as well as seat components; and E-Systems, which consists of the design, development, engineering and manufacture of complete electrical distribution systems, as well as electronic control modules, electrification products and connectivity products.

Recent Developments: For the quarter ended Sep 28 2019, net income decreased 13.1% to US$238.6 million from US$274.7 million in the year-earlier quarter. Revenues were US$4.83 billion, down 1.4% from US$4.89 billion the year before. Direct operating expenses was unchanged at US$4.37 billion versus the comparable period the year before. Indirect operating expenses decreased 2.7% to US$158.6 million from US$163.0 million in the equivalent prior-year period.

Prospects: Our evaluation of Lear Corp. as of October 4th, 2019 is the result of our systematic analysis on three basic characteristics: earnings strength, relative valuation, and recent stock price movement. The company has managed to produce a neutral trend in earnings per share over the past 5 quarters. However, recent analyst estimates for the company have been reduced while LEA has posted results that exceeded analysts' expectations. Based on operating earnings yield, the company is undervalued when compared to all of the companies we cover. Share price changes over the past year indicates that LEA will perform well over the near term.

Financial Data

(US$ in Thousands)	9 Mos	6 Mos	3 Mos	12/31/2018	12/31/2017	12/31/2016	12/31/2015	12/31/2014
Earnings Per Share	13.65	13.87	15.78	17.22	18.59	13.33	9.59	8.23
Cash Flow Per Share	25.48	23.83	25.38	27.10	26.01	22.32	16.56	11.57
Tang Book Value Per Share	42.93	43.05	45.49	44.41	41.11	27.88	25.16	28.62
Dividends Per Share	2.950	2.900	2.850	2.800	2.000	1.200	1.000	0.800
Dividend Payout %	21.61	20.91	18.06	16.26	10.76	9.00	10.43	9.72
Income Statement								
Total Revenue	14,992,700	10,167,700	5,160,100	21,148,500	20,467,000	18,557,600	18,211,400	17,727,300
EBITDA	1,270,600	851,100	431,400	2,106,900	2,040,100	1,799,000	1,466,000	1,165,800
Depn & Amortn	380,400	251,900	123,600	484,400	427,700	378,200	347,800	310,900
Income Before Taxes	820,800	553,800	286,900	1,538,400	1,526,700	1,338,300	1,031,500	787,400
Income Taxes	149,900	116,400	43,100	311,900	197,500	370,200	285,500	121,400
Net Income	627,600	411,700	228,900	1,149,800	1,313,400	975,100	745,500	672,400
Average Shares	61,330	62,354	63,123	66,161	69,277	73,124	77,767	81,728
Balance Sheet								
Current Assets	6,618,000	6,736,300	6,597,600	6,280,500	6,613,000	5,649,300	5,286,600	5,379,600
Total Assets	12,753,300	12,847,700	12,362,000	11,600,700	11,945,900	9,900,600	9,405,800	9,150,200
Current Liabilities	4,907,800	5,027,000	4,914,400	4,500,600	4,854,300	4,182,300	3,839,600	3,957,800
Long-Term Obligations	2,297,600	2,300,100	1,938,600	1,941,000	1,951,500	1,898,000	1,931,700	1,475,000
Total Liabilities	8,549,500	8,611,300	8,116,700	7,400,000	7,795,400	6,843,400	6,478,400	6,191,400
Stockholders' Equity	4,203,800	4,236,400	4,245,300	4,200,700	4,150,500	3,057,200	2,927,400	2,958,800
Shares Outstanding	60,644	61,237	62,415	62,939	66,873	69,431	74,464	78,021
Statistical Record								
Return on Assets %	6.78	6.97	8.19	9.77	12.02	10.07	8.04	7.69
Return on Equity %	19.77	20.53	23.71	27.54	36.44	32.50	25.33	22.40
EBITDA Margin %	8.47	8.37	8.36	9.96	9.97	9.69	8.05	6.58
Net Margin %	4.19	4.05	4.44	5.44	6.42	5.25	4.09	3.79
Asset Turnover	1.61	1.59	1.64	1.80	1.87	1.92	1.96	2.03
Current Ratio	1.35	1.34	1.34	1.40	1.36	1.35	1.38	1.36
Debt to Equity	0.55	0.54	0.46	0.46	0.47	0.62	0.66	0.50
Price Range	158.79-106.01	192.47-116.96	205.34-116.96	205.34-116.96	180.89-132.08	138.80-94.98	126.34-93.40	103.28-71.97
P/E Ratio	11.63-7.77	13.88-8.43	13.01-7.41	11.92-6.79	9.73-7.10	10.41-7.13	13.17-9.74	12.55-8.74
Average Yield %	2.18	1.96	1.76	1.63	1.31	1.05	0.90	0.90

Address: 21557 Telegraph Road, Southfield, MI 48033	Web Site: www.lear.com	Auditors: Ernst & Young LLP
Telephone: 248-447-1500	Officers: Raymond E. Scott - President, Chief Executive Officer, Executive Vice President, Senior Vice President, Division Officer Terrence B. Larkin - Executive Vice President, Senior Vice President, General Counsel, Corporate Secretary	Investor Contact: 248-447-1500
Fax: 248-447-5250		Transfer Agents: Computershare Trust Company, Canton, MA

LEGG MASON, INC.

Exchange	Symbol	Price	52Wk Range	Yield	P/E
NYS	LM	$35.91 (12/31/2019)	39.99-25.51	4.46	N/A

*7 Year Price Score 73.58 ***NYSE Composite Index=100** ***12 Month Price Score 104.31**

Interim Earnings (Per Share)

Qtr.	Jun	Sep	Dec	Mar
2016-17	0.31	0.63	0.50	0.75
2017-18	0.52	0.78	1.58	0.15
2018-19	0.75	0.82	(2.55)	0.57
2019-20	0.51	0.74	...	...

Interim Dividends (Per Share)

Amt	Decl	Ex	Rec	Pay
0.34Q	02/11/2019	03/25/2019	03/26/2019	04/29/2019
0.40Q	05/13/2019	07/01/2019	07/02/2019	07/22/2019
0.40Q	08/01/2019	10/09/2019	10/10/2019	10/28/2019
0.40Q	11/05/2019	12/23/2019	12/24/2019	01/20/2020

Indicated Div: $1.60

Valuation Analysis

		Institutional Holding	
Forecast EPS	$3.64	No of Institutions	577
	(01/17/2020)		
Market Cap	$3.1 Billion	Shares	
Book Value	$3.7 Billion		111,164,848
Price/Book	0.84	% Held	
Price/Sales	1.10		81.64

Business Summary: Wealth Management (MIC: 5.5.2 SIC: 6282 NAIC: 523930)

Legg Mason is a holding company. Through its subsidiaries, Co. is an asset management company that provides investment management and related products and services. Co.'s investment advisory services include discretionary and non-discretionary management of separate investment accounts for institutional and individual investors. Co.'s investment products include proprietary mutual funds ranging from money market and other liquidity products to fixed income, equity and alternative funds managed in various investment styles. Co. also provides other domestic and offshore funds to both retail and institutional investors, privately placed real estate funds, hedge funds, and funds-of-hedge funds.

Recent Developments: For the quarter ended Sep 30 2019, net income decreased 5.6% to US$76.5 million from US$81.1 million in the year-earlier quarter. Revenues were US$743.3 million, down 2.0% from US$758.4 million the year before. Operating income was US$125.0 million versus US$135.7 million in the prior-year quarter, a decrease of 7.9%. Indirect operating expenses decreased 0.7% to US$618.3 million from US$622.7 million in the equivalent prior-year period.

Prospects: Our evaluation of Legg Mason Inc. as of October 4th, 2019 is the result of our systematic analysis on three basic characteristics: earnings strength, relative valuation, and recent stock price movement. The company has enjoyed a very positive trend in earnings per share over the past 5 quarters. However, recent analyst estimates for the company have been unchanged, while LM has posted results that exceeded analysts' expectations. Based on operating earnings yield, the company is undervalued when compared to all of the companies we cover. Share price changes over the past year indicates that LM will perform well over the near term.

Financial Data

(US$ in Thousands)	6 Mos	3 Mos	03/31/2019	03/31/2018	03/31/2017	03/31/2016	03/31/2015	03/31/2014
Earnings Per Share	(0.73)	(0.65)	(0.38)	3.01	2.18	(0.25)	2.04	2.33
Cash Flow Per Share	4.78	5.51	6.57	5.43	5.37	4.22	5.07	3.59
Tang Book Value Per Share	N.M.	N.M.	N.M.	N.M.	N.M.	N.M.	N.M.	2.67
Dividends Per Share	1.420	1.020	1.360	1.120	0.880	0.800	0.640	0.520
Dividend Payout %	...	...	...	37.21	40.37	...	31.37	22.32
Income Statement								
Total Revenue	1,448,624	705,360	2,903,259	3,140,322	2,886,902	2,660,844	2,819,106	2,741,757
EBITDA	256,470	115,243	206,455	417,592	557,449	77,908	473,913	529,030
Depn & Amortn	22,411	11,148	72,795	72,986	80,213	60,297	55,086	62,845
Income Before Taxes	184,902	79,617	28,495	233,840	370,878	(25,218)	367,993	419,641
Income Taxes	46,802	18,048	20,561	(102,510)	84,175	7,692	125,284	137,805
Net Income	112,433	45,350	(28,508)	285,075	227,256	(25,032)	237,080	284,784
Average Shares	87,127	86,494	85,423	91,194	100,799	107,406	113,246	122,383
Balance Sheet								
Current Assets	1,743,679	1,745,864	2,019,856	1,928,382	1,801,747	2,385,128	1,922,035	2,128,383
Total Assets	7,802,302	7,845,841	7,794,122	8,152,534	8,290,415	7,520,446	7,073,977	7,111,349
Current Liabilities	785,733	866,881	1,109,744	982,042	809,387	841,553	815,046	821,245
Long-Term Obligations	1,972,092	1,971,772	1,971,451	2,221,810	2,221,867	1,740,985	1,058,089	1,038,826
Total Liabilities	4,082,980	4,145,058	4,134,367	4,328,129	4,307,041	3,306,883	2,589,076	2,386,625
Stockholders' Equity	3,719,322	3,700,783	3,659,755	3,824,405	3,983,374	4,213,563	4,484,901	4,724,724
Shares Outstanding	86,783	86,656	85,556	84,606	95,726	107,011	111,469	117,173
Statistical Record								
Return on Assets %	N.M.	N.M.	N.M.	3.47	2.87	N.M.	3.34	3.96
Return on Equity %	N.M.	N.M.	N.M.	7.30	5.54	N.M.	5.15	5.97
EBITDA Margin %	17.70	16.34	7.11	13.30	19.31	2.93	16.81	19.30
Net Margin %	7.76	6.43	N.M.	9.08	7.87	N.M.	8.41	10.39
Asset Turnover	0.36	0.36	0.36	0.38	0.37	0.36	0.40	0.38
Current Ratio	2.22	2.01	1.82	1.96	2.23	2.83	2.36	2.59
Debt to Equity	0.53	0.53	0.54	0.58	0.56	0.41	0.24	0.22
Price Range	39.99-23.51	38.28-23.51	40.71-23.51	46.14-35.65	37.72-27.77	55.58-25.20	58.92-43.36	49.04-29.76
P/E Ratio	...	...	...	15.33-11.84	17.30-12.74	...	28.88-21.25	21.05-12.77
Average Yield %	4.39	3.30	4.28	2.86	2.67	1.83	1.24	1.39

Address: 100 International Drive, Baltimore, MD 21202 **Telephone:** 410-539-0000	**Web Site:** www.leggmason.com **Officers:** Joseph A. Sullivan - Chairman, President, Chief Executive Officer, Acting Chief Executive Officer, Senior Executive Vice President, Chief Administrative Officer Peter H. Nachtwey - Senior Executive Vice President, Chief Financial Officer	**Auditors:** PricewaterhouseCoopers LLP **Investor Contact:** 410-454-5246 **Transfer Agents:** American Stock Transfer & Trust Company, New York, NY

LEGGETT & PLATT, INC.

*7 Year Price Score 83.65   ***NYSE Composite Index=100**   ***12 Month Price Score 117.38**

Interim Earnings (Per Share)

Qtr.	Mar	Jun	Sep	Dec
2016	0.63	0.87	0.67	0.59
2017	0.62	0.64	0.60	0.27
2018	0.57	.0.63	0.67	0.39
2019	0.45	0.64	0.74	...

Interim Dividends (Per Share)

Amt	Decl	Ex	Rec	Pay
0.38Q	02/27/2019	03/14/2019	03/15/2019	04/15/2019
0.40Q	05/07/2019	06/13/2019	06/14/2019	07/15/2019
0.40Q	08/06/2019	09/12/2019	09/13/2019	10/15/2019
0.40Q	11/05/2019	12/12/2019	12/13/2019	01/15/2020

Indicated Div: $1.60

Valuation Analysis

		Institutional Holding	
Forecast EPS	$2.56	No of Institutions	
	(01/15/2020)	682	
Market Cap	$6.7 Billion	Shares	
Book Value	$1.3 Billion	139,808,480	
Price/Book	5.33	% Held	
Price/Sales	1.44	77.52	

Business Summary: Furniture (MIC: 1.6.2 SIC: 2519 NAIC: 337121)

Leggett & Platt designs and produces engineered components and products in homes, offices, automobiles and aircraft. Co.'s segments are: Residential Products, which supplies components and machinery used by bedding manufacturers in the production and assembly of their finished products, as well as producing private-label finished mattresses for bedding brands; Industrial Products, which supplies high-carbon drawn steel wire; Furniture Products, which supplies components used by home and work furniture manufacturers; and Specialized Products, which designs, manufactures and sells products including automotive seating components, tubing and fabricated assemblies, and hydraulic cylinders.

Recent Developments: For the quarter ended Sep 30 2019, net income increased 10.7% to US$99.6 million from US$90.0 million in the year-earlier quarter. Revenues were US$1.24 billion, up 13.5% from US$1.09 billion the year before. Operating income was US$144.1 million versus US$124.4 million in the prior-year quarter, an increase of 15.8%. Direct operating expenses rose 11.5% to US$963.8 million from US$864.4 million in the comparable period the year before. Indirect operating expenses increased 27.9% to US$131.4 million from US$102.7 million in the equivalent prior-year period.

Prospects: Our evaluation of Leggett & Platt Inc. as of October 4th, 2019 is the result of our systematic analysis on three basic characteristics: earnings strength, relative valuation, and recent stock price movement. The company has produced a positive trend in earnings per share over the past 5 quarters. However, recent analyst estimates for the company have been unchanged, and LEG has posted results in line with analysts' expectations. Based on operating earnings yield, the company is undervalued when compared to all of the companies we cover. Share price changes over the past year indicates that LEG will perform poorly over the near term.

Financial Data
(US$ in Thousands)

	9 Mos	6 Mos	3 Mos	12/31/2018	12/31/2017	12/31/2016	12/31/2015	12/31/2014
Earnings Per Share	2.22	2.15	2.14	2.26	2.13	2.76	2.28	0.68
Cash Flow Per Share	4.49	3.86	3.18	3.28	3.26	4.00	2.55	2.70
Tang Book Value Per Share	N.M.	N.M.	N.M.	1.11	1.51	1.01	0.64	0.89
Dividends Per Share	1.560	1.540	1.520	1.500	1.420	1.340	1.260	1.220
Dividend Payout %	70.27	71.63	71.03	66.37	66.67	48.55	55.26	179.41
Income Statement								
Total Revenue	3,607,600	2,368,300	1,155,100	4,269,500	3,943,800	3,749,900	3,917,200	3,782,300
EBITDA	523,000	330,500	144,500	561,700	583,900	628,700	590,800	441,100
Depn & Amortn	144,700	96,300	46,300	124,800	116,000	106,700	104,300	109,600
Income Before Taxes	315,300	192,300	78,200	384,400	432,000	487,100	449,800	295,500
Income Taxes	68,300	44,900	17,100	78,300	138,400	120,000	121,800	70,300
Net Income	247,000	147,400	61,200	305,900	292,600	385,800	325,100	98,000
Average Shares	135,400	135,200	135,000	135,200	137,300	140,000	142,900	143,200
Balance Sheet								
Current Assets	1,604,600	1,703,000	1,659,000	1,524,600	1,766,500	1,324,900	1,311,200	1,429,600
Total Assets	4,857,800	5,002,000	4,953,800	3,382,000	3,550,800	2,984,100	2,967,600	3,140,600
Current Liabilities	920,800	900,300	867,000	815,700	976,200	706,600	701,200	992,200
Long-Term Obligations	2,316,100	2,494,900	2,528,700	1,167,800	1,097,900	956,200	945,400	766,700
Total Liabilities	3,602,600	3,763,800	3,759,100	2,225,000	2,360,600	1,892,500	1,882,000	1,994,100
Stockholders' Equity	1,255,200	1,238,200	1,194,700	1,157,000	1,190,200	1,091,600	1,085,600	1,146,500
Shares Outstanding	131,602	131,470	131,268	130,500	131,900	133,500	135,600	137,800
Statistical Record								
Return on Assets %	7.14	6.72	6.69	8.82	8.95	12.93	10.64	3.14
Return on Equity %	24.79	24.54	24.19	26.07	25.65	35.34	29.13	7.72
EBITDA Margin %	14.50	13.96	12.51	13.16	14.81	16.77	15.08	11.66
Net Margin %	6.85	6.22	5.30	7.16	7.42	10.29	8.30	2.59
Asset Turnover	1.11	1.04	1.02	1.23	1.21	1.26	1.28	1.21
Current Ratio	1.74	1.89	1.91	1.87	1.81	1.88	1.87	1.44
Debt to Equity	1.85	2.01	2.12	1.01	0.92	0.88	0.87	0.67
Price Range	46.07-33.97	46.40-33.97	46.40-33.97	48.80-33.97	54.04-43.50	54.53-37.79	51.00-40.68	42.95-29.06
P/E Ratio	20.75-15.30	21.58-15.80	21.68-15.87	21.59-15.03	25.37-20.42	19.76-13.69	22.37-17.84	63.16-42.74
Average Yield %	3.93	3.75	3.62	3.49	2.89	2.80	2.76	3.53

Address: No. 1 Leggett Road, Carthage, MO 64836
Telephone: 417-358-8131

Web Site: www.leggett.com
Officers: Karl G. Glassman - Chairman, President, Chief Executive Officer, Executive Vice President, Chief Operating Officer J. Mitchell Dolloff - President, Executive Vice President, Chief Operating Officer, Division Officer

Auditors: PricewaterhouseCoopers LLP
Investor Contact: 417-358-8131
Transfer Agents: Wells Fargo Shareowner Services, St. Paul, MN

LEIDOS HOLDINGS INC

Exchange	Symbol	Price	52Wk Range	Yield	P/E
NYS	LDOS	$97.89 (12/31/2019)	98.53-51.33	1.39	21.37

*7 Year Price Score 119.97 *NYSE Composite Index=100 *12 Month Price Score 112.26

TRADING VOLUME (thousand shares)

Interim Earnings (Per Share)

Qtr.	Mar	Jun	Sep	Dec
2016	0.66	0.55	0.80	0.22
2017	0.47	0.64	0.53	0.73
2018	0.66	0.94	0.96	1.25
2019	1.29	0.93	1.11	...

Interim Dividends (Per Share)

Amt	Decl	Ex	Rec	Pay
0.32Q	02/15/2019	03/14/2019	03/15/2019	03/29/2019
0.32Q	04/26/2019	06/13/2019	06/14/2019	06/28/2019
0.34Q	07/29/2019	09/13/2019	09/16/2019	09/30/2019
0.34Q	10/25/2019	12/13/2019	12/16/2019	12/27/2019

Indicated Div: $1.36 (Div. Reinv. Plan)

Valuation Analysis Institutional Holding

Forecast EPS	$5.00	No of Institutions
(01/16/2020)		693
Market Cap	$13.8 Billion	Shares
Book Value	$3.2 Billion	150,108,256
Price/Book	4.25	% Held
Price/Sales	1.28	N/A

Business Summary: IT Services (MIC: 6.3.1 SIC: 7373 NAIC: 541330)

Leidos Holdings is a holding company, engaged in a science, engineering and information technology that provides services and solutions in the defense, intelligence, civil and health markets. Co.'s segments are: defense solutions, which deploys solutions in the areas of intelligence surveillance and reconnaissance, enterprise information technology, integrated systems, cybersecurity and global services; civil, which is focused on integrating and protecting physical, digital and data domains; and health, which is focused on delivering solutions to federal and commercial customers that are responsible for the health and well-being of people including service members and veterans.

Recent Developments: For the quarter ended Sep 27 2019, net income increased 10.2% to US$162.0 million from US$147.0 million in the year-earlier quarter. Revenues were US$2.84 billion, up 10.1% from US$2.58 billion the year before. Operating income was US$249.0 million versus US$203.0 million in the prior-year quarter, an increase of 22.7%. Direct operating expenses rose 12.7% to US$2.45 billion from US$2.17 billion in the comparable period the year before. Indirect operating expenses decreased 31.3% to US$136.0 million from US$198.0 million in the equivalent prior-year period.

Prospects: Our evaluation of Leidos Holdings Inc. as of October 4th, 2019 is the result of our systematic analysis on three basic characteristics: earnings strength, relative valuation, and recent stock price movement. The company has managed to produce a neutral trend in earnings per share over the past 5 quarters. However, recent analyst estimates for the company have been raised and LDOS has posted results that exceeded analysts' expectations. Based on operating earnings yield, the company is undervalued when compared to all of the companies we cover. Share price changes over the past year indicates that LDOS will perform over the near term.

Financial Data

(US$ in Millions)	9 Mos	6 Mos	3 Mos	12/28/2018	12/29/2017	12/30/2016	01/01/2016	01/30/2015
Earnings Per Share	4.58	4.43	4.44	3.80	2.38	2.35	3.27	(4.36)
Cash Flow Per Share	6.48	6.59	7.13	5.10	3.47	4.38	5.94	5.37
Dividends Per Share	1.300	1.280	1.280	1.280	1.280	14.920	1.280	1.280
Dividend Payout %	28.38	28.89	28.83	33.68	53.78	634.89	39.14	...
Income Statement								
Total Revenue	8,140	5,305	2,577	10,194	10,170	7,043	4,712	5,063
EBITDA	767	515	295	785	575	432	437	(162)
Depn & Amortn	45	29	15	55	55	38	33	47
Income Before Taxes	623	415	242	592	380	308	355	(283)
Income Taxes	150	98	57	28	29	72	112	47
Net Income	486	325	189	581	366	244	242	(323)
Average Shares	145	146	147	153	154	104	74	74
Balance Sheet								
Current Assets	2,924	2,914	2,860	2,839	2,674	2,381	1,793	1,618
Total Assets	9,410	9,327	9,360	8,770	8,990	9,132	3,377	3,281
Current Liabilities	2,527	2,246	2,322	2,059	2,202	2,016	1,040	951
Long-Term Obligations	2,939	2,954	2,966	3,052	3,056	3,225	1,086	1,164
Total Liabilities	6,164	5,968	6,066	5,462	5,620	5,997	2,309	2,283
Stockholders' Equity	3,246	3,359	3,294	3,308	3,370	3,135	1,068	998
Shares Outstanding	141	144	144	146	151	150	72	74
Statistical Record								
Return on Assets %	7.36	7.29	7.31	6.56	4.05	3.91	6.97	N.M.
Return on Equity %	20.12	19.48	19.87	17.45	11.28	11.64	19.74	N.M.
EBITDA Margin %	9.42	9.71	11.45	7.70	5.65	6.13	9.27	N.M.
Net Margin %	5.97	6.13	7.33	5.70	3.60	3.46	5.14	N.M.
Asset Turnover	1.18	1.16	1.13	1.15	1.13	1.13	1.36	1.36
Current Ratio	1.16	1.30	1.23	1.38	1.21	1.18	1.72	1.70
Debt to Equity	0.91	0.88	0.90	0.92	0.91	1.03	1.02	1.17
Price Range	88.82-50.54	79.85-50.54	71.99-50.54	71.99-50.54	65.22-48.31	56.19-38.50	59.05-38.05	46.07-33.21
P/E Ratio	19.39-11.03	18.02-11.41	16.21-11.38	18.94-13.30	27.40-20.30	23.91-16.38	18.06-11.64	...
Average Yield %	1.86	1.94	2.02	1.98	2.29	31.53	2.83	3.26

Address: 11951 Freedom Drive, Reston, VA 20190	**Web Site:** www.leidos.com	**Auditors:** Deloitte & Touche LLP
Telephone: 571-526-6000	**Officers:** Roger A. Krone - Chairman, Chief Executive Officer James C. Reagan - Executive Vice President, Chief Financial Officer	**Investor Contact:** 703-676-2283 **Transfer Agents:** BNY Mellon Shareowner Services

LENNAR CORP

Exchange	Symbol	Price	52Wk Range	Yield	P/E
NYS	LEN	$55.79 (12/31/2019)	61.97-39.15	0.90	9.10

*7 Year Price Score 91.74   *NYSE Composite Index=100   ***12 Month Price Score 106.79**

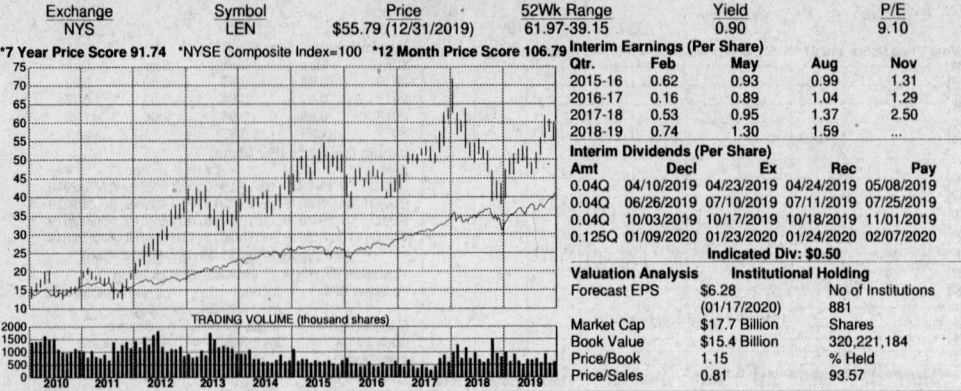

Interim Earnings (Per Share)

Qtr.	Feb	May	Aug	Nov
2015-16	0.62	0.93	0.99	1.31
2016-17	0.16	0.89	1.04	1.29
2017-18	0.53	0.95	1.37	2.50
2018-19	0.74	1.30	1.59	...

Interim Dividends (Per Share)

Amt	Decl	Ex	Rec	Pay
0.04Q	04/10/2019	04/23/2019	04/24/2019	05/08/2019
0.04Q	06/26/2019	07/10/2019	07/11/2019	07/25/2019
0.04Q	10/03/2019	10/17/2019	10/18/2019	11/01/2019
0.125Q	01/09/2020	01/23/2020	01/24/2020	02/07/2020

Indicated Div: $0.50

Valuation Analysis

		Institutional Holding	
Forecast EPS	$6.28	No of Institutions	
	(01/17/2020)	881	
Market Cap	$17.7 Billion	Shares	
Book Value	$15.4 Billion	320,221,184	
Price/Book	1.15	% Held	
Price/Sales	0.81	93.57	

TRADING VOLUME (thousand shares)

Business Summary: Builders (MIC: 2.2.5 SIC: 1521 NAIC: 236115)

Lennar is a homebuilder in the U.S., an originator of residential and commercial mortgage loans, and a developer of multifamily rental properties. In addition, Co. is involved in ventures, and has interests in companies, that are engaged in applying technology to purchasing, residing in and selling homes. Co.'s homebuilding operations include the construction and sale of single-family attached and detached homes as well as the purchase, development and sale of residential land directly and through unconsolidated entities in which it has investments. Co. primarily sell single-family attached and detached homes in communities targeted to first-time, move-up, and active adult, homebuyers.

Recent Developments: For the quarter ended Aug 31 2019, net income increased 9.6% to US$512.6 million from US$467.6 million in the year-earlier quarter. Revenues were US$5.86 billion, up 3.3% from US$5.67 billion the year before. Direct operating expenses rose 2.5% to US$5.12 billion from US$4.99 billion in the comparable period the year before. Indirect operating expenses decreased 14.5% to US$92.6 million from US$108.3 million in the equivalent prior-year period.

Prospects: Our evaluation of Lennar Corp. as of October 4th, 2019 is the result of our systematic analysis on three basic characteristics: earnings strength, relative valuation, and recent stock price movement. The company has enjoyed a very positive trend in earnings per share over the past 5 quarters. In addition, recent analyst estimates for the company have been raised, and LEN has posted results that exceeded analysts' expectations. Based on operating earnings yield, the company is undervalued when compared to all of the companies we cover. Share price changes over the past year indicates that LEN will perform poorly over the near term.

Financial Data

(US$ in Thousands)	9 Mos	6 Mos	3 Mos	11/30/2018	11/30/2017	11/30/2016	11/30/2015	11/30/2014
Earnings Per Share	6.13	5.91	5.56	5.44	3.38	3.85	3.39	2.75
Cash Flow Per Share	3.96	3.89	4.14	5.56	4.20	2.27	(2.01)	(3.82)
Tang Book Value Per Share	36.88	35.70	34.44	33.62	31.99	29.80	26.05	23.08
Dividends Per Share	0.160	0.160	0.160	0.160	0.160	0.160	0.160	0.160
Dividend Payout %	2.61	2.71	2.88	2.94	4.73	4.15	4.72	5.83
Income Statement								
Total Revenue	15,288,030	9,430,972	3,868,082	20,571,631	12,646,365	10,949,999	9,474,008	7,779,812
EBITDA	1,502,665	848,415	306,921	2,345,098	1,217,769	1,344,728	1,180,426	992,888
Depn & Amortn	(19,841)	(13,335)	(7,048)	67,637	77,636	64,838	63,540	59,929
Income Before Taxes	1,522,506	861,750	313,969	2,277,461	1,140,133	1,275,264	1,104,432	896,408
Income Taxes	374,670	220,230	79,700	545,171	417,857	417,378	390,416	341,091
Net Income	1,174,748	661,382	239,910	1,695,831	810,480	911,844	802,894	638,916
Average Shares	318,104	320,330	321,349	308,565	237,156	235,326	235,428	232,804
Balance Sheet								
Current Assets	19,996,050	19,875,829	19,345,895	19,193,787	13,762,319	10,911,843	10,171,054	9,230,259
Total Assets	29,459,447	29,583,064	28,749,926	28,566,181	18,745,034	15,361,781	14,419,509	12,958,267
Current Liabilities	1,092,708	1,067,984	1,025,286	1,154,782	604,953	478,546	475,909	412,558
Long-Term Obligations	10,282,365	10,659,798	10,381,632	8,543,868	6,410,003	4,575,977	5,025,130	4,690,213
Total Liabilities	14,087,509	14,423,760	13,963,112	13,984,646	10,872,717	8,335,739	8,770,565	8,131,247
Stockholders' Equity	15,371,938	15,159,304	14,786,814	14,581,535	7,872,317	7,026,042	5,648,944	4,827,020
Shares Outstanding	317,619	322,146	323,174	324,238	239,964	234,475	215,368	209,140
Statistical Record								
Return on Assets %	6.83	6.60	6.35	7.17	4.75	6.11	5.87	5.27
Return on Equity %	13.41	13.29	12.92	15.11	10.88	14.35	15.33	14.20
EBITDA Margin %	9.83	9.00	7.93	11.40	9.63	12.28	12.46	12.76
Net Margin %	7.68	7.01	6.20	8.24	6.41	8.33	8.47	8.21
Asset Turnover	0.75	0.74	0.76	0.87	0.74	0.73	0.69	0.64
Current Ratio	18.30	18.61	18.87	16.62	22.75	22.80	21.37	22.37
Debt to Equity	0.67	0.70	0.70	0.59	0.81	0.65	0.89	0.97
Price Range	53.66-38.06	55.55-38.06	64.00-38.06	71.82-38.84	62.78-41.29	51.42-37.16	54.64-40.62	46.70-33.64
P/E Ratio	8.75-6.21	9.40-6.44	11.51-6.85	13.20-7.14	18.57-12.22	13.36-9.65	16.12-11.98	16.98-12.23
Average Yield %	0.34	0.33	0.32	0.29	0.32	0.36	0.33	0.41

Address: 700 Northwest 107th Avenue, Miami, FL 33172 Telephone: 305-559-4000	Web Site: www.lennar.com Officers: Jeff J. McCall - Senior Vice President Stuart A. Miller - President, Chief Executive Officer, Executive Chairman	Auditors: DELOITTE & TOUCHE LLP Investor Contact: 305-559-4000 Transfer Agents: ComputerShare Investor Services, Providence, RI

LENNOX INTERNATIONAL INC

Exchange	Symbol	Price	52Wk Range	Yield	P/E
NYS	LII	$243.97 (12/31/2019)	292.70-212.25	1.26	26.09

*7 Year Price Score 139.41 ***NYSE Composite Index=100** ***12 Month Price Score 93.53**

Interim Earnings (Per Share)

Qtr.	Mar	Jun	Sep	Dec
2016	0.56	2.51	2.33	0.94
2017	1.00	2.69	2.44	1.02
2018	0.90	3.35	2.65	1.88
2019	1.73	2.80	2.94	...

Interim Dividends (Per Share)

Amt	Decl	Ex	Rec	Pay
0.64Q	03/15/2019	03/29/2019	04/01/2019	04/15/2019
0.77Q	05/22/2019	06/27/2019	06/28/2019	07/15/2019
0.77Q	09/19/2019	09/30/2019	10/01/2019	10/15/2019
0.77Q	12/13/2019	12/30/2019	12/31/2019	01/15/2020

Indicated Div: $3.08

Valuation Analysis | **Institutional Holding**

Forecast EPS	$11.20	No of Institutions
	(01/17/2020)	569
Market Cap	$9.4 Billion	Shares
Book Value	N/A	35,621,880
Price/Book	N/A	% Held
Price/Sales	2.50	62.77

Business Summary: Industrial Machinery & Equipment (MIC: 7.2.1 SIC: 3585 NAIC: 333415)

Lennox International provides climate control solutions. Co. designs, manufactures and markets products for the heating, ventilation, air conditioning and refrigeration markets. Co.'s segments are: Residential Heating and Cooling, which manufactures and markets furnaces, air conditioners, heat pumps, packaged heating and cooling systems, equipment and accessories, comfort control products, and replacement parts and supplies; Commercial Heating and Cooling, which manufactures and sells unitary heating and cooling equipment; and Refrigeration, which provides condensing units, unit coolers, fluid coolers, air-cooled condensers, air handlers, display cases and refrigeration rack systems.

Recent Developments: For the quarter ended Sep 30 2019, income from continuing operations increased 6.2% to US$114.7 million from US$108.0 million in the year-earlier quarter. Net income increased 6.2% to US$114.7 million from US$108.0 million in the year-earlier quarter. Revenues were US$1.03 billion, unchanged from the year before. Operating income was US$156.8 million versus US$145.2 million in the prior-year quarter, an increase of 8.0%. Direct operating expenses rose 0.9% to US$734.6 million from US$728.3 million in the comparable period the year before. Indirect operating expenses decreased 9.7% to US$141.5 million from US$156.7 million in the equivalent prior-year period.

Prospects: Our evaluation of Lennox International Inc. as of October 4th, 2019 is the result of our systematic analysis on three basic characteristics: earnings strength, relative valuation, and recent stock price movement. The company has generated a negative trend in earnings per share over the past 5 quarters. In addition, recent analyst estimates for the company have been reduced and LII has posted results that fell short of analysts' expectations. Based on operating earnings yield, the company is fairly valued when compared to all of the companies we cover. Share price changes over the past year indicates that LII will perform over the near term.

Financial Data

(US$ in Thousands)	9 Mos	6 Mos	3 Mos	12/31/2018	12/31/2017	12/31/2016	12/31/2015	12/31/2014
Earnings Per Share	9.35	9.06	9.61	8.74	7.14	6.32	4.09	4.23
Cash Flow Per Share	10.07	10.73	11.03	12.20	7.70	8.15	7.38	3.86
Dividends Per Share	2.820	2.690	2.560	2.430	1.960	1.650	1.380	1.140
Dividend Payout %	30.16	29.69	26.64	27.80	27.45	26.11	33.74	26.95
Income Statement								
Total Revenue	2,922,200	1,889,400	790,300	3,883,900	3,839,600	3,641,600	3,467,400	3,367,400
EBITDA	445,600	274,400	109,500	560,200	540,800	469,400	355,600	381,800
Depn & Amortn	53,100	34,900	18,200	66,000	64,600	58,100	62,800	60,800
Income Before Taxes	356,000	215,600	80,400	455,900	445,600	384,300	269,200	303,800
Income Taxes	71,500	42,400	13,600	107,600	156,900	124,100	95,400	109,500
Net Income	294,700	180,000	69,300	359,000	305,700	277,800	186,600	205,800
Average Shares	39,000	39,500	40,100	41,100	42,800	44,000	45,600	48,600
Balance Sheet								
Current Assets	1,317,300	1,443,900	1,220,900	1,089,400	1,137,300	1,005,900	938,200	1,014,000
Total Assets	2,214,800	2,340,400	2,105,700	1,817,200	1,891,500	1,760,300	1,680,200	1,764,300
Current Liabilities	1,109,900	1,075,000	917,400	1,008,500	654,500	888,600	824,000	827,300
Long-Term Obligations	1,056,800	1,155,800	1,059,000	740,500	970,500	615,700	508,600	675,000
Total Liabilities	2,492,100	2,557,900	2,310,500	1,966,800	1,841,400	1,722,700	1,579,000	1,755,900
Stockholders' Equity	(277,300)	(217,500)	(204,800)	(149,600)	50,100	37,600	101,200	8,400
Shares Outstanding	38,527	39,025	39,560	39,857	41,809	42,974	44,678	44,635
Statistical Record								
Return on Assets %	17.95	16.38	18.63	19.36	16.74	16.10	10.83	12.14
Return on Equity %	...	...	...	...	697.15	399.19	340.51	83.44
EBITDA Margin %	15.25	14.52	13.86	14.42	14.08	12.89	10.26	11.34
Net Margin %	10.08	9.53	8.77	9.24	7.96	7.63	5.38	6.11
Asset Turnover	1.83	1.70	1.83	2.09	2.10	2.11	2.01	1.99
Current Ratio	1.19	1.34	1.33	1.08	1.74	1.13	1.14	1.23
Debt to Equity	...	...	...	...	19.37	16.38	5.03	80.36
Price Range	292.70-193.12	285.50-193.12	264.40-189.28	228.62-189.28	210.66-148.51	163.16-113.97	137.79-93.85	96.04-73.66
P/E Ratio	31.30-20.65	31.51-21.32	27.51-19.70	26.16-21.66	29.50-20.80	25.82-18.03	33.69-22.95	22.70-17.41
Average Yield %	1.15	1.14	1.18	1.16	1.11	1.16	1.20	1.31

Address: 2140 Lake Park Blvd., Richardson, TX 75080 **Telephone:** 972-497-5000	**Web Site:** www.lennoxinternational.com **Officers:** Todd M. Bluedorn - Chairman, Chief Executive Officer Joseph William Reitmeier - Executive Vice President, Chief Financial Officer	**Auditors:** KPMG LLP **Investor Contact:** 972-497-6670 **Transfer Agents:** Computershare, Providence, RI

LIBERTY PROPERTY TRUST

Exchange	Symbol	Price	52Wk Range	Yield	P/E
NYS	LPT	$60.05 (12/31/2019)	62.23-40.65	2.73	21.07

*7 Year Price Score 105.84 *NYSE Composite Index=100 *12 Month Price Score 110.97

Interim Earnings (Per Share)

Qtr.	Mar	Jun	Sep	Dec
2016	0.39	0.34	0.37	1.33
2017	0.29	0.35	0.40	0.87
2018	0.95	0.13	1.01	1.15
2019	0.37	0.67	0.66	...

Interim Dividends (Per Share)

Amt	Decl	Ex	Rec	Pay
0.41Q	02/21/2019	03/29/2019	04/01/2019	04/15/2019
0.41Q	06/14/2019	06/28/2019	07/01/2019	07/15/2019
0.41Q	09/16/2019	09/30/2019	10/01/2019	10/15/2019
0.41Q	12/09/2019	12/31/2019	01/02/2020	01/15/2020

Indicated Div: $1.64 (Div. Reinv. Plan)

Valuation Analysis / **Institutional Holding**

Forecast EPS	$1.68	No of Institutions	
	(01/14/2020)	604	
Market Cap	$9.5 Billion	Shares	
Book Value	$3.8 Billion	191,470,384	
Price/Book	2.47	% Held	
Price/Sales	14.35	97.80	

Business Summary: REITs (MIC: 5.3.1 SIC: 6798 NAIC: 525930)

Liberty Property Trust is a self-administered and self-managed real estate investment trust. Substantially all of Co.'s operations are conducted directly or indirectly, by its subsidiary, Liberty Property Limited Partnership. Co. provides leasing, property management, development and other tenant-related services for its industrial and office properties. Co.'s reportable segments are: Carolinas/Richmond; Chicago/Minneapolis; Florida; Houston; Lehigh/Central PA; Philadelphia; Southeastern PA; Southern California; and the U.K. Certain other segments are aggregated into an Other category which includes: Arizona; Atlanta; Cincinnati/Columbus/Indianapolis; Dallas; DC Metro; and New Jersey.

Recent Developments: For the quarter ended Sep 30 2019, net income decreased 33.4% to US$102.7 million from US$154.1 million in the year-earlier quarter. Revenues were US$163.2 million, up 1.2% from US$161.3 million the year before.

Prospects: Our evaluation of Liberty Property Trust as of October 4th, 2019 is the result of our systematic analysis on three basic characteristics: earnings strength, relative valuation, and recent stock price movement. The company has enjoyed a very positive trend in earnings per share over the past 5 quarters. However, recent analyst estimates for the company have been mixed and LPT has posted results that fell short of analysts' expectations. Based on operating earnings yield, the company is fairly valued when compared to all of the companies we cover. Share price changes over the past year indicates that LPT will perform very well over the near term.

Financial Data
(US$ in Thousands)

	9 Mos	6 Mos	3 Mos	12/31/2018	12/31/2017	12/31/2016	12/31/2015	12/31/2014
Earnings Per Share	2.85	3.20	2.66	3.24	1.91	2.43	1.60	1.47
Cash Flow Per Share	2.09	2.01	2.33	2.60	2.29	2.27	2.60	2.29
Tang Book Value Per Share	24.36	22.63	22.48	22.88	21.32	20.77	20.35	20.70
Dividends Per Share	1.630	1.620	1.610	1.600	1.600	1.900	1.900	1.900
Dividend Payout %	57.19	50.63	60.53	49.38	83.77	78.19	118.75	129.25
Income Statement								
Total Revenue	481,743	318,574	157,750	704,889	719,778	746,708	808,773	792,631
EBITDA	211,594	127,657	58,111	373,029	485,882	614,073	538,446	481,553
Depn & Amortn	3,498	2,311	1,201	143,400	148,900	166,800	181,000	179,100
Income Before Taxes	145,339	85,699	34,785	152,047	255,903	346,146	244,530	168,235
Income Taxes	1,449	571	832	7,364	1,992	1,971	3,233	2,967
Net Income	254,465	154,100	54,330	479,607	282,340	356,817	238,039	217,910
Average Shares	150,979	148,668	148,540	148,221	147,541	146,889	148,843	147,886
Balance Sheet								
Current Assets	545,863	50,889	130,637	235,330	152,056	179,264	177,501	213,061
Total Assets	7,338,732	6,882,259	6,938,579	6,934,394	6,439,757	5,992,813	6,557,629	6,625,536
Current Liabilities	157,404	136,667	150,732	148,460	161,731	159,293	149,323	148,809
Long-Term Obligations	3,031,267	3,084,374	3,128,779	3,092,746	2,909,545	2,556,936	3,147,016	3,163,395
Total Liabilities	3,495,877	3,527,011	3,605,730	3,604,533	3,352,399	2,989,422	3,604,701	3,597,864
Stockholders' Equity	3,842,855	3,355,248	3,332,849	3,329,861	3,087,358	3,003,391	2,952,928	3,027,672
Shares Outstanding	157,755	148,297	148,258	147,899	147,450	146,993	147,577	148,557
Statistical Record								
Return on Assets %	5.99	7.06	5.90	7.17	4.54	5.67	3.61	3.25
Return on Equity %	12.00	14.60	12.08	14.95	9.27	11.95	7.96	7.19
EBITDA Margin %	43.92	40.07	36.84	52.92	67.50	82.24	66.58	60.75
Net Margin %	52.82	48.37	34.44	68.04	39.23	47.79	29.43	27.49
Asset Turnover	0.09	0.10	0.10	0.11	0.12	0.12	0.12	0.12
Current Ratio	3.47	0.37	0.87	1.59	0.94	1.13	1.19	1.43
Debt to Equity	0.79	0.92	0.94	0.93	0.94	0.85	1.07	1.04
Price Range	53.13-40.13	51.16-40.13	49.09-38.91	46.46-38.63	45.29-37.56	42.25-27.30	41.42-29.91	40.08-32.77
P/E Ratio	18.64-14.08	15.99-12.54	18.45-14.63	14.34-11.92	23.71-19.66	17.39-11.23	25.89-18.69	27.27-22.29
Average Yield %	3.43	3.56	3.67	3.78	3.87	5.20	5.49	5.24

Address: 650 East Swedesford Road, Wayne, PA 19087 **Telephone:** 610-648-1700	**Web Site:** www.libertyproperty.com **Officers:** William P. Hankowsky - Chairman, President, Chief Executive Officer Michael T. Hagan - Executive Vice President, Chief Investment Officer	**Auditors:** Ernst & Young LLP **Investor Contact:** 610-648-1704 **Transfer Agents:** Wells Fargo Shareholder Services, St. Paul, MN

LIFE STORAGE INC

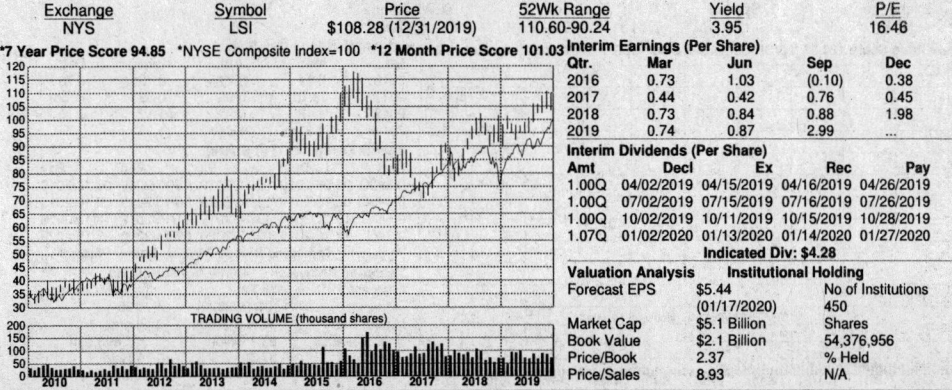

Exchange	Symbol	Price	52Wk Range	Yield	P/E
NYS	LSI	$108.28 (12/31/2019)	110.60-90.24	3.95	16.46

*7 Year Price Score 94.85   ***NYSE Composite Index=100**   ***12 Month Price Score 101.03**

Interim Earnings (Per Share)

Qtr.	Mar	Jun	Sep	Dec
2016	0.73	1.03	(0.10)	0.38
2017	0.44	0.42	0.76	0.45
2018	0.73	0.84	0.88	1.98
2019	0.74	0.87	2.99	...

Interim Dividends (Per Share)

Amt	Decl	Ex	Rec	Pay
1.00Q	04/02/2019	04/15/2019	04/16/2019	04/26/2019
1.00Q	07/02/2019	07/15/2019	07/16/2019	07/26/2019
1.00Q	10/02/2019	10/11/2019	10/15/2019	10/28/2019
1.07Q	01/02/2020	01/13/2020	01/14/2020	01/27/2020

Indicated Div: $4.28

Valuation Analysis / Institutional Holding

Valuation Analysis		Institutional Holding	
Forecast EPS	$5.44	No of Institutions	
	(01/17/2020)	450	
Market Cap	$5.1 Billion	Shares	
Book Value	$2.1 Billion	54,376,956	
Price/Book	2.37	% Held	
Price/Sales	8.93	N/A	

Business Summary: REITs (MIC: 5.3.1 SIC: 6798 NAIC: 525930)

Life Storage is a self-administered and self-managed real estate investment company that acquires, owns and manages self-storage properties. Co. owns its assets and conducts its operations through Life Storage LP (the Operating Partnership), and subsidiaries of the Operating Partnership. In addition, Co. has an ownership interest in and/or manages self-storage properties in various states under the name Life Storage®. Co.'s self-storage facilities provide storage space to residential and commercial users on a month-to-month basis. Individual storage spaces are secured by a lock furnished by the customer to provide the customer with control of access to the space.

Recent Developments: For the quarter ended Sep 30 2019, net income increased 240.7% to US$140.7 million from US$41.3 million in the year-earlier quarter. Revenues were US$145.6 million, up 2.9% from US$141.5 million the year before. Revenues from property income fell 0.2% to US$128.6 million from US$128.8 million in the corresponding quarter a year earlier.

Prospects: Our evaluation of Life Storage Inc. as of October 4th, 2019 is the result of our systematic analysis on three basic characteristics: earnings strength, relative valuation, and recent stock price movement. The company has produced a positive trend in earnings per share over the past 5 quarters. However, recent analyst estimates for the company have been mixed and LSI has posted results that fell short of analysts' expectations. Based on operating earnings yield, the company is fairly valued when compared to all of the companies we cover. Share price changes over the past year indicates that LSI will perform well over the near term.

Financial Data

(US$ in Thousands)	9 Mos	6 Mos	3 Mos	12/31/2018	12/31/2017	12/31/2016	12/31/2015	12/31/2014
Earnings Per Share	6.58	4.47	4.44	4.43	2.07	1.96	3.16	2.67
Cash Flow Per Share	5.99	5.81	5.75	5.64	5.36	5.21	5.26	4.42
Tang Book Value Per Share	45.41	43.42	43.54	44.14	43.57	44.96	32.75	28.61
Dividends Per Share	4.000	4.000	4.000	4.000	3.950	3.700	3.200	2.720
Dividend Payout %	60.79	89.49	90.09	90.29	190.82	188.78	101.27	101.87
Income Statement								
Total Revenue	427,186	281,552	136,522	550,850	529,750	462,608	366,602	326,080
EBITDA	278,250	112,052	52,543	380,246	299,624	262,497	206,481	174,200
Depn & Amortn	9,000	1,846	903	106,151	131,774	126,769	59,690	52,691
Income Before Taxes	213,251	73,679	33,826	203,436	93,495	81,291	109,672	86,971
Net Income	215,198	75,196	34,454	206,590	96,365	85,225	112,524	88,531
Average Shares	46,657	46,631	46,636	46,597	46,490	43,407	35,601	33,191
Balance Sheet								
Current Assets	37,834	65,414	30,222	29,622	24,857	37,026	20,747	21,417
Total Assets	4,188,740	4,034,777	3,958,803	3,892,212	3,876,774	3,857,984	2,122,172	1,854,800
Current Liabilities	99,337	90,344	77,513	96,637	102,315	84,832	55,350	50,841
Long-Term Obligations	1,917,640	1,869,083	1,800,548	1,714,122	1,726,763	1,653,552	830,993	801,127
Total Liabilities	2,053,422	1,992,857	1,911,912	1,834,475	1,848,451	1,769,490	919,857	878,931
Stockholders' Equity	2,135,318	2,041,920	2,046,891	2,057,737	2,028,323	2,088,494	1,202,315	975,869
Shares Outstanding	46,656	46,650	46,632	46,617	46,552	46,454	36,710	34,105
Statistical Record								
Return on Assets %	7.63	5.28	5.29	5.32	2.49	2.84	5.66	5.18
Return on Equity %	14.84	10.29	10.19	10.11	4.68	5.17	10.33	9.59
EBITDA Margin %	65.14	39.80	38.49	69.03	56.56	56.74	56.32	53.42
Net Margin %	50.38	26.71	25.24	37.50	18.19	18.42	30.69	27.15
Asset Turnover	0.14	0.14	0.14	0.14	0.14	0.15	0.18	0.19
Current Ratio	0.38	0.72	0.39	0.31	0.24	0.44	0.37	0.42
Debt to Equity	0.90	0.92	0.88	0.83	0.85	0.79	0.69	0.82
Price Range	105.96-89.73	102.24-89.73	102.24-83.52	102.24-76.97	91.12-70.59	117.95-79.15	110.00-86.13	88.94-63.30
P/E Ratio	16.10-13.64	22.87-20.07	23.03-18.81	23.08-17.37	44.02-34.10	60.18-40.38	34.81-27.26	33.31-23.71
Average Yield %	4.11	4.16	4.22	4.38	4.89	3.73	3.40	3.55

Address: 6467 Main Street, Williamsville, NY 14221 **Telephone:** 716-633-1850 **Fax:** 716-633-1860	**Web Site:** www.unclebobs.com **Officers:** Mark G. Barberio - Chairman Joseph V. Saffire - Chief Executive Officer, Chief Investment Officer	**Auditors:** Ernst & Young LLP **Investor Contact:** 716-633-1850 **Transfer Agents:** American Stock Transfer & Trust Company, Brooklyn, NY

LILLY (ELI) & CO

Exchange	Symbol	Price	52Wk Range	Yield	P/E
NYS	LLY	$131.43 (12/31/2019)	132.43-106.79	2.25	15.99

*7 Year Price Score 120.09 *NYSE Composite Index=100 *12 Month Price Score 96.65

Interim Earnings (Per Share)

Qtr.	Mar	Jun	Sep	Dec
2016	0.41	0.71	0.73	0.73
2017	(0.10)	0.95	0.53	(1.56)
2018	1.16	(0.25)	1.12	1.10
2019	4.31	1.44	1.37	...

Interim Dividends (Per Share)

Amt	Decl	Ex	Rec	Pay
0.645Q	05/06/2019	05/16/2019	05/17/2019	06/10/2019
0.645Q	06/19/2019	08/14/2019	08/15/2019	09/10/2019
0.645Q	10/21/2019	11/14/2019	11/15/2019	12/10/2019
0.74Q	12/16/2019	02/13/2020	02/14/2020	03/10/2020

Indicated Div: $2.96 (Div. Reinv. Plan)

Valuation Analysis

Forecast EPS	$5.82
	(01/16/2020)
Market Cap	$126.2 Billion
Book Value	$3.4 Billion
Price/Book	37.30
Price/Sales	5.57

Institutional Holding

No of Institutions	2125
Shares	917,603,520
% Held	66.66

Business Summary: Pharmaceuticals (MIC: 4.1.1 SIC: 2834 NAIC: 325412)

Eli Lilly and Company is engaged in discovering, developing, manufacturing, and marketing products in two business segments: human pharmaceutical products; and animal health products. Co.'s human pharmaceutical products include: cardiovascular, endocrinology, immunology, neuroscience and oncology products. Co.'s animal health products are comprised of products for animals, among others, which include Clynav™, a vaccine to control pancreas disease in salmon; Coban®, Maxiban®, and Monteban®, anticoccidial agents for use in poultry; as well as products for companion animals, which include Comfortis®, a chewable tablet that kills fleas and prevents flea infestations on dogs.

Recent Developments: For the quarter ended Sep 30 2019, income from continuing operations increased 14.7% to US$1.25 billion from US$1.09 billion in the year-earlier quarter. Net income increased 9.1% to US$1.25 billion from US$1.15 billion in the year-earlier quarter. Revenues were US$5.48 billion, up 3.2% from US$5.31 billion the year before. Direct operating expenses rose 1.9% to US$1.18 billion from US$1.15 billion in the comparable period the year before. Indirect operating expenses increased 2.1% to US$2.87 billion from US$2.81 billion in the equivalent prior-year period.

Prospects: Our evaluation of Lilly (Eli) & Co. as of October 4th, 2019 is the result of our systematic analysis on three basic characteristics: earnings strength, relative valuation, and recent stock price movement. The company has produced a positive trend in earnings per share over the past 5 quarters. However, recent analyst estimates for the company have been unchanged, while LLY has posted results that exceeded analysts' expectations. Based on operating earnings yield, the company is fairly valued when compared to all of the companies we cover. Share price changes over the past year indicates that LLY will perform well over the near term.

Financial Data

(US$ in Thousands)	9 Mos	6 Mos	3 Mos	12/31/2018	12/31/2017	12/31/2016	12/31/2015	12/31/2014
Earnings Per Share	8.22	7.97	6.28	3.13	(0.19)	2.58	2.26	2.23
Cash Flow Per Share	4.73	5.36	5.51	5.38	5.34	4.57	2.61	4.08
Tang Book Value Per Share	N.M.	N.M.	N.M.	1.85	2.90	5.16	4.97	9.66
Dividends Per Share	2.498	2.415	2.333	2.250	2.080	2.040	2.000	1.960
Dividend Payout %	30.38	30.30	37.14	71.88	...	79.07	88.50	87.89
Income Statement								
Total Revenue	16,205,500	10,728,900	5,092,200	24,555,700	22,871,300	21,222,100	19,958,700	19,615,600
EBITDA	4,732,200	2,948,300	1,143,500	4,786,100	3,018,200	4,166,700	3,581,800	3,787,200
Depn & Amortn	891,900	603,800	356,500	879,600	763,100	716,200	717,600	759,100
Income Before Taxes	3,602,800	2,197,000	731,100	3,795,700	2,197,400	3,374,000	2,790,000	3,000,300
Income Taxes	460,600	308,700	170,000	563,700	2,401,500	636,400	381,600	609,800
Net Income	6,822,700	5,568,800	4,241,600	3,232,000	(204,100)	2,737,600	2,408,400	2,390,500
Average Shares	918,500	924,600	984,000	1,033,667	1,052,023	1,061,825	1,065,720	1,074,286
Balance Sheet								
Current Assets	12,661,800	13,454,500	12,597,500	20,549,600	19,202,100	15,101,400	12,573,600	12,179,800
Total Assets	37,893,100	38,666,400	38,006,800	43,908,400	44,981,000	38,805,900	35,568,900	37,178,200
Current Liabilities	10,828,600	11,855,400	11,236,100	11,888,100	14,535,900	10,986,600	8,229,600	11,207,500
Long-Term Obligations	13,662,200	13,717,600	13,610,200	11,639,700	9,940,500	8,367,800	7,972,400	5,367,700
Total Liabilities	34,510,600	35,885,900	35,526,500	34,079,700	33,388,800	24,798,200	20,997,600	21,805,000
Stockholders' Equity	3,382,500	2,780,500	2,480,300	9,828,700	11,592,200	14,007,700	14,571,300	15,373,200
Shares Outstanding	960,046	965,432	970,830	1,057,035	1,100,008	1,100,875	1,105,267	1,110,627
Statistical Record								
Return on Assets %	19.26	19.36	15.19	7.27	N.M.	7.34	6.62	6.60
Return on Equity %	96.58	109.42	73.57	30.18	N.M.	19.11	16.09	14.49
EBITDA Margin %	29.20	27.48	22.46	19.49	13.20	19.63	17.95	19.31
Net Margin %	42.10	51.90	83.30	13.16	N.M.	12.90	12.07	12.19
Asset Turnover	0.55	0.57	0.58	0.55	0.55	0.57	0.55	0.54
Current Ratio	1.17	1.13	1.12	1.73	1.32	1.37	1.53	1.09
Debt to Equity	4.04	4.93	5.49	1.18	0.86	0.60	0.55	0.35
Price Range	131.02-105.90	131.02-85.86	131.02-75.70	118.64-74.21	87.89-74.58	84.26-65.97	89.98-68.41	72.83-50.73
P/E Ratio	15.94-12.88	16.44-10.77	20.86-12.05	37.90-23.71	...	32.66-25.57	39.81-30.27	32.66-22.75
Average Yield %	2.16	2.14	2.25	2.40	2.53	2.67	2.54	3.18

Address: Lilly Corporate Center, Indianapolis, IN 46285 Telephone: 317-276-2000	Web Site: www.lilly.com Officers: David A. Ricks - Chairman, President, Chief Executive Officer, Senior Vice President, Division Officer Michael J. (Mike) Harrington - Executive Vice President, General Counsel	Auditors: Ernst & Young LLP Investor Contact: 317-276-2000 Transfer Agents: Wells Fargo Shareowner Services, St. Paul, MN

LINCOLN NATIONAL CORP.

Exchange	Symbol	Price	52Wk Range	Yield	P/E
NYS	LNC	$59.01 (12/31/2019)	67.15-50.84	2.71	14.79

*7 Year Price Score 88.99 ***NYSE Composite Index=100** ***12 Month Price Score 92.70**

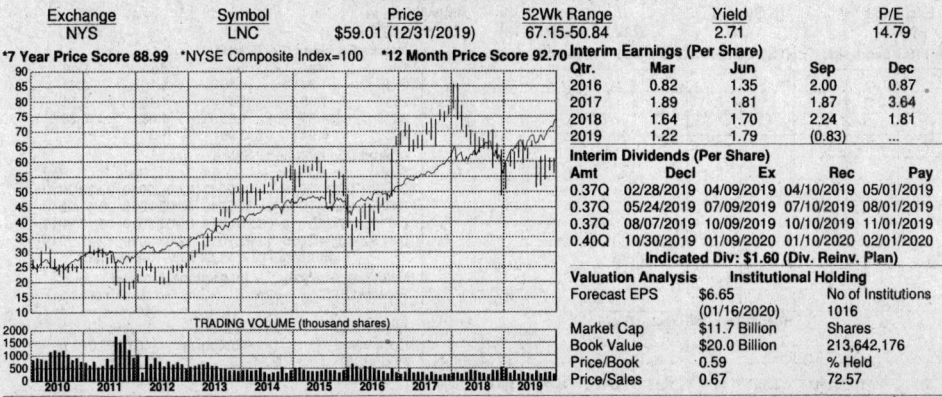

Interim Earnings (Per Share)

Qtr.	Mar	Jun	Sep	Dec
2016	0.82	1.35	2.00	0.87
2017	1.89	1.81	1.87	3.64
2018	1.64	1.70	2.24	1.81
2019	1.22	1.79	(0.83)	...

Interim Dividends (Per Share)

Amt	Decl	Ex	Rec	Pay
0.37Q	02/28/2019	04/09/2019	04/10/2019	05/01/2019
0.37Q	05/24/2019	07/09/2019	07/10/2019	08/01/2019
0.37Q	08/07/2019	10/09/2019	10/10/2019	11/01/2019
0.40Q	10/30/2019	01/09/2020	01/10/2020	02/01/2020

Indicated Div: $1.60 (Div. Reinv. Plan)

Valuation Analysis		Institutional Holding	
Forecast EPS	$6.65	No of Institutions	1016
	(01/16/2020)		
Market Cap	$11.7 Billion	Shares	
Book Value	$20.0 Billion	213,642,176	
Price/Book	0.59	% Held	
Price/Sales	0.67	72.57	

Business Summary: Life & Health (MIC: 5.2.2 SIC: 6311 NAIC: 524113)

Lincoln National is a holding company. Co. operates multiple insurance and retirement businesses through its subsidiary companies. Co. sells a range of wealth protection, accumulation and retirement income products and solutions. These products include fixed and indexed annuities, variable annuities, universal life insurance (UL), variable universal life insurance, linked-benefit UL, indexed universal life insurance, term life insurance, employer-sponsored retirement plans and services, and group life, disability and dental. Co. provides products and services through its Annuities, Retirement Plan Services, Life Insurance and Group Protection segments.

Recent Developments: For the quarter ended Sep 30 2019, net loss amounted to US$161.0 million versus net income of US$490.0 million in the year-earlier quarter. Revenues were US$4.64 billion, up 8.8% from US$4.26 billion the year before. Net premiums earned were US$1.33 billion versus US$1.32 billion in the prior-year quarter, an increase of 0.2%. Net investment income fell 2.8% to US$1.24 billion from US$1.27 billion a year ago.

Prospects: Our evaluation of Lincoln National Corp. (ID) as of October 4th, 2019 is the result of our systematic analysis on three basic characteristics: earnings strength, relative valuation, and recent stock price movement. The company has generated a negative trend in earnings per share over the past 5 quarters. In addition, recent analyst estimates for the company have been reduced and LNC has posted results that fell short of analysts' expectations. Based on operating earnings yield, the company is undervalued when compared to all of the companies we cover. Share price changes over the past year indicates that LNC will perform poorly over the near term.

Financial Data
(US$ in Thousands)

	9 Mos	6 Mos	3 Mos	12/31/2018	12/31/2017	12/31/2016	12/31/2015	12/31/2014
Earnings Per Share	3.99	7.06	6.97	7.40	9.22	5.03	4.51	5.67
Cash Flow Per Share	(9.78)	(6.21)	2.31	9.00	3.55	5.42	8.95	9.68
Tang Book Value Per Share	91.87	83.06	72.12	61.05	73.15	53.92	46.52	52.49
Dividends Per Share	1.440	1.400	1.360	1.320	1.160	1.000	0.800	0.640
Dividend Payout %	36.09	19.83	19.51	17.84	12.58	19.88	17.74	11.29
Income Statement								
Premium Income	4,170,000	2,845,000	1,446,000	4,601,000	3,256,000	2,987,000	3,246,000	2,988,000
Total Revenue	12,913,000	8,275,000	3,965,000	16,424,000	14,257,000	13,330,000	13,572,000	13,554,000
Benefits & Claims	6,112,000	3,610,000	1,757,000	6,786,000	5,160,000	4,692,000	5,044,000	4,679,000
Income Before Taxes	438,000	689,000	268,000	1,885,000	1,130,000	1,458,000	1,430,000	1,997,000
Income Taxes	(16,000)	73,000	16,000	244,000	(949,000)	266,000	276,000	483,000
Net Income	454,000	616,000	252,000	1,641,000	2,079,000	1,192,000	1,154,000	1,515,000
Average Shares	201,561	202,905	205,961	219,552	226,220	236,830	254,938	267,963
Balance Sheet								
Total Assets	325,278,000	322,259,000	314,299,000	298,147,000	281,763,000	261,627,000	251,937,000	253,377,000
Total Liabilities	305,279,000	303,804,000	297,882,000	283,797,000	264,441,000	247,149,000	238,320,000	237,637,000
Stockholders' Equity	19,999,000	18,455,000	16,417,000	14,350,000	17,322,000	14,478,000	13,617,000	15,740,000
Shares Outstanding	198,327	200,775	202,987	205,862	218,090	226,335	243,835	256,551
Statistical Record								
Return on Assets %	0.27	0.48	0.51	0.57	0.77	0.46	0.46	0.62
Return on Equity %	4.86	8.94	9.42	10.36	13.08	8.46	7.86	10.38
Loss Ratio %	146.57	126.89	121.51	147.49	158.48	157.08	155.39	156.59
Net Margin %	3.52	7.44	6.36	9.99	14.58	8.94	8.50	11.18
Price Range	70.58-48.79	70.58-48.79	72.22-48.79	85.91-48.79	78.54-63.23	68.48-30.78	61.65-46.07	58.80-45.67
P/E Ratio	17.69-12.23	10.00-6.91	10.36-7.00	11.61-6.59	8.52-6.86	13.61-6.12	13.67-10.22	10.37-8.05
Average Yield %	2.36	2.24	2.14	1.93	1.65	2.17	1.45	1.23

Address: 150 N. Radnor Chester Road,	Web Site: www.lfg.com	Auditors: Ernst & Young LLP
Suite A305, Radnor, PA 19087	Officers: Dennis R. Glass - President, Chief Executive	Transfer Agents: Computershare,
Telephone: 484-583-1400	Officer Lisa M. Buckingham - Executive Vice	Providence, RI
	President, Senior Vice President, Chief Brand Officer,	
	Chief People Officer, Place, Chief Human Resources	
	Officer	

LINDE PLC

Exchange	Symbol	Price	52Wk Range	Yield	P/E
NYS	LIN	$212.90 (12/31/2019)	212.90-152.29	1.64	18.45

*7 Year Price Score N/A *NYSE Composite Index=100 *12 Month Price Score 104.39

Interim Earnings (Per Share)

Qtr.	Mar	Jun	Sep	Dec
2016	1.24	1.39	1.18	1.41
2017	1.35	1.41	1.45	0.11
2018	1.59	1.65	1.58	8.29
2019	0.94	0.96	1.35	...

Interim Dividends (Per Share)

Amt	Decl	Ex	Rec	Pay
0.875Q	02/26/2019	03/07/2019	03/08/2019	03/22/2019
0.875Q	04/30/2019	05/31/2019	06/03/2019	06/17/2019
0.875Q	07/26/2019	08/30/2019	09/03/2019	09/17/2019
0.875Q	10/24/2019	12/02/2019	12/03/2019	12/17/2019

Indicated Div: $3.50 (Div. Reinv. Plan)

Valuation Analysis

		Institutional Holding
Forecast EPS	N/A	No of Institutions 1041
Market Cap	$114.5 Billion	Shares
Book Value	$49.0 Billion	403,899,072
Price/Book	2.34	% Held
Price/Sales	4.25	72.46

TRADING VOLUME (thousand shares)

Business Summary: Specialty Chemicals (MIC: 8.3.2 SIC: 2813 NAIC: 325120)

Linde is an industrial gas company. Co.'s main products in its industrial gases business are atmospheric gases (oxygen, nitrogen, argon, and rare gases) and process gases (carbon dioxide, helium, hydrogen, electronic gases, specialty gases, and acetylene). Co. also designs, engineers, and builds equipment that produces industrial gases for internal use and provides its customers a range of gas production and processing services such as olefin plants, natural gas plants, air separation plants, hydrogen and synthesis gas plants and other types of plants. The surface technologies segment supplies wear-resistant and high-temperature corrosion-resistant metallic and ceramic coatings and powders.

Recent Developments: For the quarter ended Sep 30 2019, income from continuing operations increased 52.3% to US$731.0 million from US$480.0 million in the year-earlier quarter. Net income increased 53.8% to US$738.0 million from US$480.0 million in the year-earlier quarter. Revenues were US$7.00 billion, up 132.7% from US$3.01 billion the year before. Operating income was US$1.00 billion versus US$669.0 million in the prior-year quarter, an increase of 49.5%. Direct operating expenses rose 139.2% to US$4.06 billion from US$1.70 billion in the comparable period the year before. Indirect operating expenses increased 202.5% to US$1.94 billion from US$641.0 million in the equivalent prior-year period.

Prospects: Our evaluation of Linde Plc as of October 4th, 2019 is the result of our systematic analysis on three basic characteristics: earnings strength, relative valuation, and recent stock price movement. The company has enjoyed a very positive trend in earnings per share over the past 5 quarters. However, recent analyst estimates for the company have been reduced, while LIN has posted results that exceeded analysts' expectations. Based on operating earnings yield, the company is overvalued when compared to all of the companies we cover. Share price changes over the past year indicates that LIN will perform well over the near term.

Financial Data

(US$ in Thousands)	9 Mos	6 Mos	3 Mos	12/31/2018	12/31/2017	12/31/2016	12/31/2015	12/31/2014
Earnings Per Share	11.54	11.77	12.46	13.11	4.32	5.21	5.35	5.73
Cash Flow Per Share	9.73	7.83	7.39	11.06	10.62	9.68	9.34	9.81
Tang Book Value Per Share	12.75	14.43	15.47	15.53	7.78	4.64	2.93	6.56
Dividends Per Share	3.450	3.400	3.350	3.300	3.150	3.000	...	...
Dividend Payout %	29.90	28.89	26.89	25.17	72.92	57.58	...	...
Income Statement								
Total Revenue	21,148,000	14,148,000	6,944,000	14,900,000	11,437,000	10,534,000	10,776,000	12,273,000
EBITDA	2,297,000	1,297,000	604,000	7,081,000	3,632,000	3,360,000	3,427,000	3,778,000
Depn & Amortn	12,000	10,000	10,000	1,830,000	1,184,000	1,122,000	1,106,000	1,170,000
Income Before Taxes	2,255,000	1,254,000	571,000	5,049,000	2,287,000	2,048,000	2,160,000	2,395,000
Income Taxes	607,000	309,000	140,000	817,000	1,026,000	551,000	612,000	691,000
Net Income	1,774,000	1,039,000	517,000	4,381,000	1,247,000	1,500,000	1,547,000	1,694,000
Average Shares	543,616	546,488	549,147	334,127	289,114	287,757	289,055	295,608
Balance Sheet								
Current Assets	9,812,000	10,681,000	15,088,000	17,272,000	3,285,000	2,880,000	2,626,000	2,839,000
Total Assets	84,394,000	87,189,000	91,641,000	93,386,000	20,436,000	19,332,000	18,319,000	19,802,000
Current Liabilities	10,883,000	10,521,000	11,140,000	12,956,000	3,307,000	2,478,000	1,893,000	2,490,000
Long-Term Obligations	10,567,000	12,255,000	12,190,000	12,288,000	7,783,000	8,917,000	8,975,000	8,669,000
Total Liabilities	35,441,000	36,625,000	40,466,000	41,790,000	14,418,000	14,311,000	13,930,000	14,179,000
Stockholders' Equity	48,953,000	50,564,000	51,175,000	51,596,000	6,018,000	5,021,000	4,389,000	5,623,000
Shares Outstanding	537,857	541,353	543,685	547,241	286,776	284,900	284,879	289,261
Statistical Record								
Return on Assets %	9.11	8.37	7.90	7.70	6.27	7.95	8.12	8.46
Return on Equity %	17.22	15.83	15.42	15.21	22.59	31.79	30.90	27.70
EBITDA Margin %	10.86	9.17	8.70	47.52	31.76	31.90	31.80	30.78
Net Margin %	8.39	7.34	7.45	29.40	10.90	14.24	14.36	13.80
Asset Turnover	0.52	0.43	0.34	0.26	0.58	0.56	0.57	0.61
Current Ratio	0.90	1.02	1.35	1.33	0.99	1.16	1.39	1.14
Debt to Equity	0.22	0.24	0.24	0.24	1.29	1.78	2.04	1.54
Price Range	206.82-148.13	204.02-148.13	176.63-148.13	166.85-148.13	...	...	...	...
P/E Ratio	17.92-12.84	17.33-12.59	14.18-11.89	12.73-11.30	...	...	...	...
Average Yield %	1.94	1.98	2.06	2.09	...	...	...	...

Address: The Priestley Centre, 10 Priestley Road, Surrey Research Park, Guildford, 06810-6268 **Telephone:** 148-324-2200	**Web Site:** www.linde.com **Officers:** Wolfgang Reitzle - Chairman Stephen F. Angel - Chairman, Chief Executive Officer	**Auditors:** PricewaterhouseCoopers LLP **Investor Contact:** 203-837-2210 **Transfer Agents:** Registrar and Transfer Company, Cranford, NJ

LINDSAY CORP

Exchange	Symbol	Price	52Wk Range	Yield	P/E	Div Acheiver
NYS	LNN	$95.99 (12/31/2019)	98.44-77.16	1.29	111.62	16 Years

*7 Year Price Score 87.90 ***NYSE Composite Index=100** ***12 Month Price Score 97.87**

Interim Earnings (Per Share)

Qtr.	Nov	Feb	May	Aug
2016-17	0.08	0.47	1.02	0.59
2017-18	0.30	0.16	0.96	0.46
2018-19	0.11	(0.32)	0.27	0.14
2019-20	0.77	...	...	...

Interim Dividends (Per Share)

Amt	Decl	Ex	Rec	Pay
0.31Q	04/01/2019	05/16/2019	05/17/2019	05/31/2019
0.31Q	07/01/2019	08/15/2019	08/16/2019	08/30/2019
0.31Q	10/30/2019	11/14/2019	11/15/2019	11/29/2019
0.31Q	01/13/2020	02/13/2020	02/14/2020	02/28/2020

Indicated Div: $1.24

Valuation Analysis / Institutional Holding

Forecast EPS	$2.65	No of Institutions	236
(01/17/2020)			
Market Cap	$1.0 Billion	Shares	
Book Value	$273.0 Million		16,548,697
Price/Book	3.80	% Held	
Price/Sales	2.35		99.37

Business Summary: Industrial Machinery & Equipment (MIC: 7.2.1 SIC: 3523 NAIC: 333111)

Lindsay is engaged in providing a variety of proprietary water management and road infrastructure products and services. Co. has operations which are categorized into two key reporting segments, Irrigation and Infrastructure. Co.'s irrigation segment includes the manufacture and marketing of center pivot, lateral move, hose reel irrigation systems, and repair and replacement parts for its irrigation systems and controls. Co.'s infrastructure segment includes the manufacture and marketing of moveable barriers, specialty barriers, crash cushions and end terminals, road marking and road safety equipment, large diameter steel tubing, and railroad signals and structures.

Recent Developments: For the quarter ended Nov 30 2019, net income increased 588.5% to US$8.3 million from US$1.2 million in the year-earlier quarter. Revenues were US$109.4 million, down 2.3% from US$112.0 million the year before. Operating income was US$12.3 million versus US$2.0 million in the prior-year quarter, an increase of 501.8%. Direct operating expenses declined 9.6% to US$75.3 million from US$83.3 million in the comparable period the year before. Indirect operating expenses decreased 18.1% to US$21.8 million from US$26.6 million in the equivalent prior-year period.

Prospects: Our evaluation of Lindsay Corp. as of October 4th, 2019 is the result of our systematic analysis on three basic characteristics: earnings strength, relative valuation, and recent stock price movement. The company has generated a negative trend in earnings per share over the past 5 quarters. However, recent analyst estimates for the company have been unchanged while LNN has posted results that fell short of analysts' expectations. Based on operating earnings yield, the company is overvalued when compared to all of the companies we cover. Share price changes over the past year indicates that LNN will perform poorly over the near term.

Financial Data

(US$ in Thousands)	3 Mos	08/31/2019	08/31/2018	08/31/2017	08/31/2016	08/31/2015	08/31/2014	08/31/2013
Earnings Per Share	0.86	0.20	1.88	2.17	1.85	2.22	4.00	5.47
Cash Flow Per Share	1.82	0.35	3.16	3.70	3.02	4.12	7.15	4.48
Tang Book Value Per Share	17.10	16.63	17.18	14.03	12.00	14.16	25.21	23.87
Dividends Per Share	1.240	1.240	1.210	1.170	1.130	1.090	0.920	0.475
Dividend Payout %	144.19	620.00	64.36	53.92	61.08	49.10	23.00	8.68
Income Statement								
Total Revenue	109,393	444,072	547,705	517,985	516,411	560,181	617,933	690,848
EBITDA	16,574	15,572	49,400	51,494	45,594	60,446	88,913	116,915
Depn & Amortn	4,748	11,100	12,500	12,200	12,200	11,700	10,800	9,800
Income Before Taxes	11,255	2,107	33,853	35,715	29,288	46,751	78,655	107,307
Income Taxes	2,910	(65)	13,576	12,536	9,021	20,442	27,143	36,737
Net Income	8,345	2,172	20,277	23,179	20,267	26,309	51,512	70,570
Average Shares	10,828	10,810	10,772	10,694	10,930	11,855	12,882	12,901
Balance Sheet								
Current Assets	316,631	313,490	331,051	292,934	292,124	322,167	374,058	368,791
Total Assets	526,811	500,314	500,256	506,032	499,565	536,468	526,551	512,296
Current Liabilities	84,801	82,131	80,094	92,037	87,870	95,112	116,367	102,092
Long-Term Obligations	115,805	115,846	116,570	116,775	116,976	117,173	...	...
Total Liabilities	253,811	232,105	223,390	235,977	247,998	247,908	143,904	131,658
Stockholders' Equity	273,000	268,209	276,866	270,055	251,567	288,560	382,647	380,638
Shares Outstanding	10,814	10,787	10,758	10,697	10,630	11,290	12,440	12,873
Statistical Record								
Return on Assets %	1.81	0.43	4.03	4.61	3.90	4.95	9.92	15.21
Return on Equity %	3.39	0.80	7.41	8.89	7.48	7.84	13.50	20.41
EBITDA Margin %	15.15	3.51	9.02	9.94	8.83	10.79	14.39	16.92
Net Margin %	7.63	0.49	3.70	4.47	3.92	4.70	8.34	10.21
Asset Turnover	0.86	0.89	1.09	1.03	0.99	1.05	1.19	1.49
Current Ratio	3.73	3.82	4.13	3.18	3.32	3.39	3.21	3.61
Debt to Equity	0.42	0.43	0.42	0.43	0.46	0.41	...	...
Price Range	103.55-77.16	108.07-77.16	101.96-84.54	94.74-69.30	78.57-64.06	89.70-73.48	92.93-72.00	94.57-65.36
P/E Ratio	120.41-89.72	540.35-385.80	54.23-44.97	43.66-31.94	42.47-34.63	40.41-33.10	23.23-18.00	17.29-11.95
Average Yield %	1.39	0.41	1.37	1.32	1.43	1.60	1.33	1.12	0.60

Address: 18135 Burke Street, Suite 100, Omaha, NE 68022	Web Site: www.lindsay.com	Auditors: KPMG LLP
Telephone: 402-829-6800	Officers: Michael C. Nahl - Chairman Timothy L. Hassinger - President, Chief Executive Officer	Investor Contact: 402-827-6579
Fax: 402-829-6834		Transfer Agents: Wells Fargo Shareowner Services, St. Paul, MN

LITHIA MOTORS INC

Exchange	Symbol	Price	52Wk Range	Yield	P/E
NYS	LAD	$147.00 (12/31/2019)	163.68-76.33	0.82	13.08

*7 Year Price Score 107.98 ***NYSE Composite Index=100** ***12 Month Price Score 124.53**

Interim Earnings (Per Share)

Qtr.	Mar	Jun	Sep	Dec
2016	1.55	2.01	2.14	2.03
2017	2.01	2.12	2.07	3.56
2018	2.07	2.44	3.84	2.55
2019	2.42	2.63	3.64	...

Interim Dividends (Per Share)

Amt	Decl	Ex	Rec	Pay
0.29Q	02/11/2019	03/07/2019	03/08/2019	03/22/2019
0.30Q	04/24/2019	05/09/2019	05/10/2019	05/24/2019
0.30Q	07/24/2019	08/08/2019	08/09/2019	08/23/2019
0.30Q	10/23/2019	11/07/2019	11/08/2019	11/22/2019

Indicated Div: $1.20

Valuation Analysis | **Institutional Holding**

Forecast EPS	$11.74	No of Institutions	413
	(01/17/2020)		
Market Cap	$3.4 Billion	Shares	
Book Value	$1.4 Billion		30,800,632
Price/Book	2.51	% Held	
Price/Sales	0.28		92.98

Business Summary: Retail - Automotive (MIC: 2.1.4 SIC: 5511 NAIC: 441110)

Lithia Motors is an automotive retailer in the U.S. Co. operates in three segments: Domestic, which is comprised of retail automotive franchises that sell new vehicles manufactured by Chrysler, General Motors and Ford; Import, which is comprised of retail automotive franchises that sell new vehicles manufactured primarily by Honda, Toyota, Subaru, Nissan and Volkswagen; and Luxury, which is comprised of retail automotive franchises that sell new vehicles manufactured primarily by BMW, Mercedes-Benz and Lexus. The franchises in each segment also sell used vehicles, parts and automotive services, and automotive finance and insurance products.

Recent Developments: For the quarter ended Sep 30 2019, net income decreased 8.5% to US$85.2 million from US$93.1 million in the year-earlier quarter. Revenues were US$3.33 billion, up 7.8% from US$3.09 billion the year before. Operating income was US$146.8 million versus US$137.6 million in the prior-year quarter, an increase of 6.7%. Direct operating expenses rose 7.5% to US$2.82 billion from US$2.63 billion in the comparable period the year before. Indirect operating expenses increased 10.8% to US$364.1 million from US$328.6 million in the equivalent prior-year period.

Prospects: Our evaluation of Lithia Motors Inc. as of October 4th, 2019 is the result of our systematic analysis on three basic characteristics: earnings strength, relative valuation, and recent stock price movement. The company has managed to produce a neutral trend in earnings per share over the past 5 quarters. However, recent analyst estimates for the company have been raised and LAD has posted results that exceeded analysts' expectations. Based on operating earnings yield, the company is undervalued when compared to all of the companies we cover. Share price changes over the past year indicates that LAD will perform over the near term.

Financial Data

(US$ in Thousands)	9 Mos	6 Mos	3 Mos	12/31/2018	12/31/2017	12/31/2016	12/31/2015	12/31/2014
Earnings Per Share	11.24	11.44	11.25	10.86	9.75	7.72	6.91	5.26
Cash Flow Per Share	25.60	22.55	23.62	21.30	5.94	3.40	2.82	1.16
Tang Book Value Per Share	38.90	35.23	34.36	20.59	25.63	18.58	17.44	12.31
Dividends Per Share	1.180	1.170	1.160	1.140	1.060	0.950	0.760	0.610
Dividend Payout %	10.50	10.23	10.31	10.50	10.87	12.31	11.00	11.60
Income Statement								
Total Revenue	9,403,800	6,071,400	2,849,700	11,821,400	10,086,510	8,678,157	7,864,252	5,390,326
EBITDA	442,100	271,100	131,000	531,200	478,903	381,630	343,329	261,461
Depn & Amortn	60,900	40,000	19,800	75,400	57,722	49,369	41,600	26,363
Income Before Taxes	280,700	163,300	77,800	337,500	347,069	283,523	262,704	210,495
Income Taxes	77,200	45,000	21,400	71,800	101,852	86,465	79,705	74,955
Net Income	203,500	118,300	56,400	265,700	245,217	197,058	182,999	138,720
Average Shares	23,400	23,500	23,200	25,500	25,145	25,521	26,490	26,382
Balance Sheet								
Current Assets	2,929,900	3,031,500	3,027,900	2,991,400	2,782,782	2,287,194	1,878,865	1,615,509
Total Assets	5,737,500	5,774,600	5,692,000	5,384,000	4,683,066	3,844,150	3,227,299	2,880,932
Current Liabilities	2,483,400	2,605,300	2,585,200	2,493,500	2,300,981	1,921,994	1,590,825	1,442,600
Long-Term Obligations	1,287,800	1,324,100	1,295,700	1,358,200	1,028,476	769,916	606,463	609,066
Total Liabilities	4,378,300	4,499,900	4,441,500	4,186,800	3,599,848	2,933,374	2,399,135	2,207,827
Stockholders' Equity	1,359,200	1,274,700	1,250,500	1,197,200	1,083,218	910,776	828,164	673,105
Shares Outstanding	23,200	23,200	23,100	23,000	24,968	25,144	26,218	26,233
Statistical Record								
Return on Assets %	4.83	4.96	5.01	5.28	5.75	5.56	5.99	6.02
Return on Equity %	20.54	22.28	22.72	23.30	24.60	22.60	24.38	22.97
EBITDA Margin %	4.70	4.47	4.60	4.49	4.75	4.40	4.37	4.85
Net Margin %	2.16	1.95	1.98	2.25	2.43	2.27	2.33	2.57
Asset Turnover	2.27	2.22	2.23	2.35	2.37	2.45	2.57	2.34
Current Ratio	1.18	1.16	1.17	1.20	1.21	1.19	1.18	1.12
Debt to Equity	0.95	1.04	1.04	1.13	0.95	0.85	0.73	0.90
Price Range	136.44-69.15	120.57-69.15	104.70-69.15	126.57-69.15	122.28-81.12	106.67-69.23	126.06-80.98	96.37-54.17
P/E Ratio	12.14-6.15	10.54-6.04	9.31-6.15	11.65-6.37	12.54-8.32	13.82-8.97	18.24-11.72	18.32-10.30
Average Yield %	1.16	1.28	1.31	1.20	1.04	1.11	0.72	0.80

Address: 150 N. Bartlett Street, Medford, OR 97501 **Telephone:** 541-776-6401	**Web Site:** www.lithia.com **Officers:** Sidney B. DeBoer - Chairman, Executive Chairman, Chief Executive Officer, Secretary Bryan B. DeBoer - President, Chief Executive Officer, Chief Operating Officer	**Auditors:** KPMG LLP **Investor Contact:** 877-331-3084 **Transfer Agents:** Broadridge Financial Solutions, Inc., Philadelphia, PA

LIVE NATION ENTERTAINMENT INC

Exchange	Symbol	Price	52Wk Range	Yield	P/E
NYS	LYV	$71.47 (12/31/2019)	73.54-47.69	N/A	7147.00

*7 Year Price Score 156.92 *NYSE Composite Index=100 *12 Month Price Score 98.03

Interim Earnings (Per Share)

Qtr.	Mar	Jun	Sep	Dec
2016	(0.29)	0.13	0.49	(0.57)
2017	(0.22)	0.29	0.53	(1.10)
2018	(0.24)	0.24	0.70	(0.80)
2019	(0.31)	0.41	0.71	...

Interim Dividends (Per Share)

No Dividends Paid

Valuation Analysis   **Institutional Holding**

Forecast EPS	$0.10	No of Institutions	
	(01/17/2020)	594	
Market Cap	$15.3 Billion	Shares	
Book Value	$1.3 Billion	171,789,120	
Price/Book	11.87	% Held	
Price/Sales	1.36	70.35	

Business Summary: Entertainment (MIC: 2.3.2 SIC: 7929 NAIC: 711410)

Live Nation Entertainment is a live entertainment company. Co. is a producer of live music concerts. Co. owns, operates, has booking rights for venues, including House of Blues® music venues and locations such as The Fillmore® in San Francisco, the Hollywood Palladium, the Ziggo Dome in Amsterdam, 3Arena in Ireland, Royal Arena in Copenhagen and Spark Arena in New Zealand. Co. is also artist management company. Co.'s artist management companies manage music artists and acts across all music genres. Co.'s segments are: Concerts, which is involved in the promotion of live music events; Sponsorship and Advertising; and Ticketing, which sells tickets for events on behalf of its clients.

Recent Developments: For the quarter ended Sep 30 2019, net income increased 5.9% to US$194.0 million from US$183.2 million in the year-earlier quarter. Revenues were US$3.77 billion, down 1.6% from US$3.84 billion the year before. Operating income was US$260.0 million versus US$234.2 million in the prior-year quarter, an increase of 11.0%. Direct operating expenses declined 4.2% to US$2.80 billion from US$2.92 billion in the comparable period the year before. Indirect operating expenses increased 5.4% to US$713.2 million from US$676.7 million in the equivalent prior-year period.

Prospects: Our evaluation of Live Nation Entertainment, Inc. as of October 4th, 2019 is the result of our systematic analysis on three basic characteristics: earnings strength, relative valuation, and recent stock price movement. The company has produced a positive trend in earnings per share over the past 5 quarters. However, recent analyst estimates for the company have been mixed and LYV has posted results that exceeded analysts' expectations. Based on operating earnings yield, the company is overvalued when compared to all of the companies we cover. Share price changes over the past year indicates that LYV will perform over the near term.

Financial Data
(US$ in Thousands)

	9 Mos	6 Mos	3 Mos	12/31/2018	12/31/2017	12/31/2016	12/31/2015	12/31/2014
Earnings Per Share	0.01	...	(0.17)	(0.09)	(0.48)	(0.23)	(0.33)	(0.49)
Cash Flow Per Share	3.41	3.41	3.04	4.54	3.04	2.95	1.49	1.35
Income Statement								
Total Revenue	8,658,521	4,884,837	1,727,828	10,787,800	10,337,448	8,354,934	7,245,731	6,866,964
EBITDA	805,677	399,389	95,689	443,278	240,098	309,349	238,352	125,888
Depn & Amortn	399,464	247,833	116,149	185,376	149,634	139,288	134,148	127,168
Income Before Taxes	308,548	84,615	(54,427)	128,358	(10,541)	66,128	4,851	(103,986)
Income Taxes	59,988	32,708	3,958	40,765	(17,154)	28,029	22,122	4,630
Net Income	229,836	50,911	(52,444)	60,249	(6,015)	2,942	(32,508)	(90,807)
Average Shares	218,957	219,977	208,908	207,441	204,923	202,076	200,973	198,874
Balance Sheet								
Current Assets	3,849,723	4,284,887	4,424,874	3,848,074	3,152,742	2,673,551	2,288,315	2,267,691
Total Assets	9,967,133	10,529,387	10,302,533	8,496,886	7,504,263	6,764,266	6,156,241	5,988,361
Current Liabilities	3,959,372	4,605,723	4,688,882	3,749,866	3,577,000	2,460,344	2,101,206	2,010,781
Long-Term Obligations	2,694,934	2,708,642	2,715,966	2,732,878	1,952,366	2,259,736	2,002,662	2,015,915
Total Liabilities	8,679,860	9,355,244	9,259,325	7,397,905	6,323,067	5,638,250	4,919,288	4,691,407
Stockholders' Equity	1,287,273	1,174,143	1,043,208	1,098,981	1,181,196	1,126,016	1,236,953	1,296,954
Shares Outstanding	213,715	213,147	211,629	210,126	208,075	204,067	202,483	201,193
Statistical Record								
Return on Assets %	0.89	0.78	0.43	0.75	N.M.	0.05	N.M.	N.M.
Return on Equity %	6.29	6.48	3.83	5.28	N.M.	0.25	N.M.	N.M.
EBITDA Margin %	9.31	8.18	5.54	4.11	2.32	3.70	3.29	1.83
Net Margin %	2.65	1.04	N.M.	0.56	N.M.	0.04	N.M.	N.M.
Asset Turnover	1.22	1.16	1.14	1.35	1.45	1.29	1.19	1.18
Current Ratio	0.97	0.93	0.94	1.03	0.88	1.09	1.09	1.13
Debt to Equity	2.09	2.31	2.60	2.49	1.65	2.01	1.62	1.55
Price Range	73.54-46.20	67.22-46.20	64.28-36.61	57.43-36.61	46.41-27.29	28.78-19.36	29.21-23.58	27.36-19.76

Address: 9348 Civic Center Drive, Beverly Hills, CA 90210 **Telephone:** 310-867-7000	**Web Site:** www.livenationentertainment.com **Officers:** Gregory B. Maffei - Chairman Joe Berchtold - President, Chief Operating Officer	**Auditors:** Ernst & Young LLP **Investor Contact:** 310-867-7000 **Transfer Agents:** Computershare, Providence, RI

LIVERAMP HOLDINGS INC

Exchange	Symbol	Price	52Wk Range	Yield	P/E
NYS	RAMP	$48.07 (12/31/2019)	62.04-37.60	N/A	3.92

*7 Year Price Score 138.64 *NYSE Composite Index=100 *12 Month Price Score 92.01

Interim Earnings (Per Share)

Qtr.	Jun	Sep	Dec	Mar
2016-17	0.05	0.09	0.01	(0.10)
2017-18	(0.02)	(0.04)	0.28	0.07
2018-19	(0.04)	0.27	13.65	(0.19)
2019-20	(0.61)	(0.59)	...	...

Interim Dividends (Per Share)

No Dividends Paid

Valuation Analysis

		Institutional Holding	
Forecast EPS	$-0.69	No of Institutions	
	(01/15/2020)	362	
Market Cap	$3.2 Billion	Shares	
Book Value	$1.2 Billion	104,393,728	
Price/Book	2.74	% Held	
Price/Sales	9.81	N/A	

Business Summary: IT Services (MIC: 6.3.1 SIC: 7374 NAIC: 541519)

LiveRamp Holdings is a global technology company. Co. provides enterprise customer management platform that help organizations utilize customer data to deliver products and experiences. A main component of Co.'s platform is the omnichannel, deterministic identity graph. Utilizing Co.'s identity graph, the LiveRamp platform resolves a customer's data (first-, second-, or third-party) to consumer identifiers that represent real people in a way that protects consumer privacy.

Recent Developments: For the quarter ended Sep 30 2019, loss from continuing operations was US$40.2 million compared with a loss of US$41.2 million in the year-earlier quarter. Net loss amounted to US$40.2 million versus net income of US$20.6 million in the year-earlier quarter. Revenues were US$90.1 million, up 39.1% from US$64.8 million the year before. Operating loss was US$50.3 million versus a loss of US$38.2 million in the prior-year quarter. Direct operating expenses rose 69.5% to US$41.5 million from US$24.5 million in the comparable period the year before. Indirect operating expenses increased 26.0% to US$99.0 million from US$78.5 million in the equivalent prior-year period.

Prospects: Our evaluation of LiveRamp Holdings Inc. as of October 4th, 2019 is the result of our systematic analysis on three basic characteristics: earnings strength, relative valuation, and recent stock price movement. The company has produced a positive trend in earnings per share over the past 5 quarters. However, recent analyst estimates for the company have been mixed and RAMP has posted results that exceeded analysts' expectations. Based on operating earnings yield, the company is overvalued when compared to all of the companies we cover. Share price changes over the past year indicates that RAMP will perform in line with the market over the near term.

Financial Data

(US$ in Thousands)	6 Mos	3 Mos	03/31/2019	03/31/2018	03/31/2017	03/31/2016	03/31/2015	03/31/2014
Earnings Per Share	12.26	13.12	13.71	0.29	0.05	0.09	(0.14)	0.11
Cash Flow Per Share	(0.25)	(0.50)	(0.03)	1.42	1.49	1.46	1.36	2.21
Tang Book Value Per Share	12.01	14.77	15.94	0.98	0.60	1.57	0.37	3.47
Income Statement								
Total Revenue	172,654	82,511	285,620	917,406	880,247	850,088	1,020,059	1,097,545
EBITDA	(77,586)	(37,193)	(163,756)	54,340	58,923	27,989	61,271	108,401
Depn & Amortn	10,400	5,300	15,600	43,500	42,900	40,600	63,200	58,300
Income Before Taxes	(87,986)	(42,493)	(179,356)	709	8,642	(20,280)	(11,979)	38,430
Income Taxes	(5,644)	(353)	(45,409)	(22,771)	4,534	(11,632)	(2,832)	29,627
Net Income	(82,342)	(42,140)	1,028,547	23,480	4,108	6,703	(11,031)	8,863
Average Shares	67,864	68,906	75,020	81,516	79,848	77,616	77,106	76,954
Balance Sheet								
Current Assets	947,139	1,138,208	1,192,076	360,345	368,519	376,010	414,054	665,525
Total Assets	1,363,230	1,439,304	1,472,911	1,209,253	1,234,538	1,149,849	1,322,424	1,323,301
Current Liabilities	123,423	121,110	95,118	178,355	230,213	224,000	248,015	249,469
Long-Term Obligations	...	...	...	227,837	189,241	157,897	254,539	289,043
Total Liabilities	176,872	167,147	142,079	460,158	495,558	450,881	619,167	640,444
Stockholders' Equity	1,186,358	1,272,157	1,330,832	749,095	738,980	698,968	703,257	682,857
Shares Outstanding	67,537	68,650	68,697	77,774	78,292	77,359	77,836	76,640
Statistical Record								
Return on Assets %	72.80	75.93	76.70	1.92	0.34	0.54	N.M.	0.71
Return on Equity %	95.39	99.23	98.90	3.16	0.57	0.95	N.M.	1.36
EBITDA Margin %	N.M.	N.M.	N.M.	5.92	6.69	3.29	6.01	9.88
Net Margin %	N.M.	N.M.	360.11	2.56	0.47	0.79	N.M.	0.81
Asset Turnover	0.26	0.23	0.21	0.75	0.74	0.69	0.77	0.87
Current Ratio	7.67	9.40	12.53	2.02	1.60	1.68	1.67	2.67
Debt to Equity	...	...	...	0.30	0.26	0.23	0.36	0.42
Price Range	62.04-36.80	62.04-34.21	62.04-21.64	32.34-21.85	29.66-19.18	22.90-16.04	35.29-16.08	38.90-18.72
P/E Ratio	5.06-3.00	4.73-2.61	4.53-1.58	111.52-75.34	593.20-383.60	254.44-178.22	...	353.64-170.18

Address: 225 Bush Street, Seventeenth Floor, San Francisco, CA 94104 **Telephone:** 866-352-3267	**Web Site:** www.liveramp.com **Officers:** Jerry D. Gramaglia - Chairman James F. Arra - President, Chief Commercial Officer	**Auditors:** KPMG LLP **Investor Contact:** 501-342-1321 **Transfer Agents:** ComputerShare Investor Services, Chicago, IL

LOCKHEED MARTIN CORP

Exchange	Symbol	Price	52Wk Range	Yield	P/E	Div Acheiver
NYS	LMT	$389.38 (12/31/2019)	397.04-258.08	2.47	18.52	16 Years

*7 Year Price Score 119.41 *NYSE Composite Index=100 *12 Month Price Score 105.27

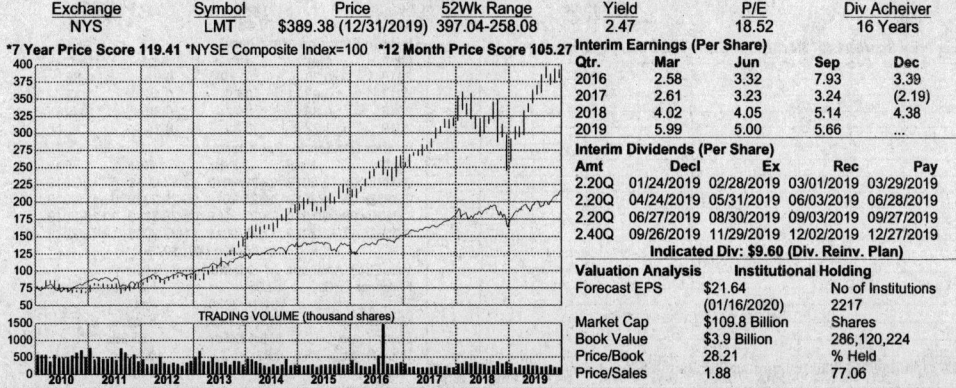

Interim Earnings (Per Share)

Qtr.	Mar	Jun	Sep	Dec
2016	2.58	3.32	7.93	3.39
2017	2.61	3.23	3.24	(2.19)
2018	4.02	4.05	5.14	4.38
2019	5.99	5.00	5.66	...

Interim Dividends (Per Share)

Amt	Decl	Ex	Rec	Pay
2.20Q	01/24/2019	02/28/2019	03/01/2019	03/29/2019
2.20Q	04/24/2019	05/31/2019	06/03/2019	06/28/2019
2.20Q	06/27/2019	08/30/2019	09/03/2019	09/27/2019
2.40Q	09/26/2019	11/29/2019	12/02/2019	12/27/2019

Indicated Div: $9.60 (Div. Reinv. Plan)

Valuation Analysis / **Institutional Holding**

Forecast EPS	$21.64 (01/16/2020)	No of Institutions	2217
Market Cap	$109.8 Billion	Shares	
Book Value	$3.9 Billion	Shares	286,120,224
Price/Book	28.21	% Held	
Price/Sales	1.88		77.06

Business Summary: Defense (MIC: 7.1.2 SIC: 3761 NAIC: 336414)

Lockheed Martin is a security and aerospace company. Co. has four segments: Aeronautics, which researches, designs, develops, manufactures, integrates, sustains, supports and upgrades military aircraft; Missiles and Fire Control, which provides air and missile defense systems, logistics, and fire control systems, among others; Rotary and Mission Systems, which provides design, manufacture, service and support for military and commercial helicopters, radar systems, and simulation and training services, among others; and Space, which researches, designs, develops, engineers and produces satellites, space transportation systems, and strategic, strike, and defensive systems.

Recent Developments: For the quarter ended Sep 29 2019, net income increased 9.2% to US$1.61 billion from US$1.47 billion in the year-earlier quarter. Revenues were US$15.17 billion, up 6.0% from US$14.32 billion the year before. Operating income was US$2.11 billion versus US$1.96 billion in the prior-year quarter, an increase of 7.2%. Direct operating expenses rose 5.7% to US$13.11 billion from US$12.40 billion in the comparable period the year before. Indirect operating income was unchanged at US$42.0 million versus the equivalent prior-year period.

Prospects: Our evaluation of Lockheed Martin Corp. as of October 4th, 2019 is the result of our systematic analysis on three basic characteristics: earnings strength, relative valuation, and recent stock price movement. The company has managed to produce a neutral trend in earnings per share over the past 5 quarters. In addition, recent analyst estimates for the company have been mixed and LMT has posted results that exceeded analysts' expectations. Based on operating earnings yield, the company is fairly valued when compared to all of the companies we cover. Share price changes over the past year indicates that LMT will perform well over the near term.

Financial Data
(US$ in Millions)

	9 Mos	6 Mos	3 Mos	12/31/2018	12/31/2017	12/31/2016	12/31/2015	12/31/2014
Earnings Per Share	21.03	20.51	19.56	17.59	6.89	17.49	11.46	11.21
Cash Flow Per Share	28.50	20.94	14.76	11.03	22.50	17.29	16.44	12.20
Dividends Per Share	8.800	8.600	8.400	8.200	7.460	6.770	6.150	5.490
Dividend Payout %	41.84	41.93	42.94	46.62	108.27	38.71	53.66	48.97
Income Statement								
Total Revenue	43,934	28,763	14,336	53,762	51,048	47,248	46,132	45,600
EBITDA	6,772	4,527	2,393	7,667	7,115	6,764	6,492	6,592
Depn & Amortn	867	565	277	1,161	1,195	1,215	1,026	994
Income Before Taxes	5,409	3,628	1,945	5,838	5,269	4,886	5,023	5,258
Income Taxes	677	504	241	792	3,340	1,133	1,418	1,644
Net Income	4,732	3,124	1,704	5,046	2,002	5,302	3,605	3,614
Average Shares	283	283	284	286	290	303	314	322
Balance Sheet								
Current Assets	19,803	18,100	18,031	16,103	17,461	15,108	16,198	12,329
Total Assets	49,275	47,840	47,684	44,876	46,521	47,806	49,128	37,073
Current Liabilities	15,515	15,132	15,403	14,398	12,637	12,542	14,057	11,112
Long-Term Obligations	12,652	12,637	12,621	12,604	13,513	14,282	14,305	6,169
Total Liabilities	45,382	44,990	45,219	43,482	47,204	46,295	46,031	33,673
Stockholders' Equity	3,893	2,850	2,465	1,394	(683)	1,511	3,097	3,400
Shares Outstanding	282	282	282	281	284	289	303	314
Statistical Record								
Return on Assets %	12.63	12.59	11.86	11.04	4.24	10.91	8.36	9.87
Return on Equity %	247.52	358.24	489.97	1,419.41	483.57	229.49	110.97	86.90
EBITDA Margin %	15.41	15.74	16.69	14.26	13.94	14.32	14.07	14.46
Net Margin %	10.77	10.86	11.89	9.39	3.92	11.22	7.81	7.93
Asset Turnover	1.23	1.24	1.20	1.18	1.08	0.97	1.07	1.24
Current Ratio	1.28	1.20	1.17	1.12	1.38	1.20	1.15	1.11
Debt to Equity	3.25	4.43	5.12	9.04	...	9.45	4.62	1.81
Price Range	397.04-245.22	363.54-245.22	358.60-245.22	361.00-245.22	322.82-250.90	267.62-206.08	226.43-185.52	196.84-146.07
P/E Ratio	18.88-11.66	17.73-11.96	18.33-12.54	20.52-13.94	46.85-36.42	15.30-11.78	19.76-16.19	17.56-13.03
Average Yield %	2.69	2.74	2.70	2.55	2.59	2.85	3.03	3.25

Address: 6801 Rockledge Drive, Bethesda, MD 20817	Web Site: www.lockheedmartin.com	Auditors: Ernst & Young LLP
Telephone: 301-897-6000	Officers: Marillyn A. Hewson - Chairman, President, President (frmr), President (frmr-frmr), Chief Executive Officer, Chief Executive Officer (frmr), Executive Vice President, Chief Operating Officer Kenneth R. Possenriede - Executive Vice President, Chief Financial Officer, Vice President, Treasurer	Investor Contact: 301-897-6584 Transfer Agents: Computershare Trust Company, N.A., Providence, RI

LOEWS CORP.

Exchange	Symbol	Price	52Wk Range	Yield	P/E
NYS	L	$52.49 (12/31/2019)	56.16-44.52	0.48	28.68

*7 Year Price Score 91.82 *NYSE Composite Index=100 *12 Month Price Score 95.37

Interim Earnings (Per Share)

Qtr.	Mar	Jun	Sep	Dec
2016	0.30	(0.19)	0.97	0.85
2017	0.87	0.69	0.46	1.43
2018	0.89	0.72	0.88	(0.50)
2019	1.27	0.82	0.24	...

Interim Dividends (Per Share)

Amt	Decl	Ex	Rec	Pay
0.063Q	02/12/2019	02/26/2019	02/27/2019	03/12/2019
0.063Q	05/14/2019	05/28/2019	05/29/2019	06/11/2019
0.063Q	08/06/2019	08/27/2019	08/28/2019	09/10/2019
0.063Q	11/12/2019	11/26/2019	11/27/2019	12/10/2019

Indicated Div: $0.25

Valuation Analysis

Forecast EPS	$2.95
	(01/16/2020)
Market Cap	$15.7 Billion
Book Value	$19.4 Billion
Price/Book	0.81
Price/Sales	1.10

Institutional Holding

No of Institutions	721
Shares	255,382,352
% Held	54.38

Business Summary: General Insurance (MIC: 5.2.1 SIC: 6331 NAIC: 524126)

Loews is a holding company. Co.'s subsidiaries are engaged in the following lines of business: commercial property and casualty insurance; operation of offshore oil and gas drilling rigs; transportation and storage of natural gas and natural gas liquids; operation of a chain of hotels; and manufacturing of plastic packaging solutions. Co.'s subsidiary, CNA Financial Corporation is an insurance holding company which provides commercial property and casualty coverages, including surety. Co.'s subsidiary, Diamond Offshore Drilling, Inc., provides contract drilling services to the energy industry with offshore drilling rigs consisting of drillships and semisubmersible rigs.

Recent Developments: For the quarter ended Sep 30 2019, net income decreased 86.5% to US$39.0 million from US$289.0 million in the year-earlier quarter. Revenues were US$3.68 billion, up 1.9% from US$3.61 billion the year before. Net premiums earned were US$1.89 billion versus US$1.85 billion in the prior-year quarter, an increase of 2.0%. Net investment income rose 6.3% to US$525.0 million from US$494.0 million a year ago.

Prospects: Our evaluation of Loews Corp. as of October 4th, 2019 is the result of our systematic analysis on three basic characteristics: earnings strength, relative valuation, and recent stock price movement. The company has produced a positive trend in earnings per share over the past 5 quarters. However, recent analyst estimates for the company have been unchanged, while L has posted results that exceeded analysts' expectations. Based on operating earnings yield, the company is fairly valued when compared to all of the companies we cover. Share price changes over the past year indicates that L will perform in line with the market over the near term.

Financial Data

(US$ in Thousands)	9 Mos	6 Mos	3 Mos	12/31/2018	12/31/2017	12/31/2016	12/31/2015	12/31/2014
Earnings Per Share	1.83	2.47	2.37	1.99	3.45	1.93	0.72	1.55
Cash Flow Per Share	6.96	8.38	12.23	13.23	7.69	6.65	9.79	7.83
Tang Book Value Per Share	62.32	61.95	60.08	57.21	55.84	52.93	50.63	50.70
Dividends Per Share	0.250	0.250	0.250	0.250	0.250	0.250	0.250	0.250
Dividend Payout %	13.66	10.12	10.55	12.56	7.25	12.95	34.72	16.13
Income Statement								
Premium Income	5,517,000	3,627,000	1,803,000	7,312,000	6,988,000	6,924,000	6,921,000	7,212,000
Total Revenue	11,055,000	7,380,000	3,757,000	14,066,000	13,735,000	13,105,000	13,415,000	14,325,000
Benefits & Claims	4,323,000	2,709,000	1,357,000	5,572,000	5,310,000	5,283,000	5,384,000	5,591,000
Income Before Taxes	843,000	783,000	508,000	834,000	1,582,000	936,000	244,000	1,810,000
Income Taxes	183,000	162,000	112,000	128,000	170,000	220,000	(43,000)	457,000
Net Income	715,000	643,000	394,000	636,000	1,164,000	654,000	260,000	591,000
Average Shares	302,350	304,540	310,360	319,930	337,500	338,310	362,690	382,550
Balance Sheet								
Total Assets	82,499,000	82,277,000	80,449,000	78,316,000	79,586,000	76,594,000	76,029,000	78,367,000
Total Liabilities	63,079,000	62,763,000	61,412,000	59,798,000	60,382,000	58,431,000	58,468,000	59,087,000
Stockholders' Equity	19,420,000	19,514,000	19,037,000	18,518,000	19,204,000	18,163,000	17,561,000	19,280,000
Shares Outstanding	299,226	302,598	305,505	312,069	332,087	336,621	339,897	372,934
Statistical Record								
Return on Assets %	0.68	0.93	0.91	0.81	1.49	0.85	0.34	0.75
Return on Equity %	2.87	3.93	3.92	3.37	6.23	3.65	1.41	3.05
Loss Ratio %	78.36	74.69	75.26	76.20	75.99	76.30	77.79	77.52
Net Margin %	6.47	8.71	10.49	4.52	8.47	4.99	1.94	4.13
Price Range	56.16-42.54	54.67-42.54	52.46-42.54	53.46-42.54	50.65-45.12	47.90-34.21	42.53-35.36	48.24-39.07
P/E Ratio	30.69-23.25	22.13-17.22	22.14-17.95	26.86-21.38	14.68-13.08	24.82-17.73	59.07-49.11	31.12-25.21
Average Yield %	0.51	0.51	0.51	0.50	0.52	0.62	0.64	0.58

Address: 667 Madison Avenue, New York, NY 10065-8087 Telephone: 212-521-2000	Web Site: www.loews.com Officers: Andrew H. Tisch - Co-Chairman Jonathan M. Tisch - Co-Chairman	Auditors: DELOITTE & TOUCHE LLP Transfer Agents: Computershare Shareowner Services, Jersey City, NJ

LOUISIANA-PACIFIC CORP

Exchange	Symbol	Price	52Wk Range	Yield	P/E
NYS	LPX	$29.67 (12/31/2019)	30.22-21.21	1.82	59.34

*7 Year Price Score 101.21 *NYSE Composite Index=100 *12 Month Price Score 108.90

TRADING VOLUME (thousand shares)

Interim Earnings (Per Share)

Qtr.	Mar	Jun	Sep	Dec
2016	0.07	0.22	0.45	0.29
2017	0.38	0.65	0.75	0.89
2018	0.62	1.11	0.86	0.14
2019	0.20	0.14	0.02	...

Interim Dividends (Per Share)

Amt	Decl	Ex	Rec	Pay
0.135Q	02/12/2019	02/25/2019	02/26/2019	03/13/2019
0.135Q	05/06/2019	05/20/2019	05/21/2019	06/03/2019
0.135Q	08/06/2019	08/16/2019	08/19/2019	09/03/2019
0.135Q	11/05/2019	11/13/2019	11/14/2019	12/04/2019

Indicated Div: $0.54

Valuation Analysis | **Institutional Holding**

Forecast EPS	$0.42	No of Institutions
(01/15/2020)		455
Market Cap	$3.5 Billion	Shares
Book Value	$1.2 Billion	149,838,704
Price/Book	2.87	% Held
Price/Sales	1.48	78.35

Business Summary: Paper & Forest Products (MIC: 8.1.2 SIC: 2493 NAIC: 321219)

Louisiana-Pacific provides building solutions. Co. designs, manufactures and markets a range of products for the new home construction, repair and remodeling and outdoor structures markets. Co. has four segments: siding, which includes LP SmartSide® Strand and Fiber trim and siding, as well as LP Outdoor Building Solutions® products for outdoor buildings; oriented strand board (OSB), which manufactures and distributes OSB structural panel products; engineered wood products, which include LP SolidStart® I-Joist, Laminated Veneer Lumber, and other related products; and South America, which manufactures and distributes OSB and siding products in South America and certain export markets.

Recent Developments: For the quarter ended Sep 30 2019, income from continuing operations decreased 99.2% to US$1.0 million from US$124.0 million in the year-earlier quarter. Net income decreased 99.2% to US$1.0 million from US$124.0 million in the year-earlier quarter. Revenues were US$603.0 million, down 18.2% from US$737.0 million the year before. Operating income was US$8.0 million versus US$168.0 million in the prior-year quarter, a decrease of 95.2%. Direct operating expenses rose 1.0% to US$529.0 million from US$524.0 million in the comparable period the year before. Indirect operating expenses increased 46.7% to US$66.0 million from US$45.0 million in the equivalent prior-year period.

Prospects: Our evaluation of Louisiana-Pacific Corp. as of October 4th, 2019 is the result of our systematic analysis on three basic characteristics: earnings strength, relative valuation, and recent stock price movement. The company has generated a negative trend in earnings per share over the past 5 quarters. In addition, recent analyst estimates for the company have been reduced and LPX has posted results that fell short of analysts' expectations. Based on operating earnings yield, the company is fairly valued when compared to all of the companies we cover. Share price changes over the past year indicates that LPX will perform in line with the market over the near term.

Financial Data

(US$ in Thousands)	9 Mos	6 Mos	3 Mos	12/31/2018	12/31/2017	12/31/2016	12/31/2015	12/31/2014
Earnings Per Share	0.50	1.34	2.31	2.73	2.66	1.03	(0.62)	(0.53)
Cash Flow Per Share	1.24	1.97	3.25	3.57	3.28	2.38	0.21	(0.37)
Tang Book Value Per Share	9.87	9.93	9.92	12.23	10.89	8.22	7.04	7.78
Dividends Per Share	0.535	0.530	0.525	0.520	...	...	...	...
Dividend Payout %	107.00	39.55	22.73	19.05				
Income Statement								
Total Revenue	1,773,000	1,170,000	582,000	2,828,000	2,733,900	2,233,400	1,892,500	1,934,800
EBITDA	151,000	113,000	69,000	659,800	652,800	309,800	37,700	25,500
Depn & Amortn	90,000	60,000	31,000	120,000	123,300	112,800	101,900	100,700
Income Before Taxes	56,000	52,000	34,000	524,000	510,200	164,900	(95,400)	(105,000)
Income Taxes	13,000	11,000	7,000	122,300	119,100	19,800	(2,700)	(27,200)
Net Income	46,000	44,000	27,000	394,600	389,800	149,800	(88,100)	(75,400)
Average Shares	122,200	124,300	132,000	144,400	146,400	145,300	142,400	141,100
Balance Sheet								
Current Assets	761,000	828,000	846,000	1,287,200	1,359,600	1,016,500	769,100	950,300
Total Assets	2,043,000	2,090,000	2,094,000	2,514,100	2,448,500	2,031,200	2,176,300	2,353,500
Current Liabilities	216,000	229,000	238,000	261,600	270,100	228,800	143,000	172,700
Long-Term Obligations	348,000	348,000	347,000	346,900	350,800	374,400	751,800	759,500
Total Liabilities	832,000	813,000	822,000	813,900	844,000	835,500	1,159,300	1,237,700
Stockholders' Equity	1,213,000	1,278,000	1,273,000	1,700,200	1,604,500	1,195,700	1,017,000	1,115,800
Shares Outstanding	117,443	123,532	123,445	136,833	144,895	144,316	142,984	142,226
Statistical Record								
Return on Assets %	2.71	7.85	14.40	15.90	17.40	7.10	N.M.	N.M.
Return on Equity %	4.17	12.16	22.46	23.88	27.84	13.50	N.M.	N.M.
EBITDA Margin %	8.52	9.66	11.86	23.33	23.88	13.87	1.99	1.32
Net Margin %	2.59	3.76	4.64	13.95	14.26	6.71	N.M.	N.M.
Asset Turnover	1.01	1.06	1.18	1.14	1.22	1.06	0.84	0.80
Current Ratio	3.52	3.62	3.55	4.92	5.03	4.44	5.38	5.50
Debt to Equity	0.29	0.27	0.27	0.20	0.22	0.31	0.74	0.68
Price Range	26.79-20.52	31.75-20.52	31.75-20.52	31.75-20.52	29.14-18.83	20.86-13.78	18.70-14.19	18.79-12.61
P/E Ratio	53.58-41.04	23.69-15.31	13.74-8.88	11.63-7.52	10.95-7.08	20.25-13.38	...	...
Average Yield %	2.22	2.12	2.01	1.92	...	...	...	...

Address: 414 Union Street, Nashville, TN 37219	**Web Site:**	**Auditors:** DELOITTE & TOUCHE LLP
Telephone: 615-986-5600	**Officers:** E. Gary Cook - Chairman William Bradley (Brad) Southern - Executive Vice President, Chief Operating Officer, Chief Executive Officer	**Transfer Agents:** Computershare Trust Company, N.A., Providence, RI

LOWE'S COMPANIES INC

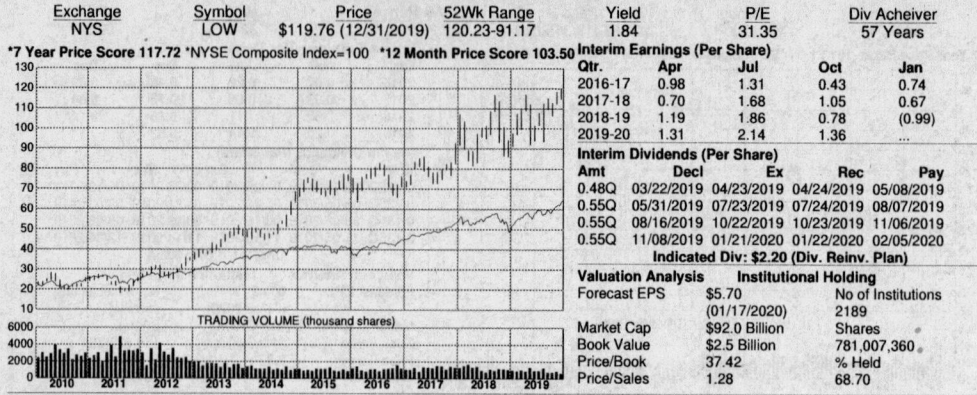

Exchange NYS	Symbol LOW	Price $119.76 (12/31/2019)	52Wk Range 120.23-91.17	Yield 1.84	P/E 31.35	Div Acheiver 57 Years

*7 Year Price Score 117.72 *NYSE Composite Index=100 *12 Month Price Score 103.50

Interim Earnings (Per Share)

Qtr.	Apr	Jul	Oct	Jan
2016-17	0.98	1.31	0.43	0.74
2017-18	0.70	1.68	1.05	0.67
2018-19	1.19	1.86	0.78	(0.99)
2019-20	1.31	2.14	1.36	...

Interim Dividends (Per Share)

Amt	Decl	Ex	Rec	Pay
0.48Q	03/22/2019	04/23/2019	04/24/2019	05/08/2019
0.55Q	05/31/2019	07/23/2019	07/24/2019	08/07/2019
0.55Q	08/16/2019	10/22/2019	10/23/2019	11/06/2019
0.55Q	11/08/2019	01/21/2020	01/22/2020	02/05/2020

Indicated Div: $2.20 (Div. Reinv. Plan)

Valuation Analysis | **Institutional Holding**
Forecast EPS $5.70 (01/17/2020)	No of Institutions 2189
Market Cap $92.0 Billion	Shares
Book Value $2.5 Billion	781,007,360
Price/Book 37.42	% Held
Price/Sales 1.28	68.70

TRADING VOLUME (thousand shares)

Business Summary: Retail - Hardware & Home Improvement (MIC: 2.1.8 SIC: 5722 NAIC: 443111)

Lowe's Companies is a home improvement retailer. Co. provides home improvement products in lumber and building materials, appliances, seasonal and outdoor living, tools and hardware, fashion fixtures, rough plumbing and electrical, paint, millwork, lawn and garden, flooring, and kitchens categories. Co. provides installation services through independent contractors in product categories, including appliances, flooring, kitchens, lumber and building materials, and millwork. Co. also provides extended protection plans for various products within the appliances, kitchens, fashion fixtures, millwork, rough plumbing and electrical, seasonal and outdoor living, and tools and hardware categories.

Recent Developments: For the quarter ended Nov 1 2019, net income increased 66.8% to US$1.05 billion from US$629.0 million in the year-earlier quarter. Revenues were US$17.39 billion, down 0.2% from US$17.42 billion the year before. Operating income was US$1.56 billion versus US$957.0 million in the prior-year quarter, an increase of 62.8%. Direct operating expenses declined 2.4% to US$11.75 billion from US$12.04 billion in the comparable period the year before. Indirect operating expenses decreased 7.6% to US$4.08 billion from US$4.42 billion in the equivalent prior-year period.

Prospects: Our evaluation of Lowe's Companies Inc. as of October 4th, 2019 is the result of our systematic analysis on three basic characteristics: earnings strength, relative valuation, and recent stock price movement. The company has enjoyed a very positive trend in earnings per share over the past 5 quarters. However, recent analyst estimates for the company have been mixed and LOW has posted results that exceeded analysts' expectations. Based on operating earnings yield, the company is fairly valued when compared to all of the companies we cover. Share price changes over the past year indicates that LOW will perform well over the near term.

Financial Data
(US$ in Thousands)

	9 Mos	6 Mos	3 Mos	02/01/2019	02/02/2018	02/03/2017	01/29/2016	01/30/2015
Earnings Per Share	3.82	3.24	2.96	2.84	4.09	3.47	2.73	2.71
Cash Flow Per Share	4.56	5.11	6.16	7.66	6.05	6.28	5.17	5.00
Tang Book Value Per Share	2.81	3.01	3.69	4.17	5.50	6.18	8.41	10.38
Dividends Per Share	2.060	1.990	1.920	1.850	1.580	1.330	1.070	0.870
Dividend Payout %	53.93	61.42	64.86	65.14	38.63	38.33	39.19	32.10
Income Statement								
Total Revenue	56,121,000	38,733,000	17,741,000	71,309,000	68,619,000	65,017,000	59,074,000	56,223,000
EBITDA	6,324,000	4,441,000	1,754,000	5,418,000	7,522,000	7,346,000	6,455,000	6,277,000
Depn & Amortn	968,000	643,000	337,000	1,400,000	1,400,000	1,500,000	1,484,000	1,485,000
Income Before Taxes	4,848,000	3,467,000	1,255,000	3,394,000	5,489,000	5,201,000	4,419,000	4,276,000
Income Taxes	1,077,000	745,000	209,000	1,080,000	2,042,000	2,108,000	1,873,000	1,578,000
Net Income	3,771,000	2,722,000	1,046,000	2,314,000	3,447,000	3,093,000	2,546,000	2,698,000
Average Shares	770,000	781,000	797,000	812,000	840,000	881,000	929,000	990,000
Balance Sheet								
Current Assets	15,662,000	16,796,000	19,335,000	14,228,000	12,772,000	12,000,000	10,561,000	10,080,000
Total Assets	39,764,000	40,695,000	43,219,000	34,508,000	35,291,000	34,408,000	31,266,000	31,827,000
Current Liabilities	15,063,000	15,835,000	17,781,000	14,497,000	12,096,000	11,974,000	10,492,000	9,348,000
Long-Term Obligations	16,635,000	16,538,000	16,542,000	14,391,000	15,564,000	14,394,000	11,545,000	10,815,000
Total Liabilities	37,306,000	38,055,000	39,983,000	30,864,000	29,418,000	27,974,000	23,612,000	21,859,000
Stockholders' Equity	2,458,000	2,640,000	3,236,000	3,644,000	5,873,000	6,434,000	7,654,000	9,968,000
Shares Outstanding	768,000	776,000	795,000	801,000	830,000	866,000	910,000	960,000
Statistical Record								
Return on Assets %	7.71	6.50	5.82	6.65	9.92	9.27	8.09	8.38
Return on Equity %	75.06	60.02	52.80	48.76	56.17	43.20	28.98	24.80
EBITDA Margin %	11.27	11.47	9.89	7.60	10.96	11.30	10.93	11.16
Net Margin %	6.72	7.03	5.90	3.25	5.02	4.76	4.31	4.80
Asset Turnover	1.88	1.85	1.76	2.05	1.97	1.95	1.88	1.75
Current Ratio	1.04	1.06	1.09	0.98	1.06	1.00	1.01	1.08
Debt to Equity	6.77	6.26	5.11	3.95	2.65	2.24	1.51	1.08
Price Range	117.18-85.96	117.18-85.96	117.18-82.83	116.84-81.48	107.40-72.24	82.94-63.40	77.61-66.25	70.44-44.63
P/E Ratio	30.68-22.50	36.17-26.53	39.59-27.98	41.14-28.69	26.26-17.66	23.90-18.27	28.43-24.27	25.99-16.47
Average Yield %	2.01	1.95	1.91	1.93	1.93	1.79	1.49	1.64

Address: 1000 Lowe's Blvd., Mooresville, NC 28117 Telephone: 704-758-1000	Web Site: www.lowes.com Officers: Richard W. Dreiling - Chairman Marvin R. Ellison - President, Chief Executive Officer	Auditors: DELOITTE & TOUCHE LLP Investor Contact: 180-081-37613 Transfer Agents: Computershare Trust Company N.A., Providence, RI

L3HARRIS TECHNOLOGIES INC

Exchange	Symbol	Price	52Wk Range	Yield	P/E	Div Acheiver
NYS	LHX	$197.87 (12/31/2019)	214.70-130.05	1.52	24.73	17 Years

*7 Year Price Score 142.73 *NYSE Composite Index=100 *12 Month Price Score 101.39

Interim Earnings (Per Share)

Qtr.	Sep	Dec	Mar	Jun
2016-17	1.27	1.40	0.69	1.07
2017-18	1.32	1.15	1.66	1.79
2018-19	1.77	1.87	2.02	2.21
2019-20	1.90	...	...	...

Interim Dividends (Per Share)

Amt	Decl	Ex	Rec	Pay
0.685Q	02/22/2019	03/07/2019	03/08/2019	03/22/2019
0.685Q	04/26/2019	05/16/2019	05/17/2019	06/04/2019
0.75Q	08/20/2019	09/03/2019	09/04/2019	09/18/2019
0.75Q	10/25/2019	11/21/2019	11/22/2019	12/06/2019

Indicated Div: $3.00 (Div. Reinv. Plan)

Valuation Analysis / Institutional Holding

Forecast EPS	$10.00	No of Institutions
(01/16/2020)		1326
Market Cap	$43.8 Billion	Shares
Book Value	$22.8 Billion	231,217,600
Price/Book	1.93	% Held
Price/Sales	4.52	N/A

Business Summary: Defense (MIC: 7.1.2 SIC: 3812 NAIC: 334511)

L3Harris Technologies, together with its subsidiaries, provides technology-based solutions. Co. has three segments: Communication Systems, which serves markets in tactical communications and defense products and in public safety networks; Electronic Systems, which provides electronic warfare, avionics, and command, control, communications, computers, intelligence, surveillance and reconnaissance solutions; and Space and Intelligence Systems, which provides intelligence, space protection, geospatial, Earth observation, universe exploration, positioning, navigation and timing, and environmental solutions for national security, defense, civil and commercial customers.

Recent Developments: For the quarter ended Sep 27 2019, income from continuing operations increased 101.4% to US$435.0 million from US$216.0 million in the year-earlier quarter. Net income increased 104.2% to US$435.0 million from US$213.0 million in the year-earlier quarter. Revenues were US$4.43 billion, up 187.4% from US$1.54 billion the year before. Direct operating expenses rose 221.0% to US$3.24 billion from US$1.01 billion in the comparable period the year before. Indirect operating expenses increased 176.0% to US$770.0 million from US$279.0 million in the equivalent prior-year period.

Prospects: Our evaluation of L3Harris Technologies Inc. as of October 4th, 2019 is the result of our systematic analysis on three basic characteristics: earnings strength, relative valuation, and recent stock price movement. The company has enjoyed a very positive trend in earnings per share over the past 5 quarters. However, recent analyst estimates for the company have been mixed and LHX has posted results that exceeded analysts' expectations. Based on operating earnings yield, the company is fairly valued when compared to all of the companies we cover. Share price changes over the past year indicates that LHX will perform well over the near term.

Financial Data

(US$ in Thousands)	3 Mos	06/28/2019	06/29/2018	06/30/2017	07/01/2016	07/03/2015	06/27/2014	06/28/2013
Earnings Per Share	8.00	7.86	5.92	4.44	2.59	3.11	4.95	1.01
Cash Flow Per Share	5.16	10.07	6.35	4.65	7.48	7.95	8.03	7.56
Dividends Per Share	2.805	2.740	2.280	2.120	2.000	1.880	1.680	1.480
Dividend Payout %	35.06	34.86	38.51	47.75	77.22	60.45	33.94	146.53
Income Statement								
Total Revenue	4,431,000	6,801,000	6,182,000	5,900,000	7,467,000	5,083,000	5,012,000	5,111,700
EBITDA	577,000	1,533,000	1,237,000	1,222,000	992,000	760,000	1,028,300	917,800
Depn & Amortn	79,000	253,000	143,000	147,000	200,000	155,000	142,100	146,400
Income Before Taxes	440,000	1,113,000	926,000	905,000	611,000	477,000	795,400	664,500
Income Taxes	5,000	160,000	205,000	267,000	266,000	143,000	256,200	202,700
Net Income	429,000	949,000	718,000	553,000	324,000	334,000	534,800	113,000
Average Shares	225,400	120,500	121,100	124,300	125,000	106,800	107,300	111,200
Balance Sheet								
Current Assets	7,027,000	2,578,000	2,223,000	2,073,000	2,608,000	3,524,000	1,991,300	1,948,100
Total Assets	38,947,000	10,117,000	9,839,000	10,090,000	11,996,000	13,129,000	4,931,200	4,858,400
Current Liabilities	4,718,000	2,268,000	1,788,000	1,926,000	1,964,000	2,281,000	1,114,600	1,297,400
Long-Term Obligations	6,307,000	2,763,000	3,408,000	3,396,000	4,120,000	5,053,000	1,575,800	1,577,100
Total Liabilities	16,174,000	6,754,000	6,517,000	7,162,000	8,940,000	9,732,000	3,105,200	3,297,100
Stockholders' Equity	22,773,000	3,363,000	3,322,000	2,928,000	3,056,000	3,397,000	1,826,000	1,561,300
Shares Outstanding	221,568	118,552	118,280	119,628	124,643	123,675	105,509	106,933
Statistical Record								
Return on Assets %	4.77	9.54	7.23	5.02	2.59	3.64	10.96	2.17
Return on Equity %	8.96	28.47	23.04	18.53	10.07	12.58	31.66	6.47
EBITDA Margin %	13.02	22.54	20.01	20.71	13.29	14.95	20.52	17.95
Net Margin %	9.68	13.95	11.61	9.37	4.34	6.57	10.67	2.21
Asset Turnover	0.40	0.68	0.62	0.54	0.60	0.55	1.03	0.98
Current Ratio	1.49	1.14	1.24	1.08	1.33	1.54	1.79	1.50
Debt to Equity	0.28	0.82	1.03	1.16	1.35	1.49	0.86	1.01
Price Range	214.70-127.26	199.40-127.26	169.00-109.08	113.82-81.54	89.48-70.28	82.46-61.52	77.55-49.08	51.97-39.95
P/E Ratio	26.84-15.91	25.37-16.19	28.55-18.43	25.64-18.36	34.55-27.14	26.51-19.78	15.67-9.92	51.46-39.55
Average Yield %	1.62	1.70	1.61	2.10	2.52	2.57	2.54	3.14

Address: 1025 West NASA Boulevard, Melbourne, FL 32919 **Telephone:** 321-727-9100	**Web Site:** www.l3harris.com **Officers:** William M. Brown - Chairman, Chief Executive Officer Christopher E. Kubasik - Vice-Chairman, President, Chief Operating Officer	**Auditors:** Ernst & Young LLP **Investor Contact:** 321-727-9383 **Transfer Agents:** Computershare, Canton, MA

M & T BANK CORP

Exchange	Symbol	Price	52Wk Range	Yield	P/E
NYS	MTB	$169.75 (12/31/2019)	176.00-142.99	2.59	12.21

*7 Year Price Score 96.68   *NYSE Composite Index=100   *12 Month Price Score 96.77

Interim Earnings (Per Share)

Qtr.	Mar	Jun	Sep	Dec
2016	1.73	1.98	2.10	1.98
2017	2.12	2.35	2.21	2.01
2018	2.23	3.26	3.53	3.74
2019	3.35	3.34	3.47	...

Interim Dividends (Per Share)

Amt	Decl	Ex	Rec	Pay
1.00Q	02/20/2019	03/01/2019	03/04/2019	03/29/2019
1.00Q	05/21/2019	05/31/2019	06/03/2019	06/28/2019
1.00Q	08/20/2019	08/30/2019	09/03/2019	09/30/2019
1.10Q	11/19/2019	11/29/2019	12/02/2019	12/31/2019

Indicated Div: $4.40 (Div. Reinv. Plan)

Valuation Analysis | **Institutional Holding**

Forecast EPS	$13.62	No of Institutions
	(01/17/2020)	961
Market Cap	$22.5 Billion	Shares
Book Value	$15.8 Billion	135,144,192
Price/Book	1.42	% Held
Price/Sales	3.24	70.62

Business Summary: Banking (MIC: 5.1.1 SIC: 6022 NAIC: 522110)

M&T Bank is a bank holding company. Through its subsidiaries, Co. provides individuals, corporations and other businesses, and institutions with commercial and retail banking services, including loans and deposits, trust, mortgage banking, asset management, insurance and other financial services. Banking activities are primarily focused on consumers residing in New York State, Maryland, New Jersey, Pennsylvania, Delaware, Connecticut, Virginia, West Virginia and the District of Columbia and on small and medium-size businesses based in those areas. Certain subsidiaries also conduct activities in other areas.

Recent Developments: For the quarter ended Sep 30 2019, net income decreased 8.7% to US$480.1 million from US$526.1 million in the year-earlier quarter. Net interest income was unchanged at US$1.03 billion versus the year-earlier quarter. Provision for loan losses was US$45.0 million versus US$16.0 million in the prior-year quarter, an increase of 181.3%. Non-interest income rose 14.9% to US$527.8 million from US$459.3 million, while non-interest expense advanced 13.1% to US$877.6 million.

Prospects: Our evaluation of M & T Bank Corp. as of October 4th, 2019 is the result of our systematic analysis on three basic characteristics: earnings strength, relative valuation, and recent stock price movement. The company has managed to produce a neutral trend in earnings per share over the past 5 quarters. However, recent analyst estimates for the company have been reduced and MTB has posted results that fell short of analysts' expectations. Based on operating earnings yield, the company is undervalued when compared to all of the companies we cover. Share price changes over the past year indicates that MTB will perform poorly over the near term.

Financial Data

(US$ in Thousands)	9 Mos	6 Mos	3 Mos	12/31/2018	12/31/2017	12/31/2016	12/31/2015	12/31/2014
Earnings Per Share	13.90	13.96	13.88	12.74	8.70	7.78	7.18	7.42
Cash Flow Per Share	13.37	15.13	14.64	14.51	18.28	7.53	12.74	8.39
Tang Book Value Per Share	74.88	73.25	71.14	69.23	68.99	67.64	63.98	57.02
Dividends Per Share	4.000	4.000	3.800	3.550	3.000	2.800	2.800	2.800
Dividend Payout %	28.78	28.65	27.38	27.86	34.48	35.99	39.00	37.74
Income Statement								
Interest Income	3,693,691	2,464,222	1,226,309	4,598,711	4,167,795	3,895,871	3,170,844	2,956,877
Interest Expense	572,260	372,681	176,249	526,409	386,751	425,984	328,257	280,431
Net Interest Income	3,121,431	2,091,541	1,050,060	4,072,302	3,781,044	3,469,887	2,842,587	2,676,446
Provision for Losses	122,000	77,000	22,000	132,000	168,000	190,000	170,000	124,000
Non-Interest Income	1,540,639	1,012,860	500,765	1,856,000	1,851,143	1,825,996	1,839,304	1,795,945
Non-Interest Expense	2,644,999	1,767,380	894,348	3,288,062	3,140,325	3,047,485	2,822,932	2,742,857
Income Before Taxes	1,895,071	1,260,021	634,477	2,508,240	2,323,862	2,058,398	1,688,959	1,605,534
Income Taxes	458,988	304,019	151,735	590,160	915,556	743,284	595,025	522,616
Net Income	1,436,083	956,002	482,742	1,918,080	1,408,306	1,315,114	1,079,667	1,066,246
Average Shares	132,999	135,464	137,920	144,151	152,551	157,304	137,533	131,844
Balance Sheet								
Net Loans & Leases	88,784,756	88,848,191	87,620,546	87,447,033	86,971,785	89,864,419	86,533,507	65,749,394
Total Assets	125,500,926	121,554,895	120,025,205	120,097,403	118,593,487	123,449,206	122,787,884	96,685,535
Total Deposits	95,113,933	91,681,024	90,469,750	90,156,572	92,432,146	95,493,876	91,957,841	73,582,053
Total Liabilities	109,721,115	105,863,068	104,437,676	104,637,212	102,342,668	106,962,584	106,614,595	84,349,639
Stockholders' Equity	15,779,811	15,691,827	15,587,529	15,460,191	16,250,819	16,486,622	16,173,289	12,335,896
Shares Outstanding	132,255	134,178	136,615	138,509	150,084	156,180	159,563	132,312
Statistical Record								
Return on Assets %	1.64	1.69	1.72	1.61	1.16	1.07	0.98	1.17
Return on Equity %	12.70	12.97	13.09	12.10	8.60	8.03	7.57	9.02
Net Interest Margin %	83.77	84.13	85.63	88.55	90.72	89.07	89.65	90.52
Efficiency Ratio %	49.94	49.89	51.78	50.94	52.17	53.26	56.34	57.71
Loans to Deposits	0.93	0.97	0.97	0.97	0.94	0.94	0.94	0.89
Price Range	176.00-135.74	179.73-135.74	187.14-135.74	196.81-135.74	173.90-142.47	158.10-100.78	133.20-112.28	128.03-109.30
P/E Ratio	12.66-9.77	12.87-9.72	13.48-9.78	15.45-10.65	19.99-16.38	20.32-12.95	18.55-15.64	17.25-14.73
Average Yield %	2.47	2.41	2.24	2.03	1.87	2.35	2.28	2.32

Address: One M & T Plaza, Buffalo, NY 14203 **Telephone:** 716-635-4000	**Web Site:** www.mtb.com **Officers:** Rene F. Jones - Chairman, Chief Executive Officer, Executive Vice President, Chief Financial Officer Richard S. Gold - President, Chief Operating Officer, Executive Vice President	**Auditors:** PricewaterhouseCoopers LLP **Investor Contact:** 716-842-5138 **Transfer Agents:** Registrar and Transfer Company, Cranford, NJ

MACERICH CO (THE)

Exchange	Symbol	Price	52Wk Range	Yield	P/E
NYS	MAC	$26.92 (12/31/2019)	46.51-25.86	11.14	47.23

*7 Year Price Score 46.58 *NYSE Composite Index=100 *12 Month Price Score 72.47

TRADING VOLUME (thousand shares)

Interim Earnings (Per Share)

Qtr.	Mar	Jun	Sep	Dec
2016	2.76	0.31	0.09	0.27
2017	0.48	0.19	0.12	0.23
2018	(0.24)	0.05	0.52	0.08
2019	0.05	0.11	0.33	...

Interim Dividends (Per Share)

Amt	Decl	Ex	Rec	Pay
0.75Q	01/31/2019	02/20/2019	02/21/2019	03/01/2019
0.75Q	04/25/2019	05/07/2019	05/08/2019	06/03/2019
0.75Q	07/25/2019	08/16/2019	08/19/2019	09/06/2019
0.75Q	10/24/2019	11/07/2019	11/08/2019	12/03/2019

Indicated Div: $3.00 (Div. Reinv. Plan)

Valuation Analysis / Institutional Holding

Forecast EPS	$0.52	No of Institutions
	(01/17/2020)	522
Market Cap	$3.8 Billion	Shares
Book Value	$2.7 Billion	200,922,128
Price/Book	1.41	% Held
Price/Sales	4.08	111.03

Business Summary: REITs (MIC: 5.3.1 SIC: 6798 NAIC: 525930)

Macerich is a self-administered and self-managed real estate investment trust. Co. is involved in the acquisition, ownership, development, redevelopment, management and leasing of regional and community/power shopping centers. Co. is the sole general partner of, and owns a majority of the ownership interests in, The Macerich Partnership, L.P. (the Operating Partnership). The Operating Partnership owns or has an ownership interest in regional shopping centers and community/power shopping centers. Co. conducts all of its operations through the Operating Partnership and its management companies, including Macerich Property Management Company, LLC and Macerich Management Company.

Recent Developments: For the quarter ended Sep 30 2019, net income decreased 38.4% to US$50.0 million from US$81.2 million in the year-earlier quarter. Revenues were US$231.1 million, down 4.6% from US$242.2 million the year before. Revenues from property income fell 4.7% to US$224.2 million from US$235.3 million in the corresponding quarter a year earlier.

Prospects: Our evaluation of Macerich Co. as of October 4th, 2019 is the result of our systematic analysis on three basic characteristics: earnings strength, relative valuation, and recent stock price movement. The company has managed to produce a neutral trend in earnings per share over the past 5 quarters. In addition, recent analyst estimates for the company have been mixed and MAC has posted results that fell short of analysts' expectations. Based on operating earnings yield, the company is overvalued when compared to all of the companies we cover. Share price changes over the past year indicates that MAC will perform poorly over the near term.

Financial Data

(US$ in Thousands)	9 Mos	6 Mos	3 Mos	12/31/2018	12/31/2017	12/31/2016	12/31/2015	12/31/2014
Earnings Per Share	0.57	0.76	0.70	0.42	1.02	3.52	3.08	10.45
Cash Flow Per Share	2.61	2.44	2.46	2.44	2.72	2.84	3.42	2.80
Tang Book Value Per Share	19.58	19.90	20.46	20.82	25.85	27.93	29.59	33.53
Dividends Per Share	3.000	2.990	2.980	2.970	2.870	2.750	6.630	2.510
Dividend Payout %	526.32	393.42	425.71	707.14	281.37	78.13	215.26	24.02
Income Statement								
Total Revenue	685,621	454,494	226,522	960,351	993,662	1,041,271	1,288,149	1,105,247
EBITDA	342,002	221,468	108,655	451,793	541,414	939,565	1,041,445	2,021,903
Depn & Amortn	211,301	141,687	73,352	275,236	277,917	277,270	354,977	289,178
Income Before Taxes	40,436	4,315	(3,054)	(6,405)	91,721	498,620	474,525	1,542,036
Income Taxes	1,703	1,025	346	(3,604)	15,594	722	(3,223)	(4,269)
Net Income	69,929	23,558	7,824	60,020	146,130	516,995	487,562	1,499,042
Average Shares	141,368	141,344	141,262	141,144	141,913	146,711	158,060	143,291
Balance Sheet								
Current Assets	246,624	283,484	273,716	272,793	255,758	280,995	257,901	230,463
Total Assets	8,775,973	8,944,099	9,002,921	9,026,808	9,605,862	9,958,148	11,258,576	13,121,778
Current Liabilities	431,913	425,900	425,778	362,443	384,113	427,481	815,382	684,122
Long-Term Obligations	5,323,965	5,433,403	5,375,240	4,982,460	5,170,264	4,965,900	5,283,742	6,292,400
Total Liabilities	6,068,762	6,179,955	6,148,208	6,076,576	5,924,284	5,852,261	6,543,162	7,481,658
Stockholders' Equity	2,707,211	2,764,144	2,854,713	2,950,232	3,681,578	4,105,887	4,715,414	5,640,120
Shares Outstanding	141,370	141,364	141,332	141,221	140,993	143,985	154,404	158,201
Statistical Record								
Return on Assets %	0.92	1.21	1.12	0.64	1.49	4.86	4.00	13.51
Return on Equity %	2.84	3.75	3.37	1.81	3.75	11.69	9.42	33.32
EBITDA Margin %	49.88	48.73	47.97	47.04	54.49	90.23	80.85	182.94
Net Margin %	10.20	5.18	3.45	6.25	14.71	49.65	37.85	135.63
Asset Turnover	0.10	0.10	0.10	0.10	0.10	0.10	0.11	0.10
Current Ratio	0.57	0.67	0.64	0.75	0.67	0.66	0.32	0.34
Debt to Equity	1.97	1.97	1.88	1.69	1.40	1.21	1.12	1.12
Price Range	54.53-27.67	60.52-32.20	60.52-41.03	68.86-41.03	72.69-52.72	89.76-67.09	94.89-72.53	84.87-55.58
P/E Ratio	95.67-48.54	79.63-42.37	86.46-58.61	163.95-97.69	71.26-51.69	25.50-19.06	30.81-23.55	8.12-5.32
Average Yield %	7.31	6.57	5.82	5.29	4.69	3.52	8.13	3.80

Address: 401 Wilshire Boulevard, Suite 700, Santa Monica, CA 90401	Web Site: www.macerich.com	Auditors: KPMG LLP
Telephone: 310-394-6000	Officers: Edward C. Coppola - President, Senior Executive Vice President, Chief Investment Officer Thomas E. O'Hern - Chief Executive Officer, Senior Executive Vice President, Executive Vice President, Senior Vice President, Chief Financial Officer, Treasurer	Transfer Agents: Computershare Trust Company, N.A., Providence, RI

MACK CALI REALTY CORP

Exchange	Symbol	Price	52Wk Range	Yield	P/E
NYS	CLI	$23.13 (12/31/2019)	24.47-19.12	3.46	11.39

*7 Year Price Score 80.46 *NYSE Composite Index=100 *12 Month Price Score 94.05

Interim Earnings (Per Share)

Qtr.	Mar	Jun	Sep	Dec
2016	0.69	0.54	(0.10)	0.17
2017	0.11	(0.44)	0.39	(0.01)
2018	0.45	(0.05)	(0.05)	0.45
2019	2.66	(0.43)	(0.65)	...

Interim Dividends (Per Share)

Amt	Decl	Ex	Rec	Pay
0.20Q	03/14/2019	04/01/2019	04/02/2019	04/12/2019
0.20Q	06/12/2019	07/01/2019	07/02/2019	07/12/2019
0.20Q	09/24/2019	10/03/2019	10/04/2019	10/11/2019
0.20Q	12/17/2019	01/02/2020	01/03/2020	01/10/2020

Indicated Div: $0.80 (Div. Reinv. Plan)

Valuation Analysis

		Institutional Holding	
Forecast EPS	$1.69	No of Institutions	
	(01/16/2020)	341	
Market Cap	$2.1 Billion	Shares	
Book Value	$1.6 Billion	111,203,512	
Price/Book	1.33	% Held	
Price/Sales	3.96	92.71	

Business Summary: REITs (MIC: 5.3.1 SIC: 6798 NAIC: 525930)

Mack-Cali Realty is a real estate investment trust. Co. owns and operates a real estate portfolio comprised of Class A office and office/flex properties located primarily in the Northeast. Co. performs substantially all real estate leasing, management, acquisition and development on an in-house basis. Co. operates in two industry segments: commercial and other real estate and multi-family real estate and services. Co. provides leasing, property management, acquisition, development, construction and tenant-related services for its commercial and other real estate and multi-family real estate portfolio. Co.'s multi-family services business also provides similar services for third parties.

Recent Developments: For the quarter ended Sep 30 2019, net loss amounted to US$56.0 million versus net income of US$1.7 million in the year-earlier quarter. Revenues were US$131.9 million, down 0.2% from US$132.1 million the year before. Revenues from property income fell 23.0% to US$3.4 million from US$4.4 million in the corresponding quarter a year earlier.

Prospects: Our evaluation of Mack Cali Realty Corp. as of October 4th, 2019 is the result of our systematic analysis on three basic characteristics: earnings strength, relative valuation, and recent stock price movement. The company has generated a negative trend in earnings per share over the past 5 quarters. However, recent analyst estimates for the company have been mixed and CLI has posted results that fell short of analysts' expectations. Based on operating earnings yield, the company is overvalued when compared to all of the companies we cover. Share price changes over the past year indicates that CLI will perform in line with the market over the near term.

Financial Data

(US$ in Thousands)	9 Mos	6 Mos	3 Mos	12/31/2018	12/31/2017	12/31/2016	12/31/2015	12/31/2014
Earnings Per Share	2.03	2.63	3.01	0.80	0.06	1.30	(1.41)	0.32
Cash Flow Per Share	1.79	1.70	1.73	1.85	2.18	1.11	1.90	1.79
Tang Book Value Per Share	17.30	18.14	18.83	16.43	16.39	16.99	16.22	18.21
Dividends Per Share	0.800	0.800	0.800	0.800	0.700	0.600	0.600	0.900
Dividend Payout %	39.41	30.42	26.58	100.00	1,166.67	46.15	...	281.25
Income Statement								
Total Revenue	396,594	264,710	134,249	530,606	616,200	613,398	594,883	636,799
EBITDA	279,393	309,095	303,187	368,658	341,349	403,616	145,276	331,703
Depn & Amortn	9,056	6,111	2,962	181,765	210,928	198,835	181,899	188,626
Income Before Taxes	200,126	256,034	276,275	106,528	39,799	111,506	(138,880)	33,814
Net Income	166,513	222,441	244,495	84,111	23,185	117,224	(125,752)	28,567
Average Shares	100,560	100,523	100,943	100,724	100,703	100,498	100,222	100,041
Balance Sheet								
Current Assets	158,891	181,330	131,670	155,663	175,600	196,232	203,420	196,255
Total Assets	5,720,935	5,327,712	5,274,284	5,060,644	4,957,885	4,296,766	4,063,490	4,192,247
Current Liabilities	278,398	267,650	265,605	240,353	267,386	230,070	224,862	221,582
Long-Term Obligations	3,151,559	2,687,642	2,686,317	2,792,651	2,809,568	2,340,009	2,154,920	2,088,654
Total Liabilities	4,151,674	3,682,125	3,570,266	3,573,986	3,481,590	2,769,595	2,607,814	2,567,466
Stockholders' Equity	1,569,261	1,645,587	1,704,018	1,486,658	1,476,295	1,527,171	1,455,676	1,624,781
Shares Outstanding	90,551	90,553	90,325	90,320	89,914	89,696	89,583	89,076
Statistical Record								
Return on Assets %	3.91	5.20	5.66	1.68	0.50	2.80	N.M.	0.66
Return on Equity %	13.85	16.90	17.78	5.68	1.54	7.84	N.M.	1.75
EBITDA Margin %	70.45	116.77	225.84	69.48	55.40	65.80	24.42	52.09
Net Margin %	41.99	84.03	182.12	15.85	3.76	19.11	N.M.	4.49
Asset Turnover	0.10	0.10	0.10	0.11	0.13	0.15	0.14	0.15
Current Ratio	0.57	0.68	0.50	0.65	0.66	0.85	0.90	0.89
Debt to Equity	2.01	1.63	1.58	1.88	1.90	1.53	1.48	1.29
Price Range	24.47-19.12	24.47-19.07	22.38-16.36	22.17-16.23	29.70-21.42	29.22-17.65	24.12-16.90	22.57-18.02
P/E Ratio	12.05-9.42	9.30-7.25	7.44-5.44	27.71-20.29	495.00-357.00	22.48-13.58	...	70.53-56.31
Average Yield %	3.70	3.78	4.00	4.10	2.73	2.38	3.02	4.38

Address: Harborside 3, 210 Hudson St., Ste. 400, Jersey City, NJ 07311 **Telephone:** 732-590-1010	**Web Site:** www.mack-cali.com **Officers:** William L. Mack - Chairman Michael J. DeMarco - President, Chief Executive Officer, Chief Operating Officer	**Auditors:** PricewaterhouseCoopers LLP **Transfer Agents:** Computershare Trust Company, N.A., Providence, RI

MACQUARIE INFRASTRUCTURE CORP

Exchange	Symbol	Price	52Wk Range	Yield	P/E
NYS	MIC	$42.84 (12/31/2019)	43.67-36.56	9.34	26.44

7 Year Price Score 54.94   **NYSE Composite Index=100**   **12 Month Price Score 98.47**

Interim Earnings (Per Share)

Qtr.	Mar	Jun	Sep	Dec
2016	0.28	0.24	0.51	0.82
2017	0.44	0.32	0.48	3.90
2018	0.88	0.45	0.25	(0.01)
2019	0.79	0.13	0.71	...

Interim Dividends (Per Share)

Amt	Decl	Ex	Rec	Pay
1.00Q	02/14/2019	03/01/2019	03/04/2019	03/07/2019
1.00Q	05/01/2019	05/10/2019	05/13/2019	05/16/2019
1.00Q	07/31/2019	08/09/2019	08/12/2019	08/15/2019
1.00Q	10/31/2019	11/07/2019	11/11/2019	11/14/2019

Indicated Div: $4.00

Valuation Analysis

		Institutional Holding	
Forecast EPS	$1.93	No of Institutions	
	(01/17/2020)	478	
Market Cap	$3.7 Billion	Shares	
Book Value	$2.9 Billion	60,344,436	
Price/Book	1.29	% Held	
Price/Sales	2.30	57.68	

Business Summary: Business Services (MIC: 7.5.2 SIC: 4581 NAIC: 488119)

Macquarie Infrastructure is a holding company. Co. owns and operates a portfolio of businesses that provide services to other businesses, government agencies and individuals primarily in the U.S. The businesses Co. owns and operate are: International-Matex Tank Terminals, which provides bulk liquid terminalling services to third parties in the U.S. and in Canada; Atlantic Aviation, which provides fuel, terminal, aircraft hangaring and other services primarily to owners and operators of general aviation jet aircraft at airports throughout the U.S.; and MIC Hawaii, which consist of energy company that processes and distributes gas and provides related services.

Recent Developments:
For the quarter ended Sep 30 2019, income from continuing operations increased 650.0% to US$15.0 million from US$2.0 million in the year-earlier quarter. Net income increased 177.3% to US$61.0 million from US$22.0 million in the year-earlier quarter. Revenues were US$405.0 million, down 3.8% from US$421.0 million the year before. Operating income was US$56.0 million versus US$53.0 million in the prior-year quarter, an increase of 5.7%. Direct operating expenses declined 4.4% to US$197.0 million from US$206.0 million in the comparable period the year before. Indirect operating expenses decreased 6.2% to US$152.0 million from US$162.0 million in the equivalent prior-year period.

Prospects:
Our evaluation of Macquarie Infrastructure Corp. as of October 4th, 2019 is the result of our systematic analysis on three basic characteristics: earnings strength, relative valuation, and recent stock price movement. The company has generated a negative trend in earnings per share over the past 5 quarters. However, recent analyst estimates for the company have been mixed and MIC has posted results that fell short of analysts' expectations. Based on operating earnings yield, the company is undervalued when compared to all of the companies we cover. Share price changes over the past year indicates that MIC will perform in line with the market over the near term.

Financial Data
(US$ in Thousands)

	9 Mos	6 Mos	3 Mos	12/31/2018	12/31/2017	12/31/2016	12/31/2015	12/31/2014
Earnings Per Share	1.62	1.16	1.48	1.60	5.13	1.85	(1.39)	16.10
Cash Flow Per Share	5.52	5.42	5.59	5.55	6.36	6.91	4.89	3.99
Tang Book Value Per Share	1.00	1.04	1.63	1.54	2.02	0.48	0.98	N.M.
Dividends Per Share	4.000	4.000	4.000	4.440	5.430	4.890	2.240	3.888
Dividend Payout %	246.91	344.83	270.27	277.50	105.85	264.32	...	24.15
Income Statement								
Income Before Taxes	118,000	96,000	88,000	114,079	221,958	226,126	(178,968)	988,518
Income Taxes	33,000	26,000	24,000	49,451	(234,154)	71,257	(65,161)	(24,374)
Net Income	142,000	81,000	70,000	136,521	451,202	156,381	(108,537)	1,042,028
Average Shares	86,303	86,099	93,913	85,249	91,073	82,218	77,997	64,925
Balance Sheet								
Total Assets	6,924,000	7,783,000	7,820,000	7,443,781	8,008,951	7,559,253	7,378,828	6,625,188
Total Liabilities	4,050,000	4,891,000	4,863,000	4,479,179	4,855,259	4,606,359	4,348,638	3,838,025
Stockholders' Equity	2,874,000	2,892,000	2,957,000	2,964,602	3,153,692	2,952,894	3,030,190	2,787,163
Shares Outstanding	86,394	86,195	85,982	85,800	84,733	82,047	80,006	71,089
Statistical Record								
Return on Assets %	1.91	1.30	1.64	1.77	5.80	2.09	N.M.	22.84
Return on Equity %	4.79	3.43	4.27	4.46	14.78	5.21	N.M.	54.42
Price Range	45.79-34.93	47.18-34.93	47.18-34.93	67.40-34.93	82.84-63.85	84.13-52.89	87.24-65.32	73.04-51.59
P/E Ratio	28.27-21.56	40.67-30.11	31.88-23.60	42.13-21.83	16.15-12.45	45.48-28.59	...	4.54-3.20
Average Yield %	9.90	9.53	9.64	9.95	7.23	6.62	2.84	6.18

Address: 125 West 55th Street, New York, NY 10019 **Telephone:** 212-231-1000	**Web Site:** www.macquarie.com/mic **Officers:** Martin Stanley - Chairman, Alternate Chairman Christopher Frost - Chief Executive Officer, President, Chief Operating Officer	**Auditors:** KPMG LLP **Investor Contact:** 212-231-1825 **Transfer Agents:** Computershare Shareowner Services LLC, Pittsburgh, PA

MACY'S INC

Exchange	Symbol	Price	52Wk Range	Yield	P/E
NYS	M	$17.00 (12/31/2019)	31.72-14.30	8.88	5.47

*7 Year Price Score 42.59 *NYSE Composite Index=100 *12 Month Price Score 72.53

TRADING VOLUME (thousand shares)

Interim Earnings (Per Share)

Qtr.	Apr	Jul	Oct	Jan
2016-17	0.37	0.03	0.05	1.53
2017-18	0.23	0.38	0.12	4.31
2018-19	0.45	0.53	0.20	2.38
2019-20	0.44	0.28	0.01	...

Interim Dividends (Per Share)

Amt	Decl	Ex	Rec	Pay
0.378Q	02/22/2019	03/14/2019	03/15/2019	04/01/2019
0.378Q	05/17/2019	06/13/2019	06/14/2019	07/01/2019
0.378Q	08/23/2019	09/12/2019	09/13/2019	10/01/2019
0.378Q	10/25/2019	12/12/2019	12/13/2019	01/02/2020

Indicated Div: $1.51 (Div. Reinv. Plan)

Valuation Analysis

		Institutional Holding	
Forecast EPS	$2.75	No of Institutions	
	(01/15/2020)	933	
Market Cap	$5.3 Billion	Shares	
Book Value	$6.1 Billion	358,190,048	
Price/Book	0.87	% Held	
Price/Sales	0.21	N/A	

Business Summary: Retail - General Merchandise/Department Stores (MIC: 2.1.1 SIC: 5311 NAIC: 452111)

Macy's is an omnichannel retail organization operating stores, websites and mobile applications under three brands (Macy's, Bloomingdale's and bluemercury) that sell merchandise, including apparel and accessories (men's, women's and children's), cosmetics, home furnishings and other consumer goods. Co.'s wholly-owned bank subsidiary, FDS Bank, provides certain collections, customer service and credit marketing services in respect of all credit card accounts that are owned either by Department Stores National Bank, a subsidiary of Citibank, N.A., or FDS Bank and that constitute a part of the credit programs of Co.'s retail operations.

Recent Developments: For the quarter ended Nov 2 2019, net income decreased 96.8% to US$2.0 million from US$62.0 million in the year-earlier quarter. Revenues were US$5.36 billion, down 4.2% from US$5.59 billion the year before. Operating income was US$52.0 million versus US$147.0 million in the prior-year quarter, a decrease of 64.6%. Direct operating expenses declined 3.7% to US$3.11 billion from US$3.23 billion in the comparable period the year before. Indirect operating expenses decreased 0.8% to US$2.20 billion from US$2.22 billion in the equivalent prior-year period.

Prospects: Our evaluation of Macy's Inc. as of October 4th, 2019 is the result of our systematic analysis on three basic characteristics: earnings strength, relative valuation, and recent stock price movement. The company has produced a positive trend in earnings per share over the past 5 quarters. However, recent analyst estimates for the company have been reduced, and M has posted results that fell short of analysts' expectations. Based on operating earnings yield, the company is undervalued when compared to all of the companies we cover. Share price changes over the past year indicates that M will perform poorly over the near term.

Financial Data

(US$ in Thousands)	9 Mos	6 Mos	3 Mos	02/02/2019	02/03/2018	01/28/2017	01/30/2016	01/31/2015
Earnings Per Share	3.11	3.30	3.55	3.56	5.04	1.99	3.22	4.22
Cash Flow Per Share	4.77	4.97	4.45	5.65	6.26	5.85	6.06	7.65
Tang Book Value Per Share	N.M.	N.M.	N.M.	6.67	4.23	N.M.	N.M.	3.34
Dividends Per Share	1.510	1.510	1.510	1.510	1.510	1.492	1.393	1.188
Dividend Payout %	48.55	45.76	42.54	42.42	29.96	75.00	43.25	28.14
Income Statement								
Total Revenue	16,754,000	11,398,000	5,676,000	25,739,000	24,837,000	25,778,000	27,079,000	28,105,000
EBITDA	423,000	375,000	446,000	2,603,000	2,763,000	2,359,000	3,086,000	3,814,000
Depn & Amortn	1,000	1,000	236,000	947,000	946,000	1,044,000	1,047,000	1,031,000
Income Before Taxes	279,000	280,000	163,000	1,420,000	1,507,000	952,000	1,678,000	2,390,000
Income Taxes	55,000	57,000	27,000	322,000	(29,000)	341,000	608,000	864,000
Net Income	224,000	223,000	136,000	1,108,000	1,547,000	619,000	1,072,000	1,526,000
Average Shares	311,000	311,600	311,400	311,400	306,800	310,800	333,000	361,700
Balance Sheet								
Current Assets	8,301,000	6,546,000	7,105,000	7,445,000	7,444,000	7,626,000	7,652,000	8,679,000
Total Assets	22,547,000	20,741,000	21,296,000	19,194,000	19,381,000	19,851,000	20,576,000	21,461,000
Current Liabilities	6,479,000	4,439,000	5,019,000	5,232,000	5,075,000	5,647,000	5,728,000	5,536,000
Long-Term Obligations	4,677,000	4,680,000	4,680,000	4,708,000	5,861,000	6,562,000	6,995,000	7,265,000
Total Liabilities	16,490,000	14,426,000	14,973,000	12,758,000	13,708,000	15,528,000	16,326,000	16,083,000
Stockholders' Equity	6,057,000	6,315,000	6,323,000	6,436,000	5,673,000	4,323,000	4,250,000	5,378,000
Shares Outstanding	308,965	308,914	308,871	307,520	304,765	304,062	310,256	340,573
Statistical Record								
Return on Assets %	4.49	5.20	5.40	5.76	7.76	3.07	5.11	7.10
Return on Equity %	16.44	16.74	18.18	18.35	30.45	14.48	22.33	26.32
EBITDA Margin %	2.52	3.29	7.86	10.11	11.12	9.15	11.40	13.57
Net Margin %	1.34	1.96	2.40	4.30	6.23	2.40	3.96	5.43
Asset Turnover	1.19	1.30	1.26	1.34	1.25	1.28	1.29	1.31
Current Ratio	1.28	1.47	1.42	1.42	1.47	1.35	1.34	1.57
Debt to Equity	0.77	0.74	0.74	0.74	1.03	1.52	1.65	1.35
Price Range	37.79-14.30	41.82-20.43	41.82-23.09	41.82-23.47	33.57-17.53	44.91-29.11	72.80-34.50	67.81-50.91
P/E Ratio	12.15-4.60	12.67-6.19	11.78-6.50	11.75-6.59	6.66-3.48	22.57-14.63	22.61-10.71	16.07-12.06
Average Yield %	6.53	5.38	4.75	4.60	6.09	3.99	2.43	2.00

Address: 7 West Seventh Street, Cincinnati, OH 45202
Telephone: 513-579-7000

Web Site: www.macys.com
Officers: Jeffrey (Jeff) Gennette - Chairman, President, Chief Executive Officer, Chief Merchandising Officer Elisa D. Garcia - Executive Vice President, Chief Legal Officer, Secretary

Auditors: KPMG LLP
Investor Contact: 513-579-7028
Transfer Agents: Computershare Shareowner Services, Pittsburgh, PA

MAGELLAN MIDSTREAM PARTNERS LP

Exchange	Symbol	Price	52Wk Range	Yield	P/E	Div Acheiver
NYS	MMP	$62.87 (12/31/2019)	67.36-56.64	6.49	13.70	17 Years

*7 Year Price Score 76.01   *NYSE Composite Index=100   *12 Month Price Score 92.06

Interim Earnings (Per Share)

Qtr.	Mar	Jun	Sep	Dec
2016	0.91	0.82	0.85	0.93
2017	0.98	0.92	0.87	1.04
2018	0.92	0.94	2.60	1.38
2019	0.91	1.11	1.19	...

Interim Dividends (Per Share)

Amt	Decl	Ex	Rec	Pay
0.998Q	01/22/2019	02/06/2019	02/07/2019	02/14/2019
1.005Q	04/25/2019	05/07/2019	05/08/2019	05/15/2019
1.013Q	07/25/2019	08/06/2019	08/07/2019	08/14/2019
1.02Q	10/24/2019	11/06/2019	11/07/2019	11/14/2019

Indicated Div: $4.08

Valuation Analysis / Institutional Holding

Forecast EPS	$4.38 (01/17/2020)	No of Institutions	868
Market Cap	$14.4 Billion	Shares	179,565,504
Book Value	N/A	% Held	64.34
Price/Book	N/A		
Price/Sales	5.03		

Business Summary: Equipment & Services (MIC: 9.1.3 SIC: 4613 NAIC: 486910)

Magellan Midstream Partners is engaged in the transportation, storage and distribution of refined petroleum products and crude oil. Co.'s segments are: refined products, which consists of its refined products pipeline system, independent terminals and ammonia pipeline system; crude oil, which comprises crude oil pipelines, condensate splitter and storage facilities and ships crude oil as a common carrier for customers including crude oil producers, end users such as refiners, and marketing and trading companies; and marine storage, which owns and operates marine storage terminals located along coastal waterways.

Recent Developments: For the quarter ended Sep 30 2019, net income decreased 54.1% to US$273.0 million from US$594.5 million in the year-earlier quarter. Revenues were US$656.6 million, up 2.9% from US$638.0 million the year before. Operating income was US$320.5 million versus US$295.6 million in the prior-year quarter, an increase of 8.4%. Direct operating expenses declined 4.9% to US$278.1 million from US$292.6 million in the comparable period the year before. Indirect operating expenses increased 16.4% to US$58.0 million from US$49.8 million in the equivalent prior-year period.

Prospects: Our evaluation of Magellan Midstream Partners L.P. as of October 4th, 2019 is the result of our systematic analysis on three basic characteristics: earnings strength, relative valuation, and recent stock price movement. The company has produced a positive trend in earnings per share over the past 5 quarters. However, recent analyst estimates for the company have been mixed and MMP has posted results that exceeded analysts' expectations. Based on operating earnings yield, the company is undervalued when compared to all of the companies we cover. Share price changes over the past year indicates that MMP will perform in line with the market over the near term.

Financial Data

(US$ in Thousands)	9 Mos	6 Mos	3 Mos	12/31/2018	12/31/2017	12/31/2016	12/31/2015	12/31/2014
Earnings Per Share	4.59	6.00	5.83	5.84	3.81	3.52	3.59	3.69
Cash Flow Per Share	6.17	5.95	5.61	5.92	4.86	4.22	4.70	4.87
Dividends Per Share	3.993	3.938	3.870	3.793	3.523	3.245	2.915	2.505
Dividend Payout %	86.98	65.63	66.38	64.94	92.45	92.19	81.20	67.89
Income Statement								
Total Revenue	1,987,230	1,330,634	628,935	2,826,573	2,507,661	2,205,410	2,188,453	2,303,723
EBITDA	769,630	497,605	233,932	1,567,793	1,142,385	1,069,403	1,062,252	1,102,931
Depn & Amortn	6,748	4,943	1,303	214,400	196,300	176,700	164,100	159,000
Income Before Taxes	614,625	391,676	177,577	1,152,879	752,367	727,293	754,975	824,745
Income Taxes	2,450	2,350	1,169	71	3,830	3,218	2,336	4,620
Net Income	734,404	461,366	207,663	1,333,925	869,531	802,771	819,122	839,519
Average Shares	228,754	228,688	228,558	228,573	228,338	228,057	227,888	227,626
Balance Sheet								
Current Assets	567,844	407,018	438,188	646,343	611,839	370,394	338,854	402,667
Total Assets	8,392,186	8,005,440	7,844,551	7,747,537	7,394,375	6,772,073	6,041,567	5,517,285
Current Liabilities	680,645	618,271	623,368	676,556	836,510	481,656	713,072	536,155
Long-Term Obligations	4,705,775	4,407,793	4,279,676	4,211,380	4,273,518	4,087,192	3,189,287	2,982,895
Total Liabilities	5,717,730	5,367,661	5,228,296	5,104,103	5,264,722	4,679,968	4,019,831	3,649,052
Shares Outstanding	228,403	228,403	228,403	228,195	228,024	227,783	227,427	227,068
Statistical Record								
Return on Assets %	13.12	17.63	17.49	17.62	12.28	12.50	14.17	16.24
EBITDA Margin %	38.73	37.40	37.19	55.47	45.56	48.49	48.54	47.88
Net Margin %	36.96	34.67	33.02	47.19	34.67	36.40	37.43	36.44
Asset Turnover	0.36	0.36	0.36	0.37	0.35	0.34	0.38	0.45
Current Ratio	0.83	0.66	0.70	0.96	0.73	0.77	0.48	0.75
Price Range	68.96-54.43	71.97-54.43	71.97-54.43	75.19-54.43	81.46-64.06	77.40-56.97	85.01-55.08	89.12-60.52
P/E Ratio	15.02-11.86	11.99-9.07	12.34-9.34	12.87-9.32	21.38-16.81	21.99-16.18	23.68-15.34	24.15-16.40
Average Yield %	6.38	6.21	5.71	4.89	4.67	3.98	3.23	

Address: One Williams Center, P.O.Box 22186, Tulsa, OK 74121-2186 Telephone: 918-574-7000	Web Site: www.magellanlp.com Officers: Michael N. Mears - Chairman, President, Chief Executive Officer Larry J. Davied - Senior Vice President	Auditors: Ernst & Young LLP Investor Contact: 918-574-7650 Transfer Agents: Computershare Trust Company, N.A., Providence, RI

441

MANPOWERGROUP INC

Exchange	Symbol	Price	52Wk Range	Yield	P/E
NYS	MAN	$97.10 (12/31/2019)	97.36-63.72	2.25	12.23

*7 Year Price Score 84.69   *NYSE Composite Index=100   *12 Month Price Score 102.21

Interim Earnings (Per Share)

Qtr.	Mar	Jun	Sep	Dec
2016	0.98	1.60	1.87	1.85
2017	1.09	1.72	2.04	3.20
2018	1.45	2.17	2.43	2.53
2019	0.88	2.11	2.42	...

Interim Dividends (Per Share)

Amt	Decl	Ex	Rec	Pay
1.01S	05/04/2018	05/31/2018	06/01/2018	06/15/2018
1.01S	11/09/2018	11/30/2018	12/03/2018	12/14/2018
1.09S	05/10/2019	05/31/2019	06/03/2019	06/14/2019
1.09S	11/07/2019	11/29/2019	12/02/2019	12/13/2019

Indicated Div: $2.18 (Div. Reinv. Plan)

Valuation Analysis

		Institutional Holding	
Forecast EPS	$7.39	No of Institutions	
	(01/17/2020)	615	
Market Cap	$5.8 Billion	Shares	
Book Value	$2.7 Billion	79,459,280	
Price/Book	2.13	% Held	
Price/Sales	0.27	81.81	

Business Summary: Business Services (MIC: 7.5.2 SIC: 7363 NAIC: 561330)

ManpowerGroup provides a range of workforce solutions and services, which include recruitment and assessment, training and development, career management, outsourcing, and workforce consulting. Co.'s family of brands and offerings includes Manpower, Experis, Right Management, and ManpowerGroup Solutions. Co.'s portfolio of recruitment services includes permanent, temporary and contract recruitment of professionals, as well as administrative and industrial positions. All of these services are provided under its Manpower and Experis brands. Co. provides services under its Experis brand, particularly in the areas of Information Technology, Engineering, and Finance.

Recent Developments: For the quarter ended Sep 30 2019, net income decreased 7.5% to US$146.1 million from US$158.0 million in the year-earlier quarter. Revenues were US$5.25 billion, down 3.1% from US$5.42 billion the year before. Operating income was US$217.0 million versus US$216.7 million in the prior-year quarter, an increase of 0.1%. Direct operating expenses declined 2.6% to US$4.41 billion from US$4.53 billion in the comparable period the year before. Indirect operating expenses decreased 7.5% to US$623.3 million from US$673.9 million in the equivalent prior-year period.

Prospects: Our evaluation of ManpowerGroup as of October 4th, 2019 is the result of our systematic analysis on three basic characteristics: earnings strength, relative valuation, and recent stock price movement. The company has generated a negative trend in earnings per share over the past 5 quarters. In addition, recent analyst estimates for the company have been reduced while MAN has posted results that exceeded analysts' expectations. Based on operating earnings yield, the company is undervalued when compared to all of the companies we cover. Share price changes over the past year indicates that MAN will perform well over the near term.

Financial Data

(US$ in Thousands)	9 Mos	6 Mos	3 Mos	12/31/2018	12/31/2017	12/31/2016	12/31/2015	12/31/2014
Earnings Per Share	7.94	7.95	8.01	8.56	8.04	6.27	5.40	5.30
Cash Flow Per Share	11.29	9.74	10.62	7.48	5.97	8.54	6.66	3.85
Tang Book Value Per Share	20.15	18.28	17.47	17.80	17.37	12.36	14.25	20.24
Dividends Per Share	2.100	2.100	2.020	2.020	1.860	1.720	1.600	0.980
Dividend Payout %	26.45	26.42	25.22	23.60	23.13	27.43	29.63	18.49
Income Statement								
Total Revenue	15,666,900	10,418,000	5,044,900	21,991,200	21,034,300	19,654,100	19,329,900	20,762,800
EBITDA	586,600	352,400	121,700	881,500	855,100	820,900	771,900	796,900
Depn & Amortn	57,100	39,000	19,400	85,800	84,400	85,300	77,700	83,800
Income Before Taxes	499,400	294,600	93,600	754,700	737,300	701,300	660,700	681,600
Income Taxes	172,500	113,800	40,100	198,000	191,900	257,600	241,500	254,000
Net Income	326,900	180,800	53,500	556,700	545,400	443,700	419,200	427,600
Average Shares	60,300	60,400	61,000	65,100	67,900	70,800	77,700	80,700
Balance Sheet								
Current Assets	6,074,800	6,376,800	6,035,400	5,997,100	6,171,200	5,132,900	5,092,500	5,033,700
Total Assets	8,753,200	9,048,300	8,818,400	8,519,800	8,883,600	7,574,200	7,517,500	7,182,500
Current Liabilities	4,111,300	4,359,900	4,216,800	4,175,900	4,810,400	3,658,800	3,451,000	3,374,400
Long-Term Obligations	983,200	1,025,800	1,003,300	1,025,300	478,100	785,600	810,900	423,900
Total Liabilities	6,055,100	6,415,800	6,242,800	5,894,900	6,108,700	5,212,300	4,892,800	4,239,500
Stockholders' Equity	2,698,100	2,632,500	2,575,600	2,624,900	2,774,900	2,361,900	2,624,700	2,943,000
Shares Outstanding	59,237	59,833	59,734	60,751	66,077	66,969	73,038	78,114
Statistical Record								
Return on Assets %	5.55	5.57	5.79	6.40	6.63	5.86	5.70	5.91
Return on Equity %	17.89	18.42	18.90	20.62	21.24	17.75	15.06	14.60
EBITDA Margin %	3.74	3.38	2.41	4.01	4.07	4.18	3.99	3.84
Net Margin %	2.09	1.74	1.06	2.53	2.59	2.26	2.17	2.06
Asset Turnover	2.41	2.38	2.43	2.53	2.56	2.60	2.63	2.87
Current Ratio	1.48	1.46	1.43	1.44	1.28	1.40	1.48	1.49
Debt to Equity	0.36	0.39	0.39	0.39	0.17	0.33	0.31	0.14
Price Range	97.16-62.59	97.16-62.59	118.66-62.59	136.02-62.59	130.38-89.81	92.83-59.90	96.56-63.79	86.73-59.00
P/E Ratio	12.24-7.88	12.22-7.87	14.81-7.81	15.89-7.31	16.22-11.17	14.81-9.55	17.88-11.81	16.36-11.13
Average Yield %	2.52	2.51	2.36	2.09	1.70	2.25	1.89	1.28

Address: 100 Manpower Place, Milwaukee, WI 53212 Telephone: 414-961-1000 Fax: 414-332-0796	Web Site: www.manpower.com Officers: Jonas Prising - Chairman, President, Chief Executive Officer, Executive Vice President John T. McGinnis - Executive Vice President, Chief Financial Officer, Principal Accounting Officer	Auditors: DELOITTE & TOUCHE LLP Investor Contact: 414-906-6807 Transfer Agents: ComputerShare, College Station, TX

MARATHON OIL CORP.

Exchange	Symbol	Price	52Wk Range	Yield	P/E
NYS	MRO	$13.58 (12/31/2019)	18.78-11.09	1.47	12.57

*7 Year Price Score 53.43   *NYSE Composite Index=100   *12 Month Price Score 82.47

Interim Earnings (Per Share)

Qtr.	Mar	Jun	Sep	Dec
2016	(0.56)	(0.20)	(0.23)	(1.66)
2017	(5.84)	(0.16)	(0.70)	(0.03)
2018	0.42	0.11	0.30	0.46
2019	0.21	0.20	0.21	...

Interim Dividends (Per Share)

Amt	Decl	Ex	Rec	Pay
0.05Q	01/30/2019	02/19/2019	02/20/2019	03/11/2019
0.05Q	04/24/2019	05/14/2019	05/15/2019	06/10/2019
0.05Q	07/31/2019	08/20/2019	08/21/2019	09/10/2019
0.05Q	10/30/2019	11/19/2019	11/20/2019	12/10/2019

Indicated Div: $0.20 (Div. Reinv. Plan)

Valuation Analysis   **Institutional Holding**

Forecast EPS	$0.78	No of Institutions
	(01/25/2020)	1080
Market Cap	$10.9 Billion	Shares
Book Value	$12.3 Billion	855,932,480
Price/Book	0.89	% Held
Price/Sales	1.90	77.22

Business Summary: Production & Extraction (MIC: 9.1.1 SIC: 1311 NAIC: 211111)

Marathon Oil is an independent exploration and production company focused on the U.S. resource plays with operations in the U.S., Europe and Africa. Co.'s U.S. segment explores for, produces and markets crude oil and condensate, natural gas liquids (NGLs) and natural gas in the U.S. Co.'s International segment explores for, produces and markets crude oil and condensate, NGLs and natural gas outside of the U.S. and produces and markets products manufactured from natural gas, such as liquefied natural gas and methanol, in Equatorial Guinea (E.G.). Co. is engaged in oil and gas development and production across its international locations primarily in E.G. and the U.K.

Recent Developments: For the quarter ended Sep 30 2019, net income decreased 35.0% to US$165.0 million from US$254.0 million in the year-earlier quarter. Revenues were US$1.35 billion, down 19.3% from US$1.67 billion the year before. Operating income was US$237.0 million versus US$423.0 million in the prior-year quarter, a decrease of 44.0%. Direct operating expenses declined 24.2% to US$163.0 million from US$215.0 million in the comparable period the year before. Indirect operating expenses decreased 8.2% to US$945.0 million from US$1.03 billion in the equivalent prior-year period.

Prospects: Our evaluation of Marathon Oil Corp. as of October 4th, 2019 is the result of our systematic analysis on three basic characteristics: earnings strength, relative valuation, and recent stock price movement. The company has generated a negative trend in earnings per share over the past 5 quarters. In addition, recent analyst estimates for the company have been reduced while MRO has posted results that exceeded analysts' expectations. Based on operating earnings yield, the company is undervalued when compared to all of the companies we cover. Share price changes over the past year indicates that MRO will perform poorly over the near term.

Financial Data

(US$ in Thousands)	9 Mos	6 Mos	3 Mos	12/31/2018	12/31/2017	12/31/2016	12/31/2015	12/31/2014
Earnings Per Share	0.21	0.20	0.21	1.29	(6.73)	(2.61)	(3.26)	4.46
Cash Flow Per Share	3.65	3.93	2.55	3.82	2.34	1.31	2.31	8.07
Tang Book Value Per Share	15.20	14.93	14.77	14.69	13.64	20.57	27.23	30.46
Dividends Per Share	0.050	0.050	0.050	0.200	0.200	0.200	0.680	0.800
Dividend Payout %	23.81	25.00	23.81	15.50	...	...	...	17.94
Income Statement								
Total Revenue	1,345,000	1,433,000	1,197,000	6,582,000	4,765,000	4,650,000	5,861,000	11,258,000
EBITDA	861,000	862,000	630,000	4,116,000	2,249,000	1,510,000	300,000	4,493,000
Depn & Amortn	622,000	605,000	554,000	2,441,000	2,372,000	2,395,000	2,957,000	2,861,000
Income Before Taxes	175,000	193,000	27,000	1,427,000	(454,000)	(1,235,000)	(2,958,000)	1,361,000
Income Taxes	10,000	32,000	(147,000)	331,000	376,000	905,000	(754,000)	392,000
Net Income	165,000	161,000	174,000	1,096,000	(5,723,000)	(2,140,000)	(2,204,000)	3,046,000
Average Shares	803,000	814,000	820,000	847,000	850,000	819,000	677,000	683,000
Balance Sheet								
Current Assets	2,520,000	2,688,000	2,776,000	2,921,000	2,566,000	3,665,000	2,590,000	4,593,000
Total Assets	20,373,000	21,282,000	21,410,000	21,321,000	22,012,000	31,094,000	32,311,000	36,011,000
Current Liabilities	2,379,000	2,471,000	1,858,000	1,832,000	1,968,000	2,240,000	1,729,000	4,379,000
Long-Term Obligations	4,903,000	4,902,000	5,501,000	5,499,000	5,494,000	6,589,000	7,276,000	5,323,000
Total Liabilities	8,102,000	9,181,000	9,202,000	9,193,000	10,304,000	13,553,000	13,758,000	14,991,000
Stockholders' Equity	12,271,000	12,101,000	12,208,000	12,128,000	11,708,000	17,541,000	18,553,000	21,020,000
Shares Outstanding	801,000	804,000	820,000	819,000	850,000	847,000	677,000	675,000
Statistical Record								
Return on Assets %	3.14	3.03	3.30	5.06	N.M.	N.M.	N.M.	8.50
Return on Equity %	5.37	5.31	5.80	9.20	N.M.	N.M.	N.M.	15.09
EBITDA Margin %	64.01	60.15	52.63	62.53	47.20	32.47	5.12	39.91
Net Margin %	12.27	11.24	14.54	16.65	N.M.	N.M.	N.M.	27.06
Asset Turnover	0.26	0.27	0.23	0.30	0.18	0.15	0.17	0.31
Current Ratio	1.06	1.09	1.49	1.59	1.30	1.64	1.50	1.05
Debt to Equity	0.40	0.41	0.45	0.45	0.47	0.38	0.39	0.25
Price Range	23.99-11.53	23.99-12.66	23.99-12.66	23.99-12.66	18.18-10.77	18.80-6.73	31.19-12.38	41.69-24.80
P/E Ratio	114.24-54.90	119.95-63.30	114.24-60.29	18.60-9.81	...	...	...	9.35-5.56
Average Yield %	0.32	0.28	0.27	1.06	1.40	1.49	2.99	2.25

Address: 5555 San Felipe Street, Houston, TX 77056-2723	Web Site: www.marathonoil.com	Auditors: PricewaterhouseCoopers LLP
Telephone: 713-629-6600	Officers: Lee M. Tillman - Chairman, President, Chief Executive Officer Patrick J. Wagner - Executive Vice President, Vice President, Interim Chief Financial Officer	Investor Contact: 713-296-4114 Transfer Agents: Computershare, Providence, RI

MARATHON PETROLEUM CORP.

Exchange	Symbol	Price	52Wk Range	Yield	P/E
NYS	MPC	$60.25 (12/31/2019)	68.02-44.63	3.52	12.90

*7 Year Price Score 94.24   ***NYSE Composite Index=100**   ***12 Month Price Score 99.93**

Interim Earnings (Per Share)

Qtr.	Mar	Jun	Sep	Dec
2016	0.00	1.51	0.27	0.43
2017	0.06	0.93	1.77	3.97
2018	0.08	2.30	1.62	1.36
2019	(0.01)	1.66	1.66	...

Interim Dividends (Per Share)

Amt	Decl	Ex	Rec	Pay
0.53Q	01/28/2019	02/19/2019	02/20/2019	03/11/2019
0.53Q	04/24/2019	05/15/2019	05/16/2019	06/10/2019
0.53Q	07/31/2019	08/20/2019	08/21/2019	09/10/2019
0.53Q	10/30/2019	11/19/2019	11/20/2019	12/10/2019

Indicated Div: $2.12 (Div. Reinv. Plan)

Valuation Analysis

		Institutional Holding	
Forecast EPS	$4.18	No of Institutions	
	(01/17/2020)	1438	
Market Cap	$39.2 Billion	Shares	
Book Value	$33.7 Billion	577,041,088	
Price/Book	1.16	% Held	
Price/Sales	0.31	71.50	

Business Summary: Refining & Marketing (MIC: 9.1.2 SIC: 1311 NAIC: 211111)

Marathon Petroleum is an independent petroleum refining and marketing, retail and midstream company. Co.'s segments include: Refining and Marketing, which refines crude oil and other feedstocks at its refineries, purchases refined products and ethanol for resale and distributes refined products; Retail, which sells transportation fuels and convenience products in the retail market across the U.S.; and Midstream, which transports, stores, distributes and markets crude oil and refined products via refining logistics assets, pipelines, terminals, towboats and barges, gathers, processes and transports natural gas, and gathers, transports, fractionates, stores and markets natural gas liquids.

Recent Developments: For the quarter ended Sep 30 2019, net income increased 45.3% to US$1.37 billion from US$941.0 million in the year-earlier quarter. Revenues were US$31.20 billion, up 34.9% from US$23.13 billion the year before. Operating income was US$2.02 billion versus US$1.40 billion in the prior-year quarter, an increase of 44.3%. Direct operating expenses rose 32.5% to US$27.30 billion from US$20.61 billion in the comparable period the year before. Indirect operating expenses increased 67.2% to US$1.88 billion from US$1.12 billion in the equivalent prior-year period.

Prospects: Our evaluation of Marathon Petroleum Corp. as of October 4th, 2019 is the result of our systematic analysis on three basic characteristics: earnings strength, relative valuation, and recent stock price movement. The company has generated a negative trend in earnings per share over the past 5 quarters. In addition, recent analyst estimates for the company have been reduced while MPC has posted results that exceeded analysts' expectations. Based on operating earnings yield, the company is undervalued when compared to all of the companies we cover. Share price changes over the past year indicates that MPC will perform very poorly over the near term.

Financial Data

(US$ in Millions)	9 Mos	6 Mos	3 Mos	12/31/2018	12/31/2017	12/31/2016	12/31/2015	12/31/2014
Earnings Per Share	4.67	4.63	5.27	5.28	6.70	2.21	5.26	4.39
Cash Flow Per Share	14.88	12.32	11.77	11.89	13.04	7.53	7.55	5.46
Tang Book Value Per Share	19.17	21.11	20.57	22.05	21.50	18.88	17.36	16.76
Dividends Per Share	2.050	1.980	1.910	1.840	1.520	1.360	1.140	0.920
Dividend Payout %	43.90	42.76	36.24	34.85	22.69	61.54	21.67	20.96
Income Statement								
Total Revenue	93,505	62,303	28,615	97,102	75,369	63,364	72,258	98,102
EBITDA	4,709	2,697	1,581	7,917	6,056	4,355	6,302	5,356
Depn & Amortn	19	9	919	2,490	2,114	2,001	1,646	1,326
Income Before Taxes	3,790	2,083	363	4,568	3,344	1,822	4,374	3,835
Income Taxes	797	457	104	962	(460)	609	1,506	1,280
Net Income	2,194	1,099	(7)	2,780	3,432	1,174	2,852	2,524
Average Shares	660	666	673	526	512	530	542	574
Balance Sheet								
Current Assets	19,139	18,396	18,151	18,023	13,401	10,401	9,471	11,339
Total Assets	98,139	96,896	96,436	92,940	49,047	44,413	43,115	30,460
Current Liabilities	15,339	14,890	15,147	13,216	10,478	7,146	6,345	8,579
Long-Term Obligations	28,282	27,853	27,565	26,980	12,322	10,544	11,896	6,610
Total Liabilities	64,401	62,689	62,485	57,765	35,014	30,856	29,878	19,709
Stockholders' Equity	33,738	34,207	33,951	35,175	14,033	13,557	13,237	10,751
Shares Outstanding	650	660	667	680	486	528	531	548
Statistical Record								
Return on Assets %	4.16	3.75	3.73	3.92	7.34	2.68	7.75	8.58
Return on Equity %	12.86	11.34	11.18	11.30	24.88	8.74	23.78	23.29
EBITDA Margin %	5.04	4.33	5.53	8.15	8.04	6.87	8.72	5.46
Net Margin %	2.35	1.76	N.M.	2.86	4.55	1.85	3.95	2.57
Asset Turnover	1.67	1.59	1.45	1.37	1.61	1.44	1.96	3.33
Current Ratio	1.25	1.24	1.20	1.36	1.28	1.46	1.49	1.32
Debt to Equity	0.84	0.81	0.81	0.77	0.88	0.78	0.90	0.61
Price Range	86.39-44.63	86.39-45.99	86.39-54.32	86.39-54.32	66.84-47.71	51.84-30.73	59.34-38.42	48.46-37.90
P/E Ratio	18.50-9.56	18.66-9.93	16.39-10.31	16.36-10.29	9.98-7.12	23.46-13.90	11.28-7.31	11.04-8.63
Average Yield %	3.44	2.99	2.66	2.51	2.81	3.38	2.25	2.11

Address: 539 South Main Street, Findlay, OH 45840-3229 **Telephone:** 419-422-2121	**Web Site:** www.marathonpetroleum.com **Officers:** Gary R. Heminger - Chairman, President, Chief Executive Officer Donald C. Templin - President, President (frmr), Executive Vice President, Senior Vice President, Chief Financial Officer, Chief Financial Officer (frmr), Division Officer, Principal Financial Officer	**Auditors:** PricewaterhouseCoopers LLP **Investor Contact:** 419-429-5640 **Transfer Agents:** Computershare, Canton, MA

MARKEL CORP (HOLDING CO)

Exchange	Symbol	Price	52Wk Range	Yield	P/E
NYS	MKL	$1143 (12/31/2019)	1196.23-957.49	N/A	29.30

*7 Year Price Score 103.15 *NYSE Composite Index=100 *12 Month Price Score 98.71

Interim Earnings (Per Share)

Qtr.	Mar	Jun	Sep	Dec
2016	11.15	5.41	5.60	9.11
2017	3.90	10.31	(18.82)	30.33
2018	(4.25)	19.97	28.50	(53.76)
2019	42.76	36.07	13.95	...

Interim Dividends (Per Share)

No Dividends Paid

Valuation Analysis / **Institutional Holding**

Forecast EPS	$37.91	No of Institutions
	(01/16/2020)	685
Market Cap	$15.8 Billion	Shares
Book Value	$10.6 Billion	13,261,407
Price/Book	1.49	% Held
Price/Sales	1.98	74.71

Business Summary: General Insurance (MIC: 5.2.1 SIC: 6331 NAIC: 524126)

Markel is a financial holding company. Co.'s business is comprised of the following types of operations: underwriting, which is comprised of risk-bearing insurance operations; investing, which is primarily related to underwriting operations; Markel Ventures, Inc., which includes controlling interests in a portfolio of businesses that operate outside of the specialty insurance marketplace; investment management, which includes investment fund managers that provide a variety of investment products, including insurance-linked securities; and program services, which serves as a fronting platform that provides other insurance companies access to the U.S. property and casualty insurance market.

Recent Developments: For the quarter ended Sep 30 2019, net income decreased 50.1% to US$204.0 million from US$409.0 million in the year-earlier quarter. Revenues were US$2.03 billion, down 9.1% from US$2.24 billion the year before. Net premiums earned were US$1.30 billion versus US$1.19 billion in the prior-year quarter, an increase of 9.7%. Net investment income rose 6.7% to US$113.4 million from US$106.3 million a year ago.

Prospects: Our evaluation of Markel Corp. as of October 4th, 2019 is the result of our systematic analysis on three basic characteristics: earnings strength, relative valuation, and recent stock price movement. The company has suffered a very negative trend in earnings per share over the past 5 quarters. In addition, recent analyst estimates for the company have been reduced while MKL has posted results that exceeded analysts' expectations. Based on operating earnings yield, the company is fairly valued when compared to all of the companies we cover. Share price changes over the past year indicates that MKL will perform in line with the market over the near term.

Financial Data
(US$ in Thousands)

	9 Mos	6 Mos	3 Mos	12/31/2018	12/31/2017	12/31/2016	12/31/2015	12/31/2014
Earnings Per Share	39.02	53.57	37.47	(9.55)	25.81	31.27	41.74	22.27
Cash Flow Per Share	60.77	60.18	61.45	64.13	61.48	38.05	46.58	51.26
Tang Book Value Per Share	490.53	470.95	423.47	368.42	458.23	472.67	420.80	418.50
Income Statement								
Premium Income	3,703,470	2,403,438	1,203,977	4,712,060	4,247,978	3,865,870	3,823,532	3,840,912
Total Revenue	6,944,662	4,911,604	2,472,488	6,841,285	6,061,659	5,612,026	5,369,983	5,133,667
Benefits & Claims	2,118,000	1,365,866	687,746	2,820,715	2,865,761	2,050,744	1,938,745	2,202,467
Income Before Taxes	1,644,798	1,382,870	732,676	(7,855)	87,295	629,920	742,105	440,378
Income Taxes	356,849	298,874	155,163	122,498	(313,463)	169,477	152,963	116,690
Net Income	1,279,362	1,073,725	576,427	(128,180)	395,269	455,689	582,772	321,182
Average Shares	13,864	13,878	13,911	13,923	14,006	14,078	14,061	14,057
Balance Sheet								
Total Assets	37,036,196	36,421,584	34,736,726	33,306,263	32,805,016	25,875,299	24,941,271	25,200,357
Total Liabilities	26,412,742	26,025,219	24,940,744	24,225,610	23,300,868	17,414,372	17,107,121	17,605,539
Stockholders' Equity	10,623,454	10,396,365	9,795,982	9,080,653	9,504,148	8,460,927	7,834,150	7,594,818
Shares Outstanding	13,815	13,826	13,856	13,887	13,903	13,954	13,959	13,961
Statistical Record								
Return on Assets %	1.49	2.10	1.52	N.M.	1.35	1.79	2.32	1.31
Return on Equity %	5.17	7.36	5.36	N.M.	4.40	5.58	7.55	4.50
Loss Ratio %	57.19	56.83	57.12	59.86	67.46	53.05	50.71	57.34
Net Margin %	18.42	21.86	23.31	(1.87)	6.52	8.12	10.85	6.26
Price Range	1196.23-954.39	1218.38-954.39	1218.38-954.39	1218.38-954.39	1147.10-891.25	982.84-810.26	934.76-662.59	703.95-529.00
P/E Ratio	30.66-24.46	22.74-17.82	32.52-25.47	...	44.44-34.53	31.43-25.91	22.39-15.87	31.61-23.75

Address: 4521 Highwoods Parkway, Glen Allen, VA 23060-6148 **Telephone:** 804-747-0136	**Web Site:** www.markelcorp.com **Officers:** Alan I. Kirshner - Executive Chairman, Chairman Emeritus, Chairman, Chief Executive Officer Steven A. Markel - Chairman, Vice-Chairman	**Auditors:** KPMG LLP **Investor Contact:** 800-446-6671 **Transfer Agents:** American Stock Transfer & Trust Co., LLC, Brooklyn, NY

MARRIOTT VACATIONS WORLDWIDE CORP.

Exchange	Symbol	Price	52Wk Range	Yield	P/E
NYS	VAC	$128.76 (12/31/2019)	130.56-68.13	1.68	38.09

*7 Year Price Score 100.65 *NYSE Composite Index=100 *12 Month Price Score 114.72

Interim Earnings (Per Share)

Qtr.	Mar	Jun	Aug	Dec
2016	0.82	1.26	0.97	1.78
Qtr.	Mar	Jun	Sep	Dec
2017	1.21	1.58	1.47	3.92
2018	1.32	0.39	(1.75)	1.98
2019	0.51	1.10	(0.21)	...

Interim Dividends (Per Share)

Amt	Decl	Ex	Rec	Pay
0.45Q	02/15/2019	02/27/2019	02/28/2019	03/14/2019
0.45Q	05/10/2019	05/22/2019	05/23/2019	06/06/2019
0.45Q	09/05/2019	09/18/2019	09/19/2019	10/03/2019
0.54Q	12/09/2019	12/20/2019	12/23/2019	01/06/2020

Indicated Div: $2.16

Valuation Analysis

		Institutional Holding	
Forecast EPS	$7.97	No of Institutions	437
	(01/16/2020)		
Market Cap	$5.5 Billion	Shares	
Book Value	$3.1 Billion		40,669,732
Price/Book	1.76	% Held	
Price/Sales	1.29		75.62

Business Summary: Hotels, Restaurants & Travel (MIC: 2.2.1 SIC: 6531 NAIC: 531311)

Marriott Vacations Worldwide is a vacation company that provides vacation ownership, exchange, rental and resort and property management, along with related businesses, products and services. Co.'s reportable segments are; Vacation Ownership, which develops, markets, sells, rents and manages vacation ownership and related products under its licensed brands; and Exchange and Third-Party Management, which includes exchange networks and membership programs comprised of exchange, getaways, interval gold and interval platinum, club interval, sales and marketing support for interval international network resorts, and operational support for interval international network resorts.

Recent Developments: For the quarter ended Sep 30 2019, net loss amounted to US$7.0 million versus a net loss of US$36.0 million in the year-earlier quarter. Revenues were US$1.08 billion, up 44.3% from US$750.0 million the year before. Revenues from property income rose 45.9% to US$499.0 million from US$342.0 million in the corresponding quarter a year earlier.

Prospects: Our evaluation of Marriott Vacations Worldwide Corp. as of October 4th, 2019 is the result of our systematic analysis on three basic characteristics: earnings strength, relative valuation, and recent stock price movement. The company has managed to produce a neutral trend in earnings per share over the past 5 quarters. However, recent analyst estimates for the company have been reduced while VAC has posted results that exceeded analysts' expectations. Based on operating earnings yield, the company is undervalued when compared to all of the companies we cover. Share price changes over the past year indicates that VAC will perform poorly over the near term.

Financial Data

(US$ in Thousands)	9 Mos	6 Mos	3 Mos	12/31/2018	12/31/2017	12/30/2016	01/01/2016	01/02/2015
Earnings Per Share	3.38	1.84	1.13	1.61	8.18	4.83	3.82	2.33
Cash Flow Per Share	4.84	2.12	2.23	2.91	5.24	5.04	3.47	8.66
Tang Book Value Per Share	N.M.	N.M.	N.M.	N.M.	39.49	33.64	33.04	33.65
Dividends Per Share	1.800	1.750	1.700	1.650	1.450	1.250	1.050	0.250
Dividend Payout %	53.25	95.11	150.44	102.48	17.73	25.88	27.49	10.73
Income Statement								
Total Revenue	3,210,000	2,128,000	1,060,000	2,968,000	1,951,945	1,811,235	1,830,463	1,736,000
EBITDA	230,000	191,000	78,000	219,000	282,172	276,525	265,978	208,000
Depn & Amortn	14,000	9,000	5,000	62,000	21,500	21,000	22,200	19,000
Income Before Taxes	116,000	113,000	39,000	103,000	225,883	222,928	206,310	151,000
Income Taxes	50,000	40,000	15,000	51,000	(895)	85,580	83,698	70,000
Net Income	64,000	73,000	24,000	55,000	226,778	137,348	122,799	81,000
Average Shares	43,400	45,200	46,100	34,000	27,733	28,422	32,168	34,600
Balance Sheet								
Current Assets	3,955,000	3,829,000	3,820,000	1,801,000	1,361,319	1,087,371	1,049,605	1,340,000
Total Assets	9,059,000	9,023,000	9,112,000	9,018,000	2,906,193	2,391,419	2,395,026	2,540,000
Current Liabilities	1,162,000	1,123,000	1,253,000	992,000	488,943	422,966	477,306	433,000
Long-Term Obligations	3,980,000	3,949,000	3,889,000	3,818,000	1,095,213	737,224	678,793	711,000
Total Liabilities	5,947,000	5,759,000	5,766,000	5,557,000	1,861,173	1,483,600	1,418,759	1,460,000
Stockholders' Equity	3,112,000	3,264,000	3,346,000	3,461,000	1,045,020	907,819	976,267	1,080,000
Shares Outstanding	42,592	43,882	44,982	45,992	26,461	26,990	29,549	32,092
Statistical Record								
Return on Assets %	1.44	1.34	0.72	0.92	8.54	5.75	4.99	3.14
Return on Equity %	3.93	3.74	1.94	2.44	23.16	14.62	11.98	7.10
EBITDA Margin %	7.17	8.98	7.36	7.38	-14.46	15.27	14.53	11.98
Net Margin %	1.99	3.43	2.26	1.85	11.62	7.58	6.71	4.67
Asset Turnover	0.47	0.65	0.58	0.50	0.73	0.76	0.74	0.67
Current Ratio	3.40	3.41	3.05	1.82	2.78	2.57	2.20	3.09
Debt to Equity	1.28	1.21	1.16	1.10	1.05	0.81	0.70	0.66
Price Range	110.40-61.33	126.33-61.33	137.49-61.33	152.51-61.33	142.12-80.67	89.52-46.60	91.88-55.98	75.92-47.30
P/E Ratio	32.66-18.14	68.66-33.33	121.67-54.27	94.73-38.09	17.37-9.86	18.53-9.65	24.05-14.65	32.58-20.30
Average Yield %	1.94	1.79	1.64	1.42	1.29	1.86	1.39	0.42

Address: 6649 Westwood Blvd.,	Web Site: www.marriottvacationsworldwide.com	Auditors: Ernst & Young LLP
Orlando, FL 32821	Officers: William J. Shaw - Chairman Stephen P.	Transfer Agents: Computershare
Telephone: 407-206-6000	Weisz - President, Chief Executive Officer	Shareowner Services, Providence, RI

MARSH & MCLENNAN COMPANIES INC.

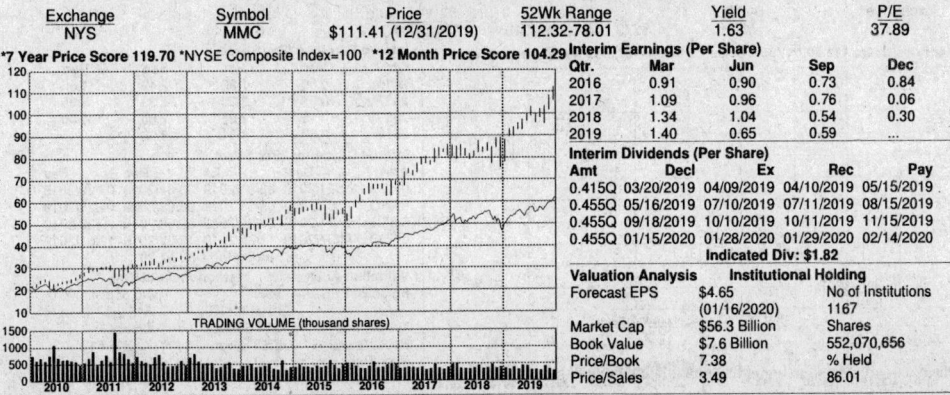

Exchange	Symbol	Price	52Wk Range	Yield	P/E
NYS	MMC	$111.41 (12/31/2019)	112.32-78.01	1.63	37.89

*7 Year Price Score 119.70 *NYSE Composite Index=100 *12 Month Price Score 104.29

Interim Earnings (Per Share)

Qtr.	Mar	Jun	Sep	Dec
2016	0.91	0.90	0.73	0.84
2017	1.09	0.96	0.76	0.06
2018	1.34	1.04	0.54	0.30
2019	1.40	0.65	0.59	...

Interim Dividends (Per Share)

Amt	Decl	Ex	Rec	Pay
0.415Q	03/20/2019	04/09/2019	04/10/2019	05/15/2019
0.455Q	05/16/2019	07/10/2019	07/11/2019	08/15/2019
0.455Q	09/18/2019	10/10/2019	10/11/2019	11/15/2019
0.455Q	01/15/2020	01/28/2020	01/29/2020	02/14/2020

Indicated Div: $1.82

Valuation Analysis — **Institutional Holding**

Forecast EPS	$4.65 (01/16/2020)	No of Institutions	1167
Market Cap	$56.3 Billion	Shares	
Book Value	$7.6 Billion	Shares	552,070,656
Price/Book	7.38	% Held	86.01
Price/Sales	3.49		

Business Summary: Brokers & Intermediaries (MIC: 5.2.3 SIC: 6411 NAIC: 524210)

Marsh & McLennan Companies is a holding company. Through its subsidiaries, Co. provides clients advice and solutions in risk, strategy and people. Co. has two segments: Risk and Insurance Services, which provides risk management, insurance broking, insurance program management services, risk consulting, analytical modeling and alternative risk financing services, as well as creates and executes reinsurance and risk management solutions for clients through risk assessment analytics, actuarial services, product knowledge and trading relationships with reinsurance markets; and Consulting, which delivers advice and digital solutions, and advisory services.

Recent Developments: For the quarter ended Sep 30 2019, net income increased 9.7% to US$306.0 million from US$279.0 million in the year-earlier quarter. Revenues were US$3.97 billion, up 13.2% from US$3.50 billion the year before.

Prospects: Our evaluation of Marsh & McLennan Cos. Inc. as of October 4th, 2019 is the result of our systematic analysis on three basic characteristics: earnings strength, relative valuation, and recent stock price movement. The company has produced a positive trend in earnings per share over the past 5 quarters. However, recent analyst estimates for the company have been mixed and MMC has posted results that exceeded analysts' expectations. Based on operating earnings yield, the company is fairly valued when compared to all of the companies we cover. Share price changes over the past year indicates that MMC will perform over the near term.

Financial Data
(US$ in Thousands)

	9 Mos	6 Mos	3 Mos	12/31/2018	12/31/2017	12/31/2016	12/31/2015	12/31/2014
Earnings Per Share	2.94	2.89	3.28	3.23	2.87	3.38	2.98	2.65
Cash Flow Per Share	4.74	4.45	4.98	4.80	3.69	3.86	3.56	3.88
Dividends Per Share	1.700	1.660	1.620	1.580	1.430	1.300	1.180	1.060
Dividend Payout %	57.82	57.44	49.39	48.92	49.83	38.46	39.60	40.00
Income Statement								
Total Revenue	12,388,000	8,420,000	4,071,000	14,950,000	14,024,000	13,211,000	12,893,000	12,951,000
EBITDA	2,503,000	2,027,000	1,155,000	2,706,000	3,040,000	2,794,000	2,566,000	2,287,000
Depn & Amortn	235,000	302,000	119,000	183,000	169,000	130,000	109,000	86,000
Income Before Taxes	1,908,000	1,494,000	944,000	2,244,000	2,643,000	2,480,000	2,307,000	2,057,000
Income Taxes	531,000	423,000	217,000	574,000	1,133,000	685,000	671,000	586,000
Net Income	1,351,000	1,048,000	716,000	1,650,000	1,492,000	1,768,000	1,599,000	1,465,000
Average Shares	511,000	512,000	511,000	511,000	519,000	524,000	536,000	553,000
Balance Sheet								
Current Assets	7,056,000	7,526,000	12,675,000	5,934,000	5,562,000	4,884,000	5,044,000	6,055,000
Total Assets	31,097,000	32,116,000	30,137,000	21,578,000	20,429,000	18,190,000	18,216,000	17,840,000
Current Liabilities	6,204,000	6,382,000	5,739,000	4,924,000	4,262,000	4,082,000	3,708,000	3,705,000
Long-Term Obligations	11,429,000	11,459,000	11,472,000	5,510,000	5,225,000	4,495,000	4,402,000	3,376,000
Total Liabilities	23,477,000	24,051,000	22,228,000	14,067,000	13,070,000	11,998,000	11,703,000	10,786,000
Stockholders' Equity	7,620,000	8,065,000	7,909,000	7,511,000	7,359,000	6,192,000	6,513,000	7,054,000
Shares Outstanding	504,997	506,568	507,017	503,837	508,711	514,491	521,897	540,142
Statistical Record								
Return on Assets %	5.76	5.54	6.51	7.86	7.73	9.69	8.87	8.41
Return on Equity %	19.96	18.72	21.15	22.19	22.02	27.76	23.57	19.59
EBITDA Margin %	20.21	24.07	28.37	18.10	21.68	21.15	19.90	17.66
Net Margin %	10.91	12.45	17.59	11.04	10.64	13.38	12.40	11.31
Asset Turnover	0.62	0.59	0.58	0.71	0.73	0.72	0.72	0.74
Current Ratio	1.14	1.18	2.21	1.21	1.31	1.20	1.36	1.63
Debt to Equity	1.50	1.42	1.45	0.73	0.71	0.73	0.68	0.48
Price Range	103.13-75.52	99.75-75.52	93.90-75.52	89.10-75.52	85.97-67.41	69.77-51.29	59.84-51.54	58.56-44.40
P/E Ratio	35.08-25.69	34.52-26.13	28.63-23.02	27.59-23.38	29.95-23.49	20.64-15.17	20.08-17.30	22.10-16.75
Average Yield %	1.85	1.89	1.92	1.90	1.85	2.04	2.10	2.07

Address: 1166 Avenue of the Americas, New York, NY 10036-2774 **Telephone:** 212-345-5000 **Fax:** 212-345-4809	**Web Site:** www.mmc.com **Officers:** H. Edward Hanway - Chairman Julio A. Portalatin - Vice-Chairman, Division Officer	**Auditors:** DELOITTE & TOUCHE LLP **Investor Contact:** 212-345-5462 **Transfer Agents:** Wells Fargo Shareowner Services, St. Paul, MN

447

MARTIN MARIETTA MATERIALS, INC.

Exchange	Symbol	Price	52Wk Range	Yield	P/E
NYS	MLM	$279.64 (12/31/2019)	279.64-170.51	0.79	30.56

*7 Year Price Score 111.20 *NYSE Composite Index=100 *12 Month Price Score 110.39

Interim Earnings (Per Share)

Qtr.	Mar	Jun	Sep	Dec
2016	0.69	1.90	2.49	1.55
2017	0.67	2.25	2.39	5.95
2018	0.16	2.92	2.85	1.50
2019	0.68	3.01	3.96	...

Interim Dividends (Per Share)

Amt	Decl	Ex	Rec	Pay
0.48Q	02/21/2019	03/01/2019	03/04/2019	03/29/2019
0.48Q	05/09/2019	05/31/2019	06/03/2019	06/28/2019
0.55Q	08/14/2019	08/30/2019	09/03/2019	09/30/2019
0.55Q	11/07/2019	11/29/2019	12/02/2019	12/31/2019

Indicated Div: $2.20

Valuation Analysis | **Institutional Holding**

Forecast EPS	$9.96	No of Institutions
	(01/17/2020)	842
Market Cap	$17.5 Billion	Shares
Book Value	$5.3 Billion	72,242,640
Price/Book	3.30	% Held
Price/Sales	3.75	98.50

Business Summary: Construction Materials (MIC: 8.5.1 SIC: 1411 NAIC: 212311)

Martin Marietta Materials is a natural resource-based building materials company. Co. supplies aggregates (crushed stone, sand and gravel) through its network of quarries, mines and distribution yards. Co. also provides cement and downstream products, namely, ready mixed concrete, asphalt and paving services. Co. conducts its Building Materials business through three segments: Mid-America Group, Southeast Group and West Group. The Mid-America and Southeast Groups provide aggregates products only. The West Group provides aggregates, cement and downstream products. Co. also has the Magnesia Specialties segment, which includes its magnesia-based chemicals and dolomitic lime businesses.

Recent Developments: For the quarter ended Sep 30 2019, net income increased 37.9% to US$248.6 million from US$180.4 million in the year-earlier quarter. Revenues were US$1.42 billion, up 16.4% from US$1.22 billion the year before. Operating income was US$345.3 million versus US$240.7 million in the prior-year quarter, an increase of 43.5%. Direct operating expenses rose 10.3% to US$999.6 million from US$906.7 million in the comparable period the year before. Indirect operating expenses increased 4.2% to US$75.4 million from US$72.3 million in the equivalent prior-year period.

Prospects: Our evaluation of Martin Marietta Materials Inc. as of October 4th, 2019 is the result of our systematic analysis on three basic characteristics: earnings strength, relative valuation, and recent stock price movement. The company has produced a positive trend in earnings per share over the past 5 quarters. However, recent analyst estimates for the company have been mixed and MLM has posted results that fell short of analysts' expectations. Based on operating earnings yield, the company is fairly valued when compared to all of the companies we cover. Share price changes over the past year indicates that MLM will perform well over the near term.

Financial Data

(US$ in Thousands)	9 Mos	6 Mos	3 Mos	12/31/2018	12/31/2017	12/31/2016	12/31/2015	12/31/2014
Earnings Per Share	9.15	8.04	7.95	7.43	11.25	6.63	4.29	2.71
Cash Flow Per Share	14.61	12.80	11.47	11.21	10.45	10.64	8.58	6.71
Tang Book Value Per Share	38.61	35.34	33.18	32.73	32.02	23.26	22.93	25.07
Dividends Per Share	1.990	1.920	1.880	1.840	1.720	1.640	1.600	1.600
Dividend Payout %	21.75	23.88	23.65	24.76	15.29	24.74	37.30	59.04
Income Statement								
Total Revenue	3,638,668	2,218,423	938,955	4,244,265	3,965,594	3,818,749	3,539,570	2,957,951
EBITDA	967,649	525,426	159,994	1,039,249	990,223	957,640	736,962	526,477
Depn & Amortn	276,974	181,986	89,211	326,099	279,808	268,935	246,874	211,242
Income Before Taxes	591,995	277,195	37,835	576,081	618,928	607,028	413,801	249,178
Income Taxes	111,077	44,899	(4,991)	105,705	(94,457)	181,584	124,863	94,847
Net Income	480,901	232,328	42,853	469,998	713,342	425,386	288,792	155,601
Average Shares	62,679	62,720	62,777	63,147	63,217	63,861	67,020	57,088
Balance Sheet								
Current Assets	1,578,398	1,533,121	1,370,111	1,365,816	2,631,160	1,086,385	1,082,168	1,288,816
Total Assets	10,223,485	10,163,657	10,048,407	9,551,419	8,992,511	7,300,905	6,961,732	7,464,392
Current Liabilities	688,982	822,216	757,637	786,750	694,216	546,588	367,191	396,648
Long-Term Obligations	2,732,815	2,732,018	2,801,228	2,730,439	2,727,294	1,506,153	1,553,649	1,571,059
Total Liabilities	4,921,513	5,068,804	5,075,933	4,605,056	4,312,911	3,160,927	2,904,448	3,113,226
Stockholders' Equity	5,301,972	5,094,853	4,972,474	4,946,363	4,679,600	4,139,978	4,057,284	4,351,166
Shares Outstanding	62,500	62,439	62,594	62,515	62,873	63,176	64,479	67,293
Statistical Record								
Return on Assets %	5.81	5.13	5.29	5.07	8.76	5.95	4.00	2.90
Return on Equity %	11.23	10.20	10.42	9.77	16.18	10.35	6.87	5.28
EBITDA Margin %	26.59	23.68	17.04	24.49	24.97	25.08	20.82	17.80
Net Margin %	13.22	10.47	4.56	11.07	17.99	11.14	8.16	5.26
Asset Turnover	0.47	0.45	0.46	0.46	0.49	0.53	0.49	0.55
Current Ratio	2.29	1.86	1.81	1.74	3.79	1.99	2.95	3.25
Debt to Equity	0.52	0.54	0.56	0.55	0.58	0.36	0.38	0.36
Price Range	274.10-153.43	230.63-153.43	230.68-153.43	239.96-153.43	242.00-195.54	233.52-117.00	176.51-104.58	134.91-98.70
P/E Ratio	29.96-16.77	28.69-19.08	29.02-19.30	32.30-20.65	21.51-17.38	35.22-17.65	41.14-24.38	49.78-36.42
Average Yield %	0.96	0.98	0.96	0.90	0.79	0.92	1.09	1.31

Address: 2710 Wycliff Road, Raleigh, NC 27607-3033
Telephone: 919-781-4550

Web Site: www.martinmarietta.com
Officers: C. Howard Nye - Chairman, President, Chief Executive Officer Roselyn R. Bar - Executive Vice President, General Counsel, Corporate Secretary, Senior Vice President

Auditors: PricewaterhouseCoopers LLP
Investor Contact: 919-781-4550
Transfer Agents: American Stock Transfer & Trust Company, LLC, Brooklyn, NY

MASCO CORP.

Exchange	Symbol	Price	52Wk Range	Yield	P/E
NYS	MAS	$47.99 (12/31/2019)	48.17-29.07	1.13	20.96

*7 Year Price Score 110.10 *NYSE Composite Index=100 *12 Month Price Score 110.57

Interim Earnings (Per Share)

Qtr.	Mar	Jun	Sep	Dec
2016	0.32	0.45	0.40	0.30
2017	0.43	0.49	0.46	0.28
2018	0.47	0.68	0.58	0.64
2019	0.39	0.82	0.44	...

Interim Dividends (Per Share)

Amt	Decl	Ex	Rec	Pay
0.12Q	03/15/2019	04/11/2019	04/12/2019	05/13/2019
0.12Q	06/21/2019	07/11/2019	07/12/2019	08/12/2019
0.135Q	09/17/2019	10/10/2019	10/11/2019	11/12/2019
0.135Q	12/18/2019	01/09/2020	01/10/2020	02/10/2020

Indicated Div: $0.54 (Div. Reinv. Plan)

Valuation Analysis | **Institutional Holding**

Forecast EPS	$2.22	No of Institutions
	(01/17/2020)	920
Market Cap	$13.7 Billion	Shares
Book Value	N/A	351,175,488
Price/Book	N/A	% Held
Price/Sales	1.68	83.87

Business Summary: Retail - Hardware & Home Improvement (MIC: 2.1.8 SIC: 2434 NAIC: 337110)

Masco designs, manufactures and distributes home improvement and building products. Co.'s segments include: Plumbing Products, which includes faucets, showerheads, handheld showers, valves, bath hardware and accessories, bathing units, shower bases and enclosures and toilets; Decorative Architectural Products, which includes paints, primers, specialty coatings, stains and waterproofing products; Cabinetry Products, which manufactures and sells semi-custom, stock and assembled cabinetry for kitchen, bath, storage, home office and home entertainment applications; and Windows and Other Specialty Products, which manufactures and sells vinyl, fiberglass and aluminum windows and patio doors.

Recent Developments: For the quarter ended Sep 30 2019, income from continuing operations increased 8.3% to US$196.0 million from US$181.0 million in the year-earlier quarter. Net income decreased 27.7% to US$138.0 million from US$191.0 million in the year-earlier quarter. Revenues were US$1.95 billion, up 2.3% from US$1.90 billion the year before. Operating income was US$316.0 million versus US$286.0 million in the prior-year quarter, an increase of 10.5%. Direct operating expenses was unchanged at US$1.28 billion versus the comparable period the year before. Indirect operating expenses increased 3.6% to US$349.0 million from US$337.0 million in the equivalent prior-year period.

Prospects: Our evaluation of Masco Corp. as of October 4th, 2019 is the result of our systematic analysis on three basic characteristics: earnings strength, relative valuation, and recent stock price movement. The company has generated a negative trend in earnings per share over the past 5 quarters. In addition, recent analyst estimates for the company have been reduced while MAS has posted results that exceeded analysts' expectations. Based on operating earnings yield, the company is undervalued when compared to all of the companies we cover. Share price changes over the past year indicates that MAS will perform in line with the market over the near term.

Financial Data

(US$ in Thousands)	9 Mos	6 Mos	3 Mos	12/31/2018	12/31/2017	12/31/2016	12/31/2015	12/31/2014
Earnings Per Share	2.29	2.43	2.29	2.37	1.66	1.47	1.02	2.38
Cash Flow Per Share	3.44	3.29	3.26	3.38	2.39	2.22	2.07	1.72
Dividends Per Share	0.480	0.465	0.450	0.435	0.405	0.385	0.365	0.330
Dividend Payout %	20.96	19.14	19.65	18.35	24.40	26.19	35.78	13.87
Income Statement								
Total Revenue	5,787,000	4,183,000	1,908,000	8,359,000	7,644,000	7,357,000	7,142,000	8,521,000
EBITDA	902,000	595,000	207,000	1,330,000	1,279,000	1,183,000	1,030,000	956,000
Depn & Amortn	...	...	...	132,000	116,000	124,000	116,000	157,000
Income Before Taxes	783,000	515,000	168,000	1,042,000	885,000	830,000	689,000	575,000
Income Taxes	202,000	136,000	41,000	258,000	305,000	296,000	293,000	(333,000)
Net Income	482,000	356,000	116,000	734,000	533,000	491,000	355,000	856,000
Average Shares	287,000	290,000	294,000	307,000	318,000	330,000	341,000	352,000
Balance Sheet								
Current Assets	2,792,000	2,843,000	2,758,000	2,766,000	3,215,000	2,934,000	3,328,000	3,863,000
Total Assets	5,520,000	5,653,000	5,602,000	5,393,000	5,488,000	5,137,000	5,680,000	7,167,000
Current Liabilities	1,909,000	1,953,000	1,929,000	1,684,000	1,628,000	1,460,000	2,506,000	2,211,000
Long-Term Obligations	2,771,000	2,771,000	2,771,000	2,971,000	2,969,000	2,995,000	2,418,000	2,919,000
Total Liabilities	5,663,000	5,744,000	5,748,000	5,504,000	5,548,000	5,435,000	5,815,000	6,243,000
Stockholders' Equity	(143,000)	(91,000)	(146,000)	(111,000)	(60,000)	(298,000)	(135,000)	924,000
Shares Outstanding	286,073	287,400	293,548	293,900	310,400	318,000	330,500	345,000
Statistical Record								
Return on Assets %	12.15	13.01	12.48	13.49	10.03	9.05	5.53	12.14
Return on Equity %	...	...	...	...	...	...	89.99	117.34
EBITDA Margin %	15.59	14.22	10.85	15.91	16.73	16.08	14.42	11.22
Net Margin %	8.33	8.51	6.08	8.78	6.97	6.67	4.97	10.05
Asset Turnover	1.47	1.48	1.49	1.54	1.44	1.36	1.11	1.21
Current Ratio	1.46	1.46	1.43	1.64	1.97	2.01	1.33	1.75
Debt to Equity	...	...	...	...	...	...	...	3.16
Price Range	43.20-27.45	40.85-27.45	41.40-27.45	46.27-27.45	44.24-31.93	36.87-23.46	30.50-20.84	22.33-17.18
P/E Ratio	18.86-11.99	16.81-11.30	18.08-11.99	19.52-11.58	26.65-19.23	25.08-15.96	29.90-20.43	9.38-7.22
Average Yield %	1.32	1.29	1.25	1.15	1.09	1.22	1.45	1.67

Address: 17450 College Parkway, Livonia, MI 48152 **Telephone:** 313-274-7400	**Web Site:** www.masco.com **Officers:** J. Michael Losh - Chairman Keith J. Allman - President, Chief Executive Officer, Group President	**Auditors:** PricewaterhouseCoopers LLP **Investor Contact:** 313-792-5500 **Transfer Agents:** Computershare, Providence, RI

MASTEC INC. (FL)

Exchange	Symbol	Price	52Wk Range	Yield	P/E
NYS	MTZ	$64.16 (12/31/2019)	72.82-40.05	N/A	15.03

*7 Year Price Score 125.11 *NYSE Composite Index=100 *12 Month Price Score 114.44

Interim Earnings (Per Share)

Qtr.	Mar	Jun	Sep	Dec
2016	(0.03)	0.30	0.69	0.65
2017	0.50	0.99	0.77	1.95
2018	0.32	1.01	1.52	0.43
2019	0.57	1.58	1.69	...

Interim Dividends (Per Share)

No Dividends Paid

Valuation Analysis — **Institutional Holding**

Forecast EPS	$5.16	No of Institutions
	(01/16/2020)	503
Market Cap	$4.9 Billion	Shares
Book Value	$1.7 Billion	74,375,960
Price/Book	2.92	% Held
Price/Sales	0.66	72.51

Business Summary: Construction Services (MIC: 7.5.4 SIC: 1623 NAIC: 237110)

MasTec is an infrastructure construction company operating mainly throughout North America across a range of industries. Co.'s segments include: Communications, which performs engineering, construction, maintenance and customer fulfillment activities related to communications infrastructure; Oil and Gas, which performs engineering, construction and maintenance services on oil and natural gas pipelines and processing facilities; Electrical Transmission, which performs engineering, construction and maintenance of electrical transmission lines and substations; and Power Generation and Industrial, which performs installation and construction of power facilities.

Recent Developments: For the quarter ended Sep 30 2019, net income increased 7.9% to US$130.1 million from US$120.5 million in the year-earlier quarter. Revenues were US$2.02 billion, up 2.0% from US$1.98 billion the year before. Direct operating expenses rose 0.5% to US$1.69 billion from US$1.68 billion in the comparable period the year before. Indirect operating expenses decreased 2.1% to US$132.3 million from US$135.2 million in the equivalent prior-year period.

Prospects: Our evaluation of MasTec Inc. as of October 4th, 2019 is the result of our systematic analysis on three basic characteristics: earnings strength, relative valuation, and recent stock price movement. The company has generated a negative trend in earnings per share over the past 5 quarters. However, recent analyst estimates for the company have been unchanged while MTZ has posted results that exceeded analysts' expectations. Based on operating earnings yield, the company is undervalued when compared to all of the companies we cover. Share price changes over the past year indicates that MTZ will perform over the near term.

Financial Data

(US$ in Thousands)	9 Mos	6 Mos	3 Mos	12/31/2018	12/31/2017	12/31/2016	12/31/2015	12/31/2014
Earnings Per Share	4.27	4.10	3.53	3.26	4.22	1.61	(0.98)	1.35
Cash Flow Per Share	12.56	11.41	5.33	6.73	1.93	2.55	4.56	4.04
Tang Book Value Per Share	4.57	2.80	1.28	1.58	1.23	N.M.	N.M.	N.M.
Income Statement								
Total Revenue	5,473,965	3,457,346	1,518,340	6,909,417	6,606,978	5,134,703	4,208,330	4,611,803
EBITDA	586,884	350,670	125,338	616,319	578,709	416,625	121,609	378,599
Depn & Amortn	160,000	109,500	54,200	192,300	167,200	143,600	141,300	129,400
Income Before Taxes	368,706	202,289	48,880	341,448	350,498	222,291	(67,746)	198,430
Income Taxes	95,073	51,770	12,033	106,072	22,942	91,784	11,957	76,429
Net Income	291,418	162,823	43,112	259,659	347,213	131,263	(79,110)	115,923
Average Shares	75,934	75,747	75,578	79,772	82,325	81,394	80,489	86,196
Balance Sheet								
Current Assets	2,198,696	2,127,012	2,262,059	2,168,989	1,852,366	1,402,486	1,132,902	1,531,751
Total Assets	4,858,652	4,797,371	4,860,393	4,439,953	4,066,576	3,183,132	2,940,197	3,563,980
Current Liabilities	1,334,506	1,391,153	1,262,652	1,283,611	963,827	839,990	752,789	980,848
Long-Term Obligations	1,221,100	2,608,500	1,539,300	1,324,223	1,280,706	961,400	945,464	1,061,159
Total Liabilities	3,184,051	3,249,250	3,428,782	3,050,055	2,635,777	2,086,601	2,000,627	2,420,319
Stockholders' Equity	1,674,601	1,548,121	1,431,611	1,389,898	1,430,799	1,096,531	939,570	1,143,661
Shares Outstanding	76,309	76,282	76,246	75,997	82,802	82,540	80,103	84,738
Statistical Record								
Return on Assets %	6.58	6.73	6.13	6.10	9.58	4.28	N.M.	3.58
Return on Equity %	20.45	21.20	19.71	18.41	27.48	12.86	N.M.	10.73
EBITDA Margin %	10.72	10.14	8.25	8.92	8.76	8.11	2.89	8.21
Net Margin %	5.32	4.71	2.84	3.76	5.26	2.56	N.M.	2.51
Asset Turnover	1.50	1.57	1.56	1.62	1.82	1.67	1.29	1.42
Current Ratio	1.65	1.53	1.79	1.69	1.92	1.67	1.50	1.56
Debt to Equity	0.73	1.68	1.08	0.95	0.90	0.88	1.01	0.93
Price Range	66.36-37.73	53.20-37.73	54.50-37.73	54.75-37.73	50.70-34.50	40.05-12.75	22.61-14.67	44.23-18.68
P/E Ratio	15.54-8.84	12.98-9.20	15.44-10.69	16.79-11.57	12.01-8.18	24.88-7.92	...	32.76-13.84

Address: 800 S. Douglas Road, 12th Floor, Coral Gables, FL 33134	Web Site: www.mastec.com	Auditors: BDO USA, LLP
Telephone: 305-599-1800	Officers: Jorge Mas - Chairman Jose Ramon Mas - Chief Executive Officer	Investor Contact: 305-406-1815 Transfer Agents: American Stock Transfer & Trust Company, Brooklyn, NY

MASTERCARD INC

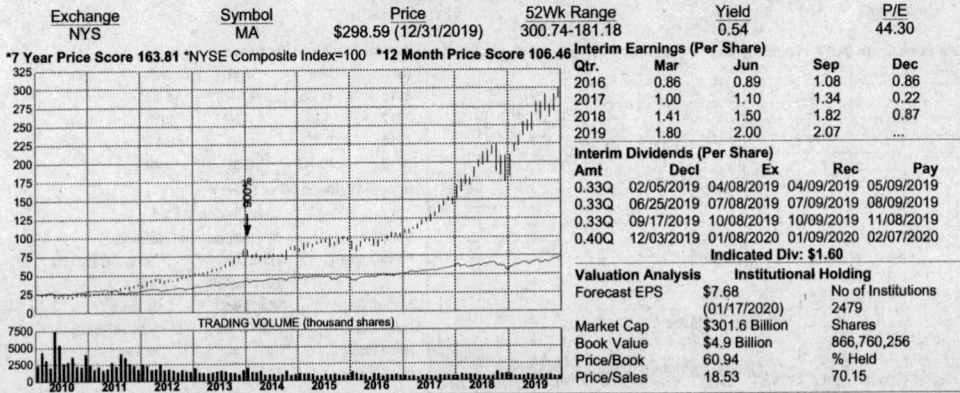

Exchange	Symbol	Price	52Wk Range	Yield	P/E
NYS	MA	$298.59 (12/31/2019)	300.74-181.18	0.54	44.30

*7 Year Price Score 163.81 *NYSE Composite Index=100 *12 Month Price Score 106.46

Interim Earnings (Per Share)

Qtr.	Mar	Jun	Sep	Dec
2016	0.86	0.89	1.08	0.86
2017	1.00	1.10	1.34	0.22
2018	1.41	1.50	1.82	0.87
2019	1.80	2.00	2.07	...

Interim Dividends (Per Share)

Amt	Decl	Ex	Rec	Pay
0.33Q	02/05/2019	04/08/2019	04/09/2019	05/09/2019
0.33Q	06/25/2019	07/08/2019	07/09/2019	08/09/2019
0.33Q	09/17/2019	10/08/2019	10/09/2019	11/08/2019
0.40Q	12/03/2019	01/08/2020	01/09/2020	02/07/2020

Indicated Div: $1.60

Valuation Analysis / Institutional Holding

Forecast EPS	$7.68	No of Institutions
	(01/17/2020)	2479
Market Cap	$301.6 Billion	Shares
Book Value	$4.9 Billion	866,760,256
Price/Book	60.94	% Held
Price/Sales	18.53	70.15

TRADING VOLUME (thousand shares)

Business Summary: Business Services (MIC: 7.5.2 SIC: 7389 NAIC: 561499)

MasterCard is a technology company, in the payments industry that connects consumers, financial institutions, merchants, governments, digital partners, businesses and other organizations worldwide, enabling them to use electronic forms of payment instead of cash and checks. Co. creates a range of payment solutions and services using its brands, including Mastercard®, Maestro® and Cirrus®. Co. facilitates the switching (authorization, clearing and settlement) of payment transactions and delivers related products and services. Co. also provides offerings such as safety and security products, information services and consulting, loyalty and reward programs and issuer and acquirer processing.

Recent Developments: For the quarter ended Sep 30 2019, net income increased 11.0% to US$2.11 billion from US$1.90 billion in the year-earlier quarter. Revenues were US$4.47 billion, up 14.6% from US$3.90 billion the year before. Operating income was US$2.66 billion versus US$2.29 billion in the prior-year quarter, an increase of 16.1%. Indirect operating expenses increased 12.5% to US$1.81 billion from US$1.61 billion in the equivalent prior-year period.

Prospects: Our evaluation of MasterCard Inc. as of October 4th, 2019 is the result of our systematic analysis on three basic characteristics: earnings strength, relative valuation, and recent stock price movement. The company has managed to produce a neutral trend in earnings per share over the past 5 quarters. Additionally, recent analyst estimates for the company have been unchanged while MA has posted results that exceeded analysts' expectations. Based on operating earnings yield, the company is fairly valued when compared to all of the companies we cover. Share price changes over the past year indicates that MA will perform over the near term.

Financial Data

(US$ in Thousands)	9 Mos	6 Mos	3 Mos	12/31/2018	12/31/2017	12/31/2016	12/31/2015	12/31/2014
Earnings Per Share	6.74	6.49	5.99	5.60	3.65	3.69	3.35	3.10
Cash Flow Per Share	6.45	6.42	6.34	5.98	5.21	4.07	3.57	2.92
Tang Book Value Per Share	N.M.	0.20	1.17	1.45	1.25	2.94	2.99	3.95
Dividends Per Share	1.240	1.160	1.080	1.000	0.880	0.760	0.640	0.440
Dividend Payout %	18.40	17.87	18.03	17.86	24.11	20.60	19.10	14.19
Income Statement								
Total Revenue	12,469,000	8,002,000	3,889,000	14,950,000	12,497,000	10,776,000	9,667,000	9,473,000
EBITDA	8,294,000	5,442,000	2,594,000	7,599,000	6,861,000	5,893,000	5,150,000	5,208,000
Depn & Amortn	878,000	623,000	345,000	209,000	185,000	152,000	131,000	107,000
Income Before Taxes	7,256,000	4,722,000	2,203,000	7,204,000	6,522,000	5,646,000	4,958,000	5,079,000
Income Taxes	1,238,000	812,000	341,000	1,345,000	2,607,000	1,587,000	1,150,000	1,462,000
Net Income	6,018,000	3,910,000	1,862,000	5,859,000	3,915,000	4,059,000	3,808,000	3,617,000
Average Shares	1,019,000	1,025,000	1,032,000	1,047,000	1,072,000	1,101,000	1,137,000	1,169,000
Balance Sheet								
Current Assets	14,847,000	14,165,000	14,396,000	16,171,000	13,797,000	13,228,000	10,985,000	10,997,000
Total Assets	25,981,000	24,731,000	23,520,000	24,860,000	21,329,000	18,675,000	16,269,000	15,329,000
Current Liabilities	10,714,000	9,497,000	10,246,000	11,593,000	8,793,000	7,206,000	6,269,000	6,222,000
Long-Term Obligations	7,735,000	7,806,000	5,799,000	5,834,000	5,424,000	5,180,000	3,287,000	1,494,000
Total Liabilities	21,032,000	19,723,000	18,352,000	19,465,000	15,861,000	13,019,000	10,241,000	8,539,000
Stockholders' Equity	4,949,000	5,008,000	5,168,000	5,395,000	5,468,000	5,656,000	6,028,000	6,790,000
Shares Outstanding	1,010,000	1,232,000	1,024,000	1,031,000	1,054,000	1,081,000	1,116,000	1,152,561
Statistical Record								
Return on Assets %	28.05	28.42	26.81	25.37	19.57	23.17	24.10	24.46
Return on Equity %	129.00	130.70	114.60	107.87	70.39	69.29	59.42	50.68
EBITDA Margin %	66.52	68.01	66.70	50.83	54.90	54.69	53.27	54.98
Net Margin %	48.26	48.86	47.88	39.19	31.33	37.67	39.39	38.18
Asset Turnover	0.66	0.67	0.66	0.65	0.62	0.62	0.61	0.64
Current Ratio	1.39	1.49	1.41	1.39	1.57	1.84	1.75	1.77
Debt to Equity	1.56	1.56	1.12	1.08	0.99	0.92	0.55	0.22
Price Range	292.08-174.65	266.79-174.65	235.87-169.70	223.77-151.91	154.19-105.00	107.02-80.65	101.50-80.74	89.08-68.68
P/E Ratio	43.34-25.91	41.11-26.91	39.38-28.33	39.96-27.13	42.24-28.77	29.00-21.86	30.30-24.10	28.74-22.15
Average Yield %	0.53	0.53	0.53	0.52	0.69	0.79	0.69	0.57

Address: 2000 Purchase Street, Purchase, NY 10577 **Telephone:** 914-249-2000	**Web Site:** www.mastercard.com **Officers:** Richard Haythornthwaite - Chairman Ann M. Cairns - Vice-Chairman, Division Officer	**Auditors:** PricewaterhouseCoopers LLP **Investor Contact:** 914-249-4565 **Transfer Agents:** Computershare, Jersey City, NJ

MATADOR RESOURCES CO

Exchange	Symbol	Price	52Wk Range	Yield	P/E
NYS	MTDR	$17.97 (12/31/2019)	21.89-12.43	N/A	10.33

*7 Year Price Score 64.97   *NYSE Composite Index=100   *12 Month Price Score 84.34

Interim Earnings (Per Share)

Qtr.	Mar	Jun	Sep	Dec
2016	(1.26)	(1.15)	0.13	1.17
2017	0.44	0.28	0.15	0.36
2018	0.55	0.53	0.15	1.20
2019	(0.15)	0.31	0.38	...

Interim Dividends (Per Share)

No Dividends Paid

Valuation Analysis

		Institutional Holding	
Forecast EPS	$1.08	No of Institutions	
	(01/17/2020)	334	
Market Cap	$2.1 Billion	Shares	
Book Value	$1.8 Billion	136,997,632	
Price/Book	1.17	% Held	
Price/Sales	2.13	104.73	

Business Summary: Production & Extraction (MIC: 9.1.1 SIC: 1311 NAIC: 211111)

Matador Resources is an independent energy company engaged in the exploration, development, production and acquisition of oil and natural gas resources in the U.S., with an emphasis on oil and natural gas shale and other unconventional plays. Co.'s operations are focused primarily on the Wolfcamp and Bone Spring plays in the Delaware Basin in Southeast New Mexico and West Texas. Co. also operates in the Eagle Ford shale play in South Texas and the Haynesville shale and Cotton Valley plays in Northwest Louisiana and East Texas. Additionally, Co. conducts midstream operations, primarily through its midstream joint venture, San Mateo Midstream, LLC.

Recent Developments: For the quarter ended Sep 30 2019, net income increased 114.0% to US$53.8 million from US$25.1 million in the year-earlier quarter. Revenues were US$279.4 million, up 34.9% from US$207.2 million the year before. Operating income was US$86.1 million versus US$67.9 million in the prior-year quarter, an increase of 26.9%. Direct operating expenses rose 59.7% to US$79.9 million from US$50.0 million in the comparable period the year before. Indirect operating expenses increased 27.0% to US$113.4 million from US$89.3 million in the equivalent prior-year period.

Prospects: Our evaluation of Matador Resources Co as of October 4th, 2019 is the result of our systematic analysis on three basic characteristics: earnings strength, relative valuation, and recent stock price movement. The company has suffered a very negative trend in earnings per share over the past 5 quarters. However, recent analyst estimates for the company have been mixed and MTDR has posted results that exceeded analysts' expectations. Based on operating earnings yield, the company is undervalued when compared to all of the companies we cover. Share price changes over the past year indicates that MTDR will perform very poorly over the near term.

Financial Data

(US$ in Thousands)	9 Mos	6 Mos	3 Mos	12/31/2018	12/31/2017	12/31/2016	12/31/2015	12/31/2014
Earnings Per Share	1.74	1.51	1.73	2.41	1.23	(1.07)	(8.34)	1.56
Cash Flow Per Share	4.65	4.71	4.61	5.36	2.93	1.47	2.56	3.58
Tang Book Value Per Share	15.39	14.89	14.53	14.52	10.66	6.94	5.70	11.81
Income Statement								
Total Revenue	694,995	415,593	173,889	899,599	544,276	264,422	316,169	431,036
EBITDA	170,661	84,618	8,074	599,899	342,385	53,302	(627,804)	313,855
Depn & Amortn	1,814	1,189	643	266,499	177,970	123,196	179,699	134,737
Income Before Taxes	114,675	47,432	(10,498)	292,073	129,850	(98,093)	(826,892)	175,129
Income Taxes	25,335	11,845	(1,013)	(7,691)	(8,157)	(1,036)	(147,368)	64,375
Net Income	63,758	19,805	(16,947)	274,207	125,867	(97,421)	(679,785)	110,771
Average Shares	116,976	116,903	115,315	113,691	102,543	91,273	81,537	70,906
Balance Sheet								
Current Assets	269,316	273,384	229,954	305,685	257,170	279,182	127,007	113,323
Total Assets	3,936,639	3,751,451	3,583,298	3,455,518	2,145,690	1,464,665	1,140,861	1,436,291
Current Liabilities	403,357	336,775	328,423	330,022	282,606	169,505	136,830	161,787
Long-Term Obligations	1,514,020	1,483,625	1,398,229	1,297,837	574,073	573,924	391,254	340,000
Total Liabilities	2,141,332	2,014,974	1,892,475	1,766,638	989,134	774,540	652,858	569,883
Stockholders' Equity	1,795,307	1,736,477	1,690,823	1,688,880	1,156,556	690,125	488,003	866,408
Shares Outstanding	116,638	116,647	116,388	116,353	108,510	99,511	85,564	73,342
Statistical Record								
Return on Assets %	5.65	5.53	6.74	9.79	6.97	N.M.	N.M.	9.52
Return on Equity %	12.00	10.69	13.50	19.27	13.63	N.M.	N.M.	15.43
EBITDA Margin %	24.56	20.36	4.64	66.69	62.91	20.16	N.M.	72.81
Net Margin %	9.17	4.77	N.M.	30.48	23.13	N.M.	N.M.	25.70
Asset Turnover	0.28	0.29	0.30	0.32	0.30	0.20	0.25	0.37
Current Ratio	0.67	0.81	0.70	0.93	0.91	1.65	0.93	0.70
Debt to Equity	0.84	0.85	0.83	0.77	0.50	0.83	0.80	0.39
Price Range	34.22-13.73	34.22-14.12	34.28-14.12	34.28-14.12	31.35-20.30	26.64-12.58	29.35-18.30	29.28-14.44
P/E Ratio	19.67-7.89	22.66-9.35	19.82-8.16	14.22-5.86	25.49-16.50	...	...	18.77-9.26

Address: 5400 LBJ Freeway, Suite 1500, Dallas, TX 75240	Web Site: www.matadorresources.com	Auditors: KPMG LLP
Telephone: 972-371-5200	Officers: Joseph Wm. Foran - Chairman, Chief Executive Officer, Secretary, President Matthew V. Hairford - President, Executive Vice President	Transfer Agents: Registrar & Transfer Company, Cranford, NJ

MAXIMUS INC.

Exchange	Symbol	Price	52Wk Range	Yield	P/E
NYS	MMS	$74.39 (12/31/2019)	81.41-64.92	1.51	20.00

*7 Year Price Score 105.43 *NYSE Composite Index=100 *12 Month Price Score 96.76

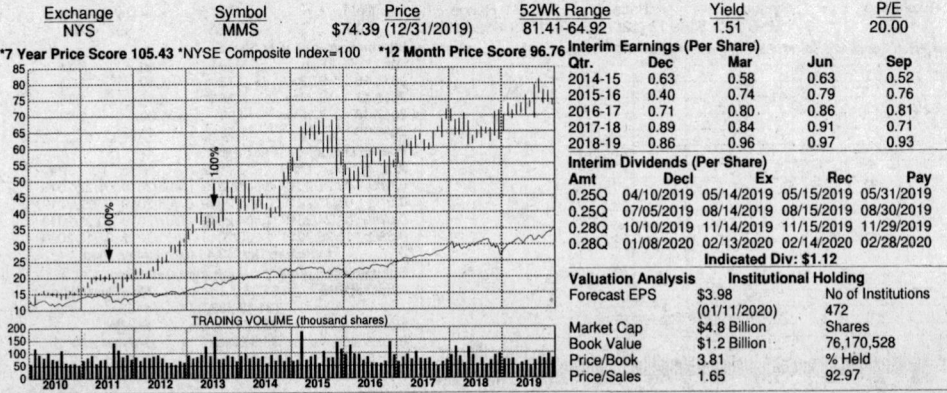

Interim Earnings (Per Share)

Qtr.	Dec	Mar	Jun	Sep
2014-15	0.63	0.58	0.63	0.52
2015-16	0.40	0.74	0.79	0.76
2016-17	0.71	0.80	0.86	0.81
2017-18	0.89	0.84	0.91	0.71
2018-19	0.86	0.96	0.97	0.93

Interim Dividends (Per Share)

Amt	Decl	Ex	Rec	Pay
0.25Q	04/10/2019	05/14/2019	05/15/2019	05/31/2019
0.25Q	07/05/2019	08/14/2019	08/15/2019	08/30/2019
0.28Q	10/10/2019	11/14/2019	11/15/2019	11/29/2019
0.28Q	01/08/2020	02/13/2020	02/14/2020	02/28/2020

Indicated Div: $1.12

Valuation Analysis

		Institutional Holding	
Forecast EPS	$3.98	No of Institutions	
	(01/11/2020)	472	
Market Cap	$4.8 Billion	Shares	
Book Value	$1.2 Billion	76,170,528	
Price/Book	3.81	% Held	
Price/Sales	1.65	92.97	

Business Summary: Business Services (MIC: 7.5.2 SIC: 7389 NAIC: 561499)

MAXIMUS is an operator of government health and human services programs worldwide. Co.'s segments are: United States Health and Human Services, which provides a variety of business process services such as program administration, appeals and assessments work and related consulting work; United States Federal Services, which provides program administration, appeals and assessments services and technology solutions, including system and software development and maintenance services; and Outside the United States, which provides business process services solutions for governments and commercial clients in geographies beyond the United States, including health and disability assessments.

Recent Developments: For the year ended Sep 30 2019, net income increased 8.9% to US$240.5 million from US$220.8 million in the prior year. Revenues were US$2.89 billion, up 20.7% from US$2.39 billion the year before. Operating income was US$317.1 million versus US$295.5 million in the prior year, an increase of 7.3%. Direct operating expenses rose 23.2% to US$2.22 billion from US$1.80 billion in the comparable period the year before. Indirect operating expenses increased 18.5% to US$354.1 million from US$298.9 million in the equivalent prior-year period.

Prospects: Our evaluation of Maximus Inc. as of October 4th, 2019 is the result of our systematic analysis on three basic characteristics: earnings strength, relative valuation, and recent stock price movement. The company has enjoyed a very positive trend in earnings per share over the past 5 quarters. However, recent analyst estimates for the company have been mixed and MMS has posted results that exceeded analysts' expectations. Based on operating earnings yield, the company is fairly valued when compared to all of the companies we cover. Share price changes over the past year indicates that MMS will perform very well over the near term.

Financial Data

(US$ in Thousands)	09/30/2019	09/30/2018	09/30/2017	09/30/2016	09/30/2015	09/30/2014	09/30/2013	09/30/2012
Earnings Per Share	3.72	3.35	3.17	2.69	2.35	2.11	1.67	1.10
Cash Flow Per Share	5.53	4.94	5.14	2.73	3.09	3.16	1.77	1.70
Tang Book Value Per Share	7.06	8.91	6.32	3.26	1.55	4.60	4.02	4.21*
Dividends Per Share	1.000	0.180	0.180	0.180	0.180	0.180	0.180	0.180
Dividend Payout %	26.88	5.37	5.68	6.69	7.66	8.53	10.78	16.44
Income Statement								
Total Revenue	2,886,815	2,392,236	2,450,961	2,403,360	2,099,821	1,700,912	1,331,279	1,050,145
EBITDA	398,531	351,217	373,805	352,679	307,565	264,098	212,508	146,375
Depn & Amortn	78,254	51,008	57,408	62,577	46,348	38,790	26,300	18,800
Income Before Taxes	317,320	299,209	314,235	285,968	259,819	227,369	189,059	131,751
Income Taxes	76,825	78,393	102,053	105,808	99,770	81,973	71,934	55,652
Net Income	240,824	220,751	209,426	178,362	157,772	145,440	116,731	76,133
Average Shares	64,820	65,932	65,632	66,229	67,275	69,087	69,893	69,612
Balance Sheet								
Current Assets	789,425	808,632	657,242	620,980	580,899	532,460	489,599	448,684
Total Assets	1,745,732	1,462,000	1,350,662	1,348,819	1,280,171	900,996	857,978	695,293
Current Liabilities	364,238	277,449	316,266	340,756	356,380	265,321	262,307	199,136
Long-Term Obligations	...	...	527	165,238	210,618	...	1,319	1,558
Total Liabilities	497,940	378,133	410,577	599,738	667,793	345,034	328,470	244,187
Stockholders' Equity	1,247,792	1,083,867	940,085	749,081	612,378	555,962	529,508	451,106
Shares Outstanding	63,979	64,371	65,137	65,223	65,437	66,613	68,525	67,970
Statistical Record								
Return on Assets %	15.02	15.70	15.52	13.53	14.47	16.54	15.03	12.05
Return on Equity %	20.66	21.81	24.80	26.13	27.01	26.80	23.81	18.39
EBITDA Margin %	13.81	14.68	15.25	14.67	14.65	15.53	15.96	13.94
Net Margin %	8.34	9.23	8.54	7.42	7.51	8.55	8.77	7.25
Asset Turnover	1.80	1.70	1.82	1.82	1.93	1.93	1.71	1.66
Current Ratio	2.17	2.91	2.08	1.82	1.63	2.01	1.87	2.25
Debt to Equity	...	...	N.M.	0.22	0.34	...	N.M.	N.M.
Price Range	81.41-61.79	72.04-60.90	65.06-45.25	69.80-45.94	69.22-39.00	50.41-38.57	45.29-27.31	29.86-16.95
P/E Ratio	21.88-16.61	21.50-18.18	20.52-14.27	25.95-17.08	29.46-16.60	23.89-18.28	27.12-16.35	27.15-15.41
Average Yield %	1.41	0.27	0.30	0.32	0.30	0.41	0.50	0.80

Address: 1891 Metro Center Drive, Reston, VA 20190 **Telephone:** 703-251-8500	**Web Site:** www.maximus.com **Officers:** Peter B. Pond - Chairman Richard A. Montoni - Vice-Chairman, President, Chief Executive Officer	**Auditors:** Ernst & Young LLP **Investor Contact:** 703-251-8637 **Transfer Agents:** American Stock Transfer & Trust Company, New York, NY

453

MCCORMICK & CO INC

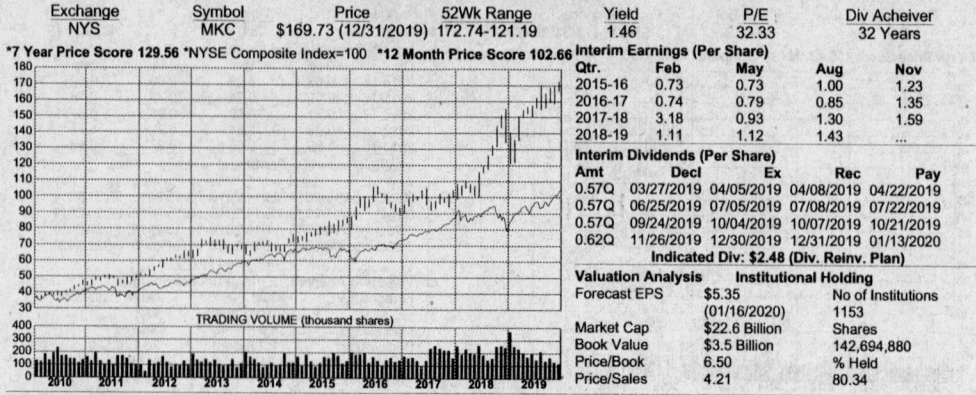

Exchange	Symbol	Price	52Wk Range	Yield	P/E	Div Achiever
NYS	MKC	$169.73 (12/31/2019)	172.74-121.19	1.46	32.33	32 Years

*7 Year Price Score 129.56 *NYSE Composite Index=100 *12 Month Price Score 102.66

Interim Earnings (Per Share)

Qtr.	Feb	May	Aug	Nov
2015-16	0.73	0.73	1.00	1.23
2016-17	0.74	0.79	0.85	1.35
2017-18	3.18	0.93	1.30	1.59
2018-19	1.11	1.12	1.43	...

Interim Dividends (Per Share)

Amt	Decl	Ex	Rec	Pay
0.57Q	03/27/2019	04/05/2019	04/08/2019	04/22/2019
0.57Q	06/25/2019	07/05/2019	07/08/2019	07/22/2019
0.57Q	09/24/2019	10/04/2019	10/07/2019	10/21/2019
0.62Q	11/26/2019	12/30/2019	12/31/2019	01/13/2020

Indicated Div: $2.48 (Div. Reinv. Plan)

Valuation Analysis

		Institutional Holding	
Forecast EPS	$5.35	No of Institutions	
	(01/16/2020)	1153	
Market Cap	$22.6 Billion	Shares	
Book Value	$3.5 Billion	142,694,880	
Price/Book	6.50	% Held	
Price/Sales	4.21	80.34	

Business Summary: Food (MIC: 1.2.1 SIC: 2099 NAIC: 311942)

McCormick & Co. manufactures, markets and distributes spices, seasoning mixes, condiments and other flavorful products to the food industry-retailers, food manufacturers and foodservice businesses. Co.'s major sales, distribution and production facilities are located in North America, Europe and China. Additional facilities are based in Australia, India, Central America, Thailand and South Africa. Co. operates in two business segments: consumer, in which Co. markets its branded products and supplies private label items; and flavor solutions, which provides a range of products flavor solutions including seasoning blends, spices and herbs, condiments, coating systems and compound flavors.

Recent Developments: For the quarter ended Aug 31 2019, net income increased 10.6% to US$191.9 million from US$173.5 million in the year-earlier quarter. Revenues were US$1.33 billion, up 0.8% from US$1.32 billion the year before. Operating income was US$253.5 million versus US$229.9 million in the prior-year quarter, an increase of 10.3%. Direct operating expenses declined 0.8% to US$789.3 million from US$795.7 million in the comparable period the year before. Indirect operating expenses decreased 2.1% to US$286.4 million from US$292.6 million in the equivalent prior-year period.

Prospects: Our evaluation of McCormick & Co. Inc. as of October 4th, 2019 is the result of our systematic analysis on three basic characteristics: earnings strength, relative valuation, and recent stock price movement. The company has managed to produce a neutral trend in earnings per share over the past 5 quarters. In addition, recent analyst estimates for the company have been mixed and MKC has posted results that exceeded analysts' expectations. Based on operating earnings yield, the company is fairly valued when compared to all of the companies we cover. Share price changes over the past year indicates that MKC will perform well over the near term.

Financial Data

(US$ in Thousands)	9 Mos	6 Mos	3 Mos	11/30/2018	11/30/2017	11/30/2016	11/30/2015	11/30/2014
Earnings Per Share	5.25	5.12	4.93	7.00	3.72	3.69	3.11	3.34
Cash Flow Per Share	6.98	6.81	7.15	6.24	6.43	5.18	4.61	3.88
Dividends Per Share	2.230	2.180	2.130	2.080	1.880	1.720	1.600	1.480
Dividend Payout %	42.48	42.58	43.20	29.71	50.54	46.61	51.45	44.31
Income Statement								
Total Revenue	3,862,600	2,533,400	1,231,500	5,408,900	4,834,100	4,411,500	4,296,300	4,243,200
EBITDA	795,800	496,400	243,300	1,066,600	836,600	753,900	655,400	706,800
Depn & Amortn	118,000	79,000	40,300	150,700	146,100	108,700	105,900	102,700
Income Before Taxes	551,100	332,000	160,000	741,300	594,800	589,200	496,200	554,400
Income Taxes	91,000	54,200	22,100	(157,300)	151,300	153,000	131,300	145,900
Net Income	489,300	297,400	148,000	933,400	477,400	472,300	401,600	437,900
Average Shares	134,200	133,900	133,800	133,200	128,400	128,000	129,200	131,000
Balance Sheet								
Current Assets	1,589,400	1,473,100	1,428,000	1,479,900	1,617,000	1,421,800	1,406,500	1,416,200
Total Assets	10,366,000	10,236,700	10,227,900	10,256,400	10,385,800	4,635,900	4,507,800	4,414,300
Current Liabilities	2,030,400	1,860,100	1,829,100	2,001,700	1,947,300	1,422,700	1,240,000	1,122,000
Long-Term Obligations	3,843,100	3,977,500	4,034,000	4,052,900	4,443,900	1,054,000	1,052,700	1,014,100
Total Liabilities	6,897,300	6,865,800	6,896,900	7,085,500	7,825,900	3,009,300	2,837,600	2,622,100
Stockholders' Equity	3,468,700	3,370,900	3,331,000	3,170,900	2,559,900	1,626,600	1,670,200	1,792,200
Shares Outstanding	132,911	132,526	132,007	132,100	131,000	125,300	127,300	128,400
Statistical Record								
Return on Assets %	6.81	6.64	6.40	9.04	6.36	10.30	9.00	9.88
Return on Equity %	21.41	21.41	20.62	32.57	22.81	28.57	23.20	23.51
EBITDA Margin %	20.60	19.59	19.76	19.72	17.31	17.09	15.25	16.66
Net Margin %	12.67	11.74	12.02	17.26	9.88	10.71	9.35	10.32
Asset Turnover	0.52	0.52	0.52	0.52	0.64	0.96	0.96	0.96
Current Ratio	0.78	0.79	0.78	0.74	0.83	1.00	1.13	1.26
Debt to Equity	1.11	1.18	1.21	1.28	1.74	0.65	0.63	0.57
Price Range	169.94-121.19	156.67-100.51	155.83-100.51	151.34-98.89	105.92-88.78	107.07-79.78	86.03-71.39	74.33-63.03
P/E Ratio	32.37-23.08	30.60-19.63	31.61-20.39	21.62-14.13	28.47-23.87	29.02-21.62	27.66-22.95	22.25-18.87
Average Yield %	1.53	1.62	1.72	1.80	1.92	1.81	2.04	2.14

Address: 24 Schilling Road, Suite 1, Hunt Valley, MD 21031
Telephone: 410-771-7301
Fax: 410-771-7462

Web Site: www.mccormickcorporation.com
Officers: Lawrence E. Kurzius - Chairman, President, Chief Executive Officer, Division Officer Michael R. Smith - Executive Vice President, Senior Vice President, Chief Financial Officer, Region Officer

Auditors: Ernst & Young LLP
Investor Contact: 410-771-7244
Transfer Agents: Wells Fargo Bank, N.A. Shareowner Services, Mendota Heights, MN

MCDONALD'S CORP

Exchange	Symbol	Price	52Wk Range	Yield	P/E	Div Acheiver
NYS	MCD	$197.61 (12/31/2019)	221.15-173.97	2.53	25.93	42 Years

*7 Year Price Score 123.22 ***NYSE Composite Index=100** ***12 Month Price Score 92.98**

Interim Earnings (Per Share)

Qtr.	Mar	Jun	Sep	Dec
2016	1.23	1.25	1.50	1.43
2017	1.47	1.70	2.32	0.89
2018	1.72	1.90	2.10	1.82
2019	1.72	1.97	2.11	...

Interim Dividends (Per Share)

Amt	Decl	Ex	Rec	Pay
1.16Q	01/24/2019	02/28/2019	03/01/2019	03/15/2019
1.16Q	05/23/2019	05/31/2019	06/03/2019	06/17/2019
1.16Q	07/18/2019	08/30/2019	09/03/2019	09/17/2019
1.25Q	09/19/2019	11/29/2019	12/02/2019	12/16/2019

Indicated Div: $5.00 (Div. Reinv. Plan)

Valuation Analysis / Institutional Holding

Forecast EPS	$7.84	No of Institutions	
	(01/17/2020)	2896	
Market Cap	$148.8 Billion	Shares	
Book Value	N/A	700,014,272	
Price/Book	N/A	% Held	
Price/Sales	7.12	63.55	

TRADING VOLUME (thousand shares)

Business Summary: Hotels, Restaurants & Travel (MIC: 2.2.1 SIC: 5812 NAIC: 722211)

McDonald's operates and franchises McDonald's restaurants, which serve a locally-relevant menu of food and beverages. Co.'s menu includes hamburgers and cheeseburgers, Big Mac, Quarter Pounder with Cheese, Filet-O-Fish, several chicken sandwiches, Chicken McNuggets, wraps, french fries, shakes, McFlurry desserts, sundaes, soft serve cones, pies, soft drinks, coffee, McCafe beverages and other beverages. The restaurants also sell other products during limited-time promotions. Co.'s restaurants in the U.S. and various international markets provide a full or limited breakfast menu. Breakfast offerings may include Sausage McMuffin with Egg, McGriddles, biscuit and bagel sandwiches and hotcakes.

Recent Developments: For the quarter ended Sep 30 2019, net income decreased 1.8% to US$1.61 billion from US$1.64 billion in the year-earlier quarter. Revenues were US$5.43 billion, up 1.1% from US$5.37 billion the year before. Operating income was US$2.41 billion versus US$2.42 billion in the prior-year quarter, a decrease of 0.3%. Direct operating expenses declined 3.9% to US$1.97 billion from US$2.05 billion in the comparable period the year before. Indirect operating expenses increased 16.6% to US$1.05 billion from US$903.8 million in the equivalent prior-year period.

Prospects: Our evaluation of McDonald's Corp. as of October 4th, 2019 is the result of our systematic analysis on three basic characteristics: earnings strength, relative valuation, and recent stock price movement. The company has managed to produce a neutral trend in earnings per share over the past 5 quarters. In addition, recent analyst estimates for the company have been mixed and MCD has posted results in line with analysts' expectations. Based on operating earnings yield, the company is fairly valued when compared to all of the companies we cover. Share price changes over the past year indicates that MCD will perform over the near term.

Financial Data

(US$ in Thousands)	9 Mos	6 Mos	3 Mos	12/31/2018	12/31/2017	12/31/2016	12/31/2015	12/31/2014
Earnings Per Share	7.62	7.61	7.54	7.54	6.37	5.44	4.80	4.82
Cash Flow Per Share	10.24	10.41	9.60	8.95	6.88	7.07	6.96	6.86
Tang Book Value Per Share	...	...	...	...	...	...	5.04	10.51
Dividends Per Share	4.640	4.490	4.340	4.190	3.830	3.610	3.440	3.280
Dividend Payout %	60.89	59.00	57.56	55.57	60.13	66.36	71.67	68.05
Income Statement								
Total Revenue	15,727,500	10,296,900	4,955,600	21,025,200	22,820,400	24,621,900	25,413,000	27,441,300
EBITDA	7,892,900	5,098,400	2,452,900	9,948,700	10,538,600	9,086,700	8,778,800	9,490,700
Depn & Amortn	1,204,300	790,900	392,600	1,302,900	1,227,500	1,390,700	1,438,000	1,539,300
Income Before Taxes	5,879,300	3,769,400	1,796,200	7,664,600	8,389,800	6,811,200	6,702,500	7,380,900
Income Taxes	1,538,100	993,800	502,900	1,891,800	3,381,200	2,179,500	2,026,400	2,614,200
Net Income	4,453,200	2,845,300	1,328,400	5,924,300	5,192,300	4,686,500	4,529,300	4,757,800
Average Shares	763,900	768,700	771,600	785,600	815,900	861,200	944,600	986,300
Balance Sheet								
Current Assets	3,604,900	3,915,400	4,964,400	4,053,200	5,327,200	4,848,600	9,643,000	4,185,500
Total Assets	45,805,000	46,199,800	46,466,600	32,811,200	33,803,700	31,023,900	37,938,700	34,281,400
Current Liabilities	4,275,600	3,240,000	3,379,600	2,973,500	2,890,600	3,468,300	2,950,400	2,747,900
Long-Term Obligations	32,850,100	32,654,300	32,892,000	31,075,300	29,536,400	25,878,500	24,122,100	14,989,700
Total Liabilities	54,404,200	53,008,600	53,017,500	39,069,600	37,071,700	33,228,200	30,850,800	21,428,000
Stockholders' Equity	(8,599,200)	(6,808,800)	(6,550,900)	(6,258,400)	(3,268,000)	(2,204,300)	7,087,900	12,853,400
Shares Outstanding	753,100	759,400	763,556	767,100	794,100	819,300	906,800	962,900
Statistical Record								
Return on Assets %	14.70	14.95	14.66	17.79	16.02	13.55	12.54	13.42
Return on Equity %	...	...	...	...	...	191.40	45.43	32.97
EBITDA Margin %	50.19	49.51	49.50	47.32	46.18	36.90	34.54	34.59
Net Margin %	28.31	27.63	26.81	28.18	22.75	19.03	17.82	17.34
Asset Turnover	0.52	0.53	0.52	0.63	0.70	0.71	0.70	0.77
Current Ratio	0.84	1.21	1.47	1.36	1.84	1.40	3.27	1.52
Debt to Equity	...	...	...	...	...	...	3.40	1.17
Price Range	221.15-162.97	207.66-155.41	189.90-155.41	189.26-148.27	174.20-119.48	131.60-110.57	120.07-88.78	103.53-88.46
P/E Ratio	29.02-21.39	27.29-20.42	25.19-20.61	25.10-19.66	27.35-18.76	24.19-20.33	25.01-18.50	21.48-18.35
Average Yield %	2.40	2.50	2.55	2.52	2.57	3.00	3.43	3.40

Address: 110 North Carpenter Street, Chicago, IL 60607 Telephone: 630-623-3000	Web Site: www.mcdonalds.com Officers: Enrique Hernandez - Chairman Christopher J. (Chris) Kempczinski - President, Chief Executive Officer, Executive Vice President, Region Officer	Auditors: Ernst & Young LLP Investor Contact: 800-228-9623 Transfer Agents: Computershare, Providence, RI

MCKESSON CORP

Exchange	Symbol	Price	52Wk Range	Yield	P/E	Div Acheiver
NYS	MCK	$138.32 (12/31/2019)	153.27-110.47	1.19	N/A	11 Years

*7 Year Price Score 69.02 *NYSE Composite Index=100 *12 Month Price Score 101.27

Interim Earnings (Per Share)

Qtr.	Jun	Sep	Dec	Mar
2016-17	2.38	1.34	2.85	16.17
2017-18	1.45	0.01	4.33	(5.44)
2018-19	(0.68)	2.51	2.40	(4.01)
2019-20	2.24	(3.99)	...	...

Interim Dividends (Per Share)

Amt	Decl	Ex	Rec	Pay
0.39Q	01/30/2019	02/28/2019	03/01/2019	04/01/2019
0.39Q	04/24/2019	05/31/2019	06/03/2019	07/01/2019
0.41Q	07/30/2019	08/30/2019	09/03/2019	10/01/2019
0.41Q	10/23/2019	11/29/2019	12/02/2019	01/02/2020

Indicated Div: $1.64

Valuation Analysis

		Institutional Holding	
Forecast EPS	$14.42	No of Institutions	
	(01/17/2020)	1309	
Market Cap	$24.9 Billion	Shares	
Book Value	$6.5 Billion	206,738,784	
Price/Book	3.85	% Held	
Price/Sales	0.11	76.14	

Business Summary: Pharmaceuticals (MIC: 4.1.1 SIC: 5122 NAIC: 325412)

McKesson provides pharmaceuticals and medical supplies and services to its customers. Co.'s segments include: U.S. Pharmaceutical and Specialty Solutions, which provides distribution and logistics services for branded, generic, specialty, biosimilar and over-the-counter pharmaceutical drugs and other healthcare-related products to customers; European Pharmaceutical Solutions, which provides distribution and services to wholesale, institutional and retail customers in European countries where it owns, partners or franchises with retail pharmacies; and Medical-Surgical Solutions, which delivers medical-supply distribution, logistics, biomedical and other services to healthcare providers.

Recent Developments: For the quarter ended Sep 30 2019, loss from continuing operations was US$676.0 million compared with income of US$552.0 million in the year-earlier quarter. Net loss amounted to US$677.0 million versus net income of US$553.0 million in the year-earlier quarter. Revenues were US$57.62 billion, up 8.6% from US$53.08 billion the year before. Operating income was US$626.0 million versus US$689.0 million in the prior-year quarter, a decrease of 9.1%. Direct operating expenses rose 8.9% to US$54.75 billion from US$50.27 billion in the comparable period the year before. Indirect operating expenses increased 6.0% to US$2.24 billion from US$2.12 billion in the equivalent prior-year period.

Prospects: Our evaluation of McKesson Corp. as of October 4th, 2019 is the result of our systematic analysis on three basic characteristics: earnings strength, relative valuation, and recent stock price movement. The company has produced a positive trend in earnings per share over the past 5 quarters. However, recent analyst estimates for the company have been unchanged, while MCK has posted results that exceeded analysts' expectations. Based on operating earnings yield, the company is undervalued when compared to all of the companies we cover. Share price changes over the past year indicates that MCK will perform over the near term.

Financial Data

(US$ in Thousands)	6 Mos	3 Mos	03/31/2019	03/31/2018	03/31/2017	03/31/2016	03/31/2015	03/31/2014
Earnings Per Share	(3.36)	3.14	0.17	0.32	22.73	9.70	6.27	5.41
Cash Flow Per Share	19.45	26.84	20.59	20.89	21.47	15.92	13.41	13.69
Dividends Per Share	1.580	1.560	1.510	1.300	1.120	1.080	0.960	0.920
Dividend Payout %	...	49.68	888.24	406.25	4.93	11.13	15.31	17.01
Income Statement								
Total Revenue	113,344,000	55,728,000	214,319,000	208,357,000	198,533,000	190,884,000	179,045,000	137,609,000
EBITDA	232,000	904,000	1,109,000	745,000	7,464,000	3,851,000	3,305,000	2,565,000
Depn & Amortn	463,000	229,000	317,000	303,000	324,000	281,000	306,000	186,000
Income Before Taxes	(351,000)	619,000	567,000	207,000	6,861,000	3,235,000	2,645,000	2,099,000
Income Taxes	(158,000)	136,000	356,000	(53,000)	1,614,000	908,000	815,000	742,000
Net Income	(307,000)	423,000	34,000	67,000	5,070,000	2,258,000	1,476,000	1,263,000
Average Shares	183,000	189,000	197,000	209,000	223,000	233,000	235,000	233,000
Balance Sheet								
Current Assets	37,353,000	38,428,000	38,465,000	37,136,000	36,948,000	38,437,000	36,670,000	32,573,000
Total Assets	58,994,000	61,680,000	59,672,000	60,381,000	60,969,000	56,563,000	53,870,000	51,759,000
Current Liabilities	37,145,000	37,952,000	37,626,000	36,685,000	35,612,000	35,071,000	33,497,000	29,501,000
Long-Term Obligations	7,342,000	7,382,000	7,265,000	6,751,000	7,305,000	6,535,000	8,180,000	8,949,000
Total Liabilities	52,512,000	53,806,000	51,578,000	50,577,000	49,874,000	47,639,000	45,869,000	43,237,000
Stockholders' Equity	6,482,000	7,874,000	8,094,000	9,804,000	11,095,000	8,924,000	8,001,000	8,522,000
Shares Outstanding	180,187	185,000	190,000	202,000	211,000	225,000	232,000	231,000
Statistical Record								
Return on Assets %	N.M.	0.97	0.06	0.11	8.63	4.08	2.79	2.92
Return on Equity %	N.M.	6.89	0.38	0.64	50.65	26.61	17.87	16.20
EBITDA Margin %	0.20	1.62	0.52	0.36	3.76	2.02	1.85	1.86
Net Margin %	N.M.	0.76	0.02	0.03	2.55	1.18	0.82	0.92
Asset Turnover	3.69	3.54	3.57	3.43	3.38	3.45	3.39	3.18
Current Ratio	1.01	1.01	1.02	1.01	1.04	1.10	1.09	1.10
Debt to Equity	1.13	0.94	0.90	0.69	0.66	0.73	1.02	1.05
Price Range	148.53-108.23	138.52-108.23	158.13-108.23	176.72-135.00	198.44-124.11	242.75-150.03	230.26-164.68	185.35-104.18
P/E Ratio	...	44.11-34.47	930.18-636.65	552.25-421.88	8.73-5.46	25.03-15.47	36.72-26.26	34.26-19.26
Average Yield %	1.23	1.24	1.15	0.85	0.68	0.54	0.48	0.66

Address: 6555 State Highway 161, Irving, TX 75039 **Telephone:** 972-446-4800	**Web Site:** www.mckesson.com **Officers:** Edward A. Mueller - Chairman Brian S. Tyler - Chief Executive Officer, President, Chief Operating Officer, Region Officer, Executive Vice President, Division Officer	**Auditors:** DELOITTE & TOUCHE LLP **Investor Contact:** 415-983-8391 **Transfer Agents:** EQ Shareowner Services, Mendota Heights, MN

MDU RESOURCES GROUP INC

Exchange	Symbol	Price	52Wk Range	Yield	P/E	Div Acheiver
NYS	MDU	$29.71 (12/31/2019)	29.77-23.56	2.79	18.45	28 Years

*7 Year Price Score 85.50 ***NYSE Composite Index=100** ***12 Month Price Score 103.19**

Interim Earnings (Per Share)

Qtr.	Mar	Jun	Sep	Dec
2016	0.13	(0.56)	0.42	0.34
2017	0.19	0.21	0.45	0.59
2018	0.22	0.22	0.55	0.40
2019	0.21	0.31	0.69	...

Interim Dividends (Per Share)

Amt	Decl	Ex	Rec	Pay
0.203Q	02/14/2019	03/13/2019	03/14/2019	04/01/2019
0.203Q	05/08/2019	06/12/2019	06/13/2019	07/01/2019
0.203Q	08/15/2019	09/11/2019	09/12/2019	10/01/2019
0.207Q	11/14/2019	12/11/2019	12/12/2019	01/01/2020

Indicated Div: $0.83 (Div. Reinv. Plan)

Valuation Analysis		Institutional Holding	
Forecast EPS	$1.59	No of Institutions	
	(01/16/2020)	549	
Market Cap	$6.0 Billion	Shares	
Book Value	$2.8 Billion	169,784,144	
Price/Book	2.13	% Held	
Price/Sales	1.15	69.79	

Business Summary: Electric Utilities (MIC: 3.1.1 SIC: 4911 NAIC: 221122)

MDU Resources Group is a regulated energy delivery and construction materials and services business. Co.'s segments are: Electric, which generates, transmits and distributes electricity in Montana, North Dakota, South Dakota and Wyoming; Natural Gas Distribution, which distributes natural gas in Idaho, Minnesota, Oregon and Washington; Pipeline and Midstream, which provides natural gas transportation, underground storage and gathering services; Construction Materials and Contracting, which operates mine, process and sell construction aggregates; produce and sell asphalt mix; and supply ready-mixed concrete; and Construction Services, which provides specialty contracting services.

Recent Developments: For the quarter ended Sep 30 2019, income from continuing operations increased 26.8% to US$136.1 million from US$107.4 million in the year-earlier quarter. Net income increased 28.3% to US$137.6 million from US$107.3 million in the year-earlier quarter. Revenues were US$1.56 billion, up 22.1% from US$1.28 billion the year before. Operating income was US$189.5 million versus US$140.0 million in the prior-year quarter, an increase of 35.3%. Direct operating expenses rose 20.6% to US$1.26 billion from US$1.05 billion in the comparable period the year before. Indirect operating expenses increased 18.7% to US$111.1 million from US$93.7 million in the equivalent prior-year period.

Prospects: Our evaluation of MDU Resources Group Inc. as of October 4th, 2019 is the result of our systematic analysis on three basic characteristics: earnings strength, relative valuation, and recent stock price movement. The company has enjoyed a very positive trend in earnings per share over the past 5 quarters. However, recent analyst estimates for the company have been unchanged, while MDU has posted results that exceeded analysts' expectations. Based on operating earnings yield, the company is undervalued when compared to all of the companies we cover. Share price changes over the past year indicates that MDU will perform in line with the market over the near term.

Financial Data

(US$ in Thousands)	9 Mos	6 Mos	3 Mos	12/31/2018	12/31/2017	12/31/2016	12/31/2015	12/31/2014
Earnings Per Share	1.61	1.47	1.38	1.39	1.43	0.33	(3.20)	1.55
Cash Flow Per Share	1.93	1.52	2.01	2.55	2.29	2.36	3.29	3.20
Tang Book Value Per Share	10.48	9.90	9.68	9.65	9.18	8.52	8.91	12.74
Dividends Per Share	0.810	0.805	0.800	0.795	0.775	0.755	0.735	0.715
Dividend Payout %	50.31	54.76	57.97	57.19	54.20	228.79	...	46.13
Income Statement								
Total Revenue	3,958,563	2,394,764	1,091,191	4,531,552	4,443,351	4,128,828	4,191,549	4,670,558
EBITDA	551,159	293,654	131,710	621,690	640,301	630,394	501,095	899,555
Depn & Amortn	187,937	122,916	59,897	220,205	207,486	216,318	227,730	401,368
Income Before Taxes	289,128	121,902	48,406	316,871	350,027	326,228	180,297	411,171
Income Taxes	48,766	17,668	7,317	47,485	65,041	93,132	65,603	119,969
Net Income	240,388	102,751	40,926	272,318	281,203	64,433	(622,435)	298,233
Average Shares	199,383	198,287	196,414	196,150	195,687	195,618	194,986	192,587
Balance Sheet								
Current Assets	1,461,815	1,444,810	1,235,229	1,184,132	1,069,995	977,475	1,021,042	1,194,973
Total Assets	7,730,611	7,591,493	7,278,923	6,988,110	6,334,666	6,284,467	6,627,608	7,809,978
Current Liabilities	1,033,677	912,602	1,062,779	986,050	812,858	669,659	947,639	968,694
Long-Term Obligations	2,180,946	2,327,984	1,946,181	1,856,841	1,566,354	1,746,561	1,627,443	1,825,278
Total Liabilities	4,935,005	4,931,192	4,673,231	4,421,335	3,905,623	3,968,223	4,231,103	4,675,937
Stockholders' Equity	2,795,606	2,660,301	2,605,692	2,566,775	2,429,043	2,316,244	2,396,505	3,134,041
Shares Outstanding	200,337	199,000	197,777	196,025	195,304	195,304	195,265	194,215
Statistical Record								
Return on Assets %	4.42	4.09	3.97	4.09	4.46	1.00	N.M.	4.01
Return on Equity %	12.01	11.30	10.76	10.90	11.85	2.73	N.M.	10.01
EBITDA Margin %	13.92	12.26	12.07	13.72	14.41	15.27	11.95	19.26
Net Margin %	6.07	4.29	3.75	6.01	6.33	1.56	N.M.	6.39
Asset Turnover	0.72	0.69	0.68	0.68	0.70	0.64	0.58	0.63
Current Ratio	1.41	1.58	1.16	1.20	1.32	1.46	1.08	1.23
Debt to Equity	0.78	0.88	0.75	0.72	0.64	0.75	0.68	0.58
Price Range	28.65-23.05	29.60-23.05	29.60-23.05	29.60-23.05	29.43-25.45	29.62-16.03	24.36-16.36	35.93-21.44
P/E Ratio	17.80-14.32	20.14-15.68	21.45-16.70	21.29-16.58	20.58-17.80	89.76-48.58	...	23.18-13.83
Average Yield %	3.12	3.07	2.98	2.93	2.88	3.34	3.70	2.31

Address: 1200 West Century Avenue, P.O. Box 5650, Bismarck, ND 58506-5650	Web Site: www.mdu.com	Auditors: DELOITTE & TOUCHE LLP
Telephone: 701-530-1000	Officers: Dennis W. Johnson - Chairman, Vice-Chairman David L. Goodin - President, Chief Executive Officer	Investor Contact: 866-866-8919
		Transfer Agents: Wells Fargo Bank, N.A., St. Paul, MN

MEDICAL PROPERTIES TRUST INC

Exchange	Symbol	Price	52Wk Range	Yield	P/E
NYS	MPW	$21.11 (12/31/2019)	21.49-15.63	4.93	26.39

*7 Year Price Score 107.82 *NYSE Composite Index=100 *12 Month Price Score 103.55

Interim Earnings (Per Share)

Qtr.	Mar	Jun	Sep	Dec
2016	0.24	0.22	0.28	0.11
2017	0.21	0.21	0.21	0.19
2018	0.25	0.30	2.00	0.20
2019	0.20	0.20	0.20	...

Interim Dividends (Per Share)

Amt	Decl	Ex	Rec	Pay
0.25Q	02/14/2019	03/13/2019	03/14/2019	04/11/2019
0.25Q	05/23/2019	06/12/2019	06/13/2019	07/11/2019
0.26Q	08/15/2019	09/11/2019	09/12/2019	10/10/2019
0.26Q	11/21/2019	12/11/2019	12/12/2019	01/09/2020

Indicated Div: $1.04

Valuation Analysis / **Institutional Holding**

Forecast EPS	$0.85	No of Institutions
	(01/17/2020)	603
Market Cap	$9.7 Billion	Shares
Book Value	$6.0 Billion	436,791,136
Price/Book	1.62	% Held
Price/Sales	12.47	71.87

Business Summary: REITs (MIC: 5.3.1 SIC: 6798 NAIC: 525930)

Medical Properties Trust is a self-advised real estate investment trust (REIT) focused on investing in and owning net-leased healthcare facilities across the U.S. and selectively in foreign jurisdictions. Co. conducts substantially all of its business through MPT Operating Partnership, L.P. Co. acquires and develops healthcare facilities and leases the facilities to healthcare operating companies. Co. also makes mortgage loans to healthcare operators collateralized by their real estate assets. In addition, Co. selectively makes loans to certain of its operators through its REIT subsidiaries.

Recent Developments: For the quarter ended Sep 30 2019, net income decreased 87.7% to US$90.3 million from US$736.5 million in the year-earlier quarter. Revenues were US$224.8 million, up 14.1% from US$197.0 million the year before. Revenues from property income rose 11.2% to US$172.9 million from US$155.5 million in the corresponding quarter a year earlier.

Prospects: Our evaluation of Medical Properties Trust Inc. as of October 4th, 2019 is the result of our systematic analysis on three basic characteristics: earnings strength, relative valuation, and recent stock price movement. The company has generated a negative trend in earnings per share over the past 5 quarters. However, recent analyst estimates for the company have been raised and MPW has posted results that exceeded analysts' expectations. Based on operating earnings yield, the company is fairly valued when compared to all of the companies we cover. Share price changes over the past year indicates that MPW will perform well over the near term.

Financial Data

(US$ in Thousands)	9 Mos	6 Mos	3 Mos	12/31/2018	12/31/2017	12/31/2016	12/31/2015	12/31/2014
Earnings Per Share	0.80	2.60	2.70	2.76	0.82	0.86	0.63	0.29
Cash Flow Per Share	1.09	1.14	1.16	1.23	1.04	1.01	0.95	0.88
Tang Book Value Per Share	12.99	12.45	12.45	12.27	10.48	10.13	8.88	8.00
Dividends Per Share	1.010	1.000	1.000	1.000	0.960	0.910	0.880	0.840
Dividend Payout %	126.25	38.46	37.04	36.23	117.07	105.81	139.68	289.66
Income Statement								
Total Revenue	597,759	373,003	180,454	784,522	704,745	541,137	441,878	312,532
EBITDA	237,784	149,259	72,065	1,391,533	599,315	485,035	336,782	201,521
Depn & Amortn	6,293	3,816	1,827	148,855	138,500	105,214	77,912	60,267
Income Before Taxes	231,491	145,443	70,238	1,019,404	283,861	220,224	138,581	48,579
Income Taxes	(3,352)	(2,607)	(2,333)	927	2,681	(6,830)	1,503	340
Net Income	245,046	155,260	75,822	1,016,685	289,793	225,048	139,598	50,522
Average Shares	440,933	395,692	381,675	366,271	350,441	261,072	218,304	170,540
Balance Sheet								
Current Assets	761,615	720,553	1,239,104	1,067,571	436,034	257,799	324,635	244,806
Total Assets	12,452,153	10,123,211	9,231,453	8,843,643	9,020,288	6,418,536	5,609,351	3,747,336
Current Liabilities	266,019	203,397	198,935	217,792	229,366	227,644	166,714	139,830
Long-Term Obligations	6,096,232	4,878,310	4,023,568	4,037,389	4,898,667	2,909,341	3,322,541	2,201,654
Total Liabilities	6,478,613	5,213,042	4,354,631	4,296,535	5,199,655	3,170,158	3,507,083	2,365,289
Stockholders' Equity	5,973,540	4,910,169	4,876,822	4,547,108	3,820,633	3,248,378	2,102,268	1,382,047
Shares Outstanding	459,778	394,425	391,839	370,637	364,424	320,514	236,744	172,743
Statistical Record								
Return on Assets %	3.05	10.17	10.97	11.38	3.75	3.73	2.98	1.52
Return on Equity %	6.19	22.19	22.99	24.30	8.20	8.39	8.01	3.71
EBITDA Margin %	39.78	40.02	39.94	177.37	85.04	89.63	76.22	64.48
Net Margin %	40.99	41.62	42.02	129.59	41.12	41.59	31.59	16.17
Asset Turnover	0.07	0.08	0.08	0.09	0.09	0.09	0.09	0.09
Current Ratio	2.86	3.54	6.23	4.90	1.90	1.13	1.95	1.75
Debt to Equity	1.02	0.99	0.83	0.89	1.28	0.90	1.58	1.59
Price Range	19.58-14.06	18.85-13.94	18.84-12.35	17.49-11.88	14.16-12.15	15.80-9.86	15.62-10.73	14.09-12.20
P/E Ratio	24.47-17.57	7.25-5.36	6.98-4.57	6.34-4.30	17.27-14.82	18.37-11.47	24.79-17.03	48.59-42.07
Average Yield %	5.77	6.04	6.52	7.08	7.31	6.78	6.70	6.36

Address: 1000 Urban Center Drive, Suite 501, Birmingham, AL 35242	Web Site: www.medicalpropertiestrust.com	Auditors: PricewaterhouseCoopers LLP
Telephone: 205-969-3755	Officers: Edward K. Aldag - Chairman, President, Chief Executive Officer Emmett E. McLean -	Investor Contact: 205-397-8897
Fax: 205-969-3756	Executive Vice President, Chief Operating Officer, Treasurer, Secretary	Transfer Agents: American Stock Transfer & Trust Company, New York, NY

MEDNAX, INC.

Exchange	Symbol	Price	52Wk Range	Yield	P/E
NYS	MD	$27.79 (12/31/2019)	36.86-20.59	N/A	N/A

*7 Year Price Score 41.06   *NYSE Composite Index=100   *12 Month Price Score 92.48

TRADING VOLUME (thousand shares)

Interim Earnings (Per Share)

Qtr.	Mar	Jun	Sep	Dec
2016	0.73	0.89	1.04	0.84
2017	0.59	0.69	0.71	1.47
2018	0.68	0.85	0.72	0.68
2019	(2.81)	(0.10)	(15.24)	...

Interim Dividends (Per Share)

No Dividends Paid

Valuation Analysis		Institutional Holding	
Forecast EPS	$3.36	No of Institutions	
	(00/25/2020)	405	
Market Cap	$2.3 Billion	Shares	
Book Value	$1.5 Billion	97,781,496	
Price/Book	1.58	% Held	
Price/Sales	0.66	N/A	

Business Summary: Diagnostic & Health Related Services (MIC: 4.2.2 SIC: 8069 NAIC: 622310)

MEDNAX provides physician services including newborn, anesthesia, maternal-fetal, radiology and teleradiology, pediatric cardiology and other pediatric subspecialty care. Co.'s network comprised of physicians, including physicians who provide neonatal clinical care, primarily within hospital-based neonatal intensive care units, to babies born prematurely or with medical complications. Co. also provides radiology services and teleradiology services. In addition to its national physician network, Co. provides services to healthcare facilities and physicians, including Co.'s, through complementary businesses, consisting of a management services organization and a consulting services company.

Recent Developments: For the quarter ended Sep 30 2019, loss from continuing operations was US$1.26 billion compared with income of US$62.2 million in the year-earlier quarter. Net loss amounted to US$1.26 billion versus net income of US$65.6 million in the year-earlier quarter. Revenues were US$888.7 million, up 4.7% from US$848.8 million the year before. Operating loss was US$1.36 billion versus an income of US$104.2 million in the prior-year quarter. Indirect operating expenses increased 202.0% to US$2.25 billion from US$744.6 million in the equivalent prior-year period.

Prospects: Our evaluation of Mednax, Inc. as of October 4th, 2019 is the result of our systematic analysis on three basic characteristics: earnings strength, relative valuation, and recent stock price movement. The company has produced a positive trend in earnings per share over the past 5 quarters. However, recent analyst estimates for the company have been mixed and MD has posted results that exceeded analysts' expectations. Based on operating earnings yield, the company is undervalued when compared to all of the companies we cover. Share price changes over the past year indicates that MD will perform very poorly over the near term.

Financial Data

(US$ in Thousands)	9 Mos	6 Mos	3 Mos	12/31/2018	12/31/2017	12/31/2016	12/31/2015	12/31/2014
Earnings Per Share	(17.47)	(1.51)	(0.56)	2.93	3.45	3.49	3.58	3.18
Cash Flow Per Share	4.20	3.98	4.03	3.18	5.53	4.79	3.96	4.29
Income Statement								
Total Revenue	2,608,167	1,719,492	851,183	3,647,123	3,458,312	3,183,159	2,779,996	2,438,913
EBITDA	(1,192,265)	164,758	81,622	489,283	517,929	602,706	581,912	531,627
Depn & Amortn	4,293	2,934	1,520	38,500	33,900	29,000	22,200	15,900
Income Before Taxes	(1,288,262)	100,021	49,379	362,014	409,470	510,614	536,602	506,836
Income Taxes	(99,710)	26,078	8,962	100,210	90,050	189,203	204,038	191,413
Net Income	(1,507,033)	(251,117)	(242,872)	268,629	320,372	324,914	336,320	317,281
Average Shares	82,441	83,689	86,545	91,606	92,958	93,109	93,960	99,887
Balance Sheet								
Current Assets	965,301	985,520	1,057,416	657,409	627,235	587,128	527,769	467,052
Total Assets	4,290,661	5,638,811	5,706,257	5,934,911	5,867,278	5,339,400	4,547,214	3,608,795
Current Liabilities	500,790	441,046	415,183	500,193	531,425	448,949	428,771	416,273
Long-Term Obligations	2,004,464	2,150,449	2,190,644	1,974,280	1,851,423	1,683,628	1,262,820	558,855
Total Liabilities	2,811,301	2,913,784	2,926,445	2,847,027	2,800,824	2,578,633	2,109,686	1,344,176
Stockholders' Equity	1,479,360	2,725,027	2,779,812	3,087,884	3,066,454	2,760,767	2,437,528	2,264,619
Shares Outstanding	84,185	84,096	86,387	87,820	93,721	93,718	93,739	96,030
Statistical Record								
Return on Assets %	N.M.	N.M.	N.M.	4.55	5.72	6.55	8.25	9.53
Return on Equity %	N.M.	N.M.	N.M.	8.73	11.00	12.47	14.30	13.77
EBITDA Margin %	N.M.	9.58	9.59	13.42	14.98	18.93	20.93	21.80
Net Margin %	N.M.	N.M.	N.M.	7.37	9.26	10.21	12.10	13.01
Asset Turnover	0.70	0.62	0.62	0.62	0.62	0.64	0.68	0.73
Current Ratio	1.93	2.23	2.55	1.31	1.18	1.31	1.23	1.12
Debt to Equity	1.35	0.79	0.79	0.64	0.60	0.61	0.52	0.25
Price Range	46.59-20.59	48.58-23.81	55.83-27.12	58.62-32.26	72.03-41.19	76.29-60.38	85.47-64.53	67.20-51.25
P/E Ratio	...	...	...	20.01-11.01	20.88-11.94	21.86-17.30	23.87-18.03	21.13-16.12

Address: 1301 Concord Terrace, Sunrise, FL 33323 Telephone: 954-384-0175	Web Site: www.mednax.com Officers: Cesar L. Alvarez - Chairman Roger J. Medel - Chief Executive Officer	Auditors: PricewaterhouseCoopers LLP Transfer Agents: ComputerShare Investor Services, Providence, RI

MEDTRONIC PLC

*7 Year Price Score 106.07 ***NYSE Composite Index=100** ***12 Month Price Score 106.26**

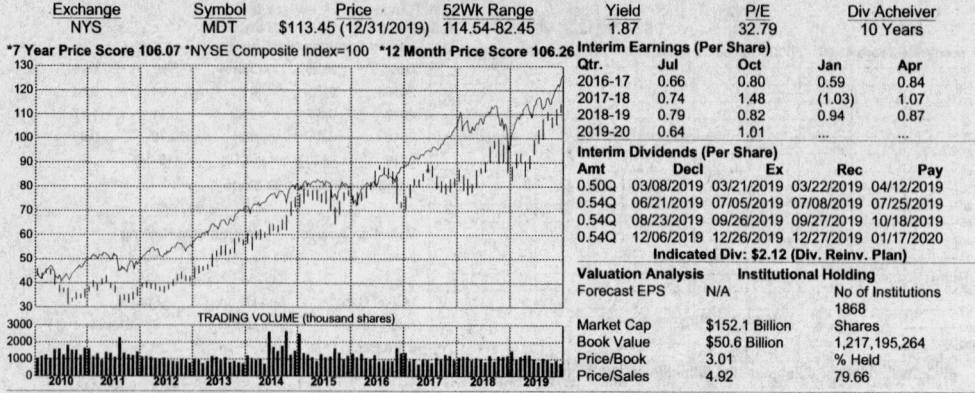

Interim Earnings (Per Share)

Qtr.	Jul	Oct	Jan	Apr
2016-17	0.66	0.80	0.59	0.84
2017-18	0.74	1.48	(1.03)	1.07
2018-19	0.79	0.82	0.94	0.87
2019-20	0.64	1.01	...	...

Interim Dividends (Per Share)

Amt	Decl	Ex	Rec	Pay
0.50Q	03/08/2019	03/21/2019	03/22/2019	04/12/2019
0.54Q	06/21/2019	07/05/2019	07/08/2019	07/25/2019
0.54Q	08/23/2019	09/26/2019	09/27/2019	10/18/2019
0.54Q	12/06/2019	12/26/2019	12/27/2019	01/17/2020

Indicated Div: $2.12 (Div. Reinv. Plan)

Valuation Analysis **Institutional Holding**

Forecast EPS	N/A	No of Institutions
		1868
Market Cap	$152.1 Billion	Shares
Book Value	$50.6 Billion	1,217,195,264
Price/Book	3.01	% Held
Price/Sales	4.92	79.66

Business Summary: Medical Instruments & Equipment (MIC: 4.3.1 SIC: 3845 NAIC: 334510)

Medtronic is a medical technology, services and solutions company. Co.'s operating segments are: Cardiac and Vascular, which is made up of the cardiac rhythm and heart failure, coronary and structural heart, and aortic, peripheral and venous divisions; Minimally Invasive Therapies, which is made up of the surgical innovations and respiratory, gastrointestinal, and renal divisions; Restorative Therapies, which is made up of the spine, brain therapies, specialty therapies, and pain therapies divisions; and Diabetes, which develops, manufactures, and markets products and services for the management of Type 1 and Type 2 diabetes.

Recent Developments: For the quarter ended Oct 25 2019, net income increased 22.4% to US$1.37 billion from US$1.12 billion in the year-earlier quarter. Revenues were US$7.71 billion, up 3.0% from US$7.48 billion the year before. Operating income was US$1.35 billion versus US$1.54 billion in the prior-year quarter, a decrease of 12.5%. Direct operating expenses rose 8.7% to US$2.39 billion from US$2.20 billion in the comparable period the year before. Indirect operating expenses increased 6.1% to US$3.96 billion from US$3.73 billion in the equivalent prior-year period.

Prospects: Our evaluation of Medtronic PLC as of October 4th, 2019 is the result of our systematic analysis on three basic characteristics: earnings strength, relative valuation, and recent stock price movement. The company has managed to produce a neutral trend in earnings per share over the past 5 quarters. In addition, recent analyst estimates for the company have been mixed and MDT has posted results that exceeded analysts' expectations. Based on operating earnings yield, the company is fairly valued when compared to all of the companies we cover. Share price changes over the past year indicates that MDT will perform in line with the market over the near term.

Financial Data

(US$ in Thousands)	6 Mos	3 Mos	04/26/2019	04/27/2018	04/28/2017	04/29/2016	04/24/2015	04/25/2014
Earnings Per Share	3.46	3.27	3.41	2.27	2.89	2.48	2.41	3.02
Cash Flow Per Share	5.61	5.08	5.22	3.45	4.99	3.64	4.49	4.96
Tang Book Value Per Share	N.M.	N.M.	N.M.	N.M.	N.M.	N.M.	N.M.	6.57
Dividends Per Share	2.080	2.040	2.000	1.840	1.720	1.520	1.220	1.120
Dividend Payout %	60.12	62.39	58.65	81.06	59.52	61.29	50.62	37.09
Income Statement								
Total Revenue	15,199,000	7,493,000	30,557,000	29,953,000	29,710,000	28,833,000	20,261,000	17,005,000
EBITDA	3,926,000	2,026,000	9,300,000	9,068,000	8,247,000	8,111,000	5,072,000	4,663,000
Depn & Amortn	881,000	440,000	2,659,000	2,644,000	2,917,000	2,820,000	1,306,000	850,000
Income Before Taxes	2,271,000	977,000	5,197,000	5,675,000	4,602,000	4,336,000	3,486,000	3,705,000
Income Taxes	23,000	100,000	547,000	2,580,000	578,000	798,000	-811,000	640,000
Net Income	2,228,000	864,000	4,631,000	3,104,000	4,028,000	3,538,000	2,675,000	3,065,000
Average Shares	1,351,400	1,351,900	1,357,500	1,368,200	1,391,400	1,425,900	1,109,000	1,013,600
Balance Sheet								
Current Assets	22,653,000	22,705,000	21,967,000	22,980,000	24,873,000	23,600,000	30,844,000	21,210,000
Total Assets	91,053,000	91,268,000	89,694,000	91,393,000	99,816,000	99,782,000	106,685,000	37,943,000
Current Liabilities	8,170,000	8,518,000	8,472,000	10,084,000	14,220,000	7,165,000	9,173,000	5,559,000
Long-Term Obligations	24,752,000	24,804,000	24,486,000	23,699,000	25,921,000	30,247,000	33,752,000	10,315,000
Total Liabilities	40,475,000	40,905,000	39,603,000	40,673,000	49,522,000	47,719,000	53,455,000	18,500,000
Stockholders' Equity	50,578,000	50,363,000	50,091,000	50,720,000	50,294,000	52,063,000	53,230,000	19,443,000
Shares Outstanding	1,340,375	1,340,797	1,340,697	1,354,218	1,369,424	1,399,018	1,421,648	998,999
Statistical Record								
Return on Assets %	5.21	4.88	5.13	3.25	4.04	3.37	3.71	8.45
Return on Equity %	9.32	8.79	9.21	6.15	7.87	6.61	7.38	16.13
EBITDA Margin %	25.83	27.04	30.43	30.27	27.76	28.13	25.03	27.42
Net Margin %	14.66	11.53	15.16	10.36	13.56	12.27	13.20	18.02
Asset Turnover	0.34	0.34	0.34	0.31	0.30	0.27	0.28	0.47
Current Ratio	2.77	2.67	2.59	2.28	1.75	3.29	3.36	3.82
Debt to Equity	0.49	0.49	0.49	0.47	0.52	0.58	0.63	0.53
Price Range	111.18-82.45	102.55-82.45	99.49-79.58	89.30-76.55	88.92-70.61	79.78-64.52	79.25-58.21	62.31-46.36
P/E Ratio	32.13-23.83	31.36-25.21	29.18-23.34	39.34-33.72	30.77-24.43	32.17-26.02	32.88-24.15	20.63-15.35
Average Yield %	2.18	2.21	2.21	2.23	2.11	2.02	1.78	2.02

MERCK & CO INC

Exchange	Symbol	Price	52Wk Range	Yield	P/E
NYS	MRK	$90.95 (12/31/2019)	91.74-72.92	2.68	25.41

*7 Year Price Score 111.61 *NYSE Composite Index=100 *12 Month Price Score 100.49

Interim Earnings (Per Share)

Qtr.	Mar	Jun	Sep	Dec
2016	0.40	0.43	0.78	(0.21)
2017	0.56	0.71	(0.02)	(0.38)
2018	0.27	0.63	0.73	0.69
2019	1.12	1.03	0.74	...

Interim Dividends (Per Share)

Amt	Decl	Ex	Rec	Pay
0.55Q	01/29/2019	03/14/2019	03/15/2019	04/05/2019
0.55Q	05/28/2019	06/14/2019	06/17/2019	07/08/2019
0.55Q	07/23/2019	09/13/2019	09/16/2019	10/07/2019
0.61Q	11/19/2019	12/13/2019	12/16/2019	01/08/2020

Indicated Div: $2.44 (Div. Reinv. Plan)

Valuation Analysis · **Institutional Holding**

Forecast EPS	$5.18
	(01/16/2020)
Market Cap	$232.0 Billion
Book Value	$26.8 Billion
Price/Book	8.64
Price/Sales	5.05

No of Institutions 3102
Shares 2,325,376,000
% Held N/A

Business Summary: Pharmaceuticals (MIC: 4.1.1 SIC: 2834 NAIC: 325412)

Merck & Co. is a global health care company that delivers health solutions through its prescription medicines, vaccines, biologic therapies and animal health products. Co.'s reportable segments are: Pharmaceutical, which includes human health pharmaceutical products that consist of therapeutic and preventive agents for the treatment of human disorders, and vaccine products that consist of preventive pediatric, adolescent and adult vaccines; and Animal Health, which discovers, develops, manufactures and markets animal health products, including pharmaceutical and vaccine products, for the prevention, treatment and control of disease in various main livestock and companion animal species.

Recent Developments: For the quarter ended Sep 30 2019, net income decreased 2.6% to US$1.91 billion from US$1.96 billion in the year-earlier quarter. Revenues were US$12.40 billion, up 14.9% from US$10.79 billion the year before. Direct operating expenses rose 10.3% to US$3.99 billion from US$3.62 billion in the comparable period the year before. Indirect operating expenses increased 28.7% to US$6.03 billion from US$4.68 billion in the equivalent prior-year period.

Prospects: Our evaluation of Merck & Co. Inc. as of October 4th, 2019 is the result of our systematic analysis on three basic characteristics: earnings strength, relative valuation, and recent stock price movement. The company has managed to produce a neutral trend in earnings per share over the past 5 quarters. In addition, recent analyst estimates for the company have been mixed and MRK has posted results that exceeded analysts' expectations. Based on operating earnings yield, the company is undervalued when compared to all of the companies we cover. Share price changes over the past year indicates that MRK will perform well over the near term.

Financial Data

(US$ in Thousands)	9 Mos	6 Mos	3 Mos	12/31/2018	12/31/2017	12/31/2016	12/31/2015	12/31/2014
Earnings Per Share	3.58	3.57	3.17	2.32	0.87	1.41	1.56	4.07
Cash Flow Per Share	4.78	4.20	4.30	4.10	2.36	3.74	4.41	2.72
Tang Book Value Per Share	N.M.	N.M.	N.M.	N.M.	0.69	1.68	1.56	5.38
Dividends Per Share	2.200	2.130	2.060	1.990	1.890	1.850	1.810	1.770
Dividend Payout %	61.45	59.66	64.98	85.78	217.24	131.21	116.03	43.49
Income Statement								
Total Revenue	34,972,000	22,575,000	10,816,000	42,294,000	40,122,000	39,807,000	39,498,000	42,237,000
EBITDA	11,838,000	8,475,000	4,085,000	10,530,000	8,348,000	6,538,000	7,179,000	19,992,000
Depn & Amortn	2,716,000	1,871,000	898,000	1,400,000	1,500,000	1,600,000	1,600,000	2,500,000
Income Before Taxes	8,673,000	6,326,000	3,067,000	8,701,000	6,479,000	4,573,000	5,196,000	17,026,000
Income Taxes	1,259,000	820,000	205,000	2,508,000	4,103,000	718,000	942,000	5,349,000
Net Income	7,487,000	5,585,000	2,915,000	6,220,000	2,394,000	3,920,000	4,442,000	11,920,000
Average Shares	2,572,000	2,588,000	2,603,000	2,679,000	2,748,000	2,787,000	2,841,000	2,928,000
Balance Sheet								
Current Assets	26,142,000	24,298,000	25,351,000	25,875,000	24,766,000	30,614,000	29,764,000	33,173,000
Total Assets	83,331,000	83,965,000	82,354,000	82,637,000	87,872,000	95,377,000	101,779,000	98,335,000
Current Liabilities	20,684,000	20,085,000	18,543,000	22,206,000	18,614,000	17,204,000	19,203,000	18,766,000
Long-Term Obligations	22,677,000	22,771,000	22,721,000	19,806,000	21,353,000	24,274,000	23,929,000	18,699,000
Total Liabilities	56,493,000	56,330,000	54,815,000	55,936,000	53,536,000	55,289,000	57,103,000	49,688,000
Stockholders' Equity	26,838,000	27,635,000	27,539,000	26,701,000	34,336,000	40,088,000	44,676,000	48,647,000
Shares Outstanding	2,550,889	2,566,795	2,583,071	2,592,560	2,696,612	2,748,732	2,781,128	2,838,140
Statistical Record								
Return on Assets %	11.06	11.08	9.98	7.30	2.61	3.97	4.44	11.69
Return on Equity %	31.43	31.12	27.44	20.38	6.43	9.22	9.52	24.22
EBITDA Margin %	33.85	37.54	37.77	24.90	20.81	16.42	18.18	47.33
Net Margin %	21.41	24.74	26.95	14.71	5.97	9.85	11.25	28.22
Asset Turnover	0.55	0.53	0.51	0.50	0.44	0.40	0.39	0.41
Current Ratio	1.26	1.21	1.37	1.17	1.33	1.78	1.55	1.77
Debt to Equity	0.84	0.82	0.83	0.74	0.62	0.61	0.54	0.38
Price Range	86.91-68.37	85.51-60.46	83.17-53.27	79.34-53.27	66.58-54.10	64.96-48.59	63.03-48.42	61.88-49.49
P/E Ratio	24.28-19.10	23.95-16.94	26.24-16.80	34.20-22.96	76.53-62.18	46.07-34.46	40.40-31.04	15.20-12.16
Average Yield %	2.78	2.85	2.97	3.10	3.04	3.22	3.20	3.10

Address: 2000 Galloping Hill Road, Kenilworth, NJ 07033 **Telephone:** 908-740-4000 **Fax:** 908-735-1500	**Web Site:** www.merck.com **Officers:** Kenneth C. Frazier - Chairman, President, Chief Executive Officer Jennifer L. Zachary - Executive Vice President, General Counsel	**Auditors:** PricewaterhouseCoopers LLP **Investor Contact:** 908-423-5881 **Transfer Agents:** Wells Fargo Shareowner Services, South St. Paul, MN

MERCURY GENERAL CORP.

Exchange	Symbol	Price	52Wk Range	Yield	P/E	Div Acheiver
NYS	MCY	$48.73 (12/31/2019)	64.81-47.29	5.17	13.10	32 Years

*7 Year Price Score 85.54   *NYSE Composite Index=100   *12 Month Price Score 86.01

Interim Earnings (Per Share)

Qtr.	Mar	Jun	Sep	Dec
2016	0.42	0.88	0.49	(0.47)
2017	0.49	0.93	0.84	0.36
2018	(0.77)	1.09	1.06	(1.48)
2019	2.45	1.50	1.25	...

Interim Dividends (Per Share)

Amt	Decl	Ex	Rec	Pay
0.627Q	02/11/2019	03/13/2019	03/14/2019	03/28/2019
0.627Q	04/29/2019	06/12/2019	06/13/2019	06/27/2019
0.627Q	07/29/2019	09/11/2019	09/12/2019	09/26/2019
0.63Q	10/28/2019	12/11/2019	12/12/2019	12/26/2019

Indicated Div: $2.52

Valuation Analysis

Forecast EPS	$2.50
	(01/17/2020)
Market Cap	$2.7 Billion
Book Value	$1.8 Billion
Price/Book	1.50
Price/Sales	0.71

Institutional Holding

No of Institutions	353
Shares	33,238,868
% Held	41.72

Business Summary: General Insurance (MIC: 5.2.1 SIC: 6331 NAIC: 524126)
Mercury General is an insurance holding company. Through its subsidiaries, Co. writes personal automobile insurance in 11 states, mainly California. Co. also writes homeowners, commercial automobile, commercial property, mechanical protection, and umbrella insurance. Co. provides the following types of automobile coverage: collision, property damage, bodily injury, comprehensive, personal injury protection, underinsured and uninsured motorist, and other hazards. Co. also provides the following types of homeowners coverage: dwelling, liability, personal property, fire, and other hazards. Co. sells its policies through independent agents, its insurance agencies, and internet sales portals.

Recent Developments: For the quarter ended Sep 30 2019, net income increased 18.3% to US$69.3 million from US$58.6 million in the year-earlier quarter. Revenues were US$987.3 million, up 10.3% from US$894.8 million the year before. Net premiums earned were US$915.0 million versus US$858.1 million in the prior-year quarter, an increase of 6.6%. Net investment income fell 4.7% to US$36.4 million from US$38.2 million a year ago.

Prospects: Our evaluation of Mercury General Corp. as of October 4th, 2019 is the result of our systematic analysis on three basic characteristics: earnings strength, relative valuation, and recent stock price movement. The company has produced a positive trend in earnings per share over the past 5 quarters. However, recent analyst estimates for the company have been reduced, and MCY has posted results that fell short of analysts' expectations. Based on operating earnings yield, the company is fairly valued when compared to all of the companies we cover. Share price changes over the past year indicates that MCY will perform over the near term.

Financial Data

(US$ in Thousands)	9 Mos	6 Mos	3 Mos	12/31/2018	12/31/2017	12/31/2016	12/31/2015	12/31/2014
Earnings Per Share	3.72	3.53	3.12	(0.10)	2.62	1.32	1.35	3.23
Cash Flow Per Share	8.52	8.40	8.67	6.93	6.17	5.19	3.45	4.48
Tang Book Value Per Share	31.58	30.93	30.03	28.18	30.69	30.46	31.66	32.60
Dividends Per Share	2.510	2.507	2.505	2.502	2.493	2.482	2.473	2.462
Dividend Payout %	67.47	71.03	80.29	...	95.13	188.07	183.15	76.24
Income Statement								
Premium Income	2,674,034	1,759,021	870,245	3,368,411	3,195,437	3,131,773	2,957,897	2,796,195
Total Revenue	2,984,525	1,997,230	1,017,743	3,380,004	3,415,962	3,227,683	3,009,300	3,011,773
Benefits & Claims	1,967,921	1,286,993	630,416	2,576,789	2,444,884	2,355,138	2,145,495	1,986,122
Income Before Taxes	349,604	268,764	167,169	(30,615)	167,085	70,724	70,567	247,425
Income Taxes	61,205	49,647	31,302	(24,887)	22,208	(2,320)	(3,912)	69,476
Net Income	288,399	219,117	135,867	(5,728)	144,877	73,044	74,479	177,949
Average Shares	55,366	55,363	55,348	55,335	55,327	55,302	55,209	55,020
Balance Sheet								
Total Assets	5,873,242	5,716,518	5,606,720	5,433,729	5,101,323	4,788,718	4,628,645	4,600,289
Total Liabilities	4,070,698	3,948,556	3,887,426	3,816,045	3,339,936	3,036,316	2,807,760	2,724,843
Stockholders' Equity	1,802,544	1,767,962	1,719,294	1,617,684	1,761,387	1,752,402	1,820,885	1,875,446
Shares Outstanding	55,355	55,355	55,350	55,340	55,332	55,289	55,164	55,121
Statistical Record								
Return on Assets %	3.69	3.59	3.22	N.M.	2.93	1.55	1.61	3.99
Return on Equity %	11.68	11.26	10.15	N.M.	8.25	4.08	4.03	9.62
Loss Ratio %	73.59	73.17	72.44	76.50	76.51	75.20	72.53	71.03
Net Margin %	9.66	10.97	13.35	(0.17)	4.24	2.26	2.47	5.91
Price Range	64.81-48.78	62.50-43.74	61.37-43.74	61.37-42.31	64.15-51.87	60.87-43.06	60.20-45.64	58.86-42.97
P/E Ratio	17.42-13.11	17.71-12.39	19.67-14.02	...	24.48-19.80	46.11-32.62	44.59-33.81	18.22-13.30
Average Yield %	4.58	4.73	4.93	5.03	4.37	4.66	4.56	5.03

Address: 4484 Wilshire Boulevard, Los Angeles, CA 90010 Telephone: 323-937-1060	Web Site: www.mercuryinsurance.com Officers: George Joseph - Chairman Gabriel Tirador - President, Chief Executive Officer	Auditors: KPMG LLP Transfer Agents: Computershare Trust Company, N.A., Canton, MA

MEREDITH CORP

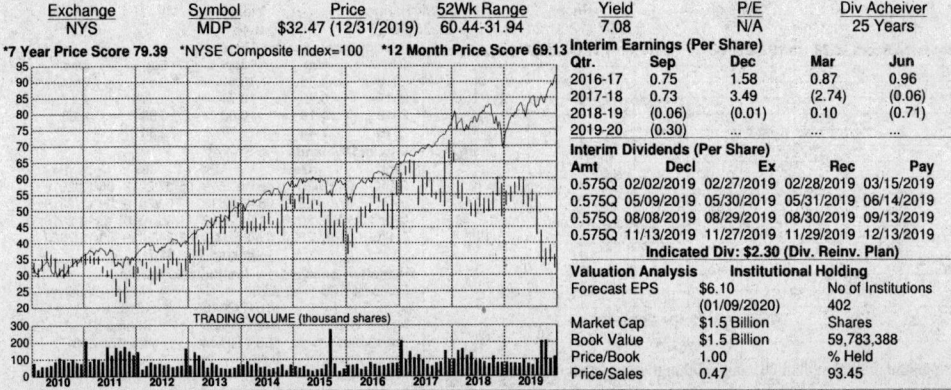

Exchange	Symbol	Price	52Wk Range	Yield	P/E	Div Acheiver
NYS	MDP	$32.47 (12/31/2019)	60.44-31.94	7.08	N/A	25 Years

*7 Year Price Score 79.39   *NYSE Composite Index=100   *12 Month Price Score 69.13

Interim Earnings (Per Share)

Qtr.	Sep	Dec	Mar	Jun
2016-17	0.75	1.58	0.87	0.96
2017-18	0.73	3.49	(2.74)	(0.06)
2018-19	(0.06)	(0.01)	0.10	(0.71)
2019-20	(0.30)	...	...	...

Interim Dividends (Per Share)

Amt	Decl	Ex	Rec	Pay
0.575Q	02/02/2019	02/27/2019	02/28/2019	03/15/2019
0.575Q	05/09/2019	05/30/2019	05/31/2019	06/14/2019
0.575Q	08/08/2019	08/29/2019	08/30/2019	09/13/2019
0.575Q	11/13/2019	11/27/2019	11/29/2019	12/13/2019

Indicated Div: $2.30 (Div. Reinv. Plan)

Valuation Analysis		Institutional Holding	
Forecast EPS	$6.10	No of Institutions	402
	(01/09/2020)		
Market Cap	$1.5 Billion	Shares	59,783,388
Book Value	$1.5 Billion	% Held	
Price/Book	1.00		93.45
Price/Sales	0.47		

Business Summary: Publishing (MIC: 2.3.3 SIC: 2721 NAIC: 511120)

Meredith is a media company. Co. is engaged in providing consumers with content and delivering the messages of its advertising and marketing partners. Co. operates two business segments: national media and local media. Co.'s national media segment includes national consumer media brands delivered via multiple media platforms including print magazines, digital and mobile media, brand licensing activities, database-related activities, affinity marketing, and business-to-business marketing products and services. Co.'s local media segment consists of television stations located across the United States in markets with related digital and mobile media assets.

Recent Developments: For the quarter ended Sep 30 2019, income from continuing operations decreased 25.3% to US$12.1 million from US$16.2 million in the year-earlier quarter. Net income decreased 64.1% to US$6.1 million from US$17.0 million in the year-earlier quarter. Revenues were US$725.2 million, down 6.4% from US$774.4 million the year before. Operating income was US$42.9 million versus US$54.2 million in the prior-year quarter, a decrease of 20.8%. Direct operating expenses declined 5.3% to US$273.7 million from US$289.1 million in the comparable period the year before. Indirect operating expenses decreased 5.2% to US$408.6 million from US$431.1 million in the equivalent prior-year period.

Prospects: Our evaluation of Meredith Corp. as of October 4th, 2019 is the result of our systematic analysis on three basic characteristics: earnings strength, relative valuation, and recent stock price movement. The company has produced a positive trend in earnings per share over the past 5 quarters. However, recent analyst estimates for the company have been reduced, and MDP has posted results that fell short of analysts' expectations. Based on operating earnings yield, the company is undervalued when compared to all of the companies we cover. Share price changes over the past year indicates that MDP will perform over the near term.

Financial Data

(US$ in Thousands)	3 Mos	06/30/2019	06/30/2018	06/30/2017	06/30/2016	06/30/2015	06/30/2014	06/30/2013
Earnings Per Share	(0.92)	(0.70)	1.47	4.16	0.75	3.02	2.50	2.74
Cash Flow Per Share	5.87	5.42	3.37	4.92	5.07	4.32	3.99	4.25
Dividends Per Share	2.270	2.240	2.130	2.030	1.905	1.780	1.680	1.580
Dividend Payout %	...	...	144.90	48.80	254.00	58.94	67.20	57.66
Income Statement								
Total Revenue	725,200	3,188,500	2,247,400	1,713,361	1,649,628	1,594,176	1,468,708	1,471,340
EBITDA	116,600	423,700	160,700	361,473	186,774	297,606	230,927	254,101
Depn & Amortn	65,100	112,500	73,400	52,350	56,165	55,494	44,412	43,267
Income Before Taxes	12,600	140,600	(9,600)	290,334	110,207	222,760	174,339	197,404
Income Taxes	500	11,500	(123,600)	101,406	76,270	85,969	60,798	73,754
Net Income	6,100	46,300	99,400	188,928	33,937	136,791	113,541	123,650
Average Shares	45,600	45,500	45,200	45,447	45,357	45,323	45,410	45,085
Balance Sheet								
Current Assets	1,326,400	1,350,100	1,979,100	505,253	481,156	482,531	470,012	407,692
Total Assets	6,595,300	6,136,900	6,727,200	2,729,623	2,628,285	2,843,282	2,543,800	2,140,059
Current Liabilities	1,170,900	1,260,800	1,190,300	459,670	477,892	531,001	483,103	456,671
Long-Term Obligations	2,394,600	2,333,300	3,117,900	635,737	620,000	732,500	627,500	300,000
Total Liabilities	5,122,000	4,622,100	5,107,100	1,733,651	1,739,242	1,891,432	1,652,148	1,285,763
Stockholders' Equity	1,473,300	1,514,800	1,620,100	995,972	889,043	951,850	891,652	854,296
Shares Outstanding	45,289	45,200	44,900	44,552	44,556	44,620	44,476	44,566
Statistical Record								
Return on Assets %	0.54	0.72	2.10	7.05	1.24	5.08	4.85	5.95
Return on Equity %	2.30	2.95	7.60	20.05	3.68	14.84	13.01	14.97
EBITDA Margin %	16.08	13.29	7.15	21.10	11.32	18.67	15.72	17.27
Net Margin %	0.84	1.45	4.42	11.03	2.06	8.58	7.73	8.40
Asset Turnover	0.48	0.50	0.48	0.64	0.60	0.59	0.63	0.71
Current Ratio	1.13	1.07	1.66	1.10	1.01	0.91	0.97	0.89
Debt to Equity	1.63	1.54	1.92	0.64	0.70	0.77	0.70	0.35
Price Range	60.44-33.68	60.44-47.85	71.80-47.85	65.70-44.15	52.76-36.46	56.96-42.33	53.34-42.96	48.04-29.68
P/E Ratio	...	...	48.84-32.55	15.79-10.61	70.35-48.61	18.86-14.02	21.34-17.18	17.53-10.83
Average Yield %	4.28	4.11	3.74	3.60	4.12	3.51	3.56	4.35

Address: 1716 Locust Street, Des Moines, IA 50309-3023	Web Site: www.meredith.com	Auditors: KPMG LLP
	Officers: D. Mell Meredith Frazier - Vice-Chairman Thomas H. Harty - President, Chief Executive Officer, Chief Operating Officer	Investor Contact: 515-284-3622
Telephone: 515-284-3000		Transfer Agents: Wells Fargo Bank, N.A., St. Paul, MN

METLIFE INC

Exchange	Symbol	Price	52Wk Range	Yield	P/E
NYS	MET	$50.97 (12/31/2019)	51.36-40.87	3.45	6.82

*7 Year Price Score 85.78 ***NYSE Composite Index=100** ***12 Month Price Score 100.22**

Interim Earnings (Per Share)

Qtr.	Mar	Jun	Sep	Dec
2016	1.98	0.06	0.51	(1.92)
2017	0.75	0.77	(0.08)	2.17
2018	1.19	0.83	0.88	2.00
2019	1.40	1.77	2.30	...

Interim Dividends (Per Share)

Amt	Decl	Ex	Rec	Pay
0.44Q	04/23/2019	05/06/2019	05/07/2019	06/13/2019
0.44Q	07/08/2019	08/05/2019	08/06/2019	09/13/2019
0.44Q	10/22/2019	11/04/2019	11/05/2019	12/13/2019
0.44Q	01/07/2020	02/03/2020	02/04/2020	03/13/2020

Indicated Div: $1.76

Valuation Analysis / **Institutional Holding**

Forecast EPS	$5.50	No of Institutions
	(01/17/2020)	1572
Market Cap	$46.9 Billion	Shares
Book Value	$68.4 Billion	862,356,288
Price/Book	0.69	% Held
Price/Sales	0.69	64.88

Business Summary: Life & Health (MIC: 5.2.2 SIC: 6311 NAIC: 524113)

MetLife is an insurance holding company. Through its subsidiaries and affiliates, Co. provides insurance, annuities, employee benefits and asset management. Co.'s segments include: U.S.; Asia; Latin America; Europe, the Middle East and Africa; and MetLife Holdings. In the U.S., Co. provides a variety of insurance and financial services products, including life, dental, disability, property and casualty, guaranteed interest, stable value and annuities to both individuals and groups. Outside the U.S., Co. provides life, medical, dental, credit and other accident and health insurance, as well as annuities, endowment and retirement and savings products to both individuals and groups.

Recent Developments: For the quarter ended Sep 30 2019, net income increased 139.3% to US$2.19 billion from US$915.0 million in the year-earlier quarter. Revenues were US$18.68 billion, up 14.7% from US$16.29 billion the year before. Net premiums earned were US$12.22 billion versus US$11.59 billion in the prior-year quarter, an increase of 5.5%. Net investment income rose 3.1% to US$4.62 billion from US$4.49 billion a year ago.

Prospects: Our evaluation of MetLife Inc. as of October 4th, 2019 is the result of our systematic analysis on three basic characteristics: earnings strength, relative valuation, and recent stock price movement. The company has generated a negative trend in earnings per share over the past 5 quarters. However, recent analyst estimates for the company have been mixed and MET has posted results that exceeded analysts' expectations. Based on operating earnings yield, the company is undervalued when compared to all of the companies we cover. Share price changes over the past year indicates that MET will perform in line with the market over the near term.

Financial Data
(US$ in Millions)

	9 Mos	6 Mos	3 Mos	12/31/2018	12/31/2017	12/31/2016	12/31/2015	12/31/2014
Earnings Per Share	7.47	6.05	5.11	4.91	3.62	0.63	4.57	5.42
Cash Flow Per Share	10.66	9.82	13.08	11.67	11.48	13.44	12.64	14.51
Tang Book Value Per Share	64.26	58.13	51.66	45.19	47.04	53.02	53.32	55.02
Dividends Per Share	1.720	1.700	1.680	1.660	1.600	1.575	1.475	1.325
Dividend Payout %	23.03	28.10	32.88	33.81	44.20	250.00	32.28	24.45
Income Statement								
Premium Income	34,532	22,311	10,770	49,342	44,502	48,359	48,052	49,013
Total Revenue	52,477	33,799	16,302	67,941	62,308	63,476	69,951	73,316
Benefits & Claims	29,713	19,065	9,072	42,656	38,313	40,804	38,714	39,102
Income Before Taxes	6,832	4,041	1,744	6,307	3,536	(195)	7,470	8,804
Income Taxes	1,511	910	359	1,179	(1,470)	(999)	2,148	2,465
Net Income	5,306	3,122	1,381	5,123	4,010	800	5,310	6,309
Average Shares	936	952	963	1,013	1,078	1,108	1,128	1,142
Balance Sheet								
Total Assets	742,812	732,167	713,188	687,538	719,892	898,764	877,933	902,337
Total Liabilities	674,444	668,356	654,679	634,797	661,216	831,455	809,907	830,185
Stockholders' Equity	68,368	63,811	58,509	52,741	58,676	67,309	68,026	72,152
Shares Outstanding	919	935	950	958	1,043	1,095	1,098	1,131
Statistical Record								
Return on Assets %	1.02	0.85	0.74	0.73	0.50	0.09	0.60	0.71
Return on Equity %	12.29	10.39	9.15	9.20	6.37	1.18	7.58	9.38
Loss Ratio %	86.04	85.45	84.23	86.45	86.09	84.38	80.57	79.78
Net Margin %	10.11	9.24	8.47	7.54	6.44	1.26	7.59	8.61
Price Range	50.92-38.24	49.67-38.24	48.79-38.24	54.77-38.24	55.73-44.39	51.14-31.38	51.42-41.05	50.99-41.94
P/E Ratio	6.82-5.12	8.21-6.32	9.55-7.48	11.15-7.79	15.40-12.26	81.18-49.80	11.25-8.98	9.41-7.74
Average Yield %	3.78	3.78	3.74	3.62	3.27	3.94	3.22	2.81

Address: 200 Park Avenue, New York, NY 10166-0188 Telephone: 212-578-9500	Web Site: www.metlife.com Officers: R. Glenn Hubbard - Chairman Michel A. Khalaf - President, Chief Executive Officer, Region Officer	Auditors: Deloitte & Touche LLP Transfer Agents: ComputerShare Investor Services, Providence, RI

METTLER-TOLEDO INTERNATIONAL, INC.

Exchange	Symbol	Price	52Wk Range	Yield	P/E
NYS	MTD	$793.28 (12/31/2019)	872.45-513.56	N/A	36.47

*7 Year Price Score 135.48 *NYSE Composite Index=100   *12 Month Price Score 97.55

Interim Earnings (Per Share)

Qtr.	Mar	Jun	Sep	Dec
2016	2.40	2.93	3.77	5.14
2017	3.48	3.84	3.99	2.93
2018	3.58	4.31	4.93	7.07
2019	4.42	5.06	5.20	...

Interim Dividends (Per Share)

No Dividends Paid

Valuation Analysis

		Institutional Holding	
Forecast EPS	$22.68	No of Institutions	
	(01/16/2020)	791	
Market Cap	$19.3 Billion	Shares	
Book Value	$438.3 Million	31,531,060	
Price/Book	44.08	% Held	
Price/Sales	6.48	91.23	

TRADING VOLUME (thousand shares)

Business Summary: Industrial Machinery & Equipment (MIC: 7.2.1 SIC: 3826 NAIC: 334516)

Mettler-Toledo International is a supplier of precision instruments and services. Co. manufactures weighing instruments for use in laboratory, industrial, packaging, logistics, and food retailing applications. Co. also manufactures several related analytical instruments and provides automated chemistry solutions used in drug and chemical compound discovery and development. In addition, Co. manufactures metal detection and other end-of-line inspection systems used in production and packaging and provides solutions for use in certain process analytics applications. Co. has five segments: U.S. Operations, Swiss Operations, Western European Operations, Chinese Operations, and Other.

Recent Developments: For the quarter ended Sep 30 2019, net income increased 2.2% to US$129.4 million from US$126.7 million in the year-earlier quarter. Revenues were US$753.9 million, up 2.6% from US$734.8 million the year before. Direct operating expenses rose 1.0% to US$318.8 million from US$315.6 million in the comparable period the year before. Indirect operating expenses increased 2.6% to US$257.9 million from US$251.4 million in the equivalent prior-year period.

Prospects: Our evaluation of Mettler-Toledo International Inc. as of October 4th, 2019 is the result of our systematic analysis on three basic characteristics: earnings strength, relative valuation, and recent stock price movement. The company has managed to produce a neutral trend in earnings per share over the past 5 quarters. In addition, recent analyst estimates for the company have been mixed and MTD has posted results that exceeded analysts' expectations. Based on operating earnings yield, the company is fairly valued when compared to all of the companies we cover. Share price changes over the past year indicates that MTD will perform well over the near term.

Financial Data

(US$ in Thousands)	9 Mos	6 Mos	3 Mos	12/31/2018	12/31/2017	12/31/2016	12/31/2015	12/31/2014
Earnings Per Share	21.75	21.48	20.73	19.88	14.24	14.22	12.48	11.44
Cash Flow Per Share	24.52	23.25	23.63	22.41	20.08	16.66	15.42	14.50
Tang Book Value Per Share	N.M.	N.M.	N.M.	N.M.	N.M.	N.M.	0.70	5.76
Income Statement								
Total Revenue	2,164,684	1,410,818	679,452	2,935,586	2,725,053	2,508,257	2,395,447	2,485,983
EBITDA	544,252	342,806	156,759	723,536	640,465	564,962	523,962	503,158
Depn & Amortn	66,225	43,938	21,989	37,167	33,458	32,743	33,087	33,617
Income Before Taxes	450,251	280,892	125,676	651,858	574,222	504,193	463,424	445,004
Income Taxes	81,891	41,927	13,871	139,247	198,250	119,823	110,604	106,763
Net Income	368,360	238,965	111,805	512,611	375,972	384,370	352,820	338,241
Average Shares	24,880	25,118	25,310	25,781	26,393	27,023	28,269	29,571
Balance Sheet								
Current Assets	963,808	981,446	969,384	1,045,860	1,006,723	896,784	862,815	849,430
Total Assets	2,635,869	2,660,858	2,636,697	2,618,847	2,549,805	2,166,777	2,018,485	2,009,110
Current Liabilities	719,255	707,251	707,964	734,434	689,673	587,515	595,127	678,890
Long-Term Obligations	1,124,279	1,087,874	1,008,485	985,021	960,170	875,056	576,984	335,790
Total Liabilities	2,197,568	2,156,772	2,074,947	2,028,784	2,002,525	1,731,834	1,438,028	1,289,515
Stockholders' Equity	438,301	504,086	561,750	590,063	547,280	434,943	580,457	719,595
Shares Outstanding	24,354	24,609	24,803	24,921	25,541	26,020	27,090	28,243
Statistical Record								
Return on Assets %	21.16	20.95	20.63	19.84	15.94	18.32	17.52	16.25
Return on Equity %	113.32	105.51	94.63	90.14	76.56	75.50	54.28	40.88
EBITDA Margin %	25.14	24.30	23.07	24.65	23.50	22.52	21.87	20.24
Net Margin %	17.02	16.94	16.46	17.46	13.80	15.32	14.73	13.61
Asset Turnover	1.15	1.14	1.15	1.14	1.16	1.20	1.19	1.19
Current Ratio	1.34	1.39	1.37	1.42	1.46	1.53	1.45	1.25
Debt to Equity	2.57	2.16	1.80	1.67	1.75	2.01	0.99	0.47
Price Range	872.45-513.56	840.00-513.56	729.72-513.56	692.30-524.03	689.11-414.52	429.91-298.14	346.92-277.62	305.89-223.80
P/E Ratio	40.11-23.61	39.11-23.91	35.20-24.77	34.82-26.36	48.39-29.11	30.23-20.97	27.80-22.25	26.74-19.56

Address: 1900 Polaris Parkway, Columbus, OH 43240 **Telephone:** 614-438-4511 **Fax:** 614-438-4646	**Web Site:** www.mt.com **Officers:** Robert F. Spoerry - Chairman Olivier A. Filliol - President, Chief Executive Officer	**Auditors:** PricewaterhouseCoopers LLP **Investor Contact:** 614-438-4748 **Transfer Agents:** Computershare Shareowner Services LLC, Jersey City, NJ

MFA FINANCIAL, INC.

Exchange	Symbol	Price	52Wk Range	Yield	P/E
NYS	MFA	$7.65 (12/31/2019)	8.00-6.68	10.46	10.77

*7 Year Price Score 78.72 *NYSE Composite Index=100 *12 Month Price Score 99.48

Interim Earnings (Per Share)

Qtr.	Mar	Jun	Sep	Dec
2016	0.20	0.20	0.21	0.19
2017	0.20	0.20	0.15	0.25
2018	0.20	0.17	0.19	0.12
2019	0.19	0.20	0.20	...

Interim Dividends (Per Share)

Amt	Decl	Ex	Rec	Pay
0.20Q	03/06/2019	03/28/2019	03/29/2019	04/30/2019
0.20Q	06/12/2019	06/28/2019	07/01/2019	07/31/2019
0.20Q	09/12/2019	09/27/2019	09/30/2019	10/31/2019
0.20Q	12/12/2019	12/27/2019	12/30/2019	01/31/2020

Indicated Div: $0.80

Valuation Analysis / Institutional Holding

Forecast EPS	$0.79	No of Institutions	
(01/10/2020)		430	
Market Cap	$3.5 Billion	Shares	
Book Value	$3.4 Billion	421,950,496	
Price/Book	1.02	% Held	
Price/Sales	5.72	90.25	

Business Summary: REITs (MIC: 5.3.1 SIC: 6798 NAIC: 525930)

MFA Financial is a holding company. Through its subsidiaries, Co. is a real estate investment trust primarily engaged in the business of investing in residential mortgage assets. Co.'s investments include the following: residential mortgage securities including Non-Agency mortgage-backed securities (MBS), Agency MBS and credit risk transfer securities; residential whole loans, including purchased performing loans, purchased credit impaired and non-performing loans; and mortgage servicing rights (MSRs)-related assets, which include term notes backed directly or indirectly by MSRs and loans to provide financing to entities that originate residential mortgage loans and own the related MSRs.

Recent Developments: For the quarter ended Sep 30 2019, net income increased 9.7% to US$95.6 million from US$87.1 million in the year-earlier quarter. Revenues were US$206.7 million, up 21.3% from US$170.3 million the year before.

Prospects: Our evaluation of MFA Financial, Inc. as of October 4th, 2019 is the result of our systematic analysis on three basic characteristics: earnings strength, relative valuation, and recent stock price movement. The company has enjoyed a very positive trend in earnings per share over the past 5 quarters. However, recent analyst estimates for the company have been mixed and MFA has posted results that exceeded analysts' expectations. Based on operating earnings yield, the company is undervalued when compared to all of the companies we cover. Share price changes over the past year indicates that MFA will perform in line with the market over the near term.

Financial Data
(US$ in Thousands)

	9 Mos	6 Mos	3 Mos	12/31/2018	12/31/2017	12/31/2016	12/31/2015	12/31/2014
Earnings Per Share	0.71	0.70	0.67	0.68	0.79	0.80	0.80	0.81
Cash Flow Per Share	0.47	0.42	0.40	0.35	0.45	0.23	0.76	0.69
Tang Book Value Per Share	4.96	4.96	5.73	7.58	8.18	8.14	7.99	8.64
Dividends Per Share	0.800	0.800	0.800	0.800	0.800	0.800	0.800	0.800
Dividend Payout %	112.68	114.29	119.40	117.65	101.27	100.00	100.00	98.77
Income Statement								
Income Before Taxes	277,496	181,897	88,857	301,801	322,393	312,668	313,226	313,504
Net Income	277,496	181,897	88,857	301,801	322,393	312,668	313,226	313,504
Average Shares	479,940	459,436	450,358	418,934	388,357	371,122	372,114	369,048
Balance Sheet								
Total Assets	13,104,821	13,208,092	12,801,613	12,420,327	10,954,734	12,484,022	13,167,323	12,354,744
Total Liabilities	9,701,395	9,804,719	9,397,082	9,004,226	7,693,098	9,450,120	10,200,062	9,151,472
Stockholders' Equity	3,403,426	3,403,373	3,404,531	3,416,101	3,261,636	3,033,902	2,967,261	3,203,272
Shares Outstanding	451,692	450,622	450,483	449,787	397,831	371,854	370,584	370,084
Statistical Record								
Return on Assets %	2.72	2.77	2.62	2.58	2.75	2.43	2.45	2.53
Return on Equity %	9.73	9.98	9.25	9.04	10.24	10.39	10.15	9.88
Price Range	7.60-6.54	8.06-6.54	8.06-6.54	8.06-6.54	8.87-7.76	8.01-5.78	8.19-6.48	8.46-7.06
P/E Ratio	10.70-9.21	11.51-9.34	12.03-9.76	11.85-9.62	11.23-9.82	10.01-7.23	10.24-8.10	10.44-8.72
Average Yield %	11.10	10.93	10.80	10.74	9.65	11.15	10.67	9.97

Address: 350 Park Avenue, 20th Floor, New York, NY 10022 **Telephone:** 212-207-6400 **Fax:** 212-207-6420	**Web Site:** www.mfafinancial.com **Officers:** George H. Krauss - Chairman Bryan Wulfsohn - Senior Vice President, Co-Chief Investment Officer	**Auditors:** KPMG LLP **Transfer Agents:** Computershare Shareowner Services LLC, Providence, RI

MGM RESORTS INTERNATIONAL

Exchange	Symbol	Price	52Wk Range	Yield	P/E
NYS	MGM	$33.27 (12/31/2019)	33.59-23.87	1.56	N/A

*7 Year Price Score 93.33   *NYSE Composite Index=100   *12 Month Price Score 106.05

Interim Earnings (Per Share)

Qtr.	Mar	Jun	Sep	Dec
2016	0.12	0.83	0.93	0.04
2017	0.36	0.36	0.26	2.38
2018	0.38	0.21	0.26	(0.05)
2019	0.05	0.08	(0.08)	...

Interim Dividends (Per Share)

Amt	Decl	Ex	Rec	Pay
0.13Q	02/13/2019	03/07/2019	03/08/2019	03/15/2019
0.13Q	04/29/2019	06/07/2019	06/10/2019	06/14/2019
0.13Q	07/25/2019	09/09/2019	09/10/2019	09/16/2019
0.13Q	10/30/2019	12/09/2019	12/10/2019	12/16/2019

Indicated Div: $0.52

Valuation Analysis   Institutional Holding

Forecast EPS	$0.35	No of Institutions	715
(01/17/2020)			
Market Cap	$17.1 Billion	Shares	
Book Value	$6.1 Billion		513,262,560
Price/Book	2.82	% Held	
Price/Sales	1.34		75.26

Business Summary: Hotels, Restaurants & Travel (MIC: 2.2.1 SIC: 7011 NAIC: 721120)

MGM Resorts International is a holding company. Through its subsidiaries, Co. owns and operates casino, hotel, and entertainment resorts, which provides gaming, hotel, convention, dining, entertainment, retail and other resort amenities. Co.'s Las Vegas Strip Resorts and Regional Operations consisted of the following casino resorts: Bellagio, MGM Grand Las Vegas, Mandalay Bay, The Mirage, Luxor, New York-New York, Excalibur, Park MGM and Circus Circus Las Vegas in Las Vegas, NV; MGM Grand Detroit in Detroit, MI; Beau Rivage in Biloxi, MS; Gold Strike in Tunica, MS; Borgata in Atlantic City, NJ; MGM National Harbor in Prince George's County, MD; and MGM Springfield in Springfield, MA.

Recent Developments: For the quarter ended Sep 30 2019, net income decreased 96.4% to US$6.1 million from US$171.4 million in the year-earlier quarter. Revenues were US$3.31 billion, up 9.4% from US$3.03 billion the year before. Operating income was US$238.4 million versus US$410.9 million in the prior-year quarter, a decrease of 42.0%. Direct operating expenses rose 8.3% to US$1.94 billion from US$1.79 billion in the comparable period the year before. Indirect operating expenses increased 37.1% to US$1.14 billion from US$831.0 million in the equivalent prior-year period.

Prospects: Our evaluation of MGM Resorts International as of October 4th, 2019 is the result of our systematic analysis on three basic characteristics: earnings strength, relative valuation, and recent stock price movement. The company has managed to produce a neutral trend in earnings per share over the past 5 quarters. However, recent analyst estimates for the company have been reduced and MGM has posted results that fell short of analysts' expectations. Based on operating earnings yield, the company is fairly valued when compared to all of the companies we cover. Share price changes over the past year indicates that MGM will perform well over the near term.

Financial Data

(US$ in Thousands)	9 Mos	6 Mos	3 Mos	12/31/2018	12/31/2017	12/31/2016	12/31/2015	12/31/2014
Earnings Per Share	...	0.34	0.47	0.81	3.35	1.92	(0.82)	(0.31)
Cash Flow Per Share	3.24	3.00	2.89	3.16	3.86	2.69	1.85	2.30
Tang Book Value Per Share	0.23	0.98	1.37	1.42	3.40	0.55	N.M.	N.M.
Dividends Per Share	0.510	0.500	0.490	0.480	0.440	...	...	...
Dividend Payout %	...	147.06	104.26	59.26	13.13	...	...	...
Income Statement								
Total Revenue	9,714,536	6,400,154	3,176,911	11,763,096	10,773,904	9,455,123	9,190,068	10,081,984
EBITDA	853,734	651,144	342,577	2,522,802	2,547,738	2,369,493	436,078	2,105,320
Depn & Amortn	29,539	19,735	9,373	1,219,146	1,026,476	890,020	866,163	853,415
Income Before Taxes	176,743	199,460	117,084	534,143	852,517	784,700	(1,227,664)	434,844
Income Taxes	75,969	83,245	71,511	50,112	(1,132,663)	22,299	(6,594)	283,708
Net Income	37,569	74,702	31,297	466,772	1,960,286	1,101,440	(447,720)	(149,873)
Average Shares	518,983	535,417	537,506	549,536	578,795	573,317	542,873	490,875
Balance Sheet								
Current Assets	2,880,746	2,040,034	2,207,135	2,526,778	2,374,627	2,229,587	2,408,749	3,027,160
Total Assets	31,168,871	30,813,715	31,146,921	30,210,706	29,159,178	28,173,301	25,215,178	26,702,511
Current Liabilities	3,293,244	2,786,539	2,812,678	2,948,882	3,092,382	2,293,421	2,237,951	3,407,925
Long-Term Obligations	14,943,874	14,661,695	14,730,829	15,088,005	12,751,052	12,979,220	12,368,311	12,913,882
Total Liabilities	25,108,319	24,293,231	24,360,717	23,698,423	21,546,526	21,953,121	20,095,251	22,611,594
Stockholders' Equity	6,060,552	6,520,484	6,786,204	6,512,283	7,612,652	6,220,180	5,119,927	4,090,917
Shares Outstanding	513,913	526,333	537,156	527,479	566,275	574,123	564,838	491,292
Statistical Record								
Return on Assets %	0.05	0.65	0.91	1.57	6.84	4.11	N.M.	N.M.
Return on Equity %	0.22	2.91	3.88	6.61	28.34	19.37	N.M.	N.M.
EBITDA Margin %	8.79	10.17	10.78	21.45	23.65	25.06	4.75	20.88
Net Margin %	0.39	1.17	0.99	3.97	18.19	11.65	N.M.	N.M.
Asset Turnover	0.42	0.42	0.40	0.40	0.38	0.35	0.35	0.38
Current Ratio	0.87	0.73	0.78	0.86	0.77	0.97	1.08	0.89
Debt to Equity	2.47	2.25	2.17	2.32	1.67	2.09	2.42	3.16
Price Range	30.55-21.84	31.52-21.84	36.41-21.84	38.03-21.84	34.27-25.43	29.95-16.56	24.14-17.57	28.39-18.01
P/E Ratio	N.M.	92.71-64.24	77.47-46.47	46.95-26.96	10.23-7.59	15.60-8.63	...	...
Average Yield %	1.87	1.83	1.71	1.57	1.43	...	...	...

Address: 3600 Las Vegas Boulevard South, Las Vegas, NV 89109 **Telephone:** 702-693-7120	**Web Site:** www.mgmresorts.com **Officers:** James J. (Jim) Murren - Chairman, Chief Executive Officer William J. Hornbuckle - President, Chief Operating Officer, Chief Marketing Officer, Division Officer	**Auditors:** Deloitte & Touche LLP **Transfer Agents:** ComputerShare Investor Services, Providence, RI

MID-AMERICA APARTMENT COMMUNITIES INC

Exchange	Symbol	Price	52Wk Range	Yield	P/E
NYS	MAA	$131.86 (12/31/2019)	139.15-92.65	3.03	57.58

*7 Year Price Score 108.62 *NYSE Composite Index=100 *12 Month Price Score 106.94

TRADING VOLUME (thousand shares)

Interim Earnings (Per Share)

Qtr.	Mar	Jun	Sep	Dec
2016	0.58	0.60	1.12	0.40
2017	0.36	0.42	1.00	1.08
2018	0.42	0.52	0.46	0.53
2019	0.55	0.53	0.68	...

Interim Dividends (Per Share)

Amt	Decl	Ex	Rec	Pay
0.96Q	03/21/2019	04/12/2019	04/15/2019	04/30/2019
0.96Q	05/21/2019	07/12/2019	07/15/2019	07/31/2019
0.96Q	09/26/2019	10/11/2019	10/15/2019	10/31/2019
1.00Q	12/10/2019	01/14/2020	01/15/2020	01/31/2020

Indicated Div: $4.00 (Div. Reinv. Plan)

Valuation Analysis

		Institutional Holding	
Forecast EPS	$2.34	No of Institutions	
	(01/17/2020)	653	
Market Cap	$15.0 Billion	Shares	
Book Value	$6.0 Billion	124,683,576	
Price/Book	2.49	% Held	
Price/Sales	9.27	93.17	

Business Summary: REITs (MIC: 5.3.1 SIC: 6798 NAIC: 525930)

Mid-America Apartment Communities is a self-administered and self-managed real estate investment trust. Co. owns, operates, acquires and develops apartment communities located in the Southeast, Southwest and Mid-Atlantic regions of the U.S. Co.'s business is conducted principally through Mid-America Apartments, L.P., in which Co. is the sole general partner.

Recent Developments: For the quarter ended Sep 30 2019, net income increased 48.9% to US$81.5 million from US$54.7 million in the year-earlier quarter. Revenues were US$415.6 million, up 4.7% from US$397.1 million the year before.

Prospects: Our evaluation of Mid-America Apartment Communities Inc. as of October 4th, 2019 is the result of our systematic analysis on three basic characteristics: earnings strength, relative valuation, and recent stock price movement. The company has enjoyed a very positive trend in earnings per share over the past 5 quarters. However, recent analyst estimates for the company have been mixed and MAA has posted results that fell short of analysts' expectations. Based on operating earnings yield, the company is overvalued when compared to all of the companies we cover. Share price changes over the past year indicates that MAA will perform well over the near term.

Financial Data

(US$ in Thousands)	9 Mos	6 Mos	3 Mos	12/31/2018	12/31/2017	12/31/2016	12/31/2015	12/31/2014
Earnings Per Share	2.29	2.07	2.06	1.93	2.86	2.69	4.41	1.97
Cash Flow Per Share	6.63	6.49	6.47	6.46	5.81	6.15	6.17	5.12
Tang Book Value Per Share	52.87	53.17	53.66	54.10	55.88	56.49	39.77	38.45
Dividends Per Share	3.803	3.765	3.728	3.690	3.480	3.280	3.080	2.920
Dividend Payout %	166.05	181.88	180.95	191.19	121.68	121.93	69.84	148.22
Income Statement								
Total Revenue	1,224,200	808,568	401,178	1,571,346	1,528,987	1,125,348	1,042,779	989,296
EBITDA	354,017	225,694	113,649	891,400	981,266	669,270	754,146	545,035
Depn & Amortn	4,706	3,468	1,747	486,005	484,730	313,463	279,382	280,462
Income Before Taxes	213,162	130,590	66,202	231,801	341,785	225,860	352,420	145,109
Income Taxes	2,814	1,323	641	2,611	2,619	1,699	1,673	2,050
Net Income	204,222	125,577	63,660	222,899	328,379	212,222	332,287	147,980
Average Shares	114,137	114,087	113,933	113,836	113,687	78,800	75,176	74,982
Balance Sheet								
Current Assets	42,682	57,684	59,387	51,673	88,867	121,800	63,641	53,582
Total Assets	11,247,754	11,274,830	11,303,762	11,323,781	11,491,919	11,604,491	6,847,781	6,831,028
Current Liabilities	...	...	...	...	...	30,799	17,545	18,921
Long-Term Obligations	4,476,114	4,539,989	4,548,098	4,528,328	4,502,057	4,499,712	3,427,568	3,524,515
Total Liabilities	5,217,646	5,211,261	5,190,595	5,164,527	5,141,599	5,190,599	3,847,434	3,934,593
Stockholders' Equity	6,030,108	6,063,569	6,113,167	6,159,254	6,350,320	6,413,892	3,000,347	2,896,435
Shares Outstanding	114,065	114,043	113,916	113,844	113,643	113,518	75,408	75,267
Statistical Record								
Return on Assets %	2.34	2.11	2.09	1.95	2.84	2.29	4.86	2.16
Return on Equity %	4.34	3.89	3.83	3.56	5.15	4.50	11.27	5.06
EBITDA Margin %	28.92	27.91	28.33	56.73	64.18	59.47	72.32	55.09
Net Margin %	16.68	15.53	15.87	14.19	21.48	18.86	31.87	14.96
Asset Turnover	0.14	0.14	0.14	0.14	0.13	0.12	0.15	0.14
Current Ratio	...	...	...	...	...	3.95	3.63	2.83
Debt to Equity	0.74	0.75	0.74	0.74	0.71	0.70	1.14	1.22
Price Range	130.46-92.23	119.98-92.23	109.62-87.93	104.49-85.39	110.32-93.78	109.67-84.64	92.40-71.15	76.24-60.74
P/E Ratio	56.97-40.28	57.96-44.56	53.21-42.68	54.14-44.24	38.57-32.79	40.77-31.46	20.95-16.13	38.70-30.83
Average Yield %	3.46	3.62	3.76	3.84	3.39	3.41	3.87	4.19

Address: 6815 Poplar Avenue, Suite 500, Germantown, TN 38138	Web Site: www.maac.com	Auditors: Ernst & Young LLP
Telephone: 901-682-6600	Officers: H. Eric Bolton - Chairman, President, Chief Executive Officer Thomas L. Grimes - Executive Vice President, Chief Operating Officer	Investor Contact: 901-682-6600
Fax: 901-682-6667		Transfer Agents: American Stock Transfer & Trust Company

MINERALS TECHNOLOGIES, INC.

Exchange	Symbol	Price	52Wk Range	Yield	P/E
NYS	MTX	$57.63 (12/31/2019)	63.20-45.55	0.35	13.89

*7 Year Price Score 74.16 *NYSE Composite Index=100 *12 Month Price Score 95.14

Interim Earnings (Per Share)

Qtr.	Mar	Jun	Sep	Dec
2016	0.97	0.60	1.18	1.04
2017	0.97	1.21	1.17	2.13
2018	1.12	1.24	1.18	1.21
2019	1.11	0.75	1.08	...

Interim Dividends (Per Share)

Amt	Decl	Ex	Rec	Pay
0.05Q	01/23/2019	02/14/2019	02/15/2019	03/07/2019
0.05Q	05/14/2019	05/29/2019	05/30/2019	06/13/2019
0.05Q	07/17/2019	08/22/2019	08/23/2019	09/05/2019
0.05Q	10/23/2019	11/01/2019	11/04/2019	12/12/2019

Indicated Div: $0.20

Valuation Analysis | **Institutional Holding**

Forecast EPS	$4.19	No of Institutions	
	(01/14/2020)	318	
Market Cap	$2.0 Billion	Shares	
Book Value	$1.4 Billion	41,883,608	
Price/Book	1.43	% Held	
Price/Sales	1.12	93.39	

Business Summary: Specialty Chemicals (MIC: 8.3.2 SIC: 2819 NAIC: 325188)

Minerals Technologies is a resource- and technology-based company. Co.'s segments are: Performance Materials, which supplies bentonite and bentonite-related products, chromite and leonardite; Specialty Minerals, which produces and sells the synthetic mineral product precipitated calcium carbonate and processed mineral product quicklime, and mines mineral ores then processes and sells natural mineral products, primarily limestone and talc; Refractories, which produces monolithic and shaped refractory materials and specialty products; and Energy Services, which provides services to improve the production, costs, compliance, and environmental impact in the oil and gas industry.

Recent Developments: For the quarter ended Sep 29 2019, net income decreased 8.9% to US$39.1 million from US$42.9 million in the year-earlier quarter. Revenues were US$449.3 million, down 3.2% from US$464.1 million the year before. Operating income was US$53.5 million versus US$68.2 million in the prior-year quarter, a decrease of 21.6%. Direct operating expenses declined 2.0% to US$338.1 million from US$344.9 million in the comparable period the year before. Indirect operating expenses increased 13.1% to US$57.7 million from US$51.0 million in the equivalent prior-year period.

Prospects: Our evaluation of Minerals Technologies Inc. as of October 4th, 2019 is the result of our systematic analysis on three basic characteristics: earnings strength, relative valuation, and recent stock price movement. The company has managed to produce a neutral trend in earnings per share over the past 5 quarters. In addition, recent analyst estimates for the company have been mixed and MTX has posted results that exceeded analysts' expectations. Based on operating earnings yield, the company is undervalued when compared to all of the companies we cover. Share price changes over the past year indicates that MTX will perform poorly over the near term.

Financial Data

(US$ in Thousands)	9 Mos	6 Mos	3 Mos	12/31/2018	12/31/2017	12/31/2016	12/31/2015	12/31/2014
Earnings Per Share	4.15	4.25	4.74	4.75	5.48	3.79	3.08	2.65
Cash Flow Per Share	6.53	6.30	5.64	5.77	5.90	6.43	7.78	9.01
Tang Book Value Per Share	11.22	10.70	10.48	9.29	7.80	0.67	N.M.	N.M.
Dividends Per Share	0.200	0.200	0.200	0.200	0.200	0.200	0.200	0.200
Dividend Payout %	4.82	4.71	4.22	4.21	3.65	5.28	6.49	7.55
Income Statement								
Total Revenue	1,350,800	901,500	437,700	1,807,600	1,675,700	1,638,000	1,797,600	1,725,000
EBITDA	165,200	110,300	64,000	330,700	309,900	300,100	283,400	246,200
Depn & Amortn	9,600	6,600	3,400	80,700	75,600	75,400	89,900	81,400
Income Before Taxes	122,300	81,400	49,200	204,100	190,900	170,300	132,600	123,000
Income Taxes	17,000	14,400	9,300	34,400	(6,600)	35,300	22,800	30,800
Net Income	103,700	65,700	39,100	169,000	195,100	133,400	107,900	92,400
Average Shares	35,100	35,300	35,300	35,600	35,600	35,200	35,000	34,800
Balance Sheet								
Current Assets	920,100	931,100	903,900	876,300	852,200	751,100	803,600	924,600
Total Assets	3,125,900	3,149,400	3,163,400	3,087,100	2,970,400	2,863,400	2,980,000	3,226,700
Current Liabilities	409,900	405,600	390,800	381,900	310,000	295,500	318,600	352,900
Long-Term Obligations	844,700	874,200	893,400	907,800	959,800	1,069,900	1,255,300	1,455,500
Total Liabilities	1,723,200	1,758,500	1,769,900	1,733,600	1,718,700	1,856,900	2,069,500	2,363,700
Stockholders' Equity	1,402,700	1,390,900	1,393,500	1,353,500	1,251,700	1,006,500	910,500	863,000
Shares Outstanding	34,854	35,062	35,235	35,190	35,374	34,969	34,784	34,649
Statistical Record								
Return on Assets %	4.71	4.80	5.45	5.58	6.69	4.55	3.48	4.16
Return on Equity %	10.82	11.25	12.48	12.97	17.28	13.88	12.17	10.80
EBITDA Margin %	12.23	12.24	14.62	18.29	18.49	18.32	15.77	14.27
Net Margin %	7.68	7.29	8.93	9.35	11.64	8.14	6.00	5.36
Asset Turnover	0.58	0.58	0.59	0.60	0.57	0.56	0.58	0.78
Current Ratio	2.24	2.30	2.31	2.29	2.75	2.54	2.52	2.62
Debt to Equity	0.60	0.63	0.64	0.67	0.77	1.06	1.38	1.69
Price Range	67.65-45.55	77.75-47.89	77.75-47.89	77.75-47.89	83.70-62.95	82.90-37.03	74.74-45.35	77.40-48.81
P/E Ratio	16.30-10.98	18.29-11.27	16.40-10.10	16.37-10.08	15.27-11.49	21.87-9.77	24.27-14.72	29.21-18.42
Average Yield %	0.36	0.33	0.31	0.30	0.27	0.33	0.32	0.32

Address: 622 Third Avenue, New York, NY 10017-6707	Web Site: www.mineralstech.com	Auditors: KPMG LLP
Telephone: 212-878-1800	Officers: Duane R. Dunham - Chairman Douglas T. Dietrich - Chief Executive Officer, Interim Co-Chief Executive Officer, Chief Financial Officer, Senior Vice President, Vice President	Investor Contact: 212-878-1831 Transfer Agents: Computershare Trust Company, N. A., Providence, RI

MOHAWK INDUSTRIES, INC.

Exchange	Symbol	Price	52Wk Range	Yield	P/E
NYS	MHK	$136.38 (12/31/2019)	156.36-110.45	N/A	14.12

*7 Year Price Score 63.45 *NYSE Composite Index=100 *12 Month Price Score 100.12

Interim Earnings (Per Share)

Qtr.	Mar	Jun	Sep	Dec
2016	2.30	3.42	3.62	3.14
2017	2.68	3.48	3.61	3.21
2018	2.78	2.62	3.02	3.05
2019	1.67	2.79	2.15	...

Interim Dividends (Per Share)

No Dividends Paid

Valuation Analysis

Valuation Analysis		Institutional Holding	
Forecast EPS	$9.97	No of Institutions	
	(01/17/2020)	735	
Market Cap	$9.8 Billion	Shares	
Book Value	$7.8 Billion	73,551,976	
Price/Book	1.26	% Held	
Price/Sales	0.98	76.60	

TRADING VOLUME (thousand shares)

Business Summary: Construction Materials (MIC: 8.5.1 SIC: 2273 NAIC: 314110)

Mohawk Industries is a global flooring manufacturer for residential and commercial spaces around the world. Co. has three reporting segments: Global Ceramic, which designs, manufactures, sources, distributes and markets a line of ceramic, porcelain and natural stone tile products used for floor and wall applications; Flooring North America, which designs, manufactures, sources and distributes carpet, carpet tile, rugs and mats, carpet pad, wood, laminate, medium-density fiberboard, luxury vinyl tile (LVT) and sheet vinyl; and Flooring Rest of the World, which designs, manufactures, sources and distributes laminate, wood flooring, LVT and sheet vinyl, broadloom carpet and carpet tile.

Recent Developments: For the quarter ended Sep 28 2019, net income decreased 31.7% to US$155.7 million from US$228.0 million in the year-earlier quarter. Revenues were US$2.52 billion, down 1.0% from US$2.55 billion the year before. Operating income was US$240.2 million versus US$287.2 million in the prior-year quarter, a decrease of 16.4%. Direct operating expenses was unchanged at US$1.83 billion versus the comparable period the year before. Indirect operating expenses increased 4.2% to US$451.5 million from US$433.2 million in the equivalent prior-year period.

Prospects: Our evaluation of Mohawk Industries Inc. as of October 4th, 2019 is the result of our systematic analysis on three basic characteristics: earnings strength, relative valuation, and recent stock price movement. The company has managed to produce a neutral trend in earnings per share over the past 5 quarters. In addition, recent analyst estimates for the company have been mixed and MHK has posted results that exceeded analysts' expectations. Based on operating earnings yield, the company is undervalued when compared to all of the companies we cover. Share price changes over the past year indicates that MHK will perform poorly over the near term.

Financial Data

(US$ in Thousands)	9 Mos	6 Mos	3 Mos	12/31/2018	12/31/2017	12/31/2016	12/31/2015	12/31/2014
Earnings Per Share	9.66	10.53	10.36	11.47	12.98	12.48	8.31	7.25
Cash Flow Per Share	17.54	15.56	16.15	15.88	16.05	17.87	12.40	9.09
Tang Book Value Per Share	60.17	59.40	56.22	54.64	49.66	35.96	21.97	28.96
Income Statement								
Total Revenue	7,546,160	5,026,975	2,442,490	9,983,634	9,491,290	8,959,087	8,071,563	7,803,446
EBITDA	1,049,174	716,747	306,357	1,575,439	1,757,614	1,647,905	1,148,433	1,077,938
Depn & Amortn	422,693	277,773	137,291	487,411	408,646	366,233	328,486	315,840
Income Before Taxes	596,171	417,980	158,593	1,049,201	1,317,857	1,241,125	748,861	663,891
Income Taxes	116,273	93,751	37,018	184,346	343,165	307,559	131,875	131,637
Net Income	479,544	324,026	121,585	861,704	971,638	930,362	615,302	531,965
Average Shares	72,392	72,680	72,646	74,773	74,839	74,568	74,043	73,363
Balance Sheet								
Current Assets	4,727,780	4,808,317	4,688,965	4,509,296	4,072,967	3,471,512	3,249,972	3,132,270
Total Assets	13,392,762	13,806,102	13,605,075	13,099,123	12,094,853	10,230,596	9,942,364	8,285,544
Current Liabilities	3,114,699	3,705,791	3,434,247	3,266,239	2,655,355	2,718,320	3,259,028	1,955,814
Long-Term Obligations	1,483,581	1,169,489	1,497,975	1,515,601	1,559,895	1,128,747	1,196,928	1,402,135
Total Liabilities	5,633,994	5,991,029	6,034,274	5,665,309	5,035,691	4,454,145	5,088,191	3,867,538
Stockholders' Equity	7,758,768	7,815,073	7,570,801	7,433,814	7,059,162	5,776,451	4,854,173	4,418,006
Shares Outstanding	71,845	72,364	72,422	72,307	74,421	74,168	73,929	72,913
Statistical Record								
Return on Assets %	5.37	5.85	5.92	6.84	8.70	9.20	6.75	6.34
Return on Equity %	9.25	10.28	10.39	11.89	15.14	17.46	13.27	11.98
EBITDA Margin %	13.90	14.26	12.54	15.78	18.52	18.39	14.23	13.81
Net Margin %	6.35	6.45	4.98	8.63	10.24	10.38	7.62	6.82
Asset Turnover	0.76	0.75	0.77	0.79	0.85	0.89	0.89	0.93
Current Ratio	1.52	1.30	1.37	1.38	1.53	1.28	1.00	1.60
Debt to Equity	0.19	0.15	0.20	0.20	0.22	0.20	0.25	0.32
Price Range	175.35-110.45	224.84-111.31	245.94-111.31	281.06-111.31	284.82-201.74	216.22-151.78	211.33-152.74	157.60-124.77
P/E Ratio	18.15-11.43	21.35-10.57	23.74-10.74	24.50-9.70	21.94-15.54	17.33-12.16	25.43-18.38	21.74-17.21

Address: 160 S. Industrial Blvd., Calhoun, GA 30701 Telephone: 706-629-7721	Web Site: www.mohawkind.com Officers: Jeffrey S. Lorberbaum - Chairman, Chief Executive Officer W. Christopher Wellborn - President, Chief Operating Officer	Auditors: KPMG LLP Investor Contact: 706-624-2695 Transfer Agents: American Stock Transfer and Trust Company, Addison, TX

MOLINA HEALTHCARE INC

Exchange	Symbol	Price	52Wk Range	Yield	P/E
NYS	MOH	$135.69 (12/31/2019)	155.28-105.90	N/A	11.49

*7 Year Price Score 152.88 *NYSE Composite Index=100 *12 Month Price Score 93.84

Interim Earnings (Per Share)

Qtr.	Mar	Jun	Sep	Dec
2016	0.43	0.58	0.76	(0.85)
2017	1.37	(4.10)	(1.70)	(4.63)
2018	1.64	3.02	2.90	3.01
2019	2.99	3.06	2.75	...

Interim Dividends (Per Share)

No Dividends Paid

Valuation Analysis / **Institutional Holding**

Forecast EPS	$11.57	No of Institutions	493
	(01/16/2020)		
Market Cap	$8.5 Billion	Shares	
Book Value	$1.8 Billion		71,232,368
Price/Book	4.67	% Held	
Price/Sales	0.50		96.85

Business Summary: Hospitals & Health Care Facilities (MIC: 4.2.1 SIC: 6324 NAIC: 524114)

Molina Healthcare is a multi-state healthcare organization, arranges for the delivery of health care services to individuals and families who receive their care through the Medicaid and Medicare programs, and through the state insurance marketplaces. Co. manages its operations through two reportable segments: Health Plans, which consists of Co.'s health plans; and Others, which includes the historical results of the Pathways Health and Community Support LLC behavioral health subsidiary, and certain corporate amounts not allocated to the Health Plans segment.

Recent Developments: For the quarter ended Sep 30 2019, net income decreased 11.2% to US$175.0 million from US$197.0 million in the year-earlier quarter. Revenues were US$4.24 billion, down 9.7% from US$4.70 billion the year before. Net premiums earned were US$4.20 billion versus US$4.45 billion in the prior-year quarter, a decrease of 5.5%.

Prospects: Our evaluation of Molina Healthcare Inc. as of October 4th, 2019 is the result of our systematic analysis on three basic characteristics: earnings strength, relative valuation, and recent stock price movement. The company has generated a negative trend in earnings per share over the past 5 quarters. However, recent analyst estimates for the company have been mixed and MOH has posted results that exceeded analysts' expectations. Based on operating earnings yield, the company is undervalued when compared to all of the companies we cover. Share price changes over the past year indicates that MOH will perform well over the near term.

Financial Data

(US$ in Thousands)	9 Mos	6 Mos	3 Mos	12/31/2018	12/31/2017	12/31/2016	12/31/2015	12/31/2014
Earnings Per Share	11.81	11.96	11.92	10.61	(9.07)	0.92	2.58	1.29
Cash Flow Per Share	4.42	(7.60)	(7.39)	(5.14)	14.36	12.20	21.63	22.59
Tang Book Value Per Share	26.27	24.70	26.19	23.50	18.03	15.60	16.36	13.06
Income Statement								
Total Revenue	12,555,000	8,312,000	4,119,000	18,890,000	19,883,000	17,782,000	14,178,000	9,666,601
EBITDA	822,000	566,000	286,000	1,150,000	(452,000)	351,000	437,000	226,715
Depn & Amortn	5,000	4,000	3,000	36,000	42,000	45,000	49,000	34,600
Income Before Taxes	750,000	517,000	260,000	999,000	(612,000)	205,000	322,000	135,304
Income Taxes	181,000	123,000	62,000	292,000	(100,000)	153,000	179,000	72,726
Net Income	569,000	394,000	198,000	707,000	(512,000)	52,000	143,000	62,223
Average Shares	63,600	64,000	66,200	66,600	56,000	56,000	56,000	48,340
Balance Sheet								
Current Assets	5,877,000	5,863,000	6,731,000	6,462,000	7,511,000	5,988,000	5,306,000	3,245,397
Total Assets	6,701,000	6,690,000	7,579,000	7,154,000	8,471,000	7,449,000	6,576,000	4,477,215
Current Liabilities	3,308,000	3,388,000	4,292,000	4,246,000	5,557,000	4,570,000	3,822,000	2,174,773
Long-Term Obligations	1,472,000	1,473,000	1,355,000	1,217,000	1,516,000	1,173,000	1,160,000	905,048
Total Liabilities	4,870,000	4,954,000	5,744,000	5,507,000	7,134,000	5,800,000	5,019,000	3,466,773
Stockholders' Equity	1,831,000	1,736,000	1,835,000	1,647,000	1,337,000	1,649,000	1,557,000	1,010,442
Shares Outstanding	63,000	63,000	63,000	62,000	60,000	57,000	56,000	49,727
Statistical Record								
Return on Assets %	10.44	10.25	9.55	9.05	N.M.	0.74	2.59	1.66
Return on Equity %	45.40	46.67	47.11	47.39	N.M.	3.24	11.14	6.54
EBITDA Margin %	6.55	6.81	6.94	6.09	N.M.	1.97	3.08	2.35
Net Margin %	4.53	4.74	4.81	3.74	N.M.	0.29	1.01	0.64
Asset Turnover	2.33	2.29	2.20	2.42	2.50	2.53	2.57	2.58
Current Ratio	1.78	1.73	1.57	1.52	1.35	1.31	1.39	1.49
Debt to Equity	0.80	0.85	0.74	0.74	1.13	0.71	0.75	0.90
Price Range	155.28-105.90	155.28-98.71	152.72-78.76	152.72-71.14	79.18-42.70	67.72-45.34	81.50-49.87	54.09-32.73
P/E Ratio	13.15-8.97	12.98-8.25	12.81-6.61	14.39-6.70	...	73.61-49.28	31.59-19.33	41.93-25.37

Address: 200 Oceangate, Suite 100, Long Beach, CA 90802 Telephone: 562-435-3666 Fax: 562-437-1335	Web Site: www.molinahealthcare.com Officers: Dale B. Wolf - Chairman Ronna E. Romney - Vice-Chairman	Auditors: Ernst & Young LLP Transfer Agents: American Stock Transfer & Trust Company, New York, NY

MOLSON COORS BEVERAGE CO

Exchange	Symbol	Price	52Wk Range	Yield	P/E
NYS	TAP A	$53.90 (12/31/2019)	66.61-50.07	4.23	75.92

*7 Year Price Score 64.79   *NYSE Composite Index=100   *12 Month Price Score 86.86

Interim Earnings (Per Share)

Qtr.	Mar	Jun	Sep	Dec
2016	0.78	0.80	0.94	6.73
2017	0.93	1.49	1.29	2.81
2018	1.28	1.96	1.56	0.35
2019	0.70	1.52	(1.86)	...

Interim Dividends (Per Share)

Amt	Decl	Ex	Rec	Pay
0.41Q	02/14/2019	03/01/2019	03/04/2019	03/15/2019
0.41Q	05/23/2019	05/31/2019	06/03/2019	06/14/2019
0.57Q	07/18/2019	08/29/2019	08/30/2019	09/13/2019
0.57Q	11/21/2019	11/29/2019	12/02/2019	12/13/2019

Indicated Div: $2.28

Valuation Analysis | **Institutional Holding**

Forecast EPS	$4.32	No of Institutions
(01/17/2020)		826
Market Cap	$11.7 Billion	Shares
Book Value	$13.2 Billion	196,029,376
Price/Book	0.89	% Held
Price/Sales	1.11	78.08

Business Summary: Beverages (MIC: 1.2.2 SIC: 2082 NAIC: 312120)

Molson Coors Brewing is a holding company. Through its subsidiaries, Co. is a brewer and has a portfolio of brands, including Blue Moon, Coors Banquet, Coors Light, Miller Lite, Staropramen, Carling, Molson Canadian and other brands, as well as craft and specialty beers such as Creemore Springs, Cobra, Doom Bar, Henry's Hard and Leinenkugel's. Co.'s segments include: MillerCoors LLC operating in the U.S.; Molson Coors Canada operating in Canada; Molson Coors Europe operating in Bulgaria, Croatia, Czech Republic, Hungary, Montenegro, the Republic of Ireland, Romania, Serbia, the U.K. and various other European countries; and Molson Coors International operating in various other countries.

Recent Developments: For the quarter ended Sep 30 2019, net loss amounted to US$399.3 million versus net income of US$345.6 million in the year-earlier quarter. Revenues were US$2.84 billion, down 3.2% from US$2.93 billion the year before. Operating loss was US$237.3 million versus an income of US$469.7 million in the prior-year quarter. Direct operating expenses declined 1.7% to US$1.69 billion from US$1.71 billion in the comparable period the year before. Indirect operating expenses increased 85.7% to US$1.39 billion from US$750.5 million in the equivalent prior-year period.

Prospects: Our evaluation of Molson Coors Brewing Co. as of October 4th, 2019 is the result of our systematic analysis on three basic characteristics: earnings strength, relative valuation, and recent stock price movement. The company has managed to produce a neutral trend in earnings per share over the past 5 quarters. In addition, recent analyst estimates for the company have been mixed and TAP has posted results that fell short of analysts' expectations. Based on operating earnings yield, the company is undervalued when compared to all of the companies we cover. Share price changes over the past year indicates that TAP will perform poorly over the near term.

Financial Data

(US$ in Thousands)	9 Mos	6 Mos	3 Mos	12/31/2018	12/31/2017	12/31/2016	12/31/2015	12/31/2014
Earnings Per Share	0.71	4.13	4.57	5.15	6.53	9.26	1.93	2.76
Cash Flow Per Share	8.44	8.59	8.86	10.79	8.66	5.30	3.76	6.88
Tang Book Value Per Share	N.M.	N.M.	N.M.	N.M.	N.M.	N.M.	1.70	N.M.
Dividends Per Share	1.800	1.640	1.640	1.640	1.640	1.640	1.640	1.480
Dividend Payout %	253.52	39.71	35.89	31.84	25.11	17.71	84.97	53.62
Income Statement								
Total Revenue	8,093,200	5,251,600	2,303,300	10,769,600	11,002,800	4,885,000	3,567,500	4,146,300
EBITDA	489,000	728,300	258,300	2,291,400	2,315,700	3,085,100	290,900	426,600
Depn & Amortn	11,200	7,500	3,700	633,400	590,700	306,300	284,500	268,400
Income Before Taxes	273,300	581,900	181,300	1,359,800	1,381,700	2,534,400	(105,600)	24,500
Income Taxes	193,300	102,600	32,200	225,200	(53,200)	1,050,700	51,800	69,000
Net Income	78,000	480,800	151,400	1,116,500	1,414,200	1,975,900	359,500	514,000
Average Shares	216,600	216,900	216,900	216,600	216,500	213,400	186,400	186,100
Balance Sheet								
Current Assets	2,286,900	2,600,400	2,338,000	2,766,300	2,189,700	2,169,600	1,258,800	1,578,900
Total Assets	28,751,600	30,061,600	29,823,600	30,109,800	30,246,900	29,341,500	12,276,300	13,996,300
Current Liabilities	3,888,600	4,088,400	4,202,400	4,300,900	3,399,300	3,157,500	1,217,200	2,325,300
Long-Term Obligations	8,058,500	8,517,900	8,484,800	8,893,800	10,598,700	11,387,700	2,908,700	2,337,100
Total Liabilities	15,589,200	16,162,200	16,176,300	16,602,400	17,020,800	17,922,800	5,233,300	6,133,000
Stockholders' Equity	13,162,400	13,899,400	13,647,300	13,507,400	13,226,100	11,418,700	7,043,000	7,863,300
Shares Outstanding	216,300	213,700	216,400	216,100	215,400	214,900	184,500	185,500
Statistical Record								
Return on Assets %	0.52	2.95	3.30	3.70	4.75	9.47	2.74	3.48
Return on Equity %	1.14	6.52	7.31	8.35	11.48	21.35	4.82	6.23
EBITDA Margin %	6.04	13.87	11.21	21.28	21.05	63.15	8.15	10.29
Net Margin %	0.96	9.16	6.57	10.37	12.85	40.45	10.08	12.40
Asset Turnover	0.35	0.35	0.36	0.36	0.37	0.23	0.27	0.28
Current Ratio	0.59	0.64	0.56	0.64	0.64	0.69	1.03	0.68
Debt to Equity	0.61	0.61	0.62	0.66	0.80	1.00	0.41	0.30
Price Range	66.61-50.07	70.62-53.66	74.10-55.15	85.21-55.15	101.59-76.52	111.25-83.63	95.14-65.19	77.75-51.32
P/E Ratio	93.82-70.52	17.10-12.99	16.21-12.07	16.55-10.71	15.56-11.72	12.01-9.03	49.30-33.78	28.17-18.59
Average Yield %	3.05	2.65	2.56	2.40	1.83	1.68	2.24	2.21

Address: 1555 Notre Dame Street East, Montreal, H2L 2R5	Web Site: www.molsoncoors.com	Auditors: PricewaterhouseCoopers LLP
Telephone: 514-521-1786	Officers: Peter H. Coors - Chairman, Chief Customer Relations Officer, Chairman (frmr), Vice-Chairman Geoffrey E. Molson - Chairman, Vice-Chairman	Investor Contact: 303-927-2448 Transfer Agents: CST Trust Company, Toronto, Ontario, Canada

MOODY'S CORP.

Exchange	Symbol	Price	52Wk Range	Yield	P/E
NYS	MCO	$237.41 (12/31/2019)	239.30-136.18	0.84	34.76

*7 Year Price Score 135.49   *NYSE Composite Index=100   *12 Month Price Score 109.14

Interim Earnings (Per Share)

Qtr.	Mar	Jun	Sep	Dec
2016	0.93	1.30	1.31	(2.19)
2017	1.78	1.61	1.63	0.13
2018	1.92	1.94	1.59	1.29
2019	1.93	1.62	1.99	...

Interim Dividends (Per Share)

Amt	Decl	Ex	Rec	Pay
0.50Q	02/12/2019	02/22/2019	02/25/2019	03/18/2019
0.50Q	04/15/2019	05/17/2019	05/20/2019	06/10/2019
0.50Q	07/09/2019	08/19/2019	08/20/2019	09/10/2019
0.50Q	10/21/2019	11/20/2019	11/21/2019	12/12/2019

Indicated Div: $2.00

Valuation Analysis

		Institutional Holding	
Forecast EPS	$8.20	No of Institutions	
	(01/16/2020)	1025	
Market Cap	$44.8 Billion	Shares	
Book Value	$472.6 Million	216,065,616	
Price/Book	94.82	% Held	
Price/Sales	9.62	88.45	

Business Summary: Business Services (MIC: 7.5.2 SIC: 7323 NAIC: 561450)

Moody's is a provider of credit ratings; credit, capital markets and economic related research, data and analytical tools; software solutions; quantitatively derived credit scores; learning solutions and certification services; offshore financial research and analytical services; and company information and business intelligence products. Co.'s segments are: Moody's Investors Service, which publishes credit ratings on a range of debt obligations and the entities that issue such obligations in markets worldwide; and Moody's Analytics, which develops products and services that support financial analysis and risk management activities of institutional participants in global financial markets.

Recent Developments: For the quarter ended Sep 30 2019, net income increased 22.6% to US$382.4 million from US$312.0 million in the year-earlier quarter. Revenues were US$1.24 billion, up 14.8% from US$1.08 billion the year before. Operating income was US$548.8 million versus US$466.8 million in the prior-year quarter, an increase of 17.6%. Direct operating expenses rose 14.3% to US$350.2 million from US$306.3 million in the comparable period the year before. Indirect operating expenses increased 11.0% to US$341.5 million from US$307.7 million in the equivalent prior-year period.

Prospects: Our evaluation of Moody's Corp. as of October 4th, 2019 is the result of our systematic analysis on three basic characteristics: earnings strength, relative valuation, and recent stock price movement. The company has produced a positive trend in earnings per share over the past 5 quarters. However, recent analyst estimates for the company have been mixed and MCO has posted results that exceeded analysts' expectations. Based on operating earnings yield, the company is fairly valued when compared to all of the companies we cover. Share price changes over the past year indicates that MCO will perform over the near term.

Financial Data

(US$ in Thousands)	9 Mos	6 Mos	3 Mos	12/31/2018	12/31/2017	12/31/2016	12/31/2015	12/31/2014
Earnings Per Share	6.83	6.43	6.75	6.74	5.15	1.36	4.63	4.61
Cash Flow Per Share	8.32	7.59	7.55	7.63	3.91	6.35	5.77	4.83
Dividends Per Share	1.940	1.880	1.820	1.760	1.520	1.480	1.360	1.120
Dividend Payout %	28.40	29.24	26.96	26.11	29.51	108.82	29.37	24.30
Income Statement								
Total Revenue	3,596,200	2,355,700	1,142,100	4,442,700	4,204,100	3,604,200	3,484,500	3,334,300
EBITDA	1,645,800	1,042,400	513,100	2,065,100	2,120,200	811,100	1,596,400	1,663,800
Depn & Amortn	149,900	101,300	50,300	191,900	158,300	126,700	113,500	95,600
Income Before Taxes	1,346,900	838,000	410,300	1,657,200	1,773,500	546,600	1,367,800	1,451,400
Income Taxes	289,600	159,200	37,900	351,600	779,100	282,200	430,000	455,000
Net Income	1,062,600	683,200	372,900	1,309,600	1,000,600	266,600	941,300	988,700
Average Shares	191,100	191,300	192,800	194,400	194,200	195,400	203,400	214,700
Balance Sheet								
Current Assets	3,042,300	3,154,600	2,898,400	3,386,900	2,580,600	3,253,100	3,243,100	2,686,400
Total Assets	9,477,800	9,591,600	9,518,100	9,526,200	8,594,200	5,327,300	5,123,400	4,669,000
Current Liabilities	2,138,000	1,839,900	2,005,600	2,098,500	2,063,300	2,428,200	1,218,500	1,199,700
Long-Term Obligations	4,736,500	5,258,000	5,752,100	5,226,100	5,111,100	3,063,000	3,401,000	2,547,300
Total Liabilities	9,005,200	9,238,800	9,394,900	9,066,300	8,921,900	6,552,300	5,688,400	4,856,800
Stockholders' Equity	472,600	352,800	123,200	459,900	(327,700)	(1,225,000)	(565,000)	(187,800)
Shares Outstanding	188,750	189,161	196,602	191,303	190,970	190,694	196,075	204,363
Statistical Record								
Return on Assets %	14.66	13.56	14.13	14.45	14.37	5.09	19.23	21.82
Return on Equity %	300.88	417.56	811.15	1,981.24	...	...	...	1,325.34
EBITDA Margin %	45.76	44.25	44.93	46.48	50.43	22.50	45.81	49.90
Net Margin %	29.55	29.00	32.65	29.48	23.80	7.40	27.01	29.65
Asset Turnover	0.52	0.49	0.48	0.49	0.60	0.69	0.71	0.74
Current Ratio	1.42	1.71	1.45	1.61	1.25	1.34	2.66	2.24
Debt to Equity	10.02	14.90	46.69	11.36	...	...	...	...
Price Range	220.54-129.35	197.35-129.35	187.02-129.35	187.02-129.35	152.57-94.67	110.16-78.45	112.90-89.32	101.84-72.65
P/E Ratio	32.29-18.94	30.69-20.12	27.71-19.16	27.75-19.19	29.63-18.38	81.00-57.68	24.38-19.29	22.09-15.76
Average Yield %	1.08	1.10	1.10	1.07	1.21	1.51	1.32	1.28

Address: 7 World Trade Center, 250 Greenwich Street, New York, NY 10007
Telephone: 212-553-0300

Web Site: www.moodys.com
Officers: Henry A. McKinnell - Chairman Raymond W. McDaniel - Chairman, President, Chief Executive Officer

Auditors: KPMG LLP
Investor Contact: 212-553-4857
Transfer Agents: American Stock Transfer & Trust Company, LLC, Brooklyn, NY

MORGAN STANLEY

Exchange	Symbol	Price	52Wk Range	Yield	P/E
NYS	MS	$51.12 (12/31/2019)	51.12-39.10	2.74	10.88

*7 Year Price Score 96.55   *NYSE Composite Index=100   *12 Month Price Score 105.44

Interim Earnings (Per Share)

Qtr.	Mar	Jun	Sep	Dec
2016	0.55	0.75	0.81	0.81
2017	1.00	0.87	0.93	0.28
2018	1.45	1.30	1.17	0.81
2019	1.39	1.23	1.27	...

Interim Dividends (Per Share)

Amt	Decl	Ex	Rec	Pay
0.30Q	04/17/2019	04/29/2019	04/30/2019	05/15/2019
0.35Q	07/18/2019	07/30/2019	07/31/2019	08/15/2019
0.35Q	10/17/2019	10/30/2019	10/31/2019	11/15/2019
0.35Q	01/16/2020	01/30/2020	01/31/2020	02/14/2020

Indicated Div: $1.40 (Div. Reinv. Plan)

Valuation Analysis

		Institutional Holding	
Forecast EPS	$5.30	No of Institutions	
	(01/17/2020)	1539	
Market Cap	$83.0 Billion	Shares	
Book Value	$82.4 Billion	1,698,990,080	
Price/Book	1.01	% Held	
Price/Sales	1.59	75.02	

Business Summary: Finance Intermediaries & Services (MIC: 5.5.1 SIC: 6211 NAIC: 523120)

Morgan Stanley is a financial holding company. Through its subsidiaries and affiliates, Co. advises, and originates, trades, manages and distributes capital for, governments, institutions and individuals. Co.'s segments are: Institutional Securities, which provides investment banking, sales and trading, lending and other services; Wealth Management, which provides brokerage and investment advisory services, financial and wealth planning services, annuity and insurance products, securities-based lending, residential real estate loans and other lending products, banking and retirement plan services; and Investment Management, which provides a range of investment strategies and products.

Recent Developments: For the quarter ended Sep 30 2019, income from continuing operations increased 2.9% to US$2.22 billion from US$2.16 billion in the year-earlier quarter. Net income increased 3.0% to US$2.22 billion from US$2.15 billion in the year-earlier quarter. Revenues were US$13.16 billion, up 4.8% from US$12.56 billion the year before. Direct operating expenses rose 16.4% to US$3.13 billion from US$2.69 billion in the comparable period the year before. Indirect operating expenses increased 4.3% to US$7.32 billion from US$7.02 billion in the equivalent prior-year period.

Prospects: Our evaluation of Morgan Stanley Dean Witter & Co. as of October 4th, 2019 is the result of our systematic analysis on three basic characteristics: earnings strength, relative valuation, and recent stock price movement. The company has produced a positive trend in earnings per share over the past 5 quarters. However, recent analyst estimates for the company have been reduced, while MS has posted results that exceeded analysts' expectations. Based on operating earnings yield, the company is undervalued when compared to all of the companies we cover. Share price changes over the past year indicates that MS will perform in line with the market over the near term.

Financial Data

(US$ in Thousands)	9 Mos	6 Mos	3 Mos	12/31/2018	12/31/2017	12/31/2016	12/31/2015	12/31/2014
Earnings Per Share	4.70	4.60	4.67	4.73	3.07	2.92	2.90	1.60
Cash Flow Per Share	21.03	21.39	7.06	4.28	(2.53)	1.32	1.92	0.59
Tang Book Value Per Share	39.73	38.44	37.62	36.99	33.46	31.97	30.26	28.26
Dividends Per Share	1.250	1.200	1.150	1.100	0.900	0.700	0.550	0.350
Dividend Payout %	26.60	26.09	24.63	23.26	29.32	23.97	18.97	21.88
Income Statement								
Interest Income	13,146,000	8,796,000	4,290,000	13,892,000	8,997,000	7,016,000	5,835,000	5,413,000
Interest Expense	9,885,000	6,753,000	3,276,000	10,086,000	5,697,000	3,318,000	2,742,000	3,678,000
Net Interest Income	3,261,000	2,043,000	1,014,000	3,806,000	3,300,000	3,698,000	3,093,000	1,735,000
Non-Interest Income	27,301,000	18,487,000	9,272,000	36,301,000	34,645,000	30,933,000	32,062,000	32,540,000
Non-Interest Expense	21,994,000	14,672,000	7,331,000	28,870,000	27,542,000	25,783,000	26,660,000	30,684,000
Income Before Taxes	8,568,000	5,858,000	2,955,000	11,237,000	10,403,000	8,848,000	8,495,000	3,591,000
Income Taxes	1,636,000	1,144,000	487,000	2,350,000	4,168,000	2,726,000	2,200,000	(90,000)
Net Income	6,803,000	4,630,000	2,429,000	8,748,000	6,111,000	5,979,000	6,127,000	3,467,000
Average Shares	1,627,000	1,655,000	1,677,000	1,738,000	1,821,000	1,887,000	1,952,815	1,970,535
Balance Sheet								
Net Loans & Leases	125,522,000	120,901,000	116,197,000	115,579,000	104,126,000	94,248,000	85,759,000	66,577,000
Total Assets	902,604,000	891,959,000	875,964,000	853,531,000	851,733,000	814,949,000	787,465,000	801,510,000
Total Deposits	180,738,000	176,593,000	179,731,000	187,820,000	159,436,000	155,863,000	156,034,000	133,544,000
Total Liabilities	820,222,000	810,235,000	795,240,000	773,285,000	774,342,000	738,899,000	712,283,000	730,610,000
Stockholders' Equity	82,382,000	81,724,000	80,724,000	80,246,000	77,391,000	76,050,000	75,182,000	70,900,000
Shares Outstanding	1,623,587	1,658,805	1,685,996	1,699,828	1,788,086	1,852,481	1,920,024	1,950,980
Statistical Record								
Return on Assets %	0.94	0.94	0.98	1.03	0.73	0.74	0.77	0.42
Return on Equity %	10.35	10.29	10.72	11.10	7.97	7.89	8.39	5.07
Net Interest Margin %	28.00	22.84	23.64	27.40	36.68	52.71	53.01	32.05
Efficiency Ratio %	55.62	53.50	54.06	57.52	63.11	67.94	70.35	80.85
Loans to Deposits	0.69	0.68	0.65	0.62	0.65	0.60	0.55	0.50
Price Range	48.46-37.01	51.05-37.01	55.22-37.01	58.91-37.01	53.85-40.69	43.73-21.69	40.54-31.01	39.00-28.47
P/E Ratio	10.31-7.87	11.10-8.05	11.82-7.93	12.45-7.82	17.54-13.25	14.98-7.43	13.98-10.69	24.38-17.79
Average Yield %	2.89	2.82	2.46	2.20	1.95	2.34	1.53	1.07

Address: 1585 Broadway, New York, NY 10036	Web Site: www.morganstanley.com	Auditors: Deloitte & Touche LLP
Telephone: 212-761-4000	Officers: James P. Gorman - Chairman, President, Chief Executive Officer Jeffrey S. Brodsky - Executive Vice President, Chief Human Resources Officer	Investor Contact: 212-761-4000 Transfer Agents: Computershare, Providence, RI

MOSAIC CO (THE)

Exchange	Symbol	Price	52Wk Range	Yield	P/E
NYS	MOS	$21.64 (12/31/2019)	33.48-17.66	0.92	N/A

*7 Year Price Score 56.60   ***NYSE Composite Index=100**   ***12 Month Price Score 77.77**

TRADING VOLUME (thousand shares)

Interim Earnings (Per Share)

Qtr.	Mar	Jun	Sep	Dec
2016	0.73	(0.03)	0.11	0.04
2017	0.00	0.28	0.65	(1.23)
2018	0.11	0.18	0.64	0.29
2019	0.34	(0.60)	(0.11)	...

Interim Dividends (Per Share)

Amt	Decl	Ex	Rec	Pay
0.05Q	05/23/2019	06/05/2019	06/06/2019	06/20/2019
0.05Q	08/14/2019	09/04/2019	09/05/2019	09/19/2019
0.05Q	10/16/2019	12/04/2019	12/05/2019	12/19/2019
0.05Q	12/19/2019	03/04/2020	03/05/2020	03/19/2020

Indicated Div: $0.20

Valuation Analysis   Institutional Holding

Forecast EPS	$0.45	No of Institutions
	(01/17/2020)	810
Market Cap	$8.2 Billion	Shares
Book Value	$10.1 Billion	339,839,872
Price/Book	0.81	% Held
Price/Sales	0.88	N/A

Business Summary: Agricultural Chemicals (MIC: 8.3.3 SIC: 2874 NAIC: 325312)

Mosaic is a producer and marketer of concentrated phosphate and potash crop nutrients. Co. is organized into three reportable business segments: Phosphates, which owns and operates mines and production facilities in Florida that produce concentrated phosphate crop nutrients and phosphate-based animal feed ingredients, and processing plants in Louisiana that produce concentrated phosphate crop nutrients; Potash, which mines and processes potash in Canada and the U.S. and sells potash in North America and internationally; and Mosaic Fertilizantes, which produces and sells concentrated phosphates crop nutrients, phosphate-based animal feed ingredients and potash fertilizer.

Recent Developments: For the quarter ended Sep 30 2019, net loss amounted to US$40.0 million versus net income of US$249.7 million in the year-earlier quarter. Revenues were US$2.75 billion, down 6.0% from US$2.93 billion the year before. Operating income was US$139.5 million versus US$393.3 million in the prior-year quarter, a decrease of 64.5%. Direct operating expenses rose 1.7% to US$2.47 billion from US$2.43 billion in the comparable period the year before. Indirect operating expenses increased 37.4% to US$140.4 million from US$102.2 million in the equivalent prior-year period.

Prospects: Our evaluation of Mosaic Co as of October 4th, 2019 is the result of our systematic analysis on three basic characteristics: earnings strength, relative valuation, and recent stock price movement. The company has generated a negative trend in earnings per share over the past 5 quarters. In addition, recent analyst estimates for the company have been reduced and MOS has posted results that fell short of analysts' expectations. Based on operating earnings yield, the company is undervalued when compared to all of the companies we cover. Share price changes over the past year indicates that MOS will perform very poorly over the near term.

Financial Data
(US$ in Thousands)

	9 Mos	6 Mos	3 Mos	12/31/2018	12/31/2017	12/31/2016	12/31/2015	12/31/2014
Earnings Per Share	(0.08)	0.67	1.45	1.22	(0.31)	0.85	2.78	2.68
Cash Flow Per Share	2.51	2.61	3.39	3.66	2.67	3.60	5.04	6.13
Tang Book Value Per Share	22.02	22.62	23.00	22.54	22.57	22.71	22.51	24.21
Dividends Per Share	0.150	0.125	0.100	0.100	0.600	1.100	1.075	1.000
Dividend Payout %	...	18.66	6.90	8.20	...	129.41	38.67	37.31
Income Statement								
Total Revenue	6,830,000	4,076,600	1,899,700	9,587,300	7,409,400	7,162,800	8,895,300	9,055,800
EBITDA	88,700	(6,500)	222,400	1,595,800	1,171,500	1,058,600	1,933,300	2,075,800
Depn & Amortn	(5,500)	(5,300)	(1,200)	878,200	659,400	703,800	732,200	750,900
Income Before Taxes	(42,000)	(94,200)	176,600	551,500	374,000	242,400	1,103,300	1,217,300
Income Taxes	64,100	(5,100)	46,600	77,100	494,900	(74,200)	99,100	184,700
Net Income	(146,400)	(102,300)	130,800	470,000	(107,200)	297,800	1,000,400	1,028,600
Average Shares	385,000	385,800	387,400	386,400	350,900	351,700	360,300	375,600
Balance Sheet								
Current Assets	4,125,300	4,228,800	4,146,300	4,237,000	4,616,500	3,057,700	4,144,700	5,364,200
Total Assets	20,440,100	20,643,900	20,445,300	20,119,200	18,633,400	16,840,700	17,412,400	18,283,000
Current Liabilities	2,724,500	2,526,900	2,397,200	2,483,700	2,031,100	1,476,800	2,048,300	1,600,400
Long-Term Obligations	4,676,100	4,705,100	4,696,700	4,491,500	4,878,100	3,779,300	3,791,100	3,778,000
Total Liabilities	10,339,700	10,170,900	9,844,100	9,721,900	9,015,900	7,256,100	7,880,600	7,579,900
Stockholders' Equity	10,100,400	10,473,000	10,601,200	10,397,300	9,617,500	9,584,600	9,531,800	10,703,100
Shares Outstanding	380,045	385,867	385,788	385,470	351,049	350,238	352,515	367,540
Statistical Record								
Return on Assets %	N.M.	1.25	2.73	2.43	N.M.	1.73	5.61	5.44
Return on Equity %	N.M.	2.49	5.30	4.70	N.M.	3.11	9.89	9.35
EBITDA Margin %	1.30	N.M.	11.71	16.64	15.81	14.78	21.73	22.92
Net Margin %	N.M.	N.M.	6.89	4.90	N.M.	4.16	11.25	11.36
Asset Turnover	0.46	0.46	0.47	0.49	0.42	0.42	0.50	0.48
Current Ratio	1.51	1.67	1.73	1.71	2.27	2.07	2.02	3.35
Debt to Equity	0.46	0.45	0.44	0.43	0.51	0.39	0.40	0.35
Price Range	36.99-17.66	36.99-21.27	36.99-23.57	36.99-23.57	34.02-19.39	31.42-22.10	53.56-27.24	50.79-40.76
P/E Ratio	...	55.21-31.75	25.51-16.32	30.32-19.32	...	36.96-26.00	19.27-9.80	18.95-15.21
Average Yield %	0.55	0.42	0.33	0.34	2.40	4.12	2.57	2.13

Address: 101 East Kennedy Blvd, Suite 2500, Tampa, FL 33602 **Telephone:** 918-918-8270 **Fax:** 763-577-2990	**Web Site:** www.mosaicco.com **Officers:** James C. (Joc) O'Rourke - President, Chief Executive Officer, Executive Vice President, Chief Operating Officer Mark J. Isaacson - Senior Vice President, Vice President, General Counsel, Corporate Secretary	**Auditors:** KPMG LLP **Investor Contact:** 763-577-8213 **Transfer Agents:** American Stock Transfer & Trust Company, New York, NY

MOTOROLA SOLUTIONS INC

Exchange	Symbol	Price	52Wk Range	Yield	P/E
NYS	MSI	$161.14 (12/31/2019)	181.16-110.76	1.59	26.86

*7 Year Price Score 144.20 *NYSE Composite Index=100   *12 Month Price Score 99.83

Interim Earnings (Per Share)

Qtr.	Mar	Jun	Sep	Dec
2016	0.10	0.61	1.13	1.42
2017	0.45	0.78	1.25	(3.43)
2018	0.69	1.05	1.43	2.45
2019	0.86	1.18	1.51	...

Interim Dividends (Per Share)

Amt	Decl	Ex	Rec	Pay
0.57Q	02/14/2019	03/14/2019	03/15/2019	04/15/2019
0.57Q	05/13/2019	06/13/2019	06/14/2019	07/15/2019
0.57Q	08/29/2019	09/12/2019	09/13/2019	10/15/2019
0.64Q	11/14/2019	12/12/2019	12/13/2019	01/15/2020

Indicated Div: $2.56

Valuation Analysis

Forecast EPS	$7.80
	(01/15/2020)
Market Cap	$27.6 Billion
Book Value	N/A
Price/Book	N/A
Price/Sales	3.55

Institutional Holding

No of Institutions	1111
Shares	335,395,328
% Held	N/A

Business Summary: Manufacturing (MIC: 6.1.1 SIC: 3663 NAIC: 334220)

Motorola Solutions is a provider of communication. Co. manages its business through two segments: Products and Systems Integration, and Services and Software Segment. The products and systems integration segment provide a portfolio of infrastructure, devices, accessories, video solutions, and the implementation, optimization, and integration of such systems, devices, and applications. The customers of the products and systems integration segment are government, public safety and first-responder agencies, municipalities, and commercial and industrial customers. The services and software segment provide a range of solution offerings for government, public safety and commercial customers.

Recent Developments: For the quarter ended Sep 28 2019, net income increased 8.1% to US$268.0 million from US$248.0 million in the year-earlier quarter. Revenues were US$1.99 billion, up 7.1% from US$1.86 billion the year before. Operating income was US$413.0 million versus US$294.0 million in the prior-year quarter, an increase of 40.5%. Direct operating expenses rose 2.7% to US$987.0 million from US$961.0 million in the comparable period the year before. Indirect operating expenses decreased 2.1% to US$594.0 million from US$607.0 million in the equivalent prior-year period.

Prospects: Our evaluation of Motorola Solutions Inc. as of October 4th, 2019 is the result of our systematic analysis on three basic characteristics: earnings strength, relative valuation, and recent stock price movement. The company has generated a negative trend in earnings per share over the past 5 quarters. However, recent analyst estimates for the company have been raised and MSI has posted results that exceeded analysts' expectations. Based on operating earnings yield, the company is fairly valued when compared to all of the companies we cover. Share price changes over the past year indicates that MSI will perform over the near term.

Financial Data

(US$ in Millions)	9 Mos	6 Mos	3 Mos	12/31/2018	12/31/2017	12/31/2016	12/31/2015	12/31/2014
Earnings Per Share	6.00	5.92	5.79	5.62	(0.95)	3.24	3.02	5.29
Cash Flow Per Share	11.04	10.02	11.13	6.62	8.26	6.85	5.04	(2.79)
Tang Book Value Per Share	...	...	...	...	...	...	...	10.60
Dividends Per Share	2.280	2.230	2.180	2.130	1.930	1.700	1.430	1.300
Dividend Payout %	38.00	37.67	37.65	37.90	...	52.47	47.35	24.57
Income Statement								
Total Revenue	5,511	3,517	1,657	7,343	6,380	6,038	5,695	5,881
EBITDA	1,106	761	284	1,684	1,620	1,344	1,240	(862)
Depn & Amortn	136	191	45	360	343	295	150	173
Income Before Taxes	805	459	184	1,102	1,076	844	917	(1,161)
Income Taxes	180	100	33	133	1,227	282	274	(465)
Net Income	625	358	151	966	(155)	560	610	1,299
Average Shares	176	176	174	172	162	173	201	245
Balance Sheet								
Current Assets	4,154	3,831	3,714	4,272	3,950	3,468	4,582	6,879
Total Assets	10,373	9,974	9,993	9,409	8,208	8,463	8,387	10,423
Current Liabilities	3,656	2,876	2,979	3,096	2,931	2,668	2,193	2,250
Long-Term Obligations	5,112	5,315	5,287	5,289	4,419	4,392	4,386	3,396
Total Liabilities	11,474	10,944	11,101	10,702	9,950	9,427	8,493	7,688
Stockholders' Equity	(1,101)	(970)	(1,108)	(1,293)	(1,742)	(964)	(106)	2,735
Shares Outstanding	171	165	164	163	161	164	174	219
Statistical Record								
Return on Assets %	10.83	10.89	10.50	10.97	N.M.	6.63	6.49	11.66
Return on Equity %	...	...	...	...	...	...	46.41	40.63
EBITDA Margin %	20.07	21.64	17.14	22.93	25.39	22.26	21.77	N.M.
Net Margin %	11.34	10.18	9.11	13.16	N.M.	9.27	10.71	22.09
Asset Turnover	0.80	0.81	0.79	0.83	0.77	0.71	0.61	0.53
Current Ratio	1.14	1.33	1.25	1.38	1.35	1.30	2.09	3.06
Debt to Equity	...	...	...	...	...	...	...	1.24
Price Range	181.16-108.97	166.86-108.97	143.61-103.98	133.79-89.91	94.53-77.34	84.00-60.36	72.45-56.79	67.87-58.50
P/E Ratio	30.19-18.16	28.19-18.41	24.80-17.96	23.81-16.00	...	25.93-18.63	23.99-18.80	12.83-11.06
Average Yield %	1.58	1.69	1.79	1.85	2.24	2.34	2.21	2.02

Address: 500 West Monroe Street, Chicago, IL 60661 Telephone: 847-576-5000 Fax: 847-576-3477	Web Site: www.motorolasolutions.com Officers: Gregory Q. Brown - Chairman, President, Chief Executive Officer, Division Officer Gino A. Bonanotte - Executive Vice President, Corporate Vice-President, Acting Chief Financial Officer, Chief Financial Officer, Acting Chief Financial Officer, Chief Financial Officer	Auditors: KPMG LLP Investor Contact: 847-576-6899 Transfer Agents: Computershare, Jersey City, NJ

MSA SAFETY INC

Exchange	Symbol	Price	52Wk Range	Yield	P/E	Div Acheiver
NYS	MSA	$126.36 (12/31/2019)	127.39-92.35	1.33	38.18	48 Years

7 Year Price Score 130.06 *NYSE Composite Index=100   *12 Month Price Score 108.99**

Interim Earnings (Per Share)

Qtr.	Mar	Jun	Sep	Dec
2016	0.31	0.82	0.63	0.66
2017	0.37	0.32	0.83	(0.85)
2018	0.83	0.85	0.86	0.63
2019	0.59	1.01	1.08	...

Interim Dividends (Per Share)

Amt	Decl	Ex	Rec	Pay
0.42Q	05/08/2019	05/17/2019	05/20/2019	06/10/2019
0.42Q	08/06/2019	08/19/2019	08/20/2019	09/10/2019
0.42Q	10/25/2019	11/06/2019	11/07/2019	12/10/2019
0.42Q	01/14/2020	02/11/2020	02/12/2020	03/10/2020

Indicated Div: $1.68

Valuation Analysis   **Institutional Holding**

Forecast EPS	$4.88	No of Institutions
(01/10/2020)		335
Market Cap	$4.9 Billion	Shares
Book Value	$702.1 Million	36,017,940
Price/Book	6.97	% Held
Price/Sales	3.53	N/A

Business Summary: Office Equipment & Furniture (MIC: 7.5.1 SIC: 3842 NAIC: 922160)

MSA Safety is engaged in the development, manufacture and supply of safety products. Co. manufactures and sells a line of safety products to protect the health and safety of workers and facility infrastructures around the world in the oil, gas and petrochemical industry, fire service, construction, industrial manufacturing applications, utilities, mining and the military. Co.'s core products include fixed gas and flame detection systems, portable gas detection instruments, industrial head protection products, firefighter helmets and protective apparel and fall protection devices. Co.'s non-core products include respirators, eye and face protection, ballistic helmets and gas masks.

Recent Developments: For the quarter ended Sep 30 2019, net income increased 25.1% to US$42.6 million from US$34.1 million in the year-earlier quarter. Revenues were US$351.0 million, up 6.0% from US$331.1 million the year before. Operating income was US$59.6 million versus US$40.0 million in the prior-year quarter, an increase of 49.0%. Direct operating expenses rose 5.2% to US$192.3 million from US$182.8 million in the comparable period the year before. Indirect operating expenses decreased 8.5% to US$99.1 million from US$108.3 million in the equivalent prior-year period.

Prospects: Our evaluation of MSA Safety Inc. as of October 4th, 2019 is the result of our systematic analysis on three basic characteristics: earnings strength, relative valuation, and recent stock price movement. The company has enjoyed a very positive trend in earnings per share over the past 5 quarters. However, recent analyst estimates for the company have been unchanged, while MSA has posted results that exceeded analysts' expectations. Based on operating earnings yield, the company is fairly valued when compared to all of the companies we cover. Share price changes over the past year indicates that MSA will perform in line with the market over the near term.

Financial Data

(US$ in Thousands)	9 Mos	6 Mos	3 Mos	12/31/2018	12/31/2017	12/31/2016	12/31/2015	12/31/2014
Earnings Per Share	3.31	3.09	2.93	3.18	0.67	2.42	1.87	2.33
Cash Flow Per Share	4.29	6.11	6.43	6.88	6.06	3.59	1.48	2.88
Tang Book Value Per Share	2.55	1.89	1.82	1.22	N.M.	3.82	2.21	6.58
Dividends Per Share	1.600	1.560	1.520	1.490	1.380	1.310	1.270	1.230
Dividend Payout %	48.34	50.49	51.88	46.86	205.97	54.13	67.91	52.79
Income Statement								
Total Revenue	1,026,726	675,713	326,038	1,358,104	1,196,809	1,149,530	1,129,922	1,136,650
EBITDA	183,441	111,351	44,065	203,528	69,539	192,495	148,780	163,246
Depn & Amortn	28,339	18,792	9,326	26,900	28,000	27,000	26,900	26,200
Income Before Taxes	144,013	85,729	32,379	162,335	29,775	151,911	111,026	127,195
Income Taxes	37,913	22,241	9,003	37,220	2,819	57,804	44,407	41,044
Net Income	105,278	63,038	23,232	124,150	26,027	91,936	70,807	88,506
Average Shares	39,144	39,160	39,084	38,961	38,697	37,986	37,710	37,728
Balance Sheet								
Current Assets	686,428	687,634	672,791	656,623	622,297	472,806	505,027	497,869
Total Assets	1,699,143	1,713,856	1,671,368	1,608,012	1,684,826	1,353,920	1,424,818	1,264,792
Current Liabilities	262,208	257,517	266,270	282,060	289,279	221,410	251,905	234,057
Long-Term Obligations	352,073	378,380	357,304	341,311	447,832	363,836	459,959	245,000
Total Liabilities	997,076	1,028,802	1,014,007	974,130	1,087,225	795,755	908,322	730,983
Stockholders' Equity	702,067	685,054	657,361	633,882	597,601	558,165	516,496	533,809
Shares Outstanding	38,737	38,711	38,682	38,526	38,222	37,736	37,372	37,448
Statistical Record								
Return on Assets %	7.77	7.23	6.83	7.54	1.71	6.60	5.27	7.08
Return on Equity %	19.19	18.45	17.79	20.16	4.50	17.06	13.48	16.09
EBITDA Margin %	17.87	16.48	13.52	14.99	5.81	16.75	13.17	14.36
Net Margin %	10.25	9.33	7.13	9.14	2.17	8.00	6.27	7.79
Asset Turnover	0.83	0.81	0.81	0.82	0.79	0.83	0.84	0.91
Current Ratio	2.62	2.67	2.53	2.33	2.15	2.14	2.00	2.13
Debt to Equity	0.50	0.55	0.54	0.54	0.75	0.65	0.89	0.46
Price Range	113.54-88.72	112.96-88.72	110.60-81.40	110.60-72.77	86.00-66.16	70.97-38.31	53.09-38.69	61.02-47.29
P/E Ratio	34.30-26.80	36.56-28.71	37.75-27.78	34.78-22.88	128.36-98.75	29.33-15.83	28.39-20.69	26.19-20.30
Average Yield %	1.55	1.53	1.54	1.59	1.83	2.49	2.72	2.28

Address: 1000 Cranberry Woods Drive, Cranberry Township, PA 16066-5207	Web Site: www.MSAsafety.com	Auditors: Ernst & Young LLP
Telephone: 724-776-8600	Officers: Nishan J. Vartanian - President, Chief Executive Officer, Senior Vice President, Chief Operating Officer, Division Officer Kenneth D. Krause - Senior Vice President, Vice President, Chief Financial Officer, Vice President (frmr), Treasurer, Principal Accounting Officer	Investor Contact: 724-741-8534
		Transfer Agents: Wells Fargo Shareowner Services, South St.Paul, MN

MSC INDUSTRIAL DIRECT CO INC

Exchange	Symbol	Price	52Wk Range	Yield	P/E	Div Acheiver
NYS	MSM	$78.47 (12/31/2019)	86.31-65.71	3.82	15.51	15 Years

*7 Year Price Score 78.29 *NYSE Composite Index=100 *12 Month Price Score 93.63

Interim Earnings (Per Share)

Qtr.	Nov	Feb	May	Aug
2016-17	0.95	0.93	1.09	1.07
2017-18	1.05	2.06	1.39	1.29
2018-19	1.33	1.24	1.44	1.20
2019-20	1.18	...	...	...

Interim Dividends (Per Share)

Amt	Decl	Ex	Rec	Pay
0.75Q	07/09/2019	07/22/2019	07/23/2019	08/06/2019
0.75Q	10/17/2019	11/08/2019	11/12/2019	11/26/2019
0.75Q	12/17/2019	01/21/2020	01/22/2020	02/05/2020
5.00Q	12/17/2019	01/21/2020	01/22/2020	02/05/2020

Indicated Div: $3.00

Valuation Analysis   **Institutional Holding**

Forecast EPS	$4.85	No of Institutions
	(01/16/2020)	499
Market Cap	$4.3 Billion	Shares
Book Value	$1.5 Billion	54,660,912
Price/Book	2.88	% Held
Price/Sales	1.30	75.14

Business Summary: Industrial Machinery & Equipment (MIC: 7.2.1 SIC: 5084 NAIC: 423830)

MSC Industrial Direct Co. is a distributor of metalworking and maintenance, repair and operations (MRO) products and services. Co. provides stock-keeping units through its eCommerce channels, including its website, mscdirect.com; its inventory management solutions; catalogs and brochures; and call-centers and branches. Co.'s range of MRO products includes cutting tools, measuring instruments, tooling components, metalworking products, fasteners, flat stock, raw materials, abrasives, machinery hand and power tools, safety and janitorial supplies, plumbing supplies, materials handling products, power transmission components, and electrical supplies.

Recent Developments: For the quarter ended Nov 30 2019, net income decreased 11.8% to US$65.5 million from US$74.2 million in the year-earlier quarter. Revenues were US$823.6 million, down 1.0% from US$831.6 million the year before. Operating income was US$90.3 million versus US$103.0 million in the prior-year quarter, a decrease of 12.3%. Direct operating expenses rose 0.6% to US$476.4 million from US$473.6 million in the comparable period the year before. Indirect operating expenses increased 0.8% to US$256.9 million from US$255.0 million in the equivalent prior-year period.

Prospects: Our evaluation of MSC Industrial Direct Co. Inc. as of October 4th, 2019 is the result of our systematic analysis on three basic characteristics: earnings strength, relative valuation, and recent stock price movement. The company has managed to produce a neutral trend in earnings per share over the past 5 quarters. In addition, recent analyst estimates for the company have been mixed and MSM has posted results that fell short of analysts' expectations. Based on operating earnings yield, the company is undervalued when compared to all of the companies we cover. Share price changes over the past year indicates that MSM will perform poorly over the near term.

Financial Data
(US$ in Thousands)

	3 Mos	08/31/2019	09/01/2018	09/02/2017	09/03/2016	08/29/2015	08/30/2014	08/31/2013
Earnings Per Share	5.06	5.20	5.80	4.05	3.77	3.74	3.76	3.75
Cash Flow Per Share	6.09	5.96	6.04	4.37	6.48	4.09	4.40	5.21
Tang Book Value Per Share	13.00	12.40	10.55	8.53	6.52	9.56	10.24	9.53
Dividends Per Share	2.760	2.640	2.220	1.800	1.720	3.160	1.320	1.200
Dividend Payout %	54.55	50.77	38.28	44.44	45.62	84.49	35.11	32.00
Income Statement								
Total Revenue	823,601	3,363,817	3,203,878	2,887,744	2,863,505	2,910,379	2,787,122	2,457,649
EBITDA	107,444	452,744	472,118	434,060	433,936	431,509	430,714	421,645
Depn & Amortn	17,025	53,243	52,113	54,356	57,052	52,799	47,729	36,169
Income Before Taxes	87,258	383,129	406,189	367,992	371,731	373,141	379,525	383,429
Income Taxes	21,806	94,332	76,966	136,561	140,515	141,833	143,458	145,434
Net Income	65,418	288,865	329,223	231,431	231,216	231,308	236,067	237,995
Average Shares	55,444	55,508	56,707	56,971	61,076	61,487	62,339	63,011
Balance Sheet								
Current Assets	1,170,820	1,199,612	1,147,507	1,005,579	981,491	1,032,076	961,415	893,489
Total Assets	2,339,765	2,311,237	2,288,727	2,098,912	2,064,951	2,101,206	2,060,747	1,943,003
Current Liabilities	403,828	446,916	490,523	557,725	478,602	422,337	309,164	213,579
Long-Term Obligations	267,583	266,431	311,236	200,991	339,772	214,789	240,235	241,566
Total Liabilities	828,902	832,687	901,473	873,772	966,575	768,336	662,184	552,620
Stockholders' Equity	1,510,863	1,478,550	1,387,254	1,225,140	1,098,376	1,332,870	1,398,563	1,390,383
Shares Outstanding	55,387	55,221	55,896	56,391	56,581	61,658	61,618	63,434
Statistical Record								
Return on Assets %	12.16	12.59	15.05	11.15	10.92	11.15	11.82	14.09
Return on Equity %	19.40	20.21	25.27	19.98	18.71	16.98	16.98	18.52
EBITDA Margin %	13.05	13.46	14.74	15.03	15.15	14.83	15.45	17.16
Net Margin %	7.94	8.59	10.28	8.01	8.07	7.95	8.47	9.68
Asset Turnover	1.46	1.47	1.46	1.39	1.35	1.40	1.40	1.45
Current Ratio	2.90	2.68	2.34	1.80	2.05	2.44	3.11	4.18
Debt to Equity	0.18	0.18	0.22	0.16	0.31	0.16	0.17	0.17
Price Range	89.31-65.71	89.82-65.71	99.26-68.81	105.50-65.62	77.76-55.01	91.09-65.04	96.13-75.55	87.79-67.18
P/E Ratio	17.65-12.99	17.27-12.64	17.11-11.86	26.05-16.20	20.63-14.59	24.36-17.39	25.57-20.09	23.41-17.91
Average Yield %	3.63	3.32	2.56	2.09	2.53	6.06	1.55	1.54

Address: 75 Maxess Road, Melville, NY 11747
Telephone: 516-812-2000
Fax: 516-349-7096

Web Site: www.mscdirect.com
Officers: Mitchell Jacobson - Chairman Erik Gershwind - President, Chief Executive Officer, Executive Vice President, Chief Operating Officer

Auditors: Ernst & Young LLP
Investor Contact: 516-812-1216
Transfer Agents: Computershare Trust Company, N.A., Providence, RI

MSCI INC

Exchange	Symbol	Price	52Wk Range	Yield	P/E
NYS	MSCI	$258.18 (12/31/2019)	266.32-141.34	1.05	37.20

*7 Year Price Score 179.42 *NYSE Composite Index=100 *12 Month Price Score 111.08

Interim Earnings (Per Share)

Qtr.	Mar	Jun	Sep	Dec
2016	0.60	0.69	0.68	0.72
2017	0.80	0.89	0.93	0.70
2018	1.24	1.28	1.36	1.79
2019	2.08	1.47	1.60	...

Interim Dividends (Per Share)

Amt	Decl	Ex	Rec	Pay
0.58Q	01/30/2019	02/21/2019	02/22/2019	03/15/2019
0.58Q	05/01/2019	05/16/2019	05/17/2019	05/31/2019
0.68Q	07/30/2019	08/15/2019	08/16/2019	08/30/2019
0.68Q	10/29/2019	11/14/2019	11/15/2019	11/27/2019

Indicated Div: $2.72

Valuation Analysis

Forecast EPS	$6.40
	(01/17/2020)
Market Cap	$21.9 Billion
Book Value	N/A
Price/Book	N/A
Price/Sales	14.46

Institutional Holding

No of Institutions	699
Shares	96,194,720
% Held	86.23

Business Summary: Publishing (MIC: 2.3.3 SIC: 7389 NAIC: 523999)

MSCI provides investment decision support tools and services. Co. operates in four segments: Index, which is primarily a provider of equity indexes that is used in many areas of the investment process, including index-linked product creation and performance benchmarking; Analytics, which provides risk management, performance attribution and portfolio management content, applications and services; environmental, social and governance (ESG), which provides products and services that help institutional investors understand how ESG factors can affect the long-term risk of their investments; and Real Estate, which provides real estate performance analysis for funds, investors and managers.

Recent Developments: For the quarter ended Sep 30 2019, net income increased 10.6% to US$137.0 million from US$123.8 million in the year-earlier quarter. Revenues were US$394.3 million, up 10.1% from US$357.9 million the year before. Operating income was US$201.2 million versus US$176.4 million in the prior-year quarter, an increase of 14.1%. Direct operating expenses declined 0.6% to US$70.5 million from US$70.9 million in the comparable period the year before. Indirect operating expenses increased 10.8% to US$122.5 million from US$110.6 million in the equivalent prior-year period.

Prospects: Our evaluation of MSCI Inc. as of October 4th, 2019 is the result of our systematic analysis on three basic characteristics: earnings strength, relative valuation, and recent stock price movement. The company has enjoyed a very positive trend in earnings per share over the past 5 quarters. However, recent analyst estimates for the company have been mixed and MSCI has posted results that exceeded analysts' expectations. Based on operating earnings yield, the company is fairly valued when compared to all of the companies we cover. Share price changes over the past year indicates that MSCI will perform very well over the near term.

Financial Data

(US$ in Thousands)	9 Mos	6 Mos	3 Mos	12/31/2018	12/31/2017	12/31/2016	12/31/2015	12/31/2014
Earnings Per Share	6.94	6.70	6.51	5.66	3.31	2.70	2.03	2.43
Cash Flow Per Share	7.54	7.01	7.26	7.03	4.47	4.52	2.80	2.64
Dividends Per Share	2.420	2.320	2.120	1.920	1.320	1.000	0.800	0.180
Dividend Payout %	34.87	34.63	32.57	33.92	39.88	37.04	39.41	7.41
Income Statement								
Total Revenue	1,151,190	756,939	371,381	1,433,984	1,274,172	1,150,669	1,075,013	996,680
EBITDA	615,056	393,512	186,383	828,830	656,630	566,016	488,585	413,624
Depn & Amortn	61,623	41,076	26,262	85,489	79,947	81,333	77,810	74,317
Income Before Taxes	456,785	288,037	128,292	629,896	466,899	385,938	349,554	308,338
Income Taxes	15,920	(15,845)	(49,900)	122,011	162,927	125,083	119,516	109,396
Net Income	440,865	303,882	178,192	507,885	303,972	260,855	223,648	284,113
Average Shares	85,550	85,393	85,649	89,701	91,914	96,540	109,926	116,706
Balance Sheet								
Current Assets	1,386,088	1,323,082	1,177,926	1,435,089	1,267,129	1,055,670	1,063,271	770,632
Total Assets	3,479,742	3,425,090	3,295,565	3,387,952	3,275,668	3,082,578	3,146,987	2,894,175
Current Liabilities	744,521	766,957	720,799	809,008	607,671	536,570	498,116	472,912
Long-Term Obligations	2,578,159	2,577,273	2,576,388	2,575,502	2,078,093	2,075,201	1,579,404	800,000
Total Liabilities	3,627,598	3,656,892	3,612,073	3,554,446	2,874,656	2,764,973	2,245,500	1,461,342
Stockholders' Equity	(147,856)	(231,802)	(316,508)	(166,494)	401,012	317,605	901,487	1,432,833
Shares Outstanding	84,707	84,694	84,675	84,174	90,104	91,279	101,013	112,072
Statistical Record								
Return on Assets %	16.28	16.08	17.20	15.24	9.56	8.35	7.40	9.43
Return on Equity %	514.34	1,011.77	1,088.98	433.13	84.60	42.68	19.16	18.88
EBITDA Margin %	53.43	51.99	50.19	57.80	51.53	49.19	45.45	41.50
Net Margin %	38.30	40.15	47.98	35.42	23.86	22.67	20.80	28.51
Asset Turnover	0.42	0.41	0.44	0.43	0.40	0.37	0.36	0.33
Current Ratio	1.86	1.73	1.63	1.77	2.09	1.97	2.13	1.63
Debt to Equity	...	...	...	...	5.18	6.53	1.75	0.56
Price Range	245.73-135.09	243.99-135.09	198.84-135.09	182.23-127.68	129.35-78.71	90.12-63.16	72.85-47.24	48.98-40.28
P/E Ratio	35.41-19.47	36.42-20.16	30.54-20.75	32.20-22.56	39.08-23.78	33.38-23.39	35.89-23.27	20.16-16.58
Average Yield %	1.24	1.28	1.29	1.22	1.24	1.29	1.29	0.40

Address: 7 World Trade Center, 250 Greenwich Street, 49th Floor, New York, NY 10007
Telephone: 212-804-3900

Web Site: www.msci.com
Officers: Henry A. Fernandez - Chairman, President, Chief Executive Officer C.D. Baer Pettit - President, Chief Operating Officer, Chief Operating Officer (frmr), Head

Auditors: PricewaterhouseCoopers LLP
Investor Contact: 212-804-3900
Transfer Agents: Broadridge Financial Solutions, Inc.

MURPHY OIL CORP

Exchange	Symbol	Price	52Wk Range	Yield	P/E
NYS	MUR	$26.80 (12/31/2019)	30.97-17.40	3.73	3.30

*7 Year Price Score 54.14   *NYSE Composite Index=100   *12 Month Price Score 92.96

Interim Earnings (Per Share)

Qtr.	Mar	Jun	Sep	Dec
2016	(1.16)	0.02	(0.09)	(0.36)
2017	0.34	(0.10)	(0.38)	(1.67)
2018	0.96	0.26	0.54	0.59
2019	0.23	0.54	6.76	...

Interim Dividends (Per Share)

Amt	Decl	Ex	Rec	Pay
0.25Q	02/06/2019	02/15/2019	02/19/2019	03/01/2019
0.25Q	04/03/2019	05/17/2019	05/20/2019	06/03/2019
0.25Q	08/07/2019	08/16/2019	08/19/2019	09/03/2019
0.25Q	10/02/2019	11/15/2019	11/18/2019	12/02/2019

Indicated Div: $1.00

Valuation Analysis   **Institutional Holding**

Forecast EPS	$0.94	No of Institutions
	(01/17/2020)	579
Market Cap	$4.2 Billion	Shares
Book Value	$5.7 Billion	180,938,976
Price/Book	0.74	% Held
Price/Sales	1.50	86.49

Business Summary: Production & Extraction (MIC: 9.1.1 SIC: 1311 NAIC: 211111)

Murphy Oil is a holding company. Through its subsidiaries, Co. is an oil and gas exploration and production company. Co. explores for and produces crude oil, natural gas and natural gas liquids worldwide. Co.'s principal exploration and production activities are conducted in the U.S. by wholly owned Murphy Exploration & Production Company - USA, in Malaysia, Australia, Brunei, Mexico and Vietnam by wholly owned Murphy Exploration & Production Company - International and its subsidiaries, and in Western Canada and offshore Eastern Canada by wholly-owned Murphy Oil Company Ltd. and its subsidiaries. Co.'s hydrocarbon production is in the U.S., Canada, Malaysia and Brunei.

Recent Developments: For the quarter ended Sep 30 2019, income from continuing operations increased 182.1% to US$158.3 million from US$56.1 million in the year-earlier quarter. Net income increased to US$1.11 billion from US$93.9 million in the year-earlier quarter. Revenues were US$817.1 million, up 66.6% from US$490.5 million the year before. Operating income was US$226.5 million versus US$122.8 million in the prior-year quarter, an increase of 84.5%. Direct operating expenses rose 86.4% to US$215.7 million from US$115.8 million in the comparable period the year before. Indirect operating expenses increased 48.8% to US$374.9 million from US$252.0 million in the equivalent prior-year period.

Prospects: Our evaluation of Murphy Oil Corp. as of October 4th, 2019 is the result of our systematic analysis on three basic characteristics: earnings strength, relative valuation, and recent stock price movement. The company has suffered a very negative trend in earnings per share over the past 5 quarters. In addition, recent analyst estimates for the company have been reduced while MUR has posted results that exceeded analysts' expectations. Based on operating earnings yield, the company is fairly valued when compared to all of the companies we cover. Share price changes over the past year indicates that MUR will perform very poorly over the near term.

Financial Data

(US$ in Thousands)	9 Mos	6 Mos	3 Mos	12/31/2018	12/31/2017	12/31/2016	12/31/2015	12/31/2014
Earnings Per Share	8.12	1.90	1.62	2.36	(1.81)	(1.60)	(13.03)	5.03
Cash Flow Per Share	8.58	7.42	6.68	7.05	6.55	3.48	6.79	17.05
Tang Book Value Per Share	36.10	29.21	25.37	27.91	26.77	28.55	30.85	48.30
Dividends Per Share	1.000	1.000	1.000	1.000	1.000	1.200	1.400	1.325
Dividend Payout %	12.32	52.63	61.73	42.37	...	...	...	26.34
Income Statement								
Total Revenue	2,191,573	1,300,053	591,004	2,570,603	2,225,129	1,874,129	3,033,080	5,476,084
EBITDA	503,709	270,715	92,607	1,626,020	1,273,080	756,347	(1,462,455)	3,357,119
Depn & Amortn	21,680	15,150	8,045	1,012,078	1,019,495	1,101,292	1,702,432	1,989,030
Income Before Taxes	318,800	141,684	33,745	432,338	71,802	(493,115)	(3,282,262)	1,252,270
Income Taxes	38,719	19,937	10,822	9,330	382,738	(219,172)	(1,026,490)	227,297
Net Income	1,221,456	132,454	40,182	411,094	(311,789)	(275,970)	(2,270,833)	905,611
Average Shares	160,980	169,272	174,491	174,209	172,524	172,173	174,351	180,070
Balance Sheet								
Current Assets	1,144,626	2,751,892	2,638,244	879,814	1,371,603	1,559,183	1,448,416	3,279,149
Total Assets	11,783,667	13,536,024	11,983,117	11,052,587	9,860,942	10,295,860	11,493,812	16,742,307
Current Liabilities	932,860	2,202,891	1,638,230	846,058	834,207	1,502,432	1,674,629	3,147,887
Long-Term Obligations	2,779,228	4,185,875	3,110,098	3,227,134	2,906,520	2,422,750	3,040,594	2,536,238
Total Liabilities	6,107,017	8,796,011	7,034,341	6,223,288	5,240,751	5,379,181	6,187,084	8,168,873
Stockholders' Equity	5,676,650	4,740,013	4,948,776	4,829,299	4,620,191	4,916,679	5,306,728	8,573,434
Shares Outstanding	157,230	162,250	195,083	173,058	172,572	172,202	172,034	177,499
Statistical Record								
Return on Assets %	12.23	2.88	2.66	3.93	N.M.	N.M.	N.M.	5.29
Return on Equity %	25.53	7.19	6.05	8.70	N.M.	N.M.	N.M.	10.55
EBITDA Margin %	22.98	20.82	15.67	63.25	57.21	40.36	N.M.	61.31
Net Margin %	55.73	10.19	6.80	15.99	N.M.	N.M.	N.M.	16.54
Asset Turnover	0.26	0.23	0.24	0.25	0.22	0.17	0.21	0.32
Current Ratio	1.23	1.25	1.61	1.04	1.64	1.04	0.86	1.04
Debt to Equity	0.49	0.88	0.63	0.67	0.63	0.49	0.57	0.30
Price Range	35.78-17.40	35.78-22.16	35.78-22.16	35.78-22.16	32.18-22.63	36.24-15.76	51.77-21.71	67.75-44.39
P/E Ratio	4.41-2.14	18.83-11.66	22.09-13.68	15.16-9.39	...	...	...	13.47-8.83
Average Yield %	3.75	3.41	3.29	3.27	3.71	4.39	3.68	2.25

Address: 300 Peach Street, El Dorado, AR 71730-7000
Telephone: 870-862-6411
Fax: 870-864-3673

Web Site: www.murphyoilcorp.com
Officers: Claiborne P. Deming - Chairman, President, Chief Executive Officer Roger W. Jenkins - President, Chief Executive Officer, Executive Vice President, Chief Operating Officer

Auditors: KPMG LLP
Investor Contact: 870-864-6501
Transfer Agents: Computershare Trust Company, N.A., Chicago, IL

MURPHY USA INC

Exchange	Symbol	Price	52Wk Range	Yield	P/E
NYS	MUSA	$117.00 (12/31/2019)	120.84-73.54	N/A	20.45

*7 Year Price Score N/A ***NYSE Composite Index=100** ***12 Month Price Score 122.93**

TRADING VOLUME (thousand shares)

Interim Earnings (Per Share)

Qtr.	Mar	Jun	Sep	Dec
2016	2.08	1.17	1.16	1.15
2017	(0.08)	1.51	1.90	3.49
2018	1.16	1.58	1.38	2.37
2019	0.16	1.01	2.18	...

Interim Dividends (Per Share)

No Dividends Paid

Valuation Analysis | Institutional Holding

Forecast EPS	$5.51	No of Institutions
	(01/17/2020)	N/A
Market Cap	$3.6 Billion	Shares
Book Value	$779.0 Million	N/A
Price/Book	4.62	% Held
Price/Sales	0.26	N/A

Business Summary: Retail - General Merchandise/Department Stores (MIC: 2.1.1 SIC: 5541 NAIC: 447110)

Murphy USA is a holding company. Through its subsidiaries, Co.'s business consists primarily of the marketing of retail motor fuel products and convenience merchandise through its retail stores. Co.'s retail stores are located in the Southeast, Southwest and Midwest U.S. Co.'s business also includes certain product supply and wholesale assets, including product distribution terminals and pipeline positions. Co. purchases fuel from oil companies, independent refiners, and other marketers, and it sells fuel to its customers. In addition to the motor fuel sold at Co.'s stores, its stores carry a selection of snacks, beverages, tobacco products and non-food merchandise.

Recent Developments: For the quarter ended Sep 30 2019, net income increased 53.8% to US$69.2 million from US$45.0 million in the year-earlier quarter. Revenues were US$3.66 billion, down 3.4% from US$3.79 billion the year before. Operating income was US$120.7 million versus US$70.0 million in the prior-year quarter, an increase of 72.4%. Direct operating expenses declined 5.4% to US$3.32 billion from US$3.51 billion in the comparable period the year before. Indirect operating expenses increased 4.8% to US$217.4 million from US$207.5 million in the equivalent prior-year period.

Prospects: Our evaluation of Murphy USA Inc. as of October 4th, 2019 is the result of our systematic analysis on three basic characteristics: earnings strength, relative valuation, and recent stock price movement. The company has suffered a very negative trend in earnings per share over the past 5 quarters. However, recent analyst estimates for the company have been unchanged while MUSA has posted results that fell short of analysts' expectations. Based on operating earnings yield, the company is undervalued when compared to all of the companies we cover. Share price changes over the past year indicates that MUSA will perform well over the near term.

Financial Data (US$ in Thousands)	9 Mos	6 Mos	3 Mos	12/31/2018	12/31/2017	12/31/2016	12/31/2015	12/31/2014
Earnings Per Share	5.72	4.92	5.49	6.48	6.78	5.59	4.02	5.26
Cash Flow Per Share	13.00	11.13	10.54	12.20	7.92	8.57	4.97	6.63
Tang Book Value Per Share	25.33	25.53	24.80	25.02	21.66	18.87	19.01	18.79
Income Statement								
Total Revenue	10,574,400	6,916,800	3,116,400	14,362,900	12,826,553	11,594,553	12,699,411	17,209,919
EBITDA	294,000	150,600	58,500	458,300	402,339	489,767	336,211	485,059
Depn & Amortn	113,800	76,200	39,700	133,000	116,966	98,610	86,568	79,234
Income Before Taxes	140,500	49,200	5,900	273,900	240,022	352,031	218,289	369,423
Income Taxes	33,300	11,200	600	60,300	(5,242)	130,539	80,698	126,341
Net Income	107,200	38,000	5,300	213,600	245,264	221,492	176,340	243,863
Average Shares	31,704	32,328	32,420	32,983	36,156	39,646	43,794	46,417
Balance Sheet								
Current Assets	664,900	656,300	612,900	570,100	614,294	515,554	435,667	665,882
Total Assets	2,616,700	2,571,300	2,504,400	2,360,800	2,331,039	2,088,740	1,886,241	1,934,257
Current Liabilities	516,900	578,800	533,300	478,100	533,351	514,560	392,292	413,080
Long-Term Obligations	966,400	833,600	838,000	842,100	860,864	629,622	490,160	492,443
Total Liabilities	1,837,700	1,755,000	1,706,600	1,553,500	1,592,637	1,391,664	1,093,951	1,075,552
Stockholders' Equity	779,000	816,300	797,800	807,300	738,402	697,076	792,290	858,705
Shares Outstanding	30,759	31,970	32,170	32,261	34,091	36,935	41,678	45,710
Statistical Record								
Return on Assets %	7.47	6.60	7.55	9.11	11.10	11.11	9.23	12.78
Return on Equity %	24.50	21.36	23.90	27.64	34.17	29.66	21.36	32.19
EBITDA Margin %	2.78	2.18	1.88	3.19	3.14	4.22	2.65	2.82
Net Margin %	1.01	0.55	0.17	1.49	1.91	1.91	1.39	1.42
Asset Turnover	5.70	5.84	5.99	6.12	5.80	5.82	6.65	9.02
Current Ratio	1.29	1.13	1.15	1.04	1.19	1.00	1.11	1.61
Debt to Equity	1.24	1.02	1.05	1.04	1.17	0.90	0.62	0.57
Price Range	93.34-70.40	88.09-70.40	88.09-62.57	88.59-62.57	81.00-61.03	79.29-54.24	73.48-48.70	69.37-37.55
P/E Ratio	16.32-12.31	17.90-14.31	16.05-11.40	13.67-9.66	11.95-9.00	14.18-9.70	18.28-12.11	13.19-7.14

Address: 200 Peach Street, El Dorado, AR 71730-5836 Telephone: 870-875-7600	Web Site: www.murphyusa.com Officers: Robert Madison Murphy - Chairman R. Andrew Clyde - President, Chief Executive Officer	Auditors: KPMG LLP Transfer Agents: Computershare Trust Company, N.A.

NABORS INDUSTRIES LTD

Exchange	Symbol	Price	52Wk Range	Yield	P/E
NYS	NBR	$2.88 (12/31/2019)	4.01-1.56	1.39	N/A

*7 Year Price Score 19.19   *NYSE Composite Index=100   *12 Month Price Score 81.90

TRADING VOLUME (thousand shares)

Interim Earnings (Per Share)

Qtr.	Mar	Jun	Sep	Dec
2016	(1.41)	(0.65)	(0.39)	(1.18)
2017	(0.52)	(0.46)	(0.52)	(0.39)
2018	(0.46)	(0.61)	(0.35)	(0.55)
2019	(0.36)	(0.61)	(0.37)	...

Interim Dividends (Per Share)

Amt	Decl	Ex	Rec	Pay
0.01Q	02/22/2019	03/11/2019	03/12/2019	04/02/2019
0.01Q	04/24/2019	06/10/2019	06/11/2019	07/02/2019
0.01Q	07/26/2019	09/10/2019	09/11/2019	10/02/2019
0.01Q	12/03/2019	12/12/2019	12/13/2019	01/03/2020

Indicated Div: $0.04

Valuation Analysis | Institutional Holding

Forecast EPS	N/A	No of Institutions 525
Market Cap	$1.0 Billion	Shares
Book Value	$2.3 Billion	362,355,776
Price/Book	0.46	% Held
Price/Sales	0.34	80.78

Business Summary: Production & Extraction (MIC: 9.1.1 SIC: 1381 NAIC: 213111)

Nabors Industries, through its subsidiaries, owns and operates land-based drilling rig fleet and is a provider of offshore platform drilling rigs in the U.S. and several international markets. Co. also provides directional drilling services, tubular services, performance tools, and technologies for its own rig fleet and those of third parties. Co.'s business is comprised of its land-based and offshore drilling rig operations and other rig related services and technologies, consisting of equipment manufacturing, rig instrumentation and optimization software. Co. has five reportable segments: U.S. Drilling, Canada Drilling, International Drilling, Drilling Solutions and Rig Technologies.

Recent Developments: For the quarter ended Sep 30 2019, loss from continuing operations was US$99.8 million compared with a loss of US$93.7 million in the year-earlier quarter. Net loss amounted to US$99.6 million versus a net loss of US$107.6 million in the year-earlier quarter. Revenues were US$756.6 million, down 2.8% from US$778.1 million the year before. Direct operating expenses declined 4.4% to US$475.5 million from US$497.2 million in the comparable period the year before. Indirect operating expenses decreased 1.9% to US$357.1 million from US$364.1 million in the equivalent prior-year period.

Prospects: Our evaluation of Nabors Industries Ltd. as of October 4th, 2019 is the result of our systematic analysis on three basic characteristics: earnings strength, relative valuation, and recent stock price movement. The company has managed to produce a neutral trend in earnings per share over the past 5 quarters. In addition, recent analyst estimates for the company have been mixed and NBR has posted results that fell short of analysts' expectations. Based on operating earnings yield, the company is overvalued when compared to all of the companies we cover. Share price changes over the past year indicates that NBR will perform well over the near term.

Financial Data
(US$ in Thousands)

	9 Mos	6 Mos	3 Mos	12/31/2018	12/31/2017	12/31/2016	12/31/2015	12/31/2014
Earnings Per Share	(1.89)	(1.87)	(1.87)	(1.99)	(1.90)	(3.64)	(1.29)	(2.28)
Cash Flow Per Share	1.93	1.48	1.36	0.97	0.22	1.92	3.03	6.13
Tang Book Value Per Share	5.95	6.30	6.62	7.05	8.70	10.85	14.64	16.36
Dividends Per Share	0.090	...	...	0.240	0.240	0.060	0.060	0.060
Income Statement								
Total Revenue	2,337,826	1,581,187	809,312	3,048,121	2,565,486	2,007,108	3,791,664	6,809,727
EBITDA	(152,534)	(135,269)	(13,495)	568,430	478,705	(157,315)	734,970	729,004
Depn & Amortn	23,197	15,868	7,730	860,100	835,900	855,400	980,577	1,155,671
Income Before Taxes	(330,865)	(254,980)	(73,577)	(518,794)	(580,084)	(1,198,075)	(427,535)	(604,615)
Income Taxes	65,100	41,197	29,799	79,269	(82,970)	(186,831)	(98,038)	62,666
Net Income	(440,201)	(321,273)	(117,709)	(640,948)	(546,811)	(1,029,742)	(372,675)	(670,659)
Average Shares	352,026	351,543	350,764	334,397	280,653	276,475	282,982	290,694
Balance Sheet								
Current Assets	1,380,348	1,466,679	1,555,903	1,593,563	1,447,336	1,155,839	1,475,897	2,741,874
Total Assets	7,273,497	7,514,503	7,773,684	7,853,944	8,401,984	8,187,015	9,537,840	11,879,942
Current Liabilities	682,304	772,167	735,802	832,077	919,476	821,934	1,006,499	1,567,475
Long-Term Obligations	3,516,592	3,550,577	3,677,580	3,585,884	4,027,766	3,578,335	3,655,200	4,348,859
Total Liabilities	5,021,792	5,132,989	5,187,349	5,153,094	5,490,168	4,939,990	5,255,130	6,971,323
Stockholders' Equity	2,251,705	2,381,514	2,586,335	2,700,850	2,911,816	3,247,025	4,282,710	4,908,619
Shares Outstanding	363,409	363,482	363,116	356,852	314,710	283,925	281,184	289,408
Statistical Record								
EBITDA Margin %	N.M.	N.M.	N.M.	18.65	18.66	N.M.	19.38	10.71
Asset Turnover	0.41	0.40	0.39	0.38	0.31	0.23	0.35	0.57
Current Ratio	2.02	1.90	2.11	1.92	1.57	1.41	1.47	1.75
Debt to Equity	1.56	1.49	1.42	1.33	1.38	1.10	0.85	0.89
Price Range	6.54-1.65	6.72-1.89	8.61-1.89	8.61-1.89	18.19-5.48	17.49-5.53	16.70-7.73	30.04-10.00
Average Yield %	2.78	...	...	3.81	2.46	0.59	0.50	0.27

Address: Crown House, Second Floor, 4 Par-la-Ville Road, Hamilton, HM08 **Telephone:** 441-292-1510	**Web Site:** www.nabors.com **Officers:** Anthony G. Petrello - Chairman, President, Chief Executive Officer, Deputy Chairman, Chief Operating Officer William J. Restrepo - Chief Financial Officer	**Auditors:** PricewaterhouseCoopers LLP **Investor Contact:** 441-292-1510 **Transfer Agents:** Computershare Trust Company, N.A., Providence, RI

482

NACCO INDUSTRIES INC

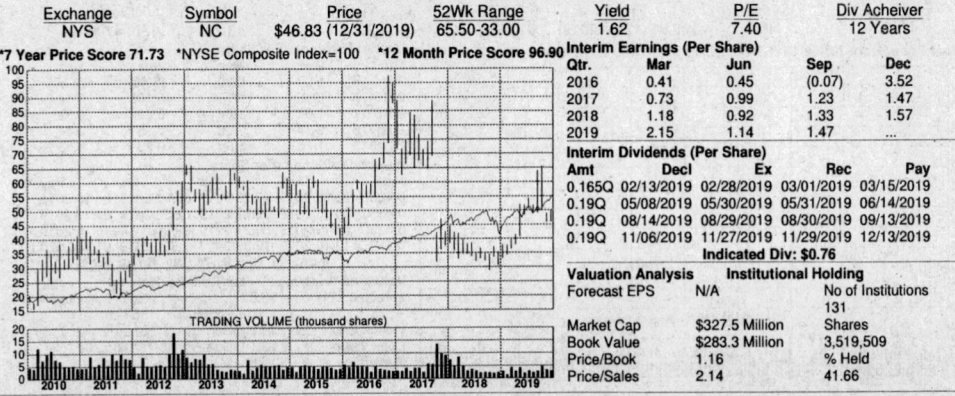

Exchange	Symbol	Price	52Wk Range	Yield	P/E	Div Acheiver
NYS	NC	$46.83 (12/31/2019)	65.50-33.00	1.62	7.40	12 Years

*7 Year Price Score 71.73   *NYSE Composite Index=100   *12 Month Price Score 96.90

Interim Earnings (Per Share)

Qtr.	Mar	Jun	Sep	Dec
2016	0.41	0.45	(0.07)	3.52
2017	0.73	0.99	1.23	1.47
2018	1.18	0.92	1.33	1.57
2019	2.15	1.14	1.47	...

Interim Dividends (Per Share)

Amt	Decl	Ex	Rec	Pay
0.165Q	02/13/2019	02/28/2019	03/01/2019	03/15/2019
0.19Q	05/08/2019	05/30/2019	05/31/2019	06/14/2019
0.19Q	08/14/2019	08/29/2019	08/30/2019	09/13/2019
0.19Q	11/06/2019	11/27/2019	11/29/2019	12/13/2019

Indicated Div: $0.76

Valuation Analysis   **Institutional Holding**

Forecast EPS   N/A   No of Institutions 131

Market Cap	$327.5 Million	Shares
Book Value	$283.3 Million	3,519,509
Price/Book	1.16	% Held
Price/Sales	2.14	41.66

Business Summary: Mining (MIC: 8.2.4 SIC: 1221 NAIC: 212111)

NACCO Industries is a public holding company for The North American Coal Corporation. The North American Coal Corporation and its affiliated companies (collectively, NACoal) operate surface mines that supply coal primarily to power generation companies under long-term contracts, and provide other services to natural resource companies. In addition, its North American Mining (NAM) business operates and maintains draglines and other equipment under contracts with sellers of aggregates. NAM primarily provides services for independently owned limestone quarries. NACoal also provides coal handling, processing and drying services for a number of customers.

Recent Developments: For the quarter ended Sep 30 2019, net income increased 11.6% to US$10.3 million from US$9.2 million in the year-earlier quarter. Revenues were US$32.6 million, up 3.7% from US$31.4 million the year before. Operating income was US$8.7 million versus US$10.5 million in the prior-year quarter, a decrease of 17.9%. Direct operating expenses rose 4.2% to US$26.4 million from US$25.3 million in the comparable period the year before. Indirect operating income amounted to US$2.5 million compared with an income of US$4.5 million in the equivalent prior-year period.

Prospects: Our evaluation of NACCO Industries Inc. as of October 4th, 2019 is the result of our systematic analysis on three basic characteristics: earnings strength, relative valuation, and recent stock price movement. The company has generated a negative trend in earnings per share over the past 5 quarters. However, recent analyst estimates for the company have been mixed and NC has posted results that fell short of analysts' expectations. Based on operating earnings yield, the company is undervalued when compared to all of the companies we cover. Share price changes over the past year indicates that NC will perform in line with the market over the near term.

Financial Data

(US$ in Thousands)	9 Mos	6 Mos	3 Mos	12/31/2018	12/31/2017	12/31/2016	12/31/2015	12/31/2014
Earnings Per Share	6.33	6.19	5.97	5.00	4.41	4.32	3.13	(5.02)
Cash Flow Per Share	9.02	8.30	8.94	7.89	6.05	13.74	15.43	2.61
Tang Book Value Per Share	35.03	33.36	32.12	30.37	25.67	23.76	20.19	19.96
Dividends Per Share	0.710	0.685	0.660	0.660	0.978	1.065	1.045	1.023
Dividend Payout %	11.22	11.07	11.06	13.20	22.17	24.65	33.39	...
Income Statement								
Total Revenue	114,052	81,449	40,097	135,375	104,778	856,438	915,860	896,782
EBITDA	(10,187)	(3,110)	1,071	(19,071)	(17,342)	2,987	4,938	(89,464)
Depn & Amortn	2,243	1,528	647	3,038	12,723	19,284	23,687	28,100
Income Before Taxes	(10,101)	(3,957)	746	(24,107)	(33,505)	(21,989)	(25,673)	(125,130)
Income Taxes	5,465	4,108	2,320	7,378	639	4,863	2,815	(38,455)
Net Income	33,257	22,993	15,018	34,785	30,337	29,607	21,984	(38,118)
Average Shares	6,991	6,986	6,998	6,960	6,873	6,854	7,022	7,590
Balance Sheet								
Current Assets	180,310	175,581	164,031	164,174	176,988	381,732	361,434	465,713
Total Assets	412,770	399,180	393,787	376,991	389,552	668,021	655,408	770,520
Current Liabilities	52,775	53,167	49,570	42,248	53,976	221,828	191,746	254,681
Long-Term Obligations	7,284	7,503	7,448	6,367	42,021	120,295	160,113	191,431
Total Liabilities	129,515	127,030	129,520	126,287	170,104	447,728	454,270	559,046
Stockholders' Equity	283,255	272,150	264,267	250,704	219,448	220,293	201,138	211,474
Shares Outstanding	6,994	6,989	6,986	6,921	6,852	6,778	6,837	7,235
Statistical Record								
Return on Assets %	11.36	11.29	10.84	9.08	5.74	4.46	3.08	N.M.
Return on Equity %	16.92	17.18	17.02	14.80	13.80	14.01	10.66	N.M.
EBITDA Margin %	N.M.	N.M.	2.67	N.M.	N.M.	0.35	0.54	N.M.
Net Margin %	29.16	28.23	37.45	25.70	28.95	3.46	2.40	N.M.
Asset Turnover	0.39	0.40	0.38	0.35	0.20	1.29	1.28	1.13
Current Ratio	3.42	3.30	3.31	3.89	3.28	1.72	1.88	1.83
Debt to Equity	0.03	0.03	0.03	0.03	0.19	0.55	0.80	0.91
Price Range	63.91-28.81	52.13-28.81	39.85-28.81	44.60-28.81	88.85-31.90	97.55-42.20	62.37-40.48	63.56-47.69
P/E Ratio	10.10-4.55	8.42-4.65	6.68-4.83	8.92-5.76	20.15-7.23	22.58-9.77	19.93-12.93	...
Average Yield %	1.68	1.82	1.89	1.84	1.51	1.70	1.99	1.87

Address: 5875 Landerbrook Drive, Suite 220, Cleveland, OH 44124-4069 **Telephone:** 440-229-5151	**Web Site:** www.nacco.com **Officers:** J. C. Butler - President, Chief Executive Officer, Senior Vice President, Vice President, Chief Administrative Officer, Treasurer John D. Neumann - Vice President, General Counsel, Secretary	**Auditors:** Ernst & Young LLP **Investor Contact:** 440-229-5130 **Transfer Agents:** Computershare, Canton, MA

NATIONAL FUEL GAS CO. (NJ)

Exchange	Symbol	Price	52Wk Range	Yield	P/E	Div Acheiver
NYS	NFG	$46.54 (12/31/2019)	61.26-43.31	3.74	13.26	47 Years

*7 Year Price Score 73.76   ***NYSE Composite Index=100**   ***12 Month Price Score 83.29**

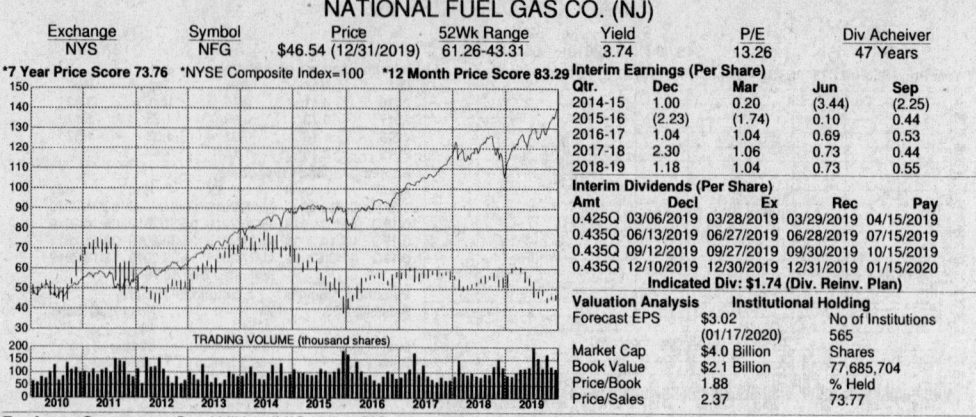

Interim Earnings (Per Share)

Qtr.	Dec	Mar	Jun	Sep
2014-15	1.00	0.20	(3.44)	(2.25)
2015-16	(2.23)	(1.74)	0.10	0.44
2016-17	1.04	1.04	0.69	0.53
2017-18	2.30	1.06	0.73	0.44
2018-19	1.18	1.04	0.73	0.55

Interim Dividends (Per Share)

Amt	Decl	Ex	Rec	Pay
0.425Q	03/06/2019	03/28/2019	03/29/2019	04/15/2019
0.435Q	06/13/2019	06/27/2019	06/28/2019	07/15/2019
0.435Q	09/12/2019	09/27/2019	09/30/2019	10/15/2019
0.435Q	12/10/2019	12/30/2019	12/31/2019	01/15/2020

Indicated Div: $1.74 (Div. Reinv. Plan)

Valuation Analysis   Institutional Holding

Forecast EPS	$3.02	No of Institutions
	(01/17/2020)	565
Market Cap	$4.0 Billion	Shares
Book Value	$2.1 Billion	77,685,704
Price/Book	1.88	% Held
Price/Sales	2.37	73.77

Business Summary: Gas Utilities (MIC: 3.3.1 SIC: 4924 NAIC: 221210)

National Fuel Gas is a holding company. Through its subsidiaries, Co. is engaged principally in the production, gathering, transportation, distribution and marketing of natural gas. Co.'s segments are: Exploration and Production, which is engaged in the exploration for, and the development and production of, natural gas and oil reserves in California and in the Appalachian region; Pipeline and Storage, which provides interstate natural gas transportation and storage services, as well as transports and stores natural gas; Gathering, which builds, owns and operates natural gas processing and pipeline gathering facilities; and Utility, which provides natural gas utility services.

Recent Developments: For the year ended Sep 30 2019, net income decreased 22.3% to US$304.3 million from US$391.5 million in the prior year. Revenues were US$1.69 billion, up 6.3% from US$1.59 billion the year before. Operating income was US$511.8 million versus US$519.7 million in the prior year, a decrease of 1.5%. Direct operating expenses rose 9.3% to US$817.0 million from US$747.6 million in the comparable period the year before. Indirect operating expenses increased 12.0% to US$364.5 million from US$325.4 million in the equivalent prior-year period.

Prospects: Our evaluation of National Fuel Gas Co. as of October 4th, 2019 is the result of our systematic analysis on three basic characteristics: earnings strength, relative valuation, and recent stock price movement. The company has managed to produce a neutral trend in earnings per share over the past 5 quarters. However, recent analyst estimates for the company have been reduced while NFG has posted results that exceeded analysts' expectations. Based on operating earnings yield, the company is undervalued when compared to all of the companies we cover. Share price changes over the past year indicates that NFG will perform well over the near term.

Financial Data

(US$ in Thousands)	09/30/2019	09/30/2018	09/30/2017	09/30/2016	09/30/2015	09/30/2014	09/30/2013	09/30/2012
Earnings Per Share	3.51	4.53	3.30	(3.43)	(4.50)	3.52	3.08	2.63
Cash Flow Per Share	8.05	7.15	8.02	6.92	10.11	10.84	8.84	7.93
Tang Book Value Per Share	24.72	22.47	19.85	17.88	23.88	28.58	26.17	23.46
Dividends Per Share	1.720	1.680	1.640	1.600	1.560	1.520	1.480	1.440
Dividend Payout %	49.00	37.09	49.70	...	...	43.18	48.05	54.75
Income Statement								
Total Revenue	1,693,332	1,592,668	1,579,881	1,452,416	1,760,913	2,113,081	1,829,551	1,626,853
EBITDA	771,927	732,744	784,083	(157,281)	(266,856)	962,915	849,295	724,712
Depn & Amortn	275,660	240,961	224,195	249,417	336,158	383,781	326,760	271,530
Income Before Taxes	389,511	384,027	444,164	(523,507)	(698,563)	489,027	432,759	370,631
Income Taxes	85,221	(7,494)	160,682	(232,549)	(319,136)	189,614	172,758	150,554
Net Income	304,290	391,521	283,482	(290,958)	(379,427)	299,413	260,001	220,077
Average Shares	86,773	86,439	86,021	84,847	84,387	84,952	84,341	83,739
Balance Sheet								
Current Assets	362,623	544,591	818,280	413,031	513,001	377,332	448,677	355,576
Total Assets	6,462,157	6,036,486	6,103,320	5,636,387	6,702,139	6,739,597	6,218,347	5,935,142
Current Liabilities	421,908	440,060	646,039	303,737	446,140	490,576	302,171	734,479
Long-Term Obligations	2,133,718	2,131,365	2,083,681	2,086,252	2,084,009	1,649,000	1,649,000	1,149,000
Total Liabilities	4,323,132	4,099,156	4,399,585	4,109,383	4,676,699	4,328,914	4,023,618	3,975,047
Stockholders' Equity	2,139,025	1,937,330	1,703,735	1,527,004	2,025,440	2,410,683	2,194,729	1,960,095
Shares Outstanding	86,315	85,956	85,543	85,118	84,594	84,157	83,661	83,330
Statistical Record								
Return on Assets %	4.87	6.45	4.83	N.M.	N.M.	4.62	4.28	3.91
Return on Equity %	14.93	21.51	17.55	N.M.	N.M.	13.00	12.52	11.40
EBITDA Margin %	45.59	46.01	49.63	N.M.	N.M.	45.57	46.42	44.55
Net Margin %	17.97	24.58	17.94	N.M.	N.M.	14.17	14.21	13.53
Asset Turnover	0.27	0.26	0.27	0.23	0.26	0.33	0.30	0.29
Current Ratio	0.86	1.24	1.27	1.36	1.15	0.77	1.48	0.48
Debt to Equity	1.00	1.10	1.22	1.37	1.03	0.68	0.75	0.59
Price Range	61.26-45.58	59.16-49.10	60.91-50.68	59.45-37.90	71.90-48.82	78.30-65.45	68.76-48.69	63.58-42.17
P/E Ratio	17.45-12.99	13.06-10.84	18.46-15.36	...	...	22.24-18.59	22.32-15.81	24.17-16.03
Average Yield %	3.15	3.11	3.13	2.49	2.10	2.52	2.85

Address: 6363 Main Street, Williamsville, NY 14221 **Telephone:** 716-857-7000	**Web Site:** www.nationalfuelgas.com **Officers:** David F. Smith - Chairman, Chief Executive Officer David P. Bauer - President, Chief Executive Officer, Treasurer, Principal Financial Officer	**Auditors:** PricewaterhouseCoopers LLP **Investor Contact:** 716-857-6987 **Transfer Agents:** Wells Fargo Shareowner Services, Saint Paul, MN

NATIONAL HEALTH INVESTORS, INC.

Exchange	Symbol	Price	52Wk Range	Yield	P/E	Div Acheiver
NYS	NHI	$81.48 (12/31/2019)	86.54-74.03	5.15	22.70	16 Years

*7 Year Price Score 94.76 *NYSE Composite Index=100 *12 Month Price Score 96.04

Interim Earnings (Per Share)

Qtr.	Mar	Jun	Sep	Dec
2016	0.85	1.16	0.83	1.03
2017	1.10	0.93	0.94	0.90
2018	0.92	0.91	0.97	0.87
2019	0.83	0.92	0.97	...

Interim Dividends (Per Share)

Amt	Decl	Ex	Rec	Pay
1.05Q	02/19/2019	03/28/2019	03/29/2019	05/10/2019
1.05Q	05/07/2019	06/27/2019	06/28/2019	08/09/2019
1.05Q	08/08/2019	09/27/2019	09/30/2019	11/08/2019
1.05Q	11/07/2019	12/30/2019	12/31/2019	01/31/2020

Indicated Div: $4.20

Valuation Analysis / **Institutional Holding**

Forecast EPS	$3.67	No of Institutions
	(01/16/2020)	344
Market Cap	$3.6 Billion	Shares
Book Value	$1.5 Billion	39,131,872
Price/Book	2.45	% Held
Price/Sales	11.56	74.63

Business Summary: REITs (MIC: 5.3.1 SIC: 6798 NAIC: 525930)

National Health Investors is a self-managed real estate investment trust (REIT) which focuses on sale-leaseback, joint-venture, mortgage and mezzanine financing of senior housing and medical investments. Co.'s portfolio consists of lease, mortgage and other note investments in independent living facilities, assisted living facilities, entrance-fee communities, senior living campuses, skilled nursing facilities, specialty hospitals and medical office buildings. Co.'s other investments have included marketable securities and a joint venture structured to comply with the provisions of the REIT Investment Diversification Empowerment Act of 2007.

Recent Developments: For the quarter ended Sep 30 2019, net income increased 4.3% to US$42.8 million from US$41.0 million in the year-earlier quarter. Revenues were US$81.7 million, up 9.0% from US$74.9 million the year before. Revenues from property income rose 5.0% to US$75.2 million from US$71.7 million in the corresponding quarter a year earlier.

Prospects: Our evaluation of National Health Investors Inc. as of October 4th, 2019 is the result of our systematic analysis on three basic characteristics: earnings strength, relative valuation, and recent stock price movement. The company has enjoyed a very positive trend in earnings per share over the past 5 quarters. However, recent analyst estimates for the company have been mixed and NHI has posted results that fell short of analysts' expectations. Based on operating earnings yield, the company is fairly valued when compared to all of the companies we cover. Share price changes over the past year indicates that NHI will perform well over the near term.

Financial Data
(US$ in Thousands)

	9 Mos	6 Mos	3 Mos	12/31/2018	12/31/2017	12/31/2016	12/31/2015	12/31/2014
Earnings Per Share	3.59	3.59	3.58	3.67	3.87	3.87	3.95	3.04
Cash Flow Per Share	5.44	5.39	5.45	4.96	4.83	4.53	4.37	3.78
Tang Book Value Per Share	33.27	32.73	32.78	32.55	31.83	30.36	29.52	27.74
Dividends Per Share	4.150	4.100	4.050	4.000	3.800	3.600	3.400	3.080
Dividend Payout %	115.60	114.21	113.13	108.99	98.19	93.02	86.08	101.32
Income Statement								
Total Revenue	235,886	154,204	76,107	294,612	278,659	248,500	228,988	177,509
EBITDA	179,525	115,861	55,482	225,682	226,538	214,244	204,537	141,201
Depn & Amortn	61,112	40,204	19,803	71,349	67,173	59,565	53,163	38,078
Income Before Taxes	118,413	75,657	35,679	154,333	159,365	154,679	151,374	103,123
Income Taxes	...	...	...	...	...	749	(707)	...
Net Income	118,417	75,658	35,679	154,333	159,365	151,540	148,862	101,609
Average Shares	43,861	43,498	43,125	42,091	41,151	39,155	37,644	33,416
Balance Sheet								
Current Assets	102,019	98,172	93,541	121,913	105,609	86,367	73,063	42,259
Total Assets	3,019,360	2,997,381	2,806,268	2,750,570	2,545,821	2,403,633	2,146,349	1,982,960
Current Liabilities	85,417	83,267	78,529	62,590	56,932	55,866	52,784	47,582
Long-Term Obligations	1,449,360	1,471,787	1,287,205	1,281,675	1,145,497	1,115,981	926,257	862,726
Total Liabilities	1,556,994	1,578,336	1,390,284	1,360,857	1,223,704	1,194,043	1,013,057	943,035
Stockholders' Equity	1,462,366	1,419,045	1,415,984	1,389,713	1,322,117	1,209,590	1,133,292	1,039,925
Shares Outstanding	43,956	43,357	43,199	42,700	41,532	39,847	38,396	37,485
Statistical Record								
Return on Assets %	5.47	5.42	5.65	5.83	6.44	6.64	7.21	5.91
Return on Equity %	11.01	11.06	11.08	11.38	12.59	12.90	13.70	11.25
EBITDA Margin %	76.11	75.13	72.90	76.60	81.30	86.21	89.32	79.55
Net Margin %	50.20	49.06	46.88	52.39	57.19	60.98	65.01	57.24
Asset Turnover	0.11	0.11	0.11	0.11	0.11	0.11	0.11	0.10
Current Ratio	1.19	1.18	1.19	1.95	1.86	1.55	1.38	0.89
Debt to Equity	0.99	1.04	0.91	0.92	0.87	0.92	0.82	0.83
Price Range	84.57-70.60	84.57-70.60	84.57-65.51	80.86-63.33	80.81-69.30	82.39-55.73	76.46-54.10	71.19-55.13
P/E Ratio	23.56-19.67	23.56-19.67	23.62-18.30	22.03-17.26	20.88-17.91	21.29-14.40	19.36-13.70	23.42-18.13
Average Yield %	5.29	5.37	5.31	5.37	5.50	4.99	5.25	4.94

Address: 222 Robert Rose Drive, Murfreesboro, TN 37129 Telephone: 615-890-9100	Web Site: www.nhireit.com Officers: W. Andrew Adams - Chairman, Chief Executive Officer Eric Mendelsohn - President, Interim President, Chief Executive Officer, Interim Chief Executive Officer	Auditors: BDO USA, LLP Transfer Agents: Computershare Trust Company, N.A., Providence, RI

NATIONAL OILWELL VARCO INC

Exchange	Symbol	Price	52Wk Range	Yield	P/E
NYS	NOV	$25.05 (12/31/2019)	30.58-18.28	0.80	N/A

*7 Year Price Score 43.92 ***NYSE Composite Index=100** ***12 Month Price Score 90.58**

Interim Earnings (Per Share)

Qtr.	Mar	Jun	Sep	Dec
2016	(0.32)	(0.58)	(3.62)	(1.88)
2017	(0.32)	(0.20)	(0.07)	(0.04)
2018	(0.18)	0.06	0.00	0.03
2019	(0.20)	(14.11)	(0.64)	...

Interim Dividends (Per Share)

Amt	Decl	Ex	Rec	Pay
0.05Q	03/01/2019	03/14/2019	03/15/2019	03/29/2019
0.05Q	05/29/2019	06/13/2019	06/14/2019	06/28/2019
0.05Q	08/15/2019	09/12/2019	09/13/2019	09/27/2019
0.05Q	11/14/2019	12/05/2019	12/06/2019	12/20/2019

Indicated Div: $0.20 (Div. Reinv. Plan)

Valuation Analysis / Institutional Holding

Forecast EPS	$0.15	No of Institutions
	(01/17/2020)	928
Market Cap	$9.7 Billion	Shares
Book Value	$8.1 Billion	439,171,296
Price/Book	1.20	% Held
Price/Sales	1.12	96.80

Business Summary: Equipment & Services (MIC: 9.1.3 SIC: 3533 NAIC: 333132)

National Oilwell Varco is an independent provider of equipment and technology to the upstream oil and gas industry. Co.'s segments include: Wellbore Technologies, which designs, manufactures, rents, and sells a variety of equipment and technologies used to perform drilling operations; Completion and Production Solutions, which designs, manufactures, and sells equipment and technologies for hydraulic fracture stimulation, well intervention, onshore production, and offshore production; and Rig Technologies, which designs, manufactures and sells land rigs, offshore drilling equipment packages, and drilling rig components that mechanize and automate the drilling process and rig functionality.

Recent Developments: For the quarter ended Sep 30 2019, net loss amounted to US$249.0 million versus net income of US$4.0 million in the year-earlier quarter. Revenues were US$2.13 billion, down 1.3% from US$2.15 billion the year before. Operating loss was US$154.0 million versus an income of US$73.0 million in the prior-year quarter. Direct operating expenses rose 12.2% to US$1.98 billion from US$1.76 billion in the comparable period the year before. Indirect operating expenses decreased 4.7% to US$305.0 million from US$320.0 million in the equivalent prior-year period.

Prospects: Our evaluation of National-Oilwell Inc. as of October 4th, 2019 is the result of our systematic analysis on three basic characteristics: earnings strength, relative valuation, and recent stock price movement. The company has produced a positive trend in earnings per share over the past 5 quarters. However, recent analyst estimates for the company have been mixed and NOV has posted results that exceeded analysts' expectations. Based on operating earnings yield, the company is overvalued when compared to all of the companies we cover. Share price changes over the past year indicates that NOV will perform very poorly over the near term.

Financial Data

(US$ in Thousands)	9 Mos	6 Mos	3 Mos	12/31/2018	12/31/2017	12/31/2016	12/31/2015	12/31/2014
Earnings Per Share	(14.92)	(14.28)	(0.11)	(0.08)	(0.63)	(6.41)	(1.99)	5.82
Cash Flow Per Share	1.21	0.79	1.61	1.38	2.21	2.55	3.44	6.11
Tang Book Value Per Share	10.25	11.16	11.74	11.83	12.01	11.47	14.78	18.40
Dividends Per Share	0.200	0.200	0.200	0.200	0.200	0.610	1.840	1.640
Dividend Payout %	...	...	...	...	...	...	...	28.18
Income Statement								
Total Revenue	6,198,000	4,072,000	1,940,000	8,453,000	7,304,000	7,251,000	14,757,000	21,440,000
EBITDA	(5,533,000)	(5,471,000)	111,000	461,000	49,000	(2,142,000)	(122,000)	3,936,000
Depn & Amortn	433,000	331,000	177,000	349,000	359,000	370,000	391,000	413,000
Income Before Taxes	(6,025,000)	(5,840,000)	(85,000)	44,000	(387,000)	(2,602,000)	(602,000)	3,436,000
Income Taxes	(323,000)	(383,000)	(10,000)	63,000	(156,000)	(207,000)	178,000	1,039,000
Net Income	(5,710,000)	(5,466,000)	(77,000)	(31,000)	(237,000)	(2,412,000)	(769,000)	2,502,000
Average Shares	382,000	382,000	380,000	378,000	377,000	376,000	387,000	430,000
Balance Sheet								
Current Assets	6,515,000	6,766,000	6,938,000	7,279,000	7,217,000	7,876,000	11,801,000	16,162,000
Total Assets	14,005,000	14,349,000	20,002,000	19,796,000	20,206,000	21,140,000	26,725,000	33,562,000
Current Liabilities	2,276,000	2,221,000	2,103,000	2,341,000	2,354,000	3,047,000	4,249,000	7,374,000
Long-Term Obligations	2,484,000	2,483,000	2,483,000	2,704,000	2,706,000	2,708,000	3,928,000	3,014,000
Total Liabilities	5,948,000	5,938,000	6,237,000	5,977,000	6,112,000	7,200,000	10,342,000	12,870,000
Stockholders' Equity	8,057,000	8,411,000	13,765,000	13,819,000	14,094,000	13,940,000	16,383,000	20,692,000
Shares Outstanding	385,850	385,904	385,932	383,426	380,104	378,637	375,764	418,977
Statistical Record								
Return on Assets %	N.M.	N.M.	N.M.	N.M.	N.M.	N.M.	N.M.	7.32
Return on Equity %	N.M.	N.M.	N.M.	N.M.	N.M.	N.M.	N.M.	11.66
EBITDA Margin %	N.M.	N.M.	5.72	5.45	0.67	N.M.	N.M.	18.36
Net Margin %	N.M.	N.M.	N.M.	N.M.	N.M.	N.M.	N.M.	11.67
Asset Turnover	0.51	0.51	0.43	0.42	0.35	0.30	0.49	0.63
Current Ratio	2.86	3.05	3.30	3.11	3.07	2.58	2.78	2.19
Debt to Equity	0.31	0.30	0.18	0.20	0.19	0.19	0.24	0.15
Price Range	45.45-18.28	48.62-20.00	48.62-24.43	48.62-24.43	41.74-29.94	40.32-26.34	65.53-33.27	86.43-61.55
P/E Ratio	...	...	...	...	...	...	...	14.85-10.58
Average Yield %	0.74	0.61	0.54	0.51	0.57	1.84	4.01	2.22

Address: 7909 Parkwood Circle Drive, Houston, TX 77036-6565 **Telephone:** 713-346-7500	**Web Site:** www.nov.com **Officers:** Clay C. Williams - Chairman, President, Chief Executive Officer, Chief Operating Officer, Chief Financial Officer, Executive Vice President, Senior Vice President Craig L. Weinstock - Senior Vice President, General Counsel, Secretary	**Auditors:** Ernst & Young LLP **Investor Contact:** 713-346-7500 **Transfer Agents:** American Stock Transfer & Trust Company, New York, NY

NATIONAL RETAIL PROPERTIES INC

Exchange	Symbol	Price	52Wk Range	Yield	P/E	Div Acheiver
NYS	NNN	$53.62 (12/31/2019)	58.91-47.29	3.84	38.58	29 Years

*7 Year Price Score 106.04 *NYSE Composite Index=100 *12 Month Price Score 96.25

Interim Earnings (Per Share)

Qtr.	Mar	Jun	Sep	Dec
2016	0.44	0.30	0.29	0.36
2017	0.35	0.33	0.35	0.42
2018	0.62	0.40	0.47	0.17
2019	0.44	0.43	0.35	...

Interim Dividends (Per Share)

Amt	Decl	Ex	Rec	Pay
0.50Q	04/15/2019	04/29/2019	04/30/2019	05/15/2019
0.515Q	07/15/2019	07/30/2019	07/31/2019	08/15/2019
0.515Q	10/15/2019	10/30/2019	10/31/2019	11/15/2019
0.515Q	01/15/2020	01/30/2020	01/31/2020	02/14/2020

Indicated Div: $2.06 (Div. Reinv. Plan)

Valuation Analysis / **Institutional Holding**

Forecast EPS	$1.63	No of Institutions	562
	(01/17/2020)		
Market Cap	$9.2 Billion	Shares	
Book Value	$4.6 Billion		198,574,736
Price/Book	1.99	% Held	
Price/Sales	14.03		N/A

Business Summary: REITs (MIC: 5.3.1 SIC: 6798 NAIC: 525930)

National Retail Properties is a real estate investment trust. Co.'s assets are primarily real estate assets. Co. acquires, owns, invests in and develops properties that are leased primarily to retail tenants under long-term net leases and are primarily held for investment.

Recent Developments: For the quarter ended Sep 30 2019, net income decreased 18.7% to US$66.7 million from US$82.0 million in the year-earlier quarter. Revenues were US$168.6 million, up 8.5% from US$155.3 million the year before. Revenues from property income rose 8.8% to US$168.2 million from US$154.7 million in the corresponding quarter a year earlier.

Prospects: Our evaluation of National Retail Properties Inc. as of October 4th, 2019 is the result of our systematic analysis on three basic characteristics: earnings strength, relative valuation, and recent stock price movement. The company has managed to produce a neutral trend in earnings per share over the past 5 quarters. In addition, recent analyst estimates for the company have been mixed and NNN has posted results that fell short of analysts' expectations. Based on operating earnings yield, the company is fairly valued when compared to all of the companies we cover. Share price changes over the past year indicates that NNN will perform over the near term.

Financial Data
(US$ in Thousands)

	9 Mos	6 Mos	3 Mos	12/31/2018	12/31/2017	12/31/2016	12/31/2015	12/31/2014
Earnings Per Share	1.39	1.51	1.48	1.65	1.45	1.38	1.20	1.24
Cash Flow Per Share	3.07	2.96	3.01	3.03	2.83	2.87	2.55	2.39
Tang Book Value Per Share	23.27	21.96	21.73	21.81	20.89	20.37	19.62	18.99
Dividends Per Share	2.015	2.000	1.975	1.950	1.860	1.780	1.710	1.650
Dividend Payout %	144.96	132.45	133.45	118.18	128.28	128.99	142.50	133.06
Income Statement								
Total Revenue	497,111	328,504	163,712	622,661	584,933	533,647	482,914	434,847
EBITDA	317,621	219,796	110,538	592,373	518,360	464,742	428,442	386,076
Depn & Amortn	4,995	3,315	2,472	185,851	180,857	156,236	140,714	121,221
Income Before Taxes	225,822	159,124	80,033	292,485	228,716	212,324	197,829	179,702
Income Taxes	...	...	...	...	...	...	10,318	(75)
Net Income	225,394	158,701	80,023	292,447	264,973	239,500	197,836	190,601
Average Shares	165,361	162,351	161,614	156,295	149,432	144,660	134,489	124,710
Balance Sheet								
Current Assets	385,140	32,914	111,551	143,451	31,597	323,059	43,133	39,276
Total Assets	7,627,684	7,252,801	7,136,988	7,103,438	6,560,534	6,334,151	5,460,044	4,926,714
Current Liabilities	45,886	81,184	47,456	19,519	140,811	19,665	20,113	17,396
Long-Term Obligations	2,853,901	2,853,053	2,852,214	2,851,395	2,459,707	2,311,689	1,975,944	1,741,054
Total Liabilities	3,001,187	3,030,352	2,984,466	2,949,188	2,719,941	2,417,352	2,117,910	1,844,199
Stockholders' Equity	4,626,497	4,222,449	4,152,522	4,154,250	3,840,593	3,916,799	3,342,134	3,082,515
Shares Outstanding	171,637	163,513	161,978	161,503	153,577	147,149	141,007	132,010
Statistical Record								
Return on Assets %	3.50	3.96	3.90	4.28	4.11	4.05	3.81	4.06
Return on Equity %	6.02	6.75	6.72	7.32	6.83	6.58	6.16	6.51
EBITDA Margin %	63.89	66.91	67.52	95.14	88.62	87.09	88.72	88.78
Net Margin %	45.34	48.31	48.88	46.97	45.30	44.88	40.97	43.83
Asset Turnover	0.09	0.09	0.09	0.09	0.09	0.09	0.09	0.09
Current Ratio	8.39	0.41	2.35	7.35	0.22	16.43	2.14	2.26
Debt to Equity	0.62	0.68	0.69	0.69	0.64	0.59	0.59	0.56
Price Range	57.68-43.24	55.71-43.24	55.71-37.18	51.16-36.52	46.13-36.72	53.46-39.00	44.24-33.99	40.34-30.33
P/E Ratio	41.50-31.11	36.89-28.64	37.64-25.12	31.01-22.13	31.81-25.32	38.74-28.26	36.87-28.33	32.53-24.46
Average Yield %	3.89	4.04	4.28	4.53	4.44	3.85	4.44	4.62

Address: 450 South Orange Avenue, Suite 900, Orlando, FL 32801 Telephone: 407-265-7348 Fax: 407-423-2894	Web Site: www.nnnreit.com Officers: Donald (Don) DeFosset - Chairman Julian E. Whitehurst - President, Chief Executive Officer, Chief Operating Officer, Executive Vice President, Secretary, General Counsel	Auditors: Ernst & Young LLP Investor Contact: 407-650-1228 Transfer Agents: American Stock Transfer & Trust Company, Brooklyn, NY

NAVISTAR INTERNATIONAL CORP.

Exchange	Symbol	Price	52Wk Range	Yield	P/E
NYS	NAV	$28.94 (12/31/2019)	39.15-21.63	N/A	13.04

*7 Year Price Score 87.36   ***NYSE Composite Index=100**   ***12 Month Price Score 95.47**

Interim Earnings (Per Share)

Qtr.	Jan	Apr	Jul	Oct
2014-15	(0.52)	(0.78)	(0.34)	(0.61)
2015-16	(0.40)	0.05	(0.42)	(0.42)
2016-17	(0.76)	(0.86)	0.38	1.47
2017-18	(0.74)	0.55	1.71	1.88
2018-19	0.11	(0.48)	1.56	1.02

Interim Dividends (Per Share)

No Dividends Paid

Valuation Analysis   **Institutional Holding**

Forecast EPS	$2.48	No of Institutions
	(01/15/2020)	300
Market Cap	$2.9 Billion	Shares
Book Value	N/A	87,596,480
Price/Book	N/A	% Held
Price/Sales	0.26	73.80

Business Summary: Autos- Manufacturing (MIC: 1.8.1 SIC: 3711 NAIC: 336211)

Navistar International is a holding company. Through its subsidiaries, Co. is a manufacturer of International® brand commercial trucks, proprietary diesel engines, and IC Bus® (IC) brand school and commercial buses. Co.'s segments include: Truck, which manufactures and distributes trucks and buses along with production of proprietary engines; Parts, which provides proprietary products to support the International commercial truck, IC Bus, proprietary engine lines, and export parts business; and Global Operations, which consists of the operations of its subsidiary, International Industria Automotiva da America do Sul Ltda that manufactures and distributes mid-range diesel engines.

Recent Developments: For the year ended Oct 31 2019, income from continuing operations decreased 34.0% to US$243.0 million from US$368.0 million a year earlier. Net income decreased 34.0% to US$243.0 million from US$368.0 million in the prior year. Revenues were US$11.25 billion, up 9.8% from US$10.25 billion the year before. Direct operating expenses rose 11.2% to US$9.25 billion from US$8.32 billion in the comparable period the year before. Indirect operating expenses increased 8.1% to US$1.58 billion from US$1.47 billion in the equivalent prior-year period.

Prospects: Our evaluation of Navistar International Corp. as of October 4th, 2019 is the result of our systematic analysis on three basic characteristics: earnings strength, relative valuation, and recent stock price movement. The company has suffered a very negative trend in earnings per share over the past 5 quarters. In addition, recent analyst estimates for the company have been reduced while NAV has posted results that exceeded analysts' expectations. Based on operating earnings yield, the company is undervalued when compared to all of the companies we cover. Share price changes over the past year indicates that NAV will perform very poorly over the near term.

Financial Data

(US$ in Millions)	10/31/2019	10/31/2018	10/31/2017	10/31/2016	10/31/2015	10/31/2014	10/31/2013	10/31/2012
Earnings Per Share	2.22	3.41	0.32	(1.19)	(2.25)	(7.60)	(11.17)	(43.56)
Cash Flow Per Share	4.53	2.72	1.17	3.26	0.56	(4.13)	1.24	8.80
Income Statement								
Total Revenue	11,251	10,250	8,570	8,111	10,140	10,806	10,775	12,948
EBITDA	631	818	482	368	274	63	(269)	(596)
Depn & Amortn	61	71	73	79	76	314	395	298
Income Before Taxes	258	420	58	(38)	(109)	(565)	(985)	(1,153)
Income Taxes	19	52	10	33	51	26	(171)	1,780
Net Income	221	340	30	(97)	(184)	(619)	(898)	(3,010)
Average Shares	99	99	93	81	81	81	80	69
Balance Sheet								
Current Assets	4,952	5,136	4,160	3,759	4,622	5,013	5,459	5,837
Total Assets	6,917	7,230	6,135	5,653	6,692	7,443	8,315	9,102
Current Liabilities	3,575	3,807	3,645	3,203	3,788	4,231	4,261	4,353
Long-Term Obligations	4,317	4,521	3,889	3,997	4,188	3,929	3,922	3,566
Total Liabilities	10,643	11,161	10,713	10,951	11,859	12,095	11,960	12,407
Stockholders' Equity	(3,726)	(3,931)	(4,578)	(5,298)	(5,167)	(4,652)	(3,645)	(3,305)
Shares Outstanding	99	98	98	81	81	81	80	79
Statistical Record								
Return on Assets %	3.12	5.09	0.51	N.M.	N.M.	N.M.	N.M.	N.M.
EBITDA Margin %	5.61	7.98	5.62	4.54	2.70	0.58	N.M.	N.M.
Net Margin %	1.96	3.32	0.35	N.M.	N.M.	N.M.	N.M.	N.M.
Asset Turnover	1.59	1.53	1.45	1.31	1.43	1.37	1.24	1.21
Current Ratio	1.39	1.35	1.14	1.17	1.22	1.18	1.28	1.34
Price Range	39.15-21.63	47.45-30.38	44.68-22.30	23.69-6.23	37.76-11.36	40.90-29.49	39.71-18.75	47.42-18.51
P/E Ratio	17.64-9.74	13.91-8.91	139.63-69.69	...	...	...	...	...

Address: 2701 Navistar Drive, Lisle, IL 60532	Web Site: www.navistar.com	Auditors: KPMG LLP
Telephone: 331-332-5000	Officers: Troy A. Clarke - Executive Chairman, Chairman, President, Chief Executive Officer, Chief Operating Officer, Division Officer Walter G. Borst - Executive Vice President, Chief Financial Officer	Investor Contact: 331-332-2143 Transfer Agents: Computershare Investor Services, Jersey City, NJ

NCR CORP

Exchange	Symbol	Price	52Wk Range	Yield	P/E
NYS	NCR	$35.16 (12/31/2019)	35.31-23.08	N/A	97.67

*7 Year Price Score 78.29   *NYSE Composite Index=100   *12 Month Price Score 102.66

Interim Earnings (Per Share)

Qtr.	Mar	Jun	Sep	Dec
2016	0.16	0.49	0.68	0.35
2017	(0.14)	0.67	0.77	(0.44)
2018	0.06	(1.33)	0.56	(0.51)
2019	0.20	0.58	0.09	...

Interim Dividends (Per Share)

No Dividends Paid

Valuation Analysis   Institutional Holding

Forecast EPS	$2.81	No of Institutions
	(01/11/2020)	590
Market Cap	$4.5 Billion	Shares
Book Value	$1.1 Billion	154,811,360
Price/Book	4.02	% Held
Price/Sales	0.66	96.16

TRADING VOLUME (thousand shares)

Business Summary: Computer Hardware & Equipment (MIC: 6.2.1 SIC: 3578 NAIC: 334119)

NCR is a software- and services-led enterprise provider in the financial, retail, hospitality and telecommunications and technology industries. Co. provides a range of solutions including software, advisory and consulting services, hardware, support and managed services. Co.'s segments include: Software, which includes software platforms such as its multi-vendor automated teller machines (ATMs) software application suite; Services, which provides end-to-end services from assessment and preparation, to staging, installation and implementation, and multivendor maintenance and support; and Hardware, which provides financial-oriented self-service hardware products, such as multi-function ATMs.

Recent Developments: For the quarter ended Sep 30 2019, income from continuing operations increased 19.5% to US$104.0 million from US$87.0 million in the year-earlier quarter. Net income increased 3.5% to US$89.0 million from US$86.0 million in the year-earlier quarter. Revenues were US$1.78 billion, up 15.0% from US$1.55 billion the year before. Operating income was US$172.0 million versus US$125.0 million in the prior-year quarter, an increase of 37.6%. Direct operating expenses rose 11.9% to US$1.28 billion from US$1.14 billion in the comparable period the year before. Indirect operating expenses increased 17.5% to US$335.0 million from US$285.0 million in the equivalent prior-year period.

Prospects: Our evaluation of NCR Corp. as of October 4th, 2019 is the result of our systematic analysis on three basic characteristics: earnings strength, relative valuation, and recent stock price movement. The company has enjoyed a very positive trend in earnings per share over the past 5 quarters. In addition, recent analyst estimates for the company have been raised, and NCR has posted results that exceeded analysts' expectations. Based on operating earnings yield, the company is undervalued when compared to all of the companies we cover. Share price changes over the past year indicates that NCR will perform very well over the near term.

Financial Data

(US$ in Thousands)	9 Mos	6 Mos	3 Mos	12/31/2018	12/31/2017	12/31/2016	12/31/2015	12/31/2014
Earnings Per Share	0.36	0.83	(1.08)	(1.16)	0.97	1.71	(1.09)	1.12
Cash Flow Per Share	5.23	4.56	4.86	4.83	6.19	7.10	4.06	3.12
Income Statement								
Total Revenue	5,029,000	3,246,000	1,536,000	6,405,000	6,516,000	6,543,000	6,373,000	6,591,000
EBITDA	650,000	400,000	173,000	283,000	728,000	635,000	164,000	395,000
Depn & Amortn	249,000	160,000	81,000	81,000	86,000	90,000	91,000	83,000
Income Before Taxes	258,000	150,000	47,000	39,000	482,000	379,000	(95,000)	137,000
Income Taxes	28,000	24,000	9,000	73,000	242,000	92,000	55,000	(48,000)
Net Income	215,000	125,000	37,000	(88,000)	232,000	270,000	(178,000)	191,000
Average Shares	123,400	152,700	122,200	118,400	127,000	157,400	167,600	171,200
Balance Sheet								
Current Assets	3,156,000	3,035,000	3,016,000	3,023,000	2,830,000	2,757,000	2,549,000	3,088,000
Total Assets	8,451,000	8,222,000	8,198,000	7,761,000	7,654,000	7,673,000	7,635,000	8,607,000
Current Liabilities	2,346,000	2,303,000	2,381,000	2,282,000	1,889,000	1,965,000	1,781,000	2,070,000
Long-Term Obligations	3,422,000	2,918,000	2,914,000	2,980,000	2,939,000	3,001,000	3,239,000	3,472,000
Total Liabilities	7,336,000	6,796,000	6,877,000	6,507,000	6,125,000	6,131,000	6,117,000	6,736,000
Stockholders' Equity	1,115,000	1,426,000	1,321,000	1,254,000	1,529,000	1,542,000	1,518,000	1,871,000
Shares Outstanding	127,400	120,300	119,800	118,700	122,000	124,600	133,000	168,600
Statistical Record								
Return on Assets %	2.11	2.08	N.M.	N.M.	3.03	3.52	N.M.	2.29
Return on Equity %	13.97	12.31	N.M.	N.M.	15.11	17.60	N.M.	10.49
EBITDA Margin %	12.93	12.32	11.26	4.42	11.17	9.71	2.57	5.99
Net Margin %	4.28	3.85	2.41	N.M.	3.56	4.13	N.M.	2.90
Asset Turnover	0.86	0.85	0.81	0.83	0.85	0.85	0.78	0.79
Current Ratio	1.35	1.32	1.27	1.32	1.50	1.40	1.43	1.49
Debt to Equity	3.07	2.05	2.21	2.38	1.92	1.95	2.13	1.86
Price Range	33.98-21.02	32.74-21.02	32.22-21.02	38.07-21.02	49.59-29.57	41.75-19.08	34.73-22.39	37.50-23.54
P/E Ratio	94.39-58.39	39.45-25.33	...	...	51.12-30.48	24.42-11.16	...	33.48-21.02

Address: 864 Spring Street N.W.,	Web Site: www.ncr.com	Auditors: PricewaterhouseCoopers LLP
Atlanta, GA 30308	Officers: Frank R. Martire - Executive Chairman	Investor Contact: 800-255-5627
Telephone: 937-445-5000	Michael D. Hayford - President, Chief Executive Officer	Transfer Agents: Wells Fargo Shareowner Services, St. Paul, MN

NEW JERSEY RESOURCES CORP

Exchange	Symbol	Price	52Wk Range	Yield	P/E	Div Acheiver
NYS	NJR	$44.57 (12/31/2019)	51.13-40.61	2.80	23.58	23 Years

*7 Year Price Score 110.51 *NYSE Composite Index=100 *12 Month Price Score 86.60

Interim Earnings (Per Share)

Qtr.	Dec	Mar	Jun	Sep
2014-15	1.44	0.71	(0.09)	0.05
2015-16	0.56	0.84	(0.20)	0.29
2016-17	0.40	1.32	0.22	(0.42)
2017-18	1.42	1.59	(0.16)	(0.20)
2018-19	0.97	0.82	(0.09)	0.20

Interim Dividends (Per Share)

Amt	Decl	Ex	Rec	Pay
0.292Q	01/22/2019	03/14/2019	03/15/2019	04/01/2019
0.292Q	05/07/2019	06/14/2019	06/17/2019	07/01/2019
0.313Q	07/09/2019	09/19/2019	09/20/2019	10/01/2019
0.313Q	11/12/2019	12/18/2019	12/19/2019	01/02/2020

Indicated Div: $1.25 (Div. Reinv. Plan)

Valuation Analysis — **Institutional Holding**

Forecast EPS	$2.13	No of Institutions
	(01/17/2020)	391
Market Cap	$4.0 Billion	Shares
Book Value	$1.6 Billion	79,254,888
Price/Book	2.59	% Held
Price/Sales	1.55	70.38

Business Summary: Gas Utilities (MIC: 3.3.1 SIC: 4924 NAIC: 221210)
New Jersey Resources is an energy services holding company whose principal business is the distribution of natural gas through a regulated utility, providing other retail and wholesale energy services to customers and investing in clean energy projects and midstream assets. Co.'s segments are: Natural Gas Distribution, which consists of regulated natural gas services, off-system sales, capacity and storage management operations; Clean Energy Ventures, which consists of capital investments in clean energy projects; Energy Services, which consists of unregulated wholesale and retail energy operations; and Midstream, which consists of investments in the midstream natural gas market.

Recent Developments: For the year ended Sep 30 2019, net income decreased 27.4% to US$169.5 million from US$233.4 million in the prior year. Revenues were US$2.59 billion, down 11.1% from US$2.92 billion the year before. Operating income was US$153.9 million versus US$199.9 million in the prior year, a decrease of 23.0%. Direct operating expenses declined 9.4% to US$2.34 billion from US$2.58 billion in the comparable period the year before. Indirect operating expenses decreased 25.3% to US$102.9 million from US$137.8 million in the equivalent prior-year period.

Prospects: Our evaluation of New Jersey Resources Corp. as of October 4th, 2019 is the result of our systematic analysis on three basic characteristics: earnings strength, relative valuation, and recent stock price movement. The company has produced a positive trend in earnings per share over the past 5 quarters. However, recent analyst estimates for the company have been reduced, and NJR has posted results that fell short of analysts' expectations. Based on operating earnings yield, the company is fairly valued when compared to all of the companies we cover. Share price changes over the past year indicates that NJR will perform well over the near term.

Financial Data

(US$ in Thousands)	09/30/2019	09/30/2018	09/30/2017	09/30/2016	09/30/2015	09/30/2014	09/30/2013	09/30/2012
Earnings Per Share	1.89	2.64	1.52	1.52	2.10	1.67	1.38	1.12
Cash Flow Per Share	2.12	4.54	2.87	1.66	4.55	4.24	1.37	0.61
Tang Book Value Per Share	17.08	15.81	13.81	13.55	12.94	11.45	10.57	9.78
Dividends Per Share	1.190	1.110	1.038	0.975	0.915	0.855	0.810	0.770
Dividend Payout %	62.96	42.05	68.26	64.14	43.57	51.20	58.91	69.06
Income Statement								
Total Revenue	2,592,045	2,915,109	2,268,617	1,880,905	2,733,987	3,738,145	3,198,068	2,248,923
EBITDA	256,908	298,629	263,281	249,431	316,395	261,483	211,324	152,461
Depn & Amortn	91,700	85,700	81,800	72,700	61,399	52,742	47,310	41,643
Income Before Taxes	118,126	166,643	136,595	145,687	227,275	183,278	140,035	89,974
Income Taxes	(37,751)	(53,785)	18,343	23,530	59,724	51,840	35,575	7,729
Net Income	169,505	233,436	132,065	131,672	180,960	141,970	114,809	92,879
Average Shares	89,616	88,315	87,144	86,731	86,265	84,922	83,628	83,264
Balance Sheet								
Current Assets	511,606	770,080	579,444	607,264	544,511	682,731	745,898	647,344
Total Assets	4,372,985	4,143,664	3,928,507	3,727,082	3,339,038	3,158,804	3,004,783	2,770,005
Current Liabilities	446,377	750,976	802,918	571,608	436,100	791,086	851,833	653,139
Long-Term Obligations	1,537,177	1,180,619	997,080	1,063,550	843,595	598,209	512,886	525,169
Total Liabilities	2,821,268	2,724,686	2,691,864	2,560,491	2,232,082	2,192,638	2,117,399	1,956,140
Stockholders' Equity	1,551,717	1,418,978	1,236,643	1,166,591	1,106,956	966,166	887,384	813,865
Shares Outstanding	89,998	88,292	86,555	86,086	85,531	84,356	83,923	83,239
Statistical Record								
Return on Assets %	3.98	5.78	3.45	3.72	5.57	4.61	3.98	3.42
Return on Equity %	11.41	17.58	10.99	11.55	17.46	15.32	13.50	11.65
EBITDA Margin %	9.91	10.24	11.61	13.26	11.57	6.99	6.61	6.78
Net Margin %	6.54	8.01	5.82	7.00	6.62	3.80	3.59	4.13
Asset Turnover	0.61	0.72	0.59	0.53	0.84	1.21	1.11	0.83
Current Ratio	1.15	1.03	0.72	1.06	1.25	0.86	0.88	0.99
Debt to Equity	0.99	0.83	0.81	0.91	0.76	0.62	0.58	0.65
Price Range	51.13-43.82	47.55-36.25	44.25-31.07	38.71-28.14	33.48-24.81	28.66-21.30	23.60-19.50	25.00-20.39
P/E Ratio	27.05-23.19	18.01-13.73	29.11-20.44	25.47-18.51	15.94-11.81	17.16-12.75	17.10-14.13	22.33-18.20
Average Yield %	2.49	2.61	2.68	2.85	3.10	3.50	3.72	3.38

Address: 1415 Wyckoff Road, Wall, NJ 07719 Telephone: 732-938-1000	Web Site: www.njresources.com Officers: Stephen D. Westhoven - President, Chief Executive Officer, Executive Vice President, Chief Operating Officer Patrick J. Migliaccio - Senior Vice President, Chief Financial Officer	Auditors: DELOITTE & TOUCHE LLP Investor Contact: 732-378-4967 Transfer Agents: Wells Fargo Shareowner Services, St. Paul, MN

NEW RELIC INC

Exchange	Symbol	Price	52Wk Range	Yield	P/E
NYS	NEWR	$65.71 (12/31/2019)	108.45-56.30	N/A	N/A

*7 Year Price Score N/A   ***NYSE Composite Index=100**   ***12 Month Price Score 74.80**

TRADING VOLUME (thousand shares)

Interim Earnings (Per Share)

Qtr.	Jun	Sep	Dec	Mar
2016-17	(0.36)	(0.28)	(0.27)	(0.28)
2017-18	(0.30)	(0.27)	(0.14)	(0.13)
2018-19	(0.10)	(0.15)	(0.18)	(0.30)
2019-20	(0.26)	(0.32)	...	...

Interim Dividends (Per Share)

No Dividends Paid

Valuation Analysis		Institutional Holding	
Forecast EPS	$0.64	No of Institutions	
	(00/22/2020)		362
Market Cap	$3.9 Billion	Shares	
Book Value	$371.2 Million		50,984,072
Price/Book	10.41	% Held	
Price/Sales	7.11		86.98

Business Summary: Internet & Software (MIC: 6.3.2 SIC: 7372 NAIC: 511210)

New Relic is a provider of an integrated, multi-tenant, cloud-based instrumentation and analytics platform that enables users to collect, store and analyze amounts of data in real time. Co.'s products include: New Relic Application Performance Management, which provides visibility into the performance and usage of server-based applications; New Relic Mobile, which provides code-level visibility into the performance and health of mobile applications running on the iOS and Android mobile operating systems; New Relic Browser; New Relic Synthetics; New Relic Infrastructure; and New Relic Insights.

Recent Developments: For the quarter ended Sep 30 2019, net loss amounted to US$19.1 million versus a net loss of US$8.5 million in the year-earlier quarter. Revenues were US$145.8 million, up 26.9% from US$114.9 million the year before. Operating loss was US$16.9 million versus a loss of US$5.5 million in the prior-year quarter. Direct operating expenses rose 36.3% to US$25.1 million from US$18.4 million in the comparable period the year before. Indirect operating expenses increased 34.9% to US$137.6 million from US$102.0 million in the equivalent prior-year period.

Prospects: Our evaluation of New Relic Inc as of October 4th, 2019 is the result of our systematic analysis on three basic characteristics: earnings strength, relative valuation, and recent stock price movement. The company has generated a negative trend in earnings per share over the past 5 quarters. In addition, recent analyst estimates for the company have been reduced while NEWR has posted results that exceeded analysts' expectations. Based on operating earnings yield, the company is overvalued when compared to all of the companies we cover. Share price changes over the past year indicates that NEWR will perform poorly over the near term.

Financial Data
(US$ in Thousands)

	6 Mos	3 Mos	03/31/2019	03/31/2018	03/31/2017	03/31/2016	03/31/2015	03/31/2014
Earnings Per Share	(1.06)	(0.89)	(0.72)	(0.83)	(1.18)	(1.39)	(1.98)	(2.58)
Cash Flow Per Share	1.76	1.75	2.03	0.65	0.37	0.08	(0.54)	(1.33)
Tang Book Value Per Share	5.39	5.22	5.06	3.61	3.24	3.56	4.47	1.98
Income Statement								
Total Revenue	286,825	141,010	479,225	355,058	263,479	181,309	110,391	63,174
EBITDA	(20,096)	(8,749)	(8,583)	(24,365)	(44,315)	(53,764)	(41,806)	(35,677)
Depn & Amortn	10,404	5,165	25,900	22,100	17,600	14,000	8,500	4,500
Income Before Taxes	(34,056)	(15,593)	(41,059)	(44,361)	(60,813)	(67,185)	(50,234)	(40,225)
Income Taxes	624	(36)	697	959	264	302	(85)	...
Net Income	(33,783)	(15,169)	(40,893)	(45,320)	(61,077)	(67,487)	(50,149)	(40,225)
Average Shares	58,372	57,944	56,884	54,814	51,715	48,410	25,290	15,596
Balance Sheet								
Current Assets	894,789	900,558	914,332	362,999	276,607	229,951	218,872	27,476
Total Assets	1,150,371	1,153,166	1,090,227	443,326	352,269	294,444	264,711	55,208
Current Liabilities	297,320	312,557	315,358	218,651	155,333	93,203	44,065	19,450
Long-Term Obligations	416,341	411,102	405,937	...	...	...	...	...
Total Liabilities	779,211	793,435	740,597	228,222	165,425	101,211	49,841	23,956
Stockholders' Equity	371,160	359,731	349,630	215,104	186,844	193,233	214,870	31,252
Shares Outstanding	58,776	58,395	58,106	55,953	53,279	49,981	47,117	15,803
Statistical Record								
Asset Turnover	0.51	0.49	0.62	0.89	0.81	0.65	0.69	0.96
Current Ratio	3.01	2.88	2.90	1.66	1.78	2.47	4.97	1.41
Debt to Equity	1.12	1.14	1.16	...	...	...	...	...
Price Range	108.45-56.30	113.44-73.50	113.44-69.45	78.52-36.95	38.54-23.95	39.91-20.83	37.25-30.33	...

Address: 188 Spear Street, Suite 1200, San Francisco, CA 94105
Telephone: 650-777-7600

Web Site: www.newrelic.com
Officers: Peter H. Fenton - Chairman Lewis Cirne - Chief Executive Officer

Auditors: DELOITTE & TOUCHE LLP
Investor Contact: 650-777-7600
Transfer Agents: Computershare Trust Company, N.A.

NEW RESIDENTIAL INVESTMENT CORP

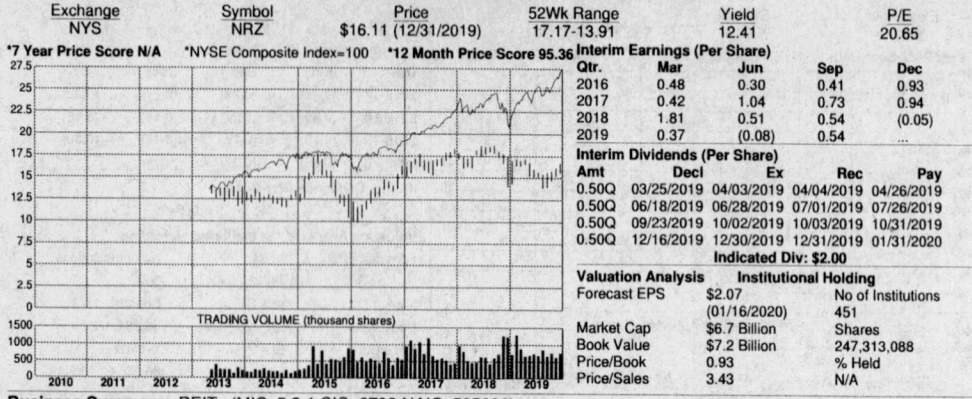

Exchange	Symbol	Price	52Wk Range	Yield	P/E
NYS	NRZ	$16.11 (12/31/2019)	17.17-13.91	12.41	20.65

*7 Year Price Score N/A   ***NYSE Composite Index=100**   ***12 Month Price Score 95.36**

Interim Earnings (Per Share)
Qtr.	Mar	Jun	Sep	Dec
2016	0.48	0.30	0.41	0.93
2017	0.42	1.04	0.73	0.94
2018	1.81	0.51	0.54	(0.05)
2019	0.37	(0.08)	0.54	...

Interim Dividends (Per Share)
Amt	Decl	Ex	Rec	Pay
0.50Q	03/25/2019	04/03/2019	04/04/2019	04/26/2019
0.50Q	06/18/2019	06/28/2019	07/01/2019	07/26/2019
0.50Q	09/23/2019	10/02/2019	10/03/2019	10/31/2019
0.50Q	12/16/2019	12/30/2019	12/31/2019	01/31/2020

Indicated Div: $2.00

Valuation Analysis
		Institutional Holding	
Forecast EPS	$2.07	No of Institutions	
	(01/16/2020)	451	
Market Cap	$6.7 Billion	Shares	
Book Value	$7.2 Billion	247,313,088	
Price/Book	0.93	% Held	
Price/Sales	3.43	N/A	

Business Summary: REITs (MIC: 5.3.1 SIC: 6798 NAIC: 525930)

New Residential Investment is a holding company. Through its subsidiaries, Co. is a real estate investment trust mainly focused on investing in, and managing investments related to residential real estate. Co. is externally managed and advised by an affiliate of Fortress Investment Group LLC. Co.'s portfolio is composed of mortgage servicing and origination related assets, residential securities (and associated call rights) and loans and other investments. A mortgage servicing right provides a mortgage servicer with the right to service a pool of residential mortgage loans in exchange for a portion of the interest payments made on the underlying residential mortgage loans.

Recent Developments: For the quarter ended Sep 30 2019, net income increased 25.2% to US$244.7 million from US$195.5 million in the year-earlier quarter. Revenues were US$630.0 million, up 21.7% from US$517.6 million the year before.

Prospects: Our evaluation of New Residential Investment Corp. as of October 4th, 2019 is the result of our systematic analysis on three basic characteristics: earnings strength, relative valuation, and recent stock price movement. The company has produced a positive trend in earnings per share over the past 5 quarters. However, recent analyst estimates for the company have been reduced, and NRZ has posted results that fell short of analysts' expectations. Based on operating earnings yield, the company is undervalued when compared to all of the companies we cover. Share price changes over the past year indicates that NRZ will perform poorly over the near term.

Financial Data
(US$ in Thousands)	9 Mos	6 Mos	3 Mos	12/31/2018	12/31/2017	12/31/2016	12/31/2015	12/31/2014
Earnings Per Share	0.78	0.78	1.37	2.81	3.15	2.12	1.32	2.53
Cash Flow Per Share	(8.35)	(10.13)	(5.26)	(3.60)	(2.98)	2.35	1.60	1.14
Tang Book Value Per Share	16.11	16.06	16.32	16.13	15.26	13.00	12.13	11.28
Dividends Per Share	1.500	2.000	1.500	2.000	1.980	1.840	1.750	0.380
Dividend Payout %	192.31	256.41	109.49	71.17	62.86	86.79	132.58	15.02
Income Statement								
Total Revenue	1,550,040	920,017	563,940	2,237,578	2,151,814	1,257,241	687,101	721,945
EBITDA	95,599	(101,643)	49,015	229,133	150,896	(126,305)	(254,417)	186,648
Depn & Amortn	(298,933)	(256,955)	(152,894)	(701,967)	(1,031,384)	(747,932)	(525,298)	(278,408)
Income Before Taxes	394,532	155,312	201,909	931,100	1,182,280	621,627	270,881	465,056
Income Taxes	18,980	24,420	45,997	(73,431)	167,628	38,911	(11,001)	22,957
Net Income	343,573	113,651	145,594	963,967	957,533	504,453	268,636	352,877
Average Shares	415,588	415,665	388,601	343,137	304,381	238,486	202,907	139,565
Balance Sheet								
Current Assets	934,487	583,984	527,825	7,454,052	2,002,241	1,978,390	1,788,417	212,985
Total Assets	41,347,925	36,792,375	33,409,568	31,691,013	22,213,562	18,365,035	15,192,722	8,093,690
Current Liabilities	33,579,937	29,696,925	26,177,510	18,230,304	10,201,086	6,805,056	4,937,019	3,301,202
Long-Term Obligations	...	...	...	7,102,266	7,084,391	7,990,605	7,249,568	2,913,209
Total Liabilities	34,169,460	30,074,410	26,587,287	25,693,343	17,523,357	15,104,935	12,396,789	6,497,601
Stockholders' Equity	7,178,465	6,717,965	6,822,281	5,997,670	4,690,205	3,260,100	2,795,933	1,596,089
Shares Outstanding	415,520	415,520	415,429	369,104	307,361	250,773	230,471	141,434
Statistical Record								
Return on Assets %	0.96	1.00	1.82	3.58	4.72	3.00	2.31	5.02
Return on Equity %	5.32	4.81	8.09	18.04	24.09	16.61	12.23	24.66
EBITDA Margin %	6.17	N.M.	8.69	10.24	7.01	N.M.	N.M.	25.85
Net Margin %	22.17	12.35	25.82	43.08	44.50	40.12	39.10	48.88
Asset Turnover	0.05	0.06	0.07	0.08	0.11	0.07	0.06	0.10
Current Ratio	0.03	0.02	0.02	0.41	0.20	0.29	0.36	0.06
Debt to Equity	...	...	...	1.18	1.51	2.45	2.59	1.83
Price Range	18.00-13.91	18.68-14.00	18.68-14.00	18.68-14.00	18.30-15.15	16.36-9.86	17.78-10.43	13.72-11.58
P/E Ratio	23.08-17.83	23.95-17.95	13.64-10.22	6.65-4.98	5.81-4.81	7.72-4.65	13.47-7.90	5.42-4.58
Average Yield %	9.29	11.78	8.67	11.48	11.84	13.97	12.18	3.00

Address: 1345 Avenue of the Americas, New York, NY 10105 **Telephone:** 212-798-3150	**Web Site:** www.newresi.com **Officers:** Michael Nierenberg - Chairman, President, Chief Executive Officer Nicholas Santoro - Chief Financial Officer, Treasurer	**Auditors:** Ernst & Young LLP **Transfer Agents:** American Stock Transfer & Trust Company, LLC

NEW YORK COMMUNITY BANCORP INC.

Exchange	Symbol	Price	52Wk Range	Yield	P/E
NYS	NYCB	$12.02 (12/31/2019)	13.69-9.41	5.66	15.82

*7 Year Price Score 67.06   *NYSE Composite Index=100   *12 Month Price Score 98.11

Interim Earnings (Per Share)

Qtr.	Mar	Jun	Sep	Dec
2016	0.27	0.26	0.26	0.23
2017	0.21	0.22	0.21	0.26
2018	0.20	0.20	0.20	0.19
2019	0.19	0.19	0.19	...

Interim Dividends (Per Share)

Amt	Decl	Ex	Rec	Pay
0.17Q	01/29/2019	02/11/2019	02/12/2019	02/26/2019
0.17Q	04/29/2019	05/13/2019	05/14/2019	05/28/2019
0.17Q	07/30/2019	08/09/2019	08/12/2019	08/26/2019
0.17Q	10/29/2019	11/07/2019	11/11/2019	11/25/2019

Indicated Div: $0.68 (Div. Reinv. Plan)

Valuation Analysis   **Institutional Holding**

Forecast EPS	$0.77	No of Institutions
	(01/15/2020)	612
Market Cap	$5.6 Billion	Shares
Book Value	$6.7 Billion	363,398,176
Price/Book	0.84	% Held
Price/Sales	2.98	57.90

Business Summary: Banking (MIC: 5.1.1 SIC: 6036 NAIC: 522120)

New York Community Bancorp is a multi-bank holding company. Through its subsidiary, New York Community Bank, Co. operates through eight local divisions: Queens County Savings Bank, Roslyn Savings Bank, Richmond County Savings Bank, Roosevelt Savings Bank, and Atlantic Bank in New York; Garden State Community Bank in New Jersey; Ohio Savings Bank in Ohio; and AmTrust Bank in Florida and Arizona. Co. is also a producer of multi-family loans in New York City, with a focus on non-luxury residential apartment buildings with rent-regulated units that feature below-market rents.

Recent Developments: For the quarter ended Sep 30 2019, net income decreased 7.2% to US$99.0 million from US$106.8 million in the year-earlier quarter. Net interest income decreased 5.4% to US$235.9 million from US$249.5 million in the year-earlier quarter. Provision for loan losses was US$4.8 million versus US$1.2 million in the prior-year quarter, an increase of 298.1%. Non-interest income rose 6.4% to US$24.4 million from US$22.9 million, while non-interest expense declined 8.3% to US$123.3 million.

Prospects: Our evaluation of New York Community Bancorp Inc. as of October 4th, 2019 is the result of our systematic analysis on three basic characteristics: earnings strength, relative valuation, and recent stock price movement. The company has managed to produce a neutral trend in earnings per share over the past 5 quarters. Additionally, recent analyst estimates for the company have been unchanged while NYCB has posted results that exceeded analysts' expectations. Based on operating earnings yield, the company is undervalued when compared to all of the companies we cover. Share price changes over the past year indicates that NYCB will perform very poorly over the near term.

Financial Data

(US$ in Thousands)	9 Mos	6 Mos	3 Mos	12/31/2018	12/31/2017	12/31/2016	12/31/2015	12/31/2014
Earnings Per Share	0.76	0.77	0.78	0.79	0.90	1.01	(0.11)	1.09
Cash Flow Per Share	1.42	0.97	1.18	1.11	2.72	1.55	(0.94)	1.64
Tang Book Value Per Share	8.06	8.01	7.92	7.85	7.88	7.09	6.70	7.03
Dividends Per Share	0.680	0.680	0.680	0.680	0.680	0.680	1.000	1.000
Dividend Payout %	89.47	88.31	87.18	86.08	75.56	67.33	...	91.74
Income Statement								
Interest Income	1,354,477	899,926	446,174	1,689,673	1,582,239	1,674,869	1,691,584	1,683,067
Interest Expense	639,547	420,911	204,849	658,678	452,236	387,487	1,283,509	542,714
Net Interest Income	714,930	479,015	241,325	1,030,995	1,130,003	1,287,382	408,075	1,140,353
Provision for Losses	5,403	622	(1,222)	18,256	37,242	4,180	(15,004)	(18,587)
Non-Interest Income	66,768	42,382	24,785	91,558	216,880	145,572	210,763	201,593
Non-Interest Expense	385,121	261,819	138,767	546,628	641,218	649,255	760,511	579,170
Income Before Taxes	391,174	258,956	128,565	557,669	668,215	777,128	(132,013)	773,066
Income Taxes	97,305	64,133	30,988	135,252	202,014	281,727	(84,857)	287,669
Net Income	293,869	194,823	97,577	422,417	466,201	495,401	(47,156)	485,397
Average Shares	465,776	465,641	465,493	487,287	487,073	485,150	448,982	440,988
Balance Sheet								
Net Loans & Leases	40,694,787	40,725,589	40,369,383	40,006,088	38,265,183	39,308,016	38,011,995	35,647,639
Total Assets	52,537,629	52,776,253	52,131,046	51,899,376	49,124,195	48,926,555	50,317,796	48,559,217
Total Deposits	31,572,176	32,332,526	31,601,125	30,764,430	29,102,163	28,887,903	28,426,758	28,328,734
Total Liabilities	45,842,622	46,101,575	45,501,976	45,244,141	42,328,819	42,802,564	44,383,100	42,777,402
Stockholders' Equity	6,695,007	6,674,678	6,629,070	6,655,235	6,795,376	6,123,991	5,934,696	5,781,815
Shares Outstanding	467,350	467,358	467,236	473,536	488,490	487,056	484,943	442,587
Statistical Record								
Return on Assets %	0.76	0.78	0.81	0.84	0.95	1.00	N.M.	1.02
Return on Equity %	5.87	5.99	6.17	6.28	7.22	8.19	N.M.	8.43
Net Interest Margin %	51.90	52.38	54.09	61.02	71.42	76.86	24.12	67.75
Efficiency Ratio %	25.74	26.11	29.46	30.69	35.64	35.66	39.98	30.73
Loans to Deposits	1.29	1.26	1.28	1.30	1.31	1.36	1.34	1.26
Price Range	13.15-8.76	12.65-8.76	12.96-8.76	14.48-8.76	16.22-11.70	17.30-13.78	19.16-15.25	17.34-14.82
P/E Ratio	17.30-11.53	16.43-11.38	16.62-11.23	18.33-11.09	18.02-13.00	17.13-13.64	...	15.91-13.60
Average Yield %	6.26	6.35	6.17	5.87	5.06	4.49	5.81	6.30

Address: 615 Merrick Avenue, Westbury, NY 11590 **Telephone:** 516-683-4100	**Web Site:** www.mynycb.com **Officers:** Dominick Ciampa - Chairman Joseph R. Ficalora - President, Chief Executive Officer, Chairman	**Auditors:** KPMG LLP **Transfer Agents:** Computershare, Providence, RI

NEW YORK TIMES CO.

Exchange	Symbol	Price	52Wk Range	Yield	P/E
NYS	NYT	$32.17 (12/31/2019)	36.07-21.39	0.62	42.33

*7 Year Price Score 146.75 *NYSE Composite Index=100 *12 Month Price Score 95.83

Interim Earnings (Per Share)

Qtr.	Mar	Jun	Sep	Dec
2016	(0.05)	0.00	0.00	0.23
2017	0.08	0.09	0.20	(0.34)
2018	0.13	0.14	0.15	0.33
2019	0.18	0.15	0.10	...

Interim Dividends (Per Share)

Amt	Decl	Ex	Rec	Pay
0.05Q	02/06/2019	04/02/2019	04/03/2019	04/18/2019
0.05Q	06/27/2019	07/09/2019	07/10/2019	07/25/2019
0.05Q	09/19/2019	10/01/2019	10/02/2019	10/17/2019
0.05Q	12/19/2019	01/07/2020	01/08/2020	01/23/2020

Indicated Div: $0.20 (Div. Reinv. Plan)

Valuation Analysis / Institutional Holding

Forecast EPS	$0.76	No of Institutions
(01/16/2020)		448
Market Cap	$5.3 Billion	Shares
Book Value	$1.1 Billion	197,771,696
Price/Book	4.87	% Held
Price/Sales	2.96	94.69

Business Summary: Publishing (MIC: 2.3.3 SIC: 2711 NAIC: 511110)

New York Times principal business consists of distributing content generated by its newsroom through its digital and print platforms. In addition, Co. distributes selected content on third-party platforms. Co.'s businesses include: newspaper, The New York Times; websites, including NYTimes.com; mobile applications, including The Times's main news applications, as well as interest-specific applications including its Crossword and Cooking products; and related businesses, such as its licensing division, its digital marketing agencies, product review and recommendation website, Wirecutter, its commercial printing operations, NYT Live and other products and services under The Times brand.

Recent Developments: For the quarter ended Sep 29 2019, net income decreased 34.2% to US$16.4 million from US$25.0 million in the year-earlier quarter. Revenues were US$428.5 million, up 2.7% from US$417.3 million the year before. Operating income was US$25.1 million versus US$41.4 million in the prior-year quarter, a decrease of 39.5%. Direct operating expenses rose 9.4% to US$178.8 million from US$163.4 million in the comparable period the year before. Indirect operating expenses increased 5.7% to US$224.6 million from US$212.5 million in the equivalent prior-year period.

Prospects: Our evaluation of New York Times Co. as of October 4th, 2019 is the result of our systematic analysis on three basic characteristics: earnings strength, relative valuation, and recent stock price movement. The company has produced a positive trend in earnings per share over the past 5 quarters. However, recent analyst estimates for the company have been reduced, while NYT has posted results that exceeded analysts' expectations. Based on operating earnings yield, the company is fairly valued when compared to all of the companies we cover. Share price changes over the past year indicates that NYT will perform over the near term.

Financial Data

(US$ in Thousands)	9 Mos	6 Mos	3 Mos	12/30/2018	12/31/2017	12/25/2016	12/27/2015	12/28/2014
Earnings Per Share	0.76	0.81	0.80	0.75	0.03	0.18	0.38	0.20
Cash Flow Per Share	0.98	0.86	0.99	0.96	0.53	0.59	1.07	0.54
Tang Book Value Per Share	5.77	5.68	5.54	5.45	4.65	4.43	4.45	4.06
Dividends Per Share	0.180	0.170	0.160	0.160	0.160	0.160	0.160	0.160
Dividend Payout %	23.68	20.99	20.00	21.33	533.33	88.89	42.11	80.00
Income Statement								
Total Revenue	1,303,821	875,320	439,062	1,748,598	1,675,639	1,555,342	1,579,215	1,588,528
EBITDA	137,663	98,961	47,681	240,904	174,237	163,327	198,182	171,403
Depn & Amortn	45,548	30,098	14,918	59,011	61,877	61,723	61,597	79,455
Income Before Taxes	88,543	66,046	31,460	165,327	92,583	66,799	97,535	38,218
Income Taxes	16,789	10,719	1,304	48,631	103,956	4,421	33,910	(3,541)
Net Income	71,754	55,327	30,156	125,684	4,296	29,068	63,246	33,307
Average Shares	167,555	167,549	167,129	166,939	164,263	162,817	166,423	161,323
Balance Sheet								
Current Assets	909,289	922,736	884,121	893,946	749,699	796,178	862,532	1,148,095
Total Assets	2,254,961	2,206,368	2,194,563	2,197,123	2,099,780	2,185,395	2,417,690	2,566,474
Current Liabilities	659,782	631,644	636,311	673,304	415,657	398,737	563,585	600,508
Long-Term Obligations	...	...	...	...	250,209	246,978	242,851	426,458
Total Liabilities	1,159,055	1,123,025	1,136,609	1,156,342	1,202,501	1,337,580	1,590,939	1,840,146
Stockholders' Equity	1,095,906	1,083,343	1,057,954	1,040,781	897,279	847,815	826,751	726,328
Shares Outstanding	166,038	166,010	165,950	165,091	162,209	161,152	161,389	150,337
Statistical Record								
Return on Assets %	5.78	6.29	6.24	5.87	0.20	1.27	2.54	1.30
Return on Equity %	12.08	13.14	13.29	13.01	0.48	3.48	8.17	4.26
EBITDA Margin %	10.56	11.31	10.86	13.78	10.40	10.50	12.55	10.79
Net Margin %	5.50	6.32	6.87	7.19	0.26	1.87	4.00	2.10
Asset Turnover	0.82	0.83	0.83	0.82	0.77	0.68	0.64	0.62
Current Ratio	1.38	1.46	1.39	1.33	1.80	2.00	1.53	1.91
Debt to Equity	...	...	...	...	0.28	0.29	0.29	0.59
Price Range	36.07-21.39	34.80-21.39	34.49-21.39	28.23-18.30	20.00-13.05	14.10-10.80	14.46-11.56	17.26-11.22
P/E Ratio	47.46-28.14	42.96-26.41	43.11-26.74	37.64-24.40	666.67-435.00	78.33-60.00	38.05-30.42	86.30-56.10
Average Yield %	0.60	0.61	0.63	0.67	0.95	1.28	1.20	1.13

Address: 620 Eighth Avenue, New York, NY 10018 **Telephone:** 212-556-1234	**Web Site:** www.nytco.com **Officers:** Arthur Sulzberger - Executive Chairman, Chairman, Publisher, Interim Chief Executive Officer Mark Thompson - President, Chief Executive Officer	**Auditors:** Ernst & Young LLP **Investor Contact:** 212-556-4317 **Transfer Agents:** Computershare, Providence, RI

NEWMARKET CORP

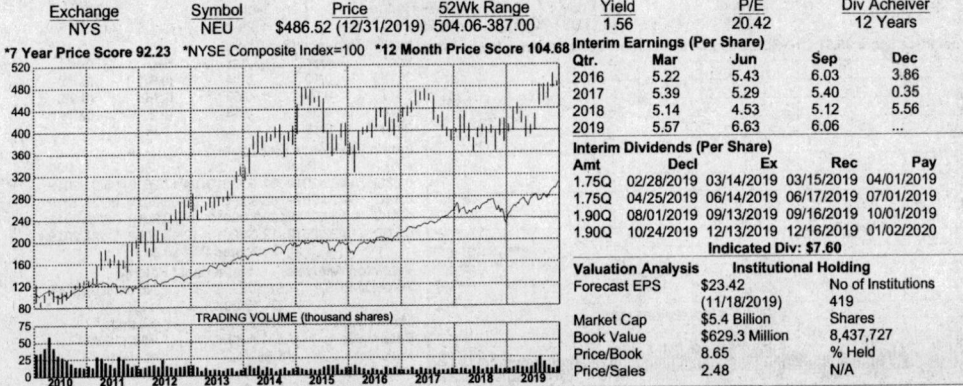

Exchange	Symbol	Price	52Wk Range	Yield	P/E	Div Acheiver
NYS	NEU	$486.52 (12/31/2019)	504.06-387.00	1.56	20.42	12 Years

*7 Year Price Score 92.23 *NYSE Composite Index=100 *12 Month Price Score 104.68

Interim Earnings (Per Share)

Qtr.	Mar	Jun	Sep	Dec
2016	5.22	5.43	6.03	3.86
2017	5.39	5.29	5.40	0.35
2018	5.14	4.53	5.12	5.56
2019	5.57	6.63	6.06	...

Interim Dividends (Per Share)

Amt	Decl	Ex	Rec	Pay
1.75Q	02/28/2019	03/14/2019	03/15/2019	04/01/2019
1.75Q	04/25/2019	06/14/2019	06/17/2019	07/01/2019
1.90Q	08/01/2019	09/13/2019	09/16/2019	10/01/2019
1.90Q	10/24/2019	12/13/2019	12/16/2019	01/02/2020

Indicated Div: $7.60

Valuation Analysis

		Institutional Holding	
Forecast EPS	$23.42	No of Institutions	419
	(11/18/2019)		
Market Cap	$5.4 Billion	Shares	
Book Value	$629.3 Million		8,437,727
Price/Book	8.65	% Held	
Price/Sales	2.48		N/A

Business Summary: Specialty Chemicals (MIC: 8.3.2 SIC: 2869 NAIC: 325199)

NewMarket is a holding company and is the parent company of Afton Chemical Corporation (Afton), Ethyl Corporation (Ethyl), NewMarket Services Corporation (NewMarket Services), and NewMarket Development Corporation (NewMarket Development). Afton manufactures and sells petroleum additives, while Ethyl represents the sale of tetraethyl lead (antiknock compounds) in North America and certain contracted manufacturing and services. NewMarket Development manages the property that Co. owns in Virginia. NewMarket Services provides various administrative services to Co., Afton, Ethyl, and NewMarket Development. Co.'s business is composed of one segment, petroleum additives.

Recent Developments: For the quarter ended Sep 30 2019, net income increased 15.9% to US$67.8 million from US$58.5 million in the year-earlier quarter. Revenues were US$555.8 million, down 1.3% from US$563.2 million the year before. Operating income was US$88.2 million versus US$68.1 million in the prior-year quarter, an increase of 29.5%. Direct operating expenses declined 6.9% to US$393.1 million from US$422.3 million in the comparable period the year before. Indirect operating expenses increased 2.4% to US$74.5 million from US$72.7 million in the equivalent prior-year period.

Prospects: Our evaluation of NewMarket Corp. as of October 4th, 2019 is the result of our systematic analysis on three basic characteristics: earnings strength, relative valuation, and recent stock price movement. The company has managed to produce a neutral trend in earnings per share over the past 5 quarters. Additionally, recent analyst estimates for the company have been unchanged while NEU has posted results that exceeded analysts' expectations. Based on operating earnings yield, the company is fairly valued when compared to all of the companies we cover. Share price changes over the past year indicates that NEU will perform well over the near term.

Financial Data

(US$ in Thousands)	9 Mos	6 Mos	3 Mos	12/31/2018	12/31/2017	12/31/2016	12/31/2015	12/31/2014
Earnings Per Share	23.82	22.88	20.78	20.34	16.08	20.54	19.45	18.38
Cash Flow Per Share	29.55	25.32	18.54	17.19	20.53	29.80	21.90	18.54
Tang Book Value Per Share	44.37	40.69	36.03	31.64	38.82	39.91	31.52	32.47
Dividends Per Share	7.150	7.000	7.000	7.000	7.000	6.400	5.800	4.700
Dividend Payout %	30.02	30.59	33.69	34.41	43.53	31.16	29.82	25.57
Income Statement								
Total Revenue	1,655,850	1,100,033	536,616	2,289,675	2,198,404	2,049,451	2,140,830	2,335,405
EBITDA	353,197	236,968	110,759	380,008	388,298	401,993	388,623	389,666
Depn & Amortn	65,500	43,716	21,939	63,000	51,000	42,000	35,000	34,000
Income Before Taxes	264,957	177,499	80,808	290,285	315,442	343,208	338,971	339,099
Income Taxes	60,773	41,120	18,603	55,551	124,933	99,767	100,368	105,844
Net Income	204,184	136,379	62,205	234,734	190,509	243,441	238,603	233,255
Average Shares	11,167	11,166	11,166	11,515	11,824	11,828	12,241	12,671
Balance Sheet								
Current Assets	826,933	829,434	856,146	813,420	833,654	836,883	774,767	797,191
Total Assets	1,770,995	1,766,985	1,798,191	1,697,274	1,712,154	1,416,436	1,289,915	1,231,925
Current Liabilities	280,478	283,479	259,973	271,301	316,793	294,590	263,680	259,674
Long-Term Obligations	639,983	678,803	782,024	770,999	602,900	507,275	494,586	363,526
Total Liabilities	1,141,657	1,177,809	1,259,995	1,207,367	1,110,505	933,185	902,351	810,884
Stockholders' Equity	629,338	589,176	538,196	489,907	601,649	483,251	387,564	421,041
Shares Outstanding	11,189	11,188	11,188	11,184	11,779	11,845	11,948	12,446
Statistical Record								
Return on Assets %	14.79	14.55	13.21	13.77	12.18	17.94	18.92	18.23
Return on Equity %	44.74	45.14	39.63	43.01	35.12	55.76	59.02	46.96
EBITDA Margin %	21.33	21.54	20.64	16.60	17.66	19.61	18.15	16.69
Net Margin %	12.33	12.40	11.59	10.25	8.67	11.88	11.15	9.99
Asset Turnover	1.22	1.24	1.25	1.34	1.41	1.51	1.70	1.83
Current Ratio	2.95	2.93	3.29	3.00	2.63	2.84	2.94	3.07
Debt to Equity	1.02	1.15	1.45	1.57	1.00	1.05	1.28	0.86
Price Range	483.94-363.17	450.07-363.17	450.07-361.42	435.54-361.42	476.18-381.23	442.62-324.89	480.33-354.59	413.39-311.61
P/E Ratio	20.32-15.25	19.67-15.87	21.66-17.39	21.41-17.77	29.61-23.71	21.55-15.82	24.70-18.23	22.49-16.95
Average Yield %	1.70	1.72	1.74	1.76	1.61	1.59	1.36	1.23

Address: 330 South Fourth Street, Richmond, VA 23219-4350
Telephone: 804-788-5000

Web Site: www.newmarket.com
Officers: Thomas E. (Teddy) Gottwald - Chairman, President, Chief Executive Officer Bruce R. Hazelgrove - Executive Vice President, Vice President, Chief Administrative Officer

Auditors: PricewaterhouseCoopers LLP
Investor Contact: 804-788-5555
Transfer Agents: ComputerShare Investor Services, Providence, RI

NEWMONT CORP

Exchange	Symbol	Price	52Wk Range	Yield	P/E
NYS	NEM	$43.45 (12/31/2019)	43.75-29.93	1.29	15.57

*7 Year Price Score 96.51   *NYSE Composite Index=100   *12 Month Price Score 102.84

Interim Earnings (Per Share)

Qtr.	Mar	Jun	Sep	Dec
2016	0.10	0.04	(0.67)	(0.65)
2017	0.09	0.33	0.38	(0.98)
2018	0.36	0.54	(0.27)	0.01
2019	0.16	(0.03)	2.65	...

Interim Dividends (Per Share)

Amt	Decl	Ex	Rec	Pay
0.88Q	03/23/2019	04/16/2019	04/17/2019	05/01/2019
0.14Q	04/24/2019	06/05/2019	06/06/2019	06/20/2019
0.14Q	07/24/2019	09/11/2019	09/12/2019	09/26/2019
0.14Q	10/22/2019	12/04/2019	12/05/2019	12/27/2019

Indicated Div: $0.56

Valuation Analysis

		Institutional Holding	
Forecast EPS	$1.30	No of Institutions	
(01/17/2020)		1136	
Market Cap	$35.6 Billion	Shares	
Book Value	$21.4 Billion	797,113,408	
Price/Book	1.66	% Held	
Price/Sales	4.04	81.08	

Business Summary: Precious Metals (MIC: 8.2.1 SIC: 1041 NAIC: 212221)

Newmont is a gold producer with operations and/or assets in the U.S., Australia, Peru, Ghana and Suriname. Co. also produces copper, principally through operations in Boddington in Australia and Phoenix in the U.S. Co.'s regions include North America, South America, Australia, and Africa. Co.'s North America segment consists primarily of Carlin, Phoenix, Twin Creeks, Long Canyon and Cripple Creek &Victor in the U.S. Co.'s South America segment consists primarily of Yanacocha in Peru and Merian in Suriname. Co.'s Australia segment consists primarily of Boddington, Tanami and Kalgoorlie in Australia. Co.'s Africa segment consists primarily of Ahafo and Akyem in Ghana.

Recent Developments: For the quarter ended Sep 30 2019, income from continuing operations was US$2.25 billion compared with a loss of US$140.0 million in the year-earlier quarter. Net income amounted to US$2.20 billion versus a net loss of US$124.0 million in the year-earlier quarter. Revenues were US$2.71 billion, up 57.2% from US$1.73 billion the year before. Direct operating expenses rose 39.9% to US$1.39 billion from US$995.0 million in the comparable period the year before. Indirect operating expenses increased 2.1% to US$863.0 million from US$845.0 million in the equivalent prior-year period.

Prospects: Our evaluation of Newmont Goldcorp Corp. as of October 4th, 2019 is the result of our systematic analysis on three basic characteristics: earnings strength, relative valuation, and recent stock price movement. The company has generated a negative trend in earnings per share over the past 5 quarters. However, recent analyst estimates for the company have been raised and NEM has posted results that fell short of analysts' expectations. Based on operating earnings yield, the company is fairly valued when compared to all of the companies we cover. Share price changes over the past year indicates that NEM will perform over the near term.

Financial Data

(US$ in Thousands)	9 Mos	6 Mos	3 Mos	12/31/2018	12/31/2017	12/31/2016	12/31/2015	12/31/2014
Earnings Per Share	2.79	(0.13)	0.44	0.64	(0.18)	(1.18)	0.43	1.02
Cash Flow Per Share	2.93	2.66	4.00	3.43	4.38	5.24	4.16	2.88
Tang Book Value Per Share	22.38	20.98	19.55	19.70	19.90	20.21	21.14	20.17
Dividends Per Share	1.440	1.440	0.560	0.560	0.250	0.125	0.100	0.225
Dividend Payout %	51.61	...	127.27	87.50	...	...	23.26	22.06
Income Statement								
Total Revenue	6,773,000	4,060,000	1,803,000	7,253,000	7,348,000	6,711,000	7,729,000	7,292,000
EBITDA	4,593,000	1,200,000	624,000	2,104,000	2,554,000	1,279,000	2,530,000	2,092,000
Depn & Amortn	1,347,000	799,000	312,000	1,215,000	1,249,000	1,220,000	1,239,000	1,229,000
Income Before Taxes	3,073,000	295,000	275,000	738,000	1,092,000	(214,000)	966,000	506,000
Income Taxes	703,000	145,000	125,000	386,000	1,125,000	563,000	644,000	133,000
Net Income	2,240,000	62,000	87,000	341,000	(98,000)	(627,000)	220,000	508,000
Average Shares	822,000	768,000	534,000	535,000	535,000	532,000	516,000	499,000
Balance Sheet								
Current Assets	5,698,000	4,638,000	5,397,000	5,277,000	5,066,000	4,677,000	4,983,000	5,439,000
Total Assets	40,763,000	36,987,000	20,880,000	20,715,000	20,563,000	21,031,000	25,182,000	24,916,000
Current Liabilities	2,611,000	2,538,000	1,815,000	1,787,000	1,395,000	1,750,000	1,416,000	2,198,000
Long-Term Obligations	6,739,000	6,057,000	3,688,000	3,608,000	4,061,000	4,049,000	6,087,000	6,480,000
Total Liabilities	19,333,000	17,633,000	10,381,000	10,213,000	9,954,000	10,310,000	13,832,000	14,642,000
Stockholders' Equity	21,430,000	19,354,000	10,499,000	10,502,000	10,609,000	10,721,000	11,350,000	10,274,000
Shares Outstanding	819,838	819,893	537,000	533,000	533,085	530,465	529,650	498,670
Statistical Record								
Return on Assets %	7.31	N.M.	1.14	1.65	N.M.	N.M.	0.88	2.05
Return on Equity %	14.00	N.M.	2.24	3.23	N.M.	N.M.	2.03	4.98
EBITDA Margin %	67.81	29.56	34.61	29.01	34.76	19.06	32.73	28.69
Net Margin %	33.07	1.53	4.83	4.70	N.M.	N.M.	2.85	6.97
Asset Turnover	0.29	0.27	0.35	0.35	0.35	0.29	0.31	0.29
Current Ratio	2.18	1.83	2.97	2.95	3.63	2.67	3.52	2.47
Debt to Equity	0.31	0.31	0.35	0.34	0.38	0.38	0.54	0.63
Price Range	41.02-29.60	38.47-29.60	41.94-29.60	41.94-29.60	39.60-31.89	45.86-16.31	27.69-15.55	27.09-17.78
P/E Ratio	14.70-10.61		95.32-67.27	65.53-46.25	...	...	64.40-36.16	26.56-17.43
Average Yield %	4.14	4.30	1.60	1.55	0.71	0.38	0.47	0.96

Address: 6363 South Fiddlers Green Circle, Greenwood Village, CO 80111	Web Site: www.newmont.com	Auditors: Ernst & Young LLP
Telephone: 303-863-7414	Officers: Noreen Doyle - Chair Thomas R. Palmer - President, Chief Operating Officer	Investor Contact: 303-837-5362
Fax: 303-837-5837		Transfer Agents: Computershare, Providence, RI

NEXTERA ENERGY INC

Exchange	Symbol	Price	52Wk Range	Yield	P/E	Div Acheiver
NYS	NEE	$242.16 (12/31/2019)	242.71-169.41	2.06	36.52	23 Years

*7 Year Price Score 131.41 *NYSE Composite Index=100 *12 Month Price Score 106.25

Interim Earnings (Per Share)

Qtr.	Mar	Jun	Sep	Dec
2016	1.41	1.16	1.62	2.06
2017	3.37	1.68	1.79	4.55
2018	9.32	1.64	2.10	0.85
2019	1.41	2.56	1.81	...

Interim Dividends (Per Share)

Amt	Decl	Ex	Rec	Pay
1.25Q	02/15/2019	02/27/2019	02/28/2019	03/15/2019
1.25Q	05/23/2019	05/31/2019	06/03/2019	06/17/2019
1.25Q	07/25/2019	08/28/2019	08/29/2019	09/16/2019
1.25Q	10/18/2019	11/27/2019	11/29/2019	12/16/2019
	Indicated Div: $5.00 (Div. Reinv. Plan)			

Valuation Analysis / **Institutional Holding**

Forecast EPS	$8.38	No of Institutions
	(01/17/2020)	2187
Market Cap	$118.4 Billion	Shares
Book Value	$36.6 Billion	464,173,568
Price/Book	3.23	% Held
Price/Sales	6.23	N/A

TRADING VOLUME (thousand shares)

Business Summary: Electric Utilities (MIC: 3.1.1 SIC: 4911 NAIC: 221121)

NextEra Energy is a holding company, engaged in electric power and energy infrastructure. Co. has two principal businesses, Florida Power & Light Company (FPL) and NextEra Energy Resources, LLC (NEER). FPL is engaged primarily in the generation, transmission, distribution and sale of electric energy in Florida. NEER is a clean energy company, which emphasizes on the development, construction and operation of long-term contracted assets with a focus on renewable projects. Through its subsidiaries, NEER owns, develops, constructs, manages and operates electric generation facilities in wholesale energy markets primarily in the U.S., as well as in Canada and Spain.

Recent Developments: For the quarter ended Sep 30 2019, net income decreased 15.2% to US$798.0 million from US$941.0 million in the year-earlier quarter. Revenues were US$5.57 billion, up 26.2% from US$4.42 billion the year before. Operating income was US$1.59 billion versus US$968.0 million in the prior-year quarter, an increase of 64.6%. Direct operating expenses rose 11.3% to US$2.13 billion from US$1.91 billion in the comparable period the year before. Indirect operating expenses increased 20.5% to US$1.85 billion from US$1.54 billion in the equivalent prior-year period.

Prospects: Our evaluation of NextEra Energy Inc. as of October 4th, 2019 is the result of our systematic analysis on three basic characteristics: earnings strength, relative valuation, and recent stock price movement. The company has produced a positive trend in earnings per share over the past 5 quarters. However, recent analyst estimates for the company have been unchanged, while NEE has posted results that exceeded analysts' expectations. Based on operating earnings yield, the company is fairly valued when compared to all of the companies we cover. Share price changes over the past year indicates that NEE will perform well over the near term.

Financial Data

(US$ in Thousands)	9 Mos	6 Mos	3 Mos	12/31/2018	12/31/2017	12/31/2016	12/31/2015	12/31/2014
Earnings Per Share	6.63	6.92	6.00	13.88	11.38	6.25	6.06	5.60
Cash Flow Per Share	15.79	14.49	14.43	13.93	13.68	13.64	13.58	12.66
Tang Book Value Per Share	66.42	65.57	64.18	71.43	59.89	52.01	48.97	44.96
Dividends Per Share	4.860	4.720	4.580	4.440	3.930	3.480	3.080	2.900
Dividend Payout %	73.30	68.21	76.33	31.99	34.53	55.68	50.83	51.79
Income Statement								
Total Revenue	14,616,000	9,044,000	4,075,000	16,727,000	17,195,000	16,155,000	17,486,000	17,021,000
EBITDA	5,090,000	3,395,000	1,456,000	12,492,000	8,540,000	8,542,000	8,141,000	7,592,000
Depn & Amortn	190,000	172,000	90,000	4,147,000	2,629,000	3,377,000	3,203,000	2,896,000
Income Before Taxes	2,880,000	1,933,000	664,000	6,994,000	4,526,000	4,240,000	3,883,000	3,552,000
Income Taxes	256,000	198,000	74,000	1,576,000	(653,000)	1,383,000	1,228,000	1,176,000
Net Income	2,794,000	1,914,000	680,000	6,638,000	5,378,000	2,912,000	2,762,000	2,469,000
Average Shares	486,000	482,800	481,800	477,000	472,500	465,800	454,000	440,100
Balance Sheet								
Current Assets	7,679,000	7,471,000	8,222,000	6,393,000	7,157,000	7,409,000	6,795,000	6,944,000
Total Assets	114,222,000	110,552,000	109,029,000	103,702,000	97,827,000	89,993,000	82,479,000	74,929,000
Current Liabilities	13,314,000	14,412,000	17,926,000	17,563,000	11,232,000	10,919,000	10,107,000	9,663,000
Long-Term Obligations	36,144,000	33,947,000	29,883,000	26,782,000	31,463,000	27,818,000	26,681,000	24,367,000
Total Liabilities	77,630,000	75,642,000	74,803,000	69,558,000	69,619,000	65,652,000	59,905,000	55,013,000
Stockholders' Equity	36,592,000	34,910,000	34,226,000	34,144,000	28,208,000	24,341,000	22,574,000	19,916,000
Shares Outstanding	488,775	479,102	478,935	478,000	471,000	468,000	461,000	443,000
Statistical Record								
Return on Assets %	3.01	3.23	2.84	6.59	5.73	3.37	3.51	3.42
Return on Equity %	9.04	9.80	8.64	21.29	20.47	12.38	13.00	13.01
EBITDA Margin %	34.82	37.54	35.73	74.68	49.67	52.88	46.56	44.60
Net Margin %	19.12	21.16	16.69	39.68	31.28	18.03	15.80	14.51
Asset Turnover	0.18	0.17	0.17	0.17	0.18	0.19	0.22	0.24
Current Ratio	0.58	0.52	0.46	0.36	0.64	0.68	0.67	0.72
Debt to Equity	0.99	0.97	0.87	0.78	1.12	1.14	1.18	1.22
Price Range	232.99-166.99	208.20-164.45	195.00-155.40	182.98-145.29	159.25-118.35	130.89-103.57	111.66-94.62	110.50-84.25
P/E Ratio	35.14-25.19	30.09-23.76	32.50-25.90	13.18-10.47	13.99-10.40	20.94-16.57	18.43-15.61	19.73-15.04
Average Yield %	2.52	2.60	2.66	2.69	2.79	2.91	3.00	3.01

Address: 700 Universe Boulevard, Juno Beach, FL 33408	Web Site: www.nexteraenergy.com	Auditors: DELOITTE & TOUCHE LLP
Telephone: 561-694-4000	Officers: James L. Robo - Chairman, President, Chief Executive Officer, Chief Operating Officer Rebecca J. Kujawa - Executive Vice President, Chief Financial Officer, Principal Financial Officer	Investor Contact: 561-694-4697
Fax: 561-694-4620		Transfer Agents: Computershare Trust Company, N.A., Canton, MA

NGL ENERGY PARTNERS LP

Exchange	Symbol	Price	52Wk Range	Yield	P/E
NYS	NGL	$11.34 (12/31/2019)	15.50-9.59	13.76	N/A

*7 Year Price Score 51.06   *NYSE Composite Index=100   *12 Month Price Score 77.44

Interim Earnings (Per Share)

Qtr.	Jun	Sep	Dec	Mar
2016-17	1.38	(0.71)	(0.07)	0.13
2017-18	(0.61)	(1.56)	0.32	0.76
2018-19	(1.55)	2.70	0.64	0.19
2019-20	(0.96)	(1.72)	...	...

Interim Dividends (Per Share)

Amt	Decl	Ex	Rec	Pay
0.39Q	01/23/2019	02/05/2019	02/06/2019	02/14/2019
0.39Q	04/24/2019	05/06/2019	05/07/2019	05/15/2019
0.39Q	07/23/2019	08/06/2019	08/07/2019	08/14/2019
0.39Q	10/24/2019	11/06/2019	11/07/2019	11/14/2019

Indicated Div: $1.56

Valuation Analysis

		Institutional Holding	
Forecast EPS	$-2.25	No of Institutions	
	(01/17/2020)	150	
Market Cap	$1.5 Billion	Shares	
Book Value	N/A	101,218,384	
Price/Book	N/A	% Held	
Price/Sales	0.06	64.28	

Business Summary: Equipment & Services (MIC: 9.1.3 SIC: 5172 NAIC: 424720)

NGL Energy Partners is a limited partnership company. Co.'s operations include: Crude Oil Logistics, which purchases crude oil from producers and transports it to refineries or for resale; Water Solutions, which provides services for the treatment and disposal of wastewater generated from crude oil and natural gas production; Liquids, which supplies natural gas liquids to retailers, wholesalers, refiners, and petrochemical plants; and Refined Products and Renewables, which conducts gasoline, diesel, ethanol, and biodiesel marketing operations, purchases refined petroleum and renewable products primarily in the Gulf Coast, Southeast and Midwest regions of the U.S.

Recent Developments: For the quarter ended Sep 30 2019, net loss amounted to US$201.4 million versus net income of US$354.9 million in the year-earlier quarter. Revenues were US$4.29 billion, down 16.2% from US$5.12 billion the year before. Operating income was US$46.4 million versus US$14.3 million in the prior-year quarter, an increase of 223.4%. Direct operating expenses declined 18.0% to US$4.06 billion from US$4.95 billion in the comparable period the year before. Indirect operating expenses increased 18.6% to US$185.6 million from US$156.4 million in the equivalent prior-year period.

Prospects: On April 17, 2017, we entered into a purchase and sale agreement with the party owning the 50% noncontrolling interest in NGL Solids Solutions, LLC. Total consideration was $23.1 million, which consisted of cash of $20.0 million and the termination of a non-compete agreement that we valued at $3.1 million and in return we received the following, the remaining 50% interest in NGL Solids Solutions, LLC; and two parcels of land to develop saltwater disposal wells.

Financial Data

(US$ in Thousands)	6 Mos	3 Mos	03/31/2019	03/31/2018	03/31/2017	03/31/2016	03/31/2015	03/31/2014
Earnings Per Share	(1.85)	2.57	2.01	(1.08)	0.95	(2.35)	(0.29)	0.51
Cash Flow Per Share	3.31	3.56	2.74	1.14	(0.25)	3.34	3.04	1.38
Dividends Per Share	1.560	1.560	1.560	1.560	1.560	2.538	2.366	2.014
Dividend Payout %	...	60.70	77.61	...	164.21	...	...	394.85
Income Statement								
Total Revenue	9,455,761	6,637,891	24,016,907	17,282,718	13,022,228	11,742,110	16,802,057	9,699,274
EBITDA	140,612	73,449	202,017	252,267	412,914	66,442	229,982	166,551
Depn & Amortn	56,790	25,821	102,314	128,808	119,707	136,938	105,700	59,900
Income Before Taxes	(1,088)	7,720	(65,023)	(76,111)	142,729	(203,585)	14,159	47,797
Income Taxes	319	(311)	1,234	1,458	1,939	(367)	(3,622)	937
Net Income	(192,930)	8,307	360,047	(70,875)	137,042	(198,929)	16,661	47,655
Average Shares	126,979	125,886	123,017	120,991	111,850	104,838	86,359	61,970
Balance Sheet								
Current Assets	1,531,198	1,649,288	1,812,673	1,799,758	1,484,207	1,028,480	1,645,344	1,309,299
Total Assets	6,664,023	6,394,905	5,902,493	6,151,122	6,320,379	5,560,155	6,547,501	4,167,223
Current Liabilities	1,298,510	1,157,438	1,251,153	1,116,382	938,598	706,017	1,112,996	995,792
Long-Term Obligations	2,773,235	2,586,954	2,160,133	2,682,628	2,963,483	2,912,837	2,745,299	1,629,834
Total Liabilities	4,669,893	4,303,120	3,533,609	4,065,954	4,116,433	3,903,797	4,421,707	2,640,644
Stockholders' Equity	...	...	149,814	82,576	63,890	...	...	...
Shares Outstanding	128,040	125,966	124,633	121,594	120,299	104,273	103,898	79,420
Statistical Record								
Return on Assets %	N.M.	8.44	5.97	N.M.	2.31	N.M.	0.31	1.48
Return on Equity %	...	...	309.86	N.M.	...	...	...	...
EBITDA Margin %	1.49	1.11	0.84	1.46	3.17	0.57	1.37	1.72
Net Margin %	N.M.	0.13	1.50	N.M.	1.05	N.M.	0.10	0.49
Asset Turnover	3.44	3.90	3.99	2.77	2.19	1.93	3.14	3.00
Current Ratio	1.18	1.42	1.45	1.61	1.58	1.46	1.48	1.31
Debt to Equity	...	...	14.42	32.49	46.38	...	...	...
Price Range	15.50-8.93	15.03-8.93	14.03-8.93	23.15-8.70	25.75-7.18	33.63-5.70	45.67-23.44	37.72-26.65
P/E Ratio	...	5.85-3.47	6.98-4.44	...	27.11-7.56	...	...	73.96-52.25
Average Yield %	12.22	12.71	13.43	11.71	8.47	12.60	6.56	6.37

Address: 6120 South Yale Avenue, Suite 805, Tulsa, OK 74136 **Telephone:** 918-481-1119	**Web Site:** www.nglenergypartners.com **Officers:** Robert W. (Trey) Karlovich - Executive Vice President, Chief Financial Officer, Treasurer, Associate/Affiliate Company Officer Kurston Patrick McMurray - Executive Vice President, Corporate Secretary, General Counsel	**Auditors:** Grant Thornton LLP **Investor Contact:** 918-481-1119 **Transfer Agents:** Wells Fargo Bank, N.A., St. Paul, MN

NIELSEN HOLDINGS PLC

Exchange	Symbol	Price	52Wk Range	Yield	P/E
NYS	NLSN	$20.30 (12/31/2019)	27.42-19.47	1.18	N/A

*7 Year Price Score 49.29   *NYSE Composite Index=100   *12 Month Price Score 83.13

Interim Earnings (Per Share)

Qtr.	Mar	Jun	Sep	Dec
2016	0.27	0.31	0.36	0.45
2017	0.20	0.37	0.41	0.23
2018	0.20	0.20	0.27	(2.67)
2019	0.12	0.34	(1.33)	...

Interim Dividends (Per Share)

Amt	Decl	Ex	Rec	Pay
0.35Q	02/22/2019	03/06/2019	03/07/2019	03/21/2019
0.35Q	04/19/2019	06/04/2019	06/05/2019	06/19/2019
0.35Q	07/18/2019	08/21/2019	08/22/2019	09/05/2019
0.06Q	11/07/2019	11/20/2019	11/21/2019	12/05/2019

Indicated Div: $0.24

Valuation Analysis   **Institutional Holding**

Forecast EPS	N/A	No of Institutions 529
Market Cap	$7.2 Billion	Shares
Book Value	$2.2 Billion	442,981,600
Price/Book	3.35	% Held
Price/Sales	1.12	N/A

Business Summary: Business Services (MIC: 7.5.2 SIC: 7389 NAIC: 561499)

Nielsen Holdings is an information and measurement company that provides clients with an understanding of consumers and consumer behavior. Co. aligns its business into two reporting segments: Buy, which provides retail transactional measurement data, consumer behavior information and analytics primarily to businesses in the consumer packaged goods industry; and Watch, which provides viewership and listening data and analytics primarily to the media and advertising industries across the television, radio, print, online, digital, mobile viewing and listening platforms.

Recent Developments: For the quarter ended Sep 30 2019, net loss amounted to US$468.0 million versus net income of US$98.0 million in the year-earlier quarter. Revenues were US$1.62 billion, up 1.0% from US$1.60 billion the year before. Operating loss was US$740.0 million versus an income of US$261.0 million in the prior-year quarter. Direct operating expenses rose 1.9% to US$694.0 million from US$681.0 million in the comparable period the year before. Indirect operating expenses increased 152.6% to US$1.66 billion from US$658.0 million in the equivalent prior-year period.

Prospects: Our evaluation of Nielsen Holdings PLC as of October 4th, 2019 is the result of our systematic analysis on three basic characteristics: earnings strength, relative valuation, and recent stock price movement. The company has produced a positive trend in earnings per share over the past 5 quarters. However, recent analyst estimates for the company have been mixed and NLSN has posted results that exceeded analysts' expectations. Based on operating earnings yield, the company is fairly valued when compared to all of the companies we cover. Share price changes over the past year indicates that NLSN will perform poorly over the near term.

Financial Data

(US$ in Millions)	9 Mos	6 Mos	3 Mos	12/31/2018	12/31/2017	12/31/2016	12/31/2015	12/31/2014
Earnings Per Share	(3.54)	(1.94)	(2.08)	(2.00)	1.20	1.39	1.54	1.00
Cash Flow Per Share	3.21	3.14	3.18	2.98	3.67	3.60	3.21	2.88
Dividends Per Share	1.400	1.400	1.400	1.390	1.330	1.210	1.090	0.950
Dividend Payout %	...	...	...	...	110.83	87.05	70.78	95.00
Income Statement								
Total Revenue	4,807	3,191	1,563	6,515	6,572	6,309	6,172	6,288
EBITDA	225	788	355	(327)	1,369	1,310	1,428	1,080
Depn & Amortn	550	364	179	169	171	165	160	162
Income Before Taxes	(620)	228	79	(882)	828	816	961	621
Income Taxes	(325)	55	32	(182)	388	309	383	236
Net Income	(306)	166	43	(712)	429	502	570	384
Average Shares	355	356	356	355	358	362	370	384
Balance Sheet								
Current Assets	1,947	2,026	2,047	2,003	2,282	2,222	1,908	2,019
Total Assets	14,343	15,588	15,742	15,179	16,866	15,730	15,303	15,376
Current Liabilities	1,775	1,889	1,917	1,657	1,697	1,594	1,687	1,798
Long-Term Obligations	8,189	8,233	8,242	8,280	8,357	7,738	7,028	6,465
Total Liabilities	12,188	12,799	12,952	12,332	12,621	11,628	10,870	10,320
Stockholders' Equity	2,155	2,789	2,790	2,847	4,245	4,102	4,433	5,056
Shares Outstanding	355	355	355	355	355	357	362	372
Statistical Record								
Return on Assets %	N.M.	N.M.	N.M.	N.M.	2.63	3.23	3.72	2.48
Return on Equity %	N.M.	N.M.	N.M.	N.M.	10.28	11.73	12.01	7.12
EBITDA Margin %	4.68	24.69	22.71	N.M.	20.83	20.76	23.14	17.18
Net Margin %	N.M.	5.20	2.75	N.M.	6.53	7.96	9.24	6.11
Asset Turnover	0.42	0.40	0.40	0.41	0.40	0.41	0.40	0.41
Current Ratio	1.10	1.07	1.07	1.21	1.34	1.39	1.13	1.12
Debt to Equity	3.80	2.95	2.95	2.91	1.97	1.89	1.59	1.28
Price Range	28.19-20.02	31.88-21.75	34.70-21.75	38.51-21.75	45.50-35.67	55.81-41.95	49.06-42.20	49.51-41.04
P/E Ratio	...	...	...	...	37.92-29.73	40.15-30.18	31.86-27.40	49.51-41.04
Average Yield %	5.72	5.44	5.09	4.69	3.32	2.42	2.39	2.10

Address: 85 Broad Street, New York, NY 10004 **Telephone:** 646-654-5000	**Web Site:** www.nielsen.com **Officers:** James A. Attwood - Executive Chairman, Chairman David W. Kenny - Chief Executive Officer, Principal Executive Officer	**Auditors:** Ernst & Young LLP **Investor Contact:** 646-654-4602 **Transfer Agents:** Computershare

499

NIKE INC

*7 Year Price Score 124.98 ***NYSE Composite Index=100** ***12 Month Price Score 103.33**

Interim Earnings (Per Share)

Qtr.	Aug	Nov	Feb	May
2016-17	0.73	0.50	0.68	0.60
2017-18	0.57	0.46	(0.57)	0.69
2018-19	0.67	0.52	0.68	0.62
2019-20	0.86	0.70	...	...

Interim Dividends (Per Share)

Amt	Decl	Ex	Rec	Pay
0.22Q	02/14/2019	03/01/2019	03/04/2019	04/01/2019
0.22Q	05/09/2019	05/31/2019	06/03/2019	07/01/2019
0.22Q	08/08/2019	08/30/2019	09/03/2019	09/30/2019
0.245Q	11/14/2019	11/29/2019	12/02/2019	01/02/2020

Indicated Div: $0.98 (Div. Reinv. Plan)

Valuation Analysis

		Institutional Holding	
Forecast EPS	$3.01	No of Institutions	
	(01/17/2020)	2241	
Market Cap	$157.9 Billion	Shares	
Book Value	$9.4 Billion	1,200,420,352	
Price/Book	16.89	% Held	
Price/Sales	3.87	62.55	

Business Summary: Apparel, Footwear & Accessories (MIC: 1.4.2 SIC: 3021 NAIC: 316211)

NIKE is engaged in the design, development and marketing and selling of athletic footwear, apparel, equipment, accessories and services. Co. focuses its NIKE Brand product offerings in Running, NIKE Basketball, the Jordan Brand, Football (Soccer), Training and Sportswear categories. Co. markets products designed for kids, as well as for other athletic and recreational uses such as American football, baseball, cricket, golf, lacrosse, tennis, walking, and other outdoor activities. Co. has license agreements that permit unaffiliated parties to manufacture and sell, using Co.-owned trademarks, certain apparel, digital devices and applications and other equipment designed for sports activities.

Recent Developments: For the quarter ended Nov 30 2019, net income increased 31.6% to US$1.12 billion from US$847.0 million in the year-earlier quarter. Revenues were US$10.33 billion, up 10.2% from US$9.37 billion the year before. Direct operating expenses rose 9.7% to US$5.78 billion from US$5.27 billion in the comparable period the year before. Indirect operating expenses increased 6.0% to US$3.30 billion from US$3.11 billion in the equivalent prior-year period.

Prospects: Our evaluation of NIKE Inc. as of October 4th, 2019 is the result of our systematic analysis on three basic characteristics: earnings strength, relative valuation, and recent stock price movement. The company has produced a positive trend in earnings per share over the past 5 quarters. In addition, recent analyst estimates for the company have been raised, and NKE has posted results that exceeded analysts' expectations. Based on operating earnings yield, the company is fairly valued when compared to all of the companies we cover. Share price changes over the past year indicates that NKE will perform poorly over the near term.

Financial Data

(US$ in Thousands)	6 Mos	3 Mos	05/31/2019	05/31/2018	05/31/2017	05/31/2016	05/31/2015	05/31/2014
Earnings Per Share	2.86	2.68	2.49	1.17	2.51	2.16	1.85	1.49
Cash Flow Per Share	2.81	3.20	3.74	3.05	2.20	1.82	2.72	1.70
Tang Book Value Per Share	5.68	5.58	5.49	5.85	7.29	7.04	7.17	5.98
Dividends Per Share	0.905	0.880	0.860	0.760	0.680	0.620	0.540	0.465
Dividend Payout %	31.64	32.84	34.54	64.96	27.09	28.70	29.19	31.31
Income Statement								
Total Revenue	20,986,000	10,660,000	39,117,000	36,397,000	34,350,000	32,376,000	30,601,000	27,799,000
EBITDA	3,199,000	1,751,000	5,555,000	5,126,000	5,651,000	5,291,000	4,839,000	4,095,000
Depn & Amortn	362,000	175,000	705,000	747,000	706,000	649,000	606,000	518,000
Income Before Taxes	2,810,000	1,561,000	4,801,000	4,325,000	4,886,000	4,623,000	4,205,000	3,544,000
Income Taxes	328,000	194,000	772,000	2,392,000	646,000	863,000	932,000	851,000
Net Income	2,482,000	1,367,000	4,029,000	1,933,000	4,240,000	3,760,000	3,273,000	2,693,000
Average Shares	1,594,400	1,597,500	1,618,400	1,659,100	1,692,000	1,742,500	1,768,800	1,811,600
Balance Sheet								
Current Assets	16,369,000	16,228,000	16,525,000	15,134,000	16,061,000	15,025,000	15,976,000	13,696,000
Total Assets	26,602,000	26,249,000	23,717,000	22,536,000	23,259,000	21,396,000	21,600,000	18,594,000
Current Liabilities	8,264,000	8,070,000	7,866,000	6,040,000	5,474,000	5,358,000	6,334,000	5,027,000
Long-Term Obligations	3,462,000	3,463,000	3,464,000	3,468,000	3,471,000	2,010,000	1,079,000	1,199,000
Total Liabilities	17,251,000	17,049,000	14,677,000	12,724,000	10,852,000	9,138,000	8,893,000	7,770,000
Stockholders' Equity	9,351,000	9,200,000	9,040,000	9,812,000	12,407,000	12,258,000	12,707,000	10,824,000
Shares Outstanding	1,559,000	1,560,000	1,568,000	1,601,000	1,643,000	1,682,000	1,714,000	1,740,000
Statistical Record								
Return on Assets %	18.56	17.66	17.42	8.44	18.99	17.44	16.29	14.89
Return on Equity %	50.58	47.32	42.74	17.40	34.38	30.04	27.82	24.50
EBITDA Margin %	15.24	16.43	14.20	14.08	16.45	16.34	15.81	14.73
Net Margin %	11.83	12.82	10.30	5.31	12.34	11.61	10.70	9.69
Asset Turnover	1.66	1.63	1.69	1.59	1.54	1.50	1.52	1.54
Current Ratio	1.98	2.01	2.10	2.51	2.93	2.80	2.52	2.72
Debt to Equity	0.37	0.38	0.38	0.35	0.28	0.16	0.08	0.11
Price Range	96.22-67.53	89.48-67.53	89.20-67.53	72.25-50.83	60.22-49.62	67.17-50.67	52.49-37.27	39.93-29.98
P/E Ratio	33.64-23.61	33.39-25.20	35.82-27.12	61.75-43.44	23.99-19.77	31.09-23.46	28.37-20.15	26.80-20.12
Average Yield %	1.07	1.08	1.08	1.23	1.25	1.04	1.21	1.22

Address: One Bowerman Drive, Beaverton, OR 97005-6453	**Web Site:** www.nike.com
Telephone: 503-671-6453	**Officers:** Mark G. Parker - Executive Chairman, Chairman, President, Chief Executive Officer John J. Donahoe - President, Chief Executive Officer

Auditors: PricewaterhouseCoopers LLP
Transfer Agents: Computershare Trust Company, N.A., Providence, RI

NISOURCE INC. (HOLDING CO.)

Exchange	Symbol	Price	52Wk Range	Yield	P/E
NYS	NI	$27.84 (12/31/2019)	30.56-25.07	2.87	22.63

*7 Year Price Score 110.73 *NYSE Composite Index=100 *12 Month Price Score 91.15

Interim Earnings (Per Share)

Qtr.	Mar	Jun	Sep	Dec
2016	0.56	0.09	0.08	0.27
2017	0.65	(0.14)	0.04	(0.16)
2018	0.81	0.07	(0.95)	(0.05)
2019	0.55	0.75	(0.02)	...

Interim Dividends (Per Share)

Amt	Decl	Ex	Rec	Pay
0.20Q	02/01/2019	02/08/2019	02/11/2019	02/20/2019
0.20Q	03/19/2019	04/29/2019	04/30/2019	05/20/2019
0.20Q	07/30/2019	07/31/2019	07/31/2019	08/20/2019
0.20Q	08/06/2019	10/30/2019	10/31/2019	11/20/2019

Indicated Div: $0.80

Valuation Analysis

		Institutional Holding	
Forecast EPS	$1.29	No of Institutions	738
	(01/17/2020)		
Market Cap	$10.4 Billion	Shares	
Book Value	$5.8 Billion		399,683,360
Price/Book	1.78	% Held	
Price/Sales	1.97		91.88

Business Summary: Gas Utilities (MIC: 3.3.1 SIC: 4924 NAIC: 221210)

NiSource is an energy holding company. Through its subsidiaries, Co. is a natural gas distribution company. Co.'s reportable segments are: Gas Distribution Operations and Electric Operations. For its gas distribution operations, through its wholly-owned subsidiary, NiSource Gas Distribution Group, Inc., Co. owns distribution subsidiaries that provide natural gas to residential, commercial and industrial customers in Ohio, Pennsylvania, Virginia, Kentucky, Maryland and Massachusetts. Through its electric operations, Co. generates, transmits and distributes electricity through its subsidiary, Northern Indiana Public Service Company LLC, and engages in wholesale and transmission transactions.

Recent Developments: For the quarter ended Sep 30 2019, net income amounted to US$6.6 million versus a net loss of US$339.5 million in the year-earlier quarter. Revenues were US$931.5 million, up 4.1% from US$895.0 million the year before. Operating income was US$91.0 million versus a loss of US$315.9 million in the prior-year quarter. Direct operating expenses declined 11.4% to US$196.7 million from US$222.0 million in the comparable period the year before. Indirect operating expenses decreased 34.9% to US$643.8 million from US$988.9 million in the equivalent prior-year period.

Prospects: Our evaluation of NiSource Inc. as of October 4th, 2019 is the result of our systematic analysis on three basic characteristics: earnings strength, relative valuation, and recent stock price movement. The company has produced a positive trend in earnings per share over the past 5 quarters. However, recent analyst estimates for the company have been mixed and NI has posted results that fell short of analysts' expectations. Based on operating earnings yield, the company is fairly valued when compared to all of the companies we cover. Share price changes over the past year indicates that NI will perform well over the near term.

Financial Data

(US$ in Thousands)	9 Mos	6 Mos	3 Mos	12/31/2018	12/31/2017	12/31/2016	12/31/2015	12/31/2014
Earnings Per Share	1.23	0.30	(0.38)	(0.18)	0.39	1.02	0.90	1.67
Cash Flow Per Share	2.26	1.76	1.48	1.52	2.25	2.49	4.58	4.19
Tang Book Value Per Share	8.21	8.55	8.02	7.95	7.11	6.62	5.95	7.10
Dividends Per Share	0.795	0.790	0.785	0.780	0.700	0.640	0.830	1.020
Dividend Payout %	64.63	263.33	...	...	179.49	62.75	92.22	61.08
Income Statement								
Total Revenue	3,811,700	2,880,200	1,869,800	5,114,500	4,874,600	4,492,500	4,651,800	6,470,600
EBITDA	1,464,200	1,189,700	548,600	677,000	1,369,400	1,411,000	1,252,400	1,849,800
Depn & Amortn	535,200	353,000	175,100	607,100	577,700	554,700	533,100	615,500
Income Before Taxes	643,400	647,000	277,900	(230,600)	443,100	510,200	339,900	794,500
Income Taxes	121,000	131,200	59,000	(180,000)	314,500	182,100	141,300	310,400
Net Income	522,400	515,800	218,900	(50,600)	128,500	331,500	286,500	530,000
Average Shares	374,100	375,232	374,656	356,500	330,800	323,500	319,836	316,600
Balance Sheet								
Current Assets	1,378,300	1,578,000	1,915,800	2,055,400	1,763,300	1,762,100	1,577,200	2,466,500
Total Assets	22,132,300	21,974,200	21,889,900	21,804,000	19,961,700	18,691,900	17,492,500	24,866,300
Current Liabilities	3,339,700	3,813,700	4,015,200	4,036,800	3,178,400	3,452,200	2,657,500	3,954,900
Long-Term Obligations	7,853,800	7,109,700	7,110,100	7,105,400	7,512,200	6,058,200	5,948,500	8,155,900
Total Liabilities	16,283,800	15,998,000	16,110,300	16,053,100	15,641,600	14,620,700	13,649,000	18,691,000
Stockholders' Equity	5,848,500	5,976,200	5,779,600	5,750,900	4,320,100	4,071,200	3,843,500	6,175,300
Shares Outstanding	373,446	373,249	373,002	372,363	337,015	323,159	319,110	316,037
Statistical Record								
Return on Assets %	2.38	0.78	N.M.	N.M.	0.66	1.83	1.35	2.23
Return on Equity %	9.35	2.88	N.M.	N.M.	3.06	8.35	5.72	8.79
EBITDA Margin %	38.41	41.31	29.34	13.24	28.09	31.41	26.92	28.59
Net Margin %	13.71	17.91	11.71	N.M.	2.64	7.38	6.16	8.19
Asset Turnover	0.25	0.25	0.25	0.24	0.25	0.25	0.22	0.27
Current Ratio	0.41	0.41	0.48	0.51	0.55	0.51	0.59	0.62
Debt to Equity	1.34	1.19	1.23	1.24	1.74	1.49	1.55	1.32
Price Range	30.56-24.31	29.44-24.31	28.82-23.27	28.08-22.51	27.58-21.84	26.77-19.46	19.83-16.10	17.41-12.69
P/E Ratio	24.85-19.76	98.13-81.03	...	...	70.72-56.00	26.25-19.08	22.03-17.88	10.43-7.60
Average Yield %	2.88	2.94	3.03	3.10	2.78	2.76	4.67	6.85

Address: 801 East 86th Avenue, Merrillville, IN 46410 Telephone: 877-647-5990	Web Site: www.nisource.com Officers: Kevin T. Kabat - Vice-Chairman, Chairman Joseph (Joe) Hamrock - President, Chief Executive Officer, Division Officer	Auditors: Deloitte & Touche LLP Investor Contact: 219-647-5200 Transfer Agents: Computershare, Providence, R.I.

NORDSTROM, INC.

Exchange	Symbol	Price	52Wk Range	Yield	P/E
NYS	JWN	$40.93 (12/31/2019)	49.29-25.15	3.62	12.00

*7 Year Price Score 56.57   *NYSE Composite Index=100   *12 Month Price Score 94.66

Interim Earnings (Per Share)

Qtr.	Apr	Jul	Oct	Jan
2016-17	0.26	0.67	(0.06)	1.15
2017-18	0.37	0.65	0.67	0.89
2018-19	0.52	0.95	0.39	1.47
2019-20	0.23	0.90	0.81	...

Interim Dividends (Per Share)

Amt	Decl	Ex	Rec	Pay
0.37Q	02/27/2019	03/08/2019	03/11/2019	03/26/2019
0.37Q	05/23/2019	05/31/2019	06/03/2019	06/18/2019
0.37Q	08/20/2019	08/29/2019	08/30/2019	09/16/2019
0.37Q	11/21/2019	11/27/2019	11/29/2019	12/16/2019

Indicated Div: $1.48

Valuation Analysis

		Institutional Holding	
Forecast EPS	$3.45	No of Institutions	
	(01/16/2020)	833	
Market Cap	$6.4 Billion	Shares	
Book Value	$851.0 Million	136,216,032	
Price/Book	7.46	% Held	
Price/Sales	0.41	61.42	

Business Summary: Retail - General Merchandise/Department Stores (MIC: 2.1.1 SIC: 5651 NAIC: 448140)

Nordstrom is a fashion retailer providing a selection of brand-name and private label apparel, shoes, cosmetics and accessories for women, men, young adults and children. Co. serves customers through two businesses: Full-Price and Off-Price. Co.'s operations consist of Co.'s Nordstrom U.S. and Canada full-line stores, U.S. and Canada Nordstrom Rack stores, Jeffrey boutiques, Last Chance clearance stores, Trunk Club clubhouses and Nordstrom Local. Additionally, customers are served online through Nordstrom.com, Nordstromrack.com, HauteLook and TrunkClub.com.

Recent Developments: For the quarter ended Nov 2 2019, net income increased 88.1% to US$126.0 million from US$67.0 million in the year-earlier quarter. Revenues were US$3.67 billion, down 2.0% from US$3.75 billion the year before. Operating income was US$193.0 million versus US$105.0 million in the prior-year quarter, an increase of 83.8%. Direct operating expenses declined 3.7% to US$2.34 billion from US$2.44 billion in the comparable period the year before. Indirect operating expenses decreased 6.0% to US$1.14 billion from US$1.21 billion in the equivalent prior-year period.

Prospects: Our evaluation of Nordstrom Inc. as of October 4th, 2019 is the result of our systematic analysis on three basic characteristics: earnings strength, relative valuation, and recent stock price movement. The company has managed to produce a neutral trend in earnings per share over the past 5 quarters. In addition, recent analyst estimates for the company have been mixed and JWN has posted results that exceeded analysts' expectations. Based on operating earnings yield, the company is undervalued when compared to all of the companies we cover. Share price changes over the past year indicates that JWN will perform very poorly over the near term.

Financial Data

(US$ in Thousands)	9 Mos	6 Mos	3 Mos	02/02/2019	02/03/2018	01/28/2017	01/30/2016	01/31/2015
Earnings Per Share	3.41	2.99	3.04	3.32	2.59	2.02	3.15	3.72
Cash Flow Per Share	7.88	8.99	8.34	7.77	8.26	9.54	13.19	6.44
Tang Book Value Per Share	N.M.	N.M.	N.M.	3.96	4.43	3.72	2.51	10.55
Dividends Per Share	1.480	1.480	1.480	1.480	1.480	1.480	6.330	1.320
Dividend Payout %	43.40	49.50	48.68	44.58	57.14	73.27	200.95	35.48
Income Statement								
Total Revenue	10,987,000	7,315,000	3,443,000	15,860,000	15,478,000	14,757,000	14,437,000	13,506,000
EBITDA	617,000	381,000	242,000	1,431,000	1,510,000	1,375,000	1,661,000	1,821,000
Depn & Amortn	132,000	89,000	165,000	594,000	584,000	570,000	560,000	498,000
Income Before Taxes	419,000	246,000	53,000	733,000	790,000	684,000	976,000	1,185,000
Income Taxes	115,000	69,000	16,000	169,000	353,000	330,000	376,000	465,000
Net Income	304,000	177,000	37,000	564,000	437,000	354,000	600,000	720,000
Average Shares	155,800	155,600	156,200	170,000	168,900	175,600	190,100	193,600
Balance Sheet								
Current Assets	3,573,000	3,483,000	2,958,000	3,374,000	3,503,000	3,242,000	3,014,000	5,224,000
Total Assets	10,075,000	9,935,000	9,338,000	7,886,000	8,115,000	7,858,000	7,698,000	9,245,000
Current Liabilities	3,981,000	4,425,000	3,892,000	3,381,000	3,289,000	3,029,000	2,911,000	2,800,000
Long-Term Obligations	2,679,000	2,178,000	2,177,000	2,677,000	2,681,000	2,763,000	2,795,000	3,123,000
Total Liabilities	9,224,000	9,176,000	8,687,000	7,013,000	7,138,000	6,988,000	6,827,000	6,805,000
Stockholders' Equity	851,000	759,000	651,000	873,000	977,000	870,000	871,000	2,440,000
Shares Outstanding	155,200	154,900	154,600	157,600	167,000	170,000	173,500	190,100
Statistical Record								
Return on Assets %	5.88	5.35	5.92	7.07	5.38	4.56	7.10	8.10
Return on Equity %	53.75	51.92	59.73	61.14	46.55	40.78	36.34	31.95
EBITDA Margin %	5.62	5.21	7.03	9.02	9.76	9.32	11.51	13.48
Net Margin %	2.77	2.42	1.07	3.56	2.82	2.40	4.16	5.33
Asset Turnover	1.65	1.69	1.81	1.99	1.91	1.90	1.71	1.52
Current Ratio	0.90	0.79	0.76	1.00	1.07	1.07	1.04	1.87
Debt to Equity	3.15	2.87	3.34	3.07	2.74	3.18	3.21	1.28
Price Range	67.46-25.15	67.46-28.76	67.46-40.29	67.46-44.19	52.82-38.30	61.49-36.20	82.32-45.45	79.78-55.38
P/E Ratio	19.78-7.38	22.56-9.62	22.19-13.25	20.32-13.31	20.39-14.79	30.44-17.92	26.13-14.43	21.45-14.89
Average Yield %	3.70	3.14	2.86	2.79	3.26	3.01	8.99	1.93

Address: 1617 Sixth Avenue, Seattle, WA 98101 **Telephone:** 206-628-2111	**Web Site:** www.nordstrom.com **Officers:** Peter E. Nordstrom - Co-President, Executive Vice President, Division Officer Erik B. Nordstrom - Co-President, Principal Executive Officer, Executive Vice President, Division Officer	**Auditors:** Deloitte & Touche LLP **Investor Contact:** 206-303-3200 **Transfer Agents:** Computershare, Providence, RI

NORFOLK SOUTHERN CORP

Exchange	Symbol	Price	52Wk Range	Yield	P/E
NYS	NSC	$194.13 (12/31/2019)	206.70-144.02	1.94	18.92

*7 Year Price Score 129.91 *NYSE Composite Index=100   *12 Month Price Score 98.07

Interim Earnings (Per Share)

Qtr.	Mar	Jun	Sep	Dec
2016	1.29	1.36	1.55	1.41
2017	1.48	1.71	1.75	13.68
2018	1.93	2.50	2.52	2.56
2019	2.51	2.70	2.49	...

Interim Dividends (Per Share)

Amt	Decl	Ex	Rec	Pay
0.86Q	01/23/2019	02/01/2019	02/04/2019	03/11/2019
0.86Q	04/23/2019	05/02/2019	05/03/2019	06/10/2019
0.94Q	07/26/2019	08/02/2019	08/05/2019	09/10/2019
0.94Q	10/22/2019	10/31/2019	11/01/2019	12/10/2019

Indicated Div: $3.76 (Div. Reinv. Plan)

Valuation Analysis   Institutional Holding

Forecast EPS	$10.01	No of Institutions
	(01/17/2020)	1870
Market Cap	$50.6 Billion	Shares
Book Value	$15.2 Billion	240,388,720
Price/Book	3.32	% Held
Price/Sales	4.40	65.19

Business Summary: Rail (MIC: 7.4.3 SIC: 4011 NAIC: 482111)

Norfolk Southern is a holding company. Through its subsidiaries, Co. is primarily engaged in the rail transportation of raw materials, intermediate products, and finished goods primarily in the Southeast, East, and Midwest and, via interchange with rail carriers, to and from the rest of the U.S. Co. also transports overseas freight through several Atlantic and Gulf Coast ports. Co. provides intermodal network in the eastern half of the U.S. Co.'s railroad operates in the states and the District of Columbia. Co.'s system reaches manufacturing plants, electric generating facilities, mines, distribution centers, transload facilities, and other businesses located in Co.'s service area.

Recent Developments: For the quarter ended Sep 30 2019, net income decreased 6.4% to US$657.0 million from US$702.0 million in the year-earlier quarter. Revenues were US$2.84 billion, down 3.6% from US$2.95 billion the year before. Operating income was US$996.0 million versus US$1.02 billion in the prior-year quarter, a decrease of 2.4%. Direct operating expenses declined 5.3% to US$877.0 million from US$926.0 million in the comparable period the year before. Indirect operating expenses decreased 3.3% to US$968.0 million from US$1.00 billion in the equivalent prior-year period.

Prospects: Our evaluation of Norfolk Southern Corp. as of October 4th, 2019 is the result of our systematic analysis on three basic characteristics: earnings strength, relative valuation, and recent stock price movement. The company has managed to produce a neutral trend in earnings per share over the past 5 quarters. However, recent analyst estimates for the company have been reduced and NSC has posted results that fell short of analysts' expectations. Based on operating earnings yield, the company is undervalued when compared to all of the companies we cover. Share price changes over the past year indicates that NSC will perform well over the near term.

Financial Data
(US$ in Thousands)

	9 Mos	6 Mos	3 Mos	12/31/2018	12/31/2017	12/31/2016	12/31/2015	12/31/2014
Earnings Per Share	10.26	10.29	10.09	9.51	18.61	5.62	5.10	6.39
Cash Flow Per Share	14.65	14.55	14.19	13.42	11.30	10.30	9.53	9.22
Tang Book Value Per Share	58.44	58.13	57.64	57.30	57.57	42.73	40.93	40.25
Dividends Per Share	3.460	3.320	3.180	3.040	2.440	2.360	2.360	2.220
Dividend Payout %	33.72	32.26	31.52	31.97	13.11	41.99	46.27	34.74
Income Statement								
Total Revenue	8,606,000	5,765,000	2,840,000	11,458,000	10,551,000	9,888,000	10,511,000	11,624,000
EBITDA	3,969,000	2,664,000	1,293,000	5,130,000	4,741,000	4,171,000	4,042,000	4,638,000
Depn & Amortn	854,000	567,000	283,000	1,104,000	1,059,000	1,030,000	1,059,000	956,000
Income Before Taxes	2,663,000	1,795,000	861,000	3,469,000	3,128,000	2,582,000	2,442,000	3,134,000
Income Taxes	607,000	396,000	184,000	803,000	(2,276,000)	914,000	886,000	1,134,000
Net Income	2,056,000	1,399,000	677,000	2,666,000	5,404,000	1,668,000	1,556,000	2,000,000
Average Shares	264,300	267,100	269,400	280,200	290,300	296,000	304,400	312,500
Balance Sheet								
Current Assets	2,016,000	1,914,000	1,922,000	1,862,000	2,149,000	2,291,000	2,633,000	2,778,000
Total Assets	37,500,000	37,172,000	37,062,000	36,239,000	35,711,000	34,892,000	34,260,000	33,241,000
Current Liabilities	2,761,000	2,451,000	2,885,000	2,591,000	2,545,000	2,339,000	2,231,000	1,780,000
Long-Term Obligations	11,085,000	11,076,000	10,569,000	10,560,000	9,136,000	9,562,000	9,393,000	8,924,000
Total Liabilities	22,262,000	21,861,000	21,731,000	20,877,000	19,352,000	22,483,000	22,072,000	20,833,000
Stockholders' Equity	15,238,000	15,311,000	15,331,000	15,362,000	16,359,000	12,409,000	12,188,000	12,408,000
Shares Outstanding	260,746	263,406	265,967	268,098	284,157	290,417	297,795	308,240
Statistical Record								
Return on Assets %	7.47	7.68	7.62	7.41	15.31	4.81	4.61	6.09
Return on Equity %	17.96	17.59	17.58	16.81	37.57	13.53	12.65	16.88
EBITDA Margin %	46.12	46.21	45.53	44.77	44.93	42.18	38.45	39.90
Net Margin %	23.89	24.27	23.84	23.27	51.22	16.87	14.80	17.21
Asset Turnover	0.31	0.32	0.32	0.32	0.30	0.29	0.31	0.35
Current Ratio	0.73	0.78	0.67	0.72	0.84	0.98	1.18	1.56
Debt to Equity	0.73	0.72	0.69	0.69	0.56	0.77	0.77	0.72
Price Range	206.70-139.79	206.70-139.79	186.89-128.92	186.71-128.92	145.91-106.99	110.69-66.60	111.73-72.44	117.20-87.76
P/E Ratio	20.15-13.62	20.09-13.59	18.52-12.78	19.63-13.56	7.84-5.75	19.70-11.85	21.91-14.20	18.34-13.73
Average Yield %	1.92	1.88	1.95	1.94	1.99	2.67	2.54	2.18

Address: Three Commercial Place, Norfolk, VA 23510-2191 **Telephone:** 757-629-2680	**Web Site:** www.norfolksouthern.com **Officers:** James A. Squires - Chairman, President, Chief Executive Officer, Executive Vice President, Chief Financial Officer, Executive Vice President Mark R. George - Executive Vice President, Chief Financial Officer, Division Officer	**Auditors:** KPMG LLP **Investor Contact:** 757-629-2861 **Transfer Agents:** American Stock Transfer & Trust Company, LLC, Brooklyn, NY

NORTHROP GRUMMAN CORP

Exchange	Symbol	Price	52Wk Range	Yield	P/E	Div Acheiver
NYS	NOC	$343.97 (12/31/2019)	382.15-239.92	1.54	17.71	15 Years

*7 Year Price Score 123.96 ***NYSE Composite Index=100** ***12 Month Price Score 102.62**

Stock price chart (2010–2019) and TRADING VOLUME (thousand shares)

Interim Earnings (Per Share)

Qtr.	Mar	Jun	Sep	Dec
2016	3.03	2.85	3.35	2.96
2017	3.63	3.15	3.68	1.01
2018	4.21	3.93	6.54	3.81
2019	5.06	5.06	5.49	...

Interim Dividends (Per Share)

Amt	Decl	Ex	Rec	Pay
1.20Q	02/12/2019	02/22/2019	02/25/2019	03/13/2019
1.32Q	05/14/2019	05/31/2019	06/03/2019	06/19/2019
1.32Q	08/21/2019	09/06/2019	09/09/2019	09/25/2019
1.32Q	11/20/2019	11/29/2019	12/02/2019	12/18/2019

Indicated Div: $5.28 (Div. Reinv. Plan)

Valuation Analysis | **Institutional Holding**

Forecast EPS	$20.35	No of Institutions
	(01/16/2020)	1493
Market Cap	$58.0 Billion	Shares
Book Value	$9.7 Billion	201,000,672
Price/Book	5.96	% Held
Price/Sales	1.74	80.11

Business Summary: Defense (MIC: 7.1.2 SIC: 3812 NAIC: 334511)

Northrop Grumman is a security company. Co.'s segments include: Aerospace Systems, which designs, develops, integrates and produces manned aircraft, autonomous systems, spacecraft, high-energy laser systems, microelectronics and other systems and subsystems; Innovation Systems, which designs, develops, integrates and produces flight, armament and space systems for national security, civil government and commercial customers; and Mission Systems, which provides end-to-end mission solutions and multifunction systems for Department of Defense, intelligence community, international, federal-civil and commercial customers.

Recent Developments: For the quarter ended Sep 30 2019, net income decreased 25.0% to US$933.0 million from US$1.24 billion in the year-earlier quarter. Revenues were US$8.48 billion, up 4.8% from US$8.09 billion the year before. Operating income was US$951.0 million versus US$1.17 billion in the prior-year quarter, a decrease of 18.9%. Direct operating expenses rose 10.7% to US$6.75 billion from US$6.10 billion in the comparable period the year before. Indirect operating expenses decreased 5.0% to US$776.0 million from US$817.0 million in the equivalent prior-year period.

Prospects: Our evaluation of Northrop Grumman Corp. as of October 4th, 2019 is the result of our systematic analysis on three basic characteristics: earnings strength, relative valuation, and recent stock price movement. The company has generated a negative trend in earnings per share over the past 5 quarters. However, recent analyst estimates for the company have been raised and NOC has posted results that exceeded analysts' expectations. Based on operating earnings yield, the company is undervalued when compared to all of the companies we cover. Share price changes over the past year indicates that NOC will perform well over the near term.

Financial Data
(US$ in Thousands)

	9 Mos	6 Mos	3 Mos	12/31/2018	12/31/2017	12/31/2016	12/31/2015	12/31/2014
Earnings Per Share	19.42	20.47	19.34	18.49	11.47	12.19	10.39	9.75
Cash Flow Per Share	24.90	22.88	18.54	22.03	14.98	15.68	11.41	12.42
Dividends Per Share	5.040	4.920	4.800	4.700	3.900	3.500	3.100	2.710
Dividend Payout %	25.95	24.04	24.82	25.42	34.00	28.71	29.84	27.79
Income Statement								
Total Revenue	25,120,000	16,645,000	8,189,000	30,095,000	25,803,000	24,508,000	23,526,000	23,979,000
EBITDA	4,252,000	2,816,000	1,406,000	5,104,000	3,884,000	3,680,000	3,558,000	3,681,000
Depn & Amortn	737,000	479,000	234,000	800,000	475,000	456,000	467,000	462,000
Income Before Taxes	3,117,000	2,062,000	1,034,000	3,742,000	3,049,000	2,923,000	2,790,000	2,937,000
Income Taxes	460,000	338,000	171,000	513,000	1,034,000	723,000	800,000	868,000
Net Income	2,657,000	1,724,000	863,000	3,229,000	2,015,000	2,200,000	1,990,000	2,069,000
Average Shares	169,900	170,300	170,700	174,600	175,600	180,500	191,600	212,100
Balance Sheet								
Current Assets	10,836,000	10,159,000	10,443,000	9,680,000	16,349,000	6,856,000	6,334,000	8,184,000
Total Assets	40,553,000	39,584,000	39,751,000	37,653,000	34,917,000	25,614,000	24,454,000	26,572,000
Current Liabilities	8,416,000	8,155,000	8,821,000	8,274,000	6,965,000	5,630,000	5,457,000	5,892,000
Long-Term Obligations	13,826,000	13,838,000	13,863,000	13,883,000	14,399,000	7,058,000	6,416,000	5,925,000
Total Liabilities	30,822,000	30,370,000	31,012,000	29,466,000	27,869,000	20,355,000	18,932,000	19,337,000
Stockholders' Equity	9,731,000	9,214,000	8,739,000	8,187,000	7,048,000	5,259,000	5,522,000	7,235,000
Shares Outstanding	168,701	169,305	169,873	170,607	174,085	175,068	181,303	198,930
Statistical Record								
Return on Assets %	8.44	9.16	9.00	8.90	6.66	8.76	7.80	7.81
Return on Equity %	35.19	40.42	40.84	42.39	32.75	40.70	31.20	23.18
EBITDA Margin %	16.93	16.92	17.17	16.96	15.05	15.02	15.12	15.35
Net Margin %	10.58	10.36	10.54	10.73	7.81	8.98	8.46	8.63
Asset Turnover	0.85	0.85	0.85	0.83	0.85	0.98	0.92	0.91
Current Ratio	1.29	1.25	1.18	1.17	2.35	1.22	1.16	1.39
Debt to Equity	1.42	1.50	1.59	1.70	2.04	1.34	1.16	0.82
Price Range	382.15-226.23	324.16-226.23	360.03-226.23	360.03-226.23	310.47-226.96	251.80-178.19	191.48-143.37	152.24-110.80
P/E Ratio	19.68-11.65	15.84-11.05	18.62-11.70	19.47-12.24	27.07-19.79	20.66-14.62	18.43-13.80	15.61-11.36
Average Yield %	1.68	1.71	1.62	1.51	1.48	1.65	1.85	2.16

Address: 2980 Fairview Park Drive, Falls Church, VA 22042 **Telephone:** 703-280-2900	**Web Site:** www.northropgrumman.com **Officers:** Kathy J. Warden - Chairman, President, Corporate Vice-President, Chief Executive Officer, Chief Operating Officer, Division Officer Lucy C. Ryan - Corporate Vice-President	**Auditors:** DELOITTE & TOUCHE LLP **Investor Contact:** 703-280-2268 **Transfer Agents:** Computershare, Providence, RI

NORTHWEST NATURAL HOLDING CO

Exchange	Symbol	Price	52Wk Range	Yield	P/E	Div Acheiver
NYS	NWN	$73.73 (12/31/2019)	73.86-57.46	2.59	34.45	63 Years

*7 Year Price Score 101.81 *NYSE Composite Index=100 ***12 Month Price Score 96.38**

Interim Earnings (Per Share)

Qtr.	Mar	Jun	Sep	Dec
2016	1.33	0.07	(0.29)	1.01
2017	1.40	0.10	(0.30)	(3.14)
2018	1.44	(0.03)	(0.41)	1.24
2019	1.49	0.04	(0.63)	...

Interim Dividends (Per Share)

Amt	Decl	Ex	Rec	Pay
0.475Q	04/04/2019	04/29/2019	04/30/2019	05/15/2019
0.475Q	07/11/2019	07/30/2019	07/31/2019	08/15/2019
0.477Q	10/03/2019	10/30/2019	10/31/2019	11/15/2019
0.477Q	01/09/2020	01/30/2020	01/31/2020	02/14/2020

Indicated Div: $1.91

Valuation Analysis / Institutional Holding

Valuation Analysis		Institutional Holding	
Forecast EPS	$2.38 (01/10/2020)	No of Institutions	N/A
Market Cap	$2.2 Billion	Shares	
Book Value	$844.7 Million	N/A	
Price/Book	2.66	% Held	
Price/Sales	3.09	N/A	

Business Summary: Gas Utilities (MIC: 3.3.1 SIC: 4924 NAIC: 221210)

Northwest Natural Holding is a holding company. Through its subsidiary, Northwest Natural Gas Company (NW Natural), Co. distributes natural gas to residential, commercial, and industrial customers in Oregon and southwest Washington. The Natural Gas Distribution (NGD) segment is the only reportable segment for Co. The NGD segment includes NW Natural local gas distribution business, NWN Gas Reserves LLC, which is a subsidiary of Northwest Energy Corporation, and the NGD-portion of NW Natural's Mist storage facility in Oregon. All other business activities, including certain gas storage activities, water businesses, and other investments and activities are aggregated and reported as other.

Recent Developments: For the quarter ended Sep 30 2019, loss from continuing operations was US$18.5 million compared with a loss of US$11.1 million in the year-earlier quarter. Net loss amounted to US$19.3 million versus a net loss of US$11.8 million in the year-earlier quarter. Revenues were US$90.3 million, down 1.0% from US$91.2 million the year before. Operating loss was US$9.6 million versus a loss of US$6.1 million in the prior-year quarter. Direct operating expenses declined 11.5% to US$22.6 million from US$25.5 million in the comparable period the year before. Indirect operating expenses increased 7.7% to US$77.3 million from US$71.8 million in the equivalent prior-year period.

Prospects: Our evaluation of Northwest Natural Holding Co. as of October 4th, 2019 is the result of our systematic analysis on three basic characteristics: earnings strength, relative valuation, and recent stock price movement. The company has produced a positive trend in earnings per share over the past 5 quarters. In addition, recent analyst estimates for the company have been raised, and NWN has posted results that exceeded analysts' expectations. Based on operating earnings yield, the company is fairly valued when compared to all of the companies we cover. Share price changes over the past year indicates that NWN will perform well over the near term.

Financial Data

(US$ in Thousands)	9 Mos	6 Mos	3 Mos	12/31/2018	12/31/2017	12/31/2016	12/31/2015	12/31/2014
Earnings Per Share	2.14	2.36	2.29	2.24	(1.94)	2.12	1.96	2.16
Cash Flow Per Share	5.44	5.50	5.85	5.86	7.21	8.01	6.75	7.94
Tang Book Value Per Share	27.75	28.82	27.42	26.10	25.85	29.71	28.47	28.12
Dividends Per Share	1.900	1.425	0.950	0.475	1.880	1.870	1.860	1.850
Dividend Payout %	88.79	60.38	41.48	21.21	...	88.21	94.90	85.65
Income Statement								
Total Revenue	499,108	408,791	285,348	706,143	762,173	675,967	723,791	754,037
EBITDA	85,459	91,386	76,025	241,528	69,343	249,849	234,422	243,426
Depn & Amortn	21,732	15,758	13,727	112,967	117,222	111,112	102,427	98,528
Income Before Taxes	31,920	54,769	52,093	91,502	(86,380)	99,609	89,456	100,335
Income Taxes	4,957	9,300	8,675	24,191	(30,757)	40,714	35,753	41,643
Net Income	24,995	44,296	43,201	64,569	(55,623)	58,895	53,703	58,692
Average Shares	30,429	29,394	28,970	28,873	28,669	27,779	27,417	27,223
Balance Sheet								
Current Assets	202,727	239,058	272,109	295,921	269,936	288,053	332,063	362,560
Total Assets	3,251,618	3,238,131	3,191,117	3,242,662	3,039,746	3,079,801	3,076,692	3,064,945
Current Liabilities	358,408	307,030	526,089	509,084	381,850	274,517	477,714	469,410
Long-Term Obligations	806,014	806,001	632,484	706,247	683,184	679,334	576,700	621,700
Total Liabilities	2,406,949	2,361,385	2,396,890	2,480,028	2,296,970	2,229,304	2,295,720	2,297,624
Stockholders' Equity	844,669	876,746	794,227	762,634	742,776	850,497	780,972	767,321
Shares Outstanding	30,435	30,422	28,962	28,880	28,736	28,630	27,427	27,284
Statistical Record								
Return on Assets %	1.92	2.20	2.13	2.06	N.M.	1.91	1.75	1.94
Return on Equity %	7.69	8.35	8.46	8.58	N.M.	7.20	6.94	7.73
EBITDA Margin %	17.12	22.36	26.64	34.20	9.10	36.96	32.39	32.28
Net Margin %	5.01	10.84	15.14	9.14	N.M.	8.71	7.42	7.78
Asset Turnover	0.23	0.23	0.23	0.22	0.25	0.22	0.24	0.25
Current Ratio	0.57	0.78	0.52	0.58	0.71	1.05	0.70	0.77
Debt to Equity	0.95	0.92	0.80	0.93	0.92	0.80	0.74	0.81
Price Range	72.03-57.46	70.71-57.46	70.71-57.20	70.71-51.95	69.15-56.85	65.60-49.44	51.98-42.18	52.46-40.36
P/E Ratio	33.66-26.85	29.96-24.35	30.88-24.98	31.57-23.19	...	30.94-23.32	26.52-21.52	24.29-18.69
Average Yield %	2.83	2.17	1.49	0.76	3.02	3.28	3.28	4.15

Address: 220 N.W. Second Avenue, Portland, OR 97209 **Telephone:** 503-226-4211	**Web Site:** www.nwnatural.com **Officers:** Tod R. Hamachek - Chairman David H. Anderson - President, Chief Executive Officer, Executive Vice President, Chief Operating Officer, Executive Vice President (frmr), Senior Vice President, Chief Financial Officer	**Auditors:** PricewaterhouseCoopers LLP **Investor Contact:** 503-226-4211ext.24 **Transfer Agents:** American Stock Transfer & Trust Company, Brooklyn, NY

NORTHWESTERN CORP.

Exchange	Symbol	Price	52Wk Range	Yield	P/E	Div Acheiver
NYS	NWE	$71.67 (12/31/2019)	76.05-58.03	3.21	17.44	13 Years

*7 Year Price Score 104.43 *NYSE Composite Index=100 *12 Month Price Score 95.67

Interim Earnings (Per Share)

Qtr.	Mar	Jun	Sep	Dec
2016	0.79	0.73	0.92	0.95
2017	1.17	0.44	0.75	0.97
2018	1.18	0.87	0.56	1.31
2019	1.44	0.94	0.42	...

Interim Dividends (Per Share)

Amt	Decl	Ex	Rec	Pay
0.575Q	02/12/2019	03/14/2019	03/15/2019	03/29/2019
0.575Q	04/23/2019	06/13/2019	06/14/2019	06/28/2019
0.575Q	07/23/2019	09/12/2019	09/13/2019	09/30/2019
0.575Q	10/29/2019	12/12/2019	12/13/2019	12/31/2019

Indicated Div: $2.30

Valuation Analysis   Institutional Holding

Forecast EPS	$3.43	No of Institutions
	(01/17/2020)	418
Market Cap	$3.9 Billion	Shares
Book Value	$2.0 Billion	64,535,960
Price/Book	1.93	% Held
Price/Sales	3.12	93.69

Business Summary: Electric Utilities (MIC: 3.1.1 SIC: 4931 NAIC: 221121)

Northwestern provides electricity and/or natural gas to customers in Montana, South Dakota and Nebraska. Co.'s segments are: electric operations; and natural gas operations. In Montana, Co.'s regulated electric utility business includes generation, transmission and distribution. Co. also transmits electricity for nonregulated entities owning generation, and utilities, cooperatives, and power marketers serving the electricity market. Co.'s regulated natural gas utility business includes production, storage, transmission and distribution. Co. transmits natural gas from production receipt points and storage facilities to distribution points and other nonaffiliated transmission systems.

Recent Developments: For the quarter ended Sep 30 2019, net income decreased 23.1% to US$21.7 million from US$28.2 million in the year-earlier quarter. Revenues were US$274.8 million, down 1.8% from US$279.9 million the year before. Operating income was US$46.4 million versus US$47.8 million in the prior-year quarter, a decrease of 3.0%. Direct operating expenses declined 11.1% to US$64.2 million from US$72.2 million in the comparable period the year before. Indirect operating expenses increased 2.8% to US$164.3 million from US$159.8 million in the equivalent prior-year period.

Prospects: Our evaluation of Northwestern Corp. as of October 4th, 2019 is the result of our systematic analysis on three basic characteristics: earnings strength, relative valuation, and recent stock price movement. The company has managed to produce a neutral trend in earnings per share over the past 5 quarters. In addition, recent analyst estimates for the company have been mixed and NWE has posted results that fell short of analysts' expectations. Based on operating earnings yield, the company is undervalued when compared to all of the companies we cover. Share price changes over the past year indicates that NWE will perform well over the near term.

Financial Data

(US$ in Thousands)	9 Mos	6 Mos	3 Mos	12/31/2018	12/31/2017	12/31/2016	12/31/2015	12/31/2014
Earnings Per Share	4.11	4.25	4.18	3.92	3.34	3.39	3.17	2.99
Cash Flow Per Share	5.74	5.54	6.36	7.64	6.66	5.97	7.18	6.23
Tang Book Value Per Share	30.49	30.60	30.23	31.49	29.19	27.28	25.79	23.93
Dividends Per Share	2.275	2.250	2.225	2.200	2.100	2.000	1.920	1.600
Dividend Payout %	55.35	52.94	53.23	56.12	62.87	59.00	60.57	53.51
Income Statement								
Total Revenue	929,775	654,939	384,220	1,192,009	1,305,652	1,257,247	1,214,299	1,204,863
EBITDA	196,545	149,433	99,326	444,714	434,471	410,831	418,101	311,992
Depn & Amortn	3,482	2,317	1,157	174,476	166,137	159,336	144,702	123,776
Income Before Taxes	122,040	99,815	74,379	178,250	176,071	156,525	181,246	110,414
Income Taxes	(20,098)	(20,653)	1,573	(18,710)	13,368	(7,647)	30,037	(10,272)
Net Income	142,138	120,468	72,806	196,960	162,703	164,172	151,209	120,686
Average Shares	50,779	50,775	50,729	50,237	48,655	48,475	47,642	40,431
Balance Sheet								
Current Assets	265,822	252,994	288,131	277,685	296,359	280,195	286,660	350,885
Total Assets	5,810,180	5,720,435	5,700,655	5,644,376	5,420,917	5,499,321	5,278,640	4,973,943
Current Liabilities	333,684	275,786	347,242	347,009	632,238	613,832	571,200	614,582
Long-Term Obligations	2,194,138	2,177,715	2,099,782	2,122,260	1,815,629	1,817,684	1,808,453	1,690,261
Total Liabilities	3,805,656	3,710,357	3,710,863	3,701,994	3,622,002	3,823,094	3,678,466	3,496,160
Stockholders' Equity	2,004,524	2,010,078	1,989,792	1,942,382	1,798,915	1,676,227	1,600,174	1,477,783
Shares Outstanding	53,996	53,996	53,996	50,323	49,372	48,331	48,172	46,914
Statistical Record								
Return on Assets %	3.69	3.86	3.81	3.56	2.98	3.04	2.95	2.78
Return on Equity %	10.69	11.01	11.05	10.53	9.36	9.99	9.83	9.62
EBITDA Margin %	21.14	22.82	25.85	37.31	33.28	32.68	34.43	25.89
Net Margin %	15.29	18.39	18.95	16.52	12.46	13.06	12.45	10.02
Asset Turnover	0.22	0.22	0.22	0.22	0.24	0.23	0.24	0.28
Current Ratio	0.80	0.92	0.83	0.80	0.47	0.46	0.50	0.57
Debt to Equity	1.09	1.08	1.06	1.09	1.01	1.08	1.13	1.14
Price Range	76.05-57.96	73.84-56.75	71.30-51.84	64.46-50.33	64.26-56.09	63.33-52.47	59.10-48.75	58.55-42.67
P/E Ratio	18.50-14.10	17.37-13.35	17.06-12.40	16.44-12.84	19.24-16.79	18.68-15.48	18.64-15.38	19.58-14.27
Average Yield %	3.37	3.50	3.70	3.86	3.52	3.44	3.60	3.31

Address: 3010 W. 69th Street, Sioux Falls, SD 57108	**Web Site:** www.northwesternenergy.com	**Auditors:** Deloitte & Touche LLP	
Telephone: 605-978-2900	**Officers:** Stephen P. Adik - Chairman Robert C. Rowe - President, Chief Executive Officer	**Investor Contact:** 605-978-2900	
		Transfer Agents: Computershare College Station, TX	

NOW INC

Exchange	Symbol	Price	52Wk Range	Yield	P/E
NYS	DNOW	$11.24 (12/31/2019)	15.86-10.05	N/A	22.04

*7 Year Price Score N/A   ***NYSE Composite Index=100**   ***12 Month Price Score 83.71**

TRADING VOLUME (thousand shares)

Interim Earnings (Per Share)

Qtr.	Mar	Jun	Sep	Dec
2016	(0.59)	(0.40)	(0.53)	(0.66)
2017	(0.21)	(0.16)	(0.08)	(0.03)
2018	0.02	0.12	0.18	0.14
2019	0.16	0.12	0.09	...

Interim Dividends (Per Share)
No Dividends Paid

Valuation Analysis / Institutional Holding

Valuation Analysis		Institutional Holding	
Forecast EPS	$0.31	No of Institutions	
	(01/16/2020)	365	
Market Cap	$1.2 Billion	Shares	
Book Value	$1.3 Billion	125,213,240	
Price/Book	0.97	% Held	
Price/Sales	0.40	102.67	

Business Summary: Equipment & Services (MIC: 9.1.3 SIC: 3533 NAIC: 333132)

NOW, through its subsidiaries, is a distributor to the oil and gas and industrial markets. Co.'s product offering includes consumable maintenance, repair and operating supplies, pipe, valves, fittings, flanges, gaskets, fasteners, electrical, instrumentation, artificial lift, pumping solutions, valve actuation and modular process, measurement and control equipment. Co. also provides warehouse and inventory management solutions as part of its supply chain and materials management offering. Co.'s solutions include outsourcing the functions of procurement, inventory and warehouse management, logistics, point of issue technology, project management, as well as business process.

Recent Developments: For the quarter ended Sep 30 2019, net income decreased 50.0% to US$10.0 million from US$20.0 million in the year-earlier quarter. Revenues were US$751.0 million, down 8.6% from US$822.0 million the year before. Operating income was US$14.0 million versus US$26.0 million in the prior-year quarter, a decrease of 46.2%. Direct operating expenses declined 8.1% to US$601.0 million from US$654.0 million in the comparable period the year before. Indirect operating expenses decreased 4.2% to US$136.0 million from US$142.0 million in the equivalent prior-year period.

Prospects: Our evaluation of NOW Inc. as of October 4th, 2019 is the result of our systematic analysis on three basic characteristics: earnings strength, relative valuation, and recent stock price movement. The company has generated a negative trend in earnings per share over the past 5 quarters. In addition, recent analyst estimates for the company have been reduced while DNOW has posted results that exceeded analysts' expectations. Based on operating earnings yield, the company is fairly valued when compared to all of the companies we cover. Share price changes over the past year indicates that DNOW will perform well over the near term.

Financial Data

(US$ in Millions)	9 Mos	6 Mos	3 Mos	12/31/2018	12/31/2017	12/31/2016	12/31/2015	12/31/2014
Earnings Per Share	0.51	0.60	0.60	0.47	(0.48)	(2.18)	(4.68)	1.06
Cash Flow Per Share	2.07	1.35	0.76	0.67	(1.06)	2.19	3.03	1.01
Tang Book Value Per Share	7.48	7.36	7.24	6.97	6.40	6.40	9.67	14.45
Income Statement								
Total Revenue	2,312	1,561	785	3,127	2,648	2,107	3,010	4,105
EBITDA	76	54	29	79	(24)	(198)	(493)	194
Depn & Amortn	30	20	10	21	28	32	25	16
Income Before Taxes	46	34	19	58	(52)	(230)	(518)	178
Income Taxes	4	2	1	6	...	4	(16)	62
Net Income	42	32	18	52	(52)	(234)	(502)	116
Average Shares	109	109	109	108	108	107	107	108
Balance Sheet								
Current Assets	1,148	1,195	1,252	1,219	1,129	959	1,292	2,047
Total Assets	1,790	1,849	1,896	1,795	1,749	1,603	1,832	2,596
Current Liabilities	470	468	475	441	394	347	307	620
Long-Term Obligations	...	62	124	132	162	65	108	...
Total Liabilities	523	585	651	581	564	420	429	630
Stockholders' Equity	1,267	1,264	1,245	1,214	1,185	1,183	1,403	1,966
Shares Outstanding	108	108	108	108	108	107	107	107
Statistical Record								
Return on Assets %	3.18	3.72	3.66	2.93	N.M.	N.M.	N.M.	4.85
Return on Equity %	4.67	5.54	5.58	4.34	N.M.	N.M.	N.M.	
EBITDA Margin %	3.29	3.46	3.69	2.53	N.M.	N.M.	N.M.	4.73
Net Margin %	1.82	2.05	2.29	1.66	N.M.	N.M.	N.M.	2.83
Asset Turnover	1.69	1.72	1.70	1.76	1.58	1.22	1.36	1.72
Current Ratio	2.44	2.55	2.64	2.76	2.87	2.76	4.21	3.30
Debt to Equity	...	0.05	0.10	0.11	0.14	0.05	0.08	...
Price Range	17.02-10.38	17.44-10.38	17.44-10.07	17.44-9.41	22.67-9.88	23.21-12.48	26.79-14.80	37.19-22.50
P/E Ratio	33.37-20.35	29.07-17.30	29.07-16.78	37.11-20.02	...	...	...	35.08-21.23

Address: 7402 North Eldridge Parkway, Houston, TX 77041	**Web Site:** www.distributionnow.com	**Auditors:** Ernst & Young LLP
Telephone: 281-823-4700	**Officers:** J. Wayne Richards - Chairman Richard J. Alario - Interim Chief Executive Officer	**Transfer Agents:** American Stock Transfer & Trust Co., LLC , Brooklyn, NY

NRG ENERGY INC

Exchange	Symbol	Price	52Wk Range	Yield	P/E
NYS	NRG	$39.75 (12/31/2019)	43.37-33.30	0.30	10.19

*7 Year Price Score 121.90 *NYSE Composite Index=100 *12 Month Price Score 96.82

Interim Earnings (Per Share)

Qtr.	Mar	Jun	Sep	Dec
2016	0.24	(0.61)	1.27	(3.13)
2017	(0.52)	(1.98)	0.53	(4.84)
2018	0.87	0.23	(0.24)	(0.02)
2019	1.72	0.75	1.45	...

Interim Dividends (Per Share)

Amt	Decl	Ex	Rec	Pay
0.03Q	01/23/2019	01/31/2019	02/01/2019	02/15/2019
0.03Q	04/08/2019	04/30/2019	05/01/2019	05/15/2019
0.03Q	07/19/2019	07/31/2019	08/01/2019	08/15/2019
0.03Q	10/17/2019	10/31/2019	11/01/2019	11/15/2019

Indicated Div: $0.12

Valuation Analysis

		Institutional Holding	
Forecast EPS	$3.37	No of Institutions	
	(01/15/2020)	727	
Market Cap	$10.0 Billion	Shares	
Book Value	N/A	311,137,440	
Price/Book	N/A	% Held	
Price/Sales	1.08	77.48	

Business Summary: Electric Utilities (MIC: 3.1.1 SIC: 4911 NAIC: 221121)

NRG Energy is an energy company, engaged in producing, selling and delivering electricity and related products and services in power markets. Co.'s Retail business provides energy and related services. Products and services range from retail energy, portable solar and battery products home services, and a variety of bundled products, which combine energy with protection products, energy efficiency and renewable energy solutions, as well as other distributed and reliability products. Co.'s wholesale power generation business includes plant operations, commercial operations, engineering, procurement and construction, asset management, energy services and other critical related functions.

Recent Developments: For the quarter ended Sep 30 2019, income from continuing operations increased 30.3% to US$374.0 million from US$287.0 million in the year-earlier quarter. Net income amounted to US$372.0 million versus a net loss of US$49.0 million in the year-earlier quarter. Revenues were US$3.00 billion, up 1.2% from US$2.96 billion the year before. Operating income was US$540.0 million versus US$398.0 million in the prior-year quarter, an increase of 35.7%. Direct operating expenses declined 3.8% to US$2.15 billion from US$2.24 billion in the comparable period the year before. Indirect operating expenses decreased 6.5% to US$303.0 million from US$324.0 million in the equivalent prior-year period.

Prospects: Our evaluation of NRG Energy Inc. as of October 4th, 2019 is the result of our systematic analysis on three basic characteristics: earnings strength, relative valuation, and recent stock price movement. The company has enjoyed a very positive trend in earnings per share over the past 5 quarters. However, recent analyst estimates for the company have been mixed and NRG has posted results that fell short of analysts' expectations. Based on operating earnings yield, the company is undervalued when compared to all of the companies we cover. Share price changes over the past year indicates that NRG will perform poorly over the near term.

Financial Data

(US$ in Thousands)	9 Mos	6 Mos	3 Mos	12/31/2018	12/31/2017	12/31/2016	12/31/2015	12/31/2014
Earnings Per Share	3.90	2.21	1.69	0.87	(6.79)	(2.22)	(19.46)	0.23
Cash Flow Per Share	4.55	4.69	3.21	4.53	4.38	6.54	3.98	4.52
Tang Book Value Per Share	...	...	...	...	...	N.M.	N.M.	14.59
Dividends Per Share	0.120	0.120	0.120	0.120	0.120	0.235	0.580	0.540
Dividend Payout %	3.08	5.43	7.10	13.79	...	...	...	234.78
Income Statement								
Total Revenue	7,626,000	4,630,000	2,165,000	9,478,000	10,629,000	12,351,000	14,674,000	15,868,000
EBITDA	1,079,000	590,000	263,000	986,000	(660,000)	250,000	(3,921,000)	1,280,000
Depn & Amortn	103,000	64,000	30,000	45,000	108,000	91,000	81,000	64,000
Income Before Taxes	658,000	307,000	119,000	458,000	(1,658,000)	(902,000)	(5,130,000)	97,000
Income Taxes	9,000	3,000	4,000	7,000	8,000	16,000	1,342,000	3,000
Net Income	1,055,000	683,000	482,000	268,000	(2,153,000)	(774,000)	(6,382,000)	134,000
Average Shares	256,000	267,000	280,000	308,000	317,000	316,000	329,000	339,000
Balance Sheet								
Current Assets	3,187,000	3,045,000	3,458,000	3,600,000	4,415,000	6,395,000	7,391,000	8,582,000
Total Assets	9,527,000	9,171,000	9,530,000	10,628,000	23,318,000	30,355,000	32,882,000	40,665,000
Current Liabilities	2,564,000	2,294,000	1,945,000	2,398,000	3,317,000	4,382,000	4,375,000	4,859,000
Long-Term Obligations	5,798,000	5,794,000	6,366,000	6,449,000	15,716,000	18,006,000	18,983,000	19,900,000
Total Liabilities	11,098,000	10,819,000	11,068,000	11,862,000	23,664,000	28,314,000	29,873,000	30,612,000
Stockholders' Equity	(1,571,000)	(1,648,000)	(1,538,000)	(1,234,000)	(346,000)	2,041,000	3,009,000	10,053,000
Shares Outstanding	251,985	258,570	267,538	283,650	316,743	315,443	314,190	336,662
Statistical Record								
Return on Assets %	9.94	3.73	2.82	1.58	N.M.	N.M.	N.M.	0.36
Return on Equity %	...	...	...	...	N.M.	N.M.	N.M.	1.35
EBITDA Margin %	14.15	12.74	12.15	10.40	N.M.	2.02	N.M.	8.07
Net Margin %	13.83	14.75	22.26	2.83	N.M.	N.M.	N.M.	0.84
Asset Turnover	0.89	0.58	0.59	0.56	0.40	0.39	0.40	0.43
Current Ratio	1.24	1.33	1.78	1.50	1.33	1.46	1.69	1.77
Debt to Equity	...	...	...	...	...	8.82	6.31	1.98
Price Range	43.37-33.30	43.37-30.57	43.37-29.96	42.68-24.00	29.49-12.30	17.90-8.98	27.50-9.00	37.66-25.83
P/E Ratio	11.12-8.54	19.62-13.83	25.66-17.73	49.06-27.59	...	...	...	..163.74-112.30
Average Yield %	0.31	0.32	0.33	0.36	0.57	1.85	2.81	1.74

Address: 804 Carnegie Center,	Web Site: www.nrgenergy.com	Auditors: KPMG LLP
Princeton, NJ 08540	Officers: Lawrence S. Coben - Chairman Mauricio	Investor Contact: 609-524-4526
Telephone: 609-524-4500	Gutierrez - President, Chief Executive Officer,	Transfer Agents: Computershare
	Executive Vice President, Chief Operating Officer	Shareowner Services LLC, College Station, TX

NU SKIN ENTERPRISES, INC.

Exchange	Symbol	Price	52Wk Range	Yield	P/E	Div Acheiver
NYS	NUS	$40.98 (12/31/2019)	69.50-37.70	3.61	19.70	17 Years

*7 Year Price Score 68.00   *NYSE Composite Index=100   *12 Month Price Score 78.81

Interim Earnings (Per Share)

Qtr.	Mar	Jun	Sep	Dec
2016	0.06	0.79	0.98	0.70
2017	0.51	0.77	0.76	0.32
2018	0.64	0.90	0.94	(0.31)
2019	0.77	0.83	0.79	...

Interim Dividends (Per Share)

Amt	Decl	Ex	Rec	Pay
0.37Q	02/13/2019	02/22/2019	02/25/2019	03/13/2019
0.37Q	04/30/2019	05/30/2019	05/31/2019	06/12/2019
0.37Q	08/06/2019	08/29/2019	08/30/2019	09/11/2019
0.37Q	11/05/2019	11/27/2019	11/29/2019	12/11/2019

Indicated Div: $1.48

Valuation Analysis

		Institutional Holding	
Forecast EPS	$3.10	No of Institutions	395
(01/15/2020)			
Market Cap	$2.3 Billion	Shares	
Book Value	$845.8 Million		50,734,516
Price/Book	2.69	% Held	
Price/Sales	0.90		76.11

Business Summary: Household & Personal Products (MIC: 1.7.1 SIC: 5122 NAIC: 424210)

Nu Skin Enterprises develops and distributes consumer products. Co. is engaged in providing a range of beauty and wellness solutions under its Nu Skin and Pharmanex category brands. Co.'s products under the Nu Skin category includes skin care devices and related consumables including ageLOC LumiSpa skin treatment and cleansing device, its ageLOC Spa systems, and its ageLOC Me customized skin care system, as well as its Epoch® products. Co.'s Pharmanex product category includes its LifePak nutritional supplements, ageLOC Youth nutritional supplement, and ageLOC TR90 weight management and body shaping system.

Recent Developments: For the quarter ended Sep 30 2019, net income decreased 17.0% to US$44.1 million from US$53.1 million in the year-earlier quarter. Revenues were US$589.9 million, down 12.6% from US$675.3 million the year before. Operating income was US$69.9 million versus US$80.7 million in the prior-year quarter, a decrease of 13.4%. Direct operating expenses declined 11.0% to US$140.2 million from US$157.5 million in the comparable period the year before. Indirect operating expenses decreased 13.1% to US$379.9 million from US$437.2 million in the equivalent prior-year period.

Prospects: Our evaluation of NU Skin Enterprises Inc. as of October 4th, 2019 is the result of our systematic analysis on three basic characteristics: earnings strength, relative valuation, and recent stock price movement. The company has managed to produce a neutral trend in earnings per share over the past 5 quarters. In addition, recent analyst estimates for the company have been mixed and NUS has posted results that exceeded analysts' expectations. Based on operating earnings yield, the company is undervalued when compared to all of the companies we cover. Share price changes over the past year indicates that NUS will perform very poorly over the near term.

Financial Data

(US$ in Thousands)	9 Mos	6 Mos	3 Mos	12/31/2018	12/31/2017	12/31/2016	12/31/2015	12/31/2014
Earnings Per Share	2.08	2.23	2.30	2.16	2.36	2.55	2.25	3.11
Cash Flow Per Share	3.91	4.06	3.53	3.67	5.73	4.95	5.55	(0.96)
Tang Book Value Per Share	10.18	9.96	9.49	8.94	9.91	9.23	11.54	12.80
Dividends Per Share	1.475	1.470	1.465	1.460	1.440	1.420	1.400	1.380
Dividend Payout %	70.91	65.92	63.70	67.59	61.02	55.69	62.22	44.37
Income Statement								
Total Revenue	1,837,057	1,247,123	623,623	2,679,008	2,279,099	2,207,797	2,247,047	2,569,495
EBITDA	259,558	175,340	85,412	276,066	323,867	273,639	273,559	345,007
Depn & Amortn	57,964	38,659	19,607	56,400	58,300	60,800	61,600	46,500
Income Before Taxes	201,594	136,681	65,805	219,666	265,567	212,839	211,959	298,507
Income Taxes	68,153	47,330	22,803	97,779	136,130	69,753	78,913	109,331
Net Income	133,441	89,351	43,002	121,887	129,437	143,086	133,046	189,176
Average Shares	55,788	55,943	56,128	56,476	54,852	56,097	59,057	60,887
Balance Sheet								
Current Assets	739,129	788,183	747,682	799,237	777,789	714,337	706,392	834,667
Total Assets	1,736,905	1,791,098	1,755,101	1,694,446	1,589,872	1,474,045	1,505,843	1,614,434
Current Liabilities	368,407	414,548	402,043	439,655	447,370	399,011	407,597	418,329
Long-Term Obligations	341,724	348,986	356,247	361,008	310,790	334,165	181,745	164,567
Total Liabilities	891,105	956,148	943,906	912,579	885,276	809,975	680,222	671,996
Stockholders' Equity	845,800	834,950	811,195	781,867	704,596	664,070	825,621	942,438
Shares Outstanding	55,600	55,600	55,600	55,400	52,700	52,600	56,000	59,000
Statistical Record								
Return on Assets %	6.64	7.05	7.33	7.42	8.45	9.58	8.53	11.01
Return on Equity %	13.79	15.23	16.07	16.40	18.91	19.16	15.05	21.01
EBITDA Margin %	14.13	14.06	13.70	10.30	14.21	12.39	12.17	13.43
Net Margin %	7.26	7.16	6.90	4.55	5.68	6.48	5.92	7.36
Asset Turnover	1.45	1.47	1.52	1.63	1.49	1.48	1.44	1.50
Current Ratio	2.01	1.90	1.86	1.82	1.74	1.79	1.73	2.00
Debt to Equity	0.40	0.42	0.44	0.46	0.44	0.50	0.22	0.17
Price Range	81.77-38.18	85.46-46.69	85.46-47.44	85.46-56.44	69.97-47.22	65.89-28.13	62.20-31.89	138.22-38.28
P/E Ratio	39.31-18.36	38.32-20.94	37.16-20.63	39.56-26.13	29.65-20.01	25.84-11.03	27.64-14.17	44.44-12.31
Average Yield %	2.68	2.27	2.05	1.98	2.45	3.05	3.04	2.09

Address: 75 West Center Street, Provo, UT 84601 **Telephone:** 801-345-1000	**Web Site:** www.nuskin.com **Officers:** Steven J. Lund - Executive Chairman, Chairman, Vice-Chairman Ryan S. Napierski - President, Region Officer, Division Officer	**Auditors:** PricewaterhouseCoopers LLP **Investor Contact:** 801-345-2657 **Transfer Agents:** American Stock Transfer & Trust Co. LLC, Brooklyn, NY

NUCOR CORP.

Exchange	Symbol	Price	52Wk Range	Yield	P/E	Div Acheiver
NYS	NUE	$56.28 (12/31/2019)	62.10-46.61	2.86	9.60	46 Years

*7 Year Price Score 86.08   *NYSE Composite Index=100   *12 Month Price Score 96.32

Interim Earnings (Per Share)

Qtr.	Mar	Jun	Sep	Dec
2016	0.22	0.73	0.84	0.69
2017	1.11	1.00	0.79	1.20
2018	1.10	2.13	2.13	2.07
2019	1.63	1.26	0.90	...

Interim Dividends (Per Share)

Amt	Decl	Ex	Rec	Pay
0.40Q	02/19/2019	03/28/2019	03/29/2019	05/10/2019
0.40Q	06/06/2019	06/27/2019	06/28/2019	08/09/2019
0.40Q	09/05/2019	09/26/2019	09/27/2019	11/08/2019
0.403Q	12/13/2019	12/30/2019	12/31/2019	02/11/2020

Indicated Div: $1.61 (Div. Reinv. Plan)

Valuation Analysis		Institutional Holding	
Forecast EPS	$4.04	No of Institutions	
	(01/17/2020)	1130	
Market Cap	$17.1 Billion	Shares	
Book Value	$10.4 Billion	323,790,688	
Price/Book	1.63	% Held	
Price/Sales	0.72	74.61	

Business Summary: Non-Precious Metals (MIC: 8.2.2 SIC: 3312 NAIC: 331111)

Nucor manufactures steel and steel products. Co.'s operations include international trading and sales companies that buy and sell steel and steel products. Co.'s segments are: steel mills, which produces sheet steel, plate steel, and structural steel, and bar steel; steel products, which produces hollow structural section steel tubing, electrical conduit, steel joists and joist girders, steel deck, cold finished steel, steel fasteners, metal building systems, and wire and wire mesh; and raw materials, which produces direct reduced iron (DRI), brokers ferrous and nonferrous metals, pig iron, hot briquetted iron and DRI, supplies ferro-alloys, and processes ferrous and nonferrous scrap metal.

Recent Developments: For the quarter ended Sep 28 2019, net income decreased 58.4% to US$293.6 million from US$706.3 million in the year-earlier quarter. Revenues were US$5.46 billion, down 19.0% from US$6.74 billion the year before. Direct operating expenses declined 10.3% to US$4.89 billion from US$5.45 billion in the comparable period the year before. Indirect operating expenses decreased 51.3% to US$160.9 million from US$330.4 million in the equivalent prior-year period.

Prospects: Our evaluation of Nucor Corp. as of October 4th, 2019 is the result of our systematic analysis on three basic characteristics: earnings strength, relative valuation, and recent stock price movement. The company has generated a negative trend in earnings per share over the past 5 quarters. In addition, recent analyst estimates for the company have been reduced and NUE has posted results that fell short of analysts' expectations. Based on operating earnings yield, the company is undervalued when compared to all of the companies we cover. Share price changes over the past year indicates that NUE will perform poorly over the near term.

Financial Data

(US$ in Thousands)	9 Mos	6 Mos	3 Mos	12/31/2018	12/31/2017	12/31/2016	12/31/2015	12/31/2014
Earnings Per Share	5.86	7.09	7.96	7.42	4.10	2.48	1.11	2.22
Cash Flow Per Share	8.58	8.88	9.51	7.58	3.29	5.42	6.73	4.20
Tang Book Value Per Share	24.73	24.17	23.37	22.18	17.70	15.56	14.58	15.18
Dividends Per Share	1.600	1.580	1.560	1.540	1.513	1.502	1.492	1.482
Dividend Payout %	27.30	22.28	19.60	20.75	36.89	60.58	134.46	66.78
Income Statement								
Total Revenue	17,457,112	11,992,610	6,096,624	25,067,279	20,252,393	16,208,122	16,439,276	21,105,141
EBITDA	2,237,489	1,646,394	894,824	3,955,565	2,517,709	2,042,338	1,503,197	2,012,328
Depn & Amortn	542,612	364,727	179,671	630,879	635,833	613,192	625,757	652,000
Income Before Taxes	1,602,118	1,220,194	686,710	3,189,151	1,708,296	1,259,902	703,909	1,191,072
Income Taxes	367,920	281,168	158,823	748,307	369,386	398,243	213,154	388,787
Net Income	1,163,320	888,289	501,806	2,360,767	1,318,688	796,271	357,659	713,946
Average Shares	304,980	305,952	307,180	316,733	320,773	319,822	320,693	320,127
Balance Sheet								
Current Assets	8,684,288	8,467,199	8,650,343	8,636,265	6,824,420	6,506,393	5,754,380	6,441,888
Total Assets	18,506,265	18,126,480	18,086,698	17,920,588	15,841,258	15,223,518	14,250,399	15,615,927
Current Liabilities	2,585,993	2,380,414	2,568,015	2,806,300	2,824,764	2,389,966	1,385,173	2,097,776
Long-Term Obligations	4,287,597	4,234,308	4,233,792	4,233,276	3,242,242	3,739,141	4,360,600	4,360,600
Total Liabilities	8,057,218	7,825,763	7,972,507	8,128,510	7,102,222	7,343,653	6,833,521	7,843,457
Stockholders' Equity	10,449,047	10,300,717	10,114,191	9,792,078	8,739,036	7,879,865	7,416,878	7,772,470
Shares Outstanding	303,215	303,157	304,804	305,592	317,969	318,737	317,962	319,033
Statistical Record								
Return on Assets %	9.93	12.43	14.67	13.98	8.49	5.39	2.40	4.63
Return on Equity %	17.89	22.48	26.28	25.48	15.87	10.38	4.71	9.26
EBITDA Margin %	12.82	13.73	14.68	15.78	12.43	12.60	9.14	9.53
Net Margin %	6.66	7.41	8.23	9.42	6.51	4.91	2.18	3.38
Asset Turnover	1.30	1.41	1.50	1.48	1.30	1.10	1.10	1.37
Current Ratio	3.36	3.56	3.37	3.08	2.42	2.72	4.15	3.07
Debt to Equity	0.41	0.41	0.42	0.43	0.37	0.47	0.59	0.56
Price Range	65.39-46.61	67.98-48.00	68.53-50.03	70.18-50.03	64.73-53.48	66.75-34.86	49.77-37.00	58.09-46.62
P/E Ratio	11.16-7.95	9.59-6.77	8.61-6.29	9.46-6.74	15.79-13.04	26.92-14.06	44.84-33.33	26.17-21.00
Average Yield %	2.84	2.67	2.54	2.43	2.58	3.06	3.34	2.87

Address: 1915 Rexford Road, Charlotte, NC 28211	Web Site: www.nucor.com	Auditors: PricewaterhouseCoopers LLP
Telephone: 704-366-7000	Officers: John J. Ferriola - Chairman, President, Chief Executive Officer, Chief Operating Officer Leon J. Topalian - President, Chief Executive Officer, Chief Operating Officer, Division Officer	Transfer Agents: American Stock Transfer & Trust Company, LLC, New York, NY
Fax: 704-362-4208		

NVR INC.

Exchange	Symbol	Price	52Wk Range	Yield	P/E
NYS	NVR	$3808 (12/31/2019)	3892.89-2381.94	N/A	17.70

*7 Year Price Score 136.13 *NYSE Composite Index=100 *12 Month Price Score 107.01

Interim Earnings (Per Share)

Qtr.	Mar	Jun	Sep	Dec
2016	15.79	22.01	28.46	37.37
2017	25.12	35.19	38.02	28.44
2018	39.34	49.05	48.28	58.27
2019	47.64	53.09	56.11	...

Interim Dividends (Per Share)

No Dividends Paid

Valuation Analysis		Institutional Holding	
Forecast EPS	$216.86	No of Institutions	
	(01/17/2020)	620	
Market Cap	$14.1 Billion	Shares	
Book Value	$2.4 Billion	4,107,368	
Price/Book	5.94	% Held	
Price/Sales	1.90	81.61	

Business Summary: Builders (MIC: 2.2.5 SIC: 1531 NAIC: 236117)

NVR is engaged in the construction and sale of single-family detached homes, townhomes and condominium buildings, all of which are primarily constructed on a pre-sold basis. Co.'s homebuilding operations include the construction and sale of single-family detached homes, townhomes and condominium buildings under three trade names: Ryan Homes, which is marketed primarily to first-time and first-time move-up buyers; and NVHomes and Heartland Homes, which are marketed primarily to move-up and luxury buyers. Co.'s mortgage banking operations also include separate subsidiaries that broker title insurance and perform title searches in connection with mortgage loan closings.

Recent Developments: For the quarter ended Sep 30 2019, net income increased 14.3% to US$223.8 million from US$195.8 million in the year-earlier quarter. Revenues were US$1.92 billion, up 3.4% from US$1.86 billion the year before. Direct operating expenses rose 3.1% to US$1.52 billion from US$1.47 billion in the comparable period the year before. Indirect operating expenses decreased 0.2% to US$130.7 million from US$130.9 million in the equivalent prior-year period.

Prospects: Our evaluation of NVR Inc. as of October 4th, 2019 is the result of our systematic analysis on three basic characteristics: earnings strength, relative valuation, and recent stock price movement. The company has managed to produce a neutral trend in earnings per share over the past 5 quarters. In addition, recent analyst estimates for the company have been mixed and NVR has posted results that exceeded analysts' expectations. Based on operating earnings yield, the company is undervalued when compared to all of the companies we cover. Share price changes over the past year indicates that NVR will perform over the near term.

Financial Data

(US$ in Thousands)	9 Mos	6 Mos	3 Mos	12/31/2018	12/31/2017	12/31/2016	12/31/2015	12/31/2014
Earnings Per Share	215.11	207.28	203.24	194.80	126.77	103.61	89.99	63.50
Cash Flow Per Share	201.73	237.07	242.02	199.15	152.40	99.67	50.57	43.14
Tang Book Value Per Share	628.02	568.26	515.17	491.82	421.72	339.27	304.87	264.25
Income Statement								
Total Revenue	5,427,684	3,505,565	1,696,120	7,189,652	6,322,274	5,834,585	5,169,562	4,453,139
EBITDA	764,671	485,981	229,884	1,004,981	893,763	705,673	648,305	494,300
Depn & Amortn	15,369	10,146	5,062	20,168	22,667	22,269	21,534	17,614
Income Before Taxes	730,493	463,319	218,607	959,732	846,911	661,697	603,212	453,546
Income Taxes	108,091	64,704	30,201	162,535	309,390	236,435	220,285	171,916
Net Income	622,402	398,615	188,406	797,197	537,521	425,262	382,927	281,630
Average Shares	3,988	3,959	3,955	4,092	4,240	4,104	4,255	4,435
Balance Sheet								
Current Assets	2,641,492	2,332,786	2,152,056	1,985,038	1,934,687	1,506,923	1,430,852	1,414,424
Total Assets	3,843,359	3,603,240	3,362,771	3,165,933	2,989,279	2,643,943	2,515,131	2,351,335
Current Liabilities	468,735	499,013	469,080	426,819	444,830	405,847	370,693	337,174
Long-Term Obligations	598,146	597,991	597,836	597,681	597,066	596,455	599,260	599,230
Total Liabilities	1,471,902	1,483,801	1,463,995	1,357,371	1,383,787	1,339,502	1,275,966	1,227,080
Stockholders' Equity	2,371,457	2,119,439	1,898,776	1,808,562	1,605,492	1,304,441	1,239,165	1,124,255
Shares Outstanding	3,698	3,643	3,590	3,577	3,691	3,693	3,890	4,049
Statistical Record								
Return on Assets %	24.65	25.00	26.40	25.90	19.08	16.44	15.74	11.64
Return on Equity %	42.16	44.36	48.70	46.70	36.94	33.35	32.40	23.61
EBITDA Margin %	14.09	13.86	13.55	13.98	14.14	12.09	12.54	11.10
Net Margin %	11.47	11.37	11.11	11.09	8.50	7.29	7.41	6.32
Asset Turnover	2.14	2.23	2.37	2.34	2.24	2.26	2.12	1.84
Current Ratio	5.64	4.67	4.59	4.65	4.35	3.71	3.86	4.19
Debt to Equity	0.25	0.28	0.31	0.33	0.37	0.46	0.48	0.53
Price Range	3766.27-2101.38	3459.62-2101.38	3210.21-2101.38	3700.00-2101.38	3525.73-1649.99	1830.00-1497.19	1720.00-1224.13	1276.68-997.49
P/E Ratio	17.51-9.77	16.69-10.14	15.80-10.34	18.99-10.79	27.81-13.02	17.66-14.45	19.11-13.60	20.11-15.71

Address: 11700 Plaza America Drive, Suite 500, Reston, VA 20190 Telephone: 703-956-4000	Web Site: www.nvrinc.com Officers: Dwight C. Schar - Chairman Paul C. Saville - President, Chief Executive Officer	Auditors: KPMG LLP Transfer Agents: Computershare Trust Company, N.A., Providence, RI

OCCIDENTAL PETROLEUM CORP

Exchange	Symbol	Price	52Wk Range	Yield	P/E	Div Acheiver
NYS	OXY	$41.21 (12/31/2019)	68.37-37.34	7.67	26.76	16 Years

*7 Year Price Score 58.93   *NYSE Composite Index=100   *12 Month Price Score 72.36

TRADING VOLUME (thousand shares)

Interim Earnings (Per Share)

Qtr.	Mar	Jun	Sep	Dec
2016	0.10	(0.18)	(0.32)	(0.35)
2017	0.15	0.66	0.25	0.64
2018	0.92	1.10	2.44	0.94
2019	0.84	0.84	(1.08)	...

Interim Dividends (Per Share)

Amt	Decl	Ex	Rec	Pay
0.78Q	02/27/2019	03/08/2019	03/11/2019	04/15/2019
0.78Q	05/09/2019	06/07/2019	06/10/2019	07/15/2019
0.79Q	07/11/2019	09/09/2019	09/10/2019	10/15/2019
0.79Q	11/06/2019	12/09/2019	12/10/2019	01/15/2020

Indicated Div: $3.16 (Div. Reinv. Plan)

Valuation Analysis / Institutional Holding

Forecast EPS	$1.92	No of Institutions
	(01/17/2020)	1690
Market Cap	$36.8 Billion	Shares
Book Value	$36.1 Billion	867,627,008
Price/Book	1.02	% Held
Price/Sales	1.91	91.60

Business Summary: Production & Extraction (MIC: 9.1.1 SIC: 1311 NAIC: 211111)

Occidental Petroleum is an oil and gas exploration and production company. Co.'s principal businesses consist of three segments: Oil and gas, which explores for, develops and produces oil and condensate, natural gas liquids (NGLs) and natural gas; Chemical, which manufactures and markets basic chemicals (chlorine, caustic soda, chlorinated organics, potassium chemicals, ethylene dichloride, chlorinated isocyanurates, sodium silicates, and calcium chloride) and vinyls (vinyl chloride monomer, precursor for polyvinyl and Ethylene); and Midstream and marketing, which purchases, markets, gathers, processes, transports and stores oil, condensate, NGL, natural gas, carbon dioxide and power.

Recent Developments: For the quarter ended Sep 30 2019, loss from continuing operations was US$737.0 million compared with income of US$1.87 billion in the year-earlier quarter. Net loss amounted to US$752.0 million versus net income of US$1.87 billion in the year-earlier quarter. Revenues were US$5.87 billion, down 4.9% from US$6.18 billion the year before. Direct operating expenses rose 33.1% to US$1.92 billion from US$1.44 billion in the comparable period the year before. Indirect operating expenses increased 107.2% to US$4.64 billion from US$2.24 billion in the equivalent prior-year period.

Prospects: Our evaluation of Occidental Petroleum Corp. as of October 4th, 2019 is the result of our systematic analysis on three basic characteristics: earnings strength, relative valuation, and recent stock price movement. The company has suffered a very negative trend in earnings per share over the past 5 quarters. In addition, recent analyst estimates for the company have been reduced while OXY has posted results that exceeded analysts' expectations. Based on operating earnings yield, the company is undervalued when compared to all of the companies we cover. Share price changes over the past year indicates that OXY will perform poorly over the near term.

Financial Data

(US$ in Thousands)	9 Mos	6 Mos	3 Mos	12/31/2018	12/31/2017	12/31/2016	12/31/2015	12/31/2014
Earnings Per Share	1.54	5.06	5.32	5.39	1.70	(0.75)	(10.23)	0.79
Cash Flow Per Share	9.30	10.51	10.16	10.07	6.53	4.42	4.38	14.17
Tang Book Value Per Share	19.99	28.53	28.40	28.46	26.89	28.13	31.89	39.26
Dividends Per Share	3.130	3.120	3.110	3.100	3.060	3.020	2.970	2.880
Dividend Payout %	203.25	61.66	58.46	57.51	180.00	...	...	364.56
Income Statement								
Total Revenue	14,436,000	8,565,000	4,089,000	18,934,000	13,274,000	10,398,000	12,699,000	21,947,000
EBITDA	5,277,000	3,882,000	1,854,000	9,643,000	5,318,000	2,715,000	(4,993,000)	5,562,000
Depn & Amortn	3,710,000	2,004,000	973,000	3,977,000	4,002,000	4,268,000	4,544,000	4,261,000
Income Before Taxes	902,000	1,627,000	783,000	5,277,000	971,000	(1,845,000)	(9,684,000)	1,224,000
Income Taxes	647,000	531,000	225,000	1,477,000	17,000	(662,000)	(1,330,000)	1,685,000
Net Income	472,000	1,266,000	631,000	4,131,000	1,311,000	(574,000)	(7,829,000)	616,000
Average Shares	845,700	749,500	750,500	763,300	765,900	763,800	765,600	781,100
Balance Sheet								
Current Assets	20,944,000	9,425,000	9,270,000	9,932,000	8,270,000	8,428,000	9,402,000	13,873,000
Total Assets	125,443,000	44,770,000	44,380,000	43,854,000	42,026,000	43,109,000	43,437,000	56,259,000
Current Liabilities	15,697,000	7,880,000	7,537,000	7,412,000	7,400,000	6,362,000	6,842,000	8,244,000
Long-Term Obligations	47,583,000	10,155,000	10,203,000	10,201,000	9,328,000	9,819,000	6,883,000	6,838,000
Total Liabilities	89,363,000	23,423,000	23,144,000	22,524,000	21,454,000	21,612,000	19,087,000	21,300,000
Stockholders' Equity	36,080,000	21,347,000	21,236,000	21,330,000	20,572,000	21,497,000	24,350,000	34,959,000
Shares Outstanding	893,317	748,304	747,877	749,389	765,104	764,237	763,678	890,557
Statistical Record								
Return on Assets %	1.38	8.65	9.30	9.62	3.08	N.M.	N.M.	0.98
Return on Equity %	4.09	18.17	19.32	19.72	6.23	N.M.	N.M.	1.58
EBITDA Margin %	36.55	45.32	45.34	50.93	40.06	26.11	N.M.	25.34
Net Margin %	3.27	14.78	15.43	21.82	9.88	N.M.	N.M.	2.81
Asset Turnover	0.23	0.44	0.44	0.44	0.31	0.24	0.25	0.35
Current Ratio	1.33	1.20	1.23	1.34	1.12	1.32	1.37	1.68
Debt to Equity	1.32	0.48	0.48	0.48	0.45	0.46	0.28	0.20
Price Range	83.13-42.13	85.70-47.43	86.48-57.11	86.48-57.11	73.70-58.02	78.31-59.60	83.08-63.61	100.90-73.13
P/E Ratio	53.98-27.36	16.94-9.37	16.26-10.73	16.04-10.60	43.35-34.13	...	...	127.73-92.57
Average Yield %	5.23	4.57	4.19	4.12	4.77	4.20	3.99	3.18

Address: 5 Greenway Plaza, Suite 110, Houston, TX 77046 Telephone: 713-215-7000	Web Site: www.oxy.com Officers: Eugene L. (Gene) Batchelder - Chairman Vicki A. Hollub - President, Chief Executive Officer, Chief Operating Officer, Senior Executive Vice President, Division Officer	Auditors: KPMG LLP Transfer Agents: American Stock Transfer and Trust Company, LLC, Brooklyn, NY

OCEANEERING INTERNATIONAL, INC.

Exchange	Symbol	Price	52Wk Range	Yield	P/E
NYS	OII	$14.91 (12/31/2019)	20.39-11.58	N/A	N/A

*7 Year Price Score 31.71 *NYSE Composite Index=100 *12 Month Price Score 86.32

Interim Earnings (Per Share)

Qtr.	Mar	Jun	Sep	Dec
2016	0.26	0.23	(0.12)	(0.11)
2017	(0.08)	0.02	(0.02)	1.75
2018	(0.50)	(0.34)	(0.67)	(0.66)
2019	(0.25)	(0.36)	(0.26)	...

TRADING VOLUME (thousand shares)

Interim Dividends (Per Share)

Dividend Payment Suspended

Valuation Analysis		Institutional Holding	
Forecast EPS	$-1.07	No of Institutions	
	(01/15/2020)	403	
Market Cap	$1.5 Billion	Shares	
Book Value	$1.3 Billion	120,267,288	
Price/Book	1.14	% Held	
Price/Sales	0.74	93.51	

Business Summary: Equipment & Services (MIC: 9.1.3 SIC: 1389 NAIC: 213112)

Oceaneering International is a provider of engineered services and products, primarily to the offshore oil and gas industry. Co. has two segments: Energy Services and Products; and Advanced Technologies. Co.'s business segments within the Energy Services and Products business are remotely operated vehicles, subsea products, subsea projects and asset integrity. Co.'s Advanced Technologies segment consists of two business units: government; and commercial. Government services and products include engineering and related manufacturing in defense and space exploration activities. Co.'s commercial business unit provides a turnkey solution that includes program management, and engineering design.

Recent Developments: For the quarter ended Sep 30 2019, net loss amounted to US$25.5 million versus a net loss of US$66.0 million in the year-earlier quarter. Revenues were US$497.6 million, down 4.2% from US$519.3 million the year before. Operating loss was US$5.2 million versus a loss of US$1.6 million in the prior-year quarter. Direct operating expenses declined 4.9% to US$448.6 million from US$471.7 million in the comparable period the year before. Indirect operating expenses increased 10.3% to US$54.3 million from US$49.2 million in the equivalent prior-year period.

Prospects: Our evaluation of Oceaneering International Inc. as of October 4th, 2019 is the result of our systematic analysis on three basic characteristics: earnings strength, relative valuation, and recent stock price movement. The company has generated a negative trend in earnings per share over the past 5 quarters. However, recent analyst estimates for the company have been mixed and OII has posted results that fell short of analysts' expectations. Based on operating earnings yield, the company is overvalued when compared to all of the companies we cover. Share price changes over the past year indicates that OII will perform poorly over the near term.

Financial Data

(US$ in Thousands)	9 Mos	6 Mos	3 Mos	12/31/2018	12/31/2017	12/31/2016	12/31/2015	12/31/2014
Earnings Per Share	(1.53)	(1.94)	(1.92)	(2.16)	1.68	0.25	2.34	4.00
Cash Flow Per Share	1.14	0.95	0.51	0.37	1.39	3.46	5.69	6.77
Tang Book Value Per Share	8.96	9.41	9.74	9.30	11.38	10.05	10.81	12.70
Dividends Per Share	...	...	...	...	0.450	0.960	1.080	1.030
Dividend Payout %	...	...	...	...	26.79	384.00	46.15	25.75
Income Statement								
Total Revenue	1,487,314	989,667	493,886	1,909,482	1,921,507	2,271,603	3,062,754	3,659,624
EBITDA	113,880	72,167	31,491	139,320	218,120	314,767	599,709	857,722
Depn & Amortn	153,357	102,790	52,486	293,590	213,519	250,247	241,235	229,779
Income Before Taxes	(63,941)	(45,794)	(27,815)	(182,050)	(15,861)	43,102	334,031	623,528
Income Taxes	21,981	14,051	(3,152)	26,494	(184,242)	18,760	105,250	195,148
Net Income	(85,532)	(60,009)	(24,827)	(212,327)	166,398	24,586	231,011	428,329
Average Shares	98,930	98,929	98,714	98,496	98,764	98,424	98,808	107,091
Balance Sheet								
Current Assets	1,167,197	1,195,193	1,220,392	1,244,889	1,187,402	1,262,595	1,517,493	1,713,550
Total Assets	2,885,692	2,938,635	2,971,518	2,824,998	3,023,950	3,130,315	3,429,536	3,511,701
Current Liabilities	510,414	491,044	500,311	494,741	435,797	508,364	615,956	679,137
Long-Term Obligations	799,855	795,639	790,969	786,580	792,312	793,058	795,836	750,000
Total Liabilities	1,588,676	1,585,665	1,586,081	1,415,763	1,364,786	1,613,672	1,850,802	1,854,081
Stockholders' Equity	1,297,016	1,352,970	1,385,437	1,409,235	1,659,164	1,516,643	1,578,734	1,657,620
Shares Outstanding	98,929	98,929	98,928	98,539	98,279	98,065	97,849	99,613
Statistical Record								
Return on Assets %	N.M.	N.M.	N.M.	N.M.	5.41	0.75	6.66	12.90
Return on Equity %	N.M.	N.M.	N.M.	N.M.	10.48	1.58	14.28	23.15
EBITDA Margin %	7.66	7.29	6.38	7.30	11.35	13.86	19.58	23.44
Net Margin %	N.M.	N.M.	N.M.	N.M.	8.66	1.08	7.54	11.70
Asset Turnover	0.68	0.69	0.67	0.65	0.62	0.69	0.88	1.10
Current Ratio	2.29	2.43	2.44	2.52	2.72	2.48	2.46	2.52
Debt to Equity	0.62	0.59	0.57	0.56	0.48	0.52	0.50	0.45
Price Range	27.40-10.96	28.49-10.96	28.49-10.96	28.49-10.96	29.35-18.28	38.78-22.75	59.12-37.06	78.88-57.49
P/E Ratio	...	...	...	...	17.47-10.88	155.12-91.00	25.26-15.84	19.72-14.37
Average Yield %	...	...	...	...	1.83	3.24	2.27	1.48

Address: 11911 FM 529, Houston, TX 77041	Web Site: www.oceaneering.com	Auditors: Ernst & Young LLP
Telephone: 713-329-4500	Officers: John R. Huff - Chairman Roderick A. Larson - President, Chief Executive Officer, Senior Vice President, Chief Operating Officer	Investor Contact: 713-329-4500 Transfer Agents: Computershare Trust Company, N.A., Providence, RI

OGE ENERGY CORP.

Exchange	Symbol	Price	52Wk Range	Yield	P/E	Div Acheiver
NYS	OGE	$44.47 (12/31/2019)	45.43-38.26	3.49	19.68	12 Years

*7 Year Price Score 101.29 *NYSE Composite Index=100 *12 Month Price Score 95.56

Interim Earnings (Per Share)

Qtr.	Mar	Jun	Sep	Dec
2016	0.13	0.35	0.92	0.29
2017	0.18	0.52	0.92	1.48
2018	0.27	0.55	1.02	0.27
2019	0.24	0.50	1.25	...

Interim Dividends (Per Share)

Amt	Decl	Ex	Rec	Pay
0.365Q	02/20/2019	04/09/2019	04/10/2019	04/30/2019
0.365Q	05/16/2019	07/09/2019	07/10/2019	07/30/2019
0.388Q	09/25/2019	10/09/2019	10/10/2019	10/30/2019
0.388Q	12/04/2019	01/09/2020	01/10/2020	01/30/2020

Indicated Div: $1.55 (Div. Reinv. Plan)

Valuation Analysis

		Institutional Holding	
Forecast EPS	$2.27	No of Institutions	
	(01/17/2020)	651	
Market Cap	$8.9 Billion	Shares	
Book Value	$4.2 Billion		174,196,672
Price/Book	2.13	% Held	
Price/Sales	3.92		65.75

Business Summary: Electric Utilities (MIC: 3.1.1 SIC: 4911 NAIC: 221121)

OGE Energy is a holding company. Through its subsidiaries, Co. is an energy and energy services provider providing physical delivery and related services for both electricity and natural gas primarily in the south central U.S. Co. conducts these activities through two business segments: electric utility, which generates, transmits, distributes and sells electric energy in Oklahoma and western Arkansas; and natural gas midstream operations, which consist of Co.'s investment in Enable Midstream Partners, LP that involves in the business of gathering, processing, transporting and storing natural gas.

Recent Developments: For the quarter ended Sep 30 2019, net income increased 22.3% to US$250.9 million from US$205.1 million in the year-earlier quarter. Revenues were US$755.4 million, up 8.1% from US$698.8 million the year before. Operating income was US$274.3 million versus US$227.3 million in the prior-year quarter, an increase of 20.7%. Direct operating expenses rose 2.0% to US$457.9 million from US$448.8 million in the comparable period the year before. Indirect operating expenses increased 2.2% to US$23.2 million from US$22.7 million in the equivalent prior-year period.

Prospects: Our evaluation of OGE Energy Corp. as of October 4th, 2019 is the result of our systematic analysis on three basic characteristics: earnings strength, relative valuation, and recent stock price movement. The company has produced a positive trend in earnings per share over the past 5 quarters. However, recent analyst estimates for the company have been mixed and OGE has posted results that fell short of analysts' expectations. Based on operating earnings yield, the company is fairly valued when compared to all of the companies we cover. Share price changes over the past year indicates that OGE will perform well over the near term.

Financial Data

(US$ in Thousands)	9 Mos	6 Mos	3 Mos	12/31/2018	12/31/2017	12/31/2016	12/31/2015	12/31/2014
Earnings Per Share	2.26	2.03	2.08	2.12	3.10	1.69	1.36	1.98
Cash Flow Per Share	3.28	3.62	4.07	4.76	3.93	3.22	4.34	3.62
Tang Book Value Per Share	20.91	20.02	19.86	20.06	19.28	17.24	16.65	16.27
Dividends Per Share	1.460	1.428	1.395	1.363	1.240	1.127	1.025	0.925
Dividend Payout %	64.60	70.32	67.07	64.27	40.00	66.72	75.37	46.72
Income Statement								
Total Revenue	1,759,100	1,003,700	490,000	2,270,300	2,261,100	2,259,200	2,196,900	2,453,100
EBITDA	690,500	323,400	127,600	822,500	865,800	849,200	810,100	825,800
Depn & Amortn	260,800	166,700	82,400	321,600	283,500	322,600	307,900	281,400
Income Before Taxes	319,600	86,200	10,600	344,900	438,500	384,500	353,200	396,000
Income Taxes	26,200	5,400	(5,800)	72,200	(49,300)	148,100	97,400	172,800
Net Income	398,200	147,300	47,100	425,500	619,000	338,200	271,300	395,800
Average Shares	200,800	200,600	200,500	200,500	200,000	199,900	199,600	199,900
Balance Sheet								
Current Assets	549,100	455,600	454,100	557,300	497,000	549,500	570,200	705,800
Total Assets	11,083,700	10,886,200	10,761,600	10,748,600	10,412,700	9,939,600	9,597,400	9,527,800
Current Liabilities	696,600	702,700	884,200	869,400	950,500	1,027,200	752,800	573,300
Long-Term Obligations	3,194,700	3,193,600	2,897,300	2,896,900	2,749,600	2,405,800	2,645,600	2,755,300
Total Liabilities	6,897,500	6,879,000	6,785,400	6,743,500	6,561,600	6,495,800	6,271,400	6,283,400
Stockholders' Equity	4,186,200	4,007,200	3,976,200	4,005,100	3,851,100	3,443,800	3,326,000	3,244,400
Shares Outstanding	200,176	200,175	200,174	199,700	199,700	199,700	199,700	199,400
Statistical Record								
Return on Assets %	4.16	3.80	3.94	4.02	6.08	3.45	2.84	4.24
Return on Equity %	11.03	10.31	10.68	10.83	16.97	9.96	8.26	12.60
EBITDA Margin %	39.25	32.22	26.04	36.23	38.29	37.59	36.87	33.66
Net Margin %	22.64	14.68	9.61	18.74	27.38	14.97	12.35	16.13
Asset Turnover	0.21	0.21	0.21	0.21	0.22	0.23	0.23	0.26
Current Ratio	0.79	0.65	0.51	0.64	0.52	0.53	0.76	1.23
Debt to Equity	0.76	0.80	0.73	0.72	0.71	0.70	0.80	0.85
Price Range	45.43-35.76	43.86-34.34	43.66-31.56	41.63-29.60	37.23-32.66	33.89-23.86	36.20-24.37	39.08-33.18
P/E Ratio	20.10-15.82	21.61-16.92	20.99-15.17	19.64-13.96	12.01-10.54	20.05-14.12	26.62-17.92	19.74-16.76
Average Yield %	3.53	3.60	3.73	3.89	3.52	3.77	3.42	2.56

Address: 321 North Harvey, P.O. Box 321, Oklahoma City, OK 73101-0321	Web Site: www.oge.com	Auditors: Ernst & Young LLP
Telephone: 405-553-3000	Officers: Sean Trauschke - Chairman, President, Chief Executive Officer Patricia D. Horn - Vice President, Corporate Secretary	Investor Contact: 405-553-3966
		Transfer Agents: Computershare, Providence, RI

OLD REPUBLIC INTERNATIONAL CORP.

Exchange	Symbol	Price	52Wk Range	Yield	P/E	Div Acheiver
NYS	ORI	$22.37 (12/31/2019)	24.07-20.00	3.58	9.99	37 Years

*7 Year Price Score 100.47   ***NYSE Composite Index=100**   ***12 Month Price Score 96.23**

Interim Earnings (Per Share)

Qtr.	Mar	Jun	Sep	Dec
2016	0.43	0.35	0.39	0.45
2017	0.39	0.35	0.17	1.01
2018	0.01	0.66	0.92	(0.35)
2019	1.37	0.55	0.67	...

Interim Dividends (Per Share)

Amt	Decl	Ex	Rec	Pay
0.20Q	05/09/2019	06/03/2019	06/04/2019	06/14/2019
0.20Q	08/21/2019	09/05/2019	09/06/2019	09/16/2019
1.00Sp	08/21/2019	09/05/2019	09/06/2019	09/16/2019
0.20Q	11/26/2019	12/05/2019	12/06/2019	12/16/2019

Indicated Div: $0.80 (Div. Reinv. Plan)

Valuation Analysis		Institutional Holding	
Forecast EPS	$1.76	No of Institutions	
	(01/15/2020)	605	
Market Cap	$6.8 Billion	Shares	
Book Value	$5.8 Billion	282,939,136	
Price/Book	1.17	% Held	
Price/Sales	1.03	86.39	

Business Summary: General Insurance (MIC: 5.2.1 SIC: 6351 NAIC: 524113)

Old Republic International is a holding company engaged in the business of insurance underwriting and related services. Through its regulated insurance company subsidiaries, Co. conducts its operations in three main segments: General Insurance Group, which is a commercial lines insurance business focused on liability insurance coverages; Title Insurance Group, which consists mainly of the issuance of policies to real estate purchasers and investors based upon searches of the public records, which contain information concerning interests in real property; and the Republic Financial Indemnity Group Run-off Business, which consists of mortgage guaranty and consumer credit indemnity operations.

Recent Developments: For the quarter ended Sep 30 2019, net income decreased 26.3% to US$202.8 million from US$275.2 million in the year-earlier quarter. Revenues were US$1.77 billion, down 0.5% from US$1.78 billion the year before. Net premiums earned were US$1.42 billion versus US$1.39 billion in the prior-year quarter, an increase of 2.5%. Net investment income rose 3.7% to US$112.6 million from US$108.6 million a year ago.

Prospects: Our evaluation of Old Republic International Corp. as of October 4th, 2019 is the result of our systematic analysis on three basic characteristics: earnings strength, relative valuation, and recent stock price movement. The company has managed to produce a neutral trend in earnings per share over the past 5 quarters. Additionally, recent analyst estimates for the company have been unchanged while ORI has posted results that fell short of analysts' expectations. Based on operating earnings yield, the company is undervalued when compared to all of the companies we cover. Share price changes over the past year indicates that ORI will perform in line with the market over the near term.

Financial Data

(US$ in Thousands)	9 Mos	6 Mos	3 Mos	12/31/2018	12/31/2017	12/31/2016	12/31/2015	12/31/2014
Earnings Per Share	2.24	2.49	2.60	1.24	1.92	1.62	1.48	1.44
Cash Flow Per Share	2.77	2.63	2.56	2.58	1.73	2.45	2.65	(0.70)
Tang Book Value Per Share	19.09	19.44	18.70	17.00	17.58	17.02	14.81	15.04
Dividends Per Share	1.795	0.790	0.785	1.780	0.760	0.750	0.740	0.730
Dividend Payout %	80.13	31.73	30.19	143.55	39.58	46.30	50.00	50.69
Income Statement								
Premium Income	4,016,500	2,593,000	1,263,400	5,253,400	5,080,200	4,868,900	4,758,800	4,446,300
Total Revenue	5,284,400	3,513,400	1,868,600	6,021,800	6,263,100	5,900,500	5,766,100	5,530,700
Benefits & Claims	...	...	...	2,440,900	2,459,200	2,329,800	2,441,300	2,500,000
Income Before Taxes	976,300	723,900	518,500	438,100	725,400	686,000	631,800	...
Income Taxes	195,600	146,100	106,200	67,500	164,800	219,000	209,600	199,700
Net Income	780,600	577,700	412,200	370,500	560,500	466,900	422,100	409,700
Average Shares	301,384	300,752	300,172	301,016	299,387	296,379	296,088	295,073
Balance Sheet								
Total Assets	21,181,800	20,987,700	20,296,900	19,327,100	19,403,500	18,591,600	17,110,500	16,988,100
Total Liabilities	15,387,900	15,093,700	14,631,300	14,180,800	14,670,200	14,119,900	13,229,600	13,064,000
Stockholders' Equity	5,793,900	5,893,900	5,665,600	5,146,200	4,733,300	4,471,600	3,880,800	3,924,000
Shares Outstanding	303,570	303,201	302,950	302,714	269,238	262,719	261,968	260,946
Statistical Record								
Return on Assets %	3.29	3.69	3.96	1.91	2.95	2.61	2.48	2.44
Return on Equity %	12.14	13.57	14.53	7.50	12.18	11.15	10.82	10.64
Loss Ratio %	...	...	...	46.46	48.41	47.85	51.30	56.23
Net Margin %	14.77	16.44	22.06	6.15	8.95	7.91	7.32	7.41
Price Range	23.77-19.65	22.95-19.65	22.95-19.65	22.95-19.65	21.46-18.11	19.98-16.58	19.02-13.87	17.27-13.74
P/E Ratio	10.61-8.77	9.22-7.89	8.83-7.56	18.51-15.85	11.18-9.43	12.33-10.23	12.85-9.37	11.99-9.54
Average Yield %	8.24	3.68	3.71	8.41	3.80	4.07	4.61	4.67

Address: 307 North Michigan Avenue, Chicago, IL 60601 Telephone: 312-346-8100	Web Site: www.oldrepublic.com Officers: Aldo C. Zucaro - Chairman, Chief Executive Officer Craig R. Smiddy - President, Chief Executive Officer, Chief Operating Officer	Auditors: KPMG LLP Investor Contact: 800-468-9716 Transfer Agents: Wells Fargo Shareholder Services, St. Paul, MN

OLIN CORP.

Exchange	Symbol	Price	52Wk Range	Yield	P/E
NYS	OLN	$17.25 (12/31/2019)	27.12-15.41	4.64	23.96

*7 Year Price Score 67.52 *NYSE Composite Index=100 *12 Month Price Score 81.22

Interim Earnings (Per Share)

Qtr.	Mar	Jun	Sep	Dec
2016	(0.23)	(0.01)	0.11	0.11
2017	0.08	(0.04)	0.31	2.90
2018	0.12	0.35	1.16	0.32
2019	0.25	(0.12)	0.27	...

Interim Dividends (Per Share)

Amt	Decl	Ex	Rec	Pay
0.20Q	01/25/2019	02/08/2019	02/11/2019	03/11/2019
0.20Q	04/25/2019	05/09/2019	05/10/2019	06/10/2019
0.20Q	07/25/2019	08/08/2019	08/09/2019	09/10/2019
0.20Q	10/23/2019	11/08/2019	11/12/2019	12/10/2019

Indicated Div: $0.80 (Div. Reinv. Plan)

Valuation Analysis

		Institutional Holding	
Forecast EPS	$0.57	No of Institutions	
	(01/17/2020)	499	
Market Cap	$2.8 Billion	Shares	
Book Value	$2.7 Billion	186,278,864	
Price/Book	1.03	% Held	
Price/Sales	0.43	86.60	

Business Summary: Diversified Chemicals (MIC: 8.3.1 SIC: 2812 NAIC: 325181)

Olin is a manufacturer and distributor of chemical products and a manufacturer of ammunition. Co.'s segments include: Chlor Alkali Products and Vinyls, which manufactures and sells chlorine and caustic soda, ethylene dichloride and vinyl chloride monomer, methyl chloride, methylene chloride, chloroform, hydrogen, bleach products and potassium hydroxide; Epoxy, which produces and sells epoxy materials, including allyl chloride, epichlorohydrin, liquid epoxy resins, solid epoxy resins and differentiated epoxy resins and additives; and Winchester, which produces and sells sporting ammunition, reloading components, small caliber military ammunition and components, and industrial cartridges.

Recent Developments: For the quarter ended Sep 30 2019, net income decreased 77.3% to US$44.2 million from US$195.1 million in the year-earlier quarter. Revenues were US$1.58 billion, down 15.8% from US$1.87 billion the year before. Operating income was US$103.4 million versus US$314.5 million in the prior-year quarter, a decrease of 67.1%. Direct operating expenses declined 5.8% to US$1.36 billion from US$1.44 billion in the comparable period the year before. Indirect operating expenses decreased 0.5% to US$115.6 million from US$116.2 million in the equivalent prior-year period.

Prospects: Our evaluation of Olin Corp. as of October 4th, 2019 is the result of our systematic analysis on three basic characteristics: earnings strength, relative valuation, and recent stock price movement. The company has suffered a very negative trend in earnings per share over the past 5 quarters. In addition, recent analyst estimates for the company have been reduced and OLN has posted results that fell short of analysts' expectations. Based on operating earnings yield, the company is undervalued when compared to all of the companies we cover. Share price changes over the past year indicates that OLN will perform poorly over the near term.

Financial Data

(US$ in Thousands)	9 Mos	6 Mos	3 Mos	12/31/2018	12/31/2017	12/31/2016	12/31/2015	12/31/2014
Earnings Per Share	0.72	1.61	2.08	1.95	3.26	(0.02)	(0.01)	1.33
Cash Flow Per Share	4.56	5.34	5.64	5.44	3.90	3.64	2.10	2.03
Tang Book Value Per Share	0.52	1.04	1.36	1.22	0.33	N.M.	N.M.	1.84
Dividends Per Share	0.800	0.800	0.800	0.800	0.800	0.800	0.800	0.800
Dividend Payout %	111.11	49.69	38.46	41.03	24.54	...	...	60.15
Income Statement								
Total Revenue	4,722,900	3,146,300	1,553,400	6,946,100	6,268,400	5,550,600	2,854,400	2,241,200
EBITDA	710,600	447,300	263,200	1,196,400	796,100	662,100	324,800	342,600
Depn & Amortn	460,300	304,300	152,900	497,800	465,100	509,500	223,900	139,100
Income Before Taxes	72,000	28,200	53,100	457,000	115,400	(35,900)	5,000	161,000
Income Taxes	6,100	6,500	11,400	109,400	(432,300)	(30,300)	8,100	57,700
Net Income	65,900	21,700	41,700	327,900	549,500	(3,900)	(1,400)	105,700
Average Shares	162,800	164,600	166,100	168,400	168,500	165,200	103,400	79,700
Balance Sheet								
Current Assets	1,769,600	1,726,200	1,684,500	1,707,400	1,699,200	1,546,200	1,933,400	816,100
Total Assets	9,232,600	9,235,300	9,169,900	8,997,400	9,218,300	8,762,600	9,321,800	2,698,100
Current Liabilities	1,077,200	1,050,100	1,139,900	1,118,300	954,300	922,600	1,147,700	377,700
Long-Term Obligations	3,587,200	3,461,900	3,273,200	3,104,400	3,611,300	3,537,100	3,675,200	658,700
Total Liabilities	6,567,900	6,464,500	6,332,300	6,165,200	6,464,600	6,489,600	6,903,000	1,684,800
Stockholders' Equity	2,664,700	2,770,800	2,837,600	2,832,200	2,753,700	2,273,000	2,418,800	1,013,300
Shares Outstanding	159,700	164,300	164,900	165,300	167,100	165,400	165,100	77,400
Statistical Record								
Return on Assets %	1.29	2.94	3.80	3.60	6.11	N.M.	N.M.	3.84
Return on Equity %	4.27	9.76	12.45	11.74	21.86	N.M.	N.M.	10.00
EBITDA Margin %	15.05	14.22	16.94	17.22	12.70	11.93	11.38	15.29
Net Margin %	1.40	0.69	2.68	4.72	8.77	N.M.	N.M.	4.72
Asset Turnover	0.69	0.72	0.74	0.76	0.70	0.61	0.47	0.81
Current Ratio	1.64	1.64	1.48	1.53	1.78	1.68	1.68	2.16
Debt to Equity	1.35	1.25	1.15	1.10	1.31	1.56	1.52	0.65
Price Range	27.12-15.41	31.58-18.09	34.18-18.09	38.60-18.09	37.15-25.98	26.83-12.78	32.41-15.82	28.85-21.22
P/E Ratio	37.67-21.40	19.61-11.24	16.43-8.70	19.79-9.28	11.40-7.97	...	...	21.69-15.95
Average Yield %	3.71	3.30	3.02	2.77	2.51	3.88	3.31	3.03

Address: 190 Carondelet Plaza, Suite 1530, Clayton, MO 63105 **Telephone:** 314-480-1400	**Web Site:** www.olin.com **Officers:** John E. Fischer - Chairman, President, Chief Executive Officer, Chief Operating Officer, Senior Vice President, Vice President, Controller, Chief Financial Officer Pat D. Dawson - Executive Vice President, Division Officer	**Auditors:** KPMG LLP **Investor Contact:** 314-480-1452 **Transfer Agents:** EQ Shareowner Services, Mendota Heights, MN

OMEGA HEALTHCARE INVESTORS, INC.

Exchange	Symbol	Price	52Wk Range	Yield	P/E	Div Acheiver
NYS	OHI	$42.35 (12/31/2019)	44.96-33.95	6.33	26.30	16 Years

*7 Year Price Score 94.62 *NYSE Composite Index=100 *12 Month Price Score 102.78

Interim Earnings (Per Share)

Qtr.	Mar	Jun	Sep	Dec
2016	0.29	0.57	0.40	0.64
2017	0.53	0.33	(0.67)	0.32
2018	0.42	0.39	0.28	0.30
2019	0.34	0.34	0.63	...

Interim Dividends (Per Share)

Amt	Decl	Ex	Rec	Pay
0.66Q	04/15/2019	04/29/2019	04/30/2019	05/15/2019
0.66Q	07/15/2019	07/30/2019	07/31/2019	08/15/2019
0.67Q	10/14/2019	10/30/2019	10/31/2019	11/15/2019
0.67Q	01/15/2020	01/30/2020	01/31/2020	02/14/2020

Indicated Div: $2.68 (Div. Reinv. Plan)

Valuation Analysis / **Institutional Holding**

Forecast EPS	$1.67
	(01/17/2020)
Market Cap	$9.3 Billion
Book Value	$3.9 Billion
Price/Book	2.38
Price/Sales	10.26

No of Institutions	669
Shares	217,404,032
% Held	82.93

Business Summary: REITs (MIC: 5.3.1 SIC: 6798 NAIC: 525930)

Omega Healthcare Investors is a real estate investment trust. Co. has one reportable segment consisting of investments in healthcare-related real estate properties located in the U.S. and the U.K. Co.'s main business is to provide financing and capital to the long-term healthcare industry with a particular focus on skilled nursing facilities, and, to a lesser extent, assisted living facilities, independent living facilities and rehabilitation and acute care facilities. Co.'s main portfolio consists of long-term leases and mortgage agreements.

Recent Developments: For the quarter ended Sep 30 2019, net income increased 142.0% to US$142.9 million from US$59.1 million in the year-earlier quarter. Revenues were US$233.2 million, up 5.1% from US$221.9 million the year before. Revenues from property income rose 5.3% to US$202.5 million from US$192.3 million in the corresponding quarter a year earlier.

Prospects: Our evaluation of Omega Healthcare Investors Inc. as of October 4th, 2019 is the result of our systematic analysis on three basic characteristics: earnings strength, relative valuation, and recent stock price movement. The company has managed to produce a neutral trend in earnings per share over the past 5 quarters. In addition, recent analyst estimates for the company have been mixed and OHI has posted results that fell short of analysts' expectations. Based on operating earnings yield, the company is fairly valued when compared to all of the companies we cover. Share price changes over the past year indicates that OHI will perform well over the near term.

Financial Data

(US$ in Thousands)	9 Mos	6 Mos	3 Mos	12/31/2018	12/31/2017	12/31/2016	12/31/2015	12/31/2014
Earnings Per Share	1.61	1.26	1.31	1.40	0.51	1.90	1.29	1.74
Cash Flow Per Share	2.56	2.59	2.72	2.49	2.92	3.25	2.69	2.67
Tang Book Value Per Share	14.82	14.62	14.02	13.84	14.68	16.39	16.50	10.98
Dividends Per Share	2.640	2.640	2.640	2.640	2.540	2.360	2.180	2.020
Dividend Payout %	163.98	209.52	201.53	188.57	498.04	124.21	168.99	116.09
Income Statement								
Total Revenue	682,162	448,967	223,688	881,682	908,385	900,827	743,617	504,787
EBITDA	658,979	394,110	193,465	777,154	636,501	838,040	661,266	482,537
Depn & Amortn	223,265	145,579	71,264	279,532	310,604	278,319	243,817	134,363
Income Before Taxes	282,724	147,721	72,200	296,513	105,921	384,333	234,526	221,349
Income Taxes	1,951	1,468	675	3,010	3,248	1,405	1,211	...
Net Income	281,583	142,843	69,702	281,578	100,419	366,415	224,524	221,349
Average Shares	226,513	220,479	213,523	209,711	206,790	201,635	180,508	127,294
Balance Sheet								
Current Assets	425,259	402,071	74,746	359,048	376,142	347,311	223,893	201,741
Total Assets	8,996,194	9,098,420	8,520,066	8,590,877	8,773,305	8,949,260	8,019,009	3,921,645
Current Liabilities	794,863	898,604	901,345	13,599	17,747	9,906	15,352	...
Long-Term Obligations	3,824,390	3,834,180	3,527,675	4,540,622	4,572,158	4,366,854	3,569,086	2,378,503
Total Liabilities	5,114,209	5,295,449	4,974,264	5,146,436	5,218,214	5,090,515	4,281,023	2,520,318
Stockholders' Equity	3,881,985	3,802,971	3,545,802	3,444,441	3,555,091	3,858,745	3,737,986	1,401,327
Shares Outstanding	218,478	216,089	207,001	202,346	198,309	196,142	187,399	127,606
Statistical Record								
Return on Assets %	3.90	2.96	3.09	3.24	1.13	4.31	3.76	6.00
Return on Equity %	9.36	7.14	7.54	8.05	2.71	9.62	8.74	16.39
EBITDA Margin %	96.60	87.78	86.49	88.14	70.07	93.03	88.93	95.59
Net Margin %	41.28	31.82	31.16	31.94	11.05	40.68	30.19	43.85
Asset Turnover	0.10	0.10	0.10	0.10	0.10	0.11	0.12	0.14
Current Ratio	0.54	0.45	0.08	26.40	21.19	35.06	14.58	...
Debt to Equity	0.99	1.01	0.99	1.32	1.29	1.13	0.95	1.70
Price Range	42.01-31.98	40.19-29.32	40.19-25.36	38.21-25.36	34.98-26.78	38.02-27.46	45.16-32.08	40.29-29.56
P/E Ratio	26.09-19.86	31.90-23.27	30.68-19.36	27.29-18.11	68.59-52.51	20.01-14.45	35.01-24.87	23.16-16.99
Average Yield %	7.17	7.54	8.00	8.67	8.06	7.12	5.91	5.68

Address: 303 International Circle, Suite 200, Hunt Valley, MD 21030 **Telephone:** 410-427-1700 **Fax:** 410-427-8800	**Web Site:** www.omegahealthcare.com **Officers:** Bernard J. Korman - Chairman, Director Emeritus C. Taylor Pickett - Chief Executive Officer	**Auditors:** Ernst & Young LLP **Investor Contact:** 410-427-1700 **Transfer Agents:** Registrar and Transfer Company, Cranford , NJ

OMNICOM GROUP, INC.

Exchange	Symbol	Price	52Wk Range	Yield	P/E
NYS	OMC	$81.02 (12/31/2019)	84.77-71.57	3.21	13.64

*7 Year Price Score 86.59 *NYSE Composite Index=100 *12 Month Price Score 96.54

Interim Earnings (Per Share)

Qtr.	Mar	Jun	Sep	Dec
2016	0.90	1.36	1.06	1.47
2017	1.02	1.40	1.13	1.10
2018	1.14	1.60	1.32	1.77
2019	1.17	1.68	1.32	...

Interim Dividends (Per Share)

Amt	Decl	Ex	Rec	Pay
0.65Q	02/11/2019	03/08/2019	03/11/2019	04/09/2019
0.65Q	05/20/2019	06/13/2019	06/14/2019	07/12/2019
0.65Q	07/15/2019	09/19/2019	09/20/2019	10/10/2019
0.65Q	12/10/2019	12/19/2019	12/20/2019	01/09/2020

Indicated Div: $2.60

Valuation Analysis   Institutional Holding

Forecast EPS	$6.00	No of Institutions	
	(01/17/2020)	1124	
Market Cap	$17.6 Billion	Shares	
Book Value	$2.5 Billion	303,091,008	
Price/Book	7.16	% Held	
Price/Sales	1.18	86.93	

Business Summary: Advertising (MIC: 2.3.4 SIC: 7311 NAIC: 541810)

Omnicom Group is a holding company, engaged in providing advertising, marketing and corporate communications services. Co.'s networks and agencies provide a range of services in the following fundamental disciplines: advertising, customer relationship management, public relations and healthcare. Service offerings includes: advertising, branding, content marketing, corporate social responsibility consulting, crisis communications, custom publishing, data analytics, database management, digital/direct marketing, digital transformation, entertainment marketing, experiential marketing, field marketing, investor relations, marketing research, among others.

Recent Developments: For the quarter ended Sep 30 2019, net income decreased 5.8% to US$312.2 million from US$331.3 million in the year-earlier quarter. Revenues were US$3.62 billion, down 2.4% from US$3.71 billion the year before. Operating income was US$473.3 million versus US$502.3 million in the prior-year quarter, a decrease of 5.8%. Direct operating expenses declined 1.2% to US$3.00 billion from US$3.03 billion in the comparable period the year before. Indirect operating expenses decreased 13.5% to US$155.1 million from US$179.4 million in the equivalent prior-year period.

Prospects: Our evaluation of Omnicom Group Inc. as of October 4th, 2019 is the result of our systematic analysis on three basic characteristics: earnings strength, relative valuation, and recent stock price movement. The company has managed to produce a neutral trend in earnings per share over the past 5 quarters. Additionally, recent analyst estimates for the company have been unchanged while OMC has posted results that exceeded analysts' expectations. Based on operating earnings yield, the company is undervalued when compared to all of the companies we cover. Share price changes over the past year indicates that OMC will perform well over the near term.

Financial Data

(US$ in Thousands)	9 Mos	6 Mos	3 Mos	12/31/2018	12/31/2017	12/31/2016	12/31/2015	12/31/2014
Earnings Per Share	5.94	5.94	5.86	5.83	4.65	4.78	4.41	4.24
Cash Flow Per Share	7.92	8.21	8.73	7.60	8.71	8.10	8.90	5.82
Dividends Per Share	2.550	2.500	2.450	2.400	2.250	2.150	2.000	1.900
Dividend Payout %	42.93	42.09	41.81	41.17	48.39	44.98	45.35	44.81
Income Statement								
Total Revenue	10,812,500	7,188,700	3,468,900	15,290,200	15,273,600	15,416,900	15,134,400	15,317,800
EBITDA	1,530,800	1,039,000	447,300	2,397,500	2,341,800	2,301,800	2,211,200	2,238,500
Depn & Amortn	54,900	36,400	18,400	264,000	282,100	292,900	291,100	294,400
Income Before Taxes	1,330,400	906,400	382,900	1,924,300	1,884,900	1,841,800	1,778,600	1,810,000
Income Taxes	345,500	233,200	102,700	492,700	696,200	600,500	583,600	593,100
Net Income	924,100	633,900	263,200	1,326,400	1,088,400	1,148,600	1,093,900	1,104,000
Average Shares	219,400	220,900	224,200	227,600	233,900	239,200	245,200	255,300
Balance Sheet								
Current Assets	11,600,900	12,802,800	13,072,200	13,726,900	14,116,000	12,722,000	11,980,500	11,190,500
Total Assets	23,653,500	25,042,100	25,211,200	24,617,000	24,931,200	23,165,400	22,110,700	21,559,700
Current Liabilities	13,259,800	15,068,100	14,913,100	15,270,200	15,108,900	14,010,900	14,219,600	12,061,100
Long-Term Obligations	4,507,000	4,025,900	4,402,000	4,384,100	4,912,900	4,920,500	3,564,200	4,562,600
Total Liabilities	21,189,400	22,631,900	22,797,900	22,069,900	22,316,100	21,003,400	19,658,300	18,709,700
Stockholders' Equity	2,464,100	2,410,200	2,413,300	2,547,100	2,615,100	2,162,000	2,452,400	2,850,000
Shares Outstanding	217,732	297,200	220,167	223,900	230,100	234,700	239,700	246,700
Statistical Record								
Return on Assets %	5.74	5.64	5.44	5.35	4.53	5.06	5.01	5.06
Return on Equity %	54.62	56.30	52.60	51.39	45.57	49.65	41.26	34.33
EBITDA Margin %	14.16	14.45	12.89	15.68	15.33	14.93	14.61	14.61
Net Margin %	8.55	8.82	7.59	8.67	7.13	7.45	7.23	7.21
Asset Turnover	0.65	0.64	0.62	0.62	0.64	0.68	0.69	0.70
Current Ratio	0.87	0.85	0.88	0.90	0.93	0.91	0.84	0.93
Debt to Equity	1.83	1.67	1.82	1.72	1.88	2.28	1.45	1.60
Price Range	84.77-68.07	83.80-67.31	78.36-67.31	82.78-67.31	87.39-65.52	88.47-67.94	80.52-64.79	78.41-64.93
P/E Ratio	14.27-11.46	14.11-11.33	13.37-11.49	14.20-11.55	18.79-14.09	18.51-14.21	18.26-14.69	18.49-15.31
Average Yield %	3.32	3.35	3.34	3.28	2.84	2.64	2.71	2.64

Address: 437 Madison Avenue, New York, NY 10022 **Telephone:** 212-415-3600 **Fax:** 212-415-3393	**Web Site:** www.omnicomgroup.com **Officers:** John D. Wren - Chairman, President, Chief Executive Officer Philip J. Angelastro - Executive Vice President, Chief Financial Officer, Senior Vice President, Controller	**Auditors:** KPMG LLP **Investor Contact:** 212-415-3393 **Transfer Agents:** Wells Fargo Bank, NA, South St. Paul, MN

ONE GAS, INC.

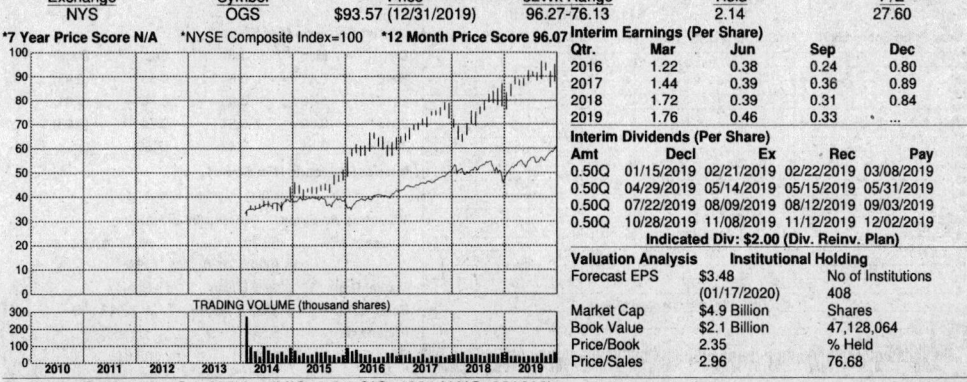

Exchange	Symbol	Price	52Wk Range	Yield	P/E
NYS	OGS	$93.57 (12/31/2019)	96.27-76.13	2.14	27.60

*7 Year Price Score N/A   *NYSE Composite Index=100   *12 Month Price Score 96.07

Interim Earnings (Per Share)

Qtr.	Mar	Jun	Sep	Dec
2016	1.22	0.38	0.24	0.80
2017	1.44	0.39	0.36	0.89
2018	1.72	0.39	0.31	0.84
2019	1.76	0.46	0.33	...

Interim Dividends (Per Share)

Amt	Decl	Ex	Rec	Pay
0.50Q	01/15/2019	02/21/2019	02/22/2019	03/08/2019
0.50Q	04/29/2019	05/14/2019	05/15/2019	05/31/2019
0.50Q	07/22/2019	08/09/2019	08/12/2019	09/03/2019
0.50Q	10/28/2019	11/08/2019	11/12/2019	12/02/2019

Indicated Div: $2.00 (Div. Reinv. Plan)

Valuation Analysis   **Institutional Holding**

Forecast EPS	$3.48	No of Institutions
	(01/17/2020)	408
Market Cap	$4.9 Billion	Shares
Book Value	$2.1 Billion	47,128,064
Price/Book	2.35	% Held
Price/Sales	2.96	76.68

Business Summary: Gas Utilities (MIC: 3.3.1 SIC: 4924 NAIC: 221210)

ONE Gas is a regulated natural gas distribution utility. Co. provides natural gas distribution services to its customers and is a natural gas distributor in Oklahoma, Kansas and Texas. Co. serves residential, commercial and industrial, transportation and wholesale, and public authority customers in the three states. Co.'s natural gas distribution markets are Oklahoma City and Tulsa, OK; Kansas City, Wichita and Topeka, KS; and Austin and El Paso, TX. Co.'s three divisions, Oklahoma Natural Gas, Kansas Gas Service and Texas Gas Service, distribute natural gas to the natural gas distribution customers in Oklahoma, Kansas and Texas.

Recent Developments: For the quarter ended Sep 30 2019, net income increased 7.3% to US$17.5 million from US$16.3 million in the year-earlier quarter. Revenues were US$248.6 million, up 4.3% from US$238.3 million the year before. Operating income was US$38.8 million versus US$36.2 million in the prior-year quarter, an increase of 7.0%. Direct operating expenses declined 3.2% to US$49.6 million from US$51.3 million in the comparable period the year before. Indirect operating expenses increased 6.2% to US$160.2 million from US$150.8 million in the equivalent prior-year period.

Prospects: Our evaluation of One Gas Inc. as of October 4th, 2019 is the result of our systematic analysis on three basic characteristics: earnings strength, relative valuation, and recent stock price movement. The company has produced a positive trend in earnings per share over the past 5 quarters. However, recent analyst estimates for the company have been reduced, while OGS has posted results that exceeded analysts' expectations. Based on operating earnings yield, the company is fairly valued when compared to all of the companies we cover. Share price changes over the past year indicates that OGS will perform in line with the market over the near term.

Financial Data

(US$ in Thousands)	9 Mos	6 Mos	3 Mos	12/31/2018	12/31/2017	12/31/2016	12/31/2015	12/31/2014
Earnings Per Share	3.39	3.37	3.30	3.25	3.08	2.65	2.24	2.07
Cash Flow Per Share	6.04	5.84	6.94	8.88	4.83	5.35	7.50	4.71
Tang Book Value Per Share	36.86	37.08	36.95	35.85	34.45	33.10	32.22	31.41
Dividends Per Share	1.960	1.920	1.880	1.840	1.680	1.400	1.200	0.840
Dividend Payout %	57.82	56.97	56.97	56.62	54.55	52.83	53.57	40.58
Income Statement								
Total Revenue	1,200,123	951,560	661,000	1,633,731	1,539,633	1,427,232	1,547,692	1,818,906
EBITDA	345,714	262,863	171,894	437,156	454,092	412,906	369,602	349,692
Depn & Amortn	134,260	88,789	43,846	160,086	151,889	143,829	133,023	125,722
Income Before Taxes	164,486	142,889	112,262	225,765	256,138	225,338	192,009	178,128
Income Taxes	28,899	24,759	18,602	53,531	93,143	85,243	72,979	68,338
Net Income	135,587	118,130	93,660	172,234	162,995	140,095	119,030	109,790
Average Shares	53,267	53,215	53,206	53,029	52,979	52,963	53,254	52,946
Balance Sheet								
Current Assets	389,683	376,812	516,270	543,287	588,994	568,923	482,845	667,501
Total Assets	5,533,180	5,446,606	5,524,292	5,468,642	5,206,878	4,942,791	4,644,410	4,649,210
Current Liabilities	677,755	578,353	658,191	698,891	673,330	443,933	304,221	392,433
Long-Term Obligations	1,285,937	1,285,811	1,285,587	1,285,483	1,193,257	1,192,446	1,201,305	1,201,311
Total Liabilities	3,431,299	3,338,143	3,419,512	3,425,986	3,246,669	3,054,511	2,802,855	2,855,173
Stockholders' Equity	2,101,881	2,108,463	2,104,780	2,042,656	1,960,209	1,888,280	1,841,555	1,794,037
Shares Outstanding	52,736	52,598	52,686	52,564	52,312	52,283	52,259	52,083
Statistical Record								
Return on Assets %	3.37	3.41	3.28	3.23	...	2.91	2.56	2.58
Return on Equity %	8.76	8.67	8.49	8.61	...	7.49	6.55	7.24
EBITDA Margin %	28.81	27.62	26.01	26.76	29.49	28.93	23.88	19.23
Net Margin %	11.30	12.41	14.17	10.54	10.59	9.82	7.69	6.04
Asset Turnover	0.31	0.31	0.31	0.31	...	0.30	0.33	0.43
Current Ratio	0.57	0.65	0.78	0.78	0.87	1.28	1.59	1.70
Debt to Equity	0.61	0.61	0.61	0.63	0.61	0.63	0.65	0.67
Price Range	96.27-76.13	92.48-74.22	90.15-65.55	87.03-62.75	79.25-62.30	66.59-48.40	51.34-39.38	44.19-32.25
P/E Ratio	28.40-22.46	27.44-22.02	27.32-19.86	26.78-19.31	25.73-20.23	25.13-18.26	22.92-17.58	21.35-15.58
Average Yield %	2.26	2.30	2.38	2.46	2.37	2.32	2.70	2.28

Address: 15 East Fifth Street, Tulsa, OK 74103 Telephone: 918-947-7000	Web Site: www.onegas.com Officers: John W. Gibson - Chairman Pierce H. Norton - President, Chief Executive Officer	Auditors: PricewaterhouseCoopers, LLP

O-I GLASS INC

Exchange	Symbol	Price	52Wk Range	Yield	P/E
NYS	OI	$11.93 (12/31/2019)	20.40-8.50	N/A	N/A

*7 Year Price Score 55.75   ***NYSE Composite Index=100**   ***12 Month Price Score 63.29**

Interim Earnings (Per Share)

Qtr.	Mar	Jun	Sep	Dec
2016	0.41	0.64	0.66	(0.43)
2017	0.30	0.85	0.76	(0.81)
2018	0.59	0.31	0.75	(0.05)
2019	0.51	0.42	(3.69)	...

Interim Dividends (Per Share)

Dividend Payment Suspended

Valuation Analysis — **Institutional Holding**

Forecast EPS	$2.20	No of Institutions
	(00/25/2020)	493
Market Cap	$1.9 Billion	Shares
Book Value	$335.0 Million	179,043,248
Price/Book	5.54	% Held
Price/Sales	0.28	86.61

Business Summary: Containers & Packaging (MIC: 8.1.3 SIC: 3221 NAIC: 327213)

Owens-Illinois is a manufacturer of glass containers. Co. has three reportable segments based on its geographic locations: Americas, Europe, and Asia Pacific. Co. produces glass containers for alcoholic beverages, including beer, flavored malt beverages, spirits and wine. Co. also produces glass packaging for a variety of food items, soft drinks, teas, juices and pharmaceuticals. Co. manufactures glass containers in a range of sizes, shapes and colors. Co. also provides engineering support for its glass manufacturing operations through facilities located in the U.S., Australia, France, Poland and Peru.

Recent Developments: For the quarter ended Sep 30 2019, loss from continuing operations was US$567.0 million compared with income of US$127.0 million in the year-earlier quarter. Net loss amounted to US$567.0 million versus net income of US$127.0 million in the year-earlier quarter. Revenues were US$1.67 billion, down 3.7% from US$1.73 billion the year before. Direct operating expenses declined 2.8% to US$1.37 billion from US$1.41 billion in the comparable period the year before. Indirect operating expenses increased 8.0% to US$190.0 million from US$176.0 million in the equivalent prior-year period.

Prospects: Our evaluation of Owens-Illinois Inc. as of October 4th, 2019 is the result of our systematic analysis on three basic characteristics: earnings strength, relative valuation, and recent stock price movement. The company has managed to produce a neutral trend in earnings per share over the past 5 quarters. However, recent analyst estimates for the company have been reduced and OI has posted results that fell short of analysts' expectations. Based on operating earnings yield, the company is undervalued when compared to all of the companies we cover. Share price changes over the past year indicates that OI will perform well over the near term.

Financial Data

(US$ in Thousands)	9 Mos	6 Mos	3 Mos	12/31/2018	12/31/2017	12/31/2016	12/31/2015	12/31/2014
Earnings Per Share	(2.81)	1.63	1.52	1.59	1.10	1.28	(0.47)	0.45
Cash Flow Per Share	2.87	1.80	3.67	4.94	4.43	4.63	3.77	4.10
Dividends Per Share	...	...	...	0.050	...	...	...	...
Dividend Payout %	...	...	...	3.14	...	...	...	...
Income Statement								
Total Revenue	5,063,000	3,393,000	1,638,000	6,877,000	6,869,000	6,702,000	6,156,000	6,784,000
EBITDA	(197,000)	283,000	147,000	861,000	865,000	956,000	573,000	719,000
Depn & Amortn	(31,000)	(20,000)	(10,000)	400,000	399,000	388,000	323,000	335,000
Income Before Taxes	(381,000)	171,000	92,000	200,000	198,000	296,000	(1,000)	154,000
Income Taxes	86,000	54,000	27,000	108,000	70,000	119,000	106,000	92,000
Net Income	(430,000)	144,000	79,000	257,000	180,000	209,000	(74,000)	75,000
Average Shares	155,536	156,471	156,635	162,088	164,647	162,825	161,169	166,047
Balance Sheet								
Current Assets	2,534,000	2,943,000	2,579,000	2,357,000	2,420,000	2,254,000	2,334,000	2,371,000
Total Assets	9,548,000	10,723,000	10,152,000	9,699,000	9,756,000	9,135,000	9,421,000	7,858,000
Current Liabilities	2,195,000	1,929,000	1,860,000	2,207,000	2,280,000	2,060,000	2,122,000	2,328,000
Long-Term Obligations	5,512,000	6,235,000	5,820,000	5,181,000	5,121,000	5,133,000	5,345,000	2,972,000
Total Liabilities	9,213,000	9,748,000	9,142,000	8,913,000	8,948,000	8,881,000	8,955,000	6,700,000
Stockholders' Equity	335,000	975,000	1,010,000	786,000	808,000	254,000	466,000	1,158,000
Shares Outstanding	155,630	155,456	155,230	155,658	163,079	162,337	160,961	164,197
Statistical Record								
Return on Assets %	N.M.	2.47	2.34	2.64	1.91	2.25	N.M.	0.92
Return on Equity %	N.M.	28.98	23.91	32.25	33.90	57.90	N.M.	5.74
EBITDA Margin %	N.M.	8.34	8.97	12.52	12.59	14.26	9.31	10.60
Net Margin %	N.M.	4.24	4.82	3.74	2.62	3.12	N.M.	1.11
Asset Turnover	0.69	0.66	0.66	0.71	0.73	0.72	0.71	0.83
Current Ratio	1.15	1.53	1.39	1.07	1.06	1.09	1.10	1.02
Debt to Equity	16.45	6.39	5.76	6.59	6.34	20.21	11.47	2.57
Price Range	20.40-9.61	20.40-15.67	21.83-15.67	23.32-15.67	25.68-17.95	20.18-12.06	26.99-16.94	35.78-23.53
P/E Ratio	...	12.52-9.61	14.36-10.31	14.67-9.86	23.35-16.32	15.77-9.42	...	79.51-52.29
Average Yield %	...	...	...	0.26	...	...	...	...

Address: One Michael Owens Way, Perrysburg, OH 43551 **Telephone:** 567-336-5000	**Web Site:** www.o-i.com **Officers:** Andres A. Lopez - President, Chief Executive Officer, Chief Operating Officer, Division Officer John A. Haudrich - Senior Vice President, Senior Vice President (frmr), Vice President, Chief Financial Officer, Interim Chief Financial Officer, Chief Strategy Officer, Chief Integration Officer, Corporate Controller	**Auditors:** Ernst & Young LLP **Investor Contact:** 567-336-2400 **Transfer Agents:** Computershare Trust Company, N.A., Providence, RI

ONEMAIN HOLDINGS INC

Exchange	Symbol	Price	52Wk Range	Yield	P/E
NYS	OMF	$42.15 (12/31/2019)	44.25-24.29	N/A	7.54

*7 Year Price Score N/A   *NYSE Composite Index=100   *12 Month Price Score 113.48

Interim Earnings (Per Share)

Qtr.	Mar	Jun	Sep	Dec
2016	1.13	0.19	0.19	0.20
2017	0.25	0.30	0.51	0.28
2018	0.91	0.05	1.09	1.24
2019	1.11	1.42	1.82	...

Interim Dividends (Per Share)

No Dividends Paid

Valuation Analysis		Institutional Holding	
Forecast EPS	$6.50	No of Institutions	
	(01/17/2020)	296	
Market Cap	$5.7 Billion	Shares	
Book Value	$4.1 Billion	132,096,368	
Price/Book	1.40	% Held	
Price/Sales	1.25	N/A	

Business Summary: Credit & Lending (MIC: 5.4.1 SIC: 6141 NAIC: 522298)

OneMain Holdings is a financial service holding company. Co. provides origination, underwriting and servicing of personal loans to non-prime customers. Within its consumer and insurance segment, Co. originates and services secured and unsecured personal loans and provides optional credit and non-credit insurance and related products through its combined branch network, its digital platform, and its centralized operations. Within its acquisitions and servicing segment, Co. services the SpringCastle Portfolio. These loans consisted of unsecured loans and loans secured by subordinate residential real estate mortgages and included both closed-end accounts and open-end lines of credit.

Recent Developments: For the quarter ended Sep 30 2019, net income increased 67.6% to US$248.0 million from US$148.0 million in the year-earlier quarter. Net interest income increased 16.3% to US$821.0 million from US$706.0 million in the year-earlier quarter. Provision for loan losses was US$282.0 million versus US$256.0 million in the prior-year quarter, an increase of 10.2%. Non-interest income rose 8.3% to US$156.0 million from US$144.0 million, while non-interest expense advanced 0.8% to US$398.0 million.

Prospects: Our evaluation of Onemain Holdings, Inc. as of October 4th, 2019 is the result of our systematic analysis on three basic characteristics: earnings strength, relative valuation, and recent stock price movement. The company has produced a positive trend in earnings per share over the past 5 quarters. However, recent analyst estimates for the company have been reduced, while OMF has posted results that exceeded analysts' expectations. Based on operating earnings yield, the company is undervalued when compared to all of the companies we cover. Share price changes over the past year indicates that OMF will perform well over the near term.

Financial Data
(US$ in Thousands)

	9 Mos	6 Mos	3 Mos	12/31/2018	12/31/2017	12/31/2016	12/31/2015	12/31/2014
Earnings Per Share	5.59	4.86	3.49	3.29	1.35	1.59	(1.89)	4.38
Cash Flow Per Share	17.04	16.51	14.99	15.08	11.50	9.82	5.71	3.49
Tang Book Value Per Share	17.05	17.32	15.84	14.64	10.46	8.54	5.59	17.45
Dividends Per Share	2.750	0.500	0.250	...	...	...	...	...
Dividend Payout %	49.19	10.29	7.16	...	...	...	...	...
Income Statement								
Total Revenue	3,480,000	2,259,000	1,104,000	4,232,000	3,756,000	3,883,000	2,192,000	2,814,104
Income Before Taxes	755,000	458,000	202,000	624,000	431,000	356,000	(269,000)	904,496
Income Taxes	161,000	112,000	50,000	177,000	248,000	113,000	(147,000)	297,046
Net Income	594,000	346,000	152,000	447,000	183,000	215,000	(242,000)	504,636
Average Shares	136,376	136,248	136,191	136,034	135,678	135,135	127,910	115,265
Balance Sheet								
Total Assets	22,410,000	21,017,000	21,358,000	20,090,000	19,433,000	18,123,000	21,056,000	11,057,864
Total Liabilities	18,316,000	16,876,000	17,408,000	16,291,000	16,155,000	15,057,000	18,305,000	9,032,595
Stockholders' Equity	4,094,000	4,141,000	3,950,000	3,799,000	3,278,000	3,066,000	2,751,000	2,025,269
Shares Outstanding	136,095	136,089	136,082	135,832	135,349	134,867	134,494	114,832
Statistical Record								
Return on Assets %	3.55	3.26	2.27	2.26	0.97	1.09	N.M.	3.81
Return on Equity %	19.71	17.35	12.96	12.63	5.77	7.37	N.M.	28.31
Net Margin %	17.07	15.32	13.77	10.56	4.87	5.54	N.M.	17.93
Asset Turnover	0.21	0.22	0.21	0.21	0.20	0.20	0.14	0.21
Price Range	42.07-23.11	36.86-23.11	36.86-23.11	36.86-23.11	32.61-22.03	41.54-16.90	53.83-31.60	39.86-22.35
P/E Ratio	7.53-4.13	7.58-4.76	10.56-6.62	11.20-7.02	24.16-16.32	26.13-10.63	...	9.10-5.10
Average Yield %	8.51	1.57	0.79	...	...	...	...	...

Address: 601 N.W. Second Street, Evansville, IN 47708 **Telephone:** 812-424-8031	**Web Site:** www.onemainfinancial.com **Officers:** Jay N. Levine - Chairman, President, Chief Executive Officer Douglas H. Shulman - President, Chief Executive Officer	**Auditors:** PricewaterhouseCoopers LLP **Transfer Agents:** American Stock Transfer & Trust Company, LLC

ONEOK INC

Exchange	Symbol	Price	52Wk Range	Yield	P/E	Div Acheiver
NYS	OKE	$75.67 (12/31/2019)	76.50-53.95	4.94	25.14	16 Years

*7 Year Price Score 104.91 *NYSE Composite Index=100 ***12 Month Price Score 99.58**

Interim Earnings (Per Share)

Qtr.	Mar	Jun	Sep	Dec
2016	0.40	0.40	0.43	0.43
2017	0.41	0.33	0.43	0.09
2018	0.64	0.68	0.75	0.71
2019	0.81	0.75	0.74	...

Interim Dividends (Per Share)

Amt	Decl	Ex	Rec	Pay
0.865Q	04/18/2019	04/26/2019	04/29/2019	05/15/2019
0.89Q	07/24/2019	08/05/2019	08/06/2019	08/14/2019
0.915Q	10/23/2019	11/01/2019	11/04/2019	11/14/2019
0.935Q	01/15/2020	01/24/2020	01/27/2020	02/14/2020

Indicated Div: $3.74 (Div. Reinv. Plan)

Valuation Analysis / Institutional Holding

Forecast EPS	$3.10	No of Institutions
	(01/17/2020)	1231
Market Cap	$31.3 Billion	Shares
Book Value	$6.2 Billion	348,115,392
Price/Book	5.03	% Held
Price/Sales	2.94	79.34

Business Summary: Production & Extraction (MIC: 9.1.1 SIC: 4924 NAIC: 221210)

Oneok is a midstream service provider. Co.'s segments include: Natural Gas Gathering and Processing, which provides midstream services to producers in North Dakota, Montana, Wyoming, Kansas and Oklahoma; natural gas liquids (NGLs), which owns and operates facilities that gather, fractionate, treat and distribute NGLs and store NGL products, primarily in Oklahoma, Kansas, Texas, New Mexico and the Rocky Mountain region; and Natural Gas Pipelines, which provides transportation and storage services to end users through its wholly owned assets and its ownership interests in Northern Border Pipeline Company and Roadrunner Gas Transmission, LLC.

Recent Developments: For the quarter ended Sep 30 2019, net income decreased 1.5% to US$309.2 million from US$313.9 million in the year-earlier quarter. Revenues were US$2.26 billion, down 33.3% from US$3.39 billion the year before. Operating income was US$482.2 million versus US$495.5 million in the prior-year quarter, a decrease of 2.7%. Direct operating expenses declined 39.0% to US$1.75 billion from US$2.87 billion in the comparable period the year before. Indirect operating expenses increased 11.9% to US$26.8 million from US$24.0 million in the equivalent prior-year period.

Prospects: Our evaluation of Oneok Inc. as of October 4th, 2019 is the result of our systematic analysis on three basic characteristics: earnings strength, relative valuation, and recent stock price movement. The company has managed to produce a neutral trend in earnings per share over the past 5 quarters. However, recent analyst estimates for the company have been raised and OKE has posted results that exceeded analysts' expectations. Based on operating earnings yield, the company is fairly valued when compared to all of the companies we cover. Share price changes over the past year indicates that OKE will perform in line with the market over the near term.

Financial Data

(US$ in Thousands)	9 Mos	6 Mos	3 Mos	12/31/2018	12/31/2017	12/31/2016	12/31/2015	12/31/2014
Earnings Per Share	3.01	3.02	2.95	2.78	1.29	1.66	1.16	1.49
Cash Flow Per Share	4.83	5.20	4.95	5.31	4.42	6.38	4.79	6.14
Tang Book Value Per Share	12.73	13.04	13.27	13.64	11.67	N.M.	N.M.	N.M.
Dividends Per Share	3.470	3.405	3.335	3.245	2.720	2.460	2.430	2.125
Dividend Payout %	115.28	112.75	113.05	116.73	210.85	148.19	209.48	142.62
Income Statement								
Total Revenue	7,500,761	5,237,533	2,779,958	12,593,196	12,173,907	8,920,934	7,763,206	12,195,091
EBITDA	1,830,427	1,210,476	601,239	2,257,729	1,773,516	1,679,502	1,167,983	1,441,071
Depn & Amortn	350,552	229,122	114,158	428,557	406,335	391,585	354,620	306,038
Income Before Taxes	1,117,385	748,441	371,661	1,359,552	881,523	818,266	396,576	778,870
Income Taxes	274,234	176,869	77,934	362,903	447,282	212,406	136,600	151,158
Net Income	958,326	649,171	337,208	1,151,703	387,841	352,039	244,977	314,107
Average Shares	415,578	415,049	415,233	414,195	299,780	212,383	210,541	210,427
Balance Sheet								
Current Assets	1,967,585	1,401,170	1,342,779	1,398,632	1,764,458	1,429,684	975,210	1,307,244
Total Assets	21,335,907	19,751,594	18,934,325	18,231,671	16,845,937	16,138,751	15,446,111	15,304,560
Current Liabilities	1,567,152	1,737,373	1,689,669	2,108,436	2,667,335	2,836,701	1,638,266	2,392,345
Long-Term Obligations	12,479,452	10,754,087	10,004,341	8,873,324	8,091,629	7,919,906	8,323,582	7,192,929
Total Liabilities	15,117,001	13,403,458	12,492,319	11,652,128	11,318,070	15,950,006	15,110,313	14,712,445
Stockholders' Equity	6,218,906	6,348,136	6,442,006	6,579,543	5,527,867	188,745	335,798	592,115
Shares Outstanding	413,076	412,964	412,752	411,532	388,703	210,681	209,731	208,322
Statistical Record								
Return on Assets %	6.38	6.85	6.92	6.57	2.35	2.22	1.59	1.90
Return on Equity %	19.44	19.29	18.63	19.02	13.57	133.86	52.80	21.44
EBITDA Margin %	24.40	23.11	21.63	17.93	14.57	18.83	15.05	11.82
Net Margin %	12.78	12.39	12.13	9.15	3.19	3.95	3.16	2.58
Asset Turnover	0.54	0.64	0.69	0.72	0.74	0.56	0.50	0.74
Current Ratio	1.26	0.81	0.79	0.66	0.66	0.50	0.60	0.55
Debt to Equity	2.01	1.69	1.55	1.35	1.46	41.96	24.79	12.15
Price Range	76.50-50.79	71.40-50.79	71.40-50.79	71.40-50.79	58.83-47.41	59.03-19.62	51.07-18.93	70.98-44.30
P/E Ratio	25.42-16.87	23.64-16.82	24.20-17.22	25.68-18.27	45.60-36.75	35.56-11.82	44.03-16.32	47.64-29.73
Average Yield %	5.23	5.18	5.14	5.14	5.08	5.99	6.22	3.44

Address: 100 West Fifth Street, Tulsa, OK 74103	Web Site: www.oneok.com	Auditors: PricewaterhouseCoopers LLP
Telephone: 918-588-7000	**Officers:** Terry K. Spencer - President, Chief Executive Officer Robert F. Martinovich - Executive Vice President, Chief Administrative Officer, Executive Vice President (frmr), Senior Vice President, Chief Financial Officer, Treasurer	**Investor Contact:** 918-588-7163
Fax: 918-588-7273		**Transfer Agents:** Wells Fargo Shareowner Services, St Paul, MN

ORACLE CORP

Exchange	Symbol	Price	52Wk Range	Yield	P/E
NYS	ORCL	$52.98 (12/31/2019)	60.15-44.78	1.81	16.98

*7 Year Price Score 102.74 *NYSE Composite Index=100 *12 Month Price Score 97.23

Interim Earnings (Per Share)

Qtr.	Aug	Nov	Feb	May
2016-17	0.43	0.48	0.53	0.76
2017-18	0.52	0.52	(0.98)	0.80
2018-19	0.57	0.61	0.76	1.04
2019-20	0.63	0.69	...	...

Interim Dividends (Per Share)

Amt	Decl	Ex	Rec	Pay
0.24Q	03/14/2019	04/10/2019	04/11/2019	04/25/2019
0.24Q	06/18/2019	07/16/2019	07/17/2019	07/31/2019
0.24Q	09/11/2019	10/09/2019	10/10/2019	10/24/2019
0.24Q	12/12/2019	01/08/2020	01/09/2020	01/23/2020

Indicated Div: $0.96

Valuation Analysis | **Institutional Holding**

Forecast EPS	$3.90	No of Institutions
(01/17/2020)		2586
Market Cap	$170.3 Billion	Shares
Book Value	$15.6 Billion	2,307,228,160
Price/Book	10.94	% Held
Price/Sales	4.30	40.43

Business Summary: Internet & Software (MIC: 6.3.2 SIC: 7372 NAIC: 511210)

Oracle provides products and services that address enterprise information technology (IT) environments. Co.'s products and services include applications and infrastructure offerings. Co.'s cloud and license business engages in the sale, marketing and delivery of its applications and infrastructure technologies through cloud and on-premise deployment models including its cloud services and license support offerings; and its cloud license and on-premise license offerings. Co.'s hardware business provides Oracle Engineered Systems, servers, storage, industry-specific hardware, operating systems, virtualization, management and other hardware-related software to support diverse IT environments.

Recent Developments: For the quarter ended Nov 30 2019, net income decreased 0.9% to US$2.31 billion from US$2.33 billion in the year-earlier quarter. Revenues were US$9.61 billion, up 0.5% from US$9.56 billion the year before. Operating income was US$3.18 billion versus US$3.10 billion in the prior-year quarter, an increase of 2.6%. Direct operating expenses rose 2.3% to US$2.05 billion from US$2.00 billion in the comparable period the year before. Indirect operating expenses decreased 1.7% to US$4.38 billion from US$4.46 billion in the equivalent prior-year period.

Prospects: Our evaluation of Oracle Corp. as of October 4th, 2019 is the result of our systematic analysis on three basic characteristics: earnings strength, relative valuation, and recent stock price movement. The company has managed to produce a neutral trend in earnings per share over the past 5 quarters. However, recent analyst estimates for the company have been raised and ORCL has posted results that exceeded analysts' expectations. Based on operating earnings yield, the company is undervalued when compared to all of the companies we cover. Share price changes over the past year indicates that ORCL will perform well over the near term.

Financial Data
(US$ in Thousands)

	6 Mos	3 Mos	05/31/2019	05/31/2018	05/31/2017	05/31/2016	05/31/2015	05/31/2014
Earnings Per Share	3.12	3.04	2.97	0.90	2.21	2.07	2.21	2.38
Cash Flow Per Share	4.25	4.17	4.00	3.73	3.43	3.20	3.26	3.30
Tang Book Value Per Share	N.M.	N.M.	N.M.	N.M.	0.76	1.88	1.88	2.48
Dividends Per Share	0.910	0.860	0.810	0.760	0.640	0.600	0.510	0.480
Dividend Payout %	29.17	28.29	27.27	84.44	28.96	28.99	23.08	20.17
Income Statement								
Total Revenue	18,832,000	9,218,000	39,506,000	39,831,000	37,728,000	37,047,000	38,226,000	38,275,000
EBITDA	7,501,000	3,576,000	16,329,000	16,635,000	15,082,000	14,996,000	16,602,000	17,361,000
Depn & Amortn	1,498,000	750,000	2,919,000	2,785,000	2,451,000	2,509,000	2,861,000	2,908,000
Income Before Taxes	5,292,000	2,482,000	12,420,000	13,026,000	11,635,000	11,558,000	12,947,000	13,802,000
Income Taxes	844,000	345,000	1,185,000	9,066,000	2,182,000	2,541,000	2,896,000	2,749,000
Net Income	4,448,000	2,137,000	11,083,000	3,825,000	9,335,000	8,901,000	9,938,000	10,955,000
Average Shares	3,331,000	3,410,000	3,732,000	4,238,000	4,217,000	4,304,999	4,502,999	4,603,999
Balance Sheet								
Current Assets	34,540,000	42,384,000	46,386,000	75,964,000	74,515,000	64,313,000	63,183,000	48,138,000
Total Assets	98,443,000	106,229,000	108,709,000	137,264,000	134,991,000	112,180,000	110,903,000	90,344,000
Current Liabilities	14,592,000	18,875,000	18,630,000	19,195,000	24,178,000	17,208,000	15,291,000	14,389,000
Long-Term Obligations	50,670,000	50,692,000	51,673,000	56,128,000	48,112,000	40,105,000	39,959,000	22,667,000
Total Liabilities	82,880,000	87,796,000	86,924,000	91,538,000	81,131,000	64,891,000	62,240,000	43,466,000
Stockholders' Equity	15,563,000	18,433,000	21,785,000	45,726,000	53,860,000	47,289,000	48,663,000	46,878,000
Shares Outstanding	3,214,000	3,296,000	3,359,000	3,997,000	4,137,000	4,131,000	4,342,999	4,463,999
Statistical Record								
Return on Assets %	10.09	9.34	9.01	2.81	7.55	7.96	9.88	12.73
Return on Equity %	47.40	38.78	32.83	7.68	18.46	18.50	20.80	23.94
EBITDA Margin %	39.83	38.79	41.33	41.76	39.98	40.48	43.43	45.36
Net Margin %	23.62	23.18	28.05	9.60	24.74	24.03	26.00	28.62
Asset Turnover	0.37	0.34	0.32	0.29	0.31	0.33	0.38	0.44
Current Ratio	2.37	2.25	2.49	3.96	3.08	3.74	4.13	3.35
Debt to Equity	3.26	2.75	2.37	1.23	0.89	0.85	0.82	0.48
Price Range	60.15-42.69	60.15-42.69	55.41-42.69	52.97-44.68	45.73-37.93	44.91-33.94	46.23-37.56	42.20-29.96
P/E Ratio	19.28-13.68	19.79-14.04	18.66-14.37	58.86-49.64	20.69-17.16	21.70-16.40	20.92-17.00	17.73-12.59
Average Yield %	1.71	1.66	1.63	1.56	1.56	1.55	1.22	1.34

Address: 500 Oracle Parkway, Redwood City, CA 94065
Telephone: 650-506-7000

Web Site: www.oracle.com
Officers: Lawrence J. Ellison - Chairman, Chief Technology Officer, Chairman (frmr), Chief Executive Officer Jeffrey O. Henley - Vice-Chairman, Chairman

Auditors: Ernst & Young LLP
Investor Contact: 650-506-4073
Transfer Agents: American Stock Transfer & Trust Company, LLC, Brooklyn, NY

OSHKOSH CORP

Exchange	Symbol	Price	52Wk Range	Yield	P/E
NYS	OSK	$94.65 (12/31/2019)	95.39-59.73	1.27	11.53

*7 Year Price Score 109.74 *NYSE Composite Index=100 *12 Month Price Score 109.37

Interim Earnings (Per Share)

Qtr.	Dec	Mar	Jun	Sep
2014-15	0.43	0.69	1.13	0.65
2015-16	0.19	0.76	1.11	0.83
2016-17	0.26	0.58	1.69	1.23
2017-18	0.74	1.47	2.05	2.04
2018-19	1.51	1.82	2.72	2.16

Interim Dividends (Per Share)

Amt	Decl	Ex	Rec	Pay
0.27Q	01/30/2019	02/14/2019	02/15/2019	03/01/2019
0.27Q	04/30/2019	05/15/2019	05/16/2019	05/30/2019
0.27Q	08/01/2019	08/16/2019	08/19/2019	09/03/2019
0.30Q	10/30/2019	11/15/2019	11/18/2019	12/02/2019

Indicated Div: $1.20 (Div. Reinv. Plan)

Valuation Analysis / **Institutional Holding**

Forecast EPS	$7.68	No of Institutions
	(01/16/2020)	608
Market Cap	$6.4 Billion	Shares
Book Value	$2.6 Billion	74,372,200
Price/Book	2.48	% Held
Price/Sales	0.77	82.15

Business Summary: Autos- Manufacturing (MIC: 1.8.1 SIC: 3711 NAIC: 336120)

Oshkosh is a designer, manufacturer and marketer of access equipment, specialty vehicles and truck bodies for the primary markets of access equipment, defense, fire and emergency and municipal, refuse hauling, concrete placement as well as airport services. Co.'s segments are: access equipment, which designs and manufactures aerial work platforms and telehandlers; defense, which designs and manufactures tactical wheeled vehicles and related service; fire and emergency, which designs and manufactures fire apparatus assembled on custom chassis; and commercial, which designs and manufactures front- and rear-discharge concrete mixers and portable and stationary concrete batch plants.

Recent Developments: For the year ended Sep 30 2019, net income increased 22.8% to US$579.4 million from US$471.9 million in the prior year. Revenues were US$8.38 billion, up 8.8% from US$7.71 billion the year before. Operating income was US$797.0 million versus US$656.0 million in the prior year, an increase of 21.5%. Direct operating expenses rose 8.2% to US$6.86 billion from US$6.35 billion in the comparable period the year before. Indirect operating expenses increased 2.5% to US$720.4 million from US$702.6 million in the equivalent prior-year period.

Prospects: Our evaluation of Oshkosh Corp. as of October 4th, 2019 is the result of our systematic analysis on three basic characteristics: earnings strength, relative valuation, and recent stock price movement. The company has generated a negative trend in earnings per share over the past 5 quarters. However, recent analyst estimates for the company have been mixed and OSK has posted results that exceeded analysts' expectations. Based on operating earnings yield, the company is undervalued when compared to all of the companies we cover. Share price changes over the past year indicates that OSK will perform in line with the market over the near term.

Financial Data

(US$ in Thousands)	09/30/2019	09/30/2018	09/30/2017	09/30/2016	09/30/2015	09/30/2014	09/30/2013	09/30/2012
Earnings Per Share	8.21	6.29	3.77	2.91	2.90	3.61	3.55	2.51
Cash Flow Per Share	8.14	5.90	3.30	7.83	1.06	2.03	4.99	2.93
Tang Book Value Per Share	17.24	14.32	10.49	5.67	4.02	3.78	4.07	0.48
Dividends Per Share	1.080	0.960	0.840	0.740	0.680	0.150	...	...
Dividend Payout %	13.15	15.26	22.28	25.43	23.45	4.16	...	...
Income Statement								
Total Revenue	8,382,000	7,705,500	6,829,600	6,279,200	6,098,100	6,808,200	7,665,100	8,180,900
EBITDA	911,900	768,300	593,500	491,100	511,800	621,900	621,500	484,100
Depn & Amortn	113,600	118,100	127,300	125,800	118,100	120,600	121,900	123,300
Income Before Taxes	750,700	594,600	411,300	307,000	326,100	431,900	445,000	286,700
Income Taxes	171,300	123,800	127,200	92,400	99,200	125,000	131,700	57,400
Net Income	579,400	471,900	285,600	216,400	229,500	309,300	318,000	230,800
Average Shares	70,558	74,981	75,790	74,432	78,981	85,457	88,953	91,893
Balance Sheet								
Current Assets	3,408,300	3,269,900	3,039,800	2,417,500	2,429,300	2,384,300	2,553,400	2,694,500
Total Assets	5,566,300	5,294,200	5,098,900	4,513,800	4,613,000	4,586,700	4,765,700	4,947,800
Current Liabilities	1,741,900	1,690,100	1,683,100	1,367,600	1,458,100	1,311,600	1,380,700	1,704,500
Long-Term Obligations	819,000	818,000	807,900	826,200	855,000	875,000	890,000	955,000
Total Liabilities	2,966,500	2,780,700	2,791,500	2,537,300	2,701,900	2,601,700	2,657,900	3,094,300
Stockholders' Equity	2,599,800	2,513,500	2,307,400	1,976,500	1,911,100	1,985,000	2,107,800	1,853,500
Shares Outstanding	67,987	72,370	75,013	73,925	75,454	79,845	86,534	91,557
Statistical Record								
Return on Assets %	10.67	9.08	5.94	4.73	4.99	6.61	6.55	4.71
Return on Equity %	22.66	19.58	13.33	11.10	11.78	15.11	16.06	13.34
EBITDA Margin %	10.88	9.97	8.69	7.82	8.39	9.13	8.11	5.92
Net Margin %	6.91	6.12	4.18	3.45	3.76	4.54	4.15	2.82
Asset Turnover	1.54	1.48	1.42	1.37	1.33	1.46	1.58	1.67
Current Ratio	1.96	1.93	1.81	1.77	1.67	1.82	1.85	1.58
Debt to Equity	0.32	0.33	0.35	0.42	0.45	0.44	0.42	0.52
Price Range	86.09-52.85	96.24-67.92	82.68-52.58	56.90-30.33	54.90-30.33	60.03-44.15	49.12-26.85	29.76-14.51
P/E Ratio	10.49-6.44	15.30-10.80	21.93-13.95	19.55-10.42	18.93-12.15	16.63-12.23	13.84-7.56	11.86-5.78
Average Yield %	1.47	1.20	1.24	1.71	1.51	0.29	...	...

Address: P.O. Box 2566, Oshkosh, WI 54903-2566	Web Site: www.oshkoshcorp.com	Auditors: DELOITTE & TOUCHE LLP
Telephone: 920-502-3009	Officers: Craig P. Omtvedt - Chairman Wilson R. Jones - President, Chief Executive Officer, Executive Vice President, Chief Operating Officer, Division Officer	Investor Contact: 920-966-5939
		Transfer Agents: Computershare Investor Services, LLC, Providence, RI

OUTFRONT MEDIA INC

Exchange	Symbol	Price	52Wk Range	Yield	P/E
NYS	OUT	$26.82 (12/31/2019)	28.32-18.12	5.37	25.30

*7 Year Price Score N/A   *NYSE Composite Index=100   *12 Month Price Score 98.49

Interim Earnings (Per Share)

Qtr.	Mar	Jun	Sep	Dec
2016	(0.02)	0.21	0.28	0.20
2017	0.02	0.27	0.36	0.25
2018	0.06	(0.04)	0.33	0.40
2019	0.04	0.35	0.27	...

Interim Dividends (Per Share)

Amt	Decl	Ex	Rec	Pay
0.36Q	02/26/2019	03/07/2019	03/08/2019	03/29/2019
0.36Q	04/26/2019	06/06/2019	06/07/2019	06/28/2019
0.36Q	07/25/2019	09/05/2019	09/06/2019	09/27/2019
0.36Q	10/22/2019	12/05/2019	12/06/2019	12/31/2019

Indicated Div: $1.44

Valuation Analysis

		Institutional Holding	
Forecast EPS	$1.08	No of Institutions	
	(01/17/2020)	368	
Market Cap	$3.8 Billion	Shares	
Book Value	$1.1 Billion	156,289,984	
Price/Book	3.44	% Held	
Price/Sales	2.15	N/A	

Business Summary: REITs (MIC: 5.3.1 SIC: 6798 NAIC: 525930)

OUTFRONT Media is a real estate investment trust that provides advertising space on out-of-home advertising structures and sites in the U.S. and Canada. Co.'s inventory consists of billboard displays, which are mainly located on the heavily traveled highways and roadways, and transit advertising displays operated under multi-year contracts with municipalities in cities across the U.S. and Canada. Co. had displays in markets in the U.S. and Canada. Co.'s portfolio includes sites such as the Bay Bridge in San Francisco, various locations along Sunset Boulevard in Los Angeles, and sites in and around both Grand Central Station and Times Square in New York.

Recent Developments: For the quarter ended Sep 30 2019, net income decreased 17.3% to US$38.7 million from US$46.8 million in the year-earlier quarter. Revenues were US$462.5 million, up 11.7% from US$414.2 million the year before.

Prospects: Our evaluation of OUTFRONT Media Inc. as of October 4th, 2019 is the result of our systematic analysis on three basic characteristics: earnings strength, relative valuation, and recent stock price movement. The company has managed to produce a neutral trend in earnings per share over the past 5 quarters. Additionally, recent analyst estimates for the company have been unchanged while OUT has posted results that fell short of analysts' expectations. Based on operating earnings yield, the company is fairly valued when compared to all of the companies we cover. Share price changes over the past year indicates that OUT will perform over the near term.

Financial Data

(US$ in Thousands)	9 Mos	6 Mos	3 Mos	12/31/2018	12/31/2017	12/31/2016	12/31/2015	12/31/2014
Earnings Per Share	1.06	1.12	0.73	0.75	0.90	0.66	(0.21)	2.67
Cash Flow Per Share	1.67	1.61	1.38	1.54	1.80	2.08	2.13	2.30
Dividends Per Share	1.440	1.440	1.440	1.440	1.440	1.360	1.420	5.670
Dividend Payout %	135.85	128.57	197.26	192.00	160.00	206.06	...	212.36
Income Statement								
Total Revenue	1,294,100	831,600	371,700	1,606,200	1,520,500	1,513,900	1,513,800	1,353,800
EBITDA	270,000	171,200	59,500	320,300	331,700	313,700	113,786,000	290,000
Depn & Amortn	69,800	45,500	22,500	85,900	89,700	108,900	113,700,000	107,200
Income Before Taxes	99,700	59,100	4,300	108,700	125,100	91,000	(28,800)	98,000
Income Taxes	8,500	5,200	(1,000)	4,900	4,100	5,400	5,400	(206,000)
Net Income	95,100	56,400	6,100	107,900	125,800	90,900	(29,400)	306,900
Average Shares	144,200	142,900	141,100	139,600	138,900	138,400	137,300	114,800
Balance Sheet								
Current Assets	460,000	846,800	351,700	429,500	376,000	378,200	416,600	355,300
Total Assets	5,320,900	5,665,000	5,077,000	3,828,700	3,808,200	3,738,500	3,845,200	4,023,600
Current Liabilities	645,100	959,300	538,500	402,600	299,600	251,500	265,600	255,200
Long-Term Obligations	2,212,500	2,245,900	2,185,700	2,149,600	2,145,300	2,136,800	2,251,700	2,198,300
Total Liabilities	4,227,900	4,567,300	4,025,700	2,725,900	2,627,100	2,505,600	2,632,600	2,578,100
Stockholders' Equity	1,093,000	1,097,700	1,051,300	1,102,800	1,181,100	1,232,900	1,212,600	1,445,500
Shares Outstanding	140,200	143,300	141,600	140,239	138,644	138,044	137,583	136,624
Statistical Record								
Return on Assets %	3.33	3.40	2.37	2.83	3.33	2.39	N.M.	8.32
Return on Equity %	14.01	14.77	9.61	9.45	10.42	7.41	N.M.	14.61
EBITDA Margin %	20.86	20.59	16.01	19.94	21.82	20.72	7,516.58	21.42
Net Margin %	7.35	6.78	1.64	6.72	8.27	6.00	N.M.	22.67
Asset Turnover	0.38	0.36	0.37	0.42	0.40	0.40	0.38	0.37
Current Ratio	0.71	0.88	0.65	1.07	1.26	1.50	1.57	1.39
Debt to Equity	2.02	2.05	2.08	1.95	1.82	1.73	1.86	1.52
Price Range	28.32-16.82	26.84-16.82	23.40-16.82	23.16-16.82	27.65-20.88	25.37-18.18	30.82-20.71	35.15-26.03
P/E Ratio	26.72-15.87	23.96-15.02	32.05-23.04	30.88-22.43	30.72-23.20	38.44-27.55	...	13.16-9.75
Average Yield %	6.22	6.53	7.19	7.21	5.95	6.10	5.50	18.34

Address: 405 Lexington Avenue, 17th Floor, New York, NY 10174 **Telephone:** 212-297-6400	**Web Site:** www.outfrontmedia.com **Officers:** Jeremy J. Male - Chairman, Chief Executive Officer Matthew Siegel - Chief Financial Officer, Executive Vice President	**Auditors:** PricewaterhouseCoopers LLP **Transfer Agents:** Wells Fargo Bank, National Association

OWENS CORNING

Exchange	Symbol	Price	52Wk Range	Yield	P/E
NYS	OC	$65.12 (12/31/2019)	68.50-43.18	1.47	14.28

*7 Year Price Score 89.22 ***NYSE Composite Index=100** ***12 Month Price Score 111.25**

Interim Earnings (Per Share)

Qtr.	Mar	Jun	Sep	Dec
2016	0.49	1.19	0.97	0.76
2017	0.89	0.85	0.85	(0.04)
2018	0.82	1.08	1.45	1.54
2019	0.40	1.26	1.36	...

Interim Dividends (Per Share)

Amt	Decl	Ex	Rec	Pay
0.22Q	02/07/2019	03/07/2019	03/08/2019	04/02/2019
0.22Q	06/20/2019	07/15/2019	07/16/2019	08/02/2019
0.22Q	09/19/2019	10/11/2019	10/15/2019	11/04/2019
0.24Q	12/05/2019	01/02/2020	01/03/2020	01/17/2020

Indicated Div: $0.96

Valuation Analysis / Institutional Holding

Forecast EPS	$4.60	No of Institutions
(01/17/2020)		552
Market Cap	$7.1 Billion	Shares
Book Value	$4.5 Billion	139,221,712
Price/Book	1.58	% Held
Price/Sales	0.99	97.48

Business Summary: Construction Materials (MIC: 8.5.1 SIC: 3292 NAIC: 327910)

Owens Corning is a holding company. Through its subsidiaries, Co. is engaging in the insulation, roofing, and fiberglass composite materials. Co. has three reporting segments: Composites, which manufactures, fabricates and sells glass reinforcements in the form of fiber; Insulation, which manufactures and sells fiberglass insulation, glass fiber pipe insulation, flexible duct media, bonded and granulated mineral wool insulation, cellular glass insulation and foam insulation; and Roofing, which manufactures and sells residential roofing shingles, oxidized asphalt materials, roofing components, and synthetic packaging materials.

Recent Developments: For the quarter ended Sep 30 2019, net income decreased 6.8% to US$151.0 million from US$162.0 million in the year-earlier quarter. Revenues were US$1.88 billion, up 3.6% from US$1.82 billion the year before. Operating income was US$275.0 million versus US$255.0 million in the prior-year quarter, an increase of 7.8%. Direct operating expenses rose 3.8% to US$1.42 billion from US$1.37 billion in the comparable period the year before. Indirect operating expenses decreased 3.6% to US$186.0 million from US$193.0 million in the equivalent prior-year period.

Prospects: Our evaluation of Owens Corning as of October 4th, 2019 is the result of our systematic analysis on three basic characteristics: earnings strength, relative valuation, and recent stock price movement. The company has generated a negative trend in earnings per share over the past 5 quarters. In addition, recent analyst estimates for the company have been reduced while OC has posted results that exceeded analysts' expectations. Based on operating earnings yield, the company is undervalued when compared to all of the companies we cover. Share price changes over the past year indicates that OC will perform poorly over the near term.

Financial Data

(US$ in Millions)	9 Mos	6 Mos	3 Mos	12/31/2018	12/31/2017	12/31/2016	12/31/2015	12/31/2014
Earnings Per Share	4.56	4.65	4.47	4.89	2.55	3.41	2.79	1.91
Cash Flow Per Share	8.18	7.19	6.78	7.27	9.11	8.22	6.33	3.75
Tang Book Value Per Share	7.89	6.54	5.24	5.07	11.61	12.20	13.57	12.79
Dividends Per Share	0.870	0.860	0.860	0.630	0.810	0.740	0.680	0.640
Dividend Payout %	19.08	18.49	19.24	12.88	31.76	21.70	24.37	33.51
Income Statement								
Total Revenue	5,468	3,585	1,667	7,057	6,384	5,677	5,350	5,276
EBITDA	930	573	231	1,205	1,006	1,016	831	629
Depn & Amortn	337	225	113	384	340	318	278	283
Income Before Taxes	492	280	82	704	559	590	453	232
Income Taxes	159	98	39	156	269	188	120	5
Net Income	332	182	44	545	289	393	330	226
Average Shares	110	109	110	111	113	115	118	118
Balance Sheet								
Current Assets	2,130	2,239	2,333	2,020	1,985	1,586	1,538	1,807
Total Assets	9,955	10,183	10,265	9,771	8,632	7,741	7,380	7,555
Current Liabilities	1,261	1,325	1,275	1,278	1,282	963	1,117	983
Long-Term Obligations	3,180	3,404	3,711	3,362	2,405	2,099	1,702	1,991
Total Liabilities	5,472	5,778	6,003	5,488	4,470	3,892	3,641	3,863
Stockholders' Equity	4,483	4,405	4,262	4,283	4,162	3,849	3,739	3,692
Shares Outstanding	108	108	108	109	111	112	115	117
Statistical Record								
Return on Assets %	5.03	5.08	4.85	5.92	3.53	5.18	4.42	2.97
Return on Equity %	11.63	12.05	11.89	12.91	7.22	10.33	8.88	6.04
EBITDA Margin %	17.01	15.98	13.86	17.08	15.76	17.90	15.53	11.92
Net Margin %	6.07	5.08	2.64	7.72	4.53	6.92	6.17	4.28
Asset Turnover	0.72	0.70	0.69	0.77	0.78	0.75	0.72	0.69
Current Ratio	1.69	1.69	1.83	1.58	1.55	1.65	1.38	1.84
Debt to Equity	0.71	0.77	0.87	0.78	0.58	0.55	0.46	0.54
Price Range	63.20-41.20	66.89-41.20	82.10-41.20	96.36-41.20	92.75-51.66	56.03-40.52	48.08-35.04	46.05-29.00
P/E Ratio	13.86-9.04	14.38-8.86	18.37-9.22	19.71-8.43	36.37-20.26	16.43-11.88	17.23-12.56	24.11-15.18
Average Yield %	1.69	1.65	1.51	0.95	1.18	1.48	1.59	1.69

Address: One Owens Corning Parkway, Toledo, OH 43659 Telephone: 419-248-8000	Web Site: www.owenscorning.com Officers: Michael H. (Mike) Thaman - Executive Chairman, Chairman, President, Chief Executive Officer Brian D. Chambers - Chairman, President, Chief Executive Officer, Vice President, Chief Operating Officer, Division Officer	Auditors: PricewaterhouseCoopers LLP Investor Contact: 419-248-5748 Transfer Agents: Wells Fargo Shareowner Services, Mendota Heights, MN

OWENS & MINOR, INC.

Exchange	Symbol	Price	52Wk Range	Yield	P/E
NYS	OMI	$5.17 (12/31/2019)	8.22-2.47	0.19	N/A

*7 Year Price Score 15.95   *NYSE Composite Index=100   *12 Month Price Score 117.90

TRADING VOLUME (thousand shares)

Interim Earnings (Per Share)

Qtr.	Mar	Jun	Sep	Dec
2016	0.39	0.45	0.48	0.44
2017	0.31	0.33	0.18	0.38
2018	0.13	(3.07)	(0.01)	(4.36)
2019	(0.23)	(0.18)	0.02	...

Interim Dividends (Per Share)

Amt	Decl	Ex	Rec	Pay
0.003Q	02/19/2019	03/14/2019	03/15/2019	03/29/2019
0.003Q	05/10/2019	06/13/2019	06/14/2019	06/28/2019
0.003Q	08/07/2019	09/13/2019	09/16/2019	09/30/2019
0.003Q	11/01/2019	12/13/2019	12/16/2019	12/31/2019

Indicated Div: $0.01 (Div. Reinv. Plan)

Valuation Analysis   Institutional Holding

Forecast EPS	$0.56 (01/17/2020)	No of Institutions 331
Market Cap	$325.0 Million	Shares
Book Value	$491.3 Million	73,790,144
Price/Book	0.66	% Held
Price/Sales	0.03	90.42

Business Summary: Medical Instruments & Equipment (MIC: 4.3.1 SIC: 5047 NAIC: 423450)

Owens & Minor is a healthcare solutions company. Co. provides products and services to healthcare provider customers either directly or indirectly via third-party distributors. Co. has two business units: Global Solutions, which provides a portfolio of medical and surgical supplies and service offerings to healthcare providers including supplier management, analytics, inventory management, and clinical supply management; and Global Products, which manufactures and sources medical surgical products via its production and kitting operations as well as provides medical supplies and solutions for the prevention of healthcare-associated infections across the acute and alternate site channels.

Recent Developments: For the quarter ended Sep 30 2019, net income amounted to US$1.2 million versus a net loss of US$565,000 in the year-earlier quarter. Revenues were US$2.40 billion, down 2.7% from US$2.46 billion the year before. Operating income was US$25.3 million versus US$21.4 million in the prior-year quarter, an increase of 18.5%. Direct operating expenses declined 3.6% to US$2.04 billion from US$2.11 billion in the comparable period the year before. Indirect operating expenses increased 1.8% to US$337.2 million from US$331.2 million in the equivalent prior-year period.

Prospects: Our evaluation of Owens & Minor Inc. as of October 4th, 2019 is the result of our systematic analysis on three basic characteristics: earnings strength, relative valuation, and recent stock price movement. The company has produced a positive trend in earnings per share over the past 5 quarters. In addition, recent analyst estimates for the company have been raised, and OMI has posted results that exceeded analysts' expectations. Based on operating earnings yield, the company is undervalued when compared to all of the companies we cover. Share price changes over the past year indicates that OMI will perform very poorly over the near term.

Financial Data

(US$ in Thousands)	9 Mos	6 Mos	3 Mos	12/31/2018	12/31/2017	12/31/2016	12/31/2015	12/31/2014
Earnings Per Share	(4.75)	(4.78)	(7.67)	(7.28)	1.20	1.76	1.65	1.06
Cash Flow Per Share	2.20	1.64	0.60	1.93	0.95	3.05	4.34	(0.06)
Tang Book Value Per Share	N.M.	N.M.	N.M.	N.M.	1.91	7.58	7.61	7.28
Dividends Per Share	0.083	0.340	0.598	0.855	1.030	1.020	1.010	1.000
Dividend Payout %	...	...	...	...	85.83	57.95	61.21	94.34
Income Statement								
Total Revenue	7,344,605	4,945,587	2,461,388	9,838,708	9,318,275	9,723,431	9,772,946	9,440,182
EBITDA	142,536	89,738	43,412	(349,274)	121,551	232,099	236,659	180,146
Depn & Amortn	88,204	58,902	28,720	42,900	32,300	32,500	36,300	35,500
Income Before Taxes	(26,386)	(25,947)	(14,409)	(469,195)	57,478	172,542	173,210	126,483
Income Taxes	(3,038)	(1,375)	(313)	(32,183)	(15,315)	63,755	69,801	59,980
Net Income	(23,348)	(24,572)	(14,096)	(437,012)	72,793	108,787	103,409	66,503
Average Shares	60,030	59,805	60,376	60,014	60,001	61,093	62,117	62,226
Balance Sheet								
Current Assets	2,251,260	2,474,629	2,465,246	2,538,578	2,181,905	1,962,039	1,974,700	1,870,706
Total Assets	3,688,419	3,896,071	3,882,364	3,773,788	3,376,293	2,717,752	2,777,840	2,735,406
Current Liabilities	1,295,789	1,470,398	1,409,676	1,472,011	1,309,733	1,034,638	1,063,589	1,004,555
Long-Term Obligations	1,553,991	1,624,692	1,685,135	1,650,582	900,744	564,583	572,559	608,551
Total Liabilities	3,197,141	3,399,170	3,380,525	3,255,369	2,360,814	1,757,714	1,785,250	1,744,568
Stockholders' Equity	491,278	496,901	501,839	518,419	1,015,479	960,038	992,590	990,838
Shares Outstanding	62,862	62,964	62,936	62,294	61,476	61,031	62,803	63,070
Statistical Record								
Return on Assets %	N.M.	N.M.	N.M.	N.M.	2.39	3.95	3.75	2.63
Return on Equity %	N.M.	N.M.	N.M.	N.M.	7.37	11.11	10.43	6.60
EBITDA Margin %	1.94	1.81	1.76	N.M.	1.30	2.39	2.42	1.91
Net Margin %	N.M.	N.M.	N.M.	N.M.	0.78	1.12	1.06	0.70
Asset Turnover	2.56	2.51	2.73	2.75	3.06	3.53	3.55	3.73
Current Ratio	1.74	1.68	1.75	1.72	1.67	1.90	1.86	1.86
Debt to Equity	3.16	3.27	3.36	3.18	0.89	0.59	0.58	0.61
Price Range	16.84-2.47	18.87-2.69	18.87-4.07	22.68-6.04	36.95-18.10	41.20-31.94	39.02-31.94	37.49-31.72
P/E Ratio	...	...	...	...	30.79-15.08	23.41-18.15	23.65-19.36	35.37-29.92
Average Yield %	1.34	3.66	4.77	5.58	3.43	2.84	2.91	2.91

Address: 9120 Lockwood Boulevard, Mechanicsville, VA 23116	Web Site: www.owens-minor.com	Auditors: KPMG LLP
Telephone: 804-723-7000	Officers: Robert C. Sledd - Chairman, Interim President, Interim Chief Executive Officer Edward A. Pesicka - President, Chief Executive Officer	Investor Contact: 804-723-7555
Fax: 804-723-7100		Transfer Agents: Computershare Shareowner Services LLC, Providence, RI

PACKAGING CORP OF AMERICA

Exchange	Symbol	Price	52Wk Range	Yield	P/E
NYS	PKG	$111.99 (12/31/2019)	113.90-82.89	2.82	13.89

*7 Year Price Score 100.83 *NYSE Composite Index=100 *12 Month Price Score 105.40

Interim Earnings (Per Share)

Qtr.	Mar	Jun	Sep	Dec
2016	1.09	1.23	1.26	1.17
2017	1.24	1.52	1.47	2.84
2018	1.48	1.97	2.18	2.16
2019	1.97	2.04	1.89	...

Interim Dividends (Per Share)

Amt	Decl	Ex	Rec	Pay
0.79Q	02/28/2019	03/14/2019	03/15/2019	04/15/2019
0.79Q	05/10/2019	06/13/2019	06/14/2019	07/15/2019
0.79Q	08/21/2019	09/12/2019	09/13/2019	10/15/2019
0.79Q	12/10/2019	12/19/2019	12/20/2019	01/15/2020

Indicated Div: $3.16

Valuation Analysis

		Institutional Holding	
Forecast EPS	$7.64	No of Institutions	
	(01/17/2020)	800	
Market Cap	$10.6 Billion	Shares	
Book Value	$3.0 Billion	128,216,624	
Price/Book	3.49	% Held	
Price/Sales	1.52	93.44	

Business Summary: Containers & Packaging (MIC: 8.1.3 SIC: 2652 NAIC: 322213)

Packaging Corporation of America is a producer of containerboard products and uncoated freesheet. Co.'s segments are: Packaging, which manufactures and sells a variety of corrugated packaging products, including conventional shipping containers as well as produces packaging for meat, fresh fruit and vegetables, processed food, beverages, and other industrial and consumer products; Paper, which manufactures and sells a range of white papers, including both commodity and specialty papers, which may have features such as colors, coatings, brightness, and recycled content; and Corporate and Other, which includes corporate support staff services and related assets and liabilities.

Recent Developments: For the quarter ended Sep 30 2019, net income decreased 13.0% to US$179.8 million from US$206.7 million in the year-earlier quarter. Revenues were US$1.75 billion, down 3.3% from US$1.81 billion the year before. Operating income was US$262.8 million versus US$298.5 million in the prior-year quarter, a decrease of 12.0%. Direct operating expenses declined 2.0% to US$1.34 billion from US$1.37 billion in the comparable period the year before. Indirect operating expenses increased 2.7% to US$148.6 million from US$144.7 million in the equivalent prior-year period.

Prospects: Our evaluation of Packaging Corp. of America as of October 4th, 2019 is the result of our systematic analysis on three basic characteristics: earnings strength, relative valuation, and recent stock price movement. The company has managed to produce a neutral trend in earnings per share over the past 5 quarters. In addition, recent analyst estimates for the company have been mixed and PKG has posted results that exceeded analysts' expectations. Based on operating earnings yield, the company is undervalued when compared to all of the companies we cover. Share price changes over the past year indicates that PKG will perform poorly over the near term.

Financial Data
(US$ in Thousands)

	9 Mos	6 Mos	3 Mos	12/31/2018	12/31/2017	12/31/2016	12/31/2015	12/31/2014
Earnings Per Share	8.06	8.35	8.28	7.80	7.07	4.75	4.47	3.99
Cash Flow Per Share	13.03	12.63	12.95	12.59	9.16	8.55	7.89	7.59
Tang Book Value Per Share	18.66	17.36	15.96	14.57	9.43	6.95	8.51	6.92
Dividends Per Share	3.160	3.160	3.160	3.000	2.520	2.360	2.200	1.600
Dividend Payout %	39.21	37.84	38.16	38.46	35.64	49.68	49.22	40.10
Income Statement								
Total Revenue	5,244,300	3,493,600	1,733,700	7,014,600	6,444,900	5,779,000	5,741,700	5,852,600
EBITDA	1,077,700	727,000	360,800	1,429,400	1,279,000	780,624	1,073,000	1,050,900
Depn & Amortn	265,100	175,300	87,400	361,700	347,800	324	323,000	348,200
Income Before Taxes	744,600	505,300	249,300	970,500	828,600	688,500	664,500	614,300
Income Taxes	184,400	124,900	62,500	232,500	160,000	238,900	227,700	221,700
Net Income	560,200	380,400	186,800	738,000	668,600	449,600	436,800	392,600
Average Shares	94,300	94,000	94,000	93,900	93,700	93,700	96,700	97,100
Balance Sheet								
Current Assets	2,531,300	2,402,700	2,262,400	2,115,100	1,915,100	1,696,300	1,554,500	1,578,600
Total Assets	7,191,100	7,074,400	6,928,600	6,569,700	6,197,500	5,777,000	5,284,600	5,348,500
Current Liabilities	770,700	729,600	740,700	693,600	832,700	625,400	561,900	611,000
Long-Term Obligations	2,680,000	2,685,600	2,667,200	2,501,300	2,499,400	2,640,300	2,324,300	2,371,700
Total Liabilities	4,156,400	4,153,200	4,134,000	3,897,300	4,014,900	4,017,200	3,651,300	3,827,100
Stockholders' Equity	3,034,700	2,921,200	2,794,600	2,672,400	2,182,600	1,759,800	1,633,300	1,521,400
Shares Outstanding	94,700	94,700	94,500	94,497	94,350	94,213	96,129	98,368
Statistical Record								
Return on Assets %	11.17	11.83	12.01	11.56	11.17	8.11	8.22	7.44
Return on Equity %	27.49	29.82	30.96	30.40	33.92	26.43	27.69	27.70
EBITDA Margin %	20.55	20.81	20.81	20.38	19.85	13.51	18.69	17.96
Net Margin %	10.68	10.89	10.77	10.52	10.37	7.78	7.61	6.71
Asset Turnover	1.02	1.05	1.08	1.10	1.08	1.04	1.08	1.11
Current Ratio	3.28	3.29	3.05	3.05	2.30	2.71	2.77	2.58
Debt to Equity	0.88	0.92	0.95	0.94	1.15	1.50	1.42	1.56
Price Range	109.98-77.95	118.16-77.95	123.78-77.95	129.58-77.95	120.92-85.00	87.51-45.15	84.24-59.34	79.69-58.61
P/E Ratio	13.65-9.67	14.15-9.34	14.95-9.41	16.61-9.99	17.10-12.02	18.42-9.51	18.85-13.28	19.97-14.69
Average Yield %	3.27	3.18	3.02	2.71	2.40	3.38	3.12	2.32

Address: 1 North Field Court, Lake Forest, IL 60045
Telephone: 847-482-3000

Web Site: www.packagingcorp.com
Officers: Mark W. Kowlzan - Chairman, Chief Executive Officer, Senior Vice President Robert P. Mundy - Senior Vice President, Chief Financial Officer, Principal Financial Officer

Auditors: KPMG LLP
Investor Contact: 877-454-2509
Transfer Agents: Computershare Trust Company N.A., Providence, RI

PALO ALTO NETWORKS, INC

Exchange	Symbol	Price	52Wk Range	Yield	P/E
NYS	PANW	$231.25 (12/31/2019)	254.88-179.70	N/A	N/A

*7 Year Price Score 130.11 *NYSE Composite Index=100 *12 Month Price Score 99.00

Interim Earnings (Per Share)

Qtr.	Oct	Jan	Apr	Jul
2016-17	(0.69)	(0.67)	(0.67)	(0.42)
2017-18	(0.70)	(0.38)	(0.51)	(0.02)
2018-19	(0.41)	(0.03)	(0.21)	(0.22)
2019-20	(0.62)	...	...	...

Interim Dividends (Per Share)

No Dividends Paid

Valuation Analysis — **Institutional Holding**

Forecast EPS	$4.95	No of Institutions
	(01/17/2020)	943
Market Cap	$22.6 Billion	Shares
Book Value	$1.5 Billion	96,815,952
Price/Book	14.88	% Held
Price/Sales	7.48	84.33

TRADING VOLUME (thousand shares)

Business Summary: Internet & Software (MIC: 6.3.2 SIC: 3577 NAIC: 423430)

Palo Alto Networks provides a platform that allows enterprises, service providers, and government entities to secure their organizations. Co.'s platform uses a traffic classification engine that identifies network traffic by application, user, and content and provides security across the network, endpoint, and cloud. Co.'s product, subscription, and support offerings include: firewall appliances and software; and Panorama, which is a centralized security management solution for global control of various firewall appliances and software deployed on an end-customer's network as well as in their instances in public or private cloud environments as a virtual appliance or a physical appliance.

Recent Developments: For the quarter ended Oct 31 2019, net loss amounted to US$59.6 million versus a net loss of US$38.3 million in the year-earlier quarter. Revenues were US$771.9 million, up 17.7% from US$656.0 million the year before. Operating loss was US$51.8 million versus a loss of US$32.1 million in the prior-year quarter. Direct operating expenses rose 18.6% to US$217.7 million from US$183.5 million in the comparable period the year before. Indirect operating expenses increased 20.1% to US$606.0 million from US$504.6 million in the equivalent prior-year period.

Prospects: Our evaluation of Palo Alto Networks, Inc as of October 4th, 2019 is the result of our systematic analysis on three basic characteristics: earnings strength, relative valuation, and recent stock price movement. The company has generated a negative trend in earnings per share over the past 5 quarters. In addition, recent analyst estimates for the company have been reduced while PANW has posted results that exceeded analysts' expectations. Based on operating earnings yield, the company is overvalued when compared to all of the companies we cover. Share price changes over the past year indicates that PANW will perform poorly over the near term.

Financial Data

(US$ in Thousands)	3 Mos	07/31/2019	07/31/2018	07/31/2017	07/31/2016	07/31/2015	07/31/2014	07/31/2013
Earnings Per Share	(1.08)	(0.87)	(1.61)	(2.39)	(2.59)	(2.02)	(3.05)	(0.43)
Cash Flow Per Share	10.65	11.17	11.31	9.59	7.54	4.29	1.19	1.67
Tang Book Value Per Share	N.M.	N.M.	3.47	5.10	6.44	4.24	3.34	3.80
Income Statement								
Total Revenue	771,900	2,899,600	2,273,100	1,761,600	1,378,500	928,052	598,179	396,107
EBITDA	70,900	79,300	(36,700)	(125,900)	(139,200)	(105,052)	(203,346)	(9,229)
Depn & Amortn	122,300	139,800	91,000	58,400	42,500	28,200	16,931	9,911
Income Before Taxes	(54,500)	(74,600)	(130,200)	(194,100)	(205,100)	(155,577)	(222,160)	(18,656)
Income Taxes	5,100	7,300	17,700	22,500	20,800	9,405	4,292	10,590
Net Income	(59,600)	(81,900)	(147,900)	(216,600)	(225,900)	(164,982)	(226,452)	(29,246)
Average Shares	96,600	94,500	91,700	90,600	87,100	81,619	74,291	68,682
Balance Sheet								
Current Assets	3,649,800	3,664,800	4,132,000	1,976,300	1,719,100	1,074,030	958,326	529,699
Total Assets	6,824,800	6,592,200	5,823,000	3,438,300	2,761,200	1,965,178	1,478,466	585,606
Current Liabilities	2,051,600	2,053,300	2,139,400	1,201,300	846,800	1,032,227	348,171	206,102
Long-Term Obligations	1,445,500	1,430,000	1,369,700	524,700	508,200	...	466,875	...
Total Liabilities	5,308,400	5,005,900	4,834,700	2,678,700	1,971,300	1,389,363	1,009,883	313,186
Stockholders' Equity	1,516,400	1,586,300	988,300	759,600	789,900	575,815	468,583	272,420
Shares Outstanding	97,600	96,800	93,600	91,500	90,500	84,788	79,519	71,612
Statistical Record								
EBITDA Margin %	9.19	2.73	N.M.	N.M.	N.M.	N.M.	N.M.	N.M.
Asset Turnover	0.48	0.47	0.49	0.57	0.58	0.54	0.58	0.80
Current Ratio	1.78	1.78	1.93	1.65	2.03	1.04	2.75	2.57
Debt to Equity	0.95	0.90	1.39	0.69	0.64	...	1.00	...
Price Range		254.88-163.44	254.88-163.44	218.32-127.72	164.15-108.01	193.54-115.69	197.09-78.67	84.21-40.99	71.75-39.56

Address: 3000 Tannery Way, Santa Clara, CA 95054 **Telephone:** 408-753-4000	**Web Site:** www.paloaltonetworks.com **Officers:** Nikesh Arora - Chairman, Chief Executive Officer Mark D. McLaughlin - Vice-Chairman, Chairman, President, Chief Executive Officer	**Auditors:** Ernst & Young LLP **Investor Contact:** 408-753-3872 **Transfer Agents:** Computershare, Canton, MA

PBF ENERGY INC

Exchange	Symbol	Price	52Wk Range	Yield	P/E
NYS	PBF	$31.37 (12/31/2019)	36.62-21.54	3.83	N/A

*7 Year Price Score 82.61   *NYSE Composite Index=100   *12 Month Price Score 99.84

Interim Earnings (Per Share)

Qtr.	Mar	Jun	Sep	Dec
2016	(0.30)	1.06	0.43	0.55
2017	(0.29)	(1.01)	2.85	2.16
2018	0.27	2.37	1.50	(3.06)
2019	1.89	(0.27)	0.57	...

Interim Dividends (Per Share)

Amt	Decl	Ex	Rec	Pay
0.30Q	02/14/2019	02/27/2019	02/28/2019	03/14/2019
0.30Q	05/01/2019	05/14/2019	05/15/2019	05/30/2019
0.30Q	08/01/2019	08/14/2019	08/15/2019	08/30/2019
0.30Q	10/31/2019	11/13/2019	11/14/2019	11/26/2019

Indicated Div: $1.20

Valuation Analysis   **Institutional Holding**

Forecast EPS	$0.85	No of Institutions
	(01/17/2020)	399
Market Cap	$3.8 Billion	Shares
Book Value	$3.0 Billion	111,494,704
Price/Book	1.26	% Held
Price/Sales	0.16	79.76

Business Summary: Refining & Marketing (MIC: 9.1.2 SIC: 2911 NAIC: 324110)

PBF Energy is a holding company. Through its subsidiaries, Co. is engaged as an independent petroleum refiner and supplier of unbranded transportation fuels, heating oil, petrochemical feedstocks, lubricants and other petroleum products in the U.S. Co. operates in two business segments: refining, which Co. produces a variety of products at each of its refineries such as gasoline, ultra-low-sulfur diesel, heating oil, jet fuel, lubricants, petrochemicals and asphalt; and logistics, which through its PBF Logistics LP subsidiary, Co. owns or leases, operates, develops and acquires crude oil and refined petroleum products terminals, pipelines, storage facilities and similar logistics assets.

Recent Developments: For the quarter ended Sep 30 2019, net income decreased 55.2% to US$86.3 million from US$192.5 million in the year-earlier quarter. Revenues were US$6.43 billion, down 15.9% from US$7.65 billion the year before. Operating income was US$151.9 million versus US$286.3 million in the prior-year quarter, a decrease of 46.9%. Direct operating expenses declined 14.8% to US$6.24 billion from US$7.33 billion in the comparable period the year before. Indirect operating expenses increased 19.2% to US$34.2 million from US$28.7 million in the equivalent prior-year period.

Prospects: Our evaluation of PBF Energy Inc as of October 4th, 2019 is the result of our systematic analysis on three basic characteristics: earnings strength, relative valuation, and recent stock price movement. The company has suffered a very negative trend in earnings per share over the past 5 quarters. In addition, recent analyst estimates for the company have been reduced and PBF has posted results that fell short of analysts' expectations. Based on operating earnings yield, the company is undervalued when compared to all of the companies we cover. Share price changes over the past year indicates that PBF will perform very poorly over the near term.

Financial Data

(US$ in Thousands)	9 Mos	6 Mos	3 Mos	12/31/2018	12/31/2017	12/31/2016	12/31/2015	12/31/2014
Earnings Per Share	(0.87)	0.06	2.70	1.10	3.73	1.74	1.65	(0.51)
Cash Flow Per Share	4.58	4.22	6.45	7.27	6.25	6.61	6.36	6.13
Tang Book Value Per Share	24.83	24.75	24.68	22.11	21.13	18.54	16.84	14.86
Dividends Per Share	1.200	1.200	1.200	1.200	1.200	1.200	1.200	1.200
Dividend Payout %	...	2,000.00	44.44	109.09	32.17	68.97	72.73	...
Income Statement								
Total Revenue	18,206,700	11,776,200	5,216,200	27,186,093	21,786,637	15,920,424	13,123,929	19,828,155
EBITDA	850,700	589,800	470,000	540,883	1,100,420	629,842	483,226	269,542
Depn & Amortn	331,300	218,400	108,600	162,174	146,978	116,629	94,781	114,919
Income Before Taxes	398,100	289,800	321,900	208,798	799,015	363,168	282,258	55,859
Income Taxes	92,000	70,000	80,500	33,507	315,584	137,650	86,725	(22,412)
Net Income	266,400	197,000	229,200	128,315	415,517	170,811	146,401	(38,237)
Average Shares	121,589	119,181	122,175	118,773	113,898	103,606	94,138	74,464
Balance Sheet								
Current Assets	3,602,900	3,599,000	3,979,300	3,236,932	3,802,959	3,407,255	3,022,011	2,346,671
Total Assets	8,917,400	8,809,700	9,126,100	8,005,415	8,117,993	7,621,927	6,105,124	5,196,288
Current Liabilities	2,312,100	2,397,800	2,606,900	2,134,515	2,418,946	2,056,547	1,495,506	1,542,822
Long-Term Obligations	2,316,400	2,185,500	2,353,500	1,931,316	2,175,042	2,108,570	1,840,355	1,260,349
Total Liabilities	5,909,700	5,842,300	6,168,400	5,328,950	5,781,339	5,596,883	4,457,827	3,978,075
Stockholders' Equity	3,007,700	2,967,400	2,957,700	2,676,465	2,336,654	2,025,044	1,647,297	1,218,213
Shares Outstanding	121,130	119,894	119,848	119,874	110,565	109,204	97,781	81,981
Statistical Record								
Return on Assets %	N.M.	0.26	3.76	1.59	5.28	2.48	2.59	N.M.
Return on Equity %	N.M.	0.82	12.33	5.12	19.05	9.28	10.22	N.M.
EBITDA Margin %	4.67	5.01	9.01	1.99	5.05	3.96	3.68	1.36
Net Margin %	1.46	1.67	4.39	0.47	1.91	1.07	1.12	N.M.
Asset Turnover	2.70	2.96	3.06	3.37	2.77	2.31	2.32	4.13
Current Ratio	1.56	1.50	1.53	1.52	1.57	1.66	2.02	1.52
Debt to Equity	0.77	0.74	0.80	0.72	0.93	1.04	1.12	1.03
Price Range	53.45-21.54	53.45-23.90	53.45-29.04	53.45-29.00	35.59-19.32	37.67-19.82	41.48-22.95	32.24-22.12
P/E Ratio	...	890.83-398.33	19.80-10.76	48.59-26.36	9.54-5.18	21.65-11.39	25.14-13.91	...
Average Yield %	3.72	3.17	2.93	2.96	4.85	4.46	3.91	4.42

Address: One Sylvan Way, Second Floor, Parsippany, NJ 07054 **Telephone:** 973-455-7500	**Web Site:** www.pbfenergy.com **Officers:** Thomas J. Nimbley - Chairman, Chief Executive Officer Matthew C. Lucey - President, Executive Vice President, Senior Vice President, Chief Financial Officer, Vice President	**Auditors:** DELOITTE & TOUCHE LLP **Investor Contact:** 973-455-7578 **Transfer Agents:** American Stock Transfer & Trust Company, Brooklyn, NY

PARAMOUNT GROUP INC

Exchange	Symbol	Price	52Wk Range	Yield	P/E
NYS	PGRE	$13.92 (12/31/2019)	14.99-12.26	2.87	174.00

*7 Year Price Score N/A   ***NYSE Composite Index=100**   ***12 Month Price Score 93.03**

Interim Earnings (Per Share)

Qtr.	Mar	Jun	Sep	Dec
2016	(0.03)	0.01	0.00	(0.03)
2017	0.00	0.44	(0.04)	(0.03)
2018	0.00	(0.14)	0.16	0.02
2019	0.02	0.01	0.03	...

Interim Dividends (Per Share)

Amt	Decl	Ex	Rec	Pay
0.10Q	03/15/2019	03/28/2019	03/29/2019	04/15/2019
0.10Q	06/14/2019	06/27/2019	06/28/2019	07/15/2019
0.10Q	09/13/2019	09/27/2019	09/30/2019	10/15/2019
0.10Q	12/13/2019	12/30/2019	12/31/2019	01/15/2020

Indicated Div: $0.40

Valuation Analysis   **Institutional Holding**

Forecast EPS	$0.03	No of Institutions
	(01/16/2020)	225
Market Cap	$3.2 Billion	Shares
Book Value	$3.9 Billion	158,514,880
Price/Book	0.82	% Held
Price/Sales	4.12	59.54

Business Summary: REITs (MIC: 5.3.1 SIC: 6798 NAIC: 525930)

Paramount Group is a real estate investment trust focused on owning, operating, managing, acquiring and redeveloping Class A office properties in select central business district submarkets of New York City, Washington, D.C. and San Francisco. Co. conducts its business through, and substantially all its interests in properties and investments are held by, Paramount Group Operating Partnership LP, a Delaware limited partnership (the Operating Partnership). Co. is the sole general partner of the Operating Partnership. Co.'s reportable segments are separated by region based on the three regions in which Co. conducts its business: New York, Washington, D.C. and San Francisco.

Recent Developments: For the quarter ended Sep 30 2019, net income decreased 75.1% to US$11.0 million from US$44.3 million in the year-earlier quarter. Revenues were US$198.3 million, up 3.0% from US$192.6 million the year before.

Prospects: Our evaluation of Paramount Group Inc as of October 4th, 2019 is the result of our systematic analysis on three basic characteristics: earnings strength, relative valuation, and recent stock price movement. The company has generated a negative trend in earnings per share over the past 5 quarters. In addition, recent analyst estimates for the company have been reduced while PGRE has posted results that exceeded analysts' expectations. Based on operating earnings yield, the company is overvalued when compared to all of the companies we cover. Share price changes over the past year indicates that PGRE will perform in line with the market over the near term.

Financial Data
(US$ in Thousands)

	9 Mos	6 Mos	3 Mos	12/31/2018	12/31/2017	12/31/2016	12/31/2015	12/31/2014
Earnings Per Share	0.08	0.21	0.06	0.04	0.37	(0.05)	(0.02)	0.27
Cash Flow Per Share	0.99	0.67	0.92	0.65	0.80	0.66	(0.08)	(3.65)
Tang Book Value Per Share	15.92	15.85	15.93	16.00	15.91	15.55	15.32	15.28
Dividends Per Share	0.400	0.400	0.400	0.400	0.380	0.380	0.419	...
Dividend Payout %	500.00	190.48	666.67	1,000.00	102.70	...	...	...
Income Statement								
Total Revenue	578,692	380,375	191,792	758,961	718,967	683,341	662,408	66,135
EBITDA	168,395	109,808	56,564	220,482	341,162	249,601	319,807	134,409
Depn & Amortn	37,580	25,663	13,333	58,814	76,016	94,935	128,603	17,260
Income Before Taxes	23,997	13,580	8,138	22,132	112,353	3,854	23,709	73,227
Income Taxes	823	1,406	1,138	3,139	5,177	1,785	2,566	505
Net Income	13,246	6,164	3,709	9,147	86,381	(9,934)	(4,419)	57,308
Average Shares	231,229	234,355	233,458	239,555	236,401	218,053	212,106	212,107
Balance Sheet								
Current Assets	639,358	615,639	659,643	675,601	517,372	393,678	295,864	530,445
Total Assets	8,579,750	8,853,875	8,721,637	8,755,978	8,917,661	8,867,168	8,794,143	9,030,441
Current Liabilities	119,362	124,460	125,599	150,236	170,140	156,346	200,758	162,966
Long-Term Obligations	3,576,734	3,741,233	3,568,933	3,566,917	3,541,300	3,594,898	2,961,524	2,852,287
Total Liabilities	4,728,960	4,903,805	4,732,760	4,755,178	4,740,920	4,877,163	5,033,126	5,119,579
Stockholders' Equity	3,850,790	3,950,070	3,988,877	4,000,800	4,176,741	3,990,005	3,761,017	3,910,862
Shares Outstanding	227,865	234,123	234,478	233,135	240,427	230,015	212,112	212,106
Statistical Record								
Return on Assets %	0.21	0.55	0.13	0.10	0.97	N.M.	N.M.	9.21
Return on Equity %	0.47	1.22	0.29	0.22	2.12	N.M.	N.M.	26.01
EBITDA Margin %	29.10	28.87	29.49	29.05	47.45	36.53	48.28	203.23
Net Margin %	2.29	1.62	1.93	1.21	12.01	N.M.	N.M.	86.65
Asset Turnover	0.09	0.09	0.09	0.09	0.08	0.08	0.07	0.11
Current Ratio	5.36	4.95	5.25	4.50	3.04	2.52	1.47	3.25
Debt to Equity	0.93	0.95	0.89	0.89	0.85	0.90	0.79	0.73
Price Range	15.00-12.26	15.97-12.26	15.97-12.26	15.97-12.30	17.52-15.23	18.25-14.38	19.75-15.72	18.80-18.06
P/E Ratio	187.50-153.25	76.05-58.38	266.17-204.33	399.25-307.50	47.35-41.16	...	...	69.63-66.89
Average Yield %	2.85	2.75	2.74	2.72	2.35	2.33	2.31	...

Address: 1633 Broadway, Suite 1801, New York, NY 10019 **Telephone:** 212-237-3100	**Web Site:** www.paramount-group.com **Officers:** Albert P. Behler - Chairman, President, Chief Executive Officer Wilbur N. Paes - Executive Vice President, Senior Vice President, Chief Financial Officer, Chief Accounting Officer, Treasurer	**Auditors:** DELOITTE & TOUCHE LLP **Transfer Agents:** Computershare Trust Company, N.A.

PARK HOTELS & RESORTS INC

Exchange	Symbol	Price	52Wk Range	Yield	P/E
NYS	PK	$25.87 (12/31/2019)	32.98-22.02	8.50	22.11

*7 Year Price Score N/A   *NYSE Composite Index=100   *12 Month Price Score 83.70

Interim Earnings (Per Share)

Qtr.	Mar	Jun	Sep	Dec
2017	11.02	0.52	0.48	0.27
2018	0.71	1.07	0.26	0.27
2019	0.48	0.40	0.02	...

Interim Dividends (Per Share)

Amt	Decl	Ex	Rec	Pay
0.45Q	02/22/2019	03/28/2019	03/29/2019	04/15/2019
0.45Q	04/26/2019	06/27/2019	06/28/2019	07/15/2019
0.45Q	07/26/2019	09/27/2019	09/30/2019	10/15/2019
0.55Q	12/09/2019	12/30/2019	12/31/2019	01/15/2020

Indicated Div: $2.20

Valuation Analysis

		Institutional Holding	
Forecast EPS	$1.24	No of Institutions	
	(01/17/2020)	381	
Market Cap	$6.2 Billion	Shares	
Book Value	$6.5 Billion		300,599,136
Price/Book	0.95	% Held	
Price/Sales	2.28		100.71

Business Summary: REITs (MIC: 5.3.1 SIC: 6798 NAIC: 525930)

Park Hotels & Resorts is a lodging real estate company with a portfolio of hotels and resorts. Co. holds investments in entities that have ownership or leasehold interests in hotels, consisting of hotels and resort sprimarily located in U.S. Co.'s portfolio includes hotels in urban and convention areas, such as New York City, Washington, D.C., Chicago, San Francisco and New Orleans; resorts in key leisure destinations, including Hawaii, Orlando and Key West; and hotels adjacent to main gateway airports, such as Los Angeles International, Boston Logan and Miami Airport, as well as hotels in select suburban locations.

Recent Developments: For the quarter ended Sep 30 2019, net income decreased 83.6% to US$9.0 million from US$55.0 million in the year-earlier quarter. Revenues were US$672.0 million, up 3.1% from US$652.0 million the year before.

Prospects: Our evaluation of Park Hotels & Resorts Inc. as of October 4th, 2019 is the result of our systematic analysis on three basic characteristics: earnings strength, relative valuation, and recent stock price movement. The company has managed to produce a neutral trend in earnings per share over the past 5 quarters. In addition, recent analyst estimates for the company have been mixed and PK has posted results that fell short of analysts' expectations. Based on operating earnings yield, the company is undervalued when compared to all of the companies we cover. Share price changes over the past year indicates that PK will perform in line with the market over the near term.

Financial Data

(US$ in Thousands)	9 Mos	6 Mos	3 Mos	12/31/2018	12/31/2017	12/31/2016	12/31/2015	12/31/2014
Earnings Per Share	1.17	1.41	2.08	2.31	12.21	...	...	...
Cash Flow Per Share	2.42	2.69	2.35	2.19	3.09	...	...	...
Tang Book Value Per Share	24.41	24.86	24.90	24.84	24.97	16.32	...	...
Dividends Per Share	2.350	2.330	2.760	2.740	4.630	...	...	...
Dividend Payout %	200.85	165.25	132.69	118.61	37.92	...	...	...
Income Statement								
Total Revenue	2,034,000	1,362,000	659,000	2,737,000	2,791,000	2,727,000	2,688,000	2,513,000
EBITDA	462,000	364,000	193,000	876,000	650,000	692,000	863,000	712,000
Depn & Amortn	185,000	124,000	63,000	273,000	283,000	295,000	283,000	245,000
Income Before Taxes	184,000	178,000	99,000	482,000	245,000	218,000	395,000	282,000
Income Taxes	12,000	12,000	7,000	23,000	(2,346,000)	82,000	118,000	117,000
Net Income	183,000	178,000	96,000	472,000	2,625,000	133,000	292,000	176,000
Average Shares	207,000	202,000	202,000	204,000	214,000			...
Balance Sheet								
Current Assets	633,000	754,000	538,000	660,000	552,000	538,000	319,000	221,000
Total Assets	11,620,000	9,431,000	9,394,000	9,363,000	9,714,000	9,834,000	9,787,000	9,714,000
Current Liabilities	500,000	460,000	407,000	455,000	494,000	468,000	333,000	284,000
Long-Term Obligations	4,100,000	2,949,000	2,949,000	2,948,000	2,961,000	3,012,000	4,057,000	4,246,000
Total Liabilities	5,123,000	3,809,000	3,766,000	3,731,000	3,703,000	5,962,000	6,966,000	7,097,000
Stockholders' Equity	6,497,000	5,622,000	5,628,000	5,632,000	6,011,000	3,872,000	2,821,000	2,617,000
Shares Outstanding	239,388	201,621	201,539	201,198	214,845	197,605	...	...
Statistical Record								
Return on Assets %	2.26	3.01	4.46	4.95	26.86	1.35	2.99	...
Return on Equity %	3.86	4.97	7.34	8.11	53.12	3.96	10.74	...
EBITDA Margin %	22.71	26.73	29.29	32.01	23.29	25.38	32.11	28.33
Net Margin %	9.00	13.07	14.57	17.25	94.05	4.88	10.86	7.00
Asset Turnover	0.26	0.29	0.29	0.29	0.29	0.28	0.28	...
Current Ratio	1.27	1.64	1.32	1.45	1.12	1.15	0.96	0.78
Debt to Equity	0.63	0.52	0.52	0.52	0.49	0.78	1.44	1.62
Price Range	32.98-23.19	34.01-25.56	34.01-25.56	34.01-24.42	29.90-24.92	...	...	...
P/E Ratio	28.19-19.82	24.12-18.13	16.35-12.29	14.72-10.57	2.45-2.04	...	...	...
Average Yield %	8.19	7.65	9.07	9.18	17.03	...	...	...

Address: 1775 Tysons Blvd., 7th Floor, Tysons, VA 22102 **Telephone:** 571-302-5757	**Web Site:** www.pkhotelsandresorts.com **Officers:** Thomas J. Baltimore - Chairman, President, Chief Executive Officer Thomas C. Morey - Executive Vice President, Senior Vice President, General Counsel, Secretary	**Auditors:** Ernst & Young LLP **Transfer Agents:** Wells Fargo Bank, N.A.

PARKER HANNIFIN CORP

Exchange	Symbol	Price	52Wk Range	Yield	P/E
NYS	PH	$205.82 (12/31/2019)	209.30-144.84	1.71	18.23

*7 Year Price Score 104.81 *NYSE Composite Index=100 *12 Month Price Score 108.47

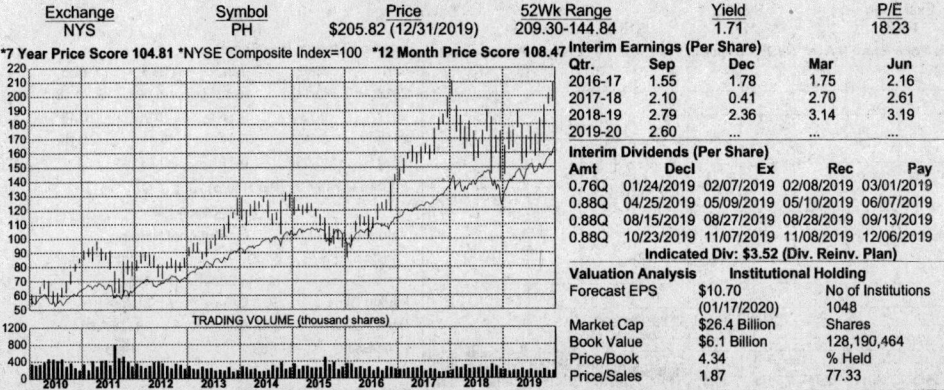

TRADING VOLUME (thousand shares)

Interim Earnings (Per Share)

Qtr.	Sep	Dec	Mar	Jun
2016-17	1.55	1.78	1.75	2.16
2017-18	2.10	0.41	2.70	2.61
2018-19	2.79	2.36	3.14	3.19
2019-20	2.60	...	...	...

Interim Dividends (Per Share)

Amt	Decl	Ex	Rec	Pay
0.76Q	01/24/2019	02/07/2019	02/08/2019	03/01/2019
0.88Q	04/25/2019	05/09/2019	05/10/2019	06/07/2019
0.88Q	08/15/2019	08/27/2019	08/28/2019	09/13/2019
0.88Q	10/23/2019	11/07/2019	11/08/2019	12/06/2019

Indicated Div: $3.52 (Div. Reinv. Plan)

Valuation Analysis | Institutional Holding

Forecast EPS	$10.70
	(01/17/2020)
Market Cap	$26.4 Billion
Book Value	$6.1 Billion
Price/Book	4.34
Price/Sales	1.87

No of Institutions	1048
Shares	
128,190,464	
% Held	77.33

Business Summary: Industrial Machinery & Equipment (MIC: 7.2.1 SIC: 3492 NAIC: 332912)

Parker Hannifin is a manufacturer of motion and control technologies and systems, providing engineered solutions for a variety of mobile, industrial and aerospace markets. Co. has two reporting segments: Diversified Industrial and Aerospace Systems. Co.'s Diversified Industrial segment products consist of a range of motion-control and fluid systems and components, which are categorized into the following groups: Engineered Materials, Filtration, Fluid Connectors, Instrumentation, and Motion Systems. Co.'s Aerospace Systems Segment products are used in commercial and military airframe and engine programs and include control actuation systems and components and pneumatic control components.

Recent Developments: For the quarter ended Sep 30 2019, net income decreased 9.8% to US$339.0 million from US$375.9 million in the year-earlier quarter. Revenues were US$3.33 billion, down 4.2% from US$3.48 billion the year before. Direct operating expenses declined 4.4% to US$2.48 billion from US$2.59 billion in the comparable period the year before. Indirect operating expenses increased 1.2% to US$399.2 million from US$394.3 million in the equivalent prior-year period.

Prospects: Our evaluation of Parker Hannifin Corp. as of October 4th, 2019 is the result of our systematic analysis on three basic characteristics: earnings strength, relative valuation, and recent stock price movement. The company has managed to produce a neutral trend in earnings per share over the past 5 quarters. In addition, recent analyst estimates for the company have been mixed and PH has posted results that exceeded analysts' expectations. Based on operating earnings yield, the company is undervalued when compared to all of the companies we cover. Share price changes over the past year indicates that PH will perform poorly over the near term.

Financial Data

(US$ in Thousands)	3 Mos	06/30/2019	06/30/2018	06/30/2017	06/30/2016	06/30/2015	06/30/2014	06/30/2013
Earnings Per Share	11.29	11.48	7.83	7.25	5.89	6.97	6.87	6.26
Cash Flow Per Share	15.72	13.31	12.03	9.77	8.62	9.11	9.31	7.98
Tang Book Value Per Share	N.M.	N.M.	N.M.	N.M.	5.59	8.29	15.44	8.20
Dividends Per Share	3.280	3.160	2.740	2.580	2.520	2.370	1.860	1.700
Dividend Payout %	29.05	27.53	34.99	35.59	42.78	34.00	27.07	27.16
Income Statement								
Total Revenue	3,334,511	14,320,324	14,302,392	12,029,312	11,360,753	12,711,744	13,215,971	13,015,704
EBITDA	612,183	2,349,238	2,153,956	1,693,945	1,441,553	1,753,422	1,854,251	1,616,275
Depn & Amortn	109,071	225,675	237,806	202,868	190,308	202,776	214,965	213,722
Income Before Taxes	433,156	1,933,425	1,702,277	1,328,641	1,114,728	1,432,240	1,556,720	1,311,001
Income Taxes	94,115	420,494	640,962	344,797	307,512	419,687	515,302	362,217
Net Income	338,898	1,512,364	1,060,801	983,412	806,840	1,012,140	1,041,048	948,427
Average Shares	130,130	131,781	135,426	135,559	136,911	145,112	151,444	151,588
Balance Sheet								
Current Assets	8,138,079	7,673,086	5,085,238	4,779,718	5,207,787	5,583,092	6,071,580	5,531,186
Total Assets	19,568,589	17,576,690	15,320,087	15,489,904	12,056,738	12,295,037	13,274,362	12,540,898
Current Liabilities	4,157,328	3,151,773	3,197,483	3,395,860	2,365,941	2,350,130	3,252,796	3,520,203
Long-Term Obligations	7,366,912	6,520,831	4,318,559	4,861,895	2,675,000	2,723,960	1,508,142	1,495,960
Total Liabilities	13,471,973	11,614,721	9,460,221	10,228,255	7,481,483	7,190,750	6,614,934	6,802,472
Stockholders' Equity	6,096,616	5,961,969	5,859,866	5,261,649	4,575,255	5,104,287	6,659,428	5,738,426
Shares Outstanding	128,464	128,480	132,414	133,191	134,012	138,558	148,902	149,288
Statistical Record								
Return on Assets %	8.43	9.19	6.89	7.14	6.61	7.92	8.07	8.00
Return on Equity %	24.19	25.59	19.08	19.99	16.63	17.21	16.79	17.84
EBITDA Margin %	18.36	16.40	15.06	14.08	12.69	13.79	14.03	12.42
Net Margin %	10.16	10.56	7.42	8.18	7.10	7.96	7.88	7.29
Asset Turnover	0.81	0.87	0.93	0.87	0.93	0.99	1.02	1.10
Current Ratio	1.96	2.43	1.59	1.41	2.20	2.38	1.87	1.57
Debt to Equity	1.21	1.09	0.74	0.92	0.58	0.53	0.23	0.26
Price Range	189.93-141.11	190.58-141.11	210.94-153.96	165.22-107.07	117.15-86.51	132.78-102.96	129.52-95.32	100.96-71.84
P/E Ratio	16.82-12.50	16.60-12.29	26.94-19.66	22.79-14.77	19.89-14.69	19.05-14.77	18.85-13.87	16.13-11.48
Average Yield %	1.96	1.88	1.55	1.84	2.38	1.96	1.61	1.95

Address: 6035 Parkland Boulevard, Cleveland, OH 44124-4141 **Telephone:** 216-896-3000	**Web Site:** www.parker.com **Officers:** Thomas L. Williams - Chairman, Chief Executive Officer, Executive Vice President Lee C. Banks - President, Executive Vice President, Chief Operating Officer	**Auditors:** DELOITTE & TOUCHE LLP **Investor Contact:** 216-896-2240 **Transfer Agents:** Wells Fargo Bank, N.A., St. Paul, MN

PARSLEY ENERGY INC

Exchange	Symbol	Price	52Wk Range	Yield	P/E
NYS	PE	$18.91 (12/31/2019)	21.77-14.13	N/A	20.12

*7 Year Price Score N/A   *NYSE Composite Index=100   *12 Month Price Score 88.26

Interim Earnings (Per Share)

Qtr.	Mar	Jun	Sep	Dec
2016	(0.14)	(0.13)	(0.02)	(0.18)
2017	0.13	0.17	(0.05)	0.18
2018	0.32	0.44	0.41	0.19
2019	(0.09)	0.41	0.43	...

Interim Dividends (Per Share)

No Dividends Paid

Valuation Analysis

		Institutional Holding	
Forecast EPS	$1.21	No of Institutions	
	(01/17/2020)	476	
Market Cap	$6.0 Billion	Shares	
Book Value	$5.8 Billion	284,952,064	
Price/Book	1.03	% Held	
Price/Sales	3.17	79.69	

Business Summary: Production & Extraction (MIC: 9.1.1 SIC: 1311 NAIC: 211111)

Parsley Energy is a holding company. Through its subsidiaries, Co. is an independent oil and natural gas company focused on the acquisition, development, exploration and production of unconventional oil and natural gas properties in the Permian Basin. The Permian Basin is located in West Texas and southeastern New Mexico. Co.'s properties are located in two sub areas of the Permian Basin, the Midland and Delaware Basins, where Co. focuses on horizontal development drilling.

Recent Developments: For the quarter ended Sep 30 2019, net income increased 4.1% to US$139.6 million from US$134.1 million in the year-earlier quarter. Revenues were US$510.2 million, down 0.2% from US$511.0 million the year before. Operating income was US$153.0 million versus US$221.0 million in the prior-year quarter, a decrease of 30.7%. Direct operating expenses rose 21.7% to US$96.0 million from US$78.9 million in the comparable period the year before. Indirect operating expenses increased 23.7% to US$261.1 million from US$211.2 million in the equivalent prior-year period.

Prospects: Our evaluation of Parsley Energy Inc as of October 4th, 2019 is the result of our systematic analysis on three basic characteristics: earnings strength, relative valuation, and recent stock price movement. The company has generated a negative trend in earnings per share over the past 5 quarters. In addition, recent analyst estimates for the company have been reduced and PE has posted results that fell short of analysts' expectations. Based on operating earnings yield, the company is undervalued when compared to all of the companies we cover. Share price changes over the past year indicates that PE will perform in line with the market over the near term.

Financial Data

(US$ in Thousands)	9 Mos	6 Mos	3 Mos	12/31/2018	12/31/2017	12/31/2016	12/31/2015	12/31/2014
Earnings Per Share	0.94	0.92	0.95	1.35	0.42	(0.46)	(0.45)	0.42
Cash Flow Per Share	4.50	4.80	4.32	4.48	2.88	1.41	1.55	3.36
Tang Book Value Per Share	18.31	17.94	17.52	17.58	14.99	10.07	7.49	5.61
Dividends Per Share	0.030	...	...	...	...	...	...	...
Dividend Payout %	3.19	...	...	...	...	...	...	...
Income Statement								
Total Revenue	1,436,363	926,212	427,671	1,826,431	967,044	457,773	266,057	301,757
EBITDA	989,969	570,317	166,818	1,247,140	559,873	176,092	122,395	132,949
Depn & Amortn	584,023	372,286	169,900	569,700	340,800	227,200	173,600	1,500
Income Before Taxes	306,379	131,826	(35,793)	551,444	129,628	(106,341)	(96,786)	92,842
Income Taxes	59,788	24,835	(7,790)	105,475	5,708	(17,424)	(23,755)	36,468
Net Income	211,581	91,871	(24,064)	369,127	106,774	(74,182)	(50,484)	23,429
Average Shares	280,547	279,768	278,794	272,884	296,512	161,793	111,271	55,239
Balance Sheet								
Current Assets	451,584	395,704	317,567	540,712	919,486	299,488	488,326	204,161
Total Assets	9,995,696	9,838,066	9,554,147	9,391,363	8,793,198	3,938,782	2,514,192	2,051,079
Current Liabilities	809,735	789,268	741,380	648,945	612,089	344,954	228,497	220,865
Long-Term Obligations	2,198,861	2,223,649	2,182,463	2,181,667	2,179,525	1,041,324	555,924	676,845
Total Liabilities	4,199,053	4,157,320	4,004,434	3,823,305	4,080,903	1,849,144	1,249,700	1,343,838
Stockholders' Equity	5,796,643	5,680,746	5,549,713	5,568,058	4,712,295	2,089,638	1,264,492	707,241
Shares Outstanding	316,658	316,655	316,694	316,753	314,388	207,599	168,768	126,046
Statistical Record								
Return on Assets %	2.76	2.73	2.84	4.06	1.68	N.M.	N.M.	1.68
Return on Equity %	4.70	4.69	4.95	7.18	3.14	N.M.	N.M.	5.75
EBITDA Margin %	68.92	61.58	39.01	68.28	57.90	38.47	46.00	44.06
Net Margin %	14.73	9.92	N.M.	20.21	11.04	N.M.	N.M.	7.76
Asset Turnover	0.20	0.20	0.20	0.20	0.15	0.14	0.12	0.22
Current Ratio	0.56	0.50	0.43	0.83	1.50	0.87	2.14	0.92
Debt to Equity	0.38	0.39	0.39	0.39	0.46	0.50	0.44	0.96
Price Range	30.70-14.13	32.87-14.51	32.87-14.51	32.87-14.51	36.88-23.86	38.27-15.66	19.82-13.50	25.16-11.26
P/E Ratio	32.66-15.03	35.73-15.77	34.60-15.27	24.35-10.75	87.81-56.81	...	...	59.90-26.81
Average Yield %	0.15	...	...	...	...	...	...	...

Address: 303 Colorado Street, Suite 3000, Austin, TX 78701 **Telephone:** 737-704-2300	**Web Site:** www.parsleyenergy.com **Officers:** Bryan Sheffield - Executive Chairman, Chairman, President, Chief Executive Officer Matthew (Matt) Gallagher - President, Chief Executive Officer, Chief Operating Officer, Vice President	**Auditors:** KPMG LLP **Transfer Agents:** American Stock Transfer & Trust Company, LLC

PAYCOM SOFTWARE INC

Exchange	Symbol	Price	52Wk Range	Yield	P/E
NYS	PAYC	$264.76 (12/31/2019)	279.66-116.50	N/A	92.90

*7 Year Price Score N/A ***NYSE Composite Index=100** ***12 Month Price Score 114.83**

TRADING VOLUME (thousand shares)

Interim Earnings (Per Share)

Qtr.	Mar	Jun	Sep	Dec
2016	0.31	0.18	0.10	0.15
2017	0.43	0.24	0.24	0.22
2018	0.70	0.61	0.49	0.54
2019	0.81	0.83	0.67	...

Interim Dividends (Per Share)

No Dividends Paid

Valuation Analysis / Institutional Holding

Valuation Analysis		Institutional Holding	
Forecast EPS	$3.42	No of Institutions	
	(00/25/2020)	568	
Market Cap	$15.3 Billion	Shares	
Book Value	$474.9 Million	45,371,176	
Price/Book	32.14	% Held	
Price/Sales	21.98	70.20	

Business Summary: Internet & Software (MIC: 6.3.2 SIC: 7372 NAIC: 541511)

Paycom Software is a holding company. Through its subsidiaries, Co. is a provider of cloud-based human capital management (HCM) solution delivered as Software-as-a-Service. Co. provides functionality and data analytics that businesses need to manage the complete employment life cycle from recruitment to retirement. Co.'s solution is based on a primary system of record maintained in a single database for various HCM functions, including talent acquisition, time and labor management, payroll, talent management and human resources management applications. Co.'s solution was developed in-house and is based on a single platform, there is no need to integrate, update or access multiple databases.

Recent Developments: For the quarter ended Sep 30 2019, net income increased 36.1% to US$39.2 million from US$28.8 million in the year-earlier quarter. Revenues were US$175.0 million, up 31.3% from US$133.3 million the year before. Operating income was US$50.6 million versus US$36.2 million in the prior-year quarter, an increase of 39.5%. Direct operating expenses rose 19.3% to US$26.4 million from US$22.1 million in the comparable period the year before. Indirect operating expenses increased 30.9% to US$98.1 million from US$74.9 million in the equivalent prior-year period.

Prospects: Our evaluation of Paycom Software Inc as of October 4th, 2019 is the result of our systematic analysis on three basic characteristics: earnings strength, relative valuation, and recent stock price movement. The company has enjoyed a very positive trend in earnings per share over the past 5 quarters. However, recent analyst estimates for the company have been unchanged, while PAYC has posted results that exceeded analysts' expectations. Based on operating earnings yield, the company is overvalued when compared to all of the companies we cover. Share price changes over the past year indicates that PAYC will perform very well over the near term.

Financial Data
(US$ in Thousands)

	9 Mos	6 Mos	3 Mos	12/31/2018	12/31/2017	12/31/2016	12/31/2015	12/31/2014
Earnings Per Share	2.85	2.67	2.45	2.34	1.13	0.74	0.36	0.11
Cash Flow Per Share	3.74	3.60	3.62	3.20	2.26	1.71	0.76	0.45
Tang Book Value Per Share	7.34	6.64	6.03	4.93	1.43	1.09	0.75	0.32
Income Statement								
Total Revenue	544,262	369,256	199,943	566,336	433,047	329,141	224,653	150,929
EBITDA	181,636	134,628	71,697	190,602	96,058	70,279	42,752	18,577
Depn & Amortn	15,874	19,617	9,309	15,125	18,500	12,000	7,800	5,500
Income Before Taxes	164,968	114,477	62,112	174,711	76,647	57,243	33,525	9,656
Income Taxes	29,772	18,433	14,830	37,646	9,840	13,403	12,580	3,993
Net Income	135,196	96,044	47,282	137,065	66,807	43,840	20,945	5,663
Average Shares	58,383	58,410	58,316	58,582	58,790	58,968	57,919	51,857
Balance Sheet								
Current Assets	1,012,975	1,287,986	1,549,484	1,064,622	1,149,862	925,583	761,138	693,393
Total Assets	1,592,027	1,826,192	2,062,828	1,521,926	1,355,164	1,078,613	876,773	798,942
Current Liabilities	918,478	1,201,278	1,483,710	1,028,682	1,140,152	898,894	727,534	678,772
Long-Term Obligations	31,293	31,727	32,179	32,614	34,414	28,711	24,974	26,123
Total Liabilities	1,117,129	1,391,430	1,664,275	1,187,173	1,219,762	962,086	778,459	724,804
Stockholders' Equity	474,898	434,762	398,553	334,753	135,402	116,527	98,314	74,138
Shares Outstanding	57,657	57,629	57,447	57,276	57,788	57,331	57,119	53,832
Statistical Record								
Return on Assets %	10.89	9.63	7.80	9.53	5.49	4.47	2.50	0.83
Return on Equity %	39.89	40.87	39.14	58.31	53.04	40.70	24.29	9.10
EBITDA Margin %	33.37	36.46	35.86	33.66	22.18	21.35	19.03	12.31
Net Margin %	24.84	26.01	23.65	24.20	15.43	13.32	9.32	3.75
Asset Turnover	0.45	0.40	0.33	0.39	0.36	0.34	0.27	0.22
Current Ratio	1.10	1.07	1.04	1.03	1.01	1.03	1.05	1.02
Debt to Equity	0.07	0.07	0.08	0.10	0.25	0.25	0.25	0.35
Price Range	255.10-111.54	230.15-100.67	190.05-97.27	163.32-80.44	85.59-43.93	52.44-22.50	45.73-23.18	28.75-12.41
P/E Ratio	89.51-39.14	86.20-37.70	77.57-39.70	69.79-34.38	75.74-38.88	70.86-30.41	127.03-64.39	261.36-112.82

Address: 7501 W. Memorial Road, Oklahoma City, OK 73142 Telephone: 405-722-6900	Web Site: www.paycom.com Officers: Chad Richison - Chairman, President, Chief Executive Officer Craig E. Boelte - Chief Financial Officer, Treasurer, Secretary	Auditors: Grant Thornton LLP Transfer Agents: American Stock Transfer & Trust Company, LLC

PENNEY (J.C.) CO.,INC. (HOLDING CO.)

Exchange	Symbol	Price	52Wk Range	Yield	P/E
NYS	JCP	$1.12 (12/31/2019)	1.85-0.55	N/A	N/A

*7 Year Price Score 13.29   *NYSE Composite Index=100   *12 Month Price Score 92.82

Interim Earnings (Per Share)

Qtr.	Apr	Jul	Oct	Jan
2016-17	(0.22)	(0.18)	(0.22)	0.62
2017-18	(0.58)	(0.20)	(0.41)	0.82
2018-19	(0.25)	(0.32)	(0.48)	0.24
2019-20	(0.48)	(0.15)	(0.29)	...

Interim Dividends (Per Share)

Dividend Payment Suspended

Valuation Analysis

		Institutional Holding	
Forecast EPS	$-1.03	No of Institutions	
	(01/14/2020)		478
Market Cap	$358.4 Million	Shares	
Book Value	$868.0 Million		266,018,416
Price/Book	0.41	% Held	
Price/Sales	0.03		61.79

Business Summary: Retail - General Merchandise/Department Stores (MIC: 2.1.1 SIC: 5311 NAIC: 452111)

J. C. Penney Company is a holding company whose principal operating subsidiary is J. C. Penney Corporation, Inc. Co.'s business consists of selling merchandise and services to consumers through its department stores and its website at jcpenney.com. Co.'s department stores and website serve the same type of customers, its website provides the same mix of merchandise as its store assortment along with other extended categories that are not provided in store, and its department stores accept returns from sales made in stores and via its website. Co. sells family apparel and footwear, accessories, jewelry, beauty products through Sephora inside JCPenney, and home furnishings.

Recent Developments: For the quarter ended Nov 2 2019, net loss amounted to US$93.0 million versus a net loss of US$151.0 million in the year-earlier quarter. Revenues were US$2.50 billion, down 8.5% from US$2.73 billion the year before. Operating loss was US$34.0 million versus a loss of US$100.0 million in the prior-year quarter. Direct operating expenses declined 14.8% to US$1.54 billion from US$1.81 billion in the comparable period the year before. Indirect operating expenses decreased 3.1% to US$993.0 million from US$1.03 billion in the equivalent prior-year period.

Prospects: Our evaluation of Penney (J.C.) Co.,Inc. as of October 4th, 2019 is the result of our systematic analysis on three basic characteristics: earnings strength, relative valuation, and recent stock price movement. The company has enjoyed a very positive trend in earnings per share over the past 5 quarters. However, recent analyst estimates for the company have been mixed and JCP has posted results that exceeded analysts' expectations. Based on operating earnings yield, the company is overvalued when compared to all of the companies we cover. Share price changes over the past year indicates that JCP will perform very poorly over the near term.

Financial Data
(US$ in Thousands)

	9 Mos	6 Mos	3 Mos	02/02/2019	02/03/2018	01/28/2017	01/30/2016	01/31/2015
Earnings Per Share	(0.68)	(0.87)	(1.04)	(0.81)	(0.37)	...	(1.68)	(2.53)
Cash Flow Per Share	1.13	1.55	1.60	1.14	1.44	1.09	1.44	0.79
Tang Book Value Per Share	2.71	3.03	3.26	1.77	2.58	2.64	2.64	4.64
Income Statement								
Total Revenue	7,674,000	5,174,000	2,555,000	12,019,000	12,506,000	12,547,000	12,625,000	12,257,000
EBITDA	345,000	235,000	67,000	598,000	653,000	974,000	517,000	289,000
Depn & Amortn	415,000	284,000	147,000	556,000	570,000	609,000	616,000	631,000
Income Before Taxes	(290,000)	(196,000)	(153,000)	(271,000)	(242,000)	2,000	(504,000)	(748,000)
Income Taxes	5,000	6,000	1,000	(16,000)	(126,000)	1,000	9,000	23,000
Net Income	(295,000)	(202,000)	(154,000)	(255,000)	(116,000)	1,000	(513,000)	(771,000)
Average Shares	320,900	319,400	317,700	315,700	311,100	313,000	305,900	305,200
Balance Sheet								
Current Assets	3,376,000	2,921,000	2,935,000	2,959,000	3,410,000	4,097,000	4,018,000	4,331,000
Total Assets	8,699,000	8,260,000	8,342,000	7,721,000	8,413,000	9,314,000	9,442,000	10,404,000
Current Liabilities	2,229,000	2,129,000	1,945,000	1,942,000	2,332,000	2,419,000	2,412,000	2,241,000
Long-Term Obligations	4,012,000	3,590,000	3,827,000	3,920,000	3,992,000	4,558,000	4,678,000	5,360,000
Total Liabilities	7,831,000	7,297,000	7,308,000	6,551,000	7,034,000	7,960,000	8,133,000	8,490,000
Stockholders' Equity	868,000	963,000	1,034,000	1,170,000	1,379,000	1,354,000	1,309,000	1,914,000
Shares Outstanding	320,000	317,700	316,800	316,100	312,000	308,300	306,100	304,900
Statistical Record								
Return on Assets %	N.M.	N.M.	N.M.	N.M.	N.M.	0.01	N.M.	N.M.
Return on Equity %	N.M.	N.M.	N.M.	N.M.	N.M.	0.08	N.M.	N.M.
EBITDA Margin %	4.50	4.54	2.62	4.98	5.22	7.76	4.10	2.36
Net Margin %	N.M.	N.M.	N.M.	N.M.	N.M.	0.01	N.M.	N.M.
Asset Turnover	1.34	1.43	1.43	1.49	1.39	1.34	1.28	1.11
Current Ratio	1.51	1.37	1.51	1.52	1.46	1.69	1.67	1.93
Debt to Equity	4.62	3.73	3.70	3.35	2.89	3.37	3.57	2.80
Price Range	1.85-0.55	2.64-0.72	3.07-0.97	4.33-0.97	7.31-2.37	11.86-6.45	9.98-6.31	11.20-5.08

Address: 6501 Legacy Drive, Plano, TX 75024-3698 Telephone: 972-431-1000	Web Site: www.jcpenney.com Officers: Ronald W. Tysoe - Non-Executive Chairman Jill A. Soltau - Chief Executive Officer	Auditors: KPMG LLP Transfer Agents: ComputerShare Investor Services, Providence, RI

PENTAIR PLC

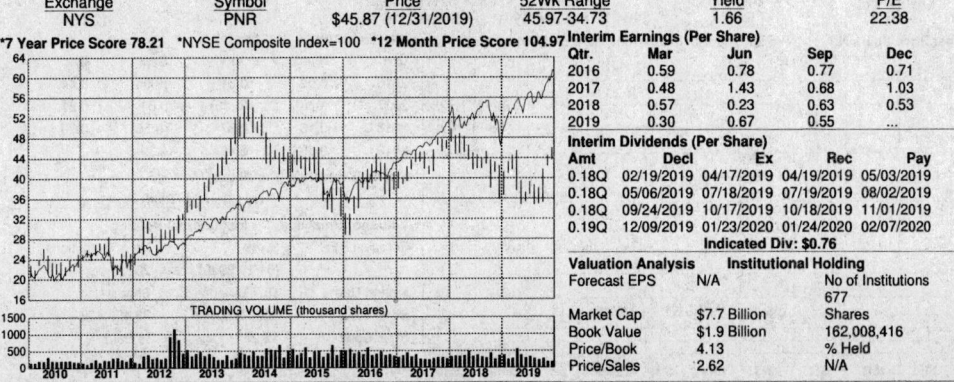

Exchange	Symbol	Price	52Wk Range	Yield	P/E
NYS	PNR	$45.87 (12/31/2019)	45.97-34.73	1.66	22.38

*7 Year Price Score 78.21 *NYSE Composite Index=100 *12 Month Price Score 104.97

Interim Earnings (Per Share)

Qtr.	Mar	Jun	Sep	Dec
2016	0.59	0.78	0.77	0.71
2017	0.48	1.43	0.68	1.03
2018	0.57	0.23	0.63	0.53
2019	0.30	0.67	0.55	...

Interim Dividends (Per Share)

Amt	Decl	Ex	Rec	Pay
0.18Q	02/19/2019	04/17/2019	04/19/2019	05/03/2019
0.18Q	05/06/2019	07/18/2019	07/19/2019	08/02/2019
0.18Q	09/24/2019	10/17/2019	10/18/2019	11/01/2019
0.19Q	12/09/2019	01/23/2020	01/24/2020	02/07/2020

Indicated Div: $0.76

Valuation Analysis

		Institutional Holding	
Forecast EPS	N/A	No of Institutions	677
Market Cap	$7.7 Billion	Shares	
Book Value	$1.9 Billion		162,008,416
Price/Book	4.13	% Held	
Price/Sales	2.62		N/A

Business Summary: Industrial Machinery & Equipment (MIC: 7.2.1 SIC: 3559 NAIC: 333298)

Pentair is a pure play water industrial manufacturing company comprised of three segments: Aquatic Systems, which manufactures and sells a line of energy-efficient residential and commercial pool equipment and accessories including pumps, filters, heaters, lights, and automatic controls; Filtration Solutions, which designs, manufactures, markets and services water solutions across residential, commercial, food and beverage and industrial applications; and Flow Technologies, which manufactures and sells products ranging from light duty diaphragm pumps to high-flow turbine pumps and solid handling pumps while serving the global residential, commercial and industrial markets.

Recent Developments: For the quarter ended Sep 30 2019, income from continuing operations increased 0.1% to US$91.3 million from US$91.2 million in the year-earlier quarter. Net income decreased 16.2% to US$92.3 million from US$110.1 million in the year-earlier quarter. Revenues were US$713.6 million, up 0.3% from US$711.4 million the year before. Operating income was US$108.8 million versus US$108.4 million in the prior-year quarter, an increase of 0.4%. Direct operating expenses declined 1.9% to US$458.6 million from US$467.6 million in the comparable period the year before. Indirect operating expenses increased 8.0% to US$146.2 million from US$135.4 million in the equivalent prior-year period.

Prospects: Our evaluation of Pentair PLC as of October 4th, 2019 is the result of our systematic analysis on three basic characteristics: earnings strength, relative valuation, and recent stock price movement. The company has managed to produce a neutral trend in earnings per share over the past 5 quarters. However, recent analyst estimates for the company have been reduced while PNR has posted results that exceeded analysts' expectations. Based on operating earnings yield, the company is undervalued when compared to all of the companies we cover. Share price changes over the past year indicates that PNR will perform poorly over the near term.

Financial Data

(US$ in Thousands)	9 Mos	6 Mos	3 Mos	12/31/2018	12/31/2017	12/31/2016	12/31/2015	12/31/2014
Earnings Per Share	2.05	2.13	1.69	1.96	3.63	2.85	(0.42)	1.11
Cash Flow Per Share	2.49	2.14	2.04	2.50	3.41	4.74	4.10	5.29
Dividends Per Share	0.715	0.710	0.880	1.050	1.380	1.340	...	...
Dividend Payout %	34.88	33.33	52.07	53.57	38.02	47.02	...	...
Income Statement								
Total Revenue	2,202,000	1,488,400	688,900	2,965,100	4,936,500	4,890,000	6,449,000	7,039,000
EBITDA	385,700	258,000	90,700	462,100	660,400	781,400	313,500	990,400
Depn & Amortn	60,500	40,900	20,200	49,700	85,200	84,600	139,500	138,700
Income Before Taxes	301,600	200,400	63,200	379,800	487,900	556,700	71,300	783,100
Income Taxes	42,800	32,900	10,800	58,100	9,200	109,400	139,100	177,300
Net Income	257,900	165,600	51,300	347,400	666,500	522,200	(76,400)	214,900
Average Shares	168,600	170,500	172,500	177,300	183,700	183,100	182,600	193,700
Balance Sheet								
Current Assets	1,002,600	1,041,500	1,251,600	1,039,400	1,748,800	2,672,000	2,780,600	2,894,100
Total Assets	4,080,400	4,170,000	4,382,200	3,806,500	8,633,700	11,534,800	11,857,000	10,655,200
Current Liabilities	694,200	710,200	705,300	818,700	1,199,400	1,471,200	1,486,500	1,639,500
Long-Term Obligations	1,118,700	1,215,100	1,370,700	787,600	1,440,700	4,278,400	4,709,300	2,997,400
Total Liabilities	2,211,600	2,363,400	2,511,800	1,970,400	3,595,900	7,280,400	7,848,200	5,991,400
Stockholders' Equity	1,868,800	1,806,600	1,870,400	1,836,100	5,037,800	4,254,400	4,008,800	4,663,800
Shares Outstanding	168,092	168,049	171,891	171,363	180,306	181,800	180,500	182,500
Statistical Record								
Return on Assets %	8.89	9.24	4.30	5.59	6.61	4.45	N.M.	1.92
Return on Equity %	18.71	19.95	8.98	10.11	14.35	12.60	N.M.	3.99
EBITDA Margin %	17.52	17.33	13.17	15.58	13.38	15.98	4.86	14.07
Net Margin %	11.71	11.13	7.45	11.72	13.50	10.68	N.M.	3.05
Asset Turnover	0.75	0.74	0.42	0.48	0.49	0.42	0.57	0.63
Current Ratio	1.44	1.47	1.77	1.27	1.46	1.82	1.87	1.77
Debt to Equity	0.60	0.67	0.73	0.43	0.29	1.01	1.17	0.64
Price Range	45.49-34.73	45.49-34.82	48.28-35.81	49.78-35.81	47.79-37.99	44.84-28.79	46.17-32.37	55.61-40.18
P/E Ratio	22.19-16.94	21.36-16.35	28.57-21.19	25.40-18.27	13.17-10.47	15.73-10.10	...	50.10-36.20
Average Yield %	1.82	1.74	2.07	2.38	3.18	3.51	...	...

Address: Regal House, 70 London Road, London, 55416-1259 **Telephone:** 749-421-6154	**Web Site:** www.pentair.com **Officers:** David A. Jones - Chairman John L. Stauch - President, Executive Vice President, Chief Executive Officer, Chief Financial Officer	**Auditors:** DELOITTE & TOUCHE LLP **Investor Contact:** 763-656-5575 **Transfer Agents:** Wells Fargo

PENUMBRA INC

Exchange	Symbol	Price	52Wk Range	Yield	P/E
NYS	PEN	$164.27 (12/31/2019)	183.40-115.84	N/A	128.34

*7 Year Price Score N/A   *NYSE Composite Index=100   *12 Month Price Score 105.36

Interim Earnings (Per Share)

Qtr.	Mar	Jun	Sep	Dec
2016	0.02	0.01	(0.04)	0.44
2017	(0.10)	(0.05)	0.01	0.27
2018	0.16	0.37	(0.55)	0.20
2019	0.30	0.46	0.32	...

Interim Dividends (Per Share)

No Dividends Paid

Valuation Analysis

		Institutional Holding	
Forecast EPS	$0.89	No of Institutions	
	(01/10/2020)	282	
Market Cap	$5.7 Billion	Shares	
Book Value	$467.3 Million	35,428,436	
Price/Book	12.27	% Held	
Price/Sales	10.97	96.92	

Business Summary: Medical Instruments & Equipment (MIC: 4.3.1 SIC: 3841 NAIC: 339112)

Penumbra is a healthcare company. Co. designs, develops, manufactures and markets medical devices. Co.'s Neuro products include Penumbra System brand of products that provides a form of mechanical thrombectomy used by specialist physicians to revascularize blood vessels that are blocked by clots in the intracranial vasculature. Co.'s Vascular products include the Ruby Coil System that consists of detachable coils and is used in clinical applications auch as active extravasations, or the escape of blood into surrounding tissue, selective embolization in patients with visceral aneurysms, embolization in patients with gastrointestinal bleeding, and high flow arterial venous malformations.

Recent Developments: For the quarter ended Sep 30 2019, net income amounted to US$11.0 million versus a net loss of US$22.4 million in the year-earlier quarter. Revenues were US$139.5 million, up 24.8% from US$111.8 million the year before. Operating income was US$13.0 million versus a loss of US$20.8 million in the prior-year quarter. Direct operating expenses rose 18.2% to US$43.5 million from US$36.8 million in the comparable period the year before. Indirect operating expenses decreased 13.4% to US$83.0 million from US$95.9 million in the equivalent prior-year period.

Prospects: Our evaluation of Penumbra Inc as of October 4th, 2019 is the result of our systematic analysis on three basic characteristics: earnings strength, relative valuation, and recent stock price movement. The company has generated a negative trend in earnings per share over the past 5 quarters. However, recent analyst estimates for the company have been unchanged while PEN has posted results that exceeded analysts' expectations. Based on operating earnings yield, the company is overvalued when compared to all of the companies we cover. Share price changes over the past year indicates that PEN will perform in line with the market over the near term.

Financial Data

(US$ in Thousands)	9 Mos	6 Mos	3 Mos	12/31/2018	12/31/2017	12/31/2016	12/31/2015	12/31/2014
Earnings Per Share	1.28	0.41	0.32	0.18	0.13	0.44	0.08	(0.18)
Cash Flow Per Share	0.84	0.51	0.46	0.84	0.38	(0.42)	(1.86)	(1.39)
Tang Book Value Per Share	12.44	12.08	11.58	11.24	10.94	8.57	7.78	20.92
Income Statement								
Total Revenue	402,142	262,640	128,439	444,938	333,764	263,317	186,095	125,510
EBITDA	41,900	27,643	12,980	3,744	3,223	(892)	5,283	3,500
Depn & Amortn	5,790	3,737	1,804	5,100	3,400	2,300	1,800	800
Income Before Taxes	38,386	25,423	11,909	1,608	2,476	(869)	4,024	3,139
Income Taxes	683	(1,280)	1,455	(4,403)	(3,611)	(15,683)	1,659	894
Net Income	38,769	27,286	10,698	6,601	4,657	14,814	2,365	2,245
Average Shares	36,271	36,214	36,213	36,086	35,319	33,478	14,219	4,609
Balance Sheet								
Current Assets	451,334	434,604	423,086	410,726	382,234	263,827	244,361	115,301
Total Assets	614,170	585,109	568,789	515,006	476,667	308,254	263,848	121,381
Current Liabilities	86,167	69,761	69,412	66,062	51,582	35,800	28,148	20,823
Total Liabilities	146,838	131,018	132,057	92,766	76,259	41,707	31,326	22,284
Stockholders' Equity	467,332	454,091	436,732	422,240	400,408	266,547	232,522	99,097
Shares Outstanding	34,910	34,792	34,737	34,437	33,685	31,108	29,897	4,736
Statistical Record								
Return on Assets %	8.15	2.77	2.23	1.33	1.19	5.16	1.23	2.33
Return on Equity %	10.36	3.42	2.77	1.60	1.40	5.92	1.43	3.05
EBITDA Margin %	10.42	10.53	10.11	0.84	0.97	N.M.	2.84	2.79
Net Margin %	9.64	10.39	8.33	1.48	1.40	5.63	1.27	1.79
Asset Turnover	0.94	0.91	0.89	0.90	0.85	0.92	0.97	1.30
Current Ratio	5.24	6.23	6.10	6.22	7.41	7.37	8.68	5.54
Price Range	183.40-113.42	167.39-113.42	165.95-112.20	165.95-84.60	115.85-64.05	79.39-42.00	55.60-36.50	...
P/E Ratio	143.28-88.61	408.27-276.63	518.59-350.63	921.94-470.00	891.15-492.69	180.43-95.45	695.00-456.25	...

Address: One Penumbra Place,	Web Site: www.penumbrainc.com	Auditors: Deloitte & Touche LLP
Alameda, CA 94502	Officers: Adam Elsesser - Chairman, President, Chief	Transfer Agents: American Stock
Telephone: 510-748-3200	Executive Officer James Pray - President	Transfer & Trust Company, LLC

PERFORMANCE FOOD GROUP CO

Exchange	Symbol	Price	52Wk Range	Yield	P/E
NYS	PFGC	$51.48 (12/31/2019)	51.51-31.64	N/A	31.01

*7 Year Price Score N/A *NYSE Composite Index=100 *12 Month Price Score 107.27

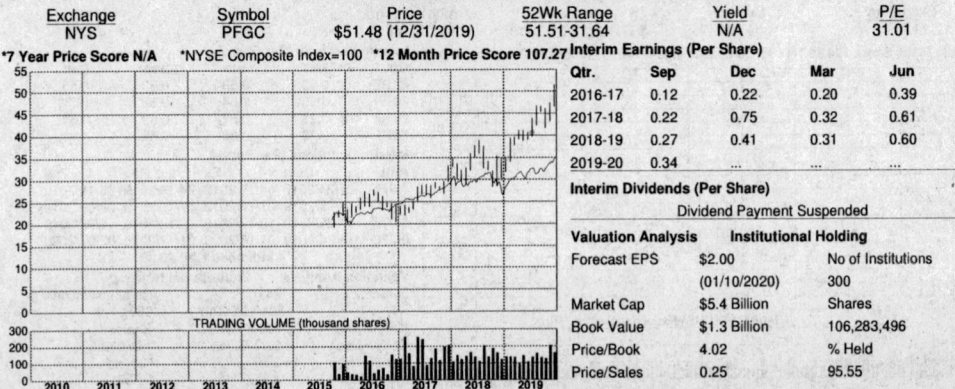

Interim Earnings (Per Share)

Qtr.	Sep	Dec	Mar	Jun
2016-17	0.12	0.22	0.20	0.39
2017-18	0.22	0.75	0.32	0.61
2018-19	0.27	0.41	0.31	0.60
2019-20	0.34	...	...	...

Interim Dividends (Per Share)

Dividend Payment Suspended

Valuation Analysis		Institutional Holding	
Forecast EPS	$2.00	No of Institutions	
	(01/10/2020)	300	
Market Cap	$5.4 Billion	Shares	
Book Value	$1.3 Billion	106,283,496	
Price/Book	4.02	% Held	
Price/Sales	0.25	95.55	

Business Summary: Retail - Food & Beverage, Drug & Tobacco (MIC: 2.1.2 SIC: 5141 NAIC: 445110)

Performance Food Group is a holding company. Through its subsidiaries, Co. markets and distributes food and food-related products. Co.'s products include frozen foods, such as meats, appetizers and entrees, fruits, vegetables, and desserts; canned and dry foods; fresh meats; dairy products; beverage products; imported specialties; fresh produce; and candy, snack, and other products. Co. also supplies non-food items including paper products such as pizza boxes, disposable napkins, plates and cups; tableware such as china and silverware; cookware such as pots, pans, and utensils; restaurant and kitchen equipment and supplies; cigarettes and other tobacco products; and cleaning supplies.

Recent Developments: For the quarter ended Sep 28 2019, net income increased 28.0% to US$36.1 million from US$28.2 million in the year-earlier quarter. Revenues were US$6.24 billion, up 37.5% from US$4.54 billion the year before. Operating income was US$63.5 million versus US$50.6 million in the prior-year quarter, an increase of 25.5%. Direct operating expenses rose 40.2% to US$5.53 billion from US$3.95 billion in the comparable period the year before. Indirect operating expenses increased 19.3% to US$647.9 million from US$543.0 million in the equivalent prior-year period.

Prospects: Our evaluation of Performance Food Group Company as of October 4th, 2019 is the result of our systematic analysis on three basic characteristics: earnings strength, relative valuation, and recent stock price movement. The company has managed to produce a neutral trend in earnings per share over the past 5 quarters. In addition, recent analyst estimates for the company have been mixed and PFGC has posted results that exceeded analysts' expectations. Based on operating earnings yield, the company is fairly valued when compared to all of the companies we cover. Share price changes over the past year indicates that PFGC will perform over the near term.

Financial Data

(US$ in Thousands)	3 Mos	06/29/2019	06/30/2018	07/01/2017	07/02/2016	06/27/2015	06/28/2014	06/29/2013
Earnings Per Share	1.66	1.59	1.90	0.93	0.70	0.64	0.18	0.10
Cash Flow Per Share	3.55	3.07	3.61	2.02	2.40	1.47	1.38	1.62
Tang Book Value Per Share	3.72	3.26	1.95	0.06	N.M.	N.M.	N.M.	
Dividends Per Share	...	...	...	...	...	...	...	2.530
Dividend Payout %	...	...	...	...	...	...	...	2,530.00
Income Statement								
Total Revenue	6,243,000	19,743,500	17,619,900	16,761,800	16,104,800	15,270,000	13,685,700	12,826,500
EBITDA	110,700	438,700	384,100	338,700	317,000	303,600	249,000	233,400
Depn & Amortn	47,200	155,000	130,100	126,100	118,600	121,300	132,700	120,000
Income Before Taxes	46,200	218,300	193,600	157,700	114,500	96,600	30,200	19,500
Income Taxes	10,100	51,500	(5,100)	61,400	46,200	40,100	14,700	11,100
Net Income	36,100	166,800	198,700	96,300	68,300	56,500	15,500	8,400
Average Shares	105,600	105,200	104,600	103,036	98,128	87,613	87,533	87,458
Balance Sheet								
Current Assets	3,769,700	2,670,600	2,203,500	2,084,900	1,938,900	1,900,300	1,727,300	...
Total Assets	6,163,000	4,653,500	4,000,900	3,804,100	3,455,400	3,390,900	3,239,800	...
Current Liabilities	1,823,000	1,699,300	1,470,000	1,383,300	1,316,700	1,277,000	1,170,400	...
Long-Term Obligations	2,360,000	1,331,800	1,175,800	1,285,900	1,143,100	1,429,600	1,449,000	...
Total Liabilities	4,829,900	3,355,300	2,865,600	2,878,600	2,652,600	2,897,900	2,805,700	...
Stockholders' Equity	1,333,100	1,298,200	1,135,300	925,500	802,800	493,000	434,100	...
Shares Outstanding	104,200	103,800	103,200	100,805	99,901	86,878	86,874	...
Statistical Record								
Return on Assets %	3.41	3.87	5.11	2.66	1.96	1.71	...	...
Return on Equity %	13.98	13.75	19.34	11.17	10.37	12.22	...	...
EBITDA Margin %	1.77	2.22	2.18	2.02	1.97	1.99	1.82	1.82
Net Margin %	0.58	0.84	1.13	0.57	0.42	0.37	0.11	0.07
Asset Turnover	4.18	4.58	4.53	4.63	4.63	4.62	...	...
Current Ratio	2.07	1.57	1.50	1.51	1.47	1.49	1.48	...
Debt to Equity	1.77	1.03	1.04	1.39	1.42	2.90	3.34	...
Price Range	46.90-28.33	41.20-28.33	37.80-25.95	28.85-20.45	27.43-19.20	...	...	...
P/E Ratio	28.25-17.07	25.91-17.82	19.89-13.66	31.02-21.99	39.19-27.43	...	...	...

Address: 12500 West Creek Parkway, Richmond, VA 23238 Telephone: 804-484-7700	Web Site: www.pfgc.com Officers: George L. Holm - Chairman, President, Chief Executive Officer Patrick T. Hagerty - Executive Vice President, Senior Vice President, Division Officer	Auditors: DELOITTE & TOUCHE LLP Transfer Agents: Computershare Trust Company, N.A.

PERKINELMER, INC.

Exchange	Symbol	Price	52Wk Range	Yield	P/E
NYS	PKI	$97.10 (12/31/2019)	101.12-72.79	0.29	46.24

*7 Year Price Score 124.79 *NYSE Composite Index=100 *12 Month Price Score 97.28

Interim Earnings (Per Share)

Qtr.	Mar	Jun	Sep	Dec
2016	0.43	0.58	0.53	0.58
2017	0.35	1.84	0.82	(0.38)
2018	0.23	0.57	0.69	0.64
2019	0.32	0.62	0.52	...

Interim Dividends (Per Share)

Amt	Decl	Ex	Rec	Pay
0.07Q	01/24/2019	04/17/2019	04/19/2019	05/10/2019
0.07Q	04/25/2019	07/18/2019	07/19/2019	08/09/2019
0.07Q	07/25/2019	10/17/2019	10/18/2019	11/08/2019
0.07Q	10/24/2019	01/16/2020	01/17/2020	02/07/2020

Indicated Div: $0.28

Valuation Analysis

		Institutional Holding	
Forecast EPS	$4.07	No of Institutions	
	(01/16/2020)	657	
Market Cap	$10.8 Billion	Shares	
Book Value	$2.7 Billion	149,082,576	
Price/Book	3.99	% Held	
Price/Sales	3.81	96.53	

Business Summary: Biotechnology (MIC: 4.1.2 SIC: 3826 NAIC: 334516)

PerkinElmer is a provider of products, services and solutions to the diagnostics, life sciences and applied markets. The principal products and services of Co.'s two operating segments are: Diagnostics, which develops diagnostics, tools and applications focused on clinically-oriented customers, particularly within the reproductive health, market diagnostics and applied genomics markets; and Discovery & Analytical Solutions, which provides products and services targeted towards the life sciences and applied markets.

Recent Developments: For the quarter ended Sep 29 2019, income from continuing operations decreased 22.3% to US$58.6 million from US$75.4 million in the year-earlier quarter. Net income decreased 23.5% to US$58.6 million from US$76.5 million in the year-earlier quarter. Revenues were US$706.9 million, up 4.8% from US$674.3 million the year before. Operating income was US$78.7 million versus US$80.2 million in the prior-year quarter, a decrease of 1.9%. Direct operating expenses rose 6.6% to US$364.6 million from US$342.0 million in the comparable period the year before. Indirect operating expenses increased 4.6% to US$263.6 million from US$252.1 million in the equivalent prior-year period.

Prospects: Our evaluation of PerkinElmer Inc. as of October 4th, 2019 is the result of our systematic analysis on three basic characteristics: earnings strength, relative valuation, and recent stock price movement. The company has managed to produce a neutral trend in earnings per share over the past 5 quarters. In addition, recent analyst estimates for the company have been mixed and PKI has posted results that fell short of analysts' expectations. Based on operating earnings yield, the company is fairly valued when compared to all of the companies we cover. Share price changes over the past year indicates that PKI will perform in line with the market over the near term.

Financial Data
(US$ in Thousands)

	9 Mos	6 Mos	3 Mos	12/30/2018	12/31/2017	01/01/2017	01/03/2016	12/28/2014
Earnings Per Share	2.10	2.27	2.22	2.13	2.64	2.12	1.87	1.39
Cash Flow Per Share	2.77	2.65	2.90	2.82	2.63	3.21	2.51	2.51
Dividends Per Share	0.280	0.280	0.280	0.280	0.280	0.280	0.280	0.280
Dividend Payout %	13.33	12.33	12.61	13.15	10.61	13.21	14.97	20.14
Income Statement								
Total Revenue	2,078,177	1,371,254	648,737	2,777,996	2,256,982	2,115,517	2,262,359	2,237,219
EBITDA	236,163	148,371	53,476	504,106	369,387	313,394	314,739	238,506
Depn & Amortn	16,036	7,355	1,144	180,588	31,300	28,500	33,400	33,300
Income Before Taxes	171,846	108,592	36,765	257,683	296,718	244,068	244,015	169,603
Income Taxes	8,642	3,998	1,312	20,208	139,828	28,362	31,327	8,437
Net Income	163,057	104,499	35,412	237,927	292,633	234,299	212,425	157,778
Average Shares	111,559	111,528	111,293	111,534	110,859	110,313	113,315	113,739
Balance Sheet								
Current Assets	1,548,405	1,337,761	1,247,646	1,234,634	1,199,955	1,189,931	1,033,161	1,068,551
Total Assets	6,489,081	6,399,072	6,086,497	5,975,522	6,091,463	4,276,683	4,166,295	4,134,075
Current Liabilities	1,188,102	706,799	742,268	771,631	950,902	603,355	561,485	597,310
Long-Term Obligations	1,750,925	2,104,466	1,848,935	1,876,624	1,788,803	1,045,254	1,011,762	1,051,892
Total Liabilities	3,782,284	3,692,205	3,448,025	3,390,567	3,588,275	2,123,113	2,055,854	2,091,973
Stockholders' Equity	2,706,797	2,706,867	2,638,472	2,584,955	2,503,188	2,153,570	2,110,441	2,042,102
Shares Outstanding	111,093	111,071	110,891	110,597	110,361	109,617	112,034	112,481
Statistical Record								
Return on Assets %	3.79	4.08	4.05	3.95	5.66	5.57	5.04	3.92
Return on Equity %	8.88	9.66	9.52	9.38	12.60	11.02	10.07	7.84
EBITDA Margin %	11.36	10.82	8.24	18.15	16.37	14.81	13.91	10.66
Net Margin %	7.85	7.62	5.46	8.56	12.97	11.08	9.39	7.05
Asset Turnover	0.46	0.45	0.46	0.46	0.44	0.50	0.54	0.56
Current Ratio	1.30	1.89	1.68	1.60	1.26	1.97	1.84	1.79
Debt to Equity	0.65	0.78	0.70	0.73	0.71	0.49	0.48	0.52
Price Range	101.12-71.87	101.12-71.87	97.50-71.87	97.27-71.87	73.84-51.57	56.92-41.45	54.36-42.66	48.25-39.83
P/E Ratio	48.15-34.22	44.55-31.66	43.92-32.37	45.67-33.74	27.97-19.53	26.85-19.55	29.07-22.81	34.71-28.65
Average Yield %	0.32	0.32	0.33	0.35	0.44	0.54	0.56	0.63

Address: 940 Winter Street, Waltham, MA 02451	**Web Site:** www.perkinelmer.com	**Auditors:** DELOITTE & TOUCHE LLP
Telephone: 781-663-6900	**Officers:** Robert F. Friel - Chairman, President, Chief Executive Officer Prahlad R. Singh - President, Chief Executive Officer, Senior Vice President, Chief Operating Officer, Division Officer	**Investor Contact:** 781-663-6900
Fax: 781-663-6052		**Transfer Agents:** Computershare, Inc., Providence , RI

PERSPECTA INC

Exchange	Symbol	Price	52Wk Range	Yield	P/E
NYS	PRSP	$26.44 (12/31/2019)	27.98-17.22	0.91	53.96

*7 Year Price Score N/A   *NYSE Composite Index=100   *12 Month Price Score 109.88

Interim Earnings (Per Share)

Qtr.	Jun	Sep	Dec	Mar
2017-18	0.22	0.28	0.00	0.00
2018-19	0.17	0.14	0.23	(0.11)
2019-20	0.19	0.18	...	...

Interim Dividends (Per Share)

Amt	Decl	Ex	Rec	Pay
0.05Q	02/13/2019	03/26/2019	03/27/2019	04/16/2019
0.06Q	05/21/2019	06/04/2019	06/05/2019	07/16/2019
0.06Q	08/13/2019	09/03/2019	09/04/2019	10/15/2019
0.06Q	11/12/2019	12/03/2019	12/04/2019	01/14/2020

Indicated Div: $0.24

Valuation Analysis

		Institutional Holding	
Forecast EPS	$2.14 (01/15/2020)	No of Institutions	471
Market Cap	$4.3 Billion	Shares	129,367,872
Book Value	$2.2 Billion	% Held	75.83
Price/Book	1.98		
Price/Sales	0.96		

TRADING VOLUME (thousand shares)

Business Summary: IT Services (MIC: 6.3.1 SIC: 7374 NAIC: 541512)

Perspecta is a provider of end-to-end enterprise information technology and operations-related services across the United States federal government as well as to certain state and local government agencies. Using its enterprise offerings and solutions, Co. assists government customers implement modern collaborative workplaces, hybrid cloud platforms and integrated digital systems of engagement with their enterprise management systems. Co.'s offerings include application services, analytics and data services, applied research, cybersecurity, cloud computing and infrastructure services, digital strategy and transformation, digital workplace, integrated solutions, and investigative services.

Recent Developments: For the quarter ended Sep 30 2019, net income increased 20.8% to US$29.0 million from US$24.0 million in the year-earlier quarter. Revenues were US$1.17 billion, up 9.7% from US$1.07 billion the year before. Direct operating expenses rose 11.7% to US$908.0 million from US$813.0 million in the comparable period the year before. Indirect operating expenses increased 3.7% to US$227.0 million from US$219.0 million in the equivalent prior-year period.

Prospects: Our evaluation of Perspecta Inc. as of October 4th, 2019 is the result of our systematic analysis on three basic characteristics: earnings strength, relative valuation, and recent stock price movement. The company has produced a positive trend in earnings per share over the past 5 quarters. However, recent analyst estimates for the company have been reduced, while PRSP has posted results that exceeded analysts' expectations. Based on operating earnings yield, the company is undervalued when compared to all of the companies we cover. Share price changes over the past year indicates that PRSP will perform in line with the market over the near term.

Financial Data

(US$ in Thousands)	6 Mos	3 Mos	03/31/2019	03/31/2018	03/31/2017	10/31/2016	10/31/2015	10/31/2014
Earnings Per Share	0.49	0.45	0.44	...	...	...	...	...
Cash Flow Per Share	3.37	2.99	2.81	...	...	...	...	...
Dividends Per Share	0.220	0.210	0.200	...	...	...	...	...
Dividend Payout %	44.90	46.67	45.45	...	...	...	...	...
Income Statement								
Total Revenue	2,279,000	1,107,000	4,030,000	2,819,000	1,073,000	2,732,000	2,585,000	2,955,000
EBITDA	341,000	178,000	359,000	280,000	137,000	327,000	131,000	421,000
Depn & Amortn	191,000	101,000	126,000	69,000	68,000	167,000	153,000	167,000
Income Before Taxes	79,000	42,000	112,000	199,000	59,000	129,000	(51,000)	221,000
Income Taxes	19,000	11,000	40,000	(9,000)	23,000	49,000	(22,000)	83,000
Net Income	60,000	31,000	72,000	208,000	36,000	80,000	(29,000)	138,000
Average Shares	162,900	163,290	164,820	...	...	...	...	...
Balance Sheet								
Current Assets	934,000	895,000	878,000	449,000	511,000	572,000	848,000	...
Total Assets	6,319,000	6,118,000	6,083,000	3,679,000	1,073,000	1,234,000	1,512,000	...
Current Liabilities	1,078,000	1,035,000	1,014,000	605,000	466,000	649,000	693,000	...
Long-Term Obligations	2,599,000	2,438,000	2,465,000	144,000	155,000	215,000	223,000	...
Total Liabilities	4,156,000	3,963,000	3,921,000	950,000	657,000	896,000	957,000	...
Stockholders' Equity	2,163,000	2,155,000	2,162,000	2,729,000	416,000	338,000	555,000	...
Shares Outstanding	161,866	162,466	163,099	165,698	...	...	...	...
Statistical Record								
Return on Assets %	1.25	1.19	1.48	8.75	7.54	5.81	...	...
Return on Equity %	3.62	3.40	2.94	13.23	23.08	17.87	...	...
EBITDA Margin %	14.96	16.08	8.91	9.93	12.77	11.97	5.07	14.25
Net Margin %	2.63	2.80	1.79	7.38	3.36	2.93	N.M.	4.67
Asset Turnover	0.71	0.70	0.83	1.19	2.25	1.98	...	...
Current Ratio	0.87	0.86	0.87	0.74	1.10	0.88	1.22	...
Debt to Equity	1.20	1.13	1.14	0.05	0.37	0.64	0.40	...
Price Range	26.41-16.16	26.14-16.16	26.14-16.16	...	...	...	...	...
P/E Ratio	53.90-32.98	58.09-35.91	59.41-36.73	...	...	...	...	...
Average Yield %	0.99	0.95	0.91	...	...	...	...	...

Address: 15052 Conference Center Drive, Chantilly, VA 20151 **Telephone:** 571-313-6000	**Web Site:** www.perspecta.com **Officers:** John Michael Lawrie - Chairman John M. Curtis - President, Chief Executive Officer	**Auditors:** DELOITTE & TOUCHE LLP **Transfer Agents:** EQ Shareowner Services

PENSKE AUTOMOTIVE GROUP INC

Exchange	Symbol	Price	52Wk Range	Yield	P/E
NYS	PAG	$50.22 (12/31/2019)	53.70-40.32	3.27	9.68

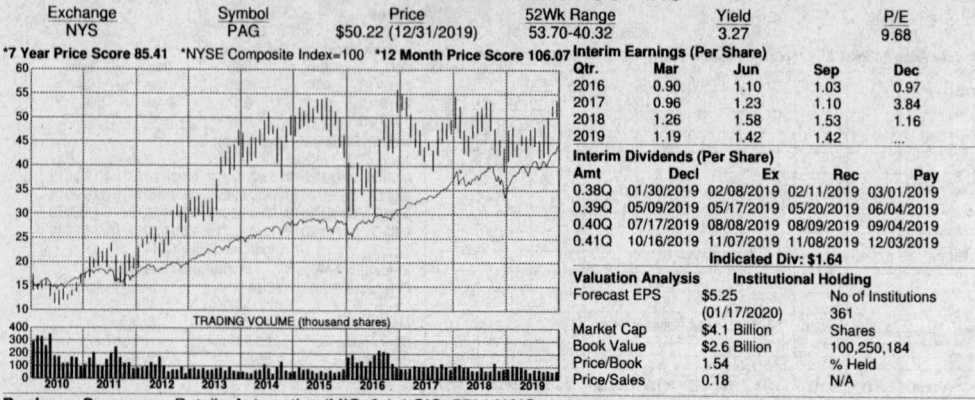

*7 Year Price Score 85.41   *NYSE Composite Index=100   *12 Month Price Score 106.07

Interim Earnings (Per Share)

Qtr.	Mar	Jun	Sep	Dec
2016	0.90	1.10	1.03	0.97
2017	0.96	1.23	1.10	3.84
2018	1.26	1.58	1.53	1.16
2019	1.19	1.42	1.42	...

Interim Dividends (Per Share)

Amt	Decl	Ex	Rec	Pay
0.38Q	01/30/2019	02/08/2019	02/11/2019	03/01/2019
0.39Q	05/09/2019	05/17/2019	05/20/2019	06/04/2019
0.40Q	07/17/2019	08/08/2019	08/09/2019	09/04/2019
0.41Q	10/16/2019	11/07/2019	11/08/2019	12/03/2019

Indicated Div: $1.64

Valuation Analysis

		Institutional Holding	
Forecast EPS	$5.25	No of Institutions	
	(01/17/2020)	361	
Market Cap	$4.1 Billion	Shares	
Book Value	$2.6 Billion	100,250,184	
Price/Book	1.54	% Held	
Price/Sales	0.18	N/A	

Business Summary: Retail - Automotive (MIC: 2.1.4 SIC: 5511 NAIC: 441110)

Penske Automotive Group is a transportation services company. Co. has four segments: Retail Automotive, consisting of its retail automotive dealership operations; Retail Commercial Truck, consisting of its retail commercial truck dealership operations in U.S. and Canada; Other, consisting of its commercial vehicle and power systems distribution operations and other non-automotive consolidated operations; and Non-Automotive Investments, consisting of its equity method investments in non-automotive operations. The Retail Automotive segment includes all automotive dealerships and all departments relevant to the operation of the dealerships and its retail automotive joint ventures.

Recent Developments: For the quarter ended Sep 30 2019, income from continuing operations decreased 10.8% to US$116.0 million from US$130.0 million in the year-earlier quarter. Net income decreased 10.8% to US$116.1 million from US$130.1 million in the year-earlier quarter. Revenues were US$5.97 billion, up 5.5% from US$5.66 billion the year before. Operating income was US$169.4 million versus US$163.9 million in the prior-year quarter, an increase of 3.4%. Direct operating expenses rose 6.1% to US$5.10 billion from US$4.81 billion in the comparable period the year before. Indirect operating expenses increased 1.7% to US$700.3 million from US$688.7 million in the equivalent prior-year period.

Prospects: Our evaluation of Penske Automotive Group Inc. as of October 4th, 2019 is the result of our systematic analysis on three basic characteristics: earnings strength, relative valuation, and recent stock price movement. The company has managed to produce a neutral trend in earnings per share over the past 5 quarters. In addition, recent analyst estimates for the company have been mixed and PAG has posted results that fell short of analysts' expectations. Based on operating earnings yield, the company is undervalued when compared to all of the companies we cover. Share price changes over the past year indicates that PAG will perform in line with the market over the near term.

Financial Data

(US$ in Thousands)	9 Mos	6 Mos	3 Mos	12/31/2018	12/31/2017	12/31/2016	12/31/2015	12/31/2014
Earnings Per Share	5.19	5.30	5.46	5.53	7.14	3.99	3.63	3.17
Cash Flow Per Share	9.05	6.06	6.29	7.21	7.25	4.24	4.36	4.06
Tang Book Value Per Share	2.65	4.95	4.70	4.39	3.04	0.46	0.66	0.00
Dividends Per Share	1.540	1.500	1.460	1.420	1.260	1.100	0.940	0.780
Dividend Payout %	29.67	28.30	26.74	25.68	17.65	27.57	25.90	24.61
Income Statement								
Total Revenue	17,287,800	11,320,200	5,564,400	22,785,100	21,386,900	20,118,500	19,284,900	17,177,200
EBITDA	580,900	384,000	185,100	768,600	706,500	664,600	644,500	590,100
Depn & Amortn	81,000	53,500	26,400	103,700	95,100	89,700	78,000	70,000
Income Before Taxes	342,500	227,400	107,000	469,300	440,600	438,600	452,600	421,200
Income Taxes	118,600	76,200	34,700	134,300	(64,800)	160,700	158,000	153,200
Net Income	334,200	218,000	100,200	471,000	613,300	342,900	326,100	286,700
Average Shares	81,683	82,912	84,418	85,165	85,877	86,000	89,759	90,354
Balance Sheet								
Current Assets	5,187,500	5,075,300	5,283,200	5,095,200	5,026,500	4,421,500	4,408,100	3,867,700
Total Assets	13,689,500	13,361,100	13,574,900	10,904,500	10,540,600	8,861,100	8,022,700	7,228,200
Current Liabilities	5,346,500	5,169,900	5,376,100	5,048,300	5,000,400	4,229,600	4,286,900	3,630,300
Long-Term Obligations	2,282,500	2,134,200	2,118,300	2,124,700	2,090,400	1,828,800	1,255,100	1,316,000
Total Liabilities	11,050,600	10,720,600	10,933,700	8,295,400	8,145,400	7,110,200	6,232,500	5,575,400
Stockholders' Equity	2,638,900	2,640,500	2,641,200	2,609,100	2,395,200	1,750,900	1,790,200	1,652,800
Shares Outstanding	81,066	81,956	83,651	84,546	85,787	85,214	89,524	90,244
Statistical Record								
Return on Assets %	3.57	3.73	3.79	4.39	6.32	4.05	4.28	4.20
Return on Equity %	16.56	17.37	18.14	18.82	29.58	19.31	18.94	18.16
EBITDA Margin %	3.36	3.39	3.33	3.37	3.30	3.30	3.34	3.44
Net Margin %	1.93	1.93	1.80	2.07	2.87	1.70	1.69	1.67
Asset Turnover	1.88	1.87	1.85	2.12	2.20	2.38	2.53	2.52
Current Ratio	0.97	0.98	0.98	1.01	1.01	1.05	1.03	1.07
Debt to Equity	0.86	0.81	0.80	0.81	0.87	1.04	0.70	0.80
Price Range	48.73-38.77	53.61-38.77	53.61-38.77	54.55-38.77	54.92-39.04	55.98-29.96	54.21-41.79	51.16-37.51
P/E Ratio	9.39-7.47	10.12-7.32	9.82-7.10	9.86-7.01	7.69-5.47	14.03-7.51	14.93-11.51	16.14-11.83
Average Yield %	3.46	3.26	3.15	2.99	2.72	2.71	1.89	1.72

Address: 2555 Telegraph Road, Bloomfield Hills, MI 48302-0954 **Telephone:** 248-648-2500 **Fax:** 248-648-2525	**Web Site:** www.penskeautomotive.com **Officers:** Roger S. Penske - Chairman, Chief Executive Officer Robert H. Kurnick - President	**Auditors:** DELOITTE & TOUCHE LLP **Investor Contact:** 866-715-5289 **Transfer Agents:** ComputerShare Investor Services, Providence, RI

PFIZER INC

Exchange	Symbol	Price	52Wk Range	Yield	P/E
NYS	PFE	$39.18 (12/31/2019)	44.40-34.24	3.88	13.60

*7 Year Price Score 96.49 *NYSE Composite Index=100 *12 Month Price Score 90.50

Interim Earnings (Per Share)

Qtr.	Mar	Jun	Sep	Dec
2016	0.49	0.33	0.21	0.14
2017	0.51	0.51	0.47	2.03
2018	0.59	0.65	0.69	(0.05)
2019	0.68	0.89	1.36	...

Interim Dividends (Per Share)

Amt	Decl	Ex	Rec	Pay
0.36Q	04/25/2019	05/09/2019	05/10/2019	06/07/2019
0.36Q	06/27/2019	08/01/2019	08/02/2019	09/03/2019
0.36Q	09/24/2019	11/07/2019	11/08/2019	12/02/2019
0.38Q	12/16/2019	01/30/2020	01/31/2020	03/06/2020

Indicated Div: $1.52

Valuation Analysis / **Institutional Holding**

Forecast EPS	$2.96	No of Institutions
	(01/16/2020)	3349
Market Cap	$216.7 Billion	Shares
Book Value	$65.1 Billion	5,230,056,448
Price/Book	3.33	% Held
Price/Sales	4.09	65.28

TRADING VOLUME (thousand shares)

Business Summary: Pharmaceuticals (MIC: 4.1.1 SIC: 2834 NAIC: 325412)

Pfizer is a research-based biopharmaceutical company. Co.'s portfolio includes medicines and vaccines, as well as consumer healthcare products. Co. manages its commercial operations through three businesses: Pfizer Biopharmaceuticals Group, which includes Co.'s health business units (except Consumer Healthcare) as well as a hospital business unit that commercializes its portfolio of sterile injectable and anti-infective medicines; Upjohn, which includes Co.'s solid oral dose brands such as Lyrica, Lipitor, Norvasc, Viagra and Celebrex, as well as certain generic medicines; and Consumer Healthcare, which is an over-the-counter medicines business.

Recent Developments: For the quarter ended Sep 29 2019, income from continuing operations increased 86.8% to US$7.68 billion from US$4.11 billion in the year-earlier quarter. Net income increased 86.4% to US$7.68 billion from US$4.12 billion in the year-earlier quarter. Revenues were US$12.68 billion, down 4.6% from US$13.30 billion the year before. Direct operating expenses declined 3.4% to US$2.60 billion from US$2.69 billion in the comparable period the year before. Indirect operating income amounted to US$641.0 million compared with an expense of US$6.50 billion in the equivalent prior-year period.

Prospects: Our evaluation of Pfizer Inc. as of October 4th, 2019 is the result of our systematic analysis on three basic characteristics: earnings strength, relative valuation, and recent stock price movement. The company has generated a negative trend in earnings per share over the past 5 quarters. However, recent analyst estimates for the company have been unchanged while PFE has posted results that exceeded analysts' expectations. Based on operating earnings yield, the company is undervalued when compared to all of the companies we cover. Share price changes over the past year indicates that PFE will perform in line with the market over the near term.

Financial Data

(US$ in Thousands)	9 Mos	6 Mos	3 Mos	12/31/2018	12/31/2017	12/31/2016	12/31/2015	12/31/2014
Earnings Per Share	2.88	2.21	1.97	1.87	3.52	1.17	1.11	1.42
Cash Flow Per Share	2.44	2.57	2.76	2.70	2.76	2.60	2.35	2.66
Dividends Per Share	1.420	1.400	1.380	1.360	1.280	1.200	1.120	1.040
Dividend Payout %	49.31	63.35	70.05	72.73	36.36	102.56	100.90	73.24
Income Statement								
Total Revenue	39,062,000	26,382,000	13,118,000	53,647,000	52,546,000	52,824,000	48,851,000	49,605,000
EBITDA	23,741,000	11,455,000	5,801,000	17,761,000	17,942,000	13,123,000	13,421,000	17,214,000
Depn & Amortn	3,578,000	2,367,000	1,183,000	4,893,000	4,758,000	4,056,000	3,728,000	4,039,000
Income Before Taxes	19,190,000	8,463,000	4,323,000	11,885,000	12,305,000	8,351,000	8,965,000	12,240,000
Income Taxes	2,566,000	(481,000)	433,000	706,000	(9,049,000)	1,123,000	1,990,000	3,120,000
Net Income	16,609,000	8,929,000	3,884,000	11,153,000	21,308,000	7,215,000	6,960,000	9,135,000
Average Shares	5,648,999	5,671,999	5,749,999	5,976,999	6,057,999	6,158,999	6,256,999	6,423,999
Balance Sheet								
Current Assets	33,459,000	47,073,000	45,290,000	49,926,000	41,141,000	38,949,000	43,804,000	57,702,000
Total Assets	170,446,000	156,199,000	155,421,000	159,422,000	171,797,000	171,615,000	167,460,000	169,274,000
Current Liabilities	36,974,000	32,030,000	29,423,000	31,858,000	30,427,000	31,115,000	29,399,000	21,631,000
Long-Term Obligations	36,044,000	36,168,000	35,733,000	32,909,000	33,538,000	31,398,000	28,818,000	31,541,000
Total Liabilities	105,344,000	96,631,000	96,615,000	96,015,000	100,489,000	112,072,000	102,741,000	97,973,000
Stockholders' Equity	65,103,000	59,568,000	58,806,000	63,407,000	71,308,000	59,544,000	64,720,000	71,301,000
Shares Outstanding	5,530,999	5,561,999	5,556,999	5,716,999	5,978,999	6,069,999	6,174,999	6,290,999
Statistical Record								
Return on Assets %	9.59	7.88	7.17	6.73	12.41	4.24	4.13	5.35
Return on Equity %	23.77	19.56	17.80	16.56	32.57	11.58	10.23	12.38
EBITDA Margin %	60.78	43.42	44.22	33.11	34.15	24.84	27.47	34.70
Net Margin %	42.52	33.85	29.61	20.79	40.55	13.66	14.25	18.42
Asset Turnover	0.31	0.33	0.34	0.32	0.31	0.31	0.29	0.29
Current Ratio	0.90	1.47	1.54	1.57	1.35	1.25	1.49	2.67
Debt to Equity	0.55	0.61	0.61	0.52	0.47	0.53	0.45	0.44
Price Range	46.23-34.24	46.23-36.33	46.23-34.76	46.23-33.63	37.20-31.15	37.31-28.56	36.15-30.82	32.75-27.70
P/E Ratio	16.05-11.89	20.92-16.44	23.47-17.64	24.72-17.98	10.57-8.85	31.89-24.41	32.57-27.77	23.06-19.51
Average Yield %	3.42	3.33	3.40	3.47	3.76	3.66	3.32	3.43

Address: 235 East 42nd Street, New York, NY 10017 **Telephone:** 212-733-2323	**Web Site:** www.pfizer.com **Officers:** Albert Bourla - Chairman, Chief Executive Officer, Chief Operating Officer, Division Officer John D. Young - Group President, Chief Business Officer, Division Officer	**Auditors:** KPMG LLP **Investor Contact:** 212-733-2323 **Transfer Agents:** Computershare Trust Company, N.A., Canton, MA

PG&E CORP (HOLDING CO)

Exchange	Symbol	Price	52Wk Range	Yield	P/E
NYS	PCG	$10.87 (12/31/2019)	24.40-3.80	N/A	N/A

*7 Year Price Score 27.19   *NYSE Composite Index=100   *12 Month Price Score 53.35

Interim Earnings (Per Share)

Qtr.	Mar	Jun	Sep	Dec
2016	0.22	0.41	0.77	1.38
2017	1.13	0.79	1.07	0.23
2018	0.86	(1.91)	1.09	(13.29)
2019	0.25	(4.83)	(3.06)	...

Interim Dividends (Per Share)

Dividend Payment Suspended

Valuation Analysis

		Institutional Holding	
Forecast EPS	$3.86	No of Institutions	
	(01/17/2020)	655	
Market Cap	$5.8 Billion	Shares	
Book Value	$8.7 Billion		549,986,176
Price/Book	0.66	% Held	
Price/Sales	0.35		92.47

Business Summary: Electric Utilities (MIC: 3.1.1 SIC: 4931 NAIC: 221122)

PG&E is a holding company that conducts its business through Pacific Gas and Electric Company (Utility), a public utility engaged in the sale and delivery of electricity and natural gas to customers. The Utility generates electricity and provides electric transmission and distribution services throughout its service territory in northern and central California to residential, commercial, industrial, and agricultural customers. The Utility provides natural gas transportation services to small commercial and residential customers and to industrial, commercial, and natural gas-fired electric generation facilities that are connected to the Utility's gas system in its service territory.

Recent Developments: For the quarter ended Sep 30 2019, net loss amounted to US$1.62 billion versus net income of US$567.0 million in the year-earlier quarter. Revenues were US$4.43 billion, up 1.2% from US$4.38 billion the year before. Operating loss was US$2.30 billion versus an income of US$696.0 million in the prior-year quarter. Direct operating expenses rose 13.9% to US$3.34 billion from US$2.94 billion in the comparable period the year before. Indirect operating expenses increased 352.3% to US$3.39 billion from US$749.0 million in the equivalent prior-year period.

Prospects: Our evaluation of PG&E Corp. as of October 4th, 2019 is the result of our systematic analysis on three basic characteristics: earnings strength, relative valuation, and recent stock price movement. The company has managed to produce a neutral trend in earnings per share over the past 5 quarters. In addition, recent analyst estimates for the company have been mixed and PCG has posted results that exceeded analysts' expectations. Based on operating earnings yield, the company is undervalued when compared to all of the companies we cover. Share price changes over the past year indicates that PCG will perform poorly over the near term.

Financial Data

(US$ in Thousands)	9 Mos	6 Mos	3 Mos	12/31/2018	12/31/2017	12/31/2016	12/31/2015	12/31/2014
Earnings Per Share	(20.93)	(16.78)	(13.86)	(13.25)	3.21	2.78	1.79	3.06
Cash Flow Per Share	8.66	8.99	10.43	9.19	11.67	8.81	7.75	7.86
Tang Book Value Per Share	16.51	19.54	24.33	24.31	37.34	35.39	33.69	33.09
Dividends Per Share	...	...	...	...	1.550	1.925	1.820	1.820
Dividend Payout %	...	...	...	...	48.29	69.24	101.68	59.48
Income Statement								
Total Revenue	12,386,000	7,954,000	4,011,000	16,759,000	17,135,000	17,666,000	16,833,000	17,090,000
EBITDA	(3,375,000)	(1,904,000)	930,000	(6,240,000)	5,882,000	5,023,000	4,237,000	4,953,000
Depn & Amortn	2,433,000	1,593,000	797,000	3,036,000	2,854,000	2,755,000	2,612,000	2,433,000
Income Before Taxes	(5,961,000)	(3,616,000)	52,000	(10,129,000)	2,171,000	1,462,000	861,000	1,795,000
Income Taxes	(1,932,000)	(1,203,000)	(84,000)	(3,292,000)	511,000	55,000	(27,000)	345,000
Net Income	(4,029,000)	(2,413,000)	136,000	(6,837,000)	1,660,000	1,407,000	888,000	1,450,000
Average Shares	529,000	529,000	527,000	517,000	513,000	501,000	487,000	470,000
Balance Sheet								
Current Assets	11,577,000	11,577,000	10,693,000	9,195,000	6,281,000	6,164,000	5,822,000	6,389,000
Total Assets	85,713,000	84,387,000	82,287,000	76,995,000	68,012,000	68,598,000	63,339,000	60,127,000
Current Liabilities	6,472,000	5,711,000	4,808,000	41,695,000	7,129,000	7,564,000	6,363,000	5,920,000
Long-Term Obligations	...	...	...	...	17,753,000	16,220,000	16,030,000	15,050,000
Total Liabilities	76,974,000	74,045,000	69,410,000	64,344,000	48,792,000	50,658,000	46,763,000	44,379,000
Stockholders' Equity	8,739,000	10,342,000	12,877,000	12,651,000	19,220,000	17,940,000	16,576,000	15,748,000
Shares Outstanding	529,229	529,223	529,210	520,338	514,755	506,891	492,025	475,913
Statistical Record								
Return on Assets %	N.M.	N.M.	N.M.	N.M.	2.43	2.13	1.44	2.51
Return on Equity %	N.M.	N.M.	N.M.	N.M.	8.93	8.13	5.49	9.64
EBITDA Margin %	N.M.	N.M.	23.19	N.M.	34.33	28.43	25.17	28.98
Net Margin %	N.M.	N.M.	3.39	N.M.	9.69	7.96	5.28	8.48
Asset Turnover	0.21	0.21	0.22	0.23	0.25	0.27	0.27	0.30
Current Ratio	1.79	2.03	2.22	0.22	0.88	0.81	0.91	1.08
Debt to Equity	...	...	...	...	0.92	0.90	0.97	0.96
Price Range	48.96-6.36	48.96-6.36	48.96-6.36	48.96-17.74	48.96-17.17	71.56-44.45	65.39-51.29	60.15-47.60	54.98-39.60
P/E Ratio	...	...	...	...	22.29-13.85	23.52-18.45	33.60-26.59	17.97-12.94
Average Yield %	...	...	...	...	2.43	3.22	3.44	3.97

Address: 77 Beale Street, P.O. Box 770000, San Francisco, CA 94177 **Telephone:** 415-973-1000 **Fax:** 415-267-7265	**Web Site:** www.pgecorp.com **Officers:** William D. Johnson - President, Chief Executive Officer John R. Simon - Interim Chief Executive Officer, Executive Vice President, Senior Vice President, Executive Vice President, General Counsel	**Auditors:** DELOITTE & TOUCHE LLP **Investor Contact:** 415-972-7080 **Transfer Agents:** American Stock Transfer and Trust Company, LLC, Brooklyn, NY

PHILIP MORRIS INTERNATIONAL INC

Exchange	Symbol	Price	52Wk Range	Yield	P/E	Div Acheiver	
NYS	PM	$85.09 (12/31/2019)	91.91-66.44	5.50	17.69	10 Years	

*7 Year Price Score 73.91   *NYSE Composite Index=100   *12 Month Price Score 98.10

Interim Earnings (Per Share)

Qtr.	Mar	Jun	Sep	Dec
2016	0.98	1.15	1.25	1.10
2017	1.02	1.14	1.27	0.45
2018	1.00	1.41	1.44	1.23
2019	0.87	1.49	1.22	...

Interim Dividends (Per Share)

Amt	Decl	Ex	Rec	Pay
1.14Q	03/07/2019	03/25/2019	03/26/2019	04/11/2019
1.14Q	06/07/2019	06/20/2019	06/21/2019	07/10/2019
1.17Q	09/11/2019	09/24/2019	09/25/2019	10/11/2019
1.17Q	12/05/2019	12/18/2019	12/19/2019	01/10/2020

Indicated Div: $4.68

Valuation Analysis   **Institutional Holding**

Forecast EPS	$5.19	No of Institutions
	(01/17/2020)	2306
Market Cap	$132.4 Billion	Shares
Book Value	N/A	1,385,064,576
Price/Book	N/A	% Held
Price/Sales	4.47	73.19

Business Summary: Tobacco Products (MIC: 1.3.1 SIC: 2111 NAIC: 312221)

Philip Morris International, through its subsidiaries, is an international tobacco company engaged in the manufacture and sale of cigarettes, smoke-free products and associated electronic devices and accessories, and other nicotine-containing products in markets outside the U.S. Co.'s portfolio comprises both international and local brands including Marlboro. Co.'s other international cigarette brands include Bond Street, Chesterfield, L&M, Lark and Philip Morris. Co. also owns a number of local cigarette brands, such as Dji Sam Soe, Sampoerna A and Sampoerna U in Indonesia; Fortune and Jackpot in the Philippines; and Belmont and Canadian Classics in Canada.

Recent Developments: For the quarter ended Sep 30 2019, net income decreased 12.6% to US$2.05 billion from US$2.34 billion in the year-earlier quarter. Revenues were US$7.64 billion, up 1.8% from US$7.50 billion the year before. Operating income was US$2.79 billion versus US$3.16 billion in the prior-year quarter, a decrease of 11.7%. Direct operating expenses declined 0.5% to US$2.61 billion from US$2.62 billion in the comparable period the year before. Indirect operating expenses increased 30.0% to US$2.25 billion from US$1.73 billion in the equivalent prior-year period.

Prospects: Our evaluation of Philip Morris International Inc. as of October 4th, 2019 is the result of our systematic analysis on three basic characteristics: earnings strength, relative valuation, and recent stock price movement. The company has managed to produce a neutral trend in earnings per share over the past 5 quarters. However, recent analyst estimates for the company have been reduced while PM has posted results that exceeded analysts' expectations. Based on operating earnings yield, the company is undervalued when compared to all of the companies we cover. Share price changes over the past year indicates that PM will perform poorly over the near term.

Financial Data

(US$ in Thousands)	9 Mos	6 Mos	3 Mos	12/31/2018	12/31/2017	12/31/2016	12/31/2015	12/31/2014
Earnings Per Share	4.81	5.03	4.95	5.08	3.88	4.48	4.42	4.76
Cash Flow Per Share	5.90	5.65	6.01	6.10	5.74	5.19	5.08	4.94
Dividends Per Share	4.590	4.560	4.560	4.490	4.220	4.120	4.040	3.880
Dividend Payout %	95.43	90.66	92.12	88.39	108.76	91.96	91.40	81.51
Income Statement								
Total Revenue	22,092,000	14,450,000	6,751,000	29,625,000	28,748,000	26,685,000	26,794,000	29,767,000
EBITDA	8,014,000	5,231,000	2,048,000	12,325,000	12,378,000	11,558,000	11,377,000	12,591,000
Depn & Amortn	50,000	35,000	19,000	989,000	875,000	743,000	754,000	889,000
Income Before Taxes	7,530,000	4,894,000	1,877,000	10,671,000	10,589,000	9,924,000	9,615,000	10,650,000
Income Taxes	1,670,000	1,035,000	424,000	2,445,000	4,307,000	2,768,000	2,688,000	3,097,000
Net Income	5,569,000	3,673,000	1,354,000	7,911,000	6,035,000	6,967,000	6,873,000	7,493,000
Average Shares	1,556,000	1,556,000	1,556,000	1,555,000	1,553,000	1,551,000	1,549,000	1,566,000
Balance Sheet								
Current Assets	19,575,000	17,163,000	15,741,000	19,442,000	21,594,000	17,608,000	15,804,000	15,484,000
Total Assets	41,420,000	39,923,000	38,042,000	39,801,000	42,968,000	36,851,000	33,956,000	35,187,000
Current Liabilities	18,045,000	18,046,000	18,486,000	17,191,000	15,962,000	16,467,000	15,386,000	15,112,000
Long-Term Obligations	26,426,000	24,858,000	23,131,000	26,975,000	31,334,000	25,851,000	25,250,000	26,929,000
Total Liabilities	52,430,000	51,122,000	50,010,000	52,260,000	55,054,000	49,539,000	47,200,000	47,816,000
Stockholders' Equity	(11,010,000)	(11,199,000)	(11,968,000)	(12,459,000)	(12,086,000)	(12,688,000)	(13,244,000)	(12,629,000)
Shares Outstanding	1,555,860	1,555,827	1,556,796	1,554,579	1,553,217	1,551,385	1,549,344	1,546,899
Statistical Record								
Return on Assets %	18.51	19.42	19.01	19.12	15.12	19.63	19.88	20.43
EBITDA Margin %	36.28	36.20	30.34	41.60	43.06	43.31	42.46	42.30
Net Margin %	25.21	25.42	20.06	26.70	20.99	26.11	25.65	25.17
Asset Turnover	0.73	0.73	0.73	0.72	0.72	0.75	0.78	0.81
Current Ratio	1.08	0.95	0.85	1.13	1.35	1.07	1.03	1.02
Price Range	91.91-65.97	91.91-65.97	103.30-65.97	110.60-65.97	122.90-90.40	103.63-85.80	90.15-75.33	91.34-75.39
P/E Ratio	19.11-13.72	18.27-13.12	20.87-13.33	21.77-12.99	31.68-23.30	23.13-19.15	20.40-17.04	19.19-15.84
Average Yield %	5.63	5.55	5.51	5.07	3.82	4.29	4.86	4.60

Address: 120 Park Avenue, New York, NY 10017	**Web Site:** www.pmi.com	**Auditors:** PricewaterhouseCoopers SA
Telephone: 917-663-2000	**Officers:** Marc S. Firestone - President, Senior Vice President, General Counsel Werner Barth - Senior Vice President, Senior Vice President (frmr)	**Investor Contact:** 191-766-32233
Fax: 917-663-5372		**Transfer Agents:** ComputerShare LLC, Providence, RI

545

PHILLIPS 66

Exchange	Symbol	Price	52Wk Range	Yield	P/E
NYS	PSX	$111.41 (12/31/2019)	119.70-80.80	3.23	11.24

*7 Year Price Score 96.97   *NYSE Composite Index=100   *12 Month Price Score 109.35

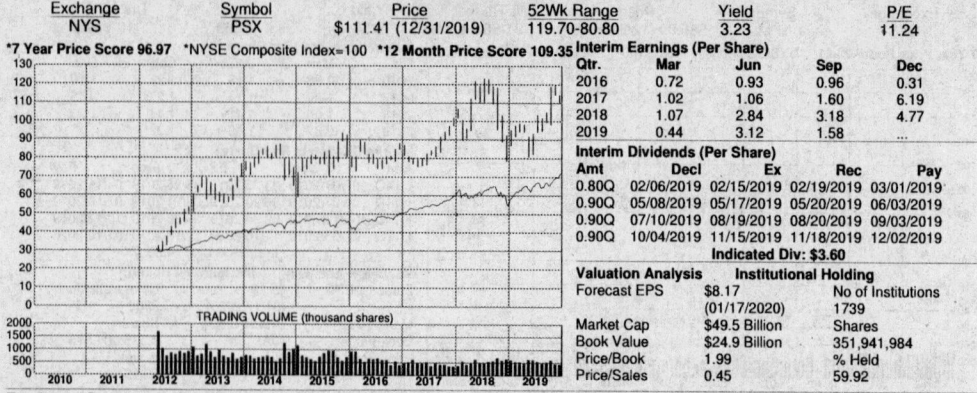

Interim Earnings (Per Share)

Qtr.	Mar	Jun	Sep	Dec
2016	0.72	0.93	0.96	0.31
2017	1.02	1.06	1.60	6.19
2018	1.07	2.84	3.18	4.77
2019	0.44	3.12	1.58	...

Interim Dividends (Per Share)

Amt	Decl	Ex	Rec	Pay
0.80Q	02/06/2019	02/15/2019	02/19/2019	03/01/2019
0.90Q	05/08/2019	05/17/2019	05/20/2019	06/03/2019
0.90Q	07/10/2019	08/19/2019	08/20/2019	09/03/2019
0.90Q	10/04/2019	11/15/2019	11/18/2019	12/02/2019

Indicated Div: $3.60

Valuation Analysis | **Institutional Holding**

Forecast EPS $8.17	No of Institutions
(01/17/2020)	1739
Market Cap $49.5 Billion	Shares
Book Value $24.9 Billion	351,941,984
Price/Book 1.99	% Held
Price/Sales 0.45	59.92

Business Summary: Refining & Marketing (MIC: 9.1.2 SIC: 2911 NAIC: 324110)

Phillips 66 is an energy manufacturing and logistics company with midstream, chemicals, refining, and marketing and specialties businesses. Co.'s segments include: Midstream, which provides crude oil and refined petroleum product transportation, terminaling and processing services, as well as natural gas and natural gas liquids transportation, storage, processing and marketing services; Chemicals, which manufactures and markets petrochemicals and plastics on a worldwide basis; Refining, which refines crude oil and other feedstocks into petroleum products; and Marketing and Specialties, which purchases for resale and markets refined petroleum products, mainly in the U.S. and Europe.

Recent Developments: For the quarter ended Sep 30 2019, net income decreased 49.4% to US$793.0 million from US$1.57 billion in the year-earlier quarter. Revenues were US$27.77 billion, down 9.2% from US$30.59 billion the year before. Direct operating expenses declined 9.3% to US$25.01 billion from US$27.59 billion in the comparable period the year before. Indirect operating expenses increased 77.0% to US$1.82 billion from US$1.03 billion in the equivalent prior-year period.

Prospects: Our evaluation of Phillips 66 Inc. as of October 4th, 2019 is the result of our systematic analysis on three basic characteristics: earnings strength, relative valuation, and recent stock price movement. The company has suffered a very negative trend in earnings per share over the past 5 quarters. However, recent analyst estimates for the company have been mixed and PSX has posted results that exceeded analysts' expectations. Based on operating earnings yield, the company is undervalued when compared to all of the companies we cover. Share price changes over the past year indicates that PSX will perform poorly over the near term.

Financial Data

(US$ in Thousands)	9 Mos	6 Mos	3 Mos	12/31/2018	12/31/2017	12/31/2016	12/31/2015	12/31/2014
Earnings Per Share	9.91	11.51	11.23	11.80	9.85	2.92	7.73	8.33
Cash Flow Per Share	16.15	13.61	14.44	16.09	7.08	5.60	10.53	6.24
Tang Book Value Per Share	46.62	45.95	44.28	44.97	41.69	35.14	35.74	31.88
Dividends Per Share	3.400	3.300	3.200	3.100	2.730	2.450	2.180	1.890
Dividend Payout %	34.31	28.67	28.50	26.27	27.72	83.90	28.20	22.69
Income Statement								
Total Revenue	79,947,000	52,176,000	23,658,000	114,217,000	104,622,000	85,777,000	100,949,000	164,093,000
EBITDA	4,456,000	3,068,000	790,000	9,305,000	5,311,000	3,697,000	7,432,000	7,007,000
Depn & Amortn	1,001,000	665,000	331,000	1,356,000	1,318,000	1,168,000	1,078,000	995,000
Income Before Taxes	3,112,000	2,169,000	340,000	7,445,000	3,555,000	2,191,000	6,044,000	5,745,000
Income Taxes	545,000	395,000	70,000	1,572,000	(1,693,000)	547,000	1,764,000	1,654,000
Net Income	2,340,000	1,628,000	204,000	5,595,000	5,106,000	1,555,000	4,227,000	4,762,000
Average Shares	451,001	455,585	459,289	474,047	518,508	530,066	546,977	571,504
Balance Sheet								
Current Assets	15,617,000	14,295,000	14,815,000	13,209,000	14,390,000	12,680,000	12,256,000	16,696,000
Total Assets	58,741,000	57,781,000	57,855,000	54,302,000	54,371,000	51,653,000	48,580,000	48,741,000
Current Liabilities	12,083,000	11,171,000	11,328,000	8,935,000	10,107,000	9,463,000	7,531,000	11,094,000
Long-Term Obligations	11,083,000	10,772,000	11,268,000	11,093,000	10,069,000	9,588,000	8,843,000	7,842,000
Total Liabilities	33,884,000	33,029,000	33,638,000	29,649,000	29,286,000	29,263,000	25,480,000	27,151,000
Stockholders' Equity	24,857,000	24,752,000	24,217,000	24,653,000	25,085,000	22,390,000	23,100,000	21,590,000
Shares Outstanding	444,357	448,541	453,551	456,165	502,270	518,766	529,410	546,381
Statistical Record								
Return on Assets %	7.99	9.52	9.59	10.30	9.63	3.09	8.69	9.67
Return on Equity %	19.01	22.67	22.87	22.50	21.51	6.82	18.92	21.87
EBITDA Margin %	5.57	5.88	3.34	8.15	5.08	4.31	7.36	4.27
Net Margin %	2.93	3.12	0.86	4.90	4.88	1.81	4.19	2.90
Asset Turnover	1.92	2.00	2.07	2.10	1.97	1.71	2.07	3.33
Current Ratio	1.29	1.28	1.31	1.48	1.42	1.34	1.63	1.50
Debt to Equity	0.45	0.44	0.47	0.45	0.40	0.43	0.38	0.36
Price Range	118.47-78.50	123.34-78.50	123.34-78.50	123.34-78.50	102.06-75.33	90.16-72.90	93.68-59.09	87.51-65.09
P/E Ratio	11.95-7.92	10.72-6.82	10.98-6.99	10.45-6.65	10.36-7.65	30.88-24.97	12.12-7.64	10.51-7.81
Average Yield %	3.55	3.31	3.04	2.93	3.22	3.03	2.74	2.40

Address: 2331 CityWest Blvd., Houston, TX 77042 **Telephone:** 281-293-6600	**Web Site:** www.Phillips66.com **Officers:** Greg C. Garland - Chairman, President, Chief Executive Officer Paula Ann Johnson - Executive Vice President, Executive Vice President (frmr), Senior Vice President, General Counsel, Corporate Secretary	**Auditors:** Ernst & Young LLP **Investor Contact:** 800-624-6440 **Transfer Agents:** Computershare, Canton, MA

PIEDMONT OFFICE REALTY TRUST INC

Exchange	Symbol	Price	52Wk Range	Yield	P/E
NYS	PDM	$22.24 (12/31/2019)	22.44-16.76	3.78	25.27

*7 Year Price Score 87.44 ***NYSE Composite Index=100** ***12 Month Price Score 100.99**

Interim Earnings (Per Share)
Qtr.	Mar	Jun	Sep	Dec
2016	0.07	0.55	(0.09)	0.21
2017	0.10	0.16	0.87	(0.21)
2018	0.42	0.09	0.13	0.35
2019	0.40	0.06	0.07	...

Interim Dividends (Per Share)
Amt	Decl	Ex	Rec	Pay
0.21Q	02/05/2019	02/27/2019	02/28/2019	03/15/2019
0.21Q	05/01/2019	05/30/2019	05/31/2019	06/21/2019
0.21Q	07/31/2019	08/29/2019	08/30/2019	09/20/2019
0.21Q	10/30/2019	11/27/2019	11/29/2019	01/03/2020

Indicated Div: $0.84

Valuation Analysis / Institutional Holding
Forecast EPS	$0.64	No of Institutions
(01/16/2020)		317
Market Cap	$2.8 Billion	Shares
Book Value	$1.7 Billion	128,150,752
Price/Book	1.67	% Held
Price/Sales	5.22	72.90

Business Summary: REITs (MIC: 5.3.1 SIC: 6798 NAIC: 525930)

Piedmont Office Realty Trust is a real estate investment trust. Co. is engaged in the acquisition, development, management, and ownership of commercial real estate properties. Co. conducts business primarily through Piedmont Operating Partnership, L.P. (Piedmont OP), as well as performing the management of its buildings through two wholly-owned subsidiaries, Piedmont Government Services, LLC and Piedmont Office Management, LLC. Co. is the sole general partner of, Piedmont OP. Co.'s portfolio of properties is primarily located in the Eastern-half of the U.S.: Atlanta, Boston, Chicago, Dallas, Minneapolis, New York, Orlando, and Washington, D.C.

Recent Developments: For the quarter ended Sep 30 2019, net income decreased 47.8% to US$8.4 million from US$16.1 million in the year-earlier quarter. Revenues were US$135.4 million, up 4.4% from US$129.7 million the year before.

Prospects: Our evaluation of Piedmont Office Realty Trust Inc. as of Jan. 21, 2018 is the result of our systematic analysis on three basic characteristics: earnings strength, relative valuation, and recent stock price movement. The company has managed to produce a neutral trend in earnings per share over the past 5 quarters. Because the company lacks sufficient analyst estimate data, we place greater weight on the historical EPS trend as the measure of earnings strength. Based on operating earnings yield, the company is overvalued when compared to all of the companies in our coverage universe. Share price changes over the past year indicates that PDM will perform in line with the market over the near

Financial Data
(US$ in Thousands)	9 Mos	6 Mos	3 Mos	12/31/2018	12/31/2017	12/31/2016	12/31/2015	12/31/2014
Earnings Per Share	0.88	0.94	0.97	1.00	0.92	0.74	1.15	0.28
Cash Flow Per Share	1.79	1.68	1.67	1.56	1.67	1.62	1.44	1.40
Tang Book Value Per Share	12.56	12.74	12.92	12.15	12.70	13.06	13.27	13.35
Dividends Per Share	0.840	0.840	0.840	0.840	1.340	0.840	0.840	0.810
Dividend Payout %	95.45	89.36	86.60	84.00	145.65	113.51	73.04	289.29
Income Statement								
Total Revenue	399,025	263,604	132,936	525,967	574,173	555,715	584,769	566,252
EBITDA	246,010	136,412	70,867	299,270	201,242	201,541	212,633	253,554
Depn & Amortn	132,480	86,784	43,052	107,956	119,288	127,733	134,503	138,679
Income Before Taxes	66,780	19,023	12,322	130,291	13,830	8,948	4,132	40,429
Net Income	66,783	58,361	50,208	130,296	133,564	107,887	172,990	43,348
Average Shares	126,239	126,490	126,180	130,635	145,379	145,634	150,880	154,585
Balance Sheet								
Current Assets	20,375	18,242	16,318	15,371	19,521	33,486	31,780	40,017
Total Assets	3,751,931	3,525,367	3,433,442	3,592,429	3,999,967	4,449,347	4,434,535	4,795,501
Current Liabilities	114,812	97,502	81,309	129,491	216,653	165,410	128,465	133,988
Long-Term Obligations	1,879,244	1,661,976	1,565,755	1,685,472	1,726,927	2,020,475	2,029,510	2,277,589
Total Liabilities	2,072,890	1,824,144	1,711,686	1,882,061	2,015,300	2,272,347	2,239,116	2,485,095
Stockholders' Equity	1,679,041	1,701,223	1,721,756	1,710,368	1,984,667	2,177,000	2,195,419	2,310,406
Shares Outstanding	125,783	125,783	125,597	126,218	142,358	145,235	145,511	154,324
Statistical Record								
Return on Assets %	3.04	3.35	3.47	3.43	3.16	2.42	3.75	0.92
Return on Equity %	6.58	6.97	6.99	7.05	6.42	4.92	7.68	1.82
EBITDA Margin %	61.65	51.75	53.31	56.90	35.05	36.27	36.36	44.78
Net Margin %	16.74	22.14	37.77	24.77	23.26	19.41	29.58	7.66
Asset Turnover	0.15	0.15	0.15	0.14	0.14	0.12	0.13	0.12
Current Ratio	0.18	0.19	0.20	0.12	0.09	0.20	0.25	0.30
Debt to Equity	1.12	0.98	0.91	0.99	0.87	0.93	0.92	0.99
Price Range	21.26-16.49	21.26-16.49	20.90-16.49	20.40-16.49	23.05-19.21	22.22-17.10	20.01-16.74	20.00-16.09
P/E Ratio	24.16-18.74	22.62-17.54	21.55-17.00	20.40-16.49	25.05-20.88	30.03-23.11	17.40-14.56	71.43-57.46
Average Yield %	4.27	4.30	4.42	4.49	6.41	4.17	4.56	4.43

Address: 5565 Glenridge Connector, Ste. 450, Atlanta, GA 30342 **Telephone:** 770-418-8800	**Web Site:** www.piedmontreit.com **Officers:** Frank C. McDowell - Chairman Dale H. Taysom - Vice-Chairman	**Auditors:** DELOITTE & TOUCHE LLP **Transfer Agents:** Computershare Inc.

PINNACLE WEST CAPITAL CORP

Exchange	Symbol	Price	52Wk Range	Yield	P/E
NYS	PNW	$89.93 (12/31/2019)	98.76-82.47	3.48	20.25

*7 Year Price Score 105.13 *NYSE Composite Index=100 *12 Month Price Score 90.52

Interim Earnings (Per Share)

Qtr.	Mar	Jun	Sep	Dec
2016	0.04	1.08	2.35	0.48
2017	0.21	1.49	2.46	0.19
2018	0.03	1.48	2.80	0.23
2019	0.16	1.28	2.77	...

Interim Dividends (Per Share)

Amt	Decl	Ex	Rec	Pay
0.738Q	04/17/2019	04/30/2019	05/01/2019	06/03/2019
0.738Q	06/19/2019	07/31/2019	08/01/2019	09/03/2019
0.782Q	10/23/2019	11/01/2019	11/04/2019	12/02/2019
0.782Q	12/19/2019	01/31/2020	02/03/2020	03/02/2020

Indicated Div: $3.13 (Div. Reinv. Plan)

Valuation Analysis   Institutional Holding

Forecast EPS	$4.68	No of Institutions
	(01/17/2020)	785
Market Cap	$10.1 Billion	Shares
Book Value	$5.6 Billion	118,480,920
Price/Book	1.82	% Held
Price/Sales	2.84	86.12

Business Summary: Electric Utilities (MIC: 3.1.1 SIC: 4911 NAIC: 221122)

Pinnacle West Capital is a holding company. Through its subsidiary, Arizona Public Service Company, Co. provides either retail or wholesale electric service to most of the State of Arizona, with the exceptions of about one-half of the Phoenix metropolitan area, the Tucson metropolitan area and Mohave County in northwestern Arizona. Co.'s business segment is its regulated electricity segment, which consists of regulated retail and wholesale electricity businesses (primarily electric service to Native Load customers) and related activities, and includes electricity generation, transmission and distribution.

Recent Developments: For the quarter ended Sep 30 2019, net income decreased 0.9% to US$317.1 million from US$319.9 million in the year-earlier quarter. Revenues were US$1.19 billion, down 6.1% from US$1.27 billion the year before. Operating income was US$403.3 million versus US$433.3 million in the prior-year quarter, a decrease of 6.9%. Direct operating expenses declined 8.3% to US$583.4 million from US$636.5 million in the comparable period the year before. Indirect operating expenses increased 2.9% to US$204.1 million from US$198.2 million in the equivalent prior-year period.

Prospects: Our evaluation of Pinnacle West Capital Corp. as of October 4th, 2019 is the result of our systematic analysis on three basic characteristics: earnings strength, relative valuation, and recent stock price movement. The company has managed to produce a neutral trend in earnings per share over the past 5 quarters. However, recent analyst estimates for the company have been reduced and PNW has posted results that fell short of analysts' expectations. Based on operating earnings yield, the company is fairly valued when compared to all of the companies we cover. Share price changes over the past year indicates that PNW will perform well over the near term.

Financial Data

(US$ in Thousands)	9 Mos	6 Mos	3 Mos	12/31/2018	12/31/2017	12/31/2016	12/31/2015	12/31/2014
Earnings Per Share	4.44	4.47	4.67	4.54	4.35	3.95	3.92	3.58
Cash Flow Per Share	10.24	10.92	11.43	11.39	10.00	9.16	9.86	9.94
Tang Book Value Per Share	49.42	46.60	46.77	46.59	44.80	43.14	41.30	39.50
Dividends Per Share	2.950	2.908	2.865	2.822	2.660	2.530	2.410	2.297
Dividend Payout %	66.44	65.04	61.35	62.17	61.15	64.05	61.48	64.18
Income Statement								
Total Revenue	2,800,818	1,610,031	740,530	3,691,247	3,565,296	3,498,682	3,495,443	3,491,632
EBITDA	753,583	316,573	89,767	1,641,785	1,556,270	1,372,772	1,344,624	1,366,128
Depn & Amortn	38,601	23,307	12,872	767,705	595,862	603,163	573,281	537,244
Income Before Taxes	561,723	191,308	25,209	664,442	766,221	584,743	593,131	644,401
Income Taxes	72,764	19,498	2,418	133,902	258,272	123,216	136,941	220,705
Net Income	474,339	162,063	17,918	511,047	488,456	442,034	437,257	397,595
Average Shares	112,746	112,651	112,735	112,550	112,367	112,046	111,552	111,178
Balance Sheet								
Current Assets	1,133,155	1,028,567	876,389	924,991	1,016,288	822,219	890,516	973,435
Total Assets	18,377,566	18,165,666	17,854,107	17,664,202	17,019,082	16,004,253	15,028,258	14,313,532
Current Liabilities	1,586,746	1,900,961	1,591,304	1,648,964	1,197,852	1,292,946	1,442,317	1,559,143
Long-Term Obligations	5,037,468	4,939,884	4,939,812	4,638,232	4,789,713	4,021,785	3,462,391	3,031,215
Total Liabilities	12,824,900	12,932,588	12,603,045	12,441,287	12,012,392	11,200,631	10,444,341	9,946,039
Stockholders' Equity	5,552,666	5,233,078	5,251,062	5,222,915	5,006,690	4,803,622	4,583,917	4,367,493
Shares Outstanding	112,345	112,303	112,277	112,101	111,751	111,336	110,980	110,571
Statistical Record								
Return on Assets %	2.78	2.82	3.00	2.95	2.96	2.84	2.98	2.86
Return on Equity %	9.18	9.80	10.24	9.99	9.96	9.39	9.77	9.29
EBITDA Margin %	26.91	19.66	12.12	44.48	43.65	39.24	38.47	39.13
Net Margin %	16.94	10.07	2.42	13.84	13.70	12.63	12.51	11.39
Asset Turnover	0.20	0.20	0.21	0.21	0.22	0.22	0.24	0.25
Current Ratio	0.71	0.54	0.55	0.56	0.85	0.64	0.62	0.62
Debt to Equity	0.91	0.94	0.94	0.89	0.96	0.84	0.76	0.69
Price Range	98.76-78.77	98.76-77.41	96.84-73.56	92.33-73.56	91.81-76.44	82.56-63.26	72.47-56.31	70.63-51.28
P/E Ratio	22.24-17.74	22.09-17.32	20.74-15.75	20.34-16.20	21.11-17.57	20.90-16.02	18.49-14.36	19.73-14.32
Average Yield %	3.22	3.30	3.42	3.49	3.11	3.42	3.83	4.05

Address: 400 North Fifth Street, P.O. Box 53999, Phoenix, AZ 85072-3999	Web Site: www.pinnaclewest.com	Auditors: Deloitte & Touche LLP
Telephone: 602-250-1000	Officers: Jeffrey B. Guldner - Chairman, President, Executive Vice President, Chief Executive Officer, General Counsel James R. Hatfield - Executive Vice President, Senior Vice President, Chief Financial Officer, Treasurer	Investor Contact: 602-250-5668
Fax: 602-379-2625		Transfer Agents: Computershare, Providence, RI

548

PIONEER NATURAL RESOURCES CO

Exchange	Symbol	Price	52Wk Range	Yield	P/E
NYS	PXD	$151.37 (12/31/2019)	175.89-118.02	1.16	35.12

*7 Year Price Score 71.70 *NYSE Composite Index=100 *12 Month Price Score 91.31

Interim Earnings (Per Share)

Qtr.	Mar	Jun	Sep	Dec
2016	(1.65)	(1.63)	0.13	(0.24)
2017	(0.25)	1.36	(0.13)	3.87
2018	1.04	0.38	2.39	1.88
2019	2.06	(1.01)	1.38	...

Interim Dividends (Per Share)

Amt	Decl	Ex	Rec	Pay
0.16Q	08/30/2018	09/27/2018	09/28/2018	10/12/2018
0.32Q	02/13/2019	03/28/2019	03/29/2019	04/12/2019
0.44Q	08/06/2019	09/26/2019	09/27/2019	10/10/2019
0.44Q	11/04/2019	12/30/2019	12/31/2019	01/14/2020

Indicated Div: $1.76

Valuation Analysis | Institutional Holding

Forecast EPS	$7.90	No of Institutions
(01/17/2020)		1066
Market Cap	$25.1 Billion	Shares
Book Value	$11.9 Billion	170,668,000
Price/Book	2.11	% Held
Price/Sales	2.69	84.80

Business Summary: Production & Extraction (MIC: 9.1.1 SIC: 1311 NAIC: 211111)

Pioneer Natural Resources is a holding company. Through its subsidiaries, Co. is engaged as an oil and gas exploration and production company that explores for, develops and produces oil, natural gas liquids and gas within the U.S., with operations primarily in the Permian Basin in West Texas.

Recent Developments: For the quarter ended Sep 30 2019, net income decreased 43.8% to US$231.0 million from US$411.0 million in the year-earlier quarter. Revenues were US$2.33 billion, down 6.1% from US$2.48 billion the year before. Direct operating expenses rose 16.1% to US$1.88 billion from US$1.62 billion in the comparable period the year before. Indirect operating expenses decreased 55.9% to US$146.0 million from US$331.0 million in the equivalent prior-year period.

Prospects: Our evaluation of Pioneer Natural Resources Co as of October 4th, 2019 is the result of our systematic analysis on three basic characteristics: earnings strength, relative valuation, and recent stock price movement. The company has enjoyed a very positive trend in earnings per share over the past 5 quarters. However, recent analyst estimates for the company have been mixed and PXD has posted results that exceeded analysts' expectations. Based on operating earnings yield, the company is fairly valued when compared to all of the companies we cover. Share price changes over the past year indicates that PXD will perform poorly over the near term.

Financial Data

(US$ in Thousands)	9 Mos	6 Mos	3 Mos	12/31/2018	12/31/2017	12/31/2016	12/31/2015	12/31/2014
Earnings Per Share	4.31	5.32	6.71	5.70	4.85	(3.34)	(1.83)	6.38
Cash Flow Per Share	19.17	18.92	19.48	18.96	12.29	9.00	8.38	16.43
Tang Book Value Per Share	70.00	69.49	70.92	69.89	64.66	59.70	54.20	55.77
Dividends Per Share	0.760	0.480	0.480	0.320	0.080	0.080	0.080	0.080
Dividend Payout %	17.63	9.02	7.15	5.61	1.65	...	...	1.25
Income Statement								
Total Revenue	6,661,000	4,336,000	2,413,000	9,415,000	5,455,000	3,824,000	4,825,000	5,055,000
EBITDA	1,979,000	1,191,000	927,000	1,820,000	1,941,000	817,000	1,241,000	2,912,000
Depn & Amortn	1,352,000	895,000	445,000	443,000	1,479,000	1,569,000	1,475,000	1,131,000
Income Before Taxes	539,000	237,000	453,000	1,251,000	309,000	(959,000)	(421,000)	1,597,000
Income Taxes	127,000	56,000	103,000	276,000	(524,000)	(403,000)	(155,000)	556,000
Net Income	412,000	181,000	350,000	978,000	833,000	(556,000)	(273,000)	930,000
Average Shares	167,000	168,000	169,000	171,000	170,000	166,000	149,000	144,000
Balance Sheet								
Current Assets	1,923,000	2,175,000	2,505,000	2,580,000	3,010,000	3,298,000	3,194,000	2,359,000
Total Assets	18,078,000	18,106,000	18,355,000	17,903,000	17,003,000	16,459,000	15,154,000	14,926,000
Current Liabilities	2,460,000	2,525,000	2,532,000	1,818,000	2,128,000	1,566,000	1,462,000	1,580,000
Long-Term Obligations	1,838,000	1,837,000	1,836,000	2,284,000	2,283,000	2,728,000	3,207,000	2,665,000
Total Liabilities	6,222,000	6,230,000	6,146,000	5,792,000	5,729,000	6,055,000	6,786,000	6,345,000
Stockholders' Equity	11,856,000	11,876,000	12,209,000	12,111,000	11,274,000	10,404,000	8,368,000	8,581,000
Shares Outstanding	165,643	167,121	168,422	169,499	170,188	169,724	149,379	149,000
Statistical Record								
Return on Assets %	4.07	5.15	6.45	5.60	4.98	N.M.	N.M.	6.83
Return on Equity %	6.19	7.83	9.74	8.36	7.69	N.M.	N.M.	12.25
EBITDA Margin %	29.71	27.47	38.42	19.33	35.58	21.37	25.72	57.61
Net Margin %	6.19	4.17	14.50	10.39	15.27	N.M.	N.M.	18.40
Asset Turnover	0.52	0.53	0.54	0.54	0.33	0.24	0.32	0.37
Current Ratio	0.78	0.86	0.99	1.42	1.41	2.11	2.18	1.49
Debt to Equity	0.16	0.15	0.15	0.19	0.20	0.26	0.38	0.31
Price Range	187.92-118.02	191.27-120.51	212.31-120.51	212.31-120.51	198.90-127.94	193.24-107.75	180.23-107.24	233.07-130.60
P/E Ratio	43.60-27.38	35.95-22.65	31.64-17.96	37.25-21.14	41.01-26.38	...	...	36.53-20.47
Average Yield %	0.52	0.31	0.29	0.18	0.05	0.05	0.06	0.04

Address: 5205 N. O'Connor Blvd., Suite 200, Irving, TX 75039	**Web Site:** www.pxd.com	**Auditors:** Ernst & Young LLP
Telephone: 972-444-9001	**Officers:** J. Kenneth Thompson - Chairman Scott D. Sheffield - Executive Chairman, Chairman, President, Chief Executive Officer, Chief Executive Officer (frmr)	**Investor Contact:** 972-444-9001
Fax: 972-969-3587		**Transfer Agents:** Continental Stock Transfer & Trust Company, New York, NY

PITNEY BOWES INC

Exchange	Symbol	Price	52Wk Range	Yield	P/E
NYS	PBI	$4.03 (12/31/2019)	7.86-3.23	4.96	11.85

*7 Year Price Score 27.15 *NYSE Composite Index=100 *12 Month Price Score 83.66

Interim Earnings (Per Share)
Qtr.	Mar	Jun	Sep	Dec
2016	0.30	0.28	0.35	(0.44)
2017	0.35	0.26	0.31	0.47
2018	0.28	0.26	0.41	0.24
2019	(0.01)	0.13	(0.02)	...

Interim Dividends (Per Share)
Amt	Decl	Ex	Rec	Pay
0.05Q	02/05/2019	02/14/2019	02/15/2019	03/11/2019
0.05Q	05/06/2019	05/23/2019	05/24/2019	06/10/2019
0.05Q	08/06/2019	08/22/2019	08/23/2019	09/11/2019
0.05Q	11/08/2019	11/18/2019	11/19/2019	12/10/2019

Indicated Div: $0.20 (Div. Reinv. Plan)

Valuation Analysis
		Institutional Holding	
Forecast EPS	$0.66	No of Institutions	
	(01/15/2020)	524	
Market Cap	$685.7 Million	Shares	
Book Value	$25.4 Million	194,602,720	
Price/Book	26.98	% Held	
Price/Sales	0.20	69.31	

TRADING VOLUME (thousand shares)

Business Summary: Office Equipment & Furniture (MIC: 7.5.1 SIC: 7372 NAIC: 511210)

Pitney Bowes is a technology company. Co.'s business segments are: Small and Medium Business Solutions, which provides a range of equipment, technology, supplies and services that enable its clients to create mail, evidence postage and help simplify and save on the sending, tracking and receiving of mail, flats and parcels; Commerce Services group, which includes its cross-border solutions, shipping solutions, fulfillment, delivery and return services and presort services; and software solutions, which provides customer information management, location intelligence and customer engagement solutions delivered as on-premise licenses or on-demand/ software-as-a-service applications.

Recent Developments: For the quarter ended Sep 30 2019, income from continuing operations decreased 88.8% to US$5.3 million from US$47.7 million in the year-earlier quarter. Net loss amounted to US$3.1 million versus net income of US$80.3 million in the year-earlier quarter. Revenues were US$790.1 million, up 3.9% from US$760.3 million the year before. Direct operating expenses rose 11.8% to US$456.8 million from US$408.5 million in the comparable period the year before. Indirect operating expenses increased 15.1% to US$352.9 million from US$306.6 million in the equivalent prior-year period.

Prospects: Our evaluation of Pitney Bowes Inc. as of October 4th, 2019 is the result of our systematic analysis on three basic characteristics: earnings strength, relative valuation, and recent stock price movement. The company has generated a negative trend in earnings per share over the past 5 quarters. However, recent analyst estimates for the company have been mixed and PBI has posted results that exceeded analysts' expectations. Based on operating earnings yield, the company is undervalued when compared to all of the companies we cover. Share price changes over the past year indicates that PBI will perform very poorly over the near term.

Financial Data
(US$ in Thousands)	9 Mos	6 Mos	3 Mos	12/31/2018	12/31/2017	12/31/2016	12/31/2015	12/31/2014
Earnings Per Share	0.34	0.77	0.90	1.19	1.39	0.49	2.03	1.64
Cash Flow Per Share	1.67	1.72	2.04	2.09	2.66	2.60	2.58	3.25
Dividends Per Share	0.338	0.475	0.613	0.750	0.750	0.750	0.750	0.750
Dividend Payout %	99.26	61.69	68.06	63.03	53.96	153.06	36.95	45.73
Income Statement								
Total Revenue	2,373,782	1,729,181	868,402	3,522,380	3,549,948	3,406,575	3,578,060	3,821,504
EBITDA	255,033	202,090	85,203	531,118	596,151	528,581	906,199	765,646
Depn & Amortn	118,514	82,813	39,365	159,000	149,000	138,000	136,000	165,000
Income Before Taxes	18,761	41,249	6,872	212,361	282,989	246,370	610,825	431,196
Income Taxes	(13,351)	12,400	8,301	12,383	21,649	131,819	189,778	112,815
Net Income	17,913	21,038	(2,659)	223,665	261,340	92,805	407,943	333,755
Average Shares	171,201	178,281	185,971	188,382	187,435	188,975	200,945	203,961
Balance Sheet								
Current Assets	2,406,762	2,161,861	2,227,109	2,324,218	2,636,508	2,325,183	2,319,808	2,760,120
Total Assets	5,597,224	5,757,987	5,806,265	5,972,903	6,678,715	5,837,133	6,141,462	6,485,693
Current Liabilities	2,145,560	1,762,323	1,774,758	1,857,140	2,054,993	2,327,619	2,279,051	2,360,623
Long-Term Obligations	2,567,363	3,029,246	3,047,661	3,066,073	3,559,278	2,750,405	2,507,912	2,927,127
Total Liabilities	5,571,812	5,705,015	5,719,909	5,733,431	6,490,154	5,940,793	5,962,740	6,408,434
Stockholders' Equity	25,412	52,972	86,356	239,472	188,561	(103,660)	178,721	77,259
Shares Outstanding	170,155	170,944	182,525	187,675	186,603	185,668	195,521	201,027
Statistical Record								
Return on Assets %	1.09	2.38	2.76	3.54	4.18	1.55	6.46	5.03
Return on Equity %	45.40	114.89	111.20	104.51	615.63	246.60	318.73	251.26
EBITDA Margin %	10.74	11.69	9.81	15.08	16.79	15.52	25.33	20.04
Net Margin %	0.75	1.22	N.M.	6.35	7.36	2.72	11.40	8.73
Asset Turnover	0.60	0.58	0.58	0.56	0.57	0.57	0.57	0.58
Current Ratio	1.12	1.23	1.25	1.25	1.28	1.00	1.02	1.17
Debt to Equity	101.03	57.19	35.29	12.80	18.88	...	14.03	37.89
Price Range	8.48-3.23	9.27-3.65	11.09-5.66	14.11-5.66	16.59-9.64	21.70-14.24	24.42-18.82	28.18-21.13
P/E Ratio	24.94-9.50	12.04-4.74	12.32-6.29	11.86-4.76	11.94-6.94	44.29-29.06	12.03-9.27	17.18-12.88
Average Yield %	5.76	6.89	7.68	8.06	5.53	4.13	3.45	2.93

Address: 3001 Summer Street, Stamford, CT 06926 Telephone: 203-356-5000 Fax: 203-351-7336	Web Site: www.pb.com Officers: Marc B. Lautenbach - President, Chief Executive Officer Michael Monahan - Executive Vice President, Chief Financial Officer, Chief Operating Officer	Auditors: PricewaterhouseCoopers LLP Investor Contact: 203-351-6349 Transfer Agents: Computershare Trust Company, N.A., Providence, RI

PLANET FITNESS INC

Exchange	Symbol	Price	52Wk Range	Yield	P/E
NYS	PLNT	$74.68 (12/31/2019)	80.90-52.80	N/A	56.58

*7 Year Price Score N/A   *NYSE Composite Index=100   *12 Month Price Score 98.16

Interim Earnings (Per Share)

Qtr.	Mar	Jun	Sep	Dec
2016	0.09	0.11	0.08	0.22
2017	0.14	0.16	0.18	(0.06)
2018	0.23	0.29	0.20	0.28
2019	0.32	0.41	0.31	...

Interim Dividends (Per Share)

Dividend Payment Suspended

Valuation Analysis   **Institutional Holding**

Forecast EPS	$1.56	No of Institutions
	(00/25/2020)	411
Market Cap	$6.7 Billion	Shares
Book Value	N/A	88,478,992
Price/Book	N/A	% Held
Price/Sales	10.04	82.71

TRADING VOLUME (thousand shares)

Business Summary: Sporting & Recreational (MIC: 2.2.4 SIC: 7991 NAIC: 713940)

Planet Fitness is a holding company. Through its subsidiaries, Co. is engaged as a franchisor and operator of fitness centers. Co.'s stores include co-branded cardio equipment, free weights, strength machines, a workout area, a small retail area and a drink cooler. Co. operates and manages its business in three business segments: Franchise, which includes operations related to its franchising business in the U.S., Puerto Rico, Canada, the Dominican Republic and Panama; Corporate-owned stores, which includes operations with respect to all corporate-owned stores throughout the U.S. and Canada; and Equipment, which includes the sale of equipment to franchisee-owned stores in the U.S.

Recent Developments: For the quarter ended Sep 30 2019, net income increased 45.0% to US$29.7 million from US$20.5 million in the year-earlier quarter. Revenues were US$166.8 million, up 22.1% from US$136.7 million the year before. Operating income was US$53.1 million versus US$43.6 million in the prior-year quarter, an increase of 21.8%. Direct operating expenses rose 23.1% to US$68.5 million from US$55.6 million in the comparable period the year before. Indirect operating expenses increased 20.8% to US$45.3 million from US$37.5 million in the equivalent prior-year period.

Prospects: Our evaluation of Planet Fitness Inc as of October 4th, 2019 is the result of our systematic analysis on three basic characteristics: earnings strength, relative valuation, and recent stock price movement. The company has generated a negative trend in earnings per share over the past 5 quarters. However, recent analyst estimates for the company have been mixed and PLNT has posted results that exceeded analysts' expectations. Based on operating earnings yield, the company is fairly valued when compared to all of the companies we cover. Share price changes over the past year indicates that PLNT will perform over the near term.

Financial Data

(US$ in Thousands)	9 Mos	6 Mos	3 Mos	12/31/2018	12/31/2017	12/31/2016	12/31/2015	12/31/2014
Earnings Per Share	1.32	1.21	1.09	1.00	0.42	0.50	0.11	...
Cash Flow Per Share	2.32	2.24	2.32	2.11	1.66	2.51	2.25	...
Dividends Per Share	...	...	...	...	...	2.780	...	...
Dividend Payout %	...	...	...	...	...	556.00	...	...
Income Statement								
Total Revenue	497,292	330,478	148,817	572,898	429,942	378,241	330,537	279,777
EBITDA	170,881	116,521	51,444	197,409	478,350	129,164	82,915	69,416
Depn & Amortn	4,192	2,832	1,577	19,540	13,886	12,131	11,088	9,138
Income Before Taxes	128,082	88,081	36,916	131,804	429,181	89,908	47,278	38,478
Income Taxes	26,924	16,615	5,277	28,642	373,580	18,661	9,148	1,183
Net Income	88,030	62,253	27,409	88,021	33,146	21,500	18,518	36,808
Average Shares	83,806	84,835	84,425	87,674	78,971	43,304	36,243	...
Balance Sheet								
Current Assets	306,270	424,123	417,436	388,540	177,001	91,225	72,945	75,318
Total Assets	1,420,232	1,523,467	1,509,592	1,353,416	1,092,465	1,001,442	699,177	609,276
Current Liabilities	135,921	125,424	134,475	131,403	112,030	83,273	66,252	60,885
Long-Term Obligations	1,155,049	1,156,792	1,158,483	1,160,127	696,576	702,003	479,779	383,220
Total Liabilities	1,858,826	1,832,582	1,855,572	1,727,990	1,211,951	1,132,201	714,557	463,756
Stockholders' Equity	(438,594)	(309,115)	(345,980)	(374,574)	(119,486)	(130,759)	(15,380)	145,520
Shares Outstanding	90,335	92,577	93,052	93,032	98,381	98,499	98,710	...
Statistical Record								
Return on Assets %	7.42	7.89	7.28	7.20	3.17	2.52	2.83	6.28
Return on Equity %	...	...	...	...	...	...	28.46	15.96
EBITDA Margin %	34.36	35.26	34.57	34.46	111.26	34.15	25.08	24.81
Net Margin %	17.70	18.84	18.42	15.36	7.71	5.68	5.60	13.16
Asset Turnover	0.44	0.48	0.46	0.47	0.41	0.44	0.51	0.48
Current Ratio	2.25	3.38	3.10	2.96	1.58	1.10	1.10	1.24
Debt to Equity	...	...	...	...	...	...	...	2.63
Price Range	80.90-45.41	80.90-44.50	68.72-36.42	56.88-29.44	34.82-18.63	24.54-13.26	19.10-14.99	...
P/E Ratio	61.29-34.40	66.86-36.78	63.05-33.41	56.88-29.44	82.90-44.36	49.08-26.52	173.64-136.27	...
Average Yield %	...	...	...	...	...	15.22	...	...

Address: 4 Liberty Lane West, Hampton, NH 03842 Telephone: 603-750-0001	Web Site: www.planetfitness.com Officers: Stephen Spinelli - Chairman Dorvin D. Lively - President, Chief Financial Officer	Auditors: KPMG LLP Transfer Agents: American Stock Transfer and Trust Company, LLC

PLANTRONICS, INC.

Exchange	Symbol	Price	52Wk Range	Yield	P/E
NYS	PLT	$27.34 (12/31/2019)	53.26-22.92	2.19	N/A

*7 Year Price Score 65.84 *NYSE Composite Index=100 *12 Month Price Score 70.45

Interim Earnings (Per Share)

Qtr.	Jun	Sep	Dec	Mar
2016-17	0.62	0.63	0.68	0.59
2017-18	0.57	0.59	(1.54)	0.30
2018-19	0.42	(2.21)	(1.06)	(0.53)
2019-20	(1.14)	(0.65)	...	...

Interim Dividends (Per Share)

Amt	Decl	Ex	Rec	Pay
0.15Q	02/05/2019	02/19/2019	02/20/2019	03/08/2019
0.15Q	05/07/2019	05/17/2019	05/20/2019	06/10/2019
0.15Q	08/06/2019	08/19/2019	08/20/2019	09/10/2019
0.15Q	11/05/2019	11/19/2019	11/20/2019	12/10/2019

Indicated Div: $0.60

Valuation Analysis / Institutional Holding

Forecast EPS	$3.17	No of Institutions
	(01/17/2020)	323
Market Cap	$1.1 Billion	Shares
Book Value	$659.1 Million	52,949,792
Price/Book	1.66	% Held
Price/Sales	0.58	101.85

Business Summary: Manufacturing (MIC: 6.1.1 SIC: 3651 NAIC: 334310)

Plantronics is a designer, manufacturer, and marketer of communications and collaboration solutions that span headsets, Open SIP desktop phones, audio and video conferencing, cloud management and analytics software solutions, and services. Co.'s main product categories are Enterprise Headsets, which includes corded and cordless communication headsets; Consumer Headsets, which includes Bluetooth and corded products for mobile device applications, personal computer and gaming; Voice, Video, and Content Sharing Solutions, which includes Open SIP desktop phones, conference room phones, and video endpoints, including cameras, speakers, and microphones.

Recent Developments: For the quarter ended Sep 28 2019, net loss amounted to US$25.9 million versus a net loss of US$86.7 million in the year-earlier quarter. Revenues were US$461.7 million, down 4.4% from US$483.1 million the year earlier. Operating loss was US$5.6 million versus a loss of US$86.0 million in the prior-year quarter. Direct operating expenses declined 22.6% to US$255.6 million from US$330.4 million in the comparable period the year before. Indirect operating expenses decreased 11.3% to US$211.7 million from US$238.6 million in the equivalent prior-year period.

Prospects: Our evaluation of Plantronics Inc. as of October 4th, 2019 is the result of our systematic analysis on three basic characteristics: earnings strength, relative valuation, and recent stock price movement. The company has produced a positive trend in earnings per share over the past 5 quarters. However, recent analyst estimates for the company have been unchanged, while PLT has posted results that fell short of analysts' expectations. Based on operating earnings yield, the company is undervalued when compared to all of the companies we cover. Share price changes over the past year indicates that PLT will perform very poorly over the near term.

Financial Data

(US$ in Thousands)	6 Mos	3 Mos	03/31/2019	03/31/2018	03/31/2017	03/31/2016	03/31/2015	03/31/2014
Earnings Per Share	(3.38)	(4.94)	(3.61)	(0.03)	2.51	1.96	2.63	2.59
Cash Flow Per Share	1.95	2.35	3.09	3.75	4.27	4.29	3.70	3.33
Tang Book Value Per Share	N.M.	N.M.	N.M.	10.15	10.97	8.90	17.10	16.00
Dividends Per Share	0.600	0.600	0.600	0.600	0.600	0.600	0.600	0.400
Dividend Payout %	...	...	...	...	23.90	30.61	22.81	15.44
Income Statement								
Total Revenue	909,476	447,767	1,674,535	856,903	881,176	856,907	865,010	818,607
EBITDA	(32,029)	(27,155)	(62,092)	150,624	151,595	127,225	167,585	155,624
Depn & Amortn	2,722	1,361	40,600	21,100	20,700	19,900	18,500	15,500
Income Before Taxes	(82,480)	(52,448)	(185,692)	100,227	101,665	82,176	145,251	141,139
Income Taxes	(11,699)	(7,577)	(50,131)	101,096	19,066	13,784	32,950	28,722
Net Income	(70,781)	(44,871)	(135,561)	(869)	82,599	68,392	112,301	112,417
Average Shares	39,584	39,239	37,569	32,345	32,963	34,938	42,643	43,364
Balance Sheet								
Current Assets	821,420	789,162	781,146	899,726	698,977	596,995	602,654	556,287
Total Assets	3,112,014	3,122,031	3,116,535	1,076,887	1,017,159	933,437	876,042	811,815
Current Liabilities	597,348	574,924	528,229	125,514	117,170	109,167	94,822	97,607
Long-Term Obligations	1,619,015	1,642,163	1,640,801	492,509	491,059	489,609	34,500	...
Total Liabilities	2,452,907	2,452,533	2,394,848	723,917	635,003	621,038	148,645	113,151
Stockholders' Equity	659,107	669,498	721,687	352,970	382,156	312,399	727,397	698,664
Shares Outstanding	39,917	39,575	39,518	33,251	33,416	33,319	41,601	42,649
Statistical Record								
Return on Assets %	N.M.	N.M.	N.M.	N.M.	8.47	7.54	13.31	14.26
Return on Equity %	N.M.	N.M.	N.M.	N.M.	23.78	13.12	15.75	16.71
EBITDA Margin %	N.M.	N.M.	N.M.	17.58	17.20	14.85	19.37	19.01
Net Margin %	N.M.	N.M.	N.M.	N.M.	9.37	7.98	12.98	13.73
Asset Turnover	0.58	0.90	0.80	0.82	0.90	0.94	1.02	1.04
Current Ratio	1.38	1.37	1.48	7.17	5.97	5.47	6.36	5.70
Debt to Equity	2.46	2.45	2.27	1.40	1.28	1.57	0.05	...
Price Range	61.90-26.45	82.21-31.24	82.21-31.24	60.37-41.36	57.47-37.28	58.09-32.55	55.45-41.57	49.56-41.41
P/E Ratio	...	...	...	...	22.90-14.85	29.64-16.61	21.08-15.81	19.14-15.99
Average Yield %	1.38	1.15	1.04	1.17	1.22	1.19	1.24	0.89

Address: 345 Encinal Street, Santa Cruz, CA 95060	**Web Site:** www.poly.com	**Auditors:** PricewaterhouseCoopers LLP
Telephone: 831-426-5858	**Officers:** Robert (Bob) C. Hagerty - Chairman Marvin Tseu - Vice-Chairman	**Investor Contact:** 831-426-5858
Fax: 831-426-6098		**Transfer Agents:** Computershare Trust Company, N.A., Providence, RI

PNC FINANCIAL SERVICES GROUP (THE)

Exchange	Symbol	Price	52Wk Range	Yield	P/E
NYS	PNC	$159.63 (12/31/2019)	161.15-116.91	2.88	14.28

7 Year Price Score 105.19 *NYSE Composite Index=100 *12 Month Price Score 107.26

Interim Earnings (Per Share)

Qtr.	Mar	Jun	Sep	Dec
2016	1.68	1.82	1.84	1.97
2017	1.96	2.10	2.16	4.15
2018	2.43	2.72	2.82	2.75
2019	2.61	2.88	2.94	...

Interim Dividends (Per Share)

Amt	Decl	Ex	Rec	Pay
0.95Q	04/04/2019	04/15/2019	04/16/2019	05/05/2019
1.15Q	07/09/2019	07/18/2019	07/19/2019	08/05/2019
1.15Q	10/03/2019	10/16/2019	10/17/2019	11/05/2019
1.15Q	01/02/2020	01/16/2020	01/17/2020	02/05/2020

Indicated Div: $4.60

Valuation Analysis

Forecast EPS	$11.80
	(01/17/2020)
Market Cap	$70.1 Billion
Book Value	$49.4 Billion
Price/Book	1.42
Price/Sales	3.28

Institutional Holding

No of Institutions	1692
Shares	441,533,184
% Held	74.34

Business Summary: Banking (MIC: 5.1.1 SIC: 6021 NAIC: 522110)

PNC Financial Services Group is a bank holding company. Co. has businesses engaged in retail banking, including residential mortgage, corporate and institutional banking and asset management, providing its products and services nationally. Co.'s segments are: Retail Banking, which provides deposit, lending, brokerage, insurance services, investment management and cash management products and services; Corporate and Institutional Banking, which provides lending, treasury management, and capital markets-related products and services; Asset Management Group, which provides personal wealth management; and BlackRock, which provides a range of investment and technology services.

Recent Developments: For the quarter ended Sep 30 2019, net income decreased 0.6% to US$1.39 billion from US$1.40 billion in the year-earlier quarter. Net interest income increased 1.5% to US$2.50 billion from US$2.47 billion in the year-earlier quarter. Provision for loan losses was US$183.0 million versus US$88.0 million in the prior-year quarter, an increase of 108.0%. Non-interest income rose 5.2% to US$1.99 billion from US$1.89 billion, while non-interest expense advanced 0.6% to US$2.62 billion.

Prospects: Our evaluation of PNC Financial Services Group as of October 4th, 2019 is the result of our systematic analysis on three basic characteristics: earnings strength, relative valuation, and recent stock price movement. The company has managed to produce a neutral trend in earnings per share over the past 5 quarters. However, recent analyst estimates for the company have been reduced while PNC has posted results that exceeded analysts' expectations. Based on operating earnings yield, the company is undervalued when compared to all of the companies we cover. Share price changes over the past year indicates that PNC will perform poorly over the near term.

Financial Data

(US$ in Thousands)	9 Mos	6 Mos	3 Mos	12/31/2018	12/31/2017	12/31/2016	12/31/2015	12/31/2014
Earnings Per Share	11.18	11.06	10.90	10.71	10.36	7.30	7.39	7.30
Cash Flow Per Share	14.38	15.40	13.89	16.79	11.85	7.34	10.69	10.50
Tang Book Value Per Share	88.16	86.11	82.98	79.93	77.18	71.83	59.89	56.71
Dividends Per Share	4.000	3.800	3.600	3.400	2.600	2.120	2.010	1.880
Dividend Payout %	35.78	34.36	33.03	31.75	25.10	29.04	27.20	25.75
Income Statement								
Interest Income	10,428,000	6,925,000	3,428,000	12,582,000	10,814,000	9,652,000	9,323,000	9,431,000
Interest Expense	2,951,000	1,952,000	953,000	2,861,000	1,706,000	1,261,000	1,045,000	906,000
Net Interest Income	7,477,000	4,973,000	2,475,000	9,721,000	9,108,000	8,391,000	8,278,000	8,525,000
Provision for Losses	552,000	369,000	189,000	408,000	441,000	433,000	255,000	273,000
Non-Interest Income	5,741,000	3,752,000	1,811,000	7,411,000	7,221,000	6,771,000	6,947,000	6,850,000
Non-Interest Expense	7,812,000	5,189,000	2,578,000	10,296,000	10,398,000	9,476,000	9,463,000	9,488,000
Income Before Taxes	4,854,000	3,167,000	1,519,000	6,428,000	5,490,000	5,253,000	5,507,000	5,614,000
Income Taxes	817,000	522,000	248,000	1,082,000	102,000	1,268,000	1,364,000	1,407,000
Net Income	4,002,000	2,623,000	1,261,000	5,301,000	5,338,000	3,903,000	4,106,000	4,184,000
Average Shares	445,000	452,000	456,000	470,000	486,000	500,000	521,000	537,000
Balance Sheet								
Net Loans & Leases	236,511,000	235,638,000	230,287,000	224,610,000	220,502,000	210,748,000	205,509,000	203,748,000
Total Assets	408,916,000	405,761,000	392,837,000	382,315,000	380,768,000	366,380,000	358,493,000	345,072,000
Total Deposits	285,583,000	273,260,000	271,221,000	267,839,000	265,053,000	257,164,000	249,002,000	232,234,000
Total Liabilities	359,496,000	356,421,000	344,301,000	334,587,000	333,255,000	320,681,000	313,783,000	300,521,000
Stockholders' Equity	49,420,000	49,340,000	48,536,000	47,728,000	47,513,000	45,699,000	44,710,000	44,551,000
Shares Outstanding	439,000	447,000	452,000	457,000	473,000	485,000	504,000	523,000
Statistical Record								
Return on Assets %	1.35	1.36	1.38	1.39	1.43	1.07	1.17	1.26
Return on Equity %	11.07	11.12	11.17	11.13	11.45	8.61	9.20	9.62
Net Interest Margin %	71.48	71.43	72.20	77.26	84.22	86.94	88.79	90.39
Efficiency Ratio %	47.76	48.01	49.21	51.50	57.65	57.70	58.16	58.28
Loans to Deposits	0.83	0.86	0.85	0.84	0.83	0.82	0.83	0.88
Price Range	142.90-109.71	146.34-109.71	152.76-109.71	162.45-109.71	146.26-113.93	118.31-77.88	99.86-82.42	92.93-76.60
P/E Ratio	12.78-9.81	13.23-9.92	14.01-10.07	15.17-10.24	14.12-11.00	16.21-10.67	13.51-11.15	12.73-10.49
Average Yield %	3.08	2.89	2.67	2.38	2.04	2.35	2.16	2.22

Address: The Tower at PNC Plaza, 300 Fifth Avenue, Pittsburgh, PA 15222-2401	**Web Site:** www.pnc.com	**Auditors:** PricewaterhouseCoopers LLP
Telephone: 412-762-2000	**Officers:** William S. Demchak - Chairman, President, Chief Executive Officer Robert Q. Reilly - Executive Vice President, Chief Financial Officer	**Investor Contact:** 412-762-8257
Fax: 412-762-5798		**Transfer Agents:** Computershare Trust Company, N. A., Canton, MA

PNM RESOURCES INC

Exchange	Symbol	Price	52Wk Range	Yield	P/E
NYS	PNM	$50.71 (12/31/2019)	52.92-40.07	2.43	N/A

*7 Year Price Score 117.32 *NYSE Composite Index=100 *12 Month Price Score 98.02

Interim Earnings (Per Share)
Qtr.	Mar	Jun	Sep	Dec
2016	0.13	0.34	0.68	0.31
2017	0.29	0.47	0.92	(0.67)
2018	0.19	0.48	1.09	(0.69)
2019	0.23	(0.95)	1.28	...

Interim Dividends (Per Share)
Amt	Decl	Ex	Rec	Pay
0.29Q	02/22/2019	05/01/2019	05/02/2019	05/16/2019
0.29Q	07/23/2019	08/05/2019	08/06/2019	08/16/2019
0.29Q	09/24/2019	10/31/2019	11/01/2019	11/15/2019
0.308Q	12/06/2019	01/31/2020	02/03/2020	02/14/2020

Indicated Div: $1.23

Valuation Analysis
		Institutional Holding	
Forecast EPS	$2.15	No of Institutions	
	(01/17/2020)	389	
Market Cap	$4.0 Billion	Shares	
Book Value	$1.7 Billion	97,096,136	
Price/Book	2.40	% Held	
Price/Sales	2.77	90.65	

TRADING VOLUME (thousand shares)

Business Summary: Electric Utilities (MIC: 3.1.1 SIC: 4911 NAIC: 221121)

PNM Resources is a holding company. Through its regulated utilities, Co. provides electricity and electric services in New Mexico and Texas. Co.'s electric utilities are Public Service Company of New Mexico (PNM) and Texas-New Mexico Power Company (TNMP). PNM is an electric utility that provides electric generation, transmission, and distribution service to its rate-regulated customers in area of north central New Mexico, including the cities of Albuquerque, Rio Rancho, and Santa Fe, and certain areas of southern New Mexico. TNMP is a regulated utility that provides transmission and distribution services in Texas under the provisions of TECA and the Texas Public Utility Regulatory Act.

Recent Developments: For the quarter ended Sep 30 2019, net income increased 16.6% to US$106.8 million from US$91.6 million in the year-earlier quarter. Revenues were US$433.6 million, up 2.6% from US$422.7 million the year before. Operating income was US$140.5 million versus US$128.0 million in the prior-year quarter, an increase of 9.8%. Direct operating expenses declined 4.0% to US$156.1 million from US$162.6 million in the comparable period the year before. Indirect operating expenses increased 3.7% to US$137.0 million from US$132.0 million in the equivalent prior-year period.

Prospects: Our evaluation of PNM Resources Inc. as of October 4th, 2019 is the result of our systematic analysis on three basic characteristics: earnings strength, relative valuation, and recent stock price movement. The company has produced a positive trend in earnings per share over the past 5 quarters. However, recent analyst estimates for the company have been unchanged, while PNM has posted results that fell short of analysts' expectations. Based on operating earnings yield, the company is fairly valued when compared to all of the companies we cover. Share price changes over the past year indicates that PNM will perform well over the near term.

Financial Data
(US$ in Thousands)	9 Mos	6 Mos	3 Mos	12/31/2018	12/31/2017	12/31/2016	12/31/2015	12/31/2014
Earnings Per Share	(0.13)	(0.32)	1.11	1.07	1.00	1.46	0.20	1.45
Cash Flow Per Share	5.79	5.83	5.68	5.36	6.56	5.19	4.85	5.20
Tang Book Value Per Share	17.63	16.89	17.80	17.85	17.93	17.69	17.43	18.26
Dividends Per Share	1.135	1.110	1.085	1.060	0.970	0.880	0.800	0.740
Dividend Payout %	...	...	97.75	99.07	97.00	60.27	400.00	51.03
Income Statement								
Total Revenue	1,113,458	679,872	349,645	1,436,613	1,445,003	1,362,951	1,439,082	1,435,853
EBITDA	330,199	110,237	124,846	496,402	605,662	543,547	377,376	521,658
Depn & Amortn	225,182	148,090	73,946	275,641	268,194	242,033	222,861	209,867
Income Before Taxes	23,721	(92,230)	22,885	109,057	225,759	195,174	46,153	200,647
Income Taxes	(32,420)	(41,608)	1,223	7,775	130,340	63,278	15,075	69,738
Net Income	45,953	(56,950)	18,832	86,170	80,402	117,377	16,168	116,782
Average Shares	80,001	79,917	79,971	80,012	80,141	80,132	80,139	80,279
Balance Sheet								
Current Assets	341,164	299,076	457,073	302,524	294,420	378,039	385,570	432,817
Total Assets	7,200,932	7,048,667	7,250,758	6,865,551	6,646,103	6,471,080	6,009,328	5,829,325
Current Liabilities	945,729	666,541	664,133	512,453	835,644	805,108	641,120	704,282
Long-Term Obligations	2,467,002	2,672,155	2,771,939	2,670,111	2,180,750	2,119,364	1,966,969	1,642,024
Total Liabilities	5,518,490	5,424,990	5,554,550	5,165,640	4,939,321	4,783,599	4,342,986	4,096,250
Stockholders' Equity	1,682,442	1,623,677	1,696,208	1,699,911	1,706,782	1,687,481	1,666,342	1,733,075
Shares Outstanding	79,653	79,653	79,653	79,653	79,653	79,653	79,653	79,653
Statistical Record								
Return on Assets %	N.M.	N.M.	1.29	1.28	1.23	1.88	0.27	2.06
Return on Equity %	N.M.	N.M.	5.30	5.06	4.74	6.98	0.95	6.83
EBITDA Margin %	29.66	16.21	35.71	34.55	41.91	39.88	26.22	36.33
Net Margin %	4.13	N.M.	5.39	6.00	5.56	8.61	1.12	8.13
Asset Turnover	0.21	0.21	0.21	0.21	0.22	0.22	0.24	0.25
Current Ratio	0.36	0.45	0.69	0.59	0.35	0.47	0.60	0.61
Debt to Equity	1.47	1.65	1.63	1.57	1.28	1.26	1.18	0.95
Price Range	52.14-38.14	51.83-37.65	47.69-35.05	44.70-33.80	45.50-33.45	36.05-29.35	31.17-24.60	31.39-23.53
P/E Ratio	...	...	42.96-31.58	41.78-31.59	45.50-33.45	24.69-20.10	155.85-123.00	21.65-16.23
Average Yield %	2.48	2.59	2.68	2.73	2.47	2.69	2.89	2.74

Address: 414 Silver Ave. SW, Albuquerque, NM 87102-3289 Telephone: 505-241-2700	Web Site: www.pnmresources.com Officers: Patricia K. Vincent-Collawn - Chairman, President, Chief Executive Officer Charles N. Eldred - Executive Vice President, Chief Financial Officer	Auditors: KPMG LLP Investor Contact: 505-241-2211 Transfer Agents: Computershare, Providence, RI

POLARIS INC

Exchange	Symbol	Price	52Wk Range	Yield	P/E	Div Acheiver
NYS	PII	$101.70 (12/31/2019)	103.44-74.73	2.40	20.02	23 Years

*7 Year Price Score 67.84   *NYSE Composite Index=100   *12 Month Price Score 105.13

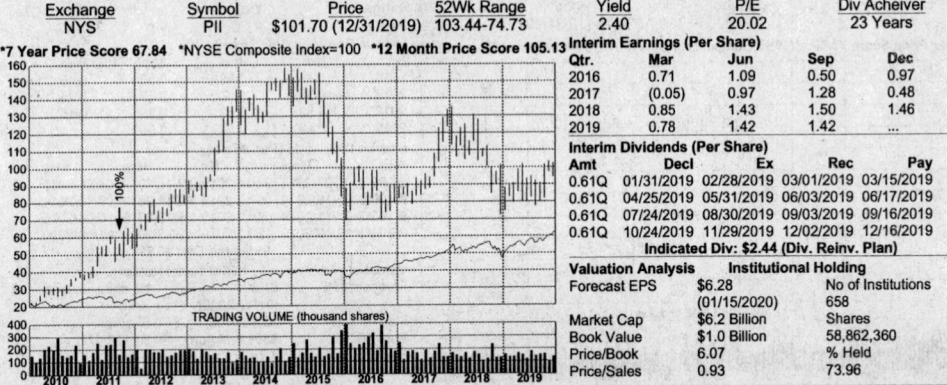

Interim Earnings (Per Share)
Qtr.	Mar	Jun	Sep	Dec
2016	0.71	1.09	0.50	0.97
2017	(0.05)	0.97	1.28	0.48
2018	0.85	1.43	1.50	1.46
2019	0.78	1.42	1.42	...

Interim Dividends (Per Share)
Amt	Decl	Ex	Rec	Pay
0.61Q	01/31/2019	02/28/2019	03/01/2019	03/15/2019
0.61Q	04/25/2019	05/31/2019	06/03/2019	06/17/2019
0.61Q	07/24/2019	08/30/2019	09/03/2019	09/16/2019
0.61Q	10/24/2019	11/29/2019	12/02/2019	12/16/2019

Indicated Div: $2.44 (Div. Reinv. Plan)

Valuation Analysis / Institutional Holding
Forecast EPS	$6.28	No of Institutions
(01/15/2020)		658
Market Cap	$6.2 Billion	Shares
Book Value	$1.0 Billion	58,862,360
Price/Book	6.07	% Held
Price/Sales	0.93	73.96

Business Summary: Autos- Manufacturing (MIC: 1.8.1 SIC: 3799 NAIC: 336999)

Polaris designs, engineers and manufactures powersports vehicles which include, Off-Road Vehicles, including All-Terrain Vehicles and side-by-side vehicles for recreational and utility use, Snowmobiles, Motorcycles, Global Adjacent Markets vehicles, including Commercial, Government and Defense vehicles, and Boats. Co.'s products, together with related Parts, Garments and Accessories, as well as aftermarket accessories and apparel, are sold through dealers, distributors and retail stores. Co.'s aftermarket portfolio of brands include Transamerican Auto Parts, which is a vertically integrated manufacturer, distributor, retailer and installer of off-road Jeep and truck accessories.

Recent Developments: For the quarter ended Sep 30 2019, net income decreased 7.5% to US$88.4 million from US$95.5 million in the year-earlier quarter. Revenues were US$1.77 billion, up 7.3% from US$1.65 billion the year before. Operating income was US$130.3 million versus US$138.9 million in the prior-year quarter, a decrease of 6.2%. Direct operating expenses rose 6.8% to US$1.34 billion from US$1.25 billion in the comparable period the year before. Indirect operating expenses increased 16.7% to US$306.3 million from US$262.4 million in the equivalent prior-year period.

Prospects: Our evaluation of Polaris Inc. as of October 4th, 2019 is the result of our systematic analysis on three basic characteristics: earnings strength, relative valuation, and recent stock price movement. The company has managed to produce a neutral trend in earnings per share over the past 5 quarters. In addition, recent analyst estimates for the company have been mixed and PII has posted results that exceeded analysts' expectations. Based on operating earnings yield, the company is undervalued when compared to all of the companies we cover. Share price changes over the past year indicates that PII will perform poorly over the near term.

Financial Data
(US$ in Thousands)	9 Mos	6 Mos	3 Mos	12/31/2018	12/31/2017	12/31/2016	12/31/2015	12/31/2014
Earnings Per Share	5.08	5.16	5.17	5.24	2.69	3.27	6.75	6.65
Cash Flow Per Share	9.09	8.38	7.21	7.63	9.22	8.87	6.67	8.00
Tang Book Value Per Share	N.M.	N.M.	N.M.	N.M.	2.58	1.31	11.56	9.82
Dividends Per Share	2.430	2.420	2.410	2.400	2.320	2.200	2.120	1.920
Dividend Payout %	47.83	46.90	46.62	45.80	86.25	67.28	31.41	28.87
Income Statement								
Total Revenue	5,046,652	3,275,005	1,495,690	6,078,540	5,428,477	4,516,629	4,719,290	4,479,648
EBITDA	525,798	332,776	139,852	726,504	548,814	503,955	856,133	842,187
Depn & Amortn	173,003	111,946	54,415	211,036	191,108	167,512	152,138	127,507
Income Before Taxes	292,023	179,791	65,018	458,501	325,551	320,124	692,539	703,441
Income Taxes	61,961	42,189	16,016	93,992	146,299	100,303	230,376	245,288
Net Income	225,029	136,641	48,378	335,257	172,492	212,948	455,361	454,029
Average Shares	62,265	62,164	62,027	63,949	64,180	65,158	67,484	68,229
Balance Sheet								
Current Assets	1,743,138	1,570,804	1,638,950	1,485,703	1,253,504	1,190,989	1,154,725	1,096,555
Total Assets	4,527,422	4,364,212	4,408,717	4,124,915	3,089,593	3,099,597	2,387,462	2,074,935
Current Liabilities	1,546,125	1,332,378	1,248,108	1,197,374	1,130,311	959,751	826,783	850,810
Long-Term Obligations	1,716,959	1,831,563	2,034,770	1,896,027	865,266	1,138,063	458,220	223,620
Total Liabilities	3,502,764	3,401,696	3,520,791	3,251,063	2,146,217	2,223,829	1,396,340	1,200,140
Stockholders' Equity	1,024,658	962,516	887,926	873,852	943,376	875,768	991,122	874,795
Shares Outstanding	61,169	61,119	61,051	60,890	63,075	63,109	65,309	66,307
Statistical Record								
Return on Assets %	7.30	8.51	8.60	9.29	5.57	7.74	20.41	24.15
Return on Equity %	32.76	34.94	35.02	36.90	18.96	22.75	48.81	64.00
EBITDA Margin %	10.42	10.16	9.35	11.95	10.11	11.16	18.14	18.80
Net Margin %	4.46	4.17	3.23	5.52	3.18	4.71	9.65	10.14
Asset Turnover	1.54	1.72	1.65	1.69	1.75	1.64	2.12	2.38
Current Ratio	1.13	1.18	1.31	1.24	1.11	1.24	1.40	1.29
Debt to Equity	1.68	1.90	2.29	2.17	0.92	1.30	0.46	0.26
Price Range	102.02-72.34	127.90-72.34	130.63-72.34	135.34-72.34	133.70-78.82	101.03-69.61	157.62-83.30	158.43-119.98
P/E Ratio	20.08-14.24	24.79-14.02	25.27-13.99	25.83-13.81	49.70-29.30	30.90-21.29	23.35-12.34	23.82-18.04
Average Yield %	2.76	2.56	2.39	2.19	2.41	2.56	1.59	1.37

Address: 2100 Highway 55, Medina, MN 55340
Telephone: 763-542-0500

Web Site: www.polaris.com
Officers: Scott W. Wine - Chairman, Chief Executive Officer Michael T. Speetzen - Executive Vice President, Chief Financial Officer

Auditors: Ernst & Young LLP
Investor Contact: 763-513-3477
Transfer Agents: Wells Fargo Shareowner Services, Mendota Heights, MN

POLYONE CORP.

Exchange	Symbol	Price	52Wk Range	Yield	P/E
NYS	POL	$36.79 (12/31/2019)	37.20-24.91	2.20	21.14

*7 Year Price Score 73.80   *NYSE Composite Index=100   *12 Month Price Score 101.61

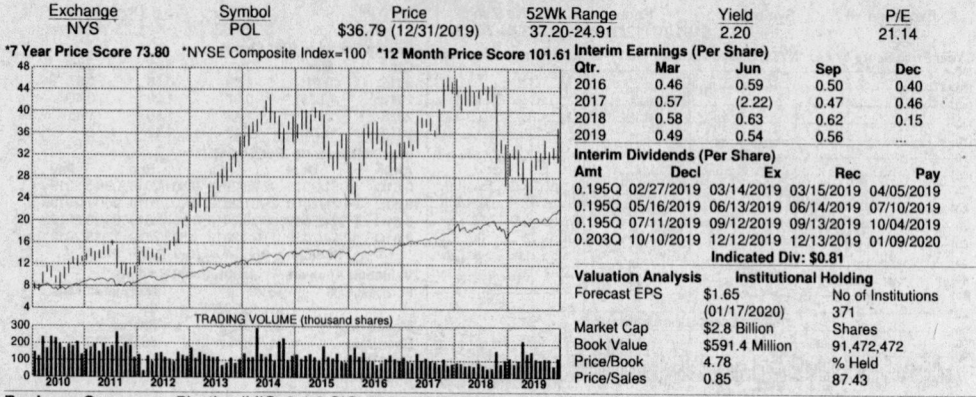

Interim Earnings (Per Share)

Qtr.	Mar	Jun	Sep	Dec
2016	0.46	0.59	0.50	0.40
2017	0.57	(2.22)	0.47	0.46
2018	0.58	0.63	0.62	0.15
2019	0.49	0.54	0.56	...

Interim Dividends (Per Share)

Amt	Decl	Ex	Rec	Pay
0.195Q	02/27/2019	03/14/2019	03/15/2019	04/05/2019
0.195Q	05/16/2019	06/13/2019	06/14/2019	07/10/2019
0.195Q	07/11/2019	09/12/2019	09/13/2019	10/04/2019
0.203Q	10/10/2019	12/12/2019	12/13/2019	01/09/2020

Indicated Div: $0.81

Valuation Analysis

	Institutional Holding	
Forecast EPS	$1.65	No of Institutions
	(01/17/2020)	371
Market Cap	$2.8 Billion	Shares
Book Value	$591.4 Million	91,472,472
Price/Book	4.78	% Held
Price/Sales	0.85	87.43

Business Summary: Plastics (MIC: 8.4.2 SIC: 2821 NAIC: 325211)

PolyOne is a provider of polymer materials, services and solutions with operations in engineered materials, composites, color and additive systems and polymer distribution. Co. is also a developer and manufacturer of additives, liquid colorants and fluoropolymers and silicone colorants. Co.'s segments include: Color, Additives and Inks, which is a provider of custom color and additive concentrates for thermoplastics, dispersions for thermosets, and specialty inks, plastisols, and vinyl slush molding solutions; and Specialty Engineered Materials, which is a provider of specialty polymer formulations, services and solutions for designers, assemblers and processors of thermoplastic materials.

Recent Developments: For the quarter ended Sep 30 2019, income from continuing operations decreased 27.4% to US$23.6 million from US$32.5 million in the year-earlier quarter. Net income decreased 14.1% to US$43.1 million from US$50.2 million in the year-earlier quarter. Revenues were US$705.3 million, down 3.3% from US$729.0 million the year before. Operating income was US$43.1 million versus US$48.7 million in the prior-year quarter, a decrease of 11.5%. Direct operating expenses declined 4.7% to US$544.8 million from US$571.8 million in the comparable period the year before. Indirect operating expenses increased 8.2% to US$117.4 million from US$108.5 million in the equivalent prior-year period.

Prospects: Our evaluation of PolyOne Corp. as of October 4th, 2019 is the result of our systematic analysis on three basic characteristics: earnings strength, relative valuation, and recent stock price movement. The company has generated a negative trend in earnings per share over the past 5 quarters. In addition, recent analyst estimates for the company have been reduced while POL has posted results that exceeded analysts' expectations. Based on operating earnings yield, the company is undervalued when compared to all of the companies we cover. Share price changes over the past year indicates that POL will perform poorly over the near term.

Financial Data

(US$ in Thousands)	9 Mos	6 Mos	3 Mos	12/31/2018	12/31/2017	12/31/2016	12/31/2015	12/31/2014
Earnings Per Share	1.74	1.80	1.89	1.99	(0.70)	1.95	1.63	0.85
Cash Flow Per Share	3.66	3.16	2.60	3.18	2.48	2.63	2.59	2.26
Dividends Per Share	0.780	0.760	0.740	0.720	0.580	0.495	0.420	0.340
Dividend Payout %	44.83	42.22	39.15	36.18	...	25.38	25.77	40.00
Income Statement								
Total Revenue	2,204,100	1,803,700	899,900	3,533,400	3,229,900	3,339,800	3,377,600	3,835,500
EBITDA	206,100	187,800	91,800	322,600	334,300	364,100	316,200	255,300
Depn & Amortn	68,400	46,900	23,300	62,600	61,200	82,000	84,400	104,700
Income Before Taxes	90,100	108,800	52,600	197,200	212,300	222,300	167,700	88,400
Income Taxes	20,800	28,400	14,300	36,400	38,700	57,300	23,000	11,200
Net Income	123,300	80,300	38,200	159,800	(57,700)	165,200	144,600	79,200
Average Shares	77,400	77,700	78,200	80,400	82,100	84,600	88,700	93,500
Balance Sheet								
Current Assets	1,173,800	1,019,800	1,034,700	998,800	1,066,600	949,500	960,800	1,042,700
Total Assets	2,946,200	2,930,600	2,961,800	2,723,300	2,705,300	2,723,300	2,595,100	2,711,200
Current Liabilities	625,500	607,300	570,300	557,600	570,600	509,600	498,100	601,200
Long-Term Obligations	1,406,300	1,392,500	1,440,700	1,336,200	1,276,400	1,239,800	1,128,000	962,000
Total Liabilities	2,354,800	2,360,200	2,393,600	2,183,300	2,106,800	1,998,600	1,890,900	1,934,900
Stockholders' Equity	591,400	570,400	568,200	540,000	598,500	724,700	704,200	776,300
Shares Outstanding	76,915	76,870	77,815	77,700	80,900	82,600	85,300	89,300
Statistical Record								
Return on Assets %	4.70	4.98	5.30	5.89	N.M.	6.20	5.45	2.80
Return on Equity %	22.36	24.38	26.22	28.07	N.M.	23.06	19.53	9.04
EBITDA Margin %	9.35	10.41	10.20	9.13	10.35	10.90	9.36	6.66
Net Margin %	5.59	4.45	4.24	4.52	N.M.	4.95	4.28	2.06
Asset Turnover	1.17	1.24	1.24	1.30	1.19	1.25	1.27	1.36
Current Ratio	1.88	1.68	1.81	1.79	1.87	1.86	1.93	1.73
Debt to Equity	2.38	2.44	2.54	2.47	2.13	1.71	1.60	1.24
Price Range	43.29-24.91	45.57-24.91	45.57-26.59	46.23-26.59	46.48-31.83	38.21-24.30	40.89-29.27	43.14-32.19
P/E Ratio	24.88-14.32	25.32-13.84	24.11-14.07	23.23-13.36	...	19.59-12.46	25.09-17.96	50.75-37.87
Average Yield %	2.50	2.22	1.95	1.76	1.53	1.53	1.17	0.90

Address: 33587 Walker Road, Avon Lake, OH 44012	Web Site:	Auditors: Ernst & Young LLP
Telephone: 440-930-1000	Officers: Robert M. Patterson - Chairman, President, President (frmr), Chief Executive Officer, Chief Executive Officer (frmr), Senior Vice President, Chief Financial Officer, Chief Operating Officer Bradley C. Richardson - Executive Vice President, Chief Financial Officer	Investor Contact: 440-930-1226 Transfer Agents: Wells Fargo Shareowner Services, Mendota Heights, MN

PORTLAND GENERAL ELECTRIC CO.

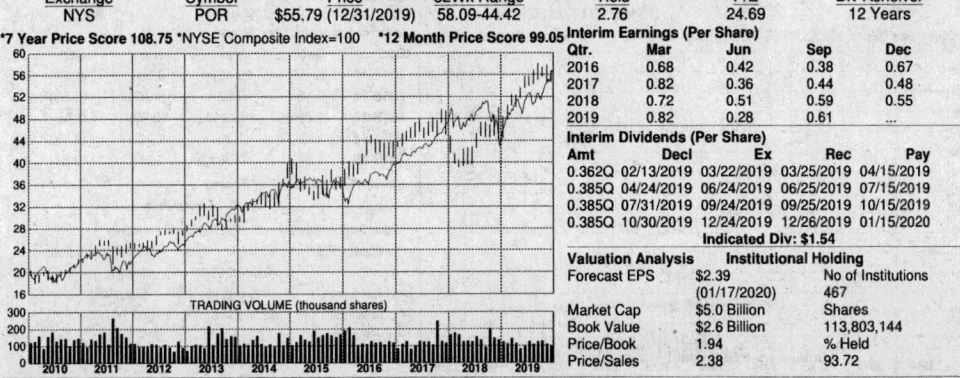

Exchange	Symbol	Price	52Wk Range	Yield	P/E	Div Acheiver
NYS	POR	$55.79 (12/31/2019)	58.09-44.42	2.76	24.69	12 Years

*7 Year Price Score 108.75 *NYSE Composite Index=100 *12 Month Price Score 99.05

Interim Earnings (Per Share)

Qtr.	Mar	Jun	Sep	Dec
2016	0.68	0.42	0.38	0.67
2017	0.82	0.36	0.44	0.48
2018	0.72	0.51	0.59	0.55
2019	0.82	0.28	0.61	...

Interim Dividends (Per Share)

Amt	Decl	Ex	Rec	Pay
0.362Q	02/13/2019	03/22/2019	03/25/2019	04/15/2019
0.385Q	04/24/2019	06/24/2019	06/25/2019	07/15/2019
0.385Q	07/31/2019	09/24/2019	09/25/2019	10/15/2019
0.385Q	10/30/2019	12/24/2019	12/26/2019	01/15/2020

Indicated Div: $1.54

Valuation Analysis   **Institutional Holding**

Forecast EPS	$2.39	No of Institutions
	(01/17/2020)	467
Market Cap	$5.0 Billion	Shares
Book Value	$2.6 Billion	113,803,144
Price/Book	1.94	% Held
Price/Sales	2.38	93.72

Business Summary: Electric Utilities (MIC: 3.1.1 SIC: 4911 NAIC: 221122)

Portland General Electric is an electric utility engaged in the generation, wholesale purchase, transmission, distribution, and retail sale of electricity in the State of Oregon. Co. meets its retail load requirement with both Co.-owned generation and power purchased in the wholesale market. Additionally, Co. participates in the wholesale market through the purchase and sale of electricity and natural gas to serve its retail customers. Co.'s state-approved service area allocation is located entirely within Oregon and includes various incorporated cities, principally in Portland and Salem.

Recent Developments: For the quarter ended Sep 30 2019, net income increased 3.8% to US$55.0 million from US$53.0 million in the year-earlier quarter. Revenues were US$542.0 million, up 3.2% from US$525.0 million the year before. Operating income was US$88.0 million versus US$91.0 million in the prior-year quarter, a decrease of 3.3%. Direct operating expenses declined 5.8% to US$243.0 million from US$258.0 million in the comparable period the year before. Indirect operating expenses increased 19.9% to US$211.0 million from US$176.0 million in the equivalent prior-year period.

Prospects: Our evaluation of Portland General Electric Co. as of October 4th, 2019 is the result of our systematic analysis on three basic characteristics: earnings strength, relative valuation, and recent stock price movement. The company has managed to produce a neutral trend in earnings per share over the past 5 quarters. In addition, recent analyst estimates for the company have been mixed and POR has posted results that fell short of analysts' expectations. Based on operating earnings yield, the company is fairly valued when compared to all of the companies we cover. Share price changes over the past year indicates that POR will perform over the near term.

Financial Data

(US$ in Millions)	9 Mos	6 Mos	3 Mos	12/31/2018	12/31/2017	12/31/2016	12/31/2015	12/31/2014
Earnings Per Share	2.26	2.24	2.47	2.37	2.10	2.16	2.04	2.18
Cash Flow Per Share	6.67	6.78	6.63	7.06	6.70	6.20	6.14	6.63
Tang Book Value Per Share	28.69	28.44	28.52	28.07	27.11	26.35	25.43	24.43
Dividends Per Share	1.495	1.472	1.450	1.428	1.340	1.260	1.180	1.115
Dividend Payout %	66.15	65.74	58.70	60.23	63.81	58.33	57.84	51.15
Income Statement								
Total Revenue	1,575	1,033	573	1,991	2,009	1,923	1,898	1,900
EBITDA	573	377	217	412	439	399	369	356
Depn & Amortn	305	202	101	59	46	44	38	25
Income Before Taxes	173	112	84	229	273	243	217	235
Income Taxes	20	14	11	17	86	50	45	61
Net Income	153	98	73	212	187	193	172	175
Average Shares	89	89	89	89	89	89	84	80
Balance Sheet								
Current Assets	416	440	596	643	526	463	557	699
Total Assets	8,154	7,997	7,948	8,110	7,838	7,527	7,221	7,042
Current Liabilities	514	440	731	791	432	577	626	873
Long-Term Obligations	2,464	2,514	2,178	2,178	2,426	2,200	2,071	2,126
Total Liabilities	5,590	5,455	5,400	5,604	5,422	5,183	4,963	5,131
Stockholders' Equity	2,564	2,542	2,548	2,506	2,416	2,344	2,258	1,911
Shares Outstanding	89	89	89	89	89	88	88	78
Statistical Record								
Return on Assets %	2.50	2.51	2.79	2.66	2.43	2.61	2.41	2.66
Return on Equity %	8.00	7.99	8.85	8.61	7.86	8.36	8.25	9.38
EBITDA Margin %	36.38	36.50	37.87	20.69	21.85	20.75	19.44	18.74
Net Margin %	9.71	9.49	12.74	10.65	9.31	10.04	9.06	9.21
Asset Turnover	0.26	0.26	0.26	0.25	0.26	0.26	0.27	0.29
Current Ratio	0.81	1.00	0.82	0.81	1.22	0.80	0.89	0.80
Debt to Equity	0.96	0.99	0.85	0.87	1.00	0.94	0.92	1.11
Price Range	58.09-44.19	55.69-42.59	52.46-39.35	49.98-39.11	49.72-42.83	45.04-35.80	40.79-33.16	40.09-29.07
P/E Ratio	25.70-19.55	24.86-19.01	21.24-15.93	21.09-16.50	23.68-20.40	20.85-16.57	20.00-16.25	18.39-13.33
Average Yield %	2.93	3.04	3.18	3.27	2.92	3.06	3.26	3.35

Address: 121 SW Salmon Street, Portland, OR 97204	**Web Site:** www.portlandgeneral.com	**Auditors:** DELOITTE & TOUCHE LLP
Telephone: 503-464-8000	**Officers:** Jack E. Davis - Chairman Maria M. Pope - Senior Vice President, Chief Financial Officer, Treasurer, President, Chief Executive Officer	**Investor Contact:** 503-464-8586
Fax: 503-464-2676		**Transfer Agents:** American Stock Transfer & Trust Company, New York, NY

POST HOLDINGS INC

Exchange	Symbol	Price	52Wk Range	Yield	P/E
NYS	POST	$109.10 (12/31/2019)	112.78-89.13	N/A	65.72

*7 Year Price Score 122.65 *NYSE Composite Index=100 *12 Month Price Score 95.54

TRADING VOLUME (thousand shares)

Interim Earnings (Per Share)

Qtr.	Dec	Mar	Jun	Sep
2014-15	(2.04)	0.45	0.33	(1.31)
2015-16	0.15	0.02	(1.92)	(0.58)
2016-17	1.22	(0.11)	(0.93)	0.16
2017-18	3.82	1.20	1.29	(0.18)
2018-19	1.67	0.58	0.21	(0.81)

Interim Dividends (Per Share)

No Dividends Paid

Valuation Analysis		Institutional Holding	
Forecast EPS	$5.07	No of Institutions	
	(01/16/2020)	446	
Market Cap	$7.9 Billion	Shares	
Book Value	$2.9 Billion	70,746,952	
Price/Book	2.69	% Held	
Price/Sales	1.38	96.14	

Business Summary: Food (MIC: 1.2.1 SIC: 2041 NAIC: 311211)

Post Holdings is a consumer packaged goods holding company. Co.'s segments are: Post Consumer Brands, which manufactures, markets and sells branded and private label ready-to-eat (RTE) cereal and hot cereal products; Weetabix, which markets and distributes branded and private label RTE cereal products; Foodservice, which produces and distributes egg and potato products; Refrigerated Retail, which produces and distributes side dishes, eggs and egg, cheese, sausage and other refrigerated products; and BellRing Brands, which markets and distributes ready-to-drink protein shakes, other RTD beverages, powders, nutrition bars and supplements in the nutrition category.

Recent Developments: For the year ended Sep 30 2019, net income decreased 73.1% to US$126.0 million from US$468.4 million in the prior year. Revenues were US$5.68 billion, down 9.2% from US$6.26 billion the year before. Operating income was US$781.0 million versus US$573.5 million in the prior year, an increase of 36.2%. Direct operating expenses declined 11.7% to US$3.89 billion from US$4.40 billion in the comparable period the year before. Indirect operating expenses decreased 21.0% to US$1.01 billion from US$1.28 billion in the equivalent prior-year period.

Prospects: Our evaluation of Post Holdings Inc. as of October 4th, 2019 is the result of our systematic analysis on three basic characteristics: earnings strength, relative valuation, and recent stock price movement. The company has managed to produce a neutral trend in earnings per share over the past 5 quarters. In addition, recent analyst estimates for the company have been mixed and POST has posted results that fell short of analysts' expectations. Based on operating earnings yield, the company is fairly valued when compared to all of the companies we cover. Share price changes over the past year indicates that POST will perform well over the near term.

Financial Data

(US$ in Thousands)	09/30/2019	09/30/2018	09/30/2017	09/30/2016	09/30/2015	09/30/2014	09/30/2013	09/30/2012
Earnings Per Share	1.66	6.16	0.50	(0.41)	(2.33)	(9.03)	0.30	1.45
Cash Flow Per Share	9.72	10.80	5.70	7.28	7.96	4.61	3.65	4.20
Income Statement								
Total Revenue	5,681,100	6,257,200	5,225,800	5,026,800	4,648,200	2,411,100	1,034,100	958,900
EBITDA	861,100	1,050,400	712,300	579,200	393,000	(87,400)	184,600	203,900
Depn & Amortn	379,600	398,400	323,100	302,800	272,800	155,800	76,800	63,200
Income Before Taxes	159,100	264,700	74,400	(30,100)	(167,300)	(426,900)	22,300	80,400
Income Taxes	(3,900)	(204,000)	26,100	(26,800)	(52,000)	(83,700)	7,100	30,500
Net Income	124,700	467,300	48,300	(3,300)	(115,300)	(343,200)	15,200	49,900
Average Shares	75,100	75,900	69,900	68,800	56,700	39,700	33,000	34,500
Balance Sheet								
Current Assets	2,126,300	2,200,300	2,615,900	2,076,900	1,781,700	1,219,000	668,100	209,700
Total Assets	11,951,600	13,057,500	11,876,800	9,360,600	9,220,400	7,731,100	3,473,800	2,732,300
Current Liabilities	802,900	792,100	704,400	634,000	611,000	519,900	146,000	126,400
Long-Term Obligations	7,066,000	7,232,100	7,149,100	4,551,200	4,511,400	3,830,500	1,408,600	930,300
Total Liabilities	9,025,700	10,007,100	9,096,800	6,352,000	6,244,400	5,447,900	1,975,200	1,500,800
Stockholders' Equity	2,925,900	3,050,400	2,780,000	3,008,600	2,976,000	2,283,200	1,498,600	1,231,500
Shares Outstanding	72,100	66,700	66,100	64,900	60,300	43,000	30,900	32,650
Statistical Record								
Return on Assets %	1.00	3.75	0.45	N.M.	N.M.	N.M.	0.49	...
Return on Equity %	4.17	16.03	1.67	N.M.	N.M.	N.M.	1.11	...
EBITDA Margin %	15.16	16.79	13.63	11.52	8.45	N.M.	17.85	21.26
Net Margin %	2.19	7.47	0.92	N.M.	N.M.	N.M.	1.47	5.20
Asset Turnover	0.45	0.50	0.49	0.54	0.55	0.43	0.33	...
Current Ratio	2.65	2.78	3.71	3.28	2.92	2.34	4.58	1.66
Debt to Equity	2.41	2.37	2.57	1.51	1.52	1.68	0.94	0.76
Price Range	112.78-84.38	100.65-71.63	88.41-70.68	87.85-53.86	69.73-31.67	60.18-33.18	49.14-30.05	33.98-26.02
P/E Ratio	67.94-50.83	16.34-11.63	176.82-141.36	...	...	...	163.80-100.17	23.43-17.94

Address: 2503 S. Hanley Road, St. Louis, MO 63144	**Web Site:** www.postholdings.com	**Auditors:** PricewaterhouseCoopers LLP
Telephone: 314-644-7600	**Officers:** Robert V. Vitale - President, Chief Executive Officer, Chief Financial Officer Diedre J. Gray - Executive Vice President, General Counsel, Chief Administrative Officer, Secretary, Senior Vice President	**Investor Contact:** 314-644-7600
		Transfer Agents: Computershare Trust Company, N.A., Providence, RI

558

PPG INDUSTRIES INC

Exchange	Symbol	Price	52Wk Range	Yield	P/E	Div Acheiver
NYS	PPG	$133.49 (12/31/2019)	133.76-97.97	1.53	26.28	47 Years

*7 Year Price Score 92.60 *NYSE Composite Index=100 *12 Month Price Score 106.12

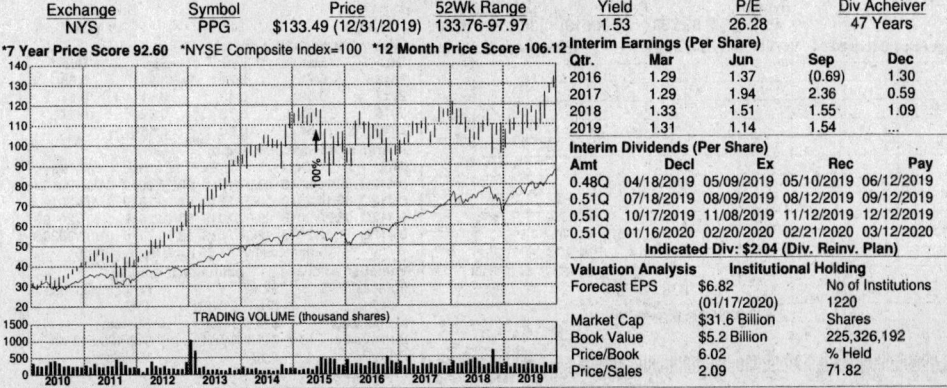

Interim Earnings (Per Share)

Qtr.	Mar	Jun	Sep	Dec
2016	1.29	1.37	(0.69)	1.30
2017	1.29	1.94	2.36	0.59
2018	1.33	1.51	1.55	1.09
2019	1.31	1.14	1.54	...

Interim Dividends (Per Share)

Amt	Decl	Ex	Rec	Pay
0.48Q	04/18/2019	05/09/2019	05/10/2019	06/12/2019
0.51Q	07/18/2019	08/09/2019	08/12/2019	09/12/2019
0.51Q	10/17/2019	11/08/2019	11/12/2019	12/12/2019
0.51Q	01/16/2020	02/20/2020	02/21/2020	03/12/2020

Indicated Div: $2.04 (Div. Reinv. Plan)

Valuation Analysis

		Institutional Holding	
Forecast EPS	$6.82	No of Institutions	
	(01/17/2020)	1220	
Market Cap	$31.6 Billion	Shares	
Book Value	$5.2 Billion	225,326,192	
Price/Book	6.02	% Held	
Price/Sales	2.09	71.82	

Business Summary: Specialty Chemicals (MIC: 8.3.2 SIC: 2851 NAIC: 325510)

PPG Industries manufactures and distributes a range of paints, coatings and specialty materials. Co.'s business is comprised of two reportable business segments: Performance Coatings, which primarily supplies a variety of protective and decorative coatings, sealants and finishes along with paint strippers, stains and related chemicals, as well as transparencies and transparent armor; and Industrial Coatings, which primarily supplies a variety of protective and decorative coatings and finishes along with adhesives, sealants, metal pretreatment products, optical monomers and coatings, precipitated silicas and other specialty materials.

Recent Developments: For the quarter ended Sep 30 2019, income from continuing operations was unchanged at US$372.0 million compared with the year-earlier quarter. Net income decreased 2.4% to US$373.0 million from US$382.0 million in the year-earlier quarter. Revenues were US$3.83 billion, up 0.2% from US$3.82 billion the year before. Direct operating expenses declined 3.2% to US$2.18 billion from US$2.25 billion in the comparable period the year before. Indirect operating expenses increased 4.6% to US$1.16 billion from US$1.11 billion in the equivalent prior-year period.

Prospects: Our evaluation of PPG Industries Inc. as of October 4th, 2019 is the result of our systematic analysis on three basic characteristics: earnings strength, relative valuation, and recent stock price movement. The company has enjoyed a very positive trend in earnings per share over the past 5 quarters. However, recent analyst estimates for the company have been reduced, while PPG has posted results that exceeded analysts' expectations. Based on operating earnings yield, the company is fairly valued when compared to all of the companies we cover. Share price changes over the past year indicates that PPG will perform in line with the market over the near term.

Financial Data

(US$ in Thousands)	9 Mos	6 Mos	3 Mos	12/31/2018	12/31/2017	12/31/2016	12/31/2015	12/31/2014
Earnings Per Share	5.08	5.09	5.46	5.47	6.17	3.28	5.14	7.51
Cash Flow Per Share	8.73	7.67	6.88	6.01	6.12	4.98	6.77	5.52
Dividends Per Share	1.950	1.920	1.890	1.860	1.700	1.560	1.415	1.310
Dividend Payout %	38.39	37.72	34.62	34.00	27.55	47.56	27.53	17.43
Income Statement								
Total Revenue	11,474,000	7,648,000	3,624,000	15,374,000	14,750,000	14,751,000	15,330,000	15,360,000
EBITDA	1,615,000	1,012,000	530,000	2,126,000	2,412,000	1,255,000	2,320,000	1,802,000
Depn & Amortn	276,000	177,000	86,000	354,000	331,000	341,000	363,000	350,000
Income Before Taxes	1,263,000	782,000	419,000	1,677,000	1,996,000	815,000	1,871,000	1,315,000
Income Taxes	297,000	188,000	102,000	353,000	616,000	241,000	456,000	259,000
Net Income	951,000	584,000	312,000	1,341,000	1,591,000	877,000	1,406,000	2,102,000
Average Shares	238,500	238,300	238,000	245,400	257,800	267,400	273,600	279,600
Balance Sheet								
Current Assets	6,817,000	6,707,000	6,409,000	5,961,000	6,477,000	6,452,000	6,554,000	6,850,000
Total Assets	18,064,000	17,955,000	17,371,000	16,015,000	16,538,000	15,769,000	17,076,000	17,583,000
Current Liabilities	4,578,000	4,706,000	4,588,000	4,373,000	3,894,000	4,240,000	4,656,000	4,876,000
Long-Term Obligations	4,885,000	4,845,000	4,626,000	4,365,000	4,134,000	3,787,000	4,042,000	3,544,000
Total Liabilities	12,817,000	12,876,000	12,467,000	11,385,000	10,980,000	10,943,000	12,093,000	12,403,000
Stockholders' Equity	5,247,000	5,079,000	4,904,000	4,630,000	5,558,000	4,826,000	4,983,000	5,180,000
Shares Outstanding	236,463	236,292	236,059	235,861	251,174	257,330	266,876	271,964
Statistical Record								
Return on Assets %	6.95	7.02	7.56	8.24	9.85	5.33	8.11	12.57
Return on Equity %	23.64	24.49	25.74	26.33	30.64	17.83	27.67	41.57
EBITDA Margin %	14.08	13.23	14.62	13.83	16.35	8.51	15.13	11.73
Net Margin %	8.29	7.64	8.61	8.72	10.79	5.95	9.17	13.68
Asset Turnover	0.87	0.87	0.87	0.94	0.91	0.90	0.88	0.92
Current Ratio	1.49	1.43	1.40	1.36	1.66	1.52	1.41	1.40
Debt to Equity	0.93	0.95	0.94	0.94	0.74	0.78	0.81	0.68
Price Range	120.69-95.09	119.86-95.09	115.98-95.09	121.47-95.09	118.67-95.25	116.55-89.27	118.85-84.51	116.23-88.30
P/E Ratio	23.76-18.72	23.55-18.68	21.24-17.42	22.21-17.38	19.23-15.44	35.53-27.22	23.12-16.44	15.48-11.76
Average Yield %	1.77	1.77	1.78	1.72	1.58	1.53	1.31	1.31

Address: One PPG Place, Pittsburgh, PA 15272	**Web Site:** www.ppg.com	**Auditors:** PricewaterhouseCoopers LLP
Telephone: 412-434-3131	**Officers:** Michael H. McGarry - Chairman, Chief Executive Officer, President, Executive Vice President, Senior Vice President, Chief Operating Officer Anne M. Foulkes - Senior Vice President, Secretary, General Counsel	**Investor Contact:** 412-434-3740 **Transfer Agents:** Computershare, Providence, R.I.

PPL CORP

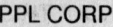

Exchange	Symbol	Price	52Wk Range	Yield	P/E	Div Acheiver
NYS	PPL	$35.88 (12/31/2019)	36.25-28.01	4.60	14.59	19 Years

*7 Year Price Score 80.54   *NYSE Composite Index=100   *12 Month Price Score 103.47

Interim Earnings (Per Share)

Qtr.	Mar	Jun	Sep	Dec
2016	0.71	0.71	0.69	0.68
2017	0.59	0.43	0.51	0.11
2018	0.65	0.73	0.62	0.57
2019	0.64	0.60	0.65	...

Interim Dividends (Per Share)

Amt	Decl	Ex	Rec	Pay
0.412Q	02/14/2019	03/07/2019	03/08/2019	04/01/2019
0.412Q	05/14/2019	06/07/2019	06/10/2019	07/01/2019
0.412Q	08/23/2019	09/09/2019	09/10/2019	10/01/2019
0.412Q	11/22/2019	12/09/2019	12/10/2019	01/02/2020

Indicated Div: $1.65 (Div. Reinv. Plan)

Valuation Analysis / Institutional Holding

Forecast EPS	$2.42	No of Institutions
	(01/17/2020)	1155
Market Cap	$25.9 Billion	Shares
Book Value	$11.9 Billion	613,408,512
Price/Book	2.18	% Held
Price/Sales	3.34	N/A

Business Summary: Electric Utilities (MIC: 3.1.1 SIC: 4911 NAIC: 221122)

PPL is a utility holding company. Through its regulated utility subsidiaries, Co. delivers electricity to customers in the U.K., Pennsylvania, Kentucky, and Virginia; delivers natural gas to customers in Kentucky; and generates electricity from power plants in Kentucky. Co. has three segments: U.K. Regulated, which has regulated electricity distribution operations in the U.K; Kentucky Regulated, which is engaged in the regulated generation, transmission, distribution and sale of electricity in Kentucky and Virginia, and the distribution and sale of natural gas in Kentucky; and Pennsylvania Regulated, which delivers electricity in eastern and central Pennsylvania.

Recent Developments: For the quarter ended Sep 30 2019, net income increased 6.7% to US$475.0 million from US$445.0 million in the year-earlier quarter. Revenues were US$1.93 billion, up 3.3% from US$1.87 billion the year before. Operating income was US$726.0 million versus US$686.0 million in the prior-year quarter, an increase of 5.8%. Direct operating expenses rose 1.9% to US$1.13 billion from US$1.11 billion in the comparable period the year before. Indirect operating expenses were unchanged at US$77.0 million versus the equivalent prior-year period.

Prospects: Our evaluation of PPL Corp. as of October 4th, 2019 is the result of our systematic analysis on three basic characteristics: earnings strength, relative valuation, and recent stock price movement. The company has managed to produce a neutral trend in earnings per share over the past 5 quarters. In addition, recent analyst estimates for the company have been mixed and PPL has posted results that exceeded analysts' expectations. Based on operating earnings yield, the company is undervalued when compared to all of the companies we cover. Share price changes over the past year indicates that PPL will perform in line with the market over the near term.

Financial Data

(US$ in Thousands)	9 Mos	6 Mos	3 Mos	12/31/2018	12/31/2017	12/31/2016	12/31/2015	12/31/2014
Earnings Per Share	2.46	2.43	2.56	2.58	1.64	2.79	1.01	2.61
Cash Flow Per Share	3.46	3.56	3.78	4.00	3.59	4.25	3.90	5.21
Tang Book Value Per Share	11.27	11.27	11.35	10.80	9.82	9.03	8.44	13.06
Dividends Per Share	1.648	1.645	1.643	1.640	1.580	1.520	1.500	1.490
Dividend Payout %	66.97	67.70	64.16	63.57	96.34	54.48	148.51	57.09
Income Statement								
Total Revenue	5,815,000	3,882,000	2,079,000	7,785,000	7,447,000	7,517,000	7,669,000	11,499,000
EBITDA	3,406,000	2,219,000	1,139,000	4,336,000	3,819,000	4,361,000	3,822,000	4,620,000
Depn & Amortn	950,000	615,000	306,000	1,094,000	1,008,000	926,000	883,000	1,237,000
Income Before Taxes	1,710,000	1,117,000	592,000	2,285,000	1,912,000	2,550,000	2,072,000	2,364,000
Income Taxes	328,000	210,000	126,000	458,000	784,000	648,000	469,000	781,000
Net Income	1,382,000	907,000	466,000	1,827,000	1,128,000	1,902,000	682,000	1,737,000
Average Shares	731,151	730,915	729,953	708,619	687,334	680,446	672,586	665,973
Balance Sheet								
Current Assets	2,534,000	2,231,000	2,429,000	2,432,000	2,294,000	2,067,000	2,646,000	6,159,000
Total Assets	44,559,000	44,204,000	44,567,000	43,396,000	41,479,000	38,315,000	39,301,000	48,864,000
Current Liabilities	3,840,000	4,063,000	4,061,000	4,563,000	4,023,000	3,837,000	3,876,000	7,443,000
Long-Term Obligations	21,547,000	20,965,000	21,114,000	20,069,000	19,847,000	17,808,000	18,563,000	18,856,000
Total Liabilities	32,657,000	32,221,000	32,395,000	31,739,000	30,718,000	28,416,000	29,382,000	35,236,000
Stockholders' Equity	11,902,000	11,983,000	12,172,000	11,657,000	10,761,000	9,899,000	9,919,000	13,628,000
Shares Outstanding	722,307	721,840	721,371	720,323	693,398	679,731	673,857	665,849
Statistical Record								
Return on Assets %	4.10	4.06	4.23	4.31	2.83	4.89	1.55	3.65
Return on Equity %	15.17	15.22	15.77	16.30	10.92	19.14	5.79	13.31
EBITDA Margin %	58.57	57.16	54.79	55.70	51.28	58.02	49.84	40.18
Net Margin %	23.77	23.36	22.41	23.47	15.15	25.30	8.89	15.11
Asset Turnover	0.18	0.18	0.18	0.18	0.19	0.19	0.17	0.24
Current Ratio	0.66	0.55	0.60	0.53	0.57	0.54	0.68	0.83
Debt to Equity	1.81	1.75	1.73	1.72	1.84	1.80	1.87	1.38
Price Range	32.74-27.59	32.74-27.59	32.74-25.61	32.27-25.61	40.06-30.76	39.68-32.19	34.75-29.14	35.21-27.46
P/E Ratio	13.31-11.22	13.47-11.35	12.79-10.00	12.51-9.93	24.43-18.76	14.22-11.54	34.41-28.85	13.49-10.52
Average Yield %	5.37	5.41	5.55	5.61	4.24	4.25	4.68	4.80

Address: Two North Ninth Street, Allentown, PA 18101-1179
Telephone: 610-774-5151

Web Site: www.pplweb.com
Officers: William H. Spence - Chairman, President, Chief Executive Officer, Chief Operating Officer Vincent Sorgi - President, Executive Vice President, Senior Vice President, Vice President, Chief Financial Officer, Chief Financial Officer (frmr), Chief Operating Officer, Controller

Auditors: DELOITTE & TOUCHE LLP
Transfer Agents: Equiniti Trust Company, Shareowner Services, Mendota Heights, MN

PRESTIGE CONSUMER HEALTHCARE INC

Exchange	Symbol	Price	52Wk Range	Yield	P/E
NYS	PBH	$40.50 (12/31/2019)	41.12-26.79	N/A	N/A

*7 Year Price Score 67.09 *NYSE Composite Index=100 ***12 Month Price Score 112.97**

Interim Earnings (Per Share)

Qtr.	Jun	Sep	Dec	Mar
2016-17	(0.10)	0.60	0.59	0.21
2017-18	0.63	0.57	5.88	(0.74)
2018-19	0.65	0.59	0.73	(2.66)
2019-20	0.65	0.65	...	...

Interim Dividends (Per Share)

No Dividends Paid

Valuation Analysis | Institutional Holding

Valuation Analysis		Institutional Holding	
Forecast EPS	$2.82	No of Institutions	
	(01/15/2020)	337	
Market Cap	$2.0 Billion	Shares	
Book Value	$1.1 Billion	75,552,024	
Price/Book	1.83	% Held	
Price/Sales	2.14	116.87	

Business Summary: Pharmaceuticals (MIC: 4.1.1 SIC: 2834 NAIC: 325412)

Prestige Consumer Healthcare is a holding company. Through its subsidiaries, Co. develops, manufactures, markets, sells and distributes over-the-counter (OTC) healthcare products to mass merchandisers and drug, food, dollar, convenience, and club stores in North America (the U.S. and Canada) and in Australia and certain other international markets. Co.'s portfolio of OTC Healthcare products includes, among others, DenTek oral care products, Monistat women's health products, Nix lice treatment products, Chloraseptic sore throat treatments, Clear Eyes eye care products, Compound W wart treatments, Luden's throat drops, BC and Goody's pain relievers and Debrox earwax remover.

Recent Developments: For the quarter ended Sep 30 2019, net income increased 7.8% to US$33.3 million from US$30.8 million in the year-earlier quarter. Revenues were US$238.1 million, down 0.5% from US$239.4 million the year before. Operating income was US$69.3 million versus US$70.9 million in the prior-year quarter, a decrease of 2.2%. Direct operating expenses declined 0.6% to US$101.3 million from US$101.9 million in the comparable period the year before. Indirect operating expenses increased 1.3% to US$67.4 million from US$66.5 million in the equivalent prior-year period.

Prospects: Our evaluation of Prestige Consumer Healthcare Inc. as of October 4th, 2019 is the result of our systematic analysis on three basic characteristics: earnings strength, relative valuation, and recent stock price movement. The company has managed to produce a neutral trend in earnings per share over the past 5 quarters. Additionally, recent analyst estimates for the company have been unchanged while PBH has posted results that exceeded analysts' expectations. Based on operating earnings yield, the company is undervalued when compared to all of the companies we cover. Share price changes over the past year indicates that PBH will perform very poorly over the near term.

Financial Data

(US$ in Thousands)	6 Mos	3 Mos	03/31/2019	03/31/2018	03/31/2017	03/31/2016	03/31/2015	03/31/2014
Earnings Per Share	(0.63)	(0.69)	(0.69)	6.34	1.30	1.88	1.49	1.39
Cash Flow Per Share	3.91	3.60	3.64	3.96	2.79	3.30	3.00	2.16
Income Statement								
Total Revenue	470,223	232,154	975,777	1,041,179	882,060	806,247	714,623	601,881
EBITDA	143,257	76,957	77,027	223,065	210,193	247,545	212,492	173,530
Depn & Amortn	3,698	5,887	10,000	10,100	6,000	5,200	3,800	3,200
Income Before Taxes	90,062	46,050	(38,055)	107,086	110,850	157,185	127,458	101,748
Income Taxes	22,885	12,125	(2,255)	(232,484)	41,455	57,278	49,198	29,133
Net Income	67,177	33,925	(35,800)	339,570	69,395	99,907	78,260	72,615
Average Shares	50,811	52,047	52,068	53,526	53,362	53,143	52,670	52,349
Balance Sheet								
Current Assets	304,886	310,521	300,938	303,477	334,434	249,013	201,707	177,185
Total Assets	3,464,760	3,460,710	3,441,036	3,760,612	3,911,348	2,948,791	2,669,405	1,795,663
Current Liabilities	146,894	143,491	126,979	123,199	162,009	106,684	99,037	84,358
Long-Term Obligations	1,754,171	1,779,380	1,798,598	1,992,952	2,193,732	1,625,309	1,588,711	934,414
Total Liabilities	2,351,970	2,359,087	2,345,205	2,582,002	3,088,799	2,204,455	2,041,781	1,232,303
Stockholders' Equity	1,112,790	1,101,623	1,095,831	1,178,610	822,549	744,336	627,624	563,360
Shares Outstanding	50,232	50,893	51,799	53,043	52,955	52,760	52,296	51,815
Statistical Record								
Return on Assets %	N.M.	N.M.	N.M.	8.85	2.02	3.55	3.51	4.11
Return on Equity %	N.M.	N.M.	N.M.	33.94	8.86	14.52	13.14	13.95
EBITDA Margin %	30.47	33.15	7.89	21.42	23.83	30.70	29.73	28.83
Net Margin %	14.29	14.61	N.M.	32.61	7.87	12.39	10.95	12.06
Asset Turnover	0.27	0.26	0.27	0.27	0.26	0.29	0.32	0.34
Current Ratio	2.08	2.16	2.37	2.46	2.06	2.33	2.04	2.10
Debt to Equity	1.58	1.62	1.64	1.69	2.67	2.18	2.53	1.66
Price Range	41.29-26.79	41.29-26.79	41.29-26.79	57.89-32.94	57.92-45.28	54.19-39.25	42.89-26.38	36.14-25.70
P/E Ratio	...	...	...	9.13-5.20	44.55-34.83	28.82-20.88	28.79-17.70	26.00-18.49

Address: 660 White Plains Road, Tarrytown, NY 10591 **Telephone:** 914-524-6800	**Web Site:** www.prestigeconsumerhealthcare.com **Officers:** Ronald M. Lombardi - Chairman, President, Chief Executive Officer, Chief Financial Officer William C. P'Pool - Senior Vice President, General Counsel, Corporate Secretary	**Auditors:** PricewaterhouseCoopers LLP **Investor Contact:** 914-524-6819 **Transfer Agents:** Computershare Ltd., Canton, MA

PRIMERICA INC

Exchange	Symbol	Price	52Wk Range	Yield	P/E
NYS	PRI	$130.56 (12/31/2019)	137.34-94.26	1.04	15.58

*7 Year Price Score 142.05 *NYSE Composite Index=100   *12 Month Price Score 102.61

Interim Earnings (Per Share)

Qtr.	Mar	Jun	Sep	Dec
2016	0.92	1.23	1.22	1.22
2017	1.11	1.36	1.46	3.68
2018	1.46	1.95	1.94	1.99
2019	1.83	2.28	2.28	...

Interim Dividends (Per Share)

Amt	Decl	Ex	Rec	Pay
0.34Q	02/07/2019	02/19/2019	02/20/2019	03/15/2019
0.34Q	05/07/2019	05/21/2019	05/22/2019	06/14/2019
0.34Q	08/07/2019	08/20/2019	08/21/2019	09/13/2019
0.34Q	11/06/2019	11/19/2019	11/20/2019	12/13/2019

Indicated Div: $1.36

Valuation Analysis — **Institutional Holding**

Forecast EPS	$8.30	No of Institutions
	(01/17/2020)	394
Market Cap	$5.4 Billion	Shares
Book Value	$1.6 Billion	44,214,548
Price/Book	3.37	% Held
Price/Sales	2.70	82.85

Business Summary: Life & Health (MIC: 5.2.2 SIC: 6311 NAIC: 524113)

Primerica is a holding company. Through its subsidiaries, Co. is a provider of financial products to households in the U.S. and Canada with licensed sales representatives. Co.'s segments are: Term Life Insurance, which provides a guaranteed death benefit if the insured dies during the fixed coverage period of an in-force policy; Investment and Savings Products, which distributes and sells to its clients a variety of mutual funds, managed investments, variable and fixed annuities, fixed indexed annuities and segregated funds; and Corporate and Other Distributed Product, which distributes prepaid legal services, auto and homeowners' insurance referrals, and home automation solutions.

Recent Developments: For the quarter ended Sep 30 2019, net income increased 13.0% to US$96.2 million from US$85.1 million in the year-earlier quarter. Revenues were US$520.7 million, up 7.4% from US$484.8 million the year before. Net premiums earned were US$303.3 million versus US$279.0 million in the prior-year quarter, an increase of 8.7%. Net investment income rose 10.0% to US$22.7 million from US$20.6 million a year ago.

Prospects: Our evaluation of Primerica Inc as of October 4th, 2019 is the result of our systematic analysis on three basic characteristics: earnings strength, relative valuation, and recent stock price movement. The company has managed to produce a neutral trend in earnings per share over the past 5 quarters. In addition, recent analyst estimates for the company have been mixed and PRI has posted results that exceeded analysts' expectations. Based on operating earnings yield, the company is undervalued when compared to all of the companies we cover. Share price changes over the past year indicates that PRI will perform in line with the market over the near term.

Financial Data

(US$ in Thousands)	9 Mos	6 Mos	3 Mos	12/31/2018	12/31/2017	12/31/2016	12/31/2015	12/31/2014
Earnings Per Share	8.38	8.04	7.71	7.33	7.61	4.59	3.70	3.29
Cash Flow Per Share	12.25	11.75	11.63	10.90	8.52	6.15	5.09	4.36
Tang Book Value Per Share	37.65	36.65	34.77	33.11	30.91	25.51	22.52	22.68
Dividends Per Share	1.270	1.180	1.090	1.000	0.780	0.700	0.640	0.480
Dividend Payout %	15.16	14.68	14.14	13.64	10.25	15.25	17.30	14.59
Income Statement								
Total Revenue	1,520,545	999,890	494,987	1,899,843	1,689,102	1,519,084	1,405,314	1,340,030
Income Before Taxes	354,967	229,828	102,368	416,084	379,520	337,595	290,981	275,722
Income Taxes	82,133	53,217	23,203	91,990	29,265	118,181	101,110	95,888
Net Income	272,834	176,611	79,165	324,094	350,255	219,414	189,871	181,412
Average Shares	42,100	42,619	42,942	43,985	45,689	47,453	50,913	54,598
Balance Sheet								
Total Assets	13,451,734	13,317,706	13,076,629	12,595,048	12,460,703	11,438,943	10,612,119	10,738,114
Total Liabilities	11,843,923	11,731,781	11,555,243	11,133,535	11,041,602	10,217,569	9,466,347	9,492,988
Stockholders' Equity	1,607,811	1,585,925	1,521,386	1,461,513	1,419,101	1,221,374	1,145,772	1,245,126
Shares Outstanding	41,492	42,008	42,399	42,694	44,251	45,721	48,297	52,169
Statistical Record								
Return on Assets %	2.75	2.70	2.64	2.59	2.93	1.98	1.78	1.72
Return on Equity %	23.56	23.32	22.90	22.50	26.53	18.49	15.88	14.71
Net Margin %	17.94	17.66	15.99	17.06	20.74	14.44	13.51	13.54
Asset Turnover	0.15	0.15	0.15	0.15	0.14	0.14	0.13	0.13
Price Range	131.56-91.38	131.56-91.38	127.79-91.38	127.70-91.38	105.30-69.95	72.50-39.93	55.09-41.01	55.60-39.51
P/E Ratio	15.70-10.90	16.36-11.37	16.57-11.85	17.42-12.47	13.84-9.19	15.80-8.70	14.89-11.08	16.90-12.01
Average Yield %	1.08	1.01	0.99	0.94	0.95	1.31	1.34	1.01

Address: 1 Primerica Parkway, Duluth, GA 30099 **Telephone:** 770-381-1000	**Web Site:** www.primerica.com **Officers:** Peter W. Schneider - President, Executive Vice President, Chief Administrative Officer, Corporate Secretary, General Counsel Glenn J. Williams - President, Chief Executive Officer	**Auditors:** KPMG LLP **Investor Contact:** 866-694-0420 **Transfer Agents:** American Stock Transfer & Trust Company, Brooklyn, NY

PROASSURANCE CORP

Exchange	Symbol	Price	52Wk Range	Yield	P/E
NYS	PRA	$36.14 (12/31/2019)	45.36-34.61	3.43	53.94

*7 Year Price Score 66.74 ***NYSE Composite Index=100** ***12 Month Price Score 91.92**

Interim Earnings (Per Share)

Qtr.	Mar	Jun	Sep	Dec
2016	0.36	0.81	0.63	1.02
2017	0.77	0.36	0.54	0.32
2018	0.22	0.53	0.58	(0.45)
2019	0.59	0.21	0.32	...

Interim Dividends (Per Share)

Amt	Decl	Ex	Rec	Pay
0.31Q	03/06/2019	03/28/2019	03/29/2019	04/22/2019
0.31Q	05/22/2019	06/13/2019	06/14/2019	07/11/2019
0.31Q	09/04/2019	09/26/2019	09/27/2019	10/11/2019
0.31Q	12/10/2019	12/26/2019	12/27/2019	01/14/2020

Indicated Div: $1.24

Valuation Analysis

		Institutional Holding	
Forecast EPS	$-1.08	No of Institutions	
	(00/25/2020)	313	
Market Cap	$1.9 Billion	Shares	
Book Value	$1.6 Billion	54,776,080	
Price/Book	1.22	% Held	
Price/Sales	2.09	84.29	

Business Summary: General Insurance (MIC: 5.2.1 SIC: 6331 NAIC: 524126)

ProAssurance is a holding company for property and casualty insurance companies. Co. has five segments: Specialty Property and Casualty, which includes its professional liability business and medical technology liability business; Workers' Compensation, which includes its workers' compensation business provided to employers with 1,000 or fewer employees; Segregated Portfolio Cell Reinsurance, which includes Co.'s Cayman Islands segregated portfolio cell operations; Lloyd's Syndicate, which includes Co.'s participation in Lloyd's of London Syndicates 1729 and 6131; and Corporate, which includes Co.'s investment operations, which are managed at the corporate level.

Recent Developments: For the quarter ended Sep 30 2019, net income decreased 44.9% to US$17.2 million from US$31.2 million in the year-earlier quarter. Revenues were US$241.9 million, down 3.0% from US$249.3 million the year before. Net premiums earned were US$215.8 million versus US$206.1 million in the prior-year quarter, an increase of 4.7%. Net investment income rose 1.8% to US$23.7 million from US$23.3 million a year ago.

Prospects: Our evaluation of ProAssurance Corp. as of October 4th, 2019 is the result of our systematic analysis on three basic characteristics: earnings strength, relative valuation, and recent stock price movement. The company has produced a positive trend in earnings per share over the past 5 quarters. However, recent analyst estimates for the company have been reduced, and PRA has posted results that fell short of analysts' expectations. Based on operating earnings yield, the company is overvalued when compared to all of the companies we cover. Share price changes over the past year indicates that PRA will perform poorly over the near term.

Financial Data

(US$ in Thousands)	9 Mos	6 Mos	3 Mos	12/31/2018	12/31/2017	12/31/2016	12/31/2015	12/31/2014
Earnings Per Share	0.67	0.93	1.25	0.88	2.00	2.83	2.11	3.30
Cash Flow Per Share	2.97	3.55	2.58	3.31	2.79	3.17	2.04	1.62
Tang Book Value Per Share	24.30	24.13	23.74	23.03	24.34	28.24	31.17	32.66
Dividends Per Share	1.740	1.740	1.740	1.740	5.930	5.930	2.240	3.860
Dividend Payout %	259.70	187.10	139.20	197.73	296.50	209.54	106.16	116.97
Income Statement								
Premium Income	633,086	417,298	208,149	818,853	738,531	733,281	694,149	699,731
Total Revenue	750,367	508,496	268,875	886,030	866,149	870,214	772,079	852,326
Benefits & Claims	489,808	328,195	159,755	...	...	515,242	456,862	379,232
Income Before Taxes	60,374	49,871	38,611	29,025	128,623	176,201	128,855	262,005
Income Taxes	(4)	6,685	6,961	(18,032)	21,359	25,120	12,658	65,440
Net Income	60,378	43,186	31,650	47,057	107,264	151,081	116,197	196,565
Average Shares	53,856	53,828	53,808	53,749	53,611	53,448	55,017	59,525
Balance Sheet								
Total Assets	4,824,359	4,786,118	4,717,108	4,600,726	4,929,197	5,065,181	4,908,163	5,169,160
Total Liabilities	3,234,901	3,204,562	3,155,212	3,077,724	3,334,402	3,266,479	2,949,809	3,011,216
Stockholders' Equity	1,589,458	1,581,556	1,561,896	1,523,002	1,594,795	1,798,702	1,958,354	2,157,944
Shares Outstanding	53,762	53,759	53,741	53,637	53,457	53,251	53,100	56,533
Statistical Record								
Return on Assets %	0.76	1.07	1.42	0.99	2.15	3.02	2.31	3.81
Return on Equity %	2.26	3.17	4.27	3.02	6.32	8.02	5.65	8.64
Loss Ratio %	77.37	78.65	76.75	...	...	70.27	65.82	54.20
Net Margin %	8.05	8.49	11.77	5.31	12.38	17.36	15.05	23.06
Price Range	46.28-34.61	49.40-34.61	49.40-34.61	56.00-35.35	63.00-51.30	62.85-46.22	53.42-43.73	48.48-42.90
P/E Ratio	69.07-51.66	53.12-37.22	39.52-27.69	63.64-40.17	31.50-25.65	22.21-16.33	25.32-20.73	14.69-13.00
Average Yield %	4.37	4.23	4.11	3.86	10.21	11.41	4.69	8.52

Address: 100 Brookwood Place, Birmingham, AL 35209
Telephone: 205-877-4400

Web Site: www.proassurance.com
Officers: W. Stancil Starnes - Executive Chairman, Chairman, Chief Executive Officer Edward L. (Ned) Rand - President, Chief Executive Officer, Executive Vice President, Senior Vice President, Chief Financial Officer, Chief Operating Officer, Chief Accounting Officer

Auditors: Ernst & Young LLP
Investor Contact: 205-877-4461
Transfer Agents: Mellon Investor Services, LLC, Ridgefield Park, NJ

PROCTER & GAMBLE COMPANY (THE)

Exchange	Symbol	Price	52Wk Range	Yield	P/E	Div Acheiver
NYS	PG	$124.90 (12/31/2019)	126.09-90.44	2.39	79.55	65 Years

*7 Year Price Score 105.82 *NYSE Composite Index=100 *12 Month Price Score 104.64

Interim Earnings (Per Share)

Qtr.	Sep	Dec	Mar	Jun
2016-17	0.96	2.88	0.93	0.83
2017-18	1.06	0.93	0.95	0.73
2018-19	1.22	1.22	1.04	(2.05)
2019-20	1.36	...	...	...

Interim Dividends (Per Share)

Amt	Decl	Ex	Rec	Pay
0.746Q	04/09/2019	04/17/2019	04/19/2019	05/15/2019
0.746Q	07/09/2019	07/18/2019	07/19/2019	08/15/2019
0.746Q	10/08/2019	10/17/2019	10/18/2019	11/15/2019
0.746Q	01/14/2020	01/23/2020	01/24/2020	02/18/2020

Indicated Div: $2.98 (Div. Reinv. Plan)

Valuation Analysis

Institutional Holding	
Forecast EPS	$4.95	No of Institutions
	(01/17/2020)	3407
Market Cap	$311.5 Billion	Shares
Book Value	$46.6 Billion	2,043,665,024
Price/Book	6.69	% Held
Price/Sales	4.53	61.73

Business Summary: Household & Personal Products (MIC: 1.7.1 SIC: 2841 NAIC: 325611)

Procter & Gamble provides consumer packaged goods. Co.'s products are sold primarily through mass merchandisers, e-commerce, grocery stores, membership club stores, drug stores, department stores, distributors, wholesalers, baby stores, beauty stores, other stores and pharmacies. Co. has five reportable segments: Beauty, which includes hair care, and skin and personal care products; Grooming, which includes shave care products; Health Care, which includes oral care and personal health care products; Fabric and Home Care, which includes fabric care and home care products; and Baby, Feminine and Family Care, which includes baby care, feminine care and family care products.

Recent Developments: For the quarter ended Sep 30 2019, net income increased 12.6% to US$3.62 billion from US$3.21 billion in the year-earlier quarter. Revenues were US$17.80 billion, up 6.6% from US$16.69 billion the year before. Operating income was US$4.29 billion versus US$3.55 billion in the prior-year quarter, an increase of 20.7%. Direct operating expenses rose 2.8% to US$8.72 billion from US$8.48 billion in the comparable period the year before. Indirect operating expenses increased 2.9% to US$4.79 billion from US$4.65 billion in the equivalent prior-year period.

Prospects: Our evaluation of Procter & Gamble Co. as of October 4th, 2019 is the result of our systematic analysis on three basic characteristics: earnings strength, relative valuation, and recent stock price movement. The company has enjoyed a very positive trend in earnings per share over the past 5 quarters. However, recent analyst estimates for the company have been unchanged, while PG has posted results that exceeded analysts' expectations. Based on operating earnings yield, the company is fairly valued when compared to all of the companies we cover. Share price changes over the past year indicates that PG will perform very well over the near term.

Financial Data
(US$ in Millions)

	3 Mos	06/30/2019	06/30/2018	06/30/2017	06/30/2016	06/30/2015	06/30/2014	06/30/2013
Earnings Per Share	1.57	1.43	3.67	5.59	3.69	2.44	4.01	3.86
Cash Flow Per Share	6.33	6.09	5.88	4.91	5.70	5.39	5.13	5.42
Dividends Per Share	2.926	2.898	2.786	2.698	2.658	2.594	2.448	2.288
Dividend Payout %	186.38	202.62	75.91	48.27	72.04	106.30	61.05	59.26
Income Statement								
Total Revenue	17,798	67,684	66,832	65,058	65,299	76,279	83,062	84,167
EBITDA	5,116	9,182	16,419	16,371	16,844	15,455	18,635	18,405
Depn & Amortn	723	2,824	2,834	2,820	3,078	3,134	3,141	2,982
Income Before Taxes	4,343	6,069	13,326	13,257	13,369	11,846	14,885	14,843
Income Taxes	726	2,103	3,465	3,063	3,342	2,916	3,178	3,441
Net Income	3,593	3,897	9,750	15,326	10,508	7,036	11,643	11,312
Average Shares	2,648	2,540	2,657	2,741	2,845	2,884	2,905	2,931
Balance Sheet								
Current Assets	21,925	22,473	23,320	26,494	33,782	29,646	31,617	23,990
Total Assets	114,058	115,095	118,310	120,406	127,136	129,495	144,266	139,263
Current Liabilities	30,253	30,011	28,237	30,210	30,770	29,790	33,726	30,037
Long-Term Obligations	20,161	20,395	20,863	18,038	18,945	18,329	19,811	19,111
Total Liabilities	67,480	67,901	66,017	65,222	69,795	67,076	75,052	71,199
Stockholders' Equity	46,578	47,194	52,293	55,184	57,341	62,419	69,214	68,064
Shares Outstanding	2,494	2,505	2,499	2,554	2,669	2,715	2,711	2,743
Statistical Record								
Return on Assets %	3.69	3.34	8.17	12.38	8.17	5.14	8.21	8.33
Return on Equity %	8.69	7.83	18.14	27.24	17.50	10.69	16.96	17.20
EBITDA Margin %	28.74	13.57	24.57	25.16	25.80	20.26	22.44	21.87
Net Margin %	20.19	5.76	14.59	23.56	16.09	9.22	14.02	13.44
Asset Turnover	0.59	0.58	0.56	0.53	0.51	0.56	0.59	0.62
Current Ratio	0.72	0.75	0.83	0.88	1.10	1.00	0.94	0.80
Debt to Equity	0.43	0.43	0.40	0.33	0.33	0.29	0.29	0.28
Price Range	124.57-78.87	112.33-77.86	94.40-70.94	91.67-81.86	84.67-68.06	93.46-77.32	85.41-75.59	82.54-61.19
P/E Ratio	79.34-50.24	78.55-54.45	25.72-19.33	16.40-14.64	22.95-18.44	38.30-31.69	21.30-18.85	21.38-15.85
Average Yield %	2.84	3.09	3.28	3.09	3.39	3.09	3.06	3.18

Address: One Procter & Gamble Plaza, Cincinnati, OH 45202	Web Site: www.pg.com	Auditors: DELOITTE & TOUCHE LLP
Telephone: 513-983-1100	Officers: David S. Taylor - Chairman, President, Chief Executive Officer Jon R. Moeller - Vice-Chairman, Chief Financial Officer	Investor Contact: 800-742-6253 Transfer Agents: Computershare, Canton, MA

PROGRESSIVE CORP. (OH)

Exchange	Symbol	Price	52Wk Range	Yield		P/E
NYS	PGR	$72.39 (12/31/2019)	84.39-58.23	0.55		13.53

*7 Year Price Score 146.15 *NYSE Composite Index=100 *12 Month Price Score 91.76

Interim Earnings (Per Share)
Qtr.	Mar	Jun	Sep	Dec
2016	0.44	0.33	0.34	0.65
2017	0.73	0.63	0.38	0.99
2018	1.22	1.19	1.57	0.44
2019	1.83	1.66	1.42	...

Interim Dividends (Per Share)
Amt	Decl	Ex	Rec	Pay
0.10Q	05/10/2019	07/03/2019	07/05/2019	07/15/2019
0.10Q	08/02/2019	10/04/2019	10/07/2019	10/15/2019
0.10Q	12/06/2019	01/07/2020	01/08/2020	01/15/2020
2.25Q	12/06/2019	01/07/2020	01/08/2020	01/15/2020

Indicated Div: $0.40

Valuation Analysis / Institutional Holding
Valuation Analysis		Institutional Holding	
Forecast EPS	$5.16	No of Institutions	1200
	(01/16/2020)		
Market Cap	$42.3 Billion	Shares	
Book Value	$14.1 Billion		567,920,384
Price/Book	3.00	% Held	
Price/Sales	1.17		79.05

Business Summary: General Insurance (MIC: 5.2.1 SIC: 6331 NAIC: 524126)

Progressive is an insurance holding company. Co.'s insurance subsidiaries and affiliates provide personal and commercial auto insurance, residential property insurance, and other insurance and related services. Co.'s Personal Lines segment writes insurance for personal autos and recreational and other vehicles. The Commercial Lines segment writes primary liability, physical damage, and other auto-related insurance for automobiles and trucks owned and/or operated by small businesses as a part of the commercial auto market. Co. is engaged in property insurance for homes, condos, manufactured homes, and renters, as well as personal umbrella insurance and primary and excess flood insurance.

Recent Developments: For the quarter ended Sep 30 2019, net income decreased 9.3% to US$843.6 million from US$930.2 million in the year-earlier quarter. Revenues were US$9.53 billion, up 12.2% from US$8.50 billion the year before. Net premiums earned were US$9.01 billion versus US$7.93 billion in the prior-year quarter, an increase of 13.6%. Net investment income rose 20.6% to US$263.0 million from US$218.1 million a year ago.

Prospects: Our evaluation of Progressive Corp. as of October 4th, 2019 is the result of our systematic analysis on three basic characteristics: earnings strength, relative valuation, and recent stock price movement. The company has generated a negative trend in earnings per share over the past 5 quarters. In addition, recent analyst estimates for the company have been reduced and PGR has posted results that fell short of analysts' expectations. Based on operating earnings yield, the company is undervalued when compared to all of the companies we cover. Share price changes over the past year indicates that PGR will perform well over the near term.

Financial Data
(US$ in Thousands)

	9 Mos	6 Mos	3 Mos	12/31/2018	12/31/2017	12/31/2016	12/31/2015	12/31/2014
Earnings Per Share	5.35	5.50	5.03	4.42	2.72	1.76	2.15	2.15
Cash Flow Per Share	10.64	10.58	10.98	10.79	6.47	4.63	3.92	2.92
Tang Book Value Per Share	22.12	20.76	18.64	16.43	14.55	12.20	10.88	11.79
Dividends Per Share	2.714	2.614	2.514	1.125	0.681	0.888	0.686	1.493
Dividend Payout %	50.73	47.53	49.98	25.45	25.03	50.47	31.92	69.44
Income Statement								
Premium Income	26,296,700	17,284,500	8,459,800	30,933,300	25,729,900	22,474,000	19,899,100	18,398,500
Total Revenue	28,281,200	18,750,700	9,300,000	31,979,000	26,839,000	23,441,400	20,853,800	19,391,400
Benefits & Claims	18,323,400	11,897,100	5,759,000	21,721,000	18,808,000	16,879,600	14,342,000	13,306,200
Income Before Taxes	3,821,400	2,811,100	1,567,500	3,163,600	2,138,900	1,470,700	1,911,600	1,907,400
Income Taxes	916,000	749,300	484,700	542,600	540,800	413,500	611,100	626,400
Net Income	2,899,500	2,057,800	1,078,400	2,615,300	1,592,200	1,031,000	1,267,600	1,281,000
Average Shares	587,100	586,900	586,600	586,700	585,700	585,000	589,200	594,800
Balance Sheet								
Total Assets	54,008,100	51,324,200	48,850,300	46,575,000	38,701,200	33,427,500	29,819,300	25,787,600
Total Liabilities	39,884,800	37,993,400	36,739,600	35,753,200	29,416,400	25,470,400	22,529,900	18,859,000
Stockholders' Equity	14,123,300	13,330,800	12,110,700	10,821,800	9,284,800	7,957,100	7,289,400	6,928,600
Shares Outstanding	584,600	584,100	584,000	583,200	581,700	579,900	583,600	587,800
Statistical Record								
Return on Assets %	6.36	6.87	6.60	6.13	4.41	3.25	4.56	5.10
Return on Equity %	24.36	26.72	26.53	26.01	18.47	13.49	17.83	19.53
Loss Ratio %	69.68	68.83	68.07	70.22	73.10	75.11	72.07	72.32
Net Margin %	10.25	10.97	11.60	8.18	5.93	4.40	6.08	6.61
Price Range	84.39-57.07	83.34-57.07	73.61-57.07	73.46-51.07	56.51-35.53	35.74-29.49	33.64-25.85	27.35-22.59
P/E Ratio	15.77-10.67	15.15-10.38	14.63-11.35	16.62-11.55	20.78-13.06	20.31-16.76	15.65-12.02	12.72-10.51
Average Yield %	3.73	3.78	3.86	1.80	1.53	2.72	2.37	5.96

Address: 6300 Wilson Mills Road, Mayfield Village, OH 44143 **Telephone:** 440-461-5000 **Fax:** 440-446-7168	**Web Site:** www.progressive.com **Officers:** Susan Patricia (Tricia) Griffith - President, Chief Executive Officer, Personal Lines Chief Operating Officer, Division Officer John Peter Sauerland - Vice President, Chief Financial Officer, Division Officer	**Auditors:** PricewaterhouseCoopers LLP **Investor Contact:** 440-395-2222 **Transfer Agents:** American Stock Transfer & Trust Company, Brookly, NY

PROLOGIS INC

Exchange	Symbol	Price	52Wk Range	Yield	P/E
NYS	PLD	$89.14 (12/31/2019)	92.40-56.57	2.38	31.50

*7 Year Price Score 123.29 *NYSE Composite Index=100 ***12 Month Price Score 107.01**

Interim Earnings (Per Share)

Qtr.	Mar	Jun	Sep	Dec
2016	0.39	0.52	0.52	0.83
2017	0.38	0.50	1.63	0.55
2018	0.68	0.62	0.60	0.97
2019	0.55	0.60	0.71	...

Interim Dividends (Per Share)

Amt	Decl	Ex	Rec	Pay
0.53Q	02/21/2019	03/14/2019	03/15/2019	03/29/2019
0.53Q	05/01/2019	06/12/2019	06/13/2019	06/28/2019
0.53Q	09/09/2019	09/19/2019	09/20/2019	09/30/2019
0.53Q	12/05/2019	12/18/2019	12/19/2019	12/31/2019

Indicated Div: $2.12

Valuation Analysis — **Institutional Holding**

Forecast EPS	$2.18	No of Institutions	
	(01/17/2020)	59	
Market Cap	$56.3 Billion	Shares	
Book Value	$22.5 Billion	10,207,956	
Price/Book	2.50	% Held	
Price/Sales	17.00	N/A	

Business Summary: REITs (MIC: 5.3.1 SIC: 6798 NAIC: 525930)

Prologis is a self-administered and self-managed real estate investment trust. Co. owns, manages and develops logistics facilities. The majority of Co.'s properties in the U.S. are wholly owned, while Co.'s properties outside the U.S. are generally held in co-investment ventures. Co. has two operating segments: Real Estate Operations, which represents the ownership and development of operating properties, and includes development activities that lead to rental operations, including land held for development and properties under development; and Strategic Capital, which represents the management of unconsolidated co-investment ventures.

Recent Developments: For the quarter ended Sep 30 2019, net income increased 30.8% to US$491.0 million from US$375.5 million in the year-earlier quarter. Revenues were US$942.2 million, up 38.1% from US$682.4 million the year before. Revenues from property income rose 16.7% to US$710.5 million from US$609.0 million in the corresponding quarter a year earlier.

Prospects: Our evaluation of Prologis Inc. as of October 4th, 2019 is the result of our systematic analysis on three basic characteristics: earnings strength, relative valuation, and recent stock price movement. The company has generated a negative trend in earnings per share over the past 5 quarters. However, recent analyst estimates for the company have been mixed and PLD has posted results that fell short of analysts' expectations. Based on operating earnings yield, the company is overvalued when compared to all of the companies we cover. Share price changes over the past year indicates that PLD will perform well over the near term.

Financial Data

(US$ in Thousands)	9 Mos	6 Mos	3 Mos	12/31/2018	12/31/2017	12/31/2016	12/31/2015	12/31/2014
Earnings Per Share	2.83	2.72	2.74	2.87	3.06	2.27	1.64	1.24
Cash Flow Per Share	3.45	3.23	3.10	3.18	3.18	2.69	1.85	1.41
Tang Book Value Per Share	35.53	35.28	35.30	34.59	28.86	27.70	27.82	27.28
Dividends Per Share	2.070	2.020	1.970	1.920	1.760	1.680	1.520	1.320
Dividend Payout %	73.14	74.26	71.90	66.90	57.52	74.01	92.68	106.45
Income Statement								
Total Revenue	2,504,605	1,562,424	772,052	2,804,449	2,618,134	2,533,135	2,197,074	1,760,787
EBITDA	1,279,792	783,414	359,458	2,695,437	2,626,626	2,258,082	1,853,116	1,548,602
Depn & Amortn	(64,515)	(43,506)	(23,750)	892,929	798,870	822,240	787,894	686,145
Income Before Taxes	1,177,310	719,513	330,611	1,588,030	1,567,001	1,140,797	789,343	579,340
Income Taxes	53,230	40,144	13,512	63,330	54,609	54,564	23,090	(25,656)
Net Income	1,185,968	733,822	348,546	1,649,361	1,652,325	1,209,932	869,439	636,183
Average Shares	655,259	655,447	654,359	590,239	552,300	546,666	533,944	506,391
Balance Sheet								
Current Assets	1,024,994	401,190	251,030	556,811	630,036	1,026,999	454,456	548,355
Total Assets	39,448,185	38,706,750	38,392,112	38,417,664	29,481,075	30,249,932	31,394,767	25,818,223
Current Liabilities	808,898	740,941	695,761	1,071,785	979,614	847,034	994,282	895,883
Long-Term Obligations	11,459,223	10,968,320	10,706,139	11,089,815	9,412,631	10,608,294	11,626,831	9,380,199
Total Liabilities	16,930,975	16,375,942	16,057,629	16,119,571	13,849,917	15,258,851	16,726,832	11,842,714
Stockholders' Equity	22,517,210	22,330,808	22,334,483	22,298,093	15,631,158	14,991,081	14,667,935	13,975,509
Shares Outstanding	631,743	631,054	630,743	629,616	532,186	528,671	524,512	509,498
Statistical Record								
Return on Assets %	4.59	4.93	4.79	4.86	5.53	3.91	3.04	2.53
Return on Equity %	8.01	8.85	8.58	8.70	10.79	8.14	6.07	4.60
EBITDA Margin %	51.10	50.14	46.56	96.11	100.32	89.14	84.34	87.95
Net Margin %	47.35	46.97	45.15	58.81	63.11	47.76	39.57	36.13
Asset Turnover	0.09	0.09	0.08	0.08	0.09	0.08	0.08	0.07
Current Ratio	1.27	0.54	0.36	0.52	0.64	1.21	0.46	0.61
Debt to Equity	0.51	0.49	0.48	0.50	0.60	0.71	0.79	0.67
Price Range	86.44-55.94	82.48-55.94	72.38-55.94	68.65-55.94	67.40-48.44	54.61-35.57	47.13-36.45	43.64-36.51
P/E Ratio	30.54-19.77	30.32-20.57	26.42-20.42	23.92-19.49	22.03-15.83	24.06-15.67	28.74-22.23	35.19-29.44
Average Yield %	2.83	2.94	3.00	2.99	3.01	3.52	3.67	3.26

Address: Pier 1, Bay 1, San Francisco, CA 94111
Telephone: 415-394-9000
Fax: 415-394-9001

Web Site: www.prologis.com
Officers: Hamid R. Moghadam - Chairman, Chief Executive Officer, Co-Chief Executive Officer
Deborah K. Briones - Senior Vice President, Associate General Counsel

Auditors: KPMG LLP
Investor Contact: 415-733-9565
Transfer Agents: Computershare Investor Services, Canton, MA

PROSPERITY BANCSHARES INC.

Exchange	Symbol	Price	52Wk Range	Yield	P/E	Div Acheiver
NYS	PB	$71.89 (12/31/2019)	75.27-62.30	2.56	15.17	19 Years

*7 Year Price Score 93.89 *NYSE Composite Index=100 *12 Month Price Score 96.06

Interim Earnings (Per Share)

Qtr.	Mar	Jun	Sep	Dec
2016	0.98	0.98	0.99	0.99
2017	0.99	0.99	0.98	0.97
2018	1.07	1.17	1.18	1.19
2019	1.18	1.18	1.19	...

Interim Dividends (Per Share)

Amt	Decl	Ex	Rec	Pay
0.41Q	01/22/2019	03/14/2019	03/15/2019	04/01/2019
0.41Q	04/16/2019	06/13/2019	06/14/2019	07/01/2019
0.41Q	07/24/2019	09/13/2019	09/16/2019	10/01/2019
0.46Q	10/23/2019	12/13/2019	12/16/2019	01/02/2020

Indicated Div: $1.84

Valuation Analysis — **Institutional Holding**

Forecast EPS	$4.78	No of Institutions
(01/17/2020)		400
Market Cap	$4.9 Billion	Shares
Book Value	$4.1 Billion	73,278,280
Price/Book	1.19	% Held
Price/Sales	5.68	85.05

Business Summary: Banking (MIC: 5.1.1 SIC: 6022 NAIC: 522110)

Prosperity Bancshares is a holding company. Through its subsidiary, Prosperity Bank®, Co. provides financial products and services to small and medium-sized businesses and consumers. Co. is a real estate lender with commercial real estate (including multifamily residential), one-to-four family residential and construction, land development and other land loans. Co. also provides commercial loans, agricultural loans, loans for automobiles and other consumer durables, home equity loans, debit and credit cards, internet banking and other cash management services, mobile banking, trust and wealth management, retail brokerage services, mortgage banking services and automated telephone banking.

Recent Developments: For the quarter ended Sep 30 2019, net income decreased 0.9% to US$81.8 million from US$82.5 million in the year-earlier quarter. Net interest income decreased 2.1% to US$154.0 million from US$157.3 million in the year-earlier quarter. Provision for loan losses was US$1.1 million versus US$2.4 million in the prior-year quarter, a decrease of 53.2%. Non-interest income rose 0.2% to US$30.7 million from US$30.6 million, while non-interest expense declined 1.3% to US$80.7 million.

Prospects: Our evaluation of Prosperity Bancshares Inc. as of October 4th, 2019 is the result of our systematic analysis on three basic characteristics: earnings strength, relative valuation, and recent stock price movement. The company has managed to produce a neutral trend in earnings per share over the past 5 quarters. However, recent analyst estimates for the company have been reduced and PB has posted results in line with analysts' expectations. Based on operating earnings yield, the company is undervalued when compared to all of the companies we cover. Share price changes over the past year indicates that PB will perform poorly over the near term.

Financial Data

(US$ in Thousands)	9 Mos	6 Mos	3 Mos	12/31/2018	12/31/2017	12/31/2016	12/31/2015	12/31/2014
Earnings Per Share	4.74	4.73	4.72	4.61	3.92	3.94	4.09	4.32
Cash Flow Per Share	6.45	5.28	5.39	4.59	5.62	4.79	4.44	5.06
Tang Book Value Per Share	32.12	31.72	31.17	30.34	27.12	24.40	22.06	18.80
Dividends Per Share	1.640	1.590	1.540	1.490	1.380	1.240	1.117	0.993
Dividend Payout %	34.60	33.62	32.63	32.32	35.20	31.47	27.32	22.97
Income Statement								
Interest Income	560,080	373,902	186,115	727,209	677,355	675,779	669,701	714,795
Interest Expense	96,341	64,153	31,204	97,616	60,492	43,159	39,191	43,641
Net Interest Income	463,739	309,749	154,911	629,593	616,863	632,620	630,510	671,154
Provision for Losses	2,600	1,500	700	16,350	14,325	24,000	7,560	18,275
Non-Interest Income	88,775	58,102	28,144	116,012	116,633	118,425	120,781	120,832
Non-Interest Expense	240,091	159,392	78,571	326,220	313,101	318,387	313,536	327,962
Income Before Taxes	309,823	206,959	103,784	403,035	406,070	408,658	430,195	445,749
Income Taxes	63,405	42,299	21,382	81,223	133,905	134,192	143,549	148,308
Net Income	246,418	164,660	82,402	321,812	272,165	274,466	286,646	297,441
Average Shares	68,738	69,806	69,847	69,821	69,484	69,680	70,049	68,911
Balance Sheet								
Net Loans & Leases	10,586,284	10,500,369	10,327,931	10,283,873	9,936,732	9,536,734	9,357,205	9,163,421
Total Assets	22,092,817	22,375,221	22,354,241	22,693,402	22,587,292	22,331,072	22,037,216	21,507,733
Total Deposits	16,929,920	16,887,629	17,197,770	17,256,558	17,821,460	17,307,302	17,681,119	17,693,158
Total Liabilities	17,966,011	18,247,326	18,244,451	18,640,578	18,763,138	18,688,761	18,574,306	18,262,907
Stockholders' Equity	4,126,806	4,127,895	4,109,790	4,052,824	3,824,154	3,642,311	3,462,910	3,244,826
Shares Outstanding	68,396	69,261	69,845	69,846	69,490	69,491	70,021	69,779
Statistical Record								
Return on Assets %	1.48	1.47	1.47	1.42	1.21	1.23	1.32	1.48
Return on Equity %	8.12	8.20	8.26	8.17	7.29	7.70	8.55	9.86
Net Interest Margin %	82.71	82.45	83.23	86.58	91.07	93.61	94.15	93.89
Efficiency Ratio %	37.21	37.12	36.67	38.69	39.43	40.09	39.66	39.25
Loans to Deposits	0.63	0.62	0.60	0.60	0.56	0.55	0.53	0.52
Price Range	75.27-57.46	76.00-57.46	76.05-57.46	78.70-57.46	77.47-56.46	73.20-33.73	59.23-45.79	67.00-53.21
P/E Ratio	15.88-12.12	16.07-12.15	16.11-12.17	17.07-12.46	19.76-14.40	18.58-8.56	14.48-11.20	15.51-12.32
Average Yield %	2.40	2.28	2.18	2.28	2.09	2.06	2.38	2.13	1.65

Address: Prosperity Bank Plaza, 4295 San Felipe, Houston, TX 77027 **Telephone:** 281-269-7199	**Web Site:** www.prosperitybankusa.com **Officers:** H. E. Timanus - Chairman, Vice-Chairman David Zalman - Chairman, Senior Chairman, President, Chief Executive Officer	**Auditors:** DELOITTE & TOUCHE LLP **Investor Contact:** 713-693-9300 **Transfer Agents:** Computershare Investor Services, Golden, Co

PRUDENTIAL FINANCIAL INC

Exchange	Symbol	Price	52Wk Range	Yield	P/E	Div Acheiver
NYS	PRU	$93.74 (12/31/2019)	105.71-78.29	4.27	10.01	10 Years

*7 Year Price Score 86.45 *NYSE Composite Index=100 *12 Month Price Score 94.37

Interim Earnings (Per Share)

Qtr.	Mar	Jun	Sep	Dec
2016	2.93	2.04	4.07	0.69
2017	3.09	1.12	5.09	8.57
2018	3.14	0.46	3.90	1.99
2019	2.22	1.71	3.44	...

Interim Dividends (Per Share)

Amt	Decl	Ex	Rec	Pay
1.00Q	02/06/2019	02/19/2019	02/20/2019	03/14/2019
1.00Q	05/14/2019	05/24/2019	05/28/2019	06/20/2019
1.00Q	08/06/2019	08/19/2019	08/20/2019	09/12/2019
1.00Q	11/11/2019	11/25/2019	11/26/2019	12/12/2019

Indicated Div: $4.00

Valuation Analysis

		Institutional Holding	
Forecast EPS	$11.40	No of Institutions	
	(01/16/2020)	9	
Market Cap	$37.3 Billion	Shares	
Book Value	$65.8 Billion	126,178	
Price/Book	0.57	% Held	
Price/Sales	0.58	60.50	

Business Summary: Life & Health (MIC: 5.2.2 SIC: 6311 NAIC: 524113)

Prudential Financial is a holding company. Through its subsidiaries and affiliates, Co. provides a range of insurance, investment management, and other financial products and services to individual and institutional customers throughout the U.S. and other countries. Co. operates five divisions. The PGIM division consists of the PGIM segment. The U.S. Workplace Solutions division consists of the Retirement and Group Insurance segments. The U.S. Individual Solutions division consists of the Individual Annuities and Individual Life segments. The International Insurance division consists of the International Insurance segment. Corporate and Other operations include the Closed Block division.

Recent Developments: For the quarter ended Sep 30 2019, net income decreased 14.9% to US$1.43 billion from US$1.68 billion in the year-earlier quarter. Revenues were US$15.11 billion, down 6.5% from US$16.15 billion the year before. Net premiums earned were US$6.94 billion versus US$8.81 billion in the prior-year quarter, a decrease of 21.3%. Net investment income rose 9.7% to US$4.44 billion from US$4.05 billion a year ago.

Prospects: Our evaluation of Prudential Financial Inc. as of October 4th, 2019 is the result of our systematic analysis on three basic characteristics: earnings strength, relative valuation, and recent stock price movement. The company has managed to produce a neutral trend in earnings per share over the past 5 quarters. In addition, recent analyst estimates for the company have been mixed and PRU has posted results that fell short of analysts' expectations. Based on operating earnings yield, the company is undervalued when compared to all of the companies we cover. Share price changes over the past year indicates that PRU will perform poorly over the near term.

Financial Data
(US$ in Millions)

	9 Mos	6 Mos	3 Mos	12/31/2018	12/31/2017	12/31/2016	12/31/2015	12/31/2014
Earnings Per Share	9.36	9.82	8.57	9.50	17.86	9.71	12.17	3.23
Cash Flow Per Share	66.90	57.52	54.86	51.88	31.49	33.63	30.76	42.30
Tang Book Value Per Share	165.20	153.01	135.04	118.37	127.96	106.76	93.69	91.84
Dividends Per Share	3.900	3.800	3.700	3.600	3.000	2.800	2.440	2.170
Dividend Payout %	41.67	38.70	43.17	37.89	16.80	28.84	20.05	67.18
Income Statement								
Premium Income	22,972	16,035	7,900	35,779	32,091	30,964	28,521	29,293
Total Revenue	45,584	30,479	15,091	62,992	59,689	58,779	57,119	54,105
Benefits & Claims	25,037	17,315	8,438	39,404	33,794	33,632	30,627	31,587
Income Before Taxes	3,741	2,016	1,140	4,834	6,487	5,705	7,769	1,759
Income Taxes	726	394	232	822	(1,438)	1,335	2,072	349
Net Income	3,058	1,640	932	4,074	7,863	4,368	5,642	1,381
Average Shares	408	413	417	426	436	446	460	467
Balance Sheet								
Total Assets	885,626	873,825	849,324	815,078	831,921	783,962	757,388	766,655
Total Liabilities	819,828	812,165	794,314	766,461	777,852	738,099	715,498	724,885
Stockholders' Equity	65,798	61,660	55,010	48,617	54,069	45,863	41,890	41,770
Shares Outstanding	398	402	407	410	422	429	447	454
Statistical Record								
Return on Assets %	0.46	0.49	0.43	0.49	0.97	0.57	0.74	0.18
Return on Equity %	6.93	7.56	6.82	7.93	15.74	9.93	13.49	3.58
Loss Ratio %	108.99	107.98	106.81	110.13	105.31	108.62	107.38	107.83
Net Margin %	6.71	5.38	6.18	6.47	13.17	7.43	9.88	2.55
Price Range	105.99-76.83	105.99-76.83	107.62-76.83	126.02-76.83	117.15-98.65	107.10-58.00	91.68-74.22	93.16-77.61
P/E Ratio	11.32-8.21	10.79-7.82	12.56-8.96	13.27-8.09	6.56-5.52	11.03-5.97	7.53-6.10	28.84-24.03
Average Yield %	4.16	3.97	3.85	3.56	2.77	3.53	2.93	2.51

Address: 751 Broad Street, Newark, NJ 07102 **Telephone:** 973-802-6000	**Web Site:** www.investor.prudential.com **Officers:** Charles F. Lowrey - Executive Vice President, Division Officer, Executive Vice President (frmr), Co-Chief Operating Officer, Region Officer, Chairman, President, Chief Executive Officer Mark B. Grier - Vice-Chairman	**Auditors:** PricewaterhouseCoopers LLP **Transfer Agents:** Computershare Trust Company, N.A., Providence, RI

PS BUSINESS PARKS INC

Exchange	Symbol	Price	52Wk Range	Yield	P/E
NYS	PSB	$24.79 (12/31/2019)	25.18-24.52	16.94	6.03

*7 Year Price Score N/A *NYSE Composite Index=100 *12 Month Price Score N/A

TRADING VOLUME (thousand shares)

2010 2011 2012 2013 2014 2015 2016 2017 2018 2019

Interim Earnings (Per Share)

Qtr.	Mar	Jun	Sep	Dec
2016	0.54	0.58	0.72	0.47
2017	0.97	0.90	0.66	0.77
2018	1.69	2.56	0.92	1.15
2019	0.96	1.04	0.96	...

Interim Dividends (Per Share)

Amt	Decl	Ex	Rec	Pay
1.05Q	02/20/2019	03/12/2019	03/13/2019	03/28/2019
1.05Q	04/23/2019	06/11/2019	06/12/2019	06/27/2019
1.05Q	07/23/2019	09/11/2019	09/12/2019	09/27/2019
1.05Q	10/22/2019	12/12/2019	12/13/2019	12/30/2019

Indicated Div: $4.20

Valuation Analysis / Institutional Holding

Forecast EPS	N/A	No of Institutions 334
Market Cap	$680.1 Million	Shares
Book Value	$1.8 Billion	25,477,388
Price/Book	0.39	% Held
Price/Sales	1.59	70.95

Business Summary: REITs (MIC: 5.3.1 SIC: 6798 NAIC: 525930)

PS Business Parks is a self-advised and self-managed real estate investment trust that owns, operates, acquires and develops commercial properties, primarily multi-tenant industrial, flex and office space. Substantially all of Co.'s assets are held, and its business conducted, through PS Business Parks, L.P. Co. owns and operates commercial space, comprising business parks, in California, Texas, Virginia, Florida, Maryland and Washington. Co. owns flex space, representing industrial buildings that are configured with a combination of warehouse and office space and can be designed to fit a variety of uses.

Recent Developments: For the quarter ended Sep 30 2019, net income increased 3.7% to US$46.5 million from US$44.8 million in the year-earlier quarter. Revenues were US$108.1 million, up 4.1% from US$103.8 million the year before.

Prospects: Our evaluation of PS Business Parks Inc. as of October 4th, 2019 is the result of our systematic analysis on three basic characteristics: earnings strength, relative valuation, and recent stock price movement. The company has enjoyed a very positive trend in earnings per share over the past 5 quarters. However, recent analyst estimates for the company have been mixed and PSB has posted results that fell short of analysts' expectations. Based on operating earnings yield, the company is overvalued when compared to all of the companies we cover. Share price changes over the past year indicates that PSB will perform very well over the near term.

Financial Data

(US$ in Thousands)	9 Mos	6 Mos	3 Mos	12/31/2018	12/31/2017	12/31/2016	12/31/2015	12/31/2014
Earnings Per Share	4.11	4.07	5.59	6.31	3.30	2.31	2.52	4.19
Cash Flow Per Share	10.69	10.41	10.12	10.11	9.98	9.22	8.83	8.47
Tang Book Value Per Share	29.15	29.21	29.19	29.44	26.92	27.03	27.39	26.68
Dividends Per Share	4.200	4.200	4.000	3.800	3.400	3.000	2.200	4.750
Dividend Payout %	102.19	103.19	71.56	60.22	103.03	129.87	87.30	113.37
Income Statement								
Total Revenue	323,671	215,607	107,825	413,516	402,179	387,389	373,675	376,915
EBITDA	140,586	95,123	46,260	370,835	275,209	249,419	267,104	328,278
Depn & Amortn	410	272	136	99,779	94,745	99,486	105,394	110,357
Income Before Taxes	142,458	95,948	46,575	271,901	180,121	144,984	148,970	204,700
Net Income	120,788	81,298	39,548	226,702	155,037	128,029	130,475	173,971
Average Shares	27,543	27,532	27,479	27,422	27,412	27,179	27,051	27,000
Balance Sheet								
Current Assets	44,049	78,926	76,737	70,687	146,944	158,399	217,239	178,517
Total Assets	2,117,734	2,057,544	2,056,619	2,068,594	2,100,159	2,119,371	2,186,658	2,227,114
Current Liabilities	...	...	...	...	130,000	230,000	...	...
Long-Term Obligations	50,000	...	...	...	...	...	250,000	250,000
Total Liabilities	358,175	296,694	296,581	303,232	406,848	506,112	526,162	513,833
Stockholders' Equity	1,759,559	1,760,850	1,760,038	1,765,362	1,693,311	1,613,259	1,660,496	1,713,281
Shares Outstanding	27,435	27,429	27,417	27,362	27,254	27,138	27,034	26,919
Statistical Record								
Return on Assets %	7.92	7.96	10.18	10.88	7.35	5.93	5.91	7.79
Return on Equity %	9.41	9.33	11.89	13.11	9.38	7.80	7.73	10.14
EBITDA Margin %	43.43	44.12	42.90	89.68	68.43	64.38	71.48	87.10
Net Margin %	37.32	37.71	36.68	54.82	38.55	33.05	34.92	46.16
Asset Turnover	0.20	0.21	0.21	0.20	0.19	0.18	0.17	0.17
Current Ratio	...	...	...	...	1.13	0.69	...	...
Debt to Equity	0.03	...	...	...	...	...	0.15	0.15

Address: 701 Western Avenue, Glendale, CA 91201-2349 **Telephone:** 818-244-8080 **Fax:** 818-242-0566	**Web Site:** www.psbusinessparks.com **Officers:** Ronald L. Havner - Chairman Maria R. Hawthorne - President, Chief Executive Officer, Executive Vice President, Chief Administrative Officer	**Auditors:** Ernst & Young LLP **Transfer Agents:** American Stock Transfer & Trust Company, Brooklyn, NY

PUBLIC SERVICE ENTERPRISE GROUP INC

Exchange	Symbol	Price	52Wk Range	Yield	P/E
NYS	PEG	$59.05 (12/31/2019)	63.31-50.75	3.18	20.65

*7 Year Price Score 109.06 ***NYSE Composite Index=100** ***12 Month Price Score 95.99**

Interim Earnings (Per Share)

Qtr.	Mar	Jun	Sep	Dec
2016	0.93	0.37	0.64	(0.19)
2017	0.23	0.22	0.78	1.88
2018	1.10	0.53	0.81	0.39
2019	1.38	0.30	0.79	...

Interim Dividends (Per Share)

Amt	Decl	Ex	Rec	Pay
0.47Q	02/19/2019	03/07/2019	03/08/2019	03/29/2019
0.47Q	04/16/2019	06/06/2019	06/07/2019	06/28/2019
0.47Q	07/16/2019	09/06/2019	09/09/2019	09/30/2019
0.47Q	11/19/2019	12/09/2019	12/10/2019	12/31/2019

Indicated Div: $1.88

Valuation Analysis

		Institutional Holding	
Forecast EPS	$3.24	No of Institutions	
	(01/17/2020)	1170	
Market Cap	$29.8 Billion	Shares	
Book Value	$14.9 Billion	429,112,512	
Price/Book	1.99	% Held	
Price/Sales	2.96	69.42	

Business Summary: Electric Utilities (MIC: 3.1.1 SIC: 4911 NAIC: 221119)

Public Service Enterprise Group is a holding company. Through its subsidiaries, Co. is engaged in the energy industry. Co. conducts its business through two subsidiaries, Public Service Electric and Gas Company (PSE&G) and PSEG Power LLC (Power). PSE&G is a public utility, which is engaged in the transmission of electricity and distribution of electricity and natural gas in certain areas of New Jersey, and Power is a multi-regional energy supply company that integrates the operations of its merchant nuclear and fossil generating assets with its power marketing businesses and fuel supply functions through energy sales in energy markets primarily in the Northeast and Mid-Atlantic U.S.

Recent Developments: For the quarter ended Sep 30 2019, net income decreased 2.2% to US$403.0 million from US$412.0 million in the year-earlier quarter. Revenues were US$2.30 billion, down 3.8% from US$2.39 billion the year before. Operating income was US$490.0 million versus US$554.0 million in the prior-year quarter, a decrease of 11.6%. Direct operating expenses declined 3.1% to US$1.50 billion from US$1.55 billion in the comparable period the year before. Indirect operating expenses increased 6.8% to US$314.0 million from US$294.0 million in the equivalent prior-year period.

Prospects: Our evaluation of Public Service Enterprise Group Inc. as of October 4th, 2019 is the result of our systematic analysis on three basic characteristics: earnings strength, relative valuation, and recent stock price movement. The company has managed to produce a neutral trend in earnings per share over the past 5 quarters. In addition, recent analyst estimates for the company have been mixed and PEG has posted results that fell short of analysts' expectations. Based on operating earnings yield, the company is fairly valued when compared to all of the companies we cover. Share price changes over the past year indicates that PEG will perform well over the near term.

Financial Data

(US$ in Thousands)	9 Mos	6 Mos	3 Mos	12/31/2018	12/31/2017	12/31/2016	12/31/2015	12/31/2014
Earnings Per Share	2.86	2.88	3.11	2.83	3.10	1.75	3.30	2.99
Cash Flow Per Share	6.21	6.16	5.93	5.78	6.46	6.54	7.76	6.25
Tang Book Value Per Share	29.21	28.92	29.05	28.21	27.16	25.78	25.63	23.89
Dividends Per Share	1.860	1.840	1.820	1.800	1.720	1.640	1.560	1.480
Dividend Payout %	65.03	63.89	58.52	63.60	55.48	93.71	47.27	49.50
Income Statement								
Total Revenue	7,598,000	5,296,000	2,980,000	9,696,000	9,084,000	9,061,000	10,415,000	10,886,000
EBITDA	1,959,000	1,269,000	996,000	3,404,000	3,408,000	2,945,000	4,114,000	3,816,000
Depn & Amortn	137,000	89,000	47,000	1,158,000	1,986,000	1,476,000	1,214,000	1,227,000
Income Before Taxes	1,405,000	975,000	847,000	1,840,000	1,254,000	1,202,000	2,668,000	2,443,000
Income Taxes	159,000	129,000	149,000	417,000	(306,000)	326,000	1,001,000	938,000
Net Income	1,256,000	853,000	700,000	1,438,000	1,574,000	887,000	1,679,000	1,518,000
Average Shares	507,000	507,000	507,000	507,000	507,000	508,000	508,000	508,000
Balance Sheet								
Current Assets	3,059,000	3,156,000	3,027,000	3,507,000	3,312,000	3,254,000	3,494,000	4,119,000
Total Assets	46,815,000	46,280,000	45,756,000	45,326,000	42,716,000	40,070,000	37,535,000	35,333,000
Current Liabilities	4,067,000	3,982,000	4,473,000	4,935,000	4,168,000	3,276,000	3,575,000	3,478,000
Long-Term Obligations	14,448,000	14,301,000	13,216,000	13,168,000	12,068,000	10,895,000	8,834,000	8,261,000
Total Liabilities	31,890,000	31,526,000	30,942,000	30,949,000	28,869,000	26,940,000	24,469,000	23,148,000
Stockholders' Equity	14,925,000	14,754,000	14,814,000	14,377,000	13,847,000	13,130,000	13,066,000	12,185,000
Shares Outstanding	504,000	504,000	504,000	504,000	505,000	504,866	505,282	505,836
Statistical Record								
Return on Assets %	3.17	3.25	3.57	3.27	3.80	2.28	4.61	4.47
Return on Equity %	9.94	10.13	10.93	10.19	11.67	6.75	13.30	12.76
EBITDA Margin %	25.78	23.96	33.42	35.11	37.52	32.50	39.50	35.05
Net Margin %	16.53	16.11	23.49	14.83	17.33	9.79	16.12	13.94
Asset Turnover	0.22	0.23	0.22	0.22	0.22	0.23	0.29	0.32
Current Ratio	0.75	0.79	0.68	0.71	0.79	0.99	0.98	1.18
Debt to Equity	0.97	0.97	0.89	0.92	0.87	0.83	0.68	0.68
Price Range	62.26-49.89	61.38-49.89	59.92-49.38	56.37-46.38	53.07-41.85	47.32-38.42	44.30-37.02	43.53-31.33
P/E Ratio	21.77-17.44	21.31-17.32	19.27-15.88	19.92-16.39	17.12-13.50	27.04-21.95	13.42-11.22	14.56-10.48
Average Yield %	3.25	3.32	3.32	3.48	3.74	3.78	4.24	3.93

Address: 80 Park Plaza, Newark, NJ 07102	**Web Site:** www.pseg.com	**Auditors:** DELOITTE & TOUCHE LLP
	Officers: Ralph Izzo - Chairman, President, Chief Executive Officer Kim C. Hanemann - President, Chief Operating Officer	**Investor Contact:** 973-430-6565
Telephone: 973-430-7000		**Transfer Agents:** Wells Fargo Bank, N.A., Mendota Heights, MN

PULTEGROUP INC

Exchange	Symbol	Price	52Wk Range	Yield	P/E
NYS	PHM	$38.80 (12/31/2019)	41.03-25.80	1.24	11.83

*7 Year Price Score 115.26 *NYSE Composite Index=100 *12 Month Price Score 113.80

Interim Earnings (Per Share)

Qtr.	Mar	Jun	Sep	Dec
2016	0.24	0.34	0.37	0.81
2017	0.28	0.32	0.58	0.26
2018	0.59	1.12	1.01	0.84
2019	0.59	0.86	0.99	...

Interim Dividends (Per Share)

Amt	Decl	Ex	Rec	Pay
0.11Q	02/06/2019	03/14/2019	03/15/2019	04/03/2019
0.11Q	05/09/2019	06/13/2019	06/14/2019	07/03/2019
0.11Q	09/05/2019	09/17/2019	09/18/2019	10/03/2019
0.12Q	12/05/2019	12/17/2019	12/18/2019	01/03/2020

Indicated Div: $0.48

Valuation Analysis

		Institutional Holding	
Forecast EPS	$3.55	No of Institutions	838
	(01/17/2020)		
Market Cap	$10.5 Billion	Shares	
Book Value	$5.2 Billion	Shares	292,233,824
Price/Book	2.03	% Held	
Price/Sales	1.03		79.28

Business Summary: Builders (MIC: 2.2.5 SIC: 1531 NAIC: 236117)

PulteGroup throughg its subsidiaries is engaged in the homebuilding business. Co. also has mortgage banking operations, conducted principally through its susidiary, Pulte Mortgage LLC, and title and insurance brokerage operations. Co. provides a range of product line to meet the needs of homebuyers in its targeted markets. Through its brands, which include Centex, Pulte Homes, Del Webb, DiVosta Homes, and John Wieland Homes and Neighborhoods, Co. provides a range of home designs, including single-family detached, townhouses, condominiums, and duplexes at different prices and with varying levels of options and amenities to its customer groups: first-time, move-up, and active adult.

Recent Developments: For the quarter ended Sep 30 2019, net income decreased 5.7% to US$273.1 million from US$289.5 million in the year-earlier quarter. Revenues were US$2.71 billion, up 2.3% from US$2.65 billion the year before. Direct operating expenses rose 3.0% to US$2.07 billion from US$2.01 billion in the comparable period the year before. Indirect operating expenses increased 7.6% to US$275.7 million from US$256.2 million in the equivalent prior-year period.

Prospects: Our evaluation of Pultegroup Inc. as of October 4th, 2019 is the result of our systematic analysis on three basic characteristics: earnings strength, relative valuation, and recent stock price movement. The company has managed to produce a neutral trend in earnings per share over the past 5 quarters. Additionally, recent analyst estimates for the company have been unchanged while PHM has posted results that exceeded analysts' expectations. Based on operating earnings yield, the company is undervalued when compared to all of the companies we cover. Share price changes over the past year indicates that PHM will perform well over the near term.

Financial Data

(US$ in Thousands)	9 Mos	6 Mos	3 Mos	12/31/2018	12/31/2017	12/31/2016	12/31/2015	12/31/2014
Earnings Per Share	3.28	3.30	3.56	3.55	1.44	1.75	1.36	1.26
Cash Flow Per Share	3.73	4.37	5.19	5.11	2.17	0.20	(0.98)	0.83
Tang Book Value Per Share	18.65	17.96	17.35	16.93	13.99	14.12	13.32	12.67
Dividends Per Share	0.440	0.420	0.400	0.380	0.360	0.360	0.330	0.230
Dividend Payout %	13.41	12.73	11.24	10.70	25.00	20.57	24.26	18.25
Income Statement								
Total Revenue	7,196,044	4,485,679	1,996,693	10,188,331	8,573,250	7,668,476	5,981,964	5,822,363
EBITDA	901,311	535,184	215,311	1,387,275	989,779	976,963	852,549	717,400
Depn & Amortn	10,600	7,000	3,450	49,400	51,000	54,000	46,200	39,833
Income Before Taxes	903,248	537,314	216,666	1,344,850	940,813	925,513	808,668	681,350
Income Taxes	222,723	129,681	49,946	325,517	491,607	331,147	321,933	215,420
Net Income	680,902	407,798	166,757	1,022,023	447,221	602,703	494,090	474,338
Average Shares	273,632	277,584	278,640	284,865	306,814	342,123	359,793	374,102
Balance Sheet								
Current Assets	8,598,703	8,461,766	8,587,496	8,481,992	7,528,646	7,534,903	6,332,065	5,854,026
Total Assets	10,264,513	10,095,537	10,207,336	10,172,976	9,686,649	10,178,200	8,967,160	8,569,410
Current Liabilities	762,139	742,760	756,978	749,908	854,848	745,133	652,636	547,715
Long-Term Obligations	2,993,541	2,974,511	3,246,552	3,376,478	3,444,771	3,460,919	2,387,982	1,981,057
Total Liabilities	5,082,921	5,025,730	5,273,897	5,355,194	5,532,623	5,518,837	4,207,835	3,764,456
Stockholders' Equity	5,181,592	5,069,807	4,933,439	4,817,782	4,154,026	4,659,363	4,759,325	4,804,954
Shares Outstanding	270,971	274,975	277,256	277,109	286,752	319,089	349,148	369,458
Statistical Record								
Return on Assets %	9.04	9.39	10.22	10.29	4.50	6.28	5.63	5.48
Return on Equity %	18.54	19.49	22.11	22.78	10.15	12.76	10.33	10.03
EBITDA Margin %	12.53	11.93	10.78	13.62	11.54	12.74	14.25	12.32
Net Margin %	9.46	9.09	8.35	10.03	5.22	7.86	8.26	8.15
Asset Turnover	1.00	1.02	1.03	1.03	0.86	0.80	0.68	0.67
Current Ratio	11.28	11.39	11.34	11.31	8.81	10.11	9.70	10.69
Debt to Equity	0.58	0.59	0.66	0.70	0.83	0.74	0.50	0.41
Price Range	36.55-20.88	32.90-20.88	32.98-20.88	35.15-20.88	34.44-18.46	22.11-15.36	23.24-17.18	21.72-16.66
P/E Ratio	11.14-6.37	9.97-6.33	9.26-5.87	9.90-5.88	23.92-12.82	12.63-8.78	17.09-12.63	17.24-13.22
Average Yield %	1.51	1.51	1.45	1.33	1.42	1.91	1.63	1.18

Address: 3350 Peachtree Road N.E., Suite 150, Atlanta, GA 30326 **Telephone:** 404-978-6400	**Web Site:** www.pultegroupinc.com **Officers:** Ryan R. Marshall - President, Region Officer, Chief Executive Officer Robert T. O'Shaughnessy - Executive Vice President, Chief Financial Officer	**Auditors:** Ernst & Young LLP **Investor Contact:** 248-433-4502 **Transfer Agents:** Computershare Trust Company N.A., Providence, RI

PURE STORAGE INC

Exchange	Symbol	Price	52Wk Range	Yield	P/E
NYS	PSTG	$17.11 (12/31/2019)	23.38-13.01	N/A	N/A

*7 Year Price Score N/A   *NYSE Composite Index=100   *12 Month Price Score 91.93

Interim Earnings (Per Share)

Qtr.	Apr	Jul	Oct	Jan
2016-17	(0.34)	(0.31)	(0.40)	(0.21)
2017-18	(0.30)	(0.29)	(0.20)	(0.05)
2018-19	(0.29)	(0.26)	(0.12)	(0.11)
2019-20	(0.41)	(0.26)	(0.12)	...

Interim Dividends (Per Share)

No Dividends Paid

Valuation Analysis

		Institutional Holding	
Forecast EPS	$0.25	No of Institutions	
	(00/22/2020)	316	
Market Cap	$4.4 Billion	Shares	
Book Value	$777.9 Million	249,597,824	
Price/Book	5.72	% Held	
Price/Sales	2.83	95.25	

Business Summary: Internet & Software (MIC: 6.3.2 SIC: 3572 NAIC: 334112)

Pure Storage is engaged in developing data platform. Co.'s data platform replaces storage systems designed for mechanical disk with all-flash systems for solid-state memory. Co.'s Pure1 cloud-based support and management platform simplifies storage administration, while real-time scanning enables it to find and fix issues. Co.'s business model replaces the forklift upgrade cycle with an Evergreen Storage subscription model. Co.'s offerings include its FlashArray and FlashBlade products, inclusive of its Purity Operating Environment software, FlashStack and Artificial Intelligence Ready Infrastructure (AIRI), Cloud Data Services, FlashArray//X, and AIRI Mini.

Recent Developments: For the quarter ended Oct 31 2019, net loss amounted to US$30.0 million versus a net loss of US$28.2 million in the year-earlier quarter. Revenues were US$428.4 million, up 14.9% from US$372.8 million the year before. Operating loss was US$28.3 million versus a loss of US$27.2 million in the prior-year quarter. Direct operating expenses rose 3.3% to US$127.8 million from US$123.7 million in the comparable period the year before. Indirect operating expenses increased 19.0% to US$328.9 million from US$276.3 million in the equivalent prior-year period.

Prospects: Our evaluation of Pure Storage Inc as of October 4th, 2019 is the result of our systematic analysis on three basic characteristics: earnings strength, relative valuation, and recent stock price movement. The company has enjoyed a very positive trend in earnings per share over the past 5 quarters. However, recent analyst estimates for the company have been mixed and PSTG has posted results that exceeded analysts' expectations. Based on operating earnings yield, the company is overvalued when compared to all of the companies we cover. Share price changes over the past year indicates that PSTG will perform very poorly over the near term.

Financial Data

(US$ in Thousands)	9 Mos	6 Mos	3 Mos	01/31/2019	01/31/2018	01/31/2017	01/31/2016	01/31/2015
Earnings Per Share	(0.90)	(0.90)	(0.90)	(0.77)	(0.84)	(1.26)	(2.59)	(6.56)
Cash Flow Per Share	0.79	0.77	0.62	0.71	0.34	(0.07)	(0.10)	(5.15)
Tang Book Value Per Share	2.62	2.49	2.57	2.90	2.23	2.31	2.92	6.47
Income Statement								
Total Revenue	1,151,436	723,027	326,700	1,359,824	1,023,019	727,977	440,333	174,451
EBITDA	(112,562)	(111,765)	(72,950)	(108,973)	(113,513)	(194,379)	(181,183)	(167,294)
Depn & Amortn	80,486	52,990	26,290	68,300	60,200	48,800	31,000	14,600
Income Before Taxes	(193,048)	(164,797)	(99,240)	(177,273)	(173,713)	(243,179)	(212,183)	(181,894)
Income Taxes	3,288	1,557	1,096	1,089	3,889	1,887	1,569	1,337
Net Income	(196,336)	(166,354)	(100,336)	(178,362)	(177,602)	(245,066)	(213,752)	(183,231)
Average Shares	255,047	251,298	245,334	232,042	211,609	194,714	82,460	27,925
Balance Sheet								
Current Assets	1,722,180	1,649,945	1,607,031	1,701,827	944,833	780,081	788,070	293,970
Total Assets	2,192,779	2,115,974	2,069,189	1,973,025	1,079,407	899,745	870,783	361,819
Current Liabilities	520,295	514,553	479,960	509,816	380,844	273,125	184,532	75,437
Long-Term Obligations	470,014	463,118	456,318	449,828	...	...	...	...
Total Liabilities	1,414,829	1,378,435	1,325,213	1,235,245	581,501	421,315	307,429	117,709
Stockholders' Equity	777,950	737,539	743,976	737,780	497,906	478,430	563,354	244,110
Shares Outstanding	259,920	255,752	252,853	243,523	220,979	204,364	190,509	36,465
Statistical Record								
Asset Turnover	0.79	0.81	0.78	0.89	1.03	0.82	0.71	0.64
Current Ratio	3.31	3.21	3.35	3.34	2.48	2.86	4.27	3.90
Debt to Equity	0.60	0.63	0.61	0.61	...	...	...	...
Price Range	23.38-13.01	28.66-14.80	28.66-14.80	28.66-14.80	20.37-9.40	15.71-9.77	19.74-12.91	...

Address: 650 Castro Street, Suite 400, Mountain View, CA 94041 Telephone: 800-379-7873	Web Site: www.purestorage.com Officers: Scott Dietzen - Chairman, Chief Executive Officer David M. Hatfield - President	Auditors: Deloitte & Touche LLP Investor Contact: 800-379-7873 Transfer Agents: American Stock Transfer & Trust Company, LLC, Brooklyn, NY

PVH CORP

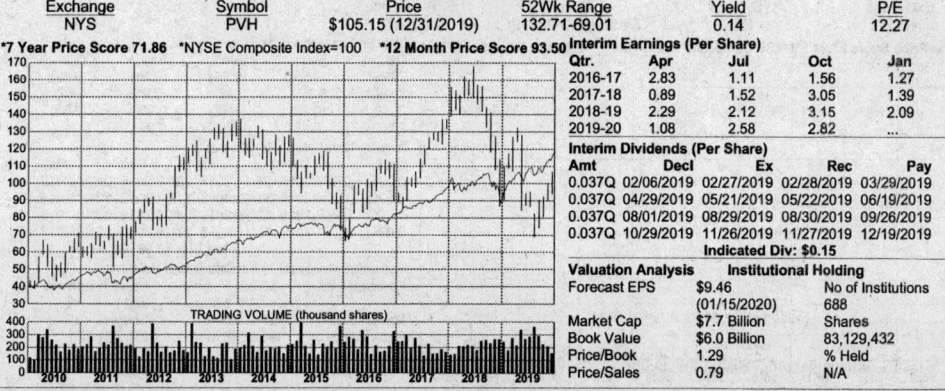

Exchange	Symbol	Price	52Wk Range	Yield	P/E
NYS	PVH	$105.15 (12/31/2019)	132.71-69.01	0.14	12.27

*7 Year Price Score 71.86 *NYSE Composite Index=100 *12 Month Price Score 93.50

Interim Earnings (Per Share)

Qtr.	Apr	Jul	Oct	Jan
2016-17	2.83	1.11	1.56	1.27
2017-18	0.89	1.52	3.05	1.39
2018-19	2.29	2.12	3.15	2.09
2019-20	1.08	2.58	2.82	...

Interim Dividends (Per Share)

Amt	Decl	Ex	Rec	Pay
0.037Q	02/06/2019	02/27/2019	02/28/2019	03/29/2019
0.037Q	04/29/2019	05/21/2019	05/22/2019	06/19/2019
0.037Q	08/01/2019	08/29/2019	08/30/2019	09/26/2019
0.037Q	10/29/2019	11/26/2019	11/27/2019	12/19/2019

Indicated Div: $0.15

Valuation Analysis

		Institutional Holding	
Forecast EPS	$9.46 (01/15/2020)	No of Institutions	688
Market Cap	$7.7 Billion	Shares	
Book Value	$6.0 Billion		83,129,432
Price/Book	1.29	% Held	
Price/Sales	0.79		N/A

Business Summary: Apparel, Footwear & Accessories (MIC: 1.4.2 SIC: 2321 NAIC: 315211)

PVH is a branded apparel company. Co. designs and markets branded dress shirts, neckwear, sportswear, jeanswear, performance apparel, intimate apparel, underwear, swimwear, swim products, handbags, accessories, footwear and other related products. Co. also licenses the use of its trademarks to third parties and joint ventures. Co.'s businesses include: Tommy Hilfiger, which consists of the Tommy Hilfiger North America and Tommy Hilfiger International segments; Calvin Klein, which consists of the Calvin Klein North America and Calvin Klein International segments; and Heritage Brands, which consists of the Heritage Brands Wholesale and Heritage Brands Retail segments.

Recent Developments: For the quarter ended Nov 3 2019, net income decreased 13.9% to US$208.9 million from US$242.6 million in the year-earlier quarter. Revenues were US$2.59 billion, up 2.5% from US$2.52 billion the year before. Direct operating expenses rose 1.9% to US$1.18 billion from US$1.16 billion in the comparable period the year before. Indirect operating expenses increased 4.7% to US$1.14 billion from US$1.09 billion in the equivalent prior-year period.

Prospects: Our evaluation of PVH Corp. as of October 4th, 2019 is the result of our systematic analysis on three basic characteristics: earnings strength, relative valuation, and recent stock price movement. The company has managed to produce a neutral trend in earnings per share over the past 5 quarters. However, recent analyst estimates for the company have been reduced while PVH has posted results that exceeded analysts' expectations. Based on operating earnings yield, the company is undervalued when compared to all of the companies we cover. Share price changes over the past year indicates that PVH will perform very poorly over the near term.

Financial Data
(US$ in Thousands)

	9 Mos	6 Mos	3 Mos	02/03/2019	02/04/2018	01/29/2017	01/31/2016	02/01/2015
Earnings Per Share	8.57	8.90	8.44	9.65	6.84	6.79	6.89	5.27
Cash Flow Per Share	13.25	11.49	12.03	11.17	8.87	11.94	10.95	9.60
Dividends Per Share	0.150	0.150	0.150	0.150	0.150	0.150	0.150	0.150
Dividend Payout %	1.75	1.69	1.78	1.55	2.19	2.21	2.18	2.85
Income Statement								
Total Revenue	7,308,200	4,720,500	2,356,300	9,656,800	8,914,800	8,203,100	8,020,300	8,241,200
EBITDA	883,400	535,200	207,900	1,134,300	874,500	1,017,500	954,700	713,800
Depn & Amortn	236,500	154,900	76,500	263,900	252,200	228,400	210,800	193,800
Income Before Taxes	562,200	323,400	101,500	754,300	500,100	674,100	630,900	381,500
Income Taxes	86,100	53,300	23,600	31,000	(25,900)	125,500	75,100	(47,500)
Net Income	484,700	275,500	82,000	746,400	537,800	549,000	572,400	439,000
Average Shares	74,200	75,100	75,900	77,300	78,600	80,900	83,100	83,300
Balance Sheet								
Current Assets	3,582,100	3,398,600	3,253,400	3,238,600	3,030,800	2,879,600	2,812,600	2,901,200
Total Assets	14,019,200	13,820,900	13,355,000	11,863,700	11,885,700	11,067,900	10,696,400	10,931,800
Current Liabilities	2,552,700	2,427,700	2,206,600	1,893,900	1,871,600	1,564,800	1,527,200	1,428,600
Long-Term Obligations	2,738,400	2,743,000	2,759,400	2,819,400	3,061,300	3,197,300	3,054,300	3,438,700
Total Liabilities	8,034,100	7,949,200	7,593,500	6,035,900	6,349,300	6,263,400	6,144,100	6,567,500
Stockholders' Equity	5,985,100	5,871,700	5,761,500	5,827,800	5,536,400	4,804,500	4,552,300	4,364,300
Shares Outstanding	73,302	74,451	75,115	75,403	77,178	78,551	81,487	82,512
Statistical Record								
Return on Assets %	4.98	5.31	5.18	6.30	4.61	5.06	5.31	3.91
Return on Equity %	11.03	11.84	11.46	13.17	10.23	11.77	12.87	10.12
EBITDA Margin %	12.09	11.34	8.82	11.75	9.81	12.40	11.90	8.66
Net Margin %	6.63	5.84	3.48	7.73	6.03	6.69	7.14	5.33
Asset Turnover	0.76	0.76	0.77	0.82	0.76	0.76	0.74	0.73
Current Ratio	1.40	1.40	1.47	1.71	1.62	1.84	1.84	2.03
Debt to Equity	0.46	0.47	0.48	0.48	0.55	0.67	0.67	0.79
Price Range	132.71-69.01	156.67-80.50	168.16-86.83	168.16-86.83	156.25-85.48	114.00-70.46	118.98-66.41	133.66-107.87
P/E Ratio	15.49-8.05	17.60-9.04	19.92-10.29	17.43-9.00	22.84-12.50	16.79-10.38	17.27-9.64	25.36-20.47
Average Yield %	0.15	0.13	0.12	0.11	0.13	0.15	0.15	0.12

Address: 200 Madison Avenue, New York, NY 10016	**Web Site:** www.pvh.com	**Auditors:** Ernst & Young LLP
Telephone: 212-381-3500	**Officers:** Emanuel (Manny) Chirico - Chairman, Chief Executive Officer Stefan Larsson - President	**Investor Contact:** 212-381-3500
		Transfer Agents: Wells Fargo Bank, N.A., St. Paul, MN

QEP RESOURCES INC

Exchange	Symbol	Price	52Wk Range	Yield	P/E
NYS	QEP	$4.50 (12/31/2019)	9.00-2.71	1.78	N/A

*7 Year Price Score 27.91   *NYSE Composite Index=100   **12 Month Price Score 59.07

Interim Earnings (Per Share)

Qtr.	Mar	Jun	Sep	Dec
2016	(4.55)	(0.90)	(0.21)	(0.47)
2017	0.32	0.19	(0.01)	0.63
2018	(0.22)	(1.42)	0.03	(2.65)
2019	(0.49)	0.20	0.34	...

Interim Dividends (Per Share)

Amt	Decl	Ex	Rec	Pay
0.02Q	07/27/2015	08/14/2015	08/18/2015	09/04/2015
0.02Q	10/26/2015	11/13/2015	11/17/2015	12/07/2015
0.02Q	08/07/2019	08/19/2019	08/20/2019	09/10/2019
0.02Q	10/21/2019	11/14/2019	11/15/2019	12/06/2019

Indicated Div: $0.08

Valuation Analysis

		Institutional Holding	
Forecast EPS	$0.23	No of Institutions	
	(00/25/2020)	380	
Market Cap	$1.1 Billion	Shares	
Book Value	$2.8 Billion	292,481,600	
Price/Book	0.39	% Held	
Price/Sales	0.83	106.93	

Business Summary: Production & Extraction (MIC: 9.1.1 SIC: 1311 NAIC: 211111)

QEP Resources is an independent crude oil and natural gas exploration and production company with operations in two regions of the U.S.: the Southern Region (primarily in Texas) and the Northern Region (primarily in North Dakota). Co. has an inventory of developed and identified undeveloped drilling locations in the Permian Basin in western Texas and the Williston Basin in North Dakota. Co. sells oil and condensate and natural gas liquids volumes to refiners, marketers, midstream service providers and other companies. In addition, Co. sells gas volumes to wholesale marketers, industrial users, local distribution companies, midstream service providers and utility companies.

Recent Developments: For the quarter ended Sep 30 2019, net income increased to US$81.0 million from US$7.3 million in the year-earlier quarter. Revenues were US$307.5 million, down 45.2% from US$560.8 million the year before. Operating income was US$52.1 million versus US$156.8 million in the prior-year quarter, a decrease of 66.8%. Direct operating expenses declined 46.2% to US$79.5 million from US$147.9 million in the comparable period the year before. Indirect operating expenses decreased 31.3% to US$175.9 million from US$256.1 million in the equivalent prior-year period.

Prospects: Our evaluation of QEP Resources Inc. as of October 4th, 2019 is the result of our systematic analysis on three basic characteristics: earnings strength, relative valuation, and recent stock price movement. The company has suffered a very negative trend in earnings per share over the past 5 quarters. In addition, recent analyst estimates for the company have been reduced and QEP has posted results that fell short of analysts' expectations. Based on operating earnings yield, the company is undervalued when compared to all of the companies we cover. Share price changes over the past year indicates that QEP will perform over the near term.

Financial Data

(US$ in Thousands)	9 Mos	6 Mos	3 Mos	12/31/2018	12/31/2017	12/31/2016	12/31/2015	12/31/2014
Earnings Per Share	(2.60)	(2.91)	(4.53)	(4.25)	1.12	(5.62)	(0.85)	4.36
Cash Flow Per Share	2.03	2.67	3.10	3.43	2.49	2.99	2.73	8.58
Tang Book Value Per Share	11.65	11.30	11.07	11.62	15.76	14.62	22.33	23.23
Dividends Per Share	0.020	...	...	...	...	...	0.080	0.080
Dividend Payout %	...	...	...	...	...	...	...	1.83
Income Statement								
Total Revenue	884,300	576,800	280,600	1,932,600	1,622,900	1,377,100	2,018,600	3,414,300
EBITDA	56,800	(84,000)	(196,200)	(307,500)	854,000	(958,100)	786,900	561,300
Depn & Amortn	4,000	2,700	1,300	862,500	760,700	877,500	887,300	1,047,300
Income Before Taxes	(42,600)	(150,200)	(228,700)	(1,329,000)	(42,900)	(1,953,200)	(243,000)	(642,300)
Income Taxes	(55,700)	(82,300)	(112,000)	(317,400)	(312,200)	(708,200)	(93,600)	(232,500)
Net Income	13,100	(67,900)	(116,700)	(1,011,600)	269,300	(1,245,000)	(149,400)	784,400
Average Shares	237,900	238,000	237,100	237,900	240,600	221,700	176,600	179,800
Balance Sheet								
Current Assets	350,100	271,400	246,400	280,600	165,400	640,100	931,800	2,001,500
Total Assets	5,570,600	5,504,300	5,470,200	6,117,800	7,394,800	7,245,400	8,425,500	9,286,800
Current Liabilities	335,200	376,500	419,300	334,300	577,300	514,800	641,600	1,344,800
Long-Term Obligations	2,029,400	2,028,100	2,026,700	2,507,100	2,160,800	2,020,900	2,042,000	2,218,100
Total Liabilities	2,800,600	2,815,000	2,834,100	3,366,900	3,596,900	3,742,700	4,477,600	5,211,500
Stockholders' Equity	2,770,000	2,689,300	2,636,100	2,750,900	3,797,900	3,502,700	3,947,900	4,075,300
Shares Outstanding	237,800	237,912	238,100	236,700	241,000	239,600	176,800	175,400
Statistical Record								
Return on Assets %	N.M.	N.M.	N.M.	N.M.	3.68	N.M.	N.M.	8.41
Return on Equity %	N.M.	N.M.	N.M.	N.M.	7.38	N.M.	N.M.	21.05
EBITDA Margin %	6.42	N.M.	N.M.	N.M.	52.62	N.M.	38.98	16.44
Net Margin %	1.48	N.M.	N.M.	N.M.	16.59	N.M.	N.M.	22.97
Asset Turnover	0.20	0.24	0.27	0.29	0.22	0.18	0.23	0.37
Current Ratio	1.04	0.72	0.59	0.84	0.29	1.24	1.45	1.49
Debt to Equity	0.73	0.75	0.77	0.91	0.57	0.58	0.52	0.54
Price Range	11.87-3.51	13.37-5.11	13.56-5.11	13.56-5.11	19.23-7.09	20.45-9.29	23.76-11.31	35.57-18.64
P/E Ratio	...	...	...	...	17.17-6.33	...	...	8.16-4.28
Average Yield %	0.28	...	...	...	...	...	0.46	0.27

Address: 1050 17th Street, Suite 800, Denver, CO 80265	**Web Site:** www.qepres.com	**Auditors:** PricewaterhouseCoopers LLP
Telephone: 303-672-6900	**Officers:** David A. Trice - Chairman Timothy J. Cutt - President, Chief Executive Officer	**Investor Contact:** 303-405-6665
		Transfer Agents: Wells Fargo Shareowner Services, Saint Paul, MN

QUAKER CHEMICAL CORP.

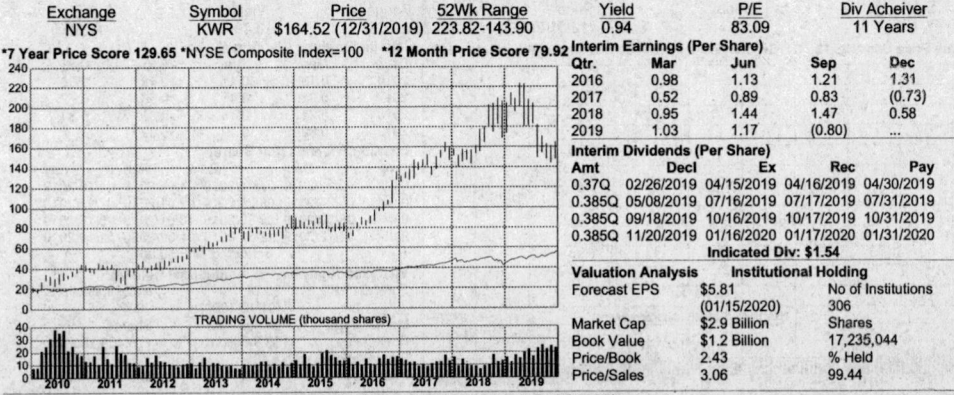

Exchange	Symbol	Price	52Wk Range	Yield	P/E	Div Acheiver
NYS	KWR	$164.52 (12/31/2019)	223.82-143.90	0.94	83.09	11 Years

*7 Year Price Score 129.65 ***NYSE Composite Index=100** ***12 Month Price Score 79.92**

Interim Earnings (Per Share)

Qtr.	Mar	Jun	Sep	Dec
2016	0.98	1.13	1.21	1.31
2017	0.52	0.89	0.83	(0.73)
2018	0.95	1.44	1.47	0.58
2019	1.03	1.17	(0.80)	...

Interim Dividends (Per Share)

Amt	Decl	Ex	Rec	Pay
0.37Q	02/26/2019	04/15/2019	04/16/2019	04/30/2019
0.385Q	05/08/2019	07/16/2019	07/17/2019	07/31/2019
0.385Q	09/18/2019	10/16/2019	10/17/2019	10/31/2019
0.385Q	11/20/2019	01/16/2020	01/17/2020	01/31/2020

Indicated Div: $1.54

Valuation Analysis / **Institutional Holding**

Forecast EPS	$5.81	No of Institutions
	(01/15/2020)	306
Market Cap	$2.9 Billion	Shares
Book Value	$1.2 Billion	17,235,044
Price/Book	2.43	% Held
Price/Sales	3.06	99.44

Business Summary: Specialty Chemicals (MIC: 8.3.2 SIC: 2999 NAIC: 324199)

Quaker Chemical develops, produces, and markets a range of formulated chemical specialty products and provides chemical management services for various heavy industrial and manufacturing applications in a global portfolio throughout its four regions: the North America region, the Europe, Middle East and Africa region, the Asia/Pacific and the South America region. Co.'s products and services include: rolling lubricants, machining and grinding compounds, corrosion preventives, hydraulic fluids, specialty greases, metal finishing compounds, forming compounds, chemical milling maskants, coatings for metal and concrete products, construction products, bio-lubricants and die casting lubricants.

Recent Developments: For the quarter ended Sep 30 2019, net loss amounted to US$13.0 million versus net income of US$19.8 million in the year-earlier quarter. Revenues were US$325.1 million, up 46.4% from US$222.0 million the year before. Operating loss was US$14.5 million versus an income of US$24.9 million in the prior-year quarter. Direct operating expenses rose 56.2% to US$220.1 million from US$140.9 million in the comparable period the year before. Indirect operating expenses increased 112.8% to US$119.6 million from US$56.2 million in the equivalent prior-year period.

Prospects: Our evaluation of Quaker Chemical Corp. as of October 4th, 2019 is the result of our systematic analysis on three basic characteristics: earnings strength, relative valuation, and recent stock price movement. The company has managed to produce a neutral trend in earnings per share over the past 5 quarters. However, recent analyst estimates for the company have been raised and KWR has posted results that fell short of analysts' expectations. Based on operating earnings yield, the company is fairly valued when compared to all of the companies we cover. Share price changes over the past year indicates that KWR will perform well over the near term.

Financial Data

(US$ in Thousands)	9 Mos	6 Mos	3 Mos	12/31/2018	12/31/2017	12/31/2016	12/31/2015	12/31/2014
Earnings Per Share	1.98	4.25	4.52	4.45	1.52	4.63	3.84	4.26
Cash Flow Per Share	3.91	6.12	5.72	5.94	4.90	5.60	5.56	4.17
Tang Book Value Per Share	N.M.	23.49	22.53	21.60	18.79	18.74	16.60	15.72
Dividends Per Share	1.495	1.480	1.465	1.450	1.400	1.330	1.240	1.100
Dividend Payout %	75.51	34.82	32.41	32.58	92.11	28.73	32.29	25.82
Income Statement								
Total Revenue	742,209	417,079	211,210	867,520	820,082	746,665	737,555	765,860
EBITDA	26,261	49,470	24,053	106,676	81,871	104,302	90,198	94,521
Depn & Amortn	792	9,702	4,859	19,537	19,845	19,441	19,007	16,398
Income Before Taxes	17,858	38,259	18,418	83,098	60,668	84,009	70,230	78,293
Income Taxes	4,096	9,729	4,929	25,050	41,653	23,226	17,785	23,539
Net Income	16,382	29,435	13,844	59,473	20,278	61,403	51,180	56,492
Average Shares	16,185	13,352	13,338	13,304	13,245	13,160	13,214	13,148
Balance Sheet								
Current Assets	724,562	412,179	391,313	418,510	406,586	376,468	365,853	351,518
Total Assets	2,724,496	724,530	708,523	709,665	722,126	692,028	685,513	665,526
Current Liabilities	345,760	153,188	147,508	151,470	154,743	127,411	124,555	124,901
Long-Term Obligations	826,503	11,788	11,720	35,934	61,068	65,769	81,439	75,328
Total Liabilities	1,522,478	268,023	263,532	274,613	314,454	289,268	312,468	308,051
Stockholders' Equity	1,202,018	456,507	444,991	435,052	407,672	402,760	373,045	357,475
Shares Outstanding	17,730	13,337	13,333	13,338	13,307	13,277	13,288	13,300
Statistical Record								
Return on Assets %	1.40	7.86	8.34	8.31	2.87	8.89	7.58	9.04
Return on Equity %	2.96	12.97	13.98	14.11	5.00	15.79	14.01	16.29
EBITDA Margin %	3.54	11.86	11.39	12.30	9.98	13.97	12.23	12.34
Net Margin %	2.21	7.06	6.55	6.86	2.47	8.22	6.94	7.38
Asset Turnover	0.55	1.17	1.19	1.21	1.16	1.08	1.09	1.23
Current Ratio	2.10	2.69	2.65	2.76	2.63	2.95	2.94	2.81
Debt to Equity	0.69	0.03	0.03	0.08	0.15	0.16	0.22	0.21
Price Range	223.82-149.49	223.82-155.37	214.18-143.52	208.99-140.74	164.78-125.48	135.85-69.57	93.16-75.74	92.67-66.71
P/E Ratio	113.04-75.50	52.66-36.56	47.38-31.75	46.96-31.63	108.41-82.55	29.34-15.03	24.26-19.72	21.75-15.66
Average Yield %	0.78	0.77	0.82	0.86	0.98	1.40	1.49	1.44

Address: One Quaker Park, 901 E. Hector Street, Conshohocken, PA 19428-2380 Telephone: 610-832-4000 Fax: 610-832-8682	Web Site: www.quakerchem.com Officers: Michael F. Barry - Chairman, President, Chief Executive Officer, Interim Chief Financial Officer Robert T. Traub - Senior Vice President, Vice President, General Counsel, Corporate Secretary	Auditors: PricewaterhouseCoopers LLP Transfer Agents: American Stock Transfer & Trust Company, LLC, Brooklyn, NY

QUANTA SERVICES, INC.

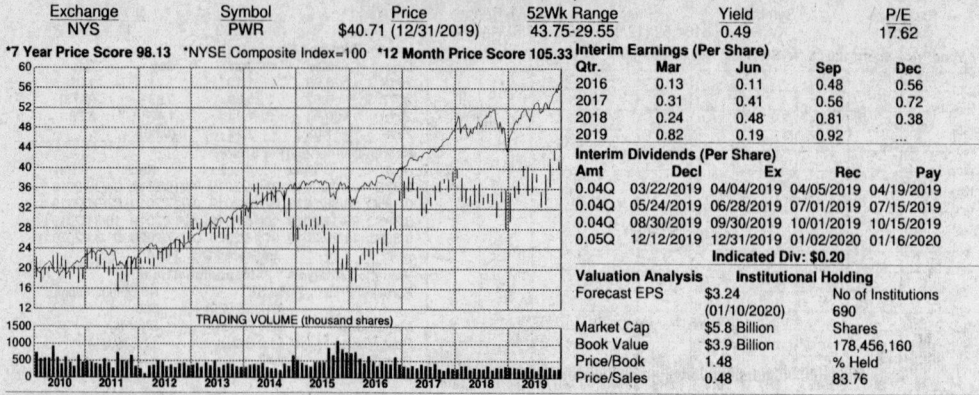

Exchange	Symbol	Price	52Wk Range	Yield	P/E
NYS	PWR	$40.71 (12/31/2019)	43.75-29.55	0.49	17.62

*7 Year Price Score 98.13 *NYSE Composite Index=100 *12 Month Price Score 105.33

Interim Earnings (Per Share)

Qtr.	Mar	Jun	Sep	Dec
2016	0.13	0.11	0.48	0.56
2017	0.31	0.41	0.56	0.72
2018	0.24	0.48	0.81	0.38
2019	0.82	0.19	0.92	...

Interim Dividends (Per Share)

Amt	Decl	Ex	Rec	Pay
0.04Q	03/22/2019	04/04/2019	04/05/2019	04/19/2019
0.04Q	05/24/2019	06/28/2019	07/01/2019	07/15/2019
0.04Q	08/30/2019	09/30/2019	10/01/2019	10/15/2019
0.05Q	12/12/2019	12/31/2019	01/02/2020	01/16/2020

Indicated Div: $0.20

Valuation Analysis

		Institutional Holding	
Forecast EPS	$3.24	No of Institutions	
	(01/10/2020)	690	
Market Cap	$5.8 Billion	Shares	
Book Value	$3.9 Billion	178,456,160	
Price/Book	1.48	% Held	
Price/Sales	0.48	83.76	

Business Summary: Construction Services (MIC: 7.5.4 SIC: 1731 NAIC: 238210)

Quanta Services is a provider of contracting services, delivering infrastructure solutions for the electric power, energy and communications industries in the U.S., Canada, Australia, Latin America and select other international markets. The services Co. provides include the design, installation, upgrade, repair and maintenance of infrastructure within each of the industries it serves, such as electric power transmission and distribution networks; substation facilities; and pipeline transmission and distribution systems and facilities, among others. Co. has two reportable segments: Electric Power Infrastructure Services; and Pipeline and Industrial Infrastructure Services.

Recent Developments: For the quarter ended Sep 30 2019, net income increased 9.7% to US$137.0 million from US$124.9 million in the year-earlier quarter. Revenues were US$3.35 billion, up 12.3% from US$2.99 billion the year before. Operating income was US$209.4 million versus US$192.6 million in the prior-year quarter, an increase of 8.7%. Direct operating expenses rose 12.5% to US$2.88 billion from US$2.56 billion in the comparable period the year before. Indirect operating expenses increased 13.2% to US$264.1 million from US$233.3 million in the equivalent prior-year period.

Prospects: Our evaluation of Quanta Services Inc. as of October 4th, 2019 is the result of our systematic analysis on three basic characteristics: earnings strength, relative valuation, and recent stock price movement. The company has generated a negative trend in earnings per share over the past 5 quarters. However, recent analyst estimates for the company have been raised and PWR has posted results that fell short of analysts' expectations. Based on operating earnings yield, the company is undervalued when compared to all of the companies we cover. Share price changes over the past year indicates that PWR will perform in line with the market over the near term.

Financial Data

(US$ in Thousands)	9 Mos	6 Mos	3 Mos	12/31/2018	12/31/2017	12/31/2016	12/31/2015	12/31/2014
Earnings Per Share	2.31	2.20	2.49	1.90	2.00	1.26	1.59	1.35
Cash Flow Per Share	0.25	(0.10)	1.72	2.35	2.39	2.42	3.17	1.41
Tang Book Value Per Share	10.35	11.10	10.70	10.06	10.79	10.24	8.31	10.65
Dividends Per Share	0.160	0.120	0.040	0.040	...	...	...	...
Dividend Payout %	6.93	5.45	1.61	2.11	...	...	...	...
Income Statement								
Total Revenue	8,999,353	5,646,458	2,807,259	11,171,423	9,466,478	7,651,319	7,572,436	7,851,250
EBITDA	677,073	395,670	243,740	739,556	589,876	523,014	433,320	668,480
Depn & Amortn	203,415	132,123	65,294	246,500	216,005	201,885	197,648	194,007
Income Before Taxes	426,354	234,426	164,879	457,666	353,757	308,665	229,141	473,449
Income Taxes	139,838	84,932	43,844	161,659	35,532	107,246	97,472	157,408
Net Income	283,900	147,832	120,488	293,346	314,978	198,383	310,907	296,714
Average Shares	147,438	147,241	146,458	154,226	157,155	157,288	195,120	219,690
Balance Sheet								
Current Assets	4,301,927	3,751,932	3,554,544	3,326,104	2,869,907	2,288,745	2,277,519	2,553,976
Total Assets	8,865,093	8,021,817	7,652,516	7,075,787	6,480,154	5,354,059	5,213,543	6,312,024
Current Liabilities	2,357,523	1,906,233	1,778,737	1,806,127	1,492,067	1,205,228	1,203,744	1,137,325
Long-Term Obligations	1,810,480	1,517,272	1,344,999	1,040,532	670,721	353,562	475,364	72,489
Total Liabilities	4,957,687	4,246,894	3,928,772	3,471,628	2,688,583	2,014,632	2,128,049	1,797,551
Stockholders' Equity	3,907,406	3,774,923	3,723,744	3,604,159	3,791,571	3,339,427	3,085,494	4,514,473
Shares Outstanding	142,273	142,166	142,081	141,590	153,828	151,226	159,783	218,145
Statistical Record								
Return on Assets %	4.24	4.44	5.26	4.33	5.32	3.74	5.40	4.90
Return on Equity %	8.82	8.82	10.21	7.93	8.83	6.16	8.18	6.78
EBITDA Margin %	7.52	7.01	8.68	6.62	6.23	6.84	5.72	8.51
Net Margin %	3.15	2.62	4.29	2.63	3.33	2.59	4.11	3.78
Asset Turnover	1.51	1.59	1.62	1.65	1.60	1.44	1.31	1.30
Current Ratio	1.82	1.97	2.00	1.84	1.92	1.90	1.89	2.25
Debt to Equity	0.46	0.40	0.36	0.29	0.18	0.11	0.15	0.02
Price Range	40.60-27.93	40.60-27.93	37.74-27.93	39.86-27.93	39.50-30.66	35.67-17.29	30.41-18.74	37.20-25.53
P/E Ratio	17.58-12.09	18.45-12.70	15.16-11.22	20.98-14.70	19.75-15.33	28.31-13.72	19.13-11.79	27.56-18.91
Average Yield %	0.45	0.34	0.12	0.12	...	...	...	...

Address: 2800 Post Oak Boulevard, Suite 2600, Houston, TX 77056 **Telephone:** 713-629-7600	**Web Site:** www.quantaservices.com **Officers:** David M. McClanahan - Chairman Earl C. (Duke) Austin - President, Chief Executive Officer, Chief Operating Officer, Division Officer	**Auditors:** PricewaterhouseCoopers LLP **Investor Contact:** 713-341-7260 **Transfer Agents:** American Stock Transfer & Trust Company, New York, NY

QUEST DIAGNOSTICS, INC.

Exchange	Symbol	Price	52Wk Range	Yield	P/E
NYS	DGX	$106.79 (12/31/2019)	107.99-80.68	1.99	20.00

*7 Year Price Score 98.95   *NYSE Composite Index=100   *12 Month Price Score 102.47

Interim Earnings (Per Share)

Qtr.	Mar	Jun	Sep	Dec
2016	0.70	1.37	1.34	1.09
2017	1.16	1.37	1.15	1.82
2018	1.27	1.57	1.53	0.92
2019	1.20	1.66	1.56	...

Interim Dividends (Per Share)

Amt	Decl	Ex	Rec	Pay
0.53Q	03/01/2019	04/05/2019	04/08/2019	04/22/2019
0.53Q	05/14/2019	07/05/2019	07/08/2019	07/22/2019
0.53Q	08/14/2019	10/03/2019	10/04/2019	10/21/2019
0.53Q	11/20/2019	01/13/2020	01/14/2020	01/29/2020

Indicated Div: $2.12

Valuation Analysis   **Institutional Holding**

Forecast EPS	$6.50	No of Institutions
	(01/16/2020)	1001
Market Cap	$14.4 Billion	Shares
Book Value	$5.6 Billion	165,552,240
Price/Book	2.57	% Held
Price/Sales	1.89	87.21

Business Summary: Diagnostic & Health Related Services (MIC: 4.2.2 SIC: 8071 NAIC: 621511)

Quest Diagnostics is a provider of diagnostic information services. Co. is comprised of two businesses: Diagnostic Information Services and Diagnostic Solutions. Co.'s Diagnostic Information Services business develops and delivers diagnostic testing information and services, providing insights that empower and enable a range of customers, including patients, clinicians, hospitals, IDNs, health plans, employers and accountable care organizations. Co.'s Diagnostic Solutions group includes its risk assessment services business, which provides solutions for insurers, and its healthcare information technology businesses, which provides solutions for healthcare providers.

Recent Developments: For the quarter ended Sep 30 2019, income from continuing operations decreased 0.4% to US$226.0 million from US$227.0 million in the year-earlier quarter. Net income decreased 0.4% to US$226.0 million from US$227.0 million in the year-earlier quarter. Revenues were US$1.96 billion, up 3.5% from US$1.89 billion the year before. Operating income was US$313.0 million versus US$304.0 million in the prior-year quarter, an increase of 3.0%. Direct operating expenses rose 3.4% to US$1.26 billion from US$1.22 billion in the comparable period the year before. Indirect operating expenses increased 4.4% to US$379.0 million from US$363.0 million in the equivalent prior-year period.

Prospects: Our evaluation of Quest Diagnostics Inc. as of October 4th, 2019 is the result of our systematic analysis on three basic characteristics: earnings strength, relative valuation, and recent stock price movement. The company has produced a positive trend in earnings per share over the past 5 quarters. However, recent analyst estimates for the company have been mixed and DGX has posted results that exceeded analysts' expectations. Based on operating earnings yield, the company is undervalued when compared to all of the companies we cover. Share price changes over the past year indicates that DGX will perform in line with the market over the near term.

Financial Data

(US$ in Thousands)	9 Mos	6 Mos	3 Mos	12/31/2018	12/31/2017	12/31/2016	12/31/2015	12/31/2014
Earnings Per Share	5.34	5.31	5.22	5.29	5.50	4.51	4.87	3.81
Cash Flow Per Share	8.81	9.58	9.66	8.82	8.58	7.61	5.63	6.47
Dividends Per Share	2.090	2.060	2.030	1.950	1.800	1.580	1.470	1.290
Dividend Payout %	39.14	38.79	38.89	36.86	32.73	35.03	30.18	33.86
Income Statement								
Total Revenue	5,800,000	3,844,000	1,891,000	7,531,000	7,709,000	7,515,000	7,493,000	7,435,000
EBITDA	1,128,000	732,000	341,000	1,183,000	1,255,000	1,301,000	1,337,000	1,081,000
Depn & Amortn	247,000	165,000	84,000	90,000	74,000	72,000	81,000	94,000
Income Before Taxes	748,000	478,000	213,000	926,000	1,030,000	1,086,000	1,103,000	823,000
Income Taxes	175,000	113,000	50,000	182,000	241,000	429,000	373,000	262,000
Net Income	605,000	390,000	164,000	736,000	772,000	645,000	709,000	556,000
Average Shares	137,000	136,000	136,000	139,000	140,000	142,000	145,000	145,000
Balance Sheet								
Current Assets	1,779,000	1,566,000	1,778,000	1,390,000	1,306,000	1,531,000	1,501,000	1,603,000
Total Assets	12,019,000	11,760,000	11,937,000	11,003,000	10,503,000	10,100,000	9,962,000	9,877,000
Current Liabilities	2,011,000	1,904,000	2,282,000	1,485,000	1,057,000	981,000	1,173,000	1,709,000
Long-Term Obligations	3,188,000	3,169,000	3,131,000	3,429,000	3,748,000	3,728,000	3,492,000	3,244,000
Total Liabilities	6,414,000	6,301,000	6,647,000	5,787,000	5,582,000	5,472,000	5,278,000	5,576,000
Stockholders' Equity	5,605,000	5,459,000	5,290,000	5,216,000	4,921,000	4,628,000	4,684,000	4,301,000
Shares Outstanding	135,000	135,000	134,000	135,000	135,000	137,000	143,000	144,000
Statistical Record								
Return on Assets %	6.36	6.49	6.39	6.84	7.49	6.41	7.15	5.91
Return on Equity %	13.40	13.67	14.01	14.52	16.17	13.82	15.78	13.48
EBITDA Margin %	19.45	19.04	18.03	15.71	16.28	17.31	17.84	14.54
Net Margin %	10.43	10.15	8.67	9.77	10.01	8.58	9.46	7.48
Asset Turnover	0.66	0.67	0.67	0.70	0.75	0.75	0.76	0.79
Current Ratio	0.88	0.82	0.78	0.94	1.24	1.56	1.28	0.94
Debt to Equity	0.57	0.58	0.59	0.66	0.76	0.81	0.75	0.75
Price Range	108.38-79.75	114.99-79.75	114.99-79.75	114.99-79.75	111.16-90.54	92.60-60.54	79.60-60.51	68.10-50.80
P/E Ratio	20.30-14.93	21.66-15.02	22.03-15.28	21.74-15.08	20.21-16.46	20.53-13.42	16.34-12.43	17.87-13.33
Average Yield %	2.20	2.13	2.06	1.90	1.79	2.01	2.08	2.18

Address: 500 Plaza Drive, Secaucus, NJ 07094	Web Site: www.QuestDiagnostics.com	Auditors: PricewaterhouseCoopers LLP
Telephone: 973-520-2700	Officers: Stephen H. Ruscowski - Chairman, President, Chief Executive Officer Stephen H. Ruscowski - Chairman, President, Chief Executive Officer	Investor Contact: 973-520-2900
		Transfer Agents: Computershare, Providence, RI

RALPH LAUREN CORP

Exchange	Symbol	Price	52Wk Range	Yield	P/E
NYS	RL	$117.22 (12/31/2019)	132.09-83.63	2.35	20.53

*7 Year Price Score 72.45 *NYSE Composite Index=100 *12 Month Price Score 93.93

TRADING VOLUME (thousand shares)

Interim Earnings (Per Share)

Qtr.	Jun	Sep	Dec	Mar
2016-17	(0.27)	0.55	0.98	(2.45)
2017-18	0.72	1.75	(1.00)	0.50
2018-19	1.31	2.07	1.48	0.42
2019-20	1.47	2.34	...	...

Interim Dividends (Per Share)

Amt	Decl	Ex	Rec	Pay
0.625Q	03/15/2019	03/28/2019	03/29/2019	04/12/2019
0.688Q	05/14/2019	06/27/2019	06/28/2019	07/12/2019
0.688Q	09/13/2019	09/26/2019	09/27/2019	10/11/2019
0.688Q	12/13/2019	12/26/2019	12/27/2019	01/10/2020

Indicated Div: $2.75

Valuation Analysis   Institutional Holding

Forecast EPS	$7.74	No of Institutions
(01/16/2020)		671
Market Cap	$8.7 Billion	Shares
Book Value	$2.9 Billion	67,342,400
Price/Book	3.00	% Held
Price/Sales	1.37	N/A

Business Summary: Apparel, Footwear & Accessories (MIC: 1.4.2 SIC: 2329 NAIC: 315211)

Ralph Lauren designs, markets, and distributes lifestyle products, including apparel, accessories, home furnishings, and other licensed product categories. Co.'s brand names include Ralph Lauren, Ralph Lauren Collection, Ralph Lauren Purple Label, Polo Ralph Lauren, Double RL, Lauren Ralph Lauren, Polo Ralph Lauren Children, Chaps, and Club Monaco, among others. Co. sells directly to customers via its retail stores, concession-based shop-within-shops, and through its own digital commerce sites; while its international licensing partners operated Ralph Lauren stores, Ralph Lauren concession shops, and Club Monaco stores and shops. Co. has three segments: North America ; Europe; and Asia.

Recent Developments: For the quarter ended Sep 28 2019, net income increased 6.9% to US$182.1 million from US$170.3 million in the year-earlier quarter. Revenues were US$1.71 billion, up 0.9% from US$1.69 billion the year before. Operating income was US$233.1 million versus US$210.0 million in the prior-year quarter, an increase of 11.0%. Direct operating expenses declined 0.7% to US$657.2 million from US$661.6 million in the comparable period the year before. Indirect operating expenses decreased 0.4% to US$815.9 million from US$819.3 million in the equivalent prior-year period.

Prospects: Our evaluation of Ralph Lauren Corp. as of October 4th, 2019 is the result of our systematic analysis on three basic characteristics: earnings strength, relative valuation, and recent stock price movement. The company has managed to produce a neutral trend in earnings per share over the past 5 quarters. In addition, recent analyst estimates for the company have been mixed and RL has posted results that exceeded analysts' expectations. Based on operating earnings yield, the company is undervalued when compared to all of the companies we cover. Share price changes over the past year indicates that RL will perform poorly over the near term.

Financial Data

(US$ in Thousands)	6 Mos	3 Mos	03/30/2019	03/31/2018	04/01/2017	04/02/2016	03/28/2015	03/29/2014
Earnings Per Share	5.71	5.44	5.27	1.97	(1.20)	4.62	7.88	8.43
Cash Flow Per Share	10.10	9.60	9.75	11.97	11.55	11.63	10.16	10.03
Tang Book Value Per Share	24.77	24.99	28.22	28.52	26.85	31.15	31.53	31.24
Dividends Per Share	2.625	2.563	2.500	2.000	2.000	2.000	1.850	1.700
Dividend Payout %	45.97	47.10	47.44	101.52	...	43.29	23.48	20.17
Income Statement								
Total Revenue	3,135,000	1,428,800	6,313,000	6,182,300	6,652,800	7,405,000	7,620,000	7,450,000
EBITDA	491,600	199,500	843,700	790,300	(69,600)	602,000	1,034,000	1,157,000
Depn & Amortn	121,000	60,300	281,300	295,200	24,100	24,000	25,000	35,000
Income Before Taxes	383,200	146,600	582,500	489,200	(99,700)	563,000	998,000	1,105,000
Income Taxes	84,000	29,500	151,600	326,400	(5,600)	156,000	285,000	320,000
Net Income	299,200	117,100	430,900	162,800	(99,300)	396,000	702,000	776,000
Average Shares	77,900	79,900	81,700	82,500	82,700	85,900	89,100	92,000
Balance Sheet								
Current Assets	3,386,700	3,654,100	3,594,800	3,548,400	2,954,500	3,053,000	3,324,000	3,329,000
Total Assets	7,228,500	7,343,700	5,942,800	6,143,300	5,652,000	6,213,000	6,106,000	6,090,000
Current Liabilities	1,736,000	1,591,000	1,200,100	1,587,200	1,159,900	1,198,000	1,186,000	970,000
Long-Term Obligations	592,200	891,500	901,700	524,400	839,100	863,000	536,000	555,000
Total Liabilities	4,314,900	4,330,900	2,655,600	2,685,900	2,352,400	2,469,000	2,215,000	2,056,000
Stockholders' Equity	2,913,600	3,012,800	3,287,200	3,457,400	3,299,600	3,744,000	3,891,000	4,034,000
Shares Outstanding	74,600	77,200	78,100	81,300	81,000	82,900	86,300	88,700
Statistical Record								
Return on Assets %	6.74	6.56	7.15	2.77	N.M.	6.33	11.54	13.52
Return on Equity %	14.14	13.65	12.81	4.83	N.M.	10.21	17.76	19.90
EBITDA Margin %	15.68	13.96	13.36	12.78	N.M.	8.13	13.57	15.53
Net Margin %	9.54	8.20	6.83	2.63	N.M.	5.35	9.21	10.42
Asset Turnover	0.95	0.95	1.05	1.05	1.12	1.18	1.25	1.30
Current Ratio	1.95	2.30	3.00	2.24	2.55	2.55	2.80	3.43
Debt to Equity	0.20	0.30	0.27	0.15	0.25	0.23	0.14	0.14
Price Range	137.55-83.63	139.41-96.20	142.90-96.20	118.87-66.11	113.68-75.98	140.26-83.18	186.73-127.66	189.56-148.71
P/E Ratio	24.09-14.65	25.63-17.68	27.12-18.25	60.34-33.56	...	30.36-18.00	23.70-16.20	22.49-17.64
Average Yield %	2.30	2.09	2.03	2.24	2.12	1.70	1.15	1.00

Address: 650 Madison Avenue, New York, NY 10022
Telephone: 212-318-7000

Web Site: www.RalphLauren.com
Officers: Ralph Lauren - Executive Chairman, Chairman, Chief Executive Officer, Chief Creative Officer David R. Lauren - Vice-Chairman, Chief Innovation Officer, Executive Vice President

Auditors: Ernst & Young LLP
Transfer Agents: The Bank of New York Mellon, Jersey City, NJ

RANGE RESOURCES CORP

Exchange	Symbol	Price	52Wk Range	Yield	P/E
NYS	RRC	$4.85 (12/31/2019)	11.87-3.33	1.65	N/A

*7 Year Price Score 14.51 *NYSE Composite Index=100 *12 Month Price Score 55.28

Interim Earnings (Per Share)

Qtr.	Mar	Jun	Sep	Dec
2016	(0.55)	(1.35)	(0.23)	(0.66)
2017	0.69	0.28	(0.52)	0.89
2018	0.20	(0.32)	0.19	(7.17)
2019	0.01	0.46	(0.11)	...

Interim Dividends (Per Share)

Amt	Decl	Ex	Rec	Pay
0.02Q	03/01/2019	03/14/2019	03/15/2019	03/29/2019
0.02Q	05/31/2019	06/13/2019	06/14/2019	06/28/2019
0.02Q	08/30/2019	09/12/2019	09/13/2019	09/30/2019
0.02Q	12/02/2019	12/12/2019	12/13/2019	12/30/2019

Indicated Div: $0.08

Valuation Analysis

		Institutional Holding	
Forecast EPS	$0.33 (01/17/2020)	No of Institutions	604
Market Cap	$1.2 Billion	Shares	
Book Value	$4.2 Billion	330,965,888	
Price/Book	0.29	% Held	
Price/Sales	0.37	111.60	

Business Summary: Production & Extraction (MIC: 9.1.1 SIC: 1311 NAIC: 211111)

Range Resources is a holding company. Through its subsidiaries, Co. is an independent natural gas, natural gas liquids and oil company, engaged in the exploration, development and acquisition of natural gas and oil properties. Co.'s principal areas of operation are the Marcellus Shale in Pennsylvania and the Lower Cotton Valley formation in North Louisiana. Co.'s reserves are primarily in the Marcellus Shale formation but also include the Utica, Upper Devonian and Medina formations.

Recent Developments: For the quarter ended Sep 30 2019, net loss amounted to US$27.6 million versus net income of US$48.5 million in the year-earlier quarter. Revenues were US$622.4 million, down 23.3% from US$811.2 million the year before. Direct operating expenses declined 9.1% to US$418.9 million from US$461.0 million in the comparable period the year before. Indirect operating expenses increased 0.3% to US$278.3 million from US$277.6 million in the equivalent prior-year period.

Prospects: Our evaluation of Range Resources Corp. as of October 4th, 2019 is the result of our systematic analysis on three basic characteristics: earnings strength, relative valuation, and recent stock price movement. The company has suffered a very negative trend in earnings per share over the past 5 quarters. In addition, recent analyst estimates for the company have been reduced while RRC has posted results that exceeded analysts' expectations. Based on operating earnings yield, the company is undervalued when compared to all of the companies we cover. Share price changes over the past year indicates that RRC will perform poorly over the near term.

Financial Data

(US$ in Thousands)	9 Mos	6 Mos	3 Mos	12/31/2018	12/31/2017	12/31/2016	12/31/2015	12/31/2014
Earnings Per Share	(6.81)	(6.51)	(7.29)	(7.10)	1.34	(2.75)	(4.29)	3.79
Cash Flow Per Share	3.08	3.59	3.55	4.02	3.33	2.03	4.11	5.83
Tang Book Value Per Share	16.54	16.64	16.18	16.27	16.66	15.19	16.30	20.50
Dividends Per Share	0.080	0.080	0.080	0.080	0.080	0.080	0.160	0.160
Dividend Payout %	...	...	...	...	5.97	...	...	4.22
Income Statement								
Total Revenue	2,222,011	1,599,566	748,137	3,282,645	2,611,030	1,099,939	1,598,068	2,711,695
EBITDA	660,688	549,121	199,169	(1,560,761)	285,499	(625,525)	(874,023)	1,212,762
Depn & Amortn	422,836	283,466	140,525	6,000	7,700	8,400	11,900	12,900
Income Before Taxes	87,591	162,391	7,107	(1,776,970)	82,120	(802,138)	(1,052,362)	1,030,885
Income Taxes	(1,432)	45,787	5,688	(30,489)	(251,026)	(280,750)	(338,677)	396,503
Net Income	89,023	116,604	1,419	(1,746,481)	333,146	(521,388)	(713,685)	634,382
Average Shares	248,082	248,436	249,154	246,171	245,458	189,868	166,389	164,403
Balance Sheet								
Current Assets	412,458	459,099	388,478	602,185	429,234	281,883	439,074	570,292
Total Assets	8,854,199	9,728,308	9,635,064	9,708,154	11,728,841	11,282,245	6,900,031	8,746,780
Current Liabilities	557,430	613,631	670,800	754,811	755,473	702,653	351,720	755,264
Long-Term Obligations	3,133,990	3,792,455	3,790,649	3,836,861	4,108,806	3,773,517	2,651,303	3,073,000
Total Liabilities	4,696,007	5,546,055	5,572,401	5,648,723	5,954,569	5,873,877	4,140,373	5,289,351
Stockholders' Equity	4,158,192	4,182,253	4,062,663	4,059,431	5,774,272	5,408,368	2,759,658	3,457,429
Shares Outstanding	251,417	251,343	251,138	249,510	248,129	247,144	169,316	168,628
Statistical Record								
Return on Assets %	N.M.	N.M.	N.M.	N.M.	2.90	N.M.	N.M.	7.91
Return on Equity %	N.M.	N.M.	N.M.	N.M.	5.96	N.M.	N.M.	21.61
EBITDA Margin %	29.73	34.33	26.62	N.M.	10.93	N.M.	N.M.	44.72
Net Margin %	4.01	7.29	0.19	N.M.	12.76	N.M.	N.M.	23.39
Asset Turnover	0.32	0.32	0.31	0.31	0.23	0.12	0.20	0.34
Current Ratio	0.74	0.75	0.58	0.80	0.57	0.40	1.25	0.76
Debt to Equity	0.75	0.91	0.93	0.95	0.71	0.70	0.96	0.89
Price Range	18.48-3.39	18.48-6.53	18.48-9.42	18.48-9.42	35.71-15.63	46.45-20.45	64.75-21.17	93.70-52.28
P/E Ratio	...	...	...	...	26.65-11.66	...	...	24.72-13.79
Average Yield %	0.81	0.63	0.56	0.52	0.34	0.22	0.37	0.20

Address: 100 Throckmorton Street, Suite 1200, Fort Worth, TX 76102 **Telephone:** 817-870-2601	**Officers:** Greg G. Maxwell - Chairman Jeffrey L. (Jeff) Ventura - Chairman, President, Chief Executive Officer, Chief Operating Officer	**Auditors:** Ernst & Young LLP **Investor Contact:** 817-870-2601 **Transfer Agents:** Computershare Investor Services, LLC, Cleveland, OH

RAYMOND JAMES FINANCIAL, INC.

Exchange	Symbol	Price	52Wk Range	Yield	P/E
NYS	RJF	$89.46 (12/31/2019)	91.59-71.54	1.65	12.48

7 Year Price Score 104.23 *NYSE Composite Index=100* **12 Month Price Score 101.17**

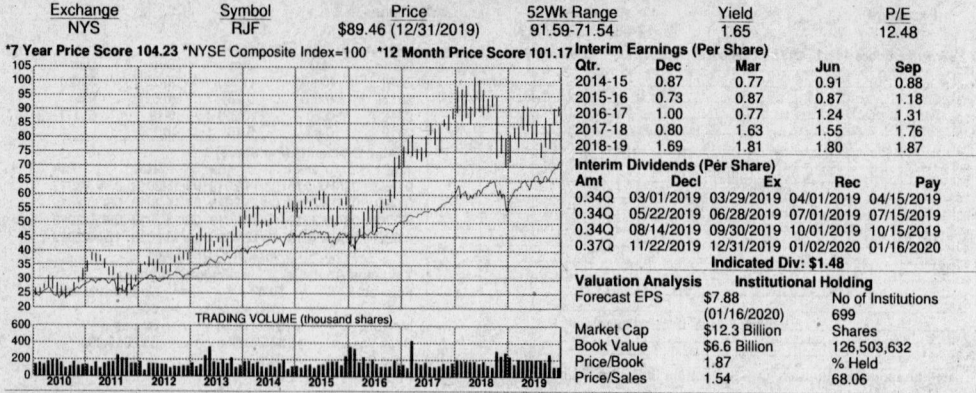

Interim Earnings (Per Share)

Qtr.	Dec	Mar	Jun	Sep
2014-15	0.87	0.77	0.91	0.88
2015-16	0.73	0.87	0.87	1.18
2016-17	1.00	0.77	1.24	1.31
2017-18	0.80	1.63	1.55	1.76
2018-19	1.69	1.81	1.80	1.87

Interim Dividends (Per Share)

Amt	Decl	Ex	Rec	Pay
0.34Q	03/01/2019	03/29/2019	04/01/2019	04/15/2019
0.34Q	05/22/2019	06/28/2019	07/01/2019	07/15/2019
0.34Q	08/14/2019	09/30/2019	10/01/2019	10/15/2019
0.37Q	11/22/2019	12/31/2019	01/02/2020	01/16/2020

Indicated Div: $1.48

Valuation Analysis

		Institutional Holding	
Forecast EPS	$7.88	No of Institutions	
	(01/16/2020)	699	
Market Cap	$12.3 Billion	Shares	
Book Value	$6.6 Billion	126,503,632	
Price/Book	1.87	% Held	
Price/Sales	1.54	68.06	

Business Summary: Finance Intermediaries & Services (MIC: 5.5.1 SIC: 6211 NAIC: 523110)

Raymond James Financial is a bank holding company and financial holding company. Through its subsidiaries, Co. is engaged in financial services activities. Co.'s segments include: Private Client Group, which provides financial planning and securities transaction services through a branch office network; Capital Markets, which conducts institutional sales, securities trading, equity research, investment banking and the syndication and management of investments that qualify for tax credits; Asset Management, which provides portfolio management and related administrative services for retail and institutional clients; and Raymond James Bank, N.A., which provides loans such as corporate loans.

Recent Developments: For the year ended Sep 30 2019, net income increased 20.7% to US$1.03 billion from US$857.0 million in the prior year. Revenues were US$8.02 billion, up 7.3% from US$7.48 billion the year before. Direct operating expenses rose 40.1% to US$283.0 million from US$202.0 million in the comparable period the year before. Indirect operating expenses increased 6.7% to US$6.37 billion from US$5.96 billion in the equivalent prior-year period.

Prospects: Our evaluation of Raymond James Financial Inc. as of October 4th, 2019 is the result of our systematic analysis on three basic characteristics: earnings strength, relative valuation, and recent stock price movement. The company has enjoyed a very positive trend in earnings per share over the past 5 quarters. However, recent analyst estimates for the company have been reduced, and RJF has posted results that fell short of analysts' expectations. Based on operating earnings yield, the company is undervalued when compared to all of the companies we cover. Share price changes over the past year indicates that RJF will perform in line with the market over the near term.

Financial Data

(US$ in Thousands)	09/30/2019	09/30/2018	09/30/2017	09/30/2016	09/30/2015	09/30/2014	09/30/2013	09/30/2012
Earnings Per Share	7.17	5.75	4.33	3.65	3.43	3.32	2.58	2.20
Cash Flow Per Share	4.09	13.10	9.11	(3.65)	6.31	3.63	4.79	2.98
Tang Book Value Per Share	43.31	39.34	35.31	31.15	29.00	26.82	23.66	21.11
Dividends Per Share	1.360	1.100	0.880	0.800	0.720	0.640	0.560	0.520
Dividend Payout %	18.97	19.13	20.32	21.92	20.99	19.28	21.71	23.64
Income Statement								
Total Revenue	8,023,000	7,475,821	6,524,875	5,520,344	5,308,164	4,965,460	4,595,798	3,897,900
EBITDA	1,472,000	1,424,670	984,538	824,744	802,483	757,307	579,638	483,904
Depn & Amortn	97,000	119,793	56,560	47,373	25,771	41,359	(14,272)	15,983
Income Before Taxes	1,375,000	1,304,877	927,978	777,371	776,712	715,948	593,910	467,921
Income Taxes	341,000	453,960	289,111	271,293	296,034	267,797	197,033	175,656
Net Income	1,034,000	856,695	636,235	529,350	502,140	480,248	367,154	295,869
Average Shares	144,000	148,838	146,647	144,513	145,939	143,589	140,541	131,791
Balance Sheet								
Current Assets	11,098,000	11,686,267	12,249,371	11,515,382	9,427,793	8,496,359	10,560,162	8,694,956
Total Assets	38,830,000	37,412,924	34,883,456	31,593,733	26,479,684	23,325,652	23,186,122	21,160,265
Current Liabilities	29,743,000	28,511,883	26,737,453	24,142,242	19,930,688	17,157,683	17,930,339	16,069,177
Long-Term Obligations	2,444,000	2,448,695	2,452,652	2,301,575	1,762,898	1,734,713	1,257,446	1,410,806
Total Liabilities	32,249,000	31,044,463	29,301,743	26,679,637	21,957,653	19,184,416	19,523,198	17,891,325
Stockholders' Equity	6,581,000	6,368,461	5,581,713	4,914,096	4,522,031	4,141,236	3,662,924	3,268,940
Shares Outstanding	137,841	145,642	144,096	141,544	142,918	141,203	139,557	137,736
Statistical Record								
Return on Assets %	2.71	2.37	1.91	1.82	2.02	2.07	1.66	1.51
Return on Equity %	15.97	14.34	12.12	11.19	11.59	12.31	10.59	10.08
EBITDA Margin %	18.35	19.06	15.09	14.94	15.12	15.25	12.61	12.41
Net Margin %	12.89	11.46	9.75	9.59	9.46	9.67	7.99	7.59
Asset Turnover	0.21	0.21	0.20	0.19	0.21	0.21	0.21	0.20
Current Ratio	0.37	0.41	0.46	0.48	0.47	0.50	0.59	0.54
Debt to Equity	0.37	0.38	0.44	0.47	0.39	0.42	0.34	0.43
Price Range	94.82-69.71	101.73-82.79	85.37-57.41	59.32-40.43	61.29-48.56	56.07-40.04	48.12-36.54	38.59-24.11
P/E Ratio	13.22-9.72	17.69-14.40	19.72-13.26	16.25-11.08	17.87-14.16	16.89-12.06	18.65-14.16	17.54-10.96
Average Yield %	1.66	1.18	1.18	1.53	1.28	1.27	1.33	1.56

Address: 880 Carillon Parkway, St. Petersburg, FL 33716 Telephone: 727-567-1000	Web Site: www.raymondjames.com Officers: Paul C. Reilly - Chairman, Chief Executive Officer Francis S. Godbold - Vice-Chairman	Auditors: KPMG LLP Investor Contact: 727-567-5133 Transfer Agents: Computershare Inc., College Station, TX

RAYONIER INC.

Exchange	Symbol	Price	52Wk Range	Yield	P/E
NYS	RYN	$32.76 (12/31/2019)	32.78-26.06	3.30	93.60

*7 Year Price Score 79.05 *NYSE Composite Index=100 *12 Month Price Score 98.12

Interim Earnings (Per Share)

Qtr.	Mar	Jun	Sep	Dec
2016	0.12	0.89	0.32	0.40
2017	0.27	0.20	0.19	0.49
2018	0.31	0.28	0.18	0.02
2019	0.19	0.19	0.00	...

Interim Dividends (Per Share)

Amt	Decl	Ex	Rec	Pay
0.27Q	02/22/2019	03/14/2019	03/15/2019	03/29/2019
0.27Q	05/17/2019	06/13/2019	06/14/2019	06/28/2019
0.27Q	07/19/2019	09/12/2019	09/13/2019	09/27/2019
0.27Q	10/18/2019	12/16/2019	12/17/2019	12/31/2019

Indicated Div: $1.08

Valuation Analysis **Institutional Holding**

Forecast EPS	$0.42 (01/17/2020)	No of Institutions 475
Market Cap	$4.2 Billion	Shares
Book Value	$1.4 Billion	147,849,488
Price/Book	2.97	% Held
Price/Sales	6.06	87.47

Business Summary: REITs (MIC: 5.3.1 SIC: 6798 NAIC: 525930)

Rayonier is a timberland real estate investment trust with assets located in the timber growing regions in the U.S. and New Zealand. Co. operates in five reportable business segments: Southern Timber, Pacific Northwest Timber, New Zealand Timber, Real Estate and Trading. The Southern Timber, Pacific Northwest Timber and New Zealand Timber segments include all activities related to the harvesting of timber in addition to lease and license activities, other non-timber activities and carbon credit sales. Co.'s Real Estate segment reflects all of its land or leasehold sales. The Trading segment reflects the log trading activities conducted by its New Zealand subsidiary.

Recent Developments: For the quarter ended Sep 30 2019, net income decreased 95.0% to US$1.5 million from US$30.6 million in the year-earlier quarter. Revenues were US$156.4 million, down 22.1% from US$200.9 million the year before.

Prospects: Our evaluation of Rayonier Inc. as of October 4th, 2019 is the result of our systematic analysis on three basic characteristics: earnings strength, relative valuation, and recent stock price movement. The company has produced a positive trend in earnings per share over the past 5 quarters. However, recent analyst estimates for the company have been reduced, while RYN has posted results that exceeded analysts' expectations. Based on operating earnings yield, the company is overvalued when compared to all of the companies we cover. Share price changes over the past year indicates that RYN will perform poorly over the near term.

Financial Data

(US$ in Thousands)	9 Mos	6 Mos	3 Mos	12/31/2018	12/31/2017	12/31/2016	12/31/2015	12/31/2014
Earnings Per Share	0.35	0.53	0.67	0.79	1.16	1.73	0.37	0.76
Cash Flow Per Share	1.65	1.90	2.34	2.40	2.01	1.66	1.41	2.50
Tang Book Value Per Share	11.02	11.58	11.91	12.02	12.35	11.49	10.49	11.74
Dividends Per Share	1.080	1.080	1.080	1.060	1.000	1.000	1.000	2.030
Dividend Payout %	308.57	203.77	161.19	134.18	86.21	57.80	270.27	267.11
Income Statement								
Total Revenue	532,764	376,346	191,546	816,138	819,596	788,278	544,874	603,521
EBITDA	81,237	70,137	38,632	314,864	343,522	372,970	195,499	264,622
Depn & Amortn	337	224	112	144,796	128,031	117,193	117,715	166,333
Income Before Taxes	60,449	56,671	32,142	142,566	183,260	222,834	43,082	44,842
Income Taxes	10,208	7,958	4,349	25,236	21,681	5,064	(859)	(9,601)
Net Income	43,112	43,546	24,794	102,216	148,842	211,972	46,165	99,337
Average Shares	129,325	129,643	129,750	129,690	127,809	122,812	125,900	131,038
Balance Sheet								
Current Assets	106,530	220,755	230,886	207,853	183,527	164,804	105,685	214,363
Total Assets	2,767,078	2,861,051	2,884,210	2,780,666	2,858,481	2,685,760	2,319,263	2,453,115
Current Liabilities	83,769	86,085	78,342	63,541	68,548	91,966	59,457	202,002
Long-Term Obligations	972,989	972,848	972,707	972,567	1,022,004	1,030,205	833,879	621,849
Total Liabilities	1,342,014	1,360,201	1,341,643	1,223,793	1,265,458	1,274,150	1,031,179	964,645
Stockholders' Equity	1,425,064	1,500,850	1,542,567	1,556,873	1,593,023	1,411,610	1,288,084	1,488,470
Shares Outstanding	129,311	129,629	129,513	129,488	128,970	122,904	122,770	126,773
Statistical Record								
Return on Assets %	1.61	2.41	3.00	3.63	5.37	8.45	1.93	3.24
Return on Equity %	2.98	4.43	5.45	6.49	9.91	15.66	3.33	6.31
EBITDA Margin %	15.25	18.64	20.17	38.58	41.91	47.31	35.88	43.85
Net Margin %	8.09	11.57	12.94	12.52	18.16	26.89	8.47	16.46
Asset Turnover	0.25	0.26	0.28	0.29	0.30	0.31	0.23	0.20
Current Ratio	1.27	2.56	2.95	3.27	2.68	1.79	1.78	1.06
Debt to Equity	0.68	0.65	0.63	0.62	0.64	0.73	0.65	0.42
Price Range	33.01-26.06	39.41-26.65	39.55-26.65	39.55-26.65	31.78-27.03	28.25-18.63	29.87-21.97	36.35-25.91
P/E Ratio	94.31-74.46	74.36-50.28	59.03-39.78	50.06-33.73	27.40-23.30	16.33-10.77	80.73-59.38	47.83-34.09
Average Yield %	3.63	3.42	3.42	3.09	3.45	3.98	3.97	6.20

Address: 1 Rayonier Way, Wildlight, FL 32097	Web Site: www.rayonier.com	Auditors: Ernst & Young LLP
Telephone: 904-357-9100	Officers: Richard D. Kincaid - Chairman David L. Nunes - President, Chief Executive Officer, Chief Operating Officer	Investor Contact: 904-357-9177 Transfer Agents: Computershare, Providence, R.I.

RAYTHEON CO.

Exchange	Symbol	Price	52Wk Range	Yield	P/E	Div Acheiver
NYS	RTN	$219.74 (12/31/2019)	221.02-149.79	1.72	18.80	14 Years

*7 Year Price Score 112.70 *NYSE Composite Index=100 *12 Month Price Score 109.16

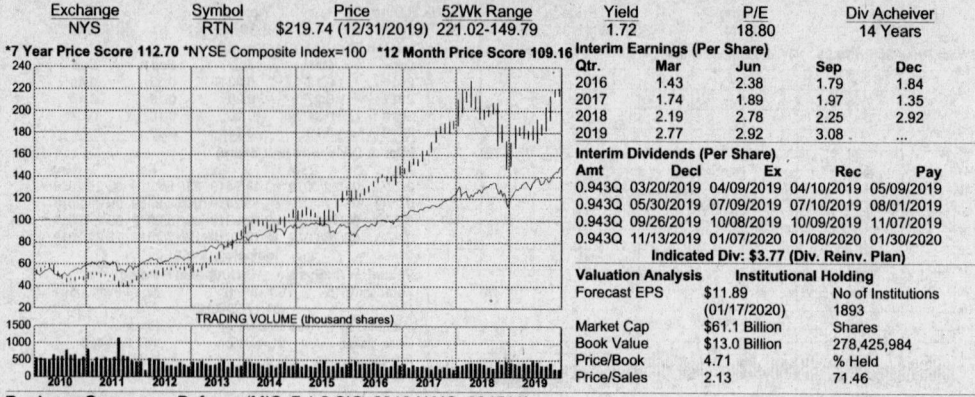

Interim Earnings (Per Share)

Qtr.	Mar	Jun	Sep	Dec
2016	1.43	2.38	1.79	1.84
2017	1.74	1.89	1.97	1.35
2018	2.19	2.78	2.25	2.92
2019	2.77	2.92	3.08	...

Interim Dividends (Per Share)

Amt	Decl	Ex	Rec	Pay
0.943Q	03/20/2019	04/09/2019	04/10/2019	05/09/2019
0.943Q	05/30/2019	07/09/2019	07/10/2019	08/01/2019
0.943Q	09/26/2019	10/08/2019	10/09/2019	11/07/2019
0.943Q	11/13/2019	01/07/2020	01/08/2020	01/30/2020

Indicated Div: $3.77 (Div. Reinv. Plan)

Valuation Analysis / **Institutional Holding**

Forecast EPS	$11.89	No of Institutions	
	(01/17/2020)	1893	
Market Cap	$61.1 Billion	Shares	
Book Value	$13.0 Billion	278,425,984	
Price/Book	4.71	% Held	
Price/Sales	2.13	71.46	

Business Summary: Defense (MIC: 7.1.2 SIC: 3812 NAIC: 334511)

Raytheon, together with its subsidiaries, is a technology company, focused on defense and other government markets. Co. has five segments: Integrated Defense Systems, which is engaged in integrated air and missile defense; large land- and sea-based radar solutions; command, control, communications, computers, cyber and intelligence solutions; Intelligence, Information and Services, which provides technical services to intelligence, defense, federal and commercial customers; Missile Systems, which produces missile and combat systems; Space and Airborne Systems, which develops integrated sensor and communication systems for missions; and Forcepoint, which develops cybersecurity products.

Recent Developments: For the quarter ended Sep 29 2019, income from continuing operations increased 34.3% to US$861.0 million from US$641.0 million in the year-earlier quarter. Net income increased 34.2% to US$860.0 million from US$641.0 million in the year-earlier quarter. Revenues were US$7.45 billion, up 9.4% from US$6.81 billion the year before. Operating income was US$1.21 billion versus US$1.18 billion in the prior-year quarter, an increase of 1.9%. Direct operating expenses rose 12.9% to US$5.50 billion from US$4.87 billion in the comparable period the year before. Indirect operating expenses decreased 1.5% to US$741.0 million from US$752.0 million in the equivalent prior-year period.

Prospects: Our evaluation of Raytheon Co. as of October 4th, 2019 is the result of our systematic analysis on three basic characteristics: earnings strength, relative valuation, and recent stock price movement. The company has managed to produce a neutral trend in earnings per share over the past 5 quarters. In addition, recent analyst estimates for the company have been mixed and RTN has posted results that exceeded analysts' expectations. Based on operating earnings yield, the company is undervalued when compared to all of the companies we cover. Share price changes over the past year indicates that RTN will perform very poorly over the near term.

Financial Data

(US$ in Thousands)	9 Mos	6 Mos	3 Mos	12/31/2018	12/31/2017	12/31/2016	12/31/2015	12/31/2014
Earnings Per Share	11.69	10.86	10.72	10.15	6.95	7.44	6.80	7.18
Cash Flow Per Share	14.77	8.58	9.69	11.97	9.43	9.59	7.74	7.00
Dividends Per Share	3.620	3.545	3.470	3.190	3.125	2.868	2.615	2.365
Dividend Payout %	30.97	32.64	32.37	31.43	44.96	38.55	38.46	32.94
Income Statement								
Total Revenue	21,334,000	13,888,000	6,729,000	27,058,000	25,348,000	24,069,000	23,247,000	22,826,000
EBITDA	3,472,000	2,246,000	1,092,000	3,674,000	3,647,000	3,562,000	3,316,000	3,487,000
Depn & Amortn	446,000	291,000	140,000	374,000	350,000	316,000	307,000	301,000
Income Before Taxes	2,922,000	1,886,000	921,000	3,147,000	3,113,000	3,030,000	2,787,000	2,983,000
Income Taxes	473,000	298,000	146,000	264,000	1,114,000	857,000	733,000	790,000
Net Income	2,458,000	1,598,000	781,000	2,909,000	2,024,000	2,211,000	2,074,000	2,244,000
Average Shares	279,400	279,900	282,200	286,800	291,400	296,800	305,200	312,600
Balance Sheet								
Current Assets	12,029,000	11,526,000	10,956,000	12,136,000	11,326,000	10,678,000	9,812,000	10,292,000
Total Assets	32,817,000	32,186,000	31,576,000	31,864,000	30,860,000	30,052,000	29,281,000	27,900,000
Current Liabilities	7,815,000	7,871,000	7,680,000	8,288,000	7,348,000	6,427,000	6,126,000	5,930,000
Long-Term Obligations	4,258,000	4,257,000	4,256,000	4,755,000	4,750,000	5,335,000	5,330,000	5,330,000
Total Liabilities	19,835,000	19,982,000	19,868,000	20,392,000	20,897,000	19,986,000	19,153,000	18,375,000
Stockholders' Equity	12,982,000	12,204,000	11,708,000	11,472,000	9,963,000	10,066,000	10,128,000	9,525,000
Shares Outstanding	278,000	278,000	280,000	282,000	288,000	293,000	299,000	307,000
Statistical Record								
Return on Assets %	10.45	9.77	9.85	9.28	6.65	7.43	7.25	8.33
Return on Equity %	27.09	26.95	27.86	27.14	20.21	21.84	21.11	21.83
EBITDA Margin %	16.27	16.17	16.23	13.58	14.39	14.80	14.26	15.28
Net Margin %	11.52	11.51	11.61	10.75	7.98	9.19	8.92	9.83
Asset Turnover	0.91	0.89	0.89	0.86	0.83	0.81	0.81	0.85
Current Ratio	1.54	1.46	1.43	1.46	1.54	1.66	1.60	1.74
Debt to Equity	0.33	0.35	0.36	0.41	0.48	0.53	0.53	0.56
Price Range	208.21-146.67	208.21-146.67	228.13-146.67	228.13-146.67	191.38-142.90	150.54-117.52	127.95-95.57	110.47-88.13
P/E Ratio	17.81-12.55	19.17-13.51	21.28-13.68	22.48-14.45	27.54-20.56	20.23-15.81	18.82-14.05	15.39-12.27
Average Yield %	2.02	1.94	1.82	1.70	1.87	2.14	2.39	1.19

Address: 870 Winter Street, Waltham, MA 02451 **Telephone:** 781-522-3000	**Web Site:** www.raytheon.com **Officers:** Thomas Anthony Kennedy - Chairman, Chief Executive Officer, Executive Vice President, Chief Operating Officer, Vice President, Division Officer Anthony F. O'Brien - Vice President, Chief Financial Officer	**Auditors:** PricewaterhouseCoopers LLP **Investor Contact:** 877-786-7070 **Transfer Agents:** American Stock Transfer & Trust Co. Brooklyn, NY

REALOGY HOLDINGS CORP

Exchange	Symbol	Price	52Wk Range	Yield	P/E
NYS	RLGY	$9.68 (12/31/2019)	18.40-4.48	3.72	N/A

*7 Year Price Score 25.65 *NYSE Composite Index=100 *12 Month Price Score 93.87

Interim Earnings (Per Share)

Qtr.	Mar	Jun	Sep	Dec
2016	(0.29)	0.63	0.73	0.40
2017	(0.20)	0.78	0.69	1.85
2018	(0.51)	0.96	0.83	(0.16)
2019	(0.87)	0.60	(0.61)	...

Interim Dividends (Per Share)

Amt	Decl	Ex	Rec	Pay
0.09Q	11/02/2018	11/14/2018	11/15/2018	11/29/2018
0.09Q	02/25/2019	03/08/2019	03/11/2019	03/25/2019
0.09Q	05/02/2019	05/14/2019	05/15/2019	05/29/2019
0.09Q	08/06/2019	08/20/2019	08/21/2019	09/04/2019

Indicated Div: $0.36

Valuation Analysis | **Institutional Holding**

Forecast EPS	$0.95
	(01/10/2020)
Market Cap	$1.1 Billion
Book Value	$2.2 Billion
Price/Book	0.51
Price/Sales	0.19

No of Institutions 338
Shares 169,462,512
% Held 82.85

Business Summary: Property, Real Estate & Development (MIC: 5.3.2 SIC: 6531 NAIC: 531210)

Realogy Holdings is a holding company. Through its subsidiaries, Co. is a provider of residential real estate services. Co. reports four segments: Real Estate Franchise Services, which include brokerage brands such as Century 21®, Coldwell Banker Commercial®, ERA® and Better Homes and Gardens® Real Estate; Co.-Owned Real Estate Brokerage Services, which own and operate under the Coldwell Banker®, Corcoran®, Sotheby's International Realty®, ZipRealty® and Citi HabitatsSM brand names; Relocation Services, which is a provider of relocation services; and Title and Settlement Services, which assist with the closing of real estate transactions by providing title and settlement services.

Recent Developments: For the quarter ended Sep 30 2019, net loss amounted to US$69.0 million versus net income of US$104.0 million in the year-earlier quarter. Revenues were US$1.63 billion, down 2.8% from US$1.68 billion the year before.

Prospects: Our evaluation of Realogy Holdings Corp as of October 4th, 2019 is the result of our systematic analysis on three basic characteristics: earnings strength, relative valuation, and recent stock price movement. The company has enjoyed a very positive trend in earnings per share over the past 5 quarters. However, recent analyst estimates for the company have been mixed and RLGY has posted results that exceeded analysts' expectations. Based on operating earnings yield, the company is undervalued when compared to all of the companies we cover. Share price changes over the past year indicates that RLGY will perform very poorly over the near term.

Financial Data
(US$ in Millions)

	9 Mos	6 Mos	3 Mos	12/31/2018	12/31/2017	12/31/2016	12/31/2015	12/31/2014
Earnings Per Share	(1.04)	0.40	0.76	1.09	3.11	1.46	1.24	0.97
Cash Flow Per Share	3.50	3.86	3.69	3.18	4.88	4.05	3.71	2.90
Dividends Per Share	0.360	0.360	0.360	0.360	0.360	0.180	...	...
Dividend Payout %	...	90.00	47.37	33.03	11.58	12.33	...	...
Income Statement								
Total Revenue	4,478	2,849	1,114	6,079	6,114	5,810	5,706	5,328
EBITDA	95	111	(69)	497	605	612	597	566
Depn & Amortn	7	5	3	98	96	89	84	74
Income Before Taxes	(122)	(38)	(135)	209	351	349	282	225
Income Taxes	(9)	(1)	(35)	65	(65)	144	110	87
Net Income	(100)	(30)	(99)	137	431	213	184	143
Average Shares	114	114	114	125	138	145	148	147
Balance Sheet								
Current Assets	862	910	771	768	789	818	961	1,026
Total Assets	7,717	7,954	7,811	7,290	7,337	7,421	7,531	7,538
Current Liabilities	1,218	1,280	1,257	1,527	955	1,050	1,605	878
Long-Term Obligations	3,221	3,325	3,335	2,800	3,221	3,265	2,962	3,891
Total Liabilities	5,538	5,704	5,625	4,979	4,719	4,957	5,113	5,359
Stockholders' Equity	2,179	2,250	2,186	2,311	2,618	2,464	2,418	2,179
Shares Outstanding	114	114	114	114	131	140	146	146
Statistical Record								
Return on Assets %	N.M.	0.66	1.39	1.87	5.84	2.84	2.44	1.92
Return on Equity %	N.M.	2.18	4.55	5.56	16.96	8.70	8.01	6.83
EBITDA Margin %	2.12	3.90	N.M.	8.18	9.90	10.53	10.46	10.62
Net Margin %	N.M.	N.M.	N.M.	2.25	7.05	3.67	3.22	2.68
Asset Turnover	0.77	0.76	0.79	0.83	0.83	0.78	0.76	0.72
Current Ratio	0.71	0.71	0.61	0.50	0.83	0.78	0.60	1.17
Debt to Equity	1.48	1.48	1.53	1.21	1.23	1.33	1.22	1.79
Price Range	20.64-4.48	23.96-6.55	27.65-11.23	27.75-14.68	34.98-25.41	36.96-22.20	49.53-36.48	49.98-33.86
P/E Ratio	...	59.90-16.38	36.38-14.78	25.46-13.47	11.25-8.17	25.32-15.21	39.94-29.42	51.53-34.91
Average Yield %	2.97	2.22	1.79	1.58	1.20	0.61	...	...

Address: 175 Park Avenue, Madison, NJ 07940
Telephone: 973-407-2000

Web Site: www.realogy.com
Officers: Michael J. Williams - Chairman Ryan M. Schneider - President, President (frmr), Chief Executive Officer, Chief Operating Officer

Auditors: PricewaterhouseCoopers LLP
Investor Contact: 973-407-4669
Transfer Agents: Computershare Trust Company, N.A.

REALTY INCOME CORP

Exchange	Symbol	Price	52Wk Range	Yield	P/E	Div Acheiver
NYS	O	$73.63 (12/31/2019)	81.94-61.93	3.79	57.08	24 Years

*7 Year Price Score 108.85 *NYSE Composite Index=100 *12 Month Price Score 100.09

Interim Earnings (Per Share)

Qtr.	Mar	Jun	Sep	Dec
2016	0.25	0.27	0.27	0.33
2017	0.27	0.30	0.32	0.21
2018	0.29	0.34	0.34	0.29
2019	0.37	0.31	0.32	...

Interim Dividends (Per Share)

Amt	Decl	Ex	Rec	Pay
0.227M	10/15/2019	10/31/2019	11/01/2019	11/15/2019
0.227M	11/20/2019	11/29/2019	12/02/2019	12/13/2019
0.228M	12/10/2019	12/31/2019	01/02/2020	01/15/2020
0.233M	01/14/2020	01/31/2020	02/03/2020	02/14/2020

Indicated Div: $2.79

Valuation Analysis

		Institutional Holding	
Forecast EPS	$1.34	No of Institutions	
	(01/17/2020)	1042	
Market Cap	$24.0 Billion	Shares	
Book Value	$9.3 Billion	288,930,176	
Price/Book	2.58	% Held	
Price/Sales	16.70	85.50	

Business Summary: REITs (MIC: 5.3.1 SIC: 6798 NAIC: 525930)

Realty Income is a real estate investment trust. Co. invests in commercial real estate. Co. owns a portfolio of properties located in various states and Puerto Rico.

Recent Developments: For the quarter ended Sep 30 2019, net income increased 2.0% to US$101.3 million from US$99.3 million in the year-earlier quarter. Revenues were US$374.2 million, up 10.7% from US$338.1 million the year before. Revenues from property income rose 10.4% to US$372.3 million from US$337.3 million in the corresponding quarter a year earlier.

Prospects: Our evaluation of Realty Income Corp. as of October 4th, 2019 is the result of our systematic analysis on three basic characteristics: earnings strength, relative valuation, and recent stock price movement. The company has produced a positive trend in earnings per share over the past 5 quarters. However, recent analyst estimates for the company have been mixed and O has posted results that fell short of analysts' expectations. Based on operating earnings yield, the company is overvalued when compared to all of the companies we cover. Share price changes over the past year indicates that O will perform well over the near term.

Financial Data

(US$ in Thousands)	9 Mos	6 Mos	3 Mos	12/31/2018	12/31/2017	12/31/2016	12/31/2015	12/31/2014
Earnings Per Share	1.29	1.31	1.34	1.26	1.10	1.13	1.09	1.04
Cash Flow Per Share	3.21	3.06	3.09	3.25	3.20	3.14	2.94	2.87
Tang Book Value Per Share	24.44	23.61	22.26	22.63	21.68	21.79	21.89	20.27
Dividends Per Share	2.697	2.678	2.659	2.639	2.537	2.403	2.279	2.193
Dividend Payout %	209.11	204.43	198.40	209.44	230.64	212.65	209.08	210.85
Income Statement								
Total Revenue	1,094,062	719,815	354,365	1,327,838	1,215,768	1,103,172	1,023,285	933,505
EBITDA	323,720	217,193	115,597	937,890	840,744	783,917	706,023	651,204
Depn & Amortn	15,795	10,543	4,367	573,292	521,426	467,440	421,168	382,064
Income Before Taxes	307,925	206,650	111,230	364,598	319,318	316,477	284,855	269,140
Net Income	307,185	206,136	110,942	363,614	318,798	315,571	283,766	270,635
Average Shares	320,263	311,322	303,819	289,923	273,936	255,624	236,208	218,767
Balance Sheet								
Current Assets	413,634	204,049	171,243	155,378	126,431	114,004	121,972	68,238
Total Assets	17,179,904	16,748,630	15,762,908	15,260,483	14,058,166	13,152,871	11,865,870	11,012,622
Current Liabilities	220,215	213,817	183,483	328,663	287,191	262,007	220,135	213,357
Long-Term Obligations	7,037,389	7,074,288	7,015,427	6,499,976	6,111,471	5,839,605	4,841,486	4,930,947
Total Liabilities	7,886,485	7,911,128	7,779,013	7,171,741	6,686,665	6,386,067	5,334,274	5,399,221
Stockholders' Equity	9,293,419	8,837,502	7,983,895	8,088,742	7,371,501	6,766,804	6,531,596	5,613,401
Shares Outstanding	325,910	318,218	303,807	303,742	284,213	260,168	250,416	224,881
Statistical Record								
Return on Assets %	2.43	2.48	2.59	2.48	2.34	2.52*	2.48	2.59
Return on Equity %	4.62	4.78	5.13	4.70	4.51	4.73	4.67	4.92
EBITDA Margin %	29.59	30.17	32.62	70.63	69.15	71.06	69.00	69.76
Net Margin %	28.08	28.64	31.31	27.38	26.22	28.61	27.73	28.99
Asset Turnover	0.09	0.09	0.09	0.09	0.09	0.09	0.09	0.09
Current Ratio	1.88	0.95	0.93	0.47	0.44	0.44	0.55	0.32
Debt to Equity	0.76	0.80	0.88	0.80	0.83	0.86	0.74	0.88
Price Range	77.28-55.85	73.98-53.28	73.98-49.13	66.34-47.56	63.19-53.21	72.14-51.17	55.14-43.38	49.57-37.33
P/E Ratio	59.91-43.29	56.47-40.67	55.21-36.66	52.65-37.75	57.45-48.37	63.84-45.28	50.59-39.80	47.66-35.89
Average Yield %	3.95	4.16	4.45	4.75	4.41	3.90	4.68	5.05

Address: 11995 El Camino Real, San Diego, CA 92130 **Telephone:** 858-284-5000	**Web Site:** www.realtyincome.com **Officers:** Sumit Roy - President, Chief Investment Officer, Chief Executive Officer, Chief Operating Officer, Executive Vice President Paul M. Meurer - Executive Vice President, Chief Financial Officer, Treasurer	**Auditors:** KPMG LLP **Investor Contact:** 760-741-2111 **Transfer Agents:** Wells Fargo Shareowner Services, St. Paul, MN

REGAL BELOIT CORP

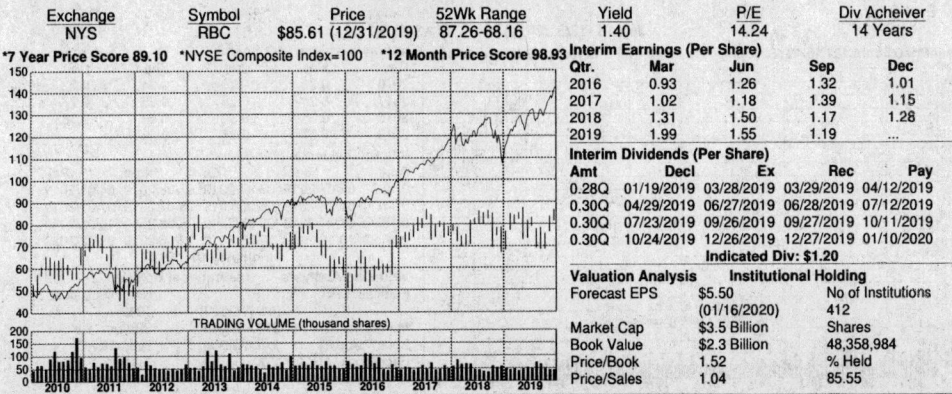

Exchange	Symbol	Price	52Wk Range	Yield	P/E	Div Acheiver
NYS	RBC	$85.61 (12/31/2019)	87.26-68.16	1.40	14.24	14 Years

*7 Year Price Score 89.10 *NYSE Composite Index=100 *12 Month Price Score 98.93

Interim Earnings (Per Share)

Qtr.	Mar	Jun	Sep	Dec
2016	0.93	1.26	1.32	1.01
2017	1.02	1.18	1.39	1.15
2018	1.31	1.50	1.17	1.28
2019	1.99	1.55	1.19	...

Interim Dividends (Per Share)

Amt	Decl	Ex	Rec	Pay
0.28Q	01/19/2019	03/28/2019	03/29/2019	04/12/2019
0.30Q	04/29/2019	06/27/2019	06/28/2019	07/12/2019
0.30Q	07/23/2019	09/26/2019	09/27/2019	10/11/2019
0.30Q	10/24/2019	12/26/2019	12/27/2019	01/10/2020

Indicated Div: $1.20

Valuation Analysis

		Institutional Holding	
Forecast EPS	$5.50	No of Institutions	
	(01/16/2020)	412	
Market Cap	$3.5 Billion	Shares	
Book Value	$2.3 Billion	48,358,984	
Price/Book	1.52	% Held	
Price/Sales	1.04	85.55	

Business Summary: Electrical Equipment (MIC: 7.3.1 SIC: 3621 NAIC: 335312)

Regal Beloit is a manufacturer of electric motors, electrical motion controls, power generation and power transmission products. Co. is comprised of three operating segments: Commercial and Industrial Systems, which designs, manufactures and sells primarily fractional, integral and large horsepower AC and DC motors and controls for commercial and industrial applications; Climate Solutions, which designs, manufactures and sells primarily fractional motors, electronic variable speed controls and blowers used in a variety of residential and light commercial air moving applications; and Power Transmission Solutions, which designs, manufactures and sells primarily mounted and unmounted bearings.

Recent Developments: For the quarter ended Sep 28 2019, net income decreased 3.6% to US$50.8 million from US$52.7 million in the year-earlier quarter. Revenues were US$772.3 million, down 16.5% from US$925.4 million the year before. Operating income was US$72.8 million versus US$69.4 million in the prior-year quarter, an increase of 4.9%. Direct operating expenses declined 16.5% to US$570.4 million from US$682.8 million in the comparable period the year before. Indirect operating expenses decreased 25.5% to US$129.1 million from US$173.2 million in the equivalent prior-year period.

Prospects: Our evaluation of Regal Beloit Corp. as of October 4th, 2019 is the result of our systematic analysis on three basic characteristics: earnings strength, relative valuation, and recent stock price movement. The company has managed to produce a neutral trend in earnings per share over the past 5 quarters. In addition, recent analyst estimates for the company have been mixed and RBC has posted results that fell short of analysts' expectations. Based on operating earnings yield, the company is undervalued when compared to all of the companies we cover. Share price changes over the past year indicates that RBC will perform in line with the market over the near term.

Financial Data
(US$ in Thousands)

	9 Mos	6 Mos	3 Mos	12/29/2018	12/30/2017	12/31/2016	01/02/2016	01/03/2015
Earnings Per Share	6.01	5.99	5.94	5.26	4.74	4.52	3.18	0.69
Cash Flow Per Share	9.24	8.19	7.91	8.34	6.54	9.86	8.55	6.52
Tang Book Value Per Share	5.56	7.10	7.04	4.11	4.02	N.M.	N.M.	16.29
Dividends Per Share	1.160	1.140	1.120	1.100	1.020	0.950	0.910	0.860
Dividend Payout %	19.30	19.03	18.86	20.91	21.52	21.02	28.62	124.64
Income Statement								
Total Revenue	2,499,800	1,727,500	853,800	3,645,600	3,360,300	3,224,500	3,509,700	3,257,100
EBITDA	389,400	282,800	154,800	433,000	412,100	414,000	348,300	213,500
Depn & Amortn	100,400	66,500	34,300	87,500	82,000	93,400	95,500	92,000
Income Before Taxes	252,500	191,800	108,000	292,200	277,200	266,400	196,900	90,300
Income Taxes	47,500	37,600	21,200	56,400	59,100	57,100	48,400	54,200
Net Income	202,200	152,500	85,900	231,200	213,000	203,400	143,300	31,000
Average Shares	41,700	43,000	43,100	43,900	44,900	45,000	45,100	45,300
Balance Sheet								
Current Assets	1,667,900	1,802,900	1,836,500	1,817,700	1,574,400	1,532,000	1,635,200	1,652,000
Total Assets	4,478,300	4,660,300	4,705,900	4,623,800	4,388,200	4,358,500	4,591,700	3,407,600
Current Liabilities	589,200	645,300	676,500	683,500	712,000	701,600	612,800	561,300
Long-Term Obligations	1,200,300	1,222,700	1,213,200	1,306,600	1,039,900	1,310,900	1,715,600	625,400
Total Liabilities	2,177,000	2,259,300	2,291,000	2,313,300	2,062,700	2,319,700	2,654,400	1,473,200
Stockholders' Equity	2,301,300	2,401,000	2,414,900	2,310,500	2,325,500	2,038,800	1,937,300	1,934,400
Shares Outstanding	40,900	42,200	42,800	42,800	44,300	44,800	44,700	44,700
Statistical Record								
Return on Assets %	5.68	5.58	5.62	5.15	4.87	4.56	3.59	0.87
Return on Equity %	11.13	11.01	10.77	10.00	9.76	10.26	7.42	1.53
EBITDA Margin %	15.58	16.37	18.13	11.88	12.26	12.84	9.92	6.55
Net Margin %	8.09	8.83	10.06	6.34	6.34	6.31	4.08	0.95
Asset Turnover	0.74	0.76	0.79	0.81	0.77	0.72	0.88	0.91
Current Ratio	2.83	2.79	2.71	2.66	2.21	2.18	2.67	2.94
Debt to Equity	0.52	0.51	0.50	0.57	0.45	0.64	0.89	0.32
Price Range	87.26-66.93	87.26-66.93	86.10-66.93	86.10-66.93	86.75-69.45	75.10-49.38	80.95-55.46	80.02-63.13
P/E Ratio	14.52-11.14	14.57-11.17	14.49-11.27	16.37-12.72	18.30-14.65	16.62-10.92	25.46-17.44	115.97-91.49
Average Yield %	1.49	1.43	1.42	1.41	1.31	1.57	1.30	1.18

Address: 200 State Street, Beloit, WI 53511	Web Site: www.regal-beloit.com	Auditors: DELOITTE & TOUCHE LLP
Telephone: 608-364-8800	Officers: Rakesh Sachdev - Chairman Louis V. Pinkham - Chief Executive Officer	Investor Contact: 608-364-8800
		Transfer Agents: ComputerShare Investor Services, Providence, RI

REGIONS FINANCIAL CORP

Exchange	Symbol	Price	52Wk Range	Yield	P/E
NYS	RF	$17.16 (12/31/2019)	17.43-13.38	3.61	11.36

*7 Year Price Score 102.16 *NYSE Composite Index=100 *12 Month Price Score 103.77

Interim Earnings (Per Share)

Qtr.	Mar	Jun	Sep	Dec
2016	0.20	0.20	0.24	0.22
2017	0.24	0.25	0.25	0.27
2018	0.35	0.32	0.50	0.38
2019	0.37	0.37	0.39	...

Interim Dividends (Per Share)

Amt	Decl	Ex	Rec	Pay
0.14Q	02/07/2019	03/07/2019	03/08/2019	04/01/2019
0.14Q	04/24/2019	06/06/2019	06/07/2019	07/01/2019
0.155Q	07/24/2019	09/05/2019	09/06/2019	10/01/2019
0.155Q	10/16/2019	12/05/2019	12/06/2019	01/02/2020

Indicated Div: $0.62

Valuation Analysis / **Institutional Holding**

Forecast EPS	$1.51	No of Institutions
	(01/17/2020)	1049
Market Cap	$16.6 Billion	Shares
Book Value	$16.6 Billion	908,019,712
Price/Book	1.00	% Held
Price/Sales	2.46	58.91

Business Summary: Banking (MIC: 5.1.1 SIC: 6021 NAIC: 522110)

Regions Financial is a financial holding company. Through its subsidiaries, Co. operates in three segments: Corporate Bank, which represents Co.'s commercial banking functions including commercial and industrial, commercial real estate and investor real estate lending; Consumer Bank, which represents Co.'s branch network, including consumer banking products and services related to residential first mortgages, home equity lines and loans, branch small business loans, indirect loans, and other consumer loans; and Wealth Management, which provides credit related products, trust and investment management, asset management, retirement and savings solutions, and estate planning.

Recent Developments: For the quarter ended Sep 30 2019, net income decreased 27.5% to US$409.0 million from US$564.0 million in the year-earlier quarter. Net interest income decreased 0.9% to US$947.0 million from US$956.0 million in the year-earlier quarter. Provision for loan losses was US$108.0 million versus US$84.0 million in the prior-year quarter, an increase of 28.6%. Non-interest income rose 7.5% to US$558.0 million from US$519.0 million, while non-interest expense declined 5.9% to US$881.0 million.

Prospects: Our evaluation of Regions Financial Corp. as of October 4th, 2019 is the result of our systematic analysis on three basic characteristics: earnings strength, relative valuation, and recent stock price movement. The company has managed to produce a neutral trend in earnings per share over the past 5 quarters. In addition, recent analyst estimates for the company have been mixed and RF has posted results that fell short of analysts' expectations. Based on operating earnings yield, the company is undervalued when compared to all of the companies we cover. Share price changes over the past year indicates that RF will perform very poorly over the near term.

Financial Data

(US$ in Thousands)	9 Mos	6 Mos	3 Mos	12/31/2018	12/31/2017	12/31/2016	12/31/2015	12/31/2014
Earnings Per Share	1.51	1.62	1.57	1.54	1.00	0.87	0.75	0.80
Cash Flow Per Share	3.13	2.91	2.65	2.08	1.92	1.55	1.19	1.52
Tang Book Value Per Share	10.38	9.99	9.25	8.69	8.78	8.56	8.20	7.94
Dividends Per Share	0.575	0.560	0.510	0.460	0.315	0.255	0.230	0.180
Dividend Payout %	38.08	34.57	32.48	29.87	31.50	29.31	30.67	22.50
Income Statement								
Interest Income	3,531,000	2,371,000	1,183,000	4,393,000	3,988,000	3,814,000	3,603,000	3,588,000
Interest Expense	671,000	458,000	223,000	602,000	373,000	313,000	268,000	309,000
Net Interest Income	2,860,000	1,913,000	960,000	3,791,000	3,615,000	3,501,000	3,335,000	3,279,000
Provision for Losses	291,000	183,000	91,000	229,000	150,000	262,000	241,000	69,000
Non-Interest Income	1,554,000	996,000	502,000	2,019,000	2,105,000	2,153,000	2,071,000	1,821,000
Non-Interest Expense	2,625,000	1,744,000	872,000	3,626,000	3,699,000	3,720,000	3,635,000	3,432,000
Income Before Taxes	1,498,000	982,000	499,000	1,955,000	1,871,000	1,672,000	1,530,000	1,599,000
Income Taxes	305,000	198,000	105,000	387,000	614,000	514,000	455,000	457,000
Net Income	1,193,000	784,000	394,000	1,759,000	1,263,000	1,163,000	1,062,000	1,155,000
Average Shares	991,000	1,012,000	1,028,000	1,102,000	1,198,000	1,261,000	1,334,000	1,387,000
Balance Sheet								
Net Loans & Leases	82,465,000	83,208,000	83,895,000	82,616,000	79,361,000	79,722,000	80,504,000	76,745,000
Total Assets	128,147,000	127,518,000	128,802,000	125,688,000	124,294,000	125,968,000	126,050,000	119,679,000
Total Deposits	94,305,000	94,971,000	95,720,000	94,491,000	96,889,000	99,035,000	98,430,000	94,200,000
Total Liabilities	111,566,000	110,910,000	113,290,000	110,598,000	108,102,000	109,304,000	109,206,000	102,690,000
Stockholders' Equity	16,581,000	16,608,000	15,512,000	15,090,000	16,192,000	16,664,000	16,844,000	16,989,000
Shares Outstanding	964,470	1,003,820	1,012,934	1,024,826	1,134,068	1,214,580	1,297,330	1,353,941
Statistical Record								
Return on Assets %	1.27	1.39	1.38	1.41	1.01	0.92	0.86	0.97
Return on Equity %	10.20	10.83	11.08	11.25	7.69	6.92	6.28	7.05
Net Interest Margin %	81.64	80.22	81.15	86.30	90.65	91.79	92.56	91.39
Efficiency Ratio %	51.28	51.84	51.75	56.55	60.71	62.34	64.06	63.45
Loans to Deposits	0.87	0.88	0.88	0.87	0.82	0.80	0.82	0.81
Price Range	18.69-12.57	19.93-12.57	19.93-12.57	20.11-12.57	17.49-13.17	14.64-7.08	10.80-8.70	11.30-9.06
P/E Ratio	12.38-8.32	12.30-7.76	12.69-8.01	13.06-8.16	17.49-13.17	16.83-8.14	14.40-11.60	14.13-11.33
Average Yield %	3.75	3.45	2.96	2.54	2.13	2.63	2.36	1.75

Address: 1900 Fifth Avenue North, Birmingham, AL 35203	Web Site: www.regions.com	Auditors: Ernst & Young LLP
Telephone: 205-581-7890	Officers: Charles D. McCrary - Chairman John M. Turner - President, Senior Executive Vice President, Head, Chief Executive Officer	Investor Contact: 205-264-7040
		Transfer Agents: Computershare Trust Company, N.A., Providence, RI

REINSURANCE GROUP OF AMERICA, INC.

Exchange	Symbol	Price	52Wk Range	Yield	P/E
NYS	RGA	$163.06 (12/31/2019)	168.32-137.84	1.72	14.00

*7 Year Price Score 114.07 *NYSE Composite Index=100 *12 Month Price Score 102.37

Interim Earnings (Per Share)

Qtr.	Mar	Jun	Sep	Dec
2016	1.17	3.64	3.07	2.92
2017	2.22	3.54	3.47	18.48
2018	1.52	3.13	4.68	1.70
2019	2.65	3.18	4.12	...

Interim Dividends (Per Share)

Amt	Decl	Ex	Rec	Pay
0.60Q	01/24/2019	02/06/2019	02/07/2019	02/28/2019
0.60Q	04/29/2019	05/08/2019	05/09/2019	05/30/2019
0.70Q	07/29/2019	08/07/2019	08/08/2019	08/29/2019
0.70Q	10/30/2019	11/08/2019	11/12/2019	12/03/2019

Indicated Div: $2.80

Valuation Analysis

		Institutional Holding	
Forecast EPS	$13.60	No of Institutions	
	(01/17/2020)	30	
Market Cap	$10.2 Billion	Shares	
Book Value	$11.5 Billion	784,655	
Price/Book	0.89	% Held	
Price/Sales	0.74	N/A	

Business Summary: Life & Health (MIC: 5.2.2 SIC: 6311 NAIC: 524130)

Reinsurance Group of America is an insurance holding company. Through its subsidiaries, Co. is engaged in providing reinsurance, which includes individual and group life and health, disability, and critical illness reinsurance. Co. also provides financial solutions, which includes longevity reinsurance, asset-intensive products, primarily annuities, and financial reinsurance and other products. Co. has five geographic-based and business-based operational segments: U.S. and Latin America; Canada; Europe, Middle East and Africa; Asia Pacific; and Corporate and Other. Geographic-based operations are further segmented into traditional and financial solutions businesses.

Recent Developments: For the quarter ended Sep 30 2019, net income decreased 12.8% to US$262.8 million from US$301.2 million in the year-earlier quarter. Revenues were US$3.63 billion, up 12.4% from US$3.23 billion the year before. Net premiums earned were US$2.81 billion versus US$2.56 billion in the prior-year quarter, an increase of 9.7%. Net investment income rose 18.5% to US$678.8 million from US$572.7 million a year ago.

Prospects: Our evaluation of Reinsurance Group of America Inc. as of October 4th, 2019 is the result of our systematic analysis on three basic characteristics: earnings strength, relative valuation, and recent stock price movement. The company has generated a negative trend in earnings per share over the past 5 quarters. In addition, recent analyst estimates for the company have been reduced and RGA has posted results that fell short of analysts' expectations. Based on operating earnings yield, the company is undervalued when compared to all of the companies we cover. Share price changes over the past year indicates that RGA will perform well over the near term.

Financial Data
(US$ in Thousands)

	9 Mos	6 Mos	3 Mos	12/31/2018	12/31/2017	12/31/2016	12/31/2015	12/31/2014
Earnings Per Share	11.65	12.21	12.16	11.00	27.71	10.79	7.46	9.78
Cash Flow Per Share	35.81	31.40	27.06	24.84	30.77	22.74	31.38	33.74
Tang Book Value Per Share	184.06	170.64	154.61	134.53	148.48	110.31	94.09	102.13
Dividends Per Share	2.500	2.400	2.300	2.200	1.820	1.560	1.400	1.260
Dividend Payout %	21.46	19.66	18.91	20.00	6.57	14.46	18.77	12.88
Income Statement								
Premium Income	8,311,240	5,501,599	2,737,813	10,543,776	9,841,130	9,248,871	8,570,741	8,669,854
Total Revenue	10,515,004	6,887,439	3,420,031	12,875,664	12,515,769	11,521,511	10,418,178	10,904,194
Benefits & Claims	...	...	...	9,318,929	8,518,917	7,993,375	7,489,382	7,406,641
Income Before Taxes	823,731	476,641	216,564	845,820	1,142,815	1,043,946	744,795	1,008,533
Income Taxes	188,761	104,436	47,057	129,978	(679,366)	342,503	242,629	324,486
Net Income	634,970	372,205	169,507	715,842	1,822,181	701,443	502,166	684,047
Average Shares	63,789	63,698	64,027	65,094	65,753	64,989	67,292	69,962
Balance Sheet								
Total Assets	75,773,985	72,043,816	66,692,481	64,535,245	60,514,818	53,097,879	50,383,152	44,679,611
Total Liabilities	64,250,251	61,334,805	57,022,373	56,084,692	50,945,283	46,004,797	44,247,771	37,656,159
Stockholders' Equity	11,523,734	10,709,011	9,670,108	8,450,553	9,569,535	7,093,082	6,135,381	7,023,452
Shares Outstanding	62,609	62,758	62,544	62,814	64,452	64,302	65,204	68,772
Statistical Record								
Return on Assets %	1.07	1.19	1.23	1.14	3.21	1.35	1.06	1.62
Return on Equity %	7.41	8.11	8.41	7.94	21.87	10.58	7.63	10.56
Loss Ratio %	...	...	...	88.38	86.56	86.43	87.38	85.43
Net Margin %	6.04	5.40	4.96	5.56	14.56	6.09	4.82	6.27
Price Range	162.99-128.18	156.03-128.18	159.32-128.18	163.98-128.18	164.17-122.13	128.28-78.61	98.57-82.81	89.22-71.51
P/E Ratio	13.99-11.00	12.78-10.50	13.10-10.54	14.91-11.65	5.92-4.41	11.89-7.29	13.21-11.10	9.12-7.31
Average Yield %	1.69	1.66	1.60	1.49	1.35	1.55	1.53	1.58

Address: 16600 Swingley Ridge Road, Chesterfield, MO 63017 Telephone: 636-736-7000	Web Site: www.rgare.com Officers: J. Cliff Eason - Chairman Anna Manning - President, Chief Executive Officer, Senior Executive Vice President	Auditors: DELOITTE & TOUCHE LLP Investor Contact: 636-300-8828

RELIANCE STEEL & ALUMINUM CO.

Exchange	Symbol	Price	52Wk Range	Yield	P/E
NYS	RS	$119.76 (12/31/2019)	121.33-69.70	1.84	13.09

*7 Year Price Score 105.39 *NYSE Composite Index=100 *12 Month Price Score 115.35

Interim Earnings (Per Share)

Qtr.	Mar	Jun	Sep	Dec
2016	1.27	1.38	0.68	0.84
2017	1.52	1.40	1.32	4.10
2018	2.30	3.16	2.03	1.26
2019	2.80	2.69	2.40	...

Interim Dividends (Per Share)

Amt	Decl	Ex	Rec	Pay
0.55Q	02/19/2019	03/14/2019	03/15/2019	03/29/2019
0.55Q	04/23/2019	05/23/2019	05/24/2019	06/14/2019
0.55Q	07/23/2019	08/15/2019	08/16/2019	09/06/2019
0.55Q	10/22/2019	11/14/2019	11/15/2019	12/06/2019

Indicated Div: $2.20

Valuation Analysis / **Institutional Holding**

Forecast EPS	$9.60	No of Institutions
	(01/17/2020)	558
Market Cap	$8.0 Billion	Shares
Book Value	$5.1 Billion	68,002,808
Price/Book	1.57	% Held
Price/Sales	0.70	76.01

Business Summary: Non-Precious Metals (MIC: 8.2.2 SIC: 5051 NAIC: 423510)

Reliance Steel & Aluminum is a metals service center company. Co. provides metals processing services and distributes a line of metal products, including alloy, aluminum, brass, copper, carbon steel, stainless steel, titanium and specialty steel products, to its customers in a range of industries, including general manufacturing, non-residential construction (including infrastructure), transportation (rail, truck trailer and shipbuilding), aerospace and defense, energy (oil and gas), electronics and semiconductor fabrication, and heavy industry (agricultural, construction and mining equipment). Co. also services the auto industry, primarily through its toll processing operations.

Recent Developments: For the quarter ended Sep 30 2019, net income increased 9.0% to US$163.9 million from US$150.3 million in the year-earlier quarter. Revenues were US$2.69 billion, down 9.7% from US$2.97 billion the year before. Operating income was US$241.2 million versus US$214.4 million in the prior-year quarter, an increase of 12.5%. Direct operating expenses declined 12.6% to US$1.87 billion from US$2.14 billion in the comparable period the year before. Indirect operating expenses decreased 7.5% to US$573.5 million from US$619.9 million in the equivalent prior-year period.

Prospects: Our evaluation of Reliance Steel & Aluminum Co. as of October 4th, 2019 is the result of our systematic analysis on three basic characteristics: earnings strength, relative valuation, and recent stock price movement. The company has generated a negative trend in earnings per share over the past 5 quarters. However, recent analyst estimates for the company have been mixed and RS has posted results that exceeded analysts' expectations. Based on operating earnings yield, the company is undervalued when compared to all of the companies we cover. Share price changes over the past year indicates that RS will perform well over the near term.

Financial Data

(US$ in Thousands)	9 Mos	6 Mos	3 Mos	12/31/2018	12/31/2017	12/31/2016	12/31/2015	12/31/2014
Earnings Per Share	9.15	8.78	9.25	8.75	8.34	4.16	4.16	4.73
Cash Flow Per Share	20.78	15.37	11.45	9.28	5.48	8.63	13.83	4.58
Tang Book Value Per Share	32.40	30.23	28.20	25.85	23.58	16.10	14.83	14.49
Dividends Per Share	2.150	2.100	2.050	2.000	1.800	1.650	1.600	1.400
Dividend Payout %	23.50	23.92	22.16	22.86	21.58	39.66	38.46	29.60
Income Statement								
Total Revenue	8,526,000	5,840,100	2,956,600	11,534,500	9,721,000	8,613,400	9,350,500	10,451,600
EBITDA	919,000	636,100	322,900	1,222,100	942,600	796,200	817,900	890,900
Depn & Amortn	130,900	86,900	43,200	215,200	218,400	222,000	218,500	213,800
Income Before Taxes	719,700	501,300	255,500	850,600	583,800	428,500	458,700	544,100
Income Taxes	179,900	125,400	63,900	208,800	(37,200)	120,100	142,500	170,000
Net Income	535,900	373,200	190,100	633,700	613,400	304,300	311,500	371,500
Average Shares	67,704	67,977	67,926	72,441	73,539	73,120	74,902	78,615
Balance Sheet								
Current Assets	3,165,000	3,365,900	3,560,800	3,285,000	3,051,300	2,688,500	2,554,200	3,121,100
Total Assets	8,130,900	8,327,100	8,504,200	8,044,900	7,751,000	7,411,300	7,121,600	7,836,600
Current Liabilities	788,500	760,800	877,400	699,100	703,700	656,000	989,700	662,800
Long-Term Obligations	1,578,200	1,944,900	2,122,200	2,138,500	1,809,400	1,846,700	1,427,900	2,222,300
Total Liabilities	3,057,500	3,386,100	3,674,400	3,373,300	3,083,900	3,262,500	3,207,500	3,737,600
Stockholders' Equity	5,073,400	4,941,000	4,829,800	4,671,600	4,667,100	4,148,800	3,914,100	4,099,000
Shares Outstanding	66,656	66,654	67,235	66,882	72,609	72,682	71,739	77,337
Statistical Record								
Return on Assets %	7.53	7.28	7.86	8.02	8.09	4.18	4.16	4.90
Return on Equity %	12.34	12.28	13.67	13.57	13.92	7.53	7.77	9.32
EBITDA Margin %	10.78	10.89	10.92	10.60	9.70	9.24	8.75	8.52
Net Margin %	6.29	6.39	6.43	5.49	6.31	3.53	3.33	3.55
Asset Turnover	1.37	1.39	1.41	1.46	1.28	1.18	1.25	1.38
Current Ratio	4.01	4.42	4.06	4.70	4.34	4.10	2.58	4.71
Debt to Equity	0.31	0.39	0.44	0.46	0.39	0.45	0.36	0.54
Price Range	103.74-69.47	94.62-69.47	96.56-69.47	96.56-69.47	87.62-69.11	86.34-51.75	66.33-52.37	76.12-57.14
P/E Ratio	11.34-7.59	10.78-7.91	10.44-7.51	11.04-7.94	10.51-8.29	20.75-12.44	15.94-12.59	16.09-12.08
Average Yield %	2.46	2.47	2.40	2.30	2.33	2.31	2.71	2.02

Address: 350 South Grand Avenue, Suite 5100, Los Angeles, CA 90071 **Telephone:** 213-687-7700	**Web Site:** www.rsac.com **Officers:** James D. Hoffman - President, Chief Executive Officer, Executive Vice President, Chief Operating Officer, Executive Vice President (frmr), Senior Vice President Karla R. Lewis - Senior Executive Vice President, Chief Financial Officer, Executive Vice President	**Auditors:** KPMG LLP **Investor Contact:** 213-576-2428 **Transfer Agents:** American Stock Transfer & Trust Company, Brooklyn, NY

RENAISSANCERE HOLDINGS LTD.

Exchange	Symbol	Price	52Wk Range	Yield	P/E	Div Acheiver
NYS	RNR	$196.02 (12/31/2019)	200.82-128.31	0.69	14.52	23 Years

*7 Year Price Score 115.57 ***NYSE Composite Index=100** ***12 Month Price Score 105.92**

Interim Earnings (Per Share)

Qtr.	Mar	Jun	Sep	Dec
2016	2.95	3.22	3.56	1.72
2017	2.25	4.24	(12.75)	(0.11)
2018	1.42	4.78	0.82	(2.11)
2019	6.43	8.35	0.83	...

Interim Dividends (Per Share)

Amt	Decl	Ex	Rec	Pay
0.34Q	02/07/2019	03/14/2019	03/15/2019	03/29/2019
0.34Q	05/15/2019	06/13/2019	06/14/2019	06/28/2019
0.34Q	07/30/2019	09/12/2019	09/13/2019	09/30/2019
0.34Q	11/13/2019	12/12/2019	12/13/2019	12/31/2019

Indicated Div: $1.36

Valuation Analysis | **Institutional Holding**

Forecast EPS	N/A	No of Institutions
		507
Market Cap	$8.7 Billion	Shares
Book Value	$6.0 Billion	55,261,532
Price/Book	1.45	% Held
Price/Sales	2.37	92.86

Business Summary: General Insurance (MIC: 5.2.1 SIC: 6331 NAIC: 524126)

RenaissanceRe Holdings is a holding company. Together with its subsidiaries, Co. is a global provider of reinsurance and insurance. Co.'s segments are: Property, which includes its catastrophe class of business, comprising excess of loss reinsurance and excess of loss retrocessional reinsurance to insure insurance and reinsurance companies against natural and man-made catastrophes, and its other property class of business, comprising proportional reinsurance, property per risk, property (re)insurance, binding facilities and regional U.S. multi-line reinsurance; and Casualty and Specialty, in which Co. provides its casualty and specialty reinsurance products and excess of loss coverage.

Recent Developments: For the quarter ended Sep 30 2019, net income increased 121.1% to US$107.9 million from US$48.8 million in the year-earlier quarter. Revenues were US$1.05 billion, up 66.9% from US$629.8 million the year before. Net premiums earned were US$906.7 million versus US$531.8 million in the prior-year quarter, an increase of 70.5%. Net investment income rose 41.1% to US$113.8 million from US$80.7 million a year ago.

Prospects: Our evaluation of RenaissanceRe Holdings Ltd. as of October 4th, 2019 is the result of our systematic analysis on three basic characteristics: earnings strength, relative valuation, and recent stock price movement. The company has enjoyed a very positive trend in earnings per share over the past 5 quarters. However, recent analyst estimates for the company have been mixed and RNR has posted results that exceeded analysts' expectations. Based on operating earnings yield, the company is undervalued when compared to all of the companies we cover. Share price changes over the past year indicates that RNR will perform very well over the near term.

Financial Data
(US$ in Thousands)

	9 Mos	6 Mos	3 Mos	12/31/2018	12/31/2017	12/31/2016	12/31/2015	12/31/2014
Earnings Per Share	13.50	13.49	9.92	4.91	(6.15)	11.43	9.28	12.60
Cash Flow Per Share	36.76	38.10	38.90	30.75	26.24	11.34	9.61	16.76
Tang Book Value Per Share	114.11	113.17	105.00	98.51	93.65	102.35	93.06	89.95
Dividends Per Share	1.350	1.340	1.330	1.320	1.280	1.240	1.200	1.160
Dividend Payout %	10.00	9.93	13.41	26.88	...	10.85	12.93	9.21
Income Statement								
Premium Income	2,368,278	1,461,530	550,028	1,976,129	1,717,575	1,403,430	1,400,551	1,062,416
Total Revenue	3,096,649	2,045,501	807,121	2,074,941	2,103,679	1,727,837	1,515,102	1,260,077
Income Before Taxes	930,597	818,989	360,659	262,615	(328,184)	630,388	496,376	686,864
Income Taxes	20,670	17,006	7,531	(6,302)	26,487	340	(45,866)	608
Net Income	705,836	659,949	282,906	227,364	(222,389)	502,962	431,192	532,718
Average Shares	43,537	43,521	42,091	39,755	39,854	41,559	43,526	39,968
Balance Sheet								
Total Assets	25,644,210	26,086,961	24,559,600	18,676,196	15,226,131	12,352,082	11,560,871	8,203,550
Total Liabilities	19,692,975	20,174,119	19,005,567	13,631,116	10,834,756	7,485,505	6,828,687	4,337,835
Stockholders' Equity	5,951,235	5,912,842	5,554,033	5,045,080	4,391,375	4,866,577	4,732,184	3,865,715
Shares Outstanding	44,151	44,162	44,159	42,207	40,023	41,187	43,701	38,441
Statistical Record								
Return on Assets %	2.95	2.91	2.21	1.34	N.M.	4.20	4.36	6.50
Return on Equity %	11.65	11.65	8.97	4.82	N.M.	10.45	10.03	13.71
Net Margin %	22.79	32.26	35.05	10.96	(10.57)	29.11	28.46	42.28
Price Range	193.58-119.93	182.93-119.93	147.05-118.65	140.67-116.61	150.35-123.88	136.45-108.93	115.47-94.50	108.42-89.80
P/E Ratio	14.34-8.88	13.56-8.89	14.82-11.96	28.65-23.75	...	11.94-9.53	12.44-10.18	8.60-7.13
Average Yield %	0.86	0.88	1.00	1.03	0.92	1.05	1.15	1.16

Address: Renaissance House, 12 Crow Lane, Pembroke, HM 19
Telephone: 441-295-4513
Fax: 441-295-9453

Web Site: www.renre.com
Officers: Kevin J. O'Donnell - President, Chief Executive Officer Robert (Bob) Qutub - Executive Vice President, Chief Financial Officer

Auditors: Ernst & Young Ltd.
Investor Contact: 441-295-4513
Transfer Agents: Computershare Shareowner Services LLC, Jersey City, NJ

REPUBLIC SERVICES INC

Exchange	Symbol	Price	52Wk Range	Yield	P/E	Div Acheiver
NYS	RSG	$89.63 (12/31/2019)	90.35-71.36	1.81	26.68	15 Years

*7 Year Price Score 128.42 *NYSE Composite Index=100 *12 Month Price Score 99.13

Interim Earnings (Per Share)

Qtr.	Mar	Jun	Sep	Dec
2016	0.45	0.52	0.25	0.55
2017	0.55	0.60	0.66	1.96
2018	0.72	0.71	0.81	0.93
2019	0.72	0.78	0.93	...

Interim Dividends (Per Share)

Amt	Decl	Ex	Rec	Pay
0.375Q	02/07/2019	03/29/2019	04/01/2019	04/15/2019
0.375Q	04/25/2019	06/28/2019	07/01/2019	07/15/2019
0.405Q	07/25/2019	09/30/2019	10/01/2019	10/15/2019
0.405Q	10/22/2019	12/31/2019	01/02/2020	01/15/2020

Indicated Div: $1.62

Valuation Analysis / Institutional Holding

Valuation Analysis		Institutional Holding	
Forecast EPS	$3.29	No of Institutions	
	(01/17/2020)	957	
Market Cap	$31.7 Billion	Shares	
Book Value	$8.0 Billion	302,068,352	
Price/Book	3.97	% Held	
Price/Sales	3.09	54.87	

Business Summary: Sanitation Services (MIC: 7.5.3 SIC: 4953 NAIC: 562219)

Republic Services is a provider of non-hazardous solid waste collection, transfer, disposal, recycling, and energy services. Co. operates through collection operations, transfer stations, active landfills, recycling processing centers, treatment, recovery and disposal facilities, and salt water disposal wells. Co. is engaged in landfill gas-to-energy and renewable energy projects and had post-closure responsibility for closed landfills. Co.'s operations primarily consist of providing collection, transfer and disposal of non-hazardous solid waste, recovering and recycling of certain materials, and energy services.

Recent Developments: For the quarter ended Sep 30 2019, net income increased 13.4% to US$298.0 million from US$262.9 million in the year-earlier quarter. Revenues were US$2.65 billion, up 3.2% from US$2.57 billion the year before. Operating income was US$467.8 million versus US$440.3 million in the prior-year quarter, an increase of 6.2%. Direct operating expenses rose 3.4% to US$1.63 billion from US$1.58 billion in the comparable period the year before. Indirect operating expenses decreased 0.1% to US$547.7 million from US$548.0 million in the equivalent prior-year period.

Prospects: Our evaluation of Republic Services Inc. as of October 4th, 2019 is the result of our systematic analysis on three basic characteristics: earnings strength, relative valuation, and recent stock price movement. The company has managed to produce a neutral trend in earnings per share over the past 5 quarters. Additionally, recent analyst estimates for the company have been unchanged while RSG has posted results that exceeded analysts' expectations. Based on operating earnings yield, the company is fairly valued when compared to all of the companies we cover. Share price changes over the past year indicates that RSG will perform over the near term.

Financial Data

(US$ in Thousands)	9 Mos	6 Mos	3 Mos	12/31/2018	12/31/2017	12/31/2016	12/31/2015	12/31/2014
Earnings Per Share	3.36	3.24	3.17	3.16	3.77	1.78	2.13	1.53
Cash Flow Per Share	7.12	6.80	6.87	6.86	5.67	5.37	4.80	4.29
Dividends Per Share	1.530	1.500	1.470	1.440	1.330	1.240	1.160	1.080
Dividend Payout %	45.54	46.30	46.37	45.57	35.28	69.66	54.46	70.59
Income Statement								
Total Revenue	7,722,700	5,075,900	2,470,600	10,040,900	10,041,500	9,387,700	9,115,000	8,788,300
EBITDA	2,174,100	1,416,800	661,700	2,712,100	2,635,700	2,261,100	2,458,700	2,071,900
Depn & Amortn	844,500	556,700	238,800	977,000	965,300	919,800	898,700	838,500
Income Before Taxes	1,038,100	664,500	324,400	1,352,900	1,309,500	970,900	1,195,900	885,300
Income Taxes	227,100	155,600	77,900	279,500	3,100	351,600	445,500	337,400
Net Income	784,000	485,700	234,200	1,036,900	1,278,400	612,600	749,900	547,600
Average Shares	321,710	322,765	323,450	328,383	339,000	344,400	351,400	358,100
Balance Sheet								
Current Assets	1,473,900	1,474,100	1,444,600	1,564,400	1,436,800	1,284,500	1,230,300	1,391,000
Total Assets	22,329,100	21,996,800	21,782,000	21,617,000	21,147,000	20,629,600	20,577,200	20,094,000
Current Liabilities	2,997,400	3,571,000	3,467,900	2,718,600	2,634,800	1,812,000	1,834,800	1,826,000
Long-Term Obligations	7,705,800	6,883,900	6,801,500	7,646,800	7,480,700	7,653,100	7,568,700	7,050,800
Total Liabilities	14,352,600	14,043,900	13,862,500	13,689,900	13,188,200	12,938,300	12,803,100	12,348,700
Stockholders' Equity	7,976,500	7,952,900	7,919,500	7,927,100	7,958,800	7,691,300	7,774,100	7,745,300
Shares Outstanding	353,300	353,000	352,800	322,500	331,700	339,400	345,600	352,700
Statistical Record								
Return on Assets %	4.96	4.86	4.82	4.85	6.12	2.97	3.69	2.74
Return on Equity %	13.65	13.29	13.06	13.05	16.34	7.90	9.66	7.00
EBITDA Margin %	28.15	27.91	26.78	27.01	26.25	24.09	26.97	23.58
Net Margin %	10.15	9.57	9.48	10.33	12.73	6.53	8.23	6.23
Asset Turnover	0.47	0.47	0.47	0.47	0.48	0.45	0.45	0.44
Current Ratio	0.49	0.41	0.42	0.58	0.55	0.71	0.67	0.76
Debt to Equity	0.97	0.87	0.86	0.96	0.94	1.00	0.97	0.91
Price Range	90.35-68.36	87.30-68.25	80.61-64.37	77.35-61.96	67.61-56.42	57.50-42.20	45.25-39.04	40.89-31.53
P/E Ratio	26.89-20.35	26.94-21.06	25.43-20.31	24.48-19.61	17.93-14.97	32.30-23.71	21.24-18.33	26.73-20.61
Average Yield %	1.90	1.96	2.03	2.06	2.11	2.50	2.80	2.95

Address: 18500 North Allied Way, Phoenix, AZ 85054 Telephone: 480-627-2700	Web Site: www.republicservices.com Officers: Manuel Kadre - Chairman Jon Vander Ark - President, Executive Vice President, Chief Operating Officer	Auditors: Ernst & Young LLP Transfer Agents: Wachovia Corp., Charlotte, NC

RESMED INC.

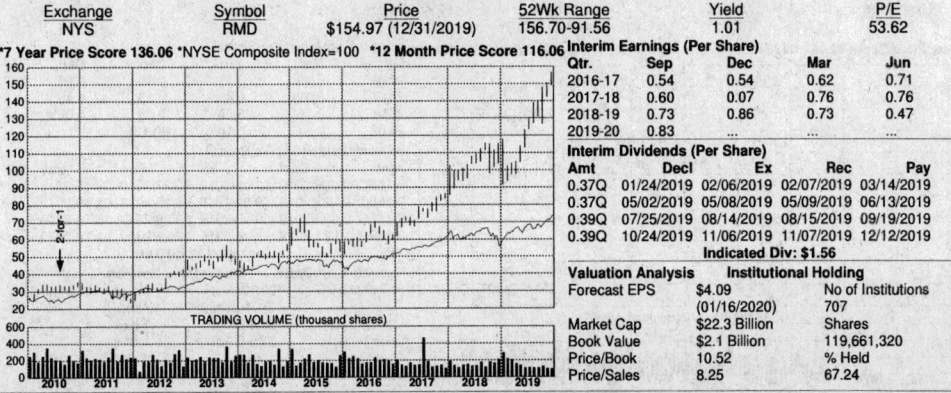

Exchange	Symbol	Price	52Wk Range	Yield	P/E
NYS	RMD	$154.97 (12/31/2019)	156.70-91.56	1.01	53.62

*7 Year Price Score 136.06 *NYSE Composite Index=100 *12 Month Price Score 116.06

Interim Earnings (Per Share)

Qtr.	Sep	Dec	Mar	Jun
2016-17	0.54	0.54	0.62	0.71
2017-18	0.60	0.07	0.76	0.76
2018-19	0.73	0.86	0.73	0.47
2019-20	0.83	...	...	...

Interim Dividends (Per Share)

Amt	Decl	Ex	Rec	Pay
0.37Q	01/24/2019	02/06/2019	02/07/2019	03/14/2019
0.37Q	05/02/2019	05/08/2019	05/09/2019	06/13/2019
0.39Q	07/25/2019	08/14/2019	08/15/2019	09/19/2019
0.39Q	10/24/2019	11/06/2019	11/07/2019	12/12/2019

Indicated Div: $1.56

Valuation Analysis

		Institutional Holding	
Forecast EPS	$4.09 (01/16/2020)	No of Institutions	707
Market Cap	$22.3 Billion	Shares	119,661,320
Book Value	$2.1 Billion	% Held	67.24
Price/Book	10.52		
Price/Sales	8.25		

Business Summary: Medical Instruments & Equipment (MIC: 4.3.1 SIC: 3841 NAIC: 339112)

ResMed is a holding company. Through its operating subsidiaries, Co. is engaged in the development, manufacturing, distribution and marketing of medical devices and cloud-based software solutions that diagnose, treat and manage respiratory disorders including sleep disordered breathing, chronic obstructive pulmonary disease, neuromuscular disease and other chronic diseases. Co. has two operating segments: Sleep and Respiratory Care and Software-as-a-Solutions. Co.'s portfolio of products includes devices, diagnostic products, mask systems, headgear and other accessories, dental devices, portable oxygen concentrators and cloud-based software informatics solutions.

Recent Developments: For the quarter ended Sep 30 2019, net income increased 13.6% to US$120.1 million from US$105.7 million in the year-earlier quarter. Revenues were US$681.1 million, up 15.8% from US$588.3 million the year before. Operating income was US$171.1 million versus US$144.1 million in the prior-year quarter, an increase of 18.7%. Direct operating expenses rose 12.6% to US$276.0 million from US$245.2 million in the comparable period the year before. Indirect operating expenses increased 17.6% to US$234.0 million from US$199.0 million in the equivalent prior-year period.

Prospects: Our evaluation of ResMed Inc. as of October 4th, 2019 is the result of our systematic analysis on three basic characteristics: earnings strength, relative valuation, and recent stock price movement. The company has enjoyed a very positive trend in earnings per share over the past 5 quarters. However, recent analyst estimates for the company have been mixed and RMD has posted results that exceeded analysts' expectations. Based on operating earnings yield, the company is fairly valued when compared to all of the companies we cover. Share price changes over the past year indicates that RMD will perform well over the near term.

Financial Data

(US$ in Thousands)	3 Mos	06/30/2019	06/30/2018	06/30/2017	06/30/2016	06/30/2015	06/30/2014	06/30/2013
Earnings Per Share	2.89	2.80	2.19	2.40	2.49	2.47	2.39	2.10
Cash Flow Per Share	3.99	3.21	3.54	2.93	3.90	2.73	2.77	2.82
Tang Book Value Per Share	N.M.	N.M.	5.43	4.46	2.39	9.08	10.15	9.06
Dividends Per Share	1.500	1.480	1.400	1.320	1.200	1.120	1.000	0.680
Dividend Payout %	51.90	52.86	63.93	55.00	48.19	45.34	41.84	32.38
Income Statement								
Total Revenue	681,056	2,606,572	2,340,196	2,066,737	1,838,713	1,678,912	1,554,973	1,514,457
EBITDA	173,956	643,475	579,672	476,472	457,835	424,154	415,704	362,775
Depn & Amortn	5,963	74,938	46,383	46,578	23,923	8,668	9,733	10,142
Income Before Taxes	157,450	534,680	521,312	418,743	439,566	435,916	431,078	385,119
Income Taxes	30,439	114,255	205,724	76,459	87,157	83,030	85,805	77,986
Net Income	120,148	404,592	315,588	342,284	352,409	352,886	345,273	307,133
Average Shares	145,099	144,484	143,987	142,453	141,669	142,687	144,359	146,410
Balance Sheet								
Current Assets	1,161,098	1,145,366	1,065,717	1,644,003	1,419,719	1,444,182	1,556,209	1,448,849
Total Assets	4,154,558	4,107,682	3,063,923	3,468,487	3,258,935	2,184,260	2,360,962	2,210,721
Current Liabilities	550,457	555,991	511,249	360,126	638,551	267,259	269,558	574,049
Long-Term Obligations	1,208,210	1,258,861	269,988	1,078,611	875,000	300,594	300,770	769
Total Liabilities	2,037,307	2,035,489	1,004,943	1,508,221	1,564,104	596,953	602,714	600,205
Stockholders' Equity	2,117,251	2,072,193	2,058,980	1,960,266	1,694,831	1,587,307	1,758,248	1,610,516
Shares Outstanding	143,769	143,654	142,679	142,174	140,660	140,474	140,304	142,013
Statistical Record								
Return on Assets %	11.60	11.28	9.66	10.18	12.91	15.53	15.10	14.13
Return on Equity %	20.86	19.59	15.70	18.73	21.42	21.10	20.50	19.09
EBITDA Margin %	25.54	24.69	24.77	23.05	24.90	25.26	26.73	23.95
Net Margin %	17.64	15.52	13.49	16.56	19.17	21.02	22.20	20.28
Asset Turnover	0.75	0.73	0.72	0.61	0.67	0.74	0.68	0.70
Current Ratio	2.11	2.06	2.08	4.57	2.22	5.40	5.77	2.52
Debt to Equity	0.57	0.61	0.13	0.55	0.52	0.19	0.17	N.M.
Price Range	140.33-91.56	123.27-91.56	107.93-72.44	78.91-57.34	64.08-49.43	74.82-46.25	57.11-42.03	51.17-30.63
P/E Ratio	48.56-31.68	44.02-32.70	49.28-33.08	32.88-23.89	25.73-19.85	30.29-18.72	23.90-17.59	24.37-14.59
Average Yield %	1.33	1.37	1.58	1.97	2.13	1.94	2.06	1.62

Address: 9001 Spectrum Center Blvd., San Diego, CA 92123	**Web Site:** www.resmed.com	**Auditors:** KPMG LLP
Telephone: 858-836-5000	**Officers:** Peter C. Farrell - Chairman, President, Chief Executive Officer Robert Andrew Douglas - President, Chief Operating Officer, Region Officer	**Investor Contact:** 858-836-5971
		Transfer Agents: Computershare Trust Company N.A., Canton, MA

RETAIL PROPERTIES OF AMERICA INC

Exchange	Symbol	Price	52Wk Range	Yield	P/E
NYS	RPAI	$13.40 (12/31/2019)	14.23-10.62	4.94	103.08

*7 Year Price Score 72.96 *NYSE Composite Index=100 *12 Month Price Score 104.78

Interim Earnings (Per Share)

Qtr.	Mar	Jun	Sep	Dec
2016	0.19	0.11	0.30	0.06
2017	(0.05)	0.48	0.15	0.46
2018	0.19	0.05	0.06	0.05
2019	0.11	0.10	(0.13)	...

Interim Dividends (Per Share)

Amt	Decl	Ex	Rec	Pay
0.166Q	02/06/2019	03/26/2019	03/27/2019	04/10/2019
0.166Q	04/23/2019	06/24/2019	06/25/2019	07/10/2019
0.166Q	07/23/2019	09/25/2019	09/26/2019	10/10/2019
0.166Q	10/23/2019	12/24/2019	12/26/2019	01/10/2020

Indicated Div: $0.66

Valuation Analysis

		Institutional Holding	
Forecast EPS	$0.12	No of Institutions	
	(01/16/2020)	N/A	
Market Cap	$2.9 Billion	Shares	
Book Value	$1.6 Billion	N/A	
Price/Book	1.74	% Held	
Price/Sales	5.96	N/A	

Business Summary: REITs (MIC: 5.3.1 SIC: 6798 NAIC: 525930)

Retail Properties of America is a real estate investment trust that owns and operates shopping centers, including properties with a mixed-use component. Co. owns retail operating properties. Co.'s retail operating portfolio includes neighborhood and community centers, power centers, and lifestyle centers and multi-tenant retail-focused mixed-use properties, as well as single-user retail properties.

Recent Developments: For the quarter ended Sep 30 2019, net loss amounted to US$28.2 million versus net income of US$12.8 million in the year-earlier quarter. Revenues were US$119.7 million, up 0.5% from US$119.1 million the year before.

Prospects: Our evaluation of Retail Properties of America as of October 4th, 2019 is the result of our systematic analysis on three basic characteristics: earnings strength, relative valuation, and recent stock price movement. The company has managed to produce a neutral trend in earnings per share over the past 5 quarters. However, recent analyst estimates for the company have been raised and RPAI has posted results that exceeded analysts' expectations. Based on operating earnings yield, the company is overvalued when compared to all of the companies we cover. Share price changes over the past year indicates that RPAI will perform poorly over the near term.

Financial Data

(US$ in Thousands)	9 Mos	6 Mos	3 Mos	12/31/2018	12/31/2017	12/31/2016	12/31/2015	12/31/2014
Earnings Per Share	0.13	0.32	0.27	0.35	1.03	0.66	0.49	0.14
Cash Flow Per Share	1.05	1.01	0.97	0.94	1.07	1.11	1.12	1.08
Tang Book Value Per Share	7.30	7.60	7.68	7.74	8.04	8.49	8.50	8.72
Dividends Per Share	0.662	0.662	0.662	0.662	0.662	0.662	0.662	0.662
Dividend Payout %	509.62	207.03	245.37	189.29	64.32	100.38	135.20	473.21
Income Statement								
Total Revenue	360,869	241,152	122,703	482,497	538,139	583,143	603,960	600,614
EBITDA	64,815	67,688	34,953	300,560	277,188	384,260	373,360	357,412
Depn & Amortn	7,585	5,420	2,764	186,385	217,580	237,420	230,590	220,892
Income Before Taxes	(2,647)	27,475	14,759	40,429	(86,484)	37,110	3,832	2,685
Net Income	16,225	44,378	23,208	77,640	251,491	166,817	125,096	43,300
Average Shares	212,995	213,090	213,223	218,231	230,927	236,951	236,382	236,187
Balance Sheet								
Current Assets	93,695	105,793	84,149	93,120	96,863	132,060	134,228	198,305
Total Assets	3,600,540	3,653,079	3,668,439	3,647,470	3,918,264	4,452,973	4,621,251	4,803,860
Current Liabilities	105,844	93,328	87,530	118,329	119,009	122,307	109,097	100,316
Long-Term Obligations	1,631,085	1,640,385	1,647,583	1,622,049	1,746,086	1,997,925	2,166,238	2,334,465
Total Liabilities	1,956,202	1,939,903	1,936,595	1,900,879	2,032,564	2,300,887	2,465,914	2,615,979
Stockholders' Equity	1,644,338	1,713,176	1,731,844	1,746,591	1,885,700	2,152,086	2,155,337	2,187,881
Shares Outstanding	213,655	213,662	213,585	213,176	219,237	236,770	237,267	236,602
Statistical Record								
Return on Assets %	0.78	1.89	1.59	2.05	6.01	3.67	2.65	0.89
Return on Equity %	1.64	3.87	3.26	4.27	12.46	7.72	5.76	1.93
EBITDA Margin %	17.96	28.07	28.49	62.29	51.51	65.89	61.82	59.51
Net Margin %	4.50	18.40	18.91	16.09	46.73	28.61	20.71	7.21
Asset Turnover	0.13	0.13	0.13	0.13	0.13	0.13	0.13	0.12
Current Ratio	0.89	1.13	0.96	0.79	0.81	1.08	1.23	1.98
Debt to Equity	0.99	0.96	0.95	0.93	0.93	0.93	1.01	1.07
Price Range	13.29-10.62	13.29-10.62	13.29-10.62	13.34-10.75	15.69-11.83	17.74-14.16	18.21-13.19	16.87-12.30
P/E Ratio	102.23-81.69	41.53-33.19	49.22-39.33	38.11-30.71	15.23-11.49	26.88-21.45	37.16-26.92	120.50-87.86
Average Yield %	5.51	5.44	5.44	5.46	4.90	4.16	4.34	4.48

Address: 2021 Spring Road, Suite 200, Oak Brook, IL 60523 **Telephone:** 630-634-4200	**Web Site:** www.rpai.com **Officers:** Gerald M. Gorski - Chairman Shane C. Garrison - President, Chief Operating Officer, Executive Vice President, Chief Investment Officer	**Auditors:** DELOITTE & TOUCHE LLP **Transfer Agents:** Registrar & Transfer Company, Cranford, NJ

RINGCENTRAL INC

Exchange	Symbol	Price	52Wk Range	Yield	P/E
NYS	RNG	$168.67 (12/31/2019)	176.70-78.42	N/A	N/A

*7 Year Price Score N/A   *NYSE Composite Index=100   *12 Month Price Score 123.63

Interim Earnings (Per Share)

Qtr.	Mar	Jun	Sep	Dec
2016	(0.09)	(0.11)	(0.11)	(0.09)
2017	(0.10)	(0.09)	(0.07)	(0.08)
2018	(0.03)	(0.10)	(0.12)	(0.07)
2019	(0.08)	(0.11)	(0.15)	...

Interim Dividends (Per Share)

No Dividends Paid

Valuation Analysis		Institutional Holding	
Forecast EPS	$0.81	No of Institutions	
	(01/17/2020)	398	
Market Cap	$14.1 Billion	Shares	
Book Value	$369.5 Million	79,079,816	
Price/Book	38.24	% Held	
Price/Sales	16.85	89.96	

Business Summary: Internet & Software (MIC: 6.3.2 SIC: 7374 NAIC: 518210)

RingCentral is a provider of software-as-a-service solutions. Co.'s product portfolio, among others, includes: RingCentral Office, which provides a unified activity for communication and collaboration across multiple modes; RingCentral Meetings, which is a collaborative meetings solution that provides web meetings, video conferencing, and screen sharing integrated with team messaging; RingCentral Professional, which is a cloud based virtual telephone service offering designed for personnel who are on the go; and RingCentral Fax, which provides online fax capabilities that allow businesses to send and receive fax documents without the need for a fax machine.

Recent Developments: For the quarter ended Sep 30 2019, net loss amounted to US$12.7 million versus a net loss of US$9.5 million in the year-earlier quarter. Revenues were US$233.4 million, up 34.2% from US$173.8 million the year before. Operating loss was US$10.7 million versus a loss of US$7.0 million in the prior-year quarter. Direct operating expenses rose 52.0% to US$59.7 million from US$39.3 million in the comparable period the year before. Indirect operating expenses increased 30.2% to US$184.3 million from US$141.6 million in the equivalent prior-year period.

Prospects: Our evaluation of RingCentral Inc as of October 4th, 2019 is the result of our systematic analysis on three basic characteristics: earnings strength, relative valuation, and recent stock price movement. The company has enjoyed a very positive trend in earnings per share over the past 5 quarters. However, recent analyst estimates for the company have been unchanged, while RNG has posted results that exceeded analysts' expectations. Based on operating earnings yield, the company is overvalued when compared to all of the companies we cover. Share price changes over the past year indicates that RNG will perform well over the near term.

Financial Data

(US$ in Thousands)	9 Mos	6 Mos	3 Mos	12/31/2018	12/31/2017	12/31/2016	12/31/2015	12/31/2014
Earnings Per Share	(0.41)	(0.38)	(0.37)	(0.33)	(0.34)	(0.40)	(0.46)	(0.72)
Cash Flow Per Share	1.13	1.06	0.98	0.91	0.54	0.41	0.07	(0.17)
Tang Book Value Per Share	3.45	3.28	3.00	3.29	2.07	1.59	1.35	1.41
Income Statement								
Total Revenue	649,993	416,641	201,489	673,624	501,526	379,724	296,228	219,887
EBITDA	9,912	8,049	3,288	8,939	(10,384)	(14,727)	(18,739)	(35,858)
Depn & Amortn	26,100	16,500	7,700	18,900	15,400	13,600	13,500	10,378
Income Before Taxes	(31,468)	(18,571)	(9,444)	(26,063)	(25,883)	(29,073)	(33,362)	(48,243)
Income Taxes	(3,118)	(2,970)	(3,086)	140	258	236	(1,263)	97
Net Income	(28,350)	(15,601)	(6,358)	(26,203)	(26,141)	(29,309)	(32,099)	(48,340)
Average Shares	83,283	82,339	81,400	79,500	76,281	72,994	70,069	66,818
Balance Sheet								
Current Assets	765,045	735,106	704,368	707,514	248,043	205,911	171,046	159,789
Total Assets	1,059,479	1,012,200	965,702	894,326	305,168	252,629	214,813	188,337
Current Liabilities	268,137	245,598	228,557	199,359	126,714	116,000	80,574	76,276
Long-Term Obligations	381,701	376,583	371,534	366,552	...	312	15,021	8,348
Total Liabilities	689,985	656,633	634,478	576,717	132,966	122,588	104,681	91,832
Stockholders' Equity	369,494	355,567	331,224	317,609	172,202	130,041	110,132	96,505
Shares Outstanding	83,776	82,874	81,828	81,046	78,054	74,383	71,963	68,559
Statistical Record								
EBITDA Margin %	1.52	1.93	1.63	1.33	N.M.	N.M.	N.M.	N.M.
Asset Turnover	0.88	0.85	0.83	1.12	1.80	1.62	1.47	1.32
Current Ratio	2.85	2.99	3.08	3.55	1.96	1.78	2.12	2.09
Debt to Equity	1.03	1.06	1.12	1.15	...	N.M.	0.14	0.09
Price Range	143.09-68.86	124.59-68.86	111.57-61.85	96.85-47.30	49.65-21.25	24.15-14.38	25.47-13.50	23.52-10.17

Address: 20 Davis Drive, Belmont, CA 94002	Web Site: www.ringcentral.com	Auditors: KPMG LLP
Telephone: 650-472-4100	Officers: Vladimir Shmunis - Chairman, Chief Executive Officer David Sipes - Chief Operating Officer, Executive Vice President, Chief Revenue Officer	Transfer Agents: Computershare Trust Company, N.A., Canton, MA

RITE AID CORP

Exchange	Symbol	Price	52Wk Range	Yield	P/E
NYS	RAD	$15.47 (12/31/2019)	20.30-5.18	N/A	N/A

*7 Year Price Score 9.86   *NYSE Composite Index=100   *12 Month Price Score 107.58

Interim Earnings (Per Share)

Qtr.	May	Aug	Nov	Feb
2016-17	0.00	0.20	0.20	(0.40)
2017-18	(1.40)	3.20	1.60	14.60
2018-19	4.00	(6.80)	0.00	(5.19)
2019-20	(1.88)	(1.49)	0.96	...

Interim Dividends (Per Share)

No Dividends Paid

Valuation Analysis	Institutional Holding	
Forecast EPS	$0.34	No of Institutions
	(01/15/2020)	380
Market Cap	$848.7 Million	Shares
Book Value	$1.0 Billion	184,049,824
Price/Book	0.84	% Held
Price/Sales	0.04	N/A

Business Summary: Retail - Food & Beverage, Drug & Tobacco (MIC: 2.1.2 SIC: 5912 NAIC: 446110)

Rite Aid is a pharmacy retail healthcare company. Co.'s Retail Pharmacy segment sells brand and generic prescription drugs, as well as an assortment of front-end products including health and beauty aids, personal care products, seasonal merchandise, and a private brand product line. Co.'s Pharmacy Services segment provides pharmacy benefit management (PBM) options through its EnvisionRxOptions and MedTrak PBMs, respectively. EnvisionRxOptions also provides mail-order and specialty pharmacy services through EnvisionPharmacies; a claims adjudication software platform in Laker Software; and a national Medicare Part D prescription drug plan through its EnvisionRx Plus product offering.

Recent Developments: For the quarter ended Nov 30 2019, income from continuing operations was US$52.3 million compared with a loss of US$17.3 million in the year-earlier quarter. Net income amounted to US$51.5 million versus a net loss of US$4.5 million in the year-earlier quarter. Revenues were US$5.46 billion, up 0.2% from US$5.45 billion the year before. Direct operating expenses was unchanged at US$4.27 billion versus the comparable period the year before. Indirect operating expenses decreased 5.4% to US$1.14 billion from US$1.20 billion in the equivalent prior-year period.

Prospects: Our evaluation of Rite Aid Corp. as of October 4th, 2019 is the result of our systematic analysis on three basic characteristics: earnings strength, relative valuation, and recent stock price movement. The company has enjoyed a very positive trend in earnings per share over the past 5 quarters. However, recent analyst estimates for the company have been mixed and RAD has posted results that exceeded analysts' expectations. Based on operating earnings yield, the company is overvalued when compared to all of the companies we cover. Share price changes over the past year indicates that RAD will perform very poorly over the near term.

Financial Data

(US$ in Thousands)	9 Mos	6 Mos	3 Mos	03/02/2019	03/03/2018	03/04/2017	02/27/2016	02/28/2015
Earnings Per Share	(7.60)	(8.56)	(13.88)	(7.99)	18.00	...	3.20	41.60
Cash Flow Per Share	(2.29)	(3.67)	...	(3.14)	8.33	4.26	19.53	13.40
Income Statement								
Total Revenue	16,201,151	10,738,853	5,372,589	21,639,557	21,528,968	32,845,073	30,736,657	26,528,377
EBITDA	335,325	142,300	50,231	(129,507)	397,541	826,517	1,050,374	1,122,955
Depn & Amortn	248,977	166,970	83,926	232,242	238,318	346,081	322,396	298,523
Income Before Taxes	(89,880)	(143,042)	(91,965)	(589,477)	(43,545)	48,445	278,404	426,820
Income Taxes	35,878	35,002	7,374	77,477	305,987	44,392	112,939	(1,682,353)
Net Income	(127,453)	(178,938)	(99,659)	(422,213)	943,470	4,053	165,465	2,109,173
Average Shares	53,584	53,041	52,976	52,854	52,481	53,041	52,118	50,893
Balance Sheet								
Current Assets	4,216,267	4,385,359	4,128,743	4,101,719	4,735,291	5,065,288	4,550,727	4,221,758
Total Assets	10,428,791	10,673,213	10,529,689	7,591,367	8,989,327	11,593,752	11,277,010	8,863,252
Current Liabilities	2,886,648	2,859,739	2,845,143	2,443,135	3,464,065	3,005,248	2,996,895	2,485,000
Long-Term Obligations	3,586,868	3,857,145	3,604,716	3,478,649	3,370,874	7,307,358	6,967,288	5,544,567
Total Liabilities	9,412,933	9,712,627	9,494,472	6,404,677	7,388,317	10,979,682	10,695,582	8,806,196
Stockholders' Equity	1,015,858	960,586	1,035,217	1,186,690	1,601,010	614,070	581,428	57,056
Shares Outstanding	54,862	54,896	53,833	54,016	53,365	52,684	52,387	49,427
Statistical Record								
Return on Assets %	N.M.	N.M.	...	N.M.	7.84	0.03	1.65	26.76
Return on Equity %	N.M.	N.M.	...	N.M.	72.82	0.67	51.97	...
EBITDA Margin %	2.07	1.33	0.93	N.M.	1.85	2.52	3.42	4.23
Net Margin %	N.M.	N.M.	N.M.	N.M.	4.38	0.01	0.54	7.95
Asset Turnover	2.33	2.29	...	2.62	1.79	2.83	3.06	3.37
Current Ratio	1.46	1.53	1.45	1.68	1.37	1.69	1.52	1.70
Debt to Equity	3.53	4.02	3.48	2.93	2.11	11.90	11.98	97.18
Price Range	22.20-5.18	27.40-5.18	42.20-7.24	42.20-12.89	104.60-28.60	174.00-105.00	186.40-121.00	170.00-90.20
P/E Ratio	...	...	...	...	5.81-1.59	N.M.	58.25-37.81	4.09-2.17

Address: 30 Hunter Lane, Camp Hill, PA 17011 **Telephone:** 717-761-2633 **Fax:** 717-975-5905	**Web Site:** www.riteaid.com **Officers:** Bruce G. Bodaken - Chairman James Peters - Chief Operating Officer	**Auditors:** Deloitte & Touche LLP **Investor Contact:** 717-214-8867 **Transfer Agents:** American Stock Transfer & Trust Company, Brooklyn, NY

RLI CORP

*7 Year Price Score 117.26 *NYSE Composite Index=100 *12 Month Price Score 105.30

Interim Earnings (Per Share)
Qtr.	Mar	Jun	Sep	Dec
2016	0.71	0.65	0.50	0.73
2017	0.45	0.59	0.04	1.29
2018	0.27	0.74	0.88	(0.47)
2019	1.46	0.89	0.71	...

Interim Dividends (Per Share)
Amt	Decl	Ex	Rec	Pay
0.23Q	05/02/2019	05/30/2019	05/31/2019	06/20/2019
0.23Q	08/14/2019	08/29/2019	08/30/2019	09/20/2019
1.00Q	11/13/2019	11/27/2019	11/29/2019	12/20/2019
0.23Q	11/13/2019	11/27/2019	11/29/2019	12/20/2019

Indicated Div: $0.92 (Div. Reinv. Plan)

Valuation Analysis
		Institutional Holding	
Forecast EPS	$2.50 (01/17/2020)	No of Institutions	334
Market Cap	$4.0 Billion	Shares	
Book Value	$999.6 Million	48,303,176	
Price/Book	4.04	% Held	
Price/Sales	4.43	88.01	

Business Summary: General Insurance (MIC: 5.2.1 SIC: 6331 NAIC: 524126)

RLI is an insurance holding company. Through its subsidiaries collectively known as RLI Insurance Group, Co. is engaged in underwriting selected property and casualty insurance. Co. has three segments: casualty, which includes commercial excess and personal umbrella, general liability, commercial transportation, professional services, small commercial, executive products, medical professional liability, and other casualty; property, which includes commercial property, marine, specialty personal and other property coverages; and surety; which includes miscellaneous surety coverage, bonds for small to medium-sized contractors, commercial surety bonds and energy surety coverages.

Recent Developments: For the quarter ended Sep 30 2019, net income decreased 17.9% to US$32.3 million from US$39.4 million in the year-earlier quarter. Revenues were US$236.9 million, down 1.5% from US$240.6 million the year before. Net premiums earned were US$211.3 million versus US$200.8 million in the prior-year quarter, an increase of 5.2%. Net investment income rose 7.5% to US$17.5 million from US$16.3 million a year ago.

Prospects: Our evaluation of RLI Corp. as of October 4th, 2019 is the result of our systematic analysis on three basic characteristics: earnings strength, relative valuation, and recent stock price movement. The company has enjoyed a very positive trend in earnings per share over the past 5 quarters. However, recent analyst estimates for the company have been mixed and RLI has posted results that exceeded analysts' expectations. Based on operating earnings yield, the company is overvalued when compared to all of the companies we cover. Share price changes over the past year indicates that RLI will perform well over the near term.

Financial Data
(US$ in Thousands)	9 Mos	6 Mos	3 Mos	12/31/2018	12/31/2017	12/31/2016	12/31/2015	12/31/2014
Earnings Per Share	2.59	2.76	2.61	1.43	2.36	2.59	3.12	3.09
Cash Flow Per Share	5.37	4.98	5.22	4.89	4.49	3.97	3.52	2.86
Tang Book Value Per Share	21.09	20.22	18.86	16.90	17.99	17.28	17.27	17.92
Dividends Per Share	1.900	1.890	1.880	1.870	2.580	2.790	2.750	3.710
Dividend Payout %	73.36	68.48	72.03	130.77	109.32	107.72	88.14	120.06
Income Statement								
Premium Income	623,485	412,230	204,689	791,366	737,937	728,608	700,161	687,375
Total Revenue	738,837	501,933	263,820	818,123	797,224	816,328	794,634	775,165
Benefits & Claims	307,206	198,216	94,297	428,193	401,584	349,778	299,045	296,609
Income Before Taxes	151,723	116,787	76,427	51,525	67,365	146,249	185,768	177,149
Income Taxes	31,252	24,629	16,268	3,402	(20,439)	42,162	59,138	54,042
Net Income	138,264	105,940	65,473	64,179	105,028	114,920	137,544	135,445
Average Shares	45,349	45,219	44,887	44,835	44,500	44,432	44,131	43,819
Balance Sheet								
Total Assets	3,505,064	3,375,109	3,236,875	3,105,065	2,947,244	2,777,633	2,736,579	2,775,542
Total Liabilities	2,505,444	2,415,161	2,342,170	2,298,223	2,093,646	1,954,061	1,913,110	1,930,480
Stockholders' Equity	999,620	959,948	894,705	806,842	853,598	823,572	823,469	845,062
Shares Outstanding	44,832	44,787	44,554	44,504	44,148	43,944	43,544	43,102
Statistical Record								
Return on Assets %	3.58	3.91	3.83	2.12	3.67	4.16	4.99	4.91
Return on Equity %	12.57	13.78	13.59	7.73	12.52	13.92	16.49	16.18
Loss Ratio %	49.27	48.08	46.07	54.11	54.42	48.01	42.71	43.15
Net Margin %	18.71	21.11	24.82	7.84	13.17	14.08	17.31	17.47
Price Range	93.96-64.57	89.94-64.57	79.86-61.74	79.86-58.71	61.61-51.02	71.00-54.60	63.02-46.91	50.54-40.31
P/E Ratio	36.28-24.93	32.59-23.39	30.60-23.66	55.85-41.06	26.11-21.62	27.41-21.08	20.20-15.04	16.36-13.05
Average Yield %	2.41	2.53	2.66	2.72	4.50	4.31	5.14	8.25

Address: 9025 North Lindbergh Drive, Peoria, IL 61615 **Telephone:** 309-692-1000 **Fax:** 309-692-1068	**Web Site:** www.rlicorp.com **Officers:** Jonathan E. Michael - Chairman, Chief Executive Officer, President Jeffrey D. Fick - Senior Vice President, Chief Legal Officer, Vice President	**Auditors:** DELOITTE & TOUCHE LLP **Investor Contact:** 309-693-5880 **Transfer Agents:** Wells Fargo Shareholder Services, St. Paul, MN

ROBERT HALF INTERNATIONAL INC.

Exchange	Symbol	Price	52Wk Range	Yield	P/E	Div Acheiver
NYS	RHI	$63.15 (12/31/2019)	68.79-52.13	1.96	16.32	14 Years

*7 Year Price Score 97.63 *NYSE Composite Index=100 *12 Month Price Score 94.15

Interim Earnings (Per Share)

Qtr.	Mar	Jun	Sep	Dec
2016	0.64	0.71	0.71	0.61
2017	0.62	0.64	0.68	0.39
2018	0.78	0.89	0.95	0.95
2019	0.93	0.98	1.01	...

Interim Dividends (Per Share)

Amt	Decl	Ex	Rec	Pay
0.31Q	02/12/2019	02/22/2019	02/25/2019	03/15/2019
0.31Q	05/02/2019	05/23/2019	05/24/2019	06/14/2019
0.31Q	08/01/2019	08/22/2019	08/23/2019	09/16/2019
0.31Q	11/06/2019	11/22/2019	11/25/2019	12/13/2019

Indicated Div: $1.24

Valuation Analysis

		Institutional Holding	
Forecast EPS	$3.90	No of Institutions	
	(01/15/2020)	703	
Market Cap	$7.3 Billion	Shares	
Book Value	$1.1 Billion	142,437,808	
Price/Book	6.59	% Held	
Price/Sales	1.22	88.03	

Business Summary: Business Services (MIC: 7.5.2 SIC: 7363 NAIC: 561320)

Robert Half International provides staffing and risk consulting services Co., through its Accountemps, Robert Half Finance & Accounting, and Robert Half Management Resources divisions, is a provider of temporary, full-time, and project personnel in accounting and finance fields. Co.'s OfficeTeam division places office and administrative personnel, ranging from executive and administrative assistants to receptionists and customer service representatives. The Robert Half Technology division provides information technology contract consultants, places employees, and provides managed services in areas ranging from multiple platform systems integration to end-user technical and desktop support.

Recent Developments: For the quarter ended Sep 30 2019, net income increased 1.7% to US$117.2 million from US$115.2 million in the year-earlier quarter. Revenues were US$1.55 billion, up 5.9% from US$1.47 billion the year before. Direct operating expenses rose 5.8% to US$905.7 million from US$855.8 million in the comparable period the year before. Indirect operating expenses increased 5.3% to US$482.7 million from US$458.6 million in the equivalent prior-year period.

Prospects: Our evaluation of Robert Half International Inc. as of October 4th, 2019 is the result of our systematic analysis on three basic characteristics: earnings strength, relative valuation, and recent stock price movement. The company has managed to produce a neutral trend in earnings per share over the past 5 quarters. In addition, recent analyst estimates for the company have been mixed and RHI has posted results in line with analysts' expectations. Based on operating earnings yield, the company is undervalued when compared to all of the companies we cover. Share price changes over the past year indicates that RHI will perform poorly over the near term.

Financial Data

(US$ in Thousands)	9 Mos	6 Mos	3 Mos	12/31/2018	12/31/2017	12/31/2016	12/31/2015	12/31/2014
Earnings Per Share	3.87	3.81	3.72	3.57	2.33	2.67	2.69	2.26
Cash Flow Per Share	4.88	4.78	4.98	4.75	3.65	3.44	3.33	2.54
Tang Book Value Per Share	7.75	7.63	7.30	7.14	7.16	6.83	6.03	5.77
Dividends Per Share	1.210	1.180	1.150	1.120	0.960	0.880	0.800	0.720
Dividend Payout %	31.27	30.97	30.91	31.37	41.20	32.96	29.74	31.86
Income Statement								
Total Revenue	4,537,047	2,984,915	1,468,530	5,800,271	5,266,789	5,250,399	5,094,933	4,695,014
EBITDA	517,007	337,371	161,881	653,169	581,210	617,537	633,945	546,306
Depn & Amortn	49,507	32,423	15,994	65,949	65,493	64,315	53,465	49,681
Income Before Taxes	471,268	307,486	147,383	591,602	517,516	554,110	581,030	497,349
Income Taxes	129,677	83,076	37,585	157,314	226,932	210,721	223,234	191,421
Net Income	341,591	224,410	109,798	434,288	290,584	343,389	357,796	305,928
Average Shares	115,868	116,988	117,966	121,602	124,892	128,766	132,930	135,541
Balance Sheet								
Current Assets	1,631,183	1,564,919	1,532,017	1,473,610	1,431,869	1,284,234	1,343,681	1,323,283
Total Assets	2,311,570	2,239,419	2,204,607	1,903,097	1,867,454	1,777,971	1,702,960	1,647,267
Current Liabilities	977,440	909,510	900,730	819,536	747,896	679,896	655,549	623,362
Long-Term Obligations	295	350	404	457	657	840	1,007	1,159
Total Liabilities	1,199,740	1,130,192	1,127,578	839,899	762,189	691,372	699,179	667,409
Stockholders' Equity	1,111,830	1,109,227	1,077,029	1,063,198	1,105,265	1,086,599	1,003,781	979,858
Shares Outstanding	116,096	117,561	118,320	119,078	124,261	127,796	131,156	135,134
Statistical Record								
Return on Assets %	20.94	21.72	21.86	23.04	15.94	19.68	21.36	19.50
Return on Equity %	40.80	40.85	40.87	40.05	26.51	32.76	36.07	32.21
EBITDA Margin %	11.40	11.30	11.02	11.26	11.04	11.76	12.44	11.64
Net Margin %	7.53	7.52	7.48	7.49	5.52	6.54	7.02	6.52
Asset Turnover	2.77	2.84	2.87	3.08	2.89	3.01	3.04	2.99
Current Ratio	1.67	1.72	1.70	1.80	1.91	1.89	2.05	2.12
Price Range	69.40-52.13	79.64-52.86	79.64-52.86	79.64-52.26	57.04-43.24	49.24-34.57	63.00-44.95	58.99-39.17
P/E Ratio	17.93-13.47	20.90-13.87	21.41-14.21	22.31-14.64	24.48-18.56	18.44-12.95	23.42-16.71	26.10-17.33
Average Yield %	2.01	1.83	1.76	1.75	1.97	2.15	1.45	1.52

Address: 2884 Sand Hill Road, Suite 200, Menlo Park, CA 94025 **Telephone:** 650-234-6000	**Web Site:** www.roberthalf.com **Officers:** Harold M. Messmer - Executive Chairman, Chairman, President, Chief Executive Officer, Principal Executive Officer M. Keith Waddell - Vice-Chairman, President, Chief Executive Officer, Chief Financial Officer, Treasurer, Principal Financial Officer	**Auditors:** PricewaterhouseCoopers LLP **Transfer Agents:** Computershare Trust Company, N.A., Canton, MA

ROCKWELL AUTOMATION, INC.

Exchange	Symbol	Price	52Wk Range	Yield	P/E
NYS	ROK	$202.67 (12/31/2019)	205.47-144.55	2.01	34.76

*7 Year Price Score 102.77 *NYSE Composite Index=100 *12 Month Price Score 108.30

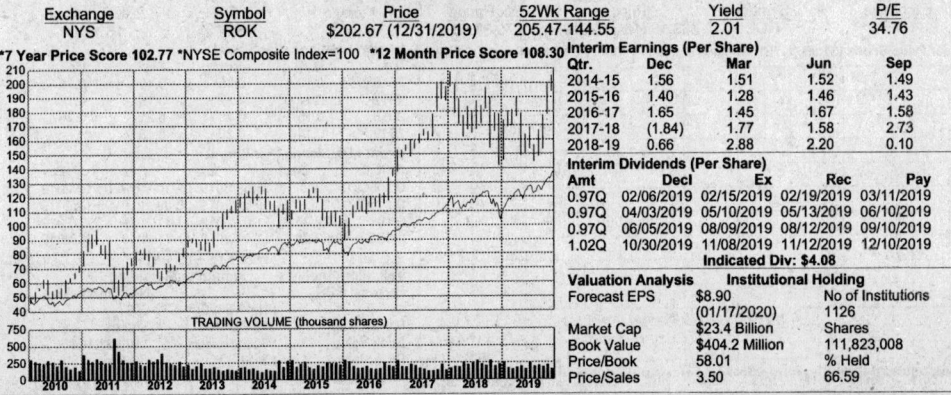

Interim Earnings (Per Share)

Qtr.	Dec	Mar	Jun	Sep
2014-15	1.56	1.51	1.52	1.49
2015-16	1.40	1.28	1.46	1.43
2016-17	1.65	1.45	1.67	1.58
2017-18	(1.84)	1.77	1.58	2.73
2018-19	0.66	2.88	2.20	0.10

Interim Dividends (Per Share)

Amt	Decl	Ex	Rec	Pay
0.97Q	02/06/2019	02/15/2019	02/19/2019	03/11/2019
0.97Q	04/03/2019	05/10/2019	05/13/2019	06/10/2019
0.97Q	06/05/2019	08/09/2019	08/12/2019	09/10/2019
1.02Q	10/30/2019	11/08/2019	11/12/2019	12/10/2019

Indicated Div: $4.08

Valuation Analysis | **Institutional Holding**

Forecast EPS	$8.90 (01/17/2020)	No of Institutions 1126
Market Cap	$23.4 Billion	Shares
Book Value	$404.2 Million	111,823,008
Price/Book	58.01	% Held
Price/Sales	3.50	66.59

Business Summary: Electrical Equipment (MIC: 7.3.1 SIC: 3829 NAIC: 334519)

Rockwell Automation is a provider of industrial automation and digital transformation. Co.'s segments include: Architecture and Software, which contains automation and information platforms, including hardware and software; and Control Products and Solutions, which combines motor control and industrial control products, other solutions and a portfolio of lifecycle services. Co.'s automation platform products include programmable automation controllers, design, networking products, sensing devices, machine safety devices, motion control products, and independent cart technology products. Co.'s information platform includes manufacturing execution system software and analytics software.

Recent Developments: For the year ended Sep 30 2019, net income increased 29.9% to US$695.8 million from US$535.5 million in the prior year. Revenues were US$6.69 billion, up 0.4% from US$6.67 billion the year before. Direct operating expenses rose 0.4% to US$3.79 billion from US$3.78 billion in the comparable period the year before. Indirect operating expenses increased 1.2% to US$1.64 billion from US$1.62 billion in the equivalent prior-year period.

Prospects: Our evaluation of Rockwell Automation Inc. as of October 4th, 2019 is the result of our systematic analysis on three basic characteristics: earnings strength, relative valuation, and recent stock price movement. The company has managed to produce a neutral trend in earnings per share over the past 5 quarters. However, recent analyst estimates for the company have been reduced while ROK has posted results that exceeded analysts' expectations. Based on operating earnings yield, the company is undervalued when compared to all of the companies we cover. Share price changes over the past year indicates that ROK will perform poorly over the near term.

Financial Data

(US$ in Thousands)	09/30/2019	09/30/2018	09/30/2017	09/30/2016	09/30/2015	09/30/2014	09/30/2013	09/30/2012
Earnings Per Share	5.83	4.21	6.35	5.56	6.09	5.91	5.36	5.13
Cash Flow Per Share	9.99	10.37	8.05	7.26	8.83	7.49	7.29	5.07
Tang Book Value Per Share	N.M.	2.70	10.50	5.14	7.54	9.96	9.72	4.96
Dividends Per Share	3.880	3.510	3.040	2.900	2.600	2.320	1.980	1.745
Dividend Payout %	66.55	83.37	47.87	52.16	42.69	39.26	36.94	34.02
Income Statement								
Total Revenue	6,694,800	6,666,000	6,311,300	5,879,500	6,307,900	6,623,500	6,351,900	6,259,400
EBITDA	1,140,300	1,544,000	1,262,900	1,173,900	1,343,000	1,336,500	1,177,200	1,156,800
Depn & Amortn	152,200	164,600	168,900	172,200	162,500	152,500	145,200	138,600
Income Before Taxes	901,000	1,330,800	1,037,400	943,100	1,127,500	1,134,200	980,900	965,900
Income Taxes	205,200	795,300	211,700	213,400	299,900	307,400	224,600	228,900
Net Income	695,800	535,500	825,700	729,700	827,600	826,800	756,300	737,000
Average Shares	119,300	126,900	129,900	131,100	135,700	139,700	140,900	143,400
Balance Sheet								
Current Assets	2,985,700	2,830,700	4,420,700	4,185,000	4,048,000	3,934,200	3,679,900	3,387,500
Total Assets	6,113,000	6,262,000	7,161,700	7,101,200	6,404,700	6,229,500	5,844,600	5,636,500
Current Liabilities	1,936,800	2,236,900	2,145,800	1,975,900	1,327,700	1,692,100	1,544,700	1,531,600
Long-Term Obligations	1,956,400	1,225,200	1,243,400	1,516,300	1,500,900	905,600	905,100	905,000
Total Liabilities	5,708,800	4,644,500	4,498,100	5,111,100	4,147,900	3,571,400	3,259,100	3,784,800
Stockholders' Equity	404,200	1,617,500	2,663,600	1,990,100	2,256,800	2,658,100	2,585,500	1,851,700
Shares Outstanding	115,700	121,100	128,400	128,500	132,400	136,700	138,900	139,800
Statistical Record								
Return on Assets %	11.25	7.98	11.58	10.78	13.10	13.70	13.17	13.46
Return on Equity %	68.83	25.02	35.49	34.27	33.68	31.54	34.09	40.84
EBITDA Margin %	17.03	23.16	20.01	19.97	21.29	20.18	18.53	18.48
Net Margin %	10.39	8.03	13.08	12.41	13.12	12.48	11.91	11.77
Asset Turnover	1.08	0.99	0.88	0.87	1.00	1.10	1.11	1.14
Current Ratio	1.54	1.27	2.06	2.12	3.05	2.33	2.38	2.21
Debt to Equity	4.84	0.76	0.47	0.76	0.67	0.34	0.35	0.49
Price Range	189.92-141.77	207.92-162.01	178.21-115.20	122.34-89.71	126.89-98.60	127.83-104.39	109.13-68.73	84.55-54.55
P/E Ratio	32.58-24.32	49.39-38.48	28.06-18.14	22.00-16.13	20.84-16.19	21.63-17.66	20.36-12.82	16.48-10.63
Average Yield %	2.34	1.92	2.02	2.65	2.28	1.97	2.27	2.39

Address: 1201 South Second Street, Milwaukee, WI 53204	**Web Site:** www.rockwellautomation.com	**Auditors:** DELOITTE & TOUCHE LLP
Telephone: 414-382-2000	**Officers:** Blake D. Moret - Chairman, President, Chief Executive Officer, Senior Vice President Patrick P. Goris - Senior Vice President, Chief Financial Officer	**Investor Contact:** 414-382-8510
		Transfer Agents: Wells Fargo Shareowner Services, St. Paul, MN

ROLLINS, INC.

Exchange	Symbol	Price	52Wk Range	Yield	P/E	Div Acheiver
NYS	ROL	$33.16 (12/31/2019)	43.75-31.53	1.27	52.63	16 Years

*7 Year Price Score 131.39 *NYSE Composite Index=100 *12 Month Price Score 91.64

Interim Earnings (Per Share)

Qtr.	Mar	Jun	Sep	Dec
2016	0.10	0.15	0.15	0.12
2017	0.12	0.17	0.16	0.10
2018	0.15	0.20	0.21	0.16
2019	0.14	0.20	0.13	...

Interim Dividends (Per Share)

Amt	Decl	Ex	Rec	Pay
0.105Q	04/23/2019	05/09/2019	05/10/2019	06/10/2019
0.105Q	07/23/2019	08/08/2019	08/09/2019	09/10/2019
0.105Q	10/22/2019	11/07/2019	11/11/2019	12/10/2019
0.05Q	10/22/2019	11/07/2019	11/11/2019	12/10/2019

Indicated Div: $0.42

Valuation Analysis / **Institutional Holding**

Forecast EPS	$0.73	No of Institutions
(01/17/2020)		516
Market Cap	$10.9 Billion	Shares
Book Value	$806.9 Million	159,433,104
Price/Book	13.46	% Held
Price/Sales	5.56	63.62

Business Summary: Business Services (MIC: 7.5.2 SIC: 7342 NAIC: 561710)

Rollins is an international service company providing pest and termite control services via its subsidiaries in North America, Australia, and Europe with international franchises in Central America, the Caribbean, the Middle East, Asia, the Mediterranean, Europe, Africa, Canada, Australia, and Mexico. Co.'s subsidiary, Orkin, LLC provides pest control services and protection against termite damage, rodents and insects to homes and businesses. Co.'s other subsidiaries include Orkin Canada, a pest control provider in Canada; Western Pest Services, a commercial pest control service company; and The Industrial Fumigant Company, a provider of pest management and sanitation services and products.

Recent Developments: For the quarter ended Sep 30 2019, net income decreased 33.9% to US$44.1 million from US$66.6 million in the year-earlier quarter. Revenues were US$556.5 million, up 14.1% from US$487.7 million the year before. Direct operating expenses rose 34.8% to US$318.6 million from US$236.3 million in the comparable period the year before. Indirect operating expenses increased 18.7% to US$191.7 million from US$161.6 million in the equivalent prior-year period.

Prospects: Our evaluation of Rollins Inc. as of October 4th, 2019 is the result of our systematic analysis on three basic characteristics: earnings strength, relative valuation, and recent stock price movement. The company has managed to produce a neutral trend in earnings per share over the past 5 quarters. In addition, recent analyst estimates for the company have been mixed and ROL has posted results that fell short of analysts' expectations. Based on operating earnings yield, the company is overvalued when compared to all of the companies we cover. Share price changes over the past year indicates that ROL will perform in line with the market over the near term.

Financial Data
(US$ in Thousands)

	9 Mos	6 Mos	3 Mos	12/31/2018	12/31/2017	12/31/2016	12/31/2015	12/31/2014
Earnings Per Share	0.63	0.70	0.70	0.71	0.55	0.51	0.47	0.42
Cash Flow Per Share	0.93	0.89	0.83	0.87	0.72	0.69	0.60	0.59
Tang Book Value Per Share	N.M.	N.M.	0.33	0.31	0.28	0.46	0.41	0.22
Dividends Per Share	0.502	0.490	0.478	0.467	0.373	0.333	0.280	0.231
Dividend Payout %	80.05	69.66	68.00	65.73	68.29	64.94	60.00	55.32
Income Statement								
Total Revenue	1,509,492	953,026	429,069	1,821,565	1,673,957	1,573,477	1,485,305	1,411,566
EBITDA	252,107	181,452	72,462	340,913	321,643	285,176	262,418	235,857
Depn & Amortn	58,505	36,815	16,683	30,400	27,400	24,700	19,400	16,627
Income Before Taxes	189,151	143,012	56,053	310,733	294,502	260,636	243,178	219,484
Income Taxes	36,569	34,491	11,827	79,070	115,378	93,267	91,029	81,820
Net Income	152,582	108,521	44,226	231,663	179,124	167,369	152,149	137,664
Average Shares	327,459	327,506	327,506	327,291	326,982	327,366	327,874	328,041
Balance Sheet								
Current Assets	324,188	319,845	289,939	286,021	262,795	290,171	313,879	283,958
Total Assets	1,764,793	1,729,777	1,272,072	1,094,124	1,033,663	916,538	852,431	808,162
Current Liabilities	410,880	414,341	352,712	299,029	294,569	276,991	252,986	252,679
Long-Term Obligations	313,500	335,375	...	...	...	...	...	...
Total Liabilities	957,896	977,513	552,948	382,216	379,739	347,993	328,402	345,486
Stockholders' Equity	806,897	752,264	719,124	711,908	653,924	568,545	524,029	462,676
Shares Outstanding	327,441	327,486	327,529	327,308	326,988	326,687	328,129	327,724
Statistical Record								
Return on Assets %	14.07	15.95	19.58	21.78	18.37	18.87	18.32	17.79
Return on Equity %	26.41	31.23	32.91	33.92	29.31	30.55	30.84	30.56
EBITDA Margin %	16.70	19.04	16.89	18.72	19.21	18.12	17.67	16.71
Net Margin %	10.11	11.39	10.31	12.72	10.70	10.64	10.24	9.75
Asset Turnover	1.35	1.33	1.59	1.71	1.72	1.77	1.79	1.82
Current Ratio	0.79	0.77	0.82	0.96	0.89	1.05	1.24	1.12
Debt to Equity	0.39	0.45	...	...	...	...	...	...
Price Range	43.75-31.53	43.75-33.79	42.77-32.35	42.77-30.31	31.87-21.94	22.73-16.05	20.23-14.18	15.02-12.07
P/E Ratio	69.44-50.05	62.50-48.27	61.10-46.21	60.24-42.69	57.95-39.89	44.56-31.48	43.05-30.17	35.76-28.73
Average Yield %	1.33	1.24	1.26	1.27	1.29	1.35	1.75	1.72

Address: 2170 Piedmont Road, N.E., Atlanta, GA 30324 **Telephone:** 404-888-2000	**Web Site:** www.rollins.com **Officers:** R. Randall Rollins - Chairman Gary W. Rollins - Vice-Chairman, President, Chief Executive Officer, Chief Operating Officer	**Auditors:** Grant Thornton LLP **Investor Contact:** 404-888-2000 **Transfer Agents:** American Stock Transfer and Trust, Brooklyn, NY

ROPER TECHNOLOGIES INC

Exchange	Symbol	Price	52Wk Range	Yield	P/E	Div Acheiver
NYS	ROP	$354.23 (12/31/2019)	384.45-258.80	0.58	32.14	26 Years

*7 Year Price Score 134.62   *NYSE Composite Index=100   *12 Month Price Score 96.88

Interim Earnings (Per Share)

Qtr.	Mar	Jun	Sep	Dec
2016	1.48	1.54	1.63	1.78
2017	1.53	1.74	1.84	4.28
2018	2.03	2.19	2.37	2.47
2019	3.53	2.38	2.64	...

Interim Dividends (Per Share)

Amt	Decl	Ex	Rec	Pay
0.463Q	03/18/2019	04/05/2019	04/08/2019	04/22/2019
0.463Q	06/17/2019	07/05/2019	07/08/2019	07/24/2019
0.463Q	09/20/2019	10/03/2019	10/04/2019	10/22/2019
0.512Q	11/15/2019	01/08/2020	01/09/2020	01/23/2020

Indicated Div: $2.05

Valuation Analysis / Institutional Holding

Forecast EPS	$13.00	No of Institutions
	(01/17/2020)	1095
Market Cap	$36.9 Billion	Shares
Book Value	$8.6 Billion	121,021,896
Price/Book	4.30	% Held
Price/Sales	6.89	93.90

Business Summary: Electrical Equipment (MIC: 7.3.1 SIC: 3823 NAIC: 334513)

Roper Technologies designs and develops software (both license and software-as-a-service) and products and solutions for a variety of end markets. Co.'s operations are reported in four segments: Radio Frequency Technology, which provides radio frequency identification communication technology and software solutions; Medical and Scientific Imaging, which provides products and software in medical applications, and digital imaging products; Industrial Technology, which produces primarily water meter and meter reading technology, fluid handling pumps, and materials analysis solutions; and Energy Systems and Controls, which produces control systems, testing equipment, valves and sensors.

Recent Developments:
For the quarter ended Sep 30 2019, net income increased 12.1% to US$277.5 million from US$247.6 million in the year-earlier quarter. Revenues were US$1.35 billion, up 2.7% from US$1.32 billion the year before. Operating income was US$385.2 million versus US$377.5 million in the prior-year quarter, an increase of 2.0%. Direct operating expenses rose 0.5% to US$480.9 million from US$478.7 million in the comparable period the year before. Indirect operating expenses increased 5.6% to US$488.4 million from US$462.5 million in the equivalent prior-year period.

Prospects:
Our evaluation of Roper Technologies Inc. as of October 4th, 2019 is the result of our systematic analysis on three basic characteristics: earnings strength, relative valuation, and recent stock price movement. The company has managed to produce a neutral trend in earnings per share over the past 5 quarters. In addition, recent analyst estimates for the company have been mixed and ROP has posted results that exceeded analysts' expectations. Based on operating earnings yield, the company is fairly valued when compared to all of the companies we cover. Share price changes over the past year indicates that ROP will perform over the near term.

Financial Data
(US$ in Thousands)

	9 Mos	6 Mos	3 Mos	12/31/2018	12/31/2017	12/31/2016	12/31/2015	12/31/2014
Earnings Per Share	11.02	10.75	10.56	9.05	9.39	6.43	6.85	6.40
Cash Flow Per Share	14.04	14.18	13.89	13.86	12.08	9.49	9.23	8.41
Dividends Per Share	1.800	1.750	1.700	1.650	1.400	1.200	1.000	0.800
Dividend Payout %	16.33	16.28	16.10	18.23	14.91	18.66	14.60	12.50
Income Statement								
Total Revenue	3,972,000	2,617,500	1,287,200	5,191,200	4,607,471	3,789,925	3,582,395	3,549,494
EBITDA	1,485,400	1,003,000	547,500	1,747,500	1,560,254	1,292,664	1,290,831	1,197,377
Depn & Amortn	268,400	172,700	84,600	367,000	344,965	240,453	204,261	197,284
Income Before Taxes	1,079,400	741,500	419,200	1,198,400	1,034,723	940,652	1,002,345	921,456
Income Taxes	182,600	122,200	49,600	254,000	62,951	282,007	306,278	275,423
Net Income	896,800	619,300	369,600	944,400	971,772	658,645	696,067	646,033
Average Shares	105,200	105,100	104,700	104,400	103,522	102,464	101,597	100,884
Balance Sheet								
Current Assets	1,619,400	1,602,300	1,586,000	1,610,700	1,759,402	1,776,501	1,618,047	1,512,105
Total Assets	17,819,100	15,908,300	15,414,100	15,249,500	14,316,413	14,324,927	10,168,365	8,412,934
Current Liabilities	1,500,900	1,443,200	1,444,700	1,448,200	2,029,409	1,445,272	720,128	627,947
Long-Term Obligations	6,195,100	4,718,900	4,487,000	4,940,200	4,354,611	5,808,561	3,264,417	2,203,031
Total Liabilities	9,247,800	7,557,300	7,276,700	7,511,000	7,452,849	8,536,062	4,869,418	3,657,574
Stockholders' Equity	8,571,300	8,351,000	8,137,400	7,738,500	6,863,564	5,788,865	5,298,947	4,755,360
Shares Outstanding	104,057	104,001	103,841	103,400	102,493	101,672	100,870	100,126
Statistical Record								
Return on Assets %	6.98	7.19	7.48	6.39	6.79	5.36	7.49	7.78
Return on Equity %	14.31	14.36	14.42	12.94	15.36	11.85	13.85	14.41
EBITDA Margin %	37.40	38.32	42.53	33.66	33.86	34.11	36.03	33.73
Net Margin %	22.58	23.66	28.71	18.19	21.09	17.38	19.43	18.20
Asset Turnover	0.32	0.34	0.36	0.35	0.32	0.31	0.39	0.43
Current Ratio	1.08	1.11	1.10	1.11	0.87	1.23	2.25	2.41
Debt to Equity	0.72	0.57	0.55	0.64	0.63	1.00	0.62	0.46
Price Range	384.45-247.01	367.61-247.01	341.97-247.01	311.51-247.01	267.21-184.93	189.79-158.89	194.83-145.75	160.48-128.99
P/E Ratio	34.89-22.41	34.20-22.98	32.38-23.39	34.42-27.29	28.46-19.69	29.52-24.71	28.44-21.28	25.07-20.15
Average Yield %	0.55	0.57	0.59	0.58	0.61	0.68	0.58	0.56

Address: 6901 Professional Parkway East, Suite 200, Sarasota, FL 34240 Telephone: 941-556-2601	Web Site: www.ropertech.com Officers: Wilbur J. Prezzano - Chairman L. Neil Hunn - President, Chief Executive Officer, Executive Vice President, Chief Operating Officer	Auditors: PricewaterhouseCoopers LLP Investor Contact: 941-556-2601 Transfer Agents: American Stock Transfer & Trust Company, New York, NY

ROYAL CARIBBEAN CRUISES LTD

Exchange	Symbol	Price	52Wk Range	Yield	P/E
NYS	RCL	$133.51 (12/31/2019)	134.17-92.55	2.34	14.59

*7 Year Price Score 111.56 *NYSE Composite Index=100 *12 Month Price Score 99.36

Interim Earnings (Per Share)

Qtr.	Mar	Jun	Sep	Dec
2016	0.46	1.06	3.21	1.21
2017	0.99	1.71	3.49	1.34
2018	1.02	2.19	3.86	1.51
2019	1.19	2.25	4.20	...

Interim Dividends (Per Share)

Amt	Decl	Ex	Rec	Pay
0.70Q	02/13/2019	03/06/2019	03/07/2019	04/05/2019
0.70Q	05/10/2019	06/03/2019	06/04/2019	07/03/2019
0.78Q	09/06/2019	09/19/2019	09/20/2019	10/11/2019
0.78Q	12/05/2019	12/19/2019	12/20/2019	01/06/2020

Indicated Div: $3.12

Valuation Analysis

		Institutional Holding	
Forecast EPS	N/A	No of Institutions	918
Market Cap	$28.0 Billion	Shares	
Book Value	$12.0 Billion		180,283,088
Price/Book	2.34	% Held	
Price/Sales	2.60		71.27

Business Summary: Hotels, Restaurants & Travel (MIC: 2.2.1 SIC: 4489 NAIC: 487210)

Royal Caribbean Cruises is a cruise company. Co. controls and operates four cruise brands: Royal Caribbean International, Celebrity Cruises, Azamara Club Cruises and Silversea Cruises. Co. also owns a joint venture interest in the German brand TUI Cruises, and an interest in the Spanish brand Pullmantur. Co.'s cruise brands provide a range of onboard services, amenities and activities, including gaming, the sale of alcoholic and other beverages, internet and other telecommunication services, gift shop items, shore excursions, photography, spa/salon and fitness services, art auctions, retail shops and a variety of restaurants and dining options.

Recent Developments: For the quarter ended June 30 2019, net income increased 2.9% to US$480.0 million from US$466.3 million in the year-earlier quarter. Revenues were US$2.81 billion, up 20.1% from US$2.34 billion the year before. Operating income was US$573.7 million versus US$456.9 million in the prior-year quarter, an increase of 25.6%. Direct operating expenses rose 17.5% to US$1.54 billion from US$1.31 billion in the comparable period the year before. Indirect operating expenses increased 21.6% to US$688.5 million from US$566.3 million in the equivalent prior-year period.

Prospects: Our evaluation of Royal Caribbean Cruises Ltd. as of October 4th, 2019 is the result of our systematic analysis on three basic characteristics: earnings strength, relative valuation, and recent stock price movement. The company has enjoyed a very positive trend in earnings per share over the past 5 quarters. However, recent analyst estimates for the company have been reduced, while RCL has posted results that exceeded analysts' expectations. Based on operating earnings yield, the company is undervalued when compared to all of the companies we cover. Share price changes over the past year indicates that RCL will perform in line with the market over the near term.

Financial Data

(US$ in Thousands)	9 Mos	6 Mos	3 Mos	12/31/2018	12/31/2017	12/31/2016	12/31/2015	12/31/2014
Earnings Per Share	9.15	8.81	8.75	8.56	7.53	5.93	3.02	3.43
Cash Flow Per Share	18.32	17.86	17.36	16.52	13.39	11.65	8.87	7.87
Tang Book Value Per Share	50.59	48.52	47.20	46.54	48.81	41.16	35.67	35.86
Dividends Per Share	2.880	2.800	2.700	2.600	2.160	1.710	1.350	1.100
Dividend Payout %	31.48	31.78	30.86	30.37	28.69	28.84	44.70	32.07
Income Statement								
Total Revenue	8,433,248	5,246,398	2,439,767	9,493,849	8,777,845	8,496,401	8,299,074	8,073,855
EBITDA	1,796,476	886,082	324,109	3,192,339	2,892,151	2,517,612	1,758,491	1,784,546
Depn & Amortn	47,737	20,467	10,366	1,075,675	997,137	947,710	827,008	772,445
Income Before Taxes	1,456,733	670,022	223,112	1,815,792	1,625,133	1,283,388	665,783	764,146
Net Income	1,605,751	722,511	249,681	1,811,042	1,625,133	1,283,388	665,783	764,146
Average Shares	210,121	210,052	209,874	211,554	215,694	216,316	220,689	223,044
Balance Sheet								
Current Assets	1,203,957	1,282,967	1,333,122	1,242,044	843,028	748,305	837,022	801,083
Total Assets	29,825,461	29,808,962	28,720,049	27,698,270	22,296,317	22,310,324	20,921,855	20,713,190
Current Liabilities	7,113,534	7,586,140	8,105,943	7,112,165	4,790,264	4,441,601	4,292,827	3,849,247
Long-Term Obligations	9,439,782	9,566,099	8,234,701	8,355,370	6,350,937	8,101,701	7,767,378	7,644,318
Total Liabilities	17,848,554	18,270,559	17,450,979	16,592,809	11,594,014	13,188,912	12,858,816	12,428,831
Stockholders' Equity	11,976,907	11,538,403	11,269,070	11,105,461	10,702,303	9,121,412	8,063,039	8,284,359
Shares Outstanding	209,607	209,518	209,549	209,016	213,337	214,594	217,993	219,297
Statistical Record								
Return on Assets %	6.77	6.88	7.01	7.24	7.29	5.92	3.20	3.75
Return on Equity %	16.52	16.61	16.85	16.61	16.40	14.90	8.15	8.94
EBITDA Margin %	21.30	16.89	13.28	33.63	32.95	29.63	21.19	22.10
Net Margin %	19.04	13.77	10.23	19.08	18.51	15.11	8.02	9.46
Asset Turnover	0.38	0.39	0.38	0.38	0.39	0.39	0.40	0.40
Current Ratio	0.17	0.17	0.16	0.17	0.18	0.17	0.19	0.21
Debt to Equity	0.79	0.83	0.73	0.75	0.59	0.89	0.96	0.92
Price Range	130.89-89.48	132.14-89.48	132.14-89.48	134.98-89.48	129.23-83.87	101.21-65.45	102.73-66.69	83.56-46.06
P/E Ratio	14.30-9.78	15.00-10.16	15.10-10.23	15.77-10.45	17.16-11.14	17.07-11.04	34.02-22.08	24.36-13.43
Average Yield %	2.61	2.44	2.44	2.25	1.96	2.25	1.59	1.86

Address: 1050 Caribbean Way, Miami, FL 33132	**Web Site:** www.royalcaribbean.com	**Auditors:** PricewaterhouseCoopers LLP
Telephone: 305-539-6000	**Officers:** Richard D. Fain - Chairman, Chief Executive Officer Adam M. Goldstein - President, Chief Operating Officer, Division Officer, Vice-Chairman	**Investor Contact:** 305-982-2625 **Transfer Agents:** American Stock Transfer and Trust Company, Brooklyn, NY

RPC, INC.

Exchange	Symbol	Price	52Wk Range	Yield	P/E
NYS	RES	$5.24 (12/31/2019)	12.89-3.45	3.82	N/A

*7 Year Price Score 40.67 *NYSE Composite Index=100 *12 Month Price Score 52.37

Interim Earnings (Per Share)

Qtr.	Mar	Jun	Sep	Dec
2016	(0.15)	(0.23)	(0.18)	(0.10)
2017	0.02	0.20	0.26	0.27
2018	0.24	0.28	0.23	0.07
2019	0.00	0.03	(0.33)	...

Interim Dividends (Per Share)

Amt	Decl	Ex	Rec	Pay
0.07Q	10/24/2018	11/08/2018	11/09/2018	12/10/2018
0.10Q	10/24/2018	11/08/2018	11/09/2018	12/10/2018
0.10Q	01/23/2019	02/08/2019	02/11/2019	03/11/2019
0.05Q	04/24/2019	05/09/2019	05/10/2019	06/10/2019

Indicated Div: $0.20

Valuation Analysis | **Institutional Holding**

Forecast EPS	$-0.17	No of Institutions
	(00/24/2020)	312
Market Cap	$1.1 Billion	Shares
Book Value	$855.2 Million	89,191,720
Price/Book	1.31	% Held
Price/Sales	0.82	36.78

Business Summary: Equipment & Services (MIC: 9.1.3 SIC: 1389 NAIC: 213112)

RPC is a holding company for several oilfield services companies. Co. provides oilfield services and equipment to oil and gas companies engaged in the exploration, production and development of oil and gas properties throughout the U.S., including the southwest, mid-continent, Gulf of Mexico, Rocky Mountain and Appalachian regions, and in selected international markets. The services provided are: Technical Services, which include pressure pumping, downhole tools, coiled tubing, snubbing, nitrogen, well control, wireline services, and fishing; and Support Services, which include rental tools, oilfield pipe inspection services, well control school and energy personnel international.

Recent Developments: For the quarter ended Sep 30 2019, net loss amounted to US$69.2 million versus net income of US$50.0 million in the year-earlier quarter. Revenues were US$293.2 million, down 33.4% from US$440.0 million the year before. Operating loss was US$92.6 million versus an income of US$54.6 million in the prior-year quarter. Direct operating expenses declined 25.2% to US$225.2 million from US$300.9 million in the comparable period the year before. Indirect operating expenses increased 90.1% to US$160.6 million from US$84.5 million in the equivalent prior-year period.

Prospects: Our evaluation of RPC Inc. as of October 4th, 2019 is the result of our systematic analysis on three basic characteristics: earnings strength, relative valuation, and recent stock price movement. The company has generated a negative trend in earnings per share over the past 5 quarters. In addition, recent analyst estimates for the company have been reduced and RES has posted results that fell short of analysts' expectations. Based on operating earnings yield, the company is overvalued when compared to all of the companies we cover. Share price changes over the past year indicates that RES will perform very poorly over the near term.

Financial Data

(US$ in Thousands)	9 Mos	6 Mos	3 Mos	12/31/2018	12/31/2017	12/31/2016	12/31/2015	12/31/2014
Earnings Per Share	(0.23)	0.33	0.58	0.82	0.75	(0.66)	(0.47)	1.14
Cash Flow Per Share	1.12	1.19	1.68	1.83	0.62	0.47	2.22	1.50
Tang Book Value Per Share	3.84	4.15	4.16	4.28	4.06	3.56	4.24	4.83
Dividends Per Share	0.320	0.420	0.470	0.470	0.200	0.050	0.155	0.420
Dividend Payout %	...	...	...	57.32	26.67	...	...	36.84
Income Statement								
Total Revenue	986,412	693,172	334,656	1,721,005	1,595,227	728,974	1,263,840	2,337,413
EBITDA	45,557	93,427	41,346	385,543	398,648	(18,546)	123,308	634,198
Depn & Amortn	132,515	86,809	43,062	166,200	166,900	220,600	274,400	233,400
Income Before Taxes	(85,643)	7,759	(1,005)	221,280	232,816	(239,360)	(153,041)	399,386
Income Taxes	(21,894)	2,327	(266)	45,878	70,305	(98,114)	(53,480)	154,193
Net Income	(63,749)	5,432	(739)	175,402	162,511	(141,246)	(99,561)	245,193
Average Shares	212,025	212,339	212,491	212,745	214,303	214,227	213,632	215,889
Balance Sheet								
Current Assets	481,111	540,127	577,852	618,938	640,135	479,057	492,208	851,628
Total Assets	1,109,863	1,223,967	1,226,492	1,199,580	1,147,224	1,035,452	1,237,094	1,759,358
Current Liabilities	136,220	172,384	163,527	143,237	145,360	101,468	107,464	239,012
Long-Term Obligations	30,165	31,624	34,348	...	...	...	...	224,500
Total Liabilities	254,688	302,292	298,629	249,161	235,527	228,653	284,813	680,976
Stockholders' Equity	855,175	921,675	927,863	950,419	911,697	806,799	952,281	1,078,382
Shares Outstanding	214,500	214,579	215,142	214,543	216,543	217,489	216,991	216,539
Statistical Record								
Return on Assets %	N.M.	5.63	10.18	14.95	14.89	N.M.	N.M.	15.60
Return on Equity %	N.M.	7.37	13.31	18.84	18.91	N.M.	N.M.	23.96
EBITDA Margin %	4.62	13.48	12.35	22.40	24.99	N.M.	9.76	27.13
Net Margin %	N.M.	0.78	N.M.	10.19	10.19	N.M.	N.M.	10.49
Asset Turnover	1.16	1.24	1.35	1.47	1.46	0.64	0.84	1.49
Current Ratio	3.53	3.13	3.53	4.32	4.40	4.72	4.58	3.56
Debt to Equity	0.04	0.03	0.04	...	...	...	...	0.21
Price Range	16.91-4.90	16.91-6.83	19.56-9.53	26.59-9.53	26.73-16.83	21.63-10.35	16.27-8.54	24.91-11.86
P/E Ratio	...	51.24-20.00	32.72-16.43	32.43-11.62	35.64-22.44	...	...	21.85-10.40
Average Yield %	3.23	3.46	3.34	2.84	0.95	0.33	1.22	2.15

Address: 2801 Buford Highway, Suite 300, Atlanta, GA 30329
Telephone: 404-321-2140

Web Site: www.rpc.net
Officers: R. Randall Rollins - Chairman Richard A. Hubbell - President, Chief Executive Officer

Auditors: Grant Thornton LLP
Investor Contact: 404-321-2140
Transfer Agents: American Stock Transfer & Trust Company, Brooklyn, NY

RPM INTERNATIONAL INC (DE)

Exchange	Symbol	Price	52Wk Range	Yield	P/E	Div Acheiver
NYS	RPM	$76.76 (12/31/2019)	76.76-52.26	1.88	30.34	45 Years

*7 Year Price Score 105.88 *NYSE Composite Index=100 *12 Month Price Score 110.30

Interim Earnings (Per Share)

Qtr.	Aug	Nov	Feb	May
2016-17	0.83	(0.54)	0.09	0.95
2017-18	0.86	0.70	0.30	0.63
2018-19	0.52	0.37	0.11	1.01
2019-20	0.82	0.59	...	...

Interim Dividends (Per Share)

Amt	Decl	Ex	Rec	Pay
0.35Q	04/03/2019	04/15/2019	04/16/2019	04/30/2019
0.35Q	07/03/2019	07/15/2019	07/16/2019	07/31/2019
0.36Q	10/03/2019	10/11/2019	10/15/2019	10/31/2019
0.36Q	01/02/2020	01/15/2020	01/16/2020	01/31/2020

Indicated Div: $1.44 (Div. Reinv. Plan)

Valuation Analysis / **Institutional Holding**

Forecast EPS	$3.36	No of Institutions
	(01/17/2020)	716
Market Cap	$10.0 Billion	Shares
Book Value	$1.4 Billion	125,464,320
Price/Book	7.11	% Held
Price/Sales	1.77	73.80

Business Summary: Specialty Chemicals (MIC: 8.3.2 SIC: 2851 NAIC: 325510)

RPM International manufactures, markets and sells various chemical product lines, including paints, infrastructure rehab and repair products, protective coatings, roofing systems, sealants and adhesives. Co.'s segments include: industrial, which includes maintenance and protection products and services for roofing and waterproofing systems; specialty, which includes industrial cleaners, restoration services equipment, colorants, exterior finishes, edible coatings and other coatings; and consumer, which includes rust-preventative, special purpose and decorative paints, caulks, sealants, primers, nail enamels, cement cleaners, floor sealers and woodcare coatings and other consumer products.

Recent Developments: For the quarter ended Aug 31 2019, net income increased 51.7% to US$106.5 million from US$70.2 million in the year-earlier quarter. Revenues were US$1.47 billion, up 0.9% from US$1.46 billion the year before. Direct operating expenses declined 1.4% to US$898.0 million from US$910.6 million in the comparable period the year before. Indirect operating expenses decreased 6.4% to US$407.2 million from US$435.1 million in the equivalent prior-year period.

Prospects: Our evaluation of RPM Inc. as of October 4th, 2019 is the result of our systematic analysis on three basic characteristics: earnings strength, relative valuation, and recent stock price movement. The company has enjoyed a very positive trend in earnings per share over the past 5 quarters. However, recent analyst estimates for the company have been unchanged, while RPM has posted results that exceeded analysts' expectations. Based on operating earnings yield, the company is fairly valued when compared to all of the companies we cover. Share price changes over the past year indicates that RPM will perform in line with the market over the near term.

Financial Data

(US$ in Thousands)	6 Mos	3 Mos	05/31/2019	05/31/2018	05/31/2017	05/31/2016	05/31/2015	05/31/2014
Earnings Per Share	2.53	2.31	2.01	2.50	1.36	2.63	1.78	2.18
Cash Flow Per Share	3.46	3.45	2.24	2.98	2.96	3.66	2.54	2.15
Dividends Per Share	1.410	1.400	1.370	1.260	1.175	1.085	1.020	0.945
Dividend Payout %	55.73	60.61	68.16	50.40	86.40	41.25	57.30	43.35
Income Statement								
Total Revenue	2,874,056	1,472,764	5,564,551	5,321,643	4,958,175	4,813,649	4,594,550	4,376,353
EBITDA	374,081	205,748	576,163	640,766	449,424	674,326	625,629	582,966
Depn & Amortn	77,572	35,839	139,143	125,176	113,770	107,232	95,088	86,743
Income Before Taxes	244,627	142,940	339,513	416,046	243,320	481,386	451,230	421,599
Income Taxes	60,784	36,353	72,158	77,791	59,662	126,008	224,925	118,503
Net Income	183,218	106,188	266,558	337,770	181,823	354,725	239,484	291,660
Average Shares	129,079	129,504	134,333	137,171	135,165	136,716	134,893	132,288
Balance Sheet								
Current Assets	2,360,265	2,416,269	2,518,092	2,470,931	2,397,436	2,138,342	2,099,846	2,062,295
Total Assets	5,580,998	5,596,425	5,441,355	5,271,822	5,090,449	4,776,041	4,694,240	4,378,365
Current Liabilities	984,068	1,496,572	1,539,405	1,006,726	1,235,394	1,002,191	903,236	937,086
Long-Term Obligations	2,421,339	2,018,185	1,973,462	2,170,643	1,836,437	1,646,332	1,654,037	1,345,965
Total Liabilities	4,180,306	4,253,033	4,035,403	3,641,049	3,654,388	3,403,706	3,402,848	2,995,521
Stockholders' Equity	1,400,692	1,343,392	1,405,952	1,630,773	1,436,061	1,372,335	1,291,392	1,382,844
Shares Outstanding	129,767	129,669	130,995	133,647	133,563	132,944	133,203	133,273
Statistical Record								
Return on Assets %	6.11	5.60	4.98	6.52	3.69	7.47	5.28	6.87
Return on Equity %	22.55	20.51	17.56	22.03	12.95	26.56	17.91	22.58
EBITDA Margin %	13.02	13.97	10.35	12.04	9.06	14.01	13.62	13.32
Net Margin %	6.37	7.21	4.79	6.35	3.67	7.37	5.21	6.66
Asset Turnover	1.04	1.03	1.04	1.03	1.01	1.01	1.01	1.03
Current Ratio	2.40	1.61	1.64	2.45	1.94	2.13	2.32	2.20
Debt to Equity	1.73	1.50	1.40	1.33	1.28	1.20	1.28	0.97
Price Range	75.62-52.26	69.51-52.26	68.05-49.39	56.01-46.92	56.26-46.29	51.45-37.38	51.82-40.22	44.14-31.20
P/E Ratio	29.89-20.66	30.09-22.62	33.86-24.57	22.40-18.77	41.37-34.04	19.56-14.21	29.11-22.60	20.25-14.31
Average Yield %	2.25	2.30	2.30	2.45	2.25	2.38	2.17	2.46

Address: P.O. Box 777, 2628 Pearl Road, Medina, OH 44258	**Web Site:** www.rpminc.com	**Auditors:** DELOITTE & TOUCHE LLP
Telephone: 330-273-5090	**Officers:** Frank C. Sullivan - Chairman, President, Chief Executive Officer Edward W. Moore - Senior	**Investor Contact:** 800-776-4488
Fax: 330-225-8743	Vice President, Vice President, Chief Compliance Officer, General Counsel, Secretary	**Transfer Agents:** EQ Shareowner Services, St. Paul, MN

RYDER SYSTEM, INC.

Exchange	Symbol	Price	52Wk Range	Yield	P/E	Div Acheiver
NYS	R	$54.31 (12/31/2019)	67.19-45.12	4.12	20.89	14 Years

*7 Year Price Score 64.42   *NYSE Composite Index=100   *12 Month Price Score 89.82

Interim Earnings (Per Share)

Qtr.	Mar	Jun	Sep	Dec
2016	1.04	1.38	1.59	0.90
2017	0.71	0.96	1.11	12.10
2018	0.63	0.80	1.68	2.06
2019	0.86	1.43	(1.75)	...

Interim Dividends (Per Share)

Amt	Decl	Ex	Rec	Pay
0.54Q	02/08/2019	02/15/2019	02/19/2019	03/15/2019
0.54Q	05/03/2019	05/17/2019	05/20/2019	06/21/2019
0.56Q	07/11/2019	08/16/2019	08/19/2019	09/20/2019
0.56Q	10/04/2019	11/15/2019	11/18/2019	12/20/2019

Indicated Div: $2.24 (Div. Reinv. Plan)

Valuation Analysis

		Institutional Holding	
Forecast EPS	$1.05	No of Institutions	
	(01/15/2020)	513	
Market Cap	$2.9 Billion	Shares	
Book Value	$2.5 Billion	64,116,212	
Price/Book	1.17	% Held	
Price/Sales	0.32	89.55	

Business Summary: Trucking (MIC: 7.4.1 SIC: 7513 NAIC: 532120)

Ryder System is engaged in transportation and supply chain management solutions. Co.'s segments include: Fleet Management Solutions, which provides full service leasing and leasing with maintenance options, commercial rental, contract or transactional maintenance services, and fleet support services such as insurance, vehicle administration and fuel services; Dedicated Transportation Solutions, which combines equipment, maintenance, drivers, administrative services and additional services to provide a dedicated transportation solution; and Supply Chain Solutions, which provides logistics management services, including distribution management, transportation management and other services.

Recent Developments: For the quarter ended Sep 30 2019, loss from continuing operations was US$91.5 million compared with income of US$91.6 million in the year-earlier quarter. Net loss amounted to US$91.5 million versus net income of US$90.8 million in the year-earlier quarter. Revenues were US$2.22 billion, up 3.0% from US$2.16 billion the year before. Direct operating expenses rose 12.5% to US$1.97 billion from US$1.75 billion in the comparable period the year before. Indirect operating expenses increased 19.2% to US$349.1 million from US$292.8 million in the equivalent prior-year period.

Prospects: Our evaluation of Ryder System Inc. as of October 4th, 2019 is the result of our systematic analysis on three basic characteristics: earnings strength, relative valuation, and recent stock price movement. The company has managed to produce a neutral trend in earnings per share over the past 5 quarters. However, recent analyst estimates for the company have been reduced while R has posted results that exceeded analysts' expectations. Based on operating earnings yield, the company is undervalued when compared to all of the companies we cover. Share price changes over the past year indicates that R will perform in line with the market over the near term.

Financial Data

(US$ in Thousands)	9 Mos	6 Mos	3 Mos	12/31/2018	12/31/2017	12/31/2016	12/31/2015	12/31/2014
Earnings Per Share	2.60	6.03	5.40	5.17	14.87	4.90	5.71	4.11
Cash Flow Per Share	38.45	35.53	34.45	31.21	29.42	30.12	27.30	26.08
Tang Book Value Per Share	36.58	38.96	38.18	44.73	45.26	30.25	28.84	25.64
Dividends Per Share	2.180	2.160	2.140	2.120	1.800	1.700	1.560	1.420
Dividend Payout %	83.85	35.82	39.63	41.01	12.10	34.69	27.32	34.55
Income Statement								
Total Revenue	6,649,252	4,425,320	2,180,327	8,409,215	7,329,599	6,786,984	6,571,893	6,638,774
EBITDA	1,726,565	1,137,930	549,366	653,421	548,136	642,224	703,649	1,520,883
Depn & Amortn	1,468,035	850,615	425,879	101,000	94,000	88,000	84,000	1,040,259
Income Before Taxes	79,960	171,220	68,151	373,861	313,786	406,381	469,215	338,549
Income Taxes	50,156	49,878	22,261	98,254	(477,229)	141,741	163,226	118,090
Net Income	29,076	120,531	45,316	273,298	790,558	262,477	304,768	218,575
Average Shares	52,319	52,549	52,641	52,696	52,988	53,361	53,260	53,036
Balance Sheet								
Current Assets	1,572,138	1,571,448	1,557,785	1,568,391	1,322,282	1,101,557	1,098,302	1,076,197
Total Assets	14,482,844	14,522,054	13,948,985	13,051,084	11,452,231	10,902,454	10,967,809	9,675,986
Current Liabilities	2,532,852	2,641,149	2,754,579	2,292,321	2,012,778	1,744,069	1,680,255	1,093,591
Long-Term Obligations	6,805,886	6,619,060	6,025,679	5,693,646	4,583,582	4,599,864	4,883,326	4,500,275
Total Liabilities	12,005,857	11,914,348	11,382,181	10,140,757	8,617,215	8,850,179	8,980,698	7,856,512
Stockholders' Equity	2,476,987	2,607,706	2,566,804	2,910,327	2,835,016	2,052,275	1,987,111	1,819,474
Shares Outstanding	53,292	53,334	53,300	53,116	52,955	53,463	53,490	53,039
Statistical Record								
Return on Assets %	1.01	2.38	2.22	2.23	7.07	2.39	2.95	2.33
Return on Equity %	5.11	11.67	10.51	9.51	32.35	12.96	16.01	11.76
EBITDA Margin %	25.97	25.71	25.20	7.77	7.48	9.46	10.71	22.91
Net Margin %	0.44	2.72	2.08	3.25	10.79	3.87	4.64	3.29
Asset Turnover	0.66	0.66	0.68	0.69	0.66	0.62	0.64	0.71
Current Ratio	0.62	0.59	0.57	0.68	0.66	0.63	0.65	0.98
Debt to Equity	2.75	2.54	2.35	1.96	1.62	2.24	2.46	2.47
Price Range	73.22-45.12	79.01-45.15	79.01-45.15	89.82-45.15	85.02-63.04	84.69-47.79	99.58-54.03	95.52-68.76
P/E Ratio	28.16-17.35	13.10-7.49	14.63-8.36	17.37-8.73	5.72-4.24	17.28-9.75	17.44-9.46	23.24-16.73
Average Yield %	3.83	3.43	3.26	2.99	2.38	2.59	1.85	1.69

Address: 11690 N.W., 105th Street, Miami, FL 33178 Telephone: 305-500-3726	Web Site: www.ryder.com Officers: Robert E. Sanchez - Chairman, President, President (frmr), Chief Executive Officer, Chief Operating Officer, Division Officer Robert D. Fatovic - Executive Vice President, Chief Legal Officer, Corporate Secretary	Auditors: PricewaterhouseCoopers LLP Investor Contact: 305-500-4053 Transfer Agents: Wells Fargo Bank, N.A., St. Paul, MN

S&P GLOBAL INC

Exchange	Symbol	Price	52Wk Range	Yield	P/E	Div Acheiver
NYS	SPGI	$273.05 (12/31/2019)	274.38-164.37	0.84	32.43	45 Years

*7 Year Price Score 145.25 *NYSE Composite Index=100 *12 Month Price Score 108.72

Interim Earnings (Per Share)

Qtr.	Mar	Jun	Sep	Dec
2016	1.10	1.44	3.36	2.05
2017	1.53	1.62	1.61	1.03
2018	1.93	1.82	1.95	2.03
2019	1.65	2.24	2.50	...

Interim Dividends (Per Share)

Amt	Decl	Ex	Rec	Pay
0.57Q	01/30/2019	02/25/2019	02/26/2019	03/12/2019
0.57Q	05/09/2019	05/28/2019	05/29/2019	06/12/2019
0.57Q	06/25/2019	08/26/2019	08/27/2019	09/11/2019
0.57Q	11/05/2019	11/25/2019	11/25/2019	12/11/2019

Indicated Div: $2.28 (Div. Reinv. Plan)

Valuation Analysis / **Institutional Holding**

Forecast EPS	$9.40	No of Institutions	
	(01/15/2020)	1377	
Market Cap	$66.7 Billion	Shares	
Book Value	$346.0 Million	266,727,456	
Price/Book	192.87	% Held	
Price/Sales	10.27	N/A	

Business Summary: Finance Intermediaries & Services (MIC: 5.5.1 SIC: 7323 NAIC: 561450)

S&P Global is a provider of transparent and independent ratings, benchmarks, analytics and data to the capital and commodity markets worldwide. Co.'s segments include: S&P Global Ratings, which provides credit ratings, research and analytics; S&P Global Market Intelligence, which provides multi-asset-class data, research and analytical capabilities that integrate cross-asset analytics and desktop services; S&P Global Platts, which provides information and benchmark prices for the commodity and energy markets; and S&P Dow Jones Indices, which provides a variety of valuation and index benchmarks for investment advisors, wealth managers and institutional investors.

Recent Developments: For the quarter ended Sep 30 2019, net income increased 23.7% to US$662.0 million from US$535.0 million in the year-earlier quarter. Revenues were US$1.69 billion, up 9.2% from US$1.55 billion the year before. Operating income was US$891.0 million versus US$704.0 million in the prior-year quarter, an increase of 26.6%. Direct operating expenses rose 6.8% to US$438.0 million from US$410.0 million in the comparable period the year before. Indirect operating expenses decreased 16.7% to US$360.0 million from US$432.0 million in the equivalent prior-year period.

Prospects: Our evaluation of S&P Global Inc. as of October 4th, 2019 is the result of our systematic analysis on three basic characteristics: earnings strength, relative valuation, and recent stock price movement. The company has managed to produce a neutral trend in earnings per share over the past 5 quarters. However, recent analyst estimates for the company have been raised and SPGI has posted results that exceeded analysts' expectations. Based on operating earnings yield, the company is fairly valued when compared to all of the companies we cover. Share price changes over the past year indicates that SPGI will perform over the near term.

Financial Data

(US$ in Thousands)	9 Mos	6 Mos	3 Mos	12/31/2018	12/31/2017	12/31/2016	12/31/2015	12/31/2014
Earnings Per Share	8.42	7.87	7.45	7.73	5.78	7.94	4.21	(0.42)
Cash Flow Per Share	9.94	8.82	8.09	8.23	7.87	5.56	0.72	4.45
Dividends Per Share	2.210	2.140	2.070	2.000	1.640	1.440	1.320	1.200
Dividend Payout %	26.25	27.19	27.79	25.87	28.37	18.14	31.35	...
Income Statement								
Total Revenue	4,964,000	3,275,000	1,571,000	6,258,000	6,063,000	5,661,000	5,313,000	5,051,000
EBITDA	2,457,000	1,525,000	654,000	3,021,000	2,790,000	3,550,000	2,074,000	247,000
Depn & Amortn	153,000	104,000	52,000	206,000	180,000	181,000	157,000	134,000
Income Before Taxes	2,199,000	1,348,000	566,000	2,681,000	2,461,000	3,188,000	1,815,000	54,000
Income Taxes	482,000	293,000	113,000	560,000	823,000	960,000	547,000	245,000
Net Income	1,582,000	965,000	410,000	1,958,000	1,496,000	2,106,000	1,156,000	(115,000)
Average Shares	246,500	247,400	248,300	253,200	258,900	265,200	274,600	271,500
Balance Sheet								
Current Assets	3,722,000	3,694,000	3,182,000	3,604,000	4,324,000	3,671,000	3,296,000	3,966,000
Total Assets	10,188,000	10,185,000	9,720,000	9,458,000	9,425,000	8,669,000	8,183,000	6,771,000
Current Liabilities	3,373,000	2,699,000	2,655,000	2,629,000	3,214,000	2,611,000	2,908,000	3,967,000
Long-Term Obligations	2,966,000	3,664,000	3,663,000	3,662,000	3,170,000	3,564,000	3,468,000	799,000
Total Liabilities	9,842,000	9,673,000	9,393,000	8,830,000	8,714,000	8,019,000	7,989,000	6,283,000
Stockholders' Equity	346,000	512,000	327,000	628,000	711,000	650,000	194,000	488,000
Shares Outstanding	244,400	246,300	246,100	248,400	253,700	258,300	265,200	272,000
Statistical Record								
Return on Assets %	21.39	20.32	20.61	20.74	16.54	24.93	15.46	N.M.
Return on Equity %	334.61	360.00	1,123.95	292.46	219.84	497.69	339.00	N.M.
EBITDA Margin %	49.50	46.56	41.63	48.27	46.02	62.71	39.04	4.89
Net Margin %	31.87	29.47	26.10	31.29	24.67	37.20	21.76	N.M.
Asset Turnover	0.66	0.66	0.69	0.66	0.67	0.67	0.71	0.79
Current Ratio	1.10	1.37	1.20	1.37	1.35	1.41	1.13	1.00
Debt to Equity	8.57	7.16	11.20	5.83	4.46	5.48	17.88	1.64
Price Range	267.75-159.00	231.28-159.00	214.78-159.00	214.78-159.00	172.57-108.39	127.56-80.77	108.59-85.40	93.71-71.98
P/E Ratio	31.80-18.88	29.39-20.20	28.83-21.34	27.79-20.57	29.86-18.75	16.07-10.17	25.79-20.29	...
Average Yield %	1.05	1.07	1.07	1.04	1.13	1.32	1.33	1.47

Address: 55 Water Street, New York, NY 10041 Telephone: 212-438-1000	Web Site: www.spglobal.com Officers: Douglas L. Peterson - President, Chief Executive Officer, Division Officer Ewout L. Steenbergen - Executive Vice President, Chief Financial Officer	Auditors: Ernst & Young LLP Investor Contact: 866-436-8502,21243 Transfer Agents: Computershare, Louisville, KY

SALESFORCE.COM INC

Exchange	Symbol	Price	52Wk Range	Yield	P/E
NYS	CRM	$162.64 (12/31/2019)	166.95-130.40	N/A	173.02

*7 Year Price Score 143.39 *NYSE Composite Index=100 *12 Month Price Score 98.09

TRADING VOLUME (thousand shares)

Interim Earnings (Per Share)

Qtr.	Apr	Jul	Oct	Jan
2016-17	0.06	0.33	(0.05)	(0.07)
2017-18	(0.01)	0.02	0.07	0.09
2018-19	0.46	0.39	0.13	0.46
2019-20	0.49	0.11	(0.12)	...

Interim Dividends (Per Share)

No Dividends Paid

Valuation Analysis		Institutional Holding	
Forecast EPS	$2.89	No of Institutions	1823
	(01/17/2020)		
Market Cap	$144.1 Billion	Shares	
Book Value	$33.3 Billion		799,585,856
Price/Book	4.33	% Held	
Price/Sales	9.09		98.69

Business Summary: Internet & Software (MIC: 6.3.2 SIC: 7372 NAIC: 511210)

Salesforce.Com is engaged in customer relationship management technology. The Salesforce Customer Success Platform delivers services spanning sales, service, marketing, commerce, engagement, integration, analytics, industries, communities, enablement and collaboration, which operate on a single trusted cloud platform. Through its platform and other developer tools, Co. also enables third parties to develop additional functionality and applications, or apps, that run on its platform, which are sold separately from or in conjunction with Co.'s service offerings. Co.'s cloud service offerings include sales cloud, service cloud, marketing and commerce cloud, and salesforce platform and other.

Recent Developments: For the quarter ended Oct 31 2019, net loss amounted to US$109.0 million versus net income of US$105.0 million in the year-earlier quarter. Revenues were US$4.51 billion, up 33.0% from US$3.39 billion the year before. Operating income was US$65.0 million versus US$92.0 million in the prior-year quarter, a decrease of 29.3%. Direct operating expenses rose 27.6% to US$1.13 billion from US$889.0 million in the comparable period the year before. Indirect operating expenses increased 37.5% to US$3.31 billion from US$2.41 billion in the equivalent prior-year period.

Prospects: Our evaluation of Salesforce.com Inc. as of October 4th, 2019 is the result of our systematic analysis on three basic characteristics: earnings strength, relative valuation, and recent stock price movement. The company has generated a negative trend in earnings per share over the past 5 quarters. However, recent analyst estimates for the company have been unchanged while CRM has posted results that exceeded analysts' expectations. Based on operating earnings yield, the company is overvalued when compared to all of the companies we cover. Share price changes over the past year indicates that CRM will perform well over the near term.

Financial Data

(US$ in Thousands)	9 Mos	6 Mos	3 Mos	01/31/2019	01/31/2018	01/31/2017	01/31/2016	01/31/2015
Earnings Per Share	0.94	1.19	1.47	1.43	0.17	0.26	(0.07)	(0.42)
Cash Flow Per Share	4.58	4.99	5.05	4.52	3.83	3.14	2.44	1.88
Tang Book Value Per Share	3.69	2.87	2.32	0.88	1.52	N.M.	0.74	N.M.
Income Statement								
Total Revenue	12,247,000	7,734,000	3,737,000	13,282,000	10,480,012	8,391,984	6,667,216	5,373,586
EBITDA	1,357,000	1,072,000	691,000	1,548,000	661,851	437,171	438,764	106,752
Depn & Amortn	647,000	426,000	209,000	411,000	372,800	322,800	302,000	246,600
Income Before Taxes	710,000	646,000	482,000	983,000	202,108	25,383	64,279	(213,085)
Income Taxes	336,000	163,000	90,000	(127,000)	74,630	(154,249)	111,705	49,603
Net Income	374,000	483,000	392,000	1,110,000	127,478	179,632	(47,426)	(262,688)
Average Shares	879,000	795,000	793,000	775,000	734,598	700,217	661,647	624,148
Balance Sheet								
Current Assets	11,026,000	9,903,000	10,035,000	10,683,000	9,290,371	5,996,827	4,347,327	3,550,072
Total Assets	49,942,000	33,336,000	33,154,000	30,737,000	21,009,802	17,584,923	12,770,772	10,692,982
Current Liabilities	10,474,000	10,195,000	10,488,000	11,255,000	10,129,518	7,258,353	5,617,005	4,390,103
Long-Term Obligations	2,824,000	2,973,000	3,173,000	3,173,000	694,781	2,008,391	1,293,947	1,370,692
Total Liabilities	16,663,000	16,170,000	16,708,000	15,132,000	11,617,439	10,084,796	7,767,903	6,717,799
Stockholders' Equity	33,279,000	17,166,000	16,446,000	15,605,000	9,392,363	7,500,127	5,002,869	3,975,183
Shares Outstanding	886,000	780,000	775,000	770,000	729,853	707,460	670,929	650,596
Statistical Record								
Return on Assets %	1.92	3.21	4.13	4.29	0.66	1.18	N.M.	N.M.
Return on Equity %	3.07	6.19	8.42	8.88	1.51	2.87	N.M.	N.M.
EBITDA Margin %	11.08	13.86	18.49	11.65	6.32	5.21	6.58	1.99
Net Margin %	3.05	6.25	10.49	8.36	1.22	2.14	N.M.	N.M.
Asset Turnover	0.41	0.50	0.50	0.50	0.54	0.55	0.57	0.54
Current Ratio	1.05	0.97	0.96	0.95	0.92	0.83	0.77	0.81
Debt to Equity	0.08	0.17	0.19	0.20	0.07	0.27	0.26	0.34
Price Range	166.95-120.67	166.95-120.67	166.95-120.67	160.43-104.03	113.91-78.58	83.77-54.05	82.14-57.28	66.22-49.13
P/E Ratio	177.61-128.37	140.29-101.40	113.57-82.09	112.19-72.75	670.06-462.24	322.19-207.88	...	...

Address: Salesforce Tower, 415 Mission Street, 3rd Fl, San Francisco, CA 94105 Telephone: 415-901-7000	Web Site: www.salesforce.com Officers: Marc Benioff - Chairman, Chief Executive Officer, Co-Chief Executive Officer Keith G. Block - Vice-Chairman, President, Co-Chief Executive Officer, Chief Operating Officer	Auditors: Ernst & Young LLP Investor Contact: 415-536-6250 Transfer Agents: Computershare, Providence, RI

SALLY BEAUTY HOLDINGS INC

Exchange	Symbol	Price	52Wk Range	Yield	P/E
NYS	SBH	$18.25 (12/31/2019)	20.00-11.73	N/A	8.08

*7 Year Price Score 55.87 *NYSE Composite Index=100 *12 Month Price Score 105.87

Interim Earnings (Per Share)

Qtr.	Dec	Mar	Jun	Sep
2014-15	0.35	0.39	0.39	0.36
2015-16	0.28	0.41	0.46	0.36
2016-17	0.39	0.41	0.49	0.28
2017-18	0.65	0.49	0.48	0.46
2018-19	0.54	0.54	0.59	0.58

Interim Dividends (Per Share)

No Dividends Paid

Valuation Analysis | **Institutional Holding**

Forecast EPS	$2.33	No of Institutions	
	(01/10/2020)	355	
Market Cap	$2.1 Billion	Shares	
Book Value	N/A		174,550,336
Price/Book	N/A	% Held	
Price/Sales	0.55		77.78

Business Summary: Retail - Specialty (MIC: 2.1.3 SIC: 5999 NAIC: 446120)

Sally Beauty Holdings is a holding company. Through its subsidiaries, Co. is an international retailer and distributor of beauty supplies with operations in North America, South America and Europe. Co.'s business segments are: Sally Beauty Supply (SBS), which is an open-line retailer of beauty supplies; and Beauty Systems Group (BSG), which is a beauty supply distributor. SBS stores and websites carry beauty supplies, featuring beauty products across product categories including hair color and care, and skin and nail care. Co. features beauty products in its BSG stores across product categories including hair color and care, skin and nail care, styling tools and other beauty items.

Recent Developments: For the year ended Sep 30 2019, net income increased 5.3% to US$271.6 million from US$258.0 million in the prior year. Revenues were US$3.88 billion, down 1.4% from US$3.93 billion the year before. Operating income was US$458.5 million versus US$426.6 million in the prior year, an increase of 7.5%. Direct operating expenses declined 1.1% to US$1.97 billion from US$1.99 billion in the comparable period the year before. Indirect operating expenses decreased 4.3% to US$1.45 billion from US$1.52 billion in the equivalent prior-year period.

Prospects: Our evaluation of Sally Beauty Holdings Inc. as of October 4th, 2019 is the result of our systematic analysis on three basic characteristics: earnings strength, relative valuation, and recent stock price movement. The company has managed to produce a neutral trend in earnings per share over the past 5 quarters. Additionally, recent analyst estimates for the company have been unchanged while SBH has posted results that exceeded analysts' expectations. Based on operating earnings yield, the company is undervalued when compared to all of the companies we cover. Share price changes over the past year indicates that SBH will perform very poorly over the near term.

Financial Data
(US$ in Thousands)

	09/30/2019	09/30/2018	09/30/2017	09/30/2016	09/30/2015	09/30/2014	09/30/2013	09/30/2012
Earnings Per Share	2.26	2.08	1.56	1.50	1.49	1.51	1.48	1.24
Cash Flow Per Share	2.68	3.03	2.50	2.38	1.92	1.98	1.81	1.62
Income Statement								
Total Revenue	3,876,411	3,932,565	3,938,317	3,952,618	3,834,343	3,753,498	3,622,216	3,523,644
EBITDA	554,573	523,789	577,797	584,597	570,426	572,096	579,762	550,355
Depn & Amortn	96,100	97,200	99,200	86,300	75,100	65,100	59,400	51,000
Income Before Taxes	362,164	328,427	345,698	354,060	378,484	390,679	412,667	360,943
Income Taxes	90,541	70,380	130,622	131,118	143,397	144,686	151,516	127,879
Net Income	271,623	258,047	215,076	222,942	235,087	245,993	261,151	233,064
Average Shares	120,283	123,832	138,176	148,803	158,226	163,419	176,159	188,610
Balance Sheet								
Current Assets	1,163,553	1,155,083	1,170,503	1,172,827	1,187,102	1,104,149	1,015,817	1,163,907
Total Assets	2,098,446	2,097,414	2,123,093	2,132,063	2,094,351	2,029,973	1,950,086	2,065,800
Current Liabilities	456,079	491,173	574,565	488,665	491,699	463,537	542,653	477,388
Long-Term Obligations	1,594,542	1,768,808	1,771,853	1,783,294	1,786,839	1,810,667	1,612,685	1,615,322
Total Liabilities	2,158,769	2,365,970	2,486,709	2,408,229	2,392,172	2,377,026	2,253,565	2,180,885
Stockholders' Equity	(60,323)	(268,556)	(363,616)	(276,166)	(297,821)	(347,053)	(303,479)	(115,085)
Shares Outstanding	116,725	119,926	129,585	144,571	151,452	154,668	164,425	180,241
Statistical Record								
Return on Assets %	12.95	12.23	10.11	10.52	11.40	12.36	13.01	12.25
EBITDA Margin %	14.31	13.32	14.67	14.79	14.88	15.24	16.01	15.62
Net Margin %	7.01	6.56	5.46	5.64	6.13	6.55	7.21	6.61
Asset Turnover	1.85	1.86	1.85	1.87	1.86	1.89	1.80	1.85
Current Ratio	2.55	2.35	2.04	2.40	2.41	2.38	1.87	2.44
Price Range	22.59-11.73	19.91-13.89	29.12-17.38	32.75-22.13	34.88-23.44	30.67-24.14	31.57-22.76	28.07-16.28
P/E Ratio	10.00-5.19	9.57-6.68	18.67-11.14	21.83-14.75	23.41-15.73	20.31-15.99	21.33-15.38	22.64-13.13

Address: 3001 Colorado Boulevard, Denton, TX 76210 Telephone: 940-898-7500	Web Site: www.sallybeautyholdings.com Officers: Robert R. (Bob) McMaster - Chairman Christian A. Brickman - President, Chief Executive Officer, Chief Operating Officer	Auditors: KPMG LLP Investor Contact: 940-297-3877 Transfer Agents: Computershare Trust Company N.A., Providence, RI

SANTANDER CONSUMER USA HOLDINGS INC

Exchange	Symbol	Price	52Wk Range	Yield	P/E
NYS	SC	$23.37 (12/31/2019)	27.51-17.59	3.77	8.59

*7 Year Price Score N/A *NYSE Composite Index=100 *12 Month Price Score 97.74

Interim Earnings (Per Share)

Qtr.	Mar	Jun	Sep	Dec
2016	0.56	0.79	0.59	0.17
2017	0.40	0.74	0.55	1.61
2018	0.67	0.92	0.64	0.30
2019	0.70	1.05	0.67	...

Interim Dividends (Per Share)

Amt	Decl	Ex	Rec	Pay
0.20Q	01/30/2019	02/08/2019	02/11/2019	02/21/2019
0.20Q	04/30/2019	05/09/2019	05/10/2019	05/20/2019
0.22Q	07/12/2019	08/02/2019	08/05/2019	08/15/2019
0.22Q	10/29/2019	11/08/2019	11/12/2019	11/22/2019

Indicated Div: $0.88

Valuation Analysis

		Institutional Holding	
Forecast EPS	$2.80	No of Institutions	275
	(01/17/2020)		
Market Cap	$8.0 Billion	Shares	
Book Value	$7.3 Billion		358,736,672
Price/Book	1.09	% Held	
Price/Sales	1.03		95.55

TRADING VOLUME (thousand shares)

Business Summary: Credit & Lending (MIC: 5.4.1 SIC: 6141 NAIC: 522298)

Santander Consumer USA Holdings is a holding company, focused on vehicle finance and third-party servicing. Co. is engaged in the indirect origination and securitization of retail installment contracts through manufacturer-franchised dealers in connection with their sale of new and used vehicles. Uder the Chrysler Agreement with FCA US LLC (FCA), Co. operates as FCA's preferred provider for consumer loans, leases and Dealer Loans and provides services to FCA customers and dealers. These products and services include consumer retail installment contracts and leases, as well as Dealer Loans for inventory, construction, real estate, working capital and revolving lines of credit.

Recent Developments: For the quarter ended Sep 30 2019, net income increased 0.3% to US$232.5 million from US$231.9 million in the year-earlier quarter. Net interest income increased 4.7% to US$1.20 billion from US$1.14 billion in the year-earlier quarter. Provision for loan losses was US$566.8 million versus US$597.9 million in the prior-year quarter, a decrease of 5.2%. Non-interest income rose 27.0% to US$31.3 million from US$24.6 million, while non-interest expense advanced 26.9% to US$347.6 million.

Prospects: Our evaluation of Santander Consumer USA Holdings Inc as of October 4th, 2019 is the result of our systematic analysis on three basic characteristics: earnings strength, relative valuation, and recent stock price movement. The company has produced a positive trend in earnings per share over the past 5 quarters. However, recent analyst estimates for the company have been mixed and SC has posted results that exceeded analysts' expectations. Based on operating earnings yield, the company is undervalued when compared to all of the companies we cover. Share price changes over the past year indicates that SC will perform over the near term.

Financial Data
(US$ in Thousands)

	9 Mos	6 Mos	3 Mos	12/31/2018	12/31/2017	12/31/2016	12/31/2015	12/31/2014
Earnings Per Share	2.72	2.69	2.56	2.54	3.30	2.13	2.31	2.15
Cash Flow Per Share	15.56	16.22	16.74	17.35	10.47	12.45	10.98	11.18
Tang Book Value Per Share	21.10	20.77	20.02	19.61	17.69	14.30	12.01	9.83
Dividends Per Share	0.820	0.800	0.650	0.500	0.030	...	...	0.150
Dividend Payout %	30.15	29.74	25.39	19.69	0.91	...	...	6.98
Income Statement								
Total Revenue	5,964,197	3,943,654	1,964,472	7,172,178	6,665,126	6,623,142	6,697,184	6,127,331
Income Before Taxes	1,131,992	817,298	337,267	1,192,268	823,514	1,160,711	1,285,325	1,209,988
Income Taxes	283,684	201,528	89,764	276,342	(364,092)	394,245	458,032	443,639
Net Income	848,308	615,770	247,503	915,926	1,187,606	766,466	827,293	766,349
Average Shares	345,956	351,556	352,051	360,672	360,292	359,078	358,887	355,722
Balance Sheet								
Total Assets	47,279,015	46,416,093	45,045,906	43,959,855	39,422,304	38,539,104	36,570,373	32,342,176
Total Liabilities	39,933,813	39,078,832	37,887,376	36,941,497	32,941,803	33,300,485	32,145,410	28,783,827
Stockholders' Equity	7,345,202	7,337,261	7,158,530	7,018,358	6,480,501	5,238,619	4,424,963	3,558,349
Shares Outstanding	342,864	348,130	351,728	352,302	360,527	358,907	357,945	348,977
Statistical Record								
Return on Assets %	2.11	2.17	2.16	2.20	3.05	2.04	2.40	2.61
Return on Equity %	13.15	13.24	13.23	13.57	20.27	15.82	20.73	24.54
Net Margin %	14.22	15.61	12.60	12.77	17.82	11.57	12.35	12.51
Asset Turnover	0.17	0.17	0.17	0.17	0.17	0.18	0.19	0.21
Price Range	27.51-16.14	23.96-16.14	21.72-15.60	21.72-15.60	18.62-11.17	15.85-8.87	26.52-15.15	25.90-16.85
P/E Ratio	10.11-5.93	8.91-6.00	8.48-6.09	8.55-6.14	5.64-3.38	7.44-4.16	11.48-6.56	12.05-7.84
Average Yield %	3.77	3.94	3.37	2.68	0.21	...	...	0.73

Address: 1601 Elm Street, Suite 800, Dallas, TX 75201 **Telephone:** 214-634-1110	**Web Site:** www.santanderconsumerusa.com **Officers:** William J. Rainer - Chairman Stephen A. Ferriss - Chairman, Vice-Chairman	**Auditors:** PricewaterhouseCoopers LLP **Transfer Agents:** Computershare Trust Company, N.A.

SCHLUMBERGER LTD

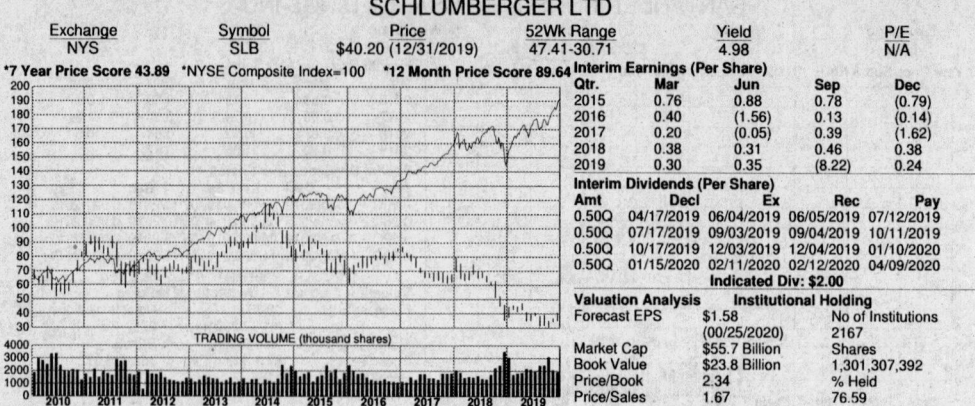

Exchange	Symbol	Price	52Wk Range	Yield	P/E
NYS	SLB	$40.20 (12/31/2019)	47.41-30.71	4.98	N/A

*7 Year Price Score 43.89 *NYSE Composite Index=100 *12 Month Price Score 89.64

Interim Earnings (Per Share)

Qtr.	Mar	Jun	Sep	Dec
2015	0.76	0.88	0.78	(0.79)
2016	0.40	(1.56)	0.13	(0.14)
2017	0.20	(0.05)	0.39	(1.62)
2018	0.38	0.31	0.46	0.38
2019	0.30	0.35	(8.22)	0.24

Interim Dividends (Per Share)

Amt	Decl	Ex	Rec	Pay
0.50Q	04/17/2019	06/04/2019	06/05/2019	07/12/2019
0.50Q	07/17/2019	09/03/2019	09/04/2019	10/11/2019
0.50Q	10/17/2019	12/03/2019	12/04/2019	01/10/2020
0.50Q	01/15/2020	02/11/2020	02/12/2020	04/09/2020
		Indicated Div: $2.00		

Valuation Analysis / Institutional Holding

Valuation Analysis		Institutional Holding	
Forecast EPS	$1.58	No of Institutions	
	(00/25/2020)	2167	
Market Cap	$55.7 Billion	Shares	
Book Value	$23.8 Billion	1,301,307,392	
Price/Book	2.34	% Held	
Price/Sales	1.67	76.59	

Business Summary: Equipment & Services (MIC: 9.1.3 SIC: 1389 NAIC: 213112)

Schlumberger provides technology for reservoir characterization, drilling, production and processing to the oil and gas industry. Co. has four segments: Reservoir Characterization, which consists of the principal technologies involved in finding and defining hydrocarbon resources; Drilling, which consists of the principal technologies involved in the drilling and positioning of oil and gas wells; Production, which consists of the principal technologies involved in the lifetime production of oil and gas reservoirs; and Cameron, which consists of the principal technologies involved in pressure and flow control for drilling and intervention rigs, oil and gas wells and production facilities.

Recent Developments: For the year ended Dec 31 2019, net loss amounted to US$10.11 billion versus net income of US$2.18 billion in the prior year. Revenues were US$33.25 billion, up 0.2% from US$33.18 billion the year before. Direct operating expenses rose 0.8% to US$28.72 billion from US$28.48 billion in the comparable period the year before. Indirect operating expenses increased 619.7% to US$14.95 billion from US$2.08 billion in the equivalent prior-year period.

Prospects: Our evaluation of Schlumberger Ltd. as of October 4th, 2019 is the result of our systematic analysis on three basic characteristics: earnings strength, relative valuation, and recent stock price movement. The company has enjoyed a very positive trend in earnings per share over the past 5 quarters. However, recent analyst estimates for the company have been reduced, while SLB has posted results that exceeded analysts' expectations. Based on operating earnings yield, the company is fairly valued when compared to all of the companies we cover. Share price changes over the past year indicates that SLB will perform poorly over the near term.

Financial Data

(US$ in Thousands)	12/31/2019	12/31/2018	12/31/2017	12/31/2016	12/31/2015	12/31/2014	12/31/2013	12/31/2012
Earnings Per Share	(7.32)	1.53	(1.08)	(1.24)	1.63	4.16	5.05	4.10
Cash Flow Per Share	3.92	4.12	4.08	4.60	6.95	8.64	7.40	5.11
Tang Book Value Per Share	0.45	1.81	1.71	4.48	12.30	13.89	15.34	11.57
Dividends Per Share	2.000	2.000	2.000	2.000	2.000	1.600	1.250	1.100
Dividend Payout %	...	130.72	...	...	122.70	38.46	24.75	26.83
Income Statement								
Total Revenue	33,250,000	33,179,000	30,664,000	28,010,000	35,711,000	48,871,000	46,459,000	42,321,000
EBITDA	(7,809,000)	5,299,000	1,683,000	1,365,000	6,427,000	11,208,000	12,182,000	10,431,000
Depn & Amortn	2,000,000	2,100,000	2,300,000	2,700,000	3,200,000	3,200,000	3,100,000	2,900,000
Income Before Taxes	(10,418,000)	2,624,000	(1,183,000)	(1,905,000)	2,881,000	7,639,000	8,691,000	7,191,000
Income Taxes	(311,000)	447,000	330,000	(278,000)	746,000	1,928,000	1,848,000	1,723,000
Net Income	(10,137,000)	2,138,000	(1,505,000)	(1,687,000)	2,072,000	5,438,000	6,732,000	5,490,000
Average Shares	1,385,000	1,393,000	1,388,000	1,357,000	1,275,000	1,308,000	1,333,000	1,339,000
Balance Sheet								
Current Assets	15,530,000	15,731,000	18,497,000	23,927,000	26,912,000	24,694,000	26,225,000	24,156,000
Total Assets	56,312,000	70,507,000	71,987,000	77,956,000	68,005,000	66,904,000	67,100,000	61,547,000
Current Liabilities	13,098,000	13,486,000	15,282,000	15,059,000	14,121,000	14,176,000	13,525,000	12,368,000
Long-Term Obligations	14,770,000	14,644,000	14,875,000	16,463,000	14,442,000	10,565,000	10,393,000	9,509,000
Total Liabilities	32,552,000	34,345,000	35,145,000	36,878,000	32,372,000	29,054,000	27,631,000	26,796,000
Stockholders' Equity	23,760,000	36,162,000	36,842,000	41,078,000	35,633,000	37,850,000	39,469,000	34,751,000
Shares Outstanding	1,384,515	1,382,964	1,383,932	1,391,475	1,256,367	1,275,312	1,307,330	1,328,255
Statistical Record								
Return on Assets %	N.M.	3.00	N.M.	N.M.	3.07	8.12	10.47	9.38
Return on Equity %	N.M.	5.86	N.M.	N.M.	5.64	14.07	18.14	16.59
EBITDA Margin %	N.M.	15.97	5.49	4.87	18.00	22.93	26.22	24.65
Net Margin %	N.M.	6.44	N.M.	N.M.	5.80	11.13	14.49	12.97
Asset Turnover	0.52	0.47	0.41	0.38	0.53	0.73	0.72	0.72
Current Ratio	1.19	1.17	1.21	1.59	1.91	1.74	1.94	1.95
Debt to Equity	0.62	0.40	0.40	0.40	0.41	0.28	0.26	0.27
Price Range	47.41-30.71	79.79-35.19	87.48-61.31	86.38-61.06	94.61-67.34	117.95-79.90	94.46-69.30	79.85-59.67
P/E Ratio	...	52.15-23.00	...	...	58.04-41.31	28.35-19.21	18.70-13.72	19.48-14.55
Average Yield %	5.14	3.17	2.82	2.59	2.44	1.62	1.54	1.55

Address: 42 Rue Saint-Dominique, Paris, 75007	**Web Site:** www.slb.com	**Auditors:** PricewaterhouseCoopers LLP
Telephone: 713-513-2000	**Officers:** Mark G. Papa - Chairman Olivier Le Peuch - Chief Executive Officer, Chief Operating Officer, Region Officer	**Investor Contact:** 713-375-3535
		Transfer Agents: Computershare Trust Company, N.A., Providence, RI

SCHWAB (CHARLES) CORP (THE)

Exchange	Symbol	Price	52Wk Range	Yield	P/E
NYS	SCHW	$47.56 (12/31/2019)	51.07-35.10	1.43	17.55

*7 Year Price Score 102.17 *NYSE Composite Index=100 *12 Month Price Score 103.81

Interim Earnings (Per Share)

Qtr.	Mar	Jun	Sep	Dec
2016	0.29	0.30	0.35	0.36
2017	0.39	0.39	0.42	0.40
2018	0.55	0.60	0.65	0.66
2019	0.69	0.66	0.70	...

Interim Dividends (Per Share)

Amt	Decl	Ex	Rec	Pay
0.17Q	01/30/2019	02/13/2019	02/14/2019	02/28/2019
0.17Q	04/30/2019	05/14/2019	05/15/2019	05/29/2019
0.17Q	07/24/2019	08/08/2019	08/09/2019	08/23/2019
0.17Q	10/23/2019	11/07/2019	11/08/2019	11/22/2019

Indicated Div: $0.68

Valuation Analysis / Institutional Holding

Forecast EPS	$2.56	No of Institutions	1517
(01/17/2020)			
Market Cap	$61.3 Billion	Shares	
Book Value	$21.4 Billion		1,210,368,896
Price/Book	2.87	% Held	
Price/Sales	5.12		75.32

Business Summary: Finance Intermediaries & Services (MIC: 5.5.1 SIC: 6211 NAIC: 523120)

Charles Schwab is a savings and loan holding company. Co. is engaged, through its subsidiaries, in wealth management, securities brokerage, banking, asset management, custody, and financial advisory services. Co. provides financial services to individuals and institutional clients in two segments: Investor Services, which provides retail brokerage and banking services to individual investors and retirement plan services, as well as other corporate brokerage services, to businesses and their employees; and Advisor Services, which provides custodial, trading, banking and support services as well as retirement business services to independent registered investment advisors and recordkeepers.

Recent Developments: For the quarter ended Sep 30 2019, net income increased 3.0% to US$951.0 million from US$923.0 million in the year-earlier quarter. Revenues were US$2.97 billion, up 5.9% from US$2.81 billion the year before. Direct operating expenses rose 14.5% to US$261.0 million from US$228.0 million in the comparable period the year before. Indirect operating expenses increased 8.5% to US$1.48 billion from US$1.36 billion in the equivalent prior-year period.

Prospects: Our evaluation of Schwab (Charles) Corp. as of October 4th, 2019 is the result of our systematic analysis on three basic characteristics: earnings strength, relative valuation, and recent stock price movement. The company has managed to produce a neutral trend in earnings per share over the past 5 quarters. However, recent analyst estimates for the company have been reduced while SCHW has posted results that exceeded analysts' expectations. Based on operating earnings yield, the company is undervalued when compared to all of the companies we cover. Share price changes over the past year indicates that SCHW will perform well over the near term.

Financial Data

(US$ in Thousands)	9 Mos	6 Mos	3 Mos	12/31/2018	12/31/2017	12/31/2016	12/31/2015	12/31/2014
Earnings Per Share	2.71	2.66	2.60	2.45	1.61	1.31	1.03	0.95
Cash Flow Per Share	9.86	6.55	7.21	9.24	0.94	2.01	0.95	1.80
Tang Book Value Per Share	13.45	13.22	13.19	12.38	10.70	9.20	7.98	7.23
Dividends Per Share	0.640	0.600	0.530	0.460	0.320	0.270	0.240	0.240
Dividend Payout %	23.62	22.56	20.38	18.78	19.88	20.61	23.30	25.26
Income Statement								
Total Revenue	9,011,000	6,039,000	3,040,000	10,989,000	8,960,000	7,649,000	6,512,000	6,160,000
EBITDA	4,018,000	2,659,000	1,332,000	4,839,000	3,882,000	3,190,000	2,458,000	2,270,000
Depn & Amortn	282,000	159,000	68,000	277,000	232,000	197,000	179,000	155,000
Income Before Taxes	3,736,000	2,500,000	1,264,000	4,562,000	3,650,000	2,993,000	2,279,000	2,115,000
Income Taxes	884,000	599,000	300,000	1,055,000	1,296,000	1,104,000	832,000	794,000
Net Income	2,852,000	1,901,000	964,000	3,507,000	2,354,000	1,889,000	1,447,000	1,321,000
Average Shares	1,308,000	1,337,000	1,344,000	1,361,000	1,353,000	1,334,000	1,327,000	1,315,000
Balance Sheet								
Current Assets	42,638,000	46,090,000	53,703,000	64,244,000	51,120,000	51,334,000	50,004,000	48,798,000
Total Assets	278,987,000	276,321,000	282,815,000	296,482,000	243,274,000	223,383,000	183,718,000	154,642,000
Current Liabilities	246,685,000	244,010,000	250,757,000	265,980,000	217,186,000	201,755,000	165,275,000	139,124,000
Long-Term Obligations	7,427,000	7,424,000	6,829,000	6,878,000	4,753,000	2,876,000	2,890,000	1,899,000
Total Liabilities	257,633,000	255,001,000	261,190,000	275,812,000	224,749,000	206,962,000	170,316,000	142,839,000
Stockholders' Equity	21,354,000	21,320,000	21,625,000	20,670,000	18,525,000	16,421,000	13,402,000	11,803,000
Shares Outstanding	1,288,931	1,308,504	1,334,401	1,332,426	1,345,332	1,332,749	1,320,337	1,310,722
Statistical Record								
Return on Assets %	1.37	1.40	1.39	1.30	1.01	0.93	0.86	0.89
Return on Equity %	17.95	18.15	18.01	17.90	13.47	12.63	11.48	11.91
EBITDA Margin %	44.59	44.03	43.82	44.03	43.33	41.70	37.75	36.85
Net Margin %	31.65	31.48	31.71	31.91	26.27	24.70	22.22	21.44
Asset Turnover	0.04	0.04	0.04	0.04	0.04	0.04	0.04	0.04
Current Ratio	0.17	0.19	0.21	0.24	0.24	0.25	0.30	0.35
Debt to Equity	0.35	0.35	0.32	0.33	0.26	0.18	0.22	0.16
Price Range	52.17-36.12	54.22-38.25	59.59-38.25	59.59-38.25	52.28-37.53	40.47-22.22	35.42-25.96	30.78-23.65
P/E Ratio	19.25-13.33	20.38-14.38	22.92-14.71	24.32-15.61	32.47-23.31	30.89-16.96	34.39-25.20	32.40-24.89
Average Yield %	1.47	1.30	1.08	0.90	0.75	0.90	0.77	0.88

Address: 211 Main Street, San Francisco, CA 94105	Web Site: www.aboutschwab.com	Auditors: DELOITTE & TOUCHE LLP
Telephone: 415-667-7000	Officers: Charles R. Schwab - Chairman Walter W. Bettinger - President, Chief Executive Officer	Investor Contact: 415-667-1841
Fax: 415-627-8894		Transfer Agents: Wells Fargo Bank, N.A., St. Paul, MN

SCIENCE APPLICATIONS INTERNATIONAL CORP

Exchange	Symbol	Price	52Wk Range	Yield	P/E
NYS	SAIC	$87.02 (12/31/2019)	90.44-61.52	1.70	33.99

*7 Year Price Score N/A   *NYSE Composite Index=100   *12 Month Price Score 101.09

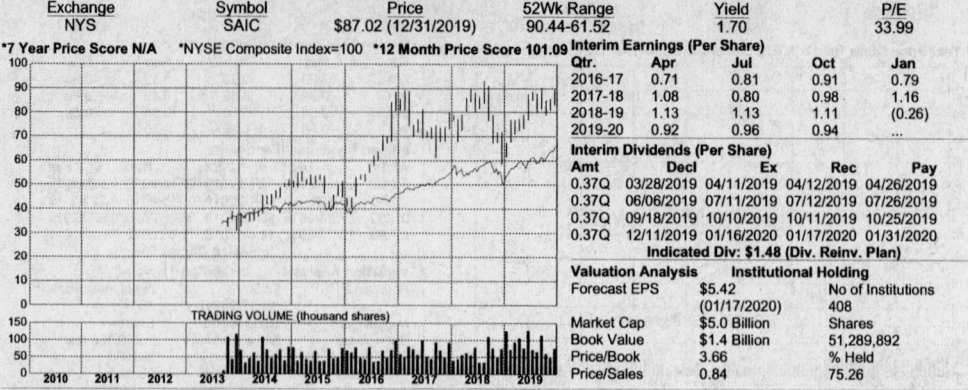

Interim Earnings (Per Share)

Qtr.	Apr	Jul	Oct	Jan
2016-17	0.71	0.81	0.91	0.79
2017-18	1.08	0.80	0.98	1.16
2018-19	1.13	1.13	1.11	(0.26)
2019-20	0.92	0.94	...	...

Interim Dividends (Per Share)

Amt	Decl	Ex	Rec	Pay
0.37Q	03/28/2019	04/11/2019	04/12/2019	04/26/2019
0.37Q	06/06/2019	07/11/2019	07/12/2019	07/26/2019
0.37Q	09/18/2019	10/10/2019	10/11/2019	10/25/2019
0.37Q	12/11/2019	01/16/2020	01/17/2020	01/31/2020

Indicated Div: $1.48 (Div. Reinv. Plan)

Valuation Analysis

		Institutional Holding	
Forecast EPS	$5.42	No of Institutions	
	(01/17/2020)	408	
Market Cap	$5.0 Billion	Shares	
Book Value	$1.4 Billion	51,289,892	
Price/Book	3.66	% Held	
Price/Sales	0.84	75.26	

Business Summary: IT Services (MIC: 6.3.1 SIC: 7373 NAIC: 541512)

Science Applications International provides technical, engineering and enterprise information technology (IT) services. Co. provides engineering, systems integration and information technology offerings for government projects and provides a range of services with an emphasis on differentiated technology services. Co.'s offerings include: engineering; technology and equipment platform integration; maintenance of ground and maritime systems; logistics; training and simulation; operation and program support services; and end-to-end services spanning the design, development, integration, deployment, management and operations, sustainment and security of its customers' entire IT infrastructure.

Recent Developments: For the quarter ended Nov 1 2019, net income increased 16.7% to US$56.0 million from US$48.0 million in the year-earlier quarter. Revenues were US$1.63 billion, up 38.5% from US$1.18 billion the year before. Operating income was US$94.0 million versus US$73.0 million in the prior-year quarter, an increase of 28.8%. Direct operating expenses rose 38.9% to US$1.46 billion from US$1.05 billion in the comparable period the year before. Indirect operating expenses increased 42.9% to US$80.0 million from US$56.0 million in the equivalent prior-year period.

Prospects: Our evaluation of Science Applications International Corp. as of October 4th, 2019 is the result of our systematic analysis on three basic characteristics: earnings strength, relative valuation, and recent stock price movement. The company has managed to produce a neutral trend in earnings per share over the past 5 quarters. In addition, recent analyst estimates for the company have been mixed and SAIC has posted results that exceeded analysts' expectations. Based on operating earnings yield, the company is undervalued when compared to all of the companies we cover. Share price changes over the past year indicates that SAIC will perform over the near term.

Financial Data
(US$ in Thousands)

	9 Mos	6 Mos	3 Mos	02/01/2019	02/02/2018	02/03/2017	01/29/2016	01/30/2015
Earnings Per Share	2.56	2.73	2.90	3.11	4.02	3.22	2.47	2.91
Cash Flow Per Share	7.12	6.50	4.62	4.25	5.03	6.04	4.95	5.92
Dividends Per Share	1.420	1.360	1.300	1.240	1.240	1.240	1.210	1.120
Dividend Payout %	55.47	49.82	44.83	39.87	30.85	38.51	48.99	38.49
Income Statement								
Total Revenue	4,839,000	3,209,000	1,615,000	4,659,000	4,454,000	4,450,000	4,315,000	3,885,000
EBITDA	389,000	261,000	131,000	246,000	281,000	296,000	253,000	259,000
Depn & Amortn	103,000	70,000	36,000	23,000	23,000	24,000	26,000	19,000
Income Before Taxes	217,000	144,000	70,000	170,000	214,000	220,000	183,000	223,000
Income Taxes	48,000	31,000	14,000	33,000	35,000	72,000	66,000	82,000
Net Income	167,000	112,000	55,000	137,000	179,000	148,000	117,000	141,000
Average Shares	58,300	59,100	60,000	44,100	44,500	45,900	47,400	48,500
Balance Sheet								
Current Assets	1,424,000	1,342,000	1,317,000	1,433,000	950,000	901,000	952,000	943,000
Total Assets	4,700,000	4,627,000	4,607,000	4,563,000	2,073,000	2,042,000	2,122,000	1,398,000
Current Liabilities	1,191,000	1,148,000	1,010,000	897,000	695,000	615,000	688,000	577,000
Long-Term Obligations	1,872,000	1,887,000	1,902,000	2,065,000	983,000	1,022,000	1,013,000	457,000
Total Liabilities	3,320,000	3,288,000	3,145,000	3,078,000	1,746,000	1,688,000	1,742,000	1,053,000
Stockholders' Equity	1,380,000	1,339,000	1,462,000	1,485,000	327,000	354,000	380,000	345,000
Shares Outstanding	58,000	58,000	59,000	60,000	43,000	44,000	45,000	46,000
Statistical Record								
Return on Assets %	4.58	4.52	4.29	4.14	8.72	6.99	6.67	9.94
Return on Equity %	17.64	17.70	16.00	15.16	52.71	39.67	32.36	39.17
EBITDA Margin %	8.04	8.13	8.11	5.28	6.31	6.65	5.86	6.67
Net Margin %	3.45	3.49	3.41	2.94	4.02	3.33	2.71	3.63
Asset Turnover	1.75	1.67	1.53	1.41	2.17	2.10	2.46	2.74
Current Ratio	1.20	1.17	1.30	1.60	1.37	1.47	1.38	1.63
Debt to Equity	1.36	1.41	1.30	1.39	3.01	2.89	2.67	1.32
Price Range	90.44-58.38	93.16-58.38	93.16-58.38	93.16-58.38	89.24-61.06	88.65-40.50	55.70-39.89	52.13-34.65
P/E Ratio	35.33-22.80	34.12-21.38	32.12-20.13	29.95-18.77	22.20-15.19	27.53-12.58	22.55-16.15	17.91-11.91
Average Yield %	1.85	1.79	1.70	1.60	1.66	1.97	2.46	2.58

Address: 12010 Sunset Hills Road, Reston, VA 20190 Telephone: 703-676-4300	Web Site: www.saic.com Officers: Donna S. Morea - Chairman Charles Alexander Mathis - Executive Vice President, Chief Financial Officer	Auditors: Ernst & Young LLP

SCOTTS MIRACLE-GRO CO (THE)

Exchange	Symbol	Price	52Wk Range	Yield	P/E
NYS	SMG	$106.18 (12/31/2019)	112.41-61.46	2.18	12.98

*7 Year Price Score 103.50 *NYSE Composite Index=100 *12 Month Price Score 104.67

Interim Earnings (Per Share)

Qtr.	Dec	Mar	Jun	Sep
2014-15	(1.23)	2.01	2.14	(0.38)
2015-16	(1.32)	3.38	3.44	(0.41)
2016-17	(1.09)	2.73	2.53	(0.53)
2017-18	(0.37)	2.59	1.47	(2.55)
2018-19	(1.44)	7.09	3.56	(1.06)

Interim Dividends (Per Share)

Amt	Decl	Ex	Rec	Pay
0.55Q	01/25/2019	02/21/2019	02/22/2019	03/08/2019
0.55Q	04/29/2019	05/24/2019	05/28/2019	06/10/2019
0.58Q	08/01/2019	08/26/2019	08/27/2019	09/10/2019
0.58Q	11/05/2019	11/25/2019	11/26/2019	12/10/2019

Indicated Div: $2.32

Valuation Analysis

		Institutional Holding	
Forecast EPS	$5.05	No of Institutions	574
	(01/17/2020)		
Market Cap	$5.9 Billion	Shares	47,640,812
Book Value	$718.7 Million	% Held	63.84
Price/Book	8.24		
Price/Sales	1.88		

Business Summary: Agricultural Chemicals (MIC: 8.3.3 SIC: 2879 NAIC: 325320)

Scotts Miracle-Gro is a manufacturer and marketer of consumer lawn and garden products in North America. Co.'s segments are: United States Consumer, which consists of Co.'s consumer lawn and garden business located in United States; Hawthorne, which consists of Co.'s indoor, urban and hydroponic gardening business; and Other, which consists of Co.'s consumer lawn and garden business in geographies other than the United States and Co.'s product sales to nurseries, greenhouses and other customers. Co. manufactures, markets and sells lawn and garden products in the following categories: lawn care, gardening and landscape, hydroponics, and controls.

Recent Developments: For the year ended Sep 30 2019, income from continuing operations increased 242.2% to US$436.7 million from US$127.6 million a year earlier. Net income increased 622.4% to US$460.2 million from US$63.7 million in the prior year. Revenues were US$3.16 billion, up 18.5% from US$2.66 billion the year before. Operating income was US$409.6 million versus US$198.9 million in the prior year, an increase of 105.9%. Direct operating expenses rose 18.8% to US$2.14 billion from US$1.80 billion in the comparable period the year before. Indirect operating expenses decreased 8.4% to US$610.0 million from US$665.7 million in the equivalent prior-year period.

Prospects: Our evaluation of Scotts Co. as of October 4th, 2019 is the result of our systematic analysis on three basic characteristics: earnings strength, relative valuation, and recent stock price movement. The company has managed to produce a neutral trend in earnings per share over the past 5 quarters. However, recent analyst estimates for the company have been raised and SMG has posted results that exceeded analysts' expectations. Based on operating earnings yield, the company is fairly valued when compared to all of the companies we cover. Share price changes over the past year indicates that SMG will perform over the near term.

Financial Data

(US$ in Thousands)	09/30/2019	09/30/2018	09/30/2017	09/30/2016	09/30/2015	09/30/2014	09/30/2013	09/30/2012
Earnings Per Share	8.18	1.12	3.63	5.09	2.57	2.65	2.57	1.71
Cash Flow Per Share	4.09	6.09	5.96	3.87	4.04	3.91	5.54	2.51
Tang Book Value Per Share	N.M.	N.M.	N.M.	N.M.	N.M.	N.M.	1.79	N.M.
Dividends Per Share	2.230	2.140	2.030	1.910	1.820	3.763	1.413	1.225
Dividend Payout %	27.26	191.07	55.92	37.52	70.82	141.98	54.96	71.64
Income Statement								
Total Revenue	3,156,000	2,663,400	2,642,100	2,836,100	3,016,500	2,841,300	2,816,500	2,826,100
EBITDA	802,300	309,500	505,700	533,500	378,200	378,500	387,500	314,200
Depn & Amortn	122,200	112,300	95,700	86,900	83,600	74,600	74,300	70,600
Income Before Taxes	578,300	110,800	343,900	384,900	244,100	256,600	254,000	181,800
Income Taxes	144,900	(11,900)	116,600	139,400	85,400	91,200	92,800	68,600
Net Income	460,700	63,700	218,300	315,300	159,800	166,500	161,100	106,500
Average Shares	56,300	57,100	60,200	62,000	62,200	62,700	62,600	62,100
Balance Sheet								
Current Assets	1,041,700	885,700	881,700	991,700	948,600	935,000	881,000	1,000,000
Total Assets	3,028,700	3,054,500	2,747,000	2,808,800	2,527,200	2,058,300	1,937,200	2,074,400
Current Liabilities	620,500	612,700	544,500	593,100	613,100	544,700	509,800	433,600
Long-Term Obligations	1,523,500	1,883,800	1,258,000	1,131,100	1,028,500	692,400	478,100	781,100
Total Liabilities	2,310,000	2,699,900	2,098,200	2,093,600	1,906,500	1,504,600	1,226,700	1,472,500
Stockholders' Equity	718,700	354,600	648,800	715,200	620,700	553,700	710,500	601,900
Shares Outstanding	55,800	55,300	58,100	60,300	61,400	60,700	62,000	61,300
Statistical Record								
Return on Assets %	15.15	2.20	7.86	11.79	6.97	8.33	8.03	5.15
Return on Equity %	85.85	12.70	32.01	47.08	27.21	26.34	24.55	18.29
EBITDA Margin %	25.42	11.62	19.14	18.81	12.54	13.32	13.76	11.12
Net Margin %	14.60	2.39	8.26	11.12	5.30	5.86	5.72	3.77
Asset Turnover	1.04	0.92	0.95	1.06	1.32	1.42	1.40	1.37
Current Ratio	1.68	1.45	1.62	1.67	1.55	1.72	1.73	2.31
Debt to Equity	2.12	5.31	1.94	1.58	1.66	1.25	0.67	1.30
Price Range	112.41-58.82	109.47-73.30	97.37-82.95	83.62-60.82	68.99-54.71	63.30-53.09	55.66-39.77	55.00-38.17
P/E Ratio	13.74-7.19	97.74-65.45	26.82-22.85	16.43-11.95	26.84-21.29	23.89-20.03	21.66-15.47	32.16-22.32
Average Yield %	2.62	2.40	2.21	2.70	2.92	6.44	3.03	2.69

Address: 14111 Scottslawn Road, Marysville, OH 43041	Web Site: www.scotts.com	Auditors: DELOITTE & TOUCHE LLP
Telephone: 937-644-0011	Officers: James Hagedorn - Chairman, Chief Executive Officer Michael C. Lukemire - President, Chief Operating Officer, Region Officer	Investor Contact: 937-644-0011
Fax: 937-644-7614		Transfer Agents: Wells Fargo Shareowner Services

SEALED AIR CORP

Exchange	Symbol	Price	52Wk Range	Yield	P/E
NYS	SEE	$39.83 (12/31/2019)	46.84-34.73	1.61	17.55

*7 Year Price Score 85.72 *NYSE Composite Index=100 *12 Month Price Score 88.55

Interim Earnings (Per Share)

Qtr.	Mar	Jun	Sep	Dec
2016	0.46	0.25	0.83	0.87
2017	(0.22)	0.45	4.15	(0.08)
2018	(1.21)	0.71	0.50	1.25
2019	0.37	0.21	0.44	...

Interim Dividends (Per Share)

Amt	Decl	Ex	Rec	Pay
0.16Q	02/14/2019	03/07/2019	03/08/2019	03/22/2019
0.16Q	05/16/2019	06/06/2019	06/07/2019	06/21/2019
0.16Q	07/11/2019	09/05/2019	09/06/2019	09/20/2019
0.16Q	10/03/2019	12/05/2019	12/06/2019	12/20/2019

Indicated Div: $0.64

Valuation Analysis

		Institutional Holding	
Forecast EPS	$2.77	No of Institutions	
	(01/16/2020)	685	
Market Cap	$6.2 Billion	Shares	
Book Value	N/A	193,926,960	
Price/Book	N/A	% Held	
Price/Sales	1.29	80.55	

Business Summary: Containers & Packaging (MIC: 8.1.3 SIC: 2671 NAIC: 322221)

Sealed Air is a holding company. Through its subsidiaries, Co. is engaged in food safety and security and product protection. Co. serves an array of end markets including food and beverage processing, food service, retail, and commercial and consumer applications. Co.'s reportable segments include: Food Care, which serves perishable food processors, primarily in red meat, smoked and processed meats, poultry and dairy (solids and liquids) markets, and provides integrated packaging materials and equipment solutions; and Product Care, which provides packaging solutions across various global markets and primarily to e-Commerce, electronics and industrial manufacturing.

Recent Developments: For the quarter ended Sep 30 2019, income from continuing operations increased 5.2% to US$79.5 million from US$75.6 million in the year-earlier quarter. Net income decreased 13.9% to US$68.0 million from US$79.0 million in the year-earlier quarter. Revenues were US$1.22 billion, up 2.7% from US$1.19 billion the year before. Operating income was US$154.0 million versus US$163.2 million in the prior-year quarter, a decrease of 5.6%. Direct operating expenses rose 0.7% to US$826.5 million from US$820.7 million in the comparable period the year before. Indirect operating expenses increased 17.6% to US$238.0 million from US$202.3 million in the equivalent prior-year period.

Prospects: Our evaluation of Sealed Air Corp. as of October 4th, 2019 is the result of our systematic analysis on three basic characteristics: earnings strength, relative valuation, and recent stock price movement. The company has managed to produce a neutral trend in earnings per share over the past 5 quarters. However, recent analyst estimates for the company have been raised and SEE has posted results that exceeded analysts' expectations. Based on operating earnings yield, the company is undervalued when compared to all of the companies we cover. Share price changes over the past year indicates that SEE will perform well over the near term.

Financial Data

(US$ in Thousands)	9 Mos	6 Mos	3 Mos	12/31/2018	12/31/2017	12/31/2016	12/31/2015	12/31/2014
Earnings Per Share	2.27	2.33	2.83	1.20	4.29	2.46	1.62	1.20
Cash Flow Per Share	3.44	3.63	3.40	2.69	2.27	4.65	4.75	(0.96)
Dividends Per Share	0.640	0.640	0.640	0.640	0.640	0.610	0.520	0.520
Dividend Payout %	28.19	27.47	22.61	53.33	14.92	24.80	32.10	43.33
Income Statement								
Total Revenue	3,492,200	2,273,700	1,112,700	4,732,700	4,461,600	6,778,300	7,031,500	7,750,500
EBITDA	478,600	286,600	172,500	767,300	697,600	981,400	853,400	806,100
Depn & Amortn	107,200	66,000	32,900	131,600	120,100	215,400	213,300	266,700
Income Before Taxes	234,800	132,500	94,700	457,800	393,300	565,900	425,900	267,200
Income Taxes	65,500	42,700	30,400	307,500	330,500	79,500	90,500	9,100
Net Income	158,700	90,700	57,500	193,100	814,900	486,400	335,400	258,100
Average Shares	154,800	155,300	155,400	160,200	188,900	197,200	206,700	213,900
Balance Sheet								
Current Assets	1,591,400	1,576,600	1,555,200	1,554,800	1,866,400	2,215,300	2,215,600	2,691,600
Total Assets	5,676,400	5,216,500	5,155,000	5,050,200	5,280,300	7,389,100	7,426,000	8,041,700
Current Liabilities	1,502,300	1,587,400	1,481,100	1,488,600	1,378,200	2,118,900	1,807,100	1,730,900
Long-Term Obligations	3,694,000	3,291,700	3,284,600	3,236,500	3,230,500	3,938,300	4,302,700	4,282,500
Total Liabilities	5,980,500	5,557,700	5,447,400	5,398,800	5,128,000	6,779,400	6,898,900	6,878,900
Stockholders' Equity	(304,100)	(341,200)	(292,400)	(348,600)	152,300	609,700	527,100	1,162,800
Shares Outstanding	154,517	154,546	155,753	155,654	168,595	193,482	196,013	210,531
Statistical Record								
Return on Assets %	6.73	7.34	8.85	3.74	12.86	6.55	4.34	3.01
Return on Equity %	...	...	...	...	213.88	85.34	39.69	20.23
EBITDA Margin %	13.70	12.61	15.50	16.21	15.64	14.48	12.14	10.40
Net Margin %	4.54	3.99	5.17	4.08	18.26	7.18	4.77	3.33
Asset Turnover	0.89	0.94	0.92	0.92	0.70	0.91	0.91	0.90
Current Ratio	1.06	0.99	1.05	1.04	1.35	1.05	1.23	1.56
Debt to Equity	...	...	...	...	21.21	6.46	8.16	3.68
Price Range	46.84-30.74	46.84-30.74	46.43-30.74	49.64-30.74	50.22-41.72	52.68-38.36	55.40-39.42	43.47-29.86
P/E Ratio	20.63-13.54	20.10-13.19	16.41-10.86	41.37-25.62	11.71-9.72	21.41-15.59	34.20-24.33	36.23-24.88
Average Yield %	1.57	1.58	1.58	1.55	1.41	1.32	1.09	1.51

Address: 2415 Cascade Pointe Boulevard, Charlotte, NC 28208	**Web Site:** www.sealedair.com	**Auditors:** PricewaterhouseCoopers LLP
Telephone: 980-221-3235	**Officers:** Jerry R. Whitaker - Chairman Edward L. (Ted) Doheny - President, Chief Executive Officer - Designate, Chief Operating Officer	**Investor Contact:** 201-791-7600
Fax: 201-703-4205		**Transfer Agents:** ComputerShare Investor Services, Providence, RI

SEMPRA ENERGY

Exchange	Symbol	Price	52Wk Range	Yield	P/E
NYS	SRE	$151.48 (12/31/2019)	152.03-106.76	2.55	17.04

*7 Year Price Score 103.24 *NYSE Composite Index=100 *12 Month Price Score 103.91

Interim Earnings (Per Share)

Qtr.	Mar	Jun	Sep	Dec
2016	1.27	0.06	2.46	1.53
2017	1.75	1.03	0.22	(1.98)
2018	1.33	(2.11)	0.99	3.20
2019	1.59	1.26	2.84	...

Interim Dividends (Per Share)

Amt	Decl	Ex	Rec	Pay
0.968Q	02/22/2019	03/21/2019	03/22/2019	04/15/2019
0.968Q	06/18/2019	07/03/2019	07/05/2019	07/15/2019
0.968Q	09/06/2019	09/19/2019	09/20/2019	10/15/2019
0.968Q	12/09/2019	12/27/2019	12/30/2019	01/15/2020

Indicated Div: $3.87

Valuation Analysis

		Institutional Holding	
Forecast EPS	$6.18 (01/16/2020)	No of Institutions	1089
Market Cap	$42.7 Billion	Shares	
Book Value	$18.6 Billion		301,142,272
Price/Book	2.29	% Held	
Price/Sales	3.85		91.22

Business Summary: Electric Utilities (MIC: 3.1.1 SIC: 4932 NAIC: 221210)

Sempra Energy is a holding company. Through its businesses, which consist of seven segments, Co. invest in, develop and operate energy infrastructure, and provide electric and gas services to customers in North and South America. Co.'s segments include: San Diego Gas & Electric Company, which provides electric service to San Diego and southern Orange counties and natural gas service to San Diego County; Southern California Gas Company, which is a natural gas distribution utility; and Sempra South American Utilities, which develops, owns and operates, or holds interests in, electric transmission, distribution and generation infrastructure in Chile and Peru.

Recent Developments: For the quarter ended Sep 30 2019, income from continuing operations increased 133.2% to US$653.0 million from US$280.0 million in the year-earlier quarter. Net income increased 172.2% to US$909.0 million from US$334.0 million in the year-earlier quarter. Revenues were US$2.76 billion, up 7.5% from US$2.57 billion the year before. Direct operating expenses declined 8.7% to US$1.47 billion from US$1.61 billion in the comparable period the year before. Indirect operating expenses increased 14.8% to US$575.0 million from US$501.0 million in the equivalent prior-year period.

Prospects: Our evaluation of Sempra Energy as of October 4th, 2019 is the result of our systematic analysis on three basic characteristics: earnings strength, relative valuation, and recent stock price movement. The company has generated a negative trend in earnings per share over the past 5 quarters. However, recent analyst estimates for the company have been raised and SRE has posted results that fell short of analysts' expectations. Based on operating earnings yield, the company is fairly valued when compared to all of the companies we cover. Share price changes over the past year indicates that SRE will perform well over the near term.

Financial Data

(US$ in Thousands)	9 Mos	6 Mos	3 Mos	12/31/2018	12/31/2017	12/31/2016	12/31/2015	12/31/2014
Earnings Per Share	8.89	7.04	3.67	3.42	1.01	5.46	5.37	4.63
Cash Flow Per Share	10.72	12.81	12.49	12.86	14.41	9.24	11.70	8.79
Tang Book Value Per Share	51.57	48.76	48.41	44.69	38.50	40.13	42.63	40.51
Dividends Per Share	3.797	2.757	3.652	3.580	3.290	3.020	2.800	2.640
Dividend Payout %	42.72	39.17	99.52	104.68	325.74	55.31	52.14	57.02
Income Statement								
Total Revenue	7,886,000	5,128,000	2,898,000	11,687,000	11,207,000	10,183,000	10,231,000	11,035,000
EBITDA	3,133,000	2,030,000	1,124,000	3,393,000	3,583,000	3,042,000	3,379,000	3,125,000
Depn & Amortn	1,174,000	772,000	383,000	1,528,000	1,422,000	1,312,000	1,250,000	1,156,000
Income Before Taxes	1,235,000	787,000	501,000	1,046,000	1,551,000	1,207,000	1,600,000	1,443,000
Income Taxes	150,000	89,000	42,000	96,000	1,276,000	389,000	341,000	300,000
Net Income	1,716,000	867,000	477,000	1,050,000	257,000	1,371,000	1,350,000	1,162,000
Average Shares	295,789	279,619	277,228	269,852	252,300	251,155	250,923	250,655
Balance Sheet								
Current Assets	3,666,000	2,783,000	3,262,000	3,645,000	3,341,000	3,110,000	2,891,000	4,184,000
Total Assets	64,585,000	62,727,000	61,618,000	60,638,000	50,454,000	47,786,000	41,150,000	39,732,000
Current Liabilities	9,498,000	8,177,000	8,612,000	7,523,000	6,635,000	5,927,000	4,612,000	5,069,000
Long-Term Obligations	21,034,000	21,237,000	19,776,000	21,611,000	16,445,000	14,429,000	13,134,000	12,167,000
Total Liabilities	45,965,000	45,287,000	44,272,000	43,500,000	37,784,000	34,835,000	29,341,000	28,406,000
Stockholders' Equity	18,620,000	17,440,000	17,346,000	17,138,000	12,670,000	12,951,000	11,809,000	11,326,000
Shares Outstanding	282,000	274,000	274,000	273,769	251,358	250,152	248,298	246,330
Statistical Record								
Return on Assets %	4.18	3.39	1.89	1.89	0.52	3.07	3.34	3.02
Return on Equity %	14.85	12.49	6.94	7.05	2.01	11.04	11.67	10.41
EBITDA Margin %	39.73	39.59	38.79	29.03	31.97	29.87	33.03	28.32
Net Margin %	21.76	16.91	16.46	8.98	2.29	13.46	13.20	10.53
Asset Turnover	0.18	0.18	0.19	0.21	0.23	0.23	0.25	0.29
Current Ratio	0.39	0.34	0.38	0.48	0.50	0.52	0.63	0.83
Debt to Equity	1.13	1.22	1.14	1.26	1.30	1.11	1.11	1.07
Price Range	147.61-106.76	141.04-106.76	126.07-100.71	118.87-100.71	122.23-100.82	114.50-87.00	115.08-90.09	115.85-88.44
P/E Ratio	16.60-12.01	20.03-15.16	34.35-27.44	34.76-29.45	121.02-99.82	20.97-15.93	21.43-16.78	25.02-19.10
Average Yield %	3.02	2.30	3.20	3.20	2.92	2.92	2.71	2.61

Address: 488 8th Avenue, San Diego, CA 92101	Web Site: www.sempra.com	Auditors: DELOITTE & TOUCHE LLP
Telephone: 619-696-2000	Officers: Jeffrey W. Martin - Chairman, Chief Executive Officer, Chief Financial Officer, Executive Vice President John Sowers - Division Officer	Transfer Agents: American Stock Transfer & Trust Company, LLC, Brooklyn, NY

SENSIENT TECHNOLOGIES CORP.

Exchange	Symbol	Price	52Wk Range	Yield	P/E	Div Acheiver
NYS	SXT	$66.09 (12/31/2019)	74.95-55.00	2.36	21.18	13 Years

*7 Year Price Score 86.01 *NYSE Composite Index=100 *12 Month Price Score 91.71

Interim Earnings (Per Share)

Qtr.	Mar	Jun	Sep	Dec
2016	0.69	0.63	0.79	0.71
2017	0.30	0.69	0.73	0.31
2018	0.89	0.92	1.12	0.78
2019	0.78	0.81	0.75	...

Interim Dividends (Per Share)

Amt	Decl	Ex	Rec	Pay
0.36Q	01/23/2019	02/01/2019	02/04/2019	03/01/2019
0.36Q	04/25/2019	05/09/2019	05/10/2019	06/03/2019
0.36Q	07/18/2019	08/01/2019	08/02/2019	09/03/2019
0.39Q	10/17/2019	11/01/2019	11/04/2019	12/02/2019

Indicated Div: $1.56

Valuation Analysis / Institutional Holding

Forecast EPS	$2.96	No of Institutions
	(01/17/2020)	374
Market Cap	$2.8 Billion	Shares
Book Value	$896.7 Million	59,423,576
Price/Book	3.12	% Held
Price/Sales	2.10	91.33

Business Summary: Specialty Chemicals (MIC: 8.3.2 SIC: 2819 NAIC: 325131)

Sensient Technologies is a manufacturer and marketer of colors, flavors and fragrances. Co.'s three reportable segments are: Flavors & Fragrances Group, which develops, manufactures, and supplies flavor and fragrance systems for the food, beverage, personal care, and household-products industries; Color Group, which provides natural and synthetic color systems for use in foods, beverages, pharmaceuticals, and nutraceuticals, colors and other ingredients for cosmetics; and Asia Pacific Group, which provides a range of products from its Flavors & Fragrances Group and Color Group, as well as products developed by regional technical teams to appeal to local preferences.

Recent Developments: For the quarter ended Sep 30 2019, net income decreased 32.5% to US$31.9 million from US$47.2 million in the year-earlier quarter. Revenues were US$317.7 million, down 7.3% from US$342.7 million the year before. Operating income was US$38.8 million versus US$50.3 million in the prior-year quarter, a decrease of 22.8%. Direct operating expenses declined 5.2% to US$215.3 million from US$227.2 million in the comparable period the year before. Indirect operating expenses decreased 2.6% to US$63.6 million from US$65.3 million in the equivalent prior-year period.

Prospects: Our evaluation of Sensient Technologies Corp. as of October 4th, 2019 is the result of our systematic analysis on three basic characteristics: earnings strength, relative valuation, and recent stock price movement. The company has managed to produce a neutral trend in earnings per share over the past 5 quarters. In addition, recent analyst estimates for the company have been mixed and SXT has posted results that fell short of analysts' expectations. Based on operating earnings yield, the company is fairly valued when compared to all of the companies we cover. Share price changes over the past year indicates that SXT will perform poorly over the near term.

Financial Data
(US$ in Thousands)

	9 Mos	6 Mos	3 Mos	12/31/2018	12/31/2017	12/31/2016	12/31/2015	12/31/2014
Earnings Per Share	3.12	3.49	3.60	3.70	2.03	2.82	2.31	1.51
Cash Flow Per Share	4.78	4.45	2.10	1.97	4.12	4.98	2.79	3.90
Tang Book Value Per Share	11.19	10.98	10.53	10.06	10.10	10.04	9.74	12.95
Dividends Per Share	1.440	1.410	1.380	1.350	1.230	1.110	1.040	0.980
Dividend Payout %	46.15	40.40	38.33	36.49	60.59	39.36	45.02	64.90
Income Statement								
Total Revenue	1,004,349	686,699	347,513	1,386,815	1,362,265	1,383,210	1,375,964	1,447,821
EBITDA	177,282	124,529	63,092	254,328	214,762	231,323	213,035	180,890
Depn & Amortn	41,706	27,741	13,672	50,950	46,956	45,714	46,694	50,225
Income Before Taxes	120,038	86,186	44,018	181,525	148,423	167,285	149,396	114,598
Income Taxes	21,029	19,048	11,211	24,165	58,823	44,372	42,149	32,827
Net Income	99,009	67,138	32,807	157,360	89,600	126,256	106,785	73,646
Average Shares	42,299	42,300	42,275	42,499	44,031	44,843	46,204	48,819
Balance Sheet								
Current Assets	792,361	812,087	826,296	822,865	733,475	717,061	753,343	759,389
Total Assets	1,778,557	1,825,495	1,840,871	1,824,940	1,724,340	1,667,860	1,711,437	1,765,206
Current Liabilities	192,191	194,669	197,452	214,700	216,323	213,675	212,922	224,905
Long-Term Obligations	616,967	656,737	688,952	689,553	604,159	582,780	613,877	451,011
Total Liabilities	881,884	928,013	963,147	964,993	872,039	832,119	866,310	718,271
Stockholders' Equity	896,673	897,482	877,724	859,947	852,301	835,741	845,127	1,046,935
Shares Outstanding	42,318	42,319	42,319	42,223	43,195	44,238	44,780	47,424
Statistical Record								
Return on Assets %	7.29	8.09	8.40	8.87	5.28	7.45	6.14	4.05
Return on Equity %	15.13	17.17	17.82	18.38	10.62	14.98	11.29	6.43
EBITDA Margin %	17.65	18.13	18.16	18.34	15.77	16.72	15.48	12.49
Net Margin %	9.86	9.78	9.44	11.35	6.58	9.13	7.76	5.09
Asset Turnover	0.73	0.74	0.76	0.78	0.80	0.82	0.79	0.80
Current Ratio	4.12	4.17	4.18	3.83	3.39	3.36	3.54	3.38
Debt to Equity	0.69	0.73	0.78	0.80	0.71	0.70	0.73	0.43
Price Range	77.82-52.81	77.82-52.81	77.82-52.81	77.82-52.81	83.35-71.84	83.11-53.92	70.25-57.39	62.98-46.74
P/E Ratio	24.94-16.93	22.30-15.13	21.62-14.67	21.03-14.27	41.06-35.39	29.47-19.12	30.41-24.84	41.71-30.95
Average Yield %	2.16	2.09	2.05	1.94	1.58	1.61	1.60	1.80

Address: 777 East Wisconsin Avenue, Milwaukee, WI 53202-5304 **Telephone:** 414-271-6755 **Fax:** 414-347-4795	**Web Site:** www.sensient.com **Officers:** Paul Manning - Chairman, President, Chief Executive Officer, Division Officer Stephen J. Rolfs - Senior Vice President, Vice President, Chief Financial Officer	**Auditors:** Ernst & Young LLP **Investor Contact:** 414-347-3779 **Transfer Agents:** Wells Fargo Bank Minnesota, N.A., St. Paul, MN

SERVICE CORP. INTERNATIONAL

Exchange	Symbol	Price	52Wk Range	Yield	P/E
NYS	SCI	$46.03 (12/31/2019)	48.56-39.08	1.56	20.64

*7 Year Price Score 122.84 ***NYSE Composite Index=100** ***12 Month Price Score 94.61**

Interim Earnings (Per Share)

Qtr.	Mar	Jun	Sep	Dec
2016	0.24	0.08	0.24	0.34
2017	0.91	0.36	0.29	1.28
2018	0.43	0.55	0.37	1.03
2019	0.43	0.39	0.38	...

Interim Dividends (Per Share)

Amt	Decl	Ex	Rec	Pay
0.18Q	02/21/2019	03/14/2019	03/15/2019	03/29/2019
0.18Q	05/08/2019	06/13/2019	06/14/2019	06/28/2019
0.18Q	08/14/2019	09/12/2019	09/13/2019	09/30/2019
0.18Q	11/13/2019	12/12/2019	12/13/2019	12/31/2019

Indicated Div: $0.72

Valuation Analysis **Institutional Holding**

Forecast EPS	$1.91	No of Institutions	
	(10/26/2019)	521	
Market Cap	$8.4 Billion	Shares	
Book Value	$1.8 Billion	189,071,408	
Price/Book	4.74	% Held	
Price/Sales	2.63	85.62	

Business Summary: Miscellaneous Consumer Services (MIC: 2.2.3 SIC: 7261 NAIC: 812210)

Service Corporation International provides deathcare products and services. Co.'s funeral service and cemetery operations consist of funeral service locations, cemeteries, funeral service/cemetery combination locations, crematoria, and other related businesses. Funeral service locations provide services related to funerals and cremations, including the use of funeral home facilities and motor vehicles, arranging and directing services, removal, preparation, embalming, cremations, memorialization, and catering. Co.'s cemeteries provide cemetery property interment rights, such as developed lots, lawn crypts, mausoleum spaces, niches, and other cremation memorialization and interment options.

Recent Developments: For the quarter ended Sep 30 2019, net income increased 2.7% to US$70.9 million from US$69.0 million in the year-earlier quarter. Revenues were US$769.2 million, down 1.2% from US$778.8 million the year before. Operating income was US$128.6 million versus US$132.3 million in the prior-year quarter, a decrease of 2.8%. Direct operating expenses declined 0.5% to US$609.5 million from US$612.6 million in the comparable period the year before. Indirect operating expenses decreased 8.0% to US$31.1 million from US$33.9 million in the equivalent prior-year period.

Prospects: Our evaluation of Service Corp. International as of October 4th, 2019 is the result of our systematic analysis on three basic characteristics: earnings strength, relative valuation, and recent stock price movement. The company has produced a positive trend in earnings per share over the past 5 quarters. However, recent analyst estimates for the company have been unchanged, and SCI has posted results in line with analysts' expectations. Based on operating earnings yield, the company is fairly valued when compared to all of the companies we cover. Share price changes over the past year indicates that SCI will perform well over the near term.

Financial Data

(US$ in Thousands)	9 Mos	6 Mos	3 Mos	12/31/2018	12/31/2017	12/31/2016	12/31/2015	12/31/2014
Earnings Per Share	2.23	2.22	2.38	2.39	2.84	0.90	1.14	0.81
Cash Flow Per Share	3.48	3.09	3.24	3.38	2.68	2.39	2.36	1.51
Dividends Per Share	0.710	0.700	0.690	0.680	0.580	0.510	0.440	0.340
Dividend Payout %	31.84	31.53	28.99	28.45	20.42	56.67	38.60	41.98
Income Statement								
Total Revenue	2,380,025	1,610,784	798,212	3,190,174	3,095,031	3,031,137	2,986,380	2,994,012
EBITDA	483,077	341,263	172,107	803,133	750,174	572,619	606,869	671,628
Depn & Amortn	72,432	50,165	24,409	179,845	180,791	178,189	172,915	167,186
Income Before Taxes	269,260	196,391	100,308	441,732	400,258	326,658	370,351	402,600
Income Taxes	46,662	44,665	21,095	(5,826)	(146,589)	149,353	135,027	225,980
Net Income	222,444	151,652	79,323	447,208	546,663	177,038	233,772	172,469
Average Shares	185,843	185,690	185,317	186,972	192,246	196,042	204,450	214,200
Balance Sheet								
Current Assets	352,179	394,217	290,052	331,232	481,296	354,396	308,409	396,856
Total Assets	13,316,321	13,360,343	13,079,061	12,693,243	12,864,503	12,038,149	11,718,888	11,923,644
Current Liabilities	563,417	614,472	604,543	555,600	828,979	537,870	519,396	552,008
Long-Term Obligations	3,466,769	3,464,902	3,409,196	3,532,182	3,135,316	3,196,616	3,071,738	2,963,794
Total Liabilities	11,540,828	11,616,115	11,378,608	11,051,340	11,455,113	10,945,436	10,534,196	10,554,918
Stockholders' Equity	1,775,493	1,744,228	1,700,453	1,641,903	1,409,390	1,092,713	1,184,692	1,368,726
Shares Outstanding	182,830	182,468	182,250	181,470	186,614	189,405	195,772	204,866
Statistical Record								
Return on Assets %	3.15	3.16	3.49	3.50	4.39	1.49	1.98	1.39
Return on Equity %	25.46	25.69	27.68	29.31	43.70	15.50	18.31	12.39
EBITDA Margin %	20.30	21.19	21.56	25.18	24.24	18.89	20.32	22.43
Net Margin %	9.35	9.41	9.94	14.02	17.66	5.84	7.83	5.76
Asset Turnover	0.24	0.24	0.25	0.25	0.25	0.25	0.25	0.24
Current Ratio	0.63	0.64	0.48	0.60	0.58	0.66	0.59	0.72
Debt to Equity	1.95	1.99	2.00	2.15	2.22	2.93	2.59	2.17
Price Range	48.56-37.71	46.97-36.09	46.97-35.30	46.97-35.30	38.00-28.81	28.67-21.65	31.94-22.29	23.22-16.82
P/E Ratio	21.78-16.91	21.16-16.26	19.74-14.83	19.65-14.77	13.38-10.14	31.86-24.06	28.02-19.55	28.67-20.77
Average Yield %	1.62	1.66	1.66	1.71	1.75	1.96	1.61	1.43

Address: 1929 Allen Parkway, Houston, TX 77019 Telephone: 713-522-5141	Web Site: www.sci-corp.com Officers: Robert L. Waltrip - Chairman Emeritus, Chairman Thomas (Tom) L. Ryan - Chairman, President, President (frmr), Chief Executive Officer	Auditors: PricewaterhouseCoopers LLP Transfer Agents: Computershare Shareowner Services, Providence, RI

SERVICEMASTER GLOBAL HOLDINGS, INC

Exchange	Symbol	Price	52Wk Range	Yield	P/E
NYS	SERV	$38.66 (12/31/2019)	58.22-33.98	N/A	N/A

*7 Year Price Score N/A   *NYSE Composite Index=100   *12 Month Price Score 75.77

Interim Earnings (Per Share)

Qtr.	Mar	Jun	Sep	Dec
2016	0.28	0.11	0.51	0.23
2017	0.29	0.63	0.59	2.25
2018	0.30	0.71	0.52	(1.82)
2019	0.51	0.43	0.19	...

Interim Dividends (Per Share)

No Dividends Paid

Valuation Analysis

		Institutional Holding	
Forecast EPS	$1.33	No of Institutions	336
	(01/17/2020)		
Market Cap	$5.2 Billion	Shares	
Book Value	$2.3 Billion		159,239,408
Price/Book	2.24	% Held	
Price/Sales	5.01		100.14

Business Summary: Miscellaneous Consumer Services (MIC: 2.2.3 SIC: 7342 NAIC: 561710)

ServiceMaster Global Holdings is a holding company. Through its subsidiaries, Co. provides services to residential and commercial customers in the termite, pest control, cleaning and restoration markets, operating through a network of company-owned locations and franchise and license agreements. Co.'s portfolio of brands includes Terminix (residential termite and pest control), Terminix Commercial (commercial termite and pest control), Copesan (commercial national accounts pest management), ServiceMaster Restore (restoration), ServiceMaster Clean (commercial cleaning), Merry Maids (residential cleaning), Furniture Medic (cabinet and furniture repair) and AmeriSpec (home inspections).

Recent Developments: For the quarter ended Sep 30 2019, income from continuing operations increased 44.4% to US$26.0 million from US$18.0 million in the year-earlier quarter. Net income decreased 64.8% to US$25.0 million from US$71.0 million in the year-earlier quarter. Revenues were US$528.0 million, up 6.5% from US$496.0 million the year before. Direct operating expenses rose 9.7% to US$305.0 million from US$278.0 million in the comparable period the year before. Indirect operating expenses increased 9.0% to US$169.0 million from US$155.0 million in the equivalent prior-year period.

Prospects: Our evaluation of ServiceMaster Global Holding as of October 4th, 2019 is the result of our systematic analysis on three basic characteristics: earnings strength, relative valuation, and recent stock price movement. The company has enjoyed a very positive trend in earnings per share over the past 5 quarters. However, recent analyst estimates for the company have been mixed and SERV has posted results that exceeded analysts' expectations. Based on operating earnings yield, the company is overvalued when compared to all of the companies we cover. Share price changes over the past year indicates that SERV will perform very well over the near term.

Financial Data

(US$ in Millions)	9 Mos	6 Mos	3 Mos	12/31/2018	12/31/2017	12/31/2016	12/31/2015	12/31/2014
Earnings Per Share	(0.69)	(0.36)	(0.08)	(0.30)	3.76	1.13	1.17	(0.50)
Cash Flow Per Share	0.57	0.79	1.30	1.69	1.53	2.40	2.49	2.24
Income Statement								
Total Revenue	1,570	1,042	482	1,900	2,912	2,746	2,594	2,457
EBITDA	343	260	136	75	592	449	475	344
Depn & Amortn	91	60	31	73	76	61	47	48
Income Before Taxes	193	159	79	(126)	370	241	270	84
Income Taxes	39	30	9	37	(139)	85	107	40
Net Income	154	129	70	(41)	510	155	160	(57)
Average Shares	136	136	136	135	135	137	136	113
Balance Sheet								
Current Assets	470	555	548	962	1,242	998	933	1,044
Total Assets	5,017	4,806	4,769	5,023	5,646	5,386	5,098	5,134
Current Liabilities	505	473	443	425	1,174	1,042	955	905
Long-Term Obligations	1,511	1,252	1,289	1,727	2,643	2,772	2,698	3,017
Total Liabilities	2,681	2,362	2,371	2,818	4,479	4,700	4,553	4,775
Stockholders' Equity	2,337	2,329	2,280	2,204	1,167	686	545	359
Shares Outstanding	135	135	136	135	135	135	135	134
Statistical Record								
Return on Assets %	N.M.	N.M.	N.M.	N.M.	4.62	2.95	3.13	N.M.
Return on Equity %	N.M.	N.M.	N.M.	N.M.	27.49	25.11	35.40	N.M.
EBITDA Margin %	21.85	24.95	28.22	3.95	20.33	16.35	18.31	14.00
Net Margin %	9.81	12.38	14.52	N.M.	17.51	5.64	6.17	N.M.
Asset Turnover	0.20	0.27	0.34	0.36	0.26	0.52	0.51	0.45
Current Ratio	0.93	1.17	1.24	2.26	1.06	0.96	0.98	1.15
Debt to Equity	0.65	0.54	0.57	0.78	2.26	4.04	4.95	8.40
Price Range	58.22-34.28	54.52-34.28	48.85-33.59	45.51-33.38	35.03-24.40	28.26-21.93	26.55-17.43	18.28-11.76
P/E Ratio	...	...	...	...	9.32-6.49	25.01-19.40	22.69-14.90	...

Address: 150 Peabody Place, Memphis, TN 38103	**Web Site:** www.servicemaster.com	**Auditors:** DELOITTE & TOUCHE LLP
Telephone: 901-597-1400	**Officers:** Nikhil Madhukar Varty - Chief Executive Officer Anthony D. (Tony) DiLucente - Senior Vice President, Chief Financial Officer	**Transfer Agents:** Computershare Trust Company, N.A.

SERVICENOW INC

Exchange	Symbol	Price	52Wk Range	Yield	P/E
NYS	NOW	$282.32 (12/31/2019)	302.31-169.12	N/A	1568.44

*7 Year Price Score 187.82 *NYSE Composite Index=100 *12 Month Price Score 99.89

TRADING VOLUME (thousand shares)

Interim Earnings (Per Share)

Qtr.	Mar	Jun	Sep	Dec
2016	(2.06)	(0.30)	(0.22)	(0.19)
2017	(0.24)	(0.33)	(0.14)	(0.16)
2018	0.06	(0.30)	0.04	0.04
2019	(0.01)	(0.06)	0.21	...

Interim Dividends (Per Share)

No Dividends Paid

Valuation Analysis		Institutional Holding	
Forecast EPS	$3.24	No of Institutions	
	(01/17/2020)	960	
Market Cap	$53.2 Billion	Shares	
Book Value	$1.4 Billion	193,337,312	
Price/Book	37.24	% Held	
Price/Sales	16.51	91.10	

Business Summary: IT Services (MIC: 6.3.1 SIC: 7372 NAIC: 511210)

ServiceNow provides enterprise cloud computing services that define, structure, manage and automate digital workflows for global enterprises. Co. markets its services to enterprises in a variety of industries, including consumer products, education, financial services, government, health care, information technology (IT) services and technology. Co. sells its subscription services through direct sales and, to a lesser extent, through indirect channel sales. Co. also provides a portfolio of personnel and other services, both directly and through its network of partners. Co.'s products include IT service management, IT operations management, IT business management, and security operations.

Recent Developments: For the quarter ended Sep 30 2019, net income increased 383.0% to US$40.6 million from US$8.4 million in the year-earlier quarter. Revenues were US$885.8 million, up 31.6% from US$673.1 million the year before. Operating income was US$56.3 million versus US$9.6 million in the prior-year quarter, an increase of 488.7%. Direct operating expenses rose 27.2% to US$200.8 million from US$157.9 million in the comparable period the year before. Indirect operating expenses increased 24.3% to US$628.7 million from US$505.7 million in the equivalent prior-year period.

Prospects: Our evaluation of ServiceNow Inc as of October 4th, 2019 is the result of our systematic analysis on three basic characteristics: earnings strength, relative valuation, and recent stock price movement. The company has produced a positive trend in earnings per share over the past 5 quarters. However, recent analyst estimates for the company have been unchanged, while NOW has posted results that exceeded analysts' expectations. Based on operating earnings yield, the company is overvalued when compared to all of the companies we cover. Share price changes over the past year indicates that NOW will perform over the near term.

Financial Data

(US$ in Thousands)	9 Mos	6 Mos	3 Mos	12/31/2018	12/31/2017	12/31/2016	12/31/2015	12/31/2014
Earnings Per Share	0.18	0.01	(0.23)	(0.15)	(0.87)	(2.75)	(1.27)	(1.23)
Cash Flow Per Share	5.87	5.57	5.06	4.56	3.76	0.97	2.02	0.96
Tang Book Value Per Share	6.17	5.26	5.15	4.78	2.11	1.42	2.91	2.13
Income Statement								
Total Revenue	2,508,663	1,622,830	788,926	2,608,816	1,933,026	1,390,513	1,005,480	682,563
EBITDA	279,408	131,869	68,989	105,774	11,486	(339,908)	(106,065)	(109,735)
Depn & Amortn	266,434	173,268	84,825	148,200	112,900	82,900	60,300	42,100
Income Before Taxes	32,999	(27,771)	(11,456)	(39,024)	(149,004)	(450,051)	(193,012)	(175,540)
Income Taxes	5,025	(15,147)	(9,911)	(12,320)	126	1,753	5,414	3,847
Net Income	27,974	(12,624)	(1,545)	(26,704)	(149,130)	(451,804)	(198,426)	(179,387)
Average Shares	197,878	186,677	182,061	177,846	171,175	164,533	155,706	145,355
Balance Sheet								
Current Assets	2,297,213	2,442,287	2,374,486	2,344,693	2,410,564	1,342,535	1,085,635	906,986
Total Assets	4,756,808	4,602,703	4,398,895	3,879,140	3,397,904	2,033,767	1,807,052	1,425,079
Current Liabilities	2,192,561	2,224,979	2,097,841	2,012,573	2,100,631	1,071,498	731,636	506,997
Long-Term Obligations	686,516	678,145	669,875	661,707	630,018	507,812	474,534	443,764
Total Liabilities	3,327,335	3,341,757	3,203,944	2,767,941	2,813,772	1,646,806	1,240,238	996,404
Stockholders' Equity	1,429,473	1,260,946	1,194,951	1,111,199	584,132	386,961	566,814	428,675
Shares Outstanding	188,559	187,461	184,739	180,175	174,275	167,430	160,785	149,509
Statistical Record								
Return on Assets %	0.84	0.07	N.M.	N.M.	N.M.	N.M.	N.M.	N.M.
Return on Equity %	2.86	0.26	N.M.	N.M.	N.M.	N.M.	N.M.	N.M.
EBITDA Margin %	11.14	8.13	8.74	4.05	0.59	N.M.	N.M.	N.M.
Net Margin %	1.12	N.M.	N.M.	N.M.	N.M.	N.M.	N.M.	N.M.
Asset Turnover	0.77	0.75	0.69	0.72	0.71	0.72	0.62	0.53
Current Ratio	1.05	1.10	1.13	1.17	1.15	1.25	1.48	1.79
Debt to Equity	0.48	0.54	0.56	0.60	1.08	1.31	1.04	1.04
Price Range	302.31-156.80	288.80-156.80	250.95-156.80	204.58-131.73	130.69-75.66	87.91-47.14	89.99-63.63	70.81-46.42

Address: 2225 Lawson Lane, Santa Clara, CA 95054 Telephone: 408-501-8550	Web Site: www.servicenow.com Officers: Frederic B. Luddy - Chief Products Officer, Chairman John J. Donahoe - President, Chief Executive Officer	Auditors: PricewaterhouseCoopers LLP Investor Contact: 408-961-2349 Transfer Agents: Computershare Trust Company, N.A

SHERWIN-WILLIAMS CO (THE)

Exchange	Symbol	Price	52Wk Range	Yield	P/E	Div Acheiver
NYS	SHW	$583.54 (12/31/2019)	593.45-380.39	0.77	39.19	39 Years

*7 Year Price Score 129.26 *NYSE Composite Index=100 *12 Month Price Score 112.26

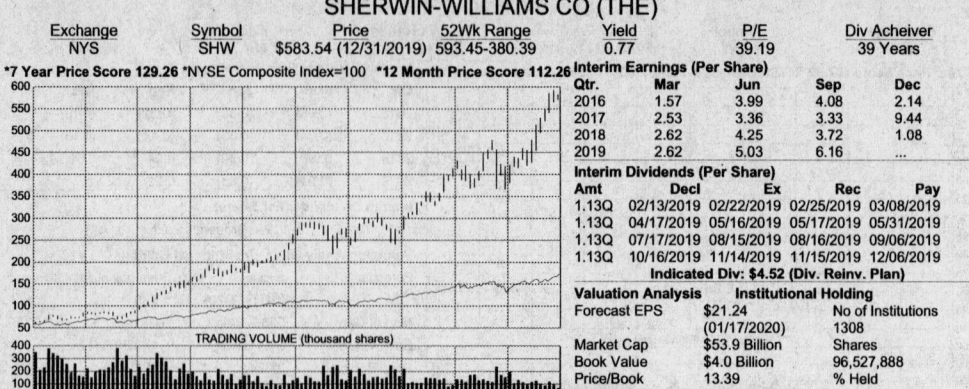

Interim Earnings (Per Share)

Qtr.	Mar	Jun	Sep	Dec
2016	1.57	3.99	4.08	2.14
2017	2.53	3.36	3.33	9.44
2018	2.62	4.25	3.72	1.08
2019	2.62	5.03	6.16	...

Interim Dividends (Per Share)

Amt	Decl	Ex	Rec	Pay
1.13Q	02/13/2019	02/22/2019	02/25/2019	03/08/2019
1.13Q	04/17/2019	05/16/2019	05/17/2019	05/31/2019
1.13Q	07/17/2019	08/15/2019	08/16/2019	09/06/2019
1.13Q	10/16/2019	11/14/2019	11/15/2019	12/06/2019

Indicated Div: $4.52 (Div. Reinv. Plan)

Valuation Analysis / Institutional Holding

Valuation Analysis		Institutional Holding	
Forecast EPS	$21.24	No of Institutions	
	(01/17/2020)	1308	
Market Cap	$53.9 Billion	Shares	
Book Value	$4.0 Billion	96,527,888	
Price/Book	13.39	% Held	
Price/Sales	3.02	75.80	

Business Summary: Specialty Chemicals (MIC: 8.3.2 SIC: 5231 NAIC: 444120)

Sherwin-Williams is engaged in the development, manufacture, distribution and sale of paint, coatings and related products to industrial, commercial and retail customers. Co.'s segments are: The Americas Group, which markets and sells Sherwin-Williams® and other controlled brand architectural paint and coatings, protective and marine products, OEM product finishes and related products; Consumer Brands Group, which supplies architectural paints, stains, varnishes, and industrial products, among others; and Performance Coatings Group, which develops and sells industrial coatings, automotive refinish, protective and marine coatings, coil coatings, packaging coatings and resins and colorants.

Recent Developments: For the quarter ended Sep 30 2019, net income increased 62.8% to US$576.4 million from US$354.0 million in the year-earlier quarter. Revenues were US$4.87 billion, up 2.9% from US$4.73 billion the year before. Direct operating expenses declined 2.9% to US$2.64 billion from US$2.72 billion in the comparable period the year before. Indirect operating expenses decreased 6.7% to US$1.40 billion from US$1.50 billion in the equivalent prior-year period.

Prospects: Our evaluation of Sherwin-Williams Co. as of October 4th, 2019 is the result of our systematic analysis on three basic characteristics: earnings strength, relative valuation, and recent stock price movement. The company has enjoyed a very positive trend in earnings per share over the past 5 quarters. However, recent analyst estimates for the company have been mixed and SHW has posted results that exceeded analysts' expectations. Based on operating earnings yield, the company is fairly valued when compared to all of the companies we cover. Share price changes over the past year indicates that SHW will perform in line with the market over the near term.

Financial Data

(US$ in Thousands)	9 Mos	6 Mos	3 Mos	12/31/2018	12/31/2017	12/31/2016	12/31/2015	12/31/2014
Earnings Per Share	14.89	12.45	11.67	11.67	18.67	11.99	11.16	8.78
Cash Flow Per Share	23.67	23.13	20.30	20.90	20.28	14.21	15.70	11.24
Tang Book Value Per Share	N.M.	N.M.	N.M.	N.M.	N.M.	5.34	N.M.	N.M.
Dividends Per Share	4.250	3.980	3.710	3.440	3.400	3.360	2.680	2.200
Dividend Payout %	28.54	31.97	31.79	29.48	18.21	28.02	24.01	25.06
Income Statement								
Total Revenue	13,786,371	8,918,721	4,040,861	17,534,493	14,983,788	11,855,602	11,339,304	11,129,533
EBITDA	2,384,942	1,444,744	535,101	2,317,379	2,274,880	1,942,072	1,807,920	1,518,381
Depn & Amortn	436,668	290,948	145,663	596,281	491,761	197,711	198,562	198,945
Income Before Taxes	1,684,388	974,555	298,854	1,359,650	1,528,219	1,595,233	1,548,966	1,258,226
Income Taxes	391,710	258,315	53,617	250,904	(285,583)	462,530	495,117	392,339
Net Income	1,292,678	716,240	245,237	1,108,746	1,772,262	1,132,703	1,053,849	865,887
Average Shares	93,604	93,561	93,668	94,988	94,927	94,488	94,024	98,075
Balance Sheet								
Current Assets	4,907,739	5,089,964	4,815,144	4,344,487	4,465,840	3,627,298	2,658,874	2,566,780
Total Assets	20,864,339	21,186,136	20,961,641	19,134,279	19,958,427	6,752,521	5,791,855	5,706,052
Current Liabilities	4,865,790	6,342,640	5,000,556	4,297,747	3,987,180	2,829,179	2,141,859	2,680,666
Long-Term Obligations	8,043,030	7,209,481	8,702,630	8,708,057	9,885,745	1,211,326	1,920,196	1,122,715
Total Liabilities	16,841,479	17,438,654	17,501,580	15,403,534	16,266,239	4,874,080	4,923,945	4,709,582
Stockholders' Equity	4,022,860	3,747,482	3,460,061	3,730,745	3,692,188	1,878,441	867,910	996,470
Shares Outstanding	92,309	92,256	92,316	93,116	93,883	93,013	92,246	94,704
Statistical Record								
Return on Assets %	6.82	5.67	5.34	5.67	13.27	18.01	18.33	14.33
Return on Equity %	34.85	31.26	30.88	29.87	63.63	82.26	113.05	62.50
EBITDA Margin %	17.30	16.20	13.24	13.22	15.18	16.38	15.94	13.64
Net Margin %	9.38	8.03	6.07	6.32	11.83	9.55	9.29	7.78
Asset Turnover	0.87	0.86	0.85	0.90	1.12	1.89	1.97	1.84
Current Ratio	1.01	0.80	0.96	1.01	1.12	1.28	1.24	0.96
Debt to Equity	2.00	1.92	2.52	2.33	2.68	0.64	2.21	1.13
Price Range	550.54-365.24	479.61-365.24	477.98-365.24	477.98-365.24	414.34-274.54	312.10-239.35	292.44-218.94	264.93-175.60
P/E Ratio	36.97-24.53	38.47-29.34	40.96-31.30	40.96-31.30	22.19-14.70	26.03-19.96	26.20-19.62	30.17-20.00
Average Yield %	0.95	0.93	0.90	0.84	0.99	1.21	0.99	1.04

Address: 101 West Prospect Avenue, Cleveland, OH 44115-1075 Telephone: 216-566-2000 Fax: 216-566-3310	Web Site: www.sherwin.com Officers: John G. Morikis - Chairman, Chief Executive Officer, President, Chief Operating Officer David B. Sewell - President, Chief Operating Officer, Division Officer	Auditors: Ernst & Young LLP Investor Contact: 216-566-2244 Transfer Agents: EQ Shareowner Services, St. Paul, MN

SIGNET JEWELERS LTD

Exchange	Symbol	Price	52Wk Range	Yield	P/E
NYS	SIG	$21.74 (12/31/2019)	37.02-11.01	6.81	N/A

*7 Year Price Score 22.06 *NYSE Composite Index=100 *12 Month Price Score 82.46

TRADING VOLUME (thousand shares)

Interim Earnings (Per Share)

Qtr.	Apr	Jul	Oct	Jan
2016-17	1.87	1.06	0.20	3.90
2017-18	1.03	1.33	(0.20)	5.20
2018-19	(8.48)	(0.56)	(0.74)	(2.31)
2019-20	(0.35)	(0.86)	(0.84)	...

Interim Dividends (Per Share)

Amt	Decl	Ex	Rec	Pay
0.37Q	04/03/2019	05/02/2019	05/03/2019	05/31/2019
0.37Q	06/06/2019	08/01/2019	08/02/2019	08/30/2019
0.37Q	09/05/2019	10/31/2019	11/01/2019	11/29/2019
0.37Q	01/16/2020	01/30/2020	01/31/2020	02/28/2020

Indicated Div: $1.48

Valuation Analysis

		Institutional Holding	
Forecast EPS	N/A	No of Institutions	336
Market Cap	$1.1 Billion	Shares	
Book Value	$1.7 Billion		87,819,424
Price/Book	0.68	% Held	
Price/Sales	0.19		N/A

Business Summary: Retail - Specialty (MIC: 2.1.3 SIC: 5944 NAIC: 448310)

Signet Jewelers is a holding company. Through its subsidiaries, Co. is a retailer of diamond jewelry. Co. operates retail jewelry stores in a variety of real estate formats including mall-based, free-standing, strip center and outlet store locations. Co. has three reportable segments: North America, which operates a variety of mall-based regional banners, including Gordon's Jewelers in the U.S. and Mappins in Canada, and JamesAllen.com; International, which stores operate in shopping malls and off-mall locations principally under the H.Samuel and Ernest Jones banners; and Other, which subsidiaries involved in the purchasing and conversion of rough diamonds to polished stones.

Recent Developments: For the quarter ended Nov 2 2019, net loss amounted to US$35.5 million versus a net loss of US$29.9 million in the year-earlier quarter. Revenues were US$1.19 billion, unchanged from the year before. Operating loss was US$39.9 million versus a loss of US$48.8 million in the prior-year quarter. Direct operating expenses declined 0.1% to US$820.0 million from US$820.5 million in the comparable period the year before. Indirect operating expenses decreased 3.0% to US$407.6 million from US$420.0 million in the equivalent prior-year period.

Prospects: Our evaluation of Signet Jewelers Limited as of October 4th, 2019 is the result of our systematic analysis on three basic characteristics: earnings strength, relative valuation, and recent stock price movement. The company has enjoyed a very positive trend in earnings per share over the past 5 quarters. However, recent analyst estimates for the company have been mixed and SIG has posted results that exceeded analysts' expectations. Based on operating earnings yield, the company is undervalued when compared to all of the companies we cover. Share price changes over the past year indicates that SIG will perform very poorly over the near term.

Financial Data

(US$ in Thousands)	9 Mos	6 Mos	3 Mos	02/02/2019	02/03/2018	01/28/2017	01/30/2016	01/31/2015
Earnings Per Share	(4.36)	(4.26)	(3.96)	(12.62)	7.44	7.08	5.87	4.75
Cash Flow Per Share	9.61	9.51	15.02	12.79	30.30	9.13	5.59	3.55
Tang Book Value Per Share	22.07	22.78	23.31	24.19	29.92	31.73	26.67	22.97
Dividends Per Share	1.480	1.480	1.480	1.480	1.240	1.040	0.880	0.720
Dividend Payout %	...	...	...	...	16.67	14.69	14.99	15.16
Income Statement								
Total Revenue	3,983,800	2,796,100	1,431,700	6,247,100	6,253,000	6,408,400	6,550,200	5,736,300
EBITDA	201,400	148,000	83,600	(606,100)	515,900	655,700	865,100	716,700
Depn & Amortn	258,800	172,500	85,900	179,600	194,100	175,000	161,400	140,100
Income Before Taxes	(85,300)	(43,800)	(11,500)	(802,600)	527,200	713,800	657,800	540,600
Income Taxes	(3,700)	2,300	(1,500)	(145,200)	7,900	170,600	189,900	159,300
Net Income	(81,600)	(46,100)	(10,000)	(657,400)	519,300	543,200	467,900	381,300
Average Shares	51,800	51,700	51,600	54,700	69,800	76,700	79,700	80,200
Balance Sheet								
Current Assets	2,938,700	2,758,600	2,822,700	2,855,800	3,446,100	4,642,600	4,589,900	4,407,300
Total Assets	6,101,600	5,965,600	6,193,300	4,420,100	5,839,600	6,597,800	6,474,400	6,327,600
Current Liabilities	1,383,100	1,311,600	1,362,200	1,033,000	1,037,200	1,203,700	1,152,900	1,338,300
Long-Term Obligations	788,800	628,200	639,000	649,600	688,200	1,317,900	1,328,700	1,363,800
Total Liabilities	4,434,400	4,261,300	4,416,200	2,603,200	2,726,200	3,495,700	3,413,700	3,517,200
Stockholders' Equity	1,667,200	1,704,300	1,777,100	1,816,900	3,113,400	3,102,100	3,060,700	2,810,400
Shares Outstanding	52,300	52,300	52,200	51,900	60,500	68,300	79,400	80,300
Statistical Record								
Return on Assets %	N.M.	N.M.	N.M.	N.M.	8.22	8.33	7.33	7.38
Return on Equity %	N.M.	N.M.	N.M.	N.M.	16.44	17.68	15.98	14.23
EBITDA Margin %	5.06	5.29	5.84	N.M.	8.25	10.23	13.21	12.49
Net Margin %	N.M.	N.M.	N.M.	N.M.	8.30	8.48	7.14	6.65
Asset Turnover	1.12	1.15	1.08	1.22	0.99	0.98	1.03	1.11
Current Ratio	2.12	2.10	2.07	2.76	3.32	3.86	3.98	3.29
Debt to Equity	0.47	0.37	0.36	0.36	0.22	0.42	0.43	0.49
Price Range	61.14-11.01	67.68-16.35	67.68-22.17	67.68-23.94	79.16-47.88	124.03-73.16	150.94-113.39	132.12-75.28
P/E Ratio	...	...	...	...	10.64-6.44	17.52-10.33	25.71-19.32	27.81-15.85
Average Yield %	5.99	4.06	3.31	3.01	1.99	1.11	0.68	0.66

Address: Clarendon House, 2 Church Street, Hamilton, HM11 Telephone: 441-296-5872	Web Site: www.signetjewelers.com Officers: H. Todd Stitzer - Chairman Virginia (Gina) C. Drosos - Chief Executive Officer	Auditors: KPMG LLP Investor Contact: 440-207-3179700 Transfer Agents: Capita Registrars, Kent, United Kingdom

SIMON PROPERTY GROUP, INC.

Exchange	Symbol	Price	52Wk Range	Yield	P/E
NYS	SPG	$148.96 (12/31/2019)	185.85-144.01	5.57	19.99

*7 Year Price Score 78.77 *NYSE Composite Index=100 *12 Month Price Score 86.40

Interim Earnings (Per Share)

Qtr.	Mar	Jun	Sep	Dec
2016	1.55	1.45	1.61	1.26
2017	1.53	1.23	1.65	1.83
2018	2.00	1.77	1.80	2.30
2019	1.78	1.60	1.77	...

Interim Dividends (Per Share)

Amt	Decl	Ex	Rec	Pay
2.05Q	02/01/2019	02/13/2019	02/14/2019	02/28/2019
2.05Q	04/30/2019	05/16/2019	05/17/2019	05/31/2019
2.10Q	07/31/2019	08/15/2019	08/16/2019	08/30/2019
2.10Q	10/30/2019	11/14/2019	11/15/2019	11/29/2019

Indicated Div: $8.30

Valuation Analysis | **Institutional Holding**

Forecast EPS	$6.73	No of Institutions
	(01/17/2020)	1163
Market Cap	$47.7 Billion	Shares
Book Value	$2.9 Billion	390,188,672
Price/Book	16.46	% Held
Price/Sales	8.33	90.68

Business Summary: REITs (MIC: 5.3.1 SIC: 6798 NAIC: 525930)

Simon Property Group is a self-administered and self-managed real estate investment trust. Simon Property Group, L.P. is Co.'s partnership subsidiary that owns all of its real estate properties and other assets. Co. owns, develops and manages shopping, dining, entertainment and mixed-use destinations, which consist of malls, Premium Outlets®, and The Mills®. In addition, Co. has redevelopment and expansion projects, including the addition of anchors, big box tenants, and restaurants, underway at several properties in the U.S., Canada, Europe and Asia. Co. has an equity stake in Klepierre SA, a Paris-based real estate company, which owns, or has an interest in, shopping centers in Europe.

Recent Developments: For the quarter ended Sep 30 2019, net income decreased 2.1% to US$628.7 million from US$642.2 million in the year-earlier quarter. Revenues were US$1.42 billion, up 0.9% from US$1.40 billion the year before. Revenues from property income rose 1.9% to US$1.31 billion from US$1.28 billion in the corresponding quarter a year earlier.

Prospects: Our evaluation of Simon Property Group Inc. as of October 4th, 2019 is the result of our systematic analysis on three basic characteristics: earnings strength, relative valuation, and recent stock price movement. The company has managed to produce a neutral trend in earnings per share over the past 5 quarters. In addition, recent analyst estimates for the company have been mixed and SPG has posted results that fell short of analysts' expectations. Based on operating earnings yield, the company is fairly valued when compared to all of the companies we cover. Share price changes over the past year indicates that SPG will perform in line with the market over the near term.

Financial Data

(US$ in Thousands)	9 Mos	6 Mos	3 Mos	12/31/2018	12/31/2017	12/31/2016	12/31/2015	12/31/2014
Earnings Per Share	7.45	7.48	7.65	7.87	6.24	5.87	5.88	4.52
Cash Flow Per Share	12.52	12.31	12.12	12.11	11.54	10.76	9.75	8.79
Tang Book Value Per Share	8.92	9.70	10.60	10.40	11.32	13.16	13.50	15.33
Dividends Per Share	8.200	8.100	8.000	7.900	7.150	6.500	6.050	5.150
Dividend Payout %	110.07	108.29	104.58	100.38	114.58	110.73	102.89	113.94
Income Statement								
Total Revenue	4,266,574	2,850,019	1,452,834	5,657,919	5,538,640	5,435,229	5,266,103	4,870,818
EBITDA	3,157,907	2,113,289	1,080,154	4,512,792	4,011,377	3,966,872	4,017,480	3,673,776
Depn & Amortn	1,055,107	711,748	339,918	1,349,776	1,357,351	1,327,946	1,239,214	1,285,784
Income Before Taxes	1,503,259	1,004,381	541,503	2,347,093	1,844,633	1,781,372	1,854,569	1,395,391
Net Income	1,590,556	1,045,468	549,309	2,440,058	1,947,962	1,838,896	1,827,720	1,408,588
Average Shares	307,275	308,708	308,978	309,627	311,517	312,690	310,102	310,731
Balance Sheet								
Current Assets	4,422,847	1,216,138	1,169,961	1,278,150	2,224,981	1,224,678	1,325,739	1,192,479
Total Assets	33,844,226	30,732,915	30,841,776	30,686,223	32,257,638	31,103,578	30,650,673	29,532,330
Current Liabilities	1,324,110	1,227,799	1,157,477	2,852,972	2,675,568	2,573,760	2,692,345	2,426,844
Long-Term Obligations	26,643,879	23,324,679	23,185,965	23,305,535	24,632,463	22,977,104	22,502,173	20,852,993
Total Liabilities	30,944,810	27,581,925	27,402,935	27,159,379	28,380,990	26,655,368	26,153,672	24,413,616
Stockholders' Equity	2,899,416	3,150,990	3,438,841	3,526,844	3,876,648	4,448,210	4,497,001	5,118,714
Shares Outstanding	320,443	320,443	320,419	320,419	320,330	313,074	309,420	310,787
Statistical Record								
Return on Assets %	7.10	7.52	7.66	7.75	6.15	5.94	6.07	4.48
Return on Equity %	71.11	68.93	66.27	65.92	46.80	41.00	38.02	25.25
EBITDA Margin %	74.02	74.15	74.35	79.76	72.43	72.98	76.29	75.42
Net Margin %	37.28	36.68	37.81	43.13	35.17	33.83	34.71	28.92
Asset Turnover	0.18	0.19	0.18	0.18	0.17	0.18	0.18	0.15
Current Ratio	3.34	0.99	1.01	0.45	0.83	0.48	0.49	0.49
Debt to Equity	9.19	7.40	6.74	6.61	6.35	5.17	5.00	4.07
Price Range	190.59-145.47	190.59-159.27	190.59-146.74	190.59-146.74	186.83-152.26	227.60-174.20	206.19-171.00	187.46-141.62
P/E Ratio	25.58-19.53	25.48-21.29	24.91-19.18	24.22-18.65	29.94-24.40	38.77-29.68	35.07-29.08	41.47-31.33
Average Yield %	4.80	4.59	4.62	4.69	4.31	3.25	3.21	3.13

Address: 225 West Washington Street, Indianapolis, IN 46204	**Web Site:** www.simon.com	**Auditors:** Ernst & Young LLP
Telephone: 317-636-1600	**Officers:** David Simon - Chairman, President, Chief Executive Officer Herbert Simon - Chairman Emeritus, Co-Chairman, Chief Executive Officer	**Investor Contact:** 800-461-3439
Fax: 317-685-7336		**Transfer Agents:** Computershare, Pittsburgh, PA

SITE CENTERS CORP

Exchange	Symbol	Price	52Wk Range	Yield	P/E
NYS	SITC	$14.02 (12/31/2019)	15.75-11.07	5.71	11.59

*7 Year Price Score 50.52   *NYSE Composite Index=100   *12 Month Price Score 99.18

Interim Earnings (Per Share)

Qtr.	Mar	Jun	Sep	Dec
2016	0.22	0.20	(0.36)	0.16
2017	(0.32)	0.12	(0.04)	(1.24)
2018	(0.34)	(0.07)	(0.09)	0.93
2019	0.15	0.05	0.08	...

Interim Dividends (Per Share)

Amt	Decl	Ex	Rec	Pay
0.20Q	02/11/2019	03/14/2019	03/15/2019	04/02/2019
0.20Q	05/09/2019	06/11/2019	06/12/2019	07/02/2019
0.20Q	09/11/2019	09/20/2019	09/23/2019	10/08/2019
0.20Q	11/07/2019	12/12/2019	12/13/2019	01/07/2020

Indicated Div: $0.80

Valuation Analysis

Valuation Analysis		Institutional Holding	
Forecast EPS	$0.30 (01/17/2020)	No of Institutions	373
Market Cap	$2.5 Billion	Shares	262,354,944
Book Value	$2.0 Billion	% Held	N/A
Price/Book	1.26		
Price/Sales	4.87		

Business Summary: REITs (MIC: 5.3.1 SIC: 6798 NAIC: 525930)

SITE Centers is a self-administered and self-managed real estate investment trust (REIT), engaged in the business of acquiring, owning, developing, redeveloping, expanding, leasing, financing and managing shopping centers. Co.'s portfolio consisted of shopping centers (including shopping centers owned through joint ventures). These centers are principally in the Southeast and Midwest, with significant concentrations in Georgia, Florida, North Carolina and Ohio.

Recent Developments: For the quarter ended Sep 30 2019, net income amounted to US$23.9 million versus a net loss of US$8.7 million in the year-earlier quarter. Revenues were US$122.5 million, down 15.0% from US$144.1 million the year before. Revenues from property income fell 14.3% to US$108.1 million from US$126.1 million in the corresponding quarter a year earlier.

Prospects: Our evaluation of SITE Centers Corp. as of October 4th, 2019 is the result of our systematic analysis on three basic characteristics: earnings strength, relative valuation, and recent stock price movement. The company has enjoyed a very positive trend in earnings per share over the past 5 quarters. However, recent analyst estimates for the company have been mixed and SITC has posted results that fell short of analysts' expectations. Based on operating earnings yield, the company is overvalued when compared to all of the companies we cover. Share price changes over the past year indicates that SITC will perform in line with the market over the near term.

Financial Data

(US$ in Thousands)	9 Mos	6 Mos	3 Mos	12/31/2018	12/31/2017	12/31/2016	12/31/2015	12/31/2014
Earnings Per Share	1.21	1.04	0.92	0.43	(1.48)	0.20	(0.54)	0.50
Cash Flow Per Share	1.42	1.24	1.38	1.44	2.23	2.53	2.41	2.35
Tang Book Value Per Share	7.90	7.97	8.09	8.09	11.87	14.48	15.34	16.85
Dividends Per Share	0.800	0.800	0.980	0.780	1.520	1.520	...	...
Dividend Payout %	66.12	76.92	106.52	181.40	...	760.00	...	...
Income Statement								
Total Revenue	382,204	259,679	131,022	707,255	921,588	1,005,805	1,028,071	985,675
EBITDA	126,284	87,020	53,466	486,926	113,244	546,096	380,784	664,370
Depn & Amortn	3,055	1,873	937	258,456	353,676	391,666	396,730	431,204
Income Before Taxes	72,914	51,376	35,324	107,602	(400,715)	(26,105)	(228,460)	11,973
Income Taxes	827	578	272	862	12,418	1,781	6,286	1,855
Net Income	76,697	53,067	35,790	114,434	(241,685)	60,012	(72,168)	117,282
Average Shares	181,507	181,209	181,091	184,535	183,681	182,780	180,473	179,061
Balance Sheet								
Current Assets	86,678	75,100	92,299	100,660	281,677	210,095	204,143	221,218
Total Assets	4,099,861	4,142,742	4,116,023	4,206,331	7,170,073	8,197,518	9,097,088	9,541,895
Current Liabilities	259,073	256,616	238,893	248,924	423,323	457,538	494,082	509,660
Long-Term Obligations	1,833,283	1,858,875	1,824,164	1,884,405	3,849,312	4,493,968	5,139,537	5,234,707
Total Liabilities	2,095,435	2,118,605	2,066,078	2,136,257	4,279,141	4,960,003	5,641,903	5,771,647
Stockholders' Equity	2,004,426	2,024,137	2,049,945	2,070,074	2,890,932	3,237,515	3,455,185	3,770,248
Shares Outstanding	180,248	180,236	180,232	181,338	183,949	182,675	182,173	179,877
Statistical Record								
Return on Assets %	5.91	4.15	3.71	2.01	N.M.	0.69	N.M.	1.22
Return on Equity %	12.96	9.55	8.49	4.61	N.M.	1.79	N.M.	3.06
EBITDA Margin %	33.04	33.51	40.81	68.85	12.29	54.29	37.04	67.40
Net Margin %	20.07	20.44	27.32	16.18	N.M.	5.97	N.M.	11.90
Asset Turnover	0.12	0.10	0.11	0.12	0.12	0.12	0.11	0.10
Current Ratio	0.33	0.29	0.39	0.40	0.67	0.46	0.41	0.43
Debt to Equity	0.91	0.92	0.89	0.91	1.33	1.39	1.49	1.39
Price Range	15.15-10.71	14.81-10.71	14.86-10.71	15.04-10.71	25.54-12.23	32.87-24.37	33.61-24.35	30.87-24.86
P/E Ratio	12.52-8.85	14.24-10.30	16.15-11.64	34.97-24.91	...	164.34-121.83	...	61.74-49.72
Average Yield %	6.11	6.11	7.58	6.04	8.69	5.38	...	...

Address: 3300 Enterprise Parkway, Beachwood, OH 44122 **Telephone:** 216-755-5500 **Fax:** 216-755-1500	**Web Site:** www.sitecenters.com **Officers:** Terrance R. Ahern - Chairman David R. Lukes - President, Chief Executive Officer	**Auditors:** PricewaterhouseCoopers LLP **Transfer Agents:** Computershare, Providence, RI

SIX FLAGS ENTERTAINMENT CORP

Exchange	Symbol	Price	52Wk Range	Yield	P/E
NYS	SIX	$45.11 (12/31/2019)	63.87-41.54	7.36	14.28

*7 Year Price Score 84.61   *NYSE Composite Index=100   *12 Month Price Score 80.75

Interim Earnings (Per Share)

Qtr.	Mar	Jun	Sep	Dec
2016	(0.51)	0.64	1.09	0.02
2017	(0.63)	0.59	2.11	1.12
2018	(0.74)	0.88	2.16	0.93
2019	(0.82)	0.94	2.11	...

Interim Dividends (Per Share)

Amt	Decl	Ex	Rec	Pay
0.82Q	02/06/2019	02/14/2019	02/18/2019	03/04/2019
0.82Q	05/01/2019	05/29/2019	05/30/2019	06/10/2019
0.82Q	08/23/2019	09/04/2019	09/05/2019	09/16/2019
0.83Q	11/18/2019	11/27/2019	11/29/2019	12/09/2019

Indicated Div: $3.32

Valuation Analysis / **Institutional Holding**

Forecast EPS	$2.41	No of Institutions
	(01/17/2020)	489
Market Cap	$3.8 Billion	Shares
Book Value	N/A	97,094,512
Price/Book	N/A	% Held
Price/Sales	2.55	N/A

Business Summary: Sporting & Recreational (MIC: 2.2.4 SIC: 7996 NAIC: 713110)

Six Flags Entertainment is a theme park operator and also an operator of waterparks. Co.'s parks provide a selection of thrill rides, water attractions, themed areas, concerts and shows, restaurants, game venues and retail outlets. Co. holds licenses for theme park usage of certain Warner Bros. and DC Comics characters throughout the U.S. (except the Las Vegas metropolitan area), Canada, Mexico and other countries. Co.'s licenses include the right to sell merchandise featuring the characters at the parks, and to use the characters in its advertising, as walk-around characters and in theming for rides, attractions and retail outlets.

Recent Developments: For the quarter ended Sep 30 2019, net income decreased 2.1% to US$200.2 million from US$204.4 million in the year-earlier quarter. Revenues were US$621.2 million, up 0.2% from US$619.8 million the year before. Direct operating expenses rose 1.9% to US$243.3 million from US$238.8 million in the comparable period the year before. Indirect operating expenses decreased 7.5% to US$87.5 million from US$94.5 million in the equivalent prior-year period.

Prospects: Our evaluation of Six Flags Entertainment Corp. as of October 4th, 2019 is the result of our systematic analysis on three basic characteristics: earnings strength, relative valuation, and recent stock price movement. The company has generated a negative trend in earnings per share over the past 5 quarters. However, recent analyst estimates for the company have been mixed and SIX has posted results that fell short of analysts' expectations. Based on operating earnings yield, the company is undervalued when compared to all of the companies we cover. Share price changes over the past year indicates that SIX will perform well over the near term.

Financial Data
(US$ in Thousands)

	9 Mos	6 Mos	3 Mos	12/31/2018	12/31/2017	12/31/2016	12/31/2015	12/31/2014
Earnings Per Share	3.16	3.21	3.15	3.23	3.09	1.25	1.58	0.77
Cash Flow Per Share	4.88	4.80	4.70	4.91	5.13	5.00	5.06	4.15
Dividends Per Share	3.280	3.240	3.200	3.160	2.620	2.380	2,140	1,930
Dividend Payout %	103.80	100.93	101.59	97.83	84.79	190.40	135.44	250.65
Income Statement								
Total Revenue	1,226,583	605,403	128,193	1,463,707	1,359,074	1,319,398	1,263,938	1,175,793
EBITDA	478,792	157,382	(35,626)	632,347	537,268	419,428	443,915	338,049
Depn & Amortn	90,919	59,680	29,815	113,246	109,206	104,290	104,788	105,449
Income Before Taxes	301,617	39,782	(93,789)	411,858	329,052	233,266	263,224	160,011
Income Taxes	70,644	9,018	(24,657)	95,855	16,026	76,539	70,369	46,522
Net Income	190,220	10,387	(69,132)	275,996	273,816	118,302	154,690	76,022
Average Shares	85,045	84,868	84,126	85,445	88,494	94,398	97,981	98,139
Balance Sheet								
Current Assets	508,385	410,053	222,616	241,929	221,072	278,791	227,977	300,924
Total Assets	3,020,703	2,938,066	2,724,907	2,517,328	2,456,676	2,487,672	2,428,440	2,534,919
Current Liabilities	410,646	476,639	531,176	368,360	297,840	315,952	272,058	231,671
Long-Term Obligations	2,268,704	2,269,761	2,064,557	2,063,512	2,021,178	1,624,487	1,498,022	1,389,215
Total Liabilities	3,655,890	3,687,873	3,490,089	3,160,421	2,961,788	2,674,162	2,404,224	2,311,024
Stockholders' Equity	(635,187)	(749,807)	(765,182)	(643,093)	(505,112)	(186,490)	24,216	223,895
Shares Outstanding	84,516	84,334	84,245	83,962	84,488	90,849	91,550	92,937
Statistical Record								
Return on Assets %	9.54	9.88	10.42	11.10	11.08	4.80	6.23	2.96
Return on Equity %	...	...	...	...	...	...	124.69	25.46
EBITDA Margin %	39.03	26.00	N.M.	43.20	39.53	31.79	35.12	28.75
Net Margin %	15.51	1.72	N.M.	18.86	20.15	8.97	12.24	6.47
Asset Turnover	0.53	0.54	0.57	0.59	0.55	0.54	0.51	0.46
Current Ratio	1.24	0.86	0.42	0.66	0.74	0.88	0.84	1.30
Debt to Equity	...	...	...	...	...	...	61.86	6.20
Price Range	69.24-46.75	71.81-46.75	72.76-46.75	72.76-50.80	67.58-51.90	61.33-46.74	54.96-42.34	43.24-33.15
P/E Ratio	21.91-14.79	22.37-14.56	23.10-14.84	22.53-15.73	21.87-16.80	49.06-37.39	34.78-26.80	56.16-43.05
Average Yield %	5.91	5.49	5.13	4.90	4.36	4.34	4.49	4.94

Address: 924 Avenue J East, Grand Prairie, TX 75050	**Web Site:** www.sixflags.com	**Auditors:** KPMG LLP
Telephone: 972-595-5000	**Officers:** Michael Spanos - President, Chief Executive Officer Lance C. Balk - Executive Vice President, General Counsel	**Investor Contact:** 972-595-5000 **Transfer Agents:** Computershare

SKECHERS USA INC

Exchange	Symbol	Price	52Wk Range	Yield	P/E
NYS	SKX	$43.19 (12/31/2019)	44.21-22.49	N/A	19.90

*7 Year Price Score 108.78 *NYSE Composite Index=100 *12 Month Price Score 114.81

Interim Earnings (Per Share)

Qtr.	Mar	Jun	Sep	Dec
2016	0.63	0.48	0.42	0.04
2017	0.60	0.38	0.59	(0.43)
2018	0.75	0.29	0.58	0.30
2019	0.71	0.49	0.67	...

Interim Dividends (Per Share)

Amt	Decl	Ex	Rec	Pay
200%	08/21/2015	10/16/2015	10/02/2015	10/15/2015

Valuation Analysis

		Institutional Holding	
Forecast EPS	$2.25	No of Institutions	446
	(01/17/2020)		
Market Cap	$6.6 Billion	Shares	138,304,784
Book Value	$2.2 Billion		
Price/Book	3.05	% Held	
Price/Sales	1.33		76.09

Business Summary: Apparel, Footwear & Accessories (MIC: 1.4.2 SIC: 3149 NAIC: 316219)

Skechers U.S.A. designs and markets Skechers-branded lifestyle footwear for men, women and children, and performance footwear for men and women under the Skechers Performance brand name. Co.'s brands are sold through department and specialty stores, athletic and independent retailers, boutiques and internet retailers. Co.'s Lifestyle Brands products include Skechers USA, Skechers Sport, Skechers Active and Skechers Sport Active, Skecher Street™, BOBS from Skechers, and Mark Nason. Co.'s Performance Brands products include Skechers GOrun, Skechers GOwalk, Skechers GOtrain, Skechers GOtrail, Skechers GO GOLF, and YOU by Skechers™.

Recent Developments: For the quarter ended Sep 30 2019, net income increased 14.8% to US$121.7 million from US$106.1 million in the year-earlier quarter. Revenues were US$1.36 billion, up 15.2% from US$1.18 billion the year before. Operating income was US$147.4 million versus US$123.9 million in the prior-year quarter, an increase of 19.0%. Direct operating expenses rose 14.4% to US$700.9 million from US$612.5 million in the comparable period the year before. Indirect operating expenses increased 15.1% to US$511.9 million from US$444.8 million in the equivalent prior-year period.

Prospects: Our evaluation of Skechers U.S.A Inc. as of October 4th, 2019 is the result of our systematic analysis on three basic characteristics: earnings strength, relative valuation, and recent stock price movement. The company has produced a positive trend in earnings per share over the past 5 quarters. However, recent analyst estimates for the company have been unchanged, while SKX has posted results that exceeded analysts' expectations. Based on operating earnings yield, the company is undervalued when compared to all of the companies we cover. Share price changes over the past year indicates that SKX will perform poorly over the near term.

Financial Data

(US$ in Thousands)	9 Mos	6 Mos	3 Mos	12/31/2018	12/31/2017	12/31/2016	12/31/2015	12/31/2014
Earnings Per Share	2.17	2.08	1.88	1.92	1.14	1.57	1.50	0.91
Cash Flow Per Share	3.29	3.64	3.27	3.65	1.02	2.34	1.52	1.08
Tang Book Value Per Share	14.18	13.91	13.46	13.26	11.70	10.35	8.64	7.05
Income Statement								
Total Revenue	3,907,146	2,546,863	1,281,957	4,662,650	4,180,826	3,577,196	3,159,068	2,386,668
EBITDA	496,464	324,938	188,299	537,283	485,027	443,750	344,030	252,466
Depn & Amortn	80,731	52,426	27,421	109,680	96,510	79,182	527	49,457
Income Before Taxes	420,039	275,539	162,743	431,884	384,260	359,484	333,497	191,380
Income Taxes	75,288	52,522	31,724	60,611	149,156	74,125	72,450	39,184
Net Income	287,028	183,938	108,758	301,041	179,190	243,493	231,912	138,811
Average Shares	153,978	153,912	154,134	156,450	156,523	155,084	154,200	153,078
Balance Sheet								
Current Assets	2,627,376	2,492,543	2,381,801	2,472,140	2,105,024	1,827,766	1,570,467	1,285,014
Total Assets	4,566,198	4,421,236	4,127,413	3,228,255	2,735,082	2,393,670	2,047,408	1,674,918
Current Liabilities	1,106,813	994,573	819,174	850,222	597,348	621,730	577,013	505,737
Long-Term Obligations	39,773	100,024	93,755	88,118	71,103	67,159	68,942	15,081
Total Liabilities	2,391,696	2,288,329	2,064,881	1,193,297	906,018	790,037	719,852	599,669
Stockholders' Equity	2,174,502	2,132,907	2,062,532	2,034,958	1,829,064	1,603,633	1,327,556	1,075,249
Shares Outstanding	153,315	153,291	153,258	153,508	156,329	154,931	153,602	152,271
Statistical Record								
Return on Assets %	8.83	8.67	8.27	10.10	6.99	10.94	12.46	9.00
Return on Equity %	15.93	15.69	14.58	15.58	10.44	16.57	19.30	13.84
EBITDA Margin %	12.71	12.76	14.69	11.52	11.60	12.40	10.89	10.58
Net Margin %	7.35	7.22	8.48	6.46	4.29	6.81	7.34	5.82
Asset Turnover	1.32	1.30	1.33	1.56	1.63	1.61	1.70	1.55
Current Ratio	2.37	2.51	2.91	2.91	3.52	2.94	2.72	2.54
Debt to Equity	0.02	0.05	0.05	0.04	0.04	0.04	0.05	0.01
Price Range	39.70-21.86	35.28-21.86	42.45-21.86	42.45-21.86	38.66-22.54	34.06-18.98	53.43-18.42	21.36-8.97
P/E Ratio	18.29-10.07	16.96-10.51	22.58-11.63	22.11-11.39	33.91-19.77	21.69-12.09	35.62-12.28	23.48-9.85

Address: 228 Manhattan Beach Blvd., Manhattan Beach, CA 90266
Telephone: 310-318-3100

Web Site: www.skechers.com
Officers: Robert Greenberg - Chairman, Chief Executive Officer Michael Greenberg - President, Chairman

Auditors: BDO USA, LLP
Investor Contact: 310-829-5400
Transfer Agents: American Stock Transfer & Trust Company, Brooklyn, NY

SJW GROUP

Exchange	Symbol	Price	52Wk Range	Yield	P/E	Div Acheiver
NYS	SJW	$71.06 (12/31/2019)	74.47-54.74	1.69	51.49	51 Years

*7 Year Price Score 121.66 *NYSE Composite Index=100 *12 Month Price Score 103.12

Interim Earnings (Per Share)

Qtr.	Mar	Jun	Sep	Dec
2016	0.16	0.82	0.92	0.67
2017	0.18	0.90	0.94	0.83
2018	0.06	0.62	0.76	0.37
2019	0.21	0.47	0.33	...

Interim Dividends (Per Share)

Amt	Decl	Ex	Rec	Pay
0.30Q	01/30/2019	02/08/2019	02/11/2019	03/01/2019
0.30Q	04/24/2019	05/03/2019	05/06/2019	06/03/2019
0.30Q	07/24/2019	08/02/2019	08/05/2019	09/03/2019
0.30Q	10/30/2019	11/07/2019	11/11/2019	12/02/2019

Indicated Div: $1.20

Valuation Analysis | **Institutional Holding**

Forecast EPS	$1.69	No of Institutions
(01/16/2020)		241
Market Cap	$2.0 Billion	Shares
Book Value	$896.7 Million	21,344,018
Price/Book	2.26	% Held
Price/Sales	5.14	93.38

Business Summary: Water Utilities (MIC: 3.2.1 SIC: 4941 NAIC: 221310)

SJW is a holding company. Through its subsidiary, San Jose Water Company, Co. is a public utility in the business of providing water service in the metropolitan San Jose, CA area. SJWTX, Inc., a subsidiary of Co., is doing business as Canyon Lake Water Service Company, which is a public utility in the business of providing water service in southern region of the Texas Hill Country in Blanco, Comal, Hays and Travis counties. SJW Land Company, another subsidiary of Co., owns undeveloped land and operates commercial buildings in Tennessee. San Jose Water Company also provides non-tariffed services including water system operations, maintenance agreements and antenna site leases.

Recent Developments: For the quarter ended Sep 30 2019, net income decreased 40.0% to US$9.5 million from US$15.8 million in the year-earlier quarter. Revenues were US$114.0 million, down 8.7% from US$124.9 million the year before. Operating income was US$17.1 million versus US$25.8 million in the prior-year quarter, a decrease of 33.9%. Direct operating expenses rose 2.2% to US$56.4 million from US$55.2 million in the comparable period the year before. Indirect operating expenses decreased 7.6% to US$40.6 million from US$43.9 million in the equivalent prior-year period.

Prospects: Our evaluation of SJW Group as of October 4th, 2019 is the result of our systematic analysis on three basic characteristics: earnings strength, relative valuation, and recent stock price movement. The company has generated a negative trend in earnings per share over the past 5 quarters. However, recent analyst estimates for the company have been unchanged while SJW has posted results that fell short of analysts' expectations. Based on operating earnings yield, the company is fairly valued when compared to all of the companies we cover. Share price changes over the past year indicates that SJW will perform well over the near term.

Financial Data

(US$ in Thousands)	9 Mos	6 Mos	3 Mos	12/31/2018	12/31/2017	12/31/2016	12/31/2015	12/31/2014
Earnings Per Share	1.38	1.81	1.96	1.82	2.86	2.57	1.85	2.54
Cash Flow Per Share	3.83	3.36	3.31	4.31	4.93	5.57	4.78	3.26
Tang Book Value Per Share	31.51	31.43	31.24	31.31	22.57	20.61	18.83	17.75
Dividends Per Share	1.180	1.160	1.140	1.120	1.040	0.810	0.780	0.750
Dividend Payout %	85.51	64.09	58.16	61.54	36.36	31.52	42.16	29.53
Income Statement								
Total Revenue	294,644	180,647	77,682	397,699	389,225	339,706	305,082	319,668
EBITDA	98,032	65,779	27,680	126,722	165,878	150,878	121,573	132,989
Depn & Amortn	47,363	31,576	15,803	53,031	46,456	42,659	38,233	35,424
Income Before Taxes	37,915	25,872	7,918	49,359	96,493	86,381	61,154	76,777
Income Taxes	8,802	6,237	2,045	10,065	35,393	33,542	23,272	24,971
Net Income	28,889	19,411	5,873	38,767	59,204	52,839	37,882	51,806
Average Shares	28,549	28,526	28,507	21,332	20,685	20,588	20,515	20,416
Balance Sheet								
Current Assets	507,814	503,919	488,456	502,722	66,858	99,611	73,376	68,093
Total Assets	2,022,382	2,003,650	1,958,807	1,956,389	1,458,001	1,443,376	1,340,963	1,269,304
Current Liabilities	144,307	127,058	86,688	163,985	85,052	63,573	79,623	44,694
Long-Term Obligations	511,076	510,859	510,903	431,424	431,092	433,335	380,825	384,365
Total Liabilities	1,125,718	1,109,655	1,070,514	1,067,077	994,792	1,021,730	957,180	909,149
Stockholders' Equity	896,664	893,995	888,293	889,312	463,209	421,646	383,783	360,155
Shares Outstanding	28,456	28,442	28,434	28,404	20,520	20,456	20,381	20,286
Statistical Record								
Return on Assets %	2.12	2.51	2.53	2.27	4.08	3.79	2.90	4.35
Return on Equity %	5.50	6.48	6.44	5.73	13.38	13.08	10.18	15.21
EBITDA Margin %	33.27	36.41	35.63	31.86	42.62	44.41	39.85	41.60
Net Margin %	9.80	10.75	7.56	9.75	15.21	15.55	12.42	16.21
Asset Turnover	0.22	0.23	0.23	0.23	0.27	0.24	0.23	0.27
Current Ratio	3.52	3.97	5.63	3.07	0.79	1.57	0.92	1.52
Debt to Equity	0.57	0.57	0.58	0.48	0.93	1.03	0.99	1.07
Price Range	69.23-52.63	67.29-52.63	68.15-51.68	68.15-51.68	68.13-45.74	56.69-29.35	35.60-27.64	32.87-25.64
P/E Ratio	50.17-38.14	37.18-29.08	34.77-26.37	37.45-28.40	23.82-15.99	22.06-11.42	19.24-14.94	12.94-10.09
Average Yield %	1.91	1.91	1.88	1.88	1.93	2.01	2.53	2.65

Address: 110 West Taylor Street, San Jose, CA 95110 Telephone: 408-279-7800	Web Site: www.sjwater.com Officers: W. Richard Roth - Chairman, President, Chief Executive Officer Eric W. Thornburg - President, Chief Executive Officer	Auditors: KPMG LLP Investor Contact: 800-250-5147 Transfer Agents: American Stock Transfer & Trust Company, LLC, Brooklyn, NY

SL GREEN REALTY CORP

Exchange	Symbol	Price	52Wk Range	Yield	P/E
NYS	SLG	$91.88 (12/31/2019)	93.47-76.79	3.85	41.95

*7 Year Price Score 70.15 *NYSE Composite Index=100 *12 Month Price Score 95.82

Interim Earnings (Per Share)

Qtr.	Mar	Jun	Sep	Dec
2016	0.23	1.33	0.34	0.44
2017	0.11	0.08	0.40	0.28
2018	1.12	1.19	1.03	(0.67)
2019	0.52	1.94	0.40	...

Interim Dividends (Per Share)

Amt	Decl	Ex	Rec	Pay
0.85Q	03/21/2019	03/28/2019	03/29/2019	04/15/2019
0.85Q	06/13/2019	06/27/2019	06/28/2019	07/15/2019
0.85Q	09/20/2019	09/27/2019	09/30/2019	10/15/2019
0.885Q	12/06/2019	12/31/2019	01/02/2020	01/15/2020

Indicated Div: $3.54

Valuation Analysis / Institutional Holding

Forecast EPS	$3.13
	(01/17/2020)
Market Cap	$7.5 Billion
Book Value	$6.0 Billion
Price/Book	1.25
Price/Sales	6.00

Institutional Holding
No of Institutions 529
Shares 122,418,128
% Held 83.63

Business Summary: REITs (MIC: 5.3.1 SIC: 6798 NAIC: 525930)

SL Green Realty is a self-managed real estate investment trust, engaged in the acquisition, development, ownership, management and operation of commercial and residential real estate properties, principally office properties, located in the New York metropolitan area. Co. has two reportable segments: real estate and debt and preferred equity investments.

Recent Developments: For the quarter ended Sep 30 2019, net income decreased 59.1% to US$40.7 million from US$99.5 million in the year-earlier quarter. Revenues were US$313.6 million, up 2.0% from US$307.5 million the year before. Revenues from property income fell 1.1% to US$248.0 million from US$250.9 million in the corresponding quarter a year earlier.

Prospects: Our evaluation of SL Green Realty Corp. as of October 4th, 2019 is the result of our systematic analysis on three basic characteristics: earnings strength, relative valuation, and recent stock price movement. The company has managed to produce a neutral trend in earnings per share over the past 5 quarters. In addition, recent analyst estimates for the company have been mixed and SLG has posted results that fell short of analysts' expectations. Based on operating earnings yield, the company is overvalued when compared to all of the companies we cover. Share price changes over the past year indicates that SLG will perform in line with the market over the near term.

Financial Data
(US$ in Thousands)

	9 Mos	6 Mos	3 Mos	12/31/2018	12/31/2017	12/31/2016	12/31/2015	12/31/2014
Earnings Per Share	2.19	2.82	2.07	2.67	0.87	2.34	2.70	5.20
Cash Flow Per Share	5.15	4.98	4.91	5.09	5.56	6.32	5.30	5.12
Tang Book Value Per Share	70.62	70.38	70.39	71.46	67.94	73.63	73.50	69.73
Dividends Per Share	3.400	3.362	3.325	3.288	3.138	2.935	2.520	2.100
Dividend Payout %	155.25	119.24	160.63	123.13	360.63	125.43	93.33	40.38
Income Statement								
Total Revenue	930,913	617,279	304,255	1,227,392	1,511,473	1,863,981	1,662,829	1,519,978
EBITDA	375,105	409,506	165,189	411,047	685,356	1,327,727	1,121,708	870,139
Depn & Amortn	7,047	143,258	71,085	242,800	365,300	783,500	523,800	338,800
Income Before Taxes	213,695	163,109	40,837	(40,422)	63,011	223,028	274,038	213,939
Net Income	249,265	212,370	47,530	247,262	101,374	249,896	284,084	518,056
Average Shares	86,714	87,398	87,810	91,530	103,403	104,881	103,734	99,696
Balance Sheet								
Current Assets	618,163	674,740	739,503	713,358	724,625	966,884	1,107,032	914,062
Total Assets	13,294,984	13,629,941	13,385,774	12,751,358	13,982,904	15,857,787	19,857,941	17,096,587
Current Liabilities	437,957	423,985	384,613	315,332	328,349	380,410	554,909	441,887
Long-Term Obligations	5,835,768	6,082,789	5,890,064	5,585,317	5,897,975	6,523,798	10,447,108	8,199,609
Total Liabilities	7,316,551	7,533,734	7,302,690	6,549,410	7,456,076	8,231,302	12,287,960	10,088,098
Stockholders' Equity	5,978,433	6,096,207	6,083,084	6,201,948	6,526,828	7,626,485	7,569,981	7,008,489
Shares Outstanding	81,515	83,465	83,272	83,684	92,803	100,562	99,975	97,325
Statistical Record								
Return on Assets %	1.43	1.81	1.41	1.85	0.68	1.40	1.54	3.23
Return on Equity %	3.07	3.92	2.94	3.89	1.43	3.28	3.90	7.63
EBITDA Margin %	40.29	66.34	54.29	33.49	45.34	71.23	67.46	57.25
Net Margin %	26.78	34.40	15.62	20.15	6.71	13.41	17.08	34.08
Asset Turnover	0.09	0.09	0.09	0.09	0.10	0.10	0.09	0.09
Current Ratio	1.41	1.59	1.92	2.26	2.21	2.54	1.99	2.07
Debt to Equity	0.98	1.00	0.97	0.90	0.90	0.86	1.38	1.17
Price Range	96.88-76.79	105.86-77.46	105.86-77.46	105.86-77.63	113.75-94.15	119.20-80.54	134.00-100.95	123.10-90.96
P/E Ratio	44.24-35.06	37.54-27.47	51.14-37.42	39.65-29.07	130.75-108.22	50.94-34.42	49.63-37.39	23.67-17.49
Average Yield %	3.91	3.63	3.49	3.39	3.03	2.83	2.12	1.97

Address: 420 Lexington Avenue, New York, NY 10170	**Web Site:** www.slgreen.com	**Auditors:** Ernst & Young LLP
Telephone: 212-594-2700	**Officers:** Stephen L. Green - Executive Chairman, Chairman Emeritus Marc Holliday - Chairman, Chief Executive Officer	**Transfer Agents:** Computershare Shareowner Services, Providence, RI

SM ENERGY CO.

Exchange	Symbol	Price	52Wk Range	Yield	P/E
NYS	SM	$11.24 (12/31/2019)	21.14-7.20	0.89	5.71

*7 Year Price Score 27.68 *NYSE Composite Index=100 *12 Month Price Score 69.31

Interim Earnings (Per Share)

Qtr.	Mar	Jun	Sep	Dec
2016	(5.10)	(2.48)	(0.52)	(2.12)
2017	0.67	(1.08)	(0.80)	(0.23)
2018	2.81	0.15	(1.21)	2.73
2019	(1.58)	0.45	0.37	...

Interim Dividends (Per Share)

Amt	Decl	Ex	Rec	Pay
0.05S	03/29/2018	04/26/2018	04/27/2018	05/09/2018
0.05S	09/28/2018	10/25/2018	10/26/2018	11/07/2018
0.05S	03/27/2019	04/25/2019	04/26/2019	05/08/2019
0.05S	09/24/2019	10/24/2019	10/25/2019	11/06/2019

Indicated Div: $0.10

Valuation Analysis / Institutional Holding

Forecast EPS	$-0.50	No. of Institutions
	(00/25/2020)	411
Market Cap	$1.3 Billion	Shares
Book Value	$2.8 Billion	131,527,664
Price/Book	0.45	% Held
Price/Sales	0.83	N/A

Business Summary: Production & Extraction (MIC: 9.1.1 SIC: 1311 NAIC: 211111)

SM Energy is an independent energy company engaged in the development, production, exploration, and acquisition of crude oil and condensate, natural gas, and natural gas liquids in onshore North America. Co.'s operations are concentrated in its onshore Permian and South Texas and Gulf Coast regions in the United States.

Recent Developments: For the quarter ended Sep 30 2019, net income amounted to US$42.2 million versus a net loss of US$135.9 million in the year-earlier quarter. Revenues were US$390.3 million, down 15.0% from US$459.4 million the year before. Operating income was US$99.5 million versus a loss of US$108.6 million in the prior-year quarter. Direct operating expenses rose 3.5% to US$340.2 million from US$328.7 million in the comparable period the year before. Indirect operating income amounted to US$49.3 million compared with an expense of US$239.3 million in the equivalent prior-year period.

Prospects: Our evaluation of SM Energy Co. as of October 4th, 2019 is the result of our systematic analysis on three basic characteristics: earnings strength, relative valuation, and recent stock price movement. The company has managed to produce a neutral trend in earnings per share over the past 5 quarters. However, recent analyst estimates for the company have been reduced while SM has posted results that exceeded analysts' expectations. Based on operating earnings yield, the company is overvalued when compared to all of the companies we cover. Share price changes over the past year indicates that SM will perform poorly over the near term.

Financial Data
(US$ in Thousands)

	9 Mos	6 Mos	3 Mos	12/31/2018	12/31/2017	12/31/2016	12/31/2015	12/31/2014
Earnings Per Share	1.97	0.39	0.09	4.48	(1.44)	(9.90)	(6.61)	9.79
Cash Flow Per Share	6.75	7.02	6.23	6.44	4.63	7.20	14.45	21.67
Tang Book Value Per Share	25.20	24.90	24.44	26.02	21.44	22.44	27.21	33.89
Dividends Per Share	0.100	0.100	0.100	0.100	0.100	0.100	0.100	0.100
Dividend Payout %	5.08	25.64	111.11	2.23	...	...	...	1.02
Income Statement								
Total Revenue	1,138,419	748,102	340,930	2,067,072	1,129,376	1,217,450	1,556,965	2,522,307
EBITDA	28,462	(74,388)	(181,837)	1,493,254	408,756	(242,548)	334,007	1,936,931
Depn & Amortn	11,554	7,633	3,789	680,571	573,312	800,683	928,719	773,678
Income Before Taxes	(101,283)	(159,628)	(223,606)	651,777	(343,813)	(1,201,916)	(722,861)	1,064,699
Income Taxes	(16,337)	(32,448)	(46,038)	143,370	(182,970)	(444,172)	(275,151)	398,648
Net Income	(84,946)	(127,180)	(177,568)	508,407	(160,843)	(757,744)	(447,710)	666,051
Average Shares	113,334	112,932	112,252	113,502	111,428	76,568	67,723	68,044
Balance Sheet								
Current Assets	311,114	288,734	221,334	429,263	549,115	224,642	518,989	745,043
Total Assets	6,453,083	6,391,939	6,286,618	6,352,862	6,176,776	6,393,511	5,621,643	6,516,700
Current Liabilities	491,042	503,945	545,342	466,052	559,212	415,172	302,525	784,660
Long-Term Obligations	2,735,769	2,721,240	2,646,287	2,596,333	2,908,770	2,897,575	2,517,970	2,366,000
Total Liabilities	3,609,333	3,590,096	3,543,393	3,432,540	3,782,168	3,896,378	3,769,242	4,230,045
Stockholders' Equity	2,843,750	2,801,843	2,743,225	2,920,322	2,394,608	2,497,133	1,852,401	2,286,655
Shares Outstanding	112,857	112,525	112,244	112,241	111,687	111,257	68,075	67,463
Statistical Record								
Return on Assets %	3.53	0.71	0.21	8.12	N.M.	N.M.	N.M.	11.87
Return on Equity %	8.26	1.68	0.49	19.13	N.M.	N.M.	N.M.	34.21
EBITDA Margin %	2.50	N.M.	N.M.	72.24	36.19	N.M.	21.45	76.79
Net Margin %	N.M.	N.M.	N.M.	24.60	N.M.	N.M.	N.M.	26.41
Asset Turnover	0.24	0.24	0.25	0.33	0.18	0.20	0.26	0.45
Current Ratio	0.63	0.57	0.41	0.92	0.98	0.54	1.72	0.95
Debt to Equity	0.96	0.97	0.96	0.89	1.21	1.16	1.36	1.03
Price Range	33.47-8.90	33.47-10.38	33.47-13.49	33.47-13.49	36.08-12.79	41.27-7.60	59.01-18.22	89.58-30.17
P/E Ratio	16.99-4.52	85.82-26.62	371.89-149.89	7.47-3.01	...	...	...	9.15-3.08
Average Yield %	0.61	0.47	0.43	0.41	0.48	0.36	0.25	0.14

Address: 1775 Sherman Street, Suite 1200, Denver, CO 80203	**Web Site:** www.sm-energy.com	**Auditors:** Ernst & Young LLP
Telephone: 303-861-8140	**Officers:** William D. Sullivan - Chairman Javan D. Ottoson - President, Chief Executive Officer,	**Investor Contact:** 303-861-8140
Fax: 303-861-0934	Executive Vice President, Chief Operating Officer	**Transfer Agents:** Computershare Trust Company NA, Golden, Co

SMITH (A O) CORP

Exchange	Symbol	Price	52Wk Range	Yield	P/E	Div Acheiver
NYS	AOS	$47.64 (12/31/2019)	56.49-40.50	2.02	19.77	26 Years

*7 Year Price Score 98.23 *NYSE Composite Index=100 *12 Month Price Score 94.92

Interim Earnings (Per Share)

Qtr.	Mar	Jun	Sep	Dec
2016	0.41	0.49	0.47	0.47
2017	0.50	0.53	0.54	0.13
2018	0.57	0.66	0.61	0.74
2019	0.53	0.61	0.53	...

Interim Dividends (Per Share)

Amt	Decl	Ex	Rec	Pay
0.22Q	04/08/2019	04/29/2019	04/30/2019	05/15/2019
0.22Q	07/08/2019	07/30/2019	07/31/2019	08/15/2019
0.24Q	10/10/2019	10/30/2019	10/31/2019	11/15/2019
0.24Q	01/16/2020	01/30/2020	01/31/2020	02/18/2020

Indicated Div: $0.96 (Div. Reinv. Plan)

Valuation Analysis

		Institutional Holding	
Forecast EPS	$2.26	No of Institutions	
	(01/15/2020)	663	
Market Cap	$7.8 Billion	Shares	
Book Value	$1.7 Billion	162,283,344	
Price/Book	4.69	% Held	
Price/Sales	2.54	75.29	

TRADING VOLUME (thousand shares)

Business Summary: Household Appliances, Electronics & Goods (MIC: 1.5.1 SIC: 3639 NAIC: 335228)

A.O. Smith is comprised of two reporting segments: North America and Rest of World. Co.'s Rest of World segment is primarily comprised of China, Europe and India. Both segments manufacture and market lines of residential and commercial gas and electric water heaters, boilers, tanks and water treatment products. Both segments primarily manufacture and market in their respective regions of the world. Co.'s Rest of World segment also manufactures and markets in-home air purification products in China. Co. serves residential and commercial end markets in North America with a range of products including water heaters, boilers, water treatment products, and other.

Recent Developments: For the quarter ended Sep 30 2019, net income decreased 16.5% to US$87.3 million from US$104.6 million in the year-earlier quarter. Revenues were US$728.2 million, down 3.4% from US$754.1 million the year before. Direct operating expenses declined 0.9% to US$444.0 million from US$448.1 million in the comparable period the year before. Indirect operating expenses decreased 1.8% to US$171.4 million from US$174.5 million in the equivalent prior-year period.

Prospects: Our evaluation of Smith (A.O.) Corp. as of October 4th, 2019 is the result of our systematic analysis on three basic characteristics: earnings strength, relative valuation, and recent stock price movement. The company has generated a negative trend in earnings per share over the past 5 quarters. However, recent analyst estimates for the company have been unchanged while AOS has posted results that fell short of analysts' expectations. Based on operating earnings yield, the company is undervalued when compared to all of the companies we cover. Share price changes over the past year indicates that AOS will perform in line with the market over the near term.

Financial Data

(US$ in Thousands)	9 Mos	6 Mos	3 Mos	12/31/2018	12/31/2017	12/31/2016	12/31/2015	12/31/2014
Earnings Per Share	2.41	2.49	2.54	2.58	1.70	1.85	1.58	1.14
Cash Flow Per Share	2.68	2.51	2.55	2.63	1.89	2.55	1.94	1.46
Tang Book Value Per Share	4.72	5.07	6.70	5.42	4.80	4.13	4.15	3.60
Dividends Per Share	0.880	0.840	0.800	0.760	0.560	0.480	0.380	0.300
Dividend Payout %	36.51	33.73	31.50	29.46	32.94	25.95	24.05	26.32
Income Statement								
Total Revenue	2,241,800	1,513,600	748,200	3,187,900	2,996,700	2,685,900	2,536,500	2,356,000
EBITDA	423,200	287,600	133,800	638,100	601,000	534,900	472,900	352,200
Depn & Amortn	58,100	38,400	20,200	71,900	70,100	65,100	63,000	59,800
Income Before Taxes	356,600	243,800	111,600	557,800	520,800	462,500	402,500	286,700
Income Taxes	77,900	52,400	22,300	113,600	224,300	136,000	119,600	78,900
Net Income	278,700	191,400	89,300	444,200	296,500	326,500	282,900	207,800
Average Shares	165,543	168,086	169,096	172,194	174,605	176,825	179,009	181,973
Balance Sheet								
Current Assets	1,504,400	1,596,600	1,658,100	1,638,500	1,766,800	1,562,000	1,455,300	1,319,000
Total Assets	3,067,900	3,175,600	3,143,500	3,071,500	3,197,300	2,891,000	2,646,500	2,515,300
Current Liabilities	730,400	730,600	737,200	785,300	788,500	765,600	653,200	605,200
Long-Term Obligations	312,400	351,800	277,600	221,400	402,900	316,400	236,100	210,100
Total Liabilities	1,411,700	1,450,500	1,394,300	1,354,500	1,548,500	1,375,700	1,204,200	1,134,000
Stockholders' Equity	1,656,200	1,725,100	1,749,200	1,717,000	1,648,800	1,515,300	1,442,300	1,381,300
Shares Outstanding	163,111	164,403	141,137	168,159	171,663	173,441	175,896	178,799
Statistical Record								
Return on Assets %	13.29	13.49	13.91	14.17	9.74	11.76	10.96	8.47
Return on Equity %	23.74	24.44	25.14	26.39	18.74	22.02	20.04	15.34
EBITDA Margin %	18.88	19.00	17.88	20.02	20.06	19.92	18.64	14.95
Net Margin %	12.43	12.65	11.94	13.93	9.89	12.16	11.15	8.82
Asset Turnover	1.00	0.98	1.01	1.02	0.98	0.97	0.98	0.96
Current Ratio	2.06	2.19	2.25	2.09	2.24	2.04	2.23	2.18
Debt to Equity	0.19	0.20	0.16	0.13	0.24	0.21	0.16	0.15
Price Range	56.49-40.50	61.39-40.50	65.86-41.41	67.84-41.41	63.42-47.19	51.41-31.03	40.43-27.11	28.40-22.34
P/E Ratio	23.44-16.80	24.65-16.27	25.93-16.30	26.29-16.05	37.31-27.76	27.79-16.77	25.59-17.16	24.91-19.60
Average Yield %	1.84	1.65	1.47	1.31	1.02	1.13	1.11	1.21

Address: 11270 West Park Place, Milwaukee, WI 53224-9508 Telephone: 414-359-4000 Fax: 414-359-4115	Web Site: www.aosmith.com Officers: Ajita G. Rajendra - Executive Chairman, Chairman, President, Chief Executive Officer, Chief Operating Officer, Executive Vice President, Senior Vice President, Division Officer Kevin J. Wheeler - President, Chief Executive Officer, Chief Operating Officer, Senior Vice President, Region Officer	Auditors: Ernst & Young LLP Investor Contact: 414-359-4130 Transfer Agents: Wells Fargo Shareowner Services, N.A., St. Paul, MN

SMUCKER (J.M.) CO.

Exchange	Symbol	Price	52Wk Range	Yield	P/E	Div Acheiver
NYS	SJM	$104.13 (12/31/2019)	127.50-93.49	3.38	21.21	21 Years

*7 Year Price Score 80.36   *NYSE Composite Index=100   *12 Month Price Score 90.14

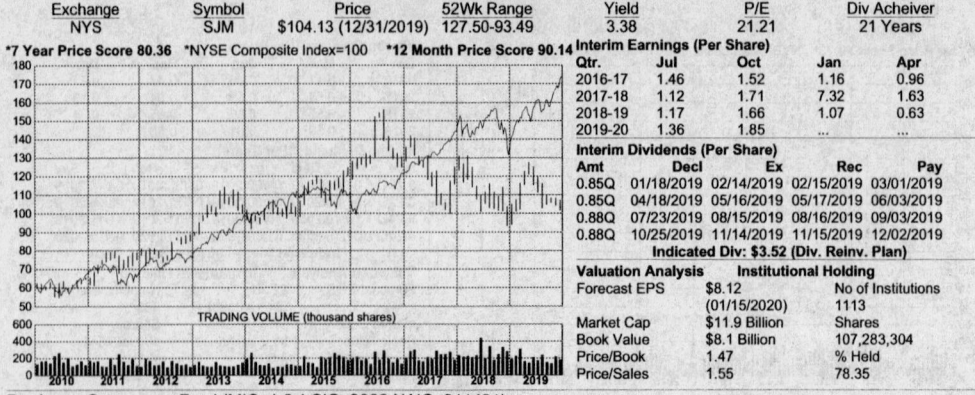

Interim Earnings (Per Share)

Qtr.	Jul	Oct	Jan	Apr
2016-17	1.46	1.52	1.16	0.96
2017-18	1.12	1.71	7.32	1.63
2018-19	1.17	1.66	1.07	0.63
2019-20	1.36	1.85	...	...

Interim Dividends (Per Share)

Amt	Decl	Ex	Rec	Pay
0.85Q	01/18/2019	02/14/2019	02/15/2019	03/01/2019
0.85Q	04/18/2019	05/16/2019	05/17/2019	06/03/2019
0.88Q	07/23/2019	08/15/2019	08/16/2019	09/03/2019
0.88Q	10/25/2019	11/14/2019	11/15/2019	12/02/2019

Indicated Div: $3.52 (Div. Reinv. Plan)

Valuation Analysis / **Institutional Holding**

Forecast EPS	$8.12	No of Institutions
	(01/15/2020)	1113
Market Cap	$11.9 Billion	Shares
Book Value	$8.1 Billion	107,283,304
Price/Book	1.47	% Held
Price/Sales	1.55	78.35

Business Summary: Food (MIC: 1.2.1 SIC: 2033 NAIC: 311421)

Smucker (J.M.) manufactures and markets food and beverage products. Co.'s principal products are coffee, dog food, pet snacks, cat food, peanut butter, fruit spreads, frozen handheld products, shortening and oils, portion control products, juices and beverages, and flour and baking ingredients. Co. has four reportable segments: U.S. Retail Coffee, U.S. Retail Consumer Foods, and U.S. Retail Pet Foods, and International and Away From Home. The U.S. retail market segments represent the sales of food and beverage products to consumers through retail outlets in North America. The International and Away From Home segment represents sales outside of the U.S. retail market segments.

Recent Developments: For the quarter ended Oct 31 2019, net income increased 12.0% to US$211.2 million from US$188.5 million in the year-earlier quarter. Revenues were US$1.96 billion, down 3.2% from US$2.02 billion the year before. Operating income was US$329.8 million versus US$330.5 million in the prior-year quarter, a decrease of 0.2%. Direct operating expenses declined 3.7% to US$1.20 billion from US$1.25 billion in the comparable period the year before. Indirect operating expenses decreased 3.8% to US$424.2 million from US$440.8 million in the equivalent prior-year period.

Prospects: Our evaluation of Smucker (J.M.) Co. as of October 4th, 2019 is the result of our systematic analysis on three basic characteristics: earnings strength, relative valuation, and recent stock price movement. The company has enjoyed a very positive trend in earnings per share over the past 5 quarters. However, recent analyst estimates for the company have been mixed and SJM has posted results that fell short of analysts' expectations. Based on operating earnings yield, the company is undervalued when compared to all of the companies we cover. Share price changes over the past year indicates that SJM will perform well over the near term.

Financial Data

(US$ in Thousands)	6 Mos	3 Mos	04/30/2019	04/30/2018	04/30/2017	04/30/2016	04/30/2015	04/30/2014
Earnings Per Share	4.91	4.72	4.52	11.78	5.10	5.76	3.33	5.42
Cash Flow Per Share	10.06	9.89	10.09	10.78	9.17	12.23	7.12	8.27
Dividends Per Share	3.430	3.400	3.330	3.090	2.920	2.650	2.500	2.260
Dividend Payout %	69.86	72.03	73.67	26.23	57.25	46.01	75.08	41.70
Income Statement								
Total Revenue	3,736,700	1,778,900	7,838,000	7,357,100	7,392,300	7,811,200	5,692,700	5,610,600
EBITDA	805,300	365,700	1,115,500	1,241,400	1,253,200	1,370,700	760,400	1,086,600
Depn & Amortn	221,000	109,600	206,000	206,300	211,700	221,700	157,500	157,500
Income Before Taxes	485,800	206,700	701,600	861,000	878,400	977,900	523,000	849,700
Income Taxes	120,000	52,100	187,200	(477,600)	286,100	289,200	178,100	284,500
Net Income	365,800	154,600	514,400	1,338,600	592,300	688,700	344,900	565,200
Average Shares	113,400	113,300	113,100	113,000	115,578	118,959	103,043	103,518
Balance Sheet								
Current Assets	1,659,200	1,613,500	1,625,200	1,555,000	1,641,800	1,573,400	2,052,300	1,539,100
Total Assets	16,791,000	16,791,600	16,711,300	15,301,200	15,639,700	15,984,100	16,882,600	9,072,100
Current Liabilities	2,310,100	2,290,800	2,341,500	1,033,800	1,832,600	1,213,000	1,022,600	891,000
Long-Term Obligations	4,584,500	4,685,300	4,686,300	4,688,000	4,445,500	5,146,000	5,944,900	1,879,800
Total Liabilities	8,695,700	8,783,900	8,740,800	7,410,100	8,789,500	8,975,600	9,795,700	4,042,500
Stockholders' Equity	8,095,300	8,007,700	7,970,500	7,891,100	6,850,200	7,008,500	7,086,900	5,029,600
Shares Outstanding	114,059	114,049	113,742	113,572	113,439	116,306	119,577	101,697
Statistical Record								
Return on Assets %	3.29	3.12	3.21	8.65	3.75	4.18	2.66	6.24
Return on Equity %	6.93	6.73	6.49	18.16	8.55	9.75	5.69	11.11
EBITDA Margin %	21.55	20.56	14.23	16.87	16.95	17.55	13.36	19.37
Net Margin %	9.79	8.69	6.56	18.19	8.01	8.82	6.06	10.07
Asset Turnover	0.45	0.45	0.49	0.48	0.47	0.47	0.44	0.62
Current Ratio	0.72	0.70	0.69	1.50	0.90	1.30	2.01	1.73
Debt to Equity	0.57	0.59	0.59	0.59	0.65	0.73	0.84	0.37
Price Range	127.50-93.16	127.50-93.16	122.79-93.16	131.53-99.99	156.23-124.74	132.52-105.59	118.20-96.45	114.36-91.81
P/E Ratio	25.97-18.97	27.01-19.74	27.17-20.61	11.17-8.49	30.63-24.46	23.01-18.33	35.50-28.96	21.10-16.94
Average Yield %	3.09	3.09	3.07	2.61	2.14	2.23	2.38	2.19

Address: One Strawberry Lane, Orrville, OH 44667-0280
Telephone: 330-682-3000

Web Site: www.jmsmucker.com
Officers: Richard K. Smucker - Executive Chairman, Executive Chairman (frmr), President, Chief Executive Officer, Co-Chief Executive Officer Timothy P. Smucker - Chairman Emeritus, Chairman, Co-Chief Executive Officer, Chairman, Co-Chief Executive Officer

Auditors: Ernst & Young LLP
Investor Contact: 330-684-3838
Transfer Agents: Computershare, Louisville, KY

SNAP-ON, INC.

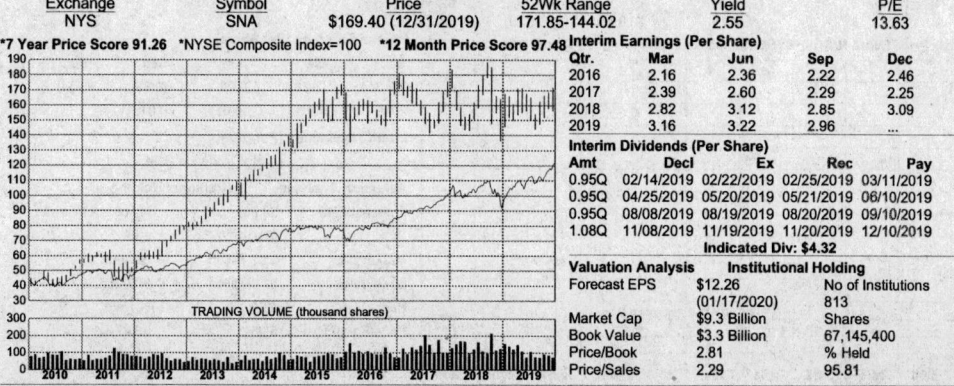

Exchange	Symbol	Price	52Wk Range	Yield	P/E
NYS	SNA	$169.40 (12/31/2019)	171.85-144.02	2.55	13.63

*7 Year Price Score 91.26 *NYSE Composite Index=100 *12 Month Price Score 97.48

Interim Earnings (Per Share)

Qtr.	Mar	Jun	Sep	Dec
2016	2.16	2.36	2.22	2.46
2017	2.39	2.60	2.29	2.25
2018	2.82	3.12	2.85	3.09
2019	3.16	3.22	2.96	...

Interim Dividends (Per Share)

Amt	Decl	Ex	Rec	Pay
0.95Q	02/14/2019	02/22/2019	02/25/2019	03/11/2019
0.95Q	04/25/2019	05/20/2019	05/21/2019	06/10/2019
0.95Q	08/08/2019	08/19/2019	08/20/2019	09/10/2019
1.08Q	11/08/2019	11/19/2019	11/20/2019	12/10/2019

Indicated Div: $4.32

Valuation Analysis / **Institutional Holding**

Forecast EPS	$12.26	No of Institutions
	(01/17/2020)	813
Market Cap	$9.3 Billion	Shares
Book Value	$3.3 Billion	67,145,400
Price/Book	2.81	% Held
Price/Sales	2.29	95.81

Business Summary: Industrial Machinery & Equipment (MIC: 7.2.1 SIC: 3429 NAIC: 332510)

Snap-on is a manufacturer and marketer of tools, equipment, diagnostics, repair information and systems solutions. Products and services include hand and power tools, tool storage, diagnostics software, handheld and PC-based diagnostic products, information and management systems, shop equipment and other solutions for vehicle dealerships and repair centers, as well as for customers in industries, such as aviation and aerospace, agriculture, construction, government and military, mining, natural resources, power generation and technical education. Co. also provides financing programs designed to facilitate the sales of its products and support its franchise business.

Recent Developments: For the quarter ended Sep 28 2019, net income increased 1.1% to US$169.2 million from US$167.4 million in the year-earlier quarter. Revenues were US$985.9 million, up 0.6% from US$980.1 million the year before. Operating income was US$228.7 million versus US$232.4 million in the prior-year quarter, a decrease of 1.6%. Direct operating expenses rose 2.1% to US$476.8 million from US$466.9 million in the comparable period the year before. Indirect operating expenses decreased 0.1% to US$280.4 million from US$280.8 million in the equivalent prior-year period.

Prospects: Our evaluation of Snap-On Inc. as of October 4th, 2019 is the result of our systematic analysis on three basic characteristics: earnings strength, relative valuation, and recent stock price movement. The company has managed to produce a neutral trend in earnings per share over the past 5 quarters. However, recent analyst estimates for the company have been reduced while SNA has posted results that exceeded analysts' expectations. Based on operating earnings yield, the company is undervalued when compared to all of the companies we cover. Share price changes over the past year indicates that SNA will perform poorly over the near term.

Financial Data

(US$ in Thousands)	9 Mos	6 Mos	3 Mos	12/29/2018	12/30/2017	12/31/2016	01/02/2016	01/03/2015
Earnings Per Share	12.43	12.32	12.22	11.87	9.52	9.20	8.10	7.14
Cash Flow Per Share	12.61	12.55	13.22	13.62	10.63	9.94	8.57	6.74
Tang Book Value Per Share	39.36	39.00	37.29	35.31	31.33	26.52	24.58	20.54
Dividends Per Share	3.800	3.670	3.540	3.410	2.950	2.540	2.200	1.850
Dividend Payout %	30.57	29.79	28.97	28.73	30.99	27.61	27.16	25.91
Income Statement								
Total Revenue	3,028,600	2,042,700	1,007,300	4,070,400	4,000,300	3,711,800	3,593,100	3,492,600
EBITDA	802,500	548,500	273,200	1,053,800	967,200	938,600	844,400	762,800
Depn & Amortn	68,500	45,600	22,600	94,100	93,200	85,600	82,500	79,500
Income Before Taxes	698,200	478,700	238,500	909,900	821,900	801,400	710,500	630,900
Income Taxes	162,900	112,500	56,900	214,400	250,900	244,300	221,200	199,500
Net Income	522,900	358,300	177,900	679,900	557,700	546,400	478,700	421,900
Average Shares	55,700	56,000	56,300	57,300	58,600	59,400	59,100	59,100
Balance Sheet								
Current Assets	2,347,900	2,306,600	2,265,300	2,216,900	2,119,300	1,884,000	1,898,700	1,858,600
Total Assets	5,596,400	5,545,400	5,490,900	5,373,100	5,249,100	4,723,200	4,486,900	4,310,100
Current Liabilities	990,100	930,800	936,000	952,000	1,193,300	989,500	670,500	718,700
Long-Term Obligations	947,500	947,900	946,700	946,000	753,600	708,800	861,700	862,700
Total Liabilities	2,292,600	2,257,300	2,293,300	2,274,300	2,295,200	2,106,000	2,074,200	2,102,300
Stockholders' Equity	3,303,800	3,288,100	3,197,600	3,098,800	2,953,900	2,617,200	2,412,700	2,207,800
Shares Outstanding	54,846	55,209	55,403	55,610	56,690	57,949	58,086	58,113
Statistical Record								
Return on Assets %	12.75	12.88	12.86	12.84	11.22	11.90	10.91	9.86
Return on Equity %	21.58	21.83	22.12	22.53	20.08	21.79	20.78	19.21
EBITDA Margin %	26.50	26.85	27.12	25.89	24.18	25.29	23.50	21.84
Net Margin %	17.27	17.54	17.66	16.70	13.94	14.72	13.32	12.08
Asset Turnover	0.74	0.75	0.75	0.77	0.80	0.81	0.82	0.82
Current Ratio	2.37	2.48	2.42	2.33	1.78	1.90	2.83	2.59
Debt to Equity	0.29	0.29	0.30	0.31	0.26	0.27	0.36	0.39
Price Range	185.54-136.13	188.46-136.13	188.46-136.13	188.46-136.13	181.53-141.51	176.20-135.41	174.09-131.45	139.35-97.23
P/E Ratio	14.93-10.95	15.30-11.05	15.42-11.14	15.88-11.47	19.07-14.86	19.15-14.72	21.49-16.23	19.52-13.62
Average Yield %	2.40	2.24	2.20	2.10	1.82	1.61	1.41	1.55

Address: 2801 80th Street, Kenosha, WI 53143	**Web Site:** www.snapon.com	**Auditors:** Deloitte & Touche LLP
	Officers: Nicholas T. Pinchuk - Chairman, President,	**Investor Contact:** 262-656-6121
Telephone: 262-656-5200	Chief Executive Officer Timothy L. Chambers - Senior	**Transfer Agents:** Computershare Trust
Fax: 262-656-5577	Vice President, Division Officer	Company, N.A., Providence, RI

SOLARWINDS CORP

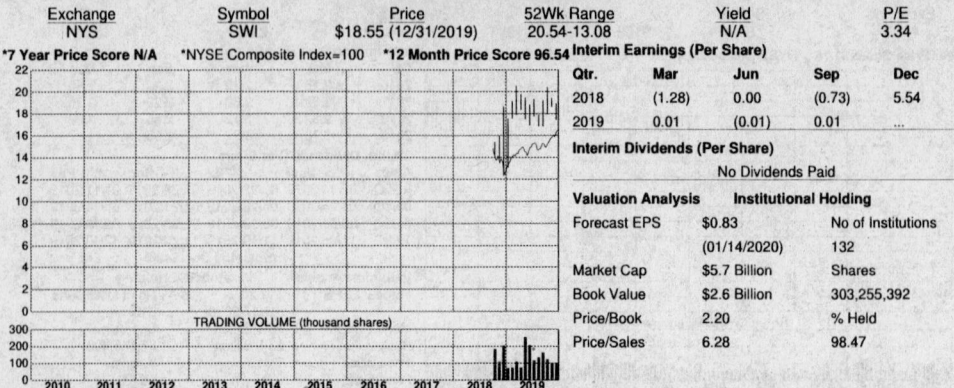

Interim Earnings (Per Share)

Qtr.	Mar	Jun	Sep	Dec
2018	(1.28)	0.00	(0.73)	5.54
2019	0.01	(0.01)	0.01	...

Interim Dividends (Per Share)

No Dividends Paid

Valuation Analysis   **Institutional Holding**

Forecast EPS	$0.83	No of Institutions
	(01/14/2020)	132
Market Cap	$5.7 Billion	Shares
Book Value	$2.6 Billion	303,255,392
Price/Book	2.20	% Held
Price/Sales	6.28	98.47

Business Summary: Internet & Software (MIC: 6.3.2 SIC: 7372 NAIC: 541512)

SolarWinds is a provider of information technology, or IT, infrastructure management software. Co.'s business is focused on building products that enable technology professionals to manage all things IT. Co.'s approach, which it calls the SolarWinds Model, enables Co. to market and sell its products directly to network and systems engineers, database administrators, storage administrators, DevOps professionals and managed service providers, Co. provides over 50 products to monitor and manage network, systems, desktop, application, storage, database and website infrastructures, whether on-premise, in the public or private cloud or in a hybrid IT infrastructure.

Recent Developments: For the quarter ended Sep 30 2019, net income amounted to US$4.4 million versus a net loss of US$398,000 in the year-earlier quarter. Revenues were US$240.5 million, up 12.8% from US$213.3 million the year before. Operating income was US$34.4 million versus US$35.1 million in the prior-year quarter, a decrease of 2.0%. Direct operating expenses rose 4.7% to US$64.8 million from US$61.9 million in the comparable period the year before. Indirect operating expenses increased 21.5% to US$141.3 million from US$116.3 million in the equivalent prior-year period.

Prospects: Our evaluation of SolarWinds Corp. as of October 4th, 2019 is the result of our systematic analysis on three basic characteristics: earnings strength, relative valuation, and recent stock price movement. The company has suffered a very negative trend in earnings per share over the past 5 quarters. However, recent analyst estimates for the company have been unchanged while SWI has posted results that exceeded analysts' expectations. Based on operating earnings yield, the company is fairly valued when compared to all of the companies we cover. Share price changes over the past year indicates that SWI will perform over the near term.

Financial Data
(US$ in Thousands)

	9 Mos	6 Mos	3 Mos	12/31/2018	12/31/2017	12/31/2016	02/04/2016
Earnings Per Share	5.55	4.81	...	2.56	(3.50)	(4.98)	(1.00)
Cash Flow Per Share	0.99	0.94	0.92	1.81	2.32	0.70	4.20
Income Statement							
Total Revenue	685,030	444,540	215,792	833,089	728,017	422,094	47,327
EBITDA	298,652	194,975	97,841	100,093	187,015	(121,721)	(122,799)
Depn & Amortn	203,602	134,631	66,749	79,795	78,697	67,624	1,695
Income Before Taxes	12,073	4,785	3,710	(121,710)	(61,468)	(359,245)	(124,967)
Income Taxes	6,654	3,759	565	(19,644)	22,398	(96,651)	(53,156)
Net Income	5,419	1,026	3,145	(102,066)	(83,866)	(262,594)	(71,811)
Average Shares	311,102	306,587	309,783	142,541	100,433	96,465	71,989
Balance Sheet							
Current Assets	348,109	280,071	566,254	500,308	388,893	239,573	...
Total Assets	5,156,076	5,207,362	5,180,472	5,194,649	5,327,064	5,202,689	...
Current Liabilities	390,265	379,899	374,778	368,102	328,394	285,653	...
Long-Term Obligations	1,896,062	1,898,713	1,901,383	1,904,072	2,245,622	2,242,892	...
Total Liabilities	2,562,517	2,573,746	2,574,095	2,578,549	2,909,938	2,842,828	...
Stockholders' Equity	2,593,559	2,633,616	2,606,377	2,616,100	2,417,126	2,359,861	...
Shares Outstanding	307,029	306,747	306,405	304,942	100,734	99,356	...
Statistical Record							
EBITDA Margin %	43.60	43.86	45.34	12.01	25.69	N.M.	N.M.
Net Margin %	0.79	0.23	1.46	N.M.	N.M.	N.M.	N.M.
Asset Turnover	0.18	0.17	...	0.16	0.14	...	...
Current Ratio	0.89	0.74	1.51	1.36	1.18	0.84	...
Debt to Equity	0.73	0.72	0.73	0.73	0.93	0.95	...
Price Range	20.54-12.35	20.54-12.35	20.54-12.35	18.66-12.35	...	...	...
P/E Ratio	3.70-2.23	4.27-2.57	...	7.29-4.82	...	...	...

SONIC AUTOMOTIVE, INC.

Exchange	Symbol	Price	52Wk Range	Yield	P/E
NYS	SAH	$31.00 (12/31/2019)	34.44-13.75	1.29	11.23

*7 Year Price Score 88.50 *NYSE Composite Index=100 *12 Month Price Score 132.11

Interim Earnings (Per Share)

Qtr.	Mar	Jun	Sep	Dec
2016	0.31	0.50	0.40	0.84
2017	(0.01)	0.27	0.44	1.39
2018	(0.05)	0.39	0.35	0.51
2019	0.98	0.61	0.66	...

Interim Dividends (Per Share)

Amt	Decl	Ex	Rec	Pay
0.10Q	02/19/2019	03/14/2019	03/15/2019	04/15/2019
0.10Q	04/25/2019	06/13/2019	06/14/2019	07/15/2019
0.10Q	07/25/2019	09/12/2019	09/13/2019	10/15/2019
0.10Q	10/24/2019	12/12/2019	12/13/2019	01/15/2020

Indicated Div: $0.40

Valuation Analysis | **Institutional Holding**

Forecast EPS	$2.53	No of Institutions
	(01/15/2020)	257
Market Cap	$1.3 Billion	Shares
Book Value	$902.4 Million	37,315,892
Price/Book	1.48	% Held
Price/Sales	0.13	82.18

Business Summary: Retail - Automotive (MIC: 2.1.4 SIC: 5511 NAIC: 441110)

Sonic Automotive is an automotive retailer in the U.S. Co. operates in two segments: Franchised Dealerships Segment; and the EchoPark Segment. The Franchised Dealerships segment is comprised of retail automotive franchises that sell new vehicles and buy and sell used vehicles, sell replacement parts, perform vehicle maintenance, warranty and repair services, and arrange finance and insurance products. The EchoPark segment is comprised of pre-owned vehicle retail locations that buy and sell used vehicles and arrange finance and insurance products.

Recent Developments: For the quarter ended Sep 30 2019, income from continuing operations increased 90.6% to US$29.2 million from US$15.3 million in the year-earlier quarter. Net income increased 91.9% to US$29.0 million from US$15.1 million in the year-earlier quarter. Revenues were US$2.70 billion, up 9.4% from US$2.47 billion the year before. Operating income was US$65.2 million versus US$48.1 million in the prior-year quarter, an increase of 35.4%. Direct operating expenses rose 9.7% to US$2.32 billion from US$2.11 billion in the comparable period the year before. Indirect operating expenses increased 3.0% to US$321.6 million from US$312.4 million in the equivalent prior-year period.

Prospects: Our evaluation of Sonic Automotive Inc. as of October 4th, 2019 is the result of our systematic analysis on three basic characteristics: earnings strength, relative valuation, and recent stock price movement. The company has produced a positive trend in earnings per share over the past 5 quarters. However, recent analyst estimates for the company have been mixed and SAH has posted results that exceeded analysts' expectations. Based on operating earnings yield, the company is undervalued when compared to all of the companies we cover. Share price changes over the past year indicates that SAH will perform well over the near term.

Financial Data
(US$ in Thousands)

	9 Mos	6 Mos	3 Mos	12/31/2018	12/31/2017	12/31/2016	12/31/2015	12/31/2014
Earnings Per Share	2.76	2.45	2.23	1.20	2.09	2.04	1.70	1.84
Cash Flow Per Share	(0.87)	1.13	(0.13)	3.36	3.70	4.73	1.38	3.09
Tang Book Value Per Share	8.13	7.52	6.98	5.70	4.32	3.86	3.54	2.10
Dividends Per Share	0.360	0.320	0.280	0.240	0.200	0.200	0.113	0.100
Dividend Payout %	13.04	13.06	12.56	20.00	9.57	9.80	6.62	5.43
Income Statement								
Total Revenue	7,705,939	5,003,219	2,389,138	9,951,630	9,867,208	9,731,779	9,624,299	9,197,099
EBITDA	217,367	151,575	88,007	274,421	289,170	314,159	289,522	295,331
Depn & Amortn	1,793	1,192	592	96,652	92,127	81,125	72,130	61,621
Income Before Taxes	138,698	98,158	61,336	75,312	108,124	155,212	145,156	161,727
Income Taxes	40,430	29,058	18,987	22,922	13,971	60,696	57,065	63,168
Net Income	97,831	68,821	42,221	51,650	92,983	93,193	86,311	97,217
Average Shares	44,203	43,230	42,888	42,950	44,358	45,948	50,883	52,563
Balance Sheet								
Current Assets	2,022,461	2,021,178	2,023,269	1,993,387	2,019,797	2,031,044	2,083,112	1,768,959
Total Assets	4,117,892	4,119,327	4,139,090	3,796,807	3,818,518	3,639,336	3,562,381	3,183,135
Current Liabilities	1,945,948	1,965,409	1,966,280	1,945,847	1,954,832	1,936,880	1,914,621	1,647,006
Long-Term Obligations	846,222	851,283	880,939	918,779	963,389	839,675	781,145	742,610
Total Liabilities	3,215,467	3,243,602	3,286,804	2,973,691	3,031,758	2,914,172	2,833,333	2,516,417
Stockholders' Equity	902,425	875,725	852,286	823,116	786,760	725,164	729,048	666,718
Shares Outstanding	43,134	43,128	43,080	42,750	43,195	44,733	49,940	50,919
Statistical Record								
Return on Assets %	3.06	2.70	2.42	1.36	2.49	2.58	2.56	3.12
Return on Equity %	14.02	12.72	11.85	6.42	12.30	12.78	12.37	15.19
EBITDA Margin %	2.82	3.03	3.68	2.76	2.93	3.23	3.01	3.21
Net Margin %	1.27	1.38	1.77	0.52	0.94	0.96	0.90	1.06
Asset Turnover	2.63	2.57	2.51	2.61	2.65	2.70	2.85	2.95
Current Ratio	1.04	1.03	1.03	1.02	1.03	1.05	1.09	1.07
Debt to Equity	0.94	0.97	1.03	1.12	1.22	1.16	1.07	1.11
Price Range	32.23-13.19	23.63-13.19	23.35-13.19	23.35-13.19	25.95-16.40	24.00-15.91	27.04-20.35	27.81-21.33
P/E Ratio	11.68-4.78	9.64-5.38	10.47-5.91	19.46-10.99	12.42-7.85	11.76-7.80	15.91-11.97	15.11-11.59
Average Yield %	1.84	1.79	1.53	1.23	1.00	1.09	0.47	0.41

Address: 4401 Colwick Road, Charlotte, NC 28211	**Web Site:** www.sonicautomotive.com	**Auditors:** KPMG LLP
Telephone: 704-566-2400	**Officers:** O. Bruton Smith - Executive Chairman, Chairman, Chief Executive Officer Jeff Dyke - President, Executive Vice President	**Investor Contact:** 888-766-4218
Fax: 704-536-5116		**Transfer Agents:** American Stock Transfer & Trust Company, New York, NY

SONOCO PRODUCTS CO.

Exchange	Symbol	Price	52Wk Range	Yield	P/E	Div Acheiver
NYS	SON	$61.72 (12/31/2019)	66.38-51.51	2.79	19.29	35 Years

*7 Year Price Score 103.48 *NYSE Composite Index=100 *12 Month Price Score 95.17

Interim Earnings (Per Share)

Qtr.	Mar	Jun	Sep	Dec
2016	0.59	0.55	0.64	1.03
2017	0.54	0.43	0.72	0.06
2018	0.73	0.88	0.72	0.76
2019	0.73	0.80	0.91	...

Interim Dividends (Per Share)

Amt	Decl	Ex	Rec	Pay
0.41Q	02/13/2019	02/26/2019	02/27/2019	03/08/2019
0.43Q	04/17/2019	05/09/2019	05/10/2019	06/10/2019
0.43Q	07/17/2019	08/08/2019	08/09/2019	09/10/2019
0.43Q	10/14/2019	11/07/2019	11/08/2019	12/10/2019

Indicated Div: $1.72 (Div. Reinv. Plan)

Valuation Analysis

		Institutional Holding	
Forecast EPS	$3.53	No of Institutions	
	(01/16/2020)	620	
Market Cap	$6.2 Billion	Shares	
Book Value	$1.8 Billion	96,705,904	
Price/Book	3.35	% Held	
Price/Sales	1.14	72.58	

Business Summary: Containers & Packaging (MIC: 8.1.3 SIC: 2671 NAIC: 322221)

Sonoco Products is a manufacturer of industrial and consumer packaging products and a provider of packaging services. Co.'s segments are: Consumer Packaging, which includes round composite cans, shaped rigid paperboard containers, fiber and plastic caulk/adhesive tubes, aluminum, steel and peelable membrane easy-open closures for composite and metal cans; Paper and Industrial Converted Products, which include recycled paperboard, chipboard, tubeboard, lightweight corestock, boxboard, linerboard, corrugating medium, edgeboard, paper grades, and adhesives; Display and Packaging, which include point-of-purchase displays; and Protective Solutions, which include packaging and components.

Recent Developments: For the quarter ended Sep 29 2019, net income increased 26.7% to US$92.3 million from US$72.8 million in the year-earlier quarter. Revenues were US$1.35 billion, down 0.8% from US$1.36 billion the year before. Operating income was US$138.5 million versus US$101.6 million in the prior-year quarter, an increase of 36.4%. Direct operating expenses declined 1.5% to US$1.09 billion from US$1.11 billion in the comparable period the year before. Indirect operating expenses decreased 19.7% to US$126.9 million from US$158.1 million in the equivalent prior-year period.

Prospects: Our evaluation of Sonoco Products Co. as of October 4th, 2019 is the result of our systematic analysis on three basic characteristics: earnings strength, relative valuation, and recent stock price movement. The company has managed to produce a neutral trend in earnings per share over the past 5 quarters. In addition, recent analyst estimates for the company have been mixed and SON has posted results that fell short of analysts' expectations. Based on operating earnings yield, the company is undervalued when compared to all of the companies we cover. Share price changes over the past year indicates that SON will perform well over the near term.

Financial Data

(US$ in Thousands)	9 Mos	6 Mos	3 Mos	12/31/2018	12/31/2017	12/31/2016	12/31/2015	12/31/2014
Earnings Per Share	3.20	3.01	3.09	3.10	1.74	2.81	2.44	2.32
Cash Flow Per Share	3.74	3.76	5.59	5.87	3.49	3.93	4.46	4.09
Tang Book Value Per Share	1.52	2.01	1.40	0.98	1.35	2.17	1.26	0.43
Dividends Per Share	1.680	1.660	1.640	1.620	1.540	1.460	1.370	1.270
Dividend Payout %	52.50	55.15	53.07	52.26	88.51	51.96	56.15	54.74
Income Statement								
Total Revenue	4,065,357	2,711,426	1,351,705	5,390,938	5,036,650	4,782,877	4,964,369	5,014,534
EBITDA	539,488	352,043	169,461	625,221	545,348	666,129	562,432	561,422
Depn & Amortn	173,085	116,978	58,614	188,533	178,049	173,295	179,888	169,911
Income Before Taxes	320,310	203,728	95,462	378,531	314,554	441,277	327,946	339,120
Income Taxes	77,213	51,115	22,624	75,008	146,589	164,631	87,738	108,922
Net Income	246,886	154,822	73,663	313,560	175,345	286,434	250,136	239,165
Average Shares	101,186	101,178	101,072	101,016	100,852	101,782	102,392	103,172
Balance Sheet								
Current Assets	1,564,022	1,579,020	1,568,491	1,519,272	1,563,636	1,348,768	1,307,378	1,390,283
Total Assets	4,986,176	4,945,564	4,941,504	4,583,465	4,557,721	3,923,203	4,020,269	4,209,996
Current Liabilities	1,307,458	1,274,888	1,156,228	1,082,930	999,970	802,616	922,516	905,445
Long-Term Obligations	1,432,681	1,446,575	1,452,078	1,189,717	1,288,002	1,020,698	1,021,854	1,200,885
Total Liabilities	3,144,501	3,105,206	3,153,328	2,824,379	2,850,655	2,390,845	2,507,340	2,702,873
Stockholders' Equity	1,841,676	1,840,358	1,788,176	1,759,086	1,707,066	1,532,358	1,512,929	1,507,123
Shares Outstanding	100,082	100,075	100,036	99,829	99,414	99,193	100,944	100,603
Statistical Record								
Return on Assets %	6.73	6.37	6.53	6.86	4.14	7.19	6.08	5.84
Return on Equity %	17.77	16.90	17.59	18.09	10.83	18.76	16.57	14.86
EBITDA Margin %	13.27	12.98	12.54	11.60	10.83	13.93	11.33	11.20
Net Margin %	6.07	5.71	5.45	5.82	3.48	5.99	5.04	4.77
Asset Turnover	1.12	1.14	1.13	1.18	1.19	1.20	1.21	1.22
Current Ratio	1.20	1.24	1.36	1.40	1.56	1.68	1.42	1.54
Debt to Equity	0.78	0.79	0.81	0.68	0.75	0.67	0.68	0.80
Price Range	66.38-50.39	65.78-50.39	61.53-47.28	58.38-46.60	55.45-47.15	55.25-37.01	47.44-37.26	44.50-37.55
P/E Ratio	20.74-15.75	21.85-16.74	19.91-15.30	18.83-15.03	31.87-27.10	19.66-13.17	19.44-15.27	19.18-16.19
Average Yield %	2.86	2.87	2.99	3.04	2.98	3.01	3.18	3.06

Address: 1 N. Second St., Hartsville, SC 29550	**Web Site:** www.sonoco.com	**Auditors:** PricewaterhouseCoopers LLP
Telephone: 843-383-7000	**Officers:** John R. Haley - Chairman, Vice-Chairman Robert C. (Rob) Tiede - President, Chief Executive Officer, Executive Vice President, Chief Operating Officer, Division Officer	**Investor Contact:** 843-339-6018
Fax: 843-383-7008		**Transfer Agents:** Continental Stock Transfer & Trust Company, New York, NY

632

SOUTH JERSEY INDUSTRIES INC

Exchange	Symbol	Price	52Wk Range	Yield	P/E	Div Acheiver
NYS	SJI	$32.98 (12/31/2019)	34.27-26.89	3.58	34.00	19 Years

*7 Year Price Score 87.59 *NYSE Composite Index=100 *12 Month Price Score 93.62

Interim Earnings (Per Share)

Qtr.	Mar	Jun	Sep	Dec
2016	0.95	(0.06)	0.12	0.59
2017	0.47	(0.10)	(0.47)	0.05
2018	1.40	(1.12)	(0.53)	0.55
2019	0.94	(0.14)	(0.38)	...

Interim Dividends (Per Share)

Amt	Decl	Ex	Rec	Pay
0.287Q	02/19/2019	03/15/2019	03/18/2019	04/02/2019
0.287Q	04/29/2019	06/07/2019	06/10/2019	07/02/2019
0.287Q	07/08/2019	09/09/2019	09/10/2019	10/02/2019
0.295Q	11/26/2019	12/09/2019	12/10/2019	12/27/2019

Indicated Div: $1.18 (Div. Reinv. Plan)

Valuation Analysis **Institutional Holding**

Forecast EPS	$1.11	No of Institutions
	(01/15/2020)	341
Market Cap	$3.0 Billion	Shares
Book Value	$1.4 Billion	91,782,104
Price/Book	2.15	% Held
Price/Sales	1.74	94.92

Business Summary: Gas Utilities (MIC: 3.3.1 SIC: 4924 NAIC: 221210)

South Jersey Industries is a holding company. Co. provides a variety of energy-related products and services through its subsidiaries. Co.'s subsidiary, SJI Utilities, Inc. owns South Jersey Gas Company, a regulated natural gas utility which distributes natural gas in the southernmost counties of New Jersey; Elizabethtown Gas Company, a regulated natural gas utility which distributes natural gas in northern and central New Jersey; and Elkton Gas Company, a regulated natural gas utility which distributes natural gas in northern Maryland. Co. also operates through its other subsidiaries, among other, South Jersey Energy Company, which acquires and markets electricity to retail end users.

Recent Developments: For the quarter ended Sep 30 2019, loss from continuing operations was US$34.7 million compared with a loss of US$45.6 million in the year-earlier quarter. Net loss amounted to US$34.8 million versus a net loss of US$45.7 million in the year-earlier quarter. Revenues were US$261.2 million, down 13.6% from US$302.5 million the year before. Operating loss was US$19.0 million versus a loss of US$38.6 million in the prior-year quarter. Direct operating expenses declined 19.8% to US$253.6 million from US$316.1 million in the comparable period the year before. Indirect operating expenses increased 6.7% to US$26.6 million from US$24.9 million in the equivalent prior-year period.

Prospects: Our evaluation of South Jersey Industries Inc. as of October 4th, 2019 is the result of our systematic analysis on three basic characteristics: earnings strength, relative valuation, and recent stock price movement. The company has produced a positive trend in earnings per share over the past 5 quarters. However, recent analyst estimates for the company have been mixed and SJI has posted results that fell short of analysts' expectations. Based on operating earnings yield, the company is fairly valued when compared to all of the companies we cover. Share price changes over the past year indicates that SJI will perform in line with the market over the near term.

Financial Data

(US$ in Thousands)	9 Mos	6 Mos	3 Mos	12/31/2018	12/31/2017	12/31/2016	12/31/2015	12/31/2014
Earnings Per Share	0.97	0.82	(0.16)	0.21	(0.04)	1.56	1.53	1.46
Cash Flow Per Share	0.99	2.24	2.85	1.72	2.39	3.42	2.72	2.43
Tang Book Value Per Share	7.70	8.36	8.44	6.23	14.79	15.96	14.19	13.65
Dividends Per Share	1.150	1.143	1.135	1.127	1.097	1.064	1.018	0.960
Dividend Payout %	118.56	139.33	...	536.90	...	68.19	66.50	65.75
Income Statement								
Total Revenue	1,165,435	904,232	637,298	1,641,338	1,243,068	1,036,500	959,568	886,996
EBITDA	200,375	193,837	160,813	199,872	120,602	289,654	238,855	202,426
Depn & Amortn	72,759	47,814	23,685	96,723	100,718	90,389	72,451	63,004
Income Before Taxes	41,672	88,936	108,475	12,853	(34,135)	167,816	134,782	109,862
Income Taxes	9,378	20,303	24,994	561	(24,937)	54,151	1,360	4,449
Net Income	37,433	72,238	85,637	17,663	(3,490)	118,810	105,107	97,046
Average Shares	92,392	92,389	91,432	84,471	79,541	76,475	68,931	66,428
Balance Sheet								
Current Assets	405,096	428,960	520,707	663,192	438,993	473,313	431,274	566,697
Total Assets	6,130,053	6,028,262	5,863,362	5,956,577	3,865,086	3,730,567	3,480,900	3,349,425
Current Liabilities	1,607,750	1,646,068	1,205,055	1,580,838	883,082	952,624	832,476	850,185
Long-Term Obligations	2,022,780	1,798,551	2,117,903	2,106,863	1,122,999	808,005	1,006,394	859,491
Total Liabilities	4,713,266	4,551,790	4,348,808	4,689,555	2,672,677	2,441,327	2,443,361	2,416,993
Stockholders' Equity	1,416,787	1,476,472	1,514,554	1,267,022	1,192,409	1,289,240	1,037,539	932,432
Shares Outstanding	92,392	92,390	92,388	85,506	79,549	79,478	70,965	68,334
Statistical Record								
Return on Assets %	1.38	1.26	N.M.	0.36	N.M.	3.29	3.08	3.09
Return on Equity %	6.29	5.21	N.M.	1.44	N.M.	10.18	10.67	11.03
EBITDA Margin %	17.19	21.44	25.23	12.18	9.70	27.95	24.89	22.82
Net Margin %	3.21	7.99	13.44	1.08	N.M.	11.46	10.95	10.94
Asset Turnover	0.29	0.31	0.36	0.33	0.33	0.29	0.28	0.28
Current Ratio	0.25	0.26	0.43	0.42	0.50	0.50	0.52	0.67
Debt to Equity	1.43	1.22	1.40	1.66	0.94	0.63	0.97	0.92
Price Range	36.13-26.78	36.13-26.78	36.13-26.78	36.13-26.11	38.12-30.78	34.68-22.63	30.30-21.37	30.61-26.00
P/E Ratio	37.25-27.61	44.06-32.66	...	172.05-124.33	...	22.23-14.51	19.80-13.97	20.97-17.81
Average Yield %	3.62	3.56	3.57	3.60	3.19	3.66	3.93	3.41

Address: 1 South Jersey Plaza, Folsom, NJ 08037	**Web Site:** www.sjiindustries.com	**Auditors:** DELOITTE & TOUCHE LLP
Telephone: 609-561-9000	**Officers:** Walter M. Higgins - Chairman Michael J. Renna - President, President (frmr), Chief Executive Officer, Vice President, Chief Operating Officer	**Investor Contact:** 609-561-9000Ext.42 **Transfer Agents:** Computershare, Canton, MA

SOUTHERN COMPANY (THE)

Exchange	Symbol	Price	52Wk Range	Yield	P/E	Div Acheiver
NYS	SO	$63.70 (12/31/2019)	63.86-43.72	3.89	14.64	17 Years

*7 Year Price Score 96.11   *NYSE Composite Index=100   *12 Month Price Score 105.37

Interim Earnings (Per Share)

Qtr.	Mar	Jun	Sep	Dec
2016	0.53	0.65	1.16	0.19
2017	0.66	(1.37)	1.06	0.49
2018	0.92	(0.15)	1.13	0.26
2019	1.99	0.85	1.25	...

Interim Dividends (Per Share)

Amt	Decl	Ex	Rec	Pay
0.62Q	04/15/2019	05/17/2019	05/20/2019	06/06/2019
0.62Q	07/15/2019	08/16/2019	08/19/2019	09/06/2019
0.62Q	10/21/2019	11/15/2019	11/18/2019	12/06/2019
0.62Q	01/17/2020	02/14/2020	02/18/2020	03/06/2020

Indicated Div: $2.48 (Div. Reinv. Plan)

Valuation Analysis

Forecast EPS	$3.10
	(01/17/2020)
Market Cap	$66.8 Billion
Book Value	$32.1 Billion
Price/Book	2.08
Price/Sales	3.06

Institutional Holding

No of Institutions	1792
Shares	735,683,648
% Held	61.61

Business Summary: Electric Utilities (MIC: 3.1.1 SIC: 4911 NAIC: 221119)

Southern is a holding company. Through its subsidiaries, Alabama Power Company, Georgia Power Company, and Mississippi Power Company, Co. is engaged in the generation, transmission, distribution, and purchase of electricity and the sale of electric service in Alabama, Georgia, and Mississippi. Co.'s Southern Power Company subsidiary develops, constructs, acquires, owns, and manages power generation assets, including renewable energy projects, and sells electricity at market-based rates in the wholesale market. Co.'s Southern Company Gas subsidiary is an energy services holding company whose primary business is the distribution of natural gas in Illinois, Georgia, Virginia, and Tennessee.

Recent Developments: For the quarter ended Sep 30 2019, net income increased 10.1% to US$1.35 billion from US$1.22 billion in the year-earlier quarter. Revenues were US$6.00 billion, down 2.7% from US$6.16 billion the year before. Operating income was US$2.01 billion versus US$2.17 billion in the prior-year quarter, a decrease of 7.4%. Direct operating expenses declined 12.0% to US$2.81 billion from US$3.20 billion in the comparable period the year before. Indirect operating expenses increased 48.2% to US$1.17 billion from US$790.0 million in the equivalent prior-year period.

Prospects: Our evaluation of Southern Company as of October 4th, 2019 is the result of our systematic analysis on three basic characteristics: earnings strength, relative valuation, and recent stock price movement. The company has enjoyed a very positive trend in earnings per share over the past 5 quarters. However, recent analyst estimates for the company have been mixed and SO has posted results that exceeded analysts' expectations. Based on operating earnings yield, the company is fairly valued when compared to all of the companies we cover. Share price changes over the past year indicates that SO will perform well over the near term.

Financial Data

(US$ in Thousands)	9 Mos	6 Mos	3 Mos	12/31/2018	12/31/2017	12/31/2016	12/31/2015	12/31/2014
Earnings Per Share	4.35	4.23	3.23	2.17	0.84	2.55	2.59	2.18
Cash Flow Per Share	5.96	5.94	5.95	6.81	6.39	5.13	6.89	6.48
Tang Book Value Per Share	25.03	24.48	20.05	18.46	17.22	17.83	22.72	22.39
Dividends Per Share	2.440	2.420	2.400	2.380	2.300	2.223	2.152	2.083
Dividend Payout %	56.09	57.21	74.30	109.68	273.81	87.16	83.11	95.53
Income Statement								
Total Revenue	16,505,000	10,510,000	5,412,000	23,495,000	23,031,000	19,896,000	17,489,000	18,467,000
EBITDA	9,895,000	6,895,000	4,652,000	7,574,000	4,690,000	7,240,000	6,841,000	6,117,000
Depn & Amortn	2,514,000	1,623,000	851,000	3,131,000	2,034,000	2,502,000	2,395,000	2,293,000
Income Before Taxes	6,087,000	4,413,000	3,371,000	2,601,000	962,000	3,421,000	3,629,000	3,008,000
Income Taxes	1,872,000	1,505,000	1,360,000	449,000	142,000	951,000	1,194,000	977,000
Net Income	4,309,000	2,989,000	2,088,000	2,242,000	880,000	2,493,000	2,421,000	2,031,000
Average Shares	1,057,000	1,052,000	1,045,000	1,025,000	1,008,000	958,000	914,000	901,000
Balance Sheet								
Current Assets	9,917,000	8,352,000	8,709,000	9,583,000	10,072,000	9,722,000	6,526,000	6,370,000
Total Assets	117,591,000	114,867,000	114,096,000	116,914,000	111,005,000	109,697,000	78,318,000	70,923,000
Current Liabilities	10,534,000	10,999,000	9,919,000	14,286,000	13,594,000	12,917,000	9,129,000	8,967,000
Long-Term Obligations	42,098,000	39,682,000	40,457,000	40,736,000	44,462,000	42,629,000	24,688,000	20,841,000
Total Liabilities	85,509,000	83,445,000	87,368,000	91,900,000	86,514,000	84,212,000	56,999,000	49,622,000
Stockholders' Equity	32,082,000	31,422,000	26,728,000	25,014,000	24,491,000	25,485,000	21,319,000	21,301,000
Shares Outstanding	1,048,733	1,045,231	1,040,295	1,033,788	1,007,603	990,394	911,721	907,777
Statistical Record								
Return on Assets %	4.01	3.90	3.00	1.97	0.80	2.64	3.24	3.00
Return on Equity %	16.03	16.03	13.10	9.06	3.52	10.62	11.36	9.80
EBITDA Margin %	59.95	65.60	85.96	32.24	20.36	36.39	39.12	33.12
Net Margin %	26.11	28.44	38.58	9.54	3.82	12.53	13.84	11.00
Asset Turnover	0.19	0.19	0.20	0.21	0.21	0.21	0.23	0.27
Current Ratio	0.94	0.76	0.88	0.67	0.74	0.75	0.71	0.71
Debt to Equity	1.31	1.26	1.51	1.63	1.82	1.67	1.16	0.98
Price Range	61.98-42.79	56.28-42.66	52.53-42.66	49.08-42.66	53.25-46.78	54.54-46.45	52.79-41.61	50.88-40.40
P/E Ratio	14.25-9.84	13.30-10.09	16.26-13.21	22.62-19.66	63.39-55.69	21.39-18.22	20.38-16.07	23.34-18.53
Average Yield %	4.73	4.99	5.18	5.27	4.62	4.43	4.78	4.70

Address: 30 Ivan Allen Jr. Boulevard, N.W., Atlanta, GA 30308 **Telephone:** 404-506-5000 **Fax:** 404-506-0455	**Web Site:** www.southerncompany.com **Officers:** Thomas A. Fanning - Chairman, President, Chief Executive Officer, Chief Operating Officer, Executive Vice President Andrew W. Evans - Executive Vice President, Chief Financial Officer	**Auditors:** Deloitte & Touche LLP **Transfer Agents:** ComputerShare, College Station, TX

SOUTHERN COPPER CORP

Exchange	Symbol	Price	52Wk Range	Yield	P/E
NYS	SCCO	$42.48 (12/31/2019)	43.19-29.21	3.77	22.36

*7 Year Price Score 87.29   *NYSE Composite Index=100   *12 Month Price Score 102.66

Interim Earnings (Per Share)

Qtr.	Mar	Jun	Sep	Dec
2016	0.24	0.29	0.26	0.22
2017	0.41	0.39	0.52	(0.37)
2018	0.61	0.53	0.48	0.38
2019	0.50	0.52	0.50	...

Interim Dividends (Per Share)

Amt	Decl	Ex	Rec	Pay
0.444Q	02/06/2019	02/08/2019	02/11/2019	02/21/2019
0.40Q	04/11/2019	05/02/2019	05/03/2019	05/17/2019
0.40Q	07/18/2019	08/07/2019	08/08/2019	08/22/2019
0.40Q	10/17/2019	11/06/2019	11/07/2019	11/21/2019

Indicated Div: $1.60

Valuation Analysis

		Institutional Holding	
Forecast EPS	$2.02	No of Institutions	
	(01/17/2020)	458	
Market Cap	$32.8 Billion	Shares	
Book Value	$6.8 Billion	65,007,284	
Price/Book	4.81	% Held	
Price/Sales	4.61	N/A	

Business Summary: Mining (MIC: 8.2.4 SIC: 1021 NAIC: 212234)

Southern Copper is a copper producer. Co.'s mining, smelting and refining facilities are located in Peru and Mexico and Co. conducts exploration activities in those countries and in Argentina, Chile and Ecuador. Co.'s Peruvian copper operations involve mining, milling and flotation of copper ore to produce copper concentrates and molybdenum concentrates, the smelting of copper concentrates to produce blister and anode copper, and the refining of anode copper to produce copper cathodes. Co.'s Mexican operations are conducted through its subsidiary, Minera Mexico, S.A. de C.V., which engages primarily in the mining and processing of copper, molybdenum, zinc, silver, gold and lead.

Recent Developments: For the quarter ended Sep 30 2019, net income increased 5.6% to US$391.3 million from US$370.7 million in the year-earlier quarter. Revenues were US$1.86 billion, up 7.9% from US$1.72 billion the year before. Operating income was US$713.8 million versus US$696.7 million in the prior-year quarter, an increase of 2.5%. Direct operating expenses rose 10.0% to US$906.5 million from US$824.0 million in the comparable period the year before. Indirect operating expenses increased 17.8% to US$239.2 million from US$203.0 million in the equivalent prior-year period.

Prospects: Our evaluation of Southern Copper Corp. as of October 4th, 2019 is the result of our systematic analysis on three basic characteristics: earnings strength, relative valuation, and recent stock price movement. The company has enjoyed a very positive trend in earnings per share over the past 5 quarters. However, recent analyst estimates for the company have been reduced, and SCCO has posted results that fell short of analysts' expectations. Based on operating earnings yield, the company is undervalued when compared to all of the companies we cover. Share price changes over the past year indicates that SCCO will perform poorly over the near term.

Financial Data

(US$ in Thousands)	9 Mos	6 Mos	3 Mos	12/31/2018	12/31/2017	12/31/2016	12/31/2015	12/31/2014
Earnings Per Share	1.90	1.88	1.89	2.00	0.94	1.00	0.93	1.61
Cash Flow Per Share	2.35	2.54	2.53	2.89	2.56	1.19	1.11	1.64
Tang Book Value Per Share	8.63	8.53	8.41	8.30	7.70	7.35	6.60	7.06
Dividends Per Share	2.044	2.044	1.944	1.400	0.590	0.180	0.340	0.460
Dividend Payout %	107.59	108.74	102.87	70.00	62.77	18.00	36.56	28.57
Income Statement								
Total Revenue	5,431,000	3,571,400	1,753,400	7,096,700	6,654,500	5,379,800	5,045,900	5,787,694
EBITDA	2,723,800	1,816,000	880,700	3,519,400	3,268,400	2,178,700	1,892,700	2,634,999
Depn & Amortn	580,600	380,400	181,600	668,900	665,200	639,100	503,600	443,000
Income Before Taxes	1,910,700	1,281,900	625,000	2,589,400	2,302,700	1,256,000	1,189,200	2,068,706
Income Taxes	730,000	489,000	237,900	1,053,500	1,593,400	501,100	464,900	754,629
Net Income	1,180,200	790,600	388,200	1,543,000	728,500	776,500	736,400	1,332,973
Average Shares	773,100	773,000	773,000	773,000	773,000	773,600	794,700	828,199
Balance Sheet								
Current Assets	4,177,600	3,098,100	3,182,400	3,180,000	3,170,100	2,566,100	2,484,200	2,489,789
Total Assets	16,494,400	15,344,600	15,542,600	14,484,800	13,780,100	13,234,300	12,593,200	11,551,910
Current Liabilities	1,432,200	1,385,400	1,123,400	1,216,300	1,168,300	999,100	920,200	1,150,905
Long-Term Obligations	7,534,900	6,573,900	6,987,600	5,960,100	5,957,100	5,954,200	5,951,500	4,006,000
Total Liabilities	9,673,100	8,604,300	8,896,100	7,917,400	7,672,400	7,402,000	7,330,300	5,747,450
Stockholders' Equity	6,821,300	6,740,300	6,646,500	6,567,400	6,107,700	5,832,300	5,262,900	5,804,460
Shares Outstanding	773,058	773,058	773,044	773,044	773,028	773,016	773,707	806,690
Statistical Record								
Return on Assets %	9.56	9.89	9.87	10.92	5.39	6.00	6.10	11.71
Return on Equity %	21.98	21.91	22.48	24.35	12.20	13.96	13.31	23.51
EBITDA Margin %	50.15	50.85	50.23	49.59	49.12	40.50	37.51	45.53
Net Margin %	21.73	22.14	22.14	21.74	10.95	14.43	14.59	23.03
Asset Turnover	0.46	0.48	0.47	0.50	0.49	0.42	0.42	0.51
Current Ratio	2.92	2.24	2.83	2.61	2.71	2.57	2.70	2.16
Debt to Equity	1.10	0.98	1.05	0.91	0.98	1.02	1.13	0.69
Price Range	43.75-29.21	49.36-29.21	57.34-29.21	57.34-29.78	47.63-32.38	34.98-22.29	33.14-24.40	33.54-26.08
P/E Ratio	23.03-15.37	26.26-15.54	30.34-15.46	28.67-14.89	50.67-34.45	34.98-22.29	35.63-26.24	20.83-16.20
Average Yield %	5.73	5.35	4.65	3.05	1.53	0.66	1.19	1.53

Address: 1440 East Missouri Avenue, Suite 160, Phoenix, AZ 85014	**Web Site:** www.southerncoppercorp.com	**Auditors:** Galaz, Yamazaki, Ruiz Urquiza, S.C.
Telephone: 602-264-1375	**Officers:** German Larrea Mota Velasco - Chairman, Holding/Parent Company Officer Oscar Gonzalez Rocha - President, Chief Executive Officer	**Investor Contact:** 602-264-1375
Fax: 602-264-1397		**Transfer Agents:** Computershare, Jersey City, NJ

SOUTHWEST AIRLINES CO

Exchange	Symbol	Price	52Wk Range	Yield	P/E
NYS	LUV	$53.98 (12/31/2019)	58.29-45.61	1.33	12.10

*7 Year Price Score 105.36 *NYSE Composite Index=100 *12 Month Price Score 100.12

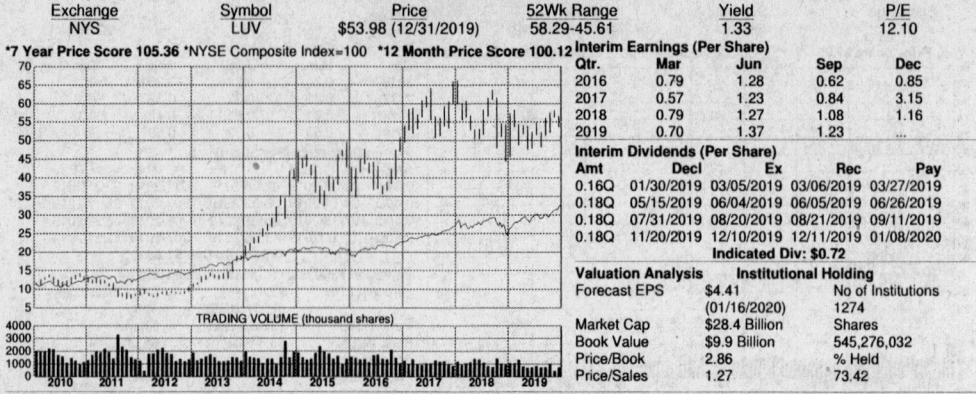

Interim Earnings (Per Share)

Qtr.	Mar	Jun	Sep	Dec
2016	0.79	1.28	0.62	0.85
2017	0.57	1.23	0.84	3.15
2018	0.79	1.27	1.08	1.16
2019	0.70	1.37	1.23	...

Interim Dividends (Per Share)

Amt	Decl	Ex	Rec	Pay
0.16Q	01/30/2019	03/05/2019	03/06/2019	03/27/2019
0.18Q	05/15/2019	06/04/2019	06/05/2019	06/26/2019
0.18Q	07/31/2019	08/20/2019	08/21/2019	09/11/2019
0.18Q	11/20/2019	12/10/2019	12/11/2019	01/08/2020

Indicated Div: $0.72

Valuation Analysis | **Institutional Holding**

Forecast EPS	$4.41	No of Institutions
	(01/16/2020)	1274
Market Cap	$28.4 Billion	Shares
Book Value	$9.9 Billion	545,276,032
Price/Book	2.86	% Held
Price/Sales	1.27	73.42

Business Summary: Airlines/Air Freight (MIC: 7.4.4 SIC: 4512 NAIC: 481111)

Southwest Airlines operates Southwest Airlines, a passenger airline that provides scheduled air transportation in the U.S. and near-international markets. Co. principally provides point-to-point service, which allows for direct nonstop routing. In addition, Co. provides a suite of digital platforms to support Customers' needs across the travel journey including Southwest.com®, mobile.southwest.com, an iOS app, and an Android app. Co. also provides Swabiz.com, a website tailored for business Customers, which provides businesses shared company credit cards, company activity reporting, and centralized traveler management.

Recent Developments: For the quarter ended Sep 30 2019, net income increased 7.2% to US$659.0 million from US$615.0 million in the year-earlier quarter. Revenues were US$5.64 billion, up 1.1% from US$5.58 billion the year before. Operating income was US$819.0 million versus US$798.0 million in the prior-year quarter, an increase of 2.6%. Direct operating expenses declined 4.2% to US$1.75 billion from US$1.83 billion in the comparable period the year before. Indirect expenses increased 4.1% to US$3.07 billion from US$2.95 billion in the equivalent prior-year period.

Prospects: Our evaluation of Southwest Airlines Co as of October 4th, 2019 is the result of our systematic analysis on three basic characteristics: earnings strength, relative valuation, and recent stock price movement. The company has generated a negative trend in earnings per share over the past 5 quarters. In addition, recent analyst estimates for the company have been reduced while LUV has posted results that exceeded analysts' expectations. Based on operating earnings yield, the company is undervalued when compared to all of the companies we cover. Share price changes over the past year indicates that LUV will perform poorly over the near term.

Financial Data

(US$ in Thousands)	9 Mos	6 Mos	3 Mos	12/31/2018	12/31/2017	12/31/2016	12/31/2015	12/31/2014
Earnings Per Share	4.46	4.31	4.21	4.29	5.79	3.55	3.27	1.64
Cash Flow Per Share	7.79	7.99	9.07	8.54	6.54	6.83	4.90	4.22
Tang Book Value Per Share	16.44	16.11	15.67	15.35	15.37	11.45	9.15	8.06
Dividends Per Share	0.680	0.660	0.640	0.605	0.475	0.375	0.285	0.220
Dividend Payout %	15.25	15.31	15.20	14.10	8.20	10.56	8.72	13.41
Income Statement								
Total Revenue	16,698,000	11,059,000	5,149,000	21,965,000	21,171,000	20,425,000	19,820,000	18,605,000
EBITDA	3,190,000	2,067,000	800,000	4,389,000	4,499,000	4,819,000	4,575,000	2,854,000
Depn & Amortn	906,000	598,000	297,000	1,201,000	1,218,000	1,221,000	1,015,000	938,000
Income Before Taxes	2,291,000	1,472,000	504,000	3,164,000	3,251,000	3,547,000	3,479,000	1,816,000
Income Taxes	504,000	344,000	117,000	699,000	(237,000)	1,303,000	1,298,000	680,000
Net Income	1,787,000	1,128,000	387,000	2,465,000	3,488,000	2,244,000	2,181,000	1,136,000
Average Shares	534,000	542,000	552,000	574,000	603,000	633,000	669,000	696,000
Balance Sheet								
Current Assets	5,650,000	5,554,000	5,483,000	5,028,000	4,815,000	4,498,000	4,024,000	4,404,000
Total Assets	26,467,000	26,374,000	26,459,000	26,243,000	25,110,000	23,286,000	21,312,000	20,200,000
Current Liabilities	8,629,000	8,611,000	8,723,000	7,905,000	6,905,000	6,844,000	7,406,000	5,923,000
Long-Term Obligations	2,398,000	2,449,000	2,602,000	2,771,000	3,320,000	2,821,000	2,541,000	2,434,000
Total Liabilities	16,536,000	16,434,000	16,668,000	16,390,000	14,680,000	14,845,000	13,954,000	13,425,000
Stockholders' Equity	9,931,000	9,940,000	9,791,000	9,853,000	10,430,000	8,441,000	7,358,000	6,775,000
Shares Outstanding	526,276	537,517	543,064	552,603	588,550	615,160	647,601	675,594
Statistical Record								
Return on Assets %	9.15	9.07	9.20	9.60	14.41	10.04	10.51	5.75
Return on Equity %	24.31	24.05	24.62	24.31	36.97	28.33	30.86	16.10
EBITDA Margin %	19.10	18.69	15.54	19.98	21.25	23.59	23.08	15.34
Net Margin %	10.70	10.20	7.52	11.22	16.48	10.99	11.00	6.11
Asset Turnover	0.84	0.85	0.85	0.86	0.87	0.91	0.95	0.94
Current Ratio	0.65	0.64	0.63	0.64	0.70	0.66	0.54	0.74
Debt to Equity	0.24	0.25	0.27	0.28	0.32	0.33	0.35	0.36
Price Range	61.70-44.40	63.77-44.40	63.77-44.40	66.29-44.40	66.09-49.46	50.89-34.72	49.58-32.36	42.32-18.84
P/E Ratio	13.83-9.96	14.80-10.30	15.15-10.55	15.45-10.35	11.41-8.54	14.34-9.78	15.16-9.90	25.80-11.49
Average Yield %	1.30	1.22	1.18	1.08	0.84	0.90	0.70	0.76

Address: P.O. Box 36611, Dallas, TX 75235-1611	**Web Site:** www.southwest.com	**Auditors:** Ernst & Young LLP
Telephone: 214-792-4000	**Officers:** Gary C. Kelly - Chairman, Chief Executive Officer, President Ron Ricks - Vice-Chairman, Executive Vice President, Chief Regulatory Officer, Executive Vice President (frmr), Corporate Secretary	**Investor Contact:** 214-792-4415
Fax: 214-792-5015		**Transfer Agents:** Wells Fargo Shareowner Services, Mendota Heights, MN

SOUTHWEST GAS HOLDINGS, INC.

Exchange	Symbol	Price	52Wk Range	Yield	P/E	Div Acheiver
NYS	SWX	$75.97 (12/31/2019)	92.14-73.92	2.87	20.81	12 Years

*7 Year Price Score 103.88 *NYSE Composite Index=100 *12 Month Price Score 88.32

Interim Earnings (Per Share)

Qtr.	Mar	Jun	Sep	Dec
2016	1.58	0.19	0.05	1.36
2017	1.45	0.37	0.21	2.01
2018	1.63	0.44	0.25	1.37
2019	1.77	0.41	0.10	...

Interim Dividends (Per Share)

Amt	Decl	Ex	Rec	Pay
0.545Q	02/25/2019	05/14/2019	05/15/2019	06/03/2019
0.545Q	05/01/2019	08/14/2019	08/15/2019	09/03/2019
0.545Q	09/25/2019	11/14/2019	11/15/2019	12/02/2019
0.545Q	11/18/2019	02/14/2020	02/18/2020	03/02/2020

Indicated Div: $2.18 (Div. Reinv. Plan)

Valuation Analysis / **Institutional Holding**

Forecast EPS	$3.71
	(01/17/2020)
Market Cap	$4.1 Billion
Book Value	$2.4 Billion
Price/Book	1.71
Price/Sales	1.36

No of Institutions	N/A
Shares	N/A
% Held	N/A

TRADING VOLUME (thousand shares)

Business Summary: Gas Utilities (MIC: 3.3.1 SIC: 4923 NAIC: 221210)

Southwest Gas Holdings is a holding company. Through its subsidiaries, Southwest Gas Corporation and Centuri Construction Group, Inc. (Centuri), Co. has two segments: Natural Gas Operations, which purchases and distributes or transports natural gas to residential, commercial, and industrial customers in portions of Arizona, Nevada, and California; and Utility Infrastructure Services, which engages in installation, replacement, repair, and maintenance of energy distribution systems, and developing industrial construction solutions. The primary focus of Centuri operations is replacement of natural gas distribution pipe and electric service lines as well as new infrastructure installations.

Recent Developments: For the quarter ended Sep 30 2019, net income decreased 47.1% to US$6.5 million from US$12.3 million in the year-earlier quarter. Revenues were US$725.2 million, up 8.5% from US$668.1 million the year before. Operating income was US$38.3 million versus US$39.7 million in the prior-year quarter, a decrease of 3.6%. Direct operating expenses rose 9.2% to US$486.6 million from US$445.8 million in the comparable period the year before. Indirect operating expenses increased 9.6% to US$200.3 million from US$182.7 million in the equivalent prior-year period.

Prospects: Our evaluation of Southwest Gas Holdings Inc. as of October 4th, 2019 is the result of our systematic analysis on three basic characteristics: earnings strength, relative valuation, and recent stock price movement. The company has produced a positive trend in earnings per share over the past 5 quarters. However, recent analyst estimates for the company have been mixed and SWX has posted results in line with analysts' expectations. Based on operating earnings yield, the company is fairly valued when compared to all of the companies we cover. Share price changes over the past year indicates that SWX will perform well over the near term.

Financial Data

(US$ in Thousands)	9 Mos	6 Mos	3 Mos	12/31/2018	12/31/2017	12/31/2016	12/31/2015	12/31/2014
Earnings Per Share	3.65	3.80	3.83	3.68	4.04	3.18	2.92	3.01
Cash Flow Per Share	9.14	10.39	10.05	10.70	7.71	12.57	11.64	7.45
Tang Book Value Per Share	38.15	38.17	37.13	35.70	34.01	32.09	30.99	28.92
Dividends Per Share	2.130	2.105	2.080	2.055	1.485	1.800	1.620	1.460
Dividend Payout %	58.36	55.39	54.31	55.84	36.76	56.60	55.48	48.50
Income Statement								
Total Revenue	2,271,780	1,546,550	833,539	2,880,013	2,548,792	2,460,490	2,463,625	2,121,707
EBITDA	455,566	345,829	222,301	515,460	518,034	515,013	486,953	483,348
Depn & Amortn	223,251	147,881	77,539	185,719	187,075	214,037	201,233	194,360
Income Before Taxes	156,593	148,139	119,962	239,178	255,682	229,165	216,014	219,521
Income Taxes	35,031	31,890	25,538	61,684	65,088	78,468	79,902	78,373
Net Income	122,218	116,865	94,809	182,277	193,841	152,041	138,317	141,126
Average Shares	54,748	54,003	53,424	49,476	47,991	47,814	47,383	46,944
Balance Sheet								
Current Assets	765,402	752,081	830,380	839,769	657,032	533,307	558,174	606,783
Total Assets	7,840,211	7,666,885	7,569,432	7,357,729	6,237,066	5,581,126	5,358,685	5,214,515
Current Liabilities	782,344	726,504	974,478	938,645	815,881	628,375	535,045	470,117
Long-Term Obligations	2,462,116	2,373,003	2,106,274	2,107,258	1,798,576	1,549,983	1,551,204	1,637,592
Total Liabilities	5,416,501	5,247,522	5,222,432	5,105,687	4,422,298	3,917,636	3,764,277	3,725,992
Stockholders' Equity	2,423,710	2,419,363	2,347,000	2,252,042	1,814,768	1,663,490	1,594,408	1,488,523
Shares Outstanding	54,624	54,321	53,391	53,026	48,090	47,482	47,377	46,523
Statistical Record								
Return on Assets %	2.64	2.81	2.85	2.68	3.28	2.77	2.62	2.89
Return on Equity %	8.77	9.12	9.37	8.96	11.15	9.31	8.97	9.72
EBITDA Margin %	20.05	22.36	26.67	17.90	20.32	20.93	19.77	22.78
Net Margin %	5.38	7.56	11.37	6.33	7.61	6.18	5.61	6.65
Asset Turnover	0.42	0.42	0.43	0.42	0.43	0.45	0.47	0.43
Current Ratio	0.98	1.04	0.85	0.89	0.81	0.85	1.04	1.29
Debt to Equity	1.02	0.98	0.90	0.94	0.99	0.99	0.97	1.10
Price Range	92.14-73.92	91.24-73.92	84.79-67.29	84.77-64.14	86.27-72.83	78.83-53.86	63.38-50.78	64.04-47.62
P/E Ratio	25.24-20.25	24.01-19.45	22.14-17.57	23.04-17.43	21.35-18.03	24.79-16.94	21.71-17.39	21.28-15.82
Average Yield %	2.54	2.60	2.67	2.71	1.85	2.61	2.86	2.72

Address: 5241 Spring Mountain Road, P.O. Box 98510, Las Vegas, NV 89193-8510 **Telephone:** 702-876-7237 **Fax:** 702-873-3820	**Web Site:** www.swgasholdings.com; www.swgas.com **Officers:** Michael J. Melarkey - Chairman John P. Hester - President, Chief Executive Officer, Executive Vice President, Senior Vice President	**Auditors:** PricewaterhouseCoopers LLP **Investor Contact:** 702-876-7237 **Transfer Agents:** Wells Fargo Shareowner Services, St. Paul, MN

SOUTHWESTERN ENERGY COMPANY

Exchange	Symbol	Price	52Wk Range	Yield	P/E
NYS	SWN	$2.42 (12/31/2019)	4.82-1.58	N/A	1.22

*7 Year Price Score 14.49   *NYSE Composite Index=100   ***12 Month Price Score 64.43**

Interim Earnings (Per Share)

Qtr.	Mar	Jun	Sep	Dec
2016	(3.03)	(1.61)	(1.52)	(0.30)
2017	0.57	0.45	0.09	0.53
2018	0.36	0.09	(0.05)	0.54
2019	1.10	0.26	0.09	...

Interim Dividends (Per Share)

No Dividends Paid

Valuation Analysis		Institutional Holding	
Forecast EPS	$0.54	No of Institutions	
	(01/15/2020)	589	
Market Cap	$1.3 Billion	Shares	
Book Value	$3.1 Billion	670,338,048	
Price/Book	0.42	% Held	
Price/Sales	0.38	99.56	

Business Summary: Production & Extraction (MIC: 9.1.1 SIC: 1311 NAIC: 211111)

Southwestern Energy is a holding company. Through its subsidiaries, Co. is an independent energy company engaged in exploration, development and production activities, including the related marketing of natural gas, oil and natural gas liquids (NGLs) produced in its operations. Co.'s primary business is the exploration for, and production of, natural gas, oil and NGLs. Co.'s operations in northeast Pennsylvania are primarily focused on the unconventional natural gas reservoir known as the Marcellus Shale, and its operations in West Virginia and southwest Pennsylvania are focused on the Marcellus Shale, the Utica and the Upper Devonian unconventional natural gas, oil and NGL reservoirs.

Recent Developments: For the quarter ended Sep 30 2019, net income amounted to US$49.0 million versus a net loss of US$29.0 million in the year-earlier quarter. Revenues were US$636.0 million, down 33.1% from US$951.0 million the year before. Operating loss was US$29.0 million versus an income of US$66.0 million in the prior-year quarter. Direct operating expenses declined 3.4% to US$477.0 million from US$494.0 million in the comparable period the year before. Indirect operating expenses decreased 51.9% to US$188.0 million from US$391.0 million in the equivalent prior-year period.

Prospects: Our evaluation of Southwestern Energy Company as of October 4th, 2019 is the result of our systematic analysis on three basic characteristics: earnings strength, relative valuation, and recent stock price movement. The company has suffered a very negative trend in earnings per share over the past 5 quarters. In addition, recent analyst estimates for the company have been reduced and SWN has posted results that fell short of analysts' expectations. Based on operating earnings yield, the company is undervalued when compared to all of the companies we cover. Share price changes over the past year indicates that SWN will perform very poorly over the near term.

Financial Data

(US$ in Thousands)	9 Mos	6 Mos	3 Mos	12/31/2018	12/31/2017	12/31/2016	12/31/2015	12/31/2014
Earnings Per Share	1.99	1.85	1.68	0.93	1.63	(6.32)	(12.25)	2.62
Cash Flow Per Share	1.84	2.04	2.41	2.13	2.20	1.14	4.15	6.64
Tang Book Value Per Share	5.79	5.70	5.43	4.32	3.86	1.85	5.85	13.15
Income Statement								
Total Revenue	2,293,000	1,657,000	990,000	3,862,000	3,203,000	2,436,000	3,133,000	4,038,000
EBITDA	783,000	585,000	295,000	1,230,000	1,601,000	(2,134,000)	(5,360,000)	2,460,000
Depn & Amortn	357,000	235,000	113,000	568,000	513,000	450,000	1,145,000	952,000
Income Before Taxes	380,000	321,000	168,000	538,000	953,000	(2,672,000)	(6,561,000)	1,449,000
Income Taxes	(401,000)	(411,000)	(426,000)	1,000	(93,000)	(29,000)	(2,005,000)	525,000
Net Income	781,000	732,000	594,000	537,000	1,046,000	(2,643,000)	(4,556,000)	924,000
Average Shares	540,038	539,947	541,320	576,642	500,804	435,337	380,521	352,410
Balance Sheet								
Current Assets	633,000	764,000	887,000	956,000	1,509,000	1,872,000	393,000	1,115,000
Total Assets	6,598,000	6,545,000	6,446,000	5,797,000	7,521,000	7,076,000	8,110,000	14,925,000
Current Liabilities	880,000	912,000	943,000	846,000	780,000	1,064,000	707,000	5,428,000
Long-Term Obligations	2,219,000	2,267,000	2,267,000	2,318,000	4,391,000	4,612,000	4,728,000	2,466,000
Total Liabilities	3,463,000	3,463,000	3,509,000	3,435,000	5,542,000	6,159,000	5,828,000	10,263,000
Stockholders' Equity	3,135,000	3,082,000	2,937,000	2,362,000	1,979,000	917,000	2,282,000	4,662,000
Shares Outstanding	541,284	541,125	541,195	546,314	512,103	495,217	390,091	354,477
Statistical Record								
Return on Assets %	15.93	14.87	13.04	8.06	14.33	N.M.	N.M.	8.04
Return on Equity %	40.75	37.88	35.98	24.74	72.24	N.M.	N.M.	22.31
EBITDA Margin %	34.15	35.30	29.80	31.85	49.98	N.M.	N.M.	60.92
Net Margin %	34.06	44.18	60.00	13.90	32.66	N.M.	N.M.	22.88
Asset Turnover	0.51	0.56	0.56	0.58	0.44	0.32	0.27	0.35
Current Ratio	0.72	0.84	0.94	1.13	1.93	1.76	0.56	0.21
Debt to Equity	0.71	0.74	0.77	0.98	2.22	5.03	2.07	0.53
Price Range	5.89-1.58	5.89-3.03	5.89-3.25	5.91-3.25	10.32-5.05	15.44-5.62	29.25-5.15	48.93-27.24
P/E Ratio	2.96-0.79	3.18-1.64	3.51-1.93	6.35-3.49	6.33-3.10	...	...	18.68-10.40

Address: 10000 Energy Drive, Spring, TX 77389	Web Site: www.swn.com	Auditors: PricewaterhouseCoopers LLP
Telephone: 832-796-1000	Officers: Catherine A. Kehr - Chairman William J. Way - President, Chief Executive Officer, Chief Operating Officer, Executive Vice President	Investor Contact: 281-.61-8.4847 Transfer Agents: Computershare Trust Company, N.A, Providence, RI

SPECTRUM BRANDS HOLDINGS INC

Exchange	Symbol	Price	52Wk Range	Yield	P/E
NYS	SPB	$64.29 (12/31/2019)	65.75-42.25	N/A	6.91

*7 Year Price Score 58.45 *NYSE Composite Index=100 *12 Month Price Score 103.33

Interim Earnings (Per Share)

Qtr.	Dec	Mar	Jun	Sep
2014-15	(3.47)	(7.19)	(2.36)	(4.46)
2015-16	(1.05)	(1.12)	(4.09)	(0.25)
2016-17	6.57	(2.54)	0.06	(0.81)
2017-18	15.57	(1.12)	11.51	(5.19)
2018-19	(2.11)	14.07	(0.53)	(2.19)

Interim Dividends (Per Share)

No Dividends Paid

Valuation Analysis		Institutional Holding	
Forecast EPS	$3.69	No of Institutions	
	(01/17/2020)	373	
Market Cap	$3.1 Billion	Shares	
Book Value	$1.7 Billion	71,997,360	
Price/Book	1.85	% Held	
Price/Sales	0.83	N/A	

Business Summary: Household & Personal Products (MIC: 1.7.1 SIC: 3639 NAIC: 335228)

Spectrum Brands Holdings manufactures, markets and/or distributes its products globally in the North America, Europe, Middle East and Africa, Latin America and Asia-Pacific regions through retailers, wholesalers and distributors, original equipment manufacturers and construction companies. Co.'s segments are: Hardware and Home Improvement, which includes security, plumbing and accessories, and builders' hardware product categories; Home and Personal Care, which includes home appliances and personal care product categories; Global Pet Care, which includes companion animal and aquatics product categories; and Home and Garden, which includes household and controls product categories.

Recent Developments: For the year ended Sep 30 2019, loss from continuing operations was US$186.7 million compared with income of US$427.0 million a year earlier. Net income decreased 45.7% to US$473.2 million from US$872.0 million in the prior year. Revenues were US$3.80 billion, down 0.2% from US$3.81 billion the year before. Operating income was US$72.2 million versus US$224.2 million in the prior year, a decrease of 67.8%. Direct operating expenses rose 0.8% to US$2.50 billion from US$2.47 billion in the comparable period the year before. Indirect operating expenses increased 11.2% to US$1.23 billion from US$1.11 billion in the equivalent prior-year period.

Prospects: Our evaluation of Spectrum Brands Holdings Inc. as of October 4th, 2019 is the result of our systematic analysis on three basic characteristics: earnings strength, relative valuation, and recent stock price movement. The company has generated a negative trend in earnings per share over the past 5 quarters. However, recent analyst estimates for the company have been mixed and SPB has posted results that exceeded analysts' expectations. Based on operating earnings yield, the company is fairly valued when compared to all of the companies we cover. Share price changes over the past year indicates that SPB will perform well over the near term.

Financial Data
(US$ in Thousands)

	09/30/2019	09/30/2018	09/30/2017	09/30/2016	09/30/2015	09/30/2014	09/30/2013	09/30/2012
Earnings Per Share	9.31	20.74	3.29	(6.14)	(17.43)	(3.16)	(4.15)	0.93
Cash Flow Per Share	0.02	9.30	26.05	28.47	8.88	23.14	23.16	27.46
Dividends Per Share	1.680	0.420	...	...	...	...	...	...
Dividend Payout %	18.05	2.03	...	...	...	...	...	...
Income Statement								
Total Revenue	3,802,100	3,145,900	5,008,500	5,215,400	5,815,900	5,963,000	5,543,400	4,480,716
EBITDA	209,100	240,000	606,500	812,700	210,800	740,200	806,600	384,068
Depn & Amortn	180,800	131,700	95,200	183,700	221,900	205,100	176,400	107,650
Income Before Taxes	(193,800)	(156,300)	151,200	231,900	(440,800)	213,200	118,300	25,386
Income Taxes	(7,100)	(460,700)	48,300	41,500	71,600	111,500	187,300	(85,282)
Net Income	471,900	768,300	106,000	(198,800)	(556,800)	(10,300)	(45,800)	89,556
Average Shares	50,700	37,000	32,249	32,508	31,951	26,275	22,552	22,546
Balance Sheet								
Current Assets	1,659,900	3,358,700	1,615,400	3,444,600	2,802,700	2,724,400	3,381,000	2,797,438
Total Assets	5,230,500	7,747,700	35,849,700	35,792,800	32,334,100	30,100,200	27,908,800	25,200,491
Current Liabilities	1,141,900	1,350,200	1,115,600	989,800	1,137,700	1,033,000	1,012,700	679,265
Long-Term Obligations	2,214,400	4,651,300	5,774,100	5,430,900	6,382,700	5,157,800	4,896,100	2,150,625
Total Liabilities	3,532,200	6,166,400	35,091,700	35,154,700	31,747,400	28,658,600	26,854,700	23,703,669
Stockholders' Equity	1,698,300	1,581,300	758,000	638,100	586,700	1,441,600	1,054,100	1,496,822
Shares Outstanding	48,800	53,400	32,351	32,378	32,474	32,621	22,959	22,605
Statistical Record								
Return on Assets %	7.27	3.52	0.30	N.M.	N.M.	N.M.	N.M.	0.37
Return on Equity %	28.78	65.69	15.19	N.M.	N.M.	N.M.	N.M.	6.67
EBITDA Margin %	5.50	7.63	12.11	15.58	3.62	12.41	14.55	8.57
Net Margin %	12.41	24.42	2.12	N.M.	N.M.	N.M.	N.M.	2.00
Asset Turnover	0.59	0.14	0.14	0.15	0.19	0.21	0.21	0.18
Current Ratio	1.45	2.49	1.45	3.48	2.46	2.64	3.34	4.12
Debt to Equity	1.30	2.94	7.62	8.51	10.88	3.58	4.64	1.44
Price Range	74.48-41.68	118.38-68.96	124.46-88.80	100.96-64.12	90.11-71.01	82.11-61.39	65.73-45.89	64.12-24.87
P/E Ratio	8.00-4.48	5.71-3.32	37.83-26.99	...	...	...	...	68.95-26.74
Average Yield %	3.02	0.45	...	...	...	...	...	...

Address: 3001 Deming Way, Middelton, WI 53562 Telephone: 608-275-3340	**Web Site:** www.spectrumbrands.com **Officers:** Andreas Rouvé - Chief Executive Officer David M. Maura - Executive Chairman, Chief Executive Officer	**Auditors:** KPMG LLP **Investor Contact:** 608-278-6148 **Transfer Agents:** American Stock Transfer & Trust, New York, NY

SPIRIT AEROSYSTEMS HOLDINGS INC

Exchange	Symbol	Price	52Wk Range	Yield	P/E
NYS	SPR	$72.88 (12/31/2019)	99.35-70.09	0.66	11.97

*7 Year Price Score 122.90 *NYSE Composite Index=100 *12 Month Price Score 94.54

Interim Earnings (Per Share)

Qtr.	Mar	Jun	Sep	Dec
2016	1.29	0.35	1.16	0.90
2017	1.17	(0.48)	1.26	1.06
2018	1.10	1.31	1.59	1.67
2019	1.55	1.61	1.26	...

Interim Dividends (Per Share)

Amt	Decl	Ex	Rec	Pay
0.12Q	01/23/2019	03/15/2019	03/18/2019	04/08/2019
0.12Q	04/24/2019	06/14/2019	06/17/2019	07/08/2019
0.12Q	07/22/2019	09/13/2019	09/16/2019	10/07/2019
0.12Q	10/23/2019	12/13/2019	12/16/2019	01/06/2020

Indicated Div: $0.48

Valuation Analysis   **Institutional Holding**

Forecast EPS	$6.43
	(01/17/2020)
Market Cap	$7.6 Billion
Book Value	$1.6 Billion
Price/Book	4.73
Price/Sales	0.99

No of Institutions	569
Shares	130,405,160
% Held	85.91

Business Summary: Aerospace (MIC: 7.1.1 SIC: 3728 NAIC: 336413)

Spirit AeroSystems Holdings is an independent non-Original Equipment Manufacturer commercial aerostructures designer and manufacturer. Co. has three segments: Fuselage Systems, which includes development, production and marketing of forward, mid and rear fuselage sections, other structure components, and related spares and maintenance, repair, and overhaul (MRO) services; Propulsion Systems, which includes development, production and marketing of nacelles, struts/pylons, other structural engine components, and related spares and MRO services; and Wing Systems, which includes development, production and marketing of flaps and slats, wing structures, and related spares and MRO services.

Recent Developments: For the quarter ended Sep 26 2019, net income decreased 22.2% to US$131.3 million from US$168.8 million in the year-earlier quarter. Revenues were US$1.92 billion, up 5.9% from US$1.81 billion the year before. Operating income was US$206.1 million versus US$222.5 million in the prior-year quarter, a decrease of 7.4%. Direct operating expenses rose 6.8% to US$1.65 billion from US$1.54 billion in the comparable period the year before. Indirect operating expenses increased 37.6% to US$66.2 million from US$48.1 million in the equivalent prior-year period.

Prospects: Our evaluation of Spirit AeroSystems Holdings Inc. as of October 4th, 2019 is the result of our systematic analysis on three basic characteristics: earnings strength, relative valuation, and recent stock price movement. The company has managed to produce a neutral trend in earnings per share over the past 5 quarters. In addition, recent analyst estimates for the company have been mixed and SPR has posted results that exceeded analysts' expectations. Based on operating earnings yield, the company is undervalued when compared to all of the companies we cover. Share price changes over the past year indicates that SPR will perform poorly over the near term.

Financial Data

(US$ in Thousands)	9 Mos	6 Mos	3 Mos	12/31/2018	12/31/2017	12/31/2016	12/31/2015	12/31/2014
Earnings Per Share	6.09	6.42	6.12	5.65	3.01	3.70	5.66	2.53
Cash Flow Per Share	8.90	8.17	8.13	7.13	4.91	5.67	9.32	2.58
Tang Book Value Per Share	15.33	13.92	12.50	11.70	15.70	15.82	15.59	11.45
Dividends Per Share	0.480	0.480	0.480	0.460	0.400	0.100	...	...
Dividend Payout %	7.88	7.48	7.84	8.14	13.29	2.70	...	...
Income Statement								
Total Revenue	5,903,800	3,983,900	1,967,800	7,222,000	6,983,000	6,792,900	6,643,900	6,799,200
EBITDA	646,600	449,800	218,200	844,900	589,100	732,800	875,600	368,200
Depn & Amortn	2,200	(600)	(600)	16,700	19,200	18,600	16,900	18,300
Income Before Taxes	587,100	414,100	203,200	756,200	534,600	660,500	808,100	262,400
Income Taxes	124,700	83,000	40,100	139,800	180,000	192,100	20,600	(95,900)
Net Income	462,400	331,100	163,100	617,000	354,900	469,700	788,700	358,800
Average Shares	104,600	104,500	105,300	109,100	117,900	127,000	139,400	141,600
Balance Sheet								
Current Assets	3,838,700	3,543,900	3,427,400	2,849,300	2,651,100	2,910,400	3,299,100	3,052,100
Total Assets	6,701,600	6,345,100	6,297,700	5,685,900	5,267,800	5,405,200	5,777,500	5,162,700
Current Liabilities	1,865,700	1,810,100	1,756,300	1,582,100	1,621,000	1,544,200	1,459,000	1,258,800
Long-Term Obligations	2,132,200	2,113,300	2,214,900	1,864,000	1,119,900	1,060,000	1,097,600	1,144,100
Total Liabilities	5,085,100	4,876,900	4,977,100	4,448,300	3,466,800	3,476,900	3,658,000	3,541,200
Stockholders' Equity	1,616,500	1,468,200	1,320,600	1,237,600	1,801,000	1,928,300	2,119,500	1,621,500
Shares Outstanding	104,888	104,855	104,876	105,461	114,447	121,642	135,617	141,089
Statistical Record								
Return on Assets %	10.34	11.33	11.22	11.27	6.65	8.38	14.42	6.99
Return on Equity %	46.85	55.94	45.26	40.61	19.03	23.14	42.17	23.13
EBITDA Margin %	10.95	11.29	11.09	11.70	8.44	10.79	13.18	5.42
Net Margin %	7.83	8.31	8.29	8.54	5.08	6.91	11.87	5.28
Asset Turnover	1.25	1.28	1.28	1.32	1.31	1.21	1.21	1.32
Current Ratio	2.06	1.96	1.95	1.80	1.64	1.88	2.26	2.42
Debt to Equity	1.32	1.44	1.68	1.51	0.62	0.55	0.52	0.71
Price Range	99.35-65.72	99.35-65.72	99.35-65.72	102.93-65.72	87.25-52.96	61.26-40.50	57.16-41.89	45.32-26.51
P/E Ratio	16.31-10.79	15.48-10.24	16.23-10.74	18.22-11.63	28.99-17.59	16.56-10.95	10.10-7.40	17.91-10.48
Average Yield %	0.58	0.58	0.56	0.53	0.60	0.21	...	...

Address: 3801 South Oliver, Wichita, KS 67210 **Telephone:** 316-526-9000	**Web Site:** www.spiritaero.com **Officers:** Robert D. Johnson - Chairman Thomas C. (Tom) Gentile - President, Chief Executive Officer, Executive Vice President, Chief Operating Officer	**Auditors:** Ernst & Young LLP **Investor Contact:** 316-523-7040 **Transfer Agents:** Computershare, Pittsburgh, PA

SPIRE INC

Exchange	Symbol	Price	52Wk Range	Yield	P/E	Div Acheiver
NYS	SR	$83.31 (12/31/2019)	87.24-72.41	2.99	23.67	15 Years

*7 Year Price Score 108.46 *NYSE Composite Index=100 *12 Month Price Score 92.73

Interim Earnings (Per Share)

Qtr.	Dec	Mar	Jun	Sep
2014-15	1.09	2.18	0.32	(0.43)
2015-16	1.08	2.31	0.24	(0.36)
2016-17	0.99	2.36	0.45	(0.32)
2017-18	2.39	2.03	0.52	(0.58)
2018-19	1.32	3.04	(0.09)	(0.75)

Interim Dividends (Per Share)

Amt	Decl	Ex	Rec	Pay
0.593Q	02/06/2019	03/08/2019	03/11/2019	04/02/2019
0.593Q	05/01/2019	06/10/2019	06/11/2019	07/02/2019
0.593Q	07/30/2019	09/10/2019	09/11/2019	10/02/2019
0.623Q	11/14/2019	12/10/2019	12/11/2019	01/03/2020

Indicated Div: $2.49

Valuation Analysis / **Institutional Holding**

Forecast EPS	$3.86 (01/16/2020)	No of Institutions	371
Market Cap	$4.2 Billion	Shares	
Book Value	$2.5 Billion	49,553,040	
Price/Book	1.67	% Held	
Price/Sales	2.18	N/A	

Business Summary: Gas Utilities (MIC: 3.3.1 SIC: 4924 NAIC: 221210)

Spire is the holding company for Spire Missouri Inc. (Spire Missouri), Spire Alabama Inc. (Spire Alabama), other gas utilities, and gas-related businesses. Co.'s segments are: Gas Utility, which includes Spire Missouri, a natural gas distribution utility system in Missouri, and Spire Alabama, a public utility engaged in the purchase, retail distribution and sale of natural gas principally in central and northern Alabama; and Gas Marketing, which includes Co.'s subsidiary, Spire Marketing Inc. that is engaged in the marketing of natural gas and providing energy services to both on-system utility transportation customers and customers outside of the service areas.

Recent Developments: For the year ended Sep 30 2019, net income decreased 13.8% to US$184.6 million from US$214.2 million in the prior year. Revenues were US$1.95 billion, down 0.6% from US$1.97 billion the year before. Operating income was US$302.3 million versus US$294.1 million in the prior year, an increase of 2.8%. Direct operating expenses declined 2.2% to US$1.47 billion from US$1.50 billion in the comparable period the year before. Indirect operating expenses increased 7.4% to US$179.4 million from US$167.0 million in the equivalent prior-year period.

Prospects: Our evaluation of Spire Inc. as of October 4th, 2019 is the result of our systematic analysis on three basic characteristics: earnings strength, relative valuation, and recent stock price movement. The company has managed to produce a neutral trend in earnings per share over the past 5 quarters. Additionally, recent analyst estimates for the company have been unchanged while SR has posted results that fell short of analysts' expectations. Based on operating earnings yield, the company is fairly valued when compared to all of the companies we cover. Share price changes over the past year indicates that SR will perform well over the near term.

Financial Data

(US$ in Thousands)	09/30/2019	09/30/2018	09/30/2017	09/30/2016	09/30/2015	09/30/2014	09/30/2013	09/30/2012
Earnings Per Share	3.52	4.33	3.43	3.24	3.16	2.35	2.02	2.79
Cash Flow Per Share	8.89	9.30	6.15	7.42	7.46	3.42	6.33	5.74
Tang Book Value Per Share	22.22	21.39	16.98	13.22	14.48	13.21	24.44	26.69
Dividends Per Share	2.370	2.250	2.100	1.960	1.840	1.760	1.700	1.660
Dividend Payout %	67.33	51.96	61.22	60.49	58.23	74.89	84.16	59.50
Income Statement								
Total Revenue	1,952,400	1,965,000	1,740,700	1,537,300	1,976,400	1,627,200	1,017,019	1,125,475
EBITDA	505,200	454,500	482,400	428,200	404,300	246,400	147,133	153,904
Depn & Amortn	181,700	168,400	154,100	137,500	130,800	83,300	49,283	41,339
Income Before Taxes	219,100	187,700	239,200	213,500	198,900	116,900	70,336	88,929
Income Taxes	34,500	(26,500)	77,600	69,300	62,000	32,300	17,578	26,289
Net Income	184,600	214,200	161,600	144,200	136,900	84,600	52,758	62,640
Average Shares	50,800	49,300	47,000	44,300	43,300	35,900	25,952	22,340
Balance Sheet								
Current Assets	614,500	659,600	725,500	569,600	530,100	604,900	475,880	343,016
Total Assets	7,619,200	6,843,600	6,546,700	6,077,400	5,290,200	5,074,000	3,125,386	1,880,262
Current Liabilities	1,468,800	1,321,700	1,097,900	1,161,300	853,800	782,800	353,178	252,124
Long-Term Obligations	2,082,600	1,900,100	1,995,000	1,833,700	1,771,500	1,851,000	912,712	339,416
Total Liabilities	5,072,800	4,588,200	4,555,400	4,309,200	3,716,600	3,565,600	2,079,104	1,278,651
Stockholders' Equity	2,546,400	2,255,400	1,991,300	1,768,200	1,573,600	1,508,400	1,046,282	601,611
Shares Outstanding	50,973	50,671	48,263	45,650	43,335	43,183	32,696	22,539
Statistical Record								
Return on Assets %	2.55	3.20	2.56	2.53	2.64	2.06	2.11	3.41
Return on Equity %	7.69	10.09	8.60	8.61	8.88	6.62	6.40	10.63
EBITDA Margin %	25.88	23.13	27.71	27.85	20.46	15.14	14.47	13.67
Net Margin %	9.46	10.90	9.28	9.38	6.93	5.20	5.19	5.57
Asset Turnover	0.27	0.29	0.28	0.27	0.38	0.40	0.41	0.61
Current Ratio	0.42	0.50	0.66	0.49	0.62	0.77	1.35	1.36
Debt to Equity	0.82	0.84	1.00	1.04	1.13	1.23	0.87	0.56
Price Range	87.24-71.15	82.25-61.30	77.40-59.97	70.84-54.53	56.02-46.15	49.56-44.24	48.16-37.70	43.27-37.37
P/E Ratio	24.78-20.21	19.00-14.16	22.57-17.48	21.86-16.83	17.73-14.60	21.09-18.83	23.84-18.66	15.51-13.39
Average Yield %	2.95	3.10	3.09	3.09	3.54	3.78	3.96	4.12

Address: 700 Market Street, St. Louis, MO 63101 **Telephone:** 314-342-0500	**Web Site:** **Officers:** Edward L. Glotzbach - Chairman Suzanne Sitherwood - President, Chief Executive Officer	**Auditors:** DELOITTE & TOUCHE LLP **Investor Contact:** 314-342-0878 **Transfer Agents:** Computershare Trust Company, N.A., Providence, RI

SPIRIT AIRLINES INC

Exchange	Symbol	Price	52Wk Range	Yield	P/E
NYS	SAVE	$40.31 (12/31/2019)	63.06-33.10	N/A	7.97

*7 Year Price Score 80.29   *NYSE Composite Index=100   *12 Month Price Score 78.87

Interim Earnings (Per Share)

Qtr.	Mar	Jun	Sep	Dec
2016	0.86	1.03	1.17	0.71
2017	0.46	1.12	0.87	3.61
2018	(0.66)	0.16	1.42	1.35
2019	0.82	1.67	1.22	...

Interim Dividends (Per Share)

No Dividends Paid

Valuation Analysis

		Institutional Holding	
Forecast EPS	$5.08	No of Institutions	
	(00/24/2020)	349	
Market Cap	$2.8 Billion	Shares	
Book Value	$2.2 Billion	77,563,056	
Price/Book	1.27	% Held	
Price/Sales	0.74	98.42	

Business Summary: Airlines/Air Freight (MIC: 7.4.4 SIC: 4512 NAIC: 481111)

Spirit Airlines is an airline that provides travel opportunities principally throughout the domestic U.S., the Caribbean and Latin America. Co.'s ultra low-cost carrier business model provides customers low, unbundled base fares with a range of optional services, allowing customers to choose their options. The majority of Co.'s tickets are sold through direct channels including online via www.spirit.com, its call center and its airport ticket counters, with spirit.com being the primary channel. Co. also partners with a number of third parties to distribute its tickets, including online and travel agents and electronic global distribution systems.

Recent Developments: For the quarter ended Sep 30 2019, net income decreased 14.4% to US$83.5 million from US$97.5 million in the year-earlier quarter. Revenues were US$992.0 million, up 9.7% from US$904.3 million the year before. Operating income was US$124.7 million versus US$145.1 million in the prior-year quarter, a decrease of 14.1%. Direct operating expenses rose 1.5% to US$438.3 million from US$431.7 million in the comparable period the year before. Indirect operating expenses increased 31.0% to US$429.0 million from US$327.5 million in the equivalent prior-year period.

Prospects: Our evaluation of Spirit Airlines Inc as of October 4th, 2019 is the result of our systematic analysis on three basic characteristics: earnings strength, relative valuation, and recent stock price movement. The company has generated a negative trend in earnings per share over the past 5 quarters. In addition, recent analyst estimates for the company have been reduced while SAVE has posted results that exceeded analysts' expectations. Based on operating earnings yield, the company is undervalued when compared to all of the companies we cover. Share price changes over the past year indicates that SAVE will perform over the near term.

Financial Data

(US$ in Thousands)	9 Mos	6 Mos	3 Mos	12/31/2018	12/31/2017	12/31/2016	12/31/2015	12/31/2014
Earnings Per Share	5.06	5.26	3.75	2.28	6.06	3.76	4.38	3.08
Cash Flow Per Share	8.13	8.72	7.90	7.42	6.14	6.72	6.55	3.58
Tang Book Value Per Share	31.85	30.61	28.90	28.25	26.06	20.12	17.13	13.78
Income Statement								
Total Revenue	2,860,720	1,868,752	855,796	3,323,034	2,647,666	2,321,956	2,141,463	1,931,580
EBITDA	382,364	255,730	89,860	445,351	536,521	550,001	584,180	399,444
Depn & Amortn	6,540	4,365	2,289	185,546	148,096	106,868	75,073	46,786
Income Before Taxes	329,663	220,650	72,081	204,976	353,652	419,460	502,403	352,994
Income Taxes	75,622	50,073	16,005	49,227	(66,954)	154,581	185,183	127,530
Net Income	254,041	170,577	56,076	155,749	420,606	264,879	317,220	225,464
Average Shares	68,545	68,620	68,516	68,430	69,377	70,508	72,426	73,294
Balance Sheet								
Current Assets	1,403,282	1,520,687	1,516,760	1,345,466	1,280,260	975,845	1,026,340	731,141
Total Assets	6,575,214	6,662,781	6,423,939	5,165,457	4,143,950	3,151,927	2,530,545	1,602,981
Current Liabilities	1,052,776	1,211,163	1,126,669	834,535	647,026	531,950	466,240	365,624
Long-Term Obligations	1,968,901	2,025,183	2,039,619	2,024,000	1,387,500	897,400	596,700	135,800
Total Liabilities	4,395,127	4,567,754	4,446,283	3,236,179	2,366,871	1,757,361	1,305,242	599,889
Stockholders' Equity	2,180,087	2,095,027	1,977,656	1,928,504	1,777,081	1,394,607	1,225,310	1,003,075
Shares Outstanding	68,448	68,440	68,438	68,269	68,196	69,326	71,541	72,775
Statistical Record								
Return on Assets %	6.09	6.35	4.64	3.35	11.53	9.30	15.35	16.20
Return on Equity %	17.24	18.81	13.89	8.41	26.52	20.17	28.47	25.44
EBITDA Margin %	13.37	13.68	10.50	13.40	20.26	23.69	27.28	20.68
Net Margin %	8.88	9.13	6.55	4.69	15.89	11.41	14.81	11.67
Asset Turnover	0.66	0.64	0.63	0.71	0.73	0.82	1.04	1.39
Current Ratio	1.33	1.26	1.35	1.61	1.98	1.83	2.20	2.00
Debt to Equity	0.90	0.97	1.03	1.05	0.78	0.64	0.49	0.14
Price Range	64.59-36.03	64.59-36.13	64.59-34.98	64.59-34.98	59.74-32.09	59.50-36.53	82.03-33.57	84.47-44.76
P/E Ratio	12.76-7.12	12.28-6.87	17.22-9.33	28.33-15.34	9.86-5.30	15.82-9.72	18.73-7.66	27.43-14.53

Address: 2800 Executive Way, Miramar, FL 33025 Telephone: 954-447-7920	Web Site: www.spirit.com Officers: H. McIntyre (Mac) Gardner - Chairman Edward M. Christie - President, Chief Executive Officer, Executive Vice President, Senior Vice President, Chief Financial Officer	Auditors: Ernst & Young LLP Investor Contact: 954-447-7920 Transfer Agents: Wells Fargo Shareholder Services

SPIRIT REALTY CAPITAL INC

Exchange	Symbol	Price	52Wk Range	Yield	P/E
NYS	SRC	$49.18 (12/31/2019)	53.05-34.63	N/A	20.24

*7 Year Price Score 74.66 *NYSE Composite Index=100 *12 Month Price Score 109.05

Interim Earnings (Per Share)

Qtr.	Mar	Jun	Sep	Dec
2016	0.30	0.50	0.30	0.00
2017	0.15	0.25	0.05	0.35
2018	0.30	0.15	0.30	0.59
2019	0.48	0.49	0.87	...

Interim Dividends (Per Share)

Amt	Decl	Ex	Rec	Pay
0.00Q	05/01/2018	06/01/2018	05/18/2018	05/31/2018
0.90Q	06/05/2018	06/28/2018	06/29/2018	07/13/2018
0.625Q	08/30/2018	09/27/2018	09/28/2018	10/15/2018
1-for-5	...	12/13/2018	...	...

Valuation Analysis

		Institutional Holding	
Forecast EPS	$2.06	No of Institutions	435
	(01/17/2020)		
Market Cap	$4.9 Billion	Shares	
Book Value	$3.3 Billion	174,987,824	
Price/Book	1.47	% Held	
Price/Sales	9.35	N/A	

Business Summary: REITs (MIC: 5.3.1 SIC: 6798 NAIC: 525930)

Spirit Realty Capital is a self-administered and self-managed real estate investment trust with in-house capabilities, including asset management, acquisition, credit, research, finance, information technology and accounting functions. Co. primarily invests in single-tenant real estate throughout the U.S., which is generally acquired through sale-leaseback transactions and subsequently leased on a long-term, triple-net basis to tenants with business operations within predominantly retail, but also office and industrial property types. Co.'s operations are carried out through Spirit Realty, L.P. (Operating Partnership).

Recent Developments: For the quarter ended Sep 30 2019, income from continuing operations increased 162.1% to US$81.3 million from US$31.0 million in the year-earlier quarter. Net income increased 170.5% to US$81.3 million from US$30.1 million in the year-earlier quarter. Revenues were US$166.9 million, up 52.3% from US$109.6 million the year before. Revenues from property income rose 52.3% to US$164.6 million from US$108.0 million in the corresponding quarter a year earlier.

Prospects: Our evaluation of Spirit Realty Capital Inc as of October 4th, 2019 is the result of our systematic analysis on three basic characteristics: earnings strength, relative valuation, and recent stock price movement. The company has managed to produce a neutral trend in earnings per share over the past 5 quarters. However, recent analyst estimates for the company have been reduced while SRC has posted results that exceeded analysts' expectations. Based on operating earnings yield, the company is fairly valued when compared to all of the companies we cover. Share price changes over the past year indicates that SRC will perform well over the near term.

Financial Data

(US$ in Thousands)	9 Mos	6 Mos	3 Mos	12/31/2018	12/31/2017	12/31/2016	12/31/2015	12/31/2014
Earnings Per Share	2.43	1.86	1.52	1.39	0.80	1.05	1.30	(0.45)
Cash Flow Per Share	4.02	3.68	3.68	3.90	4.13	3.84	4.30	2.83
Tang Book Value Per Share	26.37	24.86	24.60	24.66	27.73	30.58	30.24	29.62
Dividends Per Share	2.500	1.875	1.250	0.625	3.600	3.525	...	...
Dividend Payout %	102.88	100.81	82.24	44.96	450.00	335.71	...	...
Income Statement								
Total Revenue	395,285	228,338	112,593	445,125	668,955	685,974	667,335	602,871
EBITDA	269,917	150,073	75,146	467,610	482,050	520,195	519,458	422,864
Depn & Amortn	11,116	8,431	4,737	220,779	279,487	277,563	270,892	253,016
Income Before Taxes	182,339	89,855	43,798	149,283	12,436	46,046	25,665	(50,222)
Income Taxes	11,730	540	220	792	394	965	601	673
Net Income	170,609	89,315	43,578	132,052	77,148	97,446	114,730	(33,799)
Average Shares	90,396	87,890	85,504	86,476	93,588	93,849	86,509	77,361
Balance Sheet								
Current Assets	358,440	9,984	9,376	14,493	8,798	10,059	21,790	176,181
Total Assets	5,663,584	5,308,033	5,158,857	5,096,316	7,263,511	7,677,971	7,918,996	8,017,001
Current Liabilities	136,781	134,081	125,183	119,768	148,919	148,915	142,475	123,298
Long-Term Obligations	2,077,508	2,126,015	2,100,233	2,054,637	3,639,680	3,664,628	4,092,787	4,369,634
Total Liabilities	2,330,804	2,378,573	2,340,221	2,294,567	3,943,902	3,995,863	4,429,165	4,698,900
Stockholders' Equity	3,332,780	2,929,460	2,818,636	2,801,749	3,319,609	3,682,108	3,489,831	3,318,101
Shares Outstanding	99,730	90,110	86,811	85,787	89,773	96,724	88,363	82,270
Statistical Record								
Return on Assets %	4.18	3.40	2.34	2.14	1.03	1.25	1.44	N.M.
Return on Equity %	7.32	6.03	4.84	4.31	2.20	2.71	3.37	N.M.
EBITDA Margin %	68.28	65.72	66.74	105.05	72.06	75.83	77.84	70.14
Net Margin %	43.16	39.12	38.70	29.67	11.53	14.21	17.19	N.M.
Asset Turnover	0.10	0.09	0.07	0.07	0.09	0.09	0.08	0.08
Current Ratio	2.62	0.07	0.07	0.12	0.06	0.07	0.15	1.43
Debt to Equity	0.62	0.73	0.75	0.73	1.10	1.00	1.17	1.32
Price Range	48.87-34.29	45.14-34.29	42.50-34.29	42.50-33.25	50.50-30.06	62.19-40.77	58.20-40.50	53.86-44.04
P/E Ratio	20.11-14.11	24.27-18.44	27.96-22.56	30.58-23.92	63.12-37.58	59.23-38.83	44.77-31.16	...
Average Yield %	6.07	4.68	3.20	1.63	9.01	6.74	...	...

Address: 2727 North Harwood Street, Suite 300, Dallas, TX 75201 **Telephone:** 972-476-1900	**Web Site:** www.spiritrealty.com **Officers:** Richard I. Gilchrist - Chairman Jackson Hsieh - President, Chief Executive Officer, Chief Operating Officer	**Auditors:** Ernst & Young LLP **Investor Contact:** 480-606-0820

SPRINT CORP

Exchange	Symbol	Price	52Wk Range	Yield	P/E
NYS	S	$5.21 (12/31/2019)	7.99-5.19	N/A	N/A

*7 Year Price Score N/A ***NYSE Composite Index=100** ***12 Month Price Score 85.37**

Interim Earnings (Per Share)

Qtr.	Jun	Sep	Dec	Mar
2016-17	(0.08)	(0.04)	(0.12)	(0.07)
2017-18	0.05	(0.01)	1.76	0.06
2018-19	0.04	0.05	(0.03)	(0.54)
2019-20	(0.03)	(0.07)	...	...

Interim Dividends (Per Share)

No Dividends Paid

Valuation Analysis

		Institutional Holding	
Forecast EPS	$-0.13	No of Institutions	
	(01/17/2020)	708	
Market Cap	$21.4 Billion	Shares	
Book Value	$25.9 Billion		815,414,464
Price/Book	0.83	% Held	
Price/Sales	0.65	N/A	

Business Summary: Services (MIC: 6.1.2 SIC: 4813 NAIC: 517110)

Sprint is a holding company. Through its subsidiaries, Co. is a communications company providing wireless and wireline communications products and services to consumers, businesses, government subscribers, and resellers. Co. has two segments: Wireless, which provides wireless services on a postpaid and prepaid payment basis to retail subscribers and also on a wholesale basis, including the sale of wireless services that utilize Co.'s network but are sold under the wholesaler's brand; and Wireline, which provides a suite of wireline communication services to other communications companies and targeted business customers, as well as voice, data and internet protocol communication services.

Recent Developments: For the quarter ended Sep 30 2019, net loss amounted to US$279.0 million versus net income of US$207.0 million in the year-earlier quarter. Revenues were US$7.80 billion, down 7.6% from US$8.43 billion the year before. Operating income was US$237.0 million versus US$778.0 million in the prior-year quarter, a decrease of 69.5%. Direct operating expenses rose 0.4% to US$3.37 billion from US$3.36 billion in the comparable period the year before. Indirect operating expenses decreased 2.5% to US$4.18 billion from US$4.29 billion in the equivalent prior-year period.

Prospects: Our evaluation of Sprint Corp as of October 4th, 2019 is the result of our systematic analysis on three basic characteristics: earnings strength, relative valuation, and recent stock price movement. The company has suffered a very negative trend in earnings per share over the past 5 quarters. However, recent analyst estimates for the company have been mixed and S has posted results that exceeded analysts' expectations. Based on operating earnings yield, the company is overvalued when compared to all of the companies we cover. Share price changes over the past year indicates that S will perform over the near term.

Financial Data (US$ in Thousands)	6 Mos	3 Mos	03/31/2019	03/31/2018	03/31/2017	03/31/2016	03/31/2015	03/31/2014
Earnings Per Share	(0.67)	(0.55)	(0.48)	1.85	(0.30)	(0.50)	(0.85)	(0.04)
Cash Flow Per Share	2.41	2.51	2.57	2.52	1.05	0.98	0.62	0.54
Income Statement								
Total Revenue	15,937,000	8,142,000	33,600,000	32,406,000	33,347,000	32,180,000	34,532,000	8,875,000
EBITDA	4,973,000	2,616,000	9,368,000	10,436,000	8,822,000	6,122,000	1,929,000	1,289,000
Depn & Amortn	4,239,000	2,133,000	8,783,000	7,768,000	7,098,000	5,794,000	3,797,000	868,000
Income Before Taxes	(479,000)	(136,000)	(1,978,000)	303,000	(771,000)	(1,854,000)	(3,919,000)	(95,000)
Income Taxes	(86,000)	(22,000)	(35,000)	(7,074,000)	435,000	141,000	(574,000)	56,000
Net Income	(393,000)	(114,000)	(1,943,000)	7,389,000	(1,206,000)	(1,995,000)	(3,345,000)	(151,000)
Average Shares	4,098,000	4,087,000	4,057,000	4,078,000	3,981,000	3,969,000	3,953,000	3,949,000
Balance Sheet								
Current Assets	10,206,000	10,589,000	12,891,000	14,253,000	14,117,000	6,833,000	9,777,000	11,579,000
Total Assets	87,928,000	88,546,000	84,601,000	85,459,000	85,123,000	78,975,000	83,030,000	84,689,000
Current Liabilities	13,052,000	11,289,000	12,115,000	10,800,000	12,458,000	11,963,000	10,940,000	9,698,000
Long-Term Obligations	33,268,000	35,073,000	35,366,000	37,463,000	35,878,000	29,268,000	32,531,000	31,787,000
Total Liabilities	62,078,000	62,430,000	58,529,000	59,103,000	66,315,000	59,192,000	61,320,000	59,377,000
Stockholders' Equity	25,850,000	26,116,000	26,072,000	26,356,000	18,808,000	19,783,000	21,710,000	25,312,000
Shares Outstanding	4,106,000	4,092,000	4,081,000	4,005,000	3,989,000	3,974,000	3,966,000	3,941,000
Statistical Record								
Return on Assets %	N.M.	N.M.	N.M.	8.66	N.M.	N.M.	N.M.	N.M.
Return on Equity %	N.M.	N.M.	N.M.	32.72	N.M.	N.M.	N.M.	N.M.
EBITDA Margin %	31.20	32.13	27.88	32.20	26.46	19.02	5.59	14.52
Net Margin %	N.M.	N.M.	N.M.	22.80	N.M.	N.M.	N.M.	N.M.
Asset Turnover	0.38	0.38	0.40	0.38	0.41	0.40	0.41	0.42
Current Ratio	0.78	0.94	1.06	1.32	1.13	0.57	0.89	1.19
Debt to Equity	1.29	1.34	1.36	1.42	1.91	1.48	1.50	1.26
Price Range	7.99-5.48	7.45-5.38	6.55-4.85	9.11-4.86	9.43-3.40	5.30-2.45	9.71-3.81	10.79-5.74
P/E Ratio	...	...	...	4.92-2.63	...	...	...	...

Address: 6200 Sprint Parkway, Overland Park, KS 66251 Telephone: 913-794-1091	Web Site: www.sprint.com Officers: Raul Marcelo Claure - Executive Chairman, President, Chief Executive Officer, Associate/Affiliate Company Officer Ronald D. Fisher - Vice-Chairman	Auditors: Deloitte & Touche LLP

644

SQUARE INC

Exchange	Symbol	Price	52Wk Range	Yield	P/E
NYS	SQ	$62.56 (12/31/2019)	82.28-52.42	N/A	N/A

*7 Year Price Score N/A   *NYSE Composite Index=100   *12 Month Price Score 89.43

TRADING VOLUME (thousand shares)

Interim Earnings (Per Share)

Qtr.	Mar	Jun	Sep	Dec
2016	(0.29)	(0.08)	(0.09)	(0.04)
2017	(0.04)	(0.04)	(0.04)	(0.04)
2018	(0.06)	(0.01)	0.04	(0.06)
2019	(0.09)	(0.02)	0.06	...

Interim Dividends (Per Share)

No Dividends Paid

Valuation Analysis		Institutional Holding	
Forecast EPS	$0.78	No of Institutions	
	(01/17/2020)	867	
Market Cap	$26.8 Billion	Shares	
Book Value	$1.2 Billion	261,655,872	
Price/Book	21.48	% Held	
Price/Sales	6.20	92.28	

Business Summary: IT Services (MIC: 6.3.1 SIC: 7372 NAIC: 511210)

Square is a commerce ecosystem that combines software with hardware to enable sellers to turn mobile devices and computing devices into payment and point-of-sale solutions. With Co.'s offering, a seller can accept payments via magnetic stripe, Europay, MasterCard, and Visa, or Near Field Communication; or online via Square Invoices, Square Virtual Terminal, or the seller's website or app. Also, sellers can gain access to reporting and analytics, next-day settlements, digital receipts, payment dispute and chargeback management, security, and Payment Card Industry compliance. Co.'s Cash App enable individuals to send and receive money electronically to and from individuals and businesses.

Recent Developments: For the quarter ended Sep 30 2019, net income increased 49.7% to US$29.4 million from US$19.6 million in the year-earlier quarter. Revenues were US$1.27 billion, up 43.6% from US$882.1 million the year before. Operating income was US$32.1 million versus a loss of US$9.9 million in the prior-year quarter. Direct operating expenses rose 44.8% to US$766.4 million from US$529.4 million in the comparable period the year before. Indirect operating expenses increased 29.1% to US$467.9 million from US$362.5 million in the equivalent prior-year period.

Prospects: Our evaluation of Square Inc as of October 4th, 2019 is the result of our systematic analysis on three basic characteristics: earnings strength, relative valuation, and recent stock price movement. The company has produced a positive trend in earnings per share over the past 5 quarters. However, recent analyst estimates for the company have been mixed and SQ has posted results that exceeded analysts' expectations. Based on operating earnings yield, the company is overvalued when compared to all of the companies we cover. Share price changes over the past year indicates that SQ will perform poorly over the near term.

Financial Data
(US$ in Thousands)

	9 Mos	6 Mos	3 Mos	12/31/2018	12/31/2017	12/31/2016	12/31/2015	12/31/2014
Earnings Per Share	(0.11)	(0.13)	(0.12)	(0.09)	(0.17)	(0.50)	(1.24)	(1.08)
Cash Flow Per Share	1.36	0.92	0.66	0.73	0.34	0.07	0.16	(0.77)
Tang Book Value Per Share	2.12	1.95	1.84	1.87	1.81	1.37	1.27	...
Income Statement								
Total Revenue	3,400,071	2,133,597	959,359	3,298,177	2,214,253	1,708,721	1,267,118	850,192
EBITDA	69,771	9,240	(11,151)	28,655	(24,506)	(141,753)	(154,808)	(135,095)
Depn & Amortn	67,550	44,654	22,190	46,800	29,700	28,700	20,100	16,500
Income Before Taxes	(13,235)	(45,238)	(38,022)	(36,127)	(62,664)	(169,673)	(176,071)	(152,653)
Income Taxes	2,259	(347)	129	2,326	149	1,917	3,746	1,440
Net Income	(15,494)	(44,891)	(38,151)	(38,453)	(62,813)	(171,590)	(179,817)	(154,093)
Average Shares	466,099	423,305	419,289	405,731	379,344	341,555	170,498	142,042
Balance Sheet								
Current Assets	2,758,766	3,528,646	3,266,522	2,111,905	1,778,294	1,001,425	705,563	409,867
Total Assets	4,000,504	4,654,006	4,402,591	3,281,023	2,187,270	1,211,362	894,772	541,888
Current Liabilities	1,644,901	2,375,594	2,183,559	1,018,541	972,827	577,464	334,202	191,106
Long-Term Obligations	928,869	919,026	909,302	899,695	358,572	...	...	30,000
Total Liabilities	2,750,710	3,469,534	3,281,002	2,160,522	1,400,937	635,209	386,724	268,216
Stockholders' Equity	1,249,794	1,184,472	1,121,589	1,120,501	786,333	576,153	508,048	273,672
Shares Outstanding	429,073	426,217	421,623	417,048	395,194	364,547	334,949	154,603
Statistical Record								
EBITDA Margin %	2.05	0.43	N.M.	0.87	N.M.	N.M.	N.M.	N.M.
Asset Turnover	1.09	0.96	1.06	1.21	1.30	1.62	1.76	1.98
Current Ratio	1.68	1.49	1.50	2.07	1.83	1.73	2.11	2.14
Debt to Equity	0.74	0.78	0.81	0.80	0.46	...	...	0.11
Price Range	97.83-50.72	99.01-50.72	99.01-44.75	99.01-36.17	48.86-13.81	15.48-8.37	13.09-11.90	...

Address: 1455 Market Street, Suite 600, San Francisco, CA 94103 Telephone: 415-375-3176	Web Site: www.squareup.com Officers: Jack Dorsey - Chairman, President, Chief Executive Officer Mohit Daswani - Finance and Strategy Lead	Auditors: Ernst & Young LLP Transfer Agents: American Stock Transfer & Trust Company, LLC, Brooklyn, NY

STANLEY BLACK & DECKER INC

Exchange	Symbol	Price	52Wk Range	Yield	P/E	Div Acheiver
NYS	SWK	$165.74 (12/31/2019)	167.76-115.69	1.67	38.19	51 Years

*7 Year Price Score 100.96 ***NYSE Composite Index=100** ***12 Month Price Score 106.05**

Interim Earnings (Per Share)

Qtr.	Mar	Jun	Sep	Dec
2016	1.28	1.84	1.68	1.70
2017	2.59	1.82	1.80	1.83
2018	1.11	1.93	1.65	(0.69)
2019	1.13	2.37	1.53	...

Interim Dividends (Per Share)

Amt	Decl	Ex	Rec	Pay
0.66Q	02/12/2019	03/04/2019	03/05/2019	03/19/2019
0.66Q	04/17/2019	06/03/2019	06/04/2019	06/18/2019
0.69Q	07/17/2019	08/30/2019	09/03/2019	09/17/2019
0.69Q	10/15/2019	11/27/2019	11/29/2019	12/17/2019

Indicated Div: $2.76

Valuation Analysis

		Institutional Holding	
Forecast EPS	$8.40	No of Institutions	
	(01/17/2020)	1029	
Market Cap	$29.3 Billion	Shares	
Book Value	$8.3 Billion	156,580,128	
Price/Book	3.55	% Held	
Price/Sales	2.04	N/A	

Business Summary: Industrial Machinery & Equipment (MIC: 7.2.1 SIC: 3423 NAIC: 332212)

Stanley Black & Decker is a provider of hand tools, power tools and related accessories, engineered fastening systems and products, services and equipment for oil and gas and infrastructure applications, commercial electronic security and monitoring systems, healthcare solutions, and mechanical access solutions (primarily automatic doors). Co.'s segments include: Tools and Storage, which is comprised of the power tools and equipment and hand tools, accessories and storage businesses; Industrial, which is comprised of the engineered fastening and infrastructure businesses; and Security, which is comprised of the convergent security solutions and the mechanical access solutions businesses.

Recent Developments: For the quarter ended Sep 28 2019, net income decreased 6.9% to US$231.1 million from US$248.3 million in the year-earlier quarter. Revenues were US$3.63 billion, up 4.0% from US$3.49 billion the year before. Direct operating expenses rose 6.1% to US$2.39 billion from US$2.26 billion in the comparable period the year before. Indirect operating expenses increased 1.2% to US$944.8 million from US$933.5 million in the equivalent prior-year period.

Prospects: Our evaluation of Stanley Black & Decker, Inc. as of October 4th, 2019 is the result of our systematic analysis on three basic characteristics: earnings strength, relative valuation, and recent stock price movement. The company has managed to produce a neutral trend in earnings per share over the past 5 quarters. However, recent analyst estimates for the company have been reduced while SWK has posted results that exceeded analysts' expectations. Based on operating earnings yield, the company is undervalued when compared to all of the companies we cover. Share price changes over the past year indicates that SWK will perform poorly over the near term.

Financial Data

(US$ in Thousands)	9 Mos	6 Mos	3 Mos	12/29/2018	12/30/2017	12/31/2016	01/02/2016	01/03/2015
Earnings Per Share	4.34	4.46	4.02	3.99	8.04	6.51	5.79	4.76
Cash Flow Per Share	10.00	10.01	7.97	8.49	9.51	10.20	8.00	8.17
Dividends Per Share	2.670	2.640	2.610	2.580	2.420	2.260	2.140	2.040
Dividend Payout %	61.52	59.19	64.93	64.66	30.10	34.72	36.96	42.86
Income Statement								
Total Revenue	10,728,000	7,094,900	3,333,600	13,982,400	12,747,200	11,406,900	11,171,800	11,338,600
EBITDA	1,210,600	808,400	296,400	1,737,800	2,169,300	1,805,400	1,730,000	1,698,200
Depn & Amortn	139,600	91,800	43,800	506,500	460,700	408,000	414,000	449,800
Income Before Taxes	893,200	598,500	194,800	1,022,100	1,526,100	1,226,100	1,150,800	1,084,800
Income Taxes	135,500	76,300	24,700	416,300	300,500	261,200	248,600	227,100
Net Income	756,700	526,200	169,900	605,200	1,226,000	965,300	883,700	760,900
Average Shares	150,623	150,358	149,908	151,643	152,449	148,207	152,706	159,737
Balance Sheet								
Current Assets	5,328,000	5,345,200	5,253,900	4,569,400	4,566,100	4,788,500	3,662,100	3,948,800
Total Assets	21,322,500	21,523,600	21,460,300	19,408,000	19,079,900	15,634,900	15,172,300	15,849,100
Current Liabilities	5,441,900	5,653,100	5,766,200	4,001,600	4,361,800	2,807,500	2,802,600	2,832,000
Long-Term Obligations	3,908,800	3,909,100	3,909,400	3,819,800	2,843,000	3,815,300	3,836,600	3,839,800
Total Liabilities	13,060,200	13,295,600	13,527,800	11,571,800	10,782,800	9,267,900	9,360,700	9,420,000
Stockholders' Equity	8,262,300	8,228,000	7,932,500	7,836,200	8,297,100	6,367,000	5,811,600	6,429,100
Shares Outstanding	176,902	176,902	151,532	151,302	154,038	152,559	153,944	157,125
Statistical Record								
Return on Assets %	3.11	3.20	2.94	3.15	7.08	6.28	5.71	4.62
Return on Equity %	7.95	8.13	7.38	7.52	16.77	15.90	14.48	11.32
EBITDA Margin %	11.28	11.39	8.89	12.43	17.02	15.83	15.49	14.98
Net Margin %	7.05	7.42	5.10	4.33	9.62	8.46	7.91	6.71
Asset Turnover	0.69	0.68	0.69	0.73	0.74	0.74	0.72	0.69
Current Ratio	0.98	0.95	0.91	1.14	1.05	1.71	1.31	1.39
Debt to Equity	0.47	0.48	0.49	0.49	0.34	0.60	0.66	0.60
Price Range	153.08-108.45	154.36-108.45	157.38-108.45	175.91-108.45	170.03-115.75	125.78-90.14	110.17-90.51	97.36-75.64
P/E Ratio	35.27-24.99	34.61-24.32	39.15-26.98	44.09-27.18	21.15-14.40	19.32-13.85	19.03-15.63	20.45-15.89
Average Yield %	1.99	1.96	1.93	1.80	1.70	2.01	2.11	2.35

Address: 1000 Stanley Drive, New Britain, CT 06053 **Telephone:** 860-225-5111 **Fax:** 860-827-3895	**Web Site:** www.stanleyblackanddecker.com **Officers:** George W. Buckley - Chairman James M. Loree - President, Chief Executive Officer, Executive Vice President, Chief Operating Officer	**Auditors:** Ernst & Young LLP **Transfer Agents:** Computershare Investor Services, Canton, MA

STARWOOD PROPERTY TRUST INC.

Exchange	Symbol	Price	52Wk Range	Yield	P/E
NYS	STWD	$24.86 (12/31/2019)	25.45-19.69	7.72	16.36

7 Year Price Score 83.61 **NYSE Composite Index=100** **12 Month Price Score 100.60**

Interim Earnings (Per Share)

Qtr.	Mar	Jun	Sep	Dec
2016	0.11	0.47	0.44	0.50
2017	0.39	0.44	0.33	0.35
2018	0.38	0.40	0.31	0.33
2019	0.25	0.45	0.49	...

Interim Dividends (Per Share)

Amt	Decl	Ex	Rec	Pay
0.48Q	02/28/2019	03/28/2019	03/29/2019	04/15/2019
0.48Q	05/08/2019	06/27/2019	06/28/2019	07/15/2019
0.48Q	08/07/2019	09/27/2019	09/30/2019	10/15/2019
0.48Q	11/08/2019	12/30/2019	12/31/2019	01/15/2020

Indicated Div: $1.92

Valuation Analysis

		Institutional Holding	
Forecast EPS	$1.86 (01/15/2020)	No of Institutions	564
Market Cap	$7.0 Billion	Shares	
Book Value	$4.7 Billion	212,203,952	
Price/Book	1.51	% Held	
Price/Sales	5.82	65.38	

Business Summary: REITs (MIC: 5.3.1 SIC: 6798 NAIC: 525930)

Starwood Property Trust is a holding company. Co. conducts its operations as a real estate investment trust. Co. has four business segments: Real estate commercial and residential lending, which engages mainly in originating, acquiring, financing and managing commercial and residential first mortgages and subordinated mortgages; Infrastructure lending, which engages mainly in originating, acquiring, financing and managing infrastructure debt investments; Real estate property, which engages mainly in acquiring and managing equity interests in commercial real estate properties; and Real estate investing and servicing, which includes a servicing business in the U.S and an investment business.

Recent Developments: For the quarter ended Sep 30 2019, net income increased 67.8% to US$150.0 million from US$89.4 million in the year-earlier quarter. Revenues were US$288.3 million, up 0.9% from US$285.7 million the year before. Revenues from property income fell 7.1% to US$84.7 million from US$91.1 million in the corresponding quarter a year earlier.

Prospects: Our evaluation of Starwood Properties Trust Inc. as of October 4th, 2019 is the result of our systematic analysis on three basic characteristics: earnings strength, relative valuation, and recent stock price movement. The company has enjoyed a very positive trend in earnings per share over the past 5 quarters. However, recent analyst estimates for the company have been mixed and STWD has posted results in line with analysts' expectations. Based on operating earnings yield, the company is undervalued when compared to all of the companies we cover. Share price changes over the past year indicates that STWD will perform well over the near term.

Financial Data

(US$ in Thousands)	9 Mos	6 Mos	3 Mos	12/31/2018	12/31/2017	12/31/2016	12/31/2015	12/31/2014
Earnings Per Share	1.52	1.34	1.29	1.42	1.52	1.50	1.91	2.24
Cash Flow Per Share	(0.57)	0.90	1.44	2.21	(0.95)	2.33	2.62	1.03
Tang Book Value Per Share	15.16	15.10	15.07	15.23	15.90	16.05	15.99	16.00
Dividends Per Share	1.920	1.920	1.920	1.920	1.920	1.920	1.920	1.920
Dividend Payout %	126.32	143.28	148.84	135.21	126.32	128.00	100.52	85.71
Income Statement								
Total Revenue	909,991	621,661	310,480	1,109,280	879,888	784,667	735,877	702,875
EBITDA	374,914	217,997	80,432	586,442	545,509	453,700	505,396	548,394
Depn & Amortn	7,579	5,176	3,590	170,455	131,725	99,428	62,681	42,141
Income Before Taxes	367,335	212,821	76,842	415,987	413,784	354,272	442,715	506,253
Income Taxes	8,380	3,867	334	15,330	31,522	8,344	17,206	24,096
Net Income	337,795	197,399	70,383	385,830	400,770	365,186	450,697	495,021
Average Shares	289,912	289,072	277,698	288,484	262,079	241,794	234,142	218,781
Balance Sheet								
Current Assets	446,435	577,578	606,298	600,911	499,918	768,340	471,289	370,621
Total Assets	74,434,100	72,947,361	72,165,588	68,262,453	62,941,289	77,256,266	85,738,138	116,099,297
Current Liabilities	400,660	387,893	363,140	410,587	389,602	364,931	317,903	298,932
Long-Term Obligations	11,102,217	11,209,598	11,157,705	10,756,635	7,972,476	6,200,670	5,432,278	4,685,252
Total Liabilities	69,778,904	68,309,654	67,544,509	63,659,021	58,462,875	72,733,992	81,597,822	112,238,441
Stockholders' Equity	4,655,196	4,637,707	4,621,079	4,603,432	4,478,414	4,522,274	4,140,316	3,860,856
Shares Outstanding	281,937	281,271	280,301	275,659	261,376	259,286	237,490	223,538
Statistical Record								
Return on Assets %	0.63	0.56	0.53	0.59	0.57	0.45	0.45	0.44
Return on Equity %	9.27	8.24	7.85	8.50	8.91	8.41	11.27	12.16
EBITDA Margin %	41.20	35.07	25.91	52.87	62.00	57.82	68.68	78.02
Net Margin %	37.12	31.75	22.67	34.78	45.55	46.54	61.25	70.43
Asset Turnover	0.02	0.02	0.02	0.02	0.01	0.01	0.01	0.01
Current Ratio	1.11	1.49	1.67	1.46	1.28	2.11	1.48	1.24
Debt to Equity	2.38	2.42	2.41	2.34	1.78	1.37	1.31	1.21
Price Range	24.86-19.36	23.16-19.36	22.90-19.36	22.90-19.36	22.97-21.32	23.30-16.93	24.67-19.74	30.67-21.78
P/E Ratio	16.36-12.74	17.28-14.45	17.75-15.01	16.13-13.63	15.11-14.03	15.53-11.29	12.92-10.34	13.69-9.72
Average Yield %	8.56	8.71	8.82	8.94	8.67	9.22	8.54	8.01

Address: 591 West Putnam Avenue, Greenwich, CT 06830	Web Site: www.starwoodpropertytrust.com	Auditors: Deloitte & Touche LLP
Telephone: 203-422-7100	Officers: Barry S. Sternlicht - Chairman, Chief Executive Officer Jeffrey F. DiModica - President	Investor Contact: 202-422-7700 Transfer Agents: American Stock Transfer & Trust Company, LLC

STATE STREET CORP.

Exchange	Symbol	Price	52Wk Range	Yield	P/E
NYS	STT	$79.10 (12/31/2019)	80.42-48.81	2.63	15.69

*7 Year Price Score 71.79   *NYSE Composite Index=100   *12 Month Price Score 109.83

Interim Earnings (Per Share)

Qtr.	Mar	Jun	Sep	Dec
2016	0.79	1.47	1.29	1.43
2017	1.15	1.53	1.66	0.89
2018	1.62	1.88	1.87	1.02
2019	1.18	1.42	1.42	...

Interim Dividends (Per Share)

Amt	Decl	Ex	Rec	Pay
0.47Q	02/21/2019	03/29/2019	04/01/2019	04/15/2019
0.47Q	05/15/2019	06/28/2019	07/01/2019	07/16/2019
0.52Q	09/19/2019	09/30/2019	10/01/2019	10/15/2019
0.52Q	12/19/2019	12/31/2019	01/02/2020	01/16/2020

Indicated Div: $2.08

Valuation Analysis

		Institutional Holding	
Forecast EPS	$5.90	No of Institutions	
	(01/17/2020)	1225	
Market Cap	$28.8 Billion	Shares	
Book Value	$25.2 Billion	404,207,424	
Price/Book	1.14	% Held	
Price/Sales	2.20	88.23	

Business Summary: Banking (MIC: 5.1.1 SIC: 6022 NAIC: 522110)

State Street is a financial holding company. Through its subsidiaries, Co. provides financial products and services to institutional investors. Co. has two lines of business: Investment Servicing, which provides, among others, custody, product and participant level accounting, daily pricing and administration, master trust and master custody, depotbank services, record-keeping, cash management, foreign exchange, brokerage and other trading services; and Investment Management, which provides a range of services and solutions, including environmental, social and governance investing, defined benefit and defined contribution and Outsourced Chief Investment Officer.

Recent Developments: For the quarter ended Sep 30 2019, net income decreased 23.7% to US$583.0 million from US$764.0 million in the year-earlier quarter. Net interest income decreased 4.2% to US$644.0 million from US$672.0 million in the year-earlier quarter. Provision for loan losses was US$2.0 million versus US$5.0 million in the prior-year quarter, a decrease of 60.0%. Non-interest income fell 2.5% to US$2.26 billion from US$2.32 billion, while non-interest expense advanced 4.3% to US$2.18 billion.

Prospects: Our evaluation of State Street Corp. as of October 4th, 2019 is the result of our systematic analysis on three basic characteristics: earnings strength, relative valuation, and recent stock price movement. The company has managed to produce a neutral trend in earnings per share over the past 5 quarters. However, recent analyst estimates for the company have been reduced while STT has posted results that exceeded analysts' expectations. Based on operating earnings yield, the company is undervalued when compared to all of the companies we cover. Share price changes over the past year indicates that STT will perform very poorly over the near term.

Financial Data

(US$ in Thousands)	9 Mos	6 Mos	3 Mos	12/31/2018	12/31/2017	12/31/2016	12/31/2015	12/31/2014
Earnings Per Share	5.04	5.49	5.95	6.40	5.24	4.97	4.47	4.57
Cash Flow Per Share	17.10	18.66	13.56	28.11	18.50	5.83	(3.44)	(1.32)
Tang Book Value Per Share	32.84	32.33	30.77	29.70	31.24	27.38	27.43	28.09
Dividends Per Share	1.930	1.880	1.830	1.780	1.600	1.440	1.320	1.160
Dividend Payout %	38.29	34.24	30.76	27.81	30.53	28.97	29.53	25.38
Income Statement								
Interest Income	3,035,000	2,034,000	1,027,000	3,662,000	2,908,000	2,512,000	2,488,000	2,652,000
Interest Expense	1,105,000	748,000	354,000	991,000	604,000	428,000	400,000	392,000
Net Interest Income	1,930,000	1,286,000	673,000	2,671,000	2,304,000	2,084,000	2,088,000	2,260,000
Provision for Losses	7,000	5,000	4,000	15,000	2,000	10,000	12,000	10,000
Non-Interest Income	6,778,000	4,519,000	2,259,000	9,311,000	8,866,000	8,123,000	8,272,000	8,035,000
Non-Interest Expense	6,627,000	4,447,000	2,293,000	8,968,000	8,269,000	8,077,000	8,050,000	7,827,000
Income Before Taxes	2,074,000	1,353,000	635,000	2,999,000	2,899,000	2,120,000	2,298,000	2,458,000
Income Taxes	396,000	258,000	127,000	400,000	722,000	(22,000)	318,000	421,000
Net Income	1,678,000	1,095,000	508,000	2,599,000	2,177,000	2,143,000	1,980,000	2,037,000
Average Shares	370,595	377,577	381,703	376,476	380,213	396,090	413,638	432,007
Balance Sheet								
Net Loans & Leases	26,938,000	25,349,000	23,311,000	25,722,000	23,240,000	19,704,000	18,753,000	18,161,000
Total Assets	244,606,000	241,540,000	228,332,000	244,626,000	238,425,000	242,698,000	245,192,000	274,119,000
Total Deposits	170,886,000	170,594,000	162,471,000	180,360,000	184,896,000	187,163,000	191,627,000	209,040,000
Total Liabilities	219,397,000	216,086,000	203,294,000	219,836,000	216,108,000	221,479,000	224,089,000	252,646,000
Stockholders' Equity	25,209,000	25,454,000	25,038,000	24,790,000	22,317,000	21,219,000	21,103,000	21,473,000
Shares Outstanding	363,623	372,572	376,720	379,946	367,649	381,939	399,651	415,195
Statistical Record								
Return on Assets %	0.88	0.94	1.02	1.08	0.90	0.88	0.76	0.79
Return on Equity %	8.51	9.57	10.31	11.03	10.00	10.10	9.30	9.73
Net Interest Margin %	64.34	60.87	65.53	72.94	79.23	82.96	83.92	85.22
Efficiency Ratio %	66.87	65.93	69.78	69.13	70.23	75.95	74.81	73.24
Loans to Deposits	0.16	0.15	0.14	0.14	0.13	0.11	0.10	0.09
Price Range	87.14-48.81	95.33-54.53	104.18-59.78	112.71-59.78	99.29-75.97	81.44-50.79	80.84-64.73	80.33-63.19
P/E Ratio	17.29-9.68	17.36-9.93	17.51-10.05	17.61-9.34	18.95-14.50	16.39-10.22	18.09-14.48	17.58-13.83
Average Yield %	2.99	2.58	2.23	1.96	1.82	2.24	1.78	1.65

Address: One Lincoln Street, Boston, MA 02111	Web Site: www.statestreet.com	Auditors: Ernst & Young LLP
Telephone: 617-786-3000	Officers: Joseph L. Hooley - Chairman, Chief Executive Officer, President, Chief Operating Officer Ronald P. O'Hanley - Vice-Chairman, President, Chief Executive Officer, Chief Operating Officer	Investor Contact: 617-664-3477 Transfer Agents: American Stock Transfer & Trust Company, LLC, Brooklyn, NY

STEPAN CO.

Exchange	Symbol	Price	52Wk Range	Yield	P/E	Div Achiever
NYS	SCL	$102.44 (12/31/2019)	102.44-72.71	1.07	22.13	51 Years

*7 Year Price Score 112.07 ***NYSE Composite Index=100** ***12 Month Price Score 100.73**

Interim Earnings (Per Share)
Qtr.	Mar	Jun	Sep	Dec
2016	1.21	1.21	0.89	0.42
2017	1.37	1.19	0.94	0.42
2018	1.31	1.41	0.95	1.15
2019	1.07	1.30	1.11	...

Interim Dividends (Per Share)
Amt	Decl	Ex	Rec	Pay
0.25Q	02/20/2019	03/01/2019	03/04/2019	03/15/2019
0.25Q	04/29/2019	05/30/2019	05/31/2019	06/14/2019
0.25Q	07/23/2019	08/29/2019	08/30/2019	09/13/2019
0.275Q	10/22/2019	11/27/2019	11/29/2019	12/13/2019

Indicated Div: $1.10

Valuation Analysis
		Institutional Holding
Forecast EPS	$4.89 (11/28/2019)	No of Institutions 268
Market Cap	$2.3 Billion	Shares
Book Value	$854.2 Million	20,359,818
Price/Book	2.70	% Held
Price/Sales	1.23	73.90

Business Summary: Specialty Chemicals (MIC: 8.3.2 SIC: 2843 NAIC: 325613)

Stepan is engaged in the production and sale of specialty and intermediate chemicals, which are sold to other manufacturers for use in a variety of end products. Co. has three reportable segments: Surfactants, which are used in a variety of consumer and industrial cleaning compounds as well as in agricultural products, lubricating ingredients, oil field chemicals and other applications; Polymers, which are used primarily in plastics, building materials, refrigeration systems and coatings, adhesives, sealants and elastomers applications; and Specialty Products, which are used in food, flavoring, nutritional supplement and pharmaceutical applications.

Recent Developments: For the quarter ended Sep 30 2019, net income increased 19.0% to US$25.9 million from US$21.8 million in the year-earlier quarter. Revenues were US$451.6 million, down 11.1% from US$508.0 million the year before. Operating income was US$28.0 million versus US$27.1 million in the prior-year quarter, an increase of 3.0%. Direct operating expenses declined 11.8% to US$374.2 million from US$424.4 million in the comparable period the year before. Indirect operating expenses decreased 12.4% to US$49.4 million from US$56.4 million in the equivalent prior-year period.

Prospects: Our evaluation of Stepan Co. as of October 4th, 2019 is the result of our systematic analysis on three basic characteristics: earnings strength, relative valuation, and recent stock price movement. The company has produced a positive trend in earnings per share over the past 5 quarters. In addition, recent analyst estimates for the company have been raised, and SCL has posted results that exceeded analysts' expectations. Based on operating earnings yield, the company is fairly valued when compared to all of the companies we cover. Share price changes over the past year indicates that SCL will perform well over the near term.

Financial Data
(US$ in Thousands)	9 Mos	6 Mos	3 Mos	12/31/2018	12/31/2017	12/31/2016	12/31/2015	12/31/2014
Earnings Per Share	4.63	4.47	4.58	4.83	3.92	3.73	3.32	2.49
Cash Flow Per Share	9.02	8.49	7.56	7.43	8.67	9.28	8.06	3.60
Tang Book Value Per Share	36.46	36.44	35.17	33.17	30.94	26.17	23.69	22.61
Dividends Per Share	1.000	0.975	0.950	0.925	0.840	0.775	0.730	0.690
Dividend Payout %	21.60	21.81	20.74	19.15	21.43	20.78	21.99	27.71
Income Statement								
Total Revenue	1,413,755	962,173	489,170	1,993,857	1,925,007	1,766,166	1,776,167	1,927,213
EBITDA	161,579	113,142	52,286	231,809	229,703	201,988	191,359	155,788
Depn & Amortn	58,545	38,959	19,403	81,115	79,022	74,967	66,985	63,804
Income Before Taxes	98,013	70,564	31,030	139,923	139,237	113,816	109,841	80,543
Income Taxes	16,945	15,376	6,052	27,173	47,690	27,618	26,819	18,454
Net Income	81,091	55,202	24,984	112,762	91,578	86,191	75,968	57,101
Average Shares	23,300	23,329	23,332	23,325	23,377	23,094	22,858	22,917
Balance Sheet								
Current Assets	798,028	806,807	808,136	802,530	788,736	685,541	619,573	575,556
Total Assets	1,518,370	1,528,968	1,526,000	1,484,666	1,470,861	1,353,890	1,239,661	1,162,014
Current Liabilities	292,963	299,466	295,448	338,582	320,253	297,265	243,244	249,513
Long-Term Obligations	236,847	237,460	270,424	239,022	268,299	288,859	313,817	246,897
Total Liabilities	664,161	671,310	694,553	700,900	730,765	719,286	682,677	626,468
Stockholders' Equity	854,209	857,658	831,447	783,766	740,096	634,604	556,984	535,546
Shares Outstanding	22,505	22,556	22,613	22,505	22,509	22,424	22,280	22,255
Statistical Record								
Return on Assets %	7.18	6.98	7.12	7.63	6.48	6.63	6.33	4.90
Return on Equity %	13.24	12.89	13.33	14.80	13.32	14.43	13.91	10.50
EBITDA Margin %	11.43	11.76	10.69	11.63	11.93	11.44	10.77	8.08
Net Margin %	5.74	5.74	5.11	5.66	4.76	4.88	4.28	2.96
Asset Turnover	1.25	1.30	1.32	1.35	1.36	1.36	1.48	1.65
Current Ratio	2.72	2.69	2.74	2.37	2.46	2.31	2.55	2.31
Debt to Equity	0.28	0.28	0.33	0.30	0.36	0.46	0.56	0.46
Price Range	99.37-70.10	94.32-70.10	94.32-68.42	90.10-68.42	91.52-70.75	86.38-41.88	55.18-37.74	66.47-37.02
P/E Ratio	21.46-15.14	21.10-15.68	20.59-14.94	18.65-14.17	23.35-18.05	23.16-11.23	16.62-11.37	26.69-14.87
Average Yield %	1.14	1.14	1.15	1.15	1.03	1.23	1.57	1.31

Address: 22 West Frontage Road, Northfield, IL 60093
Telephone: 847-446-7500

Web Site: www.stepan.com
Officers: F. Quinn Stepan - Chairman, President, Chief Executive Officer Frank Pacholec - Vice President, Vice President (frmr), Chief Sustainability Officer, Interim Chief Technology Officer

Auditors: DELOITTE & TOUCHE LLP
Investor Contact: 847-446-7500
Transfer Agents: Computershare Investor Services, LLC, Chicago, IL

STERIS PLC (IRELAND)

Exchange	Symbol	Price	52Wk Range	Yield	P/E
NYS	STE	$152.42 (12/31/2019)	155.40-101.48	0.94	38.69

*7 Year Price Score 142.26 *NYSE Composite Index=100 *12 Month Price Score 103.44

Interim Earnings (Per Share)

Qtr.	Jun	Sep	Dec	Mar
2016-17	0.56	0.47	(0.06)	0.31
2017-18	0.68	0.75	1.11	0.86
2018-19	0.82	0.91	0.56	1.28
2019-20	0.99	1.11	...	...

Interim Dividends (Per Share)

Amt	Decl	Ex	Rec	Pay
0.34Q	05/07/2019	06/11/2019	06/12/2019	06/28/2019
0.37Q	08/05/2019	09/09/2019	09/10/2019	09/26/2019
0.37Q	11/04/2019	11/25/2019	11/26/2019	12/20/2019

Indicated Div: $1.44

Valuation Analysis

		Institutional Holding	
Forecast EPS	N/A	No of Institutions	N/A
Market Cap	$12.9 Billion	Shares	N/A
Book Value	$3.2 Billion	% Held	N/A
Price/Book	4.00		
Price/Sales	4.46	N/A	

Business Summary: Medical Instruments & Equipment (MIC: 4.3.1 SIC: 3842 NAIC: 339113)

STERIS is a provider of infection prevention and other procedural products and services. Co. has four segments: Healthcare Products, which provides a portfolio of infection prevention, procedural and gastrointestinal solutions including consumable products, equipment maintenance and installation services; Healthcare Specialty Services, which provides a range of solutions and managed services including hospital sterilization services and instrument and scope repairs; Life Sciences, which designs, manufactures and sells consumable products, equipment maintenance, other services and capital equipment; and Applied Sterilization Technologies, which provides contract sterilization services.

Recent Developments: For the quarter ended Sep 30 2019, net income increased 22.8% to US$95.1 million from US$77.5 million in the year-earlier quarter. Revenues were US$736.8 million, up 8.5% from US$679.0 million the year before. Operating income was US$126.7 million versus US$106.6 million in the prior-year quarter, an increase of 18.9%. Direct operating expenses rose 6.1% to US$418.2 million from US$394.3 million in the comparable period the year before. Indirect operating expenses increased 7.8% to US$191.9 million from US$178.1 million in the equivalent prior-year period.

Prospects: Our evaluation of Steris PLC (Ireland) as of October 4th, 2019 is the result of our systematic analysis on three basic characteristics: earnings strength, relative valuation, and recent stock price movement. The company has managed to produce a neutral trend in earnings per share over the past 5 quarters. In addition, recent analyst estimates for the company have been mixed and STE has posted results that exceeded analysts' expectations. Based on operating earnings yield, the company is fairly valued when compared to all of the companies we cover. Share price changes over the past year indicates that STE will perform over the near term.

Financial Data

(US$ in Thousands)	6 Mos	3 Mos	03/31/2019	03/31/2018	03/31/2017	03/31/2016	03/31/2015	03/31/2014
Earnings Per Share	3.94	3.74	3.56	3.39	1.28	1.56	2.25	2.17
Cash Flow Per Share	6.76	6.48	6.38	5.38	4.96	3.59	4.14	3.56
Tang Book Value Per Share	3.93	3.39	2.96	0.53	N.M.	N.M.	3.54	4.93
Dividends Per Share	1.390	1.360	1.330	1.210	1.090	0.980	0.900	0.820
Dividend Payout %	35.28	36.36	37.36	35.69	85.16	62.82	40.00	37.79
Income Statement								
Total Revenue	1,433,643	696,803	2,782,170	2,619,996	2,612,756	2,238,764	1,850,263	1,622,252
EBITDA	333,557	157,190	538,639	511,591	347,131	306,885	288,692	263,844
Depn & Amortn	96,736	47,102	127,174	108,137	119,536	93,958	61,481	57,037
Income Before Taxes	216,717	99,410	369,470	354,982	184,646	171,884	208,820	188,376
Income Taxes	36,798	14,633	64,394	63,360	74,015	60,299	73,756	58,934
Net Income	179,359	84,590	304,051	290,915	109,965	110,763	135,064	129,442
Average Shares	85,695	85,566	85,468	85,713	86,094	71,184	60,045	59,745
Balance Sheet								
Current Assets	1,031,954	1,044,282	1,053,735	989,657	1,017,802	972,525	720,432	674,745
Total Assets	5,185,717	5,229,723	5,073,071	5,200,334	4,924,455	5,346,416	2,099,466	1,887,162
Current Liabilities	428,023	432,774	465,196	398,462	381,583	400,606	283,331	254,506
Long-Term Obligations	1,187,195	1,210,003	1,183,227	1,316,001	1,478,361	1,567,796	623,250	493,480
Total Liabilities	1,957,049	1,992,823	1,895,261	1,994,374	2,125,853	2,323,382	1,027,834	848,457
Stockholders' Equity	3,228,668	3,236,900	3,177,810	3,205,960	2,798,602	3,023,034	1,071,632	1,038,705
Shares Outstanding	84,797	84,754	84,517	84,517	84,948	85,920	59,675	58,968
Statistical Record								
Return on Assets %	6.58	6.20	5.92	5.75	2.14	2.97	6.78	7.10
Return on Equity %	10.59	10.08	9.53	9.69	3.78	5.40	12.80	13.05
EBITDA Margin %	23.27	22.56	19.36	19.53	13.29	13.71	15.60	16.26
Net Margin %	12.51	12.14	10.93	11.10	4.21	4.95	7.30	7.98
Asset Turnover	0.57	0.55	0.54	0.52	0.51	0.60	0.93	0.89
Current Ratio	2.41	2.41	2.27	2.48	2.67	2.43	2.54	2.65
Debt to Equity	0.37	0.37	0.37	0.41	0.53	0.52	0.58	0.48
Price Range	155.40-99.58	148.88-99.58	128.03-91.02	95.85-69.22	73.90-63.28	77.73-61.96	70.38-47.64	49.76-39.02
P/E Ratio	39.44-25.27	39.81-26.63	35.96-25.57	28.27-20.42	57.73-49.44	49.83-39.72	31.28-21.17	22.93-17.98
Average Yield %	1.08	1.04	1.20	1.42	1.57	1.43	1.54	1.83

Address: 70 Sir John Rogerson's Quay, Dublin 2, 44060-1834 Telephone: 123-220-00	Web Site: www.steris-ir.com Officers: Mohsen M. Sohi - Chairman Walter M. Rosebrough - President, Chief Executive Officer	Auditors: Ernst & Young LLP Investor Contact: 440-392-7245 Transfer Agents: Computershare, Providence, RI

STERLING BANCORP (DE)

*7 Year Price Score 95.95   ***NYSE Composite Index=100**   ***12 Month Price Score 97.41**

TRADING VOLUME (thousand shares)

Interim Earnings (Per Share)

Qtr.	Mar	Jun	Sep	Dec
2016	0.18	0.29	0.29	0.31
2017	0.29	0.31	0.33	(0.35)
2018	0.43	0.50	0.52	0.50
2019	0.47	0.46	0.59	...

Interim Dividends (Per Share)

Amt	Decl	Ex	Rec	Pay
0.07Q	01/23/2019	02/01/2019	02/04/2019	02/19/2019
0.07Q	04/24/2019	05/03/2019	05/06/2019	05/20/2019
0.07Q	07/24/2019	08/02/2019	08/05/2019	08/19/2019
0.07Q	10/23/2019	11/01/2019	11/04/2019	11/18/2019

Indicated Div: $0.28

Valuation Analysis

		Institutional Holding	
Forecast EPS	$2.05	No of Institutions	
	(01/17/2020)	93	
Market Cap	$4.3 Billion	Shares	
Book Value	$4.5 Billion	15,567,962	
Price/Book	0.94	% Held	
Price/Sales	3.23	N/A	

Business Summary: Banking (MIC: 5.1.1 SIC: 6021 NAIC: 522110)

Sterling Bancorp is a bank holding company and financial holding company. Through its subsidiary, Sterling National Bank (the Bank), Co. provides commercial, business, and consumer banking products and services. The Bank's principal business is accepting deposits and, together with funds generated from operations and borrowings, investing in various types of loans and securities. The Bank also operates its commercial finance businesses, which include asset-based lending, payroll financing, factoring, warehouse lending, equipment financing, and public sector financing. Co.'s commercial banking teams focus on the origination of commercial and industria loans and commercial mortgage loans.

Recent Developments: For the quarter ended Sep 30 2019, net income increased 2.3% to US$122.4 million from US$119.7 million in the year-earlier quarter. Net interest income decreased 8.5% to US$223.3 million from US$243.9 million in the year-earlier quarter. Provision for loan losses was US$13.7 million versus US$9.5 million in the prior-year quarter, an increase of 44.2%. Non-interest income rose 114.7% to US$51.8 million from US$24.1 million, while non-interest expense declined 4.8% to US$106.5 million.

Prospects: Our evaluation of Sterling Bancorp as of October 4th, 2019 is the result of our systematic analysis on three basic characteristics: earnings strength, relative valuation, and recent stock price movement. The company has managed to produce a neutral trend in earnings per share over the past 5 quarters. However, recent analyst estimates for the company have been reduced and STL has posted results that fell short of analysts' expectations. Based on operating earnings yield, the company is undervalued when compared to all of the companies we cover. Share price changes over the past year indicates that STL will perform poorly over the near term.

Financial Data
(US$ in Thousands)

	9 Mos	6 Mos	3 Mos	12/31/2018	12/31/2017	12/31/2016	12/31/2015	12/31/2014
Earnings Per Share	2.02	1.95	1.99	1.95	0.58	1.07	0.60	0.20
Cash Flow Per Share	2.22	2.09	2.07	1.76	1.54	1.52	0.83	(1.03)
Tang Book Value Per Share	12.90	12.40	11.92	11.78	10.53	8.08	7.05	6.47
Dividends Per Share	0.280	0.280	0.280	0.280	0.280	0.280	0.280	0.070
Dividend Payout %	13.86	14.36	14.07	14.36	48.28	26.17	46.67	35.00
Income Statement								
Interest Income	907,066	611,857	309,400	1,208,473	682,449	461,551	348,141	68,087
Interest Expense	216,400	144,512	73,894	241,070	106,306	57,282	36,925	7,850
Net Interest Income	690,666	467,345	235,506	967,403	576,143	404,269	311,216	60,237
Provision for Losses	35,400	21,700	10,200	46,000	26,000	20,000	15,700	3,000
Non-Interest Income	90,172	38,342	11,284	91,397	64,202	70,987	62,751	13,957
Non-Interest Expense	345,361	239,442	114,409	458,370	433,375	247,902	260,318	45,814
Income Before Taxes	405,364	250,368	129,911	566,230	180,970	207,354	97,949	25,380
Income Taxes	85,020	52,471	28,474	118,976	87,939	67,382	31,835	8,376
Net Income	320,344	197,897	101,437	447,254	93,031	139,972	66,114	17,004
Average Shares	203,566	207,376	213,505	224,816	158,124	131,234	110,329	84,194
Balance Sheet								
Net Loans & Leases	20,730,055	20,292,863	20,058,485	20,688,832	19,936,322	9,505,497	7,843,325	4,819,866
Total Assets	30,077,665	30,237,545	29,956,607	31,383,307	30,359,541	14,178,447	11,955,952	7,424,822
Total Deposits	21,579,324	20,948,464	21,225,639	21,214,148	20,538,204	10,068,259	8,580,007	5,212,325
Total Liabilities	25,556,698	25,778,387	25,537,384	26,954,454	26,119,363	12,323,264	10,290,879	6,449,622
Stockholders' Equity	4,520,967	4,459,158	4,419,223	4,428,853	4,240,178	1,855,183	1,665,073	975,200
Shares Outstanding	202,392	205,187	209,560	216,227	224,782	135,257	130,006	83,927
Statistical Record								
Return on Assets %	1.42	1.40	1.49	1.45	0.42	1.07	0.68	1.18
Return on Equity %	9.71	9.81	10.35	10.32	3.05	7.93	5.01	9.25
Net Interest Margin %	75.65	76.65	76.12	80.05	84.42	87.59	89.39	88.47
Efficiency Ratio %	30.52	37.94	35.68	35.26	58.04	46.55	63.35	55.84
Loans to Deposits	0.96	0.97	0.95	0.98	0.97	0.94	0.91	0.92
Price Range	22.55-15.73	24.45-15.73	25.30-15.73	26.25-15.73	26.05-21.15	24.40-13.57	17.61-12.97	14.49-11.05
P/E Ratio	11.16-7.79	12.54-8.07	12.71-7.90	13.46-8.07	44.91-36.47	22.80-12.68	29.35-21.62	72.45-55.25
Average Yield %	1.43	1.38	1.33	1.25	1.19	1.62	1.93	0.55

Address: 400 Rella Boulevard, Montebello, NY 10901 Telephone: 845-369-8040	Web Site: www.sterlingbancorp.com Officers: Richard L. O'Toole - Chairman Jack L. Kopnisky - President, Chief Executive Officer	Auditors: Crowe LLP Investor Contact: 845-369-8040 Transfer Agents: Registrar and Transfer Company, Crandford, NJ

STORE CAPITAL CORP

Exchange	Symbol	Price	52Wk Range	Yield	P/E
NYS	STOR	$37.24 (12/31/2019)	40.80-27.46	3.76	30.03

*7 Year Price Score N/A *NYSE Composite Index=100 *12 Month Price Score 105.72

Interim Earnings (Per Share)

Qtr.	Mar	Jun	Sep	Dec
2016	0.18	0.21	0.24	0.20
2017	0.19	0.35	0.15	0.21
2018	0.26	0.31	0.23	0.26
2019	0.20	0.30	0.48	...

Interim Dividends (Per Share)

Amt	Decl	Ex	Rec	Pay
0.33Q	03/15/2019	03/28/2019	03/29/2019	04/15/2019
0.33Q	06/17/2019	06/27/2019	06/28/2019	07/15/2019
0.35Q	09/10/2019	09/27/2019	09/30/2019	10/15/2019
0.35Q	12/16/2019	12/30/2019	12/31/2019	01/15/2020

Indicated Div: $1.40

Valuation Analysis

		Institutional Holding	
Forecast EPS	$1.22 (01/16/2020)	No of Institutions	476
Market Cap	$8.7 Billion	Shares	
Book Value	$4.3 Billion		229,706,528
Price/Book	2.03	% Held	
Price/Sales	13.68		98.55

Business Summary: REITs (MIC: 5.3.1 SIC: 6798 NAIC: 525930)

Store Capital is an internally managed net-lease real estate investment trust, that is engaged in the acquisition, investment and management of Single Tenant Operational Real Estate properties. Co.'s customers operate across a variety of industries within the service, retail and manufacturing sectors of the U.S. economy, with restaurants, early childhood education centers, furniture stores, health clubs and movie theaters representing the main industries in Co.'s portfolio. From time to time, Co. also provides mortgage financing to its customers.

Recent Developments: For the quarter ended Sep 30 2019, net income increased 131.5% to US$111.6 million from US$48.2 million in the year-earlier quarter. Revenues were US$171.8 million, up 25.4% from US$137.0 million the year before. Revenues from property income rose 21.7% to US$158.0 million from US$129.8 million in the corresponding quarter a year earlier.

Prospects: Our evaluation of STORE Capital Corp as of October 4th, 2019 is the result of our systematic analysis on three basic characteristics: earnings strength, relative valuation, and recent stock price movement. The company has managed to produce a neutral trend in earnings per share over the past 5 quarters. Additionally, recent analyst estimates for the company have been unchanged while STOR has posted results that exceeded analysts' expectations. Based on operating earnings yield, the company is overvalued when compared to all of the companies we cover. Share price changes over the past year indicates that STOR will perform over the near term.

Financial Data

(US$ in Thousands)	9 Mos	6 Mos	3 Mos	12/31/2018	12/31/2017	12/31/2016	12/31/2015	12/31/2014
Earnings Per Share	1.24	0.99	1.00	1.06	0.90	0.82	0.68	0.61
Cash Flow Per Share	1.91	1.89	1.80	1.92	1.73	1.65	1.52	1.38
Tang Book Value Per Share	18.35	17.88	17.63	17.48	16.36	15.58	14.62	13.74
Dividends Per Share	1.340	1.320	1.300	1.280	1.200	1.120	1.040	0.114
Dividend Payout %	108.06	133.33	130.00	120.75	133.33	136.59	152.94	18.67
Income Statement								
Total Revenue	492,259	320,425	156,638	540,756	452,847	376,343	284,762	190,441
EBITDA	357,028	200,367	87,554	546,656	411,553	349,550	264,361	177,110
Depn & Amortn	14,535	9,010	3,737	199,983	168,188	133,907	99,857	66,465
Income Before Taxes	225,671	113,860	45,749	217,612	122,887	110,463	82,722	42,686
Income Taxes	533	340	193	642	453	358	274	180
Net Income	225,138	113,520	45,556	216,970	162,038	123,325	83,770	48,139
Average Shares	232,645	228,242	222,637	204,933	178,656	149,124	122,207	78,454
Balance Sheet								
Current Assets	27,553	25,368	37,352	27,511	42,937	54,200	67,115	136,313
Total Assets	7,813,427	7,699,974	7,479,342	7,113,971	5,899,777	4,941,668	3,911,388	2,913,612
Current Liabilities	82,181	76,009	74,676	207,954	350,068	94,209	246,670	43,609
Long-Term Obligations	3,287,126	3,365,682	3,298,188	2,925,312	2,306,901	2,303,671	1,597,505	1,284,151
Total Liabilities	3,504,336	3,581,485	3,490,187	3,250,470	2,728,835	2,458,413	1,851,595	1,330,928
Stockholders' Equity	4,309,091	4,118,489	3,989,155	3,863,501	3,170,942	2,483,255	2,059,793	1,582,684
Shares Outstanding	234,804	230,330	226,290	221,071	193,766	159,341	140,858	115,212
Statistical Record								
Return on Assets %	3.87	3.11	3.12	3.33	2.99	2.78	2.45	2.05
Return on Equity %	7.11	5.77	5.86	6.17	5.73	5.41	4.60	4.09
EBITDA Margin %	72.53	62.53	55.90	101.09	90.88	92.88	92.84	93.00
Net Margin %	45.74	35.43	29.08	40.12	35.78	32.77	29.42	25.28
Asset Turnover	0.09	0.09	0.08	0.08	0.08	0.08	0.08	0.08
Current Ratio	0.34	0.33	0.50	0.13	0.12	0.58	0.27	3.13
Debt to Equity	0.76	0.82	0.83	0.76	0.73	0.93	0.78	0.81
Price Range	38.72-27.40	35.46-26.96	33.97-24.14	30.85-22.52	26.37-19.77	31.19-22.38	23.77-19.79	22.04-19.50
P/E Ratio	31.23-22.10	35.82-27.23	33.97-24.14	29.10-21.25	29.30-21.97	38.04-27.29	34.96-29.10	36.13-31.97
Average Yield %	4.11	4.31	4.54	4.76	4.99	4.21	4.77	0.55

Address: 8377 East Hartford Drive, Suite 100, Scottsdale, AZ 85255
Telephone: 480-256-1100

Web Site: www.storecapital.com
Officers: Morton H. Fleischer - Chairman Christopher H. Volk - President, Chief Executive Officer

Auditors: Ernst & Young LLP
Transfer Agents: American Stock Transfer & Trust Company, LLC

STRYKER CORP

Exchange	Symbol	Price	52Wk Range	Yield	P/E	Div Acheiver
NYS	SYK	$209.94 (12/31/2019)	221.82-152.46	1.10	23.27	26 Years

*7 Year Price Score 132.82 *NYSE Composite Index=100 *12 Month Price Score 98.11

Interim Earnings (Per Share)

Qtr.	Mar	Jun	Sep	Dec
2016	1.07	1.00	0.94	1.34
2017	1.17	1.03	1.14	(0.66)
2018	1.16	1.19	1.55	5.44
2019	1.09	1.26	1.23	...

Interim Dividends (Per Share)

Amt	Decl	Ex	Rec	Pay
0.52Q	02/06/2019	03/28/2019	03/29/2019	04/30/2019
0.52Q	05/01/2019	06/27/2019	06/28/2019	07/31/2019
0.52Q	07/31/2019	09/27/2019	09/30/2019	10/31/2019
0.575Q	12/04/2019	12/30/2019	12/31/2019	01/31/2020

Indicated Div: $2.30

Valuation Analysis **Institutional Holding**

Forecast EPS	$8.23	No of Institutions
	(01/17/2020)	1807
Market Cap	$78.6 Billion	Shares
Book Value	$12.3 Billion	341,891,360
Price/Book	6.38	% Held
Price/Sales	5.40	73.24

Business Summary: Medical Instruments & Equipment (MIC: 4.3.1 SIC: 3841 NAIC: 339112)

Stryker is a medical technology company. Co. provides products and services in orthopaedics, medical and surgical, and neurotechnology and spine. Co.'s Orthopaedics products consist of implants used in hip and knee joint replacements and trauma and extremities surgeries. Co.'s MedSurg products include surgical equipment and navigation systems, endoscopic and communications systems, patient handling, emergency medical equipment and intensive care disposable products, reprocessed and remanufactured medical devices and other medical device products used in a range of medical specialties. Co.'s Neurotechnology and Spine products include neurosurgical, neurovascular, and spinal implant devices.

Recent Developments: For the quarter ended Sep 30 2019, net income decreased 21.0% to US$466.0 million from US$590.0 million in the year-earlier quarter. Revenues were US$3.59 billion, up 10.6% from US$3.24 billion the year before. Operating income was US$628.0 million versus US$576.0 million in the prior-year quarter, an increase of 9.0%. Direct operating expenses rose 15.6% to US$1.26 billion from US$1.09 billion in the comparable period the year before. Indirect operating expenses increased 7.8% to US$1.70 billion from US$1.58 billion in the equivalent prior-year period.

Prospects: Our evaluation of Stryker Corp. as of October 4th, 2019 is the result of our systematic analysis on three basic characteristics: earnings strength, relative valuation, and recent stock price movement. The company has produced a positive trend in earnings per share over the past 5 quarters. However, recent analyst estimates for the company have been mixed and SYK has posted results that exceeded analysts' expectations. Based on operating earnings yield, the company is fairly valued when compared to all of the companies we cover. Share price changes over the past year indicates that SYK will perform well over the near term.

Financial Data

(US$ in Thousands)	9 Mos	6 Mos	3 Mos	12/31/2018	12/31/2017	12/31/2016	12/31/2015	12/31/2014
Earnings Per Share	9.02	9.34	9.27	9.34	2.68	4.35	3.78	1.34
Cash Flow Per Share	6.69	6.66	7.03	6.98	4.17	4.83	2.39	4.71
Tang Book Value Per Share	N.M.	N.M.	N.M.	N.M.	N.M.	N.M.	6.92	6.33
Dividends Per Share	2.080	2.030	1.980	1.930	1.745	1.565	1.415	1.260
Dividend Payout %	23.06	21.73	21.36	20.66	65.11	35.98	37.43	94.03
Income Statement								
Total Revenue	10,753,000	7,166,000	3,516,000	13,601,000	12,444,000	11,325,000	9,946,000	9,675,000
EBITDA	2,209,000	1,434,000	670,000	3,079,000	2,705,000	2,467,000	2,132,000	1,538,000
Depn & Amortn	583,000	389,000	190,000	723,000	642,000	546,000	397,000	378,000
Income Before Taxes	1,626,000	1,045,000	480,000	2,356,000	2,063,000	1,921,000	1,735,000	1,160,000
Income Taxes	268,000	153,000	68,000	(1,197,000)	1,043,000	274,000	296,000	645,000
Net Income	1,358,000	892,000	412,000	3,553,000	1,020,000	1,647,000	1,439,000	515,000
Average Shares	380,300	379,500	379,300	380,300	380,100	378,500	380,900	382,800
Balance Sheet								
Current Assets	8,566,000	8,185,000	7,888,000	9,733,000	7,993,000	7,861,000	7,944,000	9,673,000
Total Assets	26,659,000	26,354,000	25,937,000	27,229,000	22,197,000	20,435,000	16,247,000	17,713,000
Current Liabilities	3,921,000	3,946,000	3,713,000	4,807,000	3,485,000	3,148,000	3,503,000	4,464,000
Long-Term Obligations	7,889,000	7,974,000	7,950,000	8,486,000	6,590,000	6,686,000	3,253,000	3,246,000
Total Liabilities	14,344,000	14,411,000	14,244,000	15,499,000	12,231,000	10,885,000	7,736,000	9,118,000
Stockholders' Equity	12,315,000	11,943,000	11,693,000	11,730,000	9,966,000	9,550,000	8,511,000	8,595,000
Shares Outstanding	374,400	374,100	373,810	374,400	374,400	375,000	373,000	378,000
Statistical Record								
Return on Assets %	14.06	14.82	14.65	14.38	4.79	8.96	8.47	3.08
Return on Equity %	30.90	33.17	33.69	32.75	10.45	18.19	16.82	5.84
EBITDA Margin %	20.54	20.01	19.06	22.64	21.74	21.78	21.44	15.90
Net Margin %	12.63	12.45	11.72	26.12	8.20	14.54	14.47	5.32
Asset Turnover	0.60	0.59	0.58	0.55	0.58	0.62	0.59	0.58
Current Ratio	2.18	2.07	2.12	2.02	2.29	2.50	2.27	2.17
Debt to Equity	0.64	0.67	0.68	0.72	0.66	0.70	0.38	0.38
Price Range	221.82-145.00	205.58-145.00	198.00-145.00	179.78-145.00	159.74-117.75	122.82-87.53	104.53-90.07	96.61-74.63
P/E Ratio	24.59-16.08	22.01-15.52	21.36-15.64	19.25-15.52	59.60-43.94	28.23-20.12	27.65-23.83	72.10-55.69
Average Yield %	1.10	1.15	1.15	1.16	1.25	1.42	1.48	1.52

Address: 2825 Airview Boulevard, Kalamazoo, MI 49002	Web Site: www.stryker.com	Auditors: Ernst & Young LLP
Telephone: 269-385-2600	Officers: Kevin A. Lobo - Chairman, Chief Executive Officer Timothy J. Scannell - President, Chief Operating Officer, Division Officer	Investor Contact: 269-385-2600
Fax: 269-385-1062		Transfer Agents: American Stock Transfer & Trust Company, LLC, New York, NY

SUN COMMUNITIES INC

Exchange	Symbol	Price	52Wk Range	Yield	P/E
NYS	SUI	$150.10 (12/31/2019)	165.29-97.79	2.00	94.40

*7 Year Price Score 139.34 *NYSE Composite Index=100 *12 Month Price Score 112.02

Interim Earnings (Per Share)

Qtr.	Mar	Jun	Sep	Dec
2016	0.14	(0.12)	0.27	(0.04)
2017	0.29	0.16	0.31	0.09
2018	0.38	0.25	0.56	0.10
2019	0.40	0.46	0.63	...

Interim Dividends (Per Share)

Amt	Decl	Ex	Rec	Pay
0.75Q	03/06/2019	03/28/2019	03/29/2019	04/15/2019
0.75Q	05/28/2019	06/27/2019	06/28/2019	07/15/2019
0.75Q	08/28/2019	09/27/2019	09/30/2019	10/15/2019
0.75Q	11/27/2019	12/30/2019	12/31/2019	01/15/2020

Indicated Div: $3.00

Valuation Analysis **Institutional Holding**

Forecast EPS	$1.70	No of Institutions
(01/17/2020)		512
Market Cap	$13.6 Billion	Shares
Book Value	$3.6 Billion	101,230,224
Price/Book	3.76	% Held
Price/Sales	11.01	99.27

Business Summary: REITs (MIC: 5.3.1 SIC: 6798 NAIC: 525930)

Sun Communities is a self-administered and self-managed real estate investment trust. Co. is in the business of acquiring, operating, developing and expanding manufactured housing (MH) and recreational vehicle (RV) communities. Co. leases individual parcels of land (sites) with utility access for placement of manufactured homes and RVs to its customers. Co. owns, operates, or has an interest in a portfolio of MH and RV communities. Co., through its subsidiary, Sun Home Services, Inc., is engaged in the marketing, selling and leasing of new and pre-owned homes to residents in Co.'s communities.

Recent Developments: For the quarter ended Sep 30 2019, net income increased 24.6% to US$64.5 million from US$51.7 million in the year-earlier quarter. Revenues were US$362.4 million, up 12.1% from US$323.4 million the year before. Revenues from property income rose 11.4% to US$270.9 million from US$243.2 million in the corresponding quarter a year earlier.

Prospects: Our evaluation of Sun Communities Inc. as of October 4th, 2019 is the result of our systematic analysis on three basic characteristics: earnings strength, relative valuation, and recent stock price movement. The company has enjoyed a very positive trend in earnings per share over the past 5 quarters. However, recent analyst estimates for the company have been mixed and SUI has posted results that fell short of analysts' expectations. Based on operating earnings yield, the company is overvalued when compared to all of the companies we cover. Share price changes over the past year indicates that SUI will perform very well over the near term.

Financial Data

(US$ in Thousands)	9 Mos	6 Mos	3 Mos	12/31/2018	12/31/2017	12/31/2016	12/31/2015	12/31/2014
Earnings Per Share	1.59	1.52	1.31	1.29	0.85	0.26	2.52	0.54
Cash Flow Per Share	5.12	4.87	4.51	4.46	3.44	3.61	3.39	3.23
Tang Book Value Per Share	39.91	39.95	36.94	36.71	33.15	32.27	26.35	18.36
Dividends Per Share	2.960	2.920	2.880	2.840	2.680	2.600	2.600	2.600
Dividend Payout %	186.16	192.11	219.85	220.16	315.29	1,000.00	103.17	481.48
Income Statement								
Total Revenue	962,218	599,775	287,330	1,126,825	982,570	833,778	674,731	471,675
EBITDA	479,448	304,338	148,444	254,021	213,839	168,999	435,978	241,255
Depn & Amortn	229,241	152,709	76,556	1,638	1,914	600	160,969	132,059
Income Before Taxes	146,822	81,679	36,780	119,600	81,683	46,084	164,131	32,215
Income Taxes	942	173	(3)	88	(136)	283	1,158	219
Net Income	137,646	78,617	36,086	111,715	76,764	31,321	160,419	31,444
Average Shares	90,332	87,564	86,033	82,040	76,711	66,321	53,702	41,805
Balance Sheet								
Current Assets	256,366	248,876	254,753	50,311	10,127	8,164	45,086	83,459
Total Assets	7,397,854	7,222,084	7,098,662	6,710,026	6,111,957	5,870,776	4,190,551	2,937,692
Current Liabilities	3,130,523	3,031,503	3,048,580	128,000	41,257	100,095	25,000	5,794
Long-Term Obligations	175,295	110,742	431,175	2,961,026	3,037,981	3,009,947	2,320,049	1,826,293
Total Liabilities	3,778,377	3,600,277	3,904,339	3,539,611	3,470,460	3,508,221	2,651,944	2,045,953
Stockholders' Equity	3,619,477	3,621,807	3,194,323	3,170,415	2,641,497	2,362,555	1,538,607	891,739
Shares Outstanding	90,690	90,667	86,463	86,357	79,679	73,206	58,395	48,573
Statistical Record								
Return on Assets %	2.11	2.00	1.76	1.74	1.28	0.62	4.50	1.27
Return on Equity %	4.33	4.34	4.00	3.84	3.07	1.60	13.20	4.94
EBITDA Margin %	49.83	50.74	51.66	22.54	21.76	20.27	64.62	51.15
Net Margin %	14.31	13.11	12.56	9.91	7.81	3.76	23.78	6.67
Asset Turnover	0.18	0.17	0.17	0.18	0.16	0.17	0.19	0.19
Current Ratio	0.08	0.08	0.08	0.39	0.25	0.08	1.80	14.40
Debt to Equity	0.05	0.03	0.13	0.93	1.15	1.27	1.51	2.05
Price Range	151.29-95.60	129.96-95.40	118.88-90.11	108.32-83.96	95.60-76.13	81.55-63.81	71.27-60.60	63.97-41.98
P/E Ratio	95.15-60.13	85.50-62.76	90.75-68.79	83.97-65.09	112.47-89.56	313.65-245.42	28.28-23.99	118.46-77.74
Average Yield %	2.47	2.67	2.83	2.96	3.10	3.58	3.93	5.15

Address: 27777 Franklin Rd., Suite 200, Southfield, MI 48034 **Telephone:** 248-208-2500	**Web Site:** www.suncommunities.com **Officers:** Gary A. Shiffman - Chairman, Chief Executive Officer, President John B. McLaren - President, Chief Operating Officer, Executive Vice President	**Auditors:** Grant Thornton LLP **Investor Contact:** 248-208-2500 **Transfer Agents:** Computershare Trust Company, N.A., Providence, RI

SUPERIOR ENERGY SERVICES, INC.

Exchange	Symbol	Price	52Wk Range	Yield	P/E
NBB	SPNV	$5.01 (12/31/2019)	54.80-0.85	N/A	N/A

*7 Year Price Score 10.44   ***NYSE Composite Index=100**   ***12 Month Price Score 17.76**

TRADING VOLUME (thousand shares)

Interim Earnings (Per Share)

Qtr.	Mar	Jun	Sep	Dec
2016	(5.70)	(31.10)	(7.80)	(13.90)
2017	(6.00)	(4.20)	(3.90)	0.60
2018	(3.90)	(1.70)	(1.40)	(48.60)
2019	(3.10)	(4.60)	(2.50)	...

Interim Dividends (Per Share)

Dividend Payment Suspended

Valuation Analysis		Institutional Holding	
Forecast EPS	$-10.25	No of Institutions	
	(01/15/2020)	338	
Market Cap	$78.4 Million	Shares	
Book Value	$143.1 Million	49,756,452	
Price/Book	0.55	% Held	
Price/Sales	0.04	8.22	

Business Summary: Equipment & Services (MIC: 9.1.3 SIC: 1389 NAIC: 213112)

Superior Energy Services provide services and products to the energy industry. Co. serves national and independent oil and natural gas exploration and production companies around the world. Co. reports its operating results in four business segments: Drilling Products and Services, which include downhole drilling tools and surface rentals; Onshore Completion and Workover Services, which include pressure pumping, fluid management and workover services; Production Services, which include intervention services used to maintain and extend oil and gas production; and Technical Solutions, which include include completion tools and services, well control services and subsea well intervention.

Recent Developments: For the quarter ended Sep 30 2019, loss from continuing operations was US$38.4 million compared with a loss of US$21.8 million in the year-earlier quarter. Net loss amounted to US$38.4 million versus a net loss of US$21.8 million in the year-earlier quarter. Revenues were US$425.7 million, down 25.7% from US$573.1 million the year before. Operating loss was US$8.2 million versus a loss of US$108,000 in the prior-year quarter. Direct operating expenses declined 27.2% to US$294.2 million from US$404.4 million in the comparable period the year before. Indirect operating expenses decreased 17.2% to US$139.7 million from US$168.8 million in the equivalent prior-year period.

Prospects: Our evaluation of Superior Energy Services Inc. as of Jan. 21, 2018 is the result of our systematic analysis on three basic characteristics: earnings strength, relative valuation, and recent stock price movement. The company has enjoyed a very positive trend in earnings per share over the past 5 quarters. Because the company lacks sufficient analyst estimate data, we place greater weight on the historical EPS trend as the measure of earnings strength. Based on operating earnings yield, the company is overvalued when compared to all of the companies in our coverage universe. Share price changes over the past year indicates that SPN will perform very poorly over the near term.

Financial Data

(US$ in Thousands)	9 Mos	6 Mos	3 Mos	12/31/2018	12/31/2017	12/31/2016	12/31/2015	12/31/2014
Earnings Per Share	(58.80)	(57.70)	(54.80)	(55.60)	(13.50)	(58.50)	(123.30)	16.50
Cash Flow Per Share	12.66	12.47	13.96	10.69	6.79	4.03	42.04	66.58
Tang Book Value Per Share	0.46	2.78	7.09	9.94	21.18	32.92	70.97	107.63
Dividends Per Share	...	...	...	...	...	...	0.800	2.400
Dividend Payout %	...	...	...	...	...	...	...	14.55
Income Statement								
Total Revenue	1,329,208	903,491	467,176	2,130,265	1,874,076	1,450,047	2,774,565	4,556,622
EBITDA	(54,319)	(47,803)	61,556	(428,842)	142,904	(520,688)	(1,378,365)	1,159,523
Depn & Amortn	16,341	11,286	82,439	374,500	419,200	486,900	584,100	620,600
Income Before Taxes	(144,935)	(108,860)	(46,004)	(902,819)	(377,751)	(1,100,341)	(2,059,783)	442,189
Income Taxes	12,261	9,895	1,701	(45,433)	(190,740)	(267,001)	(252,020)	161,399
Net Income	(157,196)	(118,755)	(47,705)	(858,115)	(205,921)	(886,899)	(1,854,718)	257,817
Average Shares	15,657	15,599	15,577	15,436	15,293	15,155	15,046	15,672
Balance Sheet								
Current Assets	833,019	799,770	752,266	772,905	760,819	781,551	1,295,125	1,728,811
Total Assets	2,123,751	2,146,297	2,247,335	2,215,962	3,110,225	3,470,255	4,914,244	7,377,389
Current Liabilities	338,484	322,103	354,382	362,777	375,197	344,534	448,576	712,047
Long-Term Obligations	1,285,755	1,284,814	1,283,862	1,282,921	1,279,771	1,284,600	1,588,263	1,627,842
Total Liabilities	1,980,664	1,965,906	1,999,269	1,925,223	1,977,796	2,166,335	2,703,432	3,297,651
Stockholders' Equity	143,087	180,391	248,066	290,739	1,132,429	1,303,920	2,210,812	4,079,738
Shares Outstanding	15,657	15,657	15,595	15,488	15,326	15,186	15,086	14,970
Statistical Record								
Return on Assets %	N.M.	N.M.	N.M.	N.M.	N.M.	N.M.	N.M.	3.49
Return on Equity %	N.M.	N.M.	N.M.	N.M.	N.M.	N.M.	N.M.	6.28
EBITDA Margin %	N.M.	N.M.	13.18	N.M.	7.63	N.M.	N.M.	25.45
Net Margin %	N.M.	N.M.	N.M.	N.M.	N.M.	N.M.	N.M.	5.66
Asset Turnover	0.73	0.78	0.80	0.80	0.57	0.34	0.45	0.62
Current Ratio	2.46	2.48	2.12	2.13	2.03	2.27	2.89	2.43
Debt to Equity	8.99	7.12	5.18	4.41	1.13	0.99	0.72	0.40
Price Range	108.20-0.85	108.20-12.20	124.70-30.00	124.70-30.00	190.30-78.90	195.00-85.90	262.80-125.90	366.90-171.90
P/E Ratio	...	...	...	...	...	...	...	22.24-10.42
Average Yield %	...	...	...	...	...	...	0.53	1.70	0.81

Address: 1001 Louisiana Street, Suite 2900, Houston, TX 77002	Web Site: www.superiorenergy.com	Auditors: KPMG LLP
Telephone: 713-654-2200	Officers: Terence E. Hall - Chairman, President, Chief Executive Officer David D. (Dave) Dunlap - President, Chief Executive Officer	Investor Contact: 281-999-0047
		Transfer Agents: Jones, Walker, LLP

SWITCH INC

Exchange	Symbol	Price	52Wk Range	Yield	P/E
NYS	SWCH	$14.82 (12/31/2019)	16.78-6.82	0.79	148.20

*7 Year Price Score N/A   *NYSE Composite Index=100   *12 Month Price Score 113.49

Interim Earnings (Per Share)

Qtr.	Mar	Jun	Sep	Dec
2017	0.10	0.07	0.08	(2.13)
2018	0.02	0.02	0.00	0.06
2019	0.01	0.01	0.02	...

Interim Dividends (Per Share)

Amt	Decl	Ex	Rec	Pay
0.029Q	03/12/2019	03/22/2019	03/25/2019	04/04/2019
0.029Q	05/08/2019	05/21/2019	05/22/2019	06/04/2019
0.029Q	08/07/2019	08/16/2019	08/19/2019	08/30/2019
0.029Q	11/07/2019	11/18/2019	11/19/2019	11/29/2019

Indicated Div: $0.12

Valuation Analysis | **Institutional Holding**

Forecast EPS	$0.11	No of Institutions
	(01/17/2020)	148
Market Cap	$3.6 Billion	Shares
Book Value	$210.6 Million	59,797,432
Price/Book	17.24	% Held
Price/Sales	8.27	69.14

TRADING VOLUME (thousand shares)

Business Summary: Internet & Software (MIC: 6.3.2 SIC: 7371 NAIC: 541511)

Switch is a holding company. Through its subsidiaries, Co. is engaged in technology infrastructure powering the sustainable growth of the connected world and the Internet of Everything. Co. provides colocation space and related services to global enterprises, financial companies, government agencies, and others that conduct business on the internet. Co. develops and operates data centers in Nevada, which are Tier IV Gold certified, and Michigan, and is developing data centers in Georgia, delivering redundant services with low latency and capacity transport environments.

Recent Developments: For the quarter ended Sep 30 2019, net income increased 52.2% to US$7.1 million from US$4.7 million in the year-earlier quarter. Revenues were US$117.6 million, up 14.4% from US$102.8 million the year before. Operating income was US$18.1 million versus US$12.5 million in the prior-year quarter, an increase of 44.7%. Direct operating expenses rose 5.0% to US$62.1 million from US$59.2 million in the comparable period the year before. Indirect operating expenses increased 20.0% to US$37.3 million from US$31.1 million in the equivalent prior-year period.

Prospects: Our evaluation of Switch Inc as of October 4th, 2019 is the result of our systematic analysis on three basic characteristics: earnings strength, relative valuation, and recent stock price movement. The company has suffered a very negative trend in earnings per share over the past 5 quarters. However, recent analyst estimates for the company have been mixed and SWCH has posted results that fell short of analysts' expectations. Based on operating earnings yield, the company is overvalued when compared to all of the companies we cover. Share price changes over the past year indicates that SWCH will perform over the near term.

Financial Data

(US$ in Thousands)	9 Mos	6 Mos	3 Mos	12/31/2018	12/31/2017	12/31/2016	12/31/2015
Earnings Per Share	0.10	0.08	0.09	0.09	(1.88)	0.15	0.37
Cash Flow Per Share	2.50	2.46	3.44	3.90	17.97	0.83	0.66
Tang Book Value Per Share	0.86	0.81	0.58	0.58	0.43	1.39	1.43
Dividends Per Share	0.103	0.088	0.088	0.059	0.014	...	...
Dividend Payout %	102.90	110.25	98.00	65.33	...	...	...
Income Statement							
Total Revenue	336,177	218,619	107,032	405,860	378,275	318,352	265,870
EBITDA	127,669	82,431	39,916	164,628	105,695	118,942	135,733
Depn & Amortn	89,833	59,046	28,917	106,666	89,100	66,600	55,400
Income Before Taxes	16,624	8,916	3,868	31,592	(8,484)	41,506	72,651
Income Taxes	1,249	639	197	1,943	(981)	...	...
Net Income	3,952	1,878	700	4,052	(15,208)	31,368	73,472
Average Shares	86,261	79,021	247,364	45,753	8,073	203,461	199,272
Balance Sheet							
Current Assets	80,609	81,287	106,022	108,327	288,190	37,817	28,708
Total Assets	1,639,113	1,524,877	1,463,857	1,460,030	1,434,759	921,015	647,578
Current Liabilities	105,113	84,068	72,139	75,028	65,285	145,678	52,184
Long-Term Obligations	666,137	597,435	598,734	600,032	606,031	477,203	302,625
Total Liabilities	1,428,491	1,325,867	1,320,258	1,316,820	1,325,865	642,652	362,884
Stockholders' Equity	210,622	199,010	143,599	143,210	108,894	278,363	284,694
Shares Outstanding	245,084	245,900	247,107	246,644	252,506	200,744	198,866
Statistical Record							
Return on Assets %	0.42	0.29	0.28	0.28	N.M.	3.99	...
Return on Equity %	3.82	2.67	3.17	3.21	N.M.	11.11	...
EBITDA Margin %	37.98	37.71	37.29	40.56	27.94	37.36	51.05
Net Margin %	1.18	0.86	0.65	1.00	N.M.	9.85	27.63
Asset Turnover	0.28	0.28	0.28	0.28	0.32	0.40	...
Current Ratio	0.77	0.97	1.47	1.44	4.41	0.26	0.55
Debt to Equity	3.16	3.00	4.17	4.19	5.57	1.71	1.06
Price Range	16.78-6.41	14.07-6.41	15.85-6.41	17.99-6.41	20.84-16.25	...	...
P/E Ratio	167.80-64.10	175.88-80.13	176.11-71.22	199.89-71.22	...	...	...
Average Yield %	0.94	0.86	0.82	0.47	0.08	...	...

Address: 7135 S. Decatur Boulevard,	Web Site: www.switch.com	Auditors: PricewaterhouseCoopers LLP
Las Vegas , NV 89118	Officers: Rob Roy - Chairman, Chief Executive	Transfer Agents: American Stock
Telephone: 702-444-4111	Officer Thomas Morton - President, General Counsel	Transfer & Trust Company, LLC

SYNCHRONY FINANCIAL

Exchange	Symbol	Price	52Wk Range
NYS	SYF	$36.01 (12/31/2019)	37.76-23.46

Yield	P/E
2.44	6.57

*7 Year Price Score N/A   ***NYSE Composite Index=100**   ***12 Month Price Score 103.78**

Interim Earnings (Per Share)

Qtr.	Mar	Jun	Sep	Dec
2016	0.70	0.58	0.73	0.70
2017	0.61	0.61	0.70	0.49
2018	0.83	0.92	0.91	1.08
2019	1.56	1.60	...	

Interim Dividends (Per Share)

Amt	Decl	Ex	Rec	Pay
0.21Q	01/22/2019	02/01/2019	02/04/2019	02/14/2019
0.21Q	04/24/2019	05/03/2019	05/06/2019	05/16/2019
0.22Q	07/24/2019	08/02/2019	08/05/2019	08/15/2019
0.22Q	10/23/2019	11/01/2019	11/04/2019	11/14/2019

Indicated Div: $0.88

Valuation Analysis / Institutional Holding

Forecast EPS	$4.26	No of Institutions	838
(01/17/2020)			
Market Cap	$23.5 Billion	Shares	
Book Value	$15.1 Billion		660,380,288
Price/Book	1.56	% Held	
Price/Sales	1.19		71.66

Business Summary: Banking (MIC: 5.1.1 SIC: 6141 NAIC: 522291)

Synchrony Financial is savings and loan holding company and financial holding company. Through its subsidiaries, Co. is a consumer financial services company. Co. provides a range of credit products through its financing programs which it has established with a group of national and regional retailers, local merchants, manufacturers, buying groups, industry associations and healthcare service providers. Through its wholly-owned subsidiary, Synchrony Bank, Co. provides its customers a range of Federal Deposit Insurance Corporation-insured deposit products. Co.'s deposit products include certificates of deposit, individual retirement accounts, money market accounts and savings accounts.

Recent Developments: For the quarter ended Sep 30 2019, net income increased 57.4% to US$1.06 billion from US$671.0 million in the year-earlier quarter. Net interest income increased 4.4% to US$4.39 billion from US$4.21 billion in the year-earlier quarter. Provision for loan losses was US$1.02 billion versus US$1.45 billion in the prior-year quarter, a decrease of 29.8%. Non-interest income rose 34.9% to US$85.0 million from US$63.0 million, while non-interest expense advanced 8.1% to US$2.08 billion.

Prospects: Our evaluation of Synchrony Financial as of October 4th, 2019 is the result of our systematic analysis on three basic characteristics: earnings strength, relative valuation, and recent stock price movement. The company has generated a negative trend in earnings per share over the past 5 quarters. However, recent analyst estimates for the company have been mixed and SYF has posted results that exceeded analysts' expectations. Based on operating earnings yield, the company is undervalued when compared to all of the companies we cover. Share price changes over the past year indicates that SYF will perform well over the near term.

Financial Data

(US$ in Millions)	9 Mos	6 Mos	3 Mos	12/31/2018	12/31/2017	12/31/2016	12/31/2015	12/31/2014
Earnings Per Share	5.48	4.79	4.47	3.74	2.42	2.71	2.65	2.78
Cash Flow Per Share	14.02	13.92	13.76	12.59	11.21	8.21	7.42	7.05
Tang Book Value Per Share	19.68	18.60	17.96	17.41	16.21	15.34	13.14	10.81
Dividends Per Share	0.850	0.840	0.780	0.720	0.560	0.260	...	...
Dividend Payout %	15.51	17.54	17.45	19.25	23.14	9.59	...	...
Income Statement								
Total Revenue	14,772	9,706	4,878	18,253	16,695	15,122	13,620	12,727
Income Before Taxes	3,966	2,591	1,462	3,644	3,324	3,570	3,531	3,386
Income Taxes	950	631	355	854	1,389	1,319	1,317	1,277
Net Income	3,016	1,960	1,107	2,790	1,935	2,251	2,214	2,109
Average Shares	661	686	708	746	799	831	835	757
Balance Sheet								
Total Assets	105,943	106,388	105,384	106,792	95,808	90,207	84,135	75,707
Total Liabilities	90,823	91,654	90,675	92,114	81,574	76,011	71,531	65,229
Stockholders' Equity	15,120	14,734	14,709	14,678	14,234	14,196	12,604	10,478
Shares Outstanding	653	668	688	718	770	817	833	833
Statistical Record								
Return on Assets %	3.61	3.32	3.24	2.75	2.08	2.58	2.77	3.13
Return on Equity %	26.10	23.39	22.41	19.30	13.61	16.75	19.18	25.66
Net Margin %	20.42	20.19	22.69	15.29	11.59	14.89	16.26	16.57
Asset Turnover	0.19	0.19	0.19	0.18	0.18	0.17	0.17	0.19
Price Range	36.60-22.17	35.24-22.17	36.12-22.17	40.21-22.17	38.97-26.50	37.26-23.36	35.99-28.52	30.50-22.93
P/E Ratio	6.68-4.05	7.36-4.63	8.08-4.96	10.75-5.93	16.10-10.95	13.75-8.62	13.58-10.76	10.97-8.25
Average Yield %	2.71	2.73	2.53	2.21	1.73	0.89	...	...

Address: 777 Long Ridge Road, Stamford, CT 06902 **Telephone:** 203-585-2400	**Web Site:** www.synchronyfinancial.com **Officers:** Richard C. Hartnack - Chairman Margaret M. Keane - President, Chief Executive Officer	**Auditors:** KPMG LLP **Transfer Agents:** Computershare Trust Company, N.A.

SYNNEX CORP

Exchange	Symbol	Price	52Wk Range	Yield	P/E
NYS	SNX	$128.80 (12/31/2019)	129.62-78.20	1.24	14.57

*7 Year Price Score 95.46   ***NYSE Composite Index=100**   ***12 Month Price Score 114.28**

Interim Earnings (Per Share)

Qtr.	Feb	May	Aug	Nov
2015-16	1.17	1.11	1.47	2.13
2016-17	1.54	1.83	1.87	2.27
2017-18	0.61	2.34	1.74	2.52
2018-19	1.69	2.23	2.40	...

Interim Dividends (Per Share)

Amt	Decl	Ex	Rec	Pay
0.375Q	03/27/2019	04/11/2019	04/12/2019	04/26/2019
0.375Q	06/25/2019	07/11/2019	07/12/2019	07/26/2019
0.375Q	09/24/2019	10/10/2019	10/11/2019	10/25/2019
0.40Q	01/09/2020	01/23/2020	01/24/2020	01/31/2020
		Indicated Div: $1.60		

Valuation Analysis

		Institutional Holding	
Forecast EPS	$13.86	No of Institutions	
	(01/15/2020)	433	
Market Cap	$6.5 Billion	Shares	
Book Value	$3.6 Billion	45,236,408	
Price/Book	1.81	% Held	
Price/Sales	0.29	97.19	

Business Summary: IT Services (MIC: 6.3.1 SIC: 5045 NAIC: 334119)

Synnex is a business process services company, providing a range of distribution, logistics and integration services for the technology industry and providing outsourced services focused on customer engagement to a range of enterprises. Co. has two segments: Technology Solutions, which distributes peripherals, Information Technology systems including data center server and storage solutions; and Concentrix, which provides a portfolio of strategic solutions and end-to-end business outsourcing services focused on customer engagement strategy, process optimization, technology innovation, front and back-office automation and business transformation to clients.

Recent Developments: For the quarter ended Aug 31 2019, net income increased 83.9% to US$123.1 million from US$66.9 million in the year-earlier quarter. Revenues were US$6.20 billion, up 28.6% from US$4.82 billion the year before. Operating income was US$208.9 million versus US$113.8 million in the prior-year quarter, an increase of 83.5%. Direct operating expenses rose 24.7% to US$5.48 billion from US$4.39 billion in the comparable period the year before. Indirect operating expenses increased 63.5% to US$517.1 million from US$316.3 million in the equivalent prior-year period.

Prospects: Our evaluation of Synnex Corp. as of October 4th, 2019 is the result of our systematic analysis on three basic characteristics: earnings strength, relative valuation, and recent stock price movement. The company has managed to produce a neutral trend in earnings per share over the past 5 quarters. However, recent analyst estimates for the company have been raised and SNX has posted results that exceeded analysts' expectations. Based on operating earnings yield, the company is undervalued when compared to all of the companies we cover. Share price changes over the past year indicates that SNX will perform very poorly over the near term.

Financial Data

(US$ in Thousands)	9 Mos	6 Mos	3 Mos	11/30/2018	11/30/2017	11/30/2016	11/30/2015	11/30/2014
Earnings Per Share	8.84	8.18	8.29	7.19	7.51	5.88	5.24	4.57
Cash Flow Per Share	6.79	(0.19)	(1.02)	2.44	4.47	8.29	16.48	(6.10)
Tang Book Value Per Share	3.54	1.55	N.M.	N.M.	20.87	30.17	34.04	28.51
Dividends Per Share	1.475	1.450	1.425	1.400	1.050	0.850	0.575	0.125
Dividend Payout %	16.69	17.73	17.19	19.47	13.98	14.46	10.97	2.74
Income Statement								
Total Revenue	17,176,000	10,972,341	5,249,453	20,053,764	17,045,700	14,061,837	13,338,397	13,839,590
EBITDA	688,479	441,587	202,785	643,007	590,793	450,860	457,001	401,168
Depn & Amortn	123,242	84,118	41,517	100,955	80,705	65,803	103,510	91,699
Income Before Taxes	437,542	272,719	119,662	457,377	464,731	356,064	327,195	284,282
Income Taxes	112,831	71,140	32,556	156,779	163,558	121,059	118,588	104,132
Net Income	324,711	201,579	87,106	300,598	301,173	234,946	208,525	180,034
Average Shares	50,845	50,939	50,927	41,451	39,758	39,530	39,352	38,845
Balance Sheet								
Current Assets	7,202,488	7,015,116	6,429,154	7,099,753	5,739,778	4,045,109	3,649,781	3,899,989
Total Assets	11,426,327	11,275,958	10,761,335	11,480,434	7,698,526	5,223,263	4,444,147	4,713,042
Current Liabilities	4,578,681	4,461,217	3,880,479	4,894,441	4,041,207	2,477,828	1,918,157	2,721,729
Long-Term Obligations	2,757,021	2,792,649	2,827,616	2,622,782	1,136,089	603,229	638,798	264,246
Total Liabilities	7,824,517	7,738,905	7,250,894	8,048,366	5,414,831	3,247,487	2,644,766	3,059,484
Stockholders' Equity	3,601,810	3,537,053	3,510,442	3,432,068	2,283,695	1,975,776	1,799,381	1,653,558
Shares Outstanding	50,605	50,593	50,720	50,694	39,673	39,477	39,189	38,924
Statistical Record								
Return on Assets %	4.69	4.13	3.99	3.13	4.66	4.85	4.55	4.48
Return on Equity %	14.77	13.13	12.47	10.52	14.14	12.41	12.08	11.75
EBITDA Margin %	4.01	4.02	3.86	3.21	3.47	3.21	3.43	2.90
Net Margin %	1.89	1.84	1.66	1.50	1.77	1.67	1.56	1.30
Asset Turnover	2.44	2.31	2.28	2.09	2.64	2.90	2.91	3.44
Current Ratio	1.57	1.57	1.66	1.45	1.42	1.63	1.90	1.43
Debt to Equity	0.77	0.79	0.81	0.76	0.50	0.31	0.36	0.16
Price Range	108.89-73.27	116.29-73.27	127.04-73.27	140.70-73.27	137.33-103.37	118.71-78.16	96.10-68.43	76.94-52.36
P/E Ratio	12.32-8.29	14.22-8.96	15.32-8.84	19.57-10.19	18.29-13.76	20.19-13.29	18.34-13.06	16.84-11.46
Average Yield %	1.62	1.54	1.48	1.32	0.88	0.89	0.72	0.19

Address: 44201 Nobel Drive, Fremont, CA 94538	Web Site: www.synnex.com	Auditors: KPMG LLP
Telephone: 510-656-3333	Officers: Matthew Miau - Chairman Emeritus, Chairman Kevin M. Murai - Chairman, President, Chief Executive Officer, Co-Chief Executive Officer	Transfer Agents: Computershare Trust Company, Providence, RI

SYNOVUS FINANCIAL CORP

Exchange	Symbol	Price	52Wk Range	Yield	P/E
NYS	SNV	$39.20 (12/31/2019)	40.16-31.96	3.06	11.60

*7 Year Price Score 88.96   ***NYSE Composite Index=100**   ***12 Month Price Score 99.32**

Interim Earnings (Per Share)

Qtr.	Mar	Jun	Sep	Dec
2016	0.39	0.46	0.51	0.53
2017	0.56	0.60	0.78	0.23
2018	0.84	0.91	0.84	0.87
2019	0.72	0.96	0.83	...

Interim Dividends (Per Share)

Amt	Decl	Ex	Rec	Pay
0.30Q	03/05/2019	03/20/2019	03/21/2019	04/01/2019
0.30Q	06/04/2019	06/19/2019	06/20/2019	07/01/2019
0.30Q	09/04/2019	09/18/2019	09/19/2019	10/01/2019
0.30Q	12/04/2019	12/18/2019	12/19/2019	01/02/2020

Indicated Div: $1.20 (Div. Reinv. Plan)

Valuation Analysis   **Institutional Holding**

Forecast EPS	$3.92	No of Institutions
(01/17/2020)		571
Market Cap	$5.8 Billion	Shares
Book Value	$4.9 Billion	207,555,520
Price/Book	1.19	% Held
Price/Sales	2.60	N/A

Business Summary: Banking (MIC: 5.1.1 SIC: 6021 NAIC: 522110)

Synovus Financial is a financial services company and a bank holding company. Through its subsidiary bank, Synovus Bank, Co. provides financial services, including commercial and retail banking, financial management, insurance, and mortgage services to its customers in Georgia, Alabama, South Carolina, Florida, and Tennessee. In addition to its banking operations, Co., through other non-bank subsidiaries, also provides various other financial services such as portfolio management for fixed-income securities, investment banking, the execution of securities transactions as a broker/dealer, trust, asset management, and financial planning services as well as mortgage services.

Recent Developments: For the quarter ended Sep 30 2019, net income increased 24.5% to US$135.7 million from US$109.1 million in the year-earlier quarter. Net interest income increased 37.9% to US$402.1 million from US$291.6 million in the year-earlier quarter. Provision for loan losses was US$27.6 million versus US$15.0 million in the prior-year quarter, an increase of 84.0%. Non-interest income rose 23.8% to US$88.8 million from US$71.7 million, while non-interest expense advanced 25.4% to US$276.3 million.

Prospects: Our evaluation of Synovus Financial Corp. as of October 4th, 2019 is the result of our systematic analysis on three basic characteristics: earnings strength, relative valuation, and recent stock price movement. The company has managed to produce a neutral trend in earnings per share over the past 5 quarters. However, recent analyst estimates for the company have been reduced while SNV has posted results that exceeded analysts' expectations. Based on operating earnings yield, the company is undervalued when compared to all of the companies we cover. Share price changes over the past year indicates that SNV will perform poorly over the near term.

Financial Data
(US$ in Thousands)

	9 Mos	6 Mos	3 Mos	12/31/2018	12/31/2017	12/31/2016	12/31/2015	12/31/2014
Earnings Per Share	3.38	3.39	3.34	3.47	2.17	1.89	1.62	1.33
Cash Flow Per Share	3.47	3.56	3.76	4.57	5.30	3.75	3.38	2.79
Tang Book Value Per Share	25.65	25.53	24.41	24.78	23.27	22.32	22.00	21.24
Dividends Per Share	1.150	1.100	1.050	1.000	0.600	0.480	0.420	0.240
Dividend Payout %	34.02	32.45	31.44	28.82	27.65	25.40	25.93	18.05
Income Statement								
Interest Income	1,544,385	1,020,970	504,839	1,344,305	1,162,497	1,022,803	945,962	928,692
Interest Expense	347,850	226,532	107,664	195,892	139,188	123,623	118,644	109,408
Net Interest Income	1,196,535	794,438	397,175	1,148,413	1,023,309	899,180	827,318	819,284
Provision for Losses	63,250	35,688	23,569	51,697	67,185	28,000	19,010	33,831
Non-Interest Income	257,945	169,185	79,378	280,093	345,327	273,194	267,920	260,537
Non-Interest Expense	832,847	556,537	292,410	829,455	821,313	755,923	717,655	743,431
Income Before Taxes	558,383	371,398	160,574	547,354	480,138	388,451	358,573	302,559
Income Taxes	146,287	95,028	40,388	118,878	204,664	141,667	132,491	107,310
Net Income	412,096	276,370	120,186	428,476	275,474	246,784	226,082	195,249
Average Shares	154,043	159,077	162,760	118,378	122,012	125,078	133,201	139,154
Balance Sheet								
Net Loans & Leases	36,152,813	35,881,185	35,377,465	25,696,018	24,549,552	23,604,633	22,177,069	20,839,988
Total Assets	47,661,182	47,318,203	46,630,025	32,669,192	31,221,837	30,104,002	28,792,653	27,051,231
Total Deposits	37,433,070	37,966,722	38,075,190	26,720,322	26,147,900	24,648,060	23,242,661	21,531,700
Total Liabilities	42,792,344	42,564,387	42,032,272	29,535,590	28,260,271	27,176,078	25,792,457	24,009,961
Stockholders' Equity	4,868,838	4,753,816	4,597,753	3,133,602	2,961,566	2,927,924	3,000,196	3,041,270
Shares Outstanding	147,594	156,872	157,454	115,865	118,897	122,266	129,547	136,122
Statistical Record								
Return on Assets %	1.30	1.24	1.14	1.34	0.90	0.84	0.81	0.73
Return on Equity %	13.08	12.38	11.79	14.06	9.35	8.30	7.48	6.52
Net Interest Margin %	76.82	76.97	78.67	85.43	88.03	87.91	87.46	88.22
Efficiency Ratio %	45.14	43.59	50.05	51.06	54.47	58.33	59.12	62.51
Loans to Deposits	0.97	0.95	0.93	0.96	0.94	0.96	0.95	0.97
Price Range	46.10-30.25	55.12-30.25	57.07-30.25	57.07-30.25	50.13-39.11	41.78-25.95	33.56-24.49	27.51-21.84
P/E Ratio	13.64-8.95	16.26-8.92	17.09-9.06	16.45-8.72	23.10-18.02	22.11-13.73	20.72-15.12	20.68-16.42
Average Yield %	3.17	2.76	2.36	2.09	1.38	1.51	1.42	0.99

Address: 1111 Bay Avenue, Suite 500, Columbus, GA 31901 **Telephone:** 706-649-2311	**Web Site:** www.synovus.com **Officers:** Kessel D. Stelling - Chairman, President, Chief Executive Officer Kevin S. Blair - President, Executive Vice President, Senior Executive Vice President, Chief Operating Officer, Interim Chief Financial Officer	**Auditors:** KPMG LLP **Investor Contact:** 706-649-3555 **Transfer Agents:** American Stock Transfer & Trust Company, LLC., Brooklyn, NY

SYSCO CORP

Exchange	Symbol	Price	52Wk Range	Yield	P/E	Div Acheiver
NYS	SYY	$85.54 (12/31/2019)	85.80-61.37	2.10	26.24	42 Years

*7 Year Price Score 119.29 ***NYSE Composite Index=100** ***12 Month Price Score 107.10**

Interim Earnings (Per Share)

Qtr.	Sep	Dec	Mar	Jun
2016-17	0.58	0.50	0.44	0.56
2017-18	0.69	0.54	0.63	0.85
2018-19	0.81	0.51	0.85	1.03
2019-20	0.87	...	...	...

Interim Dividends (Per Share)

Amt	Decl	Ex	Rec	Pay
0.39Q	02/21/2019	04/04/2019	04/05/2019	04/26/2019
0.39Q	05/23/2019	07/03/2019	07/05/2019	07/26/2019
0.39Q	07/26/2019	10/03/2019	10/04/2019	10/25/2019
0.45Q	11/14/2019	01/02/2020	01/03/2020	01/24/2020

Indicated Div: $1.80 (Div. Reinv. Plan)

Valuation Analysis / Institutional Holding

Valuation Analysis		Institutional Holding	
Forecast EPS	$3.80	No of Institutions	
	(01/17/2020)	1751	
Market Cap	$43.7 Billion	Shares	
Book Value	$2.5 Billion	558,877,824	
Price/Book	17.80	% Held	
Price/Sales	0.73	76.97	

Business Summary: Retail - Food & Beverage, Drug & Tobacco (MIC: 2.1.2 SIC: 5141 NAIC: 424410)

Sysco, acting through its subsidiaries and divisions, is a distributor of food and related products primarily to the foodservice or food-away-from-home industry. Co. has three reportable segments: United States Foodservice Operations, which primarily include United States Broadline operations, which distribute a line of food products, including custom-cut meat, seafood, specialty produce, specialty imports and a variety of non-food products; International Foodservice Operations, which include operations in the Americas and Europe, which distribute a line of food products and a variety of non-food products; and SYGMA, which consists of its United States customized distribution subsidiary.

Recent Developments: For the quarter ended Sep 28 2019, net income increased 5.3% to US$453.8 million from US$431.0 million in the year-earlier quarter. Revenues were US$15.30 billion, up 0.6% from US$15.22 billion the year before. Operating income was US$668.3 million versus US$628.1 million in the prior-year quarter, an increase of 6.4%. Direct operating expenses rose 0.4% to US$12.36 billion from US$12.31 billion in the comparable period the year before. Indirect operating expenses were unchanged at US$2.28 billion versus the equivalent prior-year period.

Prospects: Our evaluation of Sysco Corp. as of October 4th, 2019 is the result of our systematic analysis on three basic characteristics: earnings strength, relative valuation, and recent stock price movement. The company has produced a positive trend in earnings per share over the past 5 quarters. In addition, recent analyst estimates for the company have been raised, and SYY has posted results that exceeded analysts' expectations. Based on operating earnings yield, the company is fairly valued when compared to all of the companies we cover. Share price changes over the past year indicates that SYY will perform in line with the market over the near term.

Financial Data

(US$ in Thousands)	3 Mos	06/29/2019	06/30/2018	07/01/2017	07/02/2016	06/27/2015	06/28/2014	06/29/2013
Earnings Per Share	3.26	3.20	2.70	2.08	1.64	1.15	1.58	1.67
Cash Flow Per Share	4.50	4.68	4.14	4.02	3.32	2.63	2.55	2.57
Tang Book Value Per Share	N.M.	N.M.	N.M.	N.M.	2.06	5.29	5.36	5.29
Dividends Per Share	1.530	1.500	1.380	1.280	1.230	1.180	1.140	1.100
Dividend Payout %	46.93	46.88	51.11	61.54	75.00	102.61	72.15	65.87
Income Statement								
Total Revenue	15,303,005	60,113,922	58,727,324	55,371,139	50,366,919	48,680,752	46,516,712	44,411,233
EBITDA	697,051	3,022,859	2,966,507	2,834,508	2,347,853	1,758,754	2,093,165	2,149,450
Depn & Amortn	31,845	656,600	614,800	765,400	608,700	495,800	493,800	473,500
Income Before Taxes	581,871	2,005,836	1,956,224	1,766,230	1,433,007	1,008,147	1,475,624	1,547,455
Income Taxes	128,090	331,565	525,458	623,727	483,385	321,374	544,091	555,028
Net Income	453,781	1,674,271	1,430,766	1,142,503	949,622	686,773	931,533	992,427
Average Shares	518,761	523,381	529,089	548,545	577,391	596,849	590,216	592,675
Balance Sheet								
Current Assets	8,484,164	8,141,505	8,003,453	8,033,438	10,053,899	11,494,304	6,681,972	6,207,427
Total Assets	18,956,575	17,966,522	18,070,404	17,756,655	16,721,804	17,989,281	13,167,950	12,663,947
Current Liabilities	6,101,471	6,103,183	6,588,746	6,095,886	4,434,456	9,399,615	4,367,630	3,749,282
Long-Term Obligations	8,637,706	8,122,058	7,540,765	7,660,877	7,336,930	2,271,825	2,384,167	2,639,986
Total Liabilities	16,501,827	15,463,919	15,563,447	15,375,139	13,242,196	12,729,057	7,901,255	7,472,137
Stockholders' Equity	2,454,748	2,502,603	2,506,957	2,381,516	3,479,608	5,260,224	5,266,695	5,191,810
Shares Outstanding	510,864	512,876	520,641	530,039	559,597	594,317	586,124	586,106
Statistical Record								
Return on Assets %	9.05	9.32	8.01	6.65	5.38	4.42	7.23	8.04
Return on Equity %	66.64	67.03	58.70	39.09	21.38	13.08	17.86	20.15
EBITDA Margin %	4.55	5.03	5.05	5.12	4.66	3.61	4.50	4.84
Net Margin %	2.97	2.79	2.44	2.06	1.89	1.41	2.00	2.23
Asset Turnover	3.21	3.35	3.29	3.22	2.86	3.13	3.61	3.60
Current Ratio	1.39	1.33	1.21	1.32	2.27	1.22	1.53	1.66
Debt to Equity	3.52	3.25	3.01	3.22	2.11	0.43	0.45	0.51
Price Range	78.87-59.95	75.78-59.95	68.35-49.11	56.61-47.26	50.74-35.68	41.25-35.54	37.85-31.16	35.24-28.31
P/E Ratio	24.19-18.39	23.68-18.73	25.31-18.19	27.22-22.72	30.94-21.76	35.87-30.90	23.96-19.72	21.10-16.95
Average Yield %	2.21	2.18	2.37	2.46	2.88	3.09	3.26	3.44

Address: 1390 Enclave Parkway, Houston, TX 77077-2099	Web Site: www.sysco.com	Auditors: Ernst & Young LLP
Telephone: 281-584-1390	Officers: Edward D. Shirley - Executive Chairman	Investor Contact: 281-584-1308
Fax: 281-584-2880	Kevin P. Hourican - President, Chief Executive Officer	Transfer Agents: American Stock Transfer & Trust Company, New York, NY

TANGER FACTORY OUTLET CENTERS, INC.

Exchange	Symbol	Price	52Wk Range	Yield	P/E	Div Acheiver
NYS	SKT	$14.73 (12/31/2019)	23.06-13.82	9.64	11.69	25 Years

*7 Year Price Score 48.92 *NYSE Composite Index=100 *12 Month Price Score 83.75

Interim Earnings (Per Share)

Qtr.	Mar	Jun	Sep	Dec
2016	0.28	0.76	0.72	0.25
2017	0.23	0.31	(0.17)	0.33
2018	0.24	0.24	(0.24)	0.20
2019	0.66	0.15	0.25	...

Interim Dividends (Per Share)

Amt	Decl	Ex	Rec	Pay
0.355Q	02/13/2019	04/29/2019	04/30/2019	05/15/2019
0.355Q	07/11/2019	07/30/2019	07/31/2019	08/15/2019
0.355Q	10/10/2019	10/30/2019	10/31/2019	11/15/2019
0.355Q	01/09/2020	01/30/2020	01/31/2020	02/14/2020

Indicated Div: $1.42 (Div. Reinv. Plan)

Valuation Analysis | **Institutional Holding**

Forecast EPS	$1.28	No of Institutions
	(01/17/2020)	419
Market Cap	$1.4 Billion	Shares
Book Value	$472.9 Million	124,861,952
Price/Book	2.89	% Held
Price/Sales	2.82	106.48

Business Summary: REITs (MIC: 5.3.1 SIC: 6798 NAIC: 525930)

Tanger Factory Outlet Centers is a real estate investment trust. Co. is an owner and operator of outlet centers in the U.S. and Canada. Co. focuses on developing, acquiring, owning, operating and managing outlet shopping centers. Co.'s outlet centers and other assets are held by, and all of its operations are conducted by, Tanger Properties Limited Partnership and subsidiaries (Operating Partnership). Co. owns the majority of the units of partnership interest issued by the Operating Partnership through its subsidiaries, Tanger GP Trust and Tanger LP Trust. Tanger GP Trust controls the Operating Partnership as its sole general partner. Tanger LP Trust holds a limited partnership interest.

Recent Developments: For the quarter ended Sep 30 2019, net income amounted to US$24.8 million versus a net loss of US$23.0 million in the year-earlier quarter. Revenues were US$119.0 million, down 4.2% from US$124.2 million the year before. Revenues from property income fell 4.3% to US$115.1 million from US$120.3 million in the corresponding quarter a year earlier.

Prospects: Our evaluation of Tanger Factory Outlet Centers Inc. as of October 4th, 2019 is the result of our systematic analysis on three basic characteristics: earnings strength, relative valuation, and recent stock price movement. The company has managed to produce a neutral trend in earnings per share over the past 5 quarters. In addition, recent analyst estimates for the company have been mixed and SKT has posted results that fell short of analysts' expectations. Based on operating earnings yield, the company is undervalued when compared to all of the companies we cover. Share price changes over the past year indicates that SKT will perform poorly over the near term.

Financial Data

(US$ in Thousands)	9 Mos	6 Mos	3 Mos	12/31/2018	12/31/2017	12/31/2016	12/31/2015	12/31/2014
Earnings Per Share	1.26	0.77	0.86	0.45	0.71	2.01	2.20	0.77
Cash Flow Per Share	2.57	2.53	2.59	2.77	2.68	2.51	2.33	2.01
Tang Book Value Per Share	5.09	5.25	5.08	2.95	3.77	4.47	3.81	2.96
Dividends Per Share	1.410	1.405	1.400	1.393	1.353	1.260	1.305	0.945
Dividend Payout %	111.90	182.47	162.79	309.44	190.49	62.69	59.32	122.73
Income Statement								
Total Revenue	357,856	238,862	123,155	494,681	488,234	465,834	439,369	418,558
EBITDA	149,787	110,934	81,855	223,658	242,609	349,911	350,808	206,336
Depn & Amortn	3,646	2,470	1,336	114,198	107,845	96,813	85,900	80,100
Income Before Taxes	99,503	77,023	64,212	44,639	69,939	193,457	210,684	69,099
Net Income	99,604	76,058	62,331	43,655	68,002	193,744	211,200	74,011
Average Shares	92,514	93,187	93,303	93,310	94,522	95,345	94,759	93,839
Balance Sheet								
Current Assets	4,664	7,379	1,616	9,083	6,101	12,222	142,864	62,880
Total Assets	2,324,357	2,343,768	2,353,824	2,384,902	2,540,105	2,526,214	2,326,707	2,097,660
Current Liabilities	73,932	60,324	87,536	82,676	90,416	78,143	125,784	97,946
Long-Term Obligations	1,571,923	1,586,309	1,582,784	1,712,918	1,763,651	1,687,866	1,563,806	1,443,194
Total Liabilities	1,851,413	1,852,986	1,875,591	1,904,723	1,958,527	1,855,998	1,751,570	1,600,841
Stockholders' Equity	472,944	490,782	478,233	480,179	581,578	670,216	575,137	496,819
Shares Outstanding	92,893	93,544	94,102	93,941	94,560	96,095	95,880	95,509
Statistical Record								
Return on Assets %	5.03	3.06	3.42	1.77	2.68	7.96	9.55	3.61
Return on Equity %	24.58	14.25	15.96	8.22	10.86	31.03	39.40	14.53
EBITDA Margin %	41.86	46.44	66.47	45.21	49.69	75.11	79.84	49.30
Net Margin %	27.83	31.84	50.61	8.82	13.93	41.59	48.07	17.68
Asset Turnover	0.20	0.20	0.20	0.20	0.19	0.19	0.20	0.20
Current Ratio	0.06	0.12	0.02	0.11	0.07	0.16	1.14	0.64
Debt to Equity	3.32	3.23	3.31	3.57	3.03	2.52	2.72	2.90
Price Range	24.36-13.82	24.67-15.53	24.67-19.85	26.27-19.85	37.17-22.19	41.74-29.67	40.55-30.58	37.65-32.02
P/E Ratio	19.33-10.97	32.04-20.17	28.69-23.08	58.38-44.11	52.35-31.25	20.77-14.76	18.43-13.90	48.90-41.58
Average Yield %	7.27	6.56	6.24	6.08	4.82	3.47	3.79	2.70

Address: 3200 Northline Avenue, Suite 360, Greensboro, NC 27408	Web Site: www.tangeroutlet.com	Auditors: DELOITTE & TOUCHE LLP
Telephone: 336-292-3010	Officers: Thomas E. (Tom) McDonough - President, Executive Vice President, Chief Operating Officer James F. (Jim) Williams - Executive Vice President, Senior Vice President, Chief Financial Officer, Chief Accounting Officer, Controller	Investor Contact: 336-834-6892
Fax: 336-297-0931		Transfer Agents: Computershare Trust Company, NA, Providence, RI

TAPESTRY INC

Exchange	Symbol	Price	52Wk Range	Yield	P/E
NYS	TPR	$26.97 (12/31/2019)	39.31-19.45	5.01	14.50

*7 Year Price Score 59.88   *NYSE Composite Index=100   *12 Month Price Score 83.96

Interim Earnings (Per Share)

Qtr.	Sep	Dec	Mar	Jun
2016-17	0.42	0.71	0.43	0.53
2017-18	(0.06)	0.22	0.48	0.73
2018-19	0.42	0.88	0.40	0.51
2019-20	0.07	...	...	...

Interim Dividends (Per Share)

Amt	Decl	Ex	Rec	Pay
0.338Q	02/21/2019	03/07/2019	03/08/2019	04/01/2019
0.338Q	05/16/2019	06/06/2019	06/07/2019	07/01/2019
0.338Q	08/15/2019	09/05/2019	09/06/2019	09/30/2019
0.338Q	11/14/2019	12/05/2019	12/06/2019	12/30/2019

Indicated Div: $1.35

Valuation Analysis / **Institutional Holding**

Forecast EPS	$2.54	No of Institutions
	(01/17/2020)	985
Market Cap	$7.4 Billion	Shares
Book Value	$3.1 Billion	308,237,728
Price/Book	2.41	% Held
Price/Sales	1.24	N/A

Business Summary: Apparel, Footwear & Accessories (MIC: 1.4.2 SIC: 3199 NAIC: 316999)

Tapestry is a lifestyle company. Co.'s primary product offerings, manufactured by third-party suppliers, include women's and men's bags, small leather goods, footwear, ready-to-wear including outerwear, watches, weekend and travel accessories, scarves, eyewear, fragrance, jewelry and other lifestyle products. Co. has three reportable segments: Coach, which includes sales of Coach brand products to customers through Coach operated stores; Kate Spade, which includes sales primarily of Kate Spade New York brand products to customers through Kate Spade operated stores; and Stuart Weitzman, which includes sales of Stuart Weitzman brand products primarily through Stuart Weitzman operated stores.

Recent Developments: For the quarter ended Sep 28 2019, net income decreased 83.6% to US$20.0 million from US$122.3 million in the year-earlier quarter. Revenues were US$1.36 billion, down 1.7% from US$1.38 billion the year before. Operating income was US$51.6 million versus US$162.3 million in the prior-year quarter, a decrease of 68.2%. Direct operating expenses declined 0.6% to US$443.4 million from US$446.1 million in the comparable period the year before. Indirect operating expenses increased 11.7% to US$862.9 million from US$772.8 million in the equivalent prior-year period.

Prospects: Our evaluation of Tapestry Inc. as of October 4th, 2019 is the result of our systematic analysis on three basic characteristics: earnings strength, relative valuation, and recent stock price movement. The company has enjoyed a very positive trend in earnings per share over the past 5 quarters. However, recent analyst estimates for the company have been mixed and TPR has posted results that fell short of analysts' expectations. Based on operating earnings yield, the company is undervalued when compared to all of the companies we cover. Share price changes over the past year indicates that TPR will perform very poorly over the near term.

Financial Data

(US$ in Thousands)	3 Mos	06/29/2019	06/30/2018	07/01/2017	07/02/2016	06/27/2015	06/28/2014	06/29/2013
Earnings Per Share	1.86	2.21	1.38	2.09	1.65	1.45	2.79	3.61
Cash Flow Per Share	2.87	2.74	3.50	3.05	2.69	3.41	3.56	5.02
Tang Book Value Per Share	N.M.	0.99	0.10	7.74	6.58	6.13	7.47	7.29
Dividends Per Share	1.350	1.350	1.350	1.350	1.350	1.350	1.350	1.238
Dividend Payout %	72.58	61.09	97.83	64.59	81.82	93.10	48.39	34.28
Income Statement								
Total Revenue	1,357,900	6,027,100	5,880,000	4,488,300	4,491,800	4,191,600	4,806,226	5,075,390
EBITDA	103,100	1,082,300	931,100	1,000,200	864,100	809,800	1,309,434	1,681,144
Depn & Amortn	64,200	268,200	260,300	212,800	210,600	191,800	189,360	162,987
Income Before Taxes	26,600	766,200	596,800	759,000	626,600	611,600	1,122,255	1,520,526
Income Taxes	6,600	122,800	199,300	168,000	166,100	209,220	340,919	486,106
Net Income	20,000	643,400	397,500	591,000	460,500	402,400	781,336	1,034,420
Average Shares	285,700	290,800	288,600	282,800	279,300	277,200	280,379	286,307
Balance Sheet								
Current Assets	2,203,900	2,556,800	2,432,600	3,953,300	2,172,900	2,506,500	1,855,217	2,070,947
Total Assets	8,450,100	6,877,300	6,678,300	5,831,600	4,892,700	4,666,900	3,663,131	3,531,897
Current Liabilities	1,212,000	918,000	938,200	753,800	826,700	834,700	813,118	722,510
Long-Term Obligations	1,597,300	1,601,900	1,599,900	1,579,500	861,200	879,100	...	485
Total Liabilities	5,363,200	3,363,900	3,433,700	2,829,700	2,209,800	2,177,000	1,242,478	1,122,739
Stockholders' Equity	3,086,900	3,513,400	3,244,600	3,001,900	2,682,900	2,489,900	2,420,653	2,409,158
Shares Outstanding	275,900	286,800	288,000	281,900	278,500	276,600	274,361	281,902
Statistical Record								
Return on Assets %	7.14	9.52	6.37	11.05	9.48	9.69	21.78	31.26
Return on Equity %	16.92	19.09	12.76	20.85	17.52	16.43	32.44	47.13
EBITDA Margin %	7.59	17.96	15.84	22.28	19.24	19.32	27.24	33.12
Net Margin %	1.47	10.68	6.76	13.17	10.25	9.60	16.26	20.38
Asset Turnover	0.79	0.89	0.94	0.84	0.92	1.01	1.34	1.53
Current Ratio	1.82	2.79	2.59	5.24	2.63	3.00	2.28	2.87
Debt to Equity	0.52	0.46	0.49	0.53	0.32	0.35	...	N.M.
Price Range	50.34-19.45	53.16-28.36	54.64-38.87	47.34-34.24	42.00-27.44	43.56-33.00	59.55-34.02	62.60-46.50
P/E Ratio	27.06-10.46	24.05-12.83	39.59-28.17	22.65-16.38	25.45-16.63	30.04-22.76	21.34-12.19	17.34-12.88
Average Yield %	4.06	3.47	2.96	3.43	3.92	3.62	2.67	2.23

Address: 10 Hudson Yards, New York, NY 10001	Web Site: www.tapestry.com	Auditors: DELOITTE & TOUCHE LLP
Telephone: 212-594-1850	Officers: Jide James Zeitlin - Chairman, Chief Executive Officer Todd Kahn - President, Chief Administrative Officer, Executive Vice President, Senior Vice President, General Counsel, Chief Legal Officer, Secretary	Transfer Agents: Mellon Investor Services, Jersey City, NJ
Fax: 212-594-1682		

TARGET CORP

Exchange	Symbol	Price	52Wk Range	Yield	P/E	Div Acheiver
NYS	TGT	$128.21 (12/31/2019)	129.21-65.53	2.06	20.48	47 Years

*7 Year Price Score 104.99 *NYSE Composite Index=100 *12 Month Price Score 125.72

Interim Earnings (Per Share)

Qtr.	Apr	Jul	Oct	Jan
2016-17	1.05	1.16	1.06	1.44
2017-18	1.23	1.22	0.88	2.01
2018-19	1.33	1.49	1.17	1.52
2019-20	1.53	1.82	1.39	...

Interim Dividends (Per Share)

Amt	Decl	Ex	Rec	Pay
0.64Q	03/14/2019	05/14/2019	05/15/2019	06/10/2019
0.66Q	06/13/2019	08/20/2019	08/21/2019	09/10/2019
0.66Q	09/19/2019	11/19/2019	11/20/2019	12/10/2019
0.66Q	01/08/2020	02/18/2020	02/19/2020	03/10/2020

Indicated Div: $2.64 (Div. Reinv. Plan)

Valuation Analysis / **Institutional Holding**

Forecast EPS	$6.35	No of Institutions	
	(01/17/2020)	2000	
Market Cap	$65.0 Billion	Shares	
Book Value	$11.5 Billion	518,991,840	
Price/Book	5.63	% Held	
Price/Sales	0.84	71.63	

Business Summary: Retail - General Merchandise/Department Stores (MIC: 2.1.1 SIC: 5331 NAIC: 452990)

Target provides its customers everyday essentials and merchandise. Co. sells an assortment of general merchandise and food. The majority of Co.'s general merchandise stores provide an edited food assortment, including perishables, dry grocery, dairy, and frozen items. Co.'s small format stores provide curated general merchandise and food assortments. Co.'s digital channels include merchandise assortment, including various items found in its stores, along with a complementary assortment. Co. also sells merchandise through periodic design and partnerships. Co.'s owned brands merchandise include: A New Day™, Archer Farms®, Art Class™, Ava & Viv®, Cat & Jack™, and Cloud Island™, among others.

Recent Developments: For the quarter ended Nov 2 2019, income from continuing operations increased 14.6% to US$706.0 million from US$616.0 million in the year-earlier quarter. Net income increased 14.8% to US$714.0 million from US$622.0 million in the year-earlier quarter. Revenues were US$18.67 billion, up 4.7% from US$17.82 billion the year before. Operating income was US$1.00 billion versus US$819.0 million in the prior-year quarter, an increase of 22.3%. Direct operating expenses rose 3.2% to US$12.94 billion from US$12.54 billion in the comparable period the year before. Indirect operating expenses increased 5.8% to US$4.73 billion from US$4.47 billion in the equivalent prior-year period.

Prospects: Our evaluation of Target Corp. as of October 4th, 2019 is the result of our systematic analysis on three basic characteristics: earnings strength, relative valuation, and recent stock price movement. The company has managed to produce a neutral trend in earnings per share over the past 5 quarters. In addition, recent analyst estimates for the company have been mixed and TGT has posted results that exceeded analysts' expectations. Based on operating earnings yield, the company is undervalued when compared to all of the companies we cover. Share price changes over the past year indicates that TGT will perform in line with the market over the near term.

Financial Data

(US$ in Millions)	9 Mos	6 Mos	3 Mos	02/02/2019	02/03/2018	01/28/2017	01/30/2016	01/31/2015
Earnings Per Share	6.26	6.04	5.71	5.51	5.33	4.70	5.31	(2.56)
Cash Flow Per Share	12.77	11.84	11.21	11.33	12.46	9.44	9.34	7.01
Tang Book Value Per Share	22.79	23.15	21.70	20.47	20.17	19.23	21.06	21.39
Dividends Per Share	2.580	2.560	2.540	2.520	2.440	2.320	2.160	1.900
Dividend Payout %	41.21	42.38	44.48	45.74	45.78	49.36	40.68	...
Income Statement								
Total Revenue	54,713	36,049	17,627	75,356	71,879	69,495	73,785	72,618
EBITDA	5,403	3,752	1,791	6,597	6,741	7,249	7,721	6,643
Depn & Amortn	1,905	1,267	644	2,460	2,429	2,280	2,191	2,108
Income Before Taxes	3,139	2,239	1,021	3,676	3,646	3,965	4,923	3,653
Income Taxes	703	509	229	746	718	1,296	1,602	1,204
Net Income	2,447	1,733	795	2,937	2,934	2,737	3,363	(1,636)
Average Shares	514	516	519	533	550	582	632	640
Balance Sheet								
Current Assets	13,805	12,119	11,607	12,519	12,564	11,990	14,130	14,087
Total Assets	43,741	41,566	40,619	41,290	38,999	37,431	40,262	41,404
Current Liabilities	16,608	14,364	13,239	15,014	13,201	12,708	12,622	11,736
Long-Term Obligations	10,513	10,365	11,357	10,223	11,317	11,031	11,945	12,705
Total Liabilities	32,196	29,730	29,502	29,993	27,290	26,478	27,305	27,407
Stockholders' Equity	11,545	11,836	11,117	11,297	11,709	10,953	12,957	13,997
Shares Outstanding	506	511	512	517	541	556	602	640
Statistical Record								
Return on Assets %	7.43	7.73	7.58	7.34	7.55	7.07	8.26	N.M.
Return on Equity %	28.69	27.41	27.06	25.60	25.47	22.96	25.02	N.M.
EBITDA Margin %	9.88	10.41	10.16	8.75	9.38	10.43	10.46	9.15
Net Margin %	4.47	4.81	4.51	3.90	4.08	3.94	4.56	N.M.
Asset Turnover	1.78	1.88	1.92	1.88	1.85	1.79	1.81	1.69
Current Ratio	0.83	0.84	0.88	0.83	0.95	0.94	1.12	1.20
Debt to Equity	0.91	0.88	1.02	0.90	0.97	1.01	0.92	0.91
Price Range	113.68-61.13	89.26-61.13	89.26-61.13	89.26-61.13	78.58-50.18	83.98-63.70	85.01-67.59	77.13-55.07
P/E Ratio	18.16-9.77	14.78-10.12	15.63-10.71	16.20-11.09	14.74-9.41	17.87-13.55	16.01-12.73	...
Average Yield %	3.07	3.22	3.28	3.30	4.14	3.16	2.77	3.03

Address: 1000 Nicollet Mall, Minneapolis, MN 55403 **Telephone:** 612-304-6073	**Web Site:** www.target.com **Officers:** Brian C. Cornell - Chairman, Chief Executive Officer John J. Mulligan - Interim President, Interim Chief Executive Officer, Executive Vice President, Chief Operating Officer, Chief Financial Officer	**Auditors:** Ernst & Young LLP **Investor Contact:** 800-775-3110 **Transfer Agents:** Mellon Investor Services, South Hackensack, N.J.

TARGA RESOURCES CORP

Exchange	Symbol	Price	52Wk Range	Yield	P/E
NYS	TRGP	$40.83 (12/31/2019)	47.89-32.46	8.92	N/A

*7 Year Price Score 52.16   *NYSE Composite Index=100   *12 Month Price Score 91.60

Interim Earnings (Per Share)

Qtr.	Mar	Jun	Sep	Dec
2016	(0.06)	(0.23)	(0.23)	(1.12)
2017	(0.77)	0.14	(0.91)	1.25
2018	(0.03)	0.35	(0.24)	(0.61)
2019	(0.30)	(0.18)	(0.34)	...

Interim Dividends (Per Share)

Amt	Decl	Ex	Rec	Pay
0.91Q	04/17/2019	04/30/2019	05/01/2019	05/15/2019
0.91Q	07/17/2019	07/30/2019	07/31/2019	08/15/2019
0.91Q	10/16/2019	10/31/2019	11/01/2019	11/15/2019
0.91Q	01/16/2020	01/30/2020	01/31/2020	02/18/2020

Indicated Div: $3.64

Valuation Analysis

		Institutional Holding	
Forecast EPS	$-0.92	No of Institutions	
	(01/16/2020)	576	
Market Cap	$9.5 Billion	Shares	
Book Value	$5.6 Billion	250,141,680	
Price/Book	1.70	% Held	
Price/Sales	1.08	95.47	

Business Summary: Refining & Marketing (MIC: 9.1.2 SIC: 4922 NAIC: 486210)

Targa Resources is a provider of midstream services and is a midstream energy company. Co. operates in two segments: Gathering and Processing, which consists of gathering, compressing, dehydrating, treating, conditioning, processing, and marketing natural gas and gathering crude oil; and Logistics and Marketing, which includes activities necessary to convert mixed natural gas liquids (NGLs) into NGL products and provides certain services such as storing, fractionating, terminaling, transporting and marketing of NGLs and NGL products, storing and terminaling of refined petroleum products and crude oil and certain natural gas supply and marketing activities in support of its other businesses.

Recent Developments: For the quarter ended Sep 30 2019, net income amounted to US$32.1 million versus a net loss of US$11.2 million in the year-earlier quarter. Revenues were US$1.90 billion, down 36.3% from US$2.99 billion the year before. Operating income was US$41.6 million versus US$76.7 million in the prior-year quarter, a decrease of 45.8%. Direct operating expenses declined 40.7% to US$1.53 billion from US$2.58 billion in the comparable period the year before. Indirect operating expenses increased 0.4% to US$332.6 million from US$331.3 million in the equivalent prior-year period.

Prospects: Our evaluation of Targa Resources Corp. as of October 4th, 2019 is the result of our systematic analysis on three basic characteristics: earnings strength, relative valuation, and recent stock price movement. The company has produced a positive trend in earnings per share over the past 5 quarters. However, recent analyst estimates for the company have been reduced, while TRGP has posted results that exceeded analysts' expectations. Based on operating earnings yield, the company is overvalued when compared to all of the companies we cover. Share price changes over the past year indicates that TRGP will perform very poorly over the near term.

Financial Data
(US$ in Thousands)

	9 Mos	6 Mos	3 Mos	12/31/2018	12/31/2017	12/31/2016	12/31/2015	12/31/2014
Earnings Per Share	(1.43)	(1.33)	(0.80)	(0.53)	(0.31)	(1.80)	1.09	2.43
Cash Flow Per Share	4.94	4.96	4.73	5.10	4.54	5.41	19.34	18.14
Tang Book Value Per Share	15.84	16.60	17.31	18.53	18.18	19.36	N.M.	N.M.
Dividends Per Share	3.640	3.640	3.640	3.640	3.640	3.640	3.390	2.678
Dividend Payout %	...	...	...	...	...	...	311.01	110.19
Income Statement								
Total Revenue	6,197,200	4,294,700	2,299,400	10,484,000	8,814,900	6,690,900	6,658,600	8,616,500
EBITDA	869,900	558,600	247,200	877,700	579,100	610,300	663,000	982,900
Depn & Amortn	597,700	393,800	197,000	633,300	621,300	601,500	540,400	362,800
Income Before Taxes	30,400	12,100	(30,400)	58,600	(275,900)	(245,400)	(109,300)	473,000
Income Taxes	(10,000)	(6,200)	(2,900)	5,500	(397,100)	(100,600)	39,600	68,000
Net Income	(96,400)	(49,100)	(38,900)	1,600	54,000	(187,300)	58,300	102,300
Average Shares	232,700	232,400	232,200	224,200	206,900	154,400	53,600	42,100
Balance Sheet								
Current Assets	1,476,000	1,211,900	1,181,000	1,418,900	1,269,900	1,006,800	920,000	882,600
Total Assets	18,918,500	18,318,200	17,569,200	16,938,200	14,388,600	12,871,200	13,253,700	6,453,500
Current Liabilities	1,669,300	1,658,000	2,041,600	2,798,800	1,616,600	1,167,600	881,600	827,100
Long-Term Obligations	7,279,700	6,639,000	7,118,500	5,632,400	4,703,000	4,606,600	5,761,500	2,885,400
Total Liabilities	13,330,000	12,514,200	11,559,300	10,613,100	8,011,800	7,431,800	11,792,300	6,283,700
Stockholders' Equity	5,588,500	5,804,000	6,009,900	6,325,100	6,376,800	5,439,400	1,461,400	169,800
Shares Outstanding	232,782	232,476	232,475	231,790	217,566	184,720	56,020	42,143
Statistical Record								
Return on Assets %	N.M.	N.M.	N.M.	0.01	0.40	N.M.	0.59	1.64
Return on Equity %	N.M.	N.M.	N.M.	0.03	0.91	N.M.	7.15	64.22
EBITDA Margin %	14.04	13.01	10.75	8.37	6.57	9.12	9.96	11.41
Net Margin %	N.M.	N.M.	N.M.	0.02	0.61	N.M.	0.88	1.19
Asset Turnover	0.50	0.58	0.64	0.67	0.65	0.51	0.68	1.38
Current Ratio	0.88	0.73	0.58	0.51	0.79	0.86	1.04	1.07
Debt to Equity	1.30	1.14	1.18	0.89	0.74	0.85	3.94	16.99
Price Range	58.51-32.46	58.51-34.11	58.51-34.11	58.51-34.11	61.35-40.35	58.20-15.43	107.22-25.74	150.62-85.34
P/E Ratio	...	...	...	...	...	...	98.37-23.61	61.98-35.12
Average Yield %	8.66	7.93	7.61	7.39	7.34	9.25	4.40	2.32

Address: 811 Louisiana St., Suite 2100, Houston, TX 77002 **Telephone:** 713-584-1000 **Fax:** 713-584-1100	**Web Site:** www.targaresources.com **Officers:** James W. Whalen - Executive Chairman Joe Bob Perkins - Executive Chairman, Chief Executive Officer	**Auditors:** PricewaterhouseCoopers LLP **Investor Contact:** 713-584-1000 **Transfer Agents:** Computershare Trust Company, N.A.

TAUBMAN CENTERS INC

Exchange	Symbol	Price	52Wk Range	Yield	P/E
NYS	TCO	$31.09 (12/31/2019)	54.30-29.59	8.68	8.01

*7 Year Price Score 54.59   *NYSE Composite Index=100   *12 Month Price Score 71.91

Interim Earnings (Per Share)

Qtr.	Mar	Jun	Sep	Dec
2016	0.41	0.57	0.31	0.48
2017	0.28	0.22	0.07	0.33
2018	0.30	0.25	0.34	0.05
2019	0.25	0.10	3.48	...

Interim Dividends (Per Share)

Amt	Decl	Ex	Rec	Pay
0.675Q	03/04/2019	03/14/2019	03/15/2019	03/29/2019
0.675Q	05/30/2019	06/13/2019	06/14/2019	06/28/2019
0.675Q	09/05/2019	09/13/2019	09/16/2019	09/30/2019
0.675Q	12/05/2019	12/13/2019	12/16/2019	12/31/2019

Indicated Div: $2.70

Valuation Analysis **Institutional Holding**

Forecast EPS	$0.82	No of Institutions
	(01/17/2020)	401
Market Cap	$1.9 Billion	Shares
Book Value	$56.9 Million	81,427,960
Price/Book	33.43	% Held
Price/Sales	2.92	100.81

TRADING VOLUME (thousand shares)

Business Summary: REITs (MIC: 5.3.1 SIC: 6798 NAIC: 525930)

Taubman Centers is a self-administered and self-managed real estate investment trust. The Taubman Realty Group Limited Partnership is a majority-owned partnership subsidiary of Co. that owns direct or indirect interests in all of Co.'s real estate properties. Co. owns, leases, acquires, disposes of, develops, expands, and manages regional shopping centers and interests therein. Co.'s owned portfolio of operating centers consisted of urban and suburban shopping centers operating in U.S. states, Puerto Rico, South Korea, and China.

Recent Developments: For the quarter ended Sep 30 2019, net income increased 730.1% to US$316.4 million from US$38.1 million in the year-earlier quarter. Revenues were US$162.5 million, up 2.1% from US$159.1 million the year before. Revenues from property income rose 60.2% to US$145.1 million from US$90.6 million in the corresponding quarter a year earlier.

Prospects: Our evaluation of Taubman Centers Inc. as of October 4th, 2019 is the result of our systematic analysis on three basic characteristics: earnings strength, relative valuation, and recent stock price movement. The company has produced a positive trend in earnings per share over the past 5 quarters. However, recent analyst estimates for the company have been mixed and TCO has posted results that fell short of analysts' expectations. Based on operating earnings yield, the company is fairly valued when compared to all of the companies we cover. Share price changes over the past year indicates that TCO will perform in line with the market over the near term.

Financial Data

(US$ in Thousands)	9 Mos	6 Mos	3 Mos	12/31/2018	12/31/2017	12/31/2016	12/31/2015	12/31/2014
Earnings Per Share	3.88	0.74	0.89	0.95	0.91	1.77	1.76	13.47
Cash Flow Per Share	4.87	4.90	4.69	4.82	4.61	5.04	5.01	5.75
Tang Book Value Per Share	0.93	...	...	...	0.37	1.19	1.87	5.03
Dividends Per Share	2.680	2.660	2.640	2.620	2.500	2.380	2.260	6.910
Dividend Payout %	69.07	359.46	296.63	275.79	274.73	134.46	128.41	51.30
Income Statement								
Total Revenue	484,318	321,812	160,208	640,870	629,165	612,557	557,172	679,129
EBITDA	284,131	184,134	97,446	334,404	315,160	337,347	299,983	312,736
Depn & Amortn	137,064	89,215	44,956	155,100	161,100	130,400	98,800	110,100
Income Before Taxes	34,477	20,024	15,605	46,107	45,488	120,662	138,142	111,833
Income Taxes	4,924	2,903	539	(231)	105	2,212	2,248	2,267
Net Income	255,887	34,145	21,508	83,486	80,705	132,613	134,127	893,013
Average Shares	62,245	61,339	61,399	61,277	61,040	60,829	62,161	64,921
Balance Sheet								
Current Assets	153,360	153,471	216,424	222,477	125,172	103,812	270,107	364,002
Total Assets	4,536,852	4,485,098	4,451,394	4,344,106	4,214,592	4,010,912	3,563,380	3,214,901
Current Liabilities	750,610	755,068	704,044	814,008	801,892	817,399	798,611	769,453
Long-Term Obligations	3,634,165	3,812,538	3,846,501	3,830,195	3,555,223	3,255,512	2,643,958	2,025,505
Total Liabilities	4,479,922	4,592,377	4,568,125	4,436,979	4,192,352	3,938,832	3,450,573	2,896,538
Stockholders' Equity	56,930	(107,279)	(116,731)	(92,873)	22,240	72,080	112,807	318,363
Shares Outstanding	61,213	61,208	61,161	61,069	60,832	60,430	60,233	63,324
Statistical Record								
Return on Assets %	5.98	1.60	1.84	1.95	1.96	3.49	3.96	26.57
Return on Equity %	5,995.26	...	...	...	171.13	143.06	62.22	900.96
EBITDA Margin %	58.67	57.22	60.82	52.18	50.09	55.07	53.84	46.05
Net Margin %	52.83	10.61	13.43	13.03	12.83	21.65	24.07	131.49
Asset Turnover	0.15	0.15	0.15	0.15	0.15	0.16	0.16	0.20
Current Ratio	0.20	0.20	0.31	0.27	0.16	0.13	0.34	0.47
Debt to Equity	63.84	...	...	...	159.86	45.17	23.44	6.36
Price Range	58.71-37.88	65.00-40.13	65.00-43.72	66.39-43.72	76.17-46.30	81.63-66.67	84.70-67.14	80.06-63.34
P/E Ratio	15.13-9.76	87.84-54.23	73.03-49.12	69.88-46.02	83.70-50.88	46.12-37.67	48.13-38.15	5.94-4.70
Average Yield %	5.59	4.99	4.78	4.55	4.16	3.27	3.03	9.43

Address: 200 East Long Lake Road, Suite 300, Bloomfield Hills, MI 48304-2324
Telephone: 248-258-6800

Web Site: www.taubman.com
Officers: Robert S. Taubman - Chairman, President, Chief Executive Officer Simon J. Leopold - Executive Vice President, Chief Financial Officer, Treasurer, Principal Accounting Officer

Auditors: KPMG LLP
Investor Contact: 248-258-7367
Transfer Agents: Computershare, Providence, R.I.

TC PIPELINES, LP

Exchange	Symbol	Price	52Wk Range	Yield	P/E	Div Acheiver
NYS	TCP	$42.30 (12/31/2019)	43.62-30.47	6.15	N/A	19 Years

*7 Year Price Score 62.78 *NYSE Composite Index=100 *12 Month Price Score 101.68

Interim Earnings (Per Share)

Qtr.	Mar	Jun	Sep	Dec
2016	1.10	0.76	0.65	0.70
2017	1.05	0.73	0.61	0.78
2018	1.32	1.00	0.79	(5.79)
2019	1.28	0.75	0.76	...

Interim Dividends (Per Share)

Amt	Decl	Ex	Rec	Pay
0.65Q	01/22/2019	01/31/2019	02/01/2019	02/11/2019
0.65Q	04/23/2019	05/02/2019	05/03/2019	05/13/2019
0.65Q	07/23/2019	08/01/2019	08/02/2019	08/14/2019
0.65Q	10/22/2019	10/31/2019	11/01/2019	11/14/2019

Indicated Div: $2.60

Valuation Analysis

		Institutional Holding	
Forecast EPS	$3.68	No of Institutions	
	(01/15/2020)	205	
Market Cap	$3.0 Billion	Shares	
Book Value	N/A	68,932,832	
Price/Book	N/A	% Held	
Price/Sales	5.80	65.74	

Business Summary: Equipment & Services (MIC: 9.1.3 SIC: 4922 NAIC: 486210)

TC PipeLines is engaged in acquiring, owning and participating in the management of energy infrastructure businesses in North America. Co. has ownership interests in eight natural gas interstate pipeline systems (Gas Transmission Northwest LLC; Bison Pipeline LLC; North Baja Pipeline, LLC; Tuscarora Gas Transmission Company; Northern Border Pipeline Company; Portland Natural Gas Transmission System; Great Lakes Gas Transmission Limited Partnership; and Iroquois Gas Transmission System, L.P) that are collectively designed to transport natural gas from producing regions and import facilities to market hubs and consuming markets primarily in the Western, Midwestern and Eastern U.S.

Recent Developments: For the quarter ended Sep 30 2019, net income decreased 9.2% to US$59.0 million from US$65.0 million in the year-earlier quarter. Revenues were US$93.0 million, down 9.7% from US$103.0 million the year before. Indirect operating expenses decreased 10.5% to US$34.0 million from US$38.0 million in the equivalent prior-year period.

Prospects: Our evaluation of TC PipeLines L.P. as of October 4th, 2019 is the result of our systematic analysis on three basic characteristics: earnings strength, relative valuation, and recent stock price movement. The company has generated a negative trend in earnings per share over the past 5 quarters. However, recent analyst estimates for the company have been raised and TCP has posted results that fell short of analysts' expectations. Based on operating earnings yield, the company is undervalued when compared to all of the companies we cover. Share price changes over the past year indicates that TCP will perform well over the near term.

Financial Data
(US$ in Thousands)

	9 Mos	6 Mos	3 Mos	12/31/2018	12/31/2017	12/31/2016	12/31/2015	12/31/2014
Earnings Per Share	(3.00)	(2.97)	(2.72)	(2.68)	3.16	3.21	(0.03)	2.67
Cash Flow Per Share	7.43	7.64	7.83	7.57	5.43	5.78	4.60	4.91
Dividends Per Share	2.600	2.600	2.600	2.950	3.880	3.660	3.460	3.300
Dividend Payout %	...	...	...	...	122.78	114.02	...	123.60
Income Statement								
Total Revenue	299,000	206,000	113,000	549,000	422,000	357,000	344,000	336,000
EBITDA	170,000	120,000	89,000	(147,000)	318,000	278,000	61,000	249,000
Depn & Amortn	1,000	1,000	20,000	97,000	97,000	86,000	85,000	86,000
Income Before Taxes	102,000	74,000	46,000	(337,000)	140,000	128,000	(77,000)	116,000
Income Taxes	1,000	1,000	...	1,000	1,000	...	...	...
Net Income	204,000	148,000	93,000	(182,000)	252,000	244,000	13,000	172,000
Average Shares	71,300	71,300	71,300	71,300	69,200	67,400	63,900	62,700
Balance Sheet								
Current Assets	140,000	90,000	107,000	97,000	90,000	102,000	81,000	68,000
Total Assets	2,822,000	2,799,000	2,899,000	2,899,000	3,559,000	3,158,000	3,133,000	3,349,000
Current Liabilities	180,000	144,000	92,000	90,000	100,000	66,000	59,000	291,000
Long-Term Obligations	1,871,000	1,892,000	2,040,000	2,072,000	2,352,000	1,835,000	1,896,000	1,446,000
Total Liabilities	2,198,000	2,181,000	2,280,000	2,308,000	2,596,000	1,929,000	1,982,000	1,997,000
Stockholders' Equity	...	...	...	...	...	83,000	...	...
Shares Outstanding	71,300	73,200	71,300	73,206	72,473	69,354	66,217	63,561
Statistical Record								
Return on Assets %	N.M.	N.M.	N.M.	N.M.	7.50	7.74	0.40	5.06
EBITDA Margin %	56.86	58.25	78.76	N.M.	75.36	77.87	17.73	74.11
Net Margin %	68.23	71.84	82.30	N.M.	59.72	68.35	3.78	51.19
Asset Turnover	0.16	0.17	0.17	0.17	0.13	0.11	0.11	0.10
Current Ratio	0.78	0.63	1.16	1.08	0.90	1.55	1.37	0.23
Debt to Equity	...	...	...	...	...	22.11	...	...
Price Range	40.83-27.27	37.92-25.52	37.66-23.16	56.55-23.16	64.90-48.88	59.99-35.44	72.53-41.48	76.59-45.52
P/E Ratio	...	...	...	...	20.54-15.47	18.69-11.04	...	28.69-17.05
Average Yield %	7.45	7.88	8.43	8.51	6.94	7.04	5.94	5.92

Address: 700 Louisiana Street, Suite 700, Houston, TX 77002-2761 Telephone: 877-290-2772	Web Site: www.tcpipelineslp.com Officers: Stanley G. Chapman - Chairman, Holding/Parent Company Officer Steven D. Becker - President, Principal Executive Officer	Auditors: KPMG LLP Investor Contact: 877-.29-0.2772 Transfer Agents: Computershare

TE CONNECTIVITY LTD

Exchange	Symbol	Price	52Wk Range	Yield	P/E
NYS	TEL	$95.84 (12/31/2019)	97.35-72.43	1.92	17.68

*7 Year Price Score 103.60 *NYSE Composite Index=100   *12 Month Price Score 99.06

Interim Earnings (Per Share)

Qtr.	Dec	Mar	Jun	Sep
2014-15	1.14	1.45	0.75	2.55
2015-16	0.91	1.03	2.35	1.23
2016-17	1.14	1.13	1.22	5.92
2017-18	(0.11)	1.38	1.29	4.72
2018-19	0.80	1.29	2.23	1.10

Interim Dividends (Per Share)

Amt	Decl	Ex	Rec	Pay
0.44Q	02/11/2019	02/21/2019	02/22/2019	03/08/2019
0.46Q	05/08/2019	05/23/2019	05/24/2019	06/07/2019
0.46Q	08/08/2019	08/22/2019	08/23/2019	09/06/2019
0.46Q	11/06/2019	11/21/2019	11/22/2019	12/06/2019

Indicated Div: $1.84

Valuation Analysis — **Institutional Holding**

Forecast EPS	N/A	No of Institutions	998
Market Cap	$32.1 Billion	Shares	
Book Value	$10.6 Billion		360,680,512
Price/Book	3.04	% Held	
Price/Sales	2.39		N/A

Business Summary: Electrical Equipment (MIC: 7.3.1 SIC: 5065 NAIC: 334111)

TE Connectivity is a manufacturing company. Co. operates three segments: Transportation Solutions, which engages in connectivity and sensor technologies, focusing on terminals and connector systems and components, sensors, relays, application tooling, and wire and heat shrink tubing; Industrial Solutions, which supplies products that connect and distribute power, data and signals, focusing on terminals and connector systems and components, heat shrink tubing, relays, and wire and cable; and Communications Solutions, which supplies electronics for the data and devices and appliances markets, focusing on terminals and connector systems and components, relays, heat shrink tubing and antennas.

Recent Developments: For the year ended Sep 27 2019, income from continuing operations decreased 24.7% to US$1.95 billion from US$2.58 billion a year earlier. Net income decreased 28.1% to US$1.84 billion from US$2.57 billion in the prior year. Revenues were US$13.45 billion, down 3.9% from US$13.99 billion the year before. Operating income was US$1.98 billion versus US$2.33 billion in the prior year, a decrease of 15.1%. Direct operating expenses declined 2.0% to US$9.05 billion from US$9.24 billion in the comparable period the year before. Indirect operating expenses increased 0.1% to US$2.42 billion from US$2.41 billion in the equivalent prior-year period.

Prospects: Our evaluation of TE Connectivity Ltd. as of October 4th, 2019 is the result of our systematic analysis on three basic characteristics: earnings strength, relative valuation, and recent stock price movement. The company has produced a positive trend in earnings per share over the past 5 quarters. However, recent analyst estimates for the company have been mixed and TEL has posted results that exceeded analysts' expectations. Based on operating earnings yield, the company is undervalued when compared to all of the companies we cover. Share price changes over the past year indicates that TEL will perform well over the near term.

Financial Data

(US$ in Millions)	09/27/2019	09/28/2018	09/29/2017	09/30/2016	09/25/2015	09/26/2014	09/27/2013
Earnings Per Share	5.42	7.27	9.40	5.44	5.89	4.27	3.02
Cash Flow Per Share	7.19	7.02	6.56	5.17	4.74	5.09	4.91
Tang Book Value Per Share	9.65	9.99	6.42	3.14	8.14	7.56	6.83
Dividends Per Share	1.800	1.680	3.080	1.400	1.240	1.080	0.920
Dividend Payout %	33.21	23.11	32.77	25.74	21.05	25.29	30.46
Income Statement							
Total Revenue	13,448	13,988	25,298	12,238	12,233	13,912	13,280
EBITDA	2,490	2,819	4,780	1,706	2,157	2,610	1,869
Depn & Amortn	510	487	908	436	463	502	496
Income Before Taxes	1,931	2,240	3,648	1,162	1,575	1,996	1,248
Income Taxes	(15)	(344)	435	(779)	337	207	(29)
Net Income	1,844	2,565	3,366	2,009	2,420	1,781	1,276
Average Shares	340	353	716	369	411	417	423
Balance Sheet							
Current Assets	5,554	6,199	11,852	4,775	7,887	7,544	6,309
Total Assets	19,694	20,386	38,806	17,608	20,608	20,152	18,461
Current Liabilities	3,540	4,410	7,694	3,066	3,577	3,954	3,924
Long-Term Obligations	3,395	3,037	7,268	3,739	3,403	3,281	2,303
Total Liabilities	9,124	9,555	19,304	9,123	11,023	11,145	10,081
Stockholders' Equity	10,570	10,831	19,502	8,485	9,585	9,007	8,380
Shares Outstanding	335	344	703	355	393	407	411
Statistical Record							
Return on Assets %	9.23	8.69	11.97	10.34	11.91	9.25	6.78
Return on Equity %	17.28	16.96	24.12	21.88	26.10	20.54	15.65
EBITDA Margin %	18.52	20.15	18.89	13.94	17.63	18.76	14.07
Net Margin %	13.71	18.34	13.31	16.42	19.78	12.80	9.61
Asset Turnover	0.67	0.47	0.90	0.63	0.60	0.72	0.71
Current Ratio	1.57	1.41	1.54	1.56	2.20	1.91	1.61
Debt to Equity	0.32	0.28	0.37	0.44	0.36	0.36	0.27
Price Range	97.35-70.72	105.75-83.06	83.22-61.03	67.61-52.27	73.42-51.47	64.97-49.91	53.54-32.03
P/E Ratio	17.96-13.05	14.55-11.43	8.85-6.49	12.43-9.61	12.47-8.74	15.22-11.69	17.73-10.61
Average Yield %	2.12	1.77	4.15	2.30	1.92	1.86	2.18

Address: Rheinstrasse 20, Schaffhausen, CH-8200 **Telephone:** 526-336-661	**Web Site:** www.te.com **Officers:** Terrence R. Curtin - Chief Executive Officer, President, Executive Vice President, Vice President, Chief Financial Officer, Corporate Controller, Division Officer Mario Calastri - Senior Vice President, Treasurer, Interim Chief Financial Officer	**Auditors:** DELOITTE & TOUCHE LLP **Investor Contact:** 610-893-9551 **Transfer Agents:** Computershare Shareowner Services LLC, Jersey City, NJ

TELEDYNE TECHNOLOGIES INC

Exchange	Symbol	Price	52Wk Range	Yield	P/E
NYS	TDY	$346.54 (12/31/2019)	349.76-200.06	N/A	34.28

*7 Year Price Score 159.46 *NYSE Composite Index=100 *12 Month Price Score 117.07

Interim Earnings (Per Share)

Qtr.	Mar	Jun	Sep	Dec
2016	1.10	1.31	1.46	1.47
2017	0.84	1.66	1.90	1.85
2018	1.81	2.32	2.43	2.45
2019	2.02	2.80	2.84	...

Interim Dividends (Per Share)

No Dividends Paid

Valuation Analysis

		Institutional Holding	
Forecast EPS	$10.40	No of Institutions	
	(11/14/2019)	531	
Market Cap	$12.6 Billion	Shares	
Book Value	$2.6 Billion	42,353,056	
Price/Book	4.92	% Held	
Price/Sales	4.11	87.24	

Business Summary: Electronic Instruments & Related Products (MIC: 6.2.3 SIC: 3812 NAIC: 334511)

Teledyne Technologies provides technologies for industrial markets. These markets include aerospace and defense, factory automation, air and water quality environmental monitoring, electronics design and development, oceanographic research, deepwater oil and gas exploration and production, medical imaging and pharmaceutical research. Co.'s products include digital imaging sensors, cameras and systems within the visible, infrared and X-ray spectra, monitoring and control instrumentation for marine and environmental applications, environment interconnects, electronic test and measurement equipment, aircraft information management systems, and defense electronics, among others.

Recent Developments: For the quarter ended Sep 29 2019, net income increased 18.2% to US$106.7 million from US$90.3 million in the year-earlier quarter. Revenues were US$802.2 million, up 10.6% from US$725.3 million the year before. Operating income was US$128.7 million versus US$105.5 million in the prior-year quarter, an increase of 22.0%. Direct operating expenses rose 9.3% to US$487.7 million from US$446.2 million in the comparable period the year before. Indirect operating expenses increased 7.0% to US$185.8 million from US$173.6 million in the equivalent prior-year period.

Prospects: Our evaluation of Teledyne Technologies Inc. as of October 4th, 2019 is the result of our systematic analysis on three basic characteristics: earnings strength, relative valuation, and recent stock price movement. The company has produced a positive trend in earnings per share over the past 5 quarters. However, recent analyst estimates for the company have been mixed and TDY has posted results that exceeded analysts' expectations. Based on operating earnings yield, the company is fairly valued when compared to all of the companies we cover. Share price changes over the past year indicates that TDY will perform well over the near term.

Financial Data

(US$ in Thousands)	9 Mos	6 Mos	3 Mos	12/30/2018	12/31/2017	01/01/2017	01/03/2016	12/28/2014
Earnings Per Share	10.11	9.70	9.22	9.01	6.26	5.37	5.44	5.75
Cash Flow Per Share	12.08	11.90	12.61	12.52	10.67	9.19	5.86	7.78
Tang Book Value Per Share	3.38	5.64	2.08	4.16	N.M.	3.60	N.M.	N.M.
Income Statement								
Total Revenue	2,329,400	1,527,200	745,200	2,901,800	2,603,800	2,149,900	2,298,100	2,394,000
EBITDA	443,100	286,300	125,900	492,900	386,000	322,100	340,400	363,400
Depn & Amortn	82,600	54,700	27,600	73,500	65,900	57,600	58,300	62,300
Income Before Taxes	344,200	220,800	92,900	393,900	287,000	241,300	258,200	282,100
Income Taxes	57,600	40,900	17,600	60,100	59,800	50,400	62,700	66,500
Net Income	286,600	179,900	75,300	333,800	227,200	190,900	195,800	217,700
Average Shares	37,600	37,400	37,200	37,000	36,300	35,500	35,300	37,900
Balance Sheet								
Current Assets	1,238,100	1,161,000	1,117,500	1,114,400	1,011,900	846,200	828,200	941,700
Total Assets	4,479,600	4,200,200	4,161,700	3,809,300	3,846,400	2,774,400	2,718,500	2,862,200
Current Liabilities	835,500	711,000	723,700	720,800	540,600	501,800	393,600	539,000
Long-Term Obligations	719,300	656,200	724,600	612,300	1,069,300	515,800	762,900	618,900
Total Liabilities	1,908,600	1,727,200	1,812,200	1,579,600	1,899,100	1,220,000	1,374,400	1,434,900
Stockholders' Equity	2,571,000	2,473,000	2,349,500	2,229,700	1,947,300	1,554,400	1,344,100	1,427,300
Shares Outstanding	36,468	36,376	36,232	36,087	35,540	35,110	34,514	36,655
Statistical Record								
Return on Assets %	9.00	8.94	8.48	8.74	6.88	6.97	6.90	7.78
Return on Equity %	15.78	15.79	15.55	16.03	13.01	13.21	13.90	15.06
EBITDA Margin %	19.02	18.75	16.89	16.99	14.82	14.98	14.81	15.18
Net Margin %	12.30	11.78	10.10	11.50	8.73	8.88	8.52	9.09
Asset Turnover	0.73	0.74	0.73	0.76	0.79	0.78	0.81	0.86
Current Ratio	1.48	1.63	1.54	1.55	1.87	1.69	2.10	1.75
Debt to Equity	0.28	0.27	0.31	0.27	0.55	0.33	0.57	0.43
Price Range	321.67-191.22	273.87-191.22	247.77-179.99	247.77-175.56	186.24-121.11	128.89-76.61	111.48-83.47	108.50-88.48
P/E Ratio	31.82-18.91	28.23-19.71	26.87-19.52	27.50-19.49	29.75-19.35	24.00-14.27	20.49-15.34	18.87-15.39

Address: 1049 Camino Dos Rios, Thousand Oaks, CA 91360-2362 Telephone: 805-373-4545	Web Site: Officers: Robert Mehrabian - Executive Chairman, Chairman, President, Chief Executive Officer Aldo (Al) Pichelli - President, Chief Executive Officer, Executive Vice President, Chief Operating Officer, Division Officer	Auditors: DELOITTE & TOUCHE LLP Investor Contact: 805-373-4542 Transfer Agents: Computershare, Jersey City, NJ

TELEFLEX INCORPORATED

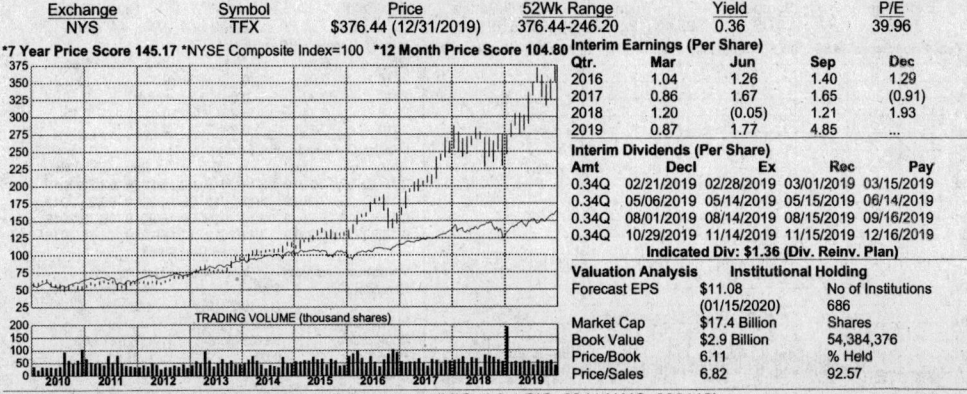

Exchange	Symbol	Price	52Wk Range	Yield	P/E
NYS	TFX	$376.44 (12/31/2019)	376.44-246.20	0.36	39.96

*7 Year Price Score 145.17 *NYSE Composite Index=100 *12 Month Price Score 104.80

Interim Earnings (Per Share)

Qtr.	Mar	Jun	Sep	Dec
2016	1.04	1.26	1.40	1.29
2017	0.86	1.67	1.65	(0.91)
2018	1.20	(0.05)	1.21	1.93
2019	0.87	1.77	4.85	...

Interim Dividends (Per Share)

Amt	Decl	Ex	Rec	Pay
0.34Q	02/21/2019	02/28/2019	03/01/2019	03/15/2019
0.34Q	05/06/2019	05/14/2019	05/15/2019	06/14/2019
0.34Q	08/01/2019	08/14/2019	08/15/2019	09/16/2019
0.34Q	10/29/2019	11/14/2019	11/15/2019	12/16/2019

Indicated Div: $1.36 (Div. Reinv. Plan)

Valuation Analysis

Forecast EPS	$11.08
	(01/15/2020)
Market Cap	$17.4 Billion
Book Value	$2.9 Billion
Price/Book	6.11
Price/Sales	6.82

Institutional Holding

No of Institutions	686
Shares	54,384,376
% Held	92.57

Business Summary: Medical Instruments & Equipment (MIC: 4.3.1 SIC: 3841 NAIC: 339112)

Teleflex is a provider of medical technology products. Co. designs, develops, manufactures and supplies single-use medical devices used by hospitals and healthcare providers for common diagnostic and therapeutic procedures in critical care and surgical applications. Co.'s segments include: Vascular North America, which provides Arrow branded catheters and related devices that are used in a range of procedures, including the administration of intravenous of intravenous therapies, the measurement of blood pressure and the withdrawal of blood samples through a single puncture site; and Interventional North America, which provides devices for treating coronary and peripheral vascular disease.

Recent Developments: For the quarter ended Sep 29 2019, income from continuing operations increased 304.9% to US$228.9 million from US$56.5 million in the year-earlier quarter. Net income increased 305.0% to US$228.9 million from US$56.5 million in the year-earlier quarter. Revenues were US$648.3 million, up 6.3% from US$609.7 million the year before. Operating income was US$117.6 million versus US$82.1 million in the prior-year quarter, an increase of 43.3%. Direct operating expenses rose 2.1% to US$272.6 million from US$267.1 million in the comparable period the year before. Indirect operating expenses decreased 0.9% to US$258.1 million from US$260.5 million in the equivalent prior-year period.

Prospects: Our evaluation of Teleflex Inc. as of October 4th, 2019 is the result of our systematic analysis on three basic characteristics: earnings strength, relative valuation, and recent stock price movement. The company has managed to produce a neutral trend in earnings per share over the past 5 quarters. However, recent analyst estimates for the company have been raised and TFX has posted results that exceeded analysts' expectations. Based on operating earnings yield, the company is fairly valued when compared to all of the companies we cover. Share price changes over the past year indicates that TFX will perform over the near term.

Financial Data

(US$ in Thousands)	9 Mos	6 Mos	3 Mos	12/31/2018	12/31/2017	12/31/2016	12/31/2015	12/31/2014
Earnings Per Share	9.42	5.78	3.96	4.29	3.27	4.98	5.10	4.04
Cash Flow Per Share	9.11	8.90	8.87	9.52	9.47	9.45	7.30	7.02
Dividends Per Share	1.360	1.360	1.360	1.360	1.360	1.360	1.360	1.360
Dividend Payout %	14.44	23.53	34.34	31.70	41.59	27.31	26.67	33.66
Income Statement								
Total Revenue	1,914,410	1,266,091	613,584	2,448,383	2,146,303	1,868,027	1,809,690	1,839,832
EBITDA	463,582	292,201	129,818	531,684	521,949	418,098	413,830	395,995
Depn & Amortn	163,260	109,500	54,575	209,980	155,263	117,906	108,393	111,133
Income Before Taxes	238,608	140,062	52,890	219,628	284,911	245,725	244,646	220,110
Income Taxes	(115,567)	14,816	10,972	23,196	129,648	8,074	7,838	28,650
Net Income	353,201	124,272	40,897	200,802	152,530	237,377	244,863	187,679
Average Shares	47,176	47,036	46,942	46,801	46,664	47,646	48,058	46,470
Balance Sheet								
Current Assets	1,237,610	1,245,141	1,182,614	1,236,169	1,128,807	1,183,393	1,006,431	1,053,209
Total Assets	6,257,182	6,314,410	6,268,069	6,277,991	6,181,492	3,891,213	3,878,516	3,977,255
Current Liabilities	530,363	493,892	520,916	582,456	483,876	427,646	666,712	634,899
Long-Term Obligations	1,949,068	2,081,372	2,072,939	2,072,200	2,162,927	850,252	646,000	700,000
Total Liabilities	3,404,206	3,649,566	3,698,191	3,738,013	3,750,961	1,751,872	1,869,244	2,065,946
Stockholders' Equity	2,852,976	2,664,844	2,569,878	2,539,978	2,430,531	2,139,341	2,009,272	1,911,309
Shares Outstanding	46,295	46,232	47,323	46,016	45,167	44,073	41,609	41,439
Statistical Record								
Return on Assets %	7.12	4.35	2.95	3.22	3.03	6.09	6.23	4.59
Return on Equity %	16.56	10.65	7.23	8.08	6.68	11.41	12.49	9.81
EBITDA Margin %	24.22	23.08	21.16	21.72	24.32	22.38	22.87	21.52
Net Margin %	18.45	9.82	6.67	8.20	7.11	12.71	13.53	10.20
Asset Turnover	0.41	0.40	0.39	0.39	0.43	0.48	0.46	0.45
Current Ratio	2.33	2.52	2.27	2.12	2.33	2.77	1.51	1.66
Debt to Equity	0.68	0.78	0.81	0.82	0.89	0.40	0.32	0.37
Price Range	371.65-229.54	336.13-228.13	304.96-228.13	287.65-228.13	270.19-158.86	188.35-126.00	140.26-109.41	119.15-90.94
P/E Ratio	39.45-24.37	58.15-39.47	77.01-57.61	67.05-53.18	82.63-48.58	37.82-25.30	27.50-21.45	29.49-22.51
Average Yield %	0.46	0.50	0.51	0.52	0.64	0.85	1.07	1.28

Address: 550 East Swedesford Road, Suite 400, Wayne, PA 19087
Telephone: 610-225-6800

Web Site: www.teleflex.com
Officers: Liam J. Kelly - President, Executive Vice President, Chief Operating Officer, Division Officer, Chief Executive Officer Thomas E. Powell - Executive Vice President, Senior Vice President, Chief Financial Officer

Auditors: PricewaterhouseCoopers LLP
Investor Contact: 610-948-2836
Transfer Agents: American Stock Transfer & Trust Company, New York, NY

TELEPHONE & DATA SYSTEMS INC

Exchange	Symbol	Price	52Wk Range	Yield	P/E	Div Acheiver
NYS	TDS	$25.43 (12/31/2019)	36.81-21.93	2.60	23.99	44 Years

*7 Year Price Score 88.66   *NYSE Composite Index=100   *12 Month Price Score 76.36

Interim Earnings (Per Share)

Qtr.	Mar	Jun	Sep	Dec
2016	0.07	0.25	0.11	(0.05)
2017	0.33	0.09	(1.64)	2.58
2018	0.34	0.29	0.41	0.13
2019	0.50	0.28	0.15	...

Interim Dividends (Per Share)

Amt	Decl	Ex	Rec	Pay
0.165Q	02/22/2019	03/14/2019	03/15/2019	03/29/2019
0.165Q	05/23/2019	06/13/2019	06/14/2019	06/28/2019
0.165Q	08/15/2019	09/13/2019	09/16/2019	09/30/2019
0.165Q	11/18/2019	12/13/2019	12/16/2019	12/30/2019

Indicated Div: $0.66

Valuation Analysis | **Institutional Holding**

Forecast EPS	$0.94	No of Institutions
	(11/19/2019)	448
Market Cap	$2.9 Billion	Shares
Book Value	$4.6 Billion	118,021,600
Price/Book	0.62	% Held
Price/Sales	0.56	N/A

Business Summary: Services (MIC: 6.1.2 SIC: 4813 NAIC: 517110)

Telephone and Data Systems is a telecommunications company. Co. conducts its wireless operations through its majority-owned subsidiary, United States Cellular Corporation. Co. provides broadband, video and voice services through its wholly-owned subsidiary, TDS Telecommunications LLC (TDS Telecom). Co. has three business segments comprised of: U.S. Cellular, which provides a range of wireless devices such as handsets, tablets, mobile hotspots, home phones and routers for use by its customers; TDS Telecom's Wireline and Cable, which provide high-speed data services bundled with video entertainment and voice services.

Recent Developments: For the quarter ended Sep 30 2019, net income decreased 56.6% to US$23.0 million from US$53.0 million in the year-earlier quarter. Revenues were US$1.32 billion, up 1.9% from US$1.30 billion the year before. Operating income was US$29.0 million versus US$51.0 million in the prior-year quarter, a decrease of 43.1%. Direct operating expenses rose 0.5% to US$608.0 million from US$605.0 million in the comparable period the year before. Indirect operating expenses increased 6.7% to US$684.0 million from US$641.0 million in the equivalent prior-year period.

Prospects: Our evaluation of Telephone and Data Systems Inc. as of October 4th, 2019 is the result of our systematic analysis on three basic characteristics: earnings strength, relative valuation, and recent stock price movement. The company has suffered a very negative trend in earnings per share over the past 5 quarters. However, recent analyst estimates for the company have been raised and TDS has posted results that fell short of analysts' expectations. Based on operating earnings yield, the company is fairly valued when compared to all of the companies we cover. Share price changes over the past year indicates that TDS will perform in line with the market over the near term.

Financial Data

(US$ in Thousands)	9 Mos	6 Mos	3 Mos	12/31/2018	12/31/2017	12/31/2016	12/31/2015	12/31/2014
Earnings Per Share	1.06	1.32	1.33	1.17	1.37	0.39	1.98	(1.26)
Cash Flow Per Share	9.38	10.05	9.91	9.08	6.99	7.09	7.27	3.64
Tang Book Value Per Share	12.56	12.25	14.32	14.06	11.25	10.97	11.25	12.91
Dividends Per Share	0.655	0.650	0.645	0.640	0.620	0.592	0.564	0.536
Dividend Payout %	61.79	49.24	48.50	54.70	45.26	151.79	28.48	...
Income Statement								
Total Revenue	3,840,000	2,518,000	1,257,000	5,109,000	5,044,000	5,104,000	5,176,241	5,009,438
EBITDA	868,000	603,000	321,000	1,046,000	713,000	880,000	1,207,962	607,851
Depn & Amortn	697,000	460,000	227,000	839,000	817,000	820,000	810,500	797,600
Income Before Taxes	67,000	74,000	60,000	61,000	(259,000)	(48,000)	294,526	(284,189)
Income Taxes	64,000	50,000	34,000	46,000	(279,000)	40,000	171,992	(4,932)
Net Income	110,000	92,000	59,000	135,000	153,000	43,000	219,037	(136,355)
Average Shares	116,000	116,000	116,000	114,000	112,000	111,000	109,910	108,485
Balance Sheet								
Current Assets	2,245,000	2,228,000	2,335,000	2,330,000	1,966,000	2,059,000	2,158,343	1,766,955
Total Assets	10,881,000	10,795,000	10,787,000	9,783,000	9,295,000	9,446,000	9,422,462	8,906,939
Current Liabilities	1,001,000	925,000	965,000	879,000	918,000	887,000	944,384	1,063,256
Long-Term Obligations	2,405,000	2,409,000	2,414,000	2,418,000	2,437,000	2,433,000	2,439,827	1,993,586
Total Liabilities	6,235,000	6,170,000	6,176,000	5,223,000	5,026,000	5,301,000	5,296,088	4,979,837
Stockholders' Equity	4,646,000	4,625,000	4,611,000	4,560,000	4,269,000	4,145,000	4,126,374	3,927,102
Shares Outstanding	114,000	114,000	114,000	114,000	111,000	110,000	108,966	107,899
Statistical Record								
Return on Assets %	1.22	1.52	1.52	1.42	1.63	0.45	2.39	N.M.
Return on Equity %	2.74	3.38	3.39	3.06	3.64	1.04	5.44	N.M.
EBITDA Margin %	22.60	23.95	25.54	20.47	14.14	17.24	23.34	12.13
Net Margin %	2.86	3.65	4.69	2.64	3.03	0.84	4.23	N.M.
Asset Turnover	0.50	0.51	0.51	0.54	0.54	0.54	0.56	0.56
Current Ratio	2.24	2.41	2.42	2.65	2.14	2.32	2.29	1.66
Debt to Equity	0.52	0.52	0.52	0.53	0.57	0.59	0.59	0.51
Price Range	36.81-24.21	36.81-24.13	36.81-24.13	35.97-24.13	32.75-24.81	31.75-20.99	30.56-23.25	27.84-22.23
P/E Ratio	34.73-22.84	27.89-18.28	27.68-18.14	30.74-20.62	23.91-18.11	81.41-53.82	15.43-11.74	...
Average Yield %	2.08	2.05	2.10	2.21	2.22	2.14	2.07	2.10

Address: 30 North LaSalle Street, Suite 4000, Chicago, IL 60602	Web Site: www.teldta.com	Auditors: PricewaterhouseCoopers LLP
Telephone: 312-630-1900	Officers: Walter C.D. Carlson - Chairman LeRoy T. Carlson - President, Chief Executive Officer	Investor Contact: 312-592-5341
Fax: 312-630-1908		Transfer Agents: Computershare Trust Company, N.A., College Station, TX

TEMPUR SEALY INTERNATIONAL, INC.

Exchange	Symbol	Price	52Wk Range	Yield	P/E
NYS	TPX	$87.06 (12/31/2019)	90.95-41.07	N/A	31.32

*7 Year Price Score 100.97 *NYSE Composite Index=100 *12 Month Price Score 116.43

Interim Earnings (Per Share)

Qtr.	Mar	Jun	Sep	Dec
2016	0.64	0.35	1.32	1.10
2017	0.62	0.45	0.81	0.88
2018	0.42	0.42	0.77	0.22
2019	0.51	0.74	1.31	...

Interim Dividends (Per Share)

No Dividends Paid

Valuation Analysis **Institutional Holding**

Forecast EPS	$3.79	No of Institutions
	(01/17/2020)	405
Market Cap	$4.7 Billion	Shares
Book Value	$336.5 Million	72,190,080
Price/Book	14.02	% Held
Price/Sales	1.62	73.88

Business Summary: Furniture (MIC: 1.6.2 SIC: 2515 NAIC: 337910)

Tempur Sealy International develops, manufactures, and markets bedding products, which it sells globally. Co.'s brand portfolio includes TEMPUR®, Tempur-Pedic®, Sealy® featuring Posturepedic® Technology, and Stearns & Foster®. Co. operates in two segments: North America and International. Co.'s North America segment consists of Tempur and Sealy manufacturing and distribution subsidiaries and licensees located in the U.S. and Canada. Co.'s International segment consists of Tempur and Sealy manufacturing and distribution subsidiaries, joint ventures and licensees located in Europe, Asia-Pacific and Latin America.

Recent Developments: For the quarter ended Sep 30 2019, income from continuing operations increased 64.2% to US$72.4 million from US$44.1 million in the year-earlier quarter. Net income increased 76.8% to US$73.2 million from US$41.4 million in the year-earlier quarter. Revenues were US$821.0 million, up 12.5% from US$729.5 million the year before. Operating income was US$120.6 million versus US$84.7 million in the prior-year quarter, an increase of 42.4%. Direct operating expenses rose 7.2% to US$460.4 million from US$429.5 million in the comparable period the year before. Indirect operating expenses increased 11.5% to US$240.0 million from US$215.3 million in the equivalent prior-year period.

Prospects: Our evaluation of Tempur-Sealy International Inc. as of October 4th, 2019 is the result of our systematic analysis on three basic characteristics: earnings strength, relative valuation, and recent stock price movement. The company has enjoyed a very positive trend in earnings per share over the past 5 quarters. However, recent analyst estimates for the company have been unchanged, while TPX has posted results that exceeded analysts' expectations. Based on operating earnings yield, the company is fairly valued when compared to all of the companies we cover. Share price changes over the past year indicates that TPX will perform very well over the near term.

Financial Data
(US$ in Thousands)

	9 Mos	6 Mos	3 Mos	12/31/2018	12/31/2017	12/31/2016	12/31/2015	12/31/2014
Earnings Per Share	2.78	2.24	1.92	1.82	2.77	3.38	1.17	1.75
Cash Flow Per Share	5.10	4.60	4.05	3.81	4.13	2.80	3.80	3.70
Income Statement								
Total Revenue	2,234,700	1,413,700	690,900	2,702,900	2,754,400	3,127,300	3,151,200	2,989,800
EBITDA	279,900	157,200	72,600	311,500	346,100	411,300	337,800	316,200
Depn & Amortn	21,700	14,400	7,200	71,800	65,300	56,100	53,500	57,700
Income Before Taxes	192,500	97,900	43,000	147,400	172,800	270,000	188,200	166,600
Income Taxes	58,800	32,700	16,900	49,600	47,700	86,800	125,400	64,900
Net Income	143,300	70,000	28,400	100,500	151,400	202,100	73,500	108,900
Average Shares	55,800	56,000	55,700	55,100	54,700	59,800	62,600	62,100
Balance Sheet								
Current Assets	960,500	891,700	853,000	805,400	607,400	671,500	809,100	766,400
Total Assets	3,103,100	3,046,700	2,965,700	2,715,400	2,694,000	2,702,600	2,655,500	2,662,600
Current Liabilities	848,000	738,700	725,500	669,000	576,900	545,500	713,000	538,300
Long-Term Obligations	1,509,500	1,585,500	1,604,100	1,599,100	1,680,700	1,817,800	1,273,300	1,535,900
Total Liabilities	2,766,600	2,740,800	2,712,200	2,500,800	2,581,500	2,717,800	2,365,300	2,459,900
Stockholders' Equity	336,500	305,900	253,500	214,600	112,500	(15,200)	290,200	202,700
Shares Outstanding	54,200	54,800	54,700	54,500	54,200	54,400	62,400	60,900
Statistical Record								
Return on Assets %	5.26	4.29	3.70	3.72	5.61	7.52	2.76	4.04
Return on Equity %	57.00	53.72	53.42	61.45	311.20	146.58	29.82	67.79
EBITDA Margin %	12.53	11.12	10.51	11.52	12.57	13.15	10.72	10.58
Net Margin %	6.41	4.95	4.11	3.72	5.50	6.46	2.33	3.64
Asset Turnover	0.98	0.97	0.97	1.00	1.02	1.16	1.19	1.11
Current Ratio	1.13	1.21	1.18	1.20	1.05	1.23	1.13	1.42
Debt to Equity	4.49	5.18	6.33	7.45	14.94	...	4.39	7.58
Price Range	81.48-39.39	74.48-39.39	59.53-39.39	64.59-39.39	69.50-40.58	82.04-50.94	81.89-49.17	61.34-45.64
P/E Ratio	29.31-14.17	33.25-17.58	31.01-20.52	35.49-21.64	25.09-14.65	24.27-15.07	69.99-42.03	35.05-26.08

Address: 1000 Tempur Way, Lexington, KY 40511 **Telephone:** 800-878-8889	**Web Site:** www.tempursealy.com **Officers:** Scott L. Thompson - Chairman, President, Chief Executive Officer Richard W. (Rick) Anderson - Executive Vice President, Region Officer	**Auditors:** Ernst & Young LLP **Investor Contact:** 800-805-3635 **Transfer Agents:** American Stock Transfer & Trust Company, LLC

TENET HEALTHCARE CORP.

Exchange	Symbol	Price	52Wk Range	Yield	P/E
NYS	THC	$38.03 (12/31/2019)	38.75-17.14	N/A	N/A

*7 Year Price Score 61.72 ***NYSE Composite Index=100** ***12 Month Price Score 124.83**

Interim Earnings (Per Share)

Qtr.	Mar	Jun	Sep	Dec
2016	(0.60)	(0.46)	(0.08)	(0.79)
2017	(0.53)	(0.55)	(3.64)	(2.27)
2018	0.96	0.25	(0.09)	(0.05)
2019	(0.18)	0.16	(2.24)	...

Interim Dividends (Per Share)

No Dividends Paid

Valuation Analysis / Institutional Holding

Valuation Analysis		Institutional Holding	
Forecast EPS	$2.65	No of Institutions	
	(01/17/2020)	438	
Market Cap	$3.9 Billion	Shares	
Book Value	N/A		195,336,384
Price/Book	N/A	% Held	
Price/Sales	0.22	N/A	

Business Summary: Hospitals & Health Care Facilities (MIC: 4.2.1 SIC: 8062 NAIC: 622110)

Tenet Healthcare is a healthcare services company. Through its subsidiaries, partnerships and joint ventures, including USPI Holding Company, Inc., Co. operates hospitals, surgical hospitals and outpatient centers. In addition, Co.'s Conifer Holdings, Inc. (Conifer) subsidiary provides healthcare business process services in the areas of hospital and physician revenue cycle management and care solutions to healthcare systems, as well as individual hospitals, physician practices, self-insured organizations, health plans and other entities. Co. has three reportable segments: Hospital Operations and other; Ambulatory Care; and Conifer.

Recent Developments: For the quarter ended Sep 30 2019, loss from continuing operations was US$153.0 million compared with income of US$65.0 million in the year-earlier quarter. Net loss amounted to US$152.0 million versus net income of US$65.0 million in the year-earlier quarter. Revenues were US$4.61 billion, up 1.9% from US$4.52 billion the year before. Operating income was US$294.0 million versus US$320.0 million in the prior-year quarter, a decrease of 8.1%. Indirect operating expenses increased 2.6% to US$4.31 billion from US$4.20 billion in the equivalent prior-year period.

Prospects: Our evaluation of Tenet Healthcare Corp. as of October 4th, 2019 is the result of our systematic analysis on three basic characteristics: earnings strength, relative valuation, and recent stock price movement. The company has enjoyed a very positive trend in earnings per share over the past 5 quarters. However, recent analyst estimates for the company have been mixed and THC has posted results that exceeded analysts' expectations. Based on operating earnings yield, the company is undervalued when compared to all of the companies we cover. Share price changes over the past year indicates that THC will perform very poorly over the near term.

Financial Data
(US$ in Millions)

	9 Mos	6 Mos	3 Mos	12/31/2018	12/31/2017	12/31/2016	12/31/2015	12/31/2014
Earnings Per Share	(2.31)	(0.16)	(0.07)	1.07	(7.00)	(1.93)	(1.41)	0.12
Cash Flow Per Share	9.30	8.55	9.20	10.27	11.93	5.60	10.35	7.02
Income Statement								
Total Revenue	13,787	9,181	4,579	18,313	19,179	19,621	18,634	16,615
EBITDA	851	733	335	2,490	1,841	2,118	1,894	1,778
Depn & Amortn	25	21	11	847	914	891	838	877
Income Before Taxes	81	214	74	639	(101)	248	144	147
Income Taxes	67	47	17	176	219	67	68	49
Net Income	(234)	(2)	(19)	111	(704)	(192)	(140)	12
Average Shares	103	104	102	103	100	99	99	100
Balance Sheet								
Current Assets	4,789	4,704	4,582	4,636	5,573	5,257	5,171	4,717
Total Assets	23,357	23,207	23,158	22,409	23,385	24,701	23,682	18,141
Current Liabilities	3,928	4,150	3,725	3,857	4,332	4,034	4,308	3,577
Long-Term Obligations	14,858	14,312	14,814	14,644	14,791	15,064	14,383	11,695
Total Liabilities	23,698	23,315	23,292	22,528	23,532	24,284	22,991	17,490
Stockholders' Equity	(341)	(108)	(134)	(119)	(147)	417	691	651
Shares Outstanding	103	103	103	102	100	99	98	98
Statistical Record								
Return on Assets %	N.M.	N.M.	N.M.	0.48	N.M.	N.M.	N.M.	0.07
Return on Equity %	...	...	...	...	N.M.	N.M.	N.M.	1.71
EBITDA Margin %	6.17	7.98	7.32	13.60	9.60	10.79	10.16	10.70
Net Margin %	N.M.	N.M.	N.M.	0.61	N.M.	N.M.	N.M.	0.07
Asset Turnover	0.80	0.80	0.78	0.80	0.80	0.81	0.89	0.97
Current Ratio	1.22	1.13	1.23	1.20	1.29	1.30	1.20	1.32
Debt to Equity	...	...	...	...	...	36.12	20.81	17.96
Price Range	31.19-16.85	38.88-16.85	38.88-16.85	38.88-14.77	22.67-12.65	32.61-14.38	60.78-27.23	63.27-38.75
P/E Ratio	...	...	...	36.34-13.80	...	...	...	527.25-322.92

Address: 1445 Ross Avenue, Suite 1400, Dallas, TX 75202 **Telephone:** 469-893-2200	**Web Site:** www.tenethealth.com **Officers:** Ronald (Ron) A. Rittenmeyer - Executive Chairman, Chief Executive Officer Saumya Sutaria - President, Chief Operating Officer	**Auditors:** DELOITTE & TOUCHE LLP **Transfer Agents:** Computershare

TENNANT CO.

Exchange	Symbol	Price	52Wk Range	Yield	P/E	Div Acheiver
NYS	TNC	$77.92 (12/31/2019)	79.23-51.19	1.13	33.73	46 Years

*7 Year Price Score 85.43   *NYSE Composite Index=100   *12 Month Price Score 108.78

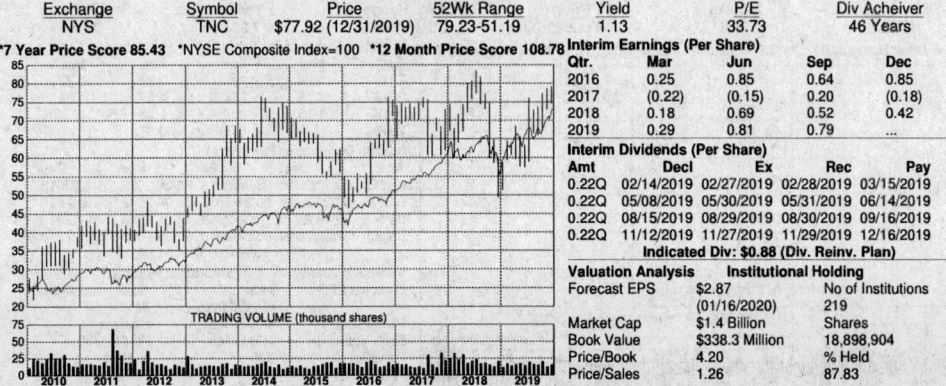

Interim Earnings (Per Share)

Qtr.	Mar	Jun	Sep	Dec
2016	0.25	0.85	0.64	0.85
2017	(0.22)	(0.15)	0.20	(0.18)
2018	0.18	0.69	0.52	0.42
2019	0.29	0.81	0.79	...

Interim Dividends (Per Share)

Amt	Decl	Ex	Rec	Pay
0.22Q	02/14/2019	02/27/2019	02/28/2019	03/15/2019
0.22Q	05/08/2019	05/30/2019	05/31/2019	06/14/2019
0.22Q	08/15/2019	08/29/2019	08/30/2019	09/16/2019
0.22Q	11/12/2019	11/27/2019	11/29/2019	12/16/2019

Indicated Div: $0.88 (Div. Reinv. Plan)

Valuation Analysis / **Institutional Holding**

Forecast EPS	$2.87	No of Institutions
	(01/16/2020)	219
Market Cap	$1.4 Billion	Shares
Book Value	$338.3 Million	18,898,904
Price/Book	4.20	% Held
Price/Sales	1.26	87.83

Business Summary: Industrial Machinery & Equipment (MIC: 7.2.1 SIC: 3589 NAIC: 333319)

Tennant is a manufacturer of floor cleaning equipment. Co. provides products and solutions consisting of mechanized cleaning equipment, detergent-free and other cleaning technologies, aftermarket parts and consumables, equipment maintenance and repair service, specialty surface coatings, and business solutions such as financing, rental and leasing programs, and machine-to-machine asset management solutions. Co.'s products are used in several types of environments including retail establishments, distribution centers, factories and warehouses, public venues such as arenas and stadiums, office buildings, schools and universities, hospitals and clinics, parking lots and streets, and more.

Recent Developments: For the quarter ended Sep 30 2019, net income increased 50.5% to US$14.6 million from US$9.7 million in the year-earlier quarter. Revenues were US$280.7 million, up 2.7% from US$273.3 million the year before. Operating income was US$21.5 million versus US$15.4 million in the prior-year quarter, an increase of 39.6%. Direct operating expenses was unchanged at US$166.7 million versus the comparable period the year before. Indirect operating expenses increased 1.4% to US$92.5 million from US$91.2 million in the equivalent prior-year period.

Prospects: Our evaluation of Tennant Co. as of October 4th, 2019 is the result of our systematic analysis on three basic characteristics: earnings strength, relative valuation, and recent stock price movement. The company has generated a negative trend in earnings per share over the past 5 quarters. However, recent analyst estimates for the company have been mixed and TNC has posted results that exceeded analysts' expectations. Based on operating earnings yield, the company is fairly valued when compared to all of the companies we cover. Share price changes over the past year indicates that TNC will perform poorly over the near term.

Financial Data

(US$ in Thousands)	9 Mos	6 Mos	3 Mos	12/31/2018	12/31/2017	12/31/2016	12/31/2015	12/31/2014
Earnings Per Share	2.31	2.04	1.92	1.82	(0.35)	2.59	1.74	2.70
Cash Flow Per Share	4.56	3.59	3.48	4.46	3.06	3.29	2.51	3.26
Tang Book Value Per Share	0.73	N.M.	N.M.	N.M.	N.M.	14.19	13.09	13.40
Dividends Per Share	0.880	0.870	0.860	0.850	0.840	0.810	0.800	0.780
Dividend Payout %	38.10	42.65	44.79	46.70	...	31.27	45.98	28.89
Income Statement								
Total Revenue	842,800	562,100	262,500	1,123,511	1,003,066	808,572	811,799	821,983
EBITDA	94,600	60,000	24,900	110,569	64,950	85,331	68,115	88,652
Depn & Amortn	41,600	28,000	14,100	54,420	43,253	17,891	16,550	17,694
Income Before Taxes	39,800	23,200	6,600	35,842	(1,292)	66,491	50,424	69,538
Income Taxes	5,000	3,000	1,200	2,304	4,913	19,877	18,336	18,887
Net Income	34,800	20,200	5,400	33,412	(6,195)	46,614	32,088	50,651
Average Shares	18,487	18,394	18,345	18,338	17,695	17,976	18,493	18,740
Balance Sheet								
Current Assets	479,500	479,400	452,400	468,644	423,115	297,922	293,644	347,089
Total Assets	1,045,100	1,070,800	1,040,700	992,544	993,977	470,037	432,295	486,932
Current Liabilities	269,900	259,700	267,200	248,874	236,507	132,829	133,216	145,630
Long-Term Obligations	322,200	346,100	330,100	328,060	345,956	32,735	21,194	24,571
Total Liabilities	706,800	737,100	722,700	678,122	697,474	191,494	180,088	206,281
Stockholders' Equity	338,300	333,700	318,000	314,422	296,503	278,543	252,207	280,651
Shares Outstanding	18,254	18,192	18,160	18,125	17,881	17,688	17,744	18,415
Statistical Record								
Return on Assets %	4.22	3.66	3.46	3.36	N.M.	10.30	6.98	10.74
Return on Equity %	13.17	11.86	11.40	10.94	N.M.	17.52	12.04	18.60
EBITDA Margin %	11.22	10.67	9.49	9.84	6.48	10.55	8.39	10.79
Net Margin %	4.13	3.59	2.06	2.97	N.M.	5.76	3.95	6.16
Asset Turnover	1.12	1.09	1.08	1.13	1.37	1.79	1.77	1.74
Current Ratio	1.78	1.85	1.69	1.88	1.79	2.24	2.20	2.38
Debt to Equity	0.95	1.04	1.04	1.04	1.17	0.12	0.08	0.09
Price Range	76.11-49.34	83.45-49.34	83.45-49.34	83.45-49.34	76.30-60.40	76.50-46.54	72.17-54.49	76.52-58.21
P/E Ratio	32.95-21.36	40.91-24.19	43.46-25.70	45.85-27.11	...	29.54-17.97	41.48-31.32	28.34-21.56
Average Yield %	1.40	1.33	1.26	1.21	1.21	1.37	1.28	1.15

Address: 701 North Lilac Drive, P.O. Box 1452, Minneapolis, MN 55440
Telephone: 763-540-1200

Web Site: www.tennantco.com
Officers: H. Chris Killingstad - President, Chief Executive Officer Keith A. Woodward - Senior Vice President, Chief Financial Officer

Auditors: KPMG LLP
Investor Contact: 763-540-1204
Transfer Agents: Equiniti Trust Company, St. Paul, MN

TENNECO INC

Exchange	Symbol	Price	52Wk Range	Yield	P/E
NYS	TEN	$13.10 (12/31/2019)	36.37-7.89	7.63	N/A

*7 Year Price Score 30.77   *NYSE Composite Index=100   *12 Month Price Score 71.53

Interim Earnings (Per Share)

Qtr.	Mar	Jun	Sep	Dec
2016	0.99	1.49	3.24	0.77
2017	1.16	(0.05)	1.57	1.31
2018	1.13	0.98	1.05	(2.23)
2019	(1.44)	0.32	0.87	...

Interim Dividends (Per Share)

Amt	Decl	Ex	Rec	Pay
0.25Q	05/16/2018	06/04/2018	06/05/2018	06/22/2018
0.25Q	07/20/2018	08/31/2018	09/04/2018	09/21/2018
0.25Q	10/10/2018	12/03/2018	12/04/2018	12/21/2018
0.25Q	02/06/2019	03/04/2019	03/05/2019	03/21/2019

Indicated Div: $1.00

Valuation Analysis

Forecast EPS	$3.34
	(01/17/2020)
Market Cap	$1.1 Billion
Book Value	$1.6 Billion
Price/Book	0.65
Price/Sales	0.06

Institutional Holding

No of Institutions	341
Shares	58,446,732
% Held	92.74

Business Summary: Auto Parts (MIC: 1.8.2 SIC: 3714 NAIC: 336399)

Tenneco designs, manufactures and sells products and services for light vehicle, commercial truck, off-highway, industrial and aftermarket customers. As a parts supplier, Co. produces individual component parts for vehicles as well as groups of components that are combined as modules or systems within vehicles. These parts, modules, and systems are sold to the light vehicle and commercial truck manufacturers as well as aftermarket customers, including independent warehouse distributors, distributors, engine rebuilders, retail parts stores, mass merchants, and service chains. Co. operates in five segments: Clean Air, Ride Performance, Aftermarket, Powertrain and Motorparts.

Recent Developments: For the quarter ended Sep 30 2019, net income increased 18.2% to US$78.0 million from US$66.0 million in the year-earlier quarter. Revenues were US$4.32 billion, up 82.2% from US$2.37 billion the year before. Direct operating expenses rose 82.5% to US$3.65 billion from US$2.00 billion in the comparable period the year before. Indirect operating expenses increased 115.0% to US$544.0 million from US$253.0 million in the equivalent prior-year period.

Prospects: Our evaluation of Tenneco Automotive Inc. as of October 4th, 2019 is the result of our systematic analysis on three basic characteristics: earnings strength, relative valuation, and recent stock price movement. The company has produced a positive trend in earnings per share over the past 5 quarters. However, recent analyst estimates for the company have been reduced, while TEN has posted results that exceeded analysts' expectations. Based on operating earnings yield, the company is undervalued when compared to all of the companies we cover. Share price changes over the past year indicates that TEN will perform very poorly over the near term.

Financial Data

(US$ in Thousands)	9 Mos	6 Mos	3 Mos	12/31/2018	12/31/2017	12/31/2016	12/31/2015	12/31/2014
Earnings Per Share	(2.48)	(2.30)	(1.64)	0.93	3.91	6.44	4.11	3.66
Cash Flow Per Share	5.76	3.23	3.57	7.49	11.91	8.72	8.66	5.61
Tang Book Value Per Share	N.M.	N.M.	N.M.	N.M.	12.15	9.44	6.09	6.63
Dividends Per Share	0.500	0.750	1.000	1.000	1.000	...	...	...
Dividend Payout %	...	...	...	107.53	25.58	...	...	...
Income Statement								
Total Revenue	13,307,000	8,988,000	4,484,000	11,763,000	9,274,000	8,599,000	8,209,000	8,420,000
EBITDA	734,000	422,000	129,000	601,000	641,000	740,000	722,000	700,000
Depn & Amortn	503,000	338,000	169,000	313,000	224,000	212,000	203,000	208,000
Income Before Taxes	(11,000)	(79,000)	(121,000)	156,000	344,000	436,000	452,000	401,000
Income Taxes	5,000	14,000	...	63,000	70,000	3,000	149,000	131,000
Net Income	(21,000)	(91,000)	(117,000)	55,000	207,000	363,000	247,000	226,000
Average Shares	80,916	80,920	80,874	58,758	53,026	56,407	60,193	61,782
Balance Sheet								
Current Assets	5,888,000	5,994,000	6,027,000	6,109,000	2,799,000	2,602,000	2,311,000	2,426,000
Total Assets	13,383,000	13,592,000	13,616,000	13,232,000	4,842,000	4,342,000	3,967,000	4,010,000
Current Liabilities	4,289,000	4,310,000	4,407,000	4,320,000	2,266,000	1,970,000	1,794,000	1,799,000
Long-Term Obligations	5,408,000	5,508,000	5,417,000	5,340,000	1,358,000	1,294,000	1,124,000	1,069,000
Total Liabilities	11,741,000	11,954,000	11,988,000	11,506,000	4,146,000	3,754,000	3,534,000	3,513,000
Stockholders' Equity	1,642,000	1,638,000	1,628,000	1,726,000	696,000	588,000	433,000	497,000
Shares Outstanding	80,920	80,947	80,950	80,876	51,440	54,235	57,593	61,209
Statistical Record								
Return on Assets %	N.M.	N.M.	N.M.	0.61	4.51	8.71	6.19	5.77
Return on Equity %	N.M.	N.M.	N.M.	4.54	32.24	70.91	53.12	48.60
EBITDA Margin %	5.52	4.70	2.88	5.11	6.91	8.61	8.80	8.31
Net Margin %	N.M.	N.M.	N.M.	0.47	2.23	4.22	3.01	2.68
Asset Turnover	1.91	1.68	1.46	1.30	2.02	2.06	2.06	2.15
Current Ratio	1.37	1.39	1.37	1.41	1.24	1.32	1.29	1.35
Debt to Equity	3.29	3.36	3.33	3.09	1.95	2.20	2.60	2.15
Price Range	42.51-7.89	46.32-9.94	57.82-21.79	64.69-26.29	68.71-51.74	66.52-35.59	61.53-42.24	68.60-47.93
P/E Ratio	...	...	...	69.56-28.27	17.57-13.23	10.33-5.53	14.97-10.28	18.74-13.10
Average Yield %	2.20	2.40	2.54	2.20	1.68	...	...	...

Address: 500 North Field Drive, Lake Forest, IL 60045 **Telephone:** 847-482-5000	**Web Site:** www.tenneco.com **Officers:** Brian J. Kesseler - Chief Executive Officer, Chief Executive Officer (frmr), Co-Chief Executive Officer, Chief Operating Officer Jason M. Hollar - Executive Vice President, Senior Vice President, Chief Financial Officer	**Auditors:** PricewaterhouseCoopers LLP **Transfer Agents:** Wells Fargo Bank, N.A. Shareowner Services, Mendota Heights, MN

TERADATA CORP (DE)

Exchange	Symbol	Price	52Wk Range	Yield	P/E
NYS	TDC	$26.77 (12/31/2019)	49.28-25.23	N/A	223.08

*7 Year Price Score 78.25   *NYSE Composite Index=100   *12 Month Price Score 70.49

Interim Earnings (Per Share)

Qtr.	Mar	Jun	Sep	Dec
2016	(0.36)	0.49	0.37	0.44
2017	(0.02)	(0.03)	0.10	(0.58)
2018	(0.06)	0.03	0.15	0.13
2019	(0.09)	(0.01)	0.09	...

Interim Dividends (Per Share)

No Dividends Paid

Valuation Analysis   Institutional Holding

Forecast EPS	$0.98	No of Institutions
	(01/17/2020)	556
Market Cap	$3.0 Billion	Shares
Book Value	$328.0 Million	135,325,760
Price/Book	9.17	% Held
Price/Sales	1.51	69.41

TRADING VOLUME (thousand shares)

Business Summary: Internet & Software (MIC: 6.3.2 SIC: 7372 NAIC: 511210)

Teradata is a cloud analytics software provider. Co.'s solutions and services comprise software, hardware, and related business consulting and support services to deliver analytics across a company's entire analytical ecosystem. Co.'s business consulting services include a range of offerings, including consulting to help organizations establish an analytic vision, identify and operationalize analytical opportunities, enable an analytical ecosystem architecture, and ensure their analytical infrastructure delivers value. Co. also provides support and maintenance services for its offerings.

Recent Developments: For the quarter ended Sep 30 2019, net income decreased 44.4% to US$10.0 million from US$18.0 million in the year-earlier quarter. Revenues were US$459.0 million, down 12.7% from US$526.0 million the year before. Operating income was US$10.0 million versus US$14.0 million in the prior-year quarter, a decrease of 28.6%. Direct operating expenses declined 19.1% to US$212.0 million from US$262.0 million in the comparable period the year before. Indirect operating expenses decreased 5.2% to US$237.0 million from US$250.0 million in the equivalent prior-year period.

Prospects: Our evaluation of Teradata Corp. as of October 4th, 2019 is the result of our systematic analysis on three basic characteristics: earnings strength, relative valuation, and recent stock price movement. The company has enjoyed a very positive trend in earnings per share over the past 5 quarters. However, recent analyst estimates for the company have been mixed and TDC has posted results that fell short of analysts' expectations. Based on operating earnings yield, the company is overvalued when compared to all of the companies we cover. Share price changes over the past year indicates that TDC will perform well over the near term.

Financial Data

(US$ in Millions)	9 Mos	6 Mos	3 Mos	12/31/2018	12/31/2017	12/31/2016	12/31/2015	12/31/2014
Earnings Per Share	0.12	0.18	0.22	0.25	(0.53)	0.95	(1.53)	2.33
Cash Flow Per Share	1.78	1.54	1.96	3.05	2.58	3.43	2.87	4.38
Tang Book Value Per Share	N.M.	N.M.	N.M.	0.10	1.03	2.93	1.97	2.87
Income Statement								
Total Revenue	1,405	946	468	2,164	2,156	2,322	2,530	2,732
EBITDA	121	77	30	102	128	350	(6)	616
Depn & Amortn	113	77	37	67	55	117	129	122
Income Before Taxes	(1)	(5)	(10)	27	58	221	(144)	494
Income Taxes	...	6	...	(3)	125	96	70	127
Net Income	(1)	(11)	(10)	30	(67)	125	(214)	367
Average Shares	114	115	117	121	125	131	139	157
Balance Sheet								
Current Assets	978	1,129	1,302	1,428	1,750	1,621	1,734	1,572
Total Assets	1,979	2,123	2,286	2,360	2,556	2,413	2,530	3,132
Current Liabilities	772	865	914	1,009	1,063	729	953	995
Long-Term Obligations	567	564	558	478	478	538	570	195
Total Liabilities	1,651	1,756	1,819	1,865	1,888	1,442	1,681	1,425
Stockholders' Equity	328	367	467	495	668	971	849	1,707
Shares Outstanding	112	114	117	116	121	130	130	147
Statistical Record								
Return on Assets %	0.68	1.02	1.16	1.22	N.M.	5.04	N.M.	11.79
Return on Equity %	3.15	4.69	4.86	5.16	N.M.	13.70	N.M.	20.59
EBITDA Margin %	8.61	8.14	6.41	4.71	5.94	15.07	N.M.	22.55
Net Margin %	N.M.	N.M.	N.M.	1.39	N.M.	5.38	N.M.	13.43
Asset Turnover	0.97	0.95	0.92	0.88	0.87	0.94	0.89	0.88
Current Ratio	1.27	1.31	1.42	1.42	1.65	2.22	1.82	1.58
Debt to Equity	1.73	1.54	1.19	0.97	0.72	0.55	0.67	0.11
Price Range	49.28-29.81	49.28-34.13	49.28-34.13	44.00-34.13	39.20-27.26	32.62-22.60	46.98-25.58	49.19-39.54
P/E Ratio	410.67-248.42	273.78-189.61	224.00-155.14	176.00-136.52	...	34.34-23.79	...	21.11-16.97

Address: 17095 Via Del Campo, San Diego, CA 92127 **Telephone:** 866-548-8348	**Web Site:** www.teradata.com **Officers:** Victor L. Lund - Executive Chairman, Interim President, Chief Executive Officer, President, Chief Financial Officer Mark A. Culhane - Chief Financial Officer	**Auditors:** PricewaterhouseCoopers LLP **Investor Contact:** 937-242-4878 **Transfer Agents:** Computershare Shareowner Services

TEREX CORP.

Exchange	Symbol	Price	52Wk Range	Yield	P/E
NYS	TEX	$29.78 (12/31/2019)	35.93-23.28	1.48	1489.00

*7 Year Price Score 76.73 *NYSE Composite Index=100 *12 Month Price Score 93.72

Interim Earnings (Per Share)
Qtr.	Mar	Jun	Sep	Dec
2016	(0.65)	0.59	0.89	(2.46)
2017	(0.04)	1.04	0.66	(0.22)
2018	0.62	0.75	0.51	(0.40)
2019	(0.93)	1.05	0.30	...

Interim Dividends (Per Share)
Amt	Decl	Ex	Rec	Pay
0.11Q	02/04/2019	03/07/2019	03/08/2019	03/19/2019
0.11Q	05/15/2019	06/06/2019	06/07/2019	06/19/2019
0.11Q	08/01/2019	08/09/2019	08/12/2019	09/19/2019
0.11Q	10/17/2019	11/07/2019	11/08/2019	12/19/2019

Indicated Div: $0.44

Valuation Analysis / Institutional Holding
Forecast EPS	$3.10	No of Institutions	
(01/17/2020)		457	
Market Cap	$2.1 Billion	Shares	
Book Value	$866.3 Million		92,924,504
Price/Book	2.43	% Held	
Price/Sales	0.45		75.79

Business Summary: Industrial Machinery & Equipment (MIC: 7.2.1 SIC: 3537 NAIC: 333924)

Terex is a global manufacturer of aerial work platforms, cranes and materials processing machinery. Co. designs, builds and supports products used in construction, maintenance, manufacturing, energy, minerals and materials management applications. Co. has three business segments include: Aerial Work Platforms, which designs, manufactures, services and markets aerial work platform equipment, telehandlers and light towers; Cranes, which designs, manufactures, services, refurbishes and markets mobile telescopic cranes, lattice boom crawler cranes, tower cranes and utility equipment; and Material Processing, which designs, manufactures and markets materials processing and specialty equipment.

Recent Developments: For the quarter ended Sep 30 2019, net income decreased 44.6% to US$21.4 million from US$38.6 million in the year-earlier quarter. Revenues were US$1.02 billion, down 6.8% from US$1.10 billion the year before. Operating income was US$86.4 million versus US$104.2 million in the prior-year quarter, a decrease of 17.1%. Direct operating expenses declined 5.1% to US$815.0 million from US$858.7 million in the comparable period the year before. Indirect operating expenses decreased 9.3% to US$123.2 million from US$135.9 million in the equivalent prior-year period.

Prospects: Our evaluation of Terex Corp. as of October 4th, 2019 is the result of our systematic analysis on three basic characteristics: earnings strength, relative valuation, and recent stock price movement. The company has enjoyed a very positive trend in earnings per share over the past 5 quarters. However, recent analyst estimates for the company have been mixed and TEX has posted results that fell short of analysts' expectations. Based on operating earnings yield, the company is undervalued when compared to all of the companies we cover. Share price changes over the past year indicates that TEX will perform poorly over the near term.

Financial Data
(US$ in Thousands)	9 Mos	6 Mos	3 Mos	12/31/2018	12/31/2017	12/31/2016	12/31/2015	12/31/2014
Earnings Per Share	0.02	0.23	(0.07)	1.48	1.36	(1.63)	1.33	2.79
Cash Flow Per Share	2.70	0.14	(1.80)	1.25	1.65	3.39	1.98	3.74
Tang Book Value Per Share	8.45	8.31	7.15	8.36	11.65	11.49	5.61	5.21
Dividends Per Share	0.430	0.420	0.410	0.400	0.320	0.280	0.240	0.200
Dividend Payout %	2,150.00	182.61	...	27.03	23.53	...	18.05	7.17
Income Statement								
Total Revenue	3,468,100	2,443,500	1,136,600	5,125,000	4,363,400	4,443,100	6,543,100	7,308,900
EBITDA	347,800	247,000	110,000	266,200	232,500	(107,500)	430,600	527,500
Depn & Amortn	38,600	25,800	13,500	53,300	59,900	65,500	98,400	110,400
Income Before Taxes	245,000	177,100	75,200	148,700	112,000	(270,700)	226,600	297,200
Income Taxes	53,800	38,300	18,000	37,400	52,000	(77,400)	81,000	37,700
Net Income	29,900	8,500	(66,600)	113,700	128,700	(176,100)	145,900	319,000
Average Shares	71,800	71,700	71,800	76,900	94,900	107,900	109,600	114,200
Balance Sheet								
Current Assets	2,034,900	2,439,600	2,508,000	2,423,000	2,383,000	2,700,500	3,144,200	3,356,200
Total Assets	3,160,700	3,603,100	3,654,800	3,485,900	3,462,500	5,006,800	5,637,100	5,928,000
Current Liabilities	922,300	1,102,000	1,103,200	1,214,700	1,035,500	1,407,000	1,458,600	1,643,100
Long-Term Obligations	1,268,800	1,445,500	1,573,500	1,214,700	979,600	1,562,000	1,751,000	1,636,300
Total Liabilities	2,294,400	2,743,000	2,873,000	2,625,400	2,240,500	3,522,100	3,759,700	3,922,100
Stockholders' Equity	866,300	860,100	781,800	860,500	1,222,000	1,484,500	1,877,400	2,005,900
Shares Outstanding	70,600	70,400	70,400	69,600	80,200	105,000	107,700	105,400
Statistical Record								
Return on Assets %	N.M.	0.41	N.M.	3.27	3.04	N.M.	2.52	5.12
Return on Equity %	N.M.	1.56	N.M.	10.92	9.51	N.M.	7.51	15.20
EBITDA Margin %	10.03	10.11	9.68	5.19	5.33	N.M.	6.58	7.22
Net Margin %	0.86	0.35	N.M.	2.22	2.95	N.M.	2.23	4.36
Asset Turnover	1.45	1.41	1.41	1.48	1.03	0.83	1.13	1.17
Current Ratio	2.21	2.21	2.27	1.99	2.30	1.92	2.16	2.04
Debt to Equity	1.46	1.68	2.01	1.41	0.80	1.05	0.93	0.82
Price Range	40.55-23.30	45.15-25.61	45.15-25.61	49.79-25.61	48.59-29.57	33.05-14.46	28.85-16.83	44.74-25.66
P/E Ratio	N.M.	196.30-111.35	...	33.64-17.30	35.73-21.74	...	21.69-12.65	16.04-9.20
Average Yield %	1.41	1.24	1.14	1.03	0.85	1.18	1.03	0.54

Address: 200 Nyala Farm Road, Westport, CT 06880	Web Site: www.terex.com	Auditors: PricewaterhouseCoopers LLP
Telephone: 203-222-7170	Officers: John L. Garrison - Chairman, President, Chief Executive Officer Kevin A. Barr - Senior Vice President	Investor Contact: 203-222-5943
Fax: 203-222-7976		Transfer Agents: American Stock Transfer & Trust Company, New York, NY

TEGNA INC

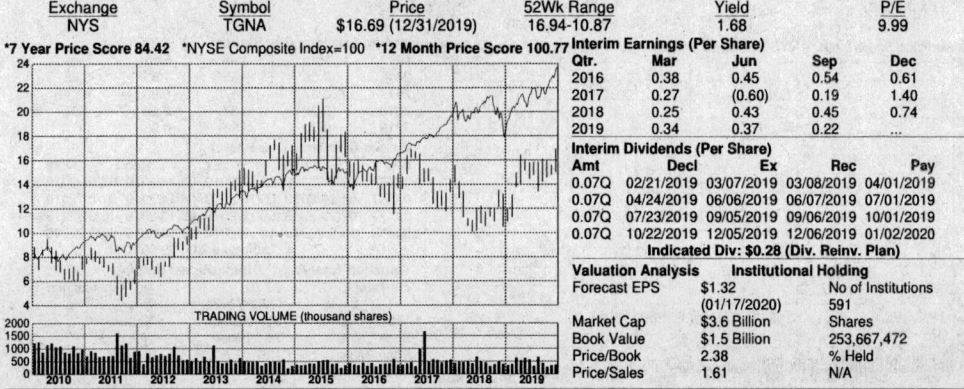

Exchange	Symbol	Price	52Wk Range	Yield	P/E
NYS	TGNA	$16.69 (12/31/2019)	16.94-10.87	1.68	9.99

*7 Year Price Score 84.42   *NYSE Composite Index=100   *12 Month Price Score 100.77

Interim Earnings (Per Share)

Qtr.	Mar	Jun	Sep	Dec
2016	0.38	0.45	0.54	0.61
2017	0.27	(0.60)	0.19	1.40
2018	0.25	0.43	0.45	0.74
2019	0.34	0.37	0.22	...

Interim Dividends (Per Share)

Amt	Decl	Ex	Rec	Pay
0.07Q	02/21/2019	03/07/2019	03/08/2019	04/01/2019
0.07Q	04/24/2019	06/06/2019	06/07/2019	07/01/2019
0.07Q	07/23/2019	09/05/2019	09/06/2019	10/01/2019
0.07Q	10/22/2019	12/05/2019	12/06/2019	01/02/2020

Indicated Div: $0.28 (Div. Reinv. Plan)

Valuation Analysis

		Institutional Holding	
Forecast EPS	$1.32	No of Institutions	
	(01/17/2020)	591	
Market Cap	$3.6 Billion	Shares	
Book Value	$1.5 Billion	253,667,472	
Price/Book	2.38	% Held	
Price/Sales	1.61	N/A	

Business Summary: Radio & Television (MIC: 2.3.1 SIC: 4833 NAIC: 515120)

Tegna is a media company. Co.'s business provides television programming and digital content. Each television station also has a digital presence across online, mobile and social platforms. Co. provides advertising & marketing services, which include local and national non-political advertising, digital marketing services (including Premion, its Over the Top advertising network), and advertising on the stations' websites and tablet and mobile products; political advertising; and other services, such as production of programming from third parties and production of advertising material. Co.'s portfolio of Big 4 NBC, CBS, ABC and FOX stations operate under long-term affiliation agreements.

Recent Developments: For the quarter ended Sep 30 2019, income from continuing operations decreased 47.9% to US$48.3 million from US$92.8 million in the year-earlier quarter. Net income decreased 50.2% to US$48.3 million from US$97.2 million in the year-earlier quarter. Revenues were US$551.9 million, up 2.4% from US$539.0 million the year before. Operating income was US$106.8 million versus US$154.3 million in the prior-year quarter, a decrease of 30.8%. Direct operating expenses rose 13.0% to US$306.5 million from US$271.2 million in the comparable period the year before. Indirect operating expenses increased 22.0% to US$138.6 million from US$113.5 million in the equivalent prior-year period.

Prospects: Our evaluation of Tegna Inc. as of October 4th, 2019 is the result of our systematic analysis on three basic characteristics: earnings strength, relative valuation, and recent stock price movement. The company has generated a negative trend in earnings per share over the past 5 quarters. However, recent analyst estimates for the company have been unchanged while TGNA has posted results that exceeded analysts' expectations. Based on operating earnings yield, the company is undervalued when compared to all of the companies we cover. Share price changes over the past year indicates that TGNA will perform over the near term.

Financial Data

(US$ in Thousands)	9 Mos	6 Mos	3 Mos	12/31/2018	12/31/2017	12/31/2016	12/31/2015	12/28/2014
Earnings Per Share	1.67	1.90	1.96	1.87	1.26	1.99	2.00	4.58
Cash Flow Per Share	1.88	2.26	2.42	2.44	1.79	3.15	2.71	3.64
Dividends Per Share	0.280	0.280	0.280	0.280	0.350	0.560	0.680	0.800
Dividend Payout %	16.77	14.74	14.29	14.97	27.78	28.14	34.00	17.47
Income Statement								
Total Revenue	1,605,542	1,053,685	516,753	2,207,282	1,903,026	3,341,198	3,050,945	6,008,174
EBITDA	466,617	329,848	154,716	773,767	647,105	1,156,125	1,163,873	1,727,709
Depn & Amortn	77,361	46,962	23,606	86,787	136,507	204,490	262,244	265,724
Income Before Taxes	244,090	190,174	84,725	494,915	300,314	719,622	628,000	1,188,741
Income Taxes	52,732	47,653	22,774	107,367	(137,246)	216,979	202,314	225,600
Net Income	202,280	153,934	73,979	405,665	273,744	436,697	459,522	1,062,171
Average Shares	218,310	217,905	217,202	216,621	217,478	219,681	229,721	231,907
Balance Sheet								
Current Assets	648,331	536,524	519,399	635,222	636,923	790,688	805,159	1,480,465
Total Assets	6,902,237	5,412,694	5,323,749	5,276,842	4,962,115	8,542,725	8,537,758	11,205,455
Current Liabilities	374,839	276,537	323,538	369,217	325,352	619,181	606,783	1,127,936
Long-Term Obligations	4,180,938	2,953,569	2,891,495	2,944,466	3,007,047	4,042,749	4,200,816	4,488,028
Total Liabilities	5,380,541	3,932,952	3,918,498	3,935,918	3,967,074	6,271,307	6,345,787	7,950,541
Stockholders' Equity	1,521,696	1,479,742	1,405,251	1,340,924	995,041	2,271,418	2,191,971	3,254,914
Shares Outstanding	216,814	216,587	216,285	215,758	214,930	214,487	219,754	226,739
Statistical Record								
Return on Assets %	6.01	7.80	8.11	7.92	4.05	5.10	4.62	10.42
Return on Equity %	26.63	31.73	34.76	34.73	16.76	19.51	16.74	35.81
EBITDA Margin %	29.06	31.30	29.94	35.06	34.00	34.60	38.15	28.76
Net Margin %	12.60	14.61	14.32	18.38	14.38	13.07	15.06	17.68
Asset Turnover	0.37	0.42	0.42	0.43	0.28	0.39	0.31	0.59
Current Ratio	1.73	1.94	1.61	1.72	1.96	1.28	1.33	1.31
Debt to Equity	2.75	2.00	2.06	2.20	3.02	1.78	1.92	1.38
Price Range	16.44-10.50	16.44-10.50	14.98-10.09	15.59-10.09	16.92-11.78	16.35-11.55	21.12-14.00	17.70-13.29
P/E Ratio	9.84-6.29	8.65-5.53	7.64-5.15	8.34-5.40	13.43-9.35	8.22-5.80	10.56-7.00	3.87-2.90
Average Yield %	2.02	2.17	2.39	2.34	2.45	3.89	3.91	5.21

Address: 8350 Broad Street, Suite 2000, Tysons, VA 22102-5151 **Telephone:** 703-873-6600	**Web Site:** www.tegna.com **Officers:** Howard D. Elias - Chairman David T. (Dave) Lougee - President, Chief Executive Officer, Division Officer	**Auditors:** Ernst & Young LLP **Investor Contact:** 703-854-6917 **Transfer Agents:** Wells Fargo Bank, N.A., St Paul, MN

TEXTRON INC

Exchange	Symbol	Price	52Wk Range	Yield	P/E
NYS	TXT	$44.60 (12/31/2019)	55.15-42.77	0.18	12.15

*7 Year Price Score 92.01 ***NYSE Composite Index=100** ***12 Month Price Score 88.00**

TRADING VOLUME (thousand shares)

Interim Earnings (Per Share)

Qtr.	Mar	Jun	Sep	Dec
2016	0.55	0.65	1.55	0.78
2017	0.37	0.57	0.60	(0.39)
2018	0.72	0.87	2.26	1.03
2019	0.76	0.93	0.95	...

Interim Dividends (Per Share)

Amt	Decl	Ex	Rec	Pay
0.02Q	02/27/2019	03/14/2019	03/15/2019	04/01/2019
0.02Q	04/24/2019	06/13/2019	06/14/2019	07/01/2019
0.02Q	07/23/2019	09/12/2019	09/13/2019	10/01/2019
0.02Q	10/23/2019	12/12/2019	12/13/2019	01/01/2020

Indicated Div: $0.08

Valuation Analysis

		Institutional Holding	
Forecast EPS	$3.70	No of Institutions	
	(00/24/2020)	N/A	
Market Cap	$10.2 Billion	Shares	
Book Value	$5.5 Billion	N/A	
Price/Book	1.87	% Held	
Price/Sales	0.76	N/A	

Business Summary: Aerospace (MIC: 7.1.1 SIC: 3721 NAIC: 336411)

Textron is a multi-industry company. Co.'s segments include: Textron Aviation, which manufactures, sells and services Beechcraft and Cessna aircraft, and services the Hawker brand of business jets; Bell, which supplies military and commercial helicopters, tiltrotor aircraft, and related spare parts and services; Textron Systems, which includes unmanned systems, marine and land systems, and simulation, training and other; Industrial, which designs and manufactures a variety of products within fuel systems and functional components and specialized vehicles product lines; and Finance, which provides financing to purchasers of new and pre-owned Textron Aviation aircraft and Bell helicopters.

Recent Developments: For the quarter ended Sep 28 2019, net income decreased 60.9% to US$220.0 million from US$563.0 million in the year-earlier quarter. Revenues were US$3.26 billion, up 1.8% from US$3.20 billion the year before. Direct operating expenses rose 2.2% to US$2.75 billion from US$2.69 billion in the comparable period the year before. Indirect operating expenses amounted to US$271.0 million compared with an income of US$115.0 million in the equivalent prior-year period.

Prospects: Our evaluation of Textron Inc. as of October 4th, 2019 is the result of our systematic analysis on three basic characteristics: earnings strength, relative valuation, and recent stock price movement. The company has generated a negative trend in earnings per share over the past 5 quarters. In addition, recent analyst estimates for the company have been reduced while TXT has posted results that exceeded analysts' expectations. Based on operating earnings yield, the company is undervalued when compared to all of the companies we cover. Share price changes over the past year indicates that TXT will perform very poorly over the near term.

Financial Data

(US$ in Millions)	9 Mos	6 Mos	3 Mos	12/29/2018	12/30/2017	12/31/2016	01/02/2016	01/03/2015
Earnings Per Share	3.67	4.98	4.92	4.83	1.14	3.53	2.50	2.13
Cash Flow Per Share	2.76	2.80	4.16	4.44	3.59	3.75	3.95	4.25
Tang Book Value Per Share	14.50	13.86	13.29	12.62	12.56	12.80	10.72	8.12
Dividends Per Share	0.080	0.080	0.080	0.080	0.080	0.080	0.080	0.080
Dividend Payout %	2.18	1.61	1.63	1.66	7.02	2.27	3.20	3.76
Income Statement								
Total Revenue	9,595	6,336	3,109	13,972	14,198	13,788	13,423	13,878
EBITDA	1,163	778	356	1,908	1,298	1,418	1,523	1,423
Depn & Amortn	302	202	102	358	362	368	383	379
Income Before Taxes	732	491	212	1,384	762	876	971	853
Income Taxes	116	95	33	162	456	33	273	248
Net Income	616	396	179	1,222	307	962	697	600
Average Shares	231	233	236	253	268	272	278	281
Balance Sheet								
Current Assets	7,241	6,914	6,587	6,614	7,027	7,053	6,478	6,273
Total Assets	15,062	14,796	14,480	14,264	15,340	15,358	14,708	14,605
Current Liabilities	3,766	3,579	3,432	3,506	3,660	3,893	3,792	3,638
Long-Term Obligations	3,604	3,613	3,523	3,526	3,898	3,317	3,348	3,866
Total Liabilities	9,610	9,460	9,247	9,072	9,693	9,784	9,744	10,333
Stockholders' Equity	5,452	5,336	5,233	5,192	5,647	5,574	4,964	4,272
Shares Outstanding	228	230	232	235	261	270	274	276
Statistical Record								
Return on Assets %	5.80	8.21	8.23	8.28	2.01	6.42	4.77	4.29
Return on Equity %	15.68	22.53	22.19	22.61	5.49	18.31	15.13	13.64
EBITDA Margin %	12.12	12.28	11.45	13.66	9.14	10.28	11.35	10.25
Net Margin %	6.42	6.25	5.76	8.75	2.16	6.98	5.19	4.32
Asset Turnover	0.90	0.91	0.94	0.95	0.93	0.92	0.92	0.99
Current Ratio	1.92	1.93	1.92	1.89	1.92	1.81	1.71	1.72
Debt to Equity	0.66	0.68	0.67	0.68	0.69	0.60	0.67	0.90
Price Range	71.82-42.77	72.30-44.16	72.30-44.16	72.30-44.16	57.18-45.37	49.04-31.11	46.86-37.00	44.23-32.28
P/E Ratio	19.57-11.65	14.52-8.87	14.70-8.98	14.97-9.14	50.16-39.80	13.89-8.81	18.74-14.80	20.77-15.15
Average Yield %	0.15	0.14	0.13	0.13	0.16	0.20	0.19	0.21

Address: 40 Westminster Street, Providence, RI 02903 **Telephone:** 401-421-2800	**Web Site:** www.textron.com **Officers:** Scott C. Donnelly - Chairman, President, Chief Executive Officer Frank T. Connor - Executive Vice President, Chief Financial Officer	**Auditors:** Ernst & Young LLP **Investor Contact:** 401-457-2288 **Transfer Agents:** American Stock Transfer & Trust Cmpany, LLC, Brooklyn, NY

678

THE GAP INC

Exchange	Symbol	Price	52Wk Range	Yield	P/E
NYS	GPS	$17.68 (12/31/2019)	29.51-15.36	5.49	8.26

*7 Year Price Score 55.34   *NYSE Composite Index=100   *12 Month Price Score 77.73

Interim Earnings (Per Share)

Qtr.	Apr	Jul	Oct	Jan
2016-17	0.32	0.31	0.51	0.55
2017-18	0.36	0.68	0.58	0.52
2018-19	0.42	0.76	0.69	0.73
2019-20	0.60	0.44	0.37	...

Interim Dividends (Per Share)

Amt	Decl	Ex	Rec	Pay
0.242Q	02/26/2019	04/09/2019	04/10/2019	05/01/2019
0.242Q	05/22/2019	07/09/2019	07/10/2019	07/31/2019
0.242Q	08/14/2019	10/08/2019	10/09/2019	10/30/2019
0.242Q	11/14/2019	01/07/2020	01/08/2020	01/29/2020

Indicated Div: $0.97

Valuation Analysis

		Institutional Holding	
Forecast EPS	$1.75 (01/17/2020)	No of Institutions	719
Market Cap	$6.6 Billion	Shares	
Book Value	$3.6 Billion		319,499,904
Price/Book	1.81	% Held	
Price/Sales	0.40		58.19

Business Summary: Retail - Apparel and Accessories (MIC: 2.1.5 SIC: 5651 NAIC: 448140)

The Gap is an apparel retail company. Co. provides apparel, accessories, and personal care products for men, women, and children under the Old Navy, Gap, Banana Republic, Athleta, Intermix, and Hill City brands. Co. has stores in the U.S., Canada, the U.K., France, Ireland, Japan, Italy, China, Hong Kong, Taiwan, and Mexico, and has franchise agreements with unaffiliated franchisees to operate Old Navy, Gap, and Banana Republic stores throughout Asia, Europe, Latin America, the Middle East, and Africa. Under these agreements, third parties operate stores that sell apparel and related products under Co.'s brand names.

Recent Developments: For the quarter ended Nov 2 2019, net income decreased 47.4% to US$140.0 million from US$266.0 million in the year-earlier quarter. Revenues were US$4.00 billion, down 2.2% from US$4.09 billion the year before. Operating income was US$221.0 million versus US$363.0 million in the prior-year quarter, a decrease of 39.1%. Direct operating expenses declined 1.1% to US$2.44 billion from US$2.47 billion in the comparable period the year before. Indirect operating expenses increased 6.2% to US$1.34 billion from US$1.26 billion in the equivalent prior-year period.

Prospects: Our evaluation of The Gap Inc. as of October 4th, 2019 is the result of our systematic analysis on three basic characteristics: earnings strength, relative valuation, and recent stock price movement. The company has generated a negative trend in earnings per share over the past 5 quarters. However, recent analyst estimates for the company have been mixed and GPS has posted results that exceeded analysts' expectations. Based on operating earnings yield, the company is undervalued when compared to all of the companies we cover. Share price changes over the past year indicates that GPS will perform poorly over the near term.

Financial Data

(US$ in Thousands)	9 Mos	6 Mos	3 Mos	02/02/2019	02/03/2018	01/28/2017	01/30/2016	01/31/2015
Earnings Per Share	2.14	2.46	2.78	2.59	2.14	1.69	2.23	2.87
Cash Flow Per Share	3.58	3.75	3.89	3.60	3.45	4.32	3.89	4.91
Tang Book Value Per Share	9.74	9.64	9.45	8.87	7.56	6.77	5.73	6.44
Dividends Per Share	0.970	0.970	0.970	0.970	0.920	0.920	0.920	0.880
Dividend Payout %	45.33	39.43	34.89	37.45	42.99	54.44	41.26	30.66
Income Statement								
Total Revenue	11,709,000	7,711,000	3,706,000	16,580,000	15,855,000	15,516,000	15,797,000	16,435,000
EBITDA	1,236,000	875,000	454,000	1,937,000	2,035,000	1,781,000	2,112,000	2,643,000
Depn & Amortn	417,000	277,000	138,000	575,000	556,000	590,000	588,000	560,000
Income Before Taxes	782,000	573,000	302,000	1,322,000	1,424,000	1,124,000	1,471,000	2,013,000
Income Taxes	247,000	178,000	75,000	319,000	576,000	448,000	551,000	751,000
Net Income	535,000	395,000	227,000	1,003,000	848,000	676,000	920,000	1,262,000
Average Shares	376,000	379,000	381,000	388,000	396,000	400,000	413,000	440,000
Balance Sheet								
Current Assets	4,572,000	4,567,000	4,212,000	4,251,000	4,568,000	4,315,000	3,985,000	4,317,000
Total Assets	14,118,000	14,043,000	13,620,000	8,049,000	7,989,000	7,610,000	7,473,000	7,690,000
Current Liabilities	3,192,000	3,134,000	2,831,000	2,174,000	2,461,000	2,453,000	2,535,000	2,234,000
Long-Term Obligations	6,899,000	6,893,000	6,846,000	1,249,000	1,249,000	1,248,000	1,310,000	1,332,000
Total Liabilities	10,484,000	10,418,000	10,049,000	4,496,000	4,845,000	4,706,000	4,928,000	4,707,000
Stockholders' Equity	3,634,000	3,625,000	3,571,000	3,553,000	3,144,000	2,904,000	2,545,000	2,983,000
Shares Outstanding	373,000	376,000	378,000	378,000	389,000	399,000	397,000	421,000
Statistical Record								
Return on Assets %	7.28	8.50	10.05	12.54	10.70	8.99	12.17	16.29
Return on Equity %	22.93	26.91	31.50	30.04	27.59	24.88	33.38	41.87
EBITDA Margin %	10.56	11.35	12.25	11.68	12.84	11.48	13.37	16.08
Net Margin %	4.57	5.12	6.13	6.05	5.35	4.36	5.82	7.68
Asset Turnover	1.47	1.49	1.56	2.07	2.00	2.06	2.09	2.12
Current Ratio	1.43	1.46	1.49	1.96	1.86	1.76	1.57	1.93
Debt to Equity	1.90	1.90	1.92	0.35	0.40	0.43	0.51	0.45
Price Range	29.51-15.36	32.70-17.49	33.75-24.52	34.59-24.60	35.48-21.20	30.71-17.09	43.45-22.45	46.59-35.74
P/E Ratio	13.79-7.18	13.29-7.11	12.14-8.82	13.36-9.50	16.58-9.91	18.17-10.11	19.48-10.07	16.23-12.45
Average Yield %	4.39	3.87	3.48	3.31	3.49	3.78	2.70	2.15

Address: Two Folsom Street, San Francisco, CA 94105 Telephone: 415-427-0100	Web Site: www.gapinc.com Officers: Robert J. (Bob) Fisher - Chairman, Interim President, Interim Chief Executive Officer Shawn Curran - Executive Vice President	Auditors: DELOITTE & TOUCHE LLP Investor Contact: 415-427-0100 Transfer Agents: Wells Fargo Bank, N.A., Mendota Heights, MN

THERMO FISHER SCIENTIFIC INC

Exchange	Symbol	Price	52Wk Range	Yield	P/E
NYS	TMO	$324.87 (12/31/2019)	328.04-212.17	0.23	36.58

*7 Year Price Score 138.82 *NYSE Composite Index=100 *12 Month Price Score 106.37

Interim Earnings (Per Share)

Qtr.	Mar	Jun	Sep	Dec
2016	1.01	1.30	1.19	1.59
2017	1.40	1.56	1.34	1.30
2018	1.43	1.85	1.75	2.21
2019	2.02	2.77	1.88	...

Interim Dividends (Per Share)

Amt	Decl	Ex	Rec	Pay
0.19Q	02/26/2019	03/14/2019	03/15/2019	04/16/2019
0.19Q	05/23/2019	06/13/2019	06/14/2019	07/16/2019
0.19Q	07/11/2019	09/16/2019	09/17/2019	10/15/2019
0.19Q	11/08/2019	12/16/2019	12/17/2019	01/15/2020

Indicated Div: $0.76

Valuation Analysis / **Institutional Holding**

Forecast EPS	$12.32	No of Institutions
	(01/16/2020)	2071
Market Cap	$141.0 Billion	Shares
Book Value	$29.4 Billion	440,151,456
Price/Book	4.80	% Held
Price/Sales	5.59	88.23

Business Summary: Biotechnology (MIC: 4.1.2 SIC: 3829 NAIC: 334519)

Thermo Fisher Scientific is engaged in serving science. Co.'s segments include: Life Sciences Solutions, which provides reagents, instruments and consumables used in biological and medical research, discovery and production of new drugs and vaccines as well as diagnosis of disease; Analytical Instruments, which provides instruments, consumables, software and services that are used for a range of applications in the laboratory, on the production line and in the field; and Specialty Diagnostics, which provides diagnostic test kits, reagents, culture media, instruments and associated products for customers in healthcare, clinical, pharmaceutical, industrial, and food safety laboratories.

Recent Developments: For the quarter ended Sep 28 2019, net income increased 7.2% to US$760.0 million from US$709.0 million in the year-earlier quarter. Revenues were US$6.27 billion, up 5.9% from US$5.92 billion the year before. Operating income was US$946.0 million versus US$912.0 million in the prior-year quarter, an increase of 3.7%. Direct operating expenses rose 6.2% to US$3.51 billion from US$3.31 billion in the comparable period the year before. Indirect operating expenses increased 6.7% to US$1.82 billion from US$1.70 billion in the equivalent prior-year period.

Prospects: Our evaluation of Thermo Fisher Scientific Inc. as of October 4th, 2019 is the result of our systematic analysis on three basic characteristics: earnings strength, relative valuation, and recent stock price movement. The company has managed to produce a neutral trend in earnings per share over the past 5 quarters. However, recent analyst estimates for the company have been raised and TMO has posted results that exceeded analysts' expectations. Based on operating earnings yield, the company is fairly valued when compared to all of the companies we cover. Share price changes over the past year indicates that TMO will perform well over the near term.

Financial Data

(US$ in Thousands)	9 Mos	6 Mos	3 Mos	12/31/2018	12/31/2017	12/31/2016	12/31/2015	12/31/2014
Earnings Per Share	8.88	8.75	7.83	7.24	5.59	5.09	4.92	4.71
Cash Flow Per Share	12.12	12.41	12.79	11.30	10.14	7.97	7.07	6.58
Dividends Per Share	0.740	0.720	0.700	0.680	0.600	0.600	0.600	0.600
Dividend Payout %	8.33	8.23	8.94	9.39	10.73	11.79	12.20	12.74
Income Statement								
Total Revenue	18,713,000	12,441,000	6,125,000	24,358,000	20,918,000	18,274,100	16,965,400	16,889,600
EBITDA	5,088,000	3,579,000	1,494,000	6,059,000	4,973,000	4,203,100	4,008,900	4,204,200
Depn & Amortn	1,701,000	1,126,000	555,000	2,267,000	2,033,000	1,758,000	1,688,200	1,684,800
Income Before Taxes	3,032,000	2,210,000	817,000	3,262,000	2,429,000	2,023,900	1,936,400	2,087,200
Income Taxes	338,000	276,000	2,000	324,000	201,000	(1,400)	(43,900)	191,700
Net Income	2,694,000	1,934,000	815,000	2,938,000	2,225,000	2,021,800	1,975,400	1,894,400
Average Shares	404,000	403,000	403,000	406,000	398,000	397,400	401,900	402,300
Balance Sheet								
Current Assets	10,514,000	11,223,000	9,939,000	10,625,000	9,421,000	7,021,000	5,741,200	6,539,800
Total Assets	56,729,000	57,970,000	55,596,000	56,232,000	56,669,000	45,907,500	40,889,000	42,852,100
Current Liabilities	5,844,000	7,509,000	5,898,000	6,147,000	7,048,000	4,865,800	4,147,300	5,349,800
Long-Term Obligations	16,392,000	16,663,000	16,812,000	17,719,000	18,873,000	15,372,400	11,473,900	12,351,600
Total Liabilities	27,374,000	29,241,000	27,903,000	28,646,000	31,256,000	24,368,200	19,538,800	22,304,000
Stockholders' Equity	29,355,000	28,729,000	27,693,000	27,586,000	25,413,000	21,539,300	21,350,200	20,548,100
Shares Outstanding	434,028	400,475	399,981	402,121	401,314	393,447	399,630	400,469
Statistical Record								
Return on Assets %	6.43	6.25	5.66	5.20	4.34	4.65	4.72	5.07
Return on Equity %	12.77	12.84	11.80	11.09	9.48	9.40	9.43	10.13
EBITDA Margin %	27.19	28.77	24.39	24.87	23.77	23.00	23.63	24.89
Net Margin %	14.40	15.55	13.31	12.06	10.64	11.06	11.64	11.22
Asset Turnover	0.45	0.44	0.44	0.43	0.41	0.42	0.41	0.45
Current Ratio	1.80	1.49	1.69	1.73	1.34	1.44	1.38	1.22
Debt to Equity	0.56	0.58	0.61	0.64	0.74	0.71	0.54	0.60
Price Range	305.43-208.47	295.55-205.57	273.72-203.14	251.98-192.98	200.37-140.98	159.56-121.94	143.03-118.13	129.29-109.63
P/E Ratio	34.40-23.48	33.78-23.49	34.96-25.94	34.80-26.65	35.84-25.22	31.35-23.96	29.07-24.01	27.45-23.28
Average Yield %	0.28	0.29	0.30	0.31	0.35	0.41	0.46	0.50

Address: 168 Third Avenue, Waltham, MA 02451	**Web Site:** www.thermofisher.com	**Auditors:** PricewaterhouseCoopers LLP
Telephone: 781-622-1000	**Officers:** Jim P. Manzi - Chairman, Chairman (frmr)	**Investor Contact:** 781-622-1111
Fax: 781-933-4476	Marc N. Casper - President, Chief Executive Officer, Executive Vice President (frmr), Senior Vice President, Chief Operating Officer	**Transfer Agents:** American Stock Transfer & Trust Company, LLC, Brooklyn, NY

THOR INDUSTRIES, INC.

Exchange	Symbol	Price	52Wk Range	Yield	P/E
NYS	THO	$74.29 (12/31/2019)	76.52-42.72	2.15	23.89

*7 Year Price Score 68.90 *NYSE Composite Index=100 *12 Month Price Score 106.65

Interim Earnings (Per Share)

Qtr.	Oct	Jan	Apr	Jul
2016-17	1.49	1.23	2.11	2.26
2017-18	2.43	1.51	2.53	1.67
2018-19	0.26	(0.10)	0.59	1.70
2019-20	0.92	...	...	...

Interim Dividends (Per Share)

Amt	Decl	Ex	Rec	Pay
0.39Q	03/21/2019	04/03/2019	04/04/2019	04/18/2019
0.39Q	06/17/2019	06/28/2019	07/01/2019	07/15/2019
0.40Q	10/10/2019	10/24/2019	10/25/2019	11/08/2019
0.40Q	12/12/2019	12/24/2019	12/26/2019	01/10/2020

Indicated Div: $1.60

Valuation Analysis **Institutional Holding**

Forecast EPS	$5.30	No of Institutions	
	(01/17/2020)	562	
Market Cap	$4.1 Billion	Shares	
Book Value	$2.1 Billion	64,626,232	
Price/Book	1.94	% Held	
Price/Sales	0.50	99.16	

TRADING VOLUME (thousand shares)

Business Summary: Autos- Manufacturing (MIC: 1.8.1 SIC: 3716 NAIC: 336213)

Thor Industries is a manufacturer of recreational vehicles. Co. has three segments: North American Towable Recreational Vehicles, which consists of: Airstream (towable), Heartland (including Bison, Cruiser RV and DRV), Jayco (including Jayco towable, Starcraft and Highland Ridge), Keystone (including CrossRoads and Dutchmen) and KZ (including Venture RV); North American Motorized Recreational Vehicle, which consists of: Airstream (motorized), Jayco (including Jayco motorized and Entegra Coach) and Thor Motor Coach; and European Recreational Vehicles, which consists of the Erwin Hymer Group business.

Recent Developments: For the quarter ended Oct 31 2019, net income increased 271.6% to US$51.8 million from US$14.0 million in the year-earlier quarter. Revenues were US$2.16 billion, up 22.9% from US$1.76 billion the year before. Direct operating expenses rose 19.5% to US$1.85 billion from US$1.55 billion in the comparable period the year before. Indirect operating expenses increased 23.4% to US$212.8 million from US$172.4 million in the equivalent prior-year period.

Prospects: Our evaluation of Thor Industries Inc. as of October 4th, 2019 is the result of our systematic analysis on three basic characteristics: earnings strength, relative valuation, and recent stock price movement. The company has enjoyed a very positive trend in earnings per share over the past 5 quarters. However, recent analyst estimates for the company have been reduced, while THO has posted results that exceeded analysts' expectations. Based on operating earnings yield, the company is undervalued when compared to all of the companies we cover. Share price changes over the past year indicates that THO will perform very poorly over the near term.

Financial Data

(US$ in Thousands)	3 Mos	07/31/2019	07/31/2018	07/31/2017	07/31/2016	07/31/2015	07/31/2014	07/31/2013
Earnings Per Share	3.11	2.47	8.14	7.09	4.88	3.74	3.35	2.88
Cash Flow Per Share	8.56	9.42	8.86	7.98	6.49	4.66	2.80	2.74
Tang Book Value Per Share	N.M.	N.M.	22.24	14.36	7.24	11.14	11.28	10.47
Dividends Per Share	1.570	1.560	1.480	1.320	1.200	1.080	1.920	2.220
Dividend Payout %	50.48	63.16	18.18	18.62	24.59	28.88	57.31	77.08
Income Statement								
Total Revenue	2,158,785	7,864,758	8,328,909	7,246,952	4,582,112	4,006,819	3,525,456	3,241,795
EBITDA	148,576	393,475	729,291	663,451	436,737	323,164	277,086	244,337
Depn & Amortn	52,892	148,777	93,223	98,258	52,575	31,381	25,834	24,987
Income Before Taxes	68,634	184,666	633,029	556,386	383,313	292,895	252,819	221,972
Income Taxes	16,789	52,201	202,878	182,132	125,291	90,886	77,303	70,296
Net Income	51,065	133,275	430,151	374,254	256,519	199,385	179,002	152,862
Average Shares	55,224	54,026	52,853	52,758	52,590	53,275	53,361	53,115
Balance Sheet								
Current Assets	1,993,483	2,037,357	1,311,674	1,180,167	1,016,858	775,841	844,049	830,704
Total Assets	5,607,541	5,660,446	2,778,665	2,557,931	2,325,464	1,503,248	1,408,718	1,328,268
Current Liabilities	1,439,385	1,448,325	769,330	781,046	651,652	378,335	370,715	361,672
Long-Term Obligations	1,780,091	1,885,253	...	145,000	360,000	...	...	...
Total Liabilities	3,494,011	3,576,021	840,924	981,391	1,060,242	438,061	431,021	435,654
Stockholders' Equity	2,113,530	2,084,425	1,937,741	1,576,540	1,265,222	1,065,187	977,697	892,614
Shares Outstanding	55,198	55,063	52,695	52,586	52,482	52,394	53,329	53,186
Statistical Record								
Return on Assets %	4.05	3.16	16.12	15.33	13.36	13.69	13.08	11.89
Return on Equity %	8.43	6.63	24.48	26.34	21.95	19.52	19.14	17.54
EBITDA Margin %	6.88	5.00	8.76	9.15	9.53	8.07	7.86	7.54
Net Margin %	2.37	1.69	5.16	5.16	5.60	4.98	5.08	4.72
Asset Turnover	1.97	1.86	3.12	2.97	2.39	2.75	2.58	2.52
Current Ratio	1.38	1.41	1.70	1.51	1.56	2.05	2.28	2.30
Debt to Equity	0.84	0.90	...	0.09	0.28	...	...	...
Price Range	74.76-42.72	105.64-48.96	157.02-90.26	115.42-74.53	76.54-48.06	64.38-50.03	64.16-49.03	55.27-27.22
P/E Ratio	24.04-13.74	42.77-19.82	19.29-11.09	16.28-10.51	15.68-9.85	17.21-13.38	19.15-14.64	19.19-9.45
Average Yield %	2.65	2.27	1.24	1.40	2.05	1.90	3.42	5.63

Address: 601 East Beardsley Ave., Elkhart, IN 46514-3305 Telephone: 574-970-7460	Web Site: www.thorindustries.com Officers: Andrew E. Graves - Chairman Peter B. Orthwein - Chairman Emeritus, Executive Chairman, Chairman, President, Chief Executive Officer	Auditors: DELOITTE & TOUCHE LLP Transfer Agents: Computershare Investor Services

3M CO

Exchange	Symbol	Price	52Wk Range	Yield	P/E	Div Acheiver
NYS	MMM	$176.42 (12/31/2019)	219.50-150.74	3.26	20.93	60 Years

*7 Year Price Score 87.99   *NYSE Composite Index=100   *12 Month Price Score 90.20

Interim Earnings (Per Share)

Qtr.	Mar	Jun	Sep	Dec
2016	2.05	2.08	2.15	1.88
2017	2.16	2.58	2.33	0.85
2018	0.98	3.07	2.58	2.28
2019	1.51	1.92	2.72	...

Interim Dividends (Per Share)

Amt	Decl	Ex	Rec	Pay
1.44Q	02/05/2019	02/14/2019	02/15/2019	03/12/2019
1.44Q	05/14/2019	05/23/2019	05/24/2019	06/12/2019
1.44Q	08/06/2019	08/15/2019	08/16/2019	09/12/2019
1.44Q	11/12/2019	11/21/2019	11/22/2019	12/12/2019

Indicated Div: $5.76 (Div. Reinv. Plan)

Valuation Analysis / Institutional Holding

Valuation Analysis		Institutional Holding	
Forecast EPS	$9.05	No of Institutions	
	(01/17/2020)	2747	
Market Cap	$101.5 Billion	Shares	
Book Value	$10.7 Billion	504,214,816	
Price/Book	9.48	% Held	
Price/Sales	3.17	64.32	

Business Summary: Medical Instruments & Equipment (MIC: 4.3.1 SIC: 3841 NAIC: 339112)

3M is a technology company. Co. has five segments: Industrial, which provides tapes, coated, non-woven and bonded abrasives, and adhesives; Safety and Graphics, which provides personal protection products, transportation safety products and commercial graphics systems; Health Care, which provides medical and surgical supplies, skin health and infection prevention products and drug delivery systems; Electronics and Energy, which provides optical films solutions for electronic displays, packaging and interconnection devices, and insulating and splicing solutions; and Consumer, which provides consumer and office tapes and adhesives, repositionable notes, and indexing systems.

Recent Developments: For the quarter ended Sep 30 2019, net income increased 2.7% to US$1.59 billion from US$1.55 billion in the year-earlier quarter. Revenues were US$7.99 billion, down 2.0% from US$8.15 billion the year before. Operating income was US$2.01 billion versus US$2.02 billion in the prior-year quarter, a decrease of 0.2%. Direct operating expenses rose 0.7% to US$4.19 billion from US$4.16 billion in the comparable period the year before. Indirect operating expenses decreased 9.4% to US$1.79 billion from US$1.98 billion in the equivalent prior-year period.

Prospects: Our evaluation of 3M Co as of October 4th, 2019 is the result of our systematic analysis on three basic characteristics: earnings strength, relative valuation, and recent stock price movement. The company has managed to produce a neutral trend in earnings per share over the past 5 quarters. However, recent analyst estimates for the company have been reduced while MMM has posted results that exceeded analysts' expectations. Based on operating earnings yield, the company is undervalued when compared to all of the companies we cover. Share price changes over the past year indicates that MMM will perform in line with the market over the near term.

Financial Data

(US$ in Millions)	9 Mos	6 Mos	3 Mos	12/31/2018	12/31/2017	12/31/2016	12/31/2015	12/31/2014
Earnings Per Share	8.43	8.29	9.44	8.89	7.93	8.16	7.58	7.49
Cash Flow Per Share	12.12	12.30	12.72	10.94	10.44	10.99	10.26	10.21
Tang Book Value Per Share	N.M.	N.M.	N.M.	N.M.	N.M.	N.M.	N.M.	7.28
Dividends Per Share	5.680	5.600	5.520	5.440	4.700	4.440	4.100	3.420
Dividend Payout %	67.38	67.55	58.47	61.19	59.27	54.41	54.09	45.66
Income Statement								
Total Revenue	24,025	16,034	7,863	32,765	31,657	30,109	30,274	31,821
EBITDA	5,890	3,462	1,547	8,768	9,364	8,697	8,381	8,543
Depn & Amortn	1,130	751	375	1,488	1,544	1,474	1,435	1,408
Income Before Taxes	4,500	2,534	1,088	7,000	7,548	7,053	6,823	7,026
Income Taxes	888	510	195	1,637	2,679	1,995	1,982	2,028
Net Income	3,601	2,018	891	5,349	4,858	5,050	4,833	4,956
Average Shares	583	586	588	602	612	618	637	662
Balance Sheet								
Current Assets	18,020	14,051	14,374	13,709	14,277	11,726	10,986	11,765
Total Assets	42,550	38,969	39,140	36,500	37,987	32,906	32,718	31,269
Current Liabilities	7,821	7,265	7,125	7,244	7,687	6,219	7,118	5,998
Long-Term Obligations	17,479	14,914	15,580	13,486	12,156	10,723	8,799	6,790
Total Liabilities	31,848	28,886	29,437	26,704	26,424	22,608	21,010	18,160
Stockholders' Equity	10,702	10,083	9,703	9,796	11,563	10,298	11,708	13,109
Shares Outstanding	575	575	576	576	594	596	609	635
Statistical Record								
Return on Assets %	12.40	12.96	14.51	14.36	13.71	15.35	15.11	15.29
Return on Equity %	47.24	48.00	54.53	50.09	44.44	45.77	38.95	32.38
EBITDA Margin %	24.52	21.59	19.67	26.76	29.58	28.89	27.68	26.85
Net Margin %	14.99	12.59	11.33	16.33	15.35	16.77	15.96	15.57
Asset Turnover	0.80	0.85	0.83	0.88	0.89	0.92	0.95	0.98
Current Ratio	2.30	1.93	2.02	1.89	1.86	1.89	1.54	1.96
Debt to Equity	1.63	1.48	1.61	1.38	1.05	1.04	0.75	0.52
Price Range	219.50-155.75	219.50-159.75	220.09-178.62	258.63-178.62	243.14-174.18	181.42-136.96	170.50-137.58	167.27-123.90
P/E Ratio	26.04-18.48	26.48-19.27	23.31-18.92	29.09-20.09	30.66-21.96	22.23-16.78	22.49-18.15	22.33-16.54
Average Yield %	3.03	2.84	2.73	2.58	2.29	2.64	2.62	2.40

Address: 3M Center, St. Paul, MN 55144-1000	**Web Site:** www.3M.com	**Auditors:** PricewaterhouseCoopers LLP
Telephone: 651-733-1110	**Officers:** Michael F. Roman - Chairman, Chief Executive Officer, Executive Vice President, Senior Vice President, Division Officer, Chief Operating Officer Denise Rutherford - Senior Vice President, Division Officer	**Investor Contact:** 651-737-8503
Fax: 651-733-9973		**Transfer Agents:** Wells Fargo Shareowner Services, St. Paul, MN

TIFFANY & CO.

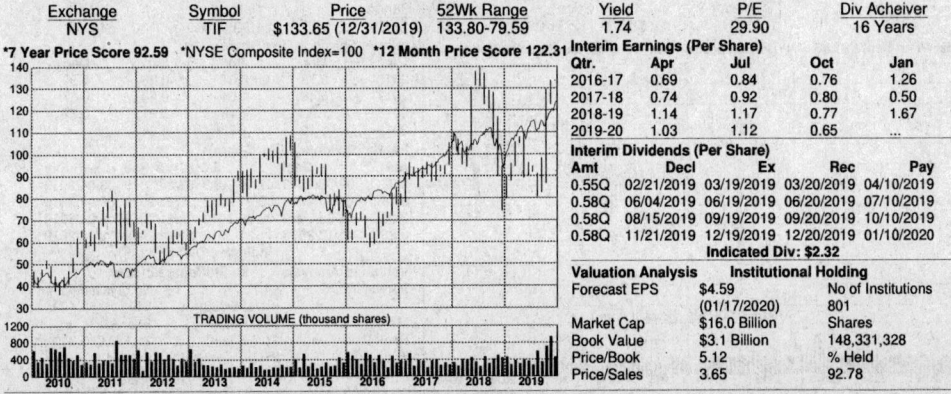

Exchange	Symbol	Price	52Wk Range	Yield	P/E	Div Acheiver
NYS	TIF	$133.65 (12/31/2019)	133.80-79.59	1.74	29.90	16 Years

*7 Year Price Score 92.59 *NYSE Composite Index=100 *12 Month Price Score 122.31

Interim Earnings (Per Share)

Qtr.	Apr	Jul	Oct	Jan
2016-17	0.69	0.84	0.76	1.26
2017-18	0.74	0.92	0.80	0.50
2018-19	1.14	1.17	0.77	1.67
2019-20	1.03	1.12	0.65	...

Interim Dividends (Per Share)

Amt	Decl	Ex	Rec	Pay
0.55Q	02/21/2019	03/19/2019	03/20/2019	04/10/2019
0.58Q	06/04/2019	06/19/2019	06/20/2019	07/10/2019
0.58Q	08/15/2019	09/19/2019	09/20/2019	10/10/2019
0.58Q	11/21/2019	12/19/2019	12/20/2019	01/10/2020

Indicated Div: $2.32

Valuation Analysis		Institutional Holding	
Forecast EPS	$4.59	No of Institutions	801
	(01/17/2020)		
Market Cap	$16.0 Billion	Shares	
Book Value	$3.1 Billion		148,331,328
Price/Book	5.12	% Held	
Price/Sales	3.65		92.78

Business Summary: Retail - Specialty (MIC: 2.1.3 SIC: 5944 NAIC: 448310)

Tiffany & Co. is a holding company that operates through its principal subsidiary, Tiffany and Company. Through its subsidiaries, Co. designs and manufactures products and operates TIFFANY & CO. retail stores worldwide, and also sells its products through Internet, catalog, business-to-business and wholesale distribution. Co.'s principal product category is jewelry. Co. provides a selection of TIFFANY & CO. brand jewelry at a range of prices. Co. also sells watches, home and accessories products and fragrances. Co. has four reportable segments: (i) Americas, (ii) Asia-Pacific, (iii) Japan and (iv) Europe.

Recent Developments: For the quarter ended Oct 31 2019, net income decreased 17.4% to US$78.4 million from US$94.9 million in the year-earlier quarter. Revenues were US$1.01 billion, unchanged from the year before. Operating income was US$118.5 million versus US$126.4 million in the prior-year quarter, a decrease of 6.3%. Direct operating expenses rose 1.5% to US$388.9 million from US$383.1 million in the comparable period the year before. Indirect operating expenses increased 0.9% to US$507.2 million from US$502.9 million in the equivalent prior-year period.

Prospects: Our evaluation of Tiffany & Co. as of October 4th, 2019 is the result of our systematic analysis on three basic characteristics: earnings strength, relative valuation, and recent stock price movement. The company has produced a positive trend in earnings per share over the past 5 quarters. However, recent analyst estimates for the company have been mixed and TIF has posted results that exceeded analysts' expectations. Based on operating earnings yield, the company is undervalued when compared to all of the companies we cover. Share price changes over the past year indicates that TIF will perform poorly over the near term.

Financial Data

(US$ in Thousands)	9 Mos	6 Mos	3 Mos	01/31/2019	01/31/2018	01/31/2017	01/31/2016	01/31/2015
Earnings Per Share	4.47	4.59	4.64	4.75	2.96	3.55	3.59	3.73
Cash Flow Per Share	5.31	4.91	3.81	4.33	7.49	5.60	6.33	4.76
Tang Book Value Per Share	26.10	26.33	26.02	25.66	25.97	24.20	22.96	21.92
Dividends Per Share	2.260	2.230	2.200	2.150	1.950	1.750	1.580	1.480
Dividend Payout %	50.56	48.58	47.41	45.26	65.88	49.30	44.01	39.68
Income Statement								
Total Revenue	3,066,100	2,051,600	1,003,100	4,442,100	4,169,800	4,001,800	4,104,900	4,249,913
EBITDA	651,300	472,700	222,800	1,006,800	1,003,300	925,100	955,200	983,201
Depn & Amortn	189,900	125,600	60,900	223,600	200,800	202,500	196,300	182,761
Income Before Taxes	432,000	326,900	151,500	743,500	760,500	676,600	709,900	737,537
Income Taxes	92,100	65,400	26,300	157,100	390,400	230,500	246,000	253,358
Net Income	339,900	261,500	125,200	586,400	370,000	446,100	463,900	484,179
Average Shares	120,600	121,400	121,900	123,500	125,100	125,500	129,100	129,918
Balance Sheet								
Current Assets	3,600,800	3,673,700	3,642,800	3,759,500	3,983,300	3,573,600	3,508,400	3,611,387
Total Assets	6,259,000	6,315,900	6,275,700	5,333,000	5,468,100	5,097,600	5,129,700	5,180,603
Current Liabilities	877,200	871,100	873,700	718,100	724,800	632,800	729,900	658,033
Long-Term Obligations	883,800	884,000	881,200	883,400	882,900	878,400	798,100	882,535
Total Liabilities	3,129,100	3,135,800	3,117,100	2,215,600	2,234,700	2,084,100	2,218,300	2,345,544
Stockholders' Equity	3,129,900	3,180,100	3,158,600	3,117,400	3,233,400	3,013,500	2,911,400	2,835,059
Shares Outstanding	119,900	120,800	121,400	121,500	124,500	124,500	126,800	129,326
Statistical Record								
Return on Assets %	9.58	9.77	9.71	10.86	7.01	8.70	9.00	9.75
Return on Equity %	17.74	17.99	17.76	18.47	11.85	15.02	16.15	17.43
EBITDA Margin %	21.24	23.04	22.21	22.66	24.06	23.12	23.27	23.13
Net Margin %	11.09	12.75	12.48	13.20	8.88	11.15	11.30	11.39
Asset Turnover	0.77	0.76	0.75	0.82	0.79	0.78	0.80	0.86
Current Ratio	4.10	4.22	4.17	5.24	5.50	5.65	4.81	5.49
Debt to Equity	0.28	0.28	0.28	0.28	0.27	0.29	0.27	0.31
Price Range	129.72-74.21	137.56-74.21	139.50-74.21	139.50-74.21	109.88-78.00	85.06-57.48	95.70-60.93	108.67-80.88
P/E Ratio	29.02-16.60	29.97-16.17	30.06-15.99	29.37-15.62	37.12-26.35	23.96-16.19	26.66-16.97	29.13-21.68
Average Yield %	2.40	2.17	1.99	1.94	2.09	2.49	1.88	1.54

Address: 727 Fifth Avenue, New York, NY 10022	Web Site: www.tiffany.com	Auditors: PricewaterhouseCoopers LLP
Telephone: 212-755-8000	Officers: Roger N. Farah - Chairman Alessandro Bogliolo - Chief Executive Officer	Investor Contact: 212-230-5301
Fax: 212-605-4465		Transfer Agents: Computershare, Providence, RI

TIMKEN CO. (THE)

Exchange	Symbol	Price	52Wk Range	Yield	P/E
NYS	TKR	$56.31 (12/31/2019)	56.92-36.39	1.99	14.08

*7 Year Price Score 91.85   *NYSE Composite Index=100   *12 Month Price Score 110.04

Interim Earnings (Per Share)

Qtr.	Mar	Jun	Sep	Dec
2016	0.78	0.57	0.26	0.30
2017	0.48	1.04	0.68	0.37
2018	1.02	1.16	0.91	0.77
2019	1.19	1.20	0.84	...

Interim Dividends (Per Share)

Amt	Decl	Ex	Rec	Pay
0.28Q	02/06/2019	02/19/2019	02/20/2019	03/04/2019
0.28Q	05/10/2019	05/21/2019	05/22/2019	06/04/2019
0.28Q	08/09/2019	08/20/2019	08/21/2019	09/04/2019
0.28Q	11/12/2019	11/21/2019	11/22/2019	12/04/2019

Indicated Div: $1.12

Valuation Analysis

		Institutional Holding	
Forecast EPS	$4.72	No of Institutions	
	(01/15/2020)	542	
Market Cap	$4.2 Billion	Shares	
Book Value	$1.7 Billion	71,170,640	
Price/Book	2.43	% Held	
Price/Sales	1.12	73.78	

Business Summary: Industrial Machinery & Equipment (MIC: 7.2.1 SIC: 3562 NAIC: 332991)

Timken designs and manages a portfolio of engineered bearings and power transmission products and services. Co.'s engineered bearing products include tapered roller bearings, spherical and cylindrical roller bearings, ball bearings and housed units. Co.'s Power Transmission products include linear motion products, gear drives, lubrication systems, belts, chain, couplings, aerospace drive systems, industrial clutches and brakes, and other products. Co. sells products and services to customers in the following market sectors: industrial distribution, general industrial, mining, construction, agriculture, rail, aerospace and defense, automotive, heavy truck, metals and energy.

Recent Developments: For the quarter ended Sep 30 2019, net income decreased 7.7% to US$66.7 million from US$72.3 million in the year-earlier quarter. Revenues were US$914.0 million, up 3.7% from US$881.3 million the year before. Operating income was US$127.9 million versus US$108.7 million in the prior-year quarter, an increase of 17.7%. Direct operating expenses rose 1.4% to US$636.5 million from US$628.0 million in the comparable period the year before. Indirect operating expenses increased 3.5% to US$149.6 million from US$144.6 million in the equivalent prior-year period.

Prospects: Our evaluation of Timken Co. as of October 4th, 2019 is the result of our systematic analysis on three basic characteristics: earnings strength, relative valuation, and recent stock price movement. The company has managed to produce a neutral trend in earnings per share over the past 5 quarters. However, recent analyst estimates for the company have been reduced and TKR has posted results that fell short of analysts' expectations. Based on operating earnings yield, the company is undervalued when compared to all of the companies we cover. Share price changes over the past year indicates that TKR will perform poorly over the near term.

Financial Data

(US$ in Thousands)	9 Mos	6 Mos	3 Mos	12/31/2018	12/31/2017	12/31/2016	12/31/2015	12/31/2014
Earnings Per Share	4.00	4.07	4.03	3.86	2.58	1.92	(0.84)	1.87
Cash Flow Per Share	6.51	6.37	5.65	4.31	3.05	5.11	4.43	3.40
Tang Book Value Per Share	1.16	0.14	N.M.	N.M.	6.57	8.35	9.04	12.16
Dividends Per Share	1.120	1.120	1.120	1.110	1.070	1.040	1.030	1.000
Dividend Payout %	28.00	27.52	27.79	28.76	41.47	54.17	...	53.48
Income Statement								
Total Revenue	2,893,700	1,979,700	979,700	3,580,800	3,003,800	2,669,800	2,872,300	3,076,200
EBITDA	539,700	381,200	192,800	556,900	391,800	349,200	(64,300)	343,800
Depn & Amortn	120,400	81,200	39,500	99,200	97,700	95,500	94,600	115,500
Income Before Taxes	367,300	265,100	136,600	408,100	259,900	222,100	(189,600)	204,000
Income Taxes	110,400	74,900	41,300	102,600	57,600	69,200	(121,600)	54,700
Net Income	248,600	184,400	91,900	302,800	203,400	152,600	(70,800)	170,800
Average Shares	76,592	77,208	77,012	78,337	78,911	79,234	84,631	91,224
Balance Sheet								
Current Assets	1,807,400	1,866,700	1,919,600	1,737,200	1,500,100	1,204,000	1,206,400	1,481,900
Total Assets	4,565,300	4,674,200	4,680,700	4,445,200	3,402,400	2,758,300	2,785,300	3,001,400
Current Liabilities	704,600	696,300	683,600	685,600	671,700	452,700	505,300	533,800
Long-Term Obligations	1,553,500	1,642,600	1,746,500	1,638,600	854,200	635,000	580,600	522,100
Total Liabilities	2,820,500	2,962,900	3,042,200	2,865,600	1,959,700	1,483,400	1,460,800	1,425,200
Stockholders' Equity	1,744,800	1,711,300	1,638,500	1,579,600	1,442,700	1,274,900	1,324,500	1,576,200
Shares Outstanding	75,324	76,041	76,119	75,953	77,703	77,449	80,263	88,591
Statistical Record								
Return on Assets %	6.81	7.71	7.64	7.72	6.60	5.49	N.M.	4.57
Return on Equity %	18.56	19.55	19.97	20.04	14.97	11.71	N.M.	8.11
EBITDA Margin %	18.65	19.26	19.68	15.55	13.04	13.08	N.M.	11.18
Net Margin %	8.59	9.31	9.38	8.46	6.77	5.72	N.M.	5.55
Asset Turnover	0.84	0.92	0.89	0.91	0.98	0.96	0.99	0.82
Current Ratio	2.57	2.68	2.81	2.53	2.23	2.66	2.39	2.78
Debt to Equity	0.89	0.96	1.07	1.04	0.59	0.50	0.44	0.33
Price Range	52.16-34.43	52.16-34.43	52.10-34.43	55.50-34.43	51.55-40.95	40.95-23.41	43.50-26.46	49.73-37.75
P/E Ratio	13.04-8.61	12.82-8.46	12.93-8.54	14.38-8.92	19.98-15.87	21.33-12.19	...	26.59-20.19
Average Yield %	2.56	2.52	2.53	2.43	2.32	3.14	2.88	2.30

Address: 4500 Mount Pleasant Street NW, North Canton, OH 44720-5450	**Web Site:** www.timken.com
Telephone: 234-262-3000	**Officers:** John M. Timken - Chairman Richard G. Kyle - President, Group President, Chief Executive Officer, Chief Operating Officer

Auditors: Ernst & Young LLP	
Investor Contact: 330-471-7446	
Transfer Agents: Wells Fargo Shareowner Services, Saint Paul, MN	

TJX COMPANIES, INC.

Exchange	Symbol	Price	52Wk Range	Yield	P/E	Div Acheiver
NYS	TJX	$61.06 (12/31/2019)	61.17-44.19	1.51	23.95	22 Years

*7 Year Price Score 117.45 *NYSE Composite Index=100 *12 Month Price Score 105.09

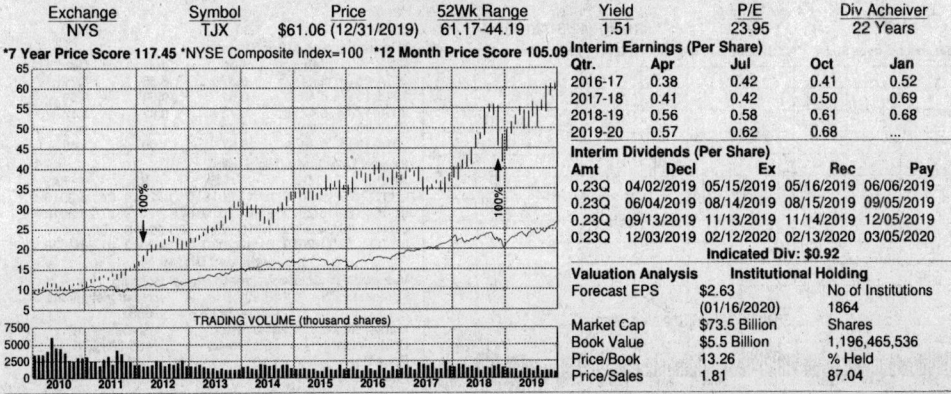

Interim Earnings (Per Share)

Qtr.	Apr	Jul	Oct	Jan
2016-17	0.38	0.42	0.41	0.52
2017-18	0.41	0.42	0.50	0.69
2018-19	0.56	0.58	0.61	0.68
2019-20	0.57	0.62	0.68	...

Interim Dividends (Per Share)

Amt	Decl	Ex	Rec	Pay
0.23Q	04/02/2019	05/15/2019	05/16/2019	06/06/2019
0.23Q	06/04/2019	08/14/2019	08/15/2019	09/05/2019
0.23Q	09/13/2019	11/13/2019	11/14/2019	12/05/2019
0.23Q	12/03/2019	02/12/2020	02/13/2020	03/05/2020

Indicated Div: $0.92

Valuation Analysis / **Institutional Holding**

Forecast EPS	$2.63	No of Institutions
	(01/16/2020)	1864
Market Cap	$73.5 Billion	Shares
Book Value	$5.5 Billion	1,196,465,536
Price/Book	13.26	% Held
Price/Sales	1.81	87.04

Business Summary: Retail - Apparel and Accessories (MIC: 2.1.5 SIC: 5651 NAIC: 448140)

TJX Companies is an off-price apparel and home fashions retailer. Co.'s segments comprised of: Marmaxx, which sells family apparel (including footwear and accessories), home fashions (including home basics, decorative accessories and giftware) and other merchandise; HomeGoods, which provides a range of home fashions, including home fashions, including furniture, rugs, lighting, soft home, decorative accessories, tabletop and cookware as well as pet, kids and gourmet food departments; TJX Canada, which operates the Winners, HomeSense and Marshalls chains in Canada; and TJX International, which operates the T.K. Maxx and HomeSense chains in Europe and the T.K. Maxx chain in Australia.

Recent Developments: For the quarter ended Nov 2 2019, net income increased 8.7% to US$828.3 million from US$762.3 million in the year-earlier quarter. Revenues were US$10.45 billion, up 6.4% from US$9.83 billion the year before. Direct operating expenses rose 6.5% to US$7.44 billion from US$6.98 billion in the comparable period the year before. Indirect operating expenses increased 7.4% to US$1.89 billion from US$1.76 billion in the equivalent prior-year period.

Prospects: Our evaluation of TJX Companies Inc. as of October 4th, 2019 is the result of our systematic analysis on three basic characteristics: earnings strength, relative valuation, and recent stock price movement. The company has managed to produce a neutral trend in earnings per share over the past 5 quarters. In addition, recent analyst estimates for the company have been mixed and TJX has posted results that fell short of analysts' expectations. Based on operating earnings yield, the company is fairly valued when compared to all of the companies we cover. Share price changes over the past year indicates that TJX will perform in line with the market over the near term.

Financial Data

(US$ in Thousands)	9 Mos	6 Mos	3 Mos	02/02/2019	02/03/2018	01/28/2017	01/30/2016	01/31/2015
Earnings Per Share	2.55	2.48	2.44	2.43	2.02	1.73	1.67	1.58
Cash Flow Per Share	2.89	2.83	2.89	3.30	2.34	2.75	2.19	2.18
Tang Book Value Per Share	4.53	4.31	4.15	4.07	4.02	3.34	2.99	2.89
Dividends Per Share	0.850	0.815	0.780	0.741	0.599	0.495	0.403	0.335
Dividend Payout %	33.33	32.86	31.90	30.50	29.64	28.61	24.17	21.27
Income Statement								
Total Revenue	29,510,515	19,059,181	9,277,585	38,972,934	35,864,664	33,183,744	30,944,938	29,078,407
EBITDA	3,727,381	2,385,703	1,146,999	5,001,726	4,614,133	4,425,373	4,321,396	4,178,646
Depn & Amortn	640,500	424,200	209,700	819,655	725,957	658,796	616,696	588,975
Income Before Taxes	3,079,908	1,957,789	936,482	4,173,211	3,856,588	3,723,043	3,658,300	3,549,884
Income Taxes	792,505	498,649	236,304	1,113,413	1,248,640	1,424,809	1,380,642	1,334,756
Net Income	2,287,403	1,459,140	700,178	3,059,798	2,607,948	2,298,234	2,277,658	2,215,128
Average Shares	1,224,288	1,228,986	1,233,407	1,259,252	1,292,210	1,328,864	1,366,502	1,407,090
Balance Sheet								
Current Assets	9,374,615	8,268,604	8,067,212	8,469,222	8,485,727	7,750,774	6,772,560	6,715,061
Total Assets	24,288,704	22,854,979	22,489,064	14,326,029	14,058,015	12,883,808	11,499,482	11,128,381
Current Liabilities	7,687,144	6,600,741	6,581,019	5,531,374	5,125,537	4,757,656	4,402,230	3,929,634
Long-Term Obligations	2,235,873	2,235,121	2,234,368	2,476,874	2,452,524	2,403,831	1,709,268	1,684,597
Total Liabilities	18,746,172	17,552,367	17,357,169	9,277,423	8,909,706	8,373,209	7,192,407	6,864,151
Stockholders' Equity	5,542,532	5,302,612	5,131,895	5,048,606	5,148,309	4,510,599	4,307,075	4,264,230
Shares Outstanding	1,203,183	1,208,932	1,212,667	1,217,182	1,256,018	1,292,638	1,326,991	1,369,466
Statistical Record								
Return on Assets %	15.92	16.57	16.68	21.62	19.05	18.90	20.19	20.83
Return on Equity %	57.95	58.18	58.56	60.18	53.13	52.27	53.29	52.30
EBITDA Margin %	12.63	12.52	12.36	12.83	12.87	13.34	13.96	14.37
Net Margin %	7.75	7.66	7.55	7.85	7.27	6.93	7.36	7.62
Asset Turnover	2.07	2.16	2.17	2.75	2.62	2.73	2.74	2.73
Current Ratio	1.22	1.25	1.23	1.53	1.66	1.63	1.54	1.71
Debt to Equity	0.40	0.42	0.44	0.49	0.48	0.53	0.40	0.40
Price Range	60.49-41.63	56.69-41.63	56.13-40.95	56.13-37.18	40.41-33.45	41.44-33.95	38.39-32.10	34.30-26.11
P/E Ratio	23.72-16.33	22.86-16.79	23.00-16.78	23.10-15.30	20.01-16.56	23.95-19.63	22.99-19.22	21.71-16.53
Average Yield %	1.62	1.57	1.56	1.57	1.61	1.30	1.16	1.12

Address: 770 Cochituate Road, Framingham, MA 01701 Telephone: 508-390-1000 Fax: 508-390-2091	Web Site: www.tjx.com Officers: Carol Meyrowitz - Executive Chairman, Chairman Ernie L. Herrman - President, Chief Executive Officer	Auditors: PricewaterhouseCoopers LLP Investor Contact: 508-390-2323 Transfer Agents: Computershare, Providence, RI

TOLL BROTHERS INC.

Exchange	Symbol	Price	52Wk Range	Yield	P/E
NYS	TOL	$39.51 (12/31/2019)	41.42-32.93	1.11	9.80

*7 Year Price Score 86.84   *NYSE Composite Index=100   *12 Month Price Score 101.11

Interim Earnings (Per Share)

Qtr.	Jan	Apr	Jul	Oct
2014-15	0.44	0.37	0.36	0.79
2015-16	0.40	0.51	0.61	0.66
2016-17	0.42	0.73	0.87	1.16
2017-18	0.83	0.72	1.26	2.04
2018-19	0.76	0.87	1.00	1.40

Interim Dividends (Per Share)

Amt	Decl	Ex	Rec	Pay
0.11Q	03/12/2019	04/11/2019	04/12/2019	04/26/2019
0.11Q	06/18/2019	07/11/2019	07/12/2019	07/26/2019
0.11Q	09/24/2019	10/10/2019	10/11/2019	10/25/2019
0.11Q	12/11/2019	01/09/2020	01/10/2020	01/24/2020

Indicated Div: $0.44

Valuation Analysis

		Institutional Holding	
Forecast EPS	$3.90	No of Institutions	
	(01/14/2020)	603	
Market Cap	$5.6 Billion	Shares	
Book Value	$5.1 Billion	155,392,576	
Price/Book	1.10	% Held	
Price/Sales	0.77	75.35	

TRADING VOLUME (thousand shares)

Business Summary: Builders (MIC: 2.2.5 SIC: 1531 NAIC: 236117)

Toll Brothers designs, builds, markets, sells, and arranges financing for residential single-family detached, attached home, master planned resort-style golf, and urban communities. Co. also designs, builds, markets, and sells urban condominiums through Toll Brothers City Living®. Co. operates its own architectural, engineering, mortgage, title, land development, golf course development, and landscaping subsidiaries. Co. also operates its own security company, TBI Smart Home Solutions, which provides homeowners with home automation and technology options. In addition, Co. operates its own lumber distribution, house component assembly, and manufacturing operations.

Recent Developments: For the year ended Oct 31 2019, net income decreased 21.1% to US$590.0 million from US$748.2 million in the prior year. Revenues were US$7.22 billion, up 1.1% from US$7.14 billion the year before. Operating income was US$680.8 million versus US$786.2 million in the prior year, a decrease of 13.4%. Direct operating expenses rose 2.4% to US$5.81 billion from US$5.67 billion in the comparable period the year before. Indirect operating expenses increased 7.4% to US$734.5 million from US$684.0 million in the equivalent prior-year period.

Prospects: Our evaluation of Toll Brothers Inc. as of October 4th, 2019 is the result of our systematic analysis on three basic characteristics: earnings strength, relative valuation, and recent stock price movement. The company has generated a negative trend in earnings per share over the past 5 quarters. However, recent analyst estimates for the company have been mixed and TOL has posted results that exceeded analysts' expectations. Based on operating earnings yield, the company is undervalued when compared to all of the companies we cover. Share price changes over the past year indicates that TOL will perform in line with the market over the near term.

Financial Data

(US$ in Thousands)	10/31/2019	10/31/2018	10/31/2017	10/31/2016	10/31/2015	10/31/2014	10/31/2013	10/31/2012
Earnings Per Share	4.03	4.85	3.17	2.18	1.97	1.84	0.97	2.86
Cash Flow Per Share	3.02	3.96	5.92	0.88	0.34	1.76	(3.36)	(1.01)
Tang Book Value Per Share	35.99	32.57	28.82	26.14	24.15	22.02	19.68	18.51
Dividends Per Share	0.440	0.410	0.240	...	...	...	...	...
Dividend Payout %	10.92	8.45	7.57	...	...	...	...	...
Income Statement								
Total Revenue	7,223,966	7,143,258	5,815,058	5,169,508	4,171,248	3,911,602	2,674,299	1,882,781
EBITDA	810,885	861,106	710,957	561,336	528,204	486,440	278,515	111,936
Depn & Amortn	67,600	21,000	18,700	15,500	15,700	22,999	25,210	22,586
Income Before Taxes	762,302	848,676	698,245	548,279	514,443	463,441	253,305	89,350
Income Taxes	197,163	185,765	278,816	206,932	172,395	164,550	97,091	(374,204)
Net Income	590,007	748,151	535,495	382,095	363,167	340,032	170,606	487,146
Average Shares	146,501	154,201	169,487	175,973	184,703	185,875	177,963	170,154
Balance Sheet								
Current Assets	9,179,853	8,780,414	7,996,764	8,186,386	8,141,760	7,357,425	5,793,960	5,384,411
Total Assets	10,828,138	10,244,590	9,445,225	9,736,789	9,206,515	8,416,902	6,827,459	6,181,044
Current Liabilities	1,788,098	1,777,502	1,688,111	1,726,136	1,188,196	1,156,619	984,631	800,229
Long-Term Obligations	3,921,347	3,698,176	3,220,024	3,775,451	3,790,240	3,399,586	2,503,664	2,252,944
Total Liabilities	5,756,322	5,484,391	4,914,031	5,507,497	4,983,958	4,562,526	3,494,472	3,059,344
Stockholders' Equity	5,071,816	4,760,199	4,531,194	4,229,292	4,222,557	3,854,376	3,332,987	3,121,700
Shares Outstanding	140,938	146,163	157,205	161,783	174,847	175,046	169,353	168,637
Statistical Record								
Return on Assets %	5.60	7.60	5.58	4.02	4.12	4.46	2.62	8.65
Return on Equity %	12.00	16.10	12.23	9.02	8.99	9.46	5.29	17.02
EBITDA Margin %	11.22	12.05	12.23	10.86	12.66	12.44	10.41	5.95
Net Margin %	8.17	10.47	9.21	7.39	8.71	8.69	6.38	25.87
Asset Turnover	0.69	0.73	0.61	0.54	0.47	0.51	0.41	0.33
Current Ratio	5.13	4.94	4.74	4.74	6.85	6.36	5.88	6.73
Debt to Equity	0.77	0.78	0.71	0.89	0.90	0.88	0.75	0.72
Price Range	41.22-29.94	52.54-28.93	46.04-27.06	38.06-24.10	41.88-30.92	39.55-29.18	37.98-29.73	36.43-17.05
P/E Ratio	10.23-7.43	10.83-5.96	14.52-8.54	17.46-11.06	21.26-15.70	21.49-15.86	39.15-30.65	12.74-5.96
Average Yield %	1.21	0.99	0.66	...	...	...	...	...

Address: 250 Gibraltar Road, Horsham, PA 19044	Web Site: www.tollbrothers.com	Auditors: Ernst & Young LLP
Telephone: 215-938-8000	Officers: Douglas C. Yearley - Chairman, President, Chief Executive Officer Martin P. Connor - Senior Vice President, Chief Financial Officer	Investor Contact: 215-938-8312
Fax: 215-938-8023		Transfer Agents: American Stock Transfer and Trust Company, New York, NY

TOOTSIE ROLL INDUSTRIES INC

Exchange	Symbol	Price	52Wk Range	Yield	P/E	Div Acheiver
NYS	TR	$34.14 (12/31/2019)	40.43-30.65	1.05	35.56	55 Years

*7 Year Price Score 98.35   *NYSE Composite Index=100   *12 Month Price Score 90.30

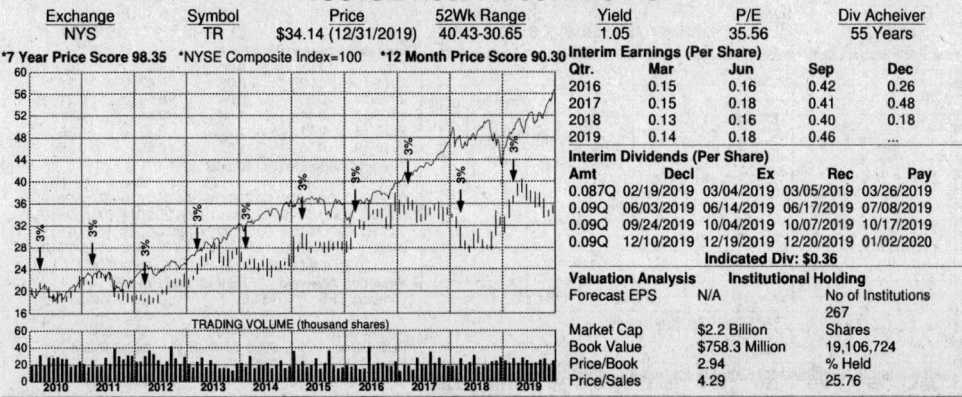

TRADING VOLUME (thousand shares)

Interim Earnings (Per Share)

Qtr.	Mar	Jun	Sep	Dec
2016	0.15	0.16	0.42	0.26
2017	0.15	0.18	0.41	0.48
2018	0.13	0.16	0.40	0.18
2019	0.14	0.18	0.46	...

Interim Dividends (Per Share)

Amt	Decl	Ex	Rec	Pay
0.087Q	02/19/2019	03/04/2019	03/05/2019	03/26/2019
0.09Q	06/03/2019	06/14/2019	06/17/2019	07/08/2019
0.09Q	09/24/2019	10/04/2019	10/07/2019	10/17/2019
0.09Q	12/10/2019	12/19/2019	12/20/2019	01/02/2020

Indicated Div: $0.36

Valuation Analysis

Forecast EPS	N/A	**Institutional Holding** No of Institutions 267
Market Cap	$2.2 Billion	Shares
Book Value	$758.3 Million	19,106,724
Price/Book	2.94	% Held
Price/Sales	4.29	25.76

Business Summary: Food (MIC: 1.2.1 SIC: 2064 NAIC: 311340)

Tootsie Roll Industries and its consolidated subsidiaries are engaged in the manufacture and sale of confectionery products. Co.'s products are marketed in a variety of packages designed to be suitable for display and sale in different types of retail outlets. They are sold through candy and grocery brokers and by Co. itself to customers throughout the U.S. These customers include wholesale distributors of candy and groceries, supermarkets, variety stores, dollar stores, chain grocers, drug chains, discount chains, cooperative grocery associations, mass merchandisers, warehouse and membership club stores, vending machine operators, the U.S. military and fund-raising charitable organizations.

Recent Developments: For the quarter ended Sep 30 2019, net income increased 14.4% to US$29.8 million from US$26.1 million in the year-earlier quarter. Revenues were US$182.7 million, up 0.2% from US$182.3 million the year before. Operating income was US$36.0 million versus US$30.2 million in the prior-year quarter, an increase of 19.2%. Direct operating expenses declined 2.0% to US$113.1 million from US$115.5 million in the comparable period the year before. Indirect operating expenses decreased 8.3% to US$33.6 million from US$36.6 million in the equivalent prior-year period.

Prospects: Our evaluation of Tootsie Roll Industries Inc. as of October 4th, 2019 is the result of our systematic analysis on three basic characteristics: earnings strength, relative valuation, and recent stock price movement. The company has managed to produce a neutral trend in earnings per share over the past 5 quarters. In addition, recent analyst estimates for the company have been mixed and TR has posted results that fell short of analysts' expectations. Based on operating earnings yield, the company is overvalued when compared to all of the companies we cover. Share price changes over the past year indicates that TR will perform over the near term.

Financial Data
(US$ in Thousands)

	9 Mos	6 Mos	3 Mos	12/31/2018	12/31/2017	12/31/2016	12/31/2015	12/31/2014
Earnings Per Share	0.96	0.90	0.88	0.86	1.21	0.99	0.96	0.91
Cash Flow Per Share	1.47	1.61	1.55	1.53	0.64	1.45	1.32	1.26
Tang Book Value Per Share	7.82	7.55	7.55	7.62	7.29	6.85	6.57	6.35
Dividends Per Share	0.352	0.352	0.350	0.347	0.337	0.327	0.309	0.274
Dividend Payout %	36.51	39.01	39.81	40.15	27.92	33.09	32.19	30.26
Income Statement								
Total Revenue	391,653	208,929	101,977	518,920	519,289	521,100	540,112	543,525
EBITDA	80,315	28,037	12,128	88,521	100,845	115,514	111,621	110,569
Depn & Amortn	15,088	694	353	18,669	18,991	19,627	20,388	20,758
Income Before Taxes	65,227	27,343	11,775	73,206	84,561	97,912	92,578	91,294
Income Taxes	14,926	6,888	2,864	16,401	3,907	30,593	26,451	28,434
Net Income	50,365	20,511	8,955	56,893	80,864	67,510	66,089	63,298
Average Shares	65,344	65,559	65,872	66,142	67,026	68,010	69,152	70,207
Balance Sheet								
Current Assets	332,306	281,089	279,976	304,046	270,920	299,300	293,806	264,621
Total Assets	982,092	948,524	940,504	947,361	930,946	920,101	908,983	910,386
Current Liabilities	77,409	60,287	53,049	61,391	63,788	63,561	72,062	64,459
Long-Term Obligations	7,500	7,500	7,500	7,500	7,500	7,730	7,883	8,194
Total Liabilities	223,763	205,720	195,676	196,739	197,106	208,737	210,800	219,577
Stockholders' Equity	758,329	742,804	744,828	750,622	733,840	711,364	698,183	690,809
Shares Outstanding	65,229	65,534	65,760	65,961	66,588	67,573	68,480	69,665
Statistical Record								
Return on Assets %	6.44	6.28	6.22	6.06	8.74	7.36	7.27	7.04
Return on Equity %	8.31	8.00	7.85	7.67	11.19	9.55	9.52	9.23
EBITDA Margin %	20.51	13.42	11.89	17.06	19.42	22.17	20.67	20.34
Net Margin %	12.86	9.82	8.78	10.96	15.57	12.96	12.24	11.65
Asset Turnover	0.53	0.55	0.56	0.55	0.56	0.57	0.59	0.60
Current Ratio	4.29	4.66	5.28	4.95	4.25	4.71	4.08	4.11
Debt to Equity	0.01	0.01	0.01	0.01	0.01	0.01	0.01	0.01
Price Range	40.43-27.58	40.43-27.58	37.45-26.94	34.67-26.94	37.11-32.47	38.02-27.02	30.69-25.22	27.25-22.56
P/E Ratio	42.11-28.73	44.92-30.65	42.56-30.62	40.31-31.33	30.67-26.84	38.41-27.29	31.97-26.27	29.95-24.79
Average Yield %	0.99	1.06	1.14	1.15	0.97	1.00	1.09	1.10

Address: 7401 South Cicero Avenue, Chicago, IL 60629 **Telephone:** 773-838-3400 **Fax:** 773-838-3534	**Web Site:** www.tootsie.com **Officers:** Ellen R. Gordon - Chairman, Chief Executive Officer G. Howard Ember - Vice President, Chief Financial Officer	**Auditors:** Grant Thornton LLP **Transfer Agents:** American Stock Transfer & Trust Company, Brooklyn, NY

TORO COMPANY (THE)

Exchange	Symbol	Price	52Wk Range	Yield	P/E	Div Acheiver
NYS	TTC	$79.67 (12/31/2019)	81.39-54.63	1.26	31.49	15 Years

*7 Year Price Score 122.46 *NYSE Composite Index=100 *12 Month Price Score 104.98

Interim Earnings (Per Share)

Qtr.	Jan	Apr	Jul	Oct
2014-15	0.27	0.82	0.47	0.21
2015-16	0.35	0.94	0.50	0.27
2016-17	0.41	1.08	0.61	0.31
2017-18	0.21	1.21	0.73	0.36
2018-19	0.55	1.07	0.56	0.35

Interim Dividends (Per Share)

Amt	Decl	Ex	Rec	Pay
0.225Q	03/19/2019	03/29/2019	04/01/2019	04/12/2019
0.225Q	05/21/2019	06/24/2019	06/25/2019	07/11/2019
0.225Q	09/17/2019	09/27/2019	09/30/2019	10/11/2019
0.25Q	12/03/2019	12/24/2019	12/26/2019	01/09/2020

Indicated Div: $1.00 (Div. Reinv. Plan)

Valuation Analysis / **Institutional Holding**

Forecast EPS	$3.35	No of Institutions
	(01/17/2020)	532
Market Cap	$8.5 Billion	Shares
Book Value	$859.6 Million	106,567,248
Price/Book	9.89	% Held
Price/Sales	2.71	82.09

Business Summary: Industrial Machinery & Equipment (MIC: 7.2.1 SIC: 3524 NAIC: 333112)

Toro designs, manufactures, and markets turf maintenance equipment and services, turf irrigation systems, landscaping equipment and lighting products, snow and ice management products, agricultural irrigation systems, rental and underground construction equipment, and residential yard and snow thrower products. Co.'s segments include: Professional, which markets its products worldwide through a network of distributors and dealers, as well as directly to government customers, rental companies, and retailers; and Residential, which markets its products to homeowners through outdoor power equipment distributors and dealers, mass retailers, hardware retailers, home centers, as well as online.

Recent Developments: For the year ended Oct 31 2019, net income increased 0.8% to US$274.0 million from US$271.9 million in the prior year. Revenues were US$3.14 billion, up 19.8% from US$2.62 billion the year before. Operating income was US$325.0 million versus US$373.1 million in the prior year, a decrease of 12.9%. Direct operating expenses rose 24.6% to US$2.09 billion from US$1.68 billion in the comparable period the year before. Indirect operating expenses increased 27.3% to US$722.9 million from US$567.9 million in the equivalent prior-year period.

Prospects: Our evaluation of Toro Co. as of October 4th, 2019 is the result of our systematic analysis on three basic characteristics: earnings strength, relative valuation, and recent stock price movement. The company has produced a positive trend in earnings per share over the past 5 quarters. However, recent analyst estimates for the company have been unchanged, while TTC has posted results that exceeded analysts' expectations. Based on operating earnings yield, the company is fairly valued when compared to all of the companies we cover. Share price changes over the past year indicates that TTC will perform well over the near term.

Financial Data

(US$ in Thousands)	10/31/2019	10/31/2018	10/31/2017	10/31/2016	10/31/2015	10/31/2014	10/31/2013	10/31/2012
Earnings Per Share	2.53	2.50	2.41	2.06	1.77	1.51	1.31	1.07
Cash Flow Per Share	3.16	3.43	3.33	3.29	2.13	1.62	1.92	1.56
Tang Book Value Per Share	1.36	3.20	2.88	2.28	1.35	2.63	2.10	1.62
Dividends Per Share	0.900	0.800	0.700	0.600	0.500	0.400	0.280	0.220
Dividend Payout %	35.57	32.00	29.05	29.13	28.17	26.49	21.37	20.56
Income Statement								
Total Revenue	3,138,084	2,618,650	2,505,176	2,392,175	2,390,875	2,172,691	2,041,431	1,958,690
EBITDA	423,951	431,387	415,657	392,736	351,263	311,280	283,586	253,226
Depn & Amortn	87,684	53,500	54,679	53,355	50,322	47,136	48,207	46,840
Income Before Taxes	310,185	361,254	343,224	320,872	282,678	249,183	219,616	190,266
Income Taxes	48,150	100,458	85,467	99,466	89,440	82,575	71,868	66,721
Net Income	273,983	271,939	267,717	230,994	201,591	173,870	154,845	129,541
Average Shares	108,090	108,657	111,252	111,987	113,514	115,256	118,210	121,236
Balance Sheet								
Current Assets	1,122,891	894,637	859,886	779,009	710,679	824,036	653,267	612,134
Total Assets	2,330,547	1,570,984	1,493,787	1,387,518	1,303,658	1,192,415	1,002,748	935,199
Current Liabilities	756,970	532,635	521,796	463,839	443,734	400,420	388,845	378,122
Long-Term Obligations	620,899	312,549	305,629	331,423	354,818	347,316	223,544	223,482
Total Liabilities	1,470,969	902,068	876,695	837,483	841,493	783,688	644,010	622,797
Stockholders' Equity	859,578	668,916	617,092	550,035	462,165	408,727	358,738	312,402
Shares Outstanding	106,742	105,600	106,882	108,427	109,301	111,356	113,577	116,532
Statistical Record								
Return on Assets %	14.04	17.75	18.58	17.12	16.15	15.84	15.98	14.31
Return on Equity %	35.85	42.29	45.88	45.52	46.30	45.31	46.14	44.61
EBITDA Margin %	13.51	16.47	16.59	16.42	14.69	14.33	13.89	12.93
Net Margin %	8.73	10.38	10.69	9.66	8.43	8.00	7.59	6.61
Asset Turnover	1.61	1.71	1.74	1.77	1.92	1.98	2.11	2.16
Current Ratio	1.48	1.68	1.65	1.68	1.60	2.06	1.68	1.62
Debt to Equity	0.72	0.47	0.50	0.60	0.77	0.85	0.62	0.72
Price Range	77.13-53.23	67.33-54.50	73.69-46.74	49.29-32.75	37.89-30.41	33.47-28.07	29.48-20.40	21.11-13.00
P/E Ratio	30.49-21.04	26.93-21.80	30.58-19.39	23.93-15.90	21.41-17.18	22.16-18.59	22.50-15.57	19.73-12.15
Average Yield %	1.34	1.30	1.12	1.41	1.48	1.29	1.18	1.25

Address: 8111 Lyndale Avenue South, Bloomington, MN 55420 Telephone: 952-888-8801	Web Site: www.thetorocompany.com Officers: Richard M. Olson - Chairman, President, Chief Executive Officer, Vice President, Chief Operating Officer Amy E. Dahl - Vice President, General Counsel, Corporate Secretary	Auditors: KPMG LLP Transfer Agents: Wells Fargo Shareowner Services, St. Paul, MN

TRANSOCEAN LTD

Exchange	Symbol	Price	52Wk Range	Yield	P/E
NYS	RIG	$6.88 (12/31/2019)	9.65-3.86	N/A	N/A

*7 Year Price Score 26.59 *NYSE Composite Index=100 *12 Month Price Score 78.54

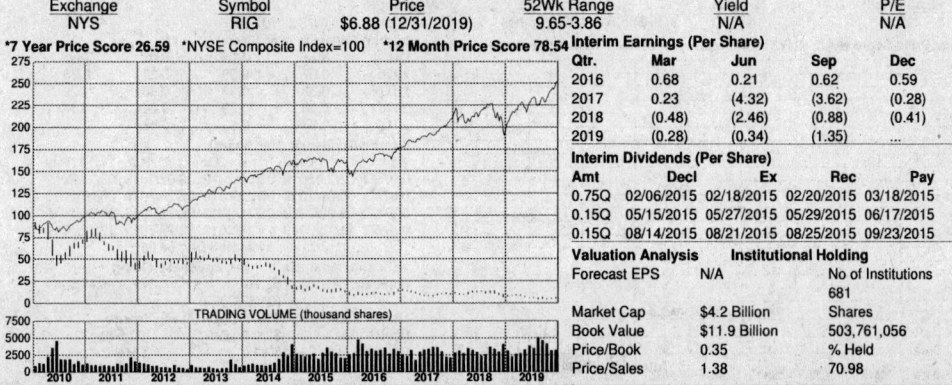

Interim Earnings (Per Share)

Qtr.	Mar	Jun	Sep	Dec
2016	0.68	0.21	0.62	0.59
2017	0.23	(4.32)	(3.62)	(0.28)
2018	(0.48)	(2.46)	(0.88)	(0.41)
2019	(0.28)	(0.34)	(1.35)	...

Interim Dividends (Per Share)

Amt	Decl	Ex	Rec	Pay
0.75Q	02/06/2015	02/18/2015	02/20/2015	03/18/2015
0.15Q	05/15/2015	05/27/2015	05/29/2015	06/17/2015
0.15Q	08/14/2015	08/21/2015	08/25/2015	09/23/2015

Valuation Analysis   Institutional Holding

Forecast EPS	N/A	No of Institutions	681
Market Cap	$4.2 Billion	Shares	
Book Value	$11.9 Billion	503,761,056	
Price/Book	0.35	% Held	
Price/Sales	1.38	70.98	

Business Summary: Equipment & Services (MIC: 9.1.3 SIC: 1381 NAIC: 213111)

Transocean is a provider of offshore contract drilling services for oil and gas wells. Co.'s primary business is to contract its drilling rigs, related equipment and work crews primarily on a dayrate basis to drill oil and gas wells. Co. focuses on ultra-deepwater and harsh environment drilling services. Co.'s mobile offshore drilling fleet consists of drillship and semisubmersible floaters used in support of offshore drilling activities and offshore support services. Also, Co.'s drilling equipment is suitable for exploration and development. Co. further categorizes the drilling units of its fleet as follows: ultra-deepwater floaters, harsh environment floaters, and midwater floaters.

Recent Developments: For the quarter ended Sep 30 2019, net loss amounted to US$825.0 million versus a net loss of US$409.0 million in the year-earlier quarter. Revenues were US$784.0 million, down 3.9% from US$816.0 million the year before. Operating loss was US$607.0 million versus a loss of US$305.0 million in the prior-year quarter. Direct operating expenses rose 22.4% to US$547.0 million from US$447.0 million in the comparable period the year before. Indirect operating expenses increased 25.2% to US$844.0 million from US$674.0 million in the equivalent prior-year period.

Prospects: Our evaluation of Transocean Ltd. as of October 4th, 2019 is the result of our systematic analysis on three basic characteristics: earnings strength, relative valuation, and recent stock price movement. The company has suffered a very negative trend in earnings per share over the past 5 quarters. However, recent analyst estimates for the company have been mixed and RIG has posted results that fell short of analysts' expectations. Based on operating earnings yield, the company is overvalued when compared to all of the companies we cover. Share price changes over the past year indicates that RIG will perform in line with the market over the near term.

Financial Data

(US$ in Millions)	9 Mos	6 Mos	3 Mos	12/31/2018	12/31/2017	12/31/2016	12/31/2015	12/31/2014
Earnings Per Share	(2.38)	(1.91)	(4.03)	(4.27)	(8.00)	2.08	2.16	(5.29)
Cash Flow Per Share	0.70	0.91	0.66	1.19	2.93	5.19	9.49	6.13
Tang Book Value Per Share	18.43	19.69	19.94	20.20	32.48	40.58	39.83	37.74
Income Statement								
Total Revenue	2,296	1,512	754	3,018	2,973	4,161	7,386	9,174
EBITDA	(512)	56	22	(278)	(1,723)	2,216	2,388	(232)
Depn & Amortn	140	92	45	930	832	893	948	1,124
Income Before Taxes	(1,119)	(348)	(179)	(1,775)	(3,003)	934	1,030	(1,800)
Income Taxes	83	29	(8)	228	94	107	206	146
Net Income	(1,204)	(379)	(171)	(1,996)	(3,127)	778	791	(1,913)
Average Shares	613	612	611	468	391	367	363	362
Balance Sheet								
Current Assets	3,771	4,208	3,792	3,948	4,606	5,098	4,785	6,001
Total Assets	24,449	25,624	25,450	25,665	22,410	26,889	26,329	28,413
Current Liabilities	1,489	1,461	1,396	1,458	1,369	1,985	2,669	3,770
Long-Term Obligations	9,041	9,378	9,071	9,605	7,146	7,740	7,397	9,059
Total Liabilities	12,516	12,876	12,504	12,558	9,703	11,087	11,831	14,742
Stockholders' Equity	11,933	12,748	12,946	13,107	12,707	15,802	14,498	13,671
Shares Outstanding	611	611	611	609	391	389	364	362
Statistical Record								
Return on Assets %	N.M.	N.M.	N.M.	N.M.	N.M.	2.92	2.89	N.M.
Return on Equity %	N.M.	N.M.	N.M.	N.M.	N.M.	5.12	5.62	N.M.
EBITDA Margin %	N.M.	3.70	2.92	N.M.	N.M.	53.26	32.33	N.M.
Net Margin %	N.M.	N.M.	N.M.	N.M.	N.M.	18.70	10.71	N.M.
Asset Turnover	0.13	0.12	0.12	0.13	0.12	0.16	0.27	0.30
Current Ratio	2.53	2.88	2.72	2.71	3.36	2.57	1.79	1.59
Debt to Equity	0.76	0.74	0.70	0.73	0.56	0.49	0.51	0.66
Price Range	14.18-3.86	14.18-5.42	14.18-6.34	14.18-6.34	15.84-7.28	15.54-8.20	21.39-11.60	49.42-16.25
P/E Ratio	...	...	...	...	...	7.47-3.94	9.90-5.37	...

Address: Turmstrasse 30, Steinhausen, 6312 **Telephone:** 417-490-500	**Web Site:** www.deepwater.com **Officers:** Chadwick C. Deaton - Chairman Jeremy D. Thigpen - President, Chief Executive Officer	**Auditors:** Ernst & Young LLP **Investor Contact:** 713-232-7551 **Transfer Agents:** Computershare Shareowner Services LLC, Pittsburgh, PA

TRANSUNION

Exchange	Symbol	Price	52Wk Range	Yield	P/E
NYS	TRU	$85.61 (12/31/2019)	87.00-54.15	0.35	44.59

*7 Year Price Score N/A   ***NYSE Composite Index=100**   ***12 Month Price Score 108.35**

Interim Earnings (Per Share)

Qtr.	Mar	Jun	Sep	Dec
2016	0.07	0.09	0.22	0.26
2017	0.33	0.34	0.36	1.29
2018	0.38	0.29	0.24	0.54
2019	0.37	0.53	0.48	...

Interim Dividends (Per Share)

Amt	Decl	Ex	Rec	Pay
0.075Q	02/21/2019	03/06/2019	03/07/2019	03/22/2019
0.075Q	05/09/2019	05/22/2019	05/23/2019	06/07/2019
0.075Q	08/08/2019	08/21/2019	08/22/2019	09/06/2019
0.075Q	11/15/2019	11/26/2019	11/27/2019	12/12/2019

Indicated Div: $0.30

Valuation Analysis

		Institutional Holding	
Forecast EPS	$2.76	No of Institutions	435
	(01/17/2020)		
Market Cap	$16.1 Billion	Shares	192,549,472
Book Value	$2.0 Billion	% Held	98.68
Price/Book	7.91		
Price/Sales	6.24		

Business Summary: Miscellaneous Consumer Services (MIC: 2.2.3 SIC: 7323 NAIC: 561450)

TransUnion is a risk and information solutions provider. Co. provides consumer reports, risk scores, analytical services and decisioning capabilities to businesses. Co.'s segments include: U.S. Information Services (USIS), which provides consumer reports, risk scores, analytical services and decisioning capabilities to businesses; International, which provides services similar to Co.'s USIS segment to businesses in select regions outside the U.S., including credit reports, analytics and decisioning services and other risk management services; and Consumer Interactive, which provides solutions that help consumers manage their personal finances and take precautions against identity theft.

Recent Developments: For the quarter ended Sep 30 2019, income from continuing operations increased 73.8% to US$88.3 million from US$50.8 million in the year-earlier quarter. Net income increased 78.7% to US$88.3 million from US$49.4 million in the year-earlier quarter. Revenues were US$689.3 million, up 14.2% from US$603.6 million the year before. Operating income was US$171.3 million versus US$122.1 million in the prior-year quarter, an increase of 40.3%. Direct operating expenses rose 6.4% to US$220.8 million from US$207.5 million in the comparable period the year before. Indirect operating expenses increased 8.4% to US$297.1 million from US$274.0 million in the equivalent prior-year period.

Prospects: Our evaluation of TransUnion as of October 4th, 2019 is the result of our systematic analysis on three basic characteristics: earnings strength, relative valuation, and recent stock price movement. The company has produced a positive trend in earnings per share over the past 5 quarters. However, recent analyst estimates for the company have been unchanged, while TRU has posted results that exceeded analysts' expectations. Based on operating earnings yield, the company is fairly valued when compared to all of the companies we cover. Share price changes over the past year indicates that TRU will perform well over the near term.

Financial Data

(US$ in Thousands)	9 Mos	6 Mos	3 Mos	12/31/2018	12/31/2017	12/31/2016	12/31/2015	12/31/2014
Earnings Per Share	1.92	1.68	1.44	1.45	2.32	0.65	0.04	(0.08)
Cash Flow Per Share	3.86	3.34	3.10	3.01	2.57	2.13	1.87	1.05
Dividends Per Share	0.300	0.300	0.300	0.225	...	...	...	...
Dividend Payout %	15.63	17.86	20.83	15.52	...	...	...	...
Income Statement								
Total Revenue	1,970,500	1,281,200	619,300	2,317,200	1,933,800	1,704,900	1,506,800	1,304,700
EBITDA	457,100	304,800	116,800	542,200	513,400	345,400	208,500	229,100
Depn & Amortn	4,700	3,200	1,600	76,600	67,900	67,700	60,300	56,700
Income Before Taxes	324,100	214,700	71,700	333,600	363,400	196,800	17,800	(14,300)
Income Taxes	64,200	39,900	600	54,500	(79,100)	74,000	11,300	2,600
Net Income	264,100	172,400	70,900	276,600	441,200	120,600	5,900	(12,500)
Average Shares	192,000	191,300	191,000	190,900	189,900	184,600	166,800	147,296
Balance Sheet								
Current Assets	892,100	869,600	893,200	841,500	588,700	550,000	427,500	401,000
Total Assets	7,022,000	7,127,300	7,175,800	7,039,800	5,118,500	4,781,200	4,446,700	4,665,800
Current Liabilities	628,100	575,700	545,900	548,500	458,400	373,300	296,000	329,900
Long-Term Obligations	3,646,000	3,831,500	3,951,800	3,976,400	2,345,300	2,325,200	2,164,600	2,865,900
Total Liabilities	4,984,600	5,116,200	5,193,900	5,150,100	3,389,800	3,418,400	3,215,300	4,078,700
Stockholders' Equity	2,037,400	2,011,100	1,981,900	1,889,700	1,728,700	1,362,800	1,231,400	587,100
Shares Outstanding	188,300	187,800	187,300	185,700	183,200	183,200	182,300	147,829
Statistical Record								
Return on Assets %	5.17	4.51	4.45	4.55	8.91	2.61	0.13	N.M.
Return on Equity %	18.76	16.77	14.38	15.29	28.54	9.27	0.65	N.M.
EBITDA Margin %	23.20	23.79	18.86	23.40	26.55	20.26	13.84	17.56
Net Margin %	13.40	13.46	11.45	11.94	22.82	7.07	0.39	N.M.
Asset Turnover	0.36	0.35	0.39	0.38	0.39	0.37	0.33	0.28
Current Ratio	1.42	1.51	1.64	1.53	1.28	1.47	1.44	1.22
Debt to Equity	1.79	1.91	1.99	2.10	1.36	1.71	1.76	4.88
Price Range	84.91-52.61	76.64-52.61	76.64-52.61	76.64-52.61	56.21-30.96	35.43-20.98	27.98-23.19	...
P/E Ratio	44.22-27.40	45.62-31.32	53.22-36.53	52.86-36.28	24.23-13.34	54.51-32.28	699.50-579.75	...
Average Yield %	0.44	0.45	0.45	0.34	...	...	...	...

Address: 555 West Adams, Chicago, IL 60661	Web Site: www.transunion.com	Auditors: Ernst & Young LLP
Telephone: 312-985-2000	Officers: Leo F. Mullin - Chairman Christopher A. Cartwright - President, Chief Executive Officer, Division Officer	Transfer Agents: American Stock Transfer & Trust Company, LLC

TRAVELERS COMPANIES INC (THE)

Exchange	Symbol	Price	52Wk Range	Yield	P/E	Div Acheiver
NYS	TRV	$136.95 (12/31/2019)	154.83-115.26	2.40	15.39	13 Years

*7 Year Price Score 101.89 *NYSE Composite Index=100 *12 Month Price Score 91.41

Interim Earnings (Per Share)

Qtr.	Mar	Jun	Sep	Dec
2016	2.30	2.24	2.45	3.28
2017	2.17	2.11	1.05	1.99
2018	2.42	1.92	2.62	2.31
2019	2.99	2.10	1.50	...

Interim Dividends (Per Share)

Amt	Decl	Ex	Rec	Pay
0.77Q	01/22/2019	03/08/2019	03/11/2019	03/29/2019
0.82Q	04/18/2019	06/07/2019	06/10/2019	06/28/2019
0.82Q	07/23/2019	09/09/2019	09/10/2019	09/30/2019
0.82Q	10/22/2019	12/09/2019	12/10/2019	12/31/2019

Indicated Div: $3.28 (Div. Reinv. Plan)

Valuation Analysis / **Institutional Holding**

Forecast EPS	$9.51	No of Institutions
	(01/17/2020)	1630
Market Cap	$35.3 Billion	Shares
Book Value	$25.6 Billion	302,034,752
Price/Book	1.38	% Held
Price/Sales	1.13	N/A

Business Summary: General Insurance (MIC: 5.2.1 SIC: 6331 NAIC: 524126)

Travelers Companies is a holding company. Through its subsidiaries, Co. is engaged in providing commercial and personal property and casualty insurance products and services to businesses, government units, associations and individuals. Co.'s segments include: Business Insurance, which provides property and casualty insurance and insurance related services; Bond and Specialty Insurance, which provides surety, fidelity, management liability, professional liability, other property and casualty coverages and related risk management services, and certain specialty insurance products; and Personal Insurance, which writes property and casualty insurance covering individuals' personal risks.

Recent Developments: For the quarter ended Sep 30 2019, net income decreased 44.1% to US$396.0 million from US$709.0 million in the year-earlier quarter. Revenues were US$8.01 billion, up 3.8% from US$7.72 billion the year before. Net premiums earned were US$7.18 billion versus US$6.88 billion in the prior-year quarter, an increase of 4.3%. Net investment income fell 3.7% to US$622.0 million from US$646.0 million a year ago.

Prospects: Our evaluation of The Travelers Companies Inc. as of October 4th, 2019 is the result of our systematic analysis on three basic characteristics: earnings strength, relative valuation, and recent stock price movement. The company has managed to produce a neutral trend in earnings per share over the past 5 quarters. However, recent analyst estimates for the company have been reduced and TRV has posted results that fell short of analysts' expectations. Based on operating earnings yield, the company is undervalued when compared to all of the companies we cover. Share price changes over the past year indicates that TRV will perform over the near term.

Financial Data

(US$ in Thousands)	9 Mos	6 Mos	3 Mos	12/31/2018	12/31/2017	12/31/2016	12/31/2015	12/31/2014
Earnings Per Share	8.90	10.02	9.84	9.28	7.33	10.28	10.88	10.70
Cash Flow Per Share	18.29	17.12	16.98	16.38	13.63	14.55	11.06	10.90
Tang Book Value Per Share	82.72	80.84	76.56	70.61	71.62	69.29	66.73	64.93
Dividends Per Share	3.180	3.130	3.080	3.030	2.830	2.620	2.380	2.150
Dividend Payout %	35.73	31.24	31.30	32.65	38.61	25.49	21.88	20.09
Income Statement								
Premium Income	21,022,000	13,843,000	6,855,000	27,059,000	25,683,000	24,534,000	23,874,000	23,713,000
Total Revenue	23,518,000	15,505,000	7,671,000	30,282,000	28,902,000	27,625,000	26,800,000	27,162,000
Benefits & Claims	14,493,000	9,263,000	4,442,000	18,291,000	17,467,000	15,070,000	13,723,000	13,870,000
Income Before Taxes	2,064,000	1,632,000	967,000	2,961,000	2,730,000	4,053,000	4,740,000	5,089,000
Income Taxes	315,000	279,000	171,000	438,000	674,000	1,039,000	1,301,000	1,397,000
Net Income	1,749,000	1,353,000	796,000	2,523,000	2,056,000	3,014,000	3,439,000	3,692,000
Average Shares	261,800	263,700	264,800	269,800	278,600	291,000	313,900	342,500
Balance Sheet								
Total Assets	110,241,000	108,572,000	107,246,000	104,233,000	103,483,000	100,245,000	100,184,000	103,078,000
Total Liabilities	84,634,000	83,251,000	82,906,000	81,339,000	79,752,000	77,024,000	76,586,000	78,242,000
Stockholders' Equity	25,607,000	25,321,000	24,340,000	22,894,000	23,731,000	23,221,000	23,598,000	24,836,000
Shares Outstanding	258,100	260,300	261,900	263,600	271,400	279,600	295,900	322,200
Statistical Record								
Return on Assets %	2.21	2.53	2.51	2.43	2.02	3.00	3.38	3.57
Return on Equity %	9.86	11.19	11.20	10.82	8.76	12.84	14.20	14.88
Loss Ratio %	68.94	66.91	64.80	67.60	68.01	61.42	57.48	58.49
Net Margin %	7.44	8.73	10.38	8.33	7.11	10.91	12.83	13.59
Price Range	154.83-112.63	153.13-112.63	139.29-112.63	150.00-112.63	136.36-115.18	122.57-102.08	115.83-96.14	106.95-80.80
P/E Ratio	17.40-12.66	15.28-11.24	14.16-11.45	16.16-12.14	18.60-15.71	11.92-9.93	10.65-8.84	10.00-7.50
Average Yield %	2.33	2.38	2.40	2.31	2.26	2.31	2.25	2.33

Address: 485 Lexington Avenue, New York, NY 10017
Telephone: 917-778-6000

Web Site: www.travelers.com
Officers: Alan D. Schnitzer - Chairman, Chief Executive Officer, Vice-Chairman, Chief Executive Officer - Designate, Executive Vice President, Chief Legal Officer Jay Steven Benet - Vice-Chairman, Chief Financial Officer

Auditors: KPMG LLP
Investor Contact: 917-778-9844
Transfer Agents: Wells Fargo Bank, N.A. Shareowner Services, St. Paul, MN

TREEHOUSE FOODS INC

Exchange	Symbol	Price	52Wk Range	Yield	P/E
NYS	THS	$48.50 (12/31/2019)	66.98-47.72	N/A	N/A

*7 Year Price Score 66.67 *NYSE Composite Index=100 *12 Month Price Score 85.37

Interim Earnings (Per Share)

Qtr.	Mar	Jun	Sep	Dec
2016	(0.06)	0.27	0.65	(4.98)
2017	0.49	(0.60)	0.50	(5.41)
2018	(0.60)	(0.36)	0.10	(0.23)
2019	(0.49)	(3.05)	(3.16)	...

Interim Dividends (Per Share)

No Dividends Paid

Valuation Analysis

		Institutional Holding	
Forecast EPS	$2.36	No of Institutions	
	(01/16/2020)	395	
Market Cap	$2.7 Billion	Shares	
Book Value	$1.8 Billion	72,724,536	
Price/Book	1.51	% Held	
Price/Sales	0.54	108.91	

Business Summary: Food (MIC: 1.2.1 SIC: 2033 NAIC: 311421)

TreeHouse Foods is a consumer packaged food and beverage manufacturer operating across the U.S., Canada, and Italy. Co.'s operating segments are: Baked Goods, which sells candy, cookies, crackers and in-store bakery products; Beverages, which sells broths, liquid non-dairy creamer, non-dairy powdered creamers, powdered drinks, single serve hot beverages, teas, and sweeteners; Condiments, which sells aseptic cheese and pudding products, jams, preserves, and jellies, mayonnaise, Mexican, barbeque, and other sauces, pickles and related products; Meals, which sells baking and mix powders, powdered soups and gravies; and Snacks, which sells bars, dried fruit and other wholesome snacks.

Recent Developments: For the quarter ended Sep 30 2019, loss from continuing operations was US$61.0 million compared with income of US$12.2 million in the year-earlier quarter. Net loss amounted to US$177.8 million versus net income of US$2.6 million in the year-earlier quarter. Revenues were US$1.06 billion, down 5.4% from US$1.12 billion the year before. Operating loss was US$55.6 million versus an income of US$39.0 million in the prior-year quarter. Direct operating expenses declined 3.6% to US$871.0 million from US$903.9 million in the comparable period the year before. Indirect operating expenses increased 38.2% to US$241.9 million from US$175.0 million in the equivalent prior-year period.

Prospects: Our evaluation of TreeHouse Foods Inc. as of October 4th, 2019 is the result of our systematic analysis on three basic characteristics: earnings strength, relative valuation, and recent stock price movement. The company has enjoyed a very positive trend in earnings per share over the past 5 quarters. However, recent analyst estimates for the company have been mixed and THS has posted results that exceeded analysts' expectations. Based on operating earnings yield, the company is fairly valued when compared to all of the companies we cover. Share price changes over the past year indicates that THS will perform well over the near term.

Financial Data

(US$ in Thousands)	9 Mos	6 Mos	3 Mos	12/31/2018	12/31/2017	12/31/2016	12/31/2015	12/31/2014
Earnings Per Share	(6.93)	(3.67)	(0.98)	(1.10)	(5.01)	(4.10)	2.63	2.23
Cash Flow Per Share	4.99	5.04	7.31	9.03	8.86	8.57	6.63	5.39
Income Statement								
Total Revenue	3,149,400	2,551,800	1,301,100	5,812,100	6,307,100	6,175,088	3,206,405	2,946,102
EBITDA	3,700	(109,500)	49,200	201,700	(228,600)	98,007	275,271	240,916
Depn & Amortn	100,900	75,200	61,900	171,900	173,500	178,400	61,500	63,300
Income Before Taxes	(175,700)	(239,500)	(39,600)	(84,800)	(524,600)	(195,363)	171,264	136,570
Income Taxes	(50,100)	(40,800)	(12,300)	(23,400)	(238,400)	33,231	56,354	46,690
Net Income	(376,500)	(198,700)	(27,300)	(61,400)	(286,200)	(228,594)	114,910	89,880
Average Shares	56,300	56,300	56,100	56,000	57,100	55,717	43,709	40,238
Balance Sheet								
Current Assets	1,269,000	1,433,300	1,379,300	1,417,100	1,484,700	1,560,749	847,203	949,436
Total Assets	5,261,200	5,592,900	5,765,000	5,599,300	5,779,300	6,545,822	3,702,796	3,903,004
Current Liabilities	851,400	836,700	841,300	835,200	599,800	693,194	275,473	,311,233
Long-Term Obligations	2,158,000	2,257,600	2,489,800	2,297,400	2,535,700	2,724,760	1,221,741	1,445,488
Total Liabilities	3,455,200	3,609,600	3,641,800	3,457,400	3,516,000	4,042,498	1,847,937	2,143,747
Stockholders' Equity	1,806,000	1,983,300	2,123,200	2,141,900	2,263,300	2,503,324	1,854,859	1,759,257
Shares Outstanding	56,200	56,200	56,200	56,000	56,638	56,759	43,125	42,662
Statistical Record								
Return on Assets %	N.M.	N.M.	N.M.	N.M.	N.M.	N.M.	3.02	2.71
Return on Equity %	N.M.	N.M.	N.M.	N.M.	N.M.	N.M.	6.36	5.93
EBITDA Margin %	0.12	N.M.	3.78	3.47	N.M.	1.59	8.59	8.18
Net Margin %	N.M.	N.M.	N.M.	N.M.	N.M.	N.M.	3.58	3.05
Asset Turnover	0.93	0.96	0.98	1.02	1.02	1.20	0.84	0.89
Current Ratio	1.49	1.71	1.64	1.70	2.48	2.25	3.08	3.05
Debt to Equity	1.19	1.14	1.17	1.07	1.12	1.09	0.66	0.82
Price Range	66.98-44.00	66.98-44.00	64.55-36.62	55.43-36.62	89.94-41.87	104.35-63.34	92.90-69.44	87.95-63.59
P/E Ratio	...	...	...	...	...	...	35.32-26.40	39.44-28.52

Address: 2021 Spring Road, Suite 600, Oak Brook, IL 60523	Web Site: www.treehousefoods.com	Auditors: DELOITTE & TOUCHE LLP
Telephone: 708-483-1300	Officers: Gary D. Smith - Chairman Steven Oakland - President, Chief Executive Officer	Transfer Agents: BNY Mellon Shareowner Services, South Hackensack, NJ

TREX CO INC

Exchange	Symbol	Price	52Wk Range	Yield	P/E
NYS	TREX	$89.88 (12/31/2019)	92.22-58.79	N/A	39.08

*7 Year Price Score 170.40 *NYSE Composite Index=100 *12 Month Price Score 108.31

Interim Earnings (Per Share)

Qtr.	Mar	Jun	Sep	Dec
2016	0.39	0.40	0.12	0.24
2017	0.47	0.48	0.34	0.31
2018	0.63	0.73	0.50	0.43
2019	0.54	0.61	0.72	...

Interim Dividends (Per Share)

Amt	Decl	Ex	Rec	Pay
100%	...	06/19/2018	05/23/2018	06/18/2018

Valuation Analysis

		Institutional Holding	
Forecast EPS	$2.42	No of Institutions	
	(01/17/2020)	434	
Market Cap	$5.2 Billion	Shares	
Book Value	$423.5 Million	68,379,976	
Price/Book	12.38	% Held	
Price/Sales	7.28	103.76	

TRADING VOLUME (thousand shares)

Business Summary: Metal Products (MIC: 8.2.3 SIC: 2499 NAIC: 321999)

Trex Company is a manufacturer of wood-alternative decking and railing products, which are marketed under the brand name Trex®. In addition, Co. is a national provider of custom-engineered railing and staging, systems for the commercial and multi-family market. Co. operates in two reportable segments: Trex Residential Products, which provides a set of product offerings in the decking, railing, fencing, steel deck framing, and outdoor lighting categories; and Trex Commercial Products, which designs and engineers custom railing solutions, which are prevalent in professional and collegiate sports facilities, standardized architectural and aluminum railing systems.

Recent Developments: For the quarter ended Sep 30 2019, net income increased 42.4% to US$42.0 million from US$29.5 million in the year-earlier quarter. Revenues were US$194.6 million, up 16.9% from US$166.4 million the year before. Operating income was US$55.0 million versus US$39.1 million in the prior-year quarter, an increase of 40.8%. Direct operating expenses rose 13.1% to US$112.1 million from US$99.2 million in the comparable period the year before. Indirect operating expenses decreased 2.6% to US$27.4 million from US$28.1 million in the equivalent prior-year period.

Prospects: Our evaluation of Trex Co. Inc. as of October 4th, 2019 is the result of our systematic analysis on three basic characteristics: earnings strength, relative valuation, and recent stock price movement. The company has managed to produce a neutral trend in earnings per share over the past 5 quarters. Additionally, recent analyst estimates for the company have been unchanged and TREX has posted results in line with analysts' expectations. Based on operating earnings yield, the company is overvalued when compared to all of the companies we cover. Share price changes over the past year indicates that TREX will perform poorly over the near term.

Financial Data

(US$ in Thousands)	9 Mos	6 Mos	3 Mos	12/31/2018	12/31/2017	12/31/2016	12/31/2015	12/31/2014
Earnings Per Share	2.30	2.08	2.20	2.28	1.61	1.15	0.76	0.64
Cash Flow Per Share	2.08	3.13	2.16	2.35	1.73	1.45	1.00	0.91
Tang Book Value Per Share	5.99	5.43	4.93	4.59	2.72	2.10	1.71	1.61
Income Statement								
Total Revenue	580,575	386,024	179,571	684,250	565,153	479,616	440,804	391,660
EBITDA	152,437	93,795	42,624	190,069	157,080	118,155	91,706	82,626
Depn & Amortn	10,477	6,857	3,425	13,400	14,700	14,200	14,300	14,800
Income Before Taxes	142,761	86,995	39,255	176,861	141,919	102,830	76,787	66,948
Income Taxes	33,520	19,730	7,700	42,289	46,791	34,983	28,689	25,427
Net Income	109,241	67,265	31,555	134,572	95,128	67,847	48,098	41,521
Average Shares	58,605	58,687	58,829	59,067	59,150	59,225	63,365	65,502
Balance Sheet								
Current Assets	307,845	286,163	291,285	270,225	148,798	105,649	99,030	85,241
Total Assets	570,770	536,198	535,645	465,122	326,227	221,430	211,998	195,824
Current Liabilities	87,524	81,469	106,575	92,775	62,509	51,385	60,449	49,454
Total Liabilities	147,220	144,665	172,488	122,159	94,977	87,269	95,535	82,439
Stockholders' Equity	423,550	391,533	363,157	342,963	231,250	134,161	116,463	113,385
Shares Outstanding	58,353	58,440	58,537	58,551	58,856	58,801	61,809	64,040
Statistical Record								
Return on Assets %	26.73	25.65	26.30	34.01	34.74	31.22	23.59	21.63
Return on Equity %	35.74	35.36	41.28	46.87	52.07	53.99	41.85	37.75
EBITDA Margin %	26.26	24.30	23.74	27.78	27.79	24.64	20.80	21.10
Net Margin %	18.82	17.43	17.57	19.67	16.83	14.15	10.91	10.60
Asset Turnover	1.43	1.46	1.41	1.73	2.06	2.21	2.16	2.04
Current Ratio	3.52	3.51	2.73	2.91	2.38	2.06	1.64	1.72
Price Range	90.93-53.61	89.15-53.61	89.15-51.94	89.15-51.70	58.88-31.36	35.48-16.10	28.44-16.07	22.07-13.22
P/E Ratio	39.53-23.31	42.86-25.77	40.52-23.61	39.10-22.68	36.57-19.48	30.85-14.00	37.42-21.15	34.48-20.66

Address: 160 Exeter Drive, Winchester, VA 22603-8605
Telephone: 540-542-6300

Web Site: www.trex.com
Officers: Ronald W. Kaplan - Chairman, President, Chief Executive Officer James E. Cline - President, Chief Executive Officer, Vice President, Chief Financial Officer

Auditors: Ernst & Young LLP
Investor Contact: 212-838-3777
Transfer Agents: Computershare, Canton, MA

TRI POINTE GROUP INC

Exchange	Symbol	Price	52Wk Range	Yield	P/E
NYS	TPH	$15.58 (12/31/2019)	16.12-10.93	N/A	11.98

*7 Year Price Score 77.79 *NSYE Composite Index=100 *12 Month Price Score 107.25

Interim Earnings (Per Share)

Qtr.	Mar	Jun	Sep	Dec
2016	0.18	0.46	0.22	0.36
2017	0.05	0.21	0.48	0.48
2018	0.28	0.42	0.43	0.68
2019	0.00	0.18	0.44	...

Interim Dividends (Per Share)

No Dividends Paid

Valuation Analysis		Institutional Holding	
Forecast EPS	$1.33	No of Institutions	
	(01/17/2020)	309	
Market Cap	$2.2 Billion	Shares	
Book Value	$2.1 Billion	168,538,112	
Price/Book	1.03	% Held	
Price/Sales	0.71	96.58	

Business Summary: Builders (MIC: 2.2.5 SIC: 1531 NAIC: 236117)

TRI Pointe Group is engaged in the design, construction and sale of single-family attached and detached homes through its portfolio of six brands across eight states, including Maracay Homes in Arizona, Pardee Homes in California and Nevada, Quadrant Homes in Washington, Trendmaker Homes in Texas, TRI Pointe Homes in California and Colorado and Winchester Homes in Maryland and Virginia. Co.'s operations are organized in two principal businesses: homebuilding, through which Co. acquires and develops land and constructs and sells single-family detached and attached homes; and financial services, which comprises of Co.'s mortgage financing operations and title services operations.

Recent Developments: For the quarter ended Sep 30 2019, net income decreased 1.7% to US$62.9 million from US$64.0 million in the year-earlier quarter. Revenues were US$748.4 million, down 3.4% from US$775.1 million the year before. Direct operating expenses declined 5.1% to US$578.7 million from US$609.9 million in the comparable period the year before. Indirect operating expenses increased 5.2% to US$87.4 million from US$83.1 million in the equivalent prior-year period.

Prospects: Our evaluation of Tri Pointe Group Inc as of October 4th, 2019 is the result of our systematic analysis on three basic characteristics: earnings strength, relative valuation, and recent stock price movement. The company has generated a negative trend in earnings per share over the past 5 quarters. However, recent analyst estimates for the company have been mixed and TPH has posted results that exceeded analysts' expectations. Based on operating earnings yield, the company is undervalued when compared to all of the companies we cover. Share price changes over the past year indicates that TPH will perform in line with the market over the near term.

Financial Data

(US$ in Thousands)	9 Mos	6 Mos	3 Mos	12/31/2018	12/31/2017	12/31/2016	12/31/2015	12/31/2014
Earnings Per Share	1.30	1.29	1.53	1.81	1.21	1.21	1.27	0.58
Cash Flow Per Share	2.04	1.45	1.03	2.10	0.66	(0.98)	0.19	(0.78)
Tang Book Value Per Share	14.02	13.54	13.34	13.39	11.70	10.51	9.29	8.00
Income Statement								
Total Revenue	1,941,741	1,193,346	494,632	3,261,009	2,808,901	2,403,922	2,400,149	1,703,616
EBITDA	125,994	39,579	2,780	397,852	364,231	312,937	336,778	148,301
Depn & Amortn	10,614	6,786	3,435	43,911	19,406	15,699	20,209	20,049
Income Before Taxes	115,380	32,793	(655)	353,941	344,825	297,238	316,569	128,252
Income Taxes	31,014	9,156	24	90,552	152,267	106,094	112,079	43,767
Net Income	89,194	26,333	71	269,911	187,191	195,171	205,461	84,197
Average Shares	141,533	142,471	142,390	149,004	155,085	161,381	162,319	145,531
Balance Sheet								
Current Assets	3,603,434	3,548,158	3,517,455	3,613,115	3,590,480	3,325,007	2,908,125	2,628,751
Total Assets	3,941,471	3,877,550	3,855,895	3,884,203	3,805,381	3,564,640	3,138,071	2,913,524
Current Liabilities	141,969	111,226	141,009	153,779	161,770	125,901	125,409	135,272
Long-Term Obligations	1,433,058	1,432,145	1,412,463	1,410,804	1,471,302	1,382,033	1,172,947	1,171,691
Total Liabilities	1,829,786	1,790,920	1,798,872	1,827,279	1,875,659	1,735,193	1,473,388	1,459,344
Stockholders' Equity	2,111,685	2,086,630	2,057,023	2,056,924	1,929,722	1,829,447	1,664,683	1,454,180
Shares Outstanding	139,237	142,258	142,210	141,661	151,162	158,626	161,813	161,355
Statistical Record								
Return on Assets %	4.82	4.89	5.90	7.02	5.08	5.81	6.79	4.92
Return on Equity %	9.26	9.21	11.30	13.54	9.96	11.14	13.18	9.48
EBITDA Margin %	6.49	3.32	0.56	12.20	12.97	13.02	14.03	8.71
Net Margin %	4.59	2.21	0.01	8.28	6.66	8.12	8.56	4.94
Asset Turnover	0.79	0.80	0.82	0.85	0.76	0.72	0.79	1.00
Current Ratio	25.38	31.90	24.94	23.50	22.19	26.41	23.19	19.43
Debt to Equity	0.68	0.69	0.69	0.69	0.76	0.76	0.70	0.81
Price Range	15.06-10.58	17.40-10.58	18.47-10.58	19.42-10.58	18.44-11.37	14.07-9.05	16.05-12.50	19.93-12.73
P/E Ratio	11.58-8.14	13.49-8.20	12.07-6.92	10.73-5.85	15.24-9.40	11.63-7.48	12.64-9.84	34.36-21.95

Address: 19540 Jamboree Road, Suite 300, Irvine, CA 92612 **Telephone:** 949-438-1400	**Web Site:** www.tripointegroup.com **Officers:** Steven J. Gilbert - Chairman Thomas J. (Tom) Mitchell - President, Chief Operating Officer	**Auditors:** Ernst & Young LLP **Investor Contact:** 949-478-8696 **Transfer Agents:** American Stock Transfer & Trust Company, LLC

TRINITY INDUSTRIES, INC.

Exchange	Symbol	Price	52Wk Range	Yield	P/E
NYS	TRN	$22.15 (12/31/2019)	25.99-16.09	3.43	20.14

*7 Year Price Score 82.81   *NYSE Composite Index=100   *12 Month Price Score 98.04

Interim Earnings (Per Share)

Qtr.	Mar	Jun	Sep	Dec
2016	0.64	0.62	0.55	0.44
2017	0.30	0.33	0.43	3.46
2018	0.26	0.43	0.19	0.20
2019	0.23	0.28	0.39	...

Interim Dividends (Per Share)

Amt	Decl	Ex	Rec	Pay
0.17Q	03/07/2019	04/12/2019	04/15/2019	04/30/2019
0.17Q	05/06/2019	07/12/2019	07/15/2019	07/31/2019
0.17Q	09/04/2019	10/11/2019	10/15/2019	10/31/2019
0.19Q	12/06/2019	01/14/2020	01/15/2020	01/31/2020

Indicated Div: $0.76

Valuation Analysis

		Institutional Holding	
Forecast EPS	$1.22	No of Institutions	
(01/17/2020)		481	
Market Cap	$2.8 Billion	Shares	
Book Value	$2.1 Billion	143,816,864	
Price/Book	1.34	% Held	
Price/Sales	1.45	73.75	

Business Summary: Construction Services (MIC: 7.5.4 SIC: 3743 NAIC: 336510)

Trinity Industries owns businesses that provide rail transportation products and services in North America. Co. has three principal business segments: the Railcar Leasing and Management Services Group, which owns and operates a fleet of railcars and provides third-party fleet leasing, management, and administrative services; the Rail Products Group, which manufactures and sells railcars and related parts and components, and provides maintenance services; and All Other, which includes Co.'s highway products business; Co.'s captive insurance and transportation companies; legal, environmental, and maintenance costs associated with non-operating facilities; and other peripheral businesses.

Recent Developments: For the quarter ended Sep 30 2019, income from continuing operations increased 68.8% to US$48.1 million from US$28.5 million in the year-earlier quarter. Net income increased 68.6% to US$47.7 million from US$28.3 million in the year-earlier quarter. Revenues were US$813.6 million, up 34.1% from US$606.9 million the year before. Operating income was US$120.3 million versus US$75.2 million in the prior-year quarter, an increase of 60.0%. Direct operating expenses rose 39.1% to US$649.1 million from US$466.5 million in the comparable period the year before. Indirect operating expenses decreased 32.2% to US$44.2 million from US$65.2 million in the equivalent prior-year period.

Prospects: Our evaluation of Trinity Industries Inc. as of October 4th, 2019 is the result of our systematic analysis on three basic characteristics: earnings strength, relative valuation, and recent stock price movement. The company has enjoyed a very positive trend in earnings per share over the past 5 quarters. However, recent analyst estimates for the company have been reduced, and TRN has posted results that fell short of analysts' expectations. Based on operating earnings yield, the company is fairly valued when compared to all of the companies we cover. Share price changes over the past year indicates that TRN will perform poorly over the near term.

Financial Data

(US$ in Thousands)	9 Mos	6 Mos	3 Mos	12/31/2018	12/31/2017	12/31/2016	12/31/2015	12/31/2014
Earnings Per Share	1.10	0.90	1.05	1.07	4.52	2.25	5.08	4.19
Cash Flow Per Share	1.79	0.26	0.61	2.63	5.13	7.33	6.26	5.43
Tang Book Value Per Share	14.87	15.40	15.05	15.02	24.66	20.79	18.97	14.28
Dividends Per Share	0.600	0.560	0.520	0.520	0.480	0.440	0.420	0.350
Dividend Payout %	54.55	62.22	49.52	48.60	10.62	19.56	8.27	8.35
Income Statement								
Total Revenue	2,154,400	1,340,800	604,800	2,509,100	3,662,800	4,588,300	6,392,700	6,170,000
EBITDA	529,400	336,700	159,000	515,600	717,700	899,500	1,586,800	1,385,600
Depn & Amortn	210,500	138,100	67,500	196,600	172,300	156,200	142,300	130,000
Income Before Taxes	158,100	91,800	40,100	151,600	372,000	566,800	1,252,000	1,064,100
Income Taxes	41,200	23,000	8,900	42,600	(341,600)	202,100	426,000	354,800
Net Income	116,000	67,000	30,600	159,300	702,500	343,600	796,500	678,200
Average Shares	126,000	129,200	132,200	146,400	152,000	148,600	152,200	156,700
Balance Sheet								
Current Assets	1,056,300	1,076,000	1,078,400	1,020,900	2,137,400	1,944,700	2,278,800	2,495,200
Total Assets	8,643,100	8,575,900	8,413,900	7,989,200	9,543,200	9,125,300	8,885,900	8,733,800
Current Liabilities	619,700	564,000	533,600	580,400	615,400	582,200	746,400	1,005,000
Long-Term Obligations	4,685,200	4,615,900	4,466,400	4,029,200	3,242,400	3,056,600	3,195,400	3,553,000
Total Liabilities	6,532,500	6,397,100	6,199,400	5,778,400	5,042,100	5,206,800	5,232,000	5,737,900
Stockholders' Equity	2,110,600	2,178,800	2,214,500	2,210,800	4,501,100	3,918,500	3,653,900	2,995,900
Shares Outstanding	127,900	127,900	133,300	133,300	150,900	152,200	152,900	155,600
Statistical Record								
Return on Assets %	1.59	1.36	1.67	1.82	7.53	3.80	9.04	8.45
Return on Equity %	4.48	3.76	4.47	4.75	16.69	9.05	23.96	25.13
EBITDA Margin %	24.57	25.11	26.29	20.55	19.59	19.60	24.82	22.46
Net Margin %	5.38	5.00	5.06	6.35	19.18	7.49	12.46	10.99
Asset Turnover	0.22	0.23	0.26	0.29	0.39	0.51	0.73	0.77
Current Ratio	1.70	1.91	2.02	1.76	3.47	3.34	3.05	2.48
Debt to Equity	2.22	2.12	2.02	1.82	0.72	0.78	0.87	1.19
Price Range	28.14-16.28	28.14-19.20	28.14-19.40	28.14-19.40	27.27-18.35	21.05-11.26	26.49-16.10	36.21-19.12
P/E Ratio	25.59-14.80	31.27-21.33	26.80-18.48	26.30-18.13	6.03-4.06	9.35-5.00	5.21-3.17	8.64-4.56
Average Yield %	2.79	2.40	2.16	2.12	2.27	2.83	2.06	1.29

Address: 2525 N. Stemmons Freeway, Dallas, TX 75207-2401 **Telephone:** 214-631-4420 **Fax:** 214-589-8501	**Web Site:** www.trin.net **Officers:** Leldon E. Echols - Chairman E. Jean Savage - President, Chief Executive Officer	**Auditors:** Ernst & Young LLP **Investor Contact:** 214-589-8909 **Transfer Agents:** American Stock Transfer & Trust Company

TRUIST FINANCIAL CORP

Exchange	Symbol	Price	52Wk Range	Yield	P/E
NYS	TFC	$56.32 (12/31/2019)	56.72-43.32	3.20	14.15

*7 Year Price Score 98.73   ***NYSE Composite Index=100**   ***12 Month Price Score 103.38**

TRADING VOLUME (thousand shares)

Interim Earnings (Per Share)

Qtr.	Mar	Jun	Sep	Dec
2016	0.67	0.66	0.73	0.72
2017	0.46	0.77	0.74	0.77
2018	0.94	0.99	1.01	0.97
2019	0.97	1.09	0.95	...

Interim Dividends (Per Share)

Amt	Decl	Ex	Rec	Pay
0.405Q	01/29/2019	02/12/2019	02/13/2019	03/01/2019
0.405Q	04/30/2019	05/14/2019	05/15/2019	06/03/2019
0.45Q	07/30/2019	08/13/2019	08/14/2019	09/03/2019
0.45Q	10/22/2019	11/07/2019	11/08/2019	12/02/2019

Indicated Div: $1.80 (Div. Reinv. Plan)

Valuation Analysis   Institutional Holding

Forecast EPS	$4.02	No of Institutions
	(01/17/2020)	1448
Market Cap	$43.2 Billion	Shares
Book Value	$32.2 Billion	650,016,704
Price/Book	1.34	% Held
Price/Sales	3.12	69.60

Business Summary: Banking (MIC: 5.1.1 SIC: 6021 NAIC: 522110)

Truist Financial is a financial holding company. Through its subsidiary, Branch Banking and Trust Company, Co. provides banking services to individuals, businesses and municipalities. Co. provides loans and lease financing, including commercial and residential mortgages; permanent commercial real estate financing arrangements; loan servicing for third-party investors; direct consumer finance loans to individuals; credit card lending; automobile financing; and equipment financing. Co. also provides other services, including deposits; discount and brokerage, annuities and mutual funds; life insurance, property and casualty insurance, health insurance and commercial general liability insurance.

Recent Developments: For the quarter ended Sep 30 2019, net income decreased 1.3% to US$828.0 million from US$839.0 million in the year-earlier quarter. Net interest income increased 0.8% to US$1.70 billion from US$1.69 billion in the year-earlier quarter. Provision for loan losses was US$117.0 million versus US$135.0 million in the prior-year quarter, a decrease of 13.3%. Non-interest income rose 5.2% to US$1.30 billion from US$1.24 billion, while non-interest expense advanced 5.6% to US$1.84 billion.

Prospects: Our evaluation of BB&T Corp. as of October 4th, 2019 is the result of our systematic analysis on three basic characteristics: earnings strength, relative valuation, and recent stock price movement. The company has managed to produce a neutral trend in earnings per share over the past 5 quarters. In addition, recent analyst estimates for the company have been mixed and BBT has posted results that exceeded analysts' expectations. Based on operating earnings yield, the company is undervalued when compared to all of the companies we cover. Share price changes over the past year indicates that BBT will perform poorly over the near term.

Financial Data

(US$ in Thousands)	9 Mos	6 Mos	3 Mos	12/31/2018	12/31/2017	12/31/2016	12/31/2015	12/31/2014
Earnings Per Share	3.98	4.04	3.94	3.91	2.74	2.77	2.56	2.75
Cash Flow Per Share	4.35	4.06	4.31	5.63	5.80	3.31	3.90	4.54
Tang Book Value Per Share	23.16	22.37	21.14	20.16	19.45	18.88	18.70	18.76
Dividends Per Share	1.665	1.620	1.590	1.560	1.260	1.150	1.050	0.950
Dividend Payout %	41.83	40.10	40.36	39.90	45.99	41.52	41.02	34.55
Income Statement								
Interest Income	6,597,000	4,379,000	2,173,000	8,120,000	7,374,000	7,066,000	6,327,000	6,142,000
Interest Expense	1,511,000	993,000	477,000	1,438,000	839,000	745,000	735,000	768,000
Net Interest Income	5,086,000	3,386,000	1,696,000	6,682,000	6,535,000	6,321,000	5,592,000	5,374,000
Provision for Losses	444,000	327,000	155,000	566,000	547,000	572,000	428,000	251,000
Non-Interest Income	3,857,000	2,554,000	1,202,000	4,876,000	4,782,000	4,472,000	4,019,000	3,784,000
Non-Interest Expense	5,359,000	3,519,000	1,768,000	6,932,000	7,444,000	6,721,000	6,266,000	5,921,000
Income Before Taxes	3,140,000	2,094,000	975,000	4,060,000	3,326,000	3,500,000	2,917,000	2,986,000
Income Taxes	629,000	411,000	177,000	803,000	911,000	1,058,000	794,000	760,000
Net Income	2,503,000	1,678,000	792,000	3,237,000	2,394,000	2,426,000	2,084,000	2,151,000
Average Shares	775,791	774,603	774,071	783,484	810,977	814,916	757,765	728,372
Balance Sheet								
Net Loans & Leases	149,282,000	152,228,000	148,330,000	148,443,000	143,310,000	143,549,000	135,526,000	119,833,000
Total Assets	236,750,000	230,872,000	227,683,000	225,697,000	221,642,000	219,276,000	209,947,000	186,814,000
Total Deposits	162,280,000	159,521,000	159,766,000	161,199,000	157,371,000	160,234,000	149,124,000	129,040,000
Total Liabilities	204,516,000	199,169,000	196,860,000	195,575,000	191,994,000	189,395,000	182,641,000	162,476,000
Stockholders' Equity	32,234,000	31,703,000	30,823,000	30,122,000	29,648,000	29,881,000	27,306,000	24,338,000
Shares Outstanding	766,303	766,010	765,920	763,326	782,006	809,475	780,337	720,698
Statistical Record								
Return on Assets %	1.44	1.46	1.45	1.45	1.09	1.13	1.05	1.16
Return on Equity %	10.62	10.76	10.73	10.83	8.04	8.46	8.07	9.13
Net Interest Margin %	76.65	76.61	78.05	82.29	88.62	89.46	88.38	87.50
Efficiency Ratio %	52.26	49.21	52.39	53.34	61.24	58.25	60.56	59.65
Loans to Deposits	0.92	0.95	0.93	0.92	0.91	0.90	0.91	0.93
Price Range	53.46-41.27	52.98-41.27	55.53-41.27	56.03-41.27	50.45-41.65	47.71-30.28	41.60-34.78	40.77-35.20
P/E Ratio	13.43-10.37	13.11-10.22	14.09-10.47	14.33-10.55	18.41-15.20	17.22-10.93	16.25-13.59	14.83-12.80
Average Yield %	3.41	3.29	3.16	3.03	2.73	3.11	2.74	2.50

Address: 200 West Second Street, Winston-Salem, NC 27101 **Telephone:** 336-733-2000 **Fax:** 336-671-2399	**Web Site:** www.bbt.com **Officers:** Kelly S. King - Chairman, Chief Executive Officer, Chief Operating Officer William H. Rogers - President, Chief Operating Officer	**Auditors:** PricewaterhouseCoopers LLP **Investor Contact:** 336-733-3021 **Transfer Agents:** Computershare Trust Company, N.A., Providence, RI

TRANSDIGM GROUP INC

Exchange	Symbol	Price	52Wk Range	Yield	P/E
NYS	TDG	$560.00 (12/31/2019)	597.78-325.55	N/A	40.46

*7 Year Price Score 148.65 *NYSE Composite Index=100 *12 Month Price Score 111.08

Interim Earnings (Per Share)

Qtr.	Dec	Mar	Jun	Sep
2014-15	1.63	1.96	1.75	2.50
2015-16	1.97	2.47	2.52	3.44
2016-17	0.41	2.78	3.08	1.65
2017-18	4.65	3.53	3.91	4.11
2018-19	3.05	3.60	2.57	4.62

Interim Dividends (Per Share)

Amt	Decl	Ex	Rec	Pay
24.00U	10/14/2016	10/20/2016	10/24/2016	11/01/2016
22.00U	08/23/2017	08/31/2017	09/05/2017	09/12/2017
30.00U	08/06/2019	08/15/2019	08/16/2019	08/23/2019
32.50U	12/20/2019	12/27/2019	12/30/2019	01/07/2020

Valuation Analysis **Institutional Holding**

Forecast EPS	$20.64	No of Institutions
	(01/17/2020)	715
Market Cap	$29.9 Billion	Shares
Book Value	N/A	63,868,328
Price/Book	N/A	% Held
Price/Sales	5.73	99.28

Business Summary: Aerospace (MIC: 7.1.1 SIC: 3728 NAIC: 336412)

TransDigm Group is a holding company. Through its subsidiaries, Co. designs, produces and supplies aircraft components for use on commercial and military aircraft. Co.'s segments are: Power and Control, which develops, produces and markets systems and components that provide power to or control power of the aircraft utilizing electronic, fluid, power and mechanical motion control technologies; Airframe, which develops, produces and markets systems and components that are used in non-power airframe applications utilizing airframe and cabin structure technologies; and Non-aviation, which develops, produces and markets products for non-aviation markets.

Recent Developments: For the year ended Sep 30 2019, income from continuing operations decreased 12.5% to US$840.9 million from US$961.5 million a year earlier. Net income decreased 6.9% to US$891.3 million from US$957.1 million in the prior year. Revenues were US$5.22 billion, up 37.1% from US$3.81 billion the year before. Operating income was US$1.93 billion versus US$1.66 billion in the prior year, an increase of 16.4%. Direct operating expenses rose 47.8% to US$2.41 billion from US$1.63 billion in the comparable period the year before. Indirect operating expenses increased 69.1% to US$882.7 million from US$522.1 million in the equivalent prior-year period.

Prospects: Our evaluation of Transdigm Group Inc. as of October 4th, 2019 is the result of our systematic analysis on three basic characteristics: earnings strength, relative valuation, and recent stock price movement. The company has produced a positive trend in earnings per share over the past 5 quarters. In addition, recent analyst estimates for the company have been raised, and TDG has posted results that exceeded analysts' expectations. Based on operating earnings yield, the company is fairly valued when compared to all of the companies we cover. Share price changes over the past year indicates that TDG will perform over the near term.

Financial Data

(US$ in Thousands)	09/30/2019	09/30/2018	09/30/2017	09/30/2016	09/30/2015	09/30/2014	09/30/2013	09/30/2012
Earnings Per Share	13.84	16.20	7.88	10.39	7.84	3.16	2.39	5.97
Cash Flow Per Share	18.05	18.39	14.20	11.88	9.20	9.50	8.54	7.66
Dividends Per Share	30.000	...	46.000	...	...	25.000	34.850	...
Dividend Payout %	216.76	...	583.76	...	...	791.14	1,458.16	...
Income Statement								
Total Revenue	5,223,203	3,811,126	3,504,286	3,171,411	2,707,115	2,372,906	1,924,400	1,700,208
EBITDA	2,148,318	1,778,409	1,580,182	1,372,866	1,149,272	892,583	792,689	768,002
Depn & Amortn	225,700	129,844	140,163	120,900	93,663	96,385	73,515	68,227
Income Before Taxes	1,062,865	985,571	837,430	768,116	636,824	448,510	448,489	487,869
Income Taxes	221,986	24,021	208,889	181,702	189,612	141,600	145,700	162,900
Net Income	889,770	957,062	596,887	586,414	447,212	306,910	302,789	324,969
Average Shares	56,265	55,597	55,530	56,157	56,606	56,993	55,080	53,882
Balance Sheet								
Current Assets	4,865,247	3,657,287	2,133,552	2,930,697	1,831,962	1,689,576	1,320,495	1,050,531
Total Assets	16,254,731	12,197,467	9,975,661	10,726,277	8,427,050	6,756,848	6,148,879	5,459,617
Current Liabilities	1,538,756	900,382	870,994	752,603	658,215	585,907	322,500	233,915
Long-Term Obligations	16,469,221	12,501,946	11,393,620	9,943,191	8,183,502	7,233,836	5,700,193	3,598,625
Total Liabilities	19,149,636	14,005,938	12,926,865	11,377,767	9,465,356	8,312,947	6,485,260	4,240,783
Stockholders' Equity	(2,894,905)	(1,808,471)	(2,951,204)	(651,490)	(1,038,306)	(1,556,099)	(336,381)	1,218,834
Shares Outstanding	53,461	52,734	51,934	53,334	53,684	52,417	52,667	51,651
Statistical Record								
Return on Assets %	6.25	8.63	5.77	6.11	5.89	4.76	5.22	6.50
Return on Equity %	...	...	...	...	...	...	68.62	31.93
EBITDA Margin %	41.13	46.66	45.09	43.29	42.45	37.62	41.19	45.17
Net Margin %	17.03	25.11	17.03	18.49	16.52	12.93	15.73	19.11
Asset Turnover	0.37	0.34	0.34	0.33	0.36	0.37	0.33	0.34
Current Ratio	3.16	4.06	2.45	3.89	2.78	2.88	4.09	4.49
Debt to Equity	...	...	...	...	...	...	...	2.95
Price Range	550.83-312.09	375.54-258.18	289.86-210.04	291.81-187.29	244.35-171.82	197.00-137.86	162.48-125.52	145.61-77.38
P/E Ratio	39.80-22.55	23.18-15.94	36.78-26.65	28.09-18.03	31.17-21.92	62.34-43.63	67.98-52.52	24.39-12.96
Average Yield %	6.93	...	17.93	...	...	14.67	24.38	...

Address: 1301 East 9th Street, Suite 3000, Cleveland, OH 44114 **Telephone:** 216-706-2960	**Web Site:** www.transdigm.com **Officers:** W. Nicholas Howley - Executive Chairman, Chairman, Chief Executive Officer Robert S. Henderson - Vice-Chairman, Executive Vice President, Division Officer	**Auditors:** Ernst & Young LLP **Investor Contact:** 216-706-2945 **Transfer Agents:** Computershare, Providence, RI

TUPPERWARE BRANDS CORP

Exchange	Symbol	Price	52Wk Range	Yield	P/E
NYS	TUP	$8.58 (12/31/2019)	38.13-7.36	N/A	4.09

*7 Year Price Score 27.55   *NYSE Composite Index=100   *12 Month Price Score 42.32

Interim Earnings (Per Share)

Qtr.	Mar	Jun	Sep	Dec
2016	0.86	1.03	0.96	1.56
2017	0.93	(0.35)	0.61	(6.41)
2018	0.70	1.26	0.79	0.37
2019	0.76	0.81	0.16	...

Interim Dividends (Per Share)

Amt	Decl	Ex	Rec	Pay
0.68Q	11/01/2018	12/18/2018	12/19/2018	01/04/2019
0.27Q	01/30/2019	03/19/2019	03/20/2019	04/05/2019
0.27Q	05/22/2019	06/18/2019	06/19/2019	07/08/2019
0.27Q	08/07/2019	09/17/2019	09/18/2019	10/04/2019

Valuation Analysis   Institutional Holding

Forecast EPS	$2.78	No of Institutions
	(00/23/2020)	445
Market Cap	$418.7 Million	Shares
Book Value	N/A	60,442,540
Price/Book	N/A	% Held
Price/Sales	0.22	82.67

Business Summary: Plastics (MIC: 8.4.2 SIC: 3089 NAIC: 326199)

Tupperware Brands is a direct-to-consumer company engaged in the manufacture and sale of Tupperware® products and cosmetics and personal care products under a range of trade names, including Avroy Shlain®, Fuller®, NaturCare®, Nutrimetics® and Nuvo®. Co.'s products include: Tupperware, which includes preparation, storage, and serving solutions for the kitchen and home, and provides a line of cookware, knives, microwave products, microfiber textiles, water-filtration related items and a range of products for on-the-go consumers; and Beauty, which manufactures and markets skin and hair care products, cosmetics, bath and body care, toiletries, fragrances, jewelry and nutritional products.

Recent Developments: For the quarter ended Sep 28 2019, net income decreased 80.1% to US$7.8 million from US$39.1 million in the year-earlier quarter. Revenues were US$418.1 million, down 13.9% from US$485.8 million the year before. Operating income was US$19.9 million versus US$67.2 million in the prior-year quarter, a decrease of 70.4%. Direct operating expenses declined 13.8% to US$141.5 million from US$164.1 million in the comparable period the year before. Indirect operating expenses increased 0.9% to US$256.7 million from US$254.5 million in the equivalent prior-year period.

Prospects: Our evaluation of Tupperware Corp. as of October 4th, 2019 is the result of our systematic analysis on three basic characteristics: earnings strength, relative valuation, and recent stock price movement. The company has managed to produce a neutral trend in earnings per share over the past 5 quarters. In addition, recent analyst estimates for the company have been mixed and TUP has posted results that fell short of analysts' expectations. Based on operating earnings yield, the company is undervalued when compared to all of the companies we cover. Share price changes over the past year indicates that TUP will perform very poorly over the near term.

Financial Data

(US$ in Thousands)	9 Mos	6 Mos	3 Mos	12/29/2018	12/30/2017	12/31/2016	12/26/2015	12/27/2014
Earnings Per Share	2.10	2.73	3.18	3.11	(5.22)	4.41	3.69	4.20
Cash Flow Per Share	2.83	3.53	2.72	2.65	4.28	4.65	4.54	5.65
Tang Book Value Per Share	...	...	...	...	...	0.25	N.M.	N.M.
Dividends Per Share	1.490	1.900	2.310	2.720	2.720	2.720	2.720	2.720
Dividend Payout %	70.95	69.60	72.64	87.46	...	61.68	73.71	64.76
Income Statement								
Total Revenue	1,380,700	962,600	487,300	2,069,700	2,255,800	2,213,100	2,283,800	2,606,100
EBITDA	157,900	134,000	61,700	370,500	279,300	396,600	357,300	393,400
Depn & Amortn	500	300	200	50,600	51,000	49,900	52,200	51,700
Income Before Taxes	127,600	113,700	51,900	276,200	185,100	301,300	259,900	298,200
Income Taxes	43,500	37,400	15,000	120,300	450,500	77,700	74,100	83,800
Net Income	84,100	76,300	36,900	155,900	(265,400)	223,600	185,800	214,400
Average Shares	48,900	48,800	48,800	50,154	50,800	50,700	50,400	51,000
Balance Sheet								
Current Assets	587,200	659,000	655,600	620,600	630,500	545,300	550,500	753,600
Total Assets	1,335,900	1,428,500	1,438,800	1,308,800	1,388,000	1,587,800	1,598,200	1,783,100
Current Liabilities	703,400	769,800	796,900	759,100	658,800	547,600	614,000	747,400
Long-Term Obligations	602,400	602,800	603,000	603,400	605,100	606,000	608,200	615,200
Total Liabilities	1,520,900	1,591,600	1,622,800	1,544,000	1,507,400	1,375,000	1,437,200	1,597,300
Stockholders' Equity	(185,000)	(163,100)	(184,000)	(235,200)	(119,400)	212,800	161,000	185,800
Shares Outstanding	48,795	48,791	48,734	48,666	51,057	50,637	50,436	49,682
Statistical Record								
Return on Assets %	7.51	9.59	10.90	11.59	N.M.	13.81	11.02	11.85
Return on Equity %	...	...	...	...	N.M.	117.70	107.45	98.01
EBITDA Margin %	11.44	13.92	12.66	17.90	12.38	17.92	15.64	15.10
Net Margin %	6.09	7.93	7.57	7.53	N.M.	10.10	8.14	8.23
Asset Turnover	1.40	1.41	1.40	1.54	1.52	1.37	1.35	1.44
Current Ratio	0.83	0.86	0.82	0.82	0.96	1.00	0.90	1.01
Debt to Equity	...	...	...	...	...	...	2.85	3.78	3.31
Price Range	38.73-12.07	42.70-18.62	48.58-24.69	65.44-30.09	73.52-53.86	66.72-43.97	72.68-48.42	95.54-59.64
P/E Ratio	18.44-5.75	15.64-6.82	15.28-7.76	21.04-9.68	...	15.13-9.97	19.70-13.12	22.75-14.20
Average Yield %	5.77	6.14	6.36	6.44	4.32	4.72	4.40	3.52

Address: 14901 South Orange Blossom Trail, Orlando, FL 32837 **Telephone:** 407-826-5050	**Web Site:** www.tupperwarebrands.com **Officers:** Susan M. Cameron - Chairman Christopher D. O'Leary - Interim Chief Executive Officer	**Auditors:** PricewaterhouseCoopers LLP **Investor Contact:** 407-826-4475 **Transfer Agents:** Equiniti Trust Company, Mendota Heights, MN

TWILIO INC

Exchange	Symbol	Price	52Wk Range	Yield	P/E
NYS	TWLO	$98.28 (12/31/2019)	149.95-81.25	N/A	N/A

*7 Year Price Score N/A   *NYSE Composite Index=100   *12 Month Price Score 78.18

Interim Earnings (Per Share)

Qtr.	Mar	Jun	Sep	Dec
2016	(0.37)	(0.45)	(0.13)	(0.10)
2017	(0.16)	(0.08)	(0.25)	(0.21)
2018	(0.25)	(0.25)	(0.28)	(0.48)
2019	(0.31)	(0.72)	(0.64)	...

Interim Dividends (Per Share)

No Dividends Paid

Valuation Analysis		Institutional Holding	
Forecast EPS	$0.13	No of Institutions	
	(01/17/2020)	673	
Market Cap	$13.5 Billion	Shares	
Book Value	$4.3 Billion	113,120,288	
Price/Book	3.14	% Held	
Price/Sales	13.37	94.32	

Business Summary: Internet & Software (MIC: 6.3.2 SIC: 7372 NAIC: 511210)

Twilio provides a cloud communications platform that enables developers to build, scale and operate communications within their software applications via Co.'s Application Programming Interfaces (APIs). Co.'s platform consists of three layers: Engagement Cloud, which provides functionality for a specific purpose, such as two-factor authentication or a contact center; Programmable Communications Cloud, which provides a range of products that enables developers to embed voice, messaging and video capabilities into their applications; and Super Network, which contains a set of API's giving Co.'s customers access to components of its platform.

Recent Developments: For the quarter ended Sep 30 2019, net loss amounted to US$87.7 million versus a net loss of US$27.1 million in the year-earlier quarter. Revenues were US$295.1 million, up 74.7% from US$168.9 million the year before. Operating loss was US$94.7 million versus a loss of US$25.0 million in the prior-year quarter. Direct operating expenses rose 77.7% to US$136.9 million from US$77.0 million in the comparable period the year before. Indirect operating expenses increased 116.3% to US$252.8 million from US$116.9 million in the equivalent prior-year period.

Prospects: Our evaluation of Twilio Inc as of October 4th, 2019 is the result of our systematic analysis on three basic characteristics: earnings strength, relative valuation, and recent stock price movement. The company has suffered a very negative trend in earnings per share over the past 5 quarters. However, recent analyst estimates for the company have been unchanged while TWLO has posted results that exceeded analysts' expectations. Based on operating earnings yield, the company is overvalued when compared to all of the companies we cover. Share price changes over the past year indicates that TWLO will perform over the near term.

Financial Data
(US$ in Thousands)

	9 Mos	6 Mos	3 Mos	12/31/2018	12/31/2017	12/31/2016	12/31/2015	12/31/2014
Earnings Per Share	(2.15)	(1.79)	(1.32)	(1.26)	(0.70)	(0.78)	(2.19)	(1.58)
Cash Flow Per Share	(0.02)	(0.19)	(0.15)	0.08	(0.04)	0.19	(1.06)	(1.03)
Tang Book Value Per Share	11.20	11.25	4.33	3.72	3.43	3.62	...	...
Income Statement								
Total Revenue	803,244	508,178	233,139	650,067	399,020	277,335	166,919	88,846
EBITDA	(216,467)	(145,110)	(70,618)	(102,258)	(49,903)	(33,598)	(31,682)	(25,045)
Depn & Amortn	56,658	37,726	17,606	18,900	13,100	7,400	3,700	1,700
Income Before Taxes	(273,125)	(182,836)	(88,224)	(121,158)	(63,003)	(40,998)	(35,382)	(26,745)
Income Taxes	(56,309)	(53,754)	(51,721)	791	705	326	122	13
Net Income	(216,816)	(129,082)	(36,503)	(121,949)	(63,708)	(41,324)	(35,504)	(26,758)
Average Shares	136,400	129,310	116,590	97,130	91,224	53,116	17,746	16,900
Balance Sheet								
Current Assets	2,068,424	2,059,513	1,063,127	872,948	353,265	353,380	136,475	46,349
Total Assets	5,110,168	5,109,105	4,120,073	1,028,710	449,782	412,694	157,516	54,974
Current Liabilities	216,228	201,781	182,339	137,810	78,527	73,704	40,443	23,198
Long-Term Obligations	452,184	448,414	443,110	436,666	...	...	...	...
Total Liabilities	825,682	812,245	792,560	590,475	89,936	83,247	40,891	23,780
Stockholders' Equity	4,284,486	4,296,860	3,327,513	438,235	359,846	329,447	116,625	31,194
Shares Outstanding	137,072	135,762	126,078	100,080	93,969	87,248	17,324	17,446
Statistical Record								
Asset Turnover	0.33	0.29	0.33	0.88	0.93	0.97	1.57	...
Current Ratio	9.57	10.21	5.83	6.33	4.50	4.79	3.37	2.00
Debt to Equity	0.11	0.10	0.13	1.00	...	...	...	...
Price Range	149.95-63.98	146.66-56.17	135.66-36.65	96.67-23.91	34.90-23.17	68.97-26.30	...	...

Address: 375 Beale Street, Suite 300, San Francisco, CA 94105 Telephone: 415-390-2337	Web Site: www.twilio.com Officers: Jeff Lawson - Chairman, Chief Executive Officer George Hu - Chief Operating Officer	Auditors: KPMG LLP Transfer Agents: Computershare Trust Company, N.A., Edison, NJ

TWITTER INC

Exchange	Symbol	Price	52Wk Range	Yield	P/E
NYS	TWTR	$32.05 (12/31/2019)	45.42-27.99	N/A	15.56

*7 Year Price Score N/A *NYSE Composite Index=100 *12 Month Price Score 81.52

TRADING VOLUME (thousand shares)

Interim Earnings (Per Share)

Qtr.	Mar	Jun	Sep	Dec
2016	(0.12)	(0.15)	(0.15)	(0.23)
2017	(0.09)	(0.16)	(0.03)	0.12
2018	0.08	0.13	1.02	0.33
2019	0.25	1.43	0.05	...

Interim Dividends (Per Share)

No Dividends Paid

Valuation Analysis | Institutional Holding

Forecast EPS	$2.40	No of Institutions
	(01/17/2020)	972
Market Cap	$24.9 Billion	Shares
Book Value	$8.4 Billion	612,179,456
Price/Book	2.95	% Held
Price/Sales	7.40	75.11

Business Summary: Internet & Software (MIC: 6.3.2 SIC: 7371 NAIC: 541511)

Twitter provides products and services for users, advertisers, developers and platform and data partners. Co.'s products and services for users include Twitter, a platform for public self-expression and conversation in real time; and Periscope, a mobile application that lets anyone broadcast and watch video live with others. Co.'s products and services for advertisers include Promoted Products such as Promoted Tweets, Promoted Accounts, and Promoted Trends. Co.'s products for developers and data partners provide tools, public APIs and embeddable widgets that developers can use to contribute their content to its platform and syndicate and distribute Twitter content across their properties.

Recent Developments: For the quarter ended Sep 30 2019, net income decreased 95.4% to US$36.5 million from US$789.2 million in the year-earlier quarter. Revenues were US$823.7 million, up 8.7% from US$758.1 million the year before. Operating income was US$44.1 million versus US$91.9 million in the prior-year quarter, a decrease of 51.9%. Direct operating expenses rose 15.4% to US$281.1 million from US$243.6 million in the comparable period the year before. Indirect operating expenses increased 18.0% to US$498.5 million from US$422.6 million in the equivalent prior-year period.

Prospects: Our evaluation of Twitter Inc as of October 4th, 2019 is the result of our systematic analysis on three basic characteristics: earnings strength, relative valuation, and recent stock price movement. The company has generated a negative trend in earnings per share over the past 5 quarters. However, recent analyst estimates for the company have been unchanged while TWTR has posted results that exceeded analysts' expectations. Based on operating earnings yield, the company is overvalued when compared to all of the companies we cover. Share price changes over the past year indicates that TWTR will perform over the near term.

Financial Data

(US$ in Thousands)	9 Mos	6 Mos	3 Mos	12/31/2018	12/31/2017	12/31/2016	12/31/2015	12/31/2014
Earnings Per Share	2.06	3.03	1.73	1.56	(0.15)	(0.65)	(0.79)	(0.96)
Cash Flow Per Share	1.76	1.91	1.89	1.78	1.13	1.08	0.58	0.14
Tang Book Value Per Share	9.19	9.12	7.58	7.24	5.10	4.61	4.47	4.51
Income Statement								
Total Revenue	2,451,988	1,628,271	786,890	3,042,359	2,443,299	2,529,619	2,218,032	1,403,002
EBITDA	313,323	239,218	124,099	851,429	359,019	(8,066)	(177,927)	(372,766)
Depn & Amortn	93,251	62,787	30,877	406,500	349,200	332,800	257,200	171,600
Income Before Taxes	232,045	184,282	96,503	423,544	(95,418)	(440,834)	(533,305)	(578,351)
Income Taxes	(1,114,841)	(1,126,082)	(94,301)	(782,052)	12,645	16,039	(12,274)	(531)
Net Income	1,346,886	1,310,364	190,804	1,205,596	(108,063)	(456,873)	(521,031)	(577,820)
Average Shares	790,523	785,056	777,689	772,686	732,702	702,135	662,424	604,990
Balance Sheet								
Current Assets	6,624,451	7,512,783	7,255,785	7,111,036	5,321,884	4,652,196	4,381,792	4,255,853
Total Assets	11,600,925	12,521,607	11,145,231	10,162,572	7,412,477	6,870,365	6,442,439	5,583,082
Current Liabilities	762,627	1,733,738	1,621,679	1,516,311	583,278	584,021	506,039	393,794
Long-Term Obligations	1,797,971	1,780,668	1,765,938	1,755,316	1,708,768	1,605,804	1,514,790	1,494,970
Total Liabilities	3,185,283	4,176,793	4,056,412	3,356,978	2,365,259	2,265,430	2,074,392	1,956,679
Stockholders' Equity	8,415,642	8,344,814	7,088,819	6,805,594	5,047,218	4,604,935	4,368,047	3,626,403
Shares Outstanding	775,718	772,393	767,913	764,257	746,902	721,572	694,132	642,385
Statistical Record								
Return on Assets %	15.01	22.03	14.29	13.72	N.M.	N.M.	N.M.	N.M.
Return on Equity %	21.55	33.84	21.72	20.34	N.M.	N.M.	N.M.	N.M.
EBITDA Margin %	12.78	14.69	15.77	27.99	14.69	N.M.	N.M.	N.M.
Net Margin %	54.93	80.48	24.25	39.63	N.M.	N.M.	N.M.	N.M.
Asset Turnover	0.31	0.31	0.34	0.35	0.34	0.38	0.37	0.23
Current Ratio	8.69	4.33	4.47	4.69	9.12	7.97	8.66	10.81
Debt to Equity	0.21	0.21	0.25	0.26	0.34	0.35	0.35	0.41
Price Range	45.42-26.45	46.65-26.45	46.76-26.45	46.76-22.16	25.20-14.29	24.87-14.01	52.87-22.14	69.00-30.50
P/E Ratio	22.05-12.84	15.40-8.73	27.03-15.29	29.97-14.21	...	...	...	...

Address: 1355 Market Street, Suite 900, San Francisco, CA 94103	Web Site: www.twitter.com	Auditors: PricewaterhouseCoopers LLP
Telephone: 415-222-9670	Officers: Omid R. Kordestani - Executive Chairman Jack Dorsey - Chairman, Chief Executive Officer, Interim Chief Executive Officer	Transfer Agents: Computershare Trust Company, N.A., Canton, MA

TYLER TECHNOLOGIES, INC.

Exchange	Symbol	Price	52Wk Range	Yield	P/E
NYS	TYL	$300.02 (12/31/2019)	300.57-176.63	N/A	90.92

*7 Year Price Score 126.11 *NYSE Composite Index=100 *12 Month Price Score 115.16

Interim Earnings (Per Share)

Qtr.	Mar	Jun	Sep	Dec
2016	0.44	0.49	0.58	1.31
2017	0.83	0.81	0.97	1.58
2018	0.95	0.97	0.96	0.81
2019	0.69	0.80	1.00	...

Interim Dividends (Per Share)

No Dividends Paid

Valuation Analysis		Institutional Holding	
Forecast EPS	$5.31	No of Institutions	
	(01/15/2020)	538	
Market Cap	$14.4 Billion	Shares	
Book Value	$1.5 Billion	45,195,960	
Price/Book	9.51	% Held	
Price/Sales	13.90	91.67	

Business Summary: Internet & Software (MIC: 6.3.2 SIC: 7372 NAIC: 511210)

Tyler Technologies provides information management solutions and services for the public sector. Co. has two segments: Enterprise Software, which provides municipal and county governments and schools with software systems and services to meet their information technology and automation needs for back-office functions such as financial management, courts and justice processes, public safety, planning, regulatory and maintenance, and land and vital records management; and Appraisal and Tax, which provides systems and software that automate the appraisal and assessment of real and personal property as well as property appraisal outsourcing services for local governments and taxing authorities.

Recent Developments: For the quarter ended Sep 30 2019, net income increased 3.8% to US$40.4 million from US$38.9 million in the year-earlier quarter. Revenues were US$275.4 million, up 16.7% from US$236.1 million the year before. Operating income was US$40.1 million versus US$37.6 million in the prior-year quarter, an increase of 6.6%. Direct operating expenses rose 16.3% to US$144.7 million from US$124.4 million in the comparable period the year before. Indirect operating expenses increased 22.5% to US$90.7 million from US$74.0 million in the equivalent prior-year period.

Prospects: Our evaluation of Tyler Technologies Inc. as of October 4th, 2019 is the result of our systematic analysis on three basic characteristics: earnings strength, relative valuation, and recent stock price movement. The company has produced a positive trend in earnings per share over the past 5 quarters. In addition, recent analyst estimates for the company have been raised, and TYL has posted results that fell short of analysts' expectations. Based on operating earnings yield, the company is overvalued when compared to all of the companies we cover. Share price changes over the past year indicates that TYL will perform in line with the market over the near term.

Financial Data

(US$ in Thousands)	9 Mos	6 Mos	3 Mos	12/31/2018	12/31/2017	12/31/2016	12/31/2015	12/31/2014
Earnings Per Share	3.30	3.26	3.43	3.68	4.18	2.82	1.77	1.66
Cash Flow Per Share	6.43	6.03	5.99	6.51	5.25	5.25	2.61	3.74
Tang Book Value Per Share	6.56	5.39	3.51	7.69	7.20	N.M.	N.M.	5.32
Income Statement								
Total Revenue	797,590	522,190	247,066	935,282	840,662	756,043	591,022	493,101
EBITDA	127,810	81,612	39,927	193,287	192,840	156,438	123,429	106,913
Depn & Amortn	15,762	10,116	4,850	37,417	31,212	27,131	15,005	12,446
Income Before Taxes	112,048	71,496	35,077	155,870	161,628	129,307	108,424	94,467
Income Taxes	12,311	12,149	7,729	8,408	(2,317)	19,450	43,555	35,527
Net Income	99,737	59,347	27,348	147,462	163,945	109,857	64,869	58,940
Average Shares	40,280	39,813	39,585	40,123	39,246	38,961	36,552	35,401
Balance Sheet								
Current Assets	569,806	453,570	402,274	518,858	496,800	282,960	268,215	346,710
Total Assets	2,055,089	1,949,431	1,909,302	1,790,963	1,589,592	1,357,945	1,356,570	573,982
Current Liabilities	476,814	453,732	403,380	423,902	382,310	361,501	337,572	232,839
Long-Term Obligations	18,134	33,769	103,956	...	...	10,000	66,000	...
Total Liabilities	535,492	527,801	550,557	466,117	422,498	442,420	497,713	237,009
Stockholders' Equity	1,519,597	1,421,630	1,358,745	1,324,846	1,167,094	915,525	858,857	336,973
Shares Outstanding	48,147	38,656	38,322	38,275	37,885	36,766	36,774	33,469
Statistical Record								
Return on Assets %	6.70	7.00	7.75	8.72	11.12	8.07	6.72	11.57
Return on Equity %	8.93	9.40	10.46	11.84	15.74	12.35	10.85	20.21
EBITDA Margin %	16.02	15.63	16.16	20.67	22.94	20.69	20.88	21.68
Net Margin %	12.50	11.37	11.07	15.77	19.50	14.53	10.98	11.95
Asset Turnover	0.53	0.54	0.54	0.55	0.57	0.56	0.61	0.97
Current Ratio	1.20	1.00	1.00	1.22	1.30	0.78	0.79	1.49
Debt to Equity	0.01	0.02	0.08	...	...	0.01	0.08	...
Price Range	263.19-173.85	250.80-173.85	250.80-173.85	250.80-173.85	184.11-144.77	175.47-119.50	180.61-104.17	114.09-76.00
P/E Ratio	79.75-52.68	76.93-53.33	73.12-50.69	68.15-47.24	44.05-34.63	62.22-42.38	102.04-58.85	68.73-45.78

Address: 5101 Tennyson Parkway,	Web Site: www.tylertech.com	Auditors: Ernst & Young LLP
Plano, TX 75024	Officers: John S. Marr - Executive Chairman,	Investor Contact: 972-713-3720
Telephone: 972-713-3700	Chairman, President, Chief Executive Officer H. Lynn	Transfer Agents: American Stock
	Moore - President, Chief Executive Officer, Executive	Transfer & Company, New York, NY
	Vice President, Secretary, General Counsel	

TYSON FOODS INC

Exchange	Symbol	Price	52Wk Range	Yield	P/E
NYS	TSN	$91.04 (12/31/2019)	93.29-53.35	1.85	16.49

*7 Year Price Score 115.93 ***NYSE Composite Index=100** ***12 Month Price Score 107.63**

Interim Earnings (Per Share)

Qtr.	Dec	Mar	Jun	Sep
2014-15	0.74	0.75	0.83	0.63
2015-16	1.15	1.10	1.25	1.03
2016-17	1.59	0.92	1.21	1.07
2017-18	4.40	0.85	1.47	1.47
2018-19	1.50	1.17	1.84	1.01

Interim Dividends (Per Share)

Amt	Decl	Ex	Rec	Pay
0.375Q	02/06/2019	05/30/2019	05/31/2019	06/14/2019
0.375Q	05/09/2019	08/29/2019	08/30/2019	09/13/2019
0.42Q	08/08/2019	11/27/2019	11/29/2019	12/13/2019
0.42Q	11/11/2019	02/27/2020	02/28/2020	03/13/2020

Indicated Div: $1.68

Valuation Analysis

		Institutional Holding	
Forecast EPS	$6.70	No of Institutions	
	(01/17/2020)	1069	
Market Cap	$33.3 Billion	Shares	
Book Value	$14.1 Billion	316,342,784	
Price/Book	2.37	% Held	
Price/Sales	0.79	68.27	

Business Summary: Food (MIC: 1.2.1 SIC: 2015 NAIC: 311615)

Tyson Foods is a food company. Co.'s operations consist of breeding stock, contract farmers, feed production, processing, further-processing, marketing and transportation of chicken and related allied products, including animal and pet food ingredients. Through its wholly-owned subsidiary, Cobb-Vantress, Inc., Co. is engaged as poultry breeding stock supplier. Co. also processes live fed cattle and hogs and fabricates dressed beef and pork carcasses into primal and sub-primal meat cuts, case-ready beef and pork and fully-cooked meats. Co. produces a range of fresh, frozen and refrigerated food products. Co. operates in Beef, Pork, Chicken and Prepared Foods segments.

Recent Developments: For the year ended Sep 28 2019, net income decreased 32.8% to US$2.04 billion from US$3.03 billion in the prior year. Revenues were US$42.41 billion, up 5.9% from US$40.05 billion the year before. Operating income was US$2.83 billion versus US$3.03 billion in the prior year, a decrease of 6.8%. Direct operating expenses rose 6.9% to US$37.38 billion from US$34.96 billion in the comparable period the year before. Indirect operating expenses increased 6.3% to US$2.20 billion from US$2.06 billion in the equivalent prior-year period.

Prospects: Our evaluation of Tyson Foods Inc. as of October 4th, 2019 is the result of our systematic analysis on three basic characteristics: earnings strength, relative valuation, and recent stock price movement. The company has managed to produce a neutral trend in earnings per share over the past 5 quarters. However, recent analyst estimates for the company have been reduced while TSN has posted results that exceeded analysts' expectations. Based on operating earnings yield, the company is undervalued when compared to all of the companies we cover. Share price changes over the past year indicates that TSN will perform over the near term.

Financial Data

(US$ in Thousands)	09/28/2019	09/29/2018	09/30/2017	10/01/2016	10/03/2015	09/27/2014	09/28/2013	09/29/2012
Earnings Per Share	5.52	8.19	4.79	4.53	2.95	2.37	2.12	1.58
Cash Flow Per Share	6.94	8.14	7.10	7.07	6.24	3.34	3.74	3.28
Tang Book Value Per Share	N.M.	N.M.	N.M.	N.M.	N.M.	N.M.	12.10	11.12
Dividends Per Share	1.500	1.200	0.900	0.600	0.400	0.300	0.300	0.160
Dividend Payout %	27.17	14.65	18.79	13.25	13.56	12.66	14.15	10.13
Income Statement								
Total Revenue	42,405,000	40,052,000	38,260,000	36,881,000	41,373,000	37,580,000	34,374,000	33,278,000
EBITDA	3,701,000	3,811,000	3,542,000	3,458,000	2,814,000	1,871,000	1,869,000	1,714,000
Depn & Amortn	819,000	723,000	642,000	617,000	609,000	494,000	474,000	443,000
Income Before Taxes	2,431,000	2,745,000	2,628,000	2,598,000	1,921,000	1,252,000	1,257,000	927,000
Income Taxes	396,000	(282,000)	850,000	826,000	697,000	396,000	409,000	351,000
Net Income	2,022,000	3,024,000	1,774,000	1,768,000	1,220,000	864,000	778,000	583,000
Average Shares	366,000	369,000	370,000	390,000	413,000	364,000	367,000	370,000
Balance Sheet								
Current Assets	7,169,000	5,688,000	6,258,000	4,888,000	5,381,000	6,221,000	5,604,000	5,403,000
Total Assets	33,097,000	29,109,000	28,066,000	22,373,000	23,004,000	23,956,000	12,177,000	11,896,000
Current Liabilities	5,513,000	5,031,000	4,032,000	2,762,000	3,535,000	3,797,000	3,010,000	2,830,000
Long-Term Obligations	9,830,000	7,962,000	9,297,000	6,200,000	6,010,000	7,535,000	1,895,000	1,917,000
Total Liabilities	19,015,000	16,306,000	17,525,000	12,765,000	13,313,000	15,066,000	5,976,000	5,884,000
Stockholders' Equity	14,082,000	12,803,000	10,541,000	9,608,000	9,691,000	8,890,000	6,201,000	6,012,000
Shares Outstanding	366,000	366,000	368,000	361,000	369,000	376,000	344,000	359,000
Statistical Record								
Return on Assets %	6.52	10.61	7.03	7.81	5.11	4.80	6.48	5.09
Return on Equity %	15.08	25.98	17.61	18.37	12.92	11.48	12.78	10.02
EBITDA Margin %	8.73	9.52	9.26	9.38	6.80	4.98	5.44	5.15
Net Margin %	4.77	7.55	4.64	4.79	2.95	2.30	2.26	1.75
Asset Turnover	1.37	1.40	1.52	1.63	1.73	2.09	2.86	2.91
Current Ratio	1.30	1.13	1.55	1.77	1.52	1.64	1.86	1.91
Debt to Equity	0.70	0.62	0.88	0.65	0.62	0.85	0.31	0.32
Price Range	93.29-50.75	83.62-57.55	75.10-56.17	76.76-43.10	45.01-37.12	44.01-27.56	31.83-16.02	20.91-14.17
P/E Ratio	16.90-9.19	10.21-7.03	15.68-11.73	16.94-9.51	15.26-12.58	18.57-11.63	15.01-7.56	13.23-8.97
Average Yield %	2.12	1.69	1.42	0.97	0.97	0.82	1.27	0.87

Address: 2200 West Don Tyson Parkway, Springdale, AR 72762-6999	Web Site: www.tyson.com	Auditors: PricewaterhouseCoopers LLP
Telephone: 479-290-4000	**Officers:** John Tyson - Chairman Noel White - President, Chief Executive Officer, Division Officer	**Investor Contact:** 479-290-4235
Fax: 479-290-7984		**Transfer Agents:** Computershare, Inc., Providence, RI

UBIQUITI INC

Exchange	Symbol	Price	52Wk Range	Yield	P/E
NYS	UI	$188.98 (12/31/2019)	198.30-95.95	0.63	39.54

*7 Year Price Score 190.67 ***NYSE Composite Index=100** ***12 Month Price Score 121.33**

Interim Earnings (Per Share)

Qtr.	Sep	Dec	Mar	Jun
2016-17	0.86	0.72	0.77	0.74
2017-18	0.92	(0.66)	1.32	0.93
2018-19	1.16	1.09	1.25	1.01
2019-20	1.43	...	...	...

Interim Dividends (Per Share)

Amt	Decl	Ex	Rec	Pay
0.25Q	02/08/2019	02/14/2019	02/18/2019	02/25/2019
0.25Q	05/10/2019	05/17/2019	05/20/2019	05/28/2019
0.30Q	08/09/2019	08/16/2019	08/19/2019	08/26/2019
0.30Q	11/05/2019	11/15/2019	11/18/2019	11/25/2019

Indicated Div: $1.20

Valuation Analysis **Institutional Holding**

Forecast EPS	$5.84	No of Institutions	
	(01/16/2020)	341	
Market Cap	$12.4 Billion	Shares	
Book Value	N/A		12,712,235
Price/Book	N/A	% Held	
Price/Sales	10.35	N/A	

Business Summary: Internet & Software (MIC: 6.3.2 SIC: 5045 NAIC: 423430)

Ubiquiti is engaged in providing portfolio of networking products and solutions for operator-owners of wireless internet services (WISP's), enterprises and smart homes. Co.'s operator-owner service provider product platforms provide carrier-class network infrastructure for fixed wireless broadband, wireless backhaul systems and routing and the related software for WISP's to control, track and bill their customers. Co.'s enterprise product platforms provide wireless LAN (WLAN) infrastructure, video surveillance products, switching and routing solutions, security gateways, and other complimentary WLAN products along with a software platform.

Recent Developments: For the quarter ended Sep 30 2019, net income increased 14.5% to US$98.1 million from US$85.7 million in the year-earlier quarter. Revenues were US$323.3 million, up 14.3% from US$282.9 million the year before. Operating income was US$120.7 million versus US$99.6 million in the prior-year quarter, an increase of 21.2%. Direct operating expenses rose 13.6% to US$171.9 million from US$151.3 million in the comparable period the year before. Indirect operating expenses decreased 4.0% to US$30.7 million from US$32.0 million in the equivalent prior-year period.

Prospects: Our evaluation of Ubiquiti Inc as of October 4th, 2019 is the result of our systematic analysis on three basic characteristics: earnings strength, relative valuation, and recent stock price movement. The company has generated a negative trend in earnings per share over the past 5 quarters. In addition, recent analyst estimates for the company have been reduced while UI has posted results that exceeded analysts' expectations. Based on operating earnings yield, the company is fairly valued when compared to all of the companies we cover. Share price changes over the past year indicates that UI will perform well over the near term.

Financial Data

(US$ in Thousands)	3 Mos	06/30/2019	06/30/2018	06/30/2017	06/30/2016	06/30/2015	06/30/2014	06/30/2013
Earnings Per Share	4.78	4.51	2.51	3.09	2.49	1.45	1.97	0.89
Cash Flow Per Share	4.17	3.63	4.30	1.38	2.33	1.53	1.38	1.49
Tang Book Value Per Share	...	1.38	4.26	7.49	5.38	4.83	3.79	1.68
Dividends Per Share	1.050	1.000	...	...	...	0.170	...	0.180
Dividend Payout %	21.97	22.17	...	...	...	11.72	...	20.22
Income Statement								
Total Revenue	323,277	1,161,733	1,016,861	865,268	666,395	595,947	572,464	320,823
EBITDA	120,928	401,797	333,327	296,561	247,755	151,578	198,545	94,404
Depn & Amortn	239	7,500	7,200	6,800	5,700	4,700	2,600	1,800
Income Before Taxes	116,036	381,489	314,142	285,024	239,940	145,748	194,611	91,753
Income Taxes	17,890	58,795	117,852	27,518	26,324	16,085	17,674	11,263
Net Income	98,146	322,694	196,290	257,506	213,616	129,663	176,937	80,490
Average Shares	68,484	71,602	78,331	83,252	85,784	89,569	89,715	90,259
Balance Sheet								
Current Assets	600,782	753,811	1,001,352	952,334	728,641	581,346	465,724	283,474
Total Assets	750,568	875,865	1,022,577	972,711	748,051	600,572	476,151	292,340
Current Liabilities	227,257	179,186	112,916	98,488	90,920	70,134	52,315	59,421
Long-Term Obligations	621,464	464,700	460,352	241,821	192,250	87,500	72,254	71,116
Total Liabilities	989,995	776,588	706,829	370,947	307,675	178,418	140,887	144,904
Stockholders' Equity	(239,427)	99,277	315,748	601,764	440,376	422,154	335,264	147,436
Shares Outstanding	65,847	69,472	74,072	80,275	81,667	87,413	88,179	87,213
Statistical Record								
Return on Assets %	38.21	34.00	19.68	29.93	31.59	24.08	46.05	31.81
Return on Equity %	2,147.49	155.51	42.79	49.42	49.40	34.24	73.31	57.83
EBITDA Margin %	37.41	34.59	32.78	34.27	37.18	25.43	34.68	29.43
Net Margin %	30.36	27.78	19.30	29.76	32.06	21.76	30.91	25.09
Asset Turnover	1.37	1.22	1.02	1.01	0.99	1.11	1.49	1.27
Current Ratio	2.64	4.21	8.87	9.67	8.01	8.29	8.90	4.77
Debt to Equity	...	4.68	1.46	0.40	0.44	0.21	0.22	0.48
Price Range	171.16-83.01	171.16-79.72	87.78-50.62	64.13-37.70	41.15-26.86	49.60-26.23	56.20-17.43	20.54-7.88
P/E Ratio	35.81-17.37	37.95-17.68	34.97-20.17	20.75-12.20	16.53-10.79	34.21-18.09	28.53-8.85	23.08-8.85
Average Yield %	0.86	0.87	...	...	...	0.50	...	1.34

Address: 685 Third Avenue, 27th Floor, New York, NY 10017 **Telephone:** 646-780-7958	**Web Site:** www.ubnt.com **Officers:** Robert J. Pera - Chairman, Chief Executive Officer Kevin Radigan - Chief Accounting Officer	**Auditors:** KPMG LLP **Investor Contact:** 646-780-7958 **Transfer Agents:** Computershare Trust Co., N.A., Canton, MA

UDR INC

Exchange	**Symbol**	**Price**	**52Wk Range**	**Yield**	**P/E**	
NYS	UDR	$46.70 (12/31/2019)	50.36-38.39	2.93	79.15	

*7 Year Price Score 109.02 ***NYSE Composite Index=100** ***12 Month Price Score 98.26**

Interim Earnings (Per Share)

Qtr.	Mar	Jun	Sep	Dec
2016	0.04	0.06	0.10	0.88
2017	0.09	0.03	0.06	0.26
2018	0.30	0.07	0.07	0.30
2019	0.08	0.12	0.09	...

Interim Dividends (Per Share)

Amt	Decl	Ex	Rec	Pay
0.343Q	03/28/2019	04/08/2019	04/09/2019	04/30/2019
0.343Q	06/20/2019	07/09/2019	07/10/2019	07/31/2019
0.343Q	09/19/2019	10/09/2019	10/10/2019	10/31/2019
0.343Q	12/12/2019	01/09/2020	01/10/2020	01/31/2020

Indicated Div: $1.37

Valuation Analysis		**Institutional Holding**	
Forecast EPS	$0.33	No of Institutions	
	(01/17/2020)	603	
Market Cap	$13.7 Billion	Shares	
Book Value	$3.2 Billion	373,281,600	
Price/Book	4.21	% Held	
Price/Sales	12.27	N/A	

Business Summary: REITs (MIC: 5.3.1 SIC: 6798 NAIC: 525930)

UDR is a real estate investment trust that owns, operates, acquires, renovates, develops, redevelops, disposes of, and manages multifamily apartment communities generally located in markets located throughout the U.S. Co. has an ownership interest in communities containing apartment homes through unconsolidated joint ventures or partnerships. Co.'s operating partnership, United Dominion Realty, L.P., has a consolidated real estate portfolio that includes communities located in several markets.

Recent Developments: For the quarter ended Sep 30 2019, net income increased 45.2% to US$29.4 million from US$20.3 million in the year-earlier quarter. Revenues were US$295.4 million, up 11.0% from US$266.1 million the year before. Revenues from property income rose 9.8% to US$289.0 million from US$263.3 million in the corresponding quarter a year earlier.

Prospects: Our evaluation of UDR Inc. as of October 4th, 2019 is the result of our systematic analysis on three basic characteristics: earnings strength, relative valuation, and recent stock price movement. The company has managed to produce a neutral trend in earnings per share over the past 5 quarters. In addition, recent analyst estimates for the company have been mixed and UDR has posted results that fell short of analysts' expectations. Based on operating earnings yield, the company is overvalued when compared to all of the companies we cover. Share price changes over the past year indicates that UDR will perform well over the near term.

Financial Data (US$ in Thousands)	9 Mos	6 Mos	3 Mos	12/31/2018	12/31/2017	12/31/2016	12/31/2015	12/31/2014
Earnings Per Share	0.59	0.57	0.52	0.74	0.44	1.08	1.29	0.59
Cash Flow Per Share	2.12	2.10	2.04	2.09	1.94	2.02	1.67	1.56
Tang Book Value Per Share	10.92	10.25	10.30	10.38	10.38	11.40	10.90	10.54
Dividends Per Share	1.330	1.310	1.290	1.278	1.225	1.163	1.093	1.015
Dividend Payout %	225.42	229.82	248.08	172.64	278.41	107.64	84.69	172.03
Income Statement								
Total Revenue	847,375	551,981	270,673	1,046,859	995,791	959,861	894,638	818,046
EBITDA	552,041	361,471	172,555	804,641	633,818	613,658	558,885	490,693
Depn & Amortn	375,766	244,052	120,061	449,923	449,324	439,036	399,294	363,929
Income Before Taxes	78,791	60,583	28,765	227,285	57,754	53,521	39,267	8,168
Income Taxes	3,836	2,337	2,212	688	(240)	(3,774)	(3,886)	(15,098)
Net Income	87,326	60,122	24,503	203,106	121,558	292,718	340,383	154,334
Average Shares	289,529	282,575	277,557	269,483	268,830	267,311	263,752	253,445
Balance Sheet								
Current Assets	23,541	24,023	24,154	208,891	21,830	22,106	27,540	37,564
Total Assets	8,697,597	8,197,266	7,955,725	7,711,728	7,733,273	7,679,584	7,663,844	6,846,534
Current Liabilities	287,609	270,031	263,816	268,424	278,108	271,654	246,002	244,999
Long-Term Obligations	3,935,897	3,870,589	3,589,829	3,547,787	3,671,663	3,401,478	3,570,795	3,583,105
Total Liabilities	5,451,035	5,247,862	5,006,743	4,806,103	4,907,473	4,586,474	4,764,089	4,111,437
Stockholders' Equity	3,246,562	2,949,404	2,948,982	2,905,625	2,825,800	3,093,110	2,899,755	2,735,097
Shares Outstanding	292,948	283,104	281,791	275,545	267,822	267,259	261,844	255,114
Statistical Record								
Return on Assets %	2.07	2.02	1.86	2.63	1.58	3.81	4.69	2.26
Return on Equity %	5.80	5.64	5.01	7.09	4.11	9.74	12.08	5.56
EBITDA Margin %	65.15	65.49	63.75	76.86	63.65	63.93	62.47	59.98
Net Margin %	10.31	10.89	9.05	19.40	12.21	30.50	38.05	18.87
Asset Turnover	0.14	0.14	0.14	0.14	0.13	0.12	0.12	0.12
Current Ratio	0.08	0.09	0.09	0.78	0.08	0.08	0.11	0.15
Debt to Equity	1.21	1.31	1.22	1.22	1.30	1.10	1.23	1.31
Price Range	48.93-38.09	46.74-36.55	45.50-34.67	42.91-32.92	40.49-34.48	38.56-33.11	37.89-30.82	31.74-23.27
P/E Ratio	82.93-64.56	82.00-64.12	87.50-66.67	57.99-44.49	92.02-78.36	35.70-30.66	29.37-23.89	53.80-39.44
Average Yield %	3.02	3.12	3.25	3.39	3.23	3.27	3.24	3.66

Address: 1745 Shea Center Drive, Suite 200, Highlands Ranch, CO 80129 **Telephone:** 720-283-6120	**Web Site:** www.udrt.com **Officers:** Thomas W. Toomey - Chairman, President, Chief Executive Officer Lynne B. Sagalyn - Vice-Chairman	**Auditors:** Ernst & Young LLP **Investor Contact:** 720-348-7762 **Transfer Agents:** Wells Fargo Shareowner Services, Saint Paul, MN

UGI CORP.

*7 Year Price Score 102.85 *NYSE Composite Index=100 *12 Month Price Score 82.24

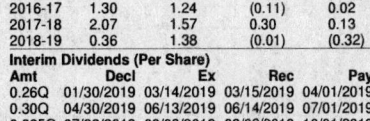

Interim Earnings (Per Share)

Qtr.	Dec	Mar	Jun	Sep
2014-15	0.19	1.40	0.05	(0.05)
2015-16	0.65	1.33	0.34	(0.25)
2016-17	1.30	1.24	(0.11)	0.02
2017-18	2.07	1.57	0.30	0.13
2018-19	0.36	1.38	(0.01)	(0.32)

Interim Dividends (Per Share)

Amt	Decl	Ex	Rec	Pay
0.26Q	01/30/2019	03/14/2019	03/15/2019	04/01/2019
0.30Q	04/30/2019	06/13/2019	06/14/2019	07/01/2019
0.325Q	07/23/2019	08/08/2019	08/09/2019	10/01/2019
0.325Q	11/22/2019	12/13/2019	12/16/2019	01/01/2020

Indicated Div: $1.30 (Div. Reinv. Plan)

Valuation Analysis — **Institutional Holding**

Forecast EPS	$2.75	No of Institutions
	(01/17/2020)	750
Market Cap	$9.4 Billion	Shares
Book Value	$3.8 Billion	194,086,336
Price/Book	2.47	% Held
Price/Sales	1.29	91.67

Business Summary: Gas Utilities (MIC: 3.3.1 SIC: 4932 NAIC: 221210)

UGI is a holding company. Through its subsidiaries and affiliates, Co. distributes, stores, transports and markets energy products and related services. Co.'s segments are: AmeriGas Propane, which distributes propane and sells, installs, and services propane appliances, including heating systems; UGI International, which includes liquefied petroleum gas distribution businesses and energy marketing business; Midstream and Marketing, which includes energy-related businesses that conduct energy marketing in the Mid-Atlantic region of the United States; and UGI Utilities, which consists of the regulated natural gas distribution businesses and the regulated electric distribution business.

Recent Developments: For the year ended Sep 30 2019, net income decreased 62.6% to US$307.9 million from US$822.4 million in the prior year. Revenues were US$7.32 billion, down 4.3% from US$7.65 billion the year before. Operating income was US$617.1 million versus US$1.06 billion in the prior year, a decrease of 42.0%. Direct operating expenses rose 6.1% to US$4.32 billion from US$4.07 billion in the comparable period the year before. Indirect operating expenses decreased 5.2% to US$2.38 billion from US$2.51 billion in the equivalent prior-year period.

Prospects: Our evaluation of UGI Corp. as of October 4th, 2019 is the result of our systematic analysis on three basic characteristics: earnings strength, relative valuation, and recent stock price movement. The company has enjoyed a very positive trend in earnings per share over the past 5 quarters. However, recent analyst estimates for the company have been reduced, and UGI has posted results that fell short of analysts' expectations. Based on operating earnings yield, the company is fairly valued when compared to all of the companies we cover. Share price changes over the past year indicates that UGI will perform in line with the market over the near term.

Financial Data

(US$ in Thousands)	09/30/2019	09/30/2018	09/30/2017	09/30/2016	09/30/2015	09/30/2014	09/30/2013	09/30/2012
Earnings Per Share	1.41	4.06	2.46	2.08	1.60	1.92	1.61	1.17
Cash Flow Per Share	6.04	6.24	5.55	5.58	6.72	5.82	4.69	4.18
Tang Book Value Per Share	N.M.	0.04	N.M.	N.M.	N.M.	N.M.	N.M.	N.M.
Dividends Per Share	1.145	1.020	0.975	0.930	0.890	0.791	0.737	0.707
Dividend Payout %	81.21	25.12	39.63	44.71	55.63	41.19	45.85	60.23
Income Statement								
Total Revenue	7,320,400	7,651,200	6,120,700	5,685,700	6,691,100	8,277,300	7,194,700	6,519,200
EBITDA	1,091,700	1,532,200	1,276,200	1,277,500	1,148,500	1,307,700	1,130,300	769,800
Depn & Amortn	448,100	455,100	357,300	338,600	313,200	305,700	301,400	264,200
Income Before Taxes	391,400	850,200	697,100	710,200	594,200	767,900	590,800	286,500
Income Taxes	92,600	32,100	177,600	221,200	179,000	235,200	162,800	99,600
Net Income	256,200	718,700	436,600	364,700	281,000	337,200	278,100	199,400
Average Shares	181,111	176,905	177,159	175,572	175,667	175,231	173,281	170,148
Balance Sheet								
Current Assets	1,566,200	1,888,100	1,697,500	1,423,800	1,459,800	1,663,000	1,627,300	1,504,500
Total Assets	13,346,600	11,980,900	11,582,200	10,847,200	10,546,600	10,093,000	10,008,800	9,709,700
Current Liabilities	2,026,900	1,732,100	1,690,100	1,442,000	1,678,900	1,430,900	1,424,900	1,487,000
Long-Term Obligations	5,779,900	4,146,500	3,994,600	3,766,000	3,441,800	3,433,600	3,542,200	3,347,600
Total Liabilities	9,529,100	8,299,500	8,418,900	7,996,300	7,854,600	7,433,900	7,516,300	7,476,600
Stockholders' Equity	3,817,500	3,681,400	3,163,300	2,850,900	2,692,000	2,659,100	2,492,500	2,233,100
Shares Outstanding	209,004	173,748	173,143	172,960	172,388	172,273	171,643	168,930
Statistical Record								
Return on Assets %	2.02	6.10	3.89	3.40	2.72	3.35	2.82	2.43
Return on Equity %	6.83	21.00	14.52	13.12	10.50	13.09	11.77	9.45
EBITDA Margin %	14.91	20.03	20.85	22.47	17.16	15.80	15.71	11.81
Net Margin %	3.50	9.39	7.13	6.41	4.20	4.07	3.87	3.06
Asset Turnover	0.58	0.65	0.55	0.53	0.65	0.82	0.73	0.79
Current Ratio	0.77	1.09	1.00	0.99	0.87	1.16	1.14	1.01
Debt to Equity	1.51	1.13	1.26	1.32	1.28	1.29	1.42	1.50
Price Range	58.96-46.50	55.58-42.53	51.68-42.07	48.05-31.67	39.60-31.78	36.33-25.50	28.69-20.33	21.17-16.59
P/E Ratio	41.82-32.98	13.69-10.48	21.01-17.10	23.10-15.23	24.75-19.86	18.92-13.28	17.82-12.63	18.09-14.18
Average Yield %	2.15	2.09	2.04	2.34	2.50	2.61	2.99	3.68

Address: 460 North Gulph Road, King of Prussia, PA 19406 Telephone: 610-337-1000	Web Site: www.ugicorp.com Officers: Frank S. Hermance - Chairman Marvin O. Schlanger - Chairman, Vice-Chairman	Auditors: Ernst & Young LLP Investor Contact: 610-337-1000 Transfer Agents: ComputerShare Investor Services, Providence, RI

UNDER ARMOUR INC

Exchange	Symbol	Price	52Wk Range	Yield	P/E
NYS	UAA	$21.60 (12/31/2019)	27.51-16.99	N/A	144.00

*7 Year Price Score 65.06 *NYSE Composite Index=100 *12 Month Price Score 86.21

Interim Earnings (Per Share)

Qtr.	Mar	Jun	Sep	Dec
2016	0.04	(0.12)	0.29	0.24
2017	(0.01)	(0.03)	0.12	(0.31)
2018	(0.07)	(0.21)	0.17	(0.09)
2019	0.05	(0.04)	0.23	...

Interim Dividends (Per Share)

No Dividends Paid

Valuation Analysis   **Institutional Holding**

Forecast EPS	$0.34	No of Institutions
	(01/17/2020)	718
Market Cap	$9.8 Billion	Shares
Book Value	$2.2 Billion	198,509,904
Price/Book	4.53	% Held
Price/Sales	1.87	96.24

Business Summary: Apparel, Footwear & Accessories (MIC: 1.4.2 SIC: 5136 NAIC: 448110)

Under Armour is engaged in the development, marketing and distribution of apparel, footwear and accessories for men, women and youth. Co. provides HEATGEAR® which is designed to be worn in warm to hot temperatures under equipment or as a single layer and COLDGEAR® which is designed to wick moisture from the body while circulating body heat from hot spots to help maintain core body temperature. Co.'s footwear offerings include running, basketball, cleated, slides and performance training, sportstyle, and outdoor footwear. Co. provides digital fitness subscriptions, along with digital advertising through its MapMyFitness, MyFitnessPal and Endomondo applications.

Recent Developments: For the quarter ended Sep 30 2019, net income increased 35.9% to US$102.3 million from US$75.3 million in the year-earlier quarter. Revenues were US$1.43 billion, down 0.9% from US$1.44 billion the year before. Operating income was US$138.9 million versus US$119.0 million in the prior-year quarter, an increase of 16.8%. Direct operating expenses declined 4.9% to US$739.6 million from US$777.8 million in the comparable period the year before. Indirect operating expenses increased 0.9% to US$551.0 million from US$546.2 million in the equivalent prior-year period.

Prospects: Our evaluation of Under Armour Inc. as of October 4th, 2019 is the result of our systematic analysis on three basic characteristics: earnings strength, relative valuation, and recent stock price movement. The company has generated a negative trend in earnings per share over the past 5 quarters. However, recent analyst estimates for the company have been unchanged while UAA has posted results that exceeded analysts' expectations. Based on operating earnings yield, the company is overvalued when compared to all of the companies we cover. Share price changes over the past year indicates that UAA will perform well over the near term.

Financial Data

(US$ in Thousands)	9 Mos	6 Mos	3 Mos	12/31/2018	12/31/2017	12/31/2016	12/31/2015	12/31/2014
Earnings Per Share	0.15	0.09	(0.08)	(0.20)	(0.22)	0.45	0.53	0.47
Cash Flow Per Share	1.36	1.32	1.15	2.84	1.07	1.39	(0.10)	0.51
Tang Book Value Per Share	3.49	3.24	3.24	3.18	3.20	3.20	2.33	2.81
Income Statement								
Total Revenue	3,825,907	2,396,451	1,204,722	5,193,185	4,976,553	4,825,335	3,963,313	3,084,370
EBITDA	160,663	22,109	34,655	139,180	188,529	545,416	488,413	411,145
Depn & Amortn	190	127	63	173,400	164,300	130,700	87,100	63,600
Income Before Taxes	144,592	11,756	30,354	(67,788)	(10,309)	388,282	386,685	342,210
Income Taxes	31,735	2,391	8,131	(20,552)	37,951	131,303	154,112	134,168
Net Income	107,443	5,128	22,477	(46,302)	(48,260)	256,979	232,573	208,042
Average Shares	454,695	451,066	453,230	221,001	219,254	221,944	441,736	438,760
Balance Sheet								
Current Assets	2,459,089	2,444,447	2,206,708	2,593,628	2,337,679	1,965,153	1,498,763	1,549,399
Total Assets	4,633,765	4,679,908	4,436,072	4,245,022	4,006,367	3,644,331	2,868,900	2,095,083
Current Liabilities	1,199,661	1,332,641	1,094,012	1,315,977	1,060,375	685,816	478,810	421,627
Long-Term Obligations	591,995	591,396	590,431	703,834	765,046	790,388	627,000	255,250
Total Liabilities	2,480,099	2,631,634	2,386,265	2,228,151	1,987,725	1,613,431	1,200,678	744,783
Stockholders' Equity	2,153,666	2,048,274	2,049,807	2,016,871	2,018,642	2,030,900	1,668,222	1,350,300
Shares Outstanding	451,532	451,247	450,918	448,582	442,082	438,438	432,192	427,791
Statistical Record								
Return on Assets %	2.52	1.90	0.15	N.M.	N.M.	7.87	9.37	11.33
Return on Equity %	5.37	4.26	0.32	N.M.	N.M.	13.86	15.41	17.31
EBITDA Margin %	4.20	0.92	2.88	2.68	3.79	11.30	12.32	13.33
Net Margin %	2.81	0.21	1.87	N.M.	N.M.	5.33	5.87	6.75
Asset Turnover	1.18	1.17	1.20	1.26	1.30	1.48	1.60	1.68
Current Ratio	2.05	1.83	2.02	1.97	2.20	2.87	3.13	3.67
Debt to Equity	0.27	0.29	0.29	0.35	0.38	0.39	0.38	0.19
Price Range	27.51-16.75	27.27-16.75	24.31-16.08	24.31-12.92	30.71-11.61	46.99-29.05	53.78-33.17	37.55-21.18
P/E Ratio	183.40-111.67	303.00-186.11	...	...	...	104.42-64.56	101.46-62.59	79.89-45.06

Address: 1020 Hull Street, Baltimore, MD 21230	**Web Site:** www.underarmour.com	**Auditors:** PricewaterhouseCoopers LLP
Telephone: 410-454-6428	**Officers:** Kevin A. Plank - Executive Chairman, Chairman, Chief Executive Officer, Brand Chief Patrik Frisk - President, Chief Executive Officer, Principal Executive Officer, Chief Operating Officer	**Investor Contact:** 410-454-6428 **Transfer Agents:** American Stock Transfer & Trust Company, New York, NY

UNION PACIFIC CORP

Exchange	Symbol	Price	52Wk Range	Yield	P/E	Div Acheiver
NYS	UNP	$180.79 (12/31/2019)	181.41-132.68	2.15	21.29	12 Years

*7 Year Price Score 123.00 *NYSE Composite Index=100 *12 Month Price Score 99.26

Interim Earnings (Per Share)

Qtr.	Mar	Jun	Sep	Dec
2016	1.16	1.17	1.36	1.39
2017	1.32	1.45	1.50	9.10
2018	1.68	1.98	2.15	2.12
2019	1.93	2.22	2.22	...

Interim Dividends (Per Share)

Amt	Decl	Ex	Rec	Pay
0.88Q	02/07/2019	02/27/2019	02/28/2019	03/29/2019
0.88Q	05/16/2019	05/30/2019	05/31/2019	06/28/2019
0.97Q	07/25/2019	08/29/2019	08/30/2019	09/30/2019
0.97Q	11/14/2019	11/27/2019	11/29/2019	12/30/2019

Indicated Div: $3.88

Valuation Analysis / Institutional Holding

Forecast EPS	$8.41	No of Institutions
	(01/17/2020)	2503
Market Cap	$125.7 Billion	Shares
Book Value	$18.0 Billion	659,539,520
Price/Book	6.98	% Held
Price/Sales	5.65	68.09

Business Summary: Rail (MIC: 7.4.3 SIC: 4011 NAIC: 482111)

Union Pacific, through its operating subsidiary, Union Pacific Railroad Company, is a Class I railroad operating in the U.S. Co.'s network included route miles, linking Pacific Coast and Gulf Coast ports with the Midwest and eastern U.S. gateways and providing several corridors to key Mexican gateways. Co. serves the western two-thirds of the country and maintains coordinated schedules with other rail carriers for the handling of freight to and from the Atlantic Coast, the Pacific Coast, the Southeast, the Southwest, Canada, and Mexico. Co.'s commodity groups includes agricultural products, energy, industrial, and premium.

Recent Developments: For the quarter ended Sep 30 2019, net income decreased 2.4% to US$1.56 billion from US$1.59 billion in the year-earlier quarter. Revenues were US$5.52 billion, down 7.0% from US$5.93 billion the year before. Operating income was US$2.23 billion versus US$2.27 billion in the prior-year quarter, a decrease of 1.5%. Direct operating expenses declined 15.9% to US$1.31 billion from US$1.56 billion in the comparable period the year before. Indirect operating expenses decreased 6.1% to US$1.97 billion from US$2.10 billion in the equivalent prior-year period.

Prospects: Our evaluation of Union Pacific Corp. as of October 4th, 2019, is the result of our systematic analysis on three basic characteristics: earnings strength, relative valuation, and recent stock price movement. The company has managed to produce a neutral trend in earnings per share over the past 5 quarters. However, recent analyst estimates for the company have been reduced while UNP has posted results that exceeded analysts' expectations. Based on operating earnings yield, the company is undervalued when compared to all of the companies we cover. Share price changes over the past year indicates that UNP will perform well over the near term.

Financial Data

(US$ in Thousands)	9 Mos	6 Mos	3 Mos	12/31/2018	12/31/2017	12/31/2016	12/31/2015	12/31/2014
Earnings Per Share	8.49	8.42	8.18	7.91	13.36	5.07	5.49	5.75
Cash Flow Per Share	12.26	12.12	12.20	11.57	9.06	9.02	8.48	8.23
Tang Book Value Per Share	25.90	25.78	25.04	28.17	31.83	24.43	24.38	23.99
Dividends Per Share	3.530	3.360	3.210	3.060	2.480	2.255	2.200	1.910
Dividend Payout %	41.58	39.90	39.24	38.69	18.56	44.48	40.07	33.22
Income Statement								
Total Revenue	16,496,000	10,980,000	5,384,000	22,832,000	21,240,000	19,941,000	21,813,000	23,988,000
EBITDA	8,273,000	5,439,000	2,577,000	10,772,000	10,440,000	9,491,000	10,285,000	10,804,000
Depn & Amortn	1,657,000	1,100,000	549,000	2,191,000	2,105,000	2,038,000	2,012,000	1,904,000
Income Before Taxes	5,869,000	3,848,000	1,790,000	7,741,000	7,632,000	6,766,000	7,656,000	8,343,000
Income Taxes	1,353,000	887,000	399,000	1,775,000	(3,080,000)	2,533,000	2,884,000	3,163,000
Net Income	4,516,000	2,961,000	1,391,000	5,966,000	10,712,000	4,233,000	4,772,000	5,180,000
Average Shares	701,900	708,000	719,500	754,300	801,700	835,400	869,400	901,100
Balance Sheet								
Current Assets	4,073,000	4,086,000	3,953,000	4,163,000	4,006,000	3,596,000	4,130,000	4,679,000
Total Assets	61,978,000	61,708,000	61,319,000	59,147,000	57,806,000	55,718,000	54,600,000	52,716,000
Current Liabilities	4,587,000	5,665,000	5,262,000	4,626,000	3,939,000	3,640,000	3,206,000	3,765,000
Long-Term Obligations	25,856,000	24,567,000	25,072,000	20,925,000	16,144,000	14,249,000	13,607,000	11,018,000
Total Liabilities	43,962,000	43,537,000	43,577,000	38,724,000	32,950,000	35,786,000	33,898,000	31,527,000
Stockholders' Equity	18,016,000	18,171,000	17,742,000	20,423,000	24,856,000	19,932,000	20,702,000	21,189,000
Shares Outstanding	695,495	704,942	708,456	725,056	780,917	815,824	849,211	883,366
Statistical Record								
Return on Assets %	10.01	10.15	10.15	10.20	18.87	7.65	8.89	10.11
Return on Equity %	31.40	32.08	28.71	26.35	47.83	20.78	22.78	24.43
EBITDA Margin %	50.15	49.54	47.86	47.18	49.15	47.60	47.15	45.04
Net Margin %	27.38	26.97	25.84	26.13	50.43	21.23	21.88	21.59
Asset Turnover	0.37	0.38	0.38	0.39	0.37	0.36	0.41	0.47
Current Ratio	0.89	0.72	0.75	0.90	1.02	0.99	1.29	1.24
Debt to Equity	1.44	1.35	1.41	1.02	0.65	0.71	0.66	0.52
Price Range	179.95-128.21	179.20-128.21	171.33-128.21	164.99-124.14	136.32-101.40	106.33-68.79	123.83-75.43	123.31-82.58
P/E Ratio	21.20-15.10	21.28-15.23	20.94-15.67	20.86-15.69	10.20-7.59	20.97-13.57	22.56-13.74	21.45-14.36
Average Yield %	2.18	2.13	2.15	2.14	2.24	2.55	2.21	1.89

Address: 1400 Douglas Street, Omaha, NE 68179	**Web Site:** www.up.com	**Auditors:** DELOITTE & TOUCHE LLP
Telephone: 402-544-5000	**Officers:** Lance M. Fritz - Chairman, President, Chief Executive Officer Robert M. Knight - Executive Vice President, Chief Financial Officer	**Investor Contact:** 187-754-77261 **Transfer Agents:** Computershare Investor Services, LLC, Providence, RI

UNITED PARCEL SERVICE INC

Exchange	Symbol	Price	52Wk Range	Yield	P/E
NYS	UPS	$117.06 (12/31/2019)	124.30-92.92	3.28	20.36

*7 Year Price Score 87.31   *NYSE Composite Index=100   *12 Month Price Score 102.33

Interim Earnings (Per Share)

Qtr.	Mar	Jun	Sep	Dec
2016	1.27	1.43	1.44	(0.26)
2017	1.32	1.58	1.45	1.27
2018	1.55	1.71	1.73	0.52
2019	1.28	1.94	2.01	...

Interim Dividends (Per Share)

Amt	Decl	Ex	Rec	Pay
0.96Q	02/15/2019	02/25/2019	02/26/2019	03/12/2019
0.96Q	05/09/2019	05/17/2019	05/20/2019	06/05/2019
0.96Q	08/08/2019	08/16/2019	08/19/2019	09/04/2019
0.96Q	11/07/2019	11/15/2019	11/18/2019	12/04/2019

Indicated Div: $3.84

Valuation Analysis / **Institutional Holding**

Forecast EPS	$7.51	No of Institutions
	(01/17/2020)	2075
Market Cap	$100.4 Billion	Shares
Book Value	$5.6 Billion	610,348,352
Price/Book	18.06	% Held
Price/Sales	1.37	55.49

Business Summary: Airlines/Air Freight (MIC: 7.4.4 SIC: 4215 NAIC: 492110)

United Parcel Service focuses its operations in the field of transportation services, primarily domestic and international letter and package delivery. Co. reports its operations in three segments: U.S. Domestic Package operations, which include the time-definite delivery of letters, documents and packages throughout the U.S.; International Package operations, which include shipments wholly outside the U.S., as well as shipments with either origin or destination outside the U.S.; and Supply Chain and Freight operations, which includes Co.'s Forwarding, Logistics, Coyote, Marken, UPS Mail Innovations, UPS Freight and other aggregated business units.

Recent Developments: For the quarter ended Sep 30 2019, net income increased 16.0% to US$1.75 billion from US$1.51 billion in the year-earlier quarter. Revenues were US$18.32 billion, up 5.0% from US$17.44 billion the year before. Operating income was US$2.13 billion versus US$1.73 billion in the prior-year quarter, an increase of 23.2%. Direct operating expenses declined 5.0% to US$4.29 billion from US$4.52 billion in the comparable period the year before. Indirect operating expenses increased 6.3% to US$11.90 billion from US$11.20 billion in the equivalent prior-year period.

Prospects: Our evaluation of United Parcel Service Inc. as of October 4th, 2019 is the result of our systematic analysis on three basic characteristics: earnings strength, relative valuation, and recent stock price movement. The company has managed to produce a neutral trend in earnings per share over the past 5 quarters. Additionally, recent analyst estimates for the company have been unchanged while UPS has posted results that exceeded analysts' expectations. Based on operating earnings yield, the company is undervalued when compared to all of the companies we cover. Share price changes over the past year indicates that UPS will perform in line with the market over the near term.

Financial Data
(US$ in Millions)

	9 Mos	6 Mos	3 Mos	12/31/2018	12/31/2017	12/31/2016	12/31/2015	12/31/2014
Earnings Per Share	5.75	5.47	5.24	5.51	5.61	3.87	5.35	3.28
Cash Flow Per Share	10.40	11.23	12.61	14.68	1.70	7.31	8.25	6.25
Dividends Per Share	3.790	3.740	3.690	3.640	3.320	3.120	2.920	2.680
Dividend Payout %	65.91	68.37	70.42	66.06	59.18	80.62	54.58	81.71
Income Statement								
Total Revenue	53,526	35,208	17,160	71,861	65,872	60,906	58,363	58,232
EBITDA	8,067	5,115	2,177	8,831	9,883	7,741	9,767	6,913
Depn & Amortn	1,730	1,143	568	2,207	2,282	2,224	2,084	1,923
Income Before Taxes	5,850	3,644	1,440	6,019	7,148	5,136	7,342	4,637
Income Taxes	1,304	848	329	1,228	2,238	1,705	2,498	1,605
Net Income	4,546	2,796	1,111	4,791	4,910	3,431	4,844	3,032
Average Shares	870	869	869	870	875	887	906	924
Balance Sheet								
Current Assets	14,184	14,843	14,904	16,210	15,548	13,849	13,208	11,808
Total Assets	53,282	52,787	52,061	50,016	45,403	40,377	38,311	35,471
Current Liabilities	12,835	13,633	13,209	14,087	12,708	11,730	10,696	8,639
Long-Term Obligations	21,740	20,427	20,377	19,931	20,278	12,394	11,316	9,864
Total Liabilities	47,724	48,382	48,594	46,995	44,403	39,972	35,841	33,330
Stockholders' Equity	5,558	4,405	3,467	3,021	1,000	405	2,470	2,141
Shares Outstanding	857	858	861	858	859	868	886	905
Statistical Record								
Return on Assets %	10.00	9.71	9.44	10.04	11.45	8.70	13.13	8.46
Return on Equity %	115.50	141.30	189.44	238.30	698.93	238.03	210.11	70.39
EBITDA Margin %	15.07	14.53	12.69	12.29	15.00	12.71	16.73	11.87
Net Margin %	8.49	7.94	6.47	6.67	7.45	5.63	8.30	5.21
Asset Turnover	1.47	1.48	1.49	1.51	1.54	1.54	1.58	1.62
Current Ratio	1.11	1.09	1.13	1.15	1.22	1.18	1.23	1.37
Debt to Equity	3.91	4.64	5.88	6.60	20.28	30.60	4.58	4.61
Price Range	122.85-89.89	124.66-89.89	124.66-89.89	134.09-89.89	123.72-102.87	120.16-88.70	114.25-94.46	112.45-93.62
P/E Ratio	21.37-15.63	22.79-16.43	23.79-17.15	24.34-16.31	22.05-18.34	31.05-22.92	21.36-17.66	34.28-28.54
Average Yield %	3.50	3.43	3.32	3.21	2.97	2.95	2.90	2.66

Address: 55 Glenlake Parkway N.E., Atlanta, GA 30328 **Telephone:** 404-828-6000	**Web Site:** www.ups.com **Officers:** David P. Abney - Chairman, Senior Vice President, Chief Executive Officer, Chief Operating Officer Norman M. Brothers - Senior Vice President, General Counsel, Corporate Secretary	**Auditors:** Deloitte & Touche LLP **Investor Contact:** 404-828-6059 **Transfer Agents:** Computershare Shareowner Services, Pittsburgh, PA

UNITED RENTALS INC

Exchange	Symbol	Price	52Wk Range	Yield	P/E
NYS	URI	$166.77 (12/31/2019)	169.82-101.98	N/A	11.51

*7 Year Price Score 102.99 *NYSE Composite Index=100 *12 Month Price Score 113.96

Interim Earnings (Per Share)

Qtr.	Mar	Jun	Sep	Dec
2016	1.01	1.52	2.16	1.79
2017	1.27	1.65	2.33	10.47
2018	2.15	3.20	4.01	3.78
2019	2.19	3.44	5.08	...

Interim Dividends (Per Share)

No Dividends Paid

Valuation Analysis

		Institutional Holding	
Forecast EPS	$19.21	No of Institutions	
	(01/17/2020)	962	
Market Cap	$12.6 Billion	Shares	
Book Value	$3.7 Billion	97,375,368	
Price/Book	3.46	% Held	
Price/Sales	1.37	78.46	

Business Summary: Construction Services (MIC: 7.5.4 SIC: 7359 NAIC: 532412)

United Rentals is an equipment rental company that operates throughout the U.S. and Canada. Co.'s segments are: general rentals, which includes the rental of construction, aerial and industrial equipment, general tools and light equipment, and related services and activities; and trench, power and fluid solutions, which includes the rental of specialty construction products and related services. The types of equipment that Co. provides include general construction and industrial equipment; aerial work platforms; trench safety equipment; power and heating, ventilating and air conditioning equipment; fluid solutions equipment; and general tools and light equipment.

Recent Developments: For the quarter ended Sep 30 2019, net income increased 17.4% to US$391.0 million from US$333.0 million in the year-earlier quarter. Revenues were US$2.49 billion, up 17.6% from US$2.12 billion the year before. Operating income was US$656.0 million versus US$578.0 million in the prior-year quarter, an increase of 13.5%. Direct operating expenses rose 23.5% to US$1.46 billion from US$1.18 billion in the comparable period the year before. Indirect operating expenses increased 4.7% to US$377.0 million from US$360.0 million in the equivalent prior-year period.

Prospects: Our evaluation of United Rentals Inc. as of October 4th, 2019 is the result of our systematic analysis on three basic characteristics: earnings strength, relative valuation, and recent stock price movement. The company has managed to produce a neutral trend in earnings per share over the past 5 quarters. Additionally, recent analyst estimates for the company have been unchanged while URI has posted results that exceeded analysts' expectations. Based on operating earnings yield, the company is undervalued when compared to all of the companies we cover. Share price changes over the past year indicates that URI will perform poorly over the near term.

Financial Data

(US$ in Thousands)	9 Mos	6 Mos	3 Mos	12/31/2018	12/31/2017	12/31/2016	12/31/2015	12/31/2014
Earnings Per Share	14.49	13.42	13.18	13.12	15.73	6.45	6.07	5.15
Cash Flow Per Share	43.18	35.70	36.25	34.52	26.36	22.33	20.96	18.47
Income Statement								
Total Revenue	6,895,000	4,407,000	2,117,000	8,047,000	6,641,000	5,762,000	5,817,000	5,685,000
EBITDA	2,781,000	1,704,000	770,000	3,320,000	2,636,000	2,410,000	2,506,000	2,326,000
Depn & Amortn	1,222,000	802,000	399,000	1,363,000	1,124,000	990,000	976,000	921,000
Income Before Taxes	1,081,000	571,000	220,000	1,476,000	1,048,000	909,000	963,000	850,000
Income Taxes	245,000	126,000	45,000	380,000	(298,000)	343,000	378,000	310,000
Net Income	836,000	445,000	175,000	1,096,000	1,346,000	566,000	585,000	540,000
Average Shares	76,857	78,467	80,047	83,530	85,562	87,775	96,379	104,956
Balance Sheet								
Current Assets	1,881,000	1,840,000	1,720,000	1,761,000	1,772,000	1,361,000	1,294,000	1,546,000
Total Assets	19,405,000	19,047,000	18,586,000	18,133,000	15,030,000	11,988,000	12,083,000	12,467,000
Current Liabilities	2,643,000	2,535,000	2,238,000	2,116,000	1,668,000	1,184,000	1,233,000	1,478,000
Long-Term Obligations	10,691,000	10,700,000	10,676,000	10,844,000	8,717,000	7,193,000	7,555,000	7,434,000
Total Liabilities	15,755,000	15,569,000	15,211,000	14,730,000	11,924,000	10,340,000	10,607,000	10,669,000
Stockholders' Equity	3,650,000	3,478,000	3,375,000	3,403,000	3,106,000	1,648,000	1,476,000	1,798,000
Shares Outstanding	75,750	77,431	78,812	79,872	84,463	84,222	91,776	97,877
Statistical Record								
Return on Assets %	6.41	6.37	6.54	6.61	9.96	4.69	4.77	4.56
Return on Equity %	32.82	32.76	33.83	33.68	56.63	36.14	35.74	29.62
EBITDA Margin %	40.33	38.67	36.37	41.26	39.69	41.83	43.08	40.91
Net Margin %	12.12	10.10	8.27	13.62	20.27	9.82	10.06	9.50
Asset Turnover	0.51	0.52	0.51	0.49	0.49	0.48	0.47	0.48
Current Ratio	0.71	0.73	0.77	0.83	1.06	1.15	1.05	1.05
Debt to Equity	2.93	3.08	3.16	3.19	2.81	4.36	5.12	4.13
Price Range	165.53-95.90	171.76-95.90	180.00-95.90	189.40-95.90	173.33-101.62	109.12-43.34	105.13-59.48	119.02-74.46
P/E Ratio	11.42-6.62	12.80-7.15	13.66-7.28	14.44-7.31	11.02-6.46	16.92-6.72	17.32-9.80	23.11-14.46

Address: 100 First Stamford Place, Suite 700, Stamford, CT 06902 Telephone: 203-622-3131	Web Site: www.unitedrentals.com Officers: Matthew J. (Matt) Flannery - President, Executive Vice President, Senior Vice President, Chief Executive Officer, Chief Operating Officer Jessica T. Graziano - Executive Vice President, Senior Vice President, Vice President, Chief Financial Officer, Controller, Principal Accounting Officer	Auditors: Ernst & Young LLP Investor Contact: 203-618-7318 Transfer Agents: American Stock Transfer & Trust Company, New York, NY

UNITED STATES STEEL CORP.

Exchange	Symbol	Price	52Wk Range	Yield	P/E
NYS	X	$11.41 (12/31/2019)	24.12-10.09	1.75	3.22

*7 Year Price Score 54.23 *NYSE Composite Index=100 *12 Month Price Score 79.17

Interim Earnings (Per Share)

Qtr.	Mar	Jun	Sep	Dec
2016	(2.32)	(0.32)	0.32	(0.59)
2017	(1.03)	1.48	0.83	0.90
2018	0.10	1.20	1.62	3.33
2019	0.31	0.39	(0.49)	...

Interim Dividends (Per Share)

Amt	Decl	Ex	Rec	Pay
0.05Q	01/30/2019	02/12/2019	02/13/2019	03/08/2019
0.05Q	05/02/2019	05/10/2019	05/13/2019	06/10/2019
0.05Q	08/01/2019	08/13/2019	08/14/2019	09/10/2019
0.05Q	10/31/2019	11/12/2019	11/13/2019	12/10/2019

Indicated Div: $0.20

Valuation Analysis

		Institutional Holding	
Forecast EPS	$-0.41	No of Institutions	593
	(01/17/2020)		
Market Cap	$1.9 Billion	Shares	148,369,408
Book Value	$4.2 Billion	% Held	68.45
Price/Book	0.46		
Price/Sales	0.14		

Business Summary: Non-Precious Metals (MIC: 8.2.2 SIC: 3312 NAIC: 331111)

United States Steel is a steel producer of flat-rolled and tubular products with production operations in the U.S. and Europe. Co. is also engaged in railroad services and real estate operations. Co.'s segments are: North American Flat-Rolled, which produces slabs, strip mill plates, sheets and tin mill products; U. S. Steel Europe, which produces and sells slabs, strip mill plate, sheet, tin mill products and spiral welded pipe, as well as heating radiators and refractory ceramic materials; and Tubular Products, which produces and sells seamless and electric resistance welded steel casing and tubing (known as oil country tubular goods), and standard and line pipe and mechanical tubing.

Recent Developments: For the quarter ended Sep 30 2019, net loss amounted to US$84.0 million versus net income of US$291.0 million in the year-earlier quarter. Revenues were US$3.07 billion, down 17.7% from US$3.73 billion the year before. Operating loss was US$80.0 million versus an income of US$373.0 million in the prior-year quarter. Direct operating expenses declined 8.5% to US$2.90 billion from US$3.17 billion in the comparable period the year before. Indirect operating expenses increased 34.2% to US$247.0 million from US$184.0 million in the equivalent prior-year period.

Prospects: Our evaluation of United States Steel Corp. as of October 4th, 2019 is the result of our systematic analysis on three basic characteristics: earnings strength, relative valuation, and recent stock price movement. The company has suffered a very negative trend in earnings per share over the past 5 quarters. In addition, recent analyst estimates for the company have been reduced while X has posted results that exceeded analysts' expectations. Based on operating earnings yield, the company is undervalued when compared to all of the companies we cover. Share price changes over the past year indicates that X will perform poorly over the near term.

Financial Data

(US$ in Millions)	9 Mos	6 Mos	3 Mos	12/31/2018	12/31/2017	12/31/2016	12/31/2015	12/31/2014
Earnings Per Share	3.54	5.65	6.46	6.25	2.19	(2.81)	(11.24)	0.69
Cash Flow Per Share	3.58	5.88	6.15	5.31	4.59	4.63	2.46	10.28
Tang Book Value Per Share	23.80	24.26	23.60	23.17	17.99	12.08	15.31	24.68
Dividends Per Share	0.200	0.200	0.200	0.200	0.200	0.200	0.200	0.200
Dividend Payout %	5.65	3.54	3.10	3.20	9.13	...	...	28.99
Income Statement								
Total Revenue	10,113	7,044	3,499	14,178	12,250	10,261	11,574	17,507
EBITDA	463	436	222	1,379	967	218	(739)	877
Depn & Amortn	454	293	143	521	501	507	547	627
Income Before Taxes	(73)	86	53	713	257	(514)	(1,497)	28
Income Taxes	(43)	1	8	(303)	(86)	24	183	68
Net Income	38	122	54	1,115	387	(440)	(1,642)	102
Average Shares	170	172	174	178	176	156	146	152
Balance Sheet								
Current Assets	4,042	4,547	4,630	4,830	4,755	4,356	3,917	6,431
Total Assets	10,917	11,291	11,152	10,982	9,862	9,160	9,190	12,314
Current Liabilities	2,850	3,223	3,140	3,197	2,721	2,331	2,148	3,569
Long-Term Obligations	2,500	2,345	2,326	2,316	2,700	2,981	3,116	3,120
Total Liabilities	6,718	6,980	6,917	6,780	6,542	6,886	6,754	8,515
Stockholders' Equity	4,199	4,311	4,235	4,202	3,320	2,274	2,436	3,799
Shares Outstanding	170	171	172	174	175	173	146	145
Statistical Record								
Return on Assets %	5.86	9.41	10.87	10.70	4.07	N.M.	N.M.	0.80
Return on Equity %	15.48	25.39	30.00	29.65	13.84	N.M.	N.M.	2.85
EBITDA Margin %	4.58	6.19	6.34	9.73	7.89	2.12	N.M.	5.01
Net Margin %	0.38	1.73	1.54	7.86	3.16	N.M.	N.M.	0.58
Asset Turnover	1.28	1.36	1.37	1.36	1.29	1.12	1.08	1.38
Current Ratio	1.42	1.41	1.47	1.51	1.75	1.87	1.82	1.80
Debt to Equity	0.60	0.54	0.55	0.55	0.81	1.31	1.28	0.82
Price Range	30.25-10.34	38.26-11.82	38.26-17.27	46.01-17.27	41.57-19.17	37.49-6.67	27.33-7.09	46.00-22.73
P/E Ratio	8.55-2.92	6.77-2.09	5.92-2.67	7.36-2.76	18.98-8.75	...	...	66.67-32.94
Average Yield %	1.08	0.85	0.70	0.60	0.71	1.08	1.07	0.66

Address: 600 Grant Street, Pittsburgh, PA 15219-2800 **Telephone:** 412-433-1121 **Fax:** 412-433-4818	**Web Site:** www.ussteel.com **Officers:** David S. Sutherland - Chairman David B. Burritt - President, Chief Executive Officer, Executive Vice President, Chief Financial Officer, Chief Operating Officer	**Auditors:** PricewaterhouseCoopers LLP **Investor Contact:** 412-433-1121 **Transfer Agents:** Wells Fargo Bank Shareowner Services, St. Paul, MN

UNITEDHEALTH GROUP INC

Exchange	Symbol	Price	52Wk Range	Yield	P/E
NYS	UNH	$293.98 (12/31/2019)	295.97-215.26	1.47	21.38

*7 Year Price Score 132.45 *NYSE Composite Index=100 *12 Month Price Score 105.34

Interim Earnings (Per Share)

Qtr.	Mar	Jun	Sep	Dec
2016	1.67	1.81	2.03	1.74
2017	2.23	2.32	2.51	3.66
2018	2.87	2.98	3.24	3.10
2019	3.56	3.42	3.67	...

Interim Dividends (Per Share)

Amt	Decl	Ex	Rec	Pay
0.90Q	02/27/2019	03/08/2019	03/11/2019	03/19/2019
1.08Q	06/05/2019	06/14/2019	06/17/2019	06/25/2019
1.08Q	08/13/2019	09/13/2019	09/16/2019	09/24/2019
1.08Q	11/08/2019	12/06/2019	12/09/2019	12/17/2019

Indicated Div: $4.32

Valuation Analysis / Institutional Holding

Forecast EPS	$16.48	No of Institutions
	(01/17/2020)	2606
Market Cap	$278.4 Billion	Shares
Book Value	$55.0 Billion	1,004,572,288
Price/Book	5.06	% Held
Price/Sales	1.16	83.52

Business Summary: Life & Health (MIC: 5.2.2 SIC: 6324 NAIC: 524114)

UnitedHealth Group is a health care company. Co. has four reportable segments across its two business platforms, UnitedHealthcare and Optum: UnitedHealthcare, which provides health care benefits to an array of customers and markets through its UnitedHealthcare Employer & Individual, UnitedHealthcare Medicare & Retirement, UnitedHealthcare Community & State and UnitedHealthcare Global; OptumHealth, which serves the physical, emotional and health-related financial needs of individuals; OptumInsight, which provides services, technology and health care knowledge to main participants in the health care industry; and OptumRx, which provides pharmacy care services and programs.

Recent Developments: For the quarter ended Sep 30 2019, net income increased 10.5% to US$3.63 billion from US$3.28 billion in the year-earlier quarter. Revenues were US$60.35 billion, up 6.7% from US$56.56 billion the year before. Net premiums earned were US$47.40 billion versus US$44.61 billion in the prior-year quarter, an increase of 6.2%.

Prospects: Our evaluation of UnitedHealth Group Inc. as of October 4th, 2019 is the result of our systematic analysis on three basic characteristics: earnings strength, relative valuation, and recent stock price movement. The company has managed to produce a neutral trend in earnings per share over the past 5 quarters. In addition, recent analyst estimates for the company have been mixed and UNH has posted results that exceeded analysts' expectations. Based on operating earnings yield, the company is undervalued when compared to all of the companies we cover. Share price changes over the past year indicates that UNH will perform in line with the market over the near term.

Financial Data
(US$ in Thousands)

	9 Mos	6 Mos	3 Mos	12/31/2018	12/31/2017	12/31/2016	12/31/2015	12/31/2014
Earnings Per Share	13.75	13.32	12.88	12.19	10.72	7.25	6.01	5.70
Cash Flow Per Share	15.44	13.10	11.04	16.32	14.10	10.26	10.22	8.28
Dividends Per Share	3.960	3.780	3.600	3.450	2.875	2.375	1.875	1.405
Dividend Payout %	28.80	28.38	27.95	28.30	26.82	32.76	31.20	24.65
Income Statement								
Total Revenue	181,254,000	120,903,000	60,308,000	226,247,000	201,159,000	184,840,000	157,107,000	130,474,000
Income Before Taxes	13,323,000	8,758,000	4,432,000	15,944,000	14,023,000	11,863,000	10,231,000	9,656,000
Income Taxes	2,752,000	1,816,000	875,000	3,562,000	3,200,000	4,790,000	4,363,000	4,037,000
Net Income	10,298,000	6,760,000	3,467,000	11,986,000	10,558,000	7,017,000	5,813,000	5,619,000
Average Shares	963,000	964,000	975,000	983,000	985,000	968,000	967,000	986,000
Balance Sheet								
Total Assets	173,709,000	167,200,000	161,197,000	152,221,000	139,058,000	122,810,000	111,383,000	86,382,000
Total Liabilities	118,713,000	114,097,000	109,473,000	100,525,000	91,282,000	84,536,000	77,553,000	53,928,000
Stockholders' Equity	54,996,000	53,103,000	51,724,000	51,696,000	47,776,000	38,274,000	33,830,000	32,454,000
Shares Outstanding	947,000	948,000	953,000	960,000	969,000	952,000	953,000	954,000
Statistical Record								
Return on Assets %	8.21	8.07	7.97	8.23	8.06	5.98	5.88	6.68
Return on Equity %	25.40	25.62	25.42	24.10	24.54	19.41	17.54	17.40
Net Margin %	5.68	5.59	5.75	5.30	5.25	3.80	3.70	4.31
Price Range	286.33-215.26	286.33-216.84	286.33-217.20	286.33-212.55	228.17-157.62	163.94-109.23	125.86-98.92	103.04-69.74
P/E Ratio	20.82-15.66	21.50-16.28	22.23-16.86	23.49-17.44	21.28-14.70	22.61-15.07	20.94-16.46	18.08-12.24
Average Yield %	1.58	1.48	1.41	1.39	1.54	1.75	1.61	1.68

Address: UnitedHealth Group Center, 9900 Bren Road East, Minnetonka, MN 55343 **Telephone:** 952-936-1300	**Web Site:** www.unitedhealthgroup.com **Officers:** Stephen J. Hemsley - Executive Chairman, Chairman, President, Chief Executive Officer, Chief Operating Officer Larry C. Renfro - Vice-Chairman, Executive Vice President, Division Officer	**Auditors:** Deloitte & Touche LLP **Investor Contact:** 800-328-5979 **Transfer Agents:** EQ Shareowner Services, St. Paul, MN

UNITED STATES CELLULAR CORP

Exchange	Symbol	Price	52Wk Range	Yield	P/E
NYS	USM	$36.23 (12/31/2019)	59.06-31.49	N/A	24.65

*7 Year Price Score 90.32   ***NYSE Composite Index=100**   ***12 Month Price Score 74.09**

Interim Earnings (Per Share)

Qtr.	Mar	Jun	Sep	Dec
2016	0.10	0.32	0.20	(0.07)
2017	0.31	0.14	(3.51)	3.21
2018	0.52	0.56	0.41	0.23
2019	0.62	0.35	0.27	...

Interim Dividends (Per Share)

Dividend Payment Suspended

Valuation Analysis

		Institutional Holding	
Forecast EPS	$1.20	No of Institutions	
	(01/09/2020)	219	
Market Cap	$3.1 Billion	Shares	
Book Value	$4.2 Billion	17,315,188	
Price/Book	0.75	% Held	
Price/Sales	0.77	17.96	

Business Summary: Services (MIC: 6.1.2 SIC: 4812 NAIC: 517212)

United States Cellular provides wireless telecommunications services. Co.'s customers are able to choose from a variety of national plans with voice, messaging and data usage options and pricing. Co.'s fourth generation Long-Term Evolution network features smartphone messaging, data and internet services that allow customers to access the internet; text, picture and video message; utilize GPS navigation; and browse and download applications to customize their wireless devices to fit their lifestyles. Co. also provides wireless solutions to consumers and business and government customers, including a suite of connected machine-to-machine solutions and software applications.

Recent Developments: For the quarter ended Sep 30 2019, net income decreased 35.1% to US$24.0 million from US$37.0 million in the year-earlier quarter. Revenues were US$1.03 billion, up 3.0% from US$1.00 billion the year before. Operating income was US$20.0 million versus US$34.0 million in the prior-year quarter, a decrease of 41.2%. Direct operating expenses rose 1.5% to US$465.0 million from US$458.0 million in the comparable period the year before. Indirect operating expenses increased 7.3% to US$546.0 million from US$509.0 million in the equivalent prior-year period.

Prospects: Our evaluation of United States Cellular Corp. as of October 4th, 2019 is the result of our systematic analysis on three basic characteristics: earnings strength, relative valuation, and recent stock price movement. The company has generated a negative trend in earnings per share over the past 5 quarters. However, recent analyst estimates for the company have been raised and USM has posted results that fell short of analysts' expectations. Based on operating earnings yield, the company is fairly valued when compared to all of the companies we cover. Share price changes over the past year indicates that USM will perform well over the near term.

Financial Data

(US$ in Thousands)	9 Mos	6 Mos	3 Mos	12/31/2018	12/31/2017	12/31/2016	12/31/2015	12/31/2014
Earnings Per Share	1.47	1.61	1.82	1.72	0.14	0.56	2.84	(0.51)
Cash Flow Per Share	9.26	9.43	9.40	8.24	5.52	5.88	6.59	2.05
Tang Book Value Per Share	19.90	19.46	22.19	21.76	17.11	16.21	16.08	17.70
Income Statement								
Total Revenue	2,970,000	1,939,000	966,000	3,967,000	3,890,000	3,939,000	3,996,853	3,892,747
EBITDA	639,000	439,000	233,000	784,000	300,000	605,000	908,908	449,970
Depn & Amortn	524,000	345,000	169,000	627,000	604,000	607,000	595,500	593,200
Income Before Taxes	42,000	47,000	41,000	56,000	(409,000)	(58,000)	263,546	(188,468)
Income Taxes	55,000	41,000	27,000	51,000	(287,000)	33,000	156,334	(11,782)
Net Income	109,000	86,000	54,000	150,000	12,000	48,000	241,347	(42,812)
Average Shares	88,000	88,000	88,000	87,000	86,000	85,000	84,891	84,213
Balance Sheet								
Current Assets	1,770,000	1,735,000	1,839,000	1,812,000	1,483,000	1,558,000	1,671,642	1,279,175
Total Assets	8,291,000	8,223,000	8,229,000	7,274,000	6,841,000	7,110,000	7,059,978	6,487,268
Current Liabilities	849,000	747,000	802,000	691,000	733,000	718,000	747,938	856,894
Long-Term Obligations	1,592,000	1,596,000	1,601,000	1,605,000	1,622,000	1,618,000	1,628,507	1,151,819
Total Liabilities	4,119,000	4,061,000	4,108,000	3,217,000	3,164,000	3,476,000	3,499,465	3,185,277
Stockholders' Equity	4,172,000	4,162,000	4,121,000	4,057,000	3,677,000	3,634,000	3,560,513	3,301,991
Shares Outstanding	86,000	87,000	86,000	86,000	85,000	85,000	84,359	84,080
Statistical Record								
Return on Assets %	1.66	1.86	2.09	2.13	0.17	0.68	3.56	N.M.
Return on Equity %	3.15	3.50	3.99	3.88	0.33	1.33	7.03	N.M.
EBITDA Margin %	21.52	22.64	24.12	19.76	7.71	15.36	22.74	11.56
Net Margin %	3.67	4.44	5.59	3.78	0.31	1.22	6.04	N.M.
Asset Turnover	0.52	0.52	0.52	0.56	0.56	0.55	0.59	0.60
Current Ratio	2.08	2.32	2.29	2.62	2.02	2.17	2.24	1.49
Debt to Equity	0.38	0.38	0.39	0.40	0.44	0.45	0.46	0.35
Price Range	59.06-34.08	59.06-32.81	59.06-32.81	58.26-32.76	45.67-32.95	45.87-33.97	43.36-34.42	44.45-31.93
P/E Ratio	40.18-23.18	36.68-20.38	32.45-18.03	33.87-19.05	326.21-235.36	81.91-60.66	15.27-12.12	...

Address: 8410 West Bryn Mawr,	Web Site: www.uscellular.com	Auditors: PricewaterhouseCoopers LLP
Chicago, IL 60631	Officers: LeRoy T. Carlson - Chairman Kenneth R.	Investor Contact: 312-592-5341
Telephone: 773-399-8900	Meyers - President, Chief Executive Officer, Vice	Transfer Agents: Computershare Trust
	President, Assistant Treasurer	Company, N.A., Louisville, KY

US BANCORP (DE)

Exchange	Symbol	Price	52Wk Range	Yield	P/E
NYS	USB	$59.29 (12/31/2019)	60.68-45.70	2.83	13.66

*7 Year Price Score 95.75   *NYSE Composite Index=100   *12 Month Price Score 105.11

Interim Earnings (Per Share)

Qtr.	Mar	Jun	Sep	Dec
2016	0.76	0.83	0.84	0.81
2017	0.82	0.85	0.88	0.96
2018	0.96	1.02	1.06	1.10
2019	1.00	1.09	1.15	...

Interim Dividends (Per Share)

Amt	Decl	Ex	Rec	Pay
0.37Q	03/19/2019	03/28/2019	03/29/2019	04/15/2019
0.37Q	06/18/2019	06/27/2019	06/28/2019	07/15/2019
0.42Q	09/17/2019	09/27/2019	09/30/2019	10/15/2019
0.42Q	12/17/2019	12/30/2019	12/31/2019	01/15/2020

Indicated Div: $1.68

Valuation Analysis / Institutional Holding

Forecast EPS	$4.39	No of Institutions
	(01/17/2020)	2141
Market Cap	$93.2 Billion	Shares
Book Value	$53.5 Billion	1,451,988,608
Price/Book	1.74	% Held
Price/Sales	3.39	70.52

Business Summary: Banking (MIC: 5.1.1 SIC: 6021 NAIC: 522110)

U.S. Bancorp is a multi-state financial services holding company. Through its subsidiaries, Co. provides a range of financial services, including lending and depository services, cash management, capital markets, and trust and investment management services. Co. also engages in credit card services, merchant and ATM processing, mortgage banking, insurance, brokerage and leasing. Co.'s subsidiary, U.S. Bank National Association, is engaged in the general banking business, principally in domestic markets. Co.'s bank and trust subsidiaries provide a range of asset management and fiduciary services for individuals, estates, foundations, business corporations and charitable organizations.

Recent Developments: For the quarter ended Sep 30 2019, net income increased 5.2% to US$1.92 billion from US$1.82 billion in the year-earlier quarter. Net interest income increased 0.9% to US$3.28 billion from US$3.25 billion in the year-earlier quarter. Provision for loan losses was US$367.0 million versus US$343.0 million in the prior-year quarter, an increase of 7.0%. Non-interest income rose 8.1% to US$2.61 billion from US$2.42 billion, while non-interest expense advanced 3.3% to US$3.14 billion.

Prospects: Our evaluation of U.S. Bancorp as of October 4th, 2019 is the result of our systematic analysis on three basic characteristics: earnings strength, relative valuation, and recent stock price movement. The company has managed to produce a neutral trend in earnings per share over the past 5 quarters. However, recent analyst estimates for the company have been reduced while USB has posted results that exceeded analysts' expectations. Based on operating earnings yield, the company is undervalued when compared to all of the companies we cover. Share price changes over the past year indicates that USB will perform in line with the market over the near term.

Financial Data

(US$ in Thousands)	9 Mos	6 Mos	3 Mos	12/31/2018	12/31/2017	12/31/2016	12/31/2015	12/31/2014
Earnings Per Share	4.34	4.25	4.18	4.14	3.51	3.24	3.16	3.08
Cash Flow Per Share	4.83	4.89	6.51	6.47	3.86	3.10	4.98	2.96
Tang Book Value Per Share	22.22	21.60	20.75	20.07	18.70	17.18	16.00	14.66
Dividends Per Share	1.530	1.480	1.410	1.340	1.160	1.070	1.010	0.965
Dividend Payout %	35.25	34.82	33.73	32.37	33.05	33.02	31.96	31.33
Income Statement								
Interest Income	13,239,000	8,802,000	4,351,000	16,173,000	14,385,000	13,167,000	12,402,000	12,228,000
Interest Expense	3,394,000	2,238,000	1,092,000	3,254,000	2,144,000	1,639,000	1,401,000	1,453,000
Net Interest Income	9,845,000	6,564,000	3,259,000	12,919,000	12,241,000	11,528,000	11,001,000	10,775,000
Provision for Losses	1,109,000	742,000	377,000	1,379,000	1,390,000	1,324,000	1,132,000	1,229,000
Non-Interest Income	7,395,000	4,781,000	2,291,000	9,602,000	9,611,000	9,577,000	9,092,000	9,164,000
Non-Interest Expense	9,384,000	6,240,000	3,087,000	12,464,000	12,945,000	11,676,000	10,931,000	10,715,000
Income Before Taxes	6,747,000	4,363,000	2,086,000	8,678,000	7,517,000	8,105,000	8,030,000	7,995,000
Income Taxes	1,294,000	827,000	378,000	1,554,000	1,264,000	2,161,000	2,097,000	2,087,000
Net Income	5,428,000	3,520,000	1,699,000	7,096,000	6,218,000	5,888,000	5,879,000	5,851,000
Average Shares	1,578,000	1,592,000	1,605,000	1,638,000	1,683,000	1,724,000	1,772,000	1,813,000
Balance Sheet								
Net Loans & Leases	295,159,000	291,828,000	286,434,000	284,893,000	280,061,000	274,220,000	260,170,000	248,604,000
Total Assets	487,671,000	481,719,000	475,775,000	467,374,000	462,040,000	445,964,000	421,853,000	402,529,000
Total Deposits	359,715,000	353,177,000	348,087,000	345,475,000	347,215,000	334,590,000	300,400,000	282,733,000
Total Liabilities	434,154,000	428,806,000	423,718,000	416,345,000	413,000,000	398,666,000	375,722,000	359,050,000
Stockholders' Equity	53,517,000	52,913,000	52,057,000	51,029,000	49,040,000	47,298,000	46,131,000	43,479,000
Shares Outstanding	1,571,142	1,584,493	1,599,037	1,608,334	1,655,645	1,696,912	1,745,190	1,785,866
Statistical Record								
Return on Assets %	1.53	1.53	1.52	1.53	1.37	1.35	1.43	1.53
Return on Equity %	14.02	14.03	14.07	14.18	12.91	12.57	13.12	13.83
Net Interest Margin %	73.95	74.25	74.90	79.88	85.10	87.55	88.70	88.12
Efficiency Ratio %	44.59	45.43	46.48	48.36	53.95	51.34	50.86	50.09
Loans to Deposits	0.82	0.83	0.82	0.82	0.81	0.82	0.87	0.88
Price Range	57.38-43.76	55.35-43.76	55.35-43.76	58.11-43.76	56.41-49.69	52.54-37.45	46.02-39.76	45.91-38.78
P/E Ratio	13.22-10.08	13.02-10.30	13.24-10.47	14.04-10.57	16.07-14.16	16.22-11.56	14.56-12.58	14.91-12.59
Average Yield %	2.95	2.87	2.75	2.55	2.20	2.49	2.33	2.30

Address: 800 Nicollet Mall, Minneapolis, MN 55402 Telephone: 651-466-3000	Web Site: www.usbank.com Officers: Andrew Cecere - Chairman, Vice-Chairman, President, Chief Executive Officer, Chief Operating Officer, Chief Financial Officer Terrance R. Dolan - Vice-Chairman, Vice-Chairman (frmr), Executive Vice President, Chief Financial Officer, Controller	Auditors: Ernst & Young LLP Investor Contact: 866-775-9668 Transfer Agents: Computershare, Providence, R.I.

UNITED TECHNOLOGIES CORP

Exchange	Symbol	Price	52Wk Range	Yield	P/E	Div Acheiver
NYS	UTX	$149.76 (12/31/2019)	150.71-103.48	1.96	25.51	25 Years

*7 Year Price Score 95.93   ***NYSE Composite Index=100**   ***12 Month Price Score 105.60**

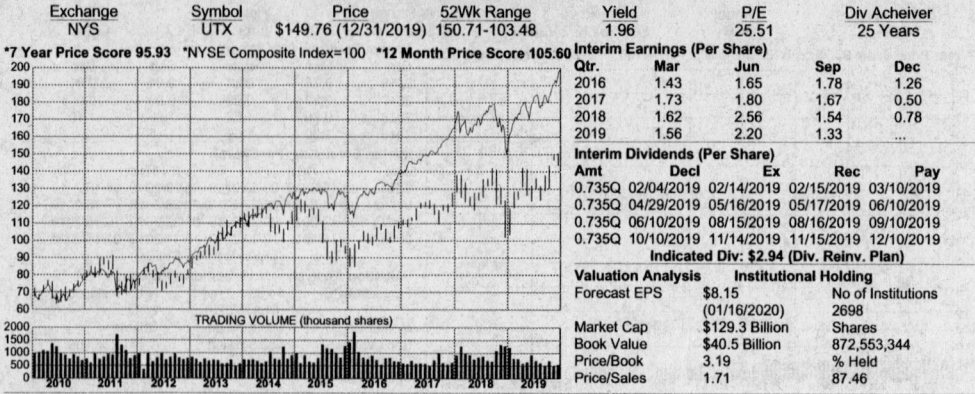

Interim Earnings (Per Share)

Qtr.	Mar	Jun	Sep	Dec
2016	1.43	1.65	1.78	1.26
2017	1.73	1.80	1.67	0.50
2018	1.62	2.56	1.54	0.78
2019	1.56	2.20	1.33	...

Interim Dividends (Per Share)

Amt	Decl	Ex	Rec	Pay
0.735Q	02/04/2019	02/14/2019	02/15/2019	03/10/2019
0.735Q	04/29/2019	05/16/2019	05/17/2019	06/10/2019
0.735Q	06/10/2019	08/15/2019	08/16/2019	09/10/2019
0.735Q	10/10/2019	11/14/2019	11/15/2019	12/10/2019

Indicated Div: $2.94 (Div. Reinv. Plan)

Valuation Analysis   **Institutional Holding**

Forecast EPS	$8.15	No of Institutions
	(01/16/2020)	2698
Market Cap	$129.3 Billion	Shares
Book Value	$40.5 Billion	872,553,344
Price/Book	3.19	% Held
Price/Sales	1.71	87.46

Business Summary: Aerospace (MIC: 7.1.1 SIC: 3724 NAIC: 336412)

United Technologies provides technology products and services to the building systems and aerospace industries. Co. has four segments: Otis, which designs, manufactures, sells and installs passenger and freight elevators; Carrier, which provides heating, ventilating, air conditioning refrigeration, fire, security and building automation products; Pratt & Whitney, which supplies aircraft engines for the commercial, military, business jet and general aviation market; and Collins Aerospace Systems, which provides aerospace products and aftermarket service solutions for aircraft manufacturers, airlines, regional, business and general aviation markets, military, space and undersea operations.

Recent Developments: For the quarter ended Sep 30 2019, net income decreased 6.8% to US$1.26 billion from US$1.35 billion in the year-earlier quarter. Revenues were US$19.50 billion, up 18.1% from US$16.51 billion the year before. Operating income was US$2.49 billion versus US$1.84 billion in the prior-year quarter, an increase of 35.3%. Direct operating expenses rose 13.4% to US$14.21 billion from US$12.54 billion in the comparable period the year before. Indirect operating expenses increased 31.0% to US$2.80 billion from US$2.14 billion in the equivalent prior-year period.

Prospects: Our evaluation of United Technologies Corp. as of October 4th, 2019 is the result of our systematic analysis on three basic characteristics: earnings strength, relative valuation, and recent stock price movement. The company has managed to produce a neutral trend in earnings per share over the past 5 quarters. In addition, recent analyst estimates for the company have been mixed and UTX has posted results that exceeded analysts' expectations. Based on operating earnings yield, the company is undervalued when compared to all of the companies we cover. Share price changes over the past year indicates that UTX will perform in line with the market over the near term.

Financial Data

(US$ in Millions)	9 Mos	6 Mos	3 Mos	12/31/2018	12/31/2017	12/31/2016	12/31/2015	12/31/2014
Earnings Per Share	5.87	6.08	6.44	6.50	5.70	6.12	8.61	6.82
Cash Flow Per Share	9.48	8.64	8.64	7.90	7.13	7.82	7.68	8.17
Dividends Per Share	2.940	2.905	2.870	2.835	2.720	2.620	2.560	2.360
Dividend Payout %	50.09	47.78	44.57	43.62	47.72	42.81	29.73	34.60
Income Statement								
Total Revenue	57,495	37,999	18,365	66,501	59,837	57,244	56,098	65,100
EBITDA	10,673	6,917	3,195	10,558	9,850	9,277	8,359	10,891
Depn & Amortn	2,831	1,864	942	1,240	1,178	1,105	1,068	1,122
Income Before Taxes	6,650	4,262	1,822	8,280	7,763	7,133	6,467	8,887
Income Taxes	1,969	838	397	2,626	2,843	1,697	2,111	2,264
Net Income	4,394	3,246	1,346	5,269	4,552	5,055	7,608	6,220
Average Shares	864	863	860	810	799	826	883	911
Balance Sheet								
Current Assets	37,816	37,058	35,402	35,503	32,858	28,550	26,706	29,758
Total Assets	139,000	138,990	137,380	134,211	96,920	89,706	87,484	91,289
Current Liabilities	35,567	35,422	31,403	31,368	24,391	21,906	22,618	22,895
Long-Term Obligations	37,782	37,910	41,004	41,192	24,989	21,697	19,320	17,872
Total Liabilities	98,541	98,236	97,642	95,765	67,310	62,127	60,126	60,076
Stockholders' Equity	40,468	40,754	39,738	38,446	29,610	27,579	27,358	31,213
Shares Outstanding	863	862	862	861	799	808	838	909
Statistical Record								
Return on Assets %	3.79	4.07	4.27	4.56	4.88	5.69	8.51	6.84
Return on Equity %	13.25	13.58	14.36	15.48	15.92	18.35	25.98	19.72
EBITDA Margin %	18.56	18.20	17.40	15.88	16.46	16.21	14.90	16.73
Net Margin %	7.64	8.54	7.33	7.92	7.61	8.83	13.56	9.55
Asset Turnover	0.59	0.60	0.59	0.58	0.64	0.64	0.63	0.72
Current Ratio	1.06	1.05	1.13	1.13	1.35	1.30	1.18	1.30
Debt to Equity	0.93	0.93	1.03	1.07	0.84	0.79	0.71	0.57
Price Range	142.61-102.06	142.61-102.06	142.08-102.06	142.08-102.06	128.12-108.18	110.98-84.66	124.11-86.82	120.09-99.17
P/E Ratio	24.29-17.39	23.46-16.79	22.06-15.85	21.86-15.70	22.48-18.98	18.13-13.83	14.41-10.08	17.61-14.54
Average Yield %	2.30	2.27	2.28	2.21	2.32	2.59	2.39	2.11

Address: 10 Farm Springs Road, Farmington, CT 06032	**Web Site:** www.utc.com	**Auditors:** PricewaterhouseCoopers LLP
Telephone: 860-728-7000	**Officers:** Thomas A. Kennedy - Executive Chairman	**Transfer Agents:** Computershare Trust
Fax: 860-728-7028	Gregory J. (Greg) Hayes - Chairman, President, Chief Executive Officer, Senior Vice President, Chief Financial Officer	Company, N. A., Canton, MA

UNIVAR SOLUTIONS INC

Exchange	Symbol	Price	52Wk Range	Yield	P/E
NYS	UNVR	$24.24 (12/31/2019)	24.45-17.53	N/A	N/A

*7 Year Price Score N/A   *NYSE Composite Index=100   *12 Month Price Score 102.32

Interim Earnings (Per Share)

Qtr.	Mar	Jun	Sep	Dec
2016	0.10	0.29	(0.46)	(0.43)
2017	0.16	0.22	0.28	0.19
2018	0.46	0.40	0.35	0.01
2019	(0.43)	0.10	0.01	...

Interim Dividends (Per Share)

No Dividends Paid

Valuation Analysis   **Institutional Holding**

Forecast EPS	$1.41	No of Institutions
	(01/17/2020)	246
Market Cap	$4.1 Billion	Shares
Book Value	$1.7 Billion	190,888,208
Price/Book	2.34	% Held
Price/Sales	0.45	108.54

Business Summary: Specialty Chemicals (MIC: 8.3.2 SIC: 5169 NAIC: 424690)

Univar Solutions is a chemical and ingredients distributor and provider of specialty services. Co. purchases chemicals from chemical producers worldwide and warehouses, repackages, blends, dilutes, transports and sells those chemicals to various customer locations across various countries. Co.'s services include e-commerce and digital marketing of chemicals for its producers, chemical waste removal and ancillary services, on-site storage of chemicals for its customers, and support services for the agricultural and pest control industries. Co.'s business is organized and managed in four geographical segments: Univar USA, Univar Canada, Univar Europe and the Middle East and Africa.

Recent Developments: For the quarter ended Sep 30 2019, income from continuing operations decreased 95.0% to US$2.5 million from US$49.6 million in the year-earlier quarter. Net income decreased 95.0% to US$2.5 million from US$49.6 million in the year-earlier quarter. Revenues were US$2.39 billion, up 12.0% from US$2.13 billion the year before. Operating income was US$88.0 million versus US$99.6 million in the prior-year quarter, a decrease of 11.6%. Direct operating expenses rose 10.9% to US$1.84 billion from US$1.66 billion in the comparable period the year before. Indirect operating expenses increased 23.8% to US$456.9 million from US$369.1 million in the equivalent prior-year period.

Prospects: Our evaluation of Univar Solutions Inc as of October 4th, 2019 is the result of our systematic analysis on three basic characteristics: earnings strength, relative valuation, and recent stock price movement. The company has managed to produce a neutral trend in earnings per share over the past 5 quarters. Additionally, recent analyst estimates for the company have been unchanged while UNVR has posted results that exceeded analysts' expectations. Based on operating earnings yield, the company is undervalued when compared to all of the companies we cover. Share price changes over the past year indicates that UNVR will perform very poorly over the near term.

Financial Data

(US$ in Thousands)	9 Mos	6 Mos	3 Mos	12/31/2018	12/31/2017	12/31/2016	12/31/2015	12/31/2014
Earnings Per Share	(0.31)	0.03	0.33	1.21	0.85	(0.50)	0.14	(0.20)
Cash Flow Per Share	1.94	0.93	2.05	2.05	1.99	3.25	2.98	1.27
Income Statement								
Total Revenue	7,131,900	4,744,600	2,160,000	8,632,500	8,253,700	8,073,700	8,981,800	10,373,900
EBITDA	256,400	92,100	(24,100)	479,800	451,800	232,600	370,200	348,200
Depn & Amortn	159,600	77,800	35,000	125,200	135,000	152,300	136,500	133,500
Income Before Taxes	(12,100)	(57,800)	(93,300)	222,200	168,800	(79,600)	26,700	(35,900)
Income Taxes	38,400	(4,800)	(23,300)	49,900	49,000	(11,200)	10,200	(15,800)
Net Income	(45,100)	(47,600)	(63,900)	172,300	119,800	(68,400)	16,500	(20,100)
Average Shares	169,500	170,700	149,200	142,200	141,400	137,800	120,100	99,718
Balance Sheet								
Current Assets	2,576,300	2,806,200	3,447,000	2,188,700	2,518,500	2,178,100	2,196,300	2,621,800
Total Assets	6,784,700	7,131,100	7,787,800	5,272,400	5,732,700	5,389,900	5,612,400	6,067,700
Current Liabilities	1,445,700	1,599,900	1,687,900	1,334,600	1,419,400	1,339,500	1,293,500	1,518,900
Long-Term Obligations	2,977,100	3,117,100	3,694,000	2,350,400	2,820,000	2,845,000	3,057,400	3,730,600
Total Liabilities	5,039,700	5,356,600	6,006,800	4,080,700	4,642,600	4,580,000	4,795,700	5,819,600
Stockholders' Equity	1,745,000	1,774,500	1,781,000	1,191,700	1,090,100	809,900	816,700	248,100
Shares Outstanding	168,600	168,600	169,700	141,700	141,100	138,800	138,000	100,190
Statistical Record								
Return on Assets %	N.M.	0.05	0.64	3.13	2.15	N.M.	0.28	N.M.
Return on Equity %	N.M.	0.22	2.92	15.10	12.61	N.M.	3.10	N.M.
EBITDA Margin %	3.60	1.94	N.M.	5.56	5.47	2.88	4.12	3.36
Net Margin %	N.M.	N.M.	N.M.	2.00	1.45	N.M.	0.18	N.M.
Asset Turnover	1.48	1.38	1.28	1.57	1.48	1.46	1.54	1.69
Current Ratio	1.78	1.75	2.04	1.64	1.77	1.63	1.70	1.73
Debt to Equity	1.71	1.76	2.07	1.97	2.59	3.51	3.74	15.04
Price Range	30.86-16.33	31.00-16.33	31.00-16.33	31.65-16.33	32.81-26.99	28.60-11.12	27.25-16.28	...
P/E Ratio	...	N.M.	93.94-49.48	26.16-13.50	38.60-31.75	...	194.64-116.29	...

Address: 3075 Highland Parkway, Suite 200, Downers Grove, IL 60515 **Telephone:** 331-777-6000	**Web Site:** www.univar.com **Officers:** Christopher D. Pappas - Chairman David C. Jukes - President, President (frmr), Chief Executive Officer, Chief Operating Officer, Region Officer	**Auditors:** Ernst & Young LLP **Transfer Agents:** Wells Fargo Shareowner Services

UNIVERSAL CORP

Exchange	Symbol	Price	52Wk Range	Yield	P/E	Div Acheiver
NYS	UVV	$57.06 (12/31/2019)	62.70-49.39	5.33	16.12	48 Years

*7 Year Price Score 82.75 *NYSE Composite Index=100 *12 Month Price Score 90.93

Interim Earnings (Per Share)

Qtr.	Jun	Sep	Dec	Mar
2016-17	(0.40)	0.90	1.92	(1.75)
2017-18	0.14	1.02	1.78	1.20
2018-19	0.52	1.24	1.11	1.24
2019-20	0.08	1.11	...	...

Interim Dividends (Per Share)

Amt	Decl	Ex	Rec	Pay
0.75Q	02/07/2019	04/05/2019	04/08/2019	05/06/2019
0.76Q	05/22/2019	07/05/2019	07/08/2019	08/05/2019
0.76Q	08/07/2019	10/04/2019	10/07/2019	11/04/2019
0.76Q	11/12/2019	01/10/2020	01/13/2020	02/03/2020

Indicated Div: $3.04 (Div. Reinv. Plan)

Valuation Analysis   **Institutional Holding**

Forecast EPS	N/A	No of Institutions
		311
Market Cap	$1.4 Billion	Shares
Book Value	$1.3 Billion	30,082,872
Price/Book	1.09	% Held
Price/Sales	0.68	85.14

Business Summary: Tobacco Products (MIC: 1.3.1 SIC: 5159 NAIC: 424590)

Universal is a holding company. Through its subsidiary, Co. is engaged in supplying leaf tobacco. Co. has the following segments: North America, South America, Africa, Europe, Asia, which are involved in flue-cured and burley leaf tobacco operations for supply to cigarette manufacturers; Dark Air-Cured, which supplies dark air-cured tobacco to manufacturers of cigars, pipe tobacco, and smokeless tobacco products; Oriental, which supplies oriental tobacco to cigarette manufacturers; and Special Services, which provides laboratory services, including physical and chemical product testing, electronic nicotine delivery system and e-liquid testing, and smoke testing for customers.

Recent Developments: For the quarter ended Sep 30 2019, net income decreased 13.3% to US$29.7 million from US$34.3 million in the year-earlier quarter. Revenues were US$475.9 million, down 11.8% from US$539.6 million the year before. Operating income was US$43.2 million versus US$54.4 million in the prior-year quarter, a decrease of 20.5%. Direct operating expenses declined 13.7% to US$379.9 million from US$440.1 million in the comparable period the year before. Indirect operating expenses increased 17.2% to US$52.8 million from US$45.1 million in the equivalent prior-year period.

Prospects: Our evaluation of Universal Corp. as of October 4th, 2019 is the result of our systematic analysis on three basic characteristics: earnings strength, relative valuation, and recent stock price movement. The company has generated a negative trend in earnings per share over the past 5 quarters. However, recent analyst estimates for the company have been mixed and UVV has posted results that fell short of analysts' expectations. Based on operating earnings yield, the company is undervalued when compared to all of the companies we cover. Share price changes over the past year indicates that UVV will perform poorly over the near term.

Financial Data
(US$ in Thousands)

	6 Mos	3 Mos	03/31/2019	03/31/2018	03/31/2017	03/31/2016	03/31/2015	03/31/2014
Earnings Per Share	3.54	3.67	4.11	4.14	0.88	3.92	4.06	5.25
Cash Flow Per Share	3.89	8.59	6.55	3.29	10.68	8.07	9.83	(0.15)
Tang Book Value Per Share	48.33	48.55	49.58	49.88	46.99	48.58	46.56	45.91
Dividends Per Share	3.010	3.000	2.800	2.170	2.130	2.090	2.050	2.010
Dividend Payout %	85.03	81.74	68.13	52.42	242.05	53.32	50.49	38.29
Income Statement								
Total Revenue	772,836	296,915	2,227,153	2,033,947	2,071,218	2,120,373	2,271,801	2,542,115
EBITDA	70,204	17,208	199,105	206,323	214,262	218,401	203,268	283,408
Depn & Amortn	18,231	9,067	37,104	34,836	35,911	36,754	35,394	37,257
Income Before Taxes	44,057	5,121	146,023	157,552	163,464	167,156	151,330	226,793
Income Taxes	15,765	4,266	41,188	50,509	56,732	54,430	38,006	75,535
Net Income	30,149	2,072	104,121	105,662	106,304	109,016	114,608	149,009
Average Shares	25,197	25,284	25,330	25,508	23,770	27,825	28,221	28,392
Balance Sheet								
Current Assets	1,649,558	1,602,058	1,588,145	1,589,043	1,561,399	1,638,546	1,634,610	1,673,247
Total Assets	2,218,232	2,177,884	2,133,184	2,168,632	2,123,405	2,232,797	2,198,473	2,270,907
Current Liabilities	352,444	290,942	253,748	267,720	267,996	246,270	270,913	454,977
Long-Term Obligations	368,633	368,568	368,503	369,086	368,733	370,000	370,000	240,000
Total Liabilities	919,573	867,543	796,097	826,203	836,916	818,575	835,748	892,677
Stockholders' Equity	1,298,659	1,310,341	1,337,087	1,342,429	1,286,489	1,414,222	1,362,725	1,378,230
Shares Outstanding	24,841	24,971	24,989	24,930	25,274	22,717	22,593	23,216
Statistical Record								
Return on Assets %	3.99	4.28	4.84	4.92	4.88	4.91	5.13	6.51
Return on Equity %	6.80	7.07	7.77	8.04	7.87	7.83	8.36	11.30
EBITDA Margin %	9.08	5.80	8.94	10.14	10.34	10.30	8.95	11.15
Net Margin %	3.90	0.70	4.68	5.19	5.13	5.14	5.04	5.86
Asset Turnover	0.93	0.99	1.04	0.95	0.95	0.95	1.02	1.11
Current Ratio	4.68	5.51	6.26	5.94	5.83	6.65	6.03	3.68
Debt to Equity	0.28	0.28	0.28	0.27	0.29	0.26	0.27	0.17
Price Range	69.91-49.39	69.91-51.02	69.91-46.60	75.60-46.35	81.35-52.33	58.41-46.80	56.82-38.53	63.36-48.43
P/E Ratio	19.75-13.95	19.05-13.90	17.01-11.34	18.26-11.20	92.44-59.47	14.90-11.94	14.00-9.49	12.07-9.22
Average Yield %	5.15	4.96	4.65	3.70	3.54	3.94	4.26	3.65

Address: 9201 Forest Hill Avenue, Richmond, VA 23235 Telephone: 804-359-9311	Web Site: www.universalcorp.com Officers: George C. Freeman - Chairman, President, Chief Executive Officer, Principal Financial Officer Airton L. Hentschke - Senior Vice President, Chief Operating Officer	Auditors: Ernst & Young LLP Investor Contact: 804-359-9311 Transfer Agents: Wells Fargo Bank, N.A., St. Paul, MN

UNIVERSAL HEALTH REALTY INCOME TRUST

Exchange	Symbol	Price	52Wk Range	Yield	P/E	Div Acheiver
NYS	UHT	$117.36 (12/31/2019)	121.97-60.24	2.33	91.69	31 Years

*7 Year Price Score 122.81 *NYSE Composite Index=100 *12 Month Price Score 122.58

Interim Earnings (Per Share)

Qtr.	Mar	Jun	Sep	Dec
2016	0.33	0.34	0.28	0.33
2017	2.32	0.30	0.29	0.44
2018	0.70	0.42	0.32	0.32
2019	0.31	0.31	0.34	...

Interim Dividends (Per Share)

Amt	Decl	Ex	Rec	Pay
0.675Q	03/06/2019	03/18/2019	03/19/2019	03/29/2019
0.68Q	06/12/2019	06/21/2019	06/24/2019	07/02/2019
0.68Q	09/04/2019	09/13/2019	09/16/2019	09/30/2019
0.685Q	12/04/2019	12/17/2019	12/18/2019	12/31/2019

Indicated Div: $2.74 (Div. Reinv. Plan)

Valuation Analysis

		Institutional Holding	
Forecast EPS	N/A	No of Institutions	231
Market Cap	$1.6 Billion	Shares	
Book Value	$184.6 Million		11,025,777
Price/Book	8.74	% Held	
Price/Sales	20.96		65.96

Business Summary: REITs (MIC: 5.3.1 SIC: 6798 NAIC: 525930)

Universal Health Realty Income Trust is real estate investment trust. Co. invests in health care and human service related facilities including acute care hospitals, rehabilitation hospitals, sub-acute facilities, medical office buildings, free-standing emergency departments and childcare centers.

Recent Developments: For the quarter ended Sep 30 2019, net income increased 6.4% to US$4.7 million from US$4.4 million in the year-earlier quarter. Revenues were US$19.9 million, up 5.5% from US$18.8 million the year before. Revenues from property income rose 4.6% to US$19.4 million from US$18.5 million in the corresponding quarter a year earlier.

Prospects: Our evaluation of Universal Health Realty Income Trust as of October 4th, 2019 is the result of our systematic analysis on three basic characteristics: earnings strength, relative valuation, and recent stock price movement. The company has managed to produce a neutral trend in earnings per share over the past 5 quarters. In addition, recent analyst estimates for the company have been mixed and UHT has posted results that fell short of analysts' expectations. Based on operating earnings yield, the company is overvalued when compared to all of the companies we cover. Share price changes over the past year indicates that UHT will perform well over the near term.

Financial Data

(US$ in Thousands)	9 Mos	6 Mos	3 Mos	12/31/2018	12/31/2017	12/31/2016	12/31/2015	12/31/2014
Earnings Per Share	1.28	1.26	1.37	1.76	3.35	1.28	1.78	3.99
Cash Flow Per Share	3.02	3.00	2.97	3.13	3.38	3.02	2.87	2.54
Tang Book Value Per Share	12.33	12.56	12.88	13.18	13.83	12.31	13.15	13.64
Dividends Per Share	2.710	2.700	2.690	2.680	2.640	2.600	2.560	2.520
Dividend Payout %	211.72	214.29	196.35	152.27	78.81	203.13	143.82	63.16
Income Statement								
Total Revenue	58,304	38,438	19,112	76,210	72,348	67,081	63,950	59,786
EBITDA	19,881	13,035	6,461	57,115	78,218	44,897	51,352	78,162
Depn & Amortn	(40)	(27)	(13)	24,713	24,952	22,783	21,973	20,663
Income Before Taxes	11,789	7,589	3,782	22,425	43,203	12,759	21,155	49,123
Net Income	13,126	8,473	4,212	24,196	45,619	17,215	23,691	51,551
Average Shares	13,757	13,749	13,747	13,722	13,625	13,468	13,301	12,934
Balance Sheet								
Current Assets	13,595	13,142	13,063	15,244	12,489	11,542	10,302	10,166
Total Assets	483,880	482,751	489,050	483,756	490,008	524,750	458,901	428,866
Current Liabilities	206,020	201,326	200,788	450	540	626	504	545
Long-Term Obligations	61,153	61,562	64,456	261,281	256,409	315,717	252,704	213,155
Total Liabilities	299,255	294,211	295,423	285,146	279,447	333,473	263,859	224,285
Stockholders' Equity	184,625	188,540	193,627	198,610	210,561	191,277	195,042	204,581
Shares Outstanding	13,757	13,756	13,747	13,746	13,735	13,599	13,327	13,301
Statistical Record								
Return on Assets %	3.61	3.55	3.84	4.97	8.99	3.49	5.34	12.86
Return on Equity %	9.04	8.71	9.29	11.83	22.71	8.89	11.86	27.85
EBITDA Margin %	34.10	33.91	33.81	74.94	108.11	66.93	80.30	130.74
Net Margin %	22.51	22.04	22.04	31.75	63.05	25.66	37.05	86.23
Asset Turnover	0.16	0.16	0.16	0.16	0.14	0.14	0.14	0.15
Current Ratio	0.07	0.07	0.07	33.88	23.13	18.44	20.44	18.65
Debt to Equity	0.33	0.33	0.33	1.32	1.22	1.65	1.30	1.04
Price Range	102.80-59.51	91.40-59.51	76.60-58.05	76.34-55.36	84.23-60.01	65.59-47.26	56.87-43.54	49.13-40.06
P/E Ratio	80.31-46.49	72.54-47.23	55.91-42.37	43.38-31.45	25.14-17.91	51.24-36.92	31.95-24.46	12.31-10.04
Average Yield %	3.43	3.70	3.97	4.09	3.67	4.58	5.13	5.75

Address: Universal Corporate Center, 367 South Gulph Road, King of Prussia, PA 19406
Telephone: 610-265-0688
Fax: 610-768-3336

Web Site: www.uhrit.com
Officers: Alan B. Miller - Chairman, President, Chief Executive Officer Charles F. Boyle - Vice President, Chief Financial Officer

Auditors: KPMG LLP
Transfer Agents: Computershare, Providence, RI

UNIVERSAL HEALTH SERVICES, INC.

Exchange	Symbol	Price	52Wk Range	Yield	P/E
NYS	UHS	$143.46 (12/31/2019)	155.37-115.98	0.56	17.84

*7 Year Price Score 100.79 *NYSE Composite Index=100 *12 Month Price Score 98.82

Interim Earnings (Per Share)

Qtr.	Mar	Jun	Sep	Dec
2016	1.93	1.89	1.54	1.78
2017	2.12	1.91	1.47	2.31
2018	2.36	2.39	1.84	1.71
2019	2.57	2.66	1.10	...

Interim Dividends (Per Share)

Amt	Decl	Ex	Rec	Pay
0.10Q	01/16/2019	02/28/2019	03/01/2019	03/15/2019
0.10Q	05/15/2019	05/31/2019	06/03/2019	06/17/2019
0.20Q	07/25/2019	08/30/2019	09/03/2019	09/16/2019
0.20Q	11/20/2019	12/04/2019	12/05/2019	12/19/2019

Indicated Div: $0.80

Valuation Analysis

Forecast EPS	$9.79
	(01/17/2020)
Market Cap	$12.6 Billion
Book Value	$5.4 Billion
Price/Book	2.33
Price/Sales	1.12

Institutional Holding

No of Institutions	695
Shares	102,608,848
% Held	79.88

TRADING VOLUME (thousand shares)

Business Summary: Hospitals & Health Care Facilities (MIC: 4.2.1 SIC: 8062 NAIC: 622110)

Universal Health Services owns and operates, through its subsidiaries, acute care hospitals and outpatient facilities and behavioral health care facilities. Co. owned and/or operated inpatient facilities and outpatient and other facilities located in several states including, Washington, D.C., the U.K., and Puerto Rico. Services provided by Co.'s hospitals include general and specialty surgery, internal medicine, obstetrics, emergency room care, radiology, oncology, diagnostic care, coronary care, pediatric services, pharmacy services and/or behavioral health services. Co.'s reportable operating segments consist of acute care hospital services and behavioral health care services.

Recent Developments: For the quarter ended Sep 30 2019, net income decreased 42.3% to US$100.9 million from US$174.9 million in the year-earlier quarter. Revenues were US$2.82 billion, up 6.6% from US$2.65 billion the year before. Operating income was US$188.9 million versus US$257.2 million in the prior-year quarter, a decrease of 26.5%. Indirect operating expenses increased 10.1% to US$2.63 billion from US$2.39 billion in the equivalent prior-year period.

Prospects: Our evaluation of Universal Health Services Inc. as of October 4th, 2019 is the result of our systematic analysis on three basic characteristics: earnings strength, relative valuation, and recent stock price movement. The company has managed to produce a neutral trend in earnings per share over the past 5 quarters. However, recent analyst estimates for the company have been raised and UHS has posted results that exceeded analysts' expectations. Based on operating earnings yield, the company is undervalued when compared to all of the companies we cover. Share price changes over the past year indicates that UHS will perform well over the near term.

Financial Data

(US$ in Thousands)	9 Mos	6 Mos	3 Mos	12/31/2018	12/31/2017	12/31/2016	12/31/2015	12/31/2014
Earnings Per Share	8.04	8.78	8.51	8.31	7.81	7.14	6.76	5.42
Cash Flow Per Share	16.09	14.99	15.07	14.38	12.36	13.22	10.33	10.48
Tang Book Value Per Share	17.83	17.51	18.04	16.91	12.36	7.75	6.65	4.51
Dividends Per Share	0.500	0.400	0.400	0.400	0.400	0.400	0.400	0.300
Dividend Payout %	6.22	4.56	4.70	4.81	5.12	5.60	5.92	5.54
Income Statement								
Total Revenue	8,482,012	5,659,559	2,804,391	10,772,278	10,409,865	9,766,210	9,043,451	8,065,326
EBITDA	1,231,489	930,439	455,976	1,599,481	1,668,578	1,632,211	1,596,895	1,377,805
Depn & Amortn	362,736	241,208	120,040	410,000	388,400	350,800	337,500	314,500
Income Before Taxes	745,179	607,104	296,296	1,034,525	1,135,009	1,156,358	1,145,901	929,667
Income Taxes	165,646	128,441	58,898	236,642	363,697	409,187	395,203	324,671
Net Income	569,678	472,488	234,168	779,705	752,303	702,409	680,528	545,343
Average Shares	88,355	89,235	90,967	93,750	96,325	98,380	100,694	100,544
Balance Sheet								
Current Assets	1,930,627	1,965,032	1,960,441	1,937,802	1,798,002	1,681,371	1,718,304	1,615,138
Total Assets	11,594,401	11,752,650	11,721,277	11,265,480	10,761,828	10,317,802	9,634,113	8,974,443
Current Liabilities	1,621,769	1,544,269	1,656,766	1,448,738	1,848,034	1,317,373	1,100,406	1,182,827
Long-Term Obligations	4,144,542	4,332,809	4,108,039	3,935,187	3,494,390	4,030,230	3,387,303	3,210,215
Total Liabilities	6,205,186	6,359,561	6,238,862	5,876,218	5,772,314	5,784,582	5,384,466	5,238,497
Stockholders' Equity	5,389,215	5,393,089	5,482,415	5,389,262	4,989,514	4,533,220	4,249,647	3,735,946
Shares Outstanding	87,582	88,488	90,140	91,349	94,227	96,630	98,296	98,716
Statistical Record								
Return on Assets %	6.36	7.03	6.95	7.08	7.14	7.02	7.31	6.31
Return on Equity %	13.54	14.98	14.77	15.02	15.80	15.95	17.04	15.61
EBITDA Margin %	14.52	16.44	16.26	14.85	16.03	16.71	17.66	17.08
Net Margin %	6.72	8.35	8.35	7.24	7.23	7.19	7.53	6.76
Asset Turnover	0.98	0.97	0.96	0.98	0.99	0.98	0.97	0.93
Current Ratio	1.19	1.27	1.18	1.34	0.97	1.28	1.56	1.37
Debt to Equity	0.77	0.80	0.75	0.73	0.70	0.89	0.80	0.86
Price Range	155.37-113.42	140.80-110.98	140.80-110.98	137.99-110.15	126.65-95.77	138.74-101.55	146.24-102.53	114.84-74.35
P/E Ratio	19.32-14.11	16.04-12.64	16.55-13.04	16.61-13.26	16.22-12.26	19.43-14.22	21.63-15.17	21.19-13.72
Average Yield %	0.38	0.32	0.32	0.33	0.35	0.33	0.32	0.32

Address: Universal Corporate Center, 367 South Gulph Road, King of Prussia, PA 19406 **Telephone:** 610-768-3300	**Web Site:** www.uhsinc.com **Officers:** Alan B. Miller - Chairman, Chief Executive Officer Marc D. Miller - President	**Auditors:** PricewaterhouseCoopers LLP **Investor Contact:** 610-768-3300 **Transfer Agents:** Computershare, Canton, MA

UNUM GROUP

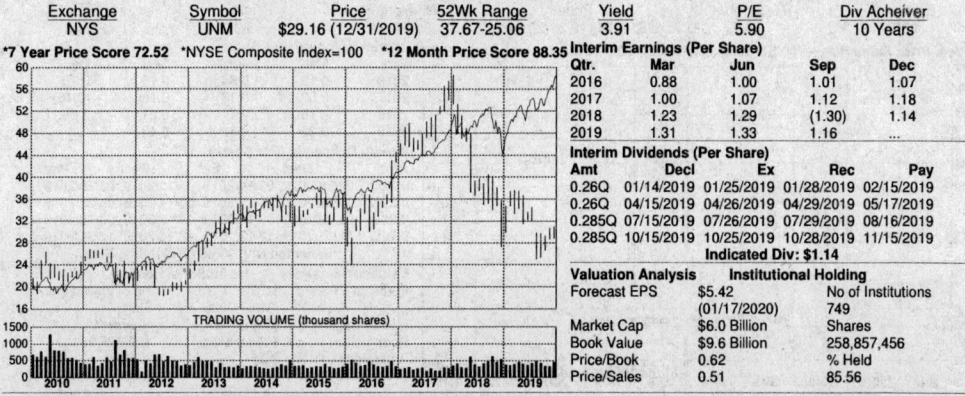

Exchange	Symbol	Price	52Wk Range	Yield	P/E	Div Acheiver
NYS	UNM	$29.16 (12/31/2019)	37.67-25.06	3.91	5.90	10 Years

*7 Year Price Score 72.52   *NYSE Composite Index=100   *12 Month Price Score 88.35

Interim Earnings (Per Share)

Qtr.	Mar	Jun	Sep	Dec
2016	0.88	1.00	1.01	1.07
2017	1.00	1.07	1.12	1.18
2018	1.23	1.29	(1.30)	1.14
2019	1.31	1.33	1.16	...

Interim Dividends (Per Share)

Amt	Decl	Ex	Rec	Pay
0.26Q	01/14/2019	01/25/2019	01/28/2019	02/15/2019
0.26Q	04/15/2019	04/26/2019	04/29/2019	05/17/2019
0.285Q	07/15/2019	07/26/2019	07/29/2019	08/16/2019
0.285Q	10/15/2019	10/25/2019	10/28/2019	11/15/2019

Indicated Div: $1.14

Valuation Analysis

		Institutional Holding	
Forecast EPS	$5.42	No of Institutions	
	(01/17/2020)	749	
Market Cap	$6.0 Billion	Shares	
Book Value	$9.6 Billion	258,857,456	
Price/Book	0.62	% Held	
Price/Sales	0.51	85.56	

Business Summary: Life & Health (MIC: 5.2.2 SIC: 6321 NAIC: 524114)

Unum Group is an insurance holding company. Through its subsidiaries, Co. is a provider of financial protection benefits in the U.S. and the U.K. Co. has three main operating business segments: Unum U.S., which includes group long-term disability, including Co.'s medical stop-loss product, and short-term disability insurance, group life and accidental death and dismemberment products; Unum International, which is comprised of Co.'s Unum U.K. line of business and Co.'s Unum Poland line of business; and Colonial Life, which includes insurance for accident, sickness, and disability products, including Co.'s dental and vision products, life products, and cancer and critical illness products.

Recent Developments: For the quarter ended Sep 30 2019, net income amounted to US$242.0 million versus a net loss of US$284.7 million in the year-earlier quarter. Revenues were US$2.96 billion, up 1.1% from US$2.93 billion the year before. Net premiums earned were US$2.33 billion versus US$2.25 billion in the prior-year quarter, an increase of 3.5%. Net investment income fell 3.2% to US$599.4 million from US$619.2 million a year ago.

Prospects: Our evaluation of UNUM Group as of October 4th, 2019 is the result of our systematic analysis on three basic characteristics: earnings strength, relative valuation, and recent stock price movement. The company has managed to produce a neutral trend in earnings per share over the past 5 quarters. In addition, recent analyst estimates for the company have been mixed and UNM has posted results that exceeded analysts' expectations. Based on operating earnings yield, the company is undervalued when compared to all of the companies we cover. Share price changes over the past year indicates that UNM will perform poorly over the near term.

Financial Data
(US$ in Thousands)

	9 Mos	6 Mos	3 Mos	12/31/2018	12/31/2017	12/31/2016	12/31/2015	12/31/2014
Earnings Per Share	4.94	2.48	2.44	2.38	4.37	3.95	3.50	1.61
Cash Flow Per Share	8.22	8.45	8.18	7.00	5.07	4.73	5.23	4.79
Tang Book Value Per Share	45.01	43.44	41.03	38.55	41.50	37.56	35.00	33.11
Dividends Per Share	1.065	1.040	1.010	0.980	0.860	0.770	0.700	0.620
Dividend Payout %	21.56	41.94	41.39	41.18	19.68	19.49	20.00	38.51
Income Statement								
Premium Income	7,013,000	4,681,800	2,338,700	8,986,100	8,597,100	8,357,700	8,082,400	7,797,200
Total Revenue	8,964,300	6,004,300	2,987,600	11,598,500	11,286,800	11,046,500	10,731,300	10,509,700
Income Before Taxes	1,004,700	705,300	353,300	627,800	1,404,000	1,347,700	1,238,300	527,200
Income Taxes	200,600	143,200	72,400	104,400	409,800	416,300	371,200	113,800
Net Income	804,100	562,100	280,900	523,400	994,200	931,400	867,100	413,400
Average Shares	208,116	211,112	214,429	220,058	227,335	235,979	247,854	256,652
Balance Sheet								
Total Assets	66,955,700	65,843,700	63,921,700	61,875,600	64,013,100	61,941,500	60,589,700	62,497,100
Total Liabilities	57,324,100	56,390,600	54,861,200	53,253,800	54,438,200	52,973,500	51,925,800	53,944,700
Stockholders' Equity	9,631,600	9,453,100	9,060,500	8,621,800	9,574,900	8,968,000	8,663,900	8,552,400
Shares Outstanding	206,228	209,575	212,290	214,553	222,547	229,822	240,917	252,309
Statistical Record								
Return on Assets %	1.63	0.82	0.84	0.83	1.58	1.52	1.41	0.68
Return on Equity %	11.61	5.57	5.72	5.75	10.72	10.54	10.07	4.80
Net Margin %	8.97	9.36	9.40	4.51	8.81	8.43	8.08	3.93
Price Range	40.23-25.06	40.51-27.24	48.92-27.24	58.59-27.24	57.49-43.80	44.60-24.07	37.61-31.05	36.81-30.71
P/E Ratio	8.14-5.07	16.33-10.98	20.05-11.16	24.62-11.45	13.16-10.02	11.29-6.09	10.75-8.87	22.86-19.07
Average Yield %	3.18	2.93	2.71	2.36	1.76	2.25	2.04	1.81

Address: 1 Fountain Square, Chattanooga, TN 37402
Telephone: 423-294-1011

Web Site: www.unum.com
Officers: Kevin T. Kabat - Chairman Richard P. McKenney - President, Chief Executive Officer, Executive Vice President, Chief Financial Officer

Auditors: Ernst & Young LLP
Transfer Agents: Computershare Trust Company, N.A., Providence, RI

URBAN EDGE PROPERTIES

Exchange	Symbol	Price	52Wk Range	Yield	P/E
NYS	UE	$19.18 (12/31/2019)	21.68-16.24	4.59	20.19

*7 Year Price Score N/A   *NYSE Composite Index=100   *12 Month Price Score 102.15

Interim Earnings (Per Share)

Qtr.	Mar	Jun	Sep	Dec
2016	0.19	0.34	0.19	0.19
2017	0.50	0.13	0.15	(0.16)
2018	0.18	0.47	0.21	0.06
2019	0.22	0.22	0.45	...

Interim Dividends (Per Share)

Amt	Decl	Ex	Rec	Pay
0.22Q	02/28/2019	03/14/2019	03/15/2019	03/29/2019
0.22Q	05/08/2019	06/13/2019	06/14/2019	06/28/2019
0.22Q	08/06/2019	09/12/2019	09/13/2019	09/30/2019
0.22Q	11/05/2019	12/13/2019	12/16/2019	12/31/2019

Indicated Div: $0.88 (Div. Reinv. Plan)

Valuation Analysis / Institutional Holding

Forecast EPS	$1.01	No of Institutions
	(01/07/2020)	257
Market Cap	$2.3 Billion	Shares
Book Value	$988.0 Million	129,825,928
Price/Book	2.35	% Held
Price/Sales	5.92	95.85

Business Summary: REITs (MIC: 5.3.1 SIC: 6798 NAIC: 525930)

Urban Edge Properties is a real estate investment trust that manages, develops, redevelops, and acquires retail real estate, primarily in the New York metropolitan area. Urban Edge Properties LP is a Delaware limited partnership formed to serve as Co.'s majority-owned partnership subsidiary and to own, through affiliates, all of Co.'s real estate and other assets. Co.'s portfolio comprises of shopping centers, malls and a warehouse park.

Recent Developments: For the quarter ended Sep 30 2019, net income increased 110.8% to US$56.7 million from US$26.9 million in the year-earlier quarter. Revenues were US$91.2 million, down 18.7% from US$112.2 million the year before.

Prospects: Our evaluation of Urban Edge Properties as of October 4th, 2019 is the result of our systematic analysis on three basic characteristics: earnings strength, relative valuation, and recent stock price movement. The company has produced a positive trend in earnings per share over the past 5 quarters. However, recent analyst estimates for the company have been unchanged, while UE has posted results that exceeded analysts' expectations. Based on operating earnings yield, the company is overvalued when compared to all of the companies we cover. Share price changes over the past year indicates that UE will perform very poorly over the near term.

Financial Data
(US$ in Thousands)

	9 Mos	6 Mos	3 Mos	12/31/2018	12/31/2017	12/31/2016	12/31/2015	12/31/2014
Earnings Per Share	0.95	0.71	0.96	0.92	0.61	0.91	0.39	...
Cash Flow Per Share	1.36	1.14	1.14	1.20	1.47	1.38	1.39	...
Tang Book Value Per Share	7.74	7.50	7.46	7.31	7.05	4.30	4.07	2.13
Dividends Per Share	0.880	0.880	0.880	0.880	0.880	0.820	0.800	...
Dividend Payout %	92.63	123.94	91.67	95.65	144.26	90.11	205.13	...
Income Statement								
Total Revenue	291,722	200,479	97,732	414,160	407,042	325,976	322,945	315,676
EBITDA	150,673	79,284	42,498	245,981	202,515	200,868	151,206	168,991
Depn & Amortn	(5,434)	(5,915)	374	68,967	75,885	52,232	53,130	46,551
Income Before Taxes	113,908	57,155	28,094	120,482	72,660	97,434	42,642	67,515
Income Taxes	1,249	1,196	202	3,519	(278)	804	1,294	1,721
Net Income	106,148	52,108	25,537	105,150	67,070	90,815	38,785	65,772
Average Shares	121,183	120,461	126,504	114,051	118,390	99,794	99,278	...
Balance Sheet								
Current Assets	650,211	578,797	578,578	581,191	617,859	245,902	285,688	123,447
Total Assets	2,873,878	2,858,419	2,874,427	2,798,994	2,820,808	1,904,138	1,918,931	1,741,529
Current Liabilities	80,161	85,034	85,424	98,517	69,595	48,842	45,331	26,924
Long-Term Obligations	1,547,486	1,548,944	1,549,479	1,550,242	1,564,542	1,197,513	1,233,983	1,288,535
Total Liabilities	1,885,829	1,898,317	1,924,760	1,894,288	1,930,889	1,443,832	1,481,011	1,483,007
Stockholders' Equity	988,049	960,102	949,667	904,706	889,919	460,306	437,920	258,522
Shares Outstanding	121,223	121,171	120,099	114,345	113,827	99,754	99,290	104,964
Statistical Record								
Return on Assets %	3.96	2.91	3.87	3.74	2.84	4.74	...	3.77
Return on Equity %	11.82	8.82	11.98	11.72	9.93	20.17	...	21.93
EBITDA Margin %	51.65	39.55	43.48	59.39	49.75	61.62	46.82	53.53
Net Margin %	36.39	25.99	26.13	25.39	16.48	27.86	12.01	20.84
Asset Turnover	0.14	0.15	0.15	0.15	0.17	0.17	...	0.18
Current Ratio	8.11	6.81	6.77	5.90	8.88	5.03	6.30	4.59
Debt to Equity	1.57	1.61	1.63	1.71	1.76	2.60	2.82	4.98
Price Range	21.80-16.24	23.28-16.40	23.28-16.40	25.59-16.40	28.85-23.44	30.15-22.22	25.00-20.12	...
P/E Ratio	22.95-17.09	32.79-23.10	24.25-17.08	27.82-17.83	47.30-38.43	33.13-24.42	64.10-51.59	...
Average Yield %	4.70	4.41	4.24	4.09	3.45	3.08	3.52	...

Address: 888 Seventh Avenue, New York, NY 10019	**Web Site:** www.uedge.com	**Auditors:** DELOITTE & TOUCHE LLP
Telephone: 212-956-2556	**Officers:** Jeffrey S. (Jeff) Olson - Chairman, Chief Executive Officer Mark J. Langer - Executive President, Chief Financial Officer	

URSTADT BIDDLE PROPERTIES INC

Exchange	Symbol	Price	52Wk Range	Yield	P/E	Div Acheiver
NYS	UBA	$24.84 (12/31/2019)	24.84-18.63	4.51	47.77	20 Years

*7 Year Price Score 86.45   ***NYSE Composite Index=100**   ***12 Month Price Score 103.51**

Interim Earnings (Per Share)

Qtr.	Jan	Apr	Jul	Oct
2014-15	0.06	0.10	0.13	0.62
2015-16	0.08	0.12	0.13	0.16
2016-17	0.08	0.57	0.14	0.01
2017-18	0.12	0.23	0.13	0.13
2018-19	0.14	0.14	0.17	0.08

Interim Dividends (Per Share)

Amt	Decl	Ex	Rec	Pay
0.275Q	03/21/2019	04/03/2019	04/04/2019	04/18/2019
0.275Q	06/03/2019	07/03/2019	07/05/2019	07/19/2019
0.275Q	09/04/2019	10/03/2019	10/04/2019	10/18/2019
0.28Q	12/18/2019	01/02/2020	01/03/2020	01/17/2020

Indicated Div: $1.12

Valuation Analysis

		Institutional Holding	
Forecast EPS	$0.89	No of Institutions	
	(01/14/2020)	41	
Market Cap	$990.0 Million	Shares	
Book Value	$579.7 Million	1,079,854	
Price/Book	1.71	% Held	
Price/Sales	7.20	3.37	

Business Summary: REITs (MIC: 5.3.1 SIC: 6798 NAIC: 525930)

Urstadt Biddle Properties is a real estate investment trust engaged in the acquisition, ownership and management of commercial real estate. Co.'s business is the ownership of real estate investments, which consist principally of investments in properties, with primary focus on neighborhood and community shopping centers in the metropolitan New York tri-state area outside of the City of New York. In addition to its business of owning and managing real estate, Co. is involved in the beer, wine and spirits retail business, through its subsidiaries. Each subsidiary corporation owns and operates a beer, wine and spirits retail store at one of its shopping centers.

Recent Developments: For the year ended Oct 31 2019, net income decreased 1.4% to US$41.6 million from US$42.2 million in the prior year. Revenues were US$137.6 million, up 1.6% from US$135.4 million the year before. Revenues from property income rose 1.1% to US$132.3 million from US$130.8 million in the corresponding earlier year.

Prospects: Our evaluation of Urstadt Biddle Properties Inc. as of October 4th, 2019 is the result of our systematic analysis on three basic characteristics: earnings strength, relative valuation, and recent stock price movement. The company has produced a positive trend in earnings per share over the past 5 quarters. However, recent analyst estimates for the company have been mixed and UBA has posted results that fell short of analysts' expectations. Based on operating earnings yield, the company is fairly valued when compared to all of the companies we cover. Share price changes over the past year indicates that UBA will perform poorly over the near term.

Financial Data

(US$ in Thousands)	10/31/2019	10/31/2018	10/31/2017	10/31/2016	10/31/2015	10/31/2014	10/31/2013	10/31/2012
Earnings Per Share	0.52	0.60	0.80	0.49	0.90	1.42	0.31	0.41
Cash Flow Per Share	1.89	1.89	1.67	1.70	1.49	1.64	1.66	1.86
Tang Book Value Per Share	8.90	9.89	10.08	10.08	9.42	8.40	7.84	9.09
Dividends Per Share	1.100	1.080	1.060	1.040	1.020	1.010	1.000	0.990
Dividend Payout %	211.54	180.00	132.50	212.24	113.33	71.13	322.58	241.46
Income Statement								
Total Revenue	137,585	135,352	123,560	116,792	115,312	102,328	94,245	91,295
EBITDA	82,017	81,750	73,778	68,352	63,576	80,837	53,352	53,875
Depn & Amortn	27,927	28,324	26,512	23,025	22,435	19,249	17,816	16,721
Income Before Taxes	40,391	40,098	34,641	32,586	27,894	51,487	27,787	28,898
Net Income	37,280	37,467	52,933	33,716	49,264	65,151	29,795	28,260
Average Shares	39,003	38,627	38,529	36,022	35,060	31,963	31,740	29,168
Balance Sheet								
Current Assets	116,933	40,999	30,612	28,185	31,167	95,513	25,515	164,614
Total Assets	1,072,304	1,008,233	996,713	931,324	861,075	819,005	650,026	724,243
Current Liabilities	11,416	3,900	4,200	4,977	3,438	1,622	1,450	1,632
Long-Term Obligations	306,606	322,396	301,071	281,016	283,207	245,697	175,496	154,836
Total Liabilities	492,580	426,092	409,483	332,291	320,297	343,962	204,112	239,725
Stockholders' Equity	579,724	582,141	587,230	599,033	540,778	475,043	445,914	484,518
Shares Outstanding	39,856	39,636	39,393	39,141	35,721	32,805	32,565	32,315
Statistical Record								
Return on Assets %	3.58	3.74	5.49	3.75	5.86	8.87	4.34	4.33
Return on Equity %	6.42	6.41	8.92	5.90	9.70	14.15	6.40	6.38
EBITDA Margin %	59.61	60.40	59.71	58.52	55.13	79.00	56.61	59.01
Net Margin %	27.10	27.68	42.84	28.87	42.72	63.67	31.61	30.95
Asset Turnover	0.13	0.14	0.13	0.13	0.14	0.14	0.14	0.14
Current Ratio	10.24	10.51	7.29	5.66	9.07	58.89	17.60	100.87
Debt to Equity	0.53	0.55	0.51	0.47	0.52	0.52	0.39	0.32
Price Range	24.43-18.63	23.75-17.50	24.33-18.41	25.13-18.57	24.22-17.43	22.08-18.13	23.05-18.12	20.78-15.61
P/E Ratio	46.98-35.83	39.58-29.17	30.41-23.01	51.29-37.90	26.91-19.37	15.55-12.77	74.35-58.45	50.68-38.07
Average Yield %	5.12	5.15	4.98	4.87	4.89	5.02	4.88	5.25

Address: 321 Railroad Avenue, Greenwich, CT 06830
Telephone: 203-863-8200

Web Site: www.ubproperties.com
Officers: Charles D. Urstadt - Chairman Willing L. Biddle - President, Chief Executive Officer, Chief Operating Officer

Auditors: PKF OíConnor Davies, LLP
Investor Contact: 203-863-8200
Transfer Agents: BNY Mellon Shareowner Services, Jersey City, N

US FOODS HOLDING CORP

Exchange	Symbol	Price	52Wk Range	Yield	P/E
NYS	USFD	$41.89 (12/31/2019)	42.81-31.52	N/A	23.40

*7 Year Price Score N/A   *NYSE Composite Index=100   *12 Month Price Score 102.70

Interim Earnings (Per Share)

Qtr.	Mar	Jun	Sep	Dec
2016	0.08	(0.07)	0.59	0.35
2017	0.12	0.29	0.42	1.14
2018	0.31	0.58	0.52	0.46
2019	0.32	0.53	0.48	...

Interim Dividends (Per Share)

No Dividends Paid

Valuation Analysis / **Institutional Holding**

Forecast EPS	$2.33	No of Institutions
(01/15/2020)		382
Market Cap	$9.2 Billion	Shares
Book Value	$3.6 Billion	214,440,144
Price/Book	2.58	% Held
Price/Sales	0.37	91.91

TRADING VOLUME (thousand shares)

Business Summary: Retail - Food & Beverage, Drug & Tobacco (MIC: 2.1.2 SIC: 5149 NAIC: 424490)

US Foods Holding is a holding company. Through its subsidiaries, Co. is engaged as a food company and foodservice distributor. Co. supplies customer locations nationwide. These customer locations include independently owned single and multi-unit restaurants, regional restaurant concepts, national restaurant chains, hospitals, nursing homes, hotels and motels, country clubs, government and military organizations, colleges and universities, and retail locations. Co. provides fresh, frozen, and dry food stock-keeping units, as well as non-food items, sourced from suppliers. Co. has distribution facilities and trucks, which allow Co. to operate and provide customer service.

Recent Developments: For the quarter ended Sep 28 2019, income from continuing operations decreased 7.9% to US$105.0 million from US$114.0 million in the year-earlier quarter. Net income decreased 7.0% to US$106.0 million from US$114.0 million in the year-earlier quarter. Revenues were US$6.53 billion, up 6.1% from US$6.15 billion the year before. Operating income was US$188.0 million versus US$179.0 million in the prior-year quarter, an increase of 5.0%. Direct operating expenses rose 6.5% to US$5.38 billion from US$5.05 billion in the comparable period the year before. Indirect operating expenses increased 4.2% to US$968.0 million from US$929.0 million in the equivalent prior-year period.

Prospects: Our evaluation of US Foods Holding Corp as of October 4th, 2019 is the result of our systematic analysis on three basic characteristics: earnings strength, relative valuation, and recent stock price movement. The company has produced a positive trend in earnings per share over the past 5 quarters. In addition, recent analyst estimates for the company have been raised, and USFD has posted results that exceeded analysts' expectations. Based on operating earnings yield, the company is fairly valued when compared to all of the companies we cover. Share price changes over the past year indicates that USFD will perform over the near term.

Financial Data

(US$ in Thousands)	9 Mos	6 Mos	3 Mos	12/29/2018	12/30/2017	12/31/2016	01/02/2016	12/27/2014
Earnings Per Share	1.79	1.83	1.88	1.87	1.97	1.03	0.98	(0.43)
Cash Flow Per Share	3.33	3.18	2.63	2.83	3.37	2.77	3.22	2.38
Income Statement								
Total Revenue	19,005,000	12,474,000	6,031,000	24,175,000	24,147,161	22,918,808	23,127,532	23,019,801
EBITDA	747,000	484,000	205,000	971,000	856,824	626,189	730,328	513,256
Depn & Amortn	231,000	155,000	72,000	300,000	283,000	266,000	253,000	261,000
Income Before Taxes	389,000	245,000	91,000	496,000	404,242	131,109	192,153	(36,946)
Income Taxes	97,000	58,000	20,000	89,000	(40,052)	(78,685)	24,635	35,968
Net Income	293,000	187,000	71,000	407,000	444,294	209,794	167,518	(72,914)
Average Shares	220,000	219,000	219,000	217,825	225,663	204,024	171,060	169,467
Balance Sheet								
Current Assets	3,560,000	3,042,000	3,081,000	2,979,000	2,819,381	2,789,171	3,060,433	2,820,099
Total Assets	11,526,000	9,339,000	9,391,000	9,186,000	9,037,158	8,944,450	9,239,359	9,022,538
Current Liabilities	2,546,000	2,216,000	2,214,000	2,076,000	2,002,882	1,969,285	1,802,823	1,825,587
Long-Term Obligations	4,788,000	3,101,000	3,275,000	3,351,000	3,648,055	3,705,751	4,682,149	4,661,697
Total Liabilities	7,969,000	5,904,000	6,081,000	5,957,000	6,285,795	6,406,800	7,327,741	7,357,822
Stockholders' Equity	3,557,000	3,435,000	3,310,000	3,229,000	2,751,363	2,537,650	1,911,618	1,664,716
Shares Outstanding	219,000	219,000	218,000	217,000	214,963	220,928	166,667	166,667
Statistical Record								
Return on Assets %	3.78	4.34	4.42	4.48	4.96	2.30	1.80	...
Return on Equity %	11.72	12.43	13.34	13.65	16.85	9.40	9.22	...
EBITDA Margin %	3.93	3.88	3.40	4.02	3.55	2.73	3.16	2.23
Net Margin %	1.54	1.50	1.18	1.68	1.84	0.92	0.72	N.M.
Asset Turnover	2.41	2.67	2.63	2.66	2.69	2.51	2.49	...
Current Ratio	1.40	1.37	1.39	1.43	1.41	1.42	1.70	1.54
Debt to Equity	1.35	0.90	0.99	1.04	1.33	1.46	2.45	2.80
Price Range	42.81-27.99	40.60-27.99	40.60-27.99	40.60-27.99	31.93-25.77	27.48-22.38	...	...
P/E Ratio	23.92-15.64	22.19-15.30	21.60-14.89	21.71-14.97	16.21-13.08	26.68-21.73	...	...

Address: 9399 W. Higgins Road, Suite 100, Rosemont, IL 60018 **Telephone:** 847-720-8000	**Web Site:** www.usfoods.com **Officers:** Pietro Satriano - Chairman, President, Chief Executive Officer Kristin M. Coleman - Executive Vice President, Chief Compliance Officer, General Counsel	**Auditors:** DELOITTE & TOUCHE LLP **Transfer Agents:** American Stock Transfer & Trust Company, LLC

VAIL RESORTS INC

Exchange	Symbol	Price	52Wk Range	Yield	P/E
NYS	MTN	$239.83 (12/31/2019)	249.25-180.81	2.94	32.67

*7 Year Price Score 121.74 *NYSE Composite Index=100 *12 Month Price Score 100.76

Interim Earnings (Per Share)

Qtr.	Oct	Jan	Apr	Jul
2016-17	(1.70)	3.63	4.40	(1.46)
2017-18	(0.71)	5.67	6.17	(2.00)
2018-19	(2.66)	5.02	7.12	(2.16)
2019-20	(2.64)	...	...	...

Interim Dividends (Per Share)

Amt	Decl	Ex	Rec	Pay
1.76Q	03/08/2019	03/26/2019	03/27/2019	04/11/2019
1.76Q	06/05/2019	06/25/2019	06/26/2019	07/11/2019
1.76Q	09/25/2019	10/07/2019	10/08/2019	10/25/2019
1.76Q	12/09/2019	12/24/2019	12/26/2019	01/09/2020

Indicated Div: $7.04

Valuation Analysis / Institutional Holding

Valuation Analysis		Institutional Holding	
Forecast EPS	$8.00	No of Institutions	
	(01/15/2020)	571	
Market Cap	$9.7 Billion	Shares	
Book Value	$1.3 Billion	46,998,312	
Price/Book	7.41	% Held	
Price/Sales	4.16	95.21	

Business Summary: Sporting & Recreational (MIC: 2.2.4 SIC: 7999 NAIC: 713990)

Vail Resorts is a holding company and operates through various subsidiaries. Co.'s business segments include: Mountain, which operates various mountain resort properties and three urban ski areas, as well as ancillary services; Lodging, which provides a range of services to guests, including owned and managed lodging properties, managed condominium units, National Park Service concessionaire properties, a resort ground transportation company, and Co.-owned mountain resort golf courses; and Real Estate, which includes the sale of land parcels to third-party developers and planning for future real estate development projects, including zoning and acquisition of applicable permits.

Recent Developments: For the quarter ended Oct 31 2019, net loss amounted to US$109.8 million versus a net loss of US$110.7 million in the year-earlier quarter. Revenues were US$267.8 million, up 21.7% from US$220.0 million the year before. Operating loss was US$135.5 million versus a loss of US$127.6 million in the prior-year quarter. Direct operating expenses rose 18.0% to US$271.7 million from US$230.4 million in the comparable period the year before. Indirect operating expenses increased 12.2% to US$131.6 million from US$117.2 million in the equivalent prior-year period.

Prospects: Our evaluation of Vail Resorts Inc. as of October 4th, 2019 is the result of our systematic analysis on three basic characteristics: earnings strength, relative valuation, and recent stock price movement. The company has generated a negative trend in earnings per share over the past 5 quarters. In addition, recent analyst estimates for the company have been reduced while MTN has posted results that exceeded analysts' expectations. Based on operating earnings yield, the company is fairly valued when compared to all of the companies we cover. Share price changes over the past year indicates that MTN will perform in line with the market over the near term.

Financial Data
(US$ in Thousands)

	3 Mos	07/31/2019	07/31/2018	07/31/2017	07/31/2016	07/31/2015	07/31/2014	07/31/2013
Earnings Per Share	7.34	7.32	9.13	5.22	4.01	3.07	0.77	1.03
Cash Flow Per Share	16.52	15.72	13.66	11.64	11.73	8.36	6.81	6.20
Tang Book Value Per Share	N.M.	N.M.	N.M.	N.M.	6.23	6.08	8.98	9.84
Dividends Per Share	6.750	6.460	5.046	3.726	2.865	2.075	1.245	0.790
Dividend Payout %	91.96	88.25	55.27	71.38	71.45	67.59	161.69	76.70
Income Statement								
Total Revenue	267,770	2,271,575	2,011,553	1,907,218	1,601,286	1,399,924	1,254,646	1,120,797
EBITDA	(75,857)	687,201	600,995	581,455	440,502	343,747	243,407	227,504
Depn & Amortn	57,845	210,700	199,200	180,800	156,800	144,000	136,600	130,200
Income Before Taxes	(156,392)	397,005	338,569	346,566	241,336	148,506	42,810	58,338
Income Taxes	(46,563)	75,472	(61,138)	116,731	93,165	34,718	15,866	21,619
Net Income	(106,475)	301,163	379,898	210,553	149,754	114,754	28,478	37,743
Average Shares	40,342	41,158	41,618	40,366	37,312	37,406	37,057	36,733
Balance Sheet								
Current Assets	428,334	527,940	538,736	433,070	322,865	288,143	275,046	343,469
Total Assets	5,157,747	4,426,077	4,064,984	4,110,718	2,482,018	2,489,621	2,173,849	2,275,422
Current Liabilities	971,500	719,133	593,620	604,557	506,481	398,647	324,206	313,335
Long-Term Obligations	2,005,057	1,527,744	1,234,277	1,234,024	686,909	806,676	625,600	795,928
Total Liabilities	3,855,259	2,925,450	2,475,550	2,539,562	1,607,478	1,623,053	1,353,006	1,451,554
Stockholders' Equity	1,302,488	1,500,627	1,589,434	1,571,156	874,540	866,568	820,843	823,868
Shares Outstanding	40,257	40,341	40,527	40,081	36,179	36,513	36,203	35,954
Statistical Record								
Return on Assets %	6.45	7.09	9.29	6.39	6.01	4.92	1.28	1.80
Return on Equity %	22.90	19.49	24.04	17.22	17.16	13.60	3.46	4.64
EBITDA Margin %	N.M.	30.25	29.88	30.49	27.51	24.55	19.40	20.30
Net Margin %	N.M.	13.26	18.89	11.04	9.35	8.20	2.27	3.37
Asset Turnover	0.49	0.54	0.49	0.58	0.64	0.60	0.56	0.53
Current Ratio	0.44	0.73	0.91	0.72	0.64	0.72	0.85	1.10
Debt to Equity	1.54	1.02	0.78	0.79	0.79	0.93	0.76	0.97
Price Range	281.41-180.81	301.42-180.81	290.38-205.66	215.36-142.60	144.80-101.26	111.48-74.23	78.79-64.90	66.98-49.00
P/E Ratio	38.34-24.63	41.18-24.70	31.81-22.53	41.26-27.32	36.11-25.25	36.31-24.18	102.32-84.29	65.03-47.57
Average Yield %	2.98	2.73	2.17	2.10	2.32	2.23	1.75	1.37

Address: 390 Interlocken Crescent, Broomfield, CO 80021 Telephone: 303-404-1800 Fax: 303-404-6415	Web Site: www.vailresorts.com Officers: Robert A. Katz - Chairman, Chief Executive Officer Michael Z. Barkin - Executive Vice President, Vice President, Chief Financial Officer	Auditors: PricewaterhouseCoopers LLP Investor Contact: 303-404-1820 Transfer Agents: Wells Fargo Shareowner Services, Saint Paul, MN

VALARIS PLC

Exchange	Symbol	Price	52Wk Range	Yield	P/E
NYS	VAL	$6.56 (12/31/2019)	19.12-3.52	N/A	N/A

*7 Year Price Score 9.49   *NYSE Composite Index=100   *12 Month Price Score 45.92

TRADING VOLUME (thousand shares)

Interim Earnings (Per Share)

Qtr.	Mar	Jun	Sep	Dec
2016	2.96	8.16	1.12	0.24
2017	(0.36)	(0.60)	(0.32)	(2.36)
2018	(1.28)	(1.40)	(1.32)	(1.84)
2019	(1.75)	2.09	(1.00)	...

Interim Dividends (Per Share)

Dividend Payment Suspended

Valuation Analysis		Institutional Holding	
Forecast EPS	N/A	No of Institutions	
		492	
Market Cap	$1.3 Billion	Shares	
Book Value	$9.5 Billion	254,792,960	
Price/Book	0.14	% Held	
Price/Sales	0.67	N/A	

Business Summary: Production & Extraction (MIC: 9.1.1 SIC: 1381 NAIC: 213111)

Valaris is an offshore contract drilling company engaged in providing offshore contract drilling services to the international oil and gas industry. The markets in which Co. operates include the Gulf of Mexico, Brazil, the Mediterranean, the North Sea, the Middle East, West Africa, Australia and Southeast Asia. Co. provides drilling services on a day rate contract basis. Co.'s business consists of three operating segments: Floaters, which includes its drillships and semisubmersible rigs; Jackups; and Other, which consists of management services on rigs owned by third-parties. Co.'s two reportable segments, Floaters and Jackups, provide one service, contract drilling.

Recent Developments: For the quarter ended Sep 30 2019, net loss amounted to US$197.5 million versus a net loss of US$142.9 million in the year-earlier quarter. Revenues were US$551.3 million, up 27.9% from US$430.9 million the year before. Operating loss was US$236.2 million versus a loss of US$41.9 million in the prior-year quarter. Direct operating expenses rose 51.8% to US$496.5 million from US$327.1 million in the comparable period the year before. Indirect operating expenses increased 99.7% to US$291.0 million from US$145.7 million in the equivalent prior-year period.

Prospects: Our evaluation of Valaris plc as of October 4th, 2019 is the result of our systematic analysis on three basic characteristics: earnings strength, relative valuation, and recent stock price movement. The company has enjoyed a very positive trend in earnings per share over the past 5 quarters. However, recent analyst estimates for the company have been mixed and VAL has posted results that fell short of analysts' expectations. Based on operating earnings yield, the company is overvalued when compared to all of the companies we cover. Share price changes over the past year indicates that VAL will perform well over the near term.

Financial Data
(US$ in Thousands)

	9 Mos	6 Mos	3 Mos	12/31/2018	12/31/2017	12/31/2016	12/31/2015	12/31/2014
Earnings Per Share	(2.50)	(2.82)	(6.31)	(5.88)	(3.64)	12.52	(27.52)	(67.52)
Cash Flow Per Share	(2.03)	(1.76)	(1.10)	(0.51)	3.12	15.40	29.25	35.54
Tang Book Value Per Share	48.08	49.08	72.25	74.01	79.98	108.90	110.60	134.73
Dividends Per Share	...	...	0.160	0.160	0.160	0.160	2.400	12.000
Dividend Payout %	...	...	...	...	...	1.28	...	...
Income Statement								
Total Revenue	1,541,100	989,800	405,900	1,705,400	1,843,000	2,776,400	4,063,400	4,564,500
EBITDA	809,400	732,300	31,500	208,200	447,200	1,657,800	(692,300)	(1,862,500)
Depn & Amortn	427,800	265,600	110,500	478,900	444,800	445,300	572,500	537,900
Income Before Taxes	90,500	282,800	(156,500)	(538,900)	(196,000)	997,500	(1,471,200)	(2,548,800)
Income Taxes	65,600	64,100	31,500	89,600	109,200	108,500	(13,900)	140,500
Net Income	18,000	215,100	(190,400)	(639,700)	(303,700)	890,200	(1,594,800)	(3,902,600)
Average Shares	197,600	188,600	108,700	108,525	83,125	69,775	58,050	57,900
Balance Sheet								
Current Assets	1,184,000	2,222,500	1,211,900	1,309,700	1,612,000	3,279,300	2,285,100	2,934,800
Total Assets	17,230,600	18,440,100	13,863,000	14,023,700	14,625,900	14,374,500	13,637,000	16,059,900
Current Liabilities	859,600	1,898,800	516,900	528,500	758,500	854,400	775,500	1,104,600
Long-Term Obligations	6,042,300	6,020,100	5,018,500	5,010,400	4,750,700	4,942,600	5,895,100	5,885,600
Total Liabilities	7,699,200	8,719,500	5,962,500	5,932,300	5,893,800	6,123,900	7,124,100	7,844,900
Stockholders' Equity	9,531,400	9,720,600	7,900,500	8,091,400	8,732,100	8,250,600	6,512,900	8,215,000
Shares Outstanding	197,950	197,750	109,350	109,287	108,987	75,762	58,837	58,562
Statistical Record								
Return on Assets %	N.M.	N.M.	N.M.	N.M.	N.M.	6.34	N.M.	N.M.
Return on Equity %	N.M.	N.M.	N.M.	N.M.	N.M.	12.03	N.M.	N.M.
EBITDA Margin %	52.52	73.98	7.76	12.21	24.26	59.71	N.M.	N.M.
Net Margin %	1.17	21.73	N.M.	N.M.	N.M.	32.06	N.M.	N.M.
Asset Turnover	0.12	0.11	0.12	0.12	0.13	0.20	0.27	0.26
Current Ratio	1.38	1.17	2.34	2.48	2.13	3.84	2.95	2.66
Debt to Equity	0.63	0.62	0.64	0.62	0.54	0.60	0.91	0.72
Price Range	37.64-3.74	37.64-6.62	37.64-13.08	37.64-13.08	47.24-16.64	63.56-26.56	127.72-54.12	229.32-105.64
P/E Ratio	...	...	...	...	...	5.08-2.12	...	...
Average Yield %	...	...	0.66	0.63	0.58	0.42	2.86	6.34

Address: 6 Chesterfield Gardens, London, W1J5BQ Telephone: 207-659-4660	Web Site: www.enscoplc.com Officers: Carl G. Trowell - Executive Chairman, President, Chief Executive Officer Thomas Peter Burke - President, Chief Executive Officer	Auditors: KPMG LLP Investor Contact: 713-430-4607 Transfer Agents: Computershare Trust Company, N.A.

VALERO ENERGY CORP

Exchange	Symbol	Price	52Wk Range	Yield	P/E
NYS	VLO	$93.65 (12/31/2019)	101.40-70.40	3.84	16.93

*7 Year Price Score 104.90 *NYSE Composite Index=100 *12 Month Price Score 107.08

Interim Earnings (Per Share)

Qtr.	Mar	Jun	Sep	Dec
2016	1.05	1.73	1.33	0.82
2017	0.68	1.23	1.91	5.36
2018	1.09	1.96	2.01	2.24
2019	0.34	1.47	1.48	...

Interim Dividends (Per Share)

Amt	Decl	Ex	Rec	Pay
0.90Q	01/24/2019	02/12/2019	02/13/2019	03/05/2019
0.90Q	04/30/2019	05/14/2019	05/15/2019	06/04/2019
0.90Q	07/18/2019	08/05/2019	08/06/2019	09/04/2019
0.90Q	10/30/2019	11/19/2019	11/20/2019	12/11/2019

Indicated Div: $3.60

Valuation Analysis **Institutional Holding**

Forecast EPS	$4.97	No of Institutions
	(01/17/2020)	1633
Market Cap	$38.5 Billion	Shares
Book Value	$21.1 Billion	410,933,344
Price/Book	1.82	% Held
Price/Sales	0.35	70.89

Business Summary: Refining & Marketing (MIC: 9.1.2 SIC: 2911 NAIC: 324110)

Valero Energy is an independent petroleum refiner and ethanol producer. Co.'s segments include: Refining, which sells refined petroleum products in the wholesale rack and bulk markets, and provides transportation and terminaling services through its subsidiary, Valero Energy Partners LP; Ethanol, which processes corn to produce ethanol, distillers grains, and corn oil, and sells its ethanol primarily to refiners and gasoline blenders; and Renewable Diesel, which includes the operations of its joint venture, Diamond Green Diesel Holdings LLC, that constructs and operates a biodiesel plant that processes animal fats, used cooking oils, and other vegetable oils into renewable green diesel.

Recent Developments: For the quarter ended Sep 30 2019, net income decreased 26.9% to US$639.0 million from US$874.0 million in the year-earlier quarter. Revenues were US$27.25 billion, down 11.7% from US$30.85 billion the year before. Operating income was US$881.0 million versus US$1.22 billion in the prior-year quarter, a decrease of 27.7%. Direct operating expenses declined 11.1% to US$26.13 billion from US$29.40 billion in the comparable period the year before. Indirect operating expenses increased 2.6% to US$238.0 million from US$232.0 million in the equivalent prior-year period.

Prospects: Our evaluation of Valero Energy Corp. as of October 4th, 2019 is the result of our systematic analysis on three basic characteristics: earnings strength, relative valuation, and recent stock price movement. The company has generated a negative trend in earnings per share over the past 5 quarters. In addition, recent analyst estimates for the company have been reduced while VLO has posted results that exceeded analysts' expectations. Based on operating earnings yield, the company is undervalued when compared to all of the companies we cover. Share price changes over the past year indicates that VLO will perform very poorly over the near term.

Financial Data

(US$ in Thousands)	9 Mos	6 Mos	3 Mos	12/31/2018	12/31/2017	12/31/2016	12/31/2015	12/31/2014
Earnings Per Share	5.53	6.06	6.55	7.29	9.16	4.94	7.99	6.85
Cash Flow Per Share	13.35	11.01	12.28	10.26	12.40	10.43	11.29	8.06
Tang Book Value Per Share	51.38	51.48	51.07	51.89	50.68	44.35	43.39	40.20
Dividends Per Share	3.500	3.400	3.300	3.200	2.800	2.400	1.700	1.050
Dividend Payout %	63.29	56.11	50.38	43.90	30.57	48.58	21.28	15.33
Income Statement								
Total Revenue	80,445,000	53,196,000	24,263,000	117,033,000	93,980,000	75,659,000	87,804,000	130,844,000
EBITDA	3,849,000	2,367,000	881,000	6,102,000	4,975,000	4,928,000	7,704,000	7,149,000
Depn & Amortn	1,684,000	1,117,000	551,000	1,400,000	1,300,000	1,300,000	1,300,000	1,200,000
Income Before Taxes	1,830,000	1,026,000	218,000	4,232,000	3,207,000	3,182,000	5,971,000	5,552,000
Income Taxes	376,000	211,000	51,000	879,000	(949,000)	765,000	1,870,000	1,777,000
Net Income	1,362,000	753,000	141,000	3,122,000	4,065,000	2,289,000	3,990,000	3,630,000
Average Shares	413,000	417,000	418,000	428,000	444,000	464,000	500,000	530,000
Balance Sheet								
Current Assets	17,033,000	17,811,000	18,480,000	17,675,000	19,312,000	16,800,000	14,972,000	16,614,000
Total Assets	51,229,000	52,022,000	52,095,000	50,155,000	50,158,000	46,173,000	44,343,000	45,550,000
Current Liabilities	12,130,000	12,548,000	12,913,000	10,724,000	11,071,000	8,328,000	7,360,000	9,980,000
Long-Term Obligations	9,170,000	9,167,000	9,006,000	8,871,000	8,750,000	7,886,000	7,250,000	5,780,000
Total Liabilities	30,122,000	30,677,000	30,786,000	28,488,000	28,167,000	26,149,000	23,816,000	24,873,000
Stockholders' Equity	21,107,000	21,345,000	21,309,000	21,667,000	21,991,000	20,024,000	20,527,000	20,677,000
Shares Outstanding	410,809	414,607	417,227	417,596	433,898	451,501	473,039	514,298
Statistical Record								
Return on Assets %	4.49	4.99	5.51	6.22	8.44	5.04	8.88	7.82
Return on Equity %	10.76	11.88	12.94	14.30	19.35	11.26	19.37	18.09
EBITDA Margin %	4.78	4.45	3.63	5.21	5.29	6.51	8.77	5.46
Net Margin %	1.69	1.42	0.58	2.67	4.33	3.03	4.54	2.77
Asset Turnover	2.12	2.20	2.26	2.33	1.95	1.67	1.95	2.82
Current Ratio	1.40	1.42	1.43	1.65	1.74	2.02	2.03	1.66
Debt to Equity	0.43	0.43	0.42	0.41	0.40	0.39	0.35	0.28
Price Range	119.99-68.94	121.21-68.94	124.44-68.94	124.44-68.94	92.30-61.47	72.09-47.24	73.03-44.07	58.51-43.76
P/E Ratio	21.70-12.47	20.00-11.38	19.00-10.53	17.07-9.46	10.08-6.71	14.59-9.56	9.14-5.52	8.54-6.39
Average Yield %	4.19	3.33	3.33	3.14	3.95	4.09	2.76	2.05

Address: One Valero Way, San Antonio, TX 78249	Web Site: www.valero.com	Auditors: KPMG LLP
Telephone: 210-345-2000	Officers: Joseph W. Gorder - Chairman, President, Chief Executive Officer, Associate/Affiliate Company Officer, Executive Vice President, Chief Operating Officer, Chief Commercial Officer Donna M. Titzman - Executive Vice President, Senior Vice President, Vice President, Chief Financial Officer, Treasurer	Investor Contact: 800-531-7911
Fax: 210-246-2646		Transfer Agents: ComputerShare Investor Services, Providence, RI

VALMONT INDUSTRIES INC

Exchange	Symbol	Price	52Wk Range	Yield	P/E
NYS	VMI	$149.78 (12/31/2019)	150.89-109.07	1.00	24.12

*7 Year Price Score 79.42 *NYSE Composite Index=100 *12 Month Price Score 103.34

TRADING VOLUME (thousand shares)

Interim Earnings (Per Share)

Qtr.	Mar	Jun	Sep	Dec
2016	1.45	1.85	1.24	3.09
2017	1.72	2.01	1.55	(0.17)
2018	1.72	1.46	0.20	0.80
2019	1.66	1.90	1.85	...

Interim Dividends (Per Share)

Amt	Decl	Ex	Rec	Pay
0.375Q	03/04/2019	03/28/2019	03/29/2019	04/15/2019
0.375Q	06/03/2019	06/27/2019	06/28/2019	07/15/2019
0.375Q	09/03/2019	09/26/2019	09/27/2019	10/15/2019
0.375Q	12/02/2019	12/26/2019	12/27/2019	01/15/2020

Indicated Div: $1.50 (Div. Reinv. Plan)

Valuation Analysis

		Institutional Holding	
Forecast EPS	$7.25	No of Institutions	
	(01/17/2020)	390	
Market Cap	$3.2 Billion	Shares	
Book Value	$1.1 Billion	25,948,026	
Price/Book	2.97	% Held	
Price/Sales	1.16	81.46	

Business Summary: Construction Materials (MIC: 8.5.1 SIC: 3499 NAIC: 332323)

Valmont Industries is a producer of fabricated metal products. Co. has four segments: Engineered Support Structures, which manufactures steel, aluminum, and composite poles and structures to which lighting and traffic control fixtures are attached for a range of outdoor lighting applications, such as streets, highways, parking lots, sports stadiums and commercial and residential developments; Utility Support Structures, which manufactures steel and concrete pole structures for electrical transmission; Coatings, which consists of galvanizing, anodizing and powder coating services; and Irrigation, which manufactures and distributes mechanical irrigation equipment and related service parts.

Recent Developments: For the quarter ended Sep 28 2019, net income increased 504.5% to US$42.3 million from US$7.0 million in the year-earlier quarter. Revenues were US$690.3 million, up 1.7% from US$678.7 million the year before. Operating income was US$63.9 million versus US$38.4 million in the prior-year quarter, an increase of 66.5%. Direct operating expenses declined 0.0% to US$514.3 million from US$514.4 million in the comparable period the year before. Indirect operating expenses decreased 10.9% to US$112.2 million from US$126.0 million in the equivalent prior-year period.

Prospects: Our evaluation of Valmont Industries Inc. as of October 4th, 2019 is the result of our systematic analysis on three basic characteristics: earnings strength, relative valuation, and recent stock price movement. The company has enjoyed a very positive trend in earnings per share over the past 5 quarters. However, recent analyst estimates for the company have been reduced, and VMI has posted results that fell short of analysts' expectations. Based on operating earnings yield, the company is undervalued when compared to all of the companies we cover. Share price changes over the past year indicates that VMI will perform in line with the market over the near term.

Financial Data

(US$ in Thousands)	9 Mos	6 Mos	3 Mos	12/29/2018	12/30/2017	12/31/2016	12/26/2015	12/27/2014
Earnings Per Share	6.21	4.56	4.12	4.20	5.11	7.63	1.71	7.09
Cash Flow Per Share	15.04	9.79	5.84	6.88	6.49	9.56	11.72	6.79
Tang Book Value Per Share	22.64	21.66	21.43	22.72	28.05	21.22	18.00	25.37
Dividends Per Share	1.500	1.500	1.500	1.500	1.500	1.500	1.500	1.375
Dividend Payout %	24.15	32.89	36.41	35.71	29.35	19.66	87.72	19.39
Income Statement								
Total Revenue	2,083,350	1,393,010	692,139	2,757,144	2,745,967	2,521,676	2,618,924	3,123,143
EBITDA	249,795	164,921	79,203	265,837	353,329	344,175	225,476	404,255
Depn & Amortn	60,424	40,583	20,253	82,827	84,957	82,417	91,144	89,328
Income Before Taxes	162,215	106,189	49,882	143,441	228,464	220,454	93,007	284,183
Income Taxes	40,151	26,388	12,427	43,135	106,145	42,063	47,427	94,894
Net Income	118,022	77,878	36,481	94,351	116,240	173,232	40,117	183,976
Average Shares	21,684	21,831	21,964	22,446	22,738	22,709	23,405	25,719
Balance Sheet								
Current Assets	1,388,404	1,347,998	1,298,900	1,340,640	1,472,565	1,253,216	1,226,852	1,392,941
Total Assets	2,725,442	2,711,739	2,645,987	2,530,274	2,602,250	2,391,731	2,399,428	2,729,668
Current Liabilities	530,947	497,301	440,839	409,035	402,998	349,848	366,554	397,214
Long-Term Obligations	764,524	765,558	741,629	741,822	753,888	754,795	763,964	766,654
Total Liabilities	1,638,751	1,629,997	1,567,722	1,470,512	1,489,414	1,448,249	1,480,987	1,527,835
Stockholders' Equity	1,086,691	1,081,742	1,078,265	1,059,762	1,112,836	943,482	918,441	1,201,833
Shares Outstanding	21,525	21,632	21,856	21,948	22,693	22,520	22,857	24,229
Statistical Record								
Return on Assets %	5.13	3.64	3.48	3.69	4.67	7.11	1.57	6.70
Return on Equity %	12.66	9.12	8.23	8.71	11.34	18.31	3.79	13.55
EBITDA Margin %	11.99	11.84	11.44	9.64	12.87	13.65	8.61	12.94
Net Margin %	5.67	5.59	5.27	3.42	4.23	6.87	1.53	5.89
Asset Turnover	1.05	1.01	1.05	1.08	1.10	1.04	1.02	1.14
Current Ratio	2.61	2.71	2.95	3.28	3.65	3.58	3.35	3.51
Debt to Equity	0.70	0.71	0.69	0.70	0.68	0.80	0.83	0.64
Price Range	146.00-104.22	156.65-104.22	156.65-104.22	171.10-104.22	172.85-136.05	155.40-98.95	130.26-93.99	161.11-123.75
P/E Ratio	23.51-16.78	34.35-22.86	38.02-25.30	40.74-24.81	33.83-26.62	20.37-12.97	76.18-54.96	22.72-17.45
Average Yield %	1.17	1.16	1.11	1.06	0.98	1.17	1.29	0.95

Address: One Valmont Plaza, Omaha, NE 68154-5215	**Web Site:** www.valmont.com	**Auditors:** DELOITTE & TOUCHE LLP
Telephone: 402-963-1000	**Officers:** Mogens C. Bay - Executive Chairman, Chairman, Chairman (frmr), President, Chief Executive Officer Stephen G. Kaniewski - President, Chief Executive Officer, Chief Operating Officer	**Investor Contact:** 402-963-1000
Fax: 402-963-1198		**Transfer Agents:** Wells Fargo Shareowner Services, Mendota Heights, MN

VALVOLINE INC

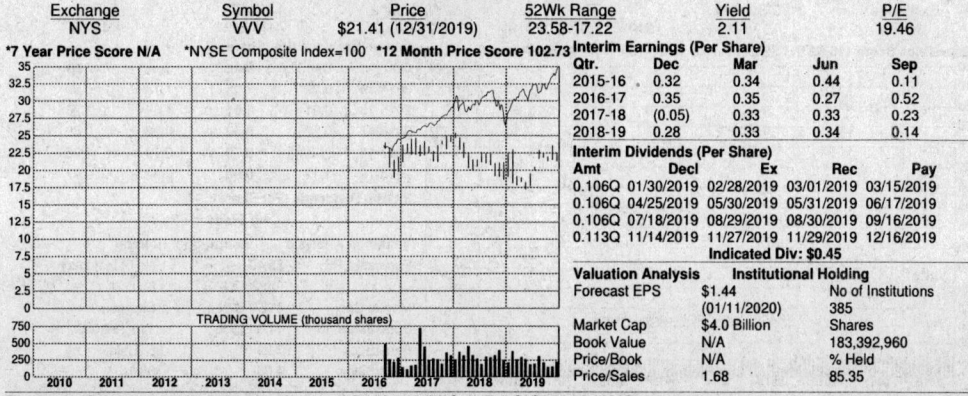

Exchange	Symbol	Price	52Wk Range	Yield	P/E
NYS	VVV	$21.41 (12/31/2019)	23.58-17.22	2.11	19.46

*7 Year Price Score N/A   *NYSE Composite Index=100   *12 Month Price Score 102.73

Interim Earnings (Per Share)
Qtr.	Dec	Mar	Jun	Sep
2015-16	0.32	0.34	0.44	0.11
2016-17	0.35	0.35	0.27	0.52
2017-18	(0.05)	0.33	0.33	0.23
2018-19	0.28	0.33	0.34	0.14

Interim Dividends (Per Share)
Amt	Decl	Ex	Rec	Pay
0.106Q	01/30/2019	02/28/2019	03/01/2019	03/15/2019
0.106Q	04/25/2019	05/30/2019	05/31/2019	06/17/2019
0.106Q	07/18/2019	08/29/2019	08/30/2019	09/16/2019
0.113Q	11/14/2019	11/27/2019	11/29/2019	12/16/2019

Indicated Div: $0.45

Valuation Analysis

		Institutional Holding	
Forecast EPS	$1.44 (01/11/2020)	No of Institutions	385
Market Cap	$4.0 Billion	Shares	
Book Value	N/A		183,392,960
Price/Book	N/A	% Held	85.35
Price/Sales	1.68		

Business Summary: Household & Personal Products (MIC: 1.7.1 SIC: 2992 NAIC: 324191)

Valvoline is a marketer and supplier of engine and automotive maintenance products and services. Co.'s segments are: Quick Lubes, which services the passenger car and light truck quick lube market via Co.-owned, independent franchises and joint venture retail quick lube service center stores, as well as independent Express Care stores that service vehicles with Co.'s products; Core North America, which sells Valvoline™ and other branded and private label engine and automotive maintenance products in the United States and Canada; and International, which sells Valvoline™ and other branded engine and automotive products for the maintenance of consumer and commercial vehicles and equipment.

Recent Developments: For the year ended Sep 30 2019, net income increased 25.3% to US$208.0 million from US$166.0 million in the prior year. Revenues were US$2.39 billion, up 4.6% from US$2.29 billion the year before. Operating income was US$398.0 million versus US$395.0 million in the prior year, an increase of 0.8%. Direct operating expenses rose 6.8% to US$1.58 billion from US$1.48 billion in the comparable period the year before. Indirect operating expenses increased 0.2% to US$412.0 million from US$411.0 million in the equivalent prior-year period.

Prospects: Our evaluation of Valvoline Inc as of October 4th, 2019 is the result of our systematic analysis on three basic characteristics: earnings strength, relative valuation, and recent stock price movement. The company has produced a positive trend in earnings per share over the past 5 quarters. However, recent analyst estimates for the company have been mixed and VVV has posted results that exceeded analysts' expectations. Based on operating earnings yield, the company is undervalued when compared to all of the companies we cover. Share price changes over the past year indicates that VVV will perform well over the near term.

Financial Data
(US$ in Thousands)

	09/30/2019	09/30/2018	09/30/2017	09/30/2016	09/30/2015	09/30/2014	09/30/2013
Earnings Per Share	1.10	0.84	1.49	1.33	...	...	...
Cash Flow Per Share	1.72	1.62	(0.64)	1.51	...	...	...
Dividends Per Share	0.424	0.298	0.196	...	...	...	...
Dividend Payout %	38.55	35.48	13.15	...	...	...	...
Income Statement							
Total Revenue	2,390,000	2,285,000	2,084,000	1,929,000	1,966,900	2,041,300	1,996,200
EBITDA	390,000	449,000	574,000	468,000	334,400	301,200	415,700
Depn & Amortn	52,000	54,000	42,000	38,000	37,600	36,500	35,100
Income Before Taxes	265,000	332,000	490,000	421,000	296,800	264,700	380,600
Income Taxes	57,000	166,000	186,000	148,000	100,700	91,300	134,500
Net Income	208,000	166,000	304,000	273,000	196,100	173,400	246,100
Average Shares	189,000	197,000	204,000	205,000	...	...	...
Balance Sheet							
Current Assets	797,000	725,000	790,000	730,000	477,300	544,700	...
Total Assets	2,064,000	1,854,000	1,915,000	1,825,000	977,900	1,082,500	...
Current Liabilities	423,000	411,000	478,000	400,000	298,600	293,500	...
Long-Term Obligations	1,327,000	1,292,000	1,034,000	724,000	...	...	...
Total Liabilities	2,322,000	2,212,000	2,032,000	2,155,000	360,800	357,700	...
Stockholders' Equity	(258,000)	(358,000)	(117,000)	(330,000)	617,100	724,800	...
Shares Outstanding	188,000	188,000	203,000	205,000	...	...	...
Statistical Record							
Return on Assets %	10.62	8.81	16.26	19.43	19.04	...	...
Return on Equity %	...	...	...	189.66	29.23	...	...
EBITDA Margin %	16.32	19.65	27.54	24.26	17.00	14.76	20.82
Net Margin %	8.70	7.26	14.59	14.15	9.97	8.49	12.33
Asset Turnover	1.22	1.21	1.11	1.37	1.91	...	...
Current Ratio	1.88	1.76	1.65	1.83	1.60	1.86	...
Price Range	22.96-17.22	25.40-20.02	24.66-18.90	23.98-23.10	...	...	...
P/E Ratio	20.87-15.65	30.24-23.83	16.55-12.68	18.03-17.37	...	...	...
Average Yield %	2.13	1.31	0.87	...	...	...	...

Address: 100 Valvoline Way, Lexington, KY 40509	**Web Site:** www.valvoline.com	**Auditors:** Ernst & Young LLP
Telephone: 859-357-7777	**Officers:** Stephen F. Kirk - Chairman Samuel J. Mitchell - President, Chief Executive Officer	**Investor Contact:** 859-357-7777
		Transfer Agents: Wells Fargo Shareowner Services

VARIAN MEDICAL SYSTEMS INC

Exchange	Symbol	Price	52Wk Range	Yield	P/E
NYS	VAR	$142.01 (12/31/2019)	143.26-105.07	N/A	44.66

*7 Year Price Score 116.62 ***NYSE Composite Index=100** ***12 Month Price Score 99.30**

Interim Earnings (Per Share)

Qtr.	Dec	Mar	Jun	Sep
2014-15	0.92	1.05	1.13	0.99
2015-16	0.91	1.01	1.04	1.24
2016-17	0.22	0.60	0.98	0.89
2017-18	(1.22)	0.79	0.79	1.26
2018-19	1.12	0.96	0.32	0.77

Interim Dividends (Per Share)

No Dividends Paid

Valuation Analysis | **Institutional Holding**

Forecast EPS	$5.40	No of Institutions
	(00/25/2020)	893
Market Cap	$12.9 Billion	Shares
Book Value	$1.8 Billion	113,189,000
Price/Book	7.29	% Held
Price/Sales	4.00	88.16

TRADING VOLUME (thousand shares)

Business Summary: Medical Instruments & Equipment (MIC: 4.3.1 SIC: 3845 NAIC: 334510)

Varian Medical Systems is a manufacturer of medical devices and software for treating cancer and other medical conditions. Co.'s segments are: Oncology Systems, which designs, manufactures, sells and services hardware and software products for treating cancer with radiotherapy, and treatments such as fixed field intensity-modulated radiation therapy, image-guided radiation therapy, volumetric modulated arc therapy, stereotactic radiosurgery, stereotactic body radiotherapy and brachytherapy, as well as associated equipment; and Proton Solutions, which develops, designs, manufactures, sells and services products and systems for delivering proton therapy, for the treatment of cancer.

Recent Developments: For the year ended Sep 27 2019, income from continuing operations increased 94.4% to US$292.2 million from US$150.3 million a year earlier. Net income increased 94.4% to US$292.2 million from US$150.3 million in the prior year. Revenues were US$3.23 billion, up 10.5% from US$2.92 billion the year before. Operating income was US$386.2 million versus US$437.4 million in the prior year, a decrease of 11.7%. Direct operating expenses rose 12.7% to US$1.85 billion from US$1.65 billion in the comparable period the year before. Indirect operating expenses increased 17.7% to US$984.1 million from US$836.2 million in the equivalent prior-year period.

Prospects: Our evaluation of Varian Medical Systems Inc. as of October 4th, 2019 is the result of our systematic analysis on three basic characteristics: earnings strength, relative valuation, and recent stock price movement. The company has produced a positive trend in earnings per share over the past 5 quarters. However, recent analyst estimates for the company have been mixed and VAR has posted results that exceeded analysts' expectations. Based on operating earnings yield, the company is fairly valued when compared to all of the companies we cover. Share price changes over the past year indicates that VAR will perform in line with the market over the near term.

Financial Data
(US$ in Thousands)

	09/27/2019	09/28/2018	09/29/2017	09/30/2016	10/02/2015	09/26/2014	09/27/2013	09/28/2012
Earnings Per Share	3.18	1.62	2.68	4.19	4.09	3.83	3.98	3.76
Cash Flow Per Share	4.10	4.99	4.33	3.75	4.63	4.33	4.21	4.44
Tang Book Value Per Share	9.42	13.04	13.09	14.31	13.82	13.22	13.98	11.77
Income Statement								
Total Revenue	3,225,100	2,919,100	2,668,200	3,217,800	3,099,111	3,049,800	2,942,897	2,807,015
EBITDA	468,300	514,300	418,800	630,600	617,487	633,612	671,749	655,056
Depn & Amortn	53,800	72,700	76,900	79,800	68,520	62,457	62,859	60,982
Income Before Taxes	420,800	452,100	344,800	556,400	554,662	574,510	612,083	595,924
Income Taxes	128,600	301,800	87,700	153,700	142,644	170,807	173,835	168,875
Net Income	291,900	149,900	249,600	402,300	411,485	403,703	438,248	427,049
Average Shares	91,900	92,500	93,200	96,000	100,552	105,271	110,053	113,473
Balance Sheet								
Current Assets	2,395,400	2,188,400	2,190,300	2,616,000	2,525,045	2,494,165	2,704,783	2,170,515
Total Assets	4,101,700	3,252,700	3,179,400	3,816,000	3,600,748	3,357,290	3,468,474	2,878,726
Current Liabilities	1,884,000	1,339,700	1,550,100	1,614,000	1,382,904	1,201,654	1,160,579	1,236,531
Long-Term Obligations	...	...	...	287,500	337,500	387,500	450,000	6,250
Total Liabilities	2,333,400	1,668,300	1,684,400	2,075,500	1,889,148	1,740,870	1,754,627	1,368,950
Stockholders' Equity	1,768,300	1,584,400	1,495,000	1,740,500	1,711,600	1,616,420	1,713,847	1,509,776
Shares Outstanding	90,800	91,200	91,700	93,700	98,070	100,942	106,491	109,407
Statistical Record								
Return on Assets %	7.96	4.67	7.16	10.88	11.64	11.86	13.85	15.93
Return on Equity %	17.46	9.76	15.47	23.37	24.33	24.31	27.26	31.10
EBITDA Margin %	14.52	17.62	15.70	19.60	19.92	20.78	22.83	23.34
Net Margin %	9.05	5.14	9.35	12.50	13.28	13.24	14.89	15.21
Asset Turnover	0.88	0.91	0.76	0.87	0.88	0.90	0.93	1.05
Current Ratio	1.27	1.63	1.41	1.62	1.83	2.08	2.33	1.76
Debt to Equity	...	...	...	0.17	0.20	0.24	0.26	N.M.
Price Range	141.98-103.97	129.46-100.06	107.87-76.57	88.16-65.55	85.14-63.26	77.50-64.20	67.54-50.55	63.49-44.37
P/E Ratio	44.65-32.69	79.91-61.77	40.25-28.57	21.04-15.64	20.82-15.47	20.24-16.76	16.97-12.70	16.89-11.80

Address: 3100 Hansen Way, Palo Alto, CA 94304-1038 Telephone: 650-493-4000	Web Site: www.varian.com Officers: R. Andrew Eckert - Chairman Timothy E. Guertin - Vice-Chairman, President, Chief Executive Officer	Auditors: PricewaterhouseCoopers LLP Investor Contact: 650-424-5782 Transfer Agents: Computershare Trust Company, N.A., Providence, RI

VECTOR GROUP LTD

Exchange	Symbol	Price	52Wk Range	Yield	P/E	Div Acheiver
NYS	VGR	$13.39 (12/31/2019)	14.14-8.52	11.95	19.13	20 Years

*7 Year Price Score 57.03 *NYSE Composite Index=100 *12 Month Price Score 110.77

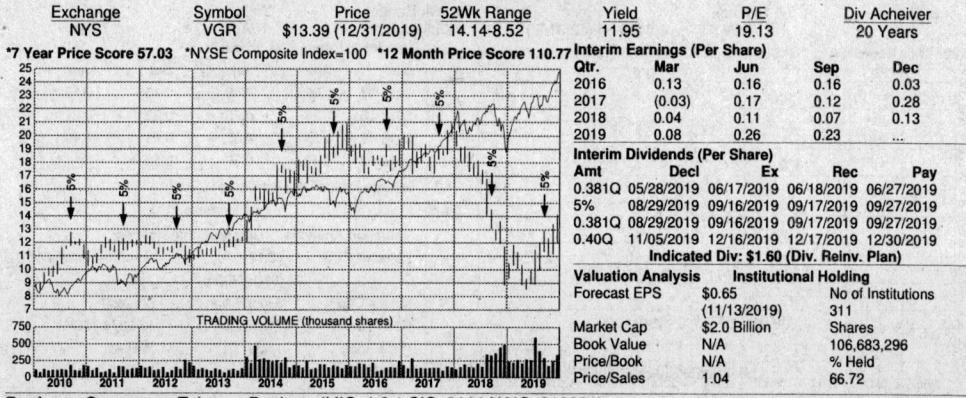

Interim Earnings (Per Share)

Qtr.	Mar	Jun	Sep	Dec
2016	0.13	0.16	0.16	0.03
2017	(0.03)	0.17	0.12	0.28
2018	0.04	0.11	0.07	0.13
2019	0.08	0.26	0.23	...

Interim Dividends (Per Share)

Amt	Decl	Ex	Rec	Pay
0.381Q	05/28/2019	06/17/2019	06/18/2019	06/27/2019
5%	08/29/2019	09/16/2019	09/17/2019	09/27/2019
0.381Q	08/29/2019	09/16/2019	09/17/2019	09/27/2019
0.40Q	11/05/2019	12/16/2019	12/17/2019	12/30/2019

Indicated Div: $1.60 (Div. Reinv. Plan)

Valuation Analysis | **Institutional Holding**

Forecast EPS	$0.65	No of Institutions
	(11/13/2019)	311
Market Cap	$2.0 Billion	Shares
Book Value	N/A	106,683,296
Price/Book	N/A	% Held
Price/Sales	1.04	66.72

Business Summary: Tobacco Products (MIC: 1.3.1 SIC: 2111 NAIC: 312221)

Vector Group is a holding company. Co. is engaged principally in the manufacture and sale of cigarettes in the U.S. through its Liggett Group LLC (Liggett) and Vector Tobacco Inc. subsidiaries; and the real estate business through its New Valley LLC (New Valley) subsidiary. Co.'s business segments were Tobacco, and Real Estate. The Tobacco segment consists of the manufacture and sale of conventional cigarettes. The Real Estate segment includes Co.'s investment in New Valley, which includes Douglas Elliman, Escena, Sagaponack and investments in real estate ventures.

Recent Developments: For the quarter ended Sep 30 2019, net income increased 139.6% to US$36.0 million from US$15.0 million in the year-earlier quarter. Revenues were US$504.8 million, down 1.8% from US$513.9 million the year before. Operating income was US$66.7 million versus US$66.0 million in the prior-year quarter, an increase of 1.1%. Direct operating expenses declined 4.1% to US$345.5 million from US$360.3 million in the comparable period the year before. Indirect operating expenses increased 5.8% to US$92.6 million from US$87.5 million in the equivalent prior-year period.

Prospects: Our evaluation of Vector Group Ltd. as of October 4th, 2019 is the result of our systematic analysis on three basic characteristics: earnings strength, relative valuation, and recent stock price movement. The company has produced a positive trend in earnings per share over the past 5 quarters. However, recent analyst estimates for the company have been unchanged, while VGR has posted results that exceeded analysts' expectations. Based on operating earnings yield, the company is fairly valued when compared to all of the companies we cover. Share price changes over the past year indicates that VGR will perform poorly over the near term.

Financial Data

(US$ in Thousands)	9 Mos	6 Mos	3 Mos	12/31/2018	12/31/2017	12/31/2016	12/31/2015	12/31/2014
Earnings Per Share	0.70	0.53	0.39	0.35	0.54	0.48	0.40	0.27
Cash Flow Per Share	1.14	1.08	1.10	1.24	0.90	0.68	1.01	0.82
Dividends Per Share	1.524	1.506	1.488	1.469	1.399	1.333	1.269	1.209
Dividend Payout %	218.72	282.28	386.17	416.97	261.52	280.53	314.89	440.87
Income Statement								
Total Revenue	1,464,146	959,356	420,924	1,870,262	1,807,476	1,690,949	1,657,197	1,591,315
EBITDA	210,887	138,845	57,171	271,892	252,311	281,729	242,461	255,976
Depn & Amortn	...	...	...	17,506	17,479	20,782	20,423	17,843
Income Before Taxes	117,081	74,919	22,859	61,955	68,538	123,983	108,385	77,142
Income Taxes	37,944	24,208	6,749	21,552	(1,582)	49,163	41,233	33,251
Net Income	90,268	54,260	14,953	58,105	84,572	71,127	59,198	36,978
Average Shares	146,736	146,521	149,399	146,484	146,271	143,845	143,177	131,447
Balance Sheet								
Current Assets	634,368	638,493	627,361	872,221	613,709	705,463	583,739	857,846
Total Assets	1,486,684	1,455,160	1,429,156	1,549,504	1,328,278	1,404,035	1,310,756	1,573,392
Current Liabilities	606,842	558,067	302,617	484,920	204,639	196,148	216,292	270,095
Long-Term Obligations	1,178,241	1,180,151	1,387,945	1,386,697	1,194,244	1,132,943	886,249	860,711
Total Liabilities	2,115,845	2,062,344	2,019,745	2,097,563	1,742,197	1,736,035	1,516,803	1,630,419
Stockholders' Equity	(629,161)	(607,184)	(590,589)	(548,059)	(413,919)	(332,000)	(206,047)	(57,027)
Shares Outstanding	147,790	148,001	147,944	147,960	148,137	147,874	143,305	146,135
Statistical Record								
Return on Assets %	7.86	6.26	4.83	4.04	6.19	5.23	4.11	2.61
EBITDA Margin %	14.40	14.47	13.58	14.54	13.96	16.66	14.63	16.09
Net Margin %	6.17	5.66	3.55	3.11	4.68	4.21	3.57	2.32
Asset Turnover	1.35	1.38	1.37	1.30	1.32	1.24	1.15	1.12
Current Ratio	1.05	1.14	2.07	1.80	3.00	3.60	2.70	3.18
Price Range	13.65-8.52	17.48-8.52	18.80-8.84	20.37-8.84	20.88-17.16	19.70-17.12	20.92-16.45	17.83-12.06
P/E Ratio	19.50-12.18	32.98-16.08	48.21-22.66	58.21-25.25	38.67-31.77	41.05-35.67	52.30-41.14	66.03-44.66
Average Yield %	14.30	12.76	10.68	9.21	7.42	7.28	6.88	7.68

Address: 4400 Biscayne Boulevard, Miami, FL 33137
Telephone: 305-579-8000

Web Site: www.vectorgroupltd.com
Officers: Bennett S. LeBow - Chairman Howard M. Lorber - President, Chief Executive Officer

Auditors: DELOITTE & TOUCHE LLP
Investor Contact: 212-687-8080
Transfer Agents: American Stock Transfer & Trust Company, LLC, Brooklyn, NY

VEEVA SYSTEMS INC

Exchange	Symbol	Price	52Wk Range	Yield	P/E
NYS	VEEV	$140.66 (12/31/2019)	175.65-84.89	N/A	72.51

*7 Year Price Score N/A *NYSE Composite Index=100 *12 Month Price Score 98.23

Interim Earnings (Per Share)

Qtr.	Apr	Jul	Oct	Jan
2016-17	0.09	0.09	0.15	0.15
2017-18	0.24	0.25	0.22	0.21
2018-19	0.29	0.32	0.41	0.45
2019-20	0.47	0.50	0.52	...

Interim Dividends (Per Share)

No Dividends Paid

Valuation Analysis **Institutional Holding**

Forecast EPS	$2.17	No of Institutions
	(01/14/2020)	742
Market Cap	$20.9 Billion	Shares
Book Value	$1.6 Billion	124,078,736
Price/Book	13.39	% Held
Price/Sales	20.36	81.38

TRADING VOLUME (thousand shares)

Business Summary: IT Services (MIC: 6.3.1 SIC: 7372 NAIC: 511210)

Veeva Systems provides industry cloud solutions for the life sciences industry. Veeva Commercial Cloud is a suite of multichannel customer relationship management applications, a commercial data warehouse, territory allocation and alignment applications, master data management applications and customer reference and data and services. Veeva Vault is Co.'s suite of cloud-based, enterprise content management applications that address the content management requirements for Co.'s customers'commercial functions, including medical and sales and marketing, and key research and development functions, including clinical, regulatory, quality, and, when available, safety.

Recent Developments: For the quarter ended Oct 31 2019, net income increased 28.3% to US$82.2 million from US$64.1 million in the year-earlier quarter. Revenues were US$280.9 million, up 25.0% from US$224.7 million the year before. Operating income was US$80.8 million versus US$63.1 million in the prior-year quarter, an increase of 28.1%. Direct operating expenses rose 19.5% to US$73.3 million from US$61.4 million in the comparable period the year before. Indirect operating expenses increased 26.5% to US$126.8 million from US$100.3 million in the equivalent prior-year period.

Prospects: Our evaluation of Veeva Systems Inc as of October 4th, 2019 is the result of our systematic analysis on three basic characteristics: earnings strength, relative valuation, and recent stock price movement. The company has managed to produce a neutral trend in earnings per share over the past 5 quarters. However, recent analyst estimates for the company have been raised and VEEV has posted results that exceeded analysts' expectations. Based on operating earnings yield, the company is overvalued when compared to all of the companies we cover. Share price changes over the past year indicates that VEEV will perform over the near term.

Financial Data

(US$ in Thousands)	9 Mos	6 Mos	3 Mos	01/31/2019	01/31/2018	01/31/2017	01/31/2016	01/31/2015
Earnings Per Share	1.94	1.83	1.65	1.47	0.92	0.47	0.38	0.28
Cash Flow Per Share	2.90	2.78	3.12	2.15	1.66	1.06	0.61	0.53
Tang Book Value Per Share	9.73	8.98	8.27	7.64	5.24	3.76	2.70	3.02
Income Statement								
Total Revenue	792,573	511,652	244,752	862,210	685,571	544,043	409,221	313,222
EBITDA	266,187	170,036	83,001	229,655	156,151	110,058	77,100	68,586
Depn & Amortn	17,728	11,518	5,671	6,400	5,900	4,900	3,100	1,400
Income Before Taxes	248,459	158,518	77,330	238,643	158,634	109,635	78,617	67,186
Income Taxes	13,523	5,827	3,881	8,811	16,668	40,831	24,157	26,803
Net Income	234,936	152,691	73,449	229,832	141,966	68,804	54,460	40,383
Average Shares	158,750	158,675	157,910	156,117	153,681	147,578	144,977	144,204
Balance Sheet								
Current Assets	1,658,121	1,620,838	1,537,851	1,433,414	1,008,136	711,865	500,964	501,837
Total Assets	1,900,441	1,859,853	1,776,104	1,653,766	1,197,008	917,700	705,799	544,890
Current Liabilities	306,897	382,941	412,587	401,022	314,676	246,784	186,279	135,523
Total Liabilities	341,876	414,836	441,001	416,017	325,481	264,722	200,550	138,057
Stockholders' Equity	1,558,565	1,445,017	1,335,103	1,237,749	871,527	652,978	505,249	406,833
Shares Outstanding	148,360	147,848	147,030	146,190	142,069	137,886	133,545	131,067
Statistical Record								
Return on Assets %	18.56	17.86	16.74	16.12	13.43	8.45	8.71	8.82
Return on Equity %	22.70	23.08	22.43	21.79	18.62	11.85	11.94	11.76
EBITDA Margin %	33.59	33.23	33.91	26.64	22.78	20.23	18.84	21.90
Net Margin %	29.64	29.84	30.01	26.66	20.71	12.65	13.31	12.89
Asset Turnover	0.62	0.60	0.59	0.60	0.65	0.67	0.65	0.68
Current Ratio	5.40	4.23	3.73	3.57	3.20	2.88	2.69	3.70
Price Range	175.65-80.01	175.65-75.63	141.55-70.13	109.20-54.32	66.82-42.33	47.36-20.61	32.69-22.83	37.80-17.87
P/E Ratio	90.54-41.24	95.98-41.33	85.79-42.50	74.29-36.95	72.63-46.01	100.77-43.85	86.03-60.08	135.00-63.82

Address: 4280 Hacienda Drive, Pleasanton, CA 94588 **Telephone:** 925-452-6500 **Fax:** 925-452-6504	**Web Site:** www.veeva.com **Officers:** Gordon Ritter - Chairman Matthew J. Wallach - President	**Auditors:** KPMG LLP **Transfer Agents:** American Stock Transfer & Trust Company, LLC, Brooklyn, NY

VENTAS INC

Exchange	Symbol	Price	52Wk Range	Yield	P/E
NYS	VTR	$57.74 (12/31/2019)	75.23-55.15	5.49	43.41

*7 Year Price Score 88.25   *NYSE Composite Index=100   *12 Month Price Score 85.64

Interim Earnings (Per Share)

Qtr.	Mar	Jun	Sep	Dec
2016	0.44	0.42	0.42	0.58
2017	0.55	0.42	1.71	1.09
2018	0.22	0.46	0.28	0.17
2019	0.35	0.58	0.23	...

Interim Dividends (Per Share)

Amt	Decl	Ex	Rec	Pay
0.792Q	02/08/2019	03/29/2019	04/01/2019	04/12/2019
0.792Q	05/15/2019	06/28/2019	07/01/2019	07/12/2019
0.792Q	09/20/2019	09/30/2019	10/01/2019	10/11/2019
0.792Q	12/06/2019	12/31/2019	01/02/2020	01/13/2020

Indicated Div: $3.17

Valuation Analysis — **Institutional Holding**

Forecast EPS	$1.43	No of Institutions
(01/17/2020)		1021
Market Cap	$21.5 Billion	Shares
Book Value	$10.7 Billion	416,918,432
Price/Book	2.02	% Held
Price/Sales	5.66	92.17

Business Summary: REITs (MIC: 5.3.1 SIC: 6798 NAIC: 525930)

Ventas is a real estate investment trust with a portfolio of seniors housing, research and innovation, and healthcare properties located throughout the U.S., Canada and the U.K. Co.'s three reportable business segments are: triple-net leased properties, which invests in and owns seniors housing and healthcare properties and leases those properties to healthcare operating companies under triple-net or absolute-net leases; senior living operations, which invests in seniors housing communities and engages independent operators to manage those communities; and office operations, which acquires, owns, develops, leases and manages medical office buildings and research and innovation centers.

Recent Developments: For the quarter ended Sep 30 2019, income from continuing operations decreased 15.8% to US$86.9 million from US$103.3 million in the year-earlier quarter. Net income decreased 15.8% to US$86.9 million from US$103.3 million in the year-earlier quarter. Revenues were US$983.2 million, up 5.0% from US$936.5 million the year before. Revenues from property income rose 5.1% to US$952.4 million from US$905.9 million in the corresponding quarter a year earlier.

Prospects: Our evaluation of Ventas Inc. as of October 4th, 2019 is the result of our systematic analysis on three basic characteristics: earnings strength, relative valuation, and recent stock price movement. The company has produced a positive trend in earnings per share over the past 5 quarters. However, recent analyst estimates for the company have been reduced, while VTR has posted results that exceeded analysts' expectations. Based on operating earnings yield, the company is overvalued when compared to all of the companies we cover. Share price changes over the past year indicates that VTR will perform over the near term.

Financial Data

(US$ in Thousands)	9 Mos	6 Mos	3 Mos	12/31/2018	12/31/2017	12/31/2016	12/31/2015	12/31/2014
Earnings Per Share	1.33	1.38	1.26	1.14	3.78	1.86	1.25	1.60
Cash Flow Per Share	3.89	3.87	3.95	3.88	4.06	3.96	4.21	4.27
Tang Book Value Per Share	25.78	26.28	25.37	26.22	28.03	27.16	26.02	28.08
Dividends Per Share	3.170	3.168	3.165	3.163	3.115	2.965	3.040	2.965
Dividend Payout %	238.35	229.53	251.19	277.41	82.41	159.41	243.20	185.31
Income Statement								
Total Revenue	2,876,746	1,893,591	942,874	3,745,810	3,574,149	3,443,522	3,286,398	3,075,746
EBITDA	717,402	510,382	241,181	1,735,187	1,916,376	1,827,193	1,673,771	1,634,643
Depn & Amortn	10,426	5,442	3,285	907,865	883,469	888,945	954,982	809,284
Income Before Taxes	372,021	283,952	127,277	384,825	584,711	518,508	351,675	448,517
Income Taxes	(57,004)	(59,009)	(1,257)	(39,953)	(59,799)	(31,343)	(39,284)	(8,732)
Net Income	421,573	336,314	125,785	409,467	1,356,470	649,231	417,843	475,767
Average Shares	376,625	365,553	360,619	359,301	358,566	348,390	334,007	296,677
Balance Sheet								
Current Assets	148,063	81,987	82,514	72,277	81,355	286,707	53,023	55,348
Total Assets	24,803,553	22,988,911	22,668,097	22,584,555	23,954,541	23,166,600	22,261,918	21,226,171
Current Liabilities	1,426,900	1,398,822	1,350,529	1,391,121	1,587,804	1,309,793	1,232,966	1,411,666
Long-Term Obligations	12,302,421	10,489,849	10,904,222	10,733,699	11,276,062	11,127,326	11,206,996	10,888,092
Total Liabilities	14,137,847	12,168,900	12,518,434	12,180,557	12,929,825	12,505,632	12,501,062	12,373,971
Stockholders' Equity	10,665,706	10,820,011	10,149,663	10,403,998	11,024,716	10,660,968	9,760,856	8,852,200
Shares Outstanding	372,723	371,478	358,387	356,572	356,186	354,124	334,342	298,471
Statistical Record								
Return on Assets %	2.04	2.19	1.98	1.76	5.76	2.85	1.92	2.32
Return on Equity %	4.58	4.67	4.37	3.82	12.51	6.34	4.49	5.34
EBITDA Margin %	24.94	26.95	25.58	46.32	53.62	53.06	50.93	53.15
Net Margin %	14.65	17.76	13.34	10.93	37.95	18.85	12.71	15.47
Asset Turnover	0.16	0.16	0.16	0.16	0.15	0.15	0.15	0.15
Current Ratio	0.10	0.06	0.06	0.05	0.05	0.22	0.04	0.04
Debt to Equity	1.15	0.97	1.07	1.03	1.02	1.04	1.15	1.23
Price Range	75.23-52.86	71.76-52.86	65.47-46.96	65.47-46.96	71.93-59.36	76.56-48.43	70.89-49.68	65.19-49.73
P/E Ratio	56.56-39.74	52.00-38.30	51.96-37.27	57.43-41.19	19.03-15.70	41.16-26.04	56.71-39.74	40.75-31.08
Average Yield %	4.95	5.21	5.47	5.71	4.80	4.59	5.14	5.23

Address: 353 N. Clark Street, Suite 3300, Chicago, IL 60654 **Telephone:** 877-483-6827	**Web Site:** www.ventasreit.com **Officers:** Debra A. Cafaro - Chairman, Chief Executive Officer Peter J. Bulgarelli - Executive Vice President	**Auditors:** KPMG LLP **Investor Contact:** 312-660-3848 **Transfer Agents:** Wells Fargo Shareowner Services, St. Paul, MN

VEREIT INC

Exchange	Symbol	Price	52Wk Range	Yield	P/E
NYS	VER	$9.24 (12/31/2019)	10.05-7.04	5.95	N/A

*7 Year Price Score 74.81 *NYSE Composite Index=100 *12 Month Price Score 100.74

Interim Earnings (Per Share)

Qtr.	Mar	Jun	Sep	Dec
2016	(0.15)	(0.02)	0.01	(0.14)
2017	0.00	0.02	0.00	(0.05)
2018	0.01	(0.09)	(0.09)	0.01
2019	0.05	0.27	(0.76)	...

Interim Dividends (Per Share)

Amt	Decl	Ex	Rec	Pay
0.138Q	02/20/2019	03/28/2019	03/29/2019	04/15/2019
0.138Q	05/06/2019	06/27/2019	06/28/2019	07/15/2019
0.138Q	08/05/2019	09/27/2019	09/30/2019	10/15/2019
0.138Q	11/05/2019	12/30/2019	12/31/2019	01/15/2020

Indicated Div: $0.55

Valuation Analysis — **Institutional Holding**

Forecast EPS	$-0.37	No of Institutions
(01/17/2020)		573
Market Cap	$9.9 Billion	Shares
Book Value	$7.0 Billion	1,103,011,584
Price/Book	1.41	% Held
Price/Sales	7.92	N/A

Business Summary: REITs (MIC: 5.3.1 SIC: 6798 NAIC: 525930)

VEREIT is a real estate operating company which owns and manages portfolios of single-tenant commercial properties in the U.S. Substantially all of Co.'s real estate operations are conducted through its Operating Partnership, VEREIT Operating Partnership, L.P. Co. is the sole general partner of the the Operating Partnership.

Recent Developments: For the quarter ended Sep 30 2019, loss from continuing operations was US$741.5 million compared with a loss of US$73.9 million in the year-earlier quarter. Net loss amounted to US$741.5 million versus a net loss of US$73.9 million in the year-earlier quarter. Revenues were US$303.0 million, down 3.5% from US$313.9 million the year before.

Prospects: Our evaluation of VEREIT Inc. as of October 4th, 2019 is the result of our systematic analysis on three basic characteristics: earnings strength, relative valuation, and recent stock price movement. The company has produced a positive trend in earnings per share over the past 5 quarters. In addition, recent analyst estimates for the company have been raised, and VER has posted results that exceeded analysts' expectations. Based on operating earnings yield, the company is overvalued when compared to all of the companies we cover. Share price changes over the past year indicates that VER will perform over the near term.

Financial Data

(US$ in Thousands)	9 Mos	6 Mos	3 Mos	12/31/2018	12/31/2017	12/31/2016	12/31/2015	12/31/2014
Earnings Per Share	(0.43)	0.24	(0.12)	(0.16)	(0.04)	(0.29)	(0.43)	(1.36)
Cash Flow Per Share	0.58	0.60	0.56	0.51	0.81	0.86	0.96	0.63
Tang Book Value Per Share	5.32	6.04	5.92	6.01	6.72	7.14	7.53	7.85
Dividends Per Share	0.550	0.550	0.550	0.550	0.550	0.550	0.275	1.076
Dividend Payout %	...	229.17	...	...	...	...	...	...
Income Statement								
Total Revenue	931,871	628,886	316,843	1,257,867	1,252,285	1,454,823	1,556,017	1,579,257
EBITDA	211,666	766,453	282,330	852,342	1,090,879	909,616	865,146	448,900
Depn & Amortn	379,133	260,771	139,394	659,948	745,499	806,548	866,549	1,007,164
Income Before Taxes	(376,413)	364,625	71,682	(88,493)	55,614	(214,308)	(359,795)	(1,010,912)
Income Taxes	3,543	2,375	1,211	5,101	6,882	(3,701)	(36,303)	...
Net Income	(371,478)	354,962	69,304	(85,774)	31,818	(195,863)	(316,353)	(977,185)
Average Shares	978,982	999,777	993,298	969,092	974,098	931,422	903,360	793,150
Balance Sheet								
Current Assets	1,356,525	533,734	349,431	90,602	98,759	350,618	128,870	479,362
Total Assets	14,455,523	13,781,884	14,053,624	13,963,493	14,705,578	15,587,574	17,405,866	20,515,139
Current Liabilities	1,327,154	315,158	331,372	332,234	327,722	308,731	292,923	173,579
Long-Term Obligations	5,633,214	5,658,260	6,024,330	6,087,922	6,073,444	6,367,248	8,059,802	10,513,781
Total Liabilities	7,438,258	6,561,488	6,961,107	6,806,434	6,821,300	7,140,213	8,881,879	11,361,251
Stockholders' Equity	7,017,265	7,220,396	7,092,517	7,157,059	7,884,278	8,447,361	8,523,987	9,153,888
Shares Outstanding	1,067,688	973,385	971,576	967,515	974,208	974,146	904,884	905,530
Statistical Record								
Return on Assets %	N.M.	2.21	N.M.	N.M.	0.21	N.M.	N.M.	N.M.
Return on Equity %	N.M.	4.21	N.M.	N.M.	0.39	N.M.	N.M.	N.M.
EBITDA Margin %	22.71	121.87	89.11	67.76	87.11	62.52	55.60	28.42
Net Margin %	N.M.	56.44	21.87	N.M.	2.54	N.M.	N.M.	N.M.
Asset Turnover	0.09	0.09	0.09	0.09	0.08	0.09	0.08	0.12
Current Ratio	1.02	1.69	1.05	0.27	0.30	1.14	0.44	2.76
Debt to Equity	0.80	0.78	0.85	0.85	0.77	0.75	0.95	1.15
Price Range	9.92-6.92	9.66-6.92	8.50-6.59	7.96-6.59	9.12-7.49	11.06-7.07	10.10-7.67	14.88-7.70
P/E Ratio	...	40.25-28.83	...	...	...	...	...	...
Average Yield %	6.56	6.94	7.33	7.54	6.60	6.00	3.13	8.72

Address: 2325 E. Camelback Road, 9th Floor, Phoenix, DE 85016 **Telephone:** 800-606-3610	**Web Site:** www.ir.vereit.com **Officers:** Glenn J. Rufrano - Chief Executive Officer Michael J. Bartolotta - Executive Vice President, Chief Financial Officer	**Auditors:** Deloitte & Touche LLP **Investor Contact:** 800-606-3610 **Transfer Agents:** DST Systems, Inc.

VERITIV CORP

Exchange	Symbol	Price	52Wk Range	Yield	P/E
NYS	VRTV	$19.67 (12/31/2019)	36.41-13.10	N/A	N/A

*7 Year Price Score N/A   *NYSE Composite Index=100   *12 Month Price Score 79.19

Interim Earnings (Per Share)

Qtr.	Mar	Jun	Sep	Dec
2016	0.21	0.49	0.34	0.26
2017	(0.14)	(0.58)	(0.91)	0.78
2018	(1.00)	(0.67)	0.09	0.59
2019	(1.68)	(0.70)	0.31	...

Interim Dividends (Per Share)

No Dividends Paid

Valuation Analysis

		Institutional Holding	
Forecast EPS	$-1.75	No of Institutions	
	(01/07/2020)	224	
Market Cap	$316.7 Million	Shares	
Book Value	$524.6 Million	17,906,328	
Price/Book	0.60	% Held	
Price/Sales	0.04	98.87	

Business Summary: Industrial Machinery & Equipment (MIC: 7.2.1 SIC: 5111 NAIC: 424110)

Veritiv is a business to business distributor of packaging, facility solutions, print and publishing products and services. Co. operates distribution centers primarily throughout the U.S., Canada and Mexico. Co.'s four reportable segments are: Packaging, which provides standard as well as custom packaging solutions; Facility Solutions, which sources and sells cleaning, break-room and other supplies; Print, which sells and distributes commercial printing, writing, copying, digital, wide format and specialty paper products, graphics consumables and graphics equipment; and Publishing and Print Management, which sells and distributes coated and uncoated commercial printing papers.

Recent Developments: For the quarter ended Sep 30 2019, net income increased 264.3% to US$5.1 million from US$1.4 million in the year-earlier quarter. Revenues were US$1.92 billion, down 12.2% from US$2.19 billion the year before. Operating income was US$19.1 million versus US$15.5 million in the prior-year quarter, an increase of 23.2%. Direct operating expenses declined 14.1% to US$1.55 billion from US$1.81 billion in the comparable period the year before. Indirect operating expenses decreased 4.5% to US$354.6 million from US$371.2 million in the equivalent prior-year period.

Prospects: Our evaluation of Veritiv Corp. as of October 4th, 2019 is the result of our systematic analysis on three basic characteristics: earnings strength, relative valuation, and recent stock price movement. The company has suffered a very negative trend in earnings per share over the past 5 quarters. However, recent analyst estimates for the company have been mixed and VRTV has posted results that fell short of analysts' expectations. Based on operating earnings yield, the company is undervalued when compared to all of the companies we cover. Share price changes over the past year indicates that VRTV will perform very poorly over the near term.

Financial Data

(US$ in Thousands)	9 Mos	6 Mos	3 Mos	12/31/2018	12/31/2017	12/31/2016	12/31/2015	12/31/2014
Earnings Per Share	(1.48)	(1.70)	(1.67)	(0.99)	(0.85)	1.30	1.67	(1.62)
Cash Flow Per Share	17.27	11.76	5.05	0.95	2.33	8.75	7.06	0.41
Tang Book Value Per Share	23.08	22.65	22.86	24.30	24.59	29.97	28.11	26.50
Income Statement								
Total Revenue	5,824,200	3,899,700	1,941,500	8,696,200	8,364,700	8,326,600	8,717,700	7,406,500
EBITDA	(300)	(22,500)	(21,500)	78,700	79,300	119,600	122,900	25,300
Depn & Amortn	1,900	1,300	600	46,600	50,000	51,300	51,000	32,900
Income Before Taxes	(32,700)	(45,400)	(33,500)	(10,200)	(1,900)	40,800	44,900	(21,600)
Income Taxes	200	(7,400)	(6,800)	5,500	11,400	19,800	18,200	(2,100)
Net Income	(32,900)	(38,000)	(26,700)	(15,700)	(13,300)	21,000	26,700	(19,600)
Average Shares	16,240	16,090	15,940	15,820	15,700	16,150	16,000	12,080
Balance Sheet								
Current Assets	1,770,700	1,833,400	1,947,500	2,084,300	2,114,100	1,948,600	1,925,200	1,959,100
Total Assets	2,637,700	2,696,800	2,820,800	2,529,700	2,708,400	2,483,700	2,476,900	2,574,500
Current Liabilities	883,200	880,400	867,100	849,700	907,400	867,800	814,200	851,100
Long-Term Obligations	726,200	815,100	944,200	987,200	1,089,900	925,300	998,300	1,067,400
Total Liabilities	2,113,100	2,178,100	2,297,200	1,986,600	2,158,700	1,941,900	1,946,800	2,062,000
Stockholders' Equity	524,600	518,700	523,600	543,100	549,700	541,800	530,100	512,500
Shares Outstanding	16,100	16,100	16,100	15,900	15,700	15,700	16,000	16,000
Statistical Record								
Return on Assets %	N.M.	N.M.	N.M.	N.M.	N.M.	0.84	1.06	N.M.
Return on Equity %	N.M.	N.M.	*N.M.	N.M.	N.M.	3.91	5.12	N.M.
EBITDA Margin %	N.M.	N.M.	N.M.	0.90	0.95	1.44	1.41	0.34
Net Margin %	N.M.	N.M.	N.M.	N.M.	N.M.	0.25	0.31	N.M.
Asset Turnover	3.06	3.16	3.09	3.32	3.22	3.35	3.45	3.91
Current Ratio	2.00	2.08	2.25	2.45	2.33	2.25	2.36	2.30
Debt to Equity	1.38	1.57	1.80	1.82	1.98	1.71	1.88	2.08
Price Range	36.46-14.22	49.20-17.66	49.20-23.71	49.20-22.65	62.25-22.70	56.40-28.00	54.11-33.06	51.87-32.50
P/E Ratio	...	...	...	...	...	43.38-21.54	32.40-19.80	...

Address: 1000 Abernathy Road N.E., Building 400, Suite 1700, Atlanta, GA 30328
Telephone: 770-391-8200

Web Site: www.veritivcorp.com
Officers: Mary A. Laschinger - Chairman, Chief Executive Officer, Holding/Parent Company Officer
Stephen Joseph Smith - Senior Vice President, Chief Financial Officer

Auditors: DELOITTE & TOUCHE LLP
Transfer Agents: Computershare Inc.

VERIZON COMMUNICATIONS INC

Exchange	Symbol	Price	52Wk Range	Yield	P/E	Div Acheiver
NYS	VZ	$61.40 (12/31/2019)	62.07-53.28	4.01	15.78	14 Years

*7 Year Price Score 94.38 ***NYSE Composite Index=100** ***12 Month Price Score 98.83**

TRADING VOLUME (thousand shares)

Interim Earnings (Per Share)

Qtr.	Mar	Jun	Sep	Dec
2016	1.06	0.17	0.89	1.10
2017	0.84	1.07	0.89	4.56
2018	1.11	1.00	1.19	0.47
2019	1.22	0.95	1.25	...

Interim Dividends (Per Share)

Amt	Decl	Ex	Rec	Pay
0.603Q	03/08/2019	04/09/2019	04/10/2019	05/01/2019
0.603Q	06/06/2019	07/09/2019	07/10/2019	08/01/2019
0.615Q	09/05/2019	10/09/2019	10/10/2019	11/01/2019
0.615Q	12/05/2019	01/09/2020	01/10/2020	02/03/2020

Indicated Div: $2.46 (Div. Reinv. Plan)

Valuation Analysis / Institutional Holding

Valuation Analysis		Institutional Holding	
Forecast EPS	$4.83	No of Institutions	
	(01/17/2020)	3258	
Market Cap	$253.9 Billion	Shares	
Book Value	$58.9 Billion	3,304,624,896	
Price/Book	4.31	% Held	
Price/Sales	1.93	66.17	

Business Summary: Services (MIC: 6.1.2 SIC: 4813 NAIC: 517110)

Verizon Communications is a holding company. Through its subsidiaries, Co. provides communications, information and entertainment products and services to consumers, businesses and governmental agencies. Co. has two reportable segments: Wireless, which provides communications products and services including wireless voice and data services and equipment sales, which are provided to consumer, business and government customers; and Wireline, which provides communications products and other services, including video and data services, corporate networking solutions, security and managed network services and local and long distance voice services.

Recent Developments: For the quarter ended Sep 30 2019, net income increased 5.4% to US$5.34 billion from US$5.06 billion in the year-earlier quarter. Revenues were US$32.89 billion, up 0.9% from US$32.61 billion the year before. Operating income was US$8.18 billion versus US$7.68 billion in the prior-year quarter, an increase of 6.6%. Direct operating expenses rose 0.4% to US$13.38 billion from US$13.33 billion in the comparable period the year before. Indirect operating expenses decreased 2.3% to US$11.33 billion from US$11.60 billion in the equivalent prior-year period.

Prospects: Our evaluation of Verizon Communications Inc. as of October 4th, 2019 is the result of our systematic analysis on three basic characteristics: earnings strength, relative valuation, and recent stock price movement. The company has managed to produce a neutral trend in earnings per share over the past 5 quarters. In addition, recent analyst estimates for the company have been mixed and VZ has posted results that exceeded analysts' expectations. Based on operating earnings yield, the company is undervalued when compared to all of the companies we cover. Share price changes over the past year indicates that VZ will perform in line with the market over the near term.

Financial Data

(US$ in Thousands)	9 Mos	6 Mos	3 Mos	12/31/2018	12/31/2017	12/31/2016	12/31/2015	12/31/2014
Earnings Per Share	3.89	3.83	3.88	3.76	7.36	3.21	4.37	2.42
Cash Flow Per Share	8.42	8.15	8.40	8.32	6.20	5.55	9.53	7.71
Dividends Per Share	2.410	2.398	2.385	2.373	2.322	2.273	2.215	2.140
Dividend Payout %	61.95	62.60	61.47	63.10	31.56	70.79	50.69	88.43
Income Statement								
Total Revenue	97,093,000	64,199,000	32,128,000	130,863,000	126,034,000	125,980,000	131,620,000	127,079,000
EBITDA	35,095,000	22,945,000	12,206,000	39,734,000	40,063,000	39,628,000	47,454,000	33,263,000
Depn & Amortn	12,577,000	8,463,000	4,231,000	15,186,000	14,741,000	14,227,000	14,323,000	14,966,000
Income Before Taxes	19,041,000	12,117,000	6,794,000	19,809,000	20,671,000	21,084,000	28,326,000	13,490,000
Income Taxes	4,450,000	2,864,000	1,628,000	3,584,000	(9,956,000)	7,378,000	9,865,000	3,314,000
Net Income	14,170,000	8,976,000	5,032,000	15,528,000	30,101,000	13,127,000	17,879,000	9,625,000
Average Shares	4,140,000	4,139,000	4,140,000	4,132,000	4,089,000	4,086,000	4,093,000	3,981,000
Balance Sheet								
Current Assets	34,895,000	33,308,000	33,397,000	34,636,000	29,913,000	26,395,000	22,280,000	29,623,000
Total Assets	284,875,000	283,108,000	283,947,000	264,829,000	257,143,000	244,180,000	244,640,000	232,708,000
Current Liabilities	39,209,000	38,214,000	38,607,000	37,930,000	33,037,000	30,340,000	35,052,000	28,064,000
Long-Term Obligations	119,983,000	122,852,000	124,016,000	105,873,000	113,642,000	105,433,000	103,705,000	110,536,000
Total Liabilities	225,954,000	226,526,000	228,091,000	211,684,000	214,047,000	221,656,000	228,212,000	220,410,000
Stockholders' Equity	58,921,000	56,582,000	55,856,000	53,145,000	43,096,000	22,524,000	16,428,000	12,298,000
Shares Outstanding	4,135,784	4,135,765	4,135,707	4,132,034	4,079,477	4,076,684	4,073,175	4,154,964
Statistical Record								
Return on Assets %	5.85	5.80	5.84	5.95	12.01	5.36	7.49	3.80
Return on Equity %	28.41	29.17	30.04	32.27	91.74	67.22	124.48	37.65
EBITDA Margin %	36.15	35.74	37.99	30.36	31.79	31.46	36.05	26.18
Net Margin %	14.59	13.98	15.66	11.87	23.88	10.42	13.58	7.57
Asset Turnover	0.48	0.48	0.48	0.50	0.50	0.51	0.55	0.50
Current Ratio	0.89	0.87	0.87	0.91	0.91	0.87	0.64	1.06
Debt to Equity	2.04	2.17	2.22	1.99	2.64	4.68	6.31	8.99
Price Range	60.88-53.05	60.88-50.42	60.88-46.38	60.65-46.29	54.64-42.89	56.53-44.15	50.55-42.84	51.97-45.42
P/E Ratio	15.65-13.64	15.90-13.16	15.69-11.95	16.13-12.31	7.42-5.83	17.61-13.75	11.57-9.80	21.48-18.77
Average Yield %	4.22	4.28	4.45	4.56	4.81	4.42	4.70	4.40

Address: 1095 Avenue of the Americas, New York, NY 10036 Telephone: 212-395-1000	Web Site: www.verizon.com Officers: Hans E. Vestberg - Chairman, Executive Vice President, Chief Executive Officer, Chief Technology Officer, Division Officer Kyle Malady - Executive Vice President, Chief Technology Officer	Auditors: Ernst & Young LLP Transfer Agents: Computershare Louisville, KY

VF CORP.

Exchange	Symbol	Price	52Wk Range	Yield	P/E	Div Acheiver
NYS	VFC	$99.66 (12/31/2019)	99.96-65.18	1.93	30.95	46 Years

*7 Year Price Score 109.28 *NYSE Composite Index=100 *12 Month Price Score 100.38

Interim Earnings (Per Share)

Qtr.	Mar	Jun	Sep	Dec
2017	0.50	0.27	0.97	(0.22)

Qtr.	Jun	Sep	Dec	Mar
2018-19	0.40	1.26	1.16	0.33
2019-20	0.12	1.61	...	...

Interim Dividends (Per Share)

Amt	Decl	Ex	Rec	Pay
0.00Q	04/29/2019	05/23/2019	05/10/2019	05/22/2019
0.51Q	05/22/2019	06/07/2019	06/10/2019	06/20/2019
0.43Q	07/24/2019	09/09/2019	09/10/2019	09/20/2019
0.48Q	10/25/2019	12/09/2019	12/10/2019	12/20/2019

Indicated Div: $1.92 (Div. Reinv. Plan)

Valuation Analysis

		Institutional Holding	
Forecast EPS	$3.36	No of Institutions	
	(01/17/2020)	1328	
Market Cap	$39.8 Billion	Shares	
Book Value	$4.6 Billion	449,256,128	
Price/Book	8.55	% Held	
Price/Sales	3.10	90.84	

TRADING VOLUME (thousand shares)

Business Summary: Apparel, Footwear & Accessories (MIC: 1.4.2 SIC: 2329 NAIC: 315228)

VF is an apparel and footwear company. Co. designs, produces, procures, markets and distributes a variety of lifestyle products, including outerwear, footwear, occupational and performance apparel, jeanswear, backpacks and luggage for consumers of all ages. Products are marketed primarily under Co.-owned brand names. Co.'s segment comprised of: Outdoor, which includes performance-based and outdoor apparel, footwear and equipment; Active, which includes active apparel, footwear and accessories; Work, which consists of work and work-inspired lifestyle apparel and footwear and occupational apparel; and Jeans, which markets denim and related casual apparel products.

Recent Developments: For the quarter ended Sep 28 2019, income from continuing operations increased 56.0% to US$649.0 million from US$416.1 million in the year-earlier quarter. Net income increased 28.0% to US$649.0 million from US$507.1 million in the year-earlier quarter. Revenues were US$3.39 billion, up 5.4% from US$3.22 billion the year before. Operating income was US$579.1 million versus US$545.0 million in the prior-year quarter, an increase of 6.3%. Direct operating expenses rose 3.4% to US$1.60 billion from US$1.55 billion in the comparable period the year before. Indirect operating expenses increased 7.8% to US$1.22 billion from US$1.13 billion in the equivalent prior-year period.

Prospects: Our evaluation of VF Corp. as of October 4th, 2019 is the result of our systematic analysis on three basic characteristics: earnings strength, relative valuation, and recent stock price movement. The company has generated a negative trend in earnings per share over the past 5 quarters. However, recent analyst estimates for the company have been mixed and VFC has posted results that exceeded analysts' expectations. Based on operating earnings yield, the company is fairly valued when compared to all of the companies we cover. Share price changes over the past year indicates that VFC will perform poorly over the near term.

Financial Data

(US$ in Thousands)	6 Mos	3 Mos	03/30/2019	03/31/2018	12/30/2017	12/31/2016	01/02/2016	01/03/2015
Earnings Per Share	3.22	2.87	3.15	0.63	1.52	2.54	2.85	2.38
Cash Flow Per Share	3.01	3.33	4.22	(2.50)	3.70	3.56	2.70	3.86
Tang Book Value Per Share	3.00	1.57	0.74	N.M.	N.M.	2.82	3.06	2.78
Dividends Per Share	1.960	1.990	1.940	0.460	1.720	1.530	1.330	1.107
Dividend Payout %	60.87	69.34	61.59	73.02	113.16	60.24	46.67	46.53
Income Statement								
Total Revenue	5,664,747	2,271,479	13,848,660	3,045,446	11,811,177	12,019,003	12,376,744	12,282,161
EBITDA	1,037,271	298,068	1,913,834	386,830	1,792,878	1,782,804	1,934,726	1,646,684
Depn & Amortn	321,129	159,178	301,005	71,532	290,503	281,577	272,075	214,504
Income Before Taxes	685,317	123,892	1,527,404	294,133	1,416,495	1,415,591	1,580,389	1,352,366
Income Taxes	(60,933)	26,643	268,400	32,969	695,286	243,064	348,796	304,861
Net Income	698,222	49,221	1,259,792	252,793	614,923	1,074,106	1,231,593	1,047,505
Average Shares	402,261	401,914	400,496	401,276	403,559	422,081	432,079	440,153
Balance Sheet								
Current Assets	4,775,207	3,990,855	4,673,457	4,683,323	4,392,124	4,293,098	4,163,136	4,185,854
Total Assets	11,270,355	10,401,964	10,356,785	10,311,310	9,958,502	9,739,287	9,639,542	9,980,140
Current Liabilities	2,404,338	1,947,145	2,661,604	3,138,829	2,745,200	1,785,400	1,941,713	1,620,241
Long-Term Obligations	2,090,922	2,126,835	2,115,884	2,212,555	2,187,789	2,039,180	1,401,820	1,423,581
Total Liabilities	6,622,736	6,250,350	6,058,269	6,623,214	6,238,602	4,798,366	4,254,704	4,349,258
Stockholders' Equity	4,647,619	4,151,614	4,298,516	3,688,096	3,719,900	4,940,921	5,384,838	5,630,882
Shares Outstanding	398,865	397,922	396,824	394,313	395,821	414,012	426,614	432,859
Statistical Record								
Return on Assets %	11.52	11.16	12.22	10.12	6.26	11.12	12.59	10.16
Return on Equity %	29.24	29.14	31.63	27.68	14.24	20.86	22.42	17.60
EBITDA Margin %	18.31	13.12	13.82	12.70	15.18	14.83	15.63	13.41
Net Margin %	12.33	2.17	9.10	8.30	5.21	8.94	9.95	8.53
Asset Turnover	1.14	1.29	1.34	1.22	1.20	1.24	1.27	1.19
Current Ratio	1.99	2.05	1.76	1.49	1.60	2.40	2.14	2.58
Debt to Equity	0.45	0.51	0.49	0.60	0.59	0.41	0.26	0.25
Price Range	90.82-63.36	90.63-63.36	90.63-63.36	79.01-68.14	70.23-45.48	62.83-49.95	73.05-58.18	71.03-52.70
P/E Ratio	28.20-19.68	31.58-22.08	28.77-20.12	125.41-108.15	46.20-29.92	24.74-19.67	25.63-20.41	29.84-22.14
Average Yield %	2.40	2.44	2.46	0.64	3.06	2.70	1.99	1.84

Address: 8505 E. Orchard Road, Greenwood Village, CO 80111
Telephone: 720-778-4000

Web Site: www.vfc.com
Officers: Steven E. Rendle - Chairman, President, Chief Executive Officer, Vice President, Chief Operating Officer, Division Officer Scott A. Roe - Vice President, Chief Financial Officer, Chief Accounting Officer, Controller

Auditors: PricewaterhouseCoopers LLP
Transfer Agents: Computershare Trust Company, N.A, Providence, RI

VICI PROPERTIES INC

Exchange	Symbol	Price	52Wk Range	Yield	P/E
NYS	VICI	$25.55 (12/31/2019)	25.55-18.48	4.66	17.99

*7 Year Price Score N/A *NYSE Composite Index=100 *12 Month Price Score 104.40

Interim Earnings (Per Share)

Qtr.	Mar	Jun	Sep	Dec
2018	0.33	0.38	0.35	0.37
2019	0.37	0.37	0.31	...

Interim Dividends (Per Share)

Amt	Decl	Ex	Rec	Pay
0.287Q	03/14/2019	03/28/2019	03/29/2019	04/11/2019
0.287Q	06/13/2019	06/27/2019	06/28/2019	07/12/2019
0.297Q	09/12/2019	09/26/2019	09/27/2019	10/10/2019
0.297Q	12/12/2019	12/26/2019	12/27/2019	01/09/2020

Indicated Div: $1.19

Valuation Analysis

		Institutional Holding	
Forecast EPS	$1.39	No of Institutions	
	(01/17/2020)	351	
Market Cap	$11.8 Billion	Shares	
Book Value	$8.0 Billion	532,800,384	
Price/Book	1.47	% Held	
Price/Sales	13.33	114.09	

TRADING VOLUME (thousand shares)

Business Summary: REITs (MIC: 5.3.1 SIC: 6798 NAIC: 525930)

VICI Properties is a holding company. Through its subsidiaries, Co. is engaged in the business of owning and acquiring gaming, hospitality and entertainment destinations. Co. conducts its real property business through VICI Properties L.P., an operating partnership and a wholly owned subsidiary of Co., and its golf course business through a real estate investment trust subsidiary, VICI Golf LLC. Co.'s portfolio consists of several properties, including Caesars Palace Las Vegas and Harrah's Las Vegas, which are entertainment facilities on the Las Vegas Strip. Co. also owns and operates golf courses located near certain of its properties, which are in close proximity to the Las Vegas Strip.

Recent Developments: For the quarter ended Sep 30 2019, net income increased 11.0% to US$146.5 million from US$132.0 million in the year-earlier quarter. Revenues were US$222.5 million, down 4.4% from US$232.7 million the year before. Revenues from property income fell 4.6% to US$216.9 million from US$227.3 million in the corresponding quarter a year earlier.

Prospects: Our evaluation of VICI Properties Inc as of October 4th, 2019 is the result of our systematic analysis on three basic characteristics: earnings strength, relative valuation, and recent stock price movement. The company has managed to produce a neutral trend in earnings per share over the past 5 quarters. However, recent analyst estimates for the company have been raised and VICI has posted results that exceeded analysts' expectations. Based on operating earnings yield, the company is undervalued when compared to all of the companies we cover. Share price changes over the past year indicates that VICI will perform in line with the market over the near term.

Financial Data

(US$ in Thousands)	9 Mos	6 Mos	3 Mos	12/31/2018	12/31/2017	12/31/2016	12/31/2015	12/31/2014
Earnings Per Share	1.42	1.46	1.47	1.43	0.19	...	...	...
Cash Flow Per Share	1.33	1.26	1.23	1.37	2.38	...	...	...
Tang Book Value Per Share	17.33	17.33	16.94	16.84	15.62	...	...	...
Dividends Per Share	1.160	1.150	1.125	0.998	...	...	...	...
Dividend Payout %	81.69	78.77	76.53	69.76	...	...	...	...
Income Statement								
Total Revenue	657,261	434,748	214,002	897,977	187,609	18,785	18,077	18,908
EBITDA	636,869	412,673	204,261	738,600	106,459	3,037	2,900	2,943
Depn & Amortn	21,128	5,312	2,395	3,686	751	3,030	2,882	2,904
Income Before Taxes	454,666	308,127	153,447	533,558	42,636	...	...	...
Income Taxes	1,098	1,074	521	1,441	(1,901)	...	(3)	(4)
Net Income	447,333	302,898	150,849	523,619	42,662	...	3	4
Average Shares	465,771	412,821	406,035	367,316	227,985	...	...	...
Balance Sheet								
Current Assets	809,805	1,333,690	986,528	1,119,324	197,406	1,644	1,042	...
Total Assets	12,581,466	12,522,046	11,448,671	11,333,368	9,739,712	90,475	92,034	...
Current Liabilities	308,074	251,570	205,478	189,537	32,157	1,024	1,224	...
Long-Term Obligations	4,125,473	4,124,448	4,123,350	4,122,264	4,785,756	...	14	...
Total Liabilities	4,591,152	4,533,309	4,486,402	4,515,919	5,048,223	6,332	6,659	...
Stockholders' Equity	7,990,314	7,988,737	6,962,269	6,817,449	4,691,489	84,143	85,375	...
Shares Outstanding	461,005	461,004	410,970	404,729	300,278	...	...	...
Statistical Record								
Return on Assets %	5.10	4.98	5.13	4.97	3.64	...	...	...
Return on Equity %	8.36	8.17	8.64	9.10	7.50	...	...	...
EBITDA Margin %	96.90	94.92	95.45	82.25	56.75	16.17	16.04	15.56
Net Margin %	68.06	69.67	70.49	58.31	22.74	...	0.02	0.02
Asset Turnover	0.08	0.08	0.08	0.09	0.16	0.21	...	...
Current Ratio	2.63	5.30	4.80	5.91	6.14	1.61	0.85	...
Debt to Equity	0.52	0.52	0.59	0.60	1.02	...	N.M.	...
Price Range	23.04-18.02	23.01-18.02	22.13-17.85	22.99-17.85	21.00-18.00	...	...	...
P/E Ratio	16.23-12.69	15.76-12.34	15.05-12.14	16.08-12.48	110.53-94.74	...	...	...
Average Yield %	5.37	5.39	5.48	4.92	...	...	...	...

Address: 430 Park Avenue, 8th Floor, New York, NY 10022	**Web Site:** www.viciproperties.com	**Auditors:** DELOITTE & TOUCHE LLP
Telephone: 646-949-4631	**Officers:** James R. Abrahamson - Chairman John Payne - President, Chief Operating Officer	**Transfer Agents:** Computershare Trust Company

VISA INC

Exchange	Symbol	Price	52Wk Range	Yield	P/E	Div Acheiver
NYS	V	$187.90 (12/31/2019)	189.39-128.13	0.64	35.32	10 Years

*7 Year Price Score 148.79 *NYSE Composite Index=100 *12 Month Price Score 104.22

TRADING VOLUME (thousand shares)

Interim Earnings (Per Share)

Qtr.	Dec	Mar	Jun	Sep
2014-15	0.63	0.63	0.69	0.62
2015-16	0.80	0.71	0.17	0.79
2016-17	0.86	0.18	0.86	0.90
2017-18	1.07	1.11	1.00	1.23
2018-19	1.30	1.31	1.37	1.35

Interim Dividends (Per Share)

Amt	Decl	Ex	Rec	Pay
0.25Q	01/29/2019	02/14/2019	02/15/2019	03/05/2019
0.25Q	04/16/2019	05/16/2019	05/17/2019	06/04/2019
0.25Q	07/15/2019	08/15/2019	08/16/2019	09/03/2019
0.30Q	10/22/2019	11/14/2019	11/15/2019	12/03/2019

Indicated Div: $1.20

Valuation Analysis / Institutional Holding

Valuation Analysis		Institutional Holding	
Forecast EPS	$6.19	No of Institutions	
	(01/17/2020)	3003	
Market Cap	$370.9 Billion	Shares	
Book Value	$34.7 Billion	1,827,034,368	
Price/Book	10.69	% Held	
Price/Sales	16.14	77.35	

Business Summary: Business Services (MIC: 7.5.2 SIC: 6159 NAIC: 522210)

Visa is engaged in digital payments. Co. facilitates payments between consumers and businesses. Co. is focused on its proprietary network, VisaNet, to provide products and services. Co. provides a portfolio of business payment solutions, including small business, corporate (travel) cards, purchasing cards, virtual cards/digital credentials, non-card cross-border business-to-business payment options and disbursement accounts, covering various main industry segments around the world. Co. also provides several capabilities and services, including fraud prevention and security, processing, loyalty, merchant and digital solutions, consulting and data solutions.

Recent Developments: For the year ended Sep 30 2019, net income increased 17.3% to US$12.08 billion from US$10.30 billion in the prior year. Revenues were US$22.98 billion, up 11.5% from US$20.61 billion the year before. Operating income was US$15.00 billion versus US$12.95 billion in the prior year, an increase of 15.8%. Indirect operating expenses increased 4.2% to US$7.98 billion from US$7.66 billion in the equivalent prior-year period.

Prospects: Our evaluation of Visa Inc. as of October 4th, 2019 is the result of our systematic analysis on three basic characteristics: earnings strength, relative valuation, and recent stock price movement. The company has managed to produce a neutral trend in earnings per share over the past 5 quarters. In addition, recent analyst estimates for the company have been mixed and V has posted results that exceeded analysts' expectations. Based on operating earnings yield, the company is fairly valued when compared to all of the companies we cover. Share price changes over the past year indicates that V will perform over the near term.

Financial Data

(US$ in Thousands)	09/30/2019	09/30/2018	09/30/2017	09/30/2016	09/30/2015	09/30/2014	09/30/2013	09/30/2012
Earnings Per Share	5.32	4.42	2.80	2.48	2.58	2.15	1.90	0.79
Cash Flow Per Share	6.40	6.20	4.38	2.56	2.96	2.34	0.95	1.54
Tang Book Value Per Share	N.M.	N.M.	N.M.	N.M.	3.00	1.39	1.23	1.40
Dividends Per Share	1.000	0.825	0.660	0.560	0.480	0.400	0.330	0.220
Dividend Payout %	18.80	18.67	23.57	22.58	18.60	18.56	17.39	27.85
Income Statement								
Total Revenue	22,977,000	20,609,000	18,358,000	15,082,000	13,880,000	12,702,000	11,778,000	10,421,000
EBITDA	16,013,000	13,976,000	12,757,000	8,891,000	9,426,000	8,093,000	7,585,000	2,426,000
Depn & Amortn	596,000	558,000	500,000	452,000	431,000	369,000	328,000	265,000
Income Before Taxes	14,884,000	12,806,000	11,694,000	8,012,000	8,995,000	7,724,000	7,257,000	2,207,000
Income Taxes	2,804,000	2,505,000	4,995,000	2,021,000	2,667,000	2,286,000	2,277,000	65,000
Net Income	12,080,000	10,301,000	6,699,000	5,991,000	6,328,000	5,438,000	4,980,000	2,144,000
Average Shares	2,272,000	2,329,000	2,395,000	2,414,000	2,457,000	2,524,000	2,624,000	2,712,000
Balance Sheet								
Current Assets	20,970,000	18,216,000	19,023,000	14,313,000	10,892,000	9,562,000	7,822,000	11,786,000
Total Assets	72,574,000	69,225,000	67,977,000	64,035,000	40,236,000	38,569,000	35,956,000	40,013,000
Current Liabilities	13,415,000	11,305,000	9,994,000	8,046,000	5,374,000	6,006,000	4,335,000	7,954,000
Long-Term Obligations	16,729,000	16,630,000	16,618,000	15,882,000	...	...	...	...
Total Liabilities	37,890,000	35,219,000	35,217,000	31,123,000	10,394,000	11,156,000	9,086,000	12,383,000
Stockholders' Equity	34,684,000	34,006,000	32,760,000	32,912,000	29,842,000	27,413,000	26,870,000	27,630,000
Shares Outstanding	1,974,000	2,025,000	2,076,000	2,133,000	2,215,000	3,048,000	3,120,000	3,244,000
Statistical Record								
Return on Assets %	17.04	15.02	10.15	11.46	16.06	14.59	13.11	5.72
Return on Equity %	35.17	30.86	20.40	19.04	22.10	20.04	18.28	7.91
EBITDA Margin %	69.69	67.82	69.49	58.95	67.91	63.71	64.40	23.28
Net Margin %	52.57	49.98	36.49	39.72	45.59	42.81	42.28	20.57
Asset Turnover	0.32	0.30	0.28	0.29	0.35	0.34	0.31	0.28
Current Ratio	1.56	1.61	1.90	1.78	2.03	1.59	1.80	1.48
Debt to Equity	0.48	0.49	0.51	0.48	...	...	...	...
Price Range	185.74-121.73	150.09-105.31	106.21-75.43	83.36-67.77	76.38-50.06	58.25-45.63	49.71-34.00	33.75-21.07
P/E Ratio	34.91-22.88	33.96-23.83	37.93-26.94	33.61-27.33	29.60-19.40	27.09-21.22	26.16-17.89	42.72-26.66
Average Yield %	0.64	0.66	0.73	0.73	0.72	0.76	0.79	0.78

Address: P.O. Box 8999, San Francisco, CA 94128-8999 **Telephone:** 650-432-3200	**Web Site:** www.corporate.visa.com **Officers:** Robert W. Matschullat - Chairman Alfred F. (Al) Kelly - Chairman, Chief Executive Officer, Chief Executive Officer - Designate	**Auditors:** KPMG LLP **Investor Contact:** 650-432-7644 **Transfer Agents:** Wells Fargo Shareowner Services, St. Paul, MN

737

VISHAY INTERTECHNOLOGY, INC.

Exchange	Symbol	Price	52Wk Range	Yield	P/E
NYS	VSH	$21.29 (12/31/2019)	22.67-14.57	1.78	12.31

*7 Year Price Score 96.66 *NYSE Composite Index=100 *12 Month Price Score 104.13

Interim Earnings (Per Share)

Qtr.	Mar	Jun	Sep	Dec
2016	0.19	0.22	0.24	(0.33)
2017	0.24	0.36	0.41	(1.15)
2018	0.39	0.65	0.51	0.69
2019	0.52	0.31	0.21	...

Interim Dividends (Per Share)

Amt	Decl	Ex	Rec	Pay
0.085Q	02/14/2019	03/13/2019	03/14/2019	03/28/2019
0.095Q	05/08/2019	06/12/2019	06/13/2019	06/27/2019
0.095Q	08/20/2019	09/11/2019	09/12/2019	09/26/2019
0.095Q	11/19/2019	12/11/2019	12/12/2019	12/23/2019

Indicated Div: $0.38

Valuation Analysis | **Institutional Holding**

Forecast EPS	$1.32	No of Institutions
	(01/17/2020)	419
Market Cap	$3.1 Billion	Shares
Book Value	$1.5 Billion	169,128,112
Price/Book	2.07	% Held
Price/Sales	1.08	86.56

Business Summary: Electrical Equipment (MIC: 7.3.1 SIC: 3679 NAIC: 334419)

Vishay Intertechnology is a manufacturer and supplier of discrete semiconductors and passive components. Co.'s semiconductor products include metal oxide semiconductor field-effect transistors, diodes, and optoelectronic components. Semiconductors are used to perform functions such as switching, amplifying, rectifying, routing, or transmitting electrical signals, power conversion, and power management. Co.'s passive components include resistors, capacitors, and magnetics such as inductors and transformers. Passive components are used to store electrical charges, to limit or resist electrical current, and to help in filtering, surge suppression, measurement, timing, and tuning applications.

Recent Developments: For the quarter ended Sep 28 2019, net income decreased 61.2% to US$30.3 million from US$78.1 million in the year-earlier quarter. Revenues were US$628.3 million, down 19.5% from US$781.0 million the year before. Operating income was US$51.0 million versus US$138.1 million in the prior-year quarter, a decrease of 63.0%. Direct operating expenses declined 12.2% to US$478.3 million from US$544.7 million in the comparable period the year before. Indirect operating expenses increased 0.9% to US$99.1 million from US$98.2 million in the equivalent prior-year period.

Prospects: Our evaluation of Vishay Intertechnology Inc. as of October 4th, 2019 is the result of our systematic analysis on three basic characteristics: earnings strength, relative valuation, and recent stock price movement. The company has generated a negative trend in earnings per share over the past 5 quarters. However, recent analyst estimates for the company have been mixed and VSH has posted results that exceeded analysts' expectations. Based on operating earnings yield, the company is undervalued when compared to all of the companies we cover. Share price changes over the past year indicates that VSH will perform very poorly over the near term.

Financial Data

(US$ in Thousands)	9 Mos	6 Mos	3 Mos	12/31/2018	12/31/2017	12/31/2016	12/31/2015	12/31/2014
Earnings Per Share	1.73	2.03	2.37	2.24	(0.14)	0.32	(0.73)	0.77
Cash Flow Per Share	2.50	2.46	2.01	1.79	2.53	2.01	1.66	2.01
Tang Book Value Per Share	8.81	8.82	8.52	8.11	8.44	9.18	9.36	10.13
Dividends Per Share	0.360	0.350	0.340	0.323	0.255	0.250	0.240	0.240
Dividend Payout %	20.81	17.24	14.35	14.40	...	78.13	...	31.17
Income Statement								
Total Revenue	2,058,728	1,430,399	745,159	3,034,689	2,603,522	2,323,431	2,300,488	2,493,282
EBITDA	355,769	264,432	146,569	591,572	455,727	260,096	250,368	347,465
Depn & Amortn	122,302	81,346	40,428	150,056	148,883	144,521	154,340	160,804
Income Before Taxes	215,018	170,836	99,948	416,776	285,476	94,216	74,740	167,143
Income Taxes	64,377	50,460	24,307	70,239	298,924	44,843	182,473	49,300
Net Income	149,974	119,936	75,459	345,758	(20,344)	48,792	(108,514)	117,629
Average Shares	145,027	145,023	145,289	154,622	145,633	150,697	147,700	153,716
Balance Sheet								
Current Assets	1,691,080	1,745,397	1,771,579	1,783,886	2,192,290	1,864,472	1,887,492	1,926,450
Total Assets	3,072,186	3,156,130	3,181,050	3,106,198	3,459,189	3,077,801	3,152,986	3,298,773
Current Liabilities	481,102	511,596	574,229	644,106	564,335	456,850	457,724	456,739
Long-Term Obligations	496,262	519,863	492,830	494,509	370,470	357,023	436,738	454,922
Total Liabilities	1,586,688	1,666,178	1,731,906	1,723,814	2,031,032	1,512,284	1,530,510	1,473,407
Stockholders' Equity	1,485,498	1,489,952	1,449,144	1,382,384	1,428,157	1,565,517	1,622,476	1,825,366
Shares Outstanding	144,445	144,445	144,435	144,215	144,003	145,976	147,590	147,453
Statistical Record								
Return on Assets %	7.86	9.16	10.63	10.53	N.M.	1.56	N.M.	3.60
Return on Equity %	17.16	20.89	24.23	24.60	N.M.	3.05	N.M.	6.36
EBITDA Margin %	17.28	18.49	19.67	19.49	17.50	11.19	10.88	13.94
Net Margin %	7.28	8.38	10.13	11.39	N.M.	2.10	N.M.	4.72
Asset Turnover	0.88	0.91	0.91	0.92	0.80	0.74	0.71	0.76
Current Ratio	3.52	3.41	3.09	2.77	3.88	4.08	4.12	4.22
Debt to Equity	0.33	0.35	0.34	0.36	0.26	0.23	0.27	0.25
Price Range	22.67-14.57	26.15-15.14	26.15-16.65	26.15-16.84	23.20-15.50	16.60-10.28	14.59-9.30	16.17-12.68
P/E Ratio	13.10-8.42	12.88-7.46	11.03-7.03	11.67-7.52	...	51.88-32.13	...	21.00-16.47
Average Yield %	1.98	1.75	1.63	1.55	1.42	1.91	1.98	1.66

Address: 63 Lancaster Avenue, Malvern, PA 19355-2143 Telephone: 610-644-1300	Web Site: Officers: Marc Zandman - Executive Chairman, Chief Business Development Officer Gerald Paul - President, Chief Executive Officer	Auditors: Ernst & Young LLP Investor Contact: 610-644-1300 Transfer Agents: American Stock Transfer & Trust Company, New York, NY

VISTRA ENERGY CORP

Exchange	Symbol	Price	52Wk Range	Yield	P/E
NYS	VST	$22.99 (12/31/2019)	27.37-4.55	2.17	22.99

*7 Year Price Score 154.72 *NYSE Composite Index=100 *12 Month Price Score 119.17

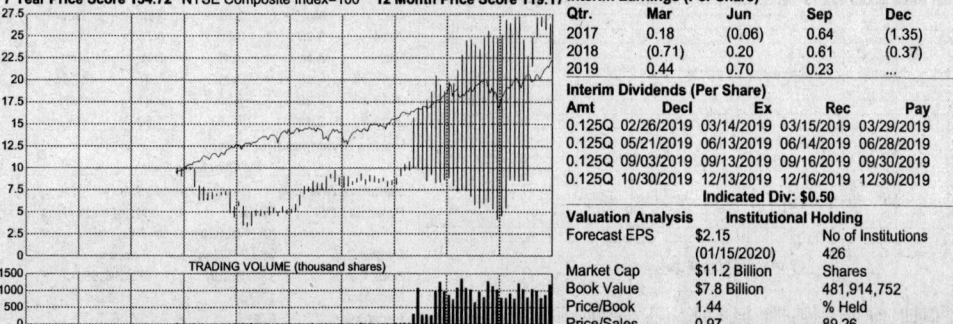

Interim Earnings (Per Share)

Qtr.	Mar	Jun	Sep	Dec
2017	0.18	(0.06)	0.64	(1.35)
2018	(0.71)	0.20	0.61	(0.37)
2019	0.44	0.70	0.23	...

Interim Dividends (Per Share)

Amt	Decl	Ex	Rec	Pay
0.125Q	02/26/2019	03/14/2019	03/15/2019	03/29/2019
0.125Q	05/21/2019	06/13/2019	06/14/2019	06/28/2019
0.125Q	09/03/2019	09/13/2019	09/16/2019	09/30/2019
0.125Q	10/30/2019	12/13/2019	12/16/2019	12/30/2019

Indicated Div: $0.50

Valuation Analysis   Institutional Holding

Forecast EPS	$2.15	No of Institutions	
	(01/15/2020)	426	
Market Cap	$11.2 Billion	Shares	
Book Value	$7.8 Billion	481,914,752	
Price/Book	1.44	% Held	
Price/Sales	0.97	89.26	

Business Summary: Electric Utilities (MIC: 3.1.1 SIC: 4911 NAIC: 221122)

Vistra Energy operates an integrated retail and generation business in markets throughout the U.S. Through its subsidiaries, Co. is engaged in electricity market activities, including electricity generation, wholesale energy sales and purchases, commodity risk management and retail sales of electricity. Co. has six segments: Retail, ERCOT, PJM, NY/NE (comprising NYISO and ISO-NE), MISO and Asset Closure. The Retail segment is engaged in retail sales of electricity and related services. The ERCOT, PJM, NY/NE and MISO segments are engaged in electricity generation, among others. The Asset Closure segment is engaged in the decommissioning and reclamation of retired plants and mines.

Recent Developments: For the quarter ended Sep 30 2019, net income decreased 65.6% to US$114.0 million from US$331.0 million in the year-earlier quarter. Revenues were US$3.19 billion, down 1.5% from US$3.24 billion the year before. Operating income was US$440.0 million versus US$650.0 million in the prior-year quarter, a decrease of 32.3%. Direct operating expenses rose 5.6% to US$2.08 billion from US$1.97 billion in the comparable period the year before. Indirect operating expenses increased 8.1% to US$670.0 million from US$620.0 million in the equivalent prior-year period.

Prospects: Our evaluation of Vistra Energy Corp as of October 4th, 2019 is the result of our systematic analysis on three basic characteristics: earnings strength, relative valuation, and recent stock price movement. The company has produced a positive trend in earnings per share over the past 5 quarters. In addition, recent analyst estimates for the company have been raised, and VST has posted results that exceeded analysts' expectations. Based on operating earnings yield, the company is fairly valued when compared to all of the companies we cover. Share price changes over the past year indicates that VST will perform poorly over the near term.

Financial Data

(US$ in Millions)	9 Mos	6 Mos	3 Mos	12/31/2018	12/31/2017	12/31/2016	10/02/2016	12/31/2015
Earnings Per Share	1.00	1.38	0.88	(0.11)	(0.59)	(0.38)	...	...
Cash Flow Per Share	4.96	4.77	3.74	2.91	3.24	0.77	...	...
Tang Book Value Per Share	5.97	7.22	6.86	6.69	4.45	3.47	...	...
Dividends Per Share	0.375	0.250	0.125	...	...	2.320	...	...
Dividend Payout %	37.50	18.12	14.20	...	...	...	...	...
Income Statement								
Total Revenue	8,949	5,755	2,923	9,144	5,430	1,191	4,255	5,704
EBITDA	2,370	1,739	900	1,460	664	(120)	23,031	(3,501)
Depn & Amortn	973	647	461	1,024	236	54	401	767
Income Before Taxes	949	793	294	(118)	250	(233)	21,584	(5,556)
Income Taxes	270	225	77	(45)	504	(70)	(1,267)	(879)
Net Income	694	581	225	(54)	(254)	(163)	22,851	(4,677)
Average Shares	493	507	509	504	427	427	...	...
Balance Sheet								
Current Assets	4,128	4,539	3,324	3,435	2,673	2,473	...	3,450
Total Assets	26,443	26,520	25,568	26,024	14,600	15,167	...	15,658
Current Liabilities	3,915	3,657	3,238	3,625	1,351	1,504	...	2,812
Long-Term Obligations	10,728	11,193	10,803	10,874	4,379	4,577	...	3
Total Liabilities	18,651	18,616	17,764	18,161	8,258	8,570	...	38,542
Stockholders' Equity	7,792	7,904	7,804	7,863	6,342	6,597	...	(22,884)
Shares Outstanding	487	476	484	493	428	427	...	...
Statistical Record								
Return on Assets %	1.94	2.74	2.36	N.M.	N.M.	N.M.	...	...
Return on Equity %	6.28	8.89	6.88	N.M.	N.M.	...	...	...
EBITDA Margin %	26.48	30.22	30.79	15.97	12.23	N.M.	541.27	N.M.
Net Margin %	7.76	10.10	7.70	N.M.	N.M.	N.M.	537.04	N.M.
Asset Turnover	0.44	0.44	0.56	0.45	0.36	0.31	...	...
Current Ratio	1.05	1.24	1.03	0.95	1.98	1.64	...	1.23
Debt to Equity	1.38	1.42	1.38	1.38	0.69	0.69	...	...
Price Range	27.25-4.09	27.25-4.09	26.89-4.09	25.62-4.09	20.49-8.10	8.89-7.86	9.36-7.73	9.76-4.91
P/E Ratio	27.25-4.09	19.75-2.96	30.56-4.65	...	...	...	...	...
Average Yield %	2.23	1.60	0.82	...	...	27.60	...	...

Address: 6555 Sierra Drive, Irving, TX 75039	**Web Site:** www.vistraenergy.com	**Auditors:** DELOITTE & TOUCHE LLP
Telephone: 214-812-4600	**Officers:** Scott B. Helm - Chairman Curtis A. (Curt) Morgan - President, Chief Executive Officer	**Investor Contact:** 214-812-0046
		Transfer Agents: American Stock Transfer & Trust Company, LLC

VMWARE INC

*7 Year Price Score 132.15 *NYSE Composite Index=100 *12 Month Price Score 90.28

TRADING VOLUME (thousand shares)

Interim Earnings (Per Share)

Qtr.	Mar	Jun	Sep	Dec
2016	0.38	0.62	0.75	1.03
Qtr.	Apr	Jul	Oct	Jan
2017-18	0.56	0.81	1.07	(1.06)
2018-19	2.29	1.56	0.81	1.21
2019-20	2.42	11.83	1.50	...

Interim Dividends (Per Share)

No Dividends Paid

Valuation Analysis / Institutional Holding

Valuation Analysis		Institutional Holding	
Forecast EPS	$6.58	No of Institutions	
	(01/17/2020)	799	
Market Cap	$62.2 Billion	Shares	
Book Value	$5.8 Billion	83,696,584	
Price/Book	10.70	% Held	
Price/Sales	6.38	17.06	

Business Summary: Internet & Software (MIC: 6.3.2 SIC: 7372 NAIC: 511210)

VMware is engaged in the development and application of technologies with x86 server-based computing, separating application software from the underlying hardware. Co.'s product and service solutions are organized into three main product groups: Software-Defined Data Center, which is designed to transform the data center into an on-demand service that addresses application requirements; Hybrid Cloud Computing, which is comprised of VMware Cloud Provider Program and VMware Cloud Services; and End-User Computing solution, which consists of VMware Workspace ONE, its digital workspace platform, that includes Unified Endpoint Management and VMware Horizon application and desktop virtualization.

Recent Developments: For the quarter ended Nov 1 2019, net income increased 85.9% to US$621.0 million from US$334.0 million in the year-earlier quarter. Revenues were US$2.46 billion, up 11.6% from US$2.20 billion the year before. Operating income was US$431.0 million versus US$495.0 million in the prior-year quarter, a decrease of 12.9%. Direct operating expenses rose 20.0% to US$378.0 million from US$315.0 million in the comparable period the year before. Indirect operating expenses increased 18.5% to US$1.65 billion from US$1.39 billion in the equivalent prior-year period.

Prospects: Our evaluation of VMware Inc. as of October 4th, 2019 is the result of our systematic analysis on three basic characteristics: earnings strength, relative valuation, and recent stock price movement. The company has generated a negative trend in earnings per share over the past 5 quarters. However, recent analyst estimates for the company have been unchanged while VMW has posted results that exceeded analysts' expectations. Based on operating earnings yield, the company is fairly valued when compared to all of the companies we cover. Share price changes over the past year indicates that VMW will perform well over the near term.

Financial Data

(US$ in Thousands)	9 Mos	6 Mos	3 Mos	02/01/2019	02/02/2018	02/03/2017	12/31/2016	12/31/2015
Earnings Per Share	16.96	16.27	6.00	5.85	1.38	(0.02)	2.78	2.34
Cash Flow Per Share	9.27	9.16	9.36	9.01	7.92	9.48	5.65	4.48
Tang Book Value Per Share	N.M.	N.M.	N.M.	N.M.	6.52	8.97	8.69	7.84
Dividends Per Share	26.810	26.810	26.810	26.810	...	...	...	...
Dividend Payout %	158.08	164.78	446.83	458.29	...	...	...	...
Income Statement								
Total Revenue	7,161,000	4,705,000	2,266,000	8,974,000	7,922,000	496,000	7,093,000	6,571,000
EBITDA	1,854,000	959,000	748,000	3,216,000	2,070,000	(3,000)	1,714,000	1,429,000
Depn & Amortn	542,000	352,000	174,000	199,000	195,000	29,000	215,000	190,000
Income Before Taxes	1,205,000	540,000	540,000	2,883,000	1,801,000	(34,000)	1,473,000	1,213,000
Income Taxes	(4,846,000)	(4,890,000)	35,000	461,000	1,231,000	(26,000)	287,000	216,000
Net Income	6,051,000	5,430,000	505,000	2,422,000	570,000	(8,000)	1,186,000	997,000
Average Shares	414,054	416,288	836,774	414,267	413,368	408,625	423,994	426,547
Balance Sheet								
Current Assets	4,641,000	5,629,000	5,288,000	5,651,000	13,734,000	9,851,000	10,335,000	9,360,000
Total Assets	22,002,000	20,372,000	14,973,000	14,662,000	20,622,000	16,397,000	16,643,000	15,746,000
Current Liabilities	7,948,000	5,858,000	5,445,000	5,696,000	5,033,000	4,289,000	4,554,000	4,129,000
Long-Term Obligations	3,000,000	4,246,000	4,244,000	4,242,000	4,234,000	1,500,000	1,500,000	1,500,000
Total Liabilities	16,188,000	15,173,000	14,412,000	14,111,000	12,846,000	8,181,000	8,546,000	7,827,000
Stockholders' Equity	5,814,000	5,199,000	561,000	551,000	7,776,000	8,216,000	8,097,000	7,919,000
Shares Outstanding	409,725	409,494	410,267	410,715	403,776	410,060	408,351	421,947
Statistical Record								
Return on Assets %	28.52	28.63	10.71	13.77	3.09	N.M.	7.30	6.44
Return on Equity %	78.37	80.39	38.84	58.33	7.15	N.M.	14.77	12.86
EBITDA Margin %	25.89	20.38	33.01	35.84	26.13	N.M.	24.16	21.75
Net Margin %	84.50	115.41	22.29	26.99	7.20	N.M.	16.72	15.17
Asset Turnover	0.42	0.43	0.50	0.51	0.43	0.32	0.44	0.42
Current Ratio	0.58	0.96	0.97	0.99	2.73	2.30	2.27	2.27
Debt to Equity	0.52	0.82	7.57	7.70	0.54	0.18	0.19	0.19
Price Range	205.52-130.56	205.52-130.67	204.13-130.67	167.34-108.46	150.00-85.89	88.95-78.88	82.58-43.84	91.14-55.42
P/E Ratio	12.12-7.70	12.63-8.03	34.02-21.78	28.61-18.54	108.70-62.24	...	29.71-15.77	38.95-23.68
Average Yield %	16.21	16.21	17.06	18.71	...	...	...	...

VORNADO REALTY TRUST

Exchange	Symbol	Price	52Wk Range	Yield	P/E
NYS	VNO	$66.50 (12/31/2019)	70.50-58.81	3.97	4.23

*7 Year Price Score 73.93 *NYSE Composite Index=100 *12 Month Price Score 93.93

Interim Earnings (Per Share)

Qtr.	Mar	Jun	Sep	Dec
2016	(0.61)	1.16	0.35	3.43
2017	0.25	0.61	(0.15)	0.14
2018	(0.09)	0.58	1.00	0.52
2019	0.95	12.56	1.69	...

Interim Dividends (Per Share)

Amt	Decl	Ex	Rec	Pay
0.66Q	10/25/2019	11/01/2019	11/04/2019	11/18/2019
1.74Q	12/18/2019	12/27/2019	12/30/2019	01/15/2020
0.21Sp	12/18/2019	12/27/2019	12/30/2019	01/15/2020
0.66Q	01/15/2020	01/24/2020	01/27/2020	02/14/2020

Indicated Div: $2.64

Valuation Analysis

		Institutional Holding	
Forecast EPS	$15.63	No of Institutions	712
	(01/16/2020)		
Market Cap	$12.7 Billion	Shares	207,944,128
Book Value	$7.1 Billion		
Price/Book	1.79	% Held	76.59
Price/Sales	6.32		

Business Summary: REITs (MIC: 5.3.1 SIC: 6798 NAIC: 525930)

Vornado Realty Trust is a real estate investment trust and conducts its business through, and substantially all of its interests in properties are held by, Vornado Realty L.P. (the Operating Partnership). Co. is the sole general partner of the common limited partnership interest in the Operating Partnership. Co. owns and operate office and retail properties with a concentration in the New York City metropolitan area. In addition, Co. has interest in Alexander's, Inc., which owns properties in the greater New York metropolitan area, as well as interests in other real estate and related investments.

Recent Developments: For the quarter ended Sep 30 2019, income from continuing operations increased 66.1% to US$363.9 million from US$219.1 million in the year-earlier quarter. Net income increased 66.0% to US$363.8 million from US$219.2 million in the year-earlier quarter. Revenues were US$466.0 million, down 14.0% from US$542.0 million the year before. Revenues from property income fell 15.1% to US$427.6 million from US$503.9 million in the corresponding quarter a year earlier.

Prospects: Our evaluation of Vornado Realty Trust as of October 4th, 2019 is the result of our systematic analysis on three basic characteristics: earnings strength, relative valuation, and recent stock price movement. The company has managed to produce a neutral trend in earnings per share over the past 5 quarters. In addition, recent analyst estimates for the company have been mixed and VNO has posted results that fell short of analysts' expectations. Based on operating earnings yield, the company is overvalued when compared to all of the companies we cover. Share price changes over the past year indicates that VNO will perform poorly over the near term.

Financial Data

(US$ in Thousands)	9 Mos	6 Mos	3 Mos	12/31/2018	12/31/2017	12/31/2016	12/31/2015	12/31/2014
Earnings Per Share	15.72	15.03	3.05	2.01	0.85	4.34	3.59	4.15
Cash Flow Per Share	3.73	4.48	3.15	4.22	4.54	5.28	3.57	6.05
Tang Book Value Per Share	32.24	31.11	18.44	18.04	17.30	29.97	27.54	27.63
Dividends Per Share	2.610	2.580	2.550	2.520	2.620	2.520	2.520	2.920
Dividend Payout %	16.60	17.17	83.61	125.37	308.24	58.06	70.19	70.36
Income Statement								
Total Revenue	1,463,732	997,771	534,668	2,163,720	2,084,126	2,506,202	2,502,267	2,635,940
EBITDA	3,406,833	2,996,773	327,125	1,278,331	1,097,835	1,761,684	1,499,334	1,377,389
Depn & Amortn	(15,561)	(11,168)	(6,525)	434,212	483,036	542,068	487,154	536,622
Income Before Taxes	3,211,854	2,852,248	235,771	539,680	300,006	841,275	661,022	400,282
Income Taxes	80,542	56,657	29,743	37,633	41,090	8,312	(84,695)	11,002
Net Income	2,942,187	2,606,749	194,022	449,954	227,416	906,917	760,434	864,852
Average Shares	191,024	191,058	190,996	191,290	191,258	190,173	189,564	188,690
Balance Sheet								
Current Assets	2,088,701	1,911,261	1,740,844	942,425	2,156,264	1,897,493	2,192,565	1,715,456
Total Assets	18,216,099	17,913,857	17,637,955	17,180,794	17,397,934	20,814,847	21,143,293	21,248,320
Current Liabilities	453,331	392,581	442,496	430,976	415,794	458,694	443,955	499,702
Long-Term Obligations	7,487,148	7,527,604	8,639,526	9,836,621	9,729,487	10,611,685	11,091,010	10,898,859
Total Liabilities	11,141,027	11,053,303	13,193,963	12,715,563	13,060,282	13,916,328	14,445,698	14,502,894
Stockholders' Equity	7,075,072	6,860,554	4,443,992	4,465,231	4,337,652	6,898,519	6,697,595	6,745,426
Shares Outstanding	190,850	190,813	190,761	190,535	189,983	189,100	188,576	187,887
Statistical Record								
Return on Assets %	17.51	16.81	3.68	2.60	1.19	4.31	3.59	4.18
Return on Equity %	53.35	52.47	14.41	10.22	4.05	13.30	11.31	12.80
EBITDA Margin %	232.75	300.35	61.18	59.08	52.68	70.29	59.92	52.25
Net Margin %	201.01	261.26	36.29	20.80	10.91	36.19	30.39	32.81
Asset Turnover	0.12	0.12	0.13	0.13	0.11	0.12	0.12	0.13
Current Ratio	4.61	4.87	3.93	2.19	5.19	4.14	4.94	3.43
Debt to Equity	1.06	1.10	1.94	2.20	2.24	1.54	1.66	1.62
Price Range	72.28-58.81	77.38-60.19	77.38-60.19	77.38-60.19	89.58-72.38	87.03-64.77	92.74-68.53	87.30-64.88
P/E Ratio	4.60-3.74	5.15-4.00	25.37-19.73	38.50-29.95	105.39-85.15	20.05-14.92	25.83-19.09	21.04-15.63
Average Yield %	3.93	3.73	3.66	3.59	3.32	3.23	3.09	3.86

Address: 888 Seventh Avenue, New York, NY 10019 **Telephone:** 212-894-7000	**Web Site:** www.vno.com **Officers:** Steven Roth - Chairman, Chief Executive Officer Michael J. Franco - President, Executive Vice President, Chief Investment Officer	**Auditors:** DELOITTE & TOUCHE LLP **Investor Contact:** 201-587-1000 **Transfer Agents:** American Stock Transfer & Trust Co., New York, NY

VOYA FINANCIAL INC

Exchange	Symbol	Price	52Wk Range	Yield	P/E
NYS	VOYA	$60.98 (12/31/2019)	61.75-39.53	0.98	17.52

*7 Year Price Score N/A   ***NYSE Composite Index=100**   ***12 Month Price Score 104.56**

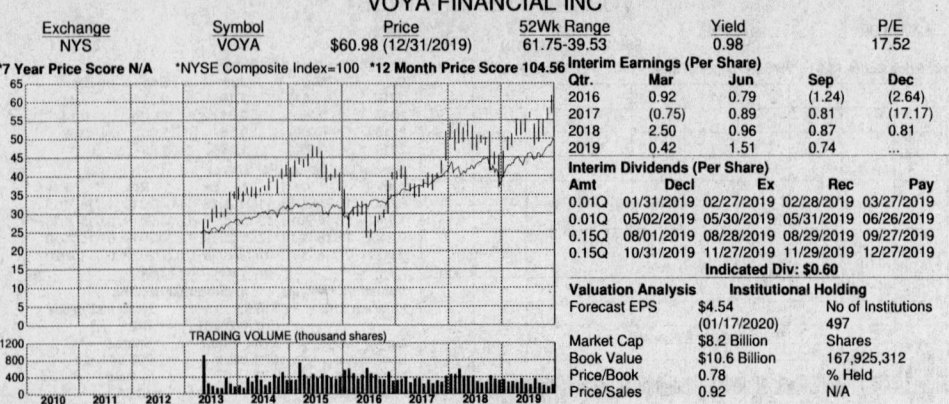

Interim Earnings (Per Share)

Qtr.	Mar	Jun	Sep	Dec
2016	0.92	0.79	(1.24)	(2.64)
2017	(0.75)	0.89	0.81	(17.17)
2018	2.50	0.96	0.87	0.81
2019	0.42	1.51	0.74	...

Interim Dividends (Per Share)

Amt	Decl	Ex	Rec	Pay
0.01Q	01/31/2019	02/27/2019	02/28/2019	03/27/2019
0.01Q	05/02/2019	05/30/2019	05/31/2019	06/26/2019
0.15Q	08/01/2019	08/28/2019	08/29/2019	09/27/2019
0.15Q	10/31/2019	11/27/2019	11/29/2019	12/27/2019

Indicated Div: $0.60

Valuation Analysis   **Institutional Holding**

Forecast EPS	$4.54	No of Institutions
	(01/17/2020)	497
Market Cap	$8.2 Billion	Shares
Book Value	$10.6 Billion	167,925,312
Price/Book	0.78	% Held
Price/Sales	0.92	N/A

Business Summary: Life & Health (MIC: 5.2.2 SIC: 6311 NAIC: 524210)

Voya Financial is a holding company. Through its subsidiaries, Co. provides a range of retirement services, investment management services, mutual funds, group insurance and supplemental health products. Co. has four segments: Retirement, which provides tax-deferred, employer-sponsored retirement savings plans and administrative services; Investment Management, which provides investment products and retirement solutions; Individual Life, which provides wealth protection and transfer opportunities through universal and variable life products; and Employee Benefits, which provides stop loss, group life, voluntary employee-paid and disability products to mid-sized and large businesses.

Recent Developments: For the quarter ended Sep 30 2019, net income decreased 15.8% to US$139.0 million from US$165.0 million in the year-earlier quarter. Revenues were US$2.24 billion, down 0.7% from US$2.25 billion the year before. Net premiums earned were US$571.0 million versus US$550.0 million in the prior-year quarter, an increase of 3.8%. Net investment income fell 0.2% to US$853.0 million from US$855.0 million a year ago.

Prospects: Our evaluation of Voya Financial Inc. as of October 4th, 2019 is the result of our systematic analysis on three basic characteristics: earnings strength, relative valuation, and recent stock price movement. The company has enjoyed a very positive trend in earnings per share over the past 5 quarters. However, recent analyst estimates for the company have been reduced, while VOYA has posted results that exceeded analysts' expectations. Based on operating earnings yield, the company is undervalued when compared to all of the companies we cover. Share price changes over the past year indicates that VOYA will perform in line with the market over the near term.

Financial Data

(US$ in Thousands)	9 Mos	6 Mos	3 Mos	12/31/2018	12/31/2017	12/31/2016	12/31/2015	12/31/2014
Earnings Per Share	3.48	3.61	3.06	5.20	(16.25)	(2.13)	1.80	9.02
Cash Flow Per Share	7.84	9.47	10.88	11.45	8.57	17.81	14.40	14.34
Tang Book Value Per Share	78.29	71.72	61.26	54.40	58.20	65.63	63.06	65.42
Dividends Per Share	0.180	0.040	0.040	0.040	0.040	0.040	0.040	0.040
Dividend Payout %	5.17	1.11	1.31	0.77	...	...	2.22	0.44
Income Statement								
Total Revenue	6,780,000	4,543,000	2,197,000	8,514,000	8,618,000	10,782,200	11,341,200	11,070,900
Income Before Taxes	618,000	475,000	177,000	610,000	528,000	(613,400)	584,500	785,200
Income Taxes	73,000	69,000	25,000	55,000	740,000	(214,700)	45,900	(1,752,200)
Net Income	420,000	300,000	74,000	875,000	(2,992,000)	(428,000)	408,300	2,299,700
Average Shares	144,300	149,900	151,300	168,200	184,100	200,800	227,400	255,100
Balance Sheet								
Total Assets	166,850,000	165,162,000	161,985,000	154,682,000	222,532,000	214,235,100	218,249,600	226,951,400
Total Liabilities	156,299,000	155,098,000	152,920,000	146,469,000	212,523,000	201,241,200	204,813,800	210,843,500
Stockholders' Equity	10,551,000	10,064,000	9,065,000	8,213,000	10,009,000	12,993,900	13,435,800	16,107,900
Shares Outstanding	134,775	140,329	147,970	150,978	171,982	194,639	209,095	241,875
Statistical Record								
Return on Assets %	0.33	0.34	0.26	0.46	N.M.	N.M.	0.18	1.03
Return on Equity %	5.67	6.08	5.45	9.60	N.M.	N.M.	2.76	15.65
Net Margin %	6.19	6.60	3.37	10.28	N.M.	N.M.	3.60	20.77
Asset Turnover	0.05	0.05	0.05	0.05	0.04	0.05	0.05	0.05
Price Range	57.29-37.06	55.30-37.06	55.15-37.06	55.15-37.06	52.07-34.18	41.00-23.38	48.14-36.04	43.07-33.11
P/E Ratio	16.46-10.65	15.32-10.27	18.02-12.11	10.61-7.13	...	...	26.74-20.02	4.77-3.67
Average Yield %	0.36	0.08	0.08	0.08	0.10	0.13	0.09	0.11

Address: 230 Park Avenue, New York, NY 10169 **Telephone:** 212-309-8200	**Web Site:** www.ing.us **Officers:** Rodney O. Martin - Chairman, Chief Executive Officer Nancy Ferrara - Executive Vice President	**Auditors:** Ernst & Young LLP **Transfer Agents:** Computershare Trust Company, N.A, Canton, MA

VULCAN MATERIALS CO (HOLDING COMPANY)

Exchange	Symbol	Price	52Wk Range	Yield	P/E
NYS	VMC	$143.99 (12/31/2019)	151.62-96.59	0.86	31.93

*7 Year Price Score 109.69 *NYSE Composite Index=100 *12 Month Price Score 102.81

Interim Earnings (Per Share)

Qtr.	Mar	Jun	Sep	Dec
2016	0.14	0.91	1.04	1.00
2017	0.33	0.89	0.81	2.43
2018	0.39	1.19	1.34	0.93
2019	0.48	1.48	1.62	...

Interim Dividends (Per Share)

Amt	Decl	Ex	Rec	Pay
0.31Q	02/08/2019	02/21/2019	02/22/2019	03/08/2019
0.31Q	05/10/2019	05/23/2019	05/24/2019	06/07/2019
0.31Q	07/12/2019	08/20/2019	08/21/2019	09/06/2019
0.31Q	10/11/2019	11/18/2019	11/19/2019	12/05/2019

Indicated Div: $1.24 (Div. Reinv. Plan)

Valuation Analysis / **Institutional Holding**

Forecast EPS	$4.80 (01/17/2020)	No of Institutions 909
Market Cap	$19.1 Billion	Shares
Book Value	$5.5 Billion	162,692,576
Price/Book	3.44	% Held
Price/Sales	3.94	92.03

TRADING VOLUME (thousand shares)

Business Summary: Mining (MIC: 8.2.4 SIC: 1429 NAIC: 212319)

Vulcan Materials is a supplier of construction aggregates and a producer of asphalt mix and ready-mixed concrete. Co. has four segments: Aggregates, which produces and sells aggregates (crushed stone, sand and gravel, sand, and other aggregates) and related products and services; Asphalt, which produces and sells asphalt mix in Alabama, Arizona, California, New Mexico, Tennessee and Texas, and includes asphalt construction paving in Alabama, Tennessee and Texas; Concrete, which produces and sells ready-mixed concrete in the U.S., Washington D.C. and in the Bahamas; and Calcium, which consists of a Florida facility that mines, produces and sells calcium products.

Recent Developments: For the quarter ended Sep 30 2019, income from continuing operations increased 21.2% to US$218.1 million from US$179.9 million in the year-earlier quarter. Net income increased 20.4% to US$215.7 million from US$179.2 million in the year-earlier quarter. Revenues were US$1.42 billion, up 14.4% from US$1.24 billion the year before. Operating income was US$303.4 million versus US$249.2 million in the prior-year quarter, an increase of 21.7%. Direct operating expenses rose 13.5% to US$1.02 billion from US$897.1 million in the comparable period the year before. Indirect operating expenses increased 3.5% to US$97.3 million from US$94.0 million in the equivalent prior-year period.

Prospects: Our evaluation of Vulcan Materials Co. as of October 4th, 2019 is the result of our systematic analysis on three basic characteristics: earnings strength, relative valuation, and recent stock price movement. The company has produced a positive trend in earnings per share over the past 5 quarters. However, recent analyst estimates for the company have been mixed and VMC has posted results that exceeded analysts' expectations. Based on operating earnings yield, the company is fairly valued when compared to all of the companies we cover. Share price changes over the past year indicates that VMC will perform well over the near term.

Financial Data
(US$ in Thousands)

	9 Mos	6 Mos	3 Mos	12/31/2018	12/31/2017	12/31/2016	12/31/2015	12/31/2014
Earnings Per Share	4.51	4.23	3.94	3.85	4.46	3.09	1.64	1.54
Cash Flow Per Share	6.84	6.49	6.48	6.29	4.87	4.83	3.78	1.98
Tang Book Value Per Share	9.85	8.53	7.34	7.15	5.92	5.35	4.45	2.45
Dividends Per Share	1.210	1.180	1.150	1.120	1.000	0.800	0.400	0.220
Dividend Payout %	26.83	27.90	29.19	29.09	22.42	25.89	24.39	14.29
Income Statement								
Total Revenue	3,742,951	2,324,193	996,511	4,382,869	3,890,296	3,592,667	3,422,181	2,994,169
EBITDA	968,761	568,779	196,743	1,037,527	903,236	918,763	776,966	780,856
Depn & Amortn	278,925	182,677	89,181	276,814	250,835	238,237	228,866	239,611
Income Before Taxes	591,671	320,133	74,628	623,290	361,316	547,257	327,857	298,838
Income Taxes	111,764	58,291	10,693	105,449	(232,075)	124,851	94,943	91,692
Net Income	476,569	260,857	63,299	515,805	601,185	419,491	221,177	204,923
Average Shares	133,375	133,354	133,054	133,926	134,878	135,790	135,093	132,991
Balance Sheet								
Current Assets	1,324,242	1,255,015	1,083,851	1,079,145	1,180,101	1,137,182	1,084,591	920,469
Total Assets	10,539,673	10,480,764	10,296,852	9,832,130	9,504,891	8,471,475	8,301,632	8,061,902
Current Liabilities	535,284	663,588	659,607	602,550	442,872	372,244	353,479	451,878
Long-Term Obligations	2,783,068	2,781,826	2,780,589	2,779,357	2,813,482	1,982,751	1,980,334	1,855,447
Total Liabilities	4,997,434	5,109,317	5,079,643	4,629,227	4,535,998	3,898,999	3,847,444	3,885,203
Stockholders' Equity	5,542,239	5,371,447	5,217,209	5,202,903	4,968,893	4,572,476	4,454,188	4,176,699
Shares Outstanding	132,350	132,231	132,069	131,762	132,324	132,339	133,172	131,907
Statistical Record								
Return on Assets %	5.88	5.55	5.33	5.33	6.69	4.99	2.70	2.51
Return on Equity %	11.24	10.86	10.39	10.14	12.60	9.27	5.13	5.05
EBITDA Margin %	25.88	24.47	19.74	23.67	23.22	25.57	22.70	26.08
Net Margin %	12.73	11.22	6.35	11.77	15.45	11.68	6.46	6.84
Asset Turnover	0.47	0.46	0.46	0.45	0.43	0.43	0.42	0.37
Current Ratio	2.47	1.89	1.64	1.79	2.66	3.05	3.07	2.04
Debt to Equity	0.50	0.52	0.53	0.53	0.57	0.43	0.44	0.44
Price Range	151.62-84.20	137.31-84.20	133.24-84.20	141.11-84.20	135.28-112.50	136.04-81.60	105.70-64.98	69.01-55.28
P/E Ratio	33.62-18.67	32.46-19.91	33.82-21.37	36.65-21.87	30.33-25.22	44.03-26.41	64.45-39.62	44.81-35.90
Average Yield %	1.01	1.04	1.02	0.96	0.82	0.72	0.45	0.35

Address: 1200 Urban Center Drive, Birmingham, AL 35242 **Telephone:** 205-298-3000 **Fax:** 205-298-2963	**Web Site:** www.vulcanmaterials.com **Officers:** J. Thomas (Tom) Hill - Chairman, President, Chief Executive Officer, Executive Vice President, Chief Operating Officer Suzanne H. Wood - Senior Vice President, Chief Financial Officer, Secretary	**Auditors:** DELOITTE & TOUCHE LLP **Investor Contact:** 205-298-3220 **Transfer Agents:** Computershare Shareowner Services LLC, Providence, RI

WABTEC CORP

Exchange	Symbol	Price	52Wk Range	Yield	P/E
NYS	WAB	$77.80 (12/31/2019)	80.97-62.31	0.62	58.50

*7 Year Price Score 76.03 ***NYSE Composite Index=100** ***12 Month Price Score 101.41**

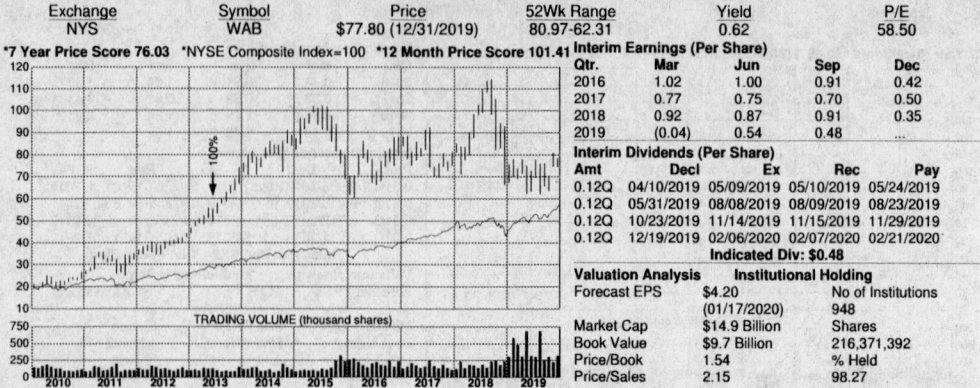

Interim Earnings (Per Share)

Qtr.	Mar	Jun	Sep	Dec
2016	1.02	1.00	0.91	0.42
2017	0.77	0.75	0.70	0.50
2018	0.92	0.87	0.91	0.35
2019	(0.04)	0.54	0.48	...

Interim Dividends (Per Share)

Amt	Decl	Ex	Rec	Pay
0.12Q	04/10/2019	05/09/2019	05/10/2019	05/24/2019
0.12Q	05/31/2019	08/08/2019	08/09/2019	08/23/2019
0.12Q	10/23/2019	11/14/2019	11/15/2019	11/29/2019
0.12Q	12/19/2019	02/06/2020	02/07/2020	02/21/2020

Indicated Div: $0.48

Valuation Analysis / Institutional Holding

Forecast EPS	$4.20	No of Institutions
	(01/17/2020)	948
Market Cap	$14.9 Billion	Shares
Book Value	$9.7 Billion	216,371,392
Price/Book	1.54	% Held
Price/Sales	2.15	98.27

Business Summary: Construction Services (MIC: 7.5.4 SIC: 3743 NAIC: 336510)

Wabtec is a provider of technology-based products and services for the global rail industry. Co. provides its products and services through two principal business segments: Transit, which manufactures and services components for new and existing passenger transit vehicles, supplies rail control and infrastructure products, builds new commuter locomotives, and refurbishes passenger transit vehicles; and Freight, which manufactures and services components for new and existing locomotives and freight cars, supplies rail control and infrastructure products, overhauls locomotives, and provides heat exchangers and cooling systems for rail and other industrial markets.

Recent Developments: For the quarter ended Sep 30 2019, net income increased 5.2% to US$90.6 million from US$86.1 million in the year-earlier quarter. Revenues were US$2.00 billion, up 85.7% from US$1.08 billion the year before. Operating income was US$169.1 million versus US$125.2 million in the prior-year quarter, an increase of 35.1%. Direct operating expenses rose 80.8% to US$1.40 billion from US$775.8 million in the comparable period the year before. Indirect operating expenses increased 143.4% to US$430.3 million from US$176.8 million in the equivalent prior-year period.

Prospects: Our evaluation of Wabtec Corp. as of October 4th, 2019 is the result of our systematic analysis on three basic characteristics: earnings strength, relative valuation, and recent stock price movement. The company has managed to produce a neutral trend in earnings per share over the past 5 quarters. However, recent analyst estimates for the company have been raised and WAB has posted results that exceeded analysts' expectations. Based on operating earnings yield, the company is undervalued when compared to all of the companies we cover. Share price changes over the past year indicates that WAB will perform poorly over the near term.

Financial Data

(US$ in Thousands)	9 Mos	6 Mos	3 Mos	12/31/2018	12/31/2017	12/31/2016	12/31/2015	12/31/2014
Earnings Per Share	1.33	1.76	2.09	3.05	2.72	3.34	4.10	3.62
Cash Flow Per Share	4.45	3.89	2.65	3.28	1.98	4.96	4.67	4.93
Tang Book Value Per Share	N.M.	N.M.	N.M.	N.M.	N.M.	N.M.	4.36	5.42
Dividends Per Share	0.480	0.480	0.480	0.480	0.440	0.360	0.280	0.200
Dividend Payout %	36.09	27.27	22.97	15.74	16.18	10.78	6.83	5.52
Income Statement								
Total Revenue	5,831,600	3,829,901	1,593,617	4,363,547	3,881,756	2,931,188	3,307,998	3,044,454
EBITDA	400,000	250,543	114,112	544,286	484,888	502,498	645,356	564,229
Depn & Amortn	(29,900)	(9,400)	55,962	66,400	66,700	47,100	43,100	38,800
Income Before Taxes	269,100	156,814	13,581	365,651	349,484	412,837	585,368	507,855
Income Taxes	82,600	59,923	18,523	75,879	89,773	99,433	186,740	156,175
Net Income	191,000	99,763	(4,472)	294,944	262,261	304,887	398,628	351,680
Average Shares	191,500	191,453	121,226	96,464	96,125	91,141	97,006	96,885
Balance Sheet								
Current Assets	4,410,400	4,229,140	4,381,137	4,449,667	2,265,113	2,867,631	1,612,448	1,637,864
Total Assets	18,900,900	18,942,593	19,077,905	8,649,234	6,579,980	6,581,018	3,300,335	3,303,841
Current Liabilities	3,198,900	3,211,315	3,254,435	1,646,690	1,573,330	1,446,639	664,776	738,802
Long-Term Obligations	4,633,500	4,528,768	4,641,286	3,792,774	1,823,303	1,762,967	695,294	520,403
Total Liabilities	9,204,500	9,140,833	9,390,059	5,784,103	3,771,112	4,375,041	1,600,728	1,496,599
Stockholders' Equity	9,696,400	9,801,760	9,687,846	2,865,131	2,808,868	2,205,977	1,699,607	1,807,242
Shares Outstanding	191,676	188,183	162,817	96,614	96,034	95,425	91,836	96,274
Statistical Record								
Return on Assets %	1.64	1.73	1.56	3.87	3.99	6.15	12.07	11.48
Return on Equity %	3.58	3.51	3.19	10.40	10.46	15.57	22.73	20.73
EBITDA Margin %	6.86	6.54	7.16	12.47	12.49	17.14	19.51	18.53
Net Margin %	3.28	2.60	N.M.	6.76	6.76	10.40	12.05	11.55
Asset Turnover	0.51	0.47	0.38	0.57	0.59	0.59	1.00	0.99
Current Ratio	1.38	1.32	1.35	2.70	1.44	1.98	2.43	2.22
Debt to Equity	0.48	0.46	0.48	1.32	0.65	0.80	0.41	0.29
Price Range	105.49-62.31	114.51-62.38	114.51-66.28	114.51-66.28	92.51-69.70	88.12-60.58	102.39-68.89	91.24-70.82
P/E Ratio	79.32-46.85	65.06-35.44	54.79-31.71	37.54-21.73	34.01-25.63	26.38-18.14	24.97-16.80	25.20-19.56
Average Yield %	0.64	0.57	0.53	0.52	0.55	0.48	0.31	0.25

Address: 1001 Air Brake Avenue, Wilmerding, PA 15148	Web Site: www.wabtec.com	Auditors: Ernst & Young LLP
Telephone: 412-825-1000	Officers: Albert J. Neupaver - Executive Chairman, Executive Chairman (frmr), Chairman, Chairman (frmr), President, Chief Executive Officer Emilio A. Fernandez - Vice-Chairman	Transfer Agents: Wells Fargo Shareowner Services, St Paul, MN
Fax: 412-825-1019		

WALMART INC

Exchange	Symbol	Price	52Wk Range	Yield	P/E	Div Acheiver
NYS	WMT	$118.84 (12/31/2019)	121.28-92.86	1.78	23.82	43 Years

*7 Year Price Score 108.73 ***NYSE Composite Index=100** ***12 Month Price Score 104.72**

Interim Earnings (Per Share)

Qtr.	Apr	Jul	Oct	Jan
2016-17	0.98	1.21	0.98	1.22
2017-18	1.00	0.96	0.58	0.74
2018-19	0.72	(0.29)	0.58	1.25
2019-20	1.33	1.26	1.15	...

Interim Dividends (Per Share)

Amt	Decl	Ex	Rec	Pay
0.53Q	02/19/2020	12/05/2019	12/06/2019	01/02/2020
0.53Q	02/19/2019	03/14/2019	03/15/2019	04/01/2019
0.53Q	02/19/2019	08/08/2019	08/09/2019	09/03/2019
0.53Q	02/19/2019	05/09/2019	05/10/2019	06/03/2019

Indicated Div: $2.12 (Div. Reinv. Plan)

Valuation Analysis		Institutional Holding	
Forecast EPS	$5.00	No of Institutions	
	(01/11/2020)	2779	
Market Cap	$337.4 Billion	Shares	
Book Value	$71.6 Billion	1,185,297,664	
Price/Book	4.71	% Held	
Price/Sales	0.65	29.19	

Business Summary: Retail - General Merchandise/Department Stores (MIC: 2.1.1 SIC: 5411 NAIC: 445110)

Walmart is engaged in global operations of retail, wholesale and other units, as well as eCommerce, located throughout the U.S., Africa, Argentina, Canada, Central America, Chile, China, India, Japan, Mexico and the U.K. Co.'s operations are conducted in three reportable segments: Walmart U.S., which is a mass merchandiser of consumer products, operating under the Walmart and Walmart Neighborhood Market brands, as well as walmart.com, jet.com and other eCommerce brands; Walmart International, which includes various formats divided into retail, wholesale and other categories; and Sam's Club, which is a membership-only warehouse club that also operates samsclub.com.

Recent Developments: For the quarter ended Oct 31 2019, net income increased 82.8% to US$3.32 billion from US$1.82 billion in the year-earlier quarter. Revenues were US$127.99 billion, up 2.5% from US$124.89 billion the year before. Operating income was US$4.72 billion versus US$4.99 billion in the prior-year quarter, a decrease of 5.4%. Direct operating expenses rose 3.0% to US$95.90 billion from US$93.12 billion in the comparable period the year before. Indirect operating expenses increased 2.2% to US$27.37 billion from US$26.79 billion in the equivalent prior-year period.

Prospects: Our evaluation of Walmart Inc. as of October 4th, 2019 is the result of our systematic analysis on three basic characteristics: earnings strength, relative valuation, and recent stock price movement. The company has managed to produce a neutral trend in earnings per share over the past 5 quarters. In addition, recent analyst estimates for the company have been mixed and WMT has posted results that exceeded analysts' expectations. Based on operating earnings yield, the company is fairly valued when compared to all of the companies we cover. Share price changes over the past year indicates that WMT will perform well over the near term.

Financial Data

(US$ in Thousands)	9 Mos	6 Mos	3 Mos	01/31/2019	01/31/2018	01/31/2017	01/31/2016	01/31/2015
Earnings Per Share	4.99	4.42	2.87	2.26	3.28	4.38	4.57	5.05
Cash Flow Per Share	8.79	9.76	9.12	9.48	9.46	10.14	8.54	8.84
Tang Book Value Per Share	14.42	13.65	12.85	14.36	20.20	19.93	20.19	19.61
Dividends Per Share	2.110	2.100	2.090	2.080	2.040	2.000	1.960	1.920
Dividend Payout %	42.28	47.51	72.82	92.04	62.20	45.66	42.89	38.02
Income Statement								
Total Revenue	382,293,000	254,302,000	123,925,000	514,405,000	500,343,000	485,873,000	482,130,000	485,651,000
EBITDA	24,401,000	16,716,000	8,496,000	24,289,000	27,801,000	32,764,000	33,505,000	36,247,000
Depn & Amortn	8,159,000	5,436,000	2,714,000	10,700,000	10,500,000	10,000,000	9,400,000	9,100,000
Income Before Taxes	14,443,000	10,070,000	5,157,000	11,460,000	15,123,000	20,497,000	21,638,000	24,799,000
Income Taxes	3,536,000	2,484,000	1,251,000	4,281,000	4,600,000	6,204,000	6,558,000	7,985,000
Net Income	10,740,000	7,452,000	3,842,000	6,670,000	9,862,000	13,643,000	14,694,000	16,363,000
Average Shares	2,861,000	2,869,000	2,886,000	2,945,000	3,010,000	3,112,000	3,217,000	3,243,000
Balance Sheet								
Current Assets	67,912,000	61,371,000	61,739,000	61,897,000	59,664,000	57,689,000	60,239,000	63,278,000
Total Assets	239,830,000	234,861,000	234,544,000	219,295,000	204,522,000	198,825,000	199,581,000	203,706,000
Current Liabilities	83,784,000	80,283,000	79,888,000	77,477,000	78,521,000	66,928,000	64,619,000	65,272,000
Long-Term Obligations	48,980,000	48,319,000	51,235,000	50,203,000	36,825,000	42,018,000	44,030,000	43,692,000
Total Liabilities	168,181,000	164,534,000	166,339,000	146,799,000	126,653,000	121,027,000	119,035,000	122,312,000
Stockholders' Equity	71,649,000	70,327,000	68,205,000	72,496,000	77,869,000	77,798,000	80,546,000	81,394,000
Shares Outstanding	2,839,000	2,847,000	2,862,000	2,878,000	2,952,000	3,048,000	3,162,000	3,228,000
Statistical Record								
Return on Assets %	6.19	5.83	3.81	3.15	4.89	6.83	7.29	8.01
Return on Equity %	20.09	18.16	11.66	8.72	12.67	17.19	18.15	20.76
EBITDA Margin %	6.38	6.57	6.86	4.72	5.56	6.74	6.95	7.46
Net Margin %	2.81	2.93	3.10	1.30	1.97	2.81	3.05	3.37
Asset Turnover	2.23	2.35	2.35	2.43	2.48	2.43	2.39	2.38
Current Ratio	0.81	0.76	0.77	0.80	0.76	0.86	0.93	0.97
Debt to Equity	0.68	0.69	0.75	0.69	0.47	0.54	0.55	0.54
Price Range	120.24-85.82	114.98-85.82	105.56-82.40	106.60-82.40	109.55-66.23	74.30-63.15	87.33-56.42	90.47-72.66
P/E Ratio	24.10-17.20	26.01-19.42	36.78-28.71	47.17-36.46	33.40-20.19	16.96-14.42	19.11-12.35	17.91-14.39
Average Yield %	2.02	2.11	2.23	2.27	2.49	2.86	2.78	2.46

Address: 702 S.W. 8th Street,	Web Site: www.stock.walmart.com	Auditors: Ernst & Young LLP
Bentonville, AR 72716	Officers: Gregory B. Penner - Chairman C. Douglas	Investor Contact: 479-273-8446
Telephone: 479-273-4000	(Doug) McMillon - President, Chief Executive Officer,	Transfer Agents: Computershare Trust
	Executive Vice President, Division Officer	Company, N.A., Providence, RI

WASTE MANAGEMENT, INC. (DE)

Exchange	Symbol	Price	52Wk Range	Yield	P/E	Div Acheiver
NYS	WM	$113.96 (12/31/2019)	120.65-88.48	1.80	27.86	15 Years

*7 Year Price Score 133.65 *NYSE Composite Index=100 ***12 Month Price Score 97.00**

Interim Earnings (Per Share)

Qtr.	Mar	Jun	Sep	Dec
2016	0.58	0.64	0.68	0.76
2017	0.67	0.81	0.87	2.05
2018	0.91	1.15	1.16	1.23
2019	0.81	0.89	1.16	...

Interim Dividends (Per Share)

Amt	Decl	Ex	Rec	Pay
0.512Q	02/19/2019	03/07/2019	03/08/2019	03/22/2019
0.512Q	05/14/2019	06/06/2019	06/07/2019	06/21/2019
0.512Q	08/19/2019	09/05/2019	09/06/2019	09/20/2019
0.512Q	11/19/2019	12/05/2019	12/06/2019	12/20/2019

Indicated Div: $2.05 (Div. Reinv. Plan)

Valuation Analysis **Institutional Holding**

Forecast EPS	$4.35	No of Institutions
	(01/17/2020)	1721
Market Cap	$48.3 Billion	Shares
Book Value	$6.8 Billion	405,640,992
Price/Book	7.12	% Held
Price/Sales	3.13	70.86

Business Summary: Sanitation Services (MIC: 7.5.3 SIC: 4953 NAIC: 562211)

Waste Management is a holding company. Through its subsidiaries, Co. is a provider of waste management environmental services. Co. partners with its residential, commercial, industrial and municipal customers and the communities it serves to manage and reduce waste at each stage from collection to disposal, while recovering resources and creating renewable energy. Co.'s Solid Waste business is operated and managed by its subsidiaries that focus on distinct geographic areas and provides collection, transfer, disposal, and recycling and resource recovery services. Through its subsidiaries, Co. is also a developer, operator and owner of landfill gas-to-energy facilities.

Recent Developments: For the quarter ended Sep 30 2019, net income decreased 0.6% to US$495.0 million from US$498.0 million in the year-earlier quarter. Revenues were US$3.97 billion, up 3.8% from US$3.82 billion the year before. Operating income was US$734.0 million versus US$699.0 million in the prior-year quarter, an increase of 5.0%. Direct operating expenses rose 2.9% to US$2.44 billion from US$2.37 billion in the comparable period the year before. Indirect operating expenses increased 5.6% to US$792.0 million from US$750.0 million in the equivalent prior-year period.

Prospects: Our evaluation of Waste Management Inc. as of October 4th, 2019 is the result of our systematic analysis on three basic characteristics: earnings strength, relative valuation, and recent stock price movement. The company has managed to produce a neutral trend in earnings per share over the past 5 quarters. Additionally, recent analyst estimates for the company have been unchanged while WM has posted results that exceeded analysts' expectations. Based on operating earnings yield, the company is fairly valued when compared to all of the companies we cover. Share price changes over the past year indicates that WM will perform over the near term.

Financial Data
(US$ in Thousands)

	9 Mos	6 Mos	3 Mos	12/31/2018	12/31/2017	12/31/2016	12/31/2015	12/31/2014
Earnings Per Share	4.09	4.09	4.35	4.45	4.41	2.65	1.65	2.79
Cash Flow Per Share	8.87	8.68	8.60	8.32	7.25	6.66	5.52	5.04
Dividends Per Share	2.002	1.955	1.908	1.860	1.700	1.640	1.540	1.500
Dividend Payout %	48.96	47.80	43.85	41.80	38.55	61.89	93.33	53.76
Income Statement								
Total Revenue	11,609,000	7,642,000	3,696,000	14,914,000	14,485,000	13,609,000	12,961,000	13,996,000
EBITDA	2,573,000	1,614,000	780,000	4,167,000	3,902,000	3,057,800	2,652,000	3,484,000
Depn & Amortn	659,000	434,000	213,000	1,376,000	1,280,000	815,800	1,169,000	1,214,000
Income Before Taxes	1,613,000	984,000	471,000	2,417,000	2,259,000	1,866,000	1,098,000	1,804,000
Income Taxes	350,000	230,000	115,000	453,000	242,000	642,000	308,000	413,000
Net Income	1,223,000	728,000	347,000	1,925,000	1,949,000	1,182,000	753,000	1,298,000
Average Shares	427,400	427,500	426,900	432,200	441,900	446,500	455,900	465,600
Balance Sheet								
Current Assets	5,560,000	4,836,000	2,488,000	2,645,000	2,624,000	2,376,000	2,345,000	3,641,000
Total Assets	27,109,000	25,986,000	23,373,000	22,650,000	21,829,000	20,859,000	20,419,000	21,412,000
Current Liabilities	2,989,000	2,846,000	3,612,000	3,108,000	3,262,000	2,794,000	2,510,000	3,485,000
Long-Term Obligations	13,147,000	12,623,000	9,323,000	9,594,000	8,752,000	8,893,000	8,728,000	8,345,000
Total Liabilities	20,324,000	19,520,000	16,958,000	16,375,000	15,810,000	15,562,000	15,074,000	15,546,000
Stockholders' Equity	6,785,000	6,466,000	6,415,000	6,275,000	6,019,000	5,297,000	5,345,000	5,866,000
Shares Outstanding	424,160	423,800	424,726	423,983	433,318	439,315	447,177	458,537
Statistical Record								
Return on Assets %	7.06	7.33	8.25	8.66	9.13	5.71	3.60	5.90
Return on Equity %	26.93	28.08	30.11	31.32	34.45	22.15	13.43	22.43
EBITDA Margin %	22.16	21.12	21.10	27.94	26.94	22.47	20.46	24.89
Net Margin %	10.53	9.53	9.39	12.91	13.46	8.69	5.81	9.27
Asset Turnover	0.62	0.64	0.66	0.67	0.68	0.66	0.62	0.64
Current Ratio	1.86	1.70	0.69	0.85	0.80	0.85	0.93	1.04
Debt to Equity	1.94	1.95	1.45	1.53	1.45	1.68	1.63	1.42
Price Range	120.65-83.70	116.97-81.49	103.91-80.00	93.75-79.12	86.30-69.18	71.14-51.52	55.18-46.35	51.58-40.41
P/E Ratio	29.50-20.46	28.60-19.92	23.89-18.39	21.07-17.78	19.57-15.69	26.85-19.44	33.44-28.09	18.49-14.48
Average Yield %	1.94	2.03	2.13	2.14	2.25	2.65	2.98	3.33

Address: 1001 Fannin Street, Houston, TX 77002	**Web Site:** www.wm.com
Telephone: 713-512-6200	**Officers:** Thomas H. Weidemeyer - Chairman John J. Morris - Executive Vice President, Senior Vice President, Chief Operating Officer

Auditors: Ernst & Young LLP	
Investor Contact: 713-265-1656	
Transfer Agents: Computershare, Canton, MA	

WATERS CORP.

Exchange	Symbol	Price	52Wk Range	Yield	P/E
NYS	WAT	$233.65 (12/31/2019)	253.15-176.34	N/A	28.85

*7 Year Price Score 119.87 *NYSE Composite Index=100 *12 Month Price Score 95.56

Interim Earnings (Per Share)

Qtr.	Mar	Jun	Sep	Dec
2016	1.15	1.57	1.53	2.15
2017	1.31	1.63	1.69	(4.38)
2018	1.40	1.98	1.83	2.44
2019	1.51	2.08	2.07	...

Interim Dividends (Per Share)

No Dividends Paid

Valuation Analysis

		Institutional Holding	
Forecast EPS	$8.81	No of Institutions	
	(01/17/2020)	828	
Market Cap	$15.2 Billion	Shares	
Book Value	$115.5 Million	85,859,632	
Price/Book	131.73	% Held	
Price/Sales	6.33	78.46	

Business Summary: Biotechnology (MIC: 4.1.2 SIC: 3826 NAIC: 334516)

Waters is a holding company. Through its subsidiaries, Co. is a specialty measurement company. Co. primarily designs, manufactures, sells and services high performance liquid chromatography, ultra performance liquid chromatography and mass spectrometry technology systems and support products, including chromatography columns, other consumable products and post-warranty service plans. In addition, Co. designs, manufactures, sells and services thermal analysis, rheometry and calorimetry instruments through its TA™ product line. Co. is also a developer and supplier of software-based products that interface with its instruments, as well as other manufacturers' instruments.

Recent Developments: For the quarter ended Sep 28 2019, net income decreased 2.0% to US$138.1 million from US$141.0 million in the year-earlier quarter. Revenues were US$577.3 million, down 0.1% from US$578.0 million the year before. Operating income was US$173.2 million versus US$171.7 million in the prior-year quarter, an increase of 0.9%. Direct operating expenses was unchanged at US$241.1 million versus the comparable period the year before. Indirect operating expenses decreased 1.3% to US$163.0 million from US$165.2 million in the equivalent prior-year period.

Prospects: Our evaluation of Waters Corp. as of October 4th, 2019 is the result of our systematic analysis on three basic characteristics: earnings strength, relative valuation, and recent stock price movement. The company has managed to produce a neutral trend in earnings per share over the past 5 quarters. In addition, recent analyst estimates for the company have been mixed and WAT has posted results that exceeded analysts' expectations. Based on operating earnings yield, the company is fairly valued when compared to all of the companies we cover. Share price changes over the past year indicates that WAT will perform in line with the market over the near term.

Financial Data

(US$ in Thousands)	9 Mos	6 Mos	3 Mos	12/31/2018	12/31/2017	12/31/2016	12/31/2015	12/31/2014
Earnings Per Share	8.10	7.86	7.76	7.65	0.25	6.41	5.65	5.07
Cash Flow Per Share	9.55	9.14	8.43	7.85	8.74	7.77	6.80	6.07
Tang Book Value Per Share	N.M.	N.M.	5.24	13.19	20.74	21.78	18.21	15.72
Income Statement								
Total Revenue	1,690,302	1,113,024	513,862	2,419,929	2,309,078	2,167,423	2,042,332	1,989,344
EBITDA	550,996	351,553	145,390	800,388	767,860	720,788	657,438	612,139
Depn & Amortn	80,319	53,615	24,764	108,408	106,002	96,449	89,987	94,231
Income Before Taxes	453,851	289,113	117,378	682,146	641,097	600,114	541,919	490,740
Income Taxes	62,322	35,717	8,392	88,352	620,786	78,611	72,866	59,120
Net Income	391,529	253,396	108,986	593,794	20,311	521,503	469,053	431,620
Average Shares	66,768	69,494	72,415	77,618	80,604	81,417	83,087	85,151
Balance Sheet								
Current Assets	1,343,906	1,620,401	2,077,791	2,663,163	4,270,134	3,635,445	3,213,533	2,853,736
Total Assets	2,561,265	2,822,922	3,249,728	3,727,426	5,324,354	4,662,059	4,268,677	3,877,934
Current Liabilities	597,153	611,696	603,279	448,931	606,157	520,321	564,076	581,595
Long-Term Obligations	1,255,601	1,048,394	1,048,283	1,148,172	1,897,501	1,701,966	1,493,027	1,240,000
Total Liabilities	2,445,765	2,266,677	2,281,986	2,160,168	3,090,566	2,360,110	2,209,826	1,983,268
Stockholders' Equity	115,500	556,245	967,742	1,567,258	2,233,788	2,301,949	2,058,851	1,894,666
Shares Outstanding	65,117	67,620	70,136	73,115	79,337	80,023	81,472	83,147
Statistical Record								
Return on Assets %	17.46	16.60	15.27	13.12	0.41	11.65	11.52	11.57
Return on Equity %	57.90	45.79	38.33	31.24	0.90	23.85	23.73	23.60
EBITDA Margin %	32.60	31.59	28.29	33.07	33.25	33.26	32.19	30.77
Net Margin %	23.16	22.77	21.21	24.54	0.88	24.06	22.97	21.70
Asset Turnover	0.73	0.69	0.62	0.53	0.46	0.48	0.50	0.53
Current Ratio	2.25	2.65	3.44	5.93	7.04	6.99	5.70	4.91
Debt to Equity	10.87	1.88	1.08	0.73	0.85	0.74	0.73	0.65
Price Range	253.15-173.54	253.15-173.54	251.71-173.54	218.70-173.54	200.27-135.49	161.82-113.62	136.50-112.53	116.98-95.08
P/E Ratio	31.25-21.42	32.21-22.08	32.44-22.36	28.59-22.68	801.08-541.96	25.24-17.73	24.16-19.92	23.07-18.75

Address: 34 Maple Street, Milford, MA 01757	**Web Site:** www.waters.com	**Auditors:** PricewaterhouseCoopers LLP
Telephone: 508-478-2000	**Officers:** Christopher J. O'Connell - Chairman, President, Chief Executive Officer Mark T. Beaudouin - Senior Vice President, Vice President, Secretary, General Counsel	**Investor Contact:** 508-482-2349
Fax: 508-872-1990		**Transfer Agents:** Computershare, Providence, RI

WATSCO INC.

Exchange	Symbol	Price	52Wk Range	Yield	P/E
NYS	WSO	$180.15 (12/31/2019)	181.94-137.24	3.55	27.55

*7 Year Price Score 99.76 *NYSE Composite Index=100 *12 Month Price Score 105.98

Interim Earnings (Per Share)

Qtr.	Mar	Jun	Sep	Dec
2016	0.71	1.82	1.78	0.83
2017	0.71	2.07	1.82	1.19
2018	0.89	2.40	2.11	1.06
2019	0.88	2.40	2.20	...

Interim Dividends (Per Share)

Amt	Decl	Ex	Rec	Pay
1.60Q	04/01/2019	04/12/2019	04/15/2019	04/30/2019
1.60Q	07/01/2019	07/15/2019	07/16/2019	07/31/2019
1.60Q	10/01/2019	10/11/2019	10/15/2019	10/31/2019
1.60Q	01/02/2020	01/15/2020	01/16/2020	01/31/2020

Indicated Div: $6.40

Valuation Analysis

		Institutional Holding	
Forecast EPS	$6.50	No of Institutions	
	(01/17/2020)	509	
Market Cap	$6.9 Billion	Shares	
Book Value	$1.4 Billion	36,040,120	
Price/Book	4.76	% Held	
Price/Sales	1.46	83.94	

Business Summary: Industrial Machinery & Equipment (MIC: 7.2.1 SIC: 5075 NAIC: 423730)

Watsco is a distributor of air conditioning, heating and refrigeration equipment and related parts and supplies (HVAC/R) in the HVAC/R distribution industry in North America. The products Co. distributes consist of: equipment, including residential ducted and ductless air conditioners, gas, electric, and oil furnaces, commercial air conditioning and heating equipment systems, and other equipment; parts, including replacement compressors, evaporator coils, motors, and other component parts; and supplies, including thermostats, insulation material, refrigerants, ductwork, grills, registers, sheet metal, tools, copper tubing, concrete pads, tape, adhesives, and other ancillary supplies.

Recent Developments: For the quarter ended Sep 30 2019, net income increased 2.9% to US$99.7 million from US$96.9 million in the year-earlier quarter. Revenues were US$1.39 billion, up 7.6% from US$1.30 billion the year before. Operating income was US$125.3 million versus US$122.3 million in the prior-year quarter, an increase of 2.5%. Direct operating expenses rose 8.5% to US$1.06 billion from US$977.0 million in the comparable period the year before. Indirect operating expenses increased 6.4% to US$209.4 million from US$196.7 million in the equivalent prior-year period.

Prospects: Our evaluation of Watsco Inc. as of October 4th, 2019 is the result of our systematic analysis on three basic characteristics: earnings strength, relative valuation, and recent stock price movement. The company has managed to produce a neutral trend in earnings per share over the past 5 quarters. In addition, recent analyst estimates for the company have been mixed and WSO has posted results that fell short of analysts' expectations. Based on operating earnings yield, the company is fairly valued when compared to all of the companies we cover. Share price changes over the past year indicates that WSO will perform in line with the market over the near term.

Financial Data

(US$ in Thousands)	9 Mos	6 Mos	3 Mos	12/31/2018	12/31/2017	12/31/2016	12/31/2015	12/31/2014
Earnings Per Share	6.54	6.45	6.45	6.49	5.81	5.15	4.90	4.32
Cash Flow Per Share	8.57	7.50	7.71	4.97	9.34	8.50	6.83	4.49
Tang Book Value Per Share	22.70	21.07	24.60	21.57	20.26	13.16	11.85	8.86
Dividends Per Share	6.250	6.100	5.950	5.600	4.600	3.600	2.800	2.000
Dividend Payout %	95.57	94.57	92.25	86.29	79.17	69.90	57.14	46.30
Income Statement								
Total Revenue	3,698,047	2,303,132	931,278	4,546,653	4,341,955	4,220,702	4,113,239	3,944,540
EBITDA	324,895	196,779	59,456	388,829	370,644	360,485	350,550	317,905
Depn & Amortn	17,983	11,656	5,768	16,747	16,770	14,853	13,802	12,158
Income Before Taxes	311,429	187,544	54,356	369,342	347,511	341,919	331,201	300,541
Income Taxes	60,060	35,830	10,552	72,813	90,221	105,936	104,677	91,839
Net Income	208,672	125,192	35,037	242,932	208,221	182,810	172,929	151,387
Average Shares	34,788	34,462	34,402	34,374	32,862	32,616	32,480	32,358
Balance Sheet								
Current Assets	1,690,827	1,695,094	1,490,384	1,441,806	1,337,397	1,240,156	1,181,265	1,157,335
Total Assets	2,693,059	2,632,434	2,398,943	2,161,033	2,046,877	1,874,649	1,788,442	1,791,067
Current Liabilities	542,288	580,518	469,773	357,566	416,477	314,888	270,301	287,022
Long-Term Obligations	171,163	221,312	139,249	135,752	22,085	235,642	245,814	303,885
Total Liabilities	1,249,950	1,276,839	1,063,731	813,184	748,924	868,821	831,132	907,107
Stockholders' Equity	1,443,109	1,355,595	1,335,212	1,347,849	1,297,953	1,005,828	957,310	883,960
Shares Outstanding	38,101	38,059	32,228	37,461	37,228	35,530	35,311	35,006
Statistical Record								
Return on Assets %	10.08	9.84	10.89	11.55	10.62	9.95	9.66	8.75
Return on Equity %	17.67	18.18	18.55	18.36	18.08	18.57	18.78	17.56
EBITDA Margin %	8.79	8.54	6.38	8.55	8.54	8.54	8.52	8.06
Net Margin %	5.64	5.44	3.76	5.34	4.80	4.33	4.20	3.84
Asset Turnover	1.90	1.85	2.03	2.16	2.21	2.30	2.30	2.28
Current Ratio	3.12	2.92	3.17	4.03	3.21	3.94	4.37	4.03
Debt to Equity	0.12	0.16	0.10	0.10	0.02	0.23	0.26	0.34
Price Range	176.40-132.59	185.73-132.59	191.35-132.59	191.35-132.59	171.38-135.45	159.03-108.09	131.89-104.92	108.20-85.53
P/E Ratio	26.97-20.27	28.80-20.56	29.67-20.56	29.48-20.43	29.50-23.31	30.88-20.99	26.92-21.41	25.05-19.80
Average Yield %	4.06	3.87	3.63	3.27	3.02	2.65	2.30	2.05

Address: 2665 South Bayshore Drive, Suite 901, Miami, FL 33133 **Telephone:** 305-714-4100	**Web Site:** www.watsco.com **Officers:** Albert H. Nahmad - Chairman, President, Chief Executive Officer Cesar L. Alvarez - Co-Vice Chairman	**Auditors:** KPMG LLP **Investor Contact:** 305-714-4100 **Transfer Agents:** American Stock Transfer & Trust Company, New York, NY

WAYFAIR INC

Exchange	Symbol	Price	52Wk Range	Yield	P/E
NYS	W	$90.37 (12/31/2019)	171.57-79.87	N/A	N/A

*7 Year Price Score N/A *NYSE Composite Index=100 *12 Month Price Score 64.34

Interim Earnings (Per Share)

Qtr.	Mar	Jun	Sep	Dec
2016	(0.49)	(0.57)	(0.72)	(0.52)
2017	(0.66)	(0.45)	(0.88)	(0.83)
2018	(1.22)	(1.13)	(1.69)	(1.59)
2019	(2.20)	(1.98)	(2.94)	...

Interim Dividends (Per Share)

No Dividends Paid

Valuation Analysis

		Institutional Holding	
Forecast EPS	$-7.91	No of Institutions	
	(01/16/2020)	389	
Market Cap	$8.4 Billion	Shares	
Book Value	N/A		79,824,120
Price/Book	N/A	% Held	
Price/Sales	0.98		86.09

Business Summary: Retail - Furniture & Home Furnishings (MIC: 2.1.6 SIC: 5961 NAIC: 454111)

Wayfair is a holding company. Through its e-commerce business model, Co. provides customers with browsing, merchandising and product discovery for products from various suppliers. Co. has online selections of furniture, decor, decorative accents, housewares, seasonal decor and other home goods. Co.'s mobile app also provides customers a way to shop for their home from their home using its View in Room 3D augmented reality tool. Co.'s sites include: Wayfair, Joss & Main, AllModern, Birch Lane, and Perigold. Wayfair is the only one of Co.'s sites that also operates internationally, operating as Wayfair.ca in Canada, Wayfair.co.uk in the U.K. and Wayfair.de in Germany.

Recent Developments: For the quarter ended Sep 30 2019, net loss amounted to US$272.0 million versus a net loss of US$151.7 million in the year-earlier quarter. Revenues were US$2.31 billion, up 35.2% from US$1.71 billion the year before. Operating loss was US$259.7 million versus a loss of US$145.3 million in the prior-year quarter. Direct operating expenses rose 34.5% to US$1.77 billion from US$1.31 billion in the comparable period the year before. Indirect operating expenses increased 48.6% to US$799.6 million from US$538.0 million in the equivalent prior-year period.

Prospects: Our evaluation of Wayfair Inc as of October 4th, 2019 is the result of our systematic analysis on three basic characteristics: earnings strength, relative valuation, and recent stock price movement. The company has produced a positive trend in earnings per share over the past 5 quarters. However, recent analyst estimates for the company have been mixed and W has posted results in line with analysts' expectations. Based on operating earnings yield, the company is overvalued when compared to all of the companies we cover. Share price changes over the past year indicates that W will perform over the near term.

Financial Data

(US$ in Thousands)	9 Mos	6 Mos	3 Mos	12/31/2018	12/31/2017	12/31/2016	12/31/2015	12/31/2014
Earnings Per Share	(8.71)	(7.46)	(6.61)	(5.63)	(2.81)	(2.29)	(0.92)	(2.97)
Cash Flow Per Share	(1.28)	(0.37)	0.18	0.95	0.39	0.74	1.61	0.08
Tang Book Value Per Share	...	...	...	...	...	0.88	2.83	3.60
Income Statement								
Total Revenue	6,593,567	4,288,080	1,944,829	6,779,174	4,720,895	3,380,360	2,249,885	1,318,951
EBITDA	(444,401)	(254,796)	(138,700)	(350,883)	(148,795)	(139,861)	(46,141)	(126,493)
Depn & Amortn	174,537	106,615	51,856	122,600	85,900	54,600	32,491	21,780
Income Before Taxes	(652,860)	(380,901)	(199,794)	(502,043)	(244,128)	(193,767)	(77,348)	(147,923)
Income Taxes	1,502	1,426	595	2,037	486	608	95	175
Net Income	(654,362)	(382,327)	(200,389)	(504,080)	(244,614)	(194,375)	(77,443)	(148,098)
Average Shares	92,540	91,802	91,104	89,472	86,983	84,977	83,726	50,641
Balance Sheet								
Current Assets	1,670,701	1,056,900	1,117,832	1,255,936	816,820	477,091	492,323	486,868
Total Assets	3,007,635	2,182,100	2,113,865	1,890,850	1,213,403	761,683	694,581	555,523
Current Liabilities	1,433,659	1,333,511	1,229,813	1,139,223	739,755	557,220	397,026	232,592
Long-Term Obligations	2,249,788	1,447,093	1,357,786	921,960	415,485	28,900	...	...
Total Liabilities	3,690,064	2,787,457	2,593,012	2,221,571	1,261,732	682,299	452,036	249,984
Stockholders' Equity	(682,429)	(605,357)	(479,147)	(330,721)	(48,329)	79,384	242,545	305,539
Shares Outstanding	92,874	92,098	91,401	90,747	88,208	85,830	84,310	83,182
Statistical Record								
Asset Turnover	4.00	4.62	4.38	4.37	4.78	4.63	3.60	3.51
Current Ratio	1.17	0.79	0.91	1.10	1.10	0.86	1.24	2.09
Debt to Equity	...	...	...	...	...	0.36	...	...
Price Range	171.57-80.44	171.57-80.44	171.57-62.30	149.92-62.30	83.77-35.18	48.25-31.89	53.58-19.12	37.72-18.40

Address: 4 Copley Place, Boston, MA 02116	**Web Site:** www.wayfair.com	**Auditors:** Ernst & Young LLP
Telephone: 617-532-6100	**Officers:** Niraj Shah - Co-Chairman, President, Chief Executive Officer Steven Conine - Co-Chairman, Chief Technology Officer	**Transfer Agents:** Computershare Trust Company, N.A.

WEBSTER FINANCIAL CORP (WATERBURY, CONN)

Exchange	Symbol	Price	52Wk Range	Yield	P/E
NYS	WBS	$53.36 (12/31/2019)	58.03-42.41	3.00	12.86

*7 Year Price Score 98.03 ***NYSE Composite Index=100** ***12 Month Price Score 93.47**

TRADING VOLUME (thousand shares)

Interim Earnings (Per Share)

Qtr.	Mar	Jun	Sep	Dec
2016	0.51	0.53	0.54	0.60
2017	0.62	0.64	0.67	0.73
2018	0.85	0.86	1.06	1.04
2019	1.06	1.05	1.00	...

Interim Dividends (Per Share)

Amt	Decl	Ex	Rec	Pay
0.33Q	01/29/2019	02/11/2019	02/12/2019	02/26/2019
0.40Q	04/22/2019	05/03/2019	05/06/2019	05/20/2019
0.40Q	07/22/2019	08/02/2019	08/05/2019	08/19/2019
0.40Q	10/29/2019	11/08/2019	11/12/2019	11/26/2019

Indicated Div: $1.60 (Div. Reinv. Plan)

Valuation Analysis   **Institutional Holding**

Forecast EPS	$4.08	No of Institutions
	(01/17/2020)	447
Market Cap	$4.9 Billion	Shares
Book Value	$3.2 Billion	100,550,360
Price/Book	1.56	% Held
Price/Sales	3.41	90.46

Business Summary: Banking (MIC: 5.1.1 SIC: 6021 NAIC: 522110)

Webster Financial is a bank holding company and financial holding company. Co., through Webster Bank, National Association, provides financial services to individuals, families, and businesses primarily from New York to Massachusetts. Co. provides business and consumer banking, mortgage lending, financial planning, trust, and investment services through banking offices, ATMs, mobile banking and its internet website. Co. also provides equipment financing, commercial real estate lending, and asset-based lending primarily across the Northeast. On a nationwide basis, Co. provides and administers health savings accounts, spending accounts, health reimbursement accounts, and commuter benefits.

Recent Developments: For the quarter ended Sep 30 2019, net income decreased 5.8% to US$93.9 million from US$99.7 million in the year-earlier quarter. Net interest income increased 4.4% to US$240.5 million from US$230.4 million in the year-earlier quarter. Provision for loan losses was US$11.3 million versus US$10.5 million in the prior-year quarter, an increase of 7.6%. Non-interest income fell 3.3% to US$69.9 million from US$72.3 million, while non-interest expense advanced 0.6% to US$179.9 million.

Prospects: Our evaluation of Webster Financial Corp. (CT) as of October 4th, 2019 is the result of our systematic analysis on three basic characteristics: earnings strength, relative valuation, and recent stock price movement. The company has managed to produce a neutral trend in earnings per share over the past 5 quarters. However, recent analyst estimates for the company have been reduced while WBS has posted results that exceeded analysts' expectations. Based on operating earnings yield, the company is undervalued when compared to all of the companies we cover. Share price changes over the past year indicates that WBS will perform poorly over the near term.

Financial Data

(US$ in Thousands)	9 Mos	6 Mos	3 Mos	12/31/2018	12/31/2017	12/31/2016	12/31/2015	12/31/2014
Earnings Per Share	4.15	4.21	4.02	3.81	2.67	2.16	2.15	2.08
Cash Flow Per Share	1.15	3.40	4.14	5.11	4.84	4.35	3.38	3.03
Tang Book Value Per Share	26.58	25.63	24.52	23.62	21.61	19.97	18.73	18.13
Dividends Per Share	1.460	1.390	1.320	1.250	1.030	0.980	0.890	0.750
Dividend Payout %	35.18	33.02	32.84	32.81	38.58	45.37	41.40	36.06
Income Statement								
Interest Income	872,583	578,447	286,190	1,055,167	913,605	821,913	760,040	718,941
Interest Expense	148,706	95,109	44,639	148,486	117,318	103,400	95,415	90,500
Net Interest Income	723,877	483,338	241,551	906,681	796,287	718,513	664,625	628,441
Provision for Losses	31,800	20,500	8,600	42,000	40,900	56,350	49,300	37,250
Non-Interest Income	214,396	144,465	68,612	282,568	259,478	264,478	239,545	202,108
Non-Interest Expense	536,220	356,326	175,686	705,616	661,075	623,191	554,554	502,138
Income Before Taxes	370,253	250,977	125,877	441,633	353,790	303,450	300,316	291,161
Income Taxes	78,003	52,592	26,141	81,215	98,351	96,323	93,976	91,409
Net Income	292,250	198,385	99,736	360,418	255,439	207,127	206,340	199,752
Average Shares	91,874	91,855	92,225	92,227	92,356	91,856	91,533	90,620
Balance Sheet								
Net Loans & Leases	19,369,555	19,077,461	18,623,516	18,265,005	17,344,752	16,899,845	15,533,836	13,808,713
Total Assets	29,895,100	28,942,043	28,238,129	27,610,315	26,487,645	26,072,529	24,677,820	22,533,010
Total Deposits	23,280,665	22,598,778	22,750,928	21,858,845	20,993,729	19,303,857	17,952,778	15,651,605
Total Liabilities	26,742,706	25,876,826	25,271,874	24,723,800	23,785,687	23,545,517	22,262,249	20,210,329
Stockholders' Equity	3,152,394	3,065,217	2,966,255	2,886,515	2,701,958	2,527,012	2,415,571	2,322,681
Shares Outstanding	92,034	92,007	92,073	92,177	92,021	91,752	91,561	90,381
Statistical Record								
Return on Assets %	1.37	1.42	1.38	1.33	0.97	0.81	0.87	0.92
Return on Equity %	13.10	13.62	13.37	12.90	9.77	8.36	8.71	8.82
Net Interest Margin %	81.78	82.73	84.40	85.93	87.16	87.42	87.45	87.41
Efficiency Ratio %	49.41	49.07	49.52	52.75	56.35	57.36	55.48	54.52
Loans to Deposits	0.83	0.84	0.82	0.84	0.83	0.88	0.87	0.88
Price Range	62.23-43.00	69.06-44.28	69.06-45.55	69.06-45.55	58.39-44.50	55.09-30.35	40.96-29.11	33.05-27.65
P/E Ratio	15.00-10.36	16.40-10.52	17.18-11.33	18.13-11.96	21.87-16.67	25.50-14.05	19.05-13.54	15.89-13.29
Average Yield %	2.80	2.46	2.21	2.07	1.98	2.55	2.43	2.46

Address: 145 Bank Street, Waterbury, CT 06702 **Telephone:** 203-578-2202	**Web Site:** www.websterbank.com **Officers:** John R. Ciulla - President, Chief Executive Officer, Executive Vice President Glenn I. MacInnes - Executive Vice President, Chief Financial Officer, Principal Accounting Officer	**Auditors:** KPMG LLP **Investor Contact:** 203-578-2202 **Transfer Agents:** Computershare, Pittsburgh, PA

WEC ENERGY GROUP INC

Exchange	Symbol	Price	52Wk Range	Yield	P/E	Div Acheiver
NYS	WEC	$92.23 (12/31/2019)	97.73-67.58	2.74	26.73	15 Years

*7 Year Price Score 118.84 *NYSE Composite Index=100 *12 Month Price Score 101.56

Interim Earnings (Per Share)

Qtr.	Mar	Jun	Sep	Dec
2016	1.09	0.57	0.68	0.61
2017	1.12	0.63	0.68	1.36
2018	1.23	0.73	0.74	0.64
2019	1.33	0.74	0.74	...

Interim Dividends (Per Share)

Amt	Decl	Ex	Rec	Pay
0.59Q	04/18/2019	05/13/2019	05/14/2019	06/01/2019
0.59Q	07/18/2019	08/13/2019	08/14/2019	09/01/2019
0.59Q	10/17/2019	11/13/2019	11/14/2019	12/01/2019
0.632Q	01/16/2020	02/13/2020	02/14/2020	03/01/2020

Indicated Div: $2.53 (Div. Reinv. Plan)

Valuation Analysis		Institutional Holding	
Forecast EPS	$3.53	No of Institutions	
	(01/17/2020)	1156	
Market Cap	$29.1 Billion	Shares	
Book Value	$10.1 Billion	291,363,200	
Price/Book	2.89	% Held	
Price/Sales	3.80	N/A	

Business Summary: Electric Utilities (MIC: 3.1.1 SIC: 4931 NAIC: 221112)

WEC Energy Group is a holding company. Through its subsidiaries, Co. provides regulated natural gas and electricity, and nonregulated renewable energy. Co.'s segments include: Wisconsin, which generates and distributes electric energy and provides retail natural gas distribution service; Illinois, which includes the natural gas utility operations; Electric Transmission, which owns, maintains, monitors, and operates electric transmission systems in Wisconsin, Michigan, Illinois, and Minnesota; and Non-Utility Energy Infrastructure, which owns and leases generating facilities to its Wisconsin Electric Power Company subsidiary and owns underground natural gas storage facilities in Michigan.

Recent Developments: For the quarter ended Sep 30 2019, net income increased 0.3% to US$234.3 million from US$233.5 million in the year-earlier quarter. Revenues were US$1.61 billion, down 2.2% from US$1.64 billion the year before. Operating income was US$310.9 million versus US$302.7 million in the prior-year quarter, an increase of 2.7%. Direct operating expenses declined 5.9% to US$1.01 billion from US$1.08 billion in the comparable period the year before. Indirect operating expenses increased 7.5% to US$283.6 million from US$263.8 million in the equivalent prior-year period.

Prospects: Our evaluation of WEC Energy Group Inc. as of October 4th, 2019 is the result of our systematic analysis on three basic characteristics: earnings strength, relative valuation, and recent stock price movement. The company has managed to produce a neutral trend in earnings per share over the past 5 quarters. In addition, recent analyst estimates for the company have been mixed and WEC has posted results that exceeded analysts' expectations. Based on operating earnings yield, the company is fairly valued when compared to all of the companies we cover. Share price changes over the past year indicates that WEC will perform over the near term.

Financial Data
(US$ in Thousands)

	9 Mos	6 Mos	3 Mos	12/31/2018	12/31/2017	12/31/2016	12/31/2015	12/31/2014
Earnings Per Share	3.45	3.45	3.44	3.34	3.79	2.96	2.34	2.59
Cash Flow Per Share	7.22	7.05	7.25	7.75	6.59	6.65	4.77	5.31
Tang Book Value Per Share	22.28	22.17	22.07	21.45	20.40	18.74	17.93	17.77
Dividends Per Share	2.322	2.285	2.248	2.210	2.080	1.980	1.743	1.560
Dividend Payout %	67.32	66.23	65.33	66.17	54.88	66.89	74.48	60.23
Income Statement								
Total Revenue	5,575,600	3,967,600	2,377,400	7,679,500	7,648,500	7,472,300	5,926,100	4,997,100
EBITDA	1,934,700	1,368,200	800,100	2,381,700	2,648,400	2,525,500	1,892,900	1,544,900
Depn & Amortn	690,100	456,300	226,400	845,800	798,600	762,600	583,500	419,400
Income Before Taxes	870,300	663,400	449,300	1,090,800	1,434,100	1,360,200	978,000	884,000
Income Taxes	91,500	80,200	65,000	167,000	383,500	566,500	433,800	361,700
Net Income	891,000	656,400	420,400	1,060,500	1,204,900	940,200	640,300	588,300
Average Shares	316,800	316,700	316,700	316,900	317,200	316,900	272,700	227,500
Balance Sheet								
Current Assets	1,773,000	1,838,700	2,008,300	2,247,600	2,213,500	2,168,700	2,206,800	1,535,400
Total Assets	34,377,200	33,934,300	33,737,100	33,475,800	31,590,500	30,123,200	29,355,200	15,163,400
Current Liabilities	2,818,400	3,362,000	2,889,900	3,331,700	3,869,300	2,431,600	2,709,000	1,668,700
Long-Term Obligations	10,897,300	9,921,000	10,326,700	9,994,000	8,746,600	9,158,200	9,124,100	4,186,400
Total Liabilities	24,295,800	23,887,700	23,722,200	23,656,500	22,098,700	21,163,000	20,670,000	10,713,300
Stockholders' Equity	10,081,400	10,046,600	10,014,900	9,819,300	9,491,800	8,960,200	8,685,200	4,450,100
Shares Outstanding	315,435	315,435	315,438	315,523	315,574	315,614	315,683	225,517
Statistical Record								
Return on Assets %	3.28	3.33	3.33	3.26	3.90	3.15	2.88	3.93
Return on Equity %	11.03	11.06	11.06	10.98	13.06	10.63	9.75	13.50
EBITDA Margin %	34.70	34.48	33.65	31.01	34.63	33.80	31.94	30.92
Net Margin %	15.98	16.54	17.68	13.81	15.75	12.58	10.80	11.77
Asset Turnover	0.23	0.23	0.24	0.24	0.25	0.25	0.27	0.33
Current Ratio	0.63	0.55	0.69	0.67	0.57	0.89	0.81	0.92
Debt to Equity	1.08	0.99	1.03	1.02	0.92	1.02	1.05	0.94
Price Range	97.73-66.65	85.42-64.03	79.90-58.60	74.96-58.60	69.53-57.03	65.82-51.31	57.47-44.97	55.23-40.31
P/E Ratio	28.33-19.32	24.76-18.56	23.23-17.03	22.44-17.54	18.35-15.05	22.24-17.33	24.56-19.22	21.32-15.56
Average Yield %	2.95	3.14	3.29	3.39	3.31	3.36	3.49	3.41

Address: 231 West Michigan Street,	Web Site: www.wecenergygroup.com	Auditors: DELOITTE & TOUCHE LLP
P.O. Box 1331, Milwaukee, WI 53201	Officers: Gale E. Klappa - Executive Chairman,	Transfer Agents: Computershare
Telephone: 414-221-2345	Chairman, President, Chief Executive Officer Joseph	Shareowner Services LLC, Providence,
Fax: 414-221-2172	Kevin Fletcher - President, Chief Executive Officer	RI

WEINGARTEN REALTY INVESTORS

Exchange	Symbol	Price	52Wk Range	Yield	P/E
NYS	WRI	$31.24 (12/31/2019)	32.10-24.34	5.06	13.41

*7 Year Price Score 73.69   ***NYSE Composite Index=100**   ***12 Month Price Score 103.03**

Interim Earnings (Per Share)

Qtr.	Mar	Jun	Sep	Dec
2016	0.85	0.28	0.40	0.34
2017	0.24	0.49	0.56	1.30
2018	1.13	0.61	0.34	0.47
2019	0.39	0.65	0.82	...

Interim Dividends (Per Share)

Amt	Decl	Ex	Rec	Pay
0.395Q	02/20/2019	03/07/2019	03/08/2019	03/15/2019
0.395Q	04/29/2019	06/06/2019	06/07/2019	06/14/2019
0.395Q	07/31/2019	09/05/2019	09/06/2019	09/13/2019
0.395Q	10/29/2019	12/05/2019	12/06/2019	12/13/2019

Indicated Div: $1.58 (Div. Reinv. Plan)

Valuation Analysis		Institutional Holding	
Forecast EPS	$2.05	No of Institutions	
	(01/17/2020)	471	
Market Cap	$4.0 Billion	Shares	
Book Value	$1.7 Billion	157,886,320	
Price/Book	2.40	% Held	
Price/Sales	8.12	78.73	

Business Summary: REITs (MIC: 5.3.1 SIC: 6798 NAIC: 525930)

Weingarten Realty Investors is a real estate investment trust, engaged in the business of owning, managing and developing retail shopping centers. Co.'s primary business is leasing space to tenants in the shopping centers it owns or leases. Co. also provides property management services to either joint ventures where Co. is partners or other outside owners. Co.'s centers are designed to attract local area customers and are anchored by a supermarket or other national tenants (such as Kroger, HEB or T.J. Maxx). The centers are primarily neighborhood and community shopping centers that often include discounters, retailers and specialty grocers as additional anchors or tenants.

Recent Developments: For the quarter ended Sep 30 2019, net income increased 103.7% to US$108.5 million from US$53.3 million in the year-earlier quarter. Revenues were US$121.4 million, down 5.8% from US$128.8 million the year before. Revenues from property income fell 6.5% to US$117.4 million from US$125.6 million in the corresponding quarter a year earlier.

Prospects: Our evaluation of Weingarten Realty Investors as of October 4th, 2019 is the result of our systematic analysis on three basic characteristics: earnings strength, relative valuation, and recent stock price movement. The company has produced a positive trend in earnings per share over the past 5 quarters. However, recent analyst estimates for the company have been mixed and WRI has posted results that fell short of analysts' expectations. Based on operating earnings yield, the company is fairly valued when compared to all of the companies we cover. Share price changes over the past year indicates that WRI will perform in line with the market over the near term.

Financial Data

(US$ in Thousands)	9 Mos	6 Mos	3 Mos	12/31/2018	12/31/2017	12/31/2016	12/31/2015	12/31/2014
Earnings Per Share	2.33	1.85	1.81	2.55	2.60	1.87	1.29	2.25
Cash Flow Per Share	2.19	2.20	2.21	2.24	2.11	1.95	1.99	1.98
Tang Book Value Per Share	13.01	12.57	12.30	12.26	12.71	12.34	11.21	12.13
Dividends Per Share	2.980	2.980	2.980	2.980	2.290	1.460	1.380	1.550
Dividend Payout %	127.90	161.08	164.64	116.86	88.08	78.07	106.98	68.89
Income Statement								
Total Revenue	367,160	245,798	123,138	531,147	573,163	549,555	512,844	514,406
EBITDA	267,275	150,917	57,739	547,176	347,315	407,862	334,163	338,013
Depn & Amortn	2,437	1,627	820	164,984	169,891	165,097	148,590	154,257
Income Before Taxes	228,185	125,353	46,014	321,651	105,013	162,331	102,353	92,787
Income Taxes	682	661	177	1,378	(17)	6,856	52	(1,261)
Net Income	240,217	133,475	49,666	327,601	335,274	238,933	174,352	288,008
Average Shares	130,137	130,135	128,590	128,441	130,071	128,569	124,329	124,370
Balance Sheet								
Current Assets	203,683	193,006	137,470	163,789	117,576	110,723	106,950	100,970
Total Assets	3,912,590	3,887,654	3,837,663	3,826,961	4,196,639	4,426,928	3,901,945	3,814,094
Current Liabilities	124,059	95,296	79,459	113,175	116,463	116,859	112,205	112,479
Long-Term Obligations	1,736,803	1,787,400	1,788,551	1,794,684	2,081,152	2,356,528	2,113,277	1,938,188
Total Liabilities	2,238,859	2,270,429	2,254,732	2,253,055	2,563,911	2,846,992	2,512,483	2,328,908
Stockholders' Equity	1,673,731	1,617,225	1,582,931	1,573,906	1,632,728	1,579,936	1,389,462	1,485,186
Shares Outstanding	128,673	128,670	128,647	128,333	128,447	128,072	123,951	122,489
Statistical Record								
Return on Assets %	7.58	5.96	5.80	8.17	7.78	5.72	4.52	7.17
Return on Equity %	17.53	14.03	13.92	20.43	20.87	16.05	12.13	20.12
EBITDA Margin %	72.80	61.40	46.89	103.02	60.60	74.22	65.16	65.71
Net Margin %	65.43	54.30	40.33	61.68	58.50	43.48	34.00	55.99
Asset Turnover	0.13	0.13	0.13	0.13	0.13	0.13	0.13	0.13
Current Ratio	1.64	2.03	1.73	1.45	1.01	0.95	0.95	0.90
Debt to Equity	1.04	1.11	1.13	1.14	1.27	1.49	1.52	1.31
Price Range	29.89-23.90	31.53-23.90	31.69-23.90	32.77-23.90	36.70-29.37	43.44-32.48	38.41-30.43	36.96-27.42
P/E Ratio	12.83-10.26	17.04-12.92	17.51-13.20	12.85-9.37	14.12-11.30	23.23-17.37	29.78-23.59	16.43-12.19
Average Yield %	10.62	10.37	10.39	10.32	6.99	3.88	3.99	4.80

Address: 2600 Citadel Plaza Drive, P.O. Box 924133, Houston, TX 77292-4133 **Telephone:** 713-866-6000	**Web Site:** www.weingarten.com **Officers:** Stanford J. Alexander - Chairman Emeritus, Chairman Andrew M. Alexander - Chairman, President, Chief Executive Officer	**Auditors:** Deloitte & Touche LLP **Investor Contact:** 713-866-6000 **Transfer Agents:** Computershare Trust Company, National Association, Canton, MA

WELBILT INC

Exchange	Symbol	Price	52Wk Range	Yield	P/E
NYS	WBT	$15.61 (12/31/2019)	19.79-10.99	N/A	34.69

*7 Year Price Score N/A   *NYSE Composite Index=100   *12 Month Price Score 101.11

Interim Earnings (Per Share)

Qtr.	Mar	Jun	Sep	Dec
2016	0.13	0.11	0.18	0.15
2017	0.04	0.21	0.24	0.46
2018	0.09	0.09	0.19	0.19
2019	(0.02)	0.14	0.14	...

Interim Dividends (Per Share)

No Dividends Paid

Valuation Analysis   **Institutional Holding**

Forecast EPS	$0.69	No of Institutions
	(00/25/2020)	275
Market Cap	$2.2 Billion	Shares
Book Value	$230.7 Million	158,354,944
Price/Book	9.55	% Held
Price/Sales	1.36	N/A

Business Summary: Industrial Machinery & Equipment (MIC: 7.2.1 SIC: 3556 NAIC: 333294)

Welbilt is a commercial foodservice equipment company. Co. designs, manufactures and supplies food and beverage equipment for the commercial foodservice market. Co.'s products are used by commercial and institutional foodservice operators including restaurants, quick-service restaurant chains, hotels, resorts, cruise ships, caterers, supermarkets, convenience stores, hospitals, schools and other institutions. Co.'s portfolio of brands includes Cleveland™, Convotherm®, Crem®, Delfield®, Frymaster®, Garland®, Kolpak®, Lincoln™, Manitowoc® Ice, Merco®, Merrychef® and Multiplex®. Co.'s products brands are supported by FitKitchen®, KitchenCare®, and KitchenConnect®.

Recent Developments: For the quarter ended Sep 30 2019, net income decreased 25.0% to US$20.1 million from US$26.8 million in the year-earlier quarter. Revenues were US$410.5 million, down 0.6% from US$412.9 million the year before. Operating income was US$54.8 million versus US$67.7 million in the prior-year quarter, a decrease of 19.1%. Direct operating expenses declined 0.1% to US$259.6 million from US$259.8 million in the comparable period the year before. Indirect operating expenses increased 12.5% to US$96.1 million from US$85.4 million in the equivalent prior-year period.

Prospects: Our evaluation of Welbilt Inc. as of October 4th, 2019 is the result of our systematic analysis on three basic characteristics: earnings strength, relative valuation, and recent stock price movement. The company has enjoyed a very positive trend in earnings per share over the past 5 quarters. However, recent analyst estimates for the company have been unchanged, while WBT has posted results that exceeded analysts' expectations. Based on operating earnings yield, the company is fairly valued when compared to all of the companies we cover. Share price changes over the past year indicates that WBT will perform very poorly over the near term.

Financial Data

(US$ in Thousands)	9 Mos	6 Mos	3 Mos	12/31/2018	12/31/2017	12/31/2016	12/31/2015	12/31/2014
Earnings Per Share	0.45	0.50	0.45	0.55	0.95	0.57	1.15	1.17
Cash Flow Per Share	(2.46)	(3.85)	(4.64)	(3.20)	0.99	0.88	1.04	1.46
Income Statement								
Total Revenue	1,212,100	801,600	375,300	1,590,100	1,445,400	1,456,600	1,570,100	1,581,300
EBITDA	173,800	105,900	37,100	233,000	253,600	238,600	232,900	224,900
Depn & Amortn	48,800	32,800	15,600	55,000	47,900	48,500	51,000	53,000
Income Before Taxes	54,100	24,600	(2,500)	89,000	118,800	104,800	196,300	187,200
Income Taxes	16,600	7,200	100	10,800	(15,200)	25,300	39,300	25,900
Net Income	37,500	17,400	(2,600)	78,200	134,000	79,500	157,100	159,800
Average Shares	141,532	141,416	140,612	141,388	140,707	139,714	137,016	137,016
Balance Sheet								
Current Assets	555,100	545,000	541,000	440,500	383,700	308,200	252,600	289,500
Total Assets	2,180,300	2,191,200	2,192,300	2,075,000	1,840,400	1,769,100	1,754,000	1,898,300
Current Liabilities	324,200	320,800	311,100	378,700	290,100	313,100	321,300	368,600
Long-Term Obligations	1,425,900	1,448,300	1,493,400	1,321,800	1,232,200	1,278,700	2,300	3,600
Total Liabilities	1,949,600	1,974,500	2,007,000	1,888,600	1,730,000	1,812,600	545,300	646,900
Stockholders' Equity	230,700	216,700	185,300	186,400	110,400	(43,500)	1,208,700	1,251,400
Shares Outstanding	141,112	141,047	140,857	140,252	139,440	138,562	137,016	...
Statistical Record								
Return on Assets %	3.02	3.31	3.09	3.99	7.42	4.50	8.60	...
Return on Equity %	32.59	39.83	39.86	52.70	400.60	13.61	12.77	...
EBITDA Margin %	14.34	13.21	9.89	14.65	17.55	16.38	14.83	14.22
Net Margin %	3.09	2.17	N.M.	4.92	9.27	5.46	10.01	10.11
Asset Turnover	0.76	0.75	0.79	0.81	0.80	0.82	0.86	...
Current Ratio	1.71	1.70	1.74	1.16	1.32	0.98	0.79	0.79
Debt to Equity	6.18	6.68	8.06	7.09	11.16	...	N.M.	N.M.
Price Range	20.49-10.82	23.59-10.82	23.59-10.82	23.60-10.82	23.51-18.25	19.33-13.80	...	...
P/E Ratio	45.53-24.04	47.18-21.64	52.42-24.04	42.91-19.67	24.75-19.21	33.91-24.21	...	...

Address: 2227 Welbilt Boulevard, New Port Richey, FL 34655 Telephone: 727-375-7010	Web Site: www.welbilt.com Officers: Cynthia M. Egnotovich - Chairperson William C. Johnson - President, Chief Executive Officer	Auditors: PricewaterhouseCoopers LLP Transfer Agents: Computershare

753

WELLCARE HEALTH PLANS INC

Exchange	Symbol	Price	52Wk Range	Yield	P/E
NYS	WCG	$330.21 (12/31/2019)	332.80-230.61	N/A	26.80

*7 Year Price Score 159.17 ***NYSE Composite Index=100** ***12 Month Price Score 107.28**

Interim Earnings (Per Share)

Qtr.	Mar	Jun	Sep	Dec
2016	0.83	2.04	1.54	1.00
2017	1.50	1.65	3.82	1.34
2018	2.25	3.35	2.70	1.00
2019	2.98	3.60	4.74	...

Interim Dividends (Per Share)

No Dividends Paid

Valuation Analysis / Institutional Holding

Valuation Analysis		Institutional Holding	
Forecast EPS	$15.70	No of Institutions	
	(01/14/2020)	621	
Market Cap	$16.6 Billion	Shares	
Book Value	$4.9 Billion		57,273,760
Price/Book	3.42	% Held	
Price/Sales	0.62		89.15

Business Summary: Hospitals & Health Care Facilities (MIC: 4.2.1 SIC: 6324 NAIC: 524114)

WellCare Health Plans is a holding company. Through its subsidiaries, Co. is a managed care company and focuses primarily on providing government-sponsored managed care services to families, children, seniors and individuals with complex medical needs primarily through Medicaid, Medicare Advantage and Medicare Prescription Drug Plans, as well as individuals in the Health Insurance Marketplace. Medicaid provides medical assistance to elderly, disabled, children and their families. The Medicare program provides health care coverage primarily to individuals age 65 or older as well as to individuals with certain disabilities and consists of four parts, labeled A through D.

Recent Developments: For the quarter ended Sep 30 2019, net income increased 84.5% to US$241.0 million from US$130.6 million in the year-earlier quarter. Revenues were US$7.14 billion, up 41.2% from US$5.06 billion the year before. Net premiums earned were US$6.97 billion versus US$4.99 billion in the prior-year quarter, an increase of 39.6%.

Prospects: Our evaluation of WellCare Health Plans Inc. as of October 4th, 2019 is the result of our systematic analysis on three basic characteristics: earnings strength, relative valuation, and recent stock price movement. The company has managed to produce a neutral trend in earnings per share over the past 5 quarters. In addition, recent analyst estimates for the company have been mixed and WCG has posted results that exceeded analysts' expectations. Based on operating earnings yield, the company is fairly valued when compared to all of the companies we cover. Share price changes over the past year indicates that WCG will perform in line with the market over the near term.

Financial Data

(US$ in Thousands)	9 Mos	6 Mos	3 Mos	12/31/2018	12/31/2017	12/31/2016	12/31/2015	12/31/2014
Earnings Per Share	12.32	10.28	10.03	9.29	8.31	5.43	2.67	1.44
Cash Flow Per Share	19.65	0.18	(3.93)	5.97	23.61	16.86	16.17	6.82
Tang Book Value Per Share	34.47	28.42	23.83	20.32	31.18	34.62	31.40	28.05
Income Statement								
Total Revenue	20,912,500	13,772,300	6,762,200	20,414,100	17,007,200	14,237,100	13,890,200	12,959,900
EBITDA	1,007,100	624,500	283,200	892,800	599,100	1,195,300	788,400	441,800
Depn & Amortn	197,600	137,700	69,600	107,000	87,700	77,200	62,000	46,800
Income Before Taxes	719,500	426,200	184,100	698,300	442,900	1,059,000	672,200	355,600
Income Taxes	167,200	94,500	33,500	253,000	87,900	287,400	217,500	114,100
Net Income	575,200	334,200	151,400	439,800	373,700	242,100	118,600	63,700
Average Shares	50,846	50,811	50,842	47,354	44,967	44,619	44,391	44,163
Balance Sheet								
Current Assets	7,400,500	7,266,700	7,780,700	6,832,400	5,819,200	5,119,600	4,268,500	3,526,300
Total Assets	13,861,700	13,205,500	13,205,900	11,764,700	8,364,600	6,152,800	5,193,600	4,495,000
Current Liabilities	6,404,000	5,930,300	6,077,300	5,015,600	4,443,200	3,055,800	2,441,600	1,935,700
Long-Term Obligations	2,029,100	2,078,200	2,127,300	2,126,400	1,182,400	997,600	912,100	900,000
Total Liabilities	9,005,300	8,602,200	8,814,700	7,524,700	5,947,900	4,152,700	3,465,300	2,899,100
Stockholders' Equity	4,856,400	4,603,300	4,391,200	4,240,000	2,416,700	2,000,100	1,728,300	1,595,900
Shares Outstanding	50,316	50,311	50,302	49,993	44,522	44,293	44,113	43,914
Statistical Record								
Return on Assets %	4.80	4.46	4.28	4.37	5.15	4.26	2.45	1.60
Return on Equity %	14.00	14.31	14.20	13.21	16.92	12.95	7.14	4.09
EBITDA Margin %	4.82	4.53	4.19	4.37	3.52	8.40	5.68	3.41
Net Margin %	2.75	2.43	2.24	2.15	2.20	1.70	0.85	0.49
Asset Turnover	2.05	2.13	1.97	2.03	2.34	2.50	2.87	3.26
Current Ratio	1.16	1.23	1.28	1.36	1.31	1.68	1.75	1.82
Debt to Equity	0.42	0.45	0.48	0.50	0.49	0.50	0.53	0.56
Price Range	321.88-221.21	321.88-221.21	321.88-189.96	321.88-188.41	212.99-136.63	141.40-70.06	98.51-72.85	84.25-56.64
P/E Ratio	26.13-17.96	31.31-21.52	32.09-18.94	34.65-20.28	25.63-16.44	26.04-12.90	36.90-27.28	58.51-39.33

Address: 8735 Henderson Road, Renaissance One, Tampa, FL 33634	**Web Site:** www.wellcare.com	**Auditors:** DELOITTE & TOUCHE LLP
Telephone: 813-290-6200	**Officers:** Christian P. (Chris) Michalik - Chairman Kenneth A. Burdick - President, Chief Executive Officer, Chief Operating Officer, Division Officer	**Investor Contact:** 813-206-3916 **Transfer Agents:** Computershare Trust Company, N.A., Providence, RI

WELLS FARGO & CO

Exchange	Symbol	Price	52Wk Range	Yield	P/E
NYS	WFC	$53.80 (12/31/2019)	54.46-43.38	3.79	11.62

*7 Year Price Score 79.81   *NYSE Composite Index=100   *12 Month Price Score 103.59

Interim Earnings (Per Share)

Qtr.	Mar	Jun	Sep	Dec
2016	0.99	1.01	1.03	0.96
2017	1.00	1.07	0.84	1.19
2018	0.96	0.98	1.13	1.21
2019	1.20	1.30	0.92	...

Interim Dividends (Per Share)

Amt	Decl	Ex	Rec	Pay
0.45Q	01/22/2019	01/31/2019	02/01/2019	03/01/2019
0.45Q	04/23/2019	05/09/2019	05/10/2019	06/01/2019
0.51Q	07/23/2019	08/08/2019	08/09/2019	09/01/2019
0.51Q	10/22/2019	11/07/2019	11/08/2019	12/01/2019

Indicated Div: $2.04 (Div. Reinv. Plan)

Valuation Analysis | **Institutional Holding**

Forecast EPS	$4.11	No of Institutions
	(01/17/2020)	2858
Market Cap	$229.7 Billion	Shares
Book Value	$193.3 Billion	4,065,860,096
Price/Book	1.19	% Held
Price/Sales	2.19	64.76

Business Summary: Banking (MIC: 5.1.1 SIC: 6021 NAIC: 522110)

Wells Fargo is a financial and bank holding company. Through its subsidiaries, Co. provides retail, commercial and corporate banking services. Co.'s segments include: Community Banking, which provides a line of financial products and services including checking and savings accounts, credit and debit cards, and automobile, student, mortgage, home equity and small business lending; Wholesale Banking, which provides a line of commercial, corporate, capital markets, cash management and real estate banking products and services; and Wealth and Investment Management, which provides a range of personalized wealth management, investment and retirement products and services.

Recent Developments: For the quarter ended Sep 30 2019, net income decreased 20.9% to US$4.81 billion from US$6.09 billion in the year-earlier quarter. Net interest income decreased 7.5% to US$11.63 billion from US$12.57 billion in the year-earlier quarter. Provision for loan losses was US$695.0 million versus US$580.0 million in the prior-year quarter, an increase of 19.8%. Non-interest income rose 10.8% to US$10.39 billion from US$9.37 billion, while non-interest expense advanced 10.4% to US$15.20 billion.

Prospects: Our evaluation of Wells Fargo & Co. as of October 4th, 2019 is the result of our systematic analysis on three basic characteristics: earnings strength, relative valuation, and recent stock price movement. The company has managed to produce a neutral trend in earnings per share over the past 5 quarters. However, recent analyst estimates for the company have been reduced while WFC has posted results that exceeded analysts' expectations. Based on operating earnings yield, the company is undervalued when compared to all of the companies we cover. Share price changes over the past year indicates that WFC will perform poorly over the near term.

Financial Data

(US$ in Thousands)	9 Mos	6 Mos	3 Mos	12/31/2018	12/31/2017	12/31/2016	12/31/2015	12/31/2014
Earnings Per Share	4.63	4.84	4.52	4.28	4.10	3.99	4.12	4.10
Cash Flow Per Share	2.14	6.48	6.33	7.52	3.77	0.03	2.88	3.35
Tang Book Value Per Share	31.02	30.69	29.46	28.35	28.28	26.17	25.21	23.42
Dividends Per Share	1.840	1.760	1.700	1.640	1.540	1.515	1.475	1.350
Dividend Payout %	39.74	36.36	37.61	38.32	37.56	37.97	35.80	32.93
Income Statement								
Interest Income	50,488,000	33,989,000	17,003,000	64,647,000	58,909,000	53,663,000	49,277,000	47,552,000
Interest Expense	14,457,000	9,583,000	4,692,000	14,652,000	9,352,000	5,909,000	3,976,000	4,025,000
Net Interest Income	36,031,000	24,406,000	12,311,000	49,995,000	49,557,000	47,754,000	45,301,000	43,527,000
Provision for Losses	2,043,000	1,348,000	845,000	1,744,000	2,528,000	3,770,000	2,442,000	1,395,000
Non-Interest Income	29,172,000	18,787,000	9,298,000	36,413,000	38,832,000	40,513,000	40,756,000	40,820,000
Non-Interest Expense	42,440,000	27,293,000	13,879,000	56,126,000	58,484,000	52,377,000	49,974,000	49,037,000
Income Before Taxes	20,596,000	14,480,000	6,848,000	28,538,000	27,377,000	32,120,000	33,641,000	33,915,000
Income Taxes	3,479,000	2,175,000	881,000	5,662,000	4,917,000	10,075,000	10,365,000	10,307,000
Net Income	16,676,000	12,066,000	5,860,000	22,393,000	22,183,000	21,938,000	22,894,000	23,057,000
Average Shares	4,389,599	4,494,999	4,583,999	4,838,399	5,017,299	5,108,329	5,209,799	5,324,399
Balance Sheet								
Net Loans & Leases	946,732,000	941,367,000	939,367,000	945,376,000	945,874,000	956,265,000	905,293,000	850,954,000
Total Assets	1,943,950,000	1,923,388,000	1,887,792,000	1,895,883,000	1,951,757,000	1,930,115,000	1,787,632,000	1,687,155,000
Total Deposits	1,308,495,000	1,288,426,000	1,264,013,000	1,286,170,000	1,335,991,000	1,306,079,000	1,223,312,000	1,168,310,000
Total Liabilities	1,750,646,000	1,724,346,000	1,689,960,000	1,699,717,000	1,744,821,000	1,730,534,000	1,594,634,000	1,502,761,000
Stockholders' Equity	193,304,000	199,042,000	197,832,000	196,166,000	206,936,000	199,581,000	192,998,000	184,394,000
Shares Outstanding	4,269,142	4,419,590	4,511,947	4,581,253	4,891,616	5,016,109	5,092,128	5,170,348
Statistical Record								
Return on Assets %	1.19	1.27	1.22	1.16	1.14	1.18	1.32	1.43
Return on Equity %	11.60	11.94	11.48	11.11	10.91	11.15	12.13	13.01
Net Interest Margin %	70.46	71.21	72.40	77.34	84.12	88.99	91.93	91.54
Efficiency Ratio %	56.34	50.67	52.77	55.54	59.84	55.62	55.51	55.49
Loans to Deposits	0.72	0.73	0.74	0.74	0.71	0.73	0.74	0.73
Price Range	54.46-43.38	59.19-43.60	59.19-43.60	65.93-43.60	61.61-49.58	57.29-43.75	58.52-50.02	55.71-44.23
P/E Ratio	11.76-9.37	12.23-9.01	13.10-9.65	15.40-10.19	15.03-12.09	14.36-10.96	14.20-12.14	13.59-10.79
Average Yield %	3.79	3.45	3.22	2.97	2.80	3.09	2.69	2.68

Address: 420 Montgomery Street, San Francisco, CA 94163 Telephone: 866-249-3302	Web Site: www.wellsfargo.com Officers: Elizabeth A. Duke - Chairman, Vice-Chairman Charles W. Scharf - President, Chief Executive Officer	Auditors: KPMG LLP Investor Contact: 415-371-2921 Transfer Agents: Wells Fargo Shareowners Services, St. Paul, MN

WELLTOWER INC

Exchange	Symbol	Price	52Wk Range	Yield	P/E	Div Acheiver
NYS	WELL	$81.78 (12/31/2019)	92.46-67.29	4.26	29.63	15 Years

*7 Year Price Score 97.64   *NYSE Composite Index=100   *12 Month Price Score 97.01

Interim Earnings (Per Share)

Qtr.	Mar	Jun	Sep	Dec
2016	0.42	0.54	0.93	0.92
2017	0.86	0.51	0.20	(0.30)
2018	1.17	0.41	0.17	0.26
2019	0.71	0.34	1.45	...

Interim Dividends (Per Share)

Amt	Decl	Ex	Rec	Pay
0.87Q	02/12/2019	02/21/2019	02/22/2019	02/28/2019
0.87Q	04/30/2019	05/13/2019	05/14/2019	05/28/2019
0.87Q	07/31/2019	08/14/2019	08/15/2019	08/22/2019
0.87Q	10/28/2019	11/12/2019	11/13/2019	11/21/2019

Indicated Div: $3.48 (Div. Reinv. Plan)

Valuation Analysis

		Institutional Holding	
Forecast EPS	$2.90	No of Institutions	
	(01/17/2020)	1114	
Market Cap	$33.2 Billion	Shares	
Book Value	$15.3 Billion	454,681,952	
Price/Book	2.17	% Held	
Price/Sales	6.51	N/A	

Business Summary: REITs (MIC: 5.3.1 SIC: 6798 NAIC: 525930)

Welltower is a real estate investment trust. Co. has three segments: Triple-Net, which includes independent living and independent supportive living (Canada), assisted living, continuing care retirement communities, Alzheimer's/dementia care and care homes with or without nursing (U.K.); Seniors Housing Operating, which includes independent living and independent supportive living, continuing care retirement communities, Alzheimer's/dementia care and include care homes with or without nursing (U.K.); and Outpatient Medical, which consists of health care related buildings that include physician offices, ambulatory surgery centers, diagnostic facilities, outpatient services and/or labs.

Recent Developments: For the quarter ended Sep 30 2019, net income increased 669.3% to US$647.9 million from US$84.2 million in the year-earlier quarter. Revenues were US$1.27 billion, up 2.4% from US$1.24 billion the year before. Revenues from property income rose 20.2% to US$412.1 million from US$342.9 million in the corresponding quarter a year earlier.

Prospects: Our evaluation of Welltower Inc. as of October 4th, 2019 is the result of our systematic analysis on three basic characteristics: earnings strength, relative valuation, and recent stock price movement. The company has managed to produce a neutral trend in earnings per share over the past 5 quarters. In addition, recent analyst estimates for the company have been mixed and WELL has posted results that fell short of analysts' expectations. Based on operating earnings yield, the company is overvalued when compared to all of the companies we cover. Share price changes over the past year indicates that WELL will perform over the near term.

Financial Data

(US$ in Thousands)	9 Mos	6 Mos	3 Mos	12/31/2018	12/31/2017	12/31/2016	12/31/2015	12/31/2014
Earnings Per Share	2.76	1.48	1.55	2.02	1.26	2.81	2.34	1.45
Cash Flow Per Share	3.91	3.95	3.98	4.24	3.91	4.53	3.94	3.72
Tang Book Value Per Share	37.46	36.83	37.18	36.09	36.68	37.87	38.10	36.80
Dividends Per Share	3.480	3.480	3.480	3.480	3.480	3.440	3.300	3.180
Dividend Payout %	126.09	235.14	224.52	172.28	276.19	122.42	141.03	219.31
Income Statement								
Total Revenue	3,858,484	2,592,351	1,272,245	4,700,499	4,316,641	4,281,160	3,859,826	3,343,546
EBITDA	390,211	308,443	142,306	1,393,557	1,238,214	1,619,639	1,471,366	1,236,053
Depn & Amortn	13,139	9,759	5,992	970,067	938,598	910,386	835,249	851,840
Income Before Taxes	377,072	298,684	136,314	423,490	299,616	709,253	636,117	384,213
Income Taxes	7,789	3,821	2,222	8,674	20,128	(19,128)	6,451	(1,267)
Net Income	1,008,108	418,232	280,470	804,954	522,774	1,077,803	883,750	512,153
Average Shares	406,891	406,673	393,452	375,250	369,001	360,227	349,424	307,747
Balance Sheet								
Current Assets	330,735	359,718	407,439	683,222	698,471	949,798	818,252	553,423
Total Assets	31,863,955	33,148,697	30,637,336	30,342,072	27,944,445	28,865,184	29,023,845	25,014,296
Long-Term Obligations	13,687,643	15,150,801	12,711,496	13,297,144	11,731,936	12,358,245	12,967,686	10,828,013
Total Liabilities	16,597,890	18,154,242	15,558,845	15,709,738	13,521,298	14,058,791	14,433,285	11,839,143
Stockholders' Equity	15,266,065	14,994,455	15,078,491	14,632,334	14,423,147	14,806,393	14,590,560	13,175,153
Shares Outstanding	405,757	405,254	403,740	383,674	371,731	362,602	354,777	328,790
Statistical Record								
Return on Assets %	3.61	2.00	2.18	2.76	1.84	3.71	3.27	2.13
Return on Equity %	7.58	4.14	4.29	5.54	3.58	7.31	6.37	4.17
EBITDA Margin %	10.11	11.90	11.19	29.65	28.68	37.83	38.12	36.97
Net Margin %	26.13	16.13	22.05	17.12	12.11	25.18	22.90	15.32
Asset Turnover	0.16	0.17	0.17	0.16	0.15	0.15	0.14	0.14
Debt to Equity	0.90	1.01	0.84	0.91	0.81	0.83	0.89	0.82
Price Range	92.46-61.60	84.63-61.60	78.72-50.01	74.72-50.01	77.66-63.27	79.61-53.68	84.31-58.21	77.98-53.05
P/E Ratio	33.50-22.32	57.18-41.62	50.79-32.26	36.99-24.76	61.63-50.21	28.33-19.10	36.03-24.88	53.78-36.59
Average Yield %	4.51	4.86	5.29	5.68	4.96	4.94	4.68	4.97

Address: 4500 Dorr Street, Toledo, OH 43615 Telephone: 419-247-2800	Web Site: www.welltower.com Officers: Jeffrey H. Donahue - Chairman Thomas J. (Tom) DeRosa - Chief Executive Officer	Auditors: Ernst & Young LLP Transfer Agents: Computershare, Providence, RI

WESCO INTERNATIONAL, INC.

Exchange	Symbol	Price	52Wk Range	Yield	P/E
NYS	WCC	$59.39 (12/31/2019)	59.99-42.59	N/A	11.51

*7 Year Price Score 65.88   *NYSE Composite Index=100   *12 Month Price Score 101.48

Interim Earnings (Per Share)

Qtr.	Mar	Jun	Sep	Dec
2016	0.77	1.02	(0.73)	0.97
2017	0.76	1.02	1.12	0.48
2018	0.93	1.22	1.41	1.26
2019	0.93	1.45	1.52	...

Interim Dividends (Per Share)

No Dividends Paid

Valuation Analysis   **Institutional Holding**

Forecast EPS	$5.22	No of Institutions
	(01/17/2020)	377
Market Cap	$2.5 Billion	Shares
Book Value	$2.2 Billion	50,443,720
Price/Book	1.13	% Held
Price/Sales	0.30	87.86

Business Summary: Electrical Equipment (MIC: 7.3.1 SIC: 5063 NAIC: 423610)

WESCO International is a distributor of products and provider of supply chain management and logistics services used primarily in industrial, construction, utility and commercial, institutional and government markets. Co. is a provider of electrical, industrial, and communications maintenance, repair and operating and original equipment manufacturers products, construction materials, and supply chain management and logistics services. Co.'s primary product categories include general supplies, wire, cable and conduit, communications and security, electrical distribution and controls, lighting and sustainability, and automation, controls and motors.

Recent Developments: For the quarter ended Sep 30 2019, net income decreased 3.5% to US$64.3 million from US$66.6 million in the year-earlier quarter. Revenues were US$2.15 billion, up 3.9% from US$2.07 billion the year before. Operating income was US$93.7 million versus US$97.5 million in the prior-year quarter, a decrease of 3.9%. Direct operating expenses rose 4.7% to US$1.75 billion from US$1.67 billion in the comparable period the year before. Indirect operating expenses increased 2.3% to US$306.5 million from US$299.7 million in the equivalent prior-year period.

Prospects: Our evaluation of Wesco International Inc. as of October 4th, 2019 is the result of our systematic analysis on three basic characteristics: earnings strength, relative valuation, and recent stock price movement. The company has managed to produce a neutral trend in earnings per share over the past 5 quarters. However, recent analyst estimates for the company have been reduced while WCC has posted results that exceeded analysts' expectations. Based on operating earnings yield, the company is undervalued when compared to all of the companies we cover. Share price changes over the past year indicates that WCC will perform poorly over the near term.

Financial Data

(US$ in Thousands)	9 Mos	6 Mos	3 Mos	12/31/2018	12/31/2017	12/31/2016	12/31/2015	12/31/2014
Earnings Per Share	5.16	5.05	4.82	4.82	3.38	2.10	4.18	5.18
Cash Flow Per Share	5.68	4.62	6.05	6.35	3.12	6.79	6.52	5.65
Tang Book Value Per Share	3.67	1.97	3.37	2.14	N.M.	N.M.	N.M.	N.M.
Income Statement								
Total Revenue	6,259,465	4,111,355	1,961,267	8,176,601	7,679,021	7,336,017	7,518,487	7,889,626
EBITDA	308,444	199,099	85,968	369,740	337,190	225,226	391,542	484,717
Depn & Amortn	46,035	30,424	15,242	17,300	16,300	17,100	17,800	18,500
Income Before Taxes	214,475	134,248	53,606	281,025	252,440	131,551	303,910	384,153
Income Taxes	44,970	29,084	11,656	55,670	89,307	30,431	95,537	108,716
Net Income	170,329	105,832	42,369	227,343	163,460	101,588	210,687	275,906
Average Shares	42,378	43,816	45,491	47,199	48,361	48,333	50,373	53,258
Balance Sheet								
Current Assets	2,578,480	2,584,864	2,513,750	2,385,640	2,408,849	2,172,457	2,257,534	2,350,338
Total Assets	5,047,411	5,067,936	4,984,638	4,605,036	4,735,468	4,490,984	4,587,425	4,754,437
Current Liabilities	1,104,524	1,124,832	1,150,722	1,061,946	1,040,969	896,797	947,801	1,063,872
Long-Term Obligations	1,346,333	1,399,486	1,214,276	1,167,311	1,313,261	1,363,135	1,456,761	1,366,430
Total Liabilities	2,854,293	2,926,861	2,782,273	2,469,726	2,615,729	2,477,703	2,810,753	2,825,785
Stockholders' Equity	2,193,118	2,141,075	2,202,365	2,135,310	2,119,739	2,013,281	1,776,672	1,928,652
Shares Outstanding	41,783	42,477	44,854	45,106	47,009	48,611	42,173	44,489
Statistical Record								
Return on Assets %	4.65	4.72	4.65	4.87	3.54	2.23	4.51	5.89
Return on Equity %	10.31	10.71	10.38	10.69	7.91	5.35	11.37	14.94
EBITDA Margin %	4.93	4.84	4.38	4.52	4.39	3.07	5.21	6.14
Net Margin %	2.72	2.57	2.16	2.78	2.13	1.38	2.80	3.50
Asset Turnover	1.68	1.67	1.68	1.75	1.66	1.61	1.61	1.68
Current Ratio	2.33	2.30	2.18	2.25	2.31	2.42	2.38	2.21
Debt to Equity	0.61	0.65	0.55	0.55	0.62	0.68	0.82	0.71
Price Range	61.12-42.59	62.40-44.09	64.00-44.09	68.75-44.09	74.45-49.60	72.15-36.05	76.21-40.04	93.81-71.18
P/E Ratio	11.84-8.25	12.36-8.73	13.28-9.15	14.26-9.15	22.03-14.67	34.36-17.17	18.23-9.58	18.11-13.74

Address: 225 West Station Square Drive, Suite 700, Pittsburgh, PA 15219 Telephone: 412-454-2200	Web Site: www.wesco.com Officers: John J. Engel - Chairman, President, Chief Executive Officer Nelson J. Squires - Senior Vice President, Chief Operating Officer	Auditors: PricewaterhouseCoopers LLP Transfer Agents: Computershare, Providence, RI

WEST PHARMACEUTICAL SERVICES, INC.

Exchange	Symbol	Price	52Wk Range	Yield	P/E	Div Acheiver
NYS	WST	$150.33 (12/31/2019)	151.21-94.53	0.43	49.29	26 Years

*7 Year Price Score 137.63 *NYSE Composite Index=100 *12 Month Price Score 110.61

Interim Earnings (Per Share)

Qtr.	Mar	Jun	Sep	Dec
2016	0.30	0.60	0.50	0.51
2017	0.81	0.51	0.67	0.00
2018	0.58	0.75	0.73	0.69
2019	0.73	0.88	0.75	...

Interim Dividends (Per Share)

Amt	Decl	Ex	Rec	Pay
0.15Q	02/21/2019	04/16/2019	04/17/2019	05/01/2019
0.15Q	05/08/2019	07/23/2019	07/24/2019	08/07/2019
0.16Q	07/25/2019	10/22/2019	10/23/2019	11/06/2019
0.16Q	12/13/2019	01/21/2020	01/22/2020	02/05/2020

Indicated Div: $0.64 (Div. Reinv. Plan)

Valuation Analysis

		Institutional Holding	
Forecast EPS	$3.15	No of Institutions	
	(11/13/2019)	545	
Market Cap	$11.1 Billion	Shares	
Book Value	$1.5 Billion	83,413,080	
Price/Book	7.48	% Held	
Price/Sales	6.21	89.81	

Business Summary: Rubber Products (MIC: 8.4.1 SIC: 3069 NAIC: 326299)

West Pharmaceutical Services is a manufacturer in the design and production of containment and delivery systems for injectable drugs and healthcare products. Co.'s products include a variety of primary packaging, containment solutions, reconstitution and transfer systems, and drug delivery systems, as well as contract manufacturing and analytical lab services. Co.'s segments include: Proprietary Products, which provides proprietary packaging, containment and drug delivery products, and analytical lab services; and Contract-Manufactured Products, which is focused on the design, manufacture, and automated assembly of devices, for pharmaceutical, diagnostic, and medical device customers.

Recent Developments: For the quarter ended Sep 30 2019, net income increased 2.0% to US$56.3 million from US$55.2 million in the year-earlier quarter. Revenues were US$456.1 million, up 5.7% from US$431.7 million the year before. Operating income was US$67.3 million versus US$60.8 million in the prior-year quarter, an increase of 10.7%. Direct operating expenses rose 4.1% to US$308.3 million from US$296.1 million in the comparable period the year before. Indirect operating expenses increased 7.6% to US$80.5 million from US$74.8 million in the equivalent prior-year period.

Prospects: Our evaluation of West Pharmaceutical Services Inc. as of October 4th, 2019 is the result of our systematic analysis on three basic characteristics: earnings strength, relative valuation, and recent stock price movement. The company has managed to produce a neutral trend in earnings per share over the past 5 quarters. In addition, recent analyst estimates for the company have been mixed and WST has posted results that exceeded analysts' expectations. Based on operating earnings yield, the company is overvalued when compared to all of the companies we cover. Share price changes over the past year indicates that WST will perform well over the near term.

Financial Data

(US$ in Thousands)	9 Mos	6 Mos	3 Mos	12/31/2018	12/31/2017	12/31/2016	12/31/2015	12/31/2014
Earnings Per Share	3.05	3.03	2.90	2.74	1.99	1.91	1.30	1.75
Cash Flow Per Share	4.51	4.26	3.93	3.91	3.56	2.99	2.95	2.58
Tang Book Value Per Share	18.28	17.74	16.94	17.14	15.57	13.56	12.20	11.31
Dividends Per Share	0.600	0.590	0.580	0.570	0.530	0.490	0.450	0.410
Dividend Payout %	19.67	19.47	20.00	20.80	26.63	25.65	34.62	23.43
Income Statement								
Total Revenue	1,369,300	913,200	443,500	1,717,400	1,599,100	1,509,100	1,399,800	1,421,400
EBITDA	295,400	204,100	96,800	348,700	323,200	284,900	214,700	266,800
Depn & Amortn	77,100	51,800	25,500	101,700	94,300	88,100	86,100	84,800
Income Before Taxes	214,400	149,500	69,900	240,700	222,400	189,800	116,100	169,000
Income Taxes	42,500	31,600	16,100	41,400	80,900	54,400	26,300	47,200
Net Income	177,800	121,500	55,400	206,900	150,700	143,600	95,600	127,100
Average Shares	75,500	75,100	75,300	75,400	75,800	75,000	73,800	72,800
Balance Sheet								
Current Assets	1,004,100	944,300	867,600	894,400	743,500	641,900	673,700	659,300
Total Assets	2,174,000	2,123,200	2,036,200	1,978,900	1,862,800	1,716,700	1,695,100	1,670,900
Current Liabilities	335,000	313,200	301,100	283,700	279,500	241,000	314,300	252,500
Long-Term Obligations	195,100	196,000	195,500	196,000	197,000	226,200	228,900	309,500
Total Liabilities	686,400	678,100	666,700	582,600	582,900	599,200	671,200	714,000
Stockholders' Equity	1,487,600	1,445,100	1,369,500	1,396,300	1,279,900	1,117,500	1,023,900	956,900
Shares Outstanding	73,990	73,700	73,500	74,100	73,900	73,100	72,300	71,300
Statistical Record								
Return on Assets %	11.16	11.44	11.20	10.77	8.42	8.39	5.68	7.61
Return on Equity %	16.19	16.77	16.35	15.46	12.57	13.38	9.65	13.64
EBITDA Margin %	21.57	22.35	21.83	20.30	20.21	18.88	15.34	18.77
Net Margin %	12.98	13.30	12.49	12.05	9.42	9.52	6.83	8.94
Asset Turnover	0.87	0.88	0.89	0.89	0.89	0.88	0.83	0.85
Current Ratio	3.00	3.02	2.88	3.15	2.66	2.66	2.14	2.61
Debt to Equity	0.13	0.14	0.14	0.14	0.15	0.20	0.22	0.32
Price Range	150.02-93.00	125.15-93.00	123.98-83.32	123.98-83.32	101.65-78.61	85.30-54.64	64.13-49.19	55.08-39.26
P/E Ratio	49.19-30.49	41.30-30.69	42.75-28.73	45.25-30.41	51.08-39.50	44.66-28.61	49.33-37.84	31.47-22.43
Average Yield %	0.51	0.53	0.56	0.56	0.58	0.67	0.79	0.90

Address: 530 Herman O. West Drive, Exton, PA 19341-0645	Web Site: www.westpharma.com	Auditors: PricewaterhouseCoopers LLP
Telephone: 610-594-2900	**Officers:** Patrick J. Zenner - Chairman Eric M. Green - President, Chief Executive Officer	**Investor Contact:** 610-594-3345
		Transfer Agents: Broadbridge Corporate Issuer Solutions, Philadelphia, PA

WABCO HOLDINGS INC

Exchange	Symbol	Price	52Wk Range	Yield	P/E
NYS	WBC	$135.50 (12/31/2019)	146.01-102.75	N/A	21.37

*7 Year Price Score 96.97   *NYSE Composite Index=100   *12 Month Price Score 97.42

Interim Earnings (Per Share)

Qtr.	Mar	Jun	Sep	Dec
2016	(0.24)	1.33	1.76	1.14
2017	1.48	1.61	1.30	3.11
2018	1.87	1.95	1.41	2.19
2019	1.64	1.38	1.13	...

Interim Dividends (Per Share)

No Dividends Paid

Valuation Analysis		Institutional Holding	
Forecast EPS	$5.80	No of Institutions	
	(01/17/2020)	483	
Market Cap	$6.9 Billion	Shares	
Book Value	$1.4 Billion	57,207,620	
Price/Book	5.11	% Held	
Price/Sales	1.95	88.87	

Business Summary: Auto Parts (MIC: 1.8.2 SIC: 3711 NAIC: 336111)

WABCO Holdings is a supplier of electronic, mechanical, electro-mechanical and aerodynamic products for manufacturers of commercial trucks, buses and trailers, as well as passenger cars. Co. engineers, develops, manufactures and sells braking, stability, suspension, steering, transmission automation and air management systems for commercial vehicles. Co.'s products are pneumatic anti-lock braking systems, electronic braking systems, electronic stability control systems, brake controls, automated manual transmission systems, air disc brakes, and a variety of mechanical products such as actuators, air compressors and air control valves for medium and heavy-duty trucks, buses and trailers.

Recent Developments: For the quarter ended Sep 30 2019, net income decreased 23.8% to US$60.8 million from US$79.8 million in the year-earlier quarter. Revenues were US$798.4 million, down 12.7% from US$914.8 million the year before. Operating income was US$80.9 million versus US$107.0 million in the prior-year quarter, a decrease of 24.4%. Direct operating expenses declined 12.5% to US$559.5 million from US$639.7 million in the comparable period the year before. Indirect operating expenses decreased 6.0% to US$158.0 million from US$168.1 million in the equivalent prior-year period.

Prospects: Our evaluation of WABCO Holdings Inc. as of October 4th, 2019 is the result of our systematic analysis on three basic characteristics: earnings strength, relative valuation, and recent stock price movement. The company has generated a negative trend in earnings per share over the past 5 quarters. In addition, recent analyst estimates for the company have been reduced and WBC has posted results that fell short of analysts' expectations. Based on operating earnings yield, the company is fairly valued when compared to all of the companies we cover. Share price changes over the past year indicates that WBC will perform well over the near term.

Financial Data

(US$ in Thousands)	9 Mos	6 Mos	3 Mos	12/31/2018	12/31/2017	12/31/2016	12/31/2015	12/31/2014
Earnings Per Share	6.34	6.62	7.19	7.43	7.50	3.98	4.72	4.81
Cash Flow Per Share	9.28	8.67	8.56	8.87	7.82	7.26	6.84	5.25
Tang Book Value Per Share	6.51	5.38	4.05	2.35	0.37	4.10	6.10	5.86
Income Statement								
Total Revenue	2,644,000	1,845,600	932,900	3,831,000	3,304,200	2,810,000	2,627,500	2,851,000
EBITDA	370,900	263,600	134,400	594,900	752,600	455,000	369,200	434,400
Depn & Amortn	100,200	69,500	35,100	124,700	107,100	98,000	96,700	101,600
Income Before Taxes	270,700	194,400	99,400	462,700	629,500	344,300	265,400	333,000
Income Taxes	48,900	33,000	12,100	49,300	229,700	121,800	11,500	55,600
Net Income	212,700	154,500	84,200	394,100	406,100	223,000	275,200	291,500
Average Shares	51,389	51,340	51,330	53,062	54,139	55,981	58,274	60,546
Balance Sheet								
Current Assets	1,945,300	1,943,300	1,991,100	1,796,900	2,394,200	1,874,000	1,386,400	1,182,500
Total Assets	3,978,800	4,012,900	4,048,200	3,738,600	4,323,400	3,056,000	2,589,900	2,432,700
Current Liabilities	646,400	652,800	765,900	596,000	1,073,300	530,900	464,800	417,700
Long-Term Obligations	808,200	839,600	829,000	845,200	1,023,300	958,900	498,700	307,100
Total Liabilities	2,620,500	2,691,700	2,797,200	2,561,800	3,202,000	2,354,600	1,803,200	1,591,100
Stockholders' Equity	1,358,300	1,321,200	1,251,000	1,176,800	1,121,400	701,400	786,700	841,600
Shares Outstanding	51,254	51,242	51,231	51,364	53,735	54,491	56,759	58,425
Statistical Record								
Return on Assets %	8.17	8.61	8.86	9.78	11.01	7.88	10.96	12.08
Return on Equity %	26.04	27.32	30.58	34.30	44.56	29.89	33.80	29.23
EBITDA Margin %	14.03	14.28	14.41	15.53	22.78	16.19	14.05	15.24
Net Margin %	8.04	8.37	9.03	10.29	12.29	7.94	10.47	10.22
Asset Turnover	0.89	0.92	0.88	0.95	0.90	0.99	1.05	1.18
Current Ratio	3.01	2.98	2.60	3.01	2.23	3.53	2.98	2.83
Debt to Equity	0.60	0.64	0.66	0.72	0.91	1.37	0.63	0.36
Price Range	146.01-100.44	146.01-100.44	146.01-100.44	161.00-100.44	155.08-104.21	113.91-84.83	133.21-94.54	110.68-84.36
P/E Ratio	23.03-15.84	22.06-15.17	20.31-13.97	21.67-13.52	20.68-13.89	28.62-21.31	28.22-20.03	23.01-17.54

Address: 1220 Pacific Drive, Auburn Hills, MI 48326-1589	Web Site: www.wabco-auto.com	Auditors: Ernst & Young Bedrijfsrevisoren
Telephone: 315-813-300	Officers: Jacques R. Esculier - Chairman, Chief Executive Officer Sean Deason - Vice President, Chief Financial Officer, Controller	BCVBA/ Reviseurs d'Entreprises SCCRL Investor Contact: 732-369-7477

WESTERN UNION CO

Exchange	Symbol	Price	52Wk Range	Yield	P/E
NYS	WU	$26.78 (12/31/2019)	27.87-16.87	2.99	10.30

*7 Year Price Score 92.82 ***NYSE Composite Index=100** ***12 Month Price Score 120.41**

Interim Earnings (Per Share)

Qtr.	Mar	Jun	Sep	Dec
2016	0.37	0.42	0.44	(0.72)
2017	0.33	0.35	0.51	(2.38)
2018	0.46	0.47	0.46	0.47
2019	0.39	1.42	0.32	...

Interim Dividends (Per Share)

Amt	Decl	Ex	Rec	Pay
0.20Q	02/07/2019	03/14/2019	03/15/2019	03/29/2019
0.20Q	05/17/2019	06/13/2019	06/14/2019	06/28/2019
0.20Q	07/18/2019	09/13/2019	09/16/2019	09/30/2019
0.20Q	12/04/2019	12/16/2019	12/17/2019	12/31/2019

Indicated Div: $0.80

Valuation Analysis

		Institutional Holding	
Forecast EPS	$1.77	No of Institutions	
	(01/15/2020)	872	
Market Cap	$11.2 Billion	Shares	
Book Value	N/A	566,396,160	
Price/Book	N/A	% Held	
Price/Sales	2.09	74.82	

Business Summary: Business Services (MIC: 7.5.2 SIC: 6099 NAIC: 522320)

Western Union is a holding company. Through its subsidiaries, Co. is engaged in money movement and payment services, providing people and businesses with ways to send money and make payments around the world. Co.'s segments are: Consumer-to-Consumer, which is focused on individual money transfers from one consumer to another; and Business Solutions, in which Co. facilitates payment and foreign exchange solutions, primarily cross-border, cross-currency transactions, for small and medium size enterprises and other organizations and individuals. Co.'s remaining businesses and services include its electronic-based and cash-based bill payment services and money order services.

Recent Developments: For the quarter ended Sep 30 2019, net income decreased 35.3% to US$135.0 million from US$208.6 million in the year-earlier quarter. Non-interest income fell 5.8% to US$1.31 billion from US$1.39 billion, while non-interest expense advanced 2.2% to US$1.11 billion.

Prospects: Our evaluation of Western Union Co as of October 4th, 2019 is the result of our systematic analysis on three basic characteristics: earnings strength, relative valuation, and recent stock price movement. The company has managed to produce a neutral trend in earnings per share over the past 5 quarters. In addition, recent analyst estimates for the company have been mixed and WU has posted results that fell short of analysts' expectations. Based on operating earnings yield, the company is undervalued when compared to all of the companies we cover. Share price changes over the past year indicates that WU will perform in line with the market over the near term.

Financial Data

(US$ in Thousands)	9 Mos	6 Mos	3 Mos	12/31/2018	12/31/2017	12/31/2016	12/31/2015	12/31/2014
Earnings Per Share	2.60	2.74	1.79	1.87	(1.19)	0.51	1.62	1.59
Cash Flow Per Share	2.29	2.15	2.12	1.82	1.57	2.12	2.09	1.96
Dividends Per Share	0.790	0.780	0.770	0.760	0.700	0.640	0.620	0.500
Dividend Payout %	30.38	28.47	43.02	40.64	...	125.49	38.27	31.45
Income Statement								
Total Revenue	3,984,400	2,677,500	1,337,000	5,589,900	5,524,300	5,422,900	5,483,700	5,607,200
EBITDA	1,424,900	1,166,500	318,500	1,213,100	561,800	564,900	1,166,500	1,199,900
Depn & Amortn	190,700	129,600	64,800	76,900	77,100	·74,200	67,700	66,600
Income Before Taxes	1,123,900	961,700	216,100	991,400	347,500	341,700	941,800	968,200
Income Taxes	201,000	173,800	43,000	139,500	904,600	88,500	104,000	115,800
Net Income	922,900	787,900	173,100	851,900	(557,100)	253,200	837,800	852,400
Average Shares	426,800	432,300	439,900	454,400	467,900	493,500	516,700	536,800
Balance Sheet								
Current Assets	1,390,900	1,210,200	833,100	1,074,700	958,700	1,004,400	1,399,300	1,846,200
Total Assets	8,803,700	9,043,300	9,432,000	8,996,800	9,231,400	9,419,600	9,458,900	9,890,400
Current Liabilities	2,018,000	1,811,400	1,616,400	1,905,000	2,143,500	1,622,800	1,090,700	1,071,700
Long-Term Obligations	2,813,000	2,812,200	3,310,300	3,308,700	3,033,600	2,786,100	3,225,600	3,720,400
Total Liabilities	8,823,400	9,013,100	9,806,200	9,306,600	9,722,800	8,517,400	8,054,000	8,590,000
Stockholders' Equity	(19,700)	30,200	(374,200)	(309,800)	(491,400)	902,200	1,404,900	1,300,400
Shares Outstanding	419,900	425,900	432,900	441,200	459,000	481,500	502,400	521,500
Statistical Record								
Return on Assets %	12.76	13.31	8.72	9.35	N.M.	2.68	8.66	8.52
Return on Equity %	...	...	...	...	N.M.	21.89	61.94	70.88
EBITDA Margin %	35.76	43.57	23.82	21.70	10.17	10.42	21.27	21.40
Net Margin %	23.16	29.43	12.95	15.24	N.M.	4.67	15.28	15.20
Asset Turnover	0.61	0.60	0.59	0.61	0.59	0.57	0.57	0.56
Current Ratio	0.69	0.67	0.52	0.56	0.45	0.62	1.28	1.72
Debt to Equity	...	93.12	...	...	...	3.09	2.30	2.86
Price Range	23.76-16.55	20.59-16.55	21.18-16.55	21.49-16.55	22.57-18.47	22.14-16.44	22.56-16.96	18.58-15.15
P/E Ratio	9.14-6.37	7.51-6.04	11.83-9.25	11.49-8.85	...	43.41-32.24	13.93-10.47	11.69-9.53
Average Yield %	4.09	4.15	4.08	3.92	3.57	3.25	3.19	2.98

Address: 7001 East Belleview Avenue, Denver, CO 80237 Telephone: 866-405-5012	Web Site: www.westernunion.com Officers: Hikmet Ersek - President, Chief Executive Officer Rajesh K. Agrawal - Executive Vice President, Chief Financial Officer, Acting Chief Financial Officer, Division Officer	Auditors: Ernst & Young LLP Transfer Agents: Wells Fargo Bank, National Association, South St. Paul, MN

WESTLAKE CHEMICAL CORP

Exchange	Symbol	Price	52Wk Range	Yield	P/E	Div Acheiver
NYS	WLK	$70.15 (12/31/2019)	80.88-56.10	1.50	19.27	14 Years

*7 Year Price Score 82.04   *NYSE Composite Index=100   *12 Month Price Score 97.74

Interim Earnings (Per Share)

Qtr.	Mar	Jun	Sep	Dec
2016	0.94	0.85	0.51	0.77
2017	1.06	1.17	1.61	6.20
2018	2.20	2.12	2.35	0.95
2019	0.55	0.92	1.22	...

Interim Dividends (Per Share)

Amt	Decl	Ex	Rec	Pay
0.25Q	02/15/2019	02/26/2019	02/27/2019	03/13/2019
0.25Q	05/17/2019	05/28/2019	05/29/2019	06/12/2019
0.263Q	08/16/2019	08/26/2019	08/27/2019	09/11/2019
0.263Q	11/15/2019	11/25/2019	11/26/2019	12/10/2019

Indicated Div: $1.05

Valuation Analysis | **Institutional Holding**

Forecast EPS	$3.71
	(01/17/2020)
Market Cap	$9.0 Billion
Book Value	$5.8 Billion
Price/Book	1.54
Price/Sales	1.09

No of Institutions 375

Shares 45,795,176

% Held 30.32

Business Summary: Specialty Chemicals (MIC: 8.3.2 SIC: 2869 NAIC: 325211)

Westlake Chemical operates a manufacturer and marketer of basic chemicals, vinyls, polymers and building products. Co. operates in two operating segments: Olefins and Vinyls. The Olefins segment manufactures and markets polyethylene, styrene monomer and various ethylene co-products. The Vinyls segment manufactures and markets polyvinyl chloride (PVC), vinyl chloride monomer, ethylene dichloride, chlor-alkali (chlorine and caustic soda), chlorinated derivative products and ethylene. Co. also manufactures and sells products fabricated from PVC, including siding, pipe, fittings, profiles, trim, mouldings, fence and decking products, window and door components and film and sheet products.

Recent Developments: For the quarter ended Sep 30 2019, net income decreased 47.8% to US$166.0 million from US$318.0 million in the year-earlier quarter. Revenues were US$2.07 billion, down 8.4% from US$2.26 billion the year before. Operating income was US$226.0 million versus US$396.0 million in the prior-year quarter, a decrease of 42.9%. Direct operating expenses declined 1.2% to US$1.70 billion from US$1.72 billion in the comparable period the year before. Indirect operating expenses increased 1.4% to US$145.0 million from US$143.0 million in the equivalent prior-year period.

Prospects: Our evaluation of Westlake Chemical Corp. as of October 4th, 2019 is the result of our systematic analysis on three basic characteristics: earnings strength, relative valuation, and recent stock price movement. The company has generated a negative trend in earnings per share over the past 5 quarters. In addition, recent analyst estimates for the company have been reduced while WLK has posted results that exceeded analysts' expectations. Based on operating earnings yield, the company is undervalued when compared to all of the companies we cover. Share price changes over the past year indicates that WLK will perform poorly over the near term.

Financial Data

(US$ In Thousands)	9 Mos	6 Mos	3 Mos	12/31/2018	12/31/2017	12/31/2016	12/31/2015	12/31/2014
Earnings Per Share	3.64	4.77	5.97	7.62	10.05	3.06	4.86	5.07
Cash Flow Per Share	9.53	10.33	10.36	10.89	11.91	6.43	8.18	7.76
Tang Book Value Per Share	31.40	30.23	29.82	30.58	23.84	13.88	23.44	20.27
Dividends Per Share	1.013	1.000	0.960	0.920	0.801	0.744	0.693	0.582
Dividend Payout %	27.82	20.96	16.08	12.07	7.97	24.32	14.26	11.48
Income Statement								
Total Revenue	6,235,000	4,169,000	2,025,000	8,635,000	8,041,000	5,075,456	4,463,336	4,415,350
EBITDA	667,000	393,000	170,000	2,039,000	1,797,000	931,091	1,195,092	1,286,092
Depn & Amortn	81,000	54,000	27,000	579,000	557,000	305,273	209,271	174,173
Income Before Taxes	497,000	281,000	113,000	1,334,000	1,081,000	554,766	957,199	1,078,035
Income Taxes	120,000	70,000	31,000	300,000	(258,000)	138,520	298,396	398,902
Net Income	349,000	191,000	72,000	996,000	1,304,000	398,859	646,010	678,523
Average Shares	128,552	128,850	128,913	129,985	129,540	129,974	132,301	133,643
Balance Sheet								
Current Assets	3,482,000	2,595,000	2,627,000	2,842,000	3,463,000	2,408,316	2,175,189	2,011,287
Total Assets	13,107,000	12,216,000	12,104,000	11,602,000	12,076,000	10,890,253	5,575,252	5,213,990
Current Liabilities	1,238,000	1,254,000	1,226,000	1,183,000	1,967,000	1,183,083	522,642	537,180
Long-Term Obligations	3,424,000	2,669,000	2,669,000	2,668,000	3,127,000	3,678,654	764,115	763,997
Total Liabilities	7,283,000	6,497,000	6,472,000	6,012,000	7,202,000	7,366,624	2,309,374	2,302,479
Stockholders' Equity	5,824,000	5,719,000	5,632,000	5,590,000	4,874,000	3,523,629	3,265,878	2,911,511
Shares Outstanding	128,136	128,268	128,592	128,468	129,418	128,925	130,218	132,891
Statistical Record								
Return on Assets %	3.80	5.28	6.59	8.41	11.36	4.83	11.98	14.63
Return on Equity %	8.26	11.23	14.50	19.04	31.06	11.72	20.92	25.46
EBITDA Margin %	10.70	9.43	8.40	23.61	22.35	18.34	26.78	29.13
Net Margin %	5.60	4.58	3.56	11.53	16.22	7.86	14.47	15.37
Asset Turnover	0.66	0.71	0.72	0.73	0.70	0.61	0.83	0.95
Current Ratio	2.81	2.07	2.14	2.40	1.76	2.04	4.16	3.74
Debt to Equity	0.59	0.47	0.47	0.48	0.64	1.04	0.23	0.26
Price Range	83.63-56.10	111.60-57.29	123.67-60.82	123.67-60.82	106.53-57.29	59.17-39.88	78.59-49.82	97.96-53.67
P/E Ratio	22.98-15.41	23.40-12.01	20.72-10.19	16.23-7.98	10.60-5.70	19.34-13.03	16.17-10.25	19.32-10.59
Average Yield %	1.47	1.29	1.18	0.94	1.09	1.53	1.10	0.78

Address: 2801 Post Oak Boulevard, Suite 600, Houston, TX 77056 **Telephone:** 713-960-9111	**Web Site:** www.westlake.com **Officers:** James Chao - Chairman Albert Chao - President, Chief Executive Officer	**Auditors:** PricewaterhouseCoopers LLP **Transfer Agents:** American Stock Transfer & Trust Company, New York, NY

WESTROCK CO

Exchange	Symbol	Price	52Wk Range	Yield	P/E
NYS	WRK	$42.91 (12/31/2019)	43.18-32.31	4.33	12.89

*7 Year Price Score N/A   ***NYSE Composite Index=100**   ***12 Month Price Score 101.81**

Interim Earnings (Per Share)

Qtr.	Dec	Mar	Jun	Sep
2014-15	0.88	0.77	1.10	0.19
2015-16	(1.76)	0.22	0.36	(0.36)
2016-17	0.32	0.40	1.29	0.76
2017-18	4.38	0.86	1.03	1.09
2018-19	0.54	0.62	0.98	1.20

Interim Dividends (Per Share)

Amt	Decl	Ex	Rec	Pay
0.455Q	02/01/2019	02/14/2019	02/15/2019	02/25/2019
0.455Q	04/26/2019	05/09/2019	05/10/2019	05/20/2019
0.455Q	07/26/2019	08/08/2019	08/09/2019	08/20/2019
0.465Q	11/07/2019	11/18/2019	11/19/2019	12/03/2019

Indicated Div: $1.86

Valuation Analysis

		Institutional Holding	
Forecast EPS	$3.35	No of Institutions	
(01/17/2020)		N/A	
Market Cap	$11.1 Billion	Shares	
Book Value	$11.7 Billion	N/A	
Price/Book	0.95	% Held	
Price/Sales	0.60	N/A	

TRADING VOLUME (thousand shares)

Business Summary: Containers & Packaging (MIC: 8.1.3 SIC: 2653 NAIC: 322211)

WestRock is a provider of paper and packaging solutions for consumer and corrugated packaging markets. Co. partners with its customers to provide paper and packaging solutions. Co.'s operating and business locations are in North America, South America, Europe, Asia and Australia. Co.'s segments include: Corrugated Packaging, which consists of Co.'s containerboard mills, corrugated packaging and distribution operations, as well as its merchandising displays and recycling procurement operations; Consumer Packaging, which consists of Co.'s consumer mills, food and beverage and partition operations; and Land and Development, which sells real estate primarily in the Charleston, SC region.

Recent Developments: For the year ended Sep 30 2019, net income decreased 54.5% to US$867.9 million from US$1.91 billion in the prior year. Revenues were US$18.29 billion, up 12.3% from US$16.29 billion the year before. Operating income was US$1.49 billion versus US$1.19 billion in the prior year, an increase of 25.9%. Direct operating expenses rose 12.5% to US$14.54 billion from US$12.92 billion in the comparable period the year before. Indirect operating expenses increased 3.7% to US$2.25 billion from US$2.17 billion in the equivalent prior-year period.

Prospects: Our evaluation of WestRock Co. as of October 4th, 2019 is the result of our systematic analysis on three basic characteristics: earnings strength, relative valuation, and recent stock price movement. The company has enjoyed a very positive trend in earnings per share over the past 5 quarters. However, recent analyst estimates for the company have been mixed and WRK has posted results that fell short of analysts' expectations. Based on operating earnings yield, the company is undervalued when compared to all of the companies we cover. Share price changes over the past year indicates that WRK will perform poorly over the near term.

Financial Data

(US$ in Thousands)	09/30/2019	09/30/2018	09/30/2017	09/30/2016	09/30/2015	09/30/2014	09/30/2013
Earnings Per Share	3.33	7.34	2.77	(1.54)	2.93	3.29	4.98
Cash Flow Per Share	9.00	9.48	7.54	6.63	7.06	8.02	7.17
Tang Book Value Per Share	1.26	10.93	5.83	9.37	9.36	12.07	...
Dividends Per Share	1.820	1.720	1.600	1.500	0.375	0.700	0.525
Dividend Payout %	54.65	23.43	57.76	...	12.80	21.28	10.54
Income Statement							
Total Revenue	18,289,000	16,285,100	14,859,700	14,171,800	11,381,300	9,895,100	9,545,400
EBITDA	2,640,500	2,218,900	1,952,200	1,340,500	1,477,700	1,338,500	1,274,300
Depn & Amortn	1,074,600	923,800	855,900	848,900	589,800	481,700	461,300
Income Before Taxes	1,134,600	1,001,300	818,600	234,900	755,200	761,500	706,100
Income Taxes	276,800	(874,500)	159,000	89,800	250,500	286,500	(21,800)
Net Income	862,900	1,906,100	708,200	(396,300)	507,100	479,700	727,300
Average Shares	259,100	259,800	255,700	257,900	173,300	146,000	146,100
Balance Sheet							
Current Assets	4,974,300	4,785,100	4,490,900	3,912,600	4,160,400	2,432,500	...
Total Assets	30,156,700	25,360,500	25,089,000	23,038,200	25,356,800	11,039,700	...
Current Liabilities	3,435,100	3,333,300	3,009,800	2,183,000	2,163,200	1,360,500	...
Long-Term Obligations	9,502,300	5,674,500	5,946,100	5,496,300	5,558,300	2,852,100	...
Total Liabilities	18,486,800	13,891,100	14,746,500	13,309,400	13,705,000	6,732,900	...
Stockholders' Equity	11,669,900	11,469,400	10,342,500	9,728,800	11,651,800	4,306,800	...
Shares Outstanding	257,800	253,500	254,500	251,000	257,000	140,000	...
Statistical Record							
Return on Assets %	3.11	7.56	2.94	N.M.	2.79	...	...
Return on Equity %	7.46	17.48	7.06	N.M.	6.36	...	...
EBITDA Margin %	14.44	13.63	13.14	9.46	12.98	13.53	13.35
Net Margin %	4.72	11.70	4.77	N.M.	4.46	4.85	7.62
Asset Turnover	0.66	0.65	0.62	0.58	0.63	...	...
Current Ratio	1.45	1.44	1.49	1.79	1.92	1.79	...
Debt to Equity	0.81	0.49	0.57	0.56	0.48	0.66	...
Price Range	53.60-32.31	70.27-53.44	59.73-45.05	51.93-27.01	58.62-45.07	...	...
P/E Ratio	16.10-9.70	9.57-7.28	21.56-16.26	...	20.01-15.38	...	...
Average Yield %	4.68	2.82	3.00	3.73	0.70	...	...

Address: 1000 Abernathy Road N.E., Atlanta, GA 30328 **Telephone:** 770-448-2193	**Web Site:** www.westrock.com **Officers:** Steven C. (Steve) Voorhees - President, Chief Executive Officer Ward H. Dickson - Executive Vice President, Chief Financial Officer	**Auditors:** Ernst & Young LLP **Investor Contact:** 770-448-2193

WESTWOOD HOLDINGS GROUP, INC.

Exchange	Symbol	Price	52Wk Range	Yield	P/E	Div Achiever
NYS	WHG	$29.62 (12/31/2019)	39.54-27.20	9.72	28.48	16 Years

*7 Year Price Score 51.40   ***NYSE Composite Index=100**   ***12 Month Price Score 88.88**

Interim Earnings (Per Share)
Qtr.	Mar	Jun	Sep	Dec
2016	0.44	0.69	0.72	0.93
2017	0.73	0.83	0.49	0.33
2018	0.93	0.94	0.62	0.64
2019	0.05	0.22	0.13	...

Interim Dividends (Per Share)
Amt	Decl	Ex	Rec	Pay
0.72Q	02/06/2019	03/07/2019	03/08/2019	04/01/2019
0.72Q	04/24/2019	06/06/2019	06/07/2019	07/01/2019
0.72Q	07/31/2019	09/05/2019	09/06/2019	10/01/2019
0.72Q	10/30/2019	12/05/2019	12/06/2019	01/02/2020

Indicated Div: $2.88

Valuation Analysis / Institutional Holding
Forecast EPS	N/A	No of Institutions 125
Market Cap	$263.8 Million	Shares 7,208,460
Book Value	$150.1 Million	% Held
Price/Book	1.76	69.75
Price/Sales	2.88	

Business Summary: Wealth Management (MIC: 5.5.2 SIC: 6282 NAIC: 523930)

Westwood Holdings Group is a holding company. Co. manages investment assets and provides for its clients through its subsidiaries, Westwood Management Corp. and Westwood Advisors, L.L.C. (Westwood Management), Westwood Trust and Westwood International Advisors Inc. (Westwood International Advisors). Westwood Management and Westwood International Advisors provide investment advisory services to institutional clients, a family of mutual funds, other mutual funds, an Irish investment company authorized pursuant to the European Communities, individuals and clients of Westwood Trust, which provides trust and custodial services and participation in self-sponsored common trust funds.

Recent Developments: For the quarter ended Sep 30 2019, net income decreased 79.2% to US$1.1 million from US$5.4 million in the year-earlier quarter. Revenues were US$19.9 million, down 33.4% from US$29.9 million the year before. Operating income was US$1.5 million versus US$7.2 million in the prior-year quarter, a decrease of 78.7%. Indirect operating expenses decreased 19.1% to US$18.4 million from US$22.7 million in the equivalent prior-year period.

Prospects: Our evaluation of Westwood Holdings Group Inc. as of October 4th, 2019 is the result of our systematic analysis on three basic characteristics: earnings strength, relative valuation, and recent stock price movement. The company has suffered a very negative trend in earnings per share over the past 5 quarters. However, recent analyst estimates for the company have been mixed and WHG has posted results that fell short of analysts' expectations. Based on operating earnings yield, the company is fairly valued when compared to all of the companies we cover. Share price changes over the past year indicates that WHG will perform poorly over the near term.

Financial Data
(US$ in Thousands)	9 Mos	6 Mos	3 Mos	12/31/2018	12/31/2017	12/31/2016	12/31/2015	12/31/2014
Earnings Per Share	1.04	1.53	2.25	3.13	2.38	2.77	3.33	3.45
Cash Flow Per Share	5.93	5.23	4.87	3.76	5.89	5.94	7.12	3.53
Tang Book Value Per Share	12.86	13.24	13.45	14.08	12.30	11.07	9.67	11.47
Dividends Per Share	2.880	2.840	2.800	2.760	2.540	2.330	2.070	1.820
Dividend Payout %	276.92	185.62	124.44	88.18	106.72	84.12	62.16	52.75
Income Statement								
Total Revenue	65,463	45,571	23,862	122,300	133,785	123,021	130,936	113,241
EBITDA	7,654	5,413	2,121	39,001	36,809	36,939	44,816	42,974
Depn & Amortn	1,943	1,261	625	2,539	2,916	2,929	2,596	938
Income Before Taxes	5,711	4,152	1,496	36,462	33,893	34,010	42,220	42,036
Income Taxes	2,341	1,899	1,104	9,711	13,904	11,363	15,115	14,787
Net Income	3,370	2,253	392	26,751	19,989	22,647	27,105	27,249
Average Shares	8,470	8,476	8,455	8,547	8,400	8,165	8,149	7,906
Balance Sheet								
Current Assets	117,661	121,094	122,071	139,739	138,114	115,957	117,604	118,764
Total Assets	177,313	179,486	181,149	190,485	192,659	179,678	181,336	139,874
Current Liabilities	17,996	16,016	15,342	25,695	31,531	29,668	44,853	27,204
Total Liabilities	27,254	25,500	25,039	29,336	36,263	33,609	47,369	29,867
Stockholders' Equity	150,059	153,986	156,110	161,149	156,396	146,069	133,967	110,007
Shares Outstanding	8,906	8,944	8,975	8,904	8,899	8,810	8,630	8,308
Statistical Record								
Return on Assets %	4.75	7.17	10.76	13.96	10.74	12.51	16.88	21.30
Return on Equity %	5.58	8.27	12.28	16.85	13.22	16.13	22.22	27.44
EBITDA Margin %	11.69	11.88	8.89	31.89	27.51	30.03	34.23	37.95
Net Margin %	5.15	4.94	1.64	21.87	14.94	18.41	20.70	24.06
Asset Turnover	0.50	0.56	0.63	0.64	0.72	0.68	0.82	0.89
Current Ratio	6.54	7.56	7.96	5.44	4.38	3.91	2.62	4.37
Price Range	51.29-27.20	61.47-28.33	61.47-33.15	69.62-33.15	70.84-51.60	63.60-42.20	64.07-50.37	67.84-51.72
P/E Ratio	49.32-26.15	40.18-18.52	27.32-14.73	22.24-10.59	29.76-21.68	22.96-15.23	19.24-15.13	19.66-14.99
Average Yield %	8.18	6.76	5.76	5.08	4.26	4.30	3.55	3.09

Address: 200 Crescent Court, Suite 1200, Dallas, TX 75201 **Telephone:** 214-756-6900	**Web Site:** www.westwoodgroup.com **Officers:** Richard M. Frank - Chairman Susan M. Byrne - Vice-Chairman, Chief Investment Officer	**Auditors:** DELOITTE & TOUCHE LLP **Investor Contact:** 214-756-6900 **Transfer Agents:** American Stock Transfer & Trust Company, Brooklyn, NY

WEX INC

Exchange	Symbol	Price	52Wk Range	Yield	P/E
NYS	WEX	$209.46 (12/31/2019)	221.02-134.58	N/A	135.14

*7 Year Price Score 131.29 *NYSE Composite Index=100 *12 Month Price Score 98.25

TRADING VOLUME (thousand shares)

Interim Earnings (Per Share)

Qtr.	Mar	Jun	Sep	Dec
2016	0.59	0.32	0.46	0.10
2017	0.68	0.40	0.79	1.85
2018	1.12	0.90	1.31	0.53
2019	0.37	0.32	0.33	...

Interim Dividends (Per Share)

No Dividends Paid

Valuation Analysis

		Institutional Holding	
Forecast EPS	$9.15	No of Institutions	
	(01/09/2020)	470	
Market Cap	$9.1 Billion	Shares	
Book Value	$1.8 Billion	55,071,836	
Price/Book	4.92	% Held	
Price/Sales	5.44	N/A	

Business Summary: Business Services (MIC: 7.5.2 SIC: 7389 NAIC: 561499)

Wex is a provider of corporate card payment solutions. Co. operates in three business segments: Fleet Solutions, which provides payment, transaction processing and information management services specifically designed for the needs of commercial and government fleets; Travel and Corporate Solutions, which focuses on the payment environment of business-to-business customers, providing customers with payment processing solutions for their corporate payment and transaction monitoring needs; and Health and Employee Benefit Solutions, which provides a software-as-a-service platform for consumer directed healthcare payments, as well as payroll related benefits to customers in Brazil.

Recent Developments: For the quarter ended Sep 30 2019, net income decreased 25.0% to US$42.4 million from US$56.6 million in the year-earlier quarter. Revenues were US$460.0 million, up 19.0% from US$386.6 million in the prior-year quarter. Operating income was US$118.3 million versus US$102.6 million in the prior-year quarter, an increase of 15.4%. Direct operating expenses rose 12.8% to US$165.7 million from US$146.8 million in the comparable period the year before. Indirect operating expenses increased 28.2% to US$176.0 million from US$137.2 million in the equivalent prior-year period.

Prospects: Our evaluation of Wex Inc. as of October 4th, 2019 is the result of our systematic analysis on three basic characteristics: earnings strength, relative valuation, and recent stock price movement. The company has enjoyed a very positive trend in earnings per share over the past 5 quarters. In addition, recent analyst estimates for the company have been raised, and WEX has posted results that exceeded analysts' expectations. Based on operating earnings yield, the company is fairly valued when compared to all of the companies we cover. Share price changes over the past year indicates that WEX will perform well over the near term.

Financial Data

(US$ in Thousands)	9 Mos	6 Mos	3 Mos	12/31/2018	12/31/2017	12/31/2016	12/31/2015	12/31/2014
Earnings Per Share	1.55	2.53	3.11	3.86	3.72	1.48	2.62	5.18
Cash Flow Per Share	9.74	12.87	8.91	9.27	3.09	(3.69)	11.48	7.62
Income Statement								
Total Revenue	1,283,646	823,683	381,876	1,492,639	1,250,548	1,018,460	854,637	817,647
EBITDA	203,625	113,828	44,634	438,419	406,901	241,137	273,613	378,456
Depn & Amortn	75,767	47,554	22,608	199,800	203,724	141,650	83,077	70,380
Income Before Taxes	127,858	66,274	22,026	238,619	178,695	87,101	184,908	301,639
Income Taxes	37,352	18,215	5,818	68,843	19,525	29,625	75,296	101,621
Net Income	44,560	29,941	16,134	168,295	160,266	60,637	111,317	202,211
Average Shares	43,811	43,761	43,572	43,574	43,105	40,914	38,843	39,000
Balance Sheet								
Current Assets	4,054,458	4,307,735	3,645,164	3,398,126	3,186,147	2,353,813	1,881,325	2,198,131
Total Assets	8,541,306	8,573,149	7,955,242	6,770,595	6,739,175	5,997,097	3,857,946	4,118,347
Current Liabilities	3,113,314	3,037,054	2,616,428	2,311,571	2,429,514	2,067,520	1,408,241	1,542,736
Long-Term Obligations	2,700,649	2,764,800	2,809,361	2,133,923	2,424,971	2,204,903	1,201,819	1,354,539
Total Liabilities	6,698,882	6,740,184	6,148,617	4,984,898	5,027,837	4,499,908	2,774,702	3,058,022
Stockholders' Equity	1,842,424	1,832,965	1,806,625	1,785,697	1,711,338	1,497,189	1,083,244	1,060,325
Shares Outstanding	43,289	43,273	43,246	43,129	43,022	42,841	38,746	38,897
Statistical Record								
Return on Assets %	0.86	1.42	1.85	2.49	2.52	1.23	2.79	5.36
Return on Equity %	3.67	6.10	7.61	9.63	9.99	4.69	10.39	20.60
EBITDA Margin %	15.86	13.82	11.69	29.37	32.54	23.68	32.02	46.29
Net Margin %	3.47	3.64	4.22	11.27	12.82	5.95	13.03	24.73
Asset Turnover	0.21	0.20	0.21	0.22	0.20	0.21	0.21	0.22
Current Ratio	1.30	1.42	1.39	1.47	1.31	1.14	1.34	1.42
Debt to Equity	1.47	1.51	1.56	1.20	1.42	1.47	1.11	1.28
Price Range	221.02-131.35	210.30-131.35	200.76-131.35	200.76-131.35	141.23-98.27	116.44-58.09	118.50-84.66	118.43-79.93
P/E Ratio	142.59-84.74	83.12-51.92	64.55-42.23	52.01-34.03	37.97-26.42	78.68-39.25	45.23-32.31	22.86-15.43

Address: 1 Hancock Street, Portland, ME 04101 Telephone: 207-773-8171	Web Site: www.wexinc.com Officers: Michael E. Dubyak - Chairman, President, Chief Executive Officer Roland T. Moriarty - Vice-Chairman	Auditors: DELOITTE & TOUCHE LLP Investor Contact: 866-230-1633 Transfer Agents: American Stock Transfer & Trust Company, Brooklyn, NY

WEYERHAEUSER CO

Exchange	Symbol	Price	52Wk Range	Yield	P/E
NYS	WY	$30.20 (12/31/2019)	30.20-21.53	4.50	N/A

*7 Year Price Score 70.50 *NYSE Composite Index=100 *12 Month Price Score 105.97

Interim Earnings (Per Share)

Qtr.	Mar	Jun	Sep	Dec
2016	0.11	0.21	0.30	0.75
2017	0.21	0.03	0.17	0.36
2018	0.35	0.42	0.34	(0.12)
2019	(0.39)	0.17	0.13	...

Interim Dividends (Per Share)

Amt	Decl	Ex	Rec	Pay
0.34Q	02/07/2019	02/28/2019	03/01/2019	03/22/2019
0.34Q	05/17/2019	06/06/2019	06/07/2019	06/21/2019
0.34Q	08/15/2019	09/05/2019	09/06/2019	09/20/2019
0.34Q	11/08/2019	12/05/2019	12/06/2019	12/20/2019

Indicated Div: $1.36

Valuation Analysis / **Institutional Holding**

Forecast EPS	$0.40 (01/17/2020)	No of Institutions	1249
Market Cap	$22.5 Billion	Shares	
Book Value	$8.6 Billion		708,350,144
Price/Book	2.62	% Held	75.40
Price/Sales	3.39		

Business Summary: REITs (MIC: 5.3.1 SIC: 6798 NAIC: 525930)

Weyerhaeuser is a real estate investment trust. Co.'s business segments are: Timberlands, which provides delivered logs (grade logs and fiber logs), timber, recreational leases and other products; Real Estate, Energy and Natural Resources (ENR), in which Real Estate sells timberland tracts for recreational, conservation, commercial or residential purposes, whereas ENR sells rights to explore and extract construction aggregates (rock, sand and gravel), coal, industrial materials and oil and natural gas for sale into energy markets; and Wood Products, which provides structural lumber, oriented strand board, wood products, other products, and complementary building products.

Recent Developments: For the quarter ended Sep 30 2019, net income decreased 61.2% to US$99.0 million from US$255.0 million in the year-earlier quarter. Revenues were US$1.67 billion, down 12.5% from US$1.91 billion the year before.

Prospects: Our evaluation of Weyerhaeuser Co. as of October 4th, 2019 is the result of our systematic analysis on three basic characteristics: earnings strength, relative valuation, and recent stock price movement. The company has produced a positive trend in earnings per share over the past 5 quarters. However, recent analyst estimates for the company have been mixed and WY has posted results that exceeded analysts' expectations. Based on operating earnings yield, the company is overvalued when compared to all of the companies we cover. Share price changes over the past year indicates that WY will perform poorly over the near term.

Financial Data

(US$ in Thousands)	9 Mos	6 Mos	3 Mos	12/31/2018	12/31/2017	12/31/2016	12/31/2015	12/31/2014
Earnings Per Share	(0.21)	...	0.25	0.99	0.77	1.39	0.89	3.18
Cash Flow Per Share	1.30	1.02	1.29	1.47	1.59	1.02	2.06	1.95
Tang Book Value Per Share	11.54	11.71	11.82	12.12	11.73	12.21	9.43	10.01
Dividends Per Share	1.360	1.360	1.340	1.320	1.250	1.240	1.200	1.020
Dividend Payout %	...	...	536.00	133.33	162.34	89.21	134.83	32.08
Income Statement								
Total Revenue	5,006,000	3,335,000	1,643,000	7,476,000	7,196,000	6,365,000	7,082,000	7,403,000
EBITDA	449,000	127,000	(173,000)	1,319,000	1,275,000	1,068,000	1,233,000	1,820,000
Depn & Amortn	382,000	247,000	123,000	197,000	206,000	198,000	314,000	500,000
Income Before Taxes	(200,000)	(302,000)	(393,000)	807,000	715,000	482,000	608,000	1,013,000
Income Taxes	(138,000)	(141,000)	(104,000)	59,000	134,000	89,000	(3,000)	185,000
Net Income	(62,000)	(161,000)	(289,000)	748,000	582,000	1,027,000	506,000	1,826,000
Average Shares	746,514	746,232	746,603	756,827	756,666	722,401	519,618	560,899
Balance Sheet								
Current Assets	1,817,000	1,696,000	1,774,000	1,602,000	1,715,000	1,622,000	2,174,000	3,033,000
Total Assets	16,832,000	17,029,000	17,132,000	17,249,000	18,059,000	19,243,000	12,486,000	13,457,000
Current Liabilities	1,169,000	1,223,000	1,201,000	1,939,000	1,165,000	1,206,000	875,000	918,000
Long-Term Obligations	6,150,000	6,153,000	6,156,000	5,419,000	6,232,000	6,840,000	5,402,000	5,402,000
Total Liabilities	8,233,000	8,305,000	8,331,000	8,203,000	9,160,000	10,063,000	7,617,000	8,153,000
Stockholders' Equity	8,599,000	8,724,000	8,801,000	9,046,000	8,899,000	9,180,000	4,869,000	5,304,000
Shares Outstanding	745,071	744,905	744,767	746,391	755,222	748,528	510,483	524,474
Statistical Record								
Return on Assets %	N.M.	0.01	1.09	4.24	3.12	6.46	3.90	13.06
Return on Equity %	N.M.	0.01	2.14	8.34	6.44	14.58	9.95	30.18
EBITDA Margin %	8.97	3.81	N.M.	17.64	17.72	16.78	17.41	24.58
Net Margin %	N.M.	N.M.	N.M.	10.01	8.09	16.14	7.14	24.67
Asset Turnover	0.39	0.39	0.41	0.42	0.39	0.40	0.55	0.53
Current Ratio	1.55	1.39	1.48	0.83	1.47	1.34	2.48	3.30
Debt to Equity	0.72	0.71	0.70	0.60	0.70	0.75	1.11	1.02
Price Range	31.98-21.10	37.27-21.10	38.36-21.10	38.36-21.10	36.55-30.21	33.12-22.22	36.69-26.87	36.64-27.72
P/E Ratio	...	N.M.	153.44-84.40	38.75-21.31	47.47-39.23	23.83-15.99	41.22-30.19	11.52-8.72
Average Yield %	5.26	4.85	4.34	3.96	3.72	4.13	3.79	3.20

Address: 220 Occidental Avenue South, Seattle, WA 98104-7800 **Telephone:** 206-539-3000	**Web Site:** www.weyerhaeuser.com **Officers:** Rick R. Holley - Chairman Devin W. Stockfish - President, Chief Executive Officer, Senior Vice President, General Counsel, Secretary, Division Officer	**Auditors:** KPMG LLP **Investor Contact:** 253-924-2058 **Transfer Agents:** Computershare Investor Services, Canton, MA

WHIRLPOOL CORP

Exchange	Symbol	Price	52Wk Range	Yield	P/E
NYS	WHR	$147.53 (12/31/2019)	162.16-106.87	3.25	9.01

*7 Year Price Score 74.39   *NYSE Composite Index=100   *12 Month Price Score 100.27

TRADING VOLUME (thousand shares)

Interim Earnings (Per Share)

Qtr.	Mar	Jun	Sep	Dec
2016	1.92	4.15	3.10	2.34
2017	2.01	2.52	3.72	(3.53)
2018	1.30	(9.50)	3.22	2.46
2019	7.31	1.04	5.57	...

Interim Dividends (Per Share)

Amt	Decl	Ex	Rec	Pay
1.15Q	02/19/2019	02/28/2019	03/01/2019	03/15/2019
1.20Q	04/15/2019	05/16/2019	05/17/2019	06/15/2019
1.20Q	08/20/2019	08/29/2019	08/30/2019	09/15/2019
1.20Q	10/14/2019	11/14/2019	11/15/2019	12/15/2019

Indicated Div: $4.80

Valuation Analysis

Forecast EPS	$15.37
	(01/17/2020)
Market Cap	$9.3 Billion
Book Value	$3.0 Billion
Price/Book	3.07
Price/Sales	0.45

Institutional Holding

No of Institutions	847
Shares	80,670,968
% Held	83.44

Business Summary: Household Appliances, Electronics & Goods (MIC: 1.5.1 SIC: 3639 NAIC: 335228)

Whirlpool is a home appliance company. Co. manufactures and markets a line of home appliances and related products. Co.'s principal products are laundry appliances, refrigerators and freezers, cooking appliances, dishwashers, mixers and other small domestic appliances. Co. also produces hermetic compressors for refrigeration systems. Co. manufactures and markets products under brand names such as Whirlpool, KitchenAid, Maytag, Consul, Brastemp, Amana, Bauknecht, JennAir, Indesit and Hotpoint. Co.'s operating segments consist of North America, Europe, Middle East and Africa, Latin America and Asia.

Recent Developments: For the quarter ended June 30 2019, net income amounted to US$72.0 million versus a net loss of US$639.0 million in the year-earlier quarter. Revenues were US$5.19 billion, up 0.9% from US$5.14 billion the year before. Operating income was US$191.0 million versus a loss of US$472.0 million in the prior-year quarter. Direct operating expenses declined 0.1% to US$4.25 billion from US$4.26 billion in the comparable period the year before. Indirect operating expenses decreased 45.2% to US$741.0 million from US$1.35 billion in the equivalent prior-year period.

Prospects: Our evaluation of Whirlpool Corp. as of October 4th, 2019 is the result of our systematic analysis on three basic characteristics: earnings strength, relative valuation, and recent stock price movement. The company has managed to produce a neutral trend in earnings per share over the past 5 quarters. In addition, recent analyst estimates for the company have been mixed and WHR has posted results that exceeded analysts' expectations. Based on operating earnings yield, the company is undervalued when compared to all of the companies we cover. Share price changes over the past year indicates that WHR will perform in line with the market over the near term.

Financial Data
(US$ in Thousands)

	9 Mos	6 Mos	3 Mos	12/31/2018	12/31/2017	12/31/2016	12/31/2015	12/31/2014
Earnings Per Share	16.38	14.03	3.49	(2.72)	4.70	11.50	9.83	8.17
Cash Flow Per Share	20.09	15.55	16.36	18.29	17.24	15.76	15.57	18.89
Dividends Per Share	4.700	4.650	4.600	4.550	4.300	3.900	3.450	2.875
Dividend Payout %	28.69	33.14	131.81	...	91.49	33.91	35.10	35.19
Income Statement								
Total Revenue	15,037,000	9,946,000	4,760,000	21,037,000	21,253,000	20,718,000	20,891,000	19,872,000
EBITDA	1,643,000	792,000	281,000	924,000	1,790,000	2,009,000	1,953,000	1,748,000
Depn & Amortn	496,000	338,000	18,000	645,000	654,000	655,000	668,000	560,000
Income Before Taxes	1,221,000	544,000	342,000	(21,000)	887,000	1,114,000	1,031,000	881,000
Income Taxes	311,000	(2,000)	(132,000)	138,000	550,000	186,000	209,000	189,000
Net Income	896,000	538,000	471,000	(183,000)	350,000	888,000	783,000	650,000
Average Shares	64,200	64,300	64,500	67,200	74,400	77,200	79,700	79,600
Balance Sheet								
Current Assets	7,375,000	8,503,000	8,236,000	7,898,000	7,930,000	7,339,000	7,325,000	8,098,000
Total Assets	18,406,000	19,855,000	19,686,000	18,347,000	20,038,000	19,153,000	19,010,000	20,002,000
Current Liabilities	8,500,000	10,094,000	9,878,000	9,678,000	8,505,000	7,662,000	7,744,000	8,403,000
Long-Term Obligations	4,105,000	4,155,000	4,137,000	4,046,000	4,392,000	3,876,000	3,470,000	3,544,000
Total Liabilities	15,378,000	17,106,000	16,884,000	16,056,000	15,840,000	14,380,000	14,267,000	15,117,000
Stockholders' Equity	3,028,000	2,749,000	2,802,000	2,291,000	4,198,000	4,773,000	4,743,000	4,885,000
Shares Outstanding	63,000	63,000	63,000	64,000	71,000	74,465	77,221	77,956
Statistical Record								
Return on Assets %	5.69	4.72	0.97	N.M.	1.79	4.64	4.01	3.66
Return on Equity %	39.57	35.67	5.47	N.M.	7.80	18.61	16.27	13.25
EBITDA Margin %	10.93	7.96	5.90	4.39	8.42	9.70	9.35	8.80
Net Margin %	5.96	5.41	9.89	N.M.	1.65	4.29	3.75	3.27
Asset Turnover	1.10	1.08	1.04	1.10	1.08	1.08	1.07	1.12
Current Ratio	0.87	0.84	0.83	0.82	0.93	0.96	0.95	0.96
Debt to Equity	1.36	1.51	1.48	1.77	1.05	0.81	0.73	0.73
Price Range	158.36-101.72	155.77-101.72	164.95-101.72	185.97-101.72	198.34-160.94	192.38-127.21	215.00-142.27	193.74-126.69
P/E Ratio	9.67-6.21	11.10-7.25	47.26-29.15	...	42.20-34.24	16.73-11.06	21.87-14.47	23.71-15.51
Average Yield %	3.59	3.63	3.47	3.23	2.43	2.33	1.93	1.88

Address: 2000 North M-63, Benton Harbor, MI 49022-2692 **Telephone:** 269-923-5000	**Web Site:** www.whirlpoolcorp.com **Officers:** Marc R. Bitzer - Chairman, Vice-Chairman, President, Chief Executive Officer, Chief Operating Officer, Region Officer James W. Peters - Executive Vice President, Chief Financial Officer, Corporate Controller, Vice President	**Auditors:** Ernst & Young LLP **Investor Contact:** 269-923-2641 **Transfer Agents:** Computershare Trust Company, N.A., Providence, RI

WHITE MOUNTAINS INSURANCE GROUP LTD

Exchange	Symbol	Price	52Wk Range	Yield	P/E
NYS	WTM	$1116 (12/31/2019)	1129.11-850.75	0.09	15.78

*7 Year Price Score 106.52 ***NYSE Composite Index=100** ***12 Month Price Score 103.24**

TRADING VOLUME (thousand shares)

Interim Earnings (Per Share)

Qtr.	Mar	Jun	Sep	Dec
2016	2.34	66.79	18.80	(3.94)
2017	7.50	3.39	130.81	11.00
2018	(12.82)	1.02	12.83	(40.68)
2019	89.64	6.44	15.29	...

Interim Dividends (Per Share)

Amt	Decl	Ex	Rec	Pay
1.00A	02/26/2016	03/17/2016	03/21/2016	03/30/2016
1.00A	03/02/2017	03/16/2017	03/20/2017	03/29/2017
1.00A	03/02/2018	03/16/2018	03/19/2018	03/28/2018
1.00A	03/01/2019	03/15/2019	03/18/2019	03/27/2019

Indicated Div: $1.00

Valuation Analysis | **Institutional Holding**

Forecast EPS	N/A	No of Institutions
		348
Market Cap	$3.6 Billion	Shares
Book Value	$3.2 Billion	3,772,151
Price/Book	1.11	% Held
Price/Sales	4.91	72.59

Business Summary: General Insurance (MIC: 5.2.1 SIC: 6331 NAIC: 524126)

White Mountains Insurance Group is an insurance holding company. Through its subsidiaries, Co. conducts its business in municipal bond insurance, specialty insurance distribution, marketing technology (for insurance and other verticals) and other operations areas. Co.'s municipal bond insurance business is conducted through its subsidiary HG Global Ltd. and its reinsurance subsidiary HG Re Ltd., (collectively, HG Global). HG Global funds the startup of and provides reinsurance to Build America Mutual Assurance Company, a mutual municipal bond insurance company. Co.'s specialty insurance distribution business is conducted through its subsidiary NSM Insurance HoldCo, LLC.

Recent Developments: For the quarter ended Sep 30 2019, income from continuing operations decreased 11.7% to US$42.3 million from US$47.9 million in the year-earlier quarter. Net income increased 41.2% to US$43.2 million from US$30.6 million in the year-earlier quarter. Revenues were US$155.5 million, down 21.7% from US$198.7 million the year before. Net premiums earned were US$5.2 million versus US$3.3 million in the prior-year quarter, an increase of 57.6%. Net investment income rose 37.3% to US$18.4 million from US$13.4 million a year ago.

Prospects: Our evaluation of White Mountains Insurance Group Ltd. as of October 4th, 2019 is the result of our systematic analysis on three basic characteristics: earnings strength, relative valuation, and recent stock price movement. The company has generated a negative trend in earnings per share over the past 5 quarters. However, recent analyst estimates for the company have been unchanged while WTM has posted results that exceeded analysts' expectations. Based on operating earnings yield, the company is overvalued when compared to all of the companies we cover. Share price changes over the past year indicates that WTM will perform well over the near term.

Financial Data
(US$ in Thousands)

	9 Mos	6 Mos	3 Mos	12/31/2018	12/31/2017	12/31/2016	12/31/2015	12/31/2014
Earnings Per Share	70.69	68.23	62.81	(41.76)	146.06	82.19	50.60	51.21
Cash Flow Per Share	(23.27)	(1.24)	(8.76)	(9.30)	22.31	(31.29)	30.23	19.71
Tang Book Value Per Share	795.05	777.53	821.01	726.60	914.73	777.29	629.03	606.43
Dividends Per Share	...	...	...	1.000	1.000	1.000	1.000	1.000
Dividend Payout %	...	...	...	...	0.68	1.22	1.98	1.95
Income Statement								
Premium Income	13,700	8,500	4,200	13,900	10,400	1,114,000	1,188,200	2,058,900
Total Revenue	718,100	562,600	433,600	369,100	373,800	1,360,700	1,808,600	2,510,200
Benefits & Claims	...	...	...	...	1,100	664,000	708,900	1,169,300
Income Before Taxes	348,600	297,500	281,700	(178,200)	7,800	(40,400)	154,900	301,700
Income Taxes	18,900	10,100	10,200	(4,000)	(7,800)	(45,400)	(700)	53,300
Net Income	353,600	304,900	284,400	(141,200)	627,200	412,500	297,600	312,700
Average Shares	3,142	3,140	3,139	3,342	4,239	4,953	5,811	6,026
Balance Sheet								
Total Assets	3,836,300	3,752,200	3,629,700	3,362,600	3,659,200	6,544,700	10,284,500	10,456,900
Total Liabilities	642,900	607,900	507,700	519,500	166,700	2,941,400	6,371,300	6,460,300
Stockholders' Equity	3,193,400	3,144,300	3,122,000	2,843,100	3,492,500	3,603,300	3,913,200	3,996,600
Shares Outstanding	3,185	3,185	3,181	3,173	3,750	4,563	5,623	5,986
Statistical Record								
Return on Assets %	5.95	5.85	5.30	N.M.	12.29	4.89	2.87	2.77
Return on Equity %	7.00	6.84	5.83	N.M.	17.68	10.95	7.52	7.91
Loss Ratio %	...	...	...	...	10.58	59.61	59.66	56.79
Net Margin %	49.24	54.19	65.59	(38.26)	167.79	30.32	16.45	12.46
Price Range	1093.91-834.13	1038.20-834.13	979.01-806.17	979.01-789.05	947.00-839.51	868.00-699.47	808.00-618.00	674.71-559.26
P/E Ratio	15.47-11.80	15.22-12.23	15.59-12.84	...	6.48-5.75	10.56-8.51	15.97-12.21	13.18-10.92
Average Yield %	...	...	...	0.11	0.11	0.12	0.14	0.16

Address: 26 Reid Street, Hamilton, HM 11
Telephone: 441-278-3160
Fax: 441-278-3170

Web Site: www.whitemountains.com
Officers: Morgan W. Davis - Chairman George
Manning Rountree - Chief Executive Officer

Auditors: PricewaterhouseCoopers LLP
Investor Contact: 203-458-5850
Transfer Agents: Computershare Trust Company, N.A., Providence, RI, United States

WHITING PETROLEUM CORP

Exchange	Symbol	Price	52Wk Range	Yield	P/E
NYS	WLL	$7.34 (12/31/2019)	30.35-4.49	N/A	6.17

*7 Year Price Score 13.61   ***NYSE Composite Index=100**   ***12 Month Price Score 34.05**

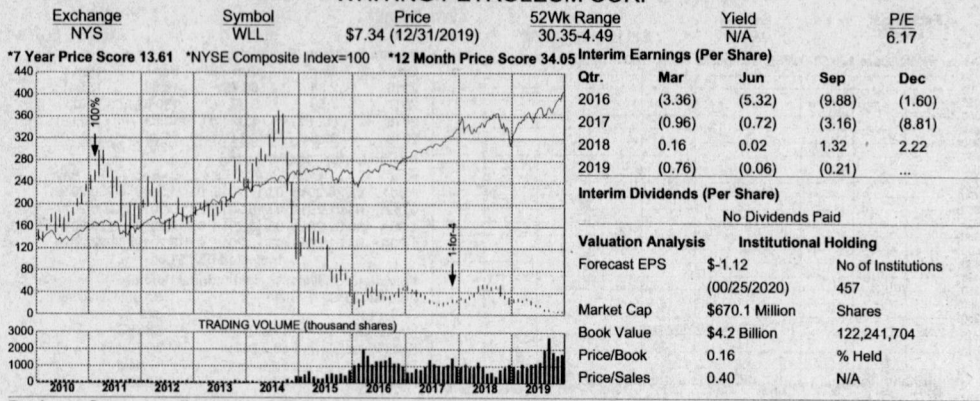

Interim Earnings (Per Share)

Qtr.	Mar	Jun	Sep	Dec
2016	(3.36)	(5.32)	(9.88)	(1.60)
2017	(0.96)	(0.72)	(3.16)	(8.81)
2018	0.16	0.02	1.32	2.22
2019	(0.76)	(0.06)	(0.21)	...

Interim Dividends (Per Share)

No Dividends Paid

Valuation Analysis / Institutional Holding

Valuation Analysis		Institutional Holding	
Forecast EPS	$-1.12	No of Institutions	
	(00/25/2020)	457	
Market Cap	$670.1 Million	Shares	
Book Value	$4.2 Billion	122,241,704	
Price/Book	0.16	% Held	
Price/Sales	0.40	N/A	

Business Summary: Production & Extraction (MIC: 9.1.1 SIC: 1311 NAIC: 211111)

Whiting Petroleum is an independent oil and gas company engaged in development, production, acquisition, and exploration activities primarily in the Rocky Mountains region of the U.S. Co.'s existing operations and capital programs are focused on organic drilling activities and on the development of previously acquired properties, while selectively pursuing acquisitions that complement its existing properties. Co. principally sells its oil and gas production to end users, marketers and other purchasers that have access to nearby pipeline or rail takeaway. In areas with no access to gathering pipelines, oil is trucked or transported to terminals, market hubs, refineries or storage facilities.

Recent Developments: For the quarter ended Sep 30 2019, net loss amounted to US$19.1 million versus net income of US$121.4 million in the year-earlier quarter. Revenues were US$375.9 million, down 33.7% from US$566.7 million the year before. Operating income was US$24.6 million versus US$169.4 million in the prior-year quarter, a decrease of 85.5%. Direct operating expenses rose 14.2% to US$85.3 million from US$74.7 million in the comparable period the year before. Indirect operating expenses decreased 17.6% to US$265.9 million from US$322.6 million in the equivalent prior-year period.

Prospects: Our evaluation of Whiting Petroleum Corp. as of October 4th, 2019 is the result of our systematic analysis on three basic characteristics: earnings strength, relative valuation, and recent stock price movement. The company has suffered a very negative trend in earnings per share over the past 5 quarters. In addition, recent analyst estimates for the company have been reduced and WLL has posted results that fell short of analysts' expectations. Based on operating earnings yield, the company is overvalued when compared to all of the companies we cover. Share price changes over the past year indicates that WLL will perform very poorly over the near term.

Financial Data

(US$ in Thousands)	9 Mos	6 Mos	3 Mos	12/31/2018	12/31/2017	12/31/2016	12/31/2015	12/31/2014
Earnings Per Share	1.19	2.72	2.80	3.73	(13.65)	(21.28)	(45.40)	2.12
Cash Flow Per Share	8.83	10.19	11.04	12.01	6.36	9.42	21.51	59.45
Tang Book Value Per Share	45.67	46.01	46.04	46.92	43.21	56.81	93.08	115.51
Income Statement								
Total Revenue	1,191,644	815,753	389,489	2,081,414	1,481,435	1,284,982	2,050,798	3,085,097
EBITDA	70,030	36,740	(39,170)	547,836	(1,522,017)	(860,671)	(2,649,706)	320,051
Depn & Amortn	20,910	16,856	6,827	6,495	7,536	8,479	9,664	5,494
Income Before Taxes	(95,052)	(75,985)	(93,780)	343,867	(1,720,641)	(1,426,770)	(2,993,495)	143,915
Income Taxes	(1,373)	(1,373)	(24,855)	1,373	(482,979)	(87,646)	(774,227)	79,170
Net Income	(93,679)	(74,612)	(68,925)	342,494	(1,237,648)	(1,339,102)	(2,219,182)	64,807
Average Shares	91,299	91,286	91,235	91,869	90,683	62,967	48,868	30,629
Balance Sheet								
Current Assets	355,314	343,050	305,036	398,426	1,189,628	622,602	535,190	842,999
Total Assets	7,774,881	7,775,726	7,751,795	7,759,573	8,403,034	9,876,142	11,389,085	14,019,504
Current Liabilities	806,513	1,094,916	527,797	536,931	1,553,328	478,331	599,813	1,208,516
Long-Term Obligations	2,605,023	2,303,864	2,839,402	2,792,321	2,764,716	3,535,303	5,197,704	5,628,782
Total Liabilities	3,604,924	3,575,099	3,549,446	3,489,257	4,483,892	4,734,912	6,638,481	8,324,530
Stockholders' Equity	4,169,957	4,200,627	4,202,349	4,270,316	3,919,142	5,141,230	4,750,604	5,694,974
Shares Outstanding	91,299	91,298	91,279	91,018	90,698	90,503	51,036	41,722
Statistical Record								
Return on Assets %	1.42	3.27	3.38	4.24	N.M.	N.M.	N.M.	0.57
Return on Equity %	2.68	6.16	6.35	8.36	N.M.	N.M.	N.M.	1.36
EBITDA Margin %	5.88	4.50	N.M.	26.32	N.M.	N.M.	N.M.	10.37
Net Margin %	N.M.	N.M.	N.M.	16.45	N.M.	N.M.	N.M.	2.10
Asset Turnover	0.22	0.24	0.26	0.26	0.16	0.12	0.16	0.27
Current Ratio	0.44	0.31	0.58	0.74	0.77	1.30	0.89	0.70
Debt to Equity	0.62	0.55	0.68	0.65	0.71	0.69	1.09	0.99
Price Range	54.51-6.27	54.51-15.89	55.46-18.89	55.46-18.89	52.40-16.00	55.40-14.12	163.80-33.24	370.64-100.16
P/E Ratio	45.81-5.27	20.04-5.84	19.81-6.75	14.87-5.06	...	...	...	174.83-47.25

Address: 1700 Lincoln Street, Suite 4700, Denver, CO 80203-4547	Web Site: www.whiting.com	Auditors: DELOITTE & TOUCHE LLP
Telephone: 303-837-1661	Officers: Bradley J. Holly - Chairman, President, Chief Executive Officer Peter W. Hagist - Senior Vice President, Vice President	Investor Contact: 303-390-4051
Fax: 303-861-4023		

WILEY (JOHN) & SONS INC.

Exchange	Symbol	Price	52Wk Range	Yield	P/E	Div Acheiver
NYS	JW A	$48.52 (12/31/2019)	52.68-41.23	2.80	18.95	25 Years

*7 Year Price Score 72.65 *NYSE Composite Index=100 *12 Month Price Score 97.31

Interim Earnings (Per Share)

Qtr.	Jul	Oct	Jan	Apr
2016-17	0.53	(0.20)	0.82	0.80
2017-18	0.16	1.06	1.19	0.93
2018-19	0.45	0.76	0.61	1.10
2019-20	0.06	0.79	...	...

Interim Dividends (Per Share)

Amt	Decl	Ex	Rec	Pay
0.33Q	03/21/2019	04/01/2019	04/02/2019	04/17/2019
0.34Q	06/28/2019	07/09/2019	07/10/2019	07/24/2019
0.34Q	09/25/2019	10/07/2019	10/08/2019	10/23/2019
0.34Q	12/19/2019	12/31/2019	01/02/2020	01/16/2020

Indicated Div: $1.36

Valuation Analysis | **Institutional Holding**

Forecast EPS	$2.42	No of Institutions	381
	(01/16/2020)		
Market Cap	$2.7 Billion	Shares	53,756,968
Book Value	$1.2 Billion		
Price/Book	2.31	% Held	72.06
Price/Sales	1.49		

Business Summary: Publishing (MIC: 2.3.3 SIC: 2731 NAIC: 511130)

John Wiley & Sons is a research and learning company. Co.'s segments are: Research, which provides scientific, technical, medical, and scholarly journals, as well as related content and services, to academic, corporate, and government libraries, learned societies, and individual researchers; Publishing, which acquires, develops and publishes scientific, professional and education books and related content, as well as test preparation services and course workflow tools, to libraries, corporations, students, and researchers; and Solutions, which provides online program management services for higher education institutions and learning, development, and assessment services for businesses.

Recent Developments: For the quarter ended Oct 31 2019, net income increased 2.1% to US$44.7 million from US$43.8 million in the year-earlier quarter. Revenues were US$466.2 million, up 3.9% from US$448.6 million the year before. Operating income was US$63.4 million versus US$57.5 million in the prior-year quarter, an increase of 10.3%. Direct operating expenses rose 8.2% to US$143.4 million from US$132.6 million in the comparable period the year before. Indirect operating expenses increased 0.3% to US$259.4 million from US$258.6 million in the equivalent prior-year period.

Prospects: Our evaluation of Wiley (John) & Sons Inc. as of October 4th, 2019 is the result of our systematic analysis on three basic characteristics: earnings strength, relative valuation, and recent stock price movement. The company has generated a negative trend in earnings per share over the past 5 quarters. In addition, recent analyst estimates for the company have been reduced and JW.A has posted results that fell short of analysts' expectations. Based on operating earnings yield, the company is undervalued when compared to all of the companies we cover. Share price changes over the past year indicates that JW.A will perform in line with the market over the near term.

Financial Data
(US$ in Thousands)

	6 Mos	3 Mos	04/30/2019	04/30/2018	04/30/2017	04/30/2016	04/30/2015	04/30/2014
Earnings Per Share	2.56	2.53	2.91	3.32	1.95	2.48	2.97	2.70
Cash Flow Per Share	4.84	5.42	4.39	6.69	5.49	6.02	6.05	5.94
Dividends Per Share	1.340	1.330	1.320	1.280	1.240	1.200	1.160	1.000
Dividend Payout %	52.34	52.57	45.36	38.55	63.59	48.39	39.06	37.04
Income Statement								
Total Revenue	889,735	423,530	1,800,069	1,796,103	1,718,530	1,727,037	1,822,440	1,775,195
EBITDA	115,540	30,895	272,631	339,273	322,926	304,777	352,767	309,665
Depn & Amortn	47,606	23,684	54,658	112,557	116,352	116,191	113,286	103,000
Income Before Taxes	60,440	3,967	212,952	213,931	191,116	174,793	225,461	195,534
Income Taxes	12,126	343	44,689	21,745	77,473	29,011	48,593	35,024
Net Income	48,314	3,624	168,263	192,186	113,643	145,782	176,868	160,510
Average Shares	56,664	56,905	57,840	57,888	58,199	58,734	59,594	59,514
Balance Sheet								
Current Assets	447,168	491,183	490,780	479,971	359,735	670,679	740,919	789,662
Total Assets	3,082,771	3,120,073	2,937,002	2,839,451	2,606,217	2,921,096	3,004,243	3,077,365
Current Liabilities	585,642	732,825	870,562	874,311	787,856	781,807	803,683	729,587
Long-Term Obligations	788,360	724,291	478,790	360,000	365,000	605,007	650,090	700,100
Total Liabilities	1,903,775	1,988,067	1,755,655	1,648,894	1,603,080	1,883,990	1,949,203	1,895,117
Stockholders' Equity	1,178,996	1,132,006	1,181,347	1,190,557	1,003,137	1,037,106	1,055,040	1,182,248
Shares Outstanding	56,157	56,468	56,630	57,410	57,167	57,564	58,838	59,052
Statistical Record								
Return on Assets %	5.08	4.94	5.83	7.06	4.11	4.91	5.82	5.46
Return on Equity %	12.48	12.63	14.19	17.52	11.14	13.90	15.81	14.79
EBITDA Margin %	12.99	7.29	15.15	18.89	18.79	17.65	19.36	17.44
Net Margin %	5.43	0.86	9.35	10.70	6.61	8.44	9.71	9.04
Asset Turnover	0.64	0.62	0.62	0.66	0.62	0.58	0.60	0.60
Current Ratio	0.76	0.67	0.56	0.55	0.46	0.86	0.92	1.08
Debt to Equity	0.67	0.64	0.41	0.30	0.36	0.58	0.62	0.59
Price Range	56.63-41.23	65.15-41.78	70.80-43.21	67.85-49.75	58.80-48.46	58.66-40.21	65.21-51.45	58.83-38.15
P/E Ratio	22.12-16.11	25.75-16.51	24.33-14.85	20.44-14.98	30.15-24.85	23.65-16.21	21.96-17.32	21.79-14.13
Average Yield %	2.84	2.60	2.34	2.20	2.31	2.40	1.97	2.04

Address: 111 River Street, Hoboken, NJ 07030	**Web Site:** www.wiley.com	**Auditors:** KPMG LLP
Telephone: 201-748-6000	**Officers:** Jesse C. Wiley - Chairman Matthew S. Kissner - Chairman, Interim President, Executive Vice President, Interim Chief Executive Officer, Group Executive	**Investor Contact:** 201-748-6874
		Transfer Agents: Registrar and Transfer Company, Cranford, NJ

WILLIAMS COS INC (THE)

Exchange	Symbol	Price	52Wk Range	Yield	P/E
NYS	WMB	$23.72 (12/31/2019)	29.35-21.95	6.41	N/A

*7 Year Price Score 62.69 *NYSE Composite Index=100 *12 Month Price Score 84.43

Interim Earnings (Per Share)

Qtr.	Mar	Jun	Sep	Dec
2016	(0.09)	(0.54)	0.08	(0.02)
2017	0.45	0.10	0.04	2.03
2018	0.18	0.16	0.13	(0.62)
2019	0.16	0.26	0.18	...

Interim Dividends (Per Share)

Amt	Decl	Ex	Rec	Pay
0.38Q	02/20/2019	03/07/2019	03/08/2019	03/25/2019
0.38Q	05/09/2019	06/06/2019	06/07/2019	06/24/2019
0.38Q	08/14/2019	09/12/2019	09/13/2019	09/30/2019
0.38Q	11/07/2019	12/12/2019	12/13/2019	12/30/2019

Indicated Div: $1.52 (Div. Reinv. Plan)

Valuation Analysis / Institutional Holding

Valuation Analysis		Institutional Holding	
Forecast EPS	$0.99	No of Institutions	
	(01/17/2020)	1265	
Market Cap	$28.7 Billion	Shares	
Book Value	$13.6 Billion	1,208,566,144	
Price/Book	2.11	% Held	
Price/Sales	3.46	86.80	

Business Summary: Equipment & Services (MIC: 9.1.3 SIC: 4922 NAIC: 486210)

Williams Companies is an energy infrastructure company. Co.'s segments include: Northeast G&P, which includes its natural gas gathering, compression, processing, and natural gas liquids (NGLs) fractionation business in the Marcellus and Utica Shale regions; Atlantic-Gulf, which includes natural gas gathering, processing and treating, crude oil production handling, and NGL fractionation assets within the onshore, offshore shelf, and deepwater areas in and around the Gulf Coast states of Texas, Louisiana, Mississippi, and Alabama; and West, which includes natural gas gathering, processing, and treating assets in Colorado, Wyoming, Louisiana, Texas, Arkansas, and Oklahoma.

Recent Developments: For the quarter ended Sep 30 2019, net income increased 21.0% to US$242.0 million from US$200.0 million in the year-earlier quarter. Revenues were US$2.00 billion, down 13.2% from US$2.30 billion the year before. Operating income was US$628.0 million versus US$501.0 million in the prior-year quarter, an increase of 25.3%. Direct operating expenses declined 32.4% to US$817.0 million from US$1.21 billion in the comparable period the year before. Indirect operating expenses decreased 6.6% to US$554.0 million from US$593.0 million in the equivalent prior-year period.

Prospects: Our evaluation of Williams Cos Inc. as of October 4th, 2019 is the result of our systematic analysis on three basic characteristics: earnings strength, relative valuation, and recent stock price movement. The company has produced a positive trend in earnings per share over the past 5 quarters. In addition, recent analyst estimates for the company have been raised, and WMB has posted results that exceeded analysts' expectations. Based on operating earnings yield, the company is fairly valued when compared to all of the companies we cover. Share price changes over the past year indicates that WMB will perform in line with the market over the near term.

Financial Data

(US$ in Thousands)	9 Mos	6 Mos	3 Mos	12/31/2018	12/31/2017	12/31/2016	12/31/2015	12/31/2014
Earnings Per Share	(0.02)	(0.07)	(0.17)	(0.16)	2.62	(0.57)	(0.76)	2.92
Cash Flow Per Share	3.02	2.93	2.79	3.38	3.09	4.87	3.57	2.94
Tang Book Value Per Share	4.58	4.70	5.04	5.67	1.05	N.M.	N.M.	N.M.
Dividends Per Share	1.480	1.440	1.400	1.360	1.200	1.680	2.450	1.958
Dividend Payout %	...	...	...	...	45.80	...	...	67.04
Income Statement								
Total Revenue	6,094,000	4,095,000	2,054,000	8,686,000	8,031,000	7,499,000	7,360,000	7,637,000
EBITDA	1,696,000	1,160,000	513,000	2,471,000	2,573,000	2,244,000	(981,000)	2,610,000
Depn & Amortn	44,000	30,000	14,000	1,392,000	1,389,000	1,407,000	1,382,000	967,000
Income Before Taxes	764,000	538,000	203,000	(33,000)	101,000	(342,000)	(3,407,000)	896,000
Income Taxes	244,000	167,000	69,000	138,000	(1,974,000)	(25,000)	(399,000)	1,249,000
Net Income	726,000	505,000	195,000	(155,000)	2,174,000	(424,000)	(571,000)	2,114,000
Average Shares	1,214,165	1,214,065	1,213,592	973,626	828,518	750,673	749,271	723,641
Balance Sheet								
Current Assets	1,434,000	2,028,000	1,287,000	1,464,000	2,179,000	1,462,000	1,527,000	1,890,000
Total Assets	46,281,000	46,509,000	45,970,000	45,302,000	46,352,000	46,835,000	49,020,000	50,563,000
Current Liabilities	3,324,000	3,389,000	4,169,000	1,811,000	2,646,000	2,949,000	2,497,000	2,567,000
Long-Term Obligations	20,719,000	20,711,000	20,703,000	22,367,000	20,434,000	22,624,000	23,812,000	20,888,000
Total Liabilities	32,660,000	32,661,000	31,564,000	30,642,000	36,696,000	42,192,000	42,872,000	41,786,000
Stockholders' Equity	13,621,000	13,848,000	14,406,000	14,660,000	9,656,000	4,643,000	6,148,000	8,777,000
Shares Outstanding	1,212,000	1,211,000	1,246,000	1,210,000	826,000	750,000	749,000	747,000
Statistical Record								
Return on Assets %	0.33	0.14	N.M.	N.M.	4.67	N.M.	N.M.	5.44
Return on Equity %	1.06	0.54	N.M.	N.M.	30.41	N.M.	N.M.	30.99
EBITDA Margin %	27.83	28.33	24.98	28.45	32.04	29.92	N.M.	34.18
Net Margin %	11.91	12.33	9.49	N.M.	27.07	N.M.	N.M.	27.68
Asset Turnover	0.18	0.19	0.19	0.19	0.17	0.16	0.15	0.20
Current Ratio	0.43	0.60	0.31	0.81	0.82	0.50	0.61	0.74
Debt to Equity	1.52	1.50	1.44	1.53	2.12	4.87	3.87	2.38
Price Range	29.35-20.58	31.79-20.58	31.79-20.58	33.21-20.58	32.42-27.02	31.78-11.16	60.86-21.54	59.44-38.03
P/E Ratio	...	...	...	...	12.37-10.31	...	...	20.36-13.02
Average Yield %	5.65	5.30	5.22	4.95	4.06	7.14	5.37	4.00

Address: One Williams Center, Tulsa, OK 74172-0172 Telephone: 918-573-2000	Web Site: www.williams.com Officers: Stephen W. Bergstrom - Chairman Joshua H. De Rienzis - Vice President, Corporate Secretary	Auditors: Ernst & Young LLP Transfer Agents: Computershare Trust Company, N.A., College Station, TX

WILLIAMS SONOMA INC

Exchange	Symbol	Price	52Wk Range	Yield	P/E	Div Acheiver
NYS	WSM	$73.44 (12/31/2019)	74.01-49.84	2.61	17.12	12 Years

*7 Year Price Score 85.84 *NYSE Composite Index=100 *12 Month Price Score 107.09

Interim Earnings (Per Share)

Qtr.	Apr	Jul	Oct	Jan
2016-17	0.44	0.58	0.78	1.63
2017-18	0.45	0.61	0.84	1.13
2018-19	0.54	0.62	1.00	1.90
2019-20	0.66	0.79	0.94	...

Interim Dividends (Per Share)

Amt	Decl	Ex	Rec	Pay
0.48Q	03/20/2019	04/25/2019	04/26/2019	05/31/2019
0.48Q	06/21/2019	07/25/2019	07/26/2019	08/30/2019
0.48Q	09/20/2019	10/24/2019	10/25/2019	11/29/2019
0.48Q	12/20/2019	01/23/2020	01/24/2020	02/28/2020

Indicated Div: $1.92

Valuation Analysis

		Institutional Holding	
Forecast EPS	$4.75	No of Institutions	
	(01/11/2020)	626	
Market Cap	$5.7 Billion	Shares	
Book Value	$1.1 Billion	108,941,752	
Price/Book	5.04	% Held	
Price/Sales	0.97	82.69	

Business Summary: Retail - Furniture & Home Furnishings (MIC: 2.1.6 SIC: 5712 NAIC: 442110)

Williams-Sonoma is a retailer of products for the home. Co. has two reportable segments, e-commerce and retail. The e-commerce segment has the following merchandise strategies: Williams Sonoma, Pottery Barn, Pottery Barn Kids, West Elm, PBteen, Williams Sonoma Home, Rejuvenation and Mark and Graham, which sell Co.'s products through its e-commerce websites and direct-mail catalogs. The retail segment, which includes Co.'s franchise operations, has the following merchandise strategies: Williams Sonoma, Pottery Barn, Pottery Barn Kids, West Elm and Rejuvenation, which sell Co.'s products through its retail stores.

Recent Developments: For the quarter ended Nov 3 2019, net income decreased 8.3% to US$74.7 million from US$81.5 million in the year-earlier quarter. Revenues were US$1.44 billion, up 6.3% from US$1.36 billion the year before. Operating income was US$101.9 million versus US$94.4 million in the prior-year quarter, an increase of 8.0%. Direct operating expenses rose 7.2% to US$924.3 million from US$862.0 million in the comparable period the year before. Indirect operating expenses increased 3.9% to US$416.3 million from US$400.6 million in the equivalent prior-year period.

Prospects: Our evaluation of Williams-Sonoma Inc. as of October 4th, 2019 is the result of our systematic analysis on three basic characteristics: earnings strength, relative valuation, and recent stock price movement. The company has managed to produce a neutral trend in earnings per share over the past 5 quarters. In addition, recent analyst estimates for the company have been mixed and WSM has posted results that exceeded analysts' expectations. Based on operating earnings yield, the company is undervalued when compared to all of the companies we cover. Share price changes over the past year indicates that WSM will perform in line with the market over the near term.

Financial Data

(US$ in Thousands)	9 Mos	6 Mos	3 Mos	02/03/2019	01/28/2018	01/29/2017	01/31/2016	02/01/2015
Earnings Per Share	4.29	4.35	4.18	4.05	3.02	3.41	3.37	3.24
Cash Flow Per Share	6.37	5.60	6.06	7.08	5.85	5.94	6.01	4.94
Tang Book Value Per Share	13.48	13.25	13.15	13.58	14.38	14.29	13.38	13.33
Dividends Per Share	1.870	1.820	1.770	1.720	1.560	1.480	1.400	1.320
Dividend Payout %	43.59	41.84	42.34	42.47	51.66	43.40	41.54	40.74
Income Statement								
Total Revenue	4,054,418	2,611,946	1,241,132	5,671,593	5,292,359	5,083,812	4,976,090	4,698,719
EBITDA	256,203	156,069	71,826	598,562	611,516	620,582	631,673	640,119
Depn & Amortn	(5,985)	(4,228)	(2,306)	162,609	157,705	147,983	143,039	137,854
Income Before Taxes	254,702	155,375	71,879	429,247	452,439	471,911	488,007	502,203
Income Taxes	64,685	40,071	19,223	95,563	192,894	166,524	177,939	193,349
Net Income	190,017	115,304	52,656	333,684	259,545	305,387	310,068	308,854
Average Shares	79,191	79,470	79,867	82,340	86,080	89,462	92,102	95,200
Balance Sheet								
Current Assets	1,659,245	1,558,019	1,485,646	1,694,343	1,636,445	1,367,180	1,336,100	1,391,923
Total Assets	3,963,824	3,869,681	3,788,365	2,812,844	2,785,749	2,476,879	2,417,427	2,330,277
Current Liabilities	1,288,910	1,186,879	1,114,215	1,074,812	1,007,823	961,256	996,427	875,948
Long-Term Obligations	299,769	299,719	299,670	299,620	299,422	...	...	...
Total Liabilities	2,831,931	2,748,078	2,666,597	1,657,130	1,582,183	1,228,659	1,219,201	1,105,571
Stockholders' Equity	1,131,893	1,121,603	1,121,768	1,155,714	1,203,566	1,248,220	1,198,226	1,224,706
Shares Outstanding	77,612	78,189	78,808	78,813	83,726	87,325	89,563	91,891
Statistical Record								
Return on Assets %	10.34	10.87	10.59	11.73	9.89	12.51	13.10	13.27
Return on Equity %	31.06	31.97	29.42	27.83	21.23	25.03	25.66	24.97
EBITDA Margin %	6.32	5.98	5.79	10.55	11.55	12.21	12.69	13.62
Net Margin %	4.69	4.41	4.24	5.88	4.90	6.01	6.23	6.57
Asset Turnover	1.76	1.79	1.77	1.99	2.02	2.08	2.10	2.02
Current Ratio	1.29	1.31	1.33	1.58	1.62	1.42	1.34	1.59
Debt to Equity	0.26	0.27	0.27	0.26	0.25	...	...	...
Price Range	71.23-45.54	72.94-45.54	72.94-45.54	72.94-45.54	55.59-42.85	61.55-46.22	88.67-48.99	80.94-52.85
P/E Ratio	16.60-10.62	16.77-10.47	17.45-10.89	18.01-11.24	18.41-14.19	18.05-13.55	26.31-14.54	24.98-16.31
Average Yield %	3.13	3.09	3.04	3.04	3.14	...	2.80	1.87	1.96

Address: 3250 Van Ness Avenue, San Francisco, CA 94109 **Telephone:** 415-421-7900 **Fax:** 415-434-0881	**Web Site:** www.williams-sonomainc.com **Officers:** Adrian D.P. Bellamy - Chairman Laura J. Alber - President, Chief Executive Officer	**Auditors:** Deloitte & Touche LLP **Transfer Agents:** Wilson Sonsini Goodrich & Rosati Professional Corporation, Palo Alto, CA

WORLD FUEL SERVICES CORP.

Exchange	Symbol	Price	52Wk Range	Yield	P/E
NYS	INT	$43.42 (12/31/2019)	43.99-21.27	0.92	19.13

*7 Year Price Score 73.51   *NYSE Composite Index=100   *12 Month Price Score 118.51

Interim Earnings (Per Share)

Qtr.	Mar	Jun	Sep	Dec
2016	0.75	0.43	0.61	0.03
2017	0.45	0.44	(0.57)	(2.83)
2018	0.46	0.42	0.56	0.44
2019	0.55	0.55	0.73	...

Interim Dividends (Per Share)

Amt	Decl	Ex	Rec	Pay
0.06Q	03/08/2019	03/21/2019	03/22/2019	04/12/2019
0.10Q	05/29/2019	06/07/2019	06/10/2019	07/05/2019
0.10Q	09/10/2019	09/24/2019	09/25/2019	10/11/2019
0.10Q	11/22/2019	12/19/2019	12/20/2019	01/10/2020

Indicated Div: $0.40

Valuation Analysis

		Institutional Holding	
Forecast EPS	$2.48	No of Institutions	
	(01/04/2020)	403	
Market Cap	$2.8 Billion	Shares	
Book Value	$1.8 Billion	84,551,872	
Price/Book	1.54	% Held	
Price/Sales	0.08	90.16	

Business Summary: Equipment & Services (MIC: 9.1.3 SIC: 5172 NAIC: 424720)

World Fuel Services is a global fuel services company. Co.'s segments are: aviation, which provides global aviation fuel supply and service solutions to main commercial airlines, second and third-tier airlines, cargo carriers, regional and low-cost carriers, airports, fixed based operators, corporate fleets, fractional operators and private aircraft; land, which provides fuel, heating oil, propane, natural gas, lubricants and related products, advisory and fulfillment solutions, transaction management services, and transportation logistics for its product deliveries; and marine, which markets fuel, lubricants and related products and services to a base of marine customers.

Recent Developments: For the quarter ended Sep 30 2019, net income increased 27.6% to US$49.4 million from US$38.7 million in the year-earlier quarter. Revenues were US$9.32 billion, down 10.6% from US$10.43 billion the year before. Operating income was US$93.6 million versus US$78.2 million in the prior-year quarter, an increase of 19.7%. Direct operating expenses declined 11.3% to US$9.02 billion from US$10.16 billion in the comparable period the year before. Indirect operating expenses increased 12.5% to US$212.0 million from US$188.5 million in the equivalent prior-year period.

Prospects: Our evaluation of World Fuel Services Corp. as of October 4th, 2019 is the result of our systematic analysis on three basic characteristics: earnings strength, relative valuation, and recent stock price movement. The company has managed to produce a neutral trend in earnings per share over the past 5 quarters. In addition, recent analyst estimates for the company have been mixed and INT has posted results that exceeded analysts' expectations. Based on operating earnings yield, the company is undervalued when compared to all of the companies we cover. Share price changes over the past year indicates that INT will perform well over the near term.

Financial Data

(US$ in Thousands)	9 Mos	6 Mos	3 Mos	12/31/2018	12/31/2017	12/31/2016	12/31/2015	12/31/2014
Earnings Per Share	2.27	2.10	1.97	1.89	(2.50)	1.81	2.64	3.11
Cash Flow Per Share	4.63	2.73	0.85	(2.71)	3.01	2.95	6.37	2.00
Tang Book Value Per Share	15.26	14.55	14.71	14.37	5.97	9.44	12.41	11.83
Dividends Per Share	0.320	0.280	0.240	0.240	0.240	0.240	0.240	0.150
Dividend Payout %	14.10	13.33	12.18	12.70	...	13.26	9.09	4.82
Income Statement								
Total Revenue	27,460,900	18,138,200	8,678,800	39,750,300	33,695,500	27,015,800	30,379,700	43,386,389
EBITDA	303,000	191,700	93,000	301,500	83,300	223,800	284,300	325,088
Depn & Amortn	64,200	43,100	22,300	45,600	44,100	42,500	35,100	30,300
Income Before Taxes	179,800	109,000	51,300	184,900	(21,100)	142,100	219,300	269,551
Income Taxes	55,500	34,000	14,000	55,900	149,200	15,700	36,300	51,144
Net Income	122,400	74,200	37,200	127,700	(170,200)	126,500	186,900	221,747
Average Shares	65,700	67,000	67,400	67,700	68,100	69,800	70,700	71,323
Balance Sheet								
Current Assets	3,969,500	3,925,000	3,894,700	3,974,800	3,940,400	3,836,600	3,254,600	3,674,843
Total Assets	5,797,500	5,751,200	5,733,200	5,676,900	5,587,800	5,412,600	4,549,400	4,879,980
Current Liabilities	2,910,500	2,902,300	2,873,200	2,935,900	2,718,600	2,182,700	1,762,800	2,241,354
Long-Term Obligations	671,000	666,500	649,700	659,900	884,600	1,170,800	746,700	671,954
Total Liabilities	3,955,400	3,951,700	3,893,000	3,861,400	3,865,800	3,487,600	2,638,000	3,024,622
Stockholders' Equity	1,842,100	1,799,400	1,840,300	1,815,400	1,721,900	1,925,000	1,911,400	1,855,358
Shares Outstanding	65,200	65,200	67,100	67,000	67,700	69,900	70,788	72,082
Statistical Record								
Return on Assets %	2.58	2.47	2.39	2.27	N.M.	2.53	3.96	4.61
Return on Equity %	8.43	7.98	7.44	7.22	N.M.	6.58	9.92	12.57
EBITDA Margin %	1.10	1.06	1.07	0.76	0.25	0.83	0.94	0.75
Net Margin %	0.45	0.41	0.43	0.32	N.M.	0.47	0.62	0.51
Asset Turnover	6.34	6.70	7.01	7.06	6.13	5.41	6.44	9.02
Current Ratio	1.36	1.35	1.36	1.35	1.45	1.76	1.85	1.64
Debt to Equity	0.36	0.37	0.35	0.36	0.51	0.61	0.39	0.36
Price Range	41.14-19.87	35.96-19.87	32.00-19.87	32.00-19.87	47.25-26.45	50.79-36.31	58.28-34.44	49.24-36.87
P/E Ratio	18.12-8.75	17.12-9.46	16.24-10.09	16.93-10.51	...	28.06-20.06	22.08-13.05	15.83-11.86
Average Yield %	1.05	1.02	0.95	0.95	0.67	0.53	0.51	0.34

Address: 9800 Northwest 41st Street, Miami, FL 33178	**Web Site:** www.wfscorp.com	**Auditors:** PricewaterhouseCoopers LLP
Telephone: 305-428-8000	**Officers:** Michael J. Kasbar - Chairman, President, Chief Operating Officer, Chief Executive Officer Ira M. Birns - Executive Vice President, Chief Financial Officer	**Investor Contact:** 305-428-8000
Fax: 305-392-5621		**Transfer Agents:** Wells Fargo Shareowner Services, St. Paul, MN

WORLD WRESTLING ENTERTAINMENT INC

Exchange	Symbol	Price	52Wk Range	Yield	P/E
NYS	WWE	$64.87 (12/31/2019)	99.25-53.16	0.74	124.75

*7 Year Price Score 195.51 *NYSE Composite Index=100 *12 Month Price Score 76.99

Interim Earnings (Per Share)

Qtr.	Mar	Jun	Sep	Dec
2016	0.18	0.01	0.14	0.11
2017	0.01	0.06	0.28	0.06
2018	0.18	0.11	0.37	0.46
2019	(0.11)	0.11	0.06	...

Interim Dividends (Per Share)

Amt	Decl	Ex	Rec	Pay
0.12Q	01/31/2019	03/14/2019	03/15/2019	03/25/2019
0.12Q	04/18/2019	06/13/2019	06/14/2019	06/25/2019
0.12Q	07/18/2019	09/12/2019	09/13/2019	09/25/2019
0.12Q	10/23/2019	12/12/2019	12/13/2019	12/26/2019

Indicated Div: $0.48

Valuation Analysis

		Institutional Holding	
Forecast EPS	$0.85	No of Institutions	
	(01/17/2020)	399	
Market Cap	$5.1 Billion	Shares	
Book Value	$293.0 Million	66,987,264	
Price/Book	17.39	% Held	
Price/Sales	5.60	75.72	

Business Summary: Entertainment (MIC: 2.3.2 SIC: 7812 NAIC: 711320)

World Wrestling Entertainment is a media and entertainment company. Co. is engaged in the production and distribution of wrestling entertainment content through various channels, including its subscription network, content rights agreements, pay-per-view event programming, filmed entertainment, live events, licensing of various WWE themed products, and the sale of consumer products featuring its brands. Co.'s operations are organized around the following key activities: Media, which reflects media content across various platforms; Live events, which provide ongoing content for its media platforms; and The Consumer Products segment, which engages in the merchandising of WWE branded products.

Recent Developments: For the quarter ended Sep 30 2019, net income decreased 82.8% to US$5.8 million from US$33.6 million in the year-earlier quarter. Revenues were US$186.4 million, down 1.1% from US$188.4 million the year before. Operating income was US$6.4 million versus US$18.1 million in the prior-year quarter, a decrease of 64.5%. Direct operating expenses rose 10.8% to US$133.8 million from US$120.8 million in the comparable period the year before. Indirect operating expenses decreased 6.8% to US$46.1 million from US$49.5 million in the equivalent prior-year period.

Prospects: Our evaluation of World Wrestling Federation Entertainment Inc. as of October 4th, 2019 is the result of our systematic analysis on three basic characteristics: earnings strength, relative valuation, and recent stock price movement. The company has suffered a very negative trend in earnings per share over the past 5 quarters. However, recent analyst estimates for the company have been mixed and WWE has posted results that exceeded analysts' expectations. Based on operating earnings yield, the company is overvalued when compared to all of the companies we cover. Share price changes over the past year indicates that WWE will perform in line with the market over the near term.

Financial Data

(US$ in Thousands)	9 Mos	6 Mos	3 Mos	12/31/2018	12/31/2017	12/31/2016	12/31/2015	12/31/2014
Earnings Per Share	0.52	0.83	0.83	1.12	0.42	0.44	0.32	(0.40)
Cash Flow Per Share	0.86	1.40	2.45	2.41	1.26	0.74	0.65	0.73
Tang Book Value Per Share	3.73	4.17	4.01	4.05	3.28	3.14	2.76	2.73
Dividends Per Share	0.480	0.480	0.480	0.480	0.480	0.480	0.480	0.480
Dividend Payout %	92.31	57.83	57.83	42.86	114.29	109.09	150.00	...
Income Statement								
Total Revenue	637,640	451,257	182,448	930,160	800,959	729,216	658,768	542,620
EBITDA	78,465	46,268	13,611	145,618	103,476	79,428	59,700	(18,199)
Depn & Amortn	58,939	33,387	18,621	24,176	24,680	23,195	21,107	25,059
Income Before Taxes	1,344	2,533	(11,349)	106,037	64,060	53,213	36,226	(45,342)
Income Taxes	(6,464)	515	(2,953)	6,449	31,420	19,372	12,082	(19,232)
Net Income	7,808	2,018	(8,396)	99,588	32,640	33,841	24,144	(30,072)
Average Shares	89,855	91,100	78,040	88,619	78,471	77,539	76,333	75,294
Balance Sheet								
Current Assets	419,518	462,064	439,603	474,008	390,982	349,306	179,758	197,221
Total Assets	1,022,119	742,883	703,220	700,299	614,507	600,903	409,145	382,554
Current Liabilities	358,101	374,133	344,588	357,539	138,194	133,134	131,593	100,575
Long-Term Obligations	354,965	28,307	31,762	25,696	208,858	196,604	17,135	21,575
Total Liabilities	729,123	417,597	390,051	384,062	361,548	361,160	199,828	176,693
Stockholders' Equity	292,996	325,286	313,169	316,237	252,959	239,743	209,317	205,861
Shares Outstanding	78,551	78,036	78,042	78,024	77,107	76,404	75,904	75,477
Statistical Record								
Return on Assets %	5.81	10.88	11.55	15.15	5.37	6.68	6.10	N.M.
Return on Equity %	17.13	24.86	25.94	34.99	13.25	15.03	11.63	N.M.
EBITDA Margin %	12.31	10.25	7.46	15.66	12.92	10.89	9.06	N.M.
Net Margin %	1.22	0.45	N.M.	10.71	4.08	4.64	3.67	N.M.
Asset Turnover	1.08	1.29	1.40	1.41	1.32	1.44	1.66	1.43
Current Ratio	1.17	1.24	1.28	1.33	2.83	2.62	1.37	1.96
Debt to Equity	1.21	0.09	0.10	0.08	0.83	0.82	0.08	0.10
Price Range	99.25-61.69	99.25-61.69	96.73-34.94	96.73-30.77	32.92-18.24	21.30-14.65	23.01-10.05	31.39-10.81
P/E Ratio	190.87-118.63	119.58-74.33	116.54-42.10	86.37-27.47	78.38-43.43	48.41-33.30	71.91-31.41	...
Average Yield %	0.61	0.59	0.66	0.79	2.14	2.61	2.94	2.91

Address: 1241 East Main Street, Stamford, CT 06902 Telephone: 203-352-8600	Web Site: www.wwe.com Officers: Vincent K. McMahon - Chairman, Chief Executive Officer George A. Barrios - Co-President, Chief Financial Officer, Chief Strategy Officer	Auditors: DELOITTE & TOUCHE LLP Investor Contact: 203-352-8600 Transfer Agents: American Stock Transfer & Trust Company, New York, NY

WORTHINGTON INDUSTRIES, INC.

Exchange	Symbol	Price	52Wk Range	Yield	P/E
NYS	WOR	$42.18 (12/31/2019)	44.02-33.36	2.28	21.52

*7 Year Price Score 80.77   ***NYSE Composite Index=100**   ***12 Month Price Score 98.71**

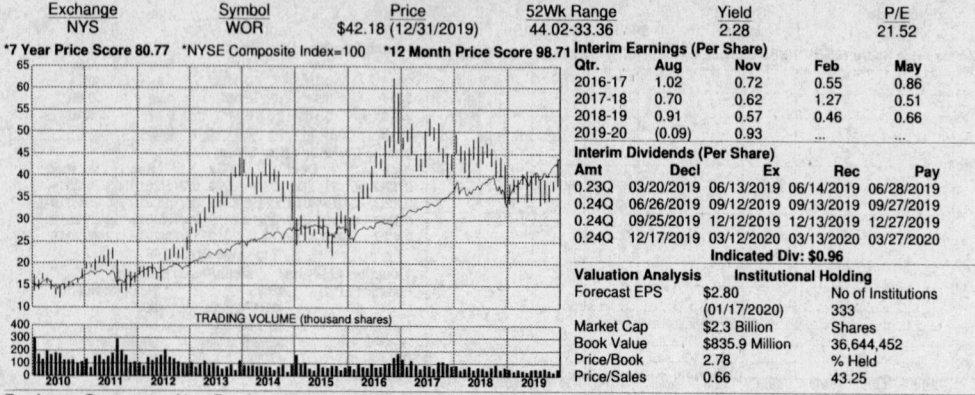

Interim Earnings (Per Share)

Qtr.	Aug	Nov	Feb	May
2016-17	1.02	0.72	0.55	0.86
2017-18	0.70	0.62	1.27	0.51
2018-19	0.91	0.57	0.46	0.66
2019-20	(0.09)	0.93	...	...

Interim Dividends (Per Share)

Amt	Decl	Ex	Rec	Pay
0.23Q	03/20/2019	06/13/2019	06/14/2019	06/28/2019
0.24Q	06/26/2019	09/12/2019	09/13/2019	09/27/2019
0.24Q	09/25/2019	12/12/2019	12/13/2019	12/27/2019
0.24Q	12/17/2019	03/12/2020	03/13/2020	03/27/2020

Indicated Div: $0.96

Valuation Analysis   **Institutional Holding**

Forecast EPS	$2.80	No of Institutions
	(01/17/2020)	333
Market Cap	$2.3 Billion	Shares
Book Value	$835.9 Million	36,644,452
Price/Book	2.78	% Held
Price/Sales	0.66	43.25

Business Summary: Non-Precious Metals (MIC: 8.2.2 SIC: 3312 NAIC: 331111)

Worthington Industries is a metals manufacturing company, focused on steel processing and manufactured metal products. Co. operates three segments: Steel Processing, which buys coils of steel from integrated steel mills and mini-mills and processes them to customer specifications; Pressure Cylinders, which manufactures and sells filled and unfilled pressure cylinders, tanks, hand torches, well water and expansion tanks, and oil and gas equipment with accessories and related products for end-use market applications; and Engineered Cabs, which designs and manufactures custom-engineered open and enclosed cabs and operator stations and custom fabrications and packaging for mobile equipment.

Recent Developments: For the quarter ended Nov 30 2019, net income increased 50.6% to US$56.9 million from US$37.8 million in the year-earlier quarter. Revenues were US$827.6 million, down 13.6% from US$958.2 million the year before. Operating income was US$32.1 million versus US$35.9 million in the prior-year quarter, a decrease of 10.4%. Direct operating expenses declined 15.6% to US$707.0 million from US$837.3 million in the comparable period the year before. Indirect operating expenses increased 4.0% to US$88.5 million from US$85.1 million in the equivalent prior-year period.

Prospects: Our evaluation of Worthington Industries Inc. as of October 4th, 2019 is the result of our systematic analysis on three basic characteristics: earnings strength, relative valuation, and recent stock price movement. The company has generated a negative trend in earnings per share over the past 5 quarters. In addition, recent analyst estimates for the company have been reduced and WOR has posted results that fell short of analysts' expectations. Based on operating earnings yield, the company is undervalued when compared to all of the companies we cover. Share price changes over the past year indicates that WOR will perform in line with the market over the near term.

Financial Data
(US$ in Thousands)

	6 Mos	3 Mos	05/31/2019	05/31/2018	05/31/2017	05/31/2016	05/31/2015	05/31/2014
Earnings Per Share	1.96	1.60	2.61	3.09	3.15	2.22	1.12	2.11
Cash Flow Per Share	5.29	4.20	3.46	4.62	5.38	6.60	3.23	3.32
Tang Book Value Per Share	5.51	4.85	5.42	6.11	9.89	7.33	6.10	6.73
Dividends Per Share	0.930	0.920	0.900	0.830	0.790	0.750	0.690	0.450
Dividend Payout %	47.45	57.50	34.48	26.86	25.08	33.78	61.61	21.33
Income Statement								
Total Revenue	1,683,496	855,859	3,759,556	3,581,620	3,014,108	2,819,714	3,384,234	3,126,426
EBITDA	61,600	6,250	227,796	228,286	290,153	202,205	126,018	215,060
Depn & Amortn	46,773	24,177	80,316	83,680	73,268	68,886	64,666	62,344
Income Before Taxes	(1,968)	(27,407)	109,417	105,931	187,089	101,649	25,552	126,045
Income Taxes	15,678	(185)	43,183	8,220	79,190	58,987	25,772	57,349
Net Income	47,310	(4,776)	153,455	194,794	204,515	143,715	76,785	151,300
Average Shares	56,072	55,241	58,823	63,042	64,874	64,755	68,483	71,664
Balance Sheet								
Current Assets	1,010,646	1,030,092	1,165,913	1,241,122	1,190,969	915,460	992,193	1,198,922
Total Assets	2,408,961	2,382,632	2,510,796	2,621,787	2,325,344	2,063,755	2,085,142	2,296,381
Current Liabilities	473,863	482,674	698,020	646,895	520,783	430,078	524,392	589,663
Long-Term Obligations	698,531	698,612	598,356	748,894	571,796	579,982	579,352	554,790
Total Liabilities	1,573,070	1,594,659	1,679,550	1,703,018	1,373,709	1,270,384	1,336,030	1,445,569
Stockholders' Equity	835,891	787,973	831,246	918,769	951,635	793,371	749,112	850,812
Shares Outstanding	55,094	54,871	55,467	58,876	62,802	61,533	64,141	67,408
Statistical Record								
Return on Assets %	4.50	3.75	5.98	7.88	9.32	6.91	3.50	7.12
Return on Equity %	13.12	10.98	17.54	20.83	23.44	18.58	9.60	17.99
EBITDA Margin %	3.66	0.73	6.06	6.37	9.63	7.17	3.72	6.88
Net Margin %	2.81	N.M.	4.08	5.44	6.79	5.10	2.27	4.84
Asset Turnover	1.41	1.45	1.46	1.45	1.37	1.36	1.54	1.47
Current Ratio	2.13	2.13	1.67	1.92	2.29	2.13	1.89	2.03
Debt to Equity	0.84	0.89	0.72	0.82	0.60	0.73	0.77	0.65
Price Range	42.58-33.36	46.58-33.36	49.01-33.36	53.14-39.65	62.35-36.26	38.26-21.88	43.85-24.18	44.05-31.35
P/E Ratio	21.72-17.02	29.11-20.85	18.78-12.91	17.20-12.83	19.79-11.51	17.23-9.86	39.15-21.59	20.88-14.86
Average Yield %	2.49	2.36	2.18	1.80	1.70	2.48	2.02	1.19

Address: 200 Old Wilson Bridge Road, Columbus, OH 43085	**Web Site:** www.worthingtonindustries.com	**Auditors:** KPMG LLP
Telephone: 614-438-3210	**Officers:** John P. McConnell - Chairman, Chief Executive Officer B. Andrew Rose - President, Chief Financial Officer, Executive Vice President, Vice President	**Investor Contact:** 614-438-3077
Fax: 614-438-3256		**Transfer Agents:** Wells Fargo Shareowner Services, Saint Paul, MN

W.P. CAREY INC

Exchange	Symbol	Price	52Wk Range	Yield	P/E	Div Acheiver
NYS	WPC	$80.04 (12/31/2019)	93.45-64.14	5.19	31.89	20 Years

*7 Year Price Score 100.63 *NYSE Composite Index=100 ***12 Month Price Score 95.89**

Interim Earnings (Per Share)

Qtr.	Mar	Jun	Sep	Dec
2016	0.54	0.48	1.03	0.44
2017	0.53	0.59	0.74	0.69
2018	0.60	0.70	0.71	1.48
2019	0.41	0.38	0.24	...

Interim Dividends (Per Share)

Amt	Decl	Ex	Rec	Pay
1.032Q	03/14/2019	03/28/2019	03/29/2019	04/15/2019
1.034Q	06/13/2019	06/27/2019	06/28/2019	07/15/2019
1.036Q	09/18/2019	09/27/2019	09/30/2019	10/15/2019
1.038Q	12/18/2019	12/30/2019	12/31/2019	01/15/2020

Indicated Div: $4.15 (Div. Reinv. Plan)

Valuation Analysis   **Institutional Holding**

Forecast EPS	$1.54	No of Institutions
(01/16/2020)		759
Market Cap	$13.8 Billion	Shares
Book Value	$7.0 Billion	110,942,160
Price/Book	1.98	% Held
Price/Sales	11.54	N/A

TRADING VOLUME (thousand shares)

Business Summary: REITs (MIC: 5.3.1 SIC: 6798 NAIC: 525930)

W. P. Carey is an internally-managed diversified real estate investment trust (REIT). Co.'s business operates in two segments: Real Estate, in which Co. invests in commercial real estate properties that are net-leased to tenants, primarily located in the U.S. and Northern and Western Europe; and Investment Management, in which Co. manages tjhe portfolios of certain non-traded investment programs through its investment management business, non-traded REITs that have invested in lodging and lodging-related properties, and a private limited partnership formed for the purpose of developing, owning, and operating student housing properties and similar investments in Europe.

Recent Developments: For the quarter ended Sep 30 2019, net income decreased 48.7% to US$41.8 million from US$81.6 million in the year-earlier quarter. Revenues were US$318.0 million, up 51.9% from US$209.4 million the year before. Revenues from property income rose 68.8% to US$302.8 million from US$179.3 million in the corresponding quarter a year earlier.

Prospects: Our evaluation of W.P.Carey Inc. as of October 4th, 2019 is the result of our systematic analysis on three basic characteristics: earnings strength, relative valuation, and recent stock price movement. The company has generated a negative trend in earnings per share over the past 5 quarters. However, recent analyst estimates for the company have been mixed and WPC has posted results that fell short of analysts' expectations. Based on operating earnings yield, the company is overvalued when compared to all of the companies we cover. Share price changes over the past year indicates that WPC will perform over the near term.

Financial Data

(US$ in Thousands)	9 Mos	6 Mos	3 Mos	12/31/2018	12/31/2017	12/31/2016	12/31/2015	12/31/2014
Earnings Per Share	2.51	2.98	3.30	3.49	2.56	2.49	1.61	2.39
Cash Flow Per Share	4.16	3.55	3.28	4.33	4.79	4.84	4.52	4.04
Tang Book Value Per Share	34.99	35.51	35.92	17.96	6.49	13.34	13.09	14.82
Dividends Per Share	4.132	4.121	4.107	4.090	4.010	3.929	3.826	3.685
Dividend Payout %	164.62	138.29	124.45	117.19	156.64	157.80	237.65	154.18
Income Statement								
Total Revenue	921,539	603,534	298,323	885,732	848,302	941,533	938,383	906,193
EBITDA	408,883	285,172	138,414	904,911	671,407	590,646	663,573	655,391
Depn & Amortn	62,537	37,675	15,925	349,298	316,466	265,179	303,906	292,606
Income Before Taxes	166,688	126,465	61,176	377,238	189,166	142,058	165,341	184,663
Income Taxes	5,147	990	(2,129)	14,411	11,609	2,711	3,288	37,621	17,609
Net Income	175,871	134,532	68,494	411,566	277,289	267,747	172,258	239,826
Average Shares	172,486	171,490	167,434	117,706	108,035	107,073	106,507	99,827
Balance Sheet								
Current Assets	331,687	202,279	243,325	292,486	267,620	455,092	219,445	233,160
Total Assets	14,083,639	14,192,007	14,155,902	14,183,039	8,231,402	8,453,954	8,754,673	8,637,328
Current Liabilities	651,337	642,082	629,885	576,050	372,819	374,007	445,089	393,924
Long-Term Obligations	6,097,189	6,177,011	6,123,488	6,378,691	4,265,267	4,440,814	4,492,793	4,088,546
Total Liabilities	7,125,533	7,207,602	7,144,605	7,358,761	5,039,141	5,152,287	5,327,430	4,886,439
Stockholders' Equity	6,958,106	6,984,405	7,011,297	6,824,278	3,192,261	3,301,667	3,427,243	3,750,889
Shares Outstanding	172,276	170,756	169,636	165,279	106,922	106,294	104,448	104,040
Statistical Record								
Return on Assets %	3.27	3.61	3.70	3.67	3.32	3.10	1.98	3.60
Return on Equity %	7.37	8.04	8.16	8.22	8.54	7.94	4.80	8.48
EBITDA Margin %	44.37	47.25	46.40	102.17	79.15	62.73	70.71	72.32
Net Margin %	19.08	22.29	22.96	46.47	32.69	28.44	18.36	26.47
Asset Turnover	0.11	0.10	0.09	0.08	0.10	0.11	0.11	0.14
Current Ratio	0.51	0.32	0.39	0.51	0.72	1.22	0.49	0.59
Debt to Equity	0.88	0.88	0.87	0.93	1.34	1.35	1.31	1.09
Price Range	91.62-62.88	86.00-62.88	78.88-61.13	70.58-59.24	72.32-59.64	72.87-51.87	73.58-56.23	72.84-57.87
P/E Ratio	36.50-25.05	28.86-21.10	23.90-18.52	20.22-16.97	28.25-23.30	29.27-20.83	45.70-34.93	30.48-24.21
Average Yield %	5.36	5.75	6.08	6.30	6.07	6.28	6.01	5.71

Address: 50 Rockefeller Plaza, New York, NY 10020
Telephone: 212-492-1100

Web Site: www.wpcarey.com
Officers: Jason E. Fox - President, Chief Executive Officer, Head John J. Park - President, Chief Financial Officer, Managing Director

Auditors: PricewaterhouseCoopers LLP
Investor Contact: 212-492-8920
Transfer Agents: Computershare Shareowner Services, LLC, Pittsburgh, PA

WPX ENERGY INC

Exchange	Symbol	Price	52Wk Range	Yield	P/E
NYS	WPX	$13.74 (12/31/2019)	15.23-8.93	N/A	7.76

*7 Year Price Score 68.43   *NYSE Composite Index=100   *12 Month Price Score 90.18

TRADING VOLUME (thousand shares)

Interim Earnings (Per Share)

Qtr.	Mar	Jun	Sep	Dec
2016	(0.06)	(0.68)	(0.72)	(0.51)
2017	0.22	0.18	(0.38)	(0.11)
2018	(0.30)	(0.21)	(0.01)	0.87
2019	(0.11)	0.72	0.29	...

Interim Dividends (Per Share)

No Dividends Paid

Valuation Analysis | Institutional Holding

Valuation Analysis		Institutional Holding	
Forecast EPS	$0.35	No of Institutions	
	(01/17/2020)	582	
Market Cap	$5.7 Billion	Shares	
Book Value	$4.6 Billion	459,011,680	
Price/Book	1.24	% Held	
Price/Sales	2.00	97.42	

Business Summary: Production & Extraction (MIC: 9.1.1 SIC: 1311 NAIC: 211111)

WPX Energy is an independent oil and natural gas exploration and production company engaged in the exploitation and development of long-life unconventional properties. Co. is focused on exploiting, developing and growing its oil positions in the Delaware Basin (a subset of the Permian Basin) in Texas and New Mexico and the Williston Basin in North Dakota.

Recent Developments: For the quarter ended Sep 30 2019, income from continuing operations was US$122.0 million compared with a loss of US$6.0 million in the year-earlier quarter. Net income amounted to US$121.0 million versus a net loss of US$7.0 million in the year-earlier quarter. Revenues were US$795.0 million, up 64.3% from US$484.0 million the year before. Operating income was US$242.0 million versus US$26.0 million in the prior-year quarter, an increase of 830.8%. Direct operating expenses rose 54.3% to US$145.0 million from US$94.0 million in the comparable period the year before. Indirect operating expenses increased 12.1% to US$408.0 million from US$364.0 million in the equivalent prior-year period.

Prospects: Our evaluation of WPX Energy Inc. as of October 4th, 2019 is the result of our systematic analysis on three basic characteristics: earnings strength, relative valuation, and recent stock price movement. The company has suffered a very negative trend in earnings per share over the past 5 quarters. However, recent analyst estimates for the company have been mixed and WPX has posted results that exceeded analysts' expectations. Based on operating earnings yield, the company is fairly valued when compared to all of the companies we cover. Share price changes over the past year indicates that WPX will perform poorly over the near term.

Financial Data

(US$ in Millions)	9 Mos	6 Mos	3 Mos	12/31/2018	12/31/2017	12/31/2016	12/31/2015	12/31/2014
Earnings Per Share	1.77	1.47	0.54	0.35	(0.08)	(2.05)	(7.42)	0.80
Cash Flow Per Share	2.70	2.58	2.40	2.16	1.28	0.83	3.46	5.28
Tang Book Value Per Share	11.10	10.80	10.06	10.23	9.78	9.38	11.60	21.20
Income Statement								
Total Revenue	1,849	1,054	359	2,310	1,336	693	1,888	3,493
EBITDA	633	425	(13)	1,298	734	(63)	(1,392)	1,226
Depn & Amortn	26	17	8	819	705	667	975	899
Income Before Taxes	488	327	(62)	316	(159)	(937)	(2,554)	204
Income Taxes	109	70	(14)	74	(148)	(325)	(915)	75
Net Income	378	257	(48)	151	(16)	(601)	(1,727)	164
Average Shares	421	423	421	411	395	313	234	206
Balance Sheet								
Current Assets	816	774	703	739	638	754	850	1,869
Total Assets	8,620	8,553	8,471	8,203	8,207	7,264	8,350	8,798
Current Liabilities	930	1,026	1,010	715	839	677	690	1,209
Long-Term Obligations	2,201	2,157	2,470	2,485	2,575	2,575	3,189	2,280
Total Liabilities	3,977	3,992	4,223	3,902	4,080	3,798	4,815	4,479
Stockholders' Equity	4,643	4,561	4,248	4,301	4,127	3,466	3,535	4,319
Shares Outstanding	418	422	422	420	398	344	275	203
Statistical Record								
Return on Assets %	8.85	7.40	2.63	1.84	N.M.	N.M.	N.M.	1.90
Return on Equity %	17.06	14.22	5.28	3.58	N.M.	N.M.	N.M.	3.89
EBITDA Margin %	34.23	40.32	N.M.	56.19	54.94	N.M.	N.M.	35.10
Net Margin %	20.44	24.38	N.M.	6.54	N.M.	N.M.	N.M.	4.70
Asset Turnover	0.35	0.31	0.28	0.28	0.17	0.09	0.22	0.41
Current Ratio	0.88	0.75	0.70	1.03	0.76	1.11	1.23	1.55
Debt to Equity	0.47	0.47	0.58	0.58	0.62	0.74	0.90	0.53
Price Range	20.53-8.93	20.53-10.10	20.53-10.10	20.53-10.10	15.26-8.71	15.54-3.56	14.55-5.16	26.62-10.27
P/E Ratio	11.60-5.05	13.97-6.87	38.02-18.70	58.66-28.86	...	...	...	33.27-12.84

Address: 3500 One Williams Center, Tulsa, OK 74172-0172 **Telephone:** 855-979-2012	**Web Site:** www.wpxenergy.com **Officers:** Richard E. (Rick) Muncrief - Chairman, President, Chief Executive Officer Clay M. Gaspar - President, Senior Vice President, Chief Operating Officer, Chief Operating Officer (frmr)	**Auditors:** Ernst & Young LLP **Investor Contact:** 539-573-9360 **Transfer Agents:** Computershare Trust Company, N.A., Canton, MA

WYNDHAM DESTINATIONS INC

Exchange	Symbol	Price	52Wk Range	Yield	P/E
NYS	WYND	$51.69 (12/31/2019)	51.91-34.83	3.48	24.27

*7 Year Price Score 95.95   ***NYSE Composite Index=100**   ***12 Month Price Score 104.90**

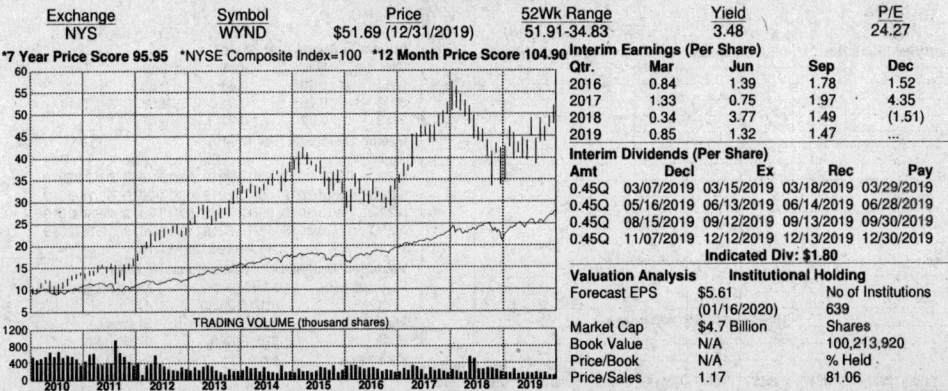

Interim Earnings (Per Share)

Qtr.	Mar	Jun	Sep	Dec
2016	0.84	1.39	1.78	1.52
2017	1.33	0.75	1.97	4.35
2018	0.34	3.77	1.49	(1.51)
2019	0.85	1.32	1.47	...

Interim Dividends (Per Share)

Amt	Decl	Ex	Rec	Pay
0.45Q	03/07/2019	03/15/2019	03/18/2019	03/29/2019
0.45Q	05/16/2019	06/13/2019	06/14/2019	06/28/2019
0.45Q	08/15/2019	09/12/2019	09/13/2019	09/30/2019
0.45Q	11/07/2019	12/12/2019	12/13/2019	12/30/2019

Indicated Div: $1.80

Valuation Analysis   **Institutional Holding**

Forecast EPS	$5.61	No of Institutions	
	(01/16/2020)	639	
Market Cap	$4.7 Billion	Shares	
Book Value	N/A	100,213,920	
Price/Book	N/A	% Held	
Price/Sales	1.17	81.06	

Business Summary: Hotels, Restaurants & Travel (MIC: 2.2.1 SIC: 7011 NAIC: 721110)

Wyndham Destinations is a provider of hospitality services and products. Co. operates in two segments: Vacation Ownership and Exchange and Rentals. The Vacation Ownership segment develops, markets and sells vacation ownership interests (VOIs) to individual consumers, provides consumer financing in connection with the sale of VOIs and provides property management services at resorts. The Exchange and Rentals segment provides vacation exchange services and products to owners of VOIs and manages and markets vacation rental properties primarily on behalf of independent owners. Co.'s vacation club brands include Club Wyndham, WorldMark by Wyndham, and Margaritaville Vacation Club by Wyndham.

Recent Developments: For the quarter ended Sep 30 2019, income from continuing operations increased 3.1% to US$135.0 million from US$131.0 million in the year-earlier quarter. Revenues were US$1.11 billion, up 4.0% from US$1.06 billion the year before. Operating income was US$214.0 million versus US$197.0 million in the prior-year quarter, an increase of 8.6%. Direct operating expenses rose 5.7% to US$536.0 million from US$507.0 million in the comparable period the year before. Indirect operating expenses decreased 0.8% to US$355.0 million from US$358.0 million in the equivalent prior-year period.

Prospects: Our evaluation of Wyndham Destinations Inc. as of October 4th, 2019 is the result of our systematic analysis on three basic characteristics: earnings strength, relative valuation, and recent stock price movement. The company has generated a negative trend in earnings per share over the past 5 quarters. In addition, recent analyst estimates for the company have been reduced while WYND has posted results that exceeded analysts' expectations. Based on operating earnings yield, the company is undervalued when compared to all of the companies we cover. Share price changes over the past year indicates that WYND will perform well over the near term.

Financial Data
(US$ in Millions)

	9 Mos	6 Mos	3 Mos	12/31/2018	12/31/2017	12/31/2016	12/31/2015	12/31/2014
Earnings Per Share	2.13	2.15	4.60	4.09	8.40	5.53	5.14	4.18
Cash Flow Per Share	4.44	4.32	4.88	4.47	9.58	8.82	8.40	7.87
Dividends Per Share	1.760	1.720	1.680	1.890	2.320	2.000	1.680	1.400
Dividend Payout %	82.63	80.00	36.52	46.21	27.62	36.17	32.68	33.49
Income Statement								
Total Revenue	3,062	1,957	918	3,931	5,076	5,599	5,536	5,281
EBITDA	660	410	182	687	920	1,282	1,229	1,144
Depn & Amortn	90	59	31	126	181	214	197	196
Income Before Taxes	454	273	112	396	590	940	916	845
Income Taxes	120	74	31	130	(229)	328	304	316
Net Income	339	204	80	672	871	611	612	529
Average Shares	92	93	94	99	103	111	119	127
Balance Sheet								
Current Assets	5,060	5,008	4,948	4,908	2,964	1,812	1,869	1,867
Total Assets	7,563	7,466	7,370	7,158	10,403	9,819	9,716	9,679
Current Liabilities	802	884	320	1,588	2,539	2,032	1,957	1,859
Long-Term Obligations	5,541	5,432	5,291	5,238	5,686	5,283	4,955	4,792
Total Liabilities	8,139	8,031	7,959	7,732	9,525	9,105	8,766	8,424
Stockholders' Equity	(576)	(565)	(589)	(574)	878	714	950	1,255
Shares Outstanding	90	92	93	94	99	105	113	121
Statistical Record								
Return on Assets %	6.14	6.38	7.78	7.65	8.61	6.24	6.31	5.45
Return on Equity %	...	...	2,564.29	442.11	109.42	73.24	55.51	36.76
EBITDA Margin %	21.55	20.95	19.83	17.48	18.12	22.90	22.20	21.66
Net Margin %	11.07	10.42	8.71	17.09	17.16	10.91	11.05	10.02
Asset Turnover	0.55	0.55	0.43	0.45	0.50	0.57	0.57	0.54
Current Ratio	6.31	5.67	15.46	3.09	1.17	0.89	0.96	1.00
Debt to Equity	...	...	...	...	6.48	7.40	5.22	3.82
Price Range	49.07-33.63	47.06-33.63	53.14-33.63	57.47-33.63	52.65-34.27	36.46-27.81	42.47-31.67	39.16-30.97
P/E Ratio	23.04-15.79	21.89-15.64	11.55-7.31	14.05-8.22	6.27-4.08	6.59-5.03	8.26-6.16	9.37-7.41
Average Yield %	4.18	4.10	3.84	4.07	5.29	6.26	4.50	4.08

Address: 6277 Sea Harbor Drive, Orlando, FL 32821 **Telephone:** 407-626-5200	**Web Site:** www.wyndhamdestinations.com **Officers:** Michael D. Brown - President, Chief Executive Officer, Division Officer Michael Hug - Executive Vice President, Chief Financial Officer	**Auditors:** DELOITTE & TOUCHE LLP **Investor Contact:** 973-753-5500 **Transfer Agents:** Wells Fargo Shareowner Services, St. Paul, MN

WYNDHAM HOTELS & RESORTS INC

Exchange	Symbol	Price	52Wk Range	Yield	P/E
NYS	WH	$62.81 (12/31/2019)	63.22-44.27	1.85	45.19

*7 Year Price Score N/A *NYSE Composite Index=100 *12 Month Price Score 102.03

Interim Earnings (Per Share)

Qtr.	Mar	Jun	Sep	Dec
2017	0.00	0.48	0.58	0.00
2018	0.00	0.21	0.58	0.43
2019	0.22	0.27	0.47	...

Interim Dividends (Per Share)

Amt	Decl	Ex	Rec	Pay
0.29Q	02/27/2019	03/14/2019	03/15/2019	03/29/2019
0.29Q	05/14/2019	06/13/2019	06/14/2019	06/28/2019
0.29Q	08/13/2019	09/12/2019	09/13/2019	09/30/2019
0.29Q	11/13/2019	12/12/2019	12/13/2019	12/30/2019

Indicated Div: $1.16

Valuation Analysis

Forecast EPS	$3.27 (01/16/2020)
Market Cap	$6.0 Billion
Book Value	$1.2 Billion
Price/Book	4.81
Price/Sales	2.86

Institutional Holding

No of Institutions	471
Shares	87,591,848
% Held	87.26

TRADING VOLUME (thousand shares)

Business Summary: Hotels, Restaurants & Travel (MIC: 2.2.1 SIC: 7011 NAIC: 721110)

Wyndham Hotels & Resorts is a hotel franchisor, licensing its hotel brands to hotel owners around the world. Co. operates in the following segments: Hotel franchising, which licenses Co.'s lodging brands and provides related services to third-party hotel owners and others; and Hotel management, which provides hotel management services for full-service and limited-service hotels as well as several hotels that are owned by Co.

Recent Developments: For the quarter ended Sep 30 2019, net income decreased 22.4% to US$45.0 million from US$58.0 million in the year-earlier quarter. Revenues were US$560.0 million, down 7.3% from US$604.0 million the year before. Operating income was US$91.0 million versus US$105.0 million in the prior-year quarter, a decrease of 13.3%. Indirect operating expenses decreased 6.0% to US$469.0 million from US$499.0 million in the equivalent prior-year period.

Prospects: Our evaluation of Wyndham Hotels & Resorts Inc. as of October 4th, 2019 is the result of our systematic analysis on three basic characteristics: earnings strength, relative valuation, and recent stock price movement. The company has enjoyed a very positive trend in earnings per share over the past 5 quarters. However, recent analyst estimates for the company have been mixed and WH has posted results that exceeded analysts' expectations. Based on operating earnings yield, the company is undervalued when compared to all of the companies we cover. Share price changes over the past year indicates that WH will perform well over the near term.

Financial Data

(US$ in Millions)	9 Mos	6 Mos	3 Mos	12/31/2018	12/31/2017	12/31/2016	12/31/2015
Earnings Per Share	1.39	1.50	1.44	1.62	...	...	...
Cash Flow Per Share	1.44	0.63	2.27	2.32	...	...	...
Dividends Per Share	1.120	1.080	1.040	0.750	...	...	...
Dividend Payout %	80.58	72.00	72.22	46.30	...	...	...
Income Statement							
Total Revenue	1,561	1,001	468	1,868	1,347	1,312	1,301
EBITDA	286	168	79	351	316	343	299
Depn & Amortn	81	56	29	68	55	55	49
Income Before Taxes	129	62	26	223	255	287	249
Income Taxes	36	15	5	61	12	115	100
Net Income	93	47	21	162	243	172	149
Average Shares	96	97	98	99	...	...	...
Balance Sheet							
Current Assets	586	596	778	851	330	255	...
Total Assets	4,630	4,656	4,904	4,976	2,122	1,983	...
Current Liabilities	514	481	663	693	406	372	...
Long-Term Obligations	2,106	2,110	2,115	2,120	81	71	...
Total Liabilities	3,388	3,356	3,540	3,558	822	872	...
Stockholders' Equity	1,242	1,300	1,364	1,418	1,300	1,111	...
Shares Outstanding	95	96	97	98	...	...	...
Statistical Record							
Return on Assets %	2.83	3.11	4.08	4.56	11.84	...	...
Return on Equity %	10.13	10.89	10.92	11.92	20.16	...	...
EBITDA Margin %	18.32	16.78	16.88	18.79	23.46	26.14	22.98
Net Margin %	5.96	4.70	4.49	8.67	18.04	13.11	11.45
Asset Turnover	0.43	0.44	0.58	0.53	0.66	...	...
Current Ratio	1.14	1.24	1.17	1.23	0.81	0.69	...
Debt to Equity	1.70	1.62	1.55	1.50	0.06	0.06	...
Price Range	61.22-43.50	61.95-43.50	66.43-43.50	66.43-43.50	...	...	...
P/E Ratio	44.04-31.29	41.30-29.00	46.13-30.21	41.01-26.85	...	...	...
Average Yield %	2.15	2.05	1.96	1.39	...	...	...

Address: 22 Sylvan Way, Parsippany, NJ 07054 **Telephone:** 973-753-6000	**Web Site:** www.wyndham.com **Officers:** Geoffrey A. Ballotti - President, Chief Executive Officer David B. Wyshner - Chief Financial Officer	**Auditors:** DELOITTE & TOUCHE LLP **Transfer Agents:** Broadridge, Inc.

XEROX HOLDINGS CORP

Exchange	Symbol	Price	52Wk Range	Yield	P/E
NYS	XRX	$36.87 (12/31/2019)	39.30-19.69	2.71	13.03

*7 Year Price Score 91.01 *NYSE Composite Index=100 *12 Month Price Score 109.34

TRADING VOLUME (thousand shares)

Interim Earnings (Per Share)

Qtr.	Mar	Jun	Sep	Dec
2016	0.12	0.60	0.68	(3.32)
2017	0.04	0.63	0.68	(0.75)
2018	0.08	0.42	0.34	0.55
2019	0.55	0.77	0.96	...

Interim Dividends (Per Share)

Amt	Decl	Ex	Rec	Pay
0.25Q	08/28/2019	09/27/2019	09/30/2019	10/31/2019
0.25Q	10/24/2019	12/30/2019	12/31/2019	01/31/2020

Indicated Div: $1.00

Valuation Analysis   Institutional Holding

Forecast EPS	$3.34	No of Institutions
	(01/16/2020)	N/A
		Shares
Market Cap	$8.1 Billion	
Book Value	$5.1 Billion	N/A
Price/Book	1.59	% Held
Price/Sales	0.87	N/A

Business Summary: Peripherals (MIC: 6.2.2 SIC: 3577 NAIC: 334119)

Xerox is a provider of digital print technology and intelligent work solutions. Co. operates in three main areas: Intelligent Workplace Services, which includes a continuum of solutions and services consisting of managed print services, industry digital solutions, personalization and communication software, content management solutions, and digitization services; Workplace Solutions, which is made up of two product groups, Entry and Mid-Range, which share common technology, manufacturing and product platforms; and Production Solutions, which enable full-color, on-demand printing of a range of applications, including variable data for personalized content and one-to-one marketing.

Recent Developments: For the quarter ended Sep 30 2019, net income increased 138.7% to US$222.0 million from US$93.0 million in the year-earlier quarter. Revenues were US$2.20 billion, down 6.5% from US$2.35 billion the year before. Direct operating expenses declined 6.5% to US$1.29 billion from US$1.38 billion in the comparable period the year before. Indirect operating expenses decreased 12.8% to US$683.0 million from US$783.0 million in the equivalent prior-year period.

Prospects: Our evaluation of Xerox Holdings Corp. as of October 4th, 2019 is the result of our systematic analysis on three basic characteristics: earnings strength, relative valuation, and recent stock price movement. The company has managed to produce a neutral trend in earnings per share over the past 5 quarters. Additionally, recent analyst estimates for the company have been unchanged while XRX has posted results that exceeded analysts' expectations. Based on operating earnings yield, the company is undervalued when compared to all of the companies we cover. Share price changes over the past year indicates that XRX will perform well over the near term.

Financial Data

(US$ in Thousands)	9 Mos	6 Mos	3 Mos	12/31/2018	12/31/2017	12/31/2016	12/31/2015	12/31/2014
Earnings Per Share	2.83	2.21	1.86	1.38	0.71	(1.96)	1.68	3.24
Cash Flow Per Share	5.95	5.49	5.03	4.58	0.13	4.31	6.05	7.15
Tang Book Value Per Share	4.63	4.88	5.05	3.46	4.14	2.79	N.M.	N.M.
Dividends Per Share	0.250	...	...	1.000	1.000	1.240	1.120	1.000
Dividend Payout %	8.83	...	...	72.46	140.85	...	66.67	30.86
Income Statement								
Total Revenue	6,695,000	4,495,000	2,206,000	9,830,000	10,265,000	10,771,000	18,045,000	19,540,000
EBITDA	1,049,000	648,000	271,000	1,023,000	1,003,000	1,078,000	1,344,000	2,212,000
Depn & Amortn	367,000	254,000	133,000	196,000	189,000	206,000	587,000	639,000
Income Before Taxes	513,000	283,000	83,000	598,000	570,000	568,000	412,000	1,206,000
Income Taxes	108,000	42,000	(8,000)	257,000	481,000	62,000	(23,000)	259,000
Net Income	535,000	314,000	133,000	361,000	195,000	(477,000)	474,000	969,000
Average Shares	220,269	235,279	228,567	251,660	256,570	255,994	269,056	299,640
Balance Sheet								
Current Assets	4,340,000	4,237,000	4,313,000	4,695,000	5,230,000	6,992,000	6,685,000	8,874,000
Total Assets	14,660,000	14,684,000	14,799,000	14,874,000	15,946,000	18,145,000	24,817,000	27,658,000
Current Liabilities	3,923,000	3,176,000	2,929,000	3,251,000	2,741,000	4,654,000	5,254,000	6,076,000
Long-Term Obligations	3,230,000	3,962,000	4,268,000	4,269,000	5,235,000	5,305,000	6,382,000	6,358,000
Total Liabilities	9,591,000	9,508,000	9,558,000	9,655,000	10,476,000	13,128,000	15,394,000	16,675,000
Stockholders' Equity	5,069,000	5,176,000	5,241,000	5,219,000	5,470,000	5,017,000	9,423,000	10,983,000
Shares Outstanding	218,963	220,787	226,411	229,623	254,613	253,593	253,209	279,186
Statistical Record								
Return on Assets %	4.48	3.57	3.04	2.34	1.14	N.M.	1.81	3.42
Return on Equity %	12.84	10.03	8.56	6.75	3.72	N.M.	4.65	8.20
EBITDA Margin %	15.67	14.42	12.28	10.41	9.77	10.01	7.45	11.32
Net Margin %	7.99	6.99	6.03	3.67	1.90	N.M.	2.63	4.96
Asset Turnover	0.61	0.62	0.62	0.64	0.60	0.50	0.69	0.69
Current Ratio	1.11	1.33	1.47	1.44	1.91	1.50	1.27	1.46
Debt to Equity	0.64	0.77	0.81	0.82	0.96	1.06	0.68	0.58
Price Range	36.48-18.92	35.45-18.92	32.91-18.92	34.13-18.92	33.95-27.52	29.64-22.89	36.88-24.48	37.73-27.14
P/E Ratio	12.89-6.69	16.04-8.56	17.69-10.17	24.73-13.71	47.82-38.76	...	21.95-14.57	11.64-8.38
Average Yield %	0.84	...	...	3.60	3.36	4.82	3.71	3.04

Address: P.O. Box 4505, 201 Merritt 7, Norwalk, CT 06851-1056 **Telephone:** 203-968-3000	**Web Site:** www.xerox.com **Officers:** Keith Cozza - Chairman Giovanni (John) Visentin - Vice-Chairman, Chief Executive Officer	**Auditors:** PricewaterhouseCoopers LLP **Transfer Agents:** Computershare Trust Company, N.A., Providence, RI

XPO LOGISTICS, INC.

Exchange	Symbol	Price	52Wk Range	Yield	P/E
NYS	XPO	$79.70 (12/31/2019)	85.67-46.20	N/A	24.01

*7 Year Price Score 110.05 *NYSE Composite Index=100 *12 Month Price Score 118.85

Interim Earnings (Per Share)

Qtr.	Mar	Jun	Sep	Dec
2016	(0.21)	0.35	0.11	0.23
2017	0.16	0.38	0.44	1.46
2018	0.50	1.03	0.74	0.62
2019	0.37	1.19	1.14	...

Interim Dividends (Per Share)

No Dividends Paid

Valuation Analysis

		Institutional Holding	
Forecast EPS	$3.95	No of Institutions	
	(01/17/2020)	500	
Market Cap	$7.4 Billion	Shares	
Book Value	$2.6 Billion	121,491,584	
Price/Book	2.86	% Held	
Price/Sales	0.43	N/A	

Business Summary: Airlines/Air Freight (MIC: 7.4.4 SIC: 4789 NAIC: 488510)

XPO Logistics is a provider of supply chain solutions to various companies. Co. runs its business on a global basis, with two reporting segments: Transportation, which provides freight brokerage, last mile, less-than-truckload, full truckload, global forwarding and managed transportation services; and Logistics, which provides differentiated and data-intensive logistics services, including warehousing and distribution, e-commerce fulfillment, cold chain solutions, reverse logistics, packaging and labeling, factory support, aftermarket support, inventory management and personalization services, such as laser etching.

Recent Developments: For the quarter ended Sep 30 2019, net income increased 18.3% to US$136.0 million from US$115.0 million in the year-earlier quarter. Revenues were US$4.15 billion, down 4.2% from US$4.34 billion the year before. Operating income was US$229.0 million versus US$209.0 million in the prior-year quarter, an increase of 9.6%. Direct operating expenses declined 5.7% to US$3.47 billion from US$3.68 billion in the comparable period the year before. Indirect operating expenses increased 2.2% to US$456.0 million from US$446.0 million in the equivalent prior-year period.

Prospects: Our evaluation of XPO Logistics, Inc. as of October 4th, 2019 is the result of our systematic analysis on three basic characteristics: earnings strength, relative valuation, and recent stock price movement. The company has managed to produce a neutral trend in earnings per share over the past 5 quarters. In addition, recent analyst estimates for the company have been mixed and XPO has posted results that exceeded analysts' expectations. Based on operating earnings yield, the company is fairly valued when compared to all of the companies we cover. Share price changes over the past year indicates that XPO will perform very poorly over the near term.

Financial Data

(US$ in Thousands)	9 Mos	6 Mos	3 Mos	12/31/2018	12/31/2017	12/31/2016	12/31/2015	12/31/2014
Earnings Per Share	3.32	2.92	2.76	2.88	2.45	0.53	(2.65)	(2.00)
Cash Flow Per Share	10.95	11.07	9.58	8.96	6.95	5.66	0.98	(0.40)
Tang Book Value Per Share	N.M.	N.M.	N.M.	N.M.	N.M.	N.M.	N.M.	4.42
Income Statement								
Total Revenue	12,512,000	8,358,000	4,120,000	17,279,000	15,380,800	14,619,400	7,623,200	2,356,600
EBITDA	1,196,000	765,000	322,000	1,329,000	1,032,700	933,900	137,200	(5,900)
Depn & Amortn	546,000	360,000	180,000	546,000	487,700	466,000	203,000	35,800
Income Before Taxes	432,000	262,000	71,000	566,000	260,700	106,800	(282,500)	(89,700)
Income Taxes	99,000	65,000	19,000	122,000	(99,500)	22,300	(90,900)	(26,100)
Net Income	312,000	182,000	47,000	422,000	340,200	69,000	(191,100)	(63,600)
Average Shares	102,000	102,000	117,000	135,000	127,800	122,800	92,800	53,600
Balance Sheet								
Current Assets	3,426,000	3,790,000	3,683,000	3,688,000	3,587,900	3,073,600	2,957,200	1,233,100
Total Assets	13,916,000	14,314,000	14,196,000	12,270,000	12,601,600	11,698,400	12,643,200	2,761,200
Current Liabilities	3,207,000	3,671,000	3,441,000	3,313,000	2,997,100	2,731,600	2,694,400	381,100
Long-Term Obligations	5,121,000	5,134,000	5,362,000	3,902,000	4,417,500	4,731,500	5,272,600	592,100
Total Liabilities	11,344,000	11,809,000	11,758,000	8,695,000	8,997,200	8,998,400	9,926,100	1,106,100
Stockholders' Equity	2,572,000	2,505,000	2,438,000	3,575,000	3,604,400	2,700,000	2,717,100	1,655,100
Shares Outstanding	92,234	92,000	93,000	115,683	119,920	111,087	109,523	77,421
Statistical Record								
Return on Assets %	3.03	2.84	2.92	3.39	2.80	0.57	N.M.	N.M.
Return on Equity %	11.95	12.26	12.96	11.76	10.79	2.54	N.M.	N.M.
EBITDA Margin %	9.56	9.15	7.82	7.69	6.71	6.39	1.80	N.M.
Net Margin %	2.49	2.18	1.14	2.44	2.21	0.47	N.M.	N.M.
Asset Turnover	1.27	1.27	1.27	1.39	1.27	1.20	0.99	1.33
Current Ratio	1.07	1.03	1.07	1.11	1.20	1.13	1.10	3.24
Debt to Equity	1.99	2.05	2.20	1.09	1.23	1.75	1.94	0.36
Price Range	113.27-44.50	114.54-44.50	114.54-44.50	114.54-44.50	92.17-42.71	49.35-19.56	50.56-21.62	42.48-23.24
P/E Ratio	34.12-13.40	39.23-15.24	41.50-16.12	39.77-15.45	37.62-17.43	93.11-36.91	...	...

Address: Five American Lane, Greenwich, CT 06831	Web Site: www.xpologistics.com	Auditors: KPMG LLP
Telephone: 855-976-6951	Officers: Bradley S. Jacobs - Chairman, Chief Executive Officer AnnaMaria DeSalva - Vice-Chairman	Investor Contact: 855-976-4696 Transfer Agents: Computershare, Canton, MA

XYLEM INC

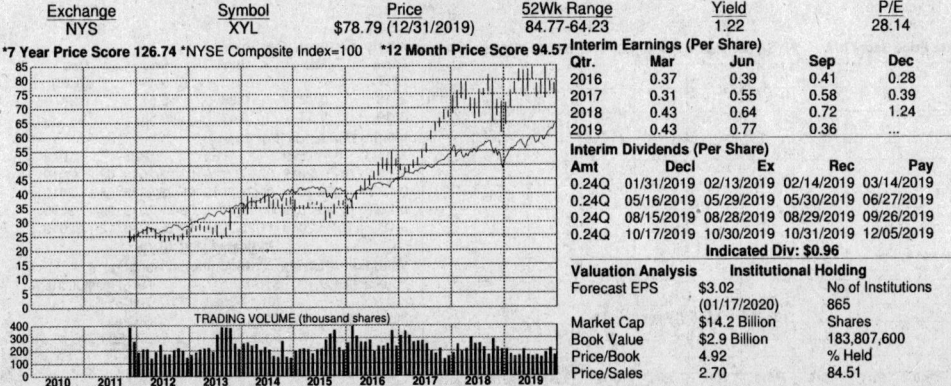

*7 Year Price Score 126.74 *NYSE Composite Index=100 *12 Month Price Score 94.57

Interim Earnings (Per Share)

Qtr.	Mar	Jun	Sep	Dec
2016	0.37	0.39	0.41	0.28
2017	0.31	0.55	0.58	0.39
2018	0.43	0.64	0.72	1.24
2019	0.43	0.57	0.36	...

Interim Dividends (Per Share)

Amt	Decl	Ex	Rec	Pay
0.24Q	01/31/2019	02/13/2019	02/14/2019	03/14/2019
0.24Q	05/16/2019	05/29/2019	05/30/2019	06/27/2019
0.24Q	08/15/2019	08/28/2019	08/29/2019	09/26/2019
0.24Q	10/17/2019	10/30/2019	10/31/2019	12/05/2019

Indicated Div: $0.96

Valuation Analysis   Institutional Holding

Forecast EPS	$3.02	No of Institutions	
	(01/17/2020)	865	
Market Cap	$14.2 Billion	Shares	
Book Value	$2.9 Billion	183,807,600	
Price/Book	4.92	% Held	
Price/Sales	2.70	84.51	

Business Summary: Industrial Machinery & Equipment (MIC: 7.2.1 SIC: 3561 NAIC: 333911)

Xylem is water technology company. Co. designs, manufactures and services engineered solutions ranging across a variety of applications primarily in the water sector, but also in electric and gas. Co.'s business segments are: water irastructure, which serves the water infrastructure sector with pump systems filtration, ultraviolet and ozone systems and pumping solutions; Applied Water, which serves the usage applications sector with water pressure boosting systems; and Measurement and Control Solutions, which serves the utility infrastructure solutions and services sector by delivering communications, smart metering, measurement and control technologies and services.

Recent Developments: For the quarter ended Sep 30 2019, net income decreased 50.0% to US$65.0 million from US$130.0 million in the year-earlier quarter. Revenues were US$1.30 billion, up 0.7% from US$1.29 billion the year before. Operating income was US$11.0 million versus US$176.0 million in the prior-year quarter, a decrease of 93.8%. Direct operating expenses rose 0.6% to US$787.0 million from US$782.0 million in the comparable period the year before. Indirect operating expenses increased 51.4% to US$498.0 million from US$329.0 million in the equivalent prior-year period.

Prospects: Our evaluation of Xylem Inc. as of October 4th, 2019 is the result of our systematic analysis on three basic characteristics: earnings strength, relative valuation, and recent stock price movement. The company has managed to produce a neutral trend in earnings per share over the past 5 quarters. In addition, recent analyst estimates for the company have been mixed and XYL has posted results that fell short of analysts' expectations. Based on operating earnings yield, the company is fairly valued when compared to all of the companies we cover. Share price changes over the past year indicates that XYL will perform in line with the market over the near term.

Financial Data

(US$ in Millions)	9 Mos	6 Mos	3 Mos	12/31/2018	12/31/2017	12/31/2016	12/31/2015	12/31/2014
Earnings Per Share	2.80	3.16	3.03	3.03	1.83	1.45	1.87	1.83
Cash Flow Per Share	3.60	3.28	3.37	3.26	3.82	2.77	2.57	2.27
Tang Book Value Per Share	N.M.	N.M.	N.M.	N.M.	N.M.	N.M.	0.36	0.33
Dividends Per Share	0.930	0.900	0.870	0.840	0.720	0.620	0.563	0.512
Dividend Payout %	33.21	28.48	28.71	27.72	39.34	42.73	30.12	27.98
Income Statement								
Total Revenue	3,878	2,582	1,237	5,207	4,707	3,771	3,653	3,916
EBITDA	482	413	176	775	651	492	541	566
Depn & Amortn	192	127	64	117	109	87	88	95
Income Before Taxes	238	250	94	580	463	337	400	419
Income Taxes	(45)	32	15	36	136	80	63	84
Net Income	283	218	79	549	331	260	340	337
Average Shares	181	181	181	181	180	180	181	184
Balance Sheet								
Current Assets	2,263	2,258	2,081	2,094	2,071	1,839	2,005	2,102
Total Assets	7,515	7,674	7,468	7,222	6,860	6,474	4,657	4,864
Current Liabilities	1,461	1,537	1,441	1,389	1,100	1,238	823	908
Long-Term Obligations	2,030	2,051	2,044	2,051	2,200	2,108	1,196	1,199
Total Liabilities	4,629	4,780	4,672	4,454	4,357	4,284	2,573	2,737
Stockholders' Equity	2,886	2,894	2,796	2,768	2,503	2,190	2,084	2,127
Shares Outstanding	180	180	179	179	179	179	178	182
Statistical Record								
Return on Assets %	6.85	7.69	7.41	7.80	4.96	4.66	7.14	6.91
Return on Equity %	18.46	21.19	20.57	20.83	14.11	12.13	16.15	15.43
EBITDA Margin %	12.43	16.00	14.23	14.88	13.83	13.05	14.81	14.45
Net Margin %	7.30	8.44	6.39	10.54	7.03	6.89	9.31	8.61
Asset Turnover	0.71	0.71	0.71	0.74	0.71	0.68	0.77	0.80
Current Ratio	1.55	1.47	1.44	1.51	1.88	1.49	2.44	2.31
Debt to Equity	0.70	0.71	0.73	0.74	0.88	0.96	0.57	0.56
Price Range	84.41-61.38	83.82-61.38	81.87-61.38	81.87-61.38	69.34-47.00	54.75-32.80	38.08-30.46	39.78-31.91
P/E Ratio	30.15-21.92	26.53-19.42	27.02-20.26	27.02-20.26	37.89-25.68	37.76-22.62	20.36-16.29	21.74-17.44
Average Yield %	1.24	1.21	1.22	1.16	1.27	1.38	1.59	1.39

Address: 1 International Drive, Rye Brook, NY 10573
Telephone: 914-323-5700
Fax: 914-323-5800

Web Site: www.xyleminc.com
Officers: Markos I. Tambakeras - Chairman Patrick K. Decker - President, Chief Executive Officer

Auditors: DELOITTE & TOUCHE LLP
Investor Contact: 914-323-5930
Transfer Agents: Wells Fargo Shareowner Services, St. Paul, MN

YUM CHINA HOLDINGS INC

Exchange	Symbol	Price	52Wk Range	Yield	P/E
NYS	YUMC	$48.01 (12/31/2019)	48.66-32.88	1.00	26.52

*7 Year Price Score N/A *NYSE Composite Index=100 *12 Month Price Score 98.15

Interim Earnings (Per Share)

Qtr.	Mar	Jun	Sep	Dec
2017	...	...	0.44	(0.26)
2018	0.72	0.36	0.51	0.20
2019	0.57	0.46	0.58	...

Interim Dividends (Per Share)

Amt	Decl	Ex	Rec	Pay
0.12Q	01/31/2019	02/27/2019	02/28/2019	03/21/2019
0.12Q	04/29/2019	05/24/2019	05/28/2019	06/17/2019
0.12Q	07/30/2019	08/26/2019	08/27/2019	09/17/2019
0.12Q	10/29/2019	11/25/2019	11/26/2019	12/17/2019

Indicated Div: $0.48

Valuation Analysis

		Institutional Holding	
Forecast EPS	$1.77	No of Institutions	
	(01/17/2020)	794	
Market Cap	$18.1 Billion	Shares	
Book Value	$3.0 Billion	376,523,776	
Price/Book	5.97	% Held	
Price/Sales	2.08	79.76	

Business Summary: Hotels, Restaurants & Travel (MIC: 2.2.1 SIC: 5812 NAIC: 722211)

Yum China Holdings is a holding company. Through its subsidiaries, Co. is a restaurant company in the People's Republic of China (China). Co.'s restaurant base consists of restaurant concepts, including KFC, Pizza Hut brands, as well as brands such as East Dawning, Little Sheep, Taco Bell and COFFii & JOY. Co. has the right to operate and sublicense the KFC, Pizza Hut and Taco Bell brands in China (excluding Hong Kong, Taiwan and Macau), and own the intellectual property of the East Dawning, Little Sheep and COFFii & JOY concepts outright. Most restaurants in the KFC, Pizza Hut, East Dawning, Taco Bell and COFFii & JOY concepts provide delivery service.

Recent Developments: For the quarter ended Sep 30 2019, net income increased 10.8% to US$235.0 million from US$212.0 million in the year-earlier quarter. Revenues were US$2.32 billion, up 4.8% from US$2.21 billion the year before. Operating income was US$300.0 million versus US$269.0 million in the prior-year quarter, an increase of 11.5%. Direct operating expenses rose 4.2% to US$1.73 billion from US$1.66 billion in the comparable period the year before. Indirect operating expenses increased 2.1% to US$294.0 million from US$288.0 million in the equivalent prior-year period.

Prospects: Our evaluation of Yum China Holdings Inc. as of October 4th, 2019 is the result of our systematic analysis on three basic characteristics: earnings strength, relative valuation, and recent stock price movement. The company has enjoyed a very positive trend in earnings per share over the past 5 quarters. In addition, recent analyst estimates for the company have been raised, and YUMC has posted results that exceeded analysts' expectations. Based on operating earnings yield, the company is fairly valued when compared to all of the companies we cover. Share price changes over the past year indicates that YUMC will perform very well over the near term.

Financial Data

(US$ in Millions)	9 Mos	6 Mos	3 Mos	12/31/2018	12/31/2017	12/31/2016	12/31/2015	12/31/2014
Earnings Per Share	1.81	1.74	1.64	1.79	1.01	1.36	...	...
Cash Flow Per Share	3.20	3.10	2.97	3.47	2.29	2.35	...	...
Tang Book Value Per Share	6.76	6.60	6.49	6.57	6.69	5.78	...	...
Dividends Per Share	0.480	0.460	0.440	0.420	0.100	...	...	...
Dividend Payout %	26.52	26.44	26.83	23.46	9.90	...	...	...
Income Statement								
Total Revenue	6,747	4,428	2,304	8,415	7,144	6,752	6,909	6,934
EBITDA	1,097	701	396	1,328	1,176	1,046	896	395
Depn & Amortn	251	167	83	414	391	385	408	392
Income Before Taxes	875	553	322	950	810	672	496	17
Income Taxes	226	139	93	214	381	158	168	54
Net Income	623	400	222	708	403	502	323	(7)
Average Shares	388	389	388	395	398	369	...	...
Balance Sheet								
Current Assets	2,256	2,137	2,067	1,952	1,802	1,426	799	648
Total Assets	6,710	6,725	6,762	4,610	4,263	3,727	3,201	3,257
Current Liabilities	1,648	1,626	1,587	1,253	1,017	1,004	948	1,040
Long-Term Obligations	23	24	23	25	21	28	34	34
Total Liabilities	3,685	3,728	3,776	1,737	1,481	1,350	1,280	1,369
Stockholders' Equity	3,025	2,997	2,986	2,873	2,782	2,377	1,921	1,888
Shares Outstanding	376	377	379	379	384	382	...	...
Statistical Record								
Return on Assets %	12.23	11.82	11.02	15.96	10.09	...	10.00	...
Return on Equity %	23.20	22.57	21.07	25.04	15.62	...	16.96	...
EBITDA Margin %	16.26	15.83	17.19	15.78	16.46	15.49	12.97	5.70
Net Margin %	9.23	9.03	9.64	8.41	5.64	7.43	4.68	N.M.
Asset Turnover	1.52	1.49	1.46	1.90	1.79	...	2.14	...
Current Ratio	1.37	1.31	1.30	1.56	1.77	1.42	0.84	0.62
Debt to Equity	0.01	0.01	0.01	0.01	0.01	0.01	0.02	0.02
Price Range	47.91-31.20	47.54-31.20	44.91-31.20	48.18-31.20	42.99-25.86	29.98-25.87	...	...
P/E Ratio	26.47-17.24	27.32-17.93	27.38-19.02	26.92-17.43	42.56-25.60	22.04-19.02	...	...
Average Yield %	1.19	1.20	1.18	1.10	0.28	...	...	...

Address: 7100 Corporate Drive, Plano, TX 75024 **Telephone:** 469-980-2898	**Web Site:** www.yumchina.com **Officers:** Fred Hu - Chairman Muktesh (Micky) Pant - Vice-Chairman, Chief Executive Officer	**Auditors:** KPMG Huazhen LLP **Transfer Agents:** American Stock Transfer & Trust Company, LLC

YUM! BRANDS INC

Exchange	Symbol	Price	52Wk Range	Yield	P/E
NYS	YUM	$100.73 (12/31/2019)	119.21-89.14	1.67	27.90

*7 Year Price Score 124.63 *NYSE Composite Index=100   *12 Month Price Score 90.84

Interim Earnings (Per Share)

Qtr.	Mar	Jun	Sep	Dec
2016	0.93	0.81	1.56	0.76
2017	0.77	0.58	1.18	1.25
2018	1.27	0.97	1.40	1.05
2019	0.83	0.92	0.81	...

Interim Dividends (Per Share)

Amt	Decl	Ex	Rec	Pay
0.42Q	01/25/2019	02/13/2019	02/14/2019	03/08/2019
0.42Q	05/06/2019	05/15/2019	05/16/2019	06/07/2019
0.42Q	08/09/2019	08/16/2019	08/19/2019	09/06/2019
0.42Q	11/11/2019	11/20/2019	11/21/2019	12/06/2019

Indicated Div: $1.68 (Div. Reinv. Plan)

Valuation Analysis   Institutional Holding

Forecast EPS	$3.70	No of Institutions
	(01/17/2020)	1491
Market Cap	$30.5 Billion	Shares
Book Value	N/A	307,619,520
Price/Book	N/A	% Held
Price/Sales	5.59	67.22

Business Summary: Hotels, Restaurants & Travel (MIC: 2.2.1 SIC: 5812 NAIC: 722211)

Yum! Brands franchises or operates a system of quick service restaurants through its KFC, Pizza Hut and Taco Bell brands. Co.'s operating segments consist of the KFC Division, the Pizza Hut Division and the Taco Bell Division. KFC restaurants provides fried and non-fried chicken products such as sandwiches, chicken strips, chicken-on-the-bone and other chicken products marketed under a variety of names. Pizza Hut is engaged in the sale of ready-to-eat pizza products. Pizza Hut operates in the delivery, carryout and casual dining segments. Taco Bell is engaged in Mexican-style food products, including various types of tacos, burritos, quesadillas, salads, nachos and other related items.

Recent Developments: For the quarter ended Sep 30 2019, net income decreased 43.8% to US$255.0 million from US$454.0 million in the year-earlier quarter. Revenues were US$1.34 billion, down 3.7% from US$1.39 billion the year before. Operating income was US$480.0 million versus US$553.0 million in the prior-year quarter, a decrease of 13.2%. Direct operating expenses declined 26.8% to US$292.0 million from US$399.0 million in the comparable period the year before. Indirect operating expenses increased 29.2% to US$567.0 million from US$439.0 million in the equivalent prior-year period.

Prospects: Our evaluation of Yum! Brands Inc. as of October 4th, 2019 is the result of our systematic analysis on three basic characteristics: earnings strength, relative valuation, and recent stock price movement. The company has produced a positive trend in earnings per share over the past 5 quarters. However, recent analyst estimates for the company have been mixed and YUM has posted results that exceeded analysts' expectations. Based on operating earnings yield, the company is fairly valued when compared to all of the companies we cover. Share price changes over the past year indicates that YUM will perform over the near term.

Financial Data

(US$ in Millions)	9 Mos	6 Mos	3 Mos	12/31/2018	12/31/2017	12/31/2016	12/26/2015	12/27/2014
Earnings Per Share	3.61	4.20	4.25	4.69	3.77	4.04	2.92	2.32
Cash Flow Per Share	4.13	4.09	4.18	3.65	2.97	3.01	4.92	4.63
Tang Book Value Per Share	...	...	...	...	...	...	N.M.	1.22
Dividends Per Share	1.620	1.560	1.500	1.440	1.200	1.890	1.690	1.520
Dividend Payout %	44.88	37.14	35.29	30.70	31.83	46.78	57.88	65.52
Income Statement								
Total Revenue	3,903	2,564	1,254	5,688	5,878	6,366	13,105	13,279
EBITDA	1,414	964	440	2,437	2,952	1,919	2,592	2,229
Depn & Amortn	84	54	26	146	238	294	712	702
Income Before Taxes	976	676	299	1,839	2,274	1,318	1,746	1,397
Income Taxes	170	125	37	297	934	324	489	406
Net Income	806	551	262	1,542	1,340	1,619	1,293	1,051
Average Shares	313	314	315	329	355	400	443	453
Balance Sheet								
Current Assets	1,548	1,122	1,186	1,207	2,507	1,482	1,688	1,646
Total Assets	5,003	4,674	4,744	4,130	5,311	5,478	8,075	8,345
Current Liabilities	987	1,186	1,327	1,301	1,512	1,369	3,088	2,411
Long-Term Obligations	10,491	9,869	9,736	9,751	9,429	9,061	3,054	3,077
Total Liabilities	13,100	12,668	12,648	12,056	11,645	11,134	7,164	6,798
Stockholders' Equity	(8,097)	(7,994)	(7,904)	(7,926)	(6,334)	(5,656)	911	1,547
Shares Outstanding	303	304	306	306	332	355	420	434
Statistical Record								
Return on Assets %	24.90	29.76	28.62	32.67	24.84	23.51	15.79	12.37
Return on Equity %	...	...	...	...	...	...	105.50	56.77
EBITDA Margin %	36.23	37.60	35.09	42.84	50.22	30.14	19.78	16.79
Net Margin %	20.65	21.49	20.89	27.11	22.80	25.43	9.87	7.91
Asset Turnover	1.19	1.23	1.16	1.20	1.09	0.92	1.60	1.56
Current Ratio	1.57	0.95	0.89	0.93	1.66	1.08	0.55	0.68
Debt to Equity	...	...	...	...	...	...	3.35	1.99
Price Range	119.21-85.47	110.67-77.74	100.90-77.74	93.46-76.30	83.47-63.18	65.62-46.91	68.22-48.26	59.89-47.57
P/E Ratio	33.02-23.68	26.35-18.51	23.74-18.29	19.93-16.27	22.14-16.76	16.24-11.61	23.36-16.53	25.81-20.51
Average Yield %	1.61	1.68	1.71	1.70	1.66	3.18	2.93	2.85

Address: 1441 Gardiner Lane, Louisville, KY 40213 **Telephone:** 502-874-8300	**Web Site:** www.yum.com **Officers:** David W. Gibbs - President, Chief Executive Officer, Chief Financial Officer, Chief Operating Officer David E. (Dave) Russell - Senior Vice President, Corporate Controller	**Auditors:** KPMG LLP **Investor Contact:** 502-874-8006 **Transfer Agents:** American Stock Transfer & Trust Company, New York, NY

ZAYO GROUP HOLDINGS INC

Exchange	Symbol	Price	52Wk Range	Yield	P/E
NYS	ZAYO	$34.65 (12/31/2019)	34.65-22.82	N/A	55.89

*7 Year Price Score N/A *NYSE Composite Index=100 *12 Month Price Score 103.57

Interim Earnings (Per Share)

Qtr.	Sep	Dec	Mar	Jun
2016-17	0.06	0.08	0.11	0.09
2017-18	0.09	0.05	0.09	0.18
2018-19	0.09	0.13	0.15	0.26
2019-20	0.08	...	...	...

Interim Dividends (Per Share)

No Dividends Paid

Valuation Analysis

		Institutional Holding	
Forecast EPS	$0.58	No of Institutions	
	(01/17/2020)	445	
Market Cap	$8.2 Billion	Shares	
Book Value	$1.4 Billion	225,983,696	
Price/Book	5.98	% Held	
Price/Sales	3.19	83.08	

Business Summary: Manufacturing (MIC: 6.1.1 SIC: 3669 NAIC: 334290)

Zayo Group Holdings is a holding company. Through its subsidiaries, Co. is a provider of communications and bandwidth infrastructure in the United States, Canada and Europe. Co. has four segments: Zayo Networks, which provides access to bandwidth infrastructure; Zayo Colocation, which provides data center and cloud infrastructure solutions to a range of enterprise, carrier, cloud and content customers; Allstream, which provides Cloud VoIP and Data Solutions; and Other, which is comprised of Zayo Professional Services that provides network and technical resources to customers. Key products include leased dark fiber, fiber to cellular towers and small cell sites and other bandwidth offering.

Recent Developments: For the year ended June 30 2019, net income increased 45.8% to US$150.0 million from US$102.9 million in the prior year. Revenues were US$2.58 billion, down 0.9% from US$2.60 billion the year before. Operating income was US$520.3 million versus US$423.2 million in the prior year, an increase of 22.9%. Direct operating expenses declined 2.8% to US$915.3 million from US$941.9 million in the comparable period the year before. Indirect operating expenses decreased 7.7% to US$1.14 billion from US$1.24 billion in the equivalent prior-year period.

Prospects: Our evaluation of Zayo Group Holdings Inc as of October 4th, 2019 is the result of our systematic analysis on three basic characteristics: earnings strength, relative valuation, and recent stock price movement. The company has produced a positive trend in earnings per share over the past 5 quarters. In addition, recent analyst estimates for the company have been raised, and ZAYO has posted results that exceeded analysts' expectations. Based on operating earnings yield, the company is overvalued when compared to all of the companies we cover. Share price changes over the past year indicates that ZAYO will perform in line with the market over the near term.

Financial Data

(US$ in Thousands)	3 Mos	06/30/2019	06/30/2018	06/30/2017	06/30/2016	06/30/2015	06/30/2014	06/30/2013
Earnings Per Share	0.62	0.62	0.41	0.35	(0.31)	(0.66)	(0.80)	(0.61)
Cash Flow Per Share	4.32	3.99	3.93	3.73	2.93	2.57	2.54	1.82
Income Statement								
Total Revenue	638,600	2,578,000	2,604,000	2,199,800	1,721,700	1,347,100	1,123,187	1,004,354
EBITDA	76,300	1,052,300	1,078,000	872,500	592,900	401,300	353,305	312,774
Depn & Amortn	(40,300)	538,300	650,200	526,900	440,500	351,400	294,125	280,128
Income Before Taxes	31,900	175,300	128,000	104,100	(67,700)	(164,100)	(144,349)	(169,818)
Income Taxes	14,000	25,300	26,100	18,400	8,500	(8,800)	37,295	(24,205)
Net Income	17,900	150,000	101,900	85,700	(76,200)	(155,300)	(179,294)	(137,217)
Average Shares	238,600	240,200	248,500	246,800	243,300	235,422	223,000	223,000
Balance Sheet								
Current Assets	531,600	485,200	630,800	514,600	397,100	567,900	544,979	303,496
Total Assets	9,881,800	9,334,600	9,216,800	8,739,400	6,727,500	6,094,600	5,049,066	4,251,240
Current Liabilities	871,900	643,500	618,200	620,300	486,500	386,900	344,886	281,760
Long-Term Obligations	5,872,100	6,011,900	5,811,700	5,626,300	4,130,200	3,680,500	3,242,529	2,821,072
Total Liabilities	8,510,500	7,993,100	7,727,700	7,328,900	5,508,300	4,883,400	4,632,681	3,644,987
Stockholders' Equity	1,371,300	1,341,500	1,489,100	1,410,500	1,219,200	1,211,200	416,385	606,253
Shares Outstanding	236,829	236,257	246,631	246,471	242,649	243,008	223,000	223,000
Statistical Record								
Return on Assets %	1.52	1.62	1.13	1.11	N.M.	N.M.	N.M.	...
Return on Equity %	9.97	10.60	7.03	6.52	N.M.	N.M.	N.M.	...
EBITDA Margin %	11.95	40.82	41.40	39.66	34.44	29.79	31.46	31.14
Net Margin %	2.80	5.82	3.91	3.90	N.M.	N.M.	N.M.	N.M.
Asset Turnover	0.27	0.28	0.29	0.28	0.27	0.24	0.24	...
Current Ratio	0.61	0.75	1.02	0.83	0.82	1.47	1.58	1.08
Debt to Equity	4.28	4.48	3.90	3.99	3.39	3.04	7.79	4.65
Price Range	34.15-20.46	39.35-20.46	37.62-29.92	35.22-27.56	29.43-21.89	32.03-22.00	...	...
P/E Ratio	55.08-33.00	63.47-33.00	91.76-72.98	100.63-78.74	...	...	...	...

Address: 1821 30th Street, Unit A, Boulder, CO 80301 **Telephone:** 303-381-4683	**Web Site:** www.zayo.com **Officers:** Daniel P. (Dan) Caruso - Chairman, Chief Executive Officer Matt Steinfort - Chief Financial Officer	**Auditors:** KPMG LLP **Transfer Agents:** American Stock Transfer & Trust Company LLC

ZENDESK INC

Exchange	Symbol	Price	52Wk Range	Yield	P/E
NYS	ZEN	$76.63 (12/31/2019)	93.74-55.54	N/A	N/A

*7 Year Price Score N/A   ***NYSE Composite Index=100**   ***12 Month Price Score 91.12**

Interim Earnings (Per Share)

Qtr.	Mar	Jun	Sep	Dec
2016	(0.30)	(0.28)	(0.27)	(0.25)
2017	(0.28)	(0.29)	(0.28)	(0.26)
2018	(0.28)	(0.33)	(0.32)	(0.31)
2019	(0.41)	(0.50)	(0.31)	...

Interim Dividends (Per Share)

No Dividends Paid

Valuation Analysis		Institutional Holding	
Forecast EPS	$0.32	No of Institutions	
	(01/16/2020)	409	
Market Cap	$8.6 Billion	Shares	
Book Value	$437.2 Million	124,565,168	
Price/Book	19.62	% Held	
Price/Sales	11.30	95.78	

Business Summary: Internet & Software (MIC: 6.3.2 SIC: 7372 NAIC: 511210)

Zendesk is a software development company that provides software as a service products to help organizations and their customers build better experiences. Co.'s family of products include: Zendesk Support, which provides organizations with the ability to track, prioritize, and solve customer support tickets; Zendesk Chat, which is a live chat software; Zendesk Talk, which is a cloud-based call center software for phone and SMS support conversations; Zendesk Guide, which is a knowledge base that powers both customer self-service and support agent productivity; Zendesk Explore, which provides analytics for businesses; and Zendesk Sell, which is a sales force automation software.

Recent Developments: For the quarter ended Sep 30 2019, net loss amounted to US$34.2 million versus a net loss of US$34.1 million in the year-earlier quarter. Revenues were US$210.5 million, up 35.9% from US$154.8 million the year before. Operating loss was US$35.4 million versus a loss of US$34.2 million in the prior-year quarter. Direct operating expenses rose 26.0% to US$59.2 million from US$47.0 million in the comparable period the year before. Indirect operating expenses increased 31.4% to US$186.7 million from US$142.0 million in the equivalent prior-year period.

Prospects: Our evaluation of Zendesk Inc as of October 4th, 2019 is the result of our systematic analysis on three basic characteristics: earnings strength, relative valuation, and recent stock price movement. The company has suffered a very negative trend in earnings per share over the past 5 quarters. However, recent analyst estimates for the company have been mixed and ZEN has posted results that exceeded analysts' expectations. Based on operating earnings yield, the company is overvalued when compared to all of the companies we cover. Share price changes over the past year indicates that ZEN will perform over the near term.

Financial Data

(US$ in Thousands)	9 Mos	6 Mos	3 Mos	12/31/2018	12/31/2017	12/31/2016	12/31/2015	12/31/2014
Earnings Per Share	(1.53)	(1.54)	(1.37)	(1.24)	(1.11)	(1.11)	(0.99)	(1.26)
Cash Flow Per Share	0.72	0.69	0.75	0.74	0.42	0.26	0.06	0.04
Tang Book Value Per Share	2.03	1.94	2.52	2.50	2.47	2.55	2.62	1.32
Income Statement								
Total Revenue	586,545	376,068	181,484	598,746	430,492	311,999	208,768	127,049
EBITDA	(71,877)	(58,840)	(25,108)	(114,495)	(91,856)	(86,606)	(72,514)	(61,578)
Depn & Amortn	56,814	37,005	18,106	23,900	20,300	16,200	11,200	6,100
Income Before Taxes	(132,824)	(98,237)	(44,286)	(143,191)	(112,156)	(102,806)	(83,714)	(67,678)
Income Taxes	661	1,024	434	(12,107)	(1,518)	993	338	(263)
Net Income	(133,485)	(99,261)	(44,720)	(131,084)	(110,638)	(103,799)	(84,052)	(67,415)
Average Shares	111,261	109,986	108,630	105,567	99,918	93,161	84,926	53,571
Balance Sheet								
Current Assets	616,708	608,910	600,335	572,596	328,207	279,818	283,231	139,005
Total Assets	1,459,458	1,438,997	1,372,678	1,237,879	560,204	475,285	422,686	205,788
Current Liabilities	449,964	907,417	389,702	342,763	230,724	167,218	117,399	78,149
Long-Term Obligations	477,007	...	464,364	458,176	...	...	...	3,911
Total Liabilities	1,022,269	1,012,020	953,733	820,958	238,563	175,857	129,396	92,082
Stockholders' Equity	437,189	426,977	418,945	416,921	321,641	299,428	293,290	113,706
Shares Outstanding	111,917	110,698	109,260	108,038	103,121	96,700	90,326	75,599
Statistical Record								
Asset Turnover	0.57	0.54	0.52	0.67	0.83	0.69	0.66	0.85
Current Ratio	1.37	0.67	1.54	1.67	1.42	1.67	2.41	1.78
Debt to Equity	1.09	...	1.11	1.10	...	...	...	0.03
Price Range	93.74-48.37	92.66-48.37	85.64-45.09	71.94-34.06	35.65-22.13	31.51-14.77	27.33-19.15	27.74-13.43

Address: 1019 Market Street, San Francisco, CA 94103 **Telephone:** 415-418-7506	**Web Site:** www.zendesk.com **Officers:** Norman Gennaro - Senior Vice President Mikkel Svane - Chairman, Chief Executive Officer	**Auditors:** Ernst & Young LLP **Transfer Agents:** Computershare Trust Company, N.A., Canton, Massachusetts

ZIMMER BIOMET HOLDINGS INC

Exchange	Symbol	Price	52Wk Range	Yield	P/E
NYS	ZBH	$149.68 (12/31/2019)	151.24-100.43	0.64	N/A

*7 Year Price Score 96.46 *NYSE Composite Index=100 *12 Month Price Score 106.68

TRADING VOLUME (thousand shares)

Interim Earnings (Per Share)

Qtr.	Mar	Jun	Sep	Dec
2016	0.52	(0.16)	0.78	0.34
2017	1.47	0.90	0.48	6.04
2018	0.85	0.90	0.79	(4.41)
2019	1.20	0.65	2.08	...

Interim Dividends (Per Share)

Amt	Decl	Ex	Rec	Pay
0.24Q	03/07/2019	03/28/2019	03/29/2019	04/30/2019
0.24Q	06/11/2019	06/27/2019	06/28/2019	07/31/2019
0.24Q	09/03/2019	09/27/2019	09/30/2019	10/31/2019
0.24Q	12/16/2019	12/26/2019	12/27/2019	01/31/2020

Indicated Div: $0.96

Valuation Analysis

		Institutional Holding	
Forecast EPS	$7.83	No of Institutions	
	(01/15/2020)	1352	
Market Cap	$30.8 Billion	Shares	
Book Value	$12.1 Billion		242,333,024
Price/Book	2.55	% Held	
Price/Sales	3.88		88.89

Business Summary: Medical Instruments & Equipment (MIC: 4.3.1 SIC: 3842 NAIC: 339113)

Zimmer Biomet Holdings is engaged in musculoskeletal healthcare. Co.'s products are: Knees, which includes knee replacement surgeries; Hips, which includes hip replacement surgeries; S.E.T., which includes surgical, sports medicine, biologics, foot and ankle, extremities and trauma products; Spine and Craniomaxillofacial and Thoracic, which designs, manufactures and distributes medical devices and surgical instruments, as well as provides face and skull reconstruction products; Dental, which manufactures and/or distributes dental reconstructive implants, dental prosthetic products and dental regenerative products; and Other, which includes bone cement and office based technology products.

Recent Developments: For the quarter ended Sep 30 2019, net income increased 166.5% to US$432.0 million from US$162.1 million in the year-earlier quarter. Revenues were US$1.89 billion, up 3.0% from US$1.84 billion the year before. Operating income was US$245.8 million versus US$223.3 million in the prior-year quarter, an increase of 10.1%. Direct operating expenses rose 1.3% to US$535.7 million from US$529.0 million in the comparable period the year before. Indirect operating expenses increased 2.4% to US$1.11 billion from US$1.08 billion in the equivalent prior-year period.

Prospects: Our evaluation of Zimmer Biomet Holdings Inc. as of October 4th, 2019 is the result of our systematic analysis on three basic characteristics: earnings strength, relative valuation, and recent stock price movement. The company has produced a positive trend in earnings per share over the past 5 quarters. However, recent analyst estimates for the company have been unchanged, while ZBH has posted results that exceeded analysts' expectations. Based on operating earnings yield, the company is undervalued when compared to all of the companies we cover. Share price changes over the past year indicates that ZBH will perform in line with the market over the near term.

Financial Data
(US$ in Thousands)

	9 Mos	6 Mos	3 Mos	12/31/2018	12/31/2017	12/31/2016	12/31/2015	12/31/2014
Earnings Per Share	(0.48)	(1.77)	(1.52)	(1.86)	8.90	1.51	0.77	4.19
Cash Flow Per Share	7.51	7.07	7.54	8.59	7.84	8.14	4.36	6.23
Tang Book Value Per Share	N.M.	N.M.	N.M.	N.M.	N.M.	N.M.	N.M.	20.05
Dividends Per Share	0.960	0.960	0.960	0.960	0.960	0.960	0.880	0.880
Dividend Payout %	...	...	...	...	10.79	63.58	114.29	21.00
Income Statement								
Total Revenue	5,856,500	3,964,100	1,975,500	7,932,900	7,824,100	7,683,900	5,997,800	4,673,300
EBITDA	1,228,000	840,000	493,100	1,056,700	1,847,900	1,787,200	1,142,800	1,263,700
Depn & Amortn	436,900	290,300	143,400	1,038,500	1,058,000	1,032,600	712,400	268,600
Income Before Taxes	616,600	432,000	291,700	(271,100)	464,600	399,600	153,200	943,900
Income Taxes	(193,500)	53,900	45,500	108,200	(1,348,800)	95,000	7,000	224,900
Net Income	810,900	379,800	246,100	(379,200)	1,813,800	305,900	147,000	720,100
Average Shares	207,000	206,200	205,800	203,500	203,700	202,400	189,800	171,700
Balance Sheet								
Current Assets	4,401,500	4,391,200	4,499,200	4,427,400	4,515,300	4,663,600	5,862,900	4,289,000
Total Assets	24,315,200	24,205,700	24,289,000	24,126,800	25,964,500	26,684,400	27,219,500	9,634,700
Current Liabilities	3,773,900	3,677,800	2,255,000	2,421,300	3,020,200	2,381,500	1,617,900	1,038,000
Long-Term Obligations	6,345,900	6,719,300	8,310,600	8,413,700	8,917,500	10,665,800	11,556,300	1,425,500
Total Liabilities	12,233,700	12,546,600	12,754,600	12,855,500	14,228,700	17,015,500	17,331,600	3,113,900
Stockholders' Equity	12,081,500	11,659,100	11,534,400	11,271,300	11,735,800	9,668,900	9,887,900	6,520,800
Shares Outstanding	205,600	204,900	204,800	204,000	202,600	200,600	202,700	169,700
Statistical Record								
Return on Assets %	N.M.	N.M.	N.M.	N.M.	6.89	1.13	0.80	7.50
Return on Equity %	N.M.	N.M.	N.M.	N.M.	16.95	3.12	1.79	11.24
EBITDA Margin %	20.97	21.19	24.96	13.32	23.62	23.26	19.05	27.04
Net Margin %	13.85	9.58	12.46	N.M.	23.18	3.98	2.45	15.41
Asset Turnover	0.32	0.32	0.31	0.32	0.30	0.28	0.33	0.49
Current Ratio	1.17	1.19	2.00	1.83	1.50	1.96	3.62	4.13
Debt to Equity	0.53	0.58	0.72	0.75	0.76	1.10	1.17	0.22
Price Range	142.61-97.23	131.47-97.23	131.47-97.23	131.47-97.23	132.61-103.33	133.09-91.68	121.76-92.41	115.05-90.87
P/E Ratio	...	...	...	...	14.90-11.61	88.14-60.72	158.13-120.01	27.46-21.69
Average Yield %	0.79	0.81	0.82	0.82	0.81	0.85	0.81	0.87

Address: 345 East Main Street,	Web Site: www.zimmer.com	Auditors: PricewaterhouseCoopers LLP
Warsaw, IN 46580	Officers: Bryan C. Hanson - President, Chief	Investor Contact: 574-267-6131
Telephone: 574-267-6131	Executive Officer Suketu P. Upadhyay - Executive	Transfer Agents: American Stock
	Vice President, Chief Financial Officer, Principal	Transfer & Trust Company LLC
	Financial Officer, Principal Accounting Officer	

ZOETIS INC

Exchange	Symbol	Price	52Wk Range	Yield	P/E
NYS	ZTS	$132.35 (12/31/2019)	133.25-81.56	0.60	43.68

*7 Year Price Score N/A   *NYSE Composite Index=100   *12 Month Price Score 106.75

Interim Earnings (Per Share)

Qtr.	Mar	Jun	Sep	Dec
2016	0.41	0.45	0.48	0.31
2017	0.48	0.50	0.61	0.16
2018	0.72	0.79	0.71	0.71
2019	0.65	0.77	0.90	...

Interim Dividends (Per Share)

Amt	Decl	Ex	Rec	Pay
0.164Q	02/12/2019	04/17/2019	04/18/2019	06/03/2019
0.164Q	05/15/2019	07/18/2019	07/19/2019	09/03/2019
0.164Q	10/03/2019	10/21/2019	10/22/2019	12/02/2019
0.20Q	12/11/2019	01/16/2020	01/17/2020	03/03/2020

Indicated Div: $0.80

Valuation Analysis   **Institutional Holding**

Forecast EPS	$3.61	No of Institutions	1319
	(01/14/2020)		
Market Cap	$63.1 Billion	Shares	
Book Value	$2.7 Billion		492,760,928
Price/Book	23.56	% Held	
Price/Sales	10.26		87.82

Business Summary: Pharmaceuticals (MIC: 4.1.1 SIC: 2834 NAIC: 325412)

Zoetis is a holding company. Through its subsidiaries, Co. is engaged in the discovery, development, manufacture and commercialization of animal health medicines, vaccines, and diagnostic products with a focus on both livestock and companion animals. Co. organizes and operates its business in two segments: the U.S. and International. Co.'s main product categories are vaccines, other pharmaceutical products, anti-infectives, parasiticides, medicated feed additives, and animal health diagnostics. Co.'s other non-pharmaceutical product categories include nutritionals and agribusiness, as well as products and services in complementary areas, including biodevices, diagnostics and genetics tests.

Recent Developments: For the quarter ended Sep 30 2019, net income increased 24.8% to US$433.0 million from US$347.0 million in the year-earlier quarter. Revenues were US$1.58 billion, up 7.0% from US$1.48 billion the year before. Direct operating expenses rose 1.3% to US$479.0 million from US$473.0 million in the comparable period the year before. Indirect operating expenses decreased 1.3% to US$547.0 million from US$554.0 million in the equivalent prior-year period.

Prospects: Our evaluation of Zoetis Inc as of October 4th, 2019 is the result of our systematic analysis on three basic characteristics: earnings strength, relative valuation, and recent stock price movement. The company has managed to produce a neutral trend in earnings per share over the past 5 quarters. However, recent analyst estimates for the company have been raised and ZTS has posted results that exceeded analysts' expectations. Based on operating earnings yield, the company is fairly valued when compared to all of the companies we cover. Share price changes over the past year indicates that ZTS will perform over the near term.

Financial Data

(US$ in Millions)	9 Mos	6 Mos	3 Mos	12/31/2018	12/31/2017	12/31/2016	12/31/2015	12/31/2014
Earnings Per Share	3.03	2.84	2.86	2.93	1.75	1.65	0.68	1.16
Cash Flow Per Share	3.76	3.85	3.73	3.71	2.75	1.43	1.33	1.25
Dividends Per Share	0.618	0.580	0.542	0.504	0.420	0.380	0.332	0.288
Dividend Payout %	20.40	20.42	18.95	17.20	24.00	23.03	48.82	24.83
Income Statement								
Total Revenue	4,586	3,002	1,455	5,825	5,307	4,888	4,765	4,785
EBITDA	1,920	1,201	563	2,134	1,933	1,624	865	1,138
Depn & Amortn	418	273	136	269	233	230	196	201
Income Before Taxes	1,364	836	381	1,690	1,525	1,228	545	820
Income Taxes	248	153	69	266	663	409	206	233
Net Income	1,116	683	312	1,428	864	821	339	583
Average Shares	481	482	483	486	493	498	502	502
Balance Sheet								
Current Assets	4,618	4,484	4,379	4,399	4,217	3,390	3,830	3,465
Total Assets	11,272	10,986	10,883	10,777	8,586	7,649	7,913	6,607
Current Liabilities	1,052	1,075	1,082	1,223	1,094	1,117	1,781	1,086
Long-Term Obligations	6,447	6,446	6,444	6,443	4,953	4,468	4,463	3,643
Total Liabilities	8,594	8,575	8,566	8,592	6,816	6,162	6,845	5,296
Stockholders' Equity	2,678	2,411	2,317	2,185	1,770	1,487	1,068	1,311
Shares Outstanding	476	477	479	479	486	492	497	501
Statistical Record								
Return on Assets %	13.45	14.04	14.18	14.75	10.64	10.52	4.67	8.86
Return on Equity %	60.93	62.77	64.91	72.21	53.05	64.09	28.50	51.80
EBITDA Margin %	41.87	40.01	38.69	36.64	36.42	33.22	18.15	23.78
Net Margin %	24.33	22.75	21.44	24.52	16.28	16.80	7.11	12.18
Asset Turnover	0.57	0.62	0.60	0.60	0.65	0.63	0.66	0.73
Current Ratio	4.39	4.17	4.05	3.60	3.85	3.03	2.15	3.19
Debt to Equity	2.41	2.67	2.78	2.95	2.80	3.00	4.18	2.78
Price Range	128.43-79.28	114.28-79.28	100.67-79.28	95.27-71.51	72.80-52.51	53.78-39.33	55.38-39.65	44.93-28.40
P/E Ratio	42.39-26.17	40.24-27.92	35.20-27.72	32.52-24.41	41.60-30.01	32.59-23.84	81.44-58.31	38.73-24.48
Average Yield %	0.61	0.62	0.61	0.59	0.69	0.79	0.72	0.85

Address: 10 Sylvan Way, Parsippany, NJ 07054	**Web Site:** www.zoetis.com	**Auditors:** KPMG LLP
Telephone: 973-822-7000	**Officers:** Michael B. McCallister - Chairman Catherine A. Knupp - President, Executive Vice President	**Transfer Agents:** Computershare Trust Company, N.A., College Station, TX

This Page Left Intentionally Blank

CONDENSED

STATISTICAL

TABULATION

The tab section consists of statistical highlights for all U.S. companies listed on the New York Stock Exchange.

Statistics for companies whose fiscal year ends prior to June 30 are listed under the prior calendar year. Statistics for companies whose fiscal year ends June 30 or after are listed under the current calendar year. Dividends and price ranges are on a calendar year basis.

Because of editorial constraints a column for fourth quarter results was not included. At fiscal year-end, full fiscal year per share earnings are listed and quarterly figures are eliminated. Quarterly per share earnings are inserted as the company reports in the current fiscal year.

NOTE: Figures listed under "Earnings Per Share" for investment companies are net asset value per share.

For abbreviations, see the blue section of the Handbook.

SYMBOL	COMPANY	NATURE OF BUSINESS	FISCAL YEAR-END	TOTAL REV. $MILL	NET INCOME $MILL	TOTAL ASSETS $MILL	NET STK EQUITY $MILL	NO OF INST	INST. HOLDINGS (SHARES)
DDD	3D Systems Corp. (DE)	Internet & Software	12/31/18	687.7	-45.5	825.8	578.4	333	112302635
MMM	3M Co	Medical Instruments & Equipment	12/31/18	32765.0	5349.0	36500.0	9796.0	2747	504214816
WBAI	500.com Ltd.	Sporting & Recreational	12/31/18	126.1	-462.6	1246.6	1116.6	28	5132133
WUBA	58.com Inc	IT Services	12/31/18	13137.8	2129.2	31830.8	23965.0	276	105718403
EGHT	8x8 Inc	Internet & Software	3/31/19	352.6	-88.7	546.4	249.4	253	106460118
ATEN	A10 Networks Inc	Internet & Software	12/31/18	232.2	-27.6	235.9	103.9	143	60087175
AIR	AAR Corp	Aerospace	5/31/19	2051.8	7.5	1517.2	905.9	284	42515272
AAN	Aaron's Inc	Retail - Furniture & Home Furnishing	12/31/18	3828.9	196.2	2826.7	1760.7	422	83826292
ABB	ABB Ltd	Electrical Equipment	12/31/18	27662.0	2173.0	44441.0	13952.0	527	147653817
ABT	Abbott Laboratories	Medical Instruments & Equipment	12/31/18	30578.0	2368.0	67173.0	30524.0	2811	1604249817
ABBV	AbbVie Inc	Pharmaceuticals	12/31/18	32753.0	5687.0	59352.0	-8446.0	2508	1209694414
ANF	Abercrombie & Fitch Co	Retail - Apparel and Accessories	2/2/19	3590.1	74.5	2385.6	1208.9	416	86220154
AGD	Aberdeen Global Dynamic Dividend	Holding and other Investment Office	10/31/19	11.2	-	140.3	139.8	55	3533650
AWP	Aberdeen Global Premier Propertie	Holding and other Investment Office	10/31/18	21.5	13.8	663.9	621.9	119	20183301
ACP	Aberdeen Income Credit Strategies	Holding and other Investment Office	10/31/19	20.2	13.7	242.5	162.9	32	3452140
JEQ	Aberdeen Japan Equity Fund Inc	Holding and other Investment Office	10/31/19	1.8	0.8	120.8	120.3	51	10249902
AOD	Aberdeen Total Dynamic Dividend F	Holding and other Investment Office	10/31/19	80.1	68.1	1009.4	1007.8	139	44112828
ABM	ABM Industries, Inc.	Sanitation Services	10/31/19	6498.6	127.4	3692.6	1542.0	310	78279801
AKR	Acadia Realty Trust	REITs	12/31/18	262.2	31.4	3958.8	1459.5	286	107383602
ACN	Accenture plc	Business Services	8/31/19	43215.0	4779.1	29789.9	14409.0	1837	554251653
ACCO	Acco Brands Corp	Office Equipment & Furniture	12/31/18	1941.2	106.7	2786.4	789.7	311	107620779
ATV	Acorn International Inc	Advertising	12/31/18	28.4	31.1	90.1	71.7	8	281159
EPAC	Actuant Corp	Industrial Machinery & Equipment	8/31/18	654.8	-249.1	1124.3	301.2	282	77773899
AYI	Acuity Brands Inc (Holding Compan	Electrical Equipment	8/31/19	3672.7	330.4	3172.4	1918.9	593	47264567
GOLF	Acushnet Holdings Corp.	Sporting & Recreational	12/31/18	1633.7	99.9	1691.6	894.9	147	38047689
ADX	Adams Diversified Equity Fund Inc	Holding and other Investment Office	12/31/18	30.7	20.6	1604.4	1580.9	161	24084297
PEO	Adams Natural Resources Fund Inc	Holding and other Investment Office	12/31/18	17.4	12.3	535.9	523.0	98	10770586
AGRO	Adecoagro SA	Agricultural Crop Production	12/31/18	808.5	-24.6	2277.4	1063.6	109	57874544
ADNT	Adient Plc	Auto Parts	9/30/19	16526.0	-491.0	10342.0	1848.0	384	97270023
ADT	ADT Inc (DE)	Services	12/31/18	4581.7	-609.2	17208.6	4224.8	194	732656866
ATGE	Adtalem Global Education Inc	Educational Services	6/30/19	1239.7	95.2	2242.7	1391.5	363	68656154
AAP	Advance Auto Parts Inc	Retail - Automotive	12/29/18	9580.6	423.8	9040.6	3550.8	740	87893152
ADSW	Advanced Disposal Services Inc (D	Miscellaneous Consumer Services	12/31/18	1558.2	9.4	3528.3	911.5	202	93286332
WMS	Advanced Drainage Systems Inc	Plastics	3/31/19	1384.7	77.8	1042.2	486.6	196	64191801
ASIX	AdvanSix Inc	Plastics	12/31/18	1515.0	66.2	1034.6	420.3	371	26760669
AVK	Advent Convertible & Income Fund	Holding and other Investment Office	10/31/19	39.3	16.3	969.1	564.1	99	9957456
ACM	AECOM	Construction Services	9/30/19	20173.3	-261.1	14461.6	3690.6	442	158613887
AEG	AEGON NV	Life & Health	12/31/18	14774.0	710.0	392633.0	22545.0	310	188028510
AER	AerCap Holdings NV	Airlines/Air Freight	12/31/18	4800.0	1015.6	43208.9	8828.0	461	134551846
AJRD	Aerojet Rocketdyne Holdings Inc	Defense	12/31/18	1895.9	137.3	2490.1	421.3	355	108293870
AES	AES Corp.	Electric Utilities	12/31/18	10736.0	1203.0	32521.0	4087.0	848	780850899
AMG	Affiliated Managers Group Inc.	Wealth Management	12/31/18	2378.4	243.6	8219.1	3457.4	627	63771470
AFL	AFLAC Inc	Life & Health	12/31/18	21758.0	2920.0	140406.0	23462.0	1501	595166098
MITT	AG Mortgage Investment Trust Inc	REITs	12/31/18	89.2	1.6	3548.9	656.0	155	24866711
AGCO	AGCO Corp.	Industrial Machinery & Equipment	12/31/18	9352.0	285.5	7626.4	2932.9	584	80972657
A	Agilent Technologies, Inc.	Medical Instruments & Equipment	10/31/19	5163.0	1071.0	9452.0	4748.0	1066	353727203
ATG PR	AGL Capital Trust II	Gas Utilities						-	0
AEM	Agnico Eagle Mines Ltd	Precious Metals	12/31/18	2191.2	-326.7	7852.8	4550.0	509	162057769
ADC	Agree Realty Corp.	REITs	12/31/18	148.2	58.2	2028.2	1236.1	333	48710886
AHC	AH Belo Corp	Publishing	12/31/18	202.3	-5.4	142.3	70.6	75	16741711
AL	Air Lease Corp	Miscellaneous Transportation Servic	12/31/18	1679.7	510.8	18481.8	4806.9	387	112959624
APD	Air Products & Chemicals Inc	Specialty Chemicals	9/30/19	8918.9	1760.0	18942.8	11053.6	1566	246845841
AYR	Aircastle Ltd.	Aerospace	12/31/18	890.4	247.9	7871.2	2008.7	219	49425928
AKS	AK Steel Holding Corp.	Non-Precious Metals	12/31/18	6818.2	186.0	4515.7	99.9	390	238585043
ALP PRQ	Alabama Power Co	Electric Utilities	12/31/18	6032.0	945.0	26730.0	7768.0		0
ALG	Alamo Group, Inc.	Industrial Machinery & Equipment	12/31/18	1008.8	73.5	721.6	507.4	224	12687205
AGI	Alamos Gold Inc (New)	Precious Metals	12/31/18	651.8	-72.6	3265.2	2602.3	215	243407528
ALK	Alaska Air Group, Inc.	Airlines/Air Freight	12/31/18	8264.0	437.0	10912.0	3751.0	715	123924093
AIN	Albany International Corp	Industrial Machinery & Equipment	12/31/18	982.5	82.9	1418.0	605.2	317	37516944
ALB	Albemarle Corp.	Specialty Chemicals	12/31/18	3374.9	693.6	7581.7	3585.3	785	122479668
AA	Alcoa Corporation	Metal Products	12/31/18	13403.0	227.0	15938.0	5389.0	412	168856797
ALC	Alcon Inc	Medical Instruments & Equipment	12/31/18	7153.0	-227.0	27062.0	22639.0	704	245751328
ALEX	Alexander & Baldwin Inc (REIT)	REITs	12/31/18	644.4	-72.0	2225.2	1210.5		0
ALX	Alexander's Inc	REITs	12/31/18	232.8	32.8	1481.3	285.1	159	2079571
ARE	Alexandria Real Estate Equities Inc	REITs	12/31/18	1327.5	379.3	14465.0	7342.0	632	135193826
AQN	Algonquin Power & Utilities Corp	Water Utilities	12/31/18	1647.4	185.0	9389.0	3177.6	168	235361409
BABA	Alibaba Group Holding Ltd	Internet & Software	3/31/19	376844.0	87886.0	965076.0	499076.0	1812	1298499925
Y	Alleghany Corp.	General Insurance	12/31/18	6887.2	39.5	25344.9	7692.7	509	15263254
ATI	Allegheny Technologies, Inc	Non-Precious Metals	12/31/18	4046.6	222.4	5501.8	1885.7	488	168900248
ALLE	Allegion Plc	Services	12/31/18	2731.7	434.9	2810.2	651.0	594	100147160
AGN	Allergan PLC	Pharmaceuticals	12/31/18	15787.4	-5096.4	101787.6	65114.1	1233	307291218
ALE	Allete Inc	Electric Utilities	12/31/18	1498.6	174.1	5165.0	2155.8	430	52100122
ADS	Alliance Data Systems Corp.	Business Services	12/31/18	7791.2	963.1	30387.7	2332.1	739	56623086
AWF	AllianceBernstein Global High Inco	Holding and other Investment Office	3/31/19	76.3	64.5	1166.5	1117.0	144	21207515
AB	AllianceBernstein Holding LP	Wealth Management	12/31/18	270.6	242.4	1490.7		312	31040644
AFB	AllianceBernstein National Municipa	Holding and other Investment Office	10/31/19	26.2	15.4	697.5	437.8	81	10896071
AIO	AllianzGI Artificial Intelligence & Tec	Holding and other Investment Office	8/26/19			0.1	0.1	-	0
CBH	AllianzGI Convertible & Income 202	Holding and other Investment Office	2/28/19	13.4	8.8	255.2	177.3		0
NCV	AllianzGI Convertible & Income Fun	Holding and other Investment Office	2/28/19	58.2	49.7	887.4	825.9	107	14231155
NCZ	AllianzGI Convertible & Income Fun	Holding and other Investment Office	2/28/19	44.1	37.8	676.5	651.4	87	13837423

T2

EARNINGS PER SHARE						P/E RATIO		DIVIDENDS PER SHARE			AV. YLD	DIV. DECLARED		PRICE RANGE	
QUARTERLY			ANNUAL					PER SHARE			%			2018	
1st	2nd	3rd	2018	2017	2016			2018	2017	2016		AMOUNT	PAYABLE		
-	-	-0.15	-0.41	-0.59	-0.35	-		-	-	-	-	-	-	14.2	6.5
-	-	2.72	8.89	7.93	8.16	24.7	17.0	5.44	4.70	4.44	3.0	1.440Y	18/53/27	219.5	150.7
-	-0.13	-	-1.10	-0.78	-0.49			-	-	-	-	-	-	15.7	7.6
-	-	0.35	6.66	4.35	-2.73	11.1	7.2	-	-	-	-	-	-	74.0	48.0
-	-0.42	-	-1.14	-0.05	-0.06			-	-	-	-	-	-	26.4	16.8
-	-	0.00	-0.38	-0.15	-0.32			-	-	-	-	-	-	7.8	6.0
-	0.40	-	0.41	1.64	1.37	126.5	73.3	0.30	0.30	0.30	0.8	0.0750Y	1/14/20	51.9	30.1
-	-	0.58	2.78	4.06	1.91	28.1	15.4	0.13	0.11	0.10	0.2	0.040Y	18/53/27	78.1	42.8
-	-	0.28	1.02	1.03	0.88	23.6	17.5	0.81	0.76	0.73	4.1	-	-	24.1	17.9
-	-	0.53	1.33	0.27	0.94	66.7	49.8	1.12	1.06	1.04	1.4	0.360Y	18/53/27	88.7	66.2
-	-	1.26	3.66	3.30	3.63	24.8	17.2	3.59	2.56	2.28	4.6	1.180Y	18/53/27	90.8	63.0
-	-	0.10	0.10	0.06	0.51	304.8	138.4	0.80	0.80	0.80	4.1	0.20Y	12/16/19	30.5	13.8
-	-	0.61	0.75	0.70		17.2	13.9	0.78	0.78	0.78	8.1	0.0650	1/28/20	10.5	8.5
-	-	-	0.08	0.11	0.17	81.5	62.4	0.60	0.60	0.60	9.9	0.040	1/28/20	6.5	5.0
-	-	-	1.55	1.49	1.46	8.4	6.8	1.44	1.44	1.44	12.0	0.120	1/28/20	13.0	10.6
-	-	-	0.07	0.07	0.08	115.1	91.7	0.48	0.32	0.31	6.7	0.1888C	1/10/20	8.1	6.4
-	-	-	0.64	0.68	0.65	14.0	11.4	0.69	0.69	0.69	8.3	0.05750	1/28/20	9.0	7.3
-	-	0.55	1.47	0.07	1.01	28.7	21.1	0.70	0.68	0.66	1.9	0.1850Y	18/53/27	42.3	30.9
-	-	0.12	0.38	0.73	0.94	78.0	61.3	1.09	1.05	1.16	3.9	0.290Z	1/15/20	29.6	23.3
2.09	-	-	6.34	5.44	6.45	-		2.66	2.42	2.20		0.80	18/53/27	-	
-	-	0.28	1.00	1.19	0.87	10.1	7.2	0.24	-	-	2.7	0.0650Y	12/18/19	10.1	7.2
-	-	-0.13	0.60	0.19	0.05	52.1	0.0	14.92	-	-	69.1	-	-	31.3	0.0
0.03	-	-	-0.36	-1.11	-1.78			0.04	0.04	0.04	0.2	0.040Y	10/14/19	27.2	20.6
1.44	-	-	8.52	7.43	6.63	17.2	13.1	0.52	0.52	0.52	0.4	0.130Y	18/53/27	146.3	111.5
-	-	0.39	1.32	1.23	0.62	24.9	15.8	0.52	0.48	-	2.0	0.140Y	12/13/19	32.8	20.9
-	-	-	0.20	0.22	0.19	83.5	61.8	2.00	1.38	0.99	13.2	0.03C	2/28/20	16.7	12.4
-	-	-	0.42	0.46	0.41	41.3	34.9	1.17	1.18	1.14	7.3	0.01C	2/28/20	17.4	14.6
-	-0.05	-	-0.21	0.08	0.02			-	-	-	-	-	-	-	
-	-	-3.43	-18.06	9.34	-16.36			0.82	0.82	-	-	0.2750	11/15/18	-	
-	-	-0.25	-0.81	0.53	-0.84			0.14	-	-	2.1	0.0350Y	18/53/27	9.6	4.3
0.26	-	-	0.54	1.91	-0.05	95.1	55.0	-	0.18	0.36	-	0.180Y	18/53/27	51.4	29.7
-	-	1.75	5.73	6.42	6.20	31.7	23.5	0.24	0.24	0.24	0.2	0.060Y	18/53/27	181.4	134.9
-	-	0.04	0.11	0.43	-0.44	299.8	211.6	-	-	-	-	-	-	33.0	23.3
-	0.10	-	0.99	0.50	0.27	40.3	24.4	0.28	0.24	0.20	0.9	0.090Y	12/13/19	39.9	24.2
-	-	0.28	2.14	4.72	1.12	16.1	9.1	-	-	-	-	-	-	34.4	19.4
-	-	-	0.51	0.69	0.75	30.5	24.5	1.40	1.24	1.13	9.6	0.11720	1/31/20	15.6	12.5
-	-	0.52	0.84	2.13	0.62	52.2	31.4	-	-	-	-	-	-	43.8	26.4
-	-	-	0.29	1.14	0.15	18.6	12.7	0.28	0.26	0.26	6.0	0.25280Z	3/16/20	5.4	3.7
1.68	-	-	6.83	6.43	5.52	-		-	-	-	-	-	-	-	
-	-	0.39	1.75	-0.13	0.27	30.0	18.3	-	-	-	-	0.030Y	5/28/04	52.5	32.0
-	-	0.32	1.81	-1.76	-1.71	11.1	7.8	0.52	0.48	0.44	3.1	0.14330Y	18/53/27	20.0	14.2
-	-	1.71	4.52	12.03	8.57	25.6	15.9	1.20	0.80	-	1.3	0.320	18/53/27	115.5	71.8
-	-	1.04	3.77	5.77	3.21	15.1	11.8	1.04	0.87	0.83	2.0	0.270Y	18/53/27	56.9	44.4
-	-	0.19	-0.42	3.77	1.80			1.98	2.00	1.90	12.2	0.450Z	1/31/20	18.4	14.7
-	-	0.10	3.58	2.32	1.96	22.5	15.2	0.60	0.56	0.52	0.8	0.160Y	18/53/27	80.7	54.4
-	-	0.60	0.97	2.10	1.40	88.1	65.2	0.60	0.53	0.46	0.8	0.180Y	18/53/27	85.5	63.3
-	0.12	-	-1.40	1.05	0.70			0.44	0.41	0.36	0.8	0.1750	12/16/19	85.2	39.0
-	-	0.48	1.78	2.08	1.97	44.3	32.4	2.15	2.02	1.92	3.1	0.5850Z	1/3/20	78.9	57.6
-	0.78	-	-0.26	0.46	-0.90			0.32	0.46	0.32	8.7	0.080Y	3/6/20	4.3	2.8
-	-	1.34	4.60	6.82	3.44	10.5	6.4	0.43	0.33	0.23	1.1	0.38440Y	18/53/27	48.4	29.6
2.14	-	-	6.78	13.65	2.89	35.6	22.8	5.20	3.62	2.53	2.5	1.340Y	18/53/27	241.3	154.6
-	-	0.57	3.17	1.87	1.92			1.14	1.06	0.98	-	0.320Y	12/13/19	-	
-	-	0.01	0.59	0.02	-0.03	6.0	2.9	-	-	-	-	0.050Y	18/53/27	3.5	1.7
-	-	-	-	-	-			1.25	0.39	-	4.8	0.31250Y	4/1/20	27.2	23.8
-	-	1.47	6.25	3.79	3.46	20.8	12.0	0.44	0.40	0.36	0.4	0.130Y	1/29/20	129.7	75.1
-	0.06	-	-0.19	0.09	-0.07			0.02	0.02	0.02	0.3	0.010	12/20/19	9.9	3.8
-	-	2.60	3.52	8.35	6.54	20.4	15.2	1.28	1.20	1.10	2.0	0.350	18/53/27	71.9	53.6
-	-	1.24	2.57	1.03	1.64	35.6	23.7	0.69	0.68	0.68	0.9	0.190Y	1/8/20	91.5	60.8
-	-	1.46	6.34	4.49	5.68	14.6	9.4	1.34	1.28	1.22	1.8	0.36750Y	18/53/27	92.3	59.3
-	-	-1.19	1.20	1.16	-2.19	25.8	13.9	-	-	-	-	-	-	31.0	16.7
-	-	-0.69	-1.02	4.34	-0.18			11.65	15.92	0.25	50.2	0.190Z	18/53/27	25.4	18.5
-	-	3.22	6.42	15.74	16.91	61.3	46.9	18.00	17.00	16.00	5.0	4.50Z	2/14/20	393.7	301.0
-	-	-0.44	3.52	1.58	-1.99	46.2	31.6	3.73	3.45	3.23	2.6	1.030Z	18/53/27	162.5	111.4
-	-	0.23	0.38	0.47	0.44	49.9	26.2	0.50	0.60	0.55	3.5	0.42970Z	4/17/20	18.9	10.0
-	3.44	-	3.06	2.12	3.49	70.7	42.7	-	-	-	-	-	-	216.4	130.6
-	-	6.27	2.62	5.85	29.59	306.1	231.2	10.00	-	-	1.4	10.0	18/53/27	802.0	605.8
-	-	0.78	1.61	-0.83	-5.97	18.2	10.7	-	-	0.24	-	0.080Y	18/53/27	29.3	17.3
-	-	1.40	4.54	2.85	2.39			0.84	0.64	0.48	-	0.270	12/30/19	-	
-	-	-2.40	-15.26	-13.19	38.18			2.88	2.80	-	-	0.740	18/53/27	-	
-	-	0.60	3.38	3.38	3.14	26.1	21.6	2.24	2.14	2.08	2.7	0.58750Y	18/53/27	88.2	73.2
-	-	-2.13	17.49	14.10	7.34	10.4	5.7	2.28	2.08	0.52	1.6	0.630	18/53/27	181.5	100.0
-	-	-	0.83	0.82	0.89	14.7	13.0	0.84	0.95	1.11	7.2	0.06550	1/17/20	12.2	10.8
-	-	0.62	2.50	2.19	2.23	12.5	10.6	2.88	2.13	1.75	9.9	0.630	11/14/19	31.2	26.4
-	-	-	0.61	0.66	0.71	23.1	20.2	0.56	0.64	0.72	4.2	0.0458M	1/17/20	14.1	12.3
-	-	-	-	-	-			-	-	-	-	0.10830	2/3/20	20.4	19.2
-	-	-	0.35	-	-	28.1	23.6	0.32	-	-	3.5	0.0460	2/3/20	9.8	8.3
-	-	-	0.69	0.73	0.83	9.5	7.7	0.78	0.78	0.93	13.4	0.05250	2/3/20	6.5	5.3
-	-	-	0.62	0.66	0.75	9.3	7.5	0.69	0.69	0.85	13.4	0.0450	2/3/20	5.8	4.6

T3

SYMBOL	COMPANY	NATURE OF BUSINESS	FISCAL YEAR-END	TOTAL REV. $MILL	NET INCOME $MILL	TOTAL ASSETS $MILL	NET STK EQUITY $MILL	NO OF INST	INST. HOLDINGS (SHARES)
ACV	AllianzGI Diversified Income & Conv	Holding and other Investment Office	1/31/19	9.7	1.7	339.2	227.3		0
NIE	AllianzGI Equity & Convertible Inco	Holding and other Investment Office	1/31/19	12.7	5.4	634.6	624.3	79	6816642
NFJ	AllianzGI NFJ Dividend Interest & P	Holding and other Investment Office	1/31/19	38.2	25.4	1294.6	1281.7	145	33368381
ALSN	Allison Transmission Holdings Inc	Auto Parts	12/31/18	2713.0	639.0	4237.0	659.0	470	208569227
ALL	Allstate Corp	General Insurance	12/31/18	39815.0	2252.0	112249.0	21312.0	1492	355062489
ALLY	Ally Financial Inc	Credit & Lending	12/31/18	10466.0	1263.0	178869.0	13268.0	602	402176826
PINE	Alpine Income Property Trust Inc	REITs	12/31/18	11.7	4.0	126.6	124.2		0
AYX	Alteryx Inc	Internet & Software	12/31/18	253.6	28.0	618.2	301.8	344	47771483
ATUS	Altice USA Inc	Radio & Television	12/31/18	9566.6	18.8	33613.8	3800.9	370	360954887
MO	Altria Group Inc	Tobacco Products	12/31/18	25364.0	6963.0	55638.0	14787.0	2362	1587560264
ACH	Aluminum Corp of China Ltd.	Non-Precious Metals	12/31/17	180.1	1378.4	200146.6	39478.4	76	2848826
ALUS	Alussa Energy Acquisition Corp	Business Services	6/30/19		-0.0	0.1	0.0		0
ABEV	Ambev SA	Beverages	12/31/18	50231.3	11024.7	94126.1	56340.6		0
AMC	AMC Entertainment Holdings Inc.	Entertainment	12/31/18	5460.8	110.1	9495.8	1398.0	228	60823078
AMCR	Amcor plc	Containers & Packaging						445	433278767
AEE	Ameren Corp	Electric Utilities	12/31/18	6291.0	815.0	27215.0	7631.0	844	229159788
AMRC	Ameresco Inc	Construction Services	12/31/18	787.1	38.0	1161.6	376.9	130	17892663
AMX	America Movil SAB de CV	Services	12/31/18	1038207.7	52566.2	1429223.4	195995.6	473	297416186
AAT	American Assets Trust Inc	REITs	12/31/18	330.9	20.0	2198.3	803.0	289	71139480
AXL	American Axle & Manufacturing Hol	Auto Parts	12/31/18	7270.4	-57.5	7510.7	1483.9	343	130680898
ACC	American Campus Communities Inc	REITs	12/31/18	880.8	117.1	7038.8	3481.1	497	161617619
AEO	American Eagle Outfitters, Inc.	Retail - Apparel and Accessories	2/2/19	4035.7	261.9	1903.4	1287.6	583	221945745
AEP	American Electric Power Co Inc	Electric Utilities	12/31/18	16195.7	1923.8	68802.8	19067.8	1534	446234596
AEL	American Equity Investment Life Ho	Life & Health	12/31/18	1547.1	458.0	61625.6	2399.1	377	104418664
AXP	American Express Co.	Credit & Lending	12/31/18	43281.0	6921.0	188602.0	22290.0	2284	869752417
AFG	American Financial Group Inc	General Insurance	12/31/18	7150.0	530.0	63456.0	4970.0	555	76767735
AMH	American Homes 4 Rent	REITs	12/31/18	1072.9	108.3	9001.5	5252.0		0
AIG	American International Group Inc	General Insurance	12/31/18	47389.0	-6.0	491984.0	56361.0	1365	1031888025
ARL	American Realty Investors, Inc.	Property, Real Estate & Developmen	12/31/18	121.0	173.7	826.1	258.3	38	349537
ARA	American Renal Associates Holding	Diagnostic & Health Related Service	12/31/18	805.8	-28.8	985.8	-58.5	90	28514538
AWR	American States Water Co	Water Utilities	12/31/18	436.8	63.9	1501.4	558.2	418	33920533
AMT	American Tower Corp (New)	REITs	12/31/18	7440.1	1236.4	33010.4	5336.1	1720	503010768
AVD	American Vanguard Corp.	Agricultural Chemicals	12/31/18	454.3	24.2	593.6	329.2	188	29536544
AWK	American Water Works Co, Inc.	Water Utilities	12/31/18	3440.0	567.0	21223.0	5864.0	1056	194241439
COLD	Americold Realty Trust	REITs	12/31/18	1603.6	48.0	2532.4	706.8	343	212702666
AMP	Ameriprise Financial Inc	Wealth Management	12/31/18	12835.0	2098.0	137216.0	5588.0	1150	150766293
ABC	AmerisourceBergen Corp.	Pharmaceuticals	9/30/19	179589.1	855.4	39172.0	2878.9	1071	191320582
AME	AMETEK Inc	Electrical Equipment	12/31/18	4845.9	777.9	8662.3	4241.9	869	239646679
RYCE	Amira Nature Foods Ltd	Food	3/31/18	418.9	-78.2	512.8	218.7	37	1611473
AMN	AMN Healthcare Services Inc	Diagnostic & Health Related Service	12/31/18	2136.1	141.7	1492.7	639.0	406	65343145
AMRX	Amneal Pharmaceuticals Inc	Pharmaceuticals	12/31/18	1663.0	-169.7	4352.7	504.8		0
AP	Ampco-Pittsburgh Corp.	Industrial Machinery & Equipment	12/31/18	419.4	-69.3	571.1	87.6	73	6773078
APH	Amphenol Corp.	Electrical Equipment	12/31/18	8202.0	1205.0	10044.9	4017.0	982	338969972
AMPY	Amplify Energy Corp (New)	Production & Extraction	12/31/18	208.6	49.8	605.5	541.7	177	61774936
AXR	AMREP Corp.	Business Services	4/30/19	12.8	1.5	100.5	89.8	35	1689371
HKIB	AMTD International Inc	Banking	12/31/18	466.8	468.1	7107.2	2651.8		0
PLAN	Anaplan Inc	IT Services	1/31/19	240.6	-131.0	528.8	307.5	257	95177008
FINS	Angel Oak Financial Strategies Inco	Finance Intermediaries & Services	4/1/19			0.1	0.1		0
AU	AngloGold Ashanti Ltd	Precious Metals	12/31/18	3943.0	133.0	6643.0	2652.0	293	222293489
BUD	Anheuser-Busch InBev SA/NV	Beverages	12/31/18	54619.0	4368.0	232103.0	64486.0		0
AXE	Anixter International Inc	Electrical Equipment	12/28/18	8400.2	156.3	4653.1	1570.4	342	41388336
NLY	Annaly Capital Management Inc	REITs	12/31/18	2279.5	54.4	105787.5	14112.1	947	968016967
AM	Antero Midstream Corp	Gas Utilities	12/31/18	142.9	66.6	47.7		312	355346207
AR	Antero Resources Corp	Production & Extraction	12/31/18	4139.6	-397.5	15519.5	7665.8	349	510626460
ANTM	Anthem Inc	Life & Health	12/31/18	92105.0	3750.0	71571.0	28541.0	1265	258901987
ANH	Anworth Mortgage Asset Corp.	REITs	12/31/18	148.8	-6.5	5037.9	581.1	224	66645364
AON	Aon Plc	Brokers & Intermediaries	12/31/18	10770.0	1134.0	26422.0	4151.0	1000	254903797
APA	Apache Corp	Production & Extraction	12/31/18	7424.0	40.0	21582.0	7130.0	1094	451786504
AIV	Apartment Investment & Manageme	REITs	12/31/18	972.4	666.2	6190.0	1699.4	560	197666155
APY	Apergy Corp	Equipment & Services	12/31/18	1216.6	94.0	1971.8	979.1	381	74929564
APHA	Aphria Inc	Pharmaceuticals	5/31/19	237.1	-16.5	2441.6	1704.7		0
ARI	Apollo Commercial Real Estate Fina	REITs	12/31/18	403.9	220.0	5095.8	2509.7	325	113205552
APO	Apollo Global Management Inc	Finance Intermediaries & Services	12/31/18	1093.1	-10.4	5991.7	1376.2	416	162886005
AFT	Apollo Senior Floating Rate Fund In	Holding and other Investment Office	12/31/18	30.1	19.5	450.0	254.4	73	5258538
AIF	Apollo Tactical Income Fund Inc	Holding and other Investment Office	12/31/18	28.8	19.2	403.4	232.4	48	4777666
APLE	Apple Hospitality REIT Inc	REITs	12/31/18	1270.6	206.1	4928.7	3409.0	306	157203605
AIT	Applied Industrial Technologies, Inc.	Industrial Machinery & Equipment	6/30/19	3472.7	144.0	2331.7	897.0	327	45830035
ATR	AptarGroup Inc.	Plastics	12/31/18	2764.8	194.7	3377.7	1422.6	560	82198755
APTV	Aptiv PLC	Auto Parts	12/31/18	14435.0	1067.0	12480.0	3459.0	734	275161867
WTR	Aqua America Inc	Water Utilities	12/31/18	838.1	192.0	6964.5	2009.4	760	169832892
WAAS	AquaVenture Holdings Ltd	Water Utilities	12/31/18	145.6	-20.7	725.5	336.6	108	14536579
ARMK	Aramark	Hotels, Restaurants & Travel	9/27/19	16227.3	448.5	13736.3	3320.0	439	275089569
ABR	Arbor Realty Trust Inc	REITs	12/31/18	484.9	180.2	4612.2	895.2	239	48107848
ARC	ARC Document Solutions, Inc.	Printing	12/31/18	400.8	8.9	339.7	140.3	118	34413741
MT	ArcelorMittal SA	Non-Precious Metals	12/31/18	76033.0	5149.0	91249.0	42086.0	8	1145871
ARCH	Arch Coal Inc	Mining	12/31/18	2451.8	312.6	1887.1	704.8	364	38948013
ADM	Archer Daniels Midland Co.	Food	12/31/18	64341.0	1810.0	40833.0	18981.0	1193	594984896
AROC	Archrock Inc	Equipment & Services	12/31/18	904.4	21.1	2552.5	841.6	300	141880935
ARNC	Arconic Inc	Non-Precious Metals	12/31/18	14014.0	642.0	18693.0	5573.0	911	505287399
ARCO	Arcos Dorados Holdings Inc	Hotels, Restaurants & Travel	12/31/18	3081.6	36.8	1578.0	392.4	148	120638125

T4

EPS 1st	EPS 2nd	EPS 3rd	EPS Ann. 2018	EPS Ann. 2017	EPS Ann. 2016	P/E High	P/E Low	Div 2018	Div 2017	Div 2016	Av. Yld %	Decl. Amount	Decl. Payable	Price High 2018	Price Low 2018
-	-	-	0.29	0.39	0.18	87.7	64.5	2.00	2.00	1.17	8.7	0.1670	2/3/20	25.4	18.7
-	-	-	0.40	0.41	0.47	58.0	46.3	1.52	1.52	1.52	7.1	0.380	1/3/20	23.2	18.5
-	-	-	0.30	0.30	0.38	44.2	35.6	1.13	1.20	1.65	9.2	0.2250	1/3/20	13.3	10.7
-	-	1.23	4.78	3.36°	1.27	10.8	8.7	0.60	0.60	0.60	1.3	0.150Y	18/53/27	51.7	41.4
-	-	2.67	5.96	8.36	4.67	18.9	13.5	1.84	1.48	1.32	1.8	0.50Y	18/53/27	112.6	80.3
-	-	0.97	2.95	2.04	2.15	11.9	7.7	0.56	0.40	0.16	1.9	0.190Y	18/53/27	35.0	22.7
-	-	-										0.058GZ	12/31/19	19.0	18.6
-	-	-0.10	0.43	-0.37	-0.95	342.3	133.3							147.2	57.3
-	-	0.12	0.03	2.18	320.00	1053.7	570.7	2.04	1.29		8.2	2.035G6	18/53/27	31.6	17.1
-	-	-1.39	3.68	5.31	7.28	15.7	10.9	3.00	2.54	2.35	6.1	0.840Y	18/53/27	57.7	40.1
-	-	0.08		0.09	0.02									11.1	7.0
-	-	-	0.70	0.46	0.79	7.7	5.8	0.50	0.50	0.59	10.9			5.4	4.0
-	-	-0.53	0.41	-3.80	1.13	40.5	17.7	2.35	0.80	0.80	20.0	0.20	12/16/19	16.6	7.2
-	-	-	0.62	0.51	0.21			0.45				0.1150	12/17/19		
-	-	1.47	3.32	2.14	2.68	24.2	19.1	1.85	1.78	1.72	2.5	0.4950Y	18/53/27	80.4	63.5
-	-	0.19	0.81	0.82	0.26	22.2	16.3							17.9	13.2
-	-	-	0.79	0.44	0.13	20.7	16.5	6.38	6.04	14.53	42.6			16.3	13.1
-	-	0.22	0.42	0.62	0.72	116.6	93.6	1.09	1.05	1.01	2.4	0.30Z	12/26/19	49.0	39.3
-	-	-1.10	-0.51	3.21	3.06							0.020Y	12/29/08	16.9	6.0
-	-	0.14	0.84	0.50	0.75	60.4	47.8	1.82	1.74	1.66	3.9	0.470Z	18/53/27	50.7	40.2
-	-	0.48	1.13	1.16	1.11	21.3	12.5	0.50	0.50	0.50	2.8	0.13750Y	18/53/27	24.1	14.1
-	-	1.48	3.90	3.88	1.24	24.5	18.7	2.53	2.39	2.27	2.9	0.70Y	18/53/27	95.7	72.8
-	-	0.41	5.01	1.93	0.97	6.6	4.1	0.28	0.26	0.24	1.0	0.30Y	18/53/27	32.9	20.7
-	-	2.08	7.91	2.97	5.65	16.3	11.8	1.44	1.31	1.19	1.2	0.430Y	18/53/27	128.6	93.4
-	-	1.62	5.85	5.28	7.33	19.1	15.2	4.45	4.79	2.15	4.4	0.450Y	18/53/27	111.6	89.1
-	-	0.08	0.08	-0.08	-0.14	338.3	243.4	0.20	0.20	0.20	0.8	0.39060Z	18/53/27	27.1	19.5
-	-	0.72	-0.01	-6.54	-0.78			1.28	1.28	1.28	2.5	0.220Y	18/53/27	57.9	38.8
-	-	-0.47	10.81	-0.61	-0.25	1.6	0.0							17.3	0.0
-	-	0.11	-0.98	-0.24	-0.28					1.30				13.9	5.8
-	-	0.76	1.72	1.88	1.62	55.3	36.8	1.06	0.99	0.91	1.4	0.3050Y	18/53/27	95.1	63.4
-	-	1.12	2.77	2.67	1.98	87.0	56.6	3.15	2.62	2.17	1.5	1.010Z	18/53/27	241.1	156.7
-	-	0.11	0.81	0.68	0.44	24.1	15.8	0.08	0.06	0.03	0.5	0.020Y	1/9/20	19.6	12.8
-	-	1.33	3.15	2.38	2.62	41.1	28.2	1.78	1.62	1.47	1.6	0.50Y	18/53/27	129.5	88.8
-	-	0.14	0.31	-0.43	-0.35	129.4	80.4	0.70	0.29	0.29	2.1	0.20Z	1/15/20	40.1	24.9
-	-	4.04	14.20	9.44	7.81	11.9	7.4	3.53	3.24	2.92	2.5	0.970Y	18/53/27	168.4	105.1
-	-	1.43	7.53	1.64	6.32	12.2	9.4	1.52	1.46	1.36	1.8	0.40Y	18/53/27	91.7	71.1
-	-	0.96	3.34	2.94	2.19	30.0	19.6	0.56	0.36	0.36	0.6	0.140Y	18/53/27	100.1	65.6
-	3.60	-	-46.00	16.80	18.00									65.2	46.0
-	-	0.49	2.91	2.68	2.15	22.4	15.8							14.8	2.3
-	-	-2.03	-0.16	-6.53	-6.63									4.8	3.0
-	-	-0.40	-5.57	-0.98	-6.68				0.18	0.45		0.090Y	4/28/17	108.3	75.1
-	-	0.92	3.85	2.06	2.61	28.1	19.5	0.88	0.70	0.58	0.9	0.250Y	18/53/27	12.8	4.2
-	-	0.15	1.91	-3.39	0.39	6.7	2.2					0.20Y	12/18/19	6.9	0.0
-	-0.27	-	0.03	0.00	-1.27	228.7	0.0					1.7	8/24/07	10.1	7.6
1.61	-	-	2.34	2.84		4.3	3.2							59.9	24.0
-	-	-0.26	-2.51	-2.92	-4.62							0.10970	1/31/20	21.3	19.7
-	-	-	0.32	-0.46	0.15	73.4	35.5	0.06	0.09		0.4			23.5	11.4
-	-	-	2.17	3.98	0.71	46.9	30.4	3.30	4.08	1.70	3.9			101.7	65.9
-	-	1.73	4.58	3.21	3.59	20.3	11.5					5.7	18/53/27	93.0	52.8
-	-	-0.54	-0.06	1.37	1.39			1.20	2.49	3.17	12.7	0.250Z	18/53/27	10.5	8.2
-	-	-0.57	0.33	0.03		43.4	13.4	0.54			5.3	0.30750Y	2/12/20	14.3	4.4
-	-	-2.86	-1.26	1.94	-2.88									10.9	1.9
-	-	4.55	14.19	14.35	9.21	22.4	16.5	3.00	2.70	2.60	1.1	0.80Y	18/53/27	317.4	234.8
-	-	-0.20	-0.16	0.47	0.17			0.56	0.60	0.60	14.6	0.090Z	1/29/20	4.5	3.1
-	-	0.93	4.59	4.70	5.16			1.56	1.41	1.29		0.440	2/14/20		
-	-	-0.45	0.11	3.41	-3.71	337.2	167.1	1.00	1.00	1.00	3.6	0.250Y	18/53/27	37.1	18.4
-	-	0.01	4.34	2.02	2.75	12.7	10.1	1.57	1.48	1.36	3.1	0.380Z	18/53/27	55.2	43.7
-	-	0.13	1.21			35.5	19.9							43.0	24.0
-	-	-0.43	0.18	0.04	0.01	78.9	21.2							14.2	3.8
-	-	0.16	1.48	1.54	1.74	13.3	11.3	1.84	1.84	1.84	10.0	0.460Z	1/15/20	19.7	16.7
-	-	1.63	-0.30	3.10	2.11			1.93	1.85	1.25	5.5	0.3984GY	12/16/19	48.3	23.9
-	-	-	1.25	1.13	1.24	12.3	11.5	1.26	1.16	1.24	8.5	0.0960	1/31/20	15.4	14.3
-	-	-	1.33	1.27	1.50	11.5	10.3	1.32	1.28	1.52	8.9	0.10	1/31/20	15.3	13.7
-	-	0.21	0.90	0.82	0.76	18.7	15.8	1.30	1.10	1.20	8.1	0.10Z	18/53/27	16.8	14.2
1.00	-	-	3.61	3.40	0.75	18.7	14.1	1.18	1.14	1.10	2.0	0.320Y	2/28/20	67.6	50.8
-	-	0.85	3.00	3.41	3.17	42.0	29.7	1.32	1.28	1.22	1.2	0.360Y	18/53/27	125.9	89.1
-	-	0.96	4.02	5.06	4.59			0.88	1.38	1.16		0.220	18/53/27		
-	-	0.38	1.08	1.35	1.32	43.6	30.4	0.85	0.79	0.74	2.1	0.23430Y	18/53/27	47.1	32.8
-	-	-0.13	-0.78	-0.98	-0.28			-	-	-		0.110Y	18/53/27	45.1	28.7
-	-	0.33	2.24	1.49	1.16	20.1	12.8	0.42	0.41	0.38	1.1	0.53130Z	12/2/19	15.5	10.2
-	-	0.35	1.50	1.12	0.83	10.4	6.8	1.13	0.72	0.62	8.7	0.01GY	2/28/20	2.8	1.1
-	-	0.02	0.20	-0.47	-1.04	13.9	5.3	-	-			0.3750Z	1/15/16	23.9	12.7
-	-	0.88	5.04	4.46	1.86	4.7	2.5	0.09			0.5	0.450Y	12/13/19	100.0	69.3
-	-	6.34	15.15	9.84	1.31	6.6	4.6	1.60	1.05		1.9	0.350Y	18/53/27	46.4	36.8
-	-	0.72	3.19	2.79	2.16	14.5	11.5	1.34	1.28	1.20	3.2	0.1450Y	2/14/20	11.0	7.9
-	-	0.14	0.19	0.26	-0.80	57.9	41.6	0.50	0.48	0.50	5.2	0.93750Y	18/53/27	31.8	17.1
-	-	0.21	1.30	-0.28	-2.31	24.5	13.1	0.24	0.24	0.09	1.0	0.030	12/12/19		
-	-	-	0.18	0.61	0.37			0.10							

SYMBOL	COMPANY	NATURE OF BUSINESS	FISCAL YEAR-END	TOTAL REV. $MILL	NET INCOME $MILL	TOTAL ASSETS $MILL	NET STK EQUITY $MILL	NO OF INST	INST. HOLDINGS (SHARES)
ACA	Arcosa Inc	Industrial Machinery & Equipment	12/31/18	1460.4	75.7	2172.2	1684.5	312	39847363
RCUS	Arcus Biosciences Inc	Biotechnology	12/31/18	8.4	-49.6	274.9	234.9	88	21236052
ARD	Ardagh Group SA	Containers & Packaging	12/31/18	9097.0	-94.0	10314.0	-1510.0	112	16560131
ASC	Ardmore Shipping Corp	Shipping	12/31/18	210.2	-42.9	844.8	346.6	132	32517540
ACRE	Ares Commercial Real Estate Corp	REITs	12/31/18	118.3	38.6	1603.3	425.6	174	24259214
ARDC	Ares Dynamic Credit Allocation Fun	Finance Intermediaries & Services	10/31/19	44.9	31.8	566.1	376.3	71	9091381
ARES	Ares Management Corp	Wealth Management	12/31/18	958.5	57.0	10154.7	587.9	199	79094503
AGX	Argan Inc	Construction Services	1/31/19	482.2	52.0	476.6	394.6	171	15714074
ARGO	Argo Group International Holdings L	General Insurance	12/31/18	1801.8	63.6	9558.2	1746.7	290	35565200
ARGD	Argo Group US Inc	General Insurance							0
ANET	Arista Networks Inc	Computer Hardware & Equipment	12/31/18	2151.4	328.1	3082.0	2143.4	666	49018444
AI	Arlington Asset Investment Corp	Holding and other Investment Office	12/31/18	7.1	-91.8	4099.4	274.4	156	35718778
ARLO	Arlo Technologies Inc	Household Appliances, Electronics &	12/31/18	464.9	-75.5	595.9	269,5	158	63027352
AHH	Armada Hoffler Properties Inc	REITs	12/31/18	193.3	17.2	1265.4	273.9	205	50673139
ARR PRC	ARMOUR Residential REIT Inc.	REITs	12/31/18	85.3	-106.0	8464.6	1125.3	216	46105932
AFI	Armstrong Flooring Inc	Plastics	12/31/18	728.2	-163.0	708.2	391.0	141	21749811
AWI	Armstrong World Industries Inc	Construction Materials	12/31/18	975.3	185.9	1873.5	261.2	379	60109869
ARW	Arrow Electronics, Inc.	Electrical Equipment	12/31/18	29676.8	716.2	17784.4	5325.0	556	106958513
APAM	Artisan Partners Asset Management	Wealth Management	12/31/18	828.6	158.3	805.0	135.0	287	52214646
ASA	ASA Gold and Precious Metals Ltd	Holding and other Investment Office	11/30/18	1	-1.4	196.1	194.8	77	7885296
ABG	Asbury Automotive Group Inc	Retail - Automotive	12/31/18	6874.4	168.0	2695.4	473.2	291	26356277
ASX	ASE Technology Holding Co Ltd	Semiconductors	12/31/18	371092.4	25262.4	533371.2	203023.4	188	120025586
ASGN	ASGN Inc	Business Services	12/31/18	3399.8	157.7	2687.9	1182.1	386	59281223
AHT	Ashford Hospitality Trust Inc	REITs	12/31/18	1430.8	-127.0	4686.0	452.5	249	90477309
ASH	Ashland Global Holdings Inc	Specialty Chemicals	9/30/19	2493.0	505.0	7251.0	3571.0		0
ASPN	Aspen Aerogels Inc	Construction Materials	12/31/18	104.4	-34.4	99.0	70.3	54	17525646
AMK	AssetMark Financial Holdings Inc	Finance Intermediaries & Services	12/31/18	363.6	37.4	1147.3	699.0	68	14956340
ASB	Associated Banc-Corp	Banking	12/31/18	1509.7	333.6	33647.9	3780.9	393	141362960
AC	Associated Capital Group Inc	Finance Intermediaries & Services	12/31/18	22.8	-58.1	954.4	866.2	70	4574958
AIZ	Assurant Inc	Life & Health	12/31/18	8057.6	251.0	41089.3	5112.0	611	73957228
AGO	Assured Guaranty Ltd	General Insurance	12/31/18	1002.0	521.0	13603.0	6555.0	423	124396381
AZN	AstraZeneca Plc	Pharmaceuticals	12/31/18	22090.0	2155.0	60651.0	12468.0	769	485815773
HOME	At Home Group Inc	Furniture	1/26/19	1165.9	49.0	1726.2	711.1	181	52362678
T	AT&T Inc	Services	12/31/18	170756.0	19370.0	531864.0	184089.0	3276	4804148810
ATTO	Atento SA	Services	12/31/18	1818.4	18.5	1213.4	331.6	59	56542575
ATH	Athene Holding Ltd	Life & Health	12/31/18	6543.0	1053.0	125505.0	8276.0	371	143801212
ATKR	Atkore International Group Inc	Electrical Equipment	9/30/19	1916.5	139.1	1437.0	232.9	220	50479242
AT	Atlantic Power Corp	Electric Utilities	12/31/18	282.3	36.8	1024.5	-6.9		0
ATO	Atmos Energy Corp.	Gas Utilities	9/30/19	2901.8	511.4	13367.6	5750.2	713	121505014
ACB	Aurora Cannabis Inc	Pharmaceuticals	6/30/19	247.9	-290.8	5502.8	4385.6		0
ATHM	Autohome Inc	IT Services	12/31/18	7233.2	2871.0	15756.2	11135.3	282	72361729
ALV	Autoliv Inc	Auto Parts	12/31/18	8678.2	190.4	6721.6	1883.7	390	46416297
AN	AutoNation, Inc.	Retail - Automotive	12/31/18	21412.8	396.0	10665.1	2716.0	437	83312884
AZO	AutoZone, Inc.	Retail - Automotive	8/31/19	11863.7	1617.2	9895.9	-1713.9	1010	28270344
AVLR	Avalara Inc	Internet & Software	12/31/18	272.1	-75.5	322.9	109.6	293	62863289
AVB	AvalonBay Communities, Inc.	REITs	12/31/18	2284.5	974.5	18380.2	10632.6	798	163624100
AGR	Avangrid Inc	Electric Utilities	12/31/18	6478.0	595.0	32167.0	15104.0	311	47926097
AVNS	Avanos Medical Inc	Medical Instruments & Equipment	12/31/18	652.3	57.5	1833.4	1297.2	402	51322964
AVTR	Avantor Inc	Specialty Chemicals	12/31/18	5864.3	-86.9	9911.6	807.6	177	445786934
AVYA	Avaya Holdings Corp	Internet & Software	9/30/19	2887.0	-671.0	6950.0	1300.0	221	122923292
AVY	Avery Dennison Corp	Containers & Packaging	12/29/18	7159.0	467.4	5177.5	955.1	805	103709190
AVH	Avianca Holdings SA	Airlines/Air Freight	12/31/18	4890.8	-24.8	7118.6	1170.5	50	8784725
AVA	Avista Corp	Electric Utilities	12/31/18	1396.9	136.4	5782.6	1773.2	380	70669871
AVX	AVX Corp.	Electrical Equipment	3/31/19	1791.8	271.8	2813.3	2384.2	235	55702941
AXTA	Axalta Coating Systems Ltd	Construction Materials	12/31/18	4696.0	207.1	6675.7	1205.1	442	250798672
AXS	AXIS Capital Holdings Ltd	General Insurance	12/31/18	5090.4	43.0	24132.6	5030.1	426	94065408
AX	Axos Financial Inc	Credit & Lending	6/30/18	647.6	155.1	11220.2	1073.1	304	55229343
AZUL	Azul SA	Airlines/Air Freight	12/31/18	9153.4	420.3	11793.2	3163.7	131	43617246
AZRE	Azure Power Global Ltd	Electric Utilities	3/31/19	9926.2	78.4	108863.8	25129.7	28	22205442
AZZ	AZZ Inc	Business Services	2/28/19	927.1	51.2	1088.6	603.7	249	27291272
BRPM	B Riley Principal Merger Corp	Services	12/31/18		-0.0	0.2	-0.0	31	6974185
BGS	B&G Foods Inc	Food	12/29/18	1700.8	172.4	3054.8	900.0	418	78791253
BW	Babcock & Wilcox Enterprises Inc	Industrial Machinery & Equipment	12/31/18	1062.4	-725.3	745.5	-286.1	134	27435104
BMI	Badger Meter Inc	Electronic Instruments & Related Pro	12/31/18	433.7	27.8	392.7	303.5	287	33369638
BCSF	Bain Capital Specialty Finance Inc	Finance Intermediaries & Services	12/31/18	99.3	55.9	1791.0	1001.6	73	18451696
BKR	Baker Hughes Company	Equipment & Services	12/31/18	22877.0	195.0	52439.0	17465.0	559	1009505945
BLL	Ball Corp	Metal Products	12/31/18	11635.0	454.0	16554.0	3458.0	882	302757491
BANC	Banc Of California Inc	Banking	12/31/18	452.2	45.5	10630.1	945.5	188	57476777
BBAR	Banco BBVA Argentina SA	Banking	12/31/18	77939.9	-1489.7	361542.4	45512.0	147	25283679
BBVA	Banco Bilbao Vizcaya Argentaria S	Banking	12/31/18	43129.0	5324.0	676689.0	47110.0	356	219171931
BBD	Banco Bradesco SA	Banking	12/31/18	145715.8	16583.9	1305543.7	124275.5	348	1033134638
BCH	Banco de Chile	Banking	12/31/18	2426357.0	603633.0	35617447.0	3673715.0	105	6167093
BLX	Banco Latinoamericano de Comerci	Banking	12/31/18	276.3	11.1	7609.2	993.6	41	9100738
BMA	Banco Macro SA	Banking	12/31/18	89160.2	-701.2	351233.0	60908.3	203	16546032
BSBR	Banco Santander Brasil SA	Banking	12/31/18	81594.3	12582.5	723865.0	91002.9	148	60830475
BSAC	Banco Santander Chile	Banking	12/31/18	2544678.0	595333.0	39132512.0	3199297.0	177	88257884
BSMX	Banco Santander Mexico SA, Institu	Banking	12/31/18	138324.0	19353.0	1408724.0	123255.0	142	48358640
SAN	Banco Santander SA (Spain)	Banking	12/31/18	76616.0	7810.0	1459271.0	96472.0	467	390780777
CIB	BanColombia SA	Banking	12/31/18	1656356.0	2658864.0	20113618.0	24848920.0	220	57317187
BXS	BancorpSouth Bank (Tupelo, MS)	Banking	12/31/18	935.5	221.3	18001.5	2205.7	289	83775762

T6

EARNINGS PER SHARE QUARTERLY			ANNUAL			P/E RATIO		DIVIDENDS PER SHARE			AV. YLD	DIV. DECLARED		PRICE RANGE 2018	
1st	2nd	3rd	2018	2017	2016			2018	2017	2016	%	AMOUNT	PAYABLE		
-	-	0.67	1.54	-	-	29.7 -	18.4	0.05	-	-	0.1	0.050Y	1/31/20	45.8 -	28.3
-	-	-0.51	-1.43	-29.03	-20.80									13.4 -	6.4
-	-	-	-0.40	-	-			0.56	0.67			0.140	11/29/19	-	
-	-	-0.37	-1.31	-0.37	0.12							0.110	8/31/16		
-	-	0.31	1.35	1.07	1.41	12.1 -	9.7	1.16	1.08	1.04	7.7	0.330Z	1/15/20	16.3 -	13.1
-	-	-	1.35	1.33	1.23	11.5 -	10.3	1.28	1.24	1.30	8.6	0.10750	3/31/20	15.5 -	13.9
-	-	0.23	0.30	0.62	1.20	119.1 -	57.0	1.33	1.13	0.83	5.0	0.43750	12/31/19	35.7 -	17.1
-	-	-0.44	4.56	4.50	2.42	11.4 -	7.5	1.00	1.00	0.70	2.3	0.250Y	1/31/20	51.9 -	34.1
-	-	-0.73	1.83	1.43	4.13			1.08	0.94	0.75		0.310	12/13/19		
-	-	-	-	-	-							0.40630Z	3/15/20	26.0 -	0.0
-	-	2.59	4.06	5.35	2.50	80.9 -	45.6	-	-	-				328.5 -	185.3
-	-	-0.23	-3.18	0.66	-1.79			1.68	2.27	2.50	24.8	0.41410Z	5/1/20	8.8 -	4.9
-	-	-0.41	-1.12	-	-									10.1 -	2.7
-	-	0.13	0.36	0.50	0.85	52.1 -	38.5	0.80	0.76	0.72	4.8	0.42190Z	1/15/20	18.8 -	13.9
-	-	-1.09	-2.92	4.17	-1.67			2.28	2.28	3.02		0.16410Z	3/27/20		
-	-	-1.44	-6.27	-1.54	0.33									15.0 -	3.6
-	-	1.48	3.56	2.86	1.87	28.8 -	16.7	0.17	-	-	0.2	0.20Y	18/53/27	102.5 -	59.4
-	-	1.10	8.10	4.48	5.68	10.6 -	7.7					0.025	18/53/27	86.1 -	62.7
-	-	0.71	2.84	0.75	1.57	11.4 -	7.7	3.19	2.76	2.80	11.8	0.650	11/29/19	32.4 -	21.7
-	-	-	-0.07	-0.09	-0.10			0.03	-	-		0.010	11/27/19		
-	-	2.33	8.28	6.62	7.40	14.8 -	8.0	-	-	-		0.2250Y	18/53/27	122.7 -	66.4
-	-	0.57	5.84	2.62	2.37	1.0 -	0.6	4.37	-	-	99.0			5.7 -	3.5
-	-	1.08	2.98	2.97	1.81	24.1 -	17.0							71.7 -	50.7
-	-	-0.42	-1.75	-1.30	-0.95			0.48	0.48	0.48	12.8	0.46880Z	1/15/20	5.6 -	2.3
-	-	1.05	1.79	0.01	-0.46	45.0 -	38.7	0.95	1.23	1.56	1.2	0.2750Y	18/53/27	80.5 -	69.3
-	-	-0.09	-1.45	-0.83	-0.52									8.4 -	2.2
-	-	-0.05	0.57	1.50	-	51.9 -	40.9	-	-	-				29.6 -	23.3
-	-	0.49	1.89	1.42	1.26	12.5 -	9.9	0.62	0.50	0.45	2.9	0.36720Y	18/53/27	23.7 -	18.6
-	-	0.26	-2.52	0.37	0.41			0.20	0.30	0.10	0.5	0.10Y	1/9/20	45.4 -	33.9
-	-	-0.96	3.98	9.39	9.13	33.6 -	22.3	2.28	2.15	2.03	2.1	1.6250Z	18/53/27	133.6 -	88.7
-	-	0.70	4.68	5.96	6.56			0.64	0.57	0.52		0.180	18/53/27		
-	-	0.54	1.70	2.37	2.76	29.7 -	20.9	1.37	1.37	1.37	3.2			50.5 -	35.5
-	-	-0.23	0.50	0.48	0.07	49.0 -	9.3	-	-	-				24.5 -	4.7
-	-	0.50	2.85	4.76	2.10	13.9 -	10.3	2.00	1.96	1.92	5.9	0.1701GHZ	18/53/27	39.6 -	29.4
-	-	-	0.28	-0.18	0.01							0.34G	11/28/17		
-	-	1.50	5.32	7.37	4.21			-	-	-		0.3945GHY	12/30/19		
-	-	0.75	2.48	1.27	0.94	17.1 -	8.2							42.3 -	20.3
-	-	0.10	0.29	-0.86	-1.02	13.1 -	7.5	-	-	-		0.030	12/31/15	3.8 -	2.2
-	-	0.68	5.43	3.73	3.38	21.1 -	16.5	1.94	1.80	1.68	1.9	0.5750Y	18/53/27	114.7 -	89.8
0.01	-	-	0.15	-0.05	-0.04	88.4 -	12.7							13.3 -	1.9
-	-	-	24.08	16.95	10.58	4.9 -	2.7	4.81	5.08	-	5.6			116.8 -	65.8
-	-	0.98	2.18	4.87	6.42	39.8 -	28.2	2.46	2.38	2.30	3.2	0.620Y	18/53/27	86.8 -	61.6
-	-	1.10	4.34	4.43	4.15	12.2 -	7.6	-	-	-				53.0 -	32.9
14.30	-	-	48.77	44.07	40.70	25.6 -	16.6							1250.0 -	811.4
-	-	-0.16	-1.95	-11.39	-10.15			-	-	-				89.5 -	31.4
-	-	2.00	7.05	6.35	7.52	31.5 -	24.0	5.88	5.68	5.40	2.9	1.520Y	18/53/27	222.0 -	169.2
-	-	0.48	1.92	1.23	2.04	27.4 -	24.9	1.74	1.73	1.73	3.5	0.440	18/53/27	52.6 -	47.8
-	-	-0.24	1.22	1.69	0.85	41.8 -	26.1	-	-	-				51.0 -	31.9
-	-	0.01	-2.69	-2.75	-0.28			-	-	-		0.780Y	5/15/20	19.2 -	13.6
-	-	-5.70	2.58	5.19	-1.54	7.5 -	3.9							19.3 -	10.1
-	-	1.71	5.28	3.13	3.54	25.4 -	16.5	2.01	1.76	1.60	1.8	0.580Y	18/53/27	133.9 -	87.1
-	-	-	-0.03	0.05	0.04			0.23	0.18	0.12	5.7			5.0 -	2.6
-	-	0.08	2.07	1.79	2.15	23.8 -	19.3	1.49	1.43	1.37	3.3	0.38750Y	12/13/19	49.2 -	40.0
-	0.20	-	0.03	0.75	0.60	684.7 -	436.3	0.45	0.43	0.42	2.7	0.1150Y	11/22/19	20.5 -	13.1
-	-	0.28	0.85	0.15	0.17			-	-	-					
-	-	0.33	0.00	-4.94	5.08			1.57	1.53	1.43		0.17571	1/17/20		
0.66	-	-	2.37	2.07	1.85	14.0 -	10.3	-	-	-				33.2 -	24.3
-	-	-	0.02	0.02	-0.55	2166.0 -	1197.0							43.3 -	23.9
-	-	-	-32.00	-111.09	1722.00			-	-	-					
-	-	0.84	1.73	2.33	2.96	28.2 -	21.4	0.68	0.64	0.60	1.6	0.170Y	2/18/20	48.9 -	37.0
-	-	-0.03	0.00	0.00				-	-	-				10.2 -	0.0
-	-	0.48	2.60	3.26	1.73	11.7 -	5.9	1.89	1.86	1.73	8.9	0.4750Y	1/30/20	30.3 -	15.4
-	-	-1.39	-57.00	-80.90	-23.10			-	-	-				7.8 -	2.3
-	-	0.44	0.95	1.19	1.11	69.6 -	50.4	0.56	0.49	0.43	1.0	0.170Y	18/53/27	66.1 -	47.9
-	-	0.41	1.45	0.73	-0.90	14.1 -	11.9	0.41	0.70	0.01	2.2	0.410Y	1/30/20	20.5 -	17.3
-	-	0.11	0.45	-0.17	-2.08	63.2 -	46.0	0.72	0.35	-	3.0	0.180Y	2/14/20	28.5 -	20.7
-	-	0.27	1.29	1.05	0.81	62.6 -	34.3	0.40	0.36	0.26	0.6	0.150Y	18/53/27	80.8 -	44.3
-	-	-0.45	0.45	0.71	1.94	38.9 -	29.4	0.52	0.52	0.49	3.5	0.43750Y	12/16/19	17.5 -	13.2
9.81	-	-	-2.43	3.34				4.56	4.44	-	55.5			14.0 -	3.1
-	-	-	0.76	0.48	0.50	8.4 -	6.1	0.25	0.30	0.37	4.5			6.4 -	4.6
-	-	-	1.97	2.23	2.12	5.3 -	3.9	0.74	0.77	0.74	8.3			10.4 -	7.6
1.01	-	-	5.98	5.62	5.51	5.4 -	3.3	467.96	463.06	508.67	1657.9			32.5 -	19.8
-	-	0.52	0.28	2.08	2.22			1.54	1.54	-		0.3850	11/19/19		
11.48	-	-	-1.06	9.43				44.86	12.07	-	101.8			76.5 -	21.9
460.51	-	-	16.04	11.32	9.29	0.9 -	0.6	1.56	1.44	0.79	13.5			13.7 -	9.8
-	-	-	3.16	2.99	2.53	10.3 -	6.6	667.38	554.23	567.70	2345.5			32.6 -	20.8
-	-	-	2.85	2.75	2.43	3.0 -	2.1	5.76	-	-	82.1			8.7 -	6.1
-	-	0.11	0.45	0.40	0.41	11.6 -	8.2	0.39	0.46	0.35	8.9	0.250	12/5/19	5.2 -	3.7
-	-	-	-2825.00	2780.00	3040.00	0.0 -	0.0	4022.48	3754.83	3500.05	8094.4			55.8 -	39.1
-	-	0.63	2.23	1.67	1.41	14.9 -	11.9	0.62	0.14	0.45	2.1	0.3438GY	18/53/27	33.2 -	26.5

SYMBOL	COMPANY	NATURE OF BUSINESS	FISCAL YEAR-END	TOTAL REV. $MILL	NET INCOME $MILL	TOTAL ASSETS $MILL	NET STK EQUITY $MILL	NO OF INST	INST. HOLDINGS (SHARES)
BAC	Bank of America Corp	Banking	12/31/18	110584.0	28147.0	2354507.0	265325.0	2979	7646970999
BOH	Bank of Hawaii Corp	Banking	12/31/18	719.1	219.6	17144.0	1268.2	434	45243534
BMO	Bank of Montreal (Quebec)	Banking	10/31/19	38747.0	5547.0	852195.0	51076.0	594	309921428
BK	Bank of New York Mellon Corp	Banking	12/31/18	19213.0	4266.0	362873.0	40638.0	1464	890267553
BNS	Bank of Nova Scotia Halifax	Banking	10/31/19	46641.0	8208.0	1086161.0	67522.0	503	688558966
NTB	Bank Of NT Butterfield & Son Ltd (T	Banking	12/31/18	535.4	195.2	10773.2	882.3	-	0
BKU	BankUnited Inc.	Banking	12/31/18	1581.2	324.9	32164.3	2923.8	328	119267846
BCS	Barclays PLC	Banking	12/31/18	28768.0	2146.0	1133283.0	62556.0	365	113562976
BBDC	Barings BDC Inc	Holding and other Investment Office	12/31/18	80.2	-0.1	1167.6	563.0	130	37537734
MCI	Barings Corporate Investors	Holding and other Investment Office	12/31/18	30.4	24.2	330.3	291.2	62	3158327
BGH	Barings Global Short Duration High	Finance Intermediaries & Services	12/31/18	50.2	38.2	528.4	366.7	-	0
MPV	Barings Participation Investors	Holding and other Investment Office	12/31/18	13.7		158.8	138.7	45	1819569
BNED	Barnes & Noble Education Inc	Retail - Specialty	4/27/19	2034.6	-24.4	946.2	450.6	164	39432364
B	Barnes Group Inc.	Industrial Machinery & Equipment	12/31/18	1495.9	166.2	2809.0	1203.1	336	59916263
GOLD	Barrick Gold Corp.	Precious Metals	12/31/18	7243.0	-1545.0	22631.0	7593.0	813	1255112259
BHC	Bausch Health Companies Inc	Pharmaceuticals	12/31/18	8380.0	-4148.0	32492.0	2733.0	487	221235966
BAX	Baxter International Inc	Medical Instruments & Equipment	12/31/18	11127.0	1624.0	15641.0	7794.0	1620	573192833
BTE	Baytex Energy Corp	Production & Extraction	12/31/18	1115.1	-325.3	6377.2	3055.4	-	0
BBX	BBX Capital Corp (New)	Hotels, Restaurants & Travel	12/31/18	947.6	35.1	1705.0	549.6	126	40139307
BCE	BCE Inc	Services	12/31/18	23468.0	2785.0	57100.0	20363.0	716	525359554
BZH	Beazer Homes USA, Inc.	Builders	9/30/19	2087.7	-79.5	1957.6	538.8	230	41629605
BDX	Becton, Dickinson & Co	Medical Instruments & Equipment	9/30/19	17290.0	1233.0	51765.0	21081.0	1891	284277390
BDC	Belden Inc	Electrical Equipment	12/31/18	2585.4	160.9	3779.3	1387.1	353	65275319
BRBR	BellRing Brands Inc	Food	9/30/19	854.4	123.1	594.5	486.4	-	0
T 28A	BellSouth Telecommunications, Inc.	Services	12/31/99	17478.0	2770.0	25295.0	8805.0	-	0
BHE	Benchmark Electronics, Inc.	Electrical Equipment	12/31/18	2566.5	22.8	1899.8	1132.2	305	50166975
WRB	Berkley (WR) Corp	General Insurance	12/31/18	7691.7	640.7	24896.0	5437.9	644	163527926
BRK A	Berkshire Hathaway Inc	General Insurance	12/31/18	247837.0	4021.0	707794.0	348703.0	3117	1065403827
BHLB	Berkshire Hills Bancorp Inc	Banking	12/31/18	581.1	105.8	12212.2	1552.9	241	41228357
BERY	Berry Global Group Inc	Plastics	9/28/19	8878.0	404.0	16469.0	1618.0	433	141568376
BBY	Best Buy Inc	Retail - Appliances and Electronics	2/2/19	42879.0	1464.0	12901.0	3306.0	983	254854692
BEST	BEST Inc	Trucking	12/31/18	27961.0	-508.0	12366.3	4138.1	100	76264289
BGSF	BG Staffing Inc	Business Services	12/30/18	286.9	17.5	100.3	65.7	101	4714153
BHP	BHP Group Ltd	Non-Precious Metals	6/30/19	44288.0	8306.0	100861.0	47240.0	663	75052741
BBL	BHP Group Plc	Production & Extraction	6/30/19	44288.0	8306.0	100861.0	47240.0	294	51100641
BIG	Big Lots, Inc.	Retail - General Merchandise/Depart	2/2/19	5238.1	156.9	2023.3	693.0	429	56201217
BH	Biglari Holdings Inc (New)	Hotels, Restaurants & Travel	12/31/18	809.9	19.4	1029.5	570.5	41	179620
BILL	Bill.com Holdings Inc	IT Services	6/30/19	108.4	-7.3	1526.3	173.7	-	0
BIO	Bio-Rad Laboratories Inc	Biotechnology	12/31/18	2289.4	365.6	5611.1	4020.3	480	23178824
BHVN	Biohaven Pharmaceutical Holding C	Pharmaceuticals	12/31/18	-	-240.9	290.0	150.9	231	50910639
BITA	Bitauto Holdings Ltd	Internet & Software	12/31/18	10579.6	-608.4	59743.9	11130.3	116	20715343
BJ	BJ's Wholesale Club Holdings Inc	Retail - General Merchandise/Depart	2/2/19	13007.3	127.3	3239.3	-202.1	258	142347284
BKH	Black Hills Corporation	Electric Utilities	12/31/18	1754.3	258.4	6963.3	2181.6	441	68732248
BKI	Black Knight Inc	Internet & Software	12/31/18	1114.0	168.5	3653.4	1786.5	444	139810212
BSM	Black Stone Minerals LP	Production & Extraction	12/31/18	609.6	295.5	1750.1	298.4	119	60385253
BB	BlackBerry Ltd	Services	2/28/19	904.0	93.0	3929.0	2636.0	492	318643312
BGIO	BlackRock 2022 Global Income Op	Holding and other Investment Office	12/31/18	17.3	13.8	252.5	198.3	30	4432308
BFZ	BlackRock California Municipal Inco	Holding and other Investment Office	7/31/19	29.5	16.6	848.5	486.6	79	7729072
BHK	BlackRock Core Bond Trust	Holding and other Investment Office	8/31/19	48.6	35.5	1158.7	851.7	118	20405246
HYT	BlackRock Corporate High Yield Fu	Holding and other Investment Office	8/31/19	128.6	97.5	1950.7	1440.4	193	38150226
BTZ	BlackRock Credit Allocation Income	Holding and other Investment Office	10/31/19	115.4	82.2	2135.3	1551.2	172	59177240
DSU	BlackRock Debt Strategies Fund Inc	Holding and other Investment Office	2/28/19	57.2	42.5	971.2	641.2	126	22446818
BGR	Blackrock Energy & Resources Trus	Holding and other Investment Office	12/31/18	13.5	8.4	359.5	357.4	102	7585776
CII	BlackRock Enhanced Capital & Inco	Holding and other Investment Office	12/31/18	14.3	7.6	689.6	674.1	95	11800235
BDJ	BlackRock Enhanced Equity Divide	Holding and other Investment Office	12/31/18	49.3	33.7	1651.1	1638.2	225	43833543
BOE	BlackRock Enhanced Global Divide	Holding and other Investment Office	12/31/18	29.1	21.2	760.9	754.6	135	25752491
EGF	BlackRock Enhanced Government	Holding and other Investment Office	12/31/18	2.6	1.7	88.1	70.9	31	4443915
BGY	BlackRock Enhanced International	Holding and other Investment Office	12/31/18	25.2	18.2	628.3	623.2	118	41578008
FRA	BlackRock Floating Rate Income Str	Holding and other Investment Office	8/31/19	43.9	30.8	767.5	526.4	130	13910685
BGT	BlackRock Floating Rate Income Tr	Holding and other Investment Office	10/31/19	26.4	18.6	473.3	321.1	105	9598013
BFO	BlackRock Florida Municipal 2020 T	Holding and other Investment Office	12/31/18	0.8	0.6	81.3	81.2	24	966123
BME	BlackRock Health Sciences Trust	Holding and other Investment Office	12/31/18	4.5	0.7	355.5	352.7	58	1791302
BLK	BlackRock Inc	Finance Intermediaries & Services	12/31/18	14198.0	4305.0	159573.0	32374.0	1660	152735899
BKT	BlackRock Income Trust Inc (The)	Holding and other Investment Office	12/31/18	8.2	5.4	684.8	398.6	97	39410670
BKN	BlackRock Investment Quality Muni	Holding and other Investment Office	4/30/19	18.8	12.2	450.4	270.7	68	2856026
BLW	Blackrock Limited Duration Income	Holding and other Investment Office	8/31/19	45.0	34.1	832.1	610.3	111	14195737
BTA	BlackRock Long-Term Municipal Ad	Holding and other Investment Office	4/30/19	12.7	8.4	280.1	167.4	40	2749266
BZM	BlackRock Maryland Municipal Bon	Holding and other Investment Office	8/31/19	1.9	1.0	51.7	32.5	20	183457
MHE	BlackRock Massachusetts Tax-Exe	Holding and other Investment Office	8/31/19	2.1	1.2	55.2	33.5	14	130050
BIT	Blackrock Multi-Sector Income Trust	Holding and other Investment Office	10/31/19	64.4	44.5	1042.6	648.6	90	13974678
MUI	BlackRock Muni Intermediate Durati	Holding and other Investment Office	4/30/19	36.5	21.4	973.7	589.9	103	15026173
MNE	BlackRock Muni New York Intermed	Holding and other Investment Office	7/31/19	3.8	1.9	108.9	65.7	24	1165970
MUA	BlackRock MuniAssets Fund, Inc.	Holding and other Investment Office	4/30/19	29.1	24.0	586.2	509.6	71	3269218
BKK	BlackRock Municipal 2020 Term Tr	Holding and other Investment Office	12/31/18	6.7	5.5	306.4	305.9	63	2513552
BTT	BlackRock Municipal 2030 Target T	Holding and other Investment Office	7/31/19	91.4	56.2	2823.3	1804.7	120	13561781
BBK	Blackrock Municipal Bond Trust	Holding and other Investment Office	8/31/19	11.5	6.9	287.1	177.0	56	1600728
BAF	BlackRock Municipal Income Invest	Holding and other Investment Office	8/31/19	9.4	5.7	234.3	137.2	41	1437607
BBF	BlackRock Municipal Income Invest	Holding and other Investment Office	7/31/19	10.9	7.0	255.3	144.7	32	646213
BYM	BlackRock Municipal Income Qualit	Holding and other Investment Office	8/31/19	26.1	16.2	673.4	415.1	90	8639786
BFK	BlackRock Municipal Income Trust	Holding and other Investment Office	4/30/19	46.2	30.4	1029.9	635.1	87	6814443

T8

1st	2nd	3rd	2018	2017	2016	P/E hi	P/E lo	2018	2017	2016	AV. YLD %	AMOUNT	PAYABLE	2018 hi	2018 lo
-	-	0.56	2.61	1.56	1.50	13.6 -	9.4	0.54	0.39	0.25	1.8	1.750Y	18/53/27	35.5 -	24.6
-	-	1.29	5.23	4.33	4.23	18.2 -	13.1	2.34	2.04	1.89	2.8	0.670Y	18/53/27	95.3 -	68.4
-	-	2.34	8.17	7.92	6.92	13.0 -	8.1	3.78	3.56	3.40	4.4	0.31870	2/25/20	106.4 -	65.8
-	-	1.07	4.04	3.72	3.15	13.4 -	10.1	1.04	0.86	0.72	2.2	0.3250Y	18/53/27	54.0 -	41.0
-	-	1.50	6.82	6.49	5.77	11.2 -	7.4	3.28	3.05	2.88	5.2	0.30310	1/29/20	76.5 -	50.3
-	-	0.90	3.50	2.76	1.18			-	1.28	0.40		0.440	11/15/19	-	
-	-	0.77	2.99	5.58	2.09	12.4 -	10.2	0.84	0.84	0.84	2.5	0.210Y	18/53/27	37.1 -	30.5
0.06	-	-	0.09	-0.10	0.10	112.7 -	73.2	0.18	0.12	0.18	2.2	-		10.1 -	6.6
-	-	0.16	-	1.55	1.62			2.21	1.65	1.89	22.1	0.150	12/18/19	10.5 -	9.3
-	-	-	1.21	2.19	1.12	14.1 -	12.3	1.20	1.20	1.20	7.5	0.30	1/17/20	17.1 -	14.8
-	-	-	1.89	1.77	1.57	10.0 -	8.5	1.78	1.63	-	10.1	0.14081	4/1/20	18.9 -	16.1
-	-	-	1.03	1.09	1.00	17.0 -	0.0	1.08	1.08	1.08	6.7	0.270	1/17/20	17.5 -	0.0
-	0.74	-	-5.40	0.11	-			-	-	-		-		7.4 -	2.9
-	-	0.89	3.15	1.09	2.48	19.9 -	13.6	0.62	0.55	0.51	1.1	0.160Y	12/10/19	62.5 -	42.8
-	0.11	-	-1.32	1.23	0.56			0.19	0.12	0.08	1.1	0.050	12/16/19	26.5 -	11.7
-	-	-0.14	-11.81	6.83	-6.94			-	-	-		1.7	12/22/10	42.0 -	18.9
-	0.66	-	2.97	1.29	9.01	30.2 -	21.7	0.73	0.61	0.51	0.9	0.220Y	18/53/27	89.8 -	64.5
-	0.14	-	-0.93	0.37	-2.29			-	-	-		0.10	9/15/15	3.1 -	1.0
-	-	0.24	0.36	0.79	0.32	18.8 -	10.7	0.04	0.03	0.01	0.8	0.01250Y	1/20/20	6.8 -	3.8
-	-	0.96	3.10	3.11	3.33	21.0 -	12.8	3.02	2.87	2.73	5.7	0.08231	2/12/20	65.1 -	39.7
-	-	0.38	-1.41	0.99	0.15			-	-	-		0.46880Z	7/15/15	16.4 -	9.1
-	-	1.51	0.60	4.60	4.49	455.8 -	352.0	3.00	2.92	2.64	1.2	0.76560Y	18/53/27	273.5 -	211.2
-	-	-6.70	3.08	1.37	2.65	20.7 -	13.5	0.21	0.20	0.20	0.4	0.050Y	18/53/27	63.8 -	41.5
-	-	-	-	-	-			-	-	-		-		23.8 -	16.0
-	-	-	-	-	-			-	-	-		-			
-	-	0.19	0.49	-0.64	1.29	72.4 -	42.1	0.60	-	-	2.2	0.150Y	1/13/20	35.5 -	20.6
-	-	0.85	3.33	2.84	3.12	21.9 -	14.3	1.39	1.03	1.01	2.2	0.757Y	18/53/27	73.0 -	47.5
-	10119.00	2446.00	7326.00	4645.00		139.2 -	117.3							340380.02 -	87000.1
-	-	0.44	2.29	1.39	1.88	14.6 -	11.5	0.88	0.84	0.80	2.9	0.230Y	11/27/19	33.4 -	26.4
-	-	0.10	3.67	2.56	1.89	16.0 -	10.2	-	-	-		-		58.8 -	37.4
-	-	1.10	3.26	3.81	2.56	27.2 -	16.1	1.36	1.57	1.43	2.0	0.50Y	18/53/27	88.6 -	52.5
-	-	-	-1.32	-8.28	-93.51			-	-	-		-		6.6 -	4.1
-	-	0.41	1.79	0.65	0.82	15.6 -	9.1	1.15	1.00	1.00	5.5	0.30	11/18/19	27.9 -	16.2
-	-	-	0.69	1.10	-1.20	85.5 -	67.2	2.94	1.62	2.34	5.6	-		59.0 -	46.4
-	-	-	0.69	1.10	-1.20	75.1 -	58.3	1.96	1.08	1.56	4.3	-		51.8 -	40.2
-	-	3.25	4.38	3.32	2.80	9.0 -	4.4	1.00	0.84	0.76	3.6	0.30Y	18/53/27	39.3 -	19.2
-	-	-0.06	66.85	40.77	81.28	2.4 -	1.2	-	-	-		-		162.0 -	81.8
-0.69	-	-	-1.01	-	-			-	-	-		-		40.0 -	35.5
-	-	-8.68	12.10	4.07	0.95	30.9 -	18.5	-	-	-		-		374.2 -	224.3
-	-	-2.04	-6.15	-5.00	-5.05			-	-	-		-			
-	-	-	-8.13	-23.16	-8.31			-	-	-		-		20.8 -	9.7
-	-	0.40	0.54	0.48	0.26	53.5 -	39.1	8.31	-	-	32.7	-		28.9 -	21.1
-	-	0.19	4.66	3.21	1.37	17.5 -	13.1	1.93	1.81	1.68	2.6	0.5350Y	18/53/27	81.6 -	61.3
-	-	0.25	1.14	1.47	0.67	56.6 -	38.7	-	-	-		-		64.5 -	44.1
-	-	0.32	1.45	1.01	0.26	12.9 -	7.9	1.33	1.20	1.10	8.6	0.370	11/21/19	18.8 -	11.4
-0.09	-	-	0.74	-2.30	-0.86	18.2 -	6.6	-	-	-		-		13.5 -	4.9
-	-	-	0.62	-	-	15.9 -	13.6	0.60	-	-	6.5	0.0177	1/9/20	9.9 -	8.4
-	-	-	0.65	0.73	0.83	21.4 -	18.8	0.67	0.77	0.86	5.1	0.038M	2/3/20	13.9 -	12.2
-	-	-	0.72	0.76	0.79	20.4 -	17.1	0.78	0.78	0.84	5.6	0.06760	1/9/20	14.7 -	12.3
-	-	-	0.83	0.85	0.82	13.7 -	11.3	0.84	0.89	0.99	8.0	0.07790	1/9/20	11.4 -	9.4
-	-	-	0.81	0.81	0.88	17.3 -	13.9	0.80	0.84	0.92	6.2	0.08390	1/9/20	14.0 -	11.3
-	-	-	0.78	0.73	0.78	14.4 -	12.8	0.82	0.21	-	7.6	0.07110	1/9/20	11.2 -	10.0
-	-	-	0.28	0.40	0.27	44.9 -	36.4	0.93	0.93	1.00	8.1	0.07760	1/31/20	12.6 -	10.2
-	-	-	0.17	0.15	0.13	101.5 -	82.2	0.99	0.99	1.15	6.2	0.08750	1/31/20	17.3 -	14.0
-	-	-	0.18	0.16	0.17	55.1 -	43.3	0.56	0.56	0.56	6.3	0.050	1/31/20	9.9 -	7.8
-	-	-	0.31	0.17	0.15	35.7 -	30.6	0.85	2.29	1.05	8.1	0.0630	1/31/20	11.1 -	9.5
-	-	-	0.30	0.28	0.36	44.2 -	0.0	0.49	0.49	0.53	3.9	0.0410	1/9/20	13.3 -	0.0
-	-	-	0.17	0.09	0.09	34.6 -	29.5	0.44	0.46	0.52	8.0	0.03380	1/31/20	5.9 -	5.0
-	-	-	0.79	0.76	0.76	17.1 -	15.2	0.74	0.81	0.75	5.8	0.07880	1/9/20	13.5 -	12.0
-	-	-	0.76	0.73	0.74	17.1 -	15.3	0.71	0.77	0.70	5.7	0.07640	1/9/20	13.0 -	11.6
-	-	-	0.11	0.37	0.46	139.4 -	0.0	0.13	0.42	0.38	1.0	0.0025M	2/3/20	15.3 -	0.0
-	-	-	0.07	0.02	0.02	607.1 -	514.3	2.40	2.40	3.00	6.2	0.20	1/31/20	42.5 -	36.0
-	-	7.15	26.58	30.23	19.04	18.9 -	14.2	12.02	10.00	9.16	2.7	3.30Y	18/53/27	503.2 -	378.0
-	-	-	0.08	0.25	0.28	76.9 -	70.8	0.17	0.32	0.34	2.8	0.03440	1/9/20	6.2 -	5.7
-	-	-	0.73	0.79	0.88	21.8 -	18.4	0.89	1.11	0.91	6.0	0.057M	2/3/20	15.9 -	13.4
-	-	-	0.95	1.01	1.32	17.3 -	14.3	0.95	1.27	1.30	6.3	0.09810	1/9/20	16.4 -	13.6
-	-	-	0.65	-	0.68	20.5 -	16.7	0.65	0.66	0.70	5.3	0.0505M	2/3/20	13.3 -	10.9
-	-	-	0.55	0.59	0.61	28.7 -	0.0	0.61	0.57	0.62	4.8	0.0395M	2/3/20	15.8 -	0.0
-	-	-	0.55	0.62	0.65	24.5 -	0.0	0.58	0.64	0.68	5.2	0.04M	2/3/20	13.5 -	0.0
-	-	-	1.38	1.51	1.69	12.7 -	11.3	1.53	1.77	1.64	9.1	0.12370	1/9/20	17.6 -	15.6
-	-	-	0.59	0.65	0.73	24.9 -	21.7	0.60	0.82	0.96	4.3	0.0445M	2/3/20	14.7 -	12.8
-	-	-	0.52	0.57	0.64	29.5 -	24.0	0.51	0.65	0.66	3.6	0.036M	2/3/20	15.3 -	12.5
-	-	-	0.68	-	0.72	23.6 -	19.4	0.68	0.70	0.74	4.5	0.0525M	2/3/20	16.1 -	13.2
-	-	-	0.27	0.55	0.57	56.0 -	54.9	0.27	0.55	0.56	1.8	0.01M	2/3/20	15.1 -	14.8
-	-	-	0.85	0.90	1.03	28.6 -	24.5	0.85	0.95	0.96	3.7	0.0624M	2/3/20	24.3 -	20.8
-	-	-	0.70	0.74	0.89	22.8 -	19.5	0.77	1.22	0.91	5.2	0.0545M	2/3/20	16.0 -	13.7
-	-	-	0.74	0.79	0.83	19.9 -	17.7	0.80	0.82	0.82	5.7	0.0515M	2/3/20	14.7 -	13.1
-	-	-	0.80	0.84	0.84	18.3 -	15.3	0.82	0.87	0.87	6.0	0.0505M	2/3/20	14.6 -	12.3
-	-	-	0.67	0.75	0.82	21.3 -	19.0	0.67	0.78	0.83	4.9	0.048M	2/3/20	14.2 -	12.7
-	-	-	0.73	0.81	0.87	19.6 -	17.0	0.77	0.84	0.90	5.6	0.0535M	2/3/20	14.3 -	12.4

SYMBOL	COMPANY	NATURE OF BUSINESS	FISCAL YEAR-END	TOTAL REV. $MILL	NET INCOME $MILL	TOTAL ASSETS $MILL	NET STK EQUITY $MILL	NO OF INST	INST. HOLDINGS (SHARES)
BLE	BlackRock Municipal Income Trust I	Holding and other Investment Office	8/31/19	25.4	16.7	569.6	356.6	63	2734276
MEN	BlackRock MuniEnhanced Fund Inc	Holding and other Investment Office	4/30/19	24.4	15.9	585.8	349.2	76	5668479
MUC	BlackRock MuniHoldings California	Holding and other Investment Office	7/31/19	38.8	23.5	1066.4	637.8	83	9178156
MUH	BlackRock MuniHoldings Fund II Inc	Holding and other Investment Office	4/30/19	13.0	8.6	283.3	173.6	51	1421289
MHD	BlackRock MuniHoldings Fund Inc	Holding and other Investment Office	4/30/19	17.2	11.5	373.0	235.0	50	1637683
MFL	BlackRock MuniHoldings Investmen	Holding and other Investment Office	8/31/19	36.1	22.2	950.9	566.3	85	8170958
MUJ	BlackRock MuniHoldings New Jerse	Holding and other Investment Office	7/31/19	31.3	19.8	779.5	481.0	48	4518282
MHN	BlackRock MuniHoldings New York	Holding and other Investment Office	8/31/19	28.6	17.2	779.3	476.5	56	7558635
MUE	BlackRock MuniHoldings Quality Fu	Holding and other Investment Office	7/31/19	20.3	12.8	508.6	313.4	69	5590879
MUS	BlackRock MuniHoldings Quality Fu	Holding and other Investment Office	4/30/19	12.0	7.6	289.5	175.9	57	3276608
MVT	BlackRock MuniVest Fund II Inc	Holding and other Investment Office	4/30/19	23.5	15.9	507.1	317.2	57	2171771
MVF	BlackRock MuniVest Fund Inc	Holding and other Investment Office	8/31/19	42.6	28.7	985.4	637.6	96	11463923
MZA	BlackRock MuniYield Arizona Fund	Holding and other Investment Office	7/31/19	4.3	2.6	111.3	68.4	18	302727
MYC	BlackRock MuniYield California Fun	Holding and other Investment Office	7/31/19	20.4	11.9	574.9	334.7	57	4015363
MCA	BlackRock MuniYield California Qua	Holding and other Investment Office	7/31/19	34.3	20.7	942.2	543.2	66	7649006
MYD	BlackRock MuniYield Fund Inc	Holding and other Investment Office	4/30/19	49.4	34.2	1075.5	682.8	86	5933416
MYF	BlackRock MuniYield Investment Fu	Holding and other Investment Office	7/31/19	15.0	10.0	330.1	198.6	43	1226749
MFT	BlackRock MuniYield Investment Q	Holding and other Investment Office	7/31/19	8.8	5.5	214.6	120.9	32	740694
MIY	BlackRock MuniYield Michigan Qual	Holding and other Investment Office	7/31/19	29.3	18.3	763.1	464.4	63	5587120
MYJ	BlackRock MuniYield New Jersey F	Holding and other Investment Office	7/31/19	26.7	17.4	632.6	388.4	39	2198092
MYN	BlackRock MuniYield New York Qu	Holding and other Investment Office	7/31/19	34.0	-	927.2	569.1	69	6864799
MPA	BlackRock MuniYield Pennsylvania	Holding and other Investment Office	7/31/19	13.6	8.4	352.6	214.4	50	1629078
MQT	BlackRock MuniYield Quality Fund I	Holding and other Investment Office	4/30/19	21.3	13.5	520.2	310.6	78	7161010
MYI	BlackRock MuniYield Quality Fund I	Holding and other Investment Office	7/31/19	62.7	39.8	1626.1	1009.4	135	22447851
MQY	BlackRock MuniYield Quality Fund I	Holding and other Investment Office	4/30/19	32.8	21.2	795.9	481.2	98	7806603
BQH	Blackrock New York Municipal Bond	Holding and other Investment Office	8/31/19	2.9	1.5	76.9	46.2	19	634620
BSE	BlackRock New York Municipal Inco	Holding and other Investment Office	8/31/19	5.9	3.3	164.3	100.0	35	2133123
BNY	Blackrock New York Municipal Inco	Holding and other Investment Office	7/31/19	12.6	7.5	333.1	195.9	37	1883952
BFY	BlackRock New York Municipal Inco	Holding and other Investment Office	8/31/19	5.2	3.0	133.5	79.7	24	786882
BCX	Blackrock Resources & Commoditie	Holding and other Investment Office	12/31/18	31.1	20.8	804.8	798.3	134	37010757
BST	BlackRock Science & Technology T	Holding and other Investment Office	12/31/18	3.1	-2.9	594.9	587.9	66	4276115
BSTZ	BlackRock Science & Technology T	Holding and other Investment Office	5/3/19	-	-	0.1	0.1	19	3771306
BSD	Blackrock Strategic Municipal Trust	Holding and other Investment Office	4/30/19	7.8	5.0	174.0	103.4	34	968435
BBN	BlackRock Taxable Municipal Bond	Holding and other Investment Office	7/31/19	112.3	79.1	2196.7	1389.0	126	11043836
BUI	BlackRock Utilities, Infrastructure &	Holding and other Investment Office	12/31/18	12.1	-	320.7	318.9	50	2386568
BHV	BlackRock Virginia Municipal Bond	Holding and other Investment Office	8/31/19	1.7	0.9	42.2	25.1	22	125478
BGX	Blackstone / GSO Long-Short Credi	Holding and other Investment Office	12/31/18	26.7	18.6	344.7	198.4	47	4336201
BSL	Blackstone / GSO Senior Floating R	Holding and other Investment Office	12/31/18	29.2	20.2	394.6	251.6	53	5868842
BGB	Blackstone / GSO Strategic Credit F	Holding and other Investment Office	12/31/18	89.7	61.7	1156.7	683.6	76	19144823
BX	Blackstone Group Inc (The)	Wealth Management	12/31/18	6833.3	1541.8	28924.6	-	1091	412345507
BXMT	Blackstone Mortgage Trust Inc	REITs	12/31/18	756.1	285.1	14467.4	3364.1	459	90618658
HRB	Block (H & R), Inc.	Miscellaneous Consumer Services	4/30/19	3094.9	422.5	3299.9	541.5	740	274481342
BE	Bloom Energy Corp	Electrical Equipment	12/31/18	742.0	-241.8	1389.7	-91.7	197	47410616
APRN	Blue Apron Holdings Inc	Food	12/31/18	667.6	-122.1	354.9	119.3	61	3328592
BCRH	Blue Capital Reinsurance Holdings	General Insurance	12/31/18	35.4	-28.6	163.3	90.7	46	7468645
BXG	Bluegreen Vacations Corp	Hotels, Restaurants & Travel	12/31/18	738.3	88.0	1346.5	429.8	85	11831862
BXC	BlueLinx Holdings Inc	Construction Materials	12/29/18	2862.8	-48.1	959.9	-14.7	104	11878034
DCF	BNY Mellon Alcentra Global Credit I	Holding and other Investment Office	8/31/19	14.5	10.3	201.0	137.6	16	2262195
DHF	BNY Mellon High Yield Strategies F	Holding and other Investment Office	3/31/19	25.9	19.0	362.6	241.2	72	9474041
DMB	BNY Mellon Municipal Bond Infrastr	Holding and other Investment Office	2/28/19	17.7	12.1	377.8	327.7	51	3882043
DSM	BNY Mellon Strategic Municipal Bon	Holding and other Investment Office	11/30/18	29.7	23.2	607.1	439.6	94	5377136
LEO	BNY Mellon Strategic Municipals In	Holding and other Investment Office	9/30/19	37.5	28.2	867.1	618.8	87	7978503
BA	Boeing Co. (The)	Aerospace	12/31/18	101127.0	10460.0	117359.0	339.0	2767	487000303
BCC	Boise Cascade Co. (DE)	Construction Materials	12/31/18	4995.3	20.5	1581.2	672.6	248	46001133
BCEI	Bonanza Creek Energy Inc	Production & Extraction	12/31/18	276.7	168.2	1061.5	863.9	203	26242169
BOOT	Boot Barn Holdings Inc	Retail - Apparel and Accessories	3/30/19	776.9	39.0	636.1	264.2	245	33888636
BAH	Booz Allen Hamilton Holding Corp.	Business Services	3/31/19	6704.0	418.5	3831.8	675.4	539	239141906
BWA	BorgWarner Inc	Auto Parts	12/31/18	10529.6	930.7	10095.3	4225.5	767	225267817
BORR	Borr Drilling Ltd	Equipment & Services	12/31/18	164.9	-190.5	2913.7	1531.8	-	0
SAM	Boston Beer Co Inc (The)	Beverages	12/29/18	995.6	92.7	639.9	460.3	398	12677785
BXP	Boston Properties Inc	REITs	12/31/18	2717.1	582.8	20256.5	5883.2	761	183266207
BSX	Boston Scientific Corp.	Medical Instruments & Equipment	12/31/18	9823.0	1671.0	20999.0	8726.0	1115	1515003026
BIF	Boulder Growth & Income Fund Inc.	Holding and other Investment Office	11/30/18	26.5	9.7	1409.1	1407.6	127	17157818
BOX	Box Inc	Internet & Software	1/31/19	608.4	-134.6	650.2	31.4	326	119391965
BYD	Boyd Gaming Corp.	Hotels, Restaurants & Travel	12/31/18	2626.7	115.0	5756.3	1145.7	359	95054487
BPMP	BP Midstream Partners LP	Equipment & Services	12/31/18	116.4	133.1	693.2	-	110	44652835
BP	BP PLC	Production & Extraction	12/31/18	303282.0	9383.0	282176.0	99444.0	1625	472625400
BPT	BP Prudhoe Bay Royalty Trust	Oil Royalty Traders	12/31/18	114.4	113.3	1.0	0.7	135	1236139
BRC	Brady Corp	Manufacturing	7/31/19	1160.6	131.3	1157.3	850.8	287	53473297
BHR	Braemar Hotels & Resorts Inc	REITs	12/31/18	431.4	1.3	1636.5	503.6	168	26841504
BDN	Brandywine Realty Trust	REITs	12/31/18	544.3	136.3	4098.5	1820.3	391	239846898
BWG	BrandywineGLOBAL Global Income	Holding and other Investment Office	10/31/19	25.9	17.2	460.0	303.6	65	11296289
LND	Brasilagro Cia Brasileira De Proprie	Agricultural Crop Production	6/30/18	384.1	126.3	1179.6	755.9	12	421927
BAK	Braskem S A	Plastics	12/31/15	47283.0	3140.3	59961.3	2022.6	48	5134500
BRFS	BRF S.A.	Food	12/31/18	30188.4	-4448.1	42382.4	6964.6	213	98814314
BGG	Briggs & Stratton Corp.	Industrial Machinery & Equipment	6/30/19	1836.6	-54.1	1551.4	446.7	281	47347349
MNRL	Brigham Minerals Inc	Production & Extraction	12/31/18	5.5	5.0	62.4	58.8	97	21980322
BFAM	Bright Horizons Family Solutions, In	Services	12/31/18	1903.2	168.9	2524.3	779.5	-	0
BEDU	Bright Scholar Education Holdings L	Educational Services	8/31/19	2563.0	241.1	7787.6	2721.4	38	13733054
BSIG	BrightSphere Investment Group Inc	Finance Intermediaries & Services	12/31/18	928.2	136.4	1553.7	103.3	-	0

EPS 1st	EPS 2nd	EPS 3rd	Ann 2018	Ann 2017	Ann 2016	P/E Hi	P/E Lo	Div 2018	Div 2017	Div 2016	Av Yld %	Amount	Payable	Price Hi	Price Lo
-	-	-	0.76	0.83	0.93	20.6	17.3	0.78	0.89	0.93	5.4	0.058M	2/3/20	15.6	13.1
-	-	-	0.59	0.70	0.70	19.5	17.1	0.64	0.68	0.73	5.8	0.039M	2/3/20	11.5	10.1
-	-	-	0.64	0.69	0.77	22.5	19.7	0.67	0.74	0.80	4.9	0.0435M	2/3/20	14.4	12.6
-	-	-	0.80	0.86	0.91	19.5	16.5	0.86	0.90	0.94	5.8	0.0565M	2/3/20	15.6	13.2
-	-	-	0.88	0.95	1.00	20.1	17.0	0.93	0.98	1.06	5.7	0.0605M	2/3/20	17.7	15.0
-	-	-	0.71	0.78	0.86	19.3	17.8	0.77	0.86	0.86	5.8	0.0455M	2/3/20	13.7	12.7
-	-	-	0.71	0.77	0.84	20.6	18.0	0.74	0.81	0.87	5.3	0.054M	2/3/20	14.6	12.8
-	-	-	0.60	0.69	0.75	23.0	20.2	0.62	0.70	0.71	4.7	0.0445M	2/3/20	13.8	12.1
-	-	-	0.69	0.75	0.78	18.8	17.0	0.72	0.77	0.81	5.8	0.044M	2/3/20	13.0	11.7
-	-	-	0.70	0.75	0.80	18.4	16.5	0.76	0.80	0.81	6.2	0.0445M	2/3/20	12.9	11.6
-	-	-	0.83	0.91	0.98	18.8	16.4	0.86	0.94	1.00	5.9	0.0555M	2/3/20	15.6	13.6
-	-	-	0.51	0.56	0.61	18.6	16.5	0.52	0.57	0.63	5.7	0.0335M	2/3/20	9.5	8.4
-	-	-	0.66	0.72	0.77	22.5	0.0	0.69	0.74	0.82	5.1	0.043M	2/3/20	14.8	0.0
-	-	-	0.66	0.74	0.86	22.4	19.8	0.75	1.10	1.01	5.4	0.043M	2/3/20	14.8	13.1
-	-	-	0.67	0.73	0.81	21.9	19.1	0.68	0.83	0.85	4.9	0.046M	2/3/20	14.7	12.8
-	-	-	0.79	0.84	0.90	19.1	16.2	0.82	0.87	0.93	5.7	0.056M	2/3/20	15.1	12.8
-	-	-	0.83	0.87	0.92	17.8	15.6	0.87	0.94	0.97	6.1	0.056M	2/3/20	14.8	12.9
-	-	-	0.74	0.79	0.83	19.4	16.9	0.80	0.83	0.85	5.9	0.05M	2/3/20	14.4	12.5
-	-	-	0.69	0.75	0.79	21.0	18.3	0.71	0.77	0.83	5.2	0.049M	2/3/20	14.5	12.6
-	-	-	0.77	0.81	0.89	20.5	17.1	0.88	0.90	0.91	6.0	0.0605M	2/3/20	15.8	13.2
-	-	-	0.58	0.64	0.70	22.8	20.1	0.59	0.65	0.73	4.7	0.0425M	2/3/20	13.2	11.6
-	-	-	0.71	0.76	0.80	20.4	18.0	0.71	0.75	0.83	5.1	0.046M	2/3/20	14.5	12.8
-	-	-	0.66	0.73	0.79	19.9	17.5	0.69	0.75	0.82	5.5	0.044M	2/3/20	13.1	11.6
-	-	-	0.68	0.77	0.84	20.2	17.9	0.74	0.82	0.88	5.6	0.0445M	2/3/20	13.7	12.1
-	-	-	0.77	0.84	0.90	19.9	17.3	0.82	0.87	0.95	5.7	0.053M	2/3/20	15.3	13.3
-	-	-	0.60	0.67	0.71	25.7	0.0	0.63	0.71	0.73	4.6	0.048M	2/3/20	15.4	0.0
-	-	-	0.55	0.63	0.68	25.4	22.2	0.56	0.63	0.68	4.2	0.0405M	2/3/20	14.0	12.2
-	-	-	0.60	0.67	0.75	24.3	20.6	0.64	0.66	0.80	4.7	0.046M	2/3/20	14.6	12.4
-	-	-	0.64	0.71	0.81	23.6	19.6	0.66	0.76	0.83	4.8	0.049M	2/3/20	15.1	12.6
-	-	-	0.22	0.20	0.14	37.9	32.5	0.62	0.61	0.58	8.0	0.05160	1/31/20	8.3	7.2
-	-	-	-0.13	-0.05	0.00			1.76	1.28	1.20	5.4	0.16550	1/31/20	34.7	27.0
												0.10	1/31/20	22.8	19.6
-	-	-	0.72	0.78	0.82	20.8	16.9	0.77	0.79	0.85	5.6	0.055M	2/3/20	15.0	12.1
-	-	-	1.47	1.58	1.63	17.3	14.1	1.57	1.58	1.58	6.7	0.11180	1/9/20	25.5	20.7
-	-	-	0.49	0.56	0.56	49.9	39.9	1.45	1.45	1.45	6.6	0.1210	1/31/20	24.5	19.5
-	-	-	0.69	0.78	0.81	25.1	0.0	0.78	0.76	0.81	5.4	0.0455M	2/3/20	17.4	0.0
-	-	-	1.46	1.34	1.40	11.2	9.6	1.61	1.24	1.43	10.4	0.1150	2/28/20	16.4	14.0
-	-	-	1.32	1.26	1.24	13.3	11.8	1.41	1.16	1.16	8.5	0.0217	1/31/20	17.6	15.6
-	-	-	1.38	1.26	1.39	10.9	9.9	1.51	1.26	1.34	10.5	0.0157	1/31/20	15.1	13.7
-	-	1.15	2.26	2.21	1.56	24.9	12.9	2.42	-	-	5.5	0.490	11/12/19	56.3	29.2
-	0.56	-	2.50	2.27	2.53	15.3	12.6	2.48	2.48	2.48	7.0	0.620Z	1/15/20	38.2	31.5
-	-0.95	-	2.91	1.91	1.49	10.1	7.9	0.96	0.88	0.80	3.8	0.260Y	18/53/27	29.3	23.0
-	-	-0.30	-4.54	-25.62	-27.84									16.3	2.7
-	-	-1.99	-9.45	-24.60	-12.60									23.9	6.4
-	-	-0.12	-3.27	-4.94	1.63			0.90	1.49	2.14		0.577	12/20/19		
-	-	0.27	1.18	1.74	9510.00	13.7	6.5	0.60	0.56	-	5.1	0.130Y	2/20/20	16.2	7.7
-	-	-0.75	-5.21	6.81	1.77							0.1250Y	12/28/07	35.1	9.5
-	-	-	0.56	-	-	17.1	13.9	0.49	-	-	5.5	0.0540	1/15/20	9.6	7.8
-	-	-	0.27	0.29	0.30	11.6	10.1	0.29	0.32	0.35	9.5	0.02150	2/21/20	3.1	2.7
-	-	-	0.69	0.68	0.71	21.6	17.6	0.64	0.71	0.75	4.7	0.053M	2/3/20	14.9	12.1
-	-	-	0.47	0.49	0.50	18.6	15.2	0.43	0.50	0.50	5.4	0.03M	1/31/20	8.7	7.1
-	-	-	0.50	0.51	0.53	17.4	14.6	0.45	0.52	0.52	5.5	0.035M	1/31/20	8.7	7.3
-	-	2.05	17.85	13.43	7.61	24.7	17.4	6.84	5.68	4.36	1.9	2.0550Y	18/53/27	440.6	310.9
-	0.69	-	0.52	2.12	0.98	76.6	42.7	1.30	0.07	-	4.4	1.6Y	12/16/19	39.9	22.2
-	1.74	-	8.16	-0.25	-4.04	3.2	2.1							26.0	17.1
0.26	-	-	1.05	0.53	0.37	42.6	16.6							44.7	17.4
0.80	-	-	2.05	1.67	1.94	37.6	21.4	0.70	0.62	0.54	1.1	0.270Y	18/53/27	77.1	44.0
-	-	0.94	4.44	2.08	0.55	10.4	7.0	0.68	0.59	0.53	1.7	0.170Y	18/53/27	46.3	30.9
-	-	-	-0.37	-0.34	-0.07									441.3	233.4
-	-	3.65	7.82	8.09	6.79	56.4	29.9								
-	-	0.70	3.70	2.93	3.26	37.8	29.5	3.50	3.05	2.70	2.7	0.32810Z	18/53/27	139.9	109.2
-	-	0.09	1.19	0.08	0.25	38.1	27.7	-	-	-				45.4	32.9
-	-	-	0.09	0.04	0.08	131.2	112.2	0.37	0.41	0.49	3.4	0.1020	1/31/20	11.8	10.1
-	-	-0.28	-1.16	-1.19	-1.67									24.9	13.0
-	-	0.35	1.00	1.64	3.63	31.1	21.1	0.23	0.15	-	0.9	0.070Y	1/15/20	31.1	21.1
-	-	0.43	1.27	0.21	-	13.7	11.0	1.01	0.36	-	6.7	0.34750	2/13/20	17.4	13.9
-	-	0.17	0.47	0.17	0.01	96.2	76.7	2.41	2.38	2.38	6.0			45.2	36.0
-	-	-	5.29	3.60	2.04	5.3	1.1	5.29	3.60	2.04	34.1	0.42420	1/21/20	27.9	5.8
0.70	-	-	1.73	1.84	1.58	34.0	24.9	0.83	0.82	0.81	1.7	0.21750Y	18/53/27	58.9	43.0
-	-	-0.37	-0.19	0.51	0.55			0.64	0.64	0.46	6.2	0.51560Z	1/15/20	13.8	8.1
-	-	0.04	0.76	0.65	0.19	21.2	16.5	0.72	0.64	0.62	4.8	0.190Z	18/53/27	16.1	12.5
-	-	-	0.85	1.04	0.92	14.9	12.2	0.93	1.08	1.30	8.0	0.070	3/2/20	12.7	10.4
-	-	-	2.35	0.47	0.18	2.0	0.0	0.21	0.49	1.36				4.8	0.0
-	-	-	-	-	-									30.0	12.5
-	-	0.33	-5.48	-1.37	-0.46			-	-	0.61				9.8	5.0
-0.81	-	-	-0.28	1.31	0.60			0.56	0.56	0.54	6.0	0.050Y	1/3/20	14.4	4.0
-	0.14	-										0.330Y	11/27/19	23.0	18.1
-	-	0.69	2.66	2.59	1.55	62.7	40.4							166.8	107.5
1.22	-	-	2.02	1.64	-0.38	6.0	4.2							12.1	8.4
-	-	0.84	1.26	0.04	1.05	11.7	6.7	0.39	-	-	3.4	0.32030Z	4/27/20	14.8	8.4

SYMBOL	COMPANY	NATURE OF BUSINESS	FISCAL YEAR-END	TOTAL REV. $MILL	NET INCOME $MILL	TOTAL ASSETS $MILL	NET STK EQUITY $MILL	NO OF INST	INST. HOLDINGS (SHARES)
BV	BrightView Holdings Inc	Services	9/30/19	2404.6	44.4	2928.6	1283.8	110	99005105
EAT	Brinker International, Inc.	Hotels, Restaurants & Travel	6/26/19	3217.9	154.9	1258.3	-778.2	467	62871051
BCO	Brinks Co (The)	Business Services	12/31/18	3488.9	-33.3	3236.0	153.7	408	64855350
BMY	Bristol-Myers Squibb Co.	Pharmaceuticals	12/31/18	22561.0	4920.0	34986.0	14031.0	2583	1638505834
BTI	British American Tobacco Plc	Tobacco Products	12/31/18	24492.0	6032.0	146342.0	65444.0	-	0
BRX	Brixmor Property Group Inc	REITs	12/31/18	1234.3	366.3	8242.4	2836.1	403	339750524
BRMK	Broadmark Realty Capital Inc	Property, Real Estate & Developmen	-	-	-	-	-	-	0
BR	Broadridge Financial Solutions Inc	Finance Intermediaries & Services	6/30/19	4362.2	482.1	3880.7	1127.5	957	141262640
BKD	Brookdale Senior Living Inc	Hospitals & Health Care Facilities	12/31/18	4531.4	-528.3	6467.3	1018.9	295	203857705
BAM	Brookfield Asset Management Inc	Property, Real Estate & Developmen	12/31/18	56771.0	3584.0	256281.0	29815.0	712	704507181
BBU	Brookfield Business Partners LP	Business Services	12/31/18	37168.0	74.0	27318.0	1548.0	87	59652835
DTLA PR	Brookfield DTLA Fund Office Trust I	REITs	12/31/18	315.7	-109.7	2795.7	220.5	2	10106
INF	Brookfield Global Listed Infrastructu	Holding and other Investment Office	12/31/18	7.7	1.6	235.5	164.1	54	3956509
BIP	Brookfield Infrastructure Partners L	Electric Utilities	12/31/18	4652.0	329.0	36580.0	5471.0	356	161838797
RA	Brookfield Real Assets Income Fun	Holding and other Investment Office	12/31/18	73.1	55.6	1092.8	805.3	108	6718361
BEP	Brookfield Renewable Partners LP	Electric Utilities	12/31/18	3032.0	24.0	34103.0	4484.0	-	0
BRO	Brown & Brown Inc	Brokers & Intermediaries	12/31/18	2014.2	344.3	6688.7	3000.6	509	228470165
BF B	Brown-Forman Corp	Beverages	4/30/19	3324.0	835.0	5139.0	1647.0	213	51209274
BRT	BRT Apartments Corp	REITs	9/30/18	119.6	23.8	1153.4	198.0	105	6696587
BC	Brunswick Corp.	Leisure Equipment	12/31/18	5159.2	265.3	4285.7	1582.6	492	99685728
BKE	Buckle, Inc. (The)	Retail - Apparel and Accessories	2/2/19	885.5	95.6	527.3	393.9	266	40410224
BBW	Build-A-Bear Workshop Inc	Retail - Specialty	2/2/19	336.6	-17.9	172.0	94.3	116	13448622
BG	Bunge Ltd.	Food	12/31/18	45743.0	267.0	19425.0	6173.0	637	135638130
BURL	Burlington Stores Inc	Retail - Apparel and Accessories	2/2/19	6668.5	414.7	3079.2	322.7	552	78635329
BWXT	BWX Technologies inc	Industrial Machinery & Equipment	12/31/18	1799.9	227.0	1655.1	235.7	393	117975909
BY	Byline Bancorp Inc	Banking	12/31/18	258.6	41.2	4942.6	650.7	98	13074264
CABO	Cable One Inc	Business Services	12/31/18	1072.3	164.8	2303.2	775.4	369	5249613
CBT	Cabot Corp.	Specialty Chemicals	9/30/19	3337.0	157.0	3004.0	998.0	432	63251579
COG	Cabot Oil & Gas Corp.	Production & Extraction	12/31/18	2188.1	557.0	4198.8	2088.2	854	462745572
CACI	CACI International Inc	IT Services	6/30/19	4986.3	265.6	5086.8	2371.3	516	31201265
WHD	Cactus Inc	Equipment & Services	12/31/18	544.1	51.7	584.7	177.7	205	49500478
CADE	Cadence Bancorporation	Banking	12/31/18	607.3	166.3	12730.3	1438.3	276	125784212
CAE	CAE Inc	Aerospace	3/31/19	3304.1	330.0	7165.5	2331.3	252	154944048
CAI	CAI International Inc	Miscellaneous Transportation Servic	12/31/18	432.1	78.6	3012.6	701.1	143	17125625
CAL	Caleres Inc	Retail - Apparel and Accessories	2/2/19	2834.8	-5.4	1838.6	634.1	276	54641701
CRC	California Resources Corp	Production & Extraction	12/31/18	3064.0	328.0	7158.0	-361.0	330	42885238
CWT	California Water Service Group (DE	Water Utilities	12/31/18	698.2	65.6	2837.7	730.2	369	44181923
CALX	Calix Inc	Services	12/31/18	441.3	-19.3	317.1	151.9	143	43013969
ELY	Callaway Golf Co (DE)	Leisure Equipment	12/31/18	1242.8	104.7	1052.9	724.6	366	113900270
CPE	Callon Petroleum Co. (DE)	Production & Extraction	12/31/18	587.6	300.4	3979.2	2445.2	411	374662428
CPT	Camden Property Trust	REITs	12/31/18	957.3	156.1	6219.6	3311.4	553	112108303
CCJ	Cameco Corp.	Mining	12/31/18	2091.7	166.3	8018.6	4993.3	440	283356002
CPB	Campbell Soup Co	Food	7/28/19	8107.0	211.0	13148.0	1103.0	870	206451408
CWH	Camping World Holdings Inc	Retail - Automotive	12/31/18	4792.0	10.4	2806.7	44.5	162	38205890
GOOS	Canada Goose Holdings Inc	Apparel, Footwear & Accessories	3/31/19	830.5	143.6	725.4	399.1	232	63041855
CM	Canadian Imperial Bank Of Comme	Banking	10/31/19	28757.0	5096.0	651604.0	38394.0	493	226576006
CNI	Canadian National Railway Co	Rail	12/31/18	14321.0	4328.0	41214.0	17641.0	890	470703239
CNQ	Canadian Natural Resources Ltd	Production & Extraction	12/31/18	21027.0	2591.0	71559.0	31974.0	572	864458372
CP	Canadian Pacific Railway Ltd	Rail	12/31/18	7316.0	1951.0	21254.0	6636.0	642	120783297
CANG	Cango Inc	IT Services	12/31/18	1091.4	302.7	7301.1	5251.8	5	33018791
CNNE	Cannae Holdings Inc	Property, Real Estate & Developmen	12/31/18	1205.4	27.6	1459.5	1124.6	-	0
CTST	CannTrust Holdings Inc	Biotechnology	12/31/18	45.6	-13.6	202.3	174.0	116	33561900
CAJ	Canon Inc	Leisure Equipment	12/31/18	3951937.0	252755.0	4899465.0	2827602.0	243	15974016
CGC	Canopy Growth Corp	Pharmaceuticals	3/31/18	77.9	-70.4	1436.8	1158.8	-	0
CMD	Cantel Medical Corp	Medical Instruments & Equipment	7/31/19	918.2	55.0	1070.4	661.5	350	47057340
COF	Capital One Financial Corp	Banking	12/31/18	32377.0	6015.0	372538.0	51668.0	1363	508151431
CSU	Capital Senior Living Corp.	Hospitals & Health Care Facilities	12/31/18	460.0	-53.6	1149.1	35.3	119	31155587
CPRI	Capri Holdings Ltd	Retail - Apparel and Accessories	3/30/19	5238.0	543.0	6650.0	2429.0	515	164248721
CMO	Capstead Mortgage Corp.	REITs	12/31/18	276.9	50.1	12186.5	1059.1	277	100010634
CAH	Cardinal Health, Inc.	Pharmaceuticals	6/30/19	145534.0	1363.0	40963.0	6328.0	1055	326381829
CRCM	Care.com Inc	Services	12/29/18	192.3	52.9	268.1	215.2	195	32390962
CSL	Carlisle Companies Inc.	Rubber Products	12/31/18	4479.5	611.1	5249.2	2597.4	564	60458536
KMX	Carmax Inc.	Retail - Automotive	2/28/19	18173.1	842.4	18717.9	3357.0	837	215253344
CCL	Carnival Corp	Hotels, Restaurants & Travel	11/30/18	18881.0	3152.0	42401.0	24443.0	1167	504795455
CUK	Carnival Plc	Hotels, Restaurants & Travel	11/30/18	18881.0	3152.0	42401.0	24443.0	186	13367248
CRS	Carpenter Technology Corp.	Non-Precious Metals	6/30/19	2380.2	167.0	3187.8	1520.1	366	52682650
CSV	Carriage Services, Inc.	Miscellaneous Consumer Services	12/31/18	268.0	11.6	917.5	221.5	151	16233063
CARS	Cars.com Inc	IT Services	12/31/18	662.1	38.8	2600.5	1626.9	308	72783395
CRI	Carter's Inc	Apparel, Footwear & Accessories	12/29/18	3462.3	282.1	2058.9	869.4	474	63909298
CVNA	Carvana Co	Retail - Automotive	12/31/18	1955.5	-61.8	991.0	73.4	264	64898250
CSLT	Castlight Health Inc	Internet & Software	12/31/18	156.4	-39.7	253.5	194.7	139	87064921
CTLT	Catalent Inc	Pharmaceuticals	6/30/19	2518.0	137.4	6184.0	2288.2	376	171336450
CTT	Catchmark Timber Trust Inc	REITs	12/31/18	97.9	-122.0	804.8	321.7	174	46150138
CAT	Caterpillar Inc.	Construction Services	12/31/18	54722.0	6147.0	78509.0	14039.0	2193	472843020
CATO	Cato Corp.	Retail - Apparel and Accessories	2/2/19	829.7	30.5	497.9	316.8	231	23091505
CBZ	CBIZ Inc	Business Services	12/31/18	922.0	61.6	1183.0	593.7	216	59358340
CBL	CBL & Associates Properties Inc	REITs	12/31/18	858.6	-78.6	5340.9	964.1	319	155261065
IGR	CBRE Clarion Global Real Estate In	Holding and other Investment Office	12/31/18	37.4	22.4	965.4	880.6	176	35395793
CBRE	CBRE Group Inc	Property, Real Estate & Developmen	12/31/18	21340.1	1063.2	13456.8	4938.8	860	394533100
FUN	Cedar Fair LP	Sporting & Recreational	12/31/18	1348.5	126.7	2024.2	-	304	41622604

EARNINGS PER SHARE						P/E RATIO		DIVIDENDS PER SHARE			AV. YLD %	DIV. DECLARED		PRICE RANGE 2018	
QUARTERLY			ANNUAL												
1st	2nd	3rd	2018	2017	2016			2018	2017	2016		AMOUNT	PAYABLE		
-	-	0.31	-0.18	-0.18	-0.67	-								19.8	10.6
0.39	-	-	2.72	2.94	3.42	18.8 -	13.6	1.52	1.36	1.28	3.6	0.380Y	18/53/27	51.0	37.0
-	-	0.10	-0.65	0.32	0.68	-		0.60	0.55	0.40	0.7	0.150Y	18/53/27	94.3	64.2
-	-	0.83	3.01	0.61	2.65	21.3 -	14.2	1.60	1.56	1.14	3.2	0.450Y	18/53/27	64.2	42.8
-	-	-	2.63	18.30	2.49	16.3 -	11.9	1.91	2.27	1.58	5.1			42.8	31.4
-	-	0.27	1.21	0.98	0.91	18.8 -	11.7	1.10	1.04	0.98	5.8	0.2850Z	18/53/27	22.7	14.2
-	-	-	-	-	-	-						0.080Z	2/14/20	12.8	10.9
0.48	-	-	3.56	2.70	2.53	37.9 -	26.3	1.46	1.32	1.20	1.2	0.540Y	18/53/27	134.9	93.7
-	-0.42	-	-2.82	-3.07	-2.18	-						0.250Y	18/53/27	8.7	6.0
-	-	-	3.40	1.34	1.55	22.8 -	11.1	0.60	0.56	0.52	1.0	0.28130	12/31/19	77.6	37.9
-	-	-	1.11	-1.04	0.06	-		-				0.06250	12/31/19		
-	-	-	-	-	-	-		-				2.25GJ	1/4/16	22.0	0.0
-	-	-	0.12	0.19	0.18	118.7 -	84.8	0.98	1.05	1.40	7.7	0.08170	3/26/20	14.2	10.2
-	-	0.07	0.59	-0.04	1.13	-		-				0.31870	12/31/19		
-	-	-	1.52	1.74	0.15	15.1 -	12.8	2.39	2.39	0.20	10.9	0.1990	3/26/20	23.0	19.4
-	0.03	-	0.13	-0.18	-0.23	-		-				0.35940	4/30/20		
-	-	0.41	1.22	1.41	0.91	33.0 -	21.9	0.30	0.28	0.25	0.9	0.0850Y	18/53/27	40.3	26.7
-	0.59	-	1.48	1.37	2.09	46.5 -	30.6	1.61	0.56	0.52	2.9	0.17430Y	18/53/27	68.8	45.4
-	-	0.20	1.61	0.97	2.23	11.5 -	7.2	0.78	0.18		5.4	0.220Z	1/7/20	18.4	11.6
-	-	-2.82	3.01	1.62	3.00	20.5 -	13.8	0.78	0.69	0.61	1.5	0.240Y	18/53/27	61.6	41.5
-	-	0.53	1.85	2.03	3.06	15.4 -	8.1	2.75	1.75	1.94	13.9	1.257Y	1/24/20	28.4	15.1
-	-	-0.40	-0.06	0.50	0.09	-		-						6.2	2.3
-	-	-10.57	1.64	0.89	5.01			1.96	1.76	1.60		1.21880Z	18/53/27		
-	-	1.44	5.48	3.01	1.99	41.9 -	25.5	-				-		229.6	139.9
-	-	0.78	2.27	1.47	1.76	28.1 -	16.8	0.64	0.42	0.36	1.2	0.170Y	18/53/27	63.7	38.1
-	-	0.39	1.18	0.38	3.27	17.4 -	14.2	-				0.03GY	1/7/20	20.5	16.7
-	-	8.68	28.77	40.72	17.14	53.8 -	27.9	7.50	6.50	6.00	0.6	2.250Y	18/53/27	1547.5	803.2
-	-	0.55	-1.85	3.80	2.36	-		1.29	1.23	1.04	2.9	0.350Y	18/53/27	50.2	37.7
-	-	0.22	1.24	0.22	-0.91	22.1 -	12.7	0.25	0.17	0.08	1.2	0.10Y	18/53/27	27.4	15.7
2.66	-	-	11.93	6.53	5.76	21.1 -	11.8	-				-		251.6	140.8
-	-	0.41	1.58	1258.36	-224.00	25.0 -	15.5	-				0.09GY	12/19/19	39.5	24.5
-	-	0.34	1.97	1.25	0.87	11.7 -	7.5	0.55			3.0	0.1750Y	12/13/19	23.1	14.8
-	0.28	-	1.29	0.93	0.85	28.4 -	14.2	0.35	0.32	0.29	1.2	0.110	12/31/19	36.7	18.4
-	-	-0.40	3.71	3.68	0.31	7.9 -	4.9	-				0.53130Y	1/15/20	29.2	18.1
-	-	0.69	2.02	1.52	1.85	15.4 -	7.2	0.28	0.28	0.28	1.2	0.070Y	1/9/20	31.1	14.5
-	-	1.89	6.77	-6.26	6.76	4.3 -	0.8	-				0.010Y	10/15/15	29.4	5.6
-	-	0.88	1.36	1.40	1.01	41.9 -	33.0	0.75	0.72	0.69	1.5	0.19750Y	18/53/27	57.0	44.9
-	-	-0.06	-0.37	-1.66	-0.56	-		-						11.1	5.7
-	-	0.32	1.08	0.42	1.98	19.7 -	13.6	0.04	0.04	0.04	0.2	0.010Y	12/19/19	21.3	14.7
-	-	0.21	1.35	0.56	-0.78	6.4 -	2.7	-				1.250Y	6/28/19	8.6	3.6
-	-	0.44	1.63	2.13	9.05	70.5 -	51.7	3.08	3.00	7.25	3.0	0.80Z	18/53/27	115.0	84.3
-	-0.06	-	0.42	-0.52	-0.16	40.5 -	19.4	0.08	0.40	0.40	0.7	0.080	12/13/19	17.0	8.1
0.55	-	-	0.86	2.89	1.81	57.5 -	37.5	1.40	1.40	1.25	3.4	0.350Y	18/53/27	49.5	32.3
-	-0.82	-	0.28	1.07	0.09	57.3 -	26.4	0.61	0.74	0.08	5.1	0.07327Y	12/30/19	16.0	7.4
-0.27	-	-	0.86	0.22	0.26	91.1 -	38.3	-						78.4	32.9
-	-	3.06	11.65	11.24	10.70	9.9 -	6.3	5.32	5.08	4.75	5.6	0.3250	1/28/20	115.6	73.7
-	1.88	-	5.87	7.24	4.67	21.7 -	12.5	1.82	1.65	1.50	1.8	0.53750	12/30/19	127.4	73.2
-	-	0.87	2.12	2.03	-0.19	19.9 -	10.7	1.34	1.10	0.94	4.3	0.3750	1/1/20	42.2	22.6
-	-	4.46	13.61	16.44	10.63	24.7 -	12.8	2.51	2.19	1.85	1.0	0.830	1/27/20	336.5	174.4
0.32	-	-	1.08	1.35	0.51	9.3 -	0.0	-						10.1	0.0
-	-	0.64	0.39	1.54	-0.09	98.5 -	44.0	-						38.4	17.2
0.12	-	-	-0.14	0.09	-0.30	-		-						13.4	0.8
-	-	58.39	234.08	222.88	137.95	0.1 -	0.1	165.77	149.31	149.39	592.5			30.0	25.5
-3.70	-	-	-0.40	-0.14	-0.05	-		-						69.9	14.2
0.14	-	-	2.18	1.71	1.44	42.4 -	29.5	0.17	0.14	0.12	0.2	0.1050Y	18/53/27	92.5	64.3
-	-	2.69	11.82	3.49	6.89	8.8 -	6.4	1.60	1.60	1.60	1.8	0.2778GHY	18/53/27	104.4	76.2
-	-	-0.68	-1.80	-1.50	-0.97	-		-						8.0	3.1
-	0.47	-	3.82	3.29	4.44	-		-							
-	-	-0.02	0.34	0.65	0.70	26.9 -	19.9	0.49	0.80	0.95	6.1	0.46880Z	1/15/20	9.1	6.8
-16.65	-	-	0.81	4.03	4.32	70.1 -	51.5	1.86	1.81	1.61	3.8	0.48110Y	18/53/27	56.8	41.7
-	-	-0.09	1.29	0.22	0.10	19.8 -	6.0	-						25.5	7.7
-	-	2.40	10.02	5.71	3.82	16.3 -	9.9	1.54	1.44	1.30	1.1	0.50Y	18/53/27	163.1	99.0
-	-	1.04	3.60	3.26	3.03	27.8 -	16.2	-						100.2	58.4
-	-	2.58	4.44	3.59	3.72	13.3 -	9.0	1.95	1.60	1.35	3.9	0.50Y	18/53/27	58.9	40.1
-	-	2.58	4.44	3.59	3.72	13.1 -	8.6	1.95	1.60	1.35	4.1			58.0	38.2
0.85	-	-	3.92	0.99	0.23	14.3 -	9.2	0.72	0.72	0.72	1.5	0.20Y	18/53/27	55.9	35.9
-	-	0.03	0.63	2.09	1.12	44.9 -	24.4	0.30	0.23	0.15	1.4	0.0750Y	3/2/20	28.3	15.4
-	-	-6.38	0.55	3.13	1.37	49.8 -	15.1	-						27.4	8.3
-	-	1.34	6.00	6.24	5.08	18.5 -	13.0	1.80	1.48	1.32	1.9	0.50Y	18/53/27	111.1	78.2
-	-	-0.78	-2.24	-1.31	-1.10	-		-						98.4	30.2
-	-	-0.06	-0.29	-0.44	-0.58	-		-						4.0	1.2
-0.05	-	-	0.63	0.87	0.89	92.1 -	47.4	-						58.0	29.8
-	-	-0.42	-2.55	-0.34	-0.29	-		0.54	0.54	0.53	5.3	0.1350Z	12/13/19	12.2	7.1
-	-	2.66	10.26	1.26	-0.11	14.5 -	11.1	3.28	3.10	3.08	2.5	1.030Y	18/53/27	148.5	113.4
-	-	0.24	0.34	1.72	2.39	57.1 -	35.5	1.32	1.29	1.20	8.6	0.330Y	1/2/20	19.4	12.1
-	-	0.32	1.09	0.91	0.75	25.8 -	17.5	-						28.1	19.1
-	-	-0.52	-0.72	0.44	0.75	-		0.68	1.00	1.06	48.5	0.41410Z	9/30/19	2.5	0.8
-	-	0.19	0.27	0.26		42.4 -	32.5	0.60	0.60	0.60	8.0	0.050	1/31/20	8.1	6.2
-	-	0.75	3.10	2.03	1.69	19.8 -	12.2							61.3	37.9
-	-	3.34	2.23	3.79	3.14	27.4 -	20.4	3.60	3.46	3.33	6.7	0.9350	12/17/19	61.0	45.6

SYMBOL	COMPANY	NATURE OF BUSINESS	FISCAL YEAR-END	TOTAL REV. $MILL	NET INCOME $MILL	TOTAL ASSETS $MILL	NET STK EQUITY $MILL	NO OF INST	INST. HOLDINGS (SHARES)
CDR	Cedar Realty Trust Inc	REITs	12/31/18	152.0	3.9	1222.9	555.4	228	98748853
CE	Celanese Corp (DE)	Specialty Chemicals	12/31/18	7155.0	1207.0	9313.0	2984.0	776	144783060
CLS	Celestica Inc	Business Services	12/31/18	6633.2	98.9	3737.7	1332.3	175	101958310
CEL	Cellcom Israel Ltd	Services	12/31/18	3688.0	-62.0	6749.0	1675.0	56	12011883
CPAC	Cementos Pacasmayo SAA (Peru)	Construction Materials	12/31/18	1262.3	76.7	2863.2	1451.4	19	3377041
CX	Cemex S.A.B. de C.V.	Construction Materials	12/31/18	276855.0	10467.0	552628.0	188650.0	405	550609343
CVE	Cenovus Energy Inc.	Production & Extraction	12/31/18	20844.0	-2669.0	35174.0	17468.0	377	1006209291
CNC	Centene Corp	Hospitals & Health Care Facilities	12/31/18	60116.0	900.0	30901.0	10917.0	975	440802946
CEN	Center Coast Brookfield MLP & Ene	Holding and other Investment Office	9/30/19	5.5	-4.6	442.1	308.1	47	6130883
CNP	CenterPoint Energy, Inc	Electric Utilities	12/31/18	10589.0	368.0	27009.0	8058.0	883	484209728
EBR	Centrais Eletricas Brasileiras S.A.-E	Electric Utilities	12/31/18	24975.7	13262.4	181210.2	55542.9	103	12053588
CEE	Central & Eastern Europe Fund Inc	Holding and other Investment Office	10/31/19	11.4	8.9	213.8	212.1	39	4694465
CPF	Central Pacific Financial Corp	Banking	12/31/18	237.1	59.5	5807.0	491.7	224	44612955
CEPU	Central Puerto SA (Argentina)	Electric Utilities	12/31/18	14265.4	17519.6	57259.9	32461.2	-	0
CCS	Century Communities Inc	Construction Services	12/31/18	2147.4	96.5	2254.3	859.4	197	33492447
CTL	CenturyLink Inc	Services	12/31/18	23443.0	-1733.0	70256.0	19828.0	1074	899390189
CDAY	Ceridian HCM Holding Inc	Internet & Software	12/31/18	746.4	-63.4	5154.4	1532.0	194	119638869
CF	CF Industries Holdings Inc	Agricultural Chemicals	12/31/18	4429.0	290.0	12661.0	2958.0	794	231374245
GIB	CGI Inc	IT Services	9/30/19	12111.2	1263.2	12621.7	6884.1	325	175530744
ECOM	ChannelAdvisor Corp	Internet & Software	12/31/18	131.2	-7.6	134.3	89.6	131	27216307
CHAP	Chaparral Energy Inc (New)	Production & Extraction	12/31/18	247.4	33.4	1340.7	884.7	88	42327181
CHRA	Charah Solutions Inc	Business Services	12/31/18	740.5	-8.9	458.9	92.6	46	7005236
CRL	Charles River Laboratories Internati	Biotechnology	12/29/18	2266.1	226.4	3855.9	1317.3	577	63305342
CLDT	Chatham Lodging Trust	REITs	12/31/18	324.2	30.6	1439.7	797.5	214	46799641
CMCM	Cheetah Mobile Inc	Internet & Software	12/31/18	4981.7	1166.9	8292.6	5476.5	70	7209934
CHGG	Chegg Inc	Educational Services	12/31/18	321.1	-14.9	760.9	410.6	327	130971307
CHE	Chemed Corp	Diagnostic & Health Related Service	12/31/18	1782.6	205.5	975.5	591.3	536	20492157
CC	Chemours Co (The)	Specialty Chemicals	12/31/18	6638.0	995.0	7362.0	1014.0	598	148552842
CHMI	Cherry Hill Mortgage Investment Co	REITs	12/31/18	94.2	37.3	2153.3	360.7	118	9127318
CHK	Chesapeake Energy Corp.	Production & Extraction	12/31/18	10231.0	873.0	10947.0	344.0	772	1471592588
CHKR	Chesapeake Granite Wash Trust	Oil Royalty Traders	12/31/18	13.5	11.3	24.4	24.4	-	0
CPK	Chesapeake Utilities Corp.	Gas Utilities	12/31/18	717.5	56.6	1693.7	518.4	244	12485789
CVX	Chevron Corporation	Refining & Marketing	12/31/18	166339.0	14824.0	253863.0	154554.0	3303	1610639763
CHWY	Chewy Inc	Business Services	2/3/19	3532.8	-267.9	541.6	-335.9	201	399560702
CHS	Chico's FAS Inc	Retail - Apparel and Accessories	2/2/19	2131.1	35.6	1007.0	580.0	361	145478839
CIM	Chimera Investment Corp	REITs	12/31/18	1199.0	411.6	27708.6	3703.8	420	137751529
DL	China Distance Education Holdings	Educational Services	9/30/18	166.7	11.6	328.9	44.3	30	37346599
CEA	China Eastern Airlines Corp., Ltd.	Airlines/Air Freight	12/31/17	101721.0	6352.0	227464.0	53106.0	38	243361
CHN	China Fund, Inc. (The)	Holding and other Investment Office	10/31/19	5.2	1.6	253.0	242.9	62	8475658
CGA	China Green Agriculture Inc	Agricultural Chemicals	6/30/19	294.3	11.6	481.0	396.6	22	194844
LFC	China Life Insurance Co Ltd	Life & Health	12/31/17	135095.0	32253.0	2897591.0	320933.0	165	17787029
CHL	China Mobile Limited	Services	12/31/18	736819.0	117781.0	1535910.0	1052405.0	523	92011425
COE	China Online Education Group	Educational Services	12/31/18	1145.5	-416.7	1010.2	-962.6	9	5383916
SNP	China Petroleum & Chemical Corp	Production & Extraction	12/31/18	2891179.0	63089.0	1592308.0	718355.0	267	12418088
XRF	China Rapid Finance Ltd	Credit & Lending	12/31/18	66.6	-66.5	96.1	0.9	28	3689947
ZNH	China Southern Airlines Co Ltd	Airlines/Air Freight	12/31/17	127489.0	5914.0	218329.0	49594.0	57	1009906
CHA	China Telecom Corp Ltd	Services	12/31/16	352285.0	18004.0	652368.0	315324.0	123	4302443
CHU	China Unicom (Hong Kong) Ltd	Services	12/31/18	290877.0	10197.0	540320.0	313922.0	170	37706507
CYD	China Yuchai International Ltd.	Auto Parts	12/31/18	16263.2	695.3	21658.0	8395.8	106	10137408
CMG	Chipotle Mexican Grill Inc	Hotels, Restaurants & Travel	12/31/18	4865.0	176.6	2265.5	1441.3	880	31063211
CHH	Choice Hotels International, Inc.	Hotels, Restaurants & Travel	12/31/18	1041.3	216.4	1138.4	-183.8	309	38753245
CB	Chubb Ltd	General Insurance	12/31/18	32717.0	3962.0	167771.0	50312.0	1511	487269307
CHT	Chunghwa Telecom Co Ltd	Services	12/31/18	215483.2	35501.6	467268.7	376562.4	178	33525557
CHD	Church & Dwight Co Inc	Household & Personal Products	12/31/18	4145.9	568.6	6069.2	2453.8	1112	243381723
CCX	Churchill Capital Corp II	Services	5/1/19	-	-0.0	0.1	0.0	27	16131244
CIEN	Ciena Corp	IT Services	10/31/19	3572.1	253.4	3893.3	2172.8	640	174870013
CI	Cigna Corp (New)	Diagnostic & Health Related Service	12/31/18	48650.0	2637.0	153226.0	41028.0	-	0
XEC	Cimarex Energy Co	Production & Extraction	12/31/18	2339.0	791.9	6062.1	3329.8	685	123444250
CBB	Cincinnati Bell Inc	Services	12/31/18	1378.2	-69.8	2730.2	-75.0	242	77986641
CNK	Cinemark Holdings Inc	Entertainment	12/31/18	3221.7	213.8	4481.8	1443.7	488	144383138
CINR	Ciner Resources LP	Mining	12/31/18	486.7	49.9	434.6	-	30	2337840
CIR	Circor International Inc	Industrial Machinery & Equipment	12/31/18	1175.8	-39.4	1791.6	529.0	221	22671908
CISN	Cision Ltd	Internet & Software	12/31/18	730.4	-24.4	1866.4	288.3	148	79718664
CIT	CIT Group Inc (New)	Banking	12/31/18	3273.2	447.1	48537.4	5946.6	556	140427321
C	Citigroup Inc	Banking	12/31/18	97120.0	18045.0	1917383.0	196220.0	2426	2410993402
CFG	Citizens Financial Group Inc (New)	Banking	12/31/18	7354.0	1721.0	160518.0	20817.0	807	495904889
CIA	Citizens, Inc. (Austin, TX)	Life & Health	12/31/18	244.0	-11.1	1615.6	187.7	81	15400051
CIO	City Office REIT Inc	REITs	12/31/18	129.5	38.2	1100.4	397.4	178	39106174
CVEO	Civeo Corp (Canada)	Business Services	12/31/18	466.7	-82.2	1001.7	535.4	124	150276126
CCC	Clarivate Analytics Plc	IT Services	12/31/18	968.5	-242.2	3709.7	1050.6	93	122687889
CLH	Clean Harbors Inc	Sanitation Services	12/31/18	3300.3	65.6	3738.3	1169.8	414	65682029
CCO	Clear Channel Outdoor Holdings Inc	Advertising	12/31/18	2721.7	-218.2	4522.0	-2262.0	241	457296663
EMO	ClearBridge Energy Midstream Opp	Holding and other Investment Office	11/30/19	3.9	2.0	1138.4	736.2	84	23827391
CEM	ClearBridge MLP & Midstream Fund	Holding and other Investment Office	11/30/19	14.0	19.7	1496.7	923.5	125	22096482
CTR	ClearBridge MLP & Midstream Total	Holding and other Investment Office	11/30/19	5.6	-8.7	597.5	401.3	62	11163919
CLW	Clearwater Paper Corp	Paper & Forest Products	12/31/18	1724.2	-143.8	1788.1	426.4	182	16691189
CWEN	Clearway Energy Inc	Electrical Equipment	12/31/18	1053.0	52.0	8500.0	1822.0	218	70639251
CLF	Cleveland-Cliffs Inc (New)	Non-Precious Metals	12/31/18	2332.4	1128.1	3529.6	424.2	519	252676681
CLPR	Clipper Realty Inc	Property, Real Estate & Developmen	12/31/18	110.0	-3.6	1101.0	65.2	69	11424266
CLX	Clorox Co (The)	Household & Personal Products	6/30/19	6214.0	820.0	5116.0	559.0	1373	129340433

EARNINGS PER SHARE — QUARTERLY			EARNINGS PER SHARE — ANNUAL			P/E RATIO		DIVIDENDS PER SHARE			AV. YLD %	DIV. DECLARED		PRICE RANGE 2018	
1st	2nd	3rd	2018	2017	2016			2018	2017	2016	%	AMOUNT	PAYABLE		
		0.00	-0.13	-0.04	-0.08	-		0.20	0.20	0.20	6.7	0.40630Z	2/20/20	3.6	2.2
		2.13	8.91	6.09	6.18	14.3	9.9	2.08	1.74	1.38	1.9	0.620Y	18/53/27	127.4	87.9
	-0.05		0.70	0.72	0.95	18.7	8.8							13.1	6.2
		1.85	-0.58	1.10	1.47							0.850	12/12/13		
					0.21			1.73	1.61		25.3			10.7	0.0
			0.22	0.34	0.33	25.3	13.1							5.6	2.9
	1.45		-2.17	3.05	-0.65			0.20	0.20	0.20	1.9	0.06250	12/31/19	14.0	7.2
		0.23	2.26	2.35	1.72	29.2	18.9							65.9	42.7
			-0.25	-0.37	-0.24			0.94	1.25	1.25	12.4	0.10420	3/26/20	8.8	5.7
		0.47	0.74	4.13	1.00	42.4	33.0	1.11	1.07	1.03	3.8	0.8750Y	18/53/27	31.4	24.4
		-0.58	9.49	-1.30	2.62	1.2	0.8	0.81			8.7			11.5	7.5
			1.01	0.53	0.42	29.1	0.0	0.56	0.32	0.49	2.2	1.46280	1/30/20	29.4	0.0
		0.51	2.01	1.34	1.50	15.2	12.4	0.82	0.70	0.60	2.8	0.230Y	12/16/19	30.6	25.0
			11.64	2.33	1.17	1.0	0.2	6.14	0.85	7.40	88.5			11.4	2.6
		0.87	3.17	2.03	2.33	10.7	5.7							34.0	17.9
		0.28	-1.63	2.21	1.16			2.16	2.16	2.16	17.1	0.250Y	18/53/27	16.7	9.7
		0.42	-0.62	-0.46	-1.65									88.8	0.0
		0.29	1.24	1.53	-1.19	42.5	31.5	1.20	1.20	1.20	2.6	0.30Y	18/53/27	52.7	39.0
		1.12	3.95	3.41	3.42	28.2	15.1							111.2	59.6
		0.06	-0.28	-0.63	-0.31									13.6	8.4
	-2.86		0.73	-2.64		11.2	1.0							8.2	0.8
	-0.11		-0.33											8.2	1.8
		1.46	4.62	2.54	3.23	33.1	22.7							152.8	104.8
		0.21	0.66	0.73	0.81	32.5	24.7	1.32	1.32	1.38	7.0	0.110Z	2/28/20	21.5	16.3
			0.78	0.94	-0.06	10.0	3.9							7.8	3.0
		-0.10	-0.13	-0.20	-0.47									45.8	28.3
		3.56	12.23	5.86	6.48	36.1	21.7	1.16	1.08	1.00	0.3	0.320Y	18/53/27	441.4	265.8
		0.46	5.45	3.91	0.04	7.4	2.2	0.84	0.12	0.12	3.4	0.250	18/53/27	40.6	11.9
		-0.32	2.18	3.98	3.30	8.6	5.5	2.11	1.96	2.11	13.3	0.51560Y	1/15/20	18.8	11.9
		-0.06	0.85	0.90	-6.45	4.0	0.7					14.3750Y	18/53/27	3.4	0.6
		0.32	0.24	0.36	0.36	7.2	2.1	0.24	0.36	0.42	23.3	0.03740	11/29/19	1.7	0.5
		0.34	3.45	3.55	2.86	28.3	23.1	1.44	1.28	1.20	1.6	0.4050Y	18/53/27	97.5	79.6
		1.36	7.74	4.85	-0.27	16.4	14.0	4.48	4.32	4.29	3.7	1.190Y	18/53/27	126.7	108.6
		-0.26	3497.89	-175.65	-560.19									37.4	22.1
		-0.07	0.79	0.69	0.01	8.1	3.2	0.33	0.32	0.31	8.1	0.08750Y	12/20/19	6.4	2.5
		0.47	1.96	2.61	2.92	10.9	9.1	2.00	2.00	2.44	10.3	0.50Z	18/53/27	21.4	17.9
		0.02	0.09	0.11	0.19	100.1	46.1	0.43	0.45	0.90	6.9	0.437	1/18/18	9.0	4.2
		0.31		0.44	0.33				2.19	2.30				41.9	23.1
			0.14	0.18	0.46	159.9	117.9	0.55	0.47	1.50	2.8	1.2523C	1/10/20	22.4	16.5
-1.62			-2.16	7.92	8.04							0.1GY	1/31/15	7.4	2.5
	0.69		1.13	0.66					0.93	1.77				14.4	10.1
		5.75	5.58	5.31		9.7	6.5	12.97	23.20	10.33	28.6			55.7	37.6
-2.06			-1.37	-1.93	-3.03									10.0	0.0
		0.50	0.52	0.42	0.39	166.4	106.0	50.20	23.82	12.34	73.3			86.5	55.1
			-1.02	-2.48	-2.46									16.5	1.6
		0.40		0.60	0.51				4.33	3.48				51.5	27.8
											7.26			56.7	37.6
			0.33	0.07	0.03	41.2	25.7	0.47	0.05	1.53	4.4			13.6	8.5
			17.02	23.40	12.89			14.79				0.850	7/19/19		
		3.47	6.31	6.17	0.77	135.0	69.6							851.5	439.4
		1.36	3.80	2.02	2.46	27.6	18.4	0.86	0.86	0.83	1.0	0.2250Y	18/53/27	104.8	70.1
		2.38	8.49	8.19	8.87			2.90	2.82			0.750	18/53/27		
		1.37	4.57	5.00	5.21	8.2	7.4	37.17	39.21	43.70	104.2			37.5	33.7
		0.62	2.27	2.90	1.75	35.4	26.6	0.87	0.76	0.71	1.2	0.22750Y	18/53/27	80.3	60.5
		0.00												10.3	0.0
		0.55	-2.49	7.53	0.51									46.0	32.9
		3.57	10.54	8.77	7.19	19.6	13.8	0.04	0.04	0.04	0.0	0.04G	18/53/27	206.5	145.5
		0.39	8.32	5.19	-4.62	9.2	4.5	0.58	0.32	0.40	1.0	0.20Y	18/53/27	76.4	37.6
		-0.32	-1.73	0.58	2.18							0.84380Y	1/2/20	10.8	3.4
		0.27	1.83	2.26	2.19	23.2	18.1	1.28	1.16	1.08	3.4	0.340Y	18/53/27	42.4	33.0
		0.73	2.48	2.07	2.08	10.3	6.0	2.27	2.27	2.26	11.4	0.340	11/20/19	25.5	15.0
		-5.64	-1.99	0.70	0.61				0.15	0.15		0.03750Y	12/12/17	47.2	21.6
		0.02	-0.19	-1.63	-0.07										
		1.50	3.61	2.80	-4.20	14.8	10.6	0.82	0.61	0.60	1.7	0.4766GHY	3/16/20	53.6	38.4
		2.07	6.68	-2.98	4.72	12.0	7.9	1.54	0.96	0.42	2.3	0.53130Y	18/53/27	79.9	52.6
		0.97	3.52	3.25	1.97	11.6	8.6	0.98	0.64	0.46	2.8	0.390Y	18/53/27	40.8	30.4
		0.04	-0.22	-0.77	0.04							0.05640	3/20/79	7.8	6.2
		-0.07	0.82	-0.05	-0.13	17.6	12.6	0.94	0.94	0.94	7.6	0.41410Z	1/24/20	14.4	10.3
		0.02	-0.84	-0.82	-0.90									2.7	0.8
-36.00			-147.14	-160.83											
		0.65	1.16	1.76	-0.69	74.9	42.8							86.9	49.7
		-0.46	-0.60	-1.77	0.39			0.08			2.0			5.7	2.2
			0.06	-0.20	-0.40	163.8	125.0	1.28	1.28	1.28	14.3	0.230	2/28/20	9.8	7.5
			0.28	-0.18	-0.47	45.9	35.4	0.35	1.20		3.0	0.2950	2/28/20	12.9	9.9
			-0.23	-0.14	-0.31			0.29			3.2	0.220	2/28/20	9.9	7.7
		-0.66	-8.72	5.88	2.90									35.0	14.2
		0.72	0.46	-0.16	0.58	44.2	29.1	1.26	1.10	0.94	7.4	0.20Y	12/16/19	20.3	13.4
		0.33	3.71	1.26	0.87	3.2	1.8					0.060Y	1/15/20	11.8	6.8
		-0.01	-0.22	-0.15	-0.34			0.38	0.37		3.3	0.0950Z	12/3/19	13.4	8.6
1.59			6.26	5.33	4.92	26.6	23.2	3.48	3.20	3.08	2.3	1.060Y	18/53/27	166.3	145.0

SYMBOL	COMPANY	NATURE OF BUSINESS	FISCAL YEAR-END	TOTAL REV. $MILL	NET INCOME $MILL	TOTAL ASSETS $MILL	NET STK EQUITY $MILL	NO OF INST	INST. HOLDINGS (SHARES)
CLDR	Cloudera Inc	Internet & Software	1/31/19	479.9	-192.6	2196.6	1562.1	293	229863068
NET	CloudFlare Inc	IT Services	12/31/18	192.7	-87.2	298.4	218.0	118	53709922
CMS	CMS Energy Corp	Electric Utilities	12/31/18	6873.0	657.0	24529.0	4755.0	822	333578022
CNA	CNA Financial Corp	General Insurance	12/31/18	10134.0	813.0	57152.0	11217.0	298	275198086
CNF	CNFinance Holdings Ltd	Finance Intermediaries & Services	12/31/18		860.9	19354.7	3045.6	-	0
CNHI	CNH Industrial NV	Industrial Machinery & Equipment	12/31/18	29706.0	1068.0	46100.0	5043.0	218	335858299
CNO	CNO Financial Group Inc	Life & Health	12/31/18	4313.5	-315.0	31439.8	3370.9	371	212425164
CEO	Cnooc Ltd.	Production & Extraction	12/31/18	226963.0	52688.0	678779.0	417365.0	314	11426342
CNXM	CNX Midstream Partners LP	Equipment & Services	12/31/18	256.7	134.0	925.4		118	30873273
CNX	CNX Resources Corp	Production & Extraction	12/31/18	1730.4	796.5	8592.2	4330.0	443	229152713
KO	Coca-Cola Co (The)	Beverages	12/31/18	31856.0	6434.0	83216.0	16981.0	2945	3444001578
CCEP	Coca-Cola European Partners plc	Manufacturing	12/31/18	11518.0	909.0	18216.0	6564.0	-	0
KOF	Coca-Cola FEMSA SAB de CV	Beverages	12/31/18	182342.0	13911.0	263787.0	124944.0	171	19932224
CDE	Coeur Mining Inc	Precious Metals	12/31/18	625.9	-48.4	1712.5	852.5	295	184805358
FOF	Cohen & Steers Closed-End Opport	Holding and other Investment Office	12/31/18	15.4	11.9	318.9	318.5	57	4188463
CNS	Cohen & Steers Inc	Wealth Management	12/31/18	381.1	113.9	432.6	222.6	246	28476681
UTF	Cohen & Steers Infrastructure Fund,	Holding and other Investment Office	12/31/18	94.7	44.7	2758.6	1883.8	182	20452305
LDP	Cohen & Steers Limited Duration Pr	Holding and other Investment Office	12/31/18	56.7	39.0	988.2	670.0	75	6280665
MIE	Cohen & Steers MLP Income & Ene	Finance Intermediaries & Services	11/30/18	3.1	-4.4	381.7	258.2	46	3455978
RQI	Cohen & Steers Quality Income Re	Holding and other Investment Office	12/31/18	63.8	33.9	1742.7	1280.6	173	18086023
RNP	Cohen & Steers REIT & Preferred &	Holding and other Investment Office	12/31/18	61.2	41.6	1302.5	950.3	135	8349733
PSF	Cohen & Steers Select Preferred & I	Holding and other Investment Office	12/31/18	25.5	18.0	416.3	286.3	53	1323346
RFI	Cohen & Steers Total Return Realty	Holding and other Investment Office	12/31/18	10.9	7.9	311.1	310.7	74	3750730
CFX	Colfax Corp	Industrial Machinery & Equipment	12/31/18	3666.8	140.2	6603.9	3269.8	324	123328980
CL	Colgate-Palmolive Co.	Household & Personal Products	12/31/18	15544.0	2400.0	12161.0	-102.0	2094	796185008
CLNY	Colony Capital Inc (New)	REITs	12/31/18	2665.3	-519.6	22215.2	7006.1	334	415002510
CLNC	Colony Credit Real Estate Inc	REITs	12/31/18	477.0	-168.5	8660.7	2706.9	160	35736883
CXP	Columbia Property Trust Inc	REITs	12/31/18	297.9	9.5	4174.0	2741.0	289	107395034
STK	Columbia Seligman Premium Techn	Holding and other Investment Office	12/31/18	3.6	-0.2	279.4	265.3	51	1637427
CCZ	Comcast Holdings Corp	Radio & Television	12/31/04	8586.0	986.0	41942.0	19912.0	3	297000
CMA	Comerica, Inc.	Banking	12/31/18	3595.0	1235.0	70818.0	7507.0	831	157967629
FIX	Comfort Systems USA Inc	Construction Services	12/31/18	2182.9	112.9	1062.6	498.0	335	47889471
CMC	Commercial Metals Co.	Non-Precious Metals	8/31/19	5829.0	198.1	3758.8	1623.9	400	134506852
CBU	Community Bank System Inc	Banking	12/31/18	586.8	168.6	10607.3	1713.8	289	45723405
CYH	Community Health Systems, Inc.	Hospitals & Health Care Facilities	12/31/18	14155.0	-788.0	15859.0	-1535.0	341	142316926
CHCT	Community Healthcare Trust Inc	REITs	12/31/18	48.6	4.4	426.6	271.7	187	20194885
CBD	Companhia Brasileira de Distribuica	Retail - General Merchandise/Depart	12/31/17	44634.0	619.0	47928.0	10333.0	-	0
SBS	Companhia de Saneamento Basico	Water Utilities	12/31/18	16085.1	2835.1	43565.1	19551.7	278	124819332
CIG	Companhia Energetica de Minas G	Electric Utilities	12/31/18	22266.0	1700.0	59855.0	14579.0	238	119328182
ELP	Companhia Paranaense De Energia	Electric Utilities	12/31/16	13101.8	958.6	30434.2	14864.2	141	32903268
SID	Companhia Siderurgica Nacional	Non-Precious Metals	12/31/18	22968.9	5074.1	47327.5	8702.7	183	59691174
CCU	Compania Cervecerias Unidas S.A.	Beverages	12/31/18	1783282.3	306890.8	2405864.9	1280126.7	170	35372030
BVN	Compania de Minas Buenaventura	Precious Metals	12/31/18	1167.4	-13.4	4217.2	2808.3	252	175435767
CODI	Compass Diversified Holdings	Miscellaneous Consumer Goods	12/31/18	1691.7	-5.7	2372.3	859.4	198	23745811
CMP	Compass Minerals International Inc	Mining	12/31/18	1493.6	68.8	2367.9	540.2	459	48622863
CRK	Comstock Resources Inc	Production & Extraction	12/31/18	223.6	64.1	2187.8	569.6	183	17787564
CAG	Conagra Brands Inc	Food	5/26/19	9538.4	678.3	22213.8	7384.6	1053	540950196
CXO	Concho Resources Inc	Production & Extraction	12/31/18	4151.0	2286.0	26294.0	18768.0	717	212684249
CCM	Concord Medical Services Holdings	Diagnostic & Health Related Service	12/31/18	190.9	-234.9	4585.4	2157.8	17	21373960
COP	ConocoPhillips	Production & Extraction	12/31/18	38727.0	6257.0	69980.0	31939.0	2352	1038974829
CCR	CONSOL Coal Resources LP	Mining	12/31/18	357.2	66.6	474.6		30	6103915
CEIX	CONSOL Energy Inc (New)	Mining	12/31/18	1532.0	153.0	2760.7	409.9	226	24112418
ED	Consolidated Edison Inc	Electric Utilities	12/31/18	12337.0	1382.0	53920.0	16726.0	1318	243771933
STZ	Constellation Brands Inc	Beverages	2/28/19	8116.0	3435.9	29231.5	12551.0	1376	181309826
CSTM	Constellium SE (France)	Non-Precious Metals	12/31/18	5686.0	188.0	3901.0	-122.0	-	0
CMS PRB	Consumers Energy Co.	Electric Utilities	12/31/18	6464.0	705.0	22025.0	6920.0	-	0
TCS	Container Store Group, Inc	Retail - Furniture & Home Furnishing	3/30/19	895.1	21.7	748.7	264.7	148	45272879
CBPX	Continental Building Products Inc	Construction Materials	12/31/18	528.1	74.2	672.4	327.7	191	38253532
CLR	Continental Resources Inc	Production & Extraction	12/31/18	4709.6	988.3	15297.9	6145.1	562	84672072
VLRS	Controladora Vuela Compania De A	Airlines/Air Freight	12/31/18	27305.1	-682.5	22310.7	9171.7	-	0
CTRA	Contura Energy Inc	Mining	12/31/18	2031.2	299.2	2746.1	1071.1	128	18449025
COO	Cooper Companies, Inc. (The)	Medical Instruments & Equipment	10/31/19	2653.4	466.7	6274.5	3628.4	746	61878799
CTB	Cooper Tire & Rubber Co.	Auto Parts	12/31/18	2808.1	76.6	2634.2	1172.0	332	68917491
CPS	Cooper-Standard Holdings Inc	Auto Parts	12/31/18	3629.3	107.8	2623.1	831.5	216	19451491
CTK	Cootek Cayman Inc	IT Services	12/31/18	134.1	10.1	118.4	84.3	10	641542
CPA	Copa Holdings S.A.	Airlines/Air Freight	12/31/18	2677.6	88.1	4087.3	1840.7	341	37991604
CLB	Core Laboratories N.V. (Netherland	Equipment & Services	12/31/18	700.8	79.5	648.8	156.8	462	57011816
CXW	CoreCivic Inc	REITs	12/31/18	1835.8	159.2	3655.7	1415.1	419	132023226
CLGX	CoreLogic Inc.	IT Services	12/31/18	1788.4	121.9	4169.0	1000.5	354	86563003
CORR	CorEnergy Infrastructure Trust Inc	REITs	12/31/18	89.2	43.7	624.9	455.0	170	11980252
CPLG	CorePoint Lodging Inc	REITs	12/31/18	862.0	-262.0	2455.0	1294.0	135	49519900
COR	CoreSite Realty Corp	REITs	12/31/18	544.4	77.9	1853.7	242.6	430	42338889
CNR	Cornerstone Building Brands Inc	Metal Products	12/31/18	559.9	-76.2	5141.2	960.0	77	67757993
GLW	Corning Inc	Electrical Equipment	12/31/18	11290.0	1066.0	27505.0	13792.0	1566	803944070
CAAP	Corporacion America Airports SA	Services	12/31/18	1426.1	7.1	3845.3	768.2	57	19082353
OFC	Corporate Office Properties Trust	REITs	12/31/18	578.1	74.7	3656.0	1585.4	382	132045019
CTVA	Corteva Inc	Agricultural Crop Production	12/31/18	5646.0	-26.0	7773.0	5035.0	1136	561306553
CTVA	Corteva Inc	Agricultural Crop Production	12/31/18	5646.0	-26.0	7773.0	5035.0	1136	561306553
CZZ	Cosan Ltd	Business Services	12/31/18	16843.9	975.4	56360.7	6614.4	213	63973654
CMRE	Costamare Inc	Shipping	12/31/18	380.4	67.2	3050.8	1357.1	139	29676142

T16

EARNINGS PER SHARE						P/E RATIO	DIVIDENDS PER SHARE			AV. YLD %	DIV. DECLARED		PRICE RANGE 2018
1st	2nd	3rd	2018	2017	2016	2018	2018	2017	2016	%	AMOUNT	PAYABLE	
		-0.29	-3.38	-5.15	-6.21								15.2 - 5.0
		-0.35	-1.08	-0.14	-0.23								21.0 - 14.6
		0.73	2.32	1.64	1.98	28.0 - 20.8	1.43	1.33	1.24	2.5	0.40750Y	18/53/27	65.0 - 48.3
		0.39	2.98	3.30	3.17	16.7 - 14.2	3.30	3.10	3.00	7.2	0.350Y	18/53/27	49.9 - 42.4
			0.62	0.40	0.19	11.0 - 0.0							6.8 - 0.0
		0.47	0.78	0.22	-0.18		0.17	0.12	0.15		0.180	5/2/19	
		0.27	-1.90	1.02	2.01		0.39	0.35	0.31	2.4	0.110Y	18/53/27	19.2 - 14.1
			1.18	0.55	0.01	213.9 - 0.0	45.27	32.80	28.08	39.7			252.4 - 0.0
		0.58	1.89	1.72	1.58	9.7 - 6.9	1.32	1.15	1.00	8.9	0.41430	2/13/20	18.3 - 13.0
		0.61	3.71	1.65	-3.70	3.6 - 1.7			0.01		0.010Y	18/53/27	13.5 - 6.2
		0.60	1.50	0.29	1.49	37.2 - 29.8	1.56	1.48	1.40	3.1	0.40Y	18/53/27	55.8 - 44.7
			1.86	1.41	1.42						0.620	6/6/19	
			0.83	-0.77	0.61	82.5 - 66.2	33.02	33.37	32.53	53.7			68.5 - 55.0
		-0.06	-0.26	-0.01	0.34								8.1 - 2.8
			0.44	0.44		30.8 - 25.2	1.04	1.04	1.04	8.2	0.0870	3/31/20	13.6 - 11.1
		0.70	2.40	1.96	2.00	28.2 - 14.2	3.82	2.12	1.54	7.5	2.7Y	12/3/19	67.6 - 34.0
			0.52	0.67	0.69	52.6 - 38.8	2.00	1.77	2.03	7.9	0.1550	3/31/20	27.3 - 20.2
			1.35	1.49	1.59	20.1 - 16.4	1.87	1.97	1.88	7.6	0.1560	3/31/20	27.1 - 22.2
			-0.16	-0.15	-0.17		0.92	0.92	1.17	10.4	0.060	3/31/20	10.4 - 6.7
			0.31	0.33	0.36	51.5 - 33.1	0.96	0.96	0.96	7.0	0.080	2/28/20	15.9 - 10.3
			0.88	0.94	1.03	28.4 - 20.0	1.49	1.49	1.48	6.8	0.1240	3/31/20	25.0 - 17.6
			1.50	1.69	1.82	21.2 - 16.1	2.06	2.17	2.45	7.3	0.1720	3/31/20	31.9 - 24.1
			0.33	0.30	0.33	47.8 - 32.6	0.96	0.96	0.96	6.9	0.080	3/31/20	15.8 - 10.8
		0.08	1.16	1.22	1.04	31.4 - 17.4					1.43750Z	4/15/20	36.5 - 20.2
		0.67	2.75	2.28	2.72	27.5 - 21.4	1.66	1.59	1.55	2.4	0.430Y	18/53/27	75.6 - 59.0
		-1.16	-1.28	-0.64	0.21		0.44	2.21	0.40	8.4	0.44530Z	18/53/27	6.2 - 4.4
		-2.77	-1.41		0.85		1.60			10.6	0.10	2/10/20	17.9 - 11.3
		-0.17	0.08	1.45	0.68	288.6 - 234.1	0.80	0.80	1.20	3.7	0.210Y	18/53/27	23.1 - 18.7
			-0.01	-0.06	-0.05		2.50	2.63	1.85	11.9	0.46250	11/26/19	23.9 - 16.7
											0.37470Z	1/15/20	61.0 - 0.0
		1.96	7.20	4.14	2.68	12.3 - 8.2	1.84	1.09	0.89	2.5	0.670Y	18/53/27	88.3 - 58.8
		0.98	3.00	1.47	1.72	19.3 - 12.2	0.33	0.29	0.28	0.7	0.10Y	11/22/19	57.8 - 36.6
0.70			1.17	0.39	0.47	19.3 - 11.4	0.48	0.48	0.48	2.7	0.120Y	18/53/27	22.6 - 13.4
		0.75	3.24	3.03	2.32	21.9 - 17.6	1.44	1.32	1.26	2.2	0.410Y	18/53/27	71.1 - 56.9
		-0.15	-6.99	-22.00	-15.54						0.25G7	18/53/27	5.1 - 1.8
		0.12	0.19	0.19	0.24	257.4 - 148.6	1.61	1.56	1.52	4.1	0.4150Z	11/29/19	48.9 - 28.2
				2.18	-1.82			0.26	0.01				26.7 - 18.5
			4.15	3.69	4.31	3.7 - 2.2	0.76	0.90	0.21	6.3			15.2 - 9.0
		0.82	1.17	0.37	0.07	3.4 - 2.5	0.51	0.24	0.55	14.5			4.0 - 2.9
					3.35				1.08				17.0 - 8.2
			3.69	0.01	-0.63	1.3 - 0.7	0.65			18.4			4.7 - 2.4
		65.02	830.55	350.76	320.59	0.0 - 0.0	342.26	218.59	200.03	1364.8			29.5 - 18.0
		0.26	-0.05	0.24	-1.27		0.09	0.08	0.03	0.6	0.02250	4/21/97	17.7 - 13.8
		-1.30	-0.42	-0.44	0.51		1.44	1.44	1.44	7.8	0.3828GH	1/30/20	26.2 - 12.8
		0.31	2.02	1.25	4.79	30.2 - 19.7	2.88	2.88	2.78	5.3	0.720Y	18/53/27	61.0 - 39.8
		-0.01	0.61	-7.61	-11.52	16.7 - 7.1					0.1250	12/15/14	10.2 - 4.3
	0.53		1.98	1.46	-1.56	17.7 - 10.5	0.85	0.90	1.00	3.1	0.21250Y	18/53/27	35.1 - 20.9
		2.78	13.25	6.41	-10.85	9.5 - 4.7					0.1250Y	18/53/27	125.2 - 62.0
		0.20	-2.76	-2.19	-2.00								3.6 - 0.0
		2.74	5.32	-0.70	-2.91	13.3 - 9.5	1.16	1.06	1.00	1.9	0.420Y	18/53/27	70.7 - 50.4
		0.25	2.37	1.39	0.83	8.1 - 3.4	2.05	2.05	2.05	13.8	0.51250	2/14/20	19.2 - 8.1
		0.16	5.38	2.40		7.1 - 2.2							38.4 - 11.8
		1.42	4.42	4.94	4.12	21.4 - 16.8	2.86	2.76	2.68	3.3	0.7650Y	18/53/27	94.7 - 74.5
		1.85	11.55	7.52	5.18	18.4 - 13.1	2.08	1.60	1.24	1.1	0.680	18/53/27	212.5 - 150.9
		0.43	1.37	-0.28	-0.04		4.50	4.50	4.50	6.2	1.1250Y	1/1/20	109.6 - 0.0
	0.08		0.40	0.31	0.11	22.5 - 9.2							9.0 - 3.7
		0.39	2.01	1.54	1.08	18.4 - 11.0							37.0 - 22.0
		0.43	2.64	2.11	-1.08	19.6 - 10.3					0.05G	18/53/27	51.8 - 27.3
		-0.12	-0.67	-0.59	3.48								11.4 - 5.3
		-3.60	25.54	14.35	-1.06	2.6 - 0.2		9.00			8.9977	7/13/17	66.0 - 5.9
		2.40	2.81	7.52	5.59	121.5 - 87.6	0.06	0.06	0.06	0.0	0.030Y	18/53/27	341.5 - 246.2
		0.58	1.51	1.81	4.51	23.3 - 15.0	0.42	0.42	0.42	1.4	0.1050Y	18/53/27	35.2 - 22.7
		-0.82	5.89	7.21	7.42	13.1 - 4.6							77.2 - 27.0
		0.00	0.00	-0.03	-0.03								13.0 - 4.5
		1.36	2.07	8.72	7.90		3.48	2.52			0.650	12/13/19	
		0.53	1.79	1.88	1.46		2.20	2.20	2.20		0.250	2/14/20	
		0.41	1.34	1.50	1.87	18.0 - 11.1	1.72	1.68	2.04	9.2	0.440Z	18/53/27	24.1 - 14.9
		0.29	1.48	1.78	1.19	33.1 - 22.2					0.22GY	18/53/27	48.9 - 32.8
		-1.65	2.79	2.07	2.14	17.8 - 12.0	3.00	3.00	3.00	7.3	0.750	2/28/20	49.6 - 33.6
		-0.22	-4.47	1.30	-0.01		0.47			4.1	0.20	1/15/20	14.6 - 8.7
		0.47	2.22	1.84	1.54	55.1 - 38.1	4.14	3.58	2.39	3.7	1.220Z	18/53/27	122.4 - 84.5
		0.20	-0.71	0.77	0.70								9.1 - 3.9
		0.38	1.13	-0.66	3.23	31.0 - 24.0	0.72	0.62	0.54	2.3	0.20Y	18/53/27	35.1 - 27.1
			-0.04	0.43	0.23								
		0.19	0.69	0.57	-0.03	43.7 - 30.5	1.10	1.10	1.10	4.0	0.2750Z	18/53/27	30.1 - 21.0
		-0.66									0.130Y	12/18/19	31.6 - 24.6
		-0.66									0.130Y	12/18/19	29.0 - 27.0
		1.26	3.83	2.05	0.98		1.74	3.26			0.08220	5/17/18	
			0.33	0.52	0.79		0.40	0.40			0.55470	1/15/20	

SYMBOL	COMPANY	NATURE OF BUSINESS	FISCAL YEAR-END	TOTAL REV. $MILL	NET INCOME $MILL	TOTAL ASSETS $MILL	NET STK EQUITY $MILL	NO OF INST	INST. HOLDINGS (SHARES)
COT	Cott Corp	Beverages	12/29/18	2372.9	382.9	3175.5	1170.4	230	131933898
COTY	Coty, Inc.	Miscellaneous Consumer Goods	6/30/19	8648.5	-3784.2	17665.4	4586.9	418	315980907
CUZ	Cousins Properties Inc	REITs	12/31/18	475.2	79.2	4146.3	2765.9	473	224871204
CVA	Covanta Holding Corp	Electric Utilities	12/31/18	1868.0	152.0	3843.0	487.0	377	129562468
CVIA	Covia Holdings Corp	Non-Precious Metals	12/31/18	1842.9	-270.5	3756.1	1454.4	114	23289927
CR	Crane Co.	Industrial Machinery & Equipment	12/31/18	3345.5	335.6	4042.7	1524.2	493	52747615
CRD A	Crawford & Co.	Brokers & Intermediaries	12/31/18	1123.0	26.0	701.4	171.3	88	14369875
BAP	CrediCorp Ltd.	Banking	12/31/18	18155.9	3983.9	177263.2	23839.2	393	65209993
CS	Credit Suisse Group AG	Banking	12/31/18	20920.0	2024.0	768916.0	43922.0	294	73674692
CPG	Crescent Point Energy Corp	Production & Extraction	12/31/18	3356.6	-2616.9	12730.4	6612.8	180	197287409
CEQP	Crestwood Equity Partners LP	Equipment & Services	12/31/18	3654.1	50.8	4294.5	-	200	65013898
CRH	CRH Plc	Construction Materials	12/31/18	26790.0	2517.0	35173.0	16029.0	223	44247525
CRT	Cross Timbers Royalty Trust	Oil Royalty Traders	12/31/18	9.2	8.6	10.1	8.5	48	670932
CAPL	CrossAmerica Partners LP	Equipment & Services	12/31/18	2445.9	5.3	866.9	-	62	15978707
CCI	Crown Castle International Corp (N	REITs	12/31/18	5423.0	671.0	32785.0	12034.0	1265	449103438
CCK	Crown Holdings Inc	Metal Products	12/31/18	11151.0	439.0	15262.0	937.0	614	172963676
CRY	CryoLife, Inc.	Medical Instruments & Equipment	12/31/18	262.8	-2.8	571.1	275.1	213	36398075
CSS	CSS Industries, Inc.	Miscellaneous Consumer Goods	3/31/19	382.3	-53.5	285.6	189.9	91	6523600
CTS	CTS Corp	Electrical Equipment	12/31/18	470.5	46.5	548.3	377.9	208	39722480
CUBE	CubeSmart	REITs	12/31/18	597.9	163.9	3753.0	1709.7	410	252632044
CUB	Cubic Corp	Electronic Instruments & Related Pro	9/30/19	1496.5	49.7	1847.2	961.6	315	39898645
CFR	Cullen/Frost Bankers, Inc.	Banking	12/31/18	1402.5	454.9	32293.0	3368.9	518	67230704
CULP	Culp Inc	Textiles	4/28/19	296.7	5.7	219.7	159.9	103	13339980
CMI	Cummins, Inc.	Auto Parts	12/31/18	23771.0	2141.0	19062.0	7348.0	1494	160032358
CURO	CURO Group Holdings Corp	Finance Intermediaries & Services	12/31/18	1094.3	-22.1	919.6	-19.1	110	19122371
CW	Curtiss-Wright Corp.	Industrial Machinery & Equipment	12/31/18	2411.8	275.7	3255.4	1530.8	442	45668849
SRF	Cushing Energy Income Fund	Holding and other Investment Office	11/30/18	0.7	-0.0	27.9	22.6	27	717904
SRV	Cushing MLP & Infrastructure Total	Holding and other Investment Office	11/30/18	2.7	-0.2	103.5	76.4	37	1994657
SZC	Cushing Renaissance Fund (The)	Holding and other Investment Office	11/30/18	6.7	2.8	179.3	136.8	44	2486295
CWK	Cushman & Wakefield PLC	Property, Real Estate & Developmen	12/31/18	8219.9	-185.8	6546.0	1360.1	115	150323887
CUBI	Customers Bancorp Inc	Banking	12/31/18	476.9	71.7	9833.4	956.8	199	30747767
CVI	CVR Energy Inc	Refining & Marketing	12/31/18	7124.0	289.0	3907.0	1246.0	330	101640764
UAN	CVR Partners LP	Agricultural Crop Production	12/31/18	351.1	-50.0	1254.4	-	74	43770145
CVS	CVS Health Corporation	Diagnostic & Health Related Service	12/31/18	194579.0	-594.0	196456.0	58225.0	2453	1236740872
CELP	Cypress Energy Partners LP	Equipment & Services	12/31/18	315.0	11.4	152.9	-	20	208930
DAN	Dana Inc	Auto Parts	12/31/18	8143.0	427.0	5918.0	1345.0	418	171576345
DHR	Danaher Corp	Medical Instruments & Equipment	12/31/18	19893.0	2650.9	47832.5	28214.4	1932	654823869
DHR	Danaher Corp	Medical Instruments & Equipment	12/31/18	19893.0	2650.9	47832.5	28214.4	1932	654823869
DAC	Danaos Corp	Shipping	12/31/18	458.7	-32.9	2679.8	690.9	28	4989185
DQ	DAQO New Energy Corp	Semiconductors	12/31/18	301.6	38.1	854.9	525.1	98	5332312
DRI	Darden Restaurants, Inc.	Hotels, Restaurants & Travel	5/26/19	8510.4	713.4	5892.8	2392.6	1041	144153807
DAR	Darling Ingredients Inc	Food	12/29/18	3387.7	101.5	4889.4	2273.0	400	199692180
DVA	DaVita Inc	Diagnostic & Health Related Service	12/31/18	11404.9	159.4	19110.3	3703.4	675	150953925
DCP	DCP Midstream LP	Equipment & Services	12/31/18	9822.0	298.0	14266.0	-	223	94317505
DECK	Deckers Outdoor Corp.	Apparel, Footwear & Accessories	3/31/19	2020.4	264.3	1427.2	1045.1	529	35384007
DE	Deere & Co.	Industrial Machinery & Equipment	11/3/19	39258.0	3253.0	73011.0	11413.0	1720	271556472
DEX	Delaware Enhanced Global Dividen	Holding and other Investment Office	11/30/18	13.5	7.8	204.7	137.8	59	4115286
DDF	Delaware Investments Dividend & I	Holding and other Investment Office	11/30/18	4.3	2.1	125.8	85.2	33	612342
DKL	Delek Logistics Partners LP	Equipment & Services	12/31/18	656.7	90.2	624.6	-	66	6365637
DK	Delek US Holdings Inc (New)	Refining & Marketing	12/31/18	10233.1	340.1	5760.6	1632.6	-	0
DELL	Dell Technologies Inc	Internet & Software	2/1/19	90621.0	-2310.0	111820.0	-4569.0	704	181562539
DLPH	Delphi Technologies PLC	Manufacturing	12/31/18	4858.0	358.0	3893.0	292.0	250	75941175
DAL	Delta Air Lines Inc (DE)	Airlines/Air Freight	12/31/18	44438.0	3935.0	60266.0	13687.0	1446	726728801
DLX	Deluxe Corp	Printing	12/31/18	1998.0	149.6	2305.1	915.4	439	49426500
DNR	Denbury Resources, Inc. (DE)	Production & Extraction	12/31/18	1473.6	322.7	4723.2	1141.8	403	415993448
DBI	Designer Brands Inc	Retail - Apparel and Accessories	2/2/19	3183.7	-20.5	1620.6	832.4	374	78633542
DESP	Despegar.com Corp	Hotels, Restaurants & Travel	12/31/18	530.6	19.2	763.9	247.6	102	36627557
DB	Deutsche Bank AG	Banking	12/31/18	36917.0	267.0	1348137.0	67169.0	313	452736807
DVN	Devon Energy Corp.	Production & Extraction	12/31/18	10734.0	3064.0	19566.0	9186.0	1139	446301905
DHX	DHI Group Inc	Internet & Software	12/31/18	161.6	7.2	258.4	145.4	154	51129747
DHT	DHT Holdings Inc	Equipment & Services	12/31/18	375.9	-46.9	1863.9	861.7	185	75977784
DEO	Diageo Plc	Beverages	6/30/19	12867.0	3160.0	31296.0	8361.0	1143	85585012
DO	Diamond Offshore Drilling, Inc.	Equipment & Services	12/31/18	1083.2	-180.3	6035.7	3584.7	413	170942104
DSSI	Diamond S Shipping Inc	Miscellaneous Transportation Servic	12/31/18	161.7	9.5	679.6	600.1	87	26403729
DRH	DiamondRock Hospitality Co.	REITs	12/31/18	863.7	87.8	3197.6	1882.9	342	318111508
DSX	Diana Shipping Inc	Shipping	12/31/18	226.2	16.6	1187.8	627.7	119	40277505
DKS	Dick's Sporting Goods, Inc	Retail - Specialty	2/2/19	8436.6	319.9	4187.1	1904.2	527	93876345
DBD	Diebold Nixdorf Inc	Computer Hardware & Equipment	12/31/18	4578.6	-568.7	4311.9	-186.4	355	100172699
DLR	Digital Realty Trust Inc	REITs	12/31/18	3046.5	331.2	23766.7	9874.5	942	255983890
DDS	Dillard's Inc.	Retail - General Merchandise/Depart	2/2/19	6503.3	170.3	3431.4	1678.4	313	32958163
DIN	Dine Brands Global Inc	Retail - Food & Beverage, Drug & To	12/31/18	780.9	80.4	1774.7	-202.3	312	22668111
DPLO	Diplomat Pharmacy Inc	Diagnostic & Health Related Service	12/31/18	5492.5	-302.3	1476.4	465.1	191	76822826
DFS	Discover Financial Services	Credit & Lending	12/31/18	12848.0	2742.0	109553.0	11130.0	1210	356376715
DIS	Disney (Walt) Co. (The)	Entertainment	9/28/19	69570.0	11054.0	193984.0	88877.0	-	0
DNI	Dividend & Income Fund	Holding and other Investment Office	12/31/18	5.5	2.4	186.0	158.9	57	6375893
DNP	DNP Select Income Fund Inc	Holding and other Investment Office	10/31/19	126.9	59.7	4181.7	3158.9	285	21165518
DLB	Dolby Laboratories Inc	Manufacturing	9/27/19	1241.6	255.2	2821.7	2307.4	456	67880931
DG	Dollar General Corp	Retail - General Merchandise/Depart	2/1/19	25625.0	1589.5	13204.0	6417.4	1147	285565251
D	Dominion Energy Inc (New)	Electric Utilities	12/31/18	13366.0	2447.0	77914.0	20107.0	1820	642131129
DPZ	Dominos Pizza Inc.	Hotels, Restaurants & Travel	12/30/18	3432.9	362.0	907.4	-3039.9	661	53373590

T18

1st	2nd	3rd	2018	2017	2016	P/E RATIO		DIV 2018	DIV 2017	DIV 2016	AV. YLD %	AMOUNT	PAYABLE	PRICE 2018	
-	-	0.07	2.71	-0.01	-0.61	7.7	4.4	0.24	0.24	0.24	1.5	0.060	12/6/19	20.9	11.8
0.07	-	-	-0.23	-0.66	0.44	-		0.50	0.65	0.25	4.6	0.1250	18/53/27	13.7	6.8
-	-	0.14	0.76	2.08	1.24	54.2	40.6	1.04	1.20	0.96	2.8	0.290Z	1/13/20	41.2	30.9
-	-	0.10	1.15	0.44	-0.03	15.9	11.7	1.00	1.00	1.00	6.0	0.250Y	1/3/20	18.3	13.5
-	-	0.41	-2.16	114.71	2.73	-		-				-		7.2	1.3
-	-	1.19	5.50	2.84	2.07	16.2	12.7	1.40	1.32	1.32	1.7	0.390Y	18/53/27	88.9	69.7
-	-	0.21	0.92	0.52	0.67	12.8	8.9	0.28	0.28	0.28	2.8	0.050Y	12/6/19	11.8	8.2
-	-	-	49.99	51.35	44.23	-		20.00	14.17	-		2.38257	11/22/19		
-	0.13	-	0.77	-0.41	-1.32	17.7	14.2	0.25	1.18	0.70	2.0	-		13.6	10.9
-	-	-0.55	-4.77	-0.23	-1.81	-		0.36	0.36	0.50	8.8	0.010	1/2/20	6.3	2.5
-	-	0.12	-0.13	-3.64	-3.55	-		2.40	2.40	3.17	7.0	0.21110	2/14/20	39.6	28.6
-	-	-	3.01	2.25	1.49	13.4	8.7	0.67	0.66	0.64	2.0	-		40.4	26.1
-	-	0.19	1.43	1.01	1.06	9.4	5.2	1.43	1.01	1.06	13.4	0.10420	2/14/20	13.5	7.4
-	-	0.20	0.11	0.56	0.22	172.5	133.9	2.20	2.48	2.40	12.8	0.5250	2/10/20	19.0	14.7
-	-	0.58	1.34	1.01	0.95	111.2	78.9	4.28	3.90	3.61	3.3	1.20Y	18/53/27	149.1	105.7
-	-	1.36	3.28	2.38	3.56	23.4	12.6	-				-		76.6	41.2
-	-	0.00	-0.08	0.11	0.32	-		-				0.030Y	12/18/15	32.4	22.4
-	0.39	-	-4.01	3.13	1.87	-		0.80	0.80	0.74	14.0	0.20Y	3/15/19	11.2	3.6
-	-	0.08	1.39	0.43	1.03	24.4	18.1	0.16	0.16	0.16	0.5	0.040Y	1/31/20	34.0	25.1
-	-	0.22	0.88	0.74	0.45	41.3	31.9	1.22	1.11	0.90	3.7	0.330Z	18/53/27	36.3	28.1
-	-	0.77	0.45	-0.41	0.06	166.5	118.0	0.27	0.27	0.27	0.4	0.1350Y	9/9/19	74.9	53.1
-	-	1.73	6.90	5.51	4.70	15.3	11.6	2.58	2.25	2.15	2.7	0.33590Y	18/53/27	105.7	80.3
-	0.19	-	1.65	1.78	1.36	12.7	8.0	0.55	0.51	0.66	3.2	0.1050	1/17/20	21.0	13.2
-	-	3.97	13.15	5.97	8.23	14.2	9.9	4.44	4.21	4.00	2.7	1.3110Y	18/53/27	186.4	130.7
-	-	0.60	-0.48	1.25	1.69	-		-				-		16.2	9.2
-	-	1.92	6.22	4.80	4.15	23.1	16.0	0.60	0.56	0.52	0.5	0.170Y	18/53/27	143.5	99.5
-	-	-	-0.02	-0.49	-0.13	-		0.48	0.48	0.94	7.1	0.040	1/31/20	8.0	5.7
-	-	-	-0.04	-0.42	-0.29	-		1.08	1.08	1.08	10.8	0.09030	1/31/20	10.7	8.7
-	-	-	-0.90	-0.11	-0.01	-		1.64	1.64	1.64	11.2	0.13670	1/31/20	17.4	12.6
-	-	0.05	-1.09	-1.53	-3.18	-		-				-			
-	-	0.74	1.78	1.97	2.31	14.2	9.9	-				0.33590Y	6/30/20	25.3	17.6
-	-	1.18	3.12	2.70	0.28	17.7	11.1	2.50	2.00	2.00	5.7	0.80Y	11/12/19	55.2	34.7
-	-	-0.20	-0.44	-0.64	-0.26	-		-	0.02	0.71		0.070	11/12/19	4.2	2.7
-	-	1.17	-0.57	6.44	4.90	-		2.00	2.00	1.70	3.3	0.50Y	18/53/27	76.6	52.1
-	-	0.26	0.72	0.29	0.13	13.7	8.1	0.84	1.04	1.63	10.7	0.210	11/14/19	9.9	5.9
-	-	0.77	2.91	0.71	4.36	7.1	4.0	0.40	0.24	0.24	2.4	0.10Y	18/53/27	20.7	11.7
-	-	0.89	3.74	3.53	3.65	41.0	26.1	0.64	0.56	0.57	0.5	11.8750Y	18/53/27	153.5	97.6
-	-	0.89	3.74	3.53	3.65	40.6	40.3	0.64	0.56	0.57	0.4	11.8750Y	18/53/27	152.0	150.6
-	-	1.12	-3.08	10.64	-46.76	-		-				0.4650	11/19/08		
-	-	-	0.12	0.34	0.16	441.7	194.2	-				-		53.0	23.3
-	0.20	-	4.73	3.80	2.90	27.0	20.8	2.52	2.24	2.10	2.2	0.880Y	18/53/27	127.6	98.3
-	-	0.15	0.60	0.77	0.62	46.8	30.5	-				-		28.1	18.3
-	-	0.95	0.92	3.47	4.29	81.6	47.2	-				-		75.0	43.4
-	-	-1.59	0.61	0.43	1.64	55.7	33.8	3.12	3.12	3.12	11.0	0.49690	18/53/27	34.0	20.6
-	2.71	-	3.58	0.18	3.70	50.0	31.6	-				-		179.1	113.3
-	-	2.81	7.24	6.68	4.81	24.8	18.6	2.58	2.40	2.40	1.6	0.760Y	18/53/27	179.8	134.8
-	-	-	0.50	0.44	0.42	20.8	17.3	1.09	0.63	0.83	11.2	0.09190	1/31/20	10.4	8.6
-	-	-	0.28	0.34	0.38	55.2	40.2	1.29	0.48	0.59	9.4	0.09140	1/31/20	15.4	11.3
-	-	0.89	2.65	2.09	2.07	12.8	10.6	3.04	2.79	2.48	9.7	0.8850	2/12/20	34.0	28.1
-	-	0.68	3.95	4.00	-2.49	11.0	7.6	0.96	0.30	0.60	2.7	0.30Y	18/53/27	43.3	30.2
-	-	0.66	-7.08	-4.22	-2.72	-		-				-		69.8	42.6
-	-	0.16	4.03	3.21	1.78	-		0.68	-	-		0.170	11/14/18		
-	-	2.31	5.67	4.95	5.79	11.1	8.0	1.31	1.01	0.68	2.4	0.40250Y	18/53/27	63.2	45.6
-	-	-7.49	3.16	4.72	4.65	17.0	11.7	1.20	1.20	1.20	2.6	0.30Y	18/53/27	53.8	36.9
-	-	0.14	0.71	0.41	-2.61	3.7	1.3	-				0.06250	9/29/15	2.6	0.9
-	-	0.60	0.83	1.52	1.54	35.8	17.1	0.80	0.80	0.80	4.0	0.250Y	1/3/20	29.8	14.2
-	-	-	0.27	0.69	0.30	-		-				-			
-	-	0.10	-0.01	-0.53	-1.08	-		0.11	-	-		-			
-	-	0.27	6.10	1.70	-6.52	5.8	3.2	0.30	0.24	0.42	1.1	0.090Y	18/53/27	35.2	19.8
-	-	0.08	0.14	0.33	-0.11	30.7	12.2	-				-		4.3	1.7
-	-	-0.15	-0.33	0.05	0.10	-		0.08	0.20	-		0.050	11/14/19		
-	-	-	1.21	1.05	0.89	145.4	114.1	2.55	2.35	2.29	1.6	-		176.0	138.1
-	-	-0.69	-1.31	0.13	-2.72	-		-				0.1250Y	18/53/27	12.4	5.0
-	-	-0.65	-			-		-				-			
-	-	0.06	0.43	0.46	0.57	26.4	20.5	0.38	0.50	0.50	3.7	0.1250Z	1/13/20	11.4	8.8
-	-	-0.04	0.10	-5.41	-2.11	-		-				0.55470	1/15/20		
-	-	0.66	3.01	2.56	2.83	16.4	10.5	0.68	0.60	0.55	1.8	0.2750Y	18/53/27	49.5	31.5
-	-	-0.46	-7.48	-3.09	-0.48	-		0.10	0.40	0.96	1.0	0.10Y	18/53/27	14.2	2.6
-	-	0.24	1.21	0.99	2.20	112.2	84.2	4.04	3.72	3.52	3.4	0.2925GHZ	18/53/27	135.7	101.8
-	-	0.22	7.51	4.93	6.91	10.9	7.3	0.34	0.28	0.26	0.5	0.150Y	18/53/27	81.6	55.0
-	-	1.36	4.37	-18.28	5.33	23.7	15.7	2.52	3.88	3.73	3.0	0.690Y	1/10/20	103.4	68.7
-	-	-2.35	-4.07	0.23	0.42	-		-				-		14.5	3.1
-	-	2.36	7.79	5.42	5.77	11.9	7.5	1.50	1.30	1.16	1.9	0.440Y	18/53/27	92.9	58.4
-	-	0.97	8.36	5.69	5.73	18.1	12.7	1.68	1.56	1.42	1.3	0.880Y	18/53/27	151.6	106.3
-	-	-	0.20	0.16	0.25	67.3	47.0	0.70	0.60	1.00	6.0	0.250	12/30/20	13.5	9.4
-	-	-	0.20	0.22	0.27	65.0	52.0	0.78	0.78	0.78	6.5	0.0650	4/10/20	13.0	10.4
-	-	0.38	1.14	1.95	1.81	61.3	50.3	0.64	0.56	0.48	1.0	0.220Y	18/53/27	69.9	57.4
-	-	1.42	5.63	4.43	3.95	29.4	19.1	1.04	1.00	0.88	0.8	0.320Y	18/53/27	165.8	107.7
-	-	1.17	3.74	4.72	3.44	22.3	18.2	3.34	3.04	2.80	4.3	0.940Y	18/53/27	83.5	68.0
-	-	2.05	8.35	5.83	4.30	35.5	26.6	2.20	1.84	1.52	0.8	0.650Y	18/53/27	296.6	222.4

SYMBOL	COMPANY	NATURE OF BUSINESS	FISCAL YEAR-END	TOTAL REV. $MILL	NET INCOME $MILL	TOTAL ASSETS $MILL	NET STK EQUITY $MILL	NO OF INST	INST. HOLDINGS (SHARES)
UFS	Domtar Corp	Paper & Forest Products	12/31/18	5455.0	283.0	4925.0	2538.0	-	0
DCI	Donaldson Co. Inc.	Industrial Machinery & Equipment	7/31/19	2844.9	267.2	2142.6	897.3	511	130751068
RRD	Donnelley (RR) & Sons Company	Printing	12/31/18	6800.2	-11.0	3640.8	-260.1	361	101497112
DFIN	Donnelley Financial Solutions Inc	Business Services	12/31/18	963.0	73.6	868.7	226.0	179	35313963
LPG	Dorian LPG Ltd.	Shipping	3/31/19	158.0	-50.9	1625.4	912.7	156	40272342
DSL	DoubleLine Income Solutions Fund	Holding and other Investment Office	9/30/19	239.8	179.4	2884.4	1954.2	188	26191509
DBL	Doubleline Opportunistic Credit Fun	Holding and other Investment Office	9/30/19	27.1	20.2	392.6	310.7	89	4986535
PLOW	Douglas Dynamics, Inc.	Industrial Machinery & Equipment	12/31/18	524.1	43.9	676.2	282.8	183	22871964
DEI	Douglas Emmett Inc	REITs	12/31/18	881.3	116.1	8261.7	2402.3	401	214753249
DOV	Dover Corp	Industrial Machinery & Equipment	12/31/18	6992.1	570.3	8365.8	2768.7	1079	165114361
DVD	Dover Motorsports, Inc.	Sporting & Recreational	12/31/18	47.0	6.9	79.0	62.9	55	9401563
DOW	Dow Inc	Plastics	12/31/18	60278.0	4499.0	77378.0	26831.0	-	0
DOW	Dow Inc	Plastics	12/31/18	60278.0	4499.0	77378.0	26831.0	-	0
RDY	Dr. Reddy's Laboratories Ltd.	Pharmaceuticals	3/31/19	142028.0	9806.0	225604.0	126460.0	219	25916946
DRD	DRD Gold Ltd	Precious Metals	6/30/19	2762.1	78.5	4060.0	2688.6	53	8024361
DRQ	Dril-Quip Inc	Equipment & Services	12/31/18	384.6	-95.7	1192.5	1096.2	349	51146805
DS	Drive Shack Inc	Sporting & Recreational	12/31/18	314.4	-38.7	401.9	134.7	162	52755614
DTE	DTE Energy Co	Electric Utilities	12/31/18	14212.0	1120.0	36288.0	10237.0	943	163912219
DTF	DTF Tax-Free Income, Inc.	Holding and other Investment Office	10/31/19	7.1	3.4	200.4	134.2	44	3728556
DCO	Ducommun Inc.	Aerospace	12/31/18	629.3	9.0	648.1	256.8	182	11822389
DSE	Duff & Phelps Select MLP and Mids	Holding and other Investment Office	11/30/18	0.6	-5.7	222.8	136.3	-	0
DUC	Duff & Phelps Utility & Corporate Bo	Holding and other Investment Office	10/31/18	13.1	7.1	368.8	263.3	60	16735749
DPG	Duff & Phelps Utility & Infrastructure	Holding and other Investment Office	10/31/18	24.4	4.5	883.5	622.0	67	7009582
DUK	Duke Energy Corp	Electric Utilities	12/31/18	24521.0	2666.0	145392.0	43817.0	2003	581899868
DRE	Duke Realty Corp	REITs	12/31/18	947.9	383.7	7804.0	4658.2	650	414548506
DD	DuPont de Nemours Inc	Plastics		-	-	-	-	178	27134855
DD	DuPont de Nemours Inc	Plastics		-	-	-	-	178	27134855
KTF	DWS Municipal Income Trust (New)	Holding and other Investment Office	11/30/18	32.3	22.0	725.1	465.3	98	9838924
KSM	DWS Strategic Municipal Income Tr	Holding and other Investment Office	11/30/18	10.6	6.9	228.4	131.7	35	1132971
DXC	DXC Technology Co	IT Services	3/31/19	20753.0	1257.0	29574.0	11402.0	808	235388879
DY	Dycom Industries, Inc.	Construction Services	1/26/19	3127.7	62.9	2097.5	804.2	388	41175930
DLNG	Dynagas LNG Partners LP	Equipment & Services	12/31/18	127.1	3.6	1063.4		33	3176048
DT	Dynatrace Inc	IT Services	3/31/19	431.0	-116.2	1811.4	-390.3	84	244290424
DX	Dynex Capital, Inc.	REITs	12/31/18	110.1	7.0	3886.1	527.2	171	20454303
ELF	e.l.f. Beauty Inc	Household & Personal Products	12/31/18	267.4	15.5	435.9	229.3	169	42177499
EGIF	Eagle Growth & Income Opportuniti	Holding and other Investment Office	12/31/18	9.3	4.9	171.5	115.1	27	2662859
EXP	Eagle Materials Inc	Construction Materials	3/31/19	1393.2	68.9	2169.2	1209.5	481	51436173
ECC	Eagle Point Credit Company Inc	Holding and other Investment Office	12/31/18	69.7	34.7	476.7	287.1	49	7930556
EIC	Eagle Point Income Co Inc	Finance Intermediaries & Services		-	-	-	-	7	841701
ESTE	Earthstone Energy Inc	Production & Extraction	12/31/18	165.4	42.3	1004.3	334.6	80	14117603
DEA	Easterly Government Properties Inc	REITs	12/31/18	160.6	5.7	1861.6	894.2	249	74074319
EGP	EastGroup Properties Inc	REITs	12/31/18	300.4	88.5	2131.7	903.1	414	44662281
EMN	Eastman Chemical Co	Plastics	12/31/18	10151.0	1080.0	15995.0	5803.0	944	133854342
KODK	Eastman Kodak Co.	Leisure Equipment	12/31/18	1325.0	-16.0	1511.0	170.0	168	42250373
ETN	Eaton Corp plc	Electrical Equipment	12/31/18	21609.0	2145.0	31092.0	16107.0	1367	368267632
EV	Eaton Vance Corp	Wealth Management	10/31/18	1683.3	400.0	4253.6	1184.1	525	107426948
EOI	Eaton Vance Enhanced Equity Inco	Holding and other Investment Office	9/30/19	10.4	4.0	601.7	591.0	92	6654684
EOS	Eaton Vance Enhanced Equity Inco	Holding and other Investment Office	12/31/18	7.3	-1.3	714.0	707.6	105	8679216
EFF	Eaton Vance Floating Rate Income	Finance Intermediaries & Services	5/31/19	12.1	7.4	206.2	130.5	51	3873631
EFT	Eaton Vance Floating Rate Income	Holding and other Investment Office	5/31/19	54.0	33.8	945.7	606.4	136	18253736
EHT	Eaton Vance High Income 2021 Tar	Holding and other Investment Office	3/31/19	14.6	10.2	282.8	213.6	34	4455373
ETX	Eaton Vance Municipal Income 202	Holding and other Investment Office	1/31/19	13.4	8.4	351.6	221.4	44	2278937
EVN	Eaton Vance Municipal Income Trus	Holding and other Investment Office	11/30/18	23.5	14.5	515.0	302.0	93	7025836
EOT	Eaton Vance National Municipal Op	Holding and other Investment Office	3/31/19	17.7	14.5	370.3	321.2	45	1551194
ETJ	Eaton Vance Risk-Managed Diversif	Holding and other Investment Office	12/31/18	10.6	3.8	574.7	570.0	113	17967609
EFR	Eaton Vance Senior Floating Rate T	Holding and other Investment Office	10/31/18	51.0	36.4	856.9	610.5	136	11550213
EVF	Eaton Vance Senior Income Trust	Holding and other Investment Office	6/30/19	24.0	15.5	424.9	304.5	95	20003120
EVG	Eaton Vance Short Duration Diversif	Holding and other Investment Office	10/31/18	19.8	13.1	354.3	259.6	63	13536461
EVT	Eaton Vance Tax Advantaged Divid	Holding and other Investment Office	10/31/19	74.9	42.1	2238.8	1784.4	144	12475886
ETW	Eaton Vance Tax Managed Global	Holding and other Investment Office	12/31/18	28.1	15.1	1050.3	1040.9	151	23128307
ETG	Eaton Vance Tax-Advantage Global	Holding and other Investment Office	10/31/18	121.6	92.9	1773.2	1334.2	122	14784302
ETO	Eaton Vance Tax-Advantaged Glob	Holding and other Investment Office	10/31/19	14.6	6.6	481.3	359.8	60	1954418
ETB	Eaton Vance Tax-Managed Buy-Wri	Holding and other Investment Office	12/31/18	8.4	3.9	376.2	372.5	77	6043465
ETV	Eaton Vance Tax-Managed Buy-Wri	Holding and other Investment Office	12/31/18	17.2	5.5	1049.1	1039.1	163	13747071
EXD	Eaton Vance Tax-Managed Buy-Wri	Holding and other Investment Office	12/31/18	2.4	0.9	104.1	97.2	35	2206740
ETY	Eaton Vance Tax-Managed Diversifi	Holding and other Investment Office	10/31/19	33.9	15.1	1810.5	1782.4	162	35010331
EXG	Eaton Vance Tax-Managed Global	Holding and other Investment Office	10/31/19	57.6	30.1	2662.1	2633.9	228	56842700
ECT	ECA Marcellus Trust I	Oil Royalty Traders	12/31/18	6.9	5.5	48.9	46.9	41	846692
ECL	Ecolab Inc	Specialty Chemicals	12/31/18	14668.2	1429.1	20074.5	8003.2	1538	273685263
EC	Ecopetrol SA	Refining & Marketing	12/31/18	68603872.0	1381386.0	24643498.0	5513 7914.0	211	63238680
EPC	Edgewell Personal Care Co	Household & Personal Products	9/30/19	2141.0	-372.2	3420.9	1303.5	460	70351774
EIX	Edison International	Electric Utilities	12/31/18	12657.0	-423.0	56715.0	10459.0	928	363578633
EW	Edwards Lifesciences Corp	Medical Instruments & Equipment	12/31/18	3722.8	722.2	5323.7	3140.4	1281	202964552
EE	El Paso Electric Company	Electric Utilities	12/31/18	903.6	84.3	3628.5	1164.1	312	48307499
ELAN	Elanco Animal Health Inc	Pharmaceuticals	12/31/18	3066.8	86.5	8956.7	5197.5	447	379206700
ELAN	Elanco Animal Health Inc	Pharmaceuticals	12/31/18	3066.8	86.5	8956.7	5197.5	447	379206700
ESTC	Elastic NV	IT Services	4/30/19	271.7	-102.3	485.7	263.0	234	54386070
EGO	Eldorado Gold Corp	Precious Metals	12/31/18	459.0	-361.9	4628.9	3283.7	210	104506453
ESI	Element Solutions Inc	Specialty Chemicals	12/31/18	1961.0	-324.4	9401.5	2109.2	235	243928354
ELVT	Elevate Credit Inc	Credit & Lending	12/31/18	786.7	12.5	753.3	116.8	95	26852570

T20

| EARNINGS PER SHARE | | | | | | P/E RATIO | | DIVIDENDS PER SHARE | | | AV. YLD | DIV. DECLARED | | PRICE RANGE | |
| QUARTERLY | | | ANNUAL | | | | | | | | % | | | 2018 | |
1st	2nd	3rd	2018	2017	2016			2018	2017	2016		AMOUNT	PAYABLE		
-	-	0.32	4.48	-4.11	2.04	12.0 -	7.1	1.74	1.66	1.65	4.0	0.4550	18/53/27	53.6 -	31.9
0.51	-	-	1.36	1.74	1.42	42.8 -	30.8	0.73	0.70	0.69	1.4	0.210Y	18/53/27	58.2 -	41.9
-	-	0.18	-0.16	-0.49	-7.09			0.34	0.56	0.14	9.2	0.030Y	3/2/20	6.3 -	1.7
-	-	0.43	2.16	0.29	1.80	7.8 -	4.4							16.9 -	9.4
-	0.74	-	-0.38	-0.03	2.29										
-	-	-	1.80	1.75	1.71	11.5 -	9.9	1.84	1.81	1.89	9.3	0.150	1/31/20	20.8 -	17.8
-	-	-	1.41	1.63	1.81	15.0 -	13.6	2.00	2.00	2.53	9.8	0.110	1/31/20	21.1 -	19.2
-	-	0.53	1.89	2.40	1.70	29.9 -	18.3	1.06	0.96	0.94	2.5	0.27250Y	12/31/19	56.4 -	34.5
-	-	0.13	0.68	0.58	0.55	65.9 -	48.3	1.01	0.94	0.89	2.5	0.280Z	18/53/27	44.8 -	32.8
-	-	1.40	3.75	5.15	3.25	30.9 -	18.6	1.90	1.82	1.72	2.0	0.490Y	18/53/27	115.8 -	69.8
-	-	-0.01	0.19	0.23	0.10	11.4 -	9.5	0.08	0.08	0.05	4.0	0.10Y	12/10/19	2.2 -	1.8
-	-	0.45	-	-	-							0.70	12/13/19	59.7 -	40.7
-	-	0.45	-	-	-							0.70	12/13/19	53.5 -	48.6
-	-	-	59.00	72.09	116.98	0.7 -	0.6	18.94	18.69	18.62	49.2	-		42.8 -	34.8
-0.03	-	-	0.01	0.03	0.15	531.0 -	167.0	0.74	0.97	4.87	23.4	-		5.3 -	1.7
-	-	-0.04	-2.58	-2.69	2.47									55.6 -	30.9
-	-	-0.20	-0.66	-0.71	1.07				0.00	0.48		0.52340Z	1/31/20	5.4 -	3.6
-	-	1.73	6.17	6.32	4.83	21.7 -	17.5	3.60	3.36	3.06	2.9	1.01250Y	18/53/27	133.8 -	107.9
-	-	-	0.47	-	0.57	31.8 -	0.0	0.62	0.75	0.88	4.5	0.04M	3/31/20	14.9 -	0.0
-	-	0.70	0.77	1.74	2.24	67.3 -	45.4					0.0750Y	3/4/11	51.8 -	34.9
-	-	-	-0.22	-0.20	-0.10			0.67	0.88	0.88	14.5	0.150	11/19/19	5.3 -	3.3
-	-	-	0.30	0.34	0.38	30.8 -	27.3	0.45	0.60	0.60	5.1	0.050	3/31/20	9.3 -	8.2
-	-	-	0.19	0.41	0.67	84.1 -	63.2	1.40	1.40	1.40	9.3	0.350	3/31/20	16.0 -	12.0
-	-	1.82	3.76	4.36	3.11	25.8 -	22.3	3.63	3.49	3.36	4.0	0.35940Y	18/53/27	97.2 -	83.7
-	-	0.62	1.07	4.56	0.88	33.2 -	23.4	0.81	1.62	0.73	2.5	0.2350Z	18/53/27	35.5 -	25.0
-	-	0.50	-	-	-							0.30Y	12/13/19	84.3 -	62.0
-	-	0.50	-	-	-							0.30Y	12/13/19	65.4 -	63.4
-	-	-	0.56	0.66	0.75	21.1 -	18.8	0.24	0.78		2.1	0.040	1/31/20	11.8 -	10.6
-	-	-	0.61	0.70	0.80	20.8 -	17.4	0.25	0.67		2.1	0.04250	1/31/20	12.7 -	10.6
-	-8.19	-	6.04	-0.88	-	11.5 -	4.4	0.72	-		1.5	0.210Y	1/14/20	69.2 -	26.3
-	-	0.76	2.15	4.92	3.89	29.6 -	18.8	-	-			0.0228G	18/53/27	63.7 -	40.5
-	-	-	-0.11	0.27	1.69			1.17	-			0.56250	2/12/20		
-	-1.58	-	0.04	0.00	-	675.5 -	431.3							27.0 -	17.3
-	-	-1.65	-0.24	1.38	2.07			2.16	2.16	2.68	12.8	0.150Z	2/3/20	18.8 -	14.1
-	0.13	-	0.32	0.68	-39.47	57.6 -	22.8							18.4 -	7.3
-	-	-	0.68	0.67	0.69	25.3 -	18.9	0.90	0.98	1.13	5.8	0.0850	1/31/20	17.2 -	12.9
-	1.72	-	5.28	4.10	3.05	18.1 -	11.7	0.40	0.40	0.40	0.5	0.10Y	18/53/27	95.4 -	61.8
-	-	-	1.59	1.88	2.14	12.2 -	8.8	2.40	2.65	2.40	14.6	0.16150Y	3/31/20	19.4 -	14.1
-	-	-	-	-	-							0.13260	3/31/20	20.3 -	0.0
-	-	0.41	1.50	-0.53	-2.92	5.2 -	2.1							7.8 -	3.1
-	-	0.01	0.08	0.10	0.10	296.6 -	192.5	1.04	1.00	0.92	5.3	0.260Y	12/27/19	23.7 -	15.4
-	-	0.60	2.49	2.44	2.93	55.3 -	35.6	2.72	2.52	2.44	2.3	0.750Z	18/53/27	137.6 -	88.7
-	-	1.93	7.56	9.47	5.75	11.2 -	8.1	2.30	2.09	1.89	3.0	0.660Y	18/53/27	84.6 -	61.5
-	-	-0.23	-0.84	1.76	0.28							0.250Y	12/12/08	4.7 -	2.0
-	-	1.44	4.91	6.68	4.21			2.64	2.40	2.28		0.710	18/53/27		
-	-	0.90	3.11	2.42	2.12	15.7 -	10.9	1.28	1.15	1.08	3.0	0.3750Y	18/53/27	48.7 -	34.0
-	-	-	0.09	0.11	0.14	177.2 -	141.4	1.04	1.04	1.04	7.0	0.08980	1/31/20	15.9 -	12.7
-	-	-	-0.03	-0.02	0.03			1.05	1.05	1.05	6.2	0.09880	1/10/20	18.0 -	14.7
-	-	-	0.90	0.95	1.06	17.8 -	15.9	0.91	0.99	1.11	6.0	0.0850	1/31/20	16.0 -	14.3
-	-	-	0.79	0.86	0.91	17.5 -	16.2	0.83	0.87	0.90	6.2	0.07927	1/31/20	13.9 -	12.8
-	-	-	0.54	0.48		18.9 -	16.7	0.60	0.45		6.1	0.0370	1/21/20	10.2 -	9.0
-	-	-	0.83	0.87	0.94	26.8 -	23.3	0.85	0.85	0.85	4.1	0.0709M	1/31/20	22.3 -	19.4
-	-	-	0.61	0.69	0.77	21.3 -	18.6	0.63	0.67	0.77	5.1	0.0474M	1/21/20	13.0 -	11.3
-	-	-	0.99	1.02	1.06	24.9 -	19.2	1.15	1.24	1.03	5.2	0.0717M	1/31/20	24.7 -	19.0
-	-	-	0.06	0.08	0.11	160.7 -	132.0	0.91	0.95	1.12	9.9	0.0760	1/31/20	9.6 -	7.9
-	-	-	0.89	0.90	0.96	15.2 -	14.3	0.86	0.87	0.94	6.6	0.05437	1/10/20	13.6 -	12.7
-	-	-	0.39	0.40	0.42	16.4 -	15.2	0.36	0.39	0.41	5.8	0.0380	1/10/20	6.4 -	5.9
-	-	-	0.69	0.70	0.72	19.8 -	18.2	0.85	0.99	1.08	6.5	0.00477	1/10/20	13.6 -	12.5
-	-	-	0.07	0.82	0.74	365.7 -	271.4	2.03	1.74	1.74	8.7	0.1450	1/31/20	25.6 -	19.0
-	-	-	0.14	0.14	0.16	74.6 -	65.9	1.09	1.10	1.17	11.1	0.07270	1/31/20	10.4 -	9.2
-	-	-	0.55	1.26	1.27	33.7 -	24.6	1.23	1.23	1.23	7.7	0.10250	1/31/20	18.6 -	13.5
-	-	-	0.45	0.49	0.82	59.5 -	42.0	2.16	2.16	2.16	8.9	0.180	1/31/20	26.8 -	18.9
-	-	-	0.15	0.16	0.19	113.4 -	90.3	1.30	1.30	1.30	8.3	0.1080	1/31/20	17.0 -	13.5
-	-	-	0.08	0.09	0.12	195.1 -	167.4	1.33	1.33	1.33	9.0	0.11080	1/31/20	15.6 -	13.4
-	-	-	0.09	0.10	0.08	115.1 -	96.3	0.77	1.16	1.16	8.1	0.07080	1/31/20	10.4 -	8.7
-	-	-	0.08	0.10	0.12	158.5 -	127.3	1.01	1.01	1.01	8.6	0.08430	1/31/20	12.7 -	10.2
-	-	-	0.09	0.09	0.20	100.0 -	82.1	0.91	0.93	0.98	11.1	0.06160	1/31/20	9.0 -	7.4
-	-	0.02	0.31	0.33	0.20	6.6 -	1.7	0.27	0.33	0.19	18.2	0.0210	11/29/19	2.0 -	0.5
-	-	1.59	4.88	5.13	4.14	42.7 -	29.0	1.69	1.52	1.42	0.9	0.470Y	18/53/27	208.6 -	141.5
-	-	-	276.80	174.60	59.50	0.1 -	0.1	1668.27	447.08	-	9016.8	-		23.0 -	15.3
-	-8.16	1.90	0.10	2.99		24.4 -	14.0							46.3 -	26.6
-	-	1.35	-1.30	1.72	3.97			2.43	2.23	1.98	3.7	0.63750Y	18/53/27	76.4 -	53.5
-	-	1.30	3.38	2.70	2.61	72.9 -	42.5							246.3 -	143.7
-	-	1.91	2.07	2.42	2.39	32.8 -	23.4	1.42	1.31	1.23	2.3	0.3850Y	12/27/19	67.9 -	48.4
-	-	0.03	0.28	-	-	124.9 -	90.3							35.0 -	25.3
-	-	0.03	0.28	-	-	112.7 -	103.7							31.6 -	29.1
-	-0.64	-	-1.65	-1.71	-										
-	0.08	-	-2.28	-0.05	-2.40				0.05	-		0.020	3/16/17	13.2 -	2.6
-	-	-0.03	-1.13	-1.04	-0.65									12.2 -	8.6
-	-	0.11	0.28	-0.20	-1.74	18.3 -	13.5							5.1 -	3.8

SYMBOL	COMPANY	NATURE OF BUSINESS	FISCAL YEAR-END	TOTAL REV. $MILL	NET INCOME $MILL	TOTAL ASSETS $MILL	NET STK EQUITY $MILL	NO OF INST	INST. HOLDINGS (SHARES)
EFC	Ellington Financial Inc	REITs	12/31/18	135.0	43.1	3971.5	563.8	108	21382993
EARN	Ellington Residential Mortgaging Re	REITs	12/31/18	26.7	-11.3	1675.6	153.8	65	7866852
AKO B	Embotelladora Andina S.A.	Beverages	12/31/18	1672915.8	96603.4	2214504.7	843813.1	18	448095
ERJ	Embraer SA	Aerospace	12/31/18	5071.1	-178.2	11293.3	3845.7	234	100152591
EME	EMCOR Group, Inc.	Construction Services	12/31/18	8130.6	283.5	4088.8	1740.5	517	73284144
EEX	Emerald Expositions Events Inc	Services	12/31/18	380.7	-25.1	1580.0	708.3	112	24098760
EBS	Emergent BioSolutions Inc	Biotechnology	12/31/18	782.4	62.7	2229.4	1010.9	333	55466789
EMR	Emerson Electric Co.	Electrical Equipment	9/30/19	18372.0	2306.0	20497.0	8233.0	2048	569062982
ESRT	Empire State Realty Trust Inc	REITs	12/31/18	731.5	66.5	4195.8	1238.5	243	172982583
EIG	Employers Holdings Inc	General Insurance	12/31/18	800.4	141.3	3919.2	1018.2	250	33856062
EDN	Empresa Distribuidora y Comerciali	Electric Utilities	12/31/18	55953.6	4297.5	76992.2	30969.0	44	4405652
ENBL	Enable Midstream Partners L.P.	Equipment & Services	12/31/18	3431.0	521.0	12444.0		138	81007025
ENB	Enbridge Inc	Equipment & Services	12/31/18	46378.0	2882.0	166905.0	69470.0	1211	1186417810
EHC	Encompass Health Corp	Hospitals & Health Care Facilities	12/31/18	4277.3	292.3	5175.0	1276.7	542	121926837
DAVA	Endava PLC	IT Services	6/30/19	287.9	24.0	222.7	166.3	-	0
EXK	Endeavour Silver Corp	Precious Metals	12/31/18	150.5	-12.4	177.0	144.8	98	31469973
ENIA	Enel Americas SA	Electric Utilities	12/31/18	13184.1	1201.4	27396.4	6724.0	215	105134490
ENIC	Enel Chile SA	Electric Utilities	12/31/18	2457161.4	361709.9	7488020.2	3421228.5	118	48875605
ENR	Energizer Holdings Inc (New)	Household & Personal Products	9/30/19	2494.5	51.1	5449.6	543.8	369	82171980
TXU 19	Energy Future Holdings Corp	Electric Utilities	12/31/15	5370.0	-5342.0	23330.0	-25061.0	68	17905839
ET	Energy Transfer LP	Equipment & Services	12/31/18	54087.0	1694.0	88246.0		943	1508208673
ETP PRE	Energy Transfer Operating LP	Equipment & Services	12/31/18	54087.0	3020.0	88442.0		72	13734221
ERF	Enerplus Corp	Production & Extraction	12/31/18	1381.0	378.3	3118.3	2001.0	307	144188839
ENS	Enersys	Electrical Equipment	3/31/19	2808.0	160.2	3118.2	1282.3	389	52581650
E	ENI S.p.A.	Production & Extraction	12/31/18	76938.0	4126.0	118373.0	51016.0	253	31682550
ENLC	EnLink Midstream LLC	Equipment & Services	12/31/18	7699.0	-13.2	10694.1	1728.9	260	243896151
EBF	Ennis Inc	Printing	2/28/19	400.8	37.4	363.1	289.1	211	29610498
ENVA	Enova International Inc	Credit & Lending	12/31/18	1114.1	70.1	1328.2	347.8	235	37278389
NPO	EnPro Industries Inc	Industrial Machinery & Equipment	12/31/18	1532.0	24.6	1719.1	862.7	297	25304417
ETM	Entercom Communications Corp	Radio & Television	12/31/18	1462.6	-362.6	4020.4	1334.3	256	107548547
ETR	Entergy Corp	Electric Utilities	12/31/18	11009.5	862.6	48275.1	9063.7	929	206109827
ELC	Entergy Louisiana LLC (New)	Electric Utilities	12/31/18	4296.3	675.6	19651.8	5902.9	1	66887
ETI PR	Entergy Texas Inc	Electric Utilities	12/31/18	1605.9	162.2	4400.0	1422.4	-	0
EPD	Enterprise Products Partners L.P.	Equipment & Services	12/31/18	36534.2	4172.4	56969.8		1446	925978703
EVC	Entravision Communications Corp.	Radio & Television	12/31/18	297.8	12.2	690.4	332.7	179	68607291
ENV	Envestnet Inc	Internet & Software	12/31/18	812.4	5.8	1313.7	633.7	302	59987794
NVST	Envista Holdings Corp	Medical Instruments & Equipment	12/31/18	2844.5	230.7	5841.6	4823.1	75	33488549
NVST	Envista Holdings Corp	Medical Instruments & Equipment	12/31/18	2844.5	230.7	5841.6	4823.1	75	33488549
EVA	Enviva Partners LP	Paper & Forest Products	12/31/18	573.7	7.0	748.8		103	34845498
ENZ	Enzo Biochem, Inc.	Diagnostic & Health Related Service	7/31/19	81.2	2.5	106.6	86.0	143	38390559
EOG	EOG Resources, Inc.	Production & Extraction	12/31/18	17275.4	3419.0	33934.5	19364.2	1475	586817862
EPAM	Epam Systems, Inc.	Internet & Software	12/31/18	1842.9	240.3	1611.8	1262.6	474	56973995
EPR	EPR Properties	REITs	12/31/18	700.7	267.0	6131.4	2865.0	573	87840143
EQM	EQM Midstream Partners LP	Equipment & Services	12/31/18	1495.1	668.0	9456.1		248	89069008
EQT	EQT Corp	Production & Extraction	12/31/18	4557.9	-2244.6	20721.3	10958.2	621	269551776
EFX	Equifax Inc	Business Services	12/31/18	3412.1	299.8	7153.2	3107.8	754	162647700
EQNR	Equinor ASA	Refining & Marketing	12/31/18	79593.0	7535.0	112508.0	42971.0	345	212147322
EQH	Equitable Holdings Inc	General Insurance	12/31/18	12078.0	1820.0	220797.0	13866.0	307	309181139
ETRN	Equitrans Midstream Corp	Gas Utilities	12/31/18	1495.1	218.4	10523.8	457.8	334	221523284
EQC	Equity Commonwealth	REITs	12/31/18	197.0	272.8	3530.8	3182.8	403	154578311
ELS	Equity Lifestyle Properties Inc	REITs	12/31/18	986.7	212.6	3925.8	1121.6	464	97680839
EQR	Equity Residential	REITs	12/31/18	2578.4	657.5	20394.2	10173.2	865	440128396
EQS	Equus Total Return, Inc.	Holding and other Investment Office	12/31/18	0.5	-3.6	70.9	43.5	26	1763632
ERA	ERA Group Inc	Miscellaneous Transportation Servic	12/31/18	221.7	13.9	764.9	463.4	138	20689797
EROS	Eros International Plc	Entertainment	3/31/19	270.1	-423.9	1088.9	521.5	125	36458244
ESE	ESCO Technologies, Inc.	Industrial Machinery & Equipment	9/30/19	813.0	81.0	1466.7	826.2	278	31346678
ESNT	Essent Group Ltd	General Insurance	12/31/18	719.4	467.4	3150.0	2365.7	352	103189356
EPRT	Essential Properties Realty Trust In	REITs	12/31/18	96.2	15.6	1380.9	562.2	187	81508062
ESS	Essex Property Trust Inc	REITs	12/31/18	1400.1	390.2	12383.6	6267.1	704	78891332
ETH	Ethan Allen Interiors, Inc.	Furniture	6/30/19	746.7	25.7	510.4	363.9	251	31752382
EURN	Euronav NV	Shipping	12/31/18	600.0	-110.1	4127.4	2260.5	114	63736915
EEA	European Equity Fund Inc (The)	Holding and other Investment Office	12/31/18	1.7	0.6	70.7	70.2	43	4226874
EB	Eventbrite Inc	Internet & Software	12/31/18	291.6	-64.1	836.9	415.2	140	47482797
EVR	Evercore Inc	Finance Intermediaries & Services	12/31/18	2064.7	377.2	2125.7	758.1	460	45594343
RE	Everest Re Group Ltd	General Insurance	12/31/18	7377.2	103.6	24794.0	7903.8	650	48380725
EVRG	Evergy Inc	Electric Utilities	12/31/18	4275.9	535.8	25598.1	10028.2	-	0
EVRI	Everi Holdings Inc	Hotels, Restaurants & Travel	12/31/18	469.5	12.4	1548.3	-108.9	250	91378376
ES	Eversource Energy	Electric Utilities	12/31/18	8448.2	1033.0	38241.3	11486.8	128	24661678
EVTC	Evertec, Inc.	Business Services	12/31/18	453.9	86.3	927.3	211.5	283	63086660
EVH	Evolent Health Inc	Business Services	12/31/18	627.1	-52.7	1722.3	1143.8	229	90038814
AQUA	Evoqua Water Technologies Corp	Industrial Machinery & Equipment	9/30/19	1444.4	-9.5	1737.8	362.8	160	69455702
XAN	Exantas Capital Corp	REITs	12/31/18	122.9	27.4	2130.9	553.8	174	31041641
EXPR	Express Inc	Retail - Apparel and Accessories	2/2/19	2116.3	9.6	1086.6	585.2	229	82106029
EXTN	Exterran Corp	Equipment & Services	12/31/18	1360.9	24.9	1567.1	552.8	187	35732329
EXR	Extra Space Storage Inc	REITs	12/31/18	1196.6	415.3	7848.0	2413.7	655	164204021
XOM	Exxon Mobil Corp	Production & Extraction	12/31/18	290212.0	20840.0	346196.0	191794.0	3545	3065313158
FN	Fabrinet	Manufacturing	6/28/19	1584.3	121.0	1255.3	863.1	298	45928758
FDS	FactSet Research Systems Inc.	IT Services	8/31/19	1435.4	352.8	1560.1	672.3	683	50468153
FICO	Fair Isaac Corp	Business Services	9/30/19	1160.1	192.1	1433.4	289.8	550	36299457
SFUN	Fang Holdings Ltd	Entertainment	12/31/18	303.0	-114.9	1824.4	594.5	122	42512636

T22

1st	2nd	3rd	2018	2017	2016	P/E high	P/E low	Div 2018	Div 2017	Div 2016	AV. YLD %	AMOUNT	PAYABLE	Price High 2018	Price Low 2018
-	-	.53	1.42	1.10	1.09	13.3	10.8					0.150Z	2/25/20	18.9	15.4
-	-	.30	-.88	.93	1.31	-		1.45	1.57	1.65	13.0	0.280Z	1/27/20	12.1	9.7
-	-	15.50	97.20	118.56	91.08	0.2	0.0	401.91	480.70	361.95	2068.9	-	-	24.0	0.0
-	-	-.03	-.24	.34	.23	-		0.12	0.35	0.09	0.6	-	-	23.4	16.4
-	-	1.45	4.85	3.82	2.97	19.2	12.0	0.32	0.32	0.32	0.4	0.080Y	18/53/27	93.0	58.1
-	-	-.27	-.34	1.13	.35	-		0.29	0.21	-	2.5	0.0750Y	11/27/19	14.5	9.2
-	-	.83	1.22	1.71	1.13	54.2	32.7							66.2	39.9
-	-	.97	3.46	2.35	2.52	22.2	16.3	1.94	1.92	1.90	2.9	0.50Y	18/53/27	77.0	56.4
-	-	.09	.39	.39	.38	41.4	33.4	0.42	0.42	0.40	2.8	0.1050Z	18/53/27	16.1	13.0
-	-	1.01	4.24	3.06	3.24	10.8	9.3	0.80	0.60	0.36	1.9	0.220Y	11/20/19	46.0	39.5
-	-	-.62	4.83	.76	-1.33	6.1	0.9							29.6	4.3
-	-	.28	1.11	.92	.69	14.6	8.1	1.27	1.27	1.27	9.8	0.33050	11/26/19	16.2	8.9
-	-	.47	1.46	1.65	1.93	35.7	21.6	2.68	2.41	2.12	6.4	0.39840Z	4/15/20	52.1	31.6
-	-	.98	2.93	2.69	2.59	24.6	19.7	1.04	0.98	0.94	1.6	0.280Y	18/53/27	72.1	57.7
-	-	-	.38	.34	.34	128.6	58.7							48.9	22.3
-	-.08	-	-.10	.08	.03	-								4.0	1.7
0.00	-	-	.02	.01	7.70	551.0	384.0	0.29	0.22	204.75	3.2	-	-	11.0	7.7
-	-	1.24	5.66	7.12	6.47	1.0	0.6	123.96	104.15	76.96	2652.4	-	-	5.6	3.6
-	-	.04	1.52	3.22	2.04	34.3	22.0	1.16	1.10	1.00	2.6	1.8750	18/53/27	52.1	33.5
-	-	-	-	-	-	-									
-	-	.32	1.15	.83	.92	13.7	9.7	1.22	1.15	1.14	8.7	0.3050	18/53/27	15.7	11.2
-	-	-	-	.93	.98	-						0.4750	2/18/20	25.8	23.9
-	.36	-	1.53	.96	1.72	8.5	3.7	0.12	0.12	0.16	1.4	0.010Y	2/14/20	13.1	5.7
-	1.47	-	2.77	3.64	2.99	32.0	19.4	0.70	0.70	0.70	1.0	0.1750	18/53/27	88.7	53.9
-	-	1.10	1.15	.94	-.41	31.5	25.1	1.17	1.16	1.14	3.6	-	-	36.2	28.8
-	-	.02	-.07	1.17	-2.56	-		1.06	1.02	1.02	11.4	0.18750	2/13/20	13.0	4.4
-	-	.41	1.30	.07	1.39	17.0	14.2	0.88	2.20	0.70	4.3	0.2250Y	2/7/20	22.1	18.5
-	-	.78	1.99	.86	1.03	15.2	9.8							30.3	19.6
-	-	-.08	1.16	24.76	-1.86	64.6	47.8	0.96	0.88	0.84	1.5	0.250Y	12/18/19	74.9	55.5
-	-	.28	-2.62	4.38	.91	-		0.36	0.52	0.23	6.7	0.020Y	12/16/19	7.7	3.1
-	-	1.82	4.63	2.28	-3.26	26.3	18.1	3.58	3.50	3.42	3.4	0.930Y	18/53/27	121.6	84.0
-	-	-	-	-	-	-		1.22	1.22	0.35	4.8	0.32810Z	4/1/20	26.6	23.3
-	-	-	-	-	-	-						0.4666GHZ	1/15/20	27.1	0.0
-	-	.46	1.91	1.30	1.20	16.1	13.1	1.72	1.67	1.59	6.1	0.4450	18/53/27	30.7	25.0
-	-	-.14	.13	1.92	.22	31.1	19.6	0.20	0.16	0.13	6.4	0.050Y	12/31/19	4.0	2.5
-	-	-.06	.12	-.08	-1.30	609.7	392.8							73.2	47.1
-	-	.48	-	-	-	-								28.8	27.3
-	-	.48	-	-	-	-								30.7	26.6
-	-	.15	.04	.61	.91	940.8	701.5	2.51	2.27	2.02	7.9	0.670	11/29/19	37.6	28.1
-0.16	-	-	-.22	-.05	.97	-								4.3	2.5
-	-	1.06	5.89	4.46	-1.98	18.2	10.9	0.76	0.67	0.67	0.9	0.28750Y	18/53/27	107.1	64.4
-	-	1.16	4.24	1.32	1.87	50.9	26.5							215.9	112.3
-	-	.36	3.27	3.29	3.17	24.6	19.3	4.32	4.08	3.84	5.7	0.3750Z	18/53/27	80.3	63.1
-	-	-.18	2.43	5.19	5.21	19.5	8.9	4.29	3.65	3.05	11.3	1.160	2/13/20	47.3	21.5
-	-	-1.41	-8.60	8.04	-2.71	-		0.12	0.12	0.12	0.8	0.030Y	18/53/27	21.7	8.4
-	-	.66	2.47	4.83	4.04	59.4	37.0	1.56	1.56	1.32	1.2	0.390Y	18/53/27	146.8	91.3
-	0.44	-	2.27	1.40	-.91	10.5	7.2	0.91	0.76	0.69	4.5	-	-	23.9	16.4
-	-	-.78	3.27	1.51	2.27	7.6	5.0	0.26	-	-	1.2	0.150Y	11/25/19	25.0	16.2
-	-	-.26	.86	-.59	-	25.6	10.7	0.41	-	3.19	2.4	0.450Y	2/21/20	22.0	9.2
-	-	.18	2.15	.17	1.62	16.1	13.7	2.50	-	-	7.7	3.57	18/53/27	34.6	29.4
-	-	.35	1.19	1.09	.96	62.3	39.5	1.10	0.97	0.85	1.8	0.30630Z	18/53/27	74.1	47.0
-	-	.71	1.77	1.63	11.68	50.2	36.0	2.16	2.02	13.02	2.7	1.03620Z	18/53/27	88.8	63.8
-	-	-	-.27	-.30	-.19	-						0.1580	9/29/08	2.0	0.0
-	-	-.09	.64	-1.36	-.39	19.2	11.0							12.3	7.1
-	-.28	-	-.36	.05	.05	-									
-	-	.77	3.54	2.07	1.77	26.1	18.0	0.32	0.24	0.32	0.4	0.080Y	1/17/20	92.5	63.7
-	-	1.47	4.77	3.99	2.41	-						0.150	12/16/19		
-	-	.18	.26	-	-	102.9	52.7	0.43	-	-	2.1	0.230Z	1/15/20	26.8	13.7
-	-	1.51	5.90	6.57	6.27	56.4	40.1	7.44	7.00	6.40	2.5	1.950Z	18/53/27	332.5	236.6
0.53	-	-	1.32	1.29	2.00	17.4	12.8	1.07	0.72	0.59	5.5	0.210Y	1/23/20	23.0	16.9
-	-	-	-.57	.01	1.29	-		0.12	0.12	-					
-	-	-	.08	.06	.11	120.7	0.0	0.07	0.09	0.08	0.8	0.1321C	1/30/20	9.7	0.0
-	-	-.36	-1.71	-1.98	-2.48	-								32.4	15.7
-	-	1.01	8.33	2.80	2.43	11.8	8.8	1.90	1.42	1.27	2.3	0.580Y	18/53/27	98.0	73.3
-	-	2.56	2.53	11.36	23.68	-		5.30	5.05	4.70	-	1.550	18/53/27		
-	-	1.56	2.50	2.27	2.43	26.9	21.9	0.94	1.60	1.52	1.5	0.5050Y	12/20/19	67.3	54.8
-	-	.12	.17	-.78	-3.78	81.3	29.9							13.8	5.1
-	-	.98	3.25	3.11	2.96	26.5	19.5	2.02	1.90	1.78	2.6	0.5350Y	18/53/27	86.2	63.5
-	-	.34	1.16	.76	1.01	31.4	23.1	0.10	0.30	0.40	0.3	0.050Y	12/6/19	36.4	26.7
-	-	-.30	-.68	-.94	-3.55	-								20.9	5.8
-	-	.03	.05	.02	.11	402.2	193.2							20.1	9.7
-	-	.31	.22	.18	-1.73	54.7	45.4	0.47	0.20	1.31	4.2	0.53910Z	1/30/20	12.0	10.0
-	-	-.05	.25	.73	1.38	24.6	7.4					0.567	12/23/10	6.2	1.9
-	-	-.29	.68	.97	-6.59	29.0	7.6							19.7	5.2
-	-	.83	3.27	3.76	2.91	37.8	26.7	3.36	3.12	2.93	3.2	0.90Z	18/53/27	123.5	87.4
-	-	.75	4.88	4.63	1.88	17.1	13.7	3.23	3.06	2.98	4.4	0.870Y	18/53/27	83.4	66.7
0.69	-	-	2.21	2.57	1.68	-									
2.43	-	-	6.78	6.51	8.19	44.6	28.6	2.40	2.12	1.88	0.9	0.720Y	18/53/27	302.1	194.0
-	-	2.12	4.57	3.98	3.39	83.0	39.1	-	0.04	0.08		0.020Y	18/53/27	379.4	178.8
-	-	1.22	-1.29	.24	-1.81	-								9.8	1.5

SYMBOL	COMPANY	NATURE OF BUSINESS	FISCAL YEAR-END	TOTAL REV. $MILL	NET INCOME $MILL	TOTAL ASSETS $MILL	NET STK EQUITY $MILL	NO OF INST	INST. HOLDINGS (SHARES)
FTCH	Farfetch Ltd	Services	12/31/18	602.4	-155.6	1351.4	1128.4	170	199555802
FPI	Farmland Partners Inc	REITs	12/31/18	56.1	12.3	1139.5	438.3	148	16883933
FSLY	Fastly Inc	IT Services	12/31/18	144.6	-30.9	162.8	87.7	108	12121071
FBK	FB Financial Corp	Banking	12/31/18	370.2	80.2	5136.8	671.9	121	17001977
FFG	FBL Financial Group Inc	Life & Health	12/31/18	719.6	93.8	9833.6	1184.1	137	8591224
AGM	Federal Agricultural Mortgage Corp	Credit & Lending	12/31/18	556.0	108.1	18694.3	752.6	185	8941066
FRT	Federal Realty Investment Trust (M	REITs	12/31/18	915.4	241.9	6289.6	2345.9	622	84991720
FSS	Federal Signal Corp.	Industrial Machinery & Equipment	12/31/18	1089.5	94.0	1023.8	530.1	314	69421108
FII	Federated Investors Inc (PA)	Wealth Management	12/31/18	1135.7	220.3	1543.7	857.1	493	118249098
FMN	Federated Premier Municipal Incom	Holding and other Investment Office	11/30/18	12.2	8.6	283.6	197.6	51	2186003
FDX	FedEx Corp	Airlines/Air Freight	5/31/19	69693.0	540.0	54403.0	17757.0	1834	225956483
RACE	Ferrari NV (New)	Autos- Manufacturing	12/31/18	3420.3	784.7	4851.7	1348.7	382	69323926
FOE	Ferro Corp	Specialty Chemicals	12/31/18	1612.4	80.1	1812.5	376.6	271	90809843
FG	FGL Holdings	Life & Health	12/31/18	711.0	13.0	30945.0	890.0	154	153003321
FCAU	Fiat Chrysler Automobiles NV	Autos- Manufacturing	12/31/18	110412.0	3608.0	96873.0	24702.0	343	466393652
FNF	Fidelity National Financial Inc	General Insurance	12/31/18	7594.0	628.0	9301.0	4630.0	703	284051731
FIS	Fidelity National Information Service	Business Services	12/31/18	8423.0	846.0	23770.0	10215.0	1333	618391999
FMO	Fiduciary/Claymore Energy Infrastru	Holding and other Investment Office	11/30/18	3.7	-8.4	648.1	375.1	103	9851062
FINV	FinVolution Group	Brokers & Intermediaries	12/31/18	4350.9	2469.1	13142.5	5923.9	95	43724618
FAF	First American Financial Corp	General Insurance	12/31/18	5747.8	474.5	10630.6	3741.9	528	106861896
FBP	First Bancorp	Banking	12/31/18	707.3	201.6	12243.6	2044.7	315	227144609
FCF	First Commonwealth Financial Corp	Banking	12/31/18	380.9	107.5	7828.3	975.4	232	85187723
FHN	First Horizon National Corp	Banking	12/31/18	2268.8	545.0	40832.3	4489.9	547	302266300
FR	First Industrial Realty Trust Inc	REITs	12/31/18	404.0	163.2	3142.7	1645.5	403	164683764
AG	First Majestic Silver Corp	Precious Metals	12/31/18	300.9	-204.2	926.1	594.6	201	76167931
FRC	First Republic Bank (San Francisco,	Banking	12/31/18	3575.1	853.8	99205.2	8677.8	689	214376096
FEO	First Trust / Aberdeen Emerging Op	Holding and other Investment Office	12/31/18	5.1	3.5	79.4	73.1	36	1797910
FDEU	First Trust Dynamic Europe Equity I	Holding and other Investment Office	12/31/18	18.6	12.8	342.2	252.7	39	6422642
FIF	First Trust Energy Infrastructure Fu	Holding and other Investment Office	11/30/18	10.6	3.1	403.2	294.6	60	5655208
FFA	First Trust Enhanced Equity Income	Holding and other Investment Office	12/31/18	7.3	3.7	285.2	277.4	57	6808715
FSD	First Trust High Income Long/Short	Holding and other Investment Office	10/31/19	46.4	31.9	773.3	582.5	88	13226738
FPF	First Trust Intermediate Duration Pr	Finance Intermediaries & Services	10/31/19	137.9	100.0	2154.5	1482.4	114	11450619
FEI	First Trust MLP & Energy Income F	Finance Intermediaries & Services	10/31/19	11.6	-0.7	779.9	551.6	87	14474777
FMY	First Trust Mortgage Income Fund	Holding and other Investment Office	10/31/19	2.3	1.4	63.0	62.8	27	3206411
FPL	First Trust New Opportunities MLP	Finance Intermediaries & Services	10/31/19	5.0	3.2	332.5	241.8	60	5371057
FIV	First Trust Senior Floating Rate 202	Holding and other Investment Office	5/31/19	26.1	17.1	497.3	339.6	48	7651332
FCT	First Trust Senior Floating Rate Inco	Holding and other Investment Office	5/31/19	29.0	19.7	565.9	365.8	92	14305248
FGB	First Trust Specialty Finance and Fi	Holding and other Investment Office	11/30/18	11.5	9.4	110.7	83.0	32	2081220
FAM	First Trust/Aberdeen Global Opport	Holding and other Investment Office	11/30/18	13.3	9.0	203.0	141.4	70	6524338
FE	FirstEnergy Corp	Electric Utilities	12/31/18	11261.0	1348.0	40063.0	6814.0	936	556963097
FIT	Fitbit Inc	Computer Hardware & Equipment	12/31/18	1512.0	-185.8	1515.5	735.9	261	167367287
FPH	Five Point Holdings LLC	Property, Real Estate & Developmen	12/31/18	49.0	-34.7	2923.9	587.0	70	51100314
FVRR	Fiverr International Ltd	Services	12/31/18	75.5	-36.1	111.0	54.0	56	10551580
FBC	Flagstar Bancorp, Inc.	Credit & Lending	12/31/18	1122.0	187.0	18531.0	1570.0	237	56118923
DFP	Flaherty & Crumrine Dynamic Prefe	Finance Intermediaries & Services	11/30/18	43.7	31.7	696.2	441.2	71	3040967
PFD	Flaherty & Crumrine Preferred and I	Holding and other Investment Office	11/30/18	13.9	9.8	223.3	142.1	39	754168
PFO	Flaherty & Crumrine Preferred and I	Holding and other Investment Office	11/30/18	13.0	9.2	207.9	132.2	48	1121029
FFC	Flaherty & Crumrine Preferred and I	Holding and other Investment Office	11/30/18	77.9	58.2	1252.3	797.4	140	8361802
FLC	Flaherty & Crumrine Total Return F	Holding and other Investment Office	11/30/18	18.7	13.3	299.5	190.2	50	1846987
FLT	FleetCor Technologies Inc	Business Services	12/31/18	2433.5	811.5	11202.5	3340.2	703	91650063
FLNG	Flex LNG Ltd	Production & Extraction	12/31/18	77.2	11.8	1294.4	827.3		0
FND	Floor & Decor Holdings Inc	Construction Materials	12/27/18	1709.8	116.2	1234.1	584.3	260	106761713
FTK	Flotek Industries Inc	Specialty Chemicals	12/31/18	177.8	-70.3	285.9	201.6	147	43959819
FLO	Flowers Foods, Inc.	Food	12/29/18	3951.9	157.2	2845.5	1258.3	501	163538268
FLS	Flowserve Corp	Industrial Machinery & Equipment	12/31/18	3832.7	119.7	4616.3	1642.3	626	150020433
FLR	Fluor Corp.	Construction Services	12/31/18	19166.6	224.8	8913.6	2963.2	724	138568350
FLY	Fly Leasing Ltd	Airlines/Air Freight	12/31/18	418.3	85.7	4226.5	702.1	125	20421820
FMC	FMC Corp.	Agricultural Chemicals	12/31/18	4727.8	502.1	9974.3	3121.1	758	137465972
FNB	FNB Corp	Banking	12/31/18	1446.0	373.0	33102.0	4608.0	455	284666342
FMX	Fomento Economico Mexicano, S.A	Beverages	12/31/18	469744.0	23990.0	576381.0	257053.0	413	129340352
FL	Foot Locker, Inc.	Retail - Apparel and Accessories	2/2/19	7939.0	541.0	3820.0	2506.0	747	137509738
F	Ford Motor Co. (DE)	Autos- Manufacturing	12/31/18	160338.0	3677.0	256540.0	35932.0	1647	2821663584
F 12A	Ford Motor Credit Company LLC	Credit & Lending	12/31/18	4585.0	2224.0	162209.0	14975.0	1	2
FOR	Forestar Group Inc (New)	Property, Real Estate & Developmen	9/30/19	428.3	33.0	1455.7	808.3	146	21765370
FTS	Fortis Inc	Electric Utilities	12/31/18	8390.0	1100.0	53051.0	16533.0		0
FTV	Fortive Corp	Industrial Machinery & Equipment	12/31/18	6452.7	2913.8	12905.6	6595.5	929	301027530
FTAI	Fortress Transportation & Infrastruct	Miscellaneous Transportation Servic	12/31/18	379.9	5.9	2638.8	997.4	106	29607618
FSM	Fortuna Silver Mines Inc	Precious Metals	12/31/18	263.3	34.0	786.5	602.8	145	61761228
FBHS	Fortune Brands Home & Security, In	Household Appliances, Electronics &	12/31/18	5485.1	389.6	5964.6	2178.2	662	150286465
FET	Forum Energy Technologies Inc	Equipment & Services	12/31/18	1064.2	-374.1	1829.7	1030.1	205	101722072
FBM	Foundation Building Materials Inc	Construction Materials	12/31/18	2044.3	-12.2	1316.7	366.3	155	41014469
FCPT	Four Corners Property Trust Inc	REITs	12/31/18	143.6	82.4	1343.1	691.1	319	72066863
FEDU	Four Seasons Education (Cayman)	Educational Services	2/28/19	335.6	-0.6	932.1	712.7	14	5447762
FNV	Franco-Nevada Corp	Precious Metals	12/31/18	653.2	139.0	4931.8	4631.9		0
FI	Frank's International NV	Equipment & Services	12/31/18	522.5	-90.7	1193.9	1034.8	143	96295966
FC	Franklin Covey Co	Business Services	8/31/19	225.4	-1.0	224.9	82.0	114	8039063
FSB	Franklin Financial Network Inc	Banking	12/31/18	180.6	34.5	4249.4	372.7	137	10382548
BEN	Franklin Resources Inc	Wealth Management	9/30/19	5774.5	1195.7	14532.2	9906.5	885	292853406
FT	Franklin Universal Trust	Holding and other Investment Office	8/31/19	14.6	9.6	282.5	215.3	75	9136940
FCX	Freeport-McMoRan Inc	Mining	12/31/18	18628.0	2602.0	42216.0	9798.0	1225	1238695990

| EARNINGS PER SHARE | | | | | | P/E RATIO | | DIVIDENDS PER SHARE | | | AV. YLD | DIV. DECLARED | | PRICE RANGE | |
| QUARTERLY | | | ANNUAL | | | | | | | | % | | | 2018 | |
1st	2nd	3rd	2018	2017	2016			2018	2017	2016		AMOUNT	PAYABLE		
-	-	-0.30	-0.59	-2.62	-2.21	-								29.7 -	7.5
-	-	-0.15	-0.01	0.03	0.09			0.35	0.51	0.51	5.6	0.3750Y	12/31/19	7.0 -	5.1
-	-	-0.13	-1.27	-1.39										33.8 -	14.9
-	-	0.76	2.55	1.86	2.10	15.7 -	12.0	0.20	0.00	4.03	0.6	0.080Y	11/15/19	40.0 -	30.6
-	-	1.01	3.75	7.75	4.28	19.0 -	14.2	3.34	3.26	3.68	5.4	0.480Y	12/31/19	71.4 -	53.1
-	-	1.33	8.83	6.60	5.97	9.9 -	7.1	2.32	1.44	1.04	3.0	0.35630Y	1/17/20	87.7 -	62.5
-	-	0.84	3.18	3.97	3.50	44.4 -	36.4	4.04	3.96	3.84	3.1	0.31250Z	18/53/27	141.2 -	115.8
-	-	0.46	1.54	1.02	0.71	22.7 -	12.6	0.31	0.28	0.28	1.1	0.080Y	11/26/19	34.9 -	19.4
-	-	0.72	2.18	2.87	2.03	16.3 -	11.5	1.06	1.00	2.00	3.4	0.270Y	18/53/27	35.6 -	25.1
-	-	-	0.74	0.79	0.81	19.4 -	17.1	0.69	0.73	0.86	5.0	0.05M	2/3/20	14.3 -	12.7
-	2.13	-	16.79	11.07	6.51	11.8 -	8.2	2.00	1.60	1.00	1.2	0.650Y	18/53/27	198.2 -	138.4
-	-	1.51	4.14	2.82	2.11							1.030	5/2/19		
-	-	0.16	0.94	0.67	-0.25	22.3 -	10.5					0.010Y	3/10/09	21.0 -	9.9
-	-	0.26	-0.07	-0.49	-0.02							0.010	12/9/19		
-	-	-0.11	2.30	2.24	1.18							1.37	5/30/19		
-	-	0.90	2.26	2.38	2.34	21.3 -	13.9	1.20	1.02	0.88	2.9	0.330Y	18/53/27	48.2 -	31.4
-	-	0.29	2.55	3.93	1.72	54.8 -	38.6	1.28	1.16	1.04	1.0	0.350Y	18/53/27	139.8 -	98.3
-	-	-	-0.24	-0.14	-0.14							0.32310	11/29/19	10.9 -	6.9
-	-	-	1.54	-2.55	-0.09	3.9 -	1.3							6.0 -	2.1
-	-	1.65	4.19	3.76	3.09	15.3 -	10.5	1.60	1.44	1.20	2.9	0.440Y	18/53/27	64.2 -	44.1
-	-	0.21	0.92	0.30	0.43	12.8 -	9.2	0.03			0.3	0.14580	1/31/20	11.8 -	8.4
-	-	0.27	1.08	0.58	0.67	13.8 -	11.2	0.35	0.32	0.28	2.6	0.10Y	11/22/19	14.9 -	12.1
-	-	0.35	1.65	0.65	0.94	10.5 -	8.1	0.48	0.36	0.28	3.1	0.38750Y	18/53/27	17.3 -	13.4
-	-	0.62	1.31	1.69	1.05	32.9 -	21.4	0.87	0.84	0.76	2.3	0.230Z	18/53/27	43.1 -	28.0
-	-0.06	-	-1.11	-0.32	0.05									16.2 -	5.2
-	-	1.31	4.81	4.31	3.93	24.5 -	17.5	0.71	0.67	0.63	0.7	0.190Y	18/53/27	117.9 -	84.3
-	-	-	0.68	0.76	0.64	21.3 -	18.2	1.40	1.40	1.40	10.2	0.350	12/31/19	14.5 -	12.4
-	-	-	0.74	0.78	0.73	20.5 -	17.2	1.45	1.89	1.45	10.3	0.1210	2/18/20	15.2 -	12.7
-	-	-	0.18	0.26	0.21	94.5 -	72.7	1.21	1.21	1.21	7.7	0.110	2/18/20	17.0 -	13.1
-	-	-	0.19	0.20	0.19	90.8 -	67.7	1.14	1.11	0.95	7.3	0.2850	12/31/19	17.3 -	12.9
-	-	-	0.96	1.04	1.00	16.4 -	13.8	1.22	1.32	1.06	8.2	0.110	2/18/20	15.8 -	13.3
-	-	-	1.73	1.86	1.94	14.0 -	11.6	1.62	1.73	1.95	7.2	0.13250	2/18/20	24.3 -	20.1
-	-	-	0.20	0.05	-0.05	61.3 -	49.4	1.26	1.30	1.42	11.0	0.10	4/15/20	12.3 -	9.9
-	-	-	0.45	0.18	-0.02	31.4 -	0.0	0.69	0.71	0.91	5.1	0.060	2/18/20	14.1 -	0.0
-	-	-	-0.28	-0.02	0.91			1.10	1.16	1.26	12.2	0.0750	4/15/20	9.9 -	7.6
-	-	-	0.47	0.17		19.7 -	17.8	0.46	0.13		5.2	0.02280	2/18/20	9.3 -	8.3
-	-	-	0.70	0.78	0.83	17.9 -	16.2	0.70	0.76	0.88	5.8	0.08250	2/18/20	12.6 -	11.3
-	-	-	0.66	0.54	0.66	9.8 -	8.0	0.70	0.70	0.70	11.4	0.1350	11/29/19	6.5 -	5.3
-	-	-	0.69	0.72	0.73	16.4 -	13.6	0.88	0.90	0.90	8.5	0.080	2/18/20	11.3 -	9.3
-	-	0.72	1.99	-3.88	-14.49	24.5 -	18.4	1.44	1.44	1.44	3.3	0.390Y	18/53/27	48.8 -	36.7
-	-0.20	-	-0.76	-1.19	-0.47									7.1 -	2.9
-	-0.16	-	-0.53	0.18	-0.89									9.2 -	6.3
-1.26	-	-	-5.42	-3.04											
-	-	1.11	3.21	1.09	2.66	12.2 -	8.4					0.040Y	12/16/19	39.1 -	26.9
-	-	-	1.65	1.69	1.84	16.2 -	12.6	1.79	1.92	1.92	7.2	0.1430	4/30/20	26.8 -	20.8
-	-	-	0.87	0.93	1.09	18.8 -	13.6	0.94	1.03	1.08	6.5	0.0750	4/30/20	16.3 -	11.8
-	-	-	0.73	0.78	0.88	17.2 -	14.8	0.80	0.88	0.88	6.8	0.06250	4/30/20	12.5 -	10.8
-	-	-	1.32	1.41	1.58	16.6 -	12.9	1.38	1.50	1.63	6.9	0.1120	4/30/20	21.9 -	17.1
-	-	-	1.33	1.43	1.60	17.5 -	12.9	1.44	1.57	1.63	7.0	0.1150	4/30/20	23.3 -	17.2
-	-	2.49	8.81	7.91	4.75	35.0 -	20.6							308.4 -	181.6
-	-	-	0.29	-0.30	-0.01							0.1G	12/18/19		
-	-	0.39	1.11	1.03	0.49	46.2 -	23.6							51.3 -	26.2
-	-	-0.19	-1.21	-0.48	-0.88									3.9 -	1.1
-	-	0.20	0.74	0.71	0.78	32.8 -	24.8	0.71	1.29	0.63	3.3	0.190Y	18/53/27	24.2 -	18.4
-	-	0.52	0.91	0.02	1.11	58.7 -	40.0	0.76	0.57	0.76	1.6	0.190Y	18/53/27	53.5 -	36.4
-	-	-5.29	1.59	1.36	2.00	26.1 -	10.1	0.84	0.84	0.84	3.0	0.10Y	18/53/27	41.6 -	16.1
1.38	-	-	2.88	0.09	-0.08	7.6 -	3.7							22.0 -	10.7
-	-	0.69	3.69	3.99	1.56	27.5 -	17.1	0.90	0.66	0.66	1.1	0.440Y	18/53/27	101.5 -	63.3
-	-	0.31	1.12	0.63	0.78	11.5 -	8.9	0.48	0.48	0.48	4.1	0.45320Y	18/53/27	12.8 -	9.9
-	-	-	1.20	2.11	1.05	83.0 -	70.9	27.00	25.46	24.17	29.0			99.6 -	85.1
-	-	1.16	2.22	4.91	3.84	29.0 -	15.3	1.24	1.10	1.00	2.6	0.380Y	18/53/27	64.5 -	34.0
-	-	0.11	0.92	1.90	1.15	11.4 -	8.5	0.73	0.65	0.85	7.9	0.150Y	18/53/27	10.5 -	7.8
-	-	0.16	1.64	1.19	1.38	13.1 -	8.1							21.4 -	13.3
-	-	0.63	2.59	2.31	1.89	21.9 -	12.8	1.73	1.63	1.52	3.8	0.24460	3/1/20	56.8 -	33.0
-	-	0.56	8.21	2.96	2.51	10.8 -	7.8	0.28	0.28	0.14	0.4	12.50Y	18/53/27	89.1 -	64.2
-	-	0.30	0.07	-	-0.26	284.6 -	199.3	1.32	1.32	1.32	8.3	0.5328GH	12/16/19	19.9 -	13.9
-	0.07	-	0.21	0.42	0.13	27.5 -	11.4							5.8 -	2.4
-	-	0.75	2.66	3.03	2.62	24.8 -	14.2	0.80	0.72	0.64	1.5	0.240Y	18/53/27	66.0 -	37.7
-	-	-4.83	-3.44	-0.60	-0.90									6.8 -	0.9
-	-	0.30	-0.28	1.99	-0.95									21.7 -	8.7
-	-	0.27	1.28	1.18	2.63	23.2 -	19.8	0.82	1.00	9.29	2.9	0.3050Z	1/15/20	29.7 -	25.3
-	-	-	1.98	0.94	-2.21	1.4 -	0.0	2.52			125.5			2.8 -	0.0
-	-	0.54	0.75	1.06	0.69	180.0 -	91.3	0.95	0.91	0.87	1.0	0.250	12/19/19	135.0 -	68.5
-	-	-0.11	-0.41	-0.72	-0.77				0.23	0.45		0.0750	9/15/17		
-0.04	-	-	-0.43	-0.52	0.47									39.7 -	21.7
-	-	0.75	2.34	2.04	2.42	15.0 -	11.2					0.060Y	2/28/20	35.2 -	26.2
-	-	0.48	1.39	3.01	2.94	25.7 -	18.6	3.92	0.80	0.72	12.7	0.270Y	18/53/27	35.7 -	25.8
-	-	-	0.39	0.38	0.39	20.4 -	16.1	0.38	0.38	0.47	5.3	0.0320	2/14/20	8.0 -	6.3
-	-	-0.15	1.78	1.25	-3.16	8.0 -	4.8	0.15			1.3	0.050Y	18/53/27	14.2 -	8.5

SYMBOL	COMPANY	NATURE OF BUSINESS	FISCAL YEAR-END	TOTAL REV. $MILL	NET INCOME $MILL	TOTAL ASSETS $MILL	NET STK EQUITY $MILL	NO OF INST	INST. HOLDINGS (SHARES)
FMS	Fresenius Medical Care AG & Co K	Diagnostic & Health Related Service	12/31/18	16546.9	1981.9	26242.3	11758.4	265	10737469
FDP	Fresh Del Monte Produce Inc.	Food	12/28/18	4493.9	-21.9	3255.2	1692.0	227	40108610
RESI	Front Yard Residential Corp	REITs	12/31/18	183.0	-130.8	2270.3	471.4	149	49694236
FRO	Frontline Ltd	Miscellaneous Transportation Servic	12/31/18	752.5	-8.9	3077.8	1163.8	191	44857409
FSK	FS KKR Capital Corp	Finance Intermediaries & Services	12/31/18	394.0	205.0	7705.0	4166.0	386	171942165
FCN	FTI Consulting Inc.	Business Services	12/31/18	2027.9	150.6	2379.1	1348.8	391	49943651
FTSI	FTS International Inc	Equipment & Services	12/31/18	1543.3	258.4	743.7	106.9	128	69393194
FUL	Fuller (HB) Company	Specialty Chemicals	12/1/18	3041.0	171.2	4175.3	1151.8	318	69853519
FF	FutureFuel Corp	Specialty Chemicals	12/31/18	291.0	53.2	471.2	389.1	164	25852861
GCV	Gabelli Convertible & Income Securi	Holding and other Investment Office	12/31/18	2.5	1.2	114.9	114.7	29	4236516
GDV	Gabelli Dividend & Income Trust	Holding and other Investment Office	12/31/18	59.9	37.3	2202.1	2197.1		0
GAB	Gabelli Equity Trust Inc (The)	Holding and other Investment Office	12/31/18	37.3	17.1	1851.8	1743.5	163	20410612
GGZ	Gabelli Global Small & Mid Cap Val	Holding and other Investment Office	12/31/18	3.1	0.7	157.3	150.4	58	3028637
GRX	Gabelli Healthcare & WellnessRx Tr	Holding and other Investment Office	12/31/18	5.1	1.4	272.3	271.6	83	5837732
GGT	Gabelli Multimedia Trust Inc	Holding and other Investment Office	12/31/18	4.1	0.8	250.0	243.3	58	3026763
GUT	Gabelli Utility Trust	Holding and other Investment Office	12/31/18	10.2	6.2	350.7	348.4	65	3170099
GCAP	GAIN Capital Holdings Inc	Finance Intermediaries & Services	12/31/18	358.0	92.9	1332.5	297.8	112	22734092
GLEO	Galileo Acquisition Corp	Business Services	8/16/19		-0.0	0.1	0.0		0
AJG	Gallagher (Arthur J.) & Co.	Brokers & Intermediaries	12/31/18	6934.0	633.5	16334.0	4498.9	884	196083364
GBL	GAMCO Investors Inc	Finance Intermediaries & Services	12/31/18	341.5	117.2	134.6	9.6	105	7386597
GNT	GAMCO Natural Resources, Gold &	Holding and other Investment Office	12/31/18	3.6	1.3	168.0	149.1	44	3663057
GME	GameStop Corp	Retail - Appliances and Electronics	2/2/19	8285.3	-673.0	4044.3	1336.2	514	131653980
GCI	Gannett Co Inc (New)	Publishing	12/30/18	1526.0	18.2	1443.9	717.2	231	72414598
GDI	Gardner Denver Holdings Inc	Industrial Machinery & Equipment	12/31/18	2689.8	269.4	4487.1	1676.0	244	211476151
GTX	Garrett Motion Inc	Auto Parts	12/31/18	3375.0	1180.0	2104.0	-2593.0	465	60406999
IT	Gartner Inc	Business Services	12/31/18	3975.5	122.5	6201.5	850.8	629	152940925
GLOG	GasLog Ltd	Equipment & Services	12/31/18	618.3	47.7	5174.8	879.7		0
GLOP	GasLog Partners LP	Miscellaneous Transportation Servic	12/31/18	352.5	115.5	2488.6	1179.7	90	21695356
GTES	Gates Industrial Corp PLC	Industrial Machinery & Equipment	12/29/18	3347.6	245.3	6722.6	1947.4	130	293845976
GATX	GATX Corp	Miscellaneous Transportation Servic	12/31/18	1360.9	211.3	7616.7	1788.1	375	52140809
GCP	GCP Applied Technologies Inc	Specialty Chemicals	12/31/18	1125.4	15.2	1281.9	479.4	229	60810471
GDL	GDL Fund (The)	Holding and other Investment Office	12/31/18	5.6	-2.3	368.3	183.4	58	8430612
GEGI 26	GE Global Insurance Holdings Corp	Brokers & Intermediaries	12/31/03	11621.0	656.0	52542.0	7943.0		0
GNK	Genco Shipping & Trading Ltd	Shipping	12/31/18	367.5	-32.9	1627.5	1053.3	119	37041389
GNRC	Generac Holdings Inc	Electrical Equipment	12/31/18	2023.5	238.3	2426.3	760.5	415	71488246
GAM	General American Investors Co., In	Holding and other Investment Office	12/31/18	20.8	8.2	1108.3	1086.9	107	7827520
GD	General Dynamics Corp	Aerospace	12/31/18	36193.0	3345.0	45408.0	11732.0	1560	296319614
GE	General Electric Co	Electrical Equipment	12/31/18	121615.0	-22355.0	309129.0	30981.0	2826	6705597795
GIS	General Mills Inc	Food	5/26/19	16865.2	1752.7	30111.2	7054.5	1818	536031795
GM	General Motors Co	Autos- Manufacturing	12/31/18	147049.0	8014.0	227339.0	38860.0	1383	1241011823
GM 26	General Motors Financial Co Inc	Credit & Lending	12/31/18		1570.0	109920.0	11659.0	52	9475070
GCO	Genesco Inc.	Retail - Apparel and Accessories	2/2/19	2188.6	-51.9	1181.1	737.6	317	22665303
GEL	Genesis Energy L.P.	Equipment & Services	12/31/18	2912.8	-6.1	6479.1	761.5	213	118564809
GEN	Genesis Healthcare Inc	Hospitals & Health Care Facilities	12/31/18	4976.6	-235.2	4263.6	-1339.5	28	1463447
GNE	Genie Energy Ltd	Electric Utilities	12/31/18	280.3	22.8	146.9	103.7	103	9343747
G	Genpact Ltd	Business Services	12/31/18	3000.8	282.0	3529.4	1404.2	420	193883568
GPC	Genuine Parts Co.	Auto Parts	12/31/18	18735.1	810.5	12683.0	3450.5	1090	148050177
GNW	Genworth Financial, Inc. (Holding C	Life & Health	12/31/18	8430.0	119.0	100923.0	12450.0	506	442592571
GEO	GEO Group Inc (The) (New)	REITs	12/31/18	2331.4	145.1	4247.5	1040.5	379	125048231
GPRK	GeoPark Ltd	Production & Extraction	12/31/18	601.2	72.4	862.7	143.0		0
GGB	Gerdau S.A.	Non-Precious Metals	12/31/18	46159.5	2303.9	51281.0	25730.6	227	270114865
GTY	Getty Realty Corp.	REITs	12/31/18	136.1	47.7	1159.2	581.2	246	32482500
GIX	GigCapital2 Inc	Business Services	3/12/19		-0.0	0.2	0.0	39	6858882
GIL	Gildan Activewear Inc	Apparel, Footwear & Accessories	12/30/18	2908.6	350.8	3004.6	1936.1	378	166741979
GKOS	Glaukos Corp	Medical Instruments & Equipment	12/31/18	181.3	-13.0	207.0	173.9	222	42667647
GSK	GlaxoSmithKline Plc	Pharmaceuticals	12/31/18	30821.0	3623.0	58066.0	4360.0	1180	350208074
CO	Global Cord Blood Corp	Diagnostic & Health Related Service	3/31/19	986.8	291.1	6551.0	3417.3	55	20154396
GMRE	Global Medical REIT Inc	REITs	12/31/18	53.2	13.5	636.1	269.3	159	19609533
GNL	Global Net Lease Inc	REITs	12/31/18	282.2	10.9	3309.5	1425.5	269	86277461
GLP	Global Partners LP	Equipment & Services	12/31/18	12672.6	103.9	2424.3		93	20706158
GPN	Global Payments Inc	Business Services	12/31/18	3366.4	452.1	13230.8	3991.4	996	288788185
GSL	Global Ship Lease, Inc.	Shipping	12/31/18	157.1	-57.4	1233.5	316.4		0
GLOB	Globant SA	Internet & Software	12/31/18	522.3	51.7	437.1	337.9	257	32867316
GL	Globe Life Inc	Life & Health	12/31/18	4303.8	701.5	23095.7	5415.2	756	105417099
GMED	Globus Medical Inc	Medical Instruments & Equipment	12/31/18	713.0	156.5	1300.7	1185.5		0
GMS	GMS Inc	Construction Materials	4/30/18	3116.0	56.0	2149.6	629.2	218	39231772
GNC	GNC Holdings Inc	Retail - Food & Beverage, Drug & To	12/31/18	2353.5	69.8	1527.8	-15.5	176	54078396
GDDY	GoDaddy Inc	Internet & Software	12/31/18	2660.1	77.1	6083.4	792.7	458	175655612
GOL	Gol Linhas Aereas Inteligentes SA	Airlines/Air Freight	12/31/18	11411.4	-1085.4	10378.3	-4985.4	136	34081926
GFI	Gold Fields Ltd.	Precious Metals	12/31/18	2577.8	-348.2	6104.3	2586.1	278	435701966
GSBD	Goldman Sachs BDC Inc	Holding and other Investment Office	12/31/18	146.7	82.8	1397.0	709.9	95	14926515
GS	Goldman Sachs Group Inc	Finance Intermediaries & Services	12/31/18	52528.0	10459.0	931796.0	90185.0	1907	317696294
GER	Goldman Sachs MLP Energy Renai	Finance Intermediaries & Services	11/30/18	1.9	-12.0	704.0	460.9		0
GMZ	Goldman Sachs MLP Income Oppor	Finance Intermediaries & Services	11/30/18	3.3	-10.4	573.8	372.9	53	10153028
GRC	Gorman-Rupp Company (The)	Industrial Machinery & Equipment	12/31/18	414.3	40.0	368.3	293.1	166	16900461
GPX	GP Strategies Corp.	Business Services	12/31/18	515.2	9.8	434.7	186.6	105	16896944
GRA	Grace (WR) & Co	Specialty Chemicals	12/31/18	1932.1	167.6	3565.3	330.9	409	67603264
GGG	Graco Inc	Industrial Machinery & Equipment	12/28/18	1653.3	341.1	1472.7	751.9	605	158008434
EAF	GrafTech International Ltd	Metal Products	12/31/18	1895.9	854.2	1505.5	-1076.8	297	307333327
GHM	Graham Corp.	Industrial Machinery & Equipment	3/31/19	91.8	-0.3	156.3	99.0	123	10090440

T26

1st	2nd	3rd	2018	2017	2016	P/E RATIO		2018	2017	2016	AV. YLD %	AMOUNT	PAYABLE	PRICE RANGE 2018	
-	-	1.01	6.45	4.16	4.06	6.6 -	4.8	0.36	0.34	0.31	1.0	-	-	42.8 -	31.1
-	-	0.38	-0.45	2.39	4.33	-		0.60	0.60	0.55		0.080	12/6/19		
-	-	-0.68	-2.44	-3.47	-4.18			0.60	0.60	0.75	5.4	0.150Z	1/28/20	13.1 -	8.7
0.24	-	-	-0.05	-1.56	0.75	-		-	0.30	1.05		0.10	12/20/19		
-	-	0.14	0.82	0.83	0.85	8.0 -	6.6	0.85	0.86	0.89	14.1	0.190	1/3/20	6.6 -	5.4
-	-	1.59	3.93	2.75	2.05	29.8 -	16.3	-	-	-		-	-	117.0 -	63.9
-	-	-0.10	6.54	-0.50	-6.93	1.8 -	0.1	-	-	-		-	-	11.9 -	0.9
-	-	0.97	3.29	1.13	2.42	15.8 -	12.0	0.61	0.59	0.55	1.3	0.160Y	18/53/27	52.0 -	39.4
-	-	0.15	1.22	0.54	1.29	15.7 -	8.4	0.24	0.24	2.53	1.8	0.060Y	12/15/20	19.2 -	10.3
-	-	-	0.09	0.09	0.12	66.7 -	48.6	0.48	0.48	0.41	9.1	0.120	12/20/19	6.0 -	4.4
-	-	-	0.45	0.32	0.36	49.3 -	40.5	1.32	1.32	1.32	6.3	0.110	3/24/20	22.2 -	18.2
-	-	-	0.07	0.04	0.07	90.3 -	73.1	0.64	0.61	0.60	10.6	0.150	12/20/19	6.3 -	5.1
-	-	-	0.07	-0.01	0.10	174.9 -	142.6	-	-	0.12		0.140	12/20/19	12.2 -	10.0
-	-	-	0.07	-0.01	-0.02	164.9 -	131.1	0.52	0.52	0.52	5.0	0.140	12/20/19	11.5 -	9.2
-	-	-	0.03	0.01	0.05	289.3 -	235.0	0.90	0.88	0.83	10.9	0.220	12/20/19	8.7 -	7.0
-	-	-	0.12	0.11	0.11	68.0 -	49.4	0.60	0.60	0.60	8.5	0.050	3/24/20	8.2 -	5.9
-	-	-0.06	2.09	-0.20	0.67	3.5 -	1.8	0.24	0.24	0.21	4.7	0.060Y	12/17/19	7.3 -	3.9
-	-	-	-	-	-			-	-	-		-	-		
-	-	0.66	3.40	2.54	2.32	28.1 -	20.7	1.64	1.56	1.52	1.9	0.430Y	18/53/27	95.7 -	70.5
-	-	0.50	4.07	2.60	3.92	5.6 -	3.7	0.08	0.10	0.06	0.4	0.020Y	12/31/19	22.6 -	15.2
-	-	-	0.06	0.05	0.01	102.8 -	85.0	0.60	0.60	0.84	10.6	0.050	3/24/20	6.2 -	5.1
-	-	-1.02	0.34	3.40	3.78	47.0 -	9.4	1.52	1.48	1.44	20.1	0.380Y	18/53/27	16.0 -	3.2
-	-	-0.31	0.31	-0.02	0.70	45.2 -	19.0	1.49	1.42	1.34	15.2	0.380Y	11/12/19	14.0 -	5.9
-	-	0.20	1.29	0.10	-0.25	28.6 -	16.0	-	-	-		-	-	37.0 -	20.6
-	-	0.50	15.86	-	-	1.2 -	0.6	-	-	-		-	-	19.4 -	8.8
-	-	0.46	1.33	0.04	2.31	128.6 -	92.6	-	-	-		-	-	171.0 -	123.2
-0.17	-	-	0.46	0.07	-0.39	-		-	-	-		0.387	12/31/19	-	
-	-	-	1.76	2.09	2.17			-	-	-		0.53130Y	12/16/19		
-	-	0.12	0.84	0.60	0.18			-	-	-		-	-		
-	-	1.25	5.52	12.75	6.29	15.4 -	12.3	1.76	1.68	1.60	2.3	0.460Y	18/53/27	85.2 -	68.0
-	-	0.23	0.21	7.74	1.02	144.9 -	79.7	-	-	-		-	-	30.4 -	16.7
-	-	-	-0.14	-0.22	-0.36	-		0.40	0.58	0.64	4.3	0.10	12/20/19	9.6 -	9.0
-	-	-	-	-	-			-	-	-		-	-		
-	-	-0.35	-0.86	-1.71	-30.03	-		-	-	-		0.3257	12/5/19	-	
-	-	1.18	3.54	2.56	1.50	28.8 -	13.9	-	-	-		5.7Y	6/21/13	102.0 -	49.1
-	-	0.31	0.32	0.30	0.30	123.9 -	91.2	2.75	3.29	3.18	7.9	0.37190Y	12/24/19	38.4 -	28.3
-	-	3.14	11.18	9.56	9.52	17.2 -	13.7	3.63	3.28	2.97	2.1	1.020Y	18/53/27	192.7 -	153.4
-	-	-1.08	-2.62	-0.72	0.89			0.37	0.84	0.93	3.8	0.010Y	18/53/27	11.6 -	7.7
-	0.95	-	3.64	2.77	2.77	15.3 -	10.6	1.96	1.92	1.78	3.8	0.490Y	18/53/27	55.6 -	38.4
-	-	1.60	5.53	-2.60	6.00	7.4 -	5.8	1.52	1.52	1.52	4.0	0.380Y	18/53/27	40.9 -	32.3
-	-	-	-	-	-			-	-	-		-	-		
-	-	1.30	-5.82	4.83	4.11			-	-	-		0.3750Y	4/30/13	52.1 -	32.2
-	-	-0.01	-0.62	0.50	1.00			2.10	2.65	2.72	9.8	0.550	2/14/20	23.9 -	17.8
-	-	0.40	-2.33	-6.15	-0.82			-	-	-		-	-	1.7 -	1.0
-	-	0.18	0.83	-0.36	-1.14	14.3 -	7.7	0.30	0.30	0.24	3.5	0.15940	2/18/20	11.9 -	6.4
-	-	0.45	1.45	1.34	1.28			-	-	-		0.0850	18/53/27		
-	-	1.56	5.50	4.18	4.59	20.9 -	16.0	2.88	2.70	2.63	2.8	0.76250Y	18/53/27	115.1 -	87.7
-	-	0.04	0.24	1.63	-0.56	20.9 -	12.1	-	-	-		-	-	5.0 -	2.9
-	-	0.39	1.20	1.21	1.33	19.9 -	11.1	1.88	1.88	1.73	10.0	0.480Z	18/53/27	23.9 -	13.3
-	-	-	1.11	-0.40	-0.82			-	-	-		0.0413G	12/10/19		
-	-	0.35	1.34	-0.21	-1.70	3.7 -	2.1	0.28	0.04	0.04	7.5	-	-	4.9 -	2.8
-	-	0.28	1.17	1.26	1.12	29.2 -	24.5	1.31	1.16	1.03	4.1	0.370Z	1/9/20	34.1 -	28.7
-	-	-0.05	-	-	-			-	-	-		-	-	10.0 -	0.0
-	-	0.51	1.66	-	2.94	31.8 -	15.4	0.45	-	0.31	1.1	0.1340	12/9/19	52.7 -	25.5
-	-	-0.37	-0.37	0.00	0.12			-	-	-		-	-	83.9 -	50.8
0.17	-	-	0.73	0.31	0.19	64.8 -	51.8	1.59	1.60	1.92	3.8	-	-	47.3 -	37.8
-	-	0.70	1.99	1.59	1.25			-	-	-		0.08G	8/24/18		
-	-	0.02	0.35	-0.09	-0.68	40.4 -	25.5	0.80	0.80	0.74	7.3	0.46880Z	1/31/20	14.2 -	8.9
-	-	0.08	0.01	0.30	0.81	2055.0 -	1762.0	2.13	1.77	-	11.0	0.53250Y	1/15/20	20.6 -	17.6
-	-	0.38	2.95	1.74	-5.91	7.3 -	5.5	1.88	1.85	1.85	9.6	0.520	18/53/27	21.4 -	16.4
-	-	0.54	2.84	3.01	0.81	64.6 -	34.8	0.04	0.04	0.02	0.0	0.1950Y	18/53/27	183.5 -	98.7
-	-	1.20	-7.42	-12.88	-11.36			-	-	-		0.50Z	5/31/20		
-	-	0.40	1.41	0.84	1.01			-	-	-		-	-		
-	-	1.82	6.09	12.22	4.49	17.5 -	12.3	0.63	0.59	0.56	0.7	0.38280Z	18/53/27	106.6 -	75.0
-	-	0.38	1.54	1.10	1.08	38.6 -	24.7	-	-	-		-	-	59.5 -	38.1
-	0.68	-	1.49	1.19	0.38	21.5 -	10.0	-	-	-		-	-	32.1 -	14.9
-	-	-0.09	0.81	-2.16	-4.12	4.1 -	1.7	-	-	0.80		0.20Y	12/30/16	3.3 -	1.4
-	-	0.42	0.45	0.79	-0.21	181.7 -	133.8	-	-	-		-	-	81.8 -	60.2
-0.00	-	-	-0.09	0.00	0.04			-	-	-		-	-	22.5 -	9.9
-	-	-	-0.42	-0.02	0.20			0.04	0.06	0.04	0.8	-	-	6.7 -	3.5
-	-	0.47	1.34	1.28	1.12	16.6 -	14.0	1.80	1.80	1.80	8.9	0.450	1/15/20	22.3 -	18.7
-	-	4.79	25.27	9.01	16.29	9.1 -	6.7	3.15	2.90	2.60	1.5	1.250Y	3/30/20	231.2 -	169.5
-	-	-	-0.15	-0.21	-0.13			0.64	0.64	0.64	12.6	0.160	11/29/19	5.9 -	3.8
-	-	-	-0.24	-0.17	-0.09			0.84	0.84	0.84	11.4	0.210	11/29/19	8.8 -	5.3
-	-	0.37	1.53	1.02	0.95	25.5 -	19.0	2.51	0.47	0.43	7.5	0.1450Y	18/53/27	39.0 -	29.1
-	-	0.13	0.59	0.76	1.21	28.7 -	18.7	-	-	-		0.025	2/1/89	16.9 -	11.1
-	-	0.80	2.49	0.16	1.33	32.0 -	25.3	0.96	0.84	0.51	1.3	0.270Y	18/53/27	79.6 -	63.1
-	-	0.49	1.97	1.45	0.24	27.1 -	20.4	0.53	0.48	0.44	1.1	0.1750Y	18/53/27	53.3 -	40.3
-	-	0.61	2.87	0.03	-	5.2 -	3.5	0.93	-	-	7.5	0.0850	12/31/19	15.0 -	9.9
-	0.12	-	-1.01	0.52	0.61	-		0.36	0.36	0.33	1.7	0.110Y	11/26/19	24.5 -	17.9

SYMBOL	COMPANY	NATURE OF BUSINESS	FISCAL YEAR-END	TOTAL REV. $MILL	NET INCOME $MILL	TOTAL ASSETS $MILL	NET STK EQUITY $MILL	NO OF INST	INST. HOLDINGS (SHARES)
GHC	Graham Holdings Co.	Educational Services	12/31/18	2696.0	271.2	4764.0	2916.8	397	4804745
GWW	Grainger (W.W.) Inc.	Electrical Equipment	12/31/18	11221.0	782.0	5873.0	1921.0	965	51468654
GRAM	Grana y Montero SAA	Construction Services	12/31/18	3899.5	-83.2	7430.4	2088.4	33	21809291
GVA	Granite Construction Inc	Construction Services	12/31/18	3318.4	42.4	2476.6	1351.6	357	59617315
GPMT	Granite Point Mortgage Trust Inc	REITs	12/31/18	185.3	63.1	3361.9	828.5	225	40704752
GRP U	Granite Real Estate Investment Tru	REITs	12/31/18	247.5	465.2	4188.8	2495.5	-	0
GPK	Graphic Packaging Holding Co	Containers & Packaging	12/31/18	6023.0	221.1	7059.2	1855.3	389	477698980
GTN	Gray Television Inc	Radio & Television	12/31/18	1084.1	210.8	4213.4	1187.2	283	98109048
AJX	Great Ajax Corp	REITs	12/31/18	111.5	28.3	1602.9	300.8	110	15893981
GWB	Great Western Bancorp Inc	Banking	9/30/19	603.6	167.4	12788.3	1900.2	228	64642941
GDOT	Green Dot Corp	Credit & Lending	12/31/18	1041.8	118.7	2287.1	909.8	348	53782052
GBX	Greenbrier Companies Inc (The)	Rail	8/31/19	3033.6	71.1	2990.6	1276.7	318	37483847
GHL	Greenhill & Co Inc	Finance Intermediaries & Services	12/31/18	352.0	39.2	485.7	62.4	232	24703401
GHG	GreenTree Hospitality Group Ltd	Hotels, Restaurants & Travel	12/31/18	945.0	394.1	3014.4	1854.7	38	8849074
GEF	Greif Inc	Containers & Packaging	10/31/19	4595.0	171.0	5426.7	1154.4	314	28527366
GFF	Griffon Corp.	Miscellaneous Consumer Goods	9/30/19	2209.3	37.3	2074.9	477.8	206	38017657
GPI	Group 1 Automotive, Inc.	Retail - Automotive	12/31/18	11601.4	157.8	5001.1	1095.7	327	29903922
GRUB	GrubHub Inc	Internet & Software	12/31/18	1007.3	78.5	2065.7	1442.3	448	117014465
PAC	Grupo Aeroportuario del Pacifico, S.	Airlines/Air Freight	12/31/18	14122.9	5037.4	39550.5	20709.0	161	8449532
ASR	Grupo Aeroportuario del Sureste SA	Airlines/Air Freight	12/31/18	15410.2	4987.6	56181.8	29106.2	153	11122439
AVAL	Grupo Aval Acciones Y Valores SA	Banking	12/31/18	8356636.0	2912694.0	259675153.0	177889709.0	88	95910910
SUPV	Grupo Supervielle SA	Banking	12/31/18	35909.2	-3028.0	141734.0	16954.0	92	13545368
TV	Grupo Televisa SAB	Radio & Television	12/31/18	101282.3	6009.4	297170.6	89516.9	268	324330528
GSX	GSX Techedu Inc	Educational Services	12/31/18	397.3	19.6	338.2	-26.5	-	0
GTT	GTT Communications, Inc	Internet & Software	12/31/18	1490.8	-243.4	4537.6	414.7	155	44978964
GSH	Guangshen Railway Co., Ltd.	Rail	12/31/17	18331.4	1015.4	33994.2	28684.7	53	1652190
GES	GUESS ?, Inc.	Retail - Apparel and Accessories	2/2/19	2609.7	14.1	1649.2	837.2	302	70566476
GGM	Guggenheim Credit Allocation Fund	Holding and other Investment Office	5/31/19	18.5	14.0	207.7	146.4	30	851038
GPM	Guggenheim Enhanced Equity Inco	Holding and other Investment Office	12/31/18	10.3	-0.5	500.0	336.5	58	7015061
GOF	Guggenheim Strategic Opportunitie	Holding and other Investment Office	5/31/19	37.5	30.7	661.7	641.8	70	4964410
GBAB	Guggenheim Taxable Municipal Ma	Holding and other Investment Office	5/31/19	29.1	22.6	501.9	395.7	59	4789290
GWRE	Guidewire Software Inc	Internet & Software	7/31/19	719.5	20.7	2167.0	1574.2	412	99621023
HAE	Haemonetics Corp.	Medical Instruments & Equipment	3/30/19	967.6	55.0	1274.8	667.9	403	64306497
HAL	Halliburton Company	Equipment & Services	12/31/18	23995.0	1656.0	25982.0	9522.0	1315	853712122
HBB	Hamilton Beach Brands Holding Co	Household Appliances, Electronics &	12/31/18	743.2	21.8	330.4	65.4	91	4692559
HPS	Hancock John Preferred Income Fd	Holding and other Investment Office	7/31/19	54.6	37.9	908.0	593.2	69	3860729
HPF	Hancock John Preferred Income Fu	Holding and other Investment Office	7/31/19	41.4	28.6	691.8	449.8	66	1695164
HTD	Hancock John Tax-Advantaged Divi	Holding and other Investment Office	10/31/19	65.0	41.6	1397.9	950.0	124	7468650
HBI	HanesBrands Inc	Apparel, Footwear & Accessories	12/29/18	6804.0	553.1	7256.0	970.3	847	398788709
HNGR	Hanger Inc	Hospitals & Health Care Facilities	12/31/18	1048.8	-0.9	703.0	-21.9	182	38274181
HASI	Hannon Armstrong Sustainable Infr	REITs	12/31/18	137.8	41.6	2154.9	801.1	271	56503287
THG	Hanover Insurance Group Inc	General Insurance	12/31/18	4494.3	391.0	12399.7	2954.7	485	48684747
HOG	Harley-Davidson Inc	Autos- Manufacturing	12/31/18	5716.9	531.5	10665.7	1773.9	764	183124314
HMY	Harmony Gold Mining Co. Ltd.	Precious Metals	6/30/19	26912.0	-2607.0	36736.0	22614.0	164	188685520
HSC	Harsco Corp.	Industrial Machinery & Equipment	12/31/18	1722.4	137.1	1632.9	268.3	401	88228615
HHS	Harte Hanks Inc	Advertising	12/31/18	284.6	17.6	125.2	-9.5	87	9978461
HIG	Hartford Financial Services Group I	General Insurance	12/31/18	18955.0	1807.0	62307.0	13101.0	1033	440932324
HVT	Haverty Furniture Cos., Inc.	Retail - Furniture & Home Furnishing	12/31/18	817.8	30.3	440.2	274.6	187	20568402
HE	Hawaiian Electric Industries Inc	Electric Utilities	12/31/18	2860.8	203.7	13104.1	2196.6	460	73235270
HCHC	HC2 Holdings Inc	Business Services	12/31/18	1976.7	162.0	6503.8	108.4	3	43552
HCA	HCA Healthcare Inc	Hospitals & Health Care Facilities	12/31/18	46677.0	3787.0	39207.0	-4950.0	939	280735022
HCI	HCI Group Inc	General Insurance	12/31/18	231.3	17.7	832.9	181.4	152	6583445
HDB	HDFC Bank Ltd	Banking	3/31/19	1201837.1	220103.8	13280073.6	1632575.3	614	341633990
HR	Healthcare Realty Trust, Inc.	REITs	12/31/18	450.4	69.8	3191.2	1716.6	368	154091848
HTA	Healthcare Trust Of America Inc	REITs	12/31/18	696.4	213.5	6188.5	3256.0	425	229463176
PEAK	Healthpeak Properties Inc	REITs	12/31/18	1846.7	1061.1	12718.6	5944.4	948	579255233
HL	Hecla Mining Co	Mining	12/31/18	567.1	-26.6	2703.9	1691.0	319	347525702
HEI	HEICO Corp	Aerospace	10/31/19	2055.6	327.9	2969.2	1666.5	537	40594190
HLX	Helix Energy Solutions Group Inc	Equipment & Services	12/31/18	739.8	28.6	2347.7	1617.8	349	170357251
HP	Helmerich & Payne, Inc.	Equipment & Services	9/30/19	2798.5	-33.7	5839.5	4012.2	771	133352136
HLF	Herbalife Nutrition Ltd	Household & Personal Products	12/31/18	4891.8	296.6	2789.8	-723.4	361	136599315
HRI	Herc Holdings Inc	Miscellaneous Transportation Servic	12/31/18	1976.7	69.1	3610.2	572.7	342	174230120
HTGC	Hercules Capital Inc	Holding and other Investment Office	12/31/18	190.6	108.7	1945.2	955.4	269	43618625
HRTG	Heritage Insurance Holdings Inc	General Insurance	12/31/18	480.2	27.2	1768.7	425.3	151	22360451
PSV	Hermitage Offshore Services Ltd	Equipment & Services	12/31/18	20.7	-197.3	191.1	54.1	52	1153643
HT	Hersha Hospitality Trust	REITs	12/31/18	495.1	10.0	2138.6	892.8	256	58417547
HSY	Hershey Company (The)	Food	12/31/18	7791.1	1177.6	7703.0	1398.7	1275	142782815
HTZ	Hertz Global Holdings Inc (New)	Miscellaneous Transportation Servic	12/31/18	9504.0	-225.0	21382.0	1061.0	226	154019368
HES	Hess Corp	Production & Extraction	12/31/18	6466.0	-282.0	21433.0	9629.0	873	325316851
HESM	Hess Midstream LP	Production & Extraction	12/31/18	662.4	70.8	2819.7		84	12993761
HPE	Hewlett Packard Enterprise Co	IT Services	10/31/19	29135.0	1049.0	51803.0	17098.0	912	1181490364
HXL	Hexcel Corp.	Plastics	12/31/18	2189.1	276.6	2824.1	1322.0	613	107684385
HCR	Hi-Crush Inc	Mining	12/31/18	842.8	137.6	1433.8		128	14458451
PCF	High Income Securities Fund	Holding and other Investment Office	8/31/19	2.3	1.3	52.9	52.8	43	3260426
HPR	HighPoint Resources Corp	Production & Extraction	12/31/18	453.0	121.2	2252.5	1212.1	143	200297441
HIW	Highwoods Properties, Inc.	REITs	12/31/18	720.0	171.8	4675.0	2246.7	423	120156988
HIL	Hill International Inc	Business Services	12/31/18	428.7	-31.5	264.8	93.8	77	36631542
HRC	Hill-Rom Holdings, Inc.	Medical Instruments & Equipment	9/30/19	2907.3	152.2	4919.0	1573.3	28	4651597
HI	Hillenbrand Inc	Industrial Machinery & Equipment	9/30/19	1807.3	121.4	2228.6	754.1	376	66591952
HTH	Hilltop Holdings, Inc.	Banking	12/31/18	1602.2	121.4	13683.6	1949.5	278	69831502

T28

SYMBOL	COMPANY	NATURE OF BUSINESS	FISCAL YEAR-END	TOTAL REV. $MILL	NET INCOME $MILL	TOTAL ASSETS $MILL	NET STK EQUITY $MILL	NO OF INST	INST. HOLDINGS (SHARES)
HGV	Hilton Grand Vacations Inc	Hotels, Restaurants & Travel	12/31/18	1999.0	298.0	2753.0	616.0	264	112871765
HLT	Hilton Worldwide Holdings Inc	Hotels, Restaurants & Travel	12/31/18	8906.0	764.0	13995.0	551.0	663	404257819
HNI	HNI Corp	Office Equipment & Furniture	12/29/18	2257.9	93.4	1401.8	562.9	292	47222084
HMLP	Hoegh LNG Partners LP	Equipment & Services	12/31/18	146.6	77.6	1023.0	520.4	65	8175656
HEP	Holly Energy Partners LP	Equipment & Services	12/31/18	506.2	178.8	2102.5		159	43967050
HFC	HollyFrontier Corp	Refining & Marketing	12/31/18	17714.7	1098.0	10994.6	5918.6	727	178070983
HD	Home Depot Inc	Retail - Hardware & Home Improvem	2/3/19	108203.0	11121.0	44003.0	-1878.0	3099	1009791360
HMC	Honda Motor Co., Ltd.(Honda Giken	Autos- Manufacturing	3/31/19	15888617.0	610316.0	20419122.0	8267720.0	348	48950237
HON	Honeywell International Inc	Auto Parts	12/31/18	41802.0	6765.0	57773.0	18187.0	2526	685508738
HMN	Horace Mann Educators Corp.	General Insurance	12/31/18	1191.6	18.3	11031.9	1290.6	274	52076566
HZN	Horizon Global Corp	Auto Parts	12/31/18	849.9	-204.0	521.4	-63.7	63	14241857
HRL	Hormel Foods Corp.	Food	10/27/19	9497.3	978.8	8109.0	5921.5	799	276072158
DHI	Horton (DR) Inc	Builders	9/30/19	17592.9	1618.5	15606.6	10020.9	962	387006796
HST	Host Hotels & Resorts Inc	REITs	12/31/18	5524.0	1087.0	12090.0	7494.0	826	938156172
HLI	Houlihan Lokey Inc	Wealth Management	3/31/19	1084.4	159.1	1423.1	891.3	244	44499155
HOV	Hovnanian Enterprises, Inc.	Builders	10/31/19	2016.9	-42.1	1881.4	-490.5	142	18993179
HHC	Howard Hughes Corp	Property, Real Estate & Developmen	12/31/18	1064.5	57.0	7355.8	3132.2	352	45861241
HPQ	HP Inc	Computer Hardware & Equipment	10/31/19	58756.0	3152.0	33467.0	-1193.0	1532	1603549896
HSFC PR	HSBC Finance Corp	Credit & Lending	12/31/16	1414.0	-529.0	13882.0	5434.0		0
HSBC	HSBC Holdings Plc	Banking	12/31/18	88667.0	13637.0	2558124.0	186253.0	623	107768064
HUSI PR	HSBC USA, Inc.	Banking	12/31/18	6554.0	320.0	172448.0	20506.0	1	80000
HMI	Huami Corp	Electronic Instruments & Related Pro	12/31/18	3645.3	340.0	3258.5	1810.9		0
HNP	Huaneng Power International Inc	Electric Utilities	12/31/17	152459.4	1793.2	378693.7	75533.3	95	1820640
HUBB	Hubbell Inc	Electrical Equipment	12/31/18	4481.7	360.2	4872.1	1780.6	481	55615639
HUBS	HubSpot Inc	Internet & Software	12/31/18	513.0	-63.8	834.0	244.6	374	42098555
HBM	Hudbay Minerals Inc	Precious Metals	12/31/18	1472.4	85.4	4685.6	2178.9	147	179139971
HUD	Hudson Ltd	Retail - General Merchandise/Depart	12/31/18	1924.2	29.5	1451.2	552.1	107	39193582
HPP	Hudson Pacific Properties Inc	REITs	12/31/18	728.4	98.8	7070.9	3666.5	317	181105019
HUM	Humana Inc.	Life & Health	12/31/18	56912.0	1683.0	25413.0	10161.0	1085	158812512
HCFT	Hunt Companies Finance Trust Inc	REITs	12/31/18	47.6	-5.5	679.4	150.1	52	13453007
HII	Huntington Ingalls Industries, Inc.	Defense	12/31/18	8176.0	836.0	6383.0	1516.0	628	43230078
HUN	Huntsman Corp	Specialty Chemicals	12/31/18	9379.0	337.0	7953.0	2520.0	593	213780592
HUYA	HUYA Inc	IT Services	12/31/18	4663.4	-1937.7	7106.2	5645.0	153	58009629
H	Hyatt Hotels Corp	Hotels, Restaurants & Travel	12/31/18	4454.0	769.0	7643.0	3670.0	308	42278517
HY	Hyster-Yale Materials Handling Inc	Autos- Manufacturing	12/31/18	3174.4	34.7	1742.1	527.4	178	8471940
IAA	IAA Inc	Retail - Automotive	12/31/18	1326.8	183.7	1500.2	563.2	408	129969547
IAA	IAA Inc	Retail - Automotive	12/31/18	1326.8	183.7	1500.2	563.2	408	129969547
IAG	IAMGold Corp	Precious Metals	12/31/18	1111.0	-28.2	3961.0	2732.6	239	310260922
IBN	ICICI Bank Ltd (India)	Banking	3/31/18	1189691.0	77121.9	11242810.4	1106297.0	490	794266514
IDA	Idacorp Inc	Electric Utilities	12/31/18	1370.8	226.8	6382.8	2370.4	493	55371036
IEX	IDEX Corporation	Industrial Machinery & Equipment	12/31/18	2483.7	410.6	3473.9	1994.6	607	89791251
IDT	IDT Corp	Services	7/31/19	1409.2	0.1	443.7	56.2	127	13708700
INFO	IHS Markit Ltd	Business Services	11/30/19	4414.6	502.7	16087.2	8415.8	622	414958604
ITW	Illinois Tool Works, Inc.	Industrial Machinery & Equipment	12/31/18	14768.0	2563.0	14870.0	3254.0	1700	353604001
IMAX	IMAX Corp.	Entertainment	12/31/18	374.4	22.8	873.6	512.2	231	61845904
ICD	Independence Contract Drilling Inc	Equipment & Services	12/31/18	142.6	-20.0	584.9	391.5	103	62123644
IHC	Independence Holding Company	Life & Health	12/31/18	350.8	28.5	1037.5	448.7	87	3892506
IRT	Independence Realty Trust Inc	REITs	12/31/18	191.2	26.3	1659.3	623.0	236	87513781
IFN	India Fund, Inc. (The)	Holding and other Investment Office	12/31/18	9.0	-1.0	715.1	642.1	140	9545095
IBA	Industrias Bachoco S.A.B. de C.V.	Food	12/31/18	61052.1	3350.0	52865.6	38096.3		0
INFY	Infosys Ltd.	IT Services	3/31/18	10939.0	2486.0	12255.0	9960.0	554	779488383
ING	ING Groep NV	Banking	12/31/18	29253.0	4761.0	884603.0	49048.0	394	151351535
IR	Ingersoll-Rand Plc	Industrial Machinery & Equipment	12/31/18	15668.2	1337.6	17914.9	7022.7	1114	229480955
NGVT	Ingevity Corp	Specialty Chemicals	12/31/18	1133.6	169.1	1315.2	338.7	406	46082201
INGR	Ingredion Inc	Food	12/31/18	5841.0	443.0	5728.0	2388.0	678	82517015
IIPR	Innovative Industrial Properties Inc	Property, Real Estate & Developmen	12/31/18	14.8	7.0	281.5	264.3	273	8269090
IPHI	Inphi Corp	Semiconductors	12/31/18	294.5	-95.8	889.9	366.7	300	55401642
INSI	Insight Select Income Fund	Holding and other Investment Office	3/31/19	10.7	9.1	225.6	220.4	52	3424731
NSP	Insperity Inc	Business Services	12/31/18	3828.5	135.4	1191.8	77.7	465	40308580
INSP	Inspire Medical Systems Inc	Medical Instruments & Equipment	12/31/18	50.6	-21.8	200.1	164.0	181	22272831
IBP	Installed Building Products Inc	Construction Services	12/31/18	1336.4	54.7	834.7	182.5	200	23601816
INST	Instructure Inc	Internet & Software	12/31/18	209.5	-43.5	274.0	128.4	167	37738050
ITGR	Integer Holdings Corp	Medical Instruments & Equipment	12/28/18	1215.0	168.0	2326.7	1060.5	330	40579265
I	Intelsat SA	Services	12/31/18	2161.2	-599.6	12241.5	-4097.0		0
ICE	Intercontinental Exchange Inc	Finance Intermediaries & Services	12/31/18	6276.0	1988.0	92791.0	17201.0	1082	560364958
IHG	InterContinental Hotels Group Plc	Hotels, Restaurants & Travel	12/31/18	4337.0	351.0	3753.0	-1085.0	170	13893759
IFS	Intercorp Financial Services Inc	Banking	12/31/18	6160.5	1084.3	63744.4	7048.1		0
IBM	International Business Machines Co	IT Services	12/31/18	79591.0	8728.0	123382.0	16796.0	2880	691830949
IFF	International Flavors & Fragrances I	Specialty Chemicals	12/31/18	3977.5	337.3	12889.4	6033.0	807	126873093
IGT	International Game Technology PL	Entertainment	12/31/18	4831.3	-21.3	13648.5	1807.9		0
IP	International Paper Co	Containers & Packaging	12/31/18	23306.0	2012.0	33576.0	7362.0	1230	428494470
INSW	International Seaways Inc	Miscellaneous Transportation Servic	12/31/18	270.4	-88.9	1848.6	1009.9	107	23517700
IPG	Interpublic Group of Companies Inc.	Advertising	12/31/18	9714.4	618.9	15620.3	2393.2	779	491202004
INXN	InterXion Holding NV	IT Services	12/31/18	561.8	31.1	2262.6	633.4	316	73952741
IPI	Intrepid Potash Inc	Mining	12/31/18	208.3	11.8	525.2	417.3	202	63244193
IVC	Invacare Corp	Medical Instruments & Equipment	12/31/18	972.3	-43.9	885.9	359.1	244	50694228
VBF	Invesco Bond Fund	Holding and other Investment Office	2/28/19	10.6	9.3	221.5	216.9	50	2916333
VCV	Invesco California Value Municipal I	Holding and other Investment Office	2/28/19	41.1	27.8	986.3	613.1	58	4757200
VTA	Invesco Dynamic Credit Opportuniti	Holding and other Investment Office	2/28/19	78.9	45.3	1526.6	938.0	138	41142884
IHIT	Invesco High Income 2023 Target T	Holding and other Investment Office	2/28/19	20.8	15.2	325.2	245.0	36	4291180

1st	2nd	3rd	2018	2017	2016	P/E RATIO		DIV 2018	DIV 2017	DIV 2016	AV. YLD %	AMOUNT	PAYABLE	PRICE 2018	
-	-	0.59	3.05	3.28	1.70	11.8	8.2	-	-	-		-		35.9	25.1
-	-	1.00	2.50	3.85	1.05	45.0	26.9	0.60	0.60	0.84	0.7	0.150Y	12/27/19	112.4	67.3
-	-	1.07	2.11	2.00	1.88	19.8	14.3	1.17	1.13	1.09	3.2	0.3050Y	18/53/27	41.9	30.1
-	-	-	1.93	1.58	1.58							0.54690	2/17/20		
-	-	0.78	1.70	2.28	1.69	18.1	12.5	2.63	2.50	2.32	9.9	0.67250	18/53/27	30.7	21.3
-	-	1.58	6.19	4.52	-1.48	9.4	6.1	1.32	1.32	1.32	2.6	0.350Y	18/53/27	58.3	38.0
-	-	2.53	7.29	6.45	5.46	32.8	23.1	3.56	2.76	2.36	1.7	1.360Y	18/53/27	238.8	168.6
-	-	318.50	590.79	342.10	191.16	0.1	0.0	96.94	90.81	88.05	360.0	-		30.1	22.9
-	-	2.23	8.98	2.14	6.20	20.3	14.5	3.06	2.74	2.45	1.9	0.90Y	18/53/27	182.0	130.1
-	-	0.60	0.44	4.08	2.02	108.4	78.8	1.14	1.10	1.06	2.7	0.28750Y	12/31/19	47.7	34.7
-	-	5.74	-8.14	-0.14	-0.66							-		5.7	1.5
-	-	0.37	1.86	1.57	1.64	24.6	20.9	0.75	0.68	0.58	1.8	0.23250Y	18/53/27	45.8	38.8
-	-	1.26	3.81	2.74	2.36	14.7	9.2	0.50	0.40	0.32	1.1	0.1750Y	18/53/27	55.9	35.1
-	-	0.51	1.47	0.76	1.02	13.7	10.6	0.85	0.85	0.85	4.7	0.057Z	18/53/27	20.1	15.6
-	0.50	-	2.60	1.63	1.10	19.0	14.1	0.80	0.71	0.30	1.8	0.310Y	12/16/19	49.5	36.6
-	-	-1.27	0.75	-56.25	-0.50	39.7	7.2					0.47660Z	10/15/07	29.8	5.4
-	-	0.69	1.32	3.91	4.73	102.3	70.1					-		135.0	92.6
-	-	0.78	3.26	1.48	1.43	7.3	4.9	0.56	0.53	0.50	2.8	0.17620Y	18/53/27	23.9	16.0
-	-	-	-	-	-					0.86		0.39750Y	6/15/16		
-	-		0.63	0.48	0.07	71.0	56.4	2.55	2.55	2.55	6.4	0.50780	4/16/18	44.7	35.5
-	-		-	-	-					0.49		0.40630Y	4/1/16		
-	-	0.51	0.65	-0.22		37.4	14.4					-		19.1	7.3
-	0.12	-		0.11	0.58			-	10.16	17.18		-		26.8	17.9
-	-	2.38	6.54	4.39	5.24	22.8	14.7	3.15	2.87	2.59	2.5	0.910Y	18/53/27	148.8	96.3
-	-	-0.35	-1.66	-1.08	-1.29							-		204.9	118.8
-	-0.21	-	0.33	0.67	-0.15	30.9	9.1	0.02	0.02	0.02	0.3	0.010	9/27/19	10.2	3.0
-	-	0.29	0.32	-	-										
-	-	0.38	0.63	0.44	0.25	59.8	43.7	1.00	1.00	0.80	2.9	0.250Z	18/53/27	37.6	27.5
-	-	5.14	12.16	16.81	4.07	30.5	19.2	2.00	1.89	0.87	0.7	0.550Y	18/53/27	371.0	232.9
-	-	0.09	-0.38	0.06	-0.79			0.28	0.60	2.05	8.3	0.0750Z	1/15/20	3.6	2.9
-	-	3.74	19.09	10.46	12.14	13.5	9.9	3.02	2.52	2.10	1.4	1.030Y	18/53/27	258.1	188.8
-	-	0.13	1.39	2.61	1.36	17.9	12.5	0.65	0.50	0.50	3.0	0.16250Y	18/53/27	24.9	17.4
-	-		-15.02	-1.01	-6.26							-		30.0	15.7
-	-	2.80	6.68	1.98	1.52	13.6	9.7	0.60			0.8	0.190Y	18/53/27	90.7	64.6
-	-	0.76	2.09	2.94	2.61	36.5	21.0	1.23	1.20	1.17	2.1	0.31750Y	12/13/19	76.3	44.0
-	-	0.31	-	-	-							-		48.9	36.0
-	-	0.31	-	-	-							-		40.0	36.6
-	-0.03	-	-0.06	1.07	0.12							0.1250	7/12/13	5.4	2.3
-0.18	-	-	11.89	17.43	17.41	1.3	0.8	4.51	9.09	9.10	38.1	-		15.3	9.5
-	-	1.78	4.49	4.21	3.94	25.2	20.0	2.40	2.24	2.08	2.3	0.670Y	18/53/27	113.3	89.9
-	-	1.37	5.29	4.36	3.53	32.8	23.0	1.66	1.45	1.34	1.1	0.50Y	18/53/27	173.4	121.4
-0.06	-	-	0.17	0.35	1.03	68.9	33.6	0.56	0.76	0.75	7.2	0.090Y	6/29/18	11.7	5.7
-	-	0.10	1.33	1.00	0.48							0.17GZ	2/14/20		
-	-	2.04	7.60	4.86	5.70	23.9	16.2	3.56	2.86	2.40	2.3	1.070Y	18/53/27	181.3	123.5
-	-	0.15	0.36	0.04	0.42	70.6	51.6					-		25.4	18.6
-	-	-0.14	-0.42	-0.64	-0.67									3.6	0.7
-	-	0.41	1.89	2.63	7.09	22.4	18.0	0.15	0.16	0.15	0.4	0.20Y	1/16/20	42.4	34.0
-	-	0.05	0.30	0.41	-0.19	51.3	30.4	0.72	0.72	0.72	5.9	0.180Z	1/24/20	15.4	9.1
-	-		-0.04	-0.01	-			4.50	3.16	1.71	21.6	0.570	1/10/20	22.0	19.5
-	-	0.59	5.58	8.25	6.58	10.1	7.2	16.82	15.23	14.97	33.6	-		56.4	40.1
-	-	0.17	0.55	0.47	0.45	21.9	16.2	0.19	0.38	0.79	1.8	-		12.1	8.9
-	-		1.22	1.41	1.28	11.2	7.6	0.54	0.54	0.53	4.7	0.38280Z	4/15/20	13.7	9.2
-	-	1.88	5.35	5.05	5.65			1.96	1.70	1.36		0.530	18/53/27		
-	-	1.41	3.97	2.97	0.83	29.5	18.4							117.1	73.2
-	-	1.47	6.17	7.06	6.55	16.1	11.9	2.45	2.20	1.90	2.9	0.630Y	18/53/27	99.2	73.3
-	-	0.55	0.75	-0.13	-4.56	183.5	60.1	1.20	0.55		1.4	0.56250Z	1/15/20	137.6	45.1
-	-	-0.36	-2.19	-1.78	2.25							-		76.2	29.7
-	-		0.87	0.88	0.93	23.9	20.1	1.04	0.90	1.01	5.4	0.1315B	12/27/19	20.8	17.5
-	-	0.63	3.22	2.01	1.54	44.9	21.2	0.80	1.58	0.48	0.7	0.30Y	18/53/27	144.6	68.3
-	-	-0.34	-1.50	-14.88	-16.90							-		75.0	39.5
-	-	0.71	1.75	1.30	1.23	43.3	19.7					-		75.7	34.4
-	-	-0.56	-1.27	-1.69	-1.92									53.7	36.9
-	-	0.92	5.15	2.09	0.19	17.9	13.1					-		92.1	67.7
-	-	-1.05	-4.63	-1.50	8.36							0.71880	5/2/16		
-	-	0.94	3.43	4.23	2.37	27.7	21.0	0.96	0.80	0.68	1.1	0.2750Y	18/53/27	94.9	72.2
-	-	-	1.83	3.05	1.94	38.4	30.1	1.14	1.04	4.61	1.8	-		70.3	55.1
-	-	-	9.82	9.63	8.71							-			
-	-	1.87	9.52	6.14	12.38	15.9	11.9	6.21	5.90	5.50	4.5	1.620Y	18/53/27	151.4	112.9
-	-	1.13	3.79	3.72	5.05	40.1	28.1	2.84	2.66	2.40	2.2	0.750Y	18/53/27	152.2	106.5
-	-	0.51	-0.10	-5.26	1.05			0.80	-	-		0.20	12/13/19		
-	-	0.87	4.85	5.13	2.18	9.8	7.6	1.93	1.86	1.78	4.4	0.51250Y	18/53/27	47.8	36.7
-	-	-0.38	-3.05	-3.64	-0.62							0.53130Z	12/30/19		
-	-	0.42	1.59	1.46	1.49	14.9	12.3	0.84	0.72	0.60	3.8	0.2350Y	18/53/27	23.8	19.6
-	-	-0.24	0.43	0.55	0.56							-			
-	-	0.00	0.09	-0.20	-0.80	44.1	23.8					0.75G7	12/27/12	4.0	2.1
-	-	-0.24	-1.33	-2.34	-1.32			0.05	0.04	0.05	0.7	0.01250Z	1/17/20	11.3	4.2
-	-	-	0.82	0.83	0.84	25.4	20.7	1.01	0.84	0.95	5.3	0.0660	1/31/20	20.8	16.9
-	-	-	0.64	0.70	0.78	21.1	18.0	0.64	0.69	0.79	5.1	0.043M	1/31/20	13.5	11.5
-	-	-	0.71	0.89	0.97	16.0	14.6	0.82	0.88	0.90	7.4	0.0750	1/31/20	11.4	10.4
-	-	-	0.61	0.12	-	17.4	16.3	0.60	0.10	-	5.8	0.050	1/31/20	10.6	10.0

SYMBOL	COMPANY	NATURE OF BUSINESS	FISCAL YEAR-END	TOTAL REV. $MILL	NET INCOME $MILL	TOTAL ASSETS $MILL	NET STK EQUITY $MILL	NO OF INST	INST. HOLDINGS (SHARES)
VLT	Invesco High Income Trust II	Holding and other Investment Office	2/28/19	10.5	7.5	175.4	125.5	49	3504038
IVZ	Invesco Ltd	Wealth Management	12/31/18	5314.1	882.8	30978.4	8578.8	800	391475679
IVR	Invesco Mortgage Capital Inc	REITs	12/31/18	312.7	-70.8	17813.5	2286.7	317	112354466
OIA	Invesco Municipal Income Opportun	Holding and other Investment Office	2/28/19	23.6	17.9	464.8	348.6	79	3866630
VMO	Invesco Municipal Opportunity Trust	Holding and other Investment Office	2/28/19	64.4	41.2	1475.0	868.4	124	11389436
VKQ	Invesco Municipal Trust	Holding and other Investment Office	2/28/19	50.9	33.5	1177.8	713.4	109	10412307
VPV	Invesco Pennsylvania Value Munici	Holding and other Investment Office	2/28/19	23.3	14.6	556.3	320.1	57	2292625
IQI	Invesco Quality Municipal Income T	Holding and other Investment Office	2/29/12	23.1	19.8	524.2	443.1	-	0
VVR	Invesco Senior Income Trust	Holding and other Investment Office	2/28/19	69.2	42.3	1359.1	862.2	177	104449477
VGM	Invesco Trust for Investment Grade	Holding and other Investment Office	2/28/19	52.4	33.9	1211.6	721.9	114	10625127
VTN	Invesco Trust For Investment Grade	Holding and other Investment Office	2/28/19	18.9	12.0	451.9	270.8	41	1927779
IIM	Invesco Value Municipal Income Tr	Holding and other Investment Office	2/28/19	50.6	32.4	1211.6	737.8	104	5663096
IRET	Investors Real Estate Trust	REITs	12/31/18	121.9	-4.4	1336.0	568.8	194	20563078
NVTA	Invitae Corp	Diagnostic & Health Related Service	12/31/18	147.7	-129.4	283.0	161.8	221	98105427
INVH	Invitation Homes Inc	Property, Real Estate & Developmen	12/31/18	1723.0	-4.9	18063.4	8229.1	396	551559062
IO	ION Geophysical Corp	Production & Extraction	12/31/18	180.0	-71.2	244.7	6.2	131	14567479
IQV	IQVIA Holdings Inc	Biotechnology	12/31/18	10412.0	259.0	22549.0	6714.0	793	194030524
IRM	Iron Mountain Inc (New)	REITs	12/31/18	4225.8	363.4	11852.2	1884.2	734	272418274
IRS	IRSA Inversiones y Representacion	Property, Real Estate & Developmen	6/30/19	69767.0	-25615.0	474634.0	32075.0	77	16574901
ICL	Israel Chemicals Ltd	Agricultural Chemicals	12/31/18	5556.0	1240.0	8776.0	3781.0	123	77435485
STAR	iStar Inc	REITs	12/31/18	798.1	-32.3	5014.3	863.0	275	74522077
ITCB	Itau CorpBanca	Banking	12/31/18	1878921.0	171331.0	29323338.0	3219478.0	42	1262191
ITUB	Itau Unibanco Holding S.A.	Banking	12/31/18	195695.0	24907.0	1552797.0	136782.0	493	1286148532
ITT	ITT Inc	Industrial Machinery & Equipment	12/31/18	2745.1	333.7	3846.8	1822.4	628	116826656
IVH	Ivy High Income Opportunities Fund	Holding and other Investment Office	9/30/19	28.7	20.8	363.2	249.4	51	4709921
JAX	J Alexander's Holdings Inc	Hotels, Restaurants & Travel	12/30/18	242.3	4.0	174.5	113.8	125	12596873
JILL	J.Jill Inc	Retail - Apparel and Accessories	2/2/19	706.3	30.5	627.0	213.8	95	13058321
JBL	Jabil Inc	Electrical Equipment	8/31/19	25282.3	287.1	12970.5	1887.4	584	183121067
J	Jacobs Engineering Group, Inc.	Business Services	9/27/19	12737.9	848.0	11462.7	5714.7	853	155036957
JHX	James Hardie Industries Plc	Construction Materials	3/31/19	2506.6	228.8	4032.6	974.4	62	3301981
JHG	Janus Henderson Group Plc	Holding and other Investment Office	12/31/18	2306.4	523.8	6911.9	4839.3	244	132720858
JOF	Japan Smaller Capitalization Fund I	Holding and other Investment Office	2/28/19	6.3	2.4	289.4	288.1	67	22998014
JBGS	JBG SMITH Properties	REITs	12/31/18	644.2	39.9	5997.3	2987.1	308	117325306
JEF	Jefferies Financial Group Inc	Agricultural Livestock	11/30/18	3764.0	1026.8	47131.1	10185.9	671	258815206
JELD	JELD-WEN Holding Inc	Construction Materials	12/31/18	4346.7	144.4	3051.1	767.8	173	61638186
JCAP	Jernigan Capital Inc	REITs	12/31/18	31.2	54.4	590.4	547.9	143	15772694
JT	Jianpu Technology Inc	Services	12/31/18	2011.8	-164.6	2445.1	1588.3	39	31087828
JKS	JinkoSolar Holding Co., Ltd.	Semiconductors	12/31/18	25042.6	406.5	35853.2	7839.9	125	23485073
JMP	JMP Group LLC	Finance Intermediaries & Services	12/31/18	193.9	-2.2	1391.2	83.7	-	0
JBT	John Bean Technologies Corp	Industrial Machinery & Equipment	12/31/18	1919.7	104.1	1442.5	456.9	345	39425585
DECR 19	John Deere Capital Corp.	Credit & Lending	11/3/19	2890.3	419.2	40089.9	4127.0	-	0
BTO	John Hancock Financial Opportuniti	Holding and other Investment Office	12/31/18	20.2	7.2	663.2	542.7	98	4746572
HEQ	John Hancock Hedged Equity & Inc	Holding and other Investment Office	12/31/18	10.0	7.7	178.9	176.6	38	2249289
JHS	John Hancock Income Securities Tr	Holding and other Investment Office	10/31/19	11.3	6.9	278.8	181.4	42	3827786
HTY	John Hancock Investment Trust	Holding and other Investment Office	8/31/92	3.9	2.6	119.5	119.5	-	0
JHI	John Hancock Investors Trust	Holding and other Investment Office	10/31/19	14.5	10.4	249.8	160.0	64	2339196
HPI	John Hancock Preferred Income Fu	Holding and other Investment Office	7/31/19	50.6	34.8	855.6	558.2	78	2494260
PDT	John Hancock Premium Dividend F	Holding and other Investment Office	10/31/19	56.6	34.9	1161.8	764.5	100	4432904
JNJ	Johnson & Johnson	Pharmaceuticals	12/30/18	81581.0	15297.0	152954.0	59752.0	3795	2329753302
JCI	Johnson Controls International plc	Miscellaneous Consumer Goods	9/30/19	23968.0	5674.0	42287.0	19766.0	1126	888263782
JLL	Jones Lang LaSalle Inc	Property, Real Estate & Developmen	12/31/18	16318.4	484.5	10025.5	3691.5	611	56728730
JPM	JPMorgan Chase & Co	Banking	12/31/18	131412.0	32474.0	2622532.0	256515.0	3599	2998703928
JMEI	Jumei International Holding Ltd	Retail - Apparel and Accessories	12/31/18	4288.9	117.2	5142.2	3671.1	69	13985011
JMIA	Jumia Technologies AG	Consumer Goods	12/31/18	130.6	-170.1	142.0	50.0	-	0
JIH	Juniper Industrial Holdings Inc	Business Services	8/29/19	-	-0.0	0.1	0.0	-	0
JNPR	Juniper Networks Inc	Peripherals	12/31/18	4647.5	566.9	9363.3	4823.2	705	378973728
JP	Jupai Holdings Ltd	Wealth Management	12/31/18	1321.7	-387.7	1980.5	1339.0	25	3603378
JE	Just Energy Group Inc	Electric Utilities	3/31/19	3812.5	-122.7	1746.1	30.9	-	0
LRN	K12 Inc	Educational Services	6/30/19	1015.8	37.2	819.6	633.4	263	43471599
KAI	Kadant Inc	Industrial Machinery & Equipment	12/29/18	633.8	60.4	725.7	373.0	222	14872865
KDMN	Kadmon Holdings Inc	Pharmaceuticals	12/31/18	1.4	-54.3	144.7	88.4	106	87959409
KAMN	Kaman Corp.	Industrial Machinery & Equipment	12/31/18	1875.4	54.2	1460.3	633.2	270	30529249
KSU	Kansas City Southern	Rail	12/31/18	2714.0	627.4	9469.8	4813.0	872	118783604
KAR	KAR Auction Services Inc.	Retail - Automotive	12/31/18	3769.6	328.0	7206.2	1464.2	507	169685864
KMF	Kayne Anderson Midstream/Energy	Holding and other Investment Office	11/30/18	12.4	-4.6	917.6	614.6	96	14579769
KYN	Kayne Anderson MLP/Midstream In	Holding and other Investment Office	11/30/18	25.4	-53.1	3483.9	2066.3	288	40434749
KB	KB Financial Group, Inc.	Banking	12/31/18	29802922.0	3061191.6	79588298.0	35703916.0	209	29986095
KBH	KB HOME	Builders	11/30/18	4547.0	170.4	5073.6	2087.5	425	99424325
KBR	KBR Inc	IT Services	12/31/18	4913.0	281.0	5072.0	1718.0	409	185440436
K	Kellogg Co	Food	12/29/18	13547.0	1336.0	17780.0	2601.0	1091	447803190
KEM	KEMET Corp.	Electrical Equipment	3/31/19	1382.8	206.6	1318.1	639.4	309	63150404
KMPR	Kemper Corp (DE)	General Insurance	12/31/18	3725.1	190.1	11544.9	3050.1	383	52458960
KMT	Kennametal Inc.	Industrial Machinery & Equipment	6/30/19	2375.2	241.9	2656.3	1335.2	414	98291877
KW	Kennedy-Wilson Holdings Inc	Property, Real Estate & Developmen	12/31/18	773.5	150.0	7357.1	1246.7	4	2975087
KEN	Kenon Holdings Ltd	Energy	12/31/18	364.0	434.2	1455.1	649.0	19	857813
KDP	Keurig Dr Pepper Inc	Beverages	12/31/18	7442.0	586.0	48918.0	22533.0	577	332730983
KEY	KeyCorp	Banking	12/31/18	7393.0	1866.0	139613.0	15595.0	1116	966377815
KEYS	Keysight Technologies Inc	Industrial Machinery & Equipment	10/31/19	4303.0	621.0	6623.0	3004.0	779	182767286
KRC	Kilroy Realty Corp	REITs	12/31/18	747.3	258.4	7765.7	3929.9	415	138194964
KRP	Kimbell Royalty Partners LP	Oil Royalty Traders	12/31/18	70.3	-52.3	753.3	364.4	57	13843660

| EARNINGS PER SHARE | | | | | | P/E RATIO | | DIVIDENDS PER SHARE | | | AV. YLD | DIV. DECLARED | | PRICE RANGE | |
| QUARTERLY | | | ANNUAL | | | | | | | | % | | | 2018 | |
1st	2nd	3rd	2018	2017	2016			2018	2017	2016		AMOUNT	PAYABLE		
-	-	-	0.93	1.08	1.14	16.1 -	13.6	1.01	1.13	1.24	7.1	0.09640	1/31/20	14.9 -	12.7
-	-	0.36	2.14	2.75	2.06	-		1.19	1.15	1.11		0.310	18/53/27	-	
-	-	0.57	-1.03	2.75	1.98	-		1.68	1.63	1.60	10.5	0.48440Z	1/27/20	17.3 -	14.7
-	-	-	0.42	0.41	0.42	19.3 -	16.8	0.41	0.40	0.39	5.3	0.0316M	1/31/20	8.1 -	7.0
-	-	-	0.73	0.78	0.85	17.6 -	15.6	0.72	0.85	0.85	5.9	0.05M	1/31/20	12.9 -	11.4
-	-	-	0.71	0.76	0.83	18.2 -	15.9	0.72	0.78	0.82	5.9	0.0489M	1/31/20	12.9 -	11.3
-	-	-	0.75	0.69	0.81	18.4 -	15.7	0.63	0.70	0.78	4.9	0.0483M	1/31/20	13.8 -	11.8
-	-	-										0.0487M	1/31/20	13.0 -	11.4
-	-	-	0.23	0.29	0.31	18.9 -	17.3	0.25	0.29	0.32	6.0	0.0240	1/31/20	4.3 -	4.0
-	-	-	0.75	0.80	0.89	17.6 -	15.5	0.76	0.81	0.88	6.1	0.0516M	1/31/20	13.2 -	11.7
-	-	-	0.69	0.72	0.87	20.1 -	17.6	0.69	0.77	0.83	5.2	0.0458M	1/31/20	13.9 -	12.1
-	-	-	0.77	0.79	0.85	20.4 -	17.8	0.74	0.79	0.84	4.9	0.0588M	1/31/20	15.7 -	13.7
-	-	2.54	-0.75	2.60	4.90			0.70			1.1	0.70Z	1/15/20	78.9 -	49.9
-	-0.82	-	-1.94	-2.65	-3.02									27.5 -	10.7
-	-	0.06	-0.01	-0.26	-0.32			0.44	0.22		1.7	0.130Y	18/53/27	31.1 -	19.7
-	-0.26	-	-5.20	-2.55	-5.71									16.7 -	5.5
-	-	0.29	1.24	5.88	0.76	130.2 -	88.7							161.5 -	110.0
-	-	0.37	1.27	0.69	0.42	29.3 -	23.2	2.37	2.24	2.00	7.2	0.61850Y	18/53/27	37.2 -	29.4
0.06	-	-	25.91	5.23	-2.18	0.6 -	0.2	23.87			268.3			15.1 -	4.8
-	-	0.31	0.97	0.29	-0.10			0.18	0.13						
-	-	-0.12	-0.95	1.56	0.55						1.6	0.56250Z	12/16/19	14.5 -	7.8
-	0.13	-	0.33	0.13	0.04	47.7 -	0.0	55.66	1.25	370.32	498.2			15.7 -	0.0
-	-	0.86	2.55	2.43	2.36	4.2 -	3.0	1.90	0.83	0.78	21.2			10.8 -	7.7
-	-	1.34	3.76	1.28	2.07	19.7 -	12.5	0.54	0.51	0.37	0.9	0.1470Y	18/53/27	74.2 -	47.1
-	-	-	1.36	1.51	1.57	10.3 -	9.0	1.28	1.48	1.60	9.5	0.10	1/31/20	14.0 -	12.2
-	-	0.05	0.27	0.50	0.47	44.3 -	30.8	-	-					11.9 -	8.3
-	-	0.05	1.27	0.55	0.10	5.6 -	0.7	-	-			1.15G7Y	4/1/19	7.2 -	0.9
0.26	-	-	0.49	0.69	1.32	88.6 -	47.2	0.32	0.32	0.32	1.0	0.080Y	18/53/27	43.4 -	23.1
-	-	3.80	1.17	2.42	1.73	83.2 -	49.0	0.75	0.45		0.9	0.190Y	18/53/27	97.3 -	57.3
-	0.12	-	0.33	0.62	0.55	60.7 -	32.4	0.28	0.30	0.98	1.9			20.0 -	10.7
-	-	0.58	2.61	3.93	1.66			1.40	0.64			0.360	11/25/19		
-	-	-	0.09	0.12	0.06	106.3 -	90.1	1.88	0.94	0.88	21.6	0.1259B	12/27/19	9.6 -	8.1
-	-	0.06	0.31	-0.70	-0.29	139.3 -	110.9	1.00	0.45		2.5	0.2250Y	18/53/27	43.2 -	34.4
-	-	0.15	2.90	0.45	0.34	7.5 -	5.6	0.45	0.33	0.25	2.4	0.150Y	18/53/27	21.6 -	16.2
-	-	0.17	1.36	0.00	-2.17	17.9 -	10.8	-	-					24.4 -	14.7
-	-	0.26	2.10	1.10	2.42	10.5 -	8.2	1.40	1.40	1.40	7.0	0.43750Z	1/15/20	22.0 -	17.3
-	-	-	-0.39	-0.57	-0.53			-	-					7.8 -	1.4
-	-	1.10	2.63	1.08	14.03	9.4 -	3.8							24.7 -	10.1
-	-	-0.21	-0.10	-0.74	0.13			0.36	0.36	0.39	9.6	0.42970Z	3/30/20	4.6 -	0.0
-	-	1.04	3.23	2.53	2.27	39.1 -	21.6	0.40	0.40	0.40	0.4	0.10Y	12/30/19	126.3 -	69.7
-	-	-	0.39	0.37	0.50	93.1 -	73.9	1.66	1.48	1.48	5.0	0.550	12/31/19	36.3 -	28.8
-	-	-	0.63	0.52	0.42	23.9 -	20.5	1.50	1.66	1.50	10.6	0.3760	12/31/19	15.1 -	12.9
-	-	-	0.66	0.75	0.79	22.4 -	19.4	0.74	0.81	0.85	5.2	0.21970	12/31/19	14.8 -	12.8
-	-	-										0.37160	12/16/19	7.1 -	6.5
-	-	-	1.21	1.28	1.32	14.7 -	11.9	1.24	1.30	1.39	7.5	0.32740	12/31/19	17.8 -	14.4
-	-	-	1.51	1.61	1.60	16.1 -	12.7	1.68	1.68	1.68	7.4	0.12350	1/31/20	24.3 -	19.1
-	-	-	0.85	1.11	0.98	21.6 -	16.4	1.70	1.47	1.11	10.1	0.09750	1/31/20	18.4 -	13.9
-	-	0.66	5.61	0.47	5.93	26.1 -	22.4	3.54	3.32	3.15	2.6	0.950Y	18/53/27	146.4 -	125.7
-	-	4.79	2.32	1.71	-1.30			1.04	1.00	1.16		0.260	1/10/20		
-	-	2.47	10.54	5.55	6.98	16.5 -	11.6	0.82	0.72	0.64	0.6	0.430Y	18/53/27	174.1 -	121.9
-	-	2.68	9.00	6.31	6.19	15.5 -	10.8	2.48	2.04	1.84	2.2	0.90Y	18/53/27	139.4 -	97.1
-	-	-	0.83	-0.25	0.95	33.5 -	20.5	-	-					27.8 -	17.0
-	-	-	-1.70	-1.65				-	-					47.0 -	5.3
-	-	-						-	-					9.8 -	0.0
-	-	0.29	1.60	0.80	1.53	17.9 -	14.2	0.72	0.40	0.40	2.8	0.190	18/53/27	28.7 -	22.6
0.04	-	-	-1.93	1.99	1.03			3.68	3.31		131.6			5.5 -	1.4
-1.85	-	-	2.62	2.42	0.43	2.2 -	0.4	0.50	0.50	0.50	14.3	0.53130	9/30/19	5.8 -	1.1
-0.25	-	-	0.68	0.01	0.23	54.4 -	27.9	-	-					37.0 -	19.0
-	-	1.41	5.30	2.75	2.88	20.2 -	14.7	0.87	0.82	0.74	1.0	0.230Y	2/6/20	107.1 -	78.0
-	-	-0.49	-0.58	-1.42	-9.74			-	-		%			5.0 -	1.6
-	-	5.08	1.92	1.75	2.10	35.3 -	28.4	0.80	0.80	0.72	1.3	0.20Y	1/9/20	67.7 -	54.5
-	-	1.81	6.13	9.16	4.43	25.3 -	15.2	1.44	1.38	1.32	1.2	0.250Y	18/53/27	155.1 -	92.9
-	-	0.27	2.42	2.62	1.60	11.4 -	7.1	1.40	1.31	1.19	6.3	0.190Y	18/53/27	27.6 -	17.3
-	-	-	-0.18	0.14	-0.07			1.20	1.30	1.50	10.9	0.0750	3/31/20	12.3 -	9.5
-	-	-	-0.45	-0.45	-0.61			1.80	1.90	2.20	12.1	0.07290	3/2/20	16.4 -	12.3
-	-	-1100.00	7676.00	8257.00	5559.00	0.0 -	0.0	1924.02	1242.96	968.55	5052.2			43.5 -	30.8
-	-	0.73	1.71	1.85	1.12	21.5 -	11.4	0.10	0.10	0.10	0.4	0.090Y	18/53/27	36.8 -	19.5
-	-	0.39	1.99	3.06	-0.43	15.4 -	7.8	0.32	0.32	0.32	1.4	0.080Y	18/53/27	30.7 -	15.5
-	-	0.72	3.83	3.62	1.96	18.1 -	13.6	2.20	2.12	2.04	3.7	0.570Y	18/53/27	69.2 -	52.1
-	-0.26	-	4.34	0.87	-1.17	6.2 -	3.7	-	-			0.050Y	8/26/19	27.1 -	15.9
-	-	1.91	3.22	2.33	0.33	28.2 -	20.2	0.96	0.96	0.96	1.2	0.280Y	18/53/27	90.7 -	65.0
0.08	-	-	2.42	0.61	-2.83	17.2 -	11.5	0.80	0.80	0.80	2.3	0.20Y	18/53/27	41.5 -	27.8
-	-	0.15	1.04	0.83	0.01	22.4 -	17.3	0.78	0.70	0.56	3.7	0.220Z	1/2/20	23.3 -	18.0
-	-	-	8.07	4.40	-7.67			1.86				1.210	11/26/19		
-	-	0.21	0.53	5.89	4.54	58.9 -	47.2	104.48	2.32	2.12	372.6	0.150Y	18/53/27	31.2 -	25.0
-	-	0.39	1.71	1.13	0.80	11.9 -	8.8	0.56	0.38	0.33	3.2	0.35160Y	18/53/27	20.4 -	15.0
-	-	0.83	0.86	0.56	1.95	126.8 -	67.8	-	-					109.1 -	58.3
-	-	0.41	2.55	1.51	2.97	33.1 -	24.1	1.79	1.65	3.38	2.3	0.4850Z	18/53/27	84.5 -	61.4
-	-	-0.73	-3.08	0.10	-10.28			1.66	0.84		10.4	0.380	2/10/20	18.5 -	13.3

SYMBOL	COMPANY	NATURE OF BUSINESS	FISCAL YEAR-END	TOTAL REV. $MILL	NET INCOME $MILL	TOTAL ASSETS $MILL	NET STK EQUITY $MILL	NO OF INST	INST. HOLDINGS (SHARES)
KMB	Kimberly-Clark Corp.	Household & Personal Products	12/31/18	18486.0	1410.0	14518.0	-223.0	2070	333700565
KIM	Kimco Realty Corp	REITs	12/31/18	1164.8	497.8	10999.1	5333.8	676	460634727
KMI	Kinder Morgan Inc.	Equipment & Services	12/31/18	14144.0	1609.0	78866.0	33678.0	1437	1716658217
KFS	Kingsway Financial Services Inc (D	General Insurance	12/31/17	193.2	-15.5	484.6	44.1	32	10154020
KGC	Kinross Gold Corp.	Precious Metals	12/31/18	3212.6	-23.6	8063.8	4506.7	404	722929405
KEX	Kirby Corp.	Shipping	12/31/18	2970.7	78.5	5871.6	3213.2	413	76141922
KL	Kirkland Lake Gold Ltd	Precious Metals	12/31/18	915.9	273.9	1710.2	1263.1		0
KRG	Kite Realty Group Trust	REITs	12/31/18	354.2	-46.6	3172.0	1412.7	307	99627040
KKR	KKR & Co Inc	Finance Intermediaries & Services	12/31/18	2395.8	1131.1	50743.4	8649.6	598	460127726
KIO	KKR Income Opportunities Fund	Finance Intermediaries & Services	10/31/19	41.6	30.3	483.0	316.7	53	4926998
KREF	KKR Real Estate Finance Trust Inc	REITs	12/31/18	203.7	89.7	5231.8	1135.2	120	45372971
KNX	Knight-Swift Transportation Holding	Trucking	12/31/18	5344.1	419.3	7911.9	5460.9	458	163273952
KNL	Knoll Inc	Office Equipment & Furniture	12/31/18	1302.3	73.2	1226.9	386.3	241	59834751
KNOP	KNOT Offshore Partners LP	Equipment & Services	12/31/18	279.5	82.2	1836.8	732.0	66	13313696
KN	Knowles Corp	Electronic Instruments & Related Pro	12/31/18	826.9	67.7	1547.9	1211.6	351	113997450
KSS	Kohl's Corp.	Retail - General Merchandise/Depart	2/2/19	20229.0	801.0	12469.0	5527.0	991	200195351
PHG	Koninklijke Philips NV	Medical Instruments & Equipment	12/31/18	18121.0	1090.0	26019.0	12088.0	438	45556685
KTB	Kontoor Brands Inc	Manufacturing	12/29/18	2764.0	263.1	2458.5	1723.5	451	60324080
KTB	Kontoor Brands Inc	Manufacturing	12/29/18	2764.0	263.1	2458.5	1723.5	451	60324080
KOP	Koppers Holdings Inc	Paper & Forest Products	12/31/18	1710.2	23.4	1479.9	56.2	253	24954816
KEP	Korea Electric Power Corp	Electric Utilities	12/31/18	60627610.0	-1314567.0	85249061.0	69743925.0	166	98607093
KF	Korea Fund Inc (The)	Holding and other Investment Office	6/30/19	3.6	1.2	172.7	168.1	45	4300727
KFY	Korn Ferry	Business Services	4/30/19	1973.9	102.7	2334.9	1240.7	358	66478648
KOS	Kosmos Energy Ltd (DE)	Production & Extraction	12/31/18	902.4	-94.0	4088.2	941.5	231	508904134
KRA	Kraton Corp	Plastics	12/31/18	2011.7	67.0	2894.7	715.1	242	36193676
KR	Kroger Co (The)	Retail - Food & Beverage, Drug & To	2/2/19	121162.0	3110.0	38118.0	7886.0	1157	845073885
KRO	Kronos Worldwide Inc	Specialty Chemicals	12/31/18	1661.9	205.0	1898.1	839.8	180	27700017
KT	KT Corp (Korea)	Services	12/31/18	23460143.0	688464.0	32188830.0	13202691.0	250	217438224
LB	L Brands, Inc	Retail - Apparel and Accessories	2/2/19	13237.0	644.0	8090.0	-869.0	699	243835951
LHX	L3Harris Technologies Inc	Defense	6/28/19	6801.0	949.0	10117.0	3363.0	1326	231217593
LZB	La-Z-Boy Inc.	Furniture	4/27/19	1745.4	68.6	1059.8	682.5	312	53455861
LH	Laboratory Corporation of America	Diagnostic & Health Related Service	12/31/18	11333.4	883.7	16185.3	6971.4	1077	118016964
LADR	Ladder Capital Corp	REITs	12/31/18	595.1	180.0	6272.9	1445.2	231	66780898
LAIX	LAIX Inc	Educational Services	12/31/18	637.2	-488.1	950.4	218.9	14	6727624
LW	Lamb Weston Holdings Inc	Food	5/26/19	3756.5	478.6	3048.1	-4.6	719	143925804
LKB 04	Landesbank Baden-Wurttemberg	Banking	12/31/17	13319.0	416.0	237713.0	13331.0		0
LCI	Lannett Co., Inc.	Pharmaceuticals	6/30/19	655.4	-272.1	1187.4	334.0	237	45758738
LPI	Laredo Petroleum, Inc	Production & Extraction	12/31/18	1105.8	324.6	2420.3	1174.2	255	329507894
LVS	Las Vegas Sands Corp	Hotels, Restaurants & Travel	12/31/18	13729.0	2413.0	22547.0	5684.0	932	334239107
LTM	LATAM Airlines Group SA	Airlines/Air Freight	12/31/18	9895.5	181.9	17566.8	3666.8	122	19477701
EL	Lauder (Estee) Cos., Inc. (The)	Household & Personal Products	6/30/19	14863.0	1785.0	13156.0	4386.0	1263	247839337
LGI	Lazard Global Total Return & Incom	Holding and other Investment Office	12/31/18	5.7	2.4	172.0	146.2	52	2964704
LAZ	Lazard Ltd	Finance Intermediaries & Services	12/31/18	2884.8	527.1	4997.2	916.9	406	100013557
LCII	LCI Industries	Auto Parts	12/31/18	2475.8	148.6	1243.9	706.3	322	30217932
LEAF	Leaf Group Ltd	Internet & Software	12/31/18	155.0	-23.2	95.1	66.7		0
LEA	Lear Corp.	Auto Parts	12/31/18	21148.5	1149.8	11600.7	4200.7	688	83870568
LEE	Lee Enterprises, Inc.	Publishing	9/29/19	509.9	14.3	555.2	-38.5	163	34079521
LM	Legg Mason, Inc.	Wealth Management	3/31/19	2903.3	-28.5	7794.1	3659.8	577	111164847
LEG	Leggett & Platt, Inc.	Furniture	12/31/18	4269.5	305.9	3382.0	1157.0	682	139808483
LEH 06	Lehman Brothers, Inc.	Finance Intermediaries & Services	11/30/02	12124.0	740.0	196219.0	3152.0		0
LDOS	Leidos Holdings Inc	IT Services	12/28/18	10194.0	581.0	8770.0	3308.0	693	150108262
LEJU	Leju Holdings Ltd	Property, Real Estate & Developmen	12/31/18	462.0	-13.5	416.7	244.1	25	1683979
LC	LendingClub Corp	Credit & Lending	12/31/18	1181.1	-128.3	3819.5	869.2	174	111159200
LEN	Lennar Corp	Builders	11/30/18	20571.6	1695.8	28566.2	14581.5	881	320221184
LII	Lennox International Inc	Industrial Machinery & Equipment	12/31/18	3883.9	359.0	1817.2	-149.6	569	35621881
LEVI	Levi Strauss & Co.	Apparel, Footwear & Accessories	11/25/18	5575.4	283.1	3542.7	959.3	168	42036430
LXP	Lexington Realty Trust	REITs	12/31/18	395.3	227.4	2953.8	1329.9	403	270572906
LPL	LG Display Co Ltd	Electrical Equipment	12/31/18	24336571.0	-207239.0	33175710.0	13979189.0	130	23213680
USA	Liberty All-Star Equity Fund	Holding and other Investment Office	12/31/18	22.8	9.6	1208.4	1183.1	172	40543810
ASG	Liberty All-Star Growth Fund Inc.	Holding and other Investment Office	12/31/18	1.3	-0.8	189.5	183.4	59	5796486
LBRT	Liberty Oilfield Services Inc	Equipment & Services	12/31/18	2155.1	126.3	1116.6	433.1	138	85302647
LPT	Liberty Property Trust	REITs	12/31/18	704.9	479.6	6934.4	3329.9	604	191470380
LSI	Life Storage Inc	REITs	12/31/18	550.9	206.6	3892.2	2057.7	450	54376955
LITB	Lightinthebox Holding Co., Ltd.	Retail - Apparel and Accessories	12/31/18	227.5	-59.6	103.6	-7.8	10	5510964
LLY	Lilly (Eli) & Co	Pharmaceuticals	12/31/18	24555.7	3232.0	43908.4	9828.7	2125	917603513
LLY	Lilly (Eli) & Co	Pharmaceuticals	12/31/18	24555.7	3232.0	43908.4	9828.7	2125	917603513
LNC	Lincoln National Corp.	Life & Health	12/31/18	16424.0	1641.0	298147.0	14350.0	1016	213642183
LIN	Linde plc	Specialty Chemicals	12/31/18	14900.0	4381.0	93386.0	51596.0	1041	403899082
LNN	Lindsay Corp	Industrial Machinery & Equipment	8/31/19	444.1	2.2	500.3	268.2	236	16548697
LN	LINE Corporation	IT Services	12/31/18	207182.0	-3718.0	486587.0	189916.0	85	8390277
LINX	Linx SA	Internet & Software	12/31/18	685.6	71.1	1647.7	1057.2		0
LGF A	Lions Gate Entertainment Corp	Entertainment	3/31/19	3680.5	-284.2	8408.9	2918.7	294	90948782
LAD	Lithia Motors Inc	Retail - Automotive	12/31/18	11821.4	265.7	5384.0	1197.2	413	30800633
LAC	Lithium Americas Corp (New)	Mining	12/31/18	4.8	-28.3	103.9	82.3	59	6755235
LYV	Live Nation Entertainment Inc	Entertainment	12/31/18	10787.8	60.2	8496.9	1099.0	594	171789113
LTHM	Livent Corp	Specialty Chemicals	12/31/18	442.5	126.1	660.0	487.9	340	152254089
LTHM	Livent Corp	Specialty Chemicals	12/31/18	442.5	126.1	660.0	487.9	340	152254089
RAMP	LiveRamp Holdings Inc	IT Services	3/31/19	285.6	1028.5	1472.9	1330.8	362	104393729
LYG	Lloyds Banking Group Plc	Banking	12/31/18	26430.0	4302.0	797598.0	49925.0	415	383480028
SCD	LMP Capital & Income Fund Inc	Holding and other Investment Office	11/30/18	15.4	9.6	346.5	256.0	48	5174578

EARNINGS PER SHARE QUARTERLY			ANNUAL			P/E RATIO		DIVIDENDS PER SHARE			AV. YLD	DIV. DECLARED		PRICE RANGE 2018	
1st	2nd	3rd	2018	2017	2016			2018	2017	2016	%	AMOUNT	PAYABLE		
-	-	1.94	4.03	6.40	5.99	35.4 -	26.8	4.00	3.88	3.68	3.1	1.070Y	18/53/27	142.7 -	107.9
-	-	0.14	1.02	0.87	0.79	21.3 -	14.3	1.12	1.09	1.03	5.9	0.32810Z	18/53/27	21.8 -	14.6
-	-	0.22	0.66	0.01	0.25	32.4 -	23.8	0.72	0.50	0.50	3.6	0.250Y	18/53/27	21.4 -	15.7
-	-0.20	-	-	-0.73	0.02									3.1 -	0.0
-	0.06	-	-0.02	0.35	-0.08							0.080	3/28/13	7.2 -	3.0
-	-	0.80	1.31	5.62	2.62	68.4 -	50.8					0.05	18/53/27	89.6 -	66.6
-	-	0.83	1.29	0.63	0.34	52.4 -	19.3	0.09	0.03	-	0.2	0.060	1/13/20	67.5 -	24.9
-	-	-0.24	-0.56	0.14	0.01			1.27	1.21	1.14	7.8	0.31750Z	12/27/19	19.7 -	13.8
-	-	0.43	2.06	1.95	0.59	14.5 -	9.1	0.29	-	-	1.1	0.40630Y	18/53/27	29.8 -	18.7
-	-	-	1.51	1.59	1.61	10.6 -	9.5	1.55	1.59	1.50	10.0	0.1250	1/31/20	16.1 -	14.4
-	-	0.41	1.58	1.30	1.61	13.2 -	11.9	1.69	0.99	1.22	8.4	0.430Z	1/15/20	20.9 -	18.9
-	-	0.44	2.36	4.34	1.16	16.4 -	10.7	0.24	0.06	-	0.7	0.060Y	12/27/19	38.7 -	25.2
-	-	0.35	1.49	1.63	1.68	18.9 -	11.1	0.60	0.60	0.60	2.6	0.170Y	12/31/19	28.1 -	16.6
-	-	-	2.22	2.04	1.54			2.08	2.08	2.08		0.520	2/13/20		
-	-	0.27	0.74	0.75	-0.47	30.7 -	16.7	-						22.7 -	12.4
-	-	0.78	5.12	3.11	3.46	14.7 -	8.6	2.20	2.00	1.80	3.9	0.670Y	18/53/27	75.5 -	44.3
-	-	0.40	1.16	1.75	1.56	42.3 -	28.5	0.67	0.70	0.67	1.6			49.1 -	33.0
-	-	-	0.25	-	-			-				0.560Y	12/20/19	42.5 -	26.1
-	-	-	0.25	-	-			-				0.560Y	12/20/19	40.8 -	0.0
-	-	0.94	1.10	1.32	1.39	39.8 -	16.3	-	0.00	0.00		0.250Y	1/5/15	43.8 -	17.9
-	-	-2326.00	2048.00	2023.00	980.00			395.06	980.17	1572.05	3241.7	0.08821	4/20/97	15.8 -	10.2
-	-	-	0.20	0.16	0.11	159.0 -	0.0	4.02	0.33	4.35	14.1	0.0710	1/3/20	31.8 -	0.0
-	0.77	-	2.35	1.47	0.58	20.8 -	15.0	0.40	0.40	0.40	1.0	0.10Y	1/15/20	48.9 -	35.2
-	-	0.04	-0.23	-0.57	-0.74			-				0.04520	18/53/27	7.5 -	4.1
-	-	0.58	2.08	3.07	3.43	17.6 -	9.8	-						36.6 -	20.4
-	-	0.32	2.09	2.05	2.06	14.3 -	10.0	0.49	0.45	0.40	1.9	0.160Y	18/53/27	29.8 -	20.8
-	-	0.17	1.77	3.06	0.37	9.0 -	5.5	0.68	0.60	0.60	5.1	0.180Y	12/12/19	15.9 -	9.8
-	-	-435.00	2809.00	1945.00	2902.00	0.0 -	0.0	500.11	399.42	250.38	4110.4	-		14.7 -	11.0
-	-	-0.91	3.42	3.98	4.22	8.4 -	4.6	2.40	4.40	4.00	10.5	0.30Y	18/53/27	28.9 -	15.9
1.90	-	-	5.92	4.44	2.59	36.3 -	22.0	2.28	2.12	2.00	1.2	0.750Y	18/53/27	214.7 -	130.1
-	0.48	-	1.67	1.73	1.55	22.3 -	16.2	0.46	0.42	0.36	1.4	0.140Y	12/13/19	37.2 -	27.0
-	-	2.25	8.61	12.21	7.02	20.7 -	14.4	-				0.0826L	6/30/00	178.1 -	123.7
-	-	0.26	1.84	1.13	1.06	10.0 -	8.4	1.53	1.22	1.28	9.0	0.340Z	1/3/20	18.4 -	15.5
-	-	-	-19.17	-13.59	-5.28			-						13.2 -	0.0
-	0.95	-	2.82	2.22	-	30.5 -	20.9	0.76	0.38	-	1.1	0.230Y	2/28/20	86.2 -	59.0
-0.32	-	-	0.75	-0.02	1.20	19.3 -	7.0	-				0.0076	12/14/79	14.5 -	5.2
-	-1.14		1.39	2.29	-1.16	3.0 -	1.5	-						4.2 -	2.1
-	-	0.69	3.07	3.54	2.10	22.8 -	16.7	3.00	2.92	2.88	5.0	0.770Z	18/53/27	69.9 -	51.4
-0.10	-	-	0.30	0.26	0.13	40.8 -	25.5	0.03	0.02	-	0.3			12.3 -	7.7
1.61	-	-	2.95	3.35	2.96	70.5 -	42.3	1.48	1.32	1.14	0.8	0.480Y	18/53/27	207.9 -	124.9
-	-	-	0.25	0.21	0.40	66.2 -	52.0	2.71	0.98	0.95	17.5	0.10650	2/24/20	16.6 -	13.0
-	-	0.40	4.06	1.91	2.92			3.03	2.81	2.69		0.470	18/53/27		
-	-	1.42	5.83	5.24	5.20	18.6 -	11.2	2.35	2.05	1.40	2.6	0.650Y	12/20/19	108.7 -	65.2
-	-	-0.17	-0.94	-1.52	-0.10			-						9.1 -	2.8
-	-	3.58	17.22	18.59	13.33	9.2 -	6.2	2.80	2.00	1.20	2.1	0.750Y	18/53/27	158.8 -	106.0
-	-	0.10	0.82	0.50	0.64	4.4 -	1.5	-				0.190Y	10/1/08	3.6 -	1.2
-	0.74	-	3.01	2.18	-0.25	13.3 -	8.6	1.12	0.88	0.80	3.2	0.40Y	18/53/27	40.0 -	25.8
-	-	0.74	2.26	2.13	2.76	24.4 -	15.7	1.50	1.42	1.34	3.5	0.40Y	18/53/27	55.2 -	35.5
-	-	1.11	3.80	2.38	2.35	25.9 -	13.5	1.28	1.28	14.92	1.7	0.340Y	18/53/27	98.5 -	51.3
-	-	-	-0.10	-1.19	-0.07			-						2.1 -	0.0
-	-	0.00	-1.50	-1.90	-1.90			-						18.1 -	11.1
-	-	1.59	5.44	3.38	3.85	11.4 -	7.3	0.16	0.16	0.16	0.3	0.1250Y	18/53/27	62.0 -	39.5
-	-	2.94	8.74	7.14	6.32	33.5 -	24.3	2.43	1.96	1.65	1.0	0.770Y	18/53/27	292.7 -	212.3
-	-	0.30	-	-	-			-				0.15GY	10/17/19	24.0 -	16.1
-	-	0.59	0.93	0.33	0.37	12.0 -	8.7	0.71	0.70	0.69	7.3	0.81250Z	2/18/20	11.2 -	8.1
1770.00	-	-	-579.00	5038.00	2534.00			248.34	249.38	246.60	3409.0	-		9.8 -	5.1
-	-	-	0.05	0.04	0.04	135.4 -	105.6	0.68	0.56	0.48	10.9	0.170	3/9/20	6.8 -	5.3
-	-	-	-0.03	-0.02	-0.02			0.46	0.42	0.36	8.0	0.130	3/9/20	6.5 -	4.4
-	-	0.15	1.81	-		9.7 -	4.5	0.10	-	-	0.8	0.050Y	3/20/20	17.6 -	8.1
-	-	0.66	3.24	1.91	2.43	19.2 -	12.5	1.60	1.60	1.90	3.1	0.410Z	18/53/27	62.2 -	40.6
-	-	2.99	4.43	2.07	1.96	25.0 -	20.4	4.00	3.95	3.70	4.0	1.070Z	18/53/27	110.6 -	90.2
-	-	-0.02	-0.44	-0.07	-0.07			-						1.7 -	0.7
-	-	1.37	3.13	-0.19	2.58	42.3 -	34.1	2.25	2.08	2.04	1.9	0.740Y	18/53/27	132.4 -	106.8
-	-	1.37	3.13	-0.19	2.58	40.3 -	39.0	2.25	2.08	2.04	1.8	0.740Y	18/53/27	126.2 -	122.1
-	-	-0.83	7.40	9.22	5.03	9.1 -	6.9	1.32	1.16	1.00	2.2	0.40Y	18/53/27	67.2 -	50.8
-	-	1.35	13.11	4.32	5.21			3.30	3.15	3.00		0.8750	18/53/27		
0.77	-	-	1.88	2.17	1.85	52.4 -	41.0	1.21	1.17	1.13	1.4	0.310Y	18/53/27	98.4 -	77.2
-	-	-	-15.62	34.01	31.48			-						51.6 -	27.0
0.11	-	-	0.43	0.51	0.46	21.5 -	15.5	-						9.2 -	6.7
-	0.01	-	2.15	0.09	0.33	8.8 -	3.7	0.09	0.09	0.34	0.7	0.090Y	11/8/18	18.9 -	7.9
-	-	3.64	10.86	9.75	7.72	15.1 -	7.2	1.14	1.06	0.95	1.0	0.30Y	18/53/27	163.7 -	78.6
-	-0.07	-	-0.32	-0.44	-0.45			-						6.4 -	2.8
-	-	0.71	-0.09	-0.48	-0.23			-						73.5 -	47.7
-	-	0.12	0.99	-		14.7 -	5.7	-						14.6 -	5.6
-	-	0.12	0.99	-		13.4 -	12.8	-						13.3 -	12.7
-	-0.59	-	0.29	0.05	0.09	213.9 -	129.7	-						62.0 -	37.6
-	-	-	0.06	0.04	0.02	59.5 -	38.5	0.12	0.13	0.16	4.1	0.48440	7/15/15	3.6 -	2.3
-	-	-	0.53	0.47	0.50	29.3 -	20.4	1.24	1.24	1.24	9.2	0.310	12/31/19	15.5 -	10.8

SYMBOL	COMPANY	NATURE OF BUSINESS	FISCAL YEAR-END	TOTAL REV. $MILL	NET INCOME $MILL	TOTAL ASSETS $MILL	NET STK EQUITY $MILL	NO OF INST	INST. HOLDINGS (SHARES)
LMT	Lockheed Martin Corp	Defense	12/31/18	53762.0	5046.0	44876.0	1394.0	2217	286120215
L	Loews Corp.	General Insurance	12/31/18	14066.0	636.0	78316.0	18518.0	721	255382346
LOMA	Loma Negra Compania Industrial Ar	Manufacturing	12/31/18	26806.9	1799.9	32865.8	15178.7	108	45676476
LPX	Louisiana-Pacific Corp	Paper & Forest Products	12/31/18	2828.0	394.6	2514.1	1700.2	455	149838703
LOW	Lowe's Companies Inc	Retail - Hardware & Home Improvem	2/1/19	71309.0	2314.0	34508.0	3644.0	2189	781007392
LXU	LSB Industries, Inc.	Specialty Chemicals	12/31/18	378.2	-72.2	1148.3	544.4	170	25541353
LTC	LTC Properties, Inc.	REITs	12/31/18	168.6	155.0	1513.6	825.5	353	39950674
LUB	Luby's, Inc.	Hotels, Restaurants & Travel	8/28/19	323.5	-15.2	186.0	101.0	64	13253795
LL	Lumber Liquidators Holdings Inc	Retail - Hardware & Home Improvem	12/31/18	1084.6	-54.4	475.5	147.4	224	27888659
LXFR	Luxfer Holdings Plc	Industrial Machinery & Equipment	12/31/18	487.9	25.0	390.4	184.3	115	26960991
LDL	Lydall, Inc.	Industrial Machinery & Equipment	12/31/18	785.9	34.9	872.7	369.3	194	18018463
WLH	Lyon (William) Homes	Builders	12/31/18	2087.2	91.6	2929.8	863.3	206	33946303
LYB	LyondellBasell Industries NV	Diversified Chemicals	12/31/18	39004.0	4690.0	28278.0	10373.0	1106	270621515
MTB	M & T Bank Corp	Banking	12/31/18	6454.7	1918.1	120097.4	15460.2	961	135144193
MTB PRA	M & T Capital Trust IV	Banking						3	104665
MDC	M.D.C. Holdings, Inc.	Builders	12/31/18	3065.2	210.8	3001.1	1576.0	385	59371858
MHO	M/I Homes Inc	Builders	12/31/18	2286.3	107.7	2021.6	855.3	247	32089309
MAC	Macerich Co (The)	REITs	12/31/18	960.4	60.0	9026.8	2950.2	522	200922127
CLI	Mack Cali Realty Corp	REITs	12/31/18	530.6	84.1	5060.6	1486.7	341	111203511
MGU	Macquarie Global Infrastructure Tot	Holding and other Investment Office	11/30/18	23.4	15.0	438.8	298.3	66	5542450
MIC	Macquarie Infrastructure Corp	Business Services	12/31/18	1761.5	136.5	7443.8	2964.6	478	60344436
MFD	Macquarie/First Trust Global Infrastr	Holding and other Investment Office	11/30/18	12.5	9.4	134.9	92.1	42	1648416
M	Macy's Inc	Retail - General Merchandise/Depart	2/2/19	25739.0	1108.0	19194.0	6436.0	933	358190063
MCN	Madison Covered Call & Equity Stra	Holding and other Investment Office	12/31/18	3.1	1.2	146.6	144.7	51	4130910
MSG	Madison Square Garden Co (The) (	Sporting & Recreational	6/30/19	1631.1	11.4	3763.6	2620.5	400	18490636
MMP	Magellan Midstream Partners LP	Equipment & Services	12/31/18	2826.6	1333.9	7747.5	-	868	179565510
MGA	Magna International Inc	Auto Parts	12/31/18	40827.0	2296.0	25945.0	10701.0	588	210071495
MX	MagnaChip Semiconductor Corp	Semiconductors	12/31/18	750.9	-3.9	583.2	-17.3	117	34146191
MGY	Magnolia Oil & Gas Corp	Production & Extraction	12/31/18	433.2	39.1	3433.5	1676.8	166	179580425
MAIN	Main Street Capital Corp	Holding and other Investment Office	12/31/18	233.4	156.6	2553.4	1476.0	292	19510516
MMD	MainStay MacKay DefinedTerm Mu	Holding and other Investment Office	5/31/19	41.5	27.8	895.7	563.1		0
MNK	Mallinckrodt Plc	Pharmaceuticals	12/28/18	3215.6	-3607.0	10877.3	2887.3	427	90541071
MANU	Manchester United Plc	Sporting & Recreational	6/30/19	627.1	18.9	1496.5	415.2	85	37380370
MTW	Manitowoc Company Inc (The)	Construction Services	12/31/18	1846.8	-67.1	1541.9	601.3	295	57230723
MN	Manning & Napier Inc.	Wealth Management	12/31/18	161.3	3.2	202.6	159.8	69	8716484
MAN	ManpowerGroup Inc	Business Services	12/31/18	21991.2	556.7	8519.8	2624.9	615	79459282
MFC	Manulife Financial Corp	Life & Health	12/31/18	38972.0	4800.0	750271.0	46058.0	636	1068821549
MRO	Marathon Oil Corp.	Production & Extraction	12/31/18	6582.0	1096.0	21321.0	12128.0	1080	855932459
MPC	Marathon Petroleum Corp.	Refining & Marketing	12/31/18	97102.0	2780.0	92940.0	35175.0	1438	577041109
MMI	Marcus & Millichap Inc	Property, Real Estate & Developmen	12/31/18	814.8	87.3	566.4	409.6	218	27506358
MCS	Marcus Corp. (The)	Entertainment	12/27/18	707.1	53.4	989.3	490.0	254	24662764
MPX	Marine Products Corp	Leisure Equipment	12/31/18	298.6	28.5	100.9	75.2	86	5720520
HZO	MarineMax Inc	Retail - Specialty	9/30/19	1237.2	36.0	784.1	368.8	212	29912456
MKL	Markel Corp (Holding Co)	General Insurance	12/31/18	6841.3	-128.2	33306.3	9080.7	685	13261407
VAC	Marriott Vacations Worldwide Corp.	Hotels, Restaurants & Travel	12/31/18	2968.0	55.0	9018.0	3461.0	437	40669731
MMC	Marsh & McLennan Companies Inc.	Brokers & Intermediaries	12/31/18	14950.0	1650.0	21578.0	7511.0	1167	552070636
MLM	Martin Marietta Materials, Inc.	Construction Materials	12/31/18	4244.3	470.0	9551.4	4946.4	842	72242639
MAS	Masco Corp.	Retail - Hardware & Home Improvem	12/31/18	8359.0	734.0	5393.0	-111.0	920	351175482
DOOR	Masonite International Corp (New)	Construction Materials	12/30/18	2170.1	92.7	1778.5	610.4	205	29841641
MTZ	MasTec Inc. (FL)	Construction Services	12/31/18	6909.4	259.7	4440.0	1389.9	503	74375961
MA	Mastercard Inc	Business Services	12/31/18	14950.0	5859.0	24860.0	5395.0	2479	866760257
MTDR	Matador Resources Co	Production & Extraction	12/31/18	899.6	274.2	3455.5	1688.9	334	136997629
MTRN	Materion Corp	Metal Products	12/31/18	1207.8	20.8	800.3	553.9	273	22268212
MATX	Matson Inc	Shipping	12/31/18	2222.8	109.0	2430.4	755.3	296	48819637
MLP	Maui Land & Pineapple Co., Inc.	Property, Real Estate & Developmen	12/31/18	11.0	0.5	48.1	30.9	67	3785424
MAXR	Maxar Technologies Inc	Internet & Software	12/31/18	2141.0	-1264.0	5001.0	643.0	144	44671004
MMS	MAXIMUS Inc.	Business Services	9/30/19	2886.8	240.8	1745.7	1247.8	472	76170528
MXL	MaxLinear Inc	Semiconductors	12/31/18	385.0	-26.2	738.8	399.9	216	71011265
MEC	Mayville Engineering Co Inc	Metal Products	12/31/18	354.5	17.9	391.7	103.0	60	5830038
MBI	MBIA Inc.	General Insurance	12/31/18	162.0	-296.0	8076.0	1119.0	296	101798896
MKC	McCormick & Co Inc	Food	11/30/18	5408.9	933.4	10256.4	3170.9	1153	142694875
MCD	McDonald's Corp	Hotels, Restaurants & Travel	12/31/18	21025.2	5924.3	32811.2	-6258.4	2896	700014277
MUX	McEwen Mining Inc	Precious Metals	12/31/18	128.8	-44.9	616.9	485.9	171	113184164
MCK	McKesson Corp	Pharmaceuticals	3/31/19	214319.0	34.0	59672.0	8094.0	1309	206738776
MDU	MDU Resources Group Inc	Electric Utilities	12/31/18	4531.6	272.3	6988.1	2566.8	549	169784140
MTL	Mechel PAO	Non-Precious Metals	12/31/18	312574.0	12628.0	317625.0	-243401.0	79	14937107
MDLA	Medallia Inc	IT Services	1/31/19	313.6	-82.2	280.2	-6.6	94	76940633
MPW	Medical Properties Trust Inc	REITs	12/31/18	784.5	1016.7	8843.6	4547.1	603	436791146
MED	Medifast Inc	Household & Personal Products	12/31/18	501.0	55.8	169.4	109.1	345	16155902
MCC	Medley Capital Corp	Holding and other Investment Office	9/30/19	46.3	-20.9	486.3	216.4	98	19225616
MDLY	Medley Management Inc	Finance Intermediaries & Services	12/31/18	56.5	-2.4	78.2	-12.0	44	3010319
MD	Mednax, Inc.	Diagnostic & Health Related Service	12/31/18	3647.1	268.6	5934.9	3087.9	405	97781497
MDT	Medtronic PLC	Medical Instruments & Equipment	4/26/19	30557.0	4631.0	89694.0	50091.0	1868	1217195312
MRK	Merck & Co Inc	Pharmaceuticals	12/31/18	42294.0	6220.0	82637.0	26701.0	3102	2325375985
MCY	Mercury General Corp.	General Insurance	12/31/18	3380.0	-5.7	5433.7	1617.7	353	33238867
MDP	Meredith Corp	Publishing	6/30/19	3188.5	46.3	6136.9	1514.8	402	59783387
MTH	Meritage Homes Corp	Builders	12/31/18	3528.6	227.3	3365.5	1720.8	372	46938497
MTOR	Meritor Inc	Auto Parts	9/30/19	4388.0	291.0	2815.0	385.0	354	96050929
MTR	Mesa Royalty Trust	Oil Royalty Traders	12/31/18	2.3	2.1	3.4	2.8	28	242618
MSB	Mesabi Trust	Non-Precious Metals	1/31/19	47.3	45.6	35.5	16.8	78	2531210

T36

EARNINGS PER SHARE						P/E RATIO		DIVIDENDS PER SHARE			AV. YLD %	DIV. DECLARED		PRICE RANGE 2018	
QUARTERLY			ANNUAL					2018	2017	2016		AMOUNT	PAYABLE		
1st	2nd	3rd	2018	2017	2016										
-	-	5.66	17.59	6.89	17.49	22.6 -	14.7	8.20	7.46	6.77	2.4	2.40Y	18/53/27	397.0 -	258.1
-	-	0.24	1.99	3.45	1.93	28.2 -	22.4	0.25	0.25	0.25	0.5	0.06250Y	18/53/27	56.2 -	44.5
-	-	-	3.02	2.79	0.87	4.3 -	1.5	-	-	-	-	-	-	13.0 -	4.7
-	-	0.02	2.73	2.66	1.03	11.1 -	7.8	0.52	-	-	2.0	0.1350Y	18/53/27	30.2 -	21.2
-	-	1.36	4.09	3.47	2.73	29.4 -	22.3	1.58	1.33	1.07	1.5	0.550Y	18/53/27	120.2 -	91.2
-	-	-1.39	-3.74	-2.18	2.54	-		-	-	-	-	10.0Y	4/1/10	7.7 -	2.9
-	-	0.68	3.89	2.20	2.21	13.6 -	10.3	2.28	2.28	2.19	4.9	0.190Z	3/31/20	52.9 -	40.3
-	-	-0.18	-1.12	-0.79	-0.35	-		-	-	-	-	0.10	9/25/00	2.3 -	1.1
-	-	0.04	-1.90	-1.33	-2.51	-		-	-	-	-	-	-	13.3 -	7.4
-	-	0.21	0.90	0.43	0.82	-		0.50	0.50	0.50	-	-	-	-	
-	-	0.17	2.02	2.85	2.16	15.1 -	9.0	-	-	-	-	0.0194	9/15/82	30.4 -	18.1
-	-	0.24	2.32	1.24	1.55	9.3 -	4.8	-	-	-	-	-	-	21.5 -	11.1
-	-	2.85	12.01	12.23	9.13	-		4.00	3.55	3.33	-	1.050	12/9/19	-	
-	-	3.47	12.74	8.70	7.78	13.8 -	11.2	3.55	3.00	2.80	2.2	1.10Y	18/53/27	176.0 -	143.0
-	-	-	-	-	-	-		-	-	-	-	0.53130Z	12/16/13	-	
-	-	0.79	3.39	2.30	1.71	13.6 -	7.8	1.11	0.86	0.82	3.2	0.30Y	11/27/19	46.0 -	26.4
-	-	1.32	3.70	2.26	1.84	12.5 -	5.9	-	-	-	-	0.60940Y	9/15/17	46.1 -	21.7
-	-	0.33	0.42	1.02	3.52	110.7 -	61.6	2.97	2.87	2.75	8.4	0.750Z	18/53/27	46.5 -	25.9
-	-	-0.65	0.80	0.06	1.30	30.6 -	23.9	0.80	0.70	0.60	3.6	0.20Z	18/53/27	24.5 -	19.1
-	-	-	1.21	1.19	0.90	21.2 -	15.6	1.53	1.48	1.48	6.7	0.420	12/27/19	25.6 -	18.8
-	-	0.71	1.60	5.13	1.85	27.3 -	23.1	4.44	5.43	4.89	10.9	1.0Y	18/53/27	43.7 -	36.9
-	-	-	1.10	1.18	1.13	10.4 -	8.5	1.20	1.20	1.20	11.5	0.250	11/29/19	11.4 -	9.3
-	-	0.01	5.04	1.99	3.22	6.3 -	2.8	1.51	1.49	1.39	7.4	0.37750Y	18/53/27	31.7 -	14.3
-	-	-	0.10	0.09	0.03	69.3 -	61.5	0.72	0.72	0.72	11.0	0.180	12/30/19	6.9 -	6.2
-3.36	-	-	5.94	-3.05	-3.12	52.6 -	41.8	-	-	-	-	-	-	312.4 -	248.1
-	-	1.19	5.84	3.81	3.52	11.5 -	9.7	3.79	3.52	3.25	6.0	1.02750	18/53/27	67.4 -	56.6
-	-	-0.75	6.61	5.90	5.16	11.3 -	6.5	1.32	1.10	1.00	2.3	0.3650	12/6/19	74.7 -	42.9
-	-	-0.05	-0.11	2.02	-0.85	-		-	-	-	-	-	-	13.3 -	5.8
-	-	0.05	0.25	0.02	-	55.7 -	39.2	-	-	-	-	-	-	13.9 -	9.8
-	-	0.62	2.60	2.39	2.23	17.1 -	13.1	2.85	2.79	2.73	7.0	0.2050	3/13/20	44.3 -	34.0
-	-	-	1.05	1.08	1.11	20.4 -	18.4	1.08	1.09	1.18	5.3	0.085M	3/31/20	21.4 -	19.3
-	-	-0.01	-42.94	21.80	-1.45	-		-	-	-	-	-	-	-	
0.04	-	-	-0.23	0.24	0.22	-		0.13	0.14	0.12	-	0.090	1/6/20	-	
-	-	0.51	-1.89	0.26	-10.92	-		-	-	-	-	0.080Y	12/10/15	19.2 -	10.7
-	-	0.05	0.21	0.25	0.62	13.4 -	7.0	0.32	0.40	0.64	16.5	0.020Y	2/3/20	2.8 -	1.5
-	-	2.42	8.56	8.04	6.27	11.4 -	7.4	2.02	1.86	1.72	2.3	1.090Y	18/53/27	97.4 -	63.7
-	-	0.35	2.33	0.98	1.41	11.3 -	6.1	0.91	0.82	0.74	4.4	0.29380	12/19/19	26.4 -	14.3
-	-	0.21	1.29	-6.73	-2.61	14.6 -	8.6	0.20	0.20	0.20	1.4	0.050Y	18/53/27	18.8 -	11.1
-	-	1.66	5.28	6.70	2.21	12.9 -	8.5	1.84	1.52	1.36	3.2	0.530Y	18/53/27	68.0 -	44.6
-	-	0.49	2.22	1.32	1.66	19.5 -	13.3	-	-	-	-	-	-	43.2 -	29.5
-	-	0.89	1.86	2.29	1.36	24.1 -	16.7	0.60	0.50	0.45	1.6	0.14550Y	12/16/19	44.8 -	31.1
-	-	0.23	0.83	0.55	0.44	22.1 -	15.3	0.50	0.33	0.24	3.4	0.17Y	12/10/19	18.3 -	12.7
-	-	0.84	1.71	0.95	0.91	12.3 -	8.1	-	-	-	-	-	-	21.0 -	13.8
-	-	13.95	-9.55	25.81	31.27	-		-	-	-	-	-	-	1196.2 -	957.5
-	-	-0.21	1.61	8.18	4.83	81.1 -	42.3	1.65	1.45	1.25	1.6	0.540Y	18/53/27	130.6 -	68.1
-	-	0.59	3.23	2.87	3.38	34.8 -	24.2	1.58	1.43	1.30	1.6	0.4550Y	18/53/27	112.3 -	78.0
-	-	3.96	7.43	11.25	6.63	37.6 -	22.9	1.84	1.72	1.64	0.8	0.550Y	18/53/27	279.6 -	170.5
-	-	0.44	2.37	1.66	1.47	20.3 -	12.3	0.44	0.41	0.39	1.1	0.1350Y	18/53/27	48.2 -	29.1
-	-	0.59	3.33	5.09	3.17	22.1 -	13.8	-	-	-	-	-	-	73.4 -	46.0
-	-	1.69	3.26	4.22	1.61	22.3 -	12.3	-	-	-	-	-	-	72.8 -	40.0
-	-	2.07	5.60	3.65	3.69	53.7 -	32.4	1.00	0.88	0.76	0.4	0.40Y	18/53/27	300.7 -	181.2
-	-	0.38	2.41	1.23	-1.07	9.1 -	5.2	-	-	-	-	-	-	21.9 -	12.4
-	-	0.17	1.01	0.56	1.27	70.3 -	42.1	0.41	0.40	0.38	0.7	0.110Y	12/4/19	71.0 -	42.6
-	-	0.84	2.53	5.37	1.85	16.6 -	12.5	0.82	0.78	0.74	2.2	0.220Y	3/5/20	42.0 -	31.5
-	-	0.00	0.03	0.57	1.15	408.7 -	325.3	-	-	-	-	0.1250	3/31/00	12.3 -	9.8
-	-	-0.44	-21.76	2.43	3.74	-		1.14	-	-	12.9	0.010Y	12/31/19	21.5 -	4.0
-	-	0.97	3.35	3.17	2.69	24.3 -	19.4	0.18	0.18	0.18	0.2	0.280Y	18/53/27	81.4 -	64.9
-	-	-0.07	-0.38	-0.14	0.91	-		-	-	-	-	-	-	28.6 -	16.7
-	-	0.49	1722.53	469.90	-	0.0 -	0.0	-	-	-	-	-	-	17.1 -	7.9
-	-	0.86	-3.33	-13.50	-2.54	-		-	-	-	-	0.340Y	1/15/08	10.7 -	8.7
-	-	1.43	7.00	3.72	3.69	24.7 -	17.3	2.08	1.88	1.72	1.4	0.620Y	18/53/27	172.7 -	121.2
-	-	2.11	7.54	6.37	5.44	29.3 -	23.1	4.19	3.83	3.61	2.1	1.250Y	18/53/27	221.2 -	174.0
-	-	-0.03	-0.13	-0.03	0.07	-		0.01	0.01	0.01	0.5	0.005D	9/4/18	2.8 -	1.0
-	-3.99	-	0.32	22.73	9.70	479.0 -	349.6	1.30	1.12	1.08	1.0	0.410Y	18/53/27	153.3 -	111.9
-	-	0.69	1.39	1.43	0.33	21.4 -	16.9	0.80	0.78	0.76	3.0	0.20750Y	18/53/27	29.8 -	23.6
-	-	-	30.34	27.76	17.12	0.1 -	0.1	-	-	-	-	-	-	2.5 -	1.6
-	-	-0.31	-3.12	-	-	-		-	-	-	-	-	-	43.0 -	24.2
-	-	0.20	2.76	0.82	0.86	7.8 -	5.7	1.00	0.96	0.91	5.4	0.260Z	18/53/27	21.5 -	15.6
-	-	1.32	4.62	2.29	1.49	34.0 -	16.1	2.19	1.44	1.07	1.9	1.130Y	2/6/20	157.1 -	74.4
-	-	-0.07	0.23	0.67	0.97	15.7 -	8.4	0.52	0.76	1.12	19.2	0.40630Z	4/30/20	3.6 -	1.9
-	-	-0.09	-0.65	0.07	0.02	-		0.80	0.80	0.80	24.9	0.030Y	5/3/19	4.9 -	2.3
-	-15.24	-	2.93	3.45	3.49	12.6 -	7.0	-	-	-	-	-	-	36.9 -	20.6
-	1.01	-	2.27	2.89	2.48	-		1.84	1.72	1.52	-	0.540	18/53/27	-	
-	-	0.74	2.32	0.87	1.41	39.5 -	31.4	1.99	1.89	1.85	2.4	0.610Y	18/53/27	91.7 -	72.9
-	-	1.25	-0.10	2.62	1.32	-		2.50	2.49	2.48	4.6	0.630Y	18/53/27	64.8 -	47.3
-0.30	-	-	1.47	4.16	0.75	41.1 -	21.7	2.13	2.03	1.91	4.4	0.5750Y	18/53/27	60.4 -	31.9
-	-	1.79	5.58	3.41	3.55	13.7 -	6.7	-	-	-	-	-	-	76.4 -	37.2
-	-	1.00	1.28	3.59	6.23	20.5 -	12.6	-	-	-	-	0.10Y	12/8/08	26.2 -	16.2
-	-	0.09	1.15	1.58	0.65	13.0 -	0.0	1.19	1.51	0.65	11.7	0.07940Z	4/30/20	14.9 -	0.0
-	-	0.47	2.55	0.73	0.65	12.5 -	8.4	2.53	0.64	0.09	9.4	0.70	2/20/20	31.9 -	21.4

SYMBOL	COMPANY	NATURE OF BUSINESS	FISCAL YEAR-END	TOTAL REV. $MILL	NET INCOME $MILL	TOTAL ASSETS $MILL	NET STK EQUITY $MILL	NO OF INST	INST. HOLDINGS (SHARES)
MEI	Methode Electronics Inc	Electrical Equipment	4/27/19	1000.3	91.6	1231.7	689.7	290	42624007
MET	MetLife Inc	Life & Health	12/31/18	67941.0	5123.0	687538.0	52741.0	1572	862356287
MCB	Metropolitan Bank Holding Corp	Banking	12/31/18	96.1	25.6	2182.6	264.5	83	4456438
MTD	Mettler-Toledo International, Inc.	Industrial Machinery & Equipment	12/31/18	2935.6	512.6	2618.8	590.1	791	31531059
MXE	Mexico Equity & Income Fund Inc (	Holding and other Investment Office	7/31/19	2.1	0.6	58.0	57.1	27	3102323
MXF	Mexico Fund, Inc.	Holding and other Investment Office	10/31/19	8.1	4.3	230.8	230.5	47	7415647
MFA	MFA Financial, Inc.	REITs	12/31/18	455.7	301.8	12420.3	3416.1	430	421950501
MCR	MFS Charter Income Trust	Holding and other Investment Office	11/30/18	22.5	17.1	503.3	396.5	88	20023139
MGF	MFS Government Markets Income	Holding and other Investment Office	11/30/18	5.2	4.0	158.4	151.5	55	26828807
CXE	MFS High Income Municipal Trust	Holding and other Investment Office	11/30/18	13.8	9.2	263.0	163.3	48	3724340
CMU	MFS High Yield Municipal Trust	Holding and other Investment Office	11/30/18	11.0	7.3	209.0	132.2	47	2480172
CIF	MFS Intermediate High Income Fun	Holding and other Investment Office	11/30/18	4.1	2.9	68.8	48.5	32	1115361
MIN	MFS Intermediate Income Trust	Holding and other Investment Office	10/31/19	15.3	12.2	472.8	472.4	108	64527522
CXH	MFS Investment Grade Municipal Tr	Holding and other Investment Office	11/30/18	7.2	4.4	148.5	92.4	48	2444037
MMT	MFS Multimarket Income Trust	Holding and other Investment Office	10/31/19	24.7	18.4	519.5	407.9	119	19447861
MFM	MFS Municipal Income Trust	Holding and other Investment Office	10/31/19	20.6	14.2	428.0	306.7	90	6320254
MFV	MFS Special Value Trust	Holding and other Investment Office	10/31/19	1.7	1.1	40.9	40.3	20	332243
MTG	MGIC Investment Corp. (WI)	Credit & Lending	12/31/18	1123.8	670.1	5677.8	3581.9	519	385878123
MGP	MGM Growth Properties LLC	REITs	12/31/18	1002.4	67.1	10951.3	1566.0	238	100685470
MGM	MGM Resorts International	Hotels, Restaurants & Travel	12/31/18	11763.1	466.8	30210.7	6512.3	715	513262546
MFGP	Micro Focus International Plc	Internet & Software	10/31/18	4754.4	784.0	16780.6	7790.9	304	58968777
MAA	Mid-America Apartment Communiti	REITs	12/31/18	1571.3	222.9	11323.8	6159.3	653	124683575
MLR	Miller Industries Inc. (TN)	Auto Parts	12/31/18	711.7	33.7	368.2	227.6	147	10966682
HIE	Miller/Howard High Income Equity F	Holding and other Investment Office	10/31/19	11.5	7.1	285.0	186.9	46	3777984
MTX	Minerals Technologies, Inc.	Specialty Chemicals	12/31/18	1807.6	169.0	3087.1	1353.5	318	41883610
MP PRD	Mississippi Power Co	Electric Utilities	12/31/18	1265.0	236.0	4886.0	1609.0	-	0
MG	Mistras Group Inc	Business Services	12/31/18	742.4	6.8	694.0	270.9	130	22376173
MUFG	Mitsubishi UFJ Financial Group Inc	Banking	3/31/19	5355622.0	718645.0	05228899.0	15199548.0	319	201021823
MIXT	MiX Telematics Ltd	Miscellaneous Transportation Servic	3/31/19	1975.9	202.3	2391.4	1751.7	82	9295582
MFG	Mizuho Financial Group Inc	Banking	3/31/19		84471.0	9761195.0	8726519.0	165	73043639
MBT	Mobile TeleSystems PJSC	Services	12/31/18	480293.0	6848.0	915993.0	65274.0	348	330684467
MODN	Model N, Inc	IT Services	9/30/19	141.2	-19.3	169.6	52.7	170	32437343
MOD	Modine Manufacturing Co	Auto Parts	3/31/19	2212.7	84.8	1538.0	-533.9	225	53288892
MC	Moelis & Co	Finance Intermediaries & Services	12/31/18	885.8	140.7	914.4	404.4	253	46040557
MOGU	MOGU Inc	Business Services	3/31/19	1074.3	-486.3	4603.8	4047.7	17	29715436
MHK	Mohawk Industries, Inc.	Construction Materials	12/31/18	9983.6	861.7	13099.1	7433.8	735	73551979
MOH	Molina Healthcare Inc	Hospitals & Health Care Facilities	12/31/18	18890.0	707.0	7154.0	1647.0	493	71232368
TAP	Molson Coors Beverage Co	Beverages	12/31/18	10769.6	1116.5	30109.8	13507.4	826	196029382
MNR	Monmouth Real Estate Investment	REITs	9/30/19	158.5	29.8	1871.9	1011.0	276	75553838
MR	Montage Resource Corp	Production & Extraction	12/31/18	515.1	18.8	1433.8	687.5	134	36813086
MCO	Moody's Corp.	Business Services	12/31/18	4442.7	1309.6	9526.2	459.9	1025	216065618
MOG A	Moog Inc	Industrial Machinery & Equipment	9/28/19	2904.7	179.7	3114.2	1322.5	326	37140445
MS	Morgan Stanley	Finance Intermediaries & Services	12/31/18	50193.0	8748.0	853531.0	80246.0	1539	1698990089
CAF	Morgan Stanley China A Share Fun	Holding and other Investment Office	12/31/18	12.3	2.2	469.3	467.8	75	11152230
MSD	Morgan Stanley Emerging Markets	Holding and other Investment Office	12/31/18	12.8	10.3	202.5	198.2	64	7542314
EDD	Morgan Stanley Emerging Markets	Holding and other Investment Office	10/31/19	49.3	33.6	668.4	504.0	80	14999164
IIF	Morgan Stanley India Investment Fu	Holding and other Investment Office	12/31/18	5.1	-0.6	373.5	320.5	77	6492364
ICB	Morgan Stanley Trusts	Holding and other Investment Office	10/31/02	5.5	4.8	103.9	103.8	-	0
MOS	Mosaic Co (The)	Agricultural Chemicals	12/31/18	9587.3	470.0	20119.2	10397.3	810	339839877
MSI	Motorola Solutions Inc	Manufacturing	12/31/18	7343.0	966.0	9409.0	-1293.0	1111	335395342
MOV	Movado Group, Inc.	Miscellaneous Consumer Goods	1/31/19	679.6	61.6	759.7	496.7	247	23086058
MPLX	MPLX LP	Equipment & Services	12/31/18	6425.0	1818.0	22779.0	988.0	426	361929891
MRC	MRC Global Inc	Industrial Machinery & Equipment	12/31/18	4172.0	74.0	2434.0	1047.0	224	93715807
MSA	MSA Safety Inc	Office Equipment & Furniture	12/31/18	1358.1	124.1	1608.0	633.9	335	36017941
MSM	MSC Industrial Direct Co Inc	Industrial Machinery & Equipment	8/31/19	3363.8	288.9	2311.2	1478.6	499	54660911
MSCI	MSCI Inc	Publishing	12/31/18	1434.0	507.9	3388.0	-166.5	699	96194724
MSGN	MSG Network Inc	Radio & Television	6/30/19	720.8	186.2	866.9	-458.8	296	69285042
MLI	Mueller Industries Inc	Industrial Machinery & Equipment	12/29/18	2507.9	104.5	1369.5	548.4	293	65416662
MWA	Mueller Water Products Inc	Industrial Machinery & Equipment	9/30/19	968.0	63.8	1337.3	590.1	310	166192065
MUR	Murphy Oil Corp	Production & Extraction	12/31/18	2570.6	411.1	11052.6	4829.3	579	180938981
MUSA	Murphy USA Inc	Retail - General Merchandise/Depart	12/31/18	14362.9	213.6	2360.8	807.3	-	0
MVO	MV Oil Trust	Production & Extraction	12/31/18	17.2	16.3	17.0	17.0	38	1285274
MVC	MVC Capital Inc	Holding and other Investment Office	10/31/18	22.9	3.8	347.1	226.7	93	13437062
MYE	Myers Industries Inc.	Plastics	12/31/18	566.7	-3.3	348.6	154.6	219	37198014
MYOV	Myovant Sciences Ltd	Pharmaceuticals	3/31/19		-273.6	173.0	4.3	82	40012471
NBR	Nabors Industries Ltd	Production & Extraction	12/31/18	3048.1	-640.9	7853.9	2700.8	524	362596618
NC	NACCO Industries Inc	Mining	12/31/18	135.4	34.8	377.0	250.7	131	3519509
NTP	Nam Tai Property Inc	Property, Real Estate & Developmen	12/31/18	0.4	-13.3	318.1	227.9	66	15748970
NBHC	National Bank Holdings Corp	Banking	12/31/18	292.2	61.5	5676.7	695.0	182	36434788
NFG	National Fuel Gas Co. (NJ)	Gas Utilities	9/30/19	1693.3	304.3	6462.2	2139.0	565	77685702
NGG	National Grid plc	Electric Utilities	3/31/19	14933.0	1511.0	62963.0	19349.0	466	44157701
NHI	National Health Investors, Inc.	REITs	12/31/18	294.6	154.3	2750.6	1389.7	344	39131870
NOV	National Oilwell Varco Inc	Equipment & Services	12/31/18	8453.0	-31.0	19796.0	13819.0	928	439171295
NPK	National Presto Industries, Inc.	Defense	12/31/18	323.3	39.9	413.6	366.1	202	6414555
NNN	National Retail Properties Inc	REITs	12/31/18	622.7	292.4	7103.4	4154.3	562	198574734
NSA	National Storage Affiliates Trust	REITs	12/31/18	330.9	14.1	2729.3	916.8	255	63058964
NW PRC	National Westminster Bank Plc	Banking	12/31/18	11148.0	2619.0	309938.0	19867.0	-	0
NTCO	Natura & Co Holding SA	Retail - Apparel and Accessories						-	
NGS	Natural Gas Services Group Inc	Equipment & Services	12/31/18	65.5	0.4	305.4	260.2	121	14377405
NGVC	Natural Grocers By Vitamin Cottage	Retail - Food & Beverage, Drug & To	9/30/19	903.6	9.4	327.1	156.9	115	8872989

1st	2nd	3rd	2018	2017	2016	P/E RATIO		2018	2017	2016	AV. YLD %	AMOUNT	PAYABLE	2018	
-	0.63	-	1.52	2.48	2.20	26.9 -	15.1	0.40	0.36	0.36	1.3	0.110Y	1/31/20	41.0 -	23.0
-	-	2.30	4.91	3.62	0.63	10.5 -	8.3	1.66	1.60	1.58	3.5	0.440Y	18/53/27	51.4 -	40.9
-	-	0.90	3.06	2.34	0.43	15.8 -	9.9	-	-	-	-	-	-	48.2 -	30.3
-	-	5.20	19.88	14.24	14.22	43.9 -	25.8	-	-	-	-	-	-	872.5 -	513.6
-	-	-	0.05	0.09	0.01	234.8 -	0.0	0.05	-	0.56	0.5	0.12010	12/31/19	11.7 -	0.0
-	-	-	0.14	0.21	0.17	106.5 -	84.9	0.68	0.53	1.05	5.0	0.250	1/30/20	14.9 -	11.9
-	-	0.20	0.68	0.79	0.80	11.8 -	9.9	0.80	0.80	0.80	10.9	0.20Z	18/53/27	8.0 -	6.7
-	-	-	0.35	0.39	0.46	24.1 -	21.2	0.71	0.75	0.74	8.8	0.05980	1/31/20	8.4 -	7.4
-	-	-	0.12	0.14	0.16	38.8 -	36.5	0.35	0.38	0.41	7.7	0.02860	1/31/20	4.7 -	4.4
-	-	-	0.29	0.30	0.32	19.9 -	16.3	0.29	0.30	0.30	5.6	0.021M	1/31/20	5.8 -	4.7
-	-	-	0.26	0.27	0.29	19.0 -	16.3	0.26	0.27	0.27	5.6	0.0185M	1/31/20	5.0 -	4.3
-	-	-	0.14	0.16	0.19	20.4 -	15.5	0.25	0.27	0.26	9.7	0.02050	1/31/20	2.9 -	2.2
-	-	-	0.10	0.10	0.11	38.7 -	36.5	0.36	0.39	0.42	9.5	0.02830	1/31/20	3.9 -	3.6
-	-	-	0.47	0.48	0.53	21.5 -	19.1	0.46	0.48	0.49	4.8	0.036M	1/31/20	10.1 -	9.0
-	-	-	0.25	0.30	0.34	24.6 -	20.9	0.51	0.54	0.53	8.8	0.04260	1/31/20	6.2 -	5.2
-	-	-	0.37	0.39	0.41	19.4 -	17.2	0.37	0.38	0.38	5.4	0.027M	1/31/20	7.2 -	6.3
-	-	-	0.16	0.20	0.23	42.2 -	31.5	0.58	0.60	0.59	10.0	0.04740	1/31/20	6.8 -	5.0
-	-	0.49	1.78	0.95	0.86	8.2 -	5.9	-	-	-	-	0.060Y	11/25/19	14.6 -	10.5
-	-	0.24	0.94	0.67	0.52	35.1 -	27.9	1.74	1.60	1.04	5.7	0.470Y	1/15/20	33.0 -	26.2
-	-	-0.08	0.81	3.35	1.92	41.5 -	29.5	0.48	0.44	-	1.7	0.130	18/53/27	33.6 -	23.9
-	-	-	1.96	0.72	0.77	13.9 -	6.6	1.51	0.88	0.67	7.6	-	-	27.2 -	12.9
-	-	0.68	1.93	2.86	2.69	72.1 -	48.0	3.69	3.48	3.28	3.1	1.0Z	18/53/27	139.2 -	92.7
-	-	0.71	2.96	2.02	1.75	12.8 -	9.0	0.72	0.72	0.68	2.2	0.180Y	12/16/19	37.8 -	26.6
-	-	-	0.46	0.32	0.64	26.5 -	21.5	1.39	1.39	1.39	12.3	0.1160	3/31/20	12.2 -	9.9
-	-	1.08	4.75	5.48	3.79	13.3 -	9.6	0.20	0.20	0.20	0.4	0.050Y	18/53/27	63.2 -	45.5
-	-	-	-	-	-	-	-	1.06	1.31	1.31	-	0.32810Y	10/1/18	-	
-	-	0.11	0.23	-0.08	0.32	72.3 -	54.9	-	-	-	-	-	-	16.6 -	12.6
21.50	-	-	92.10	14.68	57.51	0.1 -	0.0	18.12	18.30	17.75	359.2	-	-	5.5 -	4.6
-	-	-	0.32	0.19	0.23	61.1 -	37.5	1.79	1.51	2.83	11.8	-	-	19.5 -	12.0
4.66	-	-	22.76	14.28	33.50	0.1 -	0.1	14.93	15.17	15.30	490.2	-	-	3.3 -	2.7
-	-	9.09	3.65	28.66	24.35	2.8 -	2.0	52.11	51.79	51.09	622.8	-	-	10.2 -	7.3
-	-0.09	-	-0.93	-1.38	-1.21	-	-	-	-	-	-	-	-	35.7 -	13.2
-	-0.09	-	0.43	0.29	-0.03	38.5 -	15.6	-	-	-	-	0.10Y	12/5/08	16.6 -	6.7
-	-	0.73	2.78	0.78	1.58	16.9 -	10.8	4.88	2.48	3.29	13.4	0.50Y	12/13/19	47.1 -	30.0
-	-	-	-2.26	-2.77	-	-	-	-	-	-	-	-	-	22.7 -	1.9
-	-	2.15	11.47	12.98	12.48	13.6 -	9.6	-	-	-	-	-	-	156.4 -	110.5
-	-	2.75	10.61	-9.07	0.92	14.6 -	10.0	-	-	-	-	-	-	155.3 -	105.9
-	-	-1.86	5.15	6.53	9.26	12.9 -	9.7	1.64	1.64	1.64	2.9	0.570Y	18/53/27	66.6 -	50.1
-	-	-0.03	0.49	0.56	0.50	31.5 -	24.4	0.68	0.64	0.64	4.9	0.38280Z	3/16/20	15.4 -	12.0
-	-	0.12	0.94	0.45	-12.60	18.7 -	2.9	-	-	-	-	-	-	17.6 -	2.7
-	-	1.99	6.74	5.15	1.36	35.5 -	20.2	1.76	1.52	1.48	0.9	0.50Y	18/53/27	239.3 -	136.2
-	-	1.35	2.68	3.90	3.47	36.4 -	27.8	0.50	-	-	0.6	0.250Y	3/2/20	97.5 -	74.5
-	-	1.27	4.73	3.07	2.92	10.8 -	8.3	1.10	0.90	0.70	2.5	0.350Y	18/53/27	51.1 -	39.1
-	-	-	0.10	0.03	0.10	244.9 -	178.3	1.73	1.22	0.80	8.1	0.7019B	12/27/19	24.5 -	17.8
-	-	-	0.50	0.58	0.62	19.5 -	16.6	0.54	0.58	0.63	5.9	0.130	1/15/20	9.8 -	8.3
-	-	-	0.68	0.63	0.78	10.5 -	9.0	0.60	0.66	0.76	8.9	0.130	1/15/20	7.1 -	6.1
-	-	-	-0.04	-0.10	-0.08	-	-	6.10	5.05	1.14	30.9	0.0279C	1/15/20	21.6 -	17.6
-	-	-	-	-	-	-	-	-	-	-	-	0.0808C	5/25/18	-	
-	-	-0.11	1.22	-0.31	0.85	27.4 -	14.5	0.10	0.60	1.10	0.4	0.050Y	18/53/27	33.5 -	17.7
-	-	1.51	5.62	-0.95	3.24	32.2 -	19.7	2.13	1.93	1.70	1.4	0.640Y	18/53/27	181.2 -	110.8
-	-	0.76	-0.66	1.51	1.90	-	-	0.52	0.52	0.44	1.8	0.20Y	12/20/19	40.1 -	18.7
-	-	0.61	2.29	1.06	-	15.6 -	9.9	2.49	2.21	2.03	8.3	0.68750	2/14/20	35.7 -	22.6
-	-	0.18	0.54	0.27	-1.10	34.9 -	20.0	-	-	-	-	-	-	18.8 -	10.8
-	-	1.08	3.18	0.67	2.42	40.1 -	29.0	1.49	1.38	1.31	1.4	0.56250Y	18/53/27	127.4 -	92.3
1.18	-	-	5.80	4.05	3.77	14.9 -	11.3	2.22	1.80	1.72	2.9	5.7Y	18/53/27	86.3 -	65.7
-	-	1.60	5.66	3.31	2.70	47.1 -	25.0	1.92	1.32	1.00	0.9	0.680	18/53/27	266.3 -	141.3
0.57	-	-	3.81	2.21	0.10	6.7 -	3.6	-	-	-	-	-	-	25.5 -	13.8
-	-	0.52	1.82	1.49	1.74	18.6 -	12.5	0.40	3.40	0.38	1.4	0.10Y	12/20/19	33.9 -	22.7
-	-	0.21	0.66	0.76	0.39	18.6 -	13.7	0.19	0.15	0.10	1.8	0.05250Y	11/20/19	12.3 -	9.0
-	-	6.76	2.36	-1.81	-1.60	13.1 -	7.4	1.00	1.00	1.20	4.0	0.250Y	18/53/27	31.0 -	17.4
-	-	2.18	6.48	6.78	5.59	18.6 -	11.3	-	-	-	-	-	-	120.8 -	73.5
-	-	0.30	0.40	0.72	0.40	22.4 -	12.3	1.42	0.72	0.40	19.0	0.190Z	1/24/20	8.9 -	4.9
-	-	-	0.20	-0.25	0.85	48.0 -	41.7	0.60	0.56	0.71	6.6	0.170	1/10/20	9.6 -	8.3
-	-	0.15	-0.10	-0.33	0.03	-	-	0.54	0.54	0.54	3.1	0.1350Y	1/3/20	19.3 -	14.7
-	-0.79	-	-2.41	-1.70	-0.04	-	-	-	-	-	-	-	-	-	
-	-	-0.37	-1.99	-1.90	-3.64	-	-	0.24	0.24	0.06	-	0.750	18/53/27	-	
-	-	1.47	5.00	4.41	4.32	13.1 -	6.6	0.66	0.98	1.06	1.4	0.190Y	18/53/27	65.5 -	33.0
-	-	0.40	-0.35	0.11	-0.26	-	-	-	0.28	0.28	-	0.070	1/19/18	-	
-	-	0.69	1.95	0.53	0.79	19.9 -	15.8	0.54	0.34	0.22	1.5	0.20Y	3/13/20	38.8 -	30.8
-	-	0.73	4.53	3.30	-3.43	13.5 -	9.6	1.68	1.64	1.60	3.2	0.4350Y	18/53/27	61.3 -	43.3
-	-	-	1.02	2.06	0.69	61.7 -	47.8	2.22	0.44	0.43	4.1	-	-	62.9 -	48.8
-	-	0.97	3.67	3.87	3.87	23.6 -	20.2	4.00	3.80	3.60	5.0	1.050Z	18/53/27	86.5 -	74.0
-	-	-0.64	-0.08	-0.63	-6.41	-	-	0.20	0.20	0.61	0.8	0.050Y	18/53/27	30.6 -	18.3
-	1.16	-	5.70	7.58	6.39	22.9 -	14.2	6.00	5.50	5.05	6.1	5.7Y	3/15/19	130.5 -	81.1
-	-	0.35	1.65	1.45	1.38	35.7 -	28.7	1.95	1.86	1.78	3.6	0.5150Z	18/53/27	58.9 -	47.3
-	-	-0.20	0.07	0.01	0.31	508.1 -	361.1	1.16	1.04	0.88	3.8	0.3750Z	12/31/19	35.6 -	25.3
-	-	-	-	-	-	-	-	-	1.27	1.54	-	-	-	-	
-	-	-0.93	0.03	1.51	0.50	634.0 -	350.3	-	-	-	-	-	-	19.0 -	10.5
-	-	0.09	0.56	0.31	0.51	29.0 -	14.7	-	-	-	-	0.07GY	12/17/19	16.3 -	8.2

SYMBOL	COMPANY	NATURE OF BUSINESS	FISCAL YEAR-END	TOTAL REV. $MILL	NET INCOME $MILL	TOTAL ASSETS $MILL	NET STK EQUITY $MILL	NO OF INST	INST. HOLDINGS (SHARES)
NRP	Natural Resource Partners LP	Mining	12/31/18	278.5	139.5	1341.6	164.6	98	13995136
NTZ	Natuzzi S.p.A.	Furniture	12/31/18	428.5	33.3	372.7	136.5	18	1985382
NLS	Nautilus Inc	Leisure Equipment	12/31/18	396.8	14.7	332.9	182.6	190	32581480
NVGS	Navigator Holdings Ltd.	Miscellaneous Transportation Servic	12/31/18	310.0	-5.7	1832.8	955.1		0
NNA	Navios Maritime Acquisition Corp	Equipment & Services	12/31/18	187.9	-86.4	1627.4	380.4	50	7591184
NM	Navios Maritime Holdings Inc	Shipping	12/31/18	546.2	-268.7	2682.5	251.9	74	11558930
NMM	Navios Maritime Partners LP	Shipping	12/31/18	231.4	-13.1	1314.1		73	17232372
NAV	Navistar International Corp.	Autos- Manufacturing	10/31/19	11251.0	221.0	6917.0	-3726.0	300	87596481
NCR	NCR Corp	Computer Hardware & Equipment	12/31/18	6405.0	-88.0	7761.0	1254.0	590	154811357
NP	Neenah Inc	Paper & Forest Products	12/31/18	1034.9	36.4	861.2	390.2	284	22953083
NNI	Nelnet Inc	Credit & Lending	12/31/18	1756.8	227.9	25221.0	2304.5	197	17268030
NPTN	NeoPhotonics Corp	Semiconductors	12/31/18	322.5	-43.6	340.6	160.2	166	43526311
NVRO	Nevro Corp	Medical Instruments & Equipment	12/31/18	387.3	-49.2	463.1	245.5	204	36773290
HYB	New America High Income Fund, In	Holding and other Investment Office	12/31/18	20.8	15.4	305.9	207.9	78	11828744
GF	New Germany Fund, Inc.	Holding and other Investment Office	12/31/18	5.5	1.7	270.3	210.6	55	11632416
IRL	New Ireland Fund Inc (The)	Holding and other Investment Office	10/31/19	1.2	0.1	54.9	54.7	35	1813274
NJR	New Jersey Resources Corp	Gas Utilities	9/30/19	2592.0	169.5	4373.0	1551.7	391	79254888
NMFC	New Mountain Finance Corp	Holding and other Investment Office	12/31/18	231.5	106.0	2448.7	1006.3	194	37303202
EDU	New Oriental Education & Technolo	Educational Services	5/31/19	3096.5	238.1	4646.6	2360.7	451	144162147
NEWR	New Relic Inc	Internet & Software	3/31/19	479.2	-40.9	1090.2	349.6	362	50984074
NRZ	New Residential Investment Corp	REITs	12/31/18	2237.6	964.0	31691.0	5997.7	451	247313080
SNR	New Senior Investment Group Inc	REITs	12/31/18	444.3	-159.4	2286.3	322.5	183	72403177
NYCB	New York Community Bancorp Inc.	Banking	12/31/18	1781.2	422.4	51899.4	6655.2	612	363398165
NYT	New York Times Co.	Publishing	12/30/18	1748.6	125.7	2197.1	1040.8	448	197771696
NEU	NewMarket Corp	Specialty Chemicals	12/31/18	2289.7	234.7	1697.3	489.9	419	8437727
NEM	Newmont Corp	Precious Metals	12/31/18	7253.0	341.0	20715.0	10502.0	1136	797113393
NR	Newpark Resources, Inc.	Equipment & Services	12/31/18	946.5	32.3	915.9	569.7	251	112092869
NEXA	Nexa Resources SA	Metal Products	12/31/18	2491.2	74.9	5735.4	2476.6	56	11538349
NXRT	NexPoint Residential Trust Inc	REITs	12/31/18	146.6	-1.6	1161.2	296.0	194	22524706
NHF	NexPoint Strategic Opportunities Fu	Holding and other Investment Office	12/31/18	40.0	21.3	1045.6	767.7	92	21686598
NEE PRK	NextEra Energy Capital Holdings In	Electric Utilities	-	-	-	-	-	-	0
NEE	NextEra Energy Inc	Electric Utilities	12/31/18	16727.0	6638.0	103702.0	34144.0	2187	464173566
NEP	NextEra Energy Partners LP	Electric Utilities	12/31/18	771.0	192.0	9405.0	2346.0	259	52691088
NEX	NexTier Oilfield Solutions Inc	Equipment & Services	12/31/18	2137.0	59.3	1054.6	487.2	176	107802852
NGL	NGL Energy Partners LP	Equipment & Services	3/31/19	24016.9	360.0	5902.5	149.8	150	101218384
NLSN	Nielsen Holdings PLC	Business Services	12/31/18	6515.0	-712.0	15179.0	2847.0	529	442981612
NKE	NIKE Inc	Apparel, Footwear & Accessories	5/31/19	39117.0	4029.0	23717.0	9040.0	2241	1200420411
NINE	Nine Energy Service Inc	Equipment & Services	12/31/18	827.2	-53.0	1141.2	594.8	86	22930441
NIO	NIO Inc	Autos- Manufacturing	12/31/18	4951.2	-9597.3	18842.6	8166.2	246	373267342
NI	NiSource Inc. (Holding Co.)	Gas Utilities	12/31/18	5114.5	-50.6	21804.0	5750.9	738	399683356
NL	NL Industries, Inc.	Electrical Equipment	12/31/18	118.2	-41.0	547.2	284.1	77	5369169
NOAH	Noah Holdings Ltd	Wealth Management	12/31/18	3289.6	811.3	8014.3	5837.7	180	34402597
NE	Noble Corp plc	Equipment & Services	12/31/18	1082.8	-885.0	9264.9	4253.2		0
NOK	Nokia Corp	Manufacturing	12/31/18	22563.0	-340.0	39517.0	15289.0	763	526807344
NOMD	Nomad Foods Ltd	Food	12/31/18	2172.8	171.2	5340.8	2059.9	252	163907371
NMR	Nomura Holdings Inc	Finance Intermediaries & Services	3/31/19	1113952.0	-100442.0	409969439.0	2631061.0	137	36536991
OSB	Norbord Inc	Paper & Forest Products	12/31/18	2424.0	371.0	1942.0	823.0		0
NAT	Nordic American Tankers Ltd	Miscellaneous Transportation Servic	12/31/18	289.0	-95.3	1071.1	602.0	210	43786966
JWN	Nordstrom, Inc.	Retail - General Merchandise/Depart	2/2/19	15860.0	564.0	7886.0	873.0	833	136216029
NSC	Norfolk Southern Corp	Rail	12/31/18	11458.0	2666.0	36239.0	15362.0	1870	240388724
NOA	North American Construction Group	Equipment & Services	12/31/18	410.1	15.3	689.8	149.7	93	16582527
NRT	North European Oil Royalty Trust	Oil Royalty Traders	10/31/19	8.4	7.6	1.6	0.1	52	1334140
NOC	Northrop Grumman Corp	Defense	12/31/18	30095.0	3229.0	37653.0	8187.0	1493	201000667
NWN	Northwest Natural Holding Co	Gas Utilities	12/31/18	706.1	64.6	3242.7	762.6		0
NWE	Northwestern Corp.	Electric Utilities	12/31/18	1192.0	197.0	5644.4	1942.4	418	64535959
NCLH	Norwegian Cruise Line Holdings Ltd	Hotels, Restaurants & Travel	12/31/18	6055.1	954.8	15206.0	5963.0	563	225283247
NVS	Novartis AG Basel	Pharmaceuticals	12/31/18	53166.0	12611.0	145563.0	78614.0	1545	298533653
NVO	Novo-Nordisk AS	Pharmaceuticals	12/31/18	111831.0	38628.0	110769.0	51839.0	781	192359588
DNOW	Now Inc	Equipment & Services	12/31/18	3127.0	52.0	1795.0	1214.0	365	125213239
NRG	NRG Energy Inc	Electric Utilities	12/31/18	9478.0	268.0	10628.0	-1234.0	727	311137435
NUS	NU Skin Enterprises, Inc.	Household & Personal Products	12/31/18	2679.0	121.9	1694.4	781.9	395	50734517
NUE	Nucor Corp.	Non-Precious Metals	12/31/18	25067.3	2360.8	17920.6	9792.1	1130	323790691
NS	NuStar Energy LP	Refining & Marketing	12/31/18	1961.8	205.8	6349.1	564.0	278	95077595
NTR	Nutrien Ltd	Agricultural Crop Production	12/31/18	19636.0	3573.0	45502.0	24425.0	602	372204794
JMLP	Nuveen All Cap Energy MLP Opport	Finance Intermediaries & Services	11/30/18	0.7	-2.4	131.5	93.4	40	2736250
NVG	Nuveen AMT-Free Municipal Credit	Holding and other Investment Office	10/31/19	243.1	160.2	5514.2	3477.0	227	20983776
NUW	Nuveen AMT-Free Municipal Value	Holding and other Investment Office	10/31/19	11.0	9.2	265.4	262.2	41	1412273
NEA	Nuveen AMT-Free Quality Municipa	Holding and other Investment Office	10/31/19	268.3	173.7	6515.9	4093.4	267	61923351
NAZ	Nuveen Arizona Quality Municipal I	Holding and other Investment Office	2/28/19	10.3	6.1	262.9	164.1	42	1169449
NKX	Nuveen California AMT-Free Qualit	Holding and other Investment Office	2/28/19	49.3	31.3	1175.3	720.8	81	7136679
NCB	Nuveen California Municipal Value	Holding and other Investment Office	2/28/19	2.6	2.2	51.9	51.6	20	266749
NCA	Nuveen California Municipal Value	Holding and other Investment Office	2/28/19	11.4	9.6	285.6	284.6	68	4025859
NAC	Nuveen California Quality Municipal	Holding and other Investment Office	2/28/19	150.0	97.4	3479.1	2163.3	118	14968196
NXC	Nuveen California Select Tax-Free I	Holding and other Investment Office	3/31/19	3.7	3.2	96.9	96.6	29	449215
JCE	Nuveen Core Equity Alpha Fund	Holding and other Investment Office	12/31/18	3.5	1.1	203.9	203.3	49	3858267
JQC	Nuveen Credit Strategies Income F	Holding and other Investment Office	7/31/19	101.9	62.6	1923.5	1151.8	193	63242555
JDD	Nuveen Diversified Dividend and In	Holding and other Investment Office	12/31/18	14.1	7.6	303.3	203.7	54	2723522
DIAX	Nuveen Dow 30SM Dynamic Overw	Holding and other Investment Office	12/31/18	15.4	9.2	619.6	610.2	93	6722642
JMF	Nuveen Energy MLP Total Return F	Holding and other Investment Office	11/30/18	2.0	15.7	594.3	407.0	85	7012898
NEV	Nuveen Enhanced Municipal Value	Holding and other Investment Office	10/31/19	24.2	18.2	503.9	380.0	60	3885572

T40

| EARNINGS PER SHARE | | | | | | P/E RATIO | | DIVIDENDS PER SHARE | | | AV. YLD | DIV. DECLARED | | PRICE RANGE | |
| QUARTERLY | | | ANNUAL | | | | | | | | % | AMOUNT | PAYABLE | 2018 | |
1st	2nd	3rd	2018	2017	2016			2018	2017	2016					
-	-	1.66	6.76	3.96	7.78	6.6 -	2.9	1.80	1.80	1.35	5.5	0.450	2/14/20	44.7 -	19.5
-	-	-0.34	0.61	-0.57	-0.11	10.2 -	0.0	-	-	-	-	-	-	6.3 -	0.0
-	-	-0.36	0.48	0.85	1.09	24.6 -	2.5	-	-	-	-	0.10Y	9/10/07	11.8 -	1.2
-	-	-	-0.10	0.10	0.80	-	-	-	-	-	-	-	-	-	
-	-6.15	-	-8.40	-7.50	6.00	-	-	1.20	3.00	3.00	-	0.30	1/9/20	-	
-	-1.49	-	-23.33	-15.00	-25.40	-	-	-	-	-	-	0.060	9/25/15	-	
-	-	-	-0.08	-0.11	-0.62	-	-	-	-	-	-	0.30	2/13/20	-	
-	-	1.56	3.41	0.32	-1.19	11.5 -	6.3	-	-	-	-	-	-	39.1 -	21.6
-	-	0.09	-1.16	0.97	1.71	-	-	-	-	-	-	-	-	35.3 -	23.1
-	-	0.84	2.12	4.68	4.24	35.2 -	27.0	1.64	1.48	1.32	2.5	0.450Y	12/3/19	74.7 -	57.2
-	-	0.83	5.57	4.14	6.02	12.4 -	9.3	0.66	0.58	0.50	1.1	0.20Y	12/13/19	69.2 -	51.7
-	-	0.05	-0.97	-1.23	0.00	-	-	-	-	-	-	-	-	8.9 -	3.6
-	-	-0.58	-1.64	-1.25	-1.12	-	-	-	-	-	-	-	-	117.5 -	35.5
-	-	-	0.66	0.71	0.75	13.9 -	11.5	0.70	0.71	0.76	8.1	0.0557	1/31/20	9.2 -	7.6
-	-	-	0.11	0.50	0.12	143.3 -	107.0	3.65	0.74	1.18	25.9	0.0681C	1/30/20	15.8 -	11.8
-	-	-	-0.03	-0.15	-0.06	-	-	1.16	1.14	2.22	13.0	0.11150	9/27/19	9.9 -	0.0
-	-	-0.09	2.64	1.52	1.52	19.4 -	15.4	1.11	1.04	0.97	2.4	0.31250Y	18/53/27	51.1 -	40.6
-	-	0.26	0.91	1.38	1.60	15.8 -	14.0	1.36	1.36	1.36	9.9	0.35940Z	4/1/20	14.4 -	12.8
0.81	-	-	1.87	1.74	1.43	68.2 -	28.9	0.43	-	0.40	0.4	-	-	127.5 -	54.0
-	-0.32	-	-0.83	-1.18	-1.39	-	-	-	-	-	-	-	-	108.5 -	56.3
-	-	0.54	2.81	3.15	2.12	6.1 -	5.0	2.00	1.98	1.84	12.6	0.44530Z	18/53/27	17.2 -	13.9
-	-	0.34	-1.94	0.15	-0.88	-	-	0.78	1.04	1.04	12.3	0.130Z	12/20/19	8.1 -	4.2
-	-	0.19	0.79	0.90	1.01	17.3 -	12.1	0.68	0.68	0.68	5.9	0.170Y	18/53/27	13.7 -	9.5
-	-	0.10	0.75	0.03	0.18	48.1 -	28.5	0.16	0.16	0.16	0.5	0.050Y	18/53/27	36.1 -	21.4
-	-	6.06	20.34	16.08	20.54	24.8 -	19.0	7.00	7.00	6.40	1.6	1.90Y	18/53/27	504.1 -	387.0
-	-	2.65	0.64	-0.18	-1.18	68.4 -	46.8	0.56	0.25	0.13	1.5	0.140Y	18/53/27	43.8 -	29.9
-	-	-0.02	0.35	-0.07	-0.49	27.6 -	16.0	-	-	-	-	-	-	9.7 -	5.6
-	-	-	0.56	1.09	-	-	-	-	-	-	-	0.52550	3/28/19	-	
-	-	4.84	-0.08	2.49	1.03	-	-	1.02	0.91	0.84	2.4	0.31250Z	12/31/19	50.2 -	33.9
-	-	-	0.75	0.93	4.08	29.5 -	21.7	2.40	2.40	2.80	12.5	0.20	1/31/20	22.1 -	16.2
-	-	-	-	-	-	-	-	-	-	-	-	0.31250Z	4/15/20	27.7 -	23.3
-	-	1.81	13.88	11.38	6.25	17.5 -	12.2	4.44	3.93	3.48	2.1	1.250Y	18/53/27	242.7 -	169.4
-	-	-1.21	2.91	-1.20	1.88	18.4 -	13.7	1.71	1.49	1.30	3.6	0.5350	2/14/20	53.6 -	39.7
-	-	0.03	0.54	-0.34	-2.14	22.6 -	7.5	-	-	-	-	-	-	12.2 -	4.1
-	-1.72	-	-1.08	0.95	-2.35	-	-	1.56	1.56	2.54	12.0	0.390	18/53/27	15.5 -	9.7
-	-	-1.33	-2.00	1.20	1.39	-	-	1.39	1.33	1.21	-	0.060	18/53/27	-	
-	0.70	-	1.17	2.51	2.16	86.8 -	62.2	0.58	0.68	0.62	0.7	0.2450Y	18/53/27	101.6 -	72.8
-	-	-0.70	-2.17	-4.55	-5.34	-	-	-	-	-	-	-	-	26.7 -	4.4
-	-	-42.59	-70.23	-346.84	-210.66	-	-	-	-	-	-	-	-	10.2 -	1.3
-	-	-0.02	-0.18	0.39	1.02	-	-	0.78	0.70	0.64	2.8	0.40630Y	18/53/27	30.6 -	25.1
-	-	-0.03	-0.84	2.38	0.31	-	-	-	-	-	-	0.1250Y	12/24/13	5.1 -	3.1
-	-	0.12	26.67	25.90	22.08	2.2 -	1.0	-	-	-	-	-	-	59.8 -	26.8
-	-	-1.79	-3.59	-2.11	-3.82	-	-	-	-	0.20	-	0.020Y	8/8/16	-	
-	-	-0.03	-0.06	-0.26	-0.13	-	-	0.19	0.17	0.26	3.7	-	-	6.6 -	3.4
-	-	0.97	0.74	0.20	-	-	-	-	-	-	-	-	-	-	
15.77	-	-	61.88	65.65	35.52	0.1 -	0.0	19.91	11.99	22.72	496.4	-	-	5.3 -	3.0
-	-	-0.21	4.27	5.03	2.13	9.2 -	4.6	4.87	1.16	0.30	16.6	0.20	12/23/19	39.5 -	19.5
-	-0.11	-	-0.67	-1.97	-0.05	-	-	0.07	0.53	1.37	-	0.020	12/18/19	-	
-	-	0.81	2.59	2.02	3.15	19.0 -	9.7	1.48	1.48	6.33	3.9	0.370Y	18/53/27	49.3 -	25.1
-	-	2.49	9.51	18.61	5.62	21.7 -	15.1	3.04	2.44	2.36	1.6	0.940Y	18/53/27	206.7 -	144.0
-	0.45	-	0.54	0.18	-0.01	33.9 -	16.7	0.08	0.08	0.08	0.6	0.040	1/3/20	18.3 -	9.0
-	-	0.22	0.70	0.76	0.67	10.9 -	7.6	0.77	0.66	0.78	11.6	0.160Z	11/27/19	7.7 -	5.3
-	-	5.49	18.49	11.47	12.19	20.7 -	13.0	4.70	3.90	3.50	1.5	1.320Y	18/53/27	382.1 -	239.9
-	-	-0.63	2.24	-1.94	2.12	33.0 -	25.7	0.47	1.88	1.87	0.7	0.47750Y	18/53/27	73.9 -	57.5
-	-	0.42	3.92	3.34	3.39	19.4 -	14.8	2.20	2.10	2.00	3.1	0.5750Y	18/53/27	76.0 -	58.0
-	-	2.09	4.25	3.31	2.78	-	-	-	-	-	-	-	-	-	
-	-	0.89	5.38	3.25	2.80	17.7 -	13.7	2.94	2.72	2.72	3.4	-	-	95.4 -	73.9
-	-	3.96	15.93	15.39	14.96	3.7 -	2.9	5.63	5.44	6.83	11.0	-	-	58.3 -	46.4
-	-	0.09	0.47	-0.48	-2.18	33.7 -	21.4	-	-	-	-	-	-	15.9 -	10.1
-	-	1.45	0.87	-6.79	-2.22	49.9 -	38.3	0.12	0.12	0.23	0.3	0.30Y	18/53/27	43.4 -	33.3
-	-	0.79	2.16	2.36	2.55	32.2 -	17.5	1.46	1.44	1.42	3.0	0.370Y	18/53/27	69.5 -	37.7
-	-	0.90	7.42	4.10	2.48	8.4 -	6.3	1.54	1.51	1.50	2.8	0.40250Y	18/53/27	62.1 -	46.6
-	-	0.11	-2.77	0.64	1.27	-	-	2.90	4.38	4.38	10.7	0.56250	12/16/19	29.5 -	21.3
-	1.47	-	5.72	-	-	12.8 -	7.9	1.63	-	-	2.8	0.450	1/16/20	73.4 -	45.0
-	-	-	-0.18	-0.07	-0.05	-	-	0.82	0.98	1.03	13.7	0.1760	2/18/20	7.0 -	4.7
-	-	-	0.81	0.84	0.73	20.9 -	17.5	0.84	0.90	0.88	5.3	0.0655M	2/3/20	16.9 -	14.2
-	-	-	0.70	0.75	0.76	25.9 -	21.3	0.90	0.73	0.79	5.4	0.039M	2/3/20	18.1 -	14.9
-	-	-	0.68	0.71	0.72	21.2 -	18.4	0.68	0.74	0.76	5.0	0.0535M	2/3/20	14.4 -	12.5
-	-	-	0.63	0.68	0.76	21.8 -	19.1	0.64	0.75	0.80	4.9	0.0438M	2/3/20	13.7 -	12.0
-	-	-	0.72	0.76	0.82	21.6 -	17.8	0.77	0.87	0.87	5.3	0.0515M	2/3/20	15.5 -	12.8
-	-	-	0.68	0.77	0.82	25.4 -	0.0	0.96	1.00	1.04	6.5	0.039M	2/3/20	17.3 -	0.0
-	-	-	0.38	0.42	0.45	28.2 -	24.3	0.40	0.44	0.47	4.0	0.0285M	2/3/20	10.7 -	9.2
-	-	-	0.72	0.78	0.88	21.5 -	17.8	0.77	0.87	0.93	5.4	0.052M	2/3/20	15.5 -	12.9
-	-	-	0.57	0.60	0.64	29.2 -	23.6	0.63	0.72	0.67	4.3	0.0437M	2/3/20	16.6 -	13.4
-	-	-	0.07	0.18	0.13	211.3 -	168.3	1.11	2.53	1.14	8.0	0.250	12/31/19	14.8 -	11.8
-	-	-	0.44	0.52	0.58	18.3 -	16.5	0.53	0.63	0.61	6.9	0.0920	2/3/20	8.1 -	7.3
-	-	-	0.38	0.47	0.46	29.6 -	23.8	0.99	1.34	1.08	9.3	0.21750	12/31/19	11.3 -	9.1
-	-	-	0.25	0.26	0.27	73.6 -	0.0	1.24	1.06	1.04	14.0	0.2950	12/31/19	18.4 -	0.0
-	-	-	0.39	-0.13	-0.12	25.7 -	18.1	1.10	1.35	1.35	12.6	0.24050	2/18/20	10.0 -	7.0
-	-	-	0.75	0.82	0.85	19.9 -	17.4	0.77	0.82	0.95	5.4	0.0565M	2/3/20	15.0 -	13.0

SYMBOL	COMPANY	NATURE OF BUSINESS	FISCAL YEAR-END	TOTAL REV. $MILL	NET INCOME $MILL	TOTAL ASSETS $MILL	NET STK EQUITY $MILL	NO OF INST	INST. HOLDINGS (SHARES)
JFR	Nuveen Floating Rate Income Fund	Holding and other Investment Office	7/31/19	61.3	39.6	1046.1	628.2	135	22035662
JRO	Nuveen Floating Rate Income Oppo	Holding and other Investment Office	7/31/19	43.4	28.6	735.6	443.7	118	14180849
NKG	Nuveen Georgia Quality Municipal I	Holding and other Investment Office	5/31/19	8.2	4.8	222.8	144.2	36	2423645
JGH	Nuveen Global High Income Fund	Holding and other Investment Office	12/31/18	39.7	29.3	546.9	371.1	77	8190989
JHY	Nuveen High Income 2020 Target T	Finance Intermediaries & Services	12/31/18	11.2	7.9	211.2	149.5	35	4012734
NID	Nuveen Intermediate Duration Muni	Finance Intermediaries & Services	5/31/19	35.6	25.4	860.0	669.4	65	10975825
NIQ	Nuveen Intermediate Duration Quali	Holding and other Investment Office	5/31/19	8.1	5.3	242.9	187.3	46	4178644
NMY	Nuveen Maryland Quality Municipal	Holding and other Investment Office	5/31/19	21.1	12.6	562.4	342.1	64	4724968
NMT	Nuveen Massachusetts Quality Mun	Holding and other Investment Office	5/31/19	8.1	4.9	212.1	137.3	34	630513
NUM	Nuveen Michigan Quality Municipal	Holding and other Investment Office	2/28/19	18.7	11.2	492.4	305.7	64	3853063
NMS	Nuveen Minnesota Quality Municipa	Holding and other Investment Office	5/31/19	5.9	3.6	141.1	87.8	19	401647
NOM	Nuveen Missouri Quality Municipal I	Holding and other Investment Office	5/31/19	2.1	1.2	52.6	32.4	13	81091
JLS	Nuveen Mortgage & Income Fund	Holding and other Investment Office	12/31/18	29.6	18.4	514.2	365.8	64	5800479
JMM	Nuveen Multi-Market Income Fund	Holding and other Investment Office	6/30/19	4.7	3.1	108.2	75.8	29	4984125
NHA	Nuveen Municipal 2021 Target Ter	Finance Intermediaries & Services	5/31/19	2.6	2.0	85.4	85.2	28	2135148
NZF	Nuveen Municipal Credit Income Fu	Holding and other Investment Office	10/31/19	166.2	106.8	3765.3	2364.0	173	16638450
NMZ	Nuveen Municipal High Income Opp	Holding and other Investment Office	10/31/18	69.1	49.7	1447.5	969.1	108	7112518
NMI	Nuveen Municipal Income Fund, Inc	Holding and other Investment Office	10/31/18	4.5	3.7	100.2	99.8	39	563395
NUV	Nuveen Municipal Value Fund, Inc.	Holding and other Investment Office	10/31/18	88.8	77.3	2236.5	2186.9	258	35850456
NJV	Nuveen New Jersey Municipal Valu	Holding and other Investment Office	2/28/19	1.1	0.8	23.8	22.7	21	255966
NXJ	Nuveen New Jersey Quality Municip	Holding and other Investment Office	2/28/19	41.4	27.7	981.9	643.0	72	5279788
NRK	Nuveen New York AMT-Free Qualit	Holding and other Investment Office	2/28/19	80.4	49.8	2011.2	1231.8	98	21616268
NYV	Nuveen New York Municipal Value	Holding and other Investment Office	2/28/19	1.5	1.2	36.2	36.1	22	330080
NNY	Nuveen New York Municipal Value	Holding and other Investment Office	2/28/19	6.3	5.4	152.7	150.3	33	998680
NAN	Nuveen New York Quality Municipal	Holding and other Investment Office	2/28/19	29.8	18.8	725.9	453.2	61	5215313
NXN	Nuveen New York Select Tax-Free I	Holding and other Investment Office	3/31/19	2.2	1.9	55.9	55.3	23	424929
NUO	Nuveen Ohio Quality Municipal Inco	Holding and other Investment Office	2/28/19	17.1		466.6	297.8	55	5596420
NPN	Nuveen Pennsylvania Municipal Val	Holding and other Investment Office	2/28/19	0.8	0.6	18.5	18.0	16	68735
NQP	Nuveen Pennsylvania Quality Munic	ETFs	2/28/19	36.6	23.1	914.8	560.4	95	7128940
JPT	Nuveen Preferred & Income 2022 T	Holding and other Investment Office	7/31/19	12.5	9.3	209.9	165.6	26	678468
JPC	Nuveen Preferred & Income Opport	Holding and other Investment Office	7/31/19	103.1	72.2	1661.1	1047.9	171	19465597
JPS	Nuveen Preferred & Income Securiti	Holding and other Investment Office	7/31/19	192.0	133.5	3154.3	2004.4	242	28543173
JPI	Nuveen Preferred & Income Term F	Holding and other Investment Office	7/31/19	52.0	37.3	840.2	561.5	85	5142758
NAD	Nuveen Quality Municipal Income F	Holding and other Investment Office	10/31/19	210.1	134.4	5097.5	3211.3	238	51994962
JRI	Nuveen Real Asset Income & Growt	Holding and other Investment Office	12/31/18	43.1	29.1	672.7	452.7	88	7282929
JRS	Nuveen Real Estate Income Fund	Holding and other Investment Office	12/31/18	16.8	9.4	400.2	273.6	82	5418743
BXMX	Nuveen S&P 500 Buy-Write Income	Holding and other Investment Office	12/31/18	28.8	15.9	1335.6	1307.7	140	22564867
SPXX	Nuveen S&P 500 Dynamic Overwrit	Holding and other Investment Office	12/31/18	5.3	2.9	242.0	238.3	57	3673191
NIM	Nuveen Select Maturities Municipal	Holding and other Investment Office	3/31/19	4.8	4.1	132.0	131.5	51	2402869
NXQ	Nuveen Select Tax Free Income Po	Holding and other Investment Office	3/31/19	10.1	9.3	264.2	263.3	70	3307264
NXP	Nuveen Select Tax-Free Income Po	Holding and other Investment Office	3/31/19	10.1	9.4	257.8	256.9	71	2014750
NXR	Nuveen Select Tax-Free Income Po	Holding and other Investment Office	3/31/19	7.9	7.3	207.5	206.8	55	2307677
NSL	Nuveen Senior Income Fund	Holding and other Investment Office	7/31/19	25.8	17.4	426.7	254.5	96	13372007
JSD	Nuveen Short Duration Credit Oppo	Holding and other Investment Office	7/31/19	18.0	12.0	291.1	170.5	52	3592377
JTD	Nuveen Tax-Advantaged Dividend	Holding and other Investment Office	12/31/18	13.1	6.2	316.6	211.3	54	3173428
JTA	Nuveen Tax-Advantaged Total Retu	Holding and other Investment Office	12/31/18	11.0	6.0	222.2	149.1	48	3586369
NBB	Nuveen Taxable Municipal Income	Holding and other Investment Office	3/31/19	40.7	30.9	756.3	584.1	87	7566060
NTX	Nuveen Texas Quality Municipal Inc	Holding and other Investment Office	2/28/19	9.1	5.5	237.9	149.3	46	1056192
NPV	Nuveen Virginia Quality Municipal In	Holding and other Investment Office	5/31/19	15.8	9.6	417.8	262.2	53	1495753
NVT	nVent Electric PLC	Electrical Equipment	12/31/18	2213.6	230.8	4552.7	2687.1	420	148501256
NVR	NVR Inc.	Builders	12/31/18	7189.7	797.2	3165.9	1808.6	620	4107368
OI	O-I Glass Inc	Containers & Packaging	12/31/18	6877.0	257.0	9699.0	786.0	493	179043249
OAC	Oaktree Acquisition Corp	Business Services	4/23/19		-0.0	0.1	0.0	11	3490783
OBE	Obsidian Energy Ltd	Production & Extraction	12/31/18	382.0	-305.0	2650.0	1868.0	179	27532426
OXY	Occidental Petroleum Corp	Production & Extraction	12/31/18	18934.0	4131.0	43854.0	21330.0	1690	867627022
OII	Oceaneering International, Inc.	Equipment & Services	12/31/18	1909.5	-212.3	2825.0	1409.2	403	120267291
OCN	Ocwen Financial Corp	Credit & Lending	12/31/18		-70.8	9394.2	554.7	212	115099667
OFG	OFG Bancorp	Banking	12/31/18	440.5	84.4	6583.4	999.9	252	63659798
OGE	OGE Energy Corp.	Electric Utilities	12/31/18	2270.3	425.5	10748.6	4005.1	651	174196664
OIBR C	Oi SA	Services	12/31/18	22060.0	27369.4	67247.6	28956.0	28	4568133
OIS	Oil States International, Inc.	Equipment & Services	12/31/18	1088.1	-19.1	2003.8	1439.8	302	75629434
ODC	Oil-Dri Corp. of America	Household & Personal Products	7/31/19	277.0	12.6	205.2	135.6	89	4191641
ORI	Old Republic International Corp.	General Insurance	12/31/18	6021.8	370.5	19327.1	5146.2	605	282939142
OLN	Olin Corp.	Diversified Chemicals	12/31/18	6946.1	327.9	8997.4	2832.2	499	186278859
OHI	Omega Healthcare Investors, Inc.	REITs	12/31/18	881.7	281.6	8590.9	3444.4	669	217404030
OMC	Omnicom Group, Inc.	Advertising	12/31/18	15290.2	1326.4	24617.0	2547.1	1124	303091012
OMN	Omnova Solutions Inc	Specialty Chemicals	11/30/18	769.8	20.7	589.2	57.6	190	44319316
ONDK	On Deck Capital Inc	Credit & Lending	12/31/18	398.4	27.7	1161.6	299.8	165	79714328
OGS	ONE Gas, Inc.	Gas Utilities	12/31/18	1633.7	172.2	5468.6	2042.7	408	47128062
OLP	One Liberty Properties, Inc.	REITs	12/31/18	79.1	20.7	780.9	297.1	165	10246794
OCFT	OneConnect Financial Technology	IT Services	12/31/18	1413.5	-1195.7	9382.6	3720.5		0
OMF	OneMain Holdings Inc	Credit & Lending	12/31/18	4232.0	447.0	20090.0	3799.0	296	132096368
OKE	ONEOK Inc	Production & Extraction	12/31/18	12593.2	1151.7	18231.7	6579.5	1231	348115392
ONE	OneSmart International Education	Educational Services	8/31/19	3993.9	245.4	6071.5	1092.3	30	62327124
ONTO	Onto Innovation Inc	Semiconductors	12/29/18	324.5	57.6	375.6	312.9	243	26191642
OOMA	OOMA Inc	Internet & Software	1/31/19	129.2	-14.6	78.4	33.0	104	16242974
OPY	Oppenheimer Holdings Inc	Finance Intermediaries & Services	12/31/18	958.2	28.9	2240.3	545.3	138	7589528
ORCL	Oracle Corp	Internet & Software	5/31/19	39506.0	11083.0	108709.0	21785.0	2586	2307228138
ORAN	Orange	Services	12/31/18	41384.0	1954.0	96592.0	30669.0	261	35459874
ORC	Orchid Island Capital, Inc.	REITs	12/31/18	37.9	-44.4	3395.6	336.1	109	27591509

T42

Table columns: **EARNINGS PER SHARE** — QUARTERLY (1st, 2nd, 3rd) and ANNUAL (2018, 2017, 2016); **P/E RATIO** (high – low); **DIVIDENDS PER SHARE** (2018, 2017, 2016); **AV. YLD %**; **DIV. DECLARED** (AMOUNT, PAYABLE); **PRICE RANGE 2018** (high – low).

1st	2nd	3rd	Ann 2018	Ann 2017	Ann 2016	P/E Hi	P/E Lo	Div 2018	Div 2017	Div 2016	AV YLD %	AMOUNT	PAYABLE	Price Hi	Price Lo
-	-	-	0.66	0.73	0.73	15.5	14.1	0.77	0.79	0.72	7.9	0.06150	2/3/20	10.2	9.3
-	-	-	0.66	0.76	0.77	15.6	14.0	0.80	0.83	0.76	8.3	0.06050	2/3/20	10.3	9.3
-	-	-	0.49	0.55	0.68	25.9	22.7	0.51	0.60	0.64	4.2	0.037M	2/3/20	12.7	11.1
-	-	-	1.26	1.42	1.47	13.1	10.9	1.35	1.44	1.54	8.8	0.1020	2/3/20	16.5	13.7
-	-	-	0.50	0.62	0.73	20.6	19.5	0.51	0.62	0.68	5.1	0.0160	2/3/20	10.3	9.7
-	-	-	0.59	0.63	0.68	23.7	21.2	0.61	0.67	0.68	4.6	0.0425M	2/3/20	14.0	12.5
-	-	-	0.45	0.49	0.53	31.0	27.7	0.46	0.51	0.58	3.5	0.0315M	2/3/20	13.9	12.5
-	-	-	0.56	0.61	0.67	24.1	21.2	0.60	0.66	0.67	4.6	0.044M	2/3/20	13.5	11.9
-	-	-	0.59	0.64	0.69	24.6	0.0	0.63	0.68	0.71	4.8	0.041M	2/3/20	14.5	0.0
-	-	-	0.61	0.68	0.76	23.5	20.6	0.63	0.78	0.78	4.6	0.0445M	2/3/20	14.4	12.6
-	-	-	0.70	0.70	0.80	21.0	0.0	0.74	0.79	0.81	5.5	0.0490	2/3/20	14.7	0.0
-	-	-	0.57	0.65	0.72	25.6	0.0	0.63	0.71	0.73	5.6	0.0405M	2/3/20	14.6	0.0
-	-	-	1.16	1.34	1.56	20.1	18.8	2.08	3.32	1.71	9.1	0.11350	2/3/20	23.4	21.8
-	-	-	0.35	0.39	0.41	21.4	0.0	0.40	0.43	0.48	5.7	0.030	2/3/20	7.5	0.0
-	-	-	0.25	0.26	0.07	39.6	0.0	0.21	0.30	0.06	2.2	0.0150	2/3/20	9.9	0.0
-	-	-	0.81	0.87	0.72	20.5	17.0	0.83	0.89	0.87	5.3	0.0625M	2/3/20	16.6	13.7
-	-	-	0.82	0.80	0.86	17.7	14.5	0.74	0.81	0.91	5.4	0.0595M	2/3/20	14.6	11.9
-	-	-	0.43	0.48	0.50	27.2	23.8	0.46	0.49	0.51	4.1	0.036M	2/3/20	11.7	10.3
-	-	-	0.38	0.40	0.40	28.2	24.8	0.39	0.39	0.39	3.8	0.031M	2/3/20	10.7	9.4
-	-	-	0.57	0.49	0.62	25.0	0.0	0.93	0.67	0.81	7.1	0.0375M	2/3/20	14.2	0.0
-	-	-	0.71	0.60	0.79	20.8	18.2	0.70	0.63	0.82	5.0	0.0515M	2/3/20	14.8	12.9
-	-	-	0.62	0.27	0.69	22.1	19.1	0.62	0.27	0.70	4.8	0.045M	2/3/20	13.7	11.8
-	-	-	0.55	0.25	0.81	27.0	0.0	0.70	0.29	0.63	5.5	0.034M	2/3/20	14.8	0.0
-	-	-	0.37	0.16	0.41	28.5	25.4	0.38	0.39	0.39	3.8	0.028M	2/3/20	10.6	9.4
-	-	-	0.67	0.29	0.65	21.3	18.5	0.70	0.76	0.79	5.1	0.048M	2/3/20	14.3	12.4
-	-	-	0.52	0.55	0.57	27.6	0.0	0.54	0.55	0.55	4.1	0.0395M	2/3/20	14.3	0.0
-	-	-	0.68	0.74	0.81	23.4	19.8	0.71	0.75	0.83	4.7	0.044M	2/3/20	15.9	13.5
-	-	-	0.55	0.51	0.68	28.5	0.0	0.77	1.12	0.62	6.0	0.038M	2/3/20	15.7	0.0
-	-	-	0.69	-	0.80	20.7	17.9	0.69	0.78	0.83	5.1	0.0505M	2/3/20	14.3	12.3
-	-	-	1.44	-	-	17.7	14.6	1.51	0.64	-	6.3	0.11850	2/3/20	25.4	21.1
-	-	-	0.76	0.72	0.77	13.8	11.2	0.77	0.78	0.80	7.9	0.0610	2/3/20	10.5	8.5
-	-	-	0.69	0.71	0.69	14.9	12.0	0.73	0.74	0.70	7.7	0.0560	2/3/20	10.3	8.3
-	-	-	1.66	1.75	1.86	15.5	12.2	1.69	1.84	2.13	7.1	0.13550	2/3/20	25.8	20.2
-	-	-	0.69	0.73	0.71	21.2	18.4	0.69	0.78	0.85	5.0	0.0535M	2/3/20	14.7	12.7
-	-	-	1.05	1.14	1.12	17.5	13.0	1.27	1.28	1.35	7.6	0.1170	2/3/20	18.4	13.7
-	-	-	0.33	0.41	0.39	33.4	25.3	0.84	1.00	0.98	8.1	0.190	12/31/19	11.0	8.3
-	-	-	0.15	0.16	0.18	92.7	80.3	0.98	0.91	0.93	7.4	0.23250	12/31/19	13.9	12.1
-	-	-	0.18	0.19	0.20	93.4	77.8	1.12	0.98	0.98	7.1	0.2650	12/31/19	16.8	14.0
-	-	-	0.33	0.32	0.32	32.3	29.2	0.31	0.32	0.33	3.0	0.0265M	2/3/20	10.7	9.6
-	-	-	0.52	0.53	0.55	29.4	26.0	0.52	0.52	0.54	3.6	0.042M	2/3/20	15.3	13.5
-	-	-	0.56	0.56	0.58	29.8	25.4	0.55	0.55	0.56	3.6	0.0455M	2/3/20	16.7	14.2
-	-	-	0.55	0.57	0.58	29.9	0.0	0.54	0.53	0.56	3.5	0.0435M	2/3/20	16.4	0.0
-	-	-	0.43	0.46	0.45	14.0	13.0	0.45	0.46	0.42	7.8	0.03650	2/3/20	6.0	5.6
-	-	-	1.19	1.29	1.21	13.6	12.2	1.30	1.25	1.19	8.5	0.09150	2/3/20	16.1	14.5
-	-	-	0.43	0.50	-	41.1	31.0	1.34	1.24	1.24	8.2	0.310	12/31/19	17.7	13.3
-	-	-	0.43	0.50	0.47	28.4	23.4	1.08	0.99	1.01	9.4	0.240	12/31/19	12.2	10.1
-	-	-	1.18	1.22	1.29	19.3	16.5	1.24	1.28	1.35	5.9	0.09250	2/3/20	22.8	19.5
-	-	-	0.57	-	-	25.4	21.9	0.64	0.65	0.65	4.7	0.0445M	2/3/20	14.5	12.5
-	-	-	0.56	0.58	0.66	26.1	21.2	0.56	0.59	0.68	4.2	0.0435M	2/3/20	14.6	11.9
-	-	0.35	1.28	-	-			0.35	-	-		0.1750	2/7/20		
-	56.11	-	194.80	126.77	103.61	20.0	12.2	-	-	-		-	-	3892.9	2381.9
-	-3.69	-	1.59	1.10	1.28	12.8	5.3	0.05	-	-	0.3	-	-	20.4	8.5
-	0.04	-	-	-	-			-	-	-		-	-		
-	-2.22	-	-4.20	-1.19	-9.73			-	-	-		0.010	10/15/15	4.8	0.5
-	-1.08	-	5.39	1.70	-0.75	12.7	6.9	3.10	3.06	3.02	5.9	0.790Y	18/53/27	68.4	37.3
-	-0.26	-	-2.16	1.68	0.25			-	0.45	0.96		0.150Y	18/53/27	20.4	11.6
-	-0.32	-	-0.53	-1.01	-1.61			-	-	-		-	-	2.4	1.3
-	0.11	-	1.52	0.88	1.03	15.9	10.8	0.25	0.24	0.24	1.2	0.14580	3/31/20	24.2	16.4
-	1.25	-	2.12	3.10	1.69	21.4	18.0	1.36	1.24	1.13	3.2	0.38750Y	18/53/27	45.4	38.3
-	-	-	18.24	-5.53	-22.94	0.1	0.0	0.01	-	-	0.6	-	-	2.5	0.8
-	-0.54	-	-0.33	-1.69	-0.92			-	-	-		-	-	20.3	12.3
0.46	-	-	1.11	1.47	1.87	34.6	23.0	0.92	0.88	0.84	2.9	0.18750Y	2/28/20	38.4	25.5
-	-	0.67	1.24	1.92	1.62	19.4	16.1	1.78	0.76	0.75	8.1	0.20Y	18/53/27	24.1	20.0
-	-	0.27	1.95	3.26	-0.02	13.9	7.9	0.80	0.80	0.80	3.9	0.20Y	18/53/27	27.1	15.4
-	-	0.63	1.40	0.51	1.90	32.1	24.3	2.64	2.54	2.36	6.8	0.670Z	18/53/27	45.0	34.0
-	-	1.32	5.83	4.65	4.78	14.5	12.3	2.40	2.25	2.15	3.1	0.650Y	18/53/27	84.8	71.6
-	-	0.01	0.46	-1.98	-0.01	22.0	12.1	-	-	-		0.050	5/31/01	10.1	5.6
-	-	0.11	0.35	-0.16	-1.17	21.5	8.7	-	-	-		-	-	7.5	3.0
-	-	0.33	3.25	3.08	2.65	29.6	23.4	1.84	1.68	1.40	2.1	0.540Y	18/53/27	96.3	76.1
-	-	0.25	1.05	1.28	1.39	29.9	22.3	1.80	1.74	1.66	6.4	0.450Z	1/7/20	31.4	23.4
-	-	-	-1.29	-0.90				-	-	-		-	-	10.1	9.8
-	1.82	-	3.29	1.35	1.59	13.4	7.5	-	-	-		0.250Y	18/53/27	44.3	24.6
-	-	0.74	2.78	1.29	1.66	27.5	19.5	3.25	2.72	2.46	4.7	0.9350Y	18/53/27	76.5	54.3
-0.30	-	-	-0.17	0.06	0.04			-	-	-		-	-	9.1	6.7
-	0.17	-	2.34	1.17	1.75	15.7	11.3	-	-	-		-	-	36.8	26.5
-	-0.32	-	-0.71	-0.74	-1.38			-	-	-		-	-	16.4	10.2
-	-	0.29	2.05	1.67	-0.09	15.3	11.9	0.44	0.44	0.44	1.6	0.120	11/22/19	31.3	24.3
-	0.69	-	0.90	2.21	2.07	66.8	49.8	0.76	0.64	0.60	1.4	0.240Y	18/53/27	60.1	44.8
-	-	-	0.62	0.62	1.04	26.9	23.5	0.70	0.65	0.61	4.5	-	-	16.7	14.6
-	-	-0.14	-0.85	0.05	0.08			1.07	1.68	1.68	17.1	0.080Z	2/26/20	7.1	5.2

SYMBOL	COMPANY	NATURE OF BUSINESS	FISCAL YEAR-END	TOTAL REV. $MILL	NET INCOME $MILL	TOTAL ASSETS $MILL	NET STK EQUITY $MILL	NO OF INST	INST. HOLDINGS (SHARES)
OEC	Orion Engineered Carbons SA	Specialty Chemicals	12/31/18	1578.2	121.3	1273.0	158.9	164	57090491
ORN	Orion Group Holdings Inc	Construction Services	12/31/18	520.9	-94.4	312.9	141.6	127	32260139
IX	Orix Corp	Credit & Lending	3/31/19	2433563.0	323745.0	12174917.0	2897074.0	173	4564712
ORA	Ormat Technologies Inc	Electric Utilities	12/31/18	719.3	98.0	3121.3	1319.8	264	43864058
OSK	Oshkosh Corp (New)	Autos- Manufacturing	9/30/19	8382.0	579.4	5566.3	2599.8	608	74372203
OR	Osisko Gold Royalties Ltd	Precious Metals	12/31/18	490.5	-105.6	2234.6	1771.6	-	0
SFTW U	Osprey Technology Acquisition Cor	IT Services	12/31/18	-	-0.0	0.2	0.0	-	0
OUT	OUTFRONT Media Inc	REITs	12/31/18	1606.2	107.9	3828.7	1102.8	368	156289977
OSG	Overseas Shipholding Group Inc (N	Equipment & Services	12/31/18	366.2	13.5	827.7	329.5	53	1749229
OVV	Ovintiv Inc	Production & Extraction	12/31/18	5939.0	1069.0	15344.0	7447.0	719	1043994935
OMI	Owens & Minor, Inc.	Medical Instruments & Equipment	12/31/18	9838.7	-437.0	3773.8	518.4	331	73790147
OC	Owens Corning	Construction Materials	12/31/18	7057.0	545.0	9771.0	4283.0	552	139221707
ORCC	Owl Rock Capital Corp	Finance Intermediaries & Services	12/31/18	388.9	245.5	5951.0	3264.8	48	51519692
OXM	Oxford Industries, Inc.	Apparel, Footwear & Accessories	2/2/19	1107.5	66.3	727.3	478.4	272	21132150
T 34D	Pacific Bell	Services	12/31/98	9406.0	1077.0	15093.0	3260.0	-	0
ROYT	Pacific Coast Oil Trust	Oil Royalty Traders	12/31/18	15.1	12.6	204.6	204.6	35	6739978
PACD	Pacific Drilling SA	Production & Extraction	12/31/18	28.5	-27.5	2748.2	1619.0	74	67425956
PKG	Packaging Corp of America	Containers & Packaging	12/31/18	7014.6	738.0	6569.7	2672.4	800	128216621
PD	PagerDuty Inc	IT Services	1/31/19	117.8	-40.7	197.2	104.1	121	41203100
PAGS	PagSeguro Digital Ltd	Internet & Software	12/31/18	4334.7	1.1	11417.3	6550.6	269	168213963
PANW	Palo Alto Networks, Inc	Internet & Software	7/31/19	2899.6	-81.9	6592.2	1586.3	943	96815954
PAM	Pampa Energia SA	Electric Utilities	12/31/18	110080.0	8435.0	213835.0	51523.0	-	0
PHX	Panhandle Oil & Gas Inc	Production & Extraction	9/30/19	66.0	-40.7	126.6	79.3	93	11082063
PARR	Par Pacific Holdings Inc	Refining & Marketing	12/31/18	3410.7	39.4	1460.7	512.3	229	53789514
PAR	Par Technology Corp.	Electronic Instruments & Related Pro	12/31/18	201.2	-24.1	94.7	45.9	101	9561855
PGRE	Paramount Group Inc	REITs	12/31/18	759.0	9.1	8756.0	4000.8	225	158514880
PKE	Park Aerospace Corp	Electrical Equipment	3/3/19	51.1	113.5	188.9	159.0	173	20709354
PK	Park Hotels & Resorts Inc	REITs	12/31/18	2737.0	472.0	9363.0	5632.0	381	300599121
PKD	Parker Drilling Co	Production & Extraction	12/31/18	480.8	-165.7	828.4	126.9	123	25513421
PH	Parker Hannifin Corp	Industrial Machinery & Equipment	6/30/19	14320.3	1512.4	17576.7	5962.0	1048	128190462
PE	Parsley Energy Inc	Production & Extraction	12/31/18	1826.4	369.1	9391.4	5568.1	476	284952051
PSN	Parsons Corp (DE)	IT Services	12/31/18	3560.5	222.3	2612.6	908.8	129	99348918
PRTY	Party City Holdco Inc	Retail - General Merchandise/Depart	12/31/18	2427.5	123.3	3642.3	1046.7	162	110616845
PAYC	Paycom Software Inc	Internet & Software	12/31/18	566.3	137.1	1521.9	334.8	568	45371175
PBF	PBF Energy Inc	Refining & Marketing	12/31/18	27186.1	128.3	8005.4	2676.5	399	111494701
PBFX	PBF Logistics LP	Equipment & Services	12/31/18	283.4	121.1	956.4	23.7	69	21038817
PCM	PCM Fund Inc	Holding and other Investment Office	6/30/19	11.9	8.0	193.9	118.2	38	1128936
BTU	Peabody Energy Corp (New)	Mining	12/31/18	5581.8	646.9	7423.7	3395.6	452	141118739
PSO	Pearson Plc	Publishing	12/31/18	4129.0	588.0	7905.0	4516.0	137	28890894
PEB	Pebblebrook Hotel Trust	REITs	12/31/18	828.7	13.4	6978.3	3759.8	345	169478577
PBA	Pembina Pipeline Corp	Equipment & Services	12/31/18	7784.0	1278.0	26664.0	14344.0	422	284277877
JCP	Penney (J.C.) Co.,Inc. (Holding Co.)	Retail - General Merchandise/Depart	2/2/19	12019.0	-255.0	7721.0	1170.0	478	266018417
PEI	Pennsylvania Real Estate Investme	REITs	12/31/18	362.4	-110.3	2405.1	440.8	284	77731658
PFSI	PennyMac Financial Services Inc (N	Credit & Lending	12/31/18	1129.2	87.7	7478.6	1653.8	-	0
PMT	Pennymac Mortgage Investment Tr	REITs	12/31/18	526.2	152.8	7813.4	1566.1	-	0
PAG	Penske Automotive Group Inc	Retail - Automotive	12/31/18	22785.1	471.0	10904.5	2609.1	361	100250186
PNR	Pentair PLC	Industrial Machinery & Equipment	12/31/18	2965.1	347.4	3806.5	1836.1	677	162008413
PEN	Penumbra Inc	Medical Instruments & Equipment	12/31/18	444.9	6.6	515.0	422.2	282	35428436
PFGC	Performance Food Group Co	Retail - Food & Beverage, Drug & To	6/29/19	19743.5	166.8	4653.5	1298.2	300	106283496
PKI	PerkinElmer, Inc.	Biotechnology	12/30/18	2778.0	237.9	5975.5	2585.0	657	149082579
PBT	Permian Basin Royalty Trust	Oil Royalty Traders	12/31/18	32.1	30.8	4.0	0.5	115	6067933
PVL	Permianville Royalty Trust	Oil Royalty Traders	12/31/18	15.9	14.4	84.1	84.1	34	21583653
PRT	PermRock Royalty Trust	Production & Extraction	12/31/18	16.2	15.6	93.6	92.2	21	6442718
PRGO	Perrigo Company plc	Pharmaceuticals	12/31/18	4731.7	131.0	10983.4	5668.0	-	0
PRSP	Perspecta Inc	IT Services	3/31/19	4030.0	72.0	6083.0	2162.0	471	129367876
PTR	PetroChina Co Ltd	Production & Extraction	12/31/17	2015890.0	22793.0	2404910.0	1193810.0	199	6457321
PBR	Petroleo Brasileiro SA	Production & Extraction	12/31/18	95584.0	7173.0	222068.0	71544.0	552	593796875
PFE	Pfizer Inc	Pharmaceuticals	12/31/18	53647.0	11153.0	159422.0	63407.0	3349	5230056545
PCG	PG&E Corp (Holding Co)	Electric Utilities	12/31/18	16759.0	-6837.0	76995.0	12651.0	655	549986181
GHY	PGIM Global High Yield Fund Inc	Finance Intermediaries & Services	7/31/19	54.2	37.4	984.2	680.9	93	20634862
ISD	PGIM High Yield Bond Fund Inc	Holding and other Investment Office	5/31/19	42.0	30.1	728.6	538.9	90	13099322
PGTI	PGT Innovations Inc	Metal Products	12/29/18	698.5	53.9	862.2	385.5	233	64987799
GLT	PH Glatfelter Co	Paper & Forest Products	12/31/18	866.3	-177.6	1339.8	538.9	225	52702262
PM	Philip Morris International Inc	Tobacco Products	12/31/18	29625.0	7911.0	39801.0	-12459.0	2306	1385064533
PSX	Phillips 66	Refining & Marketing	12/31/18	114217.0	5595.0	54302.0	24653.0	1739	351941985
PSXP	Phillips 66 Partners LP	Equipment & Services	12/31/18	1486.0	796.0	5819.0	-1.0	243	58675282
FENG	Phoenix New Media Ltd	Radio & Television	12/31/18	1377.4	-63.2	4630.7	3079.7	50	14859083
DNK	Phoenix Tree Holdings Ltd	Services						-	0
PHR	Phreesia Inc	Business Services	1/31/19	99.9	-15.1	59.3	-4.5	69	17836959
DOC	Physicians Realty Trust	REITs	12/31/18	422.6	56.2	4142.8	2379.5	351	197120796
PDM	Piedmont Office Realty Trust Inc	REITs	12/31/18	526.0	130.3	3592.4	1710.4	317	128150752
PIR	Pier 1 Imports Inc.	Retail - Furniture & Home Furnishing	3/2/19	1552.9	-198.8	656.3	89.5	157	18233020
PCQ	Pimco California Municipal Income	Holding and other Investment Office	12/31/18	22.7	17.3	493.9	370.9	40	1454497
PCK	Pimco California Municipal Income	Holding and other Investment Office	12/31/18	22.4	17.4	502.5	393.9	46	2152000
PZC	Pimco California Municipal Income	Holding and other Investment Office	12/31/18	18.8	14.3	410.7	308.8	36	1474613
PTY	PIMCO Corporate & Income Opport	Holding and other Investment Office	7/31/19	133.4	116.7	1885.3	1503.9	142	10605390
PCN	PIMCO Corporate & Income Strateg	Holding and other Investment Office	7/31/19	32.9	28.2	760.1	739.1	-	0
PCI	PIMCO Dynamic Credit & Mortgage	Holding and other Investment Office	6/30/19	406.5	258.6	6084.0	3245.0	206	28561554
PDI	PIMCO Dynamic Income Fund	Holding and other Investment Office	6/30/19	216.3	153.6	2743.6	1603.4	152	9652966
PGP	PIMCO Global StocksPLUS & Inco	Holding and other Investment Office	6/30/19	14.9	12.1	273.9	107.6	44	906418

T44

| EARNINGS PER SHARE | | | | | | P/E RATIO | DIVIDENDS PER SHARE | | | AV. YLD % | DIV. DECLARED | | PRICE RANGE |
| QUARTERLY | | | ANNUAL | | | | | | | | | | 2018 |
1st	2nd	3rd	2018	2017	2016		2018	2017	2016		AMOUNT	PAYABLE	
0.31	-	-	1.99	1.07	0.82	-	0.80	0.77	0.74			0.20	12/30/19	-
-	-	0.14	-3.31	0.01	-0.13	-	-	-	-	-	-	-	5.9 - 1.8
-	-	60.89	-244.15	208.68	198.52	0.4 - 0.3	282.18	231.75	286.77	375.5	-	-	85.7 - 68.6
-	-	0.30	1.92	3.06	1.87	40.6 - 26.5	0.53	0.41	0.52	0.8	0.110Y	12/4/19	77.9 - 50.8
-	-	2.72	6.29	3.77	2.91	15.2 - 9.5	0.96	0.84	0.74	1.2	0.30Y	18/53/27	95.4 - 59.7
-	-	-0.32	-0.67	-0.33	0.40	-	0.20	0.18	0.16	1.6	0.050	1/15/20	17.4 - 8.4
-	-	-	0.00	0.00	-	-	-	-	-	-	-	-	10.2 - 0.0
-	-	0.27	0.75	0.90	0.66	37.8 - 24.2	1.44	1.44	1.36	5.8	0.360Y	18/53/27	28.3 - 18.1
-	-	-0.04	0.15	0.64	-3.25	17.7 - 10.0	-	-	-	-	0.17970	5/13/16	2.6 - 1.5
-	-	0.11	1.11	0.85	-1.07	-	0.06	0.06	0.06	-	-	-	-
-	-	0.02	-7.28	1.20	1.76	-	0.85	1.03	1.02	16.5	0.00250Y	18/53/27	8.2 - 2.5
-	-	1.36	4.89	2.55	3.41	14.0 - 8.8	0.63	0.81	0.74	1.1	0.240Y	18/53/27	68.5 - 43.2
-	-	0.31	1.38	1.55	0.78	13.9 - 11.2	-	-	-	-	0.047Y	1/31/20	19.1 - 15.5
-	-	0.10	3.89	3.15	1.85	21.7 - 16.5	1.08	1.08	1.00	1.5	0.370Y	1/31/20	84.3 - 64.3
-	0.08	-	0.33	0.11	0.01	7.1 - 0.6	0.30	0.14	0.01	17.1	0.00390Z	1/24/20	2.4 - 0.2
-	-0.98	-	-3700.20	6400.00	7600.00	-	-	-	-	-	-	-	-
-	-	1.89	7.80	7.07	4.75	14.6 - 10.6	3.00	2.52	2.36	3.0	0.790Y	18/53/27	113.9 - 82.9
-	-	-0.20	-1.91	-	-	-	-	-	-	-	-	-	57.4 - 21.8
-	-	-	2.86	1.83	0.48	-	-	0.91	-	-	-	-	-
-0.62	-	-	-1.61	-2.39	-2.59	-	-	-	-	-	-	-	254.9 - 179.7
-	-	-	4.31	2.34	-0.01	8.9 - 2.8	-	-	-	-	-	-	38.5 - 12.2
-	-	0.28	0.86	0.21	-0.61	19.4 - 12.5	0.16	0.16	0.16	1.2	0.040Y	3/6/20	16.7 - 10.8
-	-	-1.65	0.85	1.57	-1.08	29.9 - 16.6	-	-	-	-	-	-	25.4 - 14.1
-	-	-0.36	-1.50	-0.22	0.11	-	-	-	-	-	-	-	31.3 - 20.0
-	-	0.03	0.04	0.37	-0.05	374.8 - 306.5	0.40	0.38	0.38	2.9	0.10Z	18/53/27	15.0 - 12.3
-	-	0.12	1.02	0.46	0.89	22.5 - 14.6	3.40	0.40	0.40	19.8	1.7Y	2/20/20	22.9 - 14.9
-	-	0.02	2.31	12.21	-	14.3 - 9.5	2.74	4.63	-	10.1	0.550Z	18/53/27	33.0 - 22.0
-	-	0.27	-	-13.35	-27.90	-	-	-	-	-	1.81250Y	9/30/18	22.8 - 11.3
2.60	-	-	7.83	7.25	5.89	26.7 - 18.5	2.74	2.58	2.52	1.6	0.880Y	18/53/27	209.3 - 144.8
-	-	0.43	1.35	0.42	-0.46	16.1 - 10.5	-	-	-	-	0.050Y	18/53/27	21.8 - 14.1
-	-	0.57	8.34	3.49	-0.45	5.1 - 3.6	-	-	-	-	-	-	42.4 - 30.1
-	-	-3.02	1.27	1.79	0.98	9.7 - 1.3	-	-	-	-	-	-	12.3 - 1.6
-	-	0.67	2.34	1.13	0.74	119.5 - 49.8	-	-	-	-	-	-	279.7 - 116.5
-	-	0.57	1.10	3.73	1.74	33.3 - 19.6	1.20	1.20	1.20	4.0	0.30Y	18/53/27	36.6 - 21.5
-	-	0.50	1.73	2.17	2.01	13.5 - 11.3	1.97	1.86	1.70	9.4	0.520	11/26/19	23.3 - 19.6
-	-	-	0.88	0.98	1.22	13.3 - 11.7	0.98	1.46	0.96	8.8	0.080	2/3/20	11.7 - 10.3
-	-	-0.81	4.43	3.67	-40.45	8.2 - 2.0	0.48	-	-	2.2	0.1450Y	11/29/19	36.2 - 9.0
-	-	-	0.76	0.50	-2.87	17.3 - 10.5	0.68	0.40	0.53	6.6	-	-	13.2 - 8.0
-	-	0.17	-0.06	1.19	0.64	-	1.52	1.52	1.52	5.3	0.39370Z	1/15/20	34.1 - 24.9
-	-	0.66	2.28	1.88	1.01	22.1 - 13.3	2.24	2.04	1.90	5.3	0.30630	3/2/20	50.5 - 30.4
-	-	-0.29	-0.37	0.00	-1.68	-	-	-	-	-	0.20Y	18/53/27	1.9 - 0.6
-	-	0.22	-1.98	-0.89	-0.40	-	0.84	0.84	0.84	13.9	0.42970Z	12/16/19	7.7 - 4.4
-	-	1.51	2.59	4.03	2.94	13.3 - 7.9	0.40	-	-	1.5	0.12GY	11/29/19	34.5 - 20.3
-	-	0.71	1.99	1.48	1.08	11.7 - 9.5	1.88	1.88	1.88	8.7	0.470Z	1/30/20	23.2 - 18.8
-	-	1.42	5.53	7.14	3.99	9.7 - 7.4	1.42	1.26	1.10	3.1	0.410Y	18/53/27	53.7 - 41.0
-	-	0.55	1.96	3.63	2.85	-	1.05	1.38	1.34	-	0.190	18/53/27	-
-	-	0.32	0.18	0.13	0.44	1018.9 - 643.6	-	-	-	-	-	-	183.4 - 115.8
0.34	-	-	1.90	0.93	0.70	27.1 - 16.7	-	-	-	-	0.070Y	18/53/27	51.5 - 31.6
-	-	0.52	2.13	2.64	2.12	47.5 - 34.2	0.28	0.28	0.28	0.3	0.070Y	18/53/27	101.1 - 72.8
-	-	0.13	0.66	0.63	0.42	12.9 - 5.3	0.66	0.63	0.42	11.6	0.04310	2/14/20	8.5 - 3.5
-	-	0.08	0.43	1.36	0.26	8.5 - 3.3	0.42	1.36	0.24	16.4	0.02060Z	2/14/20	3.6 - 1.4
-	-	0.21	1.28	-	-	8.2 - 4.2	1.28	-	-	16.4	0.03220	2/14/20	10.4 - 5.4
-	-	0.67	0.95	0.84	-28.01	-	0.76	0.64	0.58	-	0.210	12/17/19	-
-	0.18	-	-	-	-	-	-	-	-	-	0.060Y	18/53/27	28.0 - 17.3
-	-	0.26	-	0.12	0.04	-	-	9.26	3.91	-	-	-	68.6 - 45.3
-	-	0.01	0.55	-0.01	-0.37	32.1 - 23.3	0.10	-	-	0.7	-	-	17.6 - 12.8
-	-	1.36	1.87	3.52	1.17	23.7 - 18.3	1.36	1.28	1.20	3.4	0.380Y	18/53/27	44.4 - 34.2
-	-	-3.06	-13.25	3.21	2.78	-	-	1.55	1.93	-	0.530Y	18/53/27	24.4 - 3.8
-	-	-	0.86	0.97	1.03	17.5 - 15.1	1.04	1.19	1.34	7.3	0.1050	2/28/20	15.0 - 13.0
-	-	-	0.90	0.98	1.06	17.1 - 14.6	1.09	1.25	1.36	7.5	0.1050	2/28/20	15.4 - 13.1
-	-	0.26	1.00	0.77	0.47	18.4 - 13.4	-	-	-	-	-	-	18.4 - 13.4
-	-	0.28	-4.06	0.18	0.49	-	0.52	0.39	0.50	3.4	0.130Y	2/1/20	18.9 - 9.7
-	-	1.22	5.08	3.88	4.48	18.1 - 13.1	4.49	4.22	4.12	5.5	1.170Y	18/53/27	91.9 - 66.4
-	-	1.58	11.80	9.85	2.92	10.1 - 6.8	3.10	2.73	2.45	3.1	0.90Y	18/53/27	119.7 - 80.8
-	-	1.15	4.00	2.59	2.20	15.7 - 10.7	2.94	2.40	1.98	5.6	0.8750	2/13/20	62.8 - 42.7
-	-	0.13	-0.11	0.06	0.14	-	-	-	-	-	-	-	4.8 - 2.0
-	-	-	-	-	-	-	-	-	-	-	-	-	-
-	-	-0.07	-24.81	-	-	-	-	-	-	-	-	-	30.0 - 22.5
-	-	0.08	0.30	0.23	0.22	64.1 - 51.4	0.92	0.91	0.90	5.1	0.230Z	1/17/20	19.2 - 15.4
-	-	0.07	1.00	0.92	0.74	22.4 - 16.8	0.84	1.34	0.84	4.1	0.210Z	18/53/27	22.4 - 16.8
-	-	-14.15	2.80	7.40	9.20	10.1 - 1.1	5.60	5.60	5.60	50.3	1.40Y	1/31/18	28.4 - 3.2
-	-	-	0.92	0.97	0.95	22.5 - 17.7	0.92	0.92	0.92	4.9	0.065M	2/3/20	20.7 - 16.3
-	-	-	0.54	0.60	0.62	19.0 - 14.8	0.42	0.57	0.61	4.5	0.032M	2/3/20	10.3 - 8.0
-	-	-	0.64	0.67	0.65	18.2 - 15.2	0.54	0.63	0.72	4.9	0.038M	2/3/20	11.6 - 9.7
-	-	-	1.30	1.21	1.30	14.6 - 12.0	1.56	1.73	1.59	8.7	0.130	2/3/20	19.0 - 15.6
-	-	-	-	-	-	-	-	-	-	-	0.11250	2/3/20	19.7 - 15.3
-	-	-	1.95	1.62	2.01	13.2 - 10.8	1.97	2.60	2.18	8.2	0.1740	2/3/20	25.6 - 21.1
-	-	-	2.95	2.60	3.87	11.5 - 10.0	2.65	4.10	5.24	8.3	0.22050	2/3/20	33.8 - 29.4
-	-	-	1.09	1.15	1.15	13.9 - 10.3	1.61	1.87	2.20	12.9	0.09390	2/3/20	15.2 - 11.2

SYMBOL	COMPANY	NATURE OF BUSINESS	FISCAL YEAR-END	TOTAL REV. $MILL	NET INCOME $MILL	TOTAL ASSETS $MILL	NET STK EQUITY $MILL	NO OF INST	INST. HOLDINGS (SHARES)
PHK	Pimco High Income Fund	Holding and other Investment Office	7/31/19	94.1	79.0	1222.1	894.0	131	9758185
PKO	PIMCO Income Opportunity Fund	Holding and other Investment Office	6/30/19	42.6	31.3	627.5	410.1	75	3391204
PFL	PIMCO Income Strategy Fund	Holding and other Investment Office	7/31/19	28.6	23.8	435.3	350.7	74	4020337
PFN	PIMCO Income Strategy Fund II	Holding and other Investment Office	7/31/19	60.8	51.0	874.7	720.4	108	10536760
PMF	Pimco Municipal Income Fund	Holding and other Investment Office	12/31/18	28.6	22.9	597.2	485.0	58	2434826
PML	Pimco Municipal Income Fund II	Holding and other Investment Office	12/31/18	64.6	50.5	1397.6	1022.0	113	6626685
PMX	Pimco Municipal Income Fund III	Holding and other Investment Office	12/31/18	31.7	25.0	649.4	500.3	65	2303167
PNF	Pimco New York Municipal Income	Holding and other Investment Office	12/31/18	7.1	5.5	154.3	128.9	31	1152381
PNI	Pimco New York Municipal Income	Holding and other Investment Office	12/31/18	10.5	7.9	225.5	177.0	31	995968
PYN	Pimco New York Municipal Income	Holding and other Investment Office	12/31/18	4.4	3.3	91.9	78.9	20	162258
RCS	PIMCO Strategic Income Fund Inc	Holding and other Investment Office	6/30/19	35.8	26.0	1537.7	309.3	81	5300992
PING	Ping Identity Holding Corp	IT Services	12/31/18	201.6	-13.4	857.0	509.1	66	76667062
PNW	Pinnacle West Capital Corp	Electric Utilities	12/31/18	3691.2	511.0	17664.2	5222.9	785	118480923
PINS	Pinterest Inc	Entertainment	12/31/18	755.9	-63.0	1152.7	870.8	258	117607464
PHD	Pioneer Floating Rate Trust	Holding and other Investment Office	11/30/18	26.1	18.3	451.1	297.9	91	12670576
PHT	Pioneer High Income Trust	Holding and other Investment Office	3/31/19	30.6	23.5	421.0	289.6	64	5679630
MAV	Pioneer Municipal High Income Adv	Holding and other Investment Office	3/31/19	20.3	17.2	440.7	439.2	70	5039805
MHI	Pioneer Municipal High Income Tru	Holding and other Investment Office	4/30/19	19.7	16.8	413.4	413.0	64	5035354
PXD	Pioneer Natural Resources Co	Production & Extraction	12/31/18	9415.0	978.0	17903.0	12111.0	1066	170667992
PIPR	Piper Sandler Companies	Finance Intermediaries & Services	12/31/18	801.0	57.0	1345.3	677.4	293	15382909
PBI	Pitney Bowes Inc	Office Equipment & Furniture	12/31/18	3522.4	223.7	5972.9	239.5	528	194682706
PBI 08	Pitney-Bowes Credit Corp	Credit & Lending	12/31/01	587.8	160.1	5721.0	1476.4	-	0
PIC	Pivotal Investment Corp II	Business Services	3/31/19		-0.0	0.0	0.0	13	4307553
PJT	PJT Partners Inc	Finance Intermediaries & Services	12/31/18	580.2	27.2	671.8	-86.5	-	0
PAA	Plains All American Pipeline LP	Equipment & Services	12/31/18	34055.0	2216.0	25511.0		605	432179059
PAGP	Plains GP Holdings LP	Equipment & Services	12/31/18	34055.0	334.0	26830.0		378	171104884
PLNT	Planet Fitness Inc	Sporting & Recreational	12/31/18	572.9	88.0	1353.4	-374.6	411	88051400
PLT	Plantronics, Inc.	Manufacturing	3/31/19	1674.5	-135.6	3116.5	721.7	323	52949791
AGS	PlayAGS Inc	Industrial Machinery & Equipment	12/31/18	285.3	-20.8	731.3	135.8	136	35679808
PHI	PLDT Inc	Services	12/31/18	164752.0	18916.0	482750.0	112358.0	127	18298657
PNC	PNC Financial Services Group (The	Banking	12/31/18	19993.0	5301.0	382315.0	47728.0	1692	441533176
PNM	PNM Resources Inc	Electric Utilities	12/31/18	1436.6	86.2	6865.6	1699.9	389	97096133
PII	Polaris Inc	Autos- Manufacturing	12/31/18	6078.5	335.3	4124.9	873.9	658	58862362
POL	PolyOne Corp.	Plastics	12/31/18	3533.4	159.8	2723.3	540.0	371	91472474
POR	Portland General Electric Co.	Electric Utilities	12/31/18	1991.0	212.0	8110.0	2506.0	467	113803145
PKX	POSCO (South Korea)	Non-Precious Metals	12/31/18	64977777.4	1690612.4	78248265.2	43371259.6	256	18543869
POST	Post Holdings Inc	Food	9/30/19	5681.1	124.7	11951.6	2925.9	446	70746952
PSTL	Postal Realty Trust Inc	Property, Real Estate & Developmen	12/31/18	7.7	1.1	35.7	-5.7	43	3137472
PPG	PPG Industries Inc	Specialty Chemicals	12/31/18	15374.0	1341.0	16015.0	4630.0	1220	225326198
PPL	PPL Corp	Electric Utilities	12/31/18	7785.0	1827.0	43396.0	11657.0	1155	613408487
PQG	PQ Group Holdings Inc	Specialty Chemicals	12/31/18	1608.2	58.3	4327.4	1659.6	99	93891021
PDS	Precision Drilling Corp.	Production & Extraction	12/31/18	1541.2	-294.3	3636.0	1557.8	194	115378744
APTS	Preferred Apartment Communities I	REITs	12/31/18	397.3	43.5	4411.0	1608.1	216	30203500
PBH	Prestige Consumer Healthcare Inc	Pharmaceuticals	3/31/19	975.8	-35.8	3441.0	1095.8	337	75552024
PVG	Pretium Resources Inc	Precious Metals	12/31/18	454.6	36.6	1613.4	903.1	-	0
PRI	Primerica Inc	Life & Health	12/31/18	1899.8	324.1	12595.0	1461.5	394	44214548
PGZ	Principal Real Estate Income Fund	Finance Intermediaries & Services	10/31/19	12.7	7.7	218.3	157.7	-	0
PRA	ProAssurance Corp	General Insurance	12/31/18	886.0	47.1	4600.7	1523.0	314	54722674
PG	Procter & Gamble Company (The)	Household & Personal Products	6/30/19	67684.0	3897.0	115095.0	47194.0	3407	2043665033
PGR	Progressive Corp. (OH)	General Insurance	12/31/18	31979.0	2615.3	46575.0	10821.8	1200	567920352
PLD 29A	Prologis Euro Finance LLC	Finance Intermediaries & Services							
PLD	Prologis Inc	REITs	12/31/18	2804.4	1649.4	38417.7	22298.1	59	10207956
PUMP	ProPetro Holding Corp	Equipment & Services	12/31/18	1704.6	173.9	1274.5	797.4	304	91666633
PRO	Pros Holdings Inc	Internet & Software	12/31/18	197.0	-64.2	437.0	54.9	256	45013812
PROS	ProSight Global Inc	General Insurance	12/31/18	785.9	54.5	2577.1	389.8	52	42331945
PB	Prosperity Bancshares Inc.	Banking	12/31/18	843.2	321.8	22693.4	4052.8	400	73278281
PRLB	Proto Labs Inc	Manufacturing	12/31/18	445.6	76.6	619.0	541.5	321	32918142
PFS	Provident Financial Services Inc	Banking	12/31/18	418.5	118.4	9725.8	1359.0	243	54587357
PRU	Prudential Financial Inc	Life & Health	12/31/18	62992.0	4074.0	815078.0	48617.0	9	126178
PUK	Prudential Plc	Life & Health	12/31/18	25222.0	3010.0	508645.0	17249.0	288	29769039
PSB	PS Business Parks Inc	REITs	12/31/18	413.5	226.7	2068.6	1765.4	334	25477388
PEG 31	PSEG Power LLC	Electric Utilities	12/31/18	4146.0	365.0	12594.0	5960.0	-	0
TLK	PT Telekomunikasi Indonesia (Pers	Services	12/31/18	130788000.0	17802000.0	205900000.0	98739000.0	222	48284586
PEG	Public Service Enterprise Group Inc	Electric Utilities	12/31/18	9696.0	1438.0	45326.0	14377.0	1170	429112518
PSA	Public Storage	REITs	12/31/18	2754.3	1711.0	10928.3	9119.5	1035	177665822
PHM	PulteGroup Inc	Builders	12/31/18	10188.3	1022.0	10173.0	4817.8	838	292233838
PSTG	PURE Storage Inc	Internet & Software	1/31/19	1359.8	-178.4	1973.0	737.8	316	249597830
PMM	Putnam Managed Municipal Income	Holding and other Investment Office	10/31/19	22.7	18.9	531.9	500.6	101	6272921
PIM	Putnam Master Intermediate Incom	Holding and other Investment Office	9/30/30	14.8	12.3	486.3	250.0	81	20839737
PMO	Putnam Municipal Opportunities Tru	Holding and other Investment Office	4/30/30	26.9	21.7	669.0	595.3	104	8702447
PPT	Putnam Premier Income Trust	Holding and other Investment Office	7/31/30	33.1	27.9	942.6	562.1	149	36923638
NEW	Puxin Ltd	Educational Services	12/31/18	2228.1	-833.4	2737.0	547.9	26	8126666
PVH	PVH Corp	Apparel, Footwear & Accessories	2/3/19	9656.8	746.4	11863.7	5827.8	688	83129431
PYX	Pyxus International Inc	Tobacco Products	3/31/19	1801.6	-70.5	1859.3	183.7	50	10895447
PZN	Pzena Investment Management Inc	Wealth Management	12/31/18	153.6	13.8	171.0	33.0	109	13482713
QTWO	Q2 Holdings Inc	Internet & Software	12/31/18	241.1	-35.4	463.7	158.9	258	54751692
QEP	QEP Resources Inc	Production & Extraction	12/31/18	1932.6	-1011.6	6117.8	2750.9	383	289246614
QGEN	Qiagen NV	Biotechnology	12/31/18	1501.8	190.4	5748.3	2635.0	376	165913280
QTS	QTS Realty Trust Inc	REITs	12/31/18	450.5	-4.5	2862.0	1194.0	305	73948462
QUAD	Quad/Graphics, Inc.	Printing	12/31/18	4193.7	8.5	2469.1	442.5	180	34356292

T46

| EARNINGS PER SHARE | | | | | | P/E RATIO | | DIVIDENDS PER SHARE | | | AV. YLD | DIV. DECLARED | | PRICE RANGE | |
| QUARTERLY | | | ANNUAL | | | | | | | | % | | | 2018 | |
1st	2nd	3rd	2018	2017	2016			2018	2017	2016		AMOUNT	PAYABLE		
-	-	-	0.62	0.67	0.74	14.6 -	12.0	0.97	1.10	1.26	12.1	0.06130	2/3/20	9.0 -	7.5
-	-	-	2.18	2.28	2.33	12.8 -	11.6	2.28	2.62	2.79	8.5	0.190	2/3/20	27.9 -	25.4
-	-	-	0.87	0.88	0.88	13.9 -	12.6	1.08	1.08	1.08	9.3	0.090	2/3/20	12.1 -	11.0
-	-	-	0.79	0.80	0.87	13.6 -	12.3	0.96	0.96	1.03	9.2	0.080	2/3/20	10.8 -	9.7
-	-	-	0.89	0.91	0.90	17.6 -	14.5	0.72	0.74	0.97	5.0	0.054M	2/3/20	15.7 -	12.9
-	-	-	0.81	0.81	0.79	19.9 -	16.3	0.78	0.78	0.78	5.2	0.059M	2/3/20	16.1 -	13.2
-	-	-	0.76	0.77	0.77	17.0 -	14.9	0.78	0.68	0.75	6.3	0.046M	2/3/20	12.9 -	11.3
-	-	-	0.70	0.69	0.70	20.7 -	17.0	0.68	0.68	0.68	5.0	0.042M	2/3/20	14.5 -	11.9
-	-	-	0.71	0.72	0.72	17.3 -	15.1	0.61	0.62	0.80	5.2	0.04M	2/3/20	12.3 -	10.7
-	-	-	0.57	0.56	0.56	18.2 -	0.0	0.51	0.52	0.58	5.3	0.0355M	2/3/20	10.4 -	0.0
-	-	-	0.77	0.70	0.76	13.8 -	11.6	0.86	0.92	1.00	8.9	0.06120	2/3/20	10.6 -	8.9
-	-	-0.01	-0.21	0.29		-		-						24.9 -	15.5
-	-	2.77	4.54	4.35	3.95	21.8 -	18.2	2.82	2.66	2.53	3.0	0.78250Y	18/53/20	98.8 -	82.5
-	-	-0.23	-0.50	-1.03		-		-						36.6 -	17.4
-	-	-	0.74	0.71	0.77	14.8 -	13.6	0.72	0.73	0.72	6.8	0.06250	1/6/20	11.0 -	10.0
-	-	-	0.85	0.95	1.19	11.3 -	9.5	0.78	0.97	1.34	8.6	0.06750	1/6/20	9.6 -	8.1
-	-	-	0.73	0.80	0.83	15.3 -	14.2	0.61	0.73	0.95	5.7	0.0375M	1/31/20	11.1 -	10.3
-	-	-	0.78	0.73	0.83	16.3 -	14.3	0.61	0.69	0.84	5.1	0.045M	1/31/20	12.7 -	11.2
-	-	1.38	5.70	4.85	-3.34	30.9 -	20.7	0.32	0.08	0.08	0.2	0.440Y	18/53/20	175.9 -	118.0
-	-	3.01	3.72	-5.07	-1.73	22.1 -	17.6	3.12	1.25	-	4.2	0.3750Y	12/13/19	82.3 -	65.5
-	-	-0.02	1.19	1.39	0.49	6.6 -	2.7	0.75	0.75	0.75	14.4	0.050Y	18/53/27	7.9 -	3.2
-	-	-0.01				-								9.9 -	0.0
-	-	0.28	1.16	-1.73	-0.17	40.5 -	31.2	0.20	0.20	0.20	0.5	0.050Y	12/18/19	46.9 -	36.2
-	-	0.55	2.71	0.95	0.43	9.2 -	6.2	1.20	1.95	2.65	5.4	0.360	2/14/20	25.0 -	16.9
-	-	0.41	2.11	-5.03	0.94	12.0 -	8.1	1.20	1.95		5.4	0.360	2/14/20	25.4 -	17.0
-	-	0.31	1.00	0.42	0.50	80.9 -	52.8	-	-	2.78	-	2.78G7	18/53/27	80.9 -	52.8
-	-0.65	-	-0.03	2.51	1.96	-		0.60	0.60	0.60	1.6	0.150Y	18/53/27	53.3 -	22.9
-	-	-0.16	-0.61	-1.94	-3.51	-								27.0 -	8.3
-	-	20.78	87.28	61.61	92.33	0.3 -	0.2	63.55	76.41	106.49	283.9	0.8	10/14/94	26.1 -	19.3
-	-	2.94	10.71	10.36	7.30	15.0 -	11.0	3.40	2.60	2.12	2.5	0.33590Y	18/53/27	161.2 -	118.3
-	-	1.28	1.07	1.00	1.46	49.5 -	37.4	1.06	0.97	0.88	2.2	0.30750Y	18/53/27	52.9 -	40.1
-	-	1.42	5.24	2.69	3.27	19.7 -	14.3	2.40	2.32	2.20	2.7	0.610Y	18/53/27	103.4 -	74.7
-	-	0.56	1.99	-0.70	1.95	18.7 -	12.5	0.72	0.58	0.50	2.3	0.20250Y	18/53/27	37.2 -	24.9
-	-	0.61	2.37	2.10	2.16	24.5 -	18.7	1.43	1.34	1.26	2.7	0.3850Y	18/53/27	58.1 -	44.4
-	-	10764.00	20911.00	34464.00	56627.00	0.0 -	0.0	2117.40	2543.46	2048.71	4107.3	-	-	62.2 -	41.2
-	-	0.21	6.16	0.50	-0.41	18.3 -	14.6	-	-	-	-	0.6250	2/15/19	112.8 -	89.9
-	-	-0.06				-						0.140Z	12/2/19	17.2 -	14.3
-	-	1.54	5.47	6.17	3.28	24.5 -	17.9	1.86	1.70	1.56	1.6	0.510Y	18/53/27	133.8 -	98.0
-	-	0.65	2.58	1.64	2.79	14.1 -	10.9	1.64	1.58	1.52	5.2	0.41250Y	18/53/27	36.3 -	28.0
-	-	0.20	0.43	0.52	-21.01	40.0 -	31.2	-	-	-	-	-	-	17.2 -	13.4
-	-0.05	-	-1.00	-0.45	-0.53	-						0.070	11/18/15	3.9 -	1.0
-	-	-0.71	-1.08	-1.13	-2.11	-		1.02	0.94	0.82	6.9	0.26250Z	1/15/20	16.8 -	12.9
-	0.65	-	6.34	1.30	1.88	6.5 -	4.2	-	-	-	-	-	-	41.1 -	26.8
-	0.06	-	0.20	-0.09	-0.47	91.4 -	33.6	-	-	-	-	-	-	18.3 -	6.7
-	-	2.28	7.33	7.61	4.59	18.7 -	12.9	1.00	0.78	0.70	0.8	0.340Y	18/53/27	137.3 -	94.3
-	-	-	1.08	0.99	1.35	19.8 -	14.9	1.32	1.71	1.74	6.9	0.110	4/30/20	21.4 -	16.1
-	-	0.32	0.88	2.00	2.83	51.5 -	39.3	1.74	5.93	5.93	4.5	0.310Y	18/53/27	45.4 -	34.6
-	1.41	-	3.67	5.59	3.69	34.4 -	24.6	2.79	2.70	2.66	2.5	0.74590Y	18/53/27	126.1 -	90.4
-	-	1.42	4.42	2.72	1.76	19.1 -	13.2	1.12	0.68	0.89	1.5	2.258Y	18/53/27	84.4 -	58.2
-	-	0.71	2.87	3.06	2.27	32.2 -	19.7	1.92	1.76	1.68	2.4	1.06750Z	18/53/27	92.4 -	56.6
0.67	-	-	2.00	0.16	-1.19	12.3 -	3.7	-	-	-	-	-	-	24.7 -	7.3
-	-	-0.42	-1.86	-2.46	-2.47	-		-	-	-	-	-	-	75.1 -	29.6
-	-	0.19	8.94	-7.57	-18.32	2.3 -	1.7	-	-	-	-	-	-	20.9 -	15.5
-	-	1.19	4.61	3.92	3.94	16.3 -	13.6	1.49	1.38	1.24	2.1	0.460Y	18/53/27	75.3 -	62.5
-	-	0.62	2.81	1.93	1.61	46.3 -	32.0	-	-	-	-	-	-	130.1 -	90.0
-	-	0.49	1.82	1.45	1.38	15.3 -	12.7	0.82	0.93	0.71	3.3	0.230Y	11/29/19	27.9 -	23.1
-	-	3.44	9.50	17.86	9.71	11.1 -	8.2	3.60	3.00	2.80	3.8	1.0Y	18/53/27	105.7 -	78.3
-	-	-	1.17	0.93	0.75	39.6 -	27.8	0.94	0.94	1.00	2.4	0.40630Z	3/23/20	46.3 -	32.5
-	-	0.96	6.31	3.30	2.31	29.4 -	20.2	-	3.40	3.00	-	0.3250Z	18/53/27	185.4 -	127.7
-	-	-	179.71	223.30	195.98	0.2 -	0.1	16844.88	11746.72	11188.16	59344.7	-	-	31.4 -	24.3
-	-	0.79	2.83	3.10	1.75	22.4 -	17.9	1.80	1.72	1.64	3.1	0.470Y	18/53/27	63.3 -	50.8
-	-	1.93	8.54	6.73	6.81	31.0 -	22.8	8.00	8.00	7.30	3.5	0.369GHZ	12/30/19	264.7 -	195.1
-	-	0.99	3.55	1.44	1.75	11.6 -	7.3	0.38	0.36	0.36	1.2	0.120Y	18/53/27	41.0 -	25.8
-	-	-0.12	-0.84	-1.26	-2.59	-		-	-	-	-	-	-	23.4 -	13.0
-	-	-	0.40	0.39	0.43	20.2 -	17.2	0.37	0.40	0.44	4.8	0.032MZ	4/1/20	8.1 -	6.9
-	-	-	0.26	0.26	0.28	18.6 -	16.5	0.29	0.31	0.31	6.3	0.030Z	4/1/20	4.8 -	4.3
-	-	-	0.64	0.69	0.74	21.1 -	17.8	0.63	0.68	0.71	5.0	0.0531MZ	4/1/20	13.5 -	11.4
-	-	-	0.31	0.28	0.31	17.8 -	15.3	0.31	0.31	0.31	6.0	0.0350Z	4/1/20	5.5 -	4.7
-1.51	-	-	-5.78	-3.98	-1.29	-		-	-	-	-	-	-	13.4 -	5.2
-	-	2.82	6.84	6.79	6.89	19.4 -	10.1	0.15	0.15	0.15	0.2	0.03750Y	18/53/27	132.7 -	69.0
-	-1.81	-	5.81	-7.05	7.38	5.3 -	1.0	-	-	-	-	-	-	30.6 -	5.8
-	-	0.19	0.77	0.40	0.58	13.5 -	9.5	0.51	0.37	0.41	5.8	0.030Y	11/22/19	10.4 -	7.3
-	-	-0.39	-0.83	-0.63	-0.92	-		-	-	-	-	-	-	92.4 -	47.3
-	-	0.34	-4.25	1.12	-5.62	-		-	-	-	-	0.020Y	18/53/27	9.0 -	2.7
-	-	0.26	0.82	0.17	0.34	-		-	-	-	-	-	-		
-	-	-0.05	-0.44	0.01	0.46	-		1.64	1.56	1.44	3.5	1.6250Z	1/15/20	54.8 -	35.2
-	-	-2.52	0.16	2.07	0.90	101.6 -	23.1	1.20	1.20	1.20	12.2	0.150Y	12/6/19	16.3 -	3.7

SYMBOL	COMPANY	NATURE OF BUSINESS	FISCAL YEAR-END	TOTAL REV. $MILL	NET INCOME $MILL	TOTAL ASSETS $MILL	NET STK EQUITY $MILL	NO OF INST	INST. HOLDINGS (SHARES)
KWR	Quaker Chemical Corp.	Specialty Chemicals	12/31/18	867.5	59.5	709.7	435.1	306	17235045
NX	Quanex Building Products Corp	Construction Materials	10/31/19	893.8	-46.7	645.1	330.2	219	41953373
PWR	Quanta Services, Inc.	Construction Services	12/31/18	11171.4	293.3	7075.8	3604.2	690	178456153
QD	Qudian Inc	Finance Intermediaries & Services	12/31/18	7692.3	2491.3	16253.4	10820.6	169	115618441
DGX	Quest Diagnostics, Inc.	Diagnostic & Health Related Service	12/31/18	7531.0	736.0	11003.0	5216.0	1001	165552243
QES	Quintana Energy Services Inc	Equipment & Services	12/31/18	604.4	-18.2	324.5	201.8	37	5162405
QHC	Quorum Health Corp	Hospitals & Health Care Facilities	12/31/18	1878.6	-200.2	1574.1	-90.4	109	28297633
QUOT	Quotient Technology Inc	Internet & Software	12/31/18	387.0	-28.3	662.4	380.1	148	68484340
CTDD	Qwest Corp	Services	12/31/18	8493.0	1665.0	20583.0	9868.0	-	0
RMED	Ra Medical Systems Inc	Medical Instruments & Equipment	12/31/18	6.3	-30.8	74.0	66.7	26	2301441
RDN	Radian Group, Inc.	General Insurance	12/31/18	1273.0	606.0	6314.7	3488.7	420	233797134
RFL	Rafael Holdings Inc	Property, Real Estate & Developmen	7/31/19	4.9	-4.7	142.1	111.0	57	5405016
RL	Ralph Lauren Corp	Apparel, Footwear & Accessories	3/30/19	6313.0	430.9	5942.8	3287.2	671	67342404
RRC	Range Resources Corp	Production & Extraction	12/31/18	3282.6	-1746.5	9708.2	4059.4	604	330965888
RNGR	Ranger Energy Services Inc	Equipment & Services	12/31/18	303.1	-3.3	302.5	101.9	-	0
PACK	Ranpak Holdings Corp	Containers & Packaging	12/31/18	-	1.4	309.2	291.2	38	37183509
RJF	Raymond James Financial, Inc.	Finance Intermediaries & Services	9/30/19	8023.0	1034.0	38830.0	6581.0	699	126503630
RYAM	Rayonier Advanced Materials Inc	Specialty Chemicals	12/31/18	2134.4	128.4	2679.1	706.9	252	52499617
RYN	Rayonier Inc.	REITs	12/31/18	816.1	102.2	2780.7	1556.9	475	147849492
RTN	Raytheon Co.	Defense	12/31/18	27058.0	2909.0	31864.0	11472.0	1893	278425980
RMAX	Re/Max Holdings Inc	Property, Real Estate & Developmen	12/31/18	212.6	27.0	426.8	481.6	196	20813652
RC	Ready Capital Corp	REITs	12/31/18	295.2	59.3	3036.8	544.8	119	19209647
RLGY	Realogy Holdings Corp	Property, Real Estate & Developmen	12/31/18	6079.0	137.0	7290.0	2311.0	338	169462514
O	Realty Income Corp	REITs	12/31/18	1327.8	363.6	15260.5	8088.7	1042	288930180
RLH	Red Lions Hotels Corp	Hotels, Restaurants & Travel	12/31/18	135.8	2.0	249.8	165.8	101	21274227
RWT	Redwood Trust Inc	REITs	12/31/18	452.5	119.6	11937.4	1348.8	331	125373072
RBC	Regal Beloit Corp	Electrical Equipment	12/29/18	3645.6	231.2	4623.8	2310.5	412	48358983
RM	Regional Management Corp	Credit & Lending	12/31/18	306.7	35.3	956.4	279.2	120	11253964
RF	Regions Financial Corp (New)	Banking	12/31/18	6412.0	1759.0	125688.0	15090.0	1049	908019722
RGS	Regis Corp	Miscellaneous Consumer Services	6/30/19	1069.0	-14.2	682.8	324.2	228	52730163
RGA	Reinsurance Group of America, Inc.	Life & Health	12/31/18	12875.7	715.8	64535.2	8450.6	30	784655
RS	Reliance Steel & Aluminum Co.	Non-Precious Metals	12/31/18	11534.5	633.7	8044.9	4671.6	558	68002805
RELX	RELX PLC	Business Services	12/31/17	-	-	3232.0	3174.0	267	58543280
RNR	RenaissanceRe Holdings Ltd.	General Insurance	12/31/18	2074.9	227.4	18676.2	5045.1	507	55261532
SOL	ReneSola Ltd	Semiconductors	12/31/18	96.9	1.8	377.7	90.7	-	0
RENN	Renren Inc	Retail - Automotive	12/31/18	498.2	72.5	437.2	147.5	46	5219772
RPLA	Replay Acquisition Corp	Services	12/31/18	-	-0.0	0.1	0.0	28	14587794
RSG	Republic Services Inc	Sanitation Services	12/31/18	10040.9	1036.9	21617.0	7927.1	957	302068360
REZI	Resideo Technologies Inc	Retail - Hardware & Home Improvem	12/31/18	4827.0	405.0	4972.0	1533.0	561	105444018
RMD	ResMed Inc.	Medical Instruments & Equipment	6/30/19	2606.6	404.6	4107.7	2072.2	707	119661322
RFP	Resolute Forest Products Inc	Paper & Forest Products	12/31/18	3756.0	235.0	3935.0	1534.0	179	97651522
QSR	Restaurant Brands International Inc	Hotels, Restaurants & Travel	12/31/18	5357.0	612.0	20141.0	1611.0	460	236416809
RPAI	Retail Properties of America Inc	REITs	12/31/18	482.5	77.6	3647.5	1746.6	-	0
RVI	Retail Value Inc	REITs	12/31/18	137.3	8.9	1962.6	662.3	164	13776388
REVG	REV Group Inc	Autos- Manufacturing	10/31/19	2403.7	-12.3	1347.1	505.0	109	64520692
REV	Revlon Inc	Household & Personal Products	12/31/18	2564.5	-294.2	3016.8	-1056.8	111	13286788
RVLV	Revolve Group Inc	Retail - Specialty	12/31/18	498.7	30.7	162.1	79.8	123	17537429
REX	REX American Resources Corp	Refining & Marketing	1/31/19	486.7	31.6	471.4	392.9	189	6764666
REXR	Rexford Industrial Realty Inc	REITs	12/31/18	212.5	46.2	2787.7	1876.1	291	128556424
RXN	Rexnord Corp (New)	Industrial Machinery & Equipment	3/31/19	2050.9	34.3	3259.7	1228.6	267	140023392
RH	RH	Retail - Furniture & Home Furnishing	2/2/19	2505.7	150.6	1806.0	-23.0	376	26497005
RNG	RingCentral Inc	Internet & Software	12/31/18	673.6	-26.2	894.3	317.6	398	79079814
RIO	Rio Tinto Plc	Mining	12/31/18	40522.0	287.0	90949.0	43686.0	611	109909387
RBA	Ritchie Bros Auctioneers Inc	Business Services	12/31/18	1170.0	121.5	2052.4	830.6	306	128950931
RAD	Rite Aid Corp	Retail - Food & Beverage, Drug & To	3/2/19	21639.6	-422.2	7591.4	1186.7	380	184049821
RMM	RiverNorth Managed Duration Muni	Holding and other Investment Office	6/17/19	-	-	0.1	0.1	-	0
RSF	RiverNorth Marketplace Lending Co	Holding and other Investment Office	6/30/19	38.0	25.8	219.8	178.3	26	1192586
RMI	RiverNorth Opportunistic Municipal I	Finance Intermediaries & Services	6/30/19	5.2	2.2	225.5	144.6	15	589448
RIV	RiverNorth Opportunities Fund Inc	Finance Intermediaries & Services	7/31/19	6.2	3.6	139.5	124.7	27	900087
OPP	RiverNorth/DoubleLine Strategic Op	Holding and other Investment Office	6/30/19	16.6	10.3	274.3	199.2	42	2557257
RLI	RLI Corp	General Insurance	12/31/18	818.1	64.2	3105.1	806.8	334	48303174
RLJ	RLJ Lodging Trust	REITs	12/31/18	1761.2	190.1	6005.1	3474.2	347	192093931
RRTS	Roadrunner Transportation System	Miscellaneous Transportation Servic	12/31/18	2216.1	-165.6	853.5	-52.2	76	55484726
RHI	Robert Half International Inc.	Business Services	12/31/18	5800.3	434.3	1903.1	1063.2	703	142437805
ROK	Rockwell Automation, Inc.	Electrical Equipment	9/30/19	6694.8	695.8	6113.0	404.2	1126	111823005
RCI 14A	Rogers Cable Inc	Radio & Television	12/31/06	3201.0	177.0	5245.0	419.0	-	0
RCI	Rogers Communications Inc	Services	12/31/18	15096.0	2059.0	31918.0	8179.0	430	270062599
ROG	Rogers Corp.	Plastics	12/31/18	879.1	87.7	1279.3	848.3	340	21597134
ROL	Rollins, Inc.	Business Services	12/31/18	1821.6	231.7	1094.1	711.9	516	159433111
ROP	Roper Technologies Inc	Electrical Equipment	12/31/18	5191.2	944.4	15249.5	7738.5	1095	121021898
RST	Rosetta Stone Inc	Internet & Software	12/31/18	173.6	-21.5	187.3	-12.0	161	28590222
RY	Royal Bank of Canada (Montreal, Q	Banking	10/31/18	67586.0	12860.0	1428935.0	83523.0	712	732478994
RBS	Royal Bank of Scotland Group Plc	Banking	12/31/18	16656.0	1910.0	694235.0	45736.0	165	35549540
RCL	Royal Caribbean Cruises Ltd	Hotels, Restaurants & Travel	12/31/18	9493.8	1811.0	27698.3	11105.5	918	180283095
RDS A	Royal Dutch Shell Plc	Production & Extraction	12/31/18	396556.0	23352.0	399194.0	198646.0	1491	266648702
RGT	Royce Global Value Trust Inc	Holding and other Investment Office	12/31/18	2.6	0.4	117.7	109.3	67	4440673
RMT	Royce Micro-Cap Trust, Inc.	Holding and other Investment Office	12/31/18	6.1	1.0	368.0	345.5	108	14696332
RVT	Royce Value Trust Inc	Holding and other Investment Office	12/31/18	25.7	-16.2	1364.8	1304.1	193	28516060
RES	RPC, Inc.	Equipment & Services	12/31/18	1721.0	175.4	1199.6	950.4	312	89194738
RPM	RPM International Inc (DE)	Specialty Chemicals	5/31/19	5564.6	266.6	5441.4	1406.0	716	125464318

EARNINGS PER SHARE — QUARTERLY — 1st	2nd	3rd	ANNUAL 2018	2017	2016	P/E RATIO	DIVIDENDS PER SHARE 2018	2017	2016	AV. YLD %	DIV. DECLARED AMOUNT	PAYABLE	PRICE RANGE 2018
		-0.80	4.45	1.52	4.63	50.3 - 32.3	1.45	1.40	1.33	0.8	0.3850Y	18/53/27	223.8 - 143.9
		0.36	0.75	0.54	-0.05	26.3 - 18.6	0.20	0.16	0.16	1.2	0.080Y	12/30/19	19.8 - 14.0
		0.92	1.90	2.00	1.26	23.0 - 15.6	0.04	-	-	0.1	0.050Y	18/53/27	43.8 - 29.6
		-	7.74	7.09	1.90	1.2 - 0.5	-	-	-	-	-	-	9.1 - 4.1
		1.56	5.29	5.50	4.51	20.4 - 15.3	1.95	1.80	1.58	2.0	0.530Y	18/53/27	108.0 - 80.7
		-1.41	-0.50	-0.05	-0.37	-	-	-	-	-	-	-	5.7 - 1.2
		-2.52	-6.91	-4.06	-12.24	-	-	-	-	-	-	-	3.6 - 0.5
		-0.12	-0.30	-0.17	-0.23	-	-	-	-	-	-	-	11.9 - 7.0
		-	-	-	-	-	1.69	1.07	-	7.0	0.43750Z	5/1/20	26.3 - 19.8
		-1.30	-3.34	-2.35	-0.60	-	-	-	-	-	-	-	9.8 - 0.8
		0.83	2.77	0.55	1.37	9.5 - 5.9	0.01	0.01	0.01	0.0	0.00250Y	12/6/19	26.2 - 16.2
-0.10			-0.93	-	-	-	-	-	-	-	-	-	28.8 - 8.3
	2.34		1.97	-1.20	4.62	67.1 - 42.5	2.00	2.00	2.00	1.8	0.68750Y	18/53/27	132.1 - 83.6
		-0.11	-7.10	1.34	-2.75	-	0.08	0.08	0.08	1.1	0.020Y	18/53/27	11.9 - 3.3
		-0.06	-0.39	-0.78	-1.79	-	-	-	-	-	-	-	8.5 - 0.0
		-0.03	0.17	0.00	-	60.6 - 0.0	-	-	-	-	-	-	10.3 - 0.0
		1.80	5.75	4.33	3.65	15.9 - 12.4	1.10	0.88	0.80	1.3	0.370Y	18/53/27	91.6 - 71.5
		-0.29	1.96	5.81	1.55	7.9 - 1.3	0.28	0.28	0.28	3.5	0.070Y	6/28/19	15.5 - 2.5
		0.00	0.79	1.16	1.73	41.5 - 33.0	1.06	1.00	1.00	3.6	0.270Z	18/53/27	32.8 - 26.1
		3.08	10.15	6.95	7.44	21.8 - 14.8	4.27	2.39	3.60	2.3	0.94250Y	18/53/27	221.0 - 149.8
		0.51	1.52	0.72	1.29	28.9 - 16.4	0.80	0.72	0.60	2.3	0.210Y	11/27/19	43.9 - 25.0
		0.27	1.84	1.38	1.85	9.0 - 7.5	1.57	1.48	1.55	10.3	0.38750Z	4/30/20	16.5 - 13.8
		-0.61	1.09	3.11	1.46	16.9 - 4.1	0.36	0.36	0.18	3.7	0.090Y	18/53/27	18.4 - 4.5
		0.32	1.26	1.10	1.13	65.0 - 49.2	2.64	2.54	2.40	3.7	0.23250Z	18/53/27	81.9 - 61.9
		-0.14	0.08	0.02	-0.23	126.9 - 33.0	-	-	-	-	-	-	10.2 - 2.6
		0.31	1.34	1.60	1.54	12.9 - 11.3	1.18	1.12	1.12	7.2	0.30Z	12/30/19	17.2 - 15.2
		1.19	5.26	4.74	4.52	16.6 - 13.0	1.10	1.02	0.95	1.4	0.30Y	18/53/27	87.3 - 68.2
		1.08	2.93	2.54	1.99	11.6 - 8.0	-	-	-	-	-	-	34.0 - 23.6
		0.39	1.54	1.00	0.87	11.3 - 8.8	0.46	0.32	0.26	3.0	0.35630Y	18/53/27	17.4 - 13.5
-0.38			0.18	-0.35	-0.23	127.9 - 81.6	-	-	-	-	0.060Y	11/19/13	23.0 - 14.7
		4.12	11.00	27.71	10.79	15.3 - 12.5	2.20	1.82	1.56	1.4	0.70Y	18/53/27	168.3 - 137.8
		2.40	8.75	8.34	4.16	13.9 - 8.0	2.00	1.80	1.65	2.1	0.550Y	18/53/27	121.3 - 69.7
		-	-	-	-	-	-	0.37	0.32	-	-	-	25.3 - 20.3
		0.83	4.91	-6.15	11.43	-	-	1.28	1.24	-	0.340	18/53/27	-
		-0.10	0.00	0.14	-0.17	-	-	-	-	-	-	-	2.1 - 0.9
		-0.02	0.07	-0.11	-0.18	86.1 - 23.2	9.19	-	-	266.4	-	-	6.0 - 1.6
		0.05	0.00	-	-	-	-	-	-	-	-	-	-
		0.93	3.16	3.77	1.78	28.6 - 22.6	1.44	1.33	1.24	1.7	0.4050Y	18/53/27	90.3 - 71.4
		0.06	3.30	-	-	7.9 - 2.7	-	-	-	-	-	-	26.2 - 8.8
0.83			2.19	2.40	2.49	71.6 - 41.8	1.40	1.32	1.20	1.1	0.390Y	18/53/27	156.7 - 91.6
		-0.47	2.52	-0.93	-0.90	5.1 - 0.0	1.50	-	-	20.7	1.5G7	12/20/18	12.8 - 0.0
		0.75	2.42	2.54	1.45	43.1 - 21.2	1.80	0.78	0.62	2.3	0.50Y	1/3/20	104.4 - 51.4
		-0.13	0.35	1.03	0.66	40.7 - 30.3	0.66	0.66	0.66	5.3	0.16560Z	18/53/27	14.2 - 10.6
		3.79	0.48	-	-	80.5 - 53.2	1.30	-	-	3.8	2.050	1/8/20	38.7 - 25.6
		0.09	0.20	0.50	0.58	73.3 - 36.1	0.20	0.15	-	1.7	0.050Y	2/28/20	14.7 - 7.2
		-0.84	-5.57	-3.48	-0.42	-	-	-	-	-	0.16740Y	10/8/13	28.3 - 14.6
		0.13	0.44	0.08	-	106.7 - 33.3	-	-	-	-	-	-	47.0 - 14.7
		-0.32	6.02	4.91	4.30	15.5 - 11.1	-	-	-	-	0.3945GHY	12/31/19	93.5 - 66.8
		0.09	0.41	0.48	0.36	117.6 - 69.6	0.64	0.58	0.54	1.6	-	-	48.2 - 28.5
	0.46		0.50	0.64	0.66	66.1 - 44.2	-	-	-	-	0.71880Y	11/15/19	33.1 - 22.1
		2.17	0.07	0.13	2.16	3456.7 - 1216.4	-	-	-	-	-	-	242.0 - 85.2
		-0.15	-0.33	-0.34	-0.40	-	-	-	-	-	-	-	176.7 - 78.4
		-	7.88	4.87	2.55	8.1 - 5.9	3.08	2.37	1.51	5.5	-	-	63.7 - 46.6
		0.23	1.11	0.69	0.85	52.2 - 29.2	0.70	0.68	0.66	1.6	0.20	12/18/19	57.9 - 32.4
		0.96	18.00	0.00	3.20	1.1 - 0.3	-	-	-	-	0.1150	18/53/27	20.3 - 5.2
		-	-	-	-	-	-	-	-	-	0.09170	3/31/20	20.7 - 19.3
		-	3.12	2.32	-	6.6 - 0.0	0.82	-	-	7.9	0.36720	2/18/20	20.5 - 0.0
		-	-	-	-	-	-	-	-	-	0.0917M	3/31/20	22.8 - 19.9
		-	0.44	0.42	0.68	40.0 - 36.3	1.89	1.89	2.18	11.2	0.180	3/31/20	17.6 - 16.0
		-	1.06	0.94	-	16.8 - 15.1	1.71	0.92	-	10.1	0.180	3/31/20	17.8 - 16.0
		0.71	1.43	2.36	2.59	69.6 - 45.7	1.87	2.58	2.79	2.2	1.7Y	18/53/27	99.6 - 65.3
		0.15	0.93	0.47	1.61	20.9 - 17.0	1.32	1.32	1.32	7.5	0.48750Z	1/31/20	19.5 - 15.8
		-2.60	-107.50	-59.25	-235.00	-	-	-	-	-	-	-	13.8 - 7.5
		1.01	3.57	2.33	2.67	19.3 - 14.6	1.12	0.96	0.88	1.9	0.310Y	18/53/27	68.8 - 52.1
		2.20	4.21	6.35	5.56	48.8 - 34.3	3.51	3.04	2.90	2.1	1.020Y	18/53/27	205.5 - 144.6
	1.15		3.99	3.31	1.62	18.3 - 11.6	1.92	1.92	1.92	3.2	0.50	4/1/20	73.2 - 46.2
		1.25	4.70	4.34	2.65	41.3 - 20.0	-	-	-	-	0.0075	2/12/92	194.2 - 93.8
		0.13	0.71	0.55	0.51	61.6 - 44.4	0.47	0.37	0.33	1.3	0.057Y	18/53/27	43.8 - 31.5
		2.64	9.05	9.39	6.43	42.5 - 28.6	1.65	1.40	1.20	0.5	0.51250Y	18/53/27	384.4 - 258.8
		-0.12	-0.95	-0.07	-1.25	-	-	-	-	-	-	-	26.3 - 14.3
		2.22	8.36	7.56	6.78	13.1 - 8.2	3.77	3.48	3.24	4.2	0.27810	2/24/20	109.4 - 68.6
		-	0.13	0.06	-0.59	55.7 - 33.5	0.04	-	-	0.7	0.53130	3/31/99	7.2 - 4.3
		4.20	8.56	7.53	5.93	-	2.60	2.16	1.71	-	0.780	18/53/27	-
		0.70	2.80	1.56	0.58	23.6 - 19.6	3.76	3.76	3.76	6.2	-	-	66.0 - 55.0
		-	0.04	0.02	0.06	292.3 - 217.2	0.04	0.11	0.14	0.4	0.060	12/27/19	11.7 - 8.7
		-	0.01	0.06	0.03	889.0 - 749.0	0.75	0.69	0.64	9.1	0.160	12/27/19	8.9 - 7.5
		-	0.18	0.13	0.12	82.8 - 65.8	1.26	1.16	1.02	9.1	0.260	12/27/19	14.9 - 11.8
		-0.33	0.82	0.75	-0.66	15.7 - 4.2	0.47	0.20	0.05	6.2	0.050Y	18/53/27	12.9 - 3.5
	0.59		2.50	1.36	2.63	30.7 - 20.9	1.26	1.18	1.09	2.0	0.360Y	18/53/27	76.8 - 52.3

SYMBOL	COMPANY	NATURE OF BUSINESS	FISCAL YEAR-END	TOTAL REV. $MILL	NET INCOME $MILL	TOTAL ASSETS $MILL	NET STK EQUITY $MILL	NO OF INST	INST. HOLDINGS (SHARES)
RPT	RPT Realty	REITs	12/31/18	260.6	17.6	1928.4	812.0	238	101645593
RTW	RTW Retailwinds Inc	Retail - Apparel and Accessories	2/2/19	893.2	4.2	288.9	86.6	121	61010992
RUBI	Rubicon Project Inc	Internet & Software	12/31/18	124.7	-61.8	360.0	118.0	170	41587666
RYB	RYB Education Inc	Educational Services	12/31/18	156.5	-1.8	243.5	108.7	15	2688610
R	Ryder System, Inc.	Trucking	12/31/18	8409.2	273.3	13051.1	2910.3	513	64116212
RYI	Ryerson Holding Corp	Non-Precious Metals	12/31/18	4408.4	106.0	2086.3	73.2	132	14679787
RHP	Ryman Hospitality Properties Inc	REITs	12/31/18	1275.1	264.7	3853.9	469.6	428	54790245
SPGI	S&P Global Inc	Finance Intermediaries & Services	12/31/18	6258.0	1958.0	9458.0	628.0	1377	266727454
SBR	Sabine Royalty Trust	Oil Royalty Traders	12/31/18	52.5	49.9	9.5	5.7	115	1780315
SB	Safe Bulkers Inc	Shipping	12/31/18	193.2	27.7	1076.2	465.8	95	21239148
SFE	Safeguard Scientifics, Inc.	Venture Capital	12/31/18	-	-15.6	145.7	67.0	153	25694829
SAFE	Safehold Inc	REITs	12/31/18	49.7	11.7	979.7	355.4	92	8538882
SAIL	SailPoint Technologies Holdings Inc	Services	12/31/18	248.9	3.7	534.4	377.7	212	83189996
CRM	Salesforce.Com Inc	Internet & Software	1/31/19	13282.0	1110.0	30737.0	15605.0	1823	799585852
SMM	Salient Midstream & MLP Fund	Holding and other Investment Office	11/30/18	4.4	-2.2	252.7	177.9	50	4906035
SBH	Sally Beauty Holdings Inc	Retail - Specialty	9/30/18	3876.4	271.6	2098.4	-60.3	355	174550335
SJT	San Juan Basin Royalty Trust	Oil Royalty Traders	12/31/18	19.5	18.0	8.0	5.8	128	9613502
SD	SandRidge Energy Inc	Production & Extraction	12/31/18	349.4	-9.1	1024.3	847.7	221	57983972
PER	SandRidge Permian Trust	Oil Royalty Traders	12/31/18	29.9	25.3	115.2	115.2		0
SC	Santander Consumer USA Holdings	Credit & Lending	12/31/18	7172.2	915.9	43959.9	7018.4	275	358736668
SOV PRC	Santander Holdings USA Inc.	Banking	12/31/18	11313.4	707.4	135634.3	21321.1	56	9131130
SAP	SAP SE	Internet & Software	12/31/18	24708.0	4083.0	51491.0	28832.0	690	69216732
SAR	Saratoga Investment Corp	Holding and other Investment Office	2/28/19	47.7	18.3	470.7	180.9	56	3914651
SSL	Sasol Ltd.	Production & Extraction	6/30/18	203576.0	4298.0	469968.0	219910.0	214	24711387
BFS	Saul Centers Inc	REITs	12/31/18	227.9	50.6	1527.5	355.9	202	12881742
SCPE U	SC Health Corp	Business Services	12/31/18	-	-0.0	0.1	0.0	12	4445107
SLB	Schlumberger Ltd	Equipment & Services	12/31/18	33250.0	-10137.0	56312.0	23760.0	2167	1299750880
SNDR	Schneider National Inc (WI)	Trucking	12/31/18	4977.0	268.9	3624.5	2132.3	214	44917923
SCHW	Schwab (Charles) Corp (The)	Finance Intermediaries & Services	12/31/18	10989.0	3507.0	296482.0	20670.0	1517	1210368833
SWM	Schweitzer-Mauduit International In	Paper & Forest Products	12/31/18	1041.3	94.5	1466.5	557.9	256	34418055
SAIC	Science Applications International C	IT Services	2/1/19	4659.0	137.0	4563.0	1485.0	408	51289892
SALT	Scorpio Bulkers Inc	Shipping	12/31/18	242.5	-12.7	1703.8	860.8	115	31367576
STNG	Scorpio Tankers Inc	Miscellaneous Transportation Servic	12/31/18	585.0	-190.1	4784.2	1839.0	213	49801873
SMG	Scotts Miracle-Gro Co (The)	Agricultural Chemicals	9/30/18	3156.0	460.7	3028.7	718.7	574	47640812
SRL	Scully Royalty Ltd	Finance Intermediaries & Services	12/31/18	139.8	112.3	506.9	386.4	53	5638693
SCU	Sculptor Capital Management	Wealth Management	12/31/18	507.2	-24.3	1447.4	148.8	150	17053773
SE	Sea Ltd	IT Services	12/31/18	827.0	-961.2	2192.7	-243.1	251	210262147
SA	Seabridge Gold Inc	Precious Metals	12/31/18	-	-19.9	423.5	386.6	149	17685513
CKH	SEACOR Holdings Inc	Shipping	12/31/18	835.8	58.1	1471.0	704.2	240	21861171
SMHI	SEACOR Marine Holdings Inc	Shipping	12/31/18	253.6	-77.6	1102.9	525.5	72	17018651
SDRL	Seadrill Ltd (New)	Production & Extraction	12/31/18	541.0	-602.0	10848.0	2883.0		0
SEE	Sealed Air Corp	Containers & Packaging	12/31/18	4732.7	193.1	5050.2	-348.6	685	193926962
SSW	Seaspan Corp	Shipping	12/31/18	1096.3	278.8	7478.0	2508.1	203	112176315
SEAS	SeaWorld Entertainment Inc.	Sporting & Recreational	12/31/18	1372.3	44.8	2115.6	265.2	268	90182690
WTTR	Select Energy Services Inc	Equipment & Services	12/31/18	1528.9	36.5	1360.6	832.9	145	63002791
SEM	Select Medical Holdings Corp	Hospitals & Health Care Facilities	12/31/18	5081.3	137.8	5964.3	803.0	260	122952788
SRE	Sempra Energy	Electric Utilities	12/31/18	11687.0	1050.0	60638.0	17138.0	1089	301142286
ST	Sensata Technologies Holding PLC	Electrical Equipment	12/31/18	3521.6	599.0	6797.7	2608.4	418	197594589
SXT	Sensient Technologies Corp.	Specialty Chemicals	12/31/18	1386.8	157.4	1824.9	859.9	374	59423575
SQNS	Sequans Communications S A	Semiconductors	12/31/18	40.3	-36.2	62.6	-5.0	32	45401688
SRG	Seritage Growth Properties	REITs	12/31/18	214.8	-73.5	2876.1	780.8	166	44123045
SCI	Service Corp. International	Miscellaneous Consumer Services	12/31/18	3190.2	447.2	12693.2	1641.9	521	189071407
SERV	ServiceMaster Global Holdings, Inc	Miscellaneous Consumer Services	12/31/18	1900.0	-41.0	5023.0	2204.0	336	159239407
NOW	ServiceNow Inc	IT Services	12/31/18	2608.8	-26.7	3879.1	1111.2	960	193337308
SFL	SFL Corporation Ltd	Equipment & Services	12/31/18	418.7	73.6	3877.8	1180.0	264	50260885
SHAK	Shake Shack Inc	Hotels, Restaurants & Travel	12/26/18	459.3	15.2	610.5	226.1	291	34517030
SJR	Shaw Communications Inc	Radio & Television	8/31/19	5340.0	731.0	15646.0	6282.0	290	340613811
SHLX	Shell Midstream Partners LP	Equipment & Services	12/31/18	524.7	464.1	1913.5		200	128913045
SHW	Sherwin-Williams Co (The)	Specialty Chemicals	12/31/18	17534.5	1108.7	19134.3	3730.7	1308	96527889
SHG	Shinhan Financial Group Co. Ltd.	Banking	12/31/18			434609190.0		181	13248860
SHOP	Shopify Inc	IT Services	12/31/18	1073.2	-64.6	2254.8	2090.8	617	66744835
SSTK	Shutterstock Inc	Internet & Software	12/31/18	623.3	54.7	531.5	286.7	195	23837658
SBGL	Sibanye-Stillwater	Mining	12/31/18	50656.4	-2499.6	84923.0	23788.4	137	146475296
SIG	Signet Jewelers Ltd	Retail - Specialty	2/2/19	6247.1	-657.4	4420.1	1816.9	336	87851613
SBOW	SilverBow Resources Inc	Production & Extraction	12/31/18	257.3	74.6	777.5	274.8	149	18408581
SI	Silvergate Capital Corp	Banking	12/31/18	80.3	22.3	2004.3	191.2		0
SPG	Simon Property Group, Inc.	REITs	12/31/18	5657.9	2440.1	30686.2	3526.8	1163	390188668
SSD	Simpson Manufacturing Co., Inc. (D	Construction Materials	12/31/18	1078.8	126.6	1021.7	855.5	335	59386964
SHI	Sinopec Shanghai Petrochemical C	Refining & Marketing	12/31/17	92013.6	6141.6	39609.5	28256.3	89	1506262
SITC	SITE Centers Corp	REITs	12/31/18	707.3	114.4	4206.3	2070.1	373	262354943
SITE	SiteOne Landscape Supply Inc	Miscellaneous Consumer Services	12/30/18	2112.3	73.9	1168.5	301.8	242	52305063
SIX	Six Flags Entertainment Corp	Sporting & Recreational	12/31/18	1463.7	276.0	2517.3	-643.1	489	97094512
SJW	SJW Group	Water Utilities	12/31/18	397.7	38.8	1956.4	889.3	241	21344018
SKM	SK Telecom Co Ltd (South Korea)	Internet & Software	12/31/18	16945910.0	3127887.0	42369111.0	22470822.0	283	90345174
SKX	Skechers USA Inc	Apparel, Footwear & Accessories	12/31/18	4662.6	301.0	3228.3	2035.0	446	138304787
SKY	Skyline Champion Corp	Builders	3/30/19	1360.0	-58.2	700.0	412.0	206	56061974
SLG	SL Green Realty Corp	REITs	12/31/18	1227.4	247.3	12751.4	6201.9	529	122418128
WORK	Slack Technologies Inc	Internet & Software	1/31/19	400.6	-140.7	1199.0	831.7	313	183906098
SM	SM Energy Co.	Production & Extraction	12/31/18	2067.1	508.4	6352.9	2920.3	412	130740276
SMAR	SmartSheet Inc	IT Services	1/31/19	177.7	-53.9	308.7	167.0	283	87209528

EARNINGS PER SHARE QUARTERLY 1st	2nd	3rd	ANNUAL 2018	2017	2016	P/E RATIO		DIVIDENDS PER SHARE 2018	2017	2016	AV. YLD %	DIV. DECLARED AMOUNT	PAYABLE	PRICE RANGE 2018	
-	-	0.05	0.13	0.78	0.66	115.7	87.7	0.88	0.88	0.86	6.8	0.90630Z	1/2/20	15.0	11.4
-	-	-0.18	0.09	-0.27	-0.16	37.9	8.3	-	-	-	-	-	-	3.4	0.7
-	-	-0.12	-1.23	-3.17	-0.39	-	-	-	-	-	-	-	-	10.7	3.6
-	-	-	-0.06	0.27	0.26	-	-	-	-	-	-	-	-	9.0	5.5
-	-	-1.75	5.17	14.87	4.90	13.0	8.7	2.12	1.80	1.70	3.8	0.560Y	18/53/27	67.2	45.1
-	-	0.27	2.81	0.46	0.54	4.3	2.2	-	-	-	-	-	-	12.2	6.3
-	-	0.43	5.14	3.43	3.11	17.8	12.8	3.40	3.20	3.00	4.2	0.90	1/15/20	91.5	65.6
-	-	2.50	7.73	5.78	7.94	35.5	21.3	2.00	1.64	1.44	0.9	0.570Y	18/53/27	274.4	164.4
-	-	0.71	3.42	2.38	1.88	15.2	11.1	3.35	2.37	1.93	7.6	0.30330Z	1/29/20	51.9	38.0
0.03	-	-	0.16	-0.98	-0.83	-	-	-	-	-	-	0.50	1/30/20	-	-
-	-	-0.12	-0.76	-4.34	-1.09	-	-	-	-	-	-	1.G7	12/30/19	12.7	8.5
-	-	0.15	0.64	-0.25	-	66.8	25.9	0.60	0.31	-	2.1	0.1560Z	1/15/20	42.7	16.6
-	-	0.04	0.04	-0.55	-0.58	801.2	426.0	-	-	-	-	-	-	32.0	17.0
-	-	-0.12	0.17	0.26	-0.07	982.1	767.1	-	-	-	-	-	-	166.9	130.4
-	-	-	-0.12	0.00	0.11	-	-	0.76	0.98	1.14	9.2	0.1710	11/27/19	9.3	6.9
-	-	0.59	2.08	1.56	1.50	9.6	5.6	-	-	-	-	-	-	20.0	11.7
-	-	0.00	0.39	0.84	0.30	14.9	5.6	0.39	0.84	0.33	10.6	0.030	2/14/20	5.8	2.2
-	-	-5.12	-0.26	1.44	-17.61	-	-	-	-	-	-	4.250Y	2/16/15	9.2	3.3
-	-	0.09	0.48	0.46	0.54	5.3	1.8	0.48	0.46	0.54	26.1	0.080Z	2/28/20	2.5	0.8
-	-	0.67	2.54	3.30	2.13	10.8	7.0	0.50	0.03	-	2.2	0.220Y	18/53/27	27.5	17.9
-	-	-	-	-	-	-	-	1.37	1.83	1.83	-	0.45620Y	8/15/18	-	-
-	-	0.82	3.42	3.35	3.04	41.0	27.9	1.01	0.90	0.82	0.8	-	-	140.2	95.5
-	-	-	2.93	1.68	1.91	9.0	7.0	1.90	1.93	2.36	7.8	0.560Y	2/6/20	26.2	20.6
-	-	-	14.18	33.27	21.66	2.4	1.2	9.59	11.10	14.15	38.9	-	-	33.9	16.8
-	-	0.39	1.60	1.63	1.52	36.3	28.7	2.08	2.04	1.84	3.9	0.3750Z	1/15/20	58.1	45.9
-	-	0.04	0.00	-	-	-	-	-	-	-	-	-	-	-	-
-	-	-8.22	1.53	-1.08	-1.24	31.0	20.1	2.00	2.00	2.00	5.1	0.50	18/53/27	47.4	30.7
-	-	0.11	1.52	2.28	1.00	15.8	11.0	0.24	0.15	0.20	1.2	0.060Y	1/9/20	24.0	16.8
-	-	0.70	2.45	1.61	1.31	20.8	14.3	0.46	0.32	0.27	1.1	0.3720Y	18/53/27	51.1	35.1
-	-	0.90	3.06	1.12	2.70	14.9	8.4	1.73	1.69	1.62	4.8	0.440Y	12/20/19	45.6	25.6
-	-	0.94	4.02	3.22	2.47	22.5	15.3	1.24	1.24	1.21	1.6	0.370	18/53/27	90.4	61.5
-	-	-0.03	-0.18	-0.83	-2.22	-	-	0.88	-	-	-	0.020	12/13/19	-	-
0.30	-	-	-5.46	-7.30	-1.50	-	-	0.40	0.40	-	-	0.42190Z	5/15/20	-	-
-	-	3.56	1.12	3.63	5.09	100.4	55.3	2.14	2.03	1.91	2.3	0.580Y	18/53/27	112.4	62.0
-	0.55	-	8.96	-3.81	-2.00	-	-	-	-	-	-	-	-	-	-
-	-	-1.20	-1.26	1.00	-7.30	-	-	1.30	0.70	-	7.1	0.030	11/25/19	25.3	10.2
-	-	-	-2.84	-2.72	-1.30	-	-	-	-	-	-	-	-	40.2	10.7
-	-0.03	-	-0.34	-0.18	-0.14	-	-	-	-	-	-	-	-	21.7	11.1
-	-	0.32	3.04	3.31	-12.76	16.4	12.5	-	-	-	-	5.7Y	12/26/12	50.0	37.9
-	-	-0.78	-3.71	-1.87	-7.47	-	-	-	-	-	-	-	-	15.0	11.1
-	-	-5.21	-6.02	-5.89	-0.36	-	-	-	-	-	-	-	-	-	-
-	-	0.44	1.20	4.29	2.46	39.0	28.9	0.64	0.64	0.61	1.5	0.160Y	18/53/27	46.8	34.7
-	-	0.42	1.31	0.94	-1.89	-	-	0.50	-	-	-	0.50	1/30/20	-	-
-	-	1.24	0.52	-2.36	-0.15	65.8	44.1	-	-	0.73	-	0.10	10/7/16	34.2	22.9
-	-	0.07	0.49	-0.51	-0.05	25.6	13.9	-	-	-	-	-	-	12.6	6.8
-	-	0.23	1.02	1.33	0.87	22.9	12.9	-	-	0.00	-	0.10Y	3/11/15	23.3	13.1
-	-	2.84	3.42	1.01	5.46	44.5	31.2	3.58	3.29	3.02	2.7	1.68750Y	18/53/27	152.0	106.8
-	-	0.44	3.53	2.37	1.53	-	-	-	-	-	-	-	-	-	-
-	-	0.75	3.70	2.03	2.82	20.3	14.9	1.35	1.23	1.11	2.0	0.390Y	18/53/27	75.0	55.0
-	-	-0.10	-0.39	-0.34	-0.39	-	-	-	-	-	-	-	-	4.7	1.8
-	-	-0.33	-2.20	-2.19	-1.64	-	-	1.00	1.00	1.00	2.4	0.43750Z	1/15/20	46.5	33.0
-	-	0.38	2.39	2.84	0.90	20.3	16.4	0.68	0.58	0.51	1.5	0.180Y	18/53/27	48.6	39.1
-	-	0.19	-0.30	3.76	1.13	-	-	-	-	-	-	-	-	58.2	34.0
-	-	0.21	-0.15	-0.87	-2.75	-	-	-	-	-	-	-	-	302.3	169.1
-	-	0.28	0.69	1.03	1.50	-	-	1.40	1.60	1.80	-	0.350	12/27/19	-	-
-	-	0.31	0.52	-0.01	0.53	201.2	84.3	-	-	-	-	-	-	104.6	43.8
-	-	-0.18	0.10	1.71	2.51	280.3	182.8	1.19	1.19	1.19	5.1	0.17440	3/31/20	28.0	18.3
-	-	0.45	1.50	1.28	1.32	14.5	11.4	1.43	1.19	0.97	7.1	0.460	2/14/20	21.8	17.1
-	-	6.16	11.67	18.67	11.99	50.9	32.6	3.44	3.40	3.36	0.7	1.130Y	18/53/27	593.5	380.4
-	-1055.00	-	-	-6116.00	-5736.00	-	-	1440.02	1437.97	1191.31	3873.3	-	-	40.5	32.2
-	-	-0.64	-0.61	-0.42	-0.42	-	-	-	-	-	-	-	-	541.5	129.8
-	-	0.14	1.54	0.47	0.91	31.4	22.0	3.00	-	-	7.5	3.G7Y	8/29/18	48.4	33.9
-	-	-	-1.10	-2.29	3.78	-	-	-	1.78	5.08	-	-	-	9.9	2.7
-	-	-0.84	7.44	7.08	5.87	-	-	1.24	1.04	0.88	-	0.370	18/53/27	25.5	7.4
-	-	2.35	6.34	6.25	-15.61	4.0	1.2	-	-	-	-	-	-	16.4	12.5
-	-	0.36	1.31	0.79	-	12.5	9.6	-	-	-	-	-	-	185.8	144.0
-	-	1.77	7.87	6.24	5.87	23.6	18.3	7.90	7.15	6.50	4.8	1.04690Z	18/53/27	84.0	54.2
-	-	0.97	2.72	1.94	1.86	30.9	19.9	0.86	0.78	0.68	1.3	0.230Y	1/23/20	52.0	26.6
-	-	0.43	-	0.57	0.55	-	-	-	22.15	8.67	-	-	-	15.8	11.1
-	-	0.08	0.43	-1.48	0.20	36.6	25.9	0.78	1.52	1.52	5.7	0.20Z	18/53/27	92.2	47.5
-	-	0.81	1.73	1.29	-3.01	53.3	27.5	-	-	-	-	-	-	63.9	41.5
-	-	2.11	3.23	3.09	1.25	19.8	12.9	3.16	2.62	2.38	6.1	0.830Y	18/53/27	74.5	54.7
-	-	0.33	1.82	2.86	2.57	40.9	30.1	1.12	1.04	0.81	1.7	0.30Y	18/53/27	27.5	21.3
-	-	-7086.00	4066.08	6582.00	3497.00	0.0	0.0	1119.67	1109.69	1095.37	4710.6	-	-	44.2	22.5
-	-	0.67	1.92	1.14	1.57	23.0	11.7	-	-	-	-	-	-	35.2	14.2
-	0.31	-	-	0.00	0.20	-	-	-	-	-	-	0.62387Y	5/31/18	93.5	76.8
-	-	0.40	2.67	0.87	2.34	35.0	28.8	3.29	3.14	2.94	3.9	0.40630Z	18/53/27	38.6	20.1
-	-	-0.16	-1.47	-1.28	-	-	-	-	-	-	-	-	-	21.1	7.2
-	-	0.37	4.48	-1.44	-9.90	4.7	1.6	0.10	0.10	0.10	0.8	0.050Y	18/53/27	54.9	22.6
-	-	-0.25	-2.94	-1.00	-1.03	-	-	-	-	-	-	-	-		

SYMBOL	COMPANY	NATURE OF BUSINESS	FISCAL YEAR-END	TOTAL REV. $MILL	NET INCOME $MILL	TOTAL ASSETS $MILL	NET STK EQUITY $MILL	NO OF INST	INST. HOLDINGS (SHARES)
SNN	Smith & Nephew Plc	Medical Instruments & Equipment	12/31/18	4904.0	663.0	8059.0	4874.0	328	43435355
AOS	Smith (A O) Corp	Household Appliances, Electronics &	12/31/18	3187.9	444.2	3071.5	1717.0	663	162283341
SJM	Smucker (J.M.) Co.	Food	4/30/19	7838.0	514.4	16711.3	7970.5	1113	107283304
SNAP	Snap Inc	Internet & Software	12/31/18	1180.4	-1255.9	2714.1	2311.0	496	461464834
SNA	Snap-On, Inc.	Industrial Machinery & Equipment	12/29/18	4070.4	679.9	5373.1	3098.8	813	67145397
SNH PRZ	SNH Capital Trust I	REITs							0
SQM	Sociedad Quimica y Minera de Chil	Agricultural Chemicals	12/31/18	2265.8	439.8	4268.1	2085.5	289	36148601
SOGO	Sogou Inc	IT & Communications	12/31/18	1124.2	98.8	1462.8	1006.5	74	24925858
SOI	Solaris Oilfield Infrastructure Inc	Industrial Machinery & Equipment	12/31/18	197.2	42.4	425.2	168.5	157	31991131
SWI	SolarWinds Corp	Internet & Software	12/31/18	833.1	-102.1	5194.6	2616.1	132	303255386
SAH	Sonic Automotive, Inc.	Retail - Automotive	12/31/18	9951.6	51.6	3796.8	823.1	257	37315891
SON	Sonoco Products Co.	Containers & Packaging	12/31/18	5390.9	313.6	4583.5	1620.5	620	96705903
SNE	Sony Corp	Household Appliances, Electronics &	3/31/19	8665687.0	916271.0	20981586.0	3746377.0	535	113268099
SOR	Source Capital, Inc.	Holding and other Investment Office	12/31/18	8.2	4.7	325.8	321.9	84	2152750
SJI	South Jersey Industries Inc	Gas Utilities	12/31/18	1641.3	17.7	5956.6	1267.0	341	91782105
SO	Southern Company (The)	Electric Utilities	12/31/18	23495.0	2242.0	116914.0	25014.0	1792	735683667
SCCO	Southern Copper Corp	Mining	12/31/18	7096.7	1543.0	14484.8	6567.4	458	65007285
LUV	Southwest Airlines Co	Airlines/Air Freight	12/31/18	21965.0	2465.0	26243.0	9853.0	1274	545276017
SWX	Southwest Gas Holdings, Inc.	Gas Utilities	12/31/18	2880.0	182.3	7357.7	2252.0		0
SWN	Southwestern Energy Company	Production & Extraction	12/31/18	3862.0	537.0	5797.0	2362.0	589	670338053
SPE	Special Opportunities Fund Inc	Holding and other Investment Office	12/31/18	3.1	0.4	174.1	172.8	40	7308599
SPB	Spectrum Brands Holdings Inc (Ne	Household & Personal Products	9/30/19	3802.1	471.9	5230.5	1698.3	373	71997358
SR	Spire Inc	Gas Utilities	9/30/19	1952.4	184.6	7619.2	2546.4	371	49553038
SPR	Spirit AeroSystems Holdings Inc	Aerospace	12/31/18	7222.0	617.0	5685.9	1237.6	569	130405162
SAVE	Spirit Airlines Inc	Airlines/Air Freight	12/31/18	3323.0	155.7	5165.5	1928.5	352	78006360
SRC	Spirit Realty Capital Inc (New)	REITs	12/31/18	445.1	132.1	5096.3	2801.7	435	174987823
SPOT	Spotify Technology SA	Radio & Television	12/31/18	5259.0	-78.0	4336.0	2094.0	433	88118978
SRLP	Sprague Resources LP	Equipment & Services	12/31/18	3771.1	79.8	1245.2		49	5715011
S	Sprint Corp (New)	Services	3/31/19	33600.0	-1943.0	84601.0	26072.0	708	815414441
SPXC	SPX Corp.	Industrial Machinery & Equipment	12/31/18	1538.6	81.2	2057.5	414.9	385	53112470
FLOW	SPX Flow Inc	Industrial Machinery & Equipment	12/31/18	2090.1	44.0	2551.8	974.3	238	46793815
SQ	Square Inc	IT Services	12/31/18	3298.2	-38.5	3281.0	1120.5	867	261655876
JOE	St. Joe Co. (The)	Property, Real Estate & Developmen	12/31/18	110.3	32.4	871.0	518.2	198	87831015
STAG	STAG Industrial Inc	REITs	12/31/18	351.0	92.9	3102.5	1613.8	382	136265555
SSI	Stage Stores Inc.	Retail - Apparel and Accessories	2/2/19	1641.5	-87.7	744.2	254.5	110	18593165
SMP	Standard Motor Products, Inc.	Auto Parts	12/31/18	1092.1	43.0	843.1	467.2	222	21133104
SXI	Standex International Corp.	Industrial Machinery & Equipment	6/30/19	791.6	67.9	921.9	464.3	227	14861574
SWK	Stanley Black & Decker Inc	Industrial Machinery & Equipment	12/29/18	13982.4	605.2	19408.0	7836.2	1029	156580132
STN	Stantec Inc	Business Services	12/31/18	3355.2	47.4	4009.9	1906.9	1	6402
SGU	Star Group LP	Gas Utilities	9/30/19	1753.9	17.6	752.7		95	22442736
SCX	Starrett (LS) Co (The)	Industrial Machinery & Equipment	6/30/19	228.0	6.1	190.1	83.4	51	3048729
SRT	StarTek, Inc.	Business Services	12/31/18	420.3	-24.3	604.6	231.0	90	5910480
STWD	Starwood Property Trust Inc.	REITs	12/31/18	1109.3	385.8	68262.5	4603.4	564	212203958
STT	State Street Corp.	Banking	12/31/18	12973.0	2599.0	244626.0	24790.0	1225	404207424
SPLP PRA	Steel Partners Holdings LP	Metal Products	12/31/18	1584.6	-32.6	2356.1		31	9936084
SCS	Steelcase, Inc.	Office Equipment & Furniture	2/22/19	3443.2	126.0	2142.4	849.8	341	93977895
SCM	Stellus Capital Investment Corp	Finance Intermediaries & Services	12/31/18	53.3	22.6	526.3	224.8	66	3503207
SCL	Stepan Co.	Specialty Chemicals	12/31/18	1993.9	112.8	1484.7	783.8	268	20359818
STE	STERIS plc (Ireland)	Medical Instruments & Equipment	3/31/19	2782.2	304.1	5073.1	3177.8		0
STL	Sterling Bancorp (DE)	Banking	12/31/18	1299.9	447.3	31383.3	4428.9	93	15567962
STC	Stewart Information Services Corp	General Insurance	12/31/18	1907.7	47.5	1372.9	673.5	255	29204876
SF	Stifel Financial Corp	Finance Intermediaries & Services	12/31/18	3195.0	394.0	24519.6	3167.6	402	72000169
STM	STMicroelectronics NV	Semiconductors	12/31/18	9664.0	1287.0	10867.0	6359.0	287	31273232
EDF	Stone Harbor Emerging Markets Inc	Holding and other Investment Office	11/30/18	24.3	18.2	259.4	171.0		0
EDI	Stone Harbor Emerging Markets Tot	Finance Intermediaries & Services	11/30/18	15.1	11.0	166.2	109.7	31	947646
STON	StoneMor Inc	Miscellaneous Consumer Services	12/31/18	316.1	-72.7	1669.1		73	20053791
SRI	Stoneridge Inc.	Auto Parts	12/31/18	866.2	53.8	559.5	283.3	211	31659084
STOR	STORE Capital Corp	REITs	12/31/18	540.8	217.0	7114.0	3863.5	476	229706536
SYK	Stryker Corp	Medical Instruments & Equipment	12/31/18	13601.0	3553.0	27229.0	11730.0	1807	341891357
MSC	Studio City International Holdings Lt	Hotels, Restaurants & Travel	12/31/18	571.2	-21.6	2802.3	843.5	18	17403575
RGR	Sturm, Ruger & Co., Inc.	Leisure Equipment	12/31/18	495.6	50.9	335.5	264.2	291	17594782
SPH	Suburban Propane Partners LP	Gas Utilities	9/28/19	1267.7	68.6	1998.3		238	30355506
SMFG	Sumitomo Mitsui Financial Group In	Banking	3/31/19	4522829.0	541932.0	95503623.0	11279323.0		0
INN	Summit Hotel Properties Inc	REITs	12/31/18	567.3	90.9	2222.3	1189.8	305	129179522
SUM	Summit Materials Inc	Construction Materials	12/29/18	2101.0	36.3	3857.6	1327.7	249	140295604
SMLP	Summit Midstream Partners LP	Equipment & Services	12/31/18	506.7	42.2	3020.6		82	42153148
SUI	Sun Communities Inc	REITs	12/31/18	1126.8	111.7	6710.0	3170.4	512	101230226
SLF	Sun Life Financial Inc	Life & Health	12/31/18	26997.0	2616.0	271827.0	24570.0	423	284526328
SXC	SunCoke Energy Inc	Metal Products	12/31/18	1450.9	26.2	2045.3	463.1	266	85065442
SU	Suncor Energy Inc	Refining & Marketing	12/31/18	38986.0	3293.0	89579.0	44005.0	860	1165497153
STG	Sunlands Technology Group	IT & Communications	12/31/18	1974.0	-927.0	3739.1	-339.1		0
NOVA	Sunnova Energy International Inc	Electric Utilities	12/31/18	104.4	-74.2	1665.1	501.1	61	54733510
SUN	Sunoco LP	Equipment & Services	12/31/18	16994.0	-207.0	4879.0	784.0	177	44478300
SHO	Sunstone Hotel Investors Inc	REITs	12/31/18	1159.1	250.4	3972.8	2663.5	329	291427892
STI 15	SunTrust Bank, Middle Georgia, N.	Banking							0
SPN	Superior Energy Services, Inc.	Equipment & Services	12/31/18	2130.3	-858.1	2216.0	290.7	338	49756453
SUP	Superior Industries International, Inc	Auto Parts	12/31/18	1501.8	26.0	1451.6	531.6	191	20101167
SUZ	Suzano SA	Paper & Forest Products	12/31/11	4848.0	29.9	21657.1	9673.5		0
SWZ	Swiss Helvetia Fund Inc (The)	Holding and other Investment Office	12/31/18	7.8	3.4	105.9	105.6	56	5132330
SWCH	Switch Inc	Internet & Software	12/31/18	405.9	4.1	1460.0	143.2	148	59797433

T52

EARNINGS PER SHARE						P/E RATIO		DIVIDENDS PER SHARE			AV. YLD %	DIV. DECLARED		PRICE RANGE 2018	
QUARTERLY 1st	2nd	3rd	ANNUAL 2018	2017	2016			2018	2017	2016		AMOUNT	PAYABLE		
-	-	0.14	0.76	0.88	0.88	63.9 -	46.7	0.71	0.37	0.63	1.7	-	-	48.6 -	35.5
-	-	0.53	2.58	1.70	1.85	21.9 -	15.7	0.76	0.56	0.48	1.6	0.240Y	18/53/27	56.5 -	40.5
-	1.85	-	11.78	5.10	5.76	10.8 -	8.0	3.09	2.92	2.65	2.8	0.880Y	18/53/27	127.5 -	93.9
-	-	-0.16	-0.97	-2.95	-0.64	-		-	-	-	-	-	-	17.9 -	5.6
-	-	2.96	11.87	9.52	9.20	14.5 -	12.1	3.41	2.95	2.54	2.1	1.080Y	18/53/27	171.8 -	144.0
-	-	0.53	1.67	1.63	1.06	26.9 -	13.8	1.42	1.17	1.18	4.4	-	-	45.0 -	23.0
-0.01	-	-	0.25	0.20	0.11	27.9 -	13.6	-	-	-	-	-	-	7.0 -	3.4
-	-	0.36	1.59	0.27	-0.23	11.9 -	6.6	0.10	-	-	0.7	0.1050Y	12/26/19	18.9 -	10.5
-	-	0.01	2.56	-3.50	-4.98	8.0 -	5.1	-	-	-	-	-	-	20.5 -	13.1
-	-	0.66	1.20	2.09	2.04	28.7 -	11.5	0.24	0.20	0.20	1.0	0.10Y	18/53/27	34.4 -	13.8
-	-	0.91	3.10	1.74	2.81	21.4 -	16.6	1.62	1.54	1.46	2.7	0.430Y	18/53/27	66.4 -	51.5
-	-	330.77	379.75	56.89	117.49	0.2 -	0.1	22.69	19.67	9.98	42.2	-	-	68.3 -	42.0
-	-	-	0.55	0.50	0.40	70.8 -	59.2	4.20	1.73	35.23	11.5	0.250Y	12/15/19	38.9 -	32.5
-	-	-0.38	0.21	-0.04	1.56	163.2 -	128.0	1.13	1.10	1.06	3.6	0.2950Y	18/53/27	34.3 -	26.9
-	-	1.25	2.17	0.84	2.55	29.4 -	20.1	2.38	2.30	2.22	4.3	0.620Y	18/53/27	63.9 -	43.7
-	-	0.50	2.00	0.94	1.00	21.6 -	14.6	1.40	0.59	0.18	3.9	0.40	18/53/27	43.2 -	29.2
-	-	1.23	4.29	5.79	3.55	13.6 -	10.6	0.60	0.47	0.38	1.1	0.180Y	18/53/27	58.3 -	45.6
-	-	0.10	3.68	4.04	3.18	25.0 -	20.1	2.06	1.49	1.80	2.5	0.5450Y	18/53/27	92.1 -	73.9
-	-	0.09	0.93	1.63	-6.32	5.2 -	1.7	-	-	-	-	0.00750	18/53/27	4.8 -	1.6
-	-	-	0.18	0.44	0.63	-		1.45	1.33	0.81	10.6	0.0940	3/31/20	14.8 -	12.0
-	-	-0.53	20.74	3.29	-6.14	3.2 -	2.1	0.42	-	-	0.8	0.420Y	18/53/27	65.8 -	43.4
-	-	-0.09	4.33	3.43	3.24	20.1 -	16.7	2.25	2.10	1.96	2.7	0.36880Y	18/53/27	87.2 -	72.4
-	-	1.26	5.65	3.01	3.70	17.6 -	12.4	0.46	0.40	0.10	0.6	0.120Y	18/53/27	99.3 -	70.1
-	-	1.22	2.28	6.06	3.76	27.7 -	14.5	-	-	-	-	-	-	63.1 -	33.1
-	-	0.87	1.39	0.80	1.05	38.2 -	24.9	0.63	3.60	3.52	1.4	0.3750Z	18/53/27	53.0 -	34.6
-0.79	-	-	-0.51	-8.14	-3.63	-		-	-	-	-	-	-		
-	-	-0.43	3.16	1.13	0.38	6.4 -	4.6	2.63	2.40	2.16	15.0	0.66750	2/10/20	20.1 -	14.7
-	-0.07	-	1.85	-0.30	-0.50	4.3 -	2.8	-	-	-	-	-	-	8.0 -	5.2
-	-	0.48	1.82	2.03	-2.02	28.4 -	14.4	-	-	-	-	0.3750Y	7/1/15	51.7 -	26.3
-	-	-0.74	1.03	1.10	-9.23	48.0 -	28.9					-	-	49.5 -	29.8
-	-	0.06	-0.09	-0.17	-0.50	-						-	-	82.3 -	52.4
-	-	0.10	0.52	0.84	0.21	39.4 -	25.0					0.160Y	9/28/07	20.5 -	13.0
-	-	0.07	0.79	0.23	0.29	40.0 -	30.5	1.42	1.41	1.39	4.8	0.42970Z	3/31/20	31.6 -	24.1
-	-	-0.55	-1.37	-1.40	0.12	-		0.30	0.60	0.58	17.8	0.050Y	12/19/18	8.6 -	0.6
-	-	0.65	1.88	1.64	2.62	29.5 -	22.5	0.84	0.76	0.68	1.7	0.230Y	12/2/19	55.4 -	42.4
1.00	-	-	2.86	3.65	4.08	28.9 -	21.0	0.18	0.62	0.54	0.2	0.220Y	2/25/20	82.6 -	59.9
-	-	1.53	3.99	8.04	6.51	42.0 -	29.0	2.58	2.42	2.26	1.8	0.690Y	18/53/27	167.8 -	115.7
-	-	0.52	0.42	0.85	1.22	88.4 -	50.0	0.55	0.50	0.45	2.0	0.1450	1/15/20	37.1 -	21.0
-	-	-0.46	0.89	0.46	0.70	11.4 -	10.1	0.46	0.42	0.40	4.8	0.1250	2/4/20	10.2 -	9.0
0.11	-	-	-0.52	0.14	-2.01	-		0.20	0.40	0.40	3.1	0.10Z	12/29/17	8.5 -	5.2
-	-0.07	-	-0.80	-0.08	0.02	-		-	-	-	-	0.250Y	11/27/06	8.8 -	6.0
-	-	0.49	1.42	1.52	1.50	17.9 -	13.9	1.92	1.92	1.92	8.3	0.480Z	18/53/27	25.4 -	19.7
-	-	1.42	6.40	5.24	4.97	12.6 -	7.6	1.78	1.60	1.44	2.8	0.520Y	18/53/27	80.4 -	48.8
-	-	-0.12	-1.25	-	0.25	-		1.50	1.27	-	6.9	0.3750Z	12/15/19	23.3 -	20.6
-	-	0.46	0.68	1.03	1.36	32.7 -	21.4	0.51	0.48	0.45	3.0	0.1450Y	1/13/20	22.2 -	14.6
-	-	0.31	1.42	1.21	1.39	10.7 -	9.0	1.36	1.36	1.36	9.7	0.11330	4/15/20	15.2 -	12.8
-	-	1.11	4.83	3.92	3.73	21.2 -	15.1	0.93	0.84	0.78	1.0	0.2750Y	18/53/27	102.4 -	72.7
-	1.11	-	3.39	1.28	1.56	-		1.21	1.09	0.98	-	0.370	18/53/27		
-	-	0.59	1.95	0.58	1.07	11.3 -	8.5	0.28	0.28	0.28	1.4	0.070Y	18/53/27	22.0 -	16.7
-	-	2.78	2.01	2.06	1.85	22.3 -	16.7	1.20	1.20	1.20	2.9	0.30Y	12/31/19	44.9 -	33.6
-	-	1.34	4.73	2.14	1.00	13.3 -	8.5	0.48	0.20	-	0.9	0.3250Z	4/15/20	63.0 -	40.0
0.20	-	-	1.41	0.89	0.19	19.4 -	8.6	0.20	0.20	0.24	1.1	-	-	27.3 -	12.1
-	-	-	1.13	1.40	1.42	12.8 -	9.8	2.16	2.16	2.16	16.2	0.170	4/30/20	14.4 -	11.1
-	-	-	1.13	1.40	0.63	11.8 -	9.4	1.81	1.81	0.91	14.7	0.15110Y	4/30/20	13.4 -	10.7
-	-	-1.09	-1.90	-1.96	-0.94	-		-	0.66	2.31	-	-	-	4.5 -	1.1
-	-	0.24	1.85	1.57	2.74	18.4 -	13.6	-	-	-	-	-	-	34.0 -	25.1
-	-	0.48	1.06	0.90	0.82	38.5 -	25.9	1.28	1.20	1.12	3.7	0.350	18/53/27	40.8 -	27.5
-	-	1.23	9.34	2.68	4.35	23.7 -	16.3	1.93	1.75	1.56	1.0	0.5750Y	18/53/27	221.8 -	152.5
-	-	-	-0.114	217.90	3393.00	-		-	-	-	-	-	-	20.9 -	0.0
-	-	0.27	2.88	2.91	4.59	20.7 -	13.8	1.10	1.36	1.73	2.2	0.110Y	11/27/19	59.6 -	39.9
-	-	-0.47	1.24	0.62	0.24	19.9 -	15.7	2.40	3.55	3.55	10.4	0.60	2/11/20	24.6 -	19.4
171.14	-	-	538.43	458.18	616.83	0.0 -	0.0	31.38	29.85	30.73	444.3	-	-	7.5 -	6.4
-	-	0.07	0.68	0.79	1.00	18.5 -	14.1	0.72	0.67	0.55	6.2	0.39060Z	11/29/19	12.6 -	9.6
-	-	0.48	0.30	1.11	0.52	83.2 -	42.0	-	-	-	-	-	-	24.9 -	12.6
-	-	-0.21	0.06	0.98	-0.71	233.8 -	48.2	2.30	2.30	2.30	30.9	0.28750	11/14/19	14.0 -	2.9
-	-	0.63	1.29	0.85	0.26	128.1 -	75.8	2.84	2.68	2.60	2.1	0.750Z	18/53/27	165.3 -	97.8
-	1.00	-	4.14	3.49	4.03	14.8 -	8.0	1.91	1.75	1.62	4.0	0.23790	12/31/19	61.4 -	33.0
-	-	-1.81	0.40	1.88	0.22	28.1 -	11.8	-	-	-	-	0.060	12/2/19	11.2 -	4.7
-	-	0.67	2.02	2.68	0.28	22.9 -	13.7	1.44	1.28	1.16	3.9	0.420	12/24/19	46.2 -	27.6
-	-	-	-147.27	-2.33	-66.40	-		-	-	-	-	-	-	5.6 -	0.0
-	-0.62	-	-6.74	-6.02	-	-		-	-	-	-	-	-	12.0 -	8.7
-	-	0.57	-3.39	0.34	-5.26	-		3.30	3.30	3.27	10.7	0.82550	11/19/19	34.0 -	27.1
-	-	0.12	1.05	0.59	0.55	14.7 -	12.2	0.69	0.73	0.68	4.9	0.59HZ	1/15/20	15.4 -	12.9
-	-	-2.50	-55.60	-13.50	-58.50	-		-	-	0.80	-	0.80	18/53/27	54.8 -	0.9
-	-	-0.57	0.29	-1.01	1.62	24.5 -	8.0	0.36	0.54	0.72	9.1	0.090Y	7/19/19	7.1 -	2.3
-	-	-	-	-	-	-		-	-	-	-	-	-	13.4 -	6.8
-	-	-	0.14	0.13	0.15	60.1 -	49.1	5.11	0.13	0.51	65.5	0.0155C	12/27/19	8.4 -	6.9
-	-	0.02	0.09	-1.88	0.15	186.4 -	75.8	0.06	0.01	-	0.5	0.02940Y	18/53/27	16.8 -	6.8

SYMBOL	COMPANY	NATURE OF BUSINESS	FISCAL YEAR-END	TOTAL REV. $MILL	NET INCOME $MILL	TOTAL ASSETS $MILL	NET STK EQUITY $MILL	NO OF INST	INST. HOLDINGS (SHARES)
SBE U	Switchback Energy Acquisition Corp	Finance Intermediaries & Services	5/16/19	-	-0.0	0.1	0.0		0
SYF	Synchrony Financial	Banking	12/31/18	18253.0	2790.0	106792.0	14678.0	838	660380307
SNX	Synnex Corp	IT Services	11/30/18	20053.8	300.6	11480.4	3432.1	433	45236409
SNV	Synovus Financial Corp	Banking	12/31/18	1624.4	428.5	32669.2	3133.6	571	207555519
SYY	Sysco Corp	Retail - Food & Beverage, Drug & To	6/29/19	60113.9	1674.3	17966.5	2502.6	1751	558877799
SYX	Systemax, Inc.	Retail - Appliances and Electronics	12/31/18	896.9	224.7	530.0	137.7	135	13024696
TLRD	Tailored Brands Inc	Retail - Apparel and Accessories	2/2/19	3239.9	83.2	1820.5	3.6	307	54540838
TWN	Taiwan Fund, Inc. (The)	Holding and other Investment Office	8/31/19	4.4	1.7	167.3	159.7	39	8505791
TSM	Taiwan Semiconductor Manufacturi	Semiconductors	12/31/18	1031361.8	351130.9	2090128.0	1676817.7	1106	1200206654
TAK	Takeda Pharmaceutical Co Ltd	Pharmaceuticals	3/31/19	2097224.0	109126.0	13872322.0	5159582.0		0
TAK	Takeda Pharmaceutical Co Ltd	Pharmaceuticals	3/31/19	2097224.0	109126.0	13872322.0	5159582.0		0
TAL	TAL Education Group	Educational Services	2/28/19	2563.0	367.2	3735.1	2483.7	366	352879688
TGE	Tallgrass Energy LP	Equipment & Services	12/31/18	793.3	137.1	5893.5	-	293	182986749
TALO	Talos Energy Inc	Production & Extraction	12/31/18	891.3	221.5	2480.0	1007.5	133	53935702
SKT	Tanger Factory Outlet Centers, Inc.	REITs	12/31/18	494.7	43.7	2384.9	480.2	419	124861949
TPR	Tapestry Inc	Apparel, Footwear & Accessories	6/29/19	6027.1	643.4	6877.3	3513.4	985	308237736
TRGP	Targa Resources Corp	Refining & Marketing	12/31/18	10484.0	1.6	16938.2	6325.1	576	250141676
TGT	Target Corp	Retail - General Merchandise/Depart	2/2/19	75356.0	2937.0	41290.0	11297.0	2000	518991840
TARO	Taro Pharmaceutical Industries Ltd.	Pharmaceuticals	3/31/19	669.9	281.8	2135.3	1905.5	149	6324534
TTM	Tata Motors Ltd	Autos- Manufacturing	3/31/18	2882951.1	66660.8	3235937.2	908589.8	291	61561654
TCO	Taubman Centers Inc	REITs	12/31/18	640.9	83.5	4344.1	-92.9	401	81427963
TMHC	Taylor Morrison Home Corp (Holdin	Builders	12/31/18	4227.4	206.4	5264.4	2415.2	278	110316884
TRP	TC Energy Corp	Equipment & Services	12/31/18	13679.0	3702.0	98920.0	29338.0	616	674404685
TCP	TC PipeLines, LP	Equipment & Services	12/31/18	549.0	-182.0	2899.0		205	68932828
TSI	TCW Strategic Income Fund Inc	Holding and other Investment Office	12/31/18	16.7	14.3	277.8	269.6	91	19250716
TEL	TE Connectivity Ltd	Electrical Equipment	9/27/19	13448.0	1844.0	19694.0	10570.0	998	360680513
TISI	Team Inc	Equipment & Services	12/31/18	1246.9	-63.1	977.8	457.1	217	40155284
FTI	TechnipFMC plc	Equipment & Services	12/31/18	12552.9	-1921.6	24784.5	10399.6		0
TECK	Teck Resources Ltd	Mining	12/31/18	12564.0	3107.0	39626.0	22884.0	423	436472529
TK	Teekay Corp	Equipment & Services	12/31/18	1707.8	-79.2	8391.7	809.0	181	25729240
TGP	Teekay LNG Partners LP	Equipment & Services	12/31/18	510.8	28.4	5384.8	-	135	32570159
TNK	Teekay Tankers Ltd	Equipment & Services	12/31/18	755.8	-52.5	2161.1	946.9	163	77352145
TGNA	TEGNA Inc	Radio & Television	12/31/18	2207.3	405.7	5276.8	1340.9	591	253667479
TRC	Tejon Ranch Co	Property, Real Estate & Developmen	12/31/18	45.6	4.3	529.0	419.3	140	20721322
HQH	Tekla Healthcare Investors	Holding and other Investment Office	9/30/19	7.6	-2.9	877.8	870.8	131	10570993
THQ	Tekla Healthcare Opportunities Fun	Finance Intermediaries & Services	9/30/19	22.4	3.1	1010.1	779.7	76	8628918
HQL	Tekla Life Sciences Investors	Holding and other Investment Office	9/30/19	2.4	-2.9	387.0	383.7	79	4019277
THW	Tekla World Healthcare Fund	Holding and other Investment Office	9/30/19	12.4	1.9	530.5	407.5	52	3538545
TDOC	Teladoc Health Inc	Diagnostic & Health Related Service	12/31/18	417.9	-97.1	1528.9	1013.1	437	95477126
TLRA	Telaria Inc	Internet & Software	12/31/18	55.2	-9.4	174.7	54.4	161	37249687
TEO	Telecom Argentina SA	Services	12/31/18	168046.0	5294.0	371738.0	225686.0	143	18657014
TDY	Teledyne Technologies Inc	Electronic Instruments & Related Pro	12/30/18	2901.8	333.8	3809.3	2229.7	531	42353054
TFX	Teleflex Incorporated	Medical Instruments & Equipment	12/31/18	2448.4	200.8	6278.0	2540.0	686	54384374
VIV	Telefonica Brasil SA	Services	12/31/18	43462.7	8928.3	102561.3	71607.0	269	173028305
TEF	Telefonica SA	Services	12/31/18	48693.0	3331.0	114047.0	17947.0	330	54622283
TDS	Telephone & Data Systems Inc	Services	12/31/18	5109.0	135.0	9783.0	4560.0	448	118021603
TU	TELUS Corp	Services	12/31/18	14095.0	1600.0	33065.0	10259.0	376	354379825
TDF	Templeton Dragon Fund, Inc.	Holding and other Investment Office	12/31/18	21.6	10.8	644.7	643.8	92	20380207
EMF	Templeton Emerging Markets Fund	Holding and other Investment Office	8/31/19	7.8	3.5	280.2	268.8	75	7210974
TEI	Templeton Emerging Markets Inco	Holding and other Investment Office	12/31/18	46.2	39.7	530.1	524.5	122	15602910
GIM	Templeton Global Income Fund (DE	Holding and other Investment Office	12/31/18	56.6	49.8	957.5	945.0	186	48250842
TPX	Tempur Sealy International, Inc.	Furniture	12/31/18	2702.9	100.5	2715.4	214.6	405	72190081
TS	Tenaris SA	Equipment & Services	12/31/18	7658.6	876.1	14251.3	11782.9	277	115050685
TME	Tencent Music Entertainment Group	IT Services	12/31/18	18985.0	1833.0	44605.0	37721.0	196	210478160
THC	Tenet Healthcare Corp.	Hospitals & Health Care Facilities	12/31/18	18313.0	111.0	22409.0	-119.0	438	195336385
TNC	Tennant Co.	Industrial Machinery & Equipment	12/31/18	1123.5	33.4	992.5	314.4	219	18898903
TEN	Tenneco Inc	Auto Parts	12/31/18	11763.0	55.0	13232.0	1726.0	341	58446733
TVE	Tennessee Valley Authority	Electric Utilities	9/30/19	11318.0	1417.0	50467.0	11625.0		0
TDC	Teradata Corp (DE)	Internet & Software	12/31/18	2164.0	30.0	2360.0	495.0	556	135325753
TEX	Terex Corp.	Industrial Machinery & Equipment	12/31/18	5125.0	113.7	3485.9	860.5	457	92924502
TX	Ternium S A	Non-Precious Metals	12/31/18	11454.8	1506.6	12547.9	6393.3	179	41503806
TRNO	Terreno Realty Corp	REITs	12/31/18	151.7	63.3	1796.5	1247.8	250	72687003
TTI	TETRA Technologies, Inc.	Equipment & Services	12/31/18	998.8	-61.6	1385.5	173.4	221	133237280
TEVA	Teva Pharmaceutical Industries Ltd	Pharmaceuticals	12/31/18	18854.0	-2150.0	60683.0	14707.0	890	704292941
TPL	Texas Pacific Land Trust	Production & Extraction	12/31/18	300.2	209.7	285.1	244.7	257	6682955
TGH	Textainer Group Holdings Ltd	Shipping	12/31/18	676.9	50.4	4744.3	1206.8	156	16091418
TXT	Textron Inc	Aerospace	12/29/18	13972.0	1222.0	14264.0	5192.0	732	231884785
GPS	The Gap Inc	Retail - Apparel and Accessories	2/2/19	16580.0	1003.0	8049.0	3553.0	719	319499896
NWHM	The New Home Company Inc	Builders	12/31/18	667.6	-14.2	696.1	240.0	70	11267061
TMO	Thermo Fisher Scientific Inc	Biotechnology	12/31/18	24358.0	2938.0	56232.0	27586.0	2071	440151460
THR	Thermon Group Holdings Inc	Electrical Equipment	3/31/19	412.6	22.8	655.8	344.7	150	39118874
TPRE	Third Point Reinsurance Ltd	General Insurance	12/31/18	370.0	-317.7	3086.2	1204.6	205	71670919
TSLF	THL Credit Senior Loan Fund	Finance Intermediaries & Services	12/31/18	13.7	9.4	183.7	128.3	48	2273653
TRI	Thomson Reuters Corp	Publishing	12/31/18	5501.0	3949.0	17047.0	9226.0	450	133667897
THO	Thor Industries, Inc.	Autos- Manufacturing	7/31/19	7864.8	133.3	5660.4	2084.4	562	64626230
TDW	Tidewater Inc (New)	Equipment & Services	12/31/18	406.5	-171.5	1827.7	1143.8	256	52230162
TIF	Tiffany & Co.	Retail - Specialty	1/31/19	4442.1	586.4	5333.0	3117.4	801	148331324
TLYS	Tilly's Inc	Retail - Apparel and Accessories	2/2/19	598.5	24.9	293.2	163.3	147	22712649
TSU	TIM Participacoes S.A.	Services	12/31/18	16981.3	2545.1	31957.9	19794.8	180	64925308
TKR	Timken Co. (The)	Industrial Machinery & Equipment	12/31/18	3580.8	302.8	4445.2	1579.6	542	71170640

T54

1st	2nd	3rd	2018	2017	2016	P/E High	P/E Low	Div 2018	Div 2017	Div 2016	AV. YLD %	AMOUNT	PAYABLE	Price High	Price Low
-	-	-0.05	-	-	-	-	-	-	-	-	-	-	-	10.1	0.0
-	-	1.60	3.74	2.42	2.71	10.1	6.4	0.72	0.56	0.26	2.1	0.220Y	18/53/27	37.8	24.1
-	-	2.40	7.19	7.51	5.88	18.0	10.9	1.40	1.05	0.85	1.4	0.40Y	18/53/27	129.6	78.2
-	-	0.83	3.47	2.17	1.89	11.6	9.2	1.00	0.60	0.48	2.8	0.36720Y	18/53/27	40.2	32.0
0.87	-	-	2.70	2.08	1.64	31.8	22.7	1.38	0.97	1.23	1.9	0.450Y	18/53/27	85.8	61.4
-	-	0.33	5.93	1.07	-0.87	4.4	3.2	9.44	0.35	0.10	42.5	0.120Y	11/18/19	26.4	18.7
-	-	-1.80	1.95	0.51	-21.26	7.6	1.9	0.72	0.72	0.72	10.2	0.180Y	9/27/19	14.8	3.7
-	-	-	0.22	0.20	0.12	101.7	0.0	0.66	-	-	3.8	0.0651B	1/10/20	22.4	0.0
-	-	3.47	13.54	13.23	12.89	4.4	2.5	31.47	27.95	24.45	71.8	-	-	59.2	34.4
-	-	58.57	237.56	146.26	101.71	0.1	0.1	90.82	90.14	88.73	486.4	-	-	21.5	16.1
-	-	58.57	237.56	146.26	101.71	0.1	0.1	90.82	90.14	88.73	479.4	-	-	19.3	18.5
-	0.15	-	1.03	0.66	0.60	47.1	24.0	0.08	-	-	0.2	-	-	48.5	24.7
-	-	0.40	1.27	-2.22	0.55	20.0	11.3	1.86	1.26	0.89	8.7	0.550	11/14/19	25.4	14.4
-	-	1.35	4.81	-	-	6.4	3.6	-	-	-	-	-	-	30.6	17.4
-	-	0.25	0.45	0.71	2.01	51.2	30.7	1.39	1.35	1.26	7.9	0.3550Z	18/53/27	23.1	13.8
0.07	-	-	1.38	2.09	1.65	28.5	14.1	1.35	1.35	1.35	4.6	0.33750Y	18/53/27	39.3	19.4
-	-	-0.34	-0.53	-0.31	-1.80	-	-	3.64	3.64	3.64	9.2	23.750	18/53/27	47.9	32.5
-	-	1.39	5.33	4.70	5.31	24.2	12.3	2.44	2.32	2.16	2.7	0.660Y	18/53/27	129.2	65.5
-	1.60	-	5.26	11.05	12.62	-	-	-	-	-	-	12.86017	12/28/18	-	-
-	-	3.51	19.60	18.00	28.40	0.9	0.4	-	0.80	-	-	-	-	17.1	7.6
-	-	3.48	0.95	0.91	1.77	57.2	31.1	2.62	2.50	2.38	6.0	0.39060Z	18/53/27	54.3	29.6
-	-	0.63	1.83	1.47	1.69	15.1	8.8	-	-	-	-	-	-	27.7	16.1
-	-	0.79	3.92	3.43	0.16	17.9	9.5	2.76	2.50	2.26	4.9	0.23750	2/28/20	70.3	37.1
-	-	0.76	-2.68	3.16	3.21	-	-	2.95	3.88	3.66	7.9	0.650	18/53/27	43.6	30.5
-	-	-	0.30	0.27	0.26	19.8	17.4	0.37	0.31	0.28	6.6	0.0246B	1/10/20	5.9	5.2
-	-	2.23	7.27	9.40	5.44	-	-	1.68	3.08	1.40	-	0.460Y	18/53/27	-	-
-	-	-0.23	-2.10	-3.49	-0.45	-	-	-	-	-	-	0.010	3/1/93	19.5	14.0
-	-	-0.27	-4.20	0.28	1932.42	-	-	0.52	-	-	-	0.130	12/4/19	-	-
-	0.41	-	5.34	4.28	1.78	6.3	2.8	0.30	0.60	0.10	1.3	0.050	12/31/19	33.6	14.8
-	-	-0.12	-0.79	-1.89	-1.62	-	-	0.22	0.22	0.22	-	0.0550	2/14/19	-	-
-	-	-	0.03	0.25	1.69	-	-	0.56	0.56	-	-	0.190	2/14/20	-	-
-	-0.40	-	-1.60	-2.48	3.20	-	-	0.24	0.96	1.44	-	0.030	3/9/18	-	-
-	-	0.22	1.87	1.26	1.99	9.1	5.8	0.28	0.35	0.56	1.9	0.070Y	18/53/27	16.9	10.9
-	-	-	0.16	-0.07	0.03	122.1	99.4	-	-	-	-	0.0250	12/10/99	19.5	15.9
-	-	-	-0.10	-0.13	-0.17	-	-	1.94	1.96	3.10	9.8	0.410	12/31/19	21.4	17.9
-	-	-	0.13	0.16	0.18	147.6	125.8	1.35	1.35	1.65	7.7	0.11250	1/31/20	19.2	16.4
-	-	-	-0.16	-0.18	-0.19	-	-	1.63	1.59	2.85	9.9	0.330	12/31/19	17.9	14.6
-	-	-	0.11	0.12	0.09	127.0	105.8	1.40	1.40	1.40	10.8	0.11670	1/31/20	14.0	11.6
-	-	-	-0.28	-1.47	-1.75	-	-	-	-	-	-	-	-	85.9	46.2
-	-	-	-0.06	-0.18	0.04	-0.40	-	-	-	-	-	-	-	10.6	2.8
-	-	0.89	2.46	7.87	4.10	7.3	3.5	46.03	20.84	9.51	341.2	-	-	18.0	8.6
-	-	2.84	9.01	6.26	5.37	38.8	22.2	-	-	-	-	-	-	349.8	200.1
-	-	4.85	4.29	3.27	4.98	87.7	57.4	1.36	1.36	1.36	0.4	0.340Y	18/53/27	376.4	246.2
-	-	-	4.96	2.56	2.27	2.9	2.2	3.46	2.39	1.84	26.9	-	-	14.5	10.9
0.16	-	-	0.57	0.56	0.42	15.7	11.4	0.40	0.40	0.73	5.0	-	-	9.0	6.5
-	-	0.15	1.17	1.37	0.39	31.5	18.7	0.64	0.62	0.59	2.2	0.1650Z	18/53/27	36.8	21.9
-	-	0.72	2.68	2.46	2.06	19.2	12.4	2.10	1.97	1.84	5.0	0.58250	1/2/20	51.4	33.2
-	-	-	0.32	0.19	0.27	64.9	51.2	0.21	0.34	-	1.1	0.6804C	12/31/19	20.8	16.4
-	-	-	0.14	0.16	0.19	114.6	93.7	1.12	0.20	1.28	7.5	0.0888B	12/31/19	16.1	13.1
-	-	-	0.83	0.85	0.25	12.7	10.6	0.65	0.62	-	6.7	0.06090	1/31/20	10.5	8.8
-	-	-	0.37	0.36	0.10	17.6	15.8	0.35	0.29	0.30	5.6	0.02880Z	1/31/20	6.5	5.9
-	-	1.31	1.82	2.77	3.38	50.0	22.6	-	-	-	-	0.080Y	18/53/27	91.0	41.1
-	-	0.09	0.74	0.46	0.05	40.9	27.1	0.82	0.82	0.86	3.4	-	-	30.2	20.1
-	-	-	0.58	0.51	0.04	32.9	19.7	-	-	-	-	-	-	19.1	11.4
-	-	-2.24	1.07	-7.00	-1.93	36.2	16.4	-	-	-	-	0.0267F	18/53/27	38.8	17.6
-	-	0.79	1.82	-0.35	2.59	43.5	28.1	0.85	0.84	0.81	1.3	0.220Y	18/53/27	79.2	51.2
-	-	0.87	0.93	3.91	6.44	39.1	8.5	1.00	1.00	-	5.7	0.250	18/53/27	36.4	7.9
-	-	-	-	-	-	-	-	0.89	0.89	0.89	3.5	0.22190Z	6/1/20	26.5	24.3
-	-	0.09	0.25	-0.53	0.95	197.1	100.9	-	-	-	-	-	-	49.3	25.2
-	-	0.30	1.48	1.36	-1.63	24.3	15.7	0.40	0.32	0.28	1.4	0.110	18/53/27	35.9	23.3
-	-	0.25	0.77	0.45	0.30	41.4	21.1	1.10	1.00	0.90	4.7	-	-	31.9	16.2
-	-	0.22	1.09	0.95	0.26	53.2	31.4	0.92	0.84	0.76	1.9	0.270Z	1/14/20	58.0	34.3
-	-	-0.13	-0.50	-0.34	-1.85	-	-	-	-	-	-	-	-	2.6	1.2
-	-	-0.29	-2.35	-16.26	0.07	-	-	0.00	0.72	1.16	0.0	17.50	12/15/17	20.0	6.2
-	-	7.74	26.93	9.72	4.66	33.5	21.0	4.05	1.35	0.31	0.6	4.257Y	3/15/19	901.0	566.3
0.30	-	-	0.88	0.34	-0.89	-	-	-	-	0.51	-	0.03D	8/30/16	-	-
-	-	0.95	4.83	1.14	3.53	11.4	8.9	0.08	0.08	0.08	0.2	0.020Y	18/53/27	55.1	42.8
-	-	0.37	2.14	1.69	2.23	13.8	7.2	0.92	0.92	0.92	4.5	0.24250Y	18/53/27	29.5	15.4
-	-	-0.23	-0.69	0.82	1.01	-	-	-	-	-	-	-	-	7.1	3.5
-	-	1.88	7.24	5.59	5.09	45.3	29.3	0.68	0.60	0.60	0.2	0.190Y	18/53/27	328.0	212.2
-	0.21	-	0.36	0.45	0.71	75.9	56.9	-	-	-	-	-	-	27.3	20.5
-	-0.16	-	-3.27	2.64	0.26	-	-	-	-	-	-	-	-	-	-
-	-	-	1.27	1.26	1.37	12.6	11.3	1.16	1.22	1.27	7.7	0.1010	2/28/20	16.0	14.3
-	-	-0.09	5.91	2.14	4.55	16.2	7.9	1.39	1.52	-	2.1	0.360	12/16/19	95.8	46.9
0.92	-	-	8.14	7.09	4.88	9.4	5.2	1.48	1.32	1.20	2.5	0.40Y	18/53/27	76.5	42.7
-	-	-1.15	-6.45	-1.82	-3.41	-	-	-	-	0.75	-	-	-	24.8	13.7
-	-	0.65	2.96	3.55	3.59	45.2	26.9	1.95	1.75	1.58	1.9	0.580Y	18/53/27	133.8	79.6
-	-	0.21	0.51	0.40	0.27	25.5	15.0	0.70	-	-	6.8	1.7	2/26/20	13.0	7.6
-	0.84	-	1.05	0.51	0.31	18.4	12.3	0.89	0.50	0.89	5.8	-	-	19.3	12.9
-	-	0.84	3.86	2.58	1.92	14.7	9.4	1.11	1.07	1.04	2.4	0.280Y	18/53/27	56.9	36.4

SYMBOL	COMPANY	NATURE OF BUSINESS	FISCAL YEAR-END	TOTAL REV. $MILL	NET INCOME $MILL	TOTAL ASSETS $MILL	NET STK EQUITY $MILL	NO OF INST	INST. HOLDINGS (SHARES)
TMST	Timkensteel Corp	Metal Products	12/31/18	1610.6	-31.7	1197.6	535.2	209	36287640
TWI	Titan International Inc	Industrial Machinery & Equipment	12/31/18	1602.4	16.1	1251.3	279.0	217	68657957
TJX	TJX Companies, Inc.	Retail - Apparel and Accessories	2/2/19	38972.9	3059.8	14326.0	5048.6	1864	1196465591
TOL	Toll Brothers Inc.	Builders	10/31/19	7224.0	590.0	10828.1	5071.8	603	155392572
TR	Tootsie Roll Industries Inc	Food	12/31/18	518.9	56.9	947.4	750.6	267	19106724
BLD	TopBuild Corp	Builders	12/31/18	2384.2	134.8	2454.5	1072.1	326	38582869
TTC	Toro Company (The)	Industrial Machinery & Equipment	10/31/19	3138.1	274.0	2330.5	859.6	532	106567247
TD	Toronto Dominion Bank	Banking	10/31/18	60325.0	11416.0	1415290.0	87701.0	814	972970532
SHLL	Tortoise Acquisition Corp	Business Services		-0.0	0.4	0.0	28	12312953
NDP	Tortoise Energy Independence Fun	Holding and other Investment Office	11/30/18	0.7	-4.2	191.3	132.5	45	2918841
TYG	Tortoise Energy Infrastructure Corp	Holding and other Investment Office	11/30/18	-1.3	-25.7	2136.3	1260.3	210	21096938
NTG	Tortoise Midstream Energy Fund In	Holding and other Investment Office	11/30/18	3.0	-22.7	1506.7	915.0		0
TTP	Tortoise Pipeline & Energy Fund Inc	Holding and other Investment Office	11/30/18	4.6	-1.5	235.3	163.2	45	2921218
TPZ	Tortoise Power & Energy Infrastruct	Holding and other Investment Office	11/30/18	5.6	1.7	191.9	137.3	55	2373268
TOT	Total SA	Production & Extraction	12/31/18	184106.0	11446.0	256762.0	115640.0	921	213185017
TSQ	Townsquare Media Inc	Radio & Television	12/31/18	430.6	-32.9	987.2	340.3	74	9074570
TM	Toyota Motor Corp	Autos- Manufacturing	3/31/19	280225681.0	1882873.0	51936949.0	19846225.0	494	17192451
TRTX	TPG RE Finance Trust Inc	REITs	12/31/18	266.9	106.9	4526.8	1327.2	148	38753378
TSLX	TPG Specialty Lending Inc	Credit & Lending	12/31/18	261.9	143.9	1730.3	1063.2	159	41209321
TAC	TransAlta Corp	Electric Utilities	12/31/18	2249.0	-198.0	9428.0	2997.0	132	156228871
TCI	Transcontinental Realty Investors, I	Property, Real Estate & Developmen	12/31/18	121.0	181.4	862.4	359.7	33	200729
TDG	TransDigm Group Inc	Aerospace	9/30/19	5223.2	889.8	16254.7	-2894.9	715	63868326
RIG	Transocean Ltd	Equipment & Services	12/31/18	3018.0	-1996.0	25665.0	13107.0	681	503761052
TGS	Transportadora de Gas del Sur S.A.	Equipment & Services	12/31/18	34062.7	11415.8	61943.0	30945.3		0
TRU	TransUnion	Miscellaneous Consumer Services	12/31/18	2317.2	276.6	7039.8	1889.7	435	192549469
TRV	Travelers Companies Inc (The)	General Insurance	12/31/18	30282.0	2523.0	104233.0	22894.0	1630	302034765
TREC	Trecora Resources	Refining & Marketing	12/31/18	287.9	-2.3	330.0	184.9	79	14376741
TG	Tredegar Corp.	Plastics	12/31/18	1095.9	24.8	707.4	354.9	229	26371027
THS	TreeHouse Foods Inc	Food	12/31/18	5812.1	-61.4	5599.3	2141.9	395	72724537
TREX	Trex Co Inc	Metal Products	12/31/18	684.3	134.6	465.1	343.0	434	68379979
TPH	TRI Pointe Group Inc	Builders	12/31/18	3261.0	269.9	3884.2	2056.9	309	168538115
TY	Tri-Continental Corp.	Holding and other Investment Office	12/31/18	61.3	53.3	1474.1	1468.8	144	10301988
TRNE	Trine Acquisition Corp	Business Services	12/31/18		-0.0	0.3	-0.0	32	6579641
TNET	Trinet Group Inc.	Business Services	12/31/18	3503.0	192.0	2435.0	375.0	255	66241189
TRN	Trinity Industries, Inc.	Construction Services	12/31/18	2509.1	159.3	7989.2	2210.8	481	143816861
TSE	Trinseo SA	Synthetic Materials	12/31/18	4622.8	292.5	2726.8	768.7	257	45238415
GTS	Triple-S Management Corp	Life & Health	12/31/18	2996.1	-63.3	2760.2	822.0	162	26075752
TPVG	TriplePoint Venture Growth BDC Co	Finance Intermediaries & Services	12/31/18	64.6	35.0	467.1	334.5	88	8301240
TRTN PR	Triton International Ltd	Business Services	12/31/18	1433.3	349.6	10270.0	2203.7	236	47609325
TGI	Triumph Group Inc.	Aerospace	3/31/19	3364.9	-321.8	2854.6	-573.3	309	79816596
TROX	Tronox Holdings PLC	Specialty Chemicals	12/31/18	1819.0	-7.0	4642.0	683.0	155	93348251
TBI	TrueBlue Inc	Business Services	12/30/18	2499.2	65.8	1114.8	591.4	257	45819183
TFC	Truist Financial Corp	Banking	12/31/18	12996.0	3237.0	225697.0	30122.0	1448	650016725
TNP	Tsakos Energy Navigation Ltd	Miscellaneous Transportation Servic	12/31/18	529.9	-99.2	3205.1	1494.7	108	26499433
TUFN	Tufin Software Technologies Ltd	IT Services	12/31/18	85.0	-4.3	47.1	-3.2		0
TUP	Tupperware Brands Corp	Plastics	12/29/18	2069.7	155.9	1308.8	-235.2	448	60406610
TKC	Turkcell Iletisim Hizmetleri AS	Services	12/31/18	21292.5	2021.1	42765.3	15921.7	169	31885215
TPB	Turning Point Brands Inc	Tobacco Products	12/31/18	332.7	25.3	339.4	82.6	146	9129422
TRQ	Turquoise Hill Resources Ltd.	Precious Metals	12/31/18	1180.0	411.2	13312.0	9320.9	228	747586496
TPC	Tutor Perini Corp	Construction Services	12/31/18	4454.7	83.4	4387.8	1809.2	26	447717
TWLO	Twilio Inc	Internet & Software	12/31/18	650.1	-121.9	1028.7	438.2	673	113120287
TRWH	Twin River Worldwide Holdings Inc	Hotels, Restaurants & Travel	12/31/18	437.5	71.4	782.4	298.7	95	32984017
TWTR	Twitter Inc	Internet & Software	12/31/18	3042.4	1205.6	10162.6	6805.6	972	612179427
TWO	Two Harbors Investment Corp	REITs	12/31/18	767.0	-44.3	30132.5	4254.5	423	222143993
TYL	Tyler Technologies, Inc.	Internet & Software	12/31/18	935.3	147.5	1791.0	1324.8	538	45195959
TSN	Tyson Foods Inc	Food	9/28/19	42405.0	2022.0	33097.0	14082.0	1069	316342768
USPH	U.S. Physical Therapy, Inc.	Hospitals & Health Care Facilities	12/31/18	453.9	34.9	443.2	215.9	293	16672372
UBER	Uber Technologies Inc	IT Services	12/31/18	11270.0	997.0	23988.0	6792.0	501	782873628
UI	Ubiquiti Inc	Internet & Software	6/30/19	1161.7	322.7	875.9	99.3	341	12712235
UBS	UBS Group AG	Banking	12/31/18	43077.0	4516.0	958489.0	52927.0		0
UDR	UDR Inc	REITs	12/31/18	1046.9	203.1	7711.7	2905.6	603	373281607
UGI	UGI Corp.	Gas Utilities	9/30/19	7320.4	256.2	13346.6	3817.5	750	194086330
UGP	Ultrapar Participacoes SA	Equipment & Services	12/31/18	90698.0	1150.4	30499.4	9448.1	142	46450049
UMH	UMH Properties Inc	REITs	12/31/18	129.6	-36.2	879.0	424.7	175	28788660
UAA	Under Armour, Inc.	Apparel, Footwear & Accessories	10/31/18	5193.2	-46.3	4245.0	2016.9	718	198509910
UFI	Unifi, Inc.	Textiles	6/30/19	708.8	2.5	592.2	392.8	174	18603740
UNF	Unifirst Corp	Business Services	8/31/19	1809.4	179.1	2047.3	1641.2	358	21014457
UN	Unilever N.V.	Household & Personal Products	12/31/18	50982.0	9389.0	59456.0	11572.0	832	176536163
UL	Unilever Plc	Household & Personal Products	12/31/18	50982.0	9389.0	59456.0	11572.0	850	119764675
UNP	Union Pacific Corp	Rail	12/31/18	22832.0	5966.0	59147.0	20423.0	2503	659539541
UIS	Unisys Corp	IT Services	12/31/18	2825.0	75.5	2457.6	-1343.5	333	100601366
UNT	Unit Corp.	Production & Extraction	12/31/18	843.3	-45.3	2698.1	1390.9	284	58151783
UMC	United Microelectronics Corp	Semiconductors	12/31/18	151252.6	7073.0	364604.9	206069.7	181	173596298
UPS	United Parcel Service Inc	Airlines/Air Freight	12/31/18	71861.0	4791.0	50016.0	3021.0	2075	610348379
URI	United Rentals Inc	Construction Services	12/31/18	8047.0	1096.0	18133.0	3403.0	962	97375369
USM	United States Cellular Corp	Services	12/31/18	3967.0	150.0	7274.0	4057.0	219	17315189
X	United States Steel Corp.	Non-Precious Metals	12/31/18	14178.0	1115.0	10982.0	4202.0	593	148369402
UTX	United Technologies Corp	Aerospace	12/31/18	66501.0	5269.0	134211.0	38446.0	2698	872553328
UNH	UnitedHealth Group Inc	Life & Health	12/31/18	226247.0	11986.0	152221.0	51696.0	2606	1004572281
UTL	UNITIL Corp	Electric Utilities	12/31/18	444.1	33.0	1298.3	351.3	214	12860648

EARNINGS PER SHARE						P/E RATIO		DIVIDENDS PER SHARE			AV. YLD %	DIV. DECLARED		PRICE RANGE 2018	
QUARTERLY			ANNUAL					PER SHARE							
1st	2nd	3rd	2018	2017	2016			2018	2017	2016	%	AMOUNT	PAYABLE	2018	
-	-	-0.10	-0.71	-0.99	-2.39	-	-					0.140Y	9/10/15	13.9 -	5.0
-	-	-0.33	0.06	-1.12	-0.81	119.8 -	38.0	0.02	0.02	0.02	0.5	0.0050Y	1/15/20	7.2 -	2.3
-	-	0.68	2.02	1.73	1.67	30.3 -	21.9	0.60	0.50	0.40	1.1	0.230Y	18/53/27	61.2 -	44.2
-	-	1.00	4.85	3.17	2.18	8.5 -	6.8	0.41	0.24	-	1.1	0.110Y	18/53/27	41.4 -	33.2
-	-	0.46	0.86	1.21	0.99	47.0 -	35.6	0.35	0.34	0.33	1.0	0.090Y	18/53/27	40.4 -	30.7
-	-	1.60	3.78	4.32	1.92	29.7 -	12.0	-				-		112.3 -	45.3
-	-	0.56	2.50	2.41	2.06	32.6 -	21.9	0.80	0.70	0.60	1.1	0.250Y	18/53/27	81.4 -	54.6
-	-	1.74	6.01	5.50	4.67	12.9 -	8.3	2.61	2.35	2.16	4.0	0.31870	1/31/20	77.7 -	50.0
-	-	0.04	0.00	-	-	-						-		10.0 -	0.0
-	-	-	-0.29	-0.20	-0.12	-		1.75	1.75	1.75	27.1	0.10	11/29/19	10.3 -	3.5
-	-	-	-0.49	-0.65	-0.78	-		2.62	2.62	2.62	12.1	0.6550	11/29/19	25.4 -	16.5
-	-	-	-0.43	-0.42	-0.46	-		1.69	1.69	1.69	13.1	0.42250	11/29/19	14.8 -	9.8
-	-	-	-0.15	-0.05	0.04	-		1.63	1.63	1.63	11.7	0.2850	11/29/19	15.8 -	11.3
-	-	-	0.24	0.59	0.71	80.2 -	64.3	1.50	1.50	1.54	8.4	0.1250	2/28/20	19.2 -	15.4
-	-	1.04	4.24	3.34	2.52	13.8 -	11.3	2.95	2.82	2.70	5.5	-		58.6 -	48.0
-	-	0.30	-1.71	-0.56	0.85	-		0.30			4.7	0.0750Y	2/14/20	10.0 -	4.8
-	-	314.99	832.78	599.21	735.36	0.2 -	0.1	420.01	417.35	448.34	326.8	-		145.1 -	114.7
-	-	0.44	1.70	1.74	2.09	12.2 -	10.8	1.71	0.71	1.99	8.6	0.430Z	1/24/20	20.7 -	18.4
-	-	0.46	2.25	2.00	1.83	9.7 -	8.2	1.78	1.75	1.56	8.8	0.390Y	1/15/20	21.8 -	18.4
-	-	-	-0.86	-0.66	0.41	-		0.16	0.16	0.16	2.2	0.31180	3/31/20	10.0 -	4.2
-	-	-0.89	20.71	-1.92	-0.10	2.0 -	0.0	-				0.180	9/29/00	40.9 -	0.0
-	-	2.57	16.20	7.88	10.39	36.9 -	20.1	-	46.00	-		32.57Y	18/53/27	597.8 -	325.6
-	-	-1.35	-4.27	-8.00	2.08	-		-				0.150	18/53/27	-	
-	-	-0.06	14.48	3.52	1.17	1.1 -	0.4	22.73	-	0.39	204.4	-		16.2 -	5.6
-	-	0.48	1.45	2.32	0.65	60.0 -	37.3	0.23	-	-	0.3	0.0750Y	18/53/27	87.0 -	54.1
-	-	1.50	9.28	7.33	10.28	16.7 -	12.4	3.03	2.83	2.62	2.2	0.820Y	18/53/27	154.8 -	115.3
-	-	0.02	-0.10	0.72	0.78	-		-				-		10.3 -	7.0
-	-	0.51	0.75	1.16	0.75	31.1 -	20.8	0.44	0.44	0.44	2.4	0.120Y	1/1/20	23.3 -	15.6
-	-	-3.16	-1.10	-5.01	-4.10	-		-				-		67.0 -	47.7
-	-	0.72	2.28	1.61	1.15	40.4 -	25.8	-				-		92.2 -	58.8
-	-	0.44	1.81	1.21	1.21	8.9 -	6.2	-				-		16.1 -	11.3
-	-	-	0.99	0.93	0.90	29.1 -	23.5	1.91	1.17	0.91	7.1	0.8115C	12/26/19	28.8 -	23.3
-	-0.05	-	-0.01	-	-	-		-				-		10.0 -	0.0
-	-	0.78	2.65	2.49	0.85	29.0 -	15.0	-				-		76.8 -	39.8
-	-	0.39	1.07	4.52	2.25	24.3 -	15.0	0.52	0.48	0.44	2.5	0.190Y	18/53/27	26.0 -	16.1
-	-	0.56	6.70	7.30	6.70	-		1.56	1.38	-		0.40	1/23/20	-	
-	-	0.58	-2.76	2.26	0.71	-		-				-		26.1 -	12.9
-	-	0.29	1.71	1.61	1.42	10.0 -	6.5	1.54	1.44	1.44	10.7	0.35940Z	4/15/20	17.0 -	11.1
-	-	1.17	4.35	4.52	-0.24	-		2.01	1.80	1.35		0.1946GH	12/16/19	-	
-	0.85	-	-8.60	-0.87	-21.29	-		0.16	0.16	0.16	0.7	0.040Y	12/16/19	29.2 -	11.4
-	-	-0.09	-0.06	-2.39	-0.50	-		-	0.18	-		0.0450	12/2/19	-	
-	-	0.68	1.63	1.34	-0.37	15.7 -	11.6	-				-		25.5 -	18.9
-	-	0.95	3.91	2.74	2.77	14.5 -	11.3	1.56	1.26	1.15	3.1	0.3250Y	18/53/27	56.7 -	44.1
0.25	-	-	-1.53	-0.19	0.47	-		0.15	0.20	-		0.59380	1/30/20	-	
-	-	-	-0.53	-0.35	-	-		-				-		-	
-	-	0.16	3.11	-5.22	4.41	12.3 -	2.4	2.72	2.72	2.72	13.8	0.270Y	18/53/27	38.1 -	7.4
-	-	0.16	0.93	0.90	0.68	7.6 -	5.0	1.72	2.81	-	30.1	-		7.0 -	4.6
-	-	0.31	1.28	1.04	1.49	42.7 -	16.1	0.17	0.04	-	0.5	0.0450Y	1/10/20	54.7 -	20.6
-	-0.22	-	0.20	0.09	0.10	13.9 -	2.0	-				-		2.8 -	0.4
-	-	0.38	1.66	2.92	1.92	12.2 -	5.6	-				1.7Y	11/12/10	20.2 -	9.3
-	-	-0.64	-1.26	-0.70	-0.78	-		-				-		149.9 -	81.3
-	-	0.18	1.87	1.56	1.12	17.9 -	11.0	-				0.10Y	10/25/19	33.4 -	20.6
-	-	0.05	1.56	-0.15	-0.65	29.1 -	17.9	-				-		45.4 -	28.0
-	-	1.00	-0.53	1.81	2.02	-		1.88	0.47	1.86	13.8	0.46880Z	1/15/20	15.1 -	12.2
-	-	1.00	3.68	4.18	2.82	81.7 -	48.0	-				-		300.6 -	176.6
-	-	1.84	8.19	4.79	4.53	11.4 -	6.5	1.20	0.90	0.60	1.5	0.3780Y	18/53/27	93.3 -	53.4
-	-	0.66	1.31	1.76	1.64	112.2 -	75.9	0.92	0.80	0.68	0.8	0.30Z	12/13/19	147.0 -	99.4
-	-0.68	-	-	-9.46	-0.90	-		-				0.30Y	18/53/27	46.4 -	26.0
1.43	-	-	2.51	3.09	2.49	79.0 -	38.2	-				0.30Y	18/53/27	198.3 -	96.0
-	0.31	-	1.18	0.27	0.84	-		0.70	0.65	-		0.70	5/8/19	-	
-	-	0.09	0.74	0.44	1.08	68.1 -	51.9	1.28	1.23	1.16	2.8	0.37080Z	18/53/27	50.4 -	38.4
-	-	-0.01	4.06	2.46	2.08	14.1 -	10.2	1.02	0.97	0.93	2.0	0.3250Y	18/53/27	57.1 -	41.4
-	-	0.30	1.05	1.44	1.43	7.5 -	3.6	0.69	0.85	0.82	12.4	-		7.9 -	3.8
-	-	0.14	-0.98	0.39	0.42	-		0.72	0.72	0.72	5.2	0.39840Z	3/16/20	16.2 -	11.4
-	-	0.23	-0.20	-0.22	0.45	-		-				-		27.5 -	17.0
0.20	-	-	1.70	1.78	1.87	16.1 -	10.0	-				0.140	5/8/98	27.4 -	17.0
2.52	-	-	8.21	3.44	6.17	25.9 -	16.3	0.23	0.15	0.15	0.1	0.20Y	3/30/20	212.8 -	133.9
-	-	-	3.48	2.15	1.82	18.3 -	15.1	1.52	1.40	-	2.6	-		63.6 -	52.6
-	-	-	3.48	2.15	1.82	18.6 -	14.8	1.53	1.37	1.26	2.6	-		64.8 -	51.6
-	-	2.22	7.91	13.36	5.07	22.9 -	16.8	3.06	2.48	2.25	1.8	0.970Y	18/53/27	181.4 -	132.7
-	-	-0.23	1.30	-1.30	-0.95	11.1 -	5.0	-	-			1.56250Y	12/1/13	14.5 -	6.5
-	-	-3.91	-0.87	2.28	-2.71	-		-				-		18.1 -	0.6
-	-	0.26	0.55	0.74	0.63	5.1 -	3.1	2.48	1.76	2.03	117.4	-		2.8 -	1.7
-	-	2.01	5.51	5.61	3.87	22.6 -	16.9	3.64	3.32	3.12	3.3	0.960Y	18/53/27	124.3 -	92.9
-	-	5.08	13.12	15.73	6.45	12.9 -	7.8	-				-		169.8 -	102.0
-	-	0.27	1.72	0.14	0.56	34.3 -	18.3	-	-			5.75GY	18/53/27	59.1 -	31.5
-	-	-0.49	6.25	2.19	-2.81	3.9 -	1.6	0.20	0.20	0.20	1.3	0.050Y	18/53/27	24.1 -	10.1
-	-	1.33	6.50	5.70	6.12	23.2 -	15.9	2.84	2.72	2.62	2.1	0.7350Y	18/53/27	150.7 -	103.5
-	-	3.67	12.19	10.72	7.25	24.3 -	17.7	3.45	2.88	2.38	1.4	1.080Y	18/53/27	296.0 -	215.3
-	-	0.15	2.23	2.06	1.94	28.8 -	21.2	1.46	1.44	1.42	2.5	0.370Y	11/27/19	64.3 -	47.2

SYMBOL	COMPANY	NATURE OF BUSINESS	FISCAL YEAR-END	TOTAL REV. $MILL	NET INCOME $MILL	TOTAL ASSETS $MILL	NET STK EQUITY $MILL	NO OF INST	INST. HOLDINGS (SHARES)
UNVR	Univar Solutions Inc	Specialty Chemicals	12/31/18	8632.5	172.3	5272.4	1191.7	246	190888215
UVV	Universal Corp	Tobacco Products	3/31/19	2227.2	104.1	2133.2	1337.1	311	30082872
UHT	Universal Health Realty Income Tru	REITs	12/31/18	76.2	24.2	483.8	198.6	231	11025777
UHS	Universal Health Services, Inc.	Hospitals & Health Care Facilities	12/31/18	10772.3	779.7	11265.5	5389.3	695	102608845
UVE	Universal Insurance Holdings Inc	General Insurance	12/31/18	823.8	117.1	1858.4	501.6	240	29454704
UTI	Universal Technical Institute, Inc.	Educational Services	9/30/19	331.5	-7.9	270.5	114.3	95	20227666
UNM	Unum Group	Life & Health	12/31/18	11598.5	523.4	61875.6	8621.8	749	258857459
UE	Urban Edge Properties	REITs	12/31/18	414.2	105.1	2799.0	904.7	257	129825928
UBA	Urstadt Biddle Properties Inc	REITs	10/31/19	137.6	37.3	1072.3	579.7	41	1079854
USB	US Bancorp (DE)	Banking	12/31/18	25775.0	7096.0	467374.0	51029.0	2141	1451988546
USFD	US Foods Holding Corp	Retail - Food & Beverage, Drug & To	12/29/18	24175.0	407.0	9186.0	3229.0	382	214440143
SLCA	US Silica Holdings, Inc.	Mining	12/31/18	1577.3	-200.8	2900.8	1044.8	295	90082677
USX	US Xpress Enterprises Inc	Trucking	12/31/18	1804.9	24.9	910.5	234.9	104	18651401
USAC	USA Compression Partners LP	Equipment & Services	12/31/18	584.4	-10.6	3774.6	477.3	110	51320704
USNA	USANA Health Sciences Inc	Household & Personal Products	12/29/18	1189.2	126.2	554.5	391.1	264	13211893
USB PRI	USB Capital X	Banking						1	15070
USDP	USD Partners LP	Rail	12/31/18	119.2	21.1	287.3		41	8049665
EGY	VAALCO Energy, Inc.	Production & Extraction	12/31/18	104.9	98.2	166.3	109.8	137	40220601
MTN	Vail Resorts Inc	Sporting & Recreational	7/31/19	2271.6	301.2	4426.1	1500.6	571	46998310
VAL	Valaris plc	Production & Extraction	12/31/18	1705.4	-639.7	14023.7	8091.4	498	254822184
RIO 34	Vale Overseas Ltd	Finance Intermediaries & Services	12/31/05	84.1	0.0	1289.4	-0.0		0
VALE	Vale SA	Non-Precious Metals	12/31/18	36575.0	6860.0	88190.0	43985.0	536	1093111013
VLO	Valero Energy Corp	Refining & Marketing	12/31/18	117033.0	3122.0	50155.0	21667.0	1633	410933346
VHI	Valhi, Inc.	Specialty Chemicals	12/31/18	1889.3	262.2	2709.6	635.4	114	13217482
VMI	Valmont Industries Inc	Construction Materials	12/29/18	2757.1	94.4	2530.3	1059.8	390	25948026
VVV	Valvoline Inc	Household & Personal Products	9/30/19	2390.0	208.0	2064.0	-258.0	385	183392955
VAPO	Vapotherm Inc	Medical Instruments & Equipment	12/31/18	42.4	-42.5	97.2	51.6	69	12631350
VAR	Varian Medical Systems Inc	Medical Instruments & Equipment	9/27/19	3225.1	291.9	4101.7	1768.3	893	113189000
VGR	Vector Group Ltd	Tobacco Products	12/31/18	1870.3	58.1	1549.5	-548.1	311	106683296
VVC 13	Vectren Utility Holdings Inc.	Electric Utilities	12/31/17	1382.6	175.8	5497.8	1722.8		0
VEC	Vectrus Inc	Services	12/31/18	1279.3	35.3	572.2	221.3	211	12660137
VEDL	Vedanta Ltd	Non-Precious Metals	3/31/19	913720.0	13705.0	1764429.0	595566.0	177	46597536
VEEV	Veeva Systems Inc	IT Services	1/31/19	862.2	229.8	1653.8	1237.7	742	124078739
VEL	Velocity Financial Inc	Finance Intermediaries & Services							0
VNTR	Venator Materials Plc	Specialty Chemicals	12/31/18	2265.0	-163.0	2485.0	847.0	118	43305638
VTR	Ventas Inc	REITs	12/31/18	3745.8	409.5	22584.6	10404.0	1021	416918422
VNE	Veoneer Inc	Auto Parts	12/31/18	2228.0	-276.0	2632.0	1826.0	149	30928707
VER	VEREIT Inc	REITs	12/31/18	1257.9	-85.8	13963.5	7157.1	573	1103011575
VRTV	Veritiv Corp	Industrial Machinery & Equipment	12/31/18	8696.2	-15.7	2529.7	543.1	224	17906327
VZ	Verizon Communications Inc	Services	12/31/18	130863.0	15528.0	264829.0	53145.0	3258	3304624877
VET	Vermilion Energy Inc	Production & Extraction	12/31/18	1525.9	271.6	6270.7	2817.3		0
VRS	Verso Corp	Paper & Forest Products	12/31/18	2682.0	171.0	1699.0	906.0	201	67774920
VFC	VF Corp.	Apparel, Footwear & Accessories	3/30/19	13848.7	1259.8	10356.8	4298.5	1328	449256129
VVI	Viad Corp.	Business Services	12/31/18	1296.2	49.2	922.5	436.2	248	23741184
VICI	VICI Properties Inc	REITs	12/31/18	898.0	523.6	11333.4	6817.4	351	532800387
VNCE	Vince Holding Corp	Retail - Apparel and Accessories	2/2/19	279.0	-2.0	234.9	74.1	54	2920503
VIPS	Vipshop Holdings Ltd	Retail - Apparel and Accessories	12/31/18	84523.9	2128.8	43562.7	17261.8	325	324833763
VGI	Virtus Global Multi-Sector Income F	Holding and other Investment Office	11/30/18	13.1	8.2	212.5	150.3	31	2954588
ZTR	Virtus Total Return Fund Inc (New)	Holding and other Investment Office	11/30/18	14.7	8.2	366.6	259.0	66	6821321
V	Visa Inc	Business Services	9/30/19	22977.0	12080.0	72574.0	34684.0	3003	1827034341
VSH	Vishay Intertechnology, Inc.	Electrical Equipment	12/31/18	3034.7	345.8	3106.2	1382.4	419	169128107
VPG	Vishay Precision Group Inc.	Electronic Instruments & Related Pro	12/31/18	299.8	23.6	326.4	218.4	172	13029339
VIST	Vista Oil & Gas SAB de CV	Oil & Gas	12/31/18	331.3	-26.4	1086.1	479.7	21	16927632
VSTO	Vista Outdoor Inc	Sporting & Recreational	3/31/19	2058.5	-648.4	1738.0	609.0	209	61687667
VST	Vistra Energy Corp	Electric Utilities	12/31/18	9144.0	-54.0	26024.0	7863.0	426	481914741
VAM	Vivaldi Opportunities Fund	Holding and other Investment Office	3/31/19	5.6	2.6	116.7	81.7	7	4914211
VSLR	Vivint Solar Inc	Electrical Equipment	12/31/18	290.3	-15.6	2327.3	288.6	133	124291225
VMW	VMware Inc	Internet & Software	2/1/19	8974.0	2422.0	14662.0	551.0	799	83696585
VOC	VOC Energy Trust	Oil Royalty Traders	12/31/18	12.9	12.1	70.0	70.0	42	2889244
VCRA	Vocera Communications, Inc.	Computer Hardware & Equipment	12/31/18	179.6	-9.7	352.1	162.9	195	46585876
VNO	Vornado Realty Trust	REITs	12/31/18	2163.7	450.0	17180.8	4465.2	712	207944126
VJET	voxeljet AG	Industrial Machinery & Equipment	12/31/18	26.0	-8.7	69.4	46.4	32	5515804
IAE	VOYA Asia Pacific Dividend Equity I	Holding and other Investment Office	2/28/19	4.3	2.6	124.2	123.2	41	6024662
IHD	VOYA Emerging Markets High Divid	Holding and other Investment Office	2/28/19	6.3	3.8	169.8	169.2	47	8090540
VOYA	Voya Financial Inc	Life & Health	12/31/18	8514.0	875.0	154682.0	8213.0	497	167925312
IGA	VOYA Global Advantage & Premiu	Holding and other Investment Office	2/28/19	5.9	3.8	214.1	209.2	54	5602497
IGD	VOYA Global Equity Dividend & Pre	Holding and other Investment Office	2/28/19	22.3	13.6	691.2	681.6	114	18412591
IDE	VOYA Infrastructure Industrials & M	Holding and other Investment Office	2/28/19	8.0	4.5	269.3	264.9	48	4340135
IID	VOYA International High Dividend E	Holding and other Investment Office	2/28/19	1.7	1.1	53.8	51.9	33	720767
IRR	Voya Natural Resources Equity Inco	Holding and other Investment Office	2/28/19	3.1	1.4	112.7	112.3	56	4269061
PPR	VOYA Prime Rate Trust	Holding and other Investment Office	2/28/19	66.7	42.7	1179.3	818.1	158	69412910
VMC	Vulcan Materials Co (Holding Comp	Mining	12/31/18	4382.9	515.8	9832.1	5202.9	909	162692578
WTI	W & T Offshore Inc	Production & Extraction	12/31/18	580.7	248.8	848.9	-324.8	247	98707935
WPC	W.P. Carey Inc	REITs	12/31/18	885.7	411.6	14183.0	6824.3	759	110942161
WNC	Wabash National Corp	Autos- Manufacturing	12/31/18	2267.3	69.4	1304.4	473.8	317	76006708
WBC	WABCO Holdings Inc	Auto Parts	12/31/18	3831.0	394.1	3738.6	1176.8	483	57207620
WAB	Wabtec Corp	Construction Services	12/31/18	4363.5	294.9	8649.2	2865.1	948	216371392
WAB	Wabtec Corp	Construction Services	12/31/18	4363.5	294.9	8649.2	2865.1	948	216371392
WDR	Waddell & Reed Financial, Inc.	Finance Intermediaries & Services	12/31/18	1160.3	183.6	1344.1	883.4	391	104865038
WD	Walker & Dunlop Inc	Business Services	12/31/18	725.2	161.4	2782.1	902.1	261	30542621

T58

| EARNINGS PER SHARE | | | | | | P/E RATIO | | DIVIDENDS PER SHARE | | | AV. YLD | DIV. DECLARED | | PRICE RANGE | |
| QUARTERLY | | | ANNUAL | | | | | PER SHARE | | | % | | | 2018 | |
1st	2nd	3rd	2018	2017	2016			2018	2017	2016		AMOUNT	PAYABLE		
-	-	0.01	1.21	0.85	-0.50	20.2 -	14.5	-	-	-	-	-	-	24.4 -	17.5
-	1.11	-	4.14	0.88	3.92	15.1 -	11.9	2.17	2.13	2.09	3.9	0.760Y	18/53/27	62.7 -	49.4
-	-	0.34	1.76	3.35	1.28	69.3 -	34.2	2.68	2.64	2.60	3.0	0.6850Z	18/53/27	122.0 -	60.2
-	-	1.10	-8.31	7.81	7.14	18.7 -	14.0	0.40	0.40	0.40	0.3	0.20Y	18/53/27	155.4 -	116.0
-	-	0.59	3.27	2.99	2.79	12.5 -	7.4	0.73	0.69	0.69	2.4	0.137Y	12/20/19	40.9 -	24.1
-	-	-0.07	-1.51	-0.54	-2.02	-		-	-	0.04	-	0.020Y	3/31/16	7.8 -	3.0
-	-	1.16	2.38	4.37	3.95	15.8 -	10.5	0.98	0.86	0.77	3.1	0.2850Y	18/53/27	37.7 -	25.1
-	-	0.45	0.92	0.61	0.91	23.6 -	17.7	0.88	0.88	0.82	4.7	0.220Z	18/53/27	21.7 -	16.2
-	-	0.17	0.60	0.80	0.49	41.4 -	31.1	1.08	1.06	1.04	4.9	0.280Z	18/53/27	24.8 -	18.6
-	-	1.15	4.14	3.51	3.24	14.7 -	11.0	1.34	1.16	1.07	2.5	0.34380Y	18/53/27	60.7 -	45.7
-	-	0.48	1.87	1.97	1.03	22.9 -	16.9	-	-	-	-	-	-	42.8 -	31.5
-	-	-0.31	-2.63	1.77	-0.63	-		0.25	0.25	0.25	2.2	0.06250Y	1/3/20	18.4 -	4.5
-	-	-0.03	0.83	-0.64	-2.59	11.9 -	4.2	-	-	-	-	-	-	9.8 -	3.5
-	-	0.02	-0.43	0.16	0.27	-		2.10	2.10	2.10	12.6	0.5250	2/7/20	18.9 -	13.1
-	-	1.09	5.12	2.53	3.99	23.2 -	11.5	-	-	-	-	-	-	119.0 -	58.9
-	-	0.08	0.77	0.88	1.06	15.5 -	12.1	1.42	1.35	1.25	13.3	0.36750	11/14/19	11.9 -	9.3
-	-	-0.07	1.62	0.16	-0.45	1.6 -	0.9	-	-	-	-	0.001F	8/1/09	2.7 -	1.4
-2.64	-	-	9.13	5.22	4.01	27.3 -	19.8	5.05	3.73	2.87	2.2	1.760Z	18/53/27	249.3 -	180.8
-	-	-1.00	-5.88	-3.64	12.52	-		0.16	0.16	0.16	-	-	-	-	
-	-	0.27	1.32	1.05	0.77	11.3 -	7.8	0.43	0.34	0.04	3.4	-	-	14.9 -	10.3
-	-	1.48	7.29	9.16	4.94	13.9 -	9.7	3.20	2.80	2.40	3.8	0.980Y	18/53/27	101.4 -	70.4
-	-	0.04	0.77	0.61	-0.05	5.7 -	2.2	0.08	0.08	0.08	3.4	0.020Y	12/19/19	4.4 -	1.7
-	-	1.85	4.20	5.11	7.63	35.9 -	26.0	1.50	1.50	1.50	1.1	0.3750Y	18/53/27	150.9 -	109.1
-	-	0.34	0.84	1.49	1.33	28.1 -	20.5	0.30	0.20	-	1.5	0.1130Y	18/53/27	23.6 -	17.2
-	-	-0.65	-14.65	-44.82	-49.38	-		-	-	-	-	-	-	23.5 -	8.0
-	-	0.32	1.62	2.68	4.19	88.4 -	64.9	-	-	-	-	0.0250	18/53/27	143.3 -	105.1
-	-	0.23	0.35	0.54	0.48	40.4 -	24.4	1.47	1.40	1.33	13.7	0.40Y	18/53/27	14.1 -	8.5
-	-	0.80	3.10	5.31	2.16	17.7 -	7.1	-	-	-	-	-	-	54.8 -	21.9
-	-	-	3.69	18.60	-42.21	3.1 -	1.9	153.25	-	20.79	1665.2	-	-	11.3 -	7.2
-	-	0.52	0.92	0.47	0.38	190.9 -	92.3	-	-	-	-	-	-	175.7 -	84.9
-	-	-0.18	-1.53	1.26	-	-		-	-	-	-	-	-	-	
-	-	0.23	1.14	3.78	1.86	66.0 -	48.4	3.16	3.12	2.96	4.9	0.79250Z	18/53/27	75.2 -	55.1
-	-	-1.20	-3.17	-		-		-	-	-	-	-	-	32.8 -	13.6
-	-	-0.76	-0.16	-0.04	-0.29	-		0.55	0.55	0.55	6.2	0.13960Z	18/53/27	10.1 -	7.0
-	-	0.31	-0.99	-0.85	1.30	-		-	-	-	-	-	-	36.4 -	13.1
-	-	1.25	3.76	7.36	3.21	16.5 -	14.2	2.37	2.32	2.27	4.1	0.6150Y	18/53/27	62.1 -	53.3
-	-	-0.07	1.91	0.51	-1.38	19.2 -	6.9	2.71	2.58	2.58	11.6	0.230	2/18/20	36.7 -	13.2
-	-	0.85	4.88	-0.87	-0.93	5.3 -	2.0	-	-	-	-	0.030Y	11/25/08	25.8 -	9.9
-	1.61	-	0.63	1.52	2.54	158.7 -	103.5	0.46	1.72	1.53	0.5	0.480Y	18/53/27	100.0 -	65.2
-	-	1.53	2.40	2.83	2.09	29.8 -	20.3	0.40	0.40	0.40	0.6	0.10Y	1/2/20	71.6 -	48.7
-	-	0.31	1.43	0.19	-	17.9 -	12.9	1.00	-	-	4.5	0.29750Z	18/53/27	25.6 -	18.5
-	-	0.67	7.70	-35.00	1.40	3.2 -	1.3	-	-	-	-	-	-	24.9 -	9.9
-	-	0.25	15.61	15.94	16.86	0.9 -	0.3	-	-	-	-	-	-	14.6 -	5.3
-	-	-	0.72	0.89	0.93	18.3 -	15.8	1.69	1.87	1.87	13.5	0.1260	3/19/20	13.2 -	11.4
-	-	-	0.34	0.41	0.27	34.9 -	26.2	1.24	1.86	1.16	11.4	0.1130	3/19/20	11.9 -	8.9
-	-	1.37	4.42	2.80	2.48	42.8 -	29.0	0.82	0.66	0.56	0.5	0.30Y	18/53/27	189.4 -	128.1
-	-	0.21	2.24	-0.14	0.32	10.1 -	6.5	0.32	0.26	0.25	1.7	0.0950	18/53/27	22.7 -	14.6
-	-	0.33	1.75	1.07	0.48	23.7 -	16.7	-	-	-	-	-	-	41.4 -	29.2
-0.19	-	-	-0.37	0.14	-	-		-	-	-	-	-	-	10.1 -	4.0
-	-0.21	-	-1.05	-4.66	2.35	-		-	-	-	-	-	-	12.2 -	4.4
-	-	0.23	-0.11	-0.59	-0.38	-		-	-	-	2.32	0.1250Y	18/53/27	27.4 -	21.4
-	-	-	0.02	-	-	718.6 -	0.0	-	-	-	-	0.11680	2/14/20	14.4 -	0.0
-	-	-0.11	-0.13	1.77	0.16	-		-	-	-	-	-	-	9.4 -	3.7
-	-	1.50	1.38	-0.02	2.78	148.9 -	94.6	-	-	-	-	10.62D	18/53/27	205.5 -	130.6
-	-	0.20	0.71	0.50	0.28	9.6 -	5.4	0.71	0.50	0.28	13.9	0.110	2/14/20	6.8 -	3.8
-	-	0.01	-0.32	-0.50	-0.64	-		-	-	-	-	-	-	41.7 -	19.1
-	-	1.69	2.01	0.85	4.34	35.1 -	29.3	2.52	2.62	2.52	3.9	0.32810Z	18/53/27	70.5 -	58.8
-	-	-	-2.21	-2.29	-3.04	-		-	-	-	-	-	-	2.4 -	1.5
-	-	-	0.24	0.25	0.29	39.5 -	33.2	0.82	0.97	1.15	9.4	0.2150	1/15/20	9.5 -	8.0
-	-	-	0.18	0.18	0.20	46.9 -	38.0	0.74	0.88	1.04	9.7	0.180	1/15/20	8.4 -	6.8
-	-	0.74	5.20	-16.25	-2.13	11.9 -	7.6	0.04	0.04	0.04	0.1	0.33440Y	18/53/27	61.8 -	39.5
-	-	-	0.19	0.18	0.17	57.1 -	48.6	0.90	1.06	1.12	8.6	0.1970	1/15/20	10.9 -	9.2
-	-	-	0.15	0.19	0.18	44.6 -	39.2	0.67	0.81	0.91	10.6	0.040	2/18/20	6.7 -	5.9
-	-	-	0.20	0.20	0.23	63.8 -	54.1	1.16	1.39	1.54	9.8	0.2290	1/15/20	12.8 -	10.8
-	-	-	0.15	0.17	0.20	42.8 -	34.1	0.57	0.72	0.83	10.1	0.030	2/18/20	6.4 -	5.1
-	-	-	0.08	0.07	0.11	68.8 -	44.8	0.65	0.77	0.91	14.1	0.0770	1/15/20	5.5 -	3.6
-	-	-	0.30	0.31	0.32	16.7 -	15.1	0.29	0.32	0.33	6.1	0.02330	1/13/20	5.0 -	4.5
-	-	1.62	3.85	4.46	3.09	39.4 -	25.1	1.12	1.00	0.80	0.9	0.310Y	18/53/27	151.6 -	96.6
-	-	0.53	1.72	0.56	-2.60	4.1 -	2.3	-	-	-	-	0.10Y	12/3/14	7.1 -	4.0
-	-	0.24	3.49	2.56	2.49	26.8 -	18.4	4.09	4.01	3.93	5.0	• 1.0380Z	18/53/27	93.5 -	64.1
-	-	0.46	1.19	1.78	1.82	13.7 -	11.0	0.30	0.24	-	2.0	0.080Y	1/23/20	16.3 -	13.1
-	-	1.13	7.43	7.50	3.98	19.7 -	13.8	-	-	-	-	0.070Y	18/53/27	146.0 -	102.8
-	-	0.48	3.05	2.72	3.34	26.5 -	20.4	0.48	0.44	0.36	0.7	0.120Y	18/53/27	81.0 -	62.3
-	-	0.48	3.05	2.72	3.34	25.7 -	0.0	0.48	0.44	0.36	1.5	0.120Y	18/53/27	78.3 -	0.0
-	-	0.46	2.28	1.69	1.78	8.4 -	6.6	1.00	1.84	1.84	5.9	0.250Y	2/3/20	19.1 -	15.0
-	-	1.39	4.96	6.56	3.65	13.6 -	8.6	1.00	-	-	1.8	0.30Y	12/9/19	67.5 -	42.8

SYMBOL	COMPANY	NATURE OF BUSINESS	FISCAL YEAR-END	TOTAL REV. $MILL	NET INCOME $MILL	TOTAL ASSETS $MILL	NET STK EQUITY $MILL	NO OF INST	INST. HOLDINGS (SHARES)
WMT	Walmart Inc	Retail - General Merchandise/Depart	1/31/19	514405.0	6670.0	219295.0	72496.0	2779	1185297676
HCC	Warrior Met Coal Inc	Mining	12/31/18	1378.0	696.8	1395.0	712.6	246	57224048
WPG	Washington Prime Group (New)	REITs	12/31/18	723.3	93.6	4361.3	999.7	326	184665961
WRE	Washington Real Estate Investment	REITs	12/31/18	336.9	25.6	2417.1	1068.1	321	88659299
WCN	Waste Connections Inc (Canada)	Sanitation Services	12/31/18	4922.9	546.9	12627.3	6454.6	522	240336746
WM	Waste Management, Inc. (DE)	Sanitation Services	12/31/18	14914.0	1925.0	22650.0	6275.0	1721	405641003
WAT	Waters Corp.	Biotechnology	12/31/18	2419.9	593.8	3727.4	1567.3	828	85859635
WSO	Watsco Inc.	Industrial Machinery & Equipment	12/31/18	4546.7	242.9	2161.0	1347.8	509	36040122
WTS	Watts Water Technologies Inc	Industrial Machinery & Equipment	12/31/18	1564.9	128.0	1653.7	891.3	355	34979621
W	Wayfair Inc	Retail - Furniture & Home Furnishing	12/31/18	6779.2	-504.1	1890.8	-330.7	389	79824122
WBS	Webster Financial Corp (Waterbury,	Banking	12/31/18	1337.7	360.4	27610.3	2886.5	447	100550358
WEC	WEC Energy Group Inc	Electric Utilities	12/31/18	7679.5	1060.5	33475.8	9819.3	1156	291363184
WEI	Weidai Ltd	Finance Intermediaries & Services	12/31/18	3161.9	601.6	6316.5	2208.7	-	0
WRI	Weingarten Realty Investors	REITs	12/31/18	531.1	327.6	3827.0	1573.9	471	157886313
WMK	Weis Markets, Inc.	Retail - Food & Beverage, Drug & To	12/29/18	3509.3	62.7	1432.0	1022.9	188	13004008
WBT	Welbilt Inc	Industrial Machinery & Equipment	12/31/18	1590.1	78.2	2075.0	186.4	274	160001001
WFC	Wells Fargo & Co (New)	Banking	12/31/18	101060.0	22393.0	1895883.0	196166.0	2858	4065860090
WSF	Wells Fargo Capital IV	Banking	-	-	-	-	-	-	0
EOD	Wells Fargo Global Dividend Opport	Holding and other Investment Office	10/31/19	12.5	7.6	309.0	258.0	65	9784702
WFE PRA	Wells Fargo Real Estate Investment	REITs	12/31/18	1379.5	1237.6	35493.3	32415.3	-	0
WELL	Welltower Inc	REITs	12/31/18	4700.5	805.0	30342.1	14632.3	1114	454681947
WCC	Wesco International, Inc.	Electrical Equipment	12/31/18	8176.6	227.3	4605.0	2135.3	377	50443722
WST	West Pharmaceutical Services, Inc.	Rubber Products	12/31/18	1717.4	206.9	1978.9	1396.3	545	83413082
WAL	Western Alliance Bancorporation	Banking	12/31/18	1076.6	435.8	23109.5	2613.7	465	97421506
TLI	Western Asset Corporate Loan Fun	Holding and other Investment Office	9/30/19	9.7	6.6	177.8	108.1	54	4898558
EMD	Western Asset Emerging Markets D	Holding and other Investment Office	12/31/18	87.0	64.3	1280.9	893.3	118	26049953
GDO	Western Asset Global Credit Define	Holding and other Investment Office	10/31/19	21.0	14.8	382.5	275.1	47	4870344
EHI	Western Asset Global High Income	Holding and other Investment Office	5/31/19	43.8	32.1	673.8	464.9	79	20605014
HIX	Western Asset High Income Fund II	Holding and other Investment Office	4/30/19	60.0	44.9	901.2	622.1	106	26872881
HIO	Western Asset High Income Opport	Holding and other Investment Office	9/30/19	50.7	44.7	722.8	703.1	110	65417686
HYI	Western Asset High Yield Defined	Holding and other Investment Office	5/31/19	29.1	25.9	370.6	364.9	-	0
WIA	Western Asset Inflation-Linked Inco	Holding and other Investment Office	11/30/18	15.8	9.7	534.1	359.9	84	21038058
WIW	Western Asset Inflation-Linked Opp	Holding and other Investment Office	11/30/18	38.9	25.7	1070.5	731.6	118	42687412
SBI	Western Asset Intermediate Muni F	Holding and other Investment Office	11/30/18	7.4	5.0	186.3	137.9	71	5205360
IGI	Western Asset Investment Grade D	Holding and other Investment Office	11/30/18	11.9	10.2	212.0	208.0	31	2305518
PAI	Western Asset Investment Grade In	Holding and other Investment Office	12/31/18	7.3	6.2	132.9	132.8	34	821608
MMU	Western Asset Managed Municipals	Holding and other Investment Office	5/31/19	38.0	27.3	850.2	623.4	94	6460027
WMC	Western Asset Mortgage Capital Co	REITs	12/31/18	199.2	26.4	4497.4	503.0	161	29369831
DMO	Western Asset Mortgage Opportunit	Holding and other Investment Office	12/31/18	24.2	17.2	317.4	201.9	44	1672885
MTT	Western Asset Municipal Defined O	Holding and other Investment Office	11/30/18	13.1	11.3	255.8	247.6	47	1485355
MHF	Western Asset Municipal High Inco	Holding and other Investment Office	10/31/19	7.7	6.6	175.6	173.9	59	3204069
MNP	Western Asset Municipal Partners F	Holding and other Investment Office	11/30/18	9.8	6.6	237.9	170.3	53	1996924
WEA	Western Asset Premier Bond Fund	Holding and other Investment Office	12/31/18	12.1	9.0	217.2	154.8	47	3436196
GFY	Western Asset Variable Rate Strate	Holding and other Investment Office	9/30/19	5.6	3.8	106.4	83.0	33	5367601
WES	Western Midstream Partners LP	Equipment & Services	12/31/18	1990.3	369.4	9238.6	-	279	197396770
WU	Western Union Co	Business Services	12/31/18	5589.9	851.9	8996.8	-309.8	872	566396173
WLK	Westlake Chemical Corp	Specialty Chemicals	12/31/18	8635.0	996.0	11602.0	5590.0	375	45795177
WLKP	Westlake Chemical Partners LP	Specialty Chemicals	12/31/18	1285.6	49.3	1462.1	-	67	21943927
WBK	Westpac Banking Corp	Banking	9/30/19	36964.0	6784.0	906626.0	65454.0	205	22793134
WRK	WestRock Co	Containers & Packaging	9/30/19	18289.0	862.9	30156.7	11669.9	-	0
WHG	Westwood Holdings Group, Inc.	Wealth Management	12/31/18	122.3	26.8	190.5	161.1	125	7208460
WEX	Wex Inc	Business Services	12/31/18	1492.6	168.3	6770.6	1785.7	470	55071835
WY	Weyerhaeuser Co	REITs	12/31/18	7476.0	748.0	17249.0	9046.0	1249	708350118
WPM	Wheaton Precious Metals Corp	Precious Metals	12/31/18	794.0	427.1	6470.0	5171.9	552	270682770
WHR	Whirlpool Corp	Household Appliances, Electronics &	12/31/18	21037.0	-183.0	18347.0	2291.0	847	80670967
WTM	White Mountains Insurance Group L	General Insurance	12/31/18	369.1	-141.2	3362.6	2843.1	348	3772151
WSR	Whitestone REIT	REITs	12/31/18	119.9	21.4	1028.9	350.5	159	25710019
WLL	Whiting Petroleum Corp	Production & Extraction	12/31/18	2081.4	342.5	7759.6	4270.3	460	122069046
WOW	WideOpenWest Inc	Services	12/31/18	1153.8	-90.6	2419.6	-290.3	124	66998432
JW A	Wiley (John) & Sons Inc.	Publishing	4/30/19	1800.1	168.3	2937.0	1181.3	381	53756970
WMB	Williams Cos Inc (The)	Equipment & Services	12/31/18	8686.0	-155.0	45302.0	14660.0	1265	1208566130
WSM	Williams Sonoma Inc	Retail - Furniture & Home Furnishing	2/3/19	5671.6	333.7	2812.8	1155.7	626	108941754
WGO	Winnebago Industries, Inc.	Autos- Manufacturing	8/31/19	1985.7	111.8	1104.2	632.2	317	36471137
WIT	Wipro Ltd	IT Services	3/31/18	544871.0	80081.0	760640.0	482936.0	209	139072438
WNS	WNS (Holdings) Ltd	IT Services	3/31/19	809.1	105.4	785.6	552.4	241	52630406
WWW	Wolverine World Wide, Inc.	Apparel, Footwear & Accessories	12/29/18	2239.2	200.1	2183.1	986.0	382	109121206
WF	Woori Financial Group Inc	Banking	12/31/17	10731244.0	1512148.0	16295461.0	20365892.0	75	3261267
WF	Woori Financial Group Inc	Banking	12/31/17	10731244.0	1512148.0	16295461.0	20365892.0	75	3261267
WK	Workiva Inc	Internet & Software	12/31/18	244.3	-50.1	231.1	-9.7	223	30853640
INT	World Fuel Services Corp.	Equipment & Services	12/31/18	39750.3	127.7	5676.9	1815.4	403	84551875
WWE	World Wrestling Entertainment Inc	Entertainment	12/31/18	930.2	99.6	700.3	316.2	399	66987262
WOR	Worthington Industries, Inc.	Non-Precious Metals	5/31/19	3759.6	153.5	2510.8	831.2	333	36644452
WPP	WPP Plc (New)	Advertising	12/31/18	15602.4	1062.9	33867.7	9382.2	284	13252794
WPX	WPX Energy Inc	Production & Extraction	12/31/18	2310.0	151.0	8203.0	4301.0	582	459011680
WYND	Wyndham Destinations Inc	Hotels, Restaurants & Travel	12/31/18	3931.0	672.0	7158.0	-574.0	639	100213920
WH	Wyndham Hotels & Resorts Inc	Hotels, Restaurants & Travel	12/31/18	1868.0	162.0	4976.0	1418.0	471	87591849
XYF	X Financial	Finance Intermediaries & Services	12/31/18	3540.6	883.1	4637.0	3517.0	-	0
XFLT	XAI Octagon Floating Rate & Altern	Holding and other Investment Office	9/30/19	11.7	7.7	131.1	78.7	18	1090902
XHR	Xenia Hotels & Resorts Inc	REITs	12/31/18	1058.2	193.7	3170.1	1823.9	309	111709573
XRX	Xerox Holdings Corp	Peripherals	12/31/18	9830.0	361.0	14874.0	5219.0	-	0

1st	2nd	3rd	2018	2017	2016	P/E RATIO		2018	2017	2016	AV. YLD %	AMOUNT	PAYABLE	PRICE RANGE 2018	
-	-	1.15	3.28	4.38	4.57	37.0 -	28.3	2.04	2.00	1.96	1.9	0.530Y	18/53/27	121.3 -	92.9
-	-	0.87	13.17	8.62	-13.15	2.5 -	1.4	6.73	11.36	-	27.3	0.050Y	11/4/19	32.9 -	17.9
-	-	-0.02	0.42	0.98	0.29	13.9 -	7.6	1.00	1.00	1.00	22.7	0.42970Z	1/15/20	5.8 -	3.2
-	-	4.14	0.32	0.25	1.65	98.0 -	71.1	1.20	1.20	1.20	4.3	0.30Z	1/6/20	31.4 -	22.8
-	-	0.60	2.07	2.18	1.07	62.1 -	35.4	0.58	0.50	0.22	0.6	0.1850	11/26/19	128.5 -	73.3
-	-	1.16	4.45	4.41	2.65	27.1 -	19.9	1.86	1.70	1.64	1.7	0.51250Y	18/53/27	120.7 -	88.5
-	-	2.07	7.65	0.25	6.41	33.1 -	23.1	-	-	-	-	-	-	253.2 -	176.3
-	-	2.20	6.49	5.81	5.15	28.0 -	21.1	5.60	4.60	3.60	3.5	1.60Y	18/53/27	181.9 -	137.2
-	-	0.94	3.73	2.12	2.44	26.9 -	17.0	0.82	0.75	0.71	0.9	0.230Y	12/13/19	100.4 -	63.2
-	-	-2.94	-5.63	-2.81	-2.29	-		-	-	-	-	-	-	171.6 -	79.9
-	-	1.00	3.81	2.67	2.16	15.2 -	11.1	1.25	1.03	0.98	2.5	0.32810Y	18/53/27	58.0 -	42.4
-	-	0.74	3.34	3.79	2.96	29.3 -	20.2	2.21	2.08	1.98	2.6	0.63250Y	18/53/27	97.7 -	67.6
-	-	2.82	10.93	7.25	2.60	1.2 -	0.0	-	0.50	-	-	-	-	13.2 -	0.0
-	-	0.82	2.55	2.60	1.87	12.6 -	9.5	2.98	2.29	1.46	10.4	0.3950Z	18/53/27	32.1 -	24.3
-	-	0.53	2.33	3.66	3.24	22.7 -	15.3	1.21	1.20	1.20	3.0	0.310Y	11/25/19	52.9 -	35.6
-	-	0.14	0.55	0.95	0.57	36.0 -	20.0	-	-	-	-	-	-	19.8 -	11.0
-	-	0.92	4.28	4.10	3.99	12.7 -	10.1	1.64	1.54	1.51	3.4	0.510Y	18/53/27	54.5 -	43.4
-	-														
-	-	-	0.23	0.30	0.62	24.6 -	20.8	0.65	0.60	0.58	12.1	0.14520	1/2/20	5.7 -	4.8
-	-	9.47	35.82	35.27	37.75	0.7 -	0.7	1.59	1.59	1.59	6.2	0.39840	9/30/19	26.3 -	25.1
-	-	1.45	2.02	1.26	2.81	45.8 -	33.3	3.48	3.48	3.44	4.3	0.870Z	18/53/27	92.5 -	67.3
-	-	1.52	4.82	3.38	2.10	12.4 -	8.8	-	-	-	-	-	-	60.0 -	42.6
-	-	0.75	2.74	1.99	1.91	55.2 -	34.5	0.57	0.53	0.49	0.5	0.160Y	18/53/27	151.2 -	94.5
-	-	1.24	4.14	3.10	2.50	13.8 -	9.4	-	-	-	-	0.39060Z	4/1/20	57.3 -	39.1
-	-	-	0.64	0.71	0.71	15.9 -	14.1	0.65	0.84	0.87	6.8	0.0630	3/2/20	10.2 -	9.1
-	-	-	1.06	1.17	1.01	13.7 -	11.7	1.20	1.21	1.26	8.7	0.10	3/2/20	14.5 -	12.4
-	-	-	0.99	1.07	1.20	18.4 -	15.3	1.28	1.36	1.36	7.6	0.1010	3/2/20	18.2 -	15.1
-	-	-	0.73	0.82	0.97	13.7 -	11.5	0.78	1.04	1.16	8.1	0.0660	3/2/20	10.0 -	8.4
-	-	-	0.56	0.66	0.73	12.7 -	10.4	0.58	0.69	0.82	8.7	0.04850	3/2/20	7.1 -	5.8
-	-	-	0.33	0.35	0.39	15.7 -	13.4	0.33	0.37	-	6.7	0.0320	3/2/20	5.2 -	4.4
-	-	-	1.10	0.88	1.28	14.3 -	12.1	1.12	1.27	1.32	7.5	0.0940	3/2/20	15.7 -	13.3
-	-	-	0.33	0.41	0.27	36.8 -	32.0	0.41	0.40	0.35	3.6	0.03450	2/28/20	12.2 -	10.6
-	-	-	0.42	0.38	0.34	27.5 -	24.3	0.43	0.42	0.37	3.9	0.0360	2/28/20	11.5 -	10.2
-	-	-	0.35	0.39	0.41	27.1 -	24.2	0.37	0.43	0.48	4.1	0.0235M	3/2/20	9.5 -	8.5
-	-	-	0.94	0.99	0.98	24.4 -	19.6	1.02	1.06	1.20	4.9	0.07650	3/2/20	22.9 -	18.4
-	-	-	0.65	0.68	0.70	25.6 -	20.3	0.69	0.69	0.69	4.6	0.0550	3/2/20	16.6 -	13.2
-	-	-	0.66	0.71	0.74	23.3 -	19.4	0.76	0.77	0.78	5.6	0.045M	3/2/20	15.4 -	12.8
-	-	0.37	0.61	2.03	-0.61	17.5 -	14.0	1.24	1.24	1.38	12.4	0.310Z	1/24/20	10.7 -	8.6
-	-	-	1.65	1.57	1.47	13.5 -	12.2	3.86	3.28	3.00	18.2	0.150	3/2/20	22.4 -	20.1
-	-	-	0.93	1.00	1.04	24.0 -	21.3	0.98	1.09	1.05	4.6	0.0590	3/2/20	22.3 -	19.8
-	-	-	0.32	0.32	0.31	24.4 -	22.0	0.31	0.28	0.33	4.1	0.0243M	3/2/20	7.8 -	7.0
-	-	-	0.67	0.70	0.76	23.4 -	20.8	0.72	0.80	0.87	4.9	0.0475M	3/2/20	15.7 -	13.9
-	-	-	0.75	0.81	0.93	19.6 -	15.9	0.79	0.86	1.03	5.8	0.0660	3/2/20	14.7 -	11.9
-	-	-	0.91	0.80	0.79	18.4 -	0.0	0.93	0.93	0.93	5.8	0.07750	3/2/20	16.7 -	0.0
-	-	0.27	1.69	1.72	1.53	20.7 -	10.4	2.29	2.02	1.71	8.4	0.6220	2/13/20	34.9 -	17.6
-	-	0.32	1.87	-1.19	0.51	14.9 -	9.0	0.76	0.70	0.64	3.6	0.20Y	18/53/27	27.9 -	16.9
-	-	1.22	7.62	10.05	3.06	10.6 -	7.4	0.92	0.80	0.74	1.4	0.26250Y	18/53/27	80.9 -	56.1
-	-	0.42	1.51	1.72	1.50	17.5 -	13.9	1.61	1.44	1.29	7.0	0.46460	11/26/19	26.4 -	21.0
-	-	-	2.30	2.29	2.18	8.9 -	0.0	1.86	1.84	2.07	10.0	-	-	20.5 -	0.0
-	-	0.98	7.34	2.77	-1.54	5.9 -	4.4	1.72	1.60	1.50	4.6	0.4650	18/53/27	43.2 -	32.3
-	-	0.13	3.13	2.38	2.77	12.6 -	8.7	2.76	2.54	2.33	8.5	0.720Y	18/53/27	39.5 -	27.2
-	-	0.33	3.86	3.72	1.48	57.3 -	34.9	-	-	-	-	-	-	221.0 -	134.6
-	-	0.13	0.99	0.77	1.39	30.5 -	21.7	1.32	1.25	1.24	5.0	0.340Z	18/53/27	30.2 -	21.5
-	-0.28	-	0.96	0.13	0.45	42.4 -	19.6	0.36	0.33	0.21	1.3	0.090	12/16/19	40.8 -	18.9
-	-	5.57	-2.72	4.70	11.50	-		4.55	4.30	3.90	3.2	1.20Y	18/53/27	162.2 -	107.6
-	-	15.29	-41.76	146.06	82.19	-		1.00	1.00	1.00	-	1.0	18/53/27	-	
-	-	0.04	0.52	0.22	0.26	28.0 -	22.3	1.14	1.14	1.24	8.7	0.09050Z	3/13/20	14.5 -	11.6
-	-	-0.21	3.73	-13.65	-21.28	8.1 -	1.2	-	-	-	-	1.56250Y	6/17/13	30.4 -	4.5
-	-	0.14	-1.11	2.02		-		-	-	-	-	-	-	9.7 -	5.0
-	0.79	-	3.32	1.95	2.48	15.9 -	12.4	1.28	1.24	1.20	2.8	0.340Y	18/53/27	52.7 -	41.2
-	-	0.18	-0.16	2.62	-0.57	-		1.36	1.20	1.68	5.3	0.380Y	18/53/27	29.4 -	21.9
-	-	0.94	3.02	3.41	3.37	24.5 -	16.5	1.56	1.48	1.40	2.5	0.480Y	18/53/27	74.0 -	49.8
0.44	-	-	3.22	2.32	1.68	16.5 -	7.4	0.40	0.40	0.40	1.1	0.110Y	1/29/20	53.3 -	23.7
-	2.94	-	12.62	13.07	13.55	0.4 -	0.3	0.74	1.13	4.46	18.3	-	-	4.6 -	3.6
-	0.48	-	1.63	0.71	1.12	40.8 -	24.2	-	-	-	-	-	-	66.5 -	39.5
-	-	0.57	2.05	-	0.89	19.3 -	11.3	0.24	0.24	0.24	0.8	0.10Y	2/3/20	36.9 -	23.1
-	-	-		-1999.001567.00		-		-	600.00	400.00	-	-	-	41.3 -	27.6
-	-	-		-1999.001567.00		-		-	600.00	400.00	-	-	-	41.5 -	0.0
-	-	-0.34	-1.15	-1.07	-1.08	-		-	-	-	-	-	-	63.0 -	35.2
-	-	0.73	1.89	-2.50	1.81	23.3 -	11.3	0.24	0.24	0.24	0.7	0.10Y	18/53/27	44.0 -	21.3
-	-	0.06	1.12	0.42	0.44	88.6 -	47.5	0.48	0.48	0.48	0.6	0.120Y	18/53/27	99.3 -	53.2
-	0.93	-	3.09	3.15	2.22	14.2 -	10.8	0.83	0.79	0.75	2.2	0.240Y	18/53/27	44.0 -	33.4
-	-	-	0.84	1.42	1.08	83.7 -	61.7	3.00	3.01	2.39	5.0	-	-	70.3 -	51.8
-	-	0.29	0.35	-0.08	-2.05	43.5 -	25.5	-	-	-	-	0.78130Y	7/31/18	15.2 -	8.9
-	-	1.47	4.09	8.40	5.53	12.7 -	8.5	1.89	2.32	2.00	4.3	0.450Y	18/53/27	51.9 -	34.8
-	-	0.47	1.62	-	-	39.0 -	27.3	0.75	-	-	1.4	0.290Y	18/53/27	63.2 -	44.3
-	-	-	2.91	1.22	-0.50	2.5 -	0.6	-	-	-	-	-	-	7.4 -	1.7
-	-	-	0.64	0.00	-	15.0 -	0.0	0.76	-	-	17.3	0.0730	2/3/20	9.6 -	0.0
-	-	0.09	1.75	0.92	0.79	13.1 -	9.6	1.10	1.10	1.10	5.3	0.2750Y	1/15/20	23.0 -	16.7
-	-	0.96	1.38	0.71	-1.96	28.5 -	14.3	1.00	1.00	1.24	3.1	0.250Y	18/53/27	39.3 -	19.7

SYMBOL	COMPANY	NATURE OF BUSINESS	FISCAL YEAR-END	TOTAL REV. $MILL	NET INCOME $MILL	TOTAL ASSETS $MILL	NET STK EQUITY $MILL	NO OF INST	INST. HOLDINGS (SHARES)
XIN	Xinyuan Real Estate Co Ltd	Property, Real Estate & Developmen	12/31/18	2217.6	73.0	8033.7	680.4	69	20944996
XPO	XPO Logistics, Inc.	Airlines/Air Freight	12/31/18	17279.0	422.0	12270.0	3575.0	500	121491582
XYL	Xylem Inc	Industrial Machinery & Equipment	12/31/18	5207.0	549.0	7222.0	2768.0	865	183807607
AUY	Yamana Gold Inc	Precious Metals	12/31/18	1798.5	-284.6	8012.9	3989.3	385	491269643
YELP	Yelp Inc	Internet & Software	12/31/18	942.8	55.3	1175.6	1075.5	354	71843708
YETI	Yeti Holdings Inc	Sporting & Recreational	12/29/18	778.8	57.8	514.2	29.0	213	42803146
YEXT	Yext Inc	Internet & Software	1/31/19	228.3	-74.8	267.1	84.5	167	71726471
YRD	Yiren Digital Ltd	Finance Intermediaries & Services	12/31/18	817.5	140.6	1093.6	744.8	66	7172329
DAO	Youdao Inc	Educational Services	12/31/18	731.6	-208.9	619.6	-681.7	-	0
YPF	YPF SA	Refining & Marketing	12/31/18	435820.0	38613.0	994016.0	359200.0	233	90450356
YUMC	Yum China Holdings Inc	Hotels, Restaurants & Travel	12/31/18	8415.0	708.0	4610.0	2873.0	794	376523764
YUM	Yum! Brands Inc	Hotels, Restaurants & Travel	12/31/18	5688.0	1542.0	4130.0	-7926.0	1491	307619528
ZAYO	Zayo Group Holdings Inc	Manufacturing	6/30/19	2578.0	150.0	9334.6	1341.5	445	225983693
ZEN	Zendesk Inc	Internet & Software	12/31/18	598.7	-131.1	1237.9	416.9	409	124565170
ZBH	Zimmer Biomet Holdings Inc	Medical Instruments & Equipment	12/31/18	7932.9	-379.2	24126.8	11271.3	1352	242333024
ZTS	Zoetis Inc	Pharmaceuticals	12/31/18	5825.0	1428.0	10777.0	2185.0	1319	492760932
ZTO	ZTO Express (Cayman) Inc	Shipping	12/31/18	17604.5	4383.0	39682.9	34217.2	240	227820663
ZUO	Zuora Inc	Internet & Software	1/31/19	235.2	-77.6	299.4	153.0	203	54898252
ZYME	Zymeworks Inc	Pharmaceuticals	12/31/18	53.0	-36.6	244.4	180.5	92	19733172

| EARNINGS PER SHARE | | | | | | P/E RATIO | | DIVIDENDS PER SHARE | | | AV. YLD % | DIV. DECLARED | | PRICE RANGE |
| QUARTERLY | | | ANNUAL | | | | | | | | | | | 2018 |
1st	2nd	3rd	2018	2017	2016			2018	2017	2016		AMOUNT	PAYABLE	
-	-	0.16	0.57	0.48	0.53	8.9 -	6.4	0.39	0.39	0.29	9.0	-	-	5.0 - 3.7
-	-	1.14	2.88	2.45	0.53	29.7 -	16.0	-	-	-	-	-	-	85.7 - 46.2
-	-	0.36	3.03	1.83	1.45	28.0 -	21.2	0.84	0.72	0.62	1.1	0.240Y	18/53/27	84.8 - 64.2
-	0.01	-	-0.30	-0.21	-0.33	-		0.02	0.02	0.02	0.6	0.010	1/14/20	5.2 - 1.8
-	-	0.14	0.62	1.75	-0.06	66.1 -	48.6	-	-	-	-	-	-	41.0 - 30.1
-	-	0.25	0.69	0.19	0.58	52.7 -	21.8	-	-	-	-	-	-	36.4 - 15.0
-	-	-0.38	-0.85	-1.39	-0.89	-		-	-	-	-	-	-	23.1 - 13.7
-	-	.	1.13	1.72	1.35	15.1 -	4.0	0.40	2.23	-	3.7	-	-	17.0 - 4.5
-	-	-	-2.80	-2.04	-	-		-	-	-	-	-	-	15.5 - 12.4
-	-	3.60	98.43	31.43	-72.13	0.2 -	0.1	3.02	1.65	1.65	23.0	-	-	18.5 - 8.1
-	-	0.58	1.79	1.01	1.36	27.2 -	18.4	0.42	0.10	-	1.0	0.120Y	18/53/27	48.7 - 32.9
-	-	0.81	4.69	3.77	4.04	25.4 -	19.0	1.44	1.20	1.89	1.4	0.470Y	18/53/27	119.2 - 89.1
0.08	-	-	0.41	0.35	-0.31	84.5 -	55.7	-	-	-	-	-	-	34.6 - 22.8
-	-	-0.31	-1.24	-1.11	-1.11	-		-	-	-	-	-	-	93.7 - 55.5
-	-	2.08	-1.86	8.90	1.51	-		0.96	0.96	0.96	0.7	0.240Y	18/53/27	151.2 - 100.4
-	-	0.90	2.93	1.75	1.65	45.5 -	27.8	0.50	0.42	0.38	0.5	0.20Y	18/53/27	133.3 - 81.6
-	-	-	5.82	4.40	2.91	4.0 -	2.6	1.20	-	-	6.1	-	-	23.5 - 15.3
-	-	-0.16	-1.78	-1.64	-2.14	-		-	-	-	-	-	-	24.6 - 13.3
-	-	-0.70	-1.26	-0.64	-2.65	-		-	-	-	-	-	-	45.5 - 0.0

This Page left intentionally blank